DICTIONARY OF CANADIAN BIOGRAPHY

DICTIONARY OF CANADIAN BIOGRAPHY

DICTIONNAIRE BIOGRAPHIQUE DU CANADA

FRANCESS G. HALPENNY GENERAL EDITOR

JEAN HAMELIN DIRECTEUR GÉNÉRAL ADJOINT

VOLUME VII

TORONTO

MARY P. BENTLEY supervisory editor JANE E. GRAHAM associate editor
HENRI PILON executive officer

CHARLES DOUGALL, ROBERT LOCHIEL FRASER, STUART R. J. SUTHERLAND
senior manuscript editors
CURTIS FAHEY, DAVID ROBERTS, CATHERINE A. WAITE, ROBERT G. WUETHERICK
manuscript editors

PHYLLIS CREIGHTON translations editor
SUSAN E. BÉLANGER bibliographies editor
DEBORAH MARSHALL editorial assistant

JOANNA DAVIS, MARA L. DE DIEGO secretaries

QUEBEC

HUGUETTE FILTEAU, MICHEL PAQUIN codirecteurs de la rédaction
THÉRÈSE P. LEMAY rédactrice-historienne principale

PAULETTE M. CHIASSON, CÉLINE CYR
CHRISTIANE DEMERS, FRANCE GALARNEAU, JAMES H. LAMBERT
MICHEL DE LORIMIER, JACQUELINE ROY rédacteurs-historiens

ROGER FISET réviseur-traducteur
MARCELLE DUQUET éditrice
MICHÈLE BRASSARD chargée de recherche
RÉJEAN BANVILLE auxiliaire de recherche

PIERRETTE DESROSIERS, SUZANNE EAST, LOUISE D. BARABÉ secrétaires

TRANSLATOR J. F. FLINN

UNIVERSITY OF TORONTO PRESS

LES PRESSES DE L'UNIVERSITÉ LAVAL

DICTIONARY OF CANADIAN BIOGRAPHY

VOLUME VII

1836 TO 1850

UNIVERSITY OF TORONTO PRESS
Toronto Buffalo London

ISBN 0-8020-3452-7 (regular edition)

Canadian Cataloguing in Publication Data
Main entry under title:

Dictionary of Canadian biography.

Added t.p. in English and French.
Issued also in French.
Contents: v.1. 1000–1700. – v.2. 1701–1740. – v.3. 1741–1770. – v.4. 1771–1800. – v.5. 1801–1820. – v.6. 1821–1835. – v.7. 1836–1850. – v.8. 1851–1860. – v.9. 1861–1870. – v.10. 1871–1880. – v.11. 1881–1890.
Includes bibliographies and indexes.
ISBN 0-8020-3142-0 (v.1) ISBN 0-8020-3240-0 (v.2)
ISBN 0-8020-3314-8 (v.3) ISBN 0-8020-3351-2 (v.4)
ISBN 0-8020-3398-9 (v.5) ISBN 0-8020-3436-5 (v.6)
ISBN 0-8020-3452-7 (v.7) ISBN 0-8020-3422-5 (v.8)
ISBN 0-8020-3319-9 (v.9) ISBN 0-8020-3287-7 (v.10)
ISBN 0-8020-3267-9 (v.11)
1. Canada – Biography
FC25.D52 1966 920′.071 C66-3974-5 rev.5
F1005.D49 1966

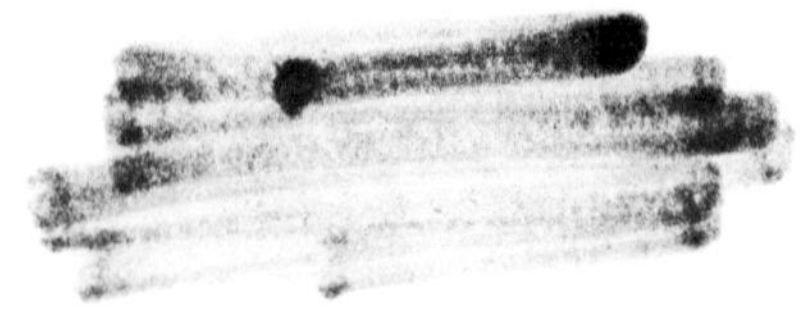

Contents

Introduction

VOLUME VII is the eleventh volume of the *Dictionary of Canadian biography/Dictionnaire biographique du Canada* to be published. Volumes I–VI appeared in 1966, 1969, 1974, 1979, 1983, and 1987, presenting persons who died or flourished between the years 1000 and 1835 (a separate *Index, volumes I to IV* was issued in 1981). Volume VII (1836–50) continues this progression, and joins it with later volumes. Volumes VIII–XI, encompassing persons who died or flourished 1851–90, have already been published, in 1985, 1976, 1972, and 1982 respectively. Volume XII (1891–1900), in preparation, will complete the 19th century. A great web of cross-references now stretches across the centuries.

The 326 contributors to volume VII, writing in either English or French, have provided 538 biographies ranging in length from fewer than 600 to more than 10,000 words. They were invited to contribute because of their special knowledge of the period and of the persons who figured in it, and have been asked to write in accordance with the DCB/DBC's *Directives to contributors*. "Biographers should endeavour to provide a readable and stimulating treatment of their subject. Factual information should come from primary sources if possible. . . . The achievements of the subjects should be seen against the background of the period in which they lived and the events in which they participated." The contributors to volume VII bring to it the benefit of new knowledge on major and minor figures and on the society in which they lived.

The lives of the people of volume VII, like those in its neighbouring volumes, reflect both historical events in Europe and North America and initiatives of the colonies of Newfoundland, Nova Scotia, Cape Breton, Prince Edward Island, New Brunswick, Lower Canada, and Upper Canada in response to their growing settlement, changing patterns in trade, and sharp questions of government. The fur trade reaches to the far north and the far west, with the settlement of Red River caught up in the struggle of rival companies. In the Arctic the exploration which features the expeditions of Sir John Franklin acquires momentum.

The major conflicts of war and allegiance repeat those of volume VI: the War of American Independence, the revolution in France, Britain's battles with revolutionary France and Napoleon, and the War of 1812 which tested and confirmed British North America's existence. The effects of these events again are everywhere evident in the volume: in the march of people northward from the Thirteen Colonies, in the disruption of religious and cultural ties caused by the French revolution, in the movements of military personnel and the consequences for civilians of armed conflict and embargo. In this volume too the great waves of immigration building up from the 1820s continue their assault upon British North America: Americans coming north for land, thousands from Britain seeking a new life in port, city, village, and farm (90,000 Irish immigrants pass through Quebec alone in 1847, the year of a fearsome experience of typhus).

A persistent theme is the debate over institutions of government. In the decades up to 1850, Newfoundland, with its population expanding especially during the Irish immigration of the twenties and thirties, moves through the successive advances of year-round governors, an improved system of colonial justice, and in 1832 representative government; ten years later a turbulent house of assembly finds itself in an amalgamated legislature. These developments are recorded in the biographies of such vigorous leaders as Peter Brown, rough-and-ready Irish merchant of Harbour Grace; William Carson, doctor, newspaperman, and agriculturist; Francis Forbes, chief justice in the Supreme Court 1816–22, reining in magistrates and the governor through his decisions; and Patrick Morris, Irish importer-exporter and passenger agent. The reactions to political events in the thirties and forties of such a powerful church leader as Bishop Michael Anthony Fleming introduce long-lived problems of denominational strife. Issues centring on reform can be viewed for Nova Scotia through Samuel George William Archibald, lawyer and high public official, imposing in his stance as a constitutionalist, or through Jotham Blanchard, editor and a radical after Joseph Hume, contending against the labyrinth of patronage and for a cheaper legal system. In New Brunswick, Richard Simonds represents debate about the recurrent issues of control of revenue, management of crown lands, and provision for King's College.

The political and social struggles that create in the Canadas an increasing turmoil of debate and explode in rebellion in 1837 and 1838 appear in one phase after another: the hotly discussed proposal for union in 1822; the crises in the legislatures over the voting of supplies; the pressure to see British parliamentary practice applied in the colonies; the attacks upon the place of judges in the legislative system; the impatience of ordinary people with procedures of land allotment and their concern with the civil status of aliens, partiality of the judiciary, the system of clergy reserves and crown lands, and favouritism in the bestowal of public office; the anxiety for French language and law among the Canadians of Lower Canada; the attempt in 1831 for a *fabriques* bill which would reduce clerical power in the parishes; the 92 Resolutions passed in 1834 and the Russell Resolutions of 1837 from Britain; the activities of the Fils de la Liberté; armed uprisings and their suppression, followed by decisions about the fate of Patriotes and other rebels and by incursions across the border; then union of the two provinces in 1841. Many biographies present this long, uncertain story that would finally arrive at responsible government. Practice of union and responsible government creates links with important themes of volume VIII and its successors.

The variety of persons and opinion may be seen in Lower Canada with Joseph Papineau, a reader of the *philosophes* and of English 18th-century theorists and an admirer of British constitutional monarchy, concerned for the Canadians but out of sympathy with his son's revolt; Ezekiel Hart, a Trois-Rivières merchant with a passion for politics, whose attempts to take his elected place in the assembly raise the question of civil rights for Jews; Herman Witsius Ryland, a colonial tory, sympathetic to the English party; Austin Cuvillier, auctioneer and associate of the British merchant community in Montreal yet one of those sent by the Canadian party to London in 1828 to complain of abuses; Elzéar Bédard, lawyer and moderate, who introduces the 92 Resolutions in the assembly and from the bench issues in November 1838 a writ of habeas corpus that brings his dismissal from office; Cyrille-Hector-Octave Côté, nationalist, calling in question the entire institutional basis of French Canadian society and finally taking up arms. For Upper Canada stand the urbane gentleman William Warren Baldwin of York, arguing from the act of 1791 for the bestowal of a constitution upon the province and from Blackstone for the liberties of subjects, and, as judge Robert Thorpe had seemed to do earlier, developing a concept of responsible government; Charles Fothergill, king's printer and journalist, raising an opposition voice for conservative reform in the 1820s in the assembly; Christopher Hagerman, lawyer, blunt yet eloquent, a strong church and state man; John Johnston Lefferty of St Catharines, doctor, a genial independent, pursuing like farmer Joseph Shepard rights for aliens. The frequent and important participation of members of the legal profession in the politics of the Canadas is illustrated by such figures as Baldwin and Hagerman and also in the complex and contrasting careers in Lower Canada of Jonathan Sewell, attorney general, chief justice 1808–38, a defender of the royal prerogative, seeking to make the colony a place of nurture for the British who had adopted it as home, and Joseph-Rémi Vallières de Saint-Réal, brilliant in the courtroom, a nationalist but a rival to Louis-Joseph Papineau in the assembly, the first Canadian to hold a chief justiceship.

The accidents of career and death have brought into volume VII a noteworthy collection of governors (or administrators) who strive to contend against, understand, compromise with, or resolve the powerful push of colonial assertion, and their biographies provide a helpful overview of differing official attitudes and initiatives: Archibald Acheson (Earl of Gosford), George Robert Ainslie, Sir Charles Bagot, Sir Archibald Campbell, Sir Colin Campbell, Sir Donald Campbell, Sir Charles Hamilton, John George Lambton (Earl of Durham), Charles Theophilus Metcalfe (Baron Metcalfe), Sir Robert Shore Milnes, George Ramsay (Earl of Dalhousie), John Ready, Hugh Swayne, Charles Edward Poulett Thomson (Baron Sydenham), Matthew Whitworth-Aylmer (Baron Aylmer). (The Colonial Office to which they, and the officials of their administrations, reported and to which public men often appealed is the subject of an introductory essay by Phillip Buckner in volume VIII.)

Journalists are another group inevitably involved with public affairs. They represent all shades of opinion, and other interests as well. In 1807 John Ryan publishes the first issue of the *Royal Gazette* in St John's, inaugurating the press, though a restricted one, in Newfoundland. Frederick John Martin Collard helps to mature political debate in Prince Edward Island. John Charlton Fisher, of the *Quebec Gazette*, eminent in the city's cultural life, is in 1824 a founder, along with William Smith and Vallières, of its Literary and Historical Society sponsored by Governor Lord Dalhousie. David Chisholme edits newspapers in Montreal and sponsors indigenous literature in his *Canadian Review*. George Perkins Bull, Orangeman, sets up the tory *Hamilton Gazette*. Thomas Dalton, publishing the *Patriot* in Kingston and York, lives up to its name in his politics, as a dreamer of a British North American union from sea to sea, and an opponent of American Methodists. Léon Gosselin is briefly editor of the radical reform paper *La Minerve* and founds the more wary *Le Populaire* in the inauspicious year 1837. Standing out as publisher of the *Quebec Gazette*, the largest weekly in the Canadas, but impressive in many fields is John Neilson, Scottish born but a resolute Canadian, printer and bookseller in English and French, supporter of education, active in agriculture and settlement, and from 1818 a leading politician in Lower Canada working for reform with the Canadian or Patriote party until in 1834 the 92 Resolutions offend his respect for the constitution and the British connection.

Inevitable for colonies in the process of settlement is a concern for land: where and how to obtain it, how to hold it, how to develop it. David William Smith, one of Simcoe's subordinates, is instrumental in the 1790s in the planning of townships for the new province of Upper Canada. A number of biographies are set amid the Lower Canadian seigneuries, inherited or purchased or managed, held by French or English, with problems of accommodating old regulations and practices to a newer age that demands access to markets: Kenelm Conor Chandler of Nicolet, Antoine-Gaspard Couillard in Rivière-du-Sud, Barthélemy Joliette at Lavaltrie. Marie-Charles-Joseph Le Moyne de Longueuil, fourth baroness of Longueuil, is the last legal French descendant of the old Le Moyne de Longueuil family. Linking qualifications as surveyor and notary to his services for land-holding religious communities and as lender to owners of property, Joseph Papineau is finally a committed and exacting seigneur himself at Petite-Nation. Undeveloped areas attract settlers significant for their future: Joseph Marshall, a loyalist officer in the Georgias, who takes up farming in the Guysborough area; William Hanington on Shediac Bay; Frederick George Heriot, a serving officer in 1812–15 and then resident on the military settlement that became Drummondville; George Hamilton, in 1815 acquiring property on the site of the city that would bear his name; Robert Nelles, of the Palatinate group in New York state, loyalist raider, with a large Niagara property on the site of Grimsby; Christian Nafziger, of the Amish group in southwestern Upper Canada. Plans for settlement on a major scale are not lacking, as with John Galt, associated by 1824 with the huge land and colonization scheme to be chartered as the Canada Company; the colourful and eccentric Dr William "Tiger" Dunlop, taken on by the company as warden of the woods and forests; Peter Robinson, impresario for the assisted emigration in the 1820s of several thousand Irish to the Bathurst and Newcastle districts and later commissioner of crown lands and clergy reserves; William Bowman Felton, hoping for a gentry in the Eastern Townships, involved with the Lower Canada Land Company. William Dickson of Niagara is one of many who eye the Grand River lands assigned to the Six Nations. The proper use of agricultural land preoccupies such farmers as Robert Wade in Hamilton Township of Upper Canada or Toler Thompson on the Tantramar marshes and prompts John Young in Nova Scotia to take up his pen as Agricola for newspaper letters in 1818–21, an initiative which leads, encouraged by Dalhousie, to the founding of agricultural societies.

The quest for the security of their own land could assume tones of desperation among native peoples, whose leaders continue to bring the encroachments of white settlers and the scarcity of provisions to Indian agents, government bodies, even personally to George IV and Queen Victoria. Bands are caught between old tribal ways and official insistence upon agricultural communities, between their own religious beliefs and efforts at conversion. Guarantees of land and help are sought by Francis Condo and Joseph Malie on the Restigouche, and by Louis-Benjamin Peminuit Paul of Shubenacadie; Peter Gonish of the Miramichi and Nicolas Vincent of Jeune-Lorette go to England on their quest. John Aisance, Ojibwa chief, Methodist from 1828 and Catholic from 1832, establishes his band, after several displacements, on Beausoleil Island; Bauzhi-geezhig-waeshikum, Ojibwa medicine man, becomes the patriarch of Walpole Island. Abishabis, a Cree at Severn House in the northwest, demonstrates with his "track to heaven" one effect of Methodist teaching. Members of the Brant family maintain its prominence. Catharine Brant (Ohtowaˀkéhson), Joseph's third wife, is an aristocratic Mohawk leader on the Grand River; William Johnson Kerr, an Indian Department officer, commands Indian forces at Queenston and Beaver Dams and acquires a respected position in the Niagara district. At the head of an Indian force at Beaver Dams also, with warriors from Lower Canada, is Jean-Baptiste de Lorimier, officer at Saint-Régis, whose mother was an Iroquois from Caughnawaga. Contacts with whites occur away from centres of settlement: for Louis Callihoo, Iroquois trader around Lesser Slave Lake, or ˀKwah, a chief of the Carriers in New Caledonia, or Eenoolooapik, Inuit guide for whalers, who makes a successful visit to Scotland, or Marguerite-Magdelaine Marcot, daughter of an Ottawa, who as a widow maintains a place in the upper Great Lakes fur trade.

Products from agriculture – flour and potash among them – increasingly move into the transatlantic trading world to join fur, fish, ships, and lumber as means of exchange for the supplies and manufactured goods required in the colonies. Despite the interruptions of wars but encouraged by military contracts, and sustained by mercantile connections in Glasgow, Liverpool, London, and the West Indies, merchandising and trading expand. Many leaders of firms are careful watchers of or participants in political debates which might affect them as citizens or entrepreneurs because of legislation (union of the Canadas being but one example) or public works such as port facilities or canals; many also are active in such joint efforts as banks, public utilities, or insurance companies, or in society through the militia, education, religious groups, or relief for the poor and immigrants. The ramifications of business activity may be sampled through Benjamin Bowring of St John's, a town grown to 10,000 in 1815, as well as Thomas Meagher, Patrick Morris, and Pierce Sweetman, these three using connections with Waterford in Ireland; Stephen Wastie Deblois and Thomas Forrester of Halifax; Thomas Barlow, John McNeil Wilmot, and John Ward of bustling Saint John; Henry Usborne, entering the timber trade at Quebec as early as 1801 and William John Chapman Benson operating at the high point of 1845 when 30 timber coves sent out 1,499 shiploads of timber products, or Allan Gilmour tapping the vastness of Miramichi forests, or George Hamilton, lumberman of the Ottawa valley and the Gatineau privilege, or Philemon Wright of Hull Township; John Forsyth in Montreal of the Forsyth, Richardson firm, a major player in the fur trade and as importer-exporter; the Canadians Joseph Masson of Montreal, with excellent business connections in Glasgow, or Claude Dénéchau of Quebec; Adam Lymburner of Quebec with a triangular fishing trade and an interest in constitutional questions; Louis-Édouard Hubert, solid bourgeois of Saint-Denis on the Richelieu; Vénérande Robichaux, Acadian, taking up business interests in Quebec after 1775, her personal contacts extending throughout Acadia; William Chisholm, building schooners and developing a harbour at Oakville; James Gray Bethune of Cobourg, a merchant-forwarder bent on improving inland water transportation; Samuel Street of Niagara, tireless in pursuit of profit, by many means; Alexander Wood of York, identified as yet one more of the chain of resourceful Scots merchants from Halifax to Detroit.

Closely allied, at times overlapping, with business activities are those of industry. William Cooper, master of York's first school, establishes mills at the Humber River and wharfage in the town; Charles Jones is equally active as a miller near Brockville. Mathew Bell brings us once more to the story of the Saint-Maurice ironworks, which as a knowledgeable manager and lessee he makes into a paternalistic community; Anthony Manahan tries to build up the Marmora Iron Works. Charles Frederick Grece and John Covert are disappointed experimenters with hemp. Henry Joseph Philips, from Hamburg, produces in his Halifax shop, with the climate in mind, the first pianos made in British North America. John Leys works on the *Frontenac* of Kingston, the first steamboat launched on the Great Lakes. Prophetic of what is to come with family enterprises and scale of operation is the history of John Molson, who at 18 emigrates to Montreal, at 21 buys a brewery to which he provides the most advanced equipment, and by 1809 is involved with steamboats.

In the fur trade, which dominates the story of the northwest, expansion is continual – into New Caledonia and down the Columbia River, into the Athabasca and the Mackenzie country. The HBC and the NWC (along with its partner companies and others it absorbed) are engaged in bitter rivalry which can pit post against post, man against man, and armed bands against Red River settlers, to be ended with amalgamation and reorganization. The strategy of rivalry and merger may be witnessed with NWC associate Simon McGillivray, Pierre de Rastel de Rocheblave and Colin Robertson of both companies, and William Williams, governor of Rupert's Land for the HBC and then of its Southern Department. Opposition is notoriously belligerent with Samuel Black and others. The experiences of the trade are made known through records kept by Daniel Williams Harmon in New Caledonia or Neil McLaren in Chicoutimi, or collected by Roderick Mackenzie. The fortunes of families resulting from marriages with Indian or Métis women recur; their welfare preoccupies such traders as William Hemmings Cook, Peter Grant, John McDonell, and John McLeod, encountering retirement and white society in Red River and in the east, and it is ignored by John George McTavish.

In societies pushed forward by the urge to settle and to expand, surveyors and engineers perform essential tasks. The thrust is felt particularly in the Canadas with surveyors represented by Joseph Bouchette, surveyor general of Lower Canada 1804–30, who surveys, makes maps, and writes topographical descriptions; William Chewett, for over 50 years prolific as a map-maker and surveyor in Upper Canada; Augustus Jones, the colourful independent figure who surveys immense tracts of Upper Canada and becomes well known for his Indian connections. Engineering carries out a major project of transportation and communication, the Rideau Canal, a story told through Sir James Carmichael Smyth and John By and associates Nicol Hugh Baird (who goes on to the Trent system and Whitby and Cobourg harbours) and John Burrows of Bytown. Elias Walker Durnford is responsible for important military works at the Citadel in Quebec, a strategic position for defence. William Redmond Casey is an anticipation of a compelling future: he is engineer for the Champlain and St Lawrence Railroad, opened July 1836, the first public railway in Canada. So too is James Cull, contractor for the first stretch of macadamized road in Upper Canada, on the Yonge Street turnpike.

The stories of wives of businessmen or landowners or office holders, hard to come by usually, can provide special insights into the life of their times. Ann Kirby, widow of John Macaulay, merchant of Kingston, assumes management of her family, advises her brother and son about business, supports worthy causes, and at 76 takes on her son's family. Anne

Murray, wife of judge William Dummer Powell in York, maintains a high social status in the town until the escapades of daughter and granddaughter, and leaves a fine set of letters. Hannah Peters Jarvis, impoverished after provincial secretary William Jarvis's death, spends her old age at Queenston with a daughter, enduring soberly a life of constant labour.

Officials of the colonies are often chosen from among merchants, landowners, the military, and lawyers but for some a career in office is their largest role and for others such as William Firth and Grant Powell one they determinedly seek. Biographies illustrate the role of the civil secretary. Herman Witsius Ryland serves in Lower Canada under several governors from Lord Dorchester on, and is also long-time clerk to the Executive Council, holding strong convictions about the role of a colonial legislature and the royal prerogative; Andrew William Cochran serves under Sherbrooke and Dalhousie; George Hillier, veteran of the Peninsular War, is a close associate of Maitland in Upper Canada and goes on to India. Charles Buller arrives as chief secretary to Durham and sits on several of his commissions. More fixed than some in their employment are such appointees as William Franklin Odell, who shares with his loyalist father for 60 years the provincial secretaryship of New Brunswick, or Charles Jeffery Peters, also of the loyalist élite, attorney general for life. John Caldwell, receiver general of Lower Canada following his father, uses public funds to help his private business, an accepted practice, but becomes embroiled in years of litigation when he cannot meet the civil list. Thomas Nickleson Jeffery is collector of customs at Halifax for 40 years, and is responsible for the care of blacks sent to Nova Scotia after the War of 1812. George Heriot, deputy postmaster general of British North America, and Andrew Porteous labour for improvement in what the British government persistently views as a source of revenue rather than service. Jean-Marie Mondelet, as coroner for Montreal, is involved with the notorious by-election disturbance of 1832 when three Canadians are shot. Service with the militia, in peace time or in war, is a short or long element in many careers and for a few may result in a senior appointment, as it does in Lower Canada for Charles-Étienne Chaussegros de Léry.

The professional military of the period know service at sea or on land during the conflicts from 1775 to 1815 – in the Thirteen Colonies, on the Atlantic stations, in the Caribbean, with Wellington's armies – and cannot forget defence in times of peace. Isaac Coffin, a career officer in the Royal Navy, ends up in 1798 absentee seigneur to the Acadians of Îles-de-la-Madeleine. During the uneasy years before 1812 Martin Hunter, when in command of the forces in the Atlantic provinces, must take emergency precautions. Robert Heriot Barclay fights a bitter, lost, naval battle on Lake Erie in 1813 as does Daniel Pring in 1814 on Lake Champlain. Phineas Riall and John Vincent are senior officers for campaigns in the Niagara peninsula during those years. Sir Richard Henry Bonnycastle of the Royal Engineers promotes works with civil uses at York and puts together an effective defence for Kingston in the troubled years of 1837 and 1838. The unusual career sometimes possible for colonials is evident with Sir William Robert Wolseley Winniett of Annapolis Royal, in the navy at 14, who becomes the Gold Coast's governor in 1845 and combats the slave trade and human sacrifice in west Africa.

Those who take up armed rebellion are, as the years assigned to volume VII would suggest, a noticeable group. Notary Chevalier de Lorimier, playing a characteristic role, participates in the political debates and public manifestations previous to the rebellion in

Lower Canada, is a combatant at Saint-Eustache, joins the Patriote army in exile, is captured at Beauharnois in the second rising, and is finally executed. Jean-Olivier Chénier, physician, a long-time Patriote, dies in the thick of the battle around the burning church of Saint-Eustache and the fate of his body becomes a *cause célèbre* to later times. Amury Girod, author, with similar persuasions and actions, commits suicide when he faces capture after the December defeats. Lucien Gagnon, a successful farmer, overwhelmed by seigneurial dues, is heavily involved in the incursions and defeats of 1838 and dies disillusioned in 1842. Examples of the composition of rebellion in Upper Canada show long-held convictions of grievance. Jacob R. Beamer of Oakland Township determines for rebellion and the raids of 1838; he is transported, as is Elijah Crocker Woodman, a sympathizer but not a rebel and a diarist of his experiences. Peter Matthews, a prosperous Pickering farmer, and Samuel Lount, a respected blacksmith from south of Lake Simcoe, both in the political union movement, lead men to join the protest march to Toronto; both are executed as examples despite petitions in their favour.

The personalities and issues surrounding development of religious groups have, as always in Canadian history of the 19th century, a major role, whether in local parishes or on a wider scene. In Newfoundland, Roman Catholic bishop Michael Anthony Fleming, from Ireland, bestrides more than 20 years in which he builds his diocese, contending with governor, colonial office, and Rome to win his causes, and with liberals in his faith as well as Protestants, labouring to erect an imposing cathedral. Contentions among priests of Scottish, Irish, or French origin recur in the Maritime provinces. The sheer size and physical difficulty of their territories afflict Antoine Gagnon when he serves among the Acadians of Richibouctou or Alexander MacDonell ("too heavy for snow shoes") among Gaelic speakers in Arisaig and Cape Breton. The frail and learned Jean-Mandé Sigogne comes to Acadia from revolutionary France in 1799 as a much-needed resident French-language priest and for 45 years takes his forceful ministry to his undisciplined and poor communities. Elsewhere, Louis-Charles Lefebvre de Bellefeuille, missionary, makes valiant travels to the Timiskaming and Abitibi country to reach Indian groups. As in other volumes, revolution in France is responsible for the presence in Lower Canada of Sulpicians such as the rigorous Charles-Vincent Fournier at Baie-du-Febvre, with a taste for church decoration. A Canadian-born Sulpician, who resists the French influence, is the incessantly active Jean-Jacques Lartigue, auxiliary bishop, then bishop, of Montreal, a dedicated ultramontanist, striving for an episcopate independent of British authorities. Walking warily through political disputes, he sees the problems of Canadians, but, as his pastoral letter of October 1837 enjoins, will have no trade with revolution. Archbishop Joseph Signay, not an ultramontanist, is pushed and pulled by the strenuous representations of Lartigue and of Ignace Bourget on external and internal church affairs. Disputatious or inflexible priests such as Louis Nau or François-Xavier Pigeon do not make religious life easy for parishioners or bishops. Alexander McDonell leads his Highlanders to a new life in Upper Canada in 1804, is involved as vicar general and bishop with York, Quebec, London, or Rome over government salaries for Catholic priests and teachers and the creation of a diocese, and stands out against all manner of political reformers and his own belligerent Irish priest in York, William John O'Grady. Michael Power, of Irish family, consecrated bishop of Toronto in 1842, develops his large diocese and cathedral until he falls victim to typhus. Women in religious orders, dedicated to education or service, hold important office, such as Eulalie Durocher (founder of the Sisters of the Holy Names of Jesus and Mary in Canada) or Marie-Marguerite Lemaire (Sisters of Charity of the Hôpital Général, Montreal).

The Church of England is served in large and isolated posts by persevering priests, such as Amos Ansley with 14 townships in the lumber area and military settlement of the Ottawa or Charles Caleb Cotton in the Eastern Townships. John Inglis at Halifax, rector of St Paul's and bishop from 1825, is a high centre of ecclesiastical concern about regulations for university education, the right to perform marriages, and resistance to evangelicals and dissent. George Mortimer, at Thornhill, Upper Canada, recipient of a Colborne rectory, has a studious and domestically comfortable life. Robert Lugger comes out to Grand River in 1827 as the New England Company's first resident missionary among the Six Nations, providing instruction in religion and in the mechanical arts. John West, made HBC chaplain in 1819, is most attracted to the Indians around Red River but finds himself providing church and school to settlers, and deploring country marriages.

Stephen Bamford spends years on circuit as a Wesleyan Methodist in Nova Scotia despite his dislike of cold and travel; Samuel Heck, farmer, is licensed as a local preacher in Augusta Township, Upper Canada, following the practice of the American Methodists; John Jones (Thayendanegea), son of Augustus Jones and brother of Peter, is a teacher and exhorter among Mississaugas at the Credit Mission. James Evans goes to Norway House in 1840 as a superintendent for the British Wesleyans, develops a Cree syllabary, and supports native right to free trade. John Burton of Halifax is apparently its only Baptist in 1794 but by 1812 has become moderator of the Nova Scotia Baptist Association. With the arrival of many Baptists among the 2,000 black refugees from the War of 1812 he strives to train black and white elders. Washington Christian, a black, establishes a church for his fellows in Toronto and becomes much respected in Baptist polity. Divisions between Calvinist and Allinite views and over close or open communion perturb many in Nova Scotia, including Joseph Dimock and Asa McGray. Benjamin Gottlieb Kohlmeister's endeavours help the firm establishment of a Moravian theocracy in northern Labrador, and Christian Frederick Denke serves as a Moravian missionary to the Delawares and Chippewas of the Thames River in Upper Canada. David Burpe, a youthful settler in Maugerville in 1763, represents the religious values of early New England puritanism among Congregationalists on the frontier. Many threads that ultimately come together in a Presbyterian union are discernible with Edward Black, minister to the Scotch Presbyterian church of Montreal, Donald Allan Fraser sent to serve Gaelic speakers in Pictou County, Nova Scotia, or Robert McDowall of the Reformed Protestant Dutch Church who comes from the Albany area to the Quinte shore. The name Pictou is firmly associated with Thomas McCulloch, doughty minister of the Secession Church, who in fighting, with true Scottish conviction, for an interdenominational academy which would give a liberal education and provide requisite training for theological candidates is opposed by Anglicans, Kirkmen, and the Council.

Other efforts to establish education are widespread. They may be attempts through supervisory bodies or normal schools such as those made by Pierre-Antoine Dorion and Hector-Simon Huot in the 1830s in Lower Canada. That colony also sees in 1821 the creation of the Education Society of the District of Quebec, in which Joseph-François

Perrault and Jacques Voyer are much involved, and other schools for poor children. Schools of note are a feature: a Baptist seminary led by Frederick William Miles at Fredericton, non-denominational, which admits women on an equal basis with men; the seminary at Nicolet, where Joseph-Onésime Leprohon as director typifies administrators who mark generations of professional men and priests; the Red River Academy of David Thomas Jones and John Macallum, the first English-speaking high school in the northwest; Alexander Skakel's Grammar School in Montreal, under the aegis of the Royal Institution for the Advancement of Learning. Walter Bromley, an evangelical half-pay officer, sets up in Nova Scotia in 1813–14, despite Anglican opposition, the non-sectarian Royal Acadian School for fee-paying children of the middle class and charity pupils, with a workshop for the unemployed. Nancy Purvis of Nova Scotia is an example of the women teachers who try to provide education for young ladies. Influential in many colonial schools is the method of instruction using senior pupils as monitors which nonconformist Joseph Lancaster develops in Britain and the British and Foreign School Society adopts. Joseph Spragg, however, applies in his Church of England school in York the monitorial method of the National Society.

Among members of the medical profession the havoc of cholera and typhus overwhelms their capacities and defeats their limited knowledge. The epidemics meet, and kill, doctors such as port health officer William Bruce Almon in Halifax and James Patrick Collins in Saint John where more than 2,000 Irish emigrants fleeing the potato famine die in 1847. Service for such unfortunate victims and the survivors, care for the poor, standards of public health to combat scourges preoccupy doctors such as Samuel Head in Halifax, who runs a seamen's and travellers' hospital and a much-needed pharmacy. Daniel Arnoldi, medical examiner in the district of Montreal, shares a frequent concern with standards of medical practice and in 1847 becomes first president of the College of Physicians and Surgeons of Lower Canada. Thomas Fargues, educated like many in London and Edinburgh, and well respected in Quebec, takes up homeopathy.

An influential protagonist in the development of the fine arts is not himself an artist but a priest, Louis-Joseph Desjardins, who in 1817 receives from France a large collection of religious pictures for distribution in the diocese of Quebec, and is a patron of local artists such as Louis-Hubert Triaud. Louis Dulongpré of Montreal is a prolific painter of portraits and religious pictures. Professional artists are not, however, numerous anywhere in British North America and their living can be precarious. James Bowman does chapel paintings and Stations of the Cross in Notre-Dame in Montreal, then portraits of family compact supporters in Toronto. William Eagar, like others, gives lessons, and takes up engravings of Nova Scotian views. Jean-Baptiste Roy-Audy turns from wood-working to copying pictures, but his portraits in a naïve style have attracted 20th-century attention. The first lithography appears in Lower Canada with views of Robert Auchmuty Sproule and in Upper Canada with the discovery of suitable lithographic stone at Kingston by Samuel Oliver Tazewell. Elizabeth Posthuma Gwillim (Mrs Simcoe), in contrast, is an accomplished example of the gentlewoman depicting in water-colours the scenes of a new environment. The training in drawing given to military men in Woolwich in England can work to the advantage of art: George Heriot and James Pattison Cockburn, familiar with English water-colourists, use their travels through the Canadas to suggest subject-matter.

John Cochrane, a Scottish sculptor, takes part in the impressive decoration of Toronto's St Lawrence Hall. Henry Musgrave Blaiklock designs neoclassical buildings at Quebec. The work relations of those who construct buildings in Lower Canada appear in the account of Charles-Simon Delorme. Laurent Amiot, with training in Paris, does important work in church and domestic silver; James J. Langford is one of the innovative Halifax silversmiths. John Geddie of Pictou builds clocks, with local scenes pictured. Thomas Nisbet makes fine furniture in Saint John.

Music and the theatre are fitfully evident. Frederick Glackemeyer teaches, sells instruments, and composes in Quebec, as does Charles Sauvageau who publishes a manual on theory. Jonathan Sewell, a patron of the arts, owns a theatre and founds a quartet in which he plays. Stephen Humbert is a singing-school leader in Saint John and compiler of Canada's first English tune-book. Frederick Brown, an itinerant actor, comes up from Boston and New York to play Shakespeare in Montreal.

The picture is somewhat different for literature. At work are a number of accomplished writers, who spend some or most of their careers in the colonies. John Galt's admired works related to Scotland have as companions in his bibliography articles, tales, and an autobiography which make use of his Canadian experiences. Dr William Dunlop of the Huron Tract writes an idiosyncratic *Statistical sketches of Upper Canada* and for the *Literary Garland* his "Recollections of the American war." Standish O'Grady composes *The emigrant*, a long poem which is still anthologized. Thomas McCulloch's vigorous satire of provincial ways in the Stepsure letters in the 1820s is enormously popular but he cannot get acceptance from British publishers for broadly humorous Scottish themes. Adam Hood Burwell composes in an 18th-century diction the first long poem of pioneer life in Upper Canada by a native-born. Sarah Herbert makes sentimental and religious tales and poems and in the 1840s owns and edits the *Olive Branch*. Unhappy circumstances of poverty or cultural isolation surround poets James Haskins and John McPherson. John MacLean (Iain MacGhillEathain), an Antigonish settler bard, writes "village verse." The experiences of life in British North America lie behind a number of valuable works of historical or descriptive non-fiction by occasional authors: Bonnycastle's books on the Canadas and Newfoundland, hard-working loyalist Peter Fisher's two histories of New Brunswick and the *Sketches and tales* of that colony by Emily Elizabeth Shaw (Mrs Beavan), Mrs Simcoe's diaries, George Heriot's *Travels*, William Smith's *History of Canada*, or Elizabeth Lichtenstein's loyalist memoirs. Jean-Baptiste Boucher writes religious commentary and Odelin participates in a vigorous controversy about the doctrines of La Mennais.

The colour and variety to be found in the biographies alluded to above pervade the volume, but strike out in some unusual vignettes: Jeanne-Charlotte Allamand (Mme Berczy) steadfast in poverty, supporting her husband through his long trials in establishing settlements; Walter Bates, author of a popular work in the manner of Daniel Defoe on an ingenious thief; William Brass, cause of a famous trial for rape and a public execution; John Church, unlettered, filling his account-books with pictographs; James Dickson, self-styled "Liberator of the Indian Nations," whose dwindling supporters journey in the 1830s by boat to the Sault and overland to Red River in winter; William Forsyth, struggling against governor and neighbours to keep the best tourist views of Niagara Falls; the symbolic life of

Sir John Franklin raising questions about how heroes are identified; Hugh Denoon, callously sending two overcrowded emigrant ships across the Atlantic; Nelson Hackett, fugitive slave, whose extradition from Canada in 1842 arouses an international furore; Henry Lamb, planning a sophisticated "Romulus" city near the great swamp in Beverly Township; Joshua Marsden, recording the outer and inner life of his simple, unadorned Methodism; François-Hyacinthe Séguin, commenting acidly in his diary on the people of Terrebonne and the manifestations of the Patriotes; the lonely priest Louis Martinet, the last surviving Recollet in Quebec; author Maria Monk, fabricating scandal about Catholic nuns and priests; Nils von Schoultz, engaging and peripatetic scoundrel, captivated by the heroics of rebellion in 1838; the wealthy old German businessman of Quebec, George Pozer, wearing 18th-century garb and sitting on his doorstep to chat; John Tanner, raised among the Shawnees from the age of nine, then an uneasy wanderer in the northwest; Thomas Irwin, constantly discouraged in his efforts to assist the Micmacs of Prince Edward Island and to teach their subtle language; Alexander Wedderburn, naval officer, following to Saint John a young lady he caught sight of on a packet; John Henry White, publisher of a religious paper in Charlottetown, and of a stereotyped Authorized Version of the Bible wonderfully illustrated but transgressing British crown copyright; John Troyer, gentle herbalist of the Baldoon settlement, reputed to have a thorough knowledge of witches and the art of expelling them.

Volume VII is a significant point of passage for contributors and for staff as attention moves from it to the last of the 19th-century volumes and the first of the 20th-century. To all who have worked so faithfully in this long and creative progression we extend our warmest thanks.

FRANCESS G. HALPENNY

JEAN HAMELIN

Acknowledgements

THE *Dictionary of Canadian biography/Dictionnaire biographique du Canada* receives assistance, advice, and encouragement from many institutions and individuals. They cannot all be named nor can their kindness and support be adequately acknowledged.

The DCB/DBC, which owes its founding to the generosity of the late James Nicholson, has been sustained over the years by its parent institutions, the University of Toronto and the University of Toronto Press and the Université Laval and Les Presses de l'université Laval. Beginning in 1973 the Canada Council provided grants to the two university presses which made possible the continuation and acceleration of the DCB/DBC's publication program, and this assistance has been maintained and amplified by the Social Sciences and Humanities Research Council of Canada, created in 1978. We should like to give special thanks to the SSHRCC not only for its financial support but also for the encouragement it has given us as we strive to complete our volumes for the 19th century. We are grateful also for the financial assistance accorded us by the Université Laval.

Of the numerous individuals who assisted in the preparation of volume VII, we owe particular thanks to our contributors. In addition, we have had the benefit of special consultation with a number of persons, some of them also contributors. We should like to acknowledge: Joyce Banks, Marie-Thérèse Béchire, Patricia Birkett, the late Phyllis R. Blakeley, Louise-Hélène Boileau, Denise Bouquet, Phillip Buckner, Susan Buggey, Susan Burke, Raymond Dumais, Micheline Fortin, Armand Gagné, Gilles Héon, H. T. Holman, Orlo Jones, Patricia Kennedy, Louis-Joseph Lépine, Allan J. MacDonald, G. Edward MacDonald, Monique Mailloux, André Martineau, the late Keith Matthews, Pamela J. Miller, Shirlee Anne Smith, George M. Story, and Lucille Vachon.

Throughout the preparation of volume VII we have enjoyed willing cooperation from libraries and archives in Canada and elsewhere. We are particularly grateful to the administrators and staffs of those institutions to which we have most frequently appealed. In addition to the National Archives of Canada in Ottawa and the provincial archives in all the provinces, they are: in Manitoba, the Hudson's Bay Company Archives (Winnipeg); in New Brunswick, the New Brunswick Museum (Saint John) and the University of New Brunswick Library (Fredericton); in Ontario, the Genealogical Library of the Church of Jesus Christ of Latter-Day Saints (Toronto), the Kingston Public Library, the Metropolitan Toronto Reference Library, and the University of Toronto Library; in Prince Edward Island, the Prince Edward Island Museum and Heritage Foundation (Charlottetown); in Quebec, the *archives civiles* and *judiciaires*, the Archives de l'archidiocèse de Québec, the Archives de la ville de Québec, the Archives de l'université de Montréal, the Bibliothèque de l'Assemblée nationale (Québec), the Bibliothèque and Archives du séminaire de Québec, the Bibliothèque générale de l'université Laval, and the McCord Museum

(Montreal). We should like to thank as well the staffs of the *archives départementales* in France, of the various record offices in the United Kingdom, and of the many archives, libraries, and historical societies in the United States who answered our numerous requests for information so kindly.

The editors of volume VII were helped in its preparation by colleagues in both offices. In Toronto, Elizabeth Hulse and Monica Sandor contributed to the final reading of the manuscript, and we were grateful for the support of Tracey Pegg during the last stages of the volume. In Quebec, Louise Boucher and Marie-Hélène Lévesque provided assistance at various times. We have also benefited from the advice of the staff of the Office de la langue française as well as that of the Translation Bureau of the Department of the Secretary of State.

We should like to recognize the guidance and encouragement we have received from the two presses with which the DCB/DBC is associated, and in particular from Harald Bohne, H. C. Van Ierssel, and Peter Scaggs at the University of Toronto Press and Marc Boucher and Denis-Marc Pinsonnault at Les Presses de l'université Laval.

DICTIONNAIRE BIOGRAPHIQUE DU CANADA DICTIONARY OF CANADIAN BIOGRAPHY

Subjects of Biographies

ABISHABIS (d. 1843)
Abrams, William (d. 1844)
Acheson, Archibald, 2nd Earl of Gosford (1776–1849)
Ainslie, George Robert (1776–1839)
Aisance, John (d. 1847)
Albro, John (1764–1839)
Allamand, Jeanne-Charlotte (Berczy) (1760–1839)
Allan, Peter John (1825–48)
Allsopp, George Waters (d. 1837)
Almon, William Bruce (1787–1840)
Amiot, Laurent (1764–1839)
Amiot, Noël-Laurent (1793–1845)
Ansley, Amos (d. 1837)
Anthony, Gabriel (d. 1846)
Archibald, Samuel George William (1777–1846)
Arnoldi, Daniel (1774–1849)
Auffray, Charles-Dominique (1794–1837)
Auldjo, George (1790–1846)

BADGLEY, Francis (1767–1841)
Bagot, Sir Charles (1781–1843)
Baird, Nicol Hugh (1796–1849)
Baldwin, William Warren (1775–1844)
Bamford, Stephen (1770–1848)
Barclay, Robert Heriot (1786–1837)
Barlow, Thomas (1788–1844)
Barnes, Richard (1805–46)
Barrett, Alfred (d. 1849)
Barrie, Sir Robert (1774–1841)
Barry, Robert (d. 1843)
Bates, Walter (1760–1842)
Baudry, Marie-Victoire, named de la Croix (1782–1846)
Bauzhi-geezhig-waeshikum (d. 1841 or 1842)
Beamer, Jacob R. (fl. 1837–47)
Beasley, Richard (1761–1842)
Beaubien, Marguerite (1797–1848)
Beauvais, *dit* Saint-James, René (1785–1837)
Bédard, Elzéar (1799–1849)
Belcher, Andrew (1763–1841)
Bell, Mathew (d. 1849)
Bell, William (1806–44)
Benson, William John Chapman (d. 1850)
Berthelot, Amable (1777–1847)
Berton, George Frederick Street (1808–40)
Bethune, James Gray (1793–1841)
Binns, Charles (d. 1847)
Black, Edward (1793–1845)
Black, Samuel (d. 1841)
Blackwood, Thomas (1773–1842)
Blaiklock, Henry Musgrave (1790–1843)
Blanchard, Jotham (1800–39)
Blanchard, Tranquille (d. 1843)
Blowers, Sampson Salter (1741/42–1842)
Bobbie. *See* Eenoolooapik
Boisseau, Nicolas-Gaspard (1765–1842)
Bonnycastle, Sir Richard Henry (1791–1847)
Bostwick, John (1780–1849)
Boucher, Jean-Baptiste (1763–1839)
Bouchette, Joseph (1774–1841)
Bourne, John Gervas Hutchinson (d. 1845)
Bowman, James (1793–1842)
Bowring, Benjamin (d. 1846)
Brant, Catharine. *See* Ohtowaʔkéhson
Brass, William (d. 1837)
Brecken, John (1800–47)
Brenton, Edward Brabazon (1763–1845)
Brien, Jean-Baptiste-Henri (1816–41)
Broke, Sir Philip Bowes Vere (1776–1841)
Bromley, Walter (d. 1838)
Brown, Frederick (d. 1838)
Brown, James (1776–1845)
Brown, Peter (d. 1845)
Buchan, David (d. in or after 1838)
Bull, George Perkins (1795–1847)
Buller, Charles (1806–48)
Bureau, Pierre (1771–1836)
Burpe, David (1752–1845)
Burrows, John (1789–1848)
Burton, John (1760–1838)
Burwell, Adam Hood (1790–1849)
Burwell, Mahlon (1783–1846)
By, John (1779–1836)

CADIEUX, Louis-Marie (1785–1838)
Caldwell, Billy (d. 1841)
Caldwell, Sir John (d. 1842)
Callihoo, Louis (fl. 1819–45)
Cameron, Duncan (d. 1848)
Campbell, Sir Archibald (1769–1843)
Campbell, Sir Colin (1776–1847)
Campbell, Sir Donald (1800–50)
Canac, *dit* Marquis, Pierre (1780–1850)

Lichtenstein, Elizabeth (Johnston) (1764–1848)
Lilly, George (d. 1846)
Lloyd, Jesse (1786–1838)
Longley, George (d. 1842)
Longworth, Francis (1766–1843)
Lorimier, Chevalier de (1803–39)
Lorimier, Jean-Baptiste de (d. 1845)
Loring, Robert Roberts (d. 1848)
Lount, Samuel (1791–1838)
Lugger, Robert (1793–1837)
Lusher, Robert Langham (d. 1849)
Lymburner, Adam (d. 1836)

MACALLUM, John (1806–49)
McConville, John (d. 1849)
McCormick, William (1784–1840)
McCulloch, Thomas (1776–1843)
Macdonald, John Small (d. 1849)
MacDonald, William Peter (1771–1847)
McDonell, Alexander (1762–1840)
MacDonell, Alexander (1782–1841)
McDonell, John (1768–1850)
McDonell (Collachie), Alexander (1762–1842)
McDouall, Robert (1774–1848)
McDowall, Robert (1768–1841)
Macfarlane, James (d. 1847)
MacGhillEathain, Iain (1787–1848)
McGillivray, Simon (d. 1840)
McGray, Asa (1780–1843)
McIntosh, John (b. 1777, d. 1845 or 1846)
McKenzie, James (d. 1849)
Mackenzie, Roderick (d. 1844)
MacKintosh, William (d. 1842)
McLaren, Neil (1766–1844)
McLeod, Alexander Roderick (d. 1840)
McLeod, John (1788–1849)
McLeod, John M. (b. 1795, fl. 1816–42)
McLoughlin, Marie-Louise, named de Saint-Henri (1780–1846)
McMahon, John Baptist (b. 1796, d. after 1840)
Macnider, Adam Lymburner (1778–1840)
McPherson, John (1817–45)
McTavish, John George (d. 1847)
Malie, Joseph (fl. 1841–46)
Manahan, Anthony (d. 1849)
Maranda, Jean-Baptiste (1803–50)
Marcot, Marguerite-Magdelaine (La Framboise) (1780–1846)
Markland, Thomas (1757–1840)
Marryat, Frederick (1792–1848)
Marsden, Joshua (1777–1837)
Marshall, Joseph (d. 1847)
Marsters, Richard Upham (1787–1845)
Martin, John Wills (fl. 1816–43)
Martinet, *dit* Bonami, Louis (1764–1848)
Masson, Joseph (1791–1847)
Matthews, Peter (d. 1838)
Meagher, Thomas (d. 1837)
Menzies, Archibald (d. 1842)
Menzies, George (d. 1847)
Merritt, Nehemiah (1770–1842)
Merritt, Thomas (1759–1842)
Metcalfe, Charles Theophilus, 1st Baron Metcalfe (1785–1846)
Meuse, Andrew James (fl. 1821–50)
Miles, Frederick William (d. 1842)
Millar, James (d. 1838)
Millidge, Thomas (1776–1838)
Milnes, Sir Robert Shore (d. 1837)
Molson, John (1763–1836)
Mondelet, Jean-Marie (d. 1843)
Monk, Maria (1816–49)
Morris, Patrick (d. 1849)
Mortimer, George (1784–1844)
Moschell, Johann Adam (1795–1849)
Munro, Hugh (d. 1846)
Murray, Anne (Powell) (1755–1849)
Murray, Sir George (1772–1846)

NAFZIGER, Christian (1776–1836)
Nau, Louis (b. 1799, d. in or after 1843)
Neilson, John (1776–1848)
Neilson, Samuel (1800–37)
Nelles, Robert (1761–1842)
Newbigging, James (d. 1838)
Nisbet, Thomas (d. 1850)

ODELIN, Jacques (1789–1841)
Odell, William Franklin (1774–1844)
O'Grady, Standish (fl. 1807–45)
O'Grady, William John (d. 1840)
Ohtowaˀkéhson (d. 1837)
O'Sullivan, Michael (d. 1839)

PAINCHAUD, Charles-François (1782–1838)
Pambrun, Pierre-Chrysologue (1792–1841)
Panet, Bonaventure (1765–1846)
Papineau, Joseph (1752–1841)
Paquin, Jacques (1791–1847)
Parent, Louis-François (1778–1850)
Parker, Snow (1760–1843)
Parkin, Edward (1791–1844)
Peabody, Francis (1760–1841)
Peminuit Paul, Louis-Benjamin (1755–1843)
Pépin, Joseph (d. 1842)
Perrault, Jean-Baptiste (1761–1844)
Perrault, Joseph-François (1753–1844)
Peters, Charles Jeffery (1773–1848)
Peters, Hannah (Jarvis) (1763–1845)
Philips, Henry Joseph (b. 1811, fl. 1845–50)
Philips, James (d. 1838)
Pienovi, Angelo (d. 1845)
Pierpoint, Richard (fl. 1779–1838)
Pigeon, François-Xavier (1778–1838)

Porteous, Andrew (d. 1849)
Post, Jordan (1767–1845)
Pothier, Toussaint (1771–1845)
Powell, Grant (d. 1838)
Power, Michael (1804–47)
Pozer, George (1752–1848)
Pring, Daniel (d. 1846)
Prophet. *See* Tenskwatawa
Proulx, Louis (1751–1838)
Purdy, William (1769–1847)
Purvis, Nancy (d. 1839)
Pushee, Nathan (1758–1838)
Putnam, William (d. 1838)

QUESNEL, Jules-Maurice (1786–1842)
Quirouet, François (1776–1844)

RADCLIFF, Thomas (1794–1841)
Raimbault, Jean (1770–1841)
Ramsay, George, 9th Earl of Dalhousie (1770–1838)
Randal, Stephen (1804–41)
Rankin, William (d. 1837)
Rastel de Rocheblave, Pierre de (1773–1840)
Raymond, Jean-Moïse (1787–1843)
Ready, John (d. 1845)
Reiffenstein, John Christopher (d. 1840)
Riall, Sir Phineas (1775–1850)
Richards, Jackson John (1787–1847)
Richardson, Samuel (d. 1843)
Robertson, Colin (1783–1842)
Robertson, William (1784–1844)
Robichaux, Vénérande (1753–1839)
Robinson, Peter (1785–1838)
Rodier, Édouard-Étienne (1804–40)
Roque, Jacques-Guillaume (1761–1840)
Roy, Thomas (d. 1842)
Roy-Audy, Jean-Baptiste (b. 1778, d. *c.* 1848)
Roy Portelance, Louis (1764–1838)
Ryan, John (d. 1847)
Ryland, Herman Witsius (d. 1838)

SAMSON, James Hunter (d. 1836)
Sattin, Antoine (1767–1836)
Sauvageau, Charles (d. 1849)
Sayer, Pierre-Guillaume (d. in or after 1849)
Sayre, James (1761–1849)
Schneider, Joseph (1772–1843)
Schoultz, Nils von (1807–38)
Secord, David (1759–1844)
Séguin, François-Hyacinthe (1787–1847)
Selee, Peet (1766–1844)
Sewell, Jonathan (d. 1839)
Shaw, Emily Elizabeth (Beavan) (fl. 1838–45)
Shawnee Prophet. *See* Tenskwatawa
Shea, William Richard (1813–44)
Shepard, Joseph (d. 1837)
Sherwood, Levius Peters (1777–1850)
Shirreff, Charles (1768–1847)
Signay, Joseph (1778–1850)
Sigogne, Jean-Mandé (1763–1844)
Simonds, Richard (1789–1836)
Simpson, Alexander (b. 1811, d. in or after 1845)
Skakel, Alexander (1776–1846)
Skerry, John (1763–1838)
Small Eyes. *See* Abishabis
Smith, Sir David William (1764–1837)
Smith, Titus (1768–1850)
Smith, William (1769–1847)
Smyth, Sir James Carmichael (1779–1838)
Somerville, James (1775–1837)
Sou-neh-hoo-way (Thomas Splitlog) (d. 1838)
Spragg, Joseph (1775–1848)
Sproule, Robert Auchmuty (d. 1845)
Stephenson, John (1796–1842)
Stewart, Charles James (1775–1837)
Stewart, Thomas Alexander (1786–1847)
Strange, James Charles Stuart (1753–1840)
Strange, Sir Thomas Andrew Lumisden (1756–1841)
Street, Samuel (1775–1844)
Stuart, Andrew (1785–1840)
Stuart, John (1780–1847)
Swayne, Hugh (d. 1836)
Sweetman, Pierce (d. 1841)

TALBOT, Edward Allen (d. 1839)
Tanner, John (d. in or after 1846)
Tazewell, Samuel Oliver (fl. 1820–38)
Tenskwatawa (d. 1836)
Thavenet, Jean-Baptiste (1763–1844)
Thom, Alexander (1775–1845)
Thompson, Hannah Maynard (Pickard) (1812–44)
Thompson, Toler (d. 1846)
Thomson, Charles Edward Poulett, 1st Baron Sydenham (1799–1841)
Thorne, Benjamin (1794–1848)
Thorpe, Robert (d. 1836)
Tiarks, Johann Ludwig (1789–1837)
Tobin, James (d. 1838)
Toler, Joseph (fl. 1831–42)
Tomah, Francis (fl. 1813–50)
Triaud, Louis-Hubert (1790–1836)
Troyer, John (1753–1842)

UNIACKE, Norman Fitzgerald (d. 1846)
Usborne, Henry (d. 1840)

VALENTINE, William (1798–1849)
Vallières de Saint-Réal, Joseph-Rémi (1787–1847)
Van Egmond, Anthony Jacob William Gysbert (1775–1838)
Vassal de Monviel, François (1759–1843)
Viau, Pierre (1784–1849)
Vincent, John (1764–1848)
Vincent, Nicolas (1769–1844)

Editorial Notes

PROPER NAMES

Persons have been entered under family name rather than title, pseudonym, popular name, nickname, or name in religion. Where possible the form of the surname is based on the signature, although contemporary usage is taken into account. Common variant spellings are included in parenthesis.

In the case of French names, "La," "Le," "Du," "Des," and sometimes "De" are considered part of the name and are capitalized. When both parts of the name are capitalized in the signature, French style treats the family name as two words; however, with individuals who were integrated into an anglophone milieu, this rule of style has been applied only when it was confirmed by a signature. Compound names occasionally appear: Joseph Le VASSEUR Borgia; Pierre de RASTEL de Rocheblave; cross-references are made in the text from the compounds to the main entry under the family name: from Borgia to Le Vasseur and from Rocheblave to Rastel.

Where a signature was not available for a subject whose name began with Mc or Mac, the form Mac, followed by a capital letter, has been used. Scottish-born immigrants who were entitled under Scottish law to a territorial designation as part of their names appear with that designation included, such as Angus Mackintosh* of Mackintosh, 26th Chief of Clan Chattan and 25th Chief of Clan Mackintosh, in volume VI. Scots for whom the designation was used merely as a convenient way of distinguishing one individual from another have the designation in parenthesis: Alexander MCDONELL (Collachie). Subjects are entered under their Gaelic names only when it is clear that they spoke Gaelic and moved in a Gaelic environment: Iain MACGHILLEATHAIN (John MacLean). In all cases, appropriate cross-references are provided.

Married women and *religieuses* have been entered under their maiden names, with cross-references to the entries from their husbands' names or their names in religion: Elizabeth Posthuma GWILLIM (Simcoe); Marie-Françoise HUOT, named Sainte-Gertrude.

Names of indigenous peoples have presented a particular problem, since a person might be known by his/her own name (written in a variety of ways by people unfamiliar with native languages) and by a nickname or baptismal name. Moreover, by the late 18th century some Indian families, such as the Tomahs [*see* Francis TOMAH], were beginning to use family surnames in the European style. Indian and Inuit names have been used when they could be found, and, because it is impossible to establish original spellings, the form generally chosen is the one found in standard sources or the one linguists now regard as correct; variants are included in parenthesis: SOUNEH-HOO-WAY (To-oo-troon-too-ra; baptized Thomas Splitlog); EENOOLOOAPIK (Bobbie). Unless they remained wholly within native cultures, persons of mixed blood are entered under their "European" name: John JONES. Appropriate cross-references are included.

For reference works useful in establishing the names of persons not receiving biographies in the DCB/DBC, the reader is referred to section III of the General Bibliography.

CROSS-REFERENCES WITHIN VOLUME VII

The first time the name of a person who has a biography in volume VII appears in another biography his or her family name is printed in capitals and level small capitals: Mathew BELL; Charles-Auguste-Marie-Joseph de FORBIN-JANSON.

CROSS-REFERENCES TO OTHER VOLUMES

An asterisk following a name indicates either that the person has a biography in a volume already published – Sir Isaac Brock*; Louis-Joseph Papineau* – or that he or she will receive a biography in a volume to be published – Sir Antoine-Aimé Dorion*; Sir John A. Macdonald*. Birth and death (or floruit) dates for such persons are given in the index as an indication of the volume in which the biography will be found.

PLACE-NAMES

Place-names are generally given in the form used at the time of reference; where necessary, the modern name and/or the present name of the province, territory, state, or country in which the place is located have been included in parenthesis: York (Toronto),

Norway House (Man.), Van Diemen's Land (Tasmania), and Danzig (Gdańsk, Poland). The English edition cites well-known place-names in their present-day English form: St Lawrence River, Montreal, Quebec, Marseilles, Geneva. The *Encyclopædia Britannica* has been followed in determining whether place-names outside Canada have accepted English forms. Cities considered to be easily recognizable (such as London, Paris, Rome, and Boston) are not identified by country; within Canada, provincial capitals and several well-known cities (such as Montreal and Vancouver) are not identified by province.

Many sources have been used as guides to establish 18th- and early 19th-century place-names: Bouchette, *Topographical description of L.C.*; *Canadian Encyclopedia*; *Docs. relating to NWC* (Wallace); *Encyclopædia Britannica*; *Encyclopedia Canadiana*; *HBRS* (several volumes in this series have been helpful); "Historic forts and trading posts of the French regime and of the English fur trading companies," comp. Ernest Voorhis (mimeograph, Ottawa, 1930); Hormisdas Magnan, *Dictionnaire historique et géographique des paroisses, missions et municipalités de la province de Québec* (Arthabaska, Qué., 1925); Morton, *Hist. of Canadian west* (Thomas; 1973); *Place-names of N.S.*; *Places in Ont.* (Mika); Rayburn, *Geographical names of N.B.* and *Geographical names of P.E.I.*; P.-G. Roy, *Inv. concessions*; W. H. Smith, *Canada: past, present and future . . .* (2v., Toronto, [1852]; repr. Belleville, Ont., 1973–74); J. T. Walbran, *British Columbia coast names, 1592–1906 . . .* (Ottawa, 1909; repr. Seattle, Wash., and London, 1972). For complete information about titles given in shortened form the reader is referred to the General Bibliography. The *Historical atlas of Canada* (1v. to date, Toronto, [1987]–) had not begun publication when the bulk of editorial work on volume VII was in progress.

Modern Canadian names are based whenever possible on the Gazetteer of Canada series issued by the Canadian Permanent Committee on Geographical Names, Ottawa, on the *Canada gazetteer atlas* (n.p., 1980), and on the *Répertoire toponymique du Québec* (Québec, 1979) published by the Commission de toponymie and the supplements published in the *Gazette officielle du Québec*. For places outside Canada the following have been major sources of reference: *Bartholomew gazetteer of Britain*, comp. Oliver Mason ([Edinburgh, 1977]); *Dictionnaire universel des noms propres . . . le Petit Robert 2*, Paul Robert *et al.*, édit. (3e éd., Paris, 1977); *Grand Larousse encyclopédique*; *National Geographic atlas of the world*, ed. W. E. Garrett *et al.* (5th ed., Washington, 1981).

CONTEMPORARY USAGE

To a large extent volume VII follows the practice of the 18th and early 19th centuries in referring to the French-speaking inhabitants of the province of Quebec simply as "Canadians." The term "French Canadian" began to be used in the 1820s, however, and has been employed in some texts for the sake of clarity. Readers should be aware that in the context of the fur trade the term "Canadian" is used, as it was at the time, to refer to Montreal-based traders, whether French- or English-speaking.

Useful reference works for contemporary usage are *A dictionary of Canadianisms on historical principles*, ed. W. S. Avis *et al.* (Toronto, 1967) and *Dictionary of Newfoundland English*, ed. G. M. Story *et al.* (Toronto, [1982]).

QUOTATIONS

Quotations have been translated when the language of the original passage is different from that of the text of the biography. Readers of the DCB may consult the DBC for the original French of quotations that have been translated into English. When a passage in French is quoted from a work that has appeared in both languages, the published English version is generally used. The wording, spelling, punctuation, and capitalization of original quotations are not altered unless it is necessary to do so for meaning, in which case the changes are made within square brackets. A name appearing within square brackets has been substituted for the original in order to identify the person more precisely or to indicate that he/she has a biography within the volume or in another volume.

DATES

If, in spite of assiduous inquiry, it is impossible to uncover a subject's birth and death dates, only the dates of his/her active career are documented. In the introductory paragraphs and in the various indexes the outside dates of activity are presented as floruit (fl.) dates.

BIBLIOGRAPHIES

Each biography is followed by a bibliography. Sources frequently used by authors and editors are cited in shortened form in individual bibliographies; the General Bibliography (pp.939–76) gives these sources in full. Many abbreviations are used in the individual bibliographies, especially for archival sources; a list of these can be found on p.2 and p.938.

The individual bibliographies are generally arranged alphabetically according to the five sections of the General Bibliography: manuscript sources, printed primary sources (including a section on contemporary newspapers), reference works, studies and theses, and journals. Wherever possible, manuscript material is cited under the location of the original documents; the location of copies used by contributors is included in the citation. In general, the items in individual bibliographies are the sources listed by the contributors, but these items have often been supplemented by bibliographic investigation in the DCB/DBC offices. Any special bibliographical comments by contributors appear within square brackets.

TRANSLATION INTO ENGLISH (a note by the translator of French biographies)

The translation of French-language biographies in volume VII presented similar challenges to those faced in volume VI. The existence in Quebec/Lower Canada of a British military establishment, a parliamentary system based on that in London, and a significant anglophone mercantile and entrepreneurial community resulted in the frequent use of English terms there; in translation these often had to be recognized under the French equivalents adopted in the province. The use of cognate terms or names in the two languages, particularly in the administrative and business worlds, which became fairly standard practice in the colony, normally caused little difficulty, as with the Union Company of Quebec/la Compagnie de l'Union de Québec, but required constant vigilance to discover the equivalent in the other language. The House of Assembly was officially bilingual and its statutes were a helpful source, as was the *Quebec Gazette/la Gazette de Québec*. A microfilm copy of the index to the commissions register (PAC, RG 68, General index, 1651–1841 and 1841–67) was used frequently in establishing the English form for official appointments. The maintenance of the seigneurial system and French civil law assured the continuing use of many of the French terms found regularly in previous volumes. For some of the more unfamiliar terminology in property transactions, translation was attempted, as in *la rente constituée* (secured annuity), in order to give readers at least an idea of the nature of the obligation involved. *A dictionary of Canadianisms on historical principles*, ed. W. S. Avis *et al.* (Toronto, 1967), was again useful in decisions relating to translation. As in volume VI the English originals of quotations in French biographies were used when available.

BIOGRAPHIES

List of Abbreviations

AAQ	Archives de l'archidiocèse de Québec	HPL	Hamilton Public Library
AC	Archives civiles	MAC-CD	Ministère des Affaires culturelles, Centre de documentation
ACAM	Archives de la chancellerie de l'archevêché de Montréal	MHA	Maritime History Archive
ACC	Anglican Church of Canada	MTRL	Metropolitan Toronto Reference Library
AD	Archives départementales	NLS	National Library of Scotland
ADB	*Australian dictionary of biography*	NMM	National Maritime Museum
ANQ	Archives nationales du Québec	NWC	North West Company
AO	Archives of Ontario	*OH*	*Ontario History*
AP	Archives paroissiales	PABC	Provincial Archives of British Columbia
ASN	Archives du séminaire de Nicolet	PAC	Public Archives of Canada/National Archives of Canada
ASQ	Archives du séminaire de Québec	PAM	Provincial Archives of Manitoba
ASSH	Archives du séminaire de Saint-Hyacinthe	PANB	Provincial Archives of New Brunswick
ASSM	Archives du séminaire de Saint-Sulpice, Montréal	PANL	Provincial Archives of Newfoundland and Labrador
ASTR	Archives du séminaire de Trois-Rivières	PANS	Public Archives of Nova Scotia
AUM	Archives de l'université de Montréal	PAPEI	Public Archives of Prince Edward Island
AVQ	Archives de la ville de Québec	PRO	Public Record Office
BL	British Library	QUA	Queen's University Archives
BRH	*Le Bulletin des recherches historiques*	*RHAF*	*Revue d'histoire de l'Amérique française*
BVM-G	Bibliothèque de la ville de Montréal, Salle Gagnon	RHL	Rhodes House Library
CCHA	Canadian Catholic Historical Association	RSC	Royal Society of Canada
CHA	Canadian Historical Association	SGCF	Société généalogique canadienne-française
CHR	*Canadian Historical Review*	*SH*	*Social History*
CTA	City of Toronto Archives	SOAS	School of Oriental and African Studies
DAB	*Dictionary of American biography*	SPG	Society for the Propagation of the Gospel in Foreign Parts
DBF	*Dictionnaire de biographie française*	SRO	Scottish Record Office
DCB	*Dictionary of Canadian biography*	UCC	United Church of Canada
DHB	*Dictionary of Hamilton biography*	UNBL	University of New Brunswick Library
DNB	*Dictionary of national biography*	UTFL	University of Toronto, Thomas Fisher Rare Book Library
DOLQ	*Dictionnaire des œuvres littéraires du Québec*	UWOL	University of Western Ontario Library
DPL	Detroit Public Library		
GRO	General Register Office		
HBC	Hudson's Bay Company		
HBCA	Hudson's Bay Company Archives		
HBRS	Hudson's Bay Record Society, *Publications*		

Biographies

A

ABISHABIS (Small Eyes), Cree religious leader; d. 30 Aug. 1843 at Severn House (Fort Severn, Ont.).

In 1842 and 1843 a powerful religious movement spread rapidly among the Cree Indians between Fort Churchill (Man.) and the Moose River (Ont.). The meteoric rise and downfall of its principal prophet, Abishabis, are traceable in some detail in contemporary Hudson's Bay Company post journals and correspondence and in the records of George Barnley, Methodist missionary at Moose Factory.

Unusual religious activity among the Crees was first recorded at Churchill and Severn in late 1842, coincident with the spreading influence of Methodist missionary James EVANS, who had been based at Norway House (Man.) since 1840. On 4 Sept. 1842 John Cromartie at Severn, for example, noted that the Indians gathered there "have been a pest to me . . . with their psalm Singing and painting Books that has been all there occupation this three weeks Back." On 15 September they were "doing nothing But Roaring and Singing night and day in place of hunting Geese." By late October more Indians had assembled, "making the woods to Ring . . . with musick and at the Same time they have Empty Stomacks and I am afraid it will be the Case with them after this if they Continue as they have done all the Fall."

On 6 Oct. 1842 Barnley at Moose Factory also encountered manifestations of religious excitement, this time linked explicitly with the activities of Evans. Two visiting Indians from Severn asked him to "decypher a piece of writing the work of an Indian. . . . and the characters employed those of the Rev J Evans' invention." Unfamiliar at the time with Evans's new syllabic writing system, Barnley failed, and thus may have enhanced the influence of those Crees who did grasp it. He later recorded how Abishabis and his associates elaborated their symbolic repertoire further with other texts and charts, and pictographs on wood.

The movement spread during the winter of 1842–43. Its strength was manifest at Fort Albany when the Indians gathered there in the spring. George Barnston*, officer in charge, thought it necessary to address his hunters on 8 June 1843 about Abishabis (who was being called Jesus Christ) and Wasiteck ("the Light") "who they believe have been in heaven, and returned to bring blessings and Knowledge to their Brethren." He asserted that "the Imposters . . . were assuming characters which were known to the Indians at first only by the preaching of the Missionaries" and that these leaders' claims – notably, of being able to map the "Track to Heaven" with lines drawn on paper or wood – were false and "wiles of the Devil." The Indians then told him they would give up "these foolish notions," and a paper portraying the road to heaven was handed to Barnston for burning by "the priestess, an elderly woman who walked from York last fall." The concern of Barnston and other HBC men about the movement was twofold: first, it distracted its converts from hunting furs so that the trade suffered; and second, some adherents reportedly were so absorbed by their new faith that they gave up all other activity and starved, as did one Albany Indian who, said Barnston, "depended on the *Charts* that he had in his possession, of the roads leading to Heaven and to hell for all his wants. On these unmeaning scratches – traced on wood or paper – . . . he did not cease to look from the moment he pitched his tent in the fall to the hour of his death."

In mid 1843 the movement became less visible in the Churchill–York area, owing in part to HBC pressures against it. Abishabis himself was said to be losing influence. As a prophet, he had gathered "tithes of clothing, arms and ammunition" in great quantities from his followers, according to James Hargrave*. When, however, he also demanded five or six wives from them, "some giving their daughters and others being obliged to surrender their wives," along with more goods, support weakened and during the spring of 1843 reports reached Hargrave at York Factory of his being "in a state of as great beggary as that from which he had at first arisen."

In July 1843 Abishabis, alienated and desperate, murdered an Indian family in the York Factory area and stole their goods, evidently to support himself on a trip to his home district of Severn. He reached Severn House on 9 August and was put in irons three days later by John Cromartie; the local Indians, knowing of his crime, were "making Complaints that he was threatning them if they Did not Comply with his Requests in Giving him food &c and in fact they was afraid to leave Place while he was hear." On 13 August he was allowed to escape, Cromartie hoping that he would "Leave the quarter when liberatted." He left but briefly; on 28 August he was in custody again. On 30 August, three of his countrymen resolved to mete out their own justice to him; they dragged him from confinement, knocked his brains out with an axe, and burned the body on a nearby island, "to secure themselves against being haunted by a 'windigo'" (a cannibalistic spirit associated with dangerous human beings).

In the Albany area his movement retained adherents through much of the next winter, especially among inland Indians unaware of his death. Thomas Corcoran, in charge at Albany, warned his colleagues at Moose Factory and Martin Falls (Ont.) to watch for its appearance and he complained to Governor Sir George Simpson* of its effects on his trade. Assured by Hargrave that the death of Abishabis had "entirely tranquilized the ferment" in the north, Simpson advised Corcoran that he now saw little cause for concern.

The movement was not forgotten, however, among the Crees. In February 1844, after an absence from Moose, Barnley returned to find the Indians under its "pernicious influence." In August he heard that "The Severn system of folly and falsehood" was spreading among the Crees of the Eastmain (Que.). At Norway House in the winter of 1847–48, the Reverend William Mason encountered a Cree, James Nanoo, who described himself as a minister ordained in the new faith. But Indian awareness of both HBC and missionary disapproval of the movement seems to have led most adherents to conceal their creative synthesis of Cree and Christian religion, and further written references are scarce. In the 1930s, however, anthropologist John Montgomery Coôper found that his Moose Factory informants had vivid oral traditions about the movement. Its expressed meaning, though, had been modified. They recollected nothing about Barnley, first missionary at Moose, except his surname and credited Abishabis and his associates with introducing them to Christianity.

JENNIFER S. H. BROWN

PAC, MG 19, A21, James Hargrave corr., Robert Harding to Hargrave, 23 June 1843; MG 24, J40 (mfm.). PAM, HBCA, B.3/a/148: f.22; 149: f.30; B.3/b/70: 9–10, 19, 27, 45; B.42/a/177: ff.3, 6, 17; B.198/a/84: ff.9–10, 13; 85: ff.5–6, 8, 13; B.239/a/157: f.50; 163: f.4; D.5/9: ff.308–9. SOAS, Methodist Missionary Soc. Arch., Wesleyan Methodist Missionary Soc., corr., Canada, William Mason, "Extracts from my journal," 1847–48 (mfm. at UCC-C). UWOL, Regional Coll., James Evans papers. J. S. H. Brown, "The track to heaven: the Hudson's Bay Cree religious movement of 1842–1843," *Papers of the thirteenth Algonquian conference*, ed. William Cowan (Ottawa, 1982), 53–63. J. S. Long, "'Shaganash': early Protestant missionaries and the adoption of Christianity by the Western James Bay Cree, 1840–1893" (D.ED. thesis, Univ. of Toronto, 1986). J. M. Cooper, "The Northern Algonquian Supreme Being," *Primitive Man* (Washington), 6 (1933): 41–111. N. J. Williamson, "Abishabis the Cree," *Studies in Religion* (Waterloo, Ont.), 9 (1980): 217–41.

ABRAMS, WILLIAM, businessman, JP, judge, office holder, and militia officer; b. *c.* 1785 in Plymouth, England; m. 1807 Sarah Trigholon, and they had two sons and eight daughters; d. 6 Feb. 1844 in Newcastle, N.B.

In 1818 William Abrams, who was in business in Greenock, Scotland, decided to open a trading establishment in the Miramichi region of New Brunswick. In February 1819 he leased some stores there for 12 months and sailed immediately for Miramichi, followed shortly afterwards by his family; they settled at Rosebank (Nordin). Within four weeks of his arrival he had purchased property to the value of over £1,300 and had established the firm of William Abrams and Company. His five partners in this venture were all resident in Scotland. After the firm was dissolved in 1830, Abrams continued in business by himself until his death.

The company had stores in both Chatham and Newcastle, but its principal establishment was at Rosebank, where Abrams had two large stores and a successful shipyard. He brought out skilled craftsmen from Scotland, and by 1825 he headed the largest shipbuilding establishment on the river. Unfortunately there are no records of vessels built before 1822, but in the years 1822–32 he built 12 ships valued at £34,570, and between 1833 and his death he built at least 15. He had two ships on the stocks at the time of the Miramichi fire in October 1825; both were destroyed along with his stores and goods worth £9,354. His total losses were estimated at £40,000, the same as those of Gilmour, Rankin and Company, the largest timber exporter in the region. More distressing were the deaths of two of his children from burns and exposure.

Abrams served with Alexander Rankin*, Francis PEABODY, and others on the relief committee aiding those who had suffered in the fire, and he set about rebuilding his business. In 1826 he launched the *Phoenix* from his re-established shipyard at Rosebank. His master builder was John Harley*. In 1834 Harley built two vessels for Abrams without the "use of ardent spirits"; it had previously been the practice to pay the men part of their wages in liquor, which was drunk on the job.

Abrams was active in the community as well as in business. He was appointed a justice of the peace in 1821 and a justice of the Inferior Court of Common Pleas in 1824. One of the organizers of the Miramichi Chamber of Commerce, he was elected its president in 1826. In 1828 he was a member of the Chatham Joint

Stock Company, which was organized to sell land in the town plot. Two years later he became a commissioner of the Seaman's Hospital in Douglastown (of which his son-in-law John Thomson* would be superintendent for many years). A commissioner for the lighthouse to be built on St Paul's Island in 1830, he would join Rankin and Joseph Cunard* in supervising the construction of another lighthouse at Point Escuminac in 1841. He was a captain in the 2nd Battalion of the Northumberland County militia in the early 1830s, and harbour-master of Miramichi from 1832 to 1835. In 1833 he was appointed to the Northumberland County Board of Health and also made commissioner of buoys for the port, harbour, and river of Miramichi. Active in establishing a branch of the Bank of British North America at Newcastle in 1836, he was also, along with his fellow shipbuilder Joseph Russell*, a promoter of the unsuccessful Miramichi Bank in the late 1830s. He was involved as well in local agricultural societies and gave land to Chatham for the establishment of a hospital.

Abrams's only venture into politics came in 1827 when he stood for one of the two Northumberland County seats in the House of Assembly. His opponents were Rankin and Richard SIMONDS, both of whom were personal friends. Soundly defeated, he never ran for office again.

Abrams was a successful merchant and community leader as well as one of the most important of the early shipbuilders in New Brunswick.

W. A. SPRAY

Northumberland Land Registry Office (Newcastle, N.B.), Registry books, 14: 248–50; 15: 116–19; 27: 437–46; 30: 193–95; 31: 309–13 (mfm. at PANB). PANB, MC 216/15, notes on William Abrams [Full of errors. W.A.S.]; RG 3, RS538, B5; RG 4, RS24, S28-P35, S36-P31; RG 10, RS108, William Abrams, 20 June 1823. Robert Cooney, *A compendious history of the northern part of the province of New Brunswick and of the district of Gaspé, in Lower Canada* (Halifax, 1832; repub. Chatham, N.B., 1896), 86, 96, 109. [Beamish Murdoch], *A narrative of the late fires at Miramichi, New Brunswick* ... (Halifax, 1825), 17, 28, 43. *Gleaner* (Miramichi [Chatham]), 14 Sept. 1830; 15 Feb., 2 Aug. 1831; 28 Feb., 3 April, 5 June 1832; 7 May 1833; 13 May 1834; 19 May, 8 Sept. 1835; 19 Dec. 1837; 7 Feb. 1844. *Mercury*, 21 Feb. 1826; 5, 26 June, 3 July 1827. *Royal Gazette* (Fredericton), 7 April, 8 Sept. 1830; 17 April 1833; 18 July 1838. J. A. Fraser, *By favourable winds: a history of Chatham, New Brunswick* ([Chatham], 1975), 30, 56, 60, 140, 157–58, 170–71. Louise Manny, *Ships of Miramichi: a history of shipbuilding on the Miramichi River, New Brunswick, Canada, 1773–1919* (Saint John, N.B., 1960).

ACHESON, ARCHIBALD, 2nd Earl of GOSFORD, colonial administrator; b. 1 Aug. 1776 in Ireland, eldest son of Arthur Acheson, 1st Earl of Gosford, and Millicent Pole; m. 20 July 1805 Mary Sparrow in London, and they had one son and two daughters; d. 27 March 1849 at his estate in Markethill (Northern Ireland).

Archibald Acheson came from a family of Scottish Protestant origin settled in Ireland since 1610. Like the sons of many Irish peers, he received an English education, the University of Oxford awarding him a BA in 1796 and an MA the following year. During the suppression of the Irish rebellion of 1798 he served as a lieutenant-colonel in the militia of County Armagh (Northern Ireland). That year he was elected to the Irish House of Commons from the family seat in this county. In 1800 he vainly opposed the act uniting Ireland and Great Britain, by the terms of which he became a member of the British House of Commons in 1801. He surrendered his seat in 1807 on succeeding his father as Earl of Gosford, and in 1811 he was elected to the House of Lords as an Irish representative peer. A brother-in-law of Lord William Cavendish Bentinck, he was connected to a powerful Whig family, and he consistently supported the Whigs in parliament. After they came to power, he received several appointments.

Although Gosford had been born into the Protestant establishment and defended "the Protestant cause," he favoured sharing power in Ireland with the Catholic majority. In 1825 he opposed a bill to outlaw the Catholic Association, led by Daniel O'Connell. Four years later he voted for Catholic emancipation, and in 1833 he defended the Whig government's assault on the privileges of the established Church of Ireland. He also supported the Whig program of introducing more Catholics into the magistracy. Known as "a good hearted, amiable and liberal gentleman," he voted for the Reform Bill of 1832 and in 1833 with the minority for the emancipation of the Jews. He was an outspoken critic of the Orange order, which he blamed for much of the religious friction in Ireland. As lord lieutenant of County Armagh from 1831 he sought to preserve peace, at a time of increasing violence, by relying on the recently formed Irish constabulary rather than on regular troops. Accused in the Commons of showing favouritism to Catholics, he was defended by Joseph Hume and by O'Connell, who declared that he had displayed "a total absence of party spirit." Since the Whigs depended on the radicals and the Irish party in that house, Gosford's popularity with both groups partly explains his appointment on 1 July 1835 as governor-in-chief of British North America. But he was also selected because the ministers hoped that he might be able to apply in Lower Canada the techniques of conciliation that he had employed so successfully in Ireland. For agreeing to accept the appointment he had been made Baron Worlingham in the United Kingdom peerage on 13 June.

A civilian, unlike his predecessors, Gosford was

not made commander of the forces in the Canadas, but he was given unusually extensive authority over the lieutenant governors of the neighbouring colonies, who were sent copies of his instructions. He was also placed at the head of a commission of inquiry into political problems in Lower Canada, on which his colleagues were Sir Charles Edward Grey, a former judge in India, and Sir George Gipps, who had served in the West Indies; Thomas Frederick Elliot, in charge of the North American Department at the Colonial Office, was seconded as secretary and became in everything but name a fourth commissioner. Their instructions from the colonial secretary, Lord Glenelg, emphasized that the commissioners were on a "mission of peace and conciliation." The function of the commission was to find a solution to the conflict between the executive and the House of Assembly which had virtually paralysed government in Lower Canada, although interference by King William IV limited the freedom of action of the commissioners by preventing them from discussing the merits of making the Legislative Council an elective body.

Gosford assumed control of the government of Lower Canada on 24 Aug. 1835. Because his predecessor, Lord Aylmer [WHITWORTH-AYLMER], had become identified with the English, or Constitutionalist, party, Gosford kept his distance from Aylmer until the latter's departure the following month. Subsequently he held a series of lavish dinner parties and balls, at which he established a reputation as a *bon vivant* and showered his attentions on the leading members of the Patriote party and their wives. Viewed with suspicion by many Patriotes, Gosford was nevertheless sufficiently popular when the assembly met in October 1835 to prevent their leader, Louis-Joseph Papineau*, from persuading the house to disband until all of the points in the 92 Resolutions were conceded. His speech opening the legislature had promised reforms "with alacrity, impartiality and firmness." During the session he responded favourably to 67 of the 72 addresses of the assembly and reserved only 1 of 59 bills. For his actions he was castigated in the anglophone press – particularly by the editor of the *Montreal Herald*, Adam Thom*, in a series of abusive "Anti-Gallic" letters. Yet Papineau and his followers were annoyed when Gosford refused to dismiss a number of unpopular officials until a full and impartial investigation had been made of their conduct. None the less, Gosford did succeed in co-opting the support of a number of moderate Patriotes [*see* George Vanfelson*], and he predicted that the assembly would vote supplies.

This assumption lay behind the first report of the Gosford commissioners, in January 1836, dealing with the critical issue of colonial finances. The report was drafted by Gipps, Gosford's intermediary in negotiations with the Patriotes over supplies and a dominant figure on the commission. Believing "the inordinate power" of the assembly to have grown out of "unwise resistance" to that house on untenable points, Gipps recommended that all crown revenues be surrendered to the assembly in return for an extremely modest civil list. In what was to become a familiar pattern, the commissioners divided; Gosford and Elliot endorsed the proposal, but Grey insisted that a much larger civil list was necessary to secure the independence of the executive and to quiet the legitimate fears of the British minority. The assembly never seriously considered the report. Early in 1836 the newly appointed lieutenant governor of Upper Canada, Sir Francis Bond Head*, released to the Upper Canadian assembly his text of Gosford's instructions. When it became known in Lower Canada that the commissioners could not accept an elective legislative council or surrender the revenues of the crown unconditionally, many moderate Patriotes drifted back into Papineau's fold. In February the feelings of the assembly "underwent a sudden change"; the house refused to vote arrears in salary due to office holders, who had gone unpaid for nearly three years, passed a six-month supply bill so objectionable that it was inevitably rejected by the Legislative Council, and reiterated its commitment to the 92 Resolutions. In March Papineau and his supporters withdrew, leaving the assembly without a quorum. Gosford prorogued the legislature on 21 March and used the casual and territorial revenues to defray the most pressing expenses. A satisfactory adjustment of the financial crisis was, he admitted, "as distant and more hopeless than ever."

The second report of the commissioners, prepared in mid March 1836, reflected this gloomy prognosis. They realistically predicted that the assembly would never vote supplies unless all its demands were met, but felt that to yield to those demands would establish "a French republic in Canada." Consequently they recommended that the Revenue Act of 1831, which had surrendered to the legislature control over the substantial revenues reserved to the crown by the Quebec Revenue Act of 1774, should be repealed to place at the disposal of the executive sufficient funds to carry on the essential services of government. The commissioners disagreed over the details; Gosford, Gipps, and Elliot believed that repeal should be for a limited time to persuade the assembly to reconsider its position, while Grey wished to make it indefinite. In London, Lord Howick, the secretary at war who, as colonial under-secretary in 1831, had drafted the bill and guided it through parliament, coerced Glenelg into refusing to repeal the act. Howick felt that the divisions among the commissioners had destroyed their usefulness, but he failed to persuade cabinet either to replace them with "a really able Governor" having large powers and clear instructions or to issue them with instructions that offered a better chance of successful negotiations with the assembly. Howick's negative influence left Gosford at the mercy of the assembly for supplies but unable to accept its conditions for a supply bill.

Gosford persevered in efforts at conciliation. In February 1836 he appointed Elzéar BÉDARD, who had moved the Patriote party's 92 Resolutions in the assembly, to a vacant judgeship, even though Bédard ranked 24th in seniority among lawyers at the bar. That April he submitted to Glenelg a list of ten candidates for the Legislative Council; seven were drawn from the majority party in the assembly. He also wished to alter the membership of the Executive Council, in which he had little confidence. At the beginning of May the commissioners, in their third report, rejected the concept that the Executive Council should be responsible to the assembly but suggested that its members should hold office at the discretion of the governor and not during good behaviour. As usual, Grey dissented; he feared that such a measure would force the governor to select his advisers from the dominant party in the assembly. Wishing to restructure the council immediately, on 5 May Gosford submitted to Glenelg a list of 14 candidates, including such prominent Patriotes as René-Édouard Caron*, Hector-Simon HUOT, Pierre-Dominique DEBARTZCH, and Augustin-Norbert Morin*, all moderate Patriotes with the possible exception of Morin, who, increasingly, was adopting Papineau's views. During the summer of 1836, while awaiting the results of his recommendations, Gosford embarked upon an extensive tour of the province, and he reported that "I never was in a Country where comfort was so generally diffused & its inhabitants so peaceable, happy, & contented." When Glenelg's instructions arrived, Gosford learned to his dismay that the colonial secretary would make no changes in the councils before the commissioners had completed their investigations and a comprehensive settlement could be offered to the assembly. On 22 September Gosford reconvened the legislature but on the 30th the assembly adjourned its proceedings until all its demands were met. Gosford prorogued the legislature and pointed out to Glenelg that important acts dealing with trade and banking would expire unless the imperial government intervened.

On 15 Nov. 1836 the Gosford commissioners completed their final report. They concluded that Britain would not be justified in altering the electoral system in the colony to increase the number of British representatives in the assembly. On the other hand, they insisted that since an elective legislative council was opposed by the British and would not, alone, satisfy the French Canadians, only minor reforms and new appointments should be made. Aware that this decision would antagonize the assembly, the commissioners reiterated that the Revenue Act of 1831 must be repealed to provide the executive with funds. They also recommended that parliament reject the extreme demands of the assembly. Predictably, Grey submitted his own report, arguing for substantial change in the electoral system to give greater weight in the assembly to the British minority.

After a lengthy debate, the cabinet accepted the Gosford commission's recommendations except that for repeal of the revenue act. On 6 March 1837 Lord John Russell introduced into the Commons ten resolutions embodying the government's program. They combined a small dose of coercion with a substantial measure of conciliation. The government did not ask parliament to give the executive a permanent source of revenue but only authority to pay from the colonial treasury arrears owed to civil servants. Glenelg promised that in future only the casual and territorial revenues would be used to defray expenses for which the assembly would not provide. The only other interference with the powers of the assembly was to be a measure extending the duration of unrenewed commercial and banking laws. Several resolutions, such as a promise not to establish land companies without the approval of the assembly, emphasized the government's desire to reach an accommodation. Although the government declared its opposition to an elected legislative council and a responsible executive council, it promised to implement the reforms recommended by the Gosford commission.

In June 1837 Gosford again submitted the names of his nominees for the councils. Although he dropped several earlier candidates because of their outspoken opposition to the Russell resolutions, the majority of those he proposed were from the Patriote party, and he predicted that if these appointments were confirmed, the assembly would vote supplies. However, Glenelg's dispatch of confirmation did not reach Gosford until after the assembly, convened to give it an opportunity to vote supplies and thus forestall parliamentary appropriation of colonial funds, had met, refused supplies, and been prorogued.

Gosford was neither a good-natured incompetent nor the "vile hypocrite" that his critics proclaimed. He hoped to create in Lower Canada an alliance of moderate politicians from both parties and to hold the balance of power as the Whig administration did in Ireland between Catholics and Protestants. Whig policy there was to distribute patronage to Catholics and liberal Protestants in order to remedy an historic imbalance in the higher levels of the administration. Gosford pursued the same goal. He increased appointments of French Canadians to the judiciary and the magistracy, insisted that a chief justice and a commissioner of crown lands should be chosen from among them, and gave them a majority on the Executive Council and a virtual majority on the Legislative

Council. He substantially increased their numbers holding offices of emolument. Moreover, he refused to allow multiple office-holding, to condone nepotism, or to appoint to prominent positions persons known to be antipathetic to them. But Lower Canada was not Ireland. In the 1830s O'Connell and the Catholic élite cooperated with the Whigs because they realized that confrontation with imperial authority was doomed to fail; lacking O'Connell's understanding of imperial politics and spurred on by English radicals, such as John Arthur Roebuck*, Papineau demanded that his party be given control over the colony through the assembly, and he foolishly believed that Britain would yield. Aware of Papineau's extremism, Gosford continued efforts to undermine his leadership by persuading the élite among French Canadians that moderation and power-sharing would achieve most of their goals. He skilfully exploited divisions within the Patriote party, an alliance of regional and local politicians differing among themselves over the extent to which the party should carry confrontation. During his first year he had co-opted politicians from Quebec. He also successfully exploited antagonism between radical Patriotes and the Roman Catholic hierarchy, by working harmoniously with Jean-Jacques LARTIGUE, whom he confirmed as the first bishop of Montreal, and Ignace Bourget*, whom he approved as Lartigue's coadjutor. Yet he failed to wrest control of the assembly from Papineau, although his tactics probably helped later to limit support for rebellion.

The vacillation of the Whig government undoubtedly contributed to Gosford's failure by confirming for many Patriotes the belief that Britain would cave in. Even without this handicap, however, Gosford was unlikely to have succeeded. He had consistently underestimated support for Papineau. Moreover, after passage of the Russell resolutions, co-opting moderates was of diminishing utility since he could not appoint to office those who rejected the resolutions, and French Canadians who defended them were marked as *vendus*. By the summer of 1837 the government could no longer maintain order in the countryside. In September Gosford dismissed 18 magistrates and 35 militia officers for attending meetings at which civil disobedience was advocated. The following month he conceded that the constitution would have to be suspended, and in November he submitted his resignation and recommended that a new governor be appointed with the authority to declare martial law.

As the government lost control in the countryside, the natural alliance between the executive and the British minority reasserted itself. Gosford viewed the English party as akin to the Orange Order in Ireland. In 1835 and 1836 he had publicly denounced the organization of rifle clubs and volunteer cavalry units by Constitutionalists in Montreal and Quebec. Later, he exploited a split in the English party between supporters and opponents of the privileged position of the established church by recommending that the clergy reserves should be applied to general education and not given solely to the Church of England. However, as the magistrate system began to collapse in 1837 the English party closed ranks, shunting the moderates aside, and Gosford was increasingly urged to seek its assistance in maintaining order. Had a larger force of British troops or an equivalent to the Irish constabulary been available, he might have resisted, but the military force in the Canadas in early 1837 was only 2,400 regulars. Although at first reluctant to increase its size, Gosford used his discretionary authority in June to transfer a regiment from Nova Scotia, an action that infuriated the commander in the Canadas, Major-General Sir John Colborne*. By October Colborne too had accepted that additional troops were needed, and Gosford requested them from the Maritimes. Under pressure from his military advisers, Gosford in November unofficially sanctioned defence preparations by the British minority. Indeed, his resignation was based in part upon the knowledge that he was *persona non grata* with the English party, whose support might be needed if a rebellion took place.

On 16 Nov. 1837, convinced that the Patriotes' grievances were "mere pretexts to clothe deeper, and darker designs," Gosford reluctantly issued 26 warrants of arrest, including one for Papineau; they supplied the spark that touched off rebellion one week later at Saint-Denis, on the Richelieu [*see* Wolfred Nelson*]. In December Gosford subjected the district of Montreal to martial law. To his credit he tried to contain the forces he had been compelled to unleash. He pleaded with Colborne to revert to civil law wherever possible. In late December, when the rebellion appeared crushed, he freed 112 habitants as an act of clemency. Although he agreed to trial by court martial for rebel leaders, he urged Colborne to proceed "with the greatest possible caution." He would not allow reprisals by the English party or persecution of non-participants.

In January 1838 Gosford learned that his resignation had been accepted. By then he was an isolated and somewhat pathetic figure. His only allies and regular companions were a few moderate French Canadians, particularly Elzéar Bédard and Étienne Parent*, editor of *Le Canadien* (Québec). He felt betrayed by Glenelg. Following termination of his appointment as a special commissioner on 18 Feb. 1837, his salary alone proved unequal to his many official expenses. He suffered increasing discomfort from gout. After a delay caused by a fall on the ice, he departed on 27 Feb. 1838, when Colborne formally took control of the administration.

Back in England, Gosford was given a vote of

thanks by the Whig ministry and awarded the GCB (civil division) on 19 July 1838. He did not lose interest in Canada. On the appointment of Lord Durham [LAMBTON] as governor he commented that "a more judicious choice could not have been made." He wrote to Durham that the majority of French Canadians had not participated in the rebellion and warned against the English party. As Durham's ethnocentricity became more pronounced, Gosford criticized him bitterly for appointing to office such outspoken opponents of French Canadians as James Stuart* and Peter McGill*. Indeed, Gosford blamed the second rebellion, in the autumn of 1838, on Durham's stupidity, and he was equally critical of Colborne and "those savage Volunteers." When Colborne suspended from office three francophone judges, Bédard, Philippe Panet*, and Joseph-Rémi VALLIÈRES de Saint-Réal, Gosford defended them at the Colonial Office and arranged for each a 12-month leave of absence at full pay. He considered the union bill of 1840 "unjust" and "arbitrary" and presented in the House of Lords a petition from Lower Canada opposing it. During the 1840s his interests again focused on Ireland, where he split with O'Connell over the issue of repeal. In his declining years he devoted his primary attention to his estates.

Gosford had left Lower Canada little loved either by the British minority or by the Patriotes. The British government ignored his advice and followed the recommendations of Durham, who declared that Gosford was "utterly ignorant . . . of all that was passing around him." The assessment is unjust. Gosford had shown considerable administrative ability, more political sensitivity than his predecessors, and greater tolerance than his immediate successors. His sincerity is unquestionable. He probably did as much to limit the severity of the rebellion as it was possible to do, and if Durham had followed his advice, the second rebellion might have been considerably less bloody. That Gosford failed to achieve his goals is self-evident; that he ever had a reasonable chance of success is doubtful.

PHILLIP BUCKNER

A portrait of Archibald Acheson, 2nd Earl of Gosford, which he presented to Jean-Jacques Lartigue at the latter's request, is reproduced in Joseph Schull, *Rebellion: the rising in French Canada, 1837* (Toronto, 1971).

National Library of Ireland (Dublin), Dept. of MSS, MSS 13345–417 (Monteagle papers). NLS, Dept. of MSS, MSS 15001–195. PAC, MG 24, A17, A19, A25, A27, A40, B1, B36, B37, B126, B127, C11. PRO, CO 42/258–80; CO 43/31–33. Univ. of Durham, Dept. of Palaeography and Diplomatic (Durham, Eng.), Earl Grey papers. Camillus [Adam Thom], *Anti-Gallic letters; addressed to His Excellency, the Earl of Gosford, governor-in-chief of the Canadas* (Montreal, 1836). G.B., Parl., *Hansard's parliamentary debates* (London), [2nd] ser., 12 (1825), 3 March; 22 (1830), 26 Feb.; 3rd ser., 2 (1831), 21 Feb.; 3 (1831), 22 March; 19 (1833), 17 July; 20 (1833), 1 Aug.; 27 (1835), 14 May; House of Commons paper, 1835, 15, no.377: 229–99, *Report from the select committee appointed to inquire into the nature, character, extent and tendency of Orange lodges, associations or societies in Ireland*. . . . L.-J.-A. Papineau, *Journal d'un Fils de la liberté*. *Quebec Gazette*, 14 Oct. 1835; 4, 8 Jan. 1836. *Times* (London), 7 April 1836, 30 March 1849. *Vindicator and Canadian Advertiser*, 30 Oct. 1835. *Burke's peerage* (1970). *Complete baronetage*, ed. G. E. Cokayne (5v., Exeter, Eng., 1900–6). *DNB*. R. B. Mosse, *The parliamentary guide: a concise history of the members of both houses* (London, 1835). George Bell, *Rough notes by an old soldier, during fifty years' service, from Ensign G.B. to Major-General C.B.* (2v., London, 1867). G. C. Bolton, *The passing of the Irish Act of Union: a study in parliamentary politics* (London, 1966). Buckner, *Transition to responsible government*. Chaussé, *Jean-Jacques Lartigue*. Christie, *Hist. of L.C.* (1848–55), vols. 3–4. G. P. Judd, *Members of parliament, 1734–1832* (Hamden, Conn., 1972). W. E. Lecky, *A history of Ireland in the eighteenth century* (new ed., 5v., London, 1892), 4: 320–21. R. B. McDowell, *Public opinion and government policy in Ireland, 1801–1846* (London, 1952). Ouellet, *Lower Canada* . Claude Thibault, "The Gosford commission, 1835–1837, and the French Canadians" (MA thesis, Bishop's Univ., Lennoxville, Que., 1963). Léon Pouliot, "Lord Gosford et Mgr Lartigue," *CHR*, 46 (1965): 238–46.

ADONWENTISHON (Ahdohwahgeseon). *See* OHTOWAˀKÉHSON

AINSLIE, GEORGE ROBERT, army officer and colonial administrator; b. 1776 near Edinburgh, eldest son of Philip Ainslie and Elizabeth Gray, daughter of Lord Gray; m. 17 Dec. 1802 Sophia Charlotte Nevile, niece of the 4th Earl of Gainsborough, and they had two sons and three daughters; d. 16 April 1839 in Edinburgh.

George Robert Ainslie entered the army as an ensign in the 19th Foot in 1793 and then served in Flanders. That same year he joined the 85th Foot as a lieutenant, and he was given a company on 15 April 1794. He served in the Netherlands, initially on Walcheren and after September 1794 on the Waal River, fighting against the French in these areas until 1799, when he was promoted major. Ainslie failed to distinguish himself in the expedition to northern Holland that year, and in January 1800 he was given the position of lieutenant-colonel in the Birmingham Fencibles, a non-regular unit. Despite his family connections his career did not advance until 1807, when he was reappointed to the regular army as a lieutenant-colonel, first in the 5th Garrison Battalion and then in the 25th Foot. On 25 July 1810 Ainslie was promoted brevet colonel.

Though Ainslie had no administrative experience, he used his family influence to obtain in 1812 the governorship of St Eustatius, in the Leeward Islands;

two months after his appointment he became lieutenant governor of Grenada. Made brigadier-general the same year, he was named governor of Dominica in April 1813. The appointment to Dominica proved unfortunate. Ainslie had an excitable temperament which did not fit him for civil administration, and he was reprimanded for suspending the secretary and registrar of the colony. More serious, he reacted with undue violence towards a maroon uprising by beheading one of the leaders and threatening to kill all runaway men, women, and children. There was an outcry in parliament, and Whitehall recalled him within a year of his appointment. In retribution he was forced to accept an inferior post, lieutenant governor of Cape Breton.

Though he was the tenth head of the colony, which had been founded in 1784, Ainslie was only the third lieutenant governor; his predecessor as lieutenant governor, William Macarmick*, had held the office *in absentia* from his departure in 1795 until his death in 1815, a succession of administrators taking his place. Ainslie was deeply disappointed by the posting, and he had had to accept a drastic reduction in pay. Moreover, his liver was in poor condition and he had amaurosis, a partial blindness – ailments which he blamed on over-exposure to the tropical sun. Since snow glare exacerbated his eye complaint, Cape Breton can hardly have appealed to him. Though he was offered the lieutenant governorship in December 1815 he did not reach Sydney until 4 Nov. 1816, having found his own passage via Paris, Amsterdam, and Halifax. His tardy arrival allowed a crisis to develop which would eventually destroy the colony.

In September 1815 Colonel Jonas Fitzherbert, the commander of the garrison, had become administrator. A former attorney general, Richard Collier Bernard DesBarres Marshall Gibbons, took advantage of Fitzherbert's lack of administrative experience to circulate a petition which demanded that a house of assembly be called. The colony had been granted an assembly at its inception, but none had ever been called because most of the island's administrators considered it could not draw upon sufficient financial resources or educated electors. The result was that no taxes had been collected until a duty on imported rum was imposed by John Despard* in 1801. The colonial élite continued to be divided over the legality of this tax, opposition to it being headed by Gibbons. In 1813 Hugh SWAYNE, the administrator, had forced Gibbons to resign as attorney general, thus putting a temporary end to the debate. Unlike Swayne, Fitzherbert was not concerned by the pro-assembly movement, and he treated Gibbons's petition lightly. Since he had suffered no reprisals, Gibbons went further and persuaded his ally Ranna Cossit, the assistant collector of the rum tax, to cease collections in June 1816. Fitzherbert realized that matters were out of hand and in August threatened Cossit with removal. Cossit backed down and began collecting taxes again, including those unpaid in the interim. The operators of the island's coal mines, Ritchie and Leaver, refused to pay the back taxes, and Fitzherbert had no alternative but to take the firm to court. There the chief justice, Archibald Charles Dodd*, agreed with the firm's lawyer, Gibbons, that taxes were illegal in Cape Breton because they had not been authorized by an assembly.

Ainslie, arriving in the midst of this crisis, found that the collection of revenues had been halted by Dodd's decision just when money was badly needed to assist destitute settlers because of the "summerless year" of 1816, when snow and frost had struck during the growing season. He could only beg the Colonial Office for assistance, which was not forthcoming. When in 1817 he began to collect a duty on exports of gypsum in order to raise funds, Gibbons protested. Ainslie's temper flared, and he asserted his authority by decreeing that Executive Council meetings would be rigidly structured and the powers of councillors limited. He dismissed from office and council, as in Dominica, those who questioned his decisions, including Thomas H. Crawley, the long-serving surveyor general, and Richard Stout*, the colony's most important merchant. There was soon warfare between Ainslie and almost all local officials, who, despite political differences, banded together against their common enemy. Ainslie could thus accomplish very little, and by 1818 he was complaining that the colonials were "linked together by . . . Roguery." Cape Bretoners also complained, probably hoping that Ainslie's reputation would lend credence to their arguments.

In the mean time, in April 1818 Gibbons had presented to parliament a petition for an assembly which claimed that all ordinances of the Executive Council were illegal since an assembly had never been called to approve them. The colonial secretary, Lord Bathurst, asked the English law officers to determine if Gibbons's position was justified, and was told it was. Ainslie, however, had previously asserted that the people of Cape Breton were too poor and illiterate to support an assembly. It was therefore decided that the colony would receive representative government by being reannexed to Nova Scotia.

When he was secretly informed of the plan early in 1819, Ainslie reacted with delight. He deeply disliked the islanders, seeing them as "the refuse of the 3 Kingdoms," and hoped that reannexation would lessen their "petty importance." His existence must have been miserable when word of the impending takeover was made public in Sydney, but permission for him to leave came too late in 1819 and he did not depart until June 1820. On 16 Oct. 1820 Lieutenant Governor Sir James Kempt* of Nova Scotia officially proclaimed the end of Cape Breton as a separate colony.

After arriving in England, Ainslie sought a retirement allowance of £500 out of the revenue from the Cape Breton coal mines, but the pension was refused because of official disapproval of his conduct in the colony. His failures haunted him for the rest of his life, and though he was promoted lieutenant-general in May 1825 he obtained no further employment. He used his leisure to pursue his hobby of numismatics, and published in 1830 a magnificent quarto volume entitled *Illustrations of the Anglo-French coinage*.

It is obvious that Ainslie was better suited to learned pursuits than to military life or to colonial administration. The industry and zeal he displayed in his study of coins soured to impatience, irascibility, and vituperation when he was dealing with people. In Dominica this attribute brought on a public outcry, and in Cape Breton it precipitated the long-delayed decision on the political fate of the island. His tenure represented a bitter end to Cape Breton's existence as a separate colony.

R. J. MORGAN

George Robert Ainslie is the author of *Illustrations of the Anglo-French coinage: taken from the cabinet of a fellow of the antiquarian societies of London, and Scotland; of the royal societies of France, Normandy, and many others, British as well as foreign* . . . (London, 1830).

PRO, CO 217/134–36, 217/138–39. *Annual reg.* (London), 1839: 333. *Gentleman's Magazine*, January–June 1814: 509. *DNB*. *The royal military calendar, containing the service of every general officer in the British army, from the date of their first commission* . . . , ed. John Philippart (3v., London, 1815–[16]), vols.2–3.

AISANCE (Aisaince, Ascance, Essens), JOHN, Ojibwa chief; b. *c.* 1790; d. in the summer of 1847 near Penetanguishene, Upper Canada.

In a treaty of 1798 by which Ojibwas ceded the territory around Penetanguishene (Penetang) Harbour to the crown, the name "Aasance" appears beside the mark of a head man of the otter clan. He was probably the father of John Aisance, described as "Young Aisaince" in the account of a council meeting conducted by officials of the Indian Department in 1811. At this ceremony land for a "wider and better path" to the king's "western children" was requested. John Aisance agreed, but asked that his people be allowed to maintain their gardens at Penetanguishene Harbour until the plots were needed by whites.

Aisance may have served the crown in the War of 1812, for it was noted in later years that he possessed a military medal. He was one of three principal men who in 1815 ratified a treaty ceding a 250,000-acre tract between Kempenfelt and Nottawasaga bays. Thirteen years later he embraced Christianity at a Methodist camp meeting. Upon his conversion he was asked to part with two of his three wives. Aisance complied, but maintained responsibility for all his children. One, John Jr, was conducting official business on behalf of the otter clan as early as 1831.

The conversion of Aisance in 1828 was part of a wave of Methodist enthusiasm which was sweeping through the Indian population of Upper Canada. Also affected were chiefs William Yellowhead [Musquakie*] and William Snake, whose people lived in close association with those of Aisance. Soon all three groups hosted active Methodist missions. These developments attracted the interest of Lieutenant Governor Sir John Colborne*. After 1830 the Upper Canadian government emphasized the settling of native groups on particular plots of land, their instruction in agriculture, and their conversion to Christianity. To help realize this aim of "civilizing" the natives, Colborne established an Indian Department station at Coldwater, around which Aisance's people developed farms with the help of the government. At the Narrows (Orillia), those who followed chiefs Yellowhead and Snake were engaged in similar activities.

Aisance soon was at odds with Thomas Gummersall Anderson*, superintendent of the Coldwater station. In 1831 the chief accused Anderson of misappropriating the payments owed his people by the crown. Anderson retaliated, characterizing Aisance as a "worthless savage" and a "great rascal." The animosity was connected with growing hostility between Methodist missionaries at Coldwater and the Narrows and the tory members of the Indian Department. These tensions Aisance partly escaped when he renounced Methodism in 1832 and joined the Roman Catholic Church. His conversion was probably influenced by the concurrent arrival in the area of Jean-Baptiste Assignack*, a devoutly Catholic Ottawa Indian who had won much fame as a warrior and orator.

Aisance served the crown loyally in the Upper Canadian uprising of 1837, leading 21 warriors into the field. He did so notwithstanding his community's sense of betrayal upon finding itself landless after the surrender of the tract from Coldwater to the Narrows, one of several territorial cessions secured from Indians by Lieutenant Governor Sir Francis Bond Head* in 1836. Evidence of fraud in the transaction is to be found in an address made six years later to Sir Charles BAGOT by Aisance and several other chiefs. They asserted that "when Sir F Bond Head insisted on our selling this Land . . . we were not made sensible of the full purport, so that we knew not the nature of the bargain."

Aisance's people remained unsettled until 1842, when land was made available for them on Beausoleil Island, in Georgian Bay. As early as 1844, however, the chief sent a group of Potawatomi Indians who were closely associated with him to hold territory on nearby Christian Island in case it should be needed by his people. This precaution indeed proved sound, since the soil at Beausoleil was not fertile. Aisance's band thus settled at Christian Island in 1856, where they remain still. By the time of this move, Aisance had been dead for nine years. Methodist sources indicate that he fell from a canoe while intoxicated. Throughout his life, he had seen his authority as a hereditary chief increasingly undermined by government and ecclesiastical officials who sought to direct the lives of Indian people.

ANTHONY J. HALL

Arch. of the Roman Catholic Archdiocese of Toronto, M (Macdonell papers), AC14.02 (mfm. at AO). PAC, RG 10, A2, 27; A4, 47, 51, 64, 68, 499. Private arch., A. J. Hall (Sudbury, Ont.), Mathew King papers. Aborigines' Protection Soc., *Report on the Indians of Upper Canada* ([London, 1839]), 21. Can., Prov. of, Legislative Assembly, *App. to the journals*, 1844–45, app.EEE, sect.II, no.1. *Canada, Indian treaties and surrenders* . . . [1680–1906] (3v., Ottawa, 1891–1912; repr. Toronto, 1971), 1: 15–17, 42–43, 203–5. *Muskoka and Haliburton, 1615–1875; a collection of documents*, ed. F. B. Murray ([Toronto], 1963), 115–16. J. [S.] Carroll, *Case and his cotemporaries* . . . (5v., Toronto, 1867–77), 3: 180–81. J. A. Clifton, *A place of refuge for all time: migration of the American Potawatomi into Upper Canada, 1830 to 1850* (National Museum of Man, *Mercury ser.*, Canadian Ethnology Service paper no.26, Ottawa, 1975), 51. Elizabeth Graham, *Medicine man to missionary: missionaries as agents of change among the Indians of southern Ontario, 1784–1867* (Toronto, 1975). A. J. Hall, "The red man's burden: land, law, and the Lord in the Indian affairs of Upper Canada, 1791–1858" (PHD thesis, Univ. of Toronto, 1984), 83–115.

ALBRO, JOHN, artisan, merchant, office holder, militia officer, and politician; b. 6 May 1764 in Newport Township, N.S., son of Samuel Albro and Jane Cole, settlers from Rhode Island; m. first 22 Oct. 1793 Elizabeth Margaret Vandergrift in Halifax, and they had two sons; m. secondly 1 Dec. 1803 Elizabeth Margaret Dupuy in Halifax; d. there 23 Oct. 1839.

At the age of 17 John Albro advertised himself as operating a tan-yard in Halifax; by 1800 he was a butcher and by 1812 a merchant. The tannery and windmill he and his brother Samuel established north of Dartmouth became a major concern, and in 1818 the Albros petitioned for government encouragement through grants of land additional to their original holdings. John's rising status in Halifax was best exemplified by the two fine Georgian stone buildings he erected on the west side of Hollis Street, near the focal point of genteel society on Sackville Street. As a merchant he eventually specialized in hardware. A willingness to work long and hard appears to explain his success in this business.

Albro was an active participant in the social and business life of the capital during the early years of the 19th century. He helped to found or was a member of the Fire Insurance Association of Halifax (1809), the Halifax Marine Insurance Company (1809), the Charitable Irish Society (1809), the Nova Scotia Philanthropic Society (1815), the Halifax Steam Boat Company (1815), and the Halifax Commercial Society (1822). Albro was also grand master of the masonic order in Nova Scotia from 1820 to 1839, acted as a vestryman at St Paul's Church in 1824 and 1825 and a churchwarden from 1828 to 1834, and for nearly 20 years was a road commissioner and fire warden in Halifax. An active militia officer, he rose to the rank of lieutenant-colonel of the 4th Regiment of Halifax militia on 21 Aug. 1828, and in later years he served as inspector and reporter of dikes and workhouse commissioner. Albro not only helped establish the Fire Insurance Association, the first fire insurance company in British North America, but he also purchased its first policy. This local competition with British-based firms had by 1817 resulted in lower insurance rates for Nova Scotians. Albro also advocated a safe water system for Halifax, joined in the unsuccessful efforts in 1822 to found a local bank, and generally could be considered an active promoter of the interests of the town.

An involvement in politics was probably an outgrowth of the increasingly important role Albro played within the community. His career in the House of Assembly was not spectacular, for he was no more than a faithful supporter of measures pursued by the Halifax business élite. Elected in 1818 for Halifax Township, he was re-elected in 1820 despite suggestions that he would be beaten, and when defeated in 1826 by Beamish Murdoch* he withdrew from active participation in politics. The contest in 1826 was a lively affair, complete with accusations that Albro's supporters had been intimidated and complaints that Albro had indulged in low and scurrilous abuse.

At times Albro does seem to have been gruff and quarrelsome. In a pique he withdrew from the Charitable Irish Society for a short time in 1820; charges he levelled against John YOUNG because of Young's conduct of an agricultural contest were found to be groundless and he conceded eventually that he had spoken "inadvisedly." He actively supported the Reverend John Thomas Twining* in the dispute of 1824–25 which divided the congregation of St Paul's, but remained a member of the church. A quarrel with Edmund Ward*, publisher of the *Free Press*, probably lessened that paper's support for him in the 1826 election. Finally, he appears to have disapproved of the style of life and marriage of his son John, and virtually disinherited him.

Albro's final years seem to have been peaceful and profitable. In Halifax, both the street and the school named after the family have long since disappeared, but in Dartmouth a street and two lakes recall the prominent role Albro and others of his family played in the growth of the town. Albro was adjudged by his peers to be of upright conduct, acting always with rectitude and independence. After he died in his 76th year, fraternal societies and a vast concourse of the inhabitants of Halifax attended him to his resting-place in St Paul's cemetery.

ALLAN C. DUNLOP

PANS, MG 3, 154; MG 9, no.315: 11; RG 20A, 70, John Albro, 1818. J. V. Duncanson, *Newport, Nova Scotia – a Rhode Island township* (Belleville, Ont., 1985). [M.] H. Creighton, *Helen Creighton: a life in folklore* (Toronto, 1975). "Masonic grand masters of the jurisdiction of Nova Scotia, 1738–1965," comp. E. T. Bliss (typescript, n.p., 1965; copy at PANS).

ALLAMAND, JEANNE-CHARLOTTE (Berczy), colonizer and teacher; b. 16 April 1760 in Lausanne, Switzerland, second daughter of Jean-Emmanuel Allamand and Judith-Henriette-Françoise David; m. 1 Nov. 1785 Albert-Guillaume (William) Berczy*, and they had two sons, William Bent* and Charles Albert*; d. 18 Sept. 1839 in Sainte-Mélanie, Lower Canada.

Jeanne-Charlotte Allamand, whose father was a draper and dyer, seems to have received a good education. She may have been employed as a governess when she met Albert-Guillaume Berczy, a painter of miniatures, who would later call himself William. They were married near Lausanne.

Until about 1790 the couple lived in Florence (Italy), though he travelled frequently. While staying in London in 1790, they exhibited paintings at the Royal Academy of Arts, he a miniature and she two "Tuscan kitchen interiors." She had perhaps received instruction in painting at Lausanne, and her husband had given her lessons in Florence. The following year he accepted the task of recruiting German colonists and accompanying them to the holdings of the Genesee Association in New York state. The Berczys and their son William Bent left with the first group of settlers in the spring of 1792.

The agent of the Genesee Association, Charles Williamson, did not fulfil the terms of the colonists' agreement with the association and Berczy left the settlement, near present-day Canaseraga, N.Y., late in 1793 to seek help. Charlotte and the Lutheran minister who had accompanied the immigrants were left in charge for the winter of 1793–94. Taking charge of the colonists was a role which Charlotte was to handle capably on several occasions. When William assisted in the formation of a new association, the German Company, to develop land in Upper Canada, she and the pastor were charged with organizing the settlers for departure without Williamson's knowledge.

Once in Upper Canada the colonists were given land in Markham Township. The Berczys themselves settled in York (Toronto). Shortages of supplies and the reluctance of Berczy's backers to commit more money forced him to travel extensively to secure tools and food, often on credit. Again Charlotte was responsible for the affairs of the settlement, although she had some assistance. She also seems to have opened a haberdashery and textile shop at this time, probably to support the family. Since little or none of the money owed to Berczy by the settlers was being paid, she lived in near poverty.

In 1797 Berczy's claim to land, as a township proprietor, was substantially reduced and in order to appeal this decision he began a series of journeys which would occupy the rest of his life. Charlotte was again left in charge during her husband's travels. At one point he sold their house and only through the sympathy of the new owner was she allowed to stay.

William moved his family to Montreal in 1798 and departed for England the following year. He did not return until 1802. Charlotte dealt with matters concerning the Markham settlement through agents, first William Weekes* and then William Willcocks*, while trying to support her family. Even when Berczy returned, he spent the years 1802 to 1804 in York and 1808–9 at Quebec. Charlotte opened an academy in her rented quarters in Montreal to teach drawing and water-colour, music, and languages. By all accounts her school was quite successful. Probably her most noted pupil was Louise-Amélie Panet, daughter of Pierre-Louis Panet*. Louise-Amélie became a painter and art teacher and married Charlotte's son William Bent in 1819. Charlotte also taught her son Charles Albert. After her husband's death in New York in 1813 she continued to teach at least until 1817.

At some time after 1817 she joined William Bent at his home in Sandwich (Windsor), Upper Canada, granted him as compensation for his father's claims. There she lived a quiet life, occasionally painting as a hobby. About 1832 William Bent and his wife moved to Sainte-Mélanie, in the seigneury of Ailleboust which Louise-Amélie had inherited, and his mother apparently went with them. Charlotte died there in 1839.

The letters between Charlotte and William are filled with expressions of love and respect. Charlotte was always a dutiful and supportive wife through all of her husband's trials and tribulations. It was clearly her strength and talent that maintained their family during his absences. Without her efforts his colonization schemes would have been much more difficult to carry out and his family might well have fallen into abject poverty.

RONALD J. STAGG

[The author wishes to thank John Andre for the information and documentation he supplied. R.J.S.]

ACC, Diocese of Montreal Arch., Christ Church (William Henry [Sorel]), parish reg., 21 Sept. 1835. AO, MS 526. AUM, P 58, S. MTRL, H. J. Cowan, MS and notes for a book on William Berczy. PAC, MG 23, HII, 6. Harper, *Early painters and engravers*. John Andre, *Infant Toronto as Simcoe's folly* (Toronto, 1971); *William Berczy, co-founder of Toronto; a sketch* (Toronto, 1967). P.-G. Roy, "Le peintre Berczy," *BRH*, 1 (1895): 172–73. John Andre, "William Bent Berczy (1791–1873)," *German-Canadian yearbook* (Toronto), 2 (1975): 167–80.

ALLAN, PETER JOHN, poet; b. 6 June 1825 in York, England, third son of Dr Colin Allan and Jane Gibbon; d. 21 Oct. 1848 in Fredericton.

Peter John Allan's father was chief medical officer at Halifax before moving to Fredericton in 1836 upon his retirement. Growing up in Fredericton, Peter John briefly attended King's College but left before completing his degree. He then turned to the study of law. About the same time, having taken up, as he put it, "the amiable foible of verse-making," he began to publish his compositions in the *New Brunswick Reporter and Fredericton Advertiser*, a local newspaper published by James Hogg*, who was himself something of a poet. Encouraged by the reception of his verses and rather bored by his legal studies, Allan began to plan the publication of a volume of poetry. He solicited enough subscriptions to underwrite the cost of publication and had completed the manuscript when he died suddenly on 21 Oct. 1848 at Fredericton, following a brief illness. His poems were posthumously published in London in the summer of 1853 by his brother, and entitled *The poetical remains of Peter John Allan*.

In reviewing the book, the London *Morning Post* stated: "His poetry may not be the best imaginable; it may not indicate the very highest order of inspiration; it may not, with propriety, be described either as vehement, overpowering, passionate, or sublime, but it is touching and contemplative; gentle humane to the heart's core; singularly sweet, elegant, and tender, and informed with a pure and lofty feeling." The assessment is reasonably fair, perhaps generous, but naturally views Allan's efforts in the light of British literary expectations rather than in the cultural context of mid-century New Brunswick. What was of passing interest to the British had a more telling effect on poetic activity in New Brunswick. At its best, Allan's verse strikes a new note in Maritime poetry:

I hear thee in the bubbling flow of springs,
The lark's ascending song of exultation,
The zephyr's sighing through the evening air;
I hear thee – thou art nature unto me;
And every worldly hope or feverish care
Vanishes still before one dream of thee,
Whose love can conquer e'en the fierce despair
Of knowing that thou never mine canst be.

Influenced by the aesthetic concepts of the Romantic poets and especially by the style and versification of Lord Byron, Allan was able in his most effective poetry to break away from the moralistic attitudes and sentimental tone that had prevailed in locally written verse since the end of the 18th century. Allan was excited by the potential of man's imagination, by the range of experience that imagination offered to human consciousness, and by the relationship between the natural world and ideal reality, which only the imagination opened to human awareness. In his best poems, Allan used this intense sensitivity to ideal reality to control the rush of emotion he felt when confronted with the sensual beauty of nature. This control gave an intellectual toughness to his verse that was missing in the verses of contemporary Maritime poets such as Joseph Howe* and Mary Jane Katzmann* (Lawson), who approached nature poetry by way of sentimentalism. The new note struck by Allan's verse was probably noticed by few. It had an immediate if muted effect on James Hogg's poetry, but it was not until the early verses of Charles George Douglas Roberts* and Bliss Carman* that once again intellectual perception and emotional sensitivity were to be found in so subtle a balance in the poetry of Maritime Canada.

THOMAS B. VINCENT

Peter John Allan is the author of *The poetical remains of Peter John Allan, esq., late of Fredericton, New Brunswick, with a short biographical notice*, ed. Henry Christmas, intro. J. M'G. Allan (London, 1853).

Church of Jesus Christ of Latter-Day Saints, Geneal. Soc. (Salt Lake City, Utah), International geneal. index. *New-Brunswick Courier*, 28 Oct. 1848. *New Brunswick Reporter and Fredericton Advertiser*, 1846–53, esp. 30 Sept. 1853 which quotes the *Morning Post* (London). *DNB*. L. M. Beckwith Maxwell, *The River St. John and its poets* ([Newcastle, N.B.], 1946).

ALLSOPP, GEORGE WATERS, businessman, seigneur, JP, politician, office holder, and militia officer; baptized 12 Oct. 1769 at Quebec, eldest son of George Allsopp* and Anna Marie Bondfield; d. 28 Sept. 1837 in Cap-Santé, Lower Canada.

In late 1784 George Waters, John, and Carleton Allsopp were taken to England by their merchant father, who enrolled George and John at "Eaton's academy," near London. Determined that George should go into business, Allsopp was frustrated by his son's imaginary ailments and slow academic progress. "Merchants accounts" was among George's studies, but Allsopp deemed experience necessary, and he frequently took his boys to dinners and meetings with commercial associates.

Returning to the province of Quebec in October 1785, George commenced training in his father's business at Quebec and extensive milling operations near Cap-Santé, in the seigneury of Jacques-Cartier. He directed the rebuilding of the main mill after it burned in 1793, and in 1795, with the family rallying around its financially troubled head, he purchased the mills and shares in the seigneury, while other shares went to his brothers and to his sister, Ann Maria, who would die in 1831.

The mills never recovered their prominence of the 1780s, but George remained attached to them after his father's death in 1805. His ownership interest in Jacques-Cartier and the seigneury of Auteuil owed more to their investment value than to social prestige. In 1808 the mills, along with houses and a wharf at Quebec, were offered for lease, a step that initiated a movement by Allsopp away from the demands and risks of direct operation; five years later war and crop failure forced the lessee of the mills, Adam Rennie, to request cancellation of his contracts with the government, then his only client. By March 1815 Allsopp had set up, under Rennie's management, a small paper-mill, the second in British North America. A grist-mill built in 1817 was leased out, as was Allsopp's banal mill on the Rivière Portneuf in 1820.

With Allsopp's entry into business had come public involvement. In 1794 he received his first commission of the peace. A member of the House of Assembly for Buckingham (1796–1800) and Hampshire (1814–20), he attended irregularly and divided his support between the English and Canadian parties. In April 1812 he became lieutenant-colonel of the Cap-Santé battalion of militia, which contained many Protestants. He also served as an extra cashier in the Army Bill Office at Quebec [*see* James Green*] in 1814 and 1815. Following the war he was instrumental as a syndic in the erection, in 1816–17, and regulation of a royal school at Cap-Santé [*see* Charles Desroches*; Joseph Langley Mills*]. Named a roads commissioner for Hampshire in 1817, Allsopp served as well from 1819 to 1825 as a commissioner of land claims in the district of Gaspé. His public and industrial interests merged in his proposals, in 1821 and 1823, for a patent office to register inventions and discoveries.

Allsopp's most persistent interest was bridging the torrents of the Rivière Jacques-Cartier. Since about 1777 his family had operated a ferry near its mouth. Between 1810 and 1822, Allsopp petitioned the government for authorization to erect with his brothers a private toll-bridge, despite the existence of other bridges. The toll-bridge was built in the late 1820s, creating a new source of family revenue.

By the 1830s the youthful closeness of the Allsopp brothers had long since given way to practical co-operation. Between 1832 and 1835, George, Carleton, Robert, and James were in partnership to produce planks, and in 1833 they jointly leased the paper-mill to Angus McDonald* and others. But family relations deteriorated during the decade as George contested his brothers' co-proprietorship of the seigneuries, and before his death in 1837 he transferred property to Adélaïde and George Alfred, his children from an unknown marriage or liaison.

Faced with the complexities of George's estate, Carleton grumbled that "GWA could never be brought to finish anything." Management of seigneurial affairs was continued by Carleton's wife, Maria Concepsion d'Alfaro, and, later, by James. The mills were evidently taken over by George Alfred. The dissensions of George's last years and a gradual Canadianization of the family were indications of how dramatically it and its enterprises had changed since the days of George Sr. As Carleton lamented to his son, in the 18th century it had mingled with the "reputed First families" of Quebec, but there had been "a falling off a new generation succeeding the old, [and] such associations were not maintained."

David Roberts

ANQ-Q, CE1-61, 12 oct. 1769, 30 sept. 1837; CN1-21, 19, 30 août 1834; 30 juill., 30 déc. 1835; 26 juin 1837; 16 janv., 8–9 mars 1838; CN1-28, 7 oct. 1835; P-240, 26; P-313; P1000-2-26. AUM, P 58, U, G. W. Allsopp à François Baby, 27 juill., 28 oct. 1812. Brome County Hist. Soc. Arch. (Knowlton, Que.), Allsopp and McCorkill family papers: 100, 105–6, 210, 214–17, 10831, 11834 (mfm. at PAC). Harvard College Library, Houghton Library, Harvard Univ. (Cambridge, Mass.), MS Can. 18 (James Monk). McGill Univ. Arch., RG 4, c.38–c.40, Allsopp to Mills, 18 April 1821, 23 Oct. 1822, 28 Sept. 1823; Hale to Mills, 23 Oct. 1823. PAC, MG 23, GIII, 1, v.2; MG 24, B1, 4: 317–18; MG 30, D1, 2: 178, 196–97, 199; RG 8, I (C ser.), 117: 83–84; 994: 79, 82; RG 9, I, A5, 4: 23; RG 68, General index, 1651–1841. Can., Prov. of, Legislative Assembly, *Journals*, 1844–45. L.C., House of Assembly, *Journals*, 1796–1800, 1805, 1808, 1810–11, 1814–20; *Statutes*, 1800, c.6; 1805, c.7; 1819, c.27; 1823, c.34. *Quebec Gazette*, 4 Nov. 1790; 18 Aug. 1791; 13 Feb. 1794; 18 July 1799; 11, 25 Jan., 8 Feb. 1810; 7, 14 March 1811; 27 April 1812; 9 Oct. 1813; 12 Jan. 1815; 28 March, 16 May, 8 Aug. 1816; 5, 26 June, 28 Aug. 1817; 13 Aug., 7, 17 Sept., 5 Oct., 16 Nov. 1818; 8, 25 Feb., 8 April, 6 May, 14 June, 13, 16 Aug., 7 Oct. 1819; 27 Jan., 25 May, 27 Nov. 1820; 24 May, 11 June, 5, 12, 16 July, 13 Sept., 8 Nov. 1821; 21 Nov., 19 Dec. 1822; 20, 24 Feb., 3 April 1823. F.-J. Audet et Fabre Surveyer, *Les députés de Saint-Maurice et de Buckinghamshire*, 59–61. Bouchette, *Topographical description of L.C.*, 386–91. Desjardins, *Guide parl.* Langelier, *Liste des terrains concédés*. *Officers of British forces in Canada* (Irving). [Madeleine Bourque *et al.*], *Livre souvenir: la vie du Cap-Santé* (s.l., 1979). George Carruthers, *Paper-making* (Toronto, 1947), 330–32. Félix Gatien et David Gosselin, *Histoire du Cap Santé . . .* (Québec, 1899), 102–3, 124, 130–31, 136–37, 148–49. Ouellet, *Lower Canada*. D. J. Roberts, "George Allsopp: Quebec merchant, 1733–1805" (MA thesis, Queen's Univ., Kingston, Ont., 1974).

ALMON, WILLIAM BRUCE, doctor, office holder, and politician; b. 25 Oct. 1787 in Halifax, son of William James Almon* and Rebecca Byles, a daughter of Mather Byles*; m. 29 Jan. 1814 Laleah Peyton Johnston, daughter of William Martin Johnston and Elizabeth LICHTENSTEIN, in Annapolis Royal, N.S.; they had 11 children, including William Johnston*; d. 12 July 1840 in Halifax.

William Bruce Almon belonged to a distinguished family which for more than a century contributed physicians and surgeons to Halifax society. Both his mother and his father were loyalists, coming to Nova Scotia in 1776 and about 1780 respectively. His father was surgeon to the Board of Ordnance and the Royal Artillery at Halifax. The entire family was staunchly tory in politics. William Bruce's sister, Amelia Elizabeth, married James William Johnston*, leader of the conservative forces in the colony and opponent of responsible government. His brother, Mather Byles Almon*, was one of the original directors of the Bank of Nova Scotia, its president from 1837 to 1870, and, like William Bruce, a member of the Legislative Council and supporter of the Johnston government.

After his education at King's College, Windsor, Almon followed in his father's footsteps and took up medicine. On 29 Oct. 1806 he began his studies at the University of Edinburgh, one of the first native Nova Scotians to travel abroad for medical training. Graduating from Edinburgh in 1809, he returned to Halifax and set up a medical practice and drug dispensary in partnership with his father. Over the next several years he assisted his father in caring for the inmates of the poor-house. In 1816 he petitioned the House of Assembly for the cost of medicine and professional services rendered to 158 refugee blacks who had been admitted to the poor-house from the ship *Chesapeake* and were suffering from dysentery and smallpox. Upon his father's death in 1817, Almon assumed the position of medical and surgical officer of the poor-house and jail, where he continued to minister to the sick and indigent.

Like many of his colleagues, Almon was concerned about improving the standards of medical treatment in Nova Scotia. He supported the passing of the Medical Act of 1828, designed to exclude "ignorant and unskilful persons from the practice of Physic and Surgery," and was a member of the province's first licensing board. Almon also apprenticed a number of young medical students, one of whom was Daniel McNeill Parker*, a founder of the Medical Society of Nova Scotia and later president of the Canadian Medical Association. Parker remembered Almon as "the warmest and kindest hearted man I ever met."

Almon invested in several companies, but he was not especially interested in business. Nor was he greatly concerned with church affairs or politics. Basically a supporter of the *status quo*, he sided with the Reverend Robert Willis* in the dispute over the rectorate of St Paul's Anglican Church that rent the congregation in 1824–25. His appointment to the Legislative Council in 1838 was probably the result of his work in the field of public health.

In August 1831 Almon had been appointed health officer of the port of Halifax. In 1832 he petitioned the assembly for payment for his services. A committee of the assembly reported that, as Almon's predecessor, Charles Wentworth Wallace, and Wallace's assistant, William Grigor*, had never received any remuneration, they should receive a fixed grant, and that thereafter health officers should be paid by the vessels they visited. It was in carrying out his duties as health officer that Almon contracted the illness that led to his death. In June 1840 a ship arrived in Halifax with a large number of passengers suffering from typhus. Almon went aboard, treated the sick as best he could, and arranged to transfer them ashore. While doing so he contracted the disease himself. He died on 12 July 1840 at the age of 52. The *Novascotian* reported that his death "spread a deep gloom over a large portion of the community."

COLIN D. HOWELL

PANS, Biog., Almon family, no.2, W. J. Almon and Son, letter-book, 1813–33 (mfm.); MG 1, 11; MG 20, 670, no.4 (typescript); RG 5, P, 80, no.2. St Luke's (Anglican) Church (Annapolis Royal, N.S.), Reg. of marriages (mfm. at PANS). N.S., House of Assembly, *Journal and proc.*, 1832. *Acadian Recorder*, 18 July 1840. *Novascotian*, 16 July 1840. A. W. H. Eaton, "Old Boston families, number four: the Byles family," *New England Hist. and Geneal. Reg.* (Boston), 69 (1915): 113. *N.S. vital statistics, 1813–22* (Punch), no.2515. R. V. Harris, *The Church of Saint Paul in Halifax, Nova Scotia: 1749–1949* (Toronto, 1949). D. A. Sutherland, "The merchants of Halifax, 1815–1850: a commercial class in pursuit of metropolitan status" (PHD thesis, Univ. of Toronto, 1975), 63, 88–89, 156–57, 177. *Evening Mail* (Halifax), 22 Dec. 1896. *Herald* (Halifax), 23 Dec. 1896. K. A. MacKenzie, "Honorable Daniel McNeill Parker, M.D. Edinburgh, D.C.L. Acadia, 1822–1907: a dean of Canadian medicine" and "The Almons," *Nova Scotia Medical Bull.* (Halifax), 29 (1950): 149–54 and 30 (1951): 31–36; "Nineteenth century physicians in Nova Scotia," N.S. Hist. Soc., *Coll.*, 31 (1957): 119–29.

AMIOT, LAURENT, gold- and silversmith; b. 10 Aug. 1764 at Quebec, son of Jean Amiot, an innkeeper, and Marie-Louise Chrestien; m. there 9 April 1793 Marguerite Levasseur, *dit* Borgia, and they had five children, including NOËL-LAURENT; d. there 3 June 1839 and was buried on 7 June in Sainte-Anne's chapel in the cathedral of Notre-Dame.

Laurent Amiot in all likelihood began his apprenticeship in the silversmith's shop of his older brother Jean-Nicolas around 1780, if it is assumed that he started at about age 16. He had studied from 1778 to 1780 at the Petit Séminaire de Québec. Despite an oral tradition transmitted by Abbé Lionel Lindsay, it is unlikely that he had worked in François Ranvoyzé*'s shop and that Ranvoyzé, sensing a potential competitor, dismissed him. If there was rivalry between the two silversmiths, it developed after Amiot returned from Europe.

Amiot spent five years in Paris to complete his training. His family almost certainly paid his living expenses, with the Séminaire de Québec serving in effect as an intermediary, as it had done some years earlier for François Baillairgé*. In all probability the young silversmith made the crossing in 1782 with Arnauld-Germain Dudevant*, a priest from the Séminaire de Québec who was returning to France. The name of the silversmith with whom he completed his training is not known. Letters from Abbé François Sorbier* de Villars, procurator of the Séminaire des Missions Étrangères in Paris, testify, however, to the young man's gifts and his development as an apprentice. "Mr Amiot continues to work successfully in Paris and behaves himself well," he noted in May 1783, adding in January 1785 that he "applies himself assiduously [and] has made considerable progress." Amiot returned to Quebec in the spring of 1787 with a fine letter from Villars which recommended him warmly to the superior of the seminary, Thomas-Laurent Bédard*, for his patronage: "I beg you to give him as much help as you can to put his talent to use." Familiar with the most recent technical innovations, Amiot was ready to promote the Louis XVI style then in fashion in Paris.

Amiot opened his first workshop at 1 Rue de la Montagne (at the foot of the Côte de la Montagne); late in his career he moved a short distance to Rue Saint-Pierre. Most of the silversmiths working at Quebec were established in this neighbourhood, including James Orkney*, Louis Robitaille, and Michel Forton*. In 1795 all of them except Robitaille signed a petition requesting exemption from an ordinance of the Court of Quarter Sessions regulating the use of forge fires [*see* Michel Forton]. Amiot maintained contact with other artists, in particular with François Baillairgé, who, like him, had been to Paris to complete his artistic training. In fact their contacts throughout their careers and in their personal lives were probably frequent. Over the years Baillairgé, who attended Amiot's wedding in 1793, furnished him with several wooden or lead models for the figure of Christ, at least one model for a jug, and numerous knobs and handles for teapots and other containers. It was also Baillairgé who made his shop sign. Amiot attended his friend's funeral in September 1830. But over and above everyday affairs, common artistic concerns brought them together.

A number of documents reveal that Amiot thought more highly of the silversmith's art and its creators than did Quebec silversmiths before him. In 1816 a notary, at Amiot's dictation, termed him a "Maître ès Art Orfèvre." In a similar situation 20 years later, when he was taking on a young apprentice, he had the word "metier" struck out and replaced by "Art d'Orfevrerie." The incident may reveal a trait peculiar to the man, but it is also proof that he was conscious of his standing as a creative artist. With Amiot, working in silver was no longer considered a craft but an art, and from then on the silversmith was no longer a craftsman but indeed an artist.

In this connection, it must be noted that Amiot was one of the few Quebec silversmiths for whom there exist drawings that show the artist's own method of creation. As with the master silversmiths in Paris at the time, who worked within the best academic tradition, the drawing suggested the work executed.

Not counting his years of apprenticeship, Amiot engaged in professional activity on a regular basis for more than 50 years; comments on his practice of his art can be found from 1788, the year after his return from Paris, until 1839, the year he died. Compared with the output of the other Quebec silversmiths active between 1790 and 1840, and particularly with that of François Ranvoyzé, who also worked at Quebec, Amiot's was without question the most important in quantity and quality. His style spread rapidly in the Quebec region, where by 1788 Ranvoyzé began to imitate him; after 1800 his influence gradually reached the Montreal region, as works by Robert Cruickshank* and Pierre Huguet*, *dit* Latour, prove in eloquent fashion.

Amiot always enjoyed the support of the clergy and it was in part the reason for his success. He initiated profound changes in church silver. By proposing new shapes, changing proportions, and introducing a new decorative idiom he attempted to redesign almost all the pieces, drawing heavily on the Louis XVI style. Between 1788 and 1795 he realized several particularly finished items that showed the path he intended to take in producing religious objects. A sanctuary lamp in the church at Repentigny executed in 1788 is worth mention. This magnificent creation, with its pure lines, marks a clear departure from the archaic style of his precursors. It is more elongated in shape than lamps produced earlier, and the decorative elements, drawn from the neoclassical repertory, are carefully grouped and perfectly combined. Paradoxically, it was during this period, in 1794, that Amiot made a ciborium which alone among his works drew upon François Ranvoyzé's decorative idiom, albeit with a quite different arrangement and rendering. The most plausible explanation for the departure from his own style in the execution of this article for the church of Saint-Marc on the Richelieu lies in the express wish of his client.

After 1800 Amiot's works show fewer striking innovations. Making hundreds of vessels for parish *fabriques*, he devoted himself to spreading an aesthetic concept. His detractors speak of repetition. Certainly, in this immense production the development becomes more subtle and more difficult to pin down. Although the outline and general appearance of the vessels scarcely vary, the arrangement of the decorative elements changes constantly, and there is thus a constant process of recreation.

Amiot did, of course, conceive other forms and new decorative effects after 1800, as in the magnificent storiated chalice that he did in 1812 for the *fabrique* of Saint-Cuthbert near Berthier-en-Haut (Berthierville). This work met with undeniable success, both in its original form and in the objects inspired by it. Under the influence of imports from France, Amiot's successors developed this type of silver article, which was still popular at the end of the 19th century. Orders from private clients enabled Amiot to create some remarkable items, such as the reliquary at Charlesbourg done in 1823. Under his impetus church silver in Lower Canada was revitalized through the introduction of an aesthetic concept originating in the Louis XVI style.

Although not as much can be learned about Amiot's domestic silver, given the difficulty of gaining access to the pieces, it is nevertheless possible to determine its essential nature. At the beginning of his career he turned out a few splendid articles in the Louis XVI style – for example, a ewer belonging to the archbishop's palace in Quebec. He also on occasion made beautiful cutlery with a shell decoration on the handle, like that being done in Paris ateliers. But overall his domestic silver was marked instead by the influence of English neoclassicism, as the teapots, sugar-bowls, and most of the flatware that came out of his workshop prove. Amiot thereby demonstrated his ability to respond to the taste of the middle class, seeking his inspiration in the hollow-ware and other articles that they imported mainly from London. Occasionally he achieved an admirable synthesis of the English rococo and the Louis XVI styles – a valuable example is the soup tureen acquired by the Baby family. To this substantial production must be added what he created as a jeweller. He in fact made numerous wedding rings – for his neighbour, printer John NEILSON, among others – and even commemorative medals.

To fill all these orders Amiot needed help. He took on at least four apprentices: Paul Morin, Jacques-Richard Filteau, Joseph Babineau, and Pierre Lespérance*. They were 16 or 17 years old, and all signed articles binding them to work for their master for a period of from four to five and a half years. Amiot probably also had close ties with François Sasseville*, who may have been his journeyman. Otherwise, there seems to be no explanation for the fact that Sasseville's nephew Lespérance did his apprenticeship with Amiot rather than with his uncle. Whatever the case, on 2 July 1839 Sasseville leased from Amiot's children the shop that he had owned and bequeathed to them. The lease stipulated that the heirs "make over to the Sieur Sasseville the entire shop in its present state as it was left by their father, with the small amount of silver that may remain included, the components and all the effects and articles pertaining to the silversmith's art." Sasseville, who had taken over his shop and clientele, was also Amiot's artistic successor for throughout his career he carried on the stylistic tradition that Amiot had begun.

It is to be regretted that historical works have thus far largely ignored Amiot, giving preference to the artists who worked under the French régime and those who carried on their tradition. Through his work Amiot was instrumental in redefining an aesthetic concept in Lower Canada in the first half of the 19th century. He was to the silversmith's art what François Baillairgé was to architecture and woodcarving.

RENÉ VILLENEUVE

Works by Laurent Amiot can be found in a great many old Quebec parishes. The two major public collections are at the Musée du Québec (Quebec) and the National Gallery of Canada (Ottawa). The Musée d'art de Saint-Laurent (Montreal) possesses some of the tools from his workshop.

ANQ-Q, CE1-1, 11 août 1764, 9 avril 1793, 16 sept. 1830, 7 juin 1839; CN1-212, 21 déc. 1816, 20 juin 1836, 2 juill. 1839; CN1-284, 10 sept. 1791, 12 janv. 1795; P-398, journal; P1000-2-34. ASQ, Fichier des anciens; Lettres, P, 22, 28–29, 35. MAC-CD, Fonds Morisset, 2, dossier Laurent Amiot. "Les dénombrements de Québec" (Plessis), ANQ *Rapport*, 1948–49: 26, 76, 125, 177. "Très humble requête des citoyens de la ville de Québec [1787]," ANQ *Rapport*, 1944–45: plate 2. *Montreal Gazette*, 4 Sept. 1834. Marius Barbeau, *Québec où survit l'ancienne France* (Québec, 1937), 61–63. J. E. Langdon, *Canadian silversmiths, 1700–1900* (Toronto, 1966), 41. *L'Abeille* (Québec), 25 avril 1878. Gérard Morisset, "Coup d'œil sur les trésors artistiques de nos paroisses," CCHA *Rapport*, 15 (1947–48): 62. P.-G. Roy, "Les canotiers entre Québec et Lévis," *BRH*, 48 (1942): 324; "La famille de Jean Amyot," *BRH*, 25 (1919): 232–34. Henri Têtu, "L'abbé André Doucet, curé de Québec, 1807–1814," *BRH*, 13 (1907): 18. Victor Tremblay, "Les archives de la Société historique du Saguenay," *RHAF*, 4 (1950–51): 12.

AMIOT, NOËL-LAURENT, Roman Catholic priest and author; b. 25 Dec. 1793 at Quebec, son of Laurent AMIOT and Marguerite Levasseur, *dit* Borgia; d. 10 Oct. 1845 in Vienna.

Noël-Laurent Amiot came from a family which had been settled at Quebec for several generations. Certain of its members had become experts in silver-work: by 1793 Laurent Amiot was considered the leading silversmith in Lower Canada. In 1808 Noël-Laurent entered the Petit Séminaire de Québec, and the prize list at school closing shows he was one of the best in his class. Influenced by the priests at the seminary and by his family, he entered the priesthood at the end of his classical studies and began at the Grand Séminaire de Québec in the autumn of 1817. The following summer Joseph-Octave Plessis*, the bishop of Quebec, sent him to the Odanak mission and the parish of Saint-François-du-Lac to assist curé Jacques PAQUIN and to learn the Abenaki language.

Amiot was ordained priest by Plessis's coadjutor, Bishop Bernard-Claude Panet*, on 13 Feb. 1820. After serving briefly as assistant priest in the parish of Sainte-Anne at Yamachiche and in that of Saint-Gervais near Quebec, Amiot was named curé of Saint-François-du-Lac and given responsibility for the Odanak mission late in 1821. He adapted quite easily to his new task, but none the less encountered difficulties with the Abenakis. He had to combat the Protestant proselytism spreading in the mission – some Abenakis even wanted to build a Protestant church there. In 1826 Amiot expressed a desire to be assigned elsewhere. Panet refused, but agreed to send him an assistant, Michael POWER. Three years later the arrival of Osunkhirhine (Pierre-Paul Masta), a young Abenaki who had become a Protestant minister, naturally aroused Amiot's wrath. With the support of the Canadian Bible societies, the young minister managed to set up a Protestant school on the mission. Amiot reacted quickly and forbad the Abenakis to send their children to it on pain of being refused the sacraments. His action even earned him Panet's approval.

Amiot struggled with several other problems. The inhabitants of the seigneury of Pierreville, who had been placed in Saint-François-du-Lac parish, often preferred the ministrations of the curé of Saint-Antoine-de-Padoue at Baie-du-Febvre (Baieville), as did the residents of Aston Township. Despite numerous discussions with these people, Amiot did not succeed in winning them back. He also had frequent altercations with Augustin Gill, the Abenakis' agent in dealings with whites, who favoured the spread of Protestantism in the mission and refused to cooperate with him.

Amiot had to leave his parish charge in the summer of 1830 following a "painful investigation" of a matter probably of a sexual nature undertaken by the bishop during his pastoral visit. Replaced by Joseph-Marie Bellenger*, he went to the United States to seek refuge with the Sulpicians in Baltimore, Md. In August 1831 Panet allowed him to return to Lower Canada, believing that he had sufficiently "made amends for the scandal that he has caused."

In October 1831 Amiot was named parish priest of Saint-Cyprien at Napierville. He was not free of trouble there, either. Napierville was by then a hive of political activity. In 1834 Amiot denounced from the pulpit the political intrigues of Dr Cyrille-Hector-Octave CÔTÉ, member of the House of Assembly for L'Acadie, who was a doctrinaire liberal and a Patriote leader in the region. Côté was organizing public meetings after mass, haranguing parishioners from the steps of the church, and inciting them to open opposition to the government. To the political confrontation with Côté was added increasing insubordination by farmers, who were protesting against tithes and seigneurial dues. Amiot was deeply worried and felt obliged to cling to a stubborn, almost blind loyalty to the authorities which was to separate him more and more from his parishioners. In this attitude he had much in common with his colleagues in the Montreal region, who implicitly followed their superiors' directions and ardently defended the established order.

Early in the autumn of 1837, a rebellious mood was developing in the parish, and Amiot did not hesitate to attack the Patriotes, who were organizing stormy meetings and anti-government demonstrations. When, on 24 October, Bishop Jean-Jacques LARTIGUE issued a pastoral letter condemning the Patriote leaders, he took an even firmer attitude. He not only read the letter from the pulpit with determination and conviction, but also spoke with unmistakable clarity about the sacred nature of the union of church and state. This definite stand marked him as one of the supporters of the British government, who were naturally suspect and the obvious target of public condemnation. Some of his parishioners reacted swiftly, organizing a political charivari against him during which they broke into the "Marseillaise," uttered threats, and threw a few stones at the presbytery windows. In 1838 the Patriotes even illegally held Amiot prisoner in his presbytery.

After the collapse of the rebellion, calm was soon restored. Amiot led a tranquil life and limited himself to carrying on his ministry zealously and assiduously. This state of affairs did not, however, last long. In November 1842 the bishop of Montreal, Ignace Bourget*, accused him of being "in open revolt" against him because he had refused assignment to another parish charge better suited to his strength. Bourget found himself obliged, therefore, to strip him of his priestly powers. It was probably this action that prompted Amiot, who had recently received a large bequest from his father, to set out late in the year on a voyage to St Peter's in Rome and the Holy Land. He kept a diary, describing his various journeys in vivid and emotional terms. He was, indeed, a pilgrim, strengthening his faith in these fervently Christian settings. He also took advantage of the trip to travel about in Europe. But an unexpected illness forced him to stop at Vienna, where he died on 10 Oct. 1845.

RICHARD CHABOT

Noël-Laurent Amiot is the author of a diary, which includes an account of his travels in Europe and the Holy Land, held at ASQ, MSS, 141.

ANQ-Q, CE1-1, 25 déc. 1793. Arch. de l'évêché de Nicolet (Nicolet, Qué.), Cartable Saint-François-du-Lac, I. Arch. du diocèse de Saint-Jean-de-Québec (Longueuil, Qué.), 13A/71–116. ASQ, C 38: 229, 243, 260, 281, 294; Lettres, P, 22, 29; Séminaire, 9, no.33; 123, nos.15–18; 128, no.7; 130, no.217. PAC, MG 8, F74; RG 4, B37, 1: 98. *L'Ami du peuple, de l'ordre et des lois*, 2 sept. 1835. Caron, "Inv. de la corr. de Mgr Panet," ANQ *Rapport*, 1933–34: 312; 1935–36: 189, 198, 200; "Inv. de la corr. de Mgr Plessis," ANQ *Rapport*, 1932–33: 121, 134, 150–51, 153. Desrosiers, "Inv. de la corr. de Mgr Bourget," ANQ *Rapport*, 1948–49: 384. T.-M. Charland, *Histoire des Abénakis d'Odanak (1675–1937)* (Montréal, 1964), 188–95; *Histoire de Saint-François-du-Lac* (Ottawa, 1942), 224–33. P.-G. Roy, "La famille de Jean Amyot," *BRH*, 25 (1919): 225–34.

ANSLEY (Annesley), AMOS, Church of England clergyman; baptized 25 Jan. 1801 in Kingston, Upper Canada, seventh child of Amos Ansley and Christina (Christian) McMichael; m. 1826 Harriet Kirkpatrick Henderson, and they had four sons and two daughters; d. 1837 in Montreal.

Amos Ansley's father, a loyalist from New York, settled in the Cataraqui (Kingston) district, where his skills as a carpenter-builder helped him play an active role in the young community. Amos was educated at the University of Edinburgh and graduated AM on 14 Jan. 1822. Stationed at Hull in Lower Canada and March Township in Upper Canada as a missionary of the Society for the Propagation of the Gospel, he was ordained deacon in 1824. In 1826 he was priested by Bishop Charles James STEWART of Quebec. His responsibilities extended to some 14 townships on both sides of the Ottawa River. Hull and March were the two principal concentrations of settlement: the village of Hull had begun at the start of the century through the economic initiatives of the American lumberman, Philemon WRIGHT; the March settlement, in contrast, was a military community where a group of retired officers and merchants tried to preserve and cultivate British social and cultural values in the wilderness of the Ottawa valley [*see* Hamnett Kirkes Pinhey*]. Ansley was active in both areas. In addition to performing the various offices – baptisms, marriages, and burials – that marked the life of an Anglican missionary, the young clergyman also helped to complete St James' Church at Hull and St Mary's at March, and took an especially active role in the promotion of schools and libraries.

The construction of the Rideau Canal [*see* John BY] added to Ansley's duties. Although Bytown (Ottawa) was not an official part of his district, he none the less assumed responsibility for the rapidly expanding population of workers, lumbermen, and military officials who were drawn to the area. The general growth of the region, in fact, led Bishop Stewart to petition the SPG to divide the missionary station. In 1829 March became a separate charge, and Ansley was left with the Lower Canadian side of the river.

This relief did not, unfortunately, betoken a prosperous future for Ansley and his family. In 1831 the bishop transferred him to Berthier-en-Haut (Berthierville) because "some untoward circumstances" had undermined his authority among his parishioners. He left Hull in 1832 but new fields did not produce the desired result. In 1834 Stewart was obliged to suspend him on account of his "habits of intemperance." At this point, Ansley seems to have suffered as well from what his wife described as an inherited "state of mental derangement." He wandered off into the United States, leaving her and their children destitute. He later returned to Montreal and died there in 1837. His wife remained extremely hard pressed to provide for their family.

The missionary reports that Ansley submitted to the SPG reveal a hard-working and dedicated priest – his bishop spoke highly of the "great diligence" with which he approached his work. His published sermon presents a man with a rational and orthodox intelligence, indeed with a sense of refinement that might seem incongruous with the emerging commercial character of the Ottawa valley. Although problems cut short his career, they were of a type that was not uncommon among missionaries who had to confront the privations of living on the very edge of Anglican civilization. While Ansley's story might not conform to the heroic tales popularized by the religious press in the Victorian era, it does reveal – in both its successes and failures – an important dimension of missionary life in the early decades of the 19th century.

WILLIAM WESTFALL

Amos Ansley is the author of *A sermon preached at the opening of St. Mary's Church, township of March, Upper-Canada* . . . (Montreal, 1828).

RHL, USPG Arch., C/CAN/Que., folders 368, 370, 384. Univ. of Edinburgh Library, Special Coll. Dept., Graduation roll, 1822; Matriculation reg., 1818–22. K. M. Bindon, "Kingston: a social history, 1785–1830" (PHD thesis, Queen's Univ., Kingston, Ont., 1979). M. S. Cross, "The dark druidical groves; the lumber community and the commercial frontier in British North America, to 1854" (PHD thesis, Univ. of Toronto, 1968). H. A. Davidson, *"Our Ansley family"* . . . (Jenkintown, Pa., 1933). H. P. Hill, *History of Christ Church Cathedral, Ottawa, 1832–1932* (Ottawa, 1932). E. G. May and W. H. Millen, *History of the parish of Hull, Que., . . . 1823–1923* (Ottawa, 1923). C. F. Pascoe, *Two hundred years of the S.P.G.* . . . (2v., London, 1901). B. S. Elliott, "'The famous township of Hull': image and aspirations of a pioneer Quebec community," *SH*, 12 (1979): 339–67.

ANTHONY, GABRIEL, Micmac chief; d. October 1846 at Bear River, N.S.

Gabriel Anthony was confirmed as chief of the Indians of Annapolis, Digby, Yarmouth, Shelburne, and Queens counties by letters patent under the Great Seal of Nova Scotia on 16 Nov. 1843. He estimated the number of people "under his charge" at 500.

Potato blight spread through Nova Scotia in 1845 and the Indians were particularly hard hit. Malnutrition prevented them from hunting effectively, and at the first appearance of fever whites refused to buy their handicrafts for fear of contagion. Local overseers of the poor did not wish to add Indians to their list of responsibilities.

In January 1846 Anthony presented a petition to the House of Assembly requesting aid for his people. He was called to the bar of the house and made a brief, dignified speech in English, carefully emphasizing his words by striking the forefinger of his right hand into the palm of his left. "Sir, I don't understand English – don't speak him very well. If I could speak my language to you, I could tell you in one word – in two words, in three words; and you would know what I have to say." He explained that as chief he was constantly travelling among his people. "I tell them not mind any one but Supreme – (Pointing upward) You understand me. (The Speaker said – Yes, we understand you)." This work, the chief continued, left him no time to look after his own affairs and he was personally destitute. At the request of several members, Anthony then addressed the house in Micmac with an eloquence that impressed members even though they could not understand a word he said. Joseph Howe*, a former commissioner of Indians for the province, explained that the gist of it was that with Indians, as with whites, those who had the most thankless duties to perform were often the worst paid. The appeal yielded 43 blankets for the Indians of the western counties. In May, Anthony tried again, with a petition directed to Lieutenant Governor Lord Falkland [Cary*] asking for £15 for 50 blankets; half of that sum was granted.

At the beginning of October 1846 there were 40 Indians living near the chapel at Bear River; 8 had already died and 29 of those remaining were sick. The fever that afflicted them was diagnosed as the result of "Vitiated Secretions and Torpor of the Liver." Pains in the chest and neck were followed by headaches, chills, fever, and spasmodic pains in the stomach and bowels. Those who were to die had greatly distended abdomens and showed "an unusual impatience and longing for Death to release them from their Suffering." Chief Gabriel Anthony was one of those who found that release.

L. F. S. Upton

PANS, MG 15, B, 3, nos.95, 102, 104. *Halifax Morning Post & Parliamentary Reporter*, 14 Jan. 1846. Upton, *Micmacs and colonists*.

ARCHIBALD, SAMUEL GEORGE WILLIAM, office holder, judge, lawyer, and politician; b. 5 Feb. 1777 in Truro, N.S., third son of Samuel Archibald of Truro and Rachel Todd of Massachusetts; m. first 16 March 1802 Elizabeth Dickson of Onslow, N.S., sister of Thomas Dickson*; m. secondly 15 Aug. 1832 Joanna Brinley, *née* Allen, widow of William Birch Brinley; d. 28 Jan. 1846 in Halifax.

Grandson of David Archibald, one of four brothers from Londonderry (Northern Ireland) who helped to found Truro in 1762, Samuel George William was apparently christened Samuel George Washington – an indication of his family's sympathies – but changed his last forename to further his chances of getting ahead. His father, a purchaser and shipper of lumber, died of fever in the Leeward Islands when Archibald was 3, and the boy was brought up by his grandfather until the age of 15. During that time he was known for his love of fun and his mischievous pranks, a forerunner of the irrepressible merriment which would let him "all through life, mingle work with play."

In 1792 Archibald went to Massachusetts, where his mother's relatives supervised his education at Haverhill and Andover until 1796. On his return he thought first of becoming a Presbyterian minister; then he served as protonotary of the Supreme Court and clerk of the peace for the district of Colchester before beginning the study of law in the office of Samuel Bradstreet Robie* about 1800. Two years later he married 15-year-old Elizabeth Dickson, a member of a family that was highly influential in public life. Within a few months he became judge of probate for the districts of Colchester and Pictou. On 16 April 1805 he was admitted as attorney and barrister and the following year elected to the House of Assembly for Halifax County, which then included the districts of Pictou and Colchester. Since his grandfather and father had been assemblymen and his eldest son, Charles Dickson*, was to be one later, four generations of the family in lineal descent served as members. Once Archibald and three of his Dickson brothers-in-law were members at the same time, and someone unkindly suggested that an Archibald–Dickson alliance engaged in log-rolling to secure road votes favourable to their constituents.

From the outset Archibald had assets that would ensure his success both as a lawyer and as an assemblyman. Peter Lynch, a Halifax lawyer and historian, remembered him as "a more than ordinarily handsome man, of great suavity of manner, with a melodious voice, fascinating address, and a thorough knowledge of human nature," who spoke "with great ease, elegance, and fluency, his periods rhythmic, and the flow of his language . . . sparkling." Archibald's first days in the assembly were marked by an almost unprecedented act, Lieutenant Governor Sir John Wentworth*'s rejection of William Cottnam Tonge* as speaker. The record does not indicate if Archibald joined in the protests, but when the new speaker, Lewis Morris WILKINS, announced that he would be absent to attend a meeting of the governors of King's College, Archibald got the house to adopt two resolutions declaring that the first duty of the speaker was to the assembly and that the summons to Wilkins was disrespectful to it. Ever the constitutionalist, he early showed his determination to resist any infringement of the lower house's rights.

More generally, Archibald's early years as an assemblyman were marked by his close attention to the improvement of roads, especially those running eastward from Halifax. A little later he gave strong support to Thomas MCCULLOCH and Pictou Academy. A secessionist Presbyterian with a deep religious faith, "he never uttered any of the cant of the day on the subject" and took no "active part in public religious exercises." But he did oppose the exclusiveness of King's College and for two decades supported McCulloch's efforts to have Pictou Academy elevated in status and given a permanent annual grant. Although he recognized McCulloch's failings – he once wrote to judge Peleg Wiswall that "the Emperor has become the real John Knox of Nova Scotia and threatens to eat you church men one and all" – he also stated more than once that he wished he had a tithe of the principal's talents. His stand on Pictou Academy not only brought him into conflict with the extremists on the Council such as Richard John Uniacke* Sr, but also prevented him from developing a genuine rapport with John YOUNG and his family, who as Kirkmen opposed the secessionist McCulloch.

By 1817 Archibald had become such a leading member of the bar that Lieutenant Governor Lord Dalhousie [RAMSAY] made him, and William Hersey Otis Haliburton*, the province's pioneer king's counsel. In the years that followed he appeared in most trials of any import. In 1819 he successfully defended William Q. Sawers on the charge of assaulting Dr Matthias Francis Hoffmann*, but a few months later he could not secure a conviction when he prosecuted Richard John Uniacke* Jr, who had killed William Bowie in the last fatal duel in Nova Scotia. In a civil suit requesting damages for assault, he admitted the guilt of his client Anthony Henry Holland*, but almost laughed the plaintiff Edmund Ward* out of court, while in a criminal libel case he took an extremely serious view of the matter and secured the conviction of Thomas FORRESTER from a jury within ten minutes. In 1835 he participated in the prosecution of Joseph Howe* for criminal libel but gave only a moderate speech to the jury, knowing full well that although Howe was guilty in law he could not get a jury to convict him. The reports of these speeches, though meagre, do show "the many sided character of his eloquence in addressing Juries."

Indeed, "in the management of causes and . . . in the management of a jury, he . . . came to be without a rival," the more so because he could "touch every emotion." Judge George Geddie Patterson called him "the greatest verdict-getter we have ever known." Both his contemporaries and more recent students have held that he was neither learned in the law nor willing to undertake the drudgery of ferreting out "the dry detail of the law connected with a cause." In particular, A. A. MacKenzie has suggested that he was "not in fact the great jurist of the family legend but a quick-witted story-telling jury lawyer, who talked himself out of scrapes when a lad, and later into the jobs he coveted." Peter Lynch, who saw him in action, noted that he made full use of the lawyers associated with him in a case, especially James F. Gray. "A hasty examination of [Gray's] briefs sufficed to give his senior as much knowledge of a case as could be obtained by others with hours of thought and labor." But Archibald's later career demonstrates that these estimates tell only part of the story.

From 1817 to 1830 the wheel of fortune turned steadily in Archibald's favour. Seldom did he spurn the mighty of the land if he could avoid it. In 1818 he acted as surrogate general of the Vice-Admiralty Court, helping to clear up the rest of the old prize cases, not so much because he wanted to, but because it was "pressed upon me under circumstances that would have rendered it impolitic to have refused." That same year he made the motion for setting up the provincial agricultural society, and in 1822 he established an oat mill in Truro at his own expense. Much later, in a barb aimed at John Young, he pointed out that he was "no theoretical speculator" in agricultural possibilities, but had spent his own money to demonstrate their practicality. From a trip to Britain and Europe in 1824 he returned, according to Thomas Chandler Haliburton*, with many anecdotes of the Old World, having seen Paris, "*touched* at Brussels, *spoke* in Strasburg, and *provisioned* at *Whitehall*." He also received an honorary LLD from the University of Glasgow and accepted the chief justiceship of Prince Edward Island after being assured that he would not have to live there. In November 1824 he spent three weeks on the Island clearing up the chaos in the Supreme Court, the objective behind his appointment.

Because of Robie's elevation to the Council in 1824, the speakership was vacant when the assembly met the following year. Archibald was elected to the office without opposition and held it until 1841. After his death Howe paid him the compliment of saying: "A more dignified and imposing Speaker, we never saw in the Chair of any Legislative Assembly." In 1824 he had been accused, along with the other lawyer-assemblymen, of unnecessarily foisting four major judicial appointments upon the province. Two years later he was to benefit from this expansion of the courts when, with the appointment of Robie to one of the new offices – the master of the rolls – he succeeded him as solicitor general. But his non-residence in Prince Edward Island was causing serious dissatisfaction with the performance of his judicial duties there. Never giving any serious thought to abandoning his large professional practice and major offices in Nova Scotia or to his hopes of becoming chief justice of that colony, he resigned his Island office in 1828.

In 1830 Archibald was at the peak of his fortunes, "the ornament of the Bar – the master spirit of the [assembly] – and the felicitous humourist of the social circle." At splendid dinner parties in his spacious residence in Halifax, his polished wit and his skill as a story-teller – perhaps the best in the province – came fully into play. His country estate at Truro, where he resided several weeks a year, was according to his biographer, Israel Longworth, a provincial show-place, "studded with gigantic elms . . . [through which] the beautiful [Salmon] river meandered in graceful curves." There the Dalhousies, the Kempts, and "the simpler inhabitants of the Country, shared his hospitality and sang his praises." Archibald's one remaining object – to be chief justice – was to be foiled by the "Brandy Dispute" of 1830 [*see* Enos Collins*]. In a series of speeches, necessarily given in committee, he argued that the power of the assembly to grant a revenue was one of substance and not form. "Consequences most serious . . . will follow, if we are to be used merely as a machine in the hands of His Majesty's Council, to prepare the revenue bills in the manner they shall dictate to us. . . . we possess a right, which to an Englishman and a freeman, is the dearest of all rights – that of *taxing ourselves, without the intervention or dictation of any power upon earth.*" Above all, he emphasized that as speaker and "the natural guardian of the rights and privileges of this House," he had a clear duty to intervene. Under this urging, the assembly stuck to its guns even though it meant the loss of the appropriation and revenue bills and all the concomitant evils. A delighted Howe stated that Archibald's speeches had placed him "on an elevation which in the whole course of his political life he never before attained," while Jotham Blanchard was almost as laudatory. In the election that followed the voters overwhelmingly condemned the Council and Archibald led the poll in Halifax County. But his stance was that of a constitutionalist, not that of a populist or reformer, and it aroused expectations that he could not fulfil.

The Council's supporters contended that even before the "Brandy Dispute" Archibald had forfeited public confidence "in consequence of his uncandid intriguing for promotion" and that in "the last storm [he had] only hurt himself while fooling others." The intrigue in question was a reference to the contention for the chief justiceship, which was in full swing by 1829. For the office held by Sampson Salter Blowers, who was ailing and approaching 90, three candidates presented themselves: Richard John Uniacke Sr, also aged and frail, but whose long-time service as attorney general gave him a special claim on the office; Brenton Halliburton*, whose judicial talents were modest and who had already done well by government in being made a puisne judge within four years of his admission to the bar, but who had strengthened his claim by performing most of the duties of the chief justice over an extended period; and Archibald, whose many services to the crown qualified him for promotion. Archibald might have had the puisne judgeship made vacant by the death of James Stewart in 1830, but he considered his existing status to be superior.

Uniacke died in October of the same year and Lieutenant Governor Sir Peregrine Maitland* made Archibald acting attorney general. But Maitland and the Council intervened in the contention for the chief justiceship by announcing that Halliburton would be sent to Britain, allegedly to remonstrate against the reduction of the duties on foreign timber imported into Great Britain. The real reason, however disguised, was to let Halliburton press his case for the chief justiceship. As a result, Archibald had no choice but to make his own trek to London. In Halifax it was wondered whether he sought the assistance of Lady Mary FitzClarence, the natural daughter of William IV whom the Archibalds had entertained royally in Halifax the previous year.

Apparently his eloquence left a mark on the Marquis of Lansdowne, who is reported to have urged him to enter the British parliament, only to draw the response: "I am already the head of one House, I do not care to become the tail of another." The decision of the colonial secretary, Viscount Goderich, delayed until 4 Dec. 1832, was to make Halliburton chief justice, allegedly because he had performed the duties of the office for so long a time, and to propose an addition to Archibald's salary as attorney general (in which office he was confirmed) until something more advantageous could be found for him. Haligonians in the know were certain that Archibald had forfeited the chief justiceship the moment he assumed the leadership of the assembly in the "Brandy Dispute."

In 1830 Archibald had suffered two other blows in the deaths of his second son and of his wife, who had borne him 15 children (among them Edward Mortimer*) and who had been an accomplished woman with the same liking for social life as himself. Less than two years later he married the widow Joanna Brinley, and they had three daughters; perhaps because Joanna did not care for social life, Archibald never got over the loss of his first wife, even though the marriage, like the first, was a happy one.

After 1830 Archibald increasingly found himself out of sympathy with the majority in the assembly. In 1832, disagreeing with both Howe and Young, he favoured the commutation of unpaid quitrents owed the crown for an annual payment by the government of £2,000. In this instance any suggestion that he had a "private and personal interest" in increasing the crown's casual revenues so that they could more readily meet the salaries borne upon them, including his own as attorney general, seems both unfair and far-fetched. Two years later Ichabod charged no less unfairly in the *Acadian Recorder* that Archibald had sought to have his salary as attorney general increased at a time "when the Treasury was drained to its very dregs, when any Money given to Roads has to be borrowed and when trade was languishing" under a general bankruptcy.

Basically Archibald was in conflict with the folklore which treated him as a supporter of popular causes. Actually, up to 1830, when the *status quo* was generally accepted, he could be counted upon to oppose any turning back of the clock, as in the "Brandy Dispute." But as the thirties advanced and Howe came to appreciate the deep-seated evils in provincial government and through the *Novascotian, or Colonial Herald* called on the voters to elect a new brand of assembly and assemblyman, Archibald found himself more and more a reluctant observer of a style of politics that was distasteful to him. By July 1836 the *Acadian Recorder* had joined fully in the attack on the existing order through the letters of Joe Warner, the pseudonym of John Young. Among other things, the letters charged Archibald with a myriad of public offences, including the condonation of waste and extravagance. Howe, who had considerable respect for Archibald, thought the criticism much too harsh since, despite "the plotting and planning" attributed to him, he had "not fared half so well" as the provincial secretary, Sir Rupert Dennis George, the collector of customs, Thomas Nickleson JEFFERY, and other major office holders. Indeed, Howe claimed, "if [Archibald] had more unscrupulously lent himself to a certain narrow party in this Province, he might have fared a good deal better."

During the 1836 election Archibald met a spirited electoral challenge in the recently created county of Colchester from Isaac Logan, one of the new breed of candidates, who mouthed Warner's arguments. In bitterness that was rare with him, he denounced Warner as "the manufacturer of slander and libel" and Logan as "the Hawker, the Pedlar, and petty Chapman of his Wares." "My name," he continued, "shall remain and stand connected with Colchester when the name of Joe Warner shall be rotten as his compost, and stink like his dunghill." Archibald also tried to "square the account" with Young in the first session of the new assembly, during which proposals were made to ban the export of grain and potatoes because of a crop failure. When, as was his wont, Young objected to interfering with the principles of political economy, Archibald scorned the idea of limiting the energies of the house in times of famine and distress by doctrines drawn from Adam Smith, asking, "Are we to be told that we are never to legislate in opposition to certain laws and rules which have been established by political theorists?" It was to be his last collision with Young, who died in October 1837.

But it was Archibald's only major contribution to the assembly that session, for although re-elected speaker he had lost the leadership of the house. Reformers, who had blossomed overnight, commanded a majority on most subjects and turned for leadership to Howe and Laurence O'Connor Doyle*. Archibald said almost nothing on Howe's 12 Resolutions, but obviously he did not look sympathetically on the reformers' disordering of the even tenor of the assembly's ways. He did not preside over the closing days of the session because of illness, which newspapers attributed to erysipelas but which resulted from a severe stroke. He never fully recovered, and during his last few years he laboured "under a paralysis of the muscles, which disturbed the expression of the face, and at times rendered articulation difficult, if not impossible." But he was restored sufficiently by December to move the major resolutions at a public meeting which deprecated the rebellion in Lower Canada and expressed a determination to look after the families of the soldiers who had left to put down the insurrection. He continued to preside over the assembly's sessions to the end of 1840, but without participating in the lower house's vigorous assertion of the popular cause.

Archibald was placed in a dilemma in 1840 when, because of the failure of Lieutenant Governor Sir Colin CAMPBELL to acknowledge that the colonial secretary's dispatch of 16 Oct. 1839 had conferred "a new and improved constitution" upon the colonies, the assembly demanded the lieutenant governor's removal. Asked by Campbell for his opinion of the dispatch, Archibald replied that, although it would be improper for him to oppose the assembly's wishes, the lieutenant governor was entitled to his views in his capacity as attorney general. Accordingly he expressed doubt that the dispatch could bear the interpretation the assembly was putting upon it, and confidence that Campbell had acted properly in awaiting further instructions from the colonial secretary. Clearly these views indicate how far "the opinions of the majority of the House, had outrun those of its Head."

When a new lieutenant governor, Lord Falkland [Cary*], reconstituted the Executive Council in October 1840, Archibald headed the list of new councillors, but following the election of the same year he could not resume the office of speaker because of a decision taken in Britain to bring Nova Scotian parliamentary practice into accord with the British. Required to choose between the speakership and the attorney generalship, Archibald retained the latter. He did not remain in the assembly much longer, however, for after the death of Charles Rufus FAIRBANKS he was sworn in as master of the rolls on 29 April 1841, a position he held until a massive stroke killed him instantly five years later. Those who feared that his lack of legal knowledge and his dislike of labour made the choice a bad one were surprised by his application to the duties of his new office. If not a great judge, he was by general agreement a very good one; certainly his performance did not suffer in comparison with those of the other masters, Robie, Fairbanks, and Alexander Stewart*.

Eloquent and imposing, Archibald brought dignity and sophistication to the Nova Scotian legislature. The Halifax newspaper the *Sun* rightly called him "one of the most amiable of men." As Howe put it: "There was no venom or malignity about Judge Archibald – to give pleasure and to share it, was a necessity of his nature – but it never gave him pleasure to give others pain." Israel Longworth is quite wrong, however, in claiming that "no other man contributed so much to mould the institutions and shape the destinies of Nova Scotia." In an assembly committed to a program of moderate reform he found himself in an altogether inhospitable environment. Yet it can at least be said of him that as a constitutionalist he prevented the reactionaries from turning back the clock.

J. MURRAY BECK

PANS, MG 1, 89, esp. no.1a; 979–80. *Acadian Recorder*, 1830–36. *Novascotian*, 1830–46. John Doull, *Sketches of attorney generals of Nova Scotia* (Halifax, 1964). Israel Longworth, *Life of S. G. W. Archibald* (Halifax, 1881). G. [G.] Patterson, *Studies in Nova Scotian history* (Halifax, 1940). Peter Lynch, "Early reminiscences of Halifax – men who have passed from us," N.S. Hist. Soc., *Coll.*, 16 (1912): 199–201.

ARNOLDI, DANIEL, physician, office holder, and JP; b. 7 March 1774 in Montreal, son of Peter Arnoldi, a soldier from Hesse (Federal Republic of Germany), and Philipina Maria (Phébé) Horn, and brother of Phebe* and Michael* Arnoldi; m. Élisabeth Franchère, and they had three sons and seven daughters; d. 19 July 1849 in Montreal.

After studying in England, Daniel Arnoldi took medical training in Montreal under Robert Sym and John Rowand. They, along with Charles Blake*, were medical examiners for the district of Montreal, and on 22 June 1795 the three signed the licence authorizing Arnoldi to practise. Arnoldi established himself in Rivière-du-Loup (Louiseville). Doubtless finding the competition too stiff and patients scarce, he moved to the Bay of Quinte region in Upper Canada around 1797. After working for three years under difficult conditions in this rather primitive area, where he used the paddle and the axe as frequently as his surgical instruments, he returned to Lower Canada and stayed at La Prairie. In 1802 he settled permanently in Montreal.

According to his friend and colleague Archibald Hall*, Arnoldi had a hard time at first, but he quickly acquired a large number of wealthy patients. In 1808 he took in John Fraser, from Upper Canada, as a student; Henry Munro, Robert Nelson*, and Andrew Fernando Holmes* also owed their medical training to him, and Holmes even became his partner.

In 1812 Arnoldi was appointed a medical examiner for the district of Montreal and took his turn in determining which candidates were qualified to practise medicine. In 1823 Lord Dalhousie [RAMSAY] modified the board of examiners and ruled that only doctors from the Montreal General Hospital could be members. Arnoldi was consequently excluded from the circle of physicians, including Holmes, John STEPHENSON, William Caldwell*, and William ROBERTSON, who now controlled entry into the medical profession. In 1823 this group founded the Montreal Medical Institution, which became the Faculty of Medicine of McGill College six years later.

Under a new medical act of 1831 the members of medical boards were no longer chosen by the governor but were elected by the licensed physicians in each district. At the first meeting of the doctors in the district of Montreal in July of that year the group from McGill College, which enjoyed the governor's patronage and had had a stranglehold on the appointment of doctors for eight years, was eliminated from the board. Arnoldi, along with Jacques Labrie*, Robert Nelson, Wolfred Nelson*, Pierre Beaubien*, Timothée Kimber*, and Jean-Baptiste Meilleur*, among other physicians, was elected. Taken by surprise, the former examiners returned to the attack when a new election was held on 7 July 1834. Wolfred Nelson, seconded by Joseph-François Davignon, nominated Arnoldi as chairman. Robertson and Stephenson fought the nomination energetically, but in vain. Arnoldi was, however, to resign from the Board of Examiners four months after joining it, since he felt himself increasingly at odds with his colleagues' political views.

In the years from 1810 to 1830 Arnoldi's political sympathies seem to have undergone a change. At first he ardently supported the authorities and in 1814 signed an address in defence of Jonathan SEWELL and James Monk*, the judges under attack by the House of Assembly [*see* James Stuart*]. Following his exclusion as a medical examiner in 1823, some members of the Canadian party used his resentment of the doctors responsible for it in an endeavour to win him to their cause. Arnoldi, making the most of the situation, supported the political thinking of his temporary allies, but never compromised himself. By May 1832 his support for the Patriote cause appeared dubious. In a by-election in Montreal West for the House of Assembly he backed Stanley Bagg, the English party candidate, rather than Patriote Daniel Tracey*, and at the time of the riot on 21 May he unreservedly approved the intervention of the military.

Other incidents were to cause the leaders of the assembly to doubt Arnoldi's sincerity. For example, his appointment by the governor as doctor to the Montreal jail in 1833 and his commission as a justice of the peace appeared suspect to many. Consequently the assembly seized upon the death of a prisoner, which it attributed to the "culpable negligence" of the jailer and Arnoldi, as a pretext to request that he be dismissed as prison doctor. Relations between Arnoldi and his former allies deteriorated. Beaubien, in a letter written to Louis-Joseph Papineau*, the head of the Patriote party, at the end of 1835, commented on Arnoldi's appointment as a justice of the peace: "Can we not say that the last administration took on some of those *raving madmen* whom it would have done better to send to the lunatic cells? Haven't we had enough of Dr Robertson? Did Dr Arnoldi have to be added to them[?]" Beaubien also blamed Arnoldi for asserting in court that Louis-Hippolyte La Fontaine* ought to have had "his skull cracked" for the part he took in the events of 21 May 1832.

Following the uprising in 1837–38 some Patriotes accused Arnoldi of having failed to look after the prisoners incarcerated in the Montreal jail for participating in the rebellion. Others, however, praised him for displaying humanity in these circumstances. Several people reproached him and his son François-Cornelius-Thomas, who was also a doctor, with having insulted the corpse of the Patriote Jean-Olivier CHÉNIER. Jacques PAQUIN, parish priest of Saint-Eustache, stated that "Dr Chénier's body was found around 6 o'clock . . . the doctors opened it up to determine the cause of death, but it is untrue that his heart was torn out and that it was made an object of curiosity." Louis-Joseph-Amédée Papineau* protested in his diary against Paquin's testimony: "To cut up a man killed on the battlefield, and riddled with bullets, and quarter his body and tear out his heart and take it to Montreal to make sure of the cause of death!!!!! Posterity! Do not forget the doctors ARNOLDI, father and son, of the city of Montreal, butchers!!!" If people at the time were not in agreement about Arnoldi's role in Chénier's autopsy, they seem at least to have concurred in recognizing the cruelty of his son, one of the leaders of a battalion of loyal volunteers from Montreal who terrorized the people of Saint-Eustache and Saint-Benoît (Mirabel).

Arnoldi's loyalty to the authorities enabled him to regain his seat on the Board of Examiners in 1839, whereas several of his former colleagues were exiled as a result of their role in the rebellion or simply ousted from office because of their indifference to the government cause. Arnoldi remained on the board until it was dissolved in 1847.

Although Arnoldi's political concepts were for the most part conservative, his participation in the movement to bring medical legislation up to date aligned him with reformers. In 1823 he took part in a meeting of doctors from the district of Montreal to address means for giving the medical profession the prestige it sadly lacked. This meeting petitioned the governor to amend the act of 1788 governing the teaching and practice of medicine. The first Lower Canadian statute to deal fully with medicine was signed in 1831. In the period of the union of the two Canadas this law, which had undergone various changes, was contested regularly in Lower Canada, particularly by the members of the Board of Examiners for the district of Montreal. It was agreed at their meeting on 4 May 1841 that a petition drawn up by doctors James Crawford, Holmes, and Arnoldi seeking amendment of the law should be sent to the assembly. In subsequent years this concern reappeared regularly on the agenda, and each time Arnoldi participated in the discussion. When the board in 1843 set up a committee to draft a bill regulating more strictly the teaching and practice of medicine, he became one of its most active members. He was, however, absent from the many doctors' meetings held between 1844 and 1847 which culminated in the passage of a bill in 1847. This act, regarded as the great charter of medicine, set up the College of Physicians and Surgeons of Lower Canada. It strengthened the power of the profession, bestowing new prestige upon it. Once the act had been passed, dissensions between doctors in the different districts and schools made the choice of the president of the college more complicated. Arnoldi was appointed finally by the governor on 10 Aug. 1847. Like most of his colleagues, Arnoldi did not limit his activities to the field of medicine. Early in his career unlucky speculations in real estate seem to have caused him financial difficulties for a time. He quickly surmounted these and in 1806 bought a fine stone house on Rue Saint-François-Xavier that was considered a model in its time. In the spring of 1829 he bought half of the seigneury of Bourg-Louis, which he later sold. On 3 Oct. 1831 there was an announcement in *La Minerve* that Arnoldi and others, in particular Joseph MASSON, Peter McGill*, and Horatio Gates*, were applying to the assembly to obtain a charter for a company to build a canal from Lac-des-Deux-Montagnes (Oka) to Lachine.

Daniel Arnoldi associated with the "best" Montreal bourgeoisie. Several of his daughters married into the upper middle class. Élisabeth wed Benjamin Holmes* and Caroline Matilda, Robert Gillespie*; Aurelia Felicite married William King McCord*, and Louise Priscille, Albert Furniss. At the time he fell victim to cholera, on 19 July 1849, Arnoldi was a justice of the peace and president of the College of Physicians and Surgeons of Lower Canada. The previous year he had been awarded a doctorate *honoris causa* by McGill College.

GILLES JANSON

ANQ-M, CE1-51, 21 août 1807, 3 août 1809, 7 juill. 1811, 9 mars 1815, 5 sept. 1816, 22 déc. 1818, 14 mai 1833, 12 juill. 1837, 16 juin 1845; CE1-63, 13 mars 1774, 19 juill. 1849; CN1-134, 30 août 1816; 13 févr. 1818; 19 avril, 5 juill. 1828; 8 oct. 1829; 18 oct. 1830; 15 sept. 1837; CN1-135, 9 août 1845, 20 févr. 1846; CN1-185, 12 avril 1806, 22 janv. 1808; CN1-187, 9, 12 oct. 1815; 31 mai 1821; CN1-216, 12 sept. 1834, 23 févr. 1837, 5 sept. 1838, 22 août 1843; P-26, 11 sept. 1832. ANQ-Q, P-69, 21, 25 déc. 1835; 16 janv., 25 févr. 1836. BVM-G, Coll. Gagnon, corr., Daniel Arnoldi à Louis Gugy, 29 mai 1821, 15 janv. 1826. PAC, MG 24, A27, ser.2, 22: 527–28; B2: 2062–64; B28, 52: 1532–39; RG 4, B28, 47: 101–2; B37, 1: 570–72; RG 68, General index, 1651–1841. Professional Corporation of Physicians of Que. Arch. (Montreal), Montreal Medical Board, minutes, 1839–47; Collège des médecins et chirurgiens du Bas-Canada, procès-verbaux, 1847–50. Émélie Berthelot-Girouard, "Les journaux d'Émélie Berthelot-Girouard," Béatrice Chassé, édit., ANQ *Rapport*, 1975: 13–20. L.C., House of Assembly, *Journals*, 9 Feb. 1833; 25 Feb., 4 March 1836; 1836, app.WW; 24 Nov. 1843. L.-J.-A. Papineau, *Journal d'un Fils de la liberté*, 2: 52. *Le Canadien*, 2 juin 1824; 4 janv., 25, 28 août 1833; 22 déc. 1837; 13 août 1845. *La Minerve*, 11 juill., 3 oct. 1831; 7, 10 juill. 1834. *Montreal Gazette*, 7 Oct. 1834. *Montreal Herald*, 25 June, 12 July 1814. *Le Populaire*, 22 déc. 1837, 3 janv. 1838. Abbott, *Hist. of medicine*. *Biographical sketch of the late Daniel Arnoldi, M.D.* ... (Montreal, 1850). Canniff, *Medical profession in U.C.* Filteau, *Hist. des patriotes* (1975). J. J. Heagerty, *Four centuries of medical history in Canada and a sketch of the medical history of Newfoundland* (2v., Toronto, 1928). Germain Lesage, *Histoire de Louiseville, 1665–1960* (Louiseville, Qué., 1961). B. [R]. Tunis, "The medical profession in Lower Canada: its evolution as a social group, 1788–1838" (BA research essay, Carleton Univ., Ottawa, 1979). Édouard Fabre Surveyer, "Une famille d'orfèvres," *BRH*, 46 (1940): 310–15. B. R. Tunis, "Medical licensing in Lower Canada: the dispute over Canada's first medical degree," *CHR*, 55 (1974): 489–504.

ASCANCE. *See* AISANCE

AUDY. *See* ROY-AUDY

AUFFRAY, CHARLES-DOMINIQUE, teacher and farmer; b. 1794 in Lamballe, France, illegitimate son of Jeanne-Mathurine Auffray; d. 28 March 1837 in Pré-d'en-Haut, N.B.

Charles-Dominique Auffray never knew his father, a soldier who died in battle several months before he was born. His mother decided to go and live with her father, Charles Auffray. She later married, but died a short time afterwards. On the death of her father in 1807, Charles-Dominique, who was only 13, was taken in by his uncle Victor Auffray.

Auffray attended the local school in his youth, and then apprenticed with master silversmiths in various French towns. In 1813 he enlisted in the Napoleonic army. After six months in the field he was wounded; subsequently, after the restoration of Louis XVIII, he was granted temporary leave. In 1816, even though he had received no discharge from active service, he left Saint-Malo for St John's with Auguste Flulin, a silversmith who had hired him. On arriving at St John's, however, Flulin, who had contraband goods with him, had all his possessions seized by customs officers, and consequently had no choice but to give his workman notice.

After spending six weeks in St John's, Auffray managed to get to Prince Edward Island, to the Acadian village of Cascumpec not far from Tignish on the northwestern coast. Since he was able to read and write, and so was considered a scholar by the villagers, he offered his services as a teacher. For the next three years, from 1816 to 1819, he taught there, but before long, according to an account written some 80 years later, he began to be distrusted: "He behaved in such a manner as to arouse suspicions, and soon his odd ways earned him the title of sorcerer. So many things were imputed to him that finally Auffray had to clear out." In fact he was brought before the justice of the peace by the parents of a girl who was carrying his child. Having made reparation to the parents, he left Cascumpec in 1819 and went to live at Barachois, another Acadian village, this time in southeastern New Brunswick, and again was hired as a teacher.

After two years, Auffray seems to have had it in mind to settle there permanently: he was engaged to a local girl, and on 12 Dec. 1821 he petitioned the lieutenant governor of the province, George Stracey Smyth*, for a grant of land in a new settlement near Barachois. His request was rejected, however, and Antoine GAGNON, the missionary responsible for Barachois, apparently refused to marry him because of insufficient proof that there were no impediments to the union. When consulted by Gagnon earlier that year, the archbishop of Quebec, Joseph-Octave Plessis*, had assented to the marriage but counselled Gagnon to seek the opinion also of his diocesan bishop, Angus Bernard MacEachern* of Charlottetown. MacEachern had already advised Gagnon that he himself would perform the ceremony only if two witnesses were able to swear on the Gospel and the crucifix that the suitor was single or a widower. As there was no one at Barachois to bear witness on his behalf, Auffray evidently had to abandon the idea of getting married.

In the autumn of 1822 Auffray was a witness at the wedding in nearby Memramcook of his friend and compatriot from Dunkirk, Gabriel Herbert, who was also a teacher. Tradition has it that he met a young lady there and fell in love with her, with the result that he moved from Barachois to Memramcook, where the missionary Louis Gingras* raised no obstacles to his plans to wed her. On 4 Nov. 1823 he married Nathalie Bourgeois, and he settled down at Pré-d'en-Haut, an Acadian village on the east bank of the Petitcodiac. Interestingly, he had stated to Gingras that he was the son of Charles-Victor Auffray and Jeanne Cantin, probably thinking that if he told the truth his marriage would not take place. At the time of the wedding he was still calling himself a "schoolmaster," but a year later, at the baptism of his first child (he would have five others in the period from 1827 to 1835), he was described as an "agricultural labourer." He remained so employed until his death on 28 March 1837. For some time he had apparently been planning to take a trip to his native land and had put a little money aside for this purpose, but death intervened unexpectedly.

Charles-Dominique Auffray figures among the first teachers or "itinerant masters" to serve in the Acadian community, both on Prince Edward Island and in New Brunswick, after the deportation of 1755. He was in some ways a precursor of Jean Leménager (the husband of his sister-in-law Élizabeth Bourgeois), Gabriel Herbert, Alexis-Théodore de La Burgue, Jacques Grenet, and Henri Renouard, Frenchmen who in the first half of the 19th century taught the Acadians in southeastern New Brunswick the rudiments of grammar and arithmetic.

R. GILLES LEBLANC

AAQ, 210 A, X: 424; 311 CN, V: 54, 56–58. Arch. of the Diocese of Saint John (Saint John, N.B.), Antoine Gagnon papers, no.126. Arch. paroissiales, Saint-Henri (Barachois, N.-B.), Reg. des baptêmes, mariages et sépultures (mfm. at Centre d'études acadiennes, univ. de Moncton, Moncton, N.-B.); Saint-Thomas (Memramcook, N.-B.), Reg. des baptêmes, mariages et sépultures (mfm. at Centre d'études acadiennes). Centre d'études acadiennes, 604-1-1 (C. Renaud, "Histoire généalogique de Dr. Jean-Marie Auffrey"); A-4-7, no.503. G. Buote, "La paroisse de Cascumpec," *L'Impartial* (Tignish, Î.-P.-É.), 17 mars 1904: 3.

AULDJO, GEORGE, businessman, militia officer, JP, and office holder; b. 2 April 1790 in Aberdeen, Scotland, son of George Auldjo, merchant, and Susan Beauvais; d. 11 April 1846 in Montreal.

George Auldjo was educated, at least in part, at the Aberdeen Grammar School before he immigrated to Montreal to join his uncle Alexander Auldjo*, a partner with William Maitland in the firm Auldjo, Maitland and Company. By 1815 it had become Maitland, Garden, and Auldjo; Maitland, and possibly Alexander Auldjo, represented it in London, while George Auldjo and George Garden* were left as the Montreal principals. Auldjo had become an agent of the Phoenix Assurance Company of London by 1816. Six years later he and Garden were apparently partners in a Quebec firm called Garden, Auldjo and Company.

Maitland, Garden, and Auldjo, meanwhile, had become a leading import-export house in Montreal, having extensive dealings in Upper Canada with merchants at Kingston and Niagara (Niagara-on-the-Lake). By 1825 it was importing large quantities of wine, port, brandy, haberdashery, indigo, gunpowder, glassware, and oil as well as cordage and other shipbuilding materials. It brought rum from Demerara (Guyana), linen from Greenock, Scotland, beer from Aberdeen, charcoal from Liverpool, England, and a wide variety of copper and iron goods from London and Dundee, Scotland; it received as well consignments of molasses, coffee, leather, and sugar from Halifax. The firm itself consigned timber pieces, staves and headings, and casks of hams, salmon, cod, and essence of spruce to these and other ports.

Auldjo often bought and sold some of these goods on his own account. He also acted as a hiring agent for Upper Canadian businessmen, including James*, Mathew, and William Crooks, who employed Canadians and immigrants in their stores and mills. On three occasions in the early 1820s Auldjo joined Horatio Gates*, among others, in planning improvements around Montreal: the construction of a new market, the building of a turnpike road to Longue-Pointe, and the extension of Rue Saint-Pierre to the St Lawrence River. He served as a director of the Bank of Montreal in 1822 at least and possibly until 1825.

The importance of his firm gave Auldjo prominence in the Montreal business community. His position was further strengthened by his marriage on 5 Oct. 1816 to 17-year-old Helen Richardson, daughter of one of the most influential businessmen-politicians of the period, John Richardson*; they would have two sons and three daughters. Like his father-in-law, Auldjo took a leading role in promoting business interests. He joined in protests against the effect of Britain's corn law on wheat exports to the mother country, and in 1822, with Richardson, Gates, and others, he organized the Committee of Trade, since "the ruinous consequences now apprehended from the growing embarrassment of Canadian commerce can no longer be averted or even delayed by the solitary exertions of individuals." He served as its president from 1825 to 1833 and in 1835–36. He had done military service during the War of 1812 as an ensign in Montreal's 1st Militia Battalion; in 1821 he reached the rank of captain in the 2nd Militia Battalion, and he was still active in the militia in 1831. In 1824 he was made an examiner of candidates for inspector of pot and pearl ashes in the district of Montreal, was appointed a commissioner to report on the state of the Montreal harbour, and received a commission of the peace. He was a prominent member of the Scotch Presbyterian Church, later known as St Gabriel Street Church. In private life he was a man of generosity and fidelity. When his cousin Thomas Thain* returned to England on the brink of a nervous breakdown in 1825, Auldjo accompanied him. "It is impossible to do justice . . . to young Auldjo," Edward Ellice* related to John FORSYTH. "He has not left Thain's bed-side, either night or day – & his attention has been both most affectionate & unremitting."

In the 1820s, borrowing in Britain, Auldjo invested heavily in shipping on behalf of Maitland, Garden, and Auldjo. In 1823 he joined a syndicate to commission construction of a steamboat engine at John Dod Ward's Eagle Foundry in Montreal. Maitland, Garden, and Auldjo also became a leading financier of sailing ships built in Montreal, William Henry (Sorel), and Quebec for export to Britain. From 1824 to 1827 its investments produced an estimated 29.4 per cent (valued at £40,000) of wind-powered tonnage constructed in Montreal yards. As the British money market tightened and demand for ships declined after 1824, this huge commitment brought ruin to the firm, and it went into receivership in 1826. Of its £242,624 in assets, about £70,800 were recovered ten years later.

The failure of his firm did not affect Auldjo's standing in the community. He retained his commissions, became a life governor of the Montreal General Hospital in 1829, and was appointed a warden of Trinity House at Montreal in 1832, a commissioner for the improvement of inland navigation the following year, a commissioner for the Lachine Canal in 1835, and by 1838 an inspector of ashes for export. His personal financial condition was partially revived in 1833 when his wife bought up some of his debts, and on her death in 1837 he inherited her valuable real estate holdings in the heart of Montreal's business district and possibly her extensive lands in Upper Canada as well.

Auldjo's fortunes in business were curiously reflected in voyages he made on its behalf. He was among the survivors when the *Lady Sherbrooke* hit rocks in the Gulf of St Lawrence in July 1831, and seven years later he was a passenger on the steamboat *Sir Robert Peel* when it was attacked and burned at Wells (Wellesley) Island, N.Y., by Upper Canadian Patriots under William Johnston*. On the latter occasion he was relieved of all his belongings and £600 which he was carrying for a colleague. Not discouraged by such episodes, in July 1843 he was among passengers on the steamer *North America*, which made an excursion to Kamouraska and Rivière-du-Loup, Lower Canada, and then up the Rivière Saguenay. This voyage was pleasantly uneventful. Auldjo's journey through life did not end blissfully, however. His business fortunes again declined, and in his last years he was reduced to living in a *déclassé* hotel on Rue Saint-Paul.

GERALD J. J. TULCHINSKY

[The author wishes to thank George A. Mackenzie for assistance in researching this biography. G.J.J.T.]

ANQ-M, CE1-126, 5 oct. 1816, 14 avril 1846. GRO (Edinburgh), Aberdeen, reg. of births and baptisms, 4 May 1790. McCord Museum, J. H. Dorwin, "Antiquarian autographs," 571. Montreal Business Hist. Project, Extracts and digests of Montreal notarial arch., W. N. Crawford: 406, 408–9, 507; N.-B. Doucet: 10170–72, 10338–39, 10669–70, 10962–63, 11696; Henry Griffin: 4158–59, 4249–50. PAC, MG 24, A2: 1060–61; D19: 78–83; RG 68, General index, 1651–1841. QUA, 2270. *Quebec Commercial List*, 14, 16–17, 21, 23 May, 23–25 June, 20, 22, 28–30 July, 17, 27 Aug., 5, 7–8, 16 Sept., 10, 18, 31 Oct., 27 Nov. 1825. *Quebec Gazette*, 31 Aug. 1815; 14 March 1816; 25 June, 5 Oct. 1818; 1 April 1819; 18 May, 26 Oct., 9 Nov. 1820; 23 April 1821; 8, 15 Aug. 1822; 13 Oct. 1823; 17 May 1824; 22 Aug. 1831; 9 Nov. 1832; 22 May 1837; 21 July 1843. Caron, "Inv. des doc. relatifs aux événements de 1837 et 1838," ANQ *Rapport*, 1925–26: 313. *Montreal almanack*, 1839: 16. *Montreal directory*, 1845: 18, 257. F. W. Terrill, *A chronology of Montreal and of Canada from A.D. 1752 to A.D. 1893* . . . (Montreal, 1893). Campbell, *Hist. of Scotch Presbyterian Church*. E. A. Collard, *The Montreal Board of Trade, 1822–1972: a story* ([Montreal], 1972), 1–7. Creighton, *Empire of St. Lawrence*. Denison, *Canada's first bank*. Robert Sweeny, *Protesting history: 4 papers* (Montreal, 1984). "Origins of the Montreal Board of Trade," *Journal of Commerce* (Gardenvale, Que.), 2nd ser., 55 (April 1927): 28–29.

AYLMER, MATTHEW WHITWORTH-AYLMER, 5th Baron. *See* WHITWORTH-AYLMER

B

BADGLEY, FRANCIS, merchant, politician, militia officer, accountant, newspaper editor, and JP; b. 26 March 1767 in London; d. 7 Oct. 1841 in Montreal.

Francis Badgley was descended from a family of small landowners and farmers on the border of Derbyshire and Cheshire, but his parents may have been London fur dealers. About 1785 he immigrated to the province of Quebec, choosing to settle in

Montreal, where he likely had family connections; a merchant named James Badgley was living there in 1784.

In 1788 Francis Badgley became the partner of Richard Dobie*, a prominent Montreal merchant, in a business which outfitted fur traders for the region southwest of Michilimackinac (Mackinac Island, Mich.) and the Great Lakes and which bought and sold furs. The partnership lasted until 1792. On 1 May of that year Badgley left with the annual spring brigade for the voyage to Grand Portage (near Grand Portage, Minn.). He had been hired to do a survey for the North West Company and during this trip he kept a diary in which he described the journey from Lachine, Lower Canada, up the Ottawa River to Lake Nipissing (Ont.) and from there to Georgian Bay and Grand Portage. The trip netted him and his former partner merely £71 but resulted in the naming of a small island near Manitoulin Island after him.

Badgley returned to Montreal in the fall of 1792 and sailed for England in late October, probably to negotiate the importation of brandy and other spirits. His Montreal connections were enhanced in 1795 when, on 27 November, he married Elizabeth Lilly, daughter of John Lilly, one of the town's more prominent merchants. From 1796 until 1799 he was in partnership with Quebec merchant Louis Dunière* and James Badgley in the firm Dunière, Badgley and Company. In 1799 he set up his own business in Montreal, Francis Badgley and Company. In that year Badgley's financial status was such that he could match his father-in-law's contribution of £20 a year towards the subscription being raised in the colony to help defray Britain's expenses in the war with France.

In 1800 Badgley contested the two-member riding of Montreal East for the House of Assembly. Both he and Pierre-Louis Panet* secured 178 votes, eliminating the third contestant. During his four years as a member of the assembly, Badgley supported the English party. He played an active role on the committee studying the demolition of Montreal's walls, was president of the committee on the abolition of slavery in the province, and supported Joseph Frobisher* and his associates in securing the incorporation of the Company of Proprietors of the Montreal Water Works. He was instrumental in having a duty imposed upon American-grown tobacco. Badgley did not seek re-election in 1804, possibly for financial reasons since members were not paid and the business of a Montreal merchant was often neglected during his absence at Quebec. Indeed, in 1803, the severe financial difficulties of a "Mr Badgley" caused serious problems for merchant Henry Joseph* of Berthier-en-Haut (Berthierville). His single term in the assembly showed him to be an energetic and responsible member, anxious to promote Montreal's commercial interests.

During the War of 1812 Badgley served as a captain in Montreal's 1st Militia Battalion. His duties were primarily with the commissariat department at La Prairie, in which his experience as a merchant and his skill in accountancy made him particularly valuable. Thomas Doige's directory of 1819 listed him as a merchant and accountant. In 1822 he became accountant for Molson's Brewery. He probably owed this appointment to his son-in-law William Molson*, who had married his eldest daughter, Elizabeth, in 1819. Of his five other children, two sons became prominent in Montreal, William* as a judge and politician and Francis* as a medical doctor. Badgley continued to be active in a variety of fields during the early 1820s. Some time between 1816 and 1822 he acted as editor of the *Montreal Gazette* [*see* James BROWN]. In 1821 he was appointed justice of the peace and was promoted major in the militia.

ELINOR KYTE SENIOR

ANQ-M, CE1-63, 11 oct. 1841. AUM, P 58. PAC, MG 11, [CO 42] Q, 24; MG 30, D1, 3: 156–95. Private arch., Mrs C. M. Badgley (Westmount, Que.), Badgley papers. *Montreal Gazette*, 3 May, 13 Dec. 1792; 30 Nov. 1795; 21 Nov. 1796; 7, 21 Oct., 2, 30 Dec. 1799; 25 June, 7, 10, 15 July 1800; 2 June 1819; 8 Oct. 1841. *Quebec Gazette*, 28 Nov. 1799. F.-J. Audet, *Les députés de Montréal*. Borthwick, *Hist. and biog. gazetteer*. E. [O.] Clark Watson, *Loyalist Clarks, Badgleys and allied families . . .* (2 parts in 1v., Rutland, Vt., [1954]). Desjardins, *Guide parl. Montreal directory*, 1819. *Officers of British forces in Canada* (Irving). W. H. Atherton, *Montreal, 1535–1914* (3v., Montreal and Vancouver, 1914), 3: 20–22. Campbell, *Hist. of Scotch Presbyterian Church*. Christie, *Hist. of L.C.* (1848–55), vol.1. Merrill Denison, *The barley and the stream: the Molson story; a footnote to Canadian history* (Toronto, 1955).

BAGOT, Sir CHARLES, colonial administrator; b. 23 Sept. 1781 at Blithfield Hall, England, second surviving son of William Bagot, 1st Baron Bagot, and Elizabeth Louisa St John, eldest daughter of John St John, 2nd Viscount St John; d. 19 May 1843 in Kingston, Upper Canada.

Charles Bagot was descended from aristocratic English families which traced their lineages to the Norman conquest. His education, at Rugby School and Christ Church College, Oxford, befitted his social position. In 1801 he was admitted to Lincoln's Inn but, disliking law, he abandoned his studies within a year. He returned to Oxford and obtained an MA in 1804. On 22 July 1806 he married Mary Charlotte Anne Wellesley-Pole, whose father, William Wellesley-Pole, later succeeded to the earldom of Mornington and whose uncle Arthur Wellesley became Duke of Wellington. Bagot and his wife were to have four sons and six daughters.

In 1807 Bagot took a seat in parliament as the member for Castle Rising, a rotten borough controlled by his uncle Richard Howard. A follower of the foreign secretary, George Canning, Bagot became under-secretary for foreign affairs in August 1807. At the end of his mentor's term of office in 1809 he found himself without a post. He also no longer held his parliamentary seat, for in 1807 he had accepted the stewardship of the Chiltern Hundreds, a legal figment which permitted him to resign from the Commons in order to assume a government office. His association with Canning, however, had developed into a close friendship which, along with his extensive family connections, would launch him on a distinguished diplomatic career.

Bagot was named minister plenipotentiary to France on 11 July 1814, but the appointment was temporary; he was replaced by Wellington later that summer. His diplomatic career began in earnest on 31 July 1815 when he was appointed minister plenipotentiary and envoy extraordinary to the United States. It was a difficult assignment, for the Americans kept grudging memories of the War of 1812, and the issues arising out of the hostilities were complicated. Although Bagot was only 34 and had little diplomatic experience, he handled the assignment with tact and sensitivity, won the respect and friendship of the American administration, and became well liked in the American capital.

He also proved to be an astute negotiator, and left his name to the Rush–Bagot agreement concerning the reduction of naval forces on the Great Lakes and Lake Champlain. Worked out during 1816 with the American secretary of state, James Monroe, the agreement was formalized by an exchange of diplomatic notes on 28 and 29 April 1817 between Bagot and the new secretary of state, Richard Rush, and was later ratified by the American Senate. It limited naval armament on the lakes to vessels of 100 tons maximum, with each side being permitted only one such vessel on lakes Champlain and Ontario and no more than two vessels on the remaining lakes. Bagot was also involved in negotiations with the American government to settle a number of other disputes concerning fisheries and the border from Lake of the Woods to the Pacific. The issues were finally resolved in London by the Convention of 1818. He returned to England the following year and, in anticipation of the coronation of King George IV, he was created a GCB on 20 May 1820. Bagot's role in the settlement of boundary issues concerning British North America did not end with his assignment in Washington. As ambassador to Russia from 1820 to 1824 he took part in the negotiations leading to the Anglo-Russian treaty of 1825 which fixed the boundaries of what is now Alaska for the next 75 years.

In the fall of 1824 Bagot was sent as ambassador to The Hague, where King Willem I of the Netherlands was attempting unsuccessfully to unify Holland and Belgium in law, language, and religion. There he became familiar with the problems posed by cultural duality within a single state and took part in the negotiations which ultimately established the independence of Belgium in 1831.

It was a measure of Bagot's high reputation that he was offered the governor generalship of India in 1828. He declined, and after his departure from The Hague in 1831 took part in only one brief mission over the next ten years, to Vienna in 1835. When Sir Robert Peel returned to office as prime minister in September 1841, Bagot agreed to succeed Lord Sydenham [THOMSON] as governor-in-chief of the recently united Province of Canada at a time when that province was undergoing a political crisis. His appointment made sense, despite his lack of parliamentary experience, for he had the personality and sound judgement required for colonial politics. Also, his knowledge of the United States was critical given that belligerent expansionism once more inflamed American politics and threatened to disrupt Anglo-American relations. Indeed, as Peel explained in reply to Charles BULLER's letter concerning the selection of a suitable candidate, "the knowledge that [Bagot] was one of the most popular ambassadors ever accredited to the United States" played an important role in his nomination. Bagot was appointed on 27 Sept. 1841 and arrived in the Canadian capital, Kingston, on 10 Jan. 1842, taking office two days later.

In the wake of the rebellions of 1837–38 the Colonial Office had decided on a policy of harmony between the executive and the legislative branches of the government which was designed to accommodate the House of Assembly but not to submit to the demands of reformers for responsible government. This policy was proving increasingly difficult to administer, for cooperation between the French- and English-speaking reformers in the province created a formidable alliance of opposition members. Sydenham had pulled together an Executive Council and maintained harmony with the assembly by offering inducements that transcended party lines, but as his promises ran out, underlying partisan alignments had begun to re-emerge.

In keeping with the strategy of assimilation proposed by Lord Durham [LAMBTON], Sydenham had taken steps to make Lower Canada essentially British. Although Bagot was to maintain this strategy, he was also instructed by the Colonial Office to try to win the Canadians' acceptance of the union of the Canadas. As a new governor, Bagot was wise enough to rely on advisers who were more familiar with the colony. Among them were Thomas William Clinton Murdoch, the civil secretary he inherited from his predecessor, who offered an expert assessment of the claims and aspirations of the Canadians, and Sir Richard Downes JACKSON, who had served as administrator since Sydenham's death and had begun a strategic distribution of government offices among Canadians as a means of winning their acceptance of the union. Bagot carried on Jackson's strategy by appointing prominent Canadians to a number of positions in the government and the judiciary; the appointees included a French-speaking Catholic deputy superintendent of education for Lower Canada, Jean-Baptiste Meilleur*. He also suspended proclamation of a decree that the Special Council of Lower Canada had passed in 1837 to introduce British common law into the courts. Such gestures he knew would reassure the Canadians that their educational and legal systems would be preserved. He then visited Montreal and Quebec, where his respectful manner, his age, grace, and charm, as well as his fluency in French did much to win over the Canadians.

In Upper Canada Bagot took his role as *ex officio* chancellor of King's College, Toronto, seriously. He urged an end to the numerous delays in opening the college [*see* John Strachan*], worked hard to find suitable professors in the colonies and in Britain [*see* Henry Holmes Croft*], and laid the college's cornerstone on 21 April 1842.

Early that summer, in an effort to strengthen his executive, Bagot appointed Francis Hincks* inspector general of public accounts. His hopes that Hincks would bring with him the support of moderate reformers and that Henry Sherwood*, sworn in as solicitor general in late July, would rally tories to the administration did not materialize. By the end of the summer it became clear that the Executive Council would barely, if at all, hold the confidence of the assembly in the session due to begin in September. Bagot took the advice of such moderate executive councillors as William Henry Draper* and Samuel Bealey Harrison* that the ministry needed the support of the French bloc. On 10 Sept. 1842 he sent for Louis-Hippolyte La Fontaine* to discuss terms for his support in the assembly. The Canadian reform leader consulted with his ally, Robert Baldwin*, the most outspoken proponent of responsible government among Upper Canadian reformers. He returned the following day with a demand for four places in the council, including a position for Baldwin. Bagot, wishing to avoid any concession towards responsible government, replied that he could accept Baldwin provided he "consider himself as brought in by the French Canadian party," not as the leader of the Upper Canadian reformers. He also offered fewer positions than the four demanded by La Fontaine, and on this point their talks broke down. At a meeting of the Executive Council on 12 September, Draper, concerned that this impasse might make possible an alliance of tory and Canadian opposition to the union, offered to resign and indicated that other councillors could be removed if it would help Bagot in his negotiations. He also threatened Bagot with mass resignations if the governor did not accept his advice. The following day Bagot offered La Fontaine the four seats he had demanded but La Fontaine surprised him by rejecting the offer.

Bagot suspected that La Fontaine's refusal came after consultation with Baldwin and was calculated to force a complete reconstruction of the Executive Council along reform party lines. His fears seemed to be confirmed later in the day when Baldwin introduced a motion of non-confidence in the assembly and reiterated his demand for responsible government. This Bagot was determined to prevent. Hoping that the backbenchers would force a compromise, he had Draper disclose the terms of his second offer to La Fontaine in the assembly. After a lively debate the reform leaders indeed succumbed to the pressure of their followers and agreed to accept Bagot's offer. Negotiations resumed on 14 September and were concluded satisfactorily. The reconstituted Executive Council eventually included La Fontaine and his supporters Augustin-Norbert Morin* and Thomas Cushing Aylwin*; Baldwin and his follower James Edward Small*; the moderate reformers Harrison, Hincks, and John Henry Dunn*; the tory Robert Baldwin Sullivan*; and the non-partisan Hamilton Hartley Killaly* and Dominick Daly*. Bagot's skill and personal prestige had salvaged the principle of harmony and, since the new executive had not been formed exclusively along party lines, appeared to have staved off responsible government. Yet Bagot himself admitted to the colonial secretary that "whether the doctrine of responsible government is openly acknowledged, or is only tacitly acquiesced in, virtually it exists."

In London, Peel was alarmed by Bagot's concessions and by a public outcry fed by opposition claims that the government of the Canadas had been handed over to ultra-radicals and former rebels who would soon sever the British connection. Bagot, however, was defended by Murdoch, now back in England, and in time the cabinet came to accept the wisdom of what Bagot had called his "great measure."

Bagot developed an amicable and productive working relationship with La Fontaine and Baldwin, but the strains of the first few months in office seem to have been too much for him. His health had been failing before he came to the Canadas. By late fall he was suffering from a combination of maladies and, too ill to play a prominent role in public affairs, he let much of the responsibility fall to La Fontaine and Baldwin. The colonial secretary accepted his resignation in January 1843. His successor, Sir Charles Theophilus METCALFE, assumed office on 30 March. By that time Bagot was too sick to return home. He died at the governor's official residence, Alwington House, less than two months later.

Bagot's "great measure" remains the most important accomplishment of his brief tenure of office. He displayed therein a fine sense of parliamentary manœuvre and a firm management of men. He was the first British statesman to bring Canadians into the government of their country, and he thus put a decisive mark on the history of constitutional government in the Canadas. As for the American issues he had been expected to address, they had already faded in the wake of the Webster-Ashburton Treaty of August 1842. Bagot deserves the credit, however, for advising the British that month to put an end to the dispute over the Oregon country before American settlement weakened their position. He did not live long enough to see his advice followed in 1845, but for this and also for his earlier contributions to British North American boundary negotiations his name and memory certainly belong to the long story of the "undefended border."

JACQUES MONET

MTRL, Robert Baldwin papers. PAC, MG 11, [CO 42] Q; MG 24, A13, B14; RG 8, I (C ser.). Egerton Ryerson, *Some remarks upon Sir Charles Bagot's Canadian government* (Kingston, [Ont.], 1843). *Statutes, treaties and documents of the Canadian constitution, 1713–1929*, ed. W. P. M. Kennedy (2nd ed., Toronto, 1930). *Burke's peerage* (1890). *DNB*. J. M. S. Careless, *The union of the Canadas: the growth of Canadian institutions, 1841–1857* (Toronto, 1967). G. P. de T. Glazebrook, *Sir Charles Bagot in Canada: a study in British colonial government* (Oxford, Eng., 1929). Monet, *Last cannon shot*. Paul Knaplund, "The Buller–Peel correspondence regarding Canada," *CHR*, 8 (1927): 41–50. J. L. Morison, "Sir Charles Bagot: an incident in Canadian parliamentary history," *Queen's Quarterly* (Kingston), 20 (1912): 1–22. W. O. Mulligan, "Sir Charles Bagot and Canadian boundary questions," CHA *Report*, 1936: 40–52.

BAIRD, NICOL HUGH, engineer and inventor; b. 26 Aug. 1796 in Glasgow, son of Hugh Baird and Margaret Burnthwaite; m. 21 Sept. 1831 in Montreal Mary White, daughter of Andrew White*, and they had four sons and four daughters; d. 18 Oct. 1849 in Brattleboro, Vt.

Relatively little is known about Nicol Hugh Baird's early life. At about the age of 16 he went to Russia where he spent several years with his uncle Charles Baird, founder of a machinery works at St Petersburg (Leningrad). Around 1816 Nicol returned to Scotland where he continued his training under his father, a canal engineer and builder. Following Hugh Baird's death in 1827, Nicol unsuccessfully sought a situation in the army and an appointment as a surveyor. In the spring of 1828, having obtained letters of recommendation from the Duke of Montrose and Thomas Telford, a prominent British engineer, he departed for the Canadas.

Baird's letters brought him quick employment. On 5 July he was received by the governor-in-chief, Lord Dalhousie [RAMSAY], who the next day ordered him to proceed to the Rideau Canal. Eight days later, at Bytown (Ottawa), arrangements were made for him to replace John Mactaggart* as clerk of works on the canal. A demanding supervisor, Baird quickly impressed his superiors with his talents. During his four years on the Rideau he became interested in the problems of bridge building in the Canadas and devised a plan for a "suspension wooden bridge," for which he received a patent in 1831. In September 1832, apparently with Lieutenant-Colonel John BY's support, he was commissioned by the provincial government to survey the mouth of the Trent River and design a bridge to span it. His professional status was recognized in Great Britain in February 1831, when he was admitted to the Institution of Civil Engineers, of which Thomas Telford was chairman.

In the spring of 1833 the lieutenant governor of Upper Canada, Sir John Colborne*, responding to local pressure to develop internal navigation in the Newcastle District, commissioned Baird to undertake a survey and prepare estimates for canals between the Bay of Quinte and Presqu'ile Bay and from the mouth of the Trent River to Rice Lake. In 1835, assisted by Frederick Preston Rubidge*, he prepared a report on the practicability of a canal between Rice Lake and Lake Simcoe. The report emphasized not only the local advantages of a line of navigation between lakes Ontario and Huron but also the commercial and military advantages that would be gained for the colony as a whole. In 1836 Baird was given the opportunity to carry out his plans when he was employed as superintending engineer by both the commissioners for the improvement of the Trent River and the commissioners for the inland waters of the Newcastle District.

Under Baird's supervision, work along the waterway progressed slowly, hindered by the rebellion of 1837–38 and by the province's financial difficulties in the late 1830s. Finally, in 1841 the government, on the recommendation of Hamilton Hartley Killaly*, concluded that the completion of the entire canal between Trent Port (Trenton) and Lake Simcoe was unwarranted. An expedient similar to one proposed by Baird in his 1835 report was adopted instead. Works that were well under way were to be completed and Scugog and Rice lakes, which formed parts of the canal route, connected to Lake Ontario by a road. Under the united province's Board of Works, formed in 1841, Baird oversaw the implementation of this scheme. With the exception of a brief period in 1842, he was employed continuously on the Trent works until October 1843.

Like many engineers of the period, Baird was inclined to over-extend himself by undertaking a number of tasks at one time. In January 1835 he examined the feasibility of constructing a canal to join Lac Saint-Louis and Lac Saint-François on the St Lawrence River. The following year he was approached by William Hamilton Merritt* to become the engineer of the Welland Canal but he demanded a salary that Merritt considered excessive. When the House of Assembly passed an act in 1837 requiring that two practical engineers do a study of the route for an enlarged Welland Canal, Baird and Killaly were chosen. Jointly they prepared a report that was presented to the assembly in February 1838. As well, Baird was involved in the survey and construction of Windsor (Whitby) harbour, improvements to Cobourg harbour, the survey of a Cobourg–Peterborough railway, the construction of Presqu'ile Point lighthouse, and the preparation of a report for the Gananoque and Wiltsie Navigation Company [*see* John McDonald*]. For a brief period in 1840 he was engineer of the Chambly Canal but was dismissed in November of that year.

Early in 1840 Baird was requested by Governor Charles Edward Poulett THOMSON to prepare a report outlining his views on water communications in Canada. He argued that the Welland and St Lawrence systems were of great importance to Canadian commerce. He felt that locks there should equal in size those of the Rideau Canal in order to accommodate large sailing vessels as well as the medium-sized steamers that made up most of the traffic on the Great Lakes. Baird saw a two-fold advantage in his system. Sailing-craft were "less subject to monopolies by wealthy Companies by whom alone Steamer transportation can be expected to be carried on." Competition between sail and steam would reduce freight rates. At the same time, with passage possible for larger vessels, lake-craft would be able to reach the West Indies and return without breaking bulk.

Despite these views, Baird soon turned his attention to finding a means of modifying steam-vessels so that they could more easily navigate existing locks. He devised a scheme for a "sweeping paddle wheel," for which he obtained an Upper Canada patent in 1842. Each of his two side-mounted paddle-wheels was narrower than normal, thus reducing the vessel's width, and each had a deeper stroke, thereby imparting greater speed and stability. Baird's proposal to have this design tested on a naval steamer had been resisted in 1841 by Williams Sandom*, the British captain commanding on the Great Lakes. However, his successor, William Newton Fowell*, was receptive and in 1845 the Admiralty authorized the alteration of the *Mohawk* at Penetanguishene to utilize Baird's paddle-wheels. With them the vessel was able to come down through the Welland Canal and so "supervise the whole of the Lakes."

With fewer opportunities for engineering work in the late 1830s and early 1840s, Baird became increasingly concerned about both recognition in the Canadas of British-born engineers and competition from Americans. When the commissioners of the Cornwall Canal explained that they had employed an American to supervise the works because there were "no Engineers in the Country known to them," Baird wrote testily in 1840 or 1841 that he would not "yield an iota of Superiority to any Engineers from the United States." He proceeded to draft an open letter to the *Montreal Gazette* showing that he was fully qualified to undertake the work.

During this period Baird ran up considerable debts, to George Strange Boulton* and John Redpath* among others, and seems to have alienated a number of people. H. H. Killaly continued to befriend him, offering advice to help him avoid mistakes, but even he was moved to warn Baird's wife not to put money or property into his hands. When the Trent works was transferred in 1843 to district engineers, under the Board of Works, Baird was passed over for a junior person. Following his departure from the Newcastle District in October of that year, Baird was unable to obtain full-time employment for some time. In June 1845 he was re-employed by the board, possibly through Killaly's influence, to lay out and superintend the construction of the Arthabaska Road, joining Quebec and Melbourne. He was also to undertake the improvement of the Kennebec Road, from Quebec to the Maine border. Baird completed the surveys by the end of the year and until the summer of 1848 supervised construction of the roads. During the following summer he was briefly employed with an American engineer examining the proposed route for a railway linking Montreal and Burlington, Vt. He was apparently unemployed at the time of his death in October 1849.

Baird's most significant contribution lies in the development of early canal and road systems in Upper and Lower Canada. Associated most frequently with local works, he none the less had the opportunity to contribute to the development of major navigation systems such as the Rideau, Trent, and Welland canals. Until some time in the early 1840s he had access to those in office, who appear to have sought and respected his opinions about public works. Baird's other, and perhaps greater, contribution is the volume of the historical record he left. Its completeness offers a rare opportunity to study early engineering in Canada.

JOHN WITHAM

AO, MS 393. Institution of Civil Engineers (London), Minute-book, no.242 (membership record of N. H. Baird, 8 Feb. 1831). PAC, RG 1, L3, 54: B17/183; RG 5, A1: 59532–33, 59542, 67405–8, 103137–54, 130725–27; RG 11, A2, 94, nos.449, 3344; 100; A3, 115: 175; RG 43, CII, 1, 2434. "Mortality schedules of Vermont, no.3: census of

1850," comp. Carrie Hollister (typescript, Rutland, Vt., 1948; copy at Vt. Hist. Soc., Montpelier), 7. U.C., House of Assembly, *App. to the journal*, 1836, 1, no.12; *Journal*, app., 1833–34: 154–61. *The valley of the Trent*, ed. and intro. E. C. Guillet (Toronto, 1957). *Montreal Witness, Weekly Review and Family Newspaper*, 5 Nov. 1849. *Patents of Canada* ... [1824–55] (2v., Toronto, 1860–65), 1: 389.

BALDWIN, WILLIAM WARREN, doctor, militia officer, JP, lawyer, office holder, judge, businessman, and politician; b. 25 April 1775 at Knockmore, the family estate south of Cork (Republic of Ireland), fifth of the 16 children of Robert Baldwin and Barbara Spread; m. 26 July 1803 Margaret Phœbe Willcocks, daughter of William Willcocks*, in York (Toronto), and they had five sons, including Robert*; d. 8 Jan. 1844 in Toronto.

Robert Baldwin Sr was a Protestant gentleman farmer who had, by the time of William Warren Baldwin's birth, acquired both office and prestige. For a time in the 1780s he published, with his brother, the *Volunteer Journal; or, Independent Gazetteer*, which William Warren later claimed had been "favorably spoken of" by Charles James Fox. In spite of continuous attention to his estates during his political involvement with the volunteer movement and despite the financial support of his patron, Sir Robert Warren, Robert slid into bankruptcy about 1788. None the less, young William received a proper education. In his will he was to leave a small sum to an heir of the Reverend Thomas Cooke, "my careful and good schoolmaster, whose attention and kindness to me demands this small acknowledgement." About 1794 he entered medical school at the University of Edinburgh, from which he graduated in 1797.

That same year, enticed by descriptions sent back by a former neighbour, Robert Baldwin resolved, contrary to his patron's advice, to emigrate to Upper Canada. He sailed in 1798 with William, one other son, and four daughters. Forced to winter in England, the family set forth again the following spring. Although family accounts give 13 July 1799 as the date of their arrival at York, Robert's first petition for land is dated 6 July. In it he expressed his desire for a grant, having heard "of the fertility of the soil & the mildness & good Government" of the province. There was, however, more to his emigration: Baldwin had been, according to the reminiscences of his youngest daughter, deeply alarmed by the persistent rumours of impending French landings in Ireland, in anticipation of which he had barricaded his house and armed his servants. The unrest preceding the uprising of the Society of United Irishmen in 1798 had also played a part in convincing him of the need to leave. William noted in 1801 that the "horrors of domestic war [had] conspired to drive us from our native country."

Robert's entry into Upper Canadian society had been well prepared. On 20 Aug. 1798 his friend Hugh Hovell Farmar wrote a letter introducing him to President Peter Russell*, another Irishman, which described him as a "Gentleman of excellent Family, of Honor & excessively clever in the farming Line, with great Industry." For his part, Russell strongly recommended Baldwin's petition to the Executive Council and he received 1,200 acres. He settled, however, on land he had purchased near an acquaintance in Clarke Township. With excellent connections, he soon acquired offices, among them the lieutenantcy of Durham County, and influence.

William found his new life in the Upper Canadian wilds unprepossessing. There, he wrote to his brother in 1801, he was "banished from all that is engaging in life, flattering to our hopes, or grateful to our industry." Although his father's appointments from Lieutenant Governor Peter Hunter* were "all honour but not profit," he found them "agreeable," assisting "in some measure to soothe the mind." He himself was appointed lieutenant-colonel of the Durham militia, a group he considered "a lawless ... damned set of villains"; he also became a justice of the peace on 1 Feb. 1800. William was concerned about unrest in the province, which he attributed to "unprincipled wretches" from the United States who "would, had they the least prospect of success, tomorrow attempt to overturn the order of things in this country."

Finding little scope for his professional ambition in the backwoods of Clarke and preferring the allures of York's small society, Baldwin moved in 1802 to the capital, where he entered the somewhat closed family world of the Russell and Willcocks households. His connections to them were established in Upper Canada but the ties went back to Cork and Hugh Farmar, who was "nearly allied" to both families. Peter Russell's "friendship" was of particular consolation to Baldwin, and Peter was a first cousin of William Willcocks, soon to be Baldwin's father-in-law. Another close friend was Joseph Willcocks*, a distant relation of William. In June 1802 Baldwin acted as Russell's intermediary with Joseph Willcocks, whose advances to Elizabeth Russell* had caused a breach in their relations. But even York offered little scope for an aspiring young doctor and in December he advertised the opening of a classical school for young gentlemen. What became of it is not known. Baldwin's career now took a new direction. The young man who had borrowed Sir William Blackstone's *Commentaries on the laws of England* from Russell became an attorney on 22 Jan. 1803 and was admitted to the bar in Easter term of the same year.

Baldwin was a visible member of York's social circle and was one of the town's most eligible bachelors, a state ended by his marriage to Phœbe Willcocks in 1803. The young couple lived briefly with the Willcockses until they moved into their own home shortly before the birth of their first child, Robert, in May 1804. In spite of the death of their second son in 1806 and the frailness of the third, William Willcocks reported in 1807 that his daughter was "happily Married." With the birth of sons in 1808 and in 1810, Baldwin's family would be complete. He was a doting father, often glimpsed in the diaries of early York making his rounds of the town with one or more children in tow.

The society of York was a cliquish world in which competition for the few profitable offices was fierce. Conventional wisdom attributes William Warren Baldwin's rise to Russell, but he was in fact in eclipse when the Baldwins arrived and they garnered most of their early rewards from Hunter. In 1806, while the vultures of official York were awaiting the fall of James Clark*, clerk of the Legislative Council, Russell was unsuccessful in persuading President Alexander Grant* that Baldwin should succeed him. For several weeks early in 1806 Baldwin had served as acting clerk of the crown and pleas. In spite of judge Robert THORPE's recommendation that he was "the only educated and qualified person in the Province" for this position, it went to John Small*. None the less, Baldwin picked up his share of plums. On 5 Feb. 1806 he followed David Burns as master in chancery, on 19 Nov. 1808 he became registrar of the Court of Probate, and on 22 July 1809 he was appointed a district court judge.

During Lieutenant Governor Francis Gore*'s first administration (1806–11), many of Baldwin's friends – Joseph Willcocks, William FIRTH, Thorpe, and Charles Burton WYATT – were either suspended or dismissed from office. Despite Baldwin's association with them and despite Gore's suspicion of him as an "Irishman, ready to join any party to make confusion," he survived. His political legerdemain was remarkable and deliberate: although it was clear who his friends were – and although he supported Thorpe during his trial for libel in 1807 – he avoided any overt demonstrations of his political sympathies. Indeed, in October 1809 he wrote to Wyatt of Gore's "disposition to befriend" him. But if William did well during this period, as his appointments to office in 1808 and 1809 evidence, others were doing better. Baldwin was not the only able and ambitious lawyer in town and he resented, although he professed not to, the meteoric ascent of John Macdonell* (Greenfield). When Greenfield made some "wanton & ungentlemanly" references about him in court, Baldwin demanded an apology and ultimately challenged him to a duel. In a note he enjoined his wife, whom he had described in a hastily made will as "unparalleled in all the excellent qualifications of her sex," "not to indulge a rash or resentful spirit, but to protect me from insults, which as a gentleman I cannot submit to." On 3 April 1812 the two men met on Toronto Island. Macdonell did not raise his pistol, which Baldwin interpreted "as an acknowledgement of his error – we joined hands thus this affair ended."

Baldwin gloried in domesticity. By the end of the War of 1812 his household included his wife, four sons, father, three sisters, sister-in-law, Elizabeth Russell, and a few servants. The extended family, usually with more relations living in close proximity, became a pattern found in several generations of Baldwins. William believed that "nature has placed the Father in the situation of absolute Governor in his own House." The centre of the household was Phœbe, whom her son Robert later described as "the master mind of our family." A sister of William's extolled Phœbe's "excellent understanding and mental attainments," which "were of the greatest consequence and assistance to him." Phœbe herself caught what marriage meant to the Baldwin men in a letter to Laurent Quetton* St George in 1815: "No real domestic comfort is to be enjoyed without a *good Wife*." She rarely emerges from the shadows (few letters from her have survived) but what gleanings there are point to a dominant figure. William himself was an urbane, polished gentleman, tough-minded and possessed of a high self-regard. Yet he harboured a vulnerability which, if trifling in comparison to his son Robert's, was more real than has often been supposed. Elizabeth Russell described him in her diary as "a poor dead hearted creature and always fears the worst." Phœbe's illness in the fall of 1809 occasioned "a gloomy mood"; as he later explained to St George, "I am an Irishman and my wife was ill." To be sure, in such a large extended family illness and death were frequent. Peter Russell died in 1808 and William Willcocks in 1813. Robert Sr, a man subject to "low spirits," died in November 1816. William himself suffered "an attack which . . . nearly carried me off" in the spring of 1817 and he was a long time recuperating. About this time his sister Alice (Ally) slipped into a sometimes violent and "unhappy insanity." After two suicide attempts, she was sent in 1819 to the Hôpital Général of Quebec (where she remained until her death in 1832). Elizabeth Russell's death in 1822 was another blow, although long expected. Most distressing were the deaths of Baldwin's children, "the greatest blessing of human life." "Sweet" Henry's death in 1820 left William grief-stricken, as did his youngest son's in 1829. In his will William would direct that his "mortal remains" be placed as close as possible to the latter "dear child."

By contrast with his family life, William's professional life was largely free of woe. It was not, however, necessarily easy. He travelled on the assize circuit, picking up business where he could and carrying out actions on behalf of various clients. In June 1814 he spent a few days at Ancaster, where the treason trials [*see* Jacob Overholser*] were in progress, but "I was not applied to in behalf of any of them." Life on circuit was hard if not on occasion harrowing. A story is told of Baldwin's becoming lost in the woods in 1815 and having to swim a swollen Credit River in the morning. Still, his practice was growing. He reckoned in 1819 that he cleared about £600 per annum, a sum sufficient – when combined with his emoluments of office and income from property – for him to have built the previous year a country house, which he called Spadina ("the Indian word for Hill – or Mont"), about three miles from York on land received as a gift from his father-in-law. Baldwin "cut an avenue through the woods all the way so that we can see the vessels passing up and down the bay." When finished, with a stable and gardens, the house cost about £1,500. By 1819 he had three clerks in his law office: James Edward Small*, his nephew Daniel Sullivan, and Simon Ebenezer WASHBURN. The following year his son Robert joined the firm as a student-at-law and in 1823 his nephew Robert Baldwin Sullivan* began his articling period. Washburn was a partner from 1820, the year he was admitted to the bar, until 1825, when Robert was admitted to the bar and became a partner.

Commerce was the basis of any Upper Canadian legal practice and William's was no exception. From 1815 he had, for instance, the principal responsibility for superintending the Upper Canadian enterprises of St George, who had returned to France. The following year he gave up the registrarship in the Court of Probate when he was appointed judge of the Surrogate Court, succeeding his father in this lucrative position. Estates inherited by the family and William's astute management of them not only added to his office's business but laid the basis for considerable wealth in the next generation. His wife and sister-in-law had inherited William Willcocks's properties, and when Maria Willcocks died in 1834 her estate went to the Baldwin family. Maria and Phœbe also inherited the vast Russell tracts after Elizabeth Russell's death. William himself was the heir to his father's property. Land acquisition and estate management were vital to Baldwin's prosperity and he amassed choice lots of both cultivated and uncultivated land. In the post-war years York was undergoing development [*see* John Ewart*] and the value of property there was increasing. Baldwin benefited. He had acquired valuable land in town, some lots through purchase, others from his father-in-law's estate. By the 1820s he had become a large landowner and a wealthy man. His practice was now worth £700 a year while his wild (uncultivated) lands yielded an annual income of £1,400 (no figure is available for his rented farms or buildings but it was doubtless considerable). Although he lacked a single, large landed estate, he none the less closely approximated the English landed gentry in his ability to derive income from his holdings. He had all the trappings and attainments of gentility: education, refinement, a country home, and independent wealth. He was, as well, the doyen of his profession, holding the esteemed treasurership of the Law Society of Upper Canada for four separate terms (1811–15, 1820–21, 1824–28, and 1832–36).

But Baldwin's stature in Canadian history has little to do with these accomplishments. Rather his eminence lies in his contribution to the development of the best known, and least understood, principle of Canadian political life, responsible government. Generations of Canadian historians have accorded the Baldwins, father and son, pride of place in the elaboration of the central doctrine of colonial evolution to nationhood, and of the transformation of empire into commonwealth.

For someone considered so essential to this process of political development, Baldwin became publicly involved with it rather late in his career, probably deliberately so. Before 1820 he was not without political opinions – his association with the pre-war opposition is evidence of that – but his views are difficult to discern. One notes, for instance, his agreement with Firth in 1812 that "a change of the Governor can effect but little change in the measures or deportment of the administration." He undoubtedly shared Wyatt's disappointment in Joseph Willcocks's treason, but he applauded his castigation of "those who persecuted him." He also shared in the dissatisfaction with the administration's favouritism. Of Gore's departure in 1817 one of Baldwin's correspondents remarked, "It's of very little consequence as the Scotch Party are at the Head yet and have it all among themselves." This complaint – it had been a tenet of the pre-war opposition that Scots monopolized both offices and executive influence – was one with which Baldwin agreed. In 1813 he had related to Wyatt a pertinent incident. An altercation between officers of the Royal Newfoundland Regiment and a brother of Alexander WOOD had resulted in criminal charges against the officers, and Baldwin defended them. When they were convicted of assault, he moved for an arrest of judgement but Chief Justice Thomas Scott* overruled him, levying "most unmeasured fines" on the officers. "Such," Baldwin reasoned, "is the consequence of touching a Scottsman."

His entry into politics came in the general election of 1820. Running in the riding of York and Simcoe and confident of success, or so Robert claimed, he was returned with Peter ROBINSON. Politically, the election came hard on the heels of Robert Gourlay*'s banishment, the prosecution of Gourlayite printer Bartemas Ferguson*, the dismissal from office of the president of the Gourlayite convention, Richard BEASLEY, and Robert Nichol*'s formidable leadership of the opposition within the House of Assembly. Baldwin considered that electors had solicited his candidacy "on the expectation of [his] rigid integrity towards the Constitution." In a broadside he professed "an affectionate regard" for British liberty and the British constitution, and "to preserve the latter ever pure," he declared, "the first must be preserved unwounded." He promised to avoid factious opposition to "legitimate objects of the Administration" while maintaining "that the purest Administration requires a vigilant activity on the part of all its constitutional checks." Thus William thought his victory had given "great public satisfaction to the independent part of the community & mortification to others." Yet one historian who has analysed his conduct in this contest has depicted him as the eloquent defender of the administration, deeply grateful to it for office. The interpretation is exaggerated. Baldwin was "thankful" to the administration that "gave it, and the Government that has continued it to me" – nothing more. Two things are clear: first, Baldwin was sufficiently prosperous to risk estrangement from government; secondly, he was not yet of a mind that such estrangement was warranted.

Baldwin was neither a manager, nor an organizer, nor a leader in the day-to-day affairs of the eighth parliament (1821–24). Nichol resumed his leadership of the opposition, although Barnabas Bidwell* was a commanding presence for the one session he was in the house. Leadership for the administration was in the hands of Attorney General John Beverley Robinson* and his principal supporters, Christopher Alexander HAGERMAN and Jonas JONES. Compared to Baldwin, assemblymen such as John Willson* or Charles JONES spoke more often in debate and produced more legislation. Baldwin's initiatives were usually confined to debate on topics that reflected his own priorities.

His privately expressed concern for the state of the economy took public shape as a motion proposing the formation of a committee to examine the agricultural depression and the collapse of British markets. The resulting committee on internal resources (which included Baldwin and was chaired by Nichol) tabled its report – the first attempt to devise a comprehensive provincial strategy for economic development – on 31 March 1821. Eight months later Baldwin supported Hagerman's resolution for encouraging hemp production, a favourite policy of the executive since Hunter's administration. Later still, in a manner calculated to advance the interests of a large landowner, he lamented "those restrictions, fees, and regulations, which operated equally against the poor as the Capitalist" in the administration of land grants, and he championed the principle that "capital ought to be blended with labour" to ensure prosperity. In 1824, and again in 1828, he was one of the most percipient critics of Robinson's acts taxing the uncultivated lands of speculators such as Baldwin himself. On both occasions, he joined forces with the Niagara area merchants Thomas Clark* and William DICKSON, who opposed the measures in the Legislative Council.

A gentleman who advocated a hierarchical society, Baldwin delivered in December 1821 the clearest enunciation of his aristocratic beliefs. The occasion was his attack on a bill sponsored by Bidwell and David McGregor Rogers* which would have eliminated the operation of primogeniture on intestate estates. This "visionary scheme," more appropriate to a republic, "aimed at a total Revolution in the laws." "Aristocracy, upon which the *happy*, *happy* Constitution of Great Britain rested, would be destroyed," and he wished to see aristocracy "supported in this Colony to preserve the constitution . . . and not [to] run into a scheme of Democracy by establishing new fangled laws." Robinson, the avatar of the *ancien régime*, was left with nothing to say but that he "agreed with every word."

Baldwin was a whig constitutionalist whose ideas on law and politics were similar to those of the pre-war opposition led by Thorpe and Willcocks and the post-war opposition initiated by Nichol. His emphasis on limited government, retrenchment of expenditures, the independence of the constitution's respective parts, and the civil rights and liberties of subjects was consistent with the country tradition in English politics. His first substantial speech in 1821 was on an attempt to repeal the Sedition Act of 1804, which – although it had been used only to banish Gourlay – had been a frequent target of Nichol's since 1817. So long as it remained law, Upper Canadians were "without a constitution; at least a *free one*." The act "remained in force, not only in the face of Magna Charta, but directly in the face of all the statutes made for the liberty and protection of the subject." He then read to the house long passages from Blackstone on the liberties of subjects. Used against British subjects, he argued, the act was "arbitrary and tyrannical." It undermined trial by jury, "the great land-mark in our constitution," and was more cruel than "the Inquisition or Star Chamber."

These utterances were commonplace and they serve only to locate Baldwin within the whig tradition. More important were his thoughts on Upper Canada's constitution. He freely invoked the solemn authority of Blackstone on liberty but preferred Irish models for the question of the sovereignty of colonial legislatures. His remarks on this subject were prompted by the report of a joint committee of the assembly and the council on commercial intercourse with Lower Canada. Chaired by William Dickson and Robinson, the committee tabled its report (written by the attorney general) in December 1821. Baldwin had specific objections to it but his salient points were matters of principle: "it admitted as a principle that . . . this legislature cannot impose duties on imports"; "it acknowledges an incapacity in ourselves to govern . . . ourselves – & in effect gives our consent to surrender our Constitution [the Constitutional Act of 1791] back to British Parliament"; and "it does not in distinct terms present what we would wish – but leaves it to the discretion of the Imperial Parliament to do with us as it may please." These principles were "subversive of every thing Valuable in our constitution. . . . The B. Parliament could not repeal that Law – the British Parlt can make and repeal the Laws of England because the parties to the making of the Law are the parties to the repealing of it, but not so here – that act gives legislative power to the inhabitants of this province – and the Law cannot be repealed without those inhabitants are parties to the repeal." "But alas," he added, "here is the point of dread."

That point became clearer, as Baldwin had anticipated, during the debate in 1823 over a proposed union of the Canadas. In his view the Constitutional Act of 1791 conferred on the province's inhabitants "the right to make laws for their peace, welfare and good government, reserving certain powers to the King and Parliament . . . to legislate in particular cases." The imperial parliament, he argued, "could not constitutionally alter *this* law without our consent; for if so, we had no constitution at all." The proposal for union had originated with a "commercial faction" in Lower Canada willing to trade "some speculative objects of imaginary advantages . . . in exchange for our Constitution." Denouncing many of the clauses of the imperial union bill as "ruinous innovations," he found "neither wisdom, good sense, nor justice evinced by the framers of that monstrous bill." The most intriguing contribution to the debate was Baldwin's statement that what the Canadas had received was not, as Lieutenant Governor John Graves Simcoe* had often averred, "the image and transcript" of the British constitution, but rather the spirit of the constitution. Why, Baldwin wondered, would restless spirits abandon the Constitutional Act just as it was about "to change the French-man into the Englishman; or rather, as it was about to change the Frenchman into the Canadian; (for there might be, and there *was*, a Canadian Character distinct from the French, and though not English was yet properly reconcilable to and perfectly consistent with English feelings, English connection, and English Constitution;)."

Baldwin stood again for York and Simcoe in the election of 1824, placing a close third in a ten-man race and thus losing his seat. Unfortunately, that defeat eliminated his participation in assembly debates, the reporting of which provides historians with a valuable source for the study of Upper Canadian political thought during the tumultuous ninth parliament (1825–28). During this period, Baldwin turned his attention to what he began to see as partiality in the provincial administration of justice; in the process he became a partisan opponent of Sir Peregrine Maitland*'s government and of his chief advisers.

In 1818 William had written of Robert's future, "I intend please God to bring him up to the bar." There was no higher calling. When stepping down as treasurer of the Law Society in 1836, William detailed in his letter of resignation the special relationship of the constitution, parliament, and the law. As embodied in the 1791 act, the constitution was decidedly aristocratic, and Baldwin was not only one of its greatest admirers but also one of its greatest defenders. His willingness to duel for the sake of his honour and his ardent defence of primogeniture were tied to the natural, political, and social inequality he wished to preserve. He had defended in 1821 a bill enabling the Law Society to raise money for offices and a library to eliminate the necessity of new lawyers conducting their business in places "unfit . . . for gentlemen." "There was," he reasoned, "no Society for which the country should feel so deep an interest. . . . Without it, whose property was safe?" As he wrote in 1836, the society "has ever appeared to me of most importance to the preservation and due administration of our Constitution." In a province lacking an aristocracy, the rule of gentlemen and the presence of a legal profession were indispensable. Crucial to gentility were rectitude, disinterested behaviour, and decorum; crucial to the legal profession was defence of the constitution and the rights which it entailed.

Baldwin's address to the jury in 1827 during George Rolph's civil suit against his assailants in a celebrated tar-and-feather incident is a specific example of Baldwin's convictions. He was disturbed that Rolph's tormentors, who were successfully defended by Allan Napier MacNab*, included several gentlemen prominent in the Gore District, "persons holding responsible offices, even occupying the seats of Justice – one of them entrusted . . . with the sword of Justice." Subsequent events served to concentrate his attention on the administration of justice. Rolph's case was followed by hotelier William FORSYTH's petition to the assembly in January 1828 complaining of Maitland's substitution of military force for legal process "to decide the question of right" in a dispute that became renowned in opposition lore as the outrage at Niagara Falls. A select committee's investigation led to a full-scale constitutional confrontation between Maitland and the assembly, which the lieutenant governor prorogued on 31 March. Then, in April at the York Assizes before John Walpole Willis*, the opposition journalist Francis Collins* reprimanded Attorney General Robinson for his partiality in the administration of justice.

In response to this charge Robinson, on 12 May 1828, sent out a letter to members of the bar raising the question of bias in his department. Baldwin replied on the 31st in a lengthy note. Although he had thus far "preserved a public silence," Robinson's circular compelled him "candidly" to state "wherein I thought you omitted your duty." The first instance he cited was the attorney general's failure "in some public and impressive manner [to] reprove your Clerks who were parties in" the riot which resulted in the destruction of William Lyon Mackenzie*'s press in 1826. Their conduct was "quite unbecoming Gentlemen and still more unbecoming them as Students at Law." The printer's conduct was "very bad" but Baldwin averred that his punishment should have been "reproof or prosecution," not "outrage." The assault on Rolph was another instance of dereliction of duty, Baldwin continued, and neither Robinson nor Solicitor General Henry John Boulton* could escape public censure for not "promptly and vigorously turning the Law against the perpetrators." It was unconscionable in his view that Boulton might later act as the public prosecutor in a criminal action against the culprits, having already defended them against Rolph's civil suit. He found the whole episode "so subversive of justice that I fully partook of the public disapprobation of that scene." The last instance he cited was the 1822–23 case of Singleton Gardiner [*see* William Dummer Powell*], who had confronted two magistrates over the performance of statute labour. Abused by them, Gardiner, with Baldwin as his counsel, had launched a civil action against them. Robinson, acting as their attorney, insisted it was his duty to protect the justices. Baldwin agreed "wherein they are in the right; but my opinion also is that it is your duty to prosecute them wherein they are grossly wrong."

Matters came to a head in June 1828. On the 16th Willis declared that, to function, the Court of King's Bench required the presence of the chief justice and the two puisne justices. With Chief Justice William Campbell* on leave, only Willis and Levius Peters SHERWOOD were sitting. With the constitutionality of the bench in doubt, the Baldwins and Washburn wrote to Willis the following day enquiring if he would invite Sherwood's consideration of the question and asking, in the event Sherwood's opinion was not immediately forthcoming, if Willis would "withhold his Judgement" in any cases involving their clients, "untill as their Counsel we be better advised as to the course to be adopted." On 23 June the Baldwins, in conjunction with John Rolph*, protested to Sherwood "against any Proceedings . . . until the Court be established according to the Provisions of the Provincial Statutes." The issue was not merely a debate about "the strictest Principles of Law." "There are no Laws," they wrote, "demanding a more religious Observance than those which limit and define the Power of Individuals forming the Government over their Fellow Creatures." The administration's decision to remove Willis in late June precipitated a political reaction unlike anything the province had known, and the sense of crisis was fuelled by the impending general election in July. The Baldwins entered the fray, William in Norfolk and Robert in the riding of York. The elder Baldwin had been "*required*, and not *invited*" to run by John Rolph, who considered him "the only person . . . combining all that is desirable in a representative of a free people." Although Robert lost, William was elected along with incumbent Duncan McCall*. Provincially the opposition gained a clear majority of members.

In York William was at the centre of a whirlwind of activity. During the campaign he had become, according to the pro-administration journalist Robert Stanton*, "a regular travelling Stump *Orator*." Stanton thought him "mad" but Baldwin's commitment to opposition was principled, and total. The legacy of the Willis agitation over the summer and fall of 1828 was multifold: formal reform organizations at York which would endure until the rebellion of 1837, sustained cooperation among pre-eminent reform leaders, and tactical planning by the opposition for the legislative session of 1829. William Baldwin loomed large in these developments as the elder statesman of the opposition coalition, and Robert was also prominent. It was not so much that the Baldwins needed other reformers; rather the reformers needed the Baldwins. The period was, after all, still the age of gentlemen, and the Baldwins were nothing if not gentlemen. And, as gentlemen, they were symbols of legitimacy for the broad reform alliance. Maitland put the point neatly in September 1828, describing Baldwin as "the only person throughout the Province, in the character of a gentleman, who has associated himself with the promoters of Mr. Hume's projects," his allusion being to the British radical Joseph Hume. The most perceptive opposition leaders, John Rolph and Marshall Spring Bidwell*, realized the importance of the Baldwins in this regard and used their organizational and manipulative talents to manœuvre the father and son into the positions to which their duty, as lawyers, Christians, and gentlemen, pointed.

Dr Baldwin addressed a constitutional meeting convened on 5 July 1828 to "complain of the arbitrary, oppressive, and high-handed conduct of the Colonial Executive" in removing Willis. The purpose of the meeting was, he said, to consider petitioning the king for redress of grievances. The alarm of those assembled sprang not from "unworthy or womanish fears" but from the concern of "men and patriots jealous of their rights and anxious to guard their liberties . . . from arbitrary power." To acquiesce in the administration's conduct would be tantamount to surrendering the constitution. He urged his listeners to be "watchful at election," for the power was in their hands to return men independent of the executive. In language faintly reminiscent of his attack on the union, he suggested that the "legislatures of these Provinces have never been formed agreeable to the spirit of our constitution." In Upper Canada, for instance, legislative councillors "are placemen and pensioners, depending upon the Executive for a living, instead of being an independent gentry." He hoped the council would be remodelled, "odious" statutes repealed, and the "laws impartially administered." Of his seven proposals for redressing the colony's grievances, his sixth is of particular interest. He called for a provincial act "to facilitate the Mode in which the present constitutional Responsibility of the Advisers of the Local Government may be carried practically into Effect, not only by the Removal of these Advisers from Office when they lose the Confidence of the People, but also by Impeachment for the heavier Offences chargeable against them."

It having been decided to memorialize the king, Baldwin presided at a meeting called on 15 August to draw up the petition. A number of resolutions were proposed and accepted. The critical 13th, moved by Robert, was an unequivocal summation of William's position on the sovereignty of the Upper Canadian legislature: "That our constitutional act . . . is a treaty between the Mother Country and us . . . pointing out and regulating the mode in which we shall exercise those rights which, independent of that act, belonged to us as British subjects, and . . . that that act, being in fact, a treaty, can only be abrogated or altered by the consent of both the parties to it."

William's outstanding contribution to Canadian and imperial history is assumed by many historians to have been the idea of responsible government. Others have stressed his role in the transition from the idea of ministerial responsibility (that is, the legal responsibility of the king's ministers to the legislature enforced by impeachment) to the idea of responsible government (which meant the political responsibility of individual ministers or the cabinet to the elected house), a change which supposedly took place in the thinking of Canadian reformers between 1822 and 1828. The former concept was commonplace in England by the 1760s, had been used by Thorpe and Pierre-Stanislas Bédard* before the War of 1812, and had been articulated by Nichol in 1820. So far as can be determined by the newspaper accounts of the debates of the eighth parliament (1821–24), Baldwin did not express himself on the matter, confining his remarks to the sovereignty of the colonial parliament as derived from its constitution; however, it would be fair to assume, given his statements on these questions, that he was familiar with the notion of ministerial responsibility. Both notions are present in his speech of 5 July 1828.

In a memorandum he penned in his copy of Charles BULLER's *Responsible government for colonies* (London, 1840), Baldwin gave an account of responsible government in Upper Canada, a "subject [that] well deserves complex elucidation in the way of an historical exposition of the evils, which early accruing and becoming inveterate led to its regeneration [there]." As the public documents for the early history of the province had, he thought, largely been lost, he began his history with a petition against union that he had drafted in 1822. He did so not because it touched on responsible government but because it presented evidence of the "constitutional rights then entertained by the people, in Contra distinction to the sentiments of the executive authorities . . . and of their dependents & partizans." He moved to the resolutions of 15 Aug. 1828 as the next bench-mark in the development of the great principle. He then proceeded to his own letters to colonial authorities which "contain the development of the nature of the responsibility required and of the means of affecting it, after the example of the British Constitution; The suggestion in its distinct shape was made by Robert Baldwin . . . in private conversation with me on the occasion of penning those letters."

William Baldwin had realized as early as 1812 that merely changing a governor did not necessarily change an administration. For a whig of an aristocratic bent, the Legislative Council was the means by which the mixed constitution was kept in balance and liberty preserved, and as late as July 1828 Baldwin seemed to be thinking of the constitution from that perspective. The new tack he adopted, whether originating with his son or not, necessitated acceptance of the executive's political responsibility to the assembly, and from it to the electorate. The electorate at issue was not the British one limited to the world of gentlemen, however, but the Upper Canadian electorate based on close to universal manhood suffrage. The great question is, why did the Baldwins think such a principle would preserve a deferential and aristocratic society? The answer, if there is one, is not clear.

Behind the scenes, Rolph and Bidwell were exerting their influence on the elder statesman of reform. On 8 Sept. 1828 Bidwell suggested to William a conference to include Rolph "on the measures to be adopted to relieve this province from the evils which a family compact have brought upon it. . . . The whole system and spirit of the present administration need to be done away." Baldwin relayed the message to Rolph who, "as one of His Majesty's faithful opposition," urged a concerted effort to choose the speaker for the forthcoming session of parliament as "a serious part of our cabinet arrangements." He also hoped that the assembly under Baldwin's "wise and prudent counsel . . . shall be enabled to carry the strongest measures and the most vital improvements."

Copies of the August petition were circulated widely for signatures through the fall and early winter of 1828. On 3 Jan. 1829 Baldwin forwarded the accumulated petitions to the British prime minister, the Duke of Wellington, inviting his "thoughts to that principle of the British Constitution, in the actual use of which the Colonists alone hope for *peace Good Government and Prosperity*" as pledged by the Constitutional Act. The principle alluded to was the "presence of a Provincial Ministry (if I may be allowed to use the term) responsible to the Provincial Parliament, and removable from Office by his Majesty's representative at his pleasure and especially when they lose the confidence of the people as expressed by the voice of their representatives in the Assembly; and that all acts of the Kings representative should have the character of local responsibility, by the signature of some member of this Ministry." Once he had adopted this language and principle, Baldwin's rhetoric became less moderate and more censorious. Bidwell had written to William on 28 May 1828 that "Power, unaccompanied with any real responsibility, any practical accountability, can never be confided safely to any man." It seems reasonable to assume that the influence of Rolph and Bidwell, whose language was much sharper, much earlier, had had an effect in showing Baldwin how executive power could be made practically accountable.

Baldwin's remarks in the house in early January 1829 on the speech from the throne highlight his new approach. Conveniently forgetting some of his own favourable statements, both private and public, about the Maitland administration, he now lumped together successive administrations from Simcoe's onward and lashed them for their pursuit of "the same injurious course." He also described as "evil" the advisers who had tried to foist union on the province. The assembly should, he thought, "be considered the great Council of the country." In a private letter to Robert on 25 January he listed the evil advisers, some of whom were on the Executive Council: Robinson and his brother Peter, John Strachan*, Henry John Boulton, and James Buchanan Macaulay*. They should be "dismissed from office and from the *Cabinet Council* – this term might be adopted with advantage." Terms such as this one he was picking up from Rolph and Bidwell. In the debate on the speech from the throne he had urged Rolph's appointment "at the top of the Treasury Bench as it had been called." It had been called that minutes earlier by Rolph himself. On the abstract level, Baldwin noted in the house that the assembly "should be placed on the same footing as the House of Commons . . . otherwise those who sat in it could not properly be called the Representatives of the people." Responsible government made the executive accountable to the assembly – suggesting parties even in an inchoate state – and the electorate. In 1836 he was to write to Robert, "It was no matter what the parties were called, whig or tory – parties will be, and must be . . . therefore it becomes important [for the executive] to have the concurrence of the Assembly." A year after the throne debate, Baldwin suggested to Joseph Hume four means for remedying the evils of Upper Canada: control of revenues by the assembly, exclusion of the judiciary from the councils, reorganization of the Legislative Council (but not on an elective principle), and the "formation of a new executive or Cabinet Council, responsible and removable as the public interest may demand – which it is anticipated would of itself indirectly lead to the removal of all our present grievances & prevent the recurrence of any such for the future."

William and Robert both contested their seats in the election of October 1830 and lost. Bitter, William withdrew from political life. In 1831 he seems to have retired from his law practice, or at least let Robert and his new partner, Robert Baldwin Sullivan, assume the greater part of the burden. That same year he and Phœbe moved back into York to live with Robert and his family. The "extreme fickleness of popular opinion" at elections weighed on his mind and in 1834, when offered an opportunity to participate in a political meeting, he declined. His public role was not in eclipse, however. The gentlemanly Baldwins were attractive to conciliatory administrators as the right sort of oppositionists. Both were considered for the Legislative Council in 1835, but neither was appointed. In that year Spadina was razed by fire. A smaller house would be erected on the site; William was also to design and build a large Georgian-style mansion in town.

The arrival of a new lieutenant governor in Toronto on 23 Jan. 1836 stirred reform hopes. Sir Francis Bond Head* made overtures to the opposition by reconstructing the Executive Council. After numerous negotiations, Head brought Robert Baldwin, Rolph, and John Henry Dunn* into the council. William, whose name had come up, was not interested. He was convinced that the answer to the colony's problems was "a responsible Government through the medium of the Executive Council . . . discharging its duties in the way analogous to the Cabinet Council of the King in England." The council's subsequent resignation in March hurled the province into its most serious political-constitutional crisis since the Willis affair. Robert, whose wife had died on 11 January, headed off to England and Ireland to be alone with his grief while William superintended family matters at home and witnessed the political desertion in March of his brother Augustus Warren* and of his nephew Robert Baldwin Sullivan to Head's council, into the arms of the "Tory junto" as he put it.

Meanwhile, no doubt at the urging of a neighbour, Francis Hincks*, Baldwin joined the executive committee of the Constitutional Reform Society of Upper Canada, where he consorted with William John O'Grady, Rolph, and others. He was given the most distinguished positions: he became president of the society and was also made chairman of the Toronto Political Union. That July Head dismissed him as district and surrogate court judge, citing as reason his signature as president on a reform society document upholding the basic doctrines of reformers. William denounced the election of July 1836 as Head's "vicious triumph over the people." Head believed Baldwin knew of the preparations for the rebellion of 1837, but Baldwin denied it and Mackenzie later corroborated his statement. On 1 Jan. 1838 Baldwin published a letter indicating his position. "Great reform" was still required but it must be "lawful and constitutional." His political activity after the election of 1836 had been "solely directed to the means of discovering the facts of unconstitutional interference in behalf of Government." When the discussions of reform groups proved "unproductive," he no longer went to meetings and could not recollect having attended any since Robert's return from England in February 1837. He deplored the "rash insurrection" which had the effect of "silencing for many years to come, the voice of Reform, even the most rational and temperate." As for the Patriot incursions, he considered them foreign invasions and was willing to take up arms against them.

Many remedies were put forward in the 1830s by various reformers to eliminate the evil rule of what most considered a corrupt oligarchy. Responsible government, the favourite of the Baldwins, was but one, albeit the least threatening – or so the Baldwins thought – to the constitution, the social order, and the British connection. William understood oligarchy in terms of classical political philosophy: it was the degenerate, or unconstitutional, form of aristocracy. He believed, even in mid 1836, that the political contention within the upper province was related "to the mere administration of affairs"; in Lower Canada, it concerned the actual "form of government." The failed rebellion eliminated more radical proposals while elevating the status of the Baldwins' moderate principle. In fact, a gesture in their direction was considered in 1835 and proffered in 1836. The Baldwins had a brief interview with Governor Lord Durham [LAMBTON] during his July tour of Upper Canada in 1838. By this time responsible government and the voluntary principle with respect to church and state had become the key articles of reform canon [*see* Francis Hincks]. The reformers' chief desire, articulated by Hincks in the *Examiner* of 18 July, was that the lieutenant governor "administer the internal affairs of the Province with the advice of a RESPONSIBLE PROVINCIAL CABINET, and not under the influence of a *Family Compact*, as at present." On 1 August William sent Durham, as did Robert, a long letter "on the subject of public discontent." Among the 20 causes he listed were the crown and clergy reserves, the land-granting department, the monopoly of the Canada Company [*see* Thomas Mercer Jones*], interference by the executive in elections, revenues of the executive independent of the assembly, parliamentary obstruction by the Legislative Council, the encouragement of Orange societies, and the "extravagant waste" on projects such as the Welland Canal [*see* John Macaulay*]. His chief recommendation was the application of "English principles of responsibility . . . to our local Executive Council." Implementation of those principles came bit by bit.

William was now too old to participate actively in politics and was content to advise the chief standard-bearer of responsible government, Robert. William's understanding of the idea had been certain for some time, and it would not change. He thought it was "conceded" by Colonial Secretary Lord John Russell's dispatch of 10 Oct. 1839 [*see* Robert Baldwin]. And he held out high hopes initially for Governor Charles Edward Poulett THOMSON's plans for a reconstituted Executive Council of the soon-to-be united province. In the late 1830s his descriptions of politics evolved, as they had in 1828, into increasingly harsh portraits. Head's interference in the election of 1836 was without parallel: "There could not be devised . . . by the most despotic Government a more wicked scheme of oppressing us." By June 1841 he saw politics as an "important struggle between good Govt. and evil govt." Several months later the contest had acquired Manichean tones: "I really believe the fight is with the powers of darkness." And he meant it. The "horrible violence from the Tories" which had so astonished him during the Yonge Street riot of November 1839 seemed to have acquired a permanency which was, as late as 1843, still upholding the "old vile Tory system."

William was an Anglican of deep personal faith, intolerant of the Orange order – he had tried to legislate its suppression in 1823 – and the clergy reserves, but tolerant of dissenters and Roman Catholics. He shared with most of his contemporaries a providential faith which focused increasingly by the late 1830s on Robert's appointed role in the divine plan. "God will direct you," he wrote to him in 1841, "therefore you cannot err." Robert believed him and agonized even more over every decision. In his will of 1842 William, who still believed firmly in primogeniture, left almost everything to Robert, explaining his decision to Phœbe in this way: "One child only can be born first – and this in all time and societies . . . has been received as the appointment of Providence. . . . It tends to preserve a reverence for the institutions of our ancestors, which though always tending to change, for by nature all human affairs must change, yet resist innovations but those only which are gradual and temperate." Perhaps William's greatest legacy was the deep personal impression he made upon his eldest son. After his father's death in 1844 Robert wrote:

"Those only who knew him intimately can appreciate the loss which we have sustained in the death of such a parent – All that is left us is to honour his memory by endeavouring to imitate his example." And honour it Robert did.

William Warren Baldwin had had a variety of social and cultural concerns. A wealthy man, he subscribed to most philanthropic bodies, and he was a director of the Bank of Upper Canada, manager of the Home District Savings Bank, and a member of both the Medical Board of Upper Canada and the York Board of Health. He was also an early president of the Toronto Mechanics' Institute, a member of St James' Church, and an advocate of missionary work among the Indians. Charles Morrison Durand, a Hamilton lawyer, remembered him as a "haughty, prejudiced, Protestant Irish gentleman . . . very rough and aristocratic in his ways." Although warm to his family, he had an aloofness that reflected a tough inner core. He knew this quality in himself. "I seem to myself quite hard – when I witness the distress of those around me – what a strange comportment is Mine – I really know nothing of myself – I wish a friend could tell me – and yet I would shrink from his candour."

ROBERT L. FRASER

[The cooperation of J. P. B. Ross and Simon Scott, who allowed access to their papers, is deeply appreciated. Acknowledgment is also due to my partner in Baldwin research, Michael S. Cross.

References to William Warren Baldwin may be found in most private manuscripts and government collections relating to the period. The essential sources are the Baldwin papers and the Laurent Quetton de St George papers at the MTRL and the Baldwin papers at AO, MS 88. The Baldwin–Ross papers at PAC, MG 24, B11, 9–10, as well as the private collection of Ross–Baldwin papers belonging to Simon Scott, are also useful. Important to this study were contemporary newspapers, among which the following were most helpful: *Canadian Freeman*, 1825–33; *Colonial Advocate*, 1824–34; *Constitution*, 1836–37; *Examiner* (Toronto), 1838–44; *Kingston Chronicle*, 1820–33, and its successor *Chronicle & Gazette*, 1833–36; *Upper Canada Gazette*, 1819–24; and *Weekly Register*, 1823–24.

Among the more thoughtful treatments of responsible government in Upper Canada are three articles by Graeme H. Patterson: "Whiggery, nationality, and the Upper Canadian reform tradition," *CHR*, 56 (1975): 25–44; "An enduring Canadian myth: responsible government and the family compact," *Journal of Canadian Studies* (Peterborough, Ont.), 12 (1977), no.2: 3–16; and "Early compact groups in the politics of York" (unpublished); and two by Paul Romney: "A conservative reformer in Upper Canada: Charles Fothergill, responsible government and the 'British Party,' 1824–1840," CHA *Hist. papers*, 1984: 42–62; and "From the types riot to the rebellion: elite ideology, anti-legal sentiment, political violence, and the rule of law in Upper Canada," *OH*, 79 (1987): 113–44. With these notable exceptions, studies of responsible government have largely isolated British North American politics from its English background. The literature here is enormous. J. C. D. Clark, *Revolution and rebellion: state and society in England in the seventeenth and eighteenth centuries* (Cambridge, Eng., 1986), is a helpful place to start. Especially worthwhile are John Brewer, *Party ideology and popular politics at the accession of George III* (Cambridge, 1976), H. T. Dickinson, *Liberty and property: political ideology in eighteenth-century Britain* (London, 1977), and J. G. A. Pocock's stimulating collection of essays, *Virtue, commerce and history; essays on political thought and history, chiefly in the eighteenth century* (Cambridge, 1985). One of the few attempts to study the development of Canadian political culture is Gordon T. Stewart's thought-provoking book, *The origins of Canadian politics: a comparative approach* (Vancouver, 1986). The best work on the Colonial Office, imperial policy, and English politics as they bore on the colonies is Buckner, *Transition to responsible government*.

There is no full-length study of Baldwin's life but aspects of it are dealt with in G. E. Wilson, *The life of Robert Baldwin; a study in the struggle for responsible government* (Toronto, 1933); R. M. and Joyce Baldwin, *The Baldwins and the great experiment* (Don Mills [Toronto], 1969); and J. M. S. Careless's "Robert Baldwin" in the volume he edited, *The pre-confederation premiers: Ontario government leaders, 1841–1867* (Toronto, 1980), 89–147. M. S. Cross and R. L. Fraser, " 'The waste that lies before me': the public and the private worlds of Robert Baldwin," CHA *Hist. papers*, 1983: 164–83, is also useful.

A fine portrait of Baldwin held in the Royal Ont. Museum, Sigmund Samuel Canadiana Building (Toronto), is reproduced opposite p.48 of the study by R. M. and Joyce Baldwin. R.L.F.]

BAMFORD, STEPHEN, soldier and Wesleyan Methodist minister; b. December 1770 near Nottingham, England; m. first 1799 in Ireland Jane —— (d. 4 June 1839); m. secondly 28 Oct. 1840 Abigail Kirk, daughter of Abdiel Kirk, a musician, and they had at least one child, Margaret; d. 14 Aug. 1848 in Digby, N.S.

Little is known about Stephen Bamford's early life until 1793 when he enlisted in the British army and was assigned to the 29th Foot. He served in the Netherlands, the West Indies, and Ireland, and from September 1802 was stationed at Halifax. While in Ireland he had become a Methodist and he was soon invited to preach in the Halifax chapel. He became a popular and effective preacher and in 1806 his friends purchased his discharge from the army. That year the Nova Scotia District recommended him to the British Wesleyan Conference and stationed him on the Cumberland circuit. Bamford was admitted to full connection by the British parent in 1810, and in the same year he was ordained in Pittsfield, Mass., by bishops Francis Asbury and William McKendree, the last missionary from the Nova Scotia District to be ordained by the Methodist Episcopal Church, an American body.

Following ordination Bamford served on several

Maritime circuits, including Liverpool, Saint John, Horton, Annapolis, Charlottetown, Halifax, and Windsor, but there is little detailed record of his work. In 1824 he became chairman of the Nova Scotia District, succeeding James Priestley. A year later Bamford assured the missionary committee in London that, despite the scandal caused by Priestley's alcoholism, "the work of the Lord is in a prosperous way." Bamford remained chairman of the Nova Scotia District after it was divided in 1826 into the New Brunswick and Nova Scotia districts. He was succeeded by William Croscombe in 1829.

By 1833 Bamford was determined to return to England. Writing in 1834 to his old friend the Reverend Robert Alder*, then the missionary secretary responsible for British North America, he exclaimed: "I cannot bear the exposure and hard travelling of this frigid country, and therefore shall not attept to take another Circuit except it be where there is no travelling." His own brethren, he wrote later, had treated him unfairly in stationing him on the comfortable Windsor circuit and then reducing his salary because "he could not stretch to the utmost bounds of a Nova-Sctia circuit!!!" Thus he was deeply grateful to Alder for arranging an appointment to Exeter, England.

Although Mrs Bamford's health prevented her from leaving Nova Scotia, Bamford did go home in 1836. After being away for more than 30 years he found England a strange and lonely place and he soon decided to return to the Maritime provinces. In 1836 he was listed on the Saint John circuit as a supernumerary, a status he retained until his death. Following his wife's death in 1839 he travelled again to England and preached for a time in Guernsey. He settled in Digby, N.S., in 1841 and preached regularly in that area. Characteristically, after he was injured in a carriage accident there he preached first in his house, and then for nine months was carried "to the Chappel by hand" and spoke from his chair. Bamford died in Digby on 14 Aug. 1848 and was buried in Saint John beside his first wife. One who was present at his death found him "as kind and considerate as ever," and indeed his simplicity, gentleness, and unassuming piety had endeared him to many.

Stephen Bamford left no record of his conversion or of his spiritual journey. His letters, which were not numerous, are those of a simple, humble man who cherished his friends, his church, his country of birth, and Nova Scotia. "I have ever endeavoured," he wrote, "to maintain the honor, and purity, of methodism, I have preached her Doctrines, enforced her Discipline and have lived a holy life." "Old England" was, he believed, the "greatest, wisest, bravest, and best of all lands"; yet, "I love Nova-Scotia, her hills, Dells, and extensive forests are all pleasing to me." Undoubtedly, he helped to establish in his adopted home a form of Methodism in which commitment to John Wesley's teaching and loyalty to England were linked inextricably.

G. S. French

An engraving by T. A. Dean of Stephen Bamford is reproduced in the *Wesleyan-Methodist Magazine*, 57 (1834), on the plate facing p.241.

SOAS, Methodist Missionary Soc. Arch., Wesleyan Methodist Missionary Soc., corr., North America (mfm. at UCC-C). Francis Asbury, *The journal and letters of Francis Asbury*, ed. E. T. Clark *et al.* (3v., London and Nashville, Tenn., 1958), 2–3. Wesleyan Methodist Church, *Minutes of the conferences* (London), 3 (1808–13): 129; 6 (1825–30), minutes for 1828–29; 7 (1831–35), minutes for 1834; 8 (1836–39): 48. *New-Brunswick Courier*, 8 June 1839, 31 Oct. 1840. *Novascotian*, 28 Aug. 1848. *N.B. vital statistics, 1840–42* (Johnson *et al.*). Smith, *Hist. of Methodist Church*. William Burt, "Memoir of the Rev. Stephen Bamford, of British North America," *Wesleyan-Methodist Magazine*, 74 (1851): 833–40.

BARCLAY, ROBERT HERIOT (Herriot), naval officer; b. 18 Sept. 1786 in Kettle (Kettlehill), Scotland, son of the Reverend Peter Barclay, minister of Kettle; brother of John*; m. 11 Aug. 1814 Agnes Cosser of Westminster (London), and they had several children; d. 8 May 1837 in Edinburgh.

Robert Heriot Barclay entered the Royal Navy as an 11-year-old in May 1798, and served as a midshipman in the 44-gun ship *Anson* until transferred to Lord Nelson's flagship, the *Victory*, in February 1805. A month later he received promotion to acting lieutenant in the *Swiftsure* (74 guns), and he was confirmed in rank ten days before taking part in the battle of Trafalgar on 21 Oct. 1805. In the storm that followed the battle the *Swiftsure* had to cut a captured French ship, the *Redoubtable*, loose from her tow, and Barclay rescued 170 of her seamen before she sank.

During 1808 and 1809 he repeatedly demonstrated a high order of bravery and skill as second lieutenant of the fifth rate *Diana* (38 guns), on service in the English Channel. In November 1809, when commanding a detachment of boats attacking a French convoy, he lost his left arm. The following year, after recuperating from the wound, he went to the North American station, apparently led to believe he would be promoted commander. Instead, he was assigned briefly to the schooner *Bream* as a lieutenant, and then served in the *Aeolus* (32 guns) and the sloop *Tartarus*. Returning to the eastern Atlantic, he was in the *Iphigenia* (36 guns) between July 1810 and October 1812.

War in North America brought Barclay to Halifax in February 1813. He conducted a small group of officers overland to Kingston, Upper Canada, and when he arrived on 5 May he took charge, as an acting commander, of all naval forces on the lakes. Superseded ten days later by Captain Sir James Lucas Yeo*, he was sent to Lake Erie as senior officer. By his own account, "This Command was offered to Captain [William Howe] Mulcaster the next in command to Sir James Yeo, who to my personal knowledge declined it in consequence of its ineffectual State and Sir James Yeo refusing to send Seamen."

When Barclay reached Amherstburg in mid June after an eventful and difficult journey, largely overland, he took command of the 16-gun ship *Queen Charlotte* and a small squadron. In vessels he was superior to the American forces, but a lack of naval stores and trained seamen, partly because of chronic shortages and partly because of Yeo's refusal to send men from Lake Ontario, placed him at a disadvantage. With extensive industrial resources and lines of communication available to him, Barclay's opponent, Captain Oliver Hazard Perry, was able to construct, arm, and man enough vessels with regular seamen to overcome Barclay's edge in numbers of ships, guns, and crews. The refusal of Major-General Francis de Rottenburg* to cooperate with Barclay in an attack left Perry's base at Erie, Pa, secure.

The American squadron concentrated there while shipwrights slaved to get the 20-gun brigs *Niagara* and *Lawrence* ready for action. Barclay looked into the harbour on 30 July, saw no sign of the ships coming out, lifted the blockade he had mounted, and bore off across the lake to Dover (Port Dover). At a public dinner there he is said to have responded to a complimentary toast, "I expect to find the Yankee brigs hard and fast on the bar at Erie when I return, in which predicament it will be but a small job to destroy them." When he went back on 4 August the *Niagara* was hard aground, but the smaller vessels and the *Lawrence* were anchored offshore. According to American master shipwright Daniel Dobbins, the southeast wind made all the vessels face in the same direction, and "viewing the coast from the offing during a southeasterly wind, the haze incident to such wind, coupled with the high land in the rear, deceives the vision." Barclay, after an hour's reconnaissance, decided that all the vessels were out, ready to do battle with his undermanned and weak little squadron. He returned to Amherstburg in order to commission his new ship, the *Detroit* (20 guns), and prepare his relatively untrained crews for the encounter he knew to be inevitable. He sailed to meet Perry on 9 September, found the American squadron among the Bass Islands soon after daylight on the 10th, and opened the engagement just before noon. "The Action Continued with great fury until half past two," reported Barclay. At that time he appeared to have won the day, but the situation was soon reversed. Every British captain and all the most experienced officers were either killed or seriously wounded by the end of the battle an hour and a half later, when Perry accepted Barclay's surrender and made prizes of all the British vessels.

Totally exonerated afterwards – his remaining arm was injured and part of his thigh was cut away, so that "he tottered before a court-martial like a Roman trophy – nothing but helm and hauberk" – he received a gift of plate from the inhabitants of Quebec and Canadian merchants in London. The Admiralty confirmed him as commander on 13 Nov. 1813, and on 7 Nov. 1815 granted him a pension of £200 in addition to the five pence a day previously allowed for his wounds.

The inhabitants of Upper Canada remembered Barclay with mixed feelings. Amelia Harris [Ryerse*] later recollected that the lifting of the blockade in July 1813 had resulted from Barclay's preoccupation with a "pretty widow." Her accusation has never been proved. Despite Barclay's undoubtedly brave fight, she added, "those who knew of his leaving the blockade could not help feeling that all the disasters of the upper part of the province lay at his door."

In the recriminations following British naval defeats during the War of 1812, Barclay became the victim of a political clash in parliament. Although the debate over Lake Erie, begun by the Marquis of Buckingham in 1815, died when Napoleon escaped from Elba, Barclay was consigned to obscurity by the Admiralty. He began to petition for employment in 1822, hoping for assistance from his supporter Buckingham, was given command of the bomb-vessel *Infernal* from 12 April to 11 Oct. 1824, and was made post-captain on 14 October. After this belated concession to his court martial's findings that "the Judgement and Gallantry of Captain Barclay . . . were highly conspicuous and entitled him to the highest Praise," he received no further employment before his death 13 years later.

W. A. B. DOUGLAS

NMM, C. G. Pitcairn-Jones, notes on sea officers. PAC, RG 8, I (C ser.), 678, 729. PRO, ADM 1/2737–38, 1/4541 (mfm. at PAC); ADM 9/4/1241; ADM 12/168/721. William L. Clements Library, Univ. of Mich. (Ann Arbor), War of 1812 coll. *Select British docs. of War of 1812* (Wood), vol.2. Marshall, *Royal naval biog.*, vol.3, pt.I. *The defended border: Upper Canada and the War of 1812 . . .* , ed. Morris Zaslow and W. B. Turner (Toronto, 1964). W. W. Dobbins, *History of the battle of Lake Erie (September 10, 1813), and reminiscences of the flagships "Lawrence" and "Niagara"* (2nd ed., Erie, Pa., 1913). B. J. Lossing, *The pictorial field-book of the War of 1812 . . .* (New York, 1869). A. T. Mahan, *Sea power in its relations to the War of 1812* (2v., London, 1905). Theodore Roosevelt, *The naval war of 1812; or, the history of the United States Navy during the last war with Great Britain; to which is appended an account of the battle of New Orleans* (3rd ed., New York, 1883). Max Rosenberg, *The building of Perry's fleet on Lake Erie, 1812–1813* (n.p., 1968). Egerton Ryerson, *The loyalists of*

America and their times: from 1620 to 1816 (2v., Toronto and Montreal, 1880). E. A. Cruikshank, "The contest for the command of Lake Ontario in 1812 and 1813," RSC *Trans.*, 3rd ser., 10 (1916), sect.II : 161–223. H. H. Peckham, "Commodore Perry's captive," *Ohio Hist.* (Columbus), 72 (1963): 220–27. C. P. Stacey, "Another look at the battle of Lake Erie," *CHR*, 39 (1958): 41–51.

BARLOW, THOMAS, businessman and politician; b. 1788 in Saint John, N.B., son of Ezekiel Barlow; m. 24 May 1834 Eliza Hoosse Morris in Halifax; d. 9 Dec. 1844 in Saint John.

Ezekiel Barlow was a Pennsylvania loyalist who settled in Parrtown (Saint John) following the American revolution. A shipwright, he eventually established himself in the West Indies trade and became a prominent liquor merchant in the city. Thomas Barlow was educated in Saint John and at the age of 20 joined his father and brother in the firm of Ezekiel Barlow. The same year he was admitted a merchant freeman of Saint John. Some time between 1813 and 1822 Thomas and Ezekiel Jr became partners with their father and the firm was reorganized as E. Barlow and Sons.

The creation of the new company occurred at the beginning of the period of most rapid growth in Saint John history. From perhaps 5,000 in 1815, the population of Saint John–Portland reached 25,000 in 1840, at which time the city was the third largest in British North America. The firm prospered with it and by the latter date was one of the largest mercantile enterprises in Saint John. The marks of the Barlows' success were the two valuable water lots off the city's market wharfs which they held on perpetual lease, and the 2,000 tons of shipping – including a steamship – owned by Thomas Barlow and by the Barlow firm in 1841. By that time, too, the Barlows were the largest private customers of the Bank of New Brunswick, their total discounts being exceeded only by those of the provincial treasurer. The firm had expanded into transatlantic commerce, coastal trading by means of steamships, and the construction of steam-engines, although the nature of the last enterprise is unclear because a second Thomas Barlow was a leading foundry owner by 1840.

Thomas Barlow was a director of the Bank of New Brunswick and of the New Brunswick Marine Assurance Company through most of the last decade of his life. He also served on the board of the New Brunswick Mining Company, which was incorporated in 1837 to develop the coal reserves of the Grand Lake area of central New Brunswick. Together with his brother and Moses Henry Perley* he was a director of the Lancaster Mill Company. A conduit for much of the American capital that flowed into the New Brunswick timber trade before the crash of 1837, the company acquired extensive timber lands and developed several large sawmilling operations in eastern Saint John County. Barlow's involvement with it brought him into conflict with many tories and small timber operators, who bitterly resented this American intrusion into the provincial economy. Barlow was an early promoter of the Saint John Water Company and served as a director of this important utility between 1836 and 1840 when it attempted to pipe water from Lily Lake to the city. In addition he was a city bondholder and participated in the 1842 meeting at which the bondholders pushed the city into bankruptcy and forced the Common Council to accept the authority of trustees appointed by the creditors.

Barlow's petitions to the House of Assembly, concentrated in the 1820s, reflect the concerns of a prominent merchant. He opposed a bill to relieve debtors from certain prison penalties in 1822 and petitioned against auction sales of foreign goods in the province in 1828. In 1829 he supported a bill permitting landlords to eject tenants. Two years later, when he was an assemblyman, he signed a petition protesting the arrival of a thousand destitute Irish immigrants at the port of Saint John.

Like most great merchants of the period Barlow participated directly in the political processes of his community. He entered the House of Assembly as a member for Saint John City in 1828, following the unseating on appeal of Gregory VanHorne, with whom he had had a fierce contest in the election of the previous year. His first term was uneventful. That he early acquired influence in the house is indicated by his serving on the committee on trade. A party system had not yet developed and Barlow's voting behaviour on assembly issues reflects the concerns of a transatlantic trader rather than those of a partisan. He favoured legislation protecting British creditors, and for reasons of economy he opposed attempts to provide missionaries to the Indians and to assist the New-Brunswick Agricultural and Emigrant Society. Re-elected in 1830, he fought every attempt to raise provincial revenues by imposing additional duties on liquor, and supported the payment of bounties for sealing voyages, for the construction of sailing vessels, and for the export of fish and the production of wheat.

During his second term Barlow was caught up in the debate over the crown lands, the issue which more than any other shaped New Brunswick politics between 1820 and 1837 [*see* Thomas Baillie*]. In the early 1830s assembly radicals headed by Charles Simonds* of Saint John disputed with the executive the control of the increasingly lucrative revenues from these lands. Initially Barlow did not agree with them. In the vote on the 1831 address to the king asking for redress of grievances against the Crown Lands Office, he joined seven other assemblymen, none from Saint John and all supporters of the prerogatives of the crown, in opposition. Subsequently, however, he grew steadily more radical. In 1832 he abandoned his traditionalist friends and joined the majority in support of a resolution asking Lieutenant Governor Sir Archibald CAMPBELL to present a statement showing the income of all office holders and the amount and expenditure of all crown revenues. During the next two years he was among the radical minority in the house – including most of the Saint John members – which attempted to deny Campbell any funds for the contingent expenses of the province. In 1834 he was a member of the majority which condemned the language of the lieutenant governor's reply to the address of the house that year. By this time Barlow was recognized throughout the province as a radical, a supporter of Simonds, and a personal opponent of Campbell. Although he did not seek re-election in 1834, he continued a vendetta against the lieutenant governor which culminated in 1836 when nine Saint John merchants petitioned the crown for Campbell's removal.

Barlow did not marry until the age of 46. At his death ten years later he left his wife and four small girls to inherit the fortune he had accumulated. Three of these children were still living at the time of his brother's death in 1853 and they became heirs to the second Barlow fortune as well.

T. W. ACHESON

City of Saint John, N.B., City Clerk's Office, Common Council, minutes, 9 Dec. 1840, 14 Jan. 1841, 7 Sept. 1842. N.B. Museum, Bank of New Brunswick, ledger, 1 April 1837–31 March 1838; Saint John, "Register of voters," 1785–1854. PANB, MC 1156; RG 2, RS7, 31, petition to the Executive Council, 16 July 1831; RG 3, RS538, B5; RG 4, RS24, S31-P23, S32-P6, S37-P6, S40-P10, S52-P80; RG 7, RS71, 1853, Ezekiel Barlow Jr. N.B., House of Assembly, *Journal*, 1828: 106; 1829: 46, 70–71, 86; 1831: 52, 110, 156; 1832: 36; 1833: 115–16; 1834; 1842, app.: cclvii–cclxxii. *A schedule of the real estate belonging to the mayor, aldermen and commonalty of the city of Saint John . . . January, 1842* (Saint John, 1849; copy at PANB). *New-Brunswick Courier*, 31 May 1834, 14 Dec. 1844. Esther Clark Wright, *The loyalists of New Brunswick* (Fredericton, 1955; repr. Hantsport, N.S., 1981).

BARNES, RICHARD, businessman and politician; b. 15 March 1805 in St John's, second son of William Barnes, merchant, and Hannah Butler; m. there 16 Dec. 1840 Eunice Alice Morris, and they had one daughter, who died in infancy, and one son; d. 3 Sept. 1846 in St John's.

At a period when most of Newfoundland's governing élite were British or Irish immigrants, Richard Barnes was acutely conscious of being native-born. His mother's family had established itself at Port de Grave in the late 1600s and his paternal grandfather, who according to family tradition came from Waterford (Republic of Ireland), had migrated in the 1760s to St John's, where he became a blockmaker. After rudimentary schooling, Barnes entered his father's shipping and carpentry business, later known as J. B. Barnes and Company. Eventually he was made a partner. He continued his education by extensive reading, and in 1835 was a founder of the St John's Reading Room and Library, serving as treasurer and secretary at various times until his death.

A founder of the Natives' Society in 1840, Barnes became actively involved in politics, for the society was intended to be not only a charitable organization but also a new political party, designed to protect and promote the interests of the native-born regardless of whether they were Irish or English, Catholic or Protestant. It was heralded by the editor of the *Newfoundland Patriot*, Robert John Parsons*, as a junction of liberal and mercantile interests. At its first meeting Barnes presented, for the society's proposed flag, an emblematic design surrounded by roses, thistles, and shamrocks, with the motto Union and Philanthropy – a forerunner of the famed "Pink white and green." The "fair native-born daughter of Terra Nova" whom he thanked for executing the design was probably his cousin and future wife, the daughter of Rachel Butler and Rutton Morris, a former minister of the Congregational Church in St John's. Barnes was himself a Congregationalist.

In the elections called in 1842, following the suspension of representative government the previous year, Barnes's main attraction for the electorate of Trinity Bay was his championship of the native-born. He took his seat in the Amalgamated Legislature the following January. However, his reputation as "the Native Member *par excellence*" suffered almost immediately when he voted with the Conservatives to oppose the appointment of a native-born candidate as clerk of the house, and a resolution condemning his action was passed by the Natives' Society. Believing that it was a lack of autonomy on the part of the members that had caused the loss of the constitution, Barnes continued to assert his own independence, opposing the appointment of a private secretary for Governor Sir John Harvey*, the granting of additional funds for expenses incurred at Government House, and the payment of elected members.

Shortly after objecting that the £350 salary for the governor's secretary would educate the children of one district for a year, Barnes introduced an education bill which would replace the public school system established by the Education Act of 1836 [*see* Charles Dalton*]. This system had been suspended after sectarian difficulties had rendered it unworkable. Barnes proposed that the responsibility for elementary schools be divided between Roman Catholics and Protestants and that each group receive equal funding. Catholic and Protestant school boards were to be appointed for each of the nine electoral districts, the majority of members on the Protestant board coming from the predominating denomination in the district. The total annual grant for elementary schools was increased from £2,100 to £5,000. The bill, passed in 1843 with a minimum of debate, established the legislative basis for a denominational system of education in the colony.

Praised by both sides of the house for his preparation of the bill and his guidance of it through the legislature, Barnes was accounted one of the most popular members by the close of the session. Already appointed a governor of the Savings Bank and secretary of the Protestant school board in St John's, in June 1843 he was elected president of the Natives' Society, which he had hitherto served as treasurer. During his two-year term of office, the building of a Natives' Hall began.

Believing the legislature should address the question of form of government, Barnes early in 1844 introduced a bill to amend the constitution imposed in 1841. Though basically it contained provision for a return to the constitution of 1832, one modification provided for an assembly of 25 members elected from 24 districts. His division and rearrangement of districts, supposedly on the basis of population distribution, aroused the anger of the Catholic Liberals who claimed that the new electoral districts were designed to diminish their influence and to create a Protestant ascendancy. Barnes, accused in the Amalgamated Legislature of being a sectarian bigot and a mercantile pawn, and also of having placed the religious bodies in hostile array by his education measure, protested that no sectarian motive was intended and that had the country been populated by Turks he would have proposed the same divisions. Attempts by the Liberals to delay the second reading failed, but only after seven divisions. Parsons, Barnes's colleague in the Natives' Society, was the only Protestant to vote with the Liberals. The lengthy and acrimonious debate ended when Barnes withdrew his bill, on learning from council members that Harvey was willing to transmit it, with some changes, to Colonial Secretary Lord Stanley for his consideration. Though the debate on the constitution resumed in 1846, Barnes's bill was the Amalgamated Legislature's only serious attempt at constitutional reform.

At a Natives' Society meeting on 15 July 1845, Barnes referred to a "preference, alike impolitic and unjust," shown in government appointments to those whose claims to consideration were "much less prominent than those of the Natives before whom they were preferred," and he urged the society to assert a more independent existence as a political party. In an era dominated by sectarian politics, however, the Natives' Society proved ineffectual as a rival to the Liberals and Conservatives. It suffered two blows in September 1846: the premature death of Barnes at the age of 41 and the collapse of its not yet completed hall. Ambrose Shea*, president of the society, eulogized Richard Barnes as "the best loved of this Society" and "the first to proclaim the rights of his countrymen." In 1878 a monument to his memory was erected by the Natives' Society in the graveyard of the Anglican cathedral.

Pamela Bruce

Cathedral of St John the Baptist (Anglican) (St John's), Reg. of burials, 1845–46. Centre for Nfld. Studies, Memorial Univ. of Nfld. Library (St John's), Biog. information on Richard Barnes. MHA, Barnes name file. PANL, P8/A/11. PRO, CO 194/120. St Thomas Parish (Anglican) Church (St John's), Reg. of marriages (copies at PANL). Nfld., General Assembly, *Journal*, 1843–46. *Courier* (St John's), 5 Sept. 1846. *Newfoundlander*, 25 May 1843; 8 Feb., 10–11, 18 April, 15 Aug. 1844; 24 July 1845. *Newfoundland Patriot*, 15 Sept., 1 Oct. 1840. *Patriot & Terra Nova Herald*, 18 Jan. 1843. *Public Ledger*, 4 Feb., 30 June 1840. *Royal Gazette and Newfoundland Advertiser*, 21 Feb., 10 Oct. 1843. *Times and General Commercial Gazette* (St John's), 9 Sept. 1846. W. M. Barnes, *Rolling home; when ships were ships and not tin pots* (London, 1931). [M. J. Bruce, named] Sister Mary Teresina, "The first forty years of educational legislation in Newfoundland" (MA thesis, Univ. of Ottawa, 1956). Garfield Fizzard, "The Amalgamated Assembly of Newfoundland, 1841–1847" (MA thesis, Memorial Univ. of Nfld., 1963). Gunn, *Political hist. of Nfld.*, 94–96. F. W. Rowe, *The development of education in Newfoundland* (Toronto, 1964). A. M. Butler, "The family of Butler in the New-Founde-Lande," *Nfld. Quarterly*, 72 (1975–76), no.1: 32–35.

BARRETT, ALFRED, engineer; b. in New England; m. and had at least one son; d. 18 July 1849 in Montreal.

About 1818 Alfred Barrett began working for the engineering staff of the Erie Canal in New York State. He gained experience there through practical work and rose rapidly, becoming an engineer by 1821. After the completion of the canal in 1825, he was appointed resident superintending engineer of the Welland Canal, in Upper Canada, on 10 May 1826. His appointment may have resulted from a visit to the Erie in 1824 by the promoter of the Welland, William Hamilton Merritt*, during which Merritt had established contact with engineers and contractors. Barrett and David Thomas, appointed chief engineer of the Welland, were probably the first American engineers to work in British North America.

After Thomas resigned in June 1827 Barrett carried on alone. Work progressed favourably until November 1828 when the steep banks of the Deep Cut at the canal summit slid into the channel. Since it was impossible to rebuild this section, the water supply system for the summit had to be redesigned. James Geddes, one of the most experienced engineers on the

Erie, was brought in to help Barrett resurvey the canal. A new source of water was found, and the canal was opened on 30 Nov. 1829. The following year Barrett surveyed the St Lawrence River from Lake Ontario to Lake St Francis with a view to improving navigation, but nothing came of the project. He returned to the Welland Canal to work on an extension at Port Colborne, Upper Canada, in 1831.

During the 1830s, with reduced opportunities for engineers in the Canadas, Barrett returned to the United States. He became the engineer of the Chenango Canal, a branch of the Erie. By 1837 he was a resident engineer on the Erie itself and the following year he became one of the five chief engineers responsible for its enlargement. Barrett resigned in 1843 because of New York laws which severely limited expenditures on the canal.

In 1841 a large imperial loan had been made available for public works in the Canadas. Much of the money was to be used to reconstruct the Canadian canal system from Lake Erie to Montreal. One of the bottlenecks was the Lachine Canal, originally built during the years 1821 to 1825. Barrett was appointed resident engineer, responsible for the canal's enlargement, soon after the end of workers' strikes there in 1843. Over the next four years he designed a larger canal prism and new lock and water control structures, while keeping the old canal open as much as possible. Some of the work necessitated construction during the winter, a rare occurrence in Canada at that time. Barrett also supervised the contractors and completed ancillary tasks such as designing basins, docks, and warehouses and developing specifications and structures for the use of surplus water as industrial power. By the 1850s water-power from the Lachine Canal had helped Montreal become the Canadas' premier industrial city.

Barrett was also responsible for work on the Chambly Canal and the dam and lock at Saint-Ours. The Department of Public Works asked him to prepare special reports on the navigation of the Grand River, Upper Canada, and the Rivière Saint-Charles at Quebec, as well as on the possibility of erecting a bridge across Lac des Deux Montagnes near Montreal. With the enlargement of the Lachine Canal completed, Barrett, in view of his previous experience, was transferred in the fall of 1848 to the Welland Canal to replace Samuel Keefer*. He did not work there long since he died in Montreal of cholera in July 1849.

Little is known of Barrett's personal life except that he was a freemason and that he helped form a total abstinence society among the Welland Canal workers in 1829. He must therefore be judged by his professional work. He held important positions on the Erie, Welland, and Lachine canals, some of the most significant and influential projects of the 19th century. The board of directors of the Welland Canal Company attributed part of his success to his ability to "combine strength with cheapness of execution" in his engineering structures. Contemporary and later engineers thought very highly of him. Only his early death prevented his acquiring a reputation equal to that of better-known colleagues.

LARRY McNALLY

AO, MS 74, package 12. PAC, MG 24, E1, 6 (mfm.); RG 11, A1, 59–65; A3, 132. Can., Parl., *Sessional papers*, 1891, 10, no.9, app.19. Can., Prov. of, Legislative Assembly, *Journals*, 1843–50. *Daylight through the mountain: letters and labours of civil engineers Walter and Francis Shanly*, ed. F. N. Walker ([Montreal], 1957). R. C. Douglas, *Confidential reports to the Hon. Sir Charles Tupper, K.C.M.G., C.B., minister of railways and canals, on the hydraulic powers situated upon the St. Lawrence and Welland canals* (Ottawa, 1882). John Mactaggart, *Three years in Canada: an account of the actual state of the country in 1826–7–8 . . .* (2v., London, 1829). *Montreal in 1856; a sketch prepared for the celebration of the opening of the Grand Trunk Railway of Canada* (Montreal, 1856). Welland Canal Company, Board of Directors, *Annual report* (St Catharines, [Ont.], 1828). *Montreal Gazette*, 19 July 1849. H. G. J. Aitken, *The Welland Canal Company: a study in Canadian enterprise* (Cambridge, Mass., 1954). J. P. Merritt, *Biography of the Hon. W. H. Merritt . . .* (St Catharines, 1875). R. E. Shaw, *Erie water west; a history of the Erie Canal, 1792–1854* ([Lexington, Ky., 1966]). N. E. Whitford, *History of the canal system of the state of New York together with brief histories of the canals of the United States and Canada . . .* (Albany, N.Y., 1906). J. P. Heisler, "The canals of Canada," *Canadian Hist. Sites*, no.8 (1973). H. C. Pentland, "The Lachine strike of 1843," *CHR*, 29 (1948): 255–77.

BARRIE, Sir ROBERT, naval officer; b. 5 May 1774 in St Augustine (Fla), only surviving child of Dr Robert Barrie of Sanquhar, Scotland, a surgeon's mate in the 31st Foot, and Dorothea (Dolly) Gardner; m. 24 Oct. 1816 Julia Wharton Ingilby, daughter of Sir John Ingilby, in Warrington (Cheshire), England, and they had one son and four daughters; d. 7 June 1841 at his seat in Swarthdale, England.

Robert Barrie's father died in 1775, and his mother left North America and returned to her relatives in Preston, Lancashire, England, where in 1784 she married George Clayton, a prosperous textile manufacturer. Young Robert attended a small school at Neston, Cheshire, and later a school at Dedham. On 5 June 1788 he entered the Royal Navy under the auspices of his uncle Captain Alan Gardner. In December 1790 Gardner, now at the Admiralty and concerned with the preparations for the voyage of Captain George Vancouver* to the Pacific, placed Barrie as a midshipman in the *Discovery*. Another young midshipman was Thomas Pitt, later Baron Camelford, who became Barrie's closest friend.

Vancouver discharged Pitt at Hawaii in 1794, but he thought well of Barrie. The latter was in charge for a time of one of the survey parties on the northern coast of what is now British Columbia. When the expedition returned to England in October 1795 he was immediately promoted lieutenant. Barrie served in the West Indies under a former *Discovery* shipmate, Thomas Manby, in 1800, and was promoted commander on 23 Oct. 1801. Seven months later he was advanced to captain, while in command of the sloop *Calypso*.

From June 1806 Barrie commanded the frigate *Pomone*, at first off the French coast and then in the Mediterranean. In June 1809 he captured the adjutant general of France, Chevalier Charles de Boissi, and in October 1810 he took Lucien Bonaparte, brother of Napoleon, who was attempting to escape to America from Italy. Barrie's most significant exploit in *Pomone* came on 1 May 1811. With two other ships under his command he entered the Golfe de Sagone, Corsica, and sank two warships and an armed merchantman as well as destroying the fortifications which protected them. Later in the year, Barrie was ordered to bring to England the British ambassador to Persia. The *Pomone* was sunk nearing Portsmouth but Barrie was acquitted of misconduct.

In October 1812 Barrie was commissioned captain of the *Dragon*, in which he took a leading part in the blockade of Chesapeake Bay on the American coast. For some months he was commodore in charge of the British squadron, which during his command took over 85 vessels. In September 1814 Barrie was part of the British attack on the Penobscot River region (Maine) [*see* Sir John Coape Sherbrooke*]. He was selected as commander of a joint expedition to capture Hampden and there to destroy the American frigate *Adams* and two other armed vessels. The British force also burned about 20 more vessels and took every town on the river from Hampden to Bangor. In a letter to his mother describing the expedition, Barrie commented, "If our Ministers be wise, the Penobscot will now be made the boundary between the Yankeys and us."

Following the peace in 1815, Barrie was placed on half pay; he then married, and went to live in France. In January 1819, after months of negotiations, he accepted the post of commissioner of the dockyard at Kingston, Upper Canada, an appointment which made him senior naval officer in the Canadas. The command, which Barrie succeeded in having detached from that of Halifax, included the inland waterways of the Canadas and the port of Quebec. The dockyard at Kingston was located on Point Frederick, the present site of the Royal Military College of Canada, and there the Barries had a house. During 1819 and 1820 Barrie built a big three-storey stone warehouse to hold the equipment of the large fleet put into reserve by the Rush–Bagot agreement of 1817. This building survives as a dormitory for cadets, and is known as the Stone Frigate.

Barrie's task as commissioner, in the face of gradual reductions in the establishment, was to have the ships under his command and their gear preserved from deterioration. He was to ensure that selected vessels could be commissioned on short notice if war with the United States was renewed. The plans for manning these ships were modified as more reserve officers and men were sent home, and after the 1830 reduction the intention was to use only former naval personnel who had settled in the Canadas.

As senior naval officer, Barrie was concerned with various matters connected with maritime affairs, such as the international boundary commission, the hydrographic survey of the Great Lakes and St Lawrence River system [*see* Henry Wolsey Bayfield*], the building of the Rideau and Welland canals [*see* John By; William Hamilton Merritt*], and relations with the United States. He was very friendly with Governor Lord Dalhousie [Ramsay] and even more so with Governor Lord Aylmer [Whitworth-Aylmer], whom he had known in Jamaica. At York (Toronto) the Barries became close friends with Sir Peregrine Maitland* and Lady Sarah Maitland, and spent long periods at the Maitlands' summer retreat near Niagara Falls. This last relationship led Barrie to sound out Sir George Cockburn at the Admiralty about the possibility of a seat on the executive councils of the Canadas, but Cockburn's response was unpromising.

At the end of 1825 Barrie was called to England for consultations with the Admiralty on the naval establishments and defences of the Canadas. Before his return to Kingston in 1827 he was promoted commodore first class. In June 1834 the inland naval establishment was abolished, and Barrie returned to England for good. King William IV immediately appointed him KCH and knighted him. He was promoted rear-admiral in 1837, and in 1840 was created KCB.

Barrie was brave in war, forthright at all times, and yet warm and generous. His copious letters now in various libraries attest to his qualities as well as to his loyalty to his subordinates, his devotion to his family, and his gift of prophecy about the future of Canada and of the United States. He is remembered in Canada in a number of place-names, which include Barrie Point and Barrie Reach, B.C., the village of Barriefield near Kingston, Barrie Island in Lake Huron, and the Ontario city of Barrie. In 1833 Barrie's wife wrote of her attraction to the newly laid out town for retirement, but her husband could not be inspired "with any of my mind."

Thomas L. Brock

[In addition to the various collections of papers now held by the archival institutions cited below, the author made use of a number of Barrie letters and artifacts obtained from Kathleen Barrie, a great-granddaughter, her sister Mrs Evelyn French, her cousin Rodney Barrie, and Captain R. L. B. Cunliffe, a great-grandson of Barrie's half-sister Frances Clayton Lyon. T.L.B.]

A portrait of Sir Robert Barrie was painted in 1967 by Cecil Jameson for the Royal Military College of Canada (Kingston, Ont.), from a miniature owned by Rodney Barrie of London. The painting is reproduced on the cover of *Historic Kingston*, no.23 (1975).

College of Arms (London), Barrie genealogy. Duke Univ. Library (Durham, N.C.), MS Dept., Sir Robert Barrie papers. Lancashire Record Office (Preston, Eng.), DDX 510/1–38 (Dolly [Gardner Barrie] Clayton, diaries, 1777, 1783, 1798, 1801–33 except 1812). NLS, Dept. of MSS, MS 2333: ff.96–110; MS 2335: ff.72–75. NMM, BIE/1–4. PAC, MG 24, F66; RG 8, III, 24–51, 72. PRO, ADM 1/417, 1/828, 1/5355, 1/5419; CO 158/16. Royal Military College of Canada, Special Coll. Division, Acc. 1032748 (transcripts of Barrie letters with biog. and notes by T. L. Brock, typescript, Montreal, 1967); Acc. 1136880 (Barrie letters). SRO, GD45/3; GD51/2/603/1–5; 51/2/622. William L. Clements Library, Univ. of Mich. (Ann Arbor), Robert Barrie papers. G.B., ADM, *Navy list*, 20 March 1838: 4–5. T. L. Brock, "H.M. Dock Yard, Kingston under Commissioner Robert Barrie, 1819–1834" and "Commodore Robert Barrie and his family in Kingston, 1819–1834," *Historic Kingston*, no.16 (1968): 3–22, and no.23: 1–18. J. W. Spurr, "The Royal Navy's presence in Kingston, part I: 1813–1836," *Historic Kingston*, no.25 (1977): 63–77.

BARRY, ROBERT, teacher, merchant, Methodist lay exhorter, office holder, and JP; b. *c.* 1759 in Kinross, Scotland, son of John Barry; m. May 1789 Mary Jessop in Delaware, and they had five sons and six daughters; d. 3 Sept. 1843 in Liverpool, N.S.

Although born in Scotland, Robert Barry was raised in Fratton, England. Through his father, a shopkeeper, he was introduced to a mercantile career. As Barry's later reminiscences indicate, he was attracted in youth to Methodist evangelicalism. About 1774 he crossed the Atlantic as an impressed seaman but made good his escape in the port of New York. Little is known of his life there beyond his participation in a business partnership, his friendship with the Reverend Charles Inglis*, the rector of Trinity Church (where Barry was a regular communicant), and his attendance at Methodist services in the John Street Chapel. This chapel, built in 1768, was the first structure in North America dedicated by its founding congregation to the Methodist movement. Here Barry is said to have started his lifelong role as an exhorter.

In the spring of 1783 some of the leading John Street Methodists, including Barry, joined the exodus of several thousand loyalists from New York to Port Roseway (Shelburne), N.S. Though the majority of these refugees eventually moved elsewhere, Barry determined to stay in the settlement. For two years he taught school in Shelburne and then became established as a merchant there in connection with his only brother, Alexander, of Portsmouth, England. Their firm, known as A. and R. Barry, engaged in the West Indies fish, lumber, sugar, and rum trade, and transported considerable quantities of agricultural produce from the Chignecto Isthmus to Halifax and St John's. British dry goods were imported from London for sale in Nova Scotia. Stores were acquired in Shelburne, in Liverpool, at the Strait of Canso, and in Dorchester, N.B., which were serviced by a small fleet of vessels owned in part or whole by A. and R. Barry.

With the dissolution of the partnership in 1810 Barry moved to Liverpool and set himself up in business there, although he still maintained his store and shipping interests in Shelburne. He was assisted by four of his sons, and saw them found their own stores in Halifax. One of them, John Alexander*, furthered family prominence by marrying in 1814 a daughter of Methodist Superintendent William Black* and by being elected in 1827 to the House of Assembly for Shelburne. Robert Barry himself served as a JP and in 1817 was appointed to the Commissioners Court, which was authorized to hold summary hearings of small claims. He joined organizations in Queens County such as the agricultural society and temperance and bible societies, and was a committee member of the Wesleyan Methodist Missionary Auxiliary Society. His business affairs were conducted with "probity, integrity and frankness," and Methodist missionary Robert Cooney* described him in 1834 as "an upright and intelligent magistrate."

Barry, whose life was guided by John Wesley's teachings, represented the important role played by merchants in Nova Scotian Methodism. These merchants – Simeon Perkins* is another example – provided leadership to the movement and at the same time enhanced its respectability. Barry himself acted as a class leader and exhorter in Shelburne, which was the headquarters of the Methodist preacher James Man*. He also advanced the sect's cause on the South Shore by participating in the construction of chapels at Shelburne, Barrington, and Sable River, and of one for blacks near Liverpool. In 1783, following a visit to Shelburne by William Black, Barry had initiated a correspondence with John Wesley. The Barry–Wesley letters offer useful insight into transatlantic Methodist ties, provide glimpses of the Shelburne Methodist society, and indicate Barry's fervent devotion to Wesleyanism. They also reveal how Nova Scotia Methodists were torn between retaining – at Wesley's insistence – their attachment to the Church of England and accepting preachers such as Freeborn Garrettson* from the Methodist Episcopal Church of the United States.

In his secular activity Barry exemplified those loyalist merchants who created a secure place for themselves in Nova Scotia. His promotion of Methodism gave him a special spiritual attachment to the colony, aided his integration into the pre-existing mercantile structure through select business ties, and kept him in touch with the greater world of transatlantic Wesleyanism. His life is a useful illustration of the dynamic impact that evangelical Protestantism has had on the formation of eastern Canadian society.

ALLEN B. ROBERTSON

In addition to the sources cited below, the records of the Nova Scotia Court of Probate for Queens (Liverpool) and Shelburne counties and of the Registry of Deeds for Halifax, Hants (Windsor), Queens, and Shelburne counties were consulted; they are available on microfilm at the PANS.

PANS, MG 1, 120, 817; MG 3, 306; MG 100, 170, doc.13 (copies); RG 34-321. UCC, Maritime Conference Arch. (Halifax), Black–McColl papers, John Wesley letters, Wesley to Robert Barry, 15 Sept. 1786; Granville Ferry Methodist Church (Granville Ferry, N.S.), board of trustees, minutes, 1887–1913, copy of letter, John Wesley to Robert Barry, 4 June 1790. *The Newlight Baptist journals of James Manning and James Innis*, ed. D. G. Bell (Saint John, N.B., 1984). John Wesley, *The letters of the Rev. John Wesley . . .*, ed. John Telford (8v., London, 1931; repr. [1960]), 7: 225, 254; 8: 12. *Christian Messenger*, 1843. *Nova-Scotia Royal Gazette*, 1802, 1806, 1812, 1814–16, 1820–21, 1824. *Times* (Halifax), 1843. G. A. Rawlyk, *Ravished by the spirit: religious revivals, Baptists, and Henry Alline* (Kingston, Ont., and Montreal, 1984). A. B. Robertson, "Loyalist, Methodist, merchant – Robert Barry – from refugee to Nova Scotian" (MA thesis, Acadia Univ., Wolfville, N.S., 1984). Marion Robertson, *King's bounty: a history of early Shelburne, Nova Scotia . . .* (Halifax, 1983). Smith, *Hist. of Methodist Church*.

BATES, WALTER, office holder and author; b. 14 March 1760 in that part of Stamford, Conn., that is now Darien, fourth son of John Bates and Sarah Bostwick; m. first 7 Oct. 1784 Abigail Lyon in Kingston, N.B., and they had four children, three of whom died in childhood; m. secondly 12 Sept. 1826 Mrs Lucy Smith in Hampton, N.B.; d. 11 Feb. 1842 in Kingston.

Walter Bates was raised as a farmer in eastern Connecticut and, given his genuine piety and reliable, unadventurous disposition, would probably have remained in that state and station had not external events compelled him to choose otherwise. His three elder brothers had become involved on the tory side of the American War of Independence, and at the age of 15 Bates was captured by rebel sympathizers, examined before a committee, subjected to indignities, and threatened with death if he did not reveal the whereabouts of one of his brothers and other leading tories suspected of being concealed in the neighbourhood. Eventually freed, he absented himself from the community for two years. He returned to find his father dying of smallpox but was obliged within three days to take refuge with the British garrison in New York. There he took the oath of allegiance to King George III.

The year 1783 found Bates among the tory farmers of Long Island (he had been teaching school there for a time) who decided to accept the king's offer of 200 acres of land in Nova Scotia plus two years' provisions and transport to their new home. He was a passenger on the *Union*, the first ship in the spring fleet of 1783 to arrive at what would become Parrtown (Saint John, N.B.). He was one of the initial group to settle at Kingston on the Belleisle (Kingston) Creek, where he would remain until his death. He became a selectman at the early age of 26 and was to serve for many years as high sheriff of Kings County.

Bates's narrative of his experiences, *Kingston and the loyalists of the "spring fleet" of A.D. 1783*, was published posthumously in 1889. It reveals a tory partisan of extreme personal modesty, much concerned with factual accuracy, who both in his conscious decisions and in the conduct of his life was greatly interested in the welfare of the Anglican church in general and of Trinity Church in Kingston in particular. Bates took a leading part in the founding of that church and involved himself in its affairs until the time of his death. He was early chosen to succeed Frederick Dibblee* as lay reader in the absence of a clergyman.

Doubtless Bates's interest in the notorious thief and confidence man Henry More Smith came from the attraction of opposites, although Smith possessed a strongly developed religious side. Be that as it may, Bates's chief claim to fame is his authorship of *The mysterious stranger; or, memoirs of Henry More Smith*, first published in 1817. This work went through many editions in North America and England and sold thousands of copies. It remains an extremely readable book. Two factors account for its attraction. The first is the remarkable character of its protagonist, the gentle, ingenious, and altogether puzzling thief, who, had he turned his attention to honest living, could quite easily have been an eminent clergyman or politician. The second is the literary skill of Bates, whose selection of circumstantial detail, concern over veracity, and modest, unassuming style are, in this book, comparable to the best work of Daniel Defoe in combining suspense with credibility.

FRED COGSWELL

Walter Bates is the author of *Kingston and the loyalists of the "spring fleet" of A.D. 1783, with reminiscenses of early days in Connecticut: a narrative . . .*, ed. W. O. Raymond (Saint John, N.B., 1889; repr. Fredericton, 1980); *The mysterious stranger; or, memoirs of Henry More Smith; alias Henry Frederick Moon; alias William Newman: who is now confined in Simbury mines, in Connecticut, for the crime of burglary; containing an account of his . . . confinement in the gaol of King's County, province of New-*

Brunswick . . . with a statement of his succeeding conduct . . . (New Haven, Conn., 1817), which was published in London the same year under the title *Companion for Caraboo: a narrative of the conduct and adventures of Henry Frederic Moon, alias Henry Frederic More Smith, alias William Newman – now under sentence of imprisonment, in Connecticut, in North America, containing an account of his unparalleled artifices, impostures, mechanical ingenuity, &c. &c. displayed during and subsequently to his confinement in one of his majesty's gaols in the province of New Brunswick, with an introductory description of New Brunswick, and a postscript containing some account of Caraboo, the late female impostor, of Bristol* (London, 1817); and *A serious conference by letters on the subject of religious worship, and of the church of God, from a member of the established episcopal Church of England, in ... New-Brunswick, to a member of the established congregational Presbyterian Church, in the state of Connecticut* . . . (Saint John, 1826).

PANB, RG 4, RS24, S24-P29, S24-P35. Saint John Regional Library, "Biographical data relating to New Brunswick families, especially of loyalist descent," comp. D. R. Jack (4v., typescript; copy at N.B. Museum). *New-Brunswick Courier*, 19 Feb. 1842. *Royal Gazette* (Fredericton), 19 Sept. 1826. *DAB*. W. G. MacFarlane, *New Brunswick bibliography: the books and writers of the province* (Saint John, 1895). G. P. Beyea, "The Canadian novel prior to confederation" (MA thesis, Univ. of N.B., Fredericton, 1950). E. B. Huntington, *History of Stamford, Connecticut* ... (Stamford, 1868; repr. with corrections, Harrison, N.Y., 1979).

BAUDRY, MARIE-VICTOIRE, named **de la Croix**, sister of the Congregation of Notre Dame, teacher, and superior of the community (superior general); b. 12 Dec. 1782 in Pointe-aux-Trembles (Montreal), daughter of Toussaint Baudry and Élisabeth Truteau; d. 10 Nov. 1846 in Montreal.

Marie-Victoire Baudry went to school at the convent in Pointe-aux-Trembles. She entered the noviciate of the Congregation of Notre Dame at Montreal in 1799 and took her vows two years later under the name of Sister de la Croix. In 1802 she began to teach at the Saint-Laurent mission on Montreal Island, and in 1804 she was responsible for a class in the Lower Town mission at Quebec.

As a member of a community primarily devoted to teaching, Sister de la Croix should have spent long years in that activity. But she was called to take charge first of the mission at Pointe-aux-Trembles (Neuville) in 1809, and then of the one at Saint-François (Saint-François-Montmagny) in 1811. Seven years later she became novice mistress at the mother house in Montreal, an office she held until she was elected superior in 1822. At the end of her six-year term she was succeeded by Marie-Catherine Huot*, named Sainte-Madeleine, and was elected councillor; she retained that post until her death.

During her six years as superior, Sister de la Croix set up three new missions: Sainte-Marie-de-la-Nouvelle-Beauce (Sainte-Marie) in 1823, Berthier-en-Haut (Berthierville) in 1825, and Terrebonne in 1826. As the sisters of the Congregation of Notre Dame were not cloistered, requests for their services in teaching and bringing up children came from a number of quarters. The superior shaped the curriculum, in which the promotion of Christian values held a large place. For example, Sister de la Croix expanded it adding, as needed, the study of English, drawing, domestic science, and various other activities.

Through Sulpician Jean-Baptiste THAVENET, the financial representative in Europe of the Lower Canadian religious communities, the Congregation of Notre Dame was able to recover the annuities that had remained in France since the French revolution [*see* Marie-Louise Compain*, named Saint-Augustin]. Sister de la Croix had a hand in the attempt to establish the Trappistine nuns in Nova Scotia. In 1822 she welcomed into the noviciate three girls chosen by Father Vincent de Paul [Jacques Merle*], who wanted to organize a branch of the order. The following year the novices returned to Nova Scotia; they remained grateful to the Congregation of Notre Dame, and especially to the superior.

Sister de la Croix was endowed with sound judgement and a strong constitution. She could show kindness while insisting firmly on obedience to the rule and adherence to the practices then in effect in the community. As a result of an accident suffered in her girlhood she limped, and later she became deaf. Despite this double infirmity she attended the spiritual exercises of the community and visited all the missions. When she died, the bishop of Montreal, Ignace Bourget*, wrote to the community: "I always admired in the good Sister de la Croix a fervent zeal for maintaining discipline and the exact observance of your holy rules; she had an abundant share of the . . . *evangelical simplicity* that your devoted founder [Marguerite Bourgeoys*] bequeathed to you. . . . [God] had given her deep understanding of all that concerns your community." Sister de la Croix's name is linked to those who in succession accomplished great deeds in responding to the call of the church and of education.

THÉRÈSE LAMBERT

ANQ-M, CE1-5, 12 déc. 1782; CE1-51, 12 nov. 1846. Arch. de la Congrégation de Notre-Dame (Montréal), Marie-Catherine Huot, dite Sainte-Madeleine, Journal et notes hist. [D.-A. Lemire-Marsolais, dite Sainte-Henriette, et] Thérèse Lambert, dite Sainte-Marie-Médiatrice , *Histoire de la Congrégation de Notre-Dame* (11v. en 13 parus, Montréal, 1941–), 6–8.

BAUZHI-GEEZHIG-WAESHIKUM (Pazhekezhikquashkum, Pechegechequistqum, Beyigishiqueshkam), chief and medicine man; b. on the Miamis

(Maumee) River (Ohio); had three sons who survived to adulthood; d. late 1841 or early 1842 on Walpole Island (Lambton County), Upper Canada.

Bauzhi-geezhig-waeshikum, whose name means "one who steps over the sky," was probably born well before the outbreak of the American revolution. As a young man he lived on the west shore of Lake St Clair in present-day Michigan, but in the late 1820s, as an elderly chief, he moved with his family across the border to Walpole Island. Alexander McKee* of the Indian Department had encouraged Britain's Ojibwa and Ottawa allies in the region to settle on the large island after the revolution, and by the time of Bauzhi-geezhig-waeshikum's arrival the island, which had never been surrendered to the crown, had a population of roughly 300.

In August 1829 the Reverend Peter Jones*, a native Methodist missionary, tried unsuccessfully to convert Bauzhi-geezhig-waeshikum to Christianity. The old chief and medicine man refused. As he explained to Jones and the Indian converts accompanying him: "The white man makes the fire-water, he drinks, and sells it to the Indians, he lies and cheats the poor Indian. I have seen him go to his prayinghouse in [Fort] Malden, and as soon as he comes out I have seen him go straight to the tavern, get drunk, quarrel, and fight. Now the white man's religion is no better than mine. I will hold fast to the religion of my forefathers." Undeterred, Jones returned on two more occasions in the early 1830s, but he made no headway. Bauzhi-geezhig-waeshikum no doubt again repeated the opinion he had expressed on the first visit: that different paths had been laid down for whites and Indians. "The Great Spirit made us all," he had said. "When [he] made the white man he gave him his worship, written in a book, and prepared a place for his soul in heaven above. He also gave him his mode of preparing and administering medicine to the sick different from that of the Indians. Brothers and friends, when the Great Spirit made the Indian he gave him his mode of worship, and the manner of administering and using medicine to the sick. The Great Spirit gave the Indian to know the virtue of roots and plants to preserve life; and by attending to these things our lives are preserved." After repeated failures Jones called the St Clair mission "the hardest I know."

Recognized as the head chief of all the Indians on Walpole Island and on the Upper Canadian side of the St Clair River, Bauzhi-geezhig-waeshikum resisted when government authorities applied pressure on him and his people to adopt Christianity and agriculture. As a protest he did not participate in a census sponsored by the Indian Department and he refused presents for several years. But, as he informed Jones in the summer of 1833, he would "agree to send our children to school that they may learn to read, put words on paper, and count, so that the white traders might not cheat them."

An intrusion of white settlers on Walpole Island infuriated him. In 1839 he told Samuel Peters Jarvis*, the chief superintendent of Indian affairs for Upper Canada, that the squatters had killed a hundred of their pigs, stolen their horses, and shot their dogs, "at the very doors of our lodges." The whites also circulated rumours that the Indians would be removed as had been done in the United States. Fortunately the Indian Department protected the Indians' title and evicted the squatters in the early 1840s.

Bauzhi-geezhig-waeshikum was a gifted orator whose speaking ability, as well as his intensive knowledge of traditional medicine, helped earn him the great respect he enjoyed among the local Indians. Jones noted that "the other chiefs never undertake anything of importance without consulting him . . . this chief is quite like a patriarch among his people."

Although the Reverend James EVANS succeeded in winning over many of the Ojibwas on the west bank of the St Clair River in the mid 1830s, neither he nor his successors made any conversions among the Indians on Walpole Island in Bauzhi-geezhig-waeshikum's lifetime. The death, shortly before 10 Jan. 1842, of one of the last great Ojibwa and Ottawa traditionalists in the area removed, in Indian agent John W. Keating's words, "a great obstacle . . . from the Missionary's war in the conversion of the Indians."

DONALD B. SMITH

[The author would like to thank Basil Johnston of the Royal Ont. Museum (Toronto) for his advice on Ojibwa names. D.B.S.]

AO, MS 296. MTRL, S. P. Jarvis papers, B57: 373–76, 381–84. PAC, RG 10, A4, 58: 59781; 67: 64211–14; 126: 70969; B3, 2022, file 8520; C1, 2, vol.569: 10. Victoria Univ. Library (Toronto), Peter Jones coll., Peter Jones papers, letter-book, 10 June 1833. Can., Prov. of, Legislative Assembly, *App. to the journals*, 1847, app.T, app.21, J. W. Keating, letter, 16 Dec. 1842. Peter Jones, *History of the Ojebway Indians; with especial reference to their conversion to Christianity . . .*, [ed. Elizabeth Field] (London, 1861); *Life and journals of Kah-ke-wa-quo-nā-by (Rev. Peter Jones), Wesleyan missionary*, [ed. Elizabeth Field and Enoch Wood] (Toronto, 1860). "Missionary intelligence," *Christian Guardian*, 27 Feb. 1830: 115. K. J. Tyler and R. T. Ryan, "The government's management of Indian trust funds: a case study of the Chippewas and Pottawatomies of Walpole Island" (report prepared for the National Indian Brotherhood, mimeograph, 1981), pp.V-2, VII-3.

BEAMER (Beemer, Bemer), JACOB R., carpenter, innkeeper, and Patriot; b. *c.* 1810 in Norfolk County, Upper Canada, son of Mary and Joseph Beamer; m. Mary ——, and they had two children; fl. 1837–47.

Jacob R. Beamer's father came to Upper Canada

from New Jersey in 1796 and was granted land in Townsend Township, Norfolk County. Here Jacob grew up, part of a large family. He became a carpenter and later, when he and his father opened a tavern at Scotland in Oakland Township, an innkeeper.

In December 1837 Beamer, who was a reformer, heard a report that the reform leader William Lyon Mackenzie* had captured Toronto and that the authorities intended arresting Charles Duncombe* and Eliakim Malcolm*, two prominent local reformers. These two determined on rebellion, and Malcolm held a meeting at the Beamers' tavern on 7 December to muster recruits. Jacob's father and his brother David supported the rebel cause, as did Jacob, who drilled and collected arms. Yet Toronto had not fallen; indeed government supporters under Allan Napier MacNab* were about to fall upon Duncombe's and Malcolm's motley army. Learning of this development on 13 December, the insurgents retreated and fled; Jacob surrendered at Simcoe. Though the authorities released him, they sent his father to the Hamilton jail. Later, when Jacob discovered that he was to be indicted, he absconded to Niagara Falls in New York State. There he continued working for the rebel cause.

In June 1838, under James Morreau, he captained a company in the "Canada Volunteer Army" of "the Patriot Service." Twenty-nine men of that "army" crossed the Niagara River into Upper Canada on 11 June, to take "arms and ammunition to the Short Hills" and to bring "independence to Canada." They soon realized that they had been misled; the Niagara area was not ripe for rebellion. Morreau wanted to turn back, but Beamer and others "determined to persevere." Consequently, on the night of 20 June the raiders descended on the village of St Johns (St Johns West). Beamer and his company plundered a few houses before the raiders, reinforced by some locals, attacked an inn housing a small contingent of the Queen's Lancers. They took the lancers prisoner, only to release them, much to Beamer's chagrin. He wanted them killed.

The raiders then scattered, but most were soon taken. Beamer was captured at St Thomas and sent to Niagara (Niagara-on-the-Lake) via London. By 17 August, the date of Beamer's trial, Morreau had already been executed. Jacob's father and two raiders, Stephen Hart and Edward Seymour, made desperate but unsuccessful attempts on the witness stand to win him acquittal. Lieutenant Governor Sir George Arthur* thought his case an aggravated one, and was therefore angered when the governor-in-chief, Lord Durham [LAMBTON], intervened to have him saved from the scaffold and transported with others to Van Diemen's Land (Tasmania) for life.

Beamer and various state prisoners were sent first to England, arriving in December 1838, and then to Van Diemen's Land, which Beamer reached in January 1840. He had now acquired bitter enemies among his fellow Short Hills prisoners. By early 1842 three of them – Samuel Chandler*, James Gammill (Gemmell, Gamble), and Benjamin Wait* – had escaped. On 28 June 1842 in the New York *Daily Plebeian* Gammill recorded for the public's disgust that Beamer had become a constable, and in his *Letters from Van Dieman's Land*, published in the United States in 1843, Wait claimed that Beamer, hoping for a reprieve, had consistently betrayed his comrades. Linus Wilson Miller* seconded Wait's accusation after his pardon in 1844. In *Notes of an exile to Van Dieman's Land* (1846) he even charged that Beamer had committed treachery as early as 1838 by revealing to the authorities a plot to rescue state prisoners from the Hamilton jail. When he had left the penal colony for the United States in 1845, Miller added, Beamer was sunk in depravity, his situation hopeless. Just before leaving Van Diemen's Land in early March 1847, another freed prisoner, Elijah Crocker WOODMAN, noted that Beamer was still "in bondage."

Beamer's eventual fate is a mystery. Perhaps he was the Jacob Bremmer sentenced in Melbourne in July 1851 to two years' hard labour for forgery, or the Jacob Beemer living in Melbourne in 1856–57. Perhaps he left Australia, perhaps not. Conceivably he returned to Upper Canada. In any case many, erstwhile comrades included, remembered him as a "traitor."

COLIN READ

[The author is grateful for information provided by the staff of the *ADB*. C.R.]

PAC, MG 24, I26, 65; RG 5, A1: esp. 104502–11, 106180–85, 108705–12, 110429–51, 110820–21, 111392–433, 111583–86, 111977–2007, 112222–36, 112458–88, 114649–51. PRO, CO 42/450 (mfm. at AO). L. W. Miller, *Notes of an exile to Van Dieman's Land: comprising incidents of the Canadian rebellion in 1838, trial of the author in Canada, and subsequent appearance before her majesty's Court of Queen's Bench, in London, imprisonment in England, and transportation to Van Dieman's Land . . .* (Fredonia, N.Y., 1846; repr. East Ardsley, Eng., 1968). Benjamin Wait, *Letters from Van Dieman's Land, written during four years imprisonment for political offences committed in Upper Canada* (Buffalo, N.Y., 1843). Guillet, *Lives and times of Patriots*. C. [F.] Read, *Rising in western U.C.*; "The Short Hills raid of June, 1838, and its aftermath," *OH*, 68 (1976): 93–115.

BEASLEY, RICHARD, office holder, fur trader, businessman, JP, politician, militia officer, and farmer; b. 21 July 1761 in the colony of New York, son of Henry Beasley and Maria Noble; m. 1791 Henrietta Springer, and they had three sons and five daughters; d. 16 Feb. 1842 in Hamilton, Upper Canada.

Richard Beasley may have been captured by rebels

on 14 Sept. 1777 during the American revolution. According to a 1795 petition, he arrived in the province of Quebec in 1777 and served two years as "Acting Commissary," presumably at Fort Niagara (near Youngstown, N.Y.). There in 1781 he witnessed a co-partnership between John Askin* and the firm of Robert Hamilton* and Richard Cartwright*, Beasley's cousin. In 1783 he formed a partnership with Peter Smith* in the Indian trade and they built trading houses at Toronto and Pemitescutiang (Port Hope). Five years later they petitioned for land at both places, but the government preferred other sites. Beasley subsequently took up land in Barton Township at the head of Lake Ontario. Patrick Campbell* visited him there in 1792 and recorded that he "keeps a shop . . . and trades much with the Indians in peltry." That same year the deputy surveyor general of the new province of Upper Canada, David William SMITH, noted that Beasley and James Wilson had a sawmill and grist-mill in Ancaster Township on a creek emptying into Burlington Bay (Hamilton Harbour).

In the early 1790s Beasley settled on the southeast end of Burlington Heights (then in Barton Township but now in Hamilton), where he built a house, stable, and barn. In spite of his improvements, the ownership of the land was disputed by another local family, the Lottridges. Situated between Burlington Bay and the marsh to the west, Coote's Paradise, the property gave its occupant control of trans-shipping there. When on 11 June 1796 Lieutenant Governor John Graves Simcoe* and his wife were in the vicinity, they set out in a boat for Beasley's. A commanding location with a beautiful view, the site was described by Elizabeth Posthuma Simcoe [GWILLIM] as "more fitt for the reception of Inhabitants than any part of the Province I have seen." Beasley used the opportunity of the visit to press his claim to the land upon the lieutenant governor, who was willing to support it if Beasley built a wharf and a storehouse. It was not until 1798, after Simcoe's departure from Upper Canada, that Beasley reached a settlement with the Lottridges. He then petitioned the Executive Council, urging official confirmation of his ownership and citing "benefit to the public as well As to himself" of the wharf and storehouse he intended to put up. He received permission to build them on the beach fronting the property and in 1799 a patent was issued.

Probably more than anyone then resident at the Head of the Lake, Beasley was in a position to reap the advantages of its growth. Aside from his enterprises, he had been appointed a magistrate in 1796, the same year he was elected to the House of Assembly for Durham, York, and 1st Lincoln. An officer of the Lincoln militia, in 1798 he was given command of the Company of the Burlington Circle in the York militia. His early political career was ordinary: in 1798 he voted for Christopher Robinson*'s bill allowing immigrants to bring slaves into the province and the following year he sided with the majority in defeating a bill allowing Methodist ministers to perform marriages. In July 1800 Beasley and Robert NELLES were elected in West York, 1st Lincoln, and Haldimand. William Claus*, who had attended the election, found "the Minds of the people there so much poisoned against the officers of Government, and that by Mr. Beasley . . . a Very troublesome man." Beasley's most notable contribution to the third parliament (1801–4) was his tenure as speaker in 1803–4. In the election of 1804 he was defeated. His re-election in 1808 for York West was contested on the ground that the returning officer had "prematurely closed the poll"; Beasley was unseated in February 1809 and succeeded by the radical agrarian John Willson*. Beasley protested to no avail.

Prosperity eluded Beasley. He had sold his share of the Ancaster mills and 400 acres of land to John Baptist Rousseaux* St John for £1,200. Despite Cartwright's warning against land speculation, he used his new-found finances in 1798 to purchase with James Wilson and Rousseaux – whom he later bought out – block 2 (Waterloo Township) of the Six Nations' lands on the Grand River for £8,887 (provincial currency). Unlike most of the speculators associated with these lands, Beasley brought in some settlers. Still, he was unable to make his mortgage payments to the Indians' trustees. In 1800 Robert Hamilton won a judgement against him for debt. To meet various obligations, he put up for sale his "valuable and pleasant property" in Barton, which included 976 acres (150 cultivated), his house, stables, a wharf, a storehouse, and timber. He managed, however, to hold on to this property and sold land in block 2 to Pennsylvania Mennonites [*see* Samuel D. Betzner*] without apprising them of the mortgage. It was several years before the tangled business was settled.

Beasley's world was collapsing on all fronts. He had recklessly abandoned milling for land speculation, only to flounder in the mire of block 2. Commercial leadership at the Head of the Lake passed to Richard Hatt* while political dominance was assumed by Willson. Beasley's life, however, was far from hard. Although he now "depended on the product" of his farm to support his family and servants, his estate included an attractive brick neoclassical style cottage, built before the War of 1812 and described in 1833 as "very roomy, being 50′ x 40′, with two wings 20′ square, and a frame kitchen 18′ x 30′." The farm had an orchard of some 200 apple trees, "a number of Choice fruit trees and a nursery of Young Apple trees," and, by the 1830s, it also included an extensive peach orchard, "said to be the best in the province." It was a suitable estate for the lieutenant-colonel of the West Riding Militia of York (commissioned on 26 May 1802).

The war and its aftermath further undercut Beasley's prestige. In the wake of the Americans' offensive along the Niagara peninsula in the spring of 1813 and the defeat that fall of Major-General Henry Procter* in the west of the province, retreating British forces and their Indian allies congregated at the depot on Burlington Heights near Beasley's farm. From June 1813 until September 1815 his home and buildings were occupied by troops, his farm encumbered with batteries and trenches, his orchards and fields rendered "useless," his garden destroyed, his fences burnt, his timber cut, his grain confiscated, and several of his buildings ruined. Damages exceeded £3,000; commissioners later awarded him over £1,300.

Worse, allegations about the ardour of his wartime conduct dogged him. His slide into disrepute was accelerated by his association with Robert Gourlay*'s post-war agitation. As Hatt's newspaper put it in 1818, in the newly formed Gore District Gourlay's "great cause of enquiry into the state of the Province has been spiritedly taken up." In December 1817 Beasley had chaired the Barton meeting responding to Gourlay's enquiries. Then, in 1818, he was elected a district representative to Gourlay's provincial convention. Opened at York (Toronto) on 6 July, it was chaired by Beasley, who began the proceedings with "a neat speech, wherein he deprecated the false and malicious insinuations and assertions thrown out before the public, as to the view and intentions of those who joined in the present business." Later that month John Strachan* damned him as a "disagreeable weak discontented Character" who had "behaved poorly during the war."

In an address to Lieutenant Governor Sir Peregrine Maitland* in October Beasley, who had been a high treason commissioner during the war, played down the need for stressing the obvious loyalty of a people "who, for three years, withstood every assault of an insidious, a daring and powerful enemy, merely for the maintenance of British Sovereignty." At issue, rather, was the colonial administration of the past 20 years which, "with little exception, only gave experience of disappointment." He looked "forward to more cheering times"; discontent, however, was real and "serious causes must exist for such agitations." Beasley went beyond the traditional call for redress of grievances. He wanted an imperial inquiry into the state of the province, a task for which the provincial House of Assembly "is not, indeed, competent." The seventh parliament had so far ignored matters "of vital import." Maitland's predecessor, Francis Gore*, had "by arbitrary acts . . . thwarted the laws of the land" and presented "just grounds for [his] impeachment." Robert Nichol*'s comprehensive resolutions in 1817 attacking Gore's administration though "excellent" had been made too late. The province suffered from the "maladministration of good laws," a check in its prosperity, and "discontent and poverty under the most genial clime, and rooted in the most fertile soil." Fearing a renewal of hostilities with the United States and possible separation from Great Britain, he urged Maitland to forward the York convention's address to the Prince Regent. The conventionists, however, had gone too far and the so-called Gagging Bill to limit such proceedings was passed on 31 October with only one dissentient vote.

The administration moved quickly against the Gourlayites. In 1819 Beasley was dropped from the magistracy and lost the command of the 2nd Regiment of Gore militia, which he had held for ten years. He demanded a court of inquiry, which was held that spring. Adjutant General Nathaniel COFFIN charged him with withdrawing from action at Lundy's Lane in 1814, disobedience, neglect of duty, and unbecoming conduct. During the farcical proceedings Beasley was not allowed to speak in his defence or call witnesses. "It has," he complained, "more the appearance of an Inquisition. . . . I might as well have been in the remotest part of India as present at Grimsby." The court of inquiry upheld his dismissal. Beasley then called for a court martial at which he could "defend himself according to the true Intent and Spirit of the British Constitution." Held at Grimsby on 24 Jan. 1820, this court found him not guilty on all but the count of neglect of duty, which it pronounced unintentional. The sentence was a mere letter of censure which Maitland wrote on 6 March informing Beasley that his services were no longer needed and that the decision bore no relation to the court martial "but is founded entirely on the prominent part taken by you in the proceedings of the late convention of Delegates, so inconsistent with your station." Beasley wrote to a friend: "I lost the Confidence of the Administration and in consequence have been put out of all the Honorable I will not say profitable appointments I held." The "times," however, had "required an inquiry" and subsequent events did not disabuse him of that notion.

Beasley contested Middlesex in 1820, losing to Mahlon BURWELL. Four years later he was elected for Halton. Given his credentials, George Tiffany, an Ancaster lawyer, suggested him to William Lyon Mackenzie* as a "partisan" of reform and as an appropriate choice for speaker. In fact, the position went to John Willson in January 1825. Beasley's time was past. In 1827 he was restored to the magistracy and from 1834 he served as an associate judge at the district assizes. Bogged down in financial difficulty since the Gourlay episode, he had been forced in 1819 to mortgage property (he then owned 11,350 acres) to the Montreal firm of François Desrivières* and Thomas BLACKWOOD. Unable to pay off the mortgage or maintain the interest payments, he sold his Burlington Heights property in 1832 to Allan Napier MacNab*. Two years later, when MacNab began building Dundurn, Beasley was still scrambling to pay his remaining debt to Blackwood. In 1842 he owned one house and two lots in Hamilton, and acted as the local agent for several firms.

ROBERT L. FRASER

AO, MS 88; MS 302; MS 502; MS 503; MS 516; MU 500, Richard Cartwright, letter-book, 1793–96; MU 2555; RG 22, ser.131; ser.155. HPL, Barton Township, census and assessment rolls, 1816–19, 1835–42. MTRL, Laurent Quetton de St George papers. PAC, RG 1, E1; L3; RG 5, A1; RG 8, I (C ser.); RG 9, I, B1; RG 19, E5(a), 3740, 3756; RG 68, General index, 1651–1841. Patrick Campbell, *Travels in the interior inhabited parts of North America in the years 1791 and 1792 . . .* , ed. H. H. Langton and W. F. Ganong (Toronto, 1937). Can., House of Commons, *Journals*, 1870, app.1. *Corr. of Hon. Peter Russell* (Cruikshank and Hunter). *Corr. of Lieut. Governor Simcoe* (Cruikshank). "District of Nassau; letter book no.2," AO *Report*, 1905: 335. [Thomas Douglas, 5th Earl of] Selkirk, *Lord Selkirk's diary, 1803–1804; a journal of his travels in British North America and the northeastern United States*, ed. P. C. T. White (Toronto, 1958; repr. New York, 1969), 303. "Grants of crown lands, etc., in Upper Canada, 1792–1796," AO *Report*, 1929. [E. P. Gwillim] Mrs Simcoe, *Mrs. Simcoe's diary*, ed. M. [E.] Quayle Innis (Toronto and New York, 1965). *John Askin papers* (Quaife), vol.1. "Journals of Legislative Assembly of U.C.," AO *Report*, 1909, 1911–13. *Kingston before the War of 1812: a collection of documents*, ed. R. A. Preston (Toronto, 1959). "Records of Niagara . . . ," ed. E. A. Cruikshank, Niagara Hist. Soc., [*Pub.*], no.40 (n.d.). *Select British docs. of War of 1812* (Wood). *Statistical account of U.C.* (Gourlay; ed. Mealing; 1974). John Strachan, *The John Strachan letter book, 1812–1834*, ed. G. W. Spragge (Toronto, 1946). *Town of York, 1793–1815* (Firth). "Upper Canada land book D, 22nd December, 1797, to 13th July, 1798," AO *Report*, 1931. *Kingston Chronicle*, 1819–20. *Kingston Gazette*, 1818. *Upper Canada Gazette*, 1794, 1801. *Death notices of Ont.* (Reid). *DHB*. Reid, *Loyalists in Ont.* Darroch Milani, *Robert Gourlay, gadfly*. Gates, *Land policies of U.C.* Johnston, *Head of the Lake* (1958). Isabel Thompson Kelsay, *Joseph Brant, 1743–1807, man of two worlds* (Syracuse, N.Y., 1984). B. G. Wilson, *Enterprises of Robert Hamilton*. Nicholas Leblovic, "The life and history of Richard Beasley, esquire," *Wentworth Bygones* (Hamilton), no.7 (1967): 3–16.

BEAUBIEN. *See also* DES RIVIÈRES

BEAUBIEN, MARGUERITE, superior of the Sisters of Charity of the Hôpital Général of Montreal; b. 29 Jan. 1797 in Nicolet, Lower Canada, daughter of Alexis Beaubien, a farmer, and Marguerite Durocher; d. 11 Aug. 1848 in Montreal.

Marguerite Beaubien's parents owned a farm on Île Moras, in the Trois-Rivières region. Since they were well off, they were able to give their daughter a good upbringing. Marguerite entered the Hôpital Général on 12 July 1816 and took her vows on 17 July 1818. She became the housemother for orphan girls, and in 1828 the pharmacist. In 1833 Sister Beaubien was chosen to replace Mother Marie-Marguerite LEMAIRE, who had just resigned as superior. Unlike her predecessors, whose term of office was indefinite, she held the superiorship for five years, and then was re-elected for a second five-year period.

On taking up her duties Mother Beaubien had a laundry with running water built beside the Hôpital Général to promote the sisters' health. The old wash-house was transformed into a store for the benefit of the poor. She had three pictures painted in France to decorate the hospital's chapel. She also had a stone porch built at the entrance to the chapel, and completed the wall around the whole property with a wrought-iron gate that was crowned with an eloquent verse from Psalm 27: "Though my father and mother forsake me, the Lord will take me into His care." The straits in which the hospital existed became even more dire as a result of a flood in January 1838.

The poor were the focus of Mother Beaubien's constant solicitude. In 1834 she ordered the community's bursar to distribute wheat to all those in need on the seigneury of Châteauguay, which belonged to the Hôpital Général, and to have the oaks on Île Saint-Bernard cut down to be sold for the poor. The seigneurial manor-house, which was run down and too cramped, was rebuilt in 1836, and the nuns used it to shelter a number of families whose heads were taking part in the rebellion of 1837–38. In 1838 Mother Beaubien presented a report to the House of Assembly asking for additional funds to assist the work for foundlings and to rebuild the lunatic cells, which had become unfit to live in. These funds were not granted and as a result the nuns stopped caring for the insane in 1844.

In 1840 Mother Beaubien had allowed the Sisters of Charity to found a house at Saint-Hyacinthe. Three years later the community adopted new rules which Sulpician Sauveur-Romain Larré drew up with Bishop Ignace Bourget*. In elections held in 1843 Mother Beaubien was chosen assistant superior. In the autumn of 1844 she was named superior of the new community of the Sisters of Charity at Bytown (Ottawa). Unfortunately a paralytic stroke forced her to resign, and she was replaced by Sister Élisabeth Bruyère*. Sister Beaubien was too ill to assume any other duties. She was to endure four years of suffering before she died.

According to one of her biographers, Marguerite Beaubien had "a gentle and peaceful disposition, a judicious and penetrating mind, and sound judgement." Sulpician Jean-Baptiste THAVENET valued "the conscientiousness and precision with which she does things." During her term of office as superior the community completed its first century. It had widened the field of its apostleship and so could look to the future with confidence.

LAURETTE DUCLOS

ANQ-M, CE1-51, 14 août 1848. ANQ-MBF, CE1-13, 29 janv. 1797. Arch. des Sœurs Grises (Montréal), Aliénés, historique; Ancien journal, I; Corr., J.-B. Thavenet; Dossier de la communauté de Saint-Hyacinthe; Dossier de sœur Marguerite Beaubien; Maison mère, corr., chapelle; Mémoire de sœur Saint-Jean-de-la-Croix; Notices biographiques (1741–1848); Reg. des affaires temporelles, I; Reg. des entrées, 1737–1889; Reg. des minutes du Conseil général. P.-G. Roy, *Inv. concessions*. É.-J.[-A.] Auclair, *Histoire de Châteauguay, 1735–1935* (Montréal, 1935). Bellemare, *Hist. de Nicolet*. [Albina Fauteux et Clémentine Drouin], *L'hôpital général des Sœurs de la charité (Sœurs Grises) depuis sa fondation jusqu'à nos jours* (3v. parus, Montréal, 1916-).

BEAUVAIS, *dit* **Saint-James, RENÉ**, woodcarver and carpenter; b. 8 Oct. 1785 in La Prairie, Que., son of Jean-Baptiste Bauvais and Marianne Lancto; d. there, unmarried, 4 Sept. 1837.

It is not known where or with whom René Beauvais, *dit* Saint-James, did his apprenticeship. There is reason to think it was with someone from Louis Quévillon*'s workshop during the first decade of the 19th century, but there is no documentary evidence to substantiate this hypothesis. Certainly by 1812 he was living at Saint-Vincent-de-Paul (Laval) and was a master woodcarver. The following year he signed a contract to do some carpentry, woodcarving, and gilding in the church at Sainte-Thérèse-de-Blainville (Sainte-Thérèse). From 1813 till 1816 he worked on the retable (the structure housing the altar), rood-loft, cornice, and vaulting of this church, tasks which woodcarver François Dugal then took up. From 1813 Saint-James also did carving, gilding, marbling, and silvering on the cornices, churchwardens' pew, and vaulting of the church in Saint-Constant. In January 1815 the *fabrique* of the parish of Sainte-Marie-de-Monnoir (Saint-Nom-de-Marie, Marieville) engaged him to do some carving.

A month later Saint-James established a partnership with Quévillon, Joseph PÉPIN, and Paul Rollin*, the four collaborating on the churches in Varennes and Pointe-Claire. In January 1817 the partnership was dissolved but Saint-James became Quévillon's partner again, and they undertook to do carving and gilding for the churches in Pointe-Claire, Verchères, Saint-Eustache, and Pierrefonds. In 1821 Saint-James joined with Rollin to do the carving, gilding, and silvering in the church in Saint-Mathias. In collaboration with Dugal he carved the pulpit, churchwardens' pew, retable, and several decorative elements in the church of La Présentation. He did some carpentry in the churches at Saint-Benoît (Mirabel) and Saint-Eustache the following year.

After Quévillon's death in 1823 Saint-James gave up several of the contracts he had made. Consequently it was Dugal who completed some of the carving at La Présentation. Saint-James went into partnership with Rollin and Dugal, and on 21 Aug. 1823 the three signed a contract to build the steeple of the church in Lachine. Rollin and Saint-James took in carpenter Simon Hogue that year in order to work on the roof of the church in Saint-Vincent-de-Paul. The firm of Rollin, Dugal, and Saint-James was dissolved on 7 April 1824. A week later Saint-James and Dugal formed another one for a ten-year period. In October 1825 a fire destroyed Saint-James's workshop. Three years later he signed a contract for the church in Rigaud, which would be completed by Nicolas Perrin. In 1831 he did some carving in the churches in Saint-Sulpice and Saint-Édouard.

Saint-James had a number of apprentices, who were taken on for about five years and were lodged with him. He taught them woodcarving, gilding, and marbling. When he died in 1837 *La Minerve* paid him this tribute: "Society has just lost one of its good citizens, Mr René St. James, architect, militia captain, and former justice of the peace and commissioner, of St. Vincent de Paul parish, where his workshop was normally located. Mr St. James for many years worked on the decoration of our churches and contributed greatly to improving this type of production, in which several of the numerous workers who were trained under him are engaging profitably at the present time." He unquestionably had an influence on woodcarving in the Montreal region. It is difficult, however, to identify his own particular work, since it is closely linked with the production of Quévillon's workshop in the period 1815–23. Thereafter he collaborated closely with Rollin and Dugal. Two madonnas at the Musée du Québec, one from the church in Chambly and the other from La Prairie, are attributed to him. The interior of the church in Saint-Mathias is a fine example of woodcarving in which he had a hand.

NICOLE CLOUTIER

ANQ-M, CE1-54, 9 oct. 1785, 6 sept. 1837; CN1-14, 12 oct. 1826, 26 juin 1832; CN1-68, 12 févr. 1817; CN1-96, 13 nov. 1812; 15 janv., 31 août, 22 oct. 1816; 3 janv. 1818; 15, 19 févr. 1820; 9 mars, 10 oct. 1821; 24 mars, 21 août, 13 oct. 1823; 7, 14 avril 1824; CN1-107, 9, 12 sept. 1813; CN1-173, 26 déc. 1833; CN1-273, 16 mai, 4 juill. 1813; 23 janv., 30 mars 1823; CN1-317, 5 mars 1820; CN1-334, 3 févr. 1815; CN1-375, 21 janv. 1815, 21 févr. 1821; CN1-383, 14 juill. 1816; CN1-391, 19 août 1817; CN2-79, 4 mars 1822; CN6-2, 12 févr. 1820; CN6-27, 1er avril 1819. MAC-CD, Fonds Morisset, 2, dossier René Beauvais, dit Saint-James. *La Minerve*, 14 sept. 1837. Émile Vaillancourt, *Une maîtrise d'art en Canada (1800–1823)*

(Montréal, 1920). Marius Barbeau, "Louis Quévillon, des Écorres," Académie canadienne-française, *Cahiers* (Montréal), 9: 142–58. Gérard Morisset, "Louis Quévillon, fondateur de l'école des Écorres, 1749–1823," *La Patrie*, 2 oct. 1949: 112.

BEAVAN, EMILY ELIZABETH. *See* SHAW

BÉDARD, ELZÉAR, lawyer, politician, and judge; b. 24 July 1799 at Quebec, second son of Pierre-Stanislas Bédard*, a lawyer and member of the House of Assembly, and Luce Lajus, daughter of François Lajus*, a Quebec doctor; m. there 15 May 1827 Julie-Henriette Marett, daughter of James Lamprière Marett, a merchant, and they had a daughter who died in infancy; d. 11 Aug. 1849 in Montreal.

Elzéar Bédard did his classical studies at the Séminaire de Nicolet from 1812 to 1814, and then at the Petit Séminaire de Québec. His studies completed in 1818, he took holy orders and, with his friend Pierre-Martial Bardy*, was tonsured by Bishop Joseph-Octave Plessis*. He afterwards abandoned this vocation and in 1819 articled with Andrew STUART, a prominent Quebec lawyer. He was called to the bar on 17 Aug. 1824.

Like many of his colleagues, Bédard soon went into provincial politics. In the 1830 general election he and Pierre Marcoux ran together in Kamouraska, but they were soundly beaten by Amable Dionne* and Charles-Eusèbe CASGRAIN. That year, along with Étienne Parent*, René-Édouard Caron*, Jean-Baptiste Fréchette, and Hector-Simon HUOT, he collected the funds to start up *Le Canadien* for the fourth time. The revived newspaper, published first on 7 May 1831, had offices at the "political centre of the Quebec district" on Rue de la Montagne (Côte de la Montagne) and represented the interests of the moderate group in the town. Bédard was returned by acclamation in a by-election on 31 July 1832 for Montmorency, a riding left vacant by the appointment of Philippe Panet* as a judge in the Court of King's Bench. He retained his seat in the 1832 general election.

Bédard joined the ranks of Louis-Joseph Papineau*'s party in the assembly, and on 17 Feb. 1834 he introduced the famous 92 Resolutions. Historians, however, have minimized his role in the development of the Patriote party's program. Thomas Chapais* asserted that the resolutions, which had been worked out at Bédard's home by Papineau, Augustin-Norbert Morin*, Louis Bourdages*, and Bédard himself, were largely inspired by Papineau and drawn up by Morin. According to François-Xavier Garneau*, the text of the resolutions was even modified to gain the support of Bédard, who was already showing a lack of enthusiasm. And on that matter Chapais added, "As there was a desire to please M. Bédard, who was somewhat vain, he was entrusted with moving them."

Having stressed the loyalty of Canadians to Britain, the 92 Resolutions mounted a thoroughgoing attack on the existing political system. They criticized the workings of the Legislative Council, which they thought should be elective, and they demanded institutions that were more popular and more in conformity with the wishes and customs of the inhabitants of Lower Canada. They denounced the working of the legal system, the exclusion of Canadians from the government, and the legislation passed by the British parliament on land tenure. In addition, they condemned the government's entire financial administration and demanded that the House of Assembly have the same powers, privileges, and immunities as did the British parliament. Finally, they requested the recall of Governor Lord Aylmer [WHITWORTH-AYLMER].

Papineau vigorously defended the 92 Resolutions in the assembly, but, as Michel Bibaud* observed, Bédard "could scarcely say a word in support of them . . . only M. Papineau seemed to have a sound knowledge of what was in them." Whatever the case, the resolutions were passed on 21 Feb. 1834, after five days of debate, by 56 votes to 23. It should be added that in December Bédard was still serving as secretary of the Quebec committee of correspondence, a body dealing with the Canadian grievances as set forth in the 92 Resolutions.

It was especially in the 1835–36 session that Bédard played a more important political role. He was regarded within the Patriote party as the leader of the moderate wing called the Quebec party, which also included René-Édouard Caron and George Vanfelson*. Bédard, who went along with the Patriote majority only reluctantly, increasingly kept his distance from Papineau. The Quebec "moderates" openly reproached Papineau for his intransigence and took a much more conciliatory approach to the new governor, Lord Gosford [ACHESON]. On the occasion of a grand ball held on 25 Nov. 1835 to mark St Catherine's Day, Lord Gosford had been particularly attentive to Mme Bédard, hoping to show his desire to establish closer relations with Bédard and his followers. Unfortunately, when on 22 Feb. 1836 he named Bédard a judge of the Court of King's Bench to replace James KERR, Bédard's adversaries, the radicals in the Patriote party, fully exploited this too-obvious appointment, considering it bribery. They derisively called Bédard and his friends, whom they thought more eager to serve their own interests than their country, the "petite famille."

Bédard had meanwhile also become concerned with municipal politics. In the first elections in the city of Quebec, held on 25 April 1833, he had been acclaimed to the council for Saint-Louis ward. On 1 May the council chose him as the first mayor over Caron by 12 votes to 8. Under Bédard's guidance the council decided how to run its affairs, adopted rules on the duties of the mayor, members of council, and secretary, and defined the responsibilities of future municipal employees. In addition the mayor and council had to deal with organizing the city's police, sanitation, and finances. In municipal elections held on 25 March 1834 Bédard retained his seat on council, but six days later he lost the mayoralty to Caron by one vote. The *Quebec Gazette* and the *Quebec Mercury* ascribed his defeat to his political conduct at the time of the debate on the 92 Resolutions. Narcisse-Eutrope Dionne* was later to comment, "It was alleged . . . that keeping a mayor in office for more than one year would have set a bad precedent." Bédard quit municipal politics on 3 April 1835.

Nor was his career as a judge free of ups and downs. On 21 Nov. 1838, during the rebellion, Bédard and Philippe Panet assented to requests for a writ of habeas corpus on behalf of John Teed, a Quebec tailor. In taking this action the two judges disregarded ordinances of the Special Council that suspended the legal provision for habeas corpus made in 1784. On 10 December Bédard and Panet were suspended from office by Sir John Colborne*.

Bédard left New York for England on 26 Dec. 1838 to defend his case. It is not known what ensued, but on 8 Aug. 1840 he and Panet were reinstated by Governor Charles Edward Poulett THOMSON. Bédard sat on the bench at Quebec until 1848. Then he went to Montreal, where he had a dispute over precedence with his junior colleague, Charles Dewey Day*, which was taken to the judicial committee of the Privy Council in London. Bédard was on his deathbed when he learned through Louis-Hippolyte La Fontaine*, the premier of the Province of Canada, that the committee had ruled in his favour. Bédard died before his time on 11 Aug. 1849 in Montreal, at age 50, during a cholera epidemic.

A leading figure of his era, who had attained high office, Elzéar Bédard had an eventful life. Whether as private individual, assemblyman, mayor, or judge, he seems to have been hounded by misfortune. This adversity can be explained partly by the fact that during the troubled period from 1834 to 1839, when exasperation and extremism prevailed, Bédard displayed moderation in the face of Papineau and his supporters, and he maintained his integrity when confronted with the decrees issued by Colborne and the Special Council. Historians have, however, played down his role in the development of the 92 Resolutions. As for the mayoralty of Quebec, it slipped out of his hands after less than a year. His appointment to the bench was greeted with derision; suspended from office, then reinstated, he died following a final quarrel over precedence. Even his death seems the final twist of fate: he was carried off by the last cholera epidemic in Lower Canada, without issue or wealth. He left his wife and an adopted daughter Hélène (born Ellen McEnes), who had married Joseph-Amable Berthelot, a lawyer and later a judge, in April 1849.

CLAUDE VACHON

AAQ, 12 A, H: 213v. ANQ-M, CE1-51, 13 août 1849. ANQ-Q, CE1-1, 24 juill. 1799, 15 mai 1827; P-144. ASQ, Fichier des anciens. PAC, MG 30, D1, 4: 1–3; RG 4, B8: 7764–70; RG 68, General index, 1651–1841. *Le Canadien*, 17 août 1849. *La Minerve*, 13 août 1849. F.-J. Audet, "Les législateurs du Bas-Canada." F.-J. Audet et Fabre Surveyer, *Les députés au premier Parl. du Bas-Canada*, 36. Desjardins, *Guide parl.* Fauteux, *Patriotes*, 379–80. Le Jeune, *Dictionnaire*, 1: 145; 2: 318. P.-G. Roy, *Les avocats de la région de Québec*; *Fils de Québec*, 3: 100–1; *Les juges de la prov. de Québec*. Wallace, *Macmillan dict.* Michel Bibaud, *Histoire du Canada et des Canadiens, sous la domination anglaise* [1830–37], J.-G. Bibaud, édit. (Montréal, 1878). Chapais, *Cours d'hist. du Canada*, 4: 15–20, 72–85, 115, 193, 225. F.-X. Chouinard *et al.*, *La ville de Québec, histoire municipale* (4v., Québec, 1963–83), 3: 136. L.-M. Côté *et al.*, *Les maires de la vieille capitale* (Québec, 1980), 1–3, 5. N.-E. Dionne, *Pierre Bédard et ses fils* (Québec, 1909), 161–217; *Les trois comédies du 'statu quo,' 1834* (Québec, 1909), 46–47. Douville, *Hist. du collège-séminaire de Nicolet.* Alfred Duclos De Celles, *Papineau, 1786–1871* (Montréal, 1905), 93–119. F.-X. Garneau, *Histoire du Canada depuis sa découverte jusqu'à nos jours*, Hector Garneau, édit. (8e éd., 9v., Montréal, 1944–46), 8: 180; 9: 20–21, 32, 38, 109. Marcel Plouffe, "Quelques particularités sociales et politiques de la charte, du système administratif et du personnel politique de la cité de Québec, 1833–1867" (thèse de MA, univ. Laval, Québec, 1971), 113. F.-J. Audet, "Les maires de Québec," *BRH*, 2 (1896): 13. Monique Duval, "Premier maire de Québec – Elzéar Bédard, digne fils du patriote Pierre Bédard," *Le Soleil* (Québec), 2 juill. 1983: E-3. Antonio Perrault, "Le Conseil spécial, 1838–1841; son œuvre législative," *La Rev. du Barreau* (Montréal), 3 (1943): 213–15. "Le premier Conseil municipal de Québec," *BRH*, 69 (1967): 37–39. "Le premier maire de Québec," *BRH*, 69: 37. Antoine Roy, "Les patriotes de la région de Québec pendant la rébellion de 1837–1838," *Cahiers des Dix*, 24 (1959): 241–54.

BEEMER. *See* BEAMER

BELCHER, ANDREW, merchant, JP, and politician; b. 22 July 1763 in Halifax, son of Jonathan Belcher* and Abigail Allen; m. 6 Sept. 1792 in Boston Mary Ann Geyer, and they had 11 children; d. 17 Nov. 1841 in Boulogne-sur-Mer, France.

The dominant influence in the early life of Andrew Belcher was not his father, Nova Scotia's chief justice from 1754 to his death in 1776, but Alexander Brymer*, a Scottish-born entrepreneur who dominated the Halifax business community through the last quarter of the 18th century. His father having died mired in debt, young Andrew's prospects were redeemed when Brymer made him his business protégé.

A more ideal patron could hardly have been secured. Brymer supposedly came to Halifax in the 1770s with £4,000 and left a quarter century later with a fortune of £250,000, the bulk of which derived from contracts to supply the Royal Navy. Having been trained to the role of merchant-gentleman, Belcher set up in trade in 1784, in partnership with a nephew of Brymer. That arrangement ended in 1795, with Belcher emerging as chief agent in Halifax for Brymer's London-based commercial empire. An indication of the scale of Brymer's operation is provided by the fact that between 1792 and 1810 the firm landed at Halifax goods valued at over £140,000. Not surprisingly, contemporaries ranked Belcher as "one of the most eminent merchants" resident in Nova Scotia.

Accumulation of wealth prompted an acquisition of civic honours. Within a couple of decades of launching his career, Belcher had become a justice of the peace, warden of St Paul's Anglican Church, president of the local grammar school, high officer in the masonic order, member of Halifax's Committee of Trade [*see* William Sabatier*], director of the abortive Shubenacadie Canal Company, and co-founder of the Fire Insurance Association of Halifax. In 1799 he sought election to the House of Assembly in Halifax Township, and on his defeat successfully petitioned to have the vote nullified. He then won the subsequent by-election, ousting a veteran incumbent who could not match his "ledger influence." Belcher's tenure in the assembly proved brief. In 1801, thanks in part to the intervention of Lieutenant Governor Sir John Wentworth*, he secured appointment to the Council, taking up the seat vacated by the departing Alexander Brymer.

Thus confirmed as a member of Halifax's oligarchy, Belcher surrounded himself with the hallmarks of gentility, including both town and country residences, large land holdings, and a portrait executed by the celebrated artist Robert Field*. His sense of achievement was lessened, however, by quarrels with other members of the Nova Scotian élite. Michael Wallace*, the provincial treasurer, repeatedly challenged Belcher's claims to precedence within the Council, a conflict that related to the question of who would succeed to control of the administration should the lieutenant governor be absent. Far more serious was the enmity shown toward Belcher by Alexander Croke, an Englishman sent out to Nova Scotia to serve as judge of the Vice-Admiralty Court. Predisposed to belittle all colonials, Croke took particular offence at Belcher, alleging that his fellow councillor was a smuggler. Croke's vindictiveness climaxed about 1805 with the circulation of a mock epic poem, using pseudonyms, entitled "The Inquisition." In it, Belcher's wife was accused of repeated adultery with military officers and members of the civil administration, including Wentworth's son. Belcher, portrayed by Croke as a "contented cuckold" who could not be certain who had fathered his children, must have been injured by this widely circulated document, but he did not retaliate, presumably because his wife had indeed engaged in compromising behaviour. Such was Croke's unpopularity, however, that the Belchers did not suffer ostracism.

Removing to England in 1811, Belcher established a residence in the London suburbs, which became a fashionable retreat for itinerant Nova Scotians. Over the next few years, in demonstration of continuing allegiance to what he termed his "native Country," Belcher donated a set of bells to St Paul's, subscribed to a fund-raising drive by King's College, and provided books to the fledgling Halifax library. More decisively, he maintained an active business presence in the Nova Scotian capital. Operating with a succession of partners, Alexander Wright, Stephen Newton Binney, and Mather Byles Almon*, Belcher functioned as a non-resident member of Halifax's merchant community. He also dabbled in the New Brunswick and Nova Scotia Land Company, a speculative venture designed to promote settlement and resource development. But for a last minute change of heart, he would have become a partner in the Halifax Banking Company, the province's pioneer banking institution established in 1825 [*see* Henry Hezekiah Cogswell*].

Apparently overextended by questionable investments, perhaps combined with a costly life-style, Belcher fell victim to the acute commercial recession of 1826. Harassed by creditors, he gave up his London house and moved to Cheltenham, Gloucestershire, a spa which offered relief from the physical and mental exhaustion felt by both Belcher and his wife. Their distress deepened in 1828 when Belcher lost his provisioning contracts at Halifax and Bermuda. In a frantic effort to avert bankruptcy, he pleaded with his Nova Scotian friends for extended credit, as well as assistance in securing some appointment – provincial agent in London or treasurer in succession to Michael Wallace. Finally, early in 1829, a desperate Belcher returned to Halifax to assume personal direction of his surviving business interests.

Assisted by a cyclical expansion in Halifax's trade, Belcher began to rebuild his battered fortunes. He still had enough influence to secure appointment as Halifax agent for the General Mining Association, a British company then launching large-scale coal exports from Nova Scotia to the United States. That lucrative office was complemented by his being named to the commission in charge of issuing provincial paper money. Belcher and his wife gained admission to the coterie surrounding Lieutenant Governor Sir Peregrine Maitland* and rumours began to circulate that Belcher might be reappointed to the Council. In 1832 he had enough capital to invest £1,000 in stock issued by the Bank of Nova Scotia, newly created as a rival to the Halifax Banking Company [*see* William LAWSON].

This success could not survive, however, in the face of commercial dislocation and rivalry from fellow entrepreneurs. Dependent on long lines of credit, Belcher lacked the means to withstand the return of hard times in 1833 and 1834. Thus weakened, he could not resist Samuel Cunard*'s drive to have himself named Halifax agent of the General Mining Association. The decisive blow came early in 1834 when three of Belcher's major creditors, Cunard included, foreclosed, demanding payment for accounts in excess of £12,000. A host of smaller creditors followed suit. One contemporary was prompted to say that among the victims of the recession "the Most Melancholy of all is poor old Belcher, who, after giving up *all* to his creditors, has had Capias after Capias served on him from Butchers, Bakers, &c." Within a year the family fled Halifax, eventually taking refuge in France, where both Belcher and his wife died in relative destitution. The remnants of prestige attaching to the family largely rested with Andrew's son Edward*, a captain in the Royal Navy and commander of the controversial Arctic expedition sent in 1852 to search for Sir John FRANKLIN.

Andrew Belcher's career went full circle, from penniless youngster to ageing absconding debtor. His failure derived from factors which went beyond personal character flaws. Belcher's success had been shaped by access to powerful friends, military contracts, and an economy sustained by the demands of war. Left on his own to survive in the unstable and competitive business climate of the 1820s and 1830s, he could not cope. As had his father, Andrew Belcher fell victim to change.

DAVID A. SUTHERLAND

Halifax County Court of Probate (Halifax), Estate papers, B37 (mfm. at PANS). Halifax County Registry of Deeds (Halifax), Deeds, 33: 238; 34: 247. PANS, MG 1, 334, nos.22a–22c; 793, nos.77, 80a, 81–83, 91–93, 99; RG 1, 172: 122; 174: 311; 305, no.56; 312, nos.3, 56; 413, no.2; RG 4, LC, 25 Feb. 1811; RG 5, P, 121, 31 Jan. 1832; RG 39, HX, J, 38: 293. PRO, CO 217/64: 97; 217/68: 197; 217/74: 11; 217/84: 92; 217/87: 127; 217/88: 102; 217/102: 241; 217/144: 143; 217/145: 320; 217/150: 351. N.S., House of Assembly, *Journal and proc.*, 21 June 1798, 21 Feb. 1800, 25 Feb. 1811. *Acadian Recorder*, 21 Feb., 18 July 1818; 20 Nov. 1824. *Novascotian, or Colonial Herald*, 20 Jan., 3 Feb., 17 March 1831; 10 May 1832; 23 Jan. 1834; 30 April 1835; 8 Aug. 1839. *Nova-Scotia Royal Gazette*, 1 Sept. 1808; 25 April 1809; 13 Feb., 27 Nov. 1811. *Royal Gazette and the Nova-Scotia Advertiser*, 16 Dec. 1794; 12 Jan. 1796; 2 April, 26 Nov. 1799; 1, 15 April 1800. *Annals, North British Society, Halifax, Nova Scotia, with portraits and biographical notes, 1768–1903*, comp. J. S. Macdonald ([3rd ed.], Halifax, 1905). *A calendar of the White collection of manuscripts in the Public Archives of Nova Scotia*, comp. Margaret Ells (Halifax, 1940). *Directory of N.S. MLAs*. *Halifax almanac*, 1797–1812. *N.-S. calendar*, 1794. R. V. Harris, *The Church of Saint Paul in Halifax, Nova Scotia: 1749–1949* (Toronto, 1949). *History of the Bank of Nova-Scotia, 1832–1900; together with copies of annual statements* ([Halifax], 1901). Murdoch, *Hist. of N.S.*, vol.3. Victor Ross and A. St L. Trigge, *A history of the Canadian Bank of Commerce, with an account of the other banks which now form part of its organization* (3v., Toronto, 1920–34), 1. C. J. Townshend, "Jonathan Belcher, first chief justice of Nova Scotia . . . ," N.S. Hist. Soc., *Coll.*, 18 (1941): 25–57. T. B. Vincent, "'The Inquisition': Alexander Croke's satire of Halifax society during the Wentworth years," *Dalhousie Rev.*, 53 (1973–74): 404–30.

BELL, MATHEW (**Matthew**; he signed M^{w} Bell), businessman, JP, office holder, politician, militia officer, and seigneur; baptized 29 June 1769 in the Church of the Holy Trinity in Berwick-upon-Tweed, England, son of James Bell and his wife Margaret; d. 24 June 1849 in Trois-Rivières, Lower Canada.

Mathew Bell, whose well-to-do father was twice mayor of Berwick-upon-Tweed, came to Quebec when he was about 15. He went to work for John Lees* as a clerk, and then around 1790 formed a partnership with David Monro*. An importer of wines and Barbados molasses, the firm of Monro and Bell leased shorelines, wharfs, and warehouses at Quebec, where it owned a store. In 1794 it bought the schooner *L'Iroquois* and the following year the sloop *Abenakis*. It seems to have grown rapidly. In the first decade of the 19th century the port registers annually recorded the arrival for the firm of such products as port, rum, shrub, lemon juice, red and white Spanish wines, raw and refined sugar, allspice, flour, and coal from Berwick-upon-Tweed.

On 5 Sept. 1805 Bell gave some indication of his prosperity when he paid Isabell Mabane £1,200 for Woodfield. This magnificent two-storey stone country house, which had been called Samos when Bishop Pierre-Herman Dosquet* occupied it, was built on 42 *arpents* of land and overlooked the St Lawrence. On 10 June 1807 Bell bought the waterfront lot "forming the frontage" of the property from the Séminaire de Québec. He seems to have lived at Woodfield only in summer and was content with making improvements to the vegetable garden. He sold the estate, including the waterfront lot, to shipbuilders William Sheppard* and John Saxton Campbell* for £3,550 on 21 Sept. 1816.

Monro and Bell apparently owed their rapid success in business to their connections with John Lees and Alexander and George* Davison, two brothers who came from the same region as Bell and were protégés of the Duke of Northumberland. Alexander had engaged in the import-export trade in partnership with Lees since 1773, and he was purveyor to the British military in North America. In addition, the firm of

Davison and Lees, together with George Davison, held leases to the king's posts on the north shore of the lower St Lawrence and to the Saint-Maurice ironworks. The brothers lived mainly in England, where they cultivated political and business contacts, and Lees ran the company in the colony. On 15 Aug. 1791 Lees and Alexander Davison ended their partnership, Lees retiring from business. Davison chose Monro and Bell to replace him and they became the brothers' agents at Quebec. They attended to buying provisions and shipping them to the British forces, and along with Peter Stuart they managed the king's posts in Alexander's name. Monro and Bell naturally became interested in the Trois-Rivières region, where the Davisons had invested heavily in property. Bell bought some land in Caxton Township in the summer of 1792, and in company with Monro and George Davison acquired a building site in Trois-Rivières in October. Alexander had settled in London at the end of the 1780s and he divested himself of his Canadian enterprises. On 6 June 1793 he made over the lease to the ironworks, valid until 10 June 1799, as well as the inventory, to his younger brother George and Monro and Bell for £4,434 11*s*. 8½*d*. George owned half the shares, but, chronically ill, he retired to England, leaving Monro and Bell to manage the operation.

The new lessees improved the existing facilities. They hired skilled labour from Europe and introduced new models of stoves and utensils. The products were sold in the company's store in Trois-Rivières, and some of the goods were taken on consignment by James Laing in Montreal and Monro and Bell at Quebec. As managers they soon ran into the problems all their predecessors had encountered: ascertaining the exact boundaries of their territory, building up the necessary reserves of ore and wood, negotiating the rent for the lease and the terms of compensation in the event of its not being renewed. These tasks gave rise to a voluminous correspondence between the lessees and the government. Mindful of the public interest, the government contemplated an auction for a 99-year lease. Bidding might increase the rent, and a longer term would induce the lessees to invest more money in the enterprise, which would be advantageous for the region. In January 1799 Governor Robert Prescott*, lacking sufficient information, made an offer to extend the lease to 1 April 1801 and authorize its holders to get their supplies of wood and ore from crown lands, as Bell had requested on several occasions. Monro and Bell accepted these generous terms. George Davison died on 21 Feb. 1799 and in June Bell and Monro became the sole lessees of the ironworks, on condition that, in accordance with an arrangement put in writing on 8 Jan. 1800, they paid Davison's heirs £10,523 18*s*. 7*d*. sterling. On 18 Dec. 1799 Monro and Bell obtained from Jesuit father Jean-Joseph Casot* a grant stretching 2 leagues along the east bank of the Saint-Maurice, with a depth of 20 *arpents*.

In June 1800, as the projected date of expiry of the lease to the ironworks, 1 April 1801, drew near, there was keen competition. Acting for the Batiscan Iron Works Company, Thomas COFFIN pushed the bid up from £25 to £500 a year. This offer was in the direction that the government had in mind. The two rival groups kept raising their bids: Coffin offered £800 and Monro and Bell offered £50 a year above the highest bid. They secured a renewal of their lease for five years, 1 April 1801 to 1 April 1806, at £850 annually. On 15 July 1805 the lease was extended for a year, in order to give the Executive Council time to gather all the information needed to develop a new policy, the basis of which would be the auction of a long-term lease, with prior notice in Canadian and British newspapers. The bidding took place at Quebec on 1 Oct. 1806. There were seemingly three rival groups: John Mure*, notary Michel Berthelot who was agent for Pierre de Sales* Laterrière and his partners, and Monro and Bell. Rather strangely the Batiscan Iron Works Company did not participate. To everyone's amazement Monro and Bell won with a bid of £60 annually. In Governor Prescott's absence the Executive Council, not knowing what to do, submitted the matter to the British government. Lord Castlereagh suspected the bidders had been in collusion. However, the president of the council, Thomas Dunn*, who held shares in the Batiscan Iron Works Company, as did his sons, saw no irregularity. The new governor, Sir James Henry Craig*, who arrived in the autumn of 1807, wanted an amicable agreement and let Monro and Bell fire up the blast-furnace, even though they had no lease. Monro and Bell argued that their low bid was justified because they had made investments to improve the ironworks and production costs had soared as a result of bad harvests and the gradual need to go farther afield for materials; furthermore, competition by British and Canadian foundries – in particular the Carron Ironworks, a Scottish company copying the products of the Saint-Maurice ironworks – was, they said, depressing prices. Betting on the impending bankruptcy of the Batiscan Iron Works Company, Monro and Bell proposed a rent of £500 annually. On 7 June 1810 the Executive Council suggested an arrangement that would include a 21-year lease from 1 Jan. 1810 to 31 March 1831 for £500 a year, and an extension of the territory towards the northwest.

Around 1810 the Saint-Maurice ironworks looked like a village, since Bell and Monro had put up 23 buildings for housing or industrial purposes in the period 1793–1807. There was a blast-furnace, a foundry, two forges, a coal crusher, a flour-mill, and a sawmill. A large house was used as the lessees' residence, and there were about 50 other dwellings for two or three hundred people, who were served by the company store. The area belonging to the ironworks covered about 120 square miles. The enterprise employed a score of skilled workmen, as well as finishers, carters, and unskilled labourers. It also gave part-time work to several hundred farmers. In early April they would go with their horses and pick up the ore lying on their own land or the company's property. During the summer they worked on their farms. Early in November some would cut about 8,000 cords of wood on the company's land, at least 5,300 of which were for conversion into charcoal; others used the ice roads to cart ore. These raw materials fed the ironworks, which operated day and night for six to eight months of the year. At the foundry the men assigned to the blast-furnace worked in teams on six-hour shifts; the casters and finishers toiled from sunrise to sunset, and there were two castings a day. In the forges the teams put in six-hour shifts. Yearly production amounted on average to 549 tons – 2¼ tons a day. The ore, when converted into pig iron, gave a 45 per cent yield. The cast iron produced was worth £12,000 a year on average. It consisted primarily of iron bars, stoves, potash or maple-sugar kettles, castings for mills and steam-engines, and forged products such as ploughshares. Bell kept another foundry going at Trois-Rivières. Equipped with two cupola-furnaces for melting pig and scrap iron, it specialized in stoves and potash kettles.

The partnership with the Davisons in the 1790s had been profitable for Bell, and it probably constituted one of the bases of his success. It had introduced him into a powerful network meshing business and politics. It had fostered the activity of Monro and Bell and led Bell to manage the ironworks. Even more important, it had provided him with a model. The Davisons owed their success to the patronage of well-placed politicians and a web of social relationships that they kept up through lavish entertaining. When he met the Davisons, Bell entered upon this same path. Politically, he was an avowed supporter of the English party. In 1794 he signed a declaration of loyalty to the British government and in 1795 a promise of fidelity to the king; in 1799 he and Monro subscribed £100 a year to support Great Britain in the war against France. In England he enjoyed Alexander Davison's protection, and at Quebec that of John Lees, his former employer who sat in the House of Assembly for Trois-Rivières and was an honorary member of the Executive Council. When he and Monro became the sole lessees of the Saint-Maurice ironworks, he began to be involved in public life. In June 1799 he obtained the first of a long series of commissions as justice of the peace which spanned the period up to 1839. In December 1799 he was appointed treasurer of the commission to erect a metropolitan church at Quebec. He was elected to the assembly for Saint-Maurice in the summer of 1800, and while he was in England in 1804 Monro held the seat. Bell ran in a by-election in Trois-Rivières in April 1807 to replace Lees, who had died. He was defeated by Ezekiel HART, but won the seat in November 1809 and represented Trois-Rivières until 22 March 1814.

As a member Bell initiated little in the assembly, for the most part simply supporting the measures put forward by the English party. He showed more interest in shipping matters. On 31 May 1802 he was appointed to the Lower Canada Board of Pilots, and on 16 May of the following year he was put on a commission to establish regulations for pilots and skippers. He became a warden of the newly founded Trinity House of Quebec on 6 May 1805, deputy master on 15 Sept. 1812, and master on 18 April 1814, a post he held until 22 Oct. 1816. The assembly and Trinity House were vantage points from which Bell served his fellow citizens while at the same time looking out for his own interests.

Bell had also become a prominent figure in society. On 17 Sept. 1799 he had married Ann MacKenzie, daughter of the late James Mackenzie, a Trois-Rivières businessman, with whom he had 12 children. Resident at Quebec, he made lengthy stays at Trois-Rivières. In Quebec he was one of the 21 members of the Barons' Club – known prior to 1800 as the Beef-Steak Club – who came from the commercial and governmental élite. He led the life of a seigneur, with a host of servants, and gave receptions and hunting parties that were famous. He was a devotee of horse-racing and an experienced horticulturist, a member of the Agriculture Society, and active in the Fire Society. In Quebec's 3rd Militia Battalion he was a captain. As soon as the War of 1812 broke out, he put himself at the service of Governor Sir George Prevost*. Prevost gave him orders on 22 April 1812 to raise a troop of light cavalry attached to the 3rd Battalion and by 27 June Bell had 34 volunteers under his command. On 27 July Major-General George Glasgow* made it an independent unit, the Quebec Volunteer Cavalry, and by early March 1813 it had about 60 men. It was quartered on Rue de la Fabrique and guarded American prisoners; in March it went to Saint-Joseph-de-Beauce to arrest some militiamen who refused to join up, and then it returned for garrison duty at Quebec.

When peace came Bell's career took a new direction. Because of his 21-year lease on the ironworks, he did not seek re-election to the assembly, counting instead on his close ties with the executive and officialdom to advance his interests. He turned his energies to reorganizing his business afairs, which had been put in jeopardy by Monro's unexpected retirement. On 31 Dec. 1815 the firm of Monro and Bell was dissolved. On 26 Oct. 1816 notary Joseph-Bernard Planté* drew up two instruments by which

Bell became sole owner of Monro and Bell for £14,350, payable in five instalments, and sole lessee of the ironworks for £13,123 10*s.* 2*d.*, payable in seven instalments from 1817 to 1823. Bell then mortgaged his assets in favour of Monro and rented out his house on Rue Saint-Pierre. These arrangements did not cover all the properties Monro and Bell owned in common. To replace Monro, Bell took John Stewart* as his partner in his import-export business. The rising star in the Quebec business community, Stewart was an old friend who had been the partner of Bell and Monro in John Stewart and Company, a firm dissolved in the autumn of 1806. Little is known about Bell and Stewart, which owned two stores, one at Quebec and the other in Trois-Rivières. It carried on the same sort of operations as Monro and Bell. The firm built a warehouse in Trois-Rivières in September 1820, but seems to have disappeared around 1825, when Stewart attained high political office. It is certain, however, that Stewart, who had been commissioner for the Jesuit estates since 1815, served as president of the Quebec Committee of Trade from 1822 to 1825, and was master of Trinity House of Quebec in 1824, was well placed to watch out for Bell's interests.

After reorganizing his business and making a visit to Great Britain – probably from the autumn of 1816 to the spring of 1819 – Bell launched into land speculation, an infrequent activity for him until then. On 23 May 1817, for example, Monro had bought jointly with the absent Bell the seigneury of Champlain for £2,520, and in August a lot in the municipality of Trois-Rivières. In the Trois-Rivières region, Edward Greive, Bell's future son-in-law and his agent, bought houses, building sites, and farms in Bell's name. More and more Bell was attracted by the townships. In December 1821 he asked for 1,200 acres in Wolfestown Township for his services as a major in the militia in 1813; he was awarded that amount on 24 Jan. 1830 in Caxton Township. He bought part of Hertel seigneury, in the parish of Notre-Dame-de-la-Visitation at Champlain, from Joseph-Rémi VALLIÈRES de Saint-Réal on 22 Feb. 1823, and successful deals in 1823 and 1831 probably made him the owner of the whole seigneury. On 20 July 1824 he purchased the seigneury of Mont-Louis, which he had changed to free and common socage in June 1839. On 15 June 1825 he took 50 shares at £100 apiece in the Lower Canada Land Company, an enterprise being set up to buy crown lands. He acquired 2,940 acres in Simpson Township on 21 Sept. 1830, and on 12 November obtained possession of 25 acres in Sillery for £566. In 1832 he began buying the properties in Aston Township that belonged to judge Anthony Gilbert Douglas, and on 11 July he authorized Frederick Griffin to buy in his name 9,100 acres that George Pyke* owned in Tingwick and Warwick townships. He obtained 526 acres in Wendover Township by letters patent on 27 Feb. 1835 and 1,181 acres in Aston on 15 April 1836. On 9 May 1837 he and Greive bought 31 parcels of 200 acres in Brompton and several others in Durham Township. Arthur William Buller*'s commission of inquiry estimated in 1838 that Bell owned 30,000 acres in addition to his seigneurial land.

These speculations remained, none the less, a marginal activity. Bell was first and foremost head of the Saint-Maurice ironworks. After Monro and Bell was dissolved, he stayed for longer periods at Trois-Rivières and he moved there permanently in 1829. By then he was 60. He had been a member of the Legislative Council since 1823; his friend Stewart had been on it since 1825 and on the Executive Council since January 1826. Public office no longer attracted Bell – he was not in good health. He continued to live as a grand seigneur, and the fate of the ironworks and his children's future were his great concerns. In the spring of 1829 he acquired three adjoining lots in Trois-Rivières for his sons who had not yet reached the age of majority; his eldest son, James, also bought one. Bell purchased another lot in the municipality for himself, and then two more in joint ownership. In October, perhaps foreseeing the prospects of the Saint-Maurice region, he made arrangements to get a sawmill built in Champlain, which was to sell part of its production on the Quebec market. In 1831 he asked for the grant of a property 84 *arpents* in area within the seigneury of Cap-de-la-Madeleine, near the Rivière Cachée, and without waiting for official confirmation he lent Greive £850 so that he could start building a dam and a sawmill. He began to participate more actively in the life of Trois-Rivières. Long a member of the district agricultural society, in 1832 he became its president. That year he was made chairman of the region's Board of Health, which had been created at his urging. From October 1833 till October 1834 he was also chairman of the local education society, and he gave £125 to support two schools. Bell apparently wanted to draw his family together at Trois-Rivières, around the ironworks, and to make the region into a kingdom for his dynasty.

It was a period when Bell emerged as the symbol of patronage. From 1829 the renewal of the lease to the Saint-Maurice ironworks, which was to run out in 1831, occasioned restlessness in the House of Assembly and in Trois-Rivières, where some people, including merchants unhappy about the monopoly on trade which Bell enjoyed in the ironworks village, maintained that it was holding back the development of their town and the settlement of the back country. There was a flood of petitions to the assembly, which, making a tougher stand against the executive, took up these grievances. In February 1829 the issues were discussed in committee of the whole. The governor,

Sir James Kempt*, had an inquiry conducted by the commissioner for crown lands. Bell pleaded his case in detailed memoranda. The Executive Council submitted the matter to the British government and simply renewed Bell's lease on a yearly basis until 1833. The 34th of the 92 Resolutions passed by the assembly in February 1834 [*see* Elzéar BÉDARD] stigmatized Bell as "a grantee of the Crown, who has been unduly and illegally favoured by the Executive." On 25 Nov. 1834 Governor Lord Aylmer [WHITWORTH-AYLMER], with London's backing, renewed the lease for the period 1 Jan. 1834–1 June 1844 at an annual rent of £500. The contract carried with it the right to build up a reserve of wood and ore from the crown lands.

When the Patriotes rose in rebellion, Bell manned the barricades. In November 1837 he administered the oath of allegiance to the officers of the 1st Battalion of Saint-Maurice militia, a unit composed of labourers from the ironworks and their sons. In December he formed two companies of volunteers and appointed his son Bryan ensign and Greive captain. Fearing for Bell's safety and wishing to maintain order in the region, the government sent some 100 soldiers with large stocks of ammunition to Trois-Rivières in January 1838. Bell was then invited to sit on the Special Council, but he declined, just as he had refused to sit on the Court of Appeal in 1831.

When he was 70, Bell slowed down his activity. He was suffering from various physical disabilities and felt lonely. His wife had died at Quebec in July 1837. One of his sons, David, had died unmarried on 25 June 1839. His friend John Stewart was still a member of the Executive Council, but his influence was declining. The political situation was changing. Bell fell back more and more on his family. For a time he continued to speculate. In the period 1839–43 he staked a large sum on his sawmill at Champlain. He bought pine and spruce logs – some 7,200 in the winter of 1843–44 alone – which he had sawn up in his mill and sent to Quebec. From 1841 the renewal of the lease to the ironworks became his major concern. There were again discussions in the assembly and the Executive Council, but the atmosphere was different – the members of both bodies were in sympathy with the people of Trois-Rivières. The government was reluctant to set a policy and simply renewed the lease from year to year. On 22 Nov. 1845 the Crown Lands Department announced that the ironworks would be auctioned on 4 Aug. 1846. The establishment and the domain, reduced to further the cultivation of new lands and the development of Trois-Rivières, would all be sold. The purchaser would have the right to buy 350 more acres at 7*s.* 6*d.* an acre to put together a reserve, and he could get his supplies of materials from the crown lands for the five years following. The former lessee would have a fortnight to vacate the premises. Bell bid £5,450, but Henry Stuart won with an offer of £5,575.

Early in the autumn of 1846 Bell left, retiring with his family to his home in Trois-Rivières. He made one final large-scale speculation on 27 May 1847, purchasing 8,800 acres in Durham Township. But his financial position seems to have been endangered. David Arthur Monro, the son of David, sued him for £60,000, claiming that in discharging the power of attorney over his ex-partner's estate, along with John Stewart, Bell had refused to give a statement of accounts. He died on 24 June 1849, leaving an estate open to dispute, which his children declined to accept.

Bell represents a generation of businessmen living in a colony in the heyday of British venture capitalism. Their operations characteristically involved sleeping partnerships, personal credit, collusion with the political powers, and participation in networks dominated by people in Great Britain. Bell himself possessed remarkable qualities: he had an imposing build, and his countenance exuded strength, perspicacity, and determination. Governor Lord Dalhousie [RAMSAY], who enjoyed his company, considered him "a very intelligent, liberal minded and honourable man."

As the son of a well-to-do merchant Bell had while very young moved in business circles and among people of status. His association with the Davisons, which thrust him into the British mercantile upper middle class, was a decisive factor. They brought him into an influential milieu, taught him the art of handling important business matters, and passed on to him operations that he had only to develop. Above all, by force of example they inspired him to take up the life of the bourgeois gentleman in which the wealthy and powerful delighted. In the large house at the ironworks, Bell had a richly furnished bedroom called the Governor's Room, spacious apartments, a ballroom, and stables full of thoroughbred horses. He could thus receive in style the leading figures in the colony and distinguished visitors. Dalhousie stated that Bell "lives and speaks more like an English gentleman than most people in this country."

To his contemporaries Mr Bell was first and foremost the head of the Saint-Maurice ironworks, a post he held for more than 47 years. He proved a knowledgeable administrator. From the first he made the investments needed to adapt production to the market. He picked the most profitable opportunities. Products of good quality and competitive prices were the bases of his strategy. He made few changes in technology, keeping the methods introduced by the company that had been founded by François-Étienne Cugnet* in 1736. His situation as a lessee and the lack of coal dissuaded him from technological innovation. To strengthen his competitive position he counted on the score of skilled workers who had acquired and passed on from father to son a competency adapted to the environment and the methods in use. He was the first to impose discipline on the employees, who lived in a remote village run in a thoroughly hierarchical fashion on the basis of their qualifications and tradition. An aristocratic type of paternalism governed working relations and even community life. Bell seems to have brought in payment for piecework and put various kinds of penalties into the employment contracts. He determined who could visit the village and what liquor and leisure activities would be permitted, and he settled quarrels between both individuals and families. He encouraged stability in his work force and preferred to ensure for his employees pleasant living conditions and a busy community life – particularly in wintertime – rather than high salaries.

In contrast with the Davisons, however, Bell had become fond of his adopted country. According to Dalhousie, he was indignant at always being considered a foreigner because of his religion and origin. Perhaps he had dreamed, as had the Hart family – and as his speculations in land and his interest in sawmills suggest – of linking his family's future with the destiny of the Saint-Maurice region, even though he was only the lessee of the ironworks. The change in the political context, the choices made by his children, and above all his extravagances as a grand seigneur, which consumed his profits and his domain, destroyed this dream, if it had ever had any reality. Instead of a kingdom he bequeathed to his children an estate so heavily mortgaged that they had no choice but to refuse it.

MICHEL BÉDARD, ANDRÉ BÉRUBÉ, and JEAN HAMELIN

[Parks Canada has computerized information on the Saint-Maurice ironworks, including a wealth of detail on Mathew Bell; it is derived mainly from the *Quebec Gazette*, the appendices to the *Journals* of the House of Assembly, minute-books of notaries of Quebec and Trois-Rivières, registry offices, the Archives judiciaires du Québec, and various collections at the ANQ and the PAC. Although substantial, this documentation on Bell does not make up for the loss of records: the financial records of Monro and Bell, Bell and Stewart, and the Saint-Maurice ironworks are all missing, and only a few fragments of Bell's own correspondence have survived. Thus, our knowledge of Bell as a person and of his activities is limited and interpretation difficult. Moreover, Bell has not been the subject of an extended study. The biography by Francis-Joseph Audet* and Édouard Fabre Surveyer in *Les députés de Saint-Maurice et de Buckinghamshire*, 26–34, is an account which does not delve beyond the main facts and events of his life. Three recent studies are, however, useful in understanding Bell's role at the Saint-Maurice ironworks: Réal Boissonneault et Michel Bédard, *La structure chronologique des forges du Saint-Maurice, des débuts à 1883* (Québec, 1980); H. C. Pentland, *Labour and capital in Canada, 1650–1860*, ed. Paul Phillips (Toronto, 1981); Roch Samson, *Les ouvriers des forges du Saint-Maurice: aspects démographiques (1762–1851)* (Parks Canada, National Hist. Parks and Sites Branch, *Microfiche report*, no.119, Ottawa, 1983). M.B., A.B., and J.H.]

ANQ-M, CN1-187, 9 avril 1837. ANQ-MBF, CN1-4, 17 sept. 1799; CN1-6, 11 avril 1831; CN1-7, 14 mai, 11 juill. 1832; 2 avril 1836; 30 sept. 1839; CN1-32, 4 nov. 1816, 23 mai 1817, 11 sept. 1820, 8 mars 1823, 21 oct. 1829, 21 sept. 1830; CN1-56, 30 mars, 4 avril 1829; CN1-62, 9–10, 24 déc. 1840; CN1-79, 6 août 1817. ANQ-Q, CN1-49, 20 juill. 1821, 27 mai 1847, 22 août 1849; CN1-208, 22 févr. 1823; CN1-230, 21 sept., 26 oct. 1816; CN1-262, 10 juin 1807. PAC, MG 24, K13: 9–17; RG 1, E11, 2; L3[L]: 20214–15, 20297–98, 20388–89, 62165–70; RG 4, A1, 283: 119; 292: 111; A2, 86; C2, 17: 334–35; RG 8, I (C ser.), 661: 87; RG 68, General index, 1651–1841. L.C., House of Assembly, *Journaux*, 1831–32, app.II, 3[e] rapport, D, no.3; 1835, app.U, no.9. *Quebec Gazette*, 3 July 1794, 18 July 1799, 13 Nov. 1806, 8 Dec. 1808, 30 Nov. 1809, 8 Oct. 1812.

BELL, WILLIAM, businessman and militia officer; b. 1 May 1806 in London, second child of William Bell* and Mary Black; m. 6 Oct. 1831 Maria Miller in Kingston, Upper Canada, and they had two sons and two daughters; d. 4 Aug. 1844 in Perth, Upper Canada.

William Bell was only 11 years old when he first gazed with his father, a Presbyterian missionary, upon the wilderness of the military settlement at Perth. After spending three years as an apprentice clerk in the general store of William Morris*, William formed a partnership with his twin brother, John, who had trained under merchant Roderick Matheson*. W. and J. Bell opened for business in Perth as general merchants on 4 Jan. 1828 and, by undercutting and selling at a lower profit, proceeded to draw the wrathful scorn of the powerful Morris. Any possibility of friendly relations between the Bell and Morris families was eroded by such mercantile competition, which ultimately divided Perth's Presbyterian congregation.

In 1829 John and his younger brother Robert* established a branch store at Morphy's Falls (Carleton Place), while William continued to expand their business as commission agents for the Montreal firm of Benjamin Hart*, among others, particularly in the supply of potash and butter. On the Tay and Mississippi rivers the Bells became directly involved in the fur and lumber trades. As well, they invested in real estate and, with James Rosamond, financed a number of early industrial operations at Carleton Place. By 1838, with activities ranging from obtaining resources in the hinterland to trading in town, William and five of his six brothers were involved in the commerce of Lanark County as merchants or clerks. Although the Bells did not participate in the Morris-controlled Tay Navigation Company, the interests of W. and J. Bell were served by the opening of both the Rideau (1832) and Tay (1834) canals. In October 1839 William represented Perth at a meeting to form the Inland Steam Transportation and Insurance Company to oppose the Ottawa and Rideau Forwarding Company, which monopolized forwarding on the Rideau Canal route to Montreal. The company never got off the ground but the Bells, envisaging a fleet of vessels based at Perth, built a barge in 1841.

The suspension of specie payments by Lower and Upper Canadian banks during the commercial crisis of 1837–38 drained merchants' supplies of coin. Already burdened by a large outstanding debt and high inventory, W. and J. Bell, like several other firms, responded in 1837 by issuing its own paper money, which could be converted into bank bills at the Perth store but not into coin. Handsomely designed and engraved in Montreal by Adolphus Bourne*, the notes, in five denominations up to a half-dollar, remained in circulation until late 1839.

A moderate reformer and supporter of Malcolm Cameron*, who had been elected to the House of Assembly for Lanark in 1836, William was a strong foe of the "family compact." He nevertheless displayed his loyalist sympathies as a captain in the 3rd Regiment of Leeds militia during the rebellion of 1837–38. Political and commercial strains after 1837 combined with personal tragedy to affect William's emotional stability. Following the birth of a son in March 1837, both his wife and the child died and William sank into a state of despondency and depression. He had married his wife, a woman of illegitimate birth, without the knowledge or sanction of his upright father. After her death, William further embarrassed him by his excessive drinking in public and on several occasions his parents looked after his children. The agitated family patriarch demanded a declaration of total abstinence by every living descendant, but to no avail.

W. and J. Bell recovered from the commercial depression in the early 1840s, but not so William Jr. His death at the age of 38, after a period of illness, deprived Perth of one of its brightest business leaders, and without his direction W. and J. Bell collapsed in 1846. In contrast to the endurance and stability of his father, William's life was one of rapid success and erratic decline.

Larry Turner

AO, MU 842, J. G. Malloch diary; RG 22, ser.155, William Bell Jr and John Bell. PAC, MG 24, D61, 2–3. Presbyterian Church in Canada Arch. (Toronto), William Bell, diary, vol.13. QUA, 2402, vols.5–12, 14–15; A. M. Campbell, "Fractional currency instituted by W. and J. Bell, Perth, Upper Canada, in 1837." *Bathurst Courier and Ottawa General Advertiser* (Perth, [Ont.]), 14 Aug. 1834, 29 Nov. 1839. *Brockville Recorder*, 16 March 1837. *Chronicle & Gazette*, 23 Oct. 1839. *Toronto Herald*, 12 Aug. 1844. Isabel [Murphy] Skelton, *A man austere: William Bell, parson and pioneer* (Toronto, 1947). Tulchinsky, *River barons*, 50. Larry Turner, *The first Tay Canal in the Rideau corridor, 1830–1850* (Parks Canada, National Hist. Parks and Sites Branch, *Microfiche report*, no.142, Ottawa, 1984); "The 'Shinplasters' of W. & J. Bell, Perth, Upper Canada, 1837–1839," *Canadian Paper Money Journal* (West Hill [Toronto]), 22 (1986): 4–13.

BELLEFEUILLE, LOUIS-CHARLES LEFEBVRE DE. *See* Lefebvre

BELLEVILLE. *See* Boucher

BEMER. *See* Beamer

BENSON, WILLIAM JOHN CHAPMAN, businessman; b. *c.* 1818, probably in London; d. 3 Dec. 1850 in Whitehall, N.Y.

William John Chapman Benson, a young man in his late twenties, arrived at Quebec from London, likely in the summer of 1845 when he leased a house on Rue Mont-Carmel in Upper Town. With £10,000 borrowed from Edward Henry Chapman of Haringey (London), Benson prepared to launch himself into the highly competitive timber trade. At Quebec, this trade, initiated on a large scale by Henry Usborne at the turn of the century, and shielded by preferential duties in Britain from competition on the part of Baltic producers, had grown by the early 1830s to become the major supplier of square timber for the large British market. While operators such as Philemon Wright continued to produce square timber, sawmills in the Ottawa valley owned by George Hamilton, for example, those around Quebec, such as the ones operated by Peter Patterson* and Sir John Caldwell, and others farther up the St Lawrence contributed deals and sawn lumber to the wood products that in some years accounted for more than three-quarters of Quebec's export business. A financial crisis in 1837 and a reduction of the preferential duty in 1842 had sent shock waves through the trade, but the effects had been short-term, and by the time of Benson's arrival Quebec was in the process of exporting a record quantity of timber; in 1845 merchants would send 1,499 shiploads of wood products from the 30 separate coves lining the St Lawrence between Cap-Rouge and the Rivière Montmorency. Exports that year of the principal product, square timber, totalled 24,000,000 cubic feet.

Having arrived late in the season in 1845, Benson began operations in 1846 after establishing his contacts. That July he contracted with an Upper Canadian lumberman from Dundas County, George Browse, to take delivery at Quebec within the season of 50 cribs of elm and white pine in return for advances of £299 to cover production costs incurred during the previous winter. In June he had agreed with the Quebec firm of

Allan Gilmour and Company [*see* Allan Gilmour*] to buy 100,000 cubic feet of red pine timber for some £4,600; the wood was to be delivered at Quebec by 31 August, and when the company failed to make the deadline Benson was awarded compensation of £591. Towards the end of the season, as was the custom among the timber merchants at Quebec, Benson began ensuring the next year's supply by financing production through the coming winter. To James Jardine of Pembroke, Upper Canada, for example, he committed advances of £1,200 at six per cent interest for the delivery of 50,000 cubic feet of red pine and an equal quantity of white. He reserved the option of purchasing the timber at the current price on its arrival in Quebec or of selling it to another merchant, the costs and Benson's commission of five per cent, along with the advances and interest, to be deducted from Jardine's account.

In October 1847 Benson consolidated his presence at Quebec with the purchase of a property on the St Lawrence opposite Sillery. Called New Liverpool, it was situated between the Chaudière and Etchemin rivers beside another establishment of the same name owned by the large firm of Hamilton and Low, which George Hamilton had founded. Benson's acquisition consisted of 66 acres of beach lot, developed as a timber cove, and 381 acres of farm land stretching back from it. With its shipyard for the construction of ocean-going vessels and its piers, wharfs, houses, and buildings on the beach, the property had been one of the major establishments in the port area, employing 60 men during the summer months. The former owners, William Price* and Peter McGill*, had been forced to put it up for sale following the tariff reductions of 1842 and financial difficulties encountered by McGill; Benson was apparently the first prospective buyer capable of assuming the price of £8,000, of which he paid £5,300 in cash.

From New Liverpool, where he also took up residence, and an office on Rue Saint-Pierre in Lower Town, Benson conducted a large shipping business. The newspapers of Quebec carried countless notices of ships arriving on his order and advertisements by him announcing charter space on ships bound for Britain, requesting space for cargoes, and offering for sale bricks or salt carried as ballast aboard inbound vessels. The papers also recorded more than 100 outgoing vessels loaded by him each year from 1846 through 1850. In 1850, when he handled the cargoes of 159 of the 1,162 ships cleared through customs, the Quebec *Morning Chronicle* listed him as the largest of the port's 47 shippers. Benson also constructed at least two vessels in his cove, the 722-ton *New Liverpool* in 1847 and the 751-ton *Harbinger* in 1848. In the latter year Benson leased the management of the cove to his agent Robert Roberts for three years at £1,500 per annum. In the summer of 1849 the shipyard was liquidated at public auction; the timber shipping operations continued under Benson's name.

Despite his youth, as a capitalist of considerable stature Benson was naturally involved in enterprises promoted by Quebec's commercial community. In 1848 he joined the board of directors of the British North American Electric Telegraph Association, which proposed to link the St Lawrence with the British market through Halifax by 1850, an undertaking vital to the commercial interests of Quebec; among the 30 parties involved in the enterprise were the timber firms of H. and E. Burstall, G. B. Symes and Company, and Sharples, Wainwright and Company and such prominent individuals as Edward Boxer*, James Gibb*, and Henry LeMesurier*. In October 1849 Benson was one of the group of subscribers promoting the Quebec and Melbourne Railway Company, later called the Quebec and Richmond Rail-road Company, a project equally important to Quebec's expansion as a port. With an investment of £1,000, second only to Peter Patterson's, he was one of the founding vice-presidents in 1850.

In December 1850 Benson was en route to England to arrange the business of the coming season, as was customary among Quebec's timber merchants, when he died suddenly in Whitehall, N.Y. His untimely death deprived Quebec of a dynamic business leader. Two other Bensons, apparently his brothers, had also come to Quebec; Thomas took over New Liverpool under the name of Benson and Company, and Willis A. joined Timothy Hibbard Dunn* in the timber business in the 1850s.

JOHN KEYES

ANQ-Q, CN1-49, 2 sept. 1846, 24–25 oct. 1848, 19 déc. 1849; CN1-67, 8 juill., 10, 25 sept., 5 oct. 1846; CN1-197, 14 oct. 1847, 6 juin 1850; P-600/4, D-362-Québec-1861. *Morning Chronicle* (Quebec), 5 July, 5 Oct., 10 Dec. 1849; 13 Dec. 1850. *Quebec Gazette*, 21 Dec. 1849. *Quebec Mercury*, 11 July, 5 Nov., 10 Dec. 1850. *Quebec directory*, 1848–49: 22, 165, 210–11, 236; 1850: 23, 252–53. J. E. Defebaugh, *History of the lumber industry of America* (2v., Chicago, 1906–7), 1: 139–40. A. R. M. Lower, *Great Britain's woodyard: British America and the timber trade, 1763–1867* (Montreal and London, 1973), 71. P. D. McClelland, "The New Brunswick economy in the nineteenth century" (PHD thesis, Harvard Univ., Cambridge, Mass., 1966), table XVIII.

BERCZY, JEANNE-CHARLOTTE. *See* ALLAMAND

BERTHELOT, AMABLE, lawyer, militia officer, politician, author, and bibliophile; b. 10 Feb. 1777 at Quebec, son of Michel-Amable Berthelot* Dartigny and Marie-Angélique Bazin; d. there unmarried 24 Nov. 1847.

The Berthelots were descended from Charles Berthelot, the son of a merchant grocer in Paris, who came to New France in 1726. At Quebec he married Thérèse Roussel, daughter of Timothée Roussel*, a surgeon there. Having a great talent for business, he became prosperous within a few years and built up a substantial fortune. In 1748 he bought the fief of Villeray, outside the Porte Saint-Louis where the Grande Allée now runs. His son, Michel-Amable Berthelot Dartigny, who inherited his land and fortune, turned to the professions of lawyer and notary. In 1792 he was elected for the riding of Quebec to the first house of assembly of Lower Canada.

Amable Berthelot was the third of seven children, four of whom died in infancy. From 1785 till 1793 he did his classical studies at the Petit Séminaire de Québec. Following in his father's footsteps he then went into law, articling in the office of Jean-Antoine Panet*, a prominent Quebec lawyer. On 17 Jan. 1799, at the age of 21, he was called to the bar. His entire training had been the customary one given to the son of a bourgeois family in the late 18th century. In his formative years he acquired a pronounced and lasting taste for research and study and began to build up an excellent private library.

As a young lawyer Berthelot settled in Trois-Rivières, where he opened an office. He soon succeeded in acquiring a good many clients and he became one of the leading citizens of his adopted town. During the War of 1812 he served as a captain in the 1st Battalion of the Trois-Rivières militia, which was under the command of Louis-Charles Foucher. He was rewarded with land grants for his services to the crown. In 1814, towards the end of the war, he too was tempted by political life; he ran for the town of Trois-Rivières and was elected to the House of Assembly along with Charles Richard Ogden*. At Quebec Berthelot, like his father before him, joined the Canadian party. He did not, however, give his support immediately to the young Louis-Joseph Papineau*, who had been an assemblyman since 1808. In the 1815 session he supported Jean-Thomas Taschereau* for the office of speaker rather than Papineau. Berthelot retained his seat until 1816.

By 1820 he had amassed a personal fortune enabling him to retire from the practice of law to concentrate on travel and study. He closed his office in Trois-Rivières and left Lower Canada for France. Europe must certainly have long held a fascination for an intellectual such as Berthelot. He lived in France for four years, from 1820 till 1824, during which he discovered the Paris of Louis XVIII and, through his fortune, had entrée to the salons of the capital. His love of books was abundantly satisfied, and it was no doubt during this stay that he in large measure built up the rich library of historical works for which he would later become known.

Shortly after returning to Lower Canada in 1824 Berthelot was again elected for Trois-Rivières, which he represented until 1827. Defeated that year when he stood for Upper Town Quebec, he retired from public life for some time. In 1831 he made plans for another trip to France. Just before sailing, he decided to put his library up for sale. The transaction was conducted by the usual auction, held on 23 Aug. 1831 in the Hôtel Malhiot at Quebec. The advertisement for this event, which appeared in the Montreal newspaper *La Minerve*, mentioned that the sale involved "a collection of nearly fifteen hundred volumes of rare and valuable books on religion, law, government, literature, and history." It is known that a catalogue of this imposing collection was published at the time, but unfortunately there is no copy of it extant. Part of the library's contents are nevertheless known through an article that Michel Bibaud* published in the Montreal *Magasin du Bas-Canada* in 1832 and a report by the House of Assembly's librarian, who bought several of the historical works. Not knowing how long he would stay in Europe, Berthelot may have preferred selling his collection to taking it with him or storing it at Quebec for several years.

Whatever the case, having returned to Lower Canada in 1834, Berthelot decided to take up permanent residence in his home town. That year he returned to politics and was elected to the assembly for Upper Town Quebec. He kept his seat until the constitution was suspended in 1838. During those critical years Berthelot, who was timid by nature and disinclined to engage in polemics, broke from the Patriote party to join the ranks of the Quebec party, in which Elzéar BÉDARD, Étienne Parent*, John NEILSON, and other moderate nationalists from the Quebec region were prominent. In February 1835, during a debate in the house, he summed up his position with the maxim: *Suaviter in modo, fortiter in re* ("Be steadfast in principle, conciliatory in action"). The aphorism does, in fact, describe Berthelot's own political activity. As an assemblyman he was especially interested in questions concerning education. Following the union of Upper and Lower Canada he concluded his political career by sitting for Kamouraska from 1841 till 1847.

Berthelot seems to have been most at ease when immersed in intellectual activity. He took an interest in history for many years and published essays on various aspects of historical archaeology. His interest in research was shared by a number of well-known Canadians in the early 19th century who were investigating the origins of New France, among them Michel Bibaud, Joseph-François PERRAULT, and Georges-Barthélemi Faribault*, and with whom Berthelot often had occasion to exchange ideas. While putting his father's papers in order, he discovered documents concerning the American invasion of

1775, including an account of the siege of Fort St John's (Saint-Jean-sur-Richelieu) by the Americans. Thanks to his efforts they have been preserved. During his second stay in France Berthelot formed a friendship with François-Xavier Garneau*, whom he met in Paris. Garneau benefited from Berthelot's experience in Europe and greatly esteemed him. Berthelot, who by then was growing old, bestowed his affection upon Garneau and later encouraged him by lending financial support to the publication of the first volume of his *Histoire du Canada depuis sa découverte jusqu'à nos jours*. Berthelot also gained recognition for his research on French grammar, and in 1843 he published an essay on grammatical analysis that attracted some attention.

Berthelot's public life is well known but his private life is much less so. He never married and in Paris he would sometimes confide to Garneau the deep loneliness of his single state. He did, however, adopt two children: Adèle, born in 1813, who married Louis-Hippolyte La Fontaine* in 1831, and Amable, born in 1815, who practised medicine at Saint-Eustache. The birth of the two children is shrouded in obscurity, and their mother's name is not given in the record of their baptism, marriage, or burial.

Nothing is known of Berthelot's relations with his family towards the end of his life. He died at Quebec on 24 Nov. 1847, at the age of 70, when he was still the sitting member for Kamouraska. The newspapers took note of his passing, and the Quebec bar formally went into mourning in his honour. In an article written at the time of Berthelot's death Garneau called him "a studious man, rather than a man of action and change." These words aptly describe Berthelot in his public career and in his personal inclinations and gifts.

GILLES GALLICHAN

In addition to two speeches, on education and on a legislative bill dealing with mortgages, Berthelot published several treatises on historical archaeology, including *Dissertation sur le canon de bronze que l'on voit dans le musée de M. Chasseur, à Québec* (Québec, 1830) and *Discours fait devant la Société de discussion de Québec, le 15 juillet 1844, sur le vaisseau trouvé à l'embouchure du ruisseau St-Michel, et que l'on prétend être la 'Petite-Hermine' de Jacques Cartier* (Québec, 1844). His research into French grammar resulted in two works: *Essai de grammaire française suivant les principes de l'abbé Girard* (Québec, 1840) and *Essai d'analyses grammaticales suivant les principes de l'abbé Girard* (Québec, 1843; nouv. éd., 1847).

The Division de la reconstitution des débats of the library of the Assemblée nationale du Québec holds files of newspaper reports on the proceedings of the House of Assembly of Lower Canada, and Berthelot's contributions in the house in 1835–37 can be found there. His speeches in the Legislative Assembly of the Province of Canada after 1841 can be followed in *Debates of the Legislative Assembly of United Canada* (Abbott Gibbs *et al.*).

ANQ-Q, CE1-1, 10 févr. 1777, 27 nov. 1847; P1000-11-184. ASQ, Fichier des anciens. PAC, MG 23, B35; MG 30, D1, 4: 498–518; RG 4, B8: 6384–87; RG 68, General index, 1651–1841. F.-X. Garneau, *Voyage en Angleterre et en France dans les années 1831, 1832 et 1833*, Paul Wyczynski, édit. (Ottawa, 1968), 282–83. L.C., House of Assembly, *Journals*, 1815; 1831–32, app.B; 1835. *Le Canadien*, 2 mars 1835; 24, 29 nov. 1847. *La Minerve*, 4 août 1831, 30 déc. 1847. F.-J. Audet, *Les députés des Trois-Rivières (1808–1838)* (Trois-Rivières, Qué., 1934); "Les législateurs du Bas-Canada." F.-J. Audet et Fabre Surveyer, *Les députés au premier Parl. du Bas-Canada*. F.-M. Bibaud, *Le panthéon canadien* (A. et V. Bibaud; 1891). Desjardins, *Guide parl.* Réginald Hamel *et al.*, *Dictionnaire pratique des auteurs québécois* (Montréal, 1976). Le Jeune, *Dictionnaire*, 1: 165. H. J. Morgan, *Bibliotheca Canadensis*. *Officers of British forces in Canada* (Irving). P.-G. Roy, *Les avocats de la région de Québec*; *Fils de Québec*, 2: 186–87. Wallace, *Macmillan dict.* Serge Gagnon, *Le Québec et ses historiens de 1840 à 1920: la Nouvelle-France de Garneau à Groulx* (Québec, 1978). Labarrère-Paulé, *Les instituteurs laïques*. Edmond Lareau, *Histoire de la littérature canadienne* (Montréal, 1874). Mason Wade, *Les Canadiens français, de 1760 à nos jours*, Adrien Venne et Francis Dufau-Labeyrie, trad. (2e éd., 2v., Ottawa, 1966). "Bibliophilie," *Magasin du Bas-Canada* (Montréal), 1 (1832): 63–65. [Hervé Biron], "Ceux qui firent notre pays: Amable Berthelot," *Le Nouvelliste* (Trois-Rivières), 10 déc. 1946: 2. "La famille Berthelot d'Artigny," *BRH*, 41 (1935): 3–38. Antoine Roy, "Sur quelques ventes aux enchères et bibliothèques privées," *Cahiers des Dix*, 26 (1961): 219–33.

BERTON, GEORGE FREDERICK STREET, lawyer and office holder; b. 10 Dec. 1808 in Burton Parish, N.B., eldest son of George Duncan Berton and Ann Frances Street; m. 28 Sept. 1833 Delia Hooke in Fredericton, and they had three children; d. there 31 Jan. 1840.

George Frederick Street Berton was born into early 19th-century New Brunswick's most extensive legal connection, and his brief but distinguished career illustrates the coalescence of the province's legal profession in the 1820s and 1830s. His maternal grandfather, Samuel Denny Street*, was New Brunswick's first lawyer. Among his lawyer uncles were George Frederick Street*, John Ambrose Sharman Street*, and Alfred Locke Street. Through his father he was related to the Ludlow family, which had provided New Brunswick with its first chief justice, George Duncan Ludlow*.

The son of the high sheriff of York County, Berton was reared in Fredericton and St Andrews. In 1822 he entered the College of New Brunswick and, taking no degree, subsequently articled for five years in the chambers of his uncle and namesake George Frederick Street. Admitted as an attorney in 1830, he went into partnership with G. F. Street and was on 3 June appointed non-resident clerk of the peace for Sunbury County in succession to his grandfather Street, who had held the office since the foundation of the province. After he was called to the bar in 1832, he established himself in Fredericton where, five years later, he commenced the successful law partnership with George Jarvis Dibblee that continued until his death. Berton filled minor public offices typical of a young lawyer with good connections and, on 15 Jan. 1838, received appointment as clerk of the crown in the Supreme Court on the ouster of William Hunter Odell*. The clerkship was a conventional stepping-stone to more prestigious legal preferment, but Berton's early death meant that his real achievements were not overshadowed by a later accumulation of offices. He is remembered today for his role in the maturation of New Brunswick's legal profession.

The death in 1821 of George Ludlow Wetmore* in a duel with Berton's uncle George Frederick Street arising out of a court-room quarrel triggered a whole series of measures to safeguard the gentlemanly image of the bar. In 1823 the Supreme Court imposed on the profession the first extensive regulations for the admission of students-at-law, attorneys, and barristers. Two years later the judges and lawyers of the province strengthened peer control through the creation of the Law Society of New Brunswick; in 1826 the society established at Fredericton its ambitious Barristers' Inn for the accommodation of out-of-town lawyers attending the sittings of the Supreme Court. Although Berton was himself too young to be involved in founding the Law Society, he did join Lemuel Allan Wilmot*, William Hayden Needham*, and Charles Fisher* as a core participant in another landmark of professionalization – the Law Students' Society, which was operating in Fredericton by 1828. In 1834 he took part in yet another professional watershed: the bar's grand remonstrance, at a meeting chaired by Attorney General Charles Jeffery PETERS, against the appointment of Englishman James Carter* to the Supreme Court in preference to New Brunswick claimants.

By 1835 the still youthful Berton had won such respect from his peers that he was given the onerous task of preparing the first thorough consolidation of New Brunswick statutes from 1786. With the careful assistance of Chief Justice Ward Chipman* he produced a meticulous edition which remains the source of first resort for pre-1836 legislation. It was in 1836 as well that his characteristic "desire to render service to my professional brethren" led Berton to begin publication of his notes on select Supreme Court appellate decisions; reports appeared first in the *Royal Gazette* and were subsequently issued in pamphlet form. The usefulness of this first New Brunswick venture into law reporting was recognized the following year when Berton – already a distributor for at least two English law-book publishers – received statutory appointment as law reporter. In 1839 he collected his reports into a one-volume consolidation. Issued at "heavy pecuniary expense," the 1839 volume was the dying Berton's intended memorial. At his death a year later Chief Justice Chipman and his colleagues publicly voiced "great regret at the loss [to] the Court, the Profession, and the Country." In less than 20 years the New Brunswick bar had moved from a homogeneous family connection to a large and rapidly professionalizing body. George Berton's pioneering labours at statute consolidation and law reporting were benchmarks in that transformation.

D. G. BELL

[Berton's compilation of the New Brunswick statutes was published as *The acts of the General Assembly of her majesty's province of New Brunswick, from the twenty sixth year of the reign of King George the Third to the sixth year of the reign of King William the Fourth* (Fredericton, 1838). His consolidated law reports, entitled *Reports of cases adjudged in the Supreme Court of the province of New Brunswick, commencing in Hilary term, 1835* (Fredericton, 1839), appeared in a second edition: *Reports of cases decided in the Supreme Court of New Brunswick, from Hilary term, 5 Wm. 4, to Hilary term, 2 Vic. . . .* , ed. A. A. Stockton (Toronto and Edinburgh, 1882). This edition is still in print. Although the earliest law report series in New Brunswick, the collection is now, for reasons not important to explain, referred to as volume 2 of the *New Brunswick reports*. D.G.B.]

N.B. Museum, A67–A71, A75, A147, A156 (Berton and Berton–Dibblee account- and process-books); Berton–Dibblee coll.; N.B. Hist. Soc. papers, packets 5, 8. PANB, MC 288; RG 2, RS7, 98: 1144–46; RG 11, RS657, Q12. *American Jurist and Law Magazine* (Boston), 19 (1838): 246–48. *Royal Gazette* (Fredericton), 4 Oct. 1833, 5 Feb. 1840. Hill, *Old Burying Ground*. *The New Brunswick militia commissioned officers' list, 1787–1867*, comp. D. R. Facey-Crowther (Fredericton, 1984). D. G. Bell, "The transformation of the New Brunswick bar, 1785–1830: from family connexion to peer control," *Papers presented at the 1987 Canadian law in history conference* (3v., Ottawa, 1987), 1: 240–56. Lawrence, *Judges of N.B*. (Stockton and Raymond). Jennifer Nedelsky and Dorothy Long, "Law reporting in the Maritime provinces: history and development" (report prepared for Canadian Law Information Council, Ottawa, 1981).

BETHUNE, JAMES GRAY, businessman, office holder, JP, and militia officer; b. 1 April 1793 in Williamstown, Upper Canada, son of John Bethune* and Véronique Waddens; m. 4 Feb. 1830 Martha Covert, and they had a daughter who died in infancy; d. 13 Oct. 1841 in Rochester, N.Y., and was buried in Cobourg, Upper Canada.

James Gray Bethune was the fourth son of the Reverend John Bethune, a prominent loyalist. About 1812, after attending John Strachan*'s school at Cornwall, he took up residence in the frontier hamlet of Hamilton (Cobourg) on the north shore of Lake Ontario. By 1817 he had opened a store, built a sawmill, was operating a distillery, and had been appointed first postmaster of Hamilton, a function he carried out in his store until 1834. As a merchant-storekeeper Bethune endured where others failed because he was able to forge a solid mercantile connection with Montreal merchants through his brother Norman, a well-placed merchant and forwarder there. But it is also clear that Bethune was an aggressive and innovative businessman who championed the economic development of the Newcastle District, and particularly trade connections through Cobourg to its hinterland.

This developmental goal was pursued in several ways. In 1826, to head off rival merchants from Port Hope, he opened a branch-store in Peterborough and later began wholesaling to inland storekeepers. He was actively interested in real estate, serving in 1819 on the first land board for the Newcastle District. Privately he acquired speculative land holdings in several parts of the district during the 1820s, including a large block in Cobourg strategically located adjacent to the harbour. In 1831 he became the local agent for the Canada Company and two years later authored a promotional pamphlet for prospective immigrants, *A schedule of real estate in the Newcastle District*. More important was his determination to develop better facilities for transportation between Cobourg and the back country. In 1827, along with John COVERT, he was a leading force in the establishment of the Cobourg harbour committee (incorporated in 1829 as the Cobourg Harbour Company), serving as its treasurer. In 1832 he began the first steamboat service on Rice Lake and the Otonabee River. A year later he opened large warehouses at Peterborough and Cobourg, launched a steamboat on Chemung Lake (north of Peterborough), and was active in having a bridge built across the Trent River, probably at the present-day village of Hastings. In addition, he led the group of investors, including Zacheus Burnham* and John Gilchrist*, which built the steamship *Cobourg* in 1833 for service on Lake Ontario and was involved in the Cobourg Rail Road Company, chartered in 1834 to build a railway between Cobourg and Rice Lake. Not surprisingly, in 1833 Bethune was appointed to the provincial commission for the improvement of navigation in the Newcastle District.

Bethune's commercial zeal and irrepressible appetite for internal improvement schemes made him a prominent and admired man in the district. As a brother of the respected Anglican cleric at Cobourg, Alexander Neil Bethune*, and as a justice of the peace and a commissioner in the district Court of Requests, he was also a trusted figure. He was appointed lieutenant-colonel of the 2nd Regiment of Northumberland militia in 1831 and was active in a number of community organizations, including the Northumberland Agricultural Society and the Newcastle District Emigrant Relief Society (formed during the cholera epidemic of 1832). With solid personal and business connections to such members of the province's commercial and political élite as John Strachan and John Macaulay*, it is not surprising that Bethune was appointed Cobourg agent for the Bank of Upper Canada in August 1830 and cashier of the branch in September 1832. However, his banking activities led to his downfall.

In the tight economy of Upper Canada, Bethune made liberal credit available to clients and to himself through such speculative practices as reciprocal note endorsements (often involving his brothers Norman and Donald*) and the issuance of accommodation drafts which lacked hard backing – all in contravention of the central bank's policy. Overextended as a result of his speculation in steamboats and hampered by tardy and defaulting debtors, he was on the road to ruin by the summer of 1833. In June his bank was mysteriously robbed of more than £3,000; according to John Langton*, some believed that Bethune had removed the money. When an investigation initiated by the bank's president, William Allan*, revealed that Bethune had allowed nearly £8,000 in credit to default, he was forced to resign in November 1833. In spite of his assets he was unable to cover his losses and in 1834 was declared bankrupt. Also hit hard by his demise were his financial guarantors (his father-in-law, John Covert, and George Strange Boulton*) and those in the district who had entrusted their savings to his care.

Undeterred, he ran as a tory for the House of Assembly in October 1834 but was defeated by John Gilchrist and Alexander McDonell*. Thereafter Bethune's financial problems hounded him and during a brief stay in debtor's prison in Amherst (now part of Cobourg) in 1836 he continued to sort out his accounts. Discredited as the "great man" of the Newcastle District, he moved to Rochester, N.Y., where, after a long illness, he died in 1841.

PETER ENNALS

J. G. Bethune, *A schedule of real estate in the Newcastle District to be disposed of at public sale; on the first day of August 1833* . . . (Cobourg, [Ont.], 1833). In the MTRL's copy, the date has been corrected in MS to read "29th day."

ACC, Diocese of Toronto Arch., Church of St Peter (Cobourg), reg. of baptisms, burials, and marriages, 1819–37; vestry minute-books, 1827–93 (mfm. at AO). AO, MS 78, William Allan to Macaulay, 31 Aug., 2 Sept. 1833; John Strachan to Macaulay, 11 Sept. 1833; MS 107, reg. of baptisms and marriages, 16; MS 524, J. G. Bethune to Peter Robinson, 6 March 1827, 19 May 1836; MU 502, Zacheus Burnham to J. G. Bethune, 25 April 1829; MU 2883; RG 1, A-I-6, 12–13; RG 22, Newcastle District, clerk of the peace, reg. of tax payments, 1821–30. MTRL, William Allan papers, John Macaulay to Allan, 5 July 1832, 2 July 1834. Northumberland West Land Registry Office (Cobourg),

Abstract index to deeds, Cobourg, vol.1, lot 16, concession A; lot 18, concessions A and B (mfm. at AO). PAC, RG 68, General index, 1651–1841: 443, 451, 466, 490. John Langton, *Early days in Upper Canada: letters of John Langton from the backwoods of Upper Canada and the Audit Office of the Province of Canada*, ed. W. A. Langton (Toronto, 1926). U.C., House of Assembly, *Journal*, app., 1828, "Report on Cobourg harbour"; 1829: 28†–29†; 1831: 97; 1833–34: 111. *Cobourg Star*, 8 Feb. 1831–20 Oct. 1841. P. [A.] Baskerville, "The entrepreneur and the metropolitan impulse: James Gray Bethune and Cobourg, 1825–1836," *Victorian Cobourg: a nineteenth century profile*, ed. Jaroslav Petryshyn *et al.* (Belleville, Ont., 1976), 56–70. E. C. Guillet, *Cobourg, 1798–1948* (Oshawa, Ont., 1948), 13. D. E. Wattie, "Cobourg, 1784–1867" (2v., MA thesis, Univ. of Toronto, 1949). P. [A.] Baskerville, "Donald Bethune's steamboat business; a study of Upper Canadian commercial and financial practice," *OH*, 67 (1975): 135–49. A. H. Young, "The Bethunes," *OH*, 27 (1931): 560.

BEYIGISHIQUESHKAM. *See* BAUZHI-GEEZHIG-WAESHIKUM

BINNS, CHARLES, businessman, lawyer, politician, office holder, and militia officer; b. *c.* 1786, perhaps in the West Riding, Yorkshire, England; m. 13 May 1809 Elizabeth Clarke in Charlottetown, and they had 12 children; d. there 28 April 1847.

Charles Binns trained as a lawyer in England and then formed a partnership with a merchant named Peter Hope. In August 1808, with the assistance of James Bardin Palmer* of Charlottetown, Binns sailed for Prince Edward Island to set up an agency to supply Hope with such local products as timber. This plan was not a success. Palmer and Binns quickly fell out, for reasons difficult to determine. Without Palmer's support, Binns drifted into financial failure in 1813, and his partnership with Hope seems to have dissolved shortly thereafter.

Binns, now married, decided to remain on the Island and enrolled as a barrister of its Supreme Court on 16 Feb. 1813. He made moderate acquisitions of land on Lot 25 and in Charlottetown and Royalty, and became a land agent for several other proprietors. At "the solicitation of some extensive Landholders," Binns opened an emigrant office at Charlottetown in 1819 but, like so many of his schemes, this one rapidly failed. Fortunately for Binns, there were few trained lawyers on the Island prior to the 1830s, and by concentrating on his modest legal talents rather than on business adventures he was able to establish a social and financial position in Charlottetown society. The shortage of lawyers also accounts in large measure for the frequency with which Binns was called upon to fill official posts under Lieutenant Governor Charles Douglass Smith*. He was deputy colonial secretary (April 1816–January 1818), solicitor general (January 1818–December 1820), and acting attorney general (November 1819–December 1820).

Although overshadowed as a lawyer by the likes of Palmer and Robert Hodgson*, Binns acted in many of the important trials of his time. The most notorious took place in October 1823 in the Court of Chancery. Binns made a futile attempt to defend the members of a committee which had framed, and a publisher who had printed, resolutions critical of Smith's administration. Ostensibly charged with contempt of chancery for accusing Smith and his family of using the court for personal gain, the defendants were really found guilty of political opposition. These proceedings were agonizing for Binns, whose natural temperament was to shun controversy. While a member of the House of Assembly for Georgetown between 1818 and 1820, he had tried to find neutral ground in the fight between Smith and the assembly. In defending Smith's opponents in court he denied any political allegiance to their cause. Preferring to move safely with the tide, Binns openly attacked Smith's administration only when the lieutenant governor departed, in 1824.

Binns's basic political timidity runs through his reaction to escheat. As an MHA for Charlottetown from 1830 to 1838 Binns shared with his electors the enthusiasm initially engendered by this proposed panacea for the Island's vexing land question. However, his conservatism reasserted itself, and in a series of ponderous and legalistic speeches Binns opposed quadrennial elections, a heavy land tax on proprietors, and eventually escheat. He was concerned that the agitation created at numerous tenant gatherings by such escheat leaders as William Cooper* threatened to subvert the legislative process. Binns led the drive which had Cooper and two of his allies committed to the custody of the assembly's sergeant-at-arms during the sessions of 1837 and 1838. Binns himself was too ill to attend most of the 1838 session, and his poor health, combined with renewed financial difficulties and the prospects of a sweeping pro-escheat victory, was probably the factor that induced him to decline nomination in the election of that year. In his last years he appeared publicly only as law clerk of the assembly for the sessions of 1844 and 1845, and as a captain of militia.

Not unlike Shakespeare's Polonius, Binns was a character of comic pretension and pathos. His speeches in court and assembly were of extraordinary length and characterized by rationalizations which exasperated his opponents and astonished even those with whom he was in agreement. His death went almost unnoticed.

M. BROOK TAYLOR

PAPEI, Acc. 2810/25; Acc. 2849/23–24, 2849/38; RG 1, commission books, 5, 10 April 1816; 22 Jan. 1818; RG 6, Supreme Court, barristers' roll; RG 16, land registry records,

1809–47; conveyance reg., liber 59: f.601. P.E.I. Museum, "Charlottetown manuscript" (n.d.); File information concerning Charles Binns. PRO, CO 226/36: 131; 226/37: 3. St Paul's Anglican Church (Charlottetown), Reg. of baptisms, marriages, and burials (mfm. at PAPEI). P.E.I., House of Assembly, *Journal*, 1818, 1820, 3 Feb. 1831, 26 Jan. 1835, 22 Jan. 1839. *Prince Edward Island Gazette*, 14 Oct., 5 Nov. 1818; 3 Sept. 1819. *Prince Edward Island Register*, 25 Oct., 1, 8 Nov. 1823; 3 Nov. 1829. *Royal Gazette* (Charlottetown), 7 Feb. 1832; 5, 19, 26 Feb., 26 Nov. 1833; 18 Feb., 2, 16 Dec. 1834; 31 March 1835; 26, 30 April 1836; 14, 21 Feb. 1837; 27 March 1838; 20 Feb., 27 Aug. 1844; 11 March 1845; 29 April 1847. A. B. Warburton, *A history of Prince Edward Island from its discovery in 1534 until the departure of Lieutenant-Governor Ready in A.D. 1831* (Saint John, N.B., 1923), 336–43.

BLACK, EDWARD, Church of Scotland minister and teacher; b. 10 Dec. 1793 in the parish of Penninghame, Scotland, third son of the Reverend James Black; m. first, before 1822, Elizabeth McCullough Craw, and they had one daughter; m. secondly *c.* 1837 Wilhemina MacMillan, and they had one son; d. 7 or 8 May 1845 in Montreal.

Edward Black was educated at local schools and from 1808 to 1815 at the University of Edinburgh. After being licensed to preach by the Presbytery of Wigtown in June 1815, he was appointed assistant to his father, but not being given his father's charge after the latter's death in 1822, he emigrated to Montreal with his wife.

It was probably an old friend, businessman Peter McGill*, who introduced Black to the Reverend Henry Esson*, minister of Montreal's most prestigious Presbyterian church, the Scotch Presbyterian Church, later known as St Gabriel Street Church. The two clergymen were unlike in appearance and ministerial style. Esson had a slender physique, was an intellectual, and probably preached at a level beyond the comprehension of at least some of his parishioners, whereas Black was a heavy-set man with Luther-like features who presented an intensely emotional, evangelical message from the pulpit. On Esson's invitation Black preached to his congregation, with such success that he was called to the pulpit on 26 Feb. 1823 as assistant to Esson and James SOMERVILLE, who had retired from active duty but remained the senior minister. At the demise of either minister, Black was to be colleague to the survivor.

Black was ordained on 4 March 1823 by an informal presbytery of Kirk ministers which had been established in the Canadas, probably in 1820. It had met periodically and had hoped to obtain statistics that would support its request for recognition of the Church of Scotland as an established church in the Canadas; recognition would bolster its claims for financial assistance from the government. The presbytery also seems to have been prepared to ordain clergymen, at least until a more official hierarchy of church courts was instituted in the Canadas. Problems ensued. John Burns, a Kirk minister of the evangelical party who arrived in Montreal in 1824 to succeed Robert Easton* as minister of St Peter Street Church, challenged the legality of Black's ordination. He complained that the presbytery did not have the power to ordain a minister because it was not directly attached to the mother church. Furthermore, he feared that by assisting Black in communion services, he would jeopardize his own position within the Church of Scotland. Members of the presbytery were furious, and resolved to send pertinent documents to Scotland and to have no further contact with Burns. Nothing more was heard of the matter, and at the end of his two-year contract Burns returned to Scotland.

Black's position at the Scotch Presbyterian Church continued to be uneasy. His salary had been guaranteed for only two years. Somerville's pension and the salaries for both Esson and Black were dependent on pew rents and church collections but this revenue was inadequate for the needs of the three. Various attempts at relieving the difficulty failed, rumours abounded, and factions arose, one supporting Esson, the other Black. At one point, in the spring of 1831, Black's supporters occupied the church, while partisans of Esson's cause tried to enter by force. Acting upon the advice of the General Assembly of the Church of Scotland, that the case should be decided by ministers in the colony, 15 Presbyterian clergymen and several elders from Upper and Lower Canada met in Kingston in early June 1831 and formed the Synod of the Presbyterian Church of Canada in connection with the Church of Scotland. The arbitrators appointed by the synod decided, on 23 May 1832, that Esson and Black should form separate congregations with Esson remaining at St Gabriel Street Church. At first Black and his congregation worshipped in a Baptist church, but on 24 Aug. 1834 they were able to assemble in the newly constructed St Paul's Church, on Rue Sainte-Hélène. During the years immediately after the separation, while his new congregation was getting established, Black had supported himself and his family by opening a school; James Moir Ferres* assisted him as teacher.

Black's wife had died in 1828, leaving one daughter. In 1837 he was granted a DD by the University of Edinburgh, and it was probably during a visit to Scotland to receive the degree that he married Wilhemina MacMillan of Wigtownshire. The couple would have one son.

Black was deeply mourned when he died at age 52. An obituary in the *Montreal Gazette* described him as "a man of powerful natural abilities, of literary accomplishments and tastes, of great and unaffected sincerity and kindness of heart, and of calm and devoted piety." He had been an outstanding minister.

He was not rigid in his beliefs, having expressed his desire to take part with other religious denominations in advancing Christendom. Furthermore, he was extremely valuable in the courts of the church because of his knowledge of forms and procedures.

ELIZABETH ANN KERR MCDOUGALL

ANQ-M, CE1-125, 12 mai 1845. QUA, 2263, Presbyterian Church of Canada in connection with the Church of Scotland, Synod papers. UCC, Montreal-Ottawa Conference Arch. (Montreal), St Gabriel Street Church, parish records, box II. *Montreal Gazette*, 13 May 1845. Borthwick, *Hist. and biog. gazetteer*. Scott *et al.*, *Fasti ecclesiæ scoticanæ*, vol.7. Campbell, *Hist. of Scotch Presbyterian Church*. Gregg, *Hist. of Presbyterian Church* (1885). E. A. [Kerr] McDougall, "The Presbyterian Church in western Lower Canada, 1815–1842" (PHD thesis, McGill Univ., Montreal, 1969).

BLACK, SAMUEL, fur trader and explorer; baptized 3 May 1780 in the parish of Pitsligo, Scotland, son of John Black and Mary Leith, who married in 1781; d. 8 Feb. 1841 at Thompson's River Post (Kamloops, B.C.).

Samuel Black was born into a Scottish trading family which had links with Canada: his maternal uncle James LEITH was involved in the New North West Company (sometimes known as the XY Company). It may have been through this association that Black came to Montreal in 1802 and was employed as a clerk by the XY Company. He showed his independent spirit by "having words" with its leading partner, Sir Alexander Mackenzie*. In 1804 the firm was absorbed by the North West Company whose service Black then entered.

During his early years in the fur trade Black distinguished himself mostly as a bravo, using his great stature and fearless mien to intimidate the rival traders of the Hudson's Bay Company, on whom he played many malicious and sometimes dangerous tricks. In 1803 he was sent to the Peace River country, where the XY Company had established itself, and then two years later to Fort Chipewyan (Alta) on Lake Athabasca to combat the incursions of the HBC men, whom he so successfully harried that in 1806 Peter Fidler* withdrew from Nottingham House. Black spent 15 years as a clerk in the Athabasca region, burning down the HBC post at Île-à-la-Crosse (Sask.) in 1811 and four years later taking part in an affray during which several HBC men were killed [*see* Joseph Howse*]. Two years afterwards he seized the rebuilt fort at Île-à-la-Crosse and later, at Fort Wedderburn (Alta) in 1818, he arrested and confined Colin ROBERTSON on the orders of William McGillivray* and under the authority of the Canada Jurisdiction Act. Black was more hated by the HBC men than any other Nor'Wester; in November 1820 George Simpson*, who had taken over from Robertson the HBC's campaign against the NWC in the Athabasca country, noted that "this Outlaw is so callous to every honourable or manly feeling that it is not unreasonable to suspect him of the blackest acts."

By this time the tide had turned against the Nor'Westers, and in June 1820 Black had fled to the NWC post at McLeod Lake in New Caledonia (B.C.) to avoid arrest. On his return to Athabasca the following winter he found Simpson in charge and in 1821, when the two fur-trading companies united [*see* Simon MCGILLIVRAY], the HBC men did not quickly forgive Black's record of violence against them. Along with Alexander Macdonell* (Greenfield), Peter Skene Ogden*, and Cuthbert Grant*, Black was at first excluded from the reconstituted HBC. In 1822 he went to England, evidently to further his cause with the HBC's London committee. Early the following year he was appointed a first-class clerk with the salary, but without the rank, of chief trader. He returned to the northwest later in 1823, assuming charge of Fort St John (near Fort St John, B.C.). The next year, when he became a chief trader, he carried out an exploration of the Finlay River and kept a journal, which was later published. His untiring curiosity and descriptive vividness make this account a valuable contribution to our knowledge of the northern regions west of the Rocky Mountains in the early days of exploration. Though his journey was partly inspired by the HBC's intention of exploring the country as far as the Russian trading territory along the coast, Black found the area too unproductive and the river route too difficult for any development of the fur trade to result from his efforts.

Black wintered in 1824–25 at Fort Dunvegan in the Peace River country, returned to York Factory (Man.), and in July 1825 was appointed to Fort Colvile (near Colville, Wash.) on the Columbia River. Shortly afterwards he was sent as chief factor to Fort Nez Percés (Walla Walla, Wash.). This was an important post which maintained the HBC's position against interloping American traders. As early as 1828 John McLoughlin*, head of the company's Columbia district, regarded Black's failure to get along with the Indians as a reason for moving him. It was not until the end of 1830, however, that he was transferred to Thompson's River Post. George Simpson, in assessing Black's nature in his celebrated "Character book" of 1832, described him as "The strangest man I ever knew. So wary & suspicious that it is scarcely possible to get a direct answer from him on any point, and when he does speak or write . . . so prolix that it is quite fatiguing to attempt following him. A perfectly honest man and his generosity might be considered indicative of a warmth of heart if he was not known to be a cold blooded fellow who could be guilty of any Cruelty and would be a perfect Tyrant if he had any power. . . . Yet his word when he can be brought to the point may be depended on. A Don Quixote in appearance Ghastly, raw boned and lanthorn jawed, yet strong vigorous and active. Has not the talent of conciliating Indians by whom he is disliked, but who are ever in dread of him, and well they may be so. as he is . . . so suspicious that offensive and defensive preparation seem to be the study of his Life having Dirks, Knives and Loaded Pistols concealed about his Person and in all directions about his Establishment even under his Table cloth at meals and in his Bed."

In 1837 Black made plans to leave the Columbia region, and was already on his way to York Factory that year when he was recalled and appointed chief factor in charge of the inland posts of the Columbia. It was a fatal turn in his fortunes, for now his failure to reach an understanding relationship with the Indians led to his death. Early in 1841 chief Tranquille of the Shuswaps quarrelled with Black over a gun, went home, and shortly afterwards died. His widow believed that Black had bewitched him and she worked on the feelings of the chief's nephew, who came to Thompson's River Post and on 8 February shot Black dead.

Black left a considerable fortune for a fur trader. He had £7,887 in credit with the HBC when he died, and this sum became the subject of lengthy litigation. His relatives in Scotland sought to appropriate it without making provision for the survivors among the eight children of Black and his two country wives, both Métis; his first wife had remarried but his second, Angélique Cameron, did not and remained a claimant. The dispute continued in and out of the courts until the 1850s, and it is not known for certain whether any provision was ever made for Angélique or any of the children. The contentiousness for which Black was notorious in life remained a feature in his affairs even after his death.

GEORGE WOODCOCK

Samuel Black is the author of *A journal of a voyage from Rocky Mountain Portage in Peace River to the sources of Finlays Branch and North West Ward in summer 1824*, ed. E. E. Rich and A. M. Johnson (*HBRS*, 18, London, 1955).

GRO (Edinburgh), Pitsligo, reg. of births and baptisms, 3 May 1780. *Docs. relating to NWC* (Wallace). *HBRS*, 1 (Rich); 2 (Rich and Fleming); 3 (Fleming); 4 (Rich); 6 (Rich). Simpson, "Character book," *HBRS*, 30 (Williams). Brown, *Strangers in blood*. Innis, *Fur trade in Canada* (1930). Morton, *Hist. of Canadian west* (Thomas; 1973). Rich, *Hist. of HBC* (1958–59), vol.2. Van Kirk, *"Many tender ties"*. J. N. Wallace, "The explorer of Finlay River in 1824," *CHR*, 9 (1928): 25–31.

BLACK DICK, RICHARD PIERPOINT, known as. *See* PIERPOINT

BLACKWOOD, THOMAS, merchant, militia officer, office holder, and JP; b. 10 Feb. 1773 in Lanarkshire, Scotland; d. 22 Nov. 1842 in Montreal.

Thomas Blackwood came to Quebec in May 1790 and was employed there until about 1795 by John Blackwood*, who is said not to have been a relative. In 1798 Thomas worked with James McGill* in establishing a French royalist colony at Windham, Upper Canada, under Joseph-Geneviève de Puisaye*, Comte de Puisaye. Two years later he joined McGill's Montreal firm of James and Andrew McGill and Company. He was at Michilimackinac (Mackinac Island, Mich.) representing the firm's interests in June and July 1806 and 1807. His letters from there give many details of the operation of early 19th-century Great Lakes trading and show that he had responsibility for considerable amounts of money and goods. In Montreal he dined often in Joseph Frobisher*'s circle of acquaintances, and on 27 Dec. 1806 Frobisher attended his wedding to Margaret Grant, the eldest daughter of John Grant of Lachine. Blackwood and his wife would have two children.

In 1810, following the dissolution of James and Andrew McGill and Company, Blackwood, François Desrivières* (McGill's stepson), and Peter Harkness formed Desrivières, Blackwood and Company. James McGill died in 1813, leaving to Blackwood £500 and an exemption from any share in the debt of McGill's late firm. Before 1815 Blackwood also partnered his brother John, trading in grain and lumber. In 1822 Thomas was among the merchants who established the Committee of Trade in Montreal [*see* John Richardson*], and he served as its first chairman until 1825. He was a director of the Montreal Savings Bank and its secretary-treasurer for a number of years from 1819. Soon after 1827 he failed in business, and he never regained his former prosperity.

Like most prominent merchants, Blackwood was active in Montreal's social and public life. By 1804 he was an ensign in Montreal's 1st Militia Battalion, and he may have served in 1812–13 as a lieutenant of artillery in the Montreal Incorporated Volunteers. He was promoted captain in the 1st Militia Battalion in 1821. In 1807 he had joined 20 other Scots in founding the Montreal Curling Club, the oldest in North America. The club's first president, he held the post again in 1815–16, 1822–23, 1829–30, and 1831–32. He was made a charter director of the Montreal General Hospital, founded in 1819 [*see* William Caldwell*], reccived a commission of the peace in 1821, and in 1824 was named an examiner of candidates for the position of inspector of pot and pearl ashes and one of five commissioners to report on the state of the Montreal harbour.

From his arrival in Montreal, Blackwood had taken a major interest in the Scotch Presbyterian Church, later known as St Gabriel Street Church. From 1808 he served often on the temporal committee and was elected its chairman annually from 1819 to 1822. He was ordained an elder in 1819 and appointed clerk of session in 1832. From 1834 he was the congregation's representative elder at all meetings of presbytery and synod. He was particularly active in seeking for Church of Scotland congregations in the Canadas privileges similar to those accorded to congregations of the Church of England. In 1828, when Archdeacon John Strachan* of York (Toronto) was pressing exclusive Anglican claims to the clergy reserves, Blackwood made public a letter Strachan had written to him in 1802 enquiring about the position of minister to the Scotch Presbyterian congregation. In 1836 he published a letter to the General Assembly of the Church of Scotland, arguing against "the false, unfounded assumption that the Church of England is the Established Church in all the British Dominions, Scotland alone excepted." Two years later, in *Remarks and observations on the constitution of the Canadas, civil and ecclesiastical*, he contended that the Church of Scotland and a few other denominations had equal claim to the rights and privileges enjoyed by the Church of England.

In this pamphlet, published anonymously and distributed only to those "upon whose opinions and decisions the settlement of Canadian affairs may be considered chiefly to depend," Blackwood discussed the causes of and possible remedies for the current political difficulties in Lower Canada. Like such conservatives as Herman Witsius RYLAND and Robert-Anne d'Estimauville*, he believed the root of the problem to be a slavish attempt by the Patriote party to make the colonial constitution a replica of the British, which had evolved through centuries to suit the British people and could fit a colony only after alteration. To solve the crisis in the Canadas he advocated a legislative union. English would be imposed as much as possible in the legislature and the courts, but he did not envisage assimilation of the Canadians. Their language should not "fall into disuse or be discouraged" more than necessary and "the free and secure exercise of their religion," not mere toleration, should be granted. Given security in their language and religion, he asserted, the Canadians would form a rampart against disloyalty and religious fanaticism introduced by "unprincipled adventurers" from Britain and, especially, the United States.

Blackwood died four years after publication of the *Remarks*. In an obituary in November 1842 the *Montreal Gazette* said that during his 47 years in Montreal Blackwood had acquired "the esteem and respect of all who knew him, consisting . . . of a very large portion of the community."

STANLEY B. FROST

Thomas Blackwood is the "Layman of the Church of Scotland" who wrote *Remarks and observations on the constitution of the Canadas, civil and ecclesiastical; with a view to its amendment* . . . (Montreal, 1838).

A portrait of Blackwood is in the Royal Montreal Curling Club and a silhouette appears in Campbell, *Hist. of Scotch Presbyterian Church*, on the plate facing p.244; a second silhouette is reproduced on p.2 of E. A. Collard's study, cited below.

McGill Univ. Arch., MG 1007, James McGill will. McGill Univ. Libraries, Dept. of Rare Books and Special Coll., MS coll., MS430, MS433, MS435. PAC, RG 4, A1, 232, 361, 403, 476; RG 68, General index, 1651–1841: 60, 186, 349. *Montreal Gazette*, 27 Nov. 1842. *Quebec Gazette*, 13 May 1790; 13 Feb. 1794; 25 July 1799; 16 Dec. 1802; 15 May 1806; 3 May 1810; 6 Sept. 1819; 24 May, 5 June, 25 Oct. 1821; 27 March 1824. *Montreal directory*, 1819. *Officers of British forces in Canada* (Irving). *Quebec almanac*, 1805: 47; 1821: 102. E. A. Collard, *The Montreal Board of Trade, 1822–1972: a story* ([Montreal], 1972), 1–7. Creighton, *Empire of St. Lawrence*. *Semi-centennial report of the Montreal Board of Trade, sketches of the growth of the city of Montreal from its foundation* . . . (Montreal, 1893).

BLAIKLOCK, HENRY MUSGRAVE, architect, civil engineer, JP, and office holder; b. 26 April 1790 in London, son of Musgrave Blaiklock and Elizabeth Harris; m. there first *c.* 1810 Catherine ——; m. secondly before 1823 Mary Morris, possibly in London, and they had three sons and a daughter; d. 9 Oct. 1843 at Quebec.

Henry Musgrave Blaiklock was born into the English middle class, judging by the professions pursued by his family. He had at least two younger brothers: George, an architect, and John, a merchant. Nothing is known of his education, but around 1812 he took up architecture in London, and he soon went into partnership with George. Subsequently George married Caroline Cecilia Price, who, according to family tradition, was the niece of Lord Dalhousie [RAMSAY]. It was supposedly at Dalhousie's invitation that George came to Quebec in 1823 or 1824, accompanied by his wife and children, his mother, and his two brothers with their families.

The contracts and lucrative offices which George and Henry managed to get in Lower Canada seem to confirm that George had a family connection with the governor, whose use of patronage was well known. In 1824 George conceived and executed plans for Holy Trinity chapel at Quebec for Jonathan SEWELL. In the winter of 1826, following a competition, he was entrusted with drawing plans for a prison in Montreal, which was, however, built by another architect, John Wells. At the governor's express request, George drew up a plan for a marine and emigrant hospital in Quebec shortly before his death on 13 Dec. 1828. Henry Musgrave had settled in the Lévis region by December 1827. He had been serving as a justice of the peace for the district of Quebec since 12 June 1826, and his commission was renewed on 15 Feb. 1828. During the years when the two brothers were establishing themselves in the province, only George seems to have been active in the field of architecture.

Henry's career as an architect and civil engineer began when he joined the Royal Engineers department on 22 July 1830. There he held the office of clerk of works until his death 13 years later. Governor Sir James Kempt* turned to him to draw up plans for the new customs building at Quebec. Presented in the autumn of 1830, they provided for an H-shaped building with two floors, the centre section to be fronted by a porch with Doric pillars. In the end, only the centre section was built, without the porch, in the period 1831–39. In 1831 Blaiklock was again called upon to design a large building. His plan for the marine and emigrant hospital called for a U-shaped three-storey building, with the wings to the rear and in front a porch having Ionic pillars, which Alfred Hawkins* claimed was modelled on a Greek temple to the Muses. This plan, which may have been inspired by George's, was chosen in preference to others because it would be less costly and would accommodate more patients. The building was constructed in part during the period 1831–43 and was completed in the 1860s; it has since been demolished.

In addition to their imposing proportions and their careful fidelity to a classical idiom, these two buildings were distinguished by numerous decorative recesses, with arched coping stones and embrasures, around the openings. In these respects they constituted excellent examples of English neoclassicism. The hospital was one of the earliest large-scale buildings in this style in Lower Canada, but the customs building, which was never completed as designed, appears to have been adapted to the local context. By multiplying the recesses Henry revealed a penchant for decoration and in this way distinguished himself from his brother, whose buildings were more severe.

From a study of Henry Musgrave Blaiklock's two main buildings one may deduce, as did historian Arthur John Hampson Richardson, that he created the plans for a house at 73 Rue Sainte-Ursule at Quebec. The façade of this residence built early in the 1830s repeats the decorative copings of the Marine and Emigrant Hospital. Later on Blaiklock was in charge of some minor works. He oversaw the renovation of the court-house in 1840 and the enlarging of the National School on Rue d'Auteuil in 1842. Maintenance of government buildings, left vacant when the capital was moved to Kingston, was entrusted to him for the period 1840–43. There remain many unanswered questions about his career at Quebec that only research into his training and his work in London might solve. Nevertheless, through the size and quality of his buildings, Blaiklock made a remarkable contribution to the development of neoclassicism in Quebec.

ANDRÉ LABERGE

ANQ-Q, CE1-61, 3, 8 déc. 1824; 17 déc. 1828; 16 janv. 1833; 19 oct. 1839; 26 avril 1842; 11 oct. 1843; CE1-68, 3 mai 1853; CE1-75, 7 janv. 1828. City of Westminster Arch. (London), Reg. of baptisms, 26 April 1790. PAC, RG 8, I (C ser.), 151: 281; RG 11, A2, 93: 188; A3, 136. Can., Prov. of, Legislative Assembly, *App. to the journals*, 1842, app.K; 1844–45, app.A. L.C., House of Assembly, *Journals*, 1826; 1827, app.H; 1828–29, app.DD; 1829–30, app.MM; 1831–32, app.H, S; 1832–33, app.I; 1835–36. Alfred Hawkins, *Hawkins's picture of Quebec; with historical recollections* (Quebec, 1834). A. J. H. Richardson *et al.*, *Quebec City: architects, artisans and builders* (Ottawa, 1984). Leslie Maitland, *L'architecture néo-classique au Canada* ([Ottawa], 1984). A. J. H. Richardson, "Guide to the architecturally and historically most significant buildings in the old city of Quebec with a biographical dictionary of architects and builders and illustrations," Assoc. for Preservation Technology, *Bull.* (Ottawa), 2 (1970), nos.3–4: 75.

BLANCHARD, JOTHAM, lawyer, editor, and politician; b. 15 March 1800 in Peterborough, N.H., eldest son of Jonathan Blanchard and Sarah Goggins; m. 7 Aug. 1832 Mrs Margaret Spears in Truro, N.S.; they had no children; d. 14 July 1839 in Pictou, N.S.

At 15 months Jotham Blanchard arrived with his parents in Truro, where his grandfather, Colonel Jotham Blanchard, had settled in 1785. While at school in Truro he fell on the ice, hurt his knee, and was left permanently lame. In 1813 the family moved to the West River of Pictou and ran Ten Mile House for seven or eight years before establishing itself in the town of Pictou. A member of the first class of Pictou Academy and one of its first graduates, Blanchard came under the lasting influence of its principal, Thomas MCCULLOCH. Following the study of law, largely in the office of Thomas Dickson* in Pictou, he was enrolled as an attorney on 18 Oct. 1821 and was admitted to the bar a year later.

According to judge George Geddie Patterson, Blanchard refused to be "cribbed, cabined and confined by the four walls of a dusty law office." Although it did not become public knowledge until 1830, he was editor of the *Colonial Patriot* of Pictou when Jacob Sparling Cunnabell and William H. Milne began to publish it on 7 Dec. 1827. The *Patriot* was the first Nova Scotian paper of any significance outside Halifax and the first to espouse liberal, even radical, principles. Although it has been suggested that the *Patriot*'s basic object was to promote the interests of Pictou Academy, that role was entirely subordinated to general political and governmental concerns. At the outset Blanchard was an ultra-liberal whig, seemingly most akin to Joseph Hume, John Arthur Roebuck*, and other British radicals. Their ideology being foreign to anything in the Nova Scotian political tradition, he was charged with republicanism and disloyalty by reactionaries such as Richard John Uniacke* Jr, who wanted him haled before the House of Assembly.

At the masthead of the *Patriot* was the motto *Pro rege, pro patria* (For king and country), and Blanchard contended that anyone who supported the dignity of the crown at the expense of the general happiness "alike commits treason against the King and his subjects." For him the root of all evils in Nova Scotian government and society was "the system which prevails among the Provincial authorities to keep all the good things among themselves and their families," in other words, the tory labyrinth of patronage distribution. Occasionally the Benthamite in him would show through, as when he maintained that the American government was the only one that had "yet acted upon the Glorious principle that the true end of Government, *is the greatest happiness to the greatest number*."

Without revealing his identity, in late May and June 1828 Blanchard entered into a wordy battle with Joseph Howe*, joint publisher of the *Acadian, and General Advertiser* in 1827 and, by the start of 1828, proprietor of the more prestigious *Novascotian, or Colonial Herald*. It began when the radical *Canadian Spectator* of Montreal published extracts from a letter of a Nova Scotian – actually it was Blanchard – to the Lower Canadian reformer James Leslie*, stating that "our papers and our parliament are servile in the extreme." An indignant Howe asked "The Writer of the Canadian Letter" to point out "one abject sentiment" in his newspaper. Still hiding his identity, Blanchard replied in the *Patriot* that the *Acadian* had been conducted by "a young man connected with the Post Office, and, of course, tied to a party" and that later he would "pull the mask from [his] face." As good as his words, he pictured Howe as the agent of a long-standing system that was designed to stifle freedom and discussion. The controversy got nastier as it proceeded: Howe accused the *Patriot*'s writers – he called them the "Pictou Scribblers" – of being "the mere speaking trumpet" of Pictou Academy; Blanchard alleged that a recent article by Howe on Lord Byron and James Henry Leigh Hunt had been purloined from *Blackwood's Edinburgh Magazine*. If nothing else, Blanchard was helping to develop Howe's talents for repartee and invective.

From March to July 1828 Blanchard was in Halifax gaining a deeper insight into the working of the province's politics, and from then until May 1829 he did the same thing in a larger sphere in Britain. McCulloch appears to have performed the editorial chores of the *Patriot* until November of that year, even though Blanchard was in Pictou in June, holding out "the olive branch of peace" to Howe – in Howe's words – and admitting that he had written the "Canadian Letter." There is no evidence at this time for the often quoted but probably apocryphal admission of Howe that the "Pictou Scribblers" had converted him from the error of his ways. But the two men did see eye to eye on the celebrated "Brandy Dispute" early in 1830 [*see* Enos Collins*] when the assembly refused to let the Council deprive it of the sole right to determine "the amount of the burthens to be borne by the people whom they represent," even at the cost of losing the appropriation bill. In the *Patriot* Blanchard called the assembly's stand the "Glorious Emancipation" of Nova Scotia and printed material from the *Novascotian* with approval. Blanchard and Howe were still far apart, however, on the remedy to be applied, for while Blanchard was thinking in terms of an "*organised party against misrule* in Nova Scotia," Howe, fearful of party and the party spirit, was still writing that "the party to which we belong is *the Province of Nova Scotia*."

Later in 1830 Blanchard decided to contest one of the four seats for Halifax County and was identified as one of the "popular" candidates in perhaps the province's best-known election. In Halifax, where "official" influence was strong, Blanchard was behind by more than 700 votes, but he received a majority of almost 1,000 in the district of Colchester. However, the real drama occurred in Pictou, where the religious differences between anti-burghers of the Secession Church who supported McCulloch and Kirkmen opposed to McCulloch and Pictou Academy led to the killing of a man and the need to protect the academy and Blanchard's home from violence. Although the Kirkmen outpolled the secessionists in Pictou, Blanchard won the county by 139 votes.

In the 1830–31 session of the legislature Blanchard exerted himself primarily as a legal reformer, wanting especially to establish the entire town of Pictou as jail limits so that, as the *Novascotian* reported, incarcerated debtors could "labour through the Town" and pay their debts during their confinement. Shocked when his efforts were blocked, he then gave his full support to a "cheap law bill," designed to reduce lawyers' fees and reform legal practice generally, which William Henry Roach of Annapolis County had been introducing for some time without success. Although as Nathaniel W. White, a tory, observed, he took "a terrible maulling" from Charles Rufus FAIRBANKS, William Blowers Bliss*, Uniacke, and Alexander Stewart*, the leading lawyer-assemblymen, he "still bellows on, nothing daunted by the array of talent marshalled against him . . . & is carrying a sweeping majority with him." Indeed, he gave as well as he got, calling his opponents "vulgar," "more . . . blackguards than gentlemen," and the champions of "a dirty, pitiful, self raised aristocracy, who want to keep down every body but themselves." Though in December 1830 Blanchard carried the assembly by 23 to 16, the Council blocked the passage of the bill. White noted that, although "a feverish agitator," Blanchard had a clear head which would prevent his espousing "ultra-liberalism" or going "beyond the constitutional barrier." Since he "speaks out boldly and shews foot, tail & all," he was not likely to be dangerous; indeed, "barring his crooked leg [he] looks somewhat like a gentleman." But he had "all the hardihood and obstinacy of . . . the Doctor [McCulloch], whose disciple he is . . . & will in following the temper of the times become the favorite of the herd."

Blanchard himself was decidedly unhappy with the session. The older assemblymen, he said in the *Patriot*, "seemed disposed to rest satisfied with previous laurels," while the newly elected were "unskilled in legislation, and distrustful of their own judgment." But, like Howe, he had misinterpreted the significance of the "Brandy Dispute," in which even the more conservative assemblymen had opposed the Council's intemperate action, and hence he expected the new assembly to be much more liberal than it actually was. During the session word had got out that McCulloch, frustrated by years of pressing the legislature unsuccessfully for an unfettered charter and permanent financial support for Pictou Academy, had decided to approach the Colonial Office directly and that Blanchard had volunteered as his emissary. As a result, a hundred "most respectable gentleman" of Pictou burned Blanchard in effigy in the middle of the town and drew his jocular response in the *Patriot* of 19 Feb. 1831: "To be ranked with Popes, and Kings, and Dukes, and Governors, is an honour which does not come the way every day to Editors."

To McCulloch and Blanchard the time seemed propitious since their counterparts, the whigs, had come to power in Britain. Leaving Halifax on 3 March, Blanchard first went to Scotland, where he secured the support of the United Associate Synod of the Secession Church for his mission. But his relations with Lord Goderich, the colonial secretary, were unexpectedly cool because he was not following recognized procedures. Consequently he had to spend some months kicking his heels in London awaiting an official statement by the Nova Scotian government before being permitted to present his own memorial. Still, according to Patterson, "he was the pioneer and Howe but his follower" in breaking the exclusive connection between the Council and the Colonial Office. Goderich eventually gave "a half and half message": he wanted a permanent grant to the academy and expected it to be made without unacceptable conditions being attached to the constitution of the academy's board of trustees, but he hoped to have it done so as to "meet and conciliate the wishes and feelings of both Parties," something that was clearly unrealizable. For Blanchard personally the trip had one significant consequence: in Scotland he had fallen ill at the home of Mrs Margaret Spears, where he was lodging; the following year his father went to Britain and brought her back to marry him.

Likely Blanchard's health was already beginning to deteriorate as the session of 1832 began and its frustrations may have accelerated a decline. Opposing him at every turn was James Boyle Uniacke*, who, he said, sought to exterminate his opponents by pure bombast and whose "low and paltry remarks" were "an insult to [the members'] understandings and feelings." Despite the implacable opposition of 15 assemblymen he got a Pictou Academy bill from the assembly that he could have lived with, only to have the Council render it utterly objectionable. As finally passed, the act not only facilitated the appointment of Kirkmen to the academy's board of trustees, but limited financial support to ten years and allocated it so as to leave only a small portion for the higher branches of learning.

Blanchard's greatest trouble in 1832, however, was with the bill to incorporate the Bank of Nova Scotia, which many of his constituents wanted him to support in order to provide competition for the private Halifax Banking Company, five of whose directors sat on the Council. When he found that the assemblymen generally knew little about banking, he resorted to a study of the authorities on the subject and then told his friends in the assembly that not until they had devoted as many hours to it as he had "will I quail before them." His particular object was to ensure a large paid-up capital and heavy shareholder liability to prevent the losses which widows and orphans in the United States had suffered because of bank failures, and to that end he engaged in vigorous debates with the assemblymen who were shareholders of the new bank. He might have spared his efforts, for on its own the Council made certain that the Bank of Nova Scotia started in August 1832 with "more safeguards against disaster than any bank of its time in British North America." But he did not escape charges of being in league with Enos Collins and the directors of the Halifax Banking Company. No less annoying was Howe's description of him and other assemblymen as "Legislative Fourteen Pounders" for voting themselves a fortnight's extra indemnity at £1 a day. Frustrated, Blanchard replied that the town of Halifax should be the last to complain since the bank bill, designed primarily to promote its interests, had unduly prolonged the session. Besides, too many non-Halifax seats were held by Haligonians and nothing should be done to discourage country residents from offering themselves as candidates.

At least the session led to acceptance of a modified

version of Roach's legal bill and, although Blanchard did not initiate them, of provisions he had long advocated for insolvent debtors which remained unaltered for many years: in future, no debtor could be kept in jail who, without fraud, had given up all his property. During the summer of 1832 Blanchard rejoiced in the reinstatement of the Grey ministry in Britain and the passage of the Reform Bill; he was also pleased to write two signed editorials advocating the introduction of the itinerating libraries he had observed working so well there. But the rest of his life brought him little satisfaction. In the autumn he was again in conflict with Howe, who accused him unfairly of upholding the abuses of the Court of Chancery. If all editors were "as ready to run a tilt" as Howe, he replied, the press would "degenerate into a mere outlet for the spleen of professional ill will."

In 1833 the economic and currency crises dominated the assembly's proceedings and Blanchard presented a logically reasoned proposal which would have forbidden banks to issue notes of less than £5 in value. This proposal was eventually incorporated in a bill which required banks to redeem their notes in specie. Late in the session, however, he accepted the Council's amendments which permitted both banks to make the redemption in provincial treasury notes. The councillors appeared to some to be legislating in their own interest, and Blanchard had scorn heaped on him for suggesting that men like Enos Collins and Samuel Cunard* would not place "their little twopenny bank" before their larger interests. Derisively Howe denounced Nova Scotia's legislators who "with a stroke of the pen turned every thing to paper." Did Blanchard not know that some assemblymen were "moved like puppets by the wires from the other end of the building – and that in no two Sessions had the ancient system of feasting and drenching with Champagne . . . been carried to such an extent" as in 1832 and 1833?

Editorially Blanchard continued to be a strong supporter of Louis-Joseph Papineau* and William Lyon Mackenzie*, contending that the North American colonies would never be "as they ought to be, until every species of internal management is transferred to the Colonists themselves." But generally his editorial writing had lost its old sting and he was showing an increasing tendency to shun extreme solutions. He thought it "brutish" to raise an outcry against such men as Earl Grey and Lord Brougham because they did not "at one swoop, destroy all existing Institutions." In July 1833 he denounced the radicals – even though "we hold the same opinions in the main, which they do" – for their "reckless course" in putting undue pressure on the whig government. That September he advocated settling the Secessionist–Kirk dispute peaceably, even to the extent of religious union, all of which was anathema to McCulloch, who privately suggested that Blanchard's manner of gaining his assembly seat would have been enough to turn anyone's head and who complained because Blanchard, after promising to present Pictou Academy's case in London for £250, had demanded £560. Because of Blanchard's almost too fulsome praise of Thomas Nickleson JEFFERY, who was acting as administrator of the province, even the Tory Hugh DENOON wondered if "the limping editor . . . expects favours from [Jeffery]."

In 1834 Blanchard still showed a few vestiges of vigour in the house. He strongly supported Fairbanks's proposal to borrow £100,000 in England to fix up the great roads once and for all: "We must come to it at last – and I think the sooner the better." He told Alexander Stewart that mere tinkering with the Council would not reform the province's constitution: "The principle of election is the only one by which [the basic defects] can be completely remedied. From this opinion I have never deviated, and am unwilling to depart." He wanted the judges' fees, which were sanctified by no law and which he contended bore most heavily on the poor, to be commuted. To Howe's disgust, he favoured acceptance of the British government's proposal to commute the quitrents for an annual payment of £2,000 to the crown as a means of relieving the minds of thousands of Nova Scotians, but he would have reduced the burden to £890 by making the payment of £2,000 bear the cost of commutation of the judges' fees and the salaries of the attorney general and solicitor general.

It was almost his last gasp. The *Patriot* ceased publication in mid 1834, perhaps because of his physical incapacity, and he did not make one appearance during the session of 1835. McCulloch, never kindly disposed towards one who failed to do his bidding, suggested privately that if Blanchard had been of "sterner stuff," he could have made himself the "first political man in the province." But he had wanted "a judgeship or something like it," and began to "puff up" Bishop John INGLIS and other academy opponents, accepted a few dinners, and became a "harmless man" without "one particle of influence" in the assembly. A much more sympathetic Howe wrote to Blanchard that he had hoped he would supply the knowledge and leadership that ordinary people lacked, and he was shocked when he seemed to become "a covert enemy to popular measures" or at least "a very suspicious and languid supporter" of principles he had long advocated. Only recently had he learned that Blanchard's health had deprived him of the energy which the times demanded and he regretted the harshness of his criticism.

Tradition has it that in 1836 Blanchard travelled to Halifax in a covered carriage equipped with a small stove and that he was content to do his constituents' business from his quarters. Actually he was in the assembly on a score of days when divisions took place, although he intervened actively only once. Fearful of an act passed the previous session in his absence which allowed a single judge to travel the Supreme Court circuits, he emphasized the danger of giving one man omnipotent power without adequate means of appeal. A sympathetic house let him speak sitting down, referred the matter to committee, but took no positive action. With that Blanchard disappeared from public view; in 1838 he lapsed into imbecility and died a year later.

Suggestions that Blanchard "left his mark writ large upon the history of Nova Scotia" are not borne out by fact; indeed, he ended up as a largely tragic figure. Starting with the belief, held also by McCulloch, that education would bring the liberalism that was dominant in everyone to the surface, he quickly found out that the factions in the legislature were impervious to facts or persuasion, and that any amount of logical argument was ineffectual against entrenched religious and economic interests. Elected one assembly too early, he was the only member of advanced political views and more often than not beat his head against a stone. Later, when he was more accommodating, deteriorating health rendered him less effective. Open-minded, he was not averse to complimenting his usual opponents when he thought they deserved it and on that account incurred criticism for inconsistency. Nevertheless, he did have at least limited success as a legal reformer, and although he did not "convert" Joseph Howe singlehanded he did contribute significantly to opening Howe's eyes to the magnitude of the province's political ills. Only his limited physical resources prevented him from being more than someone who would hint at the major political changes which were to come in the 1840s.

J. MURRAY BECK

PANS, MG 1, 553, 955. *Colonial Patriot*, 1827–34. *Novascotian, or Colonial Herald*, 1828–36. B. F. MacDonald, "Intellectual forces in Pictou, 1803–1843" (MA thesis, Univ. of N.B., Fredericton, 1977). Thomas Miller, *Historical and genealogical record of the first settlers of Colchester County* ... (Halifax, 1837; repr. Belleville, Ont., 1972). G. [G.] Patterson, "Jotham Blanchard," in his *Studies in Nova Scotian history* (Halifax, 1940), 34–46.

BLANCHARD, TRANQUILLE, merchant; b. *c.* 1773, probably in Caraquet (N.B.), son of Olivier Blanchard and Catherine-Josephe Amirault; m. *c.* 1800 Marie-Modeste Robichaux, daughter of Jean-Baptiste Robichaux*, and they had three sons and seven daughters, two of whom died in infancy; d. 21 May 1843 in Caraquet.

Tranquille Blanchard had a career linked with Charles Robin and Company. His family's connection with this powerful enterprise went back to 1766; that year his father was employed as pilot of the *Seaflower* by Charles Robin*, who came on behalf of Robin, Pipon and Company to explore commercial prospects in the Baie des Chaleurs. The master of a schooner and a carpenter, Olivier Blanchard was one of the founders of Caraquet [*see* Alexis Landry*], and as such apparently always enjoyed the greatest respect in the community.

Tranquille, the fifth of nine children, found himself the sole male heir to the family assets when he reached adulthood. In 1814 he went into business on his own, "at home." A few years later he bought a small store at Pointe de Roche which he used as a trading-post and warehouse for his goods. From 1818 he served as middleman for Charles Robin and Company in the Caraquet region. The firm, which was based at Paspébiac in Lower Canada, was the largest exporter of fish in the Baie des Chaleurs area. It had set up a system of barter, advancing fishermen the products they needed in exchange for their catch. Blanchard was responsible for delivering to its customers the salt and bales of merchandise stored for them in its two small depots at Caraquet. In return the company assisted him in his own business, selling him the goods he ordered from Paspébiac and buying the dried cod brought in by his own customers. Although regarded as the company's authorized agent for northeastern New Brunswick, Blanchard was never actually an employee. He received some remuneration for his services as its forwarding agent and warehouse man, but his income came principally from his business. Because of the concentration of the company's local trade in his hands and his high level of turnover – about £1,000 to £1,200 sterling annually in the years before 1834 – he enjoyed exceptional discount rates on the goods he bought to sell to his customers (10 per cent, except on salt).

In the period 1826–37 Blanchard provided from 500 to 2,500 quintals of dried cod a year to Charles Robin and Company, and thus was one of its major suppliers. He dealt regularly with some 30 owners of fishing establishments. His business grew steadily, reaching a peak at the end of his career: £2,200 on average from 1834 to 1836 and £2,900 in 1837. In addition to dried cod and cod liver oil he delivered rabbit, marten, fox, and lynx pelts to the company, as well as substantial quantities of maple syrup. These minor items of trade, which he tried to promote among his customers so as to lighten the burden of their debts to him, remained secondary and became rapidly less significant towards the end of the 1830s.

Blanchard's role as middleman between the company and its customers in the Caraquet region put him in an uncomfortable position. He had to apply locally the credit policy of his own creditor. Urged to be parsimonious in allocating merchandise, to press its customers to meet their obligations, and to select those to be given credit strictly on the basis of their performance in economic terms and their solvency, he claimed that his ability to carry out the task was limited by his links with the people of his community. Although he on occasion threatened to penalize his dishonest customers in order to induce them to pay their accounts, he put his main efforts into advising them to manage their family enterprises more responsibly. In hard times, when the community was having trouble securing bare necessities, Blanchard was ready to yield to the pleas of the poorest families. His creditor then reproached him for acquiring bad debts and retaining insolvent customers, but he hastily replied that this generosity was necessary to meet the competition from the other merchants and to keep the company's clients. The competition he anticipated, whether imaginary or real, sometimes served simply as a pretext for him to ask his creditor for delivery of other necessities at the end of the fishing season.

The social pressures to which Blanchard was subject as a full member of the Acadian community of Caraquet forced him to give credit to his own most impoverished customers. They explain his precarious financial position and limited economic ambitions. In 1834 Blanchard, in delicate health, drew up his will. He made over two small houses of similar size near his residence to two of his sons, Agapit and Tranquille, on condition that they live with him until they married.

In 1838 Charles Robin and Company decided to establish a company agent at Caraquet and to put up a store and warehouses there. Consequently Blanchard was delegated to prepare for the transfer and get the store built according to plans conceived by the management in Jersey; it was at this time, it seems, that he gave up his own store and went out of business. On arrival, the new manager, Francis Briard, contacted the company's clients, who had been Blanchard's customers. He soon realized how generous Blanchard had been in distributing merchandise in the course of the previous winter, and the company later blamed him for not adequately informing it about the true quality of the clientele he had encountered on arrival.

Tranquille Blanchard was a deeply religious man. The misfortunes that seemed to dog him – particularly deaths in his family – had shaken and disillusioned him, but they had also engendered real compassion for others in distress. Possessed of a keen sense of right and wrong, he had always made absolute integrity the keystone of his business activity and had reacted strongly against dishonesty on the part of his clients or any attack upon his reputation as a businessman. If he had often dared elude customs officers and engage in smuggling rum, it was because he considered the institution they represented could only be deleterious to trade and to the well-being of the people.

ANDRÉ LEPAGE and CLARENCE LEBRETON

PAC, MG 28, III18. "Document inédit," *La Rev. d'hist. de la Soc. hist. Nicolas-Denys* (Bertrand, N.-B.), 2 (1974), no.1: 22–25. Patrice Gallant, *Les registres de la Gaspésie (1752–1850)* (6v., Sayabec, Qué., 1968). Fidèle Thériault, *Les familles de Caraquet: dictionnaire généalogique . . .* (Fredericton, 1985). Antoine Bernard, *Histoire de la survivance acadienne, 1755–1935* (Montréal, 1935). W. F. Ganong, *The history of Caraquet and Pokemouche*, ed. S. B. Ganong (Saint John, N.B., 1948). David Lee, *The Robins in Gaspé, 1766–1825* (Markham, Ont., 1984). André Lepage, "Le capitalisme marchand et la pêche à la morue en Gaspésie: la Charles Robin and Company dans la baie des Chaleurs (1820–1870)" (thèse de PHD, univ. Laval, Québec, 1983). Fidèle Thériault, "Olivier Blanchard, 1726–1796," *La Rev. d'hist. de la Soc. hist. Nicolas-Denys*, 6 (1978), no.3: 9–17.

BLOWERS, SAMPSON SALTER, lawyer, office holder, politician, and judge; b. 10 March 1741/42 in Boston, son of John Blowers and Sarah Salter; m. there 5 April 1774 Sarah Kent, daughter of Benjamin Kent, a barrister of Boston; they had no children but adopted Sarah Ann Anderson; d. 25 Oct. 1842 in Halifax.

Sampson Salter Blowers's father died shortly after returning from the siege of Louisbourg, Île Royale (Cape Breton Island), in 1745, and some time afterwards the boy became an orphan. Brought up by his maternal grandfather, Sampson Salter, he attended the Boston Grammar School and graduated from Harvard College with a BA in 1763 and an MA in 1765. Blowers then studied law in the office of Thomas Hutchinson and in 1766 was admitted as an attorney in the Suffolk Inferior Court. Four years later he became a barrister in the Massachusetts Superior Court. Blowers made spectacular progress as a trial lawyer, and in 1770 was associated with John Adams and Josiah Quincy in defending the soldiers of the 29th Foot accused of murder in the Boston "massacre." By that time the income from his law practice was £400 annually, one of the largest in Boston.

In June 1774 the Boston courts were closed after the Massachusetts Government Act abrogated the colony's charter. Blowers had been much criticized for his loyalist sentiments, and this event persuaded him to leave Massachusetts. Five months later he sailed for England with his wife, Sarah. They lived on his small savings and a bequest to her of a few thousand pounds which was "chiefly secured on Mortgage." However, it became increasingly difficult to collect rents and interest on property in Massachusetts. Finding himself "without the means of earning a shilling," Blowers asked the Treasury for assistance and was granted an annual allowance of £100.

The British occupation of New York City and Newport, R.I., in 1776 made Blowers optimistic about his prospects, and he left England with his wife in 1777, believing that he would be "useful as well to

Government as to himself by residing in America." They settled in Newport. In April 1778 Blowers went to Boston, where Sarah had been taken ill during a visit. Although he had obtained a pass from the American authorities, on his arrival he was arrested and "put into a dismal stinking lower room." He refused to appeal for redress and said that his one wish "was to get out of the country as soon as possible." Exchanged to Halifax, he returned to England and was sent back to Newport with a commission as judge of the Vice-Admiralty Court. A few days after his arrival, however, the Newport garrison was evacuated to New York. On 13 March 1781 he was appointed solicitor general of New York through the influence of Lord George Germain, secretary of state for the American colonies. Blowers could not practise because New York was under military rule, but he found "sufficient and profitable employment" in the Vice-Admiralty Court. Serving as judge while the incumbent was absent in England, he made large sums from fees levied when prize ships were declared forfeit.

In September 1783 Blowers sailed for Halifax, bearing a letter of recommendation from Sir Guy Carleton*. Notwithstanding Governor John Parr*'s polite reception, Blowers was doubtful about his prospects, and commented to fellow lawyer Ward Chipman* that "there is very little business in our way to be done here, and that but indifferently paid for, and there is no want of lawyers." However, he was soon in demand. In 1785 he acted in 100 cases in the Supreme Court, about half as many as Solicitor General Richard John Uniacke*. Blowers had mixed success in recovering his wartime losses. The loyalist claims commission disallowed his claim for nearly £4,800 in real estate and personal property, but he was granted an annual pension of £100. After the peace he had obtained £1,000 in payment of debts, but in 1788 he was still trying to collect money owed on real estate, bonds, and mortgages in the United States.

Blowers's eminent position in the legal field rapidly made him the recipient of government favour. In 1784 he was appointed attorney general of the newly formed province of New Brunswick through the influence in England of Sir William Pepperrell, an important New England loyalist. However, he refused the post, explaining that he was weary of the frequent moves he had made, "and having taken up my abode in Halifax I could not subject my family to the inconvenience of beginning a new Settlement at St. John." That December he was appointed attorney general of Nova Scotia on the removal of Richard Gibbons* to Cape Breton. His promotion touched off a quarrel with Uniacke which lasted until the latter's death. Uniacke had expected to succeed Gibbons, and in compensation he was named advocate general of the Vice-Admiralty Court by Parr. Blowers objected, declaring that the attorney general should also be advocate general, and he wrote to the home secretary that no one "ever has been or will be found more deficient in Loyalty" than Uniacke. The latter retaliated by accusing Blowers of supporting smuggling. In 1790 the two clashed again when Blowers hired a black servant whom Uniacke had dismissed. Uniacke said some "rude things" and Blowers challenged him to a duel. The meeting was prevented, and Chief Justice Thomas Andrew Lumisden STRANGE bound the two men over to keep the peace. Matters ended the same way in 1798 when Blowers challenged Uniacke to a duel after Uniacke had severely beaten Jonathan Sterns, Blowers's protégé, in a street fight.

In 1785 Blowers had entered politics when he was elected to the House of Assembly for Halifax County, and he was chosen speaker when the new house met. The early years of the sixth assembly were peaceful, but in 1787 dissatisfaction with the administration of justice led the house to ask Parr for an investigation into the conduct of judge James Brenton* and acting chief justice Isaac Deschamps*. On 3 Jan. 1788 Blowers became the first loyalist to be appointed to the Council, and once there he "took a decided part" in defending the judges against the assembly's attacks. Some loyalist assemblymen were critical of his actions. Isaac Wilkins thought that he had not defended the assembly's position strongly enough in the Council, and Thomas Henry Barclay* accused him of "having tacitly sanctioned the proceedings of the house . . . and now taking distinct part on the contrary side." There was some belief that Blowers's lack of enthusiasm for the assembly's cause might have been due to personal motives. At the time of his retirement in 1797, Strange noted that if Blowers had not hoped to succeed to the then vacant chief justiceship, the attorney general "at least drew from the zeal with which he endeavoured to maintain [the judges'] innocence" the thought that he might be considered for the post.

As matters turned out, Blowers was appointed chief justice, but not until 9 Sept. 1797, after Strange's resignation had been received. He had been well recommended by Lieutenant Governor Sir John Wentworth* and by Strange, who thought him the best person the British government could "procure for the Office, from this Country." As chief justice, Blowers became president of the Council. Strange's testimony of 1797 indicates that on the Council his services had been "of real utility in conducting the business, whether of Government or Legislation." Blowers maintained a sense of his position as president, and when in 1808 a junior councillor, judge Alexander CROKE, became administrator in the absence of Lieutenant Governor Sir George Prevost*, he refused to attend Council meetings. Writing in 1826 to his fellow judge Peleg Wiswall, he commented that in the Council he confined himself "to the duty of president without entering into the debates respecting a new issue of paper money, or the mighty subject of the Shubenacadie Canal." In addition to being chief justice and councillor, Blowers served as judge of the Vice-Admiralty Court between 1821 and 1833.

Blowers was an original member of the board of governors of King's College at Windsor, and he faithfully attended meetings held in that town. As one of the committee for drafting the statutes of the college in 1803, he agreed with Croke that King's should be an institution for liberal education rather than the seminary envisaged by Bishop Charles Inglis*. All, however, agreed that students must subscribe to the Thirty-Nine Articles of the Church of England. This stipulation effectively excluded three-quarters of the population from the college, and in 1817 Lieutenant Governor Lord Dalhousie [RAMSAY] proposed that a non-denominational college be established at Halifax. Blowers recognized the threat posed to King's, and in May 1818 he and William Cochran*, vice-president of the college, submitted a resolution for repealing the statutes requiring adherence to the Thirty-Nine Articles. However, the archbishop of Canterbury, the patron of King's, refused to agree to the proposal. In 1824 an attempt was made to unite King's and the non-denominational Dalhousie College in Halifax, but Blowers objected, declaring that any such action would be too near to a breach of trust by the governors of King's.

As chief justice, Blowers commanded great respect. Looking back on the early years of the 19th century, John George Marshall* wrote that in 1804 Blowers was "truly eminent for a high standard of legal knowledge, logical skill, and power of argument and chasteness and attractiveness of language. . . . During those earliest years the Chief Justice tried all the causes, and delivered the decisions on legal argument; on these latter occasions, the two associates merely assenting." Nearly all of the cases tried before Blowers were for debt, with a few for trespass and smuggling, and some on appeal from the Inferior Court of Common Pleas. In 1809 Blowers was head of a special 15-man commission which sat to try Edward Jordan for piracy. When William Wilkie* was tried for printed libel in 1820, Blowers presided. The Halifax lawyer and historian Thomas Beamish Akins* thought that in trying this case the chief justice departed somewhat from the impartiality of the bench, but Blowers ended his address by telling the jury to acquit Wilkie if they honestly thought he had written for the public good.

Slavery was an important issue to Blowers. While attorney general he had had frequent conversations with Strange on the subject, and found that the chief justice did not want to make a decision on the legality of slavery but rather "wished to wear out the claim [of slave-holders] gradually." When Blowers became chief justice he adopted this policy. On one occasion a black woman arrested in Annapolis Royal was claimed as a slave, and Blowers hinted that an action should be brought to try this claim. The plaintiff could not prove that he had had a legal right to purchase the woman, and his case collapsed. Because in part of Blowers's demands for the proof of its legality, slavery died out in Nova Scotia relatively soon in the 19th century, in contrast to New Brunswick, where Chief Justice George Duncan Ludlow* held that slavery was legal.

In addition to sitting at Halifax, the judges of the Supreme Court went on circuit to most counties, and after 1816 to the entire province. Any two judges were authorized to hold sittings, and in order to aid with the work-load a third assistant judge was appointed in 1809 and an associate judge in 1816. Even then there were always difficulties in finding enough judges when illness or old age prevented any of them from travelling. Blowers himself was increasingly absent from circuit courts and even from the court at Halifax as the 1820s progressed. By 1830 he admitted that for several years past he had been "obliged to decline the Trial of Causes owing to the decay of my hearing and sight," but asserted that he attended the Council and considered legal matters with his fellow judges.

By this time, however, pressure was mounting on the chief justice to resign, in particular from his subordinate Brenton Halliburton*. But Blowers was not ready to step down. Writing in 1831 to his brother Henry*, William Blowers Bliss*, who had married Blowers's adopted daughter, claimed that Blowers had "no intention of resigning" and added that he was "sore at this hunting for his place." But in October 1832 Blowers accepted the inevitable and asked Lieutenant Governor Sir Peregrine Maitland*, who was returning to England, to indicate to the British government that he wished to resign. Administrator Thomas Nickleson JEFFERY was instructed by London to accept Blowers's resignation after the assembly had been asked to grant him a pension. However, the old loyalist believed that he was entitled to a pension from the crown and stepped down "without waiting for any colonial remuneration which there was little reason to expect." His prediction was accurate, for the assembly refused to grant a pension, but none was forthcoming from England. Halliburton succeeded as chief justice, and since there was now a vacancy on the Supreme Court, Blowers petitioned Jeffery and Lord Goderich, the colonial secretary, to appoint his son-in-law, Bliss, to the judgeship. Bliss did not receive the post at this time because he lacked seniority, but he was nominated on 15 May 1834.

After his retirement, Blowers continued to spend the summers at his farm in Windsor and the winters at his Halifax house. In October 1842, seven months after reaching his 100th birthday, he broke his hip in a fall and died on the 25th. He left a life interest in his property to his wife and small legacies to his sisters, nieces, and nephews, but most of his estate went to his adopted child, who "was unto him as a daughter." Her husband estimated that nearly £40,000 was involved, part of which consisted of "nearly £10,000 invested in the Funds in Great Britain and between £2000 and £3000" with London bankers.

PHYLLIS R. BLAKELEY

Sampson Salter Blowers kept a diary of his 1776 "Journey to & Thro' part of France &c," preserved in PANS, MG 1, 139B. The journal has been printed in PANS, Board of Trustees, *Report* (Halifax), 1948: 13–38.

Halifax County Court of Probate (Halifax), Estate papers, B83 (mfm. at PANS). PANS, MG 1, 979–80, esp. 979, folder 3; 1598–600; 1603, esp. nos.56, 56b; RG 39, AP, C, 1; HX, J, 12; 14–15; 17, 9 Sept. 1797; 24–26; 99–100. PRO, CO 217/37: 87–89, 123–24; 217/149: 170–77; 217/154: 715–29, 803–10. Boston, Registry Dept., *Records relating to the early history of Boston*, ed. W. H. Whitmore *et al.* (39v., Boston, 1876–1909), [24]: *Boston births, 1700–1800*, 239, 242, 251; [30]: *Boston marriages, 1752–1809*, 16, 56, 325, 393, 402. *Acadian Recorder*, 11 Nov. 1820; 16 April, 29 Oct. 1842. *Novascotian*, 7, 21 Feb. 1833; 27 Oct. 1842. E. A. Jones, *The loyalists of Massachusetts: their memorials, petitions and claims* (London, 1930; repr. Baltimore, Md., 1969). C. K. Shipton, *Sibley's Harvard graduates* . . . (17v. to date, Cambridge and Boston, Mass., 1933–), vol.15. Beck, *Government of N.S.* Cuthbertson, *Old attorney general.* John Doull, *Sketches of attorney generals of Nova Scotia* (Halifax, 1964), 19–25. H. Y. Hind, *The University of King's College, Windsor, Nova Scotia, 1790–1890* (New York, 1890), 32–34, 50–54, 60–62. J. G. Marshall, *A brief history of public proceedings and events, legal, – parliamentary, – and miscellaneous, in the province of Nova Scotia, during the earliest years of the present century* (Halifax, [1878?]). C. J. Townshend, *History of the Court of Chancery of Nova Scotia* (Toronto, 1900). Margaret Ells, "Nova Scotian 'Sparks of Liberty,'" *Dalhousie Rev.*, 16 (1936–37): 475–92. G. V. V. Nicholls, "A forerunner of Joseph Howe," *CHR*, 8 (1927): 224–32.

BOBBIE. *See* EENOOLOOAPIK

BOISSEAU, NICOLAS-GASPARD, author, notary, politician, and office holder; b. 10 Oct. 1765 in Saint-Pierre, Île d'Orléans, son of Nicolas-Gaspard Boisseau* and Claire Jolliette; m. 11 Jan. 1790 Catherine Gaspé, daughter of Ignace-Philippe Aubert* de Gaspé, in Saint-Jean-Port-Joli, Que., and they had 11 children, 4 of whom died in infancy; d. 9 March 1842 in the parish of Saint-Thomas (at Montmagny), Lower Canada.

Nicolas-Gaspard Boisseau began studies at the Petit Séminaire de Québec but had to stop when the town was besieged by the Americans in 1775 [*see* Benedict Arnold*; Richard Montgomery*]. He returned to Île d'Orléans, where his father took charge of his education. He went back to the Petit Séminaire in 1778 and studied there until 1780. He then started working for his father, who was clerk of the Court of Common Pleas in the district of Quebec and clerk of the peace.

Relying on this experience with his father, Boisseau sought a commission as notary from Governor Lord Dorchester [Carleton*] on 14 Jan. 1787. It appears that his years as a clerk could not replace articling, a normal requirement for candidates, and consequently he did not get his commission until 22 July 1791, after sitting for examinations and being interviewed at length.

From 1787 to 1789, while waiting to be licensed, Boisseau wrote memoirs. These are essentially notes based on newspapers and on books he had probably borrowed from his father's library, but they do reveal his interests. In them are to be found a little of the history of the world and of his own country, and a little geography, such as descriptions of Quebec and Montreal and of some remarkable physical features of the land. Boisseau had a predilection for information on the earth and skies. Consequently he comments on the climate, stars, volcanoes, storms, and even unusually heavy snowfalls. Only the political chronicle takes more space than the material on natural science. He relates the great political and military events, past or present, at home or abroad, and pays particular attention to the comings and goings of the governor and of Prince William Henry during his visit in 1787.

Boisseau was interested in curious facts and amusing anecdotes. A few pages of ethnography describing courtship, rural customs, tree planting in May, and the production of charcoal and maple sugar furnish some worthwhile observations – if they are his own. Boisseau, however, says little about himself. He alludes to his health and his difficulties in obtaining his notary's commission. He gives a brief self-portrait that is limited to a description of his physical features, as are the portraits he draws of his parents. This man of the *ancien régime* was less interested in people than memorialists in the romantic or modern periods would be. It may be that youth or an extrovert nature explain his silence about himself. Boisseau does include a score of letters from family correspondence, considering them worthy of publication in a personal work. But they are treated as of no greater importance than discoveries and inventions, a few statistics on shipping, population figures for the province given in the 1784 census, or the number of cords of wood used to heat homes in the colony. On the other hand, the memoirs show a new sensitivity to rigorous and objective organization and marshalling of facts.

Boisseau's discourses upon nature and the human condition are done in an ethico-philosophical style larded with fables, maxims, proverbs, and the sententious prose in vogue at the end of the 18th century, a style illustrated in France by his contemporaries

Nicolas de Chamfort, Pierre Choderlos de Laclos, and Antoine Rivarol. He may have read La Rochefoucauld's *Maximes* or La Bruyère's *Les caractères*. But it is impossible to know whether extracts from these authors and other passages were simply reprinted in the newspapers of the time and gleaned or pastiched by the apprentice notary. In that case his interest in natural science and moral dissertation would not derive from a deep-seated bent but rather from a banal encounter with ideas regularly seen in the newspapers.

In the first elections for the House of Assembly, held in 1792, Boisseau was elected for the riding of Orléans, which at that time took in the whole island. He gave up politics, however, in 1796, Jérôme Martineau* replacing him as member. From then on Boisseau devoted almost all his energies to his profession as notary. He practised first at Saint-Vallier, and then in 1799 established himself in the parish of Saint-Thomas. He was appointed commissioner for the erection of free schools in the parish in 1803, commissioner to receive the oath of allegiance in 1812, and commissioner for roads and bridges for Devon County in 1817. He thus led a professional life some distance removed from public affairs on the provincial scale. From 1818 to 1820 he had financial difficulties which forced him to part with a good deal of his property at Saint-Thomas and 500 acres in Nelson Township received in 1804.

SERGE GAGNON

Nicolas-Gaspard Boisseau's minute-book, containing instruments for the period 1791–1841, is at ANQ-Q, CN3-7. His memoirs are at PAC, MG 23, GV, 1.

ANQ-Q, CE1-12, 10 oct. 1765; CE2-7, 12 mars 1842; CE2-18, 11 janv. 1790. ASQ, Fichier des anciens. PAC, RG 68, General index, 1651–1841. *Quebec Gazette*, 24 Feb. 1791; 6 Nov. 1817; 16 April, 16 July, 9 Nov. 1818; 7 Sept., 19 Oct. 1820; 4 Jan., 29 March, 31 May, 26 July 1821. F.-J. Audet, "Les législateurs du Bas-Canada." F.-J. Audet et Fabre Surveyer, *Les députés au premier Parl. du Bas-Canada*. Desjardins, *Guide parl.* Langelier, *Liste des terrains concédés*, 1199. Wallace, *Macmillan dict.* P.-G. Roy, *La famille Aubert de Gaspé* (Lévis, Qué., 1907); *La famille Boisseau* (Lévis, 1907).

BONAMI, LOUIS MARTINET, *dit.* *See* MARTINET

BONNYCASTLE, Sir RICHARD HENRY, army officer, military engineer, artist, and author; b. 30 Sept. 1791 in Woolwich (London), England, eldest son of John Bonnycastle, professor of mathematics at the Royal Military Academy there, and his second wife, Bridget Johnstone; m. 1814 Frances Johnstone, and they had two sons and three daughters; d. 3 Nov. 1847 in Kingston, Upper Canada.

Richard Henry Bonnycastle's family was exceptional in that its middle-class status rested on the father's intellectual achievements rather than on business or inheritance and in that it was associated with a unique military institution. The Royal Military Academy was the first tertiary school in the English-speaking world to furnish advanced engineering and scientific courses to prospective officers of the artillery and the engineers, and John Bonnycastle was among the pioneers of this intellectually oriented system of military education. Academy graduates dealt not only with heavy weapons and fortifications but also with roads, harbours, and canals, with cartographical, meteorological, and geological observations, and with drawing and painting because of the need to sketch for military purposes. A place was found for Richard because his father was on the staff, and because he had the ability to fulfil the rigorous entrance requirements. The academy furnished one of the few pathways into the military and social élite, and Richard made the most of the opportunity. His career was not brilliant, but in the way he applied his education for the benefit of civilian society, especially in Upper Canada, he was the model of a helpful Board of Ordnance officer. Indeed, he and Lieutenant-Colonel John BY are the outstanding examples in Upper Canada of constructive imperial military officers.

Bonnycastle graduated as a second lieutenant of Royal Engineers on 28 Sept. 1808. In 1809 he served at the siege of Flushing (Vlissingen) in the Netherlands campaign and was promoted first lieutenant. Three years later he went to Nova Scotia and participated in the British occupation of part of Maine in 1814, acting as engineer in charge of fortifications erected on the Castine peninsula. During this service he was promoted second captain. From Maine, Bonnycastle went to the British occupation forces in France. In 1818 he was at Woolwich completing his first literary effort, a two-volume description of Spain's Latin American colonies with historical comments entitled *Spanish America* (London, 1818). He was fluent in French, and appears to have done most of his research from Spanish sources in France.

For the next few years Bonnycastle performed routine duties at home. In 1826 he was sent to Upper Canada, serving at Fort George (Niagara-on-the-Lake) and Kingston until 1832, when he was posted to York (Toronto). By that date he was already well known among the leading colonists. It appears that from the start he took a keen interest in all forms of colonial development, made information from his military surveys available to civilians, and did original research in geology and mineralogy. When he was leaving Kingston, James MACFARLANE, editor of the *Kingston Chronicle*, praised his efforts "to promote the discovery of our Canadian resources" and his geological surveying. At York, Bonnycastle became a prominent freemason, and he was also a major contributor to the artistic community. In January 1834 he was chosen president of the Society of Artists and Amateurs, the first art society in York, and a number of his paintings, depicting Lower Canadian and European subjects, were displayed that July at the society's only exhibition. Bonnycastle attributed his interest in painting to the influence of his godfather the artist Henry Fuseli.

In 1835 Bonnycastle presided over the transfer to the city of two bridges across the Don River, attracting favourable comment by the enthusiasm with which he made this donation on the part of the British government. The bridges were Ordnance property, constructed at British expense. It was departmental policy to hand over such works to civilians as their military use ceased and thus to aid worthy public causes. Bonnycastle promoted other kinds of development, urging Lieutenant Governor Sir John Colborne* in 1835 to request that the British government erect one of its proposed colonial astronomical observatories in Toronto. Such an observatory, he argued, would be invaluable to the university planned for the city, and would serve to lay the foundations for the study of science in Upper Canada. The education of the population, he asserted, would be ample compensation for the money spent. The effect of Bonnycastle's pressure is not known, but in 1840 the Ordnance set up an observatory for terrestrial magnetism and meteorology at Toronto. In 1853 it handed this institution over to the University of Toronto, where it became both a valuable weather station and a teaching department.

Bonnycastle's contributions to civil society were, however, eclipsed by his military achievements in 1837 and 1838. In 1837 he was promoted brevet major and placed in command of the engineers at Kingston, with the specific task of completing construction of the new Fort Henry, begun in 1832. By late 1837 Bonnycastle, directing a force of mostly Irish artisans and labourers, had finished work. Almost immediately afterwards came the rebellions in the Canadas. Lieutenant Governor Sir Francis Bond Head* had previously ordered most of the regulars in Upper Canada to Montreal, leaving in the Kingston area only the Ordnance personnel and a few sailors. On 6 December, Bonnycastle, the senior officer capable of duty, received a letter from Head informing him that rebellion had broken out at Toronto and ordering him to hold Fort Henry and its invaluable military stores against attacks from rebels. He set about building a garrison from local resources with energy and tact, winning strong support from the colonists. By the beginning of 1838 his force consisted of the Fort Henry workers, whom he had armed, militia from the counties around Kingston, the élite Kingstonians serving in the Frontenac Light Dragoons, a detachment of the Perth Artillery, and a unit of regular sailors called the Queen's Marine Artillery, together with some Mohawks from the Bay of Quinte region.

The threat to Kingston was now posed by about 2,000 Upper Canadian refugees and American sympathizers in New York state who sought to liberate Upper Canada. Intending to strike at Fort Henry across the frozen St Lawrence, on 22 Feb. 1838 they left Clayton, N.Y., and seized Hickory Island near Gananoque as a preliminary move. Bonnycastle and the Kingstonians expected a battle, but the Patriots, having infiltrated the defences with spies, withdrew the next day. The Kingstonians heaped praise on Bonnycastle for his vigorous leadership, which had probably persuaded the enemy that an attack would be too costly. His superiors were also impressed. In March 1840 they gave him a knighthood.

That year Sir Richard, who now regarded himself as a permanent resident of Kingston, was promoted lieutenant-colonel, and shortly afterwards he did a tour of duty as commanding engineer in Newfoundland. Between 1841 and 1846 he made his main literary contribution, publishing with Henry Colburn in London *The Canadas in 1841* (2v., 1842), *Newfoundland in 1842: a sequel to "The Canadas in 1841"* (2v., 1842), and *Canada and the Canadians, in 1846* (2v., 1846). He retired from the engineers in June 1847 and died in Kingston soon after, at the age of 56. A fellow officer and friend, Sir James Edward Alexander, edited Bonnycastle's voluminous notes and published them in *Canada as it was, is, and may be* (2v., London, 1852). These works are not great literature, but they were competent and informative tracts which helped to publicize British North America in Britain and to attract middle-class immigrants and investment capital.

Bonnycastle was an enthusiast for imperial development and a believer in progress through education and hard work. He had all the Victorian middle-class virtues, and his writings show few of the prejudices which often went with them. Although only his posthumous volumes dwelt on history in any detail, all his Canadian works are helpful sources for the period. They are equally valuable for the attitudes they reflect, which are those of an imperial official with a most useful colonial career and the founder of a respected middle-class Ontario family.

G. K. Raudzens

[The two main sources for Bonnycastle's life are compilations of information in the Bonnycastle papers at AO, MU 281. The first is a family history by a descendant, Evelyn Frances Bonnycastle Luttrell. She identifies most of her sources clearly. The second is a biography, probably based on the Luttrell document, by J. E. R. Munro, entitled "Sir Richard Henry Bonnycastle, Lieutenant-Colonel Royal Engineers." There are no dates of compilation on either document, but they appear to come from the late 1950s or early 1960s.

There are entries for Bonnycastle in the standard Canadian biographical dictionaries, in the *DNB*, and in Norah Story, *The Oxford companion to Canadian history and literature* (Toronto and London, 1967). He figures in books on the Ordnance Department such as Whitworth Porter *et al.*, *History of the Corps of Royal Engineers* (9v. to date, London and Chatham, Eng., 1899– ; vols.1–3 repr. Chatham, 1951–54), 1–2; R. [F.] Legget, *Rideau waterway* (Toronto, 1955); and G. [K.] Raudzens, *The British Ordnance Department and Canada's canals, 1815–1855* (Waterloo, Ont., 1979). His name appears regularly in the Canadian press during the 1830s and 1840s, for example in the *Kingston Chronicle* and its successor the *Chronicle & Gazette*, the *British Colonist*, the *Montreal Gazette*, and the *Toronto Patriot*. References to primary documents are cited in the works noted above. G.K.R.]

BORGIA, JOSEPH LE VASSEUR. *See* LE VASSEUR

BOSTWICK, JOHN, surveyor, office holder, militia officer, politician, JP, and businessman; b. 24 Feb. 1780 in Great Barrington, Mass., son of Gideon Bostwick and Gesie Burghardt; m. first *c.* 1802 Mary Ryerson, and they had four sons and three daughters; m. secondly after 1821 Polly ——; d. 9 Sept. 1849 in Port Stanley, Upper Canada.

In 1788 John Bostwick's father, a Church of England minister, joined Edward Jessup* and others in petitioning, unsuccessfully, for a tract on the Ottawa River. Gideon Bostwick was granted Oxford Township, in southwest Upper Canada, in 1793 but he died that year before he could move there from Great Barrington. A resourceful pioneer, John came to Upper Canada four years later, settling in the Long Point area on the north shore of Lake Erie. He became apprenticed to the surveyor William Hambly, who between 1793 and 1812 laid out more than 30 townships, including several in the London District.

Bostwick rapidly established himself in the district's incipient society, which was concentrated in the Long Point area around Vittoria, the district's capital, and included a large proportion of American-born settlers. His personal progress is reflected by his appointment as high constable of the district in October 1800 and as deputy sheriff by April 1801. He patented 600 acres at the mouth of Kettle Creek, in Yarmouth Township, in September 1804. That same year he joined three other prominent residents of the London District, including Thomas Talbot*, on a commission to recommend a route for a new road from Port Talbot to the Long Point area. The Bostwick Road, as it was called, was not completed because of a lack of funds but a trail followed its route. In 1805, at the age of 25, he succeeded as sheriff Joseph Ryerson, prominent Charlotteville loyalist whose daughter he had married.

At the outbreak of the War of 1812 Bostwick volunteered for service. As captain of a flank company of the 1st Norfolk Militia, he quickly acquired experience at the capture of Detroit in August 1812. In September Major-General Isaac Brock*, in a request for reinforcements from Talbot, who supervised the militia in the London District, declared, "You cannot send a better Capt. than Bothwick." Two months later his company took part in the battle of Frenchman Creek, near Fort Erie, suffering severe losses and earning the praise of Lieutenant-Colonel Cecil Bisshopp*. At Nanticoke 12 months later, after British regulars had withdrawn to the head of Lake Ontario, Bostwick narrowly escaped being shot in the capture of a band of marauders by a volunteer force under his brother Henry.

Bostwick continued surveying after the war but was not officially examined as a surveyor until 1819. In 1816 he performed two assignments on his own in the surveys of Westminster Township and the Talbot Road. The following year he moved from Long Point to his land at Kettle Creek. The Bostwicks were the first settlers at that location, their nearest neighbours being eight miles away on the Talbot Road east.

Bostwick remained sheriff of the London District until 1818. Two years later he and fellow surveyor Mahlon BURWELL were elected to the House of Assembly for Middlesex. Both tories and members of the regional oligarchy which supported Thomas Talbot, Bostwick and Burwell were opposed by candidates backed by the Scottish settlers of Aldborough Township, to whom Talbot had issued few deeds. Because these settlers technically held so little land, they were not allowed to vote. Bostwick did not run for election in 1824 and was defeated in 1830 and again in 1836.

In 1821 Bostwick's first wife, Mary, died, leaving him with considerable responsibilities including the care of 7 children ranging in age from 5 to 20 years and the task of settlement at Kettle Creek. That same year Bostwick received a grant of 1,200 acres as a consequence of his promotion to lieutenant-colonel of the 3rd Regiment of Middlesex militia. In 1824 he became secretary of the innovative but short-lived Talbot Dispensatory at St Thomas, a medical institution proposed by John Rolph* and Charles Duncombe*. As well, in 1829 he received his first commission as a justice of the peace. In 1837, by which time he had become colonel of his regiment, he was involved in extinguishing the uprising led by Duncombe.

Bostwick's activities at Kettle Creek harbour, first called Port Stanley in the late 1820s, were in part entrepreneurial. By 1822 he had constructed a small warehouse and was dealing in ashes, grain, and other products. Bostwick was anxious to develop the settlement into what appeared to be its rightful place as the major port for the Talbot settlement. His pressing financial needs at this time were reflected in the mortgaging of some harbour-side property in late 1827. Several small lots, some of which bordered the creek, were sold by him two years later at prices ranging from £12 10*s*. to £25. The remaining water-lots, however, he refused to sell for less than £100 each. Bostwick's role in the village's development may have been limited. The leading commercial figure there was almost certainly James Hamilton, a St Thomas merchant. Edward Ermatinger*, an early historian of the Talbot settlement, regarded Bostwick as an excessively modest man who "had no turn for speculation, and no faculty for money-making." Contemporary critics of Port Stanley's slow growth assigned varying degrees of responsibility to him because of his sale of lots at prices which reportedly discouraged commercial and residential development. Others identified the harbour as a major drawback.

The port's facilities were rudimentary in the 1820s. A provincial statute of 1827 authorized the construction of wharfs and the dredging of the shallow harbour. Supervised by a commission which included Bostwick, the building of piers was completed by 1831 but further development was delayed by gales, silting, and excessive costs. Bostwick was appointed collector of tolls in 1831; three years later, when Port Stanley became a port of entry, he became collector of customs, a post that he retained for 10 years. Though it grew gradually as a forwarding and milling centre and transfer point for immigrants, William Pope, the naturalist and artist, was disgusted in 1835 by its "dirty miserable appearance" while Henry Dalley of Malahide Township dismissed it as a "miserable abortion" with a silt-choked harbour.

By the 1840s Bostwick had accumulated considerable real property as well as varied responsibilities within his family and community. He was the head of a large household – 12 people according to the census of 1842. In 1826 he had given land for an Anglican church but a congregation was not organized until 1836. Bostwick's efforts continued with his chairmanship of the building committee in the early 1840s, leading to the completion of Christ Church in 1845. His property in several townships was by and large undeveloped for farming, because his principal efforts had been directed into Port Stanley. Trade there increased tremendously during the 1840s, but the prospect of railway communication between London, Toronto, Montreal, and New York threatened to disrupt the flow of trade through small riparian settlements such as Port Stanley. Bostwick died in 1849, never to see the new form of transportation in his area. At his death his assets were quite limited – a reflection perhaps of the diversity of his interests and the direction of his energy into a number of channels rather than into the pursuit of entrepreneurial success alone.

ALAN G. BRUNGER

AO, MU 2136, 1938, no.6; RG 1, A-I-6: 5687, 12223–32; RG 22, ser.155. Christ Church (Anglican) Cemetery (Port Stanley, Ont.), Tombstone inscription, John Bostwick. PAC, RG 1, L3, 34: B7/34; RG 5, A1: 110173–78; RG 68, General index, 1651–1841: 182, 465, 666, 668. "Minutes of the Court of General Quarter Sessions of the Peace for the London District ...," AO *Report*, 1933: 17, 81, 166. William Pope, "William Pope's journal ...," [ed. M. A. Garland], *Western Ontario Hist. Nuggets* (London), no.18 (1953): 26. *The Talbot papers*, ed. J. H. Coyne (2v., Ottawa, 1908–9). U.C., House of Assembly, *Journal*, 1828: 95–96; 1831, app.: 109–10. *Farmers' Journal and Welland Canal Intelligencer* (St Catharines, [Ont.]), 28 Jan. 1829. Armstrong, *Handbook of Upper Canadian chronology* (1967). *Land surveys of southern Ontario: an introduction and index to the field notebooks of the Ontario land surveyors, 1784–1859*, comp. [R.] L. Gentilcore and Kate Donkin, ed. C. E. Heidenreich (Toronto, 1973), 39–101. W. H. Smith, *Canada: past, present and future* ... (2v., Toronto, [1852]; repr. Belleville, Ont., 1973–74), 1: 93. "State papers, [1761–99]," PAC *Report* , 1890: 213.

Booklet on the local history of Elgin County, comp. George Thorman and Ralph Parker (St Thomas, Ont., [1965?]). A. G. Brunger, "A spatial analysis of individual settlements in southern London District, Upper Canada, 1800–1836" (PHD thesis, Univ. of Western Ont., London, 1974). Brian Dawe, *"Old Oxford is wide awake!" : pioneer settlers and politicians in Oxford County, 1793–1853* (n.p., 1980). Edward Ermatinger, *Life of Colonel Talbot, and the Talbot settlement* ... (St Thomas, 1859; repr. Belleville, 1972). D. J. Hall, *Economic development in Elgin County, 1850–1880* (Petrolia, Ont., 1972), 83–84. F. C. Hamil, *Lake Erie baron: the story of Colonel Thomas Talbot* (Toronto, 1955). *Historical sketch of the village of Port Stanley*, comp. A. M. Hepburn ([Port Stanley, 1952]). *History of the county of Middlesex, Canada* ... (Toronto and London, 1889; repr. with intro. by D. [J.] Brock, Belleville, 1972). Patterson, "Studies in elections in U.C." Read, *Rising in western U.C.* C. J. Taylor *et al.*, *History of Great Barrington (Berkshire), Massachusetts* ... ([new ed.], 2 pts. in 1, Great Barrington, 1928), pt.I: 178–79, 345. N. J. Thomas, "Port Stanley," *A pioneer history: Elgin County*, ed. J. S. Brierley (St Thomas, 1896; repr. Petrolia, 1971), 137–44. E. A. Cruikshank, "The county of Norfolk in the War of 1812," *OH*, 20 (1923): 9–40. A. M. Hepburn, "Early visitors and explorers to Port Stanley," *Western Ontario Hist. Notes* (London), 14 (1957–58), no.4: 29–30.

BOUCHER (Boucher, *dit* **Belleville), JEAN-BAPTISTE**, Roman Catholic priest and author; b. 23 July 1763 at Quebec, son of Jean-Baptiste Boucher, *dit* Belleville, and Marie Martin; d. 6 Sept. 1839 in La Prairie, Lower Canada.

Jean-Baptiste Boucher entered the second form at the Petit Séminaire de Québec in 1777, and had the good fortune to do the sixth form (Rhetoric) and the two-year Philosophy program under the expert guidance of Charles Chauveaux. Upon completing classical studies in 1784 he was admitted to the Grand Séminaire. During his final year of theology in 1786–87 the Petit Séminaire put him in charge of the pupils of the fifth form. After being ordained priest on 7 Oct. 1787, Boucher was not appointed to teach in the seminary, but instead was named assistant priest at Saint-Ours. Two years later he became the parish priest, and then was sent to take over the parish of La Nativité-de-la-Trés-Sainte-Vierge at La Prairie, where he served from 1792 until his death. For nearly half a century he devoted himself to pastoral duties, while acting as counsellor to the bishop of Quebec and the curés in the Montreal region. A distinguished intellectual, he used his leisure for study. The activity of a priest in a rural parish followed the rhythm of the seasons and the liturgy, which itself was seemingly created to accompany life in the fields. Sunday brought the entire population to mass and Boucher, who was fond of preaching, never let slip the opportunity for a sermon.

In politics Boucher was a thoroughgoing supporter of the authorities. Like the rest of the clergy, he had had his thinking shaped by the French revolution and counter-revolution. On 25 March 1810, he complied with Bishop Joseph-Octave Plessis*'s request to remind parishioners from the pulpit of their duty to King George III, and on that same Sunday he also read Governor Sir James Henry Craig*'s proclamation which, among other things, called upon the people to remain loyal. As he said in a letter to the bishop three days later, Boucher thought that in so doing the clergy would bring upon itself "the implacable hatred of the revolutionary party [the Canadian party]." On 9 April *La Gazette de Montréal* printed a letter, signed Æquitas, in which Boucher referred to the governor's "truly paternal sentiments" and declared that "the Catholic religion . . . was completely loyal to the monarchy and the established government."

The La Prairie region, south of Montreal, was of strategic importance during the War of 1812. A military camp was set up there, and in 1813 it was the scene of constant troop movements. De Meuron's Regiment proceeded to La Prairie after arriving at Quebec that summer. In its ranks were soldiers of Napoleon taken prisoner in Spain who had agreed to serve in North America provided they would not have to fight against France. The officers, on the other hand, were staunch royalists. Boucher had to billet soldiers from the regiment in his presbytery, and on some occasions he was called upon to accompany deserters of Spanish origin to the scaffold, since he had learned the language of Cervantes. He got along famously with the officers and received them at his table, but he had a great deal of trouble with certain of the men who hated priests and denigrated them when talking with people in the parish.

Bishop Plessis appreciated the talents of Boucher, with whom he had probably become friends at the seminary. As the diocese had no French books to counter possible inroads of Protestantism, Plessis asked Boucher to translate John Mannock's *The poor man's catechism: or the Christian doctrine explained, with short admonitions* (London, 1752). The translation came out at Quebec in 1806 as *Manuel abrégé de controverse: ou controverse des pauvres*. It was more a defence of Catholicism than an attack upon Protestantism, and thus avoided offending the Church of England. Boucher also translated, under the title "Fondements de la foi," Richard Challoner's *The grounds of the Catholick doctrine contain'd in the profession of faith of Pius IV* (1734), but his work remained in manuscript form and is thought to have been used only in the Grand Séminaire de Québec. Boucher had begun a treatise on the "Preuves abrégées des dogmes de la religion catholique," and here he tried to cast doubt on the apostolic succession in the Church of England. Like the "Fondements," these "Preuves," or "Lettres dogmatiques," which were sent to Plessis during the period 1801–13, remained unpublished. When the bishop turned his attention to a reworking of the longer catechism of Quebec in the period 1811–18, he appointed Jean-Charles Bédard* and Boucher to help him. Previously he had asked Boucher to translate the Douai catechism, which was used in Ireland and at Halifax.

Boucher, however, had not waited for the bishop's orders before publishing; in 1795 he had had a *Recueil de cantiques à l'usage des missions, des retraites et des catéchismes* printed by John NEILSON at Quebec. In 1817 he submitted to the same publisher a work meant to complement his *Recueil* and to be used in catechizing and in the schools. These "Extraits pieux et élégants," which never appeared in print, included the most brilliant pieces from French prose and poetry to demonstrate the truths of religion, on the model of *La bibliothèque portative des écrivains français ou Choix des meilleurs morceaux extraits de leurs ouvrages*, which had been published in London in 1800 by François Moysant.

Writing in 1921, Mgr Louis-Adolphe Paquet* remarked on Jean-Baptiste Boucher's talent and his erudition, calling it astonishing for the period. In his "Lettres dogmatiques" alone Boucher quotes and comments upon 120 authors, yet his thought remains clear and his style elegant. Such a work, dealing with theology and controversial topics, presupposes a tremendous amount of reading and a knowledge of several languages. Besides French and Latin, which he had learned at the seminary, he had studied Greek, Hebrew, English, and Spanish. This learning explains his need of books. The record of the sale of his belongings after his death reveals that he had built up a personal library of more than 800 titles and 2,000 volumes, not counting the books sold in job lots. Among them were the Latin and Greek classics and the great French, English, and Spanish authors of the 17th, 18th, and 19th centuries in the fields of theology, history and geography, science, and the arts, as well as in *belles-lettres*. He even owned a copy of St Thomas Aquinas's *Summa theologica*. The foreign-language dictionaries for use in translation and the 27 grammars for seven different languages are proof that he engaged in serious linguistic studies. In addition he subscribed to the Quebec and Montreal newspapers, and he exchanged books with Plessis and other parish priests. He was respected by the bishop and the Quebec and Montreal clergy. He was also esteemed by his father and brothers, who had come to live at La Prairie around 1800. Eager to prepare young men for the priesthood, he always lodged some at his presbytery and taught them rhetoric in particular. His attitude during the events of 1837–38 is not known, but by then he was old and he had been ill since 1834. With his death on 6 Sept. 1839 a priest of great intellectual and moral excellence was lost.

CLAUDE GALARNEAU

[Jean-Baptiste Boucher is the author of *Recueil de cantiques à l'usage des missions, des retraites et des catéchismes* (Québec, 1795), which went through numerous editions, the tenth being in 1833; a copy of the work is held in the library of the Séminaire de Québec. From 1801 to 1813 Boucher sent Bishop Plessis various "Lettres dogmatiques," which were brought together under the title "Preuves abrégées des dogmes de la religion catholique attaqués dans les trente-neuf articles de la confession de foi de l'Église anglicane, dans une suite de lettres adressées à Sa Grandeur, monseigneur J.-O. Plessis, évêque de Canath, et coadjuteur de Québec" and are held in two manuscript volumes at ASQ, MSS, 218–19. The ASQ also holds a copy of John Mannock's *Manuel abrégé de controverse: ou controverse des pauvres*, translated by Boucher and published at Quebec in 1806 (MSS, 281). C.G.]

AAQ, CD, Diocèse de Québec, V: 6; 60 CN, IV: 12–95; 26 CP, D: 62. ANQ-M, CE1-2, 9 sept. 1839; CN1-233, 23 sept.–3 oct. 1839. ANQ-Q, CE1-1, 24 juill. 1763. Arch. du diocèse de Saint-Jean-de-Québec (Longueuil, Qué.), 2A/16-123. ASQ, Fichier des anciens; Lettres, Y, 107. AUM, P 58, U, Boucher, dit Belleville, à Augustin Chaboillez, 27 mai 1834. PAC, MG 24, B1, 1–3, 7–8, 12, 18, 20. J.-B. Boucher, "Lettre de l'abbé J.-B. Boucher à John Neilson," *BRH*, 35 (1929): 255–56. Pierre Caron, "Le livre dans la vie du clergé québécois sous le Régime anglais" (thèse de MA, univ. Laval, Québec, 1980). Claude Galarneau, *La France devant l'opinion canadienne (1760–1815)* (Québec et Paris, 1970); *Les collèges classiques au Canada français (1620–1970)* (Montréal, 1978), 24. Lambert, "Joseph-Octave Plessis," 764–93, 820–25, 895–96, 948. Fernand Porter, *L'institution catéchistique au Canada; deux siècles de formation religieuse, 1633–1833* (Montréal, 1949). Luc Lacourcière, "Le général de Flipe [Phips]," *Cahiers des Dix*, 39 (1974): 256. É.-Z. Massicotte, "La complainte des 40 noyés," *BRH*, 26 (1920): 90–93. L.-A. Paquet, "Un controversiste canadien," *Le Canada français* (Québec), 2e sér., 6 (1920–21): 10–17. P.-G. Roy, "Cantique de Noël," *BRH*, 1 (1895): 77.

BOUCHETTE, JOSEPH, surveyor and militia and naval officer; b. 14 May 1774 at Quebec, eldest son of Jean-Baptiste Bouchette* and Marie-Angélique Duhamel; m. 4 July 1797 Adélaïde Chaboillez, daughter of Charles-Jean-Baptiste Chaboillez*, in Montreal, and they had five children; d. 8 April 1841 in Montreal.

Joseph Bouchette's name does not appear on the list of pupils who attended the Petit Séminaire de Québec, and a number of historians have therefore concluded that he received little schooling. Many aspects of his life and career, however, suggest otherwise. The ease with which Bouchette wrote and spoke English and his ability to assimilate in one year the knowledge required to obtain his surveyor's diploma suggest that he had some education. It is possible that he received it from his mother, who was well educated, or took lessons from an English teacher, or was able to sail on a training ship.

In 1817 Bouchette declared in one of his statements of service that he had done survey work with William CHEWETT's team in the Montreal region in 1788, and in the area between Vaudreuil and Long Sault (Ont.) the following year. In March 1790 he is listed as an employee of the Surveyor General's Office in Quebec, where he had been hired as assistant draftsman to recopy surveys of the province. That his uncle, Samuel Johannes Holland*, was surveyor general doubtless helped him obtain the post. Bouchette, who made friends with one of Holland's assistants, James Peachey*, a talented painter in water-colours, took advantage of his move to the town to attend classes given by François Baillairgé*, a well-known artist, architect, and woodcarver.

On 25 March 1791 Bouchette qualified as a surveyor, but he chose to enlist in the Provincial Marine. He went to York (Toronto) that year to serve under his father, a master and commander on the Great Lakes. Because of his skills, young Bouchette was put in charge of the hydrographic surveys of the harbour at York, which he completed in November 1792. He distinguished himself in May 1794 by refloating a schooner that had sunk near the harbour and was considered beyond recovery. The exploit earned him promotion to second lieutenant that month. The next winter he worked as a draftsman to make several copies of a map of Upper Canada. A severe reduction in the Provincial Marine in 1796 obliged him to leave that service and he then bought a lieutenant's commission in the Royal Canadian Volunteer Regiment. Returning to Lower Canada, he took up residence in Montreal, and on 1 June 1797 he received command of an armed ship and a detachment of 30 men from his regiment. He was assigned to the St Lawrence between Quebec and Montreal.

At Holland's request, during the winter of 1800–1 Bouchette acted as examiner for those seeking to become surveyors. He went to live at Quebec in the spring of 1801, and in July he returned to the Surveyor General's Office. Holland was getting old; he needed a reliable assistant who might one day replace him. He wanted his son JOHN FREDERICK to have this position but Lieutenant Governor Sir Robert Shore MILNES used his authority and influence to see that Bouchette received it in July. Milnes's choice was hardly surprising, given the importance he attached to developing the townships. Bouchette, who had shown his loyalty to the crown on many an occasion and had even made friends with the Duke of Kent [Edward* Augustus], was a man on whom the lieutenant governor could count. Holland died on 28 Dec. 1801; Bouchette took over his duties on an acting basis and his appointment as surveyor general was officially confirmed in 1804. His first task was to restore order to a department that had been rather neglected by his predecessor as a result of tensions with the Americans but probably even more because of his great age.

In March 1806 Bouchette drew up a report on the seigneury of Saint-Maurice and the land occupied by the ironworks. This document included maps and plans, which were accompanied by a detailed account of the work done by his colleagues as well as his own observations and findings. The following year Bouchette went to London to draw the authorities' attention to the importance of establishing the boundary between Lower Canada and the United States exactly. He emphasized the need to plot the 45th parallel with accuracy. After his return to Quebec late in 1807, he collected data for a map of Lower Canada and a statistical and descriptive work to go with it. This project did not prevent him from attending closely to his work as surveyor general. On 12 Dec. 1808, for instance, he submitted a report on the determination of the boundary between the United States and Lower Canada. He did topographical and hydrographic surveys of the shores of the St Lawrence from Cap-Rouge to Sillery in the summer of 1809 and of the estuary of the Saint-Charles the following summer. In 1811 he returned to the problem of the boundary with the United States.

Bouchette also had a successful military career. The War of 1812 gave him the chance to distinguish himself by carrying out important reconnaissance missions. As a surveyor he was able to describe all the approaches which a defence network would have to control. His missions took him to Lachine, the shores of Lac Saint-François, and Riviére-du-Loup, as well as to Lacolle and Odelltown. He took advantage of the war to establish links with a number of leading figures, among them Governor Sir George Prevost*. On 26 Oct. 1812 Bouchette was commissioned major of the Île d'Orléans battalion of militia. The following month he raised the Quebec Volunteers, which he subsequently commanded. He was promoted lieutenant-colonel in the Lower Canadian militia in March 1813. The termination of the war brought his military career to an end, but he retained the rank of lieutenant-colonel. He would often mention his exploits, for example when asking the government to give him a better salary.

On 18 Feb. 1814 Bouchette presented before the House of Assembly his project to produce a large-scale map of Lower Canada accompanied by a topographical dictionary; the assembly referred it to a special committee which brought in a favourable report on 23 February. Meeting in committee of the whole, the house decided to place £1,500 at Bouchette's disposal. A public subscription was also launched, the fee being five guineas payable on receipt of the map. The majority of the subscribers were English-speaking, a clear indication of the privileged links between Bouchette and this community. With the assurance of the assembly's backing, Bouchette left for England in August 1814 to arrange for publication of his work. He was counting on the support of the governor and senior office holders, as well as the friendship of a few influential persons, among them the Duke of Kent.

In London Bouchette published in 1815 a map of Lower Canada drawn on a scale of 2¾ miles to the inch, and an accompanying catalogue in French which also appeared in English under the title *A topographical description of the province of Lower Canada*. The work was evidently well received in scientific circles, since on 1 April 1816 the Society for the Encouragement of Arts, Manufactures, and Commerce in London conferred a gold medal upon him. On returning to Lower Canada, Bouchette received another mark of appreciation, this time from the seigneur Alexander Fraser, who in November 1817 donated a quarter of the seigneuries of Madawaska and Lac Témiscouata to him. In March of the following year Fraser added a twelfth in joint ownership.

During his stay in London Bouchette had been appointed special surveyor to the king, with responsibility for putting into effect article 5 of the Treaty of Ghent, which provided for the creation of commissions to settle the disputed boundary between New Brunswick and the United States [*see* Thomas Henry Barclay*]. Eager to carry out his task well, before returning to North America he had taken courses in astronomy at his own expense. He landed at Halifax in September 1816 and two months later was at Quebec, where he prepared a plan that he would personally submit to the British arbitrators.

In the spring of 1817 Bouchette went with some American surveyors to the source of the St Croix River. The boundary between New Brunswick and Maine was to be laid out from this point. He then handed the commissioners a voluminous report for which he was much praised. He left immediately for

Burlington, Vt, and there organized an expedition to plot the 45th parallel. But he caught "Lake Champlain fever"; becoming critically ill, he had himself taken back to Montreal, and in 1818 he was replaced by surveyor William Franklin ODELL.

Determining the boundary was not the only problem that Bouchette had to face at this period. He also had to try to fix the lines between crown lands and seigneuries. With this in mind he asked all the seigneurs for copies of their title deeds, to enable him to direct the work of his survey parties. Furthermore, his office was swamped with requests from men who, having served in the war, had received crown land grants and wanted them surveyed. Matters were in such a state of confusion that in 1820 the governor, Lord Dalhousie [RAMSAY], asked Bouchette to investigate the situation in the area between Lake Champlain and the American frontier and the St Lawrence River. It was necessary to identify which of the occupied lands had been surveyed and which had not. The following year Bouchette was again busy tracing the boundary and submitted a report setting out the problems. Subsequently he directed the work on a vast number of files related to the surveying of crown lands in Lower Canada. Because there was still so much confusion regarding grants to military men, in 1824 Lord Dalhousie asked Bouchette to make a tour of the various townships in which they were located. Following his round of inspection Bouchette published a report in 1825 which earned him a letter of congratulation from the governor.

From 1826 to 1829 Bouchette collected data for another book. On 29 Sept. 1829 he left for London, along with his wife and his son Robert-Shore-Milnes*. Though he was assured of the government's backing (the assembly had promised to buy 100 copies), as well as of support from his many friends in England, it still took him three years of effort to get three volumes published, this time only in English. The first two were entitled *The British dominions in North America; or a topographical description of the provinces of Lower and Upper Canada*, and the third *A topographical dictionary of the province of Lower Canada*. A map of Lower Canada showing the administrative divisions of the province came with the books and it was the one used in the 1831 census.

Bouchette remained in Europe until 1834 and took the opportunity to visit France and Italy. During this period his son Joseph, who had been deputy surveyor general for some years, replaced him and seems to have carried out his responsibilities well. On his return Bouchette resumed his duties, but he left his son in charge of a number of matters.

By then Bouchette was elderly and had difficulty putting up with the animosity shown him by his compatriots in the assembly. From the moment he entered public service he had proved a devoted and staunch servant of the crown. His association with the English party had aroused the dissatisfaction of the Canadian majority in the assembly. Bouchette had made his views quite clear. In 1822 he had helped set up a committee supporting union of the two Canadas and had indeed been the only French-speaking member on it. In a public speech on 28 November he had demonstrated the necessity of union, even if it would be greatly in Upper Canada's favour. He was sorely tried when his youngest son, Robert-Shore-Milnes, espoused the Patriote cause and was sentenced in 1838 to exile in Bermuda.

Bouchette's desire to be identified with the English-speaking community created other difficulties for him. Being an office holder, he paid great attention to his public image. He lived beyond his means, which caused him many financial troubles. For example, between 1809 and 1829 he was summoned before the courts more than 75 times for unpaid accounts. Generally small amounts owing a tailor, a shoemaker, or a general merchant were involved. From 1817 his financial problems became serious. The publication of his first work on Lower Canada had resulted in a deficit of £1,702. As the assembly had paid him only £500 of the £1,500 it had promised him before he left for England, Bouchette demanded the sum due him. His case was discussed on many occasions in the house, but the Canadian majority blocked settlement of the dispute. It was not until 1875 that the crown paid compensation to his grandsons. In 1818 Bouchette's salary had dropped from £600 a year to £400. He protested vigorously to the authorities, drawing up a list of his numerous faithful services and demanding a seat on the Legislative Council. Finding that his financial situation was worsening, he tried speculating in land. Between 1818 and 1824 a number of advertisements of houses being offered for sale or rent by Bouchette appeared in the *Quebec Gazette*. The endeavour turned out badly, however, since on three occasions his properties were put up for sale by the sheriff. His situation was so disastrous that in 1824 he had to part with the plates and the original manuscript of the work brought out in 1815. Order was apparently restored in 1829 after his lands at Lac Témiscouata were sold.

Despite his many financial problems Bouchette subscribed regularly to the Quebec Fire Society from 1803 to 1821. In 1801 he was a member of the commission managing the Jesuit estates, and in 1805 and 1806 he sat on the board of the Union Company of Quebec. He contributed financially to the Quebec Emigrants' Society in 1820. The following year he joined the district agriculture society; he was also elected member of a committee to promote education. In 1824 he contributed to the founding of the Literary and Historical Society of Quebec. It was he who was behind the establishment of the Société pour l'Encouragement des Sciences et des Arts en Canada in 1827; he was its president until 1829, when it joined with the Literary and Historical Society of Quebec.

Bouchette left Quebec in the autumn of 1840, apparently after differences with the governor, Lord Sydenham [THOMSON]. Sydenham abolished the post of surveyor general, which Bouchette was the last to hold. Henceforth its responsibilities came under the commissioner of crown lands. Bouchette took up residence in Montreal and died there on 8 April 1841. His funeral was held in the church of Notre-Dame, where he was buried.

A great man, Bouchette none the less aroused much controversy. He was admired by the colonial authorities, and as a result he was on very bad terms with the Canadian majority in the House of Assembly. His loyalty to the crown, his desire to establish a colony centred on English culture, his important office, and his stand on union all caused him to be regarded as a man who had sold out to the English.

Some of his biographers charge that Bouchette used and even plagiarized work by William Berczy* in preparing his 1815 volume. This does not seem likely however: no trace has been found of Berczy's manuscript, and through his professional activities Bouchette possessed all the material needed for his books. The work that came out in 1815 represented the first synthesis of information about the geography of Lower Canada. Bouchette was labouring in the interests of the British empire, but his works reveal a great concern for the advancement of science. His 1832 publications were even more detailed and complete than the earlier ones.

As surveyor general Joseph Bouchette was obviously in a favourable position to develop and publish his material. Nevertheless the synthesis that he produced from his labours, augmented by his personal research, rouses admiration and makes him particularly important for the history and development of Canada. In addition to completely reorganizing surveying and cartographic services in Lower Canada, he published works that demonstrate his artistic and scientific talents. He may also be judged by an impressive number of maps.

CLAUDE BOUDREAU and PIERRE LÉPINE

Joseph Bouchette is the author of *A topographical description of the province of Lower Canada, with remarks upon Upper Canada, and on the relative connexion of both provinces with the United States of America* (London, 1815; repr. Saint-Lambert, Que., 1973); *The British dominions in North America; or a topographical description of the provinces of Lower and Upper Canada . . .* (2v., London, 1832); and *A topographical dictionary of the province of Lower Canada* (London, 1832).

ANQ-M, CE1-51, 13 avril 1841; P1000-1-57. ANQ-Q, P1000-14-255. PAC, MG 11, [CO 42] Q, 81, 123, 135, 157, 159; RG 31, C1, 1831. R.-S.-M. Bouchette, *Mémoires de Robert-S.-M. Bouchette, 1805–1840* (Montréal, 1903). L.C., House of Assembly, *Journals*, 1815, 1817–19, 1821, 1823–25, 1827. *La Minerve*, 25 mai, 18 juin 1827. *Quebec Gazette*, 11 April 1805; 6 Feb. 1806; 15 March 1819; 6 April, 23 Oct., 2 Nov. 1820; 10 May, 25 June, 9 Aug. 1821; 6 June, 2, 5 Dec. 1822; 1 April 1824. [F.-M.] Bibaud, *Dict. hist.* *DOLQ*, 1: 68–71, 179–81. Le Jeune, *Dictionnaire*. H. J. Morgan, *Sketches of celebrated Canadians*. Claude Boudreau, "L'analyse de la carte ancienne, essai méthodologique: la carte du Bas-Canada de 1831, de Joseph Bouchette" (thèse de MA, univ. Laval, Québec, 1985). M.-A. Guérin, "Le lieutenant-colonel et arpenteur général du Bas-Canada, Joseph Bouchette, père" (thèse de bibliothéconomie, univ. de Montréal, 1951). Gérard Parizeau, *La société canadienne-française au XIXe siècle: essais sur le milieu* (Montréal, 1975). N.-E. Dionne, "Joseph Bouchette," *BRH*, 20 (1914): 226–30. Édouard Fabre Surveyer, "Joseph Bouchette, ses frères et sœurs," *BRH*, 47 (1941): 180–82; "The Bouchette family," RSC *Trans.*, 3rd ser., 35 (1941), sect.II: 135–40. "Joseph Bouchette en Angleterre de 1829 à 1833," *BRH*, 43 (1937): 245–46. Gérard Parizeau, "Joseph Bouchette: l'homme et le haut fonctionnaire," RSC *Trans.*, 4th ser., 9 (1971), sect.I: 95–126. Benjamin Sulte, "Jean-Baptiste Bouchette," RSC *Trans.*, 3rd ser., 2 (1908), sect.I: 67–83. Albert Tessier, "De Jacques Buteux à l'arpenteur Bouchette," *Cahiers des Dix*, 4 (1939): 223–42.

BOURNE, JOHN GERVAS HUTCHINSON, judge; baptized 1 July 1804 in Eastwood, Nottinghamshire, England, only son of John Bourne and Ruth Elizabeth ——; m. May 1831 Elizabeth ——, and they had two children; d. 21 Nov. 1845 in London.

John Gervas Hutchinson Bourne matriculated to Pembroke College, Oxford, on 17 Oct. 1821 and received a BA from Pembroke in 1825 and an MA three years later. From 1826 to 1831 he was a fellow of Magdalen College but had to resign when he married. He was admitted to the Inner Temple on 28 Nov. 1825 and was called to the bar on 20 Nov. 1829. After becoming a barrister, he practised on the Midland circuit, where he attracted the attention of Thomas Denman, a prominent Whig lawyer who became lord chief justice in 1832. Denman was involved in the dismissal of Henry John Boulton* as chief justice of Newfoundland and was undoubtedly responsible for his replacement by Bourne in July 1838. Bourne was apparently loosely associated with the reformers in Britain, but there is no evidence that he had been an active partisan. He was best known, according to Governor Henry Prescott*, as "a Scholar and a perfect Gentleman." He had published in London *The exile of Idria: a German tale* (1833) and *The picture, and the prosperous man* (1835), as well as a translation of Pierre-Jean de Béranger's songs (1837). Bourne was a competent lawyer but, as he admitted to Colonial Secretary Lord Stanley in 1843, had he "been very eminent . . . in the Law, or making a fortune by it" in England, he would not have gone to Newfoundland.

Bourne arrived in the colony in September 1838. He did not find his legal duties onerous, except for travelling the outport circuit – he suffered severely from seasickness. In his charges to the juries, he repeatedly complimented Newfoundland on its lack of serious crime. Unfortunately the cases he did have to consider often had strong political overtones. Since Boulton's removal was viewed by reformers as a victory and by conservatives as an affront, Bourne became the focal point of partisan conflict. On his arrival he had added to his unpopularity among conservatives by proclaiming himself a "zealous advocate for Catholic rights" who had married a Catholic and brought up his elder daughter in that faith. When in the *Kielley* v. *Carson* case [*see* William CARSON] Bourne upheld the right of the Newfoundland House of Assembly to the same privileges as the British House of Commons and when he supported a revision of the process of jury selection to ensure more Catholics were chosen, Henry David Winton* and his conservative *Public Ledger* accused him of throwing himself "into the arms of the radical party."

The reformers admired Bourne's "heart," yet they felt he lacked "the moral courage to be guided by its promptings" and were frequently disappointed in his judicial decisions, especially when he followed "in Boulton's path" in *Nowlan* v. *McGrath* and denied that fishing servants had first claim on the assets of a bankrupt planter. The *Newfoundland Patriot* warned, "*That* man can be no friend to Newfoundland who would register an opinion from the Bench of Justice that a *custom* which protected her fisheries, was a custom which could not be legally supported." When Bourne presided over a trial in which a verdict for libel was passed against John Kent*, a leading reformer, Kent ceased to be "on speaking terms" with him. Indeed, Bourne's decisions in several libel suits against reform journalists and his firmness during the Conception Bay riots in 1840 were praised by the conservative press.

If Bourne was innocent of partisan behaviour on the bench, he was guilty of possessing a quick temper. He frequently quarrelled with his fellow judges, especially Augustus Wallet DesBarres for whom he had scant respect. His *bête noire* was Bryan Robinson*, a prominent conservative lawyer, who successfully appealed the Kielley–Carson decision to the Privy Council. A flamboyant court-room performer, Robinson clashed with Bourne during libel trials in the early 1840s and their clashes were a source of public entertainment. Bourne became convinced that he was "the object of attack to all about him."

When accepting the position of judge of the Vice-Admiralty Court in September 1843, Bourne pleaded with Stanley for a "transfer to any European situation . . . of even considerably less than half my present pay." Robinson was equally discontented and in February 1843 had petitioned the Colonial Office to dismiss Bourne. He charged the chief justice "with evincing partiality, with warping the Law of the Land," with "ignorance in his profession," and, for good measure, with beating his wife. The legal adviser to the Colonial Office, James Stephen, found the last charge not proved but plausible; yet, "however disgraceful," wife-beating "can hardly be said to disqualify a man from being a Judge." The other complaints were so flimsily supported that Robinson was advised to "retract or greatly to qualify" them. "Reluctantly" he agreed not to pursue the matter.

Although counselled by his friend Sir Richard Henry BONNYCASTLE of the Royal Engineers to treat Robinson's complaints "with dignified contempt," Bourne over-reacted and sought retribution. In an attempt to gain conservative support for his administration, Governor Sir John Harvey* had named Robinson to the Executive Council. Since Robinson was an aggressive, high-church Anglican, the appointment appalled the colony's Presbyterians, who included Walter Grieve* and several other of Bourne's closest associates, and the low-church Anglicans, led by Charles Blackman*, whose church Bourne attended. Apparently at their urging, and with the encouragement of Winton, Bourne insisted that Robinson's appointment be cancelled. When Harvey refused, Bourne accused him of naming Robinson because Harvey owed him money. Unable to substantiate these charges to the Colonial Office, Bourne was dismissed in May 1844 and replaced temporarily by James Simms*.

Bourne returned to London where he published a lengthy poem, *England won* . . . (1845), and began to work on "some articles upon Colonial Affairs." He died on 21 Nov. 1845, from "an affection of the brain, the result perhaps of intense study conjoined to disappointed hopes," according to obituaries. To some extent Bourne was the victim of the bitter partisanship of Newfoundland politics, which had led to the departure of both of his immediate predecessors, Richard Alexander Tucker* and Boulton. But, unlike them, he was not dismissed for overtly political activities. As the *Patriot* declared in his obituary, Bourne "should have rested content with defeating Robinson's machinations; he erred when he came unnecessarily into collision with the Governor. When he did this he played into his adversary's game." In this sense Bourne's uncontrollable temper and lack of discretion were the causes of his disappointed hopes.

PHILLIP BUCKNER

PANL, GN 2/2, 40, 43–44, 46–47. PRO, CO 194/118–20. *Newfoundlander*, 1838–44. *Newfoundland Patriot*, 1838–42. *Patriot & Terra Nova Herald*, 1842–44. *Public Ledger*,

1838–44. *Royal Gazette and Newfoundland Advertiser*, 1838–44. *Times and General Commercial Gazette* (St John's), 1838–44. Gunn, *Political hist. of Nfld.* Prowse, *Hist. of Nfld.* (1895). Malcolm MacDonell, "The conflict between Sir John Harvey and Chief Justice John Gervase Hutchinson Bourne," CHA *Report*, 1956: 45–54.

BOWMAN, JAMES, painter; b. 1793 in Allegheny County, Pa; d. 18 May 1842 in Rochester, N.Y.

James Bowman typifies a number of successful American portrait painters working as itinerants in the Canadas and in the eastern United States during the 1830s and 1840s. Commencing life as a carpenter in Ohio, he learned the rudiments of painting from a local artist before painting portraits in Pittsburgh, Philadelphia, and Washington. From 1822 he spent about eight years in Europe, studying in London (under Sir Thomas Lawrence), in Paris, and in Rome. On returning to the United States about 1829, he painted in Charleston, W.Va, and Boston.

Bowman moved to Quebec City in 1831. There he had commissions for portraits of Governor Lord Aylmer [WHITWORTH-AYLMER], Lady Aylmer, and Marie-Louise de Saint-Henri [MCLOUGHLIN] of the Ursulines. In the spring of 1833 he exhibited in Montreal a diorama of the interior of the Capuchin chapel in Rome; that July it appeared in Quebec, the first diorama exhibited there. The *Quebec Mercury* praised it highly for its startling illusionistic effect, but Antoine Plamondon* criticized it in *Le Canadien*, claiming that it had "enormous faults" and that it made a "feeble impression."

While working in Montreal during 1833 and 1834, Bowman continued his portraiture, painting members of the English-speaking establishment. Soon after his arrival in 1833, he painted a view of the Sulpician mission at Lac-des-Deux-Montagnes (Oka) which depicted priests, including Joseph-Vincent Quiblier*, distributing presents from the pope to some 70 Indians. That year Quiblier commissioned Bowman to produce six paintings for the side chapels of the new church of Notre-Dame in Montreal. After accomplishing this task, Bowman was asked to execute for Notre-Dame 14 paintings representing the Stations of the Cross, in which he would be assisted by his pupil Thomas-Henri Valin. With only four of these completed, Bowman abandoned the project in 1834 and moved to Toronto. Plamondon took on the assignment in 1836, at the same time writing to Quiblier that Bowman's four Stations were bad and that they had gone to hang "in dark corridors" of the Ursuline convent in Quebec (they have since been lost). Of Bowman's six original paintings commissioned for the church, only two (*Le Christ désignant saint Roch comme patron contre la peste* and *L'éducation de la Vierge*) are preserved.

Much acclaim was heaped on Bowman by the Toronto *Patriot*, a conservative newspaper, after he moved there in October 1834. His sitters, described as the local "Gentry," were leading family-compact supporters. Perhaps these portraits were regarded as having a certain propaganda value at a time when William Lyon Mackenzie* was championing reform in Upper Canada. A subscription was set up to commission a portrait of the lieutenant governor, Sir John Colborne*. Portraits were painted of Allan Napier MacNab*, MacNab's mother-in-law (described as in Sir Thomas Lawrence's style), various MacNab family members, Colborne's son, judge Levius Peters SHERWOOD, John Strachan*, William DUNLOP, and others. The *Patriot* praised Bowman's paintings as the "best pictures that have ever been exhibited in this country," and described him as a "fine subject for moral reflection; he was literally a Backwoods-man of America, and, in the recesses of the forest, became fired with the noble ambition to rival the first in the Arts." The youthful Paul Kane* was swept up by Bowman's enthusiasm and arranged to go to Europe with him for study; plans were altered following Bowman's marriage, and Kane went overseas alone in 1841.

Bowman had left Toronto in 1835. The following year he married Julia M. Chew in Detroit and then painted in several American cities before opening a studio in Rochester, N.Y., in October 1841. There he struck up a brief but close friendship with Cornelius Krieghoff*, then working in that city. Krieghoff copied Bowman's most noted portrait, that of Danish sculptor Bertel Thorvaldsen. Bowman died suddenly in May 1842. The following year Krieghoff held an exhibition of his own paintings, proposing to use any proceeds to erect a memorial to Bowman, who had undoubtedly inspired all younger artists with whom he came in contact.

J. RUSSELL HARPER

L'Ami du peuple, de l'ordre et des lois, 11 oct. 1834. *Le Canadien*, 24 juill. 1833. *Patriot* (Toronto), 21, 28, 31 Oct., 7 Nov., 5, 23 Dec. 1834; 16 Jan. 1835. *Le Populaire*, 23 oct. 1837. *Quebec Gazette*, 30 Sept. 1831, 2 Jan. 1832, 15 July 1833. *Quebec Mercury*, 13 July 1833. *Rochester Daily Advertiser* (Rochester, N.Y.), 19 May 1842, 30 May 1843. *Rochester Daily Democrat*, 1 June 1842. *Rochester Evening Post*, 18 May 1842. G. C. Groce and D. H. Wallace, *The New-York Historical Society's dictionary of artists in America, 1564–1860* (New Haven, Conn., and London, 1957; repr. 1964). Harper, *Early painters and engravers*. Maurault, *La paroisse: hist. de Notre-Dame de Montréal* (1929), 114, 163. Morisset, *Coup d'œil sur les arts*, 80–81; *Peintres et tableaux*, 2: 82; *La peinture traditionnelle*, 138. *Paul Kane's frontier; including "Wanderings of an artist among the Indians of North America" by Paul Kane*, ed. and intro. J. R. Harper (Toronto, 1971). Yves Lacasse, "La contribution du peintre américain James Bowman (1793–1842) au premier décor intérieur de l'église Notre-Dame de

Montréal," *Journal of Canadian Art Hist.* (Montreal), 7 (1983–84): 74–91.

BOWRING, BENJAMIN, watchmaker and businessman; baptized 17 May 1778 in Exeter, England, one of three children of Nathaniel Bowring and Susannah White; m. 9 Oct. 1803 Charlotte Price in Wellington, Somerset, and they had five sons and one daughter; d. 1 June 1846 in Liverpool, England.

Benjamin Bowring came from a family that had been involved for over two centuries in the woollen industry in Exeter. After receiving his early education at the Unitarian chapel academy in his mother's native Moretonhampstead, he apprenticed to watchmaker Charles Price, whose daughter he later married. Three days before his marriage, he opened his own watchmaking shop in Exeter, and he built it into a prosperous business. A Nonconformist, Bowring was a strong supporter of the abolition of the slave trade and generally took an active role in Exeter's social life.

Looking for new opportunities for his trade, in 1811 Bowring visited Newfoundland, which at the time was experiencing substantial growth in both its population and its fishery. No doubt his knowledge of the colony came from the long-standing connection of West Country merchants with the island's fishery. During the Napoleonic Wars, St John's was a booming frontier port whose population had increased from just over 3,200 in 1794 to approximately 10,000 in 1815.

Having made several trips to St John's between 1811 and 1815, Bowring became one of the port's permanent residents in 1815; the following spring his wife and family joined him. His early years in Newfoundland were marked by a depression in the fishery and by temporary set-backs when his watchmaking shop was destroyed several times by fire during the period 1816–19. While he pursued his craft, his wife opened a small dry-goods store attached to the shop. Her business venture proved successful and Bowring decided to abandon watchmaking to concentrate on what was a growing retail trade. He was able to establish himself firmly in the uncertain St John's economy of the 1820s because of his family's business connections in England through which he bought the necessary dry goods and manufactured products. During a poor fishery many merchants would fail, but Bowring was willing to take risks and this adventurous spirit was a decided asset to him. In 1823 he was secure and bold enough to purchase two schooners to transport goods from England and return with Newfoundland cod and seal products. The following year Bowring changed the name of his firm to Benjamin Bowring and Son when his eldest son, William, became a partner.

In addition to serving on the executives of several educational and charitable societies in St John's in the early 1820s, Bowring was a strong advocate for the establishment of a municipal government to implement, among other measures, fire safety and building regulations. He and his fellow merchants believed that the existing system of government, whereby Newfoundland was administered by an imperially appointed governor, was inadequate to deal with the increasing political problems of both capital and colony. In 1826 an incorporation scheme for St John's, of which Bowring was a prominent promoter, failed because of differences within the business community as to what form of taxation the proposed municipality should adopt. Following this failure, Bowring and other community leaders renewed their efforts to secure a colonial legislature for Newfoundland, which was finally instituted in 1832. However, his enthusiasm for the new legislature quickly waned after 1833 when politicians divided along religious lines and disputed issues of patronage [*see* William CARSON]. Nevertheless, Bowring was pleased that one of the first acts of the House of Assembly in early 1833 was to provide for a compulsory fire brigade in St John's.

This new attempt at fire protection proved no help when Bowring's premises and much of the south side of Water Street were burnt on 7 July. The loss postponed for a year his decision to turn over the Newfoundland business to his son, Charles Tricks (William had drowned in 1828). It was Benjamin's intention to build up a strong English side to the firm by providing the goods St John's needed and marketing Newfoundland fishery products in England and Europe. As he still had sufficient capital to re-establish business in St John's, he decided to do so. Once the premises were nearly completed in mid 1834, he gave control of the firm to Charles and with the rest of his family returned to England. In 1835 he set up a trading company, known as Benjamin Bowring, in Liverpool. Bowring remained in regular contact with his son, offering advice and examining the accounts of Benjamin Bowring and Son. Under Charles's direction the company underwent substantial expansion during the 1830s and it entered the front ranks of the Water Street mercantile establishments. Crucial to its growth was the decision after 1834 to have the firm become directly involved in the lucrative seal fishery by providing its own vessels and building a storage vat at St John's for the oil. The increased volume in business was a boost to the Liverpool company, whose financial and business transactions were closely tied to those of the Newfoundland enterprise. In 1839 the name of the latter firm was changed to Bowring Brothers when Charles's brother Henry Price became his partner. Two years later they were joined by their brother Edward.

The association of Henry and Edward with the management of Bowring Brothers enabled Benjamin to turn over control of the Liverpool operation in 1841 to Charles, who none the less retained supervision of the Newfoundland company. Under Charles the Liverpool firm, renamed C. T. Bowring and Company, became a major international shipping and insurance business, while Bowring Brothers became one of the leading firms in the cod and seal fisheries and in the provision of foodstuffs and manufactured goods to Newfoundlanders (its expansion was continued under Charles's son Charles R.*). Benjamin Bowring's legacy is in the establishment of both businesses which, the St John's *Newfoundland Patriot* wryly noted in 1839, were passed on to the "whole 'tribe of Benjamin.'"

MELVIN BAKER

MHA, Bowring name file; Keith Matthews, "Profiles of Water Street merchants" (typescript, 1980). PRO, RG 4/965: 67. Melvin Baker, "The government of St. John's, Newfoundland, 1800–1921" (PHD thesis, Univ. of Western Ont., London, 1981). Gunn, *Political hist. of Nfld.* David Keir, *The Bowring story* (London, 1962). Paul O'Neill, *The story of St. John's, Newfoundland* (2v., Erin, Ont., 1975–76), 2. A. C. Wardle, *Benjamin Bowring and his descendants; a record of mercantile achievement* (London, 1938).

BRANT, CATHARINE. *See* OHTOWAʔKÉHSON

BRASS, WILLIAM, fur trader, merchant, and convicted rapist; baptized 8 May 1796 in Kingston, Upper Canada, son of David Brass and Mary Magdalen Mattice; m. Elizabeth ——; they had no children; d. 1 Dec. 1837 in Kingston.

Born about 1792, William Brass was the son of a respectable and wealthy loyalist settler at Kingston. In 1821 William received a grant of land north of the town, in Loughborough Township, where he carried on business as a merchant and fur trader. Little is known about his life except that he spent considerable time trading among the Indians. After one such expedition, in 1834, he was reported to have been devoured by wolves – part of a skull and some bones were found 12 miles from Kingston and identified as his. The rumour proved false, but is illustrative of his nomadic, rather wild existence.

As a result of the settlement of Loughborough in the 1820s and 1830s and the diminishing economic importance of the fur trade in the province, Brass's business began to falter. He attended the occasional reform meeting, but he seemed to care little for the social and moral conventions of most of the Upper Canadian community. He began to drink heavily, and his wife left him. In June 1835 he hired lawyer Henry Smith* to straighten out his financial problems. Instead, Smith obtained the patent for Brass's property in his own name by taking advantage of his client's excessive drinking. During one of these terrible bouts, in June 1837, he was arrested on a charge of raping eight-year-old Mary Ann Dempsey of Loughborough, who had been left in his care.

After eight days of delirium tremens Brass sobered up to what was going on around him. In September he launched three separate legal actions against Smith: one on the alleged land fraud, one for damages, and another of forcible entry into Brass's house. To defend him against the charge of rape he employed lawyers Henry Cassady and John A. Macdonald*. The Kingston *British Whig* reported that Brass had "fallen victim to an infamous conspiracy commenced by a rascally individual in whom he placed confidence, and carried into execution by wretches as worthless as himself."

The trial, which took place on 7 October before judge Jonas JONES, was a major sensation. Solicitor General William Henry Draper* prosecuted. He called the alleged victim to the stand and she described the incident. Two medical practitioners and a midwife gave evidence which established the probability of the child's having been violated. John Caswell, the last witness for the crown, claimed to have seen the rape but not to have interfered, because, he said, the defendant was armed. The "very able defence" was led by the 22-year old Macdonald, who impressed the *British Whig* as a rapidly rising young lawyer. He and Cassady tried to prove that Smith, Caswell, Stephen Acroid, and other neighbours of Brass were conspiring against him in order to deprive him of his lands. The defence attempted to show further that he was drunk at the time of the alleged rape and incapable of intercourse. Even if he had committed the crime, they argued, he was unquestionably insane at the time and therefore not accountable in law. After a little more than an hour's deliberation the jury found Brass guilty. Jones sentenced him to be hanged on 1 December.

Many people felt Brass did not deserve to hang. Lieutenant Governor Sir Francis Bond Head* was petitioned by 135 inhabitants of the Midland District, among them 18 justices of the peace, to grant Brass his life, but without success. By stressing his father's military service to the crown in Butler's Rangers the petition made clear the tension that existed in Loughborough between loyalist families and more recently arrived groups of immigrants. John Solomon CARTWRIGHT's preface to the petition reveals the preference loyalists expected from colonial administrators in matters where judicial discretion could be exercised. Meanwhile the defence tried to get a new trial, and depositions, many from loyalist descendants, were taken which discredited Caswell's testimony. Three individuals swore that he was somewhere other than Brass's house when the alleged rape took place; one deponent, Filinda Chadwick, swore to having overheard a conversation a few days before the trial in which Caswell told Mrs Brass that he could either save her husband or hang him. The controversy raged in Kingston until 1 December.

On that day Brass and his executioner, both clad in white gowns, appeared upon the temporary gallows built out of a window in the court-house. Brass, who had been vilified and feared by his neighbours, was now a public spectacle. In a resolute, calm voice he declared his innocence and repeatedly accused Smith, Acroid, and Caswell of conspiring against him. He asked if these men were present, for he hoped to look down upon them for the last time. When he finished speaking, part of the platform gave way and he dangled, suspended by it for a moment. He was then kicked from the platform and fell, not into eternity, but all the way to his coffin, waiting below. The crowd began to shout murder and a rescue was attempted, but soldiers prevented a riot. The bumbling sheriff, Richard Bullock, cut the noose from Brass's neck and dragged him up the court-house stairs. Brass shouted triumphantly to the crowd: "You see I am innocent; this gallows was not built for me – 'tis for Young Henry Smith." He was thrown from the window a second time, with a shorter rope around his neck, and he plunged to his death with Smith's name on his lips. Brass was buried the following day, not in the family plot in Kingston but on his farm in Loughborough.

Reaction to Brass's conviction and death was hotly mixed. To many farmers in Loughborough, struggling against the wilderness, Brass had seemed almost supernatural because of the ease with which he slipped in and out of that hostile environment. Reduced finally to a near animal state, he was hated as a symbol of the wilderness and this enmity possibly made the farmers more willing to believe in Brass's guilt and less receptive to evidence suggesting his innocence. Elsewhere, however, others were shocked by the uncertainties surrounding the case and by the botched execution. A letter to the *British Whig*, written from Adolphustown and requesting more information on the hanging, stated that the "intense feeling produced by the account of his m——r" surpassed any response to a crime the writer had ever witnessed in that area. It was rumoured there, he continued, that through surgical aid Brass had been resuscitated and was still alive.

WILLIAM TEATERO

PAC, RG 5, A1: 98346–93. *The parish register of Kingston, Upper Canada, 1785–1811*, ed. A. H. Young (Kingston, Ont., 1921), 89. *British Whig*, 28 Feb. 1834; 12, 28 Sept., 7 Oct., 1, 8 Dec. 1837. *Chronicle & Gazette*, 26 April, 17 May 1834; 11 Oct. 1837. *Upper Canada Herald*, 10 Oct. 1837. W. [R.] Teatero, "He worked in shadow of the gallows," *Whig-Standard* (Kingston), 13 July 1978: 7, 15.

BRECKEN, JOHN, businessman, politician, and office holder; b. 23 Feb. 1800 in Charlottetown, elder son of Ralph Brecken and Matilda Robinson; m. there 20 June 1826 Margaret Leah de St Croix, and they had three sons, including Frederick de St Croix Brecken*, and one daughter; d. there 2 Nov. 1847.

John Brecken's grandfather was a loyalist of the same name who had come to St John's (Prince Edward) Island from Shelburne, N.S., in 1784. He soon prospered as a merchant, and took John's father into the firm. Ralph died when John was only 13, leaving an estate of almost £25,000, most of which was in the form of debts owing to the business. This estate was not dispersed among his children and the business continued to be operated under his name; control seems to have been in the hands of his widow and their son John. Periodic divisions of income and capital from the estate were to be made by the Probate Court until Matilda died in 1842. Of the seven children, John received the largest share of these distributions which, combined with an income left him in 1827 by his grandfather, seems to have provided a fund of capital that he sustained and possibly added to.

Using both his own resources and those controlled by his mother, Brecken began acting as a banker for many in the colony. He served as deputy treasurer of the colony for a number of years and on several occasions was acting treasurer. He was named resident director of the Bank of British North America in 1836. Unlike other well-to-do merchants and capitalists, Brecken possessed wealth that was not directly connected with land. He held only a few small parcels that his grandfather had bequeathed to him, and there is no evidence that he engaged in land speculation or even lent money on the strength of mortgages.

Besides financial well-being Brecken inherited a relatively high place in the Island's social structure. His mother was a daughter of Joseph Robinson*, a politician, and when John was married it was to the only child of Dr Benjamin de St Croix and his wife, Margaret, a granddaughter of Thomas Desbrisay*, a former lieutenant governor. Most of John's sisters made equally advantageous and prestigious marriages, so that by 1840 an economic and social web had been woven, at the centre of which was Matilda Brecken. The web had political strands as well as social and economic ones.

Ralph Brecken had been a member of the House of Assembly for some years, serving as speaker in 1812. John's political activity began in 1829 when he defeated James Bardin Palmer* in a Charlottetown by-election; he retained his seat the following year. In January 1834 he was named to the Council by Lieutenant Governor Aretas William Young* and, when it was separated into executive and legislative components by Lieutenant Governor Sir Charles Augustus FitzRoy* in 1839, he sat as a member of each. As such he was one of the targets of the 1841 assembly resolution concerning "family connection" in the Executive Council and "connection and influence" in the Legislative Council. At the time the resolution was passed Brecken sat with two brothers-in-law, Thomas Heath Haviland*, the colonial secretary, and James Ellis Peake, the major shipbuilder in the colony, on the Executive Council. Another brother-in-law, Donald McDonald*, a prominent landowner, sat with him on the Legislative Council. He was also related somewhat more distantly to other members of both bodies. In spite of evidence that a true "family compact" existed in the colony there is little to suggest that Brecken engaged in concerted action for direct personal advantage, and his period of public service was without major incident.

John Brecken's obituaries were perfunctory. By 1847 the wealth and the family connections that had defined the boundaries of his life had been superseded in great measure by new political and social forces.

H. T. Holman

Bank of Montreal Arch., Court Committee of Directors, minute-book no.1 (mfm. at PAC). PAPEI, RG 6.2, Probate Court records, inventory of the estate of Ralph Brecken. PRO, CO 226/51: 12, 15, 103. Supreme Court of P.E.I. (Charlottetown), Estates Division, estate of Ralph Brecken. P.E.I., House of Assembly, *Journal*, 23 April 1841. *Prince Edward Island Register*, 9, 16 June 1829. *Royal Gazette* (Charlottetown), 7, 28 Sept., 12 Oct. 1830; 4 Feb. 1834; 18 Oct. 1836; 7 Jan. 1840; 9 Nov. 1847. *An Island refuge: loyalists and disbanded troops on the Island of Saint John*, ed. Orlo Jones and Doris Haslam (Charlottetown, 1983). I. L. Rogers, *Charlottetown: the life in its buildings* (Charlottetown, 1983).

BRENTON, EDWARD BRABAZON, lawyer, politician, judge, and office holder; b. 22 April 1763 in Halifax, only child of James Brenton* and his first wife, Rebecca Scott; m. 13 Jan. 1791 Catherine Taylor in Halifax, and they had one daughter; d. 11 March 1845 in Royal Leamington Spa, England.

As the eldest son of a man who was to become Nova Scotia's solicitor general, attorney general, and assistant judge of its Supreme Court, Edward Brabazon Brenton seemed destined for a career at the bar and on the bench. He studied law at Lincoln's Inn, London, to which he was admitted on 30 Oct. 1781, but he did not become a member of the English bar. Brenton was admitted to the Nova Scotia bar on 5 April 1785, and began practising in Halifax. He was probably one of the two "young gentlemen" who in 1790 acted as attorneys to James Brenton and Isaac Deschamps* when they were impeached by the House of Assembly during the so-called "judges' affair." In December 1792, bearing testimonials from Lieutenant Governor John Wentworth* and from Chief Justice Thomas Andrew Lumisden Strange, who had early marked him as "in all respects deserving of future attention," Edward Brenton went to England to solicit appointment as judge advocate of the Nova Scotia military district; he received it the following March. In July 1799 the Duke of Kent [Edward* Augustus], commander-in-chief of the forces in British North America, advanced him to the newly created position of deputy judge advocate general for British North America.

As early as 1792 Wentworth had predicted that Brenton might enter the assembly, where his father had sat for 14 years. The younger Brenton was overseas when the house was dissolved in January 1793, however, and could not stand for election. He remained high in the esteem of Wentworth, who in 1802 recommended him for a seat on the Council. The appointment was made on 13 June 1805 but Brenton took his seat only after the death of his father in December 1806. James's position on the Supreme Court did not devolve to his son. It went instead to Brenton Halliburton*, a cousin of Edward's who was some 18 years his junior at the bar.

In March 1808 Brenton was appointed a master extraordinary in the Court of Chancery, and in January 1810 he was made both a revenue commissioner and surrogate to the judge of the Vice-Admiralty Court by Wentworth's successor, Sir George Prevost*. The following year his career in Nova Scotia came to an end. He attended his last Council meeting on 16 Aug. 1811, and nine days later he embarked with Prevost for Quebec. During Prevost's term as governor-in-chief and commander of British forces in North America Brenton served as his civil secretary, replacing Herman Witsius Ryland, and his aide-de-camp. He seems to have accompanied Prevost to England upon the latter's recall in 1815, and to have spent the next decade there. It is difficult to elaborate upon this period of his life. He was superannuated in 1817 after the office of deputy judge advocate general was discontinued. When Prevost's conduct during the War of 1812 was traduced in an article in the *Quarterly Review* (London) of October 1822, Brenton wrote an anonymous reply. *Some account of the public life of the late Lieutenant-General Sir George Prevost* was a mundane apologia which did nothing to enhance Prevost's posthumous reputation.

In 1825 Brenton returned to British North America when the new governor of Newfoundland, Thomas John Cochrane*, brought him along as colonial secretary. A year later an assistant judge of the Supreme Court was forced to resign, and Brenton was appointed to succeed him. Beginning in October 1827 he acted on two occasions as head of the court while the chief justice, Richard Alexander Tucker*, administered the government during Cochrane's absence. Already over 60 years of age when he arrived in St John's, in 1838 Brenton was forced by ill health to take a leave of absence. A reputation as a philanthropist and an assiduous judge remained behind him in Newfoundland. He would retain the judgeship until his death, when he was replaced by George LILLY.

Brenton's diverse career as a public servant in British North America had spanned almost half a century. On his return to England he retired to Royal Leamington Spa, where he lived out the final seven years of his life.

J. B. CAHILL

Edward Brabazon Brenton is the anonymous author of *Some account of the public life of the late Lieutenant-General Sir George Prevost, bart., particularly of his services in the Canadas* . . . (London, 1823).

Honourable Soc. of Lincoln's Inn (London), Reg. of admissions, 30 Oct. 1781. PAC, RG 7, G15C; RG 8, I (C ser.). PANS, RG 1, 172: 173; 173: 3–4; 192: 21, 152; 525, pt.III: 41. PRO, CO 217/36: 143; 217/76: 100–1; 217/80: 255; PROB 11/2013; WO 85/2, 27 March 1793; 85/3, 19 July 1799. St Paul's Anglican Church (Halifax), Reg. of baptisms. *Gentleman's Magazine*, January–June 1845: 565. *Nova-Scotia Magazine* (Halifax), 2 (January–June 1790): 457. *Newfoundlander*, 1 May 1845. *Royal Gazette and the Nova-Scotia Advertiser*, 18 Jan. 1791. *Encyclopedia Canadiana*. G.B., WO, *Army list*, 1817–18. *N.S. vital statistics, 1769–1812* (Punch), no.199. *The book of Newfoundland*, ed. J. R. Smallwood *et al.* (6v., St John's, 1937–75), 5: 545. Prowse, *Hist. of Nfld.* (1895), 662.

BRIAND. *See* TRIAUD

BRIEN, JEAN-BAPTISTE-HENRI, physician and Patriote; b. 1816 in Saint-Martin (Laval), Lower Canada; d. 1841 in New York, supposedly unmarried.

Jean-Baptiste-Henri Brien came from a farm family, and after attending the Petit Séminaire de Montréal from 1827 till 1833 he went into medicine. He took his training with Dr William Robinson of Saint-Vincent-de-Paul (Laval), and then with Dr Charles Smallwood* of Saint-Martin. Licensed to practise in the autumn of 1837, Brien went into partnership with Jean-Baptiste Trestler, a physician in the parish of Saint-Laurent.

On 5 Sept. 1837, when the Fils de la Liberté [*see* André Ouimet*] was founded in Montreal, Brien was among the youngest of its members. In mid November he went to Saint-Eustache, where armed resistance was being mounted against the government's policy of arresting Patriote leaders, but he does not seem to have taken part in the battle there on 14 December. At the end of the month, along with Étienne Chartier*, the parish priest of Saint-Benoît (at Mirabel), and Jean-Baptiste-Chamilly de Lorimier, younger brother of CHEVALIER, Brien fled to the United States.

Brien lived first at St Albans, Vt, moving later to Plattsburgh, N.Y. He attended a meeting in Swanton, Vt, on 9 Jan. 1838 at which Robert Nelson*, Cyrille-Hector-Octave CÔTÉ, and Chevalier de Lorimier put forward a proposal to return in force to Lower Canada. Brien worked on getting ammunition ready, particularly in Plattsburgh, and on 28 Feb. 1838 participated in a raid on Caldwell's Manor, near Missisquoi Bay, during which Nelson issued a proclamation announcing the independence of Lower Canada. At St Albans shortly afterwards he was initiated into the secrets of the Association des Frères-Chasseurs and the plans to coordinate an invasion from the United States with an uprising in the colony.

Brien stayed in Montreal during the summer of 1838, and then went to live at Sainte-Martine. His task was to work towards an uprising in Beauharnois County. A general insurrection was planned for the week of 3 November. That night the insurgents in Beauharnois seized the arms held by the quartermaster of the local volunteers, took seigneur Edward Ellice*'s manor-house, and captured some prisoners, including Ellice's son and daughter-in-law. Brien himself would take them to Châteauguay. He more than other leaders (for example, Toussaint Rochon, a blacksmith in Beauharnois, and Joseph Dumouchelle, a farmer from Sainte-Martine) treated their adversaries with such delicacy that he was suspected of being on both sides. In actual fact, on returning to Sainte-Martine on 4 November he decided to abandon everything and flee to the United States. He persuaded a farmer and a merchant from Sainte-Martine to accompany him, but at nightfall the two turned back. The next day Brien, now alone, was taken prisoner by the Russeltown (Saint-Chrysostome) volunteers.

It is thought that Brien agreed, possibly at the suggestion of the younger Edward Ellice, to make a complete confession in order to save his life. Attorney General Charles Richard Ogden* issued instructions on 16 Nov. 1838, when Brien was being held in the Montreal jail, that no one was to communicate with him. Two days later Brien signed a long declaration disclosing the activities of the fugitives in the United States, the Frères-Chasseurs' regulations and plans, and what had taken place at Beauharnois and Sainte-Martine. This document was compromising for several people, among them Chevalier de Lorimier, who would share Brien's cell and would be hanged on 15 Feb. 1839.

Brien was sentenced to death for high treason by a court martial, but he escaped this penalty. The draft of a text addressed to the Executive Council on 11 Feb. 1839 says: "In consequence of information he has supplied, Jean-Baptiste-Henri Brien will not be executed." Brien remained in prison until 26 Sept. 1839, when he was released on condition of banishment. He went to the United States, travelling, it is believed, by way of Upper Canada to avoid recognition and any unwelcome encounters.

According to Louis-Joseph-Amédée Papineau*'s diary, Jean-Baptiste-Henri Brien was seen in New York in the summer of 1840 and died there in 1841, after taking a trip to Texas. The *Canadian Antiquarian and Numismatic Journal*, which published Brien's declaration in 1908, states, however, that he had died "a few years ago." In the absence of further details the first hypothesis seems more plausible.

JEAN-PAUL BERNARD

Information concerning the birth of Jean-Baptiste-Henri Brien is provided in an article which appeared in the *North American* on 4 Dec. 1839.

BVM-G, Fonds Ægidius Fauteux, notes compilées par Ægidius Fauteux sur les patriotes de 1837–38 dont les noms commencent par la lettre B. PAC, MG 24, B39. Jane Ellice, *The diary of Jane Ellice*, ed. Patricia Godsell (Ottawa, 1975). L.-J.-A. Papineau, *Journal d'un Fils de la liberté*. [Jacques Paquin], *Journal historique des événemens arrivés à Saint-Eustache, pendant la rébellion du comté du lac des Deux Montagnes, depuis les soulèvemens commencés à la fin de novembre, jusqu'au moment où la tranquillité fut parfaitement rétablie* (Montréal, 1838). *Report of state trials*, 2: 548–61. "Un document inédit sur les événements assez obscurs de l'insurrection de 1837–38," [F.-L.-G.] Baby, édit., *Canadian Antiquarian and Numismatic Journal*, 3rd ser., 1 (1908): 3–31. *Le Canadien*, 23, 25 oct. 1839. *Montreal Gazette*, 11 Oct. 1838. *North American*, 15 Nov., 11 Dec. 1839. *Le Patriote canadien* (Burlington, Vt.), 23 oct. 1839. Caron, "Inv. des doc. relatifs aux événements de 1837 et 1838," ANQ *Rapport*, 1925–26: 235, 269, 275, 279; "Papiers Duvernay," ANQ *Rapport*, 1926–27: 178–79, 182, 193, 201, 207, 209, 219, 221. F.-T. B[ègue]-Clavel, *Histoire pittoresque de la franc-maçonnerie et de sociétés secrètes anciennes et modernes* (3e éd., Paris, 1844). Fauteux, *Patriotes*, 141–43. L.-O. David, "Révélations faites en prison par le Dr Brien, le faux ami du noble de Lorimier," *L'Opinion publique*, 24 mars 1881: 133–34; 31 mars 1881: 145–46; 7 avril 1881: 157–58; 14 avril 1881: 169–70; 21 avril 1881: 181.

BROKE, Sir PHILIP BOWES VERE, naval officer; b. 9 Sept. 1776 in Broke Hall, Nacton, England, eldest son of Philip Bowes Broke and Elizabeth Beaumont; m. 25 Nov. 1802 Sarah Louisa Middleton, and they had 11 children; d. 2 Jan. 1841 in London.

Philip Bowes Vere Broke entered the Royal Naval Academy at Portsmouth in 1788 and four years later joined the *Bulldog* as a midshipman. A lieutenant from 1797, he was present at the battle of Cape St Vincent that year, and saw further service off Ireland and in the North Sea. On 14 Feb. 1801 he was promoted captain, and on 31 Aug. 1806 took command of the frigate *Shannon*. Broke was ordered to Halifax in August 1811 to join the squadron under Vice-Admiral Herbert Sawyer, and arrived there on 24 September. For the next 18 months he cruised in the western Atlantic to intercept French warships and, from mid 1812, American shipping, returning to Halifax from time to time. After assuming command of the *Shannon*, Broke had devoted his energies to raising the ship's standard of gunnery, and a well-thought-out program of training was followed with great care. These exertions were to produce one of the most efficient fighting ships in the Royal Navy at a time when naval gunnery was often poor.

On 21 March 1813 Broke sailed in company with the frigate *Tenedos* to keep watch on Boston Harbor, where several of the powerful American super-frigates had gathered. By late May, having detached the *Tenedos*, Broke was running short of fresh water, but he was anxious to engage one of the much-vaunted enemy vessels before returning to Halifax. On the morning of 1 June he closed the land and saw the frigate *Chesapeake* apparently ready for sea. He sent a written challenge to Captain James Lawrence, but before it could be delivered the American ship got under way and came up on the *Shannon*'s starboard quarter. At 5:50 P.M. the *Shannon* opened fire. The effect of her broadside was catastrophic for the *Chesapeake*. The men at her wheel were killed and sheets and brails shot away, so that she lost way and collided with the *Shannon*. The British vessel then raked her opponent, causing havoc among the enemy gun crews. Broke had the two ships lashed together and, seeing the Americans leaving their guns, led away the main deck boarders. After a brief, desperate resistance, during which Broke was badly wounded by a blow on the head from the butt of a musket, the *Chesapeake* surrendered, her captain mortally wounded and nearly one-half of her crew casualties. Eleven minutes had elapsed since the first shot. Although the American vessel was larger and carried a heavier armament, her crew had had little time to work together, and the victory was the result of Broke's leadership and excellent training. Halifax hailed the appearance of the *Shannon* and her prize with jubilation. It is said that the clergy and choir of St Paul's Church ran down George Street in their cassocks and surplices to see the ships.

Broke recovered sufficiently from his wound to be able to resume command of the *Shannon* when she sailed for England in October 1813. His victory had provided a badly needed tonic to a British public depressed by earlier American naval successes, and he was showered with honours, being made a baronet on 25 Sept. 1813 and a KCB on 3 Jan. 1815. He was also awarded the small naval gold medal given to post-captains who had distinguished themselves in action. However, much troubled by his wound, he never served at sea again, and spent most of the rest of his life at Broke Hall. There he took a keen interest in the community and was kept busy with correspondence on naval matters, chiefly gunnery. He was promoted rear-admiral of the red on 22 July 1830. In 1840 he became concerned about his health and decided to undergo an operation in London to repair the damage from his wound. He could not stand the strain and died on 2 Jan. 1841, being buried in St Martin's Church in Nacton seven days later.

H. F. PULLEN

Admiral Sir P. V. B. Broke, bart., K.C.B., &c.: a memoir, comp. J. G. Brighton (London, 1866). *DNB*. H. F. Pullen, *The "Shannon" and the "Chesapeake"* (Toronto and Montreal, 1970).

BROMLEY, WALTER, social reformer, humanitarian, and educator; baptized 27 Feb. 1775 in Keelby, England, eldest son of Robert Bromley and Jane ——; m. 1794 in Port-au-Prince (Haiti); there were at least two children of this union, one of whom, Stephen, married Ann DeLancey, daughter of James DeLancey*, and studied law with Thomas Chandler Haliburton*; m. secondly 25 Dec. 1831 Jane Ashton in Boston, England, and they had several children; found drowned 7 May 1838 in the River Torrens, South Australia.

Raised in an agrarian Lincolnshire family, Walter Bromley enlisted in the 23rd Foot as a boy. During the wars with revolutionary and Napoleonic France, he served in such diverse theatres as the West Indies, the Netherlands, Denmark, Malta, Asia Minor, Nova Scotia (1808–10), and the Iberian peninsula. After returning to England in 1811 he retired from active service in the army with the rank of captain. Drawing half pay until the 1830s, Bromley was free to indulge his propensity for social activism. This enthusiasm had been awakened by an exposure to the evangelical interests then fashionable among his senior officers and by his own enlightened reaction to the poverty, illiteracy, and exploitation he found in England and elsewhere, in city and countryside, among whites and non-whites.

Bromley's return to Nova Scotia in 1813 as a social reformer was wholly prompted by a desire to do good and spread British evangelical influences abroad. Nova Scotia had not been his first choice. After devoting his talents briefly to the study of the social ills of London, he had planned to undertake an agency for the British and Foreign Bible Society among the inhabitants of Spain and Portugal and among British soldiers involved in the Peninsular campaign. The society, however, was unwilling to encourage this bold venture, and so Bromley decided to promote the objects of the British and Foreign School Society in Nova Scotia, under the official sponsorship of the Duke of Kent [Edward* Augustus].

Bromley's Royal Acadian School, which opened in Halifax in 1813–14, represented an important departure in education for the colonies. It was non-sectarian and, like the local bible society, drew as its supporters a cross-section of local society comprised of liberal-minded elements both inside and outside the Church of England. Although the aim of the school was to attack illiteracy, encourage morality, and promote industry, it also challenged the existing notions of privilege and authority in society. The controversy inspired by Anglican opposition to its establishment – one of the school's leading critics was judge Alexander CROKE – would have daunted a lesser mortal than Bromley. Instead, acting as both teacher and administrator, he thrived on the publicity his efforts aroused. The opponents of denominational privilege, led by Thomas MCCULLOCH, rallied to his side. His school also benefited from being in the right place at the right time and proved to be an important social experiment. It combined under one roof inexpensive education for the children of the emergent middle class, free education for the children of the poor during the serious depression that followed the Napoleonic Wars, and a workshop for the unemployed at a time when local society had not yet begun to cope with the relief of the able-bodied poor.

Despite constant financial uncertainties, the school continued to attract the patronage of the city's élite and a clientele of shopkeepers and artisans whose children's educational prospects were extremely precarious in a town without public schooling. Because it was neither a charity school nor a private school, Bromley's institution represented the inauguration of a middle way in education much needed by the town's nascent bourgeoisie. The Royal Acadian School was one of the first institutions of colonial society in which middle-class self-interest and the interests of an increasingly middle-class society could be combined. Here charity pupils – black and immigrant – and fee-paying pupils – the sons and daughters of rising Halifax families (both Protestant and Catholic) – were put through their paces in the three Rs, religion, and vocational training. Parents relished the opportunity to secure a modestly priced education for their children, and for the pupils the Royal Acadian School provided an invaluable start in life. Newspaper editor George Edward Fenety*, who attended Bromley's school in the early 1820s, claimed in 1858 that besides journalists like himself his schoolmates had included "Lawyers, Statesmen, Sailors (in her Majesty's service) &c.&c." One of them was Joseph Howe*. Another was Daniel Cronan*, reputed to be Halifax's richest citizen on his death in 1892.

In addition to benefiting members of the middle and lower orders, Bromley's school made a seminal contribution to the development of the education movement. The school's success prompted the establishment, by the Church of England and other denominations and groups, of a host of somewhat similar schools whose mission to the same type of socio-economic constituency exerted continuous pressure on the provincial government to provide support for public education. Then again, the fact that it followed a specific educational philosophy helped to provoke a debate on the nature and purpose of schooling. Moreover, the monitorial method of instruction used at the school trained a new generation of common school teachers. Just as important was the technique of placing the management of the school in the hands of voluntary trustees. This arrangement assured the school of prestigious patronage, continued support from both the government and private citizens, and attractiveness to the deferential elements of a traditional society, who were favourably impressed by their employers' and rulers' interest in the school. Long after Bromley's departure from Nova Scotia, the school continued to play a central role in the campaign for free education. (It was destined to become a girls' school by the 1870s.)

The school also contributed to the debate on the political economy of poverty and was a springboard for launching Bromley into his activities as the "Poor Man's Friend." At a time when sluggish trade and substantial immigration were creating economic distress in the colony, Bromley used his school to provide opportunities for supplementing local industry. Attempts to increase employment formed an essential part of his utilitarian and energetic approach to the problems of the poor. Particularly concerned to keep the impoverished servant class of Halifax fully occupied as the most effective deterrent to mischief and vice, Bromley employed in 1823, under the direction of one of his former female monitors, 67 girls and women to spin and knit native wool in his school or in their dwellings. Most of the yarn was manufactured into socks which Bromley sold for 2*s.* a pair. As in other undertakings, he ventured into this field of private enterprise without regard for personal profit. He paid his workers 2*s.* a day, and considered that he was helping to ameliorate the problem of unemployment. The "spinning manufactory," he maintained, "is what was much wanted in Halifax, as the late war had destroyed the very sinews of industry, so that hardly a spinning-wheel could be found in the whole town, while the country abounded in wool and flax, the former article sent in quantities to the United States."

Superficially, the picture of a domestic manufactory in the school is highly reminiscent of the notorious schools of industry in 18th-century England. But, since Bromley paid his female employees a reasonable rate for piece-work, the situation was materially different, and some credence must be given to his claim that this employment "proved a blessing to many poor people, who are enabled to obtain the necessaries of life by their own industry." Because he was utilizing local products and local labour, Bromley sought in 1823 the backing of the Central Board of Agriculture [*see* John YOUNG] for his linen and woollen manufactory. That body's collapse in 1825 and Bromley's departure from the colony shortly afterwards meant that no long-term benefits accrued from these efforts, but sufficient local interest had been shown for the board to offer a premium for the manufacture of woollen garments. The bounty covered the financial loss that Bromley sustained from his manufacturing enterprise for the year, although, as one commentator put it, "he had to purchase wheels, wool-looms, flax-looms &c and could not devote as much attention to it, as an individual would have done who pursued it for profit."

Bromley's promotion of manufacturing complemented his keen participation in the Halifax Poor Man's Friend Society, organized in 1820. He was not a believer in indiscriminate charity. The pamphlets he had published in England in 1812 evinced an abhorrence of mendicity, and the Poor Man's Friend Society, of which he was a leading member, was formed "for the adoption of such measures, as would more effectually relieve the wants of the numerous poor, and destroy the system of public begging." Begging by children reflected badly on the highly moralistic education they were supposed to be receiving in the town's monitorial schools. The foundation and activities of the new society, based on British counterparts, were undoubtedly inspired by the hard times of the 1820s. The members of the society, led by the town's medical practitioners, hoped to provide a viable alternative to the existing method of offering relief under the aegis of the unsavoury poor-house. The emphasis initially placed on selective aid in the form of materials and provisions, and on finding employment for able-bodied paupers, was a feature of the society that appealed to Bromley. But the waning enthusiasm of its patrons and the consequent decline in its income meant that the Halifax Poor Man's Friend Society rapidly fell into the less constructive practice of providing indiscriminate mass relief through soup-kitchens and the much criticized poor-house.

However humane Bromley may have been, he probably deplored this turn of events and sympathized with the Malthusian criticisms voiced in the Halifax press. Indeed, his contemporaneous promotion of a domestic manufactory in the school can be interpreted as the measure of a frustrated activist designed to encourage the Poor Man's Friend Society back along the path of utilitarian self-help. In 1824 Bromley claimed that the society had agreed to adopt his economic plans for "houses of industry" as the model for its future operations. Together with his political supporter Samuel George William ARCHIBALD, John Young, the ubiquitous John Starr, a generous protagonist of all benevolent societies, and a sprinkling of dissenting clergymen, Bromley contributed to the work of the ill-fated society principally through his service on its committee of industry. The active, middle-class element in the society preferred to assist the poor to help themselves by the provision of employment and the establishment of a savings bank, which would enable them to lay aside sufficient wages in the summer months to see them through a bad winter. The collapse of these plans, and ultimately in 1827 of the society itself, must be attributed to the organization's reliance on a few individuals and to the improvement of economic conditions, not to "the doctrine of laissez faire, and the moralizing objection to poor relief as voiced by the Malthusians," as George E. Hart claims in his 1953 study of the society.

When Bromley left Halifax in 1825 he abandoned not only a declining poor relief enterprise, but also an educational experiment which had not fulfilled his expectations. He had intended to promote the establishment of British and Foreign schools throughout the Maritime colonies. His early reports to the society in London indicate that several schools were founded, and he claimed that he had trained 12 teachers by 1817. But, despite continually optimistic remarks, only the Royal Acadian School and a few Sunday schools existed at the time of Bromley's departure. The decision of the Nova Scotia House of Assembly in 1815 "that it is not expedient to extend Acadian schools throughout the province" put an end to Bromley's dream. Bromley subsequently continued as an agent of the British and Foreign School Society during the period between 1826 and 1836 from his home base near Boston in Lincolnshire. According to his own account, he successfully promoted the establishment of schools and school societies throughout the more receptive counties of England.

The other major aspect of Bromley's career in Nova Scotia was his profound interest in the welfare of the Indians. Exactly how he became aware of the Indians' circumstances is unclear, but the answer may lie in his good services to the poor and disadvantaged. In 1814 he had indicated that as soon as his work in Halifax was safely under way, he intended "to take myself to the woods among the Indians, where it is probable I may remain the remainder of my days." The Indians were certainly represented among the beggars and drunkards whom he confronted in the streets of Halifax. Although both blacks and Indians became special objects of his concern, it is the public exposure he gave to the plight of the rapidly declining Indian population of Nova Scotia and New Brunswick that particularly contributes to his historical significance.

He undertook his campaign to assist the Indians at the same time as he was launching his school. He found it impossible, however, to arouse sufficient colonial interest to sustain a voluntary local society for fostering the improvement of their conditions. To make matters worse, the assembly showed little concern for the welfare of a group of unenfranchised residents once the return of peace after 1815 removed all danger of an Indian threat. Bromley was therefore forced to seek the support of the English missionary societies. His main aid came from the New England Company, which contributed to his experiment among the Micmacs at Shubenacadie. Here, and briefly at similar settlements in Chester and Fredericton, he promoted self-help through agrarian employment as a more "civilized" occupation than hunting and as a way to keep the Indians away from the evil influences of urban life. Bromley's work could not be continued, however, without permanent funding and greater toleration for the Indians' unshakable Catholicism, with which his sponsor Lieutenant Governor Lord Dalhousie [RAMSAY] was reluctant to interfere. Ultimately Bromley's major achievement was to help expose the scandalous project supported by the New England Company at Sussex Vale (Sussex Corner), N.B., where he discovered in 1822 that exploitation of Indian children was given priority over religious instruction and vocational training [*see* Oliver Arnold*].

Despite the failure of his own scheme, Bromley's attitudes towards the Indians were singularly enlightened for his day and were later reflected in his work among the aborigines of South Australia between 1836 and his accidental death in May 1838. In both parts of Britain's empire, Bromley totally dismissed the idea that native people were naturally inferior and set out to encourage their material improvement through settlement and agriculture, their talents through education, and their pride through his own study of their languages. To mid Victorian Haligonians, however, Bromley's reputation centred not on his Indian projects but on his Royal Acadian School, a sure sign that the route to folk-hero status in the 19th century was through service to the self-interest of the middle class.

JUDITH FINGARD

For information on Bromley's own publications as well as primary printed and secondary sources relating to his career, see Judith Fingard, "English humanitarianism and the colonial mind: Walter Bromley in Nova Scotia, 1813–25," *CHR*, 54 (1973): 123–51. The major manuscript sources are as follows: British and Foreign Bible Soc. Arch. (London), Home corr., 1812, 1815, 1836; Guildhall Library (London), MSS 7920/2, 7956, 7969–70 (New England Company papers) (mfm. at PAC); Lincolnshire Arch. Office (Lincoln, Eng.), Anderson Pelham, rental books; Keelby, vestry records, 1775; Yarborough wapentake, land tax accounts; PAC, MG 24, B16; PANS, MG 15, B, 3, no.24; MG 20, 180; RG 1, 230, 305, 411; RG 5, P, 80; RG 20C, 40, no.436; PRO, CO 13/5, 13/7, 13/9, 13/11; CO 15/1; SOAS, Methodist Missionary Soc. Arch., Wesleyan Methodist Missionary Soc., corr., North America, box 4; Council for World Mission Arch., London Missionary Soc., corr., North America, folder 2, no.41, folder 5, nos.7–8, 12; and SRO,

GD45/3/18–27 (mfm. at PAC). See also Church of Jesus Christ of Latter-Day Saints, Geneal. Soc. (Salt Lake City, Utah), International geneal. index, and PRO, WO 25/751: ff.28–28v.

Relevant secondary sources found or written since the publication of the article include: J. M. Beck, *Joseph Howe* (2v., Kingston, Ont., and Montreal, 1982–83), 1; Susan Buggey, "Churchmen and dissenters: religious toleration in Nova Scotia, 1758–1835" (MA thesis, Dalhousie Univ., Halifax, 1981); Upton, *Micmacs and colonists*; *Herald* (Halifax), 23 Sept. 1892; *Morning Chronicle* (Halifax), 10 July 1868, 11 July 1874; *Morning Herald* (Halifax), 7, 12 Sept. 1885; and *Morning News* (Saint John, N.B.), 2 Aug. 1858.

BROWN, FREDERICK, actor and theatre manager; b. in London, son of D. L. Brown; d. 1838 in North Carolina.

Although known as the "Liverpool Roscius," Frederick Brown in fact never completely fulfilled his early promise as a child prodigy. Short and slight with "a face of no marked constructiveness, but rather common in form," he was considered a highly respectable and gentlemanly leading player, but was not of the highest rank. At Sunderland (Tyne and Wear) on 28 May 1814 he married the actress-dancer Sophia De Camp. His marriage connected him with prominent acting families. His wife's sister Maria Theresa (Marie Thérèse), herself a well-known actress, had married actor Charles Kemble, younger brother of the famed John Philip Kemble and Mrs Sarah Siddons.

The Browns came to North America in 1816 and starred at the Federal Street Theatre, Boston, for the 1816–17 season. Their first appearance in Lower Canada was by "special engagement" with John Duplessis Turnbull's stock company in Montreal during April 1818. That July, after a "most favourable reception" at the Fairbanks Wharf Theatre in Halifax, Brown returned to Montreal, where he remained from October to April 1819, with the exception of engagements in Kingston in February and his New York début at the Park Theatre as Hamlet on 9 March. In Montreal Brown was applauded for his versatility and was well received in his repertoire of Shakespearian roles and in the late 18th-century classics made famous by John Philip Kemble. His Othello, particularly, was closely analysed and even compared with Kemble's.

Back in Boston for the autumn of 1819, Brown raised the ire of audiences by his indifferent playing of a series of secondary roles. Fearing a row, the management allowed him to return once more to Montreal, where between mid December 1819 and mid February 1820 he played major parts, scoring a particular success with the tragic George Barnwell in George Lillo's *The London merchant*. On 4 May 1820 Turnbull's playhouse burned down and Brown would not return to Montreal until 1825. He regained the respect of his Boston audience on 25 May 1821, when he replaced the legendary Edmund Kean as Richard III, after the great star had refused to perform. Brown's name then began to appear along the eastern seaboard. In 1823 he supported the American actor Junius Brutus Booth in Philadelphia and in Richmond, Va, and during 1824–25 became, for the first time, a manager in Charleston, S.C., and Savannah, Ga. He had less success acting in New York and was harshly criticized in October 1824 and again in May and June 1825. The poor notices may have helped him to decide to apply to manage the new Theatre Royal being built in Montreal.

The 1,000-seat, Georgian-style playhouse, on the site of present-day Bonsecours market, was constructed at a cost of £7,500. John MOLSON was the principal shareholder. The theatre opened on 21 Nov. 1825, just one week behind schedule, and Brown, the lessee, "received the warmest marks of approbation" for his playing of Vapid, the playwright in Frederic Reynolds's *The dramatist*. However, the conscientious though relatively inexperienced manager was destined to lose money. The theatre's extravagant appointments, its weekly overhead, the lavish size of the company (30 actors and actresses, 14 musicians, and backstage personnel), the ambitious repertoire heavily weighted with Shakespeare and avoiding the popular melodramas, and the relatively small English-language population in Montreal (10,881) combined to defeat the enterprise. Guest stars did little to stem the tide and the poorly heated theatre was discouraging to spectators when winter temperatures hovered around −32°F. As attendance dwindled so did newspaper coverage and some actors deserted to other theatres. Brown toured to Quebec from 6 to 21 Feb. 1826, to good response but limited returns. The 24-week season ended on 8 May but Brown retained the theatre until the autumn in hopes that an appearance by Edmund Kean would reverse his fortunes. Although the renowned star attracted crowds and gave Brown's management a final flourish, his nightly fee nullified the gains. The Browns had supported Kean, playing, for example, Iago and Emilia to his Othello. On 3 November the citizens of Montreal accorded Brown a farewell dinner and gave him a gold ring in testimony of their esteem. He had played over 100 roles during the season of 1825–26.

From January to mid May 1827 Brown took many of his Montreal troupe to Charleston, where he managed the company, again unprofitably. He played at smaller theatres in New York during the summers of 1827 and 1833, although he was located primarily in the southern United States. Brown and his wife returned to Montreal several times between 1829 and 1833, a period when her brother Vincent De Camp took over the Theatre Royal for four limited summer seasons. On 9 July 1831 the *Montreal Gazette*'s theatre critic found Brown's playing "greatly improved," with "much less of the useless declamation which formerly rather injured . . . his acting." The last record of Brown's activity dates from the summer of 1834. While with comedians in Wilmington, Del., he penned some verses about the disrepair of a church which led to its restoration. Four years later he died in obscurity in North Carolina. His wife succumbed in October 1841 at Mobile, Ala.

Brown's North American vicissitudes as an actor-manager were typical of those faced by the English touring professionals of the period. As an actor in the heroic style of the Kemble tradition, he must have been something of an anachronism at a time when melodramas and equestrian shows were becoming popular. As a manager, he is remembered for his attempts to give colonial Montreal quality theatre.

DAVID GARDNER

Univ. of Pa. Library (Philadelphia), Charles Durang, "History of the Philadelphia stage between the years 1749 and 1855" (mfm.). F. C. Wemyss, *Chronology of the American stage from 1752 to 1852* (New York, [1852]; repr. 1968). Baudoin Burger, *L'activité théâtrale au Québec (1765–1825)* (Montréal, 1974). W. W. Clapp, *A record of the Boston stage* (Boston and Cambridge, Mass., 1853; repr. New York and London, [1963]). Merrill Denison, *The barley and the stream: the Molson story; a footnote to Canadian history* (Toronto, 1955). Franklin Graham, *Histrionic Montreal: annals of the Montreal stage with biographical and critical notices of the plays and players of a century* (2nd ed., Montreal, 1902; repr. New York and London, 1969). W. S. Hoole, *The ante-bellum Charleston theatre* (Tuscaloosa, Ala., 1946). Glen Hughes, *A history of the American theatre, 1700–1950* (New York, [1951]). G. C. D. Odell, *Annals of the New York stage* (15v., New York, 1927–49), 3. Y. S. Bains, "The articulate audience and the fortunes of the theatre in Halifax in 1816–1819," *Dalhousie Rev.*, 57 (1977–78): 726–35; "Canadian newspaper reviews of Frederick Brown," *Journal of Canadian Studies* (Peterborough, Ont.), 20 (1985–86), no.2: 150–58; "Frederick Brown and Montreal's doomed Theatre Royal, 1825–26," *Theatre Survey* (Albany, N.Y.), 24 (1983): 65–75; "The New Montreal Theatre: battling way back then," *Canadian Theatre Rev.* (Downsview [Toronto]), 24 (1979): 64–68. Owen Klein, "The opening of Montreal's Theatre Royal, 1825," *Theatre Hist. in Canada* (Toronto and Kingston, Ont.), 1 (1980): 24–38.

BROWN, JAMES, bookbinder and businessman; b. 1776 in Glasgow; m. *c.* 1795 and had at least four children; d. 23 May 1845 in Montreal.

James Brown arrived in Montreal in 1797 and went to work in Quebec as a bookbinder for printer John NEILSON. Several years later he returned to Montreal to set up as a bookseller and bookbinder. In November 1801 he advertised in the *Montreal Gazette*, inviting the public to come to his bookshop on Rue Saint-François-Xavier and see works he had bound as well as books for sale. Besides volumes in English and French, some of which were printed in Montreal and at Quebec, in particular in Neilson's shop, he sold office supplies and such items as stockings, mittens, barrels of coal, eyeglasses, and scrubbing-brushes.

In 1804 Brown was asked to become sales agent in Montreal for Walter Ware. Ware, who was from Massachusetts, had signed a 30-year lease in 1803 with the seigneur of Argenteuil, James Murray, to rent six acres in the village of St Andrews (Saint-André-Est), and in the summer of 1804 he built a paper-mill there. Brown accepted Ware's invitation and decided as well to collect rags, the raw material for making paper. He then asked Neilson to print 500 handbills announcing that the paper-mill in St Andrews was in business. In September 1805 he put the first wrapping-paper to come out of the paper-mill on sale in his bookshop.

In December 1806 Brown bought a share in Ware's company. He received a 5 per cent commission on the sale of paper and 25 per cent on the raw material collected. Financial difficulties, however, led to the dissolution of the company on 29 March 1809. A few days later Brown joined with John Chesser to buy the mill, and in a short time he became its sole owner. Increasingly engaged in the enterprise, he went to live at St Andrews in October 1810. His production included wrapping-paper, blue and blotting-paper, notepaper, bonnet board, printing-paper, and cartridge-paper. He had a number of workmen, some young apprentices, craftsmen, and an engineer working for him.

On 28 Feb. 1807 Brown had told Neilson that he intended to found a newspaper. He had not yet received the printing equipment he had ordered from Glasgow but being anxious not to let Nahum Mower, an American who was working on the same idea, get ahead of him, Brown asked Neilson to print a bilingual handbill announcing his new paper. In July he launched the *Canadian Gazette/Gazette canadienne*. He was assisted by his brother Charles, who took charge of the printing. The bilingual weekly contained foreign and local news, as well as some poetry, anecdotes, letters, and advertisements. Brown used about 15 agents to distribute the paper in Lower and Upper Canada. At that time two other Montreal newspapers were in circulation: Mower's *Canadian Courant and Montreal Advertiser* and Edward Edwards*'s *Montreal Gazette*. Edwards, who was heavily in debt, became unable to compete and in February 1808 sold his paper to Brown, who took the *Canadian Gazette* off the market. From 7 March it was Brown who published the *Montreal Gazette*; printing was entrusted to his brother. Beginning on 23 June he produced it in his own shop, and Charles's name no longer appeared on it.

Although Brown wanted to make certain changes in the paper, the *Montreal Gazette* retained the same format and style it had had under Edwards. It remained bilingual, and despite some criticism Brown continued to publish all pieces solely in the language in which they were written. From 1 July 1816 the title and date appeared in English only, and most of the articles were published in that language. Between 1808 and 1822 he also printed some 50 other works. They included volumes of a religious, political, or historical nature, French and Latin grammars, police regulations, and calendars.

Brown sold his newspaper and printing shop to Thomas Andrew Turner in 1822, apparently preferring to concentrate on his paper-mill. In 1824 he decided to dispose of his bookstore also and he subsequently seems to have concerned himself solely with the mill. Ten years later the new seigneur of Argenteuil, Charles Christopher Johnson, refused to renew the lease and within a few years he bought Brown out. The paper-mill then went out of production, and Brown moved to Montreal to live. In the rebellion of 1837–38 he returned to head a group of militiamen from St Andrews but afterwards he went back to Montreal, where he died on 23 May 1845.

LUCIE CHÉNÉ

ANQ-M, CE1-92, 23 mai 1845; CN1-7, 29 mars 1832; CN1-117, 31 mai 1804; CN1-185, 6 déc. 1806. ANQ-Q, CN1-262, 21 oct. 1811, 9 févr. 1815; P-193. PAC, MG 24, B1, 1: 66–67; 2: 27–29, 41–42, 115–16; 3: 336–37; 16: 22; 18: 293, 295, 297–98, 300–1, 305; 39: 1139; 137: 114; 147: 14, 114, 116, 162, 183–84, 206, 276, 310, 438, 471, 480; 148: 2, 4, 9, 20, 35, 39, 129, 193, 224, 268, 286, 301, 358, 414, 460, 497, 501; 149: 1, 6, 23, 45, 53–54, 66, 70, 82, 96, 119, 182, 187, 231, 250, 270, 281, 326, 339–40, 367, 370, 384, 411, 424; 150: 5, 10, 13, 25, 41, 60, 94, 102, 119, 135, 141, 145, 147, 153, 157, 161, 163, 210, 234, 245, 268, 270–72, 288, 311; 158: 626, 638; 184: 749–846. "Les dénombrements de Québec" (Plessis), ANQ *Rapport*, 1948–49: 125. *L'Aurore des Canadas*, 27 mai 1845. *Le Canadien*, 26 mai 1845. *La Gazette canadienne* (Montréal), juillet 1807–mars 1808. *Montreal Gazette*, 1808–45. *Quebec Gazette*, 28 May 1845. *Quebec Mercury*, 5 Jan. 1805, 27 May 1845. Beaulieu et Hamelin, *La presse québécoise*, vol.1. Borthwick, *Hist. and biog. gazetteer*. Béatrice Chassé, "Collection Neilson," ANQ *Rapport*, 1974: 25–37. Hare et Wallot, *Les imprimés dans le Bas-Canada*. Yolande Buono, "Imprimerie et diffusion de l'imprimé à Montréal, de 1776 à 1820" (thèse de MA, univ. de Montréal, 1980). George Carruthers, *Paper-making* (Toronto, 1947). E. A. Collard, *A tradition lives; the story of the "Gazette", Montreal, founded June 3, 1778* (Montreal, 1953). Ægidius Fauteux, *The introduction of printing into Canada* (Montreal, 1930). J. C. Oswald, *Printing in the Americas* (2v., Port Washington, N.Y., 1965). É.-Z. Massicotte, "Le premier moulin à papier au Canada," *BRH*, 39 (1933): 635–37.

BROWN, PETER, merchant, politician, and JP; b. *c*. 1797 in Ireland; d. 28 Dec. 1845 in Harbour Grace, Nfld.

Peter Brown passed his childhood in Ireland. He was, by trade, a carpenter. In 1817 he was settled in Harbour Grace, and by the 1820s had become established as an important fish merchant and prominent Roman Catholic. Although he appears to have received little formal schooling, in 1826 he was a member of a committee to build St Patrick's Free School in Harbour Grace, an early indication of his lifelong interest in education. (He was still involved in the affairs of the school in 1845.)

Brown was not an active participant in the Harbour Grace meetings of 1829 and 1830 which called for the establishment of a Newfoundland legislature, but in 1831 his name appears along with those of other respectable petitioners requesting the boon. When representative government was granted by Britain in 1832, he seemed initially reluctant to offer himself as a candidate for election unless a fellow merchant, Thomas Ridley*, also agreed to stand. Eventually he allowed his name to go forward without Ridley's, and he was returned as one of four members from the district of Conception Bay, the others being Robert Pack*, Charles Cozens, and James Power. The four had run as a group, apparently having pledged themselves "to oppose the imposition of any *Tax* which may have a tendency to injure the interests of the Fisheries or of Agriculture, or that may bear exclusively upon the poor"; "to procure an Act which shall cause the balance of servants' wages TO BE PAID IN CASH"; and to decline to take "any Office of emolument under Government while they sit as Representatives in the House of Assembly." The second promise is highly suggestive. It is apparent that the election of Brown and the others was one manifestation of the strength of popular feeling against the truck system in Harbour Grace and Carbonear in the early 1830s – feeling which had already broken out into dangerous riots. The reform movement in Conception Bay at that time was a movement among the masses.

When the new assembly opened on 1 Jan. 1833, Brown immediately moved that the house "do now proceed" to the election of its own officers (the clerk, the sergeant-at-arms, and the messenger). Another of his actions was to introduce a bill that would prevent government contractors and other office holders from sitting in the legislature. Both these issues were to cause controversy in Newfoundland throughout the early years of the assembly. Brown was attempting to anticipate and prevent encroachments by the crown upon the rights of the house, thus showing that in spite of his description of himself as "a true Radical," he was in fact somewhat traditional in his thinking, an old whig transplanted in the colonies. The first two sessions passed peacefully enough, and Brown's efforts demonstrated that he took seriously his pledges to work for the practical benefit of his constituents. He successfully piloted through the house bills to establish fire companies in Harbour Grace and to regulate the town's streets. However, both proved to be defective pieces of legislation and had to be quickly amended. The Harbour Grace street bill was aimed at controlling the reconstruction of the town after the fire of August 1832, in which Brown's premises had been saved. In 1833 he was accused of drafting the bill to favour his own business. He was also attacked for his proposal to change the name of the colony to Clarence Island.

It was not until William CARSON was returned in a by-election in December 1833 that the partisan divisions among members were revealed. Pack, Brown, and Power found themselves in a minority rump of reformers which included Carson and another St John's member, John Kent*. These men were loosely united in their opposition to alleged unconstitutional exertions of executive power and violations of civil rights, and in their concern to assert the authority of the legislature. Brown tended to support Carson in debates on such issues. In February 1835, for example, he spoke in favour of Carson's unsuccessful attempt to have a select committee of the house inquire into the administration of justice – really, an effort to undermine Chief Justice Henry John Boulton*. Brown's speech on that occasion was careful and moderate. He does not appear to have been dominated by Carson, even during the period 1834–36. Indeed, on such issues as establishing a classical academy, imposing taxes, and increasing the number of representatives, Brown was perhaps Carson's most persistent opponent. He feared what he described as the "preponderating influence" of St John's upon the assembly, and worried that outport interests were being overlooked in a number of measures that Carson supported. He was especially incensed over Carson's favourite scheme to create an academy for, as Brown contemptuously phrased it, "the instruction of the opulent in the learned languages, in the richest town in the Island, whilst a common English School is denied to the poor people in the outports." This theme of neglect of the outharbours became more marked in his speeches as years passed. Brown may not have been a graceful orator – he was ridiculed for "his choking and suffocating efforts to deliver himself" – but he was his own man, a rough and ready Irishman of independent means who stood his ground. In 1836, after an angry exchange in the house, Brown struck Kent and knocked his hat off. On the following morning Kent apologized for his bad behaviour.

In the stormy election of 1836 Brown, who had been appointed a justice of the peace in 1834, again ran for Conception Bay. It appears that he played no part in encouraging the tumults at the polls in his district; indeed, according to a report by magistrate Thomas Danson, he tried, without avail, "to prevent the riotous and brutal conduct of the Mob" during the polling. He was returned, and, when that election was invalidated, was elected again in 1837, finding himself now in a house for the first time controlled by reformers. Also in the new assembly were Patrick MORRIS, the brilliant John Valentine Nugent*, and, once again, Kent. With Carson as speaker, the assembly quickly adopted the abrasive tone in its dealings with the Council (or upper house) and the general combativeness that would mark its activities for the next four years. Brown was not slow to initiate contentious pieces of legislation. On opening day he was once again asserting the house's right to select its officers, and shortly afterwards he persuaded the legislature to undertake an inquiry into the activities of Harbour Grace magistrate John Stark during the 1836 election. Thus Brown was by no means out of place in the assertive assembly of 1837–41. Yet his alliance with the dominant St John's reformers was an uneasy one. He and Morris quarrelled as soon as the house opened. Brown also immediately tackled the *Newfoundland Patriot*, the newspaper normally thought of as the organ of the reformers, and made a dangerous and permanent enemy for himself in the editor, Robert John Parsons*. In August 1837 Brown angered both Nugent and Morris by introducing a justice bill that threatened to undermine the jury system and restore summary jurisdiction to the courts. He was reported as saying that he was aware of juries in Harbour Grace, "not one of whom knew that two and two made four." In effect, he was proposing a return to something resembling the old surrogate system [*see* James Lundrigan*].

Brown further angered Morris and Carson by persisting in his opposition to an academy in St John's. In 1839 Carson professed himself "astonished" that Brown could "so systematically oppose education." The charge was unjust. What Brown wanted was fair treatment of "the poor and those in the humbler walks of life . . . throughout the Island." He was, in fact, an enlightened thinker about education. It is noteworthy, for example, that he opposed religious segregation in schools, arguing that "there should be one general school for all denominations of christians, for it was by Catholics and Protestants mixing together that prejudice could be overcome." Brown was serving as a member of the board of education in Conception Bay in 1836, when Protestants, by insisting that the Bible in the King James version should be read in schools, in effect began the dissension that led to the creation of the denominational system of education in Newfoundland [*see* Charles Dalton*]. He later served as chairman of both the integrated and the Roman Catholic boards of education for the district.

Despite an occasional eccentricity such as his reactionary jury bill, Brown's instincts as a reformer were sound. In his concern for the poor – a persistent theme of his political career – he may, in fact, have been more of a social reformer than some of his high-minded urban colleagues. It seems to have been his lack of gentility, his stubborn character and earthy rhetoric, and his unyielding advocacy of outharbour interests that they objected to, rather than any slackening in principle. Brown in any case refused to play a minor role in the assembly. He became chairman of the important committee of supply and appears to have handled the responsibility well. The proceedings of the house show him occasionally impatient to get on with the practical business of running the country. Brown's general conduct in the house was thought so acceptable that his name was mentioned for possible promotion to the Council. He was also believed to be angling for the office of chief magistrate in Conception Bay – a rumour, kept alive by Parsons in the *Patriot*, which may have damaged Brown politically. Governor Henry Prescott* seemed to prefer Brown to all the other reformers, apparently viewing him as a stabilizing, moderating force in a volatile legislature. "He has a strong mind, but has had little education," Prescott wrote, adding, "He is not so tractable as others [among the reformers], and I believe regrets the composition of the present House of Assembly."

In 1841 Brown was chosen as one of four delegates to represent the views of the assembly to a select committee of the British House of Commons on Newfoundland. The four spent the summer of 1841 in London, but a change of administration in England may have prevented them from bringing effective pressure upon the imperial government. In 1842 they learned that a bill was before the Commons which in effect would destroy Newfoundland's 1832 constitution, replacing it with a peculiar legislature in which the upper and lower houses would be combined. Though the assembly had not been sitting for a year, the delegation drafted a petition of protest, which was presented to the Commons by the Irish politician Daniel O'Connell. The petition eloquently presented the case against altering the constitution in such a way as "to neutralize the influence of the people, and make a mockery of representative government in Newfoundland." However, the British government proceeded with its plan, and Newfoundland was blessed for the next five years with a legislative system that was an oddity in the colony's constitutional history.

Once the new constitution was approved, Brown ran once more for Conception Bay in the elections of December 1842. He was defeated, placing an ignominious sixth in a field of seven. He had been the object of persistent attack in the *Patriot* since 1837, and the abuse had spread to the press in Conception Bay. For this and possibly other reasons, Brown had become unpopular. Late in 1839, in a strange incident which seems to have been unconnected with politics, his house had been fired upon by four gunmen in a simultaneous discharge. Mercilessly, Parsons alleged that Brown had fired the guns himself.

In the closing years of his life, Brown maintained his interest in education, and became active in a Harbour Grace association for the repeal of the union between Britain and Ireland. In June 1844 his business premises were destroyed by fire. However, despite the loss – he was only partially insured – he remained in comfortable circumstances.

Peter Brown was the leading Conception Bay member in the Newfoundland House of Assembly from 1833 to 1841. His career is a reminder that the reform movement in the colony grew from roots in the outports as well as in the capital city, and that within that movement, once it became a powerful force in the assembly, there were conflicting regional interests. A study of Brown's career shows Carson, Kent, and Morris from a different perspective: as St John's politicians, rather than as bearers of the torch of reform for the whole island. Brown's chief contribution to the assembly was to keep it mindful of its responsibilities for all regions of the colony.

PATRICK O'FLAHERTY

NLS, Dept. of MSS, MS 2274. PANL, GN 2/1, 28–45; GN 5/1/B/1, Harbour Grace, 1813–26. PRO, CO 194/60–124. Nfld., General Assembly, *Journal*, 1843–45; House of Assembly, *Journal*, 1833–41. *Newfoundlander*, 1827–34, 1837–45. *Newfoundland Mercantile Journal*, 1816–27. *Newfoundland Patriot*, 1834–42. *Newfoundland Vindicator* (St John's), 1841–42. *Patriot & Terra Nova Herald*, 1842–47. *Public Ledger*, 1828–47. *Royal Gazette and Newfoundland Advertiser*, 1828–31, 1845. *Sentinel and Conception Bay Advertiser* (Carbonear, Nfld.), 1839–40. Gunn, *Political hist. of Nfld.*

BUCHAN, DAVID, naval officer, colonial administrator, judge, office holder, and Arctic explorer; b. 1780 in Scotland; m. 1802 or 1803 Maria Adye, and they had at least three children; d., apparently at sea, some time after 8 Dec. 1838.

In 1806 David Buchan was appointed lieutenant in the Royal Navy and two years later, as a convoy officer for the fishing fleet, he began his long association with Newfoundland. In October 1810 Governor John Thomas Duckworth* chose him to lead an expedition into the interior of the island with the aim of making contact with the Beothuks, the small native Indian tribe the government was anxious to protect. With a party of 27, mostly from his schooner *Adonis*, Buchan headed west along the Exploits River on 13 January with supplies and gifts loaded on heavy sledges. Struggling against bad weather and icy conditions, the party glimpsed increasing signs of the Indians' presence until on 24 January some members finally arrived at the Beothuks' wigwams on Red Indian Lake.

Although neither side spoke the other's language, relations between them appeared to be amicable. To cement these new relations Buchan decided to retrieve the gifts he had left with the rest of his party at a camp 12 miles down the river. Four Beothuks accompanied him on the trip and two marines remained behind. When Buchan returned two days later, he discovered the bodies of the marines. The Indians had dispersed. Concerned about the safety of his party, Buchan decided to end his mission to the Beothuks. "I could not . . . entertain any hope of securing their persons without bloodshed, which would frustrate all future expectation of their reconciliation and civilization, the grand object in view," he remarked. The exhausted group retraced their steps and reached the *Adonis* on 30 January. A second expedition was undertaken from 4 to 19 March. Its progress was obstructed by heavy storms and its members suffered from exposure. When they reached an Indian storage-wigwam pierced by arrows, Buchan deduced that the Beothuks were still inimical and retreated to the coast.

In December 1813 Buchan commanded the *Adonis* in the convoy to England and in 1815, as captain of the *Pike*, he briefly occupied Saint-Pierre. He was acting governor of Newfoundland during the winters of 1815–16 and 1816–17, when famine struck the colony and St John's endured three major fires. He once again travelled in the convoy during the fall of 1817.

Having been raised to the rank of commander on 13 April 1816, Buchan was placed in charge of the *Dorothea* on 15 Jan. 1818 to prepare for a polar expedition. Probably through the interest in Arctic exploration of John Barrow, second secretary in the Admiralty, Buchan was provided with elaborate orders to find a passage through the ice at the North Pole and then to sail through Bering Strait into the Pacific Ocean. A second vessel, the *Trent*, was commanded by John FRANKLIN. After their two whaling ships had been strengthened, Buchan and Franklin left from the Thames on 25 April. Struggling through pack-ice most of the summer, the ships skirted the western and northern harbours of Spitsbergen, probing into channels wherever the ice parted. In July the vessels were jammed at 80°34′ N, the most northerly point they were to reach. After three strenuous weeks of trying to free them, the expedition finally gained open water.

Buchan then turned west towards Greenland, but a gale forced the vessels back into the ice at the edge of the field. Within four hours they were so badly damaged that the expedition had to be abandoned. After making repairs at a quiet harbour in Spitsbergen, Buchan again headed west, examining the pack-ice until the expedition was within 12 leagues of Greenland. When the weather threatened once more, he at last turned back and reached the Thames safely on 22 Oct. 1818. Although a route across the pole had not been found, many scientific, cartographic, and natural history observations were successfully carried out by specialists assigned to the ships.

Returning to Newfoundland the next year as captain of the *Grasshopper*, Buchan served again as senior officer in the absence of the governor during the winter. On 8 Aug. 1819 he received from Governor Sir Charles HAMILTON a new assignment concerning the Beothuks. A woman, Demasduwit*, had recently been captured by whites and it was Buchan's duty to continue the attempt to reunite her with her people. However, she died of tuberculosis before he could make any move. Buchan then determined to transport her body to a Beothuk camp and on 21 January once again ascended the Exploits River. After placing her body, her possessions, and some gifts in a special tent at Red Indian Lake, the party continued west for three days. Although they saw signs of the Beothuks, they did not encounter any. The expedition regained the *Grasshopper* on 29 Feb. 1820. Three years later Buchan once more acted humanely towards the Beothuks. Three women, including Shawnadithit*, had been brought to St John's. As senior officer, Buchan ordered magistrate John Peyton Jr of Twillingate to make every effort to return them to their homes.

While serving as senior officer when the governors were not in residence, Buchan also acted as an itinerant judge, or naval surrogate, in the outports. In 1820 he was involved in a set of controversial cases. He and the Reverend John Leigh* sentenced two fishermen, Philip Butler and James Lundrigan*, to be flogged. On information subsequently filed by the fishermen, both surrogates were charged with trespass for assault and false imprisonment, but they were acquitted. Buchan was promoted captain in the Royal Navy on 12 June 1823, but, back in England that fall, was taken off the active list. Seeking some sort of employment from the colonial secretary, he was appointed high sheriff of Newfoundland on 1 March 1825. He was to remain in that position until after the introduction of representative government in 1832, officially resigning on 27 Aug. 1835.

After various tours of duty during 30 years in a rapidly changing Newfoundland, Buchan must have become involved with the East India Company, for he is last heard of on one of its ships, the *Upton Castle*, which sailed from Calcutta on 8 Dec. 1838.

WILLIAM KIRWIN

David Buchan never published accounts of his expeditions to make contact with the Beothuk Indians. They were obtained from his reports in Admiralty sources and printed, with various modifications, in the following works: [David] Buchan, "Mr. Buchan's expedition into the interior of Newfoundland," [ed. John Barrow], in Barrow, *A chronological history of voyages into the Arctic regions . . .* (London, 1818; repr., intro. Christopher Lloyd, New York, 1971), app., 1–23; "Narrative of Captain Buchan's journey up the River Exploits, in search of the native Indians, in the winter of 1810–11," *Royal Gazette and Newfoundland Advertiser*, 30 July, 6, 13 Aug. 1861; Charles Pedley, *The history of Newfoundland from the earliest times to the year 1860* (London, 1863), 482–502; and J. P. Howley, *The Beothucks or Red Indians: the aboriginal inhabitants of Newfoundland* (Cambridge, Eng., 1915; repr. Toronto, 1974, and New York, 1979), 72–90, 121–26.

Nfld. Public Library Services, Provincial Reference and Resource Library (St John's), David Buchan, journal. PRO, CO 194/50–93. John Barrow, *Voyages of discovery and research within the Arctic regions, from the year 1818 to the present time* . . . (New York, 1846), 49–61. F. W. Beechey, *A voyage of discovery towards the North Pole, performed in his majesty's ships "Dorothea" and "Trent" under the command of Captain David Buchan, R.N.; 1818 . . .* (London, 1843), 1–211. Edward Chappell, *Voyage of his majesty's ship "Rosamond" to Newfoundland and the southern coast of Labrador, of which countries no account has been published by any British traveller since the reign of Queen Elizabeth* (London, 1818), 185–87, 248–50, 259–60. *Lloyd's register of British and foreign shipping* (London), 1838–39. W. L. Clowes, *The Royal Navy; a history from the earliest times to the present* (7v., London, 1897–1903), 6: 508. B. D. Fardy, *Captain David Buchan in Newfoundland* (St John's, 1983). [This work is a readable account, but it is not historically accurate. W.K.] C. R. Fay, *Life and labour in Newfoundland* (Toronto, 1956). Prowse, *Hist. of Nfld.* (1895), 384–411. F. G. Speck, *Beothuk and Micmac* (New York, 1922; repr. 1981), 49–50. Edward Curran, "David Buchan – explorer," *Nfld. Quarterly*, 52 (1953), no.1: 26–28. L. F. S. Upton, "The extermination of the Beothucks of Newfoundland," *CHR*, 58 (1977): 133–53; "A portrait by Shanawdithit," *Nfld. Quarterly*, 73 (1977), no.2: 44.

BULL, GEORGE PERKINS (he may also have had a third Christian name, **Bothesby**), printer, newspaperman, and office holder; b. 14 June 1795 in Drogheda (Republic of Ireland), son of Captain Joseph Bull; m. 28 June 1818 Dorothea Burland, and they had four sons; d. 5 Dec. 1847 in Hamilton, Upper Canada.

George Perkins Bull came from a military family of slender means. Both his father and his brother Richard were officers in the light dragoons. George, trained in Dublin as a printer, had prospered sufficiently by 1823 to assume responsibility for the care of Richard's two children. In 1827 he became the publisher, and fellow Orangeman Ogle Robert Gowan* the editor, of the *Antidote, or Protestant Guardian*, a Dublin periodical designed to conduct an eleventh-hour defence of Protestant privileges against the threat posed by Roman Catholic emancipation. The *Antidote* collapsed when Bull served a year in prison after libelling a Catholic priest. At this time Bull broke with Gowan. Although Gowan had undoubtedly imposed upon Bull, at the root of the quarrel was a clash of personalities between the flamboyant and gifted Gowan and the hard-working but less imaginative Bull. Bull retaliated by conducting a campaign against Gowan which he was to carry into the New World.

Bull emigrated to Lower Canada late in 1831, settling in Montreal, where he opened a business as "a Printer, Stationer & Bookseller," and later began publication of the *London and Canada Record*. Gowan, who had established himself two years earlier as a gentleman farmer in Leeds County, Upper Canada, had united most of the Canadian Orangemen under his leadership in the Grand Orange Lodge of British North America (founded 1 Jan. 1830). Bull's first thought was to undo Gowan's work. He managed to convince Montreal Orangemen that Gowan was an impostor of bad character. As a result the Lower Canadian Orangemen broke with Gowan's lodge and established a direct connection with the grand lodge of the United Kingdom; Bull became temporary master of the Montreal Lodge No.434. Although Bull's charges were circulated in the Upper Canadian press, during the course of 1832 Gowan was able to answer them to the satisfaction of his Upper Canadian followers and to secure expressions of confidence from the British grand lodge.

Bull made an effort to find a place in Montreal as a supporter of the English party. He acted as a special constable during the election riots of 1832 and was a crown witness in the trials which followed. Yet, as he stated on 20 June 1833 in a petition to the lieutenant governor of Upper Canada, Sir John Colborne*, he had not "received sufficient encouragement" to remain in Montreal and had thus removed to York (Toronto). His petition to Colborne, which listed as references the names of more than 40 gentlemen, noblemen, magistrates, and clergy, all Orangemen, is a testimonial to Bull's diligence in using his Orange connections. Although he did not secure assistance from Colborne, in July 1834 Bull was able to establish the Toronto *Recorder and General Advertiser*, a substantial journal which supported the tory interests in the election of 1834.

In the *Recorder*, Bull eagerly reported the violence at the polls in Leeds County which led to Gowan's election being declared invalid. Their continuing feud may explain the invitation Bull received in 1835 from Allan Napier MacNab*, another of Gowan's staunch opponents, to establish a tory newspaper in Hamilton. Bull's *Hamilton Gazette*, published semi-weekly, was moderate in tone, represented high church toryism, and enjoyed moderate success. By the mid 1840s, however, the aggressiveness of Solomon Brega's reform *Journal and Express* convinced Hamilton tories that they needed a more active voice than the *Gazette*, which seemed to be turning more to theological concerns. On 15 July 1846 the *Hamilton Spectator, and Journal of Commerce*, established by Robert Reid Smiley*, began to champion the tory cause. Bull, who had been appointed coroner for the Gore District on 19 June 1846, continued the *Gazette* until his death the next year, at which time one of his three surviving sons, Harcourt Burland, took over its operation until it was absorbed by the *Spectator* in the mid 1850s.

The son of an army officer, George Perkins Bull was born with a status that could not be sustained by his means, and he sought to secure himself as a gentleman through political journalism. In his dispute with Gowan and in most of his writings, he adopted the tone of a decent man outraged by the presumptions of his personal and political enemies, an approach which, in combination with effective commercial journalism, enabled him to garner the security and political connections he sought.

HEREWARD SENIOR

AO, MU 1857, no.2311; RG 22, ser.205, no.740. PAC, MG 11, [CO 42] Q, 202-1: 17–18; MG 27, I, E30; RG 5, A1: 71753–56. G.B., Parl., House of Commons paper, 1835, 17, no.605, *Report from the select committee appointed to inquire into the origin, nature, extent and tendency of Orange institutions in Great Britain and the colonies*, app., no.23: 396. *Interesting trial: Hopkins against Gowan, Wexford spring assizes, March 14, 15, 1827* . . . (Dublin, 1827; repr. Kingston, [Ont.], and Toronto, 1837; copy at Queen's Univ. Library, Special Coll. Dept., Kingston). *Brockville Gazette* (Brockville, [Ont.]), 21 June, 16 Aug. 1832. *Church*, 10 Dec. 1847. *Constitution*, 14 June 1837. *Hamilton Gazette, and General Advertiser* (Hamilton, [Ont.]), 1835–47. *Recorder and General Advertiser* (Toronto), 14 May, 6 June 1835. *St. Catharines Journal*, 16 Dec. 1847. *Vindicator* (Montreal), 2 April 1832. *Death notices of Ont.* (Reid). *DHB*. Hereward Senior, *Orangeism, the Canadian phase* (Toronto, 1972), 41–42, 48.

BULLER, CHARLES, office holder and politician; b. 6 Aug. 1806 in Calcutta, eldest son of Charles Buller and Barbara Isabella Kirkpatrick; d. unmarried 29 Nov. 1848 in London.

Described by historian Thomas Carlyle as a man of "high principle and honourable conduct" with a "cheerful, good tempered winning expression," Charles Buller blended the "perfect probity, politeness," and "truthfulness" of his father, an employee of the East India Company, with the wit and imagination of his "graceful, airy, and ingeniously intelligent" mother. After attending Harrow from 1819 to 1821, Charles enrolled in several sessions at the University of Edinburgh during 1821–23. From 1822 to 1825 along with his brother Arthur William* he was privately tutored by Carlyle, who had to brush up on his Latin and Greek to keep up with Charles, "a most manageable, intelligent, cheery, and altogether welcome . . . phenomenon." After taking his BA at Trinity College, Cambridge, in 1828, Charles studied law, but, although called to the bar in 1831, he did not immediately practise that profession.

Instead Buller turned to politics and journalism. In parliament he represented his family seat, West Looe, in 1830–31 and then sat for Liskeard from 1832 to 1848. A popular Radical, he supported many reform measures. In 1836 he proposed and chaired the select committee on the state of government records and later he headed a committee inquiring into the election law in Ireland. Increasingly he demonstrated an interest in colonial questions. Although sometimes criticized for his levity in parliament, he could be earnest and dignified. His verbal facility was matched by his literary ability. Not only did he write for newspapers and in 1837 even edit with Henry Cole the *Guide to Knowledge* (London), a weekly paper, but he also contributed to the *Edinburgh Review* and the *Westminster Review* and authored numerous pamphlets.

In January 1838 Buller was offered the post of chief secretary to Lord Durham [LAMBTON], who had been appointed governor-in-chief of British North America with the special mission of inquiring into the government of Upper and Lower Canada following the rebellion of 1837. After initially refusing, Buller was persuaded by Durham to accept the post. Despite his misgivings about their postponed departure, he and his brother Arthur William left for Quebec with the governor in April 1838, after the insurrection had been suppressed. The delay had undermined the urgency of the mission and the necessity for the unusual powers it had been granted. Unlike Durham, who, he thought, "had too strong a feeling against the French Canadians on account of their recent insurrection," Buller was sympathetic, believing that the Canadians had been driven to rebellion by "long injustice" and "the deplorable imbecility of our Colonial policy." Although Durham was prepared to temper his justice with mercy, he had decided, Buller noted, "that no quarter should be shewn to the absurd pretensions of race, and that he must . . . aim at making Canada thoroughly British." Otherwise Buller reported favourably on the character, actions, and accomplishments of Durham, who had been "uniformly kind . . . to me from the first" and "very amenable to good advice."

Soon after his arrival Durham replaced the members of the Executive Council of Lower Canada and established several sub-commissions to study special problems and gather information for his final report. Appointed to the Executive Council on 2 June and to the Special Council on 28 June, Buller also headed some of these sub-commissions, but delegated the duties. Thus, although he was designated early in June head of the inquiry into crown lands and immigration in British North America, it was not he but the assistant commissioners, Richard Davies Hanson and Charles Franklin Head, who supervised the work, most of which was done by Edward Gibbon Wakefield*. Likewise, although charged with the commission on municipal institutions on 25 August, Buller had his assistants, William Kennedy and Adam Thom*, do most of the investigation and prepare the report. As chief secretary Buller's main responsibility was to assist Durham with the internal administration of the colony. He accompanied him in July to Montreal and Niagara (Niagara-on-the-Lake), but was too ill to continue the trip to Toronto, Kingston, and Prescott. Back in Montreal Buller worked out the terms for the commutation of the seigneurial rights held by the Séminaire de Saint-Sulpice. Towards the end of October he reached an agreement with the superior of the seminary, Joseph-Vincent Quiblier*.

Buller was also responsible for advising Durham concerning the fate of the prisoners of the rebellion in Lower Canada. Because a trial might trigger a public outcry and because of the difficulty of securing impartial juries, Buller and legal adviser Thomas Edward Michell Turton suggested punishment of the leaders by an *ex post facto* law. Initially Durham disapproved of the idea. Obliged to rely heavily on Buller, he eventually overcame his reservations and decided on an ordinance which would banish eight of the most guilty to Bermuda once they had confessed and which would forbid them and others exiled in the United States to return to Lower Canada. The ordinance was accompanied by a proclamation granting amnesty to the remaining prisoners, with the exception of those who had committed murder. Buller was dispatched from Quebec to Montreal to secure political support there for the measure and through the efforts of John Simpson*, a government official in whom the Patriotes had confidence, to obtain the confessions. In the end, most Lower Canadians seem to have approved of the ordinance, passed by the Special Council on 28 June.

By 7 September, however, public criticism in England and Lower Canada was mounting over a number of issues connected with Durham's mission. Buller urged his chief, sick and discouraged, not to resign. Given the high expectations everyone had entertained for his mission, Buller wrote to Durham, "the reasons which you regard as justifying failure or withdrawal . . . will not be considered sufficient." With political realism, he pointed out that Durham could not count on the support of the Tories in Britain or of Lord Melbourne's administration. Later that month Durham went ahead with his resignation on learning that his ordinance had been disallowed and that he had not been supported by the British government over the issue. Buller blamed the lack of support on Durham's failure to provide the government with adequate information. He approved of the resignation "as an act done in compliance with a stern and sad necessity." Moreover, he realized that Durham's ill health and "nervous agitation" necessitated his return to England. But he regretted his superior's decision not to return via the United States, where he would have been honoured and given greater political credibility.

Buller stayed behind in Lower Canada to collect materials for the reports of the various sub-commissions and arrived in England on 21 December. An attribution of the final report to himself, possibly by Lord Brougham, Durham's antagonist, was dismissed by him as a groundless assertion. Even though he had ably assisted his chief in compiling material and perhaps in drafting sections, the report remained Durham's. Eager to rectify the wrongs done to Durham, Buller none the less abided by his superior's wish not to imperil the interests of Canada and did not pursue a defence of Durham on his return.

Buller resumed his political career and began practising law before the Judicial Committee of the Privy Council in cases dealing with colonial and Indian appeals. He held the post of secretary to the Board of Control for part of 1841, and was appointed judge advocate general by Lord John Russell's Whig government in 1846. In 1847 he became chief poor-law commissioner, "with the hope of doing good." He spoke out in parliament on the ballot, the Irish question, church rates, national education, poor laws, corn laws, income tax, and the depreciation of gold coin.

His interest in the British colonies remained. In 1843 he spoke eloquently on colonization as "a way for colonies to enlarge at home and abroad the field of employment for capital and labour," and argued that "extensive colonization is one appropriate remedy for the ills of our social state, and a remedy which tends to promote and give efficiency to every other remedy." Possible political arrangements for the colonies were discussed in *Responsible government for colonies* (1840); for Buller "the union of the Canadas carried responsible government with it as a necessary consequence." Published anonymously so that he could be frank and outspoken, the pamphlet elaborated on those of Durham's ideas which had been most misunderstood and misrepresented. In addition to explaining and defining the role of the colonial governor under responsible government, he vigorously attacked the Colonial Office. Through his writings and parliamentary speeches Buller helped to bring about reforms in colonial policy.

When the "blunderings of a surgeon" followed by typhus cut short his life, Buller was missed by leading liberals and reformers. Carlyle eulogized him as "a fine honest fellow" and "the genialest radical I have ever met." Buller's bust was placed in Westminster Abbey and in 1860 he was commemorated in Sir Edward George Earle Lytton Bulwer-Lytton's *St. Stephens: a poem*, "Farewell, fine humorist, finer reasoner still, / Lively as Luttrell, logical as Mill."

HEATHER LYSONS-BALCON

Charles Buller is the author of "Sketch of Lord Durham's mission to Canada" in the Buller papers at the PAC (MG 24, A26); it has been published in "The Durham papers," PAC *Report*, 1923: 341–69. He also wrote *Responsible government for colonies* (London, 1840), which appeared first in the *Colonial Gazette* (London) from December 1839 to February 1840; it was reprinted in *Charles Buller and responsible government*, ed. E. M. Wrong (Oxford, 1926); chapters VI and VII were also reprinted in E. G. Wakefield, *A view of the art of colonization, with present reference to the British empire; in letters between a statesman and a colonist* (London, 1849). Other works by Buller are listed in the *British Library general catalogue*. His correspondence with British North American figures is at PAC (MG 24, A2, A17, B2, B14 (mfm.)).

[J. G. Lambton, 1st Earl of] Durham, *Lord Durham's report on the affairs of British North America*, ed. C. P. Lucas (3v., Oxford, 1912; repr. New York, 1970). Desjardins, *Guide parl. DNB*. H. J. Morgan, *Sketches of celebrated Canadians*. C. W. New, *Lord Durham; a biography of John George Lambton, first Earl of Durham* (Oxford, 1929). S. J. Reid, *Life and letters of the first Earl of Durham, 1792–1840* (London, 1906).

BUREAU, PIERRE, businessman and politician; b. 9 Oct. 1771 in L'Ancienne-Lorette, Que., son of Jean-Baptiste Bureau and Angélique Allain; m. 12 July 1791 Geneviève Gilbert at Quebec; d. 6 June 1836 in Trois-Rivières, Lower Canada.

In December 1800 Pierre Bureau put an advertisement in the *Quebec Gazette* "to inform the Public, particularly Gentlemen travelling," that at his house in Sainte-Anne-de-la-Pérade (La Pérade) they could "be accommodated with good beds, the best wines and other liquors, and every thing convenient for their reception at reasonable charges," as well as with stabling for their horses. Bureau kept this stage until 1808 and also acted as ferryman on the Rivière Sainte-Anne. In 1810 he was sued by the local seigneur, Charles-Louis Tarieu* de Lanaudière, but he won the case.

In December 1810 Bureau planned to petition the House of Assembly for the exclusive right to build a toll-bridge over the river. Apparently nothing came of the idea, however, since he went to live at Trois-Rivières a short time later. As a resident of that town he requested the assembly's permission in 1815 to build a bridge over the Rivière Champlain.

Although Bureau had set up as a merchant in Trois-Rivières, he also transacted business at Quebec and acted as attorney on certain occasions. In February 1809, for example, he sold 400 quintals of flour to a master baker in Upper Town. Seven years later the sale of a two-storey house on Rue Saint-Charles in Lower Town brought him £600. He also was involved in a few transactions with John NEILSON, the printer and owner of the *Quebec Gazette*.

Bureau's business throve, at least until 1820. In March of that year he was sued by Daniel ARNOLDI and was obliged to part with four lots and four houses in Trois-Rivières. In 1821 Quebec merchants Jacques and Joseph Leblond took legal action against him. Consequently the court issued a writ of attachment on three properties at Sainte-Anne-de-la-Pérade, one with two houses and a number of farm buildings, on part of Île Saint-Ignace, and on Île Sainte-Marguerite.

Bureau had been elected to the House of Assembly for Saint-Maurice on 18 Feb. 1819, replacing Louis GUGY, who had been appointed to the Legislative Council. He took up his duties on 19 March, but his election was disputed on 2 April. Isaac Ogden read to the house a petition from Étienne Ranvoyzé* and other voters in the riding. Bureau's opponents claimed that, although he had received the largest number of votes, he had been proclaimed elected illegally and had contravened provincial laws. He was accused of having bribed people either not to vote or to vote for him, as well as of having opened and maintained inns and taverns, serving voters at his own expense during the polling. The house then appointed three commissioners to conduct hearings, which were held in June at the presbyteries of the parishes of Champlain and Yamachiche. Bureau apparently retained his seat, and in the general election of March 1820 he was re-elected in his riding, with Louis Picotte* as running-mate. In the house the following December, Bureau opposed a motion to have the results of assembly votes published. Four years later he was involved in the debate on the Canada Trade Act. The group led by Louis Bourdages* succeeded in getting a special committee set up to study the possible repercussions of the act. A few days later Bureau aligned himself with Louis-Joseph Papineau*. He supported Papineau for speaker in 1825. In 1830 he backed a motion to compensate members for their travelling expenses and living costs at Quebec during parliamentary sessions. He also expressed himself in favour of the new militia legislation. The following year he voted for two resolutions directed against the Legislative Council, and he upheld the idea of making that body elective. In 1831 he supported a bill on the *fabriques* [*see* Louis Bourdages]. Bureau worked on 14 parliamentary committees and attended the house regularly. He was a member until his death.

SONIA CHASSÉ

ANQ-MBF, CE1-48, 8 juin 1836; CN1-32, 14 avril 1817; CN1-56, 24, 26 sept. 1823; 17 mars 1824; 1er mars 1827; 5 oct. 1829; CN1-91, 20 oct. 1801; 29 mars 1802; 18 mars 1803; 25 août, 26 oct., 9 nov. 1804; 25 janv. 1805; 4 juin, 9 août 1806; 22 févr., 21 sept., 10 déc. 1807; 24 oct. 1808; 25 févr. 1809; 25 mai, 29 juill., 22 nov. 1810; 17 sept. 1811; 22 févr., 26 avril 1812. ANQ-Q, CE1-1, 12 juill. 1791; CE1-2, 10 oct. 1771; CN1-16, 12 oct. 1808, 13 févr. 1809, 6 sept. 1816; CN1-230, 10 juill. 1791; P-192. L.C., House of Assembly, *Journals*, 1819–20. *Quebec Gazette*, 25 Dec. 1800; 14 Nov. 1805; 9 June 1808; 30 Aug. 1810; 17, 24 Jan., 11 April 1811; 14 Jan. 1813; 8 June, 23 Nov. 1815; 8 Feb., 14, 21 March, 4 April, 27 June, 7 Nov. 1816; 11 Sept., 4, 11 Dec. 1817; 5 Oct. 1818; 25 Feb., 11 March, 5, 19 April, 17, 31 May 1819; 9, 13, 16 March, 13, 20, 24 April, 10 July, 21 Aug., 11 Dec. 1820; 31 May, 2 Aug., 13 Sept., 22 Nov., 10, 17, 27 Dec. 1821; 25 July, 5 Dec. 1822; 27 Nov. 1823; 4 March 1824; 10 June 1836. F.-J. Audet, *Les députés de Saint-Maurice (1808–1838) et de Champlain (1830–1838)* (Trois-Rivières, Qué., 1934). Christine Chartré *et al.*, *Répertoire des marchés de construction et des actes de société des Archives nationales du Québec à Trois-Rivières, de 1760 à 1825* ([Ottawa], 1980). Maurice Grenier, "La chambre d'Assemblée du Bas-Canada, 1815–1837" (thèse de MA, univ. de Montréal, 1966). L.-S. Rheault, *Autrefois et aujourd'hui à Sainte-Anne de la Pérade* (Trois-Rivières, 1895).

BURPE (Burpee), DAVID, farmer, magistrate, and office holder; b. 22 April 1752 in Rowley, Mass., eldest son of Jeremiah Burpe, a carpenter, and Mary Saunders; m. 1 Jan. 1778 Elizabeth Gallishan, and they had seven sons and seven daughters; d. 31 May 1845 in Maugerville, N.B.

David Burpe must have received his formal education in Massachusetts, for there would have been few opportunities after 1763 when his father joined Israel Perley* and others in founding the settlement of Maugerville, in what was then the colony of Nova Scotia. Also in the group was David's elderly grandfather Jonathan Burpe, who became first deacon of the Congregational church that was soon organized. In its earliest years Maugerville operated as a traditional New England community, with civil authority vested in town meetings and the church responsible for social discipline.

At age 19, after the death of his parents, David became responsible for his seven surviving brothers and sisters. Active, reticent, cautious, and systematic, he already showed the characteristics of his mature years. While pursuing his farm chores he had trained himself by keeping a diary, which is literate and meticulous, but silent regarding his personal views and ambitions. An account-book that notes each item he purchased or sold from 1772 to 1784 is an important source for historians in showing how values of goods and services fluctuated during the years of the American revolution in a community where money was scarce and barter common. Historians owe him a further debt for his careful listing of the possessions left by his grandfather in 1781; it provides a rare insight into the style of living of a comparatively well-to-do frontier farmer.

The Burpe family shared the anti-British sentiments of their former compatriots in Massachusetts and David may have played some role in organizing Maugerville's support of the new Massachusetts government in 1775. Edward Burpe, a younger brother, joined Jonathan Eddy*'s expedition against Fort Cumberland (near Sackville, N.B.) the following year. In 1777 a British garrison was placed in Fort Howe (Saint John) and six years later many Maugerville farms were taken over by American loyalists. Few of the newcomers had cause to respect the feelings of "rebels," and the old families, in turn, resented the favours granted to the intruders. Disturbed by the changes in their society and inspired by the New Light ideas of Henry Alline*, who had held "reformation" services in Maugerville in 1779 and 1781, some of the old inhabitants set themselves apart by withdrawing into a sectarian world of religious fervour. Among them were the followers of Archelaus Hammond, who advocated an antinomianism that led to bizarre forms of worship.

Although Burpe, who accepted the conservative Old Light ideas of his grandfather Jonathan, was not prepared to compromise with the New Lights on theological matters, he nevertheless played a role in countering the deep divisions in his society and emerged as a moderating influence between the loyalist newcomers and the old inhabitants. In 1787 he and Jacob Barker Jr received appointments as justices of the peace for Sunbury County, of which the township of Maugerville, now divided into the parishes of Maugerville and Sheffield, formed a part. These were positions of privilege, for authority no longer rested with town meetings, as in New England, but was vested in the justices, who met in the Court of General Sessions to administer county affairs.

The division of Maugerville township that had taken place in 1786 was reinforced by denominational differences. In the parish of Maugerville loyalist Anglicans were in the majority; in Sheffield old inhabitants predominated. When the Church of England in Maugerville claimed the public lot on which the old New England meeting-house stood, Burpe and Barker took the lead in 1789 in moving the building several miles downriver to a public lot in Sheffield, using 60 teams of oxen to haul it on the ice. That year the members of the Congregational Church signed a new covenant. All came from a small number of New England families, but their church was supported by immigrant Scots and other dissenters, including a few loyalists. For reasons which are unknown, though it seems probable that he considered himself unworthy, Burpe did not become a church member in terms of

Congregational polity until 1805, yet he acted as clerk and served on all important committees. The congregation invited John James, a Calvinist Methodist from England, to be their pastor.

The appointment of this minister ended disastrously. In 1792, after being accused of drunkenness, association with persons of questionable character, and finally "scandalous Indecencies" in his behaviour towards a young woman, James embraced the Church of England. The dissenters were able to regain possession of the parsonage, and the meeting-house of which it formed a part, only on 6 Aug. 1793 when, finding the premises temporarily vacated, Burpe entered and defied the authorities to expel him. By then the rupture between Anglicans and dissenters had become unbridgeable and dissenter abhorrence of Anglican exclusivism made Sunbury County the centre of opposition to the policies of Lieutenant Governor Thomas Carleton*. It was perhaps at this time that Burpe began a mutually helpful association with Samuel Denny Street*, next to James Glenie* the leading opponent of the administration.

For the three decades ending in 1830 Burpe was one of his county's most active magistrates. He became a justice of the Inferior Court of Common Pleas and carried out a great deal of routine work, examining witnesses, signing recognizances, and binding persons to keep the peace. In 1814 he was appointed a justice of the quorum and made use of his office to get around the provision in the marriage law that required dissenters to be married by Anglican clergymen. Between January 1815 and September 1835 he performed 124 civil ceremonies in Sheffield. He also served as county auditor.

Burpe's participation in public affairs had behind it a firm commitment to the religious and social values of 17th-century New England Puritanism. While still comparatively young he became "Squire" Burpe, a patriarchal figure bent on restoring the fortunes of the dissenters' church and upholding Calvinist theology and traditional forms of worship in the face of New Light, Methodist, and Baptist appeals. His efforts reached fruition in 1820: the Sheffield congregation, reorganized and, for the time being, in communion with the Church of Scotland, was given title to a small portion of the land set aside for the church when the township of Maugerville was founded and finally obtained from Scotland a long-term resident pastor. Later, it reverted to its Congregational identity until it entered the United Church of Canada in 1925.

When Burpe's son David died in 1830, he received a long obituary in provincial papers. Although he was county treasurer and church deacon, the notice taken was really a recognition of his father, then in his 78th year and still an active magistrate. Among the documents old David left when he died at the age of 93 is one entitled "Record Book kept by the Town Clerk of Sheffield Sunbury County 1767–1835." It is a fitting memorial to his career, for he had preserved the spirit of the old Maugerville township, and by continuing its records had made it possible for the story of the persistence of a frontier community to be known to later generations.

D. M. YOUNG

[There is a thinly veiled lampoon of Burpe in Edward Winslow*'s *Substance of the debates, in the Young Robin Hood Society* . . . , a political satire that appeared in New Brunswick in 1795. Edited by Ann Gorman Condon, it appears as "'The Young Robin Hood Society' . . ." in *Acadiensis* (Fredericton), 15 (1985–86), no.2: 120–43. Dr Condon does not, however, draw attention to the parallels between Winslow's character Zedekiah T. and Burpe. D.M.Y.]

N.B. Museum, Sheffield, N.B., papers, David Burpe, "Record Book kept by the Town Clerk of Sheffield Sunbury County 1767–1835" (mfm. at PANB). PANB, MC 1, Burpee family; MC 300, MS5/144; MS33/36 ("A copy of the record book kept by the town clerk of Sheffield, Sunbury County, 1767–1835," ed. William McLeod, typescript, 1932); RG 3, RS307, C1, 10 April 1787; RG 18, RS157. UNBL, MG H9, F. M. Miles, "Maugerville School, 1763–1951" (typescript, 1951). "Documents of the Congregational Church at Maugerville," N.B. Hist. Soc., *Coll.*, 1 (1894–97), no.1: 119–52; no.2: 153–59. "Documents relating to Sunbury County: David Burpee's diary," N.B. Hist. Soc., *Coll.*, 1, no.1: 89–95. *The Newlight Baptist journals of James Manning and James Innis*, ed. D. G. Bell (Saint John, N.B., 1984). "The Pickard papers," ed. Gerald Keith, N.B. Hist. Soc., *Coll.*, no.15 (1959): 55–78. "Sunbury County documents," N.B. Hist. Soc., *Coll.*, 1, no.1: 100–18. *Head Quarters, or Literary, Political, and Commercial Journal* (Fredericton), 4 June 1845.

Early settlers of Rowley, Massachusetts: a genealogical record of the families who settled in Rowley before 1700 with several generations of their descendants, comp. G. B. Blodgette, ed. A. E. Jewett (Rowley, 1933). *The Stickney family: a genealogical memoir of the descendants of William and Elizabeth Stickney, from 1637 to 1869* (Salem, Mass., 1869). MacNutt, *New Brunswick*. W. D. Moore, "Sunbury County, 1760–1830" (MA thesis, Univ. of N.B., Fredericton, 1977). George Patterson, *Memoir of the Rev. James MacGregor, D.D.* . . . (Philadelphia, 1859). R. W. Colston, "Old Sunbury . . . ," *St. John Daily Sun*, 9 Sept. 1898: 6–7. James Hannay, "The Maugerville settlement, 1763–1824," N.B. Hist. Soc., *Coll.*, 1, no.1: 63–88. G. C. Warren, "Canada's pioneer missionary," *Tidings* (Wolfville, N.S.), 70 (1944), no.11: 3–5.

BURROWS, JOHN (originally named **John Burrows Honey**), surveyor, engineer, artist, and politician; b. 1 May 1789 possibly in the parish of Buckland Monachorum, near Plymouth, England, son of Christopher Honey and Elizabeth Burrows; m. first 7 June 1809 Ann Boden (Bowden) in the parish of Stoke Damerel (Plymouth); m. secondly 4 Feb. 1833 Maria Elizabeth Hoskin, *née* Blake; he had six sons and five daughters; d. 27 July 1848 in Kingston, Upper Canada.

John Burrows Honey first practised civil engineering in Plymouth. As well, while in England, he served in a militia unit, the Prince of Wales regiment. However, according to a grandnephew, William Thomas Rochester Preston*, he was forced to leave the country because of his political radicalism. In about 1815 he immigrated to the Canadas and settled in Nepean Township, Upper Canada. He apparently returned briefly to Plymouth but soon sailed back, arriving at Quebec on 20 Oct. 1817 and locating once again in Nepean, on the site of present-day Ottawa. Honey qualified as a land surveyor in Hull, Lower Canada, in December 1820. The following year he acquired title to 200 acres in Nepean, property which would increase greatly in value when the Rideau Canal was constructed through the lot, but he sold it, prematurely, in September 1821 for £95 to Nicholas Sparks*.

Honey made his name on the staff of Lieutenant-Colonel John BY during the construction of the canal. Taken on as an overseer of works on 1 March 1827, he held a responsible post, assisting the Royal Engineers in the measurement and assessment of the work of the various contractors and in the certification of accounts. At about this time he changed his surname to Burrows, a step the one-time radical reputedly took to avoid detection in England. When John Mactaggart*, the clerk of works, was dismissed for misconduct in June 1828, By would have named Burrows to the post instead of Nicol Hugh BAIRD had he had more experience. As it was, Burrows had assumed Mactaggart's duties on several occasions when he was ill disposed, and had acted as a draftsman and surveyor in the engineer department. In By's words Burrows had rendered himself "extremely useful on all occasions." It was not surprising therefore that, in early 1830, By recommended, though without success, that Burrows's pay be raised from 7*s.* 6*d.* to 13*s.* per day, within 1*s.* of the top pay accorded the clerk of works. In 1832, following the canal's completion, By without hesitation appointed Burrows to represent the crown before a jury investigating flood claims brought by landowners along the canal. That year he was also among the permanent appointees to the engineering staff of the British Ordnance department at Bytown (Ottawa).

Burrows had established himself as a leading citizen there soon after the commencement of the canal. From 1828 he served as a town councillor, and was nominated to council as late as 1847. In 1833 he married for the second time, and letters indicate a devoted husband and father. An ardent Methodist, he built in 1827 the first chapel in Bytown, and when this burned, made his house available to the congregation pending the building of a new chapel. Although temperate in his habits, he could enjoy a glass of wine with his wife.

By February 1837 Burrows owned no fewer than 17 houses in Bytown, an indication that he had achieved some measure of prosperity. Writing to her sister in England that year, Maria Burrows described her husband's health as poor; he had been confined to their house for most of the winter with rheumatism and lumbago. Despite failing health, Burrows continued as overseer of works in the Ordnance department's engineering office until his death. In that position he executed a series of historically useful pencil and water-colour views of various lock-sites on the canal. He died on 27 July 1848, and was buried in Hull and later reburied in New Edinburgh (Ottawa).

Burrows's service in the construction of the Rideau Canal, and his contribution to the community to which it gave rise, were considerable. His high principles and religious fervour were untainted by intolerance or Pharisaism.

E. F. BUSH

John Burrows's 1827 sketch-book or diary is in Ottawa, Hist. Soc., Bytown Museum and Arch. (Ottawa), JBUR; a photocopy of it is available at the PAC. The diary has been published in *Sights and surveys: two diarists on the Rideau*, ed. Edwin Welch (Ottawa, 1979). A number of Burrows's pencil and water-colour sketches of the Rideau Canal are reproduced in R. W. Passfield, *Building the Rideau Canal: a pictorial history* (Don Mills [Toronto], 1982).

AO, MU 938, biog. information relating to John Burrows; RG 22, ser.155. PAC, MG 29, D106; RG 5, A1: 48488, 65430; RG 8, I (C ser.), 43: 236; 45: 236. PRO, WO 44/20: 65–68; 44/23: 249–52 (copies at PAC). *Christian Guardian*, 9 Aug., 4 Oct. 1848. *Church*, 17 Aug. 1848. *Packet* (Bytown [Ottawa]), 29 July 1848. Lucien Brault, *Ottawa old & new* (Ottawa, 1946). E. F. Bush, *The builders of the Rideau Canal, 1826–32* (Can., National Hist. Parks and Sites Branch, *Manuscript report*, no.185, Ottawa, 1976), 89–93. Blodwen Davies, *The charm of Ottawa . . .* (Toronto, 1932). H. T. Douglas, "Bits and pieces, that's all; ten thousand words concerning Ottawa and the Ottawa area" (typescript, [Ottawa], 1969; copy at Ottawa, Hist. Soc., Bytown Museum and Arch.). R. [F.] Legget, *Rideau waterway* (Toronto, 1955). H. [J. W.] and Olive [Moffatt] Walker, *Carleton saga* (Ottawa, 1968).

BURTON, JOHN, Methodist and Baptist minister; b. July 1760 in County Durham, England; m. Mary ——, also of England, and they had one son and one daughter; d. 6 Feb. 1838 in Halifax.

John Burton and his family came to Halifax on 20 May 1792 while on their way to the United States. Burton had been sent to the new republic as a Methodist missionary under the auspices of the Countess of Huntingdon, a wealthy benefactress of the Methodist cause. Upon his arrival in Halifax, he was invited to fill the pulpit of Philip Marchinton*'s meeting-house. He preached there until the fall of 1793, when he made a trip to the United States. While he was in Knowlton, N.J., he embraced Baptist principles, received baptism by immersion, and was ordained a Baptist minister in January 1794. He returned to Nova Scotia that June, having apparently abandoned his original plan of settling in the United States.

In 1794 Burton seems to have been the only Baptist in Halifax. By 1795, however, his preaching had won enough converts that a church could be formed. In 1802 the tiny congregation moved into its new chapel at the corner of Barrington and Buckingham streets. The chapel had been built with funds which Burton had raised during a visit to Baptist congregations in New England. Modelled on the Regular Baptist order, Burton's church adhered to the Philadelphia Confession of Faith, a strict Calvinist creed. Among other things this creed restricted communion to those who had been baptized by immersion. The tiny church was the only Baptist church in the colony which kept to the letter of strict Baptist doctrine and practice. All the other churches in the Nova Scotia Baptist Association (formed in 1800) admitted unimmersed members. Because of his principles, Burton kept his congregation outside the Baptist association until 1811, two years after that body had finally adopted the Regular Baptist order. Still, although not in their association for many years, Burton was sought out by the Baptists to give advice and counsel on matters of doctrine and structure. In fact, so highly esteemed was he that the year after his church joined the association Burton was made its moderator.

In the early 19th century Burton was one of a group of preachers – his colleagues included Joseph DIMOCK, Edward Manning*, Harris Harding*, and Richard Preston* – who contributed to the dramatic growth of the Baptist church in Nova Scotia. As well, in his work among the colony's black Baptists, Burton helped fill the void created by the departure of David George*, a black preacher who had joined the exodus to Sierra Leone in 1792. Indeed, Burton should be seen as a bridge between George in the late 18th century and Richard Preston in the 1820s, for during that long period he was the only preacher who made the religious welfare of Nova Scotia's black Baptists one of his chief concerns. In 1811 Burton's church had 33 members, the majority of whom were free blacks from Halifax and the neighbouring settlements of Preston and Hammonds Plains. Shunned, or merely tolerated, by the rest of Christian Halifax, the blacks were from the first warmly received in the Baptist Church. Burton became known as "an apostle to the coloured people" and would often be sent out by the Baptist association on missionary visits to the black communities surrounding Halifax. He shared the extreme poverty of his congregation, and yet he was frequently seen going out to these black communities with goods and bread for the poor.

During and immediately after the War of 1812, roughly 2,000 black refugees left the southern United States under British protection to settle in Nova Scotia [*see* Thomas Nickleson JEFFERY]. Recognizing Burton's familiarity with the black community, the Nova Scotia government made him one of those in charge of the refugee settlements in Hammonds Plains and Preston, even giving him the power of magistrate to settle legal matters. Since the dislocated blacks had to contend with the smallpox epidemic of 1815, as well as with all the problems of learning to live in a new land, Burton's commission was a staggering one.

By 1819, because of Burton's work among the refugees and because most of these blacks had been Baptists in the United States, the Halifax church had swelled to a membership of 300 – more than double the size of the next largest congregation in the colonial Baptist association. Throughout this period Burton trained both black and white elders to work with him in his church and among the colony's growing black population. These elders were sent out on lengthy preaching missions which saw the formation of new black Baptist churches throughout Nova Scotia. Richard Preston was one such travelling elder.

In 1824–25 a controversy at St Paul's (Anglican) Church [*see* John Thomas Twining*] caused several members of that communion to leave and adopt the principles of the Baptist faith. These whites, who included James Walton Nutting*, James William Johnston*, and Edmund Albern Crawley*, were not anxious to join with the Halifax Baptist Church because of its congregation's low social status and what they judged to be Burton's insufficient education. After worshipping briefly at Burton's church, the new Baptists formed their own congregation in a chapel on Granville Street. This chapel became known as the First Baptist Church after the dissolution of Burton's church, and it bears that name today.

Burton's Halifax church was plagued by other dissensions; power struggles and racial tension were especially divisive. Finally, in 1832, under Richard Preston, 29 members left Burton's church to form the African Chapel, located on Cornwallis Street. In only a few years this church would become the focal point of black evangelism and ministry for the entire colony. The original Baptist church of Halifax grew smaller, and Burton's age and declining health made it impossible for him to minister regularly to it. After his death in 1838 its membership was completely absorbed in the two newer Baptist churches of Halifax.

Burton made a great impact upon the white Baptist church of Nova Scotia, and was the major influence on the structure and growth of its black Baptist church. His counsel helped to lead to the adoption of New England Baptist principles which gave Nova Scotia's white Baptists a unity in doctrine and structure. Within his own lifetime he was recognized as "a Father of the Baptist Denomination in Nova Scotia." His labours in Halifax initiated the growth of black congregations throughout the province. Among the blacks, it was he who was responsible for the training of the early black elders and the strict adherence to Baptist structural models. These twin contributions were the foundations for all subsequent development and growth in the black Baptist church of Nova Scotia.

STEPHEN DAVIDSON

A portrait of John Burton is in the Atlantic Baptist Hist. Coll. at Acadia Univ. (Wolfville, N.S.). His bible (London, 1708) is at St Paul's Anglican Church in Halifax.

Atlantic Baptist Hist. Coll., Joseph Dimock, diary; Edward Manning, corr. and journals, vols.2, 4–7; Menno [J. M. Cramp], "The Baptists of Nova Scotia (1760–1860)" (scrapbook of clippings of column by Cramp in the *Christian Messenger*, 18 Jan. 1860–23 Sept. 1863); "A sketch of the history of the Baptists in the city and county of Halifax" (typescript, [1897?]). PANS, MG 100, 115, no.15; RG 5, P, 42. David Benedict, *A general history of the Baptist denomination in America and other parts of the world* (New York, 1848). N.S. and N.B. Baptist Assoc., *Minutes* (Halifax; Saint John), 1811; 1818–19. N.S. Baptist Assoc., *Minutes* (Halifax), 1835. *Acadian Recorder*, 10 Feb. 1827. *Christian Messenger*, 16 Feb. 1838. Bill, *Fifty years with Baptist ministers*. J. M. Cramp, *Baptist history: from the foundation of the Christian church to the close of the eighteenth century* (Philadelphia, [1869]). S. E. Davidson, "Leaders of the black Baptists of Nova Scotia, 1782–1832" (BA thesis, Acadia Univ., 1975). Levy, *Baptists of the Maritime prov.* P. E. McKerrow, *A brief history of the coloured Baptists of Nova Scotia . . .* (Halifax, 1895). A. P. [Borden] Oliver, *A brief history of the colored Baptists of Nova Scotia, 1782–1953; in commemoration of centennial celebrations of the African United Baptist Association of Nova Scotia, Inc.* ([Halifax, 1953]). *Repent and believe: the Baptist experience in Maritime Canada*, ed. B. M. Moody (Hantsport, N.S., 1980). R. W. Winks, *The blacks in Canada: a history* (London and New Haven, Conn., 1971). R. M. Hattie, "Old-time Halifax churches," N.S. Hist. Soc., *Coll.*, 26 (1945): 49–103.

BURWELL, ADAM HOOD, author, journalist, and clergyman; b. 4 June 1790 near Fort Erie (Ont.), son of Adam Burwell and Sarah Veal; m. 22 Feb. 1829 Sarah Barnard in Troy, N.Y.; d. 2 Nov. 1849 in Kingston, Upper Canada.

Adam Hood Burwell spent his childhood on the family farm in Bertie Township. By 1818 the family had moved to the flourishing settlement on the north shore of Lake Erie founded by Thomas Talbot*. The settlement had been partly surveyed by Adam's elder brother, MAHLON, who had established the Talbot Road. While working on Mahlon's farm at Port Talbot, Burwell had a vision in which an oracle foretold the birth of a great poet in Upper Canada. That poet, Burwell concluded, was himself. "Talbot Road: a poem," published that same year in the *Niagara Spectator* (Niagara-on-the-Lake), is the first long poem of pioneer life in Upper Canada by a native-born author. Dedicated to Talbot, it combines aristocratic 18th-century poetic diction with local charm and colour. Erieus, Burwell's pseudonym, identifies him as the author of poems in the Niagara *Gleaner*. Other poems appeared in the *Scribbler* and the *Canadian Review and Literary and Historical Journal*. Most describe the everyday joys and sorrows of life; some display Burwell's political sentiments. His affinity for natural scenery, evident in "Talbot Road" and early poems such as "A summer's evening" and "Journal of a day's journey in Upper Canada in October, 1816," adumbrates his later theological beliefs in an apocalyptic nature. His poems display both sensitivity and a sincere commitment to literature as a means of social change. He was active in local affairs and apparently took an interest in the political issues of the day. An advertisement from 1819 announces a proposed volume of Burwell's verse including the "The Gourlay-ad," no doubt a treatment of the controversial Robert Gourlay*. It is also possible that in 1824 Burwell was the Spanish Freeholder who libelled Chief Justice William Dummer Powell* in William Lyon Mackenzie*'s *Colonial Advocate*.

Talbot eventually recommended Burwell to Bishop Jacob Mountain* as a candidate for holy orders. In March 1827, at Quebec, Burwell was ordained by Bishop Charles James STEWART as a deacon of the Church of England. His first appointment was at Lennoxville, but by 1830 he and his family had moved to Trois-Rivières. Between 1830 and 1831 Burwell edited the *Christian Sentinel and Anglo-Canadian Churchman's Magazine*, a weekly Anglican journal. He hoped to transform it into a "constitutional political paper," but he also published poems and a quantity of prose in it. After only a year of publication (and despite the moral support of Archdeacon John Strachan*), the journal succumbed to financial and administrative pressures. Burwell's writings in the early 1830s reflect an increasing propensity for evangelical politics. In spite of frail health and warnings from Stewart to curb his "Low Church calvinistic evangelism," Burwell vigorously promulgated his religious and political ideas in a series of essays published in the *Kingston Chronicle* from March 1831 to February 1832 under the pseudonym One of the People.

In May 1832 Burwell succeeded Amos ANSLEY at Hull, where he ardently advocated a controversial brand of religious fundamentalism based, in part, on the teachings of Edward Irving, the Scottish-born preacher whose movement became the Catholic Apostolic Church. Burwell published two Irvingite tracts in

1835: *Doctrine of the Holy Spirit* . . . (Toronto) and *A voice of warning and instruction concerning the signs of the time* . . . (Kingston). By October 1836 Burwell's doctrinal differences had divorced him from the Church of England; he moved to Kingston where he helped to found the first Catholic Apostolic Church in North America.

Burwell continued to write and publish (primarily in Montreal's *Literary Garland* between January and September 1849). The neoclassical emphasis of his early poetry had, however, been replaced by the intense mysticism evident in such poems as "Nebuchadnezzar's vision of the tree . . ." and "Summer evening contemplations." Essays like "On the doctrine of social unity" and "On the philosophy of human perfection and happiness" continued to reflect Burwell's commitment to the achievement of a fundamentalist Christian society. These writings did not, it seems, find a receptive audience. In 1844 Strachan tactfully praised Burwell as a writer but cautioned him that his works "may be too elaborate – too full of reasoning or too abstract for general Reading." Adam Hood Burwell served in the Catholic Apostolic Church until his death.

MICHAEL WILLIAMS

All of Adam Hood Burwell's poetry which had been traced in contemporary periodicals and newspapers by 1965 is republished in "The poems of Adam Hood Burwell, pioneer poet of Upper Canada," ed. C. F. Klinck, *Western Ontario Hist. Nuggets* (London), no.30 (1965). Fourteen additional poems appear in "'New' poems of Adam Hood Burwell," ed. M. L. MacDonald, *Canadian Poetry* (London), no.18 (spring–summer 1986): 99–117. No copy of the proposed volume advertised in the *Gleaner, and Niagara Newspaper* of 5 Aug. 1819 has come to light.

AO, MS 35, letter-books, 1844–49; MS 78, Burwell corr., 1831. *Literary Garland*, new ser., 7 (1849): 15–16, 69–73, 119–26, 178–81, 403–9, 448–57. *Daily British Whig*, 3 Nov. 1849. *Scribbler* (Montreal), 9 Aug. 1821–12 June 1823. *Upper Canada Gazette*, 1 June, 11 July 1822; 24 April, 3 July 1823. *Weekly Register*, 1 Aug. 1822. Lucien Brault, *Hull, 1800–1950* (Ottawa, 1950); *Ottawa old & new* (Ottawa, 1946). T. R. Millman, *The life of the Right Reverend, the Honourable Charles James Stewart, D.D., Oxon., second Anglican bishop of Quebec* (London, Ont., 1953). P. E. Shaw, *The Catholic Apostolic Church, sometimes called Irvingite: a historical study* (New York, 1946). Paul Romney, "The Spanish freeholder imbroglio of 1824: inter-elite and intra-elite rivalry in Upper Canada," *OH*, 76 (1984): 32–47.

BURWELL, MAHLON, surveyor, militia officer, businessman, office holder, politician, and JP; b. 18 Feb. 1783 in New Jersey, son of Adam Burwell and Sarah Veal; m. 20 April 1810 Sarah Haun in Niagara (Niagara-on-the-Lake), Upper Canada, and they had seven sons and two daughters; d. 25 Jan. 1846 in Port Talbot, Upper Canada.

Mahlon Burwell is thought to have descended from an English family with homes in Bedfordshire and Northamptonshire. Part of the family moved to North America in the 17th century, settling in Virginia. Burwell's father, a native of New Jersey, was probably a loyalist during the American Revolutionary War; in 1786 he settled in what would soon become Upper Canada and in 1797 he received 850 acres of land in Bertie Township for military service.

According to a newspaper account in 1833, Mahlon had not much more than 12 months of schooling, and when he decided to take up surveying, had little formal training in it. He failed to meet the provincial requirements for licensing as a surveyor in 1805 and had to extend his apprenticeship. Yet he acquired the minimal mathematical background necessary to use the instruments of the time: a circumferentor and a measuring chain. Despite the trying circumstances under which he worked, his field-notes, maps, and diaries are detailed and contain a remarkable amount of scientific information. Such records were obviously a requirement of surveyors' contracts, but not all supplied them. It was no doubt because of his thoroughness that Burwell was engaged to survey so much of southwestern Upper Canada. Upon the recommendation of Thomas Talbot* he was first employed by the provincial government in 1809, laying out townships (most in the Talbot settlement) and beginning the Talbot Road. Between 1809 and 1812 he moved from Bertie to Port Talbot, in Southwold Township on the north shore of Lake Erie, and later settled on the line between Southwold and Dunwich Township.

During the War of 1812 he held the rank of lieutenant-colonel in Talbot's militia regiment (1st Middlesex) but saw little action. He was ordered on duty in December 1812 and was among those who helped organize the defence of the London District. He may have taken part in the hostilities on the Niagara frontier in 1812–13 and was on duty at Otter (Big Otter) Creek, north of Lake Erie, in 1814. In August of that year he was carried off by marauders as a prisoner to the United States, and a month later his property at Port Talbot was destroyed. Taken eventually to Chillicothe, Ohio, he was released on parole in December.

Returning home, Burwell resumed surveying. Between 1814 and 1825 he surveyed all or part of 24 townships north of the Thames River and south of it, in the counties of Kent and Essex. As well, he resumed work on the Talbot Road, long considered the best road in Upper Canada, which constituted an enduring testimony to his skills as a surveyor. After 1825 his work for the government was much more dispersed geographically. By 1834 he had completed 49 surveys or resurveys, a remarkable accomplishment. The work was physically demanding and stressful because of bad weather and the lack of resources sufficient to pay, shelter, and feed his men. These hardships took their toll on Burwell, who developed rheumatism. In 1832, when he was still only 49, his health prompted a letter to William CHEWETT, acting surveyor general, requesting that he not be asked to make a resurvey of Dunwich Township should it be needed.

At first paid in cash, Burwell subsequently accepted recompense in land. Under the system of tendering to survey, his bid was invariably 4½ per cent of the area to be surveyed. As a result, he built up large holdings of land in various parts of Upper Canada, especially in the southwest. He is known to have received a total of 39,759 acres, but this figure does not include whatever compensation (possibly cash) he received for 18 surveys on which the government's record is silent. In addition, he was granted or purchased some 3,525 acres. His holdings were thus at least 43,284 acres. In 1830–31, on property at the mouth of Otter Creek, which he had received for surveying Bayham Township, Burwell and his brother John laid out a plot for a village, Port Burwell. There Mahlon later built Trinity Church (Anglican) and formed a company to promote harbour development and the shipment of timber.

Burwell had to ballot for the location of the acreages he acquired and was therefore unable to pick choice lots. Nevertheless, provided he disposed of his holdings rapidly, he was financially better off to accept land rather than monetary compensation for his services. Some insight into the process can be gained from examining his holdings in Essex County, where most of his land was located. Of the 67 properties there belonging to him or his estate between 1815 and 1854, only 6 were of good quality. Yet, between 1823 and his death in 1846, he sold 54 per cent of his holdings within 2 years of receiving them, the rest within 10. (Most was sold to fellow surveyors Benjamin Springer, Peter Carroll, and Roswell Mount*.) Moreover, he seems to have obtained the going rate. The same pattern must also have prevailed in the centrally located and more populous areas where Burwell held better endowed lands.

Still, while he waited for sales he had to pay taxes. Since his holdings were scattered, he felt he was not deriving the benefits he should. In the 1830s much of his correspondence with the government was related to the possibility of exchanging parcels. An Anglican, he was permitted in 1837 to exchange land in Caradoc Township for clergy reserves in Bayham, which he intended to donate as a glebe to the new church in Port Burwell. An earlier, more ambitious exchange had been denied. In 1829 he sought to exchange 10,000 acres, in scattered lots, for an equivalent amount south of the Huron Tract, in what is now Sarnia Township. Here he proposed to establish tenants and to entail the block to his heirs. This was financially an astute move but it failed because the lands had already been assigned and because it was held that a successful application would only induce similar applications. The problem of disposing of Burwell's scattered parcels of varying quality passed to his heirs.

Throughout his lifetime Burwell was the friend and aide of Thomas Talbot, the autocratic, Anglo-Irish colonizer who played such an important role in the settlement of southwestern Ontario. He valued Burwell for his professional skill and usefulness, and no doubt had a large say in his appointment in 1809 to the lucrative post of registrar of lands for Middlesex. In addition, he helped secure Burwell's election to the House of Assembly in 1812. Perhaps because of this assistance and the friendship between the two, Burwell bore Talbot's sarcasm towards him. Yet in 1817 Burwell publicly criticized the proposed celebration of the Talbot settlement's anniversary, an event he judged excessively expensive and "premature," in that Talbot was still alive. Resolutions were passed by the anniversary committee declaring Burwell's views "indelicate and obstructive" and written in the "most disrespectful manner." The relationship survived and Talbot was greatly grieved at Burwell's death in 1846. Edward Ermatinger*, writing about Burwell in 1859, used such words to describe him as imperious, opinionated, assiduous, ambitious, and politically consistent – qualities which may have been attractive to Talbot. But Ermatinger also described Burwell as selfish, egotistical, vindictive, intellectually dull, and given to ostentatious displays of courage, and he painted the picture of a man to whom circumstance offered the chance of rising to the "highest rank as a statesman" but whose personal qualities stood in the way. In contrast Ermatinger's son, Charles Oakes Zaccheus, saw Burwell as someone who, possessing little suavity, was essentially a man of integrity. He was a man of marked character, no one was indifferent to him, few liked him, and many resented every breath he took. His character is reflected in the names he bestowed upon his sons: Alexander, Hercules, Isaac Brock, Hannibal, John Walpole, Leonidas, and Edward.

From 1812 to 1820 he represented Oxford and Middlesex in the assembly and from 1820 to 1824 Middlesex. He was defeated by John Rolph* and John Matthews* in 1824 and again four years later but sat for Middlesex from 1830 to 1834. He lost in 1834 and did not return to the house until 1836, representing the town of London. Between 1812 and 1824 Burwell supported the government in the house, and in 1828 was described by William Lyon Mackenzie*, editor of the reform *Colonial Advocate*, as one of the "Positively Ministerial, or Court Candidates."

As a supporter and servant of the government, Burwell became the recipient of patronage. In 1813 he received the first of his many commissions as a justice of the peace and a year later he was appointed to arrest those suspected of high treason during the war. In 1820 he became collector of customs at Port Talbot; in 1821 he was a member of the assembly committee that reported on Upper Canada's financial concerns with Lower Canada. The following year he became a commissioner under the alien act for the London District and in 1824 was appointed a coroner for that district. John Matthews, his political opponent, argued in 1828 that Burwell had secured sufficient remunerative posts to be styled "Commissioner in Banco Regis." These sentiments were echoed later that year in the *Colonial Advocate*, where Mackenzie saw the actions of "the cast off Mahlon Burwell" as "profligate, abandoned and shameless." The benefits of his offices and most especially his success in securing survey contracts explained, in Mackenzie's opinion, his consistent loyalty.

Certainly by 1828 Burwell was exercising considerable power and influence. Matthews wrote to Zacariah Mudge in January 1828 that, for years, under the influence of Talbot, Burwell had controlled all the civil and military appointments within Middlesex County and, as chairman of the Court of Quarter Sessions and foreman of the grand jury, held enormous administrative and legal powers: "It becomes necessary therefore to be a sattelite of this mans, or to suffer the persecution and punishment which he assumes the power to inflict." By 1832 what the reform St Thomas *Liberal* called the "Burwell dynasty" (a group including John BOSTWICK and Burwell's brother John) had become "almost absolute" thanks to the support of Talbot. In 1833 Asahel Bradley Lewis*, the *Liberal*'s editor, reported that Middlesex was controlled as "absolutely . . . as is the petty sovereignty of a German despot."

A most important element in this control was the office of justice of the peace. Burwell worked hard to secure the appointment by the central government of those he considered appropriate. In 1835, of the 60 nominated for the London District, he recommended 20. Interestingly, four years earlier, he had seen his way clear to nominate Eliakim Malcolm*, whose politics he deemed "rather *radical*." This he did against the advice of fellow tory John Baptist Askin*, who as clerk of the peace stood on top of the district's oligarchic ladder. Burwell's tolerance, remarkable in this politically troubled period which culminated in rebellion, led to the appointment of reformers to a variety of offices. Presumably he felt, as historian Colin Frederick Read has suggested, that there was little to fear from those with the talent, social standing, and property needed to qualify for these positions. Burwell was also concerned about the geographical distribution of the magistrates. In 1835 and again in 1836 he warned the provincial government that the magistrates in and around London unduly influenced the business of the Court of Quarter Sessions because they were closer to the court and thus able to attend regularly. His advice undoubtedly influenced the decision to partition the London District in 1837.

Paradoxically, having sought to limit the influence of the town of London, he was elected its first representative in 1836. He was aided in this election by J. B. Askin, with whom he was frequently at odds. In the same year Burwell sent Civil Secretary John Joseph* a list of his supporters who would be eligible to vote if land patents were issued to them and sent immediately to Askin. They were. Yet, when Askin asked Burwell to help examine rebels from the district in January 1838, Burwell, though colonel of the 2nd Regiment of Middlesex militia, did not reply. Nor did he attend that month the Court of Quarter Sessions, of which he was chairman. He may have been ill, he may have considered events politically too explosive, or he may have decided to devote his time to the upcoming parliament. Whatever his reason, he soon came to believe that a conspiracy existed to remove him as chairman and indeed he was passed over in April in favour of Joseph Brant Clench*. Burwell was soon under attack too as registrar of lands, in which office his son Leonidas served as deputy. The officials in London sought to appoint a Londoner as registrar and to move the registry office from near Port Talbot to their town. Burwell, pointing to his long service, his expenses in building the office, and its location nearer the "geographical centre" of the district, managed to stave off the opposition for a time. Yet his influence was dwindling and he was considered derelict in his duty. No doubt he was associated in the minds of some with the abuses of office and low moral character of his fellow magistrate and brother, John. He might have looked for support to Askin had he not fought with him. He was anonymously accused of mismanaging district funds. In his defence, he argued in 1839 that the charge had been prompted by lumbermen who refused to pay him the appropriate fees for the services of the Port Burwell Harbour Company, in which he was the principal entrepreneur. In the post-rebellion era the central government could no longer afford to support the old "courtier compact." Even Thomas Talbot had his power of supervision within the Talbot settlement removed in 1838.

In 1842 Mahlon Burwell turned over his business interests at Port Burwell to his son Leonidas. He died at Port Talbot four years later. As a surveyor and registrar he had played an important role in the settlement of southwestern Ontario. As a friend and adviser of Thomas Talbot and as a magistrate and MHA, he figured significantly in the political history of the region. Some said his service was motivated by self-interest. Unfortunately, much of the documentary material which survives was written by his detractors in an emotionally charged period. Burwell was not simply a government toady. He held more liberal views than many on matters of education to the extent of demanding, in 1831, and then chairing a committee on education. He hoped to ensure a centralized, provincial system. Realizing that it required adequate financing, a need overlooked by many reformers, he proposed, in a series of forward-looking school bills in 1832, 1833, and 1837, to use local taxation for support and to introduce crown-appointed, district boards and commissioners with supervisory powers. He was capable of opposing Talbot and could see his way to recommending radicals as magistrates. Paradoxically, in a period in which all politicians claimed independence as a characteristic, he was a forceful individual demonstrably capable of it in thought and action, even if he was remarkably partisan over issues and views which he cherished. However one regards his motives, which this author does not consider base, Burwell played a significant but, as yet, largely unacknowledged role in the life of the province.

JOHN CLARKE

Mahlon Burwell's voluminous survey records are divided between two repositories. The AO's holdings include correspondence in RG 1, A-I-1, 17, and A-I-6, 4–10, 12, 16–17, 19, 24; survey diaries and field notes in RG 1, CB-1, boxes 2, 16, 19, 23–24, 26, 32, 36–37, 39–40; and numerous survey maps in the Map Coll. Additional material, including diaries, field notes, and maps, remains at the Ont., Ministry of Natural Resources, Survey Records Office (Toronto). One of Burwell's survey diaries was published as "The diary of Mahlon Burwell, January 24 to August 4, 1827," ed. R. M. Lewis, *OH*, 49 (1957): 199–219.

PAC, MG 24, G46; RG 1, E3, 87: 48–50; L1, 28: 427; 29: 57, 188, 362, 366, 487; 30: 19, 25, 405; 31: 353, 599, 604; 32: 557; 33: 418; 34: 134; 35: 321; 36: 149; 37: 224, 416; 38: 585; 39: 471; L3, 36: B9/71; 40: B11/164; 44: B13/9; 49: B15/53; 50: B15/145; 60: B20/43; 61: B20/113; 63: B21/151; 64: B22/73; 65: B22/120; RG 5, A1: 47897–99, 70880, 83070, 84377, 91306–7, 93684, 93956–57, 97746, 106552–62; B36, 1: 58; C1, 12, file 1501, no.6469; RG 8, I (C ser.), 681: 149; 685: 156; 1222: 205; RG 68, General index, 1651–1841: 122, 124, 126–27, 130–31, 133, 135–36, 138–39, 141, 144, 147, 150, 153, 156, 162, 182, 194, 245, 300, 302, 423. UWOL, Regional Coll., Burwell family papers. "Early records of St. Mark's and St. Andrew's churches, Niagara," comp. Janet Carnochan, *OH*, 3 (1901): 58. "Journals of Legislative Assembly of U.C.," AO *Report*, 1913: 111, 129, 311; 1914: 266. U.C., House of Assembly, *Journal*, 1831: 34–35; 1833–34, app.: 120–22. *Colonial Advocate*, 1 May, 5 June 1828. *Liberal* (St Thomas, [Ont.]), 29 Nov., 6 Dec. 1832; 25 July 1833. *Death notices of Ont.* (Reid). *Land surveys of southern Ontario: an introduction and index to the field notebooks of the Ontario land surveyors, 1784–1859*, comp. [R.] L. Gentilcore and Kate Donkin, ed. C. E. Heidenreich (Toronto, 1973), 39–101. A. G. Brunger, "A spatial analysis of individual settlements in southern London District, Upper Canada, 1800–1836" (PHD thesis, Univ. of Western Ont., London, 1974). *Canadian education: a history*, ed. J. D. Wilson *et al.* (Scarborough [Toronto], 1970). John Clarke, "A geographical analysis of colonial settlement in the Western District of Upper Canada, 1788–1850" (PHD thesis, Univ. of Western Ont., 1970). C. O. [Z.] Ermatinger, *The Talbot regime; or the first half century of the Talbot settlement* (St Thomas, 1904). Edward Ermatinger, *Life of Colonel Talbot, and the Talbot settlement* . . . (St Thomas, 1859; repr. Belleville, Ont., 1972). F. C. Hamil, *Lake Erie baron: the story of Colonel Thomas Talbot* (Toronto, 1955). E. N. Lewis, *Sidelights on the Talbot settlement* (St Thomas, 1938). Patterson, "Studies in elections in U.C." D. W. Thomson, *Men and meridians: the history of surveying and mapping in Canada* (3v., Ottawa, 1966–69), 1. Archibald Blue, "Colonel Mahlon Burwell, land surveyor," Canadian Institute, *Proc.* (Toronto), new ser., 2 ([1898–1905]): 41–56. John Clarke, "Mapping the lands supervised by Colonel the Honourable Thomas Talbot in the Western District of Upper Canada, 1811–1849," *Canadian Cartographer* (Toronto), 8 (1971): 8–18. R. L. Gentilcore, "Lines on the land: crown surveys and settlement in Upper Canada," *OH*, 61 (1969): 57–73. C. [F.] Read, "The London District oligarchy in the rebellion era," *OH*, 72 (1980): 195–209.

BY, JOHN, army officer and military engineer; b. in the summer of 1779, probably on 7 August, in Lambeth (London), England, second son of George By and Mary Bryan; m. first 12 Nov. 1801 Elizabeth Baines in Madron, England; m. secondly 14 March 1818 Esther March in Cheshunt, England, and they had two daughters; d. 1 Feb. 1836 in Frant, England.

John By broke with the family tradition of joining the customs service by entering the Royal Military Academy in Woolwich (London). He obtained a commission on 1 Aug. 1799 as a second lieutenant in the Royal Artillery, but transferred to the Royal Engineers on 20 December. By served first at Woolwich and then at Plymouth, becoming a first lieutenant on 18 April 1801. In August 1802 he was ordered to the Canadas. There he was engaged in a variety of duties, including work on the defences of Quebec and the construction of a new canal at the Cascades (near Île des Cascades), Lower Canada. He was also associated with Jean-Baptiste Duberger* in the building of a scale model of Quebec, which he took with him when he was recalled to England in 1810 for service in the Peninsular War. While in the Canadas he was promoted second captain on 1 March 1805 and captain on 24 June 1809. By participated with some distinction in the Peninsular War, taking part in the sieges of Badajoz, Spain, in 1811.

Recalled to England in January 1812, By was placed in charge of the gunpowder works at Waltham Abbey (London), Faversham, and Purfleet, and he carried out this assignment with credit. On 23 June 1814 he was promoted brevet major, and that year he completed the building of a new small-arms factory at Enfield Lock (London), which he had designed. In 1821, at the age of 42, he was placed on half pay in keeping with the economies of the time. Promoted lieutenant-colonel on 2 Dec. 1824, in March 1826 he was selected by General Gother Mann*, inspector general of fortifications at the Board of Ordnance, to be superintending engineer for the construction of a canal system that would link the Ottawa River and Lake Ontario by way of the Rideau and Cataraqui river systems. By landed at Quebec on 30 May 1826 and returned to England late in 1832 with the Rideau Canal complete and in operation. He took up residence at Shernfold Park, Frant, but he was a broken man in poor health. He died little more than three years later.

The War of 1812 had clearly demonstrated the vulnerability of the military supply line along the St Lawrence between Montreal and Kingston, Upper Canada. British commanders in Lower and Upper Canada had seen the need for an alternative route even before the end of the war, and late in 1814 Lieutenant-Colonel George Richard John Macdonell* had roughly surveyed the Rideau–Cataraqui line. To render the route between Montreal and Kingston by the Ottawa, Rideau, and Cataraqui rivers navigable for small naval vessels, it was necessary to build a lock at the mouth of the Ottawa River, three small canals to circumvent rapids on the Ottawa, and a canal system along the stretch from the mouth of the Rideau River to Kingston. Although representations were made to London about the necessity of these works, it was only late in 1815 that orders were given for a study of the route to be made. Lieutenant Joshua Jebb* surveyed the Rideau–Cataraqui route in the spring of 1816 but nothing further transpired. However, the entrance lock to the Ottawa was built by private interests that year.

In July 1818 the Duke of Richmond [Lennox*] arrived at Quebec to become governor-in-chief of British North America. He had been ordered to report on the defences of the colonies, and within four months he submitted a fine review and a description of necessary works. In transmitting the report to the Duke of Wellington, master general of the Ordnance, Richmond strongly urged the building of the Ottawa and Rideau canals. On his own authority, he ordered two companies of the Royal Staff Corps to begin construction of the Ottawa canals [*see* Henry Abraham DuVernet]. Unfortunately, Richmond's death in 1819 while he was inspecting the Rideau route put a halt to the Rideau project. Matters rested there until April 1825, when a commission of engineer officers headed by Sir James Carmichael Smyth was sent from England to report on the defences of British North America. The commission recommended the construction of a Rideau canal. Wellington gave his firm support, and early in 1826 a start on the project was authorized.

Late in September 1826 By arrived at the mouth of the Rideau River to begin initial preparations. In April 1827, accompanied by John Burrows and others, he made a canoe trip along the 123-mile route to see the proposed work sites, and that summer construction began at several places along the Rideau and the Cataraqui. By's instructions required him to lay out locks 100 feet long and 22 feet wide, but he realized that steam vessels were destined to change water transport completely. In July 1826, even before examining the route, By had concluded that larger locks would be needed. In submitting his first comprehensive estimates of cost for the canal in late 1827 he therefore added an alternative calculation based on locks 150 feet long and 50 feet wide, large enough to take small naval steam vessels and the spars of white pine required by the Royal Navy. At the suggestion of Governor Lord Dalhousie [Ramsay] he sent his estimates to London in the hands of a trusted assistant, with a strong plea for permission to enlarge the locks.

By's estimates were greeted in London with consternation. His advocacy of large locks was so radical, and his estimates so much higher than any previous figures, that a special board of senior engineer officers was established in January 1828 to review his submission. The board commended all that By had done and approved of the larger locks. Official doubts remained, however, and Sir James Kempt*, lieutenant governor of Nova Scotia, was requested to head another board of inquiry, which would examine the work already done and advise on the size of the locks. The board travelled the length of the works in June and completely endorsed By's actions. It recommended locks 134 feet in length and 33 feet in width, somewhat smaller than those in By's proposal but the largest in the Canadas. The Ordnance accepted the recommendations and By built all the locks to the new dimensions.

The task of building the canal was carried out in five working seasons, a start being made at ancillary works in September 1826 and the canal being effectively completed in November 1831. When finished, the system included 47 masonry locks and 52 dams; most of the dams were also of masonry, and one notable arched structure at Jones Falls was over 60 feet high, far and away the highest in North America. Eight of the locks had to be built at the northern end of the system in order to circumvent the falls at the mouth of the Rideau. The entire undertaking – a major one even by modern standards – was achieved through simple methods of construction. Not only was the drilling of rock carried out laboriously by hand, but all lifting of heavy timbers for lock gates and blocks of finished masonry for lock walls had to be done by manpower and by hand-operated winches and derricks.

The logistics of building the canal were perhaps even more remarkable. A pioneer feature of the Rideau project was the extensive use of civilian contractors, as specified in By's instructions. Five of those selected for masonry work, John Redpath*,

Robert Drummond*, Thomas Phillips, Andrew White*, and Thomas McKay*, gave such satisfaction that By presented silver cups to them on completion of the work. Contractors for excavations, on the other hand, who were generally inexperienced, caused By much worry and trouble, the more so because some contracts had to be terminated and legal problems ensued. At the peak of construction about 2,000 men, mainly labourers but including two companies of the Royal Sappers and Miners, were living in rough camps cleared in the forest along the route. All the workers and their supplies had to be brought in, generally by canoes and small bateaux. But the most serious difficulty was caused by the outbreaks of malaria at various times, especially during the summer of 1828. The disease caused work to halt and was particularly virulent along the Cataraqui River, where hundreds of workers died. By himself almost succumbed, but his iron constitution allowed him to recover and speedily resume work.

All the work was laid out and supervised by By and his able subordinates of the Royal Engineers. He must have been a splendid leader and teacher, since several of his assistants became full generals and served with distinction in high offices in British colonies around the world. A further indication of By's character is his decision to make his headquarters at the camp established at the junction of the Rideau and Ottawa rivers and to forgo the military base at Kingston. That camp developed into the small settlement of Bytown, which grew rapidly and in 1855 was renamed Ottawa. By was clearly an engineer of outstanding ability. Many features of his work on the canal were innovative, perhaps the most original being his extensive use of dams to flood major rapids, create slack-water "lakes" of navigable depth above them, and control spring run-off. Moreover, his plans for the truss framework bridge he constructed over the Chaudière Falls on the Ottawa were based on a design by Andrea Palladio, testimony to his wide reading and his intuitive sense of good design.

By traversed the finished canal with his family and friends in May 1832, but the same month trouble erupted in England over his expenditures. The British government had authorized the start of work on the canal on the basis of the very preliminary estimate of £169,000 made by the Smyth commission. Only late in 1827 could By provide a more accurate estimate of £474,000, and that figure was later increased when his recommendation for larger locks was accepted and some defence works were added. The final cost was about £800,000. However, this sum was found to include an amount that had not been approved by the Treasury. When the Ordnance received By's last estimate in the spring of 1832, it took the unusual step of submitting it direct to the Treasury. This body issued a minute on 25 May which criticized By severely for overspending and which demanded that he be recalled to answer questions about his accounts.

As it happened, By returned to England without being aware of any censure, and it was not until June 1833 that he learned of the Treasury minute. The criticism naturally affected him keenly. Since he had been given specific instructions by Wellington "not to wait for Parliamentary Grants, but to proceed with all despatch consistent with economy," he was able to answer Treasury charges that he had misspent funds; he does not seem to have been called to defend himself before any committee. By had been meticulous in maintaining financial accounts, both for individual work and for the canal as a whole, and his papers would have been available for inspection if his case had been thoroughly examined. Even though he had private support from senior officers in the Ordnance, including Kempt, not a word was said publicly in his defence, despite pleas from himself, his wife, and senior army friends. He did have the satisfaction of a few words of commendation from the king, but that was all. Despite the evidence in his favour, By died without his name being cleared officially.

The early 1830s in Britain was a time not only of political reform but also of changes in the administration of government. During this period the Treasury was attempting to achieve the commanding influence over other departments it later acquired, and as part of its campaign it was attacking the Ordnance vigorously for lack of proper control over expenditures. It seems probable that By in his remote station was made a sort of scapegoat in this exchange. The fact that his last estimate was sent direct to the Treasury and that that body issued its minute just four days later lends support to this view.

Although he was to encounter criticism in London, John By left the Canadas to general regret and with widespread tributes to his work. The citizens of Montreal, Brockville, and Kingston were among those who lauded his achievements. A part of the address presented to him by a committee of the Montreal Committee of Trade provides a fitting concluding comment: "An undertaking of great magnitude and importance, the successful accomplishment of which, in so comparatively short a period, notwithstanding the unheard of unestimable difficulties and impediments which had to be encountered and surmounted, in an almost unexplored and uninhabited wilderness . . . evinced on your part a moral courage and an undaunted spirit and combination of science and management equally exciting our admiration and deserving our praise."

ROBERT F. LEGGET

No well-authenticated portrait of John By is known to exist. Two silhouettes have been used in recent publications, but they have not been positively identified.

A full-length biography of By is available in R. [F.] Legget, *John By, lieutenant colonel, Royal Engineers, 1779–1836: builder of the Rideau Canal, founder of Ottawa* ([Ottawa], 1982). A summary biography and a description of his work in building the canal is given in the same author's *Rideau waterway* (Toronto, 1955; rev. ed., Toronto and Buffalo, N.Y., 1972; 2nd ed., Toronto, 1986). Much of the information about By's life comes from H. P. Hill, "Lieutenant-Colonel John By – a biography," *Royal Engineers Journal* (Chatham, Eng.), [new ser.], 46 (1932): 522–25, and this was supplemented by minor pieces of information such as his baptismal record in the register of St-Mary-at-Lambeth (London), 10 Aug. 1779, at the Greater London Record Office.

C

CADIEUX, LOUIS-MARIE, Roman Catholic priest, school administrator, author, and vicar general; b. 7 March 1785 in Montreal, son of Louis Cadieux and Madeleine Serre; d. 13 June 1838 in Rivière-Ouelle, Lower Canada, and was buried there two days later.

Louis-Marie Cadieux was engaged in secondary studies at the Collège Saint-Raphaël in Montreal from 1798 to 1806. He then went to the Séminaire de Nicolet, and there, while studying theology, taught in succession from 1807 until 1810 the third, fifth, and sixth years (Method, Belles-Lettres, and Rhetoric). He received the tonsure on 22 Jan. 1807 and minor orders on 31 July 1808. The seminary's superior, Jean Raimbault, who was parish priest of Saint-Jean-Baptiste at Nicolet, was impatient to see his protégé ordained, and in January 1810 told Bishop Joseph-Octave Plessis* that Cadieux was "mature, of the required age, and . . . as well prepared as he will be in six months in both learning and piety, and if ever there was a reason for advancing a deadline . . . , we have one here, I believe." Plessis did not share Raimbault's eagerness and did not ordain Cadieux until 26 August, in the church of Baie-du-Febvre (Baieville). Upon his ordination Cadieux was appointed director of the Séminaire de Nicolet, a post he held until leaving Nicolet in 1813.

That year Cadieux was sent as parish priest to La Nativité-de-Notre-Dame at Beauport, near Quebec, where he worked for six years. In 1819 he was appointed curé of Immaculée-Conception at Trois-Rivières. At first he refused to move to the town, convinced that "nothing is more contrary to my character and my ways than having so much to do . . . with people of a certain quality." He was the more opposed to being transferred since large sums had just been put into repairing the presbytery at Beauport, but in the end he accepted the appointment.

Cadieux began his ministry upon his arrival in Trois-Rivières, and he soon obtained the office of superior of the Ursulines located there; he carried on both functions until 1835. In addition he was interested in journalism and contributed to the short-lived *Ami de la religion et du roi*, which Ludger Duvernay* was publishing. It was Duvernay who in 1823 brought out the pamphlet *Observations sur un écrit intitulé "Questions sur le gouvernement ecclésiastique du district de Montréal"*, now known to have been written by Cadieux. In it Cadieux refuted assertions made by Augustin Chaboillez*, the parish priest of Saint-Antoine at Longueuil, who opposed the creation of a new bishopric in Montreal. But readers were uncertain of the authorship of the text. Indeed, Bishop Plessis was long considered its author – a view not wholly wrong, given that he made more than 144 changes in the draft Cadieux sent him before publication. Two years later Cadieux returned to writing, with a memoir proposing that in light of the dilapidated state of the building housing the Séminaire de Nicolet, the seminary be relocated at Trois-Rivières, in a former château owned by the government which had been turned into a barracks. Although it was persuasive, the memoir had little impact and failed to sway the religious authorities, who entertained no thought of such a move.

At the time of his appointment as vicar general of the diocese of Quebec on 20 Feb. 1833, Cadieux was having some difficulty in administering his parish. The leading citizens of Trois-Rivières had insisted upon their right to participate in electing the chairman for the meetings of the *fabrique*. Cadieux had rejected these claims, and his refusal led to the creation of a new council of the *fabrique* from which the parish priest was excluded. The quarrel was resolved, but there were after-effects, which showed up in the financial problems that Cadieux was encountering. On 16 Aug. 1834 he complained to the archbishop of Quebec, Joseph Signay, that the *fabrique* was irregular in its payments of sums owing him and that since coming to Trois-Rivières he had used up his entire patrimony. In the same letter he asked to be transferred to the parish of Sainte-Anne at Varennes, which paid better. Cadieux was then being seriously considered for the office of auxiliary to the archbishop of Quebec in Montreal. He refused the offer of this post, and although 400 parishioners signed a petition to keep him at Trois-Rivières, in September 1835 he accepted appointment as parish priest of Notre-Dame-de-Liesse at Rivière-Ouelle. There he was to become a founding member of the corporation of the Collège de Sainte-Anne-de-la-Pocatière.

No sooner had Cadieux been installed at Rivière-Ouelle than he asked Signay for permission to erect a new presbytery suitable for a vicar general, since, as he stressed, his parishioners were prepared to put up a fine, large building. Unfortunately he had little time to enjoy his new quarters, for he died on 13 June 1838. In his will he left everything to the corporation of the Séminaire de Nicolet, on condition, however, that it pay his sister, Rose Cadieux, an annuity of £25 for the rest of her life. The corporation refused the legacy, considering it disadvantageous. By the terms of Cadieux's will his estate went to the corporation of the Collège de Sainte-Anne-de-la-Pocatière instead.

ALAIN GAMELIN

Louis-Marie Cadieux is the co-author with J.-O. Plessis of *Observations sur un écrit intitulé "Questions sur le gouvernement ecclésiastique du district de Montréal"* (Trois-Rivières, [Qué.], 1823). He also wrote, in 1825, "Mémoire de M. Cadieux pour la translation du séminaire de Nicolet aux Trois-Rivières," which is reproduced in Douville, *Hist. du collège-séminaire de Nicolet*, 1: 173–76.

AAQ, 1 CB. ANQ-M, CE1-51, 7 mars 1785. ANQ-Q, CE3-1, 15 juin 1838. ASN, AO, Polygraphie, I–IV; Séminaire, II: 78–81; lettres de Mgr Plessis à Jean Raimbault, I, 1806–11; II, 1811–15; lettres des directeurs et autres à l'évêque de Québec, 1804–6; Transfert du séminaire de Nicolet, boîte I, no.1; AP-G, L.-É. Bois, D, 4; G, 3, 6, 9. ASTR, 0123. *L'Ami de la religion et du roi* (Trois-Rivières), juin–septembre 1820. Allaire, *Dictionnaire*. F.-M. Bibaud, *Le panthéon canadien* (A. et V. Bibaud; 1891). Caron, "Inv. de la corr. de Mgr Panet," ANQ *Rapport*, 1933–34, 1934–35, 1935–36; "Inv. de la corr. de Mgr Plessis," ANQ *Rapport*, 1927–28, 1928–29; "Inv. de la corr. de Mgr Signay," ANQ *Rapport*, 1936–37, 1937–38, 1938–39. Desrosiers, "Inv. de la corr. de Mgr Lartigue," ANQ *Rapport*, 1943–44. Wallace, *Macmillan dict*. Hervé Biron, *Grandeurs et misères de l'Église trifluvienne (1615–1947)* (Trois-Rivières, 1947). Chabot, *Le curé de campagne*. Douville, *Hist. du collège-séminaire de Nicolet*. P.-H. Hudon, *Rivière-Ouelle de la Bouteillerie; 3 siècles de vie* (Ottawa, 1972). Wilfrid Lebon, *Histoire du collège de Sainte-Anne-de-la-Pocatière* (2v., Québec, 1948–49). Lemieux, *L'établissement de la première prov. eccl.* Maurault, *Le collège de Montréal* (Dansereau; 1967). *Les ursulines des Trois-Rivières depuis leur établissement jusqu'à nos jours* (4v., Trois-Rivières, 1888–1911). Yves Tessier, "Ludger Duvernay et les débuts de la presse périodique aux Trois-Rivières," *RHAF*, 18 (1964–65): 387–404, 566–81.

CALDWELL, BILLY (possibly baptized **Thomas**, sometimes called **Sagaunash**), Indian Department official and merchant; b. 17 March, *c.* 1780, in the vicinity of Fort Niagara (near Youngstown, N.Y.); d. 27 Sept. 1841 at Trader's Point (near Council Bluffs, Iowa).

Billy Caldwell was one of the frontier personalities who were born out of passing liaisons between British men and native women and who spent their lives on the social boundary between British or American and Indian institutions. The natural son of William Caldwell*, a captain in Butler's Rangers, and a Mohawk woman whose name is unknown (she was a daughter of Rising Sun), Billy Caldwell was abandoned by his father while an infant. Ordered west to Detroit, the elder Caldwell left Billy to spend his childhood among the Mohawks near Niagara and later on the Grand River (Ont.). About 1789 he brought the boy into the family created by his marriage to Suzanne Baby at Detroit. There Billy Caldwell received a basic education aimed at making him into a family retainer, the manager of the Caldwell farm on the south side of the Detroit River. He rejected the status of second-class son, however, and crossed into American territory to enter the fur trade.

Caldwell began his 37-year association with the Thomas Forsyth–John Kinzie trading partnership in 1797, first in what is now southwestern Michigan and along the Wabash River, later in the northern part of present-day Illinois, where in 1803 he rose to the position of chief clerk in the firm's new post at Chicago. A Potawatomi woman named La Nanette, of the powerful fish clan, was his first wife; she died shortly after the marriage, whereupon he married a daughter of Robert Forsyth and an Ojibwa woman. After his second wife's death he again married, this time a person known only as the Frenchwoman, likely the daughter of an influential Métis trader in Chicago. He had some eight to ten children in all, none of whom lived to adulthood or survived him.

Until 1820 Caldwell identified himself as a "true Briton," remaining faithful to the values he had acquired in the Detroit River border communities where he was raised, in spite of the fact that his father never recognized him as his rightful eldest son. By early 1812 he was reputed to be especially influential among the powerful Potawatomi, Ottawa, and Ojibwa communities around Lake Michigan, so that both American and British officials vied for his services in the coming war. Spurning overtures from Governor William Henry Harrison of Ohio, during the winter of 1812–13 he made his way back to Amherstburg, Upper Canada, and there he obtained a commission as captain in the Indian Department. His first combat experience came at the River Raisin (Mich.) in January 1813, where he was severely wounded while attempting to rescue an injured American officer. He later served as a liaison officer with Indian forces at the sieges of Fort Meigs (near Perrysburg, Ohio) and Fort Stephenson (Fremont, Ohio), at the battle of Moraviantown, and on the Niagara frontier.

Upon the death of Matthew Elliott* in 1814, efforts were made to have Caldwell replace Elliott as superintendent of Indians for the Western District, but his father was appointed with Billy as second-in-command. Subsequently Billy collaborated with Lieutenant-Colonel Reginald James, commanding the garrison at Fort Malden (Amherstburg), in successful attempts to depose his father, and thus secured the post of superintendent. However, he proved inept in his administrative duties and was discharged from the Indian Department in September 1816. Thereafter he tried ineffectually to establish himself as a merchant in Amherstburg and vicinity. By 1820 he had left Upper Canada forever. Having immigrated to the Chicago area he worked in the Indian trade and soon became an American citizen.

It was in Chicago between 1827 and 1833 that various legends grew up concerning Caldwell's ancestry, rank, and status, which eventually made him a "half-breed principal chief" of the Potawatomis. None of the details of these fictions – that he was a Potawatomi, a chief, the saviour of the whites who survived the battle near Fort Dearborn (Chicago) in 1812 – is historically documented. They represent the fabrications of his employers, who had him appointed as an American-recognized chief the better to serve their business interests. Some legendary elements, for example the fable that he was Tecumseh*'s private secretary, represented his own embellishments. Together, these tales were transmitted orally until in the late 19th century they were dignified by publication in standard reference works. His supposed Potawatomi name, Sagaunash, as it turns out, was not a personal name at all but an ethnic label, *sakonosh*, by which these tribesmen identified him as "the English-speaking Canadian."

Caldwell was influential in aiding the negotiation of the final series of treaties signed by the United Bands of Potawatomis, Ottawas, and Ojibwas of Wisconsin and Illinois, which ended in 1833 when they ceded their last block of lands at the Treaty of Chicago. His services no longer needed, he was then abandoned by his American patrons and thereafter entered the full-time employ of the united bands. He migrated with them to western Missouri and Iowa where he made his final home, managing their business affairs and negotiating on their behalf with American officials until his death of cholera in 1841.

JAMES A. CLIFTON

An exhaustive bibliography of the primary sources relating to Billy Caldwell and of the various printed traditional sketches of him can be found in two works by the author, "Merchant, soldier, broker, chief; a corrected obituary of Billy Caldwell," Ill. State Hist. Soc., *Journal* (Springfield), 71 (1978): 185–210, and "Personal and ethnic identity on the Great Lakes frontier: the case of Billy Caldwell, Anglo-Canadian," *Ethnohistory* (Tucson, Ariz.), 25 (1978): 69–94.

Among the important manuscript sources are BL, Add. MSS 21885: 121 (copy at PAC); Chicago Hist. Soc., Billy Caldwell to Francis Caldwell, 17 March 1834; and Wis., State Hist. Soc., Draper MSS, 17S229–35, 238–40; 21S74–88. Most of the extensive correspondence from, to, and about Caldwell during his Indian Department years is found in PAC, RG 10, A1, 4, and A2, 28, 30–34; further information from these years and also concerning the 1816–19 period is in the Caldwell papers, PAC, MG 24, B147 (photocopies).

CALDWELL, Sir JOHN, lawyer, politician, office holder, businessman, and seigneur; baptized 25 Feb. 1775 at Quebec, only son of Henry Caldwell* and Ann Hamilton; m. 21 Aug. 1800 Jane Davidson at Quebec, and they had two sons and a daughter; d. 26 Oct. 1842 in Boston.

John Caldwell spent his childhood near Quebec, at the manor-house of Belmont. The estate was one of the properties on which his father had taken a 99-year lease from Lieutenant-General James Murray* in 1774 and which he was to buy in 1801. In addition to looking after his numerous fiefs, business activities, and responsibilities as a legislative councillor, Henry Caldwell served as receiver general from 1794. On 29 Jan. 1799 he decided to give his son power of attorney to administer his assets and business affairs. John, after a thorough education under Alexander Spark*, had been called to the bar on 20 June 1798, but as a result of his father's action he never practised as a lawyer.

In 1800 Caldwell went into politics when the residents of Lauzon, a seigneury also leased by his father for 99 years, urged him to run for the Lower Canadian House of Assembly. He stood for Dorchester that year and was elected along with Jean-Thomas Taschereau*. He remained a member until the 1809 elections, when some irregularities worked to his detriment. The polling officer, Jean-Baptiste Demers, whose sympathies lay with the Canadian party and Caldwell's opponents, declared Taschereau and Pierre Langlois elected before the polls were due to close. Shortly after the house opened in January 1810, Caldwell and his supporters protested against the conduct of Demers and demanded that the election be overturned. This request was rejected, then reconsidered. It was decided that the legitimacy of the election would be verified on 10 March. On 1 March, however, Governor Sir James Henry Craig* prorogued parliament, and the order died. In the following elections Caldwell defeated Taschereau, but only by 51 votes. After a decade in the house he relinquished his seat on 15 Dec. 1811. He had not played a large role, distinguishing himself more by his repeated absences than by his speeches. In general he supported the "Château clique" – the government party – but he retained a certain independence of mind. For example, he spoke in favour of pronouncing judges ineligible to be assemblymen, citing the difficulties that might arise from the simultaneous exercise of the two offices. He was called to the Legislative Council in 1811 and remained on it until 1838.

At his father's death in May 1810 Caldwell entered into possession of almost all his assets – one of the few exceptions being the seigneury of Lauzon, which was bequeathed to his young son Henry John. The distribution had been made according to a hand-written will, unsigned and undated; the only other one dated from 1799, when Henry's wife was still alive. As his son was just nine, Caldwell continued to manage Lauzon. At this time he owned Belmont and was the recognized seigneur of Gaspé and Foucault; in 1803 he had bought the seigneury of Saint-Étienne.

Joseph BOUCHETTE's descriptions of Caldwell's properties, published in 1815, give an idea of their state of development. The surveyor general paid little attention to Foucault, Gaspé, and Saint-Étienne, which had more wood than people, but he underlined the advantages of the seigneury of Lauzon. It was near Quebec, and had soils of high quality and plentiful timber. As numerous rivers flowed through it, it had three grist-mills and several sawmills. With the economic situation in his favour and a domain having highly prized and varied resources, Caldwell had not waited for his father's death to develop Lauzon, which he was managing. Using his engineering skills, he had diverted rivers to improve the output of the mills. A few years after his father's purchase of the seigneury in 1801, the two men had laid down new regulations for granting lands. Anxious to make their properties profitable and to safeguard them, they had raised the yearly payments and had added to previous contracts a series of restrictions on the building of mills. They had not, however, acted differently from other seigneurs.

In dealing with his lands, Caldwell not only kept the best locations for himself but also sought to ensure the supply of wood for his sawmills. In 1826, when he granted Pierre Lambert the sub-fief of Saint-Félix in the seigneury of Gaspé, he retained the rights to exploit any pine and spruce forests on it. Ten years earlier he had presented a request to Lord Bathurst for a change in the system of tenure on the seigneuries of Gaspé and Saint-Étienne. His proposed measure was designed to encourage the immigration of people from the British Isles, who were not eager to settle on seigneurial land. In the end the request was turned down, but if things had gone differently, Caldwell would have had sole ownership of 40,000 *arpents*, with only 4,000 cleared.

It would have taken more than one refusal to make Caldwell slow down in his initiatives. In building sawmills and flour-mills at the mouth of the Etchemin his father had encouraged the founding of a village there. This development was attractive to John, who was working along the same lines. Using his right of repurchase he had begun in 1804 to buy land along the St Lawrence now included in Notre-Dame ward at Lévis. He continued his dealings and in 1818 acquired in the space of two months the entire stretch of land above the cliff. The locality was called the town of Aubigny. Caldwell divided this magnificent domain into building lots, setting some aside for a public market and a park, and then he had a hotel and an Anglican chapel built. Wealthy people from Quebec had their summer homes there. Nevertheless the settlement never grew as Caldwell had hoped, and in Bouchette's time there were only about 40 dwellings. According to him the rents the seigneur demanded were far too high.

On 19 Nov. 1808 Caldwell had been appointed acting receiver general at the request of his father, who was gradually relinquishing his activities. The post became his officially on 6 June 1810. As receiver general he made only £400 a year, a sum he thought quite insufficient considering his heavy responsibility. His plans and his style of living required substantial capital outlays. In 1817 Caldwell sold Belmont to James Irvine* for £4,000 and then divided his time between his residence at Quebec and his seigneurial manor-house at Pointe-Lévy (Lauzon and Lévis).

Caldwell could also count on the proceeds from his lumber and flour business. He was in partnership with his brother-in-law John Davidson, who had been acting as business agent and attorney for the seigneur of Lauzon since 1811. The firm of Caldwell and Davidson specialized in dressing lumber. Caldwell got some of the wood from Upper Canada, but most of it came from the reserves on his seigneuries. He hired his *censitaires* to chop down the trees and bring the logs to his mills, where they were sawn into boards. All the facilities for shipping the product were near at hand.

Like other lumber merchants at Quebec, Caldwell and Davidson went into shipbuilding. On 28 Sept. 1816 they formed a company with Hiran Nicholas, a Montreal merchant, François LANGUEDOC, John White, and John Goudie* of Quebec, and Richard Lilliot, a merchant at Pointe-Lévy. The company was to put a steamship into passenger and freight service between the two shores of the St Lawrence. Each partner was entitled to one share. Caldwell was to import the engine and necessary fittings from Great Britain, and then have a loading wharf built. The *Lauzon* would go into service in 1818. On 28 Sept. 1816 Caldwell and Davidson had also entered partnership with Robert Armour*, George Davis (Davies), and James Macdowall, all Montreal merchants, and White, Languedoc, Goudie, Robert Melvin, and François Bélanger to form the Quebec Steamboat Company, for the purpose of running a steamship between Quebec and Montreal. Caldwell and Davidson held jointly one of the seven shares, and Caldwell was to furnish the same equipment as in the first arrangement.

In 1820, wanting to prepare for their own succession, Caldwell and Davidson brought their sons, Henry John and John, into the management of the flour-mill at Saint-Nicolas through a partnership agreement signed on 27 October. But subsequent events thwarted their plans. No matter how much profit Caldwell made from exporting flour and from his lumber business, his expenditures for Aubigny, the mills he built, and the purchases of land he was constantly making exceeded the income he could count on. His situation, like that of all the lumber merchants, remained precarious and subject to the impact of the protectionist policy of the imperial government. That the receiver general had such a grand style of living created doubt in the House of Assembly about the use he might be making of public funds. From 1815 the assembly demanded that it be kept informed of his accounts and the true financial situation of the province. The fact that Caldwell had loyal friends inside the administration did not prevent a scandal from erupting in 1823.

The receiver general was directly answerable to the British government. He had full power to levy and collect fees, taxes, and other revenues payable in the province for the maintenance of the administration of justice and the civil government. His salary was minimal, but he could dispose of the funds he held for his own purposes, on condition that he account for them on request. Caldwell had made generous use of this privilege, to the point that on 1 May 1822 he was unable to meet the expenses of the civil list. To cover his insolvency, Governor Lord Dalhousie [RAMSAY] took £30,000 out of military funds and then in January 1823 turned to the house for reimbursement. Judging that Caldwell had received a personal favour and that he ought to have had more than £100,000 to hand, the house took no action on the governor's claim and voted supplies as if there had been no deficit. The situation was becoming embarrassing for Dalhousie. He submitted the problem to the Executive Council, which questioned Caldwell. Caldwell was no more able to honour his obligations now than he had been the previous year. The council declared that the matter had to be referred to the British government and that the best solution was to postpone payment of the civil list until July and of other appropriations until November or December. This delay would give time to ascertain the crown's position and might enable Caldwell to replenish his funds.

Dalhousie sent John Davidson to England to present the facts and defend both his policy as governor and Caldwell's claims. Caldwell made a modest effort towards obtaining funds to pay his most pressing debts. To this end he parted with his shares in the *Lauzon* and the Quebec Steamboat Company and he committed to it the arrears owed by the Lauzon *censitaires* and the sale price of the Hôtel Lauzon. In addition he signed a promise to sell the seigneury of Foucault to Robert Christie*, receiving from him an initial £2,000.

Meanwhile Dalhousie was preparing to confront the house on this awkward case, which involved not only some £100,000 but also the entire machinery of colonial administration. The assembly had more than once complained that it did not have sufficient control of public revenues. The Caldwell affair provided a number of arguments in support of its point of view, beginning with the governor's complicity. In a hurry to take action Dalhousie, with the backing of the executive, appointed two controllers to assist Caldwell, and then a few days before the opening of the session on 25 Nov. 1823 he dismissed him from office. On being informed of these developments, the assembly set up a committee, chaired by Austin CUVILLIER, to examine the situation. Caldwell was called before it and questioned about the organization of the receiver general's office and the steps he intended to take to clear his debt. He proposed, among other measures, to sell his house in Lower Town Quebec, the seigneuries of Gaspé, Saint-Étienne, and Foucault, about 50 acres in the suburbs of Quebec, and some 40,000 more in various townships. The committee's report made little mention of this suggested course of action and emphasized the assembly's complaints about the colonial administration. In a message sent to London the assembly argued that the receiver general was directly responsible to the imperial government, and that London had an obligation to reimburse the province for the funds it had lost.

Caldwell wanted at all costs to be reinstated in office. Davidson went to England to plead his partner's cause once more and to inform the lords of the Treasury about the measures Caldwell had in mind to discharge his debt. Reinstatement was turned down, supposedly because Caldwell did not put up sufficient guarantees. Legal action was started: on 13 June 1825 two complaints were brought before the Court of King's Bench at Quebec. The first one involved Caldwell himself and sought recovery of the sum he owed as of 17 Nov. 1823, a little more than £219,000, plus interest. The second concerned him as heir to his father's estate and involved nearly £40,000, which the elder Caldwell had owed at his death. He contested both suits, but on 20 October the court ruled that he had to pay more than £96,000. He proposed to Dalhousie a method of reimbursement similar to the one that he had laid before the house committee, but he insisted on retaining Lauzon in return for an annual payment of £2,000. The governor submitted his proposals to the Executive Council, which suggested waiting for instructions from the Treasury. These delays antagonized the assembly, as did the attitude of

Caldwell, who at one moment made conciliatory offers and at the next rejected the accusations against him and refused adamantly to part with Lauzon. The house was well aware that Caldwell enjoyed support on both sides of the Atlantic.

Despite Caldwell's connections and all his efforts, the seigneury of Lauzon had to be put up for sale on 27 Aug. 1826. Henry John Caldwell protested the sale on grounds that the seigneury had been bequeathed to him by his grandfather and that it could not be used to clear his father's deficit. But because the will in Henry Caldwell's hand was neither signed nor dated, in June 1827 the Court of King's Bench declared it invalid. The case was appealed, and on 30 July 1828 the judgement was upheld. Henry John Caldwell decided to appeal to the Privy Council. While awaiting the final decision his father made a request to the Treasury that he might be considered the lessee of Lauzon for a period of five to seven years rather than on a yearly basis, but his request was denied.

The sale of Caldwell's other properties began on 21 Sept. 1829. Moses Hart* bought the seigneury of Gaspé, George POZER that of Saint-Étienne, and John Anthony Donegani* that of Foucault. Thomas Scott purchased the lots at Sainte-Foy, and the property in Lower Town went to John Jones. Caldwell did not remain inactive in the mean time and continued to make land grants on Lauzon until 1835. In his situation he was in a great hurry to collect annual payments and arrears due him. To satisfy his creditors he would give up a piece of land or the right to build a mill, always for monetary compensation. He took care, however, to grant the best parts of the seigneury to his children. To protect his sources of income as far as possible he even leased the communal mill to his brother-in-law Davidson for 20 years. He remained involved in the lumber business. In the Legislative Council the former receiver general, who in 1830 had inherited a baronetcy from a cousin, still enjoyed the confidence of his colleagues, and in 1831 Lord Aylmer [WHITWORTH-AYLMER] did not hesitate to appoint him acting speaker.

In January 1834, since the Privy Council had not yet given its opinion, the assembly wanted to reopen the debate and find out where matters stood. A committee of five was set up which reported on the situation, emphasizing irregularities. Among other things it questioned why Caldwell should not be required to pay interest on the amount of his default that had been recognized. In the end, the house demanded that the imperial government repay the sums owing the province, or that the remaining assets of the seigneur of Lauzon be seized. This famous scandal was reflected in the 92 Resolutions passed on 21 Feb. 1834, for Caldwell is depicted in the 34th, and the 84th gives as one of the assembly's grievances "the refusal of His Majesty's Government to reimburse to the province the amount for which the late Receiver-general was a defaulter." In June the Privy Council upheld the judgement of the Court of Appeal.

In his vexation Caldwell, who could not even make the annual payment required for the seigneury of Lauzon, wanted to resign from the Legislative Council in 1836. At that time he was living in seclusion in Boston. There being no precedent since councillors were named for life, his resignation was refused. That year the house set up a new committee to study the conditions of sale of Lauzon as well as Caldwell's proposal to make it over to the government as settlement for his debt, rather than to put it up for auction. The majority in the assembly, however, thought it more advantageous to proceed with a public sale. The debate was cut short by the turmoil of 1837–38.

The Caldwell affair was revived in 1840 in the Special Council. The former receiver general still owed the province some £78,675. He did not live to learn of the official decision. A bill passed the year after his death ordered Lauzon to be sold by the sheriff of the district of Quebec. On 17 March 1845 the government bought it for £40,500. More than 20 years of lawsuits, manœuvres, delays, and impassioned debates had been required to resolve the matter. These events revealed, of course, the ambition of one man, John Caldwell. They also reflected all the tensions that stirred up the colony in the years preceding the union of the two Canadas.

ANDRÉE HÉROUX

ANQ-Q, CE1-61, 25 févr. 1775, 21 août 1800; CN1-49, 2 juill. 1824, 22 déc. 1830; CN1-116, 23 oct. 1818; 31 août 1826; 28–29 mai 1831; 30 mars, 1er août 1832; CN1-178, 2 févr. 1801, 10 mai 1814; CN1-208, 22 avril, 13 oct., 7 nov. 1823; 1er oct. 1824; 22 mars 1825; 11 avril 1827; 19 avril, 31 oct. 1829; 17 déc. 1830; 12 avril 1832; 12, 24 sept. 1834; 17 déc. 1836; 24 sept. 1840; CN1-230, 9 janv. 1817, 13 mars 1823; CN1-262, 29 janv. 1799; 9, 21 oct. 1811; 28 sept. 1816; 18–19, 31 août, 4, 8, 14, 17, 19 sept., 23 oct. 1818; 12 nov. 1825; 21 janv. 1828; 20 janv. 1843; 8 mai 1846. Can., Prov. of, Legislative Council, *Journaux*, 1843: 12, 29, 32–33, 62, 130; *Statutes*, 1843, c.26. L.C., House of Assembly, *Journaux*, 1802: 213; 1803: 171, 173, 177; 1810: 131, 151–57, 195; 1815: 342, 344, 346, 434, 436, 494; 1820–21: 87, 107, 160–61, 280; 1823: 45, app.H; 1823–24: 23, 55, 107, 197, 230, app.E, L, S; 1825, app.O; 1826: 25, 59, 78; 1827: 23, 42, 95, 153, 187, 294; 1828–29: 212, 226, 320, 322, 346, 349–351; 1832–33: 191; 1834: 26, 31, 147, 194, 264, 482, app.CC; 1835–36: 366, 526–27, 604, 633, 645, 648; Legislative Council, *Journaux*, 1835: 22–23; 1835–36: 114, 216; Special Council, *Journals*, 1840–41, app.A. *Docs. relating to constitutional hist., 1791–1818* (Doughty and McArthur), 490–501. *Docs. relating to constitutional hist., 1819–28* (Doughty and Story), 88–89, 186–201, 315, 323–38, 453–70, 486–90. *Quebec Gazette*, 19 April 1810, 1 April 1813, 19 Dec. 1825, 31 Oct. 1842, 17 March 1845. Bouchette, *Topographical description of L.C.*

Quebec almanac, 1799, 1830, 1831. P.-G. Roy, *Les avocats de la région de Québec*; *Inv. concessions*. Turcotte, *Le Conseil législatif*. Christie, *Hist. of L.C.* (1866), vol.3. J.-E. Roy, *Hist. de Lauzon*, vols.3–5. D. T. Ruddell, "Quebec City, 1765–1831: the evolution of a colonial town" (D. ès L. thesis, Univ. Laval, Quebec, 1981). P.-G. Roy, "Le testament de l'honorable Henry Caldwell," *BRH*, 29 (1923): 202–4.

CALLIHOO (Calehue, Kalliou), LOUIS, Iroquois fur trader, trapper, and hunter; probably b. at Caughnawaga (Kahnawake), Que.; fl. 1819–45 in the vicinity of Lesser Slave Lake (Alta).

Louis Callihoo was one of many Iroquois men who travelled west with the fur trade in the late 18th and early 19th century. He probably came, like most of them, from the mission village of Caughnawaga, sometimes called Sault-Saint-Louis. An entry in its parish registers records the baptism of a Louis Karhiio, born 17 Oct. 1782 to Thomas Anatoha (Kanakonme) and Marie-Anne Tekonwakwehinni. A note beside the name indicates that he "went to the north, married there, had a family, [and] never returned." This description fits the career of Louis Callihoo; unlike most Iroquois who went to the west, he stayed there for the remainder of his life, and he founded a large and prominent family.

It has been claimed that the family name was originally Kwarakwante and that Father Albert Lacombe* was responsible for naming the branch that settled about the St Albert mission (Alta) Callioux, which later became corrupted to Callihoo. This hypothesis is not supported by the historical record. Individuals with the name Callihoo (variously spelled) appear well before Father Lacombe's time, in fur-trade records from the early 1800s and in church records from the 1840s. A Louis Cahiheue of Sault-Saint-Louis was hired in 1800 by McTavish, Frobisher and Company, agents for the North West Company, to winter in the north for two years. In 1812–13 a Louis Calihue worked for the NWC in the Athabasca district.

By the 1819–20 trading season Louis Callihoo was one of a number of Iroquois and Canadian freemen who hunted and trapped in the Smoky River area of what is now northwest Alberta and traded at posts on the Athabasca River and at Lesser Slave Lake. He was never a contract employee of the Hudson's Bay Company, although he did perform occasional services for it such as hauling goods to the Lesser Slave Lake post in 1819 or wintering company horses in 1829.

Callihoo appears to have married two sisters from one of the Smoky River families of freemen. His first wife was Josephte Patenaude and his second was Marie Patenaude; with them he had two and seven recorded children, respectively, between 1822 and 1845. Throughout the 1820s and into the 1830s he is portrayed in HBC journals as the head of a small network of free trappers and hunters living along the Smoky River. He and his family are included in an 1838 census of freemen who traded at Lesser Slave Lake. By 1842 he had moved from the Smoky River area to Shaw Point on the lake.

Callihoo was probably brought up as a Roman Catholic. The first missionary to reach the Lesser Slave Lake area was a Methodist, the Reverend Robert Terrill Rundle*, who arrived in the early 1840s. Although Callihoo associated with Rundle, even calling the missionary to attend him when ill, he did not become a Protestant convert. All his recorded children were baptized and married by priests, including six baptized in October of 1845 by Joseph Bourassa, one of the earliest Roman Catholic missionaries to reach Lesser Slave Lake.

Callihoo died some time between 1845 and 1856. His nine children survived to produce families of their own. Notable among his descendants are Michel Callihoo (Calistrois), who as chief signed an adhesion to Treaty 6 in 1878 and settled his band near St Albert, Felix Calihoo, a founder in 1932 of the Métis Association of Alberta, and John Callihoo, a founder in 1939 of the Indian Association of Alberta.

TRUDY NICKS

Arch. of the Archdiocese of Edmonton (Roman Catholic), Sainte-Anne (Lac Ste Anne), reg. des baptêmes, mariages et sépultures, 1844–59. PAM, HBCA, B.8/a/1; B.94/a/2; B.115/a/3–9; B.239/z/10; F.4/32. Provincial Arch. of Alta. (Edmonton), 71.185 (O. J. Rath, corr., reports, and geneal. charts tracing hereditary condition in descendants of Louis l'Iroquois, 1954–55); Oblats de Marie-Immaculée, Forts des Prairies/1 (reg. des baptêmes, mariages et sépultures, 1842–59); Forts des Prairies/5 (index des reg. des mariages, s.d.). R. T. Rundle, *The Rundle journals, 1840–1848*, intro. and notes G. M. Hutchinson, ed. H. A. Dempsey (Calgary, 1977). Trudy Nicks, "The Iroquois and the fur trade in western Canada," *Old trails and new directions: papers of the third North American Fur Trade Conference*, ed. C. M. Judd and A. J. Ray (Toronto, 1980), 85–101. D. I. Buchanan, "Blood genotypes -D-/-D- and CDe/-D-; transfusion therapy and some effects of multiple pregnancy," *American Journal of Clinical Pathology* (Baltimore, Md.), 26 (January–June 1956): 21–30.

CAMERON, DUNCAN, fur trader and politician; b. *c.* 1764 in Glen Moriston, Scotland, son of Alexander Cameron and Margaret McDonell; d. 15 May 1848 in Williamstown, Upper Canada.

In 1773 Duncan Cameron immigrated to New York with his parents, who settled in Tryon County; seven years later, during the American revolution, he joined a loyalist regiment, probably the King's Royal Regiment of New York [*see* Sir John Johnson*]. He came to the province of Quebec in 1785, in which year he entered the fur trade as a clerk for Alexander Shaw and

Gabriel Cotté*, independent traders in the Lake Nipigon (Ont.) region.

Cameron soon established himself as a formidable opponent to the Hudson's Bay Company as it tried to expand into the territory north and west of Lake Nipigon. When HBC man James Sutherland* wintered at Red Lake in 1790–91, he found that Cameron was already "well respected by the Indians as he has been some years at this place." With dismay, Sutherland noted how well provided his rival was with Jamaican rum, Brazilian tobacco, and elegant uniforms for the Indians; in addition Cameron sported "a large brass Blunderbuss which makes a hidious report" and "a beautiful shaloon flag" that contrasted sadly with his own "old dirty thing." The winter was not a loss for Sutherland's company "as two Houses draws more Indians," but his opponents, with their better supplies and knowledge of the area and their ostentation, kept the upper hand, trading 45 packs of fur to the HBC's 33. Yet Cameron preserved excellent relations with Sutherland, receiving the latter's appreciation for "his genteel behaviour and obliging nature" when they parted in the spring. Cameron was again at Red Lake in 1791–92, this time in opposition to HBC man John Best, with whom relations were far less cordial. As wintering agent for the Shaw–Cotté partnership, he also sent traders into the Lake Winnipeg drainage area, on the upper Bloodvein River (Man./Ont.).

In 1793–94 Cameron sent Jean-Baptiste Turcotte to trade at Big Lake (MacDowell Lake, Ont.) and maintained two posts on the Bloodvein River which cut into the HBC's trade at Red Lake. Cameron wintered in 1795–96 west of Lake Winnipeg at Partridge Crop, on the Fairford River (Man.), having as rivals John Best at Dauphin River and two independent traders, Joseph Rhéaume and Gabriel Atina Laviolette. Trade relations were tense; on 31 March 1796 Best wrote that Cameron was "constantly at variance with me concerning trade, that it is almost Impossible to get ye furrs without fighting for it."

After Gabriel Cotté died in February 1795, Cameron arranged for the firms of Forsyth, Richardson and Company and Todd, McGill and Company to supply his trade goods. When these firms temporarily withdrew from the northwest trade, a result of their rejection of the shares offered to them in 1795 by the North West Company, Cameron evidently had no choice but to join that concern, in which he became a partner. In 1796 he was placed in charge of its Nipigon department, a position he held until 1807. In 1796–98 he was at Fly Lake (Whiteloon Lake) in the Severn River headwaters, opposing HBC man David Sanderson. The two competed at Sandy Lake from 1798 to 1801, when Sanderson departed for Berens River, leaving the Severn trade largely to Cameron and his men.

In 1803–4 Cameron and 26 men overwhelmed their HBC rivals under James Peter Whitford at Island Lake (Man.). In 1804–5 Charles Thomas Isham* did little better than his predecessor against the NWC there, while Cameron himself wintered at Owl Lake (McInnes Lake, Ont.) in opposition to John Sanderson. Portions of Cameron's journal from this winter survive, along with a valuable ethnographic account of the region which he may have drafted in the same period. In 1806–7 he wintered at Trout (Big Trout) Lake, east of Lake Severn, where, according to HBC man James Swain, he "dealt with the Natives in a very extravagant way."

In 1807 Cameron and Alexander MacKay* succeeded the latter's brother William* in the charge of the Lake Winnipeg department based at Fort Bas-de-la-Rivière (Fort Alexander, Man.). The following winter Cameron traded in opposition to HBC man Alexander Kennedy at Drunken (Wrong) Lake, east of Lake Winnipeg. In July 1808, at Cameron's urging, the NWC cut the department's posts and labour force in half since its expenses had greatly exceeded returns. Cameron spent 1808–11 at Fort Alexander, as Bas-de-la-Rivière was by then named, presiding over a trade much reduced by competition and fur depletion. One of his Lake Winnipeg clerks, George Nelson* (who married a cousin of Cameron's Ojibwa wife), wrote warmly in this period of his "esteem & respect" for Cameron as his bourgeois: "we are (us Clerks) never hapier than when together & in his Company." Cameron turned his charge over to John Dugald Cameron* in 1811 and went to the Lac La Pluie department, which he managed for three years.

The most conspicuous period of Cameron's career began in 1814 when, with Alexander Macdonell* (Greenfield), he took over the Red River department and confronted the HBC colony of Red River, established two years before by Lord Selkirk [Douglas*] and governed by Miles Macdonell*. By this time the Nor'Westers had stepped up their opposition to the colony, encouraging the local freemen, mixed-bloods, and Indians to take action against it [*see* Cuthbert Grant*]. In August 1814 HBC man Peter Fidler* described the appearance of Cameron and Macdonell at Red River "dressed in regimentals" and en route to the NWC's Fort Gibraltar (Winnipeg). Styling himself a captain and Macdonell a lieutenant, Cameron asserted that he and not Miles Macdonell was the "Chief of this Country," and he sent for all the freemen in the neighbourhood, "wishing to hire them – to prevent them . . . from killing Buffalo for the support of the Settlement." On 5 September, acting on a warrant issued by Nor'Wester Archibald Norman McLeod as a magistrate for the Indian country under the Canada Jurisdiction Act, Cameron and seven armed men arrested John Spencer, sheriff of the colony, "for breaking open their stores at Brandon House last spring."

In June 1815 the Nor'Westers' continuing pressures to disperse the colony, reinforced by reports of Sioux and Métis threats against it, led to the departure of about 140 settlers and to Miles Macdonell's giving himself up to Cameron in exchange, he hoped, for the safety of the remaining colonists. When depredations against them continued, however, they too departed. They were persuaded to return to Red River by Colin ROBERTSON, who met them on their way to York Factory (Man.).

In March 1816 Robertson raided Fort Gibraltar, seizing documents which implicated the NWC in raids that had been made on the colony and arresting Cameron, who was sent to York Factory and then, after a year's detention, to England. Released without standing trial, he returned to the Canadas about 1820, when he took legal action against Robertson "for false imprisonment . . . [and] for damages to an enormous amount." Retiring from the fur trade, he settled in Glengarry County in the Williamstown area, where other Nor'Westers had also located, among them David Thompson*.

During at least the years 1807–12, Cameron had had an Indian wife and family, a connection that evidently linked him to the Ojibwas of the loon clan in the Nipigon area. A letter of 28 July 1812 contained a warning to a young relative against allowing "Love to get the better of Raison . . . if he should get Married before he is settled in a proper way, then all his future prospects are dished . . . this I too well know by dear bought experience." In the fall of 1820 Cameron married Margaret McLeod, in Upper Canada, and they had a daughter and three sons, including Sir Roderick William*, who became active in the shipping trade to Australia. Duncan Cameron represented Glengarry in the Upper Canadian House of Assembly during the ninth parliament (1825–28). He died at Williamstown on 15 May 1848.

JENNIFER S. H. BROWN

AO, MU 2102, 1812, no.14, item 2; MU 2198, no.3 (photocopy). MTRL, George Nelson papers, journal no.5: 190, 199, 206–7, 227; letter to his sister, 4 June 1811. PAC, RG 1, L3, 107: C14/252; RG 5, A1: 38177–78. PAM, HBCA, B.3/b/46: ff.32–33; B.51/a/1: f.18; B.149/a/7: f.3; B.177/a/1: ff.11–12, 16, 22–23, 26, 31–32; B.198/b/5: f.44; B.235/a/3: ff.4–5. *Les bourgeois de la Compagnie du Nord-Ouest* (Masson), vol.2. *Docs. relating to NWC* (Wallace). *HBRS*, 1 (Rich); 2 (Rich and Fleming). "United Empire Loyalists: enquiry into the losses and services in consequence of their loyalty; evidence in the Canadian claims," AO *Report*, 1904: 1093. *Legislators and legislatures of Ont.* (Forman), 1: 57. *Marriage bonds of Ont.* (T. B. Wilson), 39. H. W. Duckworth, "The Nipigon trade to 1796" (paper presented at the fifth North American Fur Trade Conference, Montreal, 1985). J. G. Harkness, *Stormont, Dundas and Glengarry: a history, 1784–1945* (Oshawa, Ont., 1946). V. P. Lytwyn, *The fur trade of the little north: Indians, pedlars, and Englishmen east of Lake Winnipeg, 1760–1821* (Winnipeg, 1986). J. A. Macdonell, *Sketches illustrating the early settlement and history of Glengarry in Canada, relating principally to the Revolutionary War of 1775–83, the War of 1812–14 and the rebellion of 1837–8* . . . (Montreal, 1893). Rich, *Fur trade* (1976).

CAMPBELL, Sir ARCHIBALD, army officer and colonial administrator; b. 12 March 1769 in Glen Lyon, Scotland, third son of Captain Archibald Campbell and Margaret Small; m. 6 July 1801 Helen Macdonald of Garth, and they had two sons and three daughters; d. 6 Oct. 1843 in Edinburgh.

Archibald Campbell took up the military profession "like a family inheritance," as one writer puts it, and on 28 Dec. 1787 became an ensign in the 77th Foot by raising 20 men for service. From 1788 until 1801 he was in the East Indies, advancing to lieutenant on 26 April 1791 and captain on 24 May 1799. In 1801 he was compelled by ill health to return to Britain and until 1804 he was employed largely in the recruiting service. After his promotion to major on 14 Sept. 1804 he was stationed variously in Guernsey, Scotland, and Ireland. In 1808 he served under Sir John Moore during the disastrous La Coruña campaign in Spain, and on 16 Feb. 1809 he was raised to the rank of lieutenant-colonel and appointed to assist in the reorganization of the Portuguese army, in which he was eventually given the rank of major-general. He commanded a brigade during all of the major battles in the Peninsula and in southern France, and received the Military Cross with one clasp, the Order of the Tower and Sword from the king of Portugal, and a knighthood on 28 April 1814. On 4 June 1814 he became a brevet colonel in the British army and was made an aide-de-camp to the Prince Regent. From 1816 he commanded the Lisbon division of the Portuguese army but he resigned following the revolution of 1820, with which he did not sympathize. Shortly after his return to England he was appointed lieutenant-colonel of the 38th Foot, which he joined at the Cape of Good Hope and accompanied to India in 1822.

Campbell's moment of glory came when he was placed in charge of the expeditionary force to Burma which sailed from the Andaman Islands on 5 May 1824. British officials were totally ignorant of the problems of tropical warfare, and one historian has described the campaign as "the worst managed of all the nineteenth-century colonial wars." Campbell must share in the responsibility since he was repeatedly guilty of over-optimism and inadequate planning, but through a mixture of luck and daring he was able to bring the campaign to a successful conclusion in February 1826. Even the military historian John William Fortescue, while critical of the expedition, admitted that Campbell had shown "an iron nerve, a strong will, high moral force and abundant moral courage." Campbell, who had become a major-general on 27 May 1825, was awarded a pension of £1,000 per annum by the East India Company, a GCB (military), and a vote of thanks by both houses of the British parliament. From 1826 until 1829 Campbell remained in command of the provinces ceded by Burma to Britain and acted as civil commissioner to that kingdom and to Siam (Thailand). Upon his return to Britain he sought another posting in the East but had to be satisfied with the lieutenant governorship of New Brunswick, a blow undoubtedly softened by his elevation as a baronet on 30 Sept. 1831.

Campbell assumed control of the administration of New Brunswick from William Black* on 8 Sept. 1831. The first issue he had to deal with was an act of "unwarrantable aggression" by Maine, whose government he believed was responsible for sending a deputation into the Madawaska settlements, the ownership of which was in dispute with New Brunswick, to elect town officers. Campbell promptly led a detachment of troops into the area and arrested a number of Americans. Although he later released those who were convicted of originating the disturbances in Madawaska, he insisted that to prevent similar acts in the future a larger force of regular troops should be stationed in New Brunswick, and he began construction of the "Royal Road" from Fredericton to Grand Falls to expedite the movement of troops and British settlers into the disputed territory. But he was unable to persuade the military authorities at Halifax to transfer to New Brunswick the number of troops he felt were needed.

Campbell was also frustrated in his efforts to improve the efficiency of the "ill organized" militia. In 1831 the House of Assembly, which did not share his concerns and sought greater control over the militia system, substantially reduced the salaries of the inspecting field officers of militia, and it only reluctantly agreed to grant the smaller amount in 1832. The following year it requested that the number of days the militia would have to serve annually be decreased from three to one and that the pay of the adjutants and sergeants-major be greatly cut. Campbell rejected both requests and persuaded the assembly to vote money for the inspecting field officers for one more year. He attributed the hostility of the house to "perverted judgement, or unnatural spirit" and protested when the Colonial Office did not include provision for the militia on the permanent civil list requested from the assembly. In March 1834 the annual vote for the inspecting field officers passed "with less opposition than is usually given," but the new assembly which met in 1835 refused to grant salaries to militia officers. Campbell fulminated against "these unpatriotic and . . . disloyal measures." Although the assembly temporarily restored the grants for the adjutants and sergeants-major, in 1837 it again rejected them and suspended the militia act. Campbell did try to improve the discipline of the militia and exercise greater control over appointments; but without adequate financial assistance from the assembly and only lukewarm support from the home government, which refused to issue the militia with arms, his efforts to create a more effective military force came to little.

The conflict over provision for the militia was only part of a broader struggle with the assembly in which Campbell was engaged soon after his arrival. In the earlier part of the 19th century New Brunswick had evolved a relatively stable political culture, but that stability had been undermined by the appointment of Thomas Baillie* as commissioner of crown lands in 1824. Baillie introduced a series of reforms which antagonized the local timber merchants and greatly increased the provincial revenues as well as his own fortune. Much of the revenue, however, was absorbed by the costs of administering his increasingly large office. Even Campbell admitted that "the *enormous* expence (without adequate advantage to the Casual Revenue) of the Crown Land Department, furnishes a ready topic for inflaming the public mind." When, early in 1832, Baillie persuaded the Colonial Office to abolish the offices of receiver general and auditor general on the grounds that they were no longer necessary, there was such an outcry against the concentration of power in Baillie's hands that Campbell had the decision reversed.

Yet despite the evidence of irregularities in Baillie's department Campbell made only minor changes in the land-granting system and vehemently objected to giving the assembly any control over land-granting policy. He denounced Baillie's detractors as "agitators" and on dividing the Council into two bodies in 1833 he promoted Baillie to the senior position in the Executive Council, to which he also appointed Baillie's father-in-law, William Franklin ODELL, and George Frederick Street*, who was closely associated with Baillie. When the assembly protested, he dismissed the complaints as arising from the frustrated ambitions of "some very troublesome and dangerous characters – two Brothers of the names of Simonds" (Charles* and RICHARD). Despite pressure from the Colonial Office he refused to appoint any of the leading members of the assembly to the Executive Council. His selections for the Legislative Council were no more judicious. In 1832 he had recommended virtually all of the members proposed for the Executive Council and only one MHA, William Crane*, who declined the appointment. In May 1833, after the council had been established, he requested that the attorney general, the solicitor general, and the advocate general be added to it to give it greater weight, but the Colonial Office refused to sanction the appointment of more officials at that time. Compelled to submit a new list, Campbell included several of the same names, among them that of the attorney general. These appointments were confirmed despite the fact that they were not acceptable to the majority in the assembly.

Campbell had even less sympathy with the desire of the assembly to gain control over the casual and territorial revenues of the crown. When the Colonial Office considered surrendering those revenues for a permanent civil list in 1832, Campbell asked that, "should such a measure ever be, *to my regret*, resolved on," a large sum should be requested for contingencies so that the government would never be dependent on the assembly. The following year he refused to provide the house with a detailed analysis of the returns from the crown revenues and described its leading members as "mischievous agitators." After the assembly had sent Charles Simonds and Edward Barron Chandler* to London in May 1833 to work out an agreement for the surrender of the casual and territorial revenues, Campbell suggested that the British government should hold out for a civil list of at least £18–20,000, a sum that the colonial secretary, Edward George Geoffrey Smith Stanley, dismissed as absurdly high. Campbell was nevertheless able to persuade the Colonial Office to demand more concessions than the assembly was willing to grant and thus secured the defeat of Stanley's offer. Campbell remained "convinced that the internal improvement of the Country . . . will be retarded" by the surrender of the crown revenues and bitterly condemned the existing system of appropriations for roads and bridges, which was controlled by the house. In November 1834 he dissolved the assembly, but the new house continued to demand control over all provincial revenues. It refused to agree to a bill providing for the commutation of quitrents, which Campbell had begun to collect, and entered into a dispute with the Legislative Council as a result of which no supply bill was passed into law. Campbell prorogued the legislature in March 1835 but reconvened it on 15 June, when it voted supplies and agreed to commute quitrents. The assembly reiterated its desire for the surrender of the casual and territorial revenues; since these revenues were rapidly increasing, however, Campbell remained opposed to any agreement.

When the assembly was again rebuffed in the 1836 session, it sent another delegation, composed of William Crane and Lemuel Allan Wilmot*, to London. Campbell argued that the appointment of the delegation was "generally deprecated *throughout* the Province," but the Whig colonial secretary, Lord Glenelg, was favourably impressed by Wilmot and Crane and negotiated a settlement with them. Campbell was dismayed by the decision to surrender the casual and territorial revenues and he delayed the implementation of his instructions to this effect by every means in his power. After the house reconvened in December 1836 it dismissed Campbell's objections as, in his words, "of trifling consequence and made from unworthy motives" and passed a civil list bill, to which he refused consent. Campbell dispatched George Frederick Street to London to justify his opposition to the bill and offered to resign if his views did not coincide with those of Lord Glenelg. Glenelg accepted his resignation and in May 1837 transferred Sir John Harvey* from Prince Edward Island to New Brunswick to negotiate a settlement with the assembly along the lines earlier agreed to by the Colonial Office.

Campbell left from Saint John on 1 June, "amidst the regret," one newspaper reported, "of a large concourse of the most respectable citizens." His departure may have been viewed with regret by the conservative faction in the colony, but it was welcomed by the great majority of New Brunswickers. On 28 June 1838 Campbell became a lieutenant-general and in August he accepted appointment as commander-in-chief in Bombay. Almost immediately he had to resign from ill health, which had also plagued him in New Brunswick. He retired to Edinburgh, where he died in 1843.

James Hannay*, in his *History of New Brunswick*, dismisses Campbell as an "old military tyrant," who was "most unfit" for office. In his conservative views Campbell differed little from the majority of army officers sent to govern the British North American colonies in the aftermath of the Napoleonic Wars. He held those views with unusual rigidity, however, perhaps because he had spent almost all of his life on service abroad, mainly in the East, where he had acquired few of the political skills required in a colony with representative institutions. Although he dismissed "the narrow views, and extremely limited knowledge and capacity of Provincial Legislators," his dispatches are littered with examples of his own prejudices. He was undoubtedly sincere when he asserted that he "had no dearer object than the inviolable preservation of the prerogative" of the crown, and, as historian William Stewart MacNutt* claims, he had every reason to be suspicious of the uses to which the assembly would put the revenues surrendered to it. But he was aloof and inflexible and he would have used those funds for equally dubious purposes: to support the clergy of the Church of England and the unpopular King's College and to increase the salaries of the small official clique which surrounded him. He foolishly interpreted all opposition as disloyalty when it was apparent even to his superiors in London that he was mistaken. As Hannay proclaims, "No Governor of New Brunswick has ever been less in sympathy with its inhabitants."

PHILLIP BUCKNER

[A portrait of Sir Archibald Campbell hangs in the National Army Museum (London).

The major source for this study was PRO, CO 188/41–56. There is a small collection of Sir Archibald Campbell papers in PAC, MG 24, A21, but they are mainly duplicates of materials in the Colonial Office files. Also useful were the *New-Brunswick Courier* from 1831 to 1837, the *Times* (Halifax), 2 May, 13, 20 June 1837, and the *Loyalist* (Fredericton), 16 Nov. 1843. Biographical details are drawn from PRO, CO 323/133: ff.353–54 and WO 211/4: ff.40–41; *Burke's peerage* (1927); Robert Chambers, *A biographical dictionary of eminent Scotsmen* (new ed., revised and continued by Thomas Thomson, 3v., London, 1870; repr. New York, 1971); *Colburn's United Service Magazine* (London), 1843, pt.III: 440–43, 480; the *DNB*; G.B., WO, *Army list*, 1788–1844; and W. A. Shaw, *The knights of England; a complete record from the earliest times to the present day* . . . (2v., London, 1906), 1: 224; 2: 313. Campbell's role in the first Burma War is examined in George Bruce, *The Burma wars, 1824–1886* (London, 1973), and J. W. Fortescue, *A history of the British army* (13v. in 14, London, 1899–1930), 11. James Hannay is very critical of Campbell in his *Hist. of N.B.*; W. S. MacNutt, *New Brunswick*, is more sympathetic. Aspects of Campbell's career are dealt with in D. R. Facey-Crowther, "The New Brunswick militia: 1784–1871" (MA thesis, Univ. of N.B., Fredericton, 1965), 118–33; Charlotte Lenentine, *Madawaska: a chapter in Maine–New Brunswick relations* (Madawaska, Maine, 1975); and Buckner, *Transition to responsible government*. P.B.]

CAMPBELL, Sir COLIN, army officer and colonial administrator; b. 1776 in Scotland, fifth son of John Campbell of Melfort and Colina Campbell of Achallader, daughter of John Campbell of Achallader; m. Jane Hendon, and they had four sons and three daughters; d. 13 June 1847 in London.

Colin Campbell was the scion of a Highland family with a strong military tradition. His father was an officer in the 42nd Foot who served in North America during the Seven Years' War, and Colin's six brothers and four sons all pursued careers in the services. In February 1792, at the age of 16, Campbell ran away from Perth Academy to join a vessel bound for the West Indies. He returned to Scotland to enter Moor's Navigation Academy in Perth but in December 1792 sailed for India as a midshipman. Appointed a lieutenant in the Breadalbane Fencibles in February 1795, he transferred in 1799 to the 1st West India Regiment as an ensign, serving as a brigade-major on St Vincent in 1800. On 21 Aug. 1801 Campbell entered the 35th Foot as a lieutenant and on 12 Feb. 1802 he joined the 78th Foot, which was in India as part of the army of Colonel Arthur Wellesley. During the attack on Ahmadnagar on 8 Aug. 1803, Campbell so impressed Wellesley by his bravery under fire that he was made a brigade-major.

Campbell, who was promoted captain on 9 Jan. 1805, returned to England as aide-de-camp to Lord Wellesley, Arthur's brother. He accompanied Arthur Wellesley on the expedition to Copenhagen in 1807 and was thanked by him in general orders. Acting successively as assistant adjutant general, assistant deputy quartermaster general, and assistant quartermaster general, he served with Wellesley (who became the Duke of Wellington) in Portugal and Spain during the Peninsular War and at Waterloo. On 2 Sept. 1808 Campbell became a major, on 3 May 1810 a lieutenant-colonel, and on 4 June 1814 a colonel. He received numerous British and foreign decorations, and on 2 Jan. 1815 he was made a KCB. From 1815 until 1818 he remained on Wellington's staff and lived at the latter's residence in Paris, and between 1819 and 1825 he did duty with his regiment in England. On 27 May 1825 he became a major-general. Although selected as lieutenant governor of Tobago in February 1828, Campbell apparently never took up the post and was appointed lieutenant governor of Portsmouth on 20 March 1828. He was made lieutenant governor of Nova Scotia in January 1834.

On 2 July 1834 Campbell took charge of the government of the colony from the administrator, Thomas Nickleson JEFFERY. Sir Colin and Lady Campbell were a great hit with "the beauty and fashion of Halifax." During the summer "scarcely a week" passed without "a Pick Nic or some convivial party" at Government House and during the winter the Campbells held a series of balls and "Private Theatricals." They sponsored local artists and writers, and Sir Colin became the patron of a host of local organizations, including the Halifax Mechanics' Institute, the Nova Scotia Horticultural Society, and the Highland Society. Haligonians praised his willingness to visit the "scenes of infection" during the cholera epidemic of 1834 and the personal interest he took in road building, and he received widespread applause for his efforts to promote economic development by requesting more free ports for Nova Scotia and changes in the imperial customs regulations to benefit the colony.

Initially Campbell's relationship with the House of Assembly was harmonious. He convened the assembly on 27 Nov. 1834 and, working through Samuel George William ARCHIBALD, the speaker, and Alexander Stewart*, a member for Cumberland County, persuaded it to grant £2,000 per annum toward his salary in order to forestall the collection of quitrents. He could not, however, convince the house that money should be set aside for "the repair of the Great Roads & Bridges, leading from the capital to the different extremities of the Province." In January 1835 he moved to remedy the complaints lodged by the Halifax grand jury against the administration of justice in the town and made substantial alterations in the bench of magistrates. After proroguing the legislature on 19 February, Campbell began a series of tours across "this beautiful and interesting Province" and on 17 Jan. 1836 informed his superiors that he found the people "moderate & tractable." The 1836 legislative session also "went off smoothly," although again Campbell could not persuade the assembly to alter the system of distributing road money and he was annoyed when it discontinued the annual grant to the inspecting field officers of militia. When he dissolved the legislature in November, the Halifax *Times* confidently predicted that Nova Scotians would rally behind the conservative faction that had hitherto controlled the house.

To the dismay of the conservatives the assembly elected in January 1837 was dominated by a loose coalition of reformers and was soon at odds with the lieutenant governor and the Council. It not only refused to make provision for the inspecting field officers but repealed the militia act and demanded control over the casual and territorial revenues. On 13 April it carried by 38 to 4 an address to the crown demanding that the Council either be made elective or be entirely reconstituted so that it was no longer controlled by the Halifax commercial élite and by supporters of the Church of England. Since the Colonial Office was already committed to substantial reform in the Canadas and New Brunswick, Campbell was aware that at the very least his Council would have to be divided into separate legislative and executive bodies but he preferred "things to remain nearly as they are." Indeed, the Colonial Office was so critical of the initial lists of names he submitted for appointment to the two new councils that he was forced to revise them. When Campbell came to make provisional appointments in January 1838, there were, as even reformer Joseph Howe* admitted, "several judicious selections," but both councils contained a clear majority of Anglicans and "not a man of liberal politics" was placed on the Executive Council save Herbert Huntington*. Campbell had also been instructed to enter into negotiations with the assembly for a civil list. In doing so he amended the Colonial Office's suggestions about salaries in order to provide "in a more liberal manner" for the judges, even though the assembly had criticized the existing scale of judicial emoluments.

Campbell's actions disappointed moderate reformers such as William Young*, but the latter vowed "to give the new body politic a fair trial" and eschewed "the reform that has broken out into rebellion" in the Canadas. On 30 March, while expressing its "regret" at Campbell's appointments, the assembly nevertheless voiced its confidence in his good intentions and even passed a civil list bill, although the amount granted was smaller than Campbell had requested and the bill was subsequently rejected by the Legislative Council. Yet when Campbell was compelled to reduce the size of the councils because of a difference between his instructions and the commission issued to the newly appointed governor-in-chief of British North America, Lord Durham [LAMBTON], he increased the proportion of Anglicans, again excluded the reform leaders, and indeed dropped Huntington. On 12 April 1838 the assembly therefore passed an address complaining that both councils contained majorities "generally hostile to the liberal party" and, fearful lest Campbell dissolve the legislature, the house immediately voted to send its own delegates to meet with Lord Durham after his arrival. Campbell described the assembly's resolutions as "insulting" and in his speech closing the session on the 17th repeated his determination to "resist any attempt to encroach upon Her Majesty's prerogative." However, he did include both reformers and conservatives in the delegation which he sent to discuss with Durham the latter's scheme for the union of British North America.

Between 1837 and 1839 Campbell's attention was increasingly distracted by the mounting crisis in Anglo-American relations triggered by the Canadian rebellions and the Maine–New Brunswick boundary dispute. During this period a large number of troops passed through Nova Scotia en route to New Brunswick or the Canadas, and Campbell personally supervised their training and the preparations for their travels west. The size of the provincial garrison also steadily increased. Campbell was promoted lieutenant-general on 28 June 1838, and by the end of 1839 he had five regiments and several companies directly under his command. As commander of the forces in the Atlantic region he was responsible for the disposition of the troops in New Brunswick, and he was frequently at loggerheads with its lieutenant governor, Sir John Harvey*, who contrary to Campbell's orders dispersed his troops in small units near the territory in dispute with Maine. Harvey appealed to London for greater autonomy. Even after his demand was rejected he continued to "pass by" Campbell and to the latter's annoyance persuaded the authorities in the Canadas to sanction his arrangements. Much of the difficulty between Harvey and Campbell arose from Harvey's wilful attempt to circumvent the normal chain of command, but a number of minor disputes occurred because of Campbell's rigidity on matters of military discipline and his desire to keep as many troops as possible directly under his control in Nova Scotia.

In August 1838 Campbell travelled to Quebec to meet Lord Durham. Although Durham had been much influenced by the opinions of William Young, one of the Nova Scotian delegates sent by Campbell, he did not see a need to replace the lieutenant governor and was content to rely on the latter's "good sense and good intentions." He even recommended that Campbell be appointed successor to Sir John Colborne* as commander of the forces in the Canadas. When the Nova Scotia assembly met in January 1839, it expressed its strong dissatisfaction with the composition of the Executive Council and refused to grant a civil list on the scale requested by Campbell, who dismissed the reformers' grievances as "imaginary" and urged the Colonial Office to resist the assembly's "onward course towards Democracy."

In April the assembly sent William Young and Huntington to London to appeal to the colonial secretary, Lord Normanby, for changes in the government along the lines adopted in New Brunswick by Harvey, who had given the dominant party in the assembly a majority of the seats in both councils and control of the casual and territorial revenues. Campbell acted somewhat disingenuously, pretending to Young and Huntington that he was unconcerned with the assembly's decision while at the same time sanctioning the dispatch of the legislative councillors Alexander Stewart and Lewis Morris Wilkins* to London to defend the *status quo*. Campbell was certain that the assembly's delegation would have little effect and he dismissed Durham's recommendation of responsible government as "absurd." In fact, Young and Huntington had considerable influence with the parliamentary under-secretary at the Colonial Office, Henry Labouchere. He prepared a dispatch from Normanby to Campbell which emphasized that the Executive Council should be composed so that "the co-operation of the popular Branch of the Constitution" would be obtained and that seats on it should be offered to leading assemblymen as the occasion arose. Yet Campbell refused to follow these instructions because he wished to show that "those who profess ultra radical principles, & systematically keep up popular agitation" would not receive government patronage, and when a vacancy occurred he appointed Alexander Stewart.

In February 1840 James Boyle Uniacke*, who had become a supporter of responsible government, resigned from the Executive Council. Campbell added a moderate liberal, James McNab, but only after McNab had indicated that he did not support responsible government. The same month the assembly insisted that Campbell use the authority given to him by the colonial secretary, Lord John Russell, to reconstruct his council, but he continued to argue that it would be "unjust" to remove councillors against whom he had no complaint. The assembly condemned Campbell for consolidating the power of a "small and exclusive party" and appealed to the Colonial Office for his dismissal. This action generated a war of petitions and over 3,000 Nova Scotians signed resolutions supporting the lieutenant governor. Campbell was confident that the Colonial Office would not yield to "Howe & his Clique" and asked for permission to dissolve the assembly, but to his consternation Russell refused and sent the new governor-in-chief, Charles Edward Poulett THOMSON, to act as arbiter between Campbell and the assembly.

Thomson arrived in Nova Scotia on 9 July 1840 and did not approve of what he found. Although he sought to "justify" Campbell's actions, he insisted that the Executive Council be remodelled to include representatives from the liberal party. Thomson hoped that Campbell might preside over the creation of the coalition council. The lieutenant governor, however, remained opposed to the appointment of Howe because of his "intemperate conduct, and offensive behaviour . . . to myself," and when Howe reported to Thomson that Campbell would not "smoke the pipe of peace" Russell selected Lord Falkland [Cary*] to implement Thomson's recommendations. Campbell was "deeply mortified," but was somewhat mollified when appointed lieutenant governor of Ceylon (Sri Lanka), "one of the best Governments under the Crown." Because the conservatives turned Campbell's departure on 3 October into a political event, the reformers, according to the *Novascotian*, "declined turning out" and only a few hundred Haligonians paid their respects. The paper expressed the hope that Campbell might be "more successful in his new Government." Campbell arrived in Ceylon on 5 April 1841, and soon revealed many of the weaknesses he had shown in Nova Scotia. He left the administration of the colony largely in the hands of his subordinates, and in 1845 James Stephen, the permanent under-secretary at the Colonial Office, described him as "an aged and feeble man" whose "judgment is not in his own keeping." Campbell left Ceylon on 19 April 1847 and returned to London, where he died on 13 June.

In its comments before Campbell's departure from Nova Scotia, the *Novascotian* had praised his "courteous" and "frank" behaviour and blamed his difficulties on "an organized party" which exercised "a most commanding influence upon his administration." Indeed, Howe professed to believe that Campbell had seen the error of his ways prior to leaving. To some extent an interpretation stressing external influences is valid. Campbell did rely for advice on men like Bishop John INGLIS and Chief Justice Brenton Halliburton*. But to exonerate Campbell from personal responsibility seems unnecessarily generous. Although an easy-going Presbyterian and far more approachable than his contemporary in New Brunswick, Sir Archibald CAMPBELL, he was also a product of the "old Wellington School" and his instinctive sympathies were with the colonial upper class. In 1837 or 1838, and probably even in 1839 or 1840, he could have become as popular as Harvey became in New Brunswick by broadening the base of his Executive Council. His prejudices, however, led to his failure. In a colony where the vast majority of the population were dissenters or Presbyterians he asserted that it was easier to find twelve churchmen fit for office than one dissenter; he believed there was only one Roman Catholic in Nova Scotia qualified for high office; and he refused to take the reformers seriously because "not one of them has one hundred pounds at stake in the province." His difficulties he ascribed to the fact that he had been "fettered by instructions which I knew to be inapplicable to the state of the Province." This claim was naïve. Substantial reform was both necessary and inevitable in Nova Scotia. Campbell asked to be misled and he was. He was thus the author of his own unpopularity.

PHILLIP BUCKNER

Harvard College Library, Houghton Library, Harvard Univ. (Cambridge, Mass.), MS Can. 58 (Joseph Howe papers) (mfm. at PAC). N.B. Museum, W. F. Ganong papers, box 42; Harvey papers, Campbell corr.; letter-books. PAC, MG 24, A17; A40. PANS, MG 2, 720, 732. PRO, CO 54/188–235; CO 217/156–75; CO 218/31–32; WO 43/529: 320–23. N.S., House of Assembly, *Journal and proc.*, 1834–40. *Novascotian*, 1834–40. *Nova-Scotia Royal Gazette*, 1834–40. *Times* (Halifax), 1834–40. F.-J. Audet, "Governors, lieutenant-governors, and administrators of Nova Scotia, 1604–1932" (typescript, n.d.; copy at PANS). *DNB*. G.B., WO, *Army list*. *A memorial history of the Campbells of Melfort, Argyllshire . . .* , comp. M. O. Campbell (London, 1882). J. M. Beck, *Government of N.S.*, 78–79; *Joseph Howe* (2v., Kingston, Ont., and Montreal, 1982–83), 1: 175–76, 186–87, 189–90, 193, 201–6, 209–10, 214–15. Buckner, *Transition to responsible government*. K. M. De Silva, *Social policy and missionary organization in Ceylon, 1840–1855* (London, 1965). H. A. J. Hulugalle, *British governors of Ceylon* (Columbo, [Sri Lanka], 1963). W. R. Livingston, *Responsible government in Nova Scotia: a study of the constitutional beginnings of the British Commonwealth* (Iowa City, 1930). W. S. MacNutt, *The Atlantic provinces: the emergence of colonial society, 1712–1857* (Toronto, 1965), 201–3, 217–18. S. W. Spavold, "Nova Scotia under the administration of Sir Colin Campbell" (MA thesis, Dalhousie Univ., Halifax, 1953). D. A. Sutherland, "J. W. Johnston and the metamorphosis of Nova Scotian conservatism" (MA thesis, Dalhousie Univ., 1967).

CAMPBELL, Sir DONALD, colonial administrator; b. 3 April 1800 in Dunstaffnage, Scotland, only son of Angus Campbell and Lillias Buchanan; m. 21 June 1825 Caroline Eliza Plomer, daughter of Sir William Plomer, and they had four sons and one daughter; d. 10 Oct. 1850 in Charlottetown.

There is no obvious reason why Sir Donald Campbell, an obscure country gentleman descended from "an ancient branch of the noble House of Campbell" in Argyll, should have been appointed lieutenant governor of Prince Edward Island on 20 Oct. 1847. Following a brief stint in the cavalry as a young man and after succeeding his uncle in 1829 as 16th captain of Dunstaffnage, Campbell appears to have dropped out of sight. On 11 March 1836 he had been created a baronet, but he had had no administrative experience and was "personally unknown" to the colonial secretary, Lord Grey. The factors most likely to have swayed Grey were Campbell's impeccable credentials as a Whig and his willingness to accept the comparatively low-paid post. Contrary to later rumours he was not the appointee of the absentee landowners, whose influence with Grey was negligible, even though, like all other lieutenant governors of the Island, he sought to protect their interests and to discourage a revival of the agitation for escheat. Nor was he chosen because of pressure from a three-man delegation of conservative politicians, including Edward Palmer* and Joseph Pope*, which travelled to London in the summer of 1847 to press for the dismissal of Campbell's predecessor, Sir Henry Vere Huntley*, already in disfavour with Grey because of his erratic and partisan behaviour. The delegation did persuade the Colonial Office to dispatch Campbell immediately, and Pope accompanied him.

The first Highlander to serve as lieutenant governor of the Island, Campbell was warmly welcomed by the Highland Society when he assumed office on 9 Dec. 1847. His appointment was also enthusiastically endorsed by the local official faction. Its members had been eager to remove Huntley and were soon assured that Campbell, although a Whig, was a Whig of a conservative bent. At the centre of this faction was the colonial secretary, Thomas Heath Haviland*, and he quickly became Campbell's chief adviser. With Haviland at his side Campbell travelled extensively across the Island in 1848, raising and distributing funds for the destitute, whose numbers had swelled after a partial failure of the potato crop, and attempting to control an outbreak of smallpox. He became a patron of local institutions, and held the largest party "ever assembled within the walls of Government House." A "practical farmer," he restored the house's garden, which Huntley had allowed to deteriorate, and established and chaired the meetings of the Royal Agricultural Society in a vain effort to promote greater interest in the development of agriculture. At least among the Island's small élite he was regarded as a "well intentioned straightforward man."

Initially even the reformers applauded the appointment of a man "with political principles closely akin to our own – as a member of the Reform Club of England." But when Campbell began to distribute patronage almost exclusively upon the advice of the old official faction his popularity was severely damaged. In his first speech to the House of Assembly, on 1 Feb. 1848, Campbell recommended a series of administrative reforms in the management of the postal service, the immigration and election laws, and local currency regulations. Virtually without exception his measures were defeated and Campbell's relations with George Coles*, the only reformer in the assembly with a seat on the Executive Council, deteriorated into nearly open hostility. In June, Campbell opposed a move to fill a vacancy on council with James Warburton, another reformer whom Huntley had nominated, and recommended Palmer instead. That

September he appointed Palmer solicitor general. Coles resigned from the council and attacked Campbell for a "want of sincerity" and for yielding his authority "to the Officials who surrounded him."

Ironically, Campbell's speech of 1 February had been so optimistic about the financial situation in the colony that Grey was moved to discontinue the British parliament's grant, and in mid January 1849 Campbell learned that thenceforth the colony would have to pay the salaries of its own officials except for that of the lieutenant governor. Even with Palmer's support Campbell could persuade the assembly to provide for the civil service only for one year and at reduced levels. A motion by the reformers for responsible government was defeated, but the conservative majority demanded that at least four members of the Executive Council should be responsible to the assembly, and they ignored Campbell's recommendations for a more highly centralized system of allocating money for roads and bridges and for the establishment of a police force in Charlottetown. Upon closing the session in May, Campbell admitted that the results of it were "not very satisfactory" and in January 1850, with little hope for a change of heart in the assembly, he dissolved the legislature in a move which caught even his supporters by surprise. When an election was called for February Campbell encouraged the rumour that the Island might be annexed to Nova Scotia if the assembly remained recalcitrant.

The reformers swept to victory in the election. When the assembly met in March it passed by 19 to 5 a vote of non-confidence in the Executive Council, which promptly resigned. Campbell met with the leaders of the reform party, Coles, Warburton, and William Swabey*, and offered them three of nine seats on the council if they would compromise over the size of the civil list, but they demanded complete control over the composition of the council and a pared-down civil list. Campbell prorogued the house until April 25 and, when the assembly then reiterated its demands and refused to vote supplies, he expressed his "disapprobation of this premeditated neglect of your legislative function." He again prorogued the house on 1 May and sought to discontinue public services, such as postal delivery, for which the assembly had not provided.

He also asked Grey for authority to dissolve the legislature in the autumn. Yet in private he admitted that responsible government was "sure to be conceded" and he appealed to Grey at least to alter the electoral system by raising the voting qualification for tenants from 40*s.* to £5 per annum to ensure that a more respectable class of men would be sent to the assembly. In fact, Grey had already prepared a dispatch instructing Campbell to grant responsible government. Whether Campbell could have come to an arrangement with the assembly is doubtful, since the reformers deeply distrusted him. But he was never forced to try because on 10 Oct. 1850, after "a very lingering and painful illness," apparently cancer of the stomach, he died. The colony was administered by Ambrose Lane* until the arrival of Campbell's successor, Sir Alexander Bannerman*.

Most Islanders probably agreed with the *Examiner*, which refused to view Campbell's death as a calamity and condemned his "love of power." That verdict may be harsh but clearly Campbell lacked the temperament to be a successful colonial governor during the transition to responsible government, and he had little understanding of how to deal with popularly elected assemblies. By the spring of 1850 he was at loggerheads even with Palmer, who later claimed to have pressed upon him "the necessity of establishing Responsible Government," and there is considerable truth in the assessment of Charles Wright Jr, a sympathetic Islander who described him as "too much of the Highland Laird."

PHILLIP BUCKNER

Court of the Lord Lyon (Edinburgh), Public reg. of all arms and bearings in Scotland, 4: f.6. GRO (Edinburgh), Kilmore and Kilbride, reg. of births and baptisms, 3, 16 April 1800. N.B. Museum, Jarvis family papers, E. J. Jarvis to William Jarvis, 14 Feb. 1848; Mrs William Jarvis to Jane Boyd, 16 Jan. 1849. PAC, MG 24, B133: 176–84, 190–218, 221–24, 228–29, 231–37, 250–56 (photocopies; copies at PAPEI). PAPEI, Acc. 2918/3. PRO, CO 226/71–79; CO 227/9–10. [H. G. Grey, 3rd] Earl Grey, *The colonial policy of Lord John Russell's administration* (2nd ed., 2v., London, 1853), 1: 349. P.E.I., House of Assembly, *Journal*, 1848–50. *Examiner* (Charlottetown), 1847–50. *Islander* , 1847–50. *Royal Gazette* (Charlottetown), 1847–50. *Burke's landed gentry* (1965–72). G.B., WO, *Army list*, 1819, 1824. *A memorial history of the Campbells of Melfort, Argyllshire . . .* , comp. M. O. Campbell (London, 1882), 81. Buckner, *Transition to responsible government*, 319–20. Duncan Campbell, *History of Prince Edward Island* (Charlottetown, 1875; repr. Belleville, Ont., 1972), 107–8. W. R. Livingston, *Responsible government in Prince Edward Island: a triumph of self-government under the crown* (Iowa City, 1931), 24, 31 *et seq.* F. MacKinnon, *Government of P.E.I.*, 66–67, 83–84. W. E. MacKinnon, *The life of the party: a history of the Liberal party in Prince Edward Island* (Summerside, P.E.I., 1973), 19–21.

CANAC, *dit* **Marquis, PIERRE** (baptized Pierre Canac, at his marriage he signed Pierre Canac *dit* Marquis and in the 1810s P. C. Marquis, but towards the end of his life he was referred to as Canac Marquis), merchant, landowner, JP, office holder, militia officer, and politician; b. 8 Oct. 1780 in Sainte-Famille, Île d'Orléans, Que., son of Jean Canac (Canac, *dit* Marquis) and Angélique (Judith) Pepin (Pepin, *dit* Lachance); d. 25 Nov. 1850 in Saint-André, near Kamouraska, Lower Canada.

Pierre Canac, *dit* Marquis, started his business career at Quebec, remaining there until he became acquainted with Marie-Salomé Michaud; still a minor, she was a daughter of Saint-André farmer Alexandre Michaud and Élisabeth Ouellet. Their meeting would make a major difference in his life. They were married in Saint-André on 15 Jan. 1810, and Canac, *dit* Marquis, then chose to live in that parish. The inhabitants of the area came to him as the leading local merchant to get supplies or sometimes to borrow money. He became the owner of a great deal of land, which he leased or sold for a good price to people eager to settle in Saint-André. In 1824 he also bought a house in the *faubourg* Saint-Roch at Quebec, which he subsequently rented to various persons.

In November 1821 Canac, *dit* Marquis, was commissioned to try minor cases in the rural parishes. He was a justice of the peace for the district of Quebec from 1821 to 1828 and thereafter for Saint-André, holding the office until it was abolished in the mid 1840s. At the time of the 1831 census Canac, *dit* Marquis, headed a family of 19, including his children and grandchildren, all Catholic, living on 785 *arpents* of land, a third of which was used to grow cereals and raise livestock. Some of the family probably attended the small private school he had established on his property. His store served as a public house. In 1831 he was appointed commissioner to receive affidavits in the seigneury of L'Islet-du-Portage, along with his friend Hypolite Sirois, *dit* Duplessis. By then he was clearly establishing himself as one of the most eminent figures in Saint-André. In 1833 he was a captain in the 1st battalion of Kamouraska militia. Promotions followed, and he rose to the rank of colonel according to his burial certificate.

He also took an interest in politics. In 1830 he was defeated in the elections for the House of Assembly, but in 1834 he was elected along with Amable Dionne* for Kamouraska. At first he played an unobtrusive part in the house, joining the Patriote majority led by Louis-Joseph Papineau*. Despite his desire to see the assembly in control of supplies, he was opposed to constitutional change, and particularly to reform of the Legislative Council. In 1836 he began to distance himself from the radicals, and the following year he voted against sending an address to the governor, Lord Gosford [Acheson], in response to the Russell Resolutions. His loyalty to colonial institutions led to his appointment as commissioner to administer oaths after the constitution was suspended on 10 Feb. 1838. During the rebellions of 1837–38 and in the early days of the United Province of Canada Marquis retained the esteem of his fellow citizens and he became mayor of Saint-André when it was incorporated in 1845. He was still active in business and remained one of the most influential figures in his region. In 1848 he was elected to the Legislative Assembly for Kamouraska. During this second term he played a bigger part in the assembly's work, in particular chairing some committees of the whole. In 1849 he voted for the controversial Rebellion Losses Bill to compensate Lower Canadians for damages suffered in 1837–38 [*see* James Bruce*]. He went to Toronto for the 1850 session and died in November of that year at Saint-André.

François Drouin

ANQ-Q, CE1-11, 9 oct. 1780; CE3-11, 15 janv. 1810, 26 nov. 1850; CN1-104, 1832–49; CN1-178, 6 oct. 1827; CN1-262, 4 juin 1805; CN3-8, 1819–29. PAC, RG 31, C1, 1831, Saint-André, Que. (mfm. at ANQ-Q); RG 68, General index, 1651–1841. Can., Prov. of, Legislative Assembly, *Journals*, 1848–50. *Debates of the Legislative Assembly of United Canada* (Abbott Gibbs *et al.*), vols.7–9. L.C., House of Assembly, *Journals*, 1835–37. F.-J. Audet, "Les législateurs du Bas-Canada." Desjardins, *Guide parl. Quebec almanac*, 1821–41. *Répertoire des mariages de Saint-André de Kamouraska, 1791–1968*, Armand Proulx, compil. (La Pocatière, Qué., [1970]). P.-H. Hudon, *Rivière-Ouelle de la Bouteillerie; 3 siècles de vie* (Ottawa, 1972), 338–40. Labarrère-Paulé, *Les instituteurs laïques*, 18, 21, 96.

CAPTAIN DICK, RICHARD PIERPOINT, known as. *See* Pierpoint

CARDINAL, JOSEPH-NARCISSE, notary, school trustee, militia officer, politician, and Patriote; b. 8 Feb. 1808 in Saint-Constant, Lower Canada, second of the eight children of Joseph Cardinal and Marguerite Cardinal; d. 21 Dec. 1838 in Montreal.

Joseph-Narcisse Cardinal came from a farm family living in comfortable circumstances in Saint-Constant, near La Prairie, at the outset of the 19th century. It seems that by 1817 his father was engaged in commerce in Montreal. Eager to have his son receive an education, he enrolled him that year in the Petit Séminaire de Montréal. Joseph-Narcisse left the seminary in 1822, and, it is thought, returned to live at home with his father, who apparently had moved to Châteauguay three years earlier, establishing himself as a farmer. In 1823 Joseph-Narcisse began articling with notary François-Georges Lepailleur in this village.

Having been licensed as a notary on 19 June 1829, Cardinal joined Lepailleur's firm as a partner. Thus, at the age of 21, he settled in Châteauguay and began practising. Through talent and honesty he acquired a great many clients. As a prominent figure in the Saint-Joachim parish Cardinal was soon called upon to deal with its affairs. In March 1829 the House of Assembly had passed a law to create schools run by trustees, a measure which intensified the struggle between the clergy and the Canadian petite bourgeoisie for control of education in several of the province's parishes. Trustees were chosen for the school in Saint-Joachim, and in the period 1829–32 they included parish priest Pierre Grenier, Lepailleur, and Cardinal. The lay trustees prepared reports for the assembly on the administration and organization of the school, in the process keeping a close watch on the teaching provided for the children. It would seem, then, that these leading citizens must have vied in influence with their priest.

There was also conflict in Saint-Joachim over where the church should be located. People in the lower end of the parish wanted simply to repair the existing church but those in the upper end urged that a new one be built in a central place. In November 1831 Cardinal acted as secretary at a meeting of community leaders which drew up a petition to the archbishop of Quebec, Bernard-Claude Panet*, asking for permission to make repairs. The petition was followed by a counter-petition in February 1834. During the discussions Cardinal tangled with Father Grenier and subsequently he came into conflict with the priest's successor, Jean-Baptiste Labelle. In a letter sent in June 1834 to the curé of Saint-François-Xavier mission at Caughnawaga (Kahnawake), Joseph Marcoux*, who had been asked by the new archbishop, Joseph SIGNAY, to investigate the matter, Cardinal criticized Labelle sharply for being biased in favour of the people living in the upper end of the parish. This petty local quarrel dragged on until the rebellions of 1837 and 1838.

According to the biography printed on 10 April 1839 in the *North American* (Swanton, Vt), Cardinal had been active in politics from the time he reached the age of majority. It is quite likely, then, that in 1830 he was involved in Jean-Moïse RAYMOND's election campaign for a seat in the assembly. Raymond, a supporter of Louis-Joseph Papineau*, was elected for the Patriote party, along with fellow candidate Austin CUVILLIER, in the new riding of Laprairie. On 31 May 1831, in Montreal, Cardinal married Eugénie Saint-Germain, a daughter of Bernard Saint-Germain, who was an interpreter with the Indian Department. They were to have four daughters and a son. Through his marriage he strengthened his position within the Canadian petite bourgeoisie in the Laprairie region. A year later he lost his father, mother, and one of his young brothers to the cholera epidemic. In 1833 he was appointed lieutenant and adjutant of the 2nd Battalion of Laprairie militia, and he was promoted captain in 1834. That year he also held the post of secretary of the county agricultural society.

At the Laprairie County meeting held at Saint-Constant in April 1834, Cardinal joined in approving the 92 Resolutions passed by the House of Assembly [*see* Elzéar BÉDARD]. He was approached then about standing in the elections the following autumn against Cuvillier, who had been attracting criticism for his moderation, and after some consideration he agreed to run for the Patriote party. Cuvillier decided not to seek re-election, supposedly out of fear that Cardinal's enormous popularity would ensure his own defeat. Early in November, during another outbreak of cholera and just a few days after the polls opened, Papineau, Denis-Benjamin Viger*, Louis-Hippolyte La Fontaine*, Augustin-Norbert Morin*, Cardinal, and several other Patriotes met in Édouard-Raymond Fabre*'s bookshop in Montreal. Probably motivated in large part by his resentment against the authorities for the death of his parents, Cardinal supported the creation of a constitutional committee "to enquire into the ravages caused last summer by that cruel disease the Asiatic cholera; into the causes of its introduction, and the participation therein, whether by act or omission, culpable and voluntary, of the present Governor-General [WHITWORTH-AYLMER] and the Provincial Executive."

In the event, in 1834 Cardinal was elected by acclamation for Laprairie, along with Raymond. According to his biographer Joseph-Alfred Mousseau*, it was a sacrifice for him to agree to serve at Quebec. A man respected by his fellow citizens and attached to his wife and children, he was not rich, and because of his stays in the capital he had to abandon his law office for several months a year and to neglect his clients and family. He none the less consented, believing he had a duty to represent his compatriots and to defend in the assembly his party's program, which included long-standing demands for reforms to improve the lot of the Canadians. In the assembly Cardinal did not stand out, but he was consistently a supporter of Papineau. He was still interested in problems related to schools and, as a member of the standing committee on education and schools in 1835, he helped prepare reports that led to the development of a bill on normal schools the following year. The national aspirations of Canadians, however, held his attention even more, and during the final sessions in the autumn of 1836 and the summer of 1837 he joined other members in refusing to vote the supplies requested by Governor Lord Gosford [ACHESON].

The adoption of Lord John Russell's resolutions by the British parliament in March 1837 made Cardinal indignant. Lord Gosford's proclamation in June prohibiting certain "seditious" public meetings further exasperated him. These measures finally convinced him that the salvation of the Canadian people as a nation would lie only in independence. Disregarding Gosford's ban, on 6 August Cardinal attended the big Laprairie County meeting held at Saint-Constant to protest against the coercive measures, and he even made a speech. Returning to Châteauguay after the assembly was dissolved on 26 August, he resumed his notarial practice. He is believed to have turned in his commission as a militia captain before summer was out to protest the dismissal of numerous Patriotes from their posts as magistrates or militia officers. By heading its delegation at the Assemblée des Six Comtés in Saint-Charles-sur-Richelieu on 23 October, Cardinal established himself as one of the Patriote leaders in Laprairie County.

According to Laurent-Olivier David*, Cardinal was "calm, thoughtful, prudent, but determined, even stubborn, once his mind was made up." He refrained from taking part in the 1837 rebellion, which he saw as a skirmish doomed to failure because it was an isolated venture unsupported by outside help. But since Cardinal did not hide his sympathies, the English party in the county threatened to denounce him to the authorities. At the urging of his wife and friends he went to the United States around mid December and stayed for a time at Fort Covington, N.Y. During his exile he travelled to Plattsburgh, where he met with Robert Nelson*. He explained to him that he wanted a real rebellion, carried out with money, muskets, and cannon, and with American assistance. Nelson convinced him that there would be substantial aid from the Americans which would ensure the success of the next uprising. On the strength of the information and the "serious" guarantees that Nelson provided, Cardinal plunged wholeheartedly into organizing a new insurrection.

Cardinal returned to Lower Canada in February or March 1838 and resumed practising clandestinely at Châteauguay in partnership with Abraham Desmarais in the house of Élisabeth Saint-Denis, the widow of J.-B. Boudria. By springtime he had joined the Association des Frères-Chasseurs, a secret society formed to foment an internal uprising that would be backed by Patriote forces invading from the United States with the support of the Americans, the goal being the establishment of an independent Lower Canada. He converted the house in which his office was located into a lodge of Frères-Chasseurs and many of his compatriots came to be sworn in. The amnesty proclaimed by Lord Durham [LAMBTON] in June enabled Cardinal to practise openly again, but did not dissuade him from his revolutionary activities. His ardour and determination led Nelson to make him one of his principal deputies around mid July and to put him in charge of organizing the uprising in Laprairie County.

When the second rebellion broke out on the night of 3 Nov. 1838, Cardinal, as brigadier-general of the Patriote army at Châteauguay, was in command of a force that disarmed and arrested the leading members of the English party in the parish. Once this part of the plans had been carried out, Cardinal, his former clerk and friend Joseph DUQUET, and his brother-in-law François-Maurice Lepailleur proceeded to Caughnawaga that night with a detachment of Patriotes to try to take badly needed weapons and ammunition from the Indians. Upon reaching the outskirts of the reserve on the morning of 4 November, the group hid in a wood, and Cardinal, Duquet, and Lepailleur went into the village, where they began discussions with the chiefs. When in the course of conversation the Indians learned of the detachment's presence, they invited the entire body of Patriotes to participate in the negotiations. The Patriotes accepted the offer but had cause to regret it, for no sooner had they entered the village than they were surrounded by the warriors from the reserve. The Patriote expedition failed because it had been ill organized, and with no means of escape Cardinal, Duquet, Lepailleur, and most of their supporters were taken captive by the Indians, who immediately escorted them to jail in Montreal. Shortly after, Cardinal's house was set on fire by supporters of the government.

On 28 Nov. 1838 Cardinal, with 11 companions, was brought before a court martial set up by Sir John Colborne*. A number of Canadian lawyers wanted to defend the accused, but some members of the court martial objected, exclaiming "Rebels cannot defend rebels!" The accused were finally able to retain Pierre Moreau and Lewis Thomas Drummond* as legal counsel. The lawyers were not allowed to argue but only to submit statements of the case. After being thoroughly advised by his attorneys, Cardinal lodged a protest challenging the competence of the court martial and asked for a jury trial. He claimed that the offence of which he was accused had been committed before the proclamation on 8 November of emergency regulations suspending habeas corpus, and that his case had to be brought before a civil court. This objection was overruled.

The trial began without further delay. Nine witnesses for the prosecution were heard, three of them Indians from Caughnawaga. Cardinal cross-examined some of them himself. By 1 December the prosecutors wound up their case. Cardinal then asked for a 72-hour delay to enable the accused to prepare their defence with their attorneys. The court complied, adjourning until 4 December. When the trial resumed, lawyer Aaron Philip Hart was admitted as a third attorney for the accused. The defendants questioned some ten witnesses, who testified in their favour. At the end of the hearings on 6 December, Drummond and Hart obtained permission to make comments on the trial as the whole. For the defence, Drummond, with Hart's help, delivered a ringing "plea" that made a strong impression on the court. Deputy judge-advocate Charles Dewey Day* replied with a long and violent summation for the prosecution, demanding that the accused be sentenced to death.

In the course of the ensuing deliberations, Major-General John Clitherow*, who was presiding at the court martial, asked the crown's legal advisers if a sentence other than the death penalty could be pronounced for the crime of high treason. Attorney General Charles Richard Ogden* was of the opinion that high treason had to be punished with death, as was Solicitor General Andrew STUART. On 8 December the court martial found all the accused guilty of high treason, except for two who were acquitted. However, the court admitted in its judgement that the sentence attached to high treason was out of all proportion to the offence. For this reason it pronounced the death sentence on only four of the accused, including Cardinal, Duquet, and Lepailleur, who were considered the leaders of the Châteauguay rebels, and it added a recommendation for executive clemency; the remaining six were sentenced to transportation. This sentence did not conform to martial law. When Colborne asked Ogden and Stuart for their opinion they of course rejected it. On 14 December Colborne therefore asked the court martial to reconsider. That very day the court sentenced all the accused to death, but again recommended executive clemency.

From then on the fate of the accused was in the hands of the authorities. On 15 December Colborne called a meeting of the Executive Council, which examined the case of Cardinal and his companions. The council reached the conclusion on 18 December that an example had to be made of the accused. It therefore decided that all of them would be executed on 21 December. But for eight of them the death sentence was at the last minute commuted to transportation.

As soon as the decision was known, Drummond and Hart stepped up their efforts with Colborne and the members of the Special Council to obtain a reprieve for Cardinal, but in vain. On 20 December, on the eve of the execution of Cardinal and Duquet, Drummond made one last attempt. In a petition sent to Colborne he voiced his doubts about the legality of the court martial and recommended that the executions be suspended until the courts had ruled on the question. He further appealed to the code of ethics adhered to by civilized nations, which prohibits judging a man under a law promulgated after the commission of the offence of which he is accused. In conclusion he maintained that if the sentence were carried out, Cardinal and Duquet would be "raised from the status of persons presumed guilty to that of martyrs to an odious persecution." On the same day the Caughnawaga Indians, who had captured Cardinal and his companions, also sent a petition to Colborne begging for mercy. Mme Cardinal herself wrote a letter that day begging Lady Colborne to intercede for her on behalf of her husband. Colborne could not be moved.

Thus, on the morning of 21 Dec. 1838 Joseph-Narcisse Cardinal walked to the scaffold with Duquet. The first to mount it, he said not a word and died bravely. To respect the wish he had apparently expressed before his execution, his body, it is said, was put in a coffin draped with a pall used for the victims of a riot on 21 May 1832 [*see* Daniel Tracey*]. He was buried in the old Catholic cemetery of Montreal, now the site of Dominion Square. In 1858 François-Maurice Lepailleur arranged for his remains to be transferred to Notre-Dame-des-Neiges cemetery, where they rest under the monument raised to the Patriotes of 1837–38. According to Ægidius Fauteux*, quoting from the *North American*, Cardinal was a man of medium height, rather slender, with black eyes and a dark complexion. History remembers him as the first martyr to the cause of independence for Lower Canada.

MICHEL DE LORIMIER

Joseph-Narcisse Cardinal's minute-book, containing notarized instruments from the years 1829–38, is at AC, Beauharnois (Valleyfield). Interesting correspondence, including letters to his wife and acquaintances written mainly during the time he spent in the Montreal jail and just before his execution, has survived. Originals and copies are held in the following collections: ANQ-M, P1000-61-1240; ANQ-Q, P-239; Arch. de la chancellerie de l'évêché de Valleyfield (Valleyfield), Saint-Joachim (Châteauguay), corr., Cardinal à Ignace Bourget, 26 nov. 1838; AUM, P 58, U, Cardinal et autres à L. T. Drummond, 24 nov. 1838. During his exile in the United States Cardinal expressed his opinions on the rebellion of 1837 to his father-in-law in a letter which is now at PAC, MG 24, B2: 2550–52.

Some of this correspondence has appeared in print. Joseph-Alfred Mousseau published extracts of letters by Cardinal in his biographical sketch, *Lecture publique sur Cardinal et Duquet, victimes de 1837–38* ... (Montréal, 1860). Laurent-Olivier David printed part of a letter in "Les hommes de 37–38: Cardinal," *La Tribune* (Montréal), 23 oct. 1880: 1–2; 27 nov. 1880: 1; this article was also published in *L'Opinion publique*, 24 févr. 1881: 85, and reproduced in *Patriotes*, 199–206. Lastly, two of Cardinal's letters were printed by Élie-Joseph-Arthur Auclair in "Un souvenir de 1838," *Rev. canadienne*, 54 (1910): 97–105, and another appears in Francis-Joseph Audet*'s "Pierre-Édouard Leclère (1798–1866)," *Cahiers des Dix*, 8 (1943): 109–40.

AAQ, 211 A, G: ff.180r–89r. AC, Beauharnois, Minutiers, Louis Demers, 15 mars 1823; F.-G. Le Pallieur, 30 mai 1831. ACAM, RLB, I: 244–45, 253. ANQ-M, CC1, 9 juill. 1839, 13 mars 1840; CE1-18, 9 févr. 1808; CE1-51, 31 mai 1831. ANQ-Q, E17/6, no.32; E17/30, nos.2231, 2239–49, 2251–52, 2254, 2257–58, 2264, 2266, 2268–70, 2274; E17/35, nos.2791–92, 2795–99; E17/39, no.3112; E17/40, nos.3176–79, 3183–87; E17/51, no.4105. Arch. de la chancellerie de l'évêché de Valleyfield, Saint-Joachim, corr., Cardinal à Joseph Marcoux, 11 juin 1834. BVM-G, Fonds Ægidius Fauteux, notes compilées par Ægidius Fauteux sur les patriotes de 1837–38 dont les noms commencent par la lettre C, carton 3. PAC, MG 24, B2, 17–21; RG 4, B8: 2884–93. *Le Boréal express, journal d'histoire du Canada* (Montréal, 1962), 529, 542–43. [A.-R. Cherrier], *Procès de Joseph N. Cardinal, et autres, auquel on a joint la requête argumentative en faveur des prisonniers, et plusieurs autres documents précieux* ... (Montréal, 1839; réimpr. 1974). [L.-]L. Ducharme, *Journal d'un exilé politique aux terres australes* (Montréal, 1845; réimpr. 1974). L.C., House of Assembly, *Journals*, 1834–37. F.-M. Lepailleur, *Journal d'exil: la vie d'un patriote de 1838 déporté en Australie* (Montréal, 1972), 191–94. L.-J.-A. Papineau, *Journal d'un Fils de la liberté*. *Report of state trials*, 1: 17–111. *La Minerve*, 31 mars, 7 avril 1834; 3, 14 août 1837. *Montreal Gazette*, 18 Dec. 1838. *North American*, 10 April, 6, 13, 20, 27 Nov. 1839.

Appletons' cyclopædia of American biography, ed. J. G. Wilson and John Fiske (7v., New York, 1888–1901), 1: 523. F.-J. Audet, "Les législateurs du Bas-Canada." Borthwick, *Hist. and biog. gazetteer*, 286–87. Desjardins, *Guide parl.* Fauteux, *Patriotes*, 65–67, 153–55. J.-J. Lefebvre, *Le Canada, l'Amérique: géographie, histoire* (éd. rév., Montréal, 1968). Le Jeune, *Dictionnaire*, 1: 303. *Quebec almanac*, 1830–38. Wallace, *Macmillan dict.* E.-J.[-A.] Auclair, *Histoire de Châteauguay, 1735–1935* (Montréal, 1935), 81–99. L.-P. Audet, *Le système scolaire*, 5: 258–87; 6: 136–37. J. D. Borthwick, *History of the Montreal prison from A.D. 1784 to A.D. 1886* ... (Montreal, 1886), 43–45, 48–49, 86–88. Chabot, *Le curé de campagne*. Christie, *Hist. of L.C.* (1866). David, *Patriotes*, 171–88, 193–97, 199–206, 216–18, 277–79. E. J. Devine, *Historic Caughnawaga* (Montreal, 1922), 358–62. Filteau, *Hist. des patriotes* (1975), 117, 207–8, 274–76, 401–9, 428–32. Labarrère-Paulé, *Les instituteurs laïques*, 17, 23, 63. Maurault, *Le collège de Montréal* (Dansereau; 1967). Ouellet, *Bas-Canada*. Francine Parent, "Les patriotes de Châteauguay (1838)" (thèse de MA, univ. de Montréal, 1984). J.-E. Roy, *Hist. du notariat*, 2: 453; 3: 7–8. Rumilly, *Papineau et son temps*. Robert Sellar, *The history of the county of Huntingdon and of the seigniories of Chateauguay and Beauharnois from their first settlement to the year 1838* (Huntingdon, Que., 1888), 505–16. André Vachon, *Histoire du notariat canadien, 1621–1960* (2e éd., Québec, 1962).

E.-J.[-A.] Auclair, "Le notaire Joseph-N. Cardinal – 1808–1838," *L'Avenir du Nord* (Saint-Jérôme, Qué.), 21 déc. 1934: 1. Ivanhoë Caron, "Une société secrète dans le Bas-Canada en 1838: l'Association des Frères Chasseurs," RSC *Trans.*, 3rd ser., 20 (1926), sect.I: 17–34. J.-J. Lefebvre, "Le notaire Joseph-Narcisse Cardinal (1808–1838), député de Laprairie en 1834; victime de l'échafaud en 1838," *BRH*, 62 (1956): 195–207. Victor Morin, "Clubs et sociétés notoires d'autrefois," *Cahiers des Dix*, 15 (1950): 185–218; "La 'République canadienne' de 1838," *RHAF*, 2 (1948–49): 483–512. Marcelle Reeves-Morache, "La canadienne pendant les troubles de 1837–1838," *RHAF*, 5 (1951–52): 99–117.

CARSON, WILLIAM, physician, author, farmer, political agitator, newspaperman, politician, and office holder; baptized 4 June 1770 in the parish of Kelton, Scotland, son of Samuel Carson and Margaret Clachertie; m. Esther (Giles?) (d. 1827), and they had five daughters and three sons; d. 26 Feb. 1843 in St John's.

William Carson attended the University of Edinburgh's Faculty of Medicine from 1787 to 1790 but, despite his later claims, it appears that he did not graduate. According to his own accounts, he practised medicine in Birmingham, England, for 13 or 14 years prior to 1808, and he is listed as a surgeon in that city's directories for the period 1800–3. While in England, Carson was not politically active; he was, however, a student of politics, choosing as his mentors Charles James Fox and Charles Grey (later Earl Grey). It was presumably from these two men that he imbibed the Whig zeal for reform and constitutional rights that he brought to bear upon the fledgling institutions of Newfoundland. Carson married while in Birmingham, and he later stated that "domestic circumstances" connected with his wife's family induced him to leave the city. After receiving the advice of "a number of influential Merchants" trading in Newfoundland, he decided to emigrate, arriving in St John's on 23 April 1808.

Carson's first appearance in public records relating to Newfoundland occurred in 1810, when he applied for letters patent entitling him to "the exclusive privilege of taking whales" in the island's coastal waters, by an elaborate, if somewhat fanciful, new method of whaling. The request, which was denied, provides an early illustration of Carson's impractical but earnest application of mind to the development of the island's resources. It was in collaboration with the merchants of St John's, who dominated the loosely regulated and mildly governed community, that Carson began his long career of agitation. In 1811 the British parliament passed an act which in effect took away the public's right to use certain ancient fishing rooms in the harbour. With the decline of the English migratory fishery, they had become commons, and local merchants and fishermen used them without fee for such purposes as building boats and storing lumber. In November 1811 a meeting of St John's merchants and other "principal inhabitants" discussed the act, and an address was sent to the Prince Regent requesting that income derived from renting the rooms be used to improve the town and that new legislation be introduced to create a "Board of Police" with the power to receive the rent and spend it for that purpose. The minutes show that those attending understood their actions did not imply "censure upon the Government" though members of the board of police were chosen by ballot. Carson was prominent in these mild transactions, which provoked a controversy in the *Royal Gazette and Newfoundland Advertiser* – the first sign of something resembling open partisan conflict in Newfoundland – but brought about no change in government policy. In 1812, before an official response to the address was received, Carson published a tract asserting that the act of 1811 had "surprised and alarmed" the inhabitants not only of St John's, but of the whole island, who held the lack of a legislature among the "misfortunes they felt severely." Drawing upon John Reeves*'s 1793 work, he described the history of the colony as one of misrepresentation and oppression of the residents by West Country merchants, charged the governors with "ignorance" and illegal, arbitrary behaviour, denounced the naval surrogates (who presided over surrogate courts around the island) as ignorant "of the most common principles of law and justice," and declaimed against the apparent policy of discouraging agriculture. In a second pamphlet (1813) he declared himself convinced of "the capability of Newfoundland to become a pastoral and agricultural country," and called for "a civil resident Governor, and a Legislative Assembly."

The pamphlets were the first literature of political protest in Newfoundland. However much they (no doubt unwittingly) distorted the colony's history and geography, they showed Carson's literary skill, his courage, and his complete possession of high-minded Whig rhetoric. It is probable, nevertheless, that Carson mistook the merchants' desire for increased influence in St John's to be evidence of a more general desire for change. The tracts infuriated local authorities, and a recommendation was made to Governor John Thomas Duckworth* that libel proceedings be initiated. This recommendation was rejected by the Colonial Office. However, Carson was immediately removed by Duckworth from his only official position, surgeon to the Loyal Volunteers of St John's. Despite angry protests to both Duckworth and the colonial secretary in London, he was not reinstated. Somewhat inexplicably, Carson always deeply resented the displeasure his behaviour inevitably provoked with a succession of governors, who identified him, not without reason, as the "root and origin" of their difficulties in regulating the colony's affairs.

Carson's activities during his early years in Newfoundland were by no means confined to politics. His medical practice in St John's was successful, and in 1810 he suggested the building of a public hospital, becoming, soon after its completion in 1814, the principal medical attendant. He was actively accumulating land for farming. In June 1812 he requested subscriptions for 20 lectures on scientific subjects, to be given the following winter. Carson's literary interests manifested themselves in a plan, outlined in 1815, to write a book on the resources and people of Newfoundland, a project he abandoned when he was denied access to government records. Court records show that he was an active litigant and an occasional advocate in popular causes. In 1814, for example, he successfully represented one John Ryan, who was charged with libelling Chief Justice Thomas Tremlett*. Journalism was yet another avocation. On the establishment of the *Newfoundland Mercantile Journal* in 1815, he contributed a series of articles under the signature Man, in one of which he stated that half of the Bible was "hurtful and useless." This view triggered a controversy culminating in a sensational libel case in 1817, with Carson as plaintiff. He lost the case, possibly because a servant testified she had heard him "ridicule the Holy Scriptures" and "deny the Divinity of our Saviour" (credible testimony since Carson, though of a Presbyterian family, admitted later to Socinian views). Carson also sounded "peals of constitutional thunder" in the *Newfoundland Sentinel, and General Commercial Register*, founded in 1818, the earliest reform journal in the colony.

The collapse of Newfoundland's economy after the Napoleonic Wars touched off debate on its future prospects and created an atmosphere in which the reform movement could grow. By 1815 it was apparent to Governor Sir Richard Goodwin Keats* that the influence of "a Party which affects a popular character" was on the increase in a "too easily agitated" St John's. Carson's solution to the growing economic difficulties was simple: an extension of the British constitution to the island and the creation of colonial equivalents to king, lords, and commons. With "a resident government and legislature," he wrote in 1817, Newfoundland could look forward to "prosperous and happy times." Exactly how a "Newfoundland Parliament" could "influence the price of fish in a foreign market" was not apparent to one sceptical observer, but by 1817 even the merchants of St John's were convinced that fundamental changes in the system of government were needed. The British government's response was to make mild concessions. In 1817 the colony was granted a year-round governor, an improvement for which Carson immediately took credit. In a letter to Colonial Secretary Lord Bathurst, furiously assaulting Governor Francis Pickmore* and giving a catalogue of grievances, he indicated more demands would follow. Yet until 1820 he could find no outrageous abuse with which to attract public attention to the need for reform.

The surrogate courts were an early and favourite object of attack by Carson, for reasons which are by no means obvious. On the whole these courts dispensed justice in a lenient and efficient fashion, calling a jury when the offender demanded one in cases involving amounts greater than 40 shillings. In July 1820, however, two Conception Bay fishermen, Philip Butler and James Lundrigan*, were called before surrogates David BUCHAN and the Reverend John Leigh*, charged with contempt of court, found guilty, and whipped. In St John's, Carson and Patrick MORRIS, an Irish merchant drawn into political agitation for the first time, turned the event into a public sensation. An action in the Supreme Court acquitted the surrogates but the judge, Francis FORBES, rebuked Buchan and Leigh for inflicting the "harsh" punishment. At a public meeting on 14 November where Morris and Carson were prominent, it was resolved to take constitutional means "to have *the law repealed*" which sanctioned "such arbitrary proceedings." A petition to the king followed, calling for reform of the system of justice and linking the Butler–Lundrigan case with other grievances, including the need for a "superintending legislature." Bathurst rejected outright the idea of a legislature, but indicated that Britain had "under consideration" altering the laws pertaining to Newfoundland.

The cause of reform now gained momentum in a city where increasing poverty seemed to underline the need for change. Some "local authority" should be granted, Governor Sir Charles HAMILTON conceded, which would "answer every good purpose of a legislature, without its evils." Throughout 1823 and 1824 Carson chaired a committee of residents pressing for changes in the new Newfoundland bill to come before parliament. When news of its contents reached St John's, the reformers learned they would have to be content with municipal institutions. Although it was not what Carson had hoped for, he accepted the idea of a corporation for the city, probably anticipating that this change would lead to the larger reform. In June 1824 new laws replaced the surrogate system by circuit courts, enlarged the Supreme Court, made provision for municipal government in the colony, and gave the governor the statutory right to dispose of unoccupied lands. The reformers had had a demonstrable influence in shaping this new constitution.

In January 1825 Carson announced he was withdrawing from politics, giving as reasons "increasing years," professional duties, and domestic responsibilities. It appears that family illness may have been a factor in his decision. In 1826, however, he was back in the political arena, this time in the bitter dispute over the form of municipal government for St John's. Carson and Morris now wished to amend the clauses in the 1824 act which authorized an appointed corporation, urging that it be replaced by an elected town council. They also urged that taxes be imposed on the rental value of property, the act having granted the corporation the right to levy "Rates and Assessments" on inhabitants and householders. This proposal angered landlords, and after a turbulent public meeting in May a petition was sent to Governor Thomas John Cochrane* by merchants, opposing incorporation. The dispute appears to have polarized opinion in the city as no other issue had done, and it is possible to see in it intimations of the cleavage between popular and mercantile interests that characterized politics in the colony after 1833. Cochrane reported that people would prefer to have regulations imposed on them by his government rather than see that "either party triumphed over the other." In effect, the corporation was scrapped. The failure to agree on some kind of municipal authority had an unexpected effect in the Colonial Office, where James Stephen used it to illustrate the need for a legislative council, with some elected members. Clearly it was but a matter of time before a legislature would be granted.

In November 1827 Carson was appointed district surgeon by his friend Chief Justice Richard Alexander Tucker*, administrator in Cochrane's absence. Out of a "desire to keep the Doctor quiet," Cochrane on his return confirmed the appointment, which brought an annual salary of £200. The duties consisted of providing medical attention to the poor. Far from keeping Carson quiet, his office seems to have given him more time for politics. In 1828 he was again in the forefront of agitation for representative institutions. Public sentiment in favour of a legislature was rapidly gaining ground in 1830 and 1831, and as it grew so did Carson's reputation as an avuncular patriot. Once again, worsening economic conditions accented the need for change. In March 1832 news reached St John's that representative government had been granted. Carson at once offered himself as a candidate in the district of St John's.

As the election of 1832 approached, the united front the colony had presented to Britain in petitioning for a legislature gave way to the sectarian rivalry which was to dominate politics for the next 50 years. In St John's the Catholic bishop, Michael Anthony FLEMING, endorsed three candidates, including John Kent*, an Irish merchant whose flamboyant electioneering among the Catholics quickly drew him into controversy, and Carson, who had been carefully cultivating Irish support since 1817. As if the endorsement of Fleming were not enough to turn Protestants against him, Carson in August and September made two public attacks upon the Anglican archdeacon, Edward Wix*, who had found heretical notions in a pamphlet by Carson on cholera. Carson replied in the *Public Ledger* that Wix was "a scourge more terrible than the Cholera itself." Thus fears of Catholic hegemony in St John's were stirred by Carson as well as Kent, and whether for this reason or because, as he later maintained in a formal protest to the house, he had been unfairly outmanœuvred at the polls, Carson was defeated in November. He responded in typical fashion. "Submission," he later wrote, "never gained a point in politics." In January 1833 the prospectus for a new weekly newspaper, the *Newfoundland Patriot*, was published. According to Robert John Parsons*, sole owner of the *Patriot* by 1840, Carson edited the paper from its inception in July 1833 until December. As late as 1835 he was still contributing occasional editorials.

The numbers of the *Patriot* issued under Carson's editorship do not survive, but from the responses of other journals and official reaction, it appears the promise made in the prospectus, that the paper would uphold "liberal and constitutional principles" in opposition to the "constituted authorities" in the colony, was fulfilled. Carson's aggressiveness succeeded in further antagonizing Cochrane and also Henry David Winton* of the *Public Ledger*; it even angered John Shea, the normally sedate editor of the *Newfoundlander*, who was advised to "think more of John Kent and Newfoundland, and less of Daniel O'Connell and the Emerald Isle." The remark reveals Carson's slight interest in Ireland, now attracting great attention among local Catholics. Nevertheless, it was to the Irish that he had to turn once again for support in a St John's by-election in December 1833. An even more bitter contest than that of 1832 ensued, with Fleming throwing his support to Carson and effectively forcing his opponent to withdraw. In a savage editorial Winton wrote that Carson's election had been brought about by the Catholic clergy's "domination" over their mentally enslaved parishioners. Hereafter, Carson would be an object of persistent attack in the *Public Ledger* and in another new paper, the *Times and General Commercial Gazette*, edited by John Williams McCoubrey*. His career as an MHA thus began inauspiciously amid much sectarian feeling.

When the house reopened in January 1834, Carson aligned himself with a minority group of "popular" members and allowed himself to be nominated for speaker, in opposition to Thomas Bennett*. Even before the vote, Carson, addressing the clerk, indicated that three members were ineligible to sit, and ought not to take part in the choice of speaker. The vote proceeded, Bennett was elected, and Carson and his friends organized a petition calling for the dissolution of the house and a new election. This first action showed well his future predilections as a legislator. Carson was a parliamentary purist, a determined defender of the rights and privileges of the house against real or imagined incursions of the Council, the governor, the Colonial Office, and private individuals. Although he was concerned with such matters as education, roads, and municipal reform, these did not engage him as much as constitutional nicety, and it is not surprising, for example, to find him in February 1834 plunging the house into a prolonged debate on the eligibility of a bankrupt to hold a seat, at a time when the colony itself was bankrupt and was forced to appeal to the British government to make up a deficiency of £4,000.

It was also clear that there was not a little hypocrisy in his argument that a government contractor such as Patrick Kough* could not sit in the house, when he himself was still district surgeon. However, Cochrane, smarting from several cuts by Carson, dismissed him from his surgeon's position in March 1834, under the pretext that the imperial treasury was no longer supplying the necessary grant. Carson then informed the governor that supplies had been voted by the house to keep the office filled, on the understanding that he should continue in it. On 9 May the house passed two resolutions of censure on Carson, in effect accusing him of lying. These proceedings evidently caused Carson considerable anguish. The loss of the office may have been a severe economic blow, since, according to Cochrane, he had given up his medical practice to his son Samuel on entering politics. In April 1834 and again in 1835 he advertised the resumption of his practice.

By 1835 partisan and sectarian feeling in St John's had reached a fever pitch, with the two objects of popular animosity being Winton and Chief Justice Henry John Boulton*. In January, Carson began his four-year assault on Boulton in a speech in the house, and on 18 February he moved for a select committee to investigate alleged breaches by Boulton of the charter under which the new Supreme Court had been established. The motion was defeated, but in May, Boulton, in a city tense over the recent mutilation of Winton, gave Carson an opportunity to renew his attack. Without bothering to call a jury, Boulton sentenced Parsons of the *Patriot* to three months in prison and a fine of £50 for contempt. This action provoked Carson and Morris to establish a Constitutional Society, and a petition against Boulton, signed by 5,000 people, was presented in the House of Commons by O'Connell. Carson added to the atmosphere of crisis by writing an open letter to Boulton in the *Patriot*, in which he affirmed that the judge was "a fit object for censure and punishment." (Boulton was in England and not expected to return.) When the tense summer was over and the colony was "subsiding into peace," Carson wrote yet another inflammatory letter to the *Patriot* which well illustrates his instincts in politics. "Agitation must be kept up – the high spirits of a high-minded people must be cherished and supported," he said. Political turmoil he welcomed as a sign of a country's growing maturity. Of all the reformers in St John's, he most closely resembled in temperament the rebels of Upper and Lower Canada.

In the general election of 1836, Carson, Kent, and Morris were successful in St John's when their opponents withdrew. Moreover, despite a grand jury inquiry into outrages committed during the polling, and the even more dramatic development of an immediate new general election made necessary by a legal technicality discovered by Boulton, the reformers had won control of the house. For five years after the new session opened in July 1837, Carson would preside as speaker in one of the most combustible assemblies in the colony's history.

Carson's influence upon the house during this period is somewhat obscured by his position as speaker, but he undoubtedly countenanced the assembly's assertiveness and helped to shape its initiatives behind the scenes. His influence may be detected in such moves as the attempt to undermine Edward Kielley*'s position as district surgeon, the awarding of an annual salary of £200 to the speaker, and the extreme step of having expunged from the journals the censure upon him of 9 May 1834. As for the principal obstinacy of the new house, its refusal to present supply bills incorporating changes by the Council, Carson made it clear to the governor that he supported the action. But perhaps his influence is most clearly seen in the assembly's pursuit of Boulton, who had unexpectedly been confirmed as chief justice and had returned to Newfoundland. At the assembly's first meeting on 3 July, Morris indicated that a committee of the whole would inquire into the administration of justice. Carson's antipathy towards Boulton and general anxiety about fairness in the courts were sharpened by three cases in 1837. In the first, Carson, Morris, and others were charged with unlawful assembly, and Carson, deeply resentful, refused to appear in court until legally compelled. In May, during an action Carson took against McCoubrey, Boulton informed the jury that the phrase "mad Dr. Carson" was not a libel. A further humiliation occurred in Samuel Carson's action against Kielley for defamation of character, also in May. In the course of this proceeding it was divulged that William Carson, to protect his son's reputation, had entered the home of a female patient and, without authorization of any kind, conducted a painful, searching examination of the most intimate kind. On learning of this invasion of privacy, Boulton was so enraged that he rebuked Carson at length on the witness stand. It was not in Carson's nature to submit to such treatment. In October the house petitioned the queen to recall Boulton, and when Carson left for England as a member of the assembly's delegation to present this and other grievances to the British government, he told the public that his "sole purpose" was the removal of Boulton, "who ought never to have been permitted to contaminate our shores." In July 1838 the judicial committee of the Privy Council recommended that it would be "inexpedient" that Boulton "should be continued in the office of Chief Justice of Newfoundland."

Carson had arrived in London in January 1838 and on 19 February departed for Liverpool to visit his brother, leaving the work of the delegation to John Valentine Nugent*. He returned to St John's in May. His visit to England having further stimulated his thinking on constitutional questions, he wrote letters to the *Newfoundlander* urging the assembly to "stick fast" to the principle that it should be modelled on the House of Commons. Carson himself adhered to the principle with great tenacity. On 9 Aug. 1838, acting on behalf of the assembly, he issued a warrant committing Kielley to jail for an alleged contempt of the house, uttered in the streets of St John's. When Kielley was released on a writ of habeas corpus issued by assistant judge George LILLY, a similar warrant was issued for the arrest of the judge and the sheriff and, on 11 August, Lilly, who resisted arrest, was taken from the court-house to the home of the sergeant-at-arms. He was kept in custody for two days, whereupon Governor Henry Prescott* prorogued the legislature and set him free. When the house reopened on 20 August, Carson was presented with a writ by the sheriff on behalf of Kielley, claiming false arrest and placing damages at £3,000. Thus began the case of *Kielley* v. *Carson*, in which the issue was the assembly's right to commit for contempt, a right Carson argued it possessed by reason of its analogy to the House of Commons [*see* Sir Bryan Robinson*]. The case went to the Newfoundland Supreme Court in December 1838, and a majority decision favoured the assembly, Lilly dissenting. Kielley gave notice of an appeal to the Privy Council. It would take over three years for the report of the judicial committee, reversing the decision, to be delivered.

The actions of the house in the Kielley affair provoked a flood of petitions to the British government calling for the abolition of the legislature and, together with the campaign against Boulton, solidified local mercantile feeling against the reformers. In 1838 the St John's Chamber of Commerce forwarded a petition to the queen that linked "some of the leading members of our House" to the Canadian rebels and called for "an immediate abolition" of representative institutions. After the Supreme Court decision in the Kielley case, Carson gave notice that when the house reconvened he had "no doubt" it would want to consider whether the petition violated "its dignity and just privileges." His letter – but one instance of Carson's choosing to act, as speaker, independently of the legislature – amounted to a threat that John Sinclair, the chamber's president, would be cited for contempt, a threat Prescott was not inclined to take lightly. There can be little doubt that the contentious activities of the house in the period 1837–39 helped to bring representative government into disrepute and paved the way for the Amalgamated Legislature. By his persistent assertion of the rights of the assembly, Carson was at least partly responsible for its diminishing reputation.

The years 1839–41 were to reveal divisions within the ranks of the reformers and bring new forces into play upon Newfoundland politics which tended to reduce Carson's significance. The proceedings of the house show heated exchanges among Carson, Kent, Peter BROWN, and Morris, and in the fall of 1839 Parsons began attacking the reformers in the *Patriot* and promoting responsible government. Carson was inclined to the view that "responsibility" had existed since 1833, an opinion Parsons scathingly rejected. But Carson persisted in his view that the constitution was "founded on a broad and liberal basis" and required only that members "put their shoulders to the wheel." Parsons was also now advocating native rights, a growing movement in which Carson, for obvious reasons, could not take a deep interest. Early in 1840 the most serious rift in the reform party occurred when Morris and Carson parted company. Clearly the solidarity of the reformers was in jeopardy, and in the event no effective opposition was mounted by them to the constitutional experiment of 1842, in which the upper and lower houses were combined. Carson himself had been frustrated by the difficulties that the Council and other members put in the way of such improvements as the creation of a St John's academy and the building of roads. In 1840 he called upon the people to "demonstrate, . . . petition" in order to preserve the assembly, but after eight years of representative government there no longer seemed to be support for such action.

In his 70th year Carson began the scientific study of agriculture, and this pursuit evidently occupied his attention more and more. It is possible that his large farm had already brought financial losses. But in agriculture Carson had found an interest which stirred him almost as much as constitutional rights. Letters on the advantages of pig farming, the preparation of compost, and the glories of the Rohan potato flowed to the press. Late in 1841 he became the first president of the Agricultural Society, and announced he would dedicate some of his leisure hours to "a few Lectures on agricultural subjects." In June 1842 he presided at the first ploughing match ever held in Newfoundland; a month later he was fined for carting rotting cods' heads. His agricultural interests had been encouraged by Sir John Harvey*, the only governor to succeed in overcoming Carson's hostility to established authority. Despite the reservations of the Colonial Office, Harvey appointed Carson to the Council in September.

In December 1842 Carson was elected in St John's, along with Nugent and Laurence O'Brien*. When the Amalgamated Legislature opened in January 1843, he unsuccessfully sought the speaker's chair, losing to James Crowdy*, an appointed member. Carson soon recognized the weak position of elected members in the new system, and in February indicated that, "if his health will permit," he would travel to England to petition against the election of Crowdy as "an uncalled for exercise of arbitrary power." Thus his political principles held firm to the last. The night before he died, he called Parsons to his side, urging him to advocate a return to representative government and "to stir up the friends of the people." According to Parsons, he had also sent for a Church of Scotland minister and relinquished his Socinian beliefs.

William Carson was a man of restless energy and driving ambition. There was in him an instinctive revulsion at the exercise of arbitrary power, together with an equally strong urge to confront such power, expose it, and defeat it. These were combined with a supreme confidence in the rightness of his own whig principles, a devastating frankness of expression, and a will of iron. When roused – and it did not take an alarming crisis to stir him – he was a formidable antagonist. He was by nature a partisan, was never inclined to compromise, and was prepared to follow his beliefs with absolute conviction into political action. He was the most radical and influential of the early Newfoundland reformers. As an agitator, he helped to undermine the ancient, paternalistic system of governing Newfoundland. As a propagandist, he disseminated views about its history, and about its potential for development, that would influence generations of writers and politicians. As a legislator, he tried to provide Newfoundland with useful social institutions and to preserve what he thought to be the rights and privileges of the House of Assembly.

PATRICK O'FLAHERTY

William Carson is the author of three pamphlets, including *A letter to the members of parliament of the United Kingdom of Great Britain and Ireland . . .* (Greenock, Scot., 1812), and *Reasons for colonizing the island of Newfoundland, in a letter addressed to the inhabitants* (Greenock, 1813); the third, on the subject of cholera, has not been located.

GRO (Edinburgh), Kelton, reg. of births and baptisms, 4 June 1770. PANL, GN 2/1, 20–45; GN 5/2/A/1, 1811–21; GN 5/2/B/1, 1819–20. PRO, CO 194/45–116; CO 195/16–20; CO 199/19. Univ. of Edinburgh Library, Special Coll. Dept., Faculty of Medicine, minutes of the proc., 1776–1811; Matriculation reg., 1786–1803; Medical matriculation index, 1783–90. *Dr William Carson, the great Newfoundland reformer: his life, letters and speeches; raw material for a biography*, comp. J. R. Smallwood (St John's, 1978). Nfld., General Assembly, *Journal*, 1843; House of Assembly, *Journal*, 1833–42. *Aris's Birmingham Gazette; or the General Correspondent* (Birmingham, Eng.), 1794–1808. *Newfoundlander*, 1827–43. *Newfoundland Mercantile Journal*, 1816–27. *Newfoundland Patriot*, 1834–42. *Newfoundland Vindicator* (St John's), 1841–42. *Patriot & Terra Nova Herald*, 1842–43. *Public Ledger*, 1827–43. *Royal Gazette and Newfoundland Advertiser*, 1810–31. Gunn, *Political hist. of Nfld.*

CARTWRIGHT, JOHN SOLOMON, lawyer, militia officer, author, judge, JP, businessman, politician, farmer, and architectural patron; b. 17 Sept. 1804 in Kingston, Upper Canada, son of Richard Cartwright* and Magdalen Secord; m. 11 Jan. 1831 in York (Toronto) Sarah Hayter Macaulay, a daughter of Dr James Macaulay*, and they had three sons and four daughters; d. 15 Jan. 1845 at Rockwood, his estate near Kingston.

From his father, who died when he was barely ten, John Solomon Cartwright inherited a fortune of about £10,000 and a position of power and influence. Yet there was a darker side to his inheritance. Four older brothers and a sister died in their teens or twenties, and another sister and brother also predeceased him. The cause of many of these early deaths was the disease which was also to kill John himself in his 41st year – pulmonary consumption.

Cartwright was educated in the Midland District Grammar School at Kingston, and in 1820 he went to York to enter the law office of John Beverley Robinson*, attorney general of Upper Canada. He was admitted to the Law Society of Upper Canada as a student in the Michaelmas term and was called to the bar in the same term, 1825. He may have returned to live at Kingston in the summer of 1822, when he was gazetted an ensign in the 1st Regiment of Frontenac militia. It is only in September 1826 however that the first newspaper account of him as counsel in court appears. In August that year he was noted as secretary of the Cataraqui Bridge Company committee. In January 1827 Cartwright's mother died, and he was thus free of immediate family ties in Kingston. He decided to continue his legal studies in England, at Lincoln's Inn, London. There he would be in easy reach of his twin brother, Robert David, who was studying for the ministry at Oxford.

Cartwright kept a journal of his trip, at least for the first months. It shows he had developed a strong and personal visual sense in his response to natural scenery and, to a lesser extent, buildings, though at times both also appealed to him for their literary or historical associations. Other qualities stand out as well: a fairness of judgement and an independence of mind. Although he had been brought up in the United Empire Loyalist tradition, he apparently bore no grudge against the Americans. On his way through New York State he stopped at Albany, which his father had left 50 years before because of the revolution, and pondered on the past, yet without a trace of rancour against his father's persecutors. "All his contemporaries," he wrote, "must like him have sunk to rest and may we not hope that they are enjoying happiness in that state where all dissensions are at an end and where all tears shall be wiped from our eyes." His first impressions of London were not favourable. After four days in the English capital Cartwright noted distastefully, "Upon the whole can't say that I admire London." Of the Court of King's Bench he remarked, "Could not perceive that the business was managed with less noise or more regularity than with us." Only when he walked to the West End did he become enthusiastic: "Was very much delighted with the appearance of [Hyde] Park which must be invaluable to the Londoner – can conceive the delight after being in the noise and smoke of London with which to enjoy in half an hours walk the clear sky and all the delights of the country." Cartwright and his brother spent July and August 1828 touring Switzerland; the following summer they travelled in Scotland.

By the autumn of 1830 Cartwright had returned to Kingston, where he resumed his law practice. His seriousness about his profession is shown by the large sum he was spending on legal books. In England he had probably laid out £250 for a "law library." In 1834 he was appointed a judge of the Midland District Court; he was elected a bencher of the Law Society of Upper Canada in 1835 and in 1838 he was made a QC.

Another activity in which Cartwright became deeply involved was banking. In May 1832 he was elected a director of the newly formed Commercial Bank of the Midland District, and when the directors met they unanimously chose him president. For the next 14 years he presided over the bank's operations. It was apparently the only bank in British North America which did not suspend specie payments during the 1837 rebellions. An aggressive institution, "the bank was by 1844 firmly established as the financial support of the eastern half of Canada West," says historian Maxwell Leroy Magill.

Cartwright also engaged in far-ranging personal business activities. In 1832 he sold a large tract of land outside Hamilton to Allan Napier MacNab*, on which the latter built Dundurn Castle. In the years 1832–33 he was involved, along with John Macaulay*, in a town-planning scheme at Niagara Falls. A grander project was a large development in Montreal, where his chief partner was his great friend James Bell Forsyth*, a Kingston-born merchant who had become a major figure in the timber trade. Their Montreal plan evolved in the years 1842–43; it seems to have collapsed because Forsyth went bankrupt from other commitments. Forsyth was able to survive, but only because Cartwright rescued him.

The land developments in which Cartwright took the most personal interest were those in and around Kingston and in Napanee. He is said to have given the land for every school, public building, and church in the latter town. To his own denomination, the Church of England, he gave not only the land but the church itself, St Mary Magdalene.

Cartwright developed a personal estate at Rockwood (he may have called it Rockhurst), to the west of Kingston as it was then. By the early 1840s his farming operations had become extensive. "Mr. Cartwright has spared no expense," reported the Kingston *Chronicle & Gazette* of 28 May 1842, "in stocking his well cultivated farm with the best breeds of cattle and sheep," and he won prizes with them at the Frontenac County cattle show in October 1841. But by the spring of 1843 Cartwright decided to give up much of his farm, subdividing it into building lots. The whole area had risen greatly in value because in 1841 Kingston had become the capital of the United Province of Canada and the property was near the governor's residence, Alwington House.

In 1834 Cartwright had entered politics, contesting

the seat of Lennox and Addington which was then held by the popular reformers Marshall Spring Bidwell* and Peter Perry*. He came in third. He tried again in July 1836 with another tory, George Hill Detlor, and they beat the reformers soundly, with Cartwright taking 475 votes to Bidwell's 370. From then until his death Cartwright represented the constituency in the assembly. He was an active member. He served on the finance committee, brought in various bills for legal reform, and sat on committees (all from 1837) concerning the Welland Canal, the improvement of the Trent River, and the survey of the Ottawa River; in 1839 he was chairman of a committee to select a site for a lunatic asylum at Kingston.

During the period of the rebellion Cartwright was a staunch supporter of the government. He was lieutenant-colonel commanding the 2nd Regiment of Lennox militia and as such was a member of the court martial in November 1838 which tried the so-called Patriots captured at the battle of Windmill Point, including the unfortunate Nils von SCHOULTZ. More cheerful duties were helping to obtain Kingston's act of incorporation as a town, and in March 1838, as chairman of the Court of Quarter Sessions, setting up procedures for the election of a town council. The council unanimously elected him mayor, but he declined. However, he did compose and read the address of the town's citizens to Lord Durham [LAMBTON] on the occasion of his brief visit of 21 July 1838.

By 1839 there was a widespread feeling in the province that major changes would have to be made in the system of government. When a select committee of the assembly recommended legislative union with Lower Canada, Cartwright proposed a set of resolutions designed to ensure English Canadian domination of any such arrangement. He believed that without these safeguards the British connection would be endangered. The terms of these resolutions, which became known as "the Cartwright conditions," enabled a majority in the assembly to vote for union, on 30 March 1839. They were rejected, however, by the new governor-in-chief, Charles Edward Poulett THOMSON (later Lord Sydenham) who demanded, and on 19 Dec. 1839 received, the assembly's unconditional assent to union. Cartwright continued his effort to protect British institutions, and on 13 Jan. 1840 moved an address insisting on certain conditions. It was carried, and Thomson agreed, among other things, that English would be the only official language of record under the union.

Cartwright was prepared to give the new constitutional arrangement a chance and for a time in 1840–41 considered supporting the efforts of William Henry Draper* to form a moderate conservative group. Under the influence of MacNab, Robinson, and others, however, he drew back and instead continued his alignment with the high tories. In the spring of 1842 Sydenham's successor, Sir Charles BAGOT, attempted to bring Cartwright into a cabinet he was trying to construct from politicians not associated with Robert Baldwin* and Louis-Hippolyte La Fontaine*. Cartwright was offered the solicitor-generalship but refused it. In a letter of 16 May to Bagot he set forth his reasons. The union appeared to be functioning in an unsatisfactory manner. "I am most anxious that it should be rendered, if possible, productive of every advantage to both sections of the Province," he said. "But I do not see how it can be possible to arrive at this desirable end, without the concert and co-operation of the French Canadians." The gerrymandering of Lower Canadian constituencies by Lord Sydenham had been reprehensible. "I cannot imagine how it could have ever been supposed that harmony could be produced by an act of the grossest injustice." Moreover, he was totally opposed to responsible government. Such a system was incompatible "with our position as a Colony, – particularly in a country where almost universal suffrage prevails, – where the great mass of the people are uneducated, – and where there is but little of that salutary influence which hereditary rank and great wealth exercises in Great Britain." Lastly, and perhaps it was the most important factor, he was unwilling to serve in the same ministry with Francis Hincks*, who "up to the very moment of the outbreak of the rebellion defended the conduct" of Louis-Joseph Papineau* and William Lyon Mackenzie*.

Conservative though he was, Cartwright was not afraid to associate himself with ameliorative measures. In October 1843 he introduced a resolution in the house concerning "Juvenile Houses of Refuge." "No greater benefit could be conferred on the country than by the establishment of institutions where the vagrant and vicious of the juvenile population would be preserved from contact with those influences which are destructive of morality, and by labor and attention to their moral culture, they would become good members of society." "Maudlin sensibility," said Dr William "Tiger" DUNLOP; he would whip the children and send them to bed. But others in the assembly, especially Thomas Cushing Aylwin*, solicitor general for Lower Canada, supported the proposal and it was referred to a select committee. When the La Fontaine–Baldwin ministry resigned in November on the issue of responsible government, Cartwright was indignant, not only because he opposed the principle – "humbug," he called it – but because he saw his cherished motion for "Juvenile Houses of Refuge" being abandoned. The idea of reform schools, as they came to be called, was not finally adopted for 15 years.

Cartwright's last political venture was also, temporarily, a failure. In November 1843 the assembly had passed a resolution moving the capital from

Kingston to Montreal. Believing that its removal to a non-British part of the union would endanger the continuation of British parliamentary institutions in Canada, on 2 March 1844 he set out for England to present a petition to the queen on behalf of 16,000 Upper Canadians requesting that the capital be retained in their half of the colony. Despite all his attachment to British institutions, however, Cartwright was first and foremost a Canadian, as a later comment by his sister-in-law shows. Unlike his twin brother, she wrote, John "ever had a warm attachment and preference for Canada and though he greatly enjoyed his abode in England and loved and admired the country, yet it never rivalled his native land in his affections."

Even before the trip Cartwright's health was deteriorating. It is a measure of his convictions, and sense of public duty, that he undertook such a journey. By October 1844 he realized that he must leave public life. Governor Sir Charles Theophilus METCALFE expressed his deep regret. Cartwright had been an adviser of his, albeit an unofficial one, and the governor had undoubtedly hoped to bring him into his cabinet. In a farewell address to his constituents Cartwright alluded to the forthcoming general election. His remarks contained no party rancour. "It is to be desired," he said, "that in the choice of their Representatives, the people of Upper Canada would keep in mind the advice given by Jethro to Moses, and select persons 'fearing God and hating covetousness.' We might then reasonably expect that our unhappy dissensions would be healed, and that we would become a virtuous, and consequently a happy and contented people."

In making John Strachan* a guardian of his children many years before, Richard Cartwright had instructed, "I am particularly anxious that the boys should have such an education as will qualify them for being useful to their friends, their country, and by a taste for literature ensure them an unfailing source of personal employment." John Solomon had clearly fulfilled his father's hopes for him. At his death he received universal praise. The Reverend Saltern Givins lamented, "Surely, Brethren, the society he was permitted to adorn for a time has lost in him no ordinary ornament – the poor and needy no common benefactor." Judge Stafford Frederick Kirkpatrick paid homage on behalf of his colleagues: "To the bar he was indeed a loss not to be replaced . . . beloved and respected by every member." At St George's Church, Kingston, in his funeral sermon, the Reverend Robert Vashon Rogers exclaimed, "A great man has fallen! – great in all that constitutes true greatness."

The only known portrait of Cartwright, painted by William Tinsley in 1842, speaks of an intellectual with scholarly interests. His library contained books on a vast range of subjects – history, literature, the classics, religion, architecture, painting, gardening, botany, optics, geology, and agriculture. It also included a substantial collection of law-books. These Cartwright saw not merely as a personal possession but as a community resource. Some months before his death he advertised in the *Chronicle & Gazette* asking borrowers to return volumes from his law library because he was selling it. The buyer was the young John A. Macdonald*, to whom it was sold at a great discount, because Cartwright characteristically hoped that it would stay in the area. But Cartwright was not just an intellectual; he was a man of action, as his careers in business, politics, and the militia show. A devoted Anglican, he was also an energetic freemason and rose to be senior warden of Ancient St John's Lodge No.3, Kingston. He liked horses and equipages and was steward of the Kingston Races in 1839. He played cards for high stakes and loved elegance and the comforts of life, including good food and wine.

As a Regency "man of taste," Cartwright had a passion for architecture which is still evident in his native town. The choice of a fine architect is not automatic; he might easily have selected lesser men. He began with commissions to Thomas Rogers*, probably the most competent and versatile architect of Upper Canada in the 1820s and 30s. From him he commissioned large town houses for himself and his brother, and likely the Commercial Bank building in Kingston and St Mary Magdalene Church in Napanee. In 1841 George Browne* came to Kingston as government architect. Cartwright recognized the superiority of this younger man, perhaps the most distinguished figure in his profession in Canada in the first half of the century. For Cartwright, Browne produced the villa of Rockwood, a masterpiece of design. Browne's greatest building is the city hall, and Cartwright almost certainly had a hand in helping him gain that commission. He may also have influenced the choice of Browne as a designer for the local branch of the Bank of Montreal and perhaps a house of John A. Macdonald's. Somc of thc fincst of the 19th-century buildings that continue to grace the city of Kingston are thus Cartwright's most visible legacy.

J. DOUGLAS STEWART and MARY STEWART

William Tinsley's portrait of John Solomon Cartwright is in the Agnes Etherington Art Centre, Queen's Univ. (Kingston, Ont.).

QUA, 2199a; 2254; 2256. Saltern Givins, *A discourse delivered in St. Mary Magdalene's Church, Napanee, on Sunday, the 2nd of February, 1845, on the occasion of the death of John Solomon Cartwright* . . . (Cobourg, [Ont.], 1845). R. V. Rogers, *Confidence in death: a sermon preached in St. George's Church, Kingston, Canada West, on Sunday, January 26th, 1845, on the occasion of the death of John Solomon Cartwright* . . . (Kingston, [1845]). *British Whig*, 6 Jan., 17 Nov. 1836. *Chronicle & Gazette*,

1833–45. *Church*, 31 Jan. 1845. *Kingston Chronicle*, 1822–33. *Heritage Kingston*, ed. J. D. Stewart and I. E. Wilson (Kingston, 1973). J. D. Stewart, "Architecture for a boom town: the primitive and the neo-baroque in George Browne's Kingston buildings" and M. L. Magill, "The failure of the Commercial Bank," *To preserve and defend: essays on Kingston in the nineteenth century*, ed. G. [J. J.] Tulchinsky (Montreal and London, 1976), 37–61 and 169–81. Adam Shortt, "Founders of Canadian banking: John Solomon Cartwright, banker, legislator and judge," Canadian Bankers' Assoc., *Journal* (Toronto), 30 (1922–23): 475–87. J. D. and Mary Stewart, "John Solomon Cartwright: Upper Canadian gentleman and Regency 'man of taste,'" *Historic Kingston*, no.27 (1979): 61–77.

CASEY, WILLIAM REDMOND, engineer; b. *c.* 1805 or *c.* 1808, probably in Brooklyn, N.Y.; d. 6 Aug. 1846 in Montreal.

William Redmond Casey began his career in the early 1830s as a sub-assistant engineer for the construction of the Philadelphia, Germantown and Norristown Railroad. He later worked in the same capacity on the Croton Aqueduct in New York State and then served as assistant engineer during the construction of the Long Island Rail Road. In the spring of 1834 he came to Lower Canada as assistant engineer for the building of the Chambly Canal.

The Company of Proprietors of the Champlain and St Lawrence Railroad, established to link Dorchester (Saint-Jean-sur-Richelieu) with La Prairie, on the St Lawrence, had been incorporated by statute in 1832. The legislation required the company to produce a plan of the line by December 1834. Two months before the deadline, with nothing having been done, Jason C. Pierce, a Dorchester merchant and one of the company's incorporators, decided to proceed at his own expense. He applied to the commissioners of the Chambly Canal for permission to employ their chief engineer, W. R. Hopkins, to undertake the necessary survey. Instead, Casey was sent. Within a month he and a surveyor had produced a map of the proposed line. In late November the company was formally organized and Casey's plan approved. By January 1835 the company had acquired the necessary financial support from subscribers such as Peter McGill* and George Simpson* and had hired Casey to superintend construction of the line. At Montreal during that winter Casey was "occupied in giving the information and specifications necessary to enable the Committee [of Management] to contract without loss of time, for the timber, iron, and materials for fencing." In April 1835 the first ground was broken. By December Casey reported "the completion of the fencing, graduation, masonry, bridges, the large wharf at Laprairie, and the frames of the station houses." All had been accomplished, he noted, "in a degree of order and harmony . . . seldom witnessed on public works." This *esprit de corps*, the directors stated in their report, was due to Casey's "tact and attention." In a period of increasing ethnic tensions, Casey's success is explained by his attitude. "The Canadians," he wrote, "formed by far the greater portion of the laborers and maintained their character for behaving with a degree of order and good nature, when working together in numbers, unequalled by any other people."

In the spring of 1836 work began on the final stage of construction, the laying of the track and superstructure. Capital was limited and Casey's expenditures remained within the established limits. He used the American method of track-laying known as "the cheap principle," which relied on the extensive use of wooden rails topped by half-inch iron straps. Such a line was less substantial than the British type which used solid iron rails; up to 1848, however, when the last of Casey's original track was replaced, no serious accidents had occurred on the line because of track failure. The Champlain and St Lawrence served as Canada's only public railway for nine years.

On 21 July 1836 the Champlain and St Lawrence Railroad was officially opened by the governor, Lord Gosford [ACHESON]. At the ceremonies held in Dorchester, Casey was especially honoured. The directors praised his work; the labourers presented him with a gold medal in appreciation of his "gentlemanly conduct towards them"; and Gosford toasted Casey, "whose abilities had been extolled by his employers and whose conduct had been approved by those under his control." In the *Vindicator and Canadian Advertiser* a few days later Thomas Storrow Brown* wrote: "We are in Canada so accustomed to see things done ill, that a work well done is a miracle."

There were no other railways about to be built in the Canadas, and so Casey went back to New York. During the next decade, he made "numerous surveys . . . in various parts of Upper and Lower Canada," but it was not until 1846 that he returned to construct a railway, the newly chartered Montreal and Lachine Rail-road. While at work on the project that summer in Montreal, he died of tuberculosis. He was buried by the Unitarian minister, John Cordner*, and rests in an unmarked grave on the mountainside in Montreal.

JOHN BESWARICK THOMPSON

ANQ-M, CE1-132, 8 août 1846. PAC, RG 30, 281. Can., Prov. of, Legislative Assembly, *App. to the journals*, 1842, app.Z. *Montreal Gazette*, 4 Dec. 1834, 25 Jan. 1845, 11 Aug. 1846, 24 Jan. 1848. *Morning Courier* (Montreal), 23 July 1836. *Vindicator and Canadian Advertiser*, 26 July 1836. *1836–1986, a tribute to Canada's first railway on its sesquicentennial* (Saint-Constant, Que., 1986). R. R. Brown, "The Champlain and St Lawrence Railroad," Railway and Locomotive Hist. Soc., *Bull.* (Boston), 39 (April 1936): 6–61. E. A. Collard, "Of many things . . . ," *Gazette* (Montreal), 30 May 1970: 6. J. B. Thompson, "William R. Casey, the forgotten engineer," *Engineering Journal* (Montreal), 54 (1971), nos.1–2: 8–9.

CASGRAIN, CHARLES-EUSÈBE, lawyer, politician, and office holder; b. 28 Dec. 1800 in Rivière-Ouelle, Lower Canada, son of Pierre Casgrain* and Marie-Marguerite Bonnenfant; m. 26 Oct. 1824 Eliza Anne Baby, daughter of James Baby*, at Quebec, and they had 14 children, among them Henri-Raymond*; d. 29 Feb. 1848 in Montreal and was buried on 9 March at Rivière-Ouelle.

Charles-Eusèbe Casgrain attended the Petit Séminaire de Québec from 1812 till 1816. He then studied at the Séminaire de Nicolet until 1818. Despite delicate health he began articling with Louis Moquin at Quebec in June of the following year and received his lawyer's commission on 7 May 1824. He practised at Quebec until 1827, when he moved to Rivière-Ouelle.

Following dissolution of the Lower Canadian House of Assembly in September 1830, Casgrain stood as a candidate in Kamouraska. He was elected along with merchant Amable Dionne*. He rarely spoke in the house, from which he was, indeed, usually absent. According to his family, he quickly took a dislike to parliamentary life and stood aloof from Louis-Joseph Papineau*'s party. Consequently he voted against the 92 Resolutions, which set out the assembly's principal grievances and demands. He was defeated in the 1834 elections.

Casgrain's lack of interest in political life did not prevent him from sitting on the Special Council, which was established on 10 Feb. 1838 and charged with administering Lower Canada after the rebellion and the suspension of the constitution. The appointment was hardly surprising, since Casgrain had openly opposed the armed uprising in 1837 and had also welcomed into his home officers of the British troops who were on the move between Quebec and Halifax. His partiality probably made him unpopular with the French-speaking élite.

In April 1839 Casgrain was commissioned to receive the oath of allegiance. Seven years later he was made deputy commissioner of public works, an appointment that was obviously connected with his services during the rebellion, and he then went to live in Montreal. One of his major responsibilities as deputy commissioner was to build the shelters at Pointe-Saint-Charles (Montreal) and Grosse Île for Irish immigrants ill with typhus. In November 1847 he caught a chill, and because of his delicate health he did not get over it. He died while still in his forties.

Charles-Eusèbe Casgrain has been described by some authors as a mediocre politician or as an opportunist intent on pleasing the British authorities. By his firmly avowed loyalty to the crown, he, like many of his contemporaries, had enabled the ruling group to legitimate its authority over the society of Lower Canada. Since he had married a woman who came from a family known since the conquest for its loyalty to the British crown, it would have been difficult for him to dissociate himself too openly from the colonial authority. The *Mémoires de famille* written by his wife many years after his death portrays Casgrain as a victim of the politics of his time whose conduct it was essential to justify to posterity. Despite the defence he remains an obscure figure in the political history of Lower Canada in the first half of the 19th century.

ANTONIO LECHASSEUR

ANQ-Q, CE1-1, 26 oct. 1824; CE3-1, 29 déc. 1800, 9 mars 1848. ASQ, Fichier des anciens. PAC, MG 29, D61: 1548–54, 1557–58, 1560–63; MG 30, D1, 7: 591–94; RG 4, B8: 7737–46; RG 11, A2, 95, 110; A3, 121; RG 68, General index, 1651–1841, 1841–67. F.-J. Audet, "Commissions d'avocats," *BRH*, 39: 583; "Les législateurs du Bas-Canada." *Cyclopædia of Canadian biog.* (Rose and Charlesworth), 1: 278. Desjardins, *Guide parl.* H. J. Morgan, *Sketches of celebrated Canadians*, 354. P.-G. Roy, *Les avocats de la région de Québec.* [E. A.] Baby, Mme C.-E. Casgrain, *Mémoires de famille: l'honorable C.-E. Casgrain* (Rivière-Ouelle, Qué., 1891). Chapais, *Cours d'hist. du Canada*, 4: 36, 209, 278, 287. Antoine Gérin-Lajoie, *Dix ans au Canada, de 1840 à 1850; histoire de l'établissement du gouvernement responsable* (Québec, 1888). P.-H. Hudon, *Rivière-Ouelle de la Bouteillerie; 3 siècles de vie* (Ottawa, 1972). [M.-E. Perreault], Mme E. Croff, *Nos ancêtres à l'œuvre à la Rivière-Ouelle* (Montréal, 1931).

CATHARINE. *See* OHTOWAʔKÉHSON

CAWDELL, JAMES MARTIN, army officer, author, teacher, secretary, librarian, and publisher; baptized 24 Feb. 1784 in Sunderland, Durham, England, son of James Cawdell and Sarah Martin; d. unmarried 13 July 1842 in a Toronto boarding-house.

By his own account James Martin Cawdell had the "Usual Classical Education" before beginning, "in compliance with my Father's Wishes, tho' repugnant to my own," the study of law. A self-declared romantic and more interested in "Rank & Honours" than wealth, he selected the Canadas as the site for his ambition. He purchased an ensigncy in the 100th Foot and joined the unit at Montreal in July 1810. What followed is largely known from his own account in a petition of December 1818.

His tour of duty took him in 1810 to York (Toronto), where his friendship with the province's discontented attorney general, William FIRTH, provoked Lieutenant Governor Francis Gore*. Brigadier-General Isaac Brock* consequently ordered the young officer to go to regimental headquarters at Fort George (Niagara-on-the-Lake). The "irritated" subaltern then wrote a satirical piece on Gore called the "'Puppet Shew.'" Brock upon learning, albeit erroneously, that he too was an object of satire banished the insubordinate ensign to St Joseph Island, "the Military Siberia of U. Canada." There, in August 1811, he posted another piece but it was removed before it had any effect.

Aggrieved, Cawdell determined to sell his commission and settle upon land he had purchased in the province. The War of 1812 interrupted his plans and he served in various capacities with the 100th until his resignation was confirmed in October 1813. Then stationed at Stoney Creek, he was anxious "to do something that would bring me forward to Notice & at the same time benefit my Country." In October he wrote to Governor Sir George Prevost* of his plan – which, Cawdell believed, "has more the Air of a Don Quixotte than of rationality" – for erecting an independent state near Fort George. Here he would raise a guerrilla band and become a "Thorn" in the Americans' side. The proposal was dismissed. Cawdell was subsequently captured by Joseph Willcocks*'s marauders. After escaping, he renewed unsuccessfully his efforts to obtain a militia commission. Several months later George Crookshank* appointed him to take charge of the commissariat's stores at Holland Landing, a position he held until the end of the war. In January 1816 Cawdell's application to succeed the ailing king's printer was rejected. Aware of his reputation for eccentricity if not lunacy, but by his own admission hot-blooded, he determined on a course which would cut him off forever from the fount of all honour and rank in the province's society. Once again, he lampooned Gore.

The resulting estrangement from government quickly reduced Cawdell to "Poverty & Obscurity." By mid 1817 he was teaching in a township school. Yet, armed with the conviction of possessing "some small portion of Genius" and anxious to avert the obscurity which was, to his mind, tantamount to death, in December 1818 he sought the favour of the new lieutenant governor, Sir Peregrine Maitland*. A political nincompoop, as vain as he was unrepentant, Cawdell passed over his satire of Gore as indignation "at being the Victim of Malice & Duplicity." In a similar vein he complained of his omission from the magistracy when "every Ignorant Clodhopper . . . who scarcely know . . . A, B from a Bull's foot" was appointed. Cawdell urged his claims, noting that he had in preparation a tract on colonization (which he stressed was "by no means Ala Gourlay [Robert Gourlay*]") and a "few trifles in verse." In a predictable, and scathing, reply Maitland refused to "patronize the publication of a person who tells me He is the lampooner of my predecessor" and affirmed the superior qualifications of farmers as magistrates over one "with that eccentricity and talent for lampooning to which You inform me You possess."

In 1822 Cawdell received a small crumb of office, the adjutancy in a York militia unit. A year later, "labouring under heavy pecuniary embarrassments," existing on his meagre teacher's salary of £16 per annum, and living from house to house, he begged Maitland for two recently vacated positions in the Western District, but without success. His long search ended in 1833 when, probably with the support of Robert Baldwin*, he became secretary and librarian of the Law Society of Upper Canada.

Although he had once chosen the military life over literature as the surest, or quickest, means of acquiring honour, it was his meagre talents for "poetical trifles" that earned him historical notice as an early Upper Canadian writer of verse. Beginning on 12 Dec. 1810, his poetry had appeared, under the pseudonym Roseharp, in the *York Gazette* for some months. Whether paeans to England's constitutional and military glories, to nature, or to women, his productions were not, it seems, well received. John Beverley Robinson* dismissed his efforts as "trash." In May 1811 Roseharp disappeared from the *Gazette*'s pages when Cawdell fell from grace. By the early 1820s, however, he had acquired a modest reputation for his talents. Charles FOTHERGILL, in publishing a poem Roseharp had written for a militia ball, referred to him as a gentleman "well known for his poetic talent." In 1826 Cawdell published a slim volume of his poetry, the proceeds from which went to one of the favourite charitable societies of gentlewomen in York.

As important to historians was his role in the province's literary beginnings. In 1823 he founded a quarterly, the *Rose Harp*. No copies are extant but a Niagara newspaper noted receipt of the first issue that July. In 1835 he launched another periodical under the same name. Believing that the colony "has now arrived at such a state of improvement in population and wealth, that we already see the dawning of the Arts and Sciences," he intended to establish a "Roseharp Patriotic Academy" to fund the periodical and to "encourage and diffuse sentiments of loyal patriotism – a taste for literature, and the fine arts." Support, however, was apparently not forthcoming and the new journal failed after one issue.

Before his death in 1842 Cawdell was quite ill, unable even to write. Estranged from both mother and sister in England, he left his most prized possessions, his books, to a small circle of friends. Life had not brought him the honour he thought his due and his self-described genius went unrecognized. Cawdell's estrangement from the society whose plaudits he coveted stemmed from his own idiosyncrasies. Unlike Gourlay, who was perceived as a critic of society, Cawdell was merely a satirist of the personalities of the powerful. He was a victim of his impetuosity. Although he became more circumspect after his brushes with Gore, he never lost altogether the romantic sensibility of his youth. The unrealized Roseharp academy was to be "tinged with the spirit of romance," and, Cawdell chided, "if its object be gained, let the cold hearted children of prudence sneer at it as they may."

ROBERT L. FRASER

James Martin Cawdell's volume of poetry, *The wandering rhymer, a fragment, with other poetical trifles*, was issued anonymously at York (Toronto) in 1826. The sole issue of his second journal, the *Roseharp: for Beauty, Loyalty and Song*, was published at Toronto on 1 Jan. 1835; it appears to have been written as well as edited by Cawdell. Copies of both items are available at the MTRL, along with the manuscript of a song, "The Raven Plume, A Romance From a Welsh Legendary Tale . . . ," which Cawdell composed for the York Bazaar Concert of 1833. His petition has been published as "The memorial of J. M. Cawdell, 1818," ed. Adam Shortt, *CHR*, 1 (1920): 289–301.

AO, MS 4, J. M. Cawdell to J. B. Robinson, 8 July 1840; MS 78, J. B. Robinson to Macaulay, 15 Feb. 1811; RG 22, ser.302, reg.6 (1838–42): 472–74. Church of Jesus Christ of Latter-Day Saints, Geneal. Soc. (Salt Lake City, Utah), International geneal. index. CTA, RG 1, B, J. M. Cawdell to T. McCord, 30 Aug. 1841 (mfm. at AO). MTRL, Robert Baldwin papers, corr. of M. A. Cawdell to Baldwin. PAC, RG 1, L3, 106: C14/7; RG 5, A1: 5026–27, 11553, 19777–91, 19795–98, 31870–72, 56711–13; RG 8, I (C ser.), 680: 322; 790: 26–34; 1015: 66; 1016: 105; 1168: 144; 1170: 327; 1171: 41; 1203½: 187, 266; 1220: 152. *Doc. hist. of campaign upon Niagara frontier* (Cruikshank), 8: 96. *John Askin papers* (Quaife), 2: 691–93, 697. *Gleaner, and Niagara Newspaper*, 19 July 1823. *Weekly Register*, 29 April 1824. *York Gazette*, 1810–11. Law Soc. of U.C., *Law Society of Upper Canada, 1797–1972 . . .* , ed. J. D. Honsberger ([Toronto], 1972), 59–60, 114.

CAWTHRA, JOSEPH, merchant and politician; b. 14 Oct. 1759 in Yeadon, England, son of Henry Cawthra and Mary Brown; m. 29 Jan. 1781 Mary Turnpenny, and they had at least nine children (six sons and three daughters); d. 15 Feb. 1842 in Toronto.

Joseph Cawthra sprang from substantial yeoman stock in Yorkshire, his forebears having dwelt in the parish of Guiseley, near Bradford, for several generations. His earliest known vocation was that of woollen manufacturer; in 1792 or 1793 he built one of the earliest steam-powered carding-, spinning-, and fulling-mills in the county. Family tradition states that he arrived in Upper Canada in 1803 after a brief stay in New York. By his own contemporary account, however, he lived in New York from 1803 until the spring of 1806, when he opened a general store, with an emphasis on apothecary's wares, at York (Toronto). Between 1806 and 1809 he was joined by his family. His profits during the War of 1812 helped to make him one of the most substantial merchants of post-war York, and in the 1820s he was a major importer of teas and other groceries.

Cawthra's first political act in Upper Canada was to sign a declaration in August 1807 hostile to the party of Robert THORPE, the recently dismissed justice of the colony's Court of King's Bench. In the 1820s and 1830s, however, he was a stalwart of anti-government politics in York. In 1828 he promoted the candidature of Thomas David Morrison* as the town's member in the House of Assembly and took part, though an Anglican, in the "Central Committee" formed at York to coordinate the campaign against King's College (University of Toronto), which reformers viewed as an element in John Strachan*'s strategy to establish the Church of England in the colony. In July of that year his name headed the petition of freeholders in the Home District to the imperial government in support of the recently dismissed justice of the Court of King's Bench, John Walpole Willis*. It was in this petition that Upper Canadian reformers first formally demanded that the provincial administration be responsible to the House of Assembly. Cawthra's prominence on this occasion provoked Lieutenant Governor Sir Peregrine Maitland* to malign him, and other leading signatories, with characteristic mendacity in a letter of 12 September to Colonial Secretary Sir George MURRAY. "Mr. Cawthra came also from the United States: he was a Shoemaker for many years in this Town, and now keeps a Shop – he can barely write." In fact, Cawthra's sojourn in the United States had been relatively brief, he had never been a shoemaker, and he could write as well as Maitland.

In electoral politics Cawthra has often been confused with his sons John and William*. John, not Joseph, was MHA for Simcoe from 1828 to 1830. Joseph, not William, was an alderman for St Lawrence Ward on Toronto's first city council, which was elected in 1834 and dominated by reformers [*see* William Lyon Mackenzie*]. He was defeated in January 1835, but William was elected an alderman for his father's old ward a year later. Joseph's spell of municipal office, his sole venture into electoral politics, reflected not only his prominence in reform circles but also his active engagement in civic affairs.

Although Cawthra was a leading merchant, his attitude towards the Bank of Upper Canada [*see* William Allan*] was for a long time consistent with his politics. In evidence given to the House of Assembly's select committee on the state of the provincial currency in 1830, he decried its privileged position as the only chartered bank in the colony and advocated a more competitive financial market. On this occasion he declared that he had never been a director or stockholder of the bank. Later that year, however, he acquired his first shares in the bank, possibly in order to stand as an "anti-establishment" candidate for its directorate, along with Jesse Ketchum*, Thomas David Morrison, and Robert Baldwin*. He was elected to the directorate in 1835, and re-elected in 1836 and 1837. He had nothing to do with founding the Bank of the People, which was set up in 1835 by other leading reformers, including James Lesslie* and John Rolph*.

This was the background to his controversial role in shoring up the Bank of Upper Canada during the financial crisis of May and June 1837. The suspension of payment in specie by banks in the United States set off a run on banks in the Canadas. The situation in Toronto was aggravated by William Lyon Mackenzie's newspaper campaign against the banks, in which he urged his readers to cash in their banknotes and withdraw their deposits in specie. On 17 May Mackenzie reported that Cawthra had visited all the banks in town the day before in order to cash in notes. Cawthra retorted that he had deposited more than £1,000 in the Bank of Upper Canada on that day and had a total of £15,000 deposited there. Francis Hincks*, the cashier of the Bank of the People, then swore an affidavit that William Cawthra, Joseph's right hand in his business, had cashed £600 of that bank's paper on the 16th and had declared his intention of cashing in paper at the city's other banks, including the Bank of Upper Canada. Joseph replied with an affidavit that he had deposited a large sum in the Bank of Upper Canada on the 16th and had withdrawn none since. At the end of June, he had to make a public denial of the rumour that his £15,000 was deposited under a private arrangement which precluded the bank from applying it to the payment of other obligations. Another report stated that Cawthra, a director, had offered to buy the bank's stock during the crisis at a discount of 20 per cent.

It seems likely that, on 16 May, the Cawthras had withdrawn specie from the Bank of the People, and perhaps from other Toronto banks, in order to shore up the Bank of Upper Canada. One might expect Mackenzie to have vilified them for doing so, and it is perhaps a measure of Joseph's prestige in reform circles that Mackenzie made excuses for the Cawthras instead, repeatedly acknowledging Joseph's long years of devotion to the reform cause and ascribing his conduct to necessity. Cawthra, explained Mackenzie, had £30,000 or more, including his deposits, tied up in the Bank of Upper Canada and was therefore compelled to defend the institution against his better judgment.

Cawthra was an anomalous and enigmatic figure in early Toronto society: anomalous in being a wealthy Anglican merchant who was involved in the Mackenzieite reform politics of Toronto and York County in the 1830s, and enigmatic because there is no surviving evidence of his reasons. Family tradition records his antipathy for the "family compact" and ascribes his adherence to the Church of England to the personal advice of John Wesley, the father of Methodism, not to leave it. It seems plausible that Cawthra was a man of independent views, with sufficient financial independence to indulge them. The financial crisis of 1837 forced him to choose between Mackenzie's anti-capitalist politics and the exigencies of capitalism in crisis, but Mackenzie's rebellion later that year made the contradiction insignificant in practical terms. At the next general election, in 1841, the reformers were led by Robert Baldwin, whose family were old and heavy investors in the Bank of Upper Canada, and their candidates in Toronto were John Henry Dunn* and Isaac Buchanan*, leading capitalists for whom Cawthra voted, probably without qualms.

PAUL ROMNEY

AO, RG 4-32, I408/1880; RG 22, ser.155. PAC, RG 1, L3, 96: C8/41; 97: C9/59. *City of Toronto poll book; exhibiting a classified list of voters, at the late great contest for responsible government* ... (Toronto, 1841). *Town of York, 1793–1815* (Firth); *1815–34* (Firth). U.C., House of Assembly, *App. to the journal*, 1835, no.3; *Journal*, 1830, app.: 21–48. *Colonial Advocate*, 14 June 1827; 2 Oct., 4 Dec. 1828; 18 Feb. 1830; 10 June 1834. *Toronto Patriot*, 16 Jan. 1835; 19, 26 May, 30 June 1837; 18 Feb. 1842. *History of Toronto and county of York, Ontario* ... (2v., Toronto, 1885), 2: 26–27. *Past and present; notes by Henry Cawthra and others*, comp. A. M. [Cawthra] Brock (Toronto, 1924).

CHALOUX, MARIE-ESTHER, named **de Saint-Joseph**, hospital nun of the Hôpital Général in Quebec and superior; b. *c.* 1770, daughter of Jean-Baptiste Chaloux and Marie-Anne Bellefontaine; d. 1 Sept. 1839 at Quebec.

A native of Quebec, Marie-Esther Chaloux's father served, whether willingly or not, as a pilot with the fleet that transported the British troops to Quebec in 1759. From 1775 he was sent to England annually, and his destitute family, reduced to living on some land at Cacouna, received only £25 in six years from the government. Their misfortune was crowned by his death in Portsmouth, England, on 7 March 1781. Mme Chaloux, who was left with five under-age children, succumbed for a time to depression, "neglecting her housekeeping, abandoning her children, giving away household articles for a pittance without rhyme or reason, often running day and night through the woods, along the roads or the beach, barefoot and barelegged in the snow, throwing herself into the water up to her waist, saying she wanted to die." In this painful situation the five children were put in the care of her son-in-law Pierre Sirois, who lived near by. On 4 March 1782 Louis Saindon was officially appointed their trustee and guardian. Mme Chaloux went to live with one relative after another. Then she went on foot to Quebec and wandered through several of the parishes roundabout. Towards the end of 1782 she was admitted to the Hôpital Général, where little by little she recovered her health. In August of the following year she was made guardian of her children.

Marie-Esther Chaloux thus grew up under difficult circumstances. On 16 Jan. 1784 she was admitted to the Hôpital Général as a boarding pupil. In recognition of the services her father had rendered, the government granted her an annuity of a little more than 400 *livres*, until at least 1787. Her mother was readmitted to the Hôpital Général on 10 Feb. 1784, and died there on 21 Sept. 1785. On 1 April 1787 Marie-Esther became a choir nun, taking the name of Saint-Joseph. Since she had no resources of her own, two-thirds of the 3,000 *livres* for her dowry was provided by Bishop Jean-Olivier Briand* and the remainder by a donor. She took her perpetual vows on 25 Sept. 1788.

Marie-Esther de Saint-Joseph served first as pharmacist and then as depositary (bursar). She had no easy task, since in the late 18th century the Hôpital Général's finances, which had been reduced to a precarious state by the conquest, were suffering from the effects of the French revolution. By 1791 the interest payments on the annuities that the nuns held in France, which had been bequeathed them by Bishop Saint-Vallier [La Croix*], their founder, were no longer reaching the community. The hospital became impoverished, and the number of women taking vows dwindled from 11 in the period 1780–89 to only 3 in the following decade. The nuns were even obliged to do much of the work in the fields.

Through the generosity and advice of a benefactress and her own management, Marie-Esther de Saint-Joseph helped get the Hôpital Général out of its straits. On 6 May 1809, in recognition of what she had accomplished, she was elected superior. But the rules did not permit any nun to hold the office for more than two consecutive three-year terms. In 1819 and 1831 she again became superior, both times for six years. In between, she resumed her duties as depositary. From 1837 till her death she served as assistant superior.

Under Marie-Esther de Saint-Joseph's direction there were soon more women taking their vows at the Hôpital Général, with 33 admissions between 1820 and 1839. Finances improved. Government aid increased, as did the work-load. In addition to running a boarding-school for girls, the nuns provided shelter to several invalid and aged persons. In 1818 the Legislative Council set up a special committee to investigate conditions in medical and welfare institutions in Lower Canada. The committee concluded in 1824 that the Hôpital Général was well run. Its report noted that there were two large rooms, one for men, the other for women, each capable of accommodating 18 or 20 patients, and it mentioned the presence of 16 "confined lunatics." Late in Marie-Esther de Saint-Joseph's life the nuns recovered some of the annuities placed in France and used them to repair their buildings.

Although her health had declined over the years, Marie-Esther de Saint-Joseph remained active until her death on 1 Sept. 1839, following a stroke. She was remembered as a gentle, charitable, and unassuming person. She had devoted herself to her community for more than half a century, and it was largely through her talents, perseverance, and prudence that the Hôpital Général was retrieved from its financial difficulties early in the 19th century.

JULIETTE CLOUTIER and RENALD LESSARD

ANQ-Q, CC1, 14 août 1783, 12 oct. 1785; CN3-11, 15 mars 1782; T11-1/2490. Arch. de l'Hôpital Général de Québec, Actes capitulaires (1739–1823), 75, 151–53, 424, 427, 700; Annales du monastère (1793–1843), 291–97; Délibérations du chapitre, 148; Reg. des élèves admises au pensionnat, nos.271, 273; Reg. des entrées des religieuses; Reg. des pauvres invalides, no.52; Reg. des pensionnaires, 144; Vêtures des novices et élections (1812–61), 1–32. BL, Add. MSS 21879 (mfm. at PAC). L.C., Legislative Council, *Journals*, 1824, app.I. [Helena O'Reilly, dite de Saint-Félix], *Monseigneur de Saint-Vallier et l'Hôpital Général de Québec: histoire du monastère de Notre-Dame des Anges* . . . (Québec, 1882).

CHANDLER, KENELM CONOR, army and militia officer, office holder, and seigneur; b. 22 Aug. 1773 at Quebec, natural son of Kenelm Chandler* and Elizabeth Conor; d. 29 Jan. 1850 in Nicolet, Lower Canada, and was buried there on 7 February.

Kenelm Conor Chandler's father came from an old family of landed proprietors at Tewkesbury, England. Kenelm Chandler settled at Quebec in 1764 and pursued a career there as a soldier and office holder in the service of the Board of Ordnance. Like others from upper class British families, he became a defender of a social order based upon the privileges of his group and advocated the maintenance of the monarchy and the seigneurial system.

Nothing is known of Kenelm Conor Chandler's childhood or youth. He entered the British army while still young, starting out in the Royal Americans (60th Foot), in which his father had served. In 1803, at 30 years of age, he was promoted captain in the regiment. His father died that year, and he, with Charlotte Dunière, his father's wife, inherited a fortune estimated at £4,730. Coming into possession of this inheritance enabled Chandler to get married. On 18 Sept. 1804 at Quebec he took as his wife Jane, daughter of fur baron Charles Grant, a senior partner in the North West Company. Several representatives of the government of Lower Canada, professional soldiers, and members of the bourgeoisie attended the wedding. The bride brought a dowry of 6,000 *livres* and a number of family possessions. This marriage was, therefore, another indication of the Chandler family's respectability. The couple would have one daughter.

In 1805 Chandler had to leave for India, where his regiment was to serve. His movements over the next five years are largely unknown, but he stayed for a time in the West Indies and there contracted an infectious disease that forced him to give up his military career. Upon Chandler's return to Lower Canada late in 1810, Governor Sir James Henry Craig* appointed him barrack master at Quebec, a post his father had held until his death. As time went on, changes occurred in Chandler's activities. He discharged his official duties satisfactorily, but also applied himself to increasing his wealth by buying land and lending money. In 1819 Thomas Trigge, his future son-in-law, replaced him as barrack master.

Chandler was on the verge of a new life. A gentleman, he was eager to move higher in the social scale, from office holder to seigneur. The ideal opportunity came in 1821, when the seigneury of Nicolet was put up for auction. No one was in a better position than he to buy it, since he was the principal creditor of its owner, Charles-François-Xavier Baby*. Consequently Chandler acquired it for the modest sum of £6,530, plus another £1,020 for the manor-house and the domanial farm. Shortly after the transaction he moved into the house, where he resided until his death.

From his arrival in Nicolet, Chandler asserted his rights as seigneur and insisted upon the honours that went with them: the seigneur's pew and the privileges of the holy water and consecrated bread in the church. He accumulated honorary posts, and in 1822 he was appointed commissioner for the summary trial of small causes at Nicolet. Also that year Governor Lord Dalhousie [RAMSAY] appointed him lieutenant-colonel of the 2nd Battalion of Buckingham militia. Full of grand ideas, Chandler dreamed of settling his seigneury with people of British stock, and so in 1823 he had an Anglican church built near his manor-house.

Eager for profit, Chandler managed his seigneury strictly. It was undergoing development and the ratio between the land and the people on it was becoming critical, so that he realized he had to pay more attention to the use of his property. If he wanted to draw maximum profit, he had to control the administration more firmly. Consequently in 1823 he hired notary Luc-Michel Cressé, whose main task was to run the seigneury efficiently. Thanks to Cressé's talents, management underwent a considerable change: the traditional ways were re-established, administrative structures were rationalized, and seigneurial demands were tightened. Under Chandler's close supervision the seigneury became a productive and highly profitable enterprise in less than ten years.

Chandler was not content with having his books kept properly. The density of population forced him from 1830 to plan a better overall organization and adopt a set of rules ensuring greater control of this small rural community. He saw the roads, village, *côtes* (concessions fronting on the water) and *censives* (seigneurial areas), mills, and lands not yet granted to tenants as a complete environment, which was both natural and man-made and which needed both formal organization and better supervision. It was necessary to preserve or re-establish certain fundamental rights, demand new services and other forms of payment, take a census of lands not yet granted, and accord tenants new terms. These tasks required that he be as well informed as possible about his entire seigneury. In order to consolidate his hold on the property, a new land roll would have to be prepared. To this end he had plans for surveying done, including a detailed survey that would provide better information about the rapid transformations occurring in the seigneury. He thereby ensured that the land roll would be drawn up on even sounder bases.

Thus in 1832 Chandler gave surveyor Jean-Baptiste Legendre, from Gentilly (Bécancour), the task of laying out survey lines, measuring every plot, and resolving certain difficulties in fixing the boundaries in the southwest corner of the seigneury. To preserve his territorial rights he then entered into a series of costly lawsuits and counter-suits that were still going on when he died. Yet he asserted himself as an all-powerful seigneur and more and more imposed respect for the boundaries of his seigneury upon his neighbours. In 1837, seasoned and meticulous, Chandler ordered his definitive land roll to be prepared. Cressé, who was entrusted with drawing it up, was not unaware of the magnitude of the task. In big registers he noted the tenants' names and marked off each parcel of land, taking into account its size, location, occupancy, state of development, frequent changes of ownership, and tenancy charges in fees and services. In this way Chandler learned all about his property: lands granted *en censive*, seigneurial domain and lands not yet ceded, income, and dues. The preparation of the land roll gave rise to much discontent among the seigneury's farmers, however. On the eve of the disturbances of 1837–38 there were even some signs of unrest and revolt in the countryside around Nicolet [*see* Jean-Baptiste Proulx*]. With the support of the curé of the parish of Saint-Jean-Baptiste, Jean RAIMBAULT, Chandler none the less succeeded in containing the Patriote movement in his region without difficulty.

After this interruption of events Chandler concentrated most of his energies on managing his principal domain, an area of nearly 300 *arpents*. It comprised a spacious manor-house, two small houses for the servants, and a well-equipped domanial farm with two barns, three stables, two storage sheds, and three outbuildings. In 1840 he began to convert some of his land into pasturage, in order to encourage the breeding of livestock on a large scale. He even installed a dairy and an abattoir to increase milk production and the sale of meat on the local markets. Chandler ran his secondary domains just as efficiently. He retained several lots near the Rivière Nicolet for himself, setting up two flour-mills and six sawmills. Similarly he seized a number of pieces of uncleared land and incorporated them into his domain with the intention of cutting wood on them. Ownership of such domanial property certainly meant prestige to him. He spent what it brought in, along with other income, on things adding social distinction – clothes for the ladies, fashionable receptions for the senior dignitaries in the government, a host of servants of every kind.

On the eve of his death in 1850 Chandler owned a large seigneury with a frontage of two leagues and a depth of five. His manor-house, a huge dwelling resembling a château, had its gold and silver plate and jewellery. His wardrobe and his wife's were filled to overflowing with fine materials and clothing of all sorts. The household linen was also indicative of the seigneur's wealth: several rooms were piled high with blankets, pillows, sheets, tablecloths, and linens. The inventory of the furniture was just as impressive: benches, chairs, buffets, wardrobes, beds. His library contained many devotional works and political writings on monarchy, as well as a number of books on the Coutume de Paris and seigneurial practices. All these appurtenances confirm that Chandler was indeed a worthy representative of the new British élite in Lower Canada in the first half of the 19th century which had adapted well to the old French institutions and had profited to the maximum from them.

RICHARD CHABOT

ANQ-MBF, CE1-12, 7 févr. 1850; CN1-21, 8 mai 1844; 13–15 mai, 3 juin 1850. ANQ-Q, CE1-61, 22 août 1773, 18 sept. 1804; CN1-230, 15 sept. 1804; CN1-262, 13 nov. 1804; P-34. ASN, AO, Polygraphie, IX: 25; Seigneurie de Nicolet, Cahier de cens et rentes, 11–18; Terrier, 2–9. PAC, RG 68, General index, 1651–1841. L.C., House of Assembly, *Journals*, 1828–29, app.R. *Quebec almanac*, 1803–5, 1810–19, 1822. P.-G. Roy, *Inv. concessions*. Bellemare, *Hist. de Nicolet*, 213–53. Richard Chabot, "Les terriers de Nicolet: une source importante pour l'histoire rurale du Québec au début du XIXe siècle," *Les Cahiers nicolétains* (Nicolet, Qué.), 6 (1984): 115–26. Denis Fréchette, "La querelle du pain bénit dans la seigneurie de Nicolet," *Les Cahiers nicolétains*, 1 (1979): 19–33. A. St-L. Trigge, "The two Kenelm Chandlers," *BRH*, 49 (1943): 108–13.

CHARRON, AMABLE, master wood-carver and merchant; b. 9 July 1785 in Varennes, Que., son of Charles Charron and Amable Bénard, *dit* Carignan; d. 8 May 1844 in Saint-Jean-Port-Joli, Lower Canada.

Amable Charron lost his father when he was five and received only a little education. He became possibly the apprentice and certainly the partner of Louis Quévillon*, a master wood-carver whose services were in wide demand. Quévillon entrusted to him the completion of some of his contracts. Thus in the period 1808–12 Charron carried out various works for the *fabriques* of Saint-Martin, on Île Jésus near Montreal, Saint-Michel, near Quebec, and Notre-Dame-de-Liesse at Rivière-Ouelle, although the agreement in the latter case may have been with Charron himself rather than with Quévillon.

The time Charron spent on the Côte-du-Sud (the area stretching from Lévis to Rivière-du-Loup) probably convinced him that he could find work there. In 1811 he had executed the retable (the structure housing the altar) and rood-screen for the church of Saint-Roch-des-Aulnaies. There was little to keep him at Saint-Vincent-de-Paul (Laval) on Île Jésus after the death in 1812 of his wife Marguerite Hogue, daughter of master carpenter Simon Hogue; they had married in 1808 and their three children had died in infancy. Consequently he decided to move to the Côte-du-Sud, where from 1812 to 1816 he executed the most important part of his artistic work. At L'Islet he panelled the church nave and carved the cornice and eight statues. In the church at Sainte-Anne-de-la-Pocatière (La Pocatière) he carved the retable, the rood-screen (identical to the one at Saint-Roch-des-Aulnaies), and four statues representing the evangelists; he is also believed to have worked on the vaulting. At Saint-Roch-des-Aulnaies he made the churchwardens' pew, altered the pulpit, and signed various pieces of carving; in a later contract he undertook to execute paintings of the four evangelists. During the years 1812–16 he had Chrysostôme Perrault and Joseph Goupil as apprentices. On 7 June 1813 at Saint-Roch-des-Aulnaies he married Marie-Geneviève Audrie, daughter of the late Jean-Baptiste Audrie, a Saint-Jean-Port-Joli merchant, from whom she had an inheritance. They moved to Saint-Jean-Port-Joli, where Charron became a general merchant, the father of a family of three, and a leading figure in the village.

The death of Marie-Geneviève in 1817 came at a turning-point in Charron's career. At that time he gave up architecture and wood-carving to concentrate on commerce. The sums he received periodically from the *fabriques* for which he had worked were unencumbered by debt, and these, with the profits from his business, enabled him to make loans to a number of people and to invest in real estate; he even tried to buy part of the seigneury of L'Islet. This affluence was accompanied by the establishment of a new family. On 18 Jan. 1819 Charron married for the third time. His bride was Marie-Anastasie Babin, daughter of merchant Jean-Marie Babin, and they were to have ten children, six of whom reached adulthood.

Charron's prosperity came to an end in the mid 1830s, when an accounting became necessary. His second wife had died intestate, and the couple had no marriage contract. On reaching the age of majority their three children demanded their share of the inheritance. Charron had difficulty reaching a settlement with his eldest son, and then suffered the misfortune in October 1832 of being widowed a third time. By the end of the decade, when all the *fabriques* had finished paying what they owed him, he had begun to sell his property, and he probably liquidated his business early in the 1840s. He sold the house in the village in 1842 and retired to his land on the 3rd concession of Saint-Jean-Port-Joli. He died there, leaving his fourth wife, Marie Pélerin, whom he had married on 18 June 1834, almost destitute.

All recollection of Amable Charron and even his name have disappeared from the Côte-du-Sud. Of the churches he helped decorate, only the one at L'Islet is still standing. He does not seem to have possessed great artistic talent. At L'Islet he merely continued the work on the cornices begun by Jean* and Pierre-Florent* Baillairgé, and his statues have for the most part disappeared. In 1814 Joseph-Octave Plessis*, the bishop of Quebec, ordered those he had carved for the church of Sainte-Anne-de-la-Pocatière to be covered up. The caryatids on the rood-screen in the church at Rivière-Ouelle ended up as "decorations" in a fives-court at the Collège de Sainte-Anne-de-la-Pocatière. Charron's friend Philippe-Joseph Aubert* de Gaspé described him as an excellent hunter with "the strength of an athlete," and some of his actions show that he had a generous spirit.

GASTON DESCHÊNES

ANQ-M, CE1-10, 10 juill. 1785, 31 août 1790; CE1-59, 3 oct. 1808; 13, 16 août 1809; 7, 9 avril 1810; 3 juill. 1811; 7 févr., 6 mai 1812; CN1-96, 1er oct. 1808; 19 févr., 13 juill. 1812. ANQ-Q, CE2-18, 18 janv. 1819, 18 juin 1834, 10 mai 1844; CE2-25, 7 juin 1813; CN2-6, 12 oct. 1822; CN2-12, 21 sept., 18 oct. 1812; 23 mai 1813; 19 nov. 1814; 8–9, 11 juill. 1817; 31 déc. 1818; 30 déc. 1821; 18 août 1826; 22 févr. 1833; 21 août 1836; 7 janv. 1839; 7 déc. 1842; CN2-21, 22 juill. 1826; CN2-24, 4 août 1836; CN2-28, 6 nov. 1842; CN2-34, 21 juin 1841, 29 janv. 1844; CN2-35, 18 oct. 1812, 2 août 1814; CN2-48, 17 juin, 31 déc. 1818; 25 juin 1819; CN3-17, 23, 28 févr. 1798; 4 août 1805. MAC-CD, Fonds Morisset, 1, dossier Saint-Roch-des-Aulnaies; 2, dossier Amable Charron. L.C., House of Assembly, *Journals*, 1817, app.B. P.[-J.] Aubert de Gaspé, *Les anciens Canadiens* (17e éd., Québec, 1971); *Mémoires* (Ottawa, 1866; réimpr. Montréal, 1971). Léon Bélanger, *L'église de L'Islet, 1768–1968* (L'Islet, Qué., 1968). Gaston Deschênes, *Amable Charron et Chrysostôme Perrault, sculpteurs de Saint-Jean-Port-Joli* (La Pocatière, Qué., 1983). P.-H. Hudon, *Rivière-Ouelle de la Bouteillerie; 3 siècles de vie* (Ottawa, 1972). Wilfrid Lebon, *Histoire du collège de Sainte-Anne-de-la-Pocatière* (2v., Québec, 1948–49). Alexis Mailloux, *Histoire de l'Île-aux-Coudres depuis son établissement jusqu'à nos jours, avec ses traditions, ses légendes, ses coutumes* (Montréal, 1879). Gérard Ouellet, *Histoire de Sainte-Anne-de-la-Pocatière, 1672–1972* (La Pocatière, 1973); *Ma paroisse: Saint-Jean Port-Joly* (Québec, 1946). Angéline Saint-Pierre, *L'église de Saint-Jean-Port-Joli* (Québec, 1977). Émile Vaillancourt, *Une maîtrise d'art en Canada (1800–1823)* (Montréal, 1920). Marius Barbeau, "Louis Quévillon (1749–1823) (école des Écorres, à Saint-Vincent-de-Paul)," *Rev. trimestrielle canadienne*, 32 (1946): 3–17. Desbras, "Un justicier de la statuaire et de la peinture dans nos vieilles églises," *BRH*, 25 (1919): 153–54. J.-M. Gauvreau, "Médard Bourgault et l'école de sculpture sur bois de Saint-Jean-Port-Joli," *Technique* (Montréal), 15 (1940): 87–98. Ramsay Traquair, "The Church of St. John the Baptist at St. Jean Port-Joli, Quebec," Royal Architectural Institute of Canada, *Journal*, (Toronto), 16 (1939): 26–34.

CHASSEUR, PIERRE, gilder, wood-carver, and founder of a museum of natural history; b. 10 Oct. 1783 at Quebec; d. there 21 May 1842.

Not much is known of Pierre Chasseur's early years except that he probably came from a humble background. He received an elementary education and did an apprenticeship somewhere in the art of gilding. In 1815 he stated that he was a gilder in business in the *faubourg* Saint-Jean at Quebec. Following the custom of the period, he also did wood-carving. In 1816 he announced in the *Quebec Gazette* that he had for sale "a collection of French and English PRINTS," which purchasers could have him frame. The following year he silvered some frames for the *fabrique* of Notre-Dame at Quebec.

In 1824 Chasseur assembled a collection of natural history specimens at the house he occupied on Rue Sainte-Hélène (Rue McMahon) in Upper Town. He did not open his museum, however, until 1826. How Chasseur, a humble artisan, had come to natural history is an interesting question. At that time Quebec was experiencing a remarkable awakening of interest in the arts, letters, and science. In 1824 the Literary and Historical Society of Quebec was founded under the patronage of Lord Dalhousie [RAMSAY]. In 1826 some young local doctors launched the *Quebec Medical Journal*, which was broadly concerned with science and natural history, and Chasseur was a subscriber. The following year the same group, with the help of prominent figures such as Joseph BOUCHETTE and merchant William Sheppard*, an enthusiastic botanist, created the Société pour l'Encouragement des Sciences et des Arts en Canada.

The Quebec public was not, however, sufficiently interested in science to ensure the success of Chasseur's undertaking. From the year he opened his museum he had to seek government assistance. His first attempt failed, but in 1828 the Lower Canadian House of Assembly, where he had the support of several members including John NEILSON and Dr François Blanchet*, granted him £350. After spending this sum and going into debt for as much again to buy and fix up the house in which he had set up his museum, Chasseur had to go back to the assembly in 1830. This time he obtained £400.

Unfortunately, Chasseur's affairs did not improve, and after several unsuccessful attempts to obtain aid from the government, the naturalist was obliged to hand his collection over to the authorities in 1836. At that time the creation of a provincial museum with the items acquired by Chasseur was considered. According to an inventory done by Dr Jean-Baptiste Meilleur*, a politician and naturalist, the collection included 500 specimens of birds, nearly 100 of mammals, and some 40 of reptiles and fish. Unfamiliar with scientific classifications, Chasseur had tried to present the specimens in ways that would evoke their natural habitat and their habits. In keeping with contemporary interests he had also accumulated Amerindian artifacts, exotic objects such as a Chinese umbrella, and a few curios such as the axe wielded by a famous murderer and a bronze cannon supposedly lost in the St Lawrence by Jacques Cartier* or Giovanni da Verrazzano*.

What happened to the collection after the government took it over is uncertain. Several sources claim that the items disappeared in a fire some time between March 1836 and November 1837, probably in the house on Rue Sainte-Hélène. Other authorities, more numerous, say that the collection had been transferred to the new parliament building in 1836. The plan for a public museum was not pursued, however, likely because political events intervened. In 1841, when the government of the province of Canada was established in Kingston, Upper Canada, the Literary and Historical Society of Quebec was offered some of the empty rooms in the parliament building at Quebec for its library and museum. At the same time the society was given charge of Chasseur's museum, which was merged with its own. On 1 Feb. 1854 fire destroyed the parliament building, and all the collections were lost.

Pierre Chasseur himself was closely involved in the events of 1837 and 1838. As early as 1826 he had paraded his convictions by adopting the motto "Dieu et la Liberté." His circle of friends and acquaintances included numerous leaders of the Patriote party. In 1830 none other than Louis-Joseph Papineau* sang his praises in *La Minerve*. During the rebellion in 1837 the Comité Permanent de Québec met at his home. These activities led to his arrest on two occasions. On 11 Nov. 1837, following an inquiry by justice of the peace Robert Symes, he was arrested and imprisoned in the Quebec jail. He was released on 18 November, through a writ of habeas corpus issued by Chief Justice Jonathan SEWELL, on payment of personal bail of £500 and two other bail-bonds of £250 posted by Narcisse-Fortunat Belleau* and Dr Jean Blanchet*. In November 1838 he was again arrested, on a charge of high treason, and he was unable to obtain his release for five months. He died on 21 May 1842 at Quebec, a ruined man.

RAYMOND DUCHESNE

ANQ-Q, CE1-1, 23 mai 1842; CN1-230, 16 oct. 1815, 12 mai 1817; P-239/21. Arch. du séminaire de Chicoutimi (Chicoutimi, Qué.), Fonds Léon Provancher, lettre de J.-B. Meilleur à Léon Provancher, 16 mars 1869. MAC-CD, Fonds Morisset, 2, dossier Pierre Chasseur. PAC, MG 24, B2, 1–3; RG 4, A1, 351. Amable Berthelot, *Dissertation sur le canon de bronze que l'on voit dans le musée de M. Chasseur, à Québec* (Québec, 1830). *Journal de médecine de Québec*, 2 (1827). L.C., House of Assembly, *Journals*, 1828–33, 1835–36. *Le Canadien*, 16 août 1833, 8 avril 1836, 24 févr. 1840, 23 mai 1842. *La Minerve*, 25 févr. 1830. *Quebec Gazette*, 6, 13 June 1816; 1 May, 19 Oct. 1826. F.-M. Bibaud, *Le panthéon canadien* (A. et V. Bibaud; 1891). Fauteux, *Patriotes*. P.-G. Roy, *Fils de Québec*, 3: 184–86. I.[-F.-T.] Lebrun, *Tableau statistique et politique des deux Canadas* (Paris, 1833). J. R. Porter, *L'art de la dorure au Québec du XVIIIe siècle à nos jours* (Québec, 1975). "Combat entre un aigle et un enfant," *La Bibliothèque canadienne* (Montréal), 5 (1827): 159. Raymond Duchesne, "Magasin de curiosités ou musée scientifique? Le musée d'histoire naturelle de Pierre Chasseur à Québec (1824–1854)," *HSTC Bull.* (Thornhill, Ont.), 7 (1983): 59–79. Damase Potvin, "Le Musée Chasseur," *Carnets de zoologie de Québec* (Québec), 12 (1952), no.2: 47–50. Antoine Roy, "Les patriotes de la région de Québec pendant la rébellion de 1837–1838," *Cahiers des Dix*, 24 (1959): 241–54. Henri Têtu, "Le Musée Chasseur à Québec," *BRH*, 8 (1902): 251–52. "Zoologie du Bas-Canada," *La Bibliothèque canadienne*, 2 (1825–26): 74–75.

CHAUSSEGROS DE LÉRY, CHARLES-ÉTIENNE, office holder, JP, seigneur, militia officer, and politician; b. 30 Sept. 1774 at Quebec, son of Gaspard-Joseph Chaussegros* de Léry and Louise Martel de Brouague; m. there 25 Nov. 1799 Josephte Fraser, daughter of the late John Fraser, a judge in the Court of King's Bench, and they had six children, three of whom died young; d. 17 Feb. 1842 at Quebec and was buried on 24 February at Saint-François (Beauceville), Lower Canada.

Charles-Étienne Chaussegros de Léry came from a respectable family that was well off financially and had close ties with the colony's government. Thus he was able at an early age to start his career on solid foundations. His father used his influence in government circles to get him the post of clerk assistant and assistant to the translator for the Legislative Council in 1793. Charles-Étienne was then only 19. In 1794 he faced a choice: to complete the articling as a student-at-law which he had begun on 1 August in the office of Michel-Amable Berthelot* Dartigny, or to continue in government service. He preferred to devote himself to his duties with the Legislative Council and at some point gave up articling. In 1797 he succeeded Jacques-François Cugnet as translator to the same body, retaining his position as clerk assistant. As the years passed, his salary went from £100 to £360. He also was made clerk of the Court of Oyer and Terminer in 1805.

Chaussegros de Léry's reputation and privileged position with the authorities gained him appointments to serve as a commissioner on various occasions: in 1815 to examine claims to compensation under the Militia Men Indemnification Act for injuries suffered in the War of 1812, in 1817 to purchase seed grain for parishes in financial straits and to improve internal communications in the district of Quebec, in 1819 to receive the oath of allegiance from office holders, and in 1830 to build churches and presbyteries. In addition he had been serving as justice of the peace since at least 1815. His appointment to the Executive Council in 1826 and to the Special Council of Lower Canada in 1838 marked the high point of a career dedicated to government service.

At the same time as he was discharging his many public functions Chaussegros de Léry had a brilliant career in the militia. During the War of 1812 he excelled in his duties as deputy quartermaster general and deputy adjutant general. His competence was highy esteemed. In 1828 he was promoted quartermaster general of the militia of Lower Canada, and in 1830 he was made colonel commanding the five militia battalions of the town of Quebec; he retained these ranks for the rest of his life.

After the death of his father in 1797 Chaussegros de Léry had inherited part of his immense estate, which included the seigneuries of Rigaud De Vaudreuil, Gentilly, Le Gardeur Belle-Plaine, Beauvais, Perthuis, and Sainte-Barbe. Later he bought the shares of several other heirs to reconstitute finally the major part of his father's patrimony in landed property. For instance, his father's house on Rue Sainte-Famille at Quebec went to him in 1800 for £460. Certain deals, however, were not so simple and even gave rise to questionable procedures. In 1809 Charles-Étienne, acting as proxy for his brother Baron François-Joseph Chaussegros de Léry, who lived in France, sold the latter's inherited rights in the seigneury of Le Gardeur Belle-Plaine to Jean-Baptiste Noël. He neglected, however, to inform his brother of the transaction. On 9 Feb. 1818, through Antoine-Louis Juchereau* Duchesnay, the baron sold Charles-Étienne the undivided half of the seigneuries of Rigaud De Vaudreuil, Perthuis, and Sainte-Barbe for £1,550. The deed was immediately followed by a counter-deed by which Charles-Étienne and Juchereau Duchesnay agreed to hide from François-Joseph the sale of Le Gardeur Belle-Plaine concluded nine years previously. These two examples show that rumours circulating in 1818 about Charles-Étienne were far from unfounded.

A descendant of a prominent family, Charles-Étienne Chaussegros de Léry followed in his father's footsteps. He too owned large landed properties until his death. Despite some questionable transactions he was a social success, owing to his personal talents and especially to his close relations with the government. Entrusted with important positions both in public administration and in the militia, he was loyal to the authorities, and this unfailing loyalty earned him appointment not only to the Executive Council but to the Special Council.

MARC DUVAL and RENALD LESSARD

ANQ-Q, CE1-1, 1er oct. 1774, 25 nov. 1799; CN1-178, 18 sept. 1818; CN1-230, 1er août 1794, 25 nov. 1799, 9 oct. 1800, 5 avril 1809, 9 févr. 1818; P-40/10; P-386/2; T11-1/207, no.162; 2734, no.129; 3611, no.162; ZQ6-45-3, 24 févr. 1842. ASQ, Séminaire, 202, nos.125–26. L.C., House of Assembly, *Journals*, 1795, 1798–1834. *Le Canadien*, 18 févr. 1842. *Quebec Gazette*, 8 June, 30 Nov. 1815; 13 March, 10 April, 1 May 1817. F.-J. Audet, "Les législateurs du Bas-Canada." Le Jeune, *Dictionnaire*, 1: 379–80. *Officers of British forces in Canada* (Irving). *Quebec almanac*, 1794. P.-G. Roy, *Inventaire des papiers de Léry conservés aux Archives de la province de Québec* (3v., Québec, 1939–40). Turcotte, *Le Conseil législatif*. [François Daniel], *Le vicomte C. de Léry, lieutenant-général de l'empire français, ingénieur en chef de la grande armée, et sa famille* (Montréal, 1867). P.-G. Roy, "La famille Chaussegros de Léry," *BRH*, 40 (1934): 577–614.

CHAZELLE, JEAN-PIERRE, Roman Catholic priest, Jesuit, and missionary; b. 12 Jan. 1789 in Saint-Just-en-Bas, France, son of Pierre Chazelle, a farm labourer, and Blandine Chalette; d. 4 Sept. 1845 in Green Bay, Wis.

Jean-Pierre Chazelle did his classical and theological studies in France at the Séminaire de Montbrison, near Lyon. He was ordained priest on 14 June 1812 and immediately began teaching philosophy, theology, and rhetoric in the seminary; he reputedly taught Jean-Baptiste-Marie Vianney, who became famous as the Curé d'Ars and was eventually canonized. Chazelle was made parish priest at Moingt in 1816, and then served as military chaplain to the 28th infantry regiment of the Légion du Gard in 1817 and to the École Royale et Militaire at La Flèche in 1819.

Wishing to become a Jesuit, on 1 March 1822, at 33 years of age, Chazelle entered the noviciate of Montrouge, near Paris. At that time the Jesuits were in wide demand for a variety of undertakings. After six months' probation Chazelle was made professor of theology at the Jesuit theological college in Paris. Appointed to the Collège de Montmorillon, near Poitiers, in 1823, he was to serve in turn as minister, assistant, and rector. In 1828 the Jesuits were excluded by ordinance from the field of teaching in France, and with the revolution in July 1830 they were expelled from the country.

Chazelle, who was then in Bordeaux, was appointed superior of Jesuit missions in North America and left for the United States on 19 Nov. 1830 with two other Jesuit priests and a brother of the order. The four were responding to a request that Benoît-Joseph Flaget, bishop of the diocese of Bardstown, Ky, had made in 1828 to the Jesuits' provincial in France, Nicolas Godinot. They arrived in New Orleans in February 1831 and were detained by the winter season. There they examined carefully Bishop Léo-Raymond de Neckère's proposals for carrying on their work in his diocese instead. When Chazelle set off again in April, he left two of his companions behind and went with the third to the diocese of Bardstown. Bishop Flaget welcomed them warmly but could no longer offer them St Joseph's College as he had promised in his letter to Godinot. Thinking that the Jesuits would not come, he had entrusted that institution to his secular clergy. Chazelle considered returning to New Orleans, but in the end Flaget put him in charge of St Mary's Seminary, which had been founded by William Byrne around 1819. Under Chazelle's guidance it soon offered more advanced courses and began to expand remarkably.

In 1839 Chazelle received a letter from Joseph-Vincent Quiblier*, the superior of the Séminaire de Saint-Sulpice in Montreal. Quiblier invited Chazelle in the name of the bishop of Montreal, Jean-Jacques LARTIGUE, to come in August as preacher for the first sacerdotal retreat to be held in the diocese. Despite the troubled times in Lower Canada and the discretion essential on Chazelle's part, his stay there did not go unnoticed. His presence rekindled memories of the Jesuits, whose past deeds had left a lasting impression. Their return to the province was keenly desired on all sides.

When Ignace Bourget* succeeded Lartigue as bishop of Montreal in 1840, he wanted to pursue his predecessor's desire to bring Jesuits to Lower Canada. In 1841 he went to Rome and sought out their general, Jean Roothaan, to request a few men for one of the Lower Canadian colleges and for the Indian missions. Chazelle was also in Rome, where he had been sent by Flaget, and he met Bourget, whom he knew from his stay in Montreal. Soon Chazelle was named superior of the Jesuits in Canada and charged with recruiting the necessary personnel.

On 31 May 1842 Chazelle arrived in Montreal at the head of a group of nine Jesuits. Staying temporarily in the bishop's palace, in July he agreed to take on the parish of Notre-Dame-de-la-Prairie-de-la-Madeleine (Nativité-de-la-Très-Sainte-Vierge) at La Prairie, near Montreal, whose curé, Michael POWER, had just been named the first bishop of Toronto and was preparing to depart for his diocese. Chazelle gave sermons, conducted retreats, and served as a military chaplain. He refused, however, to take charge of the Collège de Chambly, and the Sulpicians were very reluctant to hand over the Petit Séminaire de Montréal to him. Furthermore, the Jesuit noviciate opened in the bishop's palace attracted no candidates and had to be moved to La Prairie in July 1843.

Meanwhile, in the summer of 1842 Bishop Power and the archbishop of New York, John Joseph Hughes, were proposing to bring Jesuits into their dioceses, and General Roothaan and the provincial of France, Clément Boulanger*, were considering the matter. Early in the autumn Power invited Chazelle to come and preach a sacerdotal retreat prior to the synod marking the inauguration of his diocese. During his stay in Upper Canada Chazelle became enthusiastic about the missions to the Indians who had been evangelized by his predecessors at the time of the early Canadian martyrs [*see* Isaac Jogues*]. That November Power made a formal request to Roothaan, and in July 1843 two French Jesuits, Pierre Point and Jean-Pierre Choné, arrived in Toronto, where they were met by Chazelle. Some days later they took charge of the parish of L'Assomption at Sandwich (Windsor), the point of departure for the missions Chazelle was to found on Walpole Island, Manitoulin Island in Georgian Bay, and Sault Ste Marie, in Upper Canada. On 31 July 1844, at Power's request, the Jesuit mission in the Canadas was split: Chazelle was appointed superior of the Upper Canadian section, and Félix Martin* superior of the Lower Canadian [*see* Clément Boulanger].

On 4 Sept. 1845, in the midst of his apostolic activity, Chazelle died at Green Bay. He had been travelling through the United States on his way to Sault Ste Marie. His colleagues lost in him a totally committed person who hesitated before no task. With a temperament that seemed unable to tolerate inaction, Chazelle had a quality of obedience which was linked to an utter open-heartedness and a faith in Providence. These qualities explain the notable achievements of a life given to teaching, administrative duties, and sacerdotal retreats.

GEORGES-ÉMILE GIGUÈRE

The records relating to Jean-Pierre Chazelle and to his works are largely held at the Arch. de la Compagnie de Jésus, Prov. du Canada français (Saint-Jérôme, Qué.), Fonds général and Sér. A, B, and D. Additional material is in Archivum Romanum Societatis Iesu (Rome), Fonds Missio Kentuckeiensis and Missio Canadensis; the author has in his possession microfilm copies of many of the items from this repository.

ACAM, 465.103; 901.055, 846-13; 901.062. AD, Loire (Saint-Étienne), État civil, Saint-Just-en-Bas, 12 janv. 1789. Allaire, *Dictionnaire*. G.-É. Giguère, "La restauration de la Compagnie de Jésus au Canada, 1839–1857" (thèse de PHD, univ. de Montréal, 1965). Laval Laurent, *Québec et l'Église aux États-Unis sous Mgr Briand et Mgr Plessis* (Montréal, 1945). Édouard Lecompte, *Les jésuites du Canada au XIXe siècle* (Montréal, 1920), 27–55, 59–70, 82–84, 87–90, 116–17, 163–64. F. X. Curran, "Father Pierre Chazelle, S.J., 1789–1845," *Catholic Hist. Rev.* (Washington), 41 (1955): 1–17; "The Jesuits in Kentucky, 1831–1846," *Mid-America* (Chicago), 24 (1953): 223–46. F. J. Nelligan, "Father Pierre Chazelle, S.J., 1789–1845," *Canadian Messenger of the Sacred Heart* (Toronto), 58 (1955): 383–89. Léon Pouliot, "Notes sur le court supériorat du P. Chazelle à Montréal (1842–1844)," *Lettres du Bas-Canada* (Montréal), 11 (1957): 97–101; "La première retraite ecclésiastique du diocèse de Montréal: 21–30 août 1839," *La Semaine religieuse de Montréal* (Montréal), 98 (1939): 230–36.

CHÉNIER, JEAN-OLIVIER, physician and Patriote; b. 9 Dec. 1806, probably in Lachine, Lower

Canada, or possibly in Montreal, and baptized the following day in Montreal, son of Victor Chénier and Cécile Morel; d. 14 Dec. 1837 in Saint-Eustache, Lower Canada.

Jean-Olivier Chénier belonged to a farming family that also had some involvement in trade. His grandfather, François Chénier, had married Suzanne-Amable Blondeau, daughter of a family of wealthy merchants established in Montreal by the end of the 18th century. When Jean-Olivier was baptized, his godfather was Jean-Baptiste Trudeau (Truteau), a fur trader and explorer. Chénier seems to have owed his education to a patron, Montreal doctor René-Joseph Kimber. Wishing to follow in Kimber's footsteps, in 1820 Chénier began training under his guidance. He was licensed to practise on 20 Feb. 1828, when he was 21.

The young doctor moved that year to Saint-Benoît (Mirabel), a village in York riding, where he soon became involved in politics. The preceding year, in a confrontation between the House of Assembly and Governor Lord Dalhousie [RAMSAY] over the question of supplies, the governor had prorogued parliament in March, and called a general election for July. When the new house chose Louis-Joseph Papineau* as speaker, Dalhousie prorogued it in November, attempting thus to assert the rights of the crown and the colonial executive. Those supporting the assembly's rights retaliated by holding public meetings, organizing the famous petition to the imperial parliament bearing 80,000 signatures, and sending a delegation [*see* Denis-Benjamin Viger*] to London. York riding took an active part in this dispute. In the July elections York voters chose the Patriote party candidates, Jacques Labrie*, a doctor at Saint-Eustache, and Jean-Baptiste Lefebvre, a merchant in Vaudreuil, over those of the English party, Nicolas-Eustache Lambert* Dumont, the co-seigneur of Mille-Îles, and John Simpson*, the customs collector at Coteau-du-Lac. At Saint-Benoît in particular a symbolic gesture of opposition to the authorities was made by notary Jean-Joseph Girouard*, a captain in the Rivière-du-Chêne militia battalion, and his political friends, who neglected that summer to proceed with the annual embodying of the militia. In 1828 Chénier was one of seven persons, including Labrie and Girouard, accused of obstructionism by the officer commanding the militia, Lieutenant-Colonel Lambert Dumont.

Following the accidental death of Jean-Baptiste Lefebvre, Chénier in 1829 joined in helping William Henry Scott*, a Saint-Eustache merchant, to win election for York. In the 1830 general election, the first to be held after a redrawing of the electoral map that split York into the three ridings of Deux-Montagnes, Vaudreuil, and Ottawa, Chénier assisted Labrie and Scott in winning Deux-Montagnes. On 26 Sept. 1831, at Saint-Eustache, he married Labrie's daughter Zéphirine. Labrie died a month later, and in December 1831 Chénier was largely instrumental in getting Girouard elected for Deux-Montagnes. In June 1832, shortly after the by-election in Montreal West during which troops opened fire and killed three people [*see* Daniel Tracey*], he was one of a group of leading citizens who urged the freeholders of Deux-Montagnes County to attend a meeting at Saint-Benoît "for the purpose of agreeing upon the most effective ways of preventing monopoly, speculation, and any selective system in the matter of settling uncultivated lands." At the ensuing meeting he was appointed to a committee of 30 persons, 6 from Saint-Benoît, charged with looking out for the Canadians' interests. According to most historians, Chénier did not leave Saint-Benoît to live in Saint-Eustache until 1834.

The 1834 elections, held after the 92 Resolutions had been passed, revealed in striking fashion the popularity of the Patriote party. Scott and Girouard won in Deux-Montagnes, despite violence and intimidation. These elections demonstrated the split between the so-called lower and upper ends of the riding – the part comprising the villages of Saint-Eustache, Saint-Benoît, and Sainte-Scholastique (Mirabel), which had been settled earlier and was largely French-speaking, and the part taking in the seigneury of Argenteuil and the townships of Chatham and Grenville, which had been populated more recently and was in good measure English-speaking. In his description of the celebration that was held after the elections, the author of *Relation historique des événements de l'élection du comté du lac des Deux Montagnes en 1834; épisode propre à faire connaître l'esprit public dans le Bas-Canada* – possibly Girouard himself – mentioned Chénier as one of the principal architects of the victory of the Patriote cause. He added: "But it was to Dr Chénier especially that the voters showed how satisfied they were with his energetic and tireless leadership and his courage in the struggle; throughout, his lady, the worthy daughter of the late Dr Labrie, had unceasingly welcomed into her home, night and day, the habitants from outlying regions who came by the hundreds to ask her for shelter, since there was no inn in the village open to Canadians. They expressed their gratitude to this lady openly."

In the years following, Chénier was active in the public meetings held in Deux-Montagnes County. On 11 April 1836, for example, along with Luc-Hyacinthe Masson*, a doctor from Saint-Benoît, he served as secretary for a meeting at Saint-Benoît where one of several resolutions urged people to abstain from buying "goods and products of British factories" and the idea of founding national factories was put forward. At the big meeting held on 1 June 1837 at Sainte-Scholastique as part of the protest against Lord John Russell's resolutions, Chénier was named to the permanent committee charged with giving effect to the meeting's proceedings. He reportedly made known his determination at that time, declaring, "What I say, I think, and I shall do it; follow me and I give you permission to kill me if ever you see me flee." In the period from June to November 1837 the committee organized a dozen meetings. Chénier was one of its leading members, along with Girouard, Masson, and Joseph-Amable Berthelot, a Saint-Eustache notary.

There was constant friction in Deux-Montagnes County in the summer of 1837. The Patriotes' opponents complained that they were being subjected to harassment and even violence. They resorted to making denunciations to the authorities. The government at first intended to hold an investigation and proceed with arrests, but decided instead to brandish threats of dismissal; it succeeded mainly in prompting the resignation of some justices of the peace and militia officers. A meeting at Saint-Benoît on 1 October, described by the Montreal newspaper *Le Populaire* in an article entitled "La révolution commence," decided that the time had come to elect justices of the peace and to let the militiamen in each parish elect their officers. Chénier served as secretary for the subsequent meeting held on the Saint-Joachim concession at Sainte-Scholastique on 15 October, and he was one of the 22 magistrates who were voted in. On 23 October he participated with Girouard and Scott in the Assemblée des Six Comtés at Saint-Charles-sur-Richelieu. At that time Scott stood out as the principal Patriote leader in Saint-Eustache, with Chénier close behind. Scott, Chénier, and Joseph Robillard, a mason and merchant, were the only ones who were members of both the permanent committee and the improvised judicial and militia organizations. Among the other leaders were notary Berthelot, surveyor Émery Féré, and farmer Jean-Baptiste Bélanger.

When arrests began on 16 Nov. 1837, Chénier was on the list of people for whom warrants had been issued. The following day Amury GIROD arrived in Deux-Montagnes County and, claiming that he had the backing of Louis-Joseph Papineau and a small council of war held at Varennes, near Montreal, with Papineau, Edmund Bailey O'Callaghan*, and Jean-Philippe Boucher-Belleville*, he imposed himself as general of the forces in the county that had been mobilized to resist and to set up a provisional government. But the "general," a striking figure who was surrounded with aides-de-camp recruited from among young Montreal lawyers, had to leave a good deal of autonomy to Chénier, who was in command of the camp at Saint-Eustache, since he himself had to travel to and fro between Saint-Benoît and Saint-Eustache. Chénier had his men and Girod his own when the two groups tried to seize arms belonging to the Indians and the Hudson's Bay Company at Lac-des-Deux-Montagnes (Oka).

The purchase and seizure of arms and food and the conduct of intelligence activities and mustering, rather than actual military training, made up Chénier's day to day work as commander. After a defeat at Saint-Charles-sur-Richelieu on 25 November the Patriote leaders found it difficult to keep up their men's morale. Early in December Scott and Féré, who were against the use of arms, withdrew from the movement, considering it thenceforth hopeless. The parish priest of Saint-Eustache, Jacques PAQUIN, his assistant, François-Xavier Desève, and their friend François-Magloire Turcotte, the curé of Sainte-Rose (at Laval), tried to point out that it was madness to entertain any notion of beating the forces of the government, now preparing to attack the insurgents.

On 14 Dec. 1837 Sir John Colborne*'s troops, who had come from Montreal by way of Île Jésus, and local volunteers under Maximilien Globensky* attacked Chénier's men. They had barricaded themselves in the church, presbytery, convent, and surrounding houses in Saint-Eustache. Chénier's followers came mainly from Saint-Eustache, Sainte-Scholastique, and Saint-Jérôme. Girod had made off in the direction of Saint-Benoît, and the handful of young men from Montreal, who claimed they belonged to the central organization, had also left the scene. It was an uneven confrontation: of Chénier's force, smaller in number and relatively poorly armed, some 40 men whose names are known were killed, and there were probably as many more unknown victims. Chénier himself was killed as he was trying to get out of the burning church. He had just turned 31.

There is some question whether the victorious British army treated Chénier's body with respect [*see* Daniel ARNOLDI] . Much has been written about the matter, particularly in the period 1883–84, when Charles-Auguste-Maximilien Globensky published *La rébellion de 1837 à Saint-Eustache* and Laurent-Olivier David* *Les patriotes de 1837–1838*. In 1952–53 once more, in the *Revue de l'université Laval*, Émile Castonguay, using the pseudonym Bernard Dufebvre, defended Globensky's thesis and Robert-Lionel Séguin that of David; and as recently as the 1970s the question resurfaced in the Saint-Eustache newspaper *La Victoire*. The facts themselves are less important than the implied symbolic significance. In any event, the controversy does not concern Chénier himself so much as it does the conduct of the British soldiers.

The rather extraordinary story of the monuments proposed to Chénier's glory also demonstrates the importance that a matter of symbolic value may possess. In 1885, in the context of the David–Globensky debate and the Riel affair [*see* Louis Riel*], it was suggested that a monument be raised to Chénier at Saint-Eustache, the initiative being taken by David Marsil, a doctor who was mayor of Saint-Eustache from 1871 to 1875 and a defeated Liberal candidate in 1878, and by his political friends. But the opponents of the project used their influence to block it – and even to turn the occasion into an unveiling of a commemorative plaque in honour of Jacques Paquin. In 1891 Marsil thought that he could have Chénier's remains transferred to the monument in memory of the Patriotes who had died in 1837–38, raised in 1858 in the Catholic cemetery of Notre-Dame-des-Neiges in Montreal. He had the body exhumed from the section of the cemetery of Saint-Eustache reserved for those who had died unbaptized. The words "Here rest his remains" were even engraved under Chénier's name on the monument. But Édouard-Charles Fabre*, the archbishop of Montreal, refused to allow the transfer of the remains and the ceremony. A committee created in 1893 that Marsil served on, which could count on Honoré Mercier*'s influence, gave Chénier his monument in Square Viger in Montreal on 24 April 1895. In 1937, on the centenary of his death, a monument to Chénier was raised in Saint-Eustache. His remains were held by the Société Saint-Jean-Baptiste de Montréal until July 1987, when they were interred in the consecrated portion of the cemetery at Saint-Eustache.

Chénier left a wife and also a young daughter who lived for only a short time after his death. His wife became a schoolteacher and soon married Louis-Auguste Desrochers, an office holder and music teacher. In 1852, having examined her claims, the Rebellion Losses Commission paid her a small indemnity for her share in the property that she had owned in community with Chénier and that she had lost when their house was burned in 1837. She won her case thanks in part to Jean-Joseph Girouard and his second wife, Émélie Berthelot, with whom she was friends. Other members of his family survived Chénier: a brother, Victor, who lived at Longueuil near Montreal, two sisters who went to live at Montebello, and a cousin, Félix, a young notary at Saint-Eustache who also had been involved in the events of 1837–38.

According to an oral statement reported by Joseph-Arthur-Calixte Éthier in a lecture delivered and published in 1905, Jean-Olivier Chénier was "a little man with broad shoulders, well built, not disagreeable, polite, but hardly timid." There is no question that he died bravely. Of course, those who hold the general view that the cause was legitimate and the action right will speak of courage and sincere generosity, whereas those who hold the contrary view will speak rather of stubbornness and baneful influence. Émile Dubois, the historian of the rebellion of 1837 in the Lac-des-Deux-Montagnes region, gives a qualified but on the whole sympathetic picture of Chénier's character. Fernand Ouellet, historian of the entire insurrectional movement, though he reproaches the Patriote leaders for their ambivalence towards the resort to arms and their tendency up to the very end not to take upon themselves the consequences of the mobilization that their words and actions had led to, does make an exception for Wolfred Nelson* at Saint-Denis on the Richelieu and for Chénier at Saint-Eustache. In his view, those two distinguished themselves by the coherence and consistency of their conduct.

JEAN-PAUL BERNARD

ANQ-M, CE1-51, 10 déc. 1806; CE6-11, 26 sept. 1831, 14 déc. 1837. ANQ-Q, E17/13, nos.665, 691, 695, 744; E17/14, nos.767, 770, 773, 775, 779–81, 788, 793, 800. BVM-G, Fonds Ægidius Fauteux, notes compilées par Ægidius Fauteux sur les patriotes de 1837–38 dont les noms commencent par la lettre C, carton 3. PAC, RG 4, B28, 51: 1238–41. Émélie Berthelot-Girouard, "Les journaux d'Émélie Berthelot-Girouard," Béatrice Chassé, édit., ANQ *Rapport*, 1975: 1–104. [J.-J. Girouard], *Relation historique des événements de l'élection du comté du lac des Deux Montagnes en 1834; épisode propre à faire connaître l'esprit public dans le Bas-Canada* (Montréal, 1835; réimpr. Québec, 1968). [P.-G. Roy], *Premier rapport de la Commission des monuments historiques de la province de Québec, 1922–1923* (Québec, 1923), 182, 243–46. F.-M. Bibaud, *Le panthéon canadien* (A. et V. Bibaud; 1891), 56. Borthwick, *Hist. and biog. gazetteer*. Fauteux, *Patriotes*, 174–76. Wallace, *Macmillan dict.*

Béatrice Chassé, "Le notaire Girouard, patriote et rebelle" (thèse de D. ès L., univ. Laval, Québec, 1974). L.-O. David, *Le héros de Saint-Eustache: Jean-Olivier Chénier* (Montréal, s.d.); *Patriotes*, 45–52, 147–51. Émile Dubois, *Le feu de la Rivière-d u-Chêne; étude historique sur le mouvement insurrectionnel de 1837 au nord de Montréal* (Saint-Jérôme, Qué., 1937), 122. J.-A.-C. Éthier, *Conférence sur Chénier* (Montréal, 1905). Filteau, *Hist. des patriotes* (1975), 369–71. [C.-A.-M. Globensky], *La rébellion de 1837 à Saint-Eustache avec un exposé préliminaire de la situation politique du Bas-Canada depuis la cession* (Québec, 1883; réimpr. Montréal, 1974), 220–24. Laurin, *Girouard & les patriotes*, 45. Raymond Paiement, *La bataille de Saint-Eustache* (Montréal, [1975]). Gilles Boileau, "Mais qui donc était Chénier?" *La Victoire* (Saint-Eustache, Qué.), 14 oct. 1970: 12. C.-M. Boissonnault, "La bataille de Saint-Eustache," *Rev. de l'univ. Laval*, 6 (1951–52): 425–41. Gaston Derome, "Le patriote Chénier," *BRH*, 59 (1953): 222. Bernard Dufebvre [Émile Castonguay], "À propos du cœur de Chénier," *Rev. de l'univ. Laval*, 7 (1952–53): 905–10; "Encore à propos des patriotes," *Rev. de l'univ. Laval*, 8 (1953–54): 41–48. Ægidius Fauteux, "Le docteur Chénier," *BRH*, 38 (1932): 715–17. Clément Laurin, "David Marsil, médecin et patriote de Saint-Eustache," Soc. d'hist. de Deux-Montagnes, *Cahiers* (Saint-Eustache), été 1978: 27–37. R.-L. Séguin, "À propos du cœur de Chénier," *Rev. de l'univ. Laval*, 7: 724–29; "La dépouille de Chénier fut-elle outragée?" *BRH*, 58 (1952): 183–88; "Questions et réponses à propos des patriotes," *Rev. de l'univ. Laval*, 8: 32–40. Soc. d'hist. de Deux-Montagnes, *Cahiers*, 5 (1982), no.2.

CHEWETT (Chewitt), WILLIAM, surveyor, office holder, JP, and militia officer; b. 21 Dec. 1753 in London; m. 1791 Isabella Macdonell, and they had four children; d. 24 Sept. 1849 in Toronto.

Having graduated as a hydrographic engineer from the East India College in London, William Chewett sailed in 1771 to Quebec where, three years later, he entered the service of the deputy surveyor general, John Collins*. During the American siege of Quebec in 1775–76, Chewett drew plans of the fortifications and determined the distances of the enemy batteries. In 1777 he was appointed acting paymaster at Île aux Noix and Fort St Johns (Saint-Jean-sur-Richelieu) where he worked until 1785. He then returned to Quebec and the Surveyor General's Office.

Chewett was a dedicated office holder whose career was characterized by numerous frustrations. The Executive Council's decision in 1791 to discontinue the settlement program for military claims the next year jeopardized his position, causing the disappointed surveyor to write Collins: "I now find I have been serving my whole life for nothing, . . . there is no surveyor in the same line as myself, that has the same right to expect a continuation from having been always on service. . . . I trust you will be able to find me some employment either in our department or some other before the expiration."

That trust was well founded and by 1792 he had secured a spot in the administration of the new province of Upper Canada. Chewett had hoped for the post of surveyor general, which went instead to David William SMITH. He always maintained that Lieutenant Governor John Graves Simcoe*'s "promises to me were numerous, and well known to the principal people of almost the whole of the two provinces, from himself and all of which have ended in a mouthful of moonshine." He blamed "false insinuations and unfavourable reports" for his failure. Chewett became senior surveyor and draftsman. He lived with his family in Williamsburg Township until 1796, when they moved to the new capital at York (Toronto). He received another disappointment in 1798 when he did not succeed Christopher Robinson* as deputy surveyor of woods; President Peter Russell* would not support his appointment because he feared the additional responsibilities would hamper Chewett's effective performance in his other duties.

In 1800 Chewett became registrar of the Surrogate Court for the Home District. The following year he served as returning officer in the by-election won by Angus Macdonell* (Collachie) in Durham, Simcoe, and the East Riding of York. That same year Collachie was dismissed as clerk of the House of Assembly but Chewett's lobbying to replace him was unsuccessful, despite strong support from Smith and Chief Justice John Elmsley*. When Smith returned to England in July 1802 he left joint supervision of the surveyor general's office to Chewett and the first clerk, Thomas Ridout*. Chewett once again sought the surveyor-generalship. Smith resigned in 1804 and, although Lieutenant Governor Peter Hunter* had promised to recommend Chewett as his successor, Charles Burton WYATT was appointed. During his tenure in office Wyatt attempted to have Chewett removed from office but the Executive Council would not agree. Wyatt himself was suspended in 1807 by Lieutenant Governor Francis Gore*, whereupon Chewett and Ridout again assumed temporary responsibility for the office. In the fall of 1809 Ridout, with Gore's blessing, went to England to lobby for the vacant office. Chewett was left in sole charge until Ridout returned the following year with the surveyor general's commission. In an apparent act of compensation by Gore, Chewett received the first clerk's job to add to his collection of offices.

In addition to his various posts in the surveyor general's office, Chewett was a justice of the peace in the Home District for many years. He had a long association with the militia, serving as a captain first in the Eastern District and later at York. By the War of 1812 he commanded the 3rd York Militia. He acted as a draftsman to Major-General Isaac Brock* at Detroit and along the Niagara frontier, and when in April 1813 Major-General Sir Roger Hale Sheaffe* retreated from York, Chewett and William Allan*, the senior militia officers, negotiated the terms of capitulation with the victorious American force. During the war Chewett was also a member of the Loyal and Patriotic Society of Upper Canada. He retired from the militia in 1818 because of failing health.

As a surveyor and draftsman Chewett drew plans and elevations for, and supervised the construction of, residences for Simcoe, Elmsley, and Smith. As well, in 1796 he surveyed with Æneas Shaw* the reserves for York's church, jail, court-house, and market square. He may also have assisted Smith in the preparation of the first printed map of Upper Canada which was published in 1800. Later Chewett advised Ridout on drafting a new map of the province to replace the one destroyed during the American occupation of York in 1813. Although he frequently mapped townships and districts, as well as the province as a whole, his name is found on only one published map, issued in London in 1813. After Ridout's death in 1829 Chewett became acting surveyor general for the last time. Upon learning that Samuel Proudfoot Hurd* had succeeded Ridout, Chewett sought permission to retire. It was granted and, after Hurd took up office in 1832, he retired on full pay.

Throughout his career, William Chewett's ambition was consistently thwarted. He had been acting surveyor general often but, despite his long service, he never won the long-sought office, or a seat on the Executive Council. His last memorial, to Lieutenant

Governor Sir John Colborne* and the House of Assembly in 1831, reveals an embittered man frustrated by colonial patronage and societal barriers. Yet as a surveyor he compiled, copied, and submitted more maps than any of his contemporaries (and probably more than anyone in the history of the surveyor general's office), making in the process an extensive contribution to the settlement of Upper Canada and the permanent cartographic record of the province's development.

RICHARD J. SIMPSON

Extracts from a journal kept by William Chewett for 1792–93 comprise most of the "Biographical sketch of the late Colonel Chewett" printed in the Assoc. of Ontario Land Surveyors, *Proc.* (Toronto), 1890: 101–16. An engraving of Chewett made from a miniature on ivory by Hoppner Francis Meyer is reproduced on the frontispiece to the volume and discussed on p.101 of the biography; the original engraving is in the association's library in Toronto.

ANQ-Q, E21/356. AO, MS 35, unbound papers, William Chewitt and J. B. Robinson, report of committee of Loyal and Patriotic Society, 1 May 1815; MS 75, Russell to John Wentworth, 17 Dec. 1798; MS 537, Chewitt to Ridout, 20 April 1812; MU 2036, 1812, no.6; RG 1, A-I-1, 1: 3; 2: 55–57, 61–65; 8: 383; 14: 116, 136, 138–39, 160, 166–67; 15: 116; 16: 79, 114, 202; 17: 16; 18: 14, 20; 40: 163, 169; 49: 527, 540, 543, 639, 1071–72; A-I-2, 14: 1658; 16: 2471, 3472, 3486; 20: 3776–77; 22: 11–12; 25: 203; A-I-4; A-I-7; A-II-1; B-IV; C-I-9, 2: 9; CB-1, box 42; RG 22, ser.155. MTRL, John Elmsley letter-book, 24 Nov. 1800; Peter Russell papers, misc. letters, 7 Nov. 1796, January–May 1797; office-book, 1796; D. W. Smith papers, B7: 3, 23. PAC, RG 5, A1: 2306, 5149. *Town of York, 1793–1815* (Firth). U.C., House of Assembly, *Journal*, 1831–32, app., 176–99. Scadding, *Toronto of old* (1873).

CHINIC, MARTIN (baptized **Cheniqui**, he signed **Chinnequy** in 1791 but was using Chinic by 1794), merchant, JP, and office holder; b. 10 Jan. 1770 at Quebec, son of Martin Chenneque* and Marie-Louise Grenete; m. first 15 Nov. 1791 Julienne-Claire Enouille, *dit* Lanois, and they had a son and four daughters; m. secondly 20 Jan. 1817 Marie-Antoinette Bourdages, widow of Louis Dubord; d. 28 March 1836 in the St Lawrence River.

Martin Chinic followed his father into small-scale mercantile and shipping business in Lower Town Quebec. By July 1792 he was a merchant on the Place du Marché (Place Notre-Dame), but in June 1795 he was a clerk of "Mr. Caldwell" (probably Henry Caldwell*). During the period 1794–1806, and evidently on his own account, Chinic registered at least three vessels, one with Louis Borgia (a merchant and neighbour of his father), and conducted a trade in the sale of flour, biscuit, spirits, "imported goods," timber, cordage, sailcloth, and other commodities.

The presence of the Chinic family in Quebec's business circles, though not dominant, was constant through most of the 19th century. Martin's son, Joseph-Martin, entered business in January 1815 with a future brother-in-law, Alexandre-Augustin Vézina, as a commission merchant and auctioneer, and later with another relation, Joseph Measam. In 1816 Martin Chinic, François QUIROUET, and his brother, Olivier Quirouet, formed a partnership as auctioneers, brokers, and commission merchants, one of a number of such businesses serving Quebec's position as a major importing and trans-shipment centre. Four years later Quirouet, Chinic et Compagnie was dissolved, but Chinic and Olivier Quirouet flourished until 1826 as auctioneers, shipping agents, and commission merchants on Rue du Sault-au-Matelot under the name of Chinic et Quirouet.

By the early 1820s Chinic had achieved a position of some prestige within Quebec's community of Canadian businessmen. On about 18 occasions between October 1820 and April 1824 he was appointed weekly director of the Quebec Bank, in which he was a shareholder. (A third of this bank's directors were French-speaking between 1818, when it was founded, and 1835.) In 1826 he petitioned, unsuccessfully, for eventual appointment as king's auctioneer. He was on the committee of the Education Society of the District of Quebec [*see* Joseph-François PERRAULT] (1821), received a commission of the peace for the Quebec district (1826), and was appointed a commissioner to establish a market in the *faubourg* Saint-Roch (1831). As well, he was a trustee of the *fabrique* of Notre-Dame parish. Widely respected, Chinic was among several Canadians belonging in 1829 to a newly formed branch of the Society of the Friends of Ireland in Quebec. Six years later, he presided at a banquet which formed part of celebrations to revive devotion to St Louis.

Joseph-Martin Chinic died prematurely in 1828, leaving his father to raise his sons, Joseph-Martin and Guillaume-Eugène*; the latter became a prominent hardware merchant, the fourth generation of the family in business at Quebec. On 28 March 1836 Chinic drowned in the St Lawrence. His body was recovered on 1 April and the following day was buried in the cathedral. The inventory of his goods suggests that he was dealing in cloth, spirits, and other articles at the time of his death. Chinic evidently did not die in prosperity, since his widow renounced her succession as being "more onerous than profitable."

DAVID ROBERTS

ANQ-Q, CE1-1, 10 janv. 1770, 15 nov. 1791, 20 janv. 1817, 2 avril 1836; CN1-49, 26 sept. 1826; CN1-116, 1er mai 1820; 4 oct. 1827; 24 juill. 1834; 9, 20 avril, 3 oct. 1836. AUM, P 58, U, Chinic et Quirouet à Eustache Soupras, 27 sept. 1824. PAC, RG 8, I (C ser.), 76: 122, 162; 603: 101; 1695: 13–14; RG 42, E1, 1382: 44, 47, 56; RG 68, General index, 1651–1841: 245, 642. "Les dénombrements de Québec" (Plessis), ANQ *Rapport*, 1948–49: 32, 87, 131, 182. *Quebec Gazette*, 1794–1824. *Quebec Mercury*, 16 April 1816. *Vindicator and Canadian Advertiser*, 12 May 1829. Marianna O'Gallagher, *Saint Patrick's, Quebec: the building of a church and of a parish, 1827 to 1833* (Quebec, 1981). P.-G. Roy, *Les cimetières de Québec* (Lévis, Qué., 1941); *Toutes petites choses du Régime anglais* (2 sér., Québec, 1946), 1: 274–75; "La famille Chinic," *BRH*, 45 (1939): 207–10.

CHIPMAN, WILLIAM ALLEN, politician, merchant, office holder, JP, and judge; b. 8 Nov. 1757 in Newport, R.I., the ninth of eleven children born to Handley Chipman and Jean Allen; m. 20 Nov. 1777 Ann Osborn, daughter of a Saint John merchant, and they had at least six children; d. 28 Dec. 1845 in Cornwallis, N.S.

William Allen Chipman was the son of a Rhode Island cabinet-maker, a devout man of "strong character and great intelligence" who in May 1761 brought his wife and children to Cornwallis Township. The family established a dominant place for itself in the economic, political, and religious life of Kings County, and William, who may have lived briefly at Annapolis Royal before returning to Cornwallis, became a wealthy merchant and reputedly one of the county's largest landowners. He also held many public offices: clerk of Cornwallis Township and customs collector for the county, 1794–1845; justice of the peace, 1797–1845; judge of the Inferior Court of Common Pleas, 1821–41; and *custos rotulorum*, 1841–45. The last three posts had been held for a time by his elder brother John, a member of the House of Assembly for Cornwallis Township from 1776 to 1785.

William was also a member of the assembly. He represented Kings County, 1799–1806; Sydney County, 1807–8; Cornwallis Township, 1811–18; Kings County, 1818–26 and 1828–30. His son Samuel* succeeded him in 1830 as the member for Kings. Although not a great orator, Chipman displayed independent opinions and, as Beamish Murdoch* put it, "good sense, firmness, and a readiness to defend the public interests." In the house he opposed compulsory militia service, championed the cause of farmers, and supported free ports, tax assessments for public education, and economy in government. He espoused the cause of dissenters, but in 1823 voted against a successful motion which allowed the Roman Catholic Laurence Kavanagh* to sit in the assembly without taking the oath against transubstantiation. In his last session Chipman defended the rights of the assembly in the celebrated "Brandy Dispute" [*see* Enos Collins*]. In general he tended to support the reform coalition against the "church and state party"; indeed he played a part in bringing the coalition together, particularly through his efforts to deprive the Church of England of its special privileges and to secure public funding for Baptist and Presbyterian educational institutions, namely Horton and Pictou academies.

Chipman was a freemason who belonged to St George's Lodge No.11, organized at his home on 22 Nov. 1784. He and his family helped to establish the Baptist denomination in Nova Scotia. His brother Thomas Handley and his son William were among the first ordained Baptist ministers in the colony. An immersed member of the Cornwallis New Light Congregational Church as early as 1799, and a strong supporter of the Reverend Edward Manning* in Cornwallis, Chipman served for 20 years as treasurer of the Nova Scotia Home Missionary Society, established to secure funds for Baptist missions at home and abroad. He was also on the Board of the Nova Scotia Baptist Education Society, which founded Horton Academy in 1828 and Queen's (Acadia) College in 1838.

According to the Reverend Ingraham Ebenezer Bill*, Chipman, "a host in himself," was a man of "impetuous temperament" and one who prized his wife "above rubies." He died at the age of 88, in the florid language of the *Novascotian* "meeting the King of Terrors with the calmness and serenity that can only spring from the consciousness of a well spent life, and a full assurance of the all sufficient nature of the sacrifice made by the blessed Redeemer." As a member of what was to become known as the "Chipman compact," he did much to establish the family's ascendancy in Kings County. Its influence reached a peak with William Allen's grandson William Henry*, a prominent merchant and opponent of confederation.

CARMAN MILLER

PANS, MG 1, 184. *Novascotian*, 26 Jan. 1846. *Sun* (Halifax), 26 Jan. 1846. *A Chipman genealogy, circa 1583–1969, beginning with John Chipman (1620–1708), first of that surname to arrive in the Massachusetts Bay colony . . .* , comp. J. H. Chipman (Norwell, Mass., 1970). *Directory of N.S. MLAs*. Esther Clark Wright, *Planters and pioneers* (Hantsport, N.S., 1978). A. W. H. Eaton, *The history of Kings County, Nova Scotia . . .* (Salem, Mass., 1910; repr. Belleville, Ont., 1972). Murdoch, *Hist. of N.S.*, 3: 407, 433, 479, 494, 497, 531. G. A. Rawlyk, *Ravished by the spirit: religious revivals, Baptists, and Henry Alline* (Kingston, Ont., and Montreal, 1984). Saunders, *Hist. of Baptists*. Norah Story, "The church and state 'party' in Nova Scotia, 1749–1851," N.S. Hist. Soc., *Coll.*, 27 (1947): 33–57.

CHISHOLM, WILLIAM, militia officer, farmer, politician, office holder, JP, and businessman; b. 15 Oct. 1788 in Jordan Bay, N.S., son of George

Chisholm and Barbara McKenzie; m. 23 May 1812 Rebecca Silverthorn, and they had four daughters and seven sons; d. 4 May 1842 in Oakville, Upper Canada.

William Chisholm's father was a Highland Scot who emigrated to Tryon County, N.Y., only to be swept up in the American revolution. A loyalist and member of the Port Roseway Associates [*see* Gideon White*], he stopped with his growing family for a few years in Nova Scotia before moving by 1793 to Upper Canada, where his brother John had located. George eventually settled in the area of Burlington Bay (Hamilton Harbour), where William and his brothers grew up.

In August 1812, less than three months after his marriage, William participated as an ensign in the 2nd York Militia at the capture of Detroit. In October he fought in the battle of Queenston Heights and two months later was promoted lieutenant in his unit. Gazetted captain in the 2nd Regiment of Gore militia shortly after the war, he became lieutenant-colonel in 1824 and colonel in 1831.

By 1816 he had moved to a farm in Nelson Township, where he helped frame the local reply in 1817 to Robert Gourlay*'s enquiries about the state of affairs in Upper Canada. At the district level and at the Upper Canadian Convention of Friends to Enquiry in York (Toronto) the following summer, Chisholm was a consistent supporter of Gourlay. In 1820 he was elected in Halton to the House of Assembly, where he would vote for the repeal of the Sedition Act and against the expulsion of Barnabas Bidwell*. Although he did not run in 1824, he supported the candidacies of reformers John Rolph* and John Matthews* in Middlesex. At the same time he began to act as agent for William Lyon Mackenzie*'s *Colonial Advocate*.

In early 1826 Chisholm entered upon the road to becoming "a ratted Gourlayite, and reformed reformer," as he would later be called by Mackenzie. That January Chisholm was still railing against Lieutenant Governor Sir Peregrine Maitland*'s actions in denying to those who had participated in Gourlay's 1818 convention the Prince Regent's bounty of land for military service. "If we don rong try us by Law and punnish us," he exclaimed to Mackenzie. But at the end of May he coldly notified the editor of the *Colonial Advocate* to appoint another agent and cancel his subscription. During the 1828 election campaign, although Chisholm was not a candidate, he was included on Mackenzie's legislative "Black List." During the rebellion of 1837–38 he commanded Allan Napier MacNab*'s left flank in the advance on Mackenzie's rebels at Montgomery's Tavern.

Chisholm's political conversion may have been partly the result of his access to patronage. In 1824 he had received his lieutenant-colonelcy. He became postmaster of Nelson Township and a commissioner of the Burlington Bay Canal in 1825 [*see* James Gordon Strobridge*], and was made a magistrate in 1827. After the belated award of his militia land bounty the following year, his political sympathies clearly lay with moderate conservatism. His fortunes on the hustings – he was elected in 1830 and 1836 and defeated in 1834 and 1841 – reflected the lot of the tories provincially.

Chisholm had become a champion of the Burlington Bay Canal and a director in the nearby Desjardins Canal [*see* Peter Desjardins*] for more than reasons of patronage. Not long content with farming, he had opened a general store, and by 1827 this operation included a licence for an inn and a still. By 1822 he was engaged in the lumber trade, and began acquiring a small fleet of schooners. He had also become a partner by 1829 in the Wellington Square (Burlington) firm of McCay, Smith and Company, which had a store on Burlington Beach.

Chisholm's shipping and lumbering interests in Halton County led him to look closely at land reserved for the Mississauga Ojibwa Indians at the mouth of Sixteen Mile (Oakville) Creek. Although his interest in the area had been evident since 1822, it was not until the spring of 1827 that he made a concrete proposal to Maitland for acquiring the land. In response to this initiative, the reserve was put up for auction and purchased by Chisholm that summer for £1,029. One of his priorities for the site was the development of a shipyard and harbour. Within a year of the purchase Chisholm and his men had "laid out a town," Oakville, and "built a Warehouse for the reception of produce there." In 1828 Chisholm succeeded in having an act passed vesting in him the rights for the use of the harbour for 50 years. In August of that year, long before the harbour was complete, Chisholm's men had turned out the first in a long series of schooners. Five years later the shipyard launced its first steamer, the *Constitution*, which had been promoted by Chisholm, Colin Campbell Ferrie*, and others. Chisholm's experience in harbour development would be called upon again when he was asked to serve as a harbour commissioner for York with Hugh Richardson* and James Grant Chewett* in 1833.

As Oakville grew, Chisholm's affairs became more deeply entwined with it. He owned the first tavern (by 1828), sawmill (1830), and grist-mill (1833), and shortly afterwards was appointed collector of customs (1834) and postmaster (1835). But this façade of prosperity proved deceiving. Chisholm's Nelson Township property, mortgaged in 1829 to finance work at Oakville, was put on the market in 1834. It would be 1839, however, before he finally sold the 12-room house, its outbuildings, his merchant's shop, and a second dwelling, and moved to Oakville. The payments for the townsite were completed on schedule in 1831, but to finance the completion of the harbour Chisholm had to get a £2,500 mortgage from the government. Not long afterwards, he gave a second mortgage, for £6,500, to Forsyth, Richardson and Company, the Montreal mercantile firm. A further mortgage in 1839, to the Gore Bank (of which he had been a director), testifies to the great expense of the development and to Chisholm's difficulty in liquidating the debt.

His business investments left him by "no means in affluent circumstances," according to post-office inspector Charles Albert Berczy*, who after the rebellion also employed Chisholm for secret service surveillance. By 1841 Chisholm was devoting much of his energy to the improvement of the colonization road to the Owen Sound district, as well as to other government-sponsored schemes for development. In 1840, with others in Oakville, he had privately incorporated the Oakville Hydraulic Company, to develop further the water-power of Sixteen Mile Creek. The company failed and with it Chisholm, his brother George, and his brother-in-law Merrick Thomas. The sheriff's sale of their property was held on 2 March 1842.

Though very much a regional figure, William Chisholm, for most contemporaries, was associated with one community, Oakville. At a dinner in 1836 he was toasted by assemblyman Archibald McLean* as "a gentleman whose liberality and honourable conduct were universally known and esteemed – and to whose enterprise, energy and public spirit, Oakville was indebted for most of the advantages she at present enjoyed." The connection of the Chisholms with Oakville did not end with William. His son Robert Kerr succeeded him as postmaster and collector of customs. Another, John Alexander, took over mills there and his eldest son, George King*, became mayor in 1857.

WALTER LEWIS

AO, MS 106, "The Chisholms of the parish of Croy, Inverness-shire, Scotland," comp. Hazel [Chisholm] Mathews (typescript); MS 516, William Chisholm to W. L. Mackenzie, 28 July 1824; 10 Jan., 23 May 1826; RG 1, C-IV, Trafalgar Township, concession 3 (South Dundas Street), lot 13. Halton Land Registry Office (Milton, Ont.), Abstract index to deeds, Nelson Township, concession 1, lots 9, 14; Trafalgar Township, concession 3, lots 13–16 (mfm. at AO). Oakville Hist. Soc. Museum (Oakville, Ont.), Chisholm papers (mfm. at Oakville Public Library). PAC, RG 1, E3, 10: 120–22; L3, 89: C1/96; 108: C15/109; RG 5, A1; RG 68, General index, 1651–1841: 460. "Journals of Legislative Assembly of U.C.," AO *Report*, 1913–14. *Statistical account of U.C.* (Gourlay). U.C., House of Assembly, *Journal*, 1828, app., public accounts for 1826–27. "U.C. land book D," AO *Report*, 1931: 151, 157. *Albion of U.C.* (Toronto), 9 April 1836. *British Whig*, 30 Sept. 1836. *Colonial Advocate*, 18 May 1824; 29 Jan., 16 March 1826; 29 May, 31 July 1828; 22 Sept. 1831. *Courier of Upper Canada* (Toronto), 15 Aug. 1835. *Gore Gazette, and Ancaster, Hamilton, Dundas and Flamborough Advertiser* (Ancaster, [Ont.]), 2 June 1827. *Hamilton Free Press* (Hamilton, [Ont.]), 25 Aug. 1831. *Hamilton Journal Express*, January–February 1842. *Kingston Gazette*, 21–28 July 1818. *Toronto Herald*, 5 May 1842. *Western Mercury* (Hamilton), 22 Dec. 1831, 29 Aug. 1833. *Canadian biog. dict.*, vol.1. Hazel [Chisholm] Mathews, *Oakville and the Sixteen: the history of an Ontario port* (Toronto, 1954; repr. 1971). Marion Robertson, *King's bounty: a history of early Shelburne, Nova Scotia . . .* (Halifax, 1983).

CHISHOLME, DAVID, editor, office holder, and author; b. 1796 in Ross-shire, Scotland; m. 16 May 1822 Rachel Cuthbert Robertson in Montreal; d. there 24 Sept. 1842.

David Chisholme arrived in Lower Canada in 1822, probably under the auspices of Lord Dalhousie [RAMSAY], who was, he later said, "pleased to deem me not altogether unworthy of his friendship in private life, and of his patronage as Governor in Chief." Chisholme had studied law in Scotland and had held legal appointments there, but following his sudden immigration to the Canadas he turned his "talents" to literary and political affairs. In 1823 he became editor of the *Montreal Gazette*; at the same time he served as the first editor of the *Canadian Magazine and Literary Repository*, which began to appear in July. He left the *Montreal Gazette* after 1 March 1824 and the *Canadian Magazine* shortly afterwards because of a dispute over financial and probably political affairs with the new proprietor of both publications, Thomas Andrew Turner. He was succeeded by Alexander James CHRISTIE. In May Chisholme became editor of the *Montreal Herald* and he soon established the *Canadian Review and Literary and Historical Journal*, undoubtedly supported by Dalhousie, who had founded the Literary and Historical Society of Quebec earlier that year. Chisholme left the *Montreal Herald* in May 1826, and the *Canadian Review and Literary and Historical Journal*, which had become the *Canadian Review and Magazine*, ceased publication in September.

Chisholme was appointed clerk of the peace for the district of Trois-Rivières by Dalhousie on 11 Nov. 1826. From 1829 to November 1835 he acted as agent for the provincial secretary in issuing shop and tavern licences and on 2 April 1834 he was appointed coroner for Trois-Rivières. In November 1835 Chisholme was summoned before a select committee of the House of Assembly investigating the fees and emoluments of government officials. The assembly accused him of "fraud, oppression, malversation" in his role as clerk of the peace and demanded his dismissal. Charged, among other things, with framing indictments for more serious offences than had actually been committed (and thus obtaining higher fees), Chisholme defended himself in a lengthy address to Lord Gosford [ACHESON]. The governor-in-chief took no action but forwarded the case to the colonial secretary, Lord Glenelg, in August 1836. The following month, the provincial secretary, Dominick Daly*, became aware of complaints that during Chisholme's tenure as agent he had received payment for licences but had failed to issue them and had not reported the revenue. Another inquiry was set up and Gosford explained to Glenelg that, after studying its evidence, he had ordered Chisholme's removal from the posts of coroner and clerk of the peace. Chisholme was informed on 28 October. The administration had decided, however, not to press charges, feeling that dismissal was punishment enough. In 1839 Chisholme again defended himself in a long statement addressed to the governor-in-chief, Sir John Colborne*, giving an account of the supposed injustice and illegality of proceedings against him, but he was never reinstated.

From 1837 until his death, Chisholme was again employed as editor of the *Montreal Gazette* [*see* Robert Armour*]. He continued to pursue policies which had created antagonism towards him in the assembly and which may have prompted his summons in 1835. An extreme tory in his defence of the Legislative Council and the governor and in his opposition to any significant power for the assembly, he constantly demonstrated bias against French Canadians in linguistic, cultural, and political affairs. He supported the recommendations of Lord Durham [LAMBTON] for union of Upper and Lower Canada, trusting that union would make British interests preponderant and lead to "the entire destruction of French Canadian ignorance and prejudice."

Chisholme's view of himself as a "literary and political writer" is supported by his authorship of several works on the Canadas. According to the *Vindicator and Canadian Advertiser*, he was the author of a pseudonymous work published in 1827, *Letter from Delta to Senex*, a vituperative response to a manifesto written by Louis-Joseph Papineau* and other members of the assembly. The work that brought him the most notoriety among reformers was *The Lower-Canada watchman*, a series of 13 political essays first published in the *Kingston Chronicle* in 1828–29. As reform politician William Lyon Mackenzie* noted mildly in a letter to John NEILSON on 25 April 1830, Chisholme was "not a prudent writer" and his essays were so full of invective and abuse that he did his tory patrons more harm than good. He attacked all persons inclined to reform, but was particularly vicious in his denunciation of Papineau and of French Canadian character generally. On the other hand, he defended any action by Dalhousie, who was thought to have paid him to write the essays. In 1832 appeared Chisholme's *Observations on the rights of the British colonies to representation in the imperial parliament*, a treatise in political economy, encyclopedic in its use of classical and modern sources, its consideration of natural and constitutional rights of the colonies, and its survey of the consequences of representation. Not unexpectedly, the primary motive for such representation was to subordinate French Canadian to British interests.

Chisholme's *Annals of Canada for 1837 and 1838* was initially published serially in the *Montreal Gazette* from January 1838 to February 1840. While evidencing Chisholme's opposition to the rebellion and the destruction of life and property, it is chiefly a military history, giving much detail on persons, conditions, and objectives of various campaigns. Although the account is biased, it provides a good impression of the broadness of action and the difficulty of military engagements. The *Annals* is the most readable of Chisholme's books because of its narrative character and the relative absence of political invective. Toward the end of his life Chisholme was working on a history of Lower Canada, but he never completed the task.

Chisholme's literary interests have a more positive role in the history of Canada than his political interests. He played an important part in the development of literature in English in Montreal during the 1820s as editor, reviewer, and writer of essays. As a periodical editor he was notably successful in attracting original matter for publication, especially in the *Canadian Review*, where over 75 per cent of the articles were on British North American topics. In his own contributions to the magazines as reviewer and as essayist, he was optimistic about the development of an indigenous literature. He advocated local subjects and was convinced that "our climate, soil, productions, scenery and inhabitants are so different from those of old countries, that every work on those subjects the result of study and observation on the spot would necessarily bear the impression of its origin." He consistently urged writers to delineate the nature of the new country and to emphasize the useful and didactic in literature rather than the delightful. He disparaged the sentimental and sensational, not approving of poetry and fiction generally, although he did review favourably Oliver Goldsmith*'s *The rising village* . . . (London, 1825) and George Longmore's *The charivari* . . . (Montreal, 1824) because of their documentary nature. Although Chisholme was always an exponent of education and literature as the agents of light and morality in the conquest of darkness and ignorance, he was never able to get beyond his own singlemindedness, displaying even in the periodicals he edited his bias against French Canadians.

CARL BALLSTADT

David Chisholme is the author of *The Lower-Canada*

watchman (Kingston, [Ont.], 1829); *Observations on the rights of the British colonies to representation in the imperial parliament* (Trois-Rivières, [Que.], 1832); *Annals of Canada for 1837 and 1838* (Montreal, [1849?]); and *Memorial and case of David Chisholme* (n.p., 1839). In addition, he probably wrote *Letter from Delta to Senex* ... (Montreal, 1827). From 1823 to 1 March 1824 and from 1837 to September 1842 he was the editor of the *Montreal Gazette*, and he held the same post with the *Montreal Herald* from May 1824 to May 1826, with the *Canadian Magazine and Literary Repository* (Montreal) for issues 1 (July–December 1823) to 2 (January–June 1824), and with the *Canadian Rev. and Literary and Hist. Journal* (Montreal), no.1 (July 1824)–no.3 (March 1825), and its successor, the *Canadian Rev. and Magazine* (Montreal), no.4 (February 1826)–no.5 (September 1826).

ANQ-M, CE1-126, 16 mai 1822; CE1-130, 26 sept. 1842. PAC, MG 11, [CO 42] Q, 263–64; MG 23, GI, 3; MG 24, I9; Reference file 1974; RG 68, General index, 1651–1841. [Launcelot Longstaff] [George Longmore], *The charivari, or Canadian poetics*, intro. M. L. MacDonald (Ottawa, 1977). *Montreal Gazette*, 26 Sept. 1842. *Vindicator and Canadian Advertiser*, 13, 21 Dec. 1830; 13 Dec. 1836. H. J. Morgan, *Bibliotheca Canadensis*, 74. C. P. A. Ballstadt, "The quest for Canadian identity in pre-confederation English-Canadian literary criticism" (MA thesis, Univ. of Western Ont., London, 1959). M. L. MacDonald, "Some notes on the Montreal literary scene in the mid-1820's," *Canadian Poetry* (London, Ont.), no.5 (fall–winter 1979): 29–40.

CHRISTIAN, WASHINGTON, Baptist minister; b. *c.* 1776, reputedly in Virginia; d. 3 July 1850 in Toronto.

The facts of Washington Christian's early life all lack documentation: his birth, his ordination in the Abyssinian Baptist Church in New York, his itinerant ministry in New England, and his move in 1825 to York (Toronto) in Upper Canada. Christian, himself a black, ministered there to a small congregation of blacks and whites, and seems to have been the first Baptist pastor to officiate regularly in the provincial capital. By 1827 he had secured a permanent meeting-place, the rooms of St George's Lodge. A small frame church was built on March (Lombard) Street in 1834, by which time Christian's flock seems to have been made up entirely of blacks and the place of worship was known as the "Negro Chapel." In 1836 Thomas Rolph* wrote that the "coloured inhabitants . . . have . . . a Church, which is well attended." A year later Christian reported a membership of 66 to the Haldimand Association, the nearest Baptist church organization, centred on the Bay of Quinte. His congregation in the 1820s had probably been composed mainly of descendants of slaves brought into the Canadas between 1763 and 1793, although Rolph believed they were later arrivals, "most of them escaped from slavery." The building of the March Street church had coincided with the influx of blacks from the United States following a disturbance in 1829 in Ohio.

In 1841 Christian built a new church, at the corner of Queen and Victoria streets. A visit by him in the winter of 1843–44 to Jamaica was important since "through the liberality of the Baptists in Jamaica the chapel is free from debt." The visit also underscored the place of the West Indies in the thinking of Upper Canadian blacks. The organization of a Sunday School, a junior temperance society, and a library followed, and until his death in 1850 Christian remained in charge of the congregation, which called itself First Baptist Church from the late 1850s.

Christian was active in general Baptist Church affairs. A valued member of the Haldimand Association, he took a leading part in its deliberations and frequently preached at its opening meetings. In the late 1840s he became a visitor to the meetings of the Amherstburg Association, in the southwest of the province, and in 1848 he was made a life-member. He also maintained contacts with the United States as a member of the American Baptist Missionary Convention, an organization sponsored by the Abyssinian Baptist Church. In Upper Canada he was markedly successful in the formation of Baptist congregations among the black communities of the Niagara peninsula, notably in St Catharines (1838) and Hamilton (1847). In 1847 he made an extensive tour of the black settlements between Chatham and Sandwich (Windsor). Few would dispute the statement of historian Dorothy Shadd Shreve that he "founded more Canadian Baptist Churches than any other coloured Baptist minister." A man of force and character, Christian was a moving preacher, capable of drawing large crowds. Hearing him speak at Whitby in 1837, an observer noted that "while truth fell from his lips it reached many hearts and suffused many eyes with tears."

Disputes within his Toronto congregation caused difficulty for Christian. The trustees, who held the deeds for the property, attempted to interfere with the general operation of the church. According to the Reverend William P. Newman, editor of the *Provincial Freeman*, the trustees treated "the old man so unkindly that he died virtually of a broken heart." He certainly died in poverty. Christian was buried in Potter's Field, and 12 years later was reinterred beside his wife, Ann, in the Necropolis.

IN COLLABORATION

Information on Washington Christian is scarce and often unsubstantiated. Some of the works cited below, for example, claim without authority that he was a West Indian. A photograph of him is published in D. G. Hill, *The freedom-seekers: blacks in early Canada* (Agincourt [Toronto], 1981).

Canadian Baptist Arch., McMaster Divinity College (Hamilton, Ont.), Amherstburg Regular Baptist Assoc., minutes, 1841–79. Haldimand Baptist Assoc., *Minutes*

(Cobourg, [Ont.], *et al.*), 1837–51. Long Point Baptist Assoc., *Minutes* (London, [Ont.]), 1837–41. Thomas Rolph, *A brief account, together with observations, made during a visit in the West Indies, and a tour through the United States of America, in parts of the years 1832–3; together with a statistical account of Upper Canada* (Dundas, [Ont.], 1836). *Provincial Freeman and Weekly Advertiser* (Chatham, [Ont.]), 24 Nov. 1855. *A history of the Amherstburg Regular Missionary Baptist Association; its auxiliaries and churches . . .* , ed. Dorothy Shadd Shreve (Amherstburg, Ont., 1940). J. K. Lewis, "Religious life of fugitive slaves and rise of coloured Baptist churches, 1820–1865, in what is now known as Ontario" (BD thesis, McMaster Divinity College, 1965). *Robertson's landmarks of Toronto*, vol.4. W. J. T. Sheffield, "Background and development of Negro Baptists in Ontario" (BD thesis, McMaster Divinity College, 1952). D. G. Simpson, "Negroes in Ontario from early times to 1870" (PHD thesis, Univ. of Western Ont., London, 1971). R. W. Winks, *The blacks in Canada: a history* (Montreal, 1971). F. H. Armstrong, "The Toronto directories and the Negro community in the late 1840's," *OH*, 61 (1969): 111–19. J. K. A. Farrell [O'Farrell], "Schemes for the transplanting of refugee American Negroes from Upper Canada in the 1840's," *OH*, 52 (1960): 245–49. D. G. Hill, "Negroes in Toronto, 1793–1865," *OH*, 55 (1963): 73–91. Fred Landon, "The Negro migration to Canada after the passing of the Fugitive Slave Act," *Journal of Negro Hist.* (Washington), 5 (1920): 22–36.

CHRISTIE, ALEXANDER JAMES, doctor, newspaperman, writer, businessman, JP, notary, and office holder; b. 1787 and baptized 14 October in the parish of Fyvie, Scotland, son of the Reverend Alexander Christie, dean of Aberdeen; m. Jane Turner, and they had at least three children, including Alexander, an engineer and bridge builder; d. 13 Nov. 1843 at Bytown (Ottawa), and was buried at Glencairn, his farm in March Township, Upper Canada.

Alexander James Christie is commonly referred to as Dr Christie in earlier biographical accounts and in references to his activities as a resident of the Montreal and Bytown areas. He did indeed practise medicine and maintained a life-long interest in medical matters, but whether or not he was a fully qualified physician is not certain. He studied mathematics at Marischal College, Aberdeen, for two years and is reputed to have studied medicine at the University of Edinburgh later, but there is no firm documentation to indicate that he took a degree. He is said to have practised in the north of Scotland and, in applying in 1827 to Dr James Forbes, head of the army medical department for Upper Canada, to serve as surgeon on the Rideau Canal during its construction, he stated that he had practised as a doctor in the British navy for several years. As a man of considerable learning and wide-ranging interests, Christie probably also did some teaching in Scotland but, as with so many other aspects of his early life, the record is not precise.

The course of Christie's life becomes clearer with his immigration to Lower Canada in May 1817. He probably came at the invitation of his brother-in-law, Thomas Andrew Turner, who found him a house and medical practice in Dorchester (Saint-Jean-sur-Richelieu). Christie obtained a licence to practise in Lower Canada on 22 July, but political and literary interests soon led him in another direction. In September 1818 he became editor and part-owner, with William Gray, of the *Montreal Herald*, a venture that did not end happily. Gray ended Christie's tenure as editor on 20 Feb. 1821 and the termination was announced in the *Herald* the following day. The dismissal followed Christie's arrest for indebtedness and he was subsequently imprisoned for "above three tedious months." In a later statement on the events, Christie alleged that his bankruptcy and arrest were engineered by Gray, who proceeded illegally to dissolve the partnership between them. The statement also alleged that Christie had been obliged to perform duties not properly his according to the terms of the partnership and that because of these and other matters Gray owed him more than £2,000. At least one deponent, William Langhorne, another *Herald* employee, supported Christie in his contentions, but, whatever the truth of the matter, Christie's days with the *Herald* were over.

This early stage of Christie's years in Canada reveals all the basic characteristics of his subsequent life, for his political views, his pursuit of medical practice, his literary interests, and his involvement in public affairs and offices, all facets of his activity in Lower Canada, were sustained during his long-time residence in Bytown. In political opinions, he was conservative and imperialist. That is, he was content with the current administration, opposed to reformers such as Robert Gourlay*, and very suspicious of American intentions toward British North America. In the pages of the *Herald* and in letters to Britain, he observed the high degree of unity amongst Americans where their national interest was concerned and warned that their resources and skills were being directed to the building of a powerful navy and military facilities in the Lake Champlain area, which evidenced their intense aversion to all things British.

For these reasons Christie immediately became and remained an advocate of appropriate Canadian responses. He urged the building of strong fortifications at strategic points along the St Lawrence, the construction and improvement of canals and water-ways, and the union of the Canadas with the capital located in an easily defensible location. He therefore energetically supported the building of the Rideau Canal, for both military and economic reasons, and the location of the capital at Bytown (one of his principal platforms when he later became editor and proprietor of the weekly *Bytown Gazette, and Ottawa and Rideau Advertiser*).

Christie's view of an editor's function was that he should be wonderfully objective and eclectic because he managed a chronicle of the times. In September 1818, in the *Herald*, he defined a newspaper as "the Epitome which registers the transactions of the great and the little. . . . A newspaper in fact should reflect . . . the image of the people's feelings; it should echo the general voice; it should promulgate the best principles; it should advocate the best interests." As the editor of the *Herald*, and then of the *Montreal Gazette* (March 1824 to August 1825) and the *Bytown Gazette* (1836 to 1843), he did report and comment on a wide range of affairs of state, economics, American conduct, and social problems, but like other editors he also revealed his hobby-horses as an opponent of the reformers and of William Lyon Mackenzie* (with whom he had been briefly on friendly terms when Mackenzie wrote for the *Herald* in 1820), as a supporter of Sir Francis Bond Head*, and as a proponent of the union of the Canadas so that French power would be decreased if not destroyed.

A medical man, Christie was certainly interested in the well-being of others. In his early days in Montreal he was active in the establishment of the Montreal General Hospital and he also served as secretary to the Emigrant Society of Montreal. The latter activity led him to seek land for a place of reception for immigrants and to write his own guide, *The emigrant's assistant: or remarks on the agricultural interest of the Canadas* (Montreal, 1821). Being a newcomer himself, Christie gathered information for his book by writing letters to men of experience throughout the two provinces and, presenting "truth . . . in a plain and homely dress," he produced chapters on the story of settlement in the Canadas and the best way for emigrants to facilitate settlement, followed by a résumé of the history and political structure of Upper and Lower Canada, and chapters on land tenure, divisions of land, how to obtain land, and how to clear it. Apparently Christie intended to produce a second volume of the work, largely statistical, but there is no evidence that he ever did.

The book together with his editorship made him part of a small literary group based in Montreal. He seems to have been on good terms with Samuel Hull Wilcocke*, editor of the *Scribbler*, a journal of invective and satire. Wilcocke wrote to Christie several times and appears to have sided with him in his struggle with Gray. He also reviewed *The emigrant's assistant* favourably in the *Scribbler*. David CHISHOLME, a fellow Scot, was also on good terms with Christie initially, asking him to contribute to the pages of the *Canadian Magazine and Literary Repository*, of which he was editor in 1823, but the two became editorial competitors and exchanged insults when, in 1824, Chisholme became editor of the *Herald* and of a new journal, the *Canadian Review and Literary and Historical Journal*. Christie, who had left Montreal in 1821, had been lured back by an offer of £200 a year to become editor of the *Gazette* and the *Canadian Magazine* from March 1824 until mid 1825. Christie and Chisholme were in agreement on literary matters, however. Both encouraged indigenous literary compositions and advocated a literature that would focus on "real occurrences or tangible objects." Both discouraged the over-use of "the machinery of poetry" and the delineation of "imaginary beings from fairy land." Like Chisholme, Christie also took the occasion of the inception of the Literary and Historical Society of Quebec in 1824 to examine the role that such organizations might play in fostering the advancement of culture in a new society.

Christie left Montreal again in the summer of 1825 and returned to March Township, where he had moved with his wife and children in the summer of 1821. The family had settled first on land Christie owned on the 7th concession but, when it proved not very productive, they relocated in 1822 to a lot on the 1st concession. Here Christie built Glencairn and established a farm, which was managed by his son Thomas. In 1827 Christie, probably seeking more town activity, moved to a site which is now at the corner of Wellington and Lyon in Ottawa. In the mid 1830s he built a house on Sparks Street, with his printing offices on an adjacent property.

In addition to trying farming, Christie practised medicine, retailed various merchandise, and served as an officer of the Hull Mining Company. From September 1826 to April 1827 he had a temporary appointment as a medical attendant to the Rideau Canal workers, and through most of the rest of 1827 he served in an unofficial capacity, keeping, as he always did, detailed records of his activities. Although he applied to Lieutenant-Colonel John BY, to James Forbes, inspector of military hospitals for the province, and to Governor Lord Dalhousie [RAMSAY], he was unable to gain a permanent official position with the canal project, apparently because he was a civilian. In March 1830 he was appointed coroner for the Bathurst District (renewed in 1836 and 1839). It was not Christie's first public office. He had served as a magistrate in Bytown and was always public-spirited, being prominent in the building of St Mary's Church (Anglican), on land owned by his friend Hamnett Kirkes Pinhey*, and delivering the welcoming address to Lord Dalhousie when he visited the district in September 1826. In January 1834 Christie became an agent for the issuing of marriage licences and in September 1835 he was proclaimed public notary by Sir John Colborne*. He was secretary of the Bathurst Agricultural Society and the Ottawa Lumber Association in 1836 and the following year he served briefly as township clerk.

As coroner, Christie became secretary to the board

of health and had to contend with the cholera crisis of 1832. He tried to isolate Bytown in June by preventing the *Shannon* and other traffic from proceeding to the town, but, although the commander of the *Shannon* complied, cholera did reach Bytown and by 12 July there had been three deaths. Christie's treatment for cholera was a mixture of soft maple charcoal, hog's lard, and maple sugar. He kept financial records of the measures taken in Bytown: in 1832 the cost of building and supplying a hospital for treatment was more than £115, and in 1834, when the disease broke out again, £123 was expended.

From 9 June 1836 until his death Christie edited the *Bytown Gazette, and Ottawa and Rideau Advertiser*. Earlier that year he had purchased the press of James JOHNSTON following the early demise of Johnston's *Bytown Independent, and Farmer's Advocate*. His new position did not disturb Christie's efforts to gain government appointments or his determination to remain active in political affairs. In 1832 he had assisted Pinhey in the by-election for Carleton County. The bitter nature of the campaign can be seen in a satirical verse account published that year, *The Carleton election; or, the tale of a Bytown ram; an epic poem, in ten cantos*, sometimes attributed to Christie. Desire for public office and political involvement were both connected to his being prominent in petitioning for the formation in 1838 of the Dalhousie District out of parts of the old Bathurst, Johnstown, and Ottawa districts.

In late 1840 Christie was nominated to stand for election in March 1841 to the Legislative Assembly of the newly united Canadas, but he was persuaded to withdraw, along with James Johnston and Robert Shirreff, in favour of Stewart Derbishire*, a Montreal editor and friend to Lord Sydenham [THOMSON] who was parachuted into the riding by the governor. In May 1842, chiefly through the efforts of Derbishire, now a member of the assembly, Christie was rewarded with the office of clerk of the peace for the newly proclaimed Dalhousie District.

Although Christie had claimed illness was his reason for resigning his candidacy in the election of 1841, he remained active as an editor. He apparently fell seriously ill early in November 1843 and he died on the 13th. His newspaper was maintained by the family for a short time and was then sold.

Alexander Christie's significance derives from his status as a lively and controversial journalist and as a chronicler of the times. He was a keeper of records and journals that contain valuable detail on local history and on economic and social conditions. His journal of "Medical and Chirurgical Observations" shows his own continuing medical education as well as the nature of medical practice in a frontier area, and his letters and travel journals delineate agricultural and human resources along the Rideau Canal and in the Ottawa valley. A notebook of natural philosophy reveals his extensive curiosity concerning the physical sciences.

CARL BALLSTADT

Alexander James Christie is the author of *The emigrant's assistant: or remarks on the agricultural interest of the Canadas* . . . (Montreal, 1821).

AO, MU 934–44. McGill Univ. Libraries, Dept. of Rare Books and Special Coll., MS coll., CH202.S180. Ottawa, Hist. Soc., Bytown Museum and Arch. (Ottawa), JCHR. PAC, MG 24, B1; I9, 1–8; I102; MG 30, D1, 8. *Canadian Magazine and Literary Repository* (Montreal), 1 (July–December 1823)–4 (January–June 1825). *Canadian Rev. and Literary and Hist. Journal* (Montreal), no.1 (July 1824)–no.3 (March 1825). *The search for English-Canadian literature: an anthology of critical articles from the nineteenth and early twentieth centuries*, ed. C. [P. A.] Ballstadt (Toronto and Buffalo, N.Y., 1975). *Bytown Gazette, and Ottawa and Rideau Advertiser*, 9 June 1836–16 Nov. 1843. *Montreal Gazette*, March 1824–September 1825. *Montreal Herald*, September 1818–February 1821. *Scribbler* (Montreal), 1821–22. C. P. A. Ballstadt, "The quest for Canadian identity in pre-confederation English-Canadian literary criticism" (MA thesis, Univ. of Western Ont., London, 1959). W. P. Lett, *Recollections of old Bytown*, ed. Edwin Welch (Ottawa, 1979). H. [J. W.] Walker and Olive [Moffatt] Walker, *Carleton saga* (Ottawa, 1968). C. C. J. Bond, "Alexander James Christie, Bytown pioneer: his life and times, 1787–1843," *OH*, 56 (1964): 17–36. H. P. Hill, "The *Bytown Gazette*, a pioneer newspaper," *OH*, 27 (1931): 407–23. M. L. MacDonald, "Some notes on the Montreal literary scene in the mid-1820's," *Canadian Poetry* (London), no.5 (fall–winter 1979): 29–40.

CHRISTIE, WILLIAM PLENDERLEATH (known until 1835 as **William Plenderleath**), seigneur and politician; b. 13 Dec. 1780 in England; d. 4 May 1845 in Blackwood (Republic of Ireland).

The third son of Gabriel Christie* and his mistress Rachel Plenderleath, William Plenderleath joined his father's regiment, the 60th Foot, as an ensign on 20 April 1793 and was promoted captain on 29 May 1803. He was stationed in the West Indies during most of the Napoleonic Wars but also served in Italy and spent 18 months on Madeira as deputy assistant adjutant-general. He resigned his commission in 1810.

Perhaps as early as 1816 Plenderleath moved to Montreal, where he may have lived as a member of the Christie household. That year he filed suit against his half-brother Napier Christie Burton to collect the unpaid balance of the legacy of £1,500 sterling left to him by his father. Some time before 1820 he married Elizabeth McGinnis, the sister of Alexander McGinnis, a trader between Bristol and Dominica. After she died he remarried, taking as his wife Amelia Martha Bowman on 30 March 1835 in Montreal. Little is known of his early years in Montreal except that he acted as executor for the estates of several members of his first wife's family and that those duties sent him to Bristol in 1820.

In Montreal Christie lived at Clifton Lodge, his home in the *faubourg* Quebec. He also owned a farm in Cornwall and 1,200 acres in Ascot Township; in 1842 he purchased Joseph PAPINEAU's house in Montreal. He held shares in the Bank of England, the Bank of Montreal, the City Bank, and the British American Land Company.

When Napier Christie Burton died in 1835, Plenderleath inherited his father's entailed estate after taking the name and arms of Christie, probably on 27 June. He thereby acquired some town lots in Dorchester (Saint-Jean-sur-Richelieu) and the seigneuries of Repentigny, Bleury, Sabrevois, Noyan, Léry, and Lacolle, swearing fealty and homage on 7 Nov. 1835.

To manage his estate Christie appointed William McGinnis of L'Acadie, a nephew by his first marriage, as his land agent. After a year on salary, McGinnis was paid a 15 per cent commission on his collections of seigneurial dues. His own interests were therefore closely linked to those of the seigneur. McGinnis also shared Christie's strong tory leanings and assisted him in his attempts to promote Protestantism as well as in business matters. His services were valued: as Christie wrote to him, "I have no one who could or would perform such necessary services for me; & none other, except your Brother, in whom I could confide."

Although Christie always acted through his agent, he closely supervised the administration of his seigneuries. He completed a survey of them, establishing a separate record for each in preparation for the division of the estate. He singled out absentees, especially those who had participated in the rebellions of 1837–38, as targets of suits for arrears in rent. A drainage project in Léry increased the area of arable land in that seigneury, the ungranted portion of which became the domain of Lakefield when Christie was unable to have it commuted into free and common socage. A similar drainage project was undertaken in Noyan, with less success. Two sawmills were constructed at Saint-Valentin, but otherwise entrepreneurial activity was left to others. The most important mill sites in the seigneuries were sold; less important ones were leased and later inherited by Christie's heirs. Christie's major achievement as a seigneur, therefore, was to put order in the management of his seigneuries so that they would produce a regular income, but he did so at the cost of using sheriff sales when necessary. Although his correspondence indicates a strong prejudice in favour of English "tenants," he dealt fairly with his *censitaires*. His administrative policy was marked by the regular collection of rents, maintained at the rates which had been established by the previous administration.

Christie actively promoted schools and Protestant missionary activity in Lower Canada, taking a special interest in education for native people. He paid for the erection of Trinity Chapel in Montreal and chose its first minister, Mark WILLOUGHBY; he financed the construction of Trinity Church in Christieville (Iberville) and of a parish school there; and he donated land for a glebe and church at both Christieville and Napierville. In addition he presented land in Ascot Township to the Church Society, of which he was a founding member and vice-president. He gave his approval to the mission of Henriette Feller [Odin*] at Grande-Ligne and paid a colporteur to deliver Protestant religious tracts in Repentigny and in the seigneuries of the upper Richelieu valley. Nevertheless, he was careful to keep his involvement in these activities quiet. Although Christie, evidently a religious man, was kind in his personal relations, proselytism rather than philanthropy seems to have been the driving force behind much of his public charity.

During the rebellions of 1837–38 Christie had volunteered his services as military secretary for Lower Canada and part of Upper Canada, and he held that office for a time. From 2 April 1838 to 1 June 1838 and from 2 Nov. 1838 to 10 Feb. 1841 he served on the Special Council of Lower Canada. He then moved to the manor he had built in Christieville. In 1843 he and his wife left for Great Britain, where he hoped to find a cure for the paralysis which affected one arm. He died in Blackwood two years later.

No children were born of Christie's marriages. His wife, his universal legatee, received £4,200 according to the terms of their marriage contract, the manor in Christieville, the seigneury of Bleury, and the domains in Léry and Lacolle. Relatives inherited the other seigneuries. Properties and moveables were left to members of the McGinnis and Bowman families. Personal friends, 32 in all, received £50 each, to be paid from the arrears in rent, and the balance, if any, was to go to several missionary societies.

Christie's right to succeed to his father's estate was questioned both before and after his death and was challenged in the courts after 1864; however, on 21 July 1874 the Judicial Committee of the Privy Council confirmed his right to inherit despite his "adulterine bastard" status, and his heirs remained undisturbed.

FRANÇOISE NOËL

ANQ-M, CE1-63, 30 mars 1835; CN1-134, 24 mars 1835; CN1-175, 3 mars 1842. ANQ-Q, P-52, nos.498–511. McCord Museum, M20483. PAC, MG 8, F99, ser.1–2, 8–9; RG 1, L3[L]: 30175–77; RG 4, B53, 3; RG 8, I (C ser.), 392: 49. *King* v. *Tunstall* (1874), 7 C.R.A.C., 126. *Quebec Gazette*, 3 Sept. 1840. Elinor Kyte Senior, *British regulars in Montreal: an imperial garrison, 1832–1854* (Montreal, 1981). Françoise Noël, "Gabriel Christie's seigneuries: settlement and seigneurial administration in the upper Richelieu valley, 1764–1854" (PHD thesis, McGill Univ., Montreal, 1985). N. W. Wallace, *A regimental chronicle and list of officers of the 60th, or King's Royal Rifle Corps, formerly the 62nd, or the Royal American Regiment of Foot* (London, 1879).

CHURCH, JOHN, militia officer and businessman; b. 30 Sept. 1757; d. 19 Oct. 1839 in Churchville (Sweetsburg), Lower Canada.

Little is known of John Church's origins. He is thought to have been a descendant of a family from the Palatinate (Federal Republic of Germany) that is believed to have emigrated around 1710 to the Hudson valley in the colony of New York. The family name, it would seem, evolved from Shirts or Shertz into Church. At the time of the American revolution Church is supposed to have crossed into Quebec to offer his services to the crown. He may then have joined John Burgoyne*'s army. A year after hostilities ended, in 1784, he went to live at Caldwell's Manor, near Missisquoi Bay. He soon married Tryphena Huntington, who had also come from the Hudson valley, and they apparently had five children, a son and four daughters, all born at Caldwell's Manor.

On 5 May 1795 Church took the oath of allegiance, a necessary step to obtain land in Lower Canada. In 1799 he moved to Dunham Township with Captain Jacob Ruiter and others. There he found his brother Henry and his sister Catherine's husband, William Shufelt, who had both come a short time before by the trail John Savage* had opened up in 1795; this path became the main route between Shefford Township and Missisquoi Bay.

After buying a lot from surveyor Jesse Pennoyer* in 1800, Church decided to settle in Dunham Township. His choice of land was a good one, since it included the site on which Churchville (later the village of Sweetsburg) was to develop. He would enlarge his holdings by further purchases. Being a genuine loyalist did not, apparently, lead Church to make large claims. In 1803, however, as associates of Henry Ruiter he and his brother Henry obtained land in Potton Township. But they do not seem to have been interested in the properties and had probably acted in a nominal capacity, like many others, in return for some compensation.

Church fairly quickly set up a business in Dunham Township based upon trading ash and potash for essential articles. The enterprise, which was on a busy route, prospered and soon had a smithy, a potashery, and a distillery. In 1814 Church took his son into partnership and around 1819 with his help built a huge brick house, one of the earliest in the region. Eventually the house would become a well-known inn in which large meetings and even weddings were held, but in which gambling was never allowed.

Church's methods of doing business have remained legendary. He believed that by selling his goods for four times what they cost he was making a four per cent profit. Since he did not know how to write, indeed could barely sign his name, his account-books are full of pictographs. Around 1830 the first post office in Churchville opened in his store, with his son in charge. At that time there was a plan to build a church on an adjacent lot, but a subscription opened by Charles Caleb COTTON, an Anglican clergyman, brought in little money, despite a generous gift from Church.

On 15 May 1804 Church had been commissioned lieutenant in the militia, and in 1805 he was taken on the strength in the 1st Townships Militia Battalion, which had been formed that year; this service involved no great obligation in peace-time, and he even managed not to take part in the War of 1812. Around 1817, however, he was appointed militia captain, a responsibility he fulfilled quite faithfully, although he was forced to complain to the governor, Sir John Coape Sherbrooke*, to obtain repayment of his expenses for travelling to Montreal. It may have been as a result of this claim that he received a land grant in Brome Township.

In 1826 Church renewed the terms of the partnership with his son and he had his will drawn up. Three years later he resigned as militia captain, recommending his son as successor. He apparently retired from business at that time, and in 1830 his son acquired another partner. Unfortunately John Church Jr died in 1831, and in 1833 his wife, Elizabeth Shufelt, also died, leaving three under-age sons. Their joint estate was then sold by auction, and Church was not even present at the family council that followed.

John Church died at Churchville on 19 Oct. 1839, aged 82, surrounded by his relatives, and was buried two days later in the Ruiter family's little cemetery near his home. His remains were later transferred to their present resting-place in Christ Church cemetery, Sweetsburg. The name Churchville disappeared in 1854, but Church, an honest and good-natured man, was long remembered in the region. He had involved himself in its life and done his best to promote its progress.

MARIE-PAULE R. LABRÈQUE

ANQ-E, CE2-38, 19 oct. 1839; CN2-21, 31 mai 1810; CN2-26, 17 août 1800; 11 mars 1826; 29 janv. 1827; 24 mai 1830; 30 juin, 18 juill. 1834. Brome County Hist. Soc. Arch. (Knowlton, Que.), H. B. Shufelt papers, Harrington, "Churchville" (typescript). Missisquoi Hist. Soc. Arch. (Stanbridge East, Que.), Church file, genealogy. PAC, RG 1, L3[L]: 24874, 31112–15, 72581, 92522; RG 9, I, A5, 1: 98; RG 31, C1, 1825, 1831, Dunham. Bouchette, *Topographical description of L.C. Illustrated atlas of the Eastern*

Townships and south western Quebec ([Toronto], 1881; repr. Port Elgin, Ont., 1972). *Illustrated dictionary of place names, United States and Canada*, ed. K. B. Harder (New York, 1971). Langelier, *Liste des terrains concédés*. Hormisdas Magnan, *Dictionnaire historique et géographique des paroisses, missions et municipalités de la province de Québec* (Arthabaska, Qué., 1925). *Officers of British forces in Canada* (Irving). "Papiers d'État – Bas-Canada," PAC *Rapport*, 1892: 241–48. Ivanhoë Caron, *La colonisation de la province de Québec* (2v., Québec, 1923–27), 2. C. M. Day, *History of the Eastern Townships, province of Quebec, Dominion of Canada, civil and descriptive* . . . (Montreal, 1869); *Pioneers of the Eastern Townships* . . . (Montreal, 1863). J. C. Furnas, *The Americans: a social history of the United States, 1587–1914* (New York, 1969). B. F. Hubbard, *Forests and clearings; the history of Stanstead County, province of Quebec, with sketches of more than five hundred families*, ed. John Lawrence (Montreal, 1874; repr. 1963). *The loyalists of the Eastern Townships of Quebec, 1783–84: 1983–84, bi-centennial* (Stanbridge East, 1984). T. R. Millman, *A short history of the parish of Dunham, Quebec* (Granby, Que., 1946). H. B. Shufelt, *Along the old roads: reflections, recollections, romance of Eastern Townships history* (Knowlton, 1956). Cyrus Thomas, *Contributions to the history of the Eastern Townships* . . . (Montreal, 1866). J. P. Noyes, "The Canadian loyalists and early settlers in the district of Bedford," Missisquoi County Hist. Soc., *Report* (Saint-Jean-sur-Richelieu, Que.), 3 (1908): 90–107; "The Missisquoi German or Dutch," 2 (1907): 31–35; "The old Church Tavern," 3: 45–46. Marion Phelps, "Dunham Township's oldest brick building burned," *Eastern Townships Advertiser* (Knowlton), 3 June 1965: 3.

CLOPPER, HENRY GEORGE, office holder, banker, and magistrate; b. 25 April 1792 in Kingsclear Parish, N.B., son of Garret Clopper and Penelope Miller; m. 9 Feb. 1820 Mary Ann Ketchum in Woodstock, N.B., and they had two daughters; d. 4 Nov. 1838 in Fredericton.

Henry George Clopper's father was a New York loyalist of Dutch descent who had served with the provincial forces during the American revolution and who held minor civil offices in New Brunswick; his mother's family were genteel Massachusetts loyalists, with a connection to the family of Edward Winslow*. After attending Fredericton Academy and serving some time as an apprentice to a Halifax merchant, Henry became a clerk in the commissariat department at Fort Cumberland (near Sackville, N.B.) in 1813. He worked for the commissariat in various places at least until 1818, being for a time in charge of the depot at Presque Isle. That he remained in employment when military establishments were reduced after the War of 1812 may have been in part due to the influence of his mother's brother-in-law, Harris William Hailes, administrator of New Brunswick in 1816–17 and afterwards aide-de-camp to Lieutenant Governor George Stracey Smyth*.

Clopper was appointed in February 1821 to succeed his father as registrar of deeds and wills for York County. On his father's death in July 1823 he also replaced him in the offices of sergeant-at-arms of the House of Assembly and county clerk. Small official plums would continue to come his way, among them the post of sub-collector of customs for Fredericton in 1831. Late in 1837 he gave up the office of county clerk, whose duties included that of acting as prosecutor, and became a justice of the peace and a judge of the Inferior Court of Common Pleas. There were few community endeavours in which Clopper was not involved. In 1822 he was one of the commissioners for erecting an almshouse and workhouse in Fredericton and he served on its board for many years. He was also clerk of the vestry of the parish church, first secretary of the Fredericton Savings Bank when it was founded in 1824, and secretary and treasurer of the Fredericton Library. In 1825 he became a founding member of the Central Committee of Relief for the Miramichi Fire, and the following year he was made one of the commissioners for the allocation of the funds it collected.

A significant event in Clopper's public career was his participation in the census of 1824. Not only was he responsible, as county clerk, for coordinating the census in York, but he was chosen by the provincial secretary, William Franklin ODELL, to compile the total returns for the colony and to report to the assembly. Census takers, who were selected by the justices of the peace, recorded population numbers by sex, colour, and age (above or under 16 years), as well as numbers of families, occupied and unoccupied houses, and new houses being built. Unfortunately, the accuracy of the figures for the colony that Clopper compiled was compromised by a few late returns from remote areas and by the failure of two counties to assess the numbers employed in lumbering operations. In 1825 Archdeacon George Best* estimated the population to be 79,176, or 5,000 more than the figure shown in the assembly's published report.

In 1834 Clopper became the first president of the Central Bank of New Brunswick, located in Fredericton. It was incorporated that year by a legislature which had recently shown itself entirely unreceptive to efforts of a group of Saint John merchants to launch a second bank in that city [*see* John McNeil WILMOT]. The ease with which the Central Bank's promoters received legislative sanction was likely owing to the fact that their institution, by virtue of its location and its modest size (the initial authorized capital being only £15,000), posed no threat to the virtual monopoly of the Bank of New Brunswick, founded in Saint John in 1820. It may have helped that Charles Simonds*, an important figure in the Bank of New Brunswick and one of the most powerful politicians in the province, was Clopper's brother-in-law. Clopper's involvement with the Central Bank led to an association with other business enterprises; one was the Nashwaak Mill and Manufacturing Company, of which he became a director, along with James Taylor* and others, in 1836.

Clopper was an obstinate man who appears to have been lacking in warmth and generosity. A dispute with a maternal uncle over the sum of £35 disrupted the family in 1830. It also involved Clopper in a confrontation with lawyer George Frederick Street*, and in 1834 the public was treated to an exchange of incivilities in the correspondence columns of the *New-Brunswick Courier* between these two scions of the loyalist aristocracy. Clopper was nevertheless a man of significant abilities. When he died the *Royal Gazette*'s obituary referred to the "clear and powerful intellect" that had "enabled him to undertake and to perform duties of such varied kind and character, as will render it a matter of extreme difficulty to supply his place in this community." Years afterwards the People's Bank of New Brunswick honoured him by placing his portrait on its five-dollar notes. Since he had had no sons and his only brother had died in 1819, the Clopper name continued to be known in New Brunswick chiefly through the career of his wife's nephew Henry George Clopper Ketchum*.

D. M. YOUNG

N.B. Museum, Central Bank, solicitor's reg., 1837–43; F85; Robinson family papers, misc., H. G. Clopper, gardening diary, 1821. PAC, MG 24, L6, 1. PANB, MC 300, MS20/25; Photograph Sect., P4/2/51; RG 1, RS336; RG 2, RS7, 115: 57–89 (mfm. at PAC); RS8, Central Bank, 1836–59; RG 4, RS24, S32-B32–32.1; S47-R2; RG 7, RS75, 1840, H. G. Clopper. PRO, CO 188/32. N.B., House of Assembly, *Journal*, 1824–25, 1832–36; Legislative Council, *Journal*, 1832–36. *Winslow papers* (Raymond). *New-Brunswick Courier*, January–August 1834. *Royal Gazette* (Fredericton), 13 Feb. 1821; 1, 29 July 1823; 30 May 1826; 7 Nov. 1838. Hill, *Old Burying Ground*. L. M. Beckwith Maxwell, *An outline of the history of central New Brunswick to the time of confederation* (Sackville, N.B., 1937; repr. Fredericton, 1984). MacNutt, *New Brunswick*. W. A. Squires, *History of Fredericton: the last 200 years*, ed. J. K. Chapman (Fredericton, 1980). *Royal Gazette*, 12 July 1865.

CLOUET, MICHEL, merchant, militia officer, politician, office holder, and JP; b. 9 Jan. 1770 in Beauport, Que., son of Joseph-Marie Clouet and Marie-Joseph Bergevin; m. 15 June 1801, at Quebec, Marie-Josephte Lalime, under-age daughter of the late Michel Lépine, *dit* Lalime, a seaman; they had no children; d. 5 Jan. 1836 at Quebec and was buried four days later in Beauport.

Michel Clouet in all likelihood spent his childhood and adolescence at Beauport, but nothing is known of this period in his life. There is also a dearth of information about when and how he came to be a merchant. In 1796 he was keeping a general store on Rue de la Montagne (Côte de la Montagne) at Quebec, and in October of that year he joined merchant François Huot* to found Huot et Clouet, a retailing company. The partnership came to an end after a year, and Clouet continued in business on Rue de la Montagne for himself. In 1805 he specialized in selling hardware. His store was at the corner of Rue Buade in a house he leased from the seigneur of Sainte-Marie, Gabriel-Elzéar Taschereau*. His enterprise was soon thriving. In 1810 he was able to buy the house from Taschereau's heirs, and subsequently he took on clerks, including his nephews Étienne Parent* and Georges-Honoré Simard*.

During the War of 1812 Clouet saw service as a captain in Quebec's 2nd Militia Battalion; he was later promoted major. He also enjoyed government patronage. For example, in 1815 he became a commissioner to oversee the demolition of the old market at Quebec. In 1828 he was made a justice of the peace for the district of Quebec, an appointment renewed in 1830 and 1833. By 1833 he was a commissioner responsible for the building of the Marine and Emigrant Hospital.

Clouet was also involved in social concerns. He subscribed to the Fire Society and the Quebec Emigrant Society. In 1817 he contributed a sum for the building of a road between the Plains of Abraham and Cap-Rouge. During the terrible cholera epidemic which swept the town in 1832, he became a member of the Quebec Board of Health and headed a benevolent society that was trying to organize help for impoverished families afflicted by the dread malady.

On 22 Oct. 1822 Clouet was elected to the House of Assembly for Quebec, which he represented with John NEILSON. Although he remained a backbencher, he was assiduous in his attendance and took part in numerous committees set up to study various bills. His precarious health forced him to give up his seat on 23 Aug. 1833, at 63 years of age; he was replaced by Louis-Théodore Besserer*.

Michel Clouet died at Quebec on 5 Jan. 1836. The funeral was held in Notre-Dame cathedral, and his remains were buried in the parish church in Beauport. His wife inherited the entire estate. She gave up the retail business and put her money into *rentes constituées* (secured annuities) and bonds. She also invested in real estate, buying several properties in Beauport which she leased to farmers. Shortly before her death she moved from Rue Buade to the home of her nephew, Georges-Honoré Simard, where she died on 4 Oct. 1849. Her fortune, estimated at more than £2,500, was divided among Clouet's 8 brothers and sisters and his 45 nephews and nieces.

CÉLINE CYR

ANQ-Q, CE1-1, 15 juin 1801; CE1-5, 9 janv. 1770, 9 janv. 1836; CN1-116, 23 oct. 1849, 23 mars 1850; CN1-208, 5, 7, 15 nov. 1836; 21 janv., 2 mars, 21 juill. 1837; 13 févr., 24 mars 1838; 27 août 1844; 24 sept. 1846; CN1-230, 11 oct. 1796, 14 juin 1801, 1er déc. 1808, 7 août 1810. PAC, RG 68, General index, 1651–1841. *Le Canadien*, 4, 6, 9 juill. 1832. *Quebec Gazette*, 24 July 1794; 30 June, 7 July, 17 Nov. 1808; 13 March 1817. Desjardins, *Guide parl. Officers of British forces in Canada* (Irving), 143. F.-J. Audet, "Michel Clouet," *BRH*, 36 (1930): 28–29. "Michel Clouet, député de Québec," *BRH*, 44 (1938): 224.

COCHRAN, ANDREW WILLIAM, lawyer, office holder, militia officer, politician, JP, and judge; b. *c.* 1793 in Windsor, N.S., son of William Cochran* and Rebecca Cuppaidge; d. 11 July 1849 in Sillery, Lower Canada.

The precocious son of an Anglican cleric, Andrew William Cochran grew up in a family of modest financial means but of rich intellectual resources; his father was the first president of King's College, Windsor. After classical studies there Cochran went into law, and in 1810 a report that he and Charles Rufus FAIRBANKS had compiled on a sensational trial for murder and piracy was published in Halifax by James Bagnall*. Cochran's talents in law and languages brought him to the attention of Lieutenant Governor Sir George Prevost*, who, after his appointment as governor of Lower Canada in 1811, promised Cochran a position in the colony. Cochran was only 19 or 20 when he arrived at Quebec and, in June 1812, was appointed an assistant in the Civil Secretary's Office. The following April he was promoted assistant civil secretary.

Shortly after his arrival Cochran was commissioned an ensign in the militia; he was appointed deputy judge advocate on the militia staff in July 1813 and in November 1814 he became acting deputy judge advocate on the army staff. Meanwhile, about April 1814, he had been named clerk of the Prerogative Court, a position he would hold until it was merged with the civil secretaryship in 1827.

Cochran quickly found that, in Lower Canadian politics, although ultimate constitutional authority for colonial affairs rested with the British parliament, there was a struggle for power within the colony between the House of Assembly, controlled by the nationalist Canadian party, and the appointed Executive and Legislative councils, dominated by the English party and loosely allied with the governor. The adoption by Prevost of a conciliatory attitude towards the assembly influenced young Cochran, and when Prevost's successor as governor, Sir John Coape Sherbrooke*, chose a similar line Cochran's views and experience made him the natural selection as Sherbrooke's civil secretary; he held the post from July 1816 to the end of July 1818. Sherbrooke's successor, the Duke of Richmond [Lennox*], adopted a policy of confrontation with the assembly, and he consequently preferred to fill the sensitive office of civil secretary with his personal secretary, John READY.

Having undertaken to study the law in Lower Canada, with the assistance of Chief Justice Jonathan SEWELL, Cochran had been called to the bar on 11 June 1817 and had subsequently started a private practice. In July 1818 he was appointed advocate general *pro tempore* until replaced by George Vanfelson* in January 1819. Three more appointments in the space of three years – auditor of the land patents in 1818, law clerk of the Legislative Council in 1819, and secretary of the Clergy Reserves Corporation in 1821 – increased his legal and administrative experience of colonial affairs and added more than £300 per annum to his income.

In the mean time Richmond's successor, Lord Dalhousie [RAMSAY], who had retained Ready as civil secretary, had become dissatisfied with him, perhaps as much for political as for administrative reasons. By 1822 Dalhousie was turning increasingly to the English party, of which Sewell was a leader and with which Cochran's recent appointments had brought him into closer contact. On 4 June 1822 Cochran replaced Ready. His task, for which he received £500 sterling a year, consisted in large part of reading, arranging, and registering the governor's official mail, provincial and imperial; he thus had considerable control over the information destined for the governor. He also often replied to the governor's correspondents and wrote to "all public officials on the details of their respective duties."

Cochran's advice to the governor concentrated on administrative detail and the legal implication of proposed actions, the spheres in which he was most experienced; indeed, he once apologized for volunteering an opinion on relations with the assembly. However, the highly politicized character of the colonial administration inevitably conferred on the governor's closest collaborator duties of a political nature. Cochran sounded out the intentions of candidates for appointment, and when, in Britain in 1824–25, Dalhousie found that he had little personal influence over the colonial secretary, Lord Bathurst, Cochran, who had accompanied him, served as his representative at the Colonial Office. Cochran shared Dalhousie's sympathies with the Canadians in general, but the British background and narrowly legal constitutional views of both men had alienated them from the leaders of the Canadian party. This alienation intensified after Dalhousie's return from Britain. During his absence Lieutenant Governor Sir Francis Nathaniel Burton* had worked out a short-term compromise with the assembly on the thorny issue of government expenditures and, encouraged by Burton's attitude, the assembly increasingly resisted

Dalhousie's use of the royal prerogative and demanded changes in imperial policy and legislation. Having no influence in the assembly, which was dominated by Louis-Joseph Papineau*, Dalhousie depended all the more on the appointed councils, and on 15 May 1827 he confirmed Cochran's political role by appointing him to the Executive Council (although Cochran did not immediately take up the position). The following year Cochran probably co-authored with Dalhousie the governor's response to Patriote attacks on his administration before the Canada committee in London. After his recall in 1828 Dalhousie informed the colonial secretary, Sir George MURRAY, that during his administration Cochran had been "my best informed and most able assistant." Papineau described Cochran's role in a more sinister light: the secretary was Dalhousie's "right-hand man, vile architect of his master's plots, confidant of all his unjust schemes against the country." Shortly before he left the colony Dalhousie had rewarded Cochran with appointments as justice of the peace, king's counsel, and commissioner of escheats and forfeitures of land.

His position in government circles not being firmly established until his engagement by Dalhousie, Cochran had resided in modest rented quarters in Upper Town until 1818 at least. On 4 September of that year he had married Houstoun Thomson, daughter of the deputy commissary general, William Thomson; they would have seven children. In subsequent years Cochran became increasingly active socially. Appointed to the committee of the Quebec Emigrants' Society in 1819, he became president of the Emigrant Aid Society the following year. In 1823 he was a director of the Quebec Fire Office, a private fire insurance company. A cultivated man, Cochran participated in the activities of the Literary and Historical Society of Quebec, which Dalhousie founded in 1824; in addition to presenting papers, he was elected vice-president in 1829 and president in 1837, 1842, 1845, and 1848. He was especially interested in the collection and publication of historical texts. In the 1830s he worked to have published Indian tales collected by a personal friend and former fur trader, Roderick MACKENZIE, and a manuscript journal of the last years of the French régime by Louis-Léonard Aumasson* de Courville. In 1842 the Literary and Historical Society sent him to Albany, N.Y., to copy documents relating to New France which it intended to publish. Cochran was busy in the mid 1830s as well in completing another of Dalhousie's projects, the monument to James Wolfe* and Louis-Joseph de Montcalm*, Marquis de Montcalm. A collector of beautiful books and strange editions, Cochran gave the inaugural address to the Quebec Library Association in 1844. He was also a vice-president and honorary counsel of the incorporated Church Society of the diocese of Quebec and a member of several other institutions connected with the Church of England.

As the son of a college president, Cochran was particularly interested in the support of education. In June 1823 he had been appointed by Dalhousie to the board of the Royal Institution for the Advancement of Learning; at the time, because the institution was viewed as anti-Catholic by Canadian leaders, Dalhousie was attempting to save it from increasing irrelevance by creating a parallel Catholic board [*see* Joseph Langley Mills*]. Cochran was president of the Royal Institution from December 1834 until the autumn of 1837. In 1845 he gave influential testimony to a committee of the assembly which was arbitrating a quarrel between the Royal Institution and the governors of McGill College [*see* John Bethune*]. After the Royal Institution was reconstituted that year with members exclusively from Montreal, Cochran continued to support education as chairman of the school commissioners at Quebec and as a trustee of Bishop's College, Lennoxville.

Solidly established in the civil service and Quebec society during Dalhousie's administration, in the early 1830s Cochran purchased a "Canadian house and garden" overlooking the St Lawrence four miles west of Quebec. He called the domain – a relatively modest one – Beauvoir. During cholera and typhus attacks in the 1830s and 1840s he remained at Beauvoir and "kept away from town except when business or public duty called me there." It was at Beauvoir that his wife died in 1837. His marriage on 24 July 1843 with Magdalen Kerr, daughter of former judge James KERR of the Court of King's Bench, reflected the progress in his social status since 1818. From 1830 to 1835 Cochran had acquired, through grants, 1,521 acres of land in Leeds, Inverness, and Ireland townships.

Cochran's services as civil secretary had ended on 1 Oct. 1828, shortly after Dalhousie's departure. The governor's replacement, Sir James Kempt*, hoping to relieve the charged political atmosphere in the colony, did not wish to retain his predecessor's closest collaborator. Cochran did not retire from the public scene, however. For a time he resisted taking the oath of office as an executive councillor – the position by making him an *ex officio* member of the provincial Court of Appeals would interfere with his modest legal practice – but Kempt eventually overcame his reluctance. He attended council meetings throughout the 1830s, defending Dalhousie's policies; in letters to his former patron and to Roderick Mackenzie he expressed mistrust of the imperial government's conciliatory policy and deplored its failure to check the growth of radicalism in the assembly. In August 1837, several months before the rebellion broke out in Lower Canada, he counselled Governor Lord Gosford [ACHESON] on legal aspects of dealing with disaffected militia officers and an assembly that refused to proceed with government business. In the aftermath of the rebellions he was appointed an assistant judge in the Court of King's Bench at Quebec on 24 June 1839; judges Joseph-Rémi VALLIÈRES de Saint-Réal, Elzéar BÉDARD, and Philippe Panet* had been suspended in December 1838 for having made decisions that favoured the Patriote cause.

Among the major factors leading to the rebellions of 1837–38 had been the state of the civil service, and Cochran's career represented in microcosm the peculiarities of the provincial government. There was almost no civil administration outside Quebec. In the capital, work was distributed haphazardly; in some busy offices the incumbents' moderate emoluments had to cover their assistants' salaries and, conversely, some incumbents received large salaries (or fees) for little or no work. Looked at individually, the sinecures seemed corrupt, but they served to distribute income and perquisites to the office-holding élite in rough proportion to their usefulness to the executive. Cochran's appointments spanned the extremes of this system. As clerk of the Prerogative Court (a position which did not officially exist) he received about £200 a year to sign marriage licences for an hour a week. As commissioner of escheats he drew £500 sterling a year for duties that he did not fulfil because successive governors failed to get a court of escheats functioning. At the other extreme he earned only £100 a year sterling for the arduous tasks he performed as a member of the Executive Council and the Court of Appeals. Cochran's total income at times approached £1,000 a year in salaries and fees, roughly that of the senior judges, the bishops, and the speaker of the assembly, and more than that of almost any civil official outside the customs service.

Successive governors tried to improve this ramshackle structure, but reforms foundered on the problem of finding pensions for redundant placemen, and on the assembly's desire for sweeping changes that the Colonial Office would not contemplate. Eventually the assembly's refusal to pay official salaries in the mid 1830s, and parliament's suspension of the colonial legislature in 1838, gave the imperial authorities occasion to abolish offices and pare down the earnings of pluralists; Cochran earned nothing after 1836 from his posts of auditor of the land patents and commissioner of escheats, was placed on half pay as law clerk of the suspended Legislative Council, and lost his position as executive councillor with the union of 1841. By 1838 he had been named among office holders who were to receive a pension of £200 a year "for their public services." He was not, however, without financial resources; as a queen's counsel he handled many criminal prosecutions at Quebec until his death in 1849 at about age 56. Ironically he succumbed to cholera in his haven of Beauvoir. The four surviving children from his first marriage – of whom three were minors – inherited a modest estate.

Talent and temperament – he was a man of ready conversation with an extensive circle of acquaintances – had secured Cochran a place near the centre of the provincial administration for nearly 30 years. He was in most ways the archetypal bureaucrat of his time. He considered office holding to be a matter of class – and, in the case of important positions, to be a British prerogative. After the death of an official in the Provincial Secretary's Office in 1834 Cochran regretted that the post had not been offered to the official's son. The young man who obtained the position, he told Roderick Mackenzie, was "clever and respectable in his character, but not of that standing in Society which I think would have been desirable for so honourable and confidential an office"; however, he added, "he is better than a Canadian, for *that* office." Cochran was typical in other respects too: never elected to public position, and for the most part successful in avoiding controversy, he was a conspicuous pluralist and sinecurist. In contrast to lazy or predatory contemporaries, however, Cochran worked with diligence, discretion, and ability and took professional pride in his vocation. He considered the dismissal from office of William Bowman FELTON, who had been accused of fraud, "just and proper," he told Mackenzie in 1837; at the same time he felt for a man "who ends so discreditably a course of 30 years in public service." But, he added, "I confess I feel more for his family, & for the discredit brought on the Public Service, and on the Legislative Council than for the individual himself." It was in part conscientious men such as Cochran who prolonged the old colonial system in Lower Canada by ensuring that the bureaucracy met most of the demands that were placed upon it.

PHILIP GOLDRING

Andrew William Cochran probably co-authored with Lord Dalhousie *Observations on the petitions of grievance addressed to the imperial parliament from the districts of Quebec, Montreal, and Three Rivers* (Quebec, 1828). He presented three papers to the Literary and Hist. Soc. of Quebec, "Ancient documents relating to Acadia: notices of the families of La Tour and D'Aulnais, therein mentioned, so far as their history is connected with it"; "A collection and critical examination of the passages in Greek authors in which mention is made of the Hyperboreans (prize essay)"; and "Notes on the measures adopted by government, between 1775 and 1786, to check the St Paul's Bay disease," which were published in its *Trans.*, 3 (1832–37): 233–41; 322–46; and 4 (1843–60): 139–52, respectively, as well as two other papers which were not published, "The diversity of laws prevailing in the different colonial possessions of Great Britain" (1843) and "On the diversity of colonial laws, the etymology of Quebec" (1844). He is also the author of *Inaugural address, delivered at Quebec, before the Quebec*

Library Association, on Friday, 26th January, 1844 (Quebec, 1844).

ANQ-Q, CE1-61, 4 sept. 1818, 17 juin 1837, 24 juill. 1843, 12 juill. 1849; CN1-18, 27 juin, 21 nov. 1848; 21 nov. 1849; CN1-208, 3 déc. 1849. McGill Univ. Libraries, Dept. of Rare Books and Special Coll., MS coll., CH27.S63. PAC, MG 24, A40: 6341–49, 6658–60, 6763–65, 6798–800, 7696–99; B14: 1713–16; C37; MG 30, D1, 8: 473–76; RG 68, General index, 1651–1841. PRO, CO 42/216: 267; 42/295: 294; CO 47/122: 30; 47/123: 18; 47/126: 13; 47/128: 92, 144; 47/136: 45; 47/137: 158. SRO, GD45/3/34A–B. G.B., Parl., Command paper, 1837, 24, [no.50]: 35–37, *Report of commissioners on grievances complained of in Lower Canada*. L.C., House of Assembly, *Journals*, 1828–29, app.Ii, 28 Feb. 1829. L.-J. Papineau, "Correspondance" (Ouellet), ANQ *Rapport*, 1953–55: 269. *Morning Chronicle* (Quebec), 13 July 1849. *Quebec Gazette*, 18 June 1812; 12 June 1817; 7 Sept. 1818; 2 Aug. 1819; 23 Oct. 1820; 26 Nov. 1821; 21 July, 13 Oct. 1823; 5 Jan., 29 March 1824; 12 July 1849. F.-J. Audet, "Les législateurs du Bas-Canada." "The Durham papers," PAC *Report*, 1923: 25, 27, 38, 246. H. J. Morgan, *Bibliotheca Canadensis*; *Sketches of celebrated Canadians*. *Officers of British forces in Canada* (Irving). Ouellet, "Inv. de la saberdache," ANQ *Rapport*, 1955–57: 123, 125, 161. *Quebec almanac*, 1815: 32; 1821–27. S. B. Frost, *McGill University: for the advancement of learning* (2v., Montreal, 1980–84), 1: 65–93. Philip Goldring, "British colonists and imperial interests in Lower Canada, 1820 to 1841" (PHD thesis, Univ. of London, 1978). Taft Manning, *Revolt of French Canada*. P.-É. Vachon, *Beauvoir, le domaine, la villa* (Cap-Rouge, Qué., 1977), 59–71. Frère Marcel-Joseph, "Les Canadiens veulent conserver le régime seigneurial," *RHAF*, 7 (1953–54): 237. Séraphin Marion, "L'Institution royale, les biens des jésuites et Honoré Mercier," *Cahiers des Dix*, 35 (1970): 97–126. R. G. Thwaites, "Le journal des jésuites," *BRH*, 5 (1899): 21–22.

COCHRANE, JOHN, sculptor; baptized 31 March 1813 near Perth, Scotland, son of James Cochrane and Elizabeth Paton; d. unmarried 31 July 1850 in Toronto.

John Cochrane, accompanied by his mother and his two brothers, James and David, left Scotland for Toronto in May 1845. The three brothers had enjoyed reputations as fine craftsmen in the Perth area, and their emigration was publicly lamented. Although not the eldest, John apparently took the leading role in establishing a business that probably employed all three brothers. His advertisement in the *British Colonist* of 31 Aug. 1847 announced his field as "SCULPTURE in MARBLE AND STONE" and listed as his specialities "Statues, Coats of Arms, Monuments, Tomb Stones, Sun Dials, Fonts, Vases, Chimney Pieces, Modelling, Ornaments &c."

Very soon after his arrival, Cochrane formed an association with Toronto architect William Thomas*, who used the Cochranes on all his important commissions between 1845 and 1850. The sculptor worked with Thomas on the decorations for the interior of St Paul's Church (Anglican) in London. Cochrane was also responsible for the stone and stucco ornamentation of St Michael's Cathedral (Roman Catholic) in Toronto, and for the stone carving, including a coat of arms in the central gable, on the episcopal palace just north of the cathedral. All three Cochranes were employed in Toronto in 1850 to embellish the exterior of Thomas's masterpiece, St Lawrence Hall. Among the notable decorations are the 16 Corinthian capitals on the façade, and the elaborately carved brackets, swags, rosettes, and panels. Three heads, said to represent the river god of the St Lawrence as well as the gods of Lake Ontario and Niagara Falls, were sculpted as keystones over the three arched ground-floor entrances. The most sophisticated work in the hall was on the coats of arms. Before 1850 Cochrane had already attracted favourable attention for his carving of coats of arms, including the one that adorned the Bank of British North America (now demolished) sculpted shortly after his arrival in Toronto. The arms of the city of Toronto, combined with the royal arms and standing figures of an Indian and Britannia, all mounted on the pediment of the façade of St Lawrence Hall, was almost certainly one of his last works.

Although there is no documentation linking Cochrane's name with other buildings, it seems probable that his hand was responsible for the extensive carving that adorned Thomas's own residence, Oakham House at 322 Church Street. It is also possible that in 1848 Cochrane worked on another of Thomas's projects, the church for the congregation of John Jennings* (now demolished) at the southeast corner of Richmond and Bay streets. Thomas and Cochrane were probably not only associates, but also friends: the stone portrait of Thomas adorning one side of the main entrance of the episcopal palace displays much more character than that of the matching figure of Bishop Michael POWER on the other side. The two men were buried in adjacent plots in St James' Cemetery, Toronto.

After Cochrane's death his brothers carried on in business with a stone-cutter, Robert Pollock, in a partnership called Cochranes and Pollock, until 1852 when David Cochrane and Pollock formed a new partnership.

In 1847 at the Toronto Society of Arts exhibition, John Cochrane exhibited a Gothic head carved in stone, an angelic head designed by Thomas, and the plans for the interior of St Paul's. The next year he served on the committee of management for the exhibition, which displayed his plaster statue of Joseph Brant [Thayendanegea*]. To the 1848 Toronto Mechanics' Institute exhibition he contributed a royal arms in plaster, a rustic sun-dial, and the statue of Brant (which he owned). The statue attracted praise for its wealth of truthful detail and may have served as the model for the Indian in the St Lawrence Hall coat of arms.

Though he remains a shadowy figure whose work is often submerged in that of Cochrane Brothers, John Cochrane's surviving works suggest he was a superior craftsman. His premature death at the age of 38 no doubt robbed his adopted city of many more fine stone carvings.

C. M. PFAFF and L. R. PFAFF

MTRL, Toronto, Mechanics' Institute papers, D25. Toronto Soc. of Arts, *Toronto Society of Arts: first exhibition, 1847 . . .* ([Toronto?, 1847?]); *Toronto Society of Arts: second exhibition, 1848 . . .* ([Toronto?, 1848?]). *British Canadian, and Canada West Commercial and General Advertiser* (Toronto), 27 March 1847. *British Colonist*, 19, 26 March, 31 Aug., 3 Sept. 1847; 28 April 1848; 2 Aug. 1850. *Globe*, 1 Aug. 1850. E. [R.] Arthur, *Toronto, no mean city* ([Toronto], 1964). M. E. and Merilyn McKelvey, *Toronto, carved in stone* (Toronto, 1984). C. D. Lowrey, "The Toronto Society of Arts, 1847–48: patriotism and the pursuit of culture in Canada West," *RACAR* (Quebec and Toronto), 12 (1985): 3–44.

COCKBURN, JAMES PATTISON, army officer and water-colourist; b. 18 March 1779 in New York City, son of Colonel John Cockburn and Mary Cockburn, daughter of Colonel Sir James Cockburn; m. 1800 Elizabeth Johanna Vansittart in Cape Colony (South Africa), and they had five sons and two daughters; d. 18 March 1847 in Woolwich (London).

James Pattison Cockburn was raised in a family of soldiers. On 19 March 1793 he entered the Royal Military Academy at Woolwich as a cadet, and there he was taught drawing, in the main under the chief drawing-master, Paul Sandby. To this two-year period of training belongs *The Royal Laboratory, Woolwich*, a water-colour in which Cockburn showed himself a skilled topographer with a strong sense of perspective and a fine, precise hand in drawing. Several figures in motion give life to the composition and prevent it from being only a topographical landscape. These characteristics would be the hallmark of his style.

Cockburn participated in the taking of Cape Colony in September 1795 and in an expedition against Manila in 1798. In 1803 he was back in England, and on 1 June 1806 he obtained the rank of captain in the artillery. His company was at first stationed at Colchester, and then in August and September 1807 was sent to Denmark, where Cockburn joined in the siege of Copenhagen. In November a set of five coloured aquatints made from his drawings recording the military operation was published. These early engravings fit into a strict topographical tradition, inherited from the 17th century, in which landscape is subordinated to the representation of sites and events. Cockburn was listed as sick from 10 Sept. 1807 until late November 1808, when he was located in Norwich. His years in the garrison there, until November 1814, were quiet except for the siege of Antwerp (Belgium) in August 1809, during which he led a flotilla with distinction and thus was awarded the task of negotiating the terms of surrender. From the expedition there remains a coloured aquatint map engraved from his drawings, the work of a cartographer in the style of Dutch artists Pieter Jansz Saenredam and Gaspar Van Wittel, which well illustrates the instruction given at the Royal Military Academy.

From 31 July to 12 Aug. 1809 Cockburn, as an honorary member, exhibited 17 water-colours at the Norwich Society of Artists, including some of Cape Colony and Bengal. He was experiencing a period of vital importance in his development as an artist. Through his contacts with the landscape painters of the Norwich school, in which Dutch and Italian influences blended, and particularly with the studios of John Sell Cotman and John Thirtle (reputedly his teacher), Cockburn's technique acquired a spontaneity it had lacked. The draftsmanship is less precise, and the result is to heighten the effect of the very diffused colouring, with the sombre tones in the foreground (deep ochres to pale olive-green) shading to light in the background. The eye is drawn to the atmospheric effects, such as the great diagonals of the sun's rays.

Cockburn returned to Colchester in December 1814 with the rank of brevet-major accorded him on 4 June. He stayed there till early in 1817. A sketch-book of August 1815 gives proof of a period at Woolwich and walks along the Thames. His symmetrical use of space demonstrates his mastery of composition. These drawings also reveal his way of working in front of the subject, which did not change much subsequently. He employed graphite, on its own or retouched with pen and with a brown ink wash, or else he used a sepia wash by itself that showed the shapes and the shades of light.

The Napoleonic Wars over, Cockburn went to stay on the Continent more frequently, working for William Bernard Cooke, an English engraver and publisher. In March 1816 and again in 1817 and 1818 he was at Naples and Pompeii, doing topographical sketches of the excavations. According to German composer Louis Spohr, to whom he showed more than 200 landscapes of Naples and its surroundings, Cockburn had "extraordinary skill in catching charming views in a matter of minutes." He was becoming an indefatigable sketcher. In the period 1816–22 he produced drawings in sepia as he moved from place to place in the Alps and elsewhere in Italy and Switzerland: vast panoramas and mountain passes figured alongside scenes of streets and market places. The wealth of pictures is explained not only by Cockburn's mastery of technical means but also, according to Spohr, by his use of "a machine that projected the landscape, in reduced scale, on paper." Although it is not certain that Spohr was referring to a *camera lucida*, the sharpness of the images in several sketches done at the time he made his remark in some measure substantiates this hypothesis.

Cockburn arrived in Lower Canada in November 1822. His visit was brief, since he left again on 17 June 1823, and his company followed in August. As a result there are few sketches from this first trip. A water-colour entitled *Cape Diamond from below no 1 tower*, dated 29 Oct. 1823, suggests Cockburn did studies that he reworked in his studio according to his usual practice. Back in Woolwich, he received the rank of major in his regiment on 29 July 1825 and was promoted lieutenant-colonel the same day. On 5 April 1826, at 47 years of age, he was given command of the Royal Artillery in the Canadas, to which he returned in August.

During these years of peace Cockburn had ample leisure to sketch Quebec and its environs as well as scenes in Upper and Lower Canada where his tours of inspection took him. Thus his subjects extend from Quebec to Niagara Falls. The idiom is firmly established in the drawings in sepia or water-colour from this mature period. The order and clarity of arrangement rest upon two constants: following a classical approach, the landscape is drawn in parallel planes; and a diagonal line (street, sidewalk, path, or river) is used to organize the elements in the composition, directing the eye from the foreground straight to the background. In his drawings of Quebec streets Cockburn reveals his debt to Paul Sandby: a soft light plays over a limited range of colours forming rhythmical compositions in pale tonalities and attenuating the analytical spirit of these water-colours. The artist's interest in community life is also evident in depictions of solemn occasions (religious processions), daily activities (men cutting ice), and anecdotal scenes (market days). These drawings, however, reveal only one aspect of his personality. Cockburn looked at nature in the Canadian countryside as a true landscape artist: he was able instinctively to find the best angle of approach and arrangement of physical features. With this ability he drew picturesque and poetic compositions, which were seldom dramatic or sublime, except perhaps for certain views of Niagara Falls. Observation of small details is still present: stratified rocks, sodden roads through heavy clay, effects of light on snow and ice. In 1831 he brought out anonymously a small "picturesque guide" to the town of Quebec and its environs illustrated with seven plates. But he turned out nothing comparable to his previous publications. On 2 Aug. 1832 he left Quebec with his family.

Cockburn settled in Woolwich, where he owned a house, and on 10 Oct. 1838 became director of the Royal Laboratory of the Royal Arsenal there. He retained this post until 15 Nov. 1846, when he retired with the rank of major-general, which had been accorded him on 9 November. His health deteriorated rapidly, and he died at his residence in Woolwich on 18 March 1847.

Cockburn produced an enormous body of work. Paradoxically, it has been studied only superficially and consequently in large measure remains to be reconstructed. The reason is simple: it is sometimes difficult to distinguish between the sketch done from life and the work done in the studio. The sketch done from life seldom has any room for improvisation and already reveals the artist's poetic idiom; the work done in the studio retains the freshness of first impressions yet has been developed in the artist's mind.

After his death James Pattison Cockburn was not completely forgotten. In August 1860 nine of his water-colours were exhibited by the Norfolk and Norwich Fine Arts Association in a show to honour "local artists who were deceased." In a review in the *Norwich Mercury* his name appeared along with the famous names of the Norwich school, and he was called an "excellent artist." Time has but confirmed the esteem in which Cockburn was held during the period he spent at Quebec. Joseph Légaré*, upon whom he had a lasting effect, certainly shared this opinion. Légaré's direct copies and his occasional borrowings, his imitations of technique and his pasticcios, are indicative of an influence, rather than of intellectual affinity. Cockburn was thus one of the few British artists, if not the only one, in the early 19th century to impart his view of nature to a Quebec landscape artist.

Didier Prioul

[James Pattison Cockburn is the author of *Swiss scenery from drawings* (London, [1820]), illustrated by 60 prints from his drawings; the book was described as "nearly ready for publication" in the November 1818 issue of *Gentleman's Magazine* (p.445). An anonymous work, *Quebec and its environs; being a picturesque guide to the stranger*, published in Quebec in 1831, was attributed to him first by Lady Aylmer, in her "Recollections of Canada, 1831" (ANQ *Rapport*, 1934–35: 283), and then in *A dictionary of books relating to America, from its discovery to the present time*, comp. Joseph Sabin (29v., New York, 1868–1936; repr. 29v. in 15, Amsterdam, 1961–62), 3: 200. It was certainly in the publisher's hands by 1829: in writing *The picture of Quebec* (Quebec, 1829), George Bourne drew extensively on it, virtually to the point of plagiarism, for the chapter "Itinerary" (pp.64–71).

A number of prints based on Cockburn's drawings were brought out in London either separately or in collections. These were, in chronological order, *The siege of Copenhagen* (1807), consisting of five aquatints; *Pictural plan of the grand expedition in the West Schelt, Aug[t] 1809; shewing the difficulty of approach to Antwerp* (1809), one aquatint; *View of the Royal Artillery barracks* and *View of the Royal Military Academy* (1816), two aquatints (derived probably from drawings in his August 1815 sketch-book, from which only the two middle leaves have been removed); *Views to illustrate the route of Mont Cenis, drawn from nature* (1822), 50 plates; *Views to illustrate the route of the Simplon, drawn from nature* (1822), 50 plates (because the copy at the BL contains a text in 81 manuscript folios which describes the voyage and is entitled "Simplon," it is conceivable that Cockburn's intention was to produce a publication similar to *Swiss scenery*); *Views in the valley of Aosta, drawn from nature* (1823), 29 plates; and *Quebec* and *The falls of Niagara* (1833), two sets of six aquatints (the series *The falls of Niagara* was republished in 1857). *Montmorency waterfall & cone, near Quebec* and *Horse-Shoe Fall, Niagara*, coloured prints published in 1844 and based on drawings of William Purser and Thomas Allom, were new studies in Cockburn's style.

In addition, Cockburn contributed his drawings to various publications, the first, on which he collaborated with the English engraver William Bernard Cooke, appearing as *Delineations of the celebrated city of Pompeii* (London, 1818). Projected to comprise two volumes in four parts and to be illustrated by 50 picturesque views, the work was described in the January 1818 issue of *Gentleman's Magazine* (p.61) as being "nearly ready for publication." A comparison of copies held at the BL and at the Bibliothèque nationale in Paris (Estampes, Vf.219) suggests that there were two editions, the first probably published in 1818 or 1819, and the second in 1827 with the plates in a different order, additional prints, and a new title. Two of Cockburn's drawings were engraved for George Newenham Wright's *The Rhine, Italy, and Greece, in a series of drawings from nature ... with historical and legendary descriptions* (2v., London and Paris, [1841]).

The principal collections of Cockburn's Canadian works are those of the Royal Ont. Museum in Toronto; the National Gallery of Canada and the Picture Division of the PAC, both in Ottawa; the McCord Museum in Montreal; and, in Quebec, the Musée du Québec, the Musée du Séminaire de Québec, and the ANQ-Q. Although his European works remain for the most part in private hands, public collections are in the British Museum (London), Dept. of Prints and Drawings; the Norwich Castle Museum (Norwich, Eng.); and the Royal Military Academy (Sandhurst, Eng.). D.P.]

GRO (London), Registration of death index, no.376, 27 March 1847 (copy at Somerset Record Office (Taunton, Eng.)). MAC-CD, Fonds Morisset, 1, Montréal, île de Montréal, bibliothèque municipale et album Viger; Québec, séminaire de Québec, archives, cartes et peintures. PAC, RG 8, I (C ser.), 747: 122, 125–26a; 748: 1–109; RG 37, A2, 298, 339. PRO, PROB 11/2055: 332 [392]; WO 17/1526: 158; 17/1527: 80; 17/1530: 105; 17/1536: 119; 17/2561; 17/2582; WO 55/1225–27, esp. 55/1227: 179–80; WO 76/360: 60.

Catalogue of the fifth exhibition by the Norwich Society of Artists in oil & water colours . . . (Norwich, 1809). *Gentleman's Magazine*, 1809: 763, 863–64; January–June 1847: 550–51. *Records of the Royal Military Academy, 1741–1892*, ed. H. D. Buchanan-Dunlop (2nd ed., Woolwich [London, 1895]). *Norfolk Chronicle and Norwich Gazette* (Norwich), 29 July 1809, 1 Sept. 1860. *Norwich Mercury*, 29 July, 5, 12 Aug. 1809. *Quebec Gazette*, 19 June 1823, 23 Nov. 1829, 1 Aug. 1832, 13 Dec. 1833. *Quebec Mercury*, 8 April 1828.

Jeremy Adamson, *From ocean to ocean: nineteenth century water colour painting in Canada* (Toronto, 1976), 5. *Allgemeines Lexikon der bildenden Künstler von der Antike bis zur Gegenwart . . .*, ed. Hans Vollmer (37v., Leipzig, [German Democratic Republic], 1907–50), 7: 146–47. Mary Allodi, *Canadian watercolours and drawings in the Royal Ontario Museum* (2v., Toronto, 1974), 1, nos.270–463. *Battery records of the Royal Artillery, 1716–1859*, comp. M. E. S. Laws (Woolwich, 1952), 127–86. W. M. E. Cooke, *The last "Lion" : . . . rambles in Quebec with James Pattison Cockburn* (Kingston, Ont., 1978); *W. H. Coverdale Collection of Canadiana: paintings, water-colours and drawings (Manoir Richelieu collection)* (Ottawa, 1983), 43–60. *Dictionnaire critique et documentaire des peintres, sculpteurs, dessinateurs et graveurs de tous les temps et de tous les pays* (nouv. éd., 10v., Paris, 1976), 3: 87. *DNB*. Harper, *Early painters and engravers*, 69; *Everyman's Canada; paintings and drawings from the McCord Museum of McGill University* (Ottawa, 1962), 68–70. *Historical records of the Seventy-Ninth Regiment of Foot or Cameron Highlanders*, comp. Robert Jameson (Edinburgh and London, 1863). *List of officers of the Royal Regiment of Artillery, as they stood in the year 1763, with a continuation to the present time . . .*, comp. John Kane (Greenwich [London], 1815), 26. *List of officers of the Royal Regiment of Artillery from the year 1716 to the present date*, comp. John Kane (rev. ed., Woolwich, 1869), 25, 103. H. L. Mallalieu, *The dictionary of British water-colour artists up to 1920* (Woodbridge, Eng., 1976; repr. 1984), 63. *The New-York Historical Society's dictionary of artists in America, 1564–1860*, comp. G. C. Groce and D. H. Wallace (New Haven, Conn., and London, 1957; repr. 1964). Norfolk and Norwich Fine Arts Assoc., *Exhibition of the works of deceased local artists, at the government school of art, in the Norwich Free Library* (Norwich, 1860), 13–15. *Quebec almanac*, 1823: 198; 1827: 205, 210; 1828: 145, 150; 1829: 159, 164; 1830: 161, 166; 1831: 183, 187; 1832: 173, 177. Miklós Rajnai, *The Norwich Society of Artists, 1805–1833: a dictionary of contributors and their work* (Norwich, 1976), 27, 104, 130, 137. Samuel Redgrave, *A dictionary of artists of the English School: painters, sculptors, architects, engravers, and ornamentists; with notices of their lives and works* (2nd ed., London, 1878; repr. Bath, Eng., 1970), 89. Ann Thomas, *Fact and fiction: Canadian painting and photography, 1860–1900* (Montreal, 1979), 16–22. W. T. Vincent, *The records of the Woolwich district* (2v., Woolwich, 1888–90), 1: 368; 2: 462, 745.

Marjorie Allthorpe-Guyton, *John Thirtle, 1777–1839; drawings in Norwich Castle Museum* ([Norwich], 1977). Michael Bell, *From Annapolis Royal to the Klondike; painters in a new land* (Toronto, 1973), 11–12, 47, 49, 73–74, 221. J. A. Browne, *England's artillerymen; an historical narrative of the services of the Royal Artillery* (London, 1865). Christina Cameron et Jean Trudel, *Québec au temps de James Patterson Cockburn* (Québec, 1976). Robert and H. A. Cockburn, *The records of the Cockburn family* (Edinburgh, 1913) [containing a portrait of J. P. Cockburn, a copy of which is in the McCord Museum]. C. P. de Volpi, *The Niagara peninsula, a pictorial record . . .* (Montreal, 1966); *Quebec, a pictorial record . . ., 1608–*

1875 (n.p., 1971). Pierre Doyon, "Les aquarellistes britanniques de l'Académie royale militaire de Woolwich et la représentation du paysage québécois, de 1759 à 1871" (2v., thèse de MA, univ. de Montréal , 1982), 1: 102–30. Harper, *Painting in Canada* (1977). A. W. Moore, *The Norwich school of artists* ([Norwich], 1985), 79. Morisset, *Coup d'œil sur les arts*, 80–81; *La peinture traditionnelle*, 75–77, 84. Fulgido Pomella, *Piemonte, Valle d'Aosta, Nizza e Savoia, Valli Valdesi nelle illustrazioni di William Brockedon e William H. Bartlett* (Ivrea, Italy, 1982), 14–15. D. R. Reid, *A concise history of Canadian painting* (Toronto, 1973), 29–30, 36. F. St G. Spendlove, *The face of early Canada: pictures of Canada which have helped to make history* (Toronto, 1958), 46–51. Louis [Ludwig] Spohr, *Autobiography* (2v., London, 1865; repr. 2v. in 1, New York, 1969). B. M. Stafford, *Voyage into substance: art, science, nature and the illustrated travel account, 1760–1840* (Cambridge, Mass., and London, 1984), 83, 91, 242, 272, 420. N. P. Willis, *Canadian scenery illustrated, from drawings by W. H. Bartlett* (2v., London, 1842; repr. Toronto, 1967). T. S. R. Boase, "English artists and the Val d'Aosta," Warburg and Courtauld Institutes, *Journal* (London), 19 (1956): 288–89. W. E. Greening, "Some early recorders of the nineteenth century Canadian scene," *Canadian Geographical Journal* (Ottawa), 66 (January–June 1963), no.4: 126–27. Ignotus [Thomas Chapais], "Le monument Wolfe et Montcalm à Québec," *BRH*, 5 (1899): 305–9. *Norwich Mercury*, 22, 29 Aug. 1860. *Notes and Queries* (London), 14 Oct., 11 Nov. 1865; 9 July 1910; 31 Aug. 1912. F. St G. Spendlove, "The Canadian watercolours of James Pattison Cockburn (1779?–1847)," *Connoisseur* (London), 133 (1954), no.537: 203–7. Jean Trudel et Christina Cameron, "Québec vu par Cockburn," *Vie des Arts* (Montréal), 19 (automne 1974): 55–57.

COFFIN, Sir ISAAC, naval officer and seigneur; b. 16 May 1759 in Boston, Mass., son of Nathaniel Coffin, a customs officer, and Elizabeth Barnes; m. 3 April 1811 Elizabeth Browne Greenly and assumed the name and arms of Greenly for two years; d. 23 July 1839 in Cheltenham, England.

Isaac Coffin entered the British navy on the North American station as a volunteer in 1773 and was promoted lieutenant only three years later. He commanded the schooner *Placentia* off Newfoundland in 1778–79, survived a shipwreck in the armed vessel *Pinson*, also under his command, on the coast of Labrador late in 1779, and in 1781 was Rear-Admiral Mariot Arbuthnot*'s signal lieutenant on the *Royal Oak* during operations off Cape Henry, Va. On 3 July 1781 he received promotion to commander. In January 1782 he served as a volunteer under Sir Samuel Hood in a brilliant action off St Kitts, in the West Indies, and on 13 June of that year, through Hood's influence, was made post captain, in command of the 74-gun *Shrewsbury*.

Coffin was evidently a capable young officer, and his subsequent career bore out the energy, competence, and bravery which won him early promotion. It also revealed an affinity for controversy. Within weeks of joining the *Shrewsbury* he refused to accept three unqualified midshipmen appointed to the ship as lieutenants by Admiral Lord Rodney, commander-in-chief in the West Indies. Brought before a court martial on 29 July 1782, Coffin was acquitted. In 1783 he was given command of a smaller ship, the *Hydra*, which he paid off in England before going on half pay.

In 1786 he returned to sea in command of the *Thisbe*, in which he took Lord Dorchester [Carleton*] to Canada. Two years later he was maliciously accused by its master of signing false musters. The practice was common but Coffin claimed he had made an honest mistake. The charge was nevertheless proved, and he was sentenced by a court martial to be dismissed from his ship. The first lord of the Admiralty, Lord Howe, changed the sentence to cashiering, and Coffin successfully appealed the punishment, which was pronounced illegal. Howe then reinstated Coffin because he "did not consider it advisable to exercise the right of the Admiralty arbitrarily to dismiss him from the navy." The case established legal precedents concerning the limits of the Admiralty's interference in sentences pronounced by courts martial.

In 1790 Coffin took command of the 20-gun *Alligator*, and in 1791 he brought Dorchester back to England, going on half pay again until the resumption of war in 1793, at which time he received command of the 36-gun *Melampus*. In 1794 he aggravated an injury he had acquired around 1790, when he jumped overboard to save the life of a seaman, and was never again fit for active service. He became regulating captain at Leith, Scotland, in 1795 and in October of that year went to Corsica as a civil commissioner of the navy. Evacuated to Lisbon when Corsica fell into French hands in 1796, he served there and in 1798 on Minorca. The following year he was appointed commissioner of the dockyard at Sheerness, England, but was sent instead to Halifax, where he became acting resident commissioner of the royal dockyard. The commissioner, Henry Duncan*, who was in England for medical treatment, took up Coffin's post at Sheerness.

Admiral Lord St Vincent was to observe in 1800 that "nothing but a radical sweep of our dockyards can do any good, and that can only be accomplished in a peace." By then, Coffin had already imposed some radical reforms on the Halifax dockyard. In December 1799 he had reported extensive irregularities: "a field was consequently opened for all kinds of frauds and embezzlements." Coffin stopped warrant officers and seamen from collecting ships' stores without supervision, removed the right of ships' captains to issue orders to dockyard officers, began a monthly rather than quarterly issue of provisions and spirits in order to curb drunkenness, and insisted on adherence to Navy Board regulations in the repair and refit of ships.

He went on to pay off horses on the dockyard establishment (boats provided cheaper transportation), dismiss 50 labourers, survey the master attendant's stores, and restrict landing or embarkation in the dockyard to those on official business. He capped off these measures by discharging the master shipwright, Elias Marshall, who had 48 years of service, 37 in the Halifax yard.

In April 1800 Coffin returned to England, bringing with him the evidence on which he had acted, so that it would not be "lost," but Duncan and Admiral Sir William Parker, commander-in-chief at Halifax, reinstated some of those he had removed from office, including Marshall, "as the Public have suffered very little from his irregularity." Coffin took up his post at Sheerness, where he applied himself with such efficiency and energy that he was brought back to the sea service (not normally allowed in the case of civil commissioners). He was promoted rear-admiral of the white on 23 April 1804. On 19 May he was made a baronet and became admiral superintendent at Portsmouth, a position he held until 28 April 1808, after which he had no further employment with the navy.

Promoted vice-admiral of the blue, Coffin continued to advance on the flag list until he became admiral of the blue on 4 June 1814. From 1818 to 1826 he sat as member of parliament for Ilchester. He was made a GCH in 1832. His wife's death, on 27 Jan. 1839, was followed by his own on 23 July of the same year.

In 1787 Coffin had alerted the Legislative Council of Quebec to American exploitation of the fisheries and to the existence of a flourishing illicit trade on the Îles de la Madeleine. A committee of the council, presided over by Chief Justice William Smith*, favoured Coffin's solution, which was to become proprietor himself. The matter lay dormant until 1795, when Coffin raised it again with the Treasury in London. The Treasury having concluded that "the fishery at these islands, unless granted to an individual will remain waste and be used by Foreigners as well as the King's subjects," letters patent were issued to Coffin on 24 April 1798 for the seigneury of Îles-de-la-Madeleine. According to the terms of the grant, Coffin was obliged to allow free access to the beaches and shores for the fishery.

Because of Coffin's professional abilities and his reputed knowledge of the fisheries, much "public utility" was expected to derive from his proprietorship. As an absentee landlord acting through agents he himself obtained nothing but aggravation. Like other proprietors in British North America of British origin, he wanted English-speaking settlers, but the islands offered them little. The Acadian inhabitants, who engaged in the walrus, seal, and cod fisheries, were reluctant to accept directions from Quebec rather than from Newfoundland as they had been accustomed to doing, and also resisted paying rent. After Coffin made his first and only visit to the islands in 1806, he tried in vain to have 22 families who had come from Saint-Pierre and Miquelon in 1792 with their priest, Jean-Baptiste Allain*, deported as "*Frenchmen* Enemies to the King who . . . live in open defiance of all law & carry on a contraband trade with the Americans to the great detriment of his Majesty's subjects." In 1822, having received no return on his investment, he attempted to sell or lease the islands to the United States. Two years later he wanted to settle friends and kin from Massachusetts, and in 1828 he proposed to annex the islands to Nova Scotia, to facilitate the administration of justice. None of these ideas was adopted.

The Îles-de-la-Madeleine venture failed, largely because the seigneurial system was in a state of flux and the British government, although prepared to admit Coffin's claims, was out of sympathy with his cause. Lord Dalhousie [RAMSAY] called it "a mad speculation." After a visit to the islands in 1831 Lieutenant Frederick Henry Baddeley*, referring to criticisms of the Madelinots such as those made by Coffin, remarked that "smuggling, on these islands, is scarcely a breach of the law, for no law but the law of God is preached upon them. . . . As long as they are abandoned . . . to their own resources, it would be unjust to deprive them of the advantage which a *free* trade offers." As a seigneur, motivated no doubt by instincts natural to a naval captain who was the son of a customs officer, Coffin had good intentions but no understanding of his tenants, and he left an archaic legacy to his heirs. His situation as seigneur was ironic, because he is remembered principally for the reforming zeal that marked his naval career.

W. A. B. DOUGLAS

NMM, C. G. Pitcairn-Jones, notes on sea officers. PAC, RG 1, L3[L]: 30884–85, 30892, 30906, 30913, 30922–35. PRO, ADM 1/494–95; ADM 12/22/443; ADM 106/2027–28; CO 42/123, 42/131, 42/192, 42/202, 42/221 (mfm. at PAC). F. H. Baddeley, "On the Magdalen Islands, being the substance of four reports," Literary and Hist. Soc. of Quebec, *Trans.*, 3 (1832–37): 128–90. *Gentleman's Magazine*, January–June 1840: 205–6. [John Jervis, 1st] Earl of St Vincent, *Letters of Admiral of the Fleet the Earl of St. Vincent whilst first lord of the Admiralty, 1801–1804 . . .*, ed. D. B. Smith (2v., London, 1922–27). Ramsay, *Dalhousie journals* (Whitelaw), 1: 115–16. *DNB*. G.B., Admiralty, *The commissioned sea officers of the Royal Navy, 1660–1815*, [ed. D. B. Smith *et al.*] (3v., n.p., [1954]). Marshall, *Royal naval biog.*, 1: 229. Paul Hubert, *Les îles de la Madeleine et les Madelinots* (Rimouski, Qué., 1926). Robert Rumilly, *Les îles de la Madeleine* (Montréal, 1941; réimpr. 1951). David Spinney, *Rodney* (London, 1969).

COFFIN, JOHN, army officer, businessman, politician, JP, judge, and office holder; b. *c.* 1751 in

Boston, son of Nathaniel Coffin, the last receiver general and cashier of British customs for Boston, and Elizabeth Barnes; brother of Isaac COFFIN and nephew of John Coffin*; m. 21 Oct. 1781 Ann Mathews (Matthews) of Johns Island, S.C., and they had ten children; d. 12 May 1838 in Westfield Parish, N.B.

Born into a prosperous mercantile family that had connections with the governing élite of colonial Massachusetts, John Coffin spent his childhood in Boston, where he received a respectable education and was introduced to the doctrines of the Church of England. Coffin and his family probably had many reasons for remaining loyal to the British crown during the American revolution; certainly the family's prosperity depended on a continued attachment to the existing order.

John Coffin launched his military career on 17 June 1775 at the battle of Bunker Hill. His activities thereafter are unclear until 19 Jan. 1777, when he was commissioned a captain in a newly formed provincial corps, the Orange Rangers. After serving with the Rangers in New Jersey and New York, he exchanged into the New York Volunteers on 19 July 1778. This regiment was transferred late in 1778 to the southern colonies, where Coffin saw action in both Georgia and South Carolina. His distinguished service at the battle of Eutaw Springs in September 1781 led to his promotion as major of the King's American Regiment on 28 Aug. 1782. When his unit was disbanded in 1783 he was placed on half pay. Even though he would see only a brief period of military service following the Revolutionary War (during the War of 1812 he raised the New Brunswick Fencibles), he received regular promotions, becoming a full general on 12 Aug. 1819.

Following the withdrawal of British troops from the southern colonies, Coffin spent much of 1783 in New York attempting to secure his future once the war had officially ended. He was to relocate in territory destined to become New Brunswick. Edward Winslow* obtained property for him on the west side of what would be named Saint John Harbour, and Henry Nase, formerly under Coffin's command in the King's American Regiment, received a contract to construct the major's house. After making these preparations, Coffin and his family embarked for Parrtown (Saint John), where they landed on 26 Sept. 1783.

Coffin immediately set about establishing himself. Probably taking advantage of his position as one of the loyalist land agents, he acquired from Beamsley Perkins Glasier* an interest in Glasier's Manor, a 5,000-acre estate situated at the confluence of the Nerepis and Saint John rivers. In 1790 he obtained ownership of the property, by then enlarged to 6,000 acres. Coffin was involved in numerous other land transactions, primarily in Kings County, and erected both a grist-mill and a sawmill on the manor. Not confining his business ventures to real-estate speculation and agricultural pursuits, he also retailed fish, lumber, and rum. His shrewd business sense, drive, and financial resources ensured him considerable success, although he was never able to enjoy an aristocratic way of life or to accumulate a vast fortune.

Despite his active participation in the campaign for the partition of Nova Scotia and his association with many of the loyalist élite, Coffin had not achieved immediate political success when New Brunswick became a reality in 1784. He was not offered a high-ranking government appointment, though he would become a justice of the peace and a judge of the Inferior Court of Common Pleas. On the fringe of political preferment, he was obliged to seek election to the House of Assembly in order to have a voice in provincial affairs. Returned as a representative of Kings County in November 1785, he served for 25 years. He was twice accused of manipulation: in 1796 he was charged with distributing provisions to voters and in 1810 his seat was declared vacant because of irregularities in his election the preceding year. As a member of the assembly, Coffin emerged as a leading defender of the principles of church and state and revealed his contempt for the champions of democracy. During the legislative session of 1802 eight assembly members under his leadership passed a revenue bill despite the fact that a quorum was not present [*see* Samuel Denny Street*]. Coffin's fiery disposition involved him in several duels, one of them with the radical James Glenie*.

In Kings County, an oligarchy was established with Coffin and George Leonard* as dominant members. From 1786, when he was appointed to the bench, Coffin accumulated many county positions, including that of chief magistrate. In company with Lieutenant Governor Thomas Carleton*, Chief Justice George Duncan Ludlow*, and others he was a founding member of the New England Company's New Brunswick committee in 1786, and in 1807 he became superintendent of the Indian school the company had established at Sussex Vale (Sussex Corner) [*see* Oliver Arnold*]. His many positions, including that of assemblyman, gave Coffin great power in all matters both secular and religious within Kings County.

In 1812 Coffin received an appointment that he must have felt was long overdue: he became a member of the New Brunswick Council. As usual, controversy dogged his footsteps. In 1824 a situation arose which led the members of the Council to consider whether or not he had forfeited his seat. Coffin had moved to England in 1817, but had not relinquished his seat or received official permission to be absent. The matter was referred to the colonial secretary, who concluded that Coffin had indeed forfeited his position. After giving Lieutenant Governor Sir Howard Douglas* the impression that he would return, however, Coffin was reinstated. Though he made periodic visits to the province thereafter, he was no more attentive to his duties and was removed from the Council in 1828. John Coffin's political ascent had ended.

Coffin did eventually re-establish residence in New Brunswick, where he spent the remaining years of a life marked by a determination to succeed in every endeavour.

ROBERT S. ELLIOT

ACC, Diocese of Fredericton Arch., Greenwich and Westfield Parish Church (Kings County, N.B.), vestry minutes, 1797–1853 (mfm. at PANB); "Inglis papers, 1787–1842," comp. W. O. Raymond (copy at N.B. Museum). Kings Land Registry Office (Sussex, N.B.), Registry books, C-1: 183–85 (mfm. at PANB). N.B. Museum, Bibles, no.65 (Coffin family Bible); Coffin family, CB DOC; Jarvis family papers, E. J. Jarvis to R. F. Hazen and Munson Jarvis, 7 Sept. 1823; Nase family papers, Henry Nase diary, 20, 29 Sept. 1782; 7 Aug., 4, 26 Sept. 1783. PAC, MG 23, D1, ser.1, 7: 34, 277; D9; RG 8, I (C ser.), 719: 15–17, 23–24, 211–12; 1874: 35, 50; 1908: 4, 10, 15, 24 (mfm. at PANB). PANB, RG 7, RS66, 1838, John Coffin; RG 10, RS108, 1833. PRO, PRO 30/55, no.4088 (mfm. at UNBL). UNBL, BC-MS, Sir Howard Douglas letter-books, Douglas to William Huskisson, 31 Jan. 1828, 18 May 1829 (transcripts at N.B. Museum). *Winslow papers* (Raymond). *Royal Gazette* (Saint John, N.B.; Fredericton), 11 Nov. 1811, 23 May 1838. Lorenzo Sabine, *Biographical sketches of loyalists of the American revolution* (2v., Boston, 1864; repr. Port Washington, N.Y., 1966). J. H. Stark, *The loyalists of Massachusetts and the other side of the American revolution* (Boston, 1910). *A memoir of General John Coffin . . .*, comp. H. [E.] Coffin (Reading, Eng., 1860). R. G. Watson, "Local government in a New Brunswick county; Kings County, 1784–1850" (MA thesis, Univ. of N.B., Fredericton, 1969). Judith Fingard, "The New England Company and the New Brunswick Indians, 1786–1826: a comment on the colonial perversion of British benevolence," *Acadiensis* (Fredericton), 1 (1971–72), no.2: 29–42.

COFFIN, NATHANIEL, surveyor, politician, JP, office holder, and militia officer; b. 20 Feb. 1766 in Boston, fifth son of John Coffin* and Isabella Child; brother of THOMAS; d. 12 Aug. 1846 in Toronto, apparently unmarried.

Nathaniel Coffin left Boston in the summer of 1775 when his family fled that place for Quebec. He was commissioned an ensign in the 40th Foot on 21 March 1783, but did not join the regiment until after it had left Staten Island (New York City) for England in November. On 11 Jan. 1786 he exchanged to half pay, perhaps because of a breach of discipline committed in Ireland.

Coffin then returned to Quebec, where he was appointed a surveyor on 19 July 1790. Over the next few years he worked in various parts of the province, particularly along the Rivière Bécancour and in the Portneuf region. In 1793 he joined William Vondenvelden*, Jesse Pennoyer*, and others to organize the masonic lodge Select Surveyors No.9. The following year Coffin and his father were founding members of an association dedicated to upholding the government in Lower Canada.

Between 1795 and 1802 Coffin was active in the area around Missisquoi Bay, and he was a member of the committee formed by Pennoyer, Samuel Willard*, and others to press the government to speed the processing of applications for land. Coffin's involvement in the region's affairs was reflected in his election from Bedford County to the House of Assembly in July 1796, but he was not conspicuous during his four years in the house. On 14 Dec. 1796 he was commissioned a JP for the district of Montreal, a post he held until around 1810. Coffin was employed by Governor Robert Prescott* in 1797 to collect witnesses for the prosecution in the trial for treason of David McLane*.

On 31 Aug. 1802 Coffin was among those granted 1,200 acres in the newly established township of Compton, where he had already made a start at settling. Over the next decade his whereabouts are largely unknown. He appears to have been in Quebec in July 1812 when he was appointed provincial aide-de-camp to his brother-in-law Major-General Roger Hale Sheaffe*. For his service with Sheaffe at Queenston Heights he was mentioned in dispatches, and he was with him in the battle at York (Toronto) in April 1813.

Coffin was appointed deputy adjutant general of the Upper Canadian militia in January 1814. As such, he looked after administration from the department's office in Kingston while the adjutant general, Colley Lyons Lucas FOSTER, moved with the army headquarters. On 25 March 1815 Coffin was made adjutant general, the only militia officer retained in full-time service after the war. He kept his rank of lieutenant-colonel, which he had received in October 1812, and was promoted colonel in 1820.

In 1816 the business of the general board of militia claims, which dealt with back pay for the wartime militia, was transferred to the adjutant general's office. Accounting for pay claims and preparing payment necessitated Coffin's presence in Quebec for the first six months of 1818, and payment itself occupied much of his time over the next several years. Not until about 1821 was this duty being displaced by the problems attendant on the formation of new units and the issuing of equipment.

After the war Coffin fell increasingly into disfavour with the reform-minded House of Assembly. There were objections in 1818 to his hiring a clerk, and an act authorizing part of the adjutant general's allowances, which lapsed in 1820, was not renewed until 1822, and then only after considerable pressure from Coffin and Lieutenant Governor Sir Peregrine Maitland*. Although in 1821 a committee of the assembly investigated the duties of the adjutant general and recommended a larger staff, the necessary funds were not voted. In 1823 an assistant adjutant general, James FitzGibbon*, was appointed, but contingency funds allowing Coffin to travel were insufficient. Further financial restraints imposed in May 1825 meant that the department could not even pay its own postage, and FitzGibbon resigned in 1827 when the assembly reduced his pay. These difficulties were not eased by Coffin's long-running quarrel with the assemblyman François Baby* concerning the amount of land due to Baby for his services as a militia officer during the War of 1812. Coffin's problems with the house culminated in March 1828, when he and the superintendent of Indian affairs, James GIVINS, were summoned to appear before a select committee investigating a dispute over government land involving William FORSYTH. They were refused permission to attend by Maitland, and the reform element had them jailed for contempt until the end of the session a few days later.

Between 1833 and 1836 Coffin was increasingly involved in the affairs of the 1st Northumberland Regiment, whose commanding officer, John COVERT, was attempting to block the activities and promotions of some of his officers because he disagreed with their political views. When Covert's behaviour finally resulted in his court martial, he blamed Coffin for having let the case go that far.

Old and sick by the 1830s, Coffin applied for retirement. Although a bill providing him with a pension and making other changes in his department was passed in the assembly, it failed in the Legislative Council. Coffin was still adjutant general on the eve of the rebellion of 1837, but his assistant, Walter O'Hara*, was doing the work, and much was left undone. When revolt broke out, Lieutenant Governor Sir Francis Bond Head* replaced Coffin with FitzGibbon.

Nathaniel Coffin did not begin his militia career until he was well into middle age. He received his appointment in 1812 because of a family tie, and had little experience of leading troops in action. Consequently he appears not to have been held in very high regard as head of the Upper Canadian militia in the post-war years, whatever his merits as an administrator. He was the senior staff officer during a period of great growth for the militia, when new units were organized throughout the province as a result of the influx of settlers. However, these units were never more than nominal, being for the most part unequipped and seldom mustered.

O. A. COOKE

PAC, MG 30, D1, 8; RG 1, L6B, 1; RG 8, I (C ser.), 273: 138–39; 677: 8–9, 140; 678: 174–77; 704: 126, 246–49; 1168: 220; RG 9, I, B1, 3: 14; 42: 11–14; 43; 47–50; 52–53. Édouard Fabre Surveyer, "Nathaniel Coffin (1766–1846)," RSC *Trans.*, 3rd ser., 42 (1948), sect.II: 59–71.

COFFIN, THOMAS, businessman, seigneur, office holder, politician, and militia officer; b. 5 July 1762 in Boston, son of John Coffin* and Isabella Child; d. 18 July 1841 in Trois-Rivières, Lower Canada.

Thomas Coffin arrived at Quebec early in August 1775 with his parents and ten brothers and sisters. His father, a Boston businessman, had decided to leave the American colonies when revolution broke out. While several of Thomas's brothers took up careers in the army or public service, among them NATHANIEL, who became a provincial surveyor in 1790, he himself went into business. By November 1782 he was established in Montreal, where he sold, among other things, West India rum, French and English brandy, port, Spanish wines, molasses, tea, soap, butter, and fruit. When he met Marguerite Godefroy de Tonnancour, daughter of Louis-Joseph Godefroy* de Tonnancour, the course of his life was, however, changed.

The couple were married in Montreal on 22 Feb. 1786 by Anglican minister David Chabrand* Delisle and went to live on the seigneury of Pointe-du-Lac. Coffin then devoted himself to his new role as a seigneur, for in addition to the sum of 66,902 *livres* 5 *sols* 3 *deniers* Marguerite's dowry included a share in the seigneuries of Yamaska, Pointe-du-Lac, Roquetaillade, Gastineau, and Godefroy. Through various transactions in 1786 and 1787 Coffin became sole owner of Pointe-du-Lac. In the following years he gave his attention to developing this seigneury and made many land grants. On 8 April 1791 he donated to the *fabrique* of Pointe-du-Lac the church, the presbytery, and a property measuring 60 *arpents*. A prominent figure in his community, on 1 July 1790 Coffin obtained the office of sheriff for the district of Trois-Rivières, which he held until December 1791. Before long, however, he was facing serious financial problems. Since he could not repay a long-standing debt of £1,200, the seigneuries of Pointe-du-Lac and Gastineau were seized by the sheriff in June 1795 and sold to Nicholas Montour* on 25 October for £3,740.

While continuing to manage his much reduced estate, Coffin took part in political life. In July 1792 he had been elected to the House of Assembly for Saint-Maurice, which he represented until June 1804. He sided for the most part with the English party. In 1793 he voted against the choice of Jean-Antoine Panet* as speaker, supporting Jacob Jordan* instead. That December he succeeded in having a committee set up to draft legislation concerning highways and bridges in the province, and he was named to chair it. A bill he introduced early in 1796 to join the seigneury of Gastineau to the parish of Pointe-du-Lac aroused great anxiety, because it raised the question of the legislature's right to establish or divide parishes without the bishop's prior consent and without their being established canonically. Bishop Jean-François Hubert* saw in it an attempt to usurp episcopal powers. The assembly hesitated and finally decided to set the bill aside. But Coffin, who had been appointed a commissioner for the building of churches and presbyteries in June 1796, introduced another bill in March 1798 to set up a new parish. The coadjutor bishop designate, Joseph-Octave Plessis*, tried in vain to have it amended, even meeting with Governor Robert Prescott*, who assured him of his good intentions with regard to the church and his opposition to the bill. The ending of the session made it possible to avoid any decision on the matter, and Coffin did not succeed in getting the bill passed when he brought it before the house again in 1800.

Coffin did not seek re-election in 1804, but ran in the 1807 by-election in Trois-Rivières. Defeated by Ezekiel HART, he got Benjamin Joseph Frobisher* to present a petition for him contesting the right of Hart, a Jew, to sit in the assembly and demanding his place. Even though Hart was expelled, Coffin did not benefit in any way. The following year Coffin won the election for Saint-Maurice and he sat in the assembly until October 1809. In the ensuing election, he withdrew after seven days of polling when he saw that he had received few votes. Subsequently, he represented Trois-Rivières from April 1810 until March 1814.

While an assemblyman, Coffin continued to be interested in business. On 18 Sept. 1798, in partnership with his brother-in-law John Craigie*, he founded the Batiscan Iron Works Company to carry out ambitious plans for exploiting iron ore on the seigneury of Batiscan. In exchange for a 99-year lease to the company of four pieces of land, Coffin received a share equal to an advance of £1,000. He was also appointed manager until 1 Jan. 1800 at an annual salary of £200. From its earliest years the firm had serious problems. In December 1800 a fire destroyed the building in which the forge was located, causing a loss estimated at more than £818. In the hope of re-establishing the business, the owners tried to obtain the lease to the Saint-Maurice ironworks, which ran out in April 1801 [*see* Mathew BELL], but they did not succeed. Coffin and Craigie then decided to take in two other partners, Thomas Dunn* in 1801 and Joseph Frobisher* in 1802, each holding a one-sixth share. Through various transactions in 1802 the company also acquired at least 10,125 acres in Radnor Township, an area rich in ore and timber, and in 1803 the partners bought the seigneury of Champlain from Alexander Ellice* for £2,000.

Modelling its operation on the Saint-Maurice ironworks, the Batiscan company mainly produced stoves, which were in great demand, sugar and potash cauldrons, kitchen kettles, and bar iron. It nevertheless regularly experienced financial difficulties. Thus in December 1808 Coffin, as manager of the ironworks, acknowledged that £2,300 was owing to McTavish, Frobisher and Company for various goods purchased in the period 1804–6; to repay this sum he assigned £800 of the company's accounts receivable to them as well as all its bar and pig iron and manufactured wares, valued at £1,500. These problems were probably not unconnected with Coffin's decision to hand his share over to Craigie on 13 Nov. 1811 for £7,538. The effort to put the ironworks back on a firm footing was unsuccessful and it closed around 1814.

After leaving the company Coffin devoted himself chiefly to his role as an assemblyman and to the numerous offices he had received through government patronage. He had been a justice of the peace since 1794, and in October 1811 Sir George Prevost* appointed him chairman of the Court of Quarter Sessions in the district of Trois-Rivières, which brought him an annual salary of £200. Since 1803 he had been colonel of the three Trois-Rivières battalions of militia, and in April 1812 he became commissioner of transports in the district of Trois-Rivières. On 16 Feb. 1813 he was appointed inspector of the town's police, a responsibility he discharged for several years. Coffin was also made commissioner for numerous other matters in the district. His appointment to the Legislative Council on 8 May 1817 came in recognition of his importance in public life, and he served until March 1838.

From the autumn of 1835, however, Coffin no longer attended council meetings. He was 73 by then and in poor health. On 18 July 1841, a year after abjuring Protestantism, he died at Trois-Rivières, leaving at least one son, William Craigie Holmes. He was buried on 22 July in the Ursuline chapel, where his wife, who had died in 1839, already lay.

HUGUETTE FILTEAU

ANQ-M, CN1-29, 18 mai 1803; CN1-375, 21 févr. 1786. ANQ-MBF, CE1-48, 22 juill. 1841. ANQ-Q, CN1-230, 8 juill., 2 oct. 1807; 7 juill. 1808; 13 nov. 1811; Index des dossiers de la Cour des plaidoyers communs et de la Cour du banc du roi, district de Québec, 1765–1808; T11-1/81, no.3589; 87, no.3988; 310, no.340; 3558, no.299. ASTR, 0329. Can., Parks Canada, région de Québec (Québec), Compagnie des forges de Batiscan, reg. de lettres, août 1807–juillet 1812. PAC, RG 4, A1: 22805–8; RG 68, General index, 1651–1841. Boston, Registry Dept., *Records relating to the early history of Boston*, ed. W. H. Whitmore *et al.* (39v., Boston, 1876–1909), [24]: *Boston births, 1700–1800*, 5 July 1762. L.C., House of Assembly, *Journals*, 1793–1814. *Quebec Gazette*, 7 Nov. 1782; 13

Nov., 11 Dec. 1788; 17 July 1794; 25 June 1795; 11 Feb. 1808; 7 Dec. 1809. F.-J. Audet et Fabre Surveyer, *Les députés au premier Parl. du Bas-Canada*; *Les députés de Saint-Maurice et de Buckinghamshire*, 5–15. Bouchette, *Topographical description of L.C.* Caron, "Inv. de la corr. de Mgr Denaut," ANQ *Rapport*, 1931–32: 329–30. Desjardins, *Guide parl. Officers of British forces in Canada* (Irving). "Papiers d'État – Bas-Canada," PAC *Rapport*, 1893: 51–52. *Quebec almanac*, 1796, 1798–99. P.-G. Roy, *Inv. concessions*, 2: 48, 254; 3: 264–65. Turcotte, *Le Conseil législatif*. Alexandre Dugré, *La Pointe-du-Lac* (Trois-Rivières, 1934), 40. Lambert, "Joseph-Octave Plessis," 293–96, 335, 781, 1078, 1102–3. Ouellet, *Bas-Canada*, 317. Qué., Ministère des Affaires culturelles, Louise Trottier, "Évaluation du potentiel historique des fours à charbon de bois des Grandes-Piles en relation avec quelques sites sidérurgiques de la Mauricie: les forges Radnor, de Batiscan, L'Islet, Saint-Tite et Shawinigan" (rapport dactylographié, Québec, 1983). J. [E.] Hare, "L'Assemblée législative du Bas-Canada, 1792–1814: députation et polarisation politique," *RHAF*, 27 (1973–74): 361–95. É.-Z. Massicotte, "Notes sur les forges de Ste-Geneviève-de-Batiscan," *BRH*, 41 (1935): 708–11. P.-G. Roy, "La famille Coffin," *BRH*, 40 (1934): 229–32.

COIGNE. *See* DECOIGNE

COLLACHIE. *See* MCDONELL

COLLARD, FREDERICK JOHN MARTIN, lawyer and journalist; b. probably in Lower Canada; d. 24 March 1848 in Charlottetown.

Frederick John Martin Collard emerged suddenly in Prince Edward Island public life in September 1844 when he advertised as a lawyer in the press, describing himself as a member of the Canadian bar with 16 years' experience. One card he placed alluded to "efforts recently made to injure him," perhaps a reference to the fact that in April he had been jailed in Halifax for allegedly having committed an act of "bestiality" on a male complainant. Because of ill health he had been released in May on his own recognizance; shortly afterwards he left Nova Scotia, and he failed to appear in court in July to face the charge. In October Robert Hodgson*, the Island's attorney general, obtained certified evidence of these events, and it seems that this material was used to prevent Collard's being called to the local bar. The following summer Collard was indicted and prosecuted for an assault with intent to commit sodomy, alleged to have taken place in Charlottetown on 15 Sept. 1844. Although he won an acquittal from the jury, pleading his own case against Hodgson and the solicitor general, James Horsfield Peters*, the notoriety clung to him, and, contrary to his hopes, he failed to generate business as a land agent.

Collard does not appear to have succeeded in any field on the Island until he became involved in the feud between the "family compact" and the lieutenant governor, Sir Henry Vere Huntley*, who had formed an alliance of convenience with the reformers. Collard possessed journalistic talents the oligarchy required, and he was to work as editor of several Charlottetown newspapers. The first appears to have been the *Morning News*, but he left in the autumn of 1845 when the publisher began to tilt towards Huntley. Soon afterwards, over the signature A British Colonist, he contributed letters on the controversy to the tory *Islander* and *Royal Gazette*. A 15-page pamphlet published over the name Junius during the legislative session of 1846 has been attributed to him; it represented the colony as gripped in a struggle between a despotic governor and popular institutions. He became a particularly close associate of Joseph Pope*, the speaker of the House of Assembly, who was waging a relentless vendetta against Huntley, and in the spring of 1846 a tory assemblyman, William Douse*, described Collard as Pope's "secretary."

An important participant in the battle was the *Constitutionalist*, issued between April and October 1846; its weekly staple was vituperative criticism of Huntley, and its editor was Collard. The lieutenant governor and Edward Whelan*, the journalistic champion of reform, believed that subsequently Collard served simultaneously as editor of the *Islander* and the *Royal Gazette*. In a sense his task was to counter the brilliant Whelan, who responded by publishing poetry and prose filled with *double entendre* concerning "Big Martin." Huntley, who professed to regard Collard with abhorrence, credited him none the less with "extraordinary eloquence and great general ability."

A competent and spirited writer, although somewhat verbose, Collard would probably have continued to play an important part in Island political journalism had he not died of erysipelas on 24 March 1848 after a brief illness. Obituaries in the *Islander* and the *Royal Gazette* stated only that he had been "Queen's Counsel" for the Gaspé region of Lower Canada, but he seems to have led a troubled and unsettled life, at least in later years, for he had resided in New Brunswick and the Îles de la Madeleine, as well as Nova Scotia and Lower Canada, before arriving in Prince Edward Island. The attorney general of Nova Scotia, James William Johnston*, had favoured releasing him on his own recognizance in 1844 because he thought him unlikely to be able to find bail; on the Island, prior to becoming Pope's assistant, he was, according to Huntley, "nearly in a state of starvation"; and his property at the time of his death was valued at less than £50.

Collard's significance in Island history is his role in the maturing of political debate: he was one of the first to write regular editorial articles on local politics from a conservative perspective. His employment indicated recognition by the tories that, with growing demands for political change, it would be prudent to cultivate public opinion systematically. His death left a void which was not filled until the hiring of Duncan Maclean*, a former colleague of Whelan, by the *Islander* in March 1850.

IAN ROSS ROBERTSON

[F. J. M. Collard is identified as the author of *An address to the people of Prince Edward Island*, published under the pseudonym Junius ([Charlottetown, 1846]), in a copy at the PAPEI, which bears the handwritten notes "Collard's Pamphlet," and "low vulgar insolence and malice of an inferior mind." I.R.R.]

PAPEI, RG 6, Supreme Court, case papers, R. *v*. F. J. M. Collard, 1845; minutes, 26 June, 3 July 1845. PRO, CO 226/69: 175–77, 208–11; 226/70: 289–90; 226/71: 70–72, 120–29, 134–47, 288, 292, 481; 226/75: 19 (mfm. at PAPEI). Supreme Court of P.E.I. (Charlottetown), Estates Division, papers of administration for F. J. M. Collard estate. P.E.I., House of Assembly, *Journal*, 1846, app.R: 94, 96, 98; 1847: 142–43; Legislative Council, *Journal*, 1847: 66–67, 69. *Constitutionalist* (Charlottetown), 27 April–17 Oct. 1846 (mfm. at PAPEI). *Examiner* (Charlottetown), 18 Sept., 2 Oct., 13 Nov., 18 Dec. 1847; 11, 27 March, 18 Sept. 1848. *Islander*, 22 Nov., 6 Dec. 1845; 18 April (extra), 1 May, 23 Oct. 1846; 24 March 1848. *Morning News* (Charlottetown), 18 Sept. 1844. *Palladium* (Charlottetown), 26 Sept. 1844. *Royal Gazette* (Charlottetown), 1 Oct. 1844; 1–8 July, 2–9 Dec. 1845; 9 April 1846 (extra); 7–14, 28 Sept. 1847; 1, 15 Feb., 21, 24 (extra), 28 March 1848. W. L. Cotton, "The press in Prince Edward Island," *Past and present of Prince Edward Island* . . . , ed. D. A. MacKinnon and A. B. Warburton (Charlottetown, [1906]), 115. [This work is the only secondary source to mention Collard. I.R.R.] *Examiner*, 11 May 1863. *Islander*, 25 June 1852, 25 Jan. 1856.

COLLINS, JAMES PATRICK, physician; b. *c*. 1824 in County Cork (Republic of Ireland), eldest of four children and only son of Patrick Collins and Isabella Hughes; m. 24 Oct. 1846 Mary Quin (Quinn) in Portland (Saint John), N.B., and they had one daughter; d. 2 July 1847 on Partridge Island, N.B.

James Patrick Collins immigrated to Saint John in 1837 with his family. As a youth he apprenticed under Dr George R. Peters, a prominent Saint John physician, who at that time was superintendent of the Lunatic Asylum. Peters fostered his interest in medicine and assisted him in pursuing medical studies, which he undertook in Paris around 1844 and later in London. Collins returned to Saint John in 1846 and that August began medical practice from his family's residence on Mill Street, York Point.

Collins had been in practice only a few months when in May 1847 a typhus epidemic broke out in North America, the disease having been brought by immigrants fleeing the potato famine in Ireland. Saint John did not escape the pestilence and by early June the hospital sheds at the quarantine establishment on Partridge Island, near the city, were crowded with fever patients and the overflow was being placed in military tents. Almost 2,500 immigrants were in quarantine at this time; many of them were still on board vessels waiting to be landed. The health officer in charge, Dr George J. Harding, could no longer handle his responsibilities alone and sought help. In spite of the risk of contracting the disease, his brother Dr William S. Harding and Dr Collins went to the quarantine station as medical assistants, at a salary of £50 a month.

It was mainly at the insistence of Lewis Burns, who had served briefly as an assemblyman for Saint John, that Collins decided to go to Partridge Island. Burns convinced him that assisting the health officer would enhance his professional reputation and benefit his fledgling medical career. It is quite probable that his brothers-in-law, James and Edmond Quin, both of whom were priests active in charitable work among the immigrants, also encouraged him to go there. Distressed by "the sufferings of his countrymen," Collins agreed to take up the challenge even against the protestations of his own family, who feared, with reason, for his well-being. Collins played a prominent role in combating the disease but in less than a month fell victim to it. Around 26 June both medical assistants were attacked by typhus and one week later, on 2 July, young Collins was dead. At the urging of his friends, the Saint John Common Council granted special permission for his body to be brought from the island to the Roman Catholic cemetery in Indiantown. Because of the danger from contagion, the corpse was sealed in a lead coffin under the direction of the health officer. The funeral procession on 4 July was most impressive and showed the respect in which Collins was held by the community. Composed of nearly 4,000 persons, it was subsequently said to have been the largest ever seen in Saint John. Several years later Collins's body was moved to St Peter's burial ground (near Fort Howe) and in 1949 it was placed in a common grave in St Joseph's cemetery.

Neither the money Collins's father earned as a grocer nor that made by Collins during his brief medical career appears to have been enough to support his widow and his posthumous child. In 1847 the New Brunswick legislature justly acknowledged his work at the quarantine station by granting £50 to his estate, and from 1848 to 1855 it gave an additional £205 to his widow, in answer to her petitions for support.

Considered a humane man of much promise in the medical profession, Collins was praised by his contemporaries for his professional talents and his devotion to his native countrymen. Even today his name is revered in Saint John, especially by those of Irish descent. A Celtic cross on Partridge Island and a half-scale replica of it on the mainland commemorate his "devotion and sacrifice" and preserve the memory of more than 2,000 Irish immigrants who died during the typhus epidemic of 1847.

JAMES M. WHALEN

Arch. of the Diocese of Saint John (Saint John, N.B.), Cathedral of the Immaculate Conception (Saint John), reg. of baptisms, 22 Aug. 1847 (mfm. at PANB). City of Saint John, City Clerk's Office, Common Council, minutes, 1847 (mfm. at PANB). N.B. Museum, Reg. of marriages for the city and county of Saint John, book C: 524 (mfm. at PANB). PAC, MG 9, A10, 5. PANB, RG 3, RS266, A11b; RG 4, RS24, S61-P282, S62-P260. Partridge Island Research Project (Saint John), "The year of the fever" (uncredited article, Saint John, *c.* 1904). PRO, CO 188/100–1, 188/108 (mfm. at PAC). St Joseph's Cemetery (Roman Catholic) (Saint John), Cemetery records (mfm. at PANB). St Mary's Cemetery (Saint John), Tombstone inscription for Patrick Collins. N.B., House of Assembly, *Journal*, 1848–55. *New-Brunswick Courier*, 22–29 Aug., 19 Sept., 31 Oct. 1846; 5, 26 June, 3–10 July, 21 Aug., 4–18 Dec. 1847; 19 Nov. 1853. William Murdoch, *Poems and songs* (2nd ed., Saint John, 1872). W. K. Reynolds, "The year of the fever," *New Brunswick Magazine* (Saint John), 1 (July–December 1898): 202–14. *Telegraph-Journal* (Saint John), 10–11 Oct. 1927. J. M. Whalen, "'Allmost as bad as Ireland': Saint John, 1847," *Archivaria* (Ottawa), no.10 (summer 1980): 85–97.

CONDO, FRANCIS (the name sometimes appears as **François Est**, *dit* **Condeau**), Micmac chief; b. *c.* 1761, the son and grandson of chiefs; d. 24 July 1837 in Lower Canada or New Brunswick.

Francis Condo was third chief at the Restigouche Indian Reserve, Que., in 1786 when chief Joseph Claude* negotiated about fishing rights and land claims with Nicholas Cox*, lieutenant governor of Gaspé. In 1812 Condo was named first chief in succession to Jacques (Joseph) Gagnon on the recommendation of missionary Charles-François PAINCHAUD.

Condo was responsible for maintaining the land claims of the Restigouche Indians against white intruders, a matter that became extremely complex because of faulty surveys. The general vagueness of land titles in the region led to a law being passed in 1819 "to secure the inhabitants of the Inferior District of Gaspé in the possession and enjoyment of their lands," and claims commissioners were appointed. Their findings in the Restigouche area drew a protest from Condo in July 1820: the Indians had not been aware that Edward Isaac Mann still claimed the lands that had been the subject of negotiation in 1786. The protest was printed in the *Quebec Gazette* in June 1823 and went to formal adjudication in April of the following year. The board awarded the Restigouche Indians some 680 acres that lay between Mann's claims and those of another white, Robert Ferguson*. Visiting Restigouche in the summer of 1826, Governor Lord Dalhousie [RAMSAY] invited Condo to meet him at Quebec in the autumn. What Condo received for his journey, however, was the governor's handwritten statement that the board's decision was "now their legal title" to the land and must be considered final. The Indians continued to press for full satisfaction of their claim, petitioning Lord Durham [LAMBTON] in 1838 and sending Joseph MALIE, Pierre Basquet*, and François Labauve to London in 1841.

The Restigouche Micmacs were in an anomalous position in Lower Canada. Their kin ties lay in New Brunswick where they spent much of their time; they used their village more as a base of operations than as a residence the year round, and this village just happened to be on the north bank of the river that marked the boundary line. Lower Canada did not consider itself under the usual obligations to these Indians, who did not receive the annual presents given to other native people in the Canadas. To mark the occasion of Condo's visit to Quebec, Dalhousie ordered the distribution of some supplies, but he was careful to point out that his action was not to constitute a precedent. To a large extent, the Restigouche Micmacs fell between two governments, and the position of a chief in such a situation was particularly difficult.

In 1823 Painchaud, who was in touch with the Indians even after he moved from the reserve, had urged Condo's dismissal, describing him as a drunk who had lost the respect of his people and who no longer lived at Restigouche. Condo eventually regained the confidence of the church, however. In 1836, a little stooped under the weight of his 75 years and wearing two silver medals on his chest, he came at the head of his people to greet Bishop Pierre-Flavien Turgeon*, who visited the Restigouche area that year. After his death he was succeeded by Thomas Barnaby.

L. F. S. UPTON

Can., Prov. of, Legislative Assembly, *App. to the journals*, 1847, 1: app.T, no.96. Ramsay, *Dalhousie journals* (Whitelaw), 3: 65–66, 71. Père Pacifique [de Valigny] [H.-J.-L. Buisson], "Ristigouche, métropole des Micmacs, théâtre du 'dernier effort de la France au Canada,'" Soc. de géographie de Québec, *Bull.* (Québec), 20 (1926): 171–85.

CONNOLLY, WILLIAM, fur trader; b. *c.* 1786 in Lachine, Que.; d. 3 June 1848 in Montreal.

William Connolly entered the North West Company as a clerk in 1801 and went west, where he would remain for 30 years. In 1802–3 he was at Nelson House (Man.) and the following winter a short distance away at Rat River House. On 9 Oct. 1804 David Thompson* met him at Southern Indian Lake, where Connolly was wintering with five men, and described him as "a young man who has seen little else than bad and extravagant example." In 1810 he was again trading at Nelson House.

By 1817 Connolly had been promoted senior clerk and the following year he was made a chief trader. From 1818 to 1821 he was in charge of Cumberland House (Sask.) in opposition to the Hudson's Bay Company. In December 1819 Connolly accused the

HBC's governor, William WILLIAMS, of indirect responsibility for the extreme sufferings of Benjamin Joseph Frobisher*, the Nor'Wester who had escaped after his capture by Williams the previous summer and who Connolly believed had died.

On 1 Dec. 1820, at a time of intense rivalry between the NWC and the HBC, Connolly made an agreement with his rival at Cumberland House, Thomas Swain, by which "neither party are to have any dealings with the Indians who trade with the other . . . and neither party is to send after Indians without 12 hours previous notice to the other." The next year amalgamation ended the struggle between the companies [*see* Simon MCGILLIVRAY] and Connolly continued as a chief trader in the new organization.

In August 1821 the Council of the Northern Department placed him in charge of the Lesser Slave Lake district. There he remained until 1824, when he was given a more challenging assignment: the management, together with Chief Trader William Brown, of New Caledonia (B.C.), in which district "serious differences and insubordination" had occurred. Connolly's headquarters were first at Fraser Lake and later at Stuart Lake. Brown (who would leave the district in 1826 because of illness) was directed by Governor George Simpson* to assert the HBC's presence in the remote Babine River country. Simpson was of the opinion that the amount of furs returned from New Caledonia could be increased. A major problem was transportation. Overland travel was difficult, and horses and leather for gear were scarce. In 1825, in which year Connolly became a chief factor, Simpson obtained approval to annex New Caledonia to the Columbia district for purposes of supply and transportation. That December Connolly, with pack horses, followed the Fraser River southward, then turned northwest to follow the Chilcotin River to its upper reaches, where he discovered that horses could be sent across the Coast Mountains. This route was regarded by Chief Factor John McLoughlin* as the "Shortest communication . . . Between New Caledonia and the sea." The following spring, on instructions from Simpson, Connolly took his district's furs to Fort Vancouver (Vancouver, Wash.) instead of to Hudson Bay. In 1828 he lost three men in the Columbia River while transporting furs to the ocean, and two were killed by Indians. Writing to James Hargrave* at York Factory (Man.), Connolly said that these losses and the scarcity of provisions had made 1828 the most unhappy year of his life.

In 1829 Simpson found New Caledonia well administered. He noted in his dispatch to the HBC's London committee in March that "the present state of the affairs of New Caledonia, manifests excellent management, and if its revenue has not encreased so rapidly as could have been wished, it can alone be ascribed to misfortunes over which Chief Factor Connolly had no controul." In June the Northern Council instructed Connolly "to use his best endeavours to extend the Trade" into the region of New Caledonia "Westward and Northward of Babine and Simpsons River, which fall into the hands of the American & Russian traders." He was at Fort Vancouver in August when word was received that the HBC's cargo ship *William and Ann* had been wrecked at the mouth of the Columbia and plundered by the Clatsop Indians. McLoughlin sent Connolly with a party to reclaim the goods. Three Indians were killed in the fighting which resulted, and when the cargo was found, the Indian village in which it had been hidden was burned on Connolly's orders. Connolly turned New Caledonia over to Peter Warren Dease* in 1831, and Charles Ross, a trader there, wrote that he "leaves the district in a much more flourishing condition than he found it."

Connolly returned to Lower Canada on furlough that year, taking with him Suzanne*, the Cree woman he had married about 1803 according to the custom of the country, and their six children. On 16 May 1832, after repudiating Suzanne, he married his second cousin, Julia Woolrich. In June, while still on furlough, he was placed in charge of the 1832–33 outfit for the king's posts, a trading area which the HBC rented from the province of Lower Canada. With his new wife he left in 1832 for Tadoussac, on the north shore of the lower St Lawrence River. Six years later his territory was enlarged to include the seigneury of Mingan.

Connolly's last years in the fur trade were not ones of contentment. First there was the worry of supporting his Indian family, who lived in Montreal but were unable to adjust to white civilization. Then there was Julia, sometimes sickly and always yearning for the amenities of the city. The Connollys' frequent absences from the trading post did not meet with Simpson's approval. As well, trade at the king's posts and adjacent seigneuries, Simpson observed to Connolly in April 1841, had become "exceedingly unproductive" and was then "absolutely unworthy of attention for any other object than as a protection . . . to those parts of the Honble. Company's territories as are most contiguous to them."

On short notice later that month, Connolly asked for a furlough. Simpson was not satisfied that he was entitled to one, and proposed to the London committee that he be pushed into retirement by being asked to choose between a posting to Fort Albany (Ont.) or a two-year leave terminating in retirement. The governor knew that Julia would not allow her husband to accept an appointment to a post so distant from Montreal. Connolly accepted the leave, retiring on 1 June 1843 and retaining full interest in the outfit for 1843–44 and a half interest in the succeeding six outfits. In retirement William and Julia lived in Montreal "in great style"; Suzanne had taken up residence at a convent in St Boniface (Man.) in 1841. When Connolly died in 1848 he willed his considerable estate to Julia. In 1864 John Connolly, Suzanne's eldest son, challenged the will, thus launching a series of court actions to establish which marriage was valid. The courts supported his claim.

Connolly, who called himself a "bit of an Irishman, and . . . a most devout Catholic," was described in 1817 by Ross Cox*, a former Nor'Wester, as "a veritable bon garçon, and an Emeralder of the first order." Simpson, in his "Character book" of 1832, regarded Connolly as "an active useful man whose Zeal and exertions have generally been crowned with success, whose Word may be depended on in most things, and whom I consider incapable of doing anything that is mean or dishonorable." The governor further depicted him as "at times Hypochondriacal," proud, hot-tempered, and "rather domineering and Tyrannical."

BRUCE PEEL

PAM, HBCA, B.49/a/35–36; B.141/a/1, 4; B.179/a/5; B.188/a/5; D.4/119: ff.58–58d. *Les bourgeois de la Compagnie du Nord-Ouest* (Masson), 2: 225–26. Ross Cox, *The Columbia River; or, scenes and adventures during a residence of six years on the western side of the Rocky Mountains* . . . , ed. E. I. and J. R. Stewart (Norman, Okla., 1957). John Franklin, *Narrative of a journey to the shores of the polar sea, in the years 1819, 20, 21, and 22* . . . (London, 1823; repr. Edmonton, 1969). Hargrave, *Hargrave corr.* (Glazebrook). *HBRS*, 2 (Rich and Fleming); 3 (Fleming); 4 (Rich); 10 (Rich); 18 (Rich and Johnson); 29 (Williams). *New light on the early history of the greater northwest: the manuscript journals of Alexander Henry . . . and of David Thompson* . . . , ed. Elliott Coues (3v., New York, 1897; repr. 3v. in 2, Minneapolis, Minn., [1965]), 3. Simpson, "Character book," *HBRS*, 30 (Williams). *The Lower Canada jurist* (35v., Montreal, 1857–91), 11: 197–265. Brown, *Strangers in blood*. Rich, *Hist. of HBC* (1958–59), vol.2. Van Kirk, *"Many tender ties"*.

COOK, WILLIAM HEMMINGS, fur trader, settler, and politician; baptized 30 May 1768 in the parish of St Andrew, Holborn, London, son of John Cook and Elizabeth ——; d. 23 Feb. 1846 in the Red River settlement (Man.).

William Hemmings Cook came from London to Rupert's Land in 1786 in the service of the Hudson's Bay Company. He worked as a writer (clerk) at York Factory (Man.), starting at £15 a year, until September 1790, when he was sent inland up the Nelson River with nine company men, but only one steersman, and some Indians to establish a post at Duck Lake. The early onset of winter compelled most of the Indians to go back to their families, so he sent on a party under his one experienced man, James Spence, who wintered at Split Lake, while with one man and an Indian he returned to York. On 1 July 1791 he set off again up the Nelson and Grass rivers to Wintering Lake, where he established Chatham House in opposition to William McKay* of the North West Company.

After three years at this and other outposts in the area, Cook went back to England. Returning in 1795 as an inland trader at a salary of £60 a year, he took charge in 1797 of the HBC posts on the upper Nelson, with headquarters at Split Lake. As second in command at York in 1809, he won the approval of Chief Factor John McNab, with whom he worked in 1808–9 on a relay system of inland transportation. Appointed chief factor in 1810, Cook was responsible, under the command of William Auld*, superintendent of the Northern Department, for York's "dependencies," including Fort Severn (Ont.) and the inland posts. During the winter of 1811–12 he struggled with problems of provisioning and transport for the Selkirk settlers – Scots and Irishmen who, under Miles Macdonell* and William Hillier, were wintering at York on their way to the Red River settlement.

Cook now earned £100 a year plus at least £50 under the HBC's new "Share of Profits" scheme, but in 1813 the company's governor and committee allowed him to resign and, in view of his long and faithful service, to settle on the Nelson with his family on a private and temporary basis. They were, however, annoyed because he had absented himself from York in 1812–13 while still receiving the emoluments of a chief factor. He was at York again in 1813–14, and he seems to have been at or near Oxford House in 1815–16. From 1816 he was back in the service of the company in the Nelson River district, at half his old salary. In 1818 he was sent to the Swan River district with headquarters at Fort Hibernia (Sask.). The following year he resigned again to try his fortune once more as a settler, this time at Red River.

Cook and many of his company colleagues, including his eldest son Joseph, had long been concerned to secure "a retreat for our children." By 1815 Cook had ten sons and daughters, children of three or possibly more country wives. One of these wives had died by 1821. Another, Matthew Cocking*'s daughter Mith-coo-coo-man E'Squaw (Agathas or Mary), he married formally on 8 March 1838, thus fulfilling what Thomas Simpson had described in a private letter of 1836 as his "intention of bringing his 35 years courtship to an early close." A third wife seems also to have been one of Cocking's daughters, Wash-e-soo E'Squaw (Agathas, Aggathas).

By 1821 Cook was established in the Red River settlement, where the HBC made him a free grant of 500 acres and paid him an annuity of £100 for seven years. He apparently worked as a "petty trader" (retailer) and freighter. Appointed a councillor to the governor of Assiniboia on 29 May 1822, he attended six meetings. On 27 Feb. 1839, three years after ownership of the district passed from the estate of Lord Selkirk [Douglas*] to the HBC, he was appointed to the Council of Assiniboia in spite of the fact that in the 1820s Governor George Simpson* had considered Cook to be "timid and weak," "useless from age and want of firmness" and from fear of losing popularity, a "most extraordinary mixture of generous eccentricity, Religion, Drunkeness and Misanthropy." According to Simpson in 1822, he had changed "his residence about a Doz. different times for as many absurd reasons." Though Donald Gunn* thought of him as a "kind hearted gentleman," Cook was often at odds with other principal settlers at Red River who had been his colleagues in the HBC, and in 1838 he quarrelled with Andrew McDermot* over a freighting bill and damaged goods. By 1843, when his name last appeared in the census returns, he had only 20 acres under cultivation.

Cook's will provided an income for his "beloved wife Mary" and bequests for four sons, seven daughters, and a granddaughter. His land was divided equally among ten of his children. It was his children and their progeny who constituted his most notable contribution to western Canada. His descendants included not only countless Cooks but also Garriochs, Budds, Settees, Calders, Wrens, and Erasmuses. Recording Cook's death, Peter Garrioch, a grandson and a trader and freighter at Red River, called him "the Father of us all."

IRENE M. SPRY

Guildhall Library (London), MS 6667/11 (St Andrew, Holborn, London, reg. of baptisms, marriages, and burials), 30 May 1768. PABC, Add. MSS 345, file 56; Add. MSS 635, box 7, folder 201, Thomas Simpson to Donald Ross, 20 Feb. 1836. PAC, MG 19, El, ser.1, 1, 18, 46–47. PAM, HBCA, A.6/15–19; A.30/4–17; A.31/9; A.32/3–17; A.36/5: ff.5–72; B.32/a/1; B.159/a/7; B.235/d/19–20; B.239/b/48–86d; B.239/c/1–2; B.239/d/19–20, 124, 129–30; B.239/x/3; C.1/398; E.4/1a–2; E.5/1–11; E.6/2, 7; E.8/5; MG 2, C38, Garrioch journal, 23 Feb. 1846. *Canadian north-west* (Oliver), 1: 57, 258–60. *HBRS*, 3 (Fleming). Morton, *Hist. of Canadian west* (1939). Rich, *Hist. of HBC* (1958–59), vol.2.

COOPER, WILLIAM, teacher, businessman, and office holder; b. *c.* 1761 in Bath, England; m. first Ann —— (d. 1826), and they had one son and three daughters; m. secondly 6 Jan. 1829 Isabella Watson in York (Toronto), Upper Canada, and they had one son; d. 28 Oct. 1840 in Toronto.

William Cooper claimed to have settled in York in 1793 and built its first house; he was certainly there in 1794, and the unfinished house he sold to Abner Miles* that November was among the earliest in the new town. He was living on his lot on Yonge Street north of the town in July 1796, but was back in York the following year. In December 1797 he described himself as a schoolmaster and petitioned unsuccessfully for more land because his house and lot were "too small for his present occupation." The following November he formally opened what was probably Toronto's first school. For 8*s.* a month per pupil, he taught the children of James Macaulay*, Thomas Ridout*, William CHEWETT, John Denison, and other local citizens, and of soldiers at the garrison. Among his pupils was a black boy whose tuition was paid by Peter Russell*, administrator of the province and a slave-holder.

In 1800 Cooper was licensed as an auctioneer and was appointed a coroner of the Home District (a position he held until 1834) and usher of the Court of King's Bench. When there was no minister in York, he conducted Anglican services in the parliament building. Although he had been granted a teacher's licence in 1799, he gave up his school two years later and turned to innkeeping. Abner Miles's inn had just closed and Cooper's Toronto Coffee House replaced it as the social centre of the community.

From his arrival in Upper Canada, Cooper had speculated in land, both in the town of York and on the Humber River. In 1806 he sold his inn and began to develop his mill-site on the Humber at Dundas Street. The king's mill, near present-day Bloor Street, was then the only mill on the river; it was owned and mismanaged by the government. Cooper's mill opened on 1 Dec. 1807 with machinery the government had provided on the condition that its cost be paid or the equipment replaced within 18 months. The mill had only one run of stone, but from this beginning Cooper built the first milling empire on the Humber, covering hundreds of acres on both sides of the river. He eventually owned a grist-mill, sawmill, fulling-mill, distillery, cooperage, tannery, blacksmith's shop, store, and tavern, as well as a 40-acre farm and houses for his skilled workmen. By 1820 the dam he had built across the river between his mills got him into trouble for obstructing the run of salmon. Two years later his dam blocked the passage of lumber; in reply to a complaint from Robert Farr, Solicitor General Henry John Boulton* wrote that "works, which are a public nuisance . . . may be removed by any individual who is strong enough to keep his ground if attacked during the operation." The lumbermen promptly followed Boulton's legal advice.

As a miller, Cooper was concerned with shipping. In November 1815 he applied for a water-lot in York on which to build the town's first commercial wharf as well as a warehouse, lumberyard, and tavern, and he was granted a lot near the foot of Church Street. Cooper's wharf was finally finished in the summer of 1817, when the first steamboats began to run on Lake Ontario [*see* James McKenzie*]. At the same time the Merchants' Wharf was being built by a consortium of leading merchants headed by William Allan*.

For some years Cooper managed both his Humber mills and his wharfage business in York. In March 1827, however, he transferred most of his Humber property to his son, Thomas. He sold his waterfront property in February 1828, but a month later bought the much longer Merchants' Wharf and continued his business as a forwarder, commission merchant, and wharfinger. In his late sixties he married Isabella Watson, a protégée of John Strachan* and his family. In the spring of 1830, "finding the Wharfage business too laborious at his advanced age," he sold his waterfront holdings to the firm of Alexander Murray and James NEWBIGGING. After a long illness Cooper died in 1840, aged 79.

Cooper's career in Upper Canada demonstrates both his versatility and his opportunism. He was skilled in identifying the needs of his community, and was often the first to fulfil them. With little respect for authority, he had frequent difficulties with the magistrates over statute labour, tavern licences, taxes, and even assault and battery. He was, however, a successful entrepreneur in a new settlement, and his various enterprises benefited both himself and others.

EDITH G. FIRTH

AO, MS 75; RG 22, ser.94. MTRL, William Allan papers, account-books of Abner and [James] Miles, 1793–1809; William Cooper papers; Humber Valley archive; Abner Miles, day-book B, 1 Sept. 1795–15 Dec. 1796; Peter Russell papers. PAC, MG 23, HII, 6, 1: 131; RG 1, E3, 12: 81; 34, pt.2: 151–52, 166; L3, 89: C1/119; 98: C10/122; 147: C misc. leases/60; RG 5, A1, esp. pp.13950–52, 28570–73, 30657, 33793–95; B9, 53; RG 7, G16C, 5: 29, 38, 80, 129; 31: 203; RG 68, General index, 1651–1841: 162, 164. *Corr. of Hon. Peter Russell* (Cruikshank and Hunter). "Minutes of the Court of General Quarter Sessions of the Peace for the Home District, 13th March, 1800, to 28th December, 1811," AO *Report*, 1932. *Town of York, 1793–1815* (Firth); *1815–34* (Firth). *York, Upper Canada: minutes of town meetings and lists of inhabitants, 1797–1823*, ed. Christine Mosser (Toronto, 1984). *Canadian Freeman*, 1825–34. *Church*, 7 Nov. 1840. *Colonial Advocate*, 1824–34. *Examiner* (Toronto), 11 Nov. 1840. *Upper Canada Gazette*, 1793–1828. John Andre, *Infant Toronto as Simcoe's folly* (Toronto, 1971). S. T. Fisher, *The merchant-millers of the Humber valley: a study of the early economy of Canada* (Toronto, 1985). E. C. Guillet, *Toronto from trading post to great city* (Toronto, 1934). K. M. Lizars, *The valley of the Humber, 1615–1913* (Toronto, 1913; repr. 1974). Ont., Dept. of Planning and Development, *Humber valley report* (Toronto, 1948). *Robertson's landmarks of Toronto*. T. W. Acheson, "The nature and structure of York commerce in the 1820s," *CHR*, 50 (1969): 406–28. Douglas McCalla, "The 'loyalist' economy of Upper Canada, 1784–1806," *SH*, 16 (1983): 279–304.

CÔTÉ, CYRILLE-HECTOR-OCTAVE (baptized **Cyrille-Hector**), teacher, physician, politician, Patriote, journalist, and Baptist minister; b. 1 Sept. 1809 at Quebec, son of Charles Côté, a skipper, and Rose Duhamel; d. 4 Oct. 1850 in Hinesburg, Vt.

Cyrille-Hector-Octave Côté's Acadian ancestors emigrated to Canada in 1756, shortly after the deportation. Stripped of financial resources and in dire poverty, they settled at Quebec and had to engage in several kinds of work to survive. Côté's father was a skipper, but he also was obliged to become a carpenter or day-labourer during the off-season. While still young, Côté learned that life is harsh and demanding and that he would have to work hard if he wanted to succeed. In these circumstances he developed at an early age the ambitiousness which was one of his striking traits. Given the family's Acadian roots, it is highly likely that he was also brought up on anti-British sentiment. To escape from his environment he would take one of the few avenues available at that time: education.

In September 1818 his parents enrolled Côté in the Petit Séminaire de Québec, but the disappearance of the honour rolls for the period makes it impossible to assess his achievement. Nor is anything known of the reading he did or the people he met, factors that may have shaped his first political and religious opinions. In 1823 the family moved from Quebec to Montreal, and in September Côté entered the sixth year (Rhetoric) at the Petit Séminaire de Montréal. This period of study ended in 1826 with Côté receiving a first prize in philosophy. On leaving school, Côté was uncertain what direction to take: with his boundless curiosity, everything attracted him. None the less he had to make a living, and that was probably why he went into teaching for the time being.

Côté seems to have been sensitive to the political developments taking place in the province. From 1826 Louis-Joseph Papineau* was consolidating his political leadership of the Canadian party, which became the Patriote party that year. Côté already had an intense admiration for Papineau, whose nationalist ideas he swiftly espoused. In his eyes Papineau was the only man capable of defending the rights of the French Canadian collectivity.

Around 1830, through some meetings with lawyers Édouard-Étienne RODIER and Louis-Hippolyte La Fontaine*, Côté was able to join several groups of intellectuals who met in Édouard-Raymond Fabre*'s bookshop and Ludger Duvernay*'s printing-shop. These young men studied the 18th-century *philosophes*, defended the principles of democracy and the sovereignty of the people, affirmed their unshakeable hostility to the colonial régime, and demanded the separation of church and state. Côté's early political and social convictions were firmly rooted in these years of reading and reflection.

In 1831 Côté was suddenly attracted to the professions and registered in medicine at McGill College. After a few months there he decided to transfer to the University of Vermont, in Burlington, where in October 1831 he was awarded a certificate of medical studies recognizing his right to practise. But by obtaining his diploma in less than five years he had infringed the regulations governing medical practice in Lower Canada. At its meeting of 7 Jan. 1832 the Board of Examiners for the district of Montreal denied him the right to practise in the province. Three months later Côté was accepted none the less by the Board of Examiners for the district of Quebec, which gave him his licence on 11 April.

In the summer of 1832 Côté decided to set up at Sainte-Marguerite-de-Blairfindie (L'Acadie), where a number of Acadian families had been living for several generations. On his arrival he was put to the test by the cholera epidemic that was striking down children and old people in the parish, and in the fear-ridden community he gave medical care with exceptional zeal. At this time he learned of the death of his mother, who had also succumbed to cholera, and he drew up a will in which he made no reference to religion but commended his soul directly to God. He went to live at Napierville in 1833 and in less than a year became immensely popular because of his dedication.

On 25 June 1833, at Saint-Valentin, Côté married Margaret Yelloby Jobson, eldest daughter of one of the richest farmers, Thomas Jobson, who was also barrack master on the Île aux Noix. There was no longer any doubt that Côté belonged to the rural petite bourgeoisie. He had no land or capital, but he owned one of the finest houses in the village of Napierville, an achievement that set him apart from the craftsmen and farmers. In addition, his education gave him considerable influence in local matters. He soon came into conflict with curé Noël-Laurent AMIOT when he demanded that parish property be administered by leading figures of the laity elected by the parishioners as a whole. On the other hand, he supported the cause of the farmers, who among other things were grappling with the unending increase in seigneurial dues.

The prestige that Côté enjoyed whetted his interest in politics. In November 1834 he easily won election to the Lower Canadian House of Assembly for L'Acadie, and he retained his seat until 1838. Receptive to the constitutional demands of the assembly and angry about the seigneurs' encroachments in his region, he soon attracted the attention of the French Canadian members. His decided views on the Roman Catholic Church, the colonial government, the seigneurial régime, and the farming class also led him to some intellectual affinity with the Patriote party radicals in the house. A doctor who read the Bible and was fascinated with Jean-Jacques Rousseau and Voltaire, Côté was sensitive to issues related to colonialism and attentive to democratic and republican ideas. He took an interest in legislation concerning the seigneuries, as well as in the drawing up of lands rolls, and by this time he had personal views about the workings of the seigneurial system that seem to have shaped his democratic and social ideas.

In 1836 Côté was called to testify before a committee of the assembly investigating the land issue and the seigneurial régime. He denounced the high rents imposed in the seigneury of Léry and took exception to the numerous illegal practices of the seigneurs in his region. Not wanting to frighten the moderate group in the Patriote party, he advocated reform of the system. He continued none the less to call in question the entire institutional basis of French Canadian society: the union of church and state, the seigneurial régime, and the denominational school. As a democrat and republican he saw that the idea of national independence had to be linked with the real demands of a social revolution. Despite his profound disagreement with Papineau over the seigneurial question, Côté – probably for strategic reasons – attached himself to the moderate wing, which was dedicated primarily to the achievement of national independence.

It was mainly on the local level, however, that Côté's political endeavours carried the most weight. From 1835 till 1837 he travelled around the parishes and participated in public assemblies. By the eve of the rebellion he had become the chief spokesman for the Patriote movement in his region. On 7 May 1837 he took part in the meeting at Saint-Ours. On 17 July he presided with Papineau over the one held at Napierville. In September he joined the Fils de la Liberté, a group of revolutionaries in Montreal. On 23 October he attended the great Assemblée des Six Comtés, at which he delivered a particularly vigorous speech. Two days later he attacked the bishop of Montreal, Jean-Jacques LARTIGUE, and his pastoral letter of 24 October. Acting on his own, Côté set up a revolutionary organization in his county in November, gathering together a number of farmers and forcibly taking from the presbyteries of Napierville and Saint-Valentin the money needed for arms. Nevertheless, the set-back suffered by the Patriotes at Saint-Charles-sur-Richelieu on 25 November was confirmation for him that the rebellion would not continue in his region. Forced into exile because a price had been set on his head, he reached the United States, from which he hoped to organize another rebellion.

From late December 1837 Côté played an important role in the split between the moderate and radical elements in the Patriote movement. For him Papineau was no longer the man for the situation; his secret departure from Saint-Denis on the Richelieu on 23 November and his repeated vacillation during the events of 1837 led Côté to reject his leadership. It was at this time as well that he established an enduring friendship with Dr Robert Nelson*. At the meetings held in Middlebury and Swanton, Vt, early in January 1838, the two of them, successfully thrusting Papineau aside, imposed their views on the rebellion and made new plans for an invasion. Côté and Nelson were at the peak of their influence and in control of the Patriote movement. They took the initiative in drawing up a declaration of independence for Lower Canada evoking the broad directions that the future Patriote government would take: creation of a republic, institution of equality of rights for all citizens, separation of church and state together with establishment of religious freedom, abolition of feudal tenure and tithes, and removal of the death penalty.

On 28 Feb. 1838 Côté and Nelson set out on foot at the head of 300–400 Patriotes to conquer Lower Canada. But on crossing the border they were quickly repulsed by British troops. Back in the United States, Côté, Nelson, and several other leaders, including Chevalier de LORIMIER and Lucien GAGNON, were arrested for violating American neutrality, but they were rapidly discharged by a sympathetic Vermont court. After the failure of the February invasion Côté attempted to regroup the Patriote movement. He planned a secret military organization, the Association des Frères-Chasseurs, with branches in Lower Canada and the United States. His traces are difficult to follow closely at this period. It is certain that in April he went to live in Plattsburgh, N.Y., where he practised medicine on occasion. It was also in the spring of 1838 that his relations with the fugitives began to deteriorate. A stubborn man, Côté defended his ideas with extraordinary vehemence, often in defiance of those around him. Several times in the course of the summer he went off to Lower Canada to work on organizing the Frères-Chasseurs. All his activity was focused on preparing for a new invasion through this secret society.

Côté and Nelson set the second uprising for 3 Nov. 1838. They arrived at Napierville that night and with their men took possession of the village, where they established a camp for the insurgents. As the general in charge of the camp, Côté used every tactic to obtain arms and supplies for the Patriotes. He succeeded, for example, in wheedling £327 out of the *fabrique* of Saint-Cyprien in Napierville. On 5 November he was in command of a 500-man detachment that went to get arms stored at Rouses Point, N.Y. Once again the Patriotes were easily defeated by volunteers attached to the British army. On 9 November the decisive battle was fought at Odelltown, Lower Canada, and ended in the defeat of the insurgents [*see* Charles HINDENLANG]. Disappointed and bitter, Côté managed to return to the United States.

After the November failure Côté became touchy and distrustful of the people around him. He could not stand being annoyed, refused ever to recognize that he was wrong, and thus set a number of Patriotes against him. In meetings at Swanton on 24 Jan. 1839 and at Corbeau, N.Y., on 18 March, Côté attacked the apathy of certain insurgents and showed a deep hostility to Papineau. He demanded that the organization get rid of its former leader, whose negative attitude was in his view doing considerable harm to the movement. He also peppered his comments with often vicious attacks against the Catholic Church, which he held responsible for the collapse of the 1837–38 insurrections. Criticized by Édouard-Élisée Malhiot* and denounced by parish priest Étienne Chartier*, Côté was accused of sowing discord in the revolutionary ranks. He none the less rejected every ideological compromise. In the course of the summer of 1839 there was a rash of defections, disagreements, dirty tricks, and personality conflicts. Côté increasingly became the target for the fierce reproaches of the insurgents, who found him more execrable with every passing day. Except for Nelson and Gagnon, all were against him. In September Côté settled at Swanton to practise his profession. Eager to have revenge on Papineau and some of his former companions, he wrote several articles in the *North American*, which was published there. He was wounded by the insults heaped upon him and downcast at the failure of his dream of independence for Lower Canada, and he definitively abandoned the Patriote movement at the end of 1840.

In February 1841 Côté moved to Chazy, N.Y. There he dreamt of leading a quiet life and practising medicine with complete peace of mind. That year he met Henriette Odin* and Louis Roussy*, who converted him to Protestantism. His political failure thus resulted in withdrawal into a religious struggle. In 1843, following the amnesty, Côté returned to Lower Canada and preached in several parishes in the Saint-Hyacinthe and Dorchester (Saint-Jean-sur-Richelieu) region. A great many priests in the diocese of Montreal feared this well-educated and clever apostate, who openly attacked the Catholic Church and its institutions in his sermons. At Saint-Pie the parishioners subjected him to a charivari which lasted a week and culminated in the setting on fire of the house in which he was preaching. In 1844 Côté went back to the United States and spent a month at Savannah, Ga, where he was treated for pneumonia. He returned to Lower Canada that year, was ordained a Baptist minister, and became pastor for Saint-Pie.

Despite the contempt and insults of his compatriots, Côté continued to believe in the validity of his choice of religion and persisted in his fight against Roman Catholicism. He also managed to gather a few of the faithful about him. In 1848 he left his congregation and went to Philadelphia, where the American Baptist Publication Society asked him to help distribute proselytizing works. That year he published a French translation of Stephen Remington's *Reasons for becoming a Baptist*. In 1848 and 1849 he wrote some pamphlets stressing the basic principles of Protestantism. At that time his reflections on baptism and marriage heightened his influence in Canada and the United States.

Late in 1849 Côté was back in Lower Canada, where he was appointed minister for Sainte-Marie-de-Monnoir (Marieville). In September 1850, being recognized as a missionary of the American Baptist Home Mission Society, he planned to attend an important Baptist meeting in Hinesburg. But on the way he had a heart attack and was rushed to Hinesburg, where he died on 4 October.

Côté had doubtless been one of the most worthy representatives of the radical Patriotes. An advocate of a doctrinaire liberalism, known for his anticlericalism, he had chiefly wanted to reconcile the idea of national independence with the goals of a real social revolution. But his fierce opposition to Papineau, his incessant quarrels with the moderates, and his sharp attacks on the clergy had contributed greatly to making him vulnerable. What did it all amount to? Through his boldness and his radical ideas Côté might have shaken up his era.

RICHARD CHABOT

Among the pamphlets which Cyrille-Hector-Octave Côté wrote for the American Baptist Pub. Soc. are *Un mot en passant à ceux qui ont abandonné l'Église romaine et ses traditions* (Montréal, 1848), translated as *The basis of infant baptism; a word in passing to those who have abandoned the church of Rome and her traditions* (1853), and *Letter from Rev. Dr. C. H. O. Cote to Kirwan, (Rev. Dr. Murray,) on the subject of Christian baptism* (Elizabethtown, N.Y., 1849). He also translated Stephen Remington, *Reasons for becoming a Baptist* (Philadelphia, n.d.) into French.

ANQ-E, CN2-8, 31 oct. 1843. ANQ-M, CE4-16, 25 juin 1833; CN1-122, 1er août 1832; CN4-24, 16 oct. 1843; CN4-30, 26 juin 1834, 3 nov. 1835. ANQ-Q, CE1-1, 1er sept. 1809; E17/31, no.2437. Arch. de la chancellerie de l'évêché de Saint-Hyacinthe (Saint-Hyacinthe, Qué.), XVII.C.33, 25 mars, 22 juin 1849. Arch. du diocèse de Saint-Jean-de-Québec (Longueuil, Qué.), 13A/79–83, 13A/85–86, 13A/92, 13A/98, 16A/58. BVM-G, Fonds Ægidius Fauteux, notes compilées par Ægidius Fauteux sur les patriotes de 1837–38 dont les noms commencent par la lettre C, carton 3. PAC, MG 24, B2: 2322–25, 2350–53, 2368–71, 2381–82, 2400–3, 2412–19, 2496–99, 2515–17, 2531–38, 2550–52, 2565–68, 2591–94, 2672–75, 2721–24, 2729–32, 2735–38, 2741, 2766–73, 2826–29, 2853–56, 2965–68, 2973–78, 2983–86, 2991–3002, 3008–11, 3031–34, 3123–26, 3208–13, 3221–22, 3232–35, 3263–64, 3293–96, 3371–74, 3425–28, 3441–44, 3478–83, 3748–51, 3993–98; B18, 1: 11; B34: 34–36; C3: 47–48, 85–86, 101, 614–15, 867–68, 897–99, 919–20, 1163–67, 1201–8, 1257–61, 1318–25, 1335–50, 1356–61, 1601–4, 1616–20, 1628–29, 1668–70, 1699–1700, 1721–22, 1726–27, 1744, 1747, 1841–44, 1846, 1871–72, 1951–52, 1969–70, 2018, 2033–38, 2161–65, 2219–22; MG 29, D61, 6: 1920; MG 30, D1, 9: 47–49; RG 4, A1, 516: 1–6, 74; 524: 8; B28, 52: 1581–82; B37, 1: 111, 597, 599. Narcisse Cyr, *Memoir of the Rev. C. H. O. Cote, M.D., with a memoir of Mrs. M. Y. Cote and a history of the Grande Ligne mission, Canada East* (Philadelphia, 1852). L.C., House of Assembly, *Journaux*, 1835–36: 86; app.EEE. *Quebec Gazette*, 1 July 1833. P.-G. Roy, *Fils de Québec*, 3: 157–59. Mario Gendron, "Tenure seigneuriale et mouvement patriote: le cas du comté de L'Acadie" (thèse de MA, univ. du Québec à Montréal, 1986), 88–89, 93, 126–27, 130–32, 139–41, 156–59. Sylvio Leblond, "Docteur Cyrille-Hector-Octave Côté (1809–1850)," *L'Union médicale du Canada* (Montréal), 102 (1973): 1572–74; "Le docteur Cyrille-Hector-Octave Côté et le mouvement baptiste français au Canada," *Laval médical* (Québec), 29 (1960): 633–41.

COTTON, CHARLES CALEB, priest of the Church of England and farmer; b. 31 July 1775 in Eton, England, eldest of 13 children of Caleb Cotton and Ann Lemoine; m. 22 June 1814 Drusilla Pettis, and they had seven children, of whom three survived their parents; d. 9 Oct. 1848 in Cowansville, Lower Canada.

Charles Caleb Cotton's father was a schoolmaster and his mother a daughter of a Swiss who taught French at Eton College. After attending Eton, Cotton graduated BA from Oriel College, University of Oxford, in 1797. He was ordained deacon by Bishop George Pretyman of Lincoln on 31 Dec. 1797 and licensed a curate in Wexham. The following November he sailed to the United States. In 1799 he became a master in Charleston College, Charleston, S.C., but the pay being meagre he resigned. From 1800 to 1804 he ministered successively at New York, in New Brunswick, N.J., and near Philadelphia.

In August 1804, well recommended, Cotton presented himself at Quebec to Bishop Jacob Mountain*, a close friend of the bishop of Lincoln, and on 9 September he became the first priest ordained in the new Cathedral of the Holy Trinity. He was subsequently licensed to Missisquoi Bay, in the seigneury of Saint-Armand. Mountain recommended him to the Society for the Propagation of the Gospel as "peculiarly suited to the situation, having great simplicity, becoming gravity of manners, good ability, and much facility in communicating his thoughts, & from his residence in America, sufficient familiarity with the manners prevalent among their new settlers which are so apt to give an Englishman disgust." Cotton had been preceded at Missisquoi Bay by the SPG missionaries Robert Quirk Short* and James Marmaduke Tunstall, but he found that little had been accomplished in the rough pioneer settlement. Without church or parsonage, and with the inconveniences of primitive board and lodging, he continued for four years to give to the people of Saint-Armand, and in a measure to those of neighbouring Caldwell's Manor, the first continuous ministrations of the church. In December 1806, however, Mountain noted that Cotton was disheartened by his parishioners, "many of them . . . addicted to profane conversation & dissolute habits." To the bishop of Lincoln he acknowledged that Cotton was "a very worthy, a very pious, & a very sensible man," but added that "his weak state of health renders him incapable of any very considerable or continued exertion: his mind appears to have no peculiar firmness; & perverseness discourages, & difficulties depress him."

To relieve Cotton, Charles James STEWART was appointed to Saint-Armand in 1807. However, Cotton moved only a few miles away to Dunham Township, provoking a mild reproach from Mountain, who reminded him that clergy "were not ordained for their own convenience and comfort" but nevertheless allowed him to remain. Yet Cotton's early years in Dunham were anything but comfortable. He had to contend not only with the indifference of the people and their ignorance of Anglican ways but also with itinerant Baptist and Methodist missionaries. In addition, he ultimately experienced personally all the problems encountered by the settlers to whom he ministered. After boarding for nearly two years with eight other people in a two-room cabin, he cleared and farmed three homesteads in succession, each one costing him dearly in time, money, and physical toil. In 1812 Mountain proposed Cotton for York (Toronto), but he was rejected by Isaac Brock*, then administering Upper Canada, who obtained the appointment of John Strachan*.

Cotton had to hold services in schoolhouses and private homes until a church was built at Dunham Flats (Dunham) in 1821. The parish was erected by provincial letters patent that year, and Cotton became rector, but the ceremony of institution, because of some "informality," had to be repeated in 1829. The first All Saints' Church, a spacious wooden building somewhat clumsily designed, stood until 1846 when it was demolished to make way for a stone structure.

Possessing no outstanding gifts, and, according to one observer, "as destitute of equestrian skill as he was . . . unequalled . . . for pedestrian ability," Cotton could not provide the range of missionary services or cover the territory that Stewart could. Neither was his ministry entirely trouble-free. A man of simple habits and fond of retirement, he was in some respects eccentric, and his practice of expressing his views baldly could give offence. In 1823 Stewart had to settle a dispute between him and his parishioners, who alleged that he was inattentive to his pastoral duties and had refused to bury a young woman because she had been baptized by a dissenting minister. Stewart had more than once lost patience with Cotton, but in this instance friendly advice and warning seem to have resolved the difficulty.

In general, however, Cotton's long ministry in Dunham was calm, and despite ill health in later life he performed his clerical duties regularly, conducting a total of 617 baptisms, 656 marriages, and 187 burials and preparing 226 candidates for confirmation. As befitted a schoolmaster's son, he catechized children, established a Sunday school (in 1824), and helped to prepare two theological students, Micajah Townsend and James Reid, for ordination. He strictly observed the rubrics of the prayer book. One of the few clergy to receive a stipend of £100 from the British government, Cotton was granted another £100 from the SPG after 1814; not until 1834 when Stewart, then bishop of Quebec, urged self-financing by churches, did parishioners begin to contribute to their rector's income. "Priest Cotton," as he was known familiarly, died in 1848 after 40 years' service in Dunham.

THOMAS R. MILLMAN

Descendants of the Cotton family have in their possession extensive correspondence containing a great deal of information on Charles Caleb Cotton and his family. A typescript, 325 pages in length, of a selection of these letters was made in 1932, and a photocopy and microfilm copy of it are at the ACC, General Synod Arch. (Toronto).

ACC, Diocese of Montreal Arch., file C-18. ACC-Q, 50. All Saints (Anglican) Church (Dunham, Que.), Reg. of baptisms, marriages, and burials, 30 April 1815, 13 Oct. 1848. RHL, USPG Arch., C/CAN/folders 362, 410 (mfm. at PAC); journal of SPG, 29–43. Trinity Church (Anglican) (Frelighsburg, Que.), Reg. of baptisms, marriages, and burials, 22 June 1814. Ernest Hawkins, *Annals of the diocese of Quebec* (London, 1849), 39–41. [G. J. Mountain], *A journal of visitation in a portion of the diocese of Quebec by the lord bishop of Montreal in 1846* (London, 1847), 61–62; *A journal of visitation to a part of the diocese of Quebec by the lord bishop of Montreal in the spring of 1843* (3rd ed., London, 1846), 37–38. SPG, [*Annual report*] (London), 1830: 129–30. *Church*, 2 Nov. 1848. T. R. Millman, *A short history of the parish of Dunham, Quebec* (Granby, Que., 1946); *Jacob Mountain, first lord bishop of Quebec; a study in church and state, 1793–1825* (Toronto, 1947); *The life of the Right Reverend, the Honourable Charles James Stewart, D.D., Oxon., second Anglican bishop of Quebec* (London, Ont., 1953). Cyrus Thomas, *Contributions to the history of the Eastern Townships* . . . (Montreal, 1866), 137–43. "A brief history of the parish of Dunham," *Church Chronicle for the Diocese of Montreal* (Montreal), 1 (1860–61): 4–7, 39–41. "Historical notes," Missisquoi County Hist. Soc., *Report* (Saint-Jean-sur-Richelieu, Que.), 3 (1908): 70–81.

COUAGNE. *See* DECOIGNE

COUILLARD, ANTOINE-GASPARD, physician, surgeon, militia officer, seigneur, JP, politician, and office holder; b. 16 Feb. 1789 in Saint-Thomas-de-la-

Pointe-à-la-Caille (Montmagny), Que., son of Jean-Baptiste Couillard and Marie-Angélique Chaussegros de Léry; m. 6 Feb. 1816 Marie-Angélique-Flore Wilson, daughter of Thomas Wilson; d. 12 June 1847 in Montmagny.

On his father's side Antoine-Gaspard Couillard was a descendant of Guillaume Couillard* de Lespinay, who helped build New France in the time of Samuel de Champlain* and was ennobled by Louis XIV in 1654, and of Guillemette Hébert*, daughter of Louis Hébert*, the first farmer in the colony. His father was seigneur of Rivière-du-Sud, and his mother was the daughter of Gaspard-Joseph Chaussegros* de Léry, officer, military engineer, and the architect of many fortifications in New France, and Louise Martel de Brouague.

Couillard commenced classical studies at the Petit Séminaire de Québec, where he developed a liking for history and literature. In 1803, however, his father took him out of that institution to have him study law with Alexandre-André-Victor Chaussegros de Léry. The young man was not cut out for legal studies and did not complete his articling. Preferring to become a doctor, he began his training with Samuel Holmes and René-Joseph Kimber, and then completed it at the University of Pennsylvania in Philadelphia. He returned to Quebec in 1811 and on 12 June of that year, at 22 years of age, he was authorized by the deputy provincial secretary, Lewis Foy, to practise medicine, surgery, and pharmacy in Lower Canada.

Remaining active professionally for about 30 years, Couillard practised in both rural and urban settings, at Saint-Thomas-de-la-Pointe-à-la-Caille and Quebec. He served as a doctor to the civilian population, and also as surgeon to the 4th Select Embodied Militia Battalion of Lower Canada during the War of 1812. His professional competence was recognized when on 13 July 1831 he was elected to the medical Board of Examiners for the district of Quebec. Because of his devotion to the poor he became known as the "doctor to the needy and the poor," as an article in the *Quebec Gazette* published at the time of his death notes.

The seigneury of Rivière-du-Sud, which had been divided and subdivided several times, was of great interest to Couillard. Upon his father's death in 1808 he had come into possession of part of it, and through purchase of other parts in 1816 and 1841 he became the principal seigneur. Not lacking in ambition, he built, apparently at the time of his marriage to the daughter of a prosperous Quebec merchant, an imposing manor-house at Montmagny, to the west of the Rivière-du-Sud. It is still standing. Made of freestone, this magnificent two-storey residence overlooking the St Lawrence River has an enormous portico, crowned with a stately pediment, that is an attraction for passers-by. In its day the house was considered one of the finest in Lower Canada. Today it is used as a hotel. Unfortunately Couillard's ineptitude in financial matters made managing his seigneury a burden for him. He was owed money by *censitaires*, patients, and friends, and he himself was in debt. Furthermore, his manor-house cost far more than he had anticipated and later he had to resign himself to selling it for a mere £3,000. This was not the first piece of bad luck Couillard suffered, but it was certainly the hardest one to accept.

Couillard was a member of the Literary and Historical Society of Quebec and regularly attended its meetings. At the same time he gave some attention, perhaps reluctantly, to public administration and politics. Gradually his financial worries undermined his health, and in 1842 he had to give up almost all of his medical practice. He served as a justice of the peace, a member of the Legislative Council from 1832 to 1838, and commissioner for administering the oath of allegiance. Then in 1842 he managed, though not without some difficulty, to obtain the post of registrar for the district of Saint-Thomas. The appointment enabled him to provide decently for his numerous children, but not to meet the demands of his creditors. Nor could he prevent the sale of his estate and belongings to William Randall Patton, a wealthy Quebec merchant, shortly before his death.

Antoine-Gaspard Couillard passed away in Montmagny on 12 June 1847, at 58 years of age, and was buried there five days later. Philippe-Joseph Aubert* de Gaspé, who had maintained "a constant and untroubled" friendship with him for half a century, bade him a touching farewell in *Les anciens Canadiens*. Paying tribute to Couillard as the best and most virtuous of men, he recalled among other things that his friend, like himself, had drunk "the bitter cup of tribulations," and that he had seen his ancestors' domain pass into alien hands.

JACQUES CASTONGUAY

ANQ-Q, CE1-1, 6 févr. 1816; CE2-7, 16 févr. 1789, 17 juin 1847; CN1-230, 4 févr. 1816. PAC, RG 4, B28, 48: 297–300; RG 68, General index, 1651–1841; 1841–67. *Le Journal de Québec*, 17 juin 1847. *Quebec Gazette*, 20 June 1811, 8 Feb. 1816. F.-J. Audet, "Les législateurs du Bas-Canada." Desjardins, *Guide parl. Officers of British forces in Canada* (Irving). Turcotte, *Le Conseil législatif*, 19, 116. P.[-J.] Aubert de Gaspé, *Les anciens Canadiens* (16e éd., Québec, 1970), 304–9. Azarie Couillard-Després, *Histoire des seigneurs de la Rivière du Sud et de leurs alliés canadiens et acadiens* (Saint-Hyacinthe, Qué., 1912), 351–65. Raymonde [Landry] Gauthier, *Les manoirs du Québec* (Montréal, 1976), 172–73. P.-G. Roy, *La famille Chaussegros de Léry* (Lévis, Qué., 1934), 15–16; *Vieux manoirs, vieilles maisons* (Québec, 1927), 200–2. F.-J. Audet, "La seigneurie de la Rivière du Sud," *BRH*, 7 (1901): 117–19.

COVERT, JOHN, farmer, JP, businessman, author, and militia officer; b. *c.* 1770 in England, possibly in

Christchurch (Dorset); m. Elizabeth ——, and they had at least two sons and two daughters; d. 5 Sept. 1843 at his farm, New Lodge, near Cobourg, Upper Canada.

When John Covert came to Upper Canada in 1820 he was a man well into middle age, yet with a young family. He arrived with money, for, after looking at land in the Rice Lake area, he decided to establish himself on a developed farm in Hamilton Township – a township along the north shore of Lake Ontario that was attracting a number of British gentry and half-pay officers, among them Francis Brockell Spilsbury*. By 1821 Covert had purchased two lots at the front of the township and commenced farming. In later years he acquired neighbouring lands to create a large farm strategically placed on the Kingston road near Cobourg at a point which afforded a possible mill site.

Like many of his class, Covert quickly found himself drawn to the problems of establishing on the frontier a sound economic base and a more familiar social order. He received the first of several commissions as a magistrate on 4 Aug. 1821. Particularly interested in transportation, he was among those who petitioned the House of Assembly in 1825 for a pier or breakwater at Cobourg and two years later, as an owner of wild land in Otonabee Township, for a ferry on Rice Lake. In October 1827, continuing his efforts for improvements to the harbour at Cobourg, Covert was a leading figure in the creation of the Cobourg harbour committee. Another petition went to the assembly in January, signed by Covert and 143 others. The following month a select committee of the assembly recommended that work should be undertaken, by a private joint-stock company that would be allowed to charge tolls. The Cobourg Harbour Company was incorporated in March 1829 but Covert, though one of the first stockholders, was not a director. His son-in-law James Gray BETHUNE was to become heavily involved in the operations of the company in the 1830s.

In an effort to break free of what he considered Upper Canada's single-minded dependence on wheat production, Covert took up the cultivation and processing of hemp. This crop had been unsuccessfully attempted earlier in both Upper and Lower Canada [*see* Charles Frederick GRECE] – as Edward Allen TALBOT noted in the early 1820s, "the two Canadas cannot at present afford a sufficient quantity to hang their own malefactors." In 1830 Covert was the first to claim a government grant, under an 1822 act, for the purchase of machinery for dressing hemp. He presented documents in November 1830 attesting to his having erected a substantial water-powered mill. Four months later Lieutenant Governor Sir John Colborne* and his Executive Council acknowledged Covert's efforts by awarding him the grant but, in accordance with the act, the machinery was placed in the name of the crown to ensure that it would be available for public use. To secure a market for hemp within the colony, Covert sent a sample of his product to Commodore Robert BARRIE, the senior naval officer in the Canadas, who "pronounced it to be as good as the Riga or Peterboro' hemp" and agreed to purchase 20 tons at £50 per ton. In May 1831, hoping to ensure a steady supply of the material and thereby make Cobourg the government depot for the commissariat at Kingston, Covert presented an address on the cultivation of hemp to his fellow members of the Northumberland Agricultural Society. Citing his own experience, he claimed that hemp would "yield on an average nearly double the value of wheat" and that a few of his neighbours, all well-to-do gentry farmers, had been induced to grow it. For a moment at least Covert was the leading advocate of hemp production in British North America, and his essay on the subject brought him a medal from the Natural History Society of Montreal. Yet his efforts proved ineffectual: few answered his call and within a short time his mill had to be converted to more conventional grist-milling.

The failure of this venture foreshadowed a series of personal tragedies and defeats that plagued Covert's later life. His business affairs, which largely consisted of land speculation in and around Cobourg and in the townships to the north, became somewhat chaotic. In a particularly acrimonious will, written shortly before his death, Covert alleged that "through the misconduct if not treachery of a fancied friend," Cobourg banker Robert Henry*, "the best part of my property and prospects have been sacrificed." Moreover, James Bethune made calls on his financial surety in 1835 following Bethune's spectacular misadventures as agent in Cobourg for the Bank of Upper Canada.

An important conservative and perhaps the leading Orangeman in Cobourg, Covert was also colonel of the 1st Regiment of Northumberland militia. His conservative politics became intermingled with his militia responsibilities when, beginning in April 1832, Covert attempted to discredit reform sympathizers in his regiment, especially Captain Wilson Seymour Conger. Covert's questionable behaviour eventually led to his court martial in July–August 1836. Finding the colonel guilty of three of the eight charges brought against him by Conger, the court concluded that Covert had been "influenced by a misdirected zeal" rather than "vindictive or malignant motives." However, in a general order dated 9 September, Lieutenant Governor Sir Francis Bond Head* stated that "he cannot consider Colonel Covert as a fit person to exercise the command of a Reg[t] of Militia in this Province: and he has therefore deemed it his painful duty to direct the Adjutant General to acquaint Colonel Covert that His Majesty has no further occasion for his services in the said Militia." Covert's predicament did not prevent his sons from being active in the militia: Henry was commissioned first lieutenant in 1838 and Frederick Peechy succumbed late that year to an illness contracted while on military service.

It was no doubt the turmoil of his business and military affairs that caused Covert to retreat from Upper Canada in 1837. During his time away he arranged through Jonas JONES, aide-de-camp to Head, to do some reconnaissance work in the United States following the outbreak of rebellion in December 1837. After a year-long absence, Covert returned to find that he had been struck off the list of magistrates. For at least the next three years he continued to petition the provincial secretary protesting the injustices done to him and seeking to recover his militia commission and to be restored as a magistrate. In the latter struggle, he finally succeeded, for his name was among the list of new magistrates published in the *Cobourg Star* on 30 Aug. 1843, less than a week before his death.

In spite of his many problems, Covert was able to leave his heirs substantial legacies consisting principally of valuable town-lots and speculative housing properties in Cobourg, at a time when that town was entering a boom period. Nevertheless, it was a disappointed man who wrote in his will of his only remaining son and principal heir, "Altho' my son Henrys sentiments & feelings have not appeared congenial with my own nor respectful & affectionate toward an unfortunate & afflicted father . . . still it is a Christian duty to forgive the past . . . and I do hereby exonerate and release my son Henry from a Bond of one thousand pound value & also other monies I have loaned to him when his premature plans brought him into trouble."

PETER ENNALS

AO, RG 8, I-1-P, 3, Covert to Jonas Jones, 15 March 1838; Covert to S. B. Harrison, 27 Nov. 1840; RG 22, ser.187, reg.G (1858–62), will of John Covert, probated 8 May 1860. Northumberland West Land Registry Office (Cobourg, Ont.), Hamilton Township, abstract index to deeds (mfm. at AO). PAC, RG 1, E3, 19: 123–30, 193–202; 28: 71–74; RG 9, I, B3, 5, nos.255, 262, 265; B8, 3. *Bank of U.C.* v. *Covert* (1836–38), 5 O.S., 541. U.C., House of Assembly, *App. to the journal*, 1835, 2, app.73; *Journal*, 10 March, 9 April 1825; 28 Jan., 12 Feb. 1828; 1828, app., report on Cobourg Harbour; 12, 17–18 Dec. 1832. *Cobourg Star*, 8 Feb., 31 May 1831; 21 Aug. 1833; 20 Aug., 6, 13 Sept. 1843; 26 Aug. 1846. P. M. Ennals, "Land and society in Hamilton Township, Upper Canada, 1797–1861" (PHD thesis, Univ. of Toronto, 1978). R. L. Jones, *History of agriculture in Ontario, 1613–1880* (Toronto, 1946; repr. Toronto and Buffalo, N.Y., 1977). D. E. Wattie, "Cobourg, 1784–1867" (2v., MA thesis, Univ. of Toronto, 1949).

COY (Coye), AMASA (Amassa, Amasy), merchant; b. 31 July 1757 in Pomfret, Conn., eldest son of J. Edward Coy (McCoy) and Ama Titus; brother of Mary Coy*; m. first 1797 Elizabeth Holly, and they had one son and two daughters; m. secondly *c.* 1808 Mary Spafford Smith, *née* Barker, and they had two sons; d. 18 July 1838 in Fredericton.

In 1763 Amasa Coy went with his parents to the Maugerville settlement in what was then the colony of Nova Scotia [*see* Israel Perley*]. They remembered nearly starving in the early years. Eventually they settled in Gage Township. Like most New Englanders in the Saint John valley, the Coys were in sympathy with the American colonists at the time of the revolution, and Amasa served in Jonathan Eddy*'s unsuccessful attack on Fort Cumberland (near Sackville, N.B.) in 1776. A report on land claims and loyalty submitted to Brigade-Major Gilfred Studholme* in 1783, after listing the claim of Coy and a brother to 200 acres in Gage Township, says simply: "Amasa was in arms against the fort at Cumberland." Their father, according to the report, "was a rebel committee man."

J. Edward Coy had been one of the founders of the Congregational Church at Maugerville in the 1760s and both he and his wife were to sign the congregation's new covenant in 1789. In the early years of the settlement the church dominated community life and imposed its discipline on individuals, but under the strain of war its unity crumbled. Visits of the evangelist Henry Alline* in 1779 and 1781 led to disputes over doctrine, as well as to a renewal of interest in spiritual affairs. With the arrival of the loyalists in 1783 came a further awareness of theological differences and ecclesiastical distinctions.

When his fellow New Englanders, very much outsiders in the new loyalist society, became preoccupied with doctrinal matters, Amasa Coy followed a moderate course. He was associated both with the traditionalists who reorganized the Congregational church and moved the meeting-house to Sheffield in 1789 [*see* David BURPE] and with an Allinite group in Waterborough and Gagetown. Around the time of his marriage in 1797 he moved from Gagetown to the parish of Queensbury in York County, where in 1800 he became one of the founding members of the Calvinist Baptist church in Prince William. This congregation joined the Baptist Association of Nova Scotia and New Brunswick, an organization which came into existence that year when a number of ministers formally set themselves apart from the New Light (Allinite) movement and allied themselves with Calvinist Baptist associations in New England. Historian David G. Bell regards this development as arising in part from a desire for respectability at a time when "new dispensationalism" had led some New Lights to act out their belief that conversion had freed them from obedience to the rules of moral and religious conduct.

In 1808 Coy acquired four lots in Fredericton, conveniently located for business purposes near Province Hall and the army barracks. Two years later he moved to Fredericton and purchased rights to 37 acres along the road to the site where King's College would be built in the 1820s. As the town grew, he prospered from the development of these properties. He also opened a store on Queen Street, which in 1825 was operating under the name of Stewart and Coy, merchants. In some of his business activities he worked in partnership with his son Asa and with his son-in-law Thomas B. Smith. Amasa and Asa were among the founders of the Central Bank of New Brunswick in 1834 [*see* Henry George CLOPPER]. Two years later Asa became the first president of the Bank of Fredericton.

In 1813 Amasa Coy was among those who planned a Baptist meeting-house in Fredericton; it was built on land he made available. The Fredericton Baptist Church, with 13 members, was founded in 1814 and Coy received his dismission from Queensbury to join it two years later. At that time the Calvinist Baptist congregations were regarded by the authorities as pro-American and therefore potentially disloyal. Later their reputation suffered from their being popularly identified with other congregations in the Saint John valley which were also designated as Baptist but which did not have the formal structures of the Baptist Association's churches or follow its rule, adopted in 1809, of close communion. Gradually, however, the efforts of the Calvinist Baptists to translate a backwoods movement into an urban setting led to a recognition of their respectability. Their church grew vigorously and by the time of Coy's death they had opened a seminary in Fredericton under the Reverend Frederick William MILES to challenge Anglican domination of higher education and had established themselves as an effective force in the shaping of the provincial polity. Amasa Coy's use of his wealth had contributed to the great success of his co-religionists in their efforts to participate in and influence the course of New Brunswick life.

D. M. YOUNG

Conn. State Library (Hartford), Indexes, Barbour coll., Pomfret vital records, I: 38; Conn. church records, Abington Congregational Church (Pomfret), 3: 277. PANB, MC 1, Coy family, two files; MC 239; RG 7, RS69, A, 1795–96, J. E. Coy; RS75, 1838, Amasa Coy. PRO, CO 188/32, George Best to SPG, 27 April 1825. UNBL, MG H9, H. A. Bridges, "Brief history of the First Baptist Church of Sheffield – sometimes referred to as the Canning Church or the Waterbury Church" (typescript, n.d.); Waterborough Baptist Church records, 1800–32 (typescript, n.d.). *The Newlight Baptist journals of James Manning and James Innis*, ed. D. G. Bell (Saint John, N.B., 1984). "Sunbury County documents," N.B. Hist. Soc., *Coll.*, 1 (1894–97), no.1: 100–18. *Royal Gazette* (Fredericton), 25 July 1838. Hill, *Old Burying Ground. The old grave-yard, Fredericton, New Brunswick: epitaphs copied by the York-Sunbury Historical Society, Inc.*, comp. L. M. Beckwith Maxwell (Sackville, N.B., 1938). Bill, *Fifty years with Baptist ministers*. I. L. Hill, *Fredericton, New Brunswick, British North America* ([Fredericton?, 1968?]), 49. W. D. Moore, "Sunbury County, 1760–1830" (MA thesis, Univ. of N.B., Fredericton, 1977).

CROIX, MARIE-VICTOIRE BAUDRY, named DE LA. *See* BAUDRY

CROKE, Sir ALEXANDER, judge, politician, author, and colonial administrator; b. 22 July 1758 in Aylesbury, England, the only surviving son of Alexander Croke and his first wife, Anne Armistead; m. 11 Aug. 1796 Alice Blake; d. 27 Dec. 1842 at Studley Priory, England.

Born into the landed gentry, Alexander Croke was the heir to a substantial though unpretentious country estate. His earliest education took place at a private school in Bierton, where, he recalled, he "acquired a general love for literature and science." On 11 Oct. 1775 he matriculated as a gentleman commoner at Oriel College, Oxford, and he remained there five years. During this period he succeeded to the Studley estate. In 1780 Croke took up the study of law at the Inns of Court, and in 1786 was called to the bar. However, as he later stated, "although I had studied the theory of the law, I never engaged in the practice of it, or attended much in Westminster Hall," since he had a competence to support him. A predisposition to theoretical deliberation was to become marked in his Nova Scotian career.

Croke resumed legal studies at Oxford in 1794, "being weary of an idle life, & seeing the necessity of a profession." He obtained the degrees of BCL and DCL in 1797, and on 3 November of that year he was admitted to the College of Advocates. Choosing to practise at the bar, he was soon given a share of the increasing business of the High Court of Admiralty engendered by the French revolutionary wars. A number of his reports brought him into public notice and earned him praise from the government and such London journals as the *Anti-Jacobin Review and Magazine* and the *Gentleman's Magazine*.

In 1801 the system of vice-admiralty courts in the British colonies was restructured, and Croke was offered one of the judgeships which had become available in Jamaica, Martinique, and Nova Scotia. Preferring "the severe, but healthy climate of Nova Scotia, to all the luxuries and all the dangers of the West Indies," he arrived in Halifax on 11 Nov. 1801 with his wife and infant son and daughter. With the exception of a trip to England in 1810 to place his son in school, Croke remained in Nova Scotia until July 1815. Eight of his eleven children were born in the province.

Croke was honoured for his work in Nova Scotia by a knighthood from the Prince Regent on 5 July 1816 and retired with an annuity of £1,000 to his estate, where he "entertained his Oxford friends, amused himself with drawing and painting, and wrote a number of books." According to certain contemporaries, he was an accomplished artist, several of his paintings obtaining the approval of Benjamin West, president of the Royal Academy of Arts. Unfortunately, no trace of his efforts has been found. Croke exhibited some degree of literary and poetic skill, publishing books and pamphlets on a wide variety of subjects. His most ambitious undertaking was *The genealogical history of the Croke family, originally named LeBlount* (Oxford, 1823), a two-volume work of extensive and well-documented research. Other endeavours included legal reports, a church catechism, polemical and satirical poetry, an essay on Latin verse, and letters on political and educational subjects. Croke died at Studley Priory in his 85th year. Eight of his children reached adulthood, but none left any progeny.

Although only one-sixth of Croke's life was spent in Nova Scotia, that period constituted the major portion of his professional career. His chief and most visible role in Nova Scotia was to preside over the Vice-Admiralty Court. Since its establishment in 1749 at Halifax the court had developed into a significant force within the province, exercising the traditional Admiralty competence over all cases of a maritime origin. Its activities involved three levels of jurisdiction – the local, which covered disputes of merchants and seamen, the imperial, which concerned control of trade and the forest reserves of the navy, and the international, which came into play in wartime and gave the court authority to condemn ships and cargoes captured by privateers and the navy.

The existence of this powerful and independent institution elicited frequent and vociferous complaints from the local population, the most common being that the court's fees were exorbitant and that the mode of trial by judge alone violated the right of Englishmen to trial by their peers. In a colony where smuggling was rife, the actual motive behind the complaints was the prospect of almost certain conviction in the admiralty court as compared with the better chances afforded by lenient juries in the common courts. The House of Assembly, dominated by Halifax merchants, was the most vocal opponent of the court, and by using the issues of high fees and non-jury trials attempted to gain some control over the institution. These issues were matters of imperial policy, over which Croke had no command, but they nevertheless provided the colonists with ample motivation for disliking the official responsible.

The other main cause of contention was the court's mandate to enforce the navigation acts. With respect to the colonies, the prime object of the legislation was to confine all transportation connected with them to British shipping and so ensure that the benefits derived fell to the mother country. Because of their slow economic development, the Maritime provinces had come to depend heavily on their neighbour to the south for supplies by the beginning of the 19th century; they therefore demanded some modification of the acts in order to obtain by legal means from the United States desperately needed staples and products for re-export to other British possessions. The lieutenant governors of the provinces fatalistically accepted a certain amount of clandestine trade as natural and unavoidable, and objected that too much preventive legislation would only obstruct "the quiet current of commercial industry." Accordingly, breaches were made in the system as Sir John Wentworth*, Sir George Prevost*, Sir John Coape Sherbrooke*, and others took advantage of emergency powers to meet the needs of the colonists.

Croke represented that segment of British society which at the beginning of the 19th century still retained its belief in the value and necessity of the navigation acts. Although he had no choice but to enforce the law, a survey of his judgements reveals how strongly he maintained his convictions and how rigidly he interpreted the statutes. The case of the *Economy*, decided in March 1813, indicates the tenor of his judicial career. After the outbreak of the War of 1812 New England had shown itself willing to continue trading with the Maritime provinces, and the colonial authorities had issued licences which allowed American vessels such as the *Economy* to transport provisions to Nova Scotia. Yet the *Economy* and its cargo of livestock had been taken by the privateer *Liverpool Packet* [*see* Joseph Barss*] despite the possession of a licence from Vice-Admiral Herbert Sawyer. In condemning ship and cargo on the grounds that Sawyer could give "no legality whatever to a traffic otherwise unlawful," Croke concluded his judgement with a traditional and comprehensive defence of the navigation acts. Although he conceded the necessity of allowing the import of certain types of foodstuffs as sanctioned by British orders in council, he would not condone the admission of livestock, which he was certain was in ample supply in Nova Scotia. However, the war had resulted in a sharp increase in the number of British troops in North America, and the military commanders believed that Maritime resources were insufficient to meet the demand for provisions. Sherbrooke informed Prevost, commander-in-chief in British North America, that Croke had "given a decree . . . which If not reversed at home will I greatly fear Cause much individual mischief." The lieutenant governor's sense of harassment was probably representative of the reactions of many who suffered from Croke's severely legalistic approach, and is revealed in a further remark to Prevost, "There is a vulgar saying that the Devil Can only run the length of his Tether – That of Bonaparte snapped short at Moscow,

And I am willing to hope that Dr: Croke has nearly reached the end of his." Whatever the legal validity of Croke's decision, the British government supported Sherbrooke by allowing licences to be granted to American ships.

The popular feeling against the Vice-Admiralty Court was not mitigated by Croke's service as administrator of the colony, a duty which as senior eligible councillor he performed in the absence of the lieutenant governor from 6 Dec. 1808 to 15 April 1809 and from 25 August to 16 Oct. 1811. His very right to the position was a matter of dispute. The royal mandamus appointing him to the Council in 1802 had given him seniority after the chief justice, and his supercession of other councillors had created difficulties. Another source of friction was the lengthy satirical poem entitled "The Inquisition" which Croke wrote probably in 1805 and which was widely circulated in manuscript. In it he presented a biting commentary on the moral tone of upper-class Halifax society, striking with witty and frequently caustic criticism at leading individuals, including many Council members, who were often only thinly veiled by classical pseudonyms. Such a work could not fail to produce resentment and even animosity in the parochial capital of Halifax. These tensions were exacerbated by Croke's suspicions of and condescending attitude towards the assembly. Prevost's warning to the British government that in his absence the civil duties would fall to "an able tho' unpopular character" reflected public opinion.

Croke's first term as administrator proceeded peacefully until the most important matter of legislative business, the annual appropriations bill, became the centre of attention. Following accepted practice, the assembly made itemized proposals for expenditures, and after some negotiation the bill was approved by the Council on 20 Jan. 1809 and sent to Croke for his formal acceptance. The assembly was stunned by Croke's refusal to assent to the bill, and the resulting controversy lasted until Prevost approved it after his return.

Croke justified his rejection of the bill in a lengthy dispatch to the colonial secretary. The basis for his first objection lay in a clause authorizing the payment of 200 guineas to the commissioners appointed to correspond with the provincial agents. Seemingly innocuous, the clause contained several new appointments, a political manœuvre that Croke recognized and denounced as an encroachment upon the royal prerogative. The second reason for his dissent lay in the amount of the sums appropriated, which he claimed was excessive and likely to cause injury to the king's service. Croke suggested a return to the practice current before 1786 when no appropriations acts were passed and all money was drawn from the provincial treasury by warrant from the legislature. Because of the intransigence of both Croke and the assembly, the house was prorogued and civil administration became paralysed. Croke's attempt to obtain the Council's permission to withdraw money from the treasury failed. His efforts to protect the crown's prerogatives and save the government from a large public debt only led to turmoil in the colony's administration and intensified the popular dislike of him and his court. His second term as administrator was uneventful.

In no sphere of Nova Scotian public life did Croke exert so lasting an influence as in education. His prolific writings, published and private, give abundant evidence of his views. To Croke, the prime concerns of education were moral and spiritual – knowledge should be directed towards producing better people, not towards helping them to advance their station in life. Convinced that instruction in the Christian faith was essential in any school curriculum, Croke believed that the only interpretation tenable was that of the Church of England, "the purest and most apostolic form of religion ever established in any country." Furthermore, adherence to the Church of England would strengthen one's allegiance to the crown and government of Britain.

By virtue of his position as judge of the Vice-Admiralty Court, Croke was appointed to the board of governors of King's College by the charter of 1802. It was intended by the board that the institution's statutes be modelled after those of Oxford, and as the only Oxford graduate among the governors Croke was the logical source of information. Along with Chief Justice Sampson Salter BLOWERS and Bishop Charles Inglis* he was appointed to the committee which was to draft them. There is no evidence that the committee ever met as a body, however, and it appears that Croke took upon himself the task of framing the statutes. To later generations, their most controversial aspect was the stipulation that all matriculants subscribe to the Thirty-Nine Articles of the Church of England; in a province which was three-quarters non-Anglican, this clause effectively prohibited most Nova Scotians from attending their only post-secondary institution. The direct result of the restriction was a proliferation of denominational academic institutions during the 19th century [*see* Thomas McCULLOCH]. Although the statutes undoubtedly reflected Croke's personal attitude towards education, they received the approbation of the board of governors, the Council, and the British authorities.

Years later, Croke became embroiled in the issue of public education centring on the so-called Bromleyan controversy. In 1813 Walter BROMLEY arrived in Nova Scotia to establish an interdenominational school for the poor, and his project drew the interest and support of many influential citizens. Declining an invitation to serve on the committee for organizing the school, Croke voiced his disapproval of the scheme in a lengthy letter published in the *Acadian Recorder* of 13 Aug. 1813. He thus began a long and heated public debate over the advantages of denominational and interdenominational education. The educational efforts of the colonists became disunited: Bromley's Royal Acadian School lost valuable supporters and Anglicans intensified their own denominational endeavours. Croke's outspoken views reinforced Nova Scotians' antipathy towards him.

The intense dislike of Alexander Croke in Nova Scotia on the part both of contemporaries and of historians up to the 20th century was engendered in part by his office. As judge of the Vice-Admiralty Court he was obliged to enforce a system of laws which were becoming increasingly outdated and which he rendered more unpalatable by his inflexible interpretations. His personality was also to blame for the public perception of him, for he exhibited a lack of understanding and diplomacy in dealing with people whom he perceived to be in a lower social station. This characteristic was especially marked in his insensitivity to the rising aspirations of Nova Scotians at the opening of the 19th century, so that his involvement in the social issues of the community led only to altercations. Although Croke was a man of considerable legal knowledge, cultural and artistic abilities, and much personal integrity, the benefits deriving from them tended to be overshadowed by his less praiseworthy traits and the unpopularity of his office.

CAROL ANNE JANZEN

Sir Alexander Croke's writings include *A report of the case of Horner against Liddiard, upon the question of what consent is necessary to the marriage of illegitimate minors . . .* (London, 1800); *Remarks upon Mr. Schlegel's work, "Upon the visitation of neutral vessels under convoy"* (London, 1801); an unpublished poem entitled "The Inquisition: An Heroic Poem in Four Cantos" ([Halifax, *c.* 1805]), a transcript copy of which is preserved at PANS, MG 1, 239C; *The catechism of the Church of England, with parallel passages from the Confession of Faith, and the larger and shorter catechisms of the Church of Scotland* (Halifax, 1813); *The substance of a judgement, delivered in the Court of Vice-Admiralty, at Halifax, (in Nova Scotia), on the 5th February, 1813; in the case of Little-Joe, Fairweather, Master; upon some questions relating to droits of admiralty . . .* (Halifax, 1813); *The genealogical history of the Croke family, originally named Le Blount* (2v., Oxford, 1823); *The case of Otmoor; with the moor orders . . .* (Oxford, 1831); *Plain truths: five letters, addressed to the members of the Conservative Association of the county and city of Oxford . . .* (Oxford, 1837); and *The progress of idolatry; a poem in ten books; the three ordeals; or the triumph of virtue, in five cantos; Studley Priory, and other poems . . .* (2v., Oxford, 1841); "The three ordeals . . ." is in fact "The Inquisition," reworded for English audiences. In addition he edited *Thirteen Psalms and the first chapter of Ecclesiastes, translated into English verse by John Croke, in the reign of Henry VIII; with other documents relating to the Croke family*, along with Philip Bliss, who saw it through the press following Croke's death. It was published in London in 1844.

The reports of Croke's cases in the Halifax Court of Vice-Admiralty were issued as *Reports of cases, argued and determined in the Court of Vice-Admiralty, at Halifax, in Nova-Scotia, from . . . 1803, to the end of the year 1813, in the time of Alexander Croke . . .*, comp. James Stewart (London, 1814).

PAC, RG 8, I (C ser.), 229; IV. PANS, MG 1, 479–80 (transcripts); RG 1, 50–54, 60–63, 213–14, 278–88, 302–5, 498. PRO, CO 217/75–82 (mfm. at PANS). Univ. of King's College Library (Halifax), Univ. of King's College, Board of Governors, minutes and proc., 1 (1787–1814); statutes, rules, and ordinances, 1803, 1807. *Anti-Jacobin Rev. and Magazine* (London), 39 (September 1801). *Gentleman's Magazine*, January–June 1843. T. C. Haliburton, *An historical and statistical account of Nova-Scotia* (2v., Halifax, 1829; repr. Belleville, Ont., 1973). Beamish Murdoch, *Epitome of the laws of Nova-Scotia* (4v. in 2, Halifax, 1832–33). N.S., House of Assembly, *Journal and proc.*, 1798–1816. *Acadian Recorder*, 1813–14. *Nova-Scotia Royal Gazette*, 1811–14. *Burke's landed gentry* (1845–46). *DNB*.

T. B. Akins, *A brief account of the origin, endowment and progress of the University of King's College, Windsor, Nova Scotia* (Halifax, 1865). Beck, *Government of N.S.* J. B. Brebner, *North Atlantic triangle: the interplay of Canada, the United States and Great Britain* (Toronto, 1966). Judith Fingard, *The Anglican design in loyalist Nova Scotia, 1783–1816* (London, 1972). Grant Gilmore and C. L. Black, *The law of admiralty* (Brooklyn [New York], 1957). H. Y. Hind, *The University of King's College, Windsor, Nova Scotia, 1790–1890* (New York, 1890). C. A. Janzen, "Tentacles of power: Alexander Croke in Nova Scotia, 1801–1815" (MA thesis, Univ. of N.B., Fredericton, 1978). K. E. Knorr, *British colonial theories, 1570–1850* (Toronto, 1944). Murdoch, *Hist. of N.S.* K. E. Stokes, "Sir John Wentworth and his times, 1767–1808" (PHD thesis, Univ. of London, 1938). I. M. Sutherland, "The civil administration of Sir George Prevost, 1811–1815; a study in conciliation" (MA thesis, Queen's Univ., Kingston, Ont., 1959). P. W. Thibeau, *Education in Nova Scotia before 1811* (Washington, 1922). J. [E.] Tulloch, "Conservative opinion in Nova Scotia during an age of revolution, 1789–1815" (MA thesis, Dalhousie Univ., Halifax, 1972). Carl Ubbelonde, *The Vice-Admiralty Courts and the American revolution* (Chapel Hill, N.C., 1960). Susan Whiteside, "Colonial adolescence: a study of the Maritime colonies of British North America, 1790–1814" (MA thesis, Univ. of B.C., Vancouver, 1965). F. L. Wiswall, *The development of admiralty jurisdiction and practice since 1800; an English study with American comparisons* (Cambridge, Eng., 1970). A. G. Archibald, "Sir Alexander Croke," N.S. Hist. Soc., *Coll.*, 2 (1879–80): 110–28. C. B. Fergusson, "Inauguration of the free school system in Nova Scotia," *Journal of Education* (Halifax), 5th ser., 14 (1964): 3–28. Judith Fingard, "English humanitarianism and the colonial mind: Walter Bromley in Nova Scotia, 1813–25," *CHR*, 54 (1973): 123–51. D. G. L. Fraser, "The origin and function of the Court of Vice-Admiralty in Halifax, 1749–1759," N.S. Hist. Soc., *Coll.*, 33 (1961): 57–80. L. H. Laing, "Nova Scotia's Admiralty Court as a problem of colonial administration," *CHR*, 16 (1935): 151–61. T. B. Vincent, "'The Inquisition': Alexander Croke's satire on Halifax society during the Wentworth years," *Dalhousie Rev.*, 53 (1973–74): 404–30.

CROKE, NICHOLAS, builder and architect; b. *c.* 1800 probably in New Ross, County Wexford (Republic of Ireland); m. 8 Aug. 1821 Mary Flynn in St John's, and they had three sons and one daughter; d. there 8 Dec. 1850.

Nicholas Croke probably came to St John's as a carpenter (the trade his eldest son later followed) fairly soon before his marriage. Like fellow Wexfordman Patrick Kough*, he must have attained some standing in the building trade for by 1836 he was styling himself "architect." However, only a few of his works are known, among them the now demolished Orphan Asylum school, built in 1827 and later enlarged by James Purcell*. As a member of the Benevolent Irish Society, which sponsored the school, Croke had submitted a set of plans and, on the basis of these, had been asked to join the building committee. When the contractor was unable to complete the work, Croke agreed to take it on. A fairly simple, hip-roofed example of vernacular Georgian-style architecture, the school was described by the Reverend Michael Francis Howley* in the 1880s as "one of the neatest buildings in the city, and was much admired by the typical 'Out-harbour-man,' on his annual visit to the capital." It may be that this admiration was occasioned only by the Purcell additions, including an observatory and portico, which gave the building some sense of style. That plainness was a characteristic of Croke's work is suggested by the comment in Robert John Parsons*'s *Newfoundland Patriot* that his New Commercial Building (1842) in St John's had an "unhandsome exterior." Croke was also responsible for a number of government works. During the period 1836–38 he was contractor for the court-houses built in Brigus and other outports.

In politics Croke took a position which was quite independent of that held by the majority of the Roman Catholic population, though possibly very dependent on the realities of his trade. The Catholic bishop, Michael Anthony FLEMING, was a strong supporter of reform politics and its adherents, the largest number of whom, including Patrick MORRIS and John Kent*, were also Irish Catholics. The few who did not follow this tradition, among them Patrick Kough and Michael McLean Little, a merchant, did so sometimes at a risk to their businesses. Croke publicly supported Kough and Little, and in 1834 he opposed William CARSON's municipal corporation bill. His alignment with the conservative faction [*see* Henry David Winton*] can be seen, in part, as self-serving. The conservatives were mostly Protestant merchants who controlled many private building contracts and had strong ties to Government House and the Council, thereby influencing which builders received public contracts.

One curious aspect of Croke's life is that he does not appear to have owned any property in Newfoundland – a somewhat unusual situation for a man of his standing at the time.

SHANE O'DEA

Basilica of St John the Baptist (Roman Catholic) (St John's), St John's parish, reg. of baptisms, 1821–36: 308; reg. of marriages, 1793–1836: 21 (copies at PANL). MHA, Croke name file. PRO, CO 194/96 (mfm. at PANL). Supreme Court of Nfld. (St John's), Registry, administration of Nicholas Croke estate, 1851; probate book, 3: f.223. Nfld., House of Assembly, *Journal*, 1837: 119; 1838: 88. *Newfoundlander*, 6 Oct. 1842. *Newfoundland Patriot*, 17 Aug. 1842. *Public Ledger*, 4 April 1834. *Royal Gazette and Newfoundland Advertiser*, 10 Dec. 1850. *Centenary volume, Benevolent Irish Society of St. John's, Newfoundland, 1806–1906* (Cork, [Republic of Ire., 1906?]), 42, 45, 68, 144. Gunn, *Political hist. of Nfld.* M. F. Howley, *Ecclesiastical history of Newfoundland* (Boston, 1888; repr. Belleville, Ont., 1979). R. R. Rostecki, *The early court houses of Newfoundland* (Can., Parks Canada, National Hist. Parks and Sites Branch, *Manuscript report*, no.312, Ottawa, 1977).

CUBIT (Cubick), GEORGE, Wesleyan minister; b. *c.* 1791 in Norwich, England; m. in England and had two children; d. 13 Oct. 1850 in London.

While he was still a boy, George Cubit and his family moved to Sheffield where he attended the Carver Street Chapel. He joined the Wesleyan Methodist Conference in 1808, was ordained in 1813, and served as an itinerant minister for three years. With his wife and two fellow missionaries, John Bell* and Richard Knight*, he left Poole on 1 Aug. 1816 and arrived in Carbonear, Nfld, on 4 September.

From the beginning, Cubit displayed the marks of superior intellectual ability and, perhaps for this reason, he was assigned to St John's. On 17 September he preached at the laying of the cornerstone for a chapel to replace the one destroyed by fire almost seven months earlier. The recently appointed governor, Francis Pickmore*, and the Methodist minister William ELLIS, chairman of the Newfoundland district, were present for the ceremony. Knight served as Cubit's assistant for a few months and the chapel was opened on 26 December.

A complaint lodged in 1816 by the Anglican clergyman David Rowland resulted in Cubit and James Sabine, the Congregational minister, being summoned before Pickmore on the charge of performing marriages in areas where the Church of England had jurisdiction. Though strongly cautioned by the governor, they declared themselves unwilling to submit and took their case to the local press. They were supported by public opinion, but the governor's position was upheld by the British government, and they were forbidden to perform marriages in Newfoundland after January 1818.

As was typical of the Wesleyans, Cubit exercised an effective ministry among the military; in St John's he won more than 80 soldiers to the cause. Indeed, he was probably the ablest of the Wesleyan preachers then stationed in Newfoundland and attracted many people by his eloquent preaching and rich exposition of Scripture. However, the effects of the economic depression following the Napoleonic Wars, the poor fishery of 1817, and several major fires which destroyed a large part of St John's were disastrous to Cubit's congregation. It was saddled with heavy debts on its old chapel and the new one, and Cubit begged for funds from the missionary committee in London, at the same time apologizing for being so importunate. Matters were complicated further by the fact that many members of his church, out of financial destitution, had scattered to the outlying areas. The city itself fell victim in the winter of 1817–18 to gangs of rowdies.

The stresses and privations proved too burdensome for Cubit's sensitive mind. As early as October 1817 he began to complain of headaches, and by January 1818 he had to forego study. The death of his infant son on 11 April aggravated his distress. In May his request to be made a supernumerary was granted by the Newfoundland district. On his doctor's advice, but without the required consent of the missionary committee in London, he returned to England in December 1818. His case was before the committee for several months but censure was not imposed, probably because of his continuing concern for the struggling overseas church. By 1820 he had returned to the active ministry in England. He spent the next 16 years serving in some of the Wesleyan Church's most influential pulpits and publishing several books, sermons, and pamphlets.

In 1836 Cubit was appointed assistant editor of the Wesleyan Book Room and two years later became principal editor, thus assuming responsibility for all the literature being produced by the church. Here he found scope for his literary gifts. He refuted attacks on Methodism by Irish politician Daniel O'Connell and was highly praised by the *Times* of London for the eloquence of his arguments. In his last years Cubit withdrew into seclusion, continuing to devote himself to literary duties but suffering still from extreme sensitivity. He remained as editor until his death from a stroke in 1850.

CALVIN D. EVANS

James Sabine, *A sermon, in commemoration of the benevolence of the citizens of Boston* . . . (St John's, 1818); *A view of the moral state of Newfoundland; with a particular reference to the present state of religious toleration in the island* (Boston, 1818). *Wesleyan-Methodist Magazine*, 39 (1816): 954–55; 41 (1818); 42 (1819): 75; 47 (1824): 245; 48 (1825): 190; 59 (1836): 691; 73 (1850): 1213; 74 (1851). *Newfoundland Mercantile Journal*, 15, 18 Sept., 26, 30 Oct., 2 Nov. 1816; 11, 17 Jan., 11, 18 April 1817. *Royal Gazette and Newfoundland Advertiser*, 24 Dec. 1816; 4, 25 March, 8 April 1817. *When was that?* (Mosdell), 27. *A century of Methodism in St. John's, Newfoundland, 1815–1915*, ed. J. W. Nichols ([St John's, 1915]), 17–20. Levi Curtis, "The Methodist (now United) Church in Newfoundland," *The book of Newfoundland*, ed. J. R. Smallwood (6v., St John's, 1937–75), 2: 291. James Dove, "The Methodist Church in Newfoundland," in Prowse, *Hist. of Nfld.* (1895), supp., 40. G. G. Findlay and W. W. Holdsworth, *The history of the Wesleyan Methodist Missionary Society* (5v., London, 1921–24), 1: 276. Charles Lench, *An account of the rise and progress of Methodism on the Grand Bank and Fortune circuits from 1816 to 1916* . . . (n.p., [1916]), 10–11. D. G. Pitt, *Windows of agates; a short history of the founding and early years of Gower Street Methodist (now United) Church in St. John's, Newfoundland* (St John's, 1966), 24–41. George Smith, *History of Wesleyan Methodism* (3v., London, 1857–61), 3. T. W. Smith, *Hist. of Methodist Church*, 2: 35, 38–40, 61, 418–19. William Wilson, *Newfoundland and its missionaries . . . to which is added a chronological table of all the important events that have occurred on the island* (Cambridge, Mass., and Halifax, 1866), 230, 238, 243. Charles Lench, "The makers of Newfoundland Methodism . . . ," *Methodist Monthly Greeting* (St John's), 12 (1900), no.8: 3–4.

CULL, JAMES, engineer, businessman, newspaperman, and surveyor; b. *c.* 1779 in Dorset, England; m. Sarah ——, and they had six sons and at least two daughters; d. 5 Sept. 1849 in Kingston, Upper Canada.

A brewer, James Cull moved in 1803 from Wareham, Dorset, to Newport, Isle of Wight, where he purchased a brewery; by 1809 he had gone into innkeeping as well. He served as a highway commissioner (1813–25) and possibly as president of a mechanics' institute. The depth of his training in civil engineering remains uncertain. In an age when engineering was only starting to establish professional standards, Cull gained credibility by being an enthusiast with practical experience. He claimed to have worked as a surveyor for 25 years, to have managed a public waterworks, and to have been employed by the Liverpool and Manchester Railway. In addition, he boasted an acquaintance with gasworks, bridges, and "everything connected with steam and water power." When he decided to emigrate to the Canadas, he maintained that he and his six grown sons collectively had experience in engineering, brewing, malting, brickmaking, and "general business."

Cull had helped the emigration agent William Cattermole direct the attention of emigrants from the Isle of Wight and the Portsmouth area to Upper Canada, and he was probably among the "persons of Capital" who accompanied Cattermole to that province in the spring of 1832. Unlike most emigrants, Cull came with technical expertise, and he understood self-promotion. At York (Toronto) he presented letters of recommendation to Lieutenant Governor Sir John Colborne*, who appointed him to the Niagara Township boundary commission in August. He gained an instant reputation as a "gentleman of talent and science." His claim that he held patents on a wooden railway and his promise to lecture on pneumatics at the mechanics' institute dazzled development-conscious provincials, and he worked himself into their confidence.

After the passage of an act in 1833 to improve the approaches to York, Cull was introduced to the trustees for the Yonge Street turnpike by John Willson*, a member of the House of Assembly. The trustees accepted Cull's bid for the construction of one mile of macadamized road, the first stretch of road to be built in Upper Canada using the British invention of compacted layers of broken rock. Cull, however, had underestimated the cost of getting and crushing stone and the difficulties of cutting through hills and crossing streams. The work progressed too slowly for the trustees, who were interested in length, not quality, and they disputed Cull's billings. On 16 Sept. 1833 they took the uncompleted road out of his hands. Arbitration favoured Cull's claim for losses, a decision upheld by select committees of the assembly and the courts. The trustees, refusing to pay, produced a report in 1835 with spiteful references to Cull as one "who professed to be a Civil Engineer." The conflict brought out fundamental incongruities between British engineering practices and the technical possibilities and financial capability of a lightly settled colony in a harsh environment [*see* Thomas ROY]. At the time of this dispute Cull was listed in the Toronto directory of 1833–34 as an engineer and also as a proprietor of a wharf and warehouse.

Cull turned to publishing in 1835. Under his editorship and proprietorship, the *Albion of U.C.*, which probably commenced publication that fall, tried to distinguish itself from Toronto's characteristically partisan press by presenting articles on agriculture, science, and engineering. Strongly conservative, Cull printed pro-government broadsides during the election of 1836 but his political editorials skirted the issues of principle then disrupting the colony. Dispute was seen as an impediment to raising capital and proceeding with public works. Cull recommended, for example, that the clergy reserves should be leased to poor immigrants at low rents and the revenues applied to "Religious and Moral Education, Bridges and Roads." He ignored entirely the political reality of strong denominations struggling over the reserves.

From an office in Toronto's market building, Cull promoted several ventures related to both printing and development. As secretary of the Emigrant Society of Upper Canada, he forwarded copies of the *Albion* to societies in the United Kingdom, a ploy he hoped would attract advertising as well as alert Britons to the colony's prospects. In April 1836 he unsuccessfully attempted to raise capital for a gazette of Upper Canadian "post towns," which would have included a census and lists of institutions and manufacturers. In November he launched another newspaper, the *Royal Standard*, and, along with a publishing associate (possibly a Mr Osborne) and three reporters, he approached the House of Assembly with a proposal for preparing an official report of debates as a feature of the newspaper. Though recommended by a committee of the assembly, the scheme was narrowly defeated.

The *Albion* carried Cull in many directions, but engineering was at its heart. In February 1837, for instance, he published a plan for improvements to Toronto. Yet whatever the *Albion* might have done to restore his engineering reputation, it is clear from his published appeals for capital and the scant advertising in the newspaper that it was a financial failure. In 1836 Cull had secured a public inquiry into his conduct on the Yonge Street project and the trustees' report. The inquiry confirmed in January 1837 his ability as a road-builder, thus removing, Cull claimed, the "stigma which has been cast upon him." He closed both the faltering *Albion* and the *Royal Standard* the following month, but winding them up created a chain of claims and accusations. After withdrawing from publishing, Cull continued to strive for an engineering position, possibly his sole avenue for advancing his fortune; in March 1837 he petitioned Lieutenant Governor Sir Francis Bond Head* for an appointment.

Cull's return to road-building came under difficult circumstances: he had to supervise the macadamizing and straightening of the Kingston–Napanee road during depression years (1837–39). Undaunted, he defended the concept of public debt before sceptical agrarians, insisting that a properly constructed road would save money over the years. His 1838 report on the road, essentially a lecture on development, offers a glimpse of a headstrong engineer accenting quality and his "experience at home" while condemning Upper Canadian demands for haste and economy. His contempt for subcontracting sections of the road to farmers and his argument that damages to farms by road-crews were balanced by increased property values both had reason, but they also demonstrated his misunderstanding of local circumstances. His logic in laying out a portion of the route through a swamp was lost on farmers by-passed by the road; others alleged that Cull's men had stolen logs for the construction of marsh crossings. Such were the travails of a man of inappropriate standards and straight lines.

The upswing in public works during the 1840s briefly strengthened Cull's prospects. In the summer of 1840 he conducted a survey of the harbour at Port

Stanley, following which he returned to Toronto expecting permanent employment with a proposed gasworks. After undertaking preliminary research, including a trip to Montreal for information, he was replaced on the project in October 1841. Within a week, however, he was directing work on the London–St Thomas road as surveyor for the London and Brock districts, reporting to the provincial Board of Works. Briefly, in 1843, he assumed the direction of work on the London–Port Sarnia road (both roads were probably macadamized), but the board considered his progress too slow. He was removed in November 1843 from the road-work and probably from the district surveyor's office. His protest spilled out the discontent of a decade: he claimed that he was "discarded, deprived of the means of subsistence, and degraded." Cull nevertheless found official employment again, for in 1846 he was working as a civil engineer and surveyor with the Ordnance department at Kingston. In August of that year he attempted, evidently without success, to become licensed as a public land surveyor. He died of cholera three years later. In its obituary the *British Colonist* noted that he had founded a public bath in Toronto and had advocated a system of water, sewer, and gas utilities for the city.

Exceedingly keen, believing himself to be thoroughly knowledgeable, but perhaps only stolidly able, Cull had a destiny of modest ends to hopeful starts. He is rescued from obscurity by his supervision of the first section of macadamized road in Upper Canada. His succession of appointments reflects the colony's growing need for skilled civilians, but, in the context of that demand, he figures as a transitional character. He functioned as a conduit for British practice, with technical specifications displacing local requirements. In contrast, younger and possibly more able engineers such as Nicol Hugh Baird, John George Howard*, and Casimir Stanislaus Gzowski* knew how to blend their skills with political awareness and provincial needs. Unable to match the rising qualifications among engineers, Cull resorted to petitions and patronage to secure himself, but toward the end of his career he lacked the formal credentials that had become important.

John C. Weaver

ACC, Diocese of Toronto Arch., Church of the Holy Trinity (Toronto), reg. of baptisms, 1844–61, nos.8–9. CTA, RG 1, B, James Cull to Mayor [R. B. Sullivan] and Aldermen, 4 May 1836; Cull to Mayor [Gurnett George], 20 Feb. 1837; Cull to Mayor [George Monro], 19 Oct. 1841. Dundas Hist. Soc. Museum (Dundas, Ont.), James Lesslie diary, 28 May–2 June 1832. Isle of Wight County Record Office (Newport, Eng.), Index of deeds; Reg. of births, marriages, and burials. PAC, RG 1, E3, 19, 43; RG 5, A1: 64050–52, 73907–15; C1, 3, file 358; RG 11, A2, 93; RG 68, General index, 1651–1841: 71. J. A. Macdonald, *The letters of Sir John A. Macdonald, 1836–1857*, ed. J. K. Johnson (2v., Ottawa, 1968–69), 1: 40. U.C., House of Assembly, *App. to the journal*, 1835, 1, no.12; 2, no.44; 1837, no.29; 1839, 2, pt.i: 181–87; *Journal*, 1836–37: 41, 56, 84–85, 93–95, 166, 175, 181; 1837–38: 288. *Albion of U.C.* (Toronto), 5 Dec. 1835; 2–16 April, 21–28 May, 2 July 1836. *British Colonist*, 15 Sept. 1849. *Hamilton Gazette, and General Advertiser* (Hamilton, [Ont.]), 26 Oct. 1840. *Early Toronto newspapers* (Firth), nos.16, 19. *Toronto directory*, 1833–34, 1837. *History of the county of Middlesex, Canada ...* (Toronto and London, Ont., 1889; repr. with intro. by D. [J.] Brock, Belleville, Ont., 1972), 13, 194. *The Royal Canadian Institute, centennial volume, 1849–1949*, ed. W. S. Wallace (Toronto, 1949), 185. M. S. Cross, "The stormy history of the York roads, 1833–1865," *OH*, 54 (1962): 1–24.

CUTLER, THOMAS, lawyer, JP, office holder, judge, militia officer, politician, and merchant; b. 11 Nov. 1752 in Boston, fifth child of Thomas Cutler and Sarah Reade; m. 3 March 1783 Elizabeth Goldsbury, probably in New York City, and they had five children; d. 8 Feb. 1837 in Guysborough, N.S.

Thomas Cutler was descended from a family resident in Massachusetts for more than a century. Educated at Yale College, he graduated in 1771 and settled at Hatfield, Mass., where he is said to have studied law. He joined the British forces in Boston at the outbreak of the American revolution and in September 1778 was proscribed in the Massachusetts Banishment Act. Serving first as a captain in the Volunteers of New England, by the end of the war he was established in New York as an assistant barrack master. In September 1783 he was commissioned ensign in the Orange Rangers, apparently because regimental rank offered greater possibilities for compensation and advancement.

Cutler and his wife were evacuated to Nova Scotia late in 1783 as part of the refugee group known as the Associated Departments of the Army and Navy, composed principally of headquarters staff. The group first settled at Port Mouton on the South Shore, but after a harsh winter marked by quarrels with other loyalists moved east to Chedabucto Bay. On 21 June 1784 they landed at the head of the bay, where the village of Guysborough was already beginning to take shape. Along with his fellow veterans, Cutler was granted farm land along the Milford Haven (Guysborough) River as well as town and water lots in the village.

Cutler's legal training and administrative experience stood him in good stead in his new home. He sat as one of the justices of the peace at the first sessions for the district, held in November 1785, and served as the first town clerk for Guysborough. He was later appointed judge of probate for Sydney County and a justice of the Inferior Court of Common Pleas. For many years Cutler held a special licence to conduct marriages. He was commissioned lieutenant-colonel of the newly organized Sydney County militia in July 1794.

In 1793 Cutler was elected to the House of Assembly for Sydney County. He and fellow refugee John Stuart were the first local residents to represent the district, which had returned two Haligonians in the previous election. Cutler took little part in the work of the assembly: he attended only two sessions and did not contest the election of 1799.

Like most pioneer inhabitants of rural Nova Scotia, Cutler turned his hand to a variety of occupations. He continued his legal practice and is said to have trained William Campbell*, later chief justice of Upper Canada. Cutler is chiefly remembered, however, for his commercial activities. As early as 1792 he was listed as a merchant in the district assessment rolls, and in the 1790s he was appointed to several local customs offices usually held by prominent traders. Cutler also took an interest in the agricultural development of the district, serving as one of the first vice-presidents of the Guysborough and Manchester Farmer Society, organized in 1819 in response to the enthusiasm generated throughout the province by John YOUNG's Agricola letters.

Local tradition honoured Cutler as "King" Cutler, reflecting his widespread influence in the county. Eulogized for his "strict and known integrity, loyalty, and ability," he is remembered as one of the founders of Guysborough.

JUDITH TULLOCH

PANS, MG 100, 129, no.40; RG 1, 169, 171–73, 223. *Novascotian, or Colonial Herald*, 23 Feb. 1837. F. B. Dexter, *Biographical sketches of the graduates of Yale College, with annals of the college history* (6v., New York and New Haven, Conn., 1885–1912), 3. J. H. Stark, *The loyalists of Massachusetts and the other side of the American revolution* (Boston, [1907]). Harriet Cunningham Hart, *History of the county of Guysborough* (Belleville, Ont., 1975). A. C. Jost, *Guysborough sketches and essays* (Guysborough, N.S., 1950).

CUVILLIER, AUSTIN (baptized and early known as **Augustin**), businessman, militia officer, politician, and JP; b. 20 Aug. 1779 at Quebec, son of Augustin Cuvillier and Angélique Miot, *dit* Girard; m. 7 Nov. 1802 Marie-Claire Perrault in Montreal, and they had seven children; d. there 11 July 1849.

Augustin Cuvillier grew up in Quebec on Rue Sous-le-Fort, a short thoroughfare at the foot of Cap Diamant inhabited by small retailers and navigators. His father ran a store there until the spring of 1785 when he apparently converted his establishment into a bakery. His sudden death at age 33 in 1789 probably left Augustin, as the eldest of seven children, with heavy responsibilities for his age. Nevertheless, Cuvillier Sr had been a cultivated man with a concern for education, and in 1794 Augustin was registered at the Collège Saint-Raphaël in Montreal; the boy seems not to have completed the course of studies, however.

Cuvillier entered the employ of Henry Richard Symes, a wealthy auctioneer in Montreal. By the turn of the century he had become a dormant partner, and in May 1802 he took over the business from the retiring Symes. He subsequently went into partnership with Thomas Aylwin as Cuvillier and Aylwin and then with Aylwin and John Harkness as Cuvillier, Aylwin, and Harkness in Montreal and Aylwin, Harkness and Company at Quebec. The second partnership, for auctioneering and general merchandising, was assigned to its creditors in October 1806 with debts totalling nearly £14,000 but assets of more than £18,000; the largest creditors were Montreal merchant James Dunlop* and the London supply house of Inglis, Ellice and Company. Despite the failure, auctioneering, which involved the import wholesale of dry goods and their sale in large lots to local buyers, would continue to be central to Cuvillier's business career. Through it, he developed a knowledge of domestic and foreign markets, a network of contacts, an understanding of banking and finance, and a reputation in the world of British colonial commerce. Indeed, Cuvillier's career in the British-dominated field of business had led him increasingly from the turn of the century to adopt Austin as an abbreviated and anglicized version of his given name, at first in English and then in French.

By 1807 Cuvillier had recovered from his setback and was in possession of auction rooms on Rue Notre-Dame next to a store occupied by James McGill*. His business expanded – at least he acquired properties – but he remained mired in financial difficulties. Properties belonging to him, including two houses and a three-storey store on Rue Notre-Dame, were seized by the sheriff on suits by the merchant James Finlay (1808), Dr Jacques Dénéchaud* (1810), and Dunlop (1813). In April 1811 a company was formed under his wife's name, as Mary C. Cuvillier and Company (more commonly, M. C. Cuvillier and Company), and it may have been a front for Cuvillier's own business.

During the War of 1812 Cuvillier served in the 5th Select Embodied Militia Battalion of Lower Canada – known as the "Devil's Own" – initially as a lieutenant and adjutant. In June 1813, while under cover to find deserters from the militia, he distinguished himself by obtaining intelligence about American forces in the Salmon River area along the New York border, where he was well known as a merchant. By April 1814 he was a captain in the Chasseurs Canadiens, but he resigned that month after an officer of the line was given command of the unit in preference to one of its own officers. In recognition of his services during the war he was granted a medal with Châteauguay clasp and, later, 800 acres of land in Litchfield Township. He ultimately became a supernumerary captain, and he would be given command of a company in October 1820. After the war, in March 1815, Cuvillier had again had his properties seized by the sheriff. One night in late June 1816, while strolling in front of his store, he discovered two robbers inside. Ever combative, he blocked them within by holding tight to the street door, despite their threats of violence, until a neighbour, Joseph MASSON, came to his assistance. Soldiers arrived finally to make the arrests.

Meanwhile Cuvillier had become one of the few Canadian businessmen extensively involved in politics. In 1809 he had failed to win a seat in the House of Assembly for Huntingdon County, but he was successful on a second try, in 1814. He quickly became a rising star in the nationalist Canadian party, which dominated the assembly and which found his understanding of the colony's economy indispensable in the struggles of the house to gain control of government finances.

The business community found Cuvillier equally useful. His presence in the councils of the Canadian party mitigated the party's inherent hostility to commercial interests. In addition, he became the driving force in the assembly for the incorporation of a colonial bank when, after the war, the redemption of the army bills threatened to leave the colony once again without paper money or sufficient specie [*see* James Green*]. In February 1815 he proposed that the assembly study the possibility of establishing a bank; his resolution was discussed without any result in action. Efforts on his part in the two following years produced greater progress but were frustrated by prorogations of the legislature. Finally, in May 1817, impatient at the delay, Cuvillier's supporters in the Montreal business community, led by John Richardson*, formed the Bank of Montreal as a private association. Cuvillier was made a director and appointed to crucial committees. In early 1818 he succeeded in piloting a bill of incorporation through the legislature only to have Governor Sir John Coape Sherbrooke* set it aside for royal assent, which was not forthcoming. The whole procedure was renewed in early 1821, and finally, in the summer of 1822, a charter was granted. In September 1818 Cuvillier had become one of nine founding shareholders in the Montreal Fire Insurance Company; by 1820 he was president of the firm.

On the political scene Cuvillier made an impact in 1817 by revealing to the assembly partiality and conflict of interest on the part of judge Louis-Charles Foucher, who had recently rendered a decision adverse to Cuvillier in a business dispute. The Canadian party, having adopted a policy of harassing administrative and judicial officials, had recently impeached chief justices Jonathan SEWELL and James Monk*, and though it had failed to obtain their dismissal, it eagerly impeached Foucher in turn; however, adjudication of the charges became bogged down in politics [*see* Herman Witsius RYLAND]. In 1820 Cuvillier unsuccessfully proposed passage of a law to remunerate members of the assembly as a means of opening the house to candidates from walks of life other than the liberal professions; Louis-Joseph Papineau* opposed the project as too democratic.

During the great debates over control of the colony's finances, Cuvillier scrutinized the executive's accounts and provided figures and financial analyses while Papineau and John NEILSON argued the party's principles. In 1821 the assembly included Cuvillier among four commissioners to conduct difficult negotiations with representatives from Upper Canada over the division of customs duties between the two colonies. Two years later he chaired a committee of the assembly investigating the defalcation of Receiver General John CALDWELL. Throughout the 1820s and even beyond Cuvillier and Neilson preached fiscal responsibility on the part of the assembly and denounced what they considered to be its tendency to excessive appropriations for non-administrative expenses, such as public works.

In 1822–23 Cuvillier was active in the Canadian party's campaign against a proposed union of the Canadas. Joseph Masson, who also campaigned against union, noted at the time that he and Cuvillier benefited from their affiliation with the Canadian party, since many Canadian retailers preferred to wait for merchandise from them rather than go to a British wholesaler. Nevertheless, auctioneering was a precarious business, and Cuvillier's association with one Jacques Cartier, probably of the Richelieu valley, ran into difficulties in the summer of 1822. In early 1823 Cuvillier could not pay the firm's large promissory notes held by the Bank of Montreal, and the partnership had to be dissolved. Cuvillier bounced back once more, only to be in financial difficulties again during the commercial crisis of 1825–26. At that time he slammed the door on the Bank of Montreal over the lending practices of its president Samuel Gerrard*, but he survived the crisis.

Although Cuvillier's financial difficulties affected his attendance in the house, they did not undermine his prestige. During the absence of Governor Lord Dalhousie [RAMSAY] in Britain in 1824–25, Cuvillier, along with Neilson and Denis-Benjamin Viger*, was particularly courted by Lieutenant Governor Sir Francis Nathaniel Burton*. Cuvillier chaired the budget committee of the assembly when the house worked out with Burton a compromise supply bill which became a model for its future demands. After Dalhousie's return Cuvillier responded energetically to the governor's defiant policies, and in November 1827, when Dalhousie rejected Papineau as the duly elected speaker of the assembly, it was "the Bankrupt auctioneer," as Dalhousie disdainfully characterized Cuvillier, who moved the house's denunciation of the action. Nationalist committees counter-attacked in early 1828 by electing Cuvillier, Neilson, and Viger to take to London mammoth petitions complaining of Dalhousie's administration. Informed of his election only hours before the departure of the ship, Cuvillier hurriedly confided his business and his family to Masson.

The delegates arrived in England on 12 March 1828. Like almost all visitors from Lower Canada – of whatever political stripe – who had preceded him to London, Cuvillier was dismayed at official ignorance of and indifference to the colony's problems. Worse still, the colonial secretary, William Huskisson, initially seemed hostile. Cuvillier was soon reassured, however, by discussions with English political and business figures. Public opinion, to which the government was highly sensitive, was with the Canadians, he informed Masson. To Hugues HENEY, a prominent Canadian nationalist, he wrote (in English), "There is an inherent aversion to despotism in the great mass of the people of this Country, which will screen us from the ambition of a Minister. . . . Freedom is a root which when *taken*, will grow in spite of every obstacle, and in America, no power on Earth can root it out." In June, during the formal inquiry conducted by a committee of the House of Commons, usually known as the Canada committee, Cuvillier gave lengthy testimony on the colony's most controversial political and economic issues. He favoured the colony's system of seigneurial tenure and the traditional French civil law, and argued for a legislative council and judiciary independent of both the executive and the people. On the other hand he opposed the establishment of a colonial aristocracy and any change in what he called the constitutional "pact" of 1791 without the consent of both parties to it, Britain and the colony. While awaiting the committee's report he visited Paris, where "the state of morality is wretched and religion, of course, in the lowest state imaginable."

The Canada committee's report responded favourably to most of the delegates' demands, and on the financial issues Cuvillier enjoyed total victory. After his return to Lower Canada he hoped to translate his success into an appointment as the colony's agent in London, which, as "the nerve centre of the world," he had found to be a businessman's paradise. However, the financial question having been settled in favour of the assembly, it was thought, Papineau turned the attention of the Patriote party (as the Canadian party was known from 1826) to more strictly political objectives, such as achieving an elective legislative council. Under the circumstances he preferred Viger as agent, and a confrontation between Papineau and Cuvillier over the matter in early 1829 marked the beginning of Cuvillier's estrangement from the Patriote party. Cuvillier's alienation increased as, later that year and early in 1830, he defended the Bank of Montreal and its charter – although with uncharacteristic clumsiness on occasion – in the face of rising popular resentment of the bank and strong attacks on it by Papineau and the Patriote party. In March 1830, however, Papineau nervously noted that a group of admiring deputies was coalescing around Cuvillier.

Cuvillier was returned for Laprairie County in the elections of 1830. In January 1831, when Governor Lord Aylmer [WHITWORTH-AYLMER] was obliged to open the legislature from his sick bed, Papineau (as speaker), Louis Bourdages*, and Cuvillier alone were invited to represent the assembly at the brief ceremony. Yet the following month the Patriote Louis-Michel Viger* noted that Cuvillier was "eyed scornfully every day" and thought that he was "declining in the opinion of the members." In March the assembly finally voted on its London agent and chose D.-B. Viger; only the members from the Eastern Townships and four or five Canadians supported Cuvillier, Papineau recorded with relief. Cuvillier confronted the Patriote party again later that year when he argued that a proposed provincial board of audit should be staffed with permanent auditors rather than political appointees. At the end of 1831 Cuvillier, with Neilson, Dominique Mondelet*, and other moderates, opposed the *fabrique* bill presented by Bourdages on behalf of the Patriote party.

The rift between Cuvillier and the Patriotes appeared outside the assembly as well. In early 1832 a group of nationalists, led by Édouard-Raymond Fabre*, met to form the Maison Canadienne de Commerce as a national wholesaling enterprise; Cuvillier was conspicuous by his absence. During a hotly disputed by-election in Montreal that spring Cuvillier energetically backed the government candidate, Stanley Bagg, exhorting the electors to broaden the representation in the assembly by returning a merchant rather than the Patriote candidate, Daniel Tracey*. When a riot broke out at the poll, Cuvillier, who had been appointed a justice of the peace in 1830, was one of the magistrates considered responsible for summoning the troops to fire on the mob; three Canadians were killed. Papineau fanned the flames of public outrage, and Cuvillier found himself vilified as a "bureaucrat" by Patriote supporters.

In 1833 Cuvillier denounced in the assembly Patriote demands for an elected legislative council. The following year he was one of only six Canadians who refused to support the 92 Resolutions, which subsequently constituted the Patriotes' electoral platform. That same year the adversaries of the Patriotes formed a constitutional association in Montreal. At its first meeting Cuvillier moved support for "the continuance of the existing connection between the United Kingdom and this Province." A popular Patriote song of the time, "C'est la faute à Papineau," reviled him as a turncoat. Papineau was determined to have his head, and Cuvillier left politics at the time of the elections of 1834 after having served for 20 years in the legislature; in defeat he was disillusioned to think that he had owed his seat to the Papineau machine rather than to his own merit.

Significantly, Cuvillier's conflicts with the Patriote party had developed at the very moment that his business fortunes were improving. He had become Montreal's leading auctioneer, notably of imported manufactured goods, fish, salt, and liquors, and of the stock of bankrupt merchants; in 1836 he made costly renovations to his store, then situated on Rue Saint-Paul. In addition to auctioneering he acted as an agent, a trustee, and a stockbroker, selling the shares of various Canadian banks. In 1836 he was named a Montreal director of the Bank of British North America, founded that year to act as a colonial bank in London. During the 1830s he expanded into Upper Canada. So prominent had Cuvillier become in Montreal that he served as president of the city's Committee of Trade from 1837 to 1841 and as a member of the group that secured its incorporation as the Montreal Board of Trade in 1841–42.

During the rebellion of 1837 Cuvillier was major and commander of Montreal's 5th Militia Battalion. In November 1837 he and Turton Penn, as magistrates, signed the requisition for military assistance that enabled British troops to march on the rebel stronghold of Saint-Denis. In January 1838 he was a founder and vice-president (under Pierre de RASTEL de Rocheblave) of the Association Loyale Canadienne du District de Montréal; it denounced both the leaders of the rebellions and the supporters of a union of the Canadas and called for a continuation of political reform "particularly in conformity with the spirit of the Constitution of 1791." With the approval of the administrator and commander of the forces, Sir John Colborne*, Cuvillier issued paper currency to offset suspension of specie payments to the troops during the rebellions; the currency was redeemed after their suppression. He suffered a serious set-back in 1837–38 after the failure of a Montreal merchant cost him £3,000 and provoked a run on his bills. The Patriotes looked forward maliciously to another humiliating failure for him, but he appears to have disappointed them.

In the wake of the report of 1839 by Lord Durham [LAMBTON] on the situation in the Canadas, Cuvillier joined with Neilson and D.-B. Viger in opposing union, and in 1841, during the first elections to the assembly of the united legislature, he was returned for Huntingdon on an anti-union ticket. The leader of the Lower Canadian reform forces in the assembly was the former Patriote Louis-Hippolyte La Fontaine*, who still held a grudge against Cuvillier for his opposition to the 92 Resolutions. However, hoping to win the Neilson–Viger group in the assembly over to his strategy for the survival of the Canadians within the union, La Fontaine reluctantly allowed himself to be convinced by the Upper Canadian reformer Francis Hincks* that Cuvillier would be a better nominee for speaker than more radical reform candidates. Cuvillier could rally the tories since he spoke fluent English and had extensive business connections in both sections of the united province; at the same time his election would be a reassuring triumph for the Canadians since he had opposed union, the civil list, equal representation from both sections (Lower Canada being more populous), funding of the debt at the expense of Lower Canada, and proscription of the French language in the legislature. Cuvillier was elected.

As speaker, Cuvillier developed exceedingly cordial relations with successive governors. In 1844 he supported Governor Charles Theophilus METCALFE in his battle against La Fontaine and Robert Baldwin* for control of patronage. This decision cost him the Huntingdon seat during elections that year, and he was defeated by La Fontaine's forces in Rimouski as well. At 65 Cuvillier saw his public career at an end. He returned to his auctioneering business, now called Cuvillier and Sons, which counted among its clients the Séminaire de Saint-Sulpice. In 1845 the seminary offered at auction its domain lands closest to Montreal, and Cuvillier himself was among the largest purchasers, spending £3,220. Four years later he contracted typhus; he died on 11 July 1849 and was buried the following day in Notre-Dame church.

Cuvillier was for a time a rare figure in the history of Lower Canada. Historians have perceived the conflict between the British merchant community and the nationalist Canadian (later Patriote) party as an important cause of the rebellions of 1837–38, yet from 1814 to 1828 Cuvillier was able to reconcile the antagonistic interests of the two groups. With the radicalization of the Patriote party from the late 1820s, however, Cuvillier became representative of a number of Canadian nationalists, such as Heney, Frédéric-Auguste Quesnel*, Joseph-Rémi VALLIÈRES de Saint-Réal, Pierre-Dominique DEBARTZCH, and Jean-Marie MONDELET and his sons Dominique and Charles-Elzéar*, who dropped out of the party in alarm or were excluded as traitors. Their absence enabled radical Patriote leaders to push the reform movement ever more rapidly and surely towards disaster.

JACQUES MONET and GERALD J. J. TULCHINSKY

A portrait of Austin Cuvillier painted by Théophile Hamel*

hangs in the Speakers' Corridor of the House of Commons in Ottawa; the PAC holds a photograph of this painting. A second portrait, at the Château Ramezay in Montreal, has been reproduced in E. K. Senior, *Redcoats and Patriotes: the rebellions in Lower Canada, 1837–38* (Stittsville, Ont., 1985).

ANQ-M, CE1-51, 7 nov. 1802, 12 juill. 1849; CN1-187, 31 juill., 11, 30 août, 27 sept., 6 nov., 7 déc. 1822; 2 févr., 29 mars, 27 mai 1823; 22 mars, 19 avril, 29 mai 1825; 22 janv., 14 févr. 1826. ANQ-Q, CE1-1, 21 août 1779, 2 déc. 1789; CE1-4, 3 nov. 1778. ASQ, Fonds Viger–Verreau, sér.O, 0147: 17, 88–93, 135, 158–61. PAC, MG 24, C3: 374–77, 1053; L3: 10547–48, 10558–60, 10577–82, 10607–10, 11825–26, 12119–20, 12566–68, 12765–67, 12848–49, 18200–4 (copies); RG 68, General index, 1651–1841. "Les dénombrements de Québec" (Plessis), ANQ *Rapport*, 1948–49: 28. *Docs. relating to constitutional hist., 1819–28* (Doughty and Story), 21–22, 193–201. G.B., Parl., House of Commons paper, 1828, 7, no.569, *Report from the select committee on the civil government of Canada* (repr. Québec, 1829). "La mission de MM. Viger, Neilson et Cuvillier en Angleterre en 1828," *BRH*, 32 (1926): 651–69. Joseph Papineau, "Correspondance de Joseph Papineau (1793–1840)," Fernand Ouellet, édit., ANQ *Rapport*, 1951–53: 187, 287. L.-J. Papineau, "Correspondance" (Ouellet), ANQ *Rapport*, 1953–55 : 214, 266, 296, 302, 315–16. Ramsay, *Dalhousie journals* (Whitelaw), 3: 92. "Très humble requête des citoyens de la ville de Québec [1787]," ANQ *Rapport*, 1944–45: plate 2. *Montreal Transcript*, 29 April 1837. *Quebec Gazette*, 7 April 1785, 9 Nov. 1786, 17 April 1788, 5 March 1789, 13 May 1802, 23 Oct. 1806, 28 Jan. 1808, 23 Nov. 1809, 29 March 1810, 16 Sept. 1813, 16 March 1815, 4 July 1816, 27 Nov. 1817, 5 Oct. 1818, 26 Oct. 1820, 26 Oct. 1829. Caron, "Inv. de la corr. de Mgr Panet," ANQ *Rapport*, 1935–36: 239; "Papiers Duvernay," 1926–27: 182. *Officers of British forces in Canada* (Irving). Ouellet, "Inv. de la saberdache," ANQ *Rapport*, 1955–57: 155. Denison, *Canada's first bank*. Henri Masson, *Joseph Masson, dernier seigneur de Terrebonne, 1791–1847* (Montréal, 1972). Maurault, *Le collège de Montréal* (Dansereau; 1967). Monet, *Last cannon shot*. Ouellet, *Bas-Canada*. Rumilly, *Papineau et son temps*. Robert Sweeny, *Protesting history: 4 papers* (Montreal, 1984). Taft Manning, *Revolt of French Canada*. F.-J. Audet, "Augustin Cuvillier," *BRH*, 33 (1927): 108–20. É.-Z. Massicotte, "C'est la faute à Papineau," *BRH*, 24 (1918): 85–87. Fernand Ouellet, "Papineau et la rivalité Québec–Montréal (1820–1840)," *RHAF*, 13 (1959–60): 311–27. Adam Shortt, "Founders of Canadian banking: Austin Cuvillier, merchant, legislator and banker," Canadian Bankers' Assoc., *Journal* (Toronto), 30 (1922–23): 304–16.

D

DALHOUSIE, GEORGE RAMSAY, 9th Earl of. *See* RAMSAY

DALTON, THOMAS, businessman, author, politician, and newspaperman; b. April or May 1782, baptized 28 June in Birmingham, England, son of William Dalton and Rebecca Watson; m. first 30 May 1803 Sarah Pratt (d. 1804), and they had one son; m. secondly 9 Nov. 1805 Sophia Simms*, and they had three sons and four daughters; d. 26 Oct. 1840 in Toronto.

Thomas Dalton, the son of a Birmingham factor, claimed to possess "a portion of natural talents improved by industry, exalted to usefulness by experience," and by intensive reading, but never professed to having received much formal education. He gained some familiarity with international commerce and finance, presumably through involvement in his father's business at home and abroad, which included supplying the Newfoundland fishing trade with hardware and domestic goods.

In 1803, just 21 and newly married, he took over the business when his father was "unjustly detained" in France by Napoleon's interning all British civilians of militia age. In January 1808 Thomas was forced into bankruptcy, and about 1810 he engaged himself as Newfoundland agent to prominent merchant James Henry Attwood. With his second wife, he moved his growing family to St John's where he quickly established himself in local society. By 1814 he was back on his feet, with his own mercantile business.

Dalton soon joined forces with John Ryan, a local Irish merchant. They were successful for a year or two, but the general economic collapse that followed the wars in Europe and America left them with debts of several thousand pounds which they were unable to pay. In November 1816 Dalton found himself bankrupt for the second time in less than ten years. The following February he left Newfoundland for England, but a few months later the family, accompanied by Thomas's father and younger brother William, came out to Upper Canada prepared to try again.

In December 1817 Thomas obtained a few acres of land on Lake Ontario just west of Kingston and, after persuading a local businessman, Smith Bartlet, to come in as a partner, set up a brewery. The partnership was dissolved amicably in June 1819 and Dalton carried on the Kingston Brewery alone. The business expanded rapidly. Historian Maxwell Leroy Magill has described the brewery as "the largest and most prosperous establishment of its kind in the province" and Dalton himself boasted that it was "one of the best that was ever established in this Province."

In 1818, while awaiting royal assent to a charter for the proposed Bank of Upper Canada at Kingston, some local merchants set up a private bank of the same name. Dalton, a lifelong believer in the efficacy of banks in stimulating industry, subscribed for a modest ten shares. After being elected a director in June 1819, without his prior approval, he increased his participation significantly until he was the second largest investor, and he borrowed heavily from the bank to expand his business. With his considerable experience and forceful manner, he was able to help the bank over some rough patches in its first years but, when a combination of sloppy business practice, internal dissension, and finally a fraudulent conspiracy involving the president, Benjamin Whitney, brought the institution tumbling down in September 1822, no effort of his could save the situation.

In December, to cover his debts to the bank, Dalton posted a £7,000 personal bond and took a £3,600 mortgage on his brewery property. With such undertakings from the major debtors, the bank's reserves were sufficient to cover all its obligations. However, a banking group in York (Toronto), headed by William Allan*, had appropriated the charter being prepared for the Kingston bank and had been incorporated in 1821 as the official Bank of Upper Canada. Thus, despite the adequate reserves, in March 1823 the provincial legislature stepped in with a hastily drafted bank act declaring Kingston's "pretended" bank illegal and making its directors personally liable for its debts. Three Kingston tories, John Macaulay*, George Herchmer Markland*, and John KIRBY, were appointed to a commission – "one family-compacted junto" Dalton called them in July – to take over the bank's affairs. Hardest hit among the directors were those who were in trade, for they were prohibited from selling anything until the bank's business could be settled. This provision was repealed in a less severe bank act passed in January 1824. Although later that year Dalton and Bartlet were successfully defended by John Beverley Robinson* in suits brought by the commissioners, the bank affair effectively ruined Dalton.

The failure of the bank and the legislature's interference were heatedly debated in the newspapers of Kingston, York, and even Montreal, as well as in many privately published pamphlets. Using the pages of the *Upper Canada Herald* of Kingston and the *Free Press* and the *Scribbler* of Montreal, Dalton turned out many pieces, in a wide variety of styles. Some appeared over his own signature, and several anonymous articles clearly suggest his hand. In one of the best of the latter, published in the *Upper Canada Herald* of 11 Nov. 1823, he ridiculed the bank commissioners in a full front-page satire purporting to be their long-awaited first report. In 1824, believing that the author of the Draconian 1823 bank act had been Christopher Alexander HAGERMAN, a fellow director and the bank's solicitor, and finding himself singled out by Hagerman for much of the blame for the failure, Dalton published a long pamphlet fiercely attacking Hagerman while stoutly defending his own position.

Dalton decided that the best place to fight his battle was in the House of Assembly. He was known to have radical sympathies and, when he stood for Kingston in 1824, there was much nervous closing of ranks by tories to block his election; he dropped out at the last minute to ensure Hagerman's defeat. When he did manage to take one of the two Frontenac seats in the reform wave of 1828, he was seen by many tories as the worst of a bad lot. In March 1829 he managed to get a new bank act passed which provided for arbitration of all the old debts; but, in Dalton's case, the new commissioners (including his erstwhile friend and fellow freemason Hugh Christopher Thomson*) refused to accept the arbitration award (which had reduced Dalton's obligation to a fraction of the original amount). At this point Dalton turned his back on the whole business, claiming that the commission owed him more, for expenses and lost business, than he had ever owed the bank. Dalton left politics in 1830 but the controversy surrounding the bank continued for nearly 20 years.

To keep his brewery going, Dalton had placed it in other hands in July 1823. The less severe 1824 bank act had permitted him to take it back that July, but the interim arrangement had been costly and the manager had absconded with the books, so that many of the outstanding accounts could never be recovered. Short of capital, Dalton struggled on desperately for a few more years but in November 1828 the brewery was badly damaged by fire and he closed it down permanently. In December 1830 the bank commissioners finally released his brewery land and four months later he sold it to Thomas Molson*.

For some years Dalton had had an interest in publishing. It first appeared in 1824 when he approached Macaulay about buying the *Kingston Chronicle*, but, according to Dalton, his career as a "writer for the public" had begun around 1820 with some anonymous articles in the *Upper Canada Herald*. Nothing has been identified for this early date but within a few years, in addition to the numerous publications concerning the bank, he had produced two long Hudibrastic poems (*An address, to the liege men of every British colony and province in the world* appeared in 1822 and "Kingston" was offered for subscription in 1823). In 1824 he published *A warning to the Canadian Land Company*, a pamphlet in which he pointed out flaws, and the consequent risks for investors, in the prospectus of the Canada Company [*see* John GALT]. Sensing that his advice might be largely ignored if he used his own name, he signed the pamphlet "An Englishman resident in Upper Canada."

On 12 Nov. 1829 Dalton launched his most important project, the *Patriot and Farmer's Monitor*.

Although this weekly newspaper seems to have quickly gained a fair share of popularity, profits were slow in coming. In October 1830, in collaboration with Bishop Alexander McDONELL, Dalton began printing the *Catholic*, an official Roman Catholic weekly edited by William Peter MACDONALD, but it lasted for only one year. Dalton tried, unsuccessfully, to sell the *Patriot* in April 1832 (offering to stay on as editor until the end of the year) and that autumn he gave up on Kingston. He moved his paper and his family to York to reach a larger and, he hoped, more generous market and, of course, to be closer to the centre of political activity in the province. Publication at York began on 7 Dec. 1832 and within a year the *Patriot* was a semi-weekly.

Thomas Dalton, the editor of the *Patriot*, was not the man many thought they knew. Tom Dalton, the brewer, had supported Robert Gourlay*, joined William Lyon Mackenzie*'s circle, and counted the notorious Bidwells, Barnabas* and Marshall Spring*, among his friends. His literary assaults on the administration of Lieutenant Governor Sir Peregrine Maitland*, on the tories generally, and on the bank commissioners particularly had certainly done little to ingratiate him with either the Kingston establishment or the government leaders at York. In fact, his independence, truculent manner, and plain speech, as well as his politics, had gained him enemies in high places. Several petitions sent by him to the legislature in the 1820s, seeking redress and compensation for injuries financial, legal, and physical, received little more than the formal recognition required by official etiquette. But with the beginning of the *Patriot* in 1829, a change seemed to take place. With Common Sense as its motto, the paper had a reform, but hardly radical, editorial tone. As implied by its name, allegiance to the crown and respect for British tradition were fundamental to its policy and, though strongly critical of perceived shortcomings of the administration, it cultivated the loyal element of the population.

By the time of his move to York in 1832, Dalton had pretty well given up his former radical associates and was courting, and to some extent being courted by, many of his old adversaries. In fact, this process seems to have begun during his stint in the assembly, where he had voted against many reform amendments and obstructive riders following the passage of the revised bank act in March 1829. Mackenzie, the most visible radical, was increasingly criticized by Dalton. Perhaps surprisingly, one of Dalton's new supporters was an old enemy, John Strachan*, and fellow editors, such as Egerton Ryerson*, began to notice in print that the *Patriot* had been granted the right to speak for the Church of England. Even the breach with Hagerman was mended in 1833 when Dalton found out that it had been Henry John Boulton*, then solicitor general and a stockholder in the bank, who had drawn up and promoted the 1823 bank act, seemingly to deflect liability from himself.

Dalton's apparent political conversion has given rise to considerable speculation and comment. His detractors insisted then, as they do today, that it was a matter of self-serving opportunism rather than of principle; Mackenzie claimed that "the Editor of the *Patriot* had been hired and brought to York for the express purpose of putting down the *Advocate*." On the other hand, Dalton's friends and the contributors to his columns commended his loyalty to British traditions and his firm belief in British freedom as the "light of the world." On balance, his conversion would seem to have been no more than a growing disenchantment with old radical associates. In fact, Dalton had no objection to being labelled a reformer for, as he said, that was surely the role of every concerned citizen. So, as editor, Dalton embraced conservative principles throughout his short career, while never abandoning his rather quixotic reforming zeal, and the *Patriot* became the most influential conservative newspaper in the province.

Something of a visionary, Dalton foresaw a great future for his adopted country and he did his utmost to make his fellow citizens see it too. For example, he is credited with being, in 1834, the first to dream of a British North America spanned from sea to sea by a transportation network driven by steam. Despite his experience in Kingston, Dalton continued to believe in the value of banks and he was active in encouraging their growth; his perpetual shortage of personal funds, however, ultimately prevented the publication of his much-advertised book "Money is power."

Dalton was the sworn enemy of American Methodists and fought Ryerson's *Christian Guardian* tooth and nail from its inception in 1829. Never an admirer of the American "democratic" way of life (considering it "rule by the mob") and constantly worried about the influence it could have on the young colony, he complained that Methodist circuit riders from the United States were spreading political doctrine not far short of sedition. Perhaps more than any other subject, however, the continuing "intransigence" of the French Canadians kept Dalton's blood boiling. He saw "the perpetuation of the French language" as the "bitterest curse to the Lower Canadians . . . , the great political error of the time." By 1831 he was supporting a union of the two Canadas, to allow Upper Canada to escape from the lower province's stranglehold on customs revenue and to bury the troublesome French vote under a much larger British one. With time his vision grew wider. In October 1836 he wrote that consolidation of all five North American provinces was "the only union that ought to be considered for a single instant, and this should be effected with all possible speed." He was optimistic about the mission of Lord

Durham [LAMBTON], viewing it as recognition at last of the importance of the North American colonies to the empire, but he was disappointed with the final proposals. He launched salvo after salvo at the "Base, imbecile, treacherous, profligate Whig Govt" in London until, finally, late in 1839 the new governor-in-chief, Charles Edward Poulett THOMSON, ordered the cancellation of the *Patriot*'s contract for publishing government advertisements, thus greatly exacerbating Dalton's financial problems and adding to his frustrations.

A lifetime of struggling against all sorts of real and imagined adversaries finally proved more than even Dalton's stubborn spirit could resist and in March 1840 he suffered a serious stroke. By August he was able to resume his place at the newspaper, but he was a broken man. On 26 October a second massive stroke brought his earthly troubles swiftly to an end. The *Patriot* was carried on by his wife for another eight years and then was sold to Edward George O'Brien*.

Thomas Dalton was described in an obituary as "friendly, amiable and cheerful." In his public life he was an enthusiastic, forceful writer who took a bold stand on all the issues of the day, often using such excessively strong language that even his family objected. John George Bourinot* was to remark that "if his zeal frequently carried him into intemperate discussion of public questions, the ardour of the times must be for him . . . the best apology." Yet he was sued for libel only once during his career, for an item inserted in the *Patriot* during his absence following his stroke. A political as well as an editorial adversary, Francis Hincks* of the Toronto *Examiner*, spoke of him as "a vigorous political writer, tho' inclined to express himself with too much bitterness towards his opponents," but blamed others for that and added, "We are unconscious of having ever entertained towards him any feelings of animosity." In reporting Dalton's death, the *Cobourg Star* called him "assuredly one of the ablest and most strenuous supporters of conservative principles the provincial press has exhibited," one "whose loss is truly to be deplored by every loyal British subject." Toronto's *Commercial Herald* called him "a man of strong and fervid mind . . . an Englishman in heart and mind as well as by birth." A modern historian, Sydney Francis Wise, maintains that Dalton "had an importance in forming the conservative consciousness in Upper Canada that has never been appreciated."

IAN R. DALTON

[Thomas Dalton's pamphlet attacking Hagerman is entitled *"By the words of thy own mouth will I condemn thee"; to Christopher Alexander Hagerman, esq.* ([Kingston, Ont.?, 1824]); a copy of it is available at the MTRL. Much of Dalton's correspondence with government officials, and their responses, can be found in PAC, RG 1, E3; RG 5, A1; and RG 7, G16C; and in PRO, CO 42. Dalton's name appears in a large number of private collections, including the Macaulay family papers (MS 78), the Mackenzie–Lindsey papers (MS 516), and the journal of Matthew Teefy (MU 2113, 1858, no.16) at the AO; the W. D. Powell papers at the MTRL; and the Egerton Ryerson papers at the UCC-C.

Dalton's early years in Kingston are best described in I. R. Dalton, "The Kingston Brewery of Thomas Dalton," *Historic Kingston*, no.26 (1978): 38–50; a revised copy of this study (typescript, 1979) is available at AO, MU 7598, no.8. His connection to the bank is thoroughly covered in the same author's manuscript, "Thomas Dalton and the 'pretended' Bank" (Toronto, 1987); the surest way to follow the complicated trail in published sources is through newspapers, especially the *Upper Canada Herald* and the *Kingston Chronicle*, and through the *Journal* (and appendices) of the House of Assembly. His years as a publisher are best investigated by studying the *Patriot* itself. I.R.D.]

St James' Cemetery and Crematorium (Toronto), Record of burials. *Bytown Gazette, and Ottawa and Rideau Advertiser*, 12 Nov. 1840. *Cobourg Star*, 29 Oct. 1840. *Commercial Herald* (Toronto), 28 Oct. 1840. *Examiner* (Toronto), 28 Oct. 1840. *Toronto Patriot*, 27 Oct. 1840. J. G. Bourinot, *The intellectual development of the Canadian people: an historical review* (Toronto, 1881). Patterson, "Studies in elections in U.C." Adam Shortt, "The history of Canadian currency, banking and exchange . . . ," Canadian Bankers' Assoc., *Journal* (Toronto), 8 (1900–1): 1–15, 145–64, 227–43, 305–26. S. F. Wise, "Tory factionalism: Kingston elections and Upper Canadian politics, 1820–1836," *OH*, 57 (1965): 205–25.

DARVEAU, JEAN-ÉDOUARD, Roman Catholic priest and missionary; b. 17 March 1816 at Quebec, second son of Charles Darveau, a tanner on Rue Saint-Vallier, and Marguerite-Marie Roi, *dit* Audi; d. 4 June 1844 at Baie-des-Canards (Duck Bay, Man.).

Jean-Édouard Darveau began his classical studies at the Petit Séminaire de Québec in 1827. Having finished them, and having had some differences with his father, he became a sailor and went off to sea in October 1836. At one point he reached Havre-de-Grâce (Le Havre), France, by way of New York and New Orleans. Nothing was heard from him for 14 months.

During Darveau's final voyage the captain talked to him about his education. He decided to return to Quebec to study theology and was introduced to the archbishop of Quebec, Joseph SIGNAY, in 1838. Although his father refused to go with him to the Grand Séminaire to seek his admission, Darveau entered it on 1 Oct. 1838 upon a promise to Signay that after ordination he would devote himself to mission work. He was ordained on 21 Feb. 1841, in the presence of his family, including his father, with whom he had had a reconciliation.

A man of determined character, with an adventurous and dedicated spirit, Darveau took up the promise made to his archbishop, offering to serve in distant missions. As there was no room in the Hudson's Bay

Company brigade, he gave up the idea of leaving with the first canoes heading west and instead became assistant priest of Saint-Roch parish in Lower Town Quebec. But on 19 April 1841 he left his post to go to Lachine, near Montreal. On 1 May he set off by canoe for the Red River settlement (Man.), travelling in the place provided free of charge to priests by the governor of the HBC, Sir George Simpson*. He reached St Boniface on 22 June. Bishop Joseph-Norbert Provencher* intended to send Darveau to the missions on Lake Winnipegosis, but first the new missionary had to spend six months learning Ojibwa with George-Antoine Bellecourt*, a priest who had been serving the Red River mission since 1831 and who with Abbé Jean-Baptiste Thibault* had already visited the Maskegons (Swampy Crees), the Indians in the missions entrusted to Darveau. Darveau spent the winter with Provencher and Bellecourt.

In May 1842 Darveau left with three companions for Baie-des-Canards. The Church of England clergy, who were to make his ministry difficult, were already in the region. The local Indians were confused about what was the true religion, since the Catholic priest, just like his "rival," the Anglican Abraham Cowley*, claimed in his sermons that there was only one. Financial resources were meagre, and Darveau subjected himself to numerous privations. He was not able to pay the Indians for the services they rendered, but his devotion to catechizing them was unbounded. He made two more visits that year to these missions.

In the spring of 1843 Darveau again left St Boniface, ministering as he journeyed. When he reached his mission at Baie-des-Canards, he built a chapel dedicated to St Norbert. During a second visit from July to October he encountered more opposition to his ministry, the Indian catechist Henry Budd* being his Protestant rival at The Pas, and he also almost drowned. He made plans to rebuild the chapel at Baie-des-Canards, which had been destroyed by a storm, and then founded a temperance society at St François Xavier before returning to St Boniface.

In March 1844 Darveau set off for his mission again with a young Indian and a Métis, Jean-Baptiste Boyer, travelling through the Waterhen Lake region. He got lost on an island and nearly froze to death but somehow managed to survive. However, as they were leaving for The Pas early in June, he and his two companions disappeared. For a long time it was believed that the three had drowned, but on the basis of testimony gathered later, in particular statements from a missionary and from Indians connected directly or indirectly with the tragedy, it was concluded that they had been murdered. According to the Indians, under the influence of Budd they had come to regard Darveau as a "windigo," an evil spirit, and to hold him responsible for an epidemic that had struck them. The remains of Darveau, a victim of religious rivalries, were buried at St Boniface.

CORINNE TELLIER

Arch. de l'archevêché de Saint-Boniface (Saint-Boniface, Man.), Fonds Langevin; Fonds Provencher. Arch. de la Soc. hist. de Saint-Boniface, Dossier J.-É. Darveau. PAM, HBCA, D.5/8: ff.358–59; MG 7, D13. G.-A. [Bellecourt], "Mon itinéraire du lac des Deux Montagnes à la Rivière-Rouge," *Rev. canadienne*, 57 (1913): 1–57. Henry Budd, *The diary of the Reverend Henry Budd, 1870–1875*, ed. Katherine Pettipas (Winnipeg, 1974). *HBRS*, 29 (Williams). L.-P.-A. Langevin, "Procès-verbal de l'exhumation . . . ," *Les Cloches de Saint-Boniface* (Saint-Boniface), 8 (1909): 137–38. C.-M. Mestre, "Notes sur les missions de la Rivière-Rouge," *Les Cloches de Saint-Boniface*, 8: 101–10. *Notice sur les missions du diocèse de Québec, qui sont secourues par l'Association de la propagation de la foi* (Québec), no.4 (janvier 1842). [J.-N.] Provencher, "Lettres de Mgr Provencher à Mgr Ignace Bourget," *Les Cloches de Saint-Boniface*, 18 (1919): 192–93, 243–45, 263–65. *Rapport sur les missions du diocèse de Québec* . . . (Québec), no.6 (juillet 1845). *Recensement de Québec, 1818* (Provost), vol.2. Alexander Ross, *The Red River settlement: its rise, progress and present state; with some account of the native races and its general history, to the present day* (London, 1856; repr. Edmonton, 1972). A.-A. Sinnott, "Un monument au prêtre martyr du lac Winnipegosis; lettre de S. G. Mgr l'archevêque de Winnipeg," *Les Cloches de Saint-Boniface*, 29 (1930): 83–84. A.-A. Taché, *Vingt années de missions dans le Nord-Ouest de l'Amérique* (Montréal, 1866). Allaire, *Dictionnaire*. Morice, *Dict. hist. des Canadiens et des Métis*. Wallace, *Macmillan dict.* [J.-P.-A.] Benoît, *Vie de Mgr Taché, archevêque de Saint-Boniface* (2v., Montréal, 1904), 1. Benoît Brouillette, *La pénétration du continent américain par les Canadiens français, 1763–1846* . . . (Montréal, 1939). *Canada and its provinces; a history of the Canadian people and their institutions* . . . , ed. Adam Shortt and A. G. Doughty (23v., Toronto, 1913–17), 11. J.-É. Champagne, *Les missions catholiques dans l'Ouest canadien (1818–1875)* (Ottawa, 1949). Georges Dugas, *Monseigneur Provencher et les missions de la Rivière-Rouge* (Montréal, 1889). Donatien Frémont, *Mgr Provencher et son temps* (Winnipeg, 1935). *Georges-Antoine Belcourt* (s.l., 1984). Marcel Giraud, *The Métis in the Canadian west*, trans. George Woodcock (2v., Edmonton, 1986). A.-G. Morice, *Histoire de l'Église catholique dans l'Ouest canadien, du lac Supérieur au Pacifique (1659–1905)* (3v., Winnipeg et Montréal, 1912); *M. Darveau, martyr du Manitoba* (Winnipeg, 1934). *Reverend Henry Budd* (n.p., 1981).

Étienne Bonnald, "Notes sur Le Pas," *Les Cloches de Saint-Boniface*, 21 (1922): 211–12. T. C. B. Boon, "Henry Budd: the first native Indian ordained in the Anglican Church on the North American continent," *Manitoba Pageant* (Winnipeg), 3 (1957), no.1: 15–16. "La confession est un besoin de l'âme coupable; à propos de l'assassinat de M. l'abbé Darveau," *Les Cloches de Saint-Boniface*, 13 (1914): 220–21. "Duck Bay, Manitoba," *Home Missions* (Toronto), September 1983: 51–54. "Inhumation . . . ," *Les Cloches de Saint-Boniface*, 8: 173–76. "Le monument Darveau," *La Liberté* (Winnipeg), 20 avril 1932. A.-G. Morice, "La mort de M. l'abbé J.-E. Darveau," *Les Cloches de Saint-Boniface*, 14 (1915): 142–44; "M. Darveau, martyr inconnu du Manitoba," *La Liberté*, 9–23 avril 1930. "Mort de Monsieur Darveau," *Les Cloches de Saint-Boniface*, 78 (1979): 35–40. "Notice sur la Rivière Rouge," *Les Cloches de Saint-Boniface*, 26 (1927): 177–82. "Pèlerinage à l'endroit où fut massacré M. l'abbé Darveau et plantation d'une croix," *Les Cloches de Saint-Boniface*, 13: 185–86. "Quatre événements importants à Camperville, Man. . . . ," *Les Cloches de Saint-Boniface*, 11 (1912): 184–86. Soc. hist. de Saint-Boniface, *Bull.*, no.5 (juin 1984): 11. "Un martyr au Manitoba," *L'Ami du foyer* (Winnipeg), 45 (1949), no.4: 59.

DAVIE, ALLISON, sea captain and shipbuilder; b. 4 May 1796 and baptized privately the next day at Great Yarmouth, England, son of Captain Allison Davie (who was buried in 1818 at Gorleston, near Great Yarmouth) and Elizabeth Cock; drowned June 1836 between Quebec and Pointe-Lévy (Lauzon and Lévis), Lower Canada.

Allison Davie came from an old English family that can be traced back to 1603, when William Davie lived in Stanfield, Norfolk County. Allison was the eldest of four boys and several girls. During the Napoleonic Wars, while still young, he entered the service of the East India Company and took part in transporting British troops in the Mediterranean.

It was on a trip to Quebec in 1825 that Davie met Elizabeth Johnson Taylor, only daughter of George Taylor, a shipbuilder, and his wife Elizabeth Taylor. Born in 1803 at North Shields, England, she had left her native land aboard the *Three Brothers* with her parents on 27 May 1811 and reached Quebec on 9 August. Her father had immediately opened a shipyard on the southwest shore of the Île d'Orléans at a place known as St Patrick's Hole. Because of the war with the United States, however, Taylor had to suspend his activities in December 1812 and go with other sailors and carpenters to build ships in Upper Canada. On returning to Île d'Orléans after hostilities ended, he resumed operations. Taylor's yard was prospering when Davie, a 300-pound "giant" with an excellent reputation as a sea captain, landed at Quebec and fell in love with Elizabeth. Taylor agreed to his daughter's marriage with Davie on two conditions: that he abandon sailing and settle down as heir to the Taylor business, and that he give his children the Taylor name. Davie assented, and the marriage was performed by the Reverend James Harkness on 16 April 1825, according to the records of St Andrew's Presbyterian Church at Quebec.

On 14 May 1827 the Taylor enterprise, in which Davie was a partner, launched the *King Fisher*, a 221-ton brig with 16 guns built for the colonial government. The launching was a major event of the day, and among the many guests at the ceremony was Governor Lord Dalhousie [RAMSAY]. Dalhousie presented Taylor with a silver cup engraved with the governor's coat of arms surmounted by a unicorn, the ship's figurehead, which had been executed by silversmith Laurent AMIOT. Shortly afterwards the yard on Île d'Orléans was shut down.

On 2 Dec. 1829 Davie bought a waterfront property at the foot of the cliff at Pointe-Lévy on the south shore of the St Lawrence with a view to setting up his enterprise there. He purchased another site on 28 December of the following year. On these lots he put up the facilities needed for repairing ships. But, as the *Quebec Gazette* reported on 5 March 1832, during the violent spring break-up "the large wharf" of his shipyard, "after being thrown over by the ice, was carried down the river." Undaunted by the disaster, Davie started over again with such energy that by autumn he had the Pointe Levis Patent Slip back in operation.

Of all the qualities that contemporaries recognized in Davie, ingenuity was the one most stressed. For example, according to the *Quebec Gazette* of 29 Oct. 1832, he was the first person in the Canadas to employ a system invented in England that allowed ships to be repaired without being put into dry dock. For this purpose he had an inclined marine railway built. The vessels, "taken at high water," were hauled out of the river on a cradle "moving on iron rollers and being drawn up by an iron chain." "We believe this is the first establishment of the kind formed in British America," the newspaper added.

The ingenious Captain Davie was not destined, however, to live long after this achievement. "One evening in the month of June 1836," Joseph-Edmond Roy* recounts, "as he was moving in a rowboat past a ship anchored in mid stream, the captain of the ship threw him a package, which fell into the sea instead of into the rowboat." In leaning overboard to catch the package Davie fell in himself. He went under and did not come up. *Le Canadien* reported on 20 June that his body, with "his gold watch, some money, and the keys he had on him," had been found at Saint-Pierre, Île d'Orléans, the preceding afternoon, "a few days" after the accident "in the roads."

Elizabeth Davie, widowed with nine children at age 33, took charge of the business in order to safeguard the family's inheritance. The first woman to head a shipbuilding firm in Canada, she ran the yard and soon made a reputation for herself as a talented builder with a keen eye for the trees to be cut. On occasion she sought help from her father, who had retired but lived until 1861. Around 1850 she handed the running of the company over to her eldest son, George Taylor Davie*, who had apprenticed in John Munn*'s shipyards in the *faubourg* Saint-Roch at Quebec. He gradually bought up his brothers' and sisters' shares, with the result that on 28 May 1885 all of Allison Davie's heirs declared him sole owner of the family business. Elizabeth Davie had died in 1873, at age 70.

Thanks to George's business sense and professsional skill, the operation prospered and grew through the purchase of a site at Saint-Joseph (at Lauzon), where he founded the Davie Shipbuilding and Repairing Company Limited.

Despite his short and modest career Allison Davie had laid the foundation of an enterprise which, through his successors, won an enviable place in the shipbuilding field.

DIANE SAINT-PIERRE

ANQ-Q, CE1-66, 16 avril 1825. MIL Davie Inc. Arch. (Lauzon, Que.), "A shipbuilding dynasty," ed. E. R. Axelson, *Canada's shipyards* (photocopy); "Davie Shipbuilding Limited, Lauzon, P.Q." (typescript); "Shipbuilding industry in our district" (photocopy). Norfolk Record Office (Norwich, Eng.), Great Yarmouth, reg. of baptisms, 4–5 May 1796. Parish arch., Gorleston with South Town (Gorleston, Eng.), reg. of burials, 24 Dec. 1818. *Le Canadien*, 20 juin 1836. *Quebec Gazette*, 14 May, 20 Aug. 1827; 5 March, 29 Oct. 1832. P.-G. Roy, *Dates lévisiennes* (12v., Lévis, Qué., 1932–40), 1: 77, 101, 130–31, 177, 256, 318; 2: 17; 3: 165; 5: 257–58; 7: 259. George Gale, *Historic tales of old Quebec* (Quebec, 1923), 145. G. W. Haws, *The Haws family and their seafaring kin* (Dunfermline, Scot., 1932), 150–59. J.-E. Roy, *Hist. de Lauzon*, 5: 162–64. P.-G. Roy, *Glanures lévisiennes* (4v., Lévis, 1920–22), 1: 33–35; *Profils lévisiens* (2 sér., Lévis, 1948), 2: 74–75. "Historique du chantier," *L'Écho maritime* (s.l.), février 1945. Denis Masse, "Québec, berceau de l'industrie de la construction maritime au Canada," *Le Soleil* (Québec), 2 nov. 1957: 40, 42. "Naissance de la Davie: tout commence par un mariage," Canada Steamship Lines, *Le Monde* (s.l.), 2 (1976), no.3: 8.

DAVIS, ROBERT, farmer, author, and Patriot; b. *c.* 1800 in County Cavan (Republic of Ireland), son of Hugh Davis; m. Rosina ——, and they had several children; d. July 1838 in Malden Township, Upper Canada.

In 1819 Hugh Davis, an Irish farmer, brought his large family to North America. The Davises settled in Nissouri Township in Upper Canada's London District. In 1824 the Executive Council agreed that Hugh's son Robert be given land next to his father. Robert became a reasonably successful farmer; he married, raised a family, and became, in the words of William Proudfoot*, "a keen Methodist – an Exhorter."

Robert Davis's life was not without controversy. An imbroglio with the authorities precipitated by unknown factors landed him and others in the Court of Quarter Sessions in 1837. He was already a reformer, and this experience doubtless helped confirm his belief that a narrow clique ruled the province, persecuting its opponents and lining its own pockets. In 1836 he had journeyed to the United States, and the following year he published *The Canadian farmer's travels*. In it, he catalogued reform grievances. A Wesleyan Methodist, he decried the acceptance by his church of government funds and the alliance its leaders had struck with Lieutenant Governor Sir Francis Bond Head* in the crucial election of 1836. He also contrasted the beauties and economies of American freedom with the sorry state of affairs in Upper Canada. If the reformers ever hoped to reverse the trend of constant decline, he argued, they must be up and doing. Let Head continue on as he was, and "the reformers . . . will awake and revenge the evils done to them. . . . When the lion is once aroused who shall hush him to sleep again?" Clearly, Davis's book, which was excerpted in William Lyon Mackenzie*'s *Constitution* (Toronto), helped create the sense of urgency and crisis that made the rebellions of 1837 possible.

In the summer of 1837 Mackenzie and others began establishing political unions and planning a grand reform convention. The high point of their organizational drive in the west came in October when some 1,000 reformers gathered near London. Davis spoke to the throng. At a meeting in West Oxford Township the following month he was chosen a delegate to the proposed convention.

In late November Mackenzie at Toronto decided that the time was ripe for rebellion. He hurriedly prepared a rising there. Though it was easily crushed, one of Davis's correspondents, Oxford County MLA Charles Duncombe*, heard differently. He decided to gather rebels near Brantford to take advantage of the apparent situation and to forestall the anticipated arrests of local reformers. In mid December his force was dispersed by troops under Colonel Allan Napier MacNab*.

Before long, the militia in and about London were hunting up weapons. In Nissouri Davis began organizing men to resist the attempt "to Seize arms for the Queens service." He soon, however, fled westward to Detroit to escape the wrath of the authorities. District clerk John Baptist Askin*, who thought him a great fool and a "most consummate" poltroon, felt that, had he surrendered, he would have been granted bail, not imprisoned.

In Detroit Davis quickly fell in with refugees from Upper Canada and with Americans preparing to aid the cause of liberty by invading the province. These Patriots stole weapons from the Detroit jail and gathered along the Detroit River. On 6 Jan. 1838 they began their "invasion," setting out to capture various Upper Canadian islands. They were short of trained men, and Davis, who had no experience of sailing, captained the *Anne* until Edward Alexander Theller* assumed command. Theller was no better qualified, and on 9 January he grounded the vessel near the Upper Canadian shore. Militiamen under Colonel Thomas RADCLIFF stormed her, taking off 21 prisoners, including Theller and Davis.

Davis had been shot through the thigh and arm, injuries which were to prove fatal, and was carried to Fort Malden at Amherstburg. Here he allegedly wrote a letter to various Patriots, including younger brother Hugh, urging them to abandon their invasion plans. He lingered on in agony until July. After his death the redoubtable Colonel John Prince* recorded that "he was an intelligent & a brave but a most desperate rebel., and he died one to the last." Theller in his *Canada in 1837–38*, published in 1841, praised his fallen comrade, who evidently had earned the respect of friends and foes alike for his derring-do.

COLIN READ

Robert Davis is the author of *The Canadian farmer's travels in the United States of America, in which remarks are made on the arbitrary colonial policy practised in Canada, and the free and equal rights, and happy effects of the liberal institutions and astonishing enterprise of the United States* (Buffalo, N.Y., 1837).

PAC, RG 5, A1: esp. 98408–11, 98951, 99468, 111098; B36, 1–2. *Rebellion of 1837* (Read and Stagg). E. A. Theller, *Canada in 1837–38* . . . (2v., Philadelphia and New York, 1841). Read, *Rising in western U.C.* J. J. Talman, "The value of crown lands papers in historical research, with an illustration of their use," RSC *Trans.*, 3rd ser., 30 (1936), sect.II: 131–36.

DEBARTZCH, PIERRE-DOMINIQUE, seigneur, lawyer, politician, militia officer, office holder, and newspaper owner; b. 22 Sept. 1782 in Saint-Charles-sur-Richelieu, Que., son of Dominique Debartzch, a merchant, and Marie-Josephte Simon, *dit* Delorme; d. 6 Sept. 1846 in Saint-Marc on the Richelieu, Lower Canada.

Pierre-Dominique Debartzch's ancestor, Dominicus Bartzsch, came from the Catholic parish of St Mary in Danzig (Gdańsk, Poland). When he settled in New France is unknown, but the first mention of his presence dates back to 1752. On 16 April of that year in Montreal, Bartzsch, a merchant-furrier, signed a marriage contract with Thérèse Filiau, *dit* Dubois, daughter of François Filiau, *dit* Dubois, a merchant-carpenter. After some time Bartzsch began to spell his name Bartzch and soon, adopting a practice common among Poles who claimed to belong to the nobility and who lived in a French-speaking milieu, he added the particle "de," whence the name de Bartzch or Debartzch.

Pierre-Dominique, an only son, studied at Harvard College in Boston. Then on 28 March 1800 he contracted to article with Denis-Benjamin Viger*. His father being dead, when he went to sign the contract he was accompanied by his guardian Hyacinthe-Marie Simon, *dit* Delorme, an uncle who was to represent Richelieu in the Lower Canadian House of Assembly from 1808 till 1814. Debartzch soon began buying real estate. In 1802 he rendered fealty and homage for part of the seigneury of Saint-Hyacinthe. On 9 July 1806 he was called to the bar, and the following month he left for Europe.

Debartzch returned to Lower Canada in 1807 and immediately went into politics. He was elected, along with Louis-Joseph Papineau*, for Kent in 1809, and both were re-elected there the following year. In the assembly he sided with the Canadian party and supported the reform cause. When the division of the seigneury of Saint-Hyacinthe was settled in 1811 Debartzch inherited three-eighths [*see* Jean Dessaulles*], about 88,420 *arpents*. During the War of 1812 he served as a captain in the 5th Select Embodied Militia Battalion of Lower Canada. In October 1813 he commanded a company at the battle of Châteauguay [*see* Charles-Michel d'Irumberry* de Salaberry], demonstrating both bravery and military leadership. John Douglas Borthwick* noted, "All did their duty well and nobly that day, but let especial mention be made of captains Ferguson [George Richard Ferguson], de Bartzch and Levesque [Marc-Antoine-Louis Lévesque]."

On 17 Jan. 1814 Debartzch left the assembly for the Legislative Council, of which he remained a member until 27 March 1838. The appointment was certainly an honour – the speaker of the assembly, Jean-Antoine Panet*, was not named to the council until 1815 and Papineau was not offered a seat until seven years later. On 7 June 1815 Debartzch, along with Thomas McCord* and Louis-René Chaussegros* de Léry, was made a commissioner for the improvement of internal communications in the district of Montreal. That year, at Saint-Ours on 25 July, he married Josette de Saint-Ours. Her father was Charles de Saint-Ours*, also a legislative councillor, who was one of the richest Canadian seigneurs at the time, and her mother was Josette Murray, niece of former governor James Murray*. In 1818 Debartzch delivered a speech in the council supporting an assembly resolution that the council be constituted a high court to investigate the case of judge Louis-Charles Foucher of Montreal, who was accused of betraying his trust in the execution of his duties. The following year, on 31 May, Debartzch was appointed to a commission of inquiry concerning the titles and claims of landholders in the seigneury of La Salle in Sherrington Township.

In 1822 Debartzch was active in the huge protest movement organized against a plan to unite Lower and Upper Canada [*see* Denis-Benjamin Viger]. Those present at the first meeting of the anti-unionists, which was held in Montreal on 7 October, set up a committee of 18 leading inhabitants of Montreal and its environs, among whom were Saint-Ours, Debartzch, Irumberry de Salaberry, and Papineau. The committee was to select delegates to take to England petitions denouncing union. On the day of the meeting the residents of

Montreal also gave what they called a constitutional banquet to honour Debartzch, as representative of the Legislative Council, and Papineau, as representative of the House of Assembly. Later, in a song entitled "Les orateurs canadiens," which alludes to the council and the banquet, Michel Bibaud* wrote:

The Areopagus,
Despite itself, I am told,
Dispatches a wise man,
Here, to set the tone:
Ah! 'tis D........
He is the great orator.

The song thus celebrates Debartzch's stand in opposition to the plan for union.

In 1826 Debartzch, who was anxious to extend his holdings, purchased the seigneury of Saint-François (also called Saint-Charles) at auction. His concerns as a seigneur did not affect his support for reforms. In 1830 he was chairman of a meeting at Saint-Charles-sur-Richelieu attended by leading inhabitants of Richelieu, Verchères, Saint-Hyacinthe, Rouville, and Chambly counties, at which resolutions advocating reform of the Legislative and Executive councils were passed. In 1832, along with Louis Bourdages*, he again chaired a meeting of these counties, which unanimously adopted 21 propositions that contained the seeds of the 92 Resolutions [*see* Elzéar BÉDARD]; the principal one demanded the withdrawal of the authority of the head of the executive to appoint legislative councillors.

To further the constitutional struggle Debartzch founded *L'Écho du pays* at Saint-Charles-sur-Richelieu in 1833. The paper, which opposed the system of government, had as its first editor a Frenchman, Alfred-Xavier Rambau*. Revolutionary articles appeared in its columns, according to *Le Populaire* of Montreal of 18 Oct. 1837. Debartzch, who had not written the pieces, came down against them and refused to continue supporting the paper, which ceased publication in 1836. That year Debartzch founded *Le Glaneur* in the same village and made Jean-Philippe Boucher-Belleville* its editor. This magazine, which dealt mainly with agricultural matters, proved ephemeral, its last issue coming out in September 1837.

Since 1835 Debartzch had been carrying on what Charles-Ovide Perrault, member for Vaudreuil in the assembly, termed a "daily" correspondence with Governor Lord Gosford [ACHESON]. On 22 Aug. 1837 Debartzch was named to the Executive Council, on which he would sit until 10 Feb. 1841. The appointment seemed to indicate a change in his political attitude and led, among other things, to his being censured by *La Minerve*, the Patriotes' organ. Yet, as a result of his appointment, Canadians achieved equality in number with the English-speaking councillors.

At the time of the rebellion, Debartzch had to leave Saint-Charles-sur-Richelieu with his family and go to Montreal. *Le Canadien* on 22 Nov. 1837 noted that his house had been surrounded and ransacked by armed men. Debartzch was to file a claim for $26,000 compensation for the property losses he sustained during the rebellion. Meanwhile, in 1841, he bought the seigneury of Cournoyer, which covered the territory that was later to become the municipality of Saint-Marc. He apparently retired there with his wife and children.

Debartzch died on 6 Sept. 1846 in Saint-Marc, at 63 years of age. He was buried three days later under the seigneur's pew in the church of Saint-Charles-sur-Richelieu. In a biography published in the *Revue trimestrielle canadienne* Jean-Jacques Lefebvre was to call him "one of the most remarkable and honest figures of the first half of the 19th century in Canada." Debartzch and his wife had had four daughters. Elmire and Caroline married respectively Lewis Thomas Drummond* and Samuel Cornwallis Monk, both Montreal lawyers. Cordelia and Louise married Édouard-Sylvestre de Rottermund* and Alexandre-Édouard Kierzkowski*, Polish exiles who were to make their mark in the province of Canada.

LUDWIK KOS RABCEWICZ ZUBKOWSKI

Pierre-Dominique Debartzch is said to be the author of *Vie politique de Mr. . . . , ex-membre de la chambre d'Assemblée du B.C. . . .* ([Québec, 1811]). The speech he delivered in the Legislative Council in 1818 is printed in Christie, *Hist. of L.C.* (1866), 6: 348–52.

ANQ-M, CE2-10, 23 sept. 1782, 9 sept. 1846; CE3-6, 25 juill. 1815; CN1-16, 28 mars 1800; CN1-134, 10 avril 1841; CN1-313, 23 sept. 1811; CN2-27, 23 juill. 1815. PAC, MG 30, D1, 10: 72–87; RG 4, B8: 6491–94; RG 68, General index, 1651–1841; 1841–67. Michel Bibaud, *Épître, satire, chansons, épigrammes et autres pièces de vers* (Montréal, 1830). "Lettres de 1835 et de 1836," Alfred Duclos De Celles, édit., RSC *Trans.*, 3e sér., 7 (1913), sect.I: 174. *La Minerve*, 7 sept. 1846. *Quebec Gazette*, 8 June 1815. F.-J. Audet, "Les législateurs du Bas-Canada." Beaulieu et Hamelin, *La presse québécoise*, 1: 76–79, 91–92. F.-M. Bibaud, *Le panthéon canadien* (1858), 76–78; (A. et V. Bibaud, 1891), 68. Borthwick, *Hist. and biog. gazetteer*, 44, 46–48, 68, 214. Desjardins, *Guide parl.* *Dictionnaire historique et géographique du Canada* (Montréal, 1885), 28. H. J. Morgan, *Sketches of celebrated Canadians*, 357. *Officers of British forces in Canada* (Irving). P.-G. Roy, *Inv. concessions*, 4: 97–98, 101; 5: 66–68. Turcotte, *Le Conseil législatif*, 18, 77. Wallace, *Macmillan dict.*

Barthe, *Souvenirs d'un demi-siècle*, 359. T.-P. Bédard, *Histoire de cinquante ans (1791–1841), annales parlementaires et politiques du Bas-Canada, depuis la Constitution jusqu'à l'Union* (Québec, 1869), 29, 295–96. Chapais, *Cours d'hist. du Canada*, 2: 268; 3: 121–22; 4: 59, 114,

188–89. C.-P. Choquette, *Histoire de la ville de Saint-Hyacinthe* (Saint-Hyacinthe, Qué., 1930), 117–19, 124, 130–32; *Histoire du séminaire de Saint-Hyacinthe depuis sa fondation jusqu'à nos jours* (2v., Montréal, 1911–12), 1: 154, 170–71. Christie, *Hist. of L.C.* (1866), 4: 422; 6: 352–58. Azarie Couillard-Després, *Histoire de la seigneurie de Saint-Ours* (2v., Montréal, 1915–17), 2: 74–76, 221. [François Daniel], *Histoire des grandes familles françaises du Canada ou aperçu sur le chevalier Benoist et quelques familles contemporaines* (Montréal, 1867), 422. David, *Patriotes*, 37–38. F.-X. Garneau, *Histoire du Canada depuis sa découverte jusqu'à nos jours*, Hector Garneau, édit. (8e éd., 9v., Montréal, 1944–46), 7: 184; 8: 145. Ludwik Kos-Rabcewicz-Zubkowski, *The Poles in Canada* (Ottawa and Montreal, 1968), 10, 18–22, 27, 162. Benjamin Sulte, *Histoire des Canadiens-français, 1608–1880 . . .* (8v., Montréal, 1882–84), 8: 72. Claude de Bonnault, "Généalogie de la famille de Saint-Ours: Dauphiné et Canada," *BRH*, 56 (1950): 106–7. J.-J. Lefebvre, "Les députés de Chambly, 1792–1967," *BRH*, 70 (1968): 11–12; "Pierre-Dominique Debartzch," *Le Devoir* (Montréal), 30 oct. 1939: 6; "Pierre-Dominique Debartzch, 1782–1846," *Rev. trimestrielle canadienne*, 27 (1941): 179–200.

DEBLOIS, STEPHEN WASTIE, businessman, office holder, and politician; b. 16 Jan. 1780 in New York City, eldest son of George Deblois and Sarah Deblois*; he had two sons and a daughter with Jane Catherine Witham, whom he later married; d. 26 Dec. 1844 in Halifax.

Stephen Wastie Deblois's father, an Englishman of Huguenot descent, emigrated in 1761 from Oxford to Salem, Mass., and set up as a general merchant. Forced to flee Salem in 1775 because of his loyalist beliefs, he took refuge in Halifax and in 1777 moved to New York City, where he continued in trade. Towards the end of the war, George Deblois returned to Halifax. He resumed his career as a merchant and began to edge into the local oligarchy, becoming a justice of the peace in 1793. His premature death in 1799 precipitated a family crisis but Sarah Deblois assumed control of her husband's firm. Stephen was probably working in the family business before 1808, the year in which his name first appears in newspaper advertisements as head of the firm.

Nothing is known about Stephen's education and business training but it is apparent that he possessed the skills required to succeed in trade. His ear career undoubtedly benefited from the prosperity that Halifax enjoyed during the closing phase of the Napoleonic Wars. In 1814, as prize goods flooded onto the local market, Deblois specialized his operations by becoming an auctioneer. When peace returned he continued as an auctioneer, concentrating on the sale of foodstuffs and related commodities imported from the United States. His activities, which represented a major innovation within the Halifax market, provoked the ire of more traditional merchants, who complained that auctioneers constituted unfair competition because they required little capital in order to operate and were in effect agents for merchants outside Nova Scotia. Deblois persisted, however, and by the early 1820s was dealing with an annual turnover of goods valued at more than £10,000.

Throughout his career Deblois operated with partners. In 1816 he recruited the first, William Bowie, who probably brought the capital and connections required to survive the post-war commercial dislocation. Following Bowie's death as a result of a duel with Richard John Uniacke* Jr in 1819, Deblois was associated with his brother William Minet Deblois, then Samuel Mitchell, and finally James W. Merkel. By the mid 1840s the firm had grown to control assets in excess of £25,000, two-thirds of which belonged to Deblois as senior partner. A leading man of property on the Halifax waterfront, Deblois supplemented his income by lending money in return for mortgage securities. One of his largest transactions involved a debt of £9,000 incurred by a hard-pressed Samuel Cunard* as he fought off bankruptcy in the early 1840s.

Deblois's entrepreneurial prominence was reflected in his election to the Halifax Chamber of Commerce and a term as vice-president of that organization. He invested in and served as a director of such enterprises as the Halifax East India Company, the Shubenacadie Canal Company, the Albion Fire Insurance Company, the Nova Scotia Marine Insurance Company, and the Bank of British North America. As his business career developed, Deblois accumulated public and honorific offices such as commissioner of the Halifax Commons, commissioner of public cemeteries, marshal of the Vice-Admiralty Court, and vice-president of the St George's Society. In addition, he served one term in the House of Assembly as member for Halifax Township.

Deblois's presence in the legislature at a time of growing agitation for political reform generated the bulk of the controversy that is associated with his name. Nominated as the candidate of Halifax's oligarchy to contest the election of 1830, Deblois challenged the sitting member, Beamish Murdoch*, a lawyer then associated with the reform cause. The contest provoked physical violence and impassioned rhetoric, with Murdoch assailing the loyalists as "the scum of the United States" who, out of "pretended" allegiance to the crown, "had fled from debts and incumberances." Having won decisively, Deblois quickly achieved prominence in the assembly, employing an aggressive and hectoring oratorical style to champion vested interests. An enthusiast for progress in such areas as canal construction and steamship navigation, he insisted that monopoly and privilege were essential for Nova Scotia's economic development. For example, while in favour of a bank and paper money, Deblois opposed incorporation of the Bank of Nova Scotia on the ground that its competition with the existing Halifax Banking Company would jeopardize business stability. Similarly, he argued that Halifax, "the heart and soul of the Country," should not be deprived of its exclusive right to control the importation of goods from foreign states through its status as the only free port in the province. When hard times disrupted the local economy in the mid 1830s and intensified demands for political change, Deblois blamed commercial distress on out-port smugglers and told the public to remain faithful to their traditional leaders.

By the time of the 1836 election, Deblois had become anathema to the growing mass of reformers in Halifax. Renowned as a reactionary, he attracted further odium because his brother served in the corrupt municipal administration. A public meeting held to review the qualifications of those seeking election howled down Deblois's name when it was placed in nomination. By this time even members of the oligarchy had come to see that Deblois's extreme partisanship had made him a laughing-stock within the community. Exclusion from the legislature did not, however, end Deblois's political career. Throughout the late 1830s and early 1840s he continued to oppose all forms of constitutional change, devoting money and influence to sustain die-hard resistance to the coming of responsible government.

During the last years of his life, Deblois remained prominent within Halifax's business and social élite. His 13-room residence on Gottingen Street, valued at £1,000 and with furnishings worth over £400, embodied the contemporary definition of genteel comfort. Annual household expenditures, including pew rental at St George's Anglican Church, a subscription to the Halifax Library, and deportment classes for the children, came to more than £400. Living standards within the Halifax élite are further indicated by Deblois's will, which gave both of his sons £3,000 on their reaching maturity and £2,000 to his daughter. Deblois's wife was secured by a marriage settlement of £1,500. The heirs obtained more than paper promises, since Deblois died leaving assets of over £23,000.

An obituary said of Deblois that he had possessed "some eccentricity of disposition." One suspects from this description that he was not a likeable personality. He certainly gave offence to those in the reform movement and could also disconcert Halifax's establishment when it suited his purposes. The curious nature of his domestic affairs must have provoked comment, especially in an era of growing middle-class propriety. In short, Deblois appears to have been something of a renegade, a man guided more by ego and ambition than by any consistent intellectual design. Nevertheless, his career provides an insight into the cross-currents of change in early 19th-century Nova Scotia.

David A. Sutherland

Halifax County Court of Probate (Halifax), Estate papers, D33; no.113 (mfm. at PANS). Halifax County Registry of Deeds (Halifax), Deeds, 71: ff.323, 325 (mfm. at PANS). PANS, MG 1, 55, nos.1237, 1357; RG 1, 171: f.61; 173: f.265; 174: f.269; 244, no.103; 289, no.122; 314, no.26. PRO, CO 217/101: 50. N.S., House of Assembly, *Journal and proc.*, 18 Jan. 1821, 25 Feb. 1822. *Acadian Recorder*, 1 June 1816; 13 March, 18 Sept. 1830; 4 March, 9 Sept. 1837. *Halifax Journal*, 17 July 1820. *Halifax Morning Post & Parliamentary Reporter*, 31 Oct. 1843, 28 Dec. 1844. *Novascotian*, 15–23 Sept. 1830; 23 Feb. 1832; 18 April 1833; 23 Jan., 13–20 March 1834; 30 July 1835; 18 Feb., 17 Nov. 1836; 2 April 1840. *Nova-Scotia Royal Gazette*, 30 July 1799, 14 Feb. 1827. *Times* (Halifax), 30 March 1841; 30 Jan., 31 Dec. 1844. *Belcher's farmer's almanack*, 1824–44. W. E. Boggs, *The genealogical record of the Boggs family, the descendants of Ezekiel Boggs* (Halifax, 1916). A. W. H. Eaton, "Old Boston families, number one: the De Blois family," *New England Hist. and Geneal. Reg.* (Boston), 67 (1913): 6–13. E. A. Jones, *The loyalists of Massachusetts: their memorials, petitions and claims* (London, 1930). Wallace Brown, *The king's friends: the composition and motives of the American loyalist claimants* (Providence, R.I., 1965).

DECOIGNE (De Couagne, Couagne, Coigne, Du Coigne), PIERRE-THÉOPHILE, notary and Patriote; b. 13 March 1808 in Saint-Philippe-de-Laprairie, Lower Canada, son of Louis Decoigne and Marguerite Bezeau; m. 1832 Mary McCabe, and they had two children; d. 18 Jan. 1839 in Montreal.

Pierre-Théophile Decoigne came from a family with noble antecedents. According to historian Claude de Bonnault, the first member of the Coigne family to settle in New France was Charles de Couagne*, an illegitimate son from the parish of Clion in Berry, who was *maître d'hôtel* to Governor Frontenac [Buade*]. He went into the fur trade and became one of the richest merchants in the colony. His son Jean-Baptiste de Couagne* had a career as an officer and military engineer at Louisbourg, Île Royale (Cape Breton Island), but the other sons followed their father's example, with varying success. It is certain that by about 1780 the Decoigne family had lost some of its importance in Quebec society, as it continued to do in subsequent years.

Son of a notary who had been captain of a company of the Chasseurs de L'Acadie in the War of 1812, Pierre-Théophile also became a notary. After studying at the Petit Séminaire de Montréal he apparently articled with his brother-in-law, Jean-Baptiste Lukin. He was authorized to practise on 7 Oct. 1837 and settled in Napierville. His brother Louis-Mars, who had been admitted to the profession in 1827, had taken over their father's practice at Sainte-Marguerite-de-Blairfindie (L'Acadie) upon his death in 1832.

Pierre-Théophile, Louis-Mars, and their younger brother Olivier had early joined the Patriote movement and were closely involved in the revolutionary events of 1837–38. Louis-Mars seems to have been the most active of the three in 1837. After the Assemblée des Six Comtés at Saint-Charles-sur-Richelieu, when the decision was taken to dismiss the militia officers and justices of the peace who had been appointed by the government, Louis-Mars decorated his house with flags bearing the Patriote emblem and participated in the charivaris against those who had received government commissions, in particular Dudley Flowers, Nelson Mott, and Timoléon Quesnel. As leader of the Patriotes in Sainte-Marguerite-de-Blairfindie, he modelled himself upon Cyrille-Hector-Octave CÔTÉ, a doctor at Napierville, and Lucien GAGNON, a farmer from Pointe-à-la-Mule (Saint-Valentin). On 28 Nov. 1837 Quesnel announced that he had taken steps to arrest Louis-Mars Decoigne and François Ranger as they were attempting to reach the United States. Released on £1,000 bail, Louis-Mars helped with plans for the second insurrection.

Pierre-Théophile played an important role in the preparations for this uprising. In September 1838 he was sworn in at Champlain, N.Y., as a member of the Association des Frères-Chasseurs. He said later that his intention at the time was to infiltrate this secret society and inform the government of its activities. Yet he was to be one of the most feared leaders of Saint-Cyprien parish, at Napierville. He even suggested confiscating the property of François-Xavier Malhiot*, the seigneur of Contrecœur. As part of a plan for gathering Patriotes from 17 parishes to seize William Henry (Sorel) on the evening of 3 November, Decoigne was given the task of assembling the habitants of Verchères, Saint-Ours, and Contrecœur the day before. To any who might be tempted to remain neutral he said: "Those who refuse to march will have their properties burned and will be treated like their cruellest enemies."

During the second insurrection, on 3 Nov. 1838, Decoigne was one of the leaders of a force of 400–500 Patriotes. He exercised his command "very energetically and harshly, striking those who were in no hurry to obey," Jean-Baptiste Fredette testified. Since the Patriote plan was doomed because of faulty organization, Colonel Édouard-Élisée Malhiot* delegated Decoigne to find Eugène-Napoléon Duchesnois and Louis-Adolphe Robitaille, the doctor and notary at Varennes, in order to warn them that the attack had been put off. He recommended Decoigne to them: "The bearer of this letter is the most dependable man, you can talk with him."

On 4 Nov. 1838 Decoigne, like most of the Patriotes from the surrounding parishes, was in camp at Napierville, where he acted as captain. He was also one of the group that confronted volunteers from the English party at Odelltown on 9 November. In fact, he captained a company there that "fired several times," according to one witness. After this day, disastrous for the Patriote cause, Decoigne returned to Napierville. On 11 November his brothers Louis-Mars and Olivier succeeded in crossing the border. Pierre-Théophile was not so lucky. He in turn tried to make it to the United States but was arrested. Under examination Decoigne referred to his having the "reputation of being a supporter of the English party," and he added: "Upon reaching the battlefield, I took up a position out of harm's way and stayed there until the end without giving any order whatsoever." He was, however, sentenced to death by a court martial on 2 Jan. 1839 and was hanged on 18 January. In 1852 his widow received partial compensation for the property losses that she and her husband had suffered during the rebellion.

FERNAND OUELLET

Pierre-Théophile Decoigne's minute-book, containing instruments for the period 1837–38, is at the AC, Beauharnois (Valleyfield).

ANQ-M, CE1-54, 13 mars 1808. ANQ-Q, E17/6, nos.76a, 77; E17/7, nos.92–93, 103–9, 128, 146; E17/10, no.402; E17/19, nos.1236–37; E17/25, nos.1732–32b, 1736, 1753; E17/32, nos.2510–11; E17/33, nos.2654a, 2655–56, 2658; E17/34, nos.2675, 2700–3, 2705, 2708, 2755; E17/35, no.2787; E17/37, no.2985; E17/39, no.3114; E17/51, nos.4111–20. PAC, RG 4, B8: 5205–7. Can., Prov. of, Legislative Assembly, *App. to the journals*, 1852–53, app.VV. "Papiers Duvernay," *Canadian Antiquarian and Numismatic Journal*, 3rd ser., 7: 83–86, 92–94. *Report of state trials*, 1: 150–215. Fauteux, *Patriotes*, 200–2. *Officers of British forces in Canada* (Irving). Tanguay, *Dictionnaire*, 3: 269–70. J. D. Borthwick, *History of the Montreal prison from A.D. 1784 to A.D. 1886* . . . (Montreal, 1886), 90. David, *Patriotes*, 222. Louise Dechêne, *Habitants et marchands de Montréal au XVIIe siècle* (Paris et Montréal, 1974), 205. Maurault, *Le collège de Montréal* (Dansereau; 1967). S.-A. Moreau, *Histoire de L'Acadie, province de Québec* (Montréal, 1908), 116–17. Claude de Bonnault, "Les Coigne du Berry en Canada," *BRH*, 46 (1940): 276–84. J.-J. Lefebvre, "Les De Couagne (Decoigne)," SGCF *Mémoires*, 25 (1974): 214–27.

DELORME, CHARLES-SIMON, joiner, carpenter, building contractor, and landowner; b. 14 June 1769 in Montreal, son of Charles-Simon Delorme and Catherine Roy; m. there 22 Nov. 1802 Marie-Marguerite Dufresne, daughter of François Dufresne, a joiner; d. there 9 June 1837.

Charles-Simon Delorme studied at the Collège Saint-Raphaël in Montreal from 1783 to 1784. Then he probably apprenticed with a master craftsman, as was the practice at the time, particularly in the building trades. In 1794 he owned a small workshop in the *faubourg* Saint-Laurent where he himself made doors and windows, supplying the handful of building contractors in Montreal. He abandoned this line of work, which was not very profitable, to devote himself after 1800 primarily to building.

Taking advantage of the surge in population that Montreal was experiencing in the early 19th century, Delorme put up more than 96 houses and 30 other buildings during his career as a contractor, which lasted from 1800 to 1830. At the beginning he was involved in most stages of the work, employing small numbers of workmen when necessary in order to meet the delivery dates demanded by his clients. As a result of the rapid growth of his enterprise he was able to concentrate on organizing the process of production on the sites, gradually giving up manual tasks except those connected with putting up the joists to support the structure of the buildings. Consequently, in the course of time his main concerns became to hire workmen, supply materials, and conduct day-to-day business. In general, the sites required a mason, three to five pit-sawyers, and half a dozen carters. In this business as in others wages became the essential link between employer and employees, and the basis on which capital was accumulated. Moreover, the pit-sawyers hired by Delorme in some respects foreshadow the modern proletariat: by then they worked in teams under a foreman, were paid on a piece rate, and no longer owned their tools.

Delorme's fees ranged from £60 to £1,000. In most contracts he required a 10 per cent advance on the total price in order to raise the capital for beginning construction. From 1819, as a result of bad workmanship by subcontractors whom he engaged, Delorme went into partnership with mason Joseph Fournier. Their firm was also the product of intense activity in 1816–17, a period in which Delorme had undertaken to build 21 houses with the aid of 23 workmen. It had thus become urgent to find a partner in order to avoid postponing completion dates and paying the consequent penalties.

In addition to building luxurious residences on Rue Saint-Paul and Place d'Armes, Delorme was involved in erecting civil and religious buildings. As it became increasingly obvious in the early years of the century that Montreal was destined to become an import and export centre, Delorme built numerous warehouses and sheds for various merchants. In 1809 Louis Charland*, surveyor of highways, streets, and lanes for the town of Montreal, had him build a covered market with 14 stalls and a "weigh-house" on the Place du Vieux-Marché (Place Royale). The following year Delorme was one of the six contractors engaged to put up the church for Saint-Antoine parish at Longueuil; this was a profitable contract by which he had a share in £4,020. Probably because Delorme's work was of high quality, other *fabriques* turned to him, including Saint-Constant in 1811, and Notre-Dame in Montreal for the building of a chapel in 1816. Delorme was also one of the contractors responsible for constructing sections of Notre-Dame Church in Montreal in the period 1824–29 [*see* James O'Donnell*]. It was in civil architecture, however, that he made his greatest contribution, with the building of the Hôtel-Dieu and the adjoining nuns' residence, which he had undertaken with his partner in 1826 and 1827.

Delorme also profited from the spin-offs of urban development in Montreal during the period 1800–30. In 1805, for example, the commissioners for inland navigation chose him to remove the debris blocking the Sault-Saint-Louis (Kahnawake) channel and to build a 300-foot wharf there. Delorme seems to have had trouble carrying out this contract, since the following year the House of Assembly granted him some funds "for the extraordinary difficulties and losses in the course of his work during the summer." In the years 1807–10 he did various jobs for the commissioners in charge of removing the fortifications of Montreal. In 1818, through Jacques Viger*, surveyor of highways, streets, lanes, and bridges for the town and parish, he received the contract for building wooden sidewalks, stairs, and sewers.

Delorme had so enlarged his holdings in landed property that when he died he owned in Montreal 13 building lots, 9 houses, 12 sheds, 8 stables, a joiner's shop, and a cooper's shop. There is some evidence that he was also raising horses; in 1819 the district agricultural society had awarded him a prize of "30 *piastres*" for the best Canadian stallion shown at an exhibition. Delorme was not, however, free of financial worries. On 20 April 1820 a fire destroyed his property in the *faubourg* Des Récollets, along with five other houses. Three days later the newspapers reported that Delorme was responsible for the fire and that he had no insurance.

The surplus capital that Delorme accumulated was on the whole not put back into his enterprises; part went into short-term credit and other forms of investment, as is shown by the £4,754 owed to him when the inventory of his estate was drawn up after his death and by the £800 he had put in the Banque du Peuple as a subscriber and the £500 in the Quebec Fire Assurance Company. Delorme's progress illustrates perfectly the way in which the group on the leading edge of the community of craftsmen was busy consolidating its financial bases and creating the dynamic elements of a middle bourgeoisie shortly before the rebellion of 1837–38. Members of this middle bourgeoisie, including Delorme, were involved in a scheme for a banking firm launched in 1833 by Louis-Michel Viger* and Jacob De Witt* in order to ensure that Canadians would have financial resources committed to stimulating and encouraging trade and industry in the province. This firm opened its doors two years later under the name of the Banque du Peuple with an initial capital of £75,000. Delorme was also concerned with the problem of land transportation in the colony and in 1831 he participated in founding the

Company of Proprietors of the Champlain and St Lawrence Railroad [*see* John Molson*].

Even though Charles-Simon Delorme was not directly involved in politics, he never hid his sympathies for the Patriote party. In the early 1830s, citing the troubled circumstances in Lower Canada, he had refused a post as justice of the peace. He died on 9 June 1837 – after an illness of several months, according to his doctor, Wolfred Nelson*. At that time *La Minerve* paid him this tribute: "He was one of the sincere friends of his country's institutions and liberties."

ROBERT TREMBLAY

ANQ-M, CE1-51, 14 juin 1769, 27 nov. 1802; CN1-16, 21 nov. 1802; 25 juill. 1809; 10 févr. 1816; 21, 26 janv., 12 avril 1819; CN1-28, 12 mars, 22 mai 1818; 20 janv., 4 juin 1819; 5 juill. 1823; 7, 15 avril 1824; 5 juill. 1826; 5, 14 mai, 26 oct. 1827; 8 sept. 1837; CN1-68, 23, 30 mai 1809; 8 avril 1811; 28 avril 1813; 14 mai 1814; 3, 26 avril, 6 juin 1815; 23 janv. 1826; CN1-74, 2 août 1802, 1er mars, 20 août, 22 déc. 1803; 24 janv., 11, 15 mai 1804; 1er mars, 26 août, 21 déc. 1805; 23 juill. 1806; 2 juin 1807; 4 juill. 1809; 5 mai 1810; 20 juill. 1811; 7 sept. 1812; 13 févr. 1813; CN1-121, 13 juin 1794, 17 sept. 1803, 20 avril 1804; CN1-134, 27 sept. 1816; 1er, 5, 7, 12, 23 mai, 14 juill., 19, 23 août 1817; CN1-194, 18 juill. 1809; CN1-215, 6 mai 1815; CN1-295, 13 avril 1805, 23 déc. 1807; CN1-313, 19 juill. 1832. MAC-CD, Fonds Morisset, 2, dossier C.-S. Delorme. L.C., *Statutes*, 1832, c.58. *La Minerve*, 15 juin 1837. *Quebec Gazette*, 13 March 1806, 11 Oct. 1819, 5 Oct. 1820, 23 April 1821. André Giroux *et al.*, *Inventaire des marchés de construction des Archives nationales du Québec, à Montréal, 1800–1830* (2v., Ottawa, 1981). Maurault, *Le collège de Montréal* (Dansereau; 1967); *La paroisse: hist. de Notre-Dame de Montréal* (1957). Robert Tremblay, "La nature du procès de travail à Montréal entre 1790 et 1830" (thèse de MA, univ. de Montréal, 1979). Louis Richard, "Jacob DeWitt (1785–1859)," *RHAF*, 3 (1949–50): 537–55.

DÉNÉCHAU, CLAUDE, merchant, militia officer, politician, office holder, and JP; b. 8 March 1768 at Quebec, son of Jacques Dénéchaud*, a surgeon and apothecary, and Angélique Gastonguay; m. 23 June 1800 Marianne-Josette Delorme in Saint-Hyacinthe, Lower Canada, but she died childless the next year; m. secondly 26 May 1807 Adélaïde Gauvreau, daughter of Louis Gauvreau*, at Quebec, and they had a number of children, including three sons and four daughters who reached adulthood; d. 30 Oct. 1836 in Berthier (Berthier-sur-Mer), Lower Canada.

Claude Dénéchau was the twin brother of Charles-Denis, a priest ordained in 1793, who served in the parish of Saint-Joseph at Deschambault. Claude became interested in business at an early age. He formed a partnership with his brother Pierre, and they established themselves at Quebec on Rue de la Fabrique. Then Dénéchau went on his own, entering the import-export trade. His business enabled him to accumulate a good deal of capital rather swiftly. In a few short years he carved an enviable place for himself in Quebec society. The reputation and the confidence he enjoyed brought him an impressive list of responsibilities and offices, including a great many as trustee of estates and guardian for young children of friends and relatives.

In 1811, to mark his success in business and consolidate his commercial endeavours, Dénéchau bought an estate at Berthier for £4,000. In 1813 he took a 29-year lease on the seigneury of Bellechasse, a property owned by the nuns of the Hôpital Général of Quebec. At that time Dénéchau promised to build a communal mill and annually to remit £62 10*s*. and 480 *minots* of wheat to the nuns. To increase the return on his investment, he sought to improve the quality of the wheat grown. His efforts were rewarded in 1818 by the Agriculture Society of the district of Quebec, which awarded him prizes.

Some time after 1813 Dénéchau and his family went to live in the manor-house at Berthier so that he could oversee the development of his land more effectively. They maintained another residence at Quebec. Eager to ameliorate living conditions in his adopted region, Dénéchau went into partnership with Joseph Fraser in 1818 to operate a toll-bridge on the Rivière du Sud and was active in the local agricultural society. He served as commissioner for the summary trial of small causes at Berthier from 1821 till 1829, and for the improvement of communications in Hertford County from 1817 till 1829.

In 1794 Dénéchau had demonstrated his attachment to the crown by signing a declaration of loyalty to the constitution and the government. That year he joined a number of his fellow citizens in presenting an address to Prince Edward* Augustus (later Duke of Kent) on the occasion of his departure for the West Indies; apparently Dénéchau already enjoyed a friendship with him, and their good relations continued until the duke's death in 1820. Dénéchau also signed an address presented to Governor Robert Prescott* when he was recalled to England in 1799.

Because of his loyalty, Dénéchau benefited from government patronage. Thus, in January 1808 he was made a justice of the peace for the district of Quebec, and his commission was renewed periodically until 1830. By virtue of a law dating from 1796, justices of the peace for the districts of Quebec and Montreal were responsible for maintaining and building roads and bridges in their districts, and Dénéchau gave his attention primarily to this aspect of his duties. In 1812 he was empowered to receive the oath of allegiance. Two years later he was appointed commissioner for the relief of the insane and foundlings, and in 1818 he was entrusted with overseeing additions and repairs to the Hôpital Général of Quebec.

In January 1800 Dénéchau had become a freemason and member of St Paul's Lodge in Montreal. That year he joined Merchants' Lodge No.40 at Quebec. This association with masonry was rather an unusual step for a French Canadian, since it often led to exclusion from communion and in effect ostracism by compatriots. His action may have stemmed from his desire to make a name for himself and to succeed in the business world, which was largely controlled by the British merchants and authorities. He was sponsored by the Duke of Kent and rose rapidly in this secret organization. Treasurer of the Provincial Grand Lodge of Lower Canada in 1801, he was made grand senior warden, the third highest officer in the lodge, five years later. In 1812 he became its grand master, and in 1820 provincial grand master for the districts of Quebec and Trois-Rivières. In this capacity he was present at the laying of the foundation stone of the monument dedicated in 1827 by Governor Lord Dalhousie [RAMSAY] to James Wolfe* and Louis-Joseph de Montcalm*.

As a prominent citizen of Quebec, Dénéchau became involved in the town's social, economic, and cultural life, assuming a host of duties and offices in numerous societies and organizations. For example, from 1801 to at least 1820 he was involved in the Quebec Fire Society, of which he was secretary-treasurer from 1803 till 1805 and president in 1808. From 1805 to 1807 he was secretary-treasurer of the Union Company of Quebec, a joint-stock company founded in 1805 by some businessmen from the region to finance the purchase and refitting of the Union Hotel on Rue Sainte-Anne. This establishment rapidly became a select place for social events at Quebec; the freemasons held many meetings there. From 1811 till 1829 Dénéchau was a member of the commission to supervise the House of Correction for the district of Quebec. In 1813 he subscribed to the Loyal and Patriotic Society of the Province of Lower Canada, which aided wounded militiamen. Two years later he contributed to the Waterloo Fund, set up to help the families of men killed or wounded in the great battle. He was president in 1816 and vice-president in 1818 of the Quebec Benevolent Society, which had been founded in 1789 to establish a fund for the assistance of needy members.

Dénéchau was involved in the cause of education. In 1815 he acted as secretary-treasurer of a committee for its advancement in all classes of society, especially among the poor. That year he was treasurer of a committee working to get a free school opened in Upper Town. He was a member of the British and Canadian School Society of the District of Quebec [*see* Joseph-François PERRAULT] from 1829 to 1832.

Yielding to the entreaties of his circle, Dénéchau in 1808 had stood against Jean-Antoine Panet* for election to the House of Assembly in the riding of Upper Town Quebec. With the backing of the English party, and in particular of Pierre-Amable De Bonne* and Perrault, he was elected. He represented the riding until 29 May 1820. Members of the assembly did not at that time receive a salary, but Dénéchau had a large personal income. He participated regularly and actively in debates, meetings of all sorts, and parliamentary committees. Among the many questions on which he took a stand was Panet's appointment as speaker of the house in 1809, and his opposition to it is worth noting. That year and in 1810, he voted against making judges ineligible to sit in the house [*see* Pierre-Amable De Bonne]. In 1811 he served on a committee studying the bill to establish a workhouse in Montreal. Seven years later he fought against Denis-Benjamin Viger*'s motion to pay the costs of travel by members coming to attend sessions of the house.

Along with his activities as a businessman and politician, Dénéchau held important posts in the militia. In 1804 he was a lieutenant in Quebec's 1st Militia Battalion. Three years later he received a captaincy. He held that rank at the beginning of the War of 1812, and was transferred to the 6th Select Embodied Militia Battalion of Lower Canada on 20 March 1813. On 17 March 1814 he was appointed deputy paymaster in the Army Bill Office [*see* James Green*]. On 10 April 1826 Dalhousie made him a major in the 1st Militia Battalion of Quebec County. Dénéchau reached the summit of his military career when he became lieutenant-colonel of the 6th Battalion of Saint-Roch militia on 9 Sept. 1828.

Beginning in 1829 or 1830 Dénéchau gave up his numerous judicial, administrative, and military duties one by one. Now over 60, he left Quebec, which faced the threat of epidemics, and went to join his family at the manor-house in Berthier. The last years of his life were marked by great upheavals. He suffered serious financial reverses, probably attributable to a combination of political changes, poor harvests in 1832–36, bad debts, and also, according to several contemporaries, his own excessive generosity.

Dénéchau died on 30 Oct. 1836, succumbing to a massive stroke. A few months before, he had withdrawn from freemasonry because of the insistence of his family, in particular his brother Charles-Denis, and of the parish priest of Berthier, and perhaps also because he was tired of ostracism by his contemporaries. Having recently returned to the church, he was entitled to receive the last rites and the honours befitting his rank and he was buried in the church at Berthier.

Claude Dénéchau left an insolvent and encumbered estate which his widow and children decided to renounce. As well, Mme Dénéchau gave up her claims to the community of property stipulated in her marriage contract, but she retained her own property. She had to restore the seigneury of Bellechasse to the nuns of the Hôpital Général in 1838, before the lease had expired, and she sold the Berthier estate, mill, and manor-house a few years later. Despite this discouraging financial situation, all her children received an excellent education, went into leading professions, and made advantageous marriages.

YVES BEAUREGARD

ANQ-Q, CE1-1, 8 mars 1768, 26 mai 1807; CE2-2, 3 nov. 1836; CN1-205, 8 juill. 1813; CN1-212, 1er déc. 1836, 28 juin 1838; CN1-230, 8 juill. 1813; CN1-253, 1er mars 1826; CN1-262, 11 oct. 1811. PAC, RG 68, General index, 1651–1841. "Les dénombrements de Québec" (Plessis), ANQ *Rapport*, 1948–49: 159. L.C., House of Assembly, *Journals*, 1811, 1818. *Recensement de Québec, 1818* (Provost). *Le Canadien*, 10 janv., 13, 17 juin 1807; 24 janv., 4, 14 mars 1810; 14, 28 mars, 4 avril, 9 déc. 1818; 6 janv. 1819; 20 sept. 1820; 31 mars 1824; 29 mars 1833; 18 avril 1834; 25 nov. 1835; 2 nov. 1836. *La Gazette de Québec*, 1794–1836. *Quebec Mercury*, 30 March 1805. F.-J. Audet, "Les législateurs du Bas-Canada." Desjardins, *Guide parl. Officers of British forces in Canada* (Irving). *Quebec almanac*, 1804–32. *Quebec directory*, 1790–91, 1826. P.-G. Roy, *Inv. concessions*, vols.2, 5; *Fils de Québec*, 2: 141–43. M.-J. et George Ahern, *Notes pour servir à l'histoire de la médecine dans le Bas-Canada depuis la fondation de Québec jusqu'au commencement du XIXe siècle* (Québec, 1923), 148–50. [E. Dénéchaud], *Biographie de la famille Dénéchaud* (Québec, 1895). Bernard Dufebvre [Émile Castonguay], *Journal d'un bourgeois de Québec* (Québec, [1960]), 246–47. George Gale, *Historic tales of old Quebec* (Quebec, 1923), 109. J. H. Graham, *Outlines of the history of freemasonry in the province of Quebec* (Montreal, 1892). P.-G. Roy, *La famille Panet* (Lévis, Qué., 1906). Sulte, *Hist. de la milice*. E. Dénéchaud, "Claude Denechaud," *BRH*, 8 (1902): 271–74. Ignotus [Thomas Chapais], "Le monument Wolfe et Montcalm à Québec," *BRH*, 5 (1899): 305–9. Eugène Rouillard, "Les premiers francs-maçons canadiens," *BRH*, 4 (1898): 188–90. P.-G. Roy, "La seigneurie de Bellechasse ou Berthier," *BRH*, 27 (1921): 65–74.

DENIS, PIERRE, Malecite; fl. 1837–41 in New Brunswick.

A Malecite named Pierdeney is mentioned by schoolmaster Frederick Dibblee* as having visited his establishment at Meductic (near present-day Meductic), N.B., some time in 1788 or 1789. On Dibblee's list of visitors his name is preceded by that of Joseph Pierdeney with a wife and five children, and it is reasonable to assume that he was an unmarried adult still living with his parents. He received three pounds of powder and three of flint from Dibblee, who hoped that presents given to Indians calling at the school would encourage them to let their children attend.

It is possible that this Pierdeney was the Pierre Denis mentioned in the account by New Brunswick's commissioner of Indian affairs, Moses Henry Perley*, of a visit to the province's Indian reserves in 1841. Pierre Denis had done what people such as Dibblee had tried to get Indians to do. He had settled down, built himself a frame-house, cleared an area of land, and become a subsistence farmer. Some years later the authorities gave a licence of occupation for this land, on the Saint Basile Indian Reserve, to a white man, Simon Hébert. Denis was not pleased that his farm and the small house in which he had been living comfortably had been leased to another, and he initially refused to give up possession. Finally Hébert was ordered to pay Denis $50, the appraised value of the house, and upon promise of payment Denis left Saint Basile in 1837 and moved to the Tobique Indian Reserve. There Perley met him in 1841, "an old man, childless, and in poor circumstances." Perley asked that the government insist on payment of the $50 still owing. Denis is not listed in the census return of June 1841 for Saint Basile or Tobique, and nothing more is known about him.

Of conditions at Tobique, Perley wrote: "The Indians . . . subsist in great measure by the chase, by occasional employment in lumbering, and in piloting rafts down the Tobique and the Saint John. They seem by no means inclined to continue labor, or the cultivation of the soil – yet, from the advantages of their situation, and the value of the Salmon Fishery, they have rather comfortable dwellings, and appear in easy circumstances as compared with others of the Tribe." Pierre Denis's mistake was in adapting to the expectations of the whites too well, too early, and in the wrong community. Had he originally settled at Tobique, where property was not so avidly sought after by whites and where resources suitable for carrying out traditional subsistence pursuits were more abundant, he likely could have lived his final years in contentment.

VINCENT O. ERICKSON

N.B. Museum, W. F. Ganong papers, box 38, return of Indian families at the entrance of the little Madawaska River; Antoine Gosselin, return of Indian families at the entrance of the Tobique River, 18 June 1841. N.B., House of Assembly, *Journal*, 1842, app.: xcii–cxxvi. *Source materials relating to N.B. Indian* (Hamilton and Spray). *Royal Gazette* (Fredericton), 16 April 1842. W. O. Raymond, "The old Meductic fort," N.B. Hist. Soc., *Coll.*, 1 (1894–97), no.2: 221–72.

DENKE (Denkey), CHRISTIAN FREDERICK, Moravian missionary; b. 8 Sept. 1775 in Bethlehem, Pa, son of Jeremiah Dencke and Sara Test; m. first 7 Aug. 1803 Anna Maria Heckedorn in Lititz, Pa; m. secondly 12 Sept. 1828 Maria Steiner; d. 12 Jan. 1838 in Salem (Winston-Salem), N.C.

A native of Langenbielau (Bielawa, Poland), Christian Frederick Denke's father was a prominent Moravian minister in Bethlehem, a major Moravian settlement and centre of missionary activity. At ten years of age Christian entered Nazareth Hall, the Moravian academy at Nazareth, Pa, where his studies included Latin and other languages, theology, management, and also botany in which he took a special interest. He sent many letters and botanical specimens to the noted American botanist Gotthilf Henry Ernest Mühlenberg, first from Nazareth Hall, where Denke became a teacher, and later from Upper Canada until the War of 1812 rendered correspondence impossible.

While teaching, Denke, a deeply religious young man, felt a call to preach to the Indians and in Nazareth he heard David Zeisberger* tell about the Delaware mission at Fairfield in Upper Canada, near present-day Thamesville, and of plans to extend missionary work to the nearby Chippewas. Being a linguist, Denke might learn the Delaware and Chippewa languages in order to translate and to preach to the Indians in their own tongues. On 27 April 1800 he was ordained a deacon and was on his way to the mission fields with John Heckewelder. At Goshen (near Gnadenhutten, Ohio), he received instruction in the Delaware dialect from Zeisberger before leaving for Fairfield. For several years Denke attempted to work with the semi-nomadic Chippewas in their temporary villages on Big Bear Creek (Sydenham River) and the St Clair River. In 1806 Denke and his wife, unsuccessful in their efforts to convert the Chippewas, returned permanently to Fairfield, where they would give years of valuable service in missionary work and education.

The War of 1812 brought disaster to Fairfield. Committed to pacifism, Denke and his partner, John Schnall, tried to keep their Indians neutral but some joined the British forces. Following the battle of Moraviantown on 5 Oct. 1813 [*see* Henry Procter*], the Americans burned Fairfield, "putting the first torch to the Moravian Church." The Schnalls returned to Bethlehem leaving the Denkes to lead the Indians to a safe place near Burlington Heights (Hamilton).

For two years the Denkes, unable to communicate with Bethlehem, took full charge of the Indians, with some assistance from the Upper Canadian government. In their winter camp near Dundas there were 183 people at the end of 1813. The following spring they moved to Nelson Township. Denke also ministered to the spiritual needs of the whites in the area. In late June 1814 he began attending the eight men condemned to death for treason at the Ancaster "Bloody Assizes" [*see* Jacob Overholser*], staying with them day and night until their execution on 20 July.

On 8 May 1815 the Denkes and their converts started their return to Fairfield, a journey of 18 days on foot for the Indians. Besides overseeing the building of a new church and village, called New Fairfield, on the other side of the Thames River, Denke took on responsibilities on behalf of the region's other settlers. As a member of a committee representing six townships, he prepared pages of information for Robert Gourlay*'s *Statistical account*. From this source it is evident that Denke and the other missionaries encouraged the practice of a strict moral code while discouraging a number of traditional customs. "Other Indians have vermilion from government to paint their bodies; but the Moravians are forbidden to practise this."

Denke's health was undermined by the troubles and responsibilities of the war and reconstruction, and he developed a drinking problem. John Schnall came back to replace him in November 1818, at which time Denke, with his wife, returned to Bethlehem for rest. After two years they accepted a call to Hope Church, in the Salem area of North Carolina, and subsequently they served in Salem and nearby Friedberg. In 1828 Anna Maria Denke died at Friedberg. Three years later Denke and his second wife retired to Salem, where he died in 1838.

LESLIE R. GRAY

According to the "Memoir of the married Brother *Christian Friedrich Denke*, who went peacefully to sleep in Salem on Jan. 12, 1838," in the Moravian Arch. (Winston-Salem, N.C.), Denke published a small primer in the Chippewa language, but this has not been located. He is believed, as well, to have written a dictionary which has been published as *A Lenâpé-English dictionary; from an anonymous MS. in the archives of the Moravian Church at Bethlehem, Pa.*, ed. D. G. Brinton and A. S. Anthony (Philadelphia, 1888). Among Denke's religious works is his Delaware translation of *The three Epistles of the Apostle John* ... (New York, 1818).

American Philosophical Soc. (Philadelphia), G. H. E. Mühlenberg, corr. from C. F. Denke, 1798–1811, including "Index floræ Nazarathanæ. . . ." Moravian Arch. (Bethlehem, Pa.), Church diaries; Indian mission records, C. F. Denke, report of first visit among the Tschipues [Chippewas], June 1801; report of new Tschipue Mission, September 1802–March 1803; Fairfield Mission, boxes A–C. R. B. McAfee, "The McAfee papers: book and journal of Robt. B. McAfee's mounted company, in Col. Richard M. Johnson's regiment . . . ," Ky. State Hist. Soc., *Reg.* (Frankfort), 26 (1928): 128–29. *Statistical account of U.C.* (Gourlay; ed. Mealing; 1974), 141–42. Elizabeth Graham, *Medicine man to missionary: missionaries as agents of change among the Indians of southern Ontario, 1784–1867* (Toronto, 1975). E. E. [Lawson] Gray and L. R. Gray, *Wilderness Christians: the Moravian mission to the Delaware Indians* (Toronto and Ithaca, N.Y., 1956). E. E. [Lawson] Gray, "A missionary venture on the St. Clair," Moravian Hist. Soc., *Trans.* (Nazareth, Pa.), 14 (1951): 341–49. L. R. Gray, "The Moravian missionaries, their Indians, and the Canadian government," CHA *Report*, 1955: 96–104.

DENOON (Dunoon), HUGH, merchant, office holder, JP, judge, and emigrant contractor; b. 18 Sept. 1762, probably in the parish of Killearnan, near Redcastle, Scotland, eldest child of David Denoon and Mary Inglis; m. Catherine Fraser, and they had at least one son; d. 24 March 1836 in Pictou, N.S.

Hugh Denoon was born into an established Highland family and should have followed in the paternal footsteps by attending university in Aberdeen and entering the Church of Scotland ministry. Instead, his younger brother went to Aberdeen and eventually succeeded his father, and Hugh went off to Halifax. After engaging in business there he went to the Pictou area, took up land on the East River as early as 1784, and later lived in Merigomish, where he acquired land rights from former members of the 82nd Foot. He subsequently moved to a house about one mile south of the town centre of Pictou, gradually acquiring a number of offices, including collector of customs, deputy registrar of deeds, justice of the peace, and judge of the Court of Common Pleas, and engaging in mercantile activity.

Most of Denoon's adult life was spent in respectable obscurity in Pictou, but at the beginning of the 19th century he acquired a certain notoriety in his native land as the first and most detested of the contractors transporting emigrants from Scotland to North America in the wave of emigration between 1801 and 1803. His undertakings were not only widely known and criticized in Scotland, but made a direct contribution to remedial parliamentary legislation, which ostensibly attempted to prevent abuses of the sort Denoon was held to have perpetrated in 1801. Separating fact from fiction in Denoon's emigration ventures is no easy matter, for facts have always had a tendency to become embellished into mythology among Highlanders, and Hugh Denoon rapidly became a legendary villain for lairds and emigrants alike.

Denoon's emigrant contracting was first noticed in Scotland in early March 1801, when it was reported that he had come lately from America to recruit emigrants, and that he proposed to secure vessels to transport them in May. Opponents of emigration were unable to gain any support from the Customs Board to arrest the scheme, but a leading Inverness attorney advised an official at Fort William that Denoon's two ships could be inspected for proper accommodation and provisions and denied clearance if these were not adequate. When consulted, Scotland's lord advocate, Charles Hope, expressed the opinion that "there is no Law for keeping the People in the Country against their Will," although he was prepared to advise the board not to clear vessels until passenger lists were supplied and there was evidence that provisions were adequate for the voyage. Denoon duly handed in his lists, showing for the 350-ton *Sarah of Liverpool* 199 passengers over 16 and 151 children, and for the 186-ton *Dove of Aberdeen* 149 passengers over 16 and 60 children: a total of 559. Negotiations then ensued between Denoon and the board concerning a formula for converting the number of children under 16 into "full" passengers. The board, convinced by Denoon's arguments that his ships were carrying 428 full passengers, decided that the provisions, which the emigrants themselves had supplied, and the space were adequate, and cleared the vessels.

The ships set sail in June and almost everything that could possibly go wrong on the passage did so. The 13-week voyage was an exceptionally long one, and smallpox broke out among the passengers. According to one contemporary account, 39 children under ten died. Off the coast of Newfoundland one of the vessels was boarded by a press-gang from the Royal Navy and a number of young men were taken off; Denoon somehow persuaded the senior naval officer to release them. In Pictou, the arrivals were put in quarantine and, unable to work, they had to be relieved by a public subscription fund. They eventually settled satisfactorily into the community, however.

Denoon's venture raised enormous controversy. In its first report on emigration, issued in January 1802, the Highland Society of Edinburgh produced an allegation, never proved, that after customs officers had inspected Denoon's vessels and pronounced themselves satisfied with the two tiers of berths and the ten feet of exercise space between them, he removed a platform hiding a third tier for passengers who were to be collected after customs clearance. The society also produced a devastating critique of the method used to determine numbers aboard Denoon's vessels, comparing the results with the maximum number of passengers allowed by the slave trade legislation passed a few years earlier. By the least restrictive method, to which the society thought the Highlanders were entitled, the *Sarah of Liverpool* and the *Dove of Aberdeen* would have been allowed only 355 passengers. The society insisted that it did not wish to compare fellow Scots with slaves, but its calculations were electrifying and the implications clear. This evidence was one of the principal arguments used by a parliamentary committee in 1803 in support of its regulatory legislation (43 Geo. III, c.56).

Denoon represented an increasing trend for emigrant contractors to view their passengers merely as cargo, and to exhibit no concern for their welfare once they had been transported to and disembarked in North America. Aggravating the problems facing passengers was the growing demand in Britain at this time for timber from British North America. Within only a few years of Denoon's venture most contractors were timber merchants filling vessels with human cargo rather than with ballast for the return journey. The legislation he helped provoke may have improved conditions on board ship, but at the same time it hampered emigration by enabling the government to harass contractors and by raising fares. After 1815 Britain no longer sought to limit emigration. In 1817 a new statute (57 Geo. III, c.10) was passed superseding the previous legislation.

Although Denoon's return to the Highlands for more passengers was often rumoured, he apparently had had enough, and there is no evidence he ever again engaged in the transatlantic emigrant trade. His venture contributed not only to the British regulation of 1803, but also to the substantial influx of Highlanders to the Pictou region in the early years of the 19th century. After his brief appearance in the public spotlight Denoon returned to his former commercial activities. When he died he left over £7,000 of uncollected small debts.

J. M. BUMSTED

GRO (Edinburgh), Killearnan, reg. of births and baptisms, 19 Sept. 1762. NLS, Dept. of MSS, MS 9646 ([E. S. Fraser of Rilig], "On Emigration from the Scottish Highlands and Isles," 1802), 32–33. Pictou County Court of Probate (Pictou, N.S.), Loose estate papers, no.225 (mfm. at PANS). PRO, HO 102/18, pt.I: ff.53–54, 72, 78 (copies at SRO). Royal Highland and Agricultural Soc. of Scotland (Ingliston, Scot.), Sederunt books, III: 475–87. SRO, GD248/3410/10; 248/3416/3. G.B., Parl., House of Commons paper, 1802–3, 4, no.80: 1–14, *First report from the committee on the survey of the coasts &c. of Scotland: emigration*, 9. *Bee* (Pictou), 30 March 1836. *Novascotian, or Colonial Herald*, 6 April 1836, 22 Nov. 1838. *N.S. vital statistics, 1823–28* (Holder); *1835–39* (Holder). Scott *et al.*, *Fasti ecclesiæ scoticanæ*, vol.7. J. M. Bumsted, *The people's clearance: Highland emigration to British North America, 1770–1815* (Edinburgh and Winnipeg, 1982). George Patterson, *A history of the county of Pictou, Nova Scotia* (Montreal, 1877; repr. Belleville, Ont., 1972), 159–60, 226–28.

DENTREMONT. *See* ENTREMONT

DESJARDINS, *dit* **DESPLANTES, LOUIS-JOSEPH,** Roman Catholic priest and missionary; b. 19 March 1766 in Messas, France, son of Jacques Desjardins de Lapérière, a merchant, and Marie-Anne Baudet; d. 30 Aug. 1848 at Quebec.

Louis-Joseph Desjardins, *dit* Desplantes, studied in France at the Petit Séminaire de Meung-sur-Loire and at the Séminaire Saint-Martin in Paris; on 20 March 1790 he was ordained priest in Bayeux. During the revolution he and his brother Philippe-Jean-Louis* were imprisoned and threatened with death, as were many of their fellow priests who refused to take the oath to the Civil Constitution of the Clergy, which the Constituent Assembly required from 1 Oct. 1791. By good luck they managed to escape and cross to England late in the summer of 1792.

In 1794, abandoning all hope of returning to his native land in the near future, Desjardins resigned himself to joining his brother, who had emigrated to Lower Canada the year before. He reached Quebec in June, along with Jean-Denis Daulé*, Jean-Baptiste-Marie Castanet*, and François-Gabriel Le Courtois*. After serving as assistant priest to Joseph-Octave Plessis*, the parish priest of Quebec, in 1795 he agreed to a proposal from Bishop Jean-François Hubert* of Quebec that he and Abbé Castanet go to serve in the settlements scattered along the shores of Baie des Chaleurs, replacing Joseph-Mathurin Bourg*. The missionaries left on 21 July, at the same time as Hubert set out on a pastoral visit with Philippe-Jean-Louis, who had been made vicar general.

The two young priests were not prepared for the exhausting ministry that apostolic zeal had led them to choose. Castanet soon ruined his already delicate health and returned to Quebec, where he died on 26 Aug. 1798. Desjardins held on for three more years. He won the esteem and affection of those to whom he ministered, as is evident from a letter written in 1801 by his successor at Baie des Chaleurs, René-Pierre Joyer, to Plessis, the bishop of Quebec: "Everywhere I have been aware of people who greatly miss – and with reason – M. Desjardins, for whom I am but a pale substitute." According to Joyer, what the region needed was "a man of as amiable a nature as M. Desjardins." After his recall in 1801 Desjardins was assistant priest, and then priest, of the parish of Notre-Dame at Quebec until 15 Oct. 1807. Plessis then appointed him chaplain to the nuns of the Hôtel-Dieu in Quebec. He was also superior of the Ursulines of Quebec from 1825 till 1833.

Desjardins accompanied Plessis on his first pastoral visit to the Maritimes in the summer of 1811. It was he who organized the practical details of the trip, and in 1812 and 1815 he again looked after preparations for the bishop's visits to that part of his immense diocese. Subsequently Desjardins continued to give many missionaries moral and financial support. "I have so much writing and calculating to do," he observed in 1830, "that I scarcely know how to manage: my relations with the missions have always been a heavy burden for me."

His brother Philippe-Jean-Louis had returned to France in 1802, and in 1817 sent him nearly 200 religious pictures to make available to parishes and communities in the diocese of Quebec. Louis-Joseph conscientiously carried out his task, which led to his becoming friends with the painters Antoine Plamondon* and Joseph Légaré* and some of their pupils. He commissioned works from them and on several occasions entrusted them with touching up paintings and making copies of them. Furthermore, the Ursuline annals relate that "M. Desjardins was not satisfied with simple encouragement; through subscriptions among the clergy and his friends he obtained passage to Europe for his protégés, trying in all respects to encourage application and talent."

In 1836 age and disabilities, including a sprain

suffered in 1824 that kept him on crutches, forced Desjardins to tender his resignation as chaplain of the Hôtel-Dieu. To show their gratitude the nuns let him have the use of his rooms until his death in August 1848. He was buried in the convent chapel. Tributes to him were unanimous in their praise of his goodness of heart, gentleness, and graciousness, and his kindly, unfailing charity.

NOËL BAILLARGEON

AAQ, 311 CN, V: 150–68; VI: 4–6, 12, 19. Arch. du monastère de l'Hôtel-Dieu de Québec, Fonds L.-J. Desjardins, t.4, c.600, nos.1–5 . Arch. du monastère des ursulines (Québec), Fonds L.-J. Desjardins; Fonds P.-J.-L. Desjardins. ASQ, Fonds Viger–Verreau, sér.O, 085–86. "Quelques prêtres français en exil au Canada," ANQ *Rapport*, 1966: 141–90. *La Minerve*, 13 févr. 1834. Caron, "Inv. de la corr. de Mgr Hubert et de Mgr Bailly de Messein," ANQ *Rapport*, 1930–31. Barthe, *Souvenirs d'un demi-siècle*. Burke, *Les ursulines de Québec*, vol.4. Dionne, *Les ecclésiastiques et les royalistes français*.

DES RIVIÈRES, RODOLPHE (baptized **Michel-Rodolphe Trottier Des Rivières Beaubien**; he went by the name Rodolphe Des Rivières Beaubien or Rodolphe Des Rivières and signed R. Des Rivières or R. DesRivières), Patriote and merchant; b. 5 May 1812 and baptized four days later in Lac-des-Deux-Montagnes (Oka), Lower Canada, son of Pierre-Charles-Robert Trottier Des Rivières Beaubien and Henriette Pillet; d. probably unmarried 17 March 1847 and was buried three days later in Montreal.

The Trottier Des Rivières Beaubien family had experienced a decline as a result of the keen competition from British merchants that forced them to abandon the fur trade in the late 1780s. When Rodolphe was born in 1812, his father was running a retail business at Lac-des-Deux-Montagnes that he had probably inherited from his own father, Eustache-Ignace*. It is not known whether Rodolphe did any classical studies or whether his father took him into his establishment to teach him the rudiments of business. He certainly received some training, since he was working as a bookkeeper with the Banque du Peuple [*see* Louis-Michel Viger*] at Montreal in 1837.

Energetic and aggressive by nature, Rodolphe became interested in politics at an early age. In 1837 he joined a group of young Montreal Patriotes who were active in Louis-Joseph Papineau*'s party and frequented Édouard-Raymond Fabre*'s bookshop. That summer he distinguished himself in an exploit recounted in the memoirs of his brother, Adélard-Isidore. One evening Rodolphe and several friends attended a theatrical performance in Montreal at which the audience was largely British. When the orchestra played "God save the Queen," the young men remained seated and kept their hats on. "Hats off! Hats off!" the cry went up on all sides, but the Patriotes paid no attention. Some of the military officers and civil functionaries present took offence and wanted to throw them out of the theatre. The handful of Canadians had no choice but to leave. Des Rivières, one of the last to go, was punched on the nape of the neck. Turning around, he recognized Dr Jones, a British army surgeon. A couple of days later he sought out his assailant on Rue Notre-Dame and demanded an apology, which Jones refused to give him. Thereupon he fearlessly tackled Jones, a 6-foot 3-inch colossus weighing 230 pounds, and gave him a real thrashing.

Des Rivières participated on 5 Sept. 1837 in the meeting held at the Nelson Hotel to found the Fils de la Liberté [*see* André Ouimet*]. His great popularity and reputation for courage were factors in his appointment two weeks later as leader of section no.6 of the association's military wing, under command of General Thomas Storrow Brown*. On 4 October he was one of the 44 people signing the "Adresse des Fils de la liberté de Montréal, aux jeunes gens des colonies de l'Amérique du Nord." He had the complete confidence of Brown, who invited him to assist him in putting 600–1,200 of the members through manœuvres at Côte à Baron on 22 October. According to historian Gérard Filteau, Des Rivières attended the Assemblée des Six Comtés at Saint-Charles-sur-Richelieu the following day. On 6 November he participated in the stormy meeting of the Fils de la Liberté held in Montreal, and in the ensuing street fights that day he took on some members of the Doric Club.

To escape the warrant for his arrest that Governor Lord Gosford [ACHESON] was on the point of issuing, Des Rivières left Montreal on the night of 15 November and went to Varennes. He met Brown there, and the two moved on to Saint-Charles-sur-Richelieu. Reaching the village on 18 November, Des Rivières was then one of the group of Patriotes who seized the manor-house of Pierre-Dominique DEBARTZCH. Afterwards, along with the local Patriote leaders Siméon Marchesseault* and Jean-Philippe Boucher-Belleville*, he began setting up a fortified camp. The next day Brown proceeded to organize a military company and Des Rivières was made colonel. According to John Edward Raymo (Raymond), a cabinet-maker from Saint-Charles-sur-Richelieu, whose statement was taken down on 21 November, Des Rivières, acting as seigneurial agent, had issued receipts for the grain to be requisitioned from ten local habitants. Merchant Simon Talon Lespérance, a justice of the peace at La Présentation who was kept in detention by the Patriotes from 22 to 24 November, declared that "a detachment of brigands, with Rodolphe Dérivieres, [a] leader of the Fils de la Liberté, at the head . . . seized . . . five thousand *minots* of grain . . . my horses, [and] ten fat pigs that were slaughtered, cut up, and carried off to the camp at St Charles."

On 23 November Des Rivières and his brother Adélard-Isidore reached Saint-Denis on the Richelieu just as the battle there began. He helped Wolfred Nelson*'s supporters harass the retreating British soldiers. Two days later he was back again at Saint-Charles-sur-Richelieu and just prior to the engagement there was given command of a Patriote brigade and ordered to take up a position on a wooded hill near the camp so as to mount an attack on the enemy's flank at the right moment. When Lieutenant-Colonel George Augustus Wetherall* and his troops had advanced to within musket range, Des Rivières and his men opened a sustained fire. They held their position until Wetherall sent a company of grenadiers against them. Outnumbered, they scattered and hid in the woods.

After this defeat Des Rivières took refuge at Saint-Denis. On 29 November a price was set on his head, a reward of £100 being offered to anyone who turned him in. Two days later he fled towards the United States with Nelson and a few other Patriotes. On 7 December, however, he was arrested at Bedford along with Boucher-Belleville, Marchesseault, Timothée Kimber*, and one or two others. Des Rivières was incarcerated at Fort Lennox, on Île aux Noix, and then on 12 December was taken to the Montreal jail in a group that included Marchesseault and Robert-Shore-Milnes Bouchette*. On 26 June 1838, in return for a promised amnesty for all the political prisoners, he and seven other Patriotes agreed to sign an admission of guilt. Because of this imprudent act he was condemned to exile two days later by the terms of the proclamation issued by Lord Durham [LAMBTON]. On 4 July he left Quebec aboard the frigate *Vestal* and on 28 July he landed at Hamilton, Bermuda.

Released on 26 Oct. 1838 because Lord Durham's decree had been repudiated, Des Rivières set sail for the United States. Upon reaching American soil on 9 November, he did not seek to return immediately to Lower Canada, as did most other exiles. After the failure of the second rebellion he chose to settle in New York, where he turned to the business world. He made contact with a wealthy New York merchant named Dempsey, who took him into his firm as a partner, doubtless because of his business sense and integrity. It may have been as agent for this establishment that Des Rivières made a trip in 1842 lasting more than eight months which, according to Ægidius Fauteux*, took him to England, Italy, and France. Back in the United States, in 1843 and 1844 he intended, according to Louis-Joseph-Amédée Papineau*, to marry Dempsey's sister or daughter, but no trace of a marriage has been discovered. Shortly after the Société des Amis was founded in Montreal in November 1844 [*see* Guillaume Lévesque*], Des Rivières joined it as a corresponding member in New York.

Rodolphe Des Rivières did not return to Lower Canada until after November 1844. He set himself up as a merchant in Montreal under the name of DesRivières et Dempsey. He died on 17 March 1847 of a liver ailment, aged only 34, "just when he was beginning to attain new heights and prosperity in business," according to *La Minerve*. On 6 Dec. 1848 a large number of his friends gathered at the Catholic cemetery in Montreal to raise a magnificent marble tombstone on his grave bearing, along with other inscriptions, the words "A political exile to Bermuda in June 1838." The memory of an intrepid and generous Patriote had been honoured.

MICHEL DE LORIMIER

A portrait in crayons of Rodolphe Des Rivières, done while he was in the Montreal prison in 1837–38 by Jean-Joseph Girouard*, is at the PAC.

ANQ-M, CE1-51, 20 mars 1847; CE6-3, 9 mai 1812. ANQ-Q, E17/6, nos.1–2, 14, 18, 22; E17/9, nos.291, 352, 354–55; E17/15, nos.857–58a, 869; E17/37, no.3020; E17/39, no.3150; E17/51, no.4145; E17/52, no.6; P-409; P-417/11, no.1037; 13, nos.1113, 1141. BVM-G, Fonds Ægidius Fauteux, notes compilées par Ægidius Fauteux sur les patriotes de 1837–38 dont les noms commencent par la lettre D, carton 4. PAC, MG 24, B2, 17–21. Univ. of B.C. Library (Vancouver), Special Coll. Division, Rodolphe Des Rivières corr. R.-S.-M. Bouchette, *Mémoires de Robert-S.-M. Bouchette, 1805–1840* (Montréal, 1903), 56–60, 69–115. T. S. Brown, *1837: my connection with it* (Quebec, 1898), 16–37. A.-I. Des Rivières, "Insurection de 1837: mémoires inédites laissées par feu le docteur Adélard-Isidore Des Rivières, l'un des Fils de la liberté," *La Patrie*, 12 mars 1898: 8. "Documents inédits," Yvon Thériault, édit., *RHAF*, 16 (1962–63): 117–26, 436–40. L.-J.-A. Papineau, *Journal d'un Fils de la liberté*. *La Minerve*, 28 août, 7 sept., 5, 9 oct., 9 nov. 1837; 18, 22 mars 1847; 7 déc. 1848. Fauteux, *Patriotes*, 27–28, 38–39, 56–61, 145–46, 210–12. Tanguay, *Dictionnaire*, 7: 353–60.

Anecdotes canadiennes suivies de mœurs, coutumes et industries d'autrefois; mots historiques, miettes de l'histoire, É.-Z. Massicotte, compil. ([2e éd.], Montréal, 1925), 107–8. Jean Béraud, *350 ans de théâtre au Canada français* (Ottawa, 1958), 34. Hector Berthelot, *Montréal, le bon vieux temps*, É.-Z. Massicotte, compil. (2e éd., 2v. en 1, Montréal, 1924), 1: 47–48. J. D. Borthwick, *Jubilé de diamant; rébellion de 37–38; précis complet de cette période; rôle d'honneur ou liste complète des patriotes détenus dans les prisons de Montréal en 1837–1838–1839; date et lieux des arrestations et autres détails intéressants et inédits sur ce sujet* (Montréal, 1898), 36, 89–91. Chapais, *Cours d'hist. du Canada*, 4: 196, 206. Christie, *Hist. of L.C.* (1866). L.-O. David, *Les gerbes canadiennes* (Montréal, 1921), 163; *Patriotes*, 13–20, 37–42, 65–71, 137–40. Ægidius Fauteux, *Le duel au Canada* (Montréal, 1934), 225–31. Filteau, *Hist. des patriotes* (1975), 117, 207–8, 244, 271–76, 301–9, 336–41, 348–49, 390–93. F.-X. Garneau, *Histoire du Canada depuis sa découverte jusqu'à nos jours*, Hector Garneau, édit. (8e éd., 9v., Montréal, 1944–46), 9: 97–98. Laurin, *Girouard & les patriotes*, 51. É.-Z. Massicotte, *Faits curieux de l'histoire de Montréal* (2e éd., Montréal, 1924), 86–96. Rumilly, *Hist. de Montréal*, 2: 228, 243; *Papineau et son temps*. Mason Wade, *Les Canadiens français, de 1760 à nos jours*, Adrien Venne et Francis Dufau-Labeyrie, trad. (2e éd., 2v., Ottawa, 1966), 1: 194–95. Montarville Boucher de La Bruère, "Louis-Joseph Papineau, de Saint-Denis à Paris," *Cahiers des Dix*, 5 (1940): 79–106. Émile Chartier, "Après 'L'affaire de Saint-Denis,' 1er–12 décembre 1837, d'après un mémoire de Brown," *BRH*, 56 (1950): 130–47. Claude Faribault, "Un atlas de Napoléon 1er, Notre-Dame de Stanbridge et la famille DesRivières," SGCF *Mémoires*, 33 (1982): 26–29. L.-A. Huguet-Latour, "La Société des amis," *BRH*, 8 (1902): 121–22. J.-J. Lefebvre, "La famille Malhiot, de Montréal et de Verchères," SGCF *Mémoires*, 12 (1961): 149–54. Victor Morin, "Clubs et sociétés notoires d'autrefois," *Cahiers des Dix*, 15 (1950): 185–218. R.-L. Séguin, "Biographie d'un patriote de '37, le Dr Luc-Hyacinthe Masson (1811–1880)," *RHAF*, 3 (1949–50): 349–66. Léon Trépanier, "Figures de maires: Édouard-Raymond Fabre," *Cahiers des Dix*, 24 (1959): 189–208.

DICKSON, JAMES, self-styled "Liberator of the Indian Nations"; fl. 1835–37.

James Dickson, variously described as a gentleman, visionary, filibuster, and pirate, briefly and dramatically touched the history of Rupert's Land. Everything concerning his career prior to his appearance in Washington and New York near the end of 1835 is conjectural. His apparent education and financial backing, his impressive appearance (Hudson's Bay Company governor George Simpson* described his face as "covered with huge whiskers and mustachios and seamed with sabre wounds"), and his air of command led to rumours of a distinguished lineage. He may have had English, Scottish, or possibly Indian ancestry. By his own account, he had spent several years in Texas, and he claimed acquaintance with a number of American army officers who had served in the west.

Early in 1836 Dickson was expressing his dream of setting up an independent Indian state and, as his plan rapidly matured, the boundaries of his state became vast indeed – from Rupert's Land to Texas and California. His main destination was said to be Texas, but he frequently referred to his "California expedition." The first steps toward recruiting a military force led him northward. He may have visited Montreal himself; in any case about 30 young men from that area, many of them sons of fur traders and Indian women, were induced to join him. They were told that the expedition would follow the Great Lakes, then the fur-trade route to the Red River, and thence southward. There is no indication that Dickson gave them as much information as he volunteered to New York acquaintances: that he wanted Indian and Métis support for an attack on Santa Fe (N.Mex.) (which he expected to fall easily) and that its capture would open the way to California, where he would set up a utopian state in which Indians would hold all the property and where only a few white officials would be permitted.

The military force that was to achieve these objectives was supposed to number about 200, but when it assembled at Buffalo, N.Y., in late July 1836 with Dickson as general of the so-called Indian liberating army, it comprised only 60 men. Second in command was John George MacKenzie, a Métis son of a retired Nor'Wester and described as secretary of war with the rank of brigadier-general. Martin McLeod, whose journal gives the day-to-day record of the expedition for the next five months, was commissioned as major, and there were six captains, three lieutenants, and two ensigns. Some of the recruits were American, but almost all the officers were from the Canadas. From Buffalo the army set out in the schooner *Wave* for Sault Ste Marie (Ont.), a journey that occupied an entire month. One week was spent in Detroit repairing the damage done in a storm; two more days were lost in an encounter with law enforcement officers in Michigan before the army was able to clear itself of a charge of stealing three cows. Arriving at Sault Ste Marie on 31 August, Dickson decided to stay there for two weeks. By this time all of the American and some of the Canadian recruits had departed; the most significant loss was MacKenzie, who had been forced to return to Montreal because of bad health. Accordingly, it was a force of less than 20 men who set out by Mackinaw boat along the south shore of Lake Superior for Fond du Lac (Duluth, Minn.), dangerously late in the season.

Dickson had told William Nourse, the HBC clerk at Sault Ste Marie, that he had first intended to follow the north shore of Superior and the former trade route to Red River, but that he had now resolved on a different route, although he would still veer northward to Red River from Fond du Lac, and then go south to Santa Fe. In a manifesto intended for the inhabitants of Santa Fe, dated November 1836, he called himself Montezuma II. McLeod's journal records the grim details of the journey overland through northern Minnesota. In its last days, Dickson left his party to go on ahead without firearms, and with insufficient food, matches, and heavy clothing. Starving and nearly frozen, he reached Red River in advance of the others. Ten men joined him there on 20 December.

The reasons for struggling northward in winter are as obscure as those for the initial grand plan of attacking Santa Fe by way of Rupert's Land. In so far as any rational purpose can be discerned, it must concern the strength of the Métis community at Red River, and a hope that Cuthbert Grant*, the warden of the plains, would use his influence on behalf of the expedition. Grant was a hospitable host through the next months, but there was no possibility of providing military aid to an army that was already decimated. Each of the survivors of the venture made his personal decision and departed from Red River, some for employment hastily offered by the HBC and Martin McLeod for Minnesota, where he later served as a member of the territorial council. Dickson himself bade a dramatic farewell to Grant and presented him with his ceremonial sword (now in the Manitoba Museum of Man and Nature), then departed across the American border in the spring of 1837. While Dickson was at Red River, he had written to former associates, giving them different accounts of the route he intended to follow: one, across the Rocky Mountains to the Columbia River, the other (which it seems likely he did follow), by way of the Missouri River to Fort Leavenworth (Leavenworth, Kans.).

Some have viewed such contradictions as evidence of the sinister nature of the plan he devised; others, including William Nourse and Charles Bankhead, secretary of the British legation at Washington, have seen the project as the product of a confused mind. But two considerations continue to make the expedition worthy of attention. In its initial stages, Governor Simpson took it more seriously than might have been expected. Knowing nothing about Dickson's capabilities or the extent of the support he could call upon, Simpson was fully aware of the potential damage to his company's interests represented by men like John George MacKenzie, men with some education and organizational ability, familial ties in the northwest, and a strong sense of grievance over HBC policy in the matter of appointments and promotions and over the trade monopoly the company sought to exercise. It soon became apparent, however, that Dickson, at least by the time he lost MacKenzie at Sault Ste Marie, had no hope of success. But out of failure came a folk memory, whose significance it is difficult to estimate. Dickson's foray into the history of Rupert's Land, and his cry for the liberation of its people, was the subject of a haunting song of might-have-beens written by Pierre Falcon*, Cuthbert Grant's brother-in-law. He sang of the arrival of the great general who came to enlist the Métis, and then of Dickson's departure with only two guides. Such a ballad can be seen as an early and emotional expression of the unspecified longings of the Métis more than a decade before they could mount any effective challenge to the HBC's monopoly.

ELIZABETH ARTHUR

A copy of James Dickson's manifesto, *Articles of war and of the government of the army of the liberator* (Washington, 1836), is preserved along with several of his letters and a list of the officers in his army in the Martin McLeod papers at the Minn. Hist. Soc. (St Paul). Some of this material has been published, with notes by G. L. Nute, in "Documents relating to James Dickson's expedition," *Mississippi Valley Hist. Rev.* (Cedar Rapids, Iowa), 10 (1923–24): 173–81. McLeod's journal, in the same collection, was edited by Nute and published as "The diary of Martin McLeod" in the *Minn. Hist. Bull.* (St Paul), 4 (1921–22) : 351–439.

PAC, RG 7, G1, 78: 471–531. D. B. Sealey, *Cuthbert Grant and the Métis* (Agincourt [Toronto], 1977). Margaret Arnett MacLeod, "Dickson the liberator," *Beaver*, outfit 287 (summer 1956): 4–7. M. E. Arthur, "General Dickson and the Indian Liberating Army in the north," *OH*, 62 (1970): 151–62. J. [S. H.] Brown, "Ultimate respectability: fur-trade children in the 'civilized world,'" *Beaver*, outfit 308 (spring 1978): 51–52. G. L. Nute, "James Dickson: a filibuster in Minnesota in 1836," *Mississippi Valley Hist. Rev.*, 10: 127–40.

DICKSON, WILLIAM, businessman, lawyer, JP, office holder, colonizer, and politician; b. 13 July 1769 in Dumfries, Scotland, second of six sons of John Dickson, a merchant, and Helen Wight, daughter of a Presbyterian clergyman; m. 12 April 1794 Charlotte Adlam in Newark (Niagara-on-the-Lake), Upper Canada, and they had three sons; d. 19 Feb. 1846 in Niagara (Niagara-on-the-Lake).

Following reverses in his father's business, William Dickson arrived in western Quebec in 1785 to join his cousin, Robert Hamilton*. Under the supervision of Hamilton's partner, Richard Cartwright*, he was a forwarding agent at Carleton Island (N.Y.); later he managed Hamilton's mills and store on the Twelve Mile Creek in the Niagara peninsula. About 1790 he settled at Niagara, opposite the fort, where, as Thomas Clark* later wrote, he "sells merchandise to the Military, and trades with the Settlers for grain &c. which is bought up to supply the Garrisons – he has been but a short time in Business for himself – short as it is, he has made out excedingly well." Business was sufficiently prosperous that in 1790 the 21-year-old Dickson built the first brick house in the peninsula.

Using his profits from merchandising, Dickson moved into large-scale land speculation, often in conjunction with his cousins Clark and Hamilton. In 1792 he petitioned Lieutenant Governor John Graves Simcoe* for 48,000 acres in the "Mississauga Tract" [*see* Kineubenae*]. His request failed, and as a result his scheme to settle the land with a "decent and loyal yeomanry" recruited in Scotland came to naught. In 1793 Dickson and Samuel Street* "discovered" that the Six Nations Indians desired to sell a portion of their Grand River lands, and they asked Simcoe to allow the sale. The lieutenant governor was opposed, believing that the 570,000 acres granted to the Indians along the river was for their use alone, but his interpretation was actively resisted by Six Nations spokesman Joseph Brant [Thayendanegea*]. In 1797 Administrator Peter Russell* finally agreed that the Indians might dispose of land, and by 1798 some 350,000 acres had been divided into six blocks to be offered for sale. The story of the dealings in Grand River lands is a murky one, but a certain amount is known about Dickson's involvement, which was considerable. In 1795 he had been the agent for an American group anxious to purchase tracts of land from the Six Nations. After 1798 he often acted as the Indians' land agent, and later as their lawyer in many of the transactions involving the blocks (in 1803 the legislature passed a bill authorizing the lieutenant governor to license him to practise law). He handled the 1803 purchase by Pennsylvania Mennonites of land in block 2 [*see* Samuel D. Betzner*], as well as the dealings of Richard BEASLEY who had sold it to them. On 13 March 1809 the Six Nations surrendered 4,000 acres to Dickson at the mouth of the Grand River, adjacent to block 5, for his professional services on their behalf.

He also speculated in the Grand River lands on his own account. By 1807 he had purchased an option on block 5, valuable because it fronted on Lake Erie. But in spite of an agreement with his brother Thomas* and Hamilton that they would buy all or some of it, he sold his rights to the Earl of Selkirk [Douglas*]. Dickson had a particular interest in block 1. In 1802 he mortgaged more than 15,000 acres to Isaac Todd* for the express purpose of buying land, possibly to finance his share in one, or more, of the failed schemes to acquire block 1. In 1808 he hatched an unsuccessful plan with Augustus JONES to use Jones's father-in-law, Henry Tekarihogen* (titular head of the Six Nations), to facilitate their purchase of the block. Finally, in 1811 he purchased it with his cousin Thomas Clark, although at the time Dickson's full partnership in the deal was concealed; five years later all the lands were transferred to him.

Dickson was involved with a number of local activities. He belonged to the Niagara Agricultural Society and the Niagara Library, and was a trustee of the district grammar school. A justice of the peace, he was an associate justice in 1801 at the trial of Mary London [Osborn*]. In 1803 he was elected poundkeeper for Niagara Township. A key figure in the mercantile élite surrounding Robert Hamilton which dominated the peninsula, Dickson, with Samuel Street, represented that interest in the election of 1800. The two were defeated by Isaac Swayze* and Ralfe Clench* in spite of an address by Dickson that Robert Nichol* described as "one of the best Speeches (perhaps) ever delivered in Upper Canada."

During the Niagara assizes in 1806, William Weekes*, a lawyer prominent in the province's political opposition, made abusive remarks about the deceased lieutenant governor, Peter Hunter*. The presiding judge, Robert THORPE, allowed them to pass without censure whereupon Dickson, Weekes's fellow counsel in the cause, protested. The resulting breach between the two men could not be patched up. Weekes then demanded an apology or satisfaction and a duel was fought on 10 October on American soil in the vicinity of Fort Niagara (near Youngstown, N.Y.). Dickson was unharmed but Weekes was mortally wounded and died the next day. No legal action was taken against Dickson.

By 1812 Dickson had built a second brick house and had purchased a magnificent library of over 1,000 volumes imported from England; he estimated its worth at more than £600. Unlike his brothers Thomas and Robert*, William did not play a major part in the War of 1812. He was taken prisoner with a number of other civilians on 19 June 1813 when the Americans occupied Niagara. Confined at Albany, N.Y., he was released in January 1814. The previous December his house, valued at £1,000, was burnt by the retreating American army. Although Dickson had not participated directly in the war effort he suffered no loss of status and continued his advancement in Upper Canadian society. In November 1815 he was appointed to the Legislative Council with Clark, Thomas Fraser*, and Neil McLean*.

After the war Dickson began intensive planning to develop block 4. With his agent, Absalom Shade*, Dickson toured the lands in 1816 and authorized a survey. The first settlement began at Shade's Mills, on the future site of Galt. Dickson was frustrated in his attempts to promote settlement by a government regulation which effectively prohibited land grants to American immigrants. In 1817 he may have backed an abortive attempt in the House of Assembly, led by Robert Nichol, to overturn the offending regulation. When that tack failed, he began the same year to encourage Robert Gourlay*, whose wife was his cousin. Dickson had first met Gourlay during a trip to Scotland in 1809. Gourlay's views of the Upper Canadian situation were heavily influenced by conversations with Dickson and other land speculators in the peninsula. In the hope that it would spur British immigration, Dickson supported Gourlay's plan to produce and publish a statistical account of the province. When strong opposition to Gourlay from officialdom in York (Toronto) made any further association with him untenable, Dickson then became a firm, if opportunistic, opponent. He was instrumental in the arrest of Bartemas Ferguson*, editor of the *Niagara Spectator*, for publishing Gourlay's material and in the arrest of Gourlay himself in 1819 under the terms of the Sedition Act of 1804. Dickson, in fact, was one of the magistrates who interrogated Gourlay and then ordered him to leave the province.

After the Gourlay episode, Dickson spent his later years developing his lands in Dumfries Township. During his trip to Scotland in 1809 he had assessed attitudes there regarding emigration to Upper Canada and had also made some preliminary arrangements concerning agents. Once the initial settlement was established, he sent his Scottish agents printed prospectuses concerning his township, wrote articles to the Scottish press, and contacted leading Scots, concentrating his efforts on Dumfries and Roxburgh and Selkirk counties. In all he treated his settlers paternally. They were moved immediately to their land and provided with stock, implements, and provisions. He was noted for making large advances of money and for not requiring substantial down payments. By 1825 his settlement was doing well and Dickson moved his entire family to Galt. He retired to Niagara in 1837, leaving the administration of his lands to his sons.

BRUCE G. WILSON

AO, MU 875–77. DPL, Burton Hist. Coll., John Askin papers. PAC, MG 19, A3, 15: 5161–63; E1, ser.1: 14404–5; McDonell papers, vol.10, Baldoon settlement letter-book, McDonell to Selkirk, 28 Nov. 1808; MG 23, HI, 1, ser.3, 2: 356; ser.4, vol.6, packet A17: 5–6, 34–35 (transcripts); MG 24, B130, Thomas Clark to Samuel Clark, 12 Oct. 1792 (copy); RG 8, I (C ser.), 690: 120–24; 1225: 8–10; RG 19, E5(a), 3740, claim 5. QUA, 2199c, letter-books, Cartwright to Todd, 18 April 1801 (transcripts at AO). *John Askin papers* (Quaife). "Journals of Legislative Assembly of U.C.," AO *Report*, 1909. *Niagara Argus* (Niagara [Niagara-on-the-Lake, Ont.]), 4 March 1846. Armstrong, H*andbook of Upper Canadian chronology* (1967). Darroch Milani, *Robert Gourlay, gadfly*. James Young, *Reminiscences of the early history of Galt and the settlement of Dumfries, in the province of Ontario* (Toronto, 1880). J. E. Kerr, "Sketch of the life of Hon. William Dickson," Niagara Hist. Soc., [*Pub.*], no.30 (1917): 19–29.

DIMOCK, JOSEPH, Baptist minister; b. 11 Dec. 1768 in Newport, N.S., son of Daniel Dimock and Deborah Bailey (Baley); m. 21 Aug. 1798 Betsy Dimock, and they had at least 11 children; d. 29 June 1846 in Bridgetown, N.S.

Joseph Dimock was a member of a New England family known since the Great Awakening for its lack of religious and political orthodoxy. His grandfather Shubael Dimock* and his father ran foul of the authorities in Mansfield, Conn., and in consequence, according to family tradition, came to Nova Scotia in 1759, six months before the arrival in the colony of other New England planters [*see* John Hicks*]. They settled first in Falmouth but later moved to Newport. Both lay preachers, they were increasingly influenced by the Baptists and were soon immersed – Daniel in 1763, Shubael by 1771. The Dimocks are thus one of the earliest continuing Baptist families in Canada. Joseph received his schooling at home; his father, he said, "gave me a common Education though small, beyond any of my Associates in the village where I lived – implanted in my Nature a thirst for Education so that I do not remember to have ever been so taken up with any pastime but I would willingly leave it for a Book." His family was greatly influenced by the preaching of Henry Alline* and quickly moved to the centre of the New Light movement launched by that charismatic preacher.

Converted on 17 July 1785, Joseph Dimock was baptized by immersion on 6 May 1787 and joined the Horton Baptist Church. He began to preach in April 1790 without formal education or ordination, very much in the New Light tradition. Along with many of the other New Light leaders, such as Edward Manning* and Harris Harding*, Dimock moved quickly towards antinomianism, joining the so-called "new dispensation" movement. Like Manning, Dimock was eventually frightened by the forces unleashed and retreated to a more orthodox position. On 10 Sept. 1793 he was ordained minister of the Chester New Light church, a mixed congregation of immersed and sprinkled members, succeeding the Reverend John Seccombe*. He remained pastor of that church for the rest of his life.

Dimock played a key role in the gradual evolution of the New Lights into the Baptist movement. He was the moderator of the crucial June 1800 meeting which saw the transformation of the Congregational and Baptist Association into the Nova Scotia Baptist Association, the adoption of the Baptist principle of baptism by immersion, and the ouster of the Congregationalist John Payzant*. Although Dimock continued to minister to a mixed congregation, he used every effort to move it in a Baptist direction and at the same time he took an increasingly important part in the Baptist Association. When in 1809 the association adopted a "close communion" position, which restricted communion to those baptized by immersion, the Chester church temporarily withdrew from that body. By 1811, however, Dimock had led a "reform" of the congregation – the unimmersed members were ousted – and the church rejoined the association. Although its membership was reduced by this move, Dimock's effective evangelism quickly restored the church to its former importance.

Dimock was involved to a substantial degree in the new endeavours undertaken by Nova Scotia Baptists in the first half of the 19th century. He was a strong supporter of the establishment of Horton Academy and Queen's (Acadia) College, a denominational press, and foreign and domestic missions. He died in Bridgetown on 29 June 1846 and was buried in Chester, the service being performed by two of his Baptist colleagues, Theodore Seth Harding and Edmund Albern Crawley*.

Although viewed as one of the great "fathers" of the denomination, Dimock was pre-eminently a successful preacher, with the power, especially in his younger days, to stir his audience profoundly. He conducted extensive missionary tours, both in the Maritime colonies and in the New England states, establishing new congregations and revitalizing old ones. Amiable, compassionate, and humble – his contemporaries, according to the Reverend John Mockett Cramp*, compared him to "the Apostle John, for his loving temper and gentleness of deportment" – Dimock symbolized another side of the often harsh Calvinism of the Baptist denomination.

BARRY M. MOODY

Like most of his ministerial contemporaries, Joseph Dimock kept a diary for most of his adult life. Covering the period from 13 Oct. 1796 to 15 Dec. 1844, it is preserved in the Atlantic Baptist Hist. Coll., Acadia Univ. (Wolfville, N.S.) and has been published in *The diary and related writings of the Reverend Joseph Dimock (1768–1846)*, ed. G. E. Levy (Hantsport, N.S., 1979). A portrait of Dimock, painted by William VALENTINE, hangs in University Hall at Acadia.

Atlantic Baptist Hist. Coll., Cornwallis, N.S., Congregational (Newlight) Church, minute-book; Edward Manning, corr.; Nova Scotia Baptist Education Soc., minutes; Wolfville, United Baptist Church, minutes of Horton Church. *Baptist Missionary Magazine of Nova-Scotia and New-Brunswick* (Saint John; Halifax), 1 (1827–29): 120–21, 212–13, 280–81; 2 (1830–32): 116–17; new ser., 1 (1834): 164; 3 (1836): 171–76. *The Newlight Baptist journals of James Manning and James Innis*, ed. D. G. Bell (Saint John, 1984). *The New Light letters and spiritual songs, 1778–1793*, ed. G. A. Rawlyk (Hantsport, 1983). John Payzant, *The journal of the Reverend John Payzant (1749–1834)*, ed. B. C. Cuthbertson (Hantsport, 1981). *Christian Messenger*, 22 Dec. 1848, 16 April 1856. J. V. Duncanson, *Falmouth – a New England township in Nova Scotia, 1760–1965* (Windsor, Ont., 1965; repr., with supp., Belleville, Ont., 1983). *A genealogy of the Dimock family from the year 1637*, comp. J. D. Marsters (Windsor, N.S., 1899). Bill, *Fifty years with Baptist ministers*. Levy, *Baptists of Maritime prov*. Saunders, *Hist. of Baptists*.

DOAN (Done), JOSHUA GWILLEN (Gillam), farmer, tanner, and Patriot; b. 1811 in Sugar Loaf, Upper Canada, youngest son of Jonathan Doan; m. 29 Sept. 1836 Fanny Milard in St Thomas, and they had one son; executed 6 Feb. 1839 in London, Upper Canada.

Before the War of 1812 Jonathan Doan and his family emigrated from Pennsylvania to the Niagara District, where Joshua Gwillen was born. In 1813 the Doans moved to Yarmouth Township, near the future site of Sparta. Jonathan, an agent for the Baby family's lands in the township, settled a number of Pennsylvania residents on them. He became a "respectable farmer" as well as a miller and a tanner. A prominent Quaker, he had the local meeting-house on his farm.

Joshua also took up farming; then, when his brother Joel P. opened a new tannery in 1832, he joined the enterprise. In 1836 he married; the next year the young couple had a son. All in all, Joshua was very much a part of his community and that community was heavily reform, or "Republican," as an unfriendly source had it, in politics. He played his part in the reform agitation of the fall of 1837, attending at least one meeting designed to further the creation of the political unions advocated by William Lyon Mackenzie*.

In November and early December Mackenzie hurriedly organized a revolt at Toronto, and, though the uprising was quickly crushed, report had it otherwise. In the west Charles Duncombe*, reform MLA for Oxford County, decided to capitalize on the situation supposedly created by Mackenzie and to forestall reprisals on local reformers by mustering a second rebel force near Brantford. His call for men reached Yarmouth. At a recruiting meeting in Sparta on 9 December Joshua and Joel Doan "were very forward," and Joshua was elected lieutenant of those raised. In the next few days he joined Streetsville resident Martin Switzer* and others in persuading men to enlist and to round up arms. He also gathered ammunition, which he distributed to the approximately 50 rebels under David Anderson who set out for Scotland, near Brantford, on the 12th. Brother Joel supplied the provision wagons. Shortly after the arrival of the party at Scotland, Duncombe's forces scattered as loyalists under Allan Napier MacNab* poured in upon them. Joshua succeeded in reaching the United States, despite a government reward of £100 for his capture. Both he and Joel, who had also escaped, were indicted for their parts in the rebellion, and both were exempted from the partial amnesty issued in October 1838.

In the United States Joshua became involved with the Patriots, those Upper Canadian refugees and their American sympathizers who hoped to produce by invasion what Mackenzie and Duncombe had failed to achieve by revolt. He was at Detroit in December 1838 with the group that planned to cross over to Windsor. He and others were told that 600 residents of the Windsor area intended joining them and that settlers about London were already in revolt. Led by "generals" L. V. Bierce and William PUTNAM, the Patriots launched their raid on 4 December, burning the steamer *Thames* and killing a handful of inhabitants. (Later, some eyewitnesses insisted Doan had been implicated in at least one death, a charge he rejected.)

When the Patriots were finally dispersed by Colonel John Prince*, 25 of the invaders had lost their lives, and a number, including Doan, their freedom. Forty-four of the latter were taken to London for trial before a court martial under Henry Sherwood*. Doan was tried for treason in early January, and, though he protested his innocence, was found guilty and sentenced to death. Vainly, he petitioned Lieutenant Governor Sir George Arthur* for mercy, claiming that two witnesses had perjured themselves, and that he had been obliged to join the Patriots and had fled them at the earliest opportunity. Later, he admitted his involvement in the raid and issued a statement intended to dissuade others from invading the colony. He enjoined his wife to "think as little of my unhappy fate as you can" and bade her "meet that coming event with . . . Christian grace and fortitude."

On 6 February he and Amos Perley, another of the six raiders whose sentences were not commuted, mounted the scaffold and, according to a newspaper account, sprang "into eternity, without a struggle." Both were taken to the Quakers' burying-ground in Sparta. Joshua left a widow, eventually married by brother Joel, and a reputation as "a brave, true-hearted man."

COLIN READ

PAC, RG 5, A1: esp. 100012–14, 118327–31; B36, 1–2; B37, trial of J. G. Doan. Trinity Church (Anglican) (St Thomas, Ont.), Reg. of marriages, 29 Sept. 1836. *Rebellion of 1837* (Read and Stagg). *St. Catharines Journal*, 4 Jan. 1838, 14 Feb. 1839. Guillet, *Lives and times of Patriots*. Read, *Rising in western U.C.*

DORION, PIERRE-ANTOINE, merchant, office holder, politician, and JP; b. *c.* 1789, son of Noël Dorion and Barbe Trudelle; d. 12 Sept. 1850 in Drummondville, Lower Canada.

An active and enterprising man, Pierre-Antoine Dorion set up a flourishing lumber business at Sainte-Anne-de-la-Pérade (La Pérade) that assured him a comfortable living. In 1829 the legislature of Lower Canada passed a schools act providing for the election of syndics, or trustees, to administer schools in every community. Dorion was chosen as a trustee in Sainte-Anne-de-la-Pérade. According to a report written in 1832, there were six schools in the district; their success was probably directly related to the competence of the teachers, but also to the trustees' energy. The achievements of the 1829 legislation must be credited in part to the dedication of people like Dorion and Jean-Baptiste Meilleur*.

By taking on this initial responsibility Dorion attracted the attention of his fellow citizens. Consequently, on 26 Oct. 1830 he was elected to the Lower Canadian House of Assembly for Champlain, and he sat until 27 March 1838, when the constitution was suspended and the assembly done away with because rebellion was brewing. While he was a member, Dorion held meetings at his home of assemblymen and Patriote sympathizers and showed himself to be an ardent defender of the principles being put forward by Louis-Joseph Papineau*.

To administer the school laws of the period the assembly in 1831 had formed a standing committee on education and schools, which was to receive the annual reports of the members of the house who had been named visitors, or inspectors, of the schools in their ridings. Dorion took his task as visitor seriously. In his report for 1835–36, for example, he indicated that in Sainte-Anne-de-la-Pérade, English, French, arithmetic, bookkeeping, and geometry were taught, noting that "the school teacher is very competent." Similarly he saw to the purchase of books for impoverished pupils. He also concerned himself with the school timetable and even complained that there were too many holidays.

In August 1830 Dorion had been appointed commissioner to prepare the plans and estimates for the construction of a bridge over the Rivière Sainte-Anne. Six years later he became commissioner for erecting this bridge. On 13 April 1837 he was made justice of the peace for the district of Trois-Rivières.

Dorion seems to have had a distinct liking for lawsuits, a liking shared with the seigneur of Sainte-Anne-De La Pérade, Charles-Louis Tarieu* de Lanaudière. The two men would journey to Quebec and go their separate ways, only to meet at the courthouse. Whatever the outcome of the case, they would return home in as good a mood as when they had left. It may have been this propensity for litigation and quibbling that was at the root of the "unfortunate business affair" which almost ruined Dorion around 1837.

On 21 Feb. 1814 Dorion had married Geneviève Bureau, the daughter of Pierre BUREAU; they had ten children, among whom were Antoine-Aimé*, Jean-Baptiste-Éric*, Vincislas-Paul-Wilfrid*, and Marie-Céphise, who became superior of the Sisters of Charity of Providence.

LOUIS-PHILIPPE AUDET

ANQ-MBF, CE1-48, 21 févr. 1814; CE2-6, 14 sept. 1850. PAC, RG 68, General index, 1651–1841. L.C., House of Assembly, *Journals*, 1835–36, app.OO. F.-J. Audet et Fabre Surveyer, *Les députés de Saint-Maurice et de Buckinghamshire*. Desjardins, *Guide parl.* P.-G. Roy, *Les juges de la prov. de Québec*. L.-P. Audet, *Le système scolaire*, vol.5; 6: 35, 47, 52. Ægidius Fauteux, "Sir Antoine-Aimé Dorion," *La Rev. du droit* (Québec), 13 (1934–35): 589–97.

DUCHESNAY, MICHEL-LOUIS JUCHEREAU. *See* JUCHEREAU

DU COIGNE. *See* DECOIGNE

DULONGPRÉ, LOUIS, musician, teacher, stage manager, painter, businessman, and militia officer; b. probably 16 April 1759 in Paris, son of Louis Dulongpré, a merchant, and Marie-Jeanne Duguay; m. 5 Feb. 1787 Marguerite Campeau in Montreal, and they had 13 children, 4 of whom reached adulthood; d. 26 April 1843 in Saint-Hyacinthe, Lower Canada.

There are two versions of Louis Dulongpré's arrival in North America. According to his obituary in *La Minerve*, he came with the squadron escorting the troops sent under the Comte de Rochambeau to help the American colonies during the War of Independence, and then out of love for liberty went into the army. But according to Louis-Édouard Bois* in *Notice sur M. Jos O. Leprohon*, Dulongpré was with the squadron of French vice-admiral Jean-Baptiste-Charles d'Estaing which, after failing to engage the British fleet off Newport, R.I., sailed for the West Indies. There, it is said, he sought a job that suited him, to no avail. Following his return to the American colonies, Dulongpré, who may have been in a musical band of the colonial regulars, reputedly wanted a transfer to Rochambeau's troops, but the hostilities came to an end. This detailed version is probably the more accurate one, since Joseph-Onésime LEPROHON was the son of Jean-Philippe Leprohon, a brother-in-law and neighbour of Dulongpré. Bois also wrote a historical note about Dulongpré's relative Jean RAIMBAULT.

After he was demobilized Dulongpré visited the former colonies, probably with the idea of settling there. At Albany, N.Y., he met some Canadian merchants who urged him to come to the province of Quebec. He was in Montreal on 30 May and 21 Dec. 1785 when he became godfather to the daughters of the artisans Pierre and Jean-Louis Foureur, *dit* Champagne.

Dulongpré appeared to Montrealers as a tall, handsome, courteous, and affable figure, elegantly dressed in the style of the *ancien régime*, with glittering buckles on his shoes and his hair powdered. A man of great urbanity, he was popular with everyone and got along famously with musicians and artists. Those well acquainted with him said he was an accomplished musician who played several stringed and wind instruments. He gave harpsichord and dancing lessons. During the period 1787–92 he regularly advertised his dancing and music school for boys and girls in the *Montreal Gazette*, and in February 1791 he announced "a BOARDING SCHOOL for YOUNG LADIES, in which they will be taught READING WRITING and ARITHMETIC, the French and English Languages, MUSICK, DANCING, DRAWING and NEEDLE WORK."

Together with Jean-Guillaume De Lisle*, Pierre-Amable De Bonne*, Joseph Quesnel*, Jacques-Clément Herse, Joseph-François PERRAULT, and François Rolland, Dulongpré founded the Théâtre de Société in Montreal in November 1789. As manager he undertook to fit out the stage and hall as well as to look after the administrative details, all for £60. He had made his arrangements months before and had rented a large house on Rue Saint-Paul.

In its initial season, from December 1789 to February 1790, the Théâtre de Société put on six plays, among them *Colas et Colinette, ou le Bailli dupé*, a comic opera by Quesnel. One of the evenings included a ballet and short plays set to choral music for which it seems plausible that Dulongpré and his pupils were responsible. Before the season opened, however, on 22 November the curé of Notre-Dame in Montreal, François-Xavier Latour-Dézery, had denounced theatrical performances from the pulpit, adding that absolution would be refused those who attended. His angry outburst prompted vehement protests and a lively controversy in the *Montreal Gazette* in which even people from Quebec were involved. As a result, the second season was brief and the members of the company restricted the audience "to a very small number of persons of high birth or noble blood"; they were then accused of favouring the élite and being uninterested in educating the young.

Since Dulongpré was not getting an adequate income from his schools, he changed careers and took up painting. Encouraged by his friends and by the success of painter François Malepart* de Beaucourt, who had been established in Montreal since 1792, Dulongpré decided to go to the United States to complete his training. He stayed from June 1793 till March 1794, living mainly in Baltimore, Md.

Upon his return Dulongpré put an advertisement in the *Quebec Gazette* stating that he had "lately arrived from the Colonies, where he has improved in the Art of Drawing under the best Academicians" and announcing that he would "paint in Miniature and in Crayons, Pastels." It is astonishing that in less than one year Dulongpré had mastered his new profession and reached the degree of perfection that characterized his best productions. In addition to his natural gifts he must have possessed a solid artistic base, since he had already painted stage sets. It is not beyond the bounds of possibility that before going to the United States he had taken lessons from Beaucourt. Beaucourt, moreover, had just returned from a stay there and had been able to recommend good teachers.

Dulongpré had few competitors in Montreal other than Beaucourt, who died in 1794, John Ramage*, an excellent miniaturist of Irish descent who died in 1802, and possibly Louis-Chrétien de Heer*. William Berczy* did not take up painting seriously until some 10 years later. At Quebec the only artist who counted was François Baillairgé*.

Dulongpré was successful because he had extensive connections. Over a quarter of a century he painted more than 3,000 portraits – an average of about ten a month – a sizeable number even taking into account the copies attributable to his son Louis and his apprentice Joseph Morant. In his diary William Dunlap, a contemporary American art historian, mentioned that in 1820 Dulongpré would not do portraits and instead was painting historical pictures for Catholic churches at $100 apiece. It is certain, however, that Dulongpré continued to do portraits after this date and that he had become interested in religious art before then.

In fact, upon his return Dulongpré had painted a number of religious pictures for parish churches and convents, and he continued this work throughout his career, with the result that some 200 such items can be attributed to him. He occasionally did gilding and architectural work. He also restored paintings, touching up, for example, several canvasses from the collection sent to Lower Canada by Philippe-Jean-Louis Desjardins*. In 1809 his plan for decorating the vault of the church of Notre-Dame in Montreal was chosen by the *fabrique* over that of Sulpician Antoine-Alexis Molin.

As a good citizen Dulongpré took an interest in public matters. From 1791 he was a member of the Agriculture Society in the district of Montreal. A few years later he took charge of one of the keys to the fire station on Rue Notre-Dame, a great responsibility at a period when the entire population lived in dread of fires. He dabbled a little in politics and turned out a hundred or so innocuous political caricatures.

Dulongpré also joined the militia. At the outbreak of the War of 1812 he was a captain in the 5th Select Embodied Militia Battalion. He and his men replaced the regular troops in the garrisons of Montreal, Chambly, and Les Cèdres. Promoted a major in September 1813, he took part in the battle of Plattsburgh the following year. On 11 April 1814 he was transferred to the 3rd Select Embodied Militia Battalion. He retired on 30 Aug. 1828 with the rank of lieutenant-colonel as a reward for his loyal services.

For years Dulongpré looked after the affairs of his wife's family. The estate her father left included at least two properties in the developing Montreal suburbs and a two-storey stone house on Rue Bonsecours. Divided into lots, the properties were rented or sold, with the result that Dulongpré spent a great deal of time in notarial offices, especially as he himself moved a score of times and frequently had to get leases or loans.

Dulongpré owned a huge lot at the corner of Rue Notre-Dame and Rue Saint-Jean-Baptiste with a one-storey stone house. He set out to put a second storey on the house and to build another of similar height next to it. He supervised every detail. The contracts he signed in 1807 with two of the best craftsmen of the period, mason François-Xavier Daveluy, *dit* Larose, and carpenter François Valade, contained specifications that left nothing to their discretion. Dulongpré lived in his new house for several months, and then in 1808 sold the two buildings for three times as much as they had cost him. In 1816 he had extensive changes made to his old farmhouse in the *faubourg* Saint-Louis.

In 1812 Dulongpré opened a factory on Rue Notre-Dame for making oiled floor-cloths "as well printed as those imported from Europe . . . at prices as low as those at which they can be imported into the province." It produced pieces of various sizes: in strips for entrance halls and stairs, and in dimensions suitable for "church sanctuaries . . . with patterns appropriate for the premises." A complete assortment was available through a Quebec merchant, but Dulongpré's product apparently could not rival the Bristol one.

In 1832 the Dulongprés left Montreal to be closer to their great friends the Papineaus and Dessaulles, and they took lodgings in Saint-Hyacinthe. At that time they supported themselves mainly through the sale of their real estate in Montreal, the music lessons he gave, and his wife's modest *rentes constituées* (secured annuities). An unexpected piece of good fortune, however, soon came their way. Under the terms of a legislative measure to allocate land to veterans of the War of 1812, which was brought forward in the House of Assembly in 1819 but not implemented until 1835, Dulongpré received 1,000 acres in Tring Township.

He invested the major part of his fortune in the Maison Canadienne de Commerce, probably because he heard its praises sung in the Papineau circle. This joint stock company, which had been founded in 1832, proposed to establish a huge warehouse holding all sorts of goods for small merchants, and possibly to finance exports. The moment was ill chosen. A series of poor crops, a slump in the sale of lumber, political events in Lower Canada and abroad: from 1837 everything conduced to the failure of the company.

Mme Dulongpré had to sell her annuities in 1839; she died on 19 July 1840. Dulongpré was deeply affected by the loss of his spouse. A wife without peer for a man who was charming but unconcerned about the future, she was remarkably beautiful, to judge by one of Dulongpré's best works, *Les saisons*, which depicts her with her three daughters. As he often used her face in his religious paintings, people would say jokingly that "she had her portrait in all the churches."

Louis Dulongpré went to live with his daughters in the United States, but he was not happy there, knowing no one, and returned to Saint-Hyacinthe. At the end of 1841 he was living in the home of a Frenchman who had just opened a fine hotel but who took a job in Montreal as a cook a year later. Becoming seriously ill, Dulongpré was taken into the seigneurial manor-house of Saint-Hyacinthe by the wife of Jean Dessaulles*, Marie-Rosalie Papineau, three days before his death.

JULES BAZIN

ANQ-M, CE1-51, 11 janv. 1768, 10 déc. 1779, 5 févr. 1787, 22 nov. 1794, 7 juill. 1796, 21 nov. 1800, 23 mars 1833; CE1-63, 7 févr. 1814, 23 août 1820; CE2-1, 21 juill. 1840, 28 avril 1843; CN1-16, 24 mars, 15 mai 1804; 26 mai 1806; 11 janv., 24 mars, 17 oct. 1807; 11 oct. 1827; CN1-28, 6 oct. 1818; 24, 29 avril, 8 juin, 10–11 août 1819; 5, 7 mai 1821; CN1-74, 19 juill. 1791; 5 juill., 17 août 1811; CN1-110, 5 juin 1822; CN1-121, 28 mai 1789; 29 sept. 1791; 19 sept. 1804; 28 janv., 31 mai 1805; 24, 26 juill., 9 oct. 1811; 5 août 1815; 21 mai 1817; 7 août 1819; CN1-126, 31 déc. 1816; CN1-128, 30 sept. 1796; 29 sept. 1797; 3 avril, 3 août 1798; 28 avril 1802; CN1-134, 22 janv., 24 févr., 2 mars, 29 avril, 16 juin 1816; 22 mai, 22 oct. 1818; 21 juin, 29 sept. 1819; 5, 7 mai 1821; 1er oct. 1822; 18 juin 1824; 30 janv. 1832; 31 mai 1835; CN1-158, 3 févr. 1787; CN1-184, 22 oct. 1805, 14 août 1806, 30 avril 1808; CN1-187, 6 sept. 1832, 11 oct. 1833; CN1-243, 1er oct. 1807; 1er févr., 13 nov. 1809; 19 déc. 1810; 7 févr. 1814; CN1-255, 14 mars 1800; CN1-290, 17 août 1784; CN1-295, 23 août 1803; 11, 15 mai, 28 juill. 1804; 27 janv. 1811; CN1-313, 23 juill. 1796; 28 juill., 23 sept. 1808; CN1-383, 23 févr. 1817. AP, Notre-Dame de Montréal, Boîte 13, chemise 15; Livre de comptes, 1806–18; Plan de décoration de l'église, 27 nov. 1809. AUM, P 58, C2/299; U, Charlotte Berczy to William Berczy, 1 Sept. 1808; William Berczy to Charlotte Berczy, 18, 22 Aug. 1808; Louis Dulongpré à Étienne Guy, 3 juill. 1812; Louis Dulongpré à Hugues Heney, 5 juill. 1828; Jacques Viger à William Berczy, 12 déc. 1811. Bibliothèque nationale du Québec (Montréal), Fonds Édouard Fabre Surveyer, Dulongpré et sa famille. McCord Museum, M21411. PAC, MG 24, B46, 3. *La Minerve*, 8 mai 1843. *Montreal Gazette*, 28 Oct. 1787; 20 Oct. 1788; 30 Sept. 1790; 24 Feb., 27 Oct. 1791; 27 Sept. 1792; 4 May 1812; 7 Aug. 1814; 10 June 1816; 14 April, 9, 16 June 1819; 21 May 1825; 8 Sept. 1828. *Montreal Herald*, 25 Jan. 1816, 1 Feb. 1817. *Quebec Gazette*, 10 April 1794, 23 April 1812, 3 June 1818, 25 March 1819.

[F.-M.] Bibaud, *Dict. hist. Canada, an encyclopædia of the country: the Canadian dominion considered in its historic relations, its natural resources, its material progress, and its national development*, ed. J. C. Hopkins (6v. and 1v. index, Toronto, 1898–1900), 4: 355. Caron, "Inv. de la corr. de Mgr Hubert et de Mgr Bailly de Messein," ANQ *Rapport*, 1930–31: 223. Louis Carrier, *Catalogue of the Château de Ramezay, museum and portrait gallery* (Montreal, 1958). L.-A. Desrosiers, "Correspondance de cinq vicaires généraux avec les évêques de Québec, 1761–1816," ANQ *Rapport*, 1947–48: 114. Harper, *Early painters and engravers*. Langelier, *Liste des terrains concédés*. *Quebec almanac*, 1794. Wallace, *Macmillan dict.* [L.-É. Bois], *Notice sur M. Jos O. Leprohon, archiprêtre, directeur du collège de Nicolet . . .* (Québec, 1870). C.-P. Choquette, *Histoire de la ville de Saint-Hyacinthe* (Saint-Hyacinthe, Qué., 1930). [C.-A. Dessaules] Mme F.-L. Béique, *Quatre-vingts ans de souvenirs* (Montréal, [1939]). Émile Falardeau, *Artistes et artisans du Canada* (5 sér., Montréal, 1940–46), 2. Harper, *Painting in Canada* (1966). Maurault, *La paroisse: hist. de Notre-Dame de Montréal*. Morisset, *Coup d'œil sur les arts*; *Peintres et tableaux*; *La peinture traditionnelle*. Luc Noppen, *Les églises du Québec (1600–1850)* (Québec, 1977). Ouellet, *Hist. économique*, 419, 435, 578. D. [R.] Reid, *A concise history of Canadian painting* (Toronto, 1973). J.-L. Roy, *Édouard-Raymond Fabre, libraire et patriote canadien (1799–1854): contre l'isolement et la sujétion* (Montréal, 1974). Sulte, *Hist. de la milice*. Philéas Gagnon, "Graveurs canadiens," *BRH*, 2 (1896): 108–9. J. E. Hare, "Le Théâtre de société à Montréal, 1789–1791," Centre de recherche en civilisation canadienne-française, *Bull.* (Ottawa), 16 (1977–78), no.2: 22–26. É.-Z. Massicotte, "Le peintre Dulongpré," *BRH*, 26 (1920): 149; "Un théâtre à Montréal en 1789," *BRH*, 23 (1917): 191–92. "Le peintre Louis Dulongpré," *BRH*, 8 (1902): 119–20, 150–51.

DUMARESQ, PERRY, naval officer, office holder, JP, and judge; b. 19 Sept. 1788 on the island of Jersey, son of Philippe (Philip) Dumaresq and Jersua (Jerusha) Perry; m. 21 Nov. 1808 Louisa W. Newton in St Paul's Church (Anglican) in Halifax, and they had 13 children; m. secondly 6 Aug. 1833 Mary Stewart in Dalhousie, N.B., and they had no children; d. there 13 March 1839.

Perry Dumaresq came from a family of Jersey nobility whose titles had descended from Guillé Dumaresq, seigneur of La Haule, born in 1360 in the parish of St Brelade. Perry was the grandson of John Dumaresq, a Jersey mathematician and astronomer. The family had a tradition of military service and had supplied many officers to the Royal Navy. In the period 1800–20 Perry's father was a customs officer at Sydney, Cape Breton Island, as well as a member of the Executive Council of this colony. Perry himself followed the example of his uncles and at an early age served in the British North Atlantic fleet, stationed at Halifax.

Dumaresq saw service in turn on the *Magicienne*, the *Hawk*, and the *Epervier*, and on 14 April 1810 he was commissioned a naval lieutenant. During the War of 1812 he received command of the schooner *Paz* in a squadron under John Poo Beresford which was responsible for patrolling the east coast of North America. He distinguished himself by capturing a great many vessels. The prizes, for the most part American schooners, were taken to Halifax, to be adjudicated by the Court of Vice-Admiralty.

The high point of Dumaresq's career was the capture on 27 March 1813 of the *Montesquieu*, a large armed merchant ship bringing a valuable cargo from Canton (People's Republic of China). The ship belonged to Stephen Girard, a Philadelphia banker who was backing the American government financially during the war. Normally Dumaresq would have sailed for Halifax with his prize, but Beresford immediately entered into negotiations with Girard's agents, who, after obtaining the authorization of the American government, paid 180,000 *piastres* to recover the ship. Dumaresq never forgave Beresford for having usurped his prize, and in subsequent years made many attempts, as did his descendants, to recover what was said to be his fortune.

When he called in at Halifax, Dumaresq was in the habit of visiting a family friend, customs officer Henry Newton, whose father, Hibbert Newton, had held the same post at Annapolis Royal and Canso for many years. It was Louisa, Henry's daughter, whom Dumaresq married. Dumaresq came out of the war with a pension and, as the son and son-in-law of customs officers, soon found a post in customs, for which military service had given him good training. Around 1818, by then the father of five children born in Nova Scotia (including Perry John Newton, later customs officer at Shippegan, N.B.), Dumaresq became customs officer at St Peters (Bathurst). Six more children were born to the Dumaresqs here, and two others later in Dalhousie. The customs office at St Peters was located inside the harbour on what was formerly called Pointe aux Pères (Ferguson Point). From there Dumaresq could survey the movement of ships carrying New Brunswick lumber to Great Britain, where the preferential tariff adopted during the Napoleonic Wars favoured British North American wood.

Tired of having to refer to the county town, Newcastle, Dumaresq went to work to get Northumberland County divided. In 1825, with the cooperation of businessmen from the north end of the province, he had Hugh MUNRO, a neighbour and member of the assembly, take to the house a petition with 600 signatures, his own at the top of the list. Two years later Gloucester County was created, with Bathurst as the county town. Dumaresq became a justice of the peace, judge of the Court of Common Pleas, and member of the board of the county grammar school.

As a result of the forest fire that had laid waste both sides of the Miramichi River up to St Peters in the autumn of 1825, the port of Dalhousie at the mouth of the Restigouche had experienced a remarkable boom. The lumber business relocated in the north of the province, attracting many families from Miramichi as well as businessmen and lumber exporters. Sensing the shift, Dumaresq decided around 1830 to move to Dalhousie and take up the post of customs officer; he settled on a lot at the entrance to the harbour, where he had a little house built that he named Bellevue.

Dumaresq again could not stand having to refer matters to a county town some 50 miles distant. He joined with others seeking a new county in the north of the province, and on 5 Dec. 1836 he chaired a public meeting called to push for this proposal. His name and that of Robert Ferguson* headed the petition which he got Peter Stewart to present in the assembly, and on 1 March 1837 the house passed the bill creating Restigouche County, with Dalhousie as its county town. After the county had been officially set up the following year, Dumaresq was appointed justice of the peace and judge of the Inferior Court of Common Pleas. But his health was deteriorating, and on 13 March 1839 he died at Dalhousie, having bequeathed his estate to his wife.

A loyal, energetic, enterprising man, with a tenacity verging on stubbornness, and an excellent speaker, Perry Dumaresq had taken an interest in good causes, particularly education, public administration, and trade.

DONAT ROBICHAUD

BL, Add. MSS 21862 (mfm. at PAC). Northumberland Land Registry Office (Newcastle, N.B.), Registry books, 26: 295, no.133. PAC, RG 8, IV, 75, 79, 94, 100, 130–31. PANB, RG 2, RS8, education, 2/78; RG 3, RS538, B5: 33; RG 4, RS24, S30-R4.2; RG 7, RS70, 1839, Perry Dumaresq; RG 10, RS108. PANS, Charts, 125; MG 1, 849, Newton family; RG 20B, 5, nos.35, 73, 135, 476. Private arch., Donat Robichaud (Beresford, N.B.), Papiers Dumaresq (copies). PRO, CO 193/6: 80, 193–97. Restigouche Land Registry Office (Campbellton, N.B.), Registry books, A: 32; 553, no.261. St James Anglican Church, Rectory (Melford, N.S.), Records of Christ Church Anglican, Guysborough, N.S. (mfm. at PANS). St Paul's Anglican Church (Halifax), Reg. of marriages, 21 Nov. 1808 (mfm. at PANS). N.B., House of Assembly, *Journal*, 3 Feb. 1836, 14 Jan. 1837; 1836, app. *Gleaner* (Miramichi [Chatham, N.B.]), 1 Dec. 1829; 2 Oct. 1832; 23 July, 13 Aug. 1833; 19 Jan., 25 Oct., 20 Dec. 1836; 31 Jan. 1837; 3 July, 11, 18 Sept. 1838; 26 March 1839; 10 March, 17 Nov. 1840. *Mercury*, 29 May 1827. *Novascotian, or Colonial Herald*, 24 May 1832. *Nova-Scotia Royal Gazette*, 9 Dec. 1812, 28 April 1813. *Royal Gazette* (Fredericton), 12 Sept. 1838. *United States' Gazette* (Philadelphia), 31 March, 1, 8 April 1813. *Weekly Chronicle* (Halifax), 22 Jan. 1813. G.B., Admiralty, *The commissioned sea officers of the Royal Navy, 1660–1815*, [ed. D. B. Smith *et al.*] (3v., n.p., [1954]), 1; *Navy list*, 1803: 8, 10, 16. J. B. McMaster, *The life and times of Stephen Girard, mariner and merchant* (2v., Philadelphia and London, 1918).

DUMOUCHELLE (Dumouchel), JEAN-BAPTISTE, merchant, militia officer, JP, and Patriote; b. 5 April 1784 in Sandwich (Windsor, Ont.), son of Louis-Vital Dumouchelle and Magdeleine Goyau; d. 29 March 1844 in Saint-Benoît (Mirabel), Lower Canada.

Jean-Baptiste Dumouchelle came to Lower Canada in 1795. It is thought that he then did classical studies at the Collège Saint-Raphaël in Montreal and that on completing his course in 1803 he went to work as a clerk for Alexis Berthelot, a merchant in Sainte-Geneviève (Sainte-Geneviève and Pierrefonds). He seems to have gone into business in 1808 as a general merchant at Saint-Benoît, and he soon became one of the leading figures in the village. On 13 Feb. 1809 he married Victoire Félix, who was the sister of Maurice-Joseph Félix, parish priest of Saint-Benoît, and later the sister-in-law of notary Jean-Joseph Girouard*; they had four children. In 1812 he apparently obtained the rank of captain in the Rivière-du-Chêne battalion of militia and he served in the War of 1812 in that capacity.

At the end of the war, in 1815, Dumouchelle returned to Saint-Benoît and resumed his business. Like Girouard, his friend and relation by marriage, he took an interest in politics. During the electoral campaign of 1827 factions emerged in York riding [*see* Jacques Labrie*] and Dumouchelle took an active part in meetings held by the Patriotes. Governor Lord Dalhousie [RAMSAY] considered such meetings outrageous and through a general order for the militia dated 12 July he had Dumouchelle's commission withdrawn because of his role in them. He was reinstated, probably after Dalhousie left in 1828, and two years later he was serving as a major in the Deux-Montagnes battalion of militia.

Dumouchelle was again a target for the hostility of the authorities on the eve of the 1837 rebellion. At that time he was dismissed from his duties as a militia officer and justice of the peace because of his participation in revolutionary gatherings. At those held in Sainte-Scholastique (Mirabel) on 1 and 15 Oct. 1837 for people from Saint-Benoît and the Saint-Joachim concession respectively, the Patriotes decided, as a sign of protest, to put Dumouchelle and several colleagues dismissed with him back in office by election. The Patriotes also decided to refuse to recognize militia officers and justices of the peace appointed by the governor.

In November 1837 Dumouchelle organized the distribution of ammunition in Deux-Montagnes County and encouraged the habitants to bring him lead to be melted down for bullets. He owned a mould and made rounds of ammunition in his cellar with the help of his two sons, Hercule and Camille. Consequently, when Sir John Colborne* and his troops reached Saint-Benoît on 15 Dec. 1837, the day after the battle at Saint-Eustache, they first hunted out the Dumouchelles, who were considered the main instigators of the revolt at Saint-Benoît. Dumouchelle was imprisoned along with his sons on 17 December and was not released until 8 July 1838, on bail of £1,000.

Upon his release Dumouchelle went back to Saint-Benoît. He discovered that his home and warehouses had been burned in the pillaging by Colborne's troops in 1837. He never succeeded in re-establishing his business and died, a ruined man, on 29 March 1844, only a few weeks after the auction of his belongings.

Had he taken no part in the 1837 rebellion, Jean-Baptiste Dumouchelle would have been remembered as a well-to-do general merchant, a militia officer, and a magistrate, indeed, a leading figure in Saint-Benoît. The part he took in the revolutionary assemblies and the fact that he made munitions which he distributed to rebels from his own village and others near by place him among the most active and aggressive Patriotes in Deux-Montagnes County.

BÉATRICE CHASSÉ

ANQ-M, CE6-9, 13 févr. 1809, 29 mars 1844. ANQ-Q, E17/13, no.742; E17/14, nos.805, 824–26, 845; P-92. PAC, MG 24, A27, 34; RG 68, General index, 1651–1841. "Documents inédits," P.-A. Linteau, édit., *RHAF*, 21 (1967–68): 281–311. Alfred Dumouchel, "Notes d'Alfred Dumouchel sur la rébellion de 1837–38 à Saint-Benoît," *BRH*, 35 (1929): 31–51. Amury Girod, "Journal kept by the late Amury Girod, translated from the German and the Italian," PAC *Report*, 1923: 370–80. "Lettre de M. Girouard à M. Morin, sur les troubles de '37 dans le comté des Deux Montagnes," *L'Opinion publique*, 2 août 1877: 361–62. *La Minerve*, 9, 16, 23 oct. 1837; 1er avril 1844. *Quebec Gazette*, 14 June 1827. Fauteux, *Patriotes*, 231–33. *Officers of British forces in Canada* (Irving). *Quebec almanac*, 1813–37. G.-F. Baillairgé, *Notices biographiques et généalogiques, famille Baillairgé* ... (11 fascicules, Joliette, Qué., 1891–94), 6: 100–10, 135, 157–60. J. D. Borthwick, *History of the Montreal prison from A.D. 1784 to A.D. 1886* ... (Montreal, 1886), 63. Béatrice Chassé, "Le notaire Girouard, patriote et rebelle" (thèse de D. ès L., univ. Laval, Québec, 1974). L.-O. David, *Les gerbes canadiennes* (Montréal, 1921), 165–66; *Patriotes*, 90–93. Émile Dubois, *Le feu de la Rivière-du-Chêne; étude historique sur le mouvement insurrectionnel de 1837 au nord de Montréal* (Saint-Jérôme, Qué., 1937), 120. Filteau, *Hist. des patriotes* (1975). [C.-A.-M. Globensky], *La rébellion de 1837 à Saint-Eustache avec un exposé préliminaire de la situation politique du Bas-Canada depuis la cession* (Québec, 1883; réimpr. Montréal, 1974). Laurin, *Girouard & les patriotes*, 55–56. Maurault, *Le collège de Montréal* (Dansereau; 1967). R.-L. Séguin, *Le mouvement insurrectionnel dans la presqu'île de Vaudreuil, 1837–1838* (Montréal, 1955), 122–23. L.-O. David, "Les hommes de 37–38: Jean-Baptiste Dumouchel, père," *L'Opinion publique*, 8 mars 1877: 109–10. Madeleine Dufour-Dumouchel, "Jean-Baptiste Dumouchel, le patriote; ses antécédents et sa descendance," SGCF *Mémoires*, 29 (1978): 94–107.

DUNLOP, ROBERT GRAHAM, ship's captain, JP, office holder, and politician; b. 1 Oct. 1790 in Keppoch, Scotland, second son of Alexander Dunlop and Janet Graham; m. 4 July 1836 Louisa McColl; d. 28 Feb. 1841 at Gairbraid, near Goderich, Upper Canada.

Sent to sea at 13 as a cabin-boy in the Royal Navy, Robert Graham Dunlop rose to the rank of lieutenant during the Napoleonic Wars in a distinguished career that featured exploits on land as well as at sea. Following the war, he attended lectures at the universities in Glasgow and Edinburgh, captained mercantile voyages to the East Indies, and returned briefly to the Royal Navy (being promoted captain before retiring in 1823). In 1833 Captain Dunlop emigrated to Upper Canada. He made the trip out with his famous younger brother, Dr William DUNLOP, who was already well established in the Goderich area and who had recently been appointed general superintendent of the vast Huron Tract by the Canada Company.

Shortly after his arrival at Goderich, the captain was appointed a justice of the peace and a commissioner of the Court of Requests, and the following year he briefly commanded the Canada Company's ill-fated steamer *Menesetung*. The brothers jointly owned the farm that surrounded the doctor's estate, Gairbraid, but they seemed content to leave its development to others in the manner of gentlemen farmers. To assist in the management of what was widely regarded as an unruly household, the brothers arranged for the emigration from Scotland of Louisa McColl, an illiterate dairymaid. She served the household well but her unmarried presence in a house of men was a scandal to some. Legend has it that the brothers decided which should wed her by three tosses of the doctor's two-headed penny. The captain's wedding to her was later solemnized by the Anglican priest Robert Francis Campbell.

In the summer of 1835 Captain Dunlop, standing as a constitutionalist, won a by-election to become Huron County's first member in the House of Assembly, soundly defeating reformer Anthony Jacob William Gysbert VAN EGMOND and Canada Company employee William Bennett Rich. Although wary of the power and privilege of the tory "family compact," Dunlop was nevertheless devoted to the patriotic preservation of the British connection and generally supported the provincial administration. He also strongly believed in the development of Upper Canada through immigration and public works. During the Executive Council crisis in early 1836 [*see* Robert Baldwin*], he stood solidly behind Lieutenant Governor Sir Francis Bond Head*. In the crushing defeat of the reformers at the general election later that year, Dunlop was returned unopposed. While attending the 1836–37 session, he became closely acquainted with Orangeman Ogle Robert Gowan*. Probably as a result of this friendship, Dunlop joined the Orange lodge in 1837 and the following year was the only non-Irish member of its provincial executive. Even though Robert, unlike his Presbyterian brother, had become an Anglican, he still favoured dividing the clergy reserves amongst the leading Protestant denominations; however, in February 1837 he simply avoided a related issue by absenting himself from the debate and vote concerning the Anglican rectories created by Sir John Colborne* the previous year. During the rebellion that erupted in December 1837, the captain, though less involved than his brother, took an active interest and was named colonel of the 3rd Regiment of Huron militia, which was never actually formed. Following the rebellion, Captain Dunlop moved resolutions to thank the sheriff of the Home District for his timely presence on Yonge Street and to grant 100 acres to all who took up arms against the rebels; on the other hand, he also tried to limit the disarming of suspects to three years.

Throughout his career in the assembly the captain showed a constant interest in Huron County affairs, supporting the Huron Fishing Company and improvements to Goderich harbour. He was also in favour of increased immigration, an extended franchise, improved jails and better treatment of the insane, the establishment of mechanics' institutes and a geological survey, and the anti-slavery campaign. When attending the assembly in Toronto he participated in local activities, giving, for example, a series of lectures in the winter of 1836–37 on the utility of education for Toronto blacks.

Although Robert Graham Dunlop represented Huron County until the close of the final session of the Upper Canadian assembly in February 1840, after 1838 his health declined and he kept mainly to Gairbraid. He died there in February 1841, mourned by all as a quiet, kindly gentleman of well-proved loyalty.

PETER A. RUSSELL

NLS, Dept. of MSS, MSS 9292–96, 9303. *The Dunlop papers . . .*, ed. J. G. Dunlop (3v., Frome, Eng., and London, 1932–55), 2: 233–40, 256–68; 3: 173, 176, 185–86, 189, 197, 219, 224, 228, 233–34, 236, 287–88. *British Colonist*, 17 March 1841. *Christian Guardian*, 11 Jan. 1837. *Patriot* (Toronto), 7, 10, 14 July 1835; 5 July 1836. Gates, *Land policies of U.C.* C. [G.] Karr, *The Canada Land Company: the early years; an experiment in colonization, 1823–1843* (Ottawa, 1974). Robina and K. M. Lizars, *In the days of the Canada Company: the story of the settlement of the Huron Tract and a view of the social life of the period, 1825–1850* (Toronto, 1896; repr. Belleville, Ont., 1973). I. A. Stewart, "Robert Graham Dunlop: a Huron County anti-compact constitutionalist" (MA thesis, Univ. of Toronto, 1947).

DUNLOP, WILLIAM, known as **Tiger Dunlop**, army officer, surgeon, Canada Company official, author, JP, militia officer, politician, and office holder; b. 19 Nov. 1792 in Greenock, Scotland, third son of Alexander Dunlop and Janet Graham; d. unmarried 29 June 1848 in Côte-Saint-Paul (Montreal), and was buried first in Hamilton and then in Goderich, Upper Canada.

William Dunlop, the son of a local banker, was educated in Greenock, and pursued his medical studies at the University of Glasgow and in London. He passed his army medical examinations in December 1812 and was appointed assistant surgeon to the 89th Foot on 4 Feb. 1813. Later that year he arrived in Upper Canada, during the War of 1812, in time to treat men wounded at both Crysler's Farm and Lundy's Lane. According to his friend James FitzGibbon*, he played a more active role in the assault on Fort Erie on 15 Aug. 1814, carrying about a dozen injured men out of the range of fire and refreshing weary survivors from canteens filled with wine. He was serving with a road-cutting party near Penetanguishene in the spring of 1815 when he received "the appalling intelligence that peace had been concluded."

Despite having a "good war," Dunlop found army life not wholly to his liking, and, after retiring on half pay on 25 Jan. 1817, he led a peripatetic existence. He went first to India where, as a journalist and editor in Calcutta, he took a hand in forcing the relaxation of press censorship. His unsuccessful attempt to clear tigers from Sagar Island in the Bay of Bengal, in an effort to turn the place into a tourist resort, provided him with his famous nickname. Dunlop returned to Scotland in the spring of 1820 because of a fever contracted on Sagar. From Rothesay he contributed to *Blackwood's Edinburgh Magazine* a series of sketches based on his experiences in India. In 1823 he lectured in Edinburgh on the fledgling science of medical jurisprudence. The following year he departed for London, where he was editor, briefly, of the daily *British Press* and where, in December, he established his own paper, the *Telescope*, which ran until December 1825.

By 1824 the Scottish novelist John GALT was constructing a huge land and colonization organization intended to operate in Upper Canada. It was finally chartered in 1826 as the Canada Company and later that year Dunlop, who had submitted to Galt a plan for assisting potential emigrants, was taken on under the exalted title of warden of the woods and forests. His official task was to inspect the Canadian lands the company had contracted for (eventually they would purchase some two and a half million acres), determine which lots might be sold quickly, investigate squatters on company lands, and "stop the spoliation of the timber." The company thought Dunlop "singularly well qualified" for this enormous job; his pay was to be the equivalent of that of an infantry captain.

Dunlop arrived in the colony in late 1826 and, at least until Galt left the firm in 1829, he bustled about performing his official duties and other self-appointed tasks as a kind of travelling factotum. Present at the much-celebrated founding of Guelph in April 1827, that summer he travelled through the bush to the future site of Goderich and the following year accompanied a party of road-cutters to the spot. He soon established his own home, Gairbraid, just north of Goderich across the Maitland River, and took his place among the local élite (he had received his first of many commissions of the peace in June 1827).

In the early years of his employment, Dunlop bristled with schemes for the company's advantage. Not a few were impractical, such as his idea for the company's canalization of the Rivière de la Petite Nation between the Ottawa and the St Lawrence. Though he was never a strict party man, Dunlop's political sympathies ran to the tory side; none the less he managed to annoy leading representatives of both poles of political opinion in Upper Canada. By 1827 he was already receiving unfavourable notice in William Lyon Mackenzie*'s *Colonial Advocate*. The same year marked the appearance of John Strachan*'s *Observations on the provision made for the maintenance of a Protestant clergy*. Dunlop's contribution to the ensuing controversy took the form of a public letter, signed Peter Poundtext, in which, with a mocking grin, he addressed Strachan as "Dear Doctor," "Dear Friend," "O celestial Doctor," and "O Theophilus." His participation was no doubt motivated as much by his desire to defend the Canada Company's position as by his love of literary brawling.

In 1829, following a dispute with company directors, John Galt resigned and was replaced by William Allan*, the firm financial pillar of the "family compact," and Thomas Mercer Jones*, an energetic protégé of Edward Ellice*. The company considered recalling Dunlop along with Galt (whom he continued to support) but Allan and Jones both thought him "beneficial" and "indefatigable." So he remained in the company's service and by 1832 he was given power of attorney to execute title deeds. A year later he became resident general superintendent of the Huron Tract (at a raised salary of £400 with an additional £100 for travelling expenses).

The year 1832 saw publication of his guide for emigrants, *Statistical sketches of Upper Canada*, an event that, along with newspaper skirmishes with Mackenzie following a riot in York (Toronto) on 23 March, helped put him back on public view. This engaging book, written under the pseudonym A Backwoodsman, mixes some (small) practical advice with much tomfoolery and fully exploits the author's humorous persona. In his chapter on climate, for example, Dunlop says that Upper Canada "may be pronounced the most healthy country under the sun, considering that whisky can be procured for about one shilling sterling per gallon." The book's aim was to attract clever young people to Upper Canada, and in that it was not without success: publisher Samuel Thompson* later remarked that he had determined in 1832 to set out for Canada "in the expectation of a good deal of fun of the kind described by Dr. Dunlop." The more sober-sided directorate of the Canada Company had hoped for something a little more serious but still they underwrote it, read it, and pronounced it both "interesting" and "very amusing."

Dunlop spent the winter of 1832–33 in Britain, conferring with his superiors in the Canada Company and visiting friends and family. When he returned to Upper Canada in the spring, he brought with him his brother ROBERT GRAHAM. The pair lived more or less quietly at Gairbraid, though after briefly serving the Canada Company Robert went on to become Huron County's first member of the House of Assembly.

William was very much a company man during this period. In fact it was probably his able, precise testimony in 1835 at Mackenzie's muckraking inquiry for the assembly (resulting in *The seventh report from the select committee on grievances*) that prevented the company from being smeared and brought to Colonial Office notice. Dunlop arranged publication of his own views the following year in a pamphlet, *Defence of the Canada Company*.

In a roundabout way, however, Mackenzie would be responsible for Dunlop's breaking with the company. During the rebellion in Upper Canada in

1837–38, Dunlop raised a militia unit, whose nickname, The Bloody Useless, gives a clue to the important role it played. Dunlop, however, doubtless relishing a sense of emergency, commandeered supplies and food for the unit from Canada Company stores. Thomas Mercer Jones was incensed and demanded Dunlop's withdrawal from the militia. Dunlop, equally angered, instead quit the company in January 1838. Despite protestations from Dunlop's brother and other influential settlers, the company directors in London upheld Jones's action. Evidently the directors had decided that they wanted a lower profile in the community than the irrepressible Dunlop exhibited. He had served the company well in many capacities, and had given it credibility and colour at a time when it needed both, but as its activities became more routine and conventional he had become less enchanted with it.

Dunlop's resignation further widened a growing schism between two factions in Huron County: those for and those against the Canada Company. He became the natural leader of the anti-company faction, known as the Colbornites, since many of them lived in Colborne Township. In February 1841 Robert Dunlop, who had represented Huron in the assembly since 1835, died. In the election later that year (after the union of Upper and Lower Canada), William ran in his place against the Canada Company's choice, James McGill Strachan*, son of the bishop and brother-in-law of Jones. Despite the *British Colonist*'s assertion that Strachan had "no more chance, than a stump tailed ox in fly time," at the close of the vote he was declared elected. Dunlop, however, protested and was awarded the seat; in the general election of 1844 Dunlop ran unopposed.

In the legislature he took a moderate tory stance, and his speeches are frequently more notable for their humour than for their grasp of the issues. In 1841 he chaired a committee to hear the grievances of the exiled radical Robert Fleming Gourlay*, and the report he wrote is both temperate and humane. His most-quoted political maxim had been written, however, in October 1839. In a letter published in the Kingston *Chronicle & Gazette*, he declared that responsible government was "a trap set by knaves to catch fools." The phrase soon became something of a rallying cry for the opponents of responsible government.

During his years in parliament Dunlop also served as the first warden of the district of Huron. His methods were sometimes high-handed, and he embroiled himself and the district council in an unfortunate dispute with the Canada Company over taxation, which was finally settled to the company's advantage. Dunlop was replaced as warden in 1846. Early that year the tory ministry of William Henry Draper* and Denis-Benjamin Viger* cast about for a safe seat for Inspector General William Cayley*. Huron looked promising, and Dunlop was offered, as a sop, the superintendency of the Lachine Canal. To the shock and indignation of the opposition press, he accepted the post. He was thus to spend his last years at a distance from Huron County.

Again Dunlop shifted to relative obscurity, though in 1847 the *Literary Garland* published what is probably his best work, "Recollections of the American war." A highly personal reminiscence of the war years, it is memorable above all for its vivid character sketches and, as always, a generous sense of humour. It was little remarked at the time of its publication, though the *British Colonist* drew attention to the "plain but pleasing and attractive style." William Dunlop died the following summer near Montreal.

As surgeon, soldier, land agent, magistrate, militia colonel, politician, and member of numerous agricultural and literary organizations, Dunlop touched a great many of the central affairs of Upper Canadian life. Yet he is remembered above all for his engaging, witty, eccentric personality. Several people close to Dunlop have suggested that his comic persona was consciously created and maintained. In 1813 one of young Willy's favourite aunts writes that his eldest brother, John, holds him in affection even though "he sees your follies and absurdities as every body must do for you hold them up to view as if they were accomplishments." And in the novel *Bogle Corbet; or, the emigrants*, John Galt says of a character plainly based on Dunlop that he "had manifestly inherited from nature some excess of drollery, and conscious of this, had himself a vivid enjoyment in overcharging even to caricature his own eccentricities, in order to witness their effect on others."

How is Dunlop's eccentric character preserved? In part through his own writings. Both his longer prose works, *Statistical sketches* and "Recollections," are highly subjective pieces with a distinctive authorial voice. His many letters to newspapers frequently advertise his character, and his caustic last will and testament (including "I give my silver cup, with a sovereign in it, to my sister Janet Graham Dunlop, because she is an old maid and pious and therefore will necessarily take to horning") has been reprinted so often as to have become something of a cliché. Moreover, a great many of the people Dunlop knew could not resist trying to preserve him in print: in Britain his literary cronies, especially John Wilson and William Maginn; in Upper Canada John Mactaggart*, Samuel Strickland*, Sir James Edward Alexander, and, of course, Galt, among others; finally, and above all, Robina and Kathleen Macfarlane* Lizars (granddaughters of Dunlop's friend Daniel Horne Lizars), who published in 1896 a work called *In the days of the Canada Company*, an informal history of Huron County, of which Dunlop is the undisputed comic hero. But even before this publication, Dunlop had become something of a local folk hero. In the 1930s one Huron old-timer remembered hearing from his father a version of one of the best-known tales, and another said of the Lizarses' stories that he had "heard them from the lips of the old pioneers gathered about the fireside of a winter's night."

Dunlop's engaging character is thus his most substantial and lasting creation. What is the essence of that character? He was a wit, a storyteller, a great drinker, and a practical joker. Most of the remembered stories cannot be verified or documented: they bear the truth of fiction, or of legend.

Dunlop is said to have done everything on a grand scale, and this is nowhere more evident than in his drinking. He kept his liquor in a wheeled, wooden cabinet called "The Twelve Apostles." One bottle he kept full of water: he called it, naturally, "Judas." His reputation as a maker of punch "and other antifogmaticks" was legendary with the Blackwoodians. Once in the Canadian legislature, when he spoke of travelling about on horseback with nothing but a sack of oatmeal, some honourable members shouted, "And a horn!" Even Susanna Moodie [Strickland*] (who did not meet Dunlop) tells a story of his drinking, in which Dunlop is inadvertently served a glass of salted holy water in place of Edinburgh ale. Dunlop's consumption of snuff, which he kept in an immense box he called "the coffin," was also typical of his gargantuan appetites. An unsympathetic legislative reporter once described him as "pulling out his half-bushel snuff box and chuckling like a clown in a circus company." And, when an American border inspector doubted that the quantity of snuff he was carrying could be simply for personal use, Dunlop tossed a handful into the air and snorted it up as it fell about him, saying, "There, that's what I want it for; *that's* the way I use it."

Like an unrestrained, oversized schoolboy, Dunlop delighted in shocking people. One afternoon in a store in Goderich, he directed each newcomer to fetch him some nails from a barrel – in which Samuel Strickland had dumped a live porcupine. He treated one unhappy Canada Company official to a ride through a gauntlet of howling wolves (simulated by Strickland and himself) until the fellow was thrown from his horse, and then nursed him back to health with soft words and alcohol. And he delighted in dressing the part of the uncouth backwoodsman, and then surprising onlookers with a learned monologue.

There is a strong element of teasing in the story of how his brother Robert came to wed their housekeeper, Louisa McColl, after losing a coin toss to William's two-headed coin. Yet William was not always the winner in his own stories, as in the tale of the ship he piloted on to the rocks in Lake Huron (he called her "the Dismal"), or the story in "Recollections" of the commanding officer who repaid one of Dunlop's blunders by smacking him smartly on the head with a switch and telling him he had been shot.

There is, of course, wit as well as slapstick in the Dunlop stories. Once, travelling in the bush with a logging chain wrapped about himself, he met an old friend from Scotland. When they parted, Dunlop asked the fellow to tell his friends at home that he had been found "in chains but well and happy." At a public meeting in Goderich in 1840, he offered those assembled three good reasons for not going to church: "First that [a man] should be sure to find his wife there, secondly, he could not bear any meeting where one man engrossed the whole of the conversation, and thirdly, that he never liked singing without drinking." And once, in the assembly, a fellow member interrupted him as he spoke on the subject of taxation to ask him how he would like a tax on bachelors. "Admirably," he replied, "luxury is always a legitimate object of taxation."

Dunlop was known under a variety of names, but the one that has lasted is Tiger. In Upper Canada he was also The Doctor, occasionally Peter Poundtext or Ursa Major, and often A Backwoodsman. More than the cairn that stands in his memory at the mouth of the Maitland River, the character of the backwoods savage/sophisticate which he created is his monument.

GARY DRAPER and ROGER HALL

The most complete list of William Dunlop's publications may be found in D. G. Draper, "Tiger: a study of the legend of William Dunlop" (PHD thesis, Univ. of Western Ont., London, 1978). A select bibliography of his major Canadian works follows.

Dunlop's guide for emigrants, *Statistical sketches of Upper Canada, for the use of emigrants: by a backwoodsman*, was sufficiently popular to require three editions. The first two were published in London in 1832; the second is identical to the first except for the title-page notation "A New Edition"; the third, issued in London the following year, includes a delightful preface which does not appear elsewhere. Shortly afterwards the *Sketches* were reproduced in whole or in part in a number of Canadian newspapers, including the *Canadian Emigrant, and Western District Commercial and General Advertiser* (Sandwich [Windsor, Ont.]), the *Canadian Freeman*, and the *Montreal Gazette*. A modern edition, based on the 1832 texts, appears in *Tiger Dunlop's Upper Canada . . .*, ed. C. F. Klinck (Toronto, 1967), 63–137. His "Recollections of the American war," originally published in the *Literary Garland*, new ser., 5 (1847): 263–70, 315–21, 352–62, 493–96, subsequently reappeared as *Recollections of the American war, 1812–14 . . .*, ed. A. H. U. Colquhoun (Toronto, 1905), and in *Tiger Dunlop's Upper Canada*, 1–62. A copy of the pamphlet *Defence of the Canada Company, by Dr. Dunlop, M.P.P.*, privately issued from Gairbraid in 1836, is at the AO.

AO, Canada Company records. PAC, MG 24, I46. PRO, CO 42, esp. 42/396. Can., Prov. of, Legislative Assembly, *App. to the journals*, 1841, app.TT. *The Dunlop papers*

. . ., ed. J. G. Dunlop (3v., Frome, Eng., and London, 1932–55). John Galt, *The autobiography of John Galt* (2v., London, 1833); *Bogle Corbet; or, the emigrants* (3v., London, [1831]). [Samuel] Strickland, *Twenty-seven years in Canada West; or, the experience of an early settler*, ed. Agnes Strickland (2v., London, 1853; repr. Edmonton, 1970). [Susanna Strickland] Moodie, *Life in the clearings versus the bush* (London, 1853). *Albion* (New York), 1828–48. *British Colonist*, 1838–48. *Canadian Emigrant, and Western District Commercial and General Advertiser*, 1831–36. *Canadian Freeman*, 1827–34. *Chronicle and Gazette*, 1833–45. *Colonial Advocate*, 1826–34. *Gore Gazette, and Ancaster, Hamilton, Dundas and Flamborough Advertiser* (Ancaster, [Ont.]), 1827–29. *Kingston Chronicle*, 1826–33. *Montreal Gazette*, 1826–28, 1830–32, 1841–48. *Toronto Patriot*, 1832–44. *Western Herald, and Farmers' Magazine* (Sandwich), 1838–42. W. H. Graham, *The Tiger of Canada West* (Toronto and Vancouver, 1962). R. D. Hall, "The Canada Company, 1826–1843" (PHD thesis, Univ. of Cambridge, Cambridge, Eng., 1973). Robina and K. M. Lizars, *Humours of '37, grave, gay and grim: rebellion times in the Canadas* (Toronto, 1897); *In the days of the Canada Company: the story of the settlement of the Huron Tract and a view of the social life of the period, 1825–1850* (Toronto, 1896; repr. Belleville, Ont., 1973). I. A. Stewart, "Robert Graham Dunlop: a Huron County anti-compact constitutionalist" (MA thesis, Univ. of Toronto, 1947). *William "Tiger" Dunlop, "Blackwoodian Backwoodsman": essays by and about Dunlop*, ed. C. F. Klinck (Toronto, 1958).

DUNOON. *See* DENOON

DUQUET, JOSEPH, Patriote; b. 18 Sept. 1815 at Châteauguay, Lower Canada, son of Joseph Duquet, an innkeeper, and Louise Dandurand; d. 21 Dec. 1838 in Montreal.

Joseph Duquet began his classical studies at the Petit Séminaire de Montréal in 1829 and finished the program at the Collège de Chambly in 1835. He was attracted to the notarial profession and articled, probably that same year, with Joseph-Narcisse CARDINAL at Châteauguay; he then continued his legal education in Montreal with Chevalier de LORIMIER, likely the following year. Both of these men were Patriotes and they were destined to die on the gallows in 1838 and 1839. In October 1837 Duquet went to work in the office of his uncle Pierre-Paul Démaray*, a notary and Patriote at Dorchester (Saint-Jean-sur-Richelieu), with whom he was expecting to complete his training.

On the night of 16–17 Nov. 1837 Duquet was present when Démaray was arrested on a charge of high treason. After Bonaventure Viger* and a handful of men had succeeded in freeing Démaray by ambushing the detachment that was taking him to the Montreal jail, Duquet accompanied his uncle to the United States. On 6 December he and other Patriotes took part in a skirmish at Moore's Corner (Saint-Armand Station). Subsequently he fled to Swanton, Vt. On 28 Feb. 1838 he participated in Robert Nelson*'s attempted invasion of Lower Canada.

After the amnesty proclaimed by Lord Durham [LAMBTON], Duquet was able to return to Lower Canada in mid July 1838. He immediately undertook an intensive campaign to recruit members for the Frères-Chasseurs. He organized a lodge at Châteauguay and persuaded Cardinal to become the head of it. On the evening of 3 November, the day set for the second uprising, he left with Cardinal and a group of followers to "borrow" weapons from the Indians at Caughnawaga (Kahnawake). On reaching their destination on the morning of 4 November, Cardinal, Duquet, and François-Maurice Lepailleur, Cardinal's brother-in-law, began parleying with the Indian chiefs. The Indians invited the entire group of Patriotes to join in the negotiations, but when they entered the reserve the warriors surrounded them, taking 64 prisoners whom they immediately conducted to the Montreal jail.

On 28 Nov. 1838 Duquet and 11 of his companions were summoned before a court martial set up by Sir John Colborne*. Lewis Thomas Drummond*, a young Irishman, Pierre Moreau, a Canadian lawyer whom the court judged "acceptable," and later Aaron Philip Hart, a brilliant man of Jewish extraction, undertook to defend them. They were not allowed, however, to intervene directly through cross-examination.

From the outset Cardinal lodged a protest disputing the court's jurisdiction, since the offences had been committed before the special ordinances of 8 Nov. 1838 had been adopted. He demanded a trial before a civil court, but in vain. When the witnesses had been heard, the attorneys received permission to present their remarks. Drummond, with Hart's assistance, put forward a vigorous defence that made a strong impression on the court, which wondered whether in the case before it the death penalty would not be an excessive punishment. The president of the court martial, Major-General John Clitherow*, enquired if it was not possible to pronounce another sentence. Attorney General Charles Richard Ogden* replied that there was no choice, and Solicitor General Andrew STUART expressed a similar opinion. Consequently, on 14 December the court martial sentenced to death all those who had been found guilty.

The court's hesitations had perplexed Colborne somewhat. On 15 Dec. 1838 he asked the Executive Council to study the cases of the condemned men, in particular Duquet's. The council held that Duquet should be considered a recidivist and that justice should take its course, just as for Cardinal. The sentences of the other condemned men were commuted to transportation.

Neither the intervention of the auxiliary bishop of Montreal, Ignace Bourget*, nor a pathetic appeal by

Duquet's mother had any effect. On 20 Dec. 1838 Drummond made a final attempt, calling attention to serious doubts about the legality of the trial. He asked that action be deferred until a competent court had given its opinion, declaring that if the sentence were carried out, the condemned men would be elevated from persons presumed guilty to martyrs to arbitrariness. Nothing availed.

In accordance with the sentence of the court, Cardinal and Duquet had to mount the scaffold on the morning of 21 Dec. 1838. Cardinal was executed first. When it was his turn to climb the steps, Duquet began to shiver and his teeth chattered. He had to be supported. When the trapdoor was sprung, the noose, which had been badly adjusted by the hangman, Humphrey, slipped and caught under the nose of the condemned man, who was thrown violently to one side and hit the ironclad framework of the gallows. His face battered and bleeding profusely, the hapless Duquet had not lost consciousness and was moaning loudly. The onlookers began yelling: "Pardon! pardon!" This agony was prolonged, it was said, for some 20 minutes, the time it took for the hangman to install a new rope and cut down the original one.

Joseph Duquet's body was buried in the same grave as Cardinal's in the old cemetery of Montreal, which is now the site of Dominion Square. The two martyred Patriotes' remains were removed in 1858 to the cemetery of Notre-Dame-des-Neiges, where they rest under a monument to the Patriotes.

GÉRARD FILTEAU

AC, Beauharnois (Valleyfield), État civil, Catholiques, Saint-Joachim (Châteauguay), 18 sept. 1815. ACAM, RLB, I: 253. ANQ-Q, E17/35, nos.2793, 2795–99; E17/39, no.3112; E17/40, nos.3176–78, 3183–87. [A.-R. Cherrier], *Procès de Joseph N. Cardinal, et autres, auquel on a joint la requête argumentative en faveur des prisonniers, et plusieurs autres documents précieux* ... (Montréal, 1839; réimpr. 1974). "Papiers Duvernay," *Canadian Antiquarian and Numismatic Journal*, 3rd ser., 6: 21; 7: 40–41. F.-X. Prieur, *Notes d'un condamné politique de 1838* (Montréal, 1884; réimpr. 1974). *Report of state trials*, 1: 17–111. *Montreal Herald*, 19 Nov. 1838. *North American*, 18 April 1839. L. J. Burpee, *The Oxford encyclopædia of Canadian history* (Toronto and London, 1926), 173. Fauteux, *Patriotes*, 237–39. Michel Bibaud, *Histoire du Canada et des Canadiens, sous la domination anglaise* [1830–37], J.-G. Bibaud, édit. (Montréal, 1878). L.-N. Carrier, *Les événements de 1837–38* (2e éd., Beauceville, Qué., 1914). Christie, *Hist. of L.C.* (1866). David, *Patriotes*, 207–18, 277–79. N.-E. Dionne, *Pierre Bédard et ses fils* (Québec, 1909). Filteau, *Hist. des patriotes* (1975). William Kingsford, *The history of Canada* (10v., Toronto and London, 1887–98), 9–10. Maurault, *Le collège de Montréal* (Dansereau; 1967). J.-A. Mousseau, *Lecture publique sur Cardinal et Duquet, victimes de 37–38* . . . (Montréal, 1860). Marcelle Reeves-Morache, *Joseph Duquet, patriote et martyr* (Montréal, 1975). Léon Trépanier, *On veut savoir* (4v., Montréal, 1960–62), 3: 131–32. "Le bourreau Humphrey," *BRH*, 6 (1900): 281–82.

DURHAM, JOHN GEORGE LAMBTON, 1st Earl of. *See* LAMBTON

DURNFORD, ELIAS WALKER, army officer and military engineer; b. 28 July 1774 in Lowestoft, England, son of Elias Durnford and Rebecca Walker; d. 8 March 1850 in Tunbridge Wells (Royal Tunbridge Wells), England.

Although he was born in Suffolk, on the North Sea coast, Elias Walker Durnford spent his first years in Pensacola (Fla), where his father was commanding engineer and then lieutenant governor of the British colony of West Florida. When he was about four, he went back to England without his parents, who entrusted him to the care of an aunt. After his father also returned on the conclusion of the American revolution, Elias, who wanted to become a military engineer himself, attended a preparatory school for the Royal Military Academy in Woolwich (London) and was subsequently admitted to the academy in October 1788. He was commissioned in the Royal Artillery in April 1793, at 18 years of age, and in October was promoted second lieutenant in the Royal Engineers. His first posting took him to the West Indies to serve alongside his father. In 1794 he directed the construction of defensive works for Pointe-à-Pitre in Guadeloupe, where he was subsequently taken prisoner by the French. After 17 months of captivity he was exchanged in July 1796 for a French officer. He resumed his engineering duties in England, and then in Ireland. When he was appointed in 1808 as commanding engineer in Newfoundland, he had to give up a "deep desire" to take part in the war in Spain.

In Newfoundland Durnford was primarily occupied with maintaining and building coastal batteries; he also put up a blockhouse on Signal Hill, near St John's. In 1813 he became a major in the army and a lieutenant-colonel in the Royal Engineers, undertaking garrison duties in addition to his engineering responsibilities. He was also named aide-de-camp to the officer commanding the forces on the island. During his stay he obtained a grant of four acres on which he grew potatoes.

From 1816 to 1831 Durnford was commanding officer of the Royal Engineers in the Canadas. He lived at first in a rebuilt section of the former intendant's palace at Quebec, and then moved with his family into the official residence for the commander of the Royal Engineers on Rue Saint-Louis. The construction of the Quebec citadel was undoubtedly his major accomplishment in British North America. The work substantially completed the town's defensive system, but the classical plan he had chosen showed that the military had a constant fear of a popular uprising. At Quebec Durnford also was in charge of rebuilding the Palais gate as well as of repairing the Anglican Cathedral of the Holy Trinity. He coordinated the reorganization of the colonies' defences to fit a new plan developed after the War of 1812 by the governor, the Duke of Richmond [Lennox*], and approved by the Duke of Wellington. A number of military works were built at that time, on Île Sainte-Hélène and Île aux Noix and at Kingston, Upper Canada, among other places. In addition, Durnford worked on the construction of canal systems on the Rideau and Ottawa rivers, although the Rideau Canal was built under his friend John By in the period 1826–31 and was never under his authority. In 1823 he had signed a voluminous report on the state of the fortifications and military buildings in the Canadas. He obtained the rank of colonel in the Royal Engineers in March 1825. As such he was granted his request, made to Governor Lord Dalhousie [Ramsay], that he be appointed commander of the troops in Lower Canada while retaining his engineering post; to his chagrin, he had failed to obtain the command a few months earlier.

Durnford returned to England in 1831 and six years later was retired from service. In 1846 he obtained the supreme rank of colonel commandant in the engineers, and in the army he almost reached the top, since he was made a lieutenant-general.

Throughout his career Durnford displayed assiduity and exemplary honesty, and he apparently won the esteem of both colleagues and superiors. During the height of the construction season he visited work sites early in the morning and then busied himself in the engineers' office until supper time, late in the evening. Eager to manage public funds with economy, he behaved irreproachably in the numerous transactions that he conducted in the name of the British government to purchase properties needed for the glacis of the Quebec citadel. Despite his zeal, he was not always beyond reproach. In 1825 the Board of Ordnance accused him of being lax in his administration of the Royal Engineers, in particular because of appointments and salary arrangements made without following the usual administrative procedures. Like most military engineers of the time Durnford did a poor job of calculating the building costs for military works. The case of the citadel is especially revealing: initially estimated at £72,400, the project cost the Treasury a little more than twice this sum.

Family values, along with professional principles, were of the greatest importance for Durnford. On 30 Oct. 1798 he married Jane Sophia Mann, daughter of a lawyer in Gravesend, England. They had 13 children, of whom four were born in Newfoundland and three at Quebec. Their six sons followed in Durnford's footsteps to become officers in the British army. Three worked in turn with him as clerks in the office of the Royal Engineers at Quebec, and the eldest and the youngest joined the corps. The family followed him wherever he went, and two of his unmarried daughters remained with him even after he retired.

An ardent conservative, Durnford respected the traditional values of his station, although he did not much enjoy social gatherings. He engaged in several sports, including cricket. Whether in Newfoundland, the Canadas, or Tunbridge Wells, the village to which he retired, Durnford liked to relax by gardening and taking care of a few animals. He was fond of reading, as was his wife; he particularly enjoyed Hannah More's religious and philanthropical works, which he bought for the Garrison Library at Quebec when he was its president.

It is difficult to estimate Durnford's fortune. Certainly, his engineering officer's pay, his post as officer commanding the Royal Engineers, and the various allowances to which he was entitled put him near the top of the British army's pay structure. He regularly kept more than one servant, and sometimes three or four. His sons studied at private institutions in England, and he gave them allowances befitting their rank. Durnford also travelled a great deal. His father and one of his aunts had owned numerous lands in Florida and New Orleans which were confiscated as a result of the American revolution. He took various measures, even making a six-month trip to the United States in 1820 and going to court several times in 1838, but title had been lost and he was never able to profit from these holdings. It is not known whether he received money that had been left by his father for his mother's use, but when her second husband died, he inherited £1,000 sterling.

Elias Walker Durnford's career was centred mainly on administration and no important scientific contribution to military engineering came out it. The name Durnford remained famous in the Royal Engineers, however, through the ongoing presence for more than a century and a half of 11 members of the family. In addition to his father and two of his own sons, his brother Andrew and four of Andrew's descendants, as well as two other Durnfords whose relationship is not known, all served in the corps. Through the descendants of a third son, Philip, the Durnford line still exists in Canada today.

André Charbonneau

Elias Walker Durnford began writing his autobiography but it was never finished. The first part was published in 1850, the year in which he died, as "Scenes in an officer's early life at Martinique, Guadeloupe, &c., during the years 1794 & 1795, recalled in advanced years," *Colburn's United Service Magazine* (London), pt.II: 605–14.

ANQ-Q, CE1-71, CN1-16, CN1-49. PAC, MG 24, F73; RG 8, I (C ser.), 393–441; II, 80–81. Private arch., E. A.

Durnford (Montreal), Notes and docs. PRO, CO 42/136–200; WO 55/860–68. *Family recollections of Lieut. General Elias Walker Durnford, a colonel commandant of the Corps of Royal Engineers*, ed. Mary Durnford (Montreal, 1863). *List of officers of the Royal Regiment of Artillery from the year 1716 to the year 1899 . . .*, comp. John Kane and W. H. Askwith (4th ed., London, 1900). A. J. H. Richardson *et al.*, *Quebec City: architects, artisans and builders* (Ottawa, 1984). *Roll of officers of the Corps of Royal Engineers from 1660 to 1898 . . .*, ed. R. F. Edwards (Chatham, Eng., 1898). J. E. Candow, *A structural and narrative history of Signal Hill National Historic Park and area to 1945* (Parks Canada, National Hist. Parks and Sites Branch, *Manuscript report*, no.348, Ottawa, 1979). André Charbonneau *et al.*, *Québec ville fortifiée, du XVIIe au XIXe siècle* (Québec, 1982). Whitworth Porter *et al.*, *History of the Corps of Royal Engineers* (9v. to date, London and Chatham, 1889– ; vols.1–3 repr. Chatham, 1951–54). J.-P. Proulx, *Histoire de St-John's et de Signal Hill* (Parks Canada, National Hist. Parks and Sites Branch, *Manuscript report*, no.339, Ottawa, 1978). A. G. Durnford, "A unique record," *Royal Engineers Journal* (Brompton, Eng.), [new ser.], 2 (1909).

DUROCHER, EULALIE (baptized **Mélanie**), named **Mother Marie-Rose**, founder and first superior of the Sisters of the Holy Names of Jesus and Mary in Canada; b. 6 Oct. 1811 in Saint-Antoine-sur-Richelieu, Lower Canada, daughter of Olivier Durocher and Geneviève Durocher; d. 6 Oct. 1849 in Longueuil, Lower Canada.

Eulalie Durocher was the tenth of 11 children, 3 of whom died in infancy. Her father, a wealthy farmer, had partially completed his classical studies, and her mother had been given the most attentive schooling at the Ursuline convent in Quebec. Consequently both were in a position to ensure that their children obtained a good education. Eulalie's brothers Flavien*, Théophile, and Eusèbe entered the priesthood, and her sister Séraphine joined the Congregation of Notre-Dame.

Eulalie did not attend the village school; her paternal grandfather Olivier Durocher, a distinguished and scholarly man who served in the militia, undertook to be her teacher at home. Upon his death in 1821, however, the little girl went as a boarding-pupil to the convent run by the Congregation of Notre-Dame in Saint-Denis on the Richelieu. After taking her first communion at the age of 12, she returned home; there she was again tutored privately by Abbé Jean-Marie-Ignace Archambault, a teacher at the Collège de Saint-Hyacinthe. Eager to dedicate herself to God in the religious life, she entered the boarding-school of the Congregation of Notre-Dame in Montreal in 1827, intending to do her noviciate there as had her sister Séraphine. But after two years of study broken by long periods of rest, she had to abandon her plans for the religious life because of poor health. She went back home, to await God's good time.

At her mother's death in 1830 Eulalie took over her role and became the life and soul of the family. Of an ardent temperament, easily peremptory, deeply pious, she had a special influence on those around her. Her brother Théophile, curé of Saint-Mathieu parish in Belœil, managed to persuade his father to move from the ancestral farm to the presbytery at Belœil; Eulalie assumed the housekeeping duties, which she carried out from 1831 till 1843. In the comings and goings of the busy presbytery, Eulalie's calling gradually took shape. The serious political, educational, and religious problems of the day were freely discussed there. She took an interest in them and became aware of the urgent need to make education accessible to children in the countryside whether rich or poor. As there was an alarming shortage of schools and teachers, she began to dream of a religious community that could easily establish more convents. When in 1841 the parish priest of Longueuil, Louis-Moïse Brassard*, appealed to the Sœurs des Saints-Noms de Jésus et de Marie of Marseilles, in France, Eulalie enrolled herself in advance, with her friend Mélodie Dufresne, as a novice in this congregation. But the French sisters did not proceed. The bishop of Marseilles, Charles-Joseph-Eugène de Mazenod, who had founded the Oblates of Mary Immaculate, then advised the bishop of Montreal, Ignace Bourget*, to set up a fledgling religious community with the two women who had been eager to be part of the anticipated French group.

In the mean time an initial party of Oblates, including Father Adrien Telmon, had arrived in Montreal. Telmon came to Belœil to conduct popular missions, and he quickly recognized in Eulalie a mentor able to gather kindred souls about her and guide them in the ways of the spirit. He lost no time in encouraging her to found a religious community typically Canadian in its dedication to educating the young. She, Mélodie, and Henriette Céré, the first three candidates, began to prepare themselves for the religious life under the guidance of the Oblates in October 1843. They moved into a building in Longueuil used as a school, in which Henriette Céré taught. On 28 Feb. 1844 Bishop Bourget conducted the ceremony when the three young women took the habit. Eulalie became Sister Marie-Rose in the community, which assumed the name and the institutions of the Sœurs des Saints-Noms de Jésus et de Marie of Marseilles. On 8 December of that year Bourget received the religious vows of all three in the parish church. Marie-Rose was then named superior, mistress of novices, and depositary.

Mother Marie-Rose faced many difficulties, not the least being her community's disputes with Abbé Charles Chiniquy*. Chiniquy entered the Oblates' noviciate in 1846 and wanted to take control of the teaching in the schools established by the sisters.

When he met with refusals from the perspicacious superior, he publicly disparaged the community. Despite the storms Mother Marie-Rose stood firm. A woman of great virtue, in close communion with the Lord and a peerless educator, she gave the community an impetus that has not been lost with the passage of time. When she died on 6 Oct. 1849, on her 38th birthday, the community already had 30 teachers, 7 novices, 7 postulants, and 448 pupils in 4 convents.

After the funeral Bourget told the mourning sisters: "I confess to you with heartfelt sincerity that I was deeply moved to see so many virtues knit together in one soul. . . . I begged her to procure me the same zeal for governing my diocese as she had for directing you." Thirty years later, in 1880, Bourget was to say: "I invoke her aid as a saint for myself, and I hope that the Lord will glorify her before men by having the church award her the honours of the altar." His last wish was fulfilled on Sunday 23 May 1982 in St Peter's Square in Rome, when before a huge crowd Pope John Paul II proclaimed Marie-Rose Durocher blessed.

MARGUERITE JEAN

ACAM, 525.105. ANQ-M, CE1-3, 6 oct. 1811; CE1-12, 8 oct. 1840. M.-C. Daveluy, "Mère Marie-Rose, 1811–1849," *Dix fondatrices canadiennes* (Montréal, 1925), 27–31. P.[-J.-B.] Duchaussois, *Rose du Canada; mère Marie-Rose, fondatrice de la Congrégation des Sœurs des Saints Noms de Jésus et de Marie* (Paris, 1932). Germaine Duval, *Par le chemin du roi une femme est venue; Marie-Rose Durocher, 1811–1849* (Montréal, 1982). Marguerite Jean, *Évolution des communautés religieuses de femmes au Canada de 1639 à nos jours* (Montréal, 1977). [J.-H. Prétot], *Mère Marie-Rose, fondatrice de la Congrégation des SS. Noms de Jésus et de Marie au Canada* (Montréal, 1895). Pierre Lambert, "Eulalie Durocher et les filles de Belœil," Soc. d'hist. de Belœil–Mont-Saint-Hilaire, *Cahiers* (Belœil, Qué.), 10 (février 1983): 11–30. André Lemay, "Mère Marie Rose," *Bull. eucharistique* (Montréal), 8 (août 1945): 226–56.

DUVERNET, HENRY ABRAHAM (in 1842 he changed his name to **Henry Abraham DuVernet Grosset Muirhead**), army officer, military engineer, and JP; b. 4 April 1787, eldest of ten children of Abraham DuVernet and Miriam Grosset Muirhead; m. Martha Maria Iqualin Van Kemper, and they had three children; d. 16 Dec. 1843 at Bredisholm, his residence near Coatbridge, Scotland.

Henry Abraham DuVernet's family traced its origins in France back to 1150. After the Reformation one branch remained in France and the other, Huguenot, went first to the Low Countries and then to England. DuVernet's father, a colonel in the Royal Artillery, was an aide-de-camp to Prince William Henry. Following Abraham DuVernet's accidental death in 1806, the prince befriended his widow and obtained commissions for some of his sons.

DuVernet himself had been appointed ensign in the Royal Staff Corps on 22 Dec. 1803 and was promoted lieutenant on 12 Sept. 1805. His first active service was with Major-General Brent Spencer's expedition to the Mediterranean in 1808. He subsequently took part in the retreat to La Coruña, Spain, with Lieutenant-General Sir John Moore and was invalided home in 1809. DuVernet was made captain on 30 May of that year, major on 2 June 1825, and lieutenant-colonel on 31 Dec. 1828. Placed on half pay on 1 July 1834, he was then the longest serving officer in the Royal Staff Corps (over 30 years); he became colonel in 1840.

In 1818 the Duke of Richmond [Lennox*], governor-in-chief of British North America, submitted a masterly report on the defences of the colonies. He stressed the urgent need for an alternative route between Montreal and Kingston to obviate the possibility of supply convoys of canoes and bateaux being ambushed in the upper St Lawrence River should hostilities with the United States break out again. DuVernet was sent to the Canadas with two companies of the Royal Staff Corps to take over the project. He arrived at Quebec on 29 July 1819.

The alternative route involved the construction of three small canals around rapids in the Ottawa River, opposite present-day Hawkesbury (Ont.), and the canalization of the Rideau and Cataraqui rivers through the Rideau lakes. The Rideau Canal would be built later by John BY of the Royal Engineers; the Ottawa River canals were DuVernet's responsibility. Arriving at the site late in the summer of 1819, he expected to receive detailed instructions from Richmond, who was on a tour of inspection which was to end at the Ottawa. Unfortunately, Richmond died before reaching the river, so DuVernet had to proceed with a minimum of instructions. And until 1827 he was held to an annual expenditure of £8,000, which he only once exceeded.

Despite these limitations DuVernet soon showed himself to be an able engineer and administrator. The Grenville Canal was well advanced when, in 1826, the Duke of Wellington ordered a speeding up of this work and the building of the other canals, at Carillon and Chute-à-Blondeau. DuVernet returned from a long leave in England in July 1827 and remained in charge of the works until November 1833, when they were substantially complete. His design for the Carillon Canal provided a remarkable response to the problems posed by high land and excavation through solid rock. An entrance lock raised vessels 13 feet into a channel excavated with less difficulty farther inland and two locks at the other end brought the vessels down 23 feet to the river level. The Ottawa River canals remained in use until 1962 when they were submerged beneath the river, impounded by the Carillon Dam of Hydro-Québec.

DuVernet's official correspondence reveals him to have been an engineer greatly respected by his superiors and always solicitous of his men. He was appointed justice of the peace for the district of Montreal in 1821. During the winter months he and his wife resided in Montreal or Chambly, but while construction was in progress they camped on the site, providing welcome hospitality to such travellers on the Ottawa as Nicholas Garry*. Like numerous military officers, DuVernet was also an artist, but only one of his paintings, a fine view of the mill and tavern of Philemon WRIGHT at Chaudière Falls, has been found.

DuVernet returned to Great Britain after November 1833. Some time in 1842, after his mother's death, he changed his name and inherited the Muirhead family estate, Bredisholm. He died there in 1843.

ROBERT F. LEGGET

Henry Abraham DuVernet's painting, *Mill and tavern of Philemon Wright at the Chaudière Falls, Hull, 1823*, is at the PAC.

PAC, MG 24, F29; RG 68, General index, 1651–1841. Private arch., Florence DuVernet (Ottawa), Genealogical information. Nicholas Garry, "Diary of Nicholas Garry, deputy-governor of the Hudson's Bay Company from 1822–1835: a detailed narrative of his travels in the northwest territories of British North America in 1821 . . . ," ed. F. N. A. Garry, RSC *Trans.*, 2nd ser. 6 (1900), sect.II: 73–204. *Burke's landed gentry* (1879). G.B., WO, *Army list*, 1810. *Hart's army list*, 1840–41. R. [F.] Legget, *Ottawa waterway: gateway to a continent* (Toronto and Buffalo, N.Y., 1975).

E

EAGAR, WILLIAM, businessman, artist, and teacher; b. *c*. 1796 in Ireland, son of William Eagar; m. 23 Jan. 1819 Maria Saunders in St John's, and they had six sons and three daughters; d. 24 Nov. 1839 in Halifax at age 43.

William Eagar had settled in Newfoundland some time before he married Maria Saunders, daughter of a prominent island family. He may well have crossed the Atlantic to take an administrative position in the fishery rather than to work as an artist. The quick settling of a personal bankruptcy in 1821 and his ownership before the end of the decade of a 20-acre farm on the outskirts of St John's indicate that he had access to considerable financial resources.

By late 1829 Eagar was advertising his services as an artist and art teacher. Undoubtedly, he had learned to draw and sketch in Ireland as part of his school curriculum (there is no evidence to substantiate a claim made in 1914 that he had studied in Italy), and this training may have been augmented by work with a professional artist. His urban views demonstrate a firm understanding of the principles of topographic rendering. That he also had some knowledge of surveying is suggested by his applying to become surveyor general of Newfoundland. The post went instead to Joseph Noad* in 1832.

Eagar travelled to London in 1831, presumably to supervise the engraving of his large drawing *Town and harbour of St. John's, taken from Signal Hill, June 1st, 1831*. While there he studied the works of leading water-colour painters and, on returning late that year, rented a schoolroom and offered to teach the technique. He soon discovered that teaching was not financially practical in St John's and began advertising his willingness to do portaits in oil and water-colour. The number of portraits he painted in Newfoundland is unknown.

Eagar moved to Halifax in September 1834 and resumed teaching and painting. His students came from fashionable families who believed art was a necessary component of an upper-class education. Within a short time he had established his reputation as a teacher and his position as the foremost landscape artist in Halifax. A lengthy account of Eagar and his work appeared in Joseph Howe*'s *Novascotian, or Colonial Herald* in 1836. He subsequently expanded his classes, lectured to the Halifax Mechanics' Institute on at least one occasion, and constructed an impressive transparency of Queen Victoria as the grand finale of the fireworks display to celebrate her coronation. He also leased and operated a commission warehouse.

In 1836 Eagar announced his most ambitious project, a series of views of Nova Scotia, New Brunswick, and Upper Canada. Sir Colin CAMPBELL, the lieutenant governor of Nova Scotia, endorsed the plan and Eagar was applauded in the press. The initial portfolio of three Nova Scotia views was engraved in Edinburgh and arrived in the province in December 1837. Eagar advertised the set as "Landscape illustrations of British North America." Encouraged by favourable reviews, he announced his second volume, scenes of New Brunswick, the same month. He had stated in 1836 that, "in order to render the work more perfect," he intended to offer subscribers a description of each scene upon completion of the volume. It is doubtful whether the letterpress was ever issued.

Eagar's engravings, however, did not sell, and the

artist, with the assistance of Hugh Bell*, petitioned the Nova Scotia House of Assembly in February 1838 for financial support to subsidize them. While awaiting an answer he planned a major art exhibition in Halifax, perhaps in part to raise money. In March he displayed 125 items, including work by his students, some of his own pieces, five paintings by William VALENTINE, and European works borrowed from local collections. The following month, when it became apparent that government funding was not going to be forthcoming, Eagar withdrew his petition and decided to lithograph his remaining views. At the end of April he travelled to Boston for supplies and to engage a lithographer and a distributor. The wisdom of his decision was reinforced in October when the first two numbers of Robert Petley's *Sketches in Nova Scotia and New Brunswick, drawn from nature and on stone* arrived in town. Petley, an army officer stationed in Halifax from 1832 to 1836, had published his lithographs in London after returning home. They went on sale for half the price of Eagar's engravings.

In July 1839 his first lithographs, three views of Halifax with a title-page vignette, went on sale there. Published as *Nova Scotia illustrated in a series of views taken on the spot and on stone*, it sold at a price comparable to Petley's *Sketches*. The second part of this series, which went on sale in August, contained three illustrations of Halifax and vicinity. Parts three and four were published posthumously in May and August 1840. Eagar had prepared the stones for part three, two scenes of the Windsor area and a panorama of Grand Pré; his drawings for part four, three views of Pictou, were transferred to stone after his death from pneumonia.

Eagar's publications were seen at the time as an expression of patriotism. Although it was hoped that they would help promote the province in Europe, it was considered just as important to inform Nova Scotians of their colony's capabilities. Joseph Howe, Thomas Chandler Haliburton*, John YOUNG, and others believed a great future lay in store were the population to recognize the opportunities at hand. *Nova Scotia illustrated* gave many of Eagar's contemporaries a glimpse of parts of the province they might not otherwise have seen. It survives as a visual document of an era when Nova Scotians believed they would soon become self-reliant.

ALEXANDRA E. CARTER

[That William Eagar may have had a middle name was suggested in *200 years of art in Halifax; an exhibition prepared in honour of the bicentenary of the founding of the city of Halifax, N.S., 1749–1949* (Halifax, 1949), where he is called William H. Eagar; although the initial has occasionally been repeated, it has not yet been substantiated in primary sources. A.E.C.]

The principal collections of William Eagar's works are at Dalhousie Univ. (Halifax), Dartmouth Heritage Museum (Dartmouth, N.S.), McCord Museum, MTRL, N.B. Museum, N.S. Museum (Halifax), PAC, PANS, and Royal Ont. Museum (Toronto). The following publications reproduce one or more of his engravings, lithographs, or paintings: A. E. Carter, "William H. Eagar: drawing master of Argyle Street, Halifax," *Journal of Canadian Art Hist.* (Montreal), 7 (1983–84): 138–55; C. P. de Volpi, *Nova Scotia, a pictorial record; historical prints and illustrations of the province of Nova Scotia, Canada, 1605–1878* ([Toronto], 1974), plates 76–93 (each reproduction is accompanied by quotations from contemporary travel accounts); Harper, *Painting in Canada* (1966); *Nova Scotia scenery: an exhibition of works by William H. Eagar (1796–1839)* ([Halifax, 1983]); *A pageant of Canada; the European contribution to the iconography of Canadian history; an exhibition arranged in celebration of the centenary of confederation* (Ottawa, 1967); Harry Piers, "Artists in Nova Scotia," N.S. Hist. Soc., *Coll.*, 18 (1914): 141–45, 161–62; and Mary Sparling, *Great expectations; the European vision in Nova Scotia, 1749–1848* (Halifax, 1980).

Cathedral of St John the Baptist (Anglican) (St John's), Reg. of marriages, 23 Jan. 1819. PANL, GN 2/1, 3 April 1832. St Paul's Anglican Church (Halifax), Reg. of burials, 1839 (mfm. at PANS). *Catalogue of Mr. Eagar's exhibition of paintings* (Halifax, 1838). N.S., House of Assembly, *Journal and proc.*, 1838: 25. *Colonial Pearl* (Halifax), 16 Dec. 1837, 29 Nov. 1839. *New-Brunswick Courier*, 9 Dec. 1837. *Novascotian, or Colonial Herald*, 3 Sept. 1834; 11 May, 28 Sept. 1836; 3 July, 7 Aug., 27 Nov. 1839. *Nova-Scotia Royal Gazette*, 27 Nov. 1839. *Public Ledger*, 3 Jan., 29 June, 10 Aug. 1832. *Times* (Halifax), 21 March, 19 Dec. 1837; 10 April, 3 July, 23 Oct. 1838; 26 Nov. 1839. Harper, *Early painters and engravers*. *Landmarks of Canada; what art has done for Canadian history . . .* (2v., Toronto, 1917–21; repr. in 1v., 1967), nos.45, 2139, 2152, 2154, 2169–75, 2177–78, 2181–84, 3622, 3627, 3629. A. E. Carter, "William H. Eagar: 'sensibilities of no common order'" (MA thesis, Concordia Univ., Montreal, 1979). J. W. Reps, *Views and viewmakers of urban America . . .* (Columbia, Mo., 1984).

EENOOLOOAPIK (Bobbie), Inuit hunter, traveller, guide, and trader; probably b. *c.* 1820 at Qimisuk (Blacklead Island) in Tenudiakbeek (Cumberland Sound, N.W.T.), eldest son of his father's marriage to Noogoonik; d. in the summer of 1847.

In Eenoolooapik's youth his family and several others migrated along the coast of Baffin Island from Qimisuk to Cape Enderby, probably on the southeast coast of the Cumberland peninsula. There they met a party of British whalers with whom they travelled to Cape Searle, on the peninsula's north shore. After learning about the whalers' homeland Eenoolooapik conceived a desire to travel there. However, his father had taken a second wife from among the natives of Cape Searle, and Eenoolooapik was left as the main support of his mother. Several times he almost boarded a homeward-bound ship but each time his mother's distress at being abandoned deterred him.

In September 1839 Eenoolooapik met the forceful

whaling captain William Penny* at Durban Island. Penny had witnessed the decline of the Arctic fishery and agreed with a suggestion published by Captain James Clark Ross* that it was finished unless the whalers diversified and wintered in the north. The whalers, constantly on the lookout for new territory, had heard of a large bay, Tenudiakbeek, described by the Inuit as full of whales and supporting a numerous Inuit population. Penny felt that it might prove the perfect place for a settlement and save the fishery, but by 1839 he had failed three times to find it. When he learned that Eenoolooapik was a native of Tenudiakbeek, had a detailed knowledge of the local geography, and wished to visit Scotland, he determined to take him home to Britain. With Eenoolooapik's help, Penny hoped to persuade the Royal Navy to explore the area.

Eenoolooapik embarked upon Penny's ship *Neptune* and on the evening of 8 November arrived in Aberdeen. The next morning crowds gathered in the harbour to greet him and several days later he gave a display of his kayaking ability on the River Dee. Unfortunately he contracted pneumonia from these exertions and was, for several months, on the brink of death. The illness led to the curtailment of Penny's plans to have him taught such skills as boat building.

Eenoolooapik was an intelligent, friendly man with a sense of humour and an ability to mimic others. These qualities were important, not only in his everyday life, but also on his visit to Scotland. They endeared him to locals who were so concerned about him that the Aberdeen papers carried information about his health. They also enabled him, upon his recovery, to behave like a born gentleman at the theatre, formal dinner parties, and two balls in honour of the queen's wedding. An instance of his sense of humour which the Scots appreciated was reported in the *Aberdeen Herald* of 16 Nov. 1839: "One of the men at the Neptune's boiling-house drew the outline caricature of a broad face, and said, 'That is an Esquimaux.' Bobbie immediately borrowed the pencil, and, drawing a very long face, with a long nose, said 'That is an Englishman.'"

Penny dispatched the map he and Eenoolooapik had drawn to the navy but, although the Admiralty provided £20 to be spent on Eenoolooapik, it was not interested in an expedition to the area. On 1 April 1840, aboard the *Bon Accord*, Eenoolooapik left Scotland, sent off with many presents for himself and a china teacup and saucer for his mother. The *Bon Accord* spent the early summer whaling and then, with Eenoolooapik's help, Penny took the ship into Tenudiakbeek. Believing it to be hitherto undiscovered, he named it Hogarth's Sound after one of his financial backers. Later the sound was recognized as being the "Cumberland Gulf" visited by John Davis* in 1585.

Eenoolooapik left the whalers at his birthplace and near by rejoined his mother and siblings who had travelled overland from Cape Searle to meet him. Shortly after, he married Amitak and had a son, Angalook. To the surprise of the whalers his status was not greatly altered by his visit to a "civilized" country. Each year Penny returned, he traded baleen with him. Eenoolooapik died of consumption in the summer of 1847, before seeing the full effects of the information he had imparted to Penny. Five years after his death the first planned wintering of a whaling crew took place. Later, wintering over became standard practice and several whaling camps were based in Cumberland Sound until the final demise of Arctic whaling. Unknowingly Eenoolooapik had helped initiate the colonization of Baffin Island by non-Inuit.

Eenoolooapik was not the only traveller in his family. His brother Totocatapik was known among the Inuit as a great voyager and a sister, Kur-king, migrated to Igloolik. Another sister was the celebrated Tookoolito (Hannah), who visited England in 1853–55 and travelled extensively in the Arctic and the United States with explorer Charles Francis Hall*.

SUSAN ROWLEY

Scott Polar Research Institute (Cambridge, Eng.), MS 1424 (William and Margaret Penny, journal, 1857–58). *Arctic whalers, icy seas: narratives of the Davis Strait whale fishery*, ed. W. G. Ross (Toronto, 1985). "Davis Strait whale fishery," *Nautical Magazine* (London and Glasgow), 9 (1840): 98–103. Alexander M'Donald, *A narrative of some passages in the history of Eenoolooapik, a young Esquimaux* ... (Edinburgh, 1841). *Aberdeen Herald and General Advertiser for the Counties of Aberdeen, Banff, and Kincardine* (Aberdeen, Scot.), 1839–40. *Aberdeen Journal and General Advertiser for the North of Scotland*, 1839–40. Alan Cooke and Clive Holland, *The exploration of northern Canada, 500 to 1920: a chronology* (Toronto, 1978). C. F. Hall, *Life with the Esquimaux: the narrative of Captain Charles Francis Hall ... from the 29th May, 1860, to the 13th September, 1862* ... (2v., London, 1864). John Tillotson, *Adventures in the ice: a comprehensive summary of Arctic exploration, discovery, and adventure* ... (London, [1869]). Richard Cull, "A description of three Esquimaux from Kinnooksook, Hogarth Sound, Cumberland Strait," Ethnological Soc. of London, *Journal*, 4 (1856): 215–25. Clive Holland, "William Penny, 1809–92: Arctic whaling master," *Polar Record* (Cambridge), 15 (1970): 25–43. P. C. Sutherland, "On the Esquimaux," Ethnological Soc. of London, *Journal*, 4: 193–214.

ELDER, WILLIAM, Baptist and Anglican clergyman and author; b. 15 Dec. 1784 in Falmouth, N.S., the second of eleven children of Matthew Elder and Rebecca Jenkins; m., probably between 1811 and 1813 in Chester, N.S., Elizabeth Fraile, and they had seven children; d. 10 Nov. 1848 in Sydney Mines, N.S.

The 19th century witnessed an astonishing religious

controversy centred on the proper mode of baptism, and nowhere was this controversy more venomous and vituperative than in Nova Scotia. Scores of books and pamphlets were issued and, as Methodist historian Thomas Watson Smith* stated it, "many pens, wielded by men of no mean skill, were worn out in the contest." The genesis of the Nova Scotian debate is to be found in William Elder's 1823 pamphlet *Infant sprinkling, weighed in the balance of the sanctuary, and found wanting*. Although treatises on the subject had appeared in Nova Scotia as early as 1811, Elder's was the first work published to refute another author, and it sparked an outpouring of the printed word that filled the religious press of the Maritime provinces for the next half-century.

Elder's father, a Presbyterian from County Donegal (Republic of Ireland), immigrated to Nova Scotia some time before 1780 and became a prosperous farmer in Falmouth. The family achieved considerable prominence in the next two generations. William's brother John was a magistrate and later sat in the House of Assembly; a sister was the mother of David Allison, second president of Mount Allison Wesleyan College; a nephew, another William, became professor of natural sciences at Acadia University. Writing in 1841, Elder noted that his "early years were not spent in academic groves," and he augmented his local schooling with disciplined reading and study. Certainly his publications demonstrate a profound knowledge of the writings of both classical and modern theologians.

As a young man Elder left home for Halifax, where he obtained an important position at the dockyard and began attending services at the Baptist church of the Reverend John BURTON. He was deeply influenced by Burton and, under the latter's guidance, became a Baptist licentiate. The Baptists had continued to grow in number since 1800, when Anglican bishop Charles Inglis* had noted "a great rage for dipping" in the province. The expansion was spearheaded by a group of remarkable preachers who made up in fervour and conviction what they lacked in formal education; among these men were Joseph DIMOCK, Harris Harding*, and Edward Manning*. On 4 Jan. 1820, Elder became one of them. Before an immense audience gathered at Dimock's church in Chester, he was "set apart." The Reverend David Nutter preached the ordination sermon which lasted for over three and a half hours. According to Ingraham Ebenezer Bill*, "the stillness of death reigned in the solemn assembly, and no one complained that the discourse was too long."

Embarking immediately on evangelistic work, in 1821 Elder settled in Granville and began ministering to a church of 12 members. He was active in the Nova Scotia Baptist Association, serving as clerk and four times as moderator. Elder was diligent in touring the back settlements and his name figures prominently in the ordination of ministers and the founding of new churches. By 1823 he had moved from Granville to a new settlement soon to be named Bridgetown [*see* John Crosskill*], and was augmenting his meagre income from the church by making axes and horseshoeing. In 1828 he participated in the founding of the Nova Scotia Baptist Education Society, of which he became a director; this organization was the genesis of Horton Academy and eventually of Acadia University. In 1833 Elder and the Reverend Richard W. Cunningham made an extensive missionary tour of Cape Breton, an account of which was published in the *Baptist Missionary Magazine of Nova-Scotia and New-Brunswick*. It was the last labour of his ministry in the Baptist faith.

Elder's 1823 pamphlet was written in response to the appearance in 1822 of a work by the Reverend George Jackson, a Methodist, whose purpose was to substantiate the legitimacy of infant baptism by sprinkling. Elder's refutation was gentle and respectfully worded and in turn was skilfully rebutted by Jackson, the Presbyterian minister Duncan Ross*, and others. Now began a period of intense mental agony for Elder, culminating in 1834 with a second pamphlet and the reversal of his views – the only case on record where the great debate actually succeeded in changing someone's mind. Elder's *Reasons for relinquishing the principles of adult baptism* pleaded that his church be tolerant and recognize the legitimacy of other points of view. Baptist reaction was immediate. A council of elders convened in the same year expelled him from all Baptist fellowship in spite of his moving exposition to them. The deluge of print now began in earnest, led by Edmund Albern Crawley*'s lengthy attack and the scurrilous pro-Elder response by Thomas Taylor.

Meanwhile, Elder, after taking charge for a year of the Congregational Church at Liverpool, was ordained deacon in the Church of England and was appointed the first rector of Trinity Church, Sydney Mines, in 1841. His reasons for embracing the established church were set out in a pamphlet published that year. Elder was ordained to the priesthood by Bishop John INGLIS on 23 July 1843 at Sydney. A tribute to Elder by his son Samuel, written in 1848, paints a revealing portrait of Elder's ministry at Sydney Mines. Samuel, himself a Baptist clergyman, wrote on his first visit home in seven years: "On Sabbath morning last, I attended service in the little church, my father officiating. There was a queerness of feeling in looking at my venerable parent in his priestly robes, and somehow they did not seem to suit him. The Episcopalian character appeared on the surface but Dissent still looks through. . . . I can never see anything in my father but a Baptist minister – a bishop of Paul's liking."

Elder died suddenly on 10 Nov. 1848. The great controversy over baptism continued for many more years. Elder stands apart from others engaged in it because of his tolerance in an age of dogmatism and his ability to compromise in the face of overwhelming sectarian inflexibility.

FRANKLYN H. HICKS

In addition to his writings in the minutes of the N.S. Baptist Assoc. and in church magazines, William Elder is the author of *Infant sprinkling, weighed in the balance of the sanctuary, and found wanting, in five letters, addressed to the Rev. George Jackson . . .* (Halifax, 1823), *Reasons for relinquishing the principles of adult baptism, and embracing those of infant baptism . . .* (Halifax, 1834), and *The claims of the established Church of England to the favorable consideration and affectionate support of British Christians . . .* (Halifax, 1841).

Of the 13 books and pamphlets dealing with Elder's theology published between 1823 and 1845, the most important are the following: Alexander Crawford, *Believer immersion, as opposed to unbeliever sprinkling; in two essays . . . to which are added three letters to Mr. Ross of Pictou, containing strictures on his first letter to Mr. Elder of Annapolis* (Charlottetown, 1827); E. A. Crawley, *A treatise on baptism, as appointed by our Lord Jesus Christ . . . containing a reply, to Mr. Elder's letters on infant baptism, and a solemn appeal, in favor of a spiritual church* (Halifax, 1835); George Jackson, *A further attempt to substantiate the legitimacy of infant baptism and of sprinkling, as a mode of administering that ordinance, in a series of letters addressed to the Rev. William Elder . . .* (Halifax, [1823]); Matthew Richey, *A short and scriptural method with Antipedobaptists; containing strictures on the Rev. E. A. Crawley's treatise on baptism, in reply to the Rev. W. Elder's letters on that subject* (Halifax, 1835); James Robertson, *A treatise on infant baptism . . .* (Halifax, 1836); Duncan Ross, *Baptism considered in its subjects and mode: in three letters, to the Reverend William Elder . . .* (Pictou, N.S., 1825); and Thomas Taylor, *The Baptist commentator reviewed; two letters to the Rev. William Jackson, on Christian baptism . . .* (Halifax, 1835).

Annapolis Valley Regional Library, Bridgetown Branch (Bridgetown, N.S.), "Book of Bridgetown pictures," comp. E. R. Coward (MS photo albums, 4v., plus scrapbook, 1958), 1: 22–23. Atlantic Baptist Hist. Coll., Acadia Univ. (Wolfville, N.S.), Samuel Elder, diary. PANS, MG 100, 138, no.9 (typescript). *Baptist Missionary Magazine of Nova-Scotia and New-Brunswick* (Saint John; Halifax), 1 (1827–29): 256, 380; new ser., 1 (1834): 73, 126. Joseph Dimock, *The diary and related writings of the Reverend Joseph Dimock (1768–1846)*, ed. G. E. Levy (Hantsport, N.S., 1979). [John Inglis], *A journal of visitation in Nova Scotia, Cape Breton, and along the eastern shore of New Brunswick, by the lord bishop of Nova Scotia, in the summer and autumn of 1843* (3rd ed., London, 1846), 32–35. George Jackson, *An humble attempt to substantiate the legitimacy of infant baptism, and of sprinkling, as a scriptural mode of administering that ordinance . . .* (Halifax, 1822). N.B. and N.S. Baptist Assoc., *Minutes* (Saint John), 1820–21. N.S. Baptist Assoc., *Minutes* (Halifax), 1822–35. *Morning Courier: Parliamentary Reporter and Literary Gazette* (Halifax), 14 Nov. 1848. J. V. Duncanson, *Falmouth – a New England township in Nova Scotia, 1760–1965* (Windsor, Ont., 1965; repr. with supp., Belleville, Ont., 1983). Bill, *Fifty years with Baptist ministers*. A. W. H. Eaton, *The history of Kings County, Nova Scotia . . .* (Salem, Mass., 1910; repr. Belleville, 1972). E. E. Jackson, *Windows on the past, North Sydney, Nova Scotia* (Windsor, N.S., 1974), 95. G. E. Levy, *Baptists of Maritime prov.*; *With the pioneer Baptists in Nova Scotia; a sketch of the life of David Nutter* (Wolfville, 1929), 55. Elizabeth Ruggles Coward, *Bridgetown, Nova Scotia: its history to 1900* ([Bridgetown, 1955]), 69–70. Saunders, *Hist. of Baptists*. Smith, *Hist. of Methodist Church*, vol.2.

ELLIS, WILLIAM, Methodist clergyman; b. 1780 in County Down (Northern Ireland); married with six children; d. 21 Sept. 1837 in Harbour Grace, Nfld.

At the age of 16 William Ellis was converted to Methodism and he subsequently served the church in his native land as a class-leader and local preacher. During the Irish rebellion of 1798, he and his family narrowly escaped death. On 30 Oct. 1808 Ellis sailed from England as a Methodist missionary to Newfoundland, arriving there on 23 November. For five years, he, John Remmington, and Samuel McDowell ministered in the settlements on the north side of Conception Bay and on the south shore of Trinity Bay. Ellis was responsible for building a church at Grates Cove and was the first person to preach in it. In 1813 he went to Bonavista, a town without a minister to serve its 1,200 Protestant residents. Under his leadership, the construction of a church, which had been started 15 years earlier, was completed. He was the first Methodist to visit Catalina, and in April 1814 he delivered the first sermon heard in Bird Island Cove (Elliston).

In 1815 the Newfoundland district of the British Wesleyan Conference was organized and Ellis became its chairman. Two years later he moved to Trinity where he established a Sunday school, had a church erected, and was able to visit many communities on the north side of the bay. While he was serving in Port de Grave in 1819, Ellis baptized six Indians who had been brought to the settlement by a Labrador planter. He was then stationed at the Blackhead mission before returning to Bonavista, which had been one of his most successful fields. In 1835, in poor health, he was again sent to Trinity, the least onerous charge. The 1837 district letter to the Missionary Society in London stated: "Brother Ellis had a stroke of palsy and is unable to continue his work; he is put down as supernumerary. . . . He has a family of six children, the oldest fifteen years of age, the youngest a quarter of a year, and therefore all that can should be done to save them from the most abject poverty." Ellis's death came at Harbour Grace on 21 September; he was the first Methodist missionary to die and be buried in Newfoundland.

The Reverend William Wilson, a fellow missionary with Ellis for 14 years, wrote: "He was a kind and amiable man, of good natural abilities, and very eloquent as a speaker; he was faithful, laborious, and successful in his work." According to the Reverend Philip Tocque*, "Often theological nuggets of gold would embellish his discourses, and a stream of Irish oratory would flow from his lips."

NABOTH WINSOR

SOAS, Methodist Missionary Soc. Arch., Wesleyan Methodist Missionary Soc., corr., Nfld., 1808–37 (mfm. at PAC). *Wesleyan-Methodist Magazine*, 31 (1808)–60 (1837). Smith, *Hist. of Methodist Church*. William Wilson, *Newfoundland and its missionaries ... to which is added a chronological table of all the important events that have occurred on the island* (Cambridge, Mass., and Halifax, 1866). *Methodist Monthly Greeting* (St John's), 11 (1899), no.12; 12 (1900), no.4.

ELSKWATAWA. *See* TENSKWATAWA

EMERSON (Emmerson), THOMAS, doctor and army and militia officer; b. *c.* 1762; d. 14 Oct. 1843 in Fredericton.

Thomas Emerson arrived in New Brunswick in 1784 as a bachelor in his early twenties, having served in Nova Scotia with the Royal Fencible Americans during the period of the American revolution [*see* Joseph Goreham*]. He was granted lands along the Digdeguash and Magaguadavic rivers, but soon sold them; he settled in St Andrews, where he practised medicine.

Emerson returned to military life in 1793 when, on the outbreak of war between Britain and France, Lieutenant Governor Thomas Carleton* raised the King's New Brunswick Regiment for service within the province. Emerson became surgeon's mate, a title that was changed in 1796 for the more impressive one of assistant surgeon. He remained with the unit until it was disbanded in 1802.

When hostilities were resumed in 1803, another regiment was quickly organized. It was the New Brunswick Fencibles, renamed in 1810 the 104th Foot. Emerson signed up as assistant surgeon in August 1804. He appears to have been stationed both in Saint John, where he testified at a trial in 1806, and in Fredericton, where his silhouette was cut the following year. It was the 104th that made the famous winter march on snowshoes up the Saint John River and across to Quebec in 1813, during war with the United States. This 24-day, 350-mile trek must have proved a strenuous task for the 50-year-old Emerson. For the remainder of the conflict the regiment was stationed in Upper Canada, where it saw long and bloody service. The unit was disbanded at Quebec in 1817. Emerson was to continue his affiliation with the army to the end of his life, serving as battalion surgeon of the York County militia from 1819 to 1843.

He returned to civilian practice, in Fredericton, some time after 1817. Records of the Fredericton Emigrant Society show that he was paid £7 16*s.* 0*d.* in 1820 for tending newcomers to the province. On 31 Dec. 1825 he was awarded a military grant of 800 acres "in the Parish of Kent in the County of York" (probably Kentville). This land he exchanged in 1826 for a house and lot in Fredericton, each property being valued at £200. His new property fronted on Carleton Street; here he probably had his residence and office.

In the early 1830s Emerson entered into partnership with Dr George P. Peters, son of the attorney general, Charles Jeffery PETERS. In his autobiography William Teel Baird* remembers going to work as a boy of almost 14 in their dispensary. Baird speaks of Dr Emerson's extensive practice, noting that he was "for many years the best known man in Fredericton." He belonged to the provincial faculty of physicians and surgeons and in 1832 was one of a three-man board to license new practitioners. He must have prospered since he acquired more land. In 1833 he leased a ten-acre lot from King's College and in 1837 he bought a farm in New Maryland.

Emerson was married twice. His first wife, Rebecca, died in 1832. Two years later, on 20 May 1834, he married Ann Bailey of Fredericton. There appear to have been no children from either marriage.

Thomas Emerson died at age 80 on 14 Oct. 1843, leaving everything to his "dear wife Ann" and to Christ Church (Anglican) upon her death. The location of his grave is unknown. Ann Emerson, who died in 1873, lies in the Old Burying Ground in Fredericton.

ROSLYN ROSENFELD

Charlotte Land Registry Office (St Andrews, N.B.), Registry books, A: 38, 278, 343, 401. MTRL, Hist. Picture Coll., T 13691. PANB, RG 7, RS75, 1843, Thomas Emerson; RG 10, RS108. Saint John Regional Library (Saint John, N.B.), "Biographical data relating to New Brunswick families, especially of loyalist descent," comp. D. R. Jack (4v., typescript; mfm. at PANB). York Land Registry Office (Fredericton), Registry books, 15: 65; 21: 412, 421; 29: 144. *Royal Gazette* (Fredericton), 18 Oct. 1843. *Commissioned officers in the medical services of the British army, 1660–1960*, comp. Alfred Peterkin *et al.* (2v., London, 1968). *Merchants' & farmers' almanack*, 1843: 53. W. T. Baird, *Seventy years of New Brunswick life* ... (Saint John, 1890; repr. Fredericton, 1978), 30–31. L. M. Beckwith Maxwell, *An outline of the history of central New Brunswick to the time of confederation* (Sackville, N.B., 1937; repr. Fredericton, 1984). Esther Clark Wright, *The loyalists of New Brunswick* (Fredericton, 1955; repr. Hantsport, N.S., 1981). W. A. Squires, *The 104th Regiment of Foot (the New Brunswick Regiment), 1803–1817* (Fredericton, 1962), 189. W. B. Stewart, *Medicine in New Brunswick* ... (Moncton, 1974).

Jonas Howe, "The King's New Brunswick Regiment, 1793–1802," N.B. Hist. Soc., *Coll.*, 1 (1894–97), no.1: 15. J. W. Lawrence, "The medical men of St. John in its first half century," N.B. Hist. Soc., *Coll.*, 1, no.3: 283–84.

ENTREMONT, BENONI D' (he signed **Dentremont**), mariner, shipbuilder, office holder, JP, and militia officer; b. *c.* 1745 at Pobomcoup (Pubnico), N.S., son of Jacques Mius d'Entremont, third Baron de Pobomcoup, and Marguerite Amirault; m. July 1783 Anne-Marguerite Pothier, and they had nine children; d. 21 Feb. 1841 at Pubnico, aged 96.

Benoni d'Entremont could pride himself on being of the "noblesse" for he was a direct descendant of Philippe Mius* d'Entremont, who had arrived in Acadia from France in 1650 or 1651 and had been made Baron de Pobomcoup by Charles de Saint-Étienne* de La Tour, governor of the colony. Benoni was influenced in his early years by his French cultural inheritance but also by the exigencies of survival in a hamlet that had not changed much since the 17th century. He shared its fervent Catholicism.

For d'Entremont, as for thousands of Acadians, the mid 18th century was devastating and heart-breaking. The Anglo-French struggle for domination in North America resulted in the deportation of some 7,000 Acadians in 1755 [*see* Charles Lawrence*], most of them being removed to the Thirteen Colonies. A year later, at age 11, d'Entremont witnessed the near-destruction of his village by the English, was captured along with his family, and was transported to Marblehead, Mass.

Life for most Acadians in Massachusetts was difficult, to say the least. Deprived of priests in that Puritan colony, separated from immediate family members and prevented by law from searching for them, many lost hope of ever regaining their homesteads and way of life. Others, through mere circumstance, were better treated on the whole. This was the case with some of the people from Pobomcoup. Tradition has it that Benoni's father met a mariner in Boston whose life and ship he had saved some 35 years earlier. To repay him, the seafarer pleaded his case with Governor William Shirley; as a consequence, his family was granted food, clothing, and a degree of liberty unknown to most exiles. The d'Entremonts and a closely associated family, the Amiraults, were even permitted to build the very vessel that would transport them back to Nova Scotia.

At the age of 21 Benoni d'Entremont again saw the shores of his native land. On 29 Aug. 1766 his family, along with eight others, arrived at Pubnico. Benoni later settled on the west side of the harbour and soon began to follow in the steps of his father, first as a sea captain, transporting goods on ships he and fellow Acadians had built. Sometimes more than the elements had to be braved. In 1778, on a return voyage from Saint-Pierre and Miquelon, his ship was seized by an American privateer, but he heroically recaptured it with two other men. He also imitated his father by becoming a community leader, initially of his own people and later of the entire population of Argyle Township, which included New England settlers who had arrived after the deportation at the invitation of Charles Lawrence, former governor of Nova Scotia.

D'Entremont's position as a community leader may have been the result of his family background, of his ability to read and write in both French and English (acquired, surprisingly, while he was in exile), or of personal qualities which people admired and respected. He became an important figure in his church and an assistant to the parish priest, Jean-Mandé SIGOGNE, acting as a sort of envoy for villagers with specific requests to make of their pastor. The provincial authorities also recognized d'Entremont's leadership. After a law was passed in 1791 permitting Acadians to serve as public officials he was named first treasurer for Argyle and a justice of the peace. In addition, he demonstrated a willingness to defend his home by joining the militia, in which he became a lieutenant. A son, Simon*, made further contributions to the community as a member of the provincial legislature.

NEIL J. BOUCHER

Arch. of the Diocese of Yarmouth (Yarmouth, N.S.), Sainte-Anne-du-Ruisseau, reg. des baptêmes, mariages et sépultures, 1799–1841 (copies at Centre acadien, univ. Sainte-Anne, Pointe-de-l'Église, N.-É.). PAC, MG 30, C20, 8: 1803–4 (mfm. at Centre acadien, univ. Sainte-Anne). PANS, RG 1, 168: 434. *Acadian exiles in the colonies*, comp. Janet Jehn (Covington, Ky., 1977). Bona Arsenault, *Histoire et généalogie des Acadiens* (2v., Québec, 1965), 1; (éd. rév., 6v., [Montréal, 1978]), 4. Edwin Crowell, *A history of Barrington Township and vicinity . . . 1604–1870* (Yarmouth, [1923]; repr. Belleville, Ont., 1973). C.-J. d'Entremont, *Histoire du Cap-Sable de l'an mil au traité de Paris, 1763* (5v., Eunice, La., 1981). H. L. d'Entremont, *The Baronnie de Pombcoup and the Acadians: a history of the ancient "Department of Cape Sable," now known as Yarmouth and Shelburne counties, Nova Scotia* (Yarmouth, 1931), 44–45, 51, 53–54, 111–15, 121–22. *Vanguard* (Yarmouth), 26 Sept. 1973.

ESSENS. *See* AISANCE

EST, *dit* CONDEAU, FRANÇOIS. *See* CONDO, FRANCIS

EVANS, JAMES, teacher, Methodist minister and missionary, linguist, and author; b. 18 Jan. 1801 in Kingston upon Hull, England, son of James Evans, ship's captain, and Mary ——; m. 1822 Mary Blithe Smith, and they had two daughters, one of whom died in childhood; d. 23 Nov. 1846 in Keelby, England.

After schooling in Lincolnshire James Evans entered the grocery business, where he learned merchandising and shorthand. In 1822 he followed his parents to Lower Canada and soon found employment as a teacher near L'Orignal, Upper Canada. About three years later he and his wife moved to Augusta Township, on the St Lawrence River, where he reportedly underwent a conversion at a Methodist camp-meeting. Under the influence of William Case*, presiding elder of the Upper Canada District of the Methodist Episcopal Church, he accepted an appointment in 1828 to the Rice Lake school for Indian children. An aptitude for language facilitated his understanding of Ojibwa and enabled him to begin translating and writing. Case steadily encouraged Evans's proposed publication of a "vocabulary and Dictionary of Indian words."

In August 1830, while still at Rice Lake, Evans was accepted as a probationer in the Methodist Episcopal (later the Wesleyan Methodist) Church; between 1831 and 1833 he served on the Credit, Ancaster, and St Catharines circuits. Ordained in 1833, he was appointed to the St Clair Mission (near Port Sarnia) the following year. When he arrived in July he found many Ojibwas opposed to Christianity [*see* BAUZHI-GEEZHIG-WAESHIKUM]; in March 1835 he reported 15 converts. His work there and the encouragement he received from other Methodist missionaries provided the basis for his rapid progress in native linguistics. A committee composed of Joseph Stinson*, Peter Jones*, Case, Evans, and his brother Ephraim* was appointed by the Canada Conference of the Methodist Church to prepare an orthographic system for the Ojibwa language. By 1836 James Evans had devised an Ojibwa syllabary of eight consonants and four vowels, but it was not accepted that year for printing by the bible society in Toronto. He spent four months in New York in 1837 securing the printing of translated hymns and Scripture and of his *Speller and interpreter, in Indian and English, for the use of the mission schools*.

The following year Evans and Thomas Hurlburt*, a fellow missionary and linguist, were sent by the Canada Conference to undertake a tour of the north shore of Lake Superior. On 18 May 1839 Evans met George Simpson*, the governor of the Hudson's Bay Company, and evidently satisfied him that Methodist missionaries would not disrupt company activities in the northwest. Simpson consequently assured him that the HBC territory was open to the Methodists. Upon returning to Upper Canada that summer, Evans was appointed minister at Guelph. In January 1840 Simpson, who wished to restrict the activity of Anglican and Roman Catholic missionaries to the Red River country (Man.), announced an agreement whereby three missionaries named by the Wesleyan Methodist Missionary Society in Britain were to be placed at strategic points in the northwest. Probably at the insistence of the British Wesleyans, a superintendent's position was later added and on 7 April Evans learned of his appointment. The party increased from four to eight as a result of the inclusion of Evans's wife and daughter and native assistants Peter Jacobs [Pahtahsega*] and Henry Bird Steinhauer*. Evans arrived at Norway House (Man.) in August and by October all of the other missionaries were in place and working: George Barnley at Moose Factory (Ont.), William Mason at Rainy Lake, and Robert Terrill Rundle* at Fort Edmonton (Edmonton, Alta).

Now at the peak of his career, Evans found his mission work at Norway House and in the nearby Indian village of Rossville both satisfying and demanding. His development of the Ojibwa syllabary enabled him within two months of his arrival to prepare the basic structure of a syllabary for another Algonkian language (Cree), to begin using the new syllabic alphabet in his schools and religious services, and to initiate a program of translating and printing. Seven works, all printed in syllabics (using crude type cast by Evans, apparently from the lead linings of tea-chests), are recorded for the Rossville Mission Press during his superintendence. However, his fervour, his concerns for the native peoples, and his location at a main transfer point of the HBC led him to criticize company policy and practice, including labour on the Sabbath.

The company had its own grievances, including the cost of the missionaries' freight, Evans's ban on Sunday travel by converted Indians, and his independent conduct. In December 1842 Simpson instructed Chief Factor Donald Ross at Norway House not to allow Evans's presence at the company's Council. The next year Simpson had the Evans family moved from the fort to Rossville, to reduce the missionary's interference in company affairs and to lessen social rivalry in the small confines of the fort, particularly between the wives of Evans and Ross. By 1845 the trading monopoly of the HBC was being sorely tested by free traders [*see* Pierre-Guillaume SAYER]. That year, in a letter to Simpson, Evans defended the right of natives to exchange furs – a practice they described as gift-giving but which the HBC considered a form of trading that infringed on its monopoly – and requested authorization for them to give a fur to the mission. The governor wrote immediately, in June, to Robert Alder* of the WMMS requesting his removal from HBC territory. A response would not come until a year later.

In the mean time troubles from other directions created stress for Evans and heightened controversy. In 1844, while he was on a canoe trip to the Athabasca country to counter the efforts of the Roman Catholic missionary Jean-Baptiste Thibault*, a gun held by Evans had accidentally discharged, killing Thomas HASSALL, his most trusted teacher and interpreter.

Evans never recovered from the shock. Reports of his changed character and emotional disturbance began to appear in company correspondence. At Rossville his small house was crowded, a result of his taking in several native girls, and he was lonely for his daughter, Eugenia Clarissa, after her marriage to John McLean* on 18 Aug. 1845. By this time disputes with the HBC over free trade and travelling on the Sabbath had flared into open hostility. In June Simpson withdrew the company's provision of food for the mission's households and authorized instead an annual grant of £200 to cover "all expenses." Under the increasing stress, threats to Evans's health – kidney infections and heart problems – now became grievous.

In February 1846 rumours of sexual play with the native girls in his home became formal charges against Evans by the Indians of the Rossville community. Evans instructed William Mason to conduct a church trial under Wesleyan discipline to test the accusations. Though he was found not guilty, his caring for a sick girl in his house was judged imprudent. The issue seemed settled, but he keenly resented the judgement of imprudence and Mason's forwarding of the documents from the trial to the missionary society in London. Additional submissions and charges were sent separately to London by Governor Simpson.

Alder's letter arrived in June, bringing a response to Simpson's request for the removal of Evans. Without revealing the request, Alder invited Evans to England for talks and suggested that he return eventually to the St Clair Mission. Upon arriving in London in October, Evans was examined by the society's secretaries, Alder and John Beecham. They also found him innocent of sexual misconduct but stated that his treating the native girls in his home with the same familiarity as he treated his daughter had been unseemly and improper. Evans died suddenly of a heart attack following a missionary rally in Lincolnshire in November. After his departure from the northwest, the Wesleyan missions there declined and for some time no effort was made to revive them.

The agonizing circumstances of Evans's last year do not diminish the worth of his many achievements, most notably the invention and introduction of syllabic characters for the Cree language. This easily learned form of written Cree spread rapidly among the native communities, initially as a result of the translating and printing done at Rossville by Evans, William and Sophia* Mason, Steinhauer, John Sinclair, and others. Evans's syllabary was soon adopted and adapted by rival missionary groups, the Church Missionary Society [*see* James Hunter*; John Horden*] and the Oblates of Mary Immaculate. Their extensive work in translation and publication ensured the survival and spread of the syllabic system; that it remains in use today is strong testimony to Evans's accomplishment.

GERALD M. HUTCHINSON

James Evans is the author of *The speller and interpreter, in Indian and English, for the use of the mission schools, and such as may desire to obtain a knowledge of the Ojibway tongue* (New York, 1837). He was involved in producing Ojibwa versions of a number of Methodist publications, including *The first nine chapters of the first book of Moses, called Genesis*, translated by Evans and revised and corrected by Peter Jones (York [Toronto], 1833), a hymn-book which appeared under the Ojibwa title *Nu-gu-mo-nun O-je-boa . . .* , translated by Evans and George Henry (New York, 1837), and several other works listed in J. C. Pilling, *Bibliography of the Algonquian languages* (Washington, 1891), reprinted as J. C. Pilling, *Bibliographies of the languages of North American Indians* (9 parts in 3 vols., New York, 1973), vol.2.

The Cree translations which Evans subsequently prepared and printed at the Rossville Mission Press are listed and discussed in the studies by Peel and Nichols cited below. Portions of his correspondence have been edited by Fred Landon and printed as "Selections from the papers of James Evans, missionary to the Indians" and "Letters of Rev. James Evans, Methodist missionary, written during his journey to and residence in the Lake Superior region, 1838–39," *OH*, 26 (1930): 474–91 and 28 (1932): 47–70. The Ojibwa syllabary which he had developed by 1836 is found in the James Evans coll. at Victoria Univ. Library in Toronto (where it is incorrectly identified as his later Cree syllabary), and in the James Evans papers in the Regional Coll. at UWOL. A portrait of Evans, by John Wycliffe Lowes Forster*, is at the UCC-C.

Humberside Record Office (Beverley, Eng.), Reg. of baptisms for the parish of Sculcoates (Kingston upon Hull), 19 Feb. 1801. PABC, Add. MSS 635, box 3, folder 78, Simpson to Ross, 1, 3 Dec. 1842; folder 79; box 5, folder 176, esp. Ross to Simpson, 15 Aug. 1842. PAM, HBCA, A.12/2; B.235/c/1, no.5; D.4/25: ff.47–47d, 62d; D.4/62: ff.67d–68; D.4/68: ff.54–55d, 154d–155; D.5/8, 11–12, 14, 17–18. SOAS, Methodist Missionary Soc. Arch., Wesleyan Methodist Missionary Soc., corr., North America, Hudson's Bay territories, boxes 13, 101–5. UCC-C, John MacLean papers, doc.E99, c88m, William Mason, 30 Dec. 1886. R. M. Ballantyne, *Hudson's Bay; every day life in the wilds of North America, during six years' residence in the territories of the Honourable Hudson's Bay Company* (2nd ed., Edinburgh and London, 1848). Letitia [Mactavish] Hargrave, *The letters of Letitia Hargrave*, ed. Margaret Arnett MacLeod (Toronto, 1947). R. T. Rundle, *The Rundle journals, 1840–1848*, intro. and notes G. M. Hutchinson, ed. H. A. Dempsey (Calgary, 1977). Wesleyan Methodist Church, Missionary Soc., *Missionary Notices* (London), new ser., 2 (1844): 413. Wesleyan Methodist Church in Canada, *The minutes of twelve annual conferences . . . from 1846 to 1857 . . .* (Toronto, 1863). *Christian Guardian*, 9 Jan., 17 April, 10 May 1839; 1 April 1840. G. H. Cornish, *Cyclopædia of Methodism in Canada, containing historical, educational, and statistical information . . .* (2v., Toronto and Halifax, 1881–1903), 1. *Death notices of Ont.* (Reid).

Boon, *Anglican Church*. J. W. Grant, *Moon of winter-*

time: missionaries and the Indians of Canada in encounter since 1534 (Toronto, 1984). John McLean, *James Evans: inventor of the syllabic system of the Cree language* (Toronto, 1890). J. D. Nichols, "The composition sequence of the first Cree hymnal," *Essays in Algonquian bibliography in honour of V. M. Dechene*, ed. H. C. Wolfart (Winnipeg, 1984), 1–21. B. [B.] Peel, *Rossville Mission Press: the invention of the Cree syllabic characters, and the first printing in Rupert's Land* (Montreal, 1974). J. E. Sanderson, *The first century of Methodism in Canada* (2v., Toronto, 1908–10). Nan Shipley, *The James Evans story* (Toronto, 1966). E. R. Young, *The apostle of the north, Rev. James Evans* (Toronto, 1900). T. C. B. Boon, "The use of catechisms and syllabics by the early missionaries of Rupert's Land," UCC, Committee on Arch., *Bull.* (Toronto), no.13 (1960): 8–17. Nathanael Burwash, "The gift to a nation of a written language," RSC *Trans.*, 3rd ser., 5 (1911), sect.II: 3–21. J. [S.] Carroll, "James Evans, the planter of Methodist missions in Rupert's Land," *Canadian Methodist Magazine* (Toronto and Halifax), 16 (January–June 1883): 329–40. G. M. Hutchinson, "James Evans' last year," Canadian Church Hist. Soc., *Journal* (Sudbury, Ont.), 19 (1977)/UCC, Committee on Arch., *Bull.*, no.26 (1977): 42–56. E. R. Young, "James Evans, the inventor of the syllabic characters," *Canadian Methodist Magazine*, 16: 433–48.

F

FAIRBANKS, CHARLES RUFUS, lawyer, politician, office holder, judge, and entrepreneur; b. 25 March 1790 in Halifax, son of Rufus Fairbanks and Anne (Nancy) Prescott; d. there 15 April 1841.

Charles Rufus Fairbanks was born into Halifax's commercial gentry. His father had come from New England to Halifax in the mid 1780s to enter a family business begun by an uncle in 1749, and there he married the daughter of a prominent merchant. Three of his five sons were to become merchants, while Charles Rufus and Samuel Prescott* chose the law. Charles received his education at the Anglican King's College in Windsor and the Roman Catholic Séminaire de Québec. Returning to Halifax, he studied law under Simon Bradstreet Robie*. In 1815, four years after his admission to the bar, he married Sarah Elizabeth, the daughter of William LAWSON, a leading merchant and politician. Six of the thirteen children born to them survived into adulthood and their marriages, combined with the business and marriage partnerships negotiated by Charles's siblings, placed him firmly within the "family compact" which dominated Halifax society through the first half of the 19th century.

Social connections, plus a reputation for eloquence, provided the foundation for Fairbanks's public career, which began in 1823 when he contested a by-election in Halifax Township. After a bitter fight with John YOUNG, Fairbanks won, largely because the Halifax business élite wanted a representative who would defend their interests against attack by outport members. Fairbanks quickly emerged as a leading figure within the House of Assembly and for over a decade used his influence to champion the aspirations of Halifax capital. He advocated low tariffs on imported food-stuffs, subsidies for the fishery, incorporation of limited-liability business enterprises, inauguration of a transatlantic steamer service, and curtailment of outport trade with foreign powers. Fairbanks's performance was influenced in part by concern for his own investments. Through the 1820s and 1830s he became involved in grist- and sawmilling, marine insurance, whaling, coal mining, and land speculation.

Fairbanks's reputation as an entrepreneur rested primarily on his commitment to the Shubenacadie canal project. Since the 1790s Halifax interests had been urging construction of a water-way to link their port with the Bay of Fundy and thereby challenge Saint John, N.B., for control of Nova Scotia's hinterland [*see* Isaac Hildrith*]. Finally, in 1826, during a boom in the local economy, a company was formed to build an 8-foot-deep canal over 54 miles, following the Grand Lake–Shubenacadie River system. Total cost was placed at £60,000, the major engineering challenge involving construction of several locks to overcome the drop of 69 feet between Grand Lake and Halifax Harbour. Fairbanks, the company's secretary-treasurer, became principal spokesman for the project within the assembly. Arguing that the canal would function as "a great public road," he persuaded a somewhat dubious house to grant the company a charter of incorporation, a subsidy of £15,000, and a guarantee of a five per cent return on company stock. Work began that summer on the most ambitious public works project in Nova Scotia before the railway era. Francis Hall, a Scottish engineer, supervised construction, and Fairbanks assumed responsibility for finances. Costs quickly exceeded estimates and, after failing to win legislative approval for a scheme whereby the canal company would issue its own paper money, Fairbanks departed for London seeking additional working capital. His negotiations through 1829 and 1830 proved remarkably successful. Private investors agreed to buy some £27,000 in company stock and the British government came forward with a loan of £20,000, secured by a mortgage on the canal property.

The comment by William Blowers Bliss* that

Fairbanks had "bamboozled the John Bulls" was prophetic. Construction halted in the winter of 1831–32, funds having been exhausted by engineering blunders, frost and flood, absconding contractors, and a riotous work force. With £80,000 spent, the project remained far from complete. Assembly critics led by John Young held Fairbanks responsible for the débâcle, but he refused to admit error. Moreover, he retained his enthusiasm, to the point of investing £1,500 of his own money for surveys designed to prove the canal's viability. His lobbying through the 1830s failed to achieve a resumption of construction but did win him widespread praise as a man of "untiring industry and indomitable perseverance." In the 1850s one of Fairbanks's sons, a civil engineer, supervised completion of his father's dream. Another son bought the works in 1870 in the mistaken belief that a canal could compete with railways. Thus for some 50 years the Shubenacadie canal was bound up with the destiny of the Fairbanks family.

Fairbanks also attracted attention as an advocate of political reform. Raised as an orthodox tory, he gradually acquired enthusiasm for such innovations as compulsory mass education, reorganization of the public accounts, incorporation of Halifax as a city with elected officials, and negotiation of a civil list settlement giving the assembly control over public revenues. In private correspondence he went farther, advocating a purge of sinecurists from the colonial administration and broadened representation within the Legislative Council, with members to serve fixed, rather than life, terms. Fairbanks also urged London to reorganize the Executive Council by replacing bureaucrats with entrepreneurs and leading assemblymen. These changes would not have introduced democracy but did reveal Fairbanks to be in touch with the currents of change and ready to sacrifice tradition for the sake of efficiency and material progress.

With some justification, contemporaries attributed many of Fairbanks's actions to opportunism. The trip to London, for example, was an occasion for him to promote himself as well as the canal company. Fairbanks appears to have deliberately sought to ingratiate himself with the Whig politicians then ascendant in Britain. His success became evident soon after his return to Halifax in 1831 when, through intervention from London, he was named solicitor general and appointed to the Executive Council. Three years later he emerged from a scramble of applicants to become master of the rolls and judge of the Vice-Admiralty Court. A fellow member of the bench, Lewis Morris Wilkins, commented, "He is extremely industrious, persevering and speculative, but good judgment I fear has no dent in his brain and he thinks too highly of himself, or meanly of others to consult on any subject."

Despite this arrogance and assertiveness, Fairbanks long remained a popular figure. His absence in Britain during the fierce legislative squabbling in 1830 over the assembly's power of the purse had proved convenient for his reputation. During the wrangling over incorporation of the Bank of Nova Scotia two years later and the subsequent controversy about making bank paper convertible into specie, Fairbanks shrewdly avoided identification with any faction. When prosperity gave way to hard times in the mid 1830s and spawned demands for radical change, he argued that Nova Scotia needed not constitutional innovation but rather loans from Britain to finance a large-scale program of public works.

Eventually, however, Fairbanks became a target for the reform movement. An initial provocation was provided by his delay in resigning from the assembly following his appointment to the judiciary. This conflict of interests provoked a protest rally in Halifax which turned into a generalized attack on the "family compact." The shift within public opinion was reflected in the fact that Hugh Bell*, Fairbanks's eventual successor in the assembly, rejected whig compromise in favour of the more sweeping changes that would be associated with the campaign for responsible government.

Shortly after taking control of the assembly in the election of 1836, the reformers resumed their attack on Fairbanks, this time focusing on his judicial position. The Vice-Admiralty Court had long been unpopular for the high fees it charged litigants, and the assembly passed a bill to deny the court jurisdiction in cases involving disputes under £20. In his appeal to London to have the legislation struck down, Fairbanks noted the class bias inherent in the assembly's action. The change would effectively transfer disputes over seamen's wages to the lower courts, where merchant magistrates could be relied upon to find on behalf of their fellow employers. The controversy, eventually decided in favour of Fairbanks, confirmed his alienation from the dominant trend in provincial affairs.

Despite his political eclipse, Fairbanks retained influence in London. Such were his connections that he was one of the few colonials to be admitted to Westminster Abbey for Queen Victoria's coronation. In Halifax he enjoyed status and comfort. His judicial income exceeded £650 per year and he held property valued at about £13,000. At the same time, he incurred major expenses in maintaining a large household (15 as of 1838), serving as a governor of King's College, and acting as a prominent member of the Halifax Turf Club. His library, worth £500, was one of his principal indulgences. In addition to law books, it held works of fiction, poetry, theology, history, and travel literature and a large collection of books and periodicals on chemistry, physics, and engineering.

A sudden stroke, attributed to overwork, prematurely ended Fairbanks's career. The executors found the estate heavily encumbered with mortgages and uncollectable debts, and creditors had to settle for a 20 per cent payment on their accounts. The family survived the crisis, and several of Fairbanks's children, including Catherine, a poet, attained prominence in mid-Victorian Halifax. Their careers were overshadowed, however, by the reputation of their father, a man whose entrepreneurial and intellectual enthusiasm captured the spirit of 19th-century Nova Scotia's "intellectual awakening."

DAVID A. SUTHERLAND

Halifax County Court of Probate (Halifax), Estate papers, no.126 (C. R. Fairbanks) (mfm. at PANS). Halifax County Registry of Deeds (Halifax), Deeds, 64: f.154 (mfm. at PANS). PANS, MG 1, 979, folder 7, no.23; 1596, no.4; 1599, nos.1–2, 4, 8–9, 11, 13, 15, 26, 34, 36; 1604, no.25; MG 2, 728, nos.504, 514, 543; MG 9, 79: f.14; MG 100, 140, no.40; RG 1, 115: f.87; 228, no.124; 289, nos.122–23; 295, no.51; 312, no.86; 314, nos.27, 83; RG 2, 45; RG 40, 11, no.23; 13, no.25. PRO, CO 217/149: 308; 217/151: 130; 217/154: 145, 368; 217/159: 183; 217/168: 108, 110, 118, 124, 205; 217/172: 96. [*Charter of the Shubenacadie Canal Company with list of shareholders and act of incorporation* (Halifax, 1826)]. N.S., House of Assembly, *Journal and proc.*, 1824–35. *Acadian Recorder*, 1 April 1815; 15 Feb. 1822; 30 Aug., 13 Sept. 1823; 25 Feb., 11 March 1826; 9 March 1839. *Colonial Patriot*, 28 May 1828. *Halifax Morning Post & Parliamentary Reporter*, 20 April, 13 July 1841. *Novascotian*, 12 March 1825; 11 Feb., 1–8 April 1826; 22–29 March 1827; 20 March 1828; 18–25 March 1830; 1–8 March, 19 April 1832; 7 March, 12 Dec. 1833; 23 Jan., 27 March, 29 Dec. 1834; 8 Feb. 1838; 17 Sept. 1840; 22 April 1841. *Nova-Scotia Royal Gazette*, 26 Feb. 1798, 21 April 1841. *Times* (Halifax), 20 April 1841. *Belcher's farmer's almanack*, 1824–40. W. E. Boggs, *The genealogical record of the Boggs family, the descendants of Ezekiel Boggs* (Halifax, 1916). *Directory of N.S. MLAs*. L. S. Fairbanks, *Genealogy of the Fairbanks family in America, 1633–1897* (Boston, 1897). Barbara Grantmyre, *The river that missed the boat* (Halifax, 1975). R. V. Harris, *The Church of Saint Paul in Halifax, Nova Scotia: 1749–1949* (Toronto, 1949). Murdoch, *Hist. of N.S.*, vol.3.

FARGUES, THOMAS, physician and office holder; b. 11 Oct. 1777 at Quebec, son of Pierre Fargues and Henriette Guichaud; d. there unmarried 11 Dec. 1847.

Thomas Fargues belonged to a middle-class Quebec family. His father was a businessman and his mother, a merchant's daughter, had been educated by the Ursulines. Thomas was the seventh child, but several of his brothers and sisters died in infancy. In 1783, three years after his father's death, his mother married Thomas Dunn*, a leading figure in the province. Three sons were born of that marriage: Thomas and William, who had military careers and with whom Fargues remained in close touch, and Robert.

Fargues studied in Boston at Harvard College, where he graduated in 1797. He then went to Europe to study medicine at the universities of London and Edinburgh. On 21 June 1811 he received the degree of doctor of medicine from the University of Edinburgh after presenting a thesis in Latin on chorea, a disease commonly known as St Vitus's dance.

On returning to Quebec, Fargues requested permission from Sir George Prevost* to practise medicine in Lower Canada, but he was not granted a licence until two years later. After that his reputation spread quickly, and soon several institutions sought his services. He assumed responsibilities, for example, as surgeon general at the Hôtel-Dieu and physician to the Hôpital Général, the Ursuline convent, and the Quebec prison. Fargues also built up a large private practice. Among his patients were the Anglican bishop Jacob Mountain*, the superior of the Séminaire de Québec, Jérôme Demers*, and the archbishop of Quebec, Joseph-Octave Plessis*, whom he attended at his death in 1825.

In June 1816 Fargues was appointed a medical examiner for the district of Quebec. When the post became elective in 1831, a meeting of the district's doctors chose him as an examiner, and he served until the early 1840s. A well-informed practitioner, Fargues followed closely the evolution of his discipline; he also owned one of the best private medical libraries in the colony. Towards the end of his life the development of homeopathy was one of his concerns. Thus, in a will drawn up in 1842 he included a clause assigning £6,000 to McGill College in Montreal to establish a chair of homeopathy bearing his name.

Fargues was considered to be an intelligent, but somewhat eccentric man, pleasant to be with and well versed in metaphysics. After 1840 he was stricken with a serious illness that brought several attacks of palsy and severely affected him mentally and physically. From then on one of his nephews looked after a large part of his affairs. In June 1843 Fargues went to England with his friend the notary John Greaves Clapham, apparently to visit his half-brothers Thomas and William and to recover his health. But when he came back, he was no better and remained in feeble health until his death.

Thomas Fargues left a fortune estimated at £25,000 that was much coveted. Besides properties within and beyond the city walls, he held shares in Canadian banks and government and city of Quebec bonds worth more than £6,000; his debtors, among whom were some Quebec businessmen, owed him more than £10,000. By the terms of his last will, dated 21 April 1844, the principal heir was to be his cousin Robert Walker Stansfeld, who had lived with him for more than six years as an apprentice and had studied medicine at McGill College at his expense. Under the will, Fargues had also left £6,000 to René-Édouard Caron* and Antoine Parant* to build a home for destitute people at Quebec. The Dunn family launched an action contesting the will, and judgement was rendered on 8 July 1850. The judge ruled that Stansfeld had exerted undue influence on Fargues at the end of his life and rejected the executors' request that the will be upheld. As a result the Dunn family remained the principal depositary of his assets.

JACQUES BERNIER

Thomas Fargues is the author of *De chorea* (Edinburgh, 1811).

ANQ-Q, CE1-61, 11 oct. 1777, 12 déc. 1847; CN1-67, 2 juill. 1841; CN1-116, 20, 25 mai 1840; CN1-208, 10 sept. 1842, 21 avril 1844, 15 déc. 1847; T11-1/449, no.577. ASQ, Séminaire, 128, no.135. PAC, RG 4, B28, 48: 415–16, 418–19. James Douglas, *Journals and reminiscences of James Douglas, M.D.*, ed. James Douglas Jr (New York, 1910). *Le Journal de Québec,* 18 déc. 1854. *Quebec Gazette,* 4 Nov. 1802, 26 May 1803, 7 May 1807, 27 June 1816, 22 May 1817, 5 July 1821, 13 Dec. 1847. *Annuaire de l'Hôtel-Dieu du Précieux-Sang* (Québec, 1909). *Quebec almanac,* 1817–43. Sœur Sainte-Léonie, "L'Hôtel-Dieu de Québec, 1639–1900: notices historiques et dépouillement des registres, 2e partie: 1759–1900" (thèse de bibliothéconomie, univ. Laval, Québec, 1964). Wallace, *Macmillan dict.* M.-J. et George Ahern, *Notes pour servir à l'histoire de la médecine dans le Bas-Canada depuis la fondation de Québec jusqu'au commencement du XIXe siècle* (Québec, 1923). Burke, *Les ursulines de Québec,* 3: 226; 4: 586–88, 633. P.-G. Roy, "La famille Fargues," *BRH,* 44 (1938): 129–32.

FELTON, WILLIAM BOWMAN, landowner, office holder, JP, militia officer, and politician; b. 1782 in Gloucester, England, son of John Felton, an officer in the Royal Navy, and Elizabeth Butt; d. 30 June 1837 at Belvidere, his residence near Sherbrooke, Lower Canada.

William Bowman Felton was among the half-pay officers who came to British North America to establish themselves as landed gentry at the close of the Napoleonic Wars. He had served as purser for the British fleet in the Mediterranean between 1800 and 1812, and then as agent-victualler at Gibraltar until 1814. He resigned this permanent post on the understanding that he would become consul-general in Tuscany (Italy), but the recommendation of Lord William Cavendish Bentinck, commander of the British forces in Sicily, was rejected by the Foreign Office. At loose ends, Felton submitted a proposal to the Colonial Office whereby he and members of his family would move to, and invest £20,000 in, a large block of land in British North America. The colonial secretary, Lord Bathurst, agreed to grant 5,000 acres to Felton and 1,200 acres to each of his four associates, his brothers Charles Bridgeman and John, and his brothers-in-law William and Charles Whitcher. In the spring of 1815 Felton embarked with his wife, Anna Maria Valls, whom he had married on Minorca in 1811, and their first child, William Locker Pickmore*.

Upon arrival at Quebec, Felton was dismayed to learn that the grant had been reduced to 4,000 acres, with 2,000 for himself. Nevertheless, he proceeded to inspect the sparsely settled Eastern Townships to which Bathurst had directed his attention because of their vulnerability to American attack. Colonel Frederick George HERIOT was establishing a military settlement, Drummondville, near the mouth of the Rivière Saint-François, so Felton chose the more centrally located Ascot Township, farther upriver. In the spring of 1816 he established his family on an elevated location christened Belvidere, several miles from Hyatt's Mill (Sherbrooke). With the aid of 59 British labourers who had accompanied him on three-year contracts, as well as a number of Canadians hired at Trois-Rivières, Felton was able to claim in the fall that 1,000 acres had been cleared and tilled. Bathurst consequently authorized the granting of the other 5,800 acres which had been promised, plus 100 acres for each British labourer who wished to settle once his contract was satisfied.

Like the other farmers in this economically isolated region, Felton raised livestock, there being no means of shipping grain to markets, but his hunger for land far exceeded the requirements of any agricultural activities. By 1818 he had purchased most of Sherbrooke's mills and mill sites at a cost of over £5,000, yet he was not interested in becoming a merchant or an industrialist for he leased most of the property to Charles Frederick Henry Goodhue, a local entrepreneur. Conveniently neglecting to mention that he had already been granted all the land originally promised, in 1821 Felton began to demand more land on the grounds that he had invested the £20,000 agreed upon. Bathurst not only consented to a 5,000-acre grant to Felton the following year but in 1826 he added still another 5,000 acres with unspecified "usual reservations" for Felton's children and labourers. By 1830 Felton had patented grants for 15,813 acres, mostly in fertile Ascot Township, while 10,861 acres had been patented for his children in neighbouring Orford Township.

To develop his extensive holdings, Felton attempted to overcome the isolation of the townships. In 1817 he served as a commissioner to oversee the expenditure of £50,000 on a road from Ascot Township to Drummondville, but five years later the road was still barely passable, and his subsequent schemes to supervise road projects went nowhere. Absentee landowners and the system of crown and clergy reserves were among the chief deterrents to settlement and a viable road network, so in 1825 Felton turned to the idea of a colonization company which would acquire much of this undeveloped land and invest capital in the region. Copying the example of the newly formed Canada Company [*see* John GALT], Felton recruited prominent Lower Canadian entrepreneurs who agreed to raise £1,000,000 (sterling) locally and in Britain. The plan was for the Lower Canada Land Company, as the project was called, to obtain all the crown lands and one-third of the clergy reserves south of the St Lawrence River in the districts of Montreal and Trois-Rivières and to build roads, bridges, schools, churches, presbyteries, and mills, as well as to recruit British settlers. In London Felton negotiated a union with a sister company and an unofficial agreement with the Colonial Office, but Lord Dalhousie [RAMSAY], the governor-in-chief, took a strong stand against such monopolistic companies. The under-secretary of state for the colonies, Robert John Wilmot-Horton, was strongly committed to the project, but a financial panic in the fall of 1826 killed chances to raise the necessary capital. When it was revived as the British American Land Company in 1833, Felton was no longer involved. Not only did his appointment as commissioner of crown lands, in 1827, preclude any direct participation, but he now favoured a more active role in colonization for the Colonial Office. Its participation, of course, would enhance his own role, whereas the existence of a company would greatly reduce his importance as commissioner. Nevertheless, when requested by the Colonial Office to report upon lands suitable for the company, Felton chose the Eastern Townships, where his own investments would inevitably benefit.

Felton's road and colonization schemes may have been less than successful, but he did manage to influence the establishment of the legal institutions which would enforce law and order as well as encourage capitalist development in the region. He complained to the authorities about the widespread smuggling, counterfeiting, and livestock rustling engaged in by settlers on both sides of the border with Vermont. He and members of his clan became justices of the peace, and in 1821 he was appointed lieutenant-colonel in the local militia. In 1823 the judicial district of Saint-François was finally established, Felton's influence ensuring that Sherbrooke was designated as the seat of the court, and that his brother Charles Bridgeman became protonotary and Charles Whitcher district sheriff. In 1824 Felton, Whitcher, and Moses Nichols were commissioned to erect a permanent jail and court-house, a task which took five years at a cost of £2,660 raised by themselves. By 1832 the court tax which they had been authorized to collect as reimbursement had produced only £210, but still the Patriote leader, Louis-Joseph Papineau*, opposed any government subsidy for the building.

Papineau's intransigence was probably due in part to Felton's association with the tory element of the Legislative Council ever since his appointment to that body on 4 April 1822. His imperialist views coincided nicely with the economic interests of the Montreal and Quebec merchants, but occasionally they could clash. He was also in conflict with the more conservative members of the council when he supported a bill to provide members of the assembly with salaries, although he argued that it would work against its radical sponsors by freeing farmers from the hold of absentee lawyers, notaries, and "petty merchants." Felton again championed the free yeoman against the petit bourgeois of the assembly when he attacked that body's attempt to strengthen sanctions against agricultural labourers who broke their engagements. They were not a servile class, he proclaimed, but the sons of the poorer landed proprietors, and they would only degenerate in city prisons. Felton's agrarianism had definite limits, however, for he vehemently opposed the bill on the *fabriques* [*see* Louis Bourdages*] on the grounds that it would weaken the beneficial influence the Catholic Church exercised over the habitants. Paradoxically, especially for someone who promoted the strengthening of British influence in Lower Canada, Felton was not at all concerned about preserving the privileges of his own Church of England. He not only opposed the clergy reserves, but also took up the cause of extending the civil privileges of the Protestant sects. Felton, then, was not an arch-tory – he even tried to persuade the Colonial Office to give in to the assembly's chief demands in 1826 – but in general he took a hard line against any concessions which would weaken the political position of the Anglo-Protestant minority in Lower Canada.

Felton's most important public role was that of the province's first commissioner of crown lands. He had probably received the appointment because of his considerable experience, including that obtained in his role as local crown-lands agent since 1822, and as compensation for the scuttling of his colonization company. The public sale of crown lands, to be managed by him, was, in fact, designed as an alternative to the company. Felton, who travelled widely as commissioner, rigorously enforced the collection of payments, but he did not hesitate to ignore instructions which would have increased the hardships of settlers by the levying of interest charges and the abolition of the quitrent system for pauper immigrants. He alienated the Clergy Reserves Corporation after 1828 by charging less than the market value for the reserves he sold and by refusing to set aside parish glebes. Opposed though he was to absentee proprietorship, Felton had a natural bias towards large resident landholders. Governor Lord Durham [LAMBTON] later charged that Felton had sold most of the clergy reserves to speculators; his agents certainly did auction some 1,200-acre blocks of crown land to individual purchasers, thereby arousing resentment among local smallholders.

The governor and the colonial secretary defended Felton against attacks by the Clergy Reserves Corporation and disgruntled residents of the townships, but his greed for land eventually gave his enemies the opportunity to destroy him. In 1835 Surveyor General Joseph BOUCHETTE, whom Felton had openly accused of extreme incompetence, if not corruption, provided compromising documents to Bartholomew Conrad Augustus Gugy*, the member of the assembly for Sherbrooke, who had been feuding with the Felton clan. As chairman of the assembly's standing committee on grievances, Gugy charged that during the 1820s Felton had taken advantage of his position as local crown-lands agent to sell certain crown lots in Ascot Township as his own property. He had had the letters patent issued in the purchasers' names, explaining to those who raised questions that he had eliminated the time and expense required to have the legal title issued in his own name before transferring it to his clients. Gugy's committee and the assembly demanded his immediate dismissal, but the governor, Lord Gosford [ACHESON], gave him his first chance to defend himself. Felton replied that he had considered the lots in question part of his five per cent commission as crown-lands agent. Gosford was not convinced by Felton's story; however, it could be neither proved nor disproved because Felton had never filed a claim specifying the lots he had set aside for himself. Gosford thus had to drop the legal proceedings initiated against Felton, but in August 1836 he suspended him as commissioner of crown lands.

Felton had quite simply become a political embarrassment to the British authorities, for even the tory press in the Eastern Townships was blaming him for the growth of radicalism in the region. Felton might nevertheless have escaped the wrath of his superiors had he not alienated their trust in the process of claiming crown land for his children. In 1828 the Colonial Office had reduced from 1,200 acres to 200 Felton's request for each of his nine children. Yet the draft of patents from the attorney general's office had somehow specified nine parcels of 1,200 acres each in Orford Township, and had been signed in November 1830 by the unsuspecting, newly arrived governor, Lord Aylmer [WHITWORTH-AYLMER]. Felton had not questioned this surprising reversal, later explaining that he had assumed Governor Sir James Kempt* had undergone a last-minute change of heart before leaving Lower Canada in October 1830. The matter went unnoticed until 1834 when the colonial secretary, Edward George Geoffrey Smith Stanley, reviewed the land grants to Lower Canada's legislative councillors. Thomas Spring-Rice, Stanley's replacement, was far from impressed with Felton's explanation. He nevertheless felt that Felton was probably innocent of falsifying the documents, and he decided not to advise his dismissal provided the extra acreage be rescinded immediately. In January 1835 Felton hastened to offer his compliance, but legal complications arose in transferring titles because most of his children were still minors. The Executive Council then agreed to accept Felton's offer to pay for the land at market value. The evaluation was delayed for a year, however, and by the spring of 1836 the governor was in no position to make concessions; the assembly was demanding the dismissal of Felton as commissioner of crown lands. Gosford required a complete revocation of the excess grant, and Felton again agreed to cooperate, but his suspension in August appears to have changed his mind. Late in 1836 Felton was dismissed and by the following summer he was dead, after having endured the final humiliation of a victory by Bouchette, who had sued him for libel. The cases against his heirs dragged on for many years, until the final one was dropped in 1876.

Felton's widow was forced to sell most of the Sherbrooke properties to the British American Land Company in 1838, and in 1841 poverty forced her to rent Belvidere and move to Quebec with her dependent children (there had been a total of 12). The eldest son, William Locker Pickmore, remained in the area as a lawyer and politician, and most of the daughters married scions of the province's élite, but Felton's dream of founding a family of landed gentry died with him. In so far as his impact on the Eastern Townships is concerned, he was probably resented no more for what he did than for what he and the other English office holders represented, the British government's distrust and disdain of the founding American settlers.

J. I. LITTLE

ANQ-E, CE1-46, 3 juill. 1827; T11-501/D13, D24. ANQ-MBF, CN1-6, 1816–20. McCord Museum, M21585. PAC, MG 24, B2; RG 1, E1, 36–45; L3[L]; RG 4, A1; RG 68. Private arch., J.-P. Kesteman (Sherbrooke, Que.), J.-P. Kesteman, "Histoire de Sherbrooke . . ." (typescript, 1979), 1. PRO, CO 42; CO 324/73–102. Elmer Cushing, *An appeal addressed to a candid public* . . . (Stanstead, Que., 1826). G.B., Parl., House of Commons paper, 1826, 4, no.404: 1–381, *Report from the select committee on emigration from the United Kingdom*. L.C., House of Assembly, *Journals*, 1823, 1834–36; Legislative Council, *Journals*, 1822–37. "Parliamentary debates" (Canadian Library Assoc. mfm. project of the debates in the legislature of the Province of Canada and the parliament of Canada for 1846–74), 7 March 1855. *British Colonist and St. Francis Gazette* (Stanstead), 1823–37. *Missiskoui Standard* (Frelighsburg, Que.), 1835–37. *Montreal Gazette*, 1815–37. *Quebec Gazette*, 5 April 1821. *Sherbrooke Gazette and Townships Advertiser* (Sherbrooke), 1832–37. *Vindicator and Canadian Advertiser*, 1835–36. Joseph Bouchette, *The British dominions in North America; or a topographical description of the provinces of Lower and Upper Canada* . . . (2v., London, 1832). L.-P. Demers, *Sherbrooke, découvertes, légendes, documents, nos rues et leurs symboles* ([Sherbrooke, 1969]). Philip

Goldring, "British colonists and imperial interests in Lower Canada, 1820 to 1841" (PHD thesis, Univ. of London, 1978). Norman Macdonald, *Canada, 1763–1841, immigration and settlement; the administration of the imperial land regulations* (London and Toronto, 1939). Jules Martel, *Histoire du système routier des Cantons de l'Est avant 1855* (Victoriaville, Qué., 1960). Maurice O'Bready, *De Ktiné à Sherbrooke; esquisse historique de Sherbrooke: des origines à 1954* (Sherbrooke, 1973). Ouellet, *Bas-Canada*. Charlotte Thibault, "Samuel Brooks, entrepreneur et homme politique du XIXe siècle" (thèse de MA, univ. de Sherbrooke, 1978). Ivanhoë Caron, "Historique de la voirie dans la province de Québec," *BRH*, 39 (1933): 438–48. J. I. Little, "Imperialism and colonization in Lower Canada: the role of William Bowman Felton," *CHR*, 66 (1985): 511–40.

FERRIE, ADAM, businessman; b. 11 Dec. 1813 in Glasgow, fifth child of Adam Ferrie* and Rachel Campbell; m. Jane Kinsey, and they had two sons and a daughter; d. 5 Feb. 1849 in Preston (Cambridge), Upper Canada.

Adam Ferrie was born into a family long engaged in commerce. In 1824 his father, a successful Glasgow merchant, established an importing and general merchandising business in Montreal as a branch of his Scottish enterprise and in an attempt to stake out a future for his sons. Five years later Ferrie Sr moved to Montreal with his family to take control of the business. The following year, as part of a major expansion, two sons, Colin Campbell* and Adam, both of whom had worked in other branches of their father's business, established a wholesale and retail store in Hamilton, Upper Canada. Branch stores, superintended by resident partners, were soon set up in five promising locations in Hamilton's hinterland: Brantford, Dundas, Nelson (Burlington), Preston, and Waterloo.

In partnership with Thomas H. Mackenzie, Adam had opened the Preston branch in 1832 under the name Adam Ferrie Jr and Company. In addition to running a general merchandising and forwarding business, the firm owned a tavern, barn, and blacksmith shop. The Ferries had also intended to build a grist-mill at Preston, but were unable to obtain the necessary water-rights. Instead, in 1834 Adam purchased for the family business a 300-acre farm and sawmill about four miles from Preston on the Grand River; an adjoining 280 acres were subsequently obtained. On this property he constructed an integrated milling complex, which he named Doon Mills (Kitchener), comprising a grist-mill, sawmill, distillery, tavern, granary, cooperage, and workmen's dwellings.

Doon Mills was an impressive and expensive operation. Ferrie, who from his youth had an interest in mechanics, designed the grist-mill on a grand scale. Its masonry construction and huge stone dam contrasted with the modest wooden mills typical of rural Upper Canadian villages. Despite the proportions of the dam, it proved unsound and burst in 1840, carrying away the distillery and other buildings. Additional expenses were incurred in reconstruction. Moreover, the new distillery proved a problem since, for some reason, it did not operate efficiently. Doon Mills was substantial, but it was a poor investment. When Robert Ferrie took over management in 1847 from his brother Adam, then ailing, he explained to their father that "too much money has been laid out up here, so as to make a profitable investment," and the complex did represent a considerable cost. The buildings were insured for £6,250, an under-valuation in Robert's opinion.

The investment at Doon was jeopardized by problems in other branches of the family business. During the early 1840s in Hamilton, Colin Ferrie and Company had encountered severe financial difficulties. In the settlement of its affairs, operating capital was diverted from Doon Mills and Adam complained to Robert that for lack of cash he feared being "forced out of the market." As well, over the next few years Colin borrowed money from Adam. These loans remained unpaid in 1847, making it difficult for Robert to balance accounts.

Adam was himself partly responsible for the problems at Doon Mills. He was not an "office man." He preferred superintending the daily operations of the complex and enjoyed dealing with customers personally, partaking of the social intercourse at the general store and post office which had been added to the complex. In consequence, according to Robert in 1847, the Doon accounts were poorly kept. Consisting mainly of single-entry bookkeeping and memoranda, they defied easy scrutiny.

Personal conflict and tension between Adam and his father put severe strain on the family business. The elder Ferrie had not approved of his son's choice of a wife and had opposed their wedding. Matters were brought to a head in 1847 by Adam Jr's deteriorating health. Suffering from tuberculosis, he feared death and the consequences of his hostile family's refusal to acknowledge or support his wife and two surviving children. To protect them, he changed his will in 1847, bequeathing to them Doon Mills and the Preston property, all of which, although in his name, was legally held for the family. He also gave his son, James, his interest in the family business. The family was furious, especially Robert, who, though managing Doon Mills, was not himself a partner in the family business. For more than a year, as Adam's health worsened, his father and brothers demanded that he relinquish title to his branch. In July 1848 his mother arrived in Preston to negotiate a settlement. Adam agreed to change his will and sign over the property; in return his father granted him and his family an annuity and altered his own will to provide for Adam's children. In his remaining months, Adam was forced to borrow money from friends and to beg his family for funds to pay his bills. He died in Preston on 5 Feb. 1849 and was buried in the Galt cemetery. Operations at Doon Mills were continued by Robert.

The career of Adam Ferrie illustrates the strengths and weaknesses of the family as a form of business organization. Family ties permitted both the extension of mercantile enterprise over long distances and the diversion of family finances to branches most in need. However, successful operation depended upon amicable relations, which could be disrupted by matters not directly pertaining to business.

DAVID G. BURLEY

GRO (Edinburgh), Glasgow, reg. of births and baptisms, December 1813. HPL, Arch. file, Ferrie family papers. Adam Ferrie, *Autobiography, late Hon. Adam Ferrie* (n.p., n.d.; copy at MTRL). *British Colonist*, 20 Feb. 1849. C. S. Bean, "History of Doon," Waterloo Hist. Soc., *Annual report* (Kitchener, Ont.), 1941: 164–72. J. F. Cowan, "Extending commercial interests and public services (a brief study of the Adam Ferrie & Co. in Waterloo County, 1832–60)," Waterloo Hist. Soc., *Annual report*, 1953: 19–28.

FIRTH, WILLIAM, office holder; b. 21 July 1768 in Norwich, England, son of William and Elizabeth Firth; m. Anne Watts, and they had five children; d. 25 Feb. 1838 of influenza in Norwich.

The son of a Norwich merchant, William Firth became a barrister and in 1803 was appointed steward of the city, a post in which he acted as city counsel and presided over the sheriff's court. Probably resident in London while he held the stewardship, he resigned soon after being commissioned (19 March 1807) attorney general of Upper Canada through the influence of William Windham, colonial secretary.

He arrived at York (Toronto) in time to take up his duties in November 1807, with high expectations for what turned out to be a brief and unhappy colonial career. His office had been vacant since the appointment (22 Jan. 1806) of his predecessor, Thomas Scott*, to the chief justiceship of the province. He got on well with Scott and also – in spite of a dispute over back salary and fees – with D'Arcy Boulton*, the solicitor general, who had been performing his duties. He was, however, soon dissatisfied with most of his colleagues, with his status, his income, his prospects, and with life at York. In April 1808 he asked for a transfer to Lower Canada as chief justice. In what may have been his only exercise of tact, he first ensured that Scott did not want the Quebec post; but his application failed. Thereafter he became one of the malcontent officials who plagued Lieutenant Governor Francis Gore*'s first administration.

He was entirely without sympathy for any kind of political dissent. It was at his persistent urging that Gore agreed to the unsuccessful prosecution of Joseph Willcocks* for seditious libel. On Firth's advice, and against that of judge William Dummer Powell*, Gore also dismissed the troublesome assemblyman David McGregor Rogers* from his post as registrar of deeds for Northumberland County. When the law officers in London upheld Powell's opinion in spite of Firth's vehement objections, the attorney general's prospects of being Gore's confidant ended.

Firth's stipend was £300 sterling a year – about half the cost of his removal to Upper Canada – plus an indeterminate amount in fees. His attempts to increase his fees made him a nuisance to Gore and a target for Powell's resentment of English appointees to Upper Canadian offices. Firth began with a list of 19 minor claims, submitted for the opinion of the new chief justice of Lower Canada, Jonathan SEWELL. Sewell's reply of 22 Sept. 1809 agreed with some of the claims, but allowed no fee higher than £2. Firth next claimed fees on all the standard forms issued through his office, although they required no more than his formal signature. On 9 March 1810 the Executive Council declined to audit this last claim. The House of Assembly also asserted the right to reduce legal fees in the Court of King's Bench, from which Firth drew about three-quarters of his income, and to limit his discretion as attorney general in choosing the level of courts for public prosecutions. His protest, in which Boulton joined, that the resulting fee table was "incapable of supporting any professional character as a Gentleman," was ineffective. It was cold comfort for him when on 14 March 1811 a committee of the council did acknowledge that some of the fees of office he had demanded were in accord with Lower Canadian practice, which had been adopted for the upper province in 1802 but never specifically authorized by imperial authority.

By the time of this partial success Firth was virtually without friends in the provincial administration, Scott having decided that as a former attorney general he had a conflict of interest in assessing the fees of that office. Firth proceeded to overreach himself in March 1811 by claiming that all legal instruments under the great seal of the province were invalid without his signature. By doing so he obscured the assembly's challenge to his authority as public prosecutor and revived a dispute among officials over their shares of the fees on land grants, threatening the jurisdiction as well as the income of the provincial secretary, William Jarvis*. While maintaining that his presence was necessary for the legality of most acts of government, he asked leave to press his case in London. Gore refused: he was offended by Firth's breaches of administrative harmony, he had already consented to the absence of the solicitor general, and he was about to go on leave himself. When Firth left anyway in September 1811, Gore recommended his dismissal. Firth left his plate, crystal, and library in the care of his business agent, William Warren BALDWIN, who also took charge of his debts and his unsatisfied claims for fees.

Firth was at first confident that he would not only win his demands but also prevent the return to Upper Canada of Gore, the man who, as he told Baldwin, had "clouded my prospects in life." From his first memorial to the Colonial Office in January 1812 to the testimony that he volunteered against Gore in the libel suits later brought by Charles Burton WYATT and Robert THORPE, he identified the lieutenant governor as the deliberate and spiteful agent of his misfortunes. After Gore's departure in October 1811 the Executive Council, which Firth denounced as "abandoned and inquisitory," had added to his grievances. It twice refused, "under the very peculiar Circumstances in which Mr. Firth abandoned his Duties in this Province," to pay the travel expenses of his last judicial circuit in Upper Canada. It did at length agree on 14 March 1812, following the opinion of the law officers in London, that he should receive the fees of office that Sewell had recommended in 1809. Beyond that, all he obtained was a ruling from the secretary of state, Lord Bathurst, that he was entitled to half his salary and fees from the date he left the province until 13 April 1812, when his removal from office was confirmed.

He went back to his legal practice, being promoted to serjeant at law in 1817, and ended his career where it had begun, on the Norfolk circuit. He may not have prospered at the bar. Apart from frequent expressions of affection for his children, his long correspondence with Baldwin shows an increasingly insistent and querulous concern about money. In 1820 he applied for a land grant in Upper Canada, but was refused on the grounds that he was not a resident. For the last year of his life he may have received an income under the will of his eldest daughter, Lucy Rosalind Proctor Firth. He died intestate with assets of less than £200 sterling.

Firth wrote four political pamphlets, all published in Norwich. The first, *An address to the electors of Norwich* ... (1794), opposed war with France because it would harm trade, but in the rest he gave vent to a rigid and bitter toryism. In *A letter to Edward Rigby* . . . (1805) he complained that the mayor of Norwich had not celebrated the victory of Trafalgar enthusiastically enough. *A letter to the Right Rev. Henry Bathurst* . . . (1813) condemned the bishop of Norwich for advocating the end of civil disabilities for Roman Catholics and Protestant dissenters. *The case of Ireland set at rest* . . . (1825) attacked Robert Peel's intended Irish reforms; it had been Peel, when under-secretary of state for War and the Colonies, who informed him of his dismissal from office. The fullest expression of Firth's enduring hostility to Roman Catholicism was his book, *Remarks on the recent state trials* . . . (1818), which also argued for more severe punishment of traitors and more rigorous suppression of public disorder. He had returned to England with "joy in once more beholding this blessed Country," as he wrote to Baldwin in 1812, but he found as much there to arouse his disapproval as he had in Upper Canada.

S. R. MEALING

[Firth left no papers of his own, but his business correspondence with W. W. Baldwin, preserved in the latter's papers at the MTRL and at PAC, MG 24, B11, includes much personal and political comment. The course of his claims for fees is documented in the records of the Executive Council (PAC, RG 1, E3). His death certificate, dated 25 Feb. 1838, is in the GRO (London). The Norfolk Record Office (Norwich, Eng.) contains the administrative bond for his estate (Norwich Archdeaconry administrative bonds, 1838, no.5) and his daughter's will (Norwich Consistory Court wills, 1839: f.321). Notices relating to Firth are in the *Norfolk and Norwich Register*, 1822; the *Norfolk Chronicle: or, the Norwich Gazette*, 28 March 1807; and the *Norwich Mercury*, 3 March 1838. Information with respect to his legal career is in *Clarke's new law list* . . . , comp. Teesdale Cockell (London), 1820: 12, 24, 292; and in the volume for 1822. For secondary accounts see particularly Paul Romney, *Mr Attorney: the attorney general for Ontario in court, cabinet, and legislature, 1791–1899* (Toronto, 1986), and also two works by W. R. Riddell: "William Firth: the third attorney-general of Upper Canada, 1807–1811," *Canadian Bar Rev.* (Toronto), 1 (1923): 326–37, 404–17, and *The bar and courts of the province of Upper Canada, or Ontario* (Toronto, 1928). S.R.M.]

FISHER, JOHN CHARLTON, printer, publisher, journalist, office holder, and author; b. 23 Oct. 1794 in Carlisle, England; m. Elinor Isabella Auchmuty before coming to Lower Canada, and they had one daughter; d. 10 Aug. 1849 on the *Sarah Sands* while returning from a trip to England.

John Charlton Fisher was a brilliant student and obtained a doctorate in law. He subsequently left his native England to settle in New York City and in 1822, with John Sherren Bartlett, he there became a founding publisher of a newspaper, the *Albion*. In the summer of 1823 Fisher accepted an offer from the authorities in Lower Canada to come to Quebec and take over as publisher of the *Quebec Gazette*. Governor Lord Dalhousie [RAMSAY] deplored the indifference shown the crown's interests by publishers John NEILSON and his son SAMUEL (the manager of the *Gazette* since 1822), and he sought in this way to control the paper's contents. Fisher and Samuel Neilson engaged in lengthy negotiations from the end of August till early October 1823 over the division of responsibilities and income but came to an impasse. As a result, on 10 October the governor dismissed Samuel Neilson as king's printer and gave the post to Fisher. A few days later Fisher received permission to put out the *Quebec Gazette, published by authority/La Gazette de Québec, publiée par autorité*. Embittered, the Neilsons protested against the usurpation of their newspaper's title, but without success, and for many years two *Quebec Gazettes* were published simultaneously. From December 1823 the one under Fisher's management was printed at the New Printing Office, which was owned by Pierre-Édouard Desbarats* and Thomas Cary* Jr. In a notarized instrument Fisher had also agreed to give this house the sole right to carry out contracts for printing official documents which he, as king's printer, was to supervise. In December 1826 the arrangement was confirmed when William KEMBLE, having been appointed king's printer jointly with Fisher on 2 November, formed a partnership with Desbarats and Cary to manage the New Printing Office.

During the 1830s Fisher continued to hold the posts of joint king's printer and publisher of the *Quebec Gazette, published by authority*. He also worked as a journalist at the *Quebec Mercury*, which was printed at the New Printing Office. In 1838 he sat as clerk, and then as secretary, to the Rebellion Losses Commission. Having given up the post of publisher of the *Quebec Gazette, published by authority* in 1840, he decided to launch his own weekly, the *Conservative*, in 1841, but it was unsuccessful. With the union of the Canadas the seat of government was moved from Quebec to Kingston that year, and then to Montreal in 1844. Stewart Derbishire* and George-Paschal Desbarats* were appointed joint queen's printers in the two cities. While Fisher's duties were greatly diminished in importance, he none the less remained queen's printer in the city of Quebec until his death. His office was located on Rue de la Montagne (Côte de la Montagne) at that time.

Fisher was one of the figures of note in the English-speaking cultural milieu of Quebec throughout the second quarter of the century. He had been a member of the Literary and Historical Society of New York, and with the approval of Lord Dalhousie, who had been thinking along these lines, he promoted the founding of a similar association at Quebec. The Literary and Historical Society of Quebec came into being in January 1824, and Fisher served as its first treasurer and corresponding secretary. He was named president in 1846 and vice-president the following year. The development of the city's libraries was dear to his heart. Early in the 1830s he served as secretary and librarian of the Garrison Library. He was also involved in the administration of the Quebec Library Association, of which he became president in 1847. A member of the Church of England, for a long time he took an active part in the St George's Society of Quebec. Fisher was interested in the history of his adopted city and collaborated closely in compiling and editing *Hawkins's picture of Quebec*, a work by Alfred Hawkins* which appeared in 1834. During the 1840s Dr Fisher, as his contemporaries called him, was one of the most popular lecturers at Quebec. He spoke before the Literary and Historical Society of Quebec, the Quebec Library Association, and the Mechanics' Institute, on subjects ranging from British history to Greek and Egyptian antiquity. When Charles Dickens visited Quebec in 1842, Fisher had the honour of being his host.

Fisher went to England in the late summer or autumn of 1848. At the end of August 1849 several Quebec newspapers announced that he had died at sea on the tenth of that month on the steamship *Sarah Sands*, which he had boarded in Liverpool three days earlier to return to Quebec. In their obituaries the papers remarked that Fisher would be remembered as a true gentleman and a scholar with a passion for history. His talents as a journalist and writer and "the elegance and purity" of his style were also recalled. Nevertheless, of all Fisher's work only one sentence, written in homage to James Wolfe* and Louis-Joseph de Montcalm*, endures: *Mortem virtus communem / Famam historia / Monumentum posteritas dedit* (Their courage gave them a common death, history a common fame, posterity a common memorial). The inscription became more renowned than its author and is still to be seen on the pedestal of the famous monument that was erected in the garden of the Château Saint-Louis at Dalhousie's wish. Commemorating the two commanding officers at the battle of the Plains of Abraham and dedicated on 8 Sept. 1828, the column is a few steps from where the Château Frontenac now stands.

JEAN-MARIE LEBEL

In addition to writing articles for the newspapers which he edited, John Charlton Fisher is the author of "Notes on the ancient English and Anglo-Saxon language," published in Literary and Hist. Soc. of Quebec, *Trans.*, 3 (1832–37): 285–91. He composed a long poem read at the reopening of the theatre of Quebec's Masonic Hall in 1831; Pierre-Georges Roy* printed it in his article "Le théâtre du Marché à foin, à Québec," *BRH*, 43 (1937): 38–40. The handwritten texts of a number of his lectures are at ANQ-Q, P-78 (fonds John Charlton Fisher).

ANQ-Q, CE1-61, 27 déc. 1824, 26 juill. 1848; CE1-79, 25 janv. 1860; CN1-253, 5 déc. 1823; 13 avril, 23 juill., 11 déc. 1824; 7 juin 1825; 8 déc. 1826; 27 janv., 23 févr. 1827; 18 sept. 1828; 6 août 1829; 19 juin 1832. AVQ, I, 1, 1828–30. PAC, MG 24, B1, papers concerning the relations of the proprietors of the *Quebec Gazette* with the government, 24 Aug., 4, 6, 24 Sept., 2, 3, 10 Oct. 1823. *The centenary volume of the Literary and Historical Society of Quebec, 1824–1924*, ed. Henry Ievers (Quebec, 1924), 18, 42, 97. James Douglas, "Opening address," Literary and Hist. Soc. of Quebec, *Trans.*, new ser., 4 (1865–66): 5–18.

Le Journal de Québec, 1er sept. 1849. *Quebec Gazette*, 30 Aug. 1849. *Quebec Mercury*, 30 Aug. 1849. Beaulieu et Hamelin, *La presse québécoise*, 1: 3, 118. H. J. Morgan, *Bibliotheca Canadensis*, 124–25; *Sketches of celebrated Canadians*, 308–9. *Quebec almanac*, 1824–41. *Quebec directory*, 1847–49. Wallace, *Macmillan dict.* Ginette Bernatchez, "La Société littéraire et historique de Québec (the Literary and Historical Society of Quebec), 1824–1890" (thèse de MA, univ. Laval, Québec, 1979), 3, 9, 20, 46, 48, 138–39, 143–45. George Gale, *Historic tales of old Quebec* (Quebec, 1923), 56, 167. Alfred Hawkins, *Hawkins's picture of Quebec; with historical recollections* (Quebec, 1834), 277, 279. J. M. LeMoine, *Picturesque Quebec: a sequel to "Quebec past and present"* (Montreal, 1882), 5, 298. F. L. Mott, *A history of American magazines, 1741–1850* (Cambridge, Mass., 1966), 131. F.-J. Audet, "John Neilson," RSC *Trans.*, 3rd ser., 22 (1928), sect.I: 81–97. Bernard Dufebvre [Émile Castonguay], "La presse anglaise en 1837–38: Adam Thom, John Neilson, John Fisher," *Rev. de l'univ. Laval*, 8 (1953–54): 267–74. Ægidius Fauteux, "L'inscription du monument Wolfe et Montcalm," *BRH*, 30 (1924): 235–36. Claude Galarneau, "Les métiers du livre à Québec (1764–1859)," *Cahiers des Dix*, 43 (1983): 143–65; "La presse périodique au Québec de 1764 à 1859," RSC *Trans.*, 4th ser., 22 (1984): 163. Ignotus [Thomas Chapais], "Le monument Wolfe et Montcalm à Québec," *BRH*, 5 (1899): 305–9. J.-M. Lebel, "John C. Fisher, hôte de Charles Dickens," *Cap-aux-Diamants* (Québec), 2 (1986–87), no.3: 29–31.

FISHER, PETER, merchant and historian; b. 9 June 1782 on Staten Island, N.Y.; d. 15 Aug. 1848 in Fredericton.

Peter Fisher is renowned as "the first historian of New Brunswick." His two summary accounts of provincial life signalled the beginning of an indigenous literary tradition. The work of the son of a loyalist soldier and farmer, his sketches are particularly notable for the insights they allow into the values and aspirations of a second-generation, rank-and-file loyalist settler.

Although technically not a native of New Brunswick, Fisher spent all but the first 15 months of his life in the province, and his career was entirely shaped by its history and material circumstances. He was born in the final days of the American revolution in the British-held territory of Staten Island. He was the third child of Lewis Fisher, a member since 1776 of the New Jersey Volunteers, and his wife Mary Barbra Till, of whom little is known except that she was probably of English parentage. Lewis Fisher was of Dutch origin, and variations on the spelling of his first name include Ludovic, Ludwig, and Lodewick. Like so many of the Dutch settlers in America, he consistently supported the continuation of British rule in the colonies. He was taken prisoner for a time early in the war and then served in and around New York City. In company with many of his comrades, Fisher and his young family left New York in September 1783 on the *Esther* and sailed northward to begin a new life of exile in the Saint John River valley.

The family settled at St Anne's Point on lands set aside for the loyalist military regiments. This community would soon be renamed Fredericton and transformed into the capital of the new province of New Brunswick, but in 1783 the site was a cold, forbidding wilderness. An invaluable narrative account of the first year of settlement, based on the recollections of Peter Fisher's mother, was drawn up in the late 19th century by William Odber Raymond* from a document in the Fisher family's possession; it provides a graphic picture of the hardships of the first winter. The loyalist families lived in tents, with stones for fireplaces and no flooring to separate them from the ground. "Many women and children, and some of the men, died from cold and exposure." The survivors lived in "Indian fashion" off the natural bounty of the land and the river: "The men caught fish and hunted moose when they could. In the spring we made maple sugar. We ate fiddle heads, grapes and even the leaves of trees to allay the pangs of hunger." The arrival of provision boats in the spring blunted the sharpest needs but the task of building shelters, clearing lands, and planting crops condemned the settlers to a continuing life of hard work and minimal nourishment: "For years there were no teams. . . . In the winter time our people had sometimes to haul their provisions by hand fifty or a hundred miles over the ice or through the woods. In summer they came in slow sailing vessels." Although virtually nothing specific is known about Peter Fisher's early life, this gruelling and dangerous settlement experience clearly dominated his childhood and shaped his outlook. His writings are marked by heartfelt tributes to the loyalist founders of New Brunswick who "wore out their lives in toil and poverty, and by their unremitting exertions subdued the wilderness, and covered the face of the country with habitations, villages, and towns."

Living in Fredericton had its advantages none the less. A basic education was available and the stirrings of government stimulated an interest in the broader issues of provincial development. Fisher's teacher was Bealing Stephen Williams, an English schoolmaster and former navy clerk, who taught school in Fredericton for nearly 40 years. Fisher acquired skill in reading, writing, and mathematics as well as a keen, methodical interest in the natural world and human history. On 15 Aug. 1807 the Anglican minister George Pidgeon married Fisher and Susannah Stephens Williams, the daughter most probably of Fisher's mentor. Seven sons and four daughters were to be born to the Fishers, several of whom would make outstanding contributions to the public life of New Brunswick. As for Peter Fisher himself, disappointingly little is known about his active life. He is mentioned in several accounts as a prominent lumber merchant, and occasionally as a blacksmith and a general merchant. He doubtless also farmed, in the classic dual occupational pattern of the day. He was acclaimed by contemporaries as an omnivorous reader and a tireless walker, qualities which help to account for his remarkably specific familiarity with New Brunswick's various regions. In 1892 Senator John Glasier* reminisced about a youthful trip with Fisher which revealed the author's purposefulness. "In 1829 I had a remarkable trip up river along with the late Peter Fisher and a sturdy negro named Jacques. We took a sailing vessel up the reach [Long Reach], and made the balance of the journey on foot, across the Devil's Back and on through to Oromoncto, which place we reached that night. We only had a loaf of bread and a quart of milk in the way of food for the three of us, and we walked from eight in the morning till ten at night. I was pretty foot sore when we arrived at Oromoncto, but Mr. Fisher was fresh and wanted to push on to Fredericton after supper. And Mr. Fisher was then nearly sixty years of age. He obtained a pint of rum, part of which he shared with me, but the liquor did not agree with me. Mr. Fisher used the balance of the rum to bathe his leg and foot. When I awoke in the morning they told me that the old man was on his way to Fredericton. I was then in my twentieth year."

Substantive knowledge of Fisher comes only from his writings, which reveal a man of moderate literary skills, keen powers of observation, and intense interest in the progressive, orderly development of New Brunswick. His first known work, with its long full title, *Sketches of New-Brunswick; containing an account of the first settlement of the province, with a brief description of the country, climate, productions, inhabitants, government, rivers, towns, settlements, public institutions, trade, revenue, population, &c.*, was published anonymously "By an Inhabitant of the Province" in 1825 and was printed on the Saint John press of Henry Chubb* and James Sears. According to an advertisement in the *Royal Gazette* of 10 Feb. 1824, Fisher had published an earlier, simpler version of this work for children, entitled *The Fredericton primer*; it included reading and spelling exercises, as well as a geography and brief history of the province. No copy of this primer has been identified by modern scholars. Fisher's second extant work is both a revision and an enlargement of the first, *Notitia of New-Brunswick, for 1836, and extending into 1837; comprising historical, geographical, statistical, and commercial notices of the province*, and appeared anonymously in 1838; it too was printed by Chubb. Fisher's unwillingness to claim authorship led to considerable confusion: in the 19th century the *Notitia* was sometimes attributed to Alexander WEDDERBURN rather than Fisher. In the 20th century Fisher has occasionally been credited with a third work, *The lay of the wilderness* . . . (Saint John, 1833), an epic poem about the loyalist period. Internal evidence suggests, however, that Fisher could not have written this poem, and scholars now conclude that only the two histories – the *Sketches* and the *Notitia* – should be attributed to him.

The preface to the *Sketches* states that the aim of the author is "to diffuse a general knowledge of the Country" as precisely and impartially as its newness and inadequate records will allow. Fisher writes in the spirit of the Enlightenment, with its ideal of scientific knowledge and its concern for social betterment. His work is essentially a catalogue of the physical and human characteristics of New Brunswick. He describes and ranks everything: climate, topography, crops, fish and game, trees and minerals, forms of government, churches and their memberships, ethnic peoples and their ways of life, cities and their activities, imports, exports, architecture, schools, degrees of capital investment, natural phenomena such as fires, freshets, and earthquakes, as well as the moral character of the inhabitants. Much of the *Sketches* reads like a technical report, with an abundance of factual detail alleviated only occasionally by a spare descriptive phrase singling out a "noble river" or the "sublime and terrific appearance" of a waterfall.

Yet Fisher was not a mere gatherer of facts. His text is punctuated with clear statements of goals and sharply critical comments, both of which spring from his deep commitment to the development of his province. He is thus an ardent patriot but never a boastful one. His ideal for New Brunswick centres around the loyalist vision of an agrarian society based on a substantial yeomanry and supplemented by a thriving timber trade and growing commercial and industrial sectors. Like the founders, Fisher believes that an agricultural way of life will not only provide material self-sufficiency but also ensure order, respect for property, and personal independence. In the *Sketches*, Fisher assesses all provincial peoples, activities, and institutions with reference to their functional contribution to this ideal. The original loyalist leaders and the "paternal" first governor, Thomas Carleton*, are praised for introducing sound principles of settlement into "a desolate wilderness." Religious and ethnic groups are ranked, with a painstaking effort at objectivity, in terms of their social impact. Fisher singles out the English immigrants from Yorkshire and their descendants as "the most thriving class of settlers," whose practices of careful cultivation and husbandry have yielded abundant crops and superior cattle. He also admires the internal peace and self-sufficiency of the Acadian people, acknowledging that they are "a different race from the English" – "very lively and hospitable, but very slovenly in their houses and cookery" – and worthy of praise as quiet, constructive members of the New Brunswick community. By contrast Fisher expresses distress over the failure of both black and Indian inhabitants to become useful settlers. He is alert to the cultural origins of their difficulties and remarkably sensitive to the "bold and figurative" Indian languages, but he pessimistically predicts that failure to adapt to the settlement pattern will condemn both groups to decline and dependence. Throughout the text, Fisher's clear ideal is the pioneer backwoodsman, "a man with his axe and a few other simple tools . . . [who] feels perfectly at home in the depth of the forest" and who can supply his wants through his own exertions. With fervent, lyrical emphasis, Fisher argues that "the genius of these people differ[s] greatly from Europeans – the human mind in new countries left to itself exerts its full energy." The experience of coping successfully in the wilderness fosters "ideas of self-importance and independence" and "much native freedom in their manners . . . [which] from their veneration to their King makes them faithful subjects and good citizens, not blindly passive, but from affection adhering to that Government under which they drew their first breath."

If pioneer resourcefulness constitutes the basis of Fisher's greatest hopes for New Brunswick, his deepest apprehensions are triggered by the excesses of the timber trade. Fisher's experience as a lumber merchant makes his comments especially noteworthy. He is unsparing in his criticism of the way in which the temptation to speculate in lumber has wasted the wealth of the forest and produced a dissipated mode of living. The source of the trouble in his view is the activity of alien speculators, who originally came from the United States to exploit the forest. Although new regulations in 1825 limited the granting of timber licences to British subjects, they did nothing in Fisher's view to halt the plunder of the woods by outside profit-seekers. These adventurers "have taken no interest in the welfare of the country; but have merely occupied a spot to make what they could in the shortest possible time." In particular northeastern New Brunswick has by no means reaped its just reward from its vast timber resources: "The wealth that has come into it, has passed as through a thoroughfare to the United States. . . . the forests are stripped and nothing left in prospect," neither large towns nor improved roads nor the kind of splendid and spacious public buildings which "speak much, though silently, for the public spirit, taste, and importance of a country."

Despite these reservations, the portrait of New Brunswick that emerges from the *Sketches* is buoyantly optimistic. The vigour and health of its people can combine, Fisher is sure, to tap the riches above and below the ground and produce a flourishing trade and civilized communities. He acknowledges that much is still to be done in his young province and lays down thoughtful, practical suggestions on the most essential needs: accurate data on climate and soil to improve agriculture, a pool of capital investment and cheap labour to augment trade and explore mineral wealth, better roads and a canal for communication, and more splendid architecture for public edification. Above all, the crown lands must be reorganized to tie the development of timber resources to the permanent settlers who feel their interest identified with the country. The colony's deficiencies do not diminish Fisher's pride in New Brunswick. He rejoices particularly that "the state of learning in this Province is very flourishing" and that, between the College of New Brunswick at Fredericton and the various parish, grammar, and Madras schools, education "is brought to the doors of most of the inhabitants, who will exert themselves to partake of the public benefit."

Taken as a whole, this first history provides a vivid insight into the social philosophy and mentality of a rank-and-file loyalist descendant. There is every reason to assume that Fisher's ideals of social progress, orderly development, and personal independence were widely held in New Brunswick, and that this energetic commitment to provincial betterment accounts in no small measure for the prosperity which was achieved in the 1820s and sustained for the next three decades.

Fisher's second edition of his history, the *Notitia of New-Brunswick*, published in 1838, affords an opportunity to re-examine this mentality and note its development. Although the *Notitia* reiterates most of the data published in the original *Sketches*, the prose is more concise and the style more colourful. Equally noticeable is a change in tone. Ten years of prosperity and unprecedented cultural achievement have produced a more boastful, aggressive, and romantic response from Fisher. He boldly asserts that "in few parts of the United States do the people live as well, and perhaps in no country has the labourer better wages, or the enterprising genius a wider field for exertion." He enumerates the sources of wealth in far more confident terms and especially notes the construction of fine houses and commercial establishments in Saint John and the introduction of such organizations devoted to "pleasing arts" as floral and horticultural societies. Two social changes in particular command Fisher's attention. The first is the influx into the province of vast numbers of Irish immigrants who are, he notes, assimilating well and who will likely make Roman Catholicism the majority religion in New Brunswick in the near future. The other significant change is the establishment of King's College by royal charter in 1829. Fisher describes the curriculum of this institution with immense pride, taking particular note of the fact that no formal restrictions are placed on students respecting age, religion, or prior education.

A new, strident political note also appears in the *Notitia*. The timber regulations for the crown lands have been redefined to Fisher's satisfaction by 1837. Payment in full was now required for purchases of crown lands, a provision that favoured the local settler and ended irresponsible speculation. However, the political abuses that gave rise to "alien speculators" remain unresolved and provoke Fisher into severe criticism of the military lieutenant governor, Sir Archibald CAMPBELL, the arbitrary powers of his Executive Council, and above all the extravagant emoluments of the commissioner of crown lands, Thomas Baillie*, and his father-in-law, Provincial Secretary William Franklin ODELL. Here again Fisher is mirroring public disgust at the powers of the small "family compact" in Fredericton who used the freedom from public control afforded by their imperial appointments to encourage capitalistic exploitation of provincial resources. Although he could not know it, Fisher was writing at the very moment when a delegation from the New Brunswick House of Assembly was reaching an accord with the British government which not only settled this vexed issue but also made New Brunswick the first of the British North American colonies to achieve democratic reform, all public revenues and the membership of the Executive Council being made subject to the will of the elected representatives of the people. Fisher's sentiments were squarely on the side of popular rule but equally firm in support of the British connection, thus accurately reflecting the long-standing loyalist ambivalence between the democratic assumptions brought up from America and the historic commitment to an imperial, hierarchical structure. History does not record Fisher's opinions on the momentous changes that occurred after 1837, but it is significant that his son Charles Fisher* led the movement for responsible government in New Brunswick and later played a key role in bringing the loyalist province into confederation.

Fisher's first wife had died in 1836 and on 30 Nov. 1847, shortly before his own death, he was remarried, to Mrs Mary Valentine of Saint John. In addition to the public contribution of his son Charles, his son Henry briefly succeeded Joseph Marshall* de Brett Maréchal as superintendent of education for New Brunswick, his son William served as the Indian superintendent for some years, and his son Lewis Peter became a prominent lawyer and educational philanthropist. A daughter, Ann, married Charles Connell*, a member of the first Dominion parliament, and a granddaughter, Annie Connell Fisher, was the wife of George Robert Parkin*, the noted educator and prophet of imperialism. Thus for three generations and beyond, the Fisher family represented the backbone of the loyalist movement, the middle ranks of hard-working, self-confident settlers and citizens whose belief in progress and popular government was always framed within the context of loyalty to the empire and peaceful, moderate change.

Fisher's two contributions to New Brunswick history will always have a distinctive place as the first comprehensive reports on the state of the province by a permanent resident. They strike the 20th-century reader more as compendiums of factual material than as works of history, but they conformed to contemporary standards, which emphasized the systematic collection of past and present data fused with an assessment of the material accomplishments of human settlement. Fisher's works lack the range and subtlety of Thomas Chandler Haliburton*'s classic account *An historical and statistical account of Nova-Scotia* (2v., Halifax, 1829), although the two authors shared a common concern for precise factual detail and a profound commitment to civilized life. Among the works of early New Brunswick historians, however, his *Sketches* rank above the efforts of Robert Cooney* and Moses Henry Perley* in terms of accuracy and critical balance. Only with the publication in London of Abraham Gesner*'s *New Brunswick, with notes for emigrants* . . . in 1847 does a fuller, more complex portrait of the province emerge. Fittingly, Gesner built on Fisher's works and acknowledged the value of his pioneer contribution. Subsequent historians continue to do so.

ANN GORMAN CONDON

A limited amount of personal material on Peter Fisher and his loyalist forebears is to be found at the PANB in church records and in the probate records (RG 7, RS75) and land petitions (RG 10, RS108) for York County; a search of the timber files for the period, however, yielded no data on his business activities. His *Sketches* were republished verbatim, with notes by William Odber Raymond, in Saint John, N.B., in 1921 under the title *The first history of New Brunswick*; this work was reprinted in Woodstock, N.B., in 1980. On Fisher's supposed authorship of the epic poem, see *The lay of the wilderness by a native of New-Brunswick*, ed. T. B. Vincent (Kingston, Ont., 1982).

Robert Cooney, *A compendious history of the northern part of the province of New Brunswick and of the district of Gaspé, in Lower Canada* (Halifax, 1832; repub. Chatham, N.B., 1896). M. H. Perley, *A hand book of information for emigrants to New-Brunswick* (Saint John, 1854). *New-Brunswick Courier*, 4 Dec. 1847. *Royal Gazette* (Fredericton), 10 Feb. 1824, 23 Aug. 1848. Hill, *Old Burying Ground*. M. W. Barkley, "The loyalist tradition in New Brunswick: a study in the growth and evolution of an historical myth, 1825–1914" (MA thesis, Queen's Univ., Kingston, 1972). Lawrence, *Judges of N.B.* (Stockton and Raymond). K. F. C. MacNaughton, *The development of the theory and practice of education in New Brunswick, 1784–1900: a study in historical background*, ed. A. G. Bailey (Fredericton, 1947). M. B. Taylor, "The writing of English-Canadian history in the nineteenth century" (PHD, 2v., Univ. of Toronto, 1984), 1: 68. W. O. Raymond, "Peter Fisher, the first historian of New Brunswick," N.B. Hist. Soc., *Coll.*, 4 (1919–28), no.10: 5–56. *St. John Weekly Sun* (Saint John), 31 Aug. 1892.

FLEMING, MICHAEL ANTHONY, Franciscan, priest, and bishop; b. *c.* 1792 in Carrick on Suir, County Tipperary (Republic of Ireland); d. 14 July 1850 in St John's.

As a youth, Michael Anthony Fleming was considered to possess "an agreeable person, engaging manners, an aptitude for learning, and a mild disposition," traits not always ascribed to him in his more mature years. He was encouraged by his uncle Martin Fleming, a Franciscan priest, to enter religious life, and in 1808 was accepted by Thomas Scallan* as a Franciscan novice in the Wexford convent. Fleming received minor orders, subdiaconate, and diaconate in September 1814 and was ordained a priest on 15 Oct. 1815, apparently some months before the canonical age of 24.

Following his ordination, Fleming was assigned to the friary at Carrick on Suir, where his uncle was superior. He was associated with the removal of the dilapidated chapel there and its replacement by a fine new church, which was still unfinished when he left for Newfoundland. There were to be insinuations later that Fleming had misused funds collected for the building and that the ensuing scandal forced him to leave Ireland. The truth of such accusations is difficult to determine.

At the invitation of Scallan, now vicar apostolic of Newfoundland, Fleming went to the island in the autumn of 1823. It seems that he first had only temporary leave, to collect funds for the Carrick chapel. Through Scallan's entreaties alone did the Franciscan authorities agree to his remaining longer. For six years he served as curate to Scallan in St John's. An able and energetic assistant, he took considerable responsibility for parish affairs, especially as Scallan's health worsened. By 1824 the bishop was calling him "a real treasure," and later he declared that Fleming's collaboration was "almost as that of an associate."

Indeed, one of the most intriguing features of Fleming's career was his relationship with Scallan, given the broad differences between them in temperament and outlook. Fleming subsequently described Scallan as "the most zealous prelate that ever sat, or perhaps ever will sit, in the episcopal chair of Newfoundland." As early as 1824 the bishop had looked to Fleming as a possible successor. Yet Fleming was to note in 1835 their "repeated differences," which in the main had revolved around a party of lay Catholics in St John's termed "liberals" by Fleming. He mentioned three major conflicts. One, probably in 1829, had concerned whether he or a lay building committee should control funds collected for the enlargement of the church. The second had been over the refusal of the authorities of the Orphan Asylum Schools, where both teachers and students were Roman Catholics, to allow religious instruction by Fleming even after hours, "lest their Protestant neighbours should be displeased." When Fleming on his own prepared over 500 of these children for communion, the bishop permitted only a private ceremony. Finally Fleming had challenged the practice of Roman Catholics, including Scallan, of attending Protestant church services which, he contended, countenanced "the worship of Heretics."

Nevertheless, when Scallan petitioned the Holy See for a coadjutor in 1827 and submitted the required three names of candidates, Fleming was his clear preference: a man "gifted with all things necessary for a bishop who would be in charge of this mission." The recommendation was accepted, and on 10 July 1829 Pope Pius VIII appointed Fleming titular bishop of Carpasia and coadjutor to Scallan. The new bishop was consecrated in St John's on 28 October, Thomas Anthony Ewer* and Nicholas Devereux assisting Scallan in place of co-consecrating bishops. Scallan himself lived just seven months more, and Fleming automatically succeeded him as vicar apostolic on 28 May 1830.

One of his priorities, and a constant preoccupation throughout his episcopate, was the recruitment of clergy for his mission. Although he was later prone to claim that there had been only seven priests in Newfoundland upon his accession, in his report to Rome at that time he gave the number as nine (plus himself), distributed among five extensive parishes which had a total Catholic population variously estimated at 30,000–80,000. The clergy already on the island Fleming felt were both qualitatively and quantitatively unequal to its demands. He believed that the colony urgently required more priests, and that the financial resources were there to support them.

To secure additional clergy, Fleming several times journeyed to Ireland. He first went there before the end of 1830, obtaining four new priests, including Edward Troy*, Charles Dalton*, and Pelagius Nowlan, who had arrived by mid 1831, and two clerical students, Michael Berney and Edward Murphy, who were ordained in Newfoundland later that year. A second trip in 1833 garnered five more priests, among them James W. Duffy*. The infusion of a large group of younger clergy, coupled with the death or departure of four priests who had served under Scallan, suddenly changed the complexion of Newfoundland Roman Catholicism. Fleming's clergy were different from their predecessors in several important respects. They were more numerous: during his régime he continued to bring over clergy – 21 in the 1830s alone, and no fewer than 36 in all. Most were secular priests and ordained specifically for Newfoundland, a change which brought stability to the mission. Unlike many earlier priests who had studied at colleges on the European continent, the majority had been educated in

Ireland, largely in the diocesan colleges of the southeast. They were of a generation who could practise their religion openly, and they had seen the success of Daniel O'Connell's movement for Catholic emancipation, a campaign in which the clergy had taken a significant part. They could be expected to take a more militant stance than their predecessors in asserting Roman Catholic rights and aspirations. It is notable that Fleming abandoned the practice of the earlier bishops, such as Patrick Lambert*, who had sent candidates for the priesthood to Lower Canadian seminaries. Even more significantly, fearing too close ties to the local community, he refused to accept native Newfoundlanders as candidates for the priesthood. This policy obviously gave the local church a strong Irish cast, and was changed only after Fleming's death.

From his Irish visit of 1833, Fleming also brought back a community of Presentation nuns from Galway, the colony's first religious sisters [*see* Miss Kirwan*, named Sister Mary Bernard]. The bishop was concerned about girls and boys being educated together, as he was about the lack of religious instruction in the Orphan Asylum Schools, and these sisters were to educate girls from poorer families. The sisters were enthusiastically received, and they opened the island's first officially Roman Catholic school in St John's in October 1833. The capacity enrolment of 450 encouraged the bishop, who within a year had organized the construction of a new schoolhouse for 1,200.

Fleming was a tireless traveller, both in his vicariate and abroad. In 1834, for example, he made an extensive visitation from Conception Bay to Fogo Island, covering 46 settlements and confirming more than 3,000 people. A great compensation for the considerable hardship of the journey was the warm reception received from local settlers, Protestant and Catholic alike. In 1835 he undertook a similar two-month voyage from St John's to Bay d'Espoir. By this time he had arranged for the construction of a small schooner, the *Madonna*, for his travels. One of his principal reasons for this voyage was to visit the Micmacs at Conne River but through a misunderstanding the majority of the inhabitants had left the settlement. Upon his return to St John's in September, Fleming found that a smallpox epidemic had broken out. When the disease appeared in the nearby community of Petty Harbour that November, the bishop, convinced of the ineffectiveness of the civil authorities, went there himself and spent the winter of 1835–36 ministering to the people, as well as building a new church and clearing a cemetery.

Despite his ecclesiastical accomplishments and his unquestionable pastoral solicitude, the first decade of Fleming's episcopate was marred by political and sectarian factionalism. This led in turn to a rift between the Catholic Church and the civil authorities, the heightening of denominational fears and concerns, and deep divisions within Fleming's own congregation. The roots of these tensions antedated Fleming's episcopate. By 1830 two attempts to introduce marriage legislation prejudicial to Catholic interests, the absence of public funding for the Orphan Asylum Schools, the controversy about seating the Roman Catholic military commander on the Council, and above all the failure to apply Catholic emancipation to Newfoundland had already angered the Catholic population. Fleming himself wrote quietly to London regarding Catholic emancipation in 1831, as did Governor Thomas John Cochrane*, and although the justice of the Roman Catholic position was readily admitted, no immediate action was forthcoming. Approval was given, however, to Fleming's request for a stipend as Catholic bishop, Colonial Secretary Sir Thomas Spring-Rice observing: "To buy a bishop for £75 is cheap enough." Relief from civil disabilities came to Newfoundland Roman Catholics only on 27 Aug. 1832, together with representative government and widespread male suffrage.

In the ensuing election Fleming supported for the St John's seats William Thomas, a respected merchant, and the "radical" candidates John Kent* and William CARSON (as he later wrote, "an Englishman, an Irishman, and Scotchman, a Catholic, Protestant, and Presbyterian"). Significantly, he did not endorse Patrick Kough*, a government contractor and member of that group of Catholic laity with whom he had earlier had disagreements. Kent's qualifications were questioned by Henry David Winton*, editor of the *Public Ledger*, a challenge Kent chose to regard as an aspersion upon his Irish Catholicism. Winton thereupon demanded Fleming's dissociation from Kent. When the bishop answered by construing that the editor's remarks reflected upon clerical participation in politics, Winton directly attacked Fleming in the *Ledger* as having forfeited all claim to consideration from Protestants and "respectable" Catholics alike. Newfoundland Catholics reacted in outrage, supporting their bishop in a series of public meetings. The inconclusive results of the election itself (won by Kent, Thomas, and Kough) were not nearly so important as the fact that the sectarian tone injected into it consolidated Irish Catholic disaffection into an anti-establishment party interest. Matters worsened in 1833 with a by-election to fill the vacancy created by Thomas's appointment to the Council. Carson, a reformer detested by the local establishment, was now pitted against Timothy Hogan, another of the lay Catholic "liberals" supported by mercantile interests. Fleming gave Carson his full support, and when Hogan alleged improper clerical influence and withdrew, his business was boycotted and he was obliged to make a public apology.

In reprisal for the *Public Ledger*'s support of Hogan

and its criticism of the clergy, a Catholic mob surrounded Winton's house on Christmas night. The magistrates called out the garrison, and several persons were bayoneted. Fleming called for obedience to the law, but he protested what he thought was undue force to Governor Cochrane, and then publicly declared that the governor had not authorized use of the military. To Cochrane this was a deliberate misrepresentation of some conciliatory remarks, and he presented the affair to London as but another sign of Fleming's determination to achieve Roman Catholic political ascendancy.

Cochrane was further outraged by a series of pseudonymous letters in the *Newfoundland Patriot* early in 1834 accusing him of bigotry, and instructed Attorney General James Simms* to proceed against their author for libel. He was astonished when Father Troy admitted responsibility, for he felt that the priest dared not have written such letters without Fleming's approval. These proceedings were quashed only after Cochrane's removal in November 1834, by his successor Henry Prescott* in an attempt to diminish tension.

Acting upon Cochrane's dispatches, the British government had taken steps in 1834 to have Fleming censured by Rome for his political activism. In the Vatican the matter went to Cardinal Capaccini, under-secretary of state. He judged it inopportune to involve the pope, but he wrote a personal letter to Fleming in November, sending it through London for approval. He told Fleming that the accusations against him would certainly incur the pope's disapproval, and asked him to prevent activities "which debase the sacerdotal character." Fleming was outraged by the complaints, which he thought to have come from Chief Justice Henry John Boulton*'s wife, a new member of the anti-Fleming Catholic faction, whom the bishop considered lax in her religious practice. In two letters to Capaccini in June 1835 Fleming documented his efforts, including 1,200 conversions to Catholicism, and defended his actions. He spoke of the religious laxity prevalent in Scallan's day, and said that he had "determined to tear up with a strong hand those vices which had been so long rankling & festering in the Bosom of the Community." Fleming named as his main antagonists Kough, Hogan, Mrs Boulton, and Joseph Shea, whom he painted as Catholic "liberals," a persuasion for which the pope had no liking. He said that politically he had supported those whose election would be "advantageous to the Country," and that the press had given "burlesque versions" of anything said from the altar. Capaccini acknowledged Fleming's defence by stating that he meant no reproof, but was simply conveying a warning; he was pleased that the charges were misrepresentations. He forwarded Fleming's letters and his own reply to London.

Cochrane's departure from Newfoundland had had little effect in dissipating sectarian tensions. Indeed, the actions of Boulton, the new chief justice, inflamed them. A legal rigorist, Boulton introduced new procedures and harsh sentences, seen by many as prejudicial to Catholics. By June 1835 protests against the chief justice were being presented in the House of Commons by Daniel O'Connell, undoubtedly with Fleming's concurrence.

The deterioration was evident after an attack upon Winton on 19 May 1835 between Harbour Grace and Carbonear. Although the assailants are unknown, the crime was commonly attributed to the "religious fanaticism" created by the *Public Ledger*'s attacks on the Catholic clergy. (An equally plausible motive, however, was revenge for Winton's denunciation, as "rabble," of the sealers who had met in 1832 on the very site of the assault to unite against the merchants.) The columns of the local newspapers were filled with abusive attacks on both sides, and the Anglican archdeacon, Edward Wix*, went so far as to keep loaded pistols in his bedroom.

Meanwhile in March 1835 Governor Prescott had received a formal protest from Michael McLean Little, a Catholic shopkeeper. Because he had supported Hogan and was a *Public Ledger* subscriber, said Little, he had been denounced as an enemy of Catholicism, and his business had suffered. Little quoted Troy as saying that "untill McLean Little becomes a beggar he cannot become a good Catholic." Without a public apology, he faced ostracism and ruin. Other Catholics in St John's had had similar experiences. Prescott was advised that legal action against Fleming was useless, but so, in his opinion, was any attempt by Rome to curtail the bishop's political activities. In May the governor told London that he saw the speedy removal of both Fleming and Boulton as the only remedy for Newfoundland's troubles.

The new colonial secretary, Lord Glenelg, unwilling "to invoke the authority of the Pope in a Dependency of the British Crown," and with the understanding that denunciations from the altar had ceased, now made representations about Fleming to Bishop James Yorke Bramston of London, who, it was thought, could have some influence. Bramston wrote to his colleague as requested, but Fleming's reply, in January 1836, argued the impossibility of defending himself without seeing any charges, which Prescott had refused to show him.

Then, in February, Glenelg received word of resistance at St Mary's to constables sent to arrest those accused along with Father Duffy (who had already been apprehended) of wilful destruction of property. There was no evidence that Fleming, or even Duffy, had countenanced defiance of the law. Still, the incident was influential in prompting Glenelg to seek contact with the Vatican. The substance of his complaints against Fleming, as reported to the Foreign Office, seemed to be that the bishop did not control his priests, and that the Catholic population of Newfoundland was "driven to the most atrocious extremes by . . . [his] conduct and language." Rome, he concluded, should be asked to remove both Fleming and Troy, or at least to admonish the bishop.

The British agent in Rome warned the Vatican that "extraordinary measures" might be taken were something not done about Fleming. He was informed that Cardinal Fransoni, the prefect of the Sacred Congregation of Propaganda, would write to Fleming. This Fransoni did on 31 March 1836, in a letter again forwarded to Fleming through the British government. Fleming was obviously well regarded in Rome, and Fransoni simply informed him that the Propaganda had been made aware of the divisions provoked by clerical involvement in politics, and reminded him of Capaccini's earlier letter. Avoiding political entanglement, advised the cardinal, could only contribute to the peace of Fleming's mission and to greater attention to pastoral duties. Glenelg wrote to Prescott that he hoped Fransoni's letter would have a "salutary effect" upon Fleming, and that if Fleming were to desist from his behaviour, the past would be forgotten. The colonial secretary warned, however, that if the bishop persisted, measures would have to be taken to restore tranquillity on the island.

It is paradoxical that during this period Fleming was seeking land for a cathedral in St John's from the British government. Very soon after receiving Fransoni's letter, he left for England to defend himself, and to press his request anew. The bishop had first sought this land in November 1834, when he petitioned the king for a parcel of six or seven acres of Ordnance land called "the Barrens," no longer needed since the garrison was moving. He suggested that while Newfoundland Protestants had received many favours from government, which he did not begrudge, the claims of the Catholic majority, who had received none, were equally legitimate. In his correspondence about the land he repeatedly emphasized the wretched condition of the existing church, "little better than a stable badly built," and proposed to construct instead a "handsome building of stone," with a residence, and a school for 1,500–1,600 pupils. The land he wanted, he wrote to O'Connell, though "bleak," was a superb site overlooking the town, and a church built on it would be a commanding symbol of the Roman Catholic presence in the colony. In his determination to obtain this property Fleming was to endure, in his words, "nearly five years of vexation and annoyance."

Prescott was told to say that consideration of the request would have to be "postponed," and to add that any further request should go through the governor. He made this reply in August 1835, and Fleming did not renew his application until June 1836, about the time of Cardinal Fransoni's admonition and Prescott's instructions from Glenelg to ignore past grievances, and on the eve of Fleming's own departure for England. He noted recent Roman Catholic churches in the Newfoundland outports; just as these were assets to their communities, so would his new church be "a real and substantial improvement to St. John's." Obviously anxious to be conciliatory, Fleming asked for the governor's support at the Colonial Office and gave an extended explanation of why the original appeal had gone directly to London. This approach was wise, for meanwhile Prescott had proposed that any land vacated by the military should revert to the Newfoundland government.

No doubt Fleming's presence in England in 1836 prompted consideration of the matter by the Board of Ordnance that August. No conclusion was reached, however, and it was not until June 1837 that the bishop, now back in St John's, received notification of the British government's decision to grant him "so much of the land in question as may be necessary" for his intended buildings. Careful perusal of the documentation might have persuaded Fleming that there was real doubt as to just what was "in question": no specific reference was made to the land for which he had applied.

The difficulties stemmed largely from the authorities in Newfoundland, who now advocated that this same site be used for a court-house and a jail. Their negative attitude may have intensified with events in the colony during his absence. Troy had been named administrator of the vicariate, with limited powers, until Fleming's return. In July 1836 Fleming had asked Troy to ensure that the newspaper controversies ceased, and in September he instructed him that "should an election take place before my return, I hope you will not interfere in any public manner with it." Still, in the turbulent general election of November, the Catholic clergy, especially Troy and Dalton, were very much in evidence. Indeed their support probably helped secure the overwhelming return of "radical" candidates. Possibly Troy had not received Fleming's letter before the elections took place; when these were invalidated and new elections were held in June 1837, there was less overt clerical involvement, although the outcome was unchanged. Simultaneously, the judicial handling of Duffy's and other cases was causing growing Catholic opposition to Boulton. Prescott himself remained intent on Fleming's removal and had assembled a dossier of accusations against him.

Fleming became aware of difficulties about the land only when he met with Prescott in September 1837. At first Fleming thought that the governor agreed with him on the unsuitability of other sites, but he was recalled the next day and told that then and there he would have to select one of these properties and commit himself to building upon it. Fleming flatly declined and, irate, sailed again for London that winter. In March 1838 he wrote to Sir George Grey, under-secretary for the colonies, of all that had transpired, saying that he had acted as if the Catholics of Newfoundland should "be led to consider themselves as not under a political ban: that they should not regard themselves as Political Parias." It was the principle, he asserted, which was at stake. If the government could not see fit to grant the land, he would be willing to purchase it at full value. A month later Grey sent a terse reply that the British government had directed Prescott, "if no insuperable objection should exist," to put Fleming in immediate possession of the site. Within weeks, under Troy's direction, nine acres were fenced in less than 15 minutes.

Remarkably, Fleming made little effort to diminish the opposition to himself in government circles; convinced that Newfoundland Roman Catholics were systematically excluded from official influence and appointments, he was not about to cease his protests. He was aware, too, that his opponents within the church had the governor's ear and, as he later wrote, he felt that Prescott had "a deep and unquenchable hatred" of him. Probably little could have been done to change the governor's conviction that replacement of the vicar apostolic by one "truly pious, enlightened, upright and benevolent" was "the greatest of our wants." The Colonial Office too was intent upon pressing the Vatican authorities to keep the bishop in check. Although there were no new substantive charges against Fleming himself, during his absence in 1836–37 Troy had certainly harassed Roman Catholic opponents, in one or two cases even denying baptism and Catholic burial.

However lax he may have been in defending himself in London, Fleming took considerable pains to protect his standing in Rome. He spent some time there in 1837 and was well received. Indeed, he attributed something of the attention accorded him to the attacks of his enemies. Already in 1836 he had procured publication in Rome of his account of his mission, *Stato della religione cattolica*. The following year he prepared for the Holy See a more extensive report, his *Relazione*. In it he spoke of being persecuted and calumniated by a small group of rich and "indifferent" Catholics supported by "two or three" priests, mentioned that the government had accused him of improprieties but had refused to provide him with specific charges, and gave an impressive account of his travels and work in Newfoundland. He described his recent trials in obtaining the land for the cathedral and his future plans.

Still, some of the accusations being made against Troy involved ecclesiastical order, and Rome could not ignore them. In fact Pope Gregory XVI wrote personally to Fleming on 5 Jan. 1838, stating that on the basis of unquestionably true reports about Troy's activities he deemed it necessary that the priest be removed from office. "Take care, therefore Venerable Brother, that . . . you restore the peace which has been disturbed, avoid scandal, and ensure that nobody is given opportunity for any justified complaints about a priest committed to your authority." It appears that Fleming complied to the extent that shortly thereafter (probably upon his return from Europe in October 1838) he removed Troy from St John's and transferred him to the remote parish of Merasheen Island. Fransoni wrote from the Vatican that Fleming had acted as he thought best and that the Holy See had not altered its good opinion of him.

There followed a period of relative calm in Fleming's relationship with London. A major source of controversy had disappeared with Troy's transfer. A Newfoundland delegation made up of Carson, Patrick MORRIS, and John Valentine Nugent* had, with Fleming's help, secured Boulton's dismissal. The land issue had been settled. The government made one further conciliatory move. Fleming had repeatedly asked, in vain, to be allowed to examine the charges against him, since he was put in the untenable position of preparing a defence without knowing of what he stood accused. Eventually, in August 1838, Sir George Grey wrote that the events referred to were remote in time and that Glenelg thought any further discussion "inexpedient." Glenelg, aware that he had no authority to judge Roman Catholic clergy in the performance of their duties, realized moreover "the injury which a further agitation of this matter must cause to the public tranquillity of the Island." Accordingly he proposed to drop the matter, and expressed the hope that Fleming would do likewise.

This interlude lasted until 1840, when Fleming and the St John's clergy made a successful effort to procure the election of Laurence O'Brien*, a Roman Catholic, over James Douglas*, a staunch liberal but a Presbyterian. Prescott judged Fleming's intervention to have come from "a pure love of dissension" and he again pressed the colonial secretary, now Lord John Russell, for a more moderate bishop. In turn, it was intimated to Rome by the Foreign Office that unless Fleming were removed all grants to Catholic clergy in the colonies would cease. Through the Austrian foreign minister, Prince von Metternich, Rome was attempting to arrange for a vicar apostolic for Corfu (Kérkira, Greece), then under British control. Metternich was told that this matter would be attended to if Rome would see to the Newfoundland bishop.

Fleming learned of this effort to depose him in August 1840, while he was in England in connection with the cathedral, and immediately he wrote to Rome about this "new persecution." On his return in November, he sent a letter to Russell, complaining again about the old charges and accusing Prescott. To Rome he wrote of his efforts for the cathedral and designs against him by one of his priests, Father Timothy Browne*. The British government's failure to admit a bishop to Corfu had great impact in Rome, and so, without committing itself definitely to removal, the Vatican informed Metternich that Fleming would be called to Rome. On 24 November Fransoni wrote to tell Fleming of the pope's express wish that he come immediately, through London, if possible, where there might be an opportunity to settle the contention. Fleming claimed never to have received this letter. Still, he was aware of reports current in St John's, probably of government origin, that he had been recalled by the Holy See. He kept up his defence in letters to Rome telling of progress on the cathedral and refuting Browne's allegations.

In England, the state of Newfoundland was the cause of concern. Prompted by reports of denominational strife, in May 1841 the government permitted a select committee of the House of Commons to examine the whole situation. Although the committee received only incomplete evidence and made no report, much of the testimony that was entered concerned divisions within the Catholic Church. Further, the impartial evidence of Sir Richard Henry BONNYCASTLE suggested that whatever his faults Fleming might have been ill treated by local officialdom. Against this background, Russell decided a new governor was needed and chose Sir John Harvey*, an appointment which created a different climate in the colony. When Fransoni wrote on 12 July 1842 to ask why Fleming had not acted as instructed, pressure for the bishop's removal had subsided. Rome no longer appeared to be insisting on Fleming's appearance and although Browne's representations took longer to counteract, by 1843 Fleming seems to have exonerated himself.

Serious though they were, these troubles were only distractions from Fleming's great preoccupation and chief work, the building of a cathedral that would command attention and respect. Upon acquiring the land in 1838, he immediately obtained a design from John Philpott Jones of Clonmel (Republic of Ireland), and detailed plans from an architect named Schmidt in Hamburg (Federal Republic of Germany), and on his return home that autumn the bishop went personally to Kellys Island to supervise the cutting of the stone. In the spring he toured the nearby outharbours, enlisting the aid of shipowners, Catholic and Protestant alike, in getting the stone to St John's. The fencing of the land, the cutting of timber for the scaffolding, and the hauling of stone onto the site involved multitudes of volunteers. Thus in May 1839 thousands of men, women, and children turned out for two days to excavate over 79,000 cubic feet of earth for the foundations, the women dragging away the clay in their aprons.

A serious set-back occurred in 1840, with the failure of the bank in London which held the funds of the Newfoundland vicariate. This loss of £4,700 did not deter Fleming, and he was generously supported by his flock: when the cornerstone of the cathedral was laid on 20 May 1841 over £2,300 was given or pledged. Yet his grandiose plans did not have universal support. Henry Simms, a member of the congregation, complained to Rome in 1843 that the project "is condemned by every thinking man – it is not suited to our condition." Probably more widely held was the view expressed by the *Newfoundland Vindicator*: "The people see it with wonder – they watch its progress each week with interest – they look upon the very walls with a species of veneration." Undeterred by reaction that he was attempting the impossible, Fleming threw himself into the work heart and soul, acting as the project's chief overseer and encouraging his flock to even greater efforts. He visited Europe to secure building supplies four times in the years 1840–45. When he left Newfoundland on the last occasion he was fatigued and ill. Construction had effectively stopped in 1841, with expenses even then of more than £21,000. It was Fleming's plan to amass sufficient materials on site to ensure completion of the exterior in one season. When he returned home in September 1845 the building was ready to be roofed and was finished within weeks. Nor was the cathedral the only focus of the bishop's building efforts. He had built a convent adjacent to it for the Sisters of Mercy immediately after their arrival in 1842, and a large new residence for the Presentation nuns was completed in 1845.

On 9 June 1846, however, a fire swept through St John's, destroying the Presentation school and residence, and with them most of Fleming's own valuables and papers, which had been brought there for safe keeping. (Fleming was again in Europe on cathedral business.) The bishop estimated the losses at more than £6,000, which could hardly be replaced by a populace reduced to destitution. Fleming was irate that he received no assistance from a fire relief fund started in Britain and administered by the government. The only other ecclesiastical building destroyed in the fire was the old Anglican church which had been intended for early replacement. Nevertheless £14,000, or half the amount collected, was devoted to construction of a Church of England cathedral, and Fleming was left entirely to his own resources. Yet popular enthusiasm was undiminished and within weeks of the fire parishioners pledged support for the cathedral. Fleming returned to Europe in April 1847 to procure materials for its interior and for rebuilding the convent.

Though unfinished, the cathedral was opened for worship on 6 Jan. 1850. Ill and exhausted by his labours, the bishop celebrated mass; it was his only service in the new church. His death later that year was widely attributed to his exertions in its regard. As the *Patriot & Terra Nova Herald* put it, "The Cathedral . . . has been that building upon which he seems to have staked all." It was as much a statement about Fleming's belief in Newfoundland's future as it was an affirmation of his Roman Catholicism.

His dedication to the cathedral was closely paralleled by his attention to the education of the young. Under his care the Presentation school flourished; by 1846 there were eight sisters, a new convent, and a school accommodating 2,000, to which girls came from almost every part of the island. Nevertheless the "laxity" of middle and upper class Catholics was always on Fleming's mind, and so he resolved to establish a second institution where "respectable Catholic ladies could receive a good and religious education." This time he turned to the Sisters of Mercy in Dublin, who established a community of three in 1842, including Sister Mary Francis [Marianne Creedon*]. They opened their school in St John's in May 1843 and, although there was some initial difficulty in sustaining their community, the school was maintained for some 30 paying pupils with good results.

In 1836 the local legislature had passed the colony's first Education Act, which provided funding for the existing religious schools and for the establishment of non-denominational elementary schools to be administered by public school boards. Fleming, perhaps reluctantly, accepted this legislation. Where Roman Catholics predominated, religious instruction could be ensured through a board by-law providing for the withdrawal of students for this purpose. Most areas with Protestant majorities, however, passed by-laws enshrining the King James version of the Bible as a school text, although it would be read without comment after hours to those whose parents desired it. This model was opposed by Roman Catholics and vetoed by Prescott. Conversely, Protestants in general could not accept exclusion of the Bible, and boards in Protestant areas refused to allocate funds for the new schools. The judgement of the *Public Ledger* that the new system "would utterly fail" was amply borne out.

In 1843 a new act established separate Roman Catholic and Protestant school boards. The foundations of denominational education in the colony were now laid, and a system of Roman Catholic elementary instruction was ensured throughout the island. Oddly enough, the bishop found himself in the position of opposing separate Protestant and Roman Catholic secondary schools in 1843–44. He felt that the Roman Catholic character of the latter was not ensured by the legislation, nor was the superintendence of the bishop recognized. In the face of this opposition a non-denominational institution was established in 1844, which lasted until 1850.

The longest-standing educational difficulty Fleming faced was resolved in 1847. Although the Orphan Asylum Schools still had only Roman Catholic pupils and received annually a portion of the Catholic educational grant, they had retained non-denominational status. Fleming had never challenged this arrangement, but he was delighted when the Benevolent Irish Society, the schools' sponsors, approached him about their future direction. He had hoped, he said, to introduce religious brothers for the education of boys but did not wish to interfere with an established institution. With the society's consent, four Irish Franciscan brothers arrived in St John's in September, and henceforth the character of the schools was not in question. By the bishop's death Catholic education had become a generally established principle in Newfoundland.

Both politically and ecclesiastically Fleming gave the Roman Catholic Church in the colony a clear Irish orientation. He was a consistent supporter of Daniel O'Connell, and on several occasions enlisted the Irish patriot's help in dealing with the British government. He permitted the collection at the church doors of funds for O'Connell's campaign to repeal the legislative union between Britain and Ireland, and was a generous personal subscriber. In church affairs also, Fleming's outlook was transatlantic. Unlike his predecessors, he did not maintain contact with the church on the North American mainland, although he did have occasional correspondence with Bishop William Walsh* in Nova Scotia, also an Irishman, and had some influence on Rome's decision in 1844 to divide the Nova Scotia diocese into two. It was Walsh who had alerted him in 1843 to a proposal to unite the dioceses of British North America under an archbishopric in Montreal. Fleming forestalled this proposal by protesting to Rome, but without giving the real reason for his opposition, the dependence of the Canadian bishops for so much of their revenues on "British Protestant bounty." For similar reasons, Fleming in 1847 successfully opposed Walsh's plan for the establishment, with government assistance, of a seminary in one of the anglophone colonies.

On 4 June 1847 the vicariate of Newfoundland was raised to the status of a diocese by Pope Pius IX. It was a mixed honour, because the diocese was annexed as a suffragan to the archdiocese of Quebec. Fleming objected to this provision on the grounds of the difficulty of access to the mainland. (At the same time he observed that the inclusion of Labrador in the Newfoundland see was "unwise," since it was more easily served from Quebec.) Only under his successor, however, did Rome accept the Newfoundland position and make the diocese instead immediately subject to the Holy See.

On 18 Nov. 1847 Fleming, only 55, wrote that his "constitution [was] so broken" that he could no longer contemplate any further travel. Earlier that year he had applied to Rome for a coadjutor bishop, recommending John Thomas Mullock*, guardian of the Franciscan house in Dublin, who had been a friend and adviser for many years. Despite reservations, in that the nomination had not come from the new ecclesiastical province of Quebec, and that the episcopacy of Newfoundland should not simply be passed on within the Franciscan order, Rome approved the request and Mullock was appointed later that year. Mullock arrived in St John's in May 1848, and proceeded to take much of the responsibility for diocesan affairs. In the spring of 1850 an ailing Fleming, in semi-retirement, moved from the episcopal residence to Belvedere, the Franciscan house. There he died a few months later. Thousands turned out to pay their last respects as his body was interred in the cathedral he had struggled so hard to build.

Whatever his shortcomings Fleming was a tireless and devoted pastor. The social status of the episcopate meant nothing to him; he was more at home "living weeks together at Kelly's Island assisting the labourers quarrying building stone" than he was at dinner in Government House. The young and the poor always had his special attention, and he remembered them generously in his will. Fleming was also an able leader, far-seeing and decisive. He had a single-mindedness that refused to be compromised or to be deflected by less important matters. His writings abound in errors and inconsistencies in dates, numbers, and amounts; these were of no particular concern. What was important always was his overriding purpose of the moment. Considering its often heated nature, Fleming's correspondence is relatively free of personal rancour. He dealt in causes, not personalities, and before his death had sought reconciliation even with his great adversary Winton. Sometimes characterized as ignorant, Fleming was in reality a good organizer and an adept communicator.

Fleming was occasionally spoken of as a bigot who exploited religious divisions for political power. This comment was neither just nor accurate. What he was, rather, was a combination of Roman Catholic theological rigorist and determined opponent of Protestant (Anglican) ascendancy. He refused payment of burial and marriage fees which supported the Church of England, but he freely petitioned the legislature that Methodists should enjoy equal privileges with Anglicans and Roman Catholics in solemnizing marriages. Even in their politics, Fleming and his clergy supported Protestant liberals and opposed Roman Catholics close to the establishment. It genuinely angered him that not one Roman Catholic was appointed to the Council from 1825 until 1840, and that Catholics had nowhere near their rightful share of public appointments. Fleming was prepared to accept a politically divided colony before he would endure a flagrant injustice.

The principal source of opposition to Fleming was a group of Roman Catholic laity and clerics, and those, such as Winton, closely aligned with them. This opposition was hard for Fleming to accept, for he saw as necessary to the interests of the church a unified Catholic front under the guidance of the bishop. The majority of his flock welcomed and supported clerical leadership. The main criticism of Fleming's episcopate is usually the clergy's treatment of those who did not. Injustices and excesses undeniably occurred, but the extent of Fleming's personal responsibility remains unclear, and there are indications that he did not automatically support Troy's conduct. Nor were the issues only those of party politics; Catholics who differed from Fleming on how to vote were likely also to be at odds with him on ecclesiastical matters.

Bishop Fleming was a pivotal figure in Newfoundland history, in his own way perhaps more responsible than any other individual for its transition to a colony with institutions akin to those of Europe and the rest of British North America. Indirectly too he probably did more than any other to challenge the mercantile domination of the colony and to assure its eventual replacement by a form of government responsible to the whole community. Admittedly his episcopate left Newfoundland a legacy of division; it certainly contributed also to the coming of age of a people.

RAYMOND J. LAHEY

Michael Anthony Fleming's published works include *Letters on the state of religion in Newfoundland, addressed to the Very Rev. Dr. A. O'Connell, P.P. . . .* (Dublin, 1844); "Religion in Newfoundland" and "Newfoundland" [two letters to the Very Reverend John Spratt, Dublin, 24 Sept., 8 Oct. 1834], *Catholic Magazine and Rev.* (Birmingham, Eng.), 6 (1835): v–xii, lxxii–lxxxi; *Stato della religione cattolica in Terra-Nuova . . .* (Rome, 1836); and *Relazione della missione cattolica in Terranuova nell'America settentrionale . . .* (Rome, 1837).

Arch. of the Archdiocese of St John's, Fleming papers; Howley papers, transcripts of docs. in the Archivio della Propaganda Fide (Rome). Archivio della Propaganda Fide, Acta, 1847; Scritture riferite nei Congressi, America settentrionale, 2 (1792–1830); 5 (1842–48). Basilica of St John the Baptist (Roman Catholic) (St John's), St John's parish, reg. of baptisms, 1823. PRO, CO 194/80, 194/82, 194/85, 194/87–93, 194/96–97, 194/99, 194/102; CO 195/18; CO 197/1. *Gentlemen-bishops and faction fighters: the letters of bishops O Donel, Lambert, Scallan, and other Irish missionaries*, ed. C. J. Byrne (St John's, 1984). *Newfoundlander*, 29 Oct. 1829; 26 May, 2, 9 June, 28 July, 25 Aug., 27 Oct. 1831; 30 Aug., 13, 20, 27 Sept., 4 Oct. 1832; 14 Feb., 26 Sept. 1833; 25 Oct. 1838; 12 Jan. 1846; 24 June, 16, 23 Sept. 1847. *Newfoundland Indicator* (St John's), 16 March, 20 April, 1 June, 20, 27 July, 17 Aug. 1844. *Newfoundland Vindicator* (St John's), 27 March, 3 July 1841. *Patriot & Terra Nova Herald*, 26 July 1843; 29 July

1847; 20, 27 July 1850. *Public Ledger*, 24 Aug. 1827; 14, 21, 25 Sept., 13 Nov. 1832; 9 Feb., 18, 25 May, 19 Aug., 9 Sept., 22, 29 Nov. 1836; 25 May 1841. *Centenary volume, Benevolent Irish Society of St. John's, Newfoundland, 1806–1906* (Cork, [Republic of Ire., 1906?]). Gunn, *Political hist. of Nfld.* M. F. Howley, *Ecclesiastical history of Newfoundland* (Boston, 1888; repr. Belleville, Ont., 1979). R. J. Lahey, "The building of a cathedral, 1838–1855," *The Basilica-Cathedral of St. John the Baptist, St. John's, Newfoundland, 1855–1980*, ed. J. F. Wallis *et al.* (St John's, 1980). F. W. Rowe, *The development of education in Newfoundland* (Toronto, 1964). Hans Rollman, "*Gentlemen-bishops and faction fighters . . .*" [book review with corrections], *Nfld. Quarterly*, 81 (1985–86), no.4: 12–14.

FLETCHER, JOHN, lawyer, militia officer, judge, office holder, and JP; b. *c.* 1767 in Rochester, England; d. 11 Oct. 1844 in Sherbrooke, Lower Canada.

John Fletcher, whose father and grandfather were Church of England clergymen, attended St Paul's School in London. Later he studied law and was called to the bar in that city. A brilliant lawyer, he rapidly acquired an excellent reputation in the profession. The scientific advances of the time were of keen interest to him. He gained further renown by giving public lectures that were always well received and by publishing articles in London's major scientific journals. Given such success, it is not easy to discern what, other than a spirit of adventure, might have prompted him to come to Lower Canada in 1810. He took up residence at Quebec and was called to the bar on 4 December of that year.

In April 1814 Fletcher made an attempt to enter politics. He ran in Upper Town Quebec for election to the House of Assembly. But Jean-Antoine Panet* and Claude DÉNÉCHAU, who were both popular in the riding, proved formidable opponents, and Fletcher withdrew before the polling ended, having received only 12 votes.

On 16 May 1814, through government patronage, Fletcher was appointed coroner for the district of Quebec, and he retained this post until 24 Sept. 1815. On 6 May 1815 he was named commissioner to rebuild the court-house at Quebec, and on 22 November he became a magistrate of the Court of Quarter Sessions there. Fletcher took part in the War of 1812 as an ensign in the 6th Select Embodied Militia Battalion, and then in the 1st Militia Battalion of the town of Quebec. He was promoted captain in the latter unit on 11 May 1816.

The following October Fletcher and William Bacheler Coltman* were made justices of the peace for the Indian Territory in the northwest. A short time later they were sent to investigate the crimes brought about by the conflict between the two great fur trade rivals, the Hudson's Bay Company and the North West Company. Fletcher went to Fort William (Thunder Bay, Ont.) with a small party of soldiers in the spring of 1817. He was to have continued on to the Red River but remained at the fort, and in the end it was Coltman who carried out their commission on his own.

Having returned to Quebec in 1818, Fletcher resumed the practice of law, and on 1 May 1823 he was appointed judge of the Provincial Court for the new district of Saint-François, with residence at Sherbrooke. An eccentric man, he rightly or wrongly became known as a judge who was often biased, high-handed, and arbitrary in his decisions. In fact, the House of Assembly received many complaints about him between 1828 and 1832. One of these contentious cases, the Dickerson affair, remains famous. In the years 1826–28 Silas Horton Dickerson*, publisher of the weekly *British Colonist and St. Francis Gazette* of Stanstead, printed several disparaging articles about the Provincial Court of Saint-François and Fletcher's decisions. Consequently, on a number of occasions he was arrested on Fletcher's orders for contempt of court and sentenced to heavy fines and even to jail. This matter, and others, were brought to the attention of the assembly in 1828. Fletcher was accused of having acted as both plaintiff and judge in certain cases and of having exceeded his judicial powers in imposing fines and prison sentences for contempt of court committed outside the court-room, as judges of the higher provincial courts and in London could do.

A lengthy investigation ensued, without Fletcher being called to testify before the assembly, and in 1829 the house asked Governor Sir James Kempt* to remove him from office. This recommendation, like those made by commissions of inquiry in 1831, 1832, and 1836, was never acted upon. In the face of repeated requests from the house for his dismissal, Fletcher finally consented to explain his conduct in three long memoranda dated 13 Feb. 1832 and 20 April and 18 May 1836. In 1836, when called upon to make a decision in the case, the new governor, Lord Gosford [ACHESON], asked for a legal opinion from the attorney general, Charles Richard Ogden*, and the solicitor general, Michael O'SULLIVAN, as to the extent of a provincial court judge's powers in a case of contempt committed outside the court-room. Both decided that Fletcher was within his rights. As a final resort Lord Gosford decided, following his predecessor's example, to refer the matter to the Privy Council in London, which never acted upon it. As a result John Fletcher was able to continue exercising his judicial functions until his death.

CHRISTINE VEILLEUX

ANQ-E, CE1-41, 11 oct. 1844; E4/T/4. L.C., House of Assembly, *Journals*, 1828–29, app.MM; 1831, app.CC; 1831–32, app.W. *Quebec Gazette*, 7, 14, 21 April 1814; 16

Sept., 7 Nov. 1816; 14 Oct. 1844. F.-J. Audet, "Commissions d'avocats," *BRH*, 39: 580; "Coroners de Québec (liste revisée)," *BRH*, 8 (1902): 147. H. J. Morgan, *Sketches of celebrated Canadians*. P.-G. Roy, *Les avocats de la région de Québec*; *Les juges de la prov. de Québec*. Wallace, *Macmillan dict*. Buchanan, *Bench and bar of L.C.* Maurice O'Bready, *De Ktiné à Sherbrooke; esquisse historique de Sherbrooke: des origines à 1954* (Sherbrooke, Qué., 1973). F.-J. Audet, "Le juge Fletcher," *BRH*, 2 (1896): 109. J.-P. Kesteman, "Les premiers journaux du district de Saint-François (1823–1845)," *RHAF*, 31 (1977–78): 239–53. "Tablette commémorative érigée dans l'église Saint-Pierre, à Sherbrooke," *BRH*, 40 (1934): 124.

FORBES, Sir FRANCIS, judge; b. 1784, probably in St George, Bermuda, son of Dr Francis Forbes and Mary Tucker; m. 1813 Amelia Sophia Grant of Kingston, Jamaica, and they had three sons; d. 8 Nov. 1841 in Newtown (Sydney, Australia).

Francis Forbes was reared in Bermuda. His early life is obscure, but his family had property in the United States and it is likely that he travelled there as a youth. Sir James Dowling, his associate on the bench during his later career in New South Wales (Australia), once said of Forbes that "from early education, his mind [was] imbued with American sympathies," and another observer drew attention to his "Yankee principles."

In 1803 young Forbes went to London to study law, and he was called to the bar of Lincoln's Inn in April 1812. In March 1811 he had received the appointment of attorney general of Bermuda; two years later he was also made king's advocate in the Vice-Admiralty Court at St George, where he was "comfortably" residing with his wife. His performance in these offices was so impressive that on 24 Aug. 1816 he was appointed chief justice in the Supreme Court of Judicature in Newfoundland, succeeding Cæsar Colclough*. He was sworn in by the surrogate David Buchan in St John's on 15 July 1817. One of his first official acts was to survey the convicts in the primitive jail and make recommendations for clemency to Governor Francis Pickmore*. As there had been no chief justice in the island for 18 months, prisoners who were serving time for crimes such as larceny and perjury had endured long sentences without review. Forbes's letter on the occasion is noteworthy for its compassion and concern for justice.

In 1817 Newfoundland still lacked any form of elective government; yet a reform movement had begun in St John's, a vigorous press had sprung up, debate had started about the future prospects of the island, and a resident middle class of professionals and merchants had emerged to assert its influence in the changing society. The collapse of the fishing economy at the end of the Napoleonic Wars, together with a series of disastrous fires in St John's in 1816–19 (in one of which Forbes saw his court-house destroyed), added to the uncertainty and restiveness of the times. British authorities responded to the pressure for change by granting the island a year-round governor in 1817, yet did not choose to alter the paternalistic way he governed. But though its political system remained primitive, Newfoundland did have an elaborate and statutory judicial system, comprising courts of session, surrogate courts, a vice-admiralty court, and a supreme court. In addition, the venerable English institution of the grand jury, regarded by Forbes as "the only lawful public Body in the Island," was also a potent force. In the absence of a legislature, the Supreme Court in particular was looked to by reformers as a means of asserting constitutional rights and of curbing executive power. Thus Forbes served as chief justice at a time when, as he well knew, there was intense public interest in his decisions and in his conduct of court business. "The eyes of the country are upon us," he said in court in 1821, while correcting a decision made by two magistrates.

In December 1817 Pickmore reported that the pressure of business in the Supreme Court was "unprecedented," but that an "able" Forbes was conducting it with "application" and "dispatch." In fact, Forbes seemed to enjoy the simplicity and quickness that had come to characterize the court's proceedings. "Such is the despatch with which causes are tried," he noted, "that it is not an infrequent occurrence for a suit to be heard and determined in the Court, the same day on which it arose." There being no "privileged practitioners" at the bar, every suitor pleaded his cause personally or through an *amicus curiae*. The judge then decided summarily upon the merits of the case, or referred it to a jury, if one had been requested. The new chief justice apparently placed little stock in "settled formality" and thought that "there are so many solid advantages arising from a cheap and ready access to the fountain head of justice, that few who have experienced the practical benefits, would consent to forego them, from any imaginary fear of encouraging a spirit of litigation." It was not long before his lenient approach drew criticism from Pickmore's successor Sir Charles Hamilton.

While Forbes's earliest civil cases show a concern to recognize the legal status of special customs in the local trade and fishery, he also asserted that English laws were "a common fund, from which the Colony may draw as often and as largely as its exigences may require." This was one of his guiding principles on the bench, a principle strengthened by a clause in the 1809 legislation relating to courts in Newfoundland, where it was specified that the Supreme Court should deal with civil cases "according to the law of *England*, as far as the same can be applied to Suits and Complaints" arising on the island. Thus the years 1817–22 saw the testing of many of the assumptions, regulations, and informal structures that had grown up in the colony – in sum, "the peculiarity of the local government," as Forbes phrased it – against the principles of the English law and constitution. It was not, indeed, the first time that these local practices had been so tested, for British crown lawyers especially had already played an important role in limiting the powers of the governor. But it was to be from Forbes that the old system would receive its most determined judicial assault.

One of his first decisions to create embarrassment for Hamilton related to the payment of the Greenwich Hospital duty, a traditional levy of 6*d*. per month on fishermen and seamen. In the harsh post-war economic conditions, this fee proved difficult to collect, and Hamilton directed his officials to proceed by attachment against non-payers. The issue reached the Supreme Court in November 1818 in the case of *Le Geyt* v. *Miller, Fergus & Co*. Forbes ruled that the dues could not be applied, as they had been in this case, to sharemen upon whose fish the supplier had a lien, until the lien had been satisfied. He also cast doubts upon the applicability to Newfoundland fishermen of the acts of parliament relating to the duty. In a long letter of complaint following the judgement, Hamilton noted to the commissioners concerned that a new act was needed making the fishermen "expressly liable to the duty." His authority had in effect been checked by the court, a proceeding that a vigilant populace could not help but notice. Soon afterwards the high sheriff, John Bland*, found himself in Forbes's court charged with forcible entry into a building that had been used by citizens to house a fire-engine. In taking down the building, Bland had been acting on Hamilton's orders. In *Hoyles* v. *Bland* (April 1819) Forbes informed the jury that it could only find for the defendant, since the house in question had been built on an ancient fishing ship's room and so was "incapable of private appropriation." Yet he stated pointedly that if Bland entered property where the crown did not have title, "he is a Trespasser, however high the orders under which he may act"; further, even supposing the crown had title, if Bland entered "with force and without the solemnity of lawful proceeding, he is liable to a criminal prosecution." The episode involving the fire house caused a considerable stir in St John's.

Forbes's comments in the Hoyles–Bland case reflected his concern over land tenure in Newfoundland. Though the inhabitants of the island now functioned in many respects as normal proprietors, legal title to land was still uncertain. In *Williams* v. *Williams* (February 1818) Forbes implied that ownership of property did not exist in the colony. "The common law of descent does not apply to property in the soil of Newfoundland," he stated.

Two cases brought by the crown against what were viewed as encroachments show him reconsidering this position. In *The King* v. *Row* (November 1818) the crown's right to remove a fence which Thomas Row had placed upon a piece of ground claimed by him as private property was denied. Although Forbes did not wish on this occasion to tackle the question of "what is real property in Newfoundland" – a question which, he wryly observed, "has been carefully avoided by all my predecessors" – he nevertheless indicated that King William's Act of 1699 entitled Row to enjoy the room "peaceably and quietly." In *The King* v. *Kough* (August 1819) Forbes equivocated no longer. "Of all evils in society, uncertainty in the law is amongst the greatest, and there cannot be any uncertainty more distressing than that of the right by which a man holds his habitation." Through an analysis of pertinent British legislation, he concluded that the right to own private property in Newfoundland had in fact already been conceded, and he found for the defendants. It was a big moment in Newfoundland history. Hamilton, convinced that Forbes had "political opinions of the freest tendency," now reported to the colonial secretary, Lord Bathurst, that "almost all the cases in which the Crown has been concerned" since Forbes's arrival "have been given against it." He repeated an earlier request for the appointment of an attorney general to protect the crown's interests in court. But Forbes summarized the matter bluntly in a letter to Hamilton in 1821: "It is too late now to dispute the general right of private property in the soil of this island."

Another point of difference between Forbes and Hamilton concerned the relationship of the Supreme Court to the other courts in the island. From his arrival Forbes treated the Supreme Court as an appeal court over all other tribunals, and he was by no means disinclined to overturn or alter judgements given in lower courts, except when they were based on the decisions of juries. He was especially wary of decisions made in the surrogate courts, which were often presided over by captains of the king's ships. "I have always been anxious to correct any errors or misapprehensions by reversing the judgment of the Surrogate Court," he noted in *Roberts* v. *Simpson* (December 1817). Similarly, in *Hutton, McLea & Co.* v. *Kelly* (February 1818), he set aside a decision of a sessions court with the reminder that "if an inferior Court exceed its jurisdiction, and an injury is occasioned thereby, the party has a right of action against its members." By 1819 Hamilton was so worried about the number of appeals against judgements in the lower courts that he asked Bathurst to have the crown lawyers clarify the appellate function of the Supreme Court; they did so in September 1820, entirely to his satisfaction, arguing that this function of the court was extremely limited. However, Forbes wrote a cogently argued, dissenting opinion, and asked that it be sent back to the crown lawyers for consideration.

Several of his most important cases sprang from errors made by the inferior courts. *Jennings & Long* v. *Hunt & Beard* (October 1820) was an action provoked by a decision in Sandwich Bay, Labrador, of surrogate Hercules Robinson, a ship's captain who had enforced regulations for the salmon fishery proclaimed by Hamilton. The surrogate, Forbes noted, "had received the orders of his Commander-in-Chief, which he merely obeyed as a subordinate officer, without question as to their legal authority." But Forbes affirmed that the governor had no legislative authority to issue his proclamation. The surrogate, he said, "mistook that for law which was not law, and so for that his judgment was erroneous." This extraordinary opinion, obviously of general application, undermined in a single stroke the informal gubernatorial system of ruling Newfoundland. Hamilton was flabbergasted; yet even he, in 1822, conceded that "some local authority" would be of use. In yet another case that created a sensation in St John's, *Lundrigan* v. *Buchan & Leigh* (November 1820), Forbes rebuked the surrogates David Buchan and the Reverend John Leigh* for sentencing fisherman James Lundrigan* to be whipped for contempt of court.

It was not just the high sheriff, magistrates, surrogates, and governor who found their customary powers brought under review by Forbes; the military establishment too had its day in court. In *John F. Trimingham & Co.* v. *Gaskin* (August 1821) the practice of firing on vessels leaving the port of St John's without passes from the governor was declared illegal, and the orders on which the action was based were said to be "founded in a misapprehension of the law." The judgement against Gaskin, the gunner who had fired the shot, forced Hamilton to ask the commander of the British troops to desist from "firing to detain any vessels" until details of the case could be laid before authorities in London. But the law officers of the crown sided with Forbes. It was another striking example of arbitrary power being brought under the rule of law.

Most of the "several thousand cases" of a civil nature that came before Forbes in his five years on the bench in Newfoundland centred, not on constitutional rights, but on insolvencies, fishermen's wages, actions for debt, and similar economic issues. His difficulties in this area were compounded by outdated British legislation pertaining to the island, for conditions in the local economy were now changing rapidly. In *Trustees of Crawford & Co.* v. *Cunningham, Bell & Co.* (October 1817) Forbes complained that "Newfoundland has been considered as a mere fishery, and, by a political sort of fiction, every person in it is supposed to be either a fisherman or a supplier of fishermen." Yet this view was "a great departure from the fact," he noted, there being "a considerable Trade" from Newfoundland "independent of the Fishery." Among his many other important cases relating to the fishery were *Stuart & Rennie* v. *Walsh* (January 1818), in which he ruled that it was legal to conduct a fishing voyage upon shares rather than wages, and *Baine, Johnston & Co.* v. *Chambers* (January 1819), in which he found against a merchant in the purchase of fish from a Trinity Bay fisherman who had been advanced supplies by another company. The relationship between the fisherman and supplying merchant, said Forbes, was "a system of credit founded in good faith; and it becomes the duty of the Court to cement this necessary confidence between the parties, and to guard it with vigilance from infraction by others." The fisherman was not entitled to sell his product to any would-be purchaser who made an offer. Forbes's concerns were thus not narrowly limited to the assertion of individual rights; he could take the side of merchants (and magistrates) if some broad community interest were threatened.

Details about Forbes's personal life in Newfoundland are elusive, though his wife in her old age described her years in St John's as "happy." There is evidence that Forbes gave some attention to local happenings; in 1819, for example, he chaired a public meeting to discuss the fate of the Beothuks. He seems to have enjoyed an acquaintance with many prominent inhabitants of the town, who testified, before his departure, to the "amiable, social, and affable manners" of one who had afforded them "so many intellectual feasts." In the heated political atmosphere of the colony Forbes kept his judicial distance from the warring parties, and won respect from all hands. Even Hamilton never doubted his knowledge or sincerity. (It should be noted as well that Forbes later denied Hamilton had ever interfered with the administration of justice in Newfoundland.) According to the inhabitants' testimonial, on the bench Forbes was known for his "uprightness," "mildness," and "patience," his judgements being delivered with such clarity and persuasiveness that litigants who entered his court "confident of success in our causes, have retired from it, perfectly satisfied with judgments against us." By 1821 the incessant work in court, together with the severe climate of Newfoundland, had affected his health and he requested a leave of absence in Britain. In May 1822, supported by a letter from his physician, the reformer William Carson, Forbes reported to Hamilton that his health "has suffered and is still suffering," and asked for a leave of four months. Given permission to go, Forbes left St John's on 7 May 1822. According to the *Public Ledger*, "His Honour was attended in solemn silence to the water's edge, and entered the boat amid the tears and aspirations of the whole community."

In 1822–23 Forbes served as an adviser to the Colonial Office in London, and undoubtedly had a strong influence in shaping the new legislation for

Newfoundland that was enacted in 1824. He argued cogently against the creation of a legislature citing, among other reasons, opposition of merchants, difficulties in internal communication and transportation, and the lack of evidence indicating that a House of Assembly, even if practicable, "would be at all useful to the island." In view of certain of his decisions on the bench, this was a somewhat unexpected stand for him to take. Instead of a legislature, he advocated a form of municipal government, for St John's and elsewhere. In the event, one of the acts of 1824 made provision for such government.

On his arrival in England in 1822, Forbes had conveyed to Bathurst his "hope of removal" from Newfoundland, and it was made known to him in August that, if he wished it, he could have the appointment of chief justice in the new supreme court in New South Wales. A year later he left to take up this post, which he filled with great distinction until July 1837. A knighthood was conferred upon him in April 1837.

Francis Forbes served just under five years on the bench in Newfoundland, but his influence on the future development of the colony was profound. His judgements checked the abuse of power by officials, established Newfoundlanders' rights to own property in the island, and showed the need for a constitutional form of government. His courageous decisions made him a hero among reformers, who said with good reason that "by him the Supreme Court has been formed on the broad principles of justice and law."

PATRICK O'FLAHERTY

[Some of the legal cases over which Sir Francis Forbes presided when he was chief justice of Newfoundland can be found in *Select cases from the records of the Supreme Court of Newfoundland* . . . (St John's and London, 1829); *Decisions of the Supreme Court of Newfoundland: the reports* . . . , ed. E. P. Morris *et al.* (St John's), 1 (1817–28); and, in the State Library of New South Wales, Mitchell Library (Sydney, Australia), MS coll., A740, "Decisions of the Supreme Court of Judicature in cases connected with the trade and fisheries of Newfoundland during the time of Francis Forbes . . . ," 28 July 1817–15 Dec. 1821. Others are located both at PANL, in GN 5/2/A/1, 1817–21, and occasionally in GN 2/1/A, and at PRO, CO 194.

The main sources for Forbes's Newfoundland career are PANL, GN 2/1/A, 28–33, and PRO, CO 194/60–69; material on Forbes can also be found in CO 38/20, CO 195/17, CO 323/40–51, 323/117–18, CO 325/4, and 325/7. The Mitchell Library has information relating to Forbes's years in Newfoundland among his papers (MS coll., A1381), pp.26–42, 50; further material on Forbes, primarily concerning his Australian career, is in the State Library of New South Wales, Dixson Library (Sydney), MS coll., Add. 61, Add. 155, Add. 159; CSIL/3; MS 108; and MSQ 21.

The *DNB*, *ADB*, and *Encyclopedia of Newfoundland and Labrador*, ed. J. R. Smallwood *et al.* (2v. to date, St John's, 1981–), all contain biographical sketches of Forbes. C. H. Currey, *Sir Francis Forbes: the first chief justice of the Supreme Court of New South Wales* (Sydney, 1968), 9–20, provides a study of Forbes's years in Newfoundland, while A. H. McLintock, *The establishment of constitutional government in Newfoundland, 1783–1832: a study of retarded colonisation* (London and Toronto, 1941), gives a general background for the period. The pamphlet *A report of certain proceedings of the inhabitants of the town of St. John, in the island of Newfoundland* . . . (St John's, 1821) affords insight into the reform movement in Newfoundland and into the reformers' view of Forbes. The *Newfoundland Mercantile Journal*, 1816–24, sheds light on the social context in which his decisions were made. P.O'F.]

FORBIN-JANSON, CHARLES-AUGUSTE-MARIE-JOSEPH DE, Roman Catholic priest; b. 3 Nov. 1785 in Paris, second son of Michel-Palamède de Forbin-Janson, Comte de Forbin-Janson, and his wife Cornélie-Henriette-Sophie-Louise-Hortense-Gabrielle Galléan, Princesse de Galléan; d. 11 July 1844 in the château of Guilhermy, near Marseilles, France.

A descendant of one of the greatest noble families in Provence, Charles-Auguste-Marie-Joseph de Forbin-Janson emigrated to Bavaria with his parents during the French revolution. Subsequently he went to Switzerland, spent some time in Paris in 1795, returned to Bavaria, and did not reappear in France until 1800. His family strongly supported the royalist cause. He remained convinced that the revolution had been caused by the conspiracies of freemasons and republicans.

Forbin-Janson reluctantly accepted the Napoleonic régime when in 1805 he took a post as a junior official (*auditeur*) with the Conseil d'État. But at the same time he joined the Congrégation de la Sainte-Vierge, a religious association organized in Paris in 1801. After it was dissolved by Napoleon in 1809, Forbin-Janson joined the Chevaliers de la Foi, a royalist secret society founded by Ferdinand de Bertier in Paris in 1810.

Forbin-Janson had by then become a seminarist. Because of the hostilities instigated by Napoleon against Pope Pius VII he had given up his career in government, and in 1808 had entered the Séminaire de Saint-Sulpice in Paris. There he joined a secret devotional society of Jesuit inspiration. At that time there was a group of young clerics at Saint-Sulpice who were caught up in the idea of missionary work, and the impetuous Forbin-Janson was afire with these visions. He became close friends with Charles-Joseph-Eugène de Mazenod, who entertained similar dreams.

Forbin-Janson was ordained at Chambéry on 15 Dec. 1811. He became superior of the Grand Séminaire de Chambéry. As acting vicar general, he went to Rome in 1814, and there, after consulting Pius VII, he was persuaded to give up the hope of going to China and to dedicate himself instead to the re-evangelization of France, which in his eyes had become a godless country as a result of the revolution's excesses. With Abbé David de Rauzan, he established the Société des Missions de France, based at Mont Valérien, to the west of Paris. This was the starting-point of the famous Restoration missions. Forbin-Janson, a man gifted with extraordinary facility in speaking, prodigiously active, and convinced that the restoration of religion was inseparable from restoration of the monarchy, drew on his burning zeal and fertile imagination to organize numerous dramatic religious demonstrations at which, according to his biographer Paul Lesourd, "political clericalism" was given free rein. The climax of a mission was the raising of a Calvary. Forbin-Janson had a great attachment to the huge cross on Mont Valérien, visible from Paris and the favourite place of pilgrimage for Parisians.

Church historian Jean Leflon has aptly characterized his activity within the Société des Missions de France: "Forbin-Janson more than anyone else, it must be admitted, overdid the boisterous spectacles for which he was often criticized; more than anyone else he sought grand effects, and combined the cause of the monarchy with that of the church from a sincere conviction that without the monarchy religion could not survive. Discretion was not his greatest virtue, and he was more than once found to be lacking in judgement. Authoritarian, unyielding, autocratic, he did not acknowledge differences of temperament, or [the need for] precautions or nuances; no obstacle stopped him, no set-back taught him a lesson."

On 21 Nov. 1823 Forbin-Janson, who was much in the public eye, was named bishop of Nancy and Toul and primate of Lorraine. He was consecrated in the chapel on Mont Valérien on 6 June 1824. In Lesourd's opinion he had none of the qualities needed to make a good bishop. Temperamentally unsuited to stay quietly within the narrow confines of a diocese, impatient of all administrative constraints, tyrannical, and abrupt in his dealings with his priests, he preferred to surround himself with colleagues from the Missions de France. He incurred the hostility not only of his clergy but also of the civil authorities, and of the public, where liberal opinion opposed to the government's reactionary policy predominated. Consequently, when during the revolution of July 1830 the fall of Charles X was announced, the seminary and the bishop's palace were sacked by rioters, and Bishop Forbin-Janson, away on a round of visits for confirmations, had to resign himself to leaving the diocese. He thought his absence would be temporary, but it proved permanent because the July monarchy of Louis-Philippe, rightly considering him a resolute adversary, refused steadfastly to allow him to return to Nancy despite his repeated requests. He received another severe blow when his political enemies destroyed the Calvary on Mont Valérien, to which he had devoted much attention and money.

Now at liberty, Forbin-Janson travelled about France preaching in retreats upon the request of bishops and superiors of religious communities. As he was in close sympathy with the work of the Society for the Propagation of the Faith, which had been founded to aid missionaries in the United States, his thoughts turned to North America. He was, in fact, receiving a steady stream of invitations from compatriots holding episcopal office there. He went to Rome, where Pope Gregory XVI approved his plan to go overseas and even entrusted him with an official mission.

On 18 Oct. 1839 Bishop Forbin-Janson landed in New York. In that era the spectacular missions through which Forbin-Janson had gained fame in France had their parallels in the revivals, both Protestant and Catholic, of the United States. As American historian Jay Patrick Dolan has shown, the religion of revivalism "was not exclusively a Protestant enterprise, but . . . also swept through Catholic America" and found its expression around 1830 in parish missions lasting one or more weeks. The initiators of these missions were mainly European Jesuits and Redemptorists, so that the tradition of European Catholicism in this field was linked with the practice of American Protestantism. The message delivered was evangelical in nature: the denunciation of sin, the threat of hell, repentance, conversion. But this evangelicalism, whose characteristics were also to be found in Protestant revivalism, had a specifically Catholic aspect: repentance was to lead to confession, and then to the Eucharist. It was a sacramental form of evangelicalism. Dolan also points out the further difference that the religion preached in the missions was strongly individualistic. It gave priority to a system of morality that taught submission, acceptance, and passivity in social and political matters, unlike the Protestant revival, which looked to prospects of success and progress.

Bishop Forbin-Janson's activity in North America was thus part of an endeavour that would continue into the 20th century. After spending a little time in New York, where he came to the realization that his compatriots had no church to call their own, he initiated the building of a church dedicated to St Vincent de Paul. Then, travelling by way of Philadelphia and St Louis, he went to New Orleans, where he delivered the Lenten sermons in 1840. In a letter to a friend he noted that their success "exceeded all expectations," despite his apprehensions, which had been roused by the existence of "eight or ten masonic lodges." "In this Babylon of the New World," these organizations kept "almost all men enchained," and mounted an opposition to him that found expression in a hostile press and "anti-preaching" scenes at the very doors of the cathedral where he spoke.

After attending the fourth Provincial Council of Baltimore, held from 16 to 24 May 1840, Forbin-Janson gave free rein to the wanderlust that was well suited to his apostolic zeal, and set off again northwards, visiting various cities in the United States and Upper Canada. Next he went to Quebec, where he gave his first sermon on Sunday, 6 Sept. 1840, in the cathedral. There followed a two-week retreat with 5,000–6,000 participants regularly attending the daily sermons, each about an hour and a half long; as in the United States, it ended with the founding of a temperance society as a collective social commitment.

Many historians have examined the situation of French Canada at that time; they have remarked on the political exhaustion following the crisis of the 1830s, the apathy to religion, largely a result of the numerical and doctrinal insufficiencies of the clergy, and the upsurge of Protestant proselytism, a product of the zeal displayed since 1834 by French-speaking Swiss ministers and the founding in 1839 of the French Canadian Missionary Society [*see* Henriette Odin*]. Bishop Forbin-Janson's stirring eloquence brought about a salutary reaction, or rather a religious revival which, bearing in mind the differences already noted, was similar to those south of the border. As a victim of the French revolution and the July revolution, which had had an influence on the rebellion of 1837–38 in Lower Canada, the French prelate by his very presence could only fix more firmly in people's minds an apprehension of the misfortunes such upheavals produced. Furthermore, as an intransigent reactionary, he would prepare the way for the ultramontane clericalism that Bishop Ignace Bourget* of Montreal would use to full advantage in both the religious and the political sphere.

Forbin-Janson had agreed to preach also in Bourget's diocese, and from the start of his preaching Bourget had seen his success at Quebec as a sign. As Bourget wrote to his clergy on 6 Oct. 1840, "Divine Providence has sent us the bishop of Nancy to create here what he has instituted to such advantage elsewhere." To give the sermons more lasting impact and value, the French example of publishing reports of the Restoration missions was followed. Thus in December 1840 a weekly paper was launched, *Prémices des "Mélanges religieux"*, which from the end of January 1841 was titled *Mélanges religieux* [*see* Jean-Charles Prince*].

It would be tedious to give a detailed account of Bishop Forbin-Janson's prodigious activity in Trois-Rivières, Montreal, and the surrounding region, or at New York, where he returned periodically to preach and to monitor progress in the building of the church to St Vincent de Paul. Suffice it to say that in his sermons he employed the spectacular methods adopted during the Restoration. Wishing to call forth an act of faith, he would try to secure it as the outcome of the anguish and terror he created, in effect seeking an emotional acquiescence that often ran counter to a freely willed acceptance of the message. Forbin-Janson's theatrical eloquence drew immense crowds, and in letters to friends and in *L'Ami de la religion*, the quasi-official journal of the French clergy, he did not shy away from dithyrambic accounts of miracles of contrition (never were so many tears shed as during those weeks of retreats!), submissiveness, and fervent sympathy which consoled him for the disappointments suffered in his ungrateful native land.

The supreme consolation of Forbin-Janson's apostolate in Lower Canada and his sweetest revenge was the raising of an immense cross on Mont Saint-Hilaire that was a happy counterpart to the one on Mont Valérien which had been destroyed. He wanted to make it an imposing monument that would be at once religious and national. Through a skilled Belœil carpenter and voluntary labour parties the 100-foot cross sheathed with metal was finally raised. Its shaft 6 feet wide and 4 feet through was lit through openings and people could climb ladders to the top. The cross was inaugurated and blessed with great ceremony on 6 Oct. 1841.

This was the crowning achievement of an apostolate that Bishop Forbin-Janson had carried out at a furious pace in some 60 localities from Lower Canada to the Maritimes. His frenzied labour, on top of the journeys he had made over vast stretches of the United States, had exhausted him. He had a premonition that his days were numbered when he sailed from New York on 8 Dec. 1841 for Europe.

Bishop Forbin-Janson was returning with a glowing memory of his "dear Canadians with their hearts of gold and their silver steeples." This ardent legitimist, knight errant of the Bourbons, and reactionary supporter of the *ancien régime* against revolutionary liberals who had laid waste his homeland and destroyed his career as a bishop, had in Montreal turned his attention to the fate of the Patriotes whom agitators, acting on principles that raised his hackles, had led astray and who, after being imprisoned and sentenced to transportation, on 28 Sept. 1839 had taken the road to exile. Before leaving, the French prelate had waited in vain for the arrival of Governor Sir Charles BAGOT to plead their cause. Back in Europe, he considered that efforts there might have more chance of being effective, and on 15 Aug. 1842 he went to London. His intervention with the colonial secretary, Lord Stanley, on behalf of his "poor Canadians," probably was, as he believed, what set in motion the measures of clemency that brought an initial group of 38 exiles back to their native soil in January 1845.

Forbin-Janson's trip to England had been preceded by one to Rome in January 1842. To reward him for the marvellous achievements of his apostolate in North America, news of which had reached him, Gregory XVI named him an assistant to the papal throne and a Roman count. But the pope was unwilling to involve himself in the dispute between Louis-Philippe's government and the bishop who, blind to all opposition, was stubbornly intent upon returning to his diocese. Refusing once more to resign, Forbin-Janson would die with the official title of bishop of Nancy.

When he returned from Rome, Forbin-Janson nurtured a plan to establish a charitable work that would interest Christian children in Europe in the fate of the young Chinese. He thought of attaching it to the Society for the Propagation of the Faith, but the central council of that body at Lyon thought the project would be in competition with its own efforts. He therefore had to resign himself to founding a separate, independent organization, the Œuvre Pontificale de la Sainte-Enfance, on 19 May 1843. From then on he devoted his declining strength to travelling around France and Belgium securing approval from bishops and collecting subscriptions. Only utter exhaustion put an end to this consuming zeal. He made up his mind to go south, to rest at his brother's home near Marseilles. And he, who in so many terrifying sermons had preached on the need to prepare for death, was himself taken by surprise, without the sacraments or a will, on 11 July 1844. He was buried in the cemetery of Picpus in Paris, which was reserved for the members of the nobility who had been beheaded, their descendants, and their connections. Right to the tomb Bishop Forbin-Janson protested against the crimes of the revolution. By a strange paradox, it was Dominican Henri Lacordaire, a priest persuaded by political realism to oppose completely the deceased bishop's reactionary attitude, who was called upon to deliver the eulogy in the cathedral of Nancy on 28 Aug. 1844.

PHILIPPE SYLVAIN

Catholicisme: hier, aujourd'hui, demain (10v. parus, Paris, 1947–), 4: 1442–43 (article de Jean Leflon). *DBF*, 14: 398–99. *Dictionnaire de spiritualité ascétique et mystique: doctrine et histoire* (12v. parus, Paris, 1932–). *Dictionnaire d'histoire et de géographie ecclésiastique* (20v. parus, Paris, 1912–), 17: 1001–4. *New Catholic encyclopedia* (17v., Toronto and San Francisco, 1966–78), 5: 1001–2. N.-E. Dionne, *Mgr de Forbin-Janson, évêque de Nancy et de Toul, primat de Lorraine; sa vie, son œuvre en Canada* (Québec, 1910). J. P. Dolan, *Catholic revivalism; the American experience, 1830–1900* (Notre Dame, Ind., 1978). Claude Galarneau, "Monseigneur de Forbin-Janson au Québec en 1840–1841," *Les ultramontains canadiens-français*, sous la direction de Nive Voisine et Jean Hamelin (Montréal, 1985), 121–42. Élisabeth Germain, *Parler du salut? Aux origines d'une mentalité religieuse, la catéchèse du salut dans la France de la Restauration* . . . (Paris, 1968). M.-J. Le Guillou, "Lamennais à la lumière de Vatican II," *L'actualité de Lamennais* (Strasbourg, France, 1981). Paul Lesourd, *Un grand cœur missionnaire: Monseigneur de Forbin-Janson, 1785–1844* . . . (Paris, 1944). Léon Pouliot, *La réaction catholique de Montréal, 1840–1841* (Montréal, 1942). René Rémond, *Les États-Unis devant l'opinion française, 1815–1852* (2v., Paris, 1962), 1. Ernest Sevrin, *Les missions religieuses en France sous la Restauration (1815–1830)* (Saint-Mandé, France, 1948). Paul Catrice, "Les missionnaires de France au Mont-Valérien de 1815 à 1830," Soc. hist. de Suresne, *Bull.* (Suresne, France), 6 (1968), no.27: 49–60. Lionel Groulx, "La situation religieuse au Canada français vers 1840," CCHA *Rapport*, 9 (1941–42): 51–75. J.-M. Mayeur, "Catholicisme intransigeant, Catholicisme social, démocratie chrétienne," *Annales ESC* (Paris), 27 (1972): 483–99.

FORRESTER, THOMAS, soldier, merchant, and politician; baptized 30 Aug. 1790 in Halifax, son of Alexander Forrester and Mary —; d. there 15 Nov. 1841.

Born into what appears to have been a lower-middle-class family, Thomas Forrester received the rudiments of a formal education at the Halifax Grammar School, and while still a youth entered the British army as a soldier. During the War of 1812 he served with the Royal Artillery in British North America. Returning to Halifax at war's end, he entered the retail dry goods trade, specializing in the sale of genteel finery. A shrewd businessman, Forrester capitalized on the economic growth in Halifax during the 1820s and 1830s. His 1819 assessment rating of £300 had risen to £4,000 in 1841, by which time he could be counted among the richest of Haligonians. His property included a stone house and store on Barrington Street (described after his death as "one of the best edifices in Halifax"), urban real estate yielding an annual rent-roll of £350, more than 1,000 acres of land across the province, and £2,000 in corporate securities, including 20 shares in the Bank of Nova Scotia. As befitted a man of property, Forrester enjoyed a position of influence in St Andrew's Presbyterian Church and won such honours as the presidency of the Nova Scotia Philanthropic Society. Thus within a few years Forrester had risen from obscurity to "handsome independence." With his wife, Elizabeth Martin, whom he had married on 25 Feb. 1813, and their five children, he "surrounded himself with the evidences of prosperity."

Material success did not, however, make Forrester a satisfied man. The post-war years also established him as an irascible trouble-maker. His letters to newspapers alleging an insurance fraud by certain leading local merchants resulted in 1825 in a conviction for libel and a fine of £100. Five years later, after a number of other clashes with the local gentry, Forrester consolidated his reputation by complaining that Halifax lawyers, judges, and officials had conspired to deny him justice in a debt action he had brought against a British army officer. Convinced that he had been victimized, Forrester petitioned Lieutenant Governor Sir Peregrine Maitland* for redress, and when rebuffed wrote directly to the Colonial Office, demanding vengeance. In the words of a contemporary, these were the actions of a man both "headstrong and intractable." An outraged Maitland described Forrester as "one of those unfortunate persons who just approach the verge of insanity without being sufficiently disordered to have the protection which declared lunatics enjoy." The attitude of local moneyed interests toward Forrester was demonstrated in 1832 when they decisively rejected his bid for election to the directorate of the Bank of Nova Scotia. Forrester's troubles reflected the difficulty a nonconforming outsider faced in attempting to penetrate the ranks of the Halifax oligarchy. An absence of deference on his part ensured that he would be excluded from public office and official patronage, a situation that could only aggravate his antagonism toward those in authority.

What transformed personal grievance into public cause was the eruption of political protest across Nova Scotia during the 1830s. Forrester's first involvement with public affairs came during the "Brandy Election" of 1830 when he backed Beamish Murdoch* in his unsuccessful attempt in Halifax Township to defeat the candidate of the oligarchy, Stephen Wastie DEBLOIS. Over the next few years, Forrester became a stock figure at meetings called to protest high official salaries, devaluation of the province's paper money, and related issues. After Joseph Howe* won acquittal in his famous 1835 trial for criminal libel, Forrester was one of the first to rally to him, seeing him as leader of an emerging reform movement. In 1836 the two stood on the reform ticket for election to the assembly and won, Forrester topping the poll in Halifax Township. Within the assembly, Forrester quickly emerged as a member of the radical wing of the amorphous reform caucus.

A man little given to abstract speculation, Forrester never defined his political principles in a systematic manner. He rarely participated in the protracted debates held to determine the precise meaning of responsible government. Instead, he concentrated on more tangible issues, such as the need for legislation that would better secure tradesmen against absconding debtors. In the promotion of one institutional innovation he assumed a leading role: the incorporation of Halifax as a city and the replacement of the appointed justices of the peace who administered civic affairs by elected officials. Using arguments that blended the self-interest of ratepayers with democratic idealism, Forrester insisted that this reform would create a municipal administration which would be honest, efficient, and cheap. The model for Halifax, he asserted, should be Boston, a city ruled by the propertied middle class, where the civic administration could both tax the affluent and impose moral discipline on the "lower orders."

Rural suspicion of urban aggrandizement and élitist opposition to the "levelling" principle of election to municipal office delayed incorporation in the assembly and councils. A charter finally passed in 1841 but it outraged Forrester, since high property qualifications for electors and office holders ensured that the new administration would remain in the hands of the élite. This caution, and the generous pensions provided for retiring municipal officials, convinced Forrester that the charter amounted to a "triumph of toryism."

By now Forrester was completely alienated from the moderate reformers. Howe had entered the coalition set up in 1840 under Lieutenant Governor Lord Falkland [Cary*] on the initiative of Governor Charles Edward Poulett THOMSON but Forrester withheld his support, arguing that the new administration involved too many compromises. His militancy may in part have stemmed from resentment over having been snubbed during negotiations leading up to the establishment of the coalition. Forrester's exclusion derived from his reputation for being irascible and erratic. Many remembered his behaviour during the financial crisis of 1837. When the panic had spread from Britain to Nova Scotia, the Halifax banks, alarmed by the prospect of runs on their cash reserves, had suspended the redemption of paper for metal. Merchants endorsed the decision but shopkeepers protested that they could not function without coinage. Possibly acting out of spite, Forrester came to the aid of Halifax retailers by launching a series of lawsuits against the Bank of Nova Scotia, claiming that its charter barred it from refusing to redeem in specie. The panic passed and payments resumed before the suits could be adjudicated, but Forrester's championing of the common man convinced respectable society that he could not be trusted with power.

Despite the break with Howe, Forrester enjoyed sufficient popularity to retain his seat in the election of 1840. In the house he played the role of radical gadfly, denouncing the legislative program of the coalition government. He widened the gap separating him from the moderates by speaking in favour of repeal of the parliamentary union between Ireland and Britain. Poor health intervened, however, to end his political career. After an illness of several months, Forrester died late in 1841. An obituary written by Howe contained the rather grudging comment that Forrester "had many good qualities for which he did not always get credit."

The chief significance of Thomas Forrester's public life lies in the extent to which it illustrated the tension generated in Halifax by Nova Scotia's "intellectual awakening." The circulation of new wealth and fresh ideas in a maturing colonial society spawned demands for change which came to be embodied in Forrester. The most significant aspect of his campaign against oligarchy was the demand for Halifax's incorporation. His ambition appeared in 1841 to have been defeated by hesitation on the part of moderates but within a decade of his death the restraints on middle-class municipal democracy had been swept aside, with the result that Halifax moved from the era of "merchantocracy" to that of "shopocracy."

DAVID A. SUTHERLAND

Halifax County Court of Probate (Halifax), Estate papers, nos.1138–39 (mfm. at PANS). PANS, RG 1, 312, nos.63, 86; RG 32, 142, 25 Feb. 1813; RG 35A, 1–3. PRO, CO 217/151: 110; 217/152: 83 *et seq.*; 217/153: 227. N.S., House of Assembly, *Journal and proc.*, 1838, app.75. *Acadian Recorder*, 29 Jan. 1825; 18 Sept. 1830; 5 Nov. 1836; 24 July 1837; 27 March, 12 June 1841. *Halifax Journal*, 20 Feb. 1837. *Novascotian*, 7, 28 June 1832; 23 Jan., 29 Dec. 1834; 11 June, 10–26 Nov. 1835; 8 Dec. 1836; 20 April 1837; 8 March 1838; 17 Oct. 1839; 9 April, 12 Nov. 1840; 18 Feb., 11 March, 29 April, 18 Nov. 1841. *Times* (Halifax), 16 Feb. 1841, 26 July 1842. *Weekly Chronicle* (Halifax), 21–28 Jan. 1825. *Belcher's farmer's almanack*, 1841. *Directory of N.S. MLAs*. *History of the Bank of Nova Scotia, 1832–1900; together with copies of annual statements* ([Toronto, 1900]).

FORSYTH, JOHN, businessman, militia officer, JP, and politician; baptized 8 Dec. 1762 in Huntly, Scotland, son of William Forsyth and Jean Phyn; d. 27 Dec. 1837 in London.

A nephew of James Phyn, who was a partner with Alexander Ellice* in Phyn, Ellice and Company of London, John Forsyth immigrated to the province of Quebec, probably in 1779, to work in that firm's Montreal office, which became Robert Ellice and Company. His brother Thomas was already employed there, and subsequently became a partner. Another brother, Joseph*, settled in Kingston, Upper Canada, ten years later and did business with Phyn, Ellices, and Inglis, successor firm to Phyn, Ellice and Company, through their Montreal branch. Following Robert Ellice*'s death in 1790 John Forsyth joined Thomas and their cousin John Richardson* in the Montreal partnership, and the company became Forsyth, Richardson and Company; Richardson immediately established his dominance. Alexander Thain would become a partner by the spring of 1816, when Thomas Forsyth retired.

Forsyth, Richardson expanded the forwarding activities of Robert Ellice and Company, operating in part through agents such as Richard Cartwright* in Kingston, Robert Hamilton* at Niagara (Niagara-on-the-Lake), and John Askin* in Detroit. Much of this business was for the fur trade. Initially operating south and west from Michilimackinac (Mackinac Island, Mich.), Forsyth, Richardson increasingly shifted its activities to the northwest, where the North West Company was seeking to establish a monopoly. In 1792 Forsyth, Richardson forced its way into the NWC but received only 2 of the 46 shares into which that copartnership was divided. Feeling its interest too small, Forsyth, Richardson left in 1795 and again traded in competition with the NWC. In 1798 it formed the nucleus of the New North West Company (sometimes called the XY Company), founded to compete with the NWC [*see* John Ogilvy*]. Reorganized and expanded in 1800 with the introduction of Alexander Mackenzie* and others, the New North West Company was, nevertheless, taken over by its more experienced rival in 1804 and Forsyth, Richardson played a leading role that year in evaluating its assets. Meanwhile, still operating south and west from Michilimackinac, Forsyth, Richardson was a major element in the formation of the Michilimackinac Company in 1806 [*see* John Ogilvy] and of the Montreal Michilimackinac Company in 1811. Although Richardson seems to have been most prominent in these developments, Forsyth was an active participant. Having travelled into the fur trade country for the first time in 1793, he had been accepted into the Beaver Club with Richardson in 1807.

Forsyth, Richardson's operations were not limited to the fur trade. In the early 1790s the firm was involved in the ill-starred Montreal Distillery Company [*see* Thomas McCord*]. It also dealt in real estate in Upper and Lower Canada and manifested interest in early plans to form the Lower Canada Land Company about 1825 [*see* William Bowman FELTON]. As well it engaged in other activities commonly conducted by Lower Canadian enterprises of the time. Through its connection with Phyn, Ellices, and Inglis it served as an agent for British merchants with Canadian business; as assignee in 1814 for the estate of Hoyle, Henderson, and Gibb of Quebec and Montreal, for example, Forsyth handled a claim from London wholesalers of more than £40,000. In December 1805 Forsyth, Richardson had received power of attorney from the executors of Alexander Ellice's will, and ten years later Forsyth was an executor of the will of James Dunlop*, a leading Montreal businessman.

Above all, however, Forsyth, Richardson was a major importer of a wide variety of merchandise for Upper Canadian wholesalers and retailers and a leading exporter of Upper Canadian produce and semi-processed goods. Imports included wines, spirits from Britain, sugar from Barbados, tea from Canton (People's Republic of China), and manufactures such as iron, steel, linen, clothing, and hardware. Exports were largely of beef, pork, fish, flour, oats, peas, staves, and horses to Barbados and wheat, deals, and staves to Greenock, Scotland. To help carry on this trade, in 1793 Forsyth, Richardson purchased a share in the *Lady Dorchester*, a 120-ton vessel serving on Lake Ontario, in which Cartwright, Hamilton, and Todd, McGill and Company of Montreal [*see* Isaac Todd*] were the principal partners. The group commissioned construction of one vessel, the *Governor Simcoe*, the same year and of another in 1794. Naturally interested in improving the navigability of the upper St Lawrence River, Forsyth was, with François Desrivières*, among 14 businessmen who in 1818 petitioned for the right to dig a canal around the Sainte-Marie current and the Lachine rapids. The following year he promoted sales of shares in the newly chartered Company of Proprietors of the Lachine Canal. He was a member of the Montreal Harbour Commission in 1824–25; it recommended major improvements and the establishment of an independent corporation to manage harbour affairs. In 1830 Forsyth was a shareholder in the Quebec and Halifax Steam Navigation Company, which had been formed that year. He had been one of 12 businessmen who, in October 1823, had planned a turnpike road from Montreal to Longue-Pointe (Montreal).

Forsyth, Richardson also took a leading part in improving financial conditions affecting trade in the colony. Forsyth played a supporting role in Richardson's abortive effort to establish the Canada Banking Company in 1792. He was among the founders, with Richardson, of the Bank of Montreal in 1817, and their firm, as well as Forsyth and Richardson individually, subscribed the maximum permissible 20 shares each. Forsyth served as a director of the bank from 1817 to 1820 and as vice-president in 1825–26. Following the bankruptcy in late 1825 of Simon McGillivray, of whom the bank, thanks to its president, Samuel Gerrard*, had become a major creditor, Forsyth supported before the board of the bank a settlement proposed by Richardson and Gerrard, who were McGillivray's trustees. In an ensuing major controversy over the financial administration of the bank, Forsyth was part of the "old guard" of former fur-trade merchants who vainly supported Gerrard's continuance as president. Forsyth had also been a founding shareholder of the Montreal Fire Insurance Company in 1818.

In the course of the daily administration of his firm, Forsyth kept abreast of affairs in Montreal, Chambly, Kingston, and other places where it did business, endorsing or protesting notes issued by traders, agents, retailers, innkeepers, and tradesmen. He occasionally, perhaps often, went into the field. In February 1817, for example, he travelled by sleigh to the customs post at Fort Saint-Jean (Saint-Jean-sur-Richelieu). Smuggling was rampant in the area, and the 19th Light Dragoons had been deployed at the border to check it. On his return Forsyth passed through La Prairie in the night, and on three different occasions he was challenged and told to stop. For whatever reason, he chose to speed on, and on the third occasion, according to the *Montreal Gazette*, "a Dragoon fired and wounded him in the arm."

From the 1790s at least, Forsyth was part of the social circuit on which the upper echelon of the Montreal business community prided itself. Anglican bishop Jacob Mountain* dined in a large company at Forsyth's home in July 1794. "The house itself is elegant, and the dinner splendid," he recorded. "People here are fond of good living and take care to want no luxury." Forsyth's political and social views and activities were representative of those of the most prominent business figures in Montreal. In the 1790s he had welcomed into his home refugees from the French revolution. He was commissioned an ensign in the Montreal Battalion of British Militia in 1797, and he reached the rank of captain in Montreal's 1st Militia Battalion in early 1812. His company formed part of the Montreal Incorporated Volunteers in 1812–13, and he was later granted land for his services during the War of 1812. Promoted major in the 1st battalion in 1821, he became lieutenant-colonel of the Royal Montreal Cavalry in June 1828. Meanwhile he had been commissioned a justice of the peace in 1821. He became a life governor of the Montreal General Hospital, which, founded in 1819, was a favourite project of the business community. Diligent in support of Richardson during the founding of the Montreal Committee of Trade in 1822, he was elected its first chairman but declined the honour and was replaced by Thomas Blackwood. On the whole, however, Forsyth's social and public involvement was restrained for a businessman of his rank; he was for example largely inactive in the affairs of his church, the Scotch Presbyterian Church, later known as St Gabriel Street Church.

Forsyth was not as active as Richardson in the turbulent politics of Lower Canada. He was, nevertheless, a steady supporter of the English party and of the policies of the colonial executive. In May 1824 he was vice-president of a dinner held on behalf of Governor Lord Dalhousie [Ramsay], and in 1827 he chaired a public dinner, attended by more than 200 people, which Dalhousie considered "a plain declaration of . . . their avowed approbation of my conduct." The same year Dalhousie made Forsyth and Richardson patrons of a subscription campaign in Montreal for the erection at Quebec of a monument to James Wolfe* and Louis-Joseph de Montcalm*. In July 1827 Forsyth was appointed to the Legislative Council on Dalhousie's recommendation. However, unlike many prominent businessmen, and most notably his partner, Forsyth was not offered, or did not accept, any great number of government appointments. In 1824 he was named to the Board of Examiners of Applicants to be

Inspectors of Pot and Pearl Ashes, and nine years later he received a commission of oyer and terminer and general jail delivery.

On 29 March 1798, in St Andrew's Church at Quebec, Forsyth had married Margaret Grant, daughter of the prominent Quebec merchant Charles Grant; three important business colleagues witnessed the ceremony – William Grant*, Robert Lester*, and John Blackwood*. Forsyth and his wife had two sons and a daughter, all of whom married within Forsyth's business circle: William (who later added Grant to his family name) married a daughter of Joseph Forsyth; John Blackwood married a daughter of Samuel Gerrard; and Jane Prescott married a son of John Gregory*, a former colleague of Forsyth in the NWC and a fellow member of the Beaver Club. A nephew, James Bell Forsyth*, represented Forsyth, Richardson at Quebec, in association with William Walker, from 1821.

Richardson died in May 1831, and for a time Forsyth carried on. In August he informed London businessman Edward Ellice* that he was "on the best of terms" with Governor Lord Aylmer [WHITWORTH-AYLMER] and "an intimate and old friend" of Aylmer's civil secretary, John Baskerville Glegg, and he offered to use these advantages to promote the development of Ellice's seigneury of Villechauve, more commonly known as Beauharnois, the management of which Forsyth, Richardson had long supervised. Forsyth spent his last years in Britain, possibly in London, where he died in 1837. Forsyth, Richardson and Company survived until 1847 when it and Forsyth, Walker and Company were dissolved.

Much more discreet in business, politics, and society than his domineering partner, John Forsyth seems to have taken responsibility for the efficient daily functioning of Forsyth, Richardson and Company, and by doing so to have freed Richardson for an active public life and to have ensured the prosperity and prestige of the commercial house that was to a large extent Richardson's power base in Lower Canadian politics. It may be speculated as well that Forsyth's less strongly anti-Canadian attitudes had a moderating effect on the political views of his impulsive and forceful associate.

GERALD J. J. TULCHINSKY

ANQ-Q, CE1-66, 29 mars 1798. GRO (Edinburgh), Aberdeen, reg. of births and baptisms, 8 Dec. 1762. Montreal Business Hist. Project, Extracts and digests of Montreal notarial arch., Henry Griffin, nos.3410, 4387, 4477, 6063, 6099, 6125, 6522. PAC, MG 24, A2: 1060–65, 1099–100, 1936–46, 1978–81; L3: 8838–39, 9159–61, 25025–38; MG 30, D1, 13: 89–107; RG 68, General index, 1651–1841. QUA, 2199c, letter-books, Richard Cartwright to Forsyth, Richardson and Company, 6 Aug., 16 Oct. 1799; 11, 17 Sept. 1800. *Les bourgeois de la Compagnie du Nord-Ouest* (Masson). *Corr. of Lieut. Governor Simcoe* (Cruikshank). *John Askin papers* (Quaife), 2: 444–45. Jacob Mountain, "From Quebec to Niagara in 1794; a diary of Bishop Jacob Mountain," ed. A. R. Kelly, ANQ *Rapport*, 1959–60: 121–65. Ramsay, *Dalhousie journals* (Whitelaw), 3: 119. John Richardson, "The John Richardson letters," ed. E. A. Cruikshank, *OH*, 6 (1905): 20–36. *Select documents in Canadian economic history*, ed. H. A. Innis and A. R. M. Lower (2v., Toronto, 1929–33), 2: 324. *Montreal Gazette*, 13 March 1838. *Quebec Commercial List*, 23 May 1825. *Quebec Gazette*, 4 July 1792; 10 Oct. 1793; 30 Jan. 1794; 30 April 1812; 14 Sept. 1815; 11 July 1816; 5 Oct., 7 Dec. 1818; 12 July, 5 Aug. 1819; 2 May, 23 Oct. 1821; 24 April, 17 July, 21 Aug., 13 Oct. 1823; 17 May 1824. *Officers of British forces in Canada* (Irving), 164. *Quebec almanac*, 1798: 106; 1810: 58. F. W. Terrill, *A chronology of Montreal and of Canada from A.D. 1752 to A.D. 1893* . . . (Montreal, 1893). Wallace, *Macmillan dict.*

Creighton, *Empire of St. Lawrence*. G. C. Davidson, *The North West Company* (Berkeley, Calif., 1918; repr. New York, 1967). Denison, *Canada's first bank*. Innis, *Fur trade in Canada* (1962). Rich, *Hist. of HBC* (1958–59). G. J. J. Tulchinsky, "The construction of the first Lachine Canal, 1815–1826" (MA thesis, McGill Univ., Montreal, 1960), 39. Wallot, *Un Québec qui bougeait*, 304. B. G. Wilson, *Enterprises of Robert Hamilton*. R. H. Fleming, "The origin of 'Sir Alexander Mackenzie and Company,'" *CHR*, 9 (1928): 137–55. "Origins of the Montreal Board of Trade," *Journal of Commerce* (Gardenvale, Que.), 2nd ser., 55 (April 1927): 28–29. Adam Shortt, "The Hon. John Richardson," Canadian Bankers' Assoc., *Journal* (Toronto), 29 (1921–22): 17–27. W. S. Wallace, "Forsyth, Richardson and Company in the fur trade," RSC *Trans.*, 3rd ser., 34 (1940), sect.II: 187–94.

FORSYTH, WILLIAM, farmer, businessman, and militiaman; b. 1771, probably in Tryon County, N.Y., son of James Forsyth and Mary ——; m. first *c.* 1795 Mary Ackler, and they had ten children; m. secondly Jane ——, and they had nine children; d. 27 Feb. 1841 in Bertie Township, Upper Canada.

In the late 18th and early 19th centuries few natural scenes then known could equal the spectacle of the great falls at Niagara. Renowned for its power and magnificence, the falls lured visitors of every sort: tourists, eccentrics, would-be poets and artists, and others less taken with the falls' majesty than with reaping a profit from nature's sublimity. These hucksters-cum-entrepreneurs have been an enduring presence at the falls and a carnival-like atmosphere and an often slatternly appearance have been their legacy. William Forsyth was such an entrepreneur, the first on the Canadian side of the Niagara River.

Forsyth's father was a loyalist farmer who in 1783 or 1784 moved his wife and five children to the west side of the Niagara River. The family made its home in Stamford Township, where William was living in 1796 when he first petitioned for land. Three years later, then described as a yeoman, he stood trial for a felony. He was acquitted but on 7 March was jailed for a capital offence. Escaping the next day, he was foiled in his attempt to reach the United States and, back in prison, he petitioned Administrator Peter Russell* for release conditional upon "his banishing himself." Despite the support of Robert Hamilton*, the most powerful man in the district and an important figure in the portaging trade around the falls, Russell hesitated since Forsyth's offence involved "so many Questions of Prudence – Policy – & Law." By mid May he had still not made a decision, after which date nothing further is known of the incident.

Forsyth next appears as a farmer living close to the Horseshoe Falls. In his reply to an 1824 query about Forsyth's claim for losses in the War of 1812, Thomas Clark*, a neighbour and commanding officer of the 2nd Lincoln Militia (Forsyth's unit), reported him "a man of uncouth behaviour." Clark remembered that he had given "some displeasure and trouble to my Officers by leaving his duty and going home at nights." On the other hand, Clark believed that at the battle of Beaver Dams in 1813 "he behaved very well in harassing the Enemy before taken prisoners." That fall American forces plundered Forsyth's home and farm. More damage was done to his house by Indians during a council convened by Major-General Phineas RIALL. Clark noted that in 1814, when Major-General Louis de WATTEVILLE was quartered there, he used Forsyth as a spy "to go across the river . . . but report says that he took over as much if not more than he brought back." Clark was not in the province at the time, however, and was unsure how true the allegation was: "Forsyth is a man not generally liked, and perhaps malice may have instigated the report – his neighbours . . . have no doubts about his loyalty – and further say that when the Enemy were in possession here, he did, and did naturally shape his Conduct as well as he could to save his property." Although Forsyth's claim of more than £425 for losses was initially rejected, upon appeal, and after Clark's review of his wartime record, he was allowed £90 in 1824.

Rumour and innuendo hung over Forsyth like the ever-present mist over the falls. The wartime stories did not impugn his character but they detracted from it, suggesting a man with a sense of what was best for himself. One popular historian, Gordon Donaldson, has hinted that Forsyth used his knowledge of the river to smuggle goods to and from the United States. There is no corroboration but Forsyth's early brushes with authority, mad escape from jail, and self-serving character suggest that there may be room for doubt.

Some time after the war Forsyth built an inn on his property. Charles FOTHERGILL stayed there in early April 1817. Two years later botanist John Goldie described it as the "nearest" to the falls of several inns along the river. In 1818 Forsyth had erected a covered stairway into the gorge for a different view at 1*s*. per person. These stairs were, he admitted, "upon the chain reserved for Military purposes, in front of . . . [his] Land between it and the River." The falls was Upper Canada's greatest scenic attraction and Forsyth's inn was the place to stay. The Duke of Richmond [Lennox*] stayed there in 1818 as did Lord Dalhousie [RAMSAY] a year later. The duke's party were less than pleased by the innkeeper's ability to accommodate them, in spite of his professed exertions, and there was a problem over the account. When Dalhousie arrived Forsyth's reputation was suspect; none the less, he found the "tavern & accommodation . . . were very good indeed, and the man himself, tho' a Yankee & reputed to be uncivil, was quite the reverse to us, obliging & attentive in every way." Visitors often seized upon other traits: Adam Fergusson* pronounced Forsyth a "personage sufficiently shrewd and well informed" whereas Samuel De Veaux found him "a man of enterprising character."

Forsyth was an aggressive entrepreneur anxious to cater to the public and expand his business as the tourist influx increased. In his situation, he needed to court the government, not run foul of it. In October 1820, through Robert Randal* (a self-styled victim of judicial partiality and executive persecution), Forsyth petitioned the Executive Council for a lease of occupation of the 66-foot-wide allowance reserved for military purposes, which fronted his property. He also wanted to secure the privilege of operating a ferry below the falls. The government, however, had no intention of leasing the military reserve, and ferry rights had already been awarded. Randal had been told that Forsyth was the "last man to look for indulgence of any Kind whatever" on account of his behaviour to Richmond. Forsyth's hurried explanation of May 1821 noted that "much has been said and that greatly misrepresented in respect to my conduct on that occasion." But his account, reasonable as it seems, availed him nothing.

Forsyth's intentions were twofold: to enlarge his accommodation for tourists and to ensure his control over the pre-eminent view of the great cataract. His own lands (inherited from his father) were just downriver from the falls, and he purchased from William DICKSON the farm adjoining his own. Forsyth's combined acreage gave him a monopoly of the best views, especially that from Table Rock, the famed outcrop near the edge of Horseshoe Falls which offered the finest prospect of it. On his newly acquired property Forsyth had built by 1822 the Pavilion Hotel, also known as the Niagara Falls Pavilion. It was described ten years later by Thomas Fowler as a "handsome frame building, . . . three stories high, with piazzas on both sides." In 1826 Forsyth added wings which were "chiefly filled with bed rooms." No expense was spared. It was, he thought, "perhaps the most splendid establishment of the kind," "unequalled in this new country" and "a place worthy of fashionable resort – whereat visitors of rank and distinction may always have suitable accomodations." An 1827 advertisement emphasized its claim as a luxury establishment "for noblemen and gentlemen of highest rank with their families, & for pleasure parties." It had "ample" rooms and one of the main rooms allowed 100 people to "dine with ease." The larder was stocked with "viands from every land," the cellars offered "the best flavoured and most costly wines and liquors," and good stabling was available across the road. As late as 1832 the approach to the falls from the Pavilion was through a forest which, as Fowler put it, "conceals the prospect till close at the place, when the scene instantaneously bursts forth with astonishing grandeur! The place at which the visitor arrives by this route is Table Rock." At the hotel, the falls was visible only from the rear balconies.

Among Forsyth's services were daily stages to Buffalo, Niagara (Niagara-on-the-Lake), Queenston, and Lewiston (he had successfully petitioned the House of Assembly, with the assistance of Robert Nichol*, to prohibit Americans from operating stages "along the Niagara Frontier"), the rental of carriages and post-horses, the stairway, and a ferry service to the United States. Table Rock was the site of the entrance to Forsyth's stairway, at the bottom of which he eventually added a tour behind the Horseshoe Falls. For 50 cents the visitor was outfitted with waxed pantaloons, frock coat, Dunstable hat, and shoes. Forsyth did everything in his power to lure tourists and to make them comfortable. "I have ever had," he said in 1826, "a great desire to add to the unrivalled natural beauties of the wild and romantic scenery in the midst of which I dwell." Accordingly, he claimed in 1829 to have spent "perhaps not less than Fifty thousand Dollars" on his operation.

By 1827 he was "reaping," as one account put it, "a fair reward from a generous public." But his dominance had been challenged: a rival, John Brown, had built a hotel upriver, although his Ontario House could not equal Forsyth's establishment, or so it was said. In 1826 it was burnt under mysterious circumstances while one of Forsyth's sons was resident. Brown rebuilt the following year. A note published in William Lyon Mackenzie*'s *Colonial Advocate* hinted that Brown was the instigator of "infamous reports" that William Forsyth had been "privy to the burning." Brown's purpose in venting the rumour, the note continued, was to deprive Forsyth – "an enterprizing individual who had done more to accommodate the public, than any other stage proprietor or tavern keeper in Canada" – of his fair share of business. To increase that share the imaginative Forsyth was planning the first in a long history of spectacles, an event calculated to draw an extraordinary number of visitors and produce an extraordinary profit. Carnival days were dawning at the falls and Forsyth would be the ring-master.

In August 1827 Forsyth, Brown, and Parkhurst Whitney, owner of a hotel on the American side, advertised that a "condemned" schooner, the *Michigan*, with a "cargo of Living Animals" would be sent "through the white tossing, and the deep rolling rapids of the Niagara and down its grand precipice, into the basin '*below*.'" When in early September the great day arrived, Mackenzie was there. The roads were jammed, the hotels and galleries "were crowded with people dressed in the pink of fashion," "every place and every corner and nook was filled." Bands played, a lion roared, and "show-men with wild beasts, gingerbread people, cake and beer stalls, wheel of fortune men" hawked their wares or plied their trades to a throng estimated by Mackenzie to have been at midday about 8,000 to 10,000. Finally, about 3:00 P.M., the ship made its appearance with its unwitting cargo: two bears, a buffalo, two foxes, a raccoon, an eagle, a dog, and 15 geese. The crew departed at Chippawa above the falls and the *Michigan* was towed closer to the rapids before being cut adrift. When it hit the first set, "there was a simultaneous shout of applause" from the appreciative crowd. In the second the ship lost its masts and several of the cargo, including a bear and the buffalo. It reached the falls rent in half and was smashed on the rocks below. One goose survived. The bear had swum to an island above the falls where it was recaptured; it was later sold to a hotel on the American side for display. Not long after, spectacular stunts by daredevils such as Sam Patch and Jean-François Gravelet* (Charles Blondin) became a regular attraction at Niagara Falls.

Forsyth's interest derives from his accomplishments in turning the sublime (the word most often used by visitors to convey the falls' majesty) into the ridiculous. But there is more to his historical reputation than his being the founder of the first tourist trap in Upper Canada. He was the central figure in the so-called Niagara Falls outrage, an event first drawn to public notice by Mackenzie in 1828 and since recounted by several historians. For John Charles Dent* writing in 1885, as for Mackenzie, the outrage was a "violent and utterly unjustifiable exercise of brute force" sanctioned and ordered by Lieutenant Governor Sir Peregrine Maitland*. And, like Mackenzie, Dent considered the outrage part of a pattern of events leading back to the attack on Mackenzie's printing-shop, the type riot of 1826. This sort of interpretation, "a simple case of Might *versus* Right," has been out of historical fashion for some time. Most recently Paul Romney has returned to this incident and others like it which "created the impression of a province ruled by men who were ready to punish any sort of opposition by violence and coercion." Indeed, it was the Forsyth affair which led to an investigation by a parliamentary committee into the administration of justice.

Fought on several fronts, the war which culminated in the outrage had its origins in a contest over tourist dollars. The major dispute focused on control of the military reserve fronting Forsyth's property, particularly the land which he had purchased from Dickson. In 1826 he applied to Dalhousie, with whom he enjoyed good relations, for a licence of occupation which would give him legal control of the reserve. He had heard rumours that "many applications" had been made for it and, "as it is the only bar between my lands and the Cascade I feel the utmost anxiety to ascertain whether it is yet indisposed of." Its loss would jeopardize his stairway (and another which he planned to build, with free use by the public, in 1827), his road from the hotel to Table Rock, and, most important, his control over the view from the latter. Dalhousie was reassuring. He did not think Maitland would grant to others a licence to a strip "so immediately convenient" to Forsyth's buildings. And, in any event, he believed there was no "intention of granting it because [it was] reserved expressly for public purposes – free from the exclusive control of any person."

Of immediate concern to Forsyth was his dispute with John Brown, who had built a plank-road to the falls from the Ontario House and constructed a stairway which, Forsyth alleged, was on his property. The stakes were high and Forsyth was not reluctant to take matters into his own hands. Brown had not only been burnt out in 1826 but had also had his road blocked by Forsyth, who fenced his property from the hotel to the falls so as to deny Brown's patrons access except across Forsyth's property. Into the fray stepped Clark, who, he later testified, had told Brown that Forsyth "had no right to put the fence where he did." Clark had his own interests in this fight. First, he was Forsyth's rival in a bitter struggle over the ferry rights below the falls which had been awarded to Clark and his partner, Samuel STREET, in 1825. Clark later complained to Attorney General John Beverley Robinson* that they had been unable to occupy the site because of Forsyth's harassment. Although he lacked direct proof, Clark blamed the Pavilion's owner for the loss of three boats in 1826 and for a broken stairway in 1827. Secondly, as was also revealed in later testimony, he had "a claim upon" Brown's hotel. It was not long after Clark's suggestion about the fence that some residents of the area complained to Maitland "of being . . . shut out from the river by the illegal act of an individual."

Thus in May 1827 Captain George Phillpotts, the commanding Royal Engineer in Upper Canada, appeared at the falls to resolve the matter. Crucial to his decision was a determination as to the exact location of the reserve. Forsyth, for instance, contended that the 66-foot allowance ran from the river's edge, thus minimizing the effect of the reserve below the falls, where some of it would be in the gorge. There were two other possible interpretations: first, that the reserve extended back from the the edge of the gorge, known to contemporaries as the lower bank; secondly, that it extended back from the edge of the escarpment (both the Pavilion and the Ontario House were near that edge), known as the upper bank. Phillpotts decided that the reserve was taken from the upper bank, and thus extended almost to Forsyth's inn and, in fact, included on it some of his out-buildings as well as his fences.

Rather than press the matter in court, in May 1827 Maitland ordered Phillpotts's party to tear down the fence "to prevent any Monopoly" – and thereby perpetrated the outrage. Forsyth put it up again, and later that month this second fence was torn down. On the second occasion a blacksmith's hut belonging to Forsyth was dumped over the escarpment. Now the various disputes went to court. On 30 Aug. 1827 Brown won a civil action against Forsyth, who was convicted of tearing up Brown's road. Then, on 3 September, Clark and Street won their suit against Forsyth for obstructing their ferry. Robinson successfully upheld the crown's claim to what it considered reserve property in a trial before James Buchanan Macaulay* (the presiding judge in the two previous cases) and associate judges Clark and William Dickson. Forsyth lost but the jury had taken 24 hours to reach a decision. He filed counter-suits against Phillpotts and sheriff Richard Leonard for trespass, but lost both actions.

The affair took a political turn when a petition from Forsyth to the House of Assembly was presented by John Matthews* on 28 Jan. 1828. It led to a major confrontation between the crown and the assembly. The gist of Forsyth's complaint was "the substitution of a military force to decide the question of right . . . in a country not under martial law." He asked the house for redress and requested it "to watch over and protect the rights of the people from the encroachment of military power." His petition went to a select committee composed of John Rolph* in the chair, Robert Randal, Matthews, and John Johnston LEFFERTY. When the committee demanded the appearance of the adjutant general of militia, Nathaniel COFFIN, and the acting superintendent of Indian affairs, James GIVINS, Maitland refused to give his permission. On 22 March the two men were jailed for contempt of the house and three days later the lieutenant governor prorogued the session. Given that Rolph had acted as Forsyth's counsel in the 1827 suits and chaired the committee, it is not surprising that Forsyth won its support. James Stephen, the colonial under-secretary, upheld the committee while the colonial secretary, Sir George MURRAY, notified Maitland's successor, Sir John

Colborne*, on 20 Oct. 1828 that Maitland "would have exercised a sounder discretion had he permitted the officers to appear before the Assembly; and I regret that he did not accomplish the object he had in view in preventing Forsyth's encroachments by means of the civil power . . . rather than by calling in military aid."

There were complications still to come. On 31 Aug. 1827 the wily Clark had obtained with Samuel Street a licence of occupation on "that part of the reserve near the ferry, up and down the river." The object, according to Solicitor General Henry John Boulton*, who granted the licence, was "to protect the lessees in the proper enjoyment of their right of ferry, and to keep the shore open and free of access to the public who had been shut out by Forsyth." The licence had been suggested by Clark in a letter to George HILLIER, Maitland's secretary, in May, not long after the outrage. Clark wanted to end Forsyth's obstruction of his ferry rights and to end Forsyth's unauthorized ferry service. The licence would allow him to take legal action against his rival although he expressed some disingenuous concern that it might have a "grasping or Monopolising appearance." Licence in hand, the partners warned Forsyth on 14 September that any subsequent incursions would render him liable to prosecution. With Forsyth at their advantage, Clark and Street did not hesitate to press their position and in December 1828 they brought, and won, two suits of trespass against him. Forsyth was badly shaken and on 16 Jan. 1829 he petitioned the Executive Council asking that the reserve "instead of being converted into a Monopoly for the benefit of speculating individuals be thrown open to the public." He thought "it hard to have his front taken from him and given to another whose lands are not adjoining." Even his stairs had been taken away by this decision and part of his meadows and buildings lost as well. The council found no irregularity in the lease of the ferry rights to Clark and Street but recommended against the continuation of the license of occupation for the reserve. Colborne himself noted that a "certain extent" near the ferry should be granted to the partners but that a one-chain strip on the top of the bank "should be thrown open to the public for a road." Council concurred.

Mackenzie was an old acquaintance of Forsyth and had the outrage raised by Joseph Hume in parliament in 1832. In the mean time, Forsyth, "harrassed by Law – injured by the Government – persecuted for the sake of his property and embarrassed in his business," sold his hotel and property to a group of investors that included Clark, Street, and William Allan*, who planned to subdivide the land for the proposed "City of the Falls." Forsyth was to remain as proprietor of his hotel (the group had also acquired the Ontario House) until December 1833. In total, he sold 407 acres plus the buildings for £10,250 which was, by his estimate, $15,000 less than what the property was worth. When Clark and Street erected a museum and baths on the reserve, Colborne took action. Phillpotts had been succeeded by Richard Henry BONNYCASTLE, who took "care not to employ the military in any shape" in ordering them to desist. The partners "now turned, full of grievance, against the government," as Bonnycastle put it, and won damages in 1833, a verdict which astounded Forsyth, not unreasonably.

Forsyth was by no means destitute. He had bought land in Bertie Township near Fort Erie in 1832. Despite the years of litigation and petitioning, he lived in comfort and elegance in Bertie Hall, his fashionable, pillared home. Yet he lived in hopes of receiving the compensation he felt was owing over the outrage. In 1835 Mackenzie raised the issue in the house, with predictable results. The select committee, which he chaired, considered that Forsyth had "sustained great injury at the hand of Sir Peregrine Maitland . . . and is entitled to compensation." On 2 April 1835 he wrote to Forsyth, "You may think that I have been neglectful in your cause, but it is not so – I have done all I could." Months later, having heard the ferry rights of Clark and Street had reverted to the crown, Forsyth applied for them but was informed that the lease had not expired. That fall he sought a licence of occupation for the portion of his lands in Bertie fronting the Niagara River; however, executive councillor Robert Baldwin Sullivan* later explained that council could not allocate "any part of the chain of reserve . . . originally made for public purpose." Squabbling over the reserve continued unabated through the 19th century, the crown contending against entrepreneurs. It was finally ended in December 1892 by a decision by John Alexander Boyd* in the High Court of Justice. With great understatement, he wrote that the "matter presented for determination has, in various forms, occasioned doubt and perplexity for some hundred years." Phillpotts's survey of 1827 was upheld.

Forsyth had fought tooth-and-nail to monopolize the tourist trade at the falls. When he failed to obtain what he wanted by lawful means, he did not hesitate to use coercion. He built a tourist empire and lost it to his most serious competitor, Clark. Unable to get redress in the courts and out-manœuvered by Clark, who was able to make his own deal for the vexed strip of military reserve, Forsyth sold out. But the river never lost its lure and Forsyth never left it. When he died in 1841 he bequeathed more than 800 acres and £1,000 to his children and wife. To one son he allowed whatever "Money as my Executors may recover or receive from Her Majesty's Government for Claims for Damages." In June 1850 Nelson Forsyth approached Mackenzie about raising the claim yet one more time but nothing came of it.

ROBERT L. FRASER

[Documents relating to William Forsyth are scattered through the major government records of the period. The most useful are: AO, RG 22, ser.96; ser.125; ser.131; ser.138; ser.155; PAC, RG 1, E3 and L3; RG 5, A1; RG 7, G1; RG 8, I (C ser.); RG 19; and PRO, CO 42. Several manuscript collections proved helpful: AO, MS 4; MS 75; MS 78; MS 88; MS 198; MS 500; MS 516; and MTRL, W. W. Baldwin papers.

The most complete documentation of the Niagara Falls outrage is found in U.C., House of Assembly, *Journal*, 1828, app., "Report of the select committee on the petition of William Forsyth"; G.B., Parl., House of Commons paper, 1833, 26, no.543: 1–28, *Upper Canada: return . . . dated 6 February 1833; – for, copy of the reports of the two select committees to whom were severally referred petitions addressed to the House of Assembly of Upper Canada . . .* (copy at AO, Imperial blue books coll.); and the report on the second Forsyth petition in the assembly's *App. to the journal*, 1835, no.22. Several maps in AO, Map Coll., D-6, depict the military reserve quite effectively. The Royal Ont. Museum, Sigmund Samuel Canadiana Building (Toronto), has a fine water-colour of the Pavilion Hotel in 1830 by James Pattison COCKBURN.

Contemporary newspapers used include the *Colonial Advocate*, 1824–33; *Niagara Gleaner*, 1824–33; and *Upper Canada Gazette*, 1823–28. Of local records, the most rewarding were the abstract indexes to deeds for Bertie and Stamford townships at the Niagara South Land Registry Office (Welland, Ont.), available on microfilm at the AO, and the surrogate court records at AO, RG 22, ser.234, vol.2. Among the printed primary sources, those worth consulting include: "District of Nassau: minutes and correspondence of the land board," AO *Report*, 1905: 303, 339; "Grants of crown lands, etc., in Upper Canada, 1792–1796," 1929: 113; "Journals of Legislative Assembly of U.C.," 1914: 157, 164; Ramsay, *Dalhousie journals* (Whitelaw), 1: 133–38; "The register of Saint Paul's Church at Fort Erie, 1836–1844," ed. E. A. Cruikshank, *OH*, 27 (1931): 150; and "Settlements and surveys," PAC *Report*, 1891, note A: 3.

Travellers' accounts of the falls abound and few fail to mention Forsyth or his hotel. The most pertinent to this biography are Charles Fothergill, "A few notes made on a journey from Montreal through the province of Upper Canada . . . ," entries for 7–14 April 1817, in his papers at UTFL, MS coll. 140, vol.21; John Goldie, *Diary of a journey through Upper Canada and some of the New England states, 1819* (Toronto, 1897); Thomas Fowler, *The journal of a tour through British America to the falls of Niagara . . . during the summer of 1831* (Aberdeen, Scot., 1832); Adam Fergusson, *Practical notes made during a tour in Canada, and a portion of the United States, in [1831]* (Edinburgh and London, 1833); W. L. Mackenzie, *Sketches of Canada and the United States* (London, 1833); Samuel De Veaux, *The falls of Niagara, or tourist's guide to this wonder of nature, including notices of the whirlpool, islands, &c., and a complete guide thro' the Canadas . . .* (Buffalo, N.Y., 1839); and R. H. Bonnycastle, *The Canadas in 1841* (2v., London, 1842). Of the numerous histories of Niagara Falls, the best, as well as the most recent, is G. A. Seibel, *Ontario's Niagara parks: 100 years; a history*, ed. O. M. Seibel (Niagara Falls, Ont., 1985). Traditional accounts of the outrage in Upper Canadian historiography are best represented in J. C. Dent, *The story of the Upper Canadian rebellion; largely derived from original sources and documents* (2v., Toronto, 1885), and Aileen Dunham, *Political unrest in Upper Canada, 1815–1836* (London, 1927; repr. Toronto, 1963). The tendency in the period after World War II to downplay the importance of the outrage is evident in Craig, *Upper Canada*. For sharply contrasting views on the government's handling of the affair, see Patrick Brode, *Sir John Beverley Robinson: bone and sinew of the compact* ([Toronto], 1984), and Paul Romney, *Mr Attorney: the attorney general for Ontario in court, cabinet, and legislature, 1791–1899* (Toronto, 1986). The best summary of Romney's position on the partiality of the administration of justice is his article "From the types riot to the rebellion: elite ideology, anti-legal sentiment, political violence, and the rule of law in Upper Canada," *OH*, 79 (1987): 113–44. R.L.F.]

FOSTER, COLLEY LYONS LUCAS, army and militia officer; b. 1778 in Ireland; m. first 1813 Elizabeth Kirkpatrick in Clonsilla parish (Republic of Ireland), and they had seven children; m. secondly 4 Feb. 1836 Ellen Humphreys in Toronto, and they had one son and two daughters; d. 7 May 1843 in Kingston, Upper Canada.

Colley Lyons Lucas Foster was commissioned in the English militia in 1798, and then entered the 52nd Foot when it raised a second battalion in 1799. He served in England and Ireland until 1804, much of the time as adjutant, and was promoted lieutenant in 1800 and captain in 1804. Between 1804 and 1811 Foster was in Jamaica as aide-de-camp and military secretary to the lieutenant governor, Sir Eyre Coote, and the governor, the Duke of Manchester. After returning to England he served briefly in Jersey, and then became aide-de-camp to Lieutenant-General Gordon Drummond* in Ireland.

In 1813 Foster accompanied Drummond to his new command in Upper Canada. He was soon immersed in the war on the Niagara frontier, and after the taking of Fort Niagara (near Youngstown), N.Y., in December, he was selected to convey the captured American colours to Governor Sir George Prevost*. On 7 Feb. 1814 Foster was appointed adjutant general of the Upper Canadian militia, and he took up additional administrative responsibilities as Drummond's military secretary. He was twice mentioned in dispatches by Drummond for his efforts in the headquarters at the siege of Fort Erie that summer.

With the conclusion of the war Foster was moved to Quebec, and gave up his militia appointment to Nathaniel COFFIN. In 1816 he was appointed assistant adjutant general to the regular forces in Upper Canada, a post he held until his death. He was promoted lieutenant-colonel in June 1815 and colonel in January 1837.

Like other officers who served in the War of 1812, Foster received extensive land grants and speculated in the undeveloped land. His grants, totalling 1,200 acres, chiefly in Ancaster, Clinton, Thorold, and Cartwright townships, were sold to finance both his purchase of a town-lot in Kingston and a small farm near the town and the construction of buildings on these properties.

From June 1824 until September 1827 Foster acted as deputy adjutant general to the army in the Canadas. In this position he was called upon to act frequently for Governor Lord Dalhousie [RAMSAY] on ceremonial occasions, and to be his military secretary. Foster petitioned for permanent appointment as deputy adjutant general, but his hopes were dashed by the arrival of Colonel Sir Thomas Noel Hill.

With the withdrawal of nearly all regular troops from Upper Canada in 1837, Foster succeeded to the command of the remaining handful of soldiers. When William Lyon Mackenzie*'s insurgents prepared to march down Yonge Street early in December, Foster played a leading part in organizing and arming a guard from among the citizens of Toronto. On 7 December, when Lieutenant Governor Sir Francis Bond Head* marched against Mackenzie with a small force, he declined Foster's services, preferring that the issue be decided by inhabitants of the province. Once Head's resignation became effective in January 1838, Foster, as senior officer, took command of the militia and regular forces in Upper Canada until the arrival of Major-General Sir George Arthur* in March. He had at times 15,000 militia under arms during this period, but he did not take the field personally. After the rebellion, Foster reassumed his duties as assistant adjutant general. In his last years he was concerned to sell his commission and retire, but he died while still on service.

Colley Lyons Lucas Foster had served out his life as a competent military administrator. He never commanded troops in the field beyond his subaltern service, but he soon caught the eye of senior commanders and rose through their personal staffs to responsible positions in war and peace.

O. A. COOKE

AO, MS 502, ser.A, C. L. L. Foster corr.; ser.B-1, B-3, C. L. L. Foster corr.; MU 1057. PAC, RG 8, I (C ser.), 187: 88–91; 237: 64–65; 685: 94–100; 704: 126; 1184: 35; 1187: 11, 88, 95; 1191: 40; 1203½M: 18–19; 1203½P: 68; 1219: 177–78, 290–93. QUA, MC, Colley Foster papers.

FOTHERGILL, CHARLES, naturalist, artist, writer, businessman, office holder, JP, printer, newspaperman, publisher, and politician; b. 23 May 1782 in York, England, son of John Fothergill and Mary Anne Forbes; m. first December 1811 Charlotte Nevins, and they had at least three sons; m. secondly 19 March 1825 Eliza Richardson at Port Hope, Upper Canada, and they had at least four sons and two daughters; d. 22 May 1840 in Toronto.

Charles Fothergill's father, a maker of ivory brushes and combs, belonged to a prominent Quaker family that had deep roots in the Yorkshire dales and claimed descent from one of William the Conqueror's generals. Fothergill's most eminent recent kinsmen were an uncle, James Forbes, author of *Oriental memoirs*, and two great-uncles: Dr John Fothergill, the naturalist and philanthropist, and Samuel Fothergill, a Quaker minister. Charles was trained to his father's business, but the ethos of trade repelled him and he rejected a commercial career in favour of scientific and artistic pursuits. He was devoted from childhood to natural history and, when only 17, published the *Ornithologia Britannica*, an 11-page folio classifying 301 species of British birds. His next publication, *The wanderer*, was a miscellany of tales, essays, and verses, typical of the debased sentimentalism of the period, which purported to show the superiority of virtuous to vicious conduct.

The young Fothergill was profligate and soon beset by debts. In 1804 he went to London and tried to make his fortune as an actor, but he abandoned this design on finding that the profession offered no security and would compel him to play second fiddle for a long time to senior but (as he thought) less talented performers. He also tried in vain to secure a commission in the Royal Navy. While in London he mixed with devotees of the "fancy" sports (including the leading prize-fighters, James and Thomas Belcher) and proceeded with various literary labours, chiefly a "Natural and civil history of Yorkshire." He spent much of 1805 in northern Yorkshire on field research for this project, and from May to November 1806 he toured the Orkney and Shetland islands to collect material for a similar work on "The northern isles of Britain." By 1812 he was employing several celebrated engravers, including Thomas Bewick, Samuel Howitt, and John Thurston, to prepare plates for these works and for a large-scale study of British fauna (chiefly birds), but he managed to publish only his *Essay on the philosophy, study, and use of natural history* (1813), which was intended partly as an advertisement for the larger treatises. From 1807 to 1812 he dwelt at various places near York or Leeds and squandered his patrimony on racehorse breeding.

In 1811 Fothergill married Charlotte Nevins, daughter of a Quaker woollen manufacturer near Leeds, after an ardent courtship which succeeded despite (or perhaps because of) her father's condemnation of him as "flighty and romantick." Fothergill claimed to be a profligate no longer, but he was constantly afflicted by financial troubles arising partly from his literary projects and partly from disastrous business deals, mainly connected with his stud. In 1813 he began to study medicine at Edinburgh but had to flee to the Isle of Man to avoid arrest as a debtor. Here, after a last attempt to publish his "Northern isles," he turned to agriculture, but his farming investment (financed by loans wheedled from his relations) was wiped out at once by the collapse of agricultural markets at the close of the Napoleonic Wars.

Fothergill had long thought of emigrating: at first to Jamaica, where an uncle was a planter, then either to the Cape of Good Hope or to Pennsylvania, where his father-in-law claimed title to large estates. He eventually chose Upper Canada, arriving there in February 1817. He presented himself to the lieutenant governor, Francis Gore*, as the precursor of a settlement of English gentlemen, and he secured the reservation of part of Monaghan Township for their settlement and a personal grant of 1,200 acres on Rice Lake. Settling at Smith's Creek (Port Hope), which he saw as the natural maritime outlet for the Rice Lake region, Fothergill opened a store and bought much realty, intending to develop the harbour commercially. He befriended the Rice Lake Ojibwas, aided humbler settlers in the newly opened townships of Cavan, Emily, and Monaghan, and began to play a leading role in the life of the Newcastle District, becoming Port Hope's first postmaster in 1817, a magistrate in 1818, and a member of the district land board in 1819. In 1818 he was personally thanked by the new lieutenant governor, Sir Peregrine Maitland*, after successfully confronting Robert Gourlay* at a public meeting at Amherst (Cobourg).

By 1820 Fothergill owned a brewery and distillery at Port Hope and a sawmill and grist-mill on the present site of Peterborough. Unfortunately, he had over-extended himself in his usual way. His store failed, his property was seized for debt, and he withdrew from Port Hope to the seclusion of his estate near Monaghan (where his "colony of gentlemen" had never materialized). At the end of 1821 he was happy to be appointed king's printer (effective 1 Jan. 1822) and move to York (Toronto). At last, in his 40th year, Fothergill possessed two objects he had long desired: a printing-press and the prospect of a steady income.

Fothergill brought to the printing business his penchant for large schemes. His predecessor, Robert Charles HORNE, had issued an unofficial newspaper supplement (the *York Weekly Post*) along with the official *Upper Canada Gazette* and published an almanac. Under Fothergill both newspaper (called from 18 April 1822 the *Weekly Register*) and almanac grew larger, affording an outlet for his literary energies. His most ambitious project, a comprehensive annual digest of political, agricultural, scientific, and cultural information to be called the "Canadian annual register," came to nothing. Even so, when Fothergill ceased to be king's printer, fellow newspaperman Francis Collins* acclaimed him for the "very superior" taste and talent he had shown as both printer and writer.

None the less, Fothergill's years in the office (January 1822 to January 1826) were fraught with calamities, both private and professional. Not all were his own fault: during the months from May to November 1822, while his wife was dying of tuberculosis, Fothergill himself suffered a prolonged illness and his infant son perished in agony from meningitis. Other disasters were of his own making, however, among them his entanglement in the "Spanish Freeholder" scandal.

In the *Weekly Register* of 7 Oct. 1824, Fothergill warmly commended a letter to him, which he cited as "A 'FREEHOLDER'S' letter to 'PAWKIE,'" but declined to publish it because he feared it was libellous. A week later, William Lyon Mackenzie* published in the *Colonial Advocate* a gross libel on the chief justice of Upper Canada, William Dummer Powell*, disguised as a letter written in 1718 by "A Spanish Freeholder" to "Lord Chief Justice Van Pawkie, at the Hague." Mackenzie claimed that this letter was the one Fothergill had praised. Powell, who for years had been at odds with Lieutenant Governor Maitland, complained to Maitland that Fothergill had given a favourable notice to the libel, but Fothergill vehemently denied that the letter in the *Advocate* was the one he had cited. When Fothergill made a public denial, Maitland refrained from making him produce his letter. Maitland may not have believed Fothergill, though, and his displeasure with the king's printer can only have been increased by the new row with Powell which Fothergill's blunder had provoked.

Fothergill's worst troubles as king's printer had to do with money. Owing to his extravagance and inefficiency, more than once he had to ask the government for an advance. His high charges in an increasingly competitive trade cost him a large amount of government business and made it hard for him to secure payment of his accounts. These financial troubles reached a climax when he presented his bill for printing the provincial statutes of 1824. Until 1823, this job had been done for a fixed tariff of £80, which for several years past had been lower than cost. In 1824 Fothergill persuaded the legislature to adopt a system of payment by the page at a rate 40 per cent higher than that allowed in the government's official schedule of charges. He then printed that session's statutes in large type, heavily leaded, a format which needed nearly twice as many pages as the old one and inflated his bill to £882. The government paid it, in response to his plea that he faced ruin, but decided later to reclaim £367 10*s*. Fothergill was forced in November 1825 to execute a bond for this sum payable on demand.

Even so, when Maitland dismissed Fothergill two months later it was for political reasons. Since the early 1820s Fothergill had made a remarkable political shift. During the general election of 1820 he had intervened in the Durham County contest by mobilizing the mainly Irish settlers of the new back townships on behalf of George Strange Boulton* (brother of Solicitor General Henry John Boulton*) against the eventual victor, Samuel Street Wilmot (the favourite candidate of the front-township "Yankees" and an associate of Surveyor General Thomas Ridout*). In the *Weekly Register*, Fothergill eulogized the lieutenant governor, defended his administration, and proclaimed Upper Canada a land of opportunity. In 1824, however, he stood for parliament against both Wilmot and Boulton, waging a campaign in which he disparaged Upper Canada's economic stagnation, denounced lawyers as parasites, and proclaimed the motto "AGRICULTURE and INTERNAL IMPROVEMENT, without the aid of those who EAT more than they EARN." Fothergill received much "Yankee" support at the poll, especially after Wilmot resigned, and fought Boulton to a tie. The returning officer cancelled three of Fothergill's votes and returned Boulton, but the House of Assembly ordered a new election at which Fothergill trounced Wilmot, who stood with Boulton's backing.

During the session of 1825–26, Fothergill emerged as a leading spokesman of the parliamentary opposition. He mounted an attack on land-granting policy and conducted a committee of the whole on the state of the province, described by Maitland as a "Committee on grievances," which adopted resolutions on such topics as the alien question, immigration, the post office, and the independence of the judiciary. For this reason, on 5 Jan. 1826 he was dismissed without notice from the king's printership (but not, as has been stated, from the postmastership of Port Hope, which he had given up six years previously). His dismissal caused a sensation, and a public subscription was taken up for his benefit. Fothergill now moved back to the neighbourhood of Port Hope.

From 1825 to 1828, Fothergill's parliamentary speeches and actions were prominently featured in the *Colonial Advocate*. Fothergill himself was recognized as a leading member of the parliamentary opposition. In 1827 it was he who was first selected, along with John Rolph*, to undertake the mission of protest (eventually executed by Robert Randal*) against the Naturalization Bill. But although Fothergill and his fellow reform leaders agreed in opposing the provincial administration, their political principles were far from identical. Fothergill idolized the "mixed" constitution of 18th-century Britain and wished Upper Canada to become a viceroyalty with a legislature that possessed the right to impeach the crown's provincial advisers for malfeasance or unconstitutional conduct. Such views alienated him from those reformers who favoured popular sovereignty, whether under American or British political institutions. Fothergill's persistent pressure for the annexation of Montreal also estranged him from an Upper Canadian opposition that was increasingly aware of French Canadian susceptibilities. In March 1829, with his capital dwindling and himself in constant fear that the government would demand payment of his bond, Fothergill wrote to the new lieutenant governor, Sir John Colborne*, and the attorney general, John Beverley Robinson*, to seek a subsidy for a pro-government newspaper that he hoped to set up at Port Hope. His application failed and the paper never appeared.

Fothergill was not re-elected to parliament in 1830. In the next year or two he moved to Pickering Township, where the family of his second wife (an Irish Quaker farmer's daughter) was settled. Here he put his remaining wealth into a scheme to erect mills and found a town (to be called Monadelphia) on the site of the present town of Pickering. Again he seriously over-extended himself, but the disaster that befell this project took the form of a fire which destroyed his mills just after their completion in 1834. Fothergill blamed this calamity on the malice of a poacher whom he had punished severely, in his capacity as magistrate, out of anxiety to save the Lake Ontario salmon fishery. At the general election of 1834, Fothergill stood as a "conservative reformer" in the riding of 3rd York but was trounced by Thomas David Morrison*, a supporter of Mackenzie.

Throughout his Upper Canadian sojourn, Fothergill pursued goals befitting the savant with a sense of public duty. Ever active as a naturalist, he continued to hope in vain that he might publish in some form his projected work on the fauna of the British empire. He did, however, complete two manuscripts of value for his time: "An essay descriptive of the quadrupeds of British North America," which won him the silver medal of the Natural History Society of Montreal in 1830, and an essay on the dangers facing the Lake Ontario salmon fishery, which was read at the Literary and Historical Society of Quebec in 1835. As a cultural entrepreneur, he joined William Rees* and William DUNLOP in 1831 to form the Literary and Philosophical Society of Upper Canada at York. To Fothergill's indignation, this short-lived institution was first spurned by John Strachan* and John Beverley Robinson and then taken over by them.

In 1835 Fothergill initiated a scheme that rivalled in grandeur the founding of King's College (University of Toronto). For two years, at first in collaboration with William Rees and then alone, he laboured to set up a "Lyceum of Natural History and the Fine Arts," which was to include a museum, an art gallery, a botanical garden, and a zoo. He invested much of his remaining wealth in this venture, but his requests for public patronage exceeded what either the government or the legislature was prepared to offer. During the last few years of his life he made plans to show in Toronto the thousands of natural history specimens he had collected for this project, but there is no evidence of a public exhibition.

Fothergill's last venture involved a return to journalism and politics. In the fall of 1837 he liquidated most of his Pickering property and bought up two Toronto newspapers (George Gurnett*'s *Courier of Upper Canada* and William John O'GRADY's *Correspondent and Advocate*) in order to set up the *Palladium of British America and Upper Canada Mercantile Advertiser* under the nominal proprietorship of his son Charles Forbes Fothergill. The first number was issued only two weeks after the Upper Canadian rebellion, and Fothergill insisted from the start that the chief cause of this calamity was the unconstitutional domination of the provincial government by the "family compact." For several months the *Palladium*, handsomely printed and the largest newspaper in the province, was the most outspoken voice of opposition in Toronto, but, according to Samuel Thompson*, who was hired to manage the paper in 1838, Fothergill lost interest in it long before it ceased to appear some time after May 1839. Fothergill died penniless less than a year later. Many of his papers and most of his museum were destroyed in a fire a month after his death.

Fothergill's career was an unbroken sequence of failures that were largely of his own making. He was well read in both general and scholarly literature but vitiated his promise by espousing projects far beyond his financial, if not his intellectual, means. He bemoaned his lack of patronage in Britain, and in Upper Canada he found it galling to be denied preferment by a clique of officials whom he thought beneath him in both breeding and education. In neither country, though, did he adopt any rational plan to achieve by his own efforts the wealth and leisure he needed for his scholarly projects, and in Upper Canada he squandered his one bite at the cherry of public patronage. His self-destructive risk-taking is probably traceable to an obsessional neurosis akin to that of the compulsive gambler.

Fothergill's writing was often ponderous and verbose, but on topics that engaged him deeply it could be forceful and direct. He also had a gift for oratory, but he lacked the coolness needed to prevail in committee and caucus and to persuade practical men to patronize his projects. His chief legislative achievement – an act promoting the formation of agricultural societies – is nowadays thought to have done little to encourage agricultural progress in the province. Fothergill was sadly out of place in the inordinately materialistic society of Upper Canada, but he also had a fatal penchant for ignoring the realities of his environment. His few surviving water-colours of the Ontario landscape are all highly idealized renderings. None the less, Fothergill's political importance in the years 1824–30 was considerable. He was then the foremost exponent of "conservative reform" views in the province, and his image of gentility and respectability was useful to the emergent reform movement at a time when many people still equated "party" activity with disloyalty.

It was not as a politician, however, but as an observer and depicter of nature that Fothergill excelled. R. Delamere Black calls Fothergill's zoological descriptions "amazing" in their minuteness and accuracy, and his water-colour studies combine the same traits with the "spirit and freedom" that Fothergill himself thought were the highest attributes of the bird-painter's art. According to James Little Baillie, "As a naturalist and an illustrator of animals, he ranked with the best of his period." Had Fothergill managed to publish his work, he might have achieved some of the fame of Thomas Bewick and John James Audubon. He found it bitterly ironic that, right at the end of his life, he was engaged in scientific correspondence by Audubon: a man who had succeeded where he himself had failed.

PAUL ROMNEY

The Charles Fothergill papers at the UTFL (MS coll. 140) comprise a miscellany of notebooks, letter-books, diaries, and rough manuscripts, with a small quantity of correspondence. They include a partial draft of his projected work on the Orkneys and Shetlands and a diary of his life in London, 1804–5. The notebooks contain all that survives of his field-work. Volumes 20, 22, 25, and 28 relate to Canada and are the subject of "Charles Fothergill's notes on the natural history of eastern Canada, 1816–1837," ed. R. D. Black, Royal Canadian Institute, *Trans.* (Toronto), 20 (1934–35): 141–68. Volumes 12, 26, 31, and 32 relate to Britain, the last two being an interleaved copy of Thomas Bewick, *History of British birds* . . . ([2nd ed.], 2v., Newcastle, Eng., and London, 1797 [actually 1798]–1805), interesting for Fothergill's water-colour embellishments of some of the plates. Volume 3 is a mutilated volume of water-colours and sketches, including a few exquisite drawings of birds. Volume 21 is a diary of his trip from Montreal to York (Toronto) by sleigh in 1817. Volumes 9–11a have been published as *The diary of Charles Fothergill, 1805: an itinerary to York, Flamborough and the north-western dales of Yorkshire*, ed. Paul Romney (Leeds, Eng., 1984). Fothergill's manuscript "An essay descriptive of the quadrupeds of British North America . . ." (1830) is at McGill Univ. Libraries, Blacker-Wood Library.

Four water-colours by Fothergill of the Upper Canadian landscape are known. The three in the Royal Ont. Museum's Sigmund Samuel Canadiana Building (Toronto) are reproduced in Mary Allodi, *Canadian watercolours and drawings in the Royal Ontario Museum* (2v., Toronto, 1974); the fourth, of Port Hope in 1819, is in family possession. The Sigmund Samuel collection also contains a portrait of Fothergill, painted around 1834, by Grove Sheldon Gilbert.

Fothergill's principal publications are *Ornithologia Britannica: or, a list of all the British birds; in Latin and English* . . . (York, Eng., 1799); *The wanderer; or, a collection of original tales and essays, founded upon facts, illustrating the virtues and vices of the present age* . . . (2v., London, 1803); *An essay on the philosophy, study, and use of natural history* (London, 1813); the *York almanac*, 1823–26; and the *Toronto almanac*, 1839. In addition, he published two newspapers: the *Upper Canada Gazette*, 1822–January 1826 (including the *Weekly Register* from 18 April 1822 until at least 29 Dec. 1825), and the *Palladium of British America and Upper Canada Mercantile Advertiser* (Toronto), 20 Dec. 1837–May 1839. He also edited and annotated W. L. Mackenzie, *Mackenzie's own narrative of the late rebellion* . . . (Toronto, 1838).

Important manuscript sources are PAC, RG 1, E3; RG 5, A1; and RG 7, G16C. The James Little Baillie papers at the UTFL (MS coll. 126), boxes 38–38a, contain Baillie's manuscript life of Fothergill and a variety of research materials. The principal secondary sources are three works by Paul Romney, "A man out of place: the life of Charles Fothergill; naturalist, businessman, journalist, politician, 1782–1840" (PHD thesis, Univ. of Toronto, 1981), "A conservative reformer in Upper Canada: Charles Fothergill, responsible government and the 'British Party,' 1824–1840," CHA *Hist. papers*, 1984: 42–62, and "The Spanish freeholder imbroglio of 1824: inter-elite and intra-elite rivalry in Upper Canada," *OH*, 76 (1984): 32–47; and one by J. L. Baillie, "Charles Fothergill, 1782–1840," *CHR*, 25 (1944): 376–96. The family background is documented in John Fothergill, *Chain of friendship: selected letters of Dr. John Fothergill of London, 1735–1780*, ed. B. C. Corner and C. C. Booth (Cambridge, Mass., 1971); R. H. Fox, *Dr. John Fothergill and his friends; chapters in eighteenth century life* (London, 1919); and Bernard Thistlethwaite, *The Thistlethwaite family; a study in genealogy* (London, 1910).

FOURNIER, CHARLES-VINCENT, Roman Catholic priest; b. 28 Jan. 1771 in Orléans, France, son of Pierre-Laurent Fournier, a starch maker, and Marie-Anne Péguy; d. 26 May 1839 in Baie-du-Febvre (Baieville), Lower Canada.

Charles-Vincent Fournier obtained his classical education in France at the Petit Séminaire de Meung-sur-Loire. In 1789 he decided to enter the priesthood and began his theological studies with the Sulpicians in his home town. He made friends with a young postulant, Jean RAIMBAULT. Driven by uncompromising zeal, they both had a burning desire to serve the church, embraced passionately the cause of the monarchy, and were bitterly opposed to the revolution. In 1790 Fournier was required to swear loyalty to the Civil Constitution of the Clergy. Like his superiors and colleagues among the Sulpicians in Orléans, he refused and chose to abandon the priesthood. He went back to his family and worked at various tasks in his father's shop.

Three years later the Constituent Assembly imposed conscription on all unmarried men between the ages of 18 and 25. Fournier and Raimbault were thus forced to enlist in a military unit from their town. Late in 1793 they joined their regiment in Paris. Despite close surveillance they managed to flee, and after many different adventures in Belgium and Germany they reached England early in 1795. Horrified at the consequences of the revolution and fearful of being persecuted in France, they decided to go to Lower Canada.

Fournier arrived at Quebec on 24 Oct. 1796. He went to live at the Collège Saint-Raphaël in Montreal, where the Sulpicians welcomed him warmly and invited him to complete his theological studies. On 23 Sept. 1797 Pierre Denaut*, the bishop of Quebec, conferred the priesthood upon him. For Fournier, a childhood dream had come true, and his satisfaction was enhanced by the fact that he was in a British colony where peace, order, and respect for the religious and civil authorities reigned.

Fournier was named assistant priest in the parish of Saint-Michel at Vaudreuil late in 1797, and in that of Saint-Joseph at Chambly a year later. In 1800 Denaut made him curé of Saint-François-d'Assise (in Montreal), which had a very plain church and a badly maintained presbytery and cemetery. Moreover, the faith of a number of his parishioners was evidently weak. Within a few years he had righted matters. He encouraged the people to rebuild the church and presbytery, tried to add lustre to religious ceremonies, set up a new school, and devoted himself to working with the destitute.

In 1810 Joseph-Octave Plessis*, bishop of Quebec, who was extremely pleased with Fournier's work, named him parish priest of Saint-Antoine-de-Padoue at Baie-du-Febvre. Upon his arrival there Fournier was faced with an epidemic of typhoid fever. He acquitted himself well in the circumstances, giving encouragement to stricken families and administering the last rites without hesitation. So great was his zeal and generosity that his parishioners praised him and afterwards never dared question his authority. Fournier emphasized the decoration of the church, for him a tangible sign of the religious vitality of the parish. He had the cornice of the sanctuary repaired in 1811. Two years later he bought velvet vestments and completed the collection of sacred vessels. From 1815 he committed the *fabrique* to even greater expenditures, in total more than 20,000 *livres*: fitting out the chapels, redoing the high altar and the structure housing it (the retable), purchasing a tabernacle, and embellishing the sanctuary. In 1818 he bought ten pictures that had been sent from France by Philippe-Jean-Louis Desjardins*. By 1825 his church was one of the most spacious and best decorated in the Trois-Rivières region.

Fournier paid particular attention to the evolution of religious practices. In 1812 he promoted the devotion termed the Way of the Cross, putting up stations that became popular for worship. Usually he preached on Sundays and feast days; he also did so occasionally in the special seasons of Advent and Lent. His sermons were uncompromising and dealt with such themes as death, sorrow, hell, sin, the Last Judgement, eternal salvation, and the chosen few. He also became known as a tenacious and demanding confessor, who sought to purge his parishioners of sin and persuade them to take Holy Communion frequently.

In 1816 Fournier drove away a liberal teacher who wanted to set up a school using the pedagogical methods of Joseph LANCASTER. From then on education was one of his main concerns. Under his supervision four schools, over which he retained control, were built in less than 15 years. Nor did he allow the leading parishioners to meddle in the business of the *fabrique* – he even refused to let them attend its meetings. After 1820 he fought against dancing and ordered his people to avoid inns whenever possible. Lust and women's dress became the focus of his preaching. These strict pastoral instructions were designed to eliminate bad influences that might taint the parish. The religious environment had a considerable impact on his flock. After 25 years of ministry Fournier must have been satisfied: his parish formed a large island of Christianity.

Fournier husbanded his assets, kept his garden well maintained, and oversaw the collection of tithes. In this wealthy parish he had a tithe of 700 *minots* of wheat and 400 of oats to count on, an income placing him well ahead of most of his parishioners. He owned a farm and some animals. His presbytery, an immense stone building, looked like a manor-house. His furnishings were splendid, and his library had an abundance of religious books and works on the revolution of 1789. His table was laden with luxury items of food and various kinds of meat. He bought a great deal of Spanish wine and West Indian rum. In income and style of life he had little in common with the majority of his parishioners. He also impressed people with his good manners, his learning, and his culture.

Fournier's authority and prestige were not confined to his parish. His colleagues who had come from France often visited him. These meetings, which were marked by cordiality and friendly understanding, occasioned numerous discussions on priestly duties. Disciplined and demanding, Fournier had the attention of his fellow clergy, who appreciated his good judgement and sensible advice. He maintained amicable relations with the priests of the Séminaire de Nicolet, who often invited him to preach there. Similarly, his frequent meetings with his friend Raimbault, its superior, who was parish priest of Nicolet and an archpriest, enabled him to develop his understanding of education and parish administration. He also involved himself in the missions set up in the Eastern Townships. He often went to the one at Drummondville, and under his influence and that of Raimbault the original chapel was built there. Sure of his devotion and loyalty, Bishop Plessis and later Bishop Bernard-Claude Panet* commissioned him to undertake several administrative tasks in the Trois-Rivières region and occasionally asked him to accompany them on their pastoral visits.

Because he was a man of outstanding mind and character who enjoyed the confidence of his superiors, Fournier won the respect of his parishioners and of the clergy in his region. Having exercised his priestly functions for nearly 40 years, he considered giving his life a new direction, or at least making a new setting for it. In 1836 he retired after a paralytic stroke. On 8 October of that year he turned over his charge to Michel Carrier*, on condition that Carrier provide him with a third of the grain collected in the parishes of Baie-du-Febvre and Saint-Zéphirin-de-Courval. He owned a magnificent house near the church, and there in silence he shut himself up and tried to make the most of the short time he had left to live. He devoted his leisure to reading, his great passion. Unable to walk or even to say mass, he took more interest in prayer. He passed away quietly on 26 May 1839 on the veranda of his house. Two days later a host of priests and laity from the Trois-Rivières region attended his funeral, a clear sign of how well known and popular he was.

A man of the 18th century, brought up in the Age of Enlightenment, profoundly marked by the revolution of 1789, Fournier remained faithful to the prescriptions and solutions of the *ancien régime*. In this context the development of liberalism in Lower Canada during the early 19th century seemed to him an outgrowth of the French revolutionary and anti-religious spirit. Not only did he fight this ideology with all his strength, but he also ensured that his parishioners were not exposed to its influence. He was better prepared than his Canadian colleagues for his pastoral task and brought greater devotion and zeal to it. Rejecting ideological compromise, and always seeking to uphold principle, he made Baie-du-Febvre a truly Christian place. His French colleagues, who had established themselves in the Trois-Rivières region after the tragic events of the 1789 revolution, served the Canadian church with the same eagerness and determination. These priests defended a form of society that belonged to the *ancien régime*, asserted their fierce hostility to liberalism, and tended to demand the union of church and state. Well trained for their parochial duties and sharing the same opinions, they became accustomed to helping one another and coordinating their efforts, concurring in the opinion of the wiser among them. They attended particularly to the spiritual welfare of their flocks, and obtained an undeniable success in shepherding the rural masses. It is not surprising that this region experienced a marked resurgence of faith and that Christianity was firmly rooted here well before the church attained a new vigour and ascendancy in the mid 19th century.

RICHARD CHABOT

ACAM, 355.107, 802-1. AD, Loiret (Orléans), État civil, Orléans, 29 janv. 1771. ANQ-M, CE3-2, 28 mai 1839. ANQ-MBF, CN1-21, 6 mars 1835. AP, Saint-Antoine-de-Padoue (Baieville), Livres de comptes, I; Saint-François-d'Assise (Montréal), Livres de comptes, I. Arch. de l'évêché de Nicolet (Nicolet, Qué.), Cartable Baie-du-Febvre, I: 77–89. ASN, AO, Polygraphie, III: 5–30; Séminaire, II: 82–101; AP-G, L.-É. Bois, G, 1: 224. Allaire, *Dictionnaire*. Caron, "Inv. de la corr. de Mgr Denaut," ANQ *Rapport*, 1931–32: 134, 137–38, 152, 178; "Inv. de la corr. de Mgr Hubert et de Mgr Bailly de Messein," 1930–31: 334–35, 347; "Inv. de la corr. de Mgr Panet," 1933–34: 393; 1935–36: 184–85; "Inv. de la corr. de Mgr Plessis," 1927–28: 256, 275; 1928–1929: 129; "Inv. de la corr. de Mgr Signay," 1936–37: 315; 1937–38: 113, 120, 128. J.-E. Bellemare, *Histoire de la Baie-Saint-Antoine, dite Baie-du-Febvre, 1683–1911* (Montréal, 1911). Dionne, *Les ecclésiastiques et les royalistes français*. Louis Martin, "Jean Raimbault, curé à Nicolet de 1806 à 1841" (thèse de MA, univ. de Montréal, 1977). "Les morts de 1839," *BRH*, 32 (1926): 18.

FRANCIS, TOMA. *See* TOMAH, FRANCIS

FRANKLIN, Sir JOHN, naval officer, Arctic explorer, and author; b. 16 April 1786 in Spilsby, England, youngest son of Willingham Franklin, mercer, and Hannah Weekes; d. 11 June 1847 off King William Island (N.W.T.).

John Franklin was educated at preparatory school in St Ives, Huntingdonshire, and, from the age of 12, at Louth grammar school near Spilsby in Lincolnshire. He was attracted to a seafaring life from an early age but met initial resistance from his father, who reluctantly permitted him a trial voyage on a merchant ship sailing between Kingston upon Hull and Lisbon. The trip confirmed his resolve to go to sea, so his father secured his appointment in the Royal Navy as a first-class volunteer on the *Polyphemus*. He set off on 23 Oct. 1800 to join the ship, which took part on 2 April 1801 in the battle of Copenhagen.

Soon afterwards Franklin was discharged and returned home, for his parents had secured, at his request, an appointment better suited to his ambitions: a commission to go with the *Investigator* under Captain Matthew Flinders on an expedition to explore the largely uncharted coast of New Holland (Australia). He joined the ship as midshipman on 27 April and sailed from Spithead on 18 July. Flinders, who was Franklin's uncle by marriage, took the boy into his care, teaching him navigation. In 1802–3 Flinders circumnavigated Australia but failed to complete his detailed survey because of scurvy among the crew and the ship's unseaworthiness. The *Investigator* was abandoned in Sydney and the crew set out for home on the *Porpoise* in August 1803. That ship, however, was wrecked on a reef six days out of Sydney, and the crew found refuge on a sandbank for six weeks while Flinders sailed for help in a boat. Franklin eventually reached Canton on a merchant ship, and then continued homewards on an East Indiaman, arriving in the summer of 1804.

After his discharge, Franklin returned to war duty on the *Bellerophon*; it was engaged first in the blockade of Brest, later as an escort for troop-ships sailing for Malta, and in October 1805 in the battle of Trafalgar, during which Franklin acted as midshipman in charge of signals. Franklin remained with the *Bellerophon*, off the coast of France, until October 1807 when he joined the *Bedford* for service off South America. He was promoted lieutenant on 11 Feb. 1808. He then saw four years' blockade duty in the North Sea before the *Bedford* sailed in September 1814 to take part in the British offensive that winter against New Orleans. During this action Franklin was wounded and was mentioned in dispatches.

When the *Bedford* returned home in May 1815 the Napoleonic Wars were drawing to an end and, after a brief and inactive service on the *Forth*, Franklin was discharged on half pay. In common with many other young officers, he found his career threatened by the coming of peace, and he now faced an indefinite period at home without prospect of employment.

The salvation of his career was the revival in 1818 of the Royal Navy's interest in exploring the Arctic. In that year John Barrow, the Admiralty's second secretary and a noted traveller, proposed Arctic exploration as an ideal means of employing naval officers and men left idle by the ending of the wars. His particular interest was in finding a navigable sea route between the Atlantic and Pacific oceans, either directly over the North Pole or through the North American Arctic between Baffin Bay and Bering Strait. The latter route, commonly known as the northwest passage, became the focus of British naval exploration for the next 36 years and the name of John Franklin is now inseparably linked with it. His appearance among the few selected to take part was probably due both to his meritorious war record and to his experience of exploration under Flinders. Two Arctic expeditions sailed in 1818: one, under Commander John Ross*, sought the northwest passage; the other, under Commander David BUCHAN, attempted to cross the Arctic Ocean from Spitsbergen with the barque *Dorothea* and brig *Trent*. Franklin was appointed to command the *Trent*. The latter expedition, taking six months, had no chance of success: the ships spent several weeks in a futile attempt to penetrate the pack-ice northwest of Spitsbergen. Its one positive result was to prove that the polar pack-ice was impenetrable.

Following the unsatisfactory outcome of both expeditions, Barrow proposed that two expeditions should continue the search for a northwest passage in 1819. William Edward Parry* was to seek an entrance to the passage from Baffin Bay; his highly successful expedition eventually determined that Lancaster Sound (N.W.T.) opened a passage towards the west. A second expedition, for which Barrow proposed Franklin as leader, would set out overland from Hudson Bay to explore and chart the north coast of the American continent eastwards from the mouth of the Coppermine River and thereby, in theory, delineate the most direct route for a northwest passage. The plan set many difficulties before Franklin. The coast had been sighted by explorers only twice before – by Samuel Hearne* at the Coppermine in 1771 and by Alexander Mackenzie* at the Mackenzie River's delta in 1789 – and it lay hundreds of miles north of the territory explored by fur traders. The Hudson's Bay and North West companies were expected to convey Franklin to the edge of unknown territory and to equip him for the coastal journey, but they were only established as far north as Great Slave Lake (N.W.T.), their supply lines were tenuous, and they were engaged in trade warfare. Franklin had just three months to prepare for an expedition that had few precedents in the history of exploration. Advice was scarce and often misleading or excessively optimistic, and he received assurances of greater assistance from the fur-trading companies than they could actually provide. The party selected to accompany him consisted of midshipmen George Back* and Robert Hood*, surgeon and naturalist John Richardson*, and seaman John Hepburn*.

The party set out from Gravesend on the HBC's supply ship *Prince of Wales* on 23 May 1819 and reached York Factory (Man.) on 30 August. The HBC could muster only one boat and one crewman, so Franklin had to leave a large part of his supplies to be forwarded later. The party struggled on with a heavily laden boat along the company's established route to Cumberland House (Sask.), where they halted for the winter on 23 October. There Franklin found that he still could not obtain sufficient information on the country to the north so, with Back and Hepburn, he set out in mid January on snowshoes for Fort Chipewyan (Alta), an NWC post, leaving Richardson and Hood to bring on the supplies in the spring. At Fort Chipewyan he made arrangements for the recruitment of Indian guides and hunters, but he again met difficulties over shortages of men, and he began to discover that the companies were unable to supply the generous quantities of provisions that had been promised in London. Shortage was to be a prevailing feature of the expedition.

After Richardson and Hood had rejoined Franklin, the expedition, reinforced by some hired voyageurs, left Fort Chipewyan on 18 July 1820. At Fort Providence (Old Fort Providence, N.W.T.), an NWC post on Great Slave Lake's North Arm, they were met by the trader Willard Ferdinand Wentzel and by Akaitcho, the Copper Indian chief whose men Wentzel had recruited as guides and hunters for the expedition. They continued along the Yellowknife River into unexplored territory, and on 20 August they reached Winter Lake, near which they built Fort Enterprise, their winter quarters.

There, Franklin encountered further problems arising mainly from the acute shortage of essential supplies. Frustrated, he began to respond with tactless and entirely uncharacteristic displays of aggression. His manner served only to diminish his authority over the Indians and voyageurs, and deprived him of much of the goodwill shown earlier by the fur traders. His demands to the companies and the Indians for supplies, accompanied by high-handed threats and accusations, met a cold, resentful response, but Back, on a winter journey to Fort Chipewyan, did manage to recover enough of the supplies left at York Factory to secure the expedition's immediate future.

They set out down the Coppermine for the coast in July 1821 with critically limited food and ammunition. Franklin's main hope of success now rested on the cooperation of the Inuit along the coast, but this hope was soon dashed. They sighted an encampment near the river's mouth, but, despite advance contact by their interpreters, Tattannoeuck* and Hoeootoerock (Junius), their approach was incautious and the Inuit fled in fear. No further opportunity to open relations arose. The coastal voyage eastwards from the Coppermine began on 21 July with the party reduced to 20 men in two Indian canoes. Their progress was slow, and by 18 August they had reached only Turnagain Point on Kent peninsula, where Franklin decided to turn back. Summer was ending, supplies were almost exhausted, and unrest among the voyageurs was turning to rebellion. The canoes were too badly damaged to permit a return by sea, so they set off with one canoe up Hood River. They were soon reduced to travelling mainly on foot. The journey quickly became a terrible ordeal. They frequently had only lichen to eat, and cold and exhaustion further weakened them. Nine men died of starvation or exposure; a man later suspected of cannibalism shot Hood and was executed by Richardson. Further distress awaited the survivors who reached Fort Enterprise, for the Indians had not stocked it with food as expected, and they lived for three more weeks on a broth of discarded deer skins, bones, and lichen. Their ordeal ended on 7 November with the arrival of Indians located by Back, who took them to Fort Providence.

The expedition spent one more winter in the north and returned to England in the autumn of 1822. It had been a failure in most respects, with much suffering and loss of life in return for limited geographical attainments. It had also exposed Franklin's weaknesses as an explorer: an inability to adapt to unexpected circumstances and a dangerously inflexible adherence to his instructions and prearranged plans. A more experienced explorer might have curtailed or postponed the expedition in the face of so much adversity. Some fur traders had questions. At a time when the HBC and the NWC were engaged in hostile trade warfare, George Simpson*, the former's governor-in-chief, resented Franklin's apparent support of the NWC and contemptuously, but quite unfairly, noted in his journal in February 1821 that the naval explorer "has not the physical powers required for the labor of moderate Voyaging in this country; he must have three meals p diem, Tea is indispensible, and with the utmost exertion he cannot walk above *Eight* miles in one day, so that it does not follow if those Gentlemen are unsuccessful that the difficulties are insurmountable."

In his own time, Franklin's shortcomings were never acknowledged, except by the fur traders. Courage rather than talent was expected in an explorer, and he had shown courage in great measure in the face of dreadful hardship. He quickly won fame and widespread respect and was established permanently as a British hero. He was promoted post-captain on 20 Nov. 1822 (having been made a commander in his absence, on 1 Jan. 1821), and he was elected a fellow of the Royal Society. Privately he resumed an old friendship with Eleanor Anne Porden, a poet, whom he married on 19 Aug. 1823. During this period, Franklin was engaged in drawing up a plan to extend the exploration of the Arctic coast by travelling east and west from the Mackenzie delta. The Admiralty accepted the plan in the autumn of 1823. Franklin proposed another overland venture, but his arrangements show considerable changes from those of his first expedition.

The main lessons that he had learned were, first, to complete his preparations well in advance and, secondly, to strive for self-sufficiency. He chose to diminish his dependence on the unpredictable reliability of fur traders, voyageurs, and Indians, and to assert his greater trust in British seamen and naval equipment and, above all, to take enough of his own supplies. In fairness, his self-sufficient approach was less necessary this time than before, for now, as a result of its union with the NWC, the HBC was a much more dependable ally and would play an essential role in conveying the expedition northwards; but Franklin's caution was to be vindicated by almost unblemished success.

The first load of provisions, together with three specially constructed boats and a party of seamen, were sent ahead through York Factory in 1824 to ensure their safe arrival in the north. Franklin set out for New York on 16 Feb. 1825, accompanied once more by Richardson and Back, and by midshipman Edward Nicholas KENDALL. Soon after his arrival in the United States, Franklin learned of the death of his wife, who had been ill since the birth of their daughter the previous year. The party travelled along fur-trading routes into the north, catching up with the seamen and boats near Methy Portage (Portage La Loche, Sask.). Early in August they reached Fort Norman (N.W.T.). From here Franklin and Kendall made a preliminary reconnaissance of the Mackenzie River down to the sea. The rest of the party went on to Great Bear Lake, where the construction of their winter quarters, near the head of Bear (Great Bear) River, was under way. On 5 September Franklin and Kendall rejoined the party at this base, named Fort Franklin.

After a comfortable winter the expedition left for the coast on 22 June 1826. At the head of the Mackenzie delta two parties were formed and separated on 4 July: Franklin, Back, and 14 men went west in two boats; Richardson and Kendall led the eastern party. Except for a skirmish with some Inuit who pillaged their boats, the coastal journey of Franklin's party was uneventful. Impeded by ice and fog, they covered little more than half the distance to Icy Cape (Alaska) before Franklin decided that, with winter approaching and his men suffering from exposure, he had no safe choice but to return. On the day he turned back, 18 August, a boat set out to meet him from the *Blossom*, which had come through Bering Strait under the command of Frederick William Beechey* and was waiting for him at Icy Cape. The boat reached Point Barrow, within 160 miles of Franklin's farthest point, Return Reef. If only he had known that, Franklin said later, nothing would have stopped him from going on. His party reached Fort Franklin on 21 September, having explored some 370 miles of uncharted coast. Richardson and Kendall, who had arrived back earlier, had successfully charted the coast east to the Coppermine.

After a second winter at Fort Franklin, the expedition set off home in 1827, reaching Liverpool on 26 September. The second of his published narratives came out the following year. Franklin again received formal honours: he won the gold medal of the Société de Géographie de Paris and, along with W. E. Parry, was knighted on 29 April 1829 and received an honorary DCL from the University of Oxford in July. Also, he renewed an acquaintance with Jane Griffin*, a friend of his late wife, and they were married in Stanmore (London) on 5 Nov. 1828. There was an endearing gaucheness in his courtship of his two wives. Though lauded, Franklin was rather awkward in some aspects of his behaviour: he was a little embarrassed by fame and not entirely at ease in society, and his writing was clumsy and tortuous. During an audience at Montreal in August 1827 Governor-in-Chief Lord Dalhousie [RAMSAY] had found him "shy and unobtrusive" but "full of general science" and capable of speaking "with slow, clear perception, with a dignified & impressive good sense, sound judgement & presence of mind." Dalhousie further described him as a "square strong man of 5′6″, dark complexion & hair, his head very round, bald, with thick curled short hair."

In the wake of his success, Franklin was invited by the Admiralty to draw up a plan for the completion of his exploration of the north coast but, when he submitted it, he was told without explanation that the Admiralty would undertake no further Arctic exploration. After years of grooming as an explorer, he once again found his future in doubt.

In 1830, following two years' idleness at home in London, Franklin gained command of the frigate *Rainbow* for duty in the Mediterranean, mainly playing a peace-keeping role along the coast of Greece during its war of independence. For his sound diplomacy in that service, he later received the Order of the Redeemer of Greece and the Royal Hanoverian Order. The *Rainbow* returned home in 1833 and was paid off on 8 Jan. 1834, and Franklin again found himself unable to obtain a new commission. Finally, in April 1836, he accepted an offer to succeed George Arthur* as lieutenant governor of Van Diemen's Land (Tasmania), a young colony with a population of colonial settlers and transported convicts.

After his arrival on 6 Jan. 1837, Franklin became caught in the bewildering factionalism that had roots in Arthur's aggressive administration. Franklin's inexperience in office, his support for the introduction of a representative assembly to an island he was obliged to maintain as a penal colony, Lady Franklin's alleged interference in government business, and the viceregal couple's preoccupation with reform (notably in education) all served to create strain between Franklin and the Colonial Office. The intrigues of Colonial Secretary Lord Stanley against him finally brought about his dismissal in 1843. Franklin's years in Van Diemen's Land were by no means fruitless: he stimulated social and cultural welfare, checked corruption, and won the affection of many convicts and settlers for his humane approach. Nevertheless, when he arrived home in June 1844 he was broken in spirit.

By chance, however, within months appeared the very tonic needed to revive him: the Admiralty's plan to renew the search for a northwest passage, and later its request to Franklin to advise on the plan's practicability. Discoveries made since the time of Franklin's overland expeditions, notably the near completion of the exploration of the Arctic mainland coast by Peter Warren Dease* and Thomas Simpson, had reduced the unexplored section of the northwest passage to a mere 300-mile strip between Barrow Strait and the mainland. There was great optimism that the passage could now be completely charted with little difficulty. From the start, Franklin was anxious to lead the expedition, and he was supported by his friends Parry, Richardson, and Sir James Clark Ross*, a veteran Arctic explorer, who persuaded the Admiralty to lay aside its concern about his age (he was then 58). He was given command on 7 Feb. 1845 and steps were taken to produce the best equipped Arctic expedition to that time.

Franklin sailed from the River Thames on 19 May 1845 with the ships *Erebus* and *Terror*, 134 men (soon after reduced to 129), and provisions for three years. The ships were the usual sturdy bomb-vessels, but for the first time they were fitted with steam-driven screw-propellers. Everything possible was done to provide for the health and comfort of the officers and men: heating was supplied by steam-boilers serving a network of pipes; each ship carried huge quantities of the latest patent preserved foods, china, cut glass, and silverware; and large libraries and other educational aids were available. Just the clothing might have seemed inadequate – standard naval cloth supplemented only by underwear and wolf-skin blankets – but then the expedition was not expected to linger in the Arctic. Franklin's instructions were to search by way of Lancaster Sound, continuing either north and west by Wellington Channel or southwest from Barrow Strait, across the unknown region towards the mainland coast, which he had already explored. He was last seen, by whalers, in northern Baffin Bay on 26 July. John Franklin was never seen again and no trace of his expedition was found for five years.

The disappearance of Franklin's expedition prompted a huge search throughout the Arctic, by both the Admiralty and private concerns, notably Lady Franklin and the HBC. The search, which led to the exploration of an enormous expanse of territory, operated most intensively between 1847 and 1859. The Admiralty stopped looking after the return of Edward Belcher*'s expedition in 1854. The main reason for the enormity of the quest and the degree of public interest was almost certainly Lady Franklin, who not only maintained a prolonged public campaign to sustain the search until her husband was found but also won extraordinary sympathy as the loyal, grieving wife of the missing hero. Interest in British North America appears not to have been as lively as in Britain, or indeed in the United States, where merchant Henry Grinnell mounted two expeditions [*see* Edwin Jesse De Haven*; Elisha Kent Kane*] and from where Charles Francis Hall* also made a search. Lady Franklin's warm reception in Montreal and British Columbia in 1860–61 indicates some interest, and much feeling for her in particular.

The reaction of fur traders to the search, however, had ranged from committed involvement to decorous disinterest. In March 1849 Letitia Hargrave [Mactavish*], the wife of an HBC chief factor, wrote from York Factory concerning the Admiralty-sponsored search by John Rae*, Sir John Richardson, and John Bell*: "The Gentlemen in the Country all looked very polite & as if Sir John [Richardson's] expedition was a very feasible exploit, but among themselves they either laughed at the whole turn out or seemed astonished that rational beings sh[d] undertake such a useless search."

Of some 30 expeditions involved in the search during the 1847–59 period, just four managed to piece together the basic facts of Franklin's last years. In 1850 the expedition of Horatio Thomas Austin* and that of William Penny* together discovered that he had spent the winter of 1845–46 at Beechey Island, in Barrow Strait. In 1854 John Rae, the HBC's most accomplished northern explorer, heard Inuit reports and found relics indicating that the expedition had come to grief in the region of King William Island. Finally, in 1859, the expedition of Francis Leopold McClintock* found further relics and human remains on King William Island, together with two brief written records, the only ones ever found, which provide almost all the known facts. They show that from Beechey Island Franklin had sailed around Cornwallis Island, then proceeded south through Peel Sound and Franklin Strait towards Victoria Strait, where in September 1846 the ships became inextricably beset in ice northwest of King William Island. Franklin died while beset with his ships in 1847; no cause of death was recorded. Led by Captain Francis Rawdon Moira Crozier, the survivors abandoned ship in 1848 and most perished of starvation and scurvy while attempting to reach the mainland. The last few died at Starvation Cove on Adelaide peninsula. By reaching the mainland those survivors effectively completed the discovery of the northwest passage. Understandably, the first claim to its discovery was made by the members of Robert John Le Mesurier McClure*'s search expedition of 1850–54, who passed through the passage partly on foot after their rescue from the ice-bound *Investigator* and who were unaware of the achievement of Franklin's men. The passage was not navigated by a single ship until Roald Amundsen* sailed through it in 1903–6. Because the fate of the Franklin expedition was not known until 1854, its officers were retained on the navy list up to that year, and Franklin was even promoted to the rank of rear-admiral on 26 Oct. 1852.

Franklin's reputation as an explorer has wavered between two extremes. Throughout the 19th century the dreadful hardships of his first expedition and the drawn-out mystery of his last bestowed upon him a popular image as the embodiment of the heroic polar explorer, just as Captain Robert Falcon Scott of the Antarctic would be to a later generation. Franklin's characteristics as a pious, diffident, gentle, and in some ways awkward man who nevertheless found great reserves of moral and physical strength in the face of terrible suffering combined to lend him an aura of greatness. To a large extent it is deserved – Franklin added more to Canada's coastal map than any other explorer except George Vancouver*. But, to more detached observers, like many of the fur traders he met and some 20th-century commentators, notably Vilhjalmur Stefansson* in *Unsolved mysteries of the Arctic*, those same characteristics have indicated his weaknesses as an explorer. His style was to lead by personal charm and by moral example, but in difficult times this was no substitute for a more authoritative kind of leadership, such as that later displayed by Amundsen. His courage was admirable, but a more accomplished explorer, Rae or Stefansson for example, would have avoided the circumstances that called for such courage. He was more willing to learn from others and from his own experiences than some of his detractors have suggested, but he was slow to learn and slower still to adapt to unexpected circumstances. His determination to succeed was unwavering but was blended with an extreme loyalty to duty – with a dangerous tendency blindly to carry out instructions. That tendency was a major failing on his first expedition and it may have contributed to the tragedy of his last. In short, Franklin is vulnerable to criticism for his record in exploration, but his defects as an explorer are quite inseparable from his considerable virtues as a man.

CLIVE HOLLAND

The personal papers of Sir John and Lady Franklin, including Franklin's expedition journals, letter-books, and other correspondence, are in the Scott Polar Research Institute (Cambridge, Eng.), MS 248. Franklin is the author of *Narrative of a journey to the shores of the polar sea, in the years 1819, 20, 21, and 22 . . .* (London, 1823; repr. Edmonton, 1969); *Narrative of a second expedition to the shores of the polar sea, in the years 1825, 1826, and 1827 . . .* (London, 1828; repr. Edmonton, 1971); and *Narrative of some passages in the history of Van Diemen's Land, during the last three years of Sir John Franklin's administration of its government* (privately printed, London, [1842]; repr. Hobart, Australia, 1967). Portraits of Franklin are in the collections of the National Portrait Gallery (London), the NMM, and the Scott Polar Research Institute. Daguerreotype photographs of Franklin and his officers, 1845, are in the NMM and the Scott Polar Research Institute.

Lincolnshire Arch. Office (Lincoln, Eng.), MISC DON 430 (transcripts and printed works relating to Sir John and Sir Willingham Franklin); MISC DON 447/1–2 ("Life and correspondence of Jane, Lady Franklin," comp. W. F. Rawnsley, vol.3, pts.1–2); Spilsby, reg. of baptisms, 18 April 1786; 2 Thimb 7/6 (15 photographic plates concerning Sir John

Franklin and clipping concerning inauguration of statue, 1861). PRO, CO 6/15–16. *HBRS*, 1 (Rich). Robert Hood, *To the Arctic by canoe, 1819–1821: the journal and paintings of Robert Hood, midshipman with Franklin*, ed. C. S. Houston (Montreal and London, 1974). Letitia [Mactavish] Hargrave, *The letters of Letitia Hargrave*, ed. Margaret Arnett MacLeod (Toronto, 1947). Ramsay, *Dalhousie journals* (Whitelaw), vol.3. John Richardson, *Arctic ordeal: the journal of John Richardson, surgeon-naturalist with Franklin, 1820–1822*, ed. C. S. Houston (Kingston, Ont., and Montreal, 1984). *ADB*. Alan Cooke and Clive Holland, *The exploration of northern Canada, 500 to 1920: a chronology* (Toronto, 1978). *DNB*. A. H. Beesly, *Sir John Franklin* (London, 1881). R. J. Cyriax, *Sir John Franklin's last Arctic expedition: a chapter in the history of the Royal Navy* (London, 1939). *The Franklin era in Canadian Arctic history, 1845–1859*, ed. P. D. Sutherland (National Museum of Man, *Mercury ser.*, Archaeological Survey of Canada paper no.131, Ottawa, 1985). G. F. Lamb, *Franklin – happy voyager – being the life and death of Sir John Franklin* (London, 1956). A. H. Markham, *Life of Sir John Franklin and the north-west passage* (London, 1891). Paul Nanton, *Arctic breakthrough: Franklin's expeditions, 1819–1847* (London, 1971). Sherard Osborn, *The career, last voyage, and fate of Captain Sir John Franklin* (London, 1860). Roderic Owen, *The fate of Franklin* (London, 1978). K. [E. Pitt] Fitzpatrick, *Sir John Franklin in Tasmania, 1837–1843* (Melbourne, Australia, 1949). Vilhjalmur Stefansson, *Unsolved mysteries of the Arctic*, intro. Stephen Leacock (New York, 1939). H. D. Traill, *The life of Sir John Franklin . . . with maps, portraits, and facsimiles* (London, 1896).

FRANKS, JACOB (John), fur trader and businessman; b. *c*. 1768, probably at Quebec, son of John Franks and Appollonia ——; d. 14 Nov. 1840 in Montreal.

Jacob Franks's ancestors, a prominent family of Bavarian Jewish merchants, came to England during the second half of the 17th century, although some branches moved on to the Orient, the West Indies, and the American colonies. Jacob's father had appeared in Halifax as a merchant by 1749, moved to Philadelphia around 1760, and settled at Quebec in 1761. In 1768 he was appointed overseer to prevent accidents by fire, the first recorded instance of an appointment by commission from the colonial government of a Jew in Canada. He was a member of the Shearith Israel congregation in Montreal [*see* Jacob Raphael Cohen*]. In his later years he was proprietor of a tavern at Quebec. He died in 1794.

By 1788 Jacob, then resident in Montreal, had become active as a fur trader in the upper Mississippi valley and at Michilimackinac (Mackinac Island, Mich.). In 1794 he was in the area of present-day Wisconsin as a clerk for Ogilvy, Gillespie and Company, settling at Green Bay on Lake Michigan. On 8 August Franks obtained a 999-year lease from the Menominee Indians of 1,200 acres, located in two parcels on either side of the Fox River at Green Bay. In 1797 he returned from a trip to Montreal with his nephew John Lawe (the son of his sister Rachel) as clerk, and purchased the store at Green Bay from Ogilvy, Gillespie. Over the next few years his business as a merchant and fur trader grew to enormous proportions because of his ability to attract the "Indian trade" to his store. In 1805 he constructed the first saw- and grist-mill in the Wisconsin area, and there is evidence that he erected a distillery as well.

Franks had reached the peak of his economic success by 1805. Cession of the southwestern fur-trade posts by the British to the United States in 1796 had finally led in 1804 to the stationing of an American customs officer on Mackinac Island to monitor the fur trade, collect duties, and issue licences. The following year the Michigan Territory (Michigan and Wisconsin) was organized and previous claims of land ownership were thrown into question. In August 1804, in the midst of these changes, four British fur traders at Prairie du Chien on the Mississippi combined their resources with Franks at Green Bay in a partnership to protect their trade in the southwest. Robert Dickson* was given two of the seven shares in the partnership; James* and George Aird, and Allen C. Wilmot, the other Prairie du Chien traders, received one share each. It was a measure of Franks's importance that he was given the remaining two shares – a position equal to Dickson's. By 1805 the partnership was known as Robert Dickson and Company.

Increasing competition from American traders, coupled with a bad winter in 1805–6, doomed the firm. By June 1806 it owed £27,000 to its supplier James and Andrew McGill and Company of Montreal, one of its many creditors. After 1807 the firm formally ended although the partners continued their association, selling their furs to the Michilimackinac Company [*see* John Ogilvy*]. The Dickson firm was reconstituted in 1810 with the addition of John Lawe and Thomas Gummersall Anderson*, who had both served it as clerks, and Jean-Joseph Rolette, a Green Bay trader.

That year, for the first time, the Americans decided to restrict traders who were British subjects from entering the Indian country within the United States. To avoid the blockade, in the fall of 1810 all eight of the associates participated in a convoy of seven armed boats, laden with goods, which paddled at night from the British post at St Joseph Island (Ont.) past the American garrison on Mackinac Island to Green Bay, where there was as yet no official American presence.

By capturing Mackinac Island from the Americans on 17 July 1812 the British regained control of the upper Great Lakes and the southwestern fur trade. Franks played a significant role in the war effort. He was the second largest provider of equipment for the Indian forces that had served under Dickson at

Mackinac. Franks himself had commanded a detachment of "Canadians or Boatmen" during the attack and a week later he provided the barge to move the British headquarters from St Joseph Island back to Mackinac. The following winter he allowed his house and store on Mackinac Island to be used by John Askin Jr as an office and commissary. During the British occupation of the island, which lasted until the summer of 1815, he supplied the garrison. He was asked to act as an evaluator of the articles found on the *Scorpion* and the *Tigress*, captured from the Americans on Lake Huron in September 1814 [*see* Miller Worsley*]. After the British gave up Mackinac Island, Franks's house was one of two "wantonly pillaged" by the inhabitants. In compensation, he was granted a building lot at the new British military post, on Drummond Island (Mich.), in 1816.

From 1813 Franks had continued in the Indian trade in partnership with Lawe and James Aird. In 1816, however, Congress declared that only Americans could conduct trade southwest of the upper lakes. By the end of June that year, when Franks arrived at Drummond Island, having wintered in Montreal, it was clear that the British fur trade south of Lake Superior had ended. In a restrictive trade climate, Franks found he could no longer rely on the North West Company (with which the Michilimackinac Company had merged) for supplies or as a market for the few furs he and his partners were able to obtain. For his supplies, he turned to David Stone and Company of New Hampshire. For his market, he chose Montreal, where he planned to sell the partnership's furs because he had "no intention of sacrificing them by selling them at Mackinac as we have formerly done for these many years past."

At the same time, he decided to marry and move permanently to Montreal. He and his country wife at Green Bay, Thérèse de Gère, *dit* Larose, had had three sons and two daughters. On 13 Nov. 1816, in Montreal, he married Mary (d. 1826), a daughter of Levy Solomons*, with whom he had a "blood connexion"; they were to have no children. In trade Franks continued in association with Lawe at Green Bay for three more years – each return being worse than the last. By 1818 Aird had quit the partnership and Franks had come to the conclusion that with "all the restrictive measures of the American government" their trade could continue only "by employing young Americans to take out the goods." On his trip to the west in the summer of 1819 he took "but very few goods" with him, those being provided by his brother-in-law Henry Joseph* and by David David* of Montreal. Franks never recovered the cost of those goods and he never again returned to the west. But he did try one more fur-trading venture, in 1819 at Lac-des-Deux-Montagnes (Oka), not far from Montreal. Within a year he had sold out to the NWC at a small loss.

Franks retired to a farm at Les Cèdres in 1820. "I certainly thought," said his wife Mary, "that after slaving so many years as he has done, he would have scraped up sufficient to enable him to live with some little ease the remaining few years he might have to live, but unfortunately its not the case and we must only do the best we can." Jacob Franks moved to Montreal in 1839, the year before he died. To the end he had retained a connection with Montreal's Jewish community, leaving a legacy to the synagogue in his will.

Throughout his career on the frontier, Franks was recognized as a Jew and treated as an equal. When Anderson first met him and his nephew at Green Bay in 1800, he noted that "an English Gentleman Jacob Frank, and his nephew John Lawe, Jews, were extensively embarked on the fur trade here." Anderson credited Franks with having given him "the first good counsel" he had heard in the west and Franks and his nephew "tendered me much friendly advice how to conduct myself with the Indians, to beware of the cunning deceit, treachery, etc., of the traders, with whom I was about to mix up."

SHELDON J. GODFREY

ANQ-M, CM1, Jacob Franks, 22 nov. 1839. Bayliss Public Library (Sault Ste Marie, Mich.), Samuel Abbot, notary-book, Mackinac, 1806–18: 33–39; Misc. coll., partnership agreement, Robert Dickson *et al.*, 16 Aug. 1804; Port Mackinac, records, 1808–9. Halifax County Registry of Deeds (Halifax), Deeds, 2: ff.41, 75, 79, 154, 202 (mfm. at PANS). PAC, MG 8, G67 (mfm.); RG 8, I (C ser.), 256: 219–23; 257: 200–1; 515: 108; 673: 230; 678: 158–59; 1219: 336–38. PANS, RG 1, 410: 1 (mfm.). Wis., State Hist. Soc., Grignon, Lawe, and Porlier papers; John Lawe papers, box 1; M. L. Martin papers, box 1. "Jacob Franks," American Jewish Hist. Soc., *Pub.* (Philadelphia), 9 (1901): 151–52. *Mich. Pioneer Coll.*, 10 (1886): 607; 15 (1889): 193–95, 246–47, 664–74; 16 (1890): 172, 307–8, 478–79; 25 (1894): 608–10. Wis., State Hist. Soc., *Coll.*, 9 (1882): 145–46, 178–79; 10 (1888): 90–91, 94–96; 15 (1900): 3–4; 18 (1908): 463; 19 (1910): 316–17, 357–60, 365–69, 461–63; 20 (1911): 34–36, 52–53. *Montreal Gazette*, 19 Nov. 1840. *Montreal Herald*, 16 Nov. 1816. *First American Jewish families: 600 genealogies, 1654–1977*, comp. M. H. Stern (Cincinnati, Ohio, 1978), 83. Jeanne Kay, "John Lawe, Green Bay trader," *Wis. Magazine of Hist.* (Madison), 64 (1980–81): 3–27.

FRASER, DONALD ALLAN, Presbyterian minister and office holder; b. 24 Nov. 1793 in the parish of Torosay, Isle of Mull, Scotland, fifth and youngest child of Alexander Fraser and Isabella Maclean; m. 3 Oct. 1814 in Crossapol, Isle of Coll, Catherine Isabella Maclean, eldest daughter of the laird of Coll, and they had ten sons and one daughter; d. 7 Feb. 1845 in St John's.

Donald Allan Fraser, son of a minister of the

Church of Scotland, was educated at the Royal High School, Edinburgh, and began study for the ministry at the age of 13 when he entered the University of Edinburgh. Following graduation he was licensed to preach on 14 Dec. 1813 by the Presbytery of Mull and was ordained on 27 March of the following year.

After brief periods as a minister on Mull, in London, and in Tain, Scotland, Fraser responded to the petition for a Gaelic-speaking minister from the Highland settlers of Pictou County, N.S. In 1817 he settled at McLellans Mountain, organizing the first Church of Scotland congregation in Pictou County. A frame church, the earliest to be built in Nova Scotia specifically for the Kirk, was erected about 1818 and served 40 families. In 1819 a church was built for a second congregation of 25 families at Frasers Mountain, six miles distant. This structure was later moved to a site at New Glasgow. Besides supplying Blue Mountain and Albion Mines (Stellarton), Fraser travelled extensively throughout the county, his fluency in Gaelic being an important asset. He undertook missionary tours to Cape Breton, Prince Edward Island, and New Brunswick but, apart from a one-year ministry at Saint John, N.B., in 1826, he remained based at McLellans Mountain, supplementing his income from his 100-acre farm, Torosay.

Fraser did not join the newly formed Presbyterian Synod of Nova Scotia in 1817, but six years later he served as the first moderator of the Church of Scotland Presbytery of Pictou. Regarded by 1833 as the "senior clergyman," he was chosen first moderator of the Synod of Nova Scotia in connection with the Church of Scotland, the establishment of which emphasized the breach among Presbyterians. Conceding privately that he loved controversy more than he ought, Fraser participated in the struggle to decide the future of Pictou Academy, set up by Thomas McCulloch as a Presbyterian college, until his departure for Lunenburg in 1838. There he served a congregation of German descent, only recently affiliated with the Church of Scotland through the efforts of his predecessor, the Reverend Johann Adam Moschell. As the sole clergyman of that denomination in Lunenburg County, Fraser travelled on horseback nearly 4,000 miles each year. Appointed a commissioner of schools, he campaigned for the financing of education by assessments and for the establishment of a county academy.

Having learned of some Scots in St John's who had neither church nor minister, Fraser travelled to Newfoundland, arriving on 24 Dec. 1841. Despite the diversity of their Presbyterianism, he succeeded in organizing them into a congregation in August 1842 and accepted its call. After his return to the island, St Andrew's Church, the first Presbyterian church to be built in Newfoundland, opened for worship in December 1843. In the pulpit Fraser was a commanding presence, being a well-built man over six feet tall, and he established a reputation as an outstanding preacher. In public he was an eloquent opponent of the two-academy system proposed for St John's. Instead of a Protestant and a Catholic college, he advocated one non-denominational institution.

Fraser was beloved by his congregations. Had he not died at the age of 52, it is unlikely that St Andrew's would have divided in 1849. His first Nova Scotia congregations showed their continuing faithfulness by sending to St John's the frame and fittings for a three-storey house. The home, also called Torosay, still stands.

Pamela Bruce

UCC, Maritime Conference Arch. (Halifax), Church of Scotland, Pictou Presbytery, minutes, 1823–77; D. A. Fraser papers, Fraser to Forrest, 14 Dec. 1839 (copies); Synod of Nova Scotia in connection with the Church of Scotland, minutes, 1833–42. *Guardian* (Halifax), 28 March, 4, 25 April 1845. *Novascotian, or Colonial Herald*, 15 March 1832. *Public Ledger*, 14 Feb., 5 Dec. 1843. Scott *et al.*, *Fasti ecclesiæ scoticanæ*, 4: 124; 7: 659. J. A. Flett, *The story of St. Andrew's Presbyterian Church, Lunenburg, N.S.* (n.p., 1970). Gregg, *Hist. of Presbyterian Church* (1885). W. M. Moncrieff, "A history of the Presbyterian Church in Newfoundland, 1622–1966" (BD thesis, Knox College, Toronto, 1966). George Patterson, *A history of the county of Pictou, Nova Scotia* (Montreal, 1877; repr. Belleville, Ont., 1972). Prowse, *Hist. of Nfld.* (1895). *Free Lance* (New Glasgow, N.S.), 12 Oct. 1917. *Presbyterian Witness* (Halifax), 15 Sept. 1889.

FRASER, PETER, merchant, magistrate, politician, and militia officer; b. 23 Sept. 1765 in Forres, Scotland, son of James Fraser, a merchant, and Jean Rose; m. Maria Berton, daughter of James Berton, an American loyalist; they had no children; d. 13 Aug. 1840 in Fredericton.

Peter Fraser arrived in Fredericton in 1784 and established himself as the leading trader on the upper Saint John River, where he gained the confidence both of the Indians and of the French-speaking settlers in the Madawaska region. Fifty years later William Teel Baird* described him as "a buyer and exporter of peltry, perhaps the principal one in the Province." In 1789 he bought one of the most desirable riverfront properties in Fredericton, where he built a wharf and a store. As an importer and agent he encountered several leading loyalists, including Edward Winslow*, with whose family he became intimate. In 1801 he was in partnership with members of two other prominent families, George Ludlow and John Robinson*. This partnership was dissolved in 1806, but Fraser maintained a connection with the Robinsons for the rest of his life.

In the general election of 1802 Fraser and his neighbour and fellow Scot Duncan McLeod stood for

York County in opposition to Archibald McLean*, Stair Agnew*, John Davidson, and Walter Price, all of whom supported the policies of Lieutenant Governor Thomas Carleton*. When the sheriff reported that the lieutenant governor's candidates were at the head of the poll, Fraser and McLeod, alleging irregularities, appealed to have the election declared invalid but lost, the deciding vote in the assembly being cast by James Fraser*, with whom Peter was connected in business. This vote was of critical importance to the lieutenant governor's faction, for it enabled them to seat members of their own group in other disputed elections and then to dominate the committees that controlled the business of the house, thus ending the political influence of James Glenie*.

In the election of 1809, however, Fraser was returned along with McLeod, and on 1 March 1810, soon after the session opened, he asked leave to prepare a bill to secure Roman Catholics in the exercise of the franchise. His action led to the passing of a measure abolishing the requirement that electors must, if called upon, take the state oaths before being allowed to vote; in their place the new act exacted a simple oath of allegiance. In 1802 French-speaking Madawaska settlers had protested when they were denied the opportunity to vote, and their petitions had been looked upon as being in support of Fraser and McLeod. Fraser continued to be returned for York County until 1827, when he retired upon his defeat in the election of that year.

Throughout his years in the house Fraser consistently voted against measures designed to strengthen the role of government officials, notably during George Stracey Smyth*'s régime, but also in 1825 when he opposed a bill, strongly recommended by Lieutenant Governor Sir Howard Douglas*, to provide funding for circuit courts. In 1821 he joined with the majority, in a close vote, to support a bill that, had it not been rejected by the Council, would have extended the authority to solemnize marriage to all ministers authorized to preach. Essentially, Fraser was an 18th-century British whig, independent in his judgements but prepared to work within the existing system. In 1808, while Winslow was administering the government, he accepted appointment as a justice of the peace, and he also served a term as warden of the Anglican parish church in Fredericton.

Although he seems to have had no military experience, in 1824 Fraser was appointed major commanding the newly formed 4th Battalion of York County militia, made up mainly of French-speaking inhabitants of the upper Saint John valley. The establishment of this unit in territory in dispute between New Brunswick and Maine was no doubt intended to confirm that most of the settlers acknowledged the New Brunswick government. Fraser was highly knowledgeable about this area. He owned a number of properties there and his business interests had included the supplying of both British and American parties engaged in the boundary survey from 1817 to 1820. He gave evidence in May 1828 at the trial of John Baker for sedition, conspiracy, and combination, a case in which New Brunswick asserted its authority in the Madawaska region [*see* Sir Howard Douglas]. Fraser retained his command when, in 1831, the upper part of York County was erected into a separate county and the 4th York Battalion was remustered as the 3rd Battalion of Carleton County militia.

Fraser was a sponsor of the Bank of New Brunswick on its incorporation in 1820 and served as vice-president in 1832. When the Fredericton Savings Bank was organized by Sir Howard Douglas in December 1824, Fraser was named vice-president, and a few weeks later was made a member of the committee to report on a site for the College of New Brunswick. Like many assemblymen in that era, he also acted as the supervisor of several roads. He was the first president of the Fredericton St Andrew's Society and presided over its convivial gatherings until 1832. He also served as a justice of the Inferior Court of Common Pleas. In 1831 the administrator, William Black*, recommended that he be made a member of the Council of New Brunswick, but the Colonial Office preferred to appoint men from sections of the province that were not already represented.

Although Fraser appears to have been regarded early in the century as a significant merchant by provincial standards, and there is no evidence that he suffered any serious reverses, by the 1830s his business and his estate were modest in comparison with those of a number of Saint John entrepreneurs. His house, which survives in Fredericton, was a combined dwelling and store, and when completed around 1816 was one of the largest privately owned buildings in the capital. "Canoes, bateaux and scows came and went continually," says a local historian, who also notes that Fraser entertained a great deal. Among his properties were a large farm and several of the most desirable intervale lots in the countryside. He died on the eve of an economic depression which reduced the value of his estate to about £8,000. It took almost three decades and an act of the legislature for his executors to settle his affairs.

D. M. Young

ACC, Diocese of Fredericton Arch., Christ Church Anglican (Fredericton), records (mfm. at PANB). GRO (Edinburgh), Forres, reg. of births and baptisms, 29 Sept. 1765. PAC, MG 11, [CO 188] New Brunswick A, 44/1: 194; MG 23, D1, ser.1, J. Johnson to Ward Chipman, 7 Aug. 1817. PANB, RG 4, RS24, esp. S16-P2, S16-P4, S16-R8; RG 7, RS75, 1840, Peter Fraser; RG 10, RS108, Peter Fraser, 1816, 1825. UNBL, MG H2, vols.11–12, 15–16, 30–31, 36; UA,

"Minute-book of the governors and trustees of the College of New Brunswick," 1800–28. York Land Registry Office (Fredericton), Registry books, 1: 224, 311, 508 (mfm. at PANB). W. T. Baird, *Seventy years of New Brunswick life* ... (Saint John, N.B., 1890; repr. Fredericton, 1978). [Ward Chipman], *Remarks upon the disputed points of boundary under the fifth article of the Treaty of Ghent, principally compiled from the statements laid by the government of Great Britain before the king of the Netherlands, as arbiter* (Saint John, 1838). N.B., House of Assembly, *Journal*, 1793; 1803; 1809–27, esp. 1810: 14, 19; 1821: 336; 1825: 60–61. *Royal Gazette* (Saint John; Fredericton), 1803–40, esp. 27 June 1820, 21 Dec. 1824, 12 May 1828, 19 Aug. 1840. *Saint John Gazette*, 26 May 1806. *The New Brunswick militia commissioned officers' list, 1787–1867*, comp. D. R. Facey-Crowther (Fredericton, 1984). I. L. Hill, *Fredericton, New Brunswick, British North America* ([Fredericton?, 1968?]). John Garner, "The enfranchisement of Roman Catholics in the Maritimes," *CHR*, 34 (1953): 203–18.

FRIAND (Friend). *See* TRIAUD

G

GAGNON, ANTOINE, Roman Catholic priest and vicar general; b. 12 Feb. 1785 in Petite-Rivière-Saint-Charles, near Quebec, son of Zacharie Gagnon and Geneviève Bouin, *dit* Dufresne; d. 2 June 1849 in Barachois, N.B.

Antoine Gagnon, who came from a family of farmers, entered the Petit Séminaire de Québec when he was ten, having first attended his parish school. Highly intelligent, he completed his classical and theological studies at the Petit Séminaire and the Grand Séminaire de Québec. On 19 Dec. 1807 he was ordained priest by Bishop Joseph-Octave Plessis* in the cathedral of Notre-Dame at Quebec. Among his classmates were Louis-Joseph Papineau*, Philippe-Joseph Aubert* de Gaspé, and Pierre-Flavien Turgeon*, all of whom were to leave their mark on 19th-century Quebec. Antoine Gagnon would leave his in Acadia.

Following ordination, Gagnon remained only two years at Quebec, serving as curate of the parish of Notre-Dame, and then in the autumn of 1809 went to Acadia. His mission, Richibouctou, covered much of the eastern seaboard of New Brunswick, taking in the Catholic villages from Baie Sainte-Anne in the north to Baie Verte in the south, a distance of more than 180 miles; he made his residence at the village of Richibouctou (Richibucto-Village). The majority of his parishioners were Acadians, for the most part descendants of people who had escaped being deported in the middle of the 18th century, but his flock also included some Micmacs, Irish, and Scots.

Because of the huge size of his mission, Gagnon was constantly on the move, and his prolonged absences created unease within the community as a whole. A dispute arose over the site of a church that Plessis ordered built when he made his pastoral visit in 1812. The arguments went on for seven years until, in June 1819, the inhabitants of Aldouane, one of the villages involved in the discussion, sent a petition to the bishop asking that the mission be split and that Gagnon minister to only one of the parts. In 1820 Plessis yielded to this request and set up two missions, Richibouctou to the north and Gédaïc to the south. Gagnon was assigned to the southern mission and established himself at the village of Gédaïc (Grande-Digue).

The results of Gagnon's 11 years of mission work were far from remarkable when, in the autumn of 1820, he went to take charge of his new mission, but the 29 years or so that followed produced a different story. Since his territory had been halved, he was able to devote greater time to his ministry and to putting more solid structures in place in his mission. From 1825 to 1848 half a dozen churches and as many presbyteries were erected in various villages. The construction of these buildings did not, however, proceed smoothly, since the Acadian faithful were as divided as ever over the choice of sites. Gagnon had to intervene, and, though he could be difficult at times, he managed to settle each dispute that arose. During the same period he took an interest in both the administration of his mission and the church affairs of his diocese.

In 1833 Angus Bernard MacEachern*, the first bishop of the diocese of Charlottetown, which at that time covered Prince Edward Island and New Brunswick, appointed Gagnon his vicar general for New Brunswick. Less than two years later MacEachern died, and as one of the longest-serving missionaries in the diocese Gagnon seemed the very man to succeed him. At least that was the opinion of Archbishop Joseph SIGNAY of Quebec, who wrote to Rome to propose Gagnon as a candidate. Shortly before his death, however, MacEachern had appointed a new vicar general in the diocese, Bernard Donald Macdonald*. Moreover, he had confided to one of his friends that he considered this young Scottish priest a worthy successor. In Rome the Scottish clergy, with the support of the British government, demanded that one of their own succeed MacEachern, and it was Macdonald whom the pope appointed bishop of Charlottetown in 1837. Gagnon was bitterly disappointed. His name was again submitted to Rome when the diocese of New Brunswick was created in 1842, but this time it was an Irishman, William Dollard*, who became bishop.

The double set-back made Gagnon very touchy and distrustful of his fellow clergy, especially of his English-speaking bishops. He nevertheless continued to serve as vicar general under them, but not without disappointments. Macdonald refused him permission to found a bilingual classical college in Barachois [*see* Joseph-Marie Paquet*], and in 1845 Dollard divided his mission into two, Barachois and Grande-Digue, removing Grande-Digue from his jurisdiction.

Since the 1820s Gagnon had acquired a great deal of property, including mills, farms, and some 14,000 acres of wooded land. The purpose of this estate was, he said, to enable him to support his college. After his plan for a classical institution fell through, he decided to make use of his holdings for the education of young clergy at Quebec who showed an interest in coming to do mission work and therefore in helping him. When this long-awaited assistance arrived in 1845, Gagnon's hopes were deceived; for it was not one of his protégés who came, but François-Magloire Turcotte, the former parish priest of Sainte-Rose (Laval), Lower Canada, who had been involved in the Patriote rebellion some years earlier.

Gagnon was upset by the appointment of Turcotte to Grande-Digue: he was losing part of his mission, and consequently his tithes, at a critical moment. The economy was in a bad state from successive slumps in the lumber trade in the 1840s, and as a result Gagnon's financial situation became increasingly difficult. He had to get rid of this intruder at all costs.

The opportunity came in 1848. That year, following complaints about a marriage solemnized by Turcotte, Bishop Dollard decided to conduct an inquiry and entrusted it to Gagnon. Using his powers as vicar general, and with the bishop's authorization, Gagnon suspended Turcotte from his duties. Turcotte's parishioners were so offended that they would not let any other priest set foot in the church, maintaining that Turcotte had been reprimanded for no reason. Neither Jean-Marie Madran*, though chosen by the bishop to succeed Turcotte, nor Gagnon, appointed to minister to the mission after Madran's hasty departure, was allowed to enter it. The inhabitants of Grande-Digue were in open revolt against the ecclesiastical authorities.

In the course of the winter of 1848–49 Gagnon's health, which had been undermined by his missionary work, became worse following an attack of dropsy, a malady he had suffered from for several years. The bitterness occasioned by his former parishioners' revolt and the precariousness of his finances hastened his end. He died on 2 June 1849 in his presbytery at Barachois and was buried three days later in the crypt of the local church. Gagnon had bequeathed his possessions to his bishop, stipulating that they were to be used to support the education of priests, but when his creditors were satisfied, there was almost nothing left.

R. GILLES LEBLANC

AAQ, 210 A, III–XXIV; 310 CN, I–II; 311 CN, I–VI. Arch. of the Diocese of Saint John (Saint John, N.B.), Dollard papers; Antoine Gagnon papers. ASQ, Lettres, N, nos.144–53; U, no.94. R. G. LeBlanc, "Antoine Gagnon and the mitre: a model of relations between *Canadien*, Scottish and Irish clergy in the early Maritime church," *Religion and identity: the experience of Irish and Scottish Catholics in Atlantic Canada*, ed. Terrence Murphy and C. J. Byrne (St John's, 1987), 98–113; "Antoine Gagnon, missionnaire auprès des Acadiens du sud-est du Nouveau-Brunswick (1809–1849)," *Sur l'empremier: la gazette de la Soc. hist. de la mer Rouge* (Robichaud, N.-B.), 1 (1984): 119–84.

GAGNON, LUCIEN (sometimes called **Julien**), farmer and Patriote; b. 8 Jan. 1793 in La Prairie, Lower Canada, son of Pierre Gagnon, a farmer, and Marie-Anne Longtin; d. 7 Jan. 1842 in Corbeau, N.Y., and was buried 11 January at Saint-Valentin, Lower Canada.

Lucien Gagnon's family had lived at La Prairie for several generations, and in all likelihood they were amongst the handful of farmers who enjoyed a fairly comfortable life. Lucien learned farm work at an early age, and like his two brothers he wanted to become the owner of a farm that would give him independence. In his last will, drawn up in 1811, Pierre Gagnon made his three sons his sole and equal heirs. Lucien therefore acquired material security while he was still young and had no difficulty in establishing himself.

On 18 Sept. 1815 Gagnon married Catherine Cartier, daughter of a prosperous farmer from Sainte-Marguerite-de-Blairfindie (L'Acadie). He already owned two properties and had at his disposal more than 14,000 *livres* of assets. His wife, who brought a large dowry, added to his fortune with money, possessions, and livestock worth 5,000 *livres*. Following his marriage, Gagnon was recognized to be a well-to-do farmer.

Gagnon led an uneventful existence until the spring of 1828, when the death of his wife upset his life and his children's. His marriage on 8 September to Sophie Régnier of Napierville led him to sell his properties at La Prairie and settle in the parish of Saint-Valentin. Land was still abundant there, but seigneurial dues were high. Gagnon rapidly became one of the major farmers in the area. Around 1830 he was producing 200 *minots* of wheat and an equally large quantity of oats and barley; he also had an impressive number of livestock.

In 1834, however, overwhelmed by seigneurial charges and in debt to Napier Christie Burton, the seigneur of Léry, Gagnon joined the Patriote movement in his parish. He became friends with Dr Cyrille-Hector-Octave CÔTÉ, who favoured a substantial reduction in seigneurial dues in Lower Canada. Thus it was essentially the conflict with the seigneurs that drew Gagnon to the radical wing of the Patriote party.

In 1837 Gagnon was one of those most active in the revolutionary organization in his region. He took part in the mass meeting at Napierville on 17 July. In September, backed by a group of Patriotes, he used threats and intimidation to secure the resignation of the justices of the peace and militia captains in L'Acadie County, all known supporters of the British government. A month later he participated in the Assemblée des Six Comtés at Saint-Charles-sur-Richelieu. Subsequently he toured the parishes in L'Acadie County in an endeavour to rally farmers to the revolutionary cause. Increasingly he displayed the makings of a leader: realistic, tenacious, inflexible, even cruel, he did not hesitate to take difficult and compromising steps when the situation demanded it.

By November 1837 Gagnon was firmly convinced that the Patriotes in his region had to act. He held an important meeting at his home which was attended by Côté, Édouard-Étienne RODIER, and Ludger Duvernay*, among others. Together they planned an attack on the village of Saint-Jean (Saint-Jean-sur-Richelieu) for late in November. On learning that the British forces were aware of their plan, the four decided to cross into the United States to await a more favourable moment. At the end of November, having just settled in at Swanton, Vt, Gagnon recrossed the border and boldly went to Saint-Valentin and the surrounding parishes to recruit support. Accompanied by about 60 men, he managed to skirt Missisquoi Bay and return to Swanton, where the main body of Patriotes was waiting for him. On 6 December the fugitives, with Gagnon at their head, attempted a new raid, this time at Moore's Corner (Saint-Armand Station). Gagnon, who was twice wounded in the battle, succeeded in getting away through the help of two comrades. This military clash, the last of the 1837 rebellion, ended in failure again for the Patriotes. Gagnon, who was taken back to Swanton, was by no means out of difficulty. Late in December he learned that volunteers attached to the British army had burnt his farm and driven his wife and eight children away. Several weeks after he moved to Corbeau, N.Y., his family came to join him.

After the collapse of the 1837 rebellion, Gagnon played an important role among the fugitives remaining in the United States. Initially just a local leader, in 1838 he became a dominant figure in the top echelons of the Patriote movement. In this period the revolutionary organization was taken in hand by Côté and Robert Nelson*, who made Gagnon their confidential agent in military matters. Gagnon's power was increased by the support given him by a small group of farmers who were demanding not only independence for Lower Canada but also the abolition of tithes and of the seigneurial régime.

On 28 Feb. 1838 Nelson, Côté, and Gagnon set out at the head of 300–400 men on a foolish escapade to conquer the colony. They had just crossed into Canadian territory when they were hemmed in and forced to return to the United States. Gagnon and several of his companions were imprisoned by the American authorities for having violated the country's neutrality law. They were nevertheless quickly released by a jury sympathetic to their cause. After this failure Nelson, Côté, and Gagnon established a secret military organization, the Association des Frères-Chasseurs, with branches on both sides of the border.

In the spring of 1838 Gagnon went incognito to Lower Canada to set up lodges of *chasseurs* and recruit members. He took advantage of the opportunity to visit his wife and children, who had moved back to Saint-Valentin. During the summer, despite the offer of a £100 reward for his capture, he travelled around the counties of Laprairie, Chambly, Beauharnois, and L'Acadie to bring farmers into the organization. He returned to the United States late in August, convinced that he had been successful in establishing an effective network of *chasseurs* in the counties he had covered.

Nelson, Côté, and Gagnon now set the second uprising for 3 Nov. 1838. Their plan was to lead their force of fugitives and American volunteers in an attack on the parishes along the south shore of the St Lawrence, and then to seize Montreal, Trois-Rivières, and Quebec. The operation again was to end in abject failure: the Patriotes would cross the American border, only to be driven back by British troops and volunteers. On 5 November Côté, Gagnon, and Philippe Touvrey, a French officer recruited by Robert Nelson, led a detachment of about 500 Patriotes to Rouses Point, N.Y., to get weapons and ammunition. They managed to repulse a picket of volunteers at the Lacolle bridge, but on their way back they were easily defeated by militiamen waiting for them. Gagnon managed to get away and reached Napierville, where the main body of Patriotes was stationed. Hearing that the regular troops under Sir John Colborne* were about to arrive, Nelson, Gagnon, and Côté led their men to Odelltown. There the decisive combat took place. On 9 November the battle ended in the defeat of the Patriotes. Gagnon conducted himself courageously till the end of the fighting, and not until the final moments, when he saw that there was no longer any hope, did he return to the United States.

It is more difficult to follow Gagnon's traces after this defeat. He certainly attended a meeting in Swanton late in December, but he displayed no enthusiasm at it. In the course of 1839 there were many disagreements, stormy debates, and personality conflicts among the insurgents. The strength of the revolutionary organization ebbed, and Gagnon was powerless to stop its decline. Bitterly disappointed by the turn of events, he quit the Patriote movement in the summer of 1840 and for several months went about Vermont villages looking for work. Early in 1841 he settled down at Champlain, N.Y. Penniless, alone, wanted by the British government which refused to extend an amnesty to him, Gagnon was unable to re-establish himself. Worn down by fever and stricken with tuberculosis, he died at Corbeau on 7 Jan. 1842. When she received the news of his death, his wife, faithful to his wish, had his body, dressed in the Patriote costume of blue tuque and garments of Canadian cloth, brought back to Saint-Valentin.

The major role played by Lucien Gagnon during the 1837–38 rebellions shows the remarkable influence that a small band of farmers had on the ideological thrust of the Patriote movement. The importance of the seigneurial question in the revolutionary program of 1838 is highly revealing in this respect. That Gagnon was a dominant figure in the Patriote organization also indicates the presence of strong grassroots leadership in the events of 1837–38.

RICHARD CHABOT

ANQ-M, CE1-2, 9 janv. 1793; CE4-1, 18 sept. 1815; CE4-6, 8 sept. 1828; CE4-16, 11 janv. 1842; CN1-200, 12 févr. 1807, 28 févr. 1811, 13 févr. 1815, 28 févr. 1817; CN1-299, 9 août 1832, 15 sept. 1837; CN4-14, 14 sept. 1815. ANQ-Q, E17. BVM-G, Fonds Ægidius Fauteux, notes compilées par Ægidius Fauteux sur les patriotes de 1837–38 dont les noms commencent par la lettre G, carton 5. PAC, MG 24, B2: 2973–78, 3243–46; B78; C3, 2: 867–68, 904–6, 1726–27; RG 1, E1, 41: 410; 62: 345; RG 4, B20, 25: 11290–92; B37, 1: 607–8; RG 31, C1, 1831, L'Acadie. Can., Prov. of, Legislative Assembly, *App. to the journals*, 1852–53, app.VV. L.C., House of Assembly, *Journals*, 1835–36. *Le Canadien*, 26 janv. 1842. *North American*, 1 May, 4 Sept. 1839; 5 May, 17 July 1841. F.-D. Brosseau, *Essai de monographie paroissiale: St-Georges d'Henryville et la seigneurie de Noyan* (Saint-Hyacinthe, Qué., 1913), 128–29, 136–37. Mario Gendron, "Tenure seigneuriale et mouvement patriote: le cas du comté de L'Acadie" (thèse de MA, univ. du Québec à Montréal, 1986), 90–91, 107, 112, 115, 148–49, 161–62, 168, 175. Rumilly, *Papineau et son temps*. Joseph Schull, *Rebellion: the rising in French Canada, 1837* (Toronto, 1971), 56, 88, 133–35, 153, 167, 169, 210. Victor Morin, "Clubs et sociétés notoires d'autrefois," *Cahiers des Dix*, 15 (1950): 199–203; "La 'République canadienne' de 1838," *RHAF*, 2 (1948–49): 491–92. Marcelle Reeves-Morache, "La Canadienne pendant les troubles de 1837–1838," *RHAF*, 5 (1951–52): 106–7.

GALT, JOHN, author and colonizer; b. 2 May 1779 in Irvine, Scotland, son of John Galt, a ship's captain, and Jean Thomson; m. 20 April 1813 Elizabeth Tilloch in London, and they had three sons, including Thomas* and Alexander Tilloch*; d. 11 April 1839 in Greenock, Scotland.

John Galt was born into a part of Scotland where class distinctions were rapidly breaking down, and where intellectual horizons were expanding as a result of the Scottish Enlightenment and the French revolution. His father's profession and the sight of vessels on the Clyde evidently expanded John's geographic horizons, but his eccentric mother, and her picturesque phraseology, were much more important in the formation of Galt's character and what he called his "hereditary predilection for oddities." Ill health cut him off from other children, fostered introspection, and threw him into the company of the old women who lived behind his grandmother's house. The young Galt listened to their recollections and stories and became an avid consumer of ballads and tales, the influence of which in his literary career he characteristically admits in his *Literary life*. Mrs Galt scorned her son's bookishness (and fascination with flowers), and she tried to direct him into more active and public pursuits. Her hopes for his worldly success counterbalanced the retiring strain in his character, and perhaps contributed to the lifelong tension he felt between literary and "active" endeavour. In his *Autobiography* Galt mentions that her death in 1826 "weakened . . . the motive that had previously impelled my energies."

Galt's physical appearance was always out of the ordinary. A schoolmate, G. J. Weir, remarked that at the age of 7 he was as tall as a boy of 14. In his youth he developed a sense that he was destined to be distinguished by other than his looks and "herculean frame." Galt was fully aware of his limitations, and was "very early impressed with the necessity of rendering myself the architect of my own elevation." His education was sporadic because of his ill health and his family's movements between Irvine and Greenock, where they finally settled around 1789. He was tutored at home and at local schools. A university education for someone of his background would not have been unusual in Ayrshire at the time, but a mercantile career seems to have been expected by both Galt and his parents. He entered the Greenock custom-house at around the age of 16 and left it soon after for a clerkship at the local firm of James Miller and Company.

Galt's informal education was greatly advanced by the formation of a literary and debating society with two schoolfellows, William Spence and James Park. In 1804 they hosted a gathering with the poet James Hogg, the celebrated Ettrick Shepherd, who reported that their conversation "was much above what I had ever been accustomed to hear." Their friendship, cut short by the ill-health and early deaths of Park and Spence, not only set Galt's priorities, in that culture and literature would follow the mercantile business of the day, but also expanded his intellectual horizons by providing a forum in which competition was encouraged and criticism dispensed. Spence was more interested in mathematics, and Park in literary criticism, than in literary creation. Galt's combative nature led him to compete with them in their own fields of endeavour. The double life Galt led at this time resulted in the development of a decisiveness and an orderly working routine which gave him "a great deal more leisure than most men." His observation in 1834 that in "considerably less than two years of great suffering, I have been enabled to dictate and publish ten volumes – much of them from bed," confirms the efficacy of his system and his "sedentary industry."

By 1804 Galt had distinguished himself by assiduity in business, by his involvement with the Greenock Library, by the publication of some poems in the *Greenock Advertiser* and the *Scots Magazine*, and by initiating a corps of volunteer sharpshooters in response to what he called the second revolutionary war in France. Yet he was restless, and when his employers received an insulting letter concerning their method of business, Galt over-reacted, pursued the culprit, and held him till he had forced a written apology from him. This incident, possibly coupled with an unhappy love affair (the girl died), resulted in Galt's decision to go to London in May 1804. The chief aim of this first and most dramatic of Galt's migrations was to go into business on his own, which, after a lonely few months, he accomplished. The factor and brokerage partnership he commenced in 1805 with a fellow Scot, John McLachlan, was soon bringing in the then considerable sum of £5,000 per annum. In 1807 he published, in the *Philosophical Magazine*, his first essay on North America, his hastily compiled "Statistical account of Upper Canada," which stemmed in part from his interest in emigration to the New World as a means of relieving over-population in Europe. For this article he drew on information supplied by William Gilkison*, a cousin and former schoolmate who had spent time as a ship's captain on the Great Lakes. Galt's commercial success must have given him a high profile in the City, and was sufficient for his father to make over to him a large sum of money. However, the complexity of the business and a correspondent's failure (described by Galt in the *Autobiography*) led to severe losses and the dissolution of the partnership in its third year.

This failure at the moment when some of Galt's "inordinate ambitions" had been realized, forced him to withdraw into the study of law at Lincoln's Inn; yet his health soon collapsed and he sought relief in travel in 1809. His wanderings did not conform to the usual grand tour but were dictated by fruitless schemes to circumvent Napoleon's blockades by establishing a trade route through the Ottoman empire. A further attempt, at Gibraltar with the firm headed by Kirkman Finlay, came to naught when Lord Wellington's Iberian victories rendered the operation unnecessary, and, as at most moments of crisis, Galt again fell ill. He returned to London in 1811, married two years later Elizabeth Tilloch, daughter of the publisher of the *Philosophical Magazine*, and turned to his pen as his main source of income.

After his return Galt produced two entertaining books of travels at his own expense, and in 1812 he brought out a collection of five of his tragedies and a well-researched *Life and administration of Cardinal Wolsey*, which went into several editions. The critics were far from kind concerning the plays: Walter Scott commented in a letter that they were "the worst ever seen." His first book of travels, however, enjoyed considerable success. Galt noted that sales had paid for his extensive touring. In 1816 he published the first part of a biography of the American painter and president of the Royal Academy of Arts, Benjamin West. Throughout this period Galt also produced numerous school textbooks, mainly under the pen-names Sir Richard Phillips and John Souter, but the exact quantity of non-fiction he wrote is hard to uncover, not least because in the course of his career Galt used at least ten pseudonyms and often published anonymously. He admitted that his early literary efforts were undertaken to "acquire the reputation of a clever fellow," but his business and literary reverses, and his desperate need for money (he had a growing family and had chosen to divide his father's estate with his mother and sister), changed his literary goal. What he later called his last work as an amateur author, *The Majolo*, a Sicilian tale, was published in 1816.

The earthquake (1820), which Galt called his first serious novel, was a commercial failure, but his play *The appeal* (1818) was performed with some success and, according to Galt, Scott contributed the epilogue. In 1820 his literary fortunes changed with the immediate popularity of William Blackwood's serialized publication of his epistolary novel *The Ayrshire legatees*, an ironic, Smollettian account of a Scottish family's voyage to London to collect an inheritance. This was followed in 1821 by the work for which Galt is still best known, *Annals of the parish*, published in book form by Blackwood to critical acclaim.

Although *Annals* was often taken for a novel, Galt referred to the group of works to which it belongs as "theoretical histories." Written in the fictional autobiographic form of which he is one of the earliest, most innovative, and prolific exponents, the book chronicles, through the eyes of a village priest, the social and industrial changes Galt observed sweeping across Ayrshire. His preservation of west country dialect was and remains relished by Scots, and the care he took is confirmed by his instruction to Blackwood "not to touch one of the Scotticisms." Yet his use of dialect somewhat hampers the modern North American reader of his Scottish works. Galt's fictional realism was maintained in *Sir Andrew Wylie* (1822), the exactitude of his portrait of Lord Sandiford being confirmed when Lord Blessington, the unsuspecting model, told Galt that he found Sandiford's character "very natural, for, in the same circumstances, he would have acted in a similar manner." Galt's documentary powers were justly praised, but his powers of imagination were sometimes criticized. In the *Autobiography* and *Literary life*, he took pains to point out that "originality" was his characteristic as a writer, and that his best works were proof that he could have done better if literature had been his sole pursuit.

The Countess of Blessington became Galt's literary patroness. Her assistance and Galt's connection with Lord Byron (with whom he had travelled in the Mediterranean in 1809–10 and of whom in 1830 he would publish a much-criticized but much-read biography) helped Galt achieve prominence. In his *Literary life*, he remarks that he knew more noblewomen than female commoners, and was acquainted with upwards of 60 members of parliament. After the success of *The Ayrshire legatees*, Galt had pursued his literary career energetically, almost all his best-known Scottish "Tales of the west" being published between 1820 and 1822. *The provost* (1822), the fictional story of a municipal politician, has been compared by literary historian Keith M. Costain with Machiavelli's *The prince*, and when taken with Galt's *The member* (1832) and *The radical* (1832) confirms his important and early contribution to the development of the political novel. The impact of Galt's work on politicians, in a century in which the power of literature was immense, is hard to assess, yet it is worth noting that George Canning read *The provost* in parliament at a single sitting. The success of Galt's Scottish stories (*The last of the lairds* was to be added in 1826) seems to have turned his head, and, boasting that his Scottish resources were superior to those of Scott, he embarked on a series of historical novels; three nearly forgotten works, *Ringan Gilhaize* (1823), *The spaewife* (1823), and *Rothelan* (1824), were the result.

By the early 1820s Galt's dormant business career was revived with his involvement in what would become the Canada Company. The firm had its origins in efforts by loyalists along the Niagara frontier of Upper Canada to gain redress for damages caused by American troops during the War of 1812. Galt had made a name for himself as a parliamentary lobbyist, particularly when his stratagems facilitated the passage of a bill to construct the Union Canal in Scotland in 1819. This renown, distant family connections in North America, and his authorship of "Statistical account of Upper Canada" a dozen years before made him a likely choice to represent loyalist interests, and the promise of a three per cent commission spurred him on. The British government, however, proved reluctant to pay reparations and subsequent efforts by Galt to raise a loan, with which to liquidate the claims, collapsed. Galt then thought, probably at the urging of an old friend and Upper Canadian resident, Roman Catholic priest Alexander McDONELL, of using the colony's own resources. The scheme: sell its crown and clergy reserves, set aside under the Constitutional Act of 1791, and use the revenue in part to pay off his constituents.

Despite Galt's high hopes, nothing much came of this plan, at least immediately, but the idea of disposing of the reserves was timely. It eventually resulted in another scheme spearheaded by Galt which saw him organize a group of City merchants and bankers into a joint-stock company to buy the reserve lands and then sell them at a profit to British emigrants. By 1824 Galt was secretary of a projected one-million-pound corporation which included some of the City's senior financial figures. Two years of wrangling with government followed before a charter was granted to the Canada Company on 19 Aug. 1826. During this time Galt devoted most of his considerable energy to the project and in the spring of 1825 he visited Upper Canada as one of five commissioners charged with evaluating the lands to be purchased. Disputes with local figures, particularly Attorney General John Beverley Robinson* and the Reverend John Strachan*, resulted in the church moiety of the reserves being replaced by a million acres of wilderness, later called the Huron Tract. The final settlement saw the company opt to purchase one and a third million acres of crown reserves throughout the colony, the Huron Tract, and scattered lands amounting to more than a million acres. The price: a uniform 3*s.* 6*d.* an acre.

Galt was charged with running the company's field operations and he took up residence in Upper Canada in December 1826. He plunged into a welter of activity. Establishing an office at York (Toronto), he attended to an accumulation of offers to purchase land. In April 1827 he founded with much ceremony the town of Guelph and, following a policy of relatively large-scale capital investment, moved rapidly to develop it as a nucleus for settlement (he was much influenced by hothouse settlements such as the Holland Land Company and the Pulteney estates, which he had visited in western New York) [*see* David Gilkison*]. Later Galt travelled to Lake Huron on an exploring expedition, arriving in late June at the camp of Canada Company warden William DUNLOP and surveyor Mahlon BURWELL. Here Galt established another instant town, Goderich. By the autumn of 1828 a road had been built to the site from Guelph. The development of the latter town had continued at a rapid pace into 1828; Samuel Strickland* was hired to manage the company's affairs there and to complete the works begun by Galt. In 1827–28 Galt was also involved in setting up company agencies elsewhere in North America.

The peculiar, inverted society of the little town of York did not know what to make of a man with Galt's vision and purpose. Galt, for his part (and curiously, since in his New World novels he was to demonstrate that he knew the peculiarities of isolated communities), blundered by associating with such political reformers as John Rolph*; by socially mingling with those out of favour with the local establishment, including the wife of John Walpole Willis*; and by rashly but understandably withholding funds due to the government in order to assist the indigent La Guayra settlers, a group of British immigrants whose attempt to settle in South America had failed and who, in the absence of official arrangements, had been directed to the Canada Company in Upper Canada. Galt, never sufficiently deferential, fell out with Lieutenant Governor Sir Peregrine Maitland*, his secretary (Major George HILLIER), Archdeacon Strachan, and the "family compact." Galt's religious tolerance and his sympathy for the Six Nations Indians, whose land claims he had represented in England in 1825 [*see* Tekarihogen* (1794–1832)], hindered his acceptance into the narrow and partisan society of York. His sense of conspiracies directed against him (as depicted in the *Autobiography*) verged on the paranoid, yet his primary problem, exacerbated by distance from London, was the fear of the company's directors that he was spending too much money and furnishing insufficient accounts. In fact, Galt was an appalling bookkeeper, and he had spent too much time on developmental schemes in the company's larger holdings, particularly the Guelph block and the million-acre Huron Tract, rather than selling off lands easily accessible from York or by road and water-way, or the scattered crown reserves. Canada Company accountant Thomas Smith was sent out in the spring of 1828, ostensibly to help him, but in actuality to investigate, and when Smith decamped to London with some of the company's papers, Galt decided to return as well to reassure the directors. On reaching New York early in 1829, he learned that he had been recalled; his replacements were Thomas Mercer Jones* and William Allan*. Galt arrived in England on 20 May. The newspapers had carried news of his recall, his creditors closed in, and he was soon imprisoned for failure to pay his sons' school fees.

As with many business failures of this nature, the facts remain murky. Galt's recall coincided with a drop in confidence in company shares on the London market. Certainly details of the dismal record of the novelist's day-to-day sales and management had not matched the showy grandeur of his spectacular road-openings and town-foundings. A more sober on-the-job superintendence would be achieved by his successors. There is no doubt, however, that Galt's prominent part in the establishment of the Canada Company was an important step in the development of the colony. Often controversial [*see* Frederick Widder*], the firm played a major role in the settlement of the province and was not wound up until its last lot was sold in the 1950s. Although Galt's business reputation had been severely injured by his recall, by 1833 – when, largely because of the efforts of Jones and Allan, company shares were the highest vendible stock on the market – he was able to float a colonial business venture, the British American Land Company, formed to develop lands in the Eastern Townships of Lower Canada. Galt served as secretary but was forced to resign in December 1832 because of his health.

While in prison, Galt had again turned to his pen for income and, with the help of old publishers such as Blackwood and new ones such as Henry Colburn and Richard Bentley, he wrote himself out of jail chiefly by putting to use his Canadian experiences. *Lawrie Todd* (1830), *Bogle Corbet* (1831), and his *Autobiography* (1833), the works by which Galt's stature as a New World author is usually judged, followed his release in November 1829 in quick succession, though he was by now severely hampered by what appears to have been arteriosclerosis. During his last five years, he was wracked with pain and was a self-admitted invalid. His literary output, however, continued strong in book form and in periodicals. In 1834 Galt and his wife moved from London to Greenock. The three-volume *Literary life* appeared that year, and *Fraser's Magazine* remained an outlet for his journalistic talents. By 1837, however, he was slowing down, producing only minor efforts, reviews, and some verse. He died at Greenock on 11 April 1839.

Canada's claim to Galt is tenuous since he was resident for less than three years. He had intended to immigrate permanently, but it was his sons who became established in the Canadas, in 1833–34 (his eldest, John, became registrar of Huron County; Thomas became a chief justice of Ontario; and the youngest, Alexander Tilloch, worked for the British American Land Company, and was a father of confederation and Canada's first high commissioner in London). John Galt's connection with the Canada Company would, he felt, be remembered "when my numerous books are forgotten." Between 1807 and 1836 (the whole of his active life) he published more than 30 items which relate to North America, the majority of them concerning the Canadas. He was well aware that the foundations of new national identities were being laid, and in his "American traditions" articles in *Fraser's Magazine* and other writings he communicates his excitement at being actual and literary midwife to a new sense of national consciousness in the Canadas. As early as 1813, in his archly titled *Letters from the Levant*, Galt mentions his interest in "everything tending to preserve, heighten, and perpetuate those public affections, which, although it has become fashionable to decry them as prejudices, are still the sources that contribute to, elevate, and sustain the dignity of nations."

With a keen eye for encouraging beneficial "national prejudices," Galt depicted North American society, from the pauper immigrants of *Lawrie Todd* to the genteel ones of *Bogle Corbet*. His use of American slang in *Lawrie Todd* and the contrast with it of the language used in the Canadas in *Bogle Corbet* (which precedes the first of Thomas Chandler Haliburton*'s Sam Slick books by five years) create important social and historical records. Galt was convinced that the accuracy of his portraits of pioneer life, which he believed were superior to those by American James Fenimore Cooper, would ensure their increasing value. Critic Elizabeth Waterston has observed that *Bogle Corbet* was the "first major work to define Canadianism by reference to an American alternative." It is also the story of an anti-hero, and Galt's frequent use of non-military male anti-heroes, especially in *Bogle Corbet* and the *Autobiography*, demonstrates a belief that " 'the man who makes a blade of corn grow where it never did before, does more good to the world than did Julius Cæsar.' " Other critics, such as Clarence G. Karr, have suggested that self-interest played a greater part in Galt's career than he would have one believe. Certainly Galt petitioned the government for a percentage commission on the sale of crown lands, but he believed that his claim was just, that he had "add[ed] to the comforts of mankind" and had helped to "build in the wilderness an asylum for the exiles of society – a refuge for the fleers from the calamities of the old world and its systems fore-doomed." As he remarks in his *Literary life*, "Nor do I ever recollect being vain of any praise that my own judgment did not in some degree ratify as deserved."

It is impossible to calculate how much Galt's efforts and ideas contributed to the creation of Canadian and American consciousness. It is, however, known that the *Autobiography* was reprinted twice in Philadelphia in the year of its publication in England, and that *Lawrie Todd* went through 17 editions by 1849. Contemporary advertisements indicate that some of Galt's works were on sale in Upper Canada, *The life of Lord Byron* actually being reprinted in Niagara (Niagara-on-the-Lake) in 1831 by Henry Chapman. The value Galt himself placed on his North American works is indicated by the large amount of space he assigns to them in his *Autobiography* and *Literary life*.

Galt's fame undoubtedly rests in Canada on his connection with the Canada Company, and in Britain on his Scottish "theoretical histories." The geographic bifurcation of his activities, and his belief that business and literature are not incompatible, contributed to the decline of his reputation after his death. The division he himself imposed by writing a business life and then a literary life one year later further hampered appreciation of the magnitude of his achievements. Galt's recall from Upper Canada at the height of his career as a colonizer crippled his North American pursuits, and his British reputation was injured by the disorganized state of his literary affairs at the time of his death. It is only recently that historians have re-established Galt's importance to Canada, a country in which the role of business has been central, and that reappraisal and republication have confirmed Galt's original and important contribution to British and North American literature. Though fine literary and historical studies of Galt exist, the definitive and well-rounded treatment of his importance to both continents and to the worlds of affairs and literature remains to be written.

ROGER HALL and NICK WHISTLER

[Most of the manuscripts of Galt's published works have been lost or destroyed; those which survive are scattered along with his other papers among a number of institutions in Canada and Great Britain. The NLS, Dept. of MSS, houses a substantial number of his letters along with some literary manuscripts; part of the miscellaneous collection of manuscripts which Mrs Galt took to Canada on her husband's death is in the Galt papers at PAC, MG 24, I4, while further material is in his papers at AO, MU 1113–15. The AO also houses a fine and voluminous collection of Canada Company records, containing the texts of many of Galt's business letters. The Colonial Office papers at the PRO, especially CO 42/367, 42/369, 42/371, 42/374, 42/376, 42/379–81, 42/383, 42/387–89, and the Upper Canada sundries at PAC, RG 5, A1, also include much material relating to Galt's colonial ventures.

The Univ. of Guelph Library, Arch. and Special Coll., in the town Galt founded, is possibly the only institution attempting to acquire any printed or manuscript material by or relating to Galt, including variant editions of his published works and critical studies about him as a literary figure and colonizer. The library holds an extensive collection of published items, including many first and rare editions, as well as a number of relevant archival collections, most notably the recently acquired H. B. Timothy coll. and a number of Galt's literary manuscripts, including his unpublished biography of Sir Walter Scott. There are smaller collections of Galt material in the Lizars family papers, the Goodwin–Haines coll., and the Canada Company papers.

Harry Lumsden, "The bibliography of John Galt," Glasgow Biblio. Soc., *Records*, 9 (1931), and I. A. Gordon, *John Galt: the life of a writer* (Toronto and Buffalo, N.Y., 1972), form the key bibliographic sources. Gordon's book, J. W. Aberdein, *John Galt* (London, 1936), and [D. M. Moir], "Biographical memoir of the author" (issued under the Greek letter delta in the 1841 edition of Galt's *The annals of the parish and the Ayrshire legatees* . . . (Edinburgh and London), i–cxiii) are the soundest works on Galt's literary career. P. H. Scott, *John Galt . . .* (Edinburgh, 1985), though limited in scope, is the first to accord the North American works their rightful place; two books of essays, *John Galt, 1779–1979*, ed. C. A. Whatley (Edinburgh, 1979), and *John Galt: reappraisals*, ed. Elizabeth Waterston (Guelph, 1985), collect the work of some recent critics of Galt.

The best scholarly guide to Galt's involvement with the Canada Company is R. D. Hall, "The Canada Company, 1826–1843" (PHD thesis, Univ. of Cambridge, Cambridge, Eng., 1973). Other sources are R. K. Gordon, *John Galt* (Toronto, 1920), H. B. Timothy, *The Galts: a Canadian odyssey; John Galt, 1779–1839* (Toronto, 1977), Thelma Coleman with James Anderson, *The Canada Company* (Stratford, Ont., 1978), and C. G. Karr, "The two sides of John Galt," *OH*, 59 (1967): 93–99.

Because Galt was so prolific, his writings on North American topics have been submerged by the weight of other material. The following chronological list of his publications relating to North America and colonial affairs extracts these titles from his other works for the first time, and while by no means exhaustive, serves as proof of his prolonged interest in New World affairs. "A statistical account of Upper Canada," *Philosophical Magazine* (London), [1st ser.], 29 (October 1807–January 1808): 3–10. *The life . . . of Benjamin West . . .* (2 pts., London and Edinburgh), first published in 1816 and 1820 respectively; the 1820 editions of both parts have been reprinted as *The life of Benjamin West (1816–20); a facsimile reproduction*, intro. Nathan Wright (2v. in 1, Gainesville, Fla., 1960). *All the voyages round the world . . .* (London, 1820), written under the pseudonym of Captain Samuel Prior. "The emigrants' voyage to Canada" and "Howison's Canada," published anonymously in *Blackwood's Edinburgh Magazine* (Edinburgh and London), 10 (August–December 1821): 455–69 and 537–45. Editor's preface to [Alexander Graydon], *Memoirs of a life, chiefly passed in Philadelphia, within the last sixty years* (Edinburgh, 1822). Three letters published under the pseudonym Bandana: "Bandana on the abandonment of the Pitt system . . . ," "Bandana on colonial undertakings," and "Bandana on emigration," *Blackwood's Edinburgh Magazine*, 13 (January–June 1823): 515–18; 20 (July–December 1826): 304–8, 470–78. "An aunt in Virginia," an unpublished play written in New York in 1828, later adapted to prose and published as "Scotch and Yankees: a caricature; by the author of 'Annals of the parish, &c.,'" *Blackwood's Edinburgh Magazine*, 33 (January–June 1833): 91–105, 188–98. Galt also wrote, but did not publish, a farce entitled "The visitors, or a trip to Quebec," described in his *Autobiography* [*see* below]. "Colonial discontent" (as Cabot), *Blackwood's Edinburgh Magazine*, 26 (July–December 1829): 332–37. "Letters from New York . . ." (signed "A."), *New Monthly Magazine and Literary Journal* (London), 26 (1829, pt.II): 130–33, 280–82, 449–51; 28 (1830, pt.I): 48–55, 239–44. *Lawrie Todd; or, the settlers in the woods* (3v., London, 1830). "The Hurons: – a Canadian tale, by the author of 'Sir Andrew Wylie,'" "Canadian sketches, – no.II . . . ," "Canadian affairs," "American traditions . . . ," "Guelph in Upper Canada," and "American traditions, – no.II . . . ," all in *Fraser's Magazine* (London), 1 (February–July 1830): 90–93, 268–70, 389–98; 2 (August 1830–January 1831): 321–28, 456–57; 4 (August 1831–January 1832): 96–100. "The colonial question" (as Agricola) and "The spectre ship of Salem" (as Nantucket), *Blackwood's Edinburgh Magazine*, 27 (January–June 1830), 455–62 and 462–65. *Bogle Corbet; or, the emigrants* (3v., London, [1831]). "The British North American provinces" (signed "Z"), and "American traditions, – no.III . . ." *Fraser's Magazine*, 5 (February–July 1832): 77–84, 275–80. *The Canadas, as they at present commend themselves to the enterprize of emigrants, colonists, and capitalists . . . ; compiled and condensed from original documents furnished by John Galt . . .*, comp. Andrew Picken (London, 1832). "Biographical sketch of William Paterson . . . ," *New Monthly Magazine and Literary Journal*, [new ser.], 35 (1832, pt.II): 168–76. "The Canada corn trade," an unsigned review in *Fraser's Magazine*, 6 (August–December 1832): 362–65. *The autobiography of John Galt* (2v., London, 1833). Introduction to Grant Thorburn, *Forty years' residence in America . . .* (London, 1834). "The metropolitan emigrant," *Fraser's Magazine*, 12 (July–December 1835): 291–99. The list concludes with a series of nine "Letters concerning projects of improvement for Upper Canada," printed in the *Cobourg Star* between 23 Nov. 1836 and 29 March 1837; these have been republished as "John Galt's *Apologia pro visione sua*," ed. Alec Lucas, *OH*, 76 (1984): 151–83. R.H. and N.W.]

GANISHE. *See* GONISH

GATIEN, FÉLIX, Roman Catholic priest, missionary, teacher, school administrator, and author; b. 28 Oct. 1776 at Quebec, son of Jean-Baptiste Gatien and Marie-Françoise Aubin-Delisle; d. 19 July 1844 in Cap-Santé, Lower Canada.

Félix Gatien entered the Petit Séminaire de Québec in 1786, and he is thought to have had some difficulties in the primary classes. But later he was more successful, since in 1790–91 he passed from the first form to the third in one year, was in the sixth form (Rhetoric) in 1793, and completed Philosophy, the final two years of the classical program, in August 1796. He had an excellent teacher, Joseph-Marie Boissonnault, in Rhetoric, and he took his philosophy and science under two *émigré* priests, Jean-Baptiste-Marie Castanet* and Jean RAIMBAULT.

Gatien studied theology while teaching at the Petit Séminaire, and on 16 Feb. 1800 he was ordained priest. After appointing him assistant priest at Saint-Eustache, Bishop Pierre Denaut* in 1801 chose him to assist Jean-Baptiste Marchand* at Sandwich (Windsor, Ont.), where Gatien carried on his ministry until 1806. On his return he was admitted to the Séminaire de Québec as a member of the community on 21 Oct. 1806. In the 11 years he spent there, he was called upon to serve as professor of theology, bursar, director of the Grand Séminaire and the Petit Séminaire, and ex-officio or appointed member of the community's council. It would have been normal for him to spend his life at the seminary and indeed on 7 Aug. 1817 the council again named him director of the Grand Séminaire. But on 29 August, in the presence of a notary, Gatien relinquished his membership in the community. The reasons for his action are not known. In a letter of 8 September to Bishop Joseph-Octave Plessis*, Bernard-Claude Panet*, his coadjutor, observed that the seminary was to be pitied upon Gatien's departure and that the way he left would do nothing to attract new members. After being a brilliant student, Gatien had proved a remarkable teacher who enjoyed the affection of his pupils.

Plessis put Gatien in charge of the parish of Cap-Santé. At the time the parish, which had a good location on the St Lawrence, took in the villages of Portneuf and Saint-Basile. Gatien, who was completely devoted to his parishioners, neglected none of his pastoral duties. Following the advice of Plessis faithfully, in 1822 he refused to serve as visitor of the school which the Royal Institution for the Advancement of Learning set up in his parish. Nor did he hesitate to speak out from the pulpit that year against the proposed union of the Canadas. In keeping with the customs of his Alma Mater, as parish priest he seldom went out and did little entertaining. He spent his spare time in the long winters reading and improving his mind. And that was how he came to write the "Mémoires historiques sur la paroisse et fabrique du Cap-Santé depuis son établissement jusqu'en 1831," which was published 40 years after his death. In so doing he had again heeded the counsels of Plessis, who encouraged priests to take an interest in Canadian history. In his *Mémoires* Gatien shows that he was well informed about the historical past of the country and keenly observant of his own times and his parishioners.

A capable administrator with solid good sense and much experience of men and events, Félix Gatien also knew how to please with the charm and finesse of his conversation, which as Louis-Jacques Casault*, his assistant priest from 1831 to 1834 and later rector of the Université Laval, would recall, was enlivened with Gallic humour. An enlightened amateur of painting, he was also one of those who believed in the talent of the young painter Antoine Plamondon*, from whom he had commissioned a large canvas for his church in 1825. Gatien belonged to a generation that had studied at Quebec or Montreal in the period 1780–1800, lived through the period of the French revolution and knew *émigré* priests, and carried on ministry under Bishop Plessis. Priests of this generation had received an excellent classical education and they shone through their qualities of mind and heart, even if they were somewhat stern. One thinks of Jérôme Demers* and Jean-Baptiste BOUCHER, to mention but two. Conscious of his responsibilities to the end, Gatien considered it necessary to tell his archbishop, Joseph SIGNAY, on 13 July 1844 that he was too ill to conduct the novena to St Anne. He died six days later.

CLAUDE GALARNEAU

Félix Gatien's "Mémoires historiques sur la paroisse et fabrique du Cap-Santé depuis son établissement jusqu'en 1831" was published at Quebec in 1884 as *Histoire de la paroisse du Cap-Santé*. In addition, François-Maximilien Bibaud, *Le panthéon canadien* (A. et V. Bibaud; 1891), credits him as author of *Manuel du chrétien* and *La semaine sainte*, about which works nothing further is known.

AAQ, 20 A, IV: 98; 61 CD, Cap-Santé, I: 22; 303 CD, I: 98. ANQ-Q, CE1-1, 29 oct. 1776; CE1-8, 22 juill. 1844. ASQ, Fichier des anciens; Lettres, O, 125; MSS, 12F: 58–63; 433; 437; MSS-M, 103–4, 140, 146, 153, 155; Séminaire, 9, nos.27–28; 40, no.2; 56, no.89; 78, no.24H; SME, 21 oct. 1806. P.-G. Roy, *Fils de Québec*, 3: 183–85. Morisset, *Peintres et tableaux*, 2: 137–38.

GEDDIE, JOHN, clockmaker; b. *c.* 1778 in Banffshire, Scotland; m. Mary Menzies, and they had one son and three daughters; d. 27 April 1843 in West River (Durham), N.S.

John Geddie, the son of a cooper, apprenticed as a clockmaker and then set up his own business in Scotland. His livelihood was threatened by the economic depression that followed the Napoleonic Wars, and in 1817 he and his family joined the tide of immigrants to Nova Scotia. Settling in Pictou, Geddie opened a shop where he offered his own clocks and watches. He also served as an elder in the Presbyterian congregation of Thomas MCCULLOCH and as an overseer of the poor. When the town council refused to pay for purchases he had made as overseer, a group of merchants secured his arrest in November 1835. Highly emotional letters and editorials, all supporting Geddie, appeared in the Pictou *Bee*, and an angry citizens' meeting demanded his release. Eventually Geddie was given his freedom and the council agreed to pay for the purchases.

It is not known how many clocks Geddie made. He was accustomed to paint "John Geddie, Pictou" on each dial, but time and repainting have removed the inscription from several clocks which may be his. At least 16 Geddie clocks can be identified as extant between 1930 and 1979. It is probable that Geddie imported the clock-works from Scotland and then assembled them. The size, material, and design of the clocks varied with the means of the prospective buyers. Some are constructed of beautifully matched mahogany, some of pine, and others of roughly finished local woods. The enamelled dial-plates depict a variety of scenes. These include a brig and small cutter under sail on a foam-capped sea, a portrait of an elegant young lady in a blue gown, and hunting scenes, both rustic and formal, of man, dog, birds, and landscape. One clock has decoration inside the case with bright flowers painted on the weights and pendulum. Another is about seven feet high, made of mahogany with inlays. On either side of the hood is a cylindrical column with brass base and capital. The broken pediment is gracefully designed. In the lunette is a hunting scene and, in each spandrel, a rose and leaves. Below the centre of the dial is a curved opening for a calendar-dial.

Museum curator Harry Piers wrote in 1936 that "Geddie was evidently the most tasteful and skilful professional clockmaker we have ever had in Nova Scotia, his productions very closely approaching those of England and Scotland in beauty of design and decoration and in thorough craftsmanship." Geddie himself would have expected his family rather than his clocks to give him a recorded niche in history. His son, John*, went to the New Hebrides (Vanuatu) to establish what was apparently the first foreign mission sponsored solely by a colonial church, and three of his granddaughters, with their husbands, were also missionaries.

Geddie made no fortune as a clockmaker. His estate assets were debts owed to him of £275 and possessions worth £252. He is buried in Laurel Hill Cemetery, Pictou. The inscription on his gravestone states: "In the several situations of Elder of the Church, Parent and Member of Society, he displayed a zeal in discharging his duties which gained the best esteem of all who knew him."

KATHRYN T. MACINTOSH

Pictou County Court of Probate (Pictou, N.S.), Letters of administration (including inventory and appraisal) for the estate of John Geddie, 1843. *Bee* (Pictou), 1835–36. *Eastern Chronicle* (Pictou), 1843. *Guardian* (Halifax), 12 May 1843. D. C. Mackay, *Silversmiths and related craftsmen of the Atlantic provinces* (Halifax, 1973). J. M. Cameron, *Pictou County's history* (Kentville, N.S., 1972). *Life of Rev. Dr. John and Mrs. Geddie, and early Presbyterian history, 1770–1845*, comp. W. E. Johnstone (Summerside, P.E.I., 1975). G. E. G. MacLaren, *Antique furniture by Nova Scotian craftsmen*, advisory ed. P. R. Blakeley (Toronto, [1961]). J. P. MacPhie, *Pictonians at home and abroad: sketches of professional men and women of Pictou County; its history and institutions* (Boston, 1914). R. S. Miller, *Misi Gete: John Geddie, pioneer missionary to the New Hebrides* (Launceston, Australia, 1975). George Patterson, *Missionary life among the cannibals: being the life of the Rev. John Geddie, D.D., first missionary to the New Hebrides; with a history of the Nova Scotia Presbyterian Mission on that group* (Toronto, 1882). "The Geddie clocks," *Eastern Chronicle* (New Glasgow, N.S.), 30 Jan. 1933. N.S., Provincial Museum and Science Library, *Report* (Halifax), 1935–36: 59; 1936–37. R. D. Steeves, "Cuckoos to weights: he found life's hobby in a maze of cogs and springs," *Chronicle-Herald* (Halifax), 22 Dec. 1964: 18. "Two old clocks," *Maclean's* (Toronto), 52 (1939), no.20: 65.

GILLESPIE, GEORGE, merchant; b. 1771 in Wiston, Scotland, son of Alexander Gillespie and Grizzel Paterson; m. 1818 Helen Hamilton, and they had five children; d. 18 Sept. 1842 at Biggar Park, Scotland.

George Gillespie was born into an active mercantile family. At least four brothers were already merchants by the time he left for the province of Quebec in 1790. Possibly he was a partner by 1796 in Dickson, Gillespie and Company of Michilimackinac (Mackinac Island, Mich.), a firm that may have been part of the North West Company operations in the Green Bay (Wis.) area, where Gillespie is said to have served for a few years. It seems more likely, however, that he was a partner, perhaps with John Ogilvy*, in Ogilvy, Gillespie and Company; this firm operated from Montreal and Michilimackinac in the years 1794–97. In 1798 Gillespie supposedly had the charge of the major NWC post at Fort St Joseph (St Joseph Island, Ont.). The following year he became a member of the Beaver Club, whose bibulous evenings he enjoyed whenever he visited Montreal.

By 1800 Gillespie and his brother John had become associates with Ogilvy, Samuel Gerrard*, John Mure*, and others in the Montreal commercial house of Parker, Gerrard, Ogilvy and Company; John handled company business in London, George at Michilimackinac. That year Gillespie was among the partners who refused to follow Ogilvy and Mure into the New North West Company (sometimes called the XY Company), formed to compete with the NWC. Gillespie moved to Montreal, probably in 1803 when Parker, Gerrard, Ogilvy and Company was reorganized to bring in Sir Alexander Mackenzie*, but he contracted to visit Michilimackinac annually on behalf of the firm. He joined the Scotch Presbyterian Church, later known as St Gabriel Street Church, which he supported generously.

In late 1806, largely through Ogilvy's work, Parker, Gerrard, Ogilvy and Company joined with three other Montreal firms trading to Michilimackinac to form the Michilimackinac Company. Shortly after, along with Josiah Bleakley* and others, Gillespie negotiated on its behalf a division of trading territory with the NWC. In 1808 after a brigade of its bateaux was seized by American customs agents at Niagara (near Youngstown), N.Y., Gillespie journeyed to Washington to protest. Two years later he accompanied Toussaint POTHIER to Michilimackinac to buy out the wintering partners; the firm was then taken over by Forsyth, Richardson and Company and McTavish, McGillivrays and Company under the name Montreal Michilimackinac Company [*see* John Richardson*].

In 1810 Gillespie and his younger brother, Robert*, established a partnership with George Moffatt*, a shrewd and aggressive Englishman; after several changes the firm became known as Gillespie, Moffatt and Company in 1816. By then Gillespie may already have returned to Scotland, where he purchased the estate of Biggar Park in his native Lanarkshire and where he lived in baronial style until his death in 1842. A son, Alexander, worked in the Quebec offices of Gillespie, Moffatt and Company from 1844 to 1849.

GERALD J. J. TULCHINSKY

ANQ-Q, P-668. PAC, MG 19, B1; B3. Private arch., Alastair Gillespie (Toronto), Diary of Alexander Gillespie, 1849–50; Diary of Marion Patterson Gillespie, 1842–49; Family trees (pedigrees) of the Gillespies (typescripts). "Dickson and Grignon papers – 1812–1815," ed. R. G. Thwaites, Wis., State Hist. Soc., *Coll.*, 11 (1888): 272. *Docs. relating to NWC* (Wallace). Augustin Grignon, "Seventy-two years' recollections of Wisconsin," Wis., State Hist. Soc., *Coll.*, 3 (1857): 250, 252. "Lawe and Grignon papers, 1794–1821," ed. L. C. Draper, Wis., State Hist. Soc., *Coll.*, 10 (1888): 90–91. *Montreal Gazette*, 4 April, 15 Aug. 1796. Campbell, *Hist. of Scotch Presbyterian Church*. D. S. Macmillan, "The 'new men' in action: Scottish mercantile and shipping operations in the North American colonies, 1760–1825," *Canadian business history; selected studies, 1497–1971*, ed. D. S. Macmillan (Toronto, 1972), 44–103. R. H. Fleming, "The origin of 'Sir Alexander Mackenzie and Company,'" *CHR*, 9 (1928): 137–55.

GILMOUR, ALLAN, lumber merchant and shipowner; b. October 1775 in Mearns parish, Renfrewshire, Scotland, eldest son of Allan Gilmour, farmer, and Elizabeth Pollok; d. unmarried 4 March 1849 at Hazeldean, Mearns.

Allan Gilmour attended the parish school in Mearns, which had an outstanding reputation among the excellent schools of the area as a nursery for future business leaders, especially in the British North American timber trade. There he received a grounding in bookkeeping and commercial practices, and by 1795 he was conducting a small-scale timber business in Mearns, supplying local and Ayrshire timber to the booming building industry of Glasgow and to the shipyards of Greenock. By 1802 he had moved to Glasgow and expanded his operations, importing deals and other lumber products from the Baltic, Russia, and Norway.

Requiring more capital to extend his business, in 1804 Gilmour entered into a loose partnership with two relations, John and Arthur Pollok, whom he had known at school. The Polloks had inherited an extensive grocery business in Glasgow from an uncle, and carried it on with success, engaging in the timber trade on the side. The new firm was capitalized at £1,500, of which Gilmour contributed two-thirds, but when the company was expanded two years later, each partner donated an equal amount.

The enterprise flourished until Napoleon's continental blockade of 1806 and 1807 which, ushering in a time of acute timber scarcity, threatened Britain's vital shipbuilding industry, and hence the navy and the merchant marine. Gilmour was one of the first to realize that the lumber resources of the British North American colonies could provide a substitute for European imports. He participated in the lobby which brought about the introduction of bounties and reduced import duties on colonial timber in 1810 and 1811 respectively, appearing before parliamentary committees in both years. He reported regularly on potential overseas supplies to the Navy Board and the Board of Trade, and to Viscount Melville, head of the Admiralty from 1812. In addition to his commercial connections in Glasgow, he had a wide range of business and political contacts in Liverpool, Manchester, London, and other trading centres. As the driving force behind Pollok, Gilmour and Company and, in effect, the managing director, he also undertook to seek out colonial timber supplies. In 1811 and early 1812 he travelled through Lower Canada, New Brunswick, and Nova Scotia, where he was well received by many influential Scottish merchants such as John Black* in Halifax and James McGill* and James Dunlop* in Montreal. These men provided him with valuable information and advice based on their own experiences in the timber trade.

After returning to Scotland, Gilmour decided to open business on the Miramichi River in New Brunswick and later in 1812 sent out his younger brother James Gilmour and Alexander Rankin*, a nephew of the Polloks. Both men had had experience in the Glasgow office and between 1812 and 1818 they made a success of the Miramichi agency. By the latter date the branch house was employing a large number of lumbermen and mill workers and Pollok, Gilmour, with a fleet of 15 vessels, was reputedly the largest operator in the British North American timber market. Gilmour pressed on with expansion; further branches were opened at Saint John (1822), Quebec (1828), Montreal (1829), Bathurst, N.B. (1832), and Dalhousie and Campbellton (1833).

All of these houses were headed by young Scots, most of whom were relatives of Gilmour or the Polloks. Each was personally selected by Gilmour, who visited North America frequently to supervise the scattered operations. John Rankin, the company historian, would later describe the detailed instructions that Gilmour left for his partners on these visits: "Before he left for home, each partner abroad would have his work for the coming winter allotted to him. . . . Nothing was too small to escape the lash of Mr Gilmour's tongue, hardly anything too big for him to adventure."

Each of these branch houses was actually organized as a separate partnership in order to limit the liability on the parent firm. The branches were, however, dependent on the Glasgow operations for financing, supplies, and manpower, and although they traded independently, they exported everything to the parent company. Within British North America there were also mutual dependencies: William Ritchie and Company of Montreal was responsible for the day-to-day trading capital of the branches, and the majority of Pollok, Gilmour's ships (which by the early 1830s were said to number 130) were built in the firm's Quebec or Saint John shipyards. The houses in Lower Canada played a middleman role in the lumbering trade, purchasing all uncontracted rafts which came down the Ottawa and St Lawrence rivers; the rest operated directly as timberers. In 1834 alone the firm exported more than 300 shiploads of timber. Appearing before the British select committee on timber duties in 1835, Gilmour stated that 5,000 men worked for the company's North American establishments, with perhaps a quarter of them employed in north-eastern New Brunswick. By 1830 Pollok, Gilmour was also acting as British agent for many shipbuilders in the Maritimes.

Between 1812 and 1838 Pollok, Gilmour made large profits, and Gilmour was able to purchase extensive estates in Scotland, including one for £200,000. Apart from the land-hunger of a farmer's son, Gilmour bought these properties to obtain the voting rights which were tied to heritable land. He used the votes to support the Whigs, who he felt were more favourable to mercantile interests and might allow the merchants a greater say in running the country.

With growing wealth, a breach developed between Gilmour and the Polloks about 1837. When they began to live for part of the year on their estates outside Glasgow, Gilmour alleged that they were shirking their responsibilities as working partners. Always a strong-willed, thrusting man, Gilmour was growing increasingly irascible, and on 5 Jan. 1838 he withdrew from the company, receiving £150,000 for his share. Robert Rankin*, the manager of the Saint John branch, succeeded him as effective manager, and the controlling partners were now Rankin, his brother Alexander, still at Miramichi, and Gilmour's nephew Allan Gilmour* of Quebec. Rankin was to reorganize the firm, now known as Rankin, Gilmour and Company, shifting the main centre of operations to Liverpool. Gilmour Sr felt strongly that he should have received a greater sum than he did for his efforts in building the company, and he tried to persuade several of the partners heading the overseas branches to join him in withdrawing from the company. Except for his nephew William Ritchie* of Montreal, they refused.

Gilmour's capacity for selecting and training promising young men for responsible positions in the firm had been highly regarded and he had been the undoubted "mainspring" of the great company he had planned and built. Into the 1840s he continued to be viewed as a celebrity in Glasgow, admired for his enterprise and verve. A systematic and precise individual, he impressed all who met him with his energy. In addition to his mercantile concerns, he was deeply involved in agricultural development. He had a keen interest in field sports as well and was an excellent shot. According to John Rankin, Gilmour was "not without kindness of disposition; but he must have been odd-tempered, susceptible to flattery, irritable and litigious, yet far-seeing and of untiring energy. In his latter days he was undoubtedly vindictive, and with feeble health came at times feeble mind; but in the main he was able to exercise his strong will to the last."

After his retirement to his estate of Hazeldean, Gilmour's health steadily declined. He had never married. When he suffered a paralytic stroke early in 1849, he bequeathed almost all of his property, including four large estates and several farms, to the sons of his brother James. He died on 4 March 1849, unquestionably one of the most successful of the Scottish-Canadian lumber magnates.

DAVID S. MACMILLAN

NLS, Dept. of MSS, MSS 6849, 6866, 6913. SRO, CE.60/1/32–69. Univ. of Glasgow Arch., Adam Smith Business Records Store, UGD/36 (family and business papers of Pollok, Gilmour & Co.). A. R. M. Lower, *Great Britain's woodyard; British America and the timber trade, 1763–1867* (Montreal and London, 1973). D. S. Macmillan, "The 'new men' in action: Scottish mercantile and shipping operations in the North American colonies, 1760–1825," *Canadian business history; selected studies, 1497–1971*, ed. D. S. Macmillan (Toronto, 1972), 44–103; "The Scot as businessman," *The Scottish tradition in Canada*, ed. W. S. Reid (Toronto, 1976; repr. 1979), 179–202. John Rankin, *A history of our firm, being some account of the firm of Pollok, Gilmour and Co. and its offshoots and connections, 1804–1920* (2nd ed., Liverpool, 1921), 12–46, 170–71. Graeme Wynn, *Timber colony: a historical geography of early nineteenth century New Brunswick* (Toronto and Buffalo, N.Y., 1981). C. R. Fay, "Mearns and the Miramichi: an episode in Canadian economic history," *CHR*, 4 (1923): 316–20.

GIROD, AMURY, farmer, author, and Patriote; b. before 1800 in Switzerland; d. 18 Dec. 1837 in Pointe-aux-Trembles (Montreal).

Nothing definite is known about Amury Girod's origins, which can only be conjectured. It is believed that he was born shortly before 1800 in a canton near the French departments of Ain, Jura, and Doubs and that he received his education at Hofwyl, Switzerland, in one of the schools created by Philipp Emanuel von Fellenberg. He is said to have gone to South America and to have served in Simón Bolívar's liberation army. Supposedly he became a cavalry lieutenant-colonel in Mexico (1828–29) and fought with the Mexicans against the Spaniards, at some point also spending a year or two in the United States. Such an extraordinary past would explain why on his arrival in

Lower Canada he knew not only French, German, and Italian but also Spanish and English.

The first traces of Girod's presence in Lower Canada date from 1831. He delivered lectures that year on the application of mathematics to mechanical engineering before the Quebec Mechanics' Institute, and in the period from September to December he published a long series of articles in *Le Canadien* on the teaching methods employed at Hofwyl. Early in 1832, when an attempt was being made at Quebec to establish an agricultural school, he signed a notarized contract with Joseph-François PERRAULT, a promoter of education, in which Perrault agreed to provide the material basis for a model farm and college and Girod to become the actual director. Enrolment was well below their expectations, and in the summer of 1832 it was rumoured that Girod might be interested in assuming the editorship of the Montreal newspaper *L'Ami du peuple, de l'ordre et des lois*. The failure of the agricultural school was evinced by the cancellation of the contract between Girod and Perrault on 19 April 1833.

Girod came to live in the Montreal area, reportedly looked at the region around Saint-Charles-sur-Richelieu where the enterprising seigneur Pierre-Dominique DEBARTZCH resided, and then rented some land at Varennes. There he became friends with Eugène-Napoléon Duchesnois, a young doctor married to Françoise Ainsse, daughter of Joseph Ainsse, the seigneur of Île-Sainte-Thérèse. On 25 Sept. 1833 in Montreal, at the Scotch Presbyterian Church (later called St Gabriel Street Church), without advance notice, ceremony, or witnesses, Girod married Françoise's sister Zoé, who was 25 and had been widowed for two years. She was the daughter of a seigneur, but his seigneury was very small. The couple took up residence on Île Sainte-Thérèse and Girod became a farmer, but he employed a hired man and preferred the pen to the plough.

In May and June 1834 Girod sent *Le Canadien* a series of articles, later reprinted in a pamphlet with a dedication to Perrault, under the title *Conversations sur l'agriculture, par un habitans de Varennes*. Then he wrote seven long essays which came out in two parts as *Notes diverses sur le Bas-Canada* in June and November 1835. In these 129 quarto pages Girod discoursed with obvious skill on social life, the administration of justice, public finances, the land question, seigneurial tenure, and the means of transportation. He also dealt with the subject of the increasing tensions between Lower Canada and Great Britain. In 1836–37 he brought out the *Traité théorique et pratique de l'agriculture* (Montréal), his translation of a work by agronomist William Evans* published in 1835. Since 1831 Girod had been contributing to *Le Canadien*, *La Minerve*, and two papers published in Saint-Charles-sur-Richelieu, *L'Écho du pays* and the *Glaneur*, under his own name and pseudonyms such as Jean-Paul, Jean-Paul Le Laboureur, Un Habitans de Varennes, Insulaire, and Lemanus. He also gave evidence before various committees of the Lower Canadian House of Assembly, particularly on land and agricultural issues, education, the proposal to set up a normal school, and even the question of penitentiaries. It is easy to understand why his farm on Île Sainte-Thérèse did not become a model of success.

In the political sphere, Girod had links with the Patriote party from the time of his arrival in the Montreal region. He was active at Varennes and more generally in Verchères County, but also at Pointe-aux-Trembles. Over the months from spring to autumn 1836 his attack on Clément-Charles Sabrevois* de Bleury, who had broken with Louis-Joseph Papineau*'s party, turned sour for him. He finally admitted his conduct had been ill-mannered, an admission which virtually proved Bleury right. In the affair Girod so lost the confidence of his political allies that he contemplated leaving Lower Canada for Mexico. His equanimity was restored by a stay in Saint-Benoît (Mirabel), where he met notary Jean-Joseph Girouard*, Étienne Chartier*, a parish priest sympathetic to the Patriotes, and Jean-Baptiste DUMOUCHELLE, and by the overture made to him at that time about launching a regional newspaper. In a quick response, Girod said that he could get a press and type, and thought of five or six young men he would need who could simultaneously master agriculture, printing techniques, and even arms drill! But the project – an original one to say the least – came to nothing.

In the wave of popular meetings that followed the news of Lord John Russell's resolutions, Girod was everywhere: at the Saint-Marc assembly on 15 May 1837 where he made a long speech, at L'Assomption in the summer, and at Sainte-Scholastique (Mirabel) in the autumn. On 6 August he was present at a gathering of the Fils de la Liberté of Laprairie County held in Saint-Constant; he was one of the group that founded the Association des Fils de la Liberté of Montreal, and he signed the manifesto of 4 October [*see* André Ouimet*]. During the period when the large assembly at Saint-Charles-sur-Richelieu was being organized for 23 October, Girod served on the sub-committee responsible for presenting to it the views of the village of Varennes. He took the floor at Saint-Charles-sur-Richelieu and with Jean-Philippe Boucher-Belleville* assumed the important office of secretary to the meeting, which brought together the representatives of six counties.

The Patriotes' activity had been more or less illegal since 15 June 1837, when Governor Lord Gosford [ACHESON] had issued a proclamation forbidding protest meetings. The government sought to rely on the justices of the peace, who could prosecute them in the name of law and order. In addition Gosford asked for military reinforcements from the Maritimes. When a new list of JPs for the district of Montreal, omitting those of dubious loyalty, was published on 13 Nov. 1837 and action by the forces of order was rumoured imminent, the Patriote leaders left Montreal before warrants of arrest could be issued against them. These were the antecedents of Girod's meeting on 15 November with Papineau and Edmund Bailey O'Callaghan*. The two had come to Varennes from Montreal via Pointe-aux-Trembles on their way to the Richelieu, and they had met Boucher-Belleville. The latter knew that Girod was at the Hôtel Girard and invited him to join their group.

According to the diary that Girod kept, being careful to write in German and Italian, the four of them then went to the home of Duchesnois, who was absent. Girod noted: "I do not remember which one of us it was, but it seems to me it was Boucher [-Belleville] who proposed that a convention be summoned and a provisional government set up. We agreed to his proposal, but we added that this first measure amounted to an act of open rebellion and that it would be advisable to look for ways to organize the populace and obtain arms and ammunition. We were all in agreement with this proposal and began to talk about our departure." Girod then proposed that his three companions go to Saint-Denis, see Wolfred Nelson* there, and try to find weapons; as for himself, he would go north and send word to them from Grand-Brûlé (Saint-Benoît). He travelled by way of Île Sainte-Thérèse, Pointe-aux-Trembles, Rivière-des-Prairies (Montreal), and Sainte-Rose (Laval), arriving in Deux-Montagnes County on 17 November. The habitants of Saint-Eustache had already taken up arms four or five days earlier.

What is known of the month that followed – Girod's last – relates mainly to his role in the military organization of Deux-Montagnes County. The sources on which an account of what took place could be based are unreliable and often contradictory. The *Journal historique des événemens arrivés à Saint-Eustache* by parish priest Jacques PAQUIN, which was published in 1838, is strongly anti-Patriote, and Paquin could not have actually seen all that he reported. The statements by witnesses made during legal proceedings after the events tend to blacken the reputation of some in order to exonerate others. The diary that Girod wrote day by day tends, naturally, to put him in the best light, although it is worth noting that the secrecy and immediacy of this record provide a certain guarantee of exactness that statements which sometimes came long after the events cannot offer.

From this material a number of general observations can be drawn. Girod had difficulty in gaining recognition or respect despite his references to his military experience and his vague claim that Papineau had given him authority. The young Montreal lawyers and notaries, many of them members of the Association des Fils de la Liberté who had fled to the region in hopes of mobilizing armed resistance, drew the same reluctant response. Moreover, whereas Girod's personal relations were quite good with the local leaders at Saint-Benoît (Girouard, the curé Chartier, and Dumouchelle), they were rather bad with those from Saint-Eustache (William Henry Scott* and Jean-Olivier CHÉNIER).

Military cadres had to be formed, volunteers recruited, defences built, arms and supplies requisitioned – all delicate matters. On 23 November, at the instance of Chevalier de LORIMIER, Girod was accepted as leader, a week after his arrival. Word of the victory at Saint-Denis came the next day, but at a council of war on 25 November Girod's idea of going on the offensive by moving on Montreal was rejected. The news of the defeat at Saint-Charles-sur-Richelieu did not help sustain mobilization. Although officially the leader, Girod had no real control, particularly at Saint-Eustache, which was of greater strategic importance than Saint-Benoît. When a party went to Lac-des-Deux-Montagnes (Oka) in order to requisition arms from the Hudson's Bay Company and persuade the Indians to give up theirs, Girod and Chénier took separate initiatives. Scott would soon withdraw from the movement. It was difficult for Girod to prevent the requisition from turning into a pillage of the families still loyal to the government and of the houses abandoned by their occupants. The final lines in his diary, written on 8 December, reveal his exhaustion and his tendency to suspect everyone.

On 14 December Major-General Sir John Colborne*'s troops, with the support of volunteers from Montreal and Saint-Eustache itself, launched an assault on the rebels barricaded in the church of Saint-Eustache. Chénier died at the head of his men in the resulting combat. Girod, who was there the evening before, had gone to Saint-Benoît to seek reinforcements. While he was on his way back to Saint-Eustache, some men he met suspected him of having slipped off and there was resistance to his orders. He then fled in the direction of Sainte-Thérèse-de-Blainville (Sainte-Thérèse) and went back along the same route that had brought him from Varennes to Deux-Montagnes County. On 17 December he was at Rivière-des-Prairies. Denounced, pursued by a party of volunteers, and discovered the next morning at Pointe-aux-Trembles, he blew his brains out. A price had been set on his head, and he had always said he did not believe that the rebels' foes would let bygones be bygones.

The following spring, settlement of Girod's estate confirmed that he had not been rich. His widow Zoé renounced the community of property, which would have been a liability, and sold her movables. It then transpired that her father, Joseph Ainsse, who was the trustee for the estate, was also guardian of "Jhuan Girod, absent, the under-age child born of the said Amury Girod's first marriage"! Another surprise was a letter from New York, written in English and dated 21 Sept. 1840, from a woman to a Catholic priest named O'Callaghan to ask him where she could get in touch with Edmund Bailey O'Callaghan, the former editor of the *Vindicator and Canadian Advertiser*, who, she believed, was acquainted with the affairs of her husband Amury Girod. She spoke of their son, of false reports of her own death, of lands that Girod was supposed to have owned in South America. In addition she declared that she had left him in 1833 because at the time she had learned of a plot and had been unwilling to denounce the persons implicated in it, including her husband, or appear to be a party to it by remaining with him. There is no other trace of this woman and this son.

According to Thomas Storrow Brown*'s statement to the librarian of McGill College around 1870, Amury Girod was a rather tall man, well built and good-looking. On the other hand, the description of his character given in historical works thus far is not pretty: he is portrayed as a man of initiative rather than perseverance, who at the last moment, through lack of courage, proved unequal to his task. This may be so. But it should also be remembered that he was a man who, having come to the colony from another culture and with other experiences, had made his contribution to Lower Canadian society. The *North American*, the newspaper of the Patriotes exiled in the United States which was published in Swanton, Vt, presented this side of the picture, describing Girod as "a gentleman of superior talents to whom the country is indebted for many valuable publications."

JEAN-PAUL BERNARD and DANIELLE GAUTHIER

Amury Girod is the author of *Conversations sur l'agriculture, par un habitans de Varennes* (Québec, 1834) and *Notes diverses sur le Bas-Canada* (Saint-Hyacinthe, Qué., 1835). He translated a work by William Evans and published it as *Traité théorique et pratique de l'agriculture, adapté à la culture et à l'économie des productions animales et végétales de cet art en Canada; avec un précis de l'histoire de l'agriculture et un aperçu de son état actuel dans quelques-uns des principaux pays, et plus particulièrement dans les Îles britanniques et le Canada* (Montréal, 1836–37). His diary for the period 15 Nov.–8 Dec. 1837 has been published as "Journal kept by the late Amury Girod, translated from the German and the Italian," PAC *Report*, 1923: 370–80. A series of articles on Girod by Gilles Boileau was published in *La Victoire* (Saint-Eustache, Qué.), 14 oct., 25 nov. 1970; 5 avril 1973; 6, 13, 20 nov. 1975; 23 dec. 1976.

Bibliothèque nationale du Québec (Montréal), Dép. des MSS, MSS-101, coll. L.-J. Ainsse, nos.152–53, 160; coll. Ainsse–Delisle, nos.9, 13–14, 125, 133, 156, 159. BVM-G, Fonds Ægidius Fauteux, étude biographique sur Amury Girod accompagnée de notes, références, copies de documents, coupures concernant ce patriote. I.[-F.-T.] Lebrun, *Tableau statistique et politique des deux Canadas* (Paris, 1833), 189, 250. [Jacques Paquin], *Journal historique des événemens arrivés à Saint-Eustache, pendant la rébellion du comté du lac des Deux Montagnes, depuis les soulèvemens commencés à la fin de novembre, jusqu'au moment où la tranquillité fut parfaitement rétablie* (Montréal, 1838). Caron, "Inv. des doc. relatifs aux événements de 1837 et 1838," ANQ *Rapport*, 1925–26: 149–50, 179–85, 187; "Papiers Duvernay," 1926–27: 159, 170, 175. Émile Dubois, *Le feu de la Rivière-du-Chêne; étude historique sur le mouvement insurrectionnel de 1837 au nord de Montréal* (Saint-Jérôme, Qué., 1937), 122–24, 177–80. Labarrère-Paulé, *Les instituteurs laïques*, 50–56. J.-C. Chapais, "Notes historiques sur les écoles d'agriculture dans Québec," *Rev. canadienne*, 70 (janvier–juin 1916): 348–50. Ægidius Fauteux, "Amury Girod ou l'homme du mystère," *La Patrie*, 19 juill. 1934: 16–17; 26 juill. 1934: 16–17; 2 août 1934: 16–17. L.-A. Huguet-Latour et L.-E. de Bellefeuille, "Amury Girod," *BRH*, 8 (1902): 139–46. William McLennan, "Amury Girod," *Canadian Antiquarian and Numismatic Journal*, 8 (1879): 70–80.

GIVINS, JAMES (early in his career he signed **Givens**), army and militia officer and Indian Department official; b. *c.* 1759, possibly in Ireland; m. Angelique Andrews in York (Toronto), and they had nine children; d. 5 March 1846 in what is now Toronto.

James Givins may have spent his early years in Ireland and was perhaps a relative of Henry Hamilton*, by whom he was "bred up" according to John Graves Simcoe*, lieutenant governor of Upper Canada. When Hamilton was appointed lieutenant governor of Detroit in 1775, young Givins accompanied him to the post. During his time there, he learned Ojibwa, an accomplishment that was to prove most useful in his later career. He was a volunteer in Hamilton's attack on Vincennes (Ind.) in 1778. Taken prisoner when the Americans regained the settlement in 1779, he spent most of the next two years interned at Williamsburg, Va.

It is thought that Givins went to England following his release, but his movements for the next decade are unknown. Then, on 30 Nov. 1791 he was appointed lieutenant in the newly formed Queen's Rangers, a corps raised to serve in Upper Canada and commanded by Simcoe. During the next several years he was engaged as a courier for confidential dispatches and as an interpreter for Simcoe in dealings with the Indians. He served in the British force sent west in 1794 during the period of international tension prior to the battle of Fallen Timbers [*see* Michikinakoua*].

As early as 1793 Simcoe had recommended Givins for a place in the Indian Department, and in June 1797 Administrator Peter Russell* named him assistant superintendent of Indian affairs for the Home District, an appointment that was finally confirmed in August 1798. He was to distribute the annual presents and to report on Indian "dispositions, movements, and intentions." His prime responsibility, however, was to prevent Joseph Brant [Thayendanegea*] and the Six Nations from forming a pan-Indian organization that would include the Mississauga Ojibwas. Brant and Givins soon clashed openly. Brant charged that Givins was restricting Indian travel in Upper Canada and was purchasing land from the Mississaugas at less than market price. The dispute became so serious that Russell instructed Givins to visit Brant personally and make amends. An uneasy *modus vivendi* was arranged, but tensions between the two did not end until Brant's death in 1807.

Following the disbanding of the Queen's Rangers, on 19 Nov. 1803 Givins had been made a captain in the 5th Foot. He subsequently left the regiment but, with the outbreak of hostilities between Britain and the United States in June 1812, he returned to active military service. He was appointed a provincial aide-de-camp to Isaac Brock* on 14 August and was gazetted a major in the militia. Although he accompanied Brock to Detroit and subsequently fought on the Niagara frontier, his finest hour came on 27 April 1813 when, with a small company of Mississaugas, he assisted in the defence of York against the invading Americans. His "spirited opposition" was noted by the British commander, Sir Roger Hale Sheaffe*. After the close of the war his association with the militia continued. On 21 Jan. 1820 he was made colonel of the 3rd Battalion of York militia and the following year he was appointed colonel of the 1st Battalion of West York militia.

Givins's greatest concern after 1814, however, was the Indian Department. With peace, the strategic military value of Indian warriors declined, while improved relations between Britain and the United States, financial retrenchment, and humanitarianism led the British government to adopt a new policy of "civilizing" the Indians. Givins was an early enthusiastic convert to one such experiment: he was instrumental in encouraging the Mississaugas and the Reverend Peter Jones* to establish a model village on the Credit River in what is now Mississauga, Ont. In 1828 when Henry Charles Darling, military secretary to Lord Dalhousie [RAMSAY], conducted an inquiry into the state of the Indians, the success of the Credit Mission was noted, and the settlement ultimately became the example for the development of the reserve system.

In April 1830 the Indian Department in the Canadas was divided into two branches, with James Givins appointed chief superintendent for Upper Canada. Despite his advanced age and his requests for retirement, he continued in office until 12 June 1837, when he left the service on full pay. He died peacefully at his home, Pine Grove, nine years later.

JOHN F. LESLIE

MTRL, James Givins papers. PAC, RG 1, L3, 203: G1/33; RG 10, 10018, general order, 13 April 1830; A1, 5, Darling to Dalhousie, 24 July 1828; B8, 737. *Corr. of Hon. Peter Russell* (Cruikshank and Hunter). *Corr. of Lieut. Governor Simcoe* (Cruikshank). *Select British docs. of War of 1812* (Wood). G.B., WO, *Army list*, 1794. *Officers of British forces in Canada* (Irving). R. S. Allen, "Red and white: the Indian tribes of the Ohio valley and Anglo-American relations, 1783–1796" (MA thesis, Dalhousie Univ., Halifax, 1971). C. W. Humphries, "The capture of York," *The defended border: Upper Canada and the War of 1812 . . .* , ed. Morris Zaslow and W. B. Turner (Toronto, 1964), 251–70. J. F. Leslie, "Commissions of inquiry into Indian affairs in the Canadas, 1828–1858: evolving a corporate memory for the Indian Department" (typescript, Indian Affairs and Northern Development Canada, Treaties and Hist. Research Centre, Ottawa, 1985). R. S. Allen, "The British Indian Department and the frontier in North America, 1755–1830," *Canadian Hist. Sites*, no.14 (1975): 5–125.

GLACKEMEYER, FREDERICK (baptized **Johann Friedrich Conrad**), musician, merchant, composer, and music teacher; b. 10 Aug. 1759 in Hanover (Federal Republic of Germany), son of Johann Wilhelm Glackemeyer and Anna Sabina Queren; m. first 25 Sept. 1784 Marie-Anne O'Neil at Quebec, and they had 16 children, including Louis-Édouard* and Henriette, who married Théodore-Frédéric Molt*; m. there secondly 2 Sept. 1813 Josephte Just, and they had a son and a daughter; d. there 13 Jan. 1836.

As available documents and Pierre-Georges Roy*'s article on the family show, little is known about Frederick Glackemeyer's life before 1784. He had enlisted in 1777 and served as bandmaster of a detachment of German troops under Lieutenant-Colonel Johann Gustav von Ehrenkrock, but there is no information about the date of his arrival in the province of Quebec. When he received his discharge from the army in 1783, Major-General Friedrich Adolph von Riedesel, the officer commanding the German troops on duty in the province, offered him a position as organist at Lauterbach (Federal Republic of Germany), but he decided to settle in the town of Quebec.

From June 1784 till September 1832 Glackemeyer was involved in activities that connected him with amateur musicians, various officials, and certain figures and institutions of the Roman Catholic Church in Quebec. In mid 1784 he began the first phase of a long career spent serving music-lovers and supporting a number of musical activities that existed somewhat precariously in the town. Throughout the period 1784–1825 he sold musical instruments imported from England at his home and also taught a variety of instruments there. In 1784 he was giving instruction on the piano, guitar, violin, and flute, to which by 1825 he had added the viola and cello. The opening of numerous commercial establishments by 1785 may have forced Glackemeyer to take on related tasks (copying music, repairing and tuning various instruments), as well as to carry a much larger quantity and diversity of instruments and accessories, including from 1788 musical scores. Like his rivals, Glackemeyer by then made use of the press. From November 1788 to November 1796 and January 1808 to April 1826, he quite regularly inserted advertisements of goods and services in the *Quebec Gazette*, the *Quebec Mercury*, the *Quebec Herald, Miscellany and Advertiser*, and from 1794 the *Times* (Quebec), of which he was a founding subscriber. He also participated in musical events in 1792 and 1831 as a singer and was the leading tenor in a concertante by Ignaz Pleyel presented on 30 Jan. 1822 by the Quebec Harmonic Society. It is likely that the £10 paid him late in 1790 by the Quebec Assembly, an association that organized dances, was for work as a professional musician.

The great frequency with which Glackemeyer moved his business from place to place – he was at 25 Côte de la Montagne in October 1790, on Rue Buade in October 1792, at 5 Rue Sainte-Famille in 1795 and at no.19 in 1798, and on Rue Saint-Joseph (Rue Garneau) from February 1814 until at least 1826 – may be related to his limited commercial success, which was not helped by the financial difficulties, uncertain health, and family problems that cast a shadow over his life around 1822. At that time Glackemeyer witnessed the temporary disappearance of the Quebec Harmonic Society. It had been founded in December 1819 and he had been made vice-president at a general meeting held in the town on 14 Nov. 1820.

Glackemeyer's name had come to public attention when on at least two occasions – in December 1785 and August 1791 – he joined other Quebec citizens in signing formal addresses published in the Montreal and Quebec periodicals. Glackemeyer had a second means of recognizing dignitaries: composing musical works with special titles, for example, "General Craigs March," a signed work written during Sir James Henry Craig*'s term as governor (1807–11), and "Chateauguay March," an arrangement for orchestra played at a dinner in honour of Lieutenant-Colonel Charles-Michel d'Irumberry* de Salaberry on 24 Sept. 1818. According to musician and journalist Nazaire Levasseur*, Glackemeyer became friends with Prince Edward* Augustus during his stay at Quebec, and as a result the prince appointed him bandmaster of a regiment from Brandenburg-Schwerin stationed at Quebec on George III's orders. As bandmaster he is said to have given open-air concerts twice weekly on the Esplanade. Levasseur's claim is, however, suspect.

An enumeration of the parish of Notre-Dame in Quebec done in the autumn of 1792 by curé Joseph-Octave Plessis* indicated that Glackemeyer resided on Rue Buade, was German, Protestant, and a musician, and that he had four parishioners, two of them communicants, living in his house. Although, according to Pierre-Georges Roy, he was not converted to Catholicism until late in life, his children, like both his wives, were practising Catholics. This situation explains why the *fabrique* hired Glackemeyer in the years from 1802 to 1824 to adjust, tune, and repair the organ, although not to play it. Glackemeyer undertook to write a "March compôsée pour le Revd. Monr. Tabeau," probably to mark the installation as organist of the young curate Pierre-Antoine Tabeau* at the end of June or beginning of July 1807. The Ursulines hail Glackemeyer as the music-master of longest standing in the annals of the convent.

Given the present state of knowledge of the period in Canadian musical history during which Glackemeyer was active at Quebec, it is scarcely possible to adjust the general appreciation put forward by his biographers, which is based more on his personal merits than on his pre-eminence or the importance of his contribution to Quebec's cultural life. Nevertheless it does seem that Glackemeyer's competence to give instruction on the various instruments he professed himself ready to teach can be called in question. Indeed, John Lambert*, who spent some time at Quebec during the first decade of the 19th century, likely had Glackemeyer in mind when he noted that "there are only two music-masters in Quebec, one of them is a good violin performer; but for any other instrument, they are very indifferent teachers." The "March compôsée pour le Revd. Monr. Tabeau" bears out this remark: the fingering scattered through the score shows an obvious lack of skill at the manual. However, such doubts do not extend to the composer's style of writing and techniques of composition in the well-structured works that have survived.

It may well be that Glackemeyer, like Marie-Hippolyte-Antoine Dessane* after him, pursued some ideal in the field of music. But judging from a passage in a letter written to Quebec lawyer Louis Moquin on 22 July 1824, he appears rather to have been a businessman anxious to augment his modest means in order to secure a good education and an honourable place in society for his numerous children.

LUCIEN POIRIER

ANQ-Q, CE1-1, 2 sept. 1813, 15 janv. 1836; CE1-61, 25 sept. 1784. AP, Notre-Dame de Québec, Enregistrement des bancs, 1813–14; Livre de comptes, 1802–24; Livre de comptes rendus par le procureur de l'œuvre et fabriques, 1814; Orgues, cloches, tableaux, 1802, 1818. Arch. of the City of Hanover (Federal Republic of Germany), Reg. of baptisms, 13 Aug. 1759. ASQ, S, carton 7, no.53; carton 11, no.39; Coll. Glackemeyer, titre de la reliure F, piano-forte, 52–53, 63–64. BVM-G, Coll. Gagnon, corr., Frederick Glackemeyer à Louis Moquin, 22 juill. 1824. Private arch., Béatrice Miller-Desmeules (Québec), Cécile Lagueux, "[Livre de musique]" (MS). John Lambert, *Travels through Canada, and the United States of North America, in the years 1806, 1807, & 1808* . . . (3rd ed., 2v., London, 1816), 1: 302. *Recensement de Québec, 1818* (Provost), 241. *Le Canadien*, 26 sept. 1818; 25 août, 1er sept. 1824. *L'Écho du pays* (Saint-Charles[-sur-Richelieu], Qué.), 21 janv. 1836. *Montreal Gazette*, 1 Dec. 1785, 2 June 1791. *Quebec Gazette*, 24 June 1784; 7 Oct. 1790; 18–19 Aug. 1791; 23 Feb., 25 Oct. 1792; 18 July 1793; 26 June 1794; 16 July 1795; 3 Nov. 1796; 14 May 1801; 13 Jan., 26 May 1803; 14 June 1804; 27 June 1805; 12 June 1806; 30 June 1808; 25 May, 14 Sept. 1809; 14 June 1810; 13 July 1815; 13 May 1819; 27 June 1822; 21 April 1823; 15 Sept. 1825; 8 June 1831. *Quebec Herald, Miscellany and Advertiser*, 24 Nov. 1788; 20 May, 9 Dec. 1790. *Quebec Mercury*, 1 May 1809; 28 June 1814; 24, 31 Jan. 1815; 12 Oct. 1819; 24 Nov. 1820; 21 June 1822; 1 June, 14, 24 Aug. 1824; 13 Sept. 1825; 11 April 1826; 7, 24, 26 Sept. 1832. *Times* (Quebec), 18 Aug. 1794; 8 June, 13 July 1795. *Dictionnaire biographique des musiciens canadiens* (2e éd., Lachine, Qué., 1935), 122–23. *Encyclopedia of music in Canada*, ed. Helmut Kallmann *et al.* (Toronto, 1981). P.-B. Marineau, "De ses archives, 'L'église paroissiale de Québec,' son service musical, 1760–1865: investigation, collection et publication" (travail présenté au Conservatoire de musique du Québec, Qué., 1977). Willy Amtmann, *La musique au Québec, 1600–1875*, Michelle Pharand, trad. (Montréal, 1976), 28, 272–81, 291, 294, 303, 407. Burke, *Les ursulines de Québec*, 4: 673–74. *Canadian musical heritage*, 4a, ed. Lucien Poirier (Ottawa, 1985), 13–15; 7, ed. Lucien Poirier (Ottawa, 1987), 78–79. V. E. DeMarce, *The settlement of former German auxiliary troops in Canada after the American revolution* (Sparta, Wis., 1984). Bernard Dufebvre [Émile Castonguay], *Cinq femmes et nous* (Québec, 1950), 102, 177–81. J. M. Gibbon, *Canadian mosaic: the making of a northern nation* (Toronto, 1938). Helmut Kallmann, *A history of music in Canada, 1534–1914* (Toronto and London, 1960), 46, 49–52, 54–55, 60–62, 67, 78, 81, 125. Marcelle Rousseau, "The rise of music in Canada" (MA thesis, Columbia Univ., New York, 1951), 44–45. Helmut Kallmann, "Frederick Glackmeyer: des données nouvelles sur sa vie et son style musical," Assoc. pour l'avancement de la recherche en musique de Québec, *Cahier* (Québec), 8 (1987): 86–92. Nazaire LeVasseur, "Musique et musiciens à Québec: souvenirs d'un amateur," *La Musique* (Québec), 1 (1919): 26–27, 52–53, 62–64, 74–75. P.-G. Roy, "La famille Glackemeyer," *BRH*, 22 (1916): 195–205.

GOESSMAN, JOHN, surveyor, office holder, and settlement agent; b. 1786 in Gronloh, Hanover (Federal Republic of Germany), and baptized **Johann Gohsmann** 22 March 1786 in the parish of Badbergen, son of Johann Henrich Gohsmann and Catharina Maria Schulte; d. unmarried 20 Jan. 1841 in Mono Township, Upper Canada.

John Goessman studied surveying and drafting at the military academy in the city of Hanover. Upon graduation he was employed for a time by the municipality's engineering department. In 1818 he immigrated to the United States, and he moved to York County, Upper Canada, in October of the following year. On 19 November he petitioned Lieutenant Governor Sir Peregrine Maitland* for a licence to practise surveying. Surveyor General Thomas Ridout* examined him and required him to serve a probationary period working in Vespra Township, under the observation of Deputy Surveyor General William CHEWETT. Goessman was granted a licence on 9 March 1821. His subsequent surveys, conducted for the government, the Canada Company, and private parties, included Burlington Beach, Mississauga Ojibwa lands on the Credit River, and the townships of Tiny, Tay, Flos, and Wilmot. He applied unsuccessfully in 1830 for a clerkship in the Surveyor General's Office. In reviewing his performance, Chewett noted that "he would have the advantage over almost all the sub-surveyors in the Province . . . [if] he governed himself with a little more regularity."

Chewett's criticism probably referred to the alcoholism that impeded Goessman's work. He was frequently involved in drink-related violence, scrapping on one occasion, in 1821 at the mouth of the Nottawasaga River, with members of the 68th Foot from Penetanguishene. On another occasion, ten years later, he appeared at the office of the clerk of the peace in York (Toronto) in "a state of great intoxication, and evidently incapable of knowing what he was about." Although he never lost his licence, he was dismissed from the office of superintendent of highways in the Home District in 1825, after less than a year of service, for absenteeism related to abuse of alcohol. Goessman seemed convinced of the propriety of his conduct, for he exposed his character to public scrutiny in 1824 by temporarily entering the general election in York and Simcoe.

During periods of unemployment as a surveyor, evidently prolonged by his alcoholism, Goessman resided in Markham Township and sought alternative means of support. In 1829 he solicited the government's sponsorship both of a German-language almanac he intended to publish and of his design for an improved stump-puller. Two years previously he had ventured into land speculation, purchasing a lot in Flos from the Canada Company. At the time he declined to mention, and the company declined to advert to, the fact that military buildings were located there. Ultimately, Goessman was blamed for the land having come into the company's hands in the first place, he having omitted to identify the buildings in his survey plan of the township. The lot escheated to the crown and he lost his purchase money of £33.

Goessman served as an agent for German-speaking settlers in Upper Canada, drafting petitions for land grants, arranging extensions of the time allowed for their performance of settlement duties, and handling other business related to land occupation and development. Among those for whom he acted were Lutherans and Anglicans in York County, including the Reverend Johann Dietrich Peterson and the Reverend Vincent Philip Mayerhoffer*. Goessman's most extensive correspondence as an agent, extending from 1828 to 1830, was conducted on behalf of Amish and Mennonite settlers in the "German Block" of Wilmot Township, which he had surveyed. These people occupied the land under an agreement that their spokesmen, Christian NAFZIGER and Jacob Erb, had made with the government, but without any written authorization such as location tickets. When the block was granted to King's College in 1828, their claims were "totally forgotten." To his credit, Goessman assisted in negotiating terms of purchase for his clients. He was less successful in promoting German immigration to Upper Canada. The only known fruit of these efforts, between 1828 and 1837, was the settlement of a few immigrants in Puslinch Township; around them a modest German community would develop, centred on the village of Morriston. Although Lieutenant Governor Sir John Colborne* had provided his "pleasing patronage" in December 1828 to Goessman's efforts to encourage German immigration, by March 1830 the government had been soured by the Wilmot experience and Colborne discouraged Goessman from placing newspaper advertisements in Buffalo, N.Y., for German immigrants.

Goessman died in 1841 in Mono Township at the home of Seneca KETCHUM. He had bequeathed his small estate to a nephew, John Gerhard Goessman, a printer in Toronto. He also left behind him an extensive correspondence that sheds significant light on German immigration and settlement patterns in Upper Canada, particularly with respect to the role of government policy. His obituary in *Der Deutsche Canadier und Neuigkeitsbote* reported that his agency on behalf of fellow Germans would be remembered "with gratitude."

E. REGINALD GOOD

AO, MU 2114, 1861, no.15; RG 1, A-I-1, 29; 45: 251–54, 263–66, 432; A-I-2, 4: 75, 136, 175–76, 180, 473, 491; C-IV, Wilmot Township, lot 5, North Erb Street; RG 22, ser.155. Evangelisch-Lutherisch Pfarrgemeinde (Badbergen, Federal Republic of Germany), Kirchenbuch, 22 March 1786. PAC, RG 1, L1, 32: 430–31, 450–51; 33: 198–99, 311; L3, 207: G13/31; 208A: G15/42; 213: G21/13; 531: W16/26, 35; RG 5, A1: 22103–4, 26689–93, 27486, 27678, 27697–720, 27894–97, 37260–63, 45679–82; 46021–24, 46103–4, 46164–66, 46356–57, 46405–7, 49872–76, 49958–60, 50555–60, 52140–42, 52557–60, 52834–55, 52926–69, 53378–81, 53498–501, 53949–54, 54183–86, 54223–26, 54605–7, 54651–59, 54903–5, 55003–5, 55029–30, 55165–74, 55289–95, 55658–60, 55728–29, 55736–38, 55889–91, 55935–38, 56389–92, 56714–16, 56723–25, 57079–83, 57287–95, 58277–79, 60473–80, 61342–52, 61509–13, 83677–78, 88115–16, 93632–35, 132391–92. *Canadian Freeman*, 22 Nov. 1832. *Colonial Advocate*, 3 April 1828. *Der Deutsche Canadier und Neuigkeitsbote* (Berlin [Kitchener, Ont.]), 12 Feb. 1841. Scadding, *Toronto of old* (Armstrong; 1966).

GOFF, FADE, businessman, politician, office holder, and JP; b. 17 Sept. 1780 in Bryanstown (Republic of Ireland), eldest son of Richard Goff and Anna Neville; m. 6 April 1809 Mary Somaindyke Ryan, and they had 11 children; d. 6 Jan. 1836 at Erinvale, Lot 34, P.E.I.

Born into a landed Anglo-Irish family of declining circumstances, Fade Goff immigrated to Newfoundland in the spring of 1809 to join his father-in-law, John RYAN, a newspaper publisher in St John's. Upon arrival Goff met John Stewart*, a landowner on Prince Edward Island, who hired Goff to be his agent there. The following spring the Goff family moved to the Island, where Fade by 1814 agreed to act also as agent for George and Alexander Birnie, a merchant house based in London.

A class of middlemen, the land agents of Prince Edward Island have been accused by historians of oppressing their tenantry while embezzling the property of their absent employers. Goff was not such an agent. His letters to George Birnie indicate that he was forced to compete for capable tenants, offering various capital improvements to induce them to settle. As for his relationship with his employers, it was that of a supplicant to his masters. Both the Birnies and John Stewart had first-hand experience of the Island, an intimate knowledge of its condition, and a wide variety of local contacts. They could not be easily deceived by an agent, and in fact quickly had Goff in a position of total dependence. When he had arrived on the Island Goff had made several bad investments in land and imported merchandise, and he had accepted large advances from his employers to cover his debts. Goff realized by 1815 that, without an upturn in the provincial economy or the acquisition of a lucrative administrative position, he was unlikely to free himself from his obligations as long as he remained on the Island. That year he applied to be agent in Newfoundland for John HILL, but Alexander Birnie sued him for payment of money owing. George Birnie smoothed matters over, apparently by holding Goff to his current post, and cut his discount at the Birnie store. In the early 1820s, believing himself "cruelly and unhandsomely used" after more than a decade of agency, Goff turned to a variety of small ventures such as the building of a flour-mill and the establishment of an emigration office, all to little advantage. Thus, while he raised his "pretty round stock" of children, Goff never managed to extricate himself from his financial predicaments, and achieved some measure of equilibrium only from political and administrative office.

Being connected with the Stewart family automatically placed Goff in a proprietorial faction often referred to by its detractors as the "cabal." Elected to the House of Assembly for Georgetown in April 1812, Goff supported this group in its assault upon the then-dominant faction known as the Loyal Electors, in which James Bardin Palmer* was prominent. That September Goff was one of six MHAS who absented themselves from the assembly in an attempt to deny a quorum and thereby prevent the passing of a supply bill sponsored by the Loyal Electors. Such tactics were part of a campaign of proprietorial pressure which had secured in August an order dismissing the lieutenant governor, Joseph Frederick Wallet DesBarres*, and which would shortly topple the Loyal Electors, who depended on his patronage.

A supporter of the proprietors, William Townshend*, became administrator when DesBarres left in October, and he used the opportunity to reward adherents of the "cabal" with office and emolument. Goff became coroner and clerk of the crown in May 1813, and proved adaptable enough to retain these offices under the new lieutenant governor, Charles Douglass Smith*, even though his previous allies in the "cabal" became disenchanted with Smith in the early 1820s. Goff twice briefly acted as colonial secretary under Smith, was created a justice of the peace in 1814, and was appointed high sheriff in 1831.

Goff had his political disappointments none the less. Perhaps because of his proximity to an unpopular lieutenant governor he failed to retain his seat in the election of 1818. He also had to wait until 1819 for confirmation of, as well as the fees for, his positions as coroner and clerk of the crown, and even then for a time had his salary garnisheed by the Birnies. (He resigned both offices in April 1830.) Appointed by Lieutenant Governor Aretas William Young* to the Council in February 1832, Goff at first attended intermittently and then ceased to do so altogether owing to his "indisposition and pecuniary embarrassment." He died after a lengthy illness.

Palmer imputed to Goff an influence "behind the curtain" of Island politics. Certainly Goff was in a position as clerk of the crown to keep such proprietors as Stewart, who could not always be present in Charlottetown, abreast of developments potentially antagonistic to their interests. A lack of sources makes Goff's precise role in influencing events difficult to define, but it appears to have been no more than ancillary to that of the proprietors themselves. Held back by financial difficulties, he was never able to secure the political and social position to which he aspired. As he wrote of himself, "Every attempt that I have made either to serve others or myself in this Island ends in loss and disappointment, and cross and unfortunate occurrences constantly have thrown me in the background."

M. BROOK TAYLOR

PAC, MG 24, D99, files 1–2. PAPEI, Acc. 2810/127, 2810/173; Acc. 2849/38, 2849/86, 2849/128; RG 1, commission books, 1812–13; 1 Feb. 1814; 3 April 1816; 22 Jan. 1818; 27 Sept., 10 Dec. 1819; 26 April 1830; 4 May 1831; 2 May 1832; RG 3, journals, 1813; RG 16, land registry records, conveyance reg., liber 17: f.328; liber 20: f.78; liber 24: ff.400, 867, 872. P.E.I. Museum, "Charlottetown manuscript" (n.d.); W. F. Goff coll., Goff family geneal. PRO, CO 226/26: 11, 112; 226/27: 82–88; 226/29: 88. St Paul's Anglican Church (Charlottetown), Reg. of baptisms, marriages, and burials, esp. 1 Aug. 1834 (mfm. at PAPEI). Supreme Court of P.E.I. (Charlottetown), Estates Division, liber 3: f.110. P.E.I., House of Assembly, *Journal*, 3–4 Nov. 1818; Legislative Council, *Journal*, 1832–36. *Prince Edward Island Gazette*, 14 Oct. 1818. *Prince Edward Island Register*, 6 May 1825, 21 March 1826, 2 Dec. 1828. *Royal Gazette* (Charlottetown), 7 Feb., 3 April 1832; 9 April 1833; 18 March 1834; 12 Jan. 1836. *Weekly Recorder of Prince Edward Island* (Charlottetown), 4 May 1812. MacKinnon, *Government of P.E.I.*, 36n. *Patriot* (Charlottetown), 6 July 1872.

GOHN. *See* JOHN

GONISH (Ganishe), PETER (Piel, Pier), Micmac captain; fl. 1841–46 in New Brunswick.

The Tabusintac Indian Reserve was created by the New Brunswick government following receipt of a memorial by 14 Indians dated September 1801. Six of those who made their marks were from the Gonish family. The family continued prominent. In 1841 John and Étienne Gonish were elected second or petit chiefs to serve under Noel Briot, grand chief of the Indians of the Miramichi; Peter Gonish was a captain.

Peter Gonish was one of those who met Captain Henry Dunn O'Halloran on his tour of New Brunswick in 1841. That evangelical army captain inspired the "three chiefs mission" which created so much displeasure at the Colonial Office in London in 1842 [*see* Joseph MALIE]. In July 1843 the government of New Brunswick learned that another Micmac was planning to go to Britain. Alarmed, the lieutenant governor's secretary, Alfred Reade, gave instructions that Indian commissioner Moses Henry Perley* should "strongly urge on him the extreme impropriety" of going, and, if he did go, Reade promised to tell the home government that he had left wife and family destitute behind him. For good measure, Reade quoted to Perley some of the acidulous comments the previous visit had elicited from the colonial secretary.

Gonish nevertheless went to Britain, accompanied by another Micmac, Joseph Dominic. Their object was to seek financial aid to improve and stock their farms. They travelled to New York, took ship to

Liverpool, and there, penniless, were forced to pawn their clothes. They then crossed to Dublin and walked through Ireland to visit O'Halloran. He received them well and sent them on to London where they were helped by, among others, the famous American ethnologist and artist George Catlin. He arranged to redeem their clothes. They were then directed to the Aborigines Protection Society where they were recognized by another visitor to London, none other than Reade, the very man who had tried to head them off. Having come so far, the two announced that they wished to go to Paris to be presented to the king of France; they would, they said, claim his assistance and the support of their French fellow Catholics. Reade gave them "present help," dissuaded them from visiting France, and kept them away from the Colonial Office.

Gonish and Dominic returned to New Brunswick, presumably at some time late in 1844. Gonish was last heard of in 1846 when he applied for relief on behalf of his band. It was a time of extreme suffering due to the failure of the potato crop, but the missionary Michael P. Egan tartly observed that Gonish had no authorization from the other Indians to ask for aid: "His object is *self*."

L. F. S. UPTON

PANB, RG 1, RS345, A2: 118–19; RG 2, RS7, 40, M. H. Perley to W. F. Odell, 2 Oct. 1843; RS8, Indians, 1/4, M. P. Egan to J. B. Toldevray, 2 March 1846. UNBL, MG H54, memorial, 26 Sept. 1801. Aborigines' Protection Soc., *Proc.* (London), 1844: 2–3. *Source materials relating to N.B. Indian* (Hamilton and Spray). Upton, *Micmacs and colonists*.

GOSFORD, ARCHIBALD ACHESON, 2nd Earl of. *See* ACHESON

GOSSELIN, LÉON (baptized **Antoine-Léon**), lawyer, journalist, newspaper proprietor, and office holder; b. 24 Dec. 1801 in L'Assomption, Lower Canada, son of Joseph Gosselin, a miller, and Thérèse Viger; m. Mary Graddon, and they had at least two children; d. 1 June 1842 in Montreal.

Through his mother Léon Gosselin was related to the powerful network of Viger, Papineau, and Cherrier families. He was the nephew of Louis-Michel Viger* and Joseph PAPINEAU, and the cousin of Louis-Joseph Papineau* and Denis-Benjamin Viger*. Having studied at the Petit Séminaire de Montréal from 1811 to 1819, he chose to go into law. He was called to the bar on 6 Dec. 1828, but it is not known if he practised at this time. In 1830 he was one of the group gathered around Ludger Duvernay*, the proprietor of *La Minerve*. He was probably already involved in editorial work for the paper, a task in which he is thought to have replaced Augustin-Norbert Morin*, who from 1830 was burdened with responsibilities as a member of the House of Assembly.

Early in 1832 Gosselin succeeded Morin as editor. Duvernay was in prison for libelling the Legislative Council. In February Gosselin believed that he too was at risk and went into hiding for a time. *La Minerve* was then the radical organ of the Patriote party in Montreal, but since the journalists did not sign their articles, it is difficult to identify what Gosselin himself wrote. In 1837 one of his critics declared in *La Quotidienne* that from his short stay at *La Minerve* Gosselin was remembered as a "confirmed revolutionary." "It was he who published the famous article signed S and thereby almost provoked an uprising among the population. Mr GOSSELIN is known to have let the author state in this article that only an immediate revolution could save the country by wresting it from the domination of the British party."

In 1832 Gosselin envisaged publishing "a gazette of the Canadian and American courts." This project, which would have allowed him to combine his legal training with his interest in journalism, was not carried out, however. In December 1832 his wife, Mary Graddon, succeeded in launching the *Montreal Museum, or Journal of Literature and Arts*, the first periodical in Lower Canada addressed to women and founded by a woman. Gosselin's role in this venture was probably minimal. At most he acted as intermediary between his wife and Duvernay, in whose shop the printing was done.

On 4 Sept. 1834 Gosselin suddenly resigned from *La Minerve* and was immediately replaced by Hyacinthe-Poirier Leblanc* de Marconnay. It is thought that he then began practising law. Late in 1835 he applied for the post of French translator to the assembly. He had the support of Louis-Joseph Papineau but ran up against the hostility of the members from Quebec city who were of more moderate political leanings. In the end he was passed over. In consequence he is believed to have begun distancing himself from the Patriotes in the course of 1836. The break, however, was apparently not final at the time Gosselin founded *Le Populaire*, which was first issued on 10 April 1837 with Leblanc de Marconnay as editor.

This bi-weekly newspaper had no distinctive character. Its four pages contained material commonly published in the newspapers of the period. Nevertheless provincial matters had the largest share of space, such a stress reflecting the many controversies of the day. The editor claimed that *Le Populaire* had reached a run of 1,400 in its second month, despite instructions from Papineau in the late spring to boycott it. The combined effects of the boycott, delivery problems connected with the uprising of November–December 1837, and the hostility of some postmasters, may, however, explain the financial difficulties that *Le Populaire* experienced in March 1838. Printers John Lovell* and Ronald Macdonald* had not been paid for some time, and on 16 March they refused to print the paper. *Le Populaire* ceased publication for nearly a month, and then came out again on 12 April, declaring that it had been the victim of a political plot. Gosselin's name was no longer on the paper, although it is not known if he had given up his ownership. On 3 Nov. 1838 the newspaper disappeared suddenly, with no explanation.

Le Populaire had suffered the repercussions of a difficult situation. Its first issue came out on the very day that news of Lord John Russell's resolutions reached Lower Canada, and its disappearance coincided with the departure for England of Lord Durham [LAMBTON]. The intervening period saw the events that culminated in the first rebellion, in November 1837. *Le Populaire* endeavoured to hold to a middle course. It favoured respect for the established authorities, but considered it had a duty to criticize and enlighten them. Consequently it supported Governor Lord Gosford [ACHESON], and then, with greater reservations, Sir John Colborne*. Lord Durham enjoyed its backing and trust. According to *Le Populaire*, all the troubles were the fault of extremists; its sympathies, therefore, did not follow ethnic lines. Having once stood up for Papineau's activity, the paper then opposed it and condemned the rebellion; under Colborne it moved closer to the Patriotes. In fact *Le Populaire* sought to defend a moderate position, but as it reacted to one situation after another, it was at times carried to the left or right.

In the Manichean context of the period such a position was not easy to maintain. Public opinion sometimes seemed bewildered by *Le Populaire*'s stance. An editorial of 12 April 1838 recognized this confusion: "Distressing circumstances and the desire to avoid calamities may for a while have misled some people about the true course of a newspaper whose title indicates its purpose clearly enough." A reiteration of principles was therefore necessary. "*Le Populaire* is *liberal* in its essence, and *loyal* in its actions; it offers good government all the support it is entitled to expect from subjects who are thinking solely of the country's prosperity." When accused of harbouring anti-Canadian sentiments, the paper proclaimed that "patriotism is not the property of a handful of individuals who could be mistaken, but resides with the mass of the people."

Its uneasy position made the paper vulnerable to hostile attack. For the *Montreal Herald* and the *Montreal Gazette*, the publishers of *Le Populaire* were "rabid enemies of all Britons." *Le Libéral* (Québec) called the paper "obscene," and *La Quotidienne* saw it as hostile to Canadian interests. With the *Vindicator and Canadian Advertiser* (Montreal) there was open warfare. Even with *L'Ami du peuple, de l'ordre et des lois*, which was of about the same tendency as *Le Populaire*, the arguments were vehement. The paper found favour only in the eyes of *Le Canadien*.

The hostility of the die-hard Patriotes may explain these generally unfavourable assessments. *Le Populaire* was also one of the few French-language newspapers never bothered by the authorities, a fact that laid it open to deep suspicion. But, above all, it seems clear that the personalities of its prime movers weighed heavily in how the paper was regarded. Gosselin and Leblanc de Marconnay were labelled traitors and turncoats for a long time. Behind them stood the figures of Clément-Charles Sabrevois* de Bleury and Pierre-Dominique DEBARTZCH, former Patriotes who had compromised themselves deeply with the government. Debartzch was often mentioned as one of the founders of *Le Populaire*, indeed as one of the secret proprietors.

In August 1840 Gosselin asked for the post of sheriff in a district court. At the time Upper and Lower Canada were united one of his articles was published in *Le Fantasque* (Québec) of 16 Nov. 1840. It attacked the views that Louis-Hippolyte La Fontaine* had earlier set out in his address to the voters of Terrebonne, published in *L'Aurore des Canadas* on 28 August. The ideas then defended by Gosselin were close to those of the young radicals who circulated this issue of *Le Fantasque* widely. In this period Gosselin reputedly refused a proposal from Governor Lord Sydenham [THOMSON] to found a newspaper defending government interests.

After a lengthy illness Gosselin died on 1 June 1842. None of the Lower Canadian newspapers carried an obituary. At the time of his death he was deputy registrar of the district of Montreal, hardly a prestigious office for a man who had taken part in the most violent controversies of his time.

Léon Gosselin, it is true, does not appear to have been a leading figure. His career as a journalist and newspaper proprietor was rather short. But although his political progress was not unusual, it is not without interest. A Patriote, then a moderate reformer during the 1837–38 rebellions, he seems to have returned to a more radical reformism. All his life he remained removed from the seat of power and seems never to have been tempted by a political career. Perhaps he died too young to show his true abilities.

GÉRARD LAURENCE

ANQ-M, CE1-51, 4 juin 1842; CE5-14, 24 déc. 1801. ANQ-Q, P-68. "Papiers Duvernay," *Canadian Antiquarian and Numismatic Journal*, 3rd ser., 6: 116. *L'Ami du peuple, de l'ordre et des lois*, 28 mars 1838. *Le Canadien*, 1er oct. 1832, 23 mars 1838. *Montreal Museum, or Journal of Literature and Arts*, December 1832–March 1834. *Le*

Populaire, 18 mai 1832; 10 avril, 15 mai, 19 juin, 13 oct. 1837; 12 avril, 28 mai, 4, 20, 25 juin 1838. *La Quotidienne* (Montréal), 28 déc. 1837. F.-J. Audet, "Commissions d'avocats," *BRH*, 39 (1933): 585. Beaulieu et Hamelin, *La presse québécoise*, vol.1. Fauteux, *Patriotes*, 157. I.[-F.-T.] Lebrun, *Tableau statistique et politique des deux Canadas* (Paris, 1833). Filteau, *Hist. des patriotes* (1938–42), 1: 213. J.-P. de Lagrave, *Les journalistes-démocrates du Bas-Canada, 1791–1840* (Montréal, 1975). J.-M. Lebel, "Ludger Duvernay et *La Minerve*: étude d'une entreprise de presse montréalaise de la première moitié du XIXe siècle" (thèse de MA, univ. Laval, Québec, 1982). Mauràult, *Le collège de Montréal* (Dansereau; 1967). Monet, *La première révolution tranquille*. Rumilly, *Papineau et son temps*, 1: 428. J.-J. Lefebvre, "La famille Viger: le maire Jacques Viger (1858); ses parents – ses descendants – ses alliés," SGCF *Mémoires*, 17 (1966): 201–38; "Pierre-Dominique Debartzch, 1782–1846," *Rev. trimestrielle canadienne*, 27 (1941): 179–200. Benjamin Sulte, "Leblanc de Marconnay," *BRH*, 18 (1912): 353–54.

GRADY. *See* O'GRADY

GRANT, COLIN P., Roman Catholic priest; b. *c.* 1784 in Glen Moriston, Scotland, son of Duncan Grant and Helena Chisholm; d. 31 March 1839 at Malignant Cove, N.S.

Colin P. Grant was the son of a Presbyterian father and a Roman Catholic mother. An excellent horseman, he first intended to join the army but was persuaded by his mother's side of the family to enter the priesthood. His theological studies were completed at the College of Killechiarain in Lismore, Scotland, where, along with Alexander MACDONELL, who would also serve in Nova Scotia, he was ordained by his cousin, Bishop John Chisholm, on Easter Sunday, 17 April 1808. Following ordination he served as a missionary in the Highlands for a period of ten years. In 1818 he decided to leave for Upper Canada, perhaps in response to one of the many calls being made for more priests in British North America. He intended to serve there under another Highland Catholic cleric, the well-known Reverend Alexander McDONELL, vicar general of Upper Canada.

Arriving in Nova Scotia in August 1818, Grant was asked by Bishop Edmund Burke* to serve temporarily at Arisaig and Antigonish, N.S. Burke's request for Grant's assistance came as the result of the death of the Reverend William Chisholm, who had been serving the Highlanders in the northeastern part of the province. In 1819 Bishop Joseph-Octave Plessis* of Quebec and McDonell of Upper Canada gave permission for Grant to serve in Nova Scotia, and in that year he was incardinated into the new vicariate. He served in Antigonish and its vicinity for almost a year and then moved to Arisaig, about 20 miles north of Antigonish, where he worked for approximately 11 years as a missionary.

From Arisaig Grant covered the territory along the gulf shore, and for some time he served the Pictou region as well. Keenly interested in education, he established a number of elementary schools in his district during the years from 1819 to 1828, including ones at Arisaig, McCara's (McArras) Brook, and Cape St George (Cape George). He enlarged the church at Arisaig and is believed to have been responsible for the building of a small chapel at North Side Cape George (Morar) on the gulf shore.

Though Grant was a man of splendid physique, the heavy labour of his large pastoral area affected his health and by 1828 he was seeking a replacement. He was praised by all as a missionary priest and had many friends among the Presbyterian Scots, who appreciated his kindness and compassion. Grant was especially friendly with the famous Gaelic bard Iain MACGHILLEATHAIN, a Presbyterian. It was stated that on one occasion Grant gave MacGhillEathain a snuff-box containing not only snuff but five pounds of gold. In February 1829 Grant resigned his charge because of poor health but agreed to attend to necessary calls until a replacement could be found. Bishop William Fraser* had many calls for pastors throughout eastern Nova Scotia, and so it was not until October 1830 that Grant was replaced by the Reverend William Bernard MacLeod, the first native-born priest of the present diocese of Antigonish.

Upon retirement Grant bought a small farm at Malignant Cove, near Arisaig. Although he was very poor his neighbours did not wish to offend his pride by offering help. Thus, his last years were sad ones; burdened with poor health and poverty, he endured further embarrassment when imprisoned briefly for debt in 1838. He died on 31 March 1839, on the 31st anniversary of his ordination to the priesthood, and was buried in the old cemetery at Lower South River. His grave was covered by an unpolished slab of stone which bore no inscription. Years after his death a subscription was raised to erect a suitable monument over his grave, and by December 1887 this goal had been accomplished.

Grant was one of a significant number of Highland priests to work in Nova Scotia during the late 18th and early 19th centuries. Through the efforts of those early missionaries, northeastern Nova Scotia became a bastion of Roman Catholicism in British North America.

R. A. MACLEAN

AAQ, 312 CN, VI: 136a (copy at Arch. of the Diocese of Antigonish, N.S.). Arch. of Scots College (Pontifical) (Rome), Vicars Apostolic, William Fraser to Angus MacDonald, 8 Oct. 1828 (copy at Arch. of the Diocese of Antigonish). Arch. of the Diocese of Antigonish, Files of the diocesan historian, A. A. Johnston, manuscript sketches, no.105 (C. P. Grant). PANS, MG 100, 103, no.34. *Colonial*

Patriot, 28 March 1828. *Filidh na coille: dain agus orain leis a bhaird Mac-Gillean, agus le Feadhainn Eile . . .* , ed. A. MacL. Sinclair (Charlottetown, 1901), 12, 103. A. A. Johnston, *A history of the Catholic Church in eastern Nova Scotia* (2v., Antigonish, 1960–71). Ronald McDonald, *The earliest Highland Catholic mission in Nova Scotia: a sermon preached at the dedication of the Church of St. Margaret's, Arisaig, July 16th, 1878* (Pictou, N.S., 1878), 10. [Sagart Arisaig (Ronald MacGillivray)], *History of Antigonish*, ed. R. A. MacLean (2v., [Antigonish], 1976), 2: 64. *Casket* (Antigonish), 8 Dec. 1887: 2. C. S. MacDonald, "Early Highland emigration to Nova Scotia and Prince Edward Island from 1770–1853" and "West Highland emigrants in eastern Nova Scotia," N.S. Hist. Soc., *Coll.*, 23 (1936): 41–48 and 32 (1959): 1–30. Sagart Arisaig [Ronald MacGillivray], "History of Antigonish, ch.XIV," *Casket*, 15 Oct. 1891: 2.

GRANT, PETER, fur trader; b. *c.* 1764 in Scotland, probably in Glen Moriston; d. 20 July 1848 in Lachine, Lower Canada.

Peter Grant joined the North West Company as a clerk in 1784, probably through the influence of John Grant, a Lachine shipper and forwarder and apparently his brother. His earliest assignments were to the Lower Red River where, according to Alexander Henry* the younger, he established the first post at Pembina (N.Dak.). In 1789 the NWC sent him to Lac Rouge (probably Red Lake, Minn.) with a trader named Desmarais and the following year, when its trader at Rainy Lake post (near Fort Frances, Ont.) became ill, it placed the two men in temporary charge of that important depot.

Passed over for promotion, Grant joined an independent venture initiated in 1792 by David Grant, whose relationship to him has not been determined. In 1790 David had become an NWC clerk, his two-year contract giving him the option on its expiry of taking £200 in wages or taking "a canoe of Merchandize on his own Account" from Grand Portage (near Grand Portage, Minn.) to any vacant post. Unsatisfactory financial returns at the contract's conclusion undoubtedly prompted the partnership in which he, Peter, and the Montreal house of Alexander and James Robertson each held a one-third interest.

In 1793 the two Grants began their adventure as free traders by staking out a site for their own depot at Grand Portage. No buildings had been erected, however, when they headed west, Peter making "his pitch" on the Qu'Appelle River some five leagues from John McDONELL's post. In 1794 Peter imprudently sent four canoes into the already over-crowded Red River region, where his posts, together with those of the Hudson's Bay and the Michilimackinac companies, numbered 14 to the NWC's 7. The Grants' ill-conceived opposition soon fell apart, with the Robertsons garnering the total returns for 1795. But in a suit launched by the NWC, the Robertsons too were to meet defeat the following year. Subsequent transactions resulted in their acquisition of the Grants' two-thirds interest but compelled them to transfer to the NWC the partnership's assets. As part of this arrangement the NWC offered Peter Grant a place in the company and £200 a year until a share fell vacant, but to David it offered nothing. Why it forgave Peter and not David, who returned to Montreal "a ruined man," is not clear.

Re-entering the NWC with a half-share, Peter became a full partner in 1797 with proprietorship of the Lac La Pluie department, then threatened by encroachments from the HBC. Grant's influence with the local Indians helped drive the intruders out of the region, into which, however, soon came another competitor, the New North West Company (sometimes called the XY Company). Departing the fray for his rotation to Montreal after the NWC's 1801 rendezvous, Grant had his leave interrupted near the end of 1802 when the company dispatched him to Sault Ste Marie (Ont.) to replace its agent there, who had drowned. In 1803 he attended the first rendezvous held at Kaministiquia (Thunder Bay, Ont.). The following year he produced a study of the Saulteaux Indians which, in the opinion of Louis-François-Rodrigue Masson*, was the "most complete and elaborate" of the accounts produced by NWC partners for Roderick MACKENZIE's intended publication on North American Indians. The study, Masson concluded, reveals Grant as "one of the keenest observers which the North-West Company had among its members."

In 1805 Grant retired, settling at Sainte-Anne-de-Bout-de-l'Île (Sainte-Anne-de-Bellevue), Lower Canada, in a great stone house now known as the Thomas Moore House. He moved around 1820 to Lachine, where he died in 1848. During his long and apparently tranquil retirement, he seems to have indulged his interest in family affairs almost exclusively; although he joined the Beaver Club in 1807, he seldom attended. Grant was the father of at least three mixed-blood children – two daughters and a son. Sharing his last decades were his daughter Mary and another son or nephew, Peter. His other daughter and her Indian mother remained at Rainy Lake and pleaded for financial support in 1816. While still in the Indian country, Grant had received similar pleas from impoverished relatives in the Highlands, where most farmers "will soon be shepherds." The sensitivity of his family correspondence and of his writings on Indians suggests his likely compliance with these appeals from his Scottish and Indian relatives.

JEAN MORRISON

[The author wishes to thank the following for their invaluable assistance: Raymond Dumais, W. Kaye Lamb, Hugh MacMillan, and Victoria Stewart. J.M.]

Peter Grant's study of the Saulteaux Indians was published with numerous editorial changes under the title "The Sauteux Indians about 1804" in *Les bourgeois de la Compagnie du Nord-Ouest* (Masson), 2: 303–66. The original manuscript, entitled "An account of the Souteux Indians" ([1804?]), is at the MTRL.

ANQ-M, CE1-124, 22 juill. 1848; CN1-29, 29 janv. 1790, 5 mars 1796. AO, MU 572. PAC, MG 19, B1, 1: 21, 41, 115, 160; B3: 7, 76; E1, ser.1: 8612; RG 8, I (C ser.), 363: 18. Presbyterian Church in Canada Arch. (Toronto), St Gabriel Street Church (Montreal), reg. of baptisms, 1798, 1804–6 (mfm. at AO). UTFL, MS coll. 31, box 24, file 7. *Les bourgeois de la Compagnie du Nord-Ouest* (Masson), 1: 32, 66, 284. *Docs. relating to NWC* (Wallace). *Five fur traders of the northwest . . .* , ed. C. M. Gates ([2nd ed.], St Paul, Minn., 1965). Simon Fraser, *The letters and journals of Simon Fraser, 1806–1808*, ed. W. K. Lamb (Toronto, 1960). Duncan McGillivray, *The journal of Duncan M'Gillivray of the North West Company at Fort George on the Saskatchewan, 1794–5*, ed. and intro. A. S. Morton (Toronto, 1929). Alexander Mackenzie, *The journals and letters of Sir Alexander Mackenzie*, ed. W. K. Lamb (Toronto, 1970). *New light on the early history of the greater northwest: the manuscript journals of Alexander Henry . . . and of David Thompson . . .* , ed. Elliott Coues (3v., New York, 1897; repr. 3v. in 2, Minneapolis, Minn., [1965]), 1: 80–81. Campbell, *Hist. of Scotch Presbyterian Church*. W. S. Wallace, *The pedlars from Quebec and other papers on the Nor'Westers* (Toronto, 1954). E. A. Mitchell, "The North West Company agreement of 1795," *CHR*, 36 (1955): 126–45.

GRECE, CHARLES FREDERICK, specialist in hemp production and JP; d. 12 March 1844 in Sainte-Thérèse-de-Blainville (Sainte-Thérèse), Lower Canada.

Charles Frederick Grece immigrated to Montreal in the autumn of 1805 as part of a costly but fruitless endeavour by the imperial and colonial governments to launch the cultivation of hemp in Lower Canada at the turn of the 19th century. Various factors underlay this interest: a growing scarcity of supplies from Europe because of war and the continental blockade, the British navy's urgent need of hemp for rope, and the necessity to diversify agricultural production in Lower Canada so that it would fit the Atlantic market economy better.

After the failure of a modest attempt under Lord Dorchester [Carleton*], the idea re-emerged under pressures at home and from abroad and by 1800 consideration was being given to making subsidies and uncultivated lands available. In 1801, while recognizing the difficulty of getting good seed, the Executive Council of Lower Canada recommended that small-scale experiments be conducted and subsidies be granted. Isaac Winslow Clarke and William Grant* were appointed agents for purchasing hemp by Lieutenant Governor Sir Robert Shore MILNES, and they carried out experiments; Clarke even sent 2,584 pounds of marketable hemp to England in 1802. Under pressure from London, Milnes set up two permanent committees, one in Montreal and the other at Quebec, gave encouragement to the agents – Clarke received a gold medal from the London Society for the Encouragement of Arts, Manufactures, and Commerce in 1804 – had the House of Assembly vote a £1,200 subsidy (the act was renewed in 1804), distributed small quantities of seed, and guaranteed producers a "generous price." Few people came forward: Clarke, Grant, and two others, Philippe Robin (from the island of Jersey) and Philemon WRIGHT, who both demanded grants and enormous areas of land – Robin wanted 20,000 acres and Wright 10,000. However, various studies were circulating around the province, John Taylor's by 1802 and Charles Taylor's from 1806, and the newspapers encouraged farmers to take up growing hemp. The government increased its pressure, on the Sulpicians among others. The agents, and even seigneurs such as Charles-Louis Tarieu* de Lanaudière, promoted the idea and two specialists arrived from London, Grece in 1805 and James Campbell* in 1806.

Grece had a brother, John William, who had been in the grain trade between England and Prussia and had offered in 1804 to launch the growing of flax and hemp in Lower Canada in exchange for a township or 50,000 acres along the Ottawa River. The Board of Trade had offered Charles Grece and James Campbell an advance of £400 and apparently 150 acres of cleared land, the advance to be repaid if the terms of the proposed agreement were not met. On arriving in Montreal, Grece was not given the cleared land that had been promised, but he received, from the date of his sailing on 17 Oct. 1805, £200 a year, in addition to 75 bushels of poor quality seed and 100 copies of Charles Taylor's brochure. In 1806 the Executive Council, which did not consider itself authorized to buy a piece of uncleared land, recommended an advance of £300 and an allowance of 10 shillings per acre for the rental of a suitable property.

This inaction in the colony prompted Grece to have his brother intervene with the British government. He sought compensation, since he had bought land near Montreal and put up buildings at great cost. Instructions were sent to the colony that 150 acres were to be bought for Grece or that he be compensated in due proportion, if he had fulfilled the terms of his contract. After an initial and detailed investigation the Executive Council concluded in September 1807 that, taking into account the circumstances, including the poor quality of the seed, Grece had indeed fulfilled his obligations. A second investigation, this time into the cost of his buildings, led the council to recommend that 75 acres be bought for Grece at a cost not to exceed £750, on condition that he pay the balance in merchandise and receive £20 a year from the government. The council considered, in fact, that he had no grounds for complaint, since the rent for his land was being paid for him above and beyond the £200 annual salary he was receiving. In 1808 Governor Sir James Henry Craig* expressed his satisfaction with Grece. Yet in 1811 Grece again had to beg for the 150 acres that had been promised by London and for compensation for the £346 he had invested in putting up his buildings. The Executive Council merely recommended that the land being worked by Grece be rented at a reasonable price for five or seven years, to allow him to present his grievances before the Board of Trade. The latter ratified this proposal, but Grece was still pressing his claims in 1814. Then his trail is all but lost, only a few further facts being known about him. In 1820 and 1824, for example, he made application for new lands at Longue-Pointe (Montreal), where he was then living. Again, he received commissions as justice of the peace in 1831, 1833, and 1837. The final renewal was on 31 Dec. 1838, and at this date all trace is lost of Grece until his death, which occurred on 12 March 1844.

Despite the injection of more than £40,000 of private and public capital between 1806 and 1809, efforts to stimulate the growing of hemp had all failed. Grece attributed the failure to the swift expansion of the lumber industry and of trade in general, whence the excessively high cost of manpower. Craig was of the same opinion. Campbell and John Lambert* would speak of conspiracy and the deliberate importation of spoiled seed. The responsibility of the imperial and colonial governments, which refused to commit themselves to an adequate financial effort, cannot be denied. These factors counted much more than the alleged opposition of the Canadians which has been attributed to their ignorance and prejudices.

JEAN-PIERRE WALLOT

Charles Frederick Grece is the author of *Essays on husbandry, addressed to the Canadian farmers* (Montreal, 1817) and *Facts and observations respecting Canada and the United States of America: affording a comparative view of the inducement to emigration in those countries . . .* (London, 1819).

PAC, MG 11, [CO 42] Q, 87-1: 243–50; 87-2: 424; 88: 2, 90, 150–55, 175; 89: 4, 70, 75, 79, 90, 249; 90: 334–45; 91: 15–18; 97A: 44; 100: 10, 241–65; 101-2: 369; 102: 44, 256; 103: 20; 104: 210–11; 105: 80–86; 106-2: 305, 395, 400–1; 107: 159, 322; 117-1: 104–9, 144–46; 117-2: 185; 119: 211; 128-1: 196; MG 17, A7-2, 5; RG 1, E1, 31; 33; L3[L]: 5428–31; 47829–910, 47913–36; RG 7, G1, 1–2; RG 68, General index, 1651–1841. UCC, Montreal Presbytery, St Therese de Blainville (Sainte-Thérèse), reg. of burials, 16 March 1844. John Lambert, *Travels through Lower Canada, and the United States of North America, in the years 1806, 1807, and 1808* . . . (3v., London, 1810), 1: 468–69. L.C., House of Assembly, *Journals*, 1800–12. Charles Taylor, *Remarks on the culture and preparation of hemp in Canada* . . . (Quebec, 1806). *Le Courier de Québec*, 1807–8. *Quebec Gazette*, 1792–1824. Hare et Wallot, *Les imprimés dans le Bas-Canada*, nos.35, 123, 137, 201(E), 250(E), 264. "Papiers d'État – Bas-Canada," PAC *Rapport*, 1892. Maurice Séguin, *La "Nation canadienne" et l'agriculture (1760–1850): essai d'histoire économique* (Trois-Rivières, Qué., 1970). Douglas Brymner, "Rapport sur les Archives du Canada," PAC *Rapport*, 1891: xlii.

GRIFFITH, JOHN, chair-manufacturer and shopkeeper; m. 18 Aug. 1825 Sarah McGinnis in Montreal, and they had ten children; fl. 1825–47.

John Griffith's origins and the date of his arrival in Montreal are obscure. His name does not appear in the Montreal directory of 1819 but by 1825, when he was married by the Reverend John Bethune* of Christ Church, he was described as a "resident of this place." It is unlikely that he was in business for himself in 1825. Within a few years, however, he had established a chair manufactory in the *faubourg* Quebec, one of Montreal's eastern suburbs. That his manufactory existed in the early 1830s is indicated by his trade cards or furniture labels; they were supplied by George Perkins BULL, a printer who worked in Montreal from 1831 to 1833.

Early Montreal chair-makers (as distinct from cabinet-makers, who worked in finer, often imported woods) produced inexpensive furniture that needed paint or varnish as a finish. They therefore almost always dealt also in paints, and Griffith followed that practice. He had begun work as a painter – he was so described at the time of his marriage – and his furniture label stressed this aspect of his activities: "John Griffith, house, sign and ornamental painter, chair maker &c." Over the years he continued to offer sign painting, "neatly executed," as one of his services. He sold paints of all kinds, including artists' supplies, but it was as a manufacturer of painted furniture, particularly chairs, that he sought to achieve prominence. In the 1830s his occupational listing in official records changed from painter to chair-maker.

By 1840 Griffith had not only a factory in the suburbs, but also a large rented furniture warehouse on Rue Saint-Paul, then Montreal's main shopping area. He launched into the wholesale as well as the retail trade. In 1843 he was advertising a stock of 2,000 chairs: cane-seated, rush-seated, and Windsor. He kept on hand bedsteads, tables, and wash-stands, and was the maker of what were called "fancy chairs." Occasional traces of the original painted decoration on these fancy chairs indicate top rails embellished with fruit or flower designs. The turned legs were sometimes meant to simulate bamboo, an imitation that would, when the chairs were new, have been emphasized by the paint work. "Many different patterns" of chairs, all warranted of superior quality, was the theme of his advertisements. He held trade auctions when as many as 700 chairs were sold at a time.

Few Montreal chair-makers of the first half of the 19th century identified their work in any way, a fact that now makes attributions hazardous. Griffith used printed labels, some of which have survived intact on the undersides of the chairs, and he also branded many of his pieces, "GRIFFITH/MONTREAL." He worked at a period when a number of chair-makers were active in Montreal, but with both a factory and a sales outlet he had facilities few of his rivals could claim. That he was well thought of by fellow workers in the trade is indicated by his appearance as a witness at baptisms and burials for a number of chair- or cabinet-makers or members of their families. Although he had been married in the Anglican faith and had his first five children baptized at Christ Church, he later turned to the St James Street Methodist Church, where many of his fellow chair- and cabinet-makers, including John Hilton*, were members.

For more than a dozen years Griffith's business prospered. He also invested in real estate. In 1846 six "valuable" building lots owned by him were offered for sale. That sale was probably a portent of financial difficulties. The next year the lease of his warehouse on Rue Saint-Paul, a "first-rate Stand" for business, was put up for auction. Griffith was bankrupt: his household furniture and all his stock were sold. There was one last echo of his days in the Montreal furniture trade. In 1850 a William Griffith who may have been his eldest son was operating a paint shop at the old address on Rue Saint-Paul, but that venture was brief.

Griffith came to the chair-making trade with large ambitions. It was his misfortune that chair-making as distinct from cabinet-making was on the way out. By the 1860s the Montreal directories, in their classification of trades, no longer regularly included chair-making as a separate category. The cabinet-maker who could offer both cheap chairs and fine furniture had already begun to absorb the chair business by the 1840s. Steam factories replaced the type of workshop Griffith had established in the 1830s. For a while, however, his name had loomed large in the Montreal trade.

ELIZABETH COLLARD

Several chairs made by John Griffith are in the Canadian Museum of Civilization (Ottawa) and there are others, including a few with their identifying label, in private collections.

ANQ-M, CE1-63, 18 août 1825, 21 mai 1826, 3 févr. 1828, 28 mars 1830, 9 avril 1831; CE1-109, 22 juin, 17 juill. 1833; 10 sept. 1835; 6 avril 1837; 17 avril 1839; 3 janv. 1844. *La Minerve*, 29 mai 1843. *Montreal Gazette*, 20 Aug. 1825; 5 Nov. 1831; 2 March, 6 April 1833; 9 May 1844; 24 May 1845; 28 April, 20 Oct. 1847; 21, 31 May 1849. *Montreal Transcript*, 2 April 1840; 14 Sept. 1843; 9, 14 May, 8 Oct. 1844; 2 May 1846; 24 April 1847. *Pilot* (Montreal), 15 April 1848. *Montreal directory*, 1842–47. Elizabeth Collard, "Montreal cabinetmakers and chairmakers, 1800–1850: a checklist," *Antiques* (New York), 105 (January–June 1974): 1132–46.

GROSSET. *See* DUVERNET

GUGY, LOUIS (Jean-Georges-Barthélemy-Guillaume-Louis), seigneur, militia officer, office holder, JP, and politician; b. January 1770 in Paris, son of Barthélemy Gugy and Jeanne-Élisabeth Teissier; m. 27 Feb. 1795 Juliana O'Connor in London, and they had nine children, including Bartholomew Conrad Augustus*; d. 17 July 1840 in Montreal.

Louis Gugy's family came from Switzerland and had a tradition of military service. It is not surprising, then, to find him serving in France in 1791 as a lieutenant of a regiment of Swiss Guards under his father's command. For political reasons Gugy had to leave France the following year. He chose to go to Switzerland, where he lived for two years. Subsequently he set off from London for Quebec, disembarking on 26 June 1794. His purpose in coming was to take possession, in his father's name, of the estate of his uncle Conrad Gugy*. Although he stayed only a couple of months, he became convinced that he should return to settle permanently. After their marriage in London, Gugy and his wife, accompanied by Barthélemy Gugy and his family, sailed on the brig *Betsey* on 30 May 1795. They reached Quebec on 8 July.

Barthélemy Gugy had inherited from his brother Conrad the seigneuries of Grandpré and Dumontier, as well as half, less seven *arpents*, of the seigneury of Grosbois. He and his family moved into the manor-house at Yamachiche. At his death on 19 April 1797, Louis became the owner of the property. He continued to live at Yamachiche until at least 1799, but then chose to settle in Trois-Rivières.

Louis's rapid rise to prominence began with his appointment as sheriff of Trois-Rivières on 13 Aug. 1805. He had been a justice of the peace for the district since 1803, and his commission was renewed in 1805. Three years later he was made a commissioner for the relief of the insane and foundlings for the district of Trois-Rivières. He was commissioned in 1808 to administer the oath to those seeking land grants.

From 1803 Gugy was also active in the militia. He served first as lieutenant and adjutant, and then as captain in the 1st battalion of Trois-Rivières militia. On 19 May 1812 he was promoted major. Transferred on 18 March 1813 to the Berthier battalion of militia, he became its lieutenant-colonel on 25 September.

Along with all these activities Gugy was involved in politics. From 23 Nov. 1809 to 1 March 1810 he represented Saint-Maurice in the House of Assembly. Associated in many people's minds with the English party, he was accused of siding with Governor Sir James Henry Craig* to the detriment of the assembly.

On 25 April 1816 Gugy was re-elected in Saint-Maurice. He held his seat until he was appointed to the Legislative Council on 10 April 1818.

One of the élite in Trois-Rivières, Gugy was appointed commissioner for the improvement of internal communications in the district of Trois-Rivières in 1815 and commissioner to erect a court-house there in 1817. The following year he was named to the board examining applicants for the various posts of inspector of flour and meal. Five years later he became commissioner to carry out repairs on the Anglican church in Trois-Rivières, and in 1826 commissioner responsible for improving the road between Saint-Grégoire (Bécancour) and Longue Pointe in Kingsey Township.

On 3 March 1827 Gugy was appointed sheriff of Montreal and gave up the similar office in Trois-Rivières. The years leading up to the rebellion of 1837–38 were scarcely happy ones for him. During an election in Montreal West there were incidents on 21 May 1832 in which three Canadians were killed by the military [*see* Daniel Tracey*], and the leaders of the Canadian party accused Gugy of partiality in carrying out his duties. The sheriff's problems, however, were only beginning.

On 2 March 1836 a committee of the house examined the initial report of a special committee investigating the fees and revenues collected by sheriffs, protonotaries, and court ushers of the courts of Appeal and of King's Bench by virtue of their respective offices. It also studied a section of the report dealing with the death of John Collins in the Montreal jail in December 1835. The debate centred on Gugy. He was accused of fraud in his financial reports, of perjury during his examination by the special committee, and of negligence, both in supervising subordinate officers and in maintaining the prison. The assembly carried out the committee's recommendation that an address be sent to Governor Lord Gosford [ACHESON] asking him to dismiss Gugy from his office as sheriff and to deny him any position of honour or profit in the future. On 6 March 1836 the governor promised to take the appropriate measures, subject first to hearing Gugy's defence. Then the case was submitted to London, which in the spring of 1837 issued instructions that Gugy was to be dismissed as sheriff. In April Roch de Saint-Ours assumed the office. Three years later Gugy died in Montreal.

Louis Gugy's loyalty to the crown had been the outstanding feature of his career, and from this attachment came both his successes and his reverses.

RENALD LESSARD

ANQ-M, CN1-192, 22 sept. 1838. ANQ-MBF, CE1-50, 6 déc. 1795, 21 avril 1797; CN1-4, 19 mars 1794; CN1-5, 17 août 1789; CN1-6, 11 mars 1803; 20 mai, 15 juill. 1823; CN1-7, 27 juill. 1840; CN1-32, 2 mai 1818; 14, 25 mai 1821; 13, 26 juin 1822; 27 août 1824. ANQ-Q, E18/201, E: 211–25; K: 158–59; E21/297, 19/55, no.145; P-98/6; 10; P-365/9. ASQ, Polygraphie, XXXVI: 18D. PAC, RG 1, L3[L]: 554, 556, 587, 4038, 48772–75, 48985–9195; RG 4, A1: 40434, 41043; B45, 1: 26; B58, 15; RG 68, General index, 1651–1841. "Documents sur la famille Gugy," *BRH*, 36 (1930): 181–82. L.C., House of Assembly, *Journals*, 1832–33, app.V; 1834, app.S; 1835–36, app.VV, WW; Legislative Council, *Journaux*, 1819: 30–31. *Le Canadien*, 22 juill. 1840. *La Minerve*, 23 mars, 10 avril 1837. *Montreal Gazette*, 4, 8, 11 April 1837. *Quebec Gazette*, 3, 24 July 1794; 9 July 1795; 2 July 1807; 30 June 1808; 22 Sept. 1814; 8 June 1815; 15 May 1817; 25 June, 3 Sept. 1818; 24 May 1821. F.-J. Audet, *Les députés de Saint-Maurice (1808–1838) et de Champlain (1830–1838)* (Trois-Rivières, Qué., 1934); "Shérifs de Montréal," *BRH*, 8 (1902): 200. Desjardins, *Guide parl.*, 140. Juliette Dubé, "Inventaire analytique du fonds Édouard-Raymond Fabre," ANQ *Rapport*, 1972: 135, 138, 141–42, 144–48, 152–53. Hare et Wallot, *Les imprimés dans le Bas-Canada*, 229–31. Le Jeune, *Dictionnaire*, 1: 723. H. J. Morgan, *Sketches of celebrated Canadians*, 518–21. "Papiers d'État – Bas-Canada," PAC *Rapport*, 1897: 283. P.-G. Roy, "Shérifs de Trois-Rivières," *BRH*, 7 (1901): 356. Turcotte, *Le Conseil législatif*, 93. Raphaël Bellemare, *Les bases de l'histoire d'Yamachiche, 1703–1903 . . .* (Montréal, [1903]), 95–100, 291–95. E. H. Bovay, *Le Canada et les Suisses, 1604–1974* (Fribourg, Suisse, 1976), 9. Napoléon Caron, *Histoire de la paroisse d'Yamachiche (précis historique)* (Trois-Rivières, 1892), 27–28. Denison, *La première banque au Canada*, 1: 293. Germain Lesage, *Histoire de Louiseville, 1665–1960* (Louiseville, Qué., 1961), 136–37. Fernand Lefebvre, "La vie à la prison de Montréal au XIXe siècle," *RHAF*, 7 (1953–54): 524–37. É.-Z. Massicotte, "Famille Gugy," *BRH*, 23 (1917): 312–14; "Les shérifs de Montréal (1763–1823)," 29 (1923): 109.

GUY, LOUIS, JP, notary, office holder, militia officer, and politician; b. 27 June 1768 in Montreal, son of merchant and landowner Pierre Guy* and Marie-Josephte Hervieux; m. 19 Oct. 1795 Josette Curot of Montreal, and they had four sons and five daughters; d. there 17 Feb. 1850.

Louis Guy's family, one of the most distinguished in Montreal, traced its lineage back to Nicolas Guy of Paris, grand chamberlain to Louis XIV. Louis originally trained as a land surveyor. He spent the winter of 1791–92 at the College of New Jersey, in Princeton, in order to learn English; his brother Étienne* would attend a few years later. On his return Louis studied law under Joseph PAPINEAU and was commissioned a notary on 31 Aug. 1801. In this profession he had great success, being appointed king's notary in 1828. As such he executed the lucrative and copious notarial work required by the government and the military.

During the War of 1812 Guy served as major with the 5th Select Embodied Militia Battalion, taking part in the battle of Châteauguay under Lieutenant-Colonel Charles-Michel d'Irumberry* de Salaberry. Guy's continued interest in the militia after the war, when he spared neither time nor money to increase its efficiency, secured his promotion to colonel in 1830. He was one of the few Canadians to achieve this rank. During the reorganization of the militia in 1830, the governor, Sir James Kempt*, frequently sought his advice on matters concerning the Montreal militia.

Guy led the opposition among Canadians to the proposed union of Upper and Lower Canada in 1822. On 7 October in Montreal he presided over the first meeting of citizens opposed to the measure. With Louis-Joseph Papineau*, Denis-Benjamin Viger*, Pierre-Dominique DEBARTZCH, and other prominent men, he organized a constitutional committee in the city to campaign against union. On 10 July 1823 Guy informed the constitutional committees throughout the province that the agents they had sent to London to represent their interests, Papineau and John NEILSON, had accomplished their mission and that the union proposal had been shelved by the British government.

Guy tended thereafter to avoid popular politics, especially as the reform movement in the province became more strident under Papineau's leadership. His competence and ready assumption of public duties brought him numerous commissions. The first had been that of justice of the peace for the district of Montreal in April 1800. Then came a steady stream of appointments, including those of commissioner of roads and bridges in and around Montreal, warden of the House of Industry, census commissioner, and commissioner for the building of churches and parsonage houses, as well as a commission of oyer and terminer. On 20 Dec. 1830 he was named to the Legislative Council by Lord Aylmer [WHITWORTH-AYLMER] who, like his predecessor Kempt, had the highest regard for Guy.

Socially and financially secure, and gifted with energy, ability, and graciousness, Guy was one of the conservative leaders of the Canadian community who supported and worked within the established political system. Like the majority of the province's inhabitants, he discountenanced illegal opposition. Yet when fighting broke out between insurgents and government forces at Saint-Denis and Saint-Charles-sur-Richelieu in late November 1837, Guy hesitated to support the justices of the peace in Montreal when they resolved to ask the governor, Lord Gosford [ACHESON], to place the district under martial law. He resembled his close friend, Jacques Viger*, Montreal's first mayor, in hoping that the insurgency would be dealt with speedily by the military forces without resort to such measures. His son Louis, then an army officer, was with the troops specially selected by Sir John Colborne* for the task of mobilizing Montreal loyalist volunteers.

Guy remained a member of the Legislative Council until March 1838 and continued to practise as a notary until 1842. With his friend Viger, he shared an interest in the history of Lower Canada, and he was said to have been a noted amateur archaeologist.

ELINOR KYTE SENIOR

ANQ-M, CE1-51, 28 juin 1768, 19 oct. 1795, 17 oct. 1850. AUM, P 58. PAC, MG 11, [CO 42] Q, 239: 382; RG 68, General index, 1651–1841. *La Minerve*, 18 févr. 1850. *Montreal Gazette*, 20 Feb. 1850. Louis Guy, "Lettre de Louis Guy, président du comité constitutionnel de Montréal aux comités des comtés," *BRH*, 38 (1932): 443–46. C.-M. d'Irumberry de Salaberry, "Lettre de Charles de Salaberry à Louis Guy," *BRH*, 38: 135. L.-J. Papineau, "Lettres de Louis-Joseph Papineau à Louis Guy," *BRH*, 34 (1928): 81–104. F.-J. Audet, "Les législateurs du Bas-Canada." F.-M. Bibaud, *Le panthéon canadien* (A. et V. Bibaud; 1891). *Officers of British forces in Canada* (Irving). Turcotte, *Le Conseil législatif*. W. H. Atherton, *Montreal, 1535–1914* (3v., Montreal and Vancouver, 1914), 3. Chapais, *Cours d'hist. du Canada*, vol.3. François Daniel, *Notice sur la famille Guy et sur quelques autres familles* (Montréal, 1867).

GWILLIM, ELIZABETH POSTHUMA (Simcoe), gentlewoman, author, and artist; baptized 22 Sept. 1762 in Aldwincle, England, daughter of Lieutenant-Colonel Thomas Gwillim and Elizabeth Spinkes; m. 30 Dec. 1782 John Graves Simcoe*, and they had 11 children; d. 17 Jan. 1850 at Wolford Lodge, near Honiton, England.

After the death of Thomas Gwillim in 1762, his widow returned to her family's home in Northamptonshire, where Elizabeth Posthuma Gwillim was born. Mrs Gwillim died in childbirth, and was buried at Aldwincle the day after her only child's baptism. The orphan was looked after by her mother's younger sister Margaret, who married Admiral Samuel Graves at Aldwincle on 14 June 1769. While living with Admiral and Mrs Graves near Honiton, Devon, Elizabeth met the admiral's godson, John Graves Simcoe, in the spring of 1782, and they were married the same year.

The Simcoes began their married life in Exeter, where their first three children were born. Elizabeth was a wealthy woman, with extensive inheritances from both her father and her mother. In 1784 she bought the Wolford estate, consisting of about 5,000 acres near Honiton, where both Simcoes spent much time in improving the property. Elizabeth lived "secluded" at Wolford, giving birth almost every year to a daughter. Finally, in June 1791, the longed-for son was born.

That same year her husband was appointed lieutenant governor of the new province of Upper Canada, and on 26 September the Simcoes with their two youngest children sailed from Weymouth, leaving their four older daughters at Wolford. On 11 November they arrived at Quebec where they passed the winter, beginning their long trip into the interior the following spring. For a year Mrs Simcoe lived in Newark (Niagara-on-the-Lake), where another daughter was born, before she moved to York (Toronto) on 30 July 1793. She had intended leaving the baby at Queenston, as "we are only going among trees & musquitos," but the child died at York in the spring of 1794, during the absence of both her father and the Simcoes' doctor. After a summer at Newark, Mrs Simcoe took her children to Quebec because of the possibility of war with the United States. She returned to Upper Canada in the spring of 1795, but in 1796 her husband was granted leave of absence, and on 10 September the Simcoes sailed from Quebec, never to return to the Canadas.

The Simcoe family were reunited at Wolford, where they now entertained lavishly. For much of 1797 Simcoe himself was in St Domingo (Haiti) but his subsequent appointment as officer in command of the Western District with headquarters in Exeter, only 14 miles from Wolford, did not break the family circle. Two sons and two daughters were born between 1798 and 1804. In July 1806 he was named commander-in-chief in India. While his wife was preparing her outfit for the East, he was suddenly sent on an expedition to Portugal, where he became ill. Brought back to England, he died at Exeter on 26 Oct. 1806. After her husband's death, Mrs Simcoe remained at Wolford with her seven daughters, none of whom married during their mother's lifetime. She had become an enthusiastic evangelical within the Church of England, and spent much of her time in good works in addition to keeping a close eye on her extensive estates and middle-aged family. Her main diversions were sketching trips in the West Country and Wales, and visits to Cornwall where her only surviving son, a clergyman, lived. Her eldest son had been killed at the siege of Badajoz, Spain, in 1812, and another son died in infancy.

The five years that Mrs Simcoe spent in the Canadas were the most exciting in her long life. She enjoyed everything – the rough North Atlantic crossing, the gaiety of Quebec, the hardships of travel in an undeveloped country, the inbred little society of Newark, the rudimentary camp life at York, and even the pursuit by the French on the voyage home. Eager to be pleased by new experiences, she usually regarded difficulties as challenging adventures. She particularly enjoyed her position as wife of the lieutenant governor; she wrote, "To have everybody I see assiduous to please me and to have nothing to do but to follow my own fancy is a satisfactory mode of living. . . . How happy I am!" She was upheld by her invincible belief in her own superiority, which was to her one of both position and talent. Her visits to settlers were made with the same sublime self-assurance as Queen Victoria's descents upon the crofters around Balmoral Castle. As to her natural superiority, Mrs Simcoe wrote, "I live with a set of people who I am sure do not know more than myself."

This attitude did not endear her to everyone; Hannah Jarvis [PETERS] called her a "little stuttering Vixon." The usual comment about Mrs Simcoe in Upper Canada, however, was that she was quiet. This quality could have been because of her slight speech impediment, as well as her traditional view of the role of women. On the voyage out, for example, she was fascinated by nautical matters, but could not find out about them. "I do not like to ask any questions," she wrote, "as I think it would look impertinent & be as bad as a woman talking politics."

Throughout her life in the Canadas, Mrs Simcoe kept a diary, writing at least three versions. The first contained brief, almost daily entries, often combined with rough sketches. The others were expanded from the first version with more detail and a smoother style, but with some omissions; they were sent back to England at every opportunity, one to Wolford and the other to Mrs Simcoe's closest friend, Mary Anne Burges, a noted author, linguist, and naturalist.

Besides recording her own activities, Mrs Simcoe wrote about her surroundings. Her descriptions are very graphic; her diaries are full of colourful vignettes, such as the Epiphany service in the Roman Catholic cathedral at Quebec or a walk through a still burning forest fire. She had, as she wrote, "the picturesque eye." She was especially interested in flora and fauna, as well as the food and medicines prepared from them. Although she was fascinated by the native peoples, her approach was anthropological or romanticized rather than personal. In general, she was not interested in people; although her marriage was a happy one, even her husband is a shadowy figure. She wrote more about her little son, Francis Gwillim, obviously his mother's favourite.

As well as her diaries, Mrs Simcoe produced a large number of water-colours depicting Canadian scenes. They also exist in several versions, from rough sketches made on the spot to finished works which were sent regularly to friends in England. After her return to Wolford, Mrs Simcoe and her daughters made further copies of her Canadian views. While in the Canadas, she experimented with etching; in her first letter to England she ordered a set of engraving tools, because she had seen Joseph Frederick Wallet DesBarres*'s engravings and was "sure I can engrave to imitate them." Apparently she etched only two small and not very successful plates, which were sent to England in 1794 and printed in Bristol and London. Mrs Simcoe had two motives in her sketching in Canada. One was artistic; she was always looking for good views, and would travel long and arduous distances to find them. The other was documentary; she was intentionally making a pictorial record of what she saw. "I took no sketch of a place I never wish to recollect," she wrote at Cap-de-la-Madeleine.

Most of the time Elizabeth Simcoe delighted in her Canadian experience. In her diaries and water-colours she has left a lively record of the Canadas in the 1790s, which is remarkable for its interest, detail, and accuracy.

EDITH G. FIRTH

[Most of Mrs Simcoe's surviving diaries are in the Simcoe papers at AO, MS 517, B3. Several were deposited in Devon Record Office (Exeter, Eng.), 1038, and were microfilmed in 1963 by the PAC as part of its collection of Simcoe papers (MG 23, H1, 1, ser.5); four of these diaries (folder 25) are now in the library at the David MacDonald Stewart Museum (Montreal). Many of her sketches are in the Picture Coll. at the AO. Two sketch-books microfilmed by the PAC (MG 23, H1, 1, ser.5, folder 26) have been presented to the Queen's York Rangers (1st American Regiment) and are in the Stewart Museum. An album of sketches is in the Picture Division at the PAC, and is described and illustrated in "Elizabeth Simcoe (1766–1850)," ed. B. G. Wilson, PAC, *Arch. Canada microfiches* ([Ottawa]), no.9 (1977) (printed pamphlet enclosing 1 fiche). Thirty-two water-colours were presented to George III and are in the BL. Mrs Simcoe's letters to Mrs Hunt at Wolford, in whose care she left her children in 1791, are in AO, MS 517, B1-1; family correspondence, especially after 1800, is on the PAC microfilm. Mary Anne Burges's diary-letters to Mrs Simcoe are divided between the AO collection (MS 517, B1-2) and the PAC microfilm (MG 23, H1, 1, ser.5, folder 29); they are useful for their picture of life at Wolford, and also because Miss Burges answered Mrs Simcoe's missing Canadian letters in detail. Information about Mrs Simcoe can also be found in her husband's papers; see the bibliography for the John Graves Simcoe sketch in *DCB*, vol.5.

Mrs Simcoe's diaries were edited by John Ross Robertson* with extensive annotation, genealogy, illustration, her funeral sermon, will, and reminiscences of a servant, John Bailey. *The diary of Mrs. John Graves Simcoe* ... was published in Toronto in 1911; a revised edition appeared in 1934, and a reprint of the original 1911 edition in 1973. A better transcription of the diaries in AO, MS 517, B3, nos.1–3, and of the letters to Mrs Hunt, was edited by Mary Emma Quayle Innis and published as *Mrs. Simcoe's diary* (Toronto and New York, 1965). Most of the secondary sources about Mrs Simcoe are based almost exclusively on the published diaries. Marian [Little] Fowler, "Portrait of Elizabeth Simcoe," *OH*, 69 (1977): 79–100, discusses her as an 18th-century woman; Ged Martin, "The Simcoes and their friends," *OH*, 69: 101–12, is based on the Bland Burges papers in the Bodleian Library, Univ. of Oxford. Hilary Arnold deals with Mrs Simcoe's birth in her typescript "[Elizabeth Posthuma Gwillim Simcoe: her birth and her Gwillim relatives]" (York, Eng., 1982), a copy of which is in AO, Pamphlet Coll., 1982, no.23. E.G.F.]

AO, MS 75. MTRL, Elizabeth Russell papers. Northamptonshire Record Office (Northampton, Eng.), All Saints Church (Aldwincle), reg. of baptisms, 22 Sept. 1762; reg. of burials, 23 Sept. 1762. PAC, MG 23, HI, 3; 5. Univ. of Guelph Library, Arch. and Special Coll. (Guelph, Ont.), J. MacI. Duff coll., Samuel Peters papers. John Blackmore, *The Christian in life and death, a sermon, preached in Dunkeswell Church on Sunday, January 27, 1850; on occasion of the death of Elizabeth Posthuma, widow of the late Lieut. General Simcoe, of Wolford Lodge, Devon* (Launceston, Eng., 1850). "Canadian letters: description of a tour thro' the provinces of Lower and Upper Canada, in the course of the years 1792 and '93," *Canadian Antiquarian and Numismatic Journal*, 3rd ser., 9 (1912): 85–168. [F.-A.-F. de La Rochefoucauld, Duc de] La Rochefoucauld-Liancourt, "La Rochefoucault-Liancourt's travels in Canada, 1795, with annotations and strictures by Sir David William Smith . . . ," ed. W. R. Riddell, AO *Report*, 1916: 39, 126, 152; *Voyage dans les États-Unis d'Amérique, fait en 1795, 1796 et 1797* (8v., Paris, [1799]), 2: 61. "Letters from the secretary of Upper Canada and Mrs. Jarvis, to her father, the Rev. Samuel Peters, D.D.," ed. A. H. Young, Women's Canadian Hist. Soc. of Toronto, *Trans.*, no.23 (1922–23): 11–63. John White, "The diary of John White, first attorney general of Upper Canada (1791–1800)," ed. William Colgate, *OH*, 47 (1955): 147–70.

H

HACKETT, NELSON, fugitive slave; b. *c.* 1810; fl. 1840–42.

To slaves in the ante-bellum United States, the Canadas were virtually synonymous with freedom and heaven. Though slavery was abolished throughout the British empire only in 1833, Canadian law and custom had long since established emancipation: by statute in 1793 in Upper Canada, and through a judicial decision in 1800 in Lower Canada. In addition, the citizenry could generally be counted on to take action if the law would not; in 1837 Solomon Molesby (Mosely) and Jesse Happy, fugitive slaves accused of horse theft by irate owners, were forcibly rescued from Upper Canadian judicial authorities, who were thereby prevented from extraditing them. So in July 1841, when Arkansan slave Nelson Hackett left home atop a stolen horse and six weeks later crossed over into Upper Canada, he had every reason to believe that freedom would be his until the day he died.

Hackett's freedom was short-lived, for his master since 1840, Alfred Wallace, determined to make an example of his handsome and articulate runaway. A wealthy merchant, Wallace was socially prominent and well connected in Fayetteville, Ark., and his influence extended to the state capital via fellow townsman Archibald Yell, the governor. Wallace and an associate, George C. Grigg, set out separately to pursue Hackett. In September, in both Windsor and Chatham, Upper Canada, Wallace swore out depositions against Hackett for the theft of his horse, as well as a saddle, coat, and gold watch. Grigg too swore out depositions, in Upper Canada and in Michigan. Wallace had Hackett arrested near Chatham and incarcerated in the Western District jail at Sandwich (Windsor). A charge of raping a "young lady of respectability," allegedly Wallace's adopted daughter, was dropped. Hackett confessed to the thefts but later denied them, claiming he had confessed because he had been "severely beaten over the head with a butt of a whip, and a large stick" during his interrogation.

Wallace set the wheels in motion for formal extradition proceedings. Before returning to Arkansas, he retained as counsel Sandwich lawyer and assemblyman John Prince*, and as collaborator Prince's Detroit friend Lewis Davenport, of Fayetteville background and owner of the Detroit–Windsor ferry. Next, on 18 September 1841, Michigan's acting governor requested the governor of the Province of Canada, Lord Sydenham [THOMSON], to release Hackett to Michigan. On the 21st Wallace petitioned Sydenham through a justice of the peace at Sandwich, Robert Mercer, who added his personal assurance that the request "is all straightforward and not a pretence for merely getting [Hackett] back again as a Slave."

Wallace's campaign for extradition was set back by the attorney general for Upper Canada, William Henry Draper*, who had serious reservations about the motives and Michigan's jurisdiction in such proceedings. Wallace persisted, and on 26 November a grand jury in Washington County, Ark., indicted Hackett for theft. The same day Wallace's friend Washington L. Wilson, owner of the stolen saddle, petitioned for Hackett's return. On 30 September Arkansas's governor, Archibald Yell, had requested that Hackett be released to Lewis Davenport, who would supervise his transfer home. Countering this blitz was a petition from Hackett, drawn up by Windsor lawyer Charles Baby. He begged to remain in Canada for upon returning to Arkansas he would be "tortured in a manner that to hang him at once would be mercy." This was to be Hackett's sole legal action.

Canada's administrator, Sir Richard Downes JACKSON, reserved a decision, but in mid January 1842 the newly arrived governor, Sir Charles BAGOT, authorized Hackett's extradition. Implementation of the order was leisurely and secretive, in part to avoid a repetition of the violent rescue of Solomon Molesby. On the night of 7–8 February, Hackett, bound and gagged, was spirited across the Detroit River and lodged in the Detroit jail, where he languished for more than two months. In April the American lawyer and abolitionist Charles Stewart visited him; abolitionists hoped to use his case as a focal point in their campaign. They soon abandoned this idea, however, because of Hackett's theft of the watch, which undermined their argument that he had merely stolen tools for escape. As well, they could find nothing out of order in the judicial proceedings. In Canada Bagot received approval from the British secretary of state, on these same grounds, for his decision to relinquish Hackett.

As soon as navigation opened in 1842, Hackett boarded a vessel, guarded by Arkansan Onesimus Evans, whom Wallace had sent to help Davenport. Aboard ship Hackett so impressed four New Yorkers that they helped him escape. Near Princeton, Ill., he wandered for two days in a forest, then was turned in by a man he had approached for food. In June 1842 Hackett was finally delivered up at Fayetteville.

Public reaction to the extradition continued strong. In June abolitionists in the British House of Commons asked questions about Hackett. In Canada, John Prince's enemy Henry C. Grant, editor of the *Western Herald*, concluded that Hackett had been entrapped by Wallace in connivance with Prince, Davenport, and deputy sheriff John Mercer. Sparked by the reaction, William DUNLOP, a member of the Legislative Assembly, put questions on the affair to the province's Executive Council. The following month a legislative debate initiated by Dunlop on the official documents of the case put the issue into the context of international law and tradition and of moral rectitude, there being no exact law in force in Canada. Extradition proceedings between Canada and the United States were based on the ambiguous Upper Canadian statute of 1833 dealing with fugitive offenders, which made no mention of escaped slaves; most Canadian MLAS doubted the act's constitutionality. The government's position, however, as voiced by Samuel Bealey Harrison* in October, was that the recent Webster–Ashburton Treaty, which had been signed in August, would put Hackett's case "on a proper footing." This was illogical, as the extradition had taken place before treaty negotiations began and was in defiance of the Canadian custom of refusing to surrender fugitive slaves.

To some the stolen watch told the tale: Hackett was a fugitive thief, and therefore eligible for extradition. To a few intimate with his case, neither the treaty nor the theft was the deciding factor. It was widely rumoured, the *Western Herald* reported, that the case and legal fees had cost Wallace $1,500, much more than Hackett's market value, and that the "principal inducement" in getting him back was to "deter other slaves from running away" by demonstrating that there was "no security for them in Canada, and that if they ran away, they could and would be brought back." This motive, widely suspected in Canada, was borne out by the testimony, later printed in Henry Walton Bibb*'s *Voice of the Fugitive*, of another slave who had escaped from Wallace. Hackett, the slave recounted, had not been tried upon returning to Fayetteville but was bound and repeatedly flogged, the first time before all the slaves. He was "then sold off to the interior of Texas." Efforts to purchase Hackett by ladies' auxiliaries of abolitionist societies in Bristol and Liverpool failed when no trace of the slave could be found.

Hackett was merely one of the countless fugitives from American slavery, yet his case provoked a public furore international in scope if brief in span. On the face of it, it was the stolen coat and watch that proved to be Hackett's undoing, but the allegation that his extradition was achieved through bribery, intrigue, and a concerted effort on the part of his powerful owner to wreak vengeance on him sheds a truer light on the case. Subsequent British policy bears out this view. When the bitterly negotiated extradition clause of the Webster–Ashburton Treaty was finalized, fugitive slaves were protected from automatic surrender to their American owners in that extradition was carefully limited to criminals. Also, the 1833 law invoked by Hackett's foes was proved *ultra vires* by article 10 of the treaty, which was specifically declared to fill a void and not to replace any existing law.

Ultimately, Hackett was returned to Arkansas in defiance of established policy, judicial precedents, civil rights guaranteed by custom, and popular views of justice and humanity. The combined resources of Wallace and his political and judicial contacts in the Arkansan slaveocracy, and of Prince and others in Canada proved so powerful that leading abolitionists despaired publicly that "Canada could no longer be looked upon as the slave's asylum." The practical consequences of the case proved to be the reverse. The publicity surrounding it brought the possibility of escape to Canada to the attention of others still in bondage, and until the end of the Civil War fugitive slaves flocked there in ever increasing numbers [*see* Henry Walton Bibb; John Anderson*].

ELIZABETH ABBOTT-NAMPHY

Library of Congress, MS Division (Washington), Lewis Tappan papers, C22/30–31 (Charles Stewart to Tappan, 9 Aug. 1842, enclosing Nelson Hackett case); C113/133 (Tappan to John Scobie, 23 July 1842). PAC, MG 24, A13, 6: 97–99. PRO, CO 42/488: 214–47. Can., Prov. of, Legislative Assembly, *App. to the journals*, 1842, app.S; *Debates of the Legislative Assembly of United Canada* (Abbott Gibbs *et al.*), 2: 361–63. G.B., Parl., *Hansard's parliamentary debates* (London), 3rd ser., 64 (1842): 640–41. *Brockville Recorder*, 28 Sept. 1837. *Montreal Gazette*, 18 June 1842. *Patriot* (Toronto), 22 Sept. 1837. *Voice of the Fugitive* (Sandwich [Windsor, Ont.]), 18 June 1851. *Western Herald, and Farmers' Magazine* (Sandwich), 30 June, 14 July, 18 Aug. 1842. R. W. Winks, *The blacks in Canada: a history* (Montreal, 1971). A. L. Murray, "The extradition of fugitive slaves from Canada: a re-evaluation," *CHR*, 43 (1962): 298–314. R. J. Zorn, "An Arkansas fugitive slave incident and its international repercussions," *Ark. Hist. Quarterly* (Fayetteville), 16 (1957): 140–49; "Criminal extradition menaces the Canadian haven for fugitive slaves, 1841–1861," *CHR*, 38 (1957): 284–94.

HAGERMAN, CHRISTOPHER ALEXANDER, militia officer, lawyer, office holder, politician, and judge; b. 28 March 1792 in Adolphustown Township, Upper Canada, son of Nicholas Hagerman and Anne Fisher; m. first 26 March 1817, in Kingston, Elizabeth Macaulay, daughter of James Macaulay*, and they had three daughters and one son; m. secondly 17 April 1834, in London, England, Elizabeth Emily Merry, and they had one daughter; m. thirdly 1846 Caroline Tysen, and they had no issue; d. 14 May 1847 in Toronto.

Few individuals in Upper Canada's at times turbulent political history provoked such extreme hostility as Christopher Alexander Hagerman. Among the men with whom historians have commonly associated him, he was the most obdurate in his defence of church and state. He evinced – by temperament more than by design – the aggressiveness lacking in a John Macaulay* and outwardly less evident in a John Beverley Robinson*. William Lyon Mackenzie*'s biographer Charles Lindsey* thought Hagerman showed "a disposition to carry the abuse of privilege as far as the most despotic sovereign had ever carried the abuse of prerogative." Charles Morrison Durand, a Hamilton lawyer prosecuted by Hagerman in the aftermath of the rebellion of 1837, depicted him as a "grim old bulldog." If Macaulay was the back-room boy of Upper Canadian administrations from Sir Peregrine Maitland*'s to Sir George Arthur*'s, Hagerman was the bully-boy.

Unlike contemporaries such as Robinson, John Macaulay, Archibald MacLean*, and Jonas JONES, all of whom moved easily, and naturally, into positions of influence and power, Hagerman started down life's path as something of an outsider – lacking what Robinson termed "interest," by which he meant a patron. It was not that Hagerman had no advantages; it was just that he did not have as many as others. His background was respectable and loyal. Nicholas Hagerman was a New Yorker of Dutch ancestry who "took an early and an Active part in favour of the British Government" during the American revolution. In 1783 he emigrated to Quebec, and the following year he settled on the Bay of Quinte in what became Adolphustown Township. He acquired a modest stature in the community as a militia captain and justice of the peace. More important professionally was his appointment in 1797 as one of Upper Canada's first barristers.

Within his closely knit family, young Christopher had an especial fondness for his brother Daniel and his sister Maria. From his father, it seems, he derived his keen sense of the loyalist legacy and an uncompromising adherence to the Church of England; it was perhaps symbolic that he had been baptized by John Langhorn*, one of the church's staunchest defenders. A boyhood acquaintance, J. Neilson, recalled to Egerton Ryerson* in 1873 that Christopher had "not . . . much early learning," and certainly, as historian Sydney Francis Wise has convincingly shown, he was never a pupil of John Strachan*. Hagerman embarked in 1807 upon a career in the law – one of the surest avenues to preferment and a comfortable life – as a student in his father's Kingston office. He would be admitted to the bar in Hilary term 1815.

His personal qualities tended to set him apart. In November 1810, from York (Toronto), Robinson wrote to John Macaulay in Kingston: "We have been favored for two or three weeks with the company of the enlightened Christopher Hagerman a Youth whose bashfulness will never stand in his way – and who you may undertake to Say will never be prevented by embarrassments from displaying his natural talents or acquired information to the best advantage – After all, tho', he has a good heart, and not a mean capacity, in short he is not So great a fool as people take him to be." There was, as Robinson's letter catches, a bravado and also an air of self-satisfaction to Hagerman, and they were as discernible in the young man as they would be characteristic of the older man.

His advance in society was effected through the good graces of outsiders, the military men who came to the province during the war years, stayed briefly, and cared little for local cliques. At the outbreak of the War of 1812 Hagerman enlisted as an officer in his father's militia company. In 1833 he would write that he had "had the good fortune to attract the notice and obtain the patronage" of Governor Sir George Prevost*, who was in Kingston between May and September 1813. Hagerman's rise in local and provincial society dates from that period. He carried dispatches for Major-General Francis de Rottenburg*, commander of the troops in Upper Canada, in August 1813. The following November he served with credit as Lieutenant-Colonel Joseph Wanton Morrison*'s aide-de-camp at the battle of Crysler's Farm. In December he was appointed provincial aide-de-camp to Lieutenant-General Gordon Drummond*, Rottenburg's successor, with the provincial rank of lieutenant-colonel. It was a rather remarkable ascent.

More good fortune was yet to come. The office of collector of customs for Kingston had been vacant since the death in September 1813 of Joseph Forsyth*, and on 27 March 1814 Hagerman received the appointment. He was with Drummond during the May attack on Oswego, N.Y., and was acknowledged in Drummond's official dispatch for having "rendered me every assistance." Present at the siege of Fort Erie in September, he again carried dispatches the following month. Drummond's high regard for his young aide was shared by his successor, Sir Frederick Philipse Robinson, who appointed Hagerman "His Majesty's Council in and for the Province of Upper Canada" on 5 Sept. 1815. Hagerman had undoubtedly arrived in Upper Canadian society, but under the unusual circumstances of wartime. When normalcy returned with the reappearance of Lieutenant Governor Francis Gore*, absent since 1811, Hagerman's appointment as counsel was undermined. Gore had wondered about it – in fact, he probably wondered who Hagerman was – and consulted the judges of the Court of King's Bench. On 4 Nov. 1815 Chief Justice Thomas Scott* reported their unanimous opinion "that under all the circumstances of the intended appointment . . . it is not expedient for the present to carry it into effect."

At the end of the war Hagerman resumed the practice of law in Kingston. His childhood friend Neilson, who observed him at the bar, remarked upon his "great powers of persuasion," and these would bring him to the fore of his profession. He found, however, that the collectorship of customs occupied him more than he had anticipated. He had been obliged to rent a house for an office, "the expense of which is greatly disproportionate to the allowance and fees attached." Accordingly, in 1816 he petitioned the Executive Council for the grant of a vacant lot in Kingston on which he could erect a house and office. He received one-fifth of an acre. He was already a landowner, having been granted in 1814 1,000 acres, which he located in Marmora Township, and another 200 as the son of a loyalist. As befitted a rising member of the bar, Hagerman involved himself in many community endeavours. Undoubtedly the "genial qualities" noted by Neilson made him an effective participant. Among the organizations to which he donated or subscribed by 1821 were the Midland District School Society, the Kingston Auxiliary Bible and Common Prayer Book Society, the Kingston Compassionate Society, the Lancasterian school, the Union Sunday School Society, the National School Society, the Society for Bettering the Condition of the Poor in the Midland District, and the Society for Promoting Christian Knowledge. He was a shareholder of the Kingston hospital, a trustee of the Midland District Grammar School, treasurer of the Midland Agricultural Society, and vice-president of the Frontenac Agricultural Society.

Most aspirants to a genteel life in Upper Canada required a wife of respectable family. Hagerman's marriage in 1817 to Elizabeth Macaulay, whose brother George he knew well, was a fine match: her father was well connected, at both York and Kingston;

her brother James Buchanan* would become an executive councillor in 1825. Hagerman himself was a good catch, securely positioned on the ladder of success. He had an affinity for women and an ease of manner which doubtless aided him in romantic endeavours; he was, as well, tall, rugged, and handsome. (Although in later life his looks were marred "by an accident to his nose which gave his face a peculiar appearance," this "facial deformity," John Ross Robertson* observed, was not "a bar to success in love:making.") Few details emerge of his personal life, for there are no family papers. What glimpses remain are incidental, but they suggest that the geniality of the public man was as apparent in the private man. He seems to have been an affectionate father and a loving husband. His first daughter was born in 1820; writing to a friend a year later, he tacked on a playful after-thought to a postscript, "Our little brat is as usual." He found amusing Chief Justice William Campbell*'s remark at an 1826 trial that "men as lords of the creation have a right to inflict a little gentle castigation on our rebellious dames." The same year he fretted when his wife was stricken with a brief but "serious attack of illness."

It was not long after his marriage that Hagerman became involved in politics. In 1828 he would declare that his chief political impulse had been "his anxiety . . . upon all occasions by supporting the views and measures of Government (emanating as he was well convinced they did from a source eminently disinterested and patriotic) to promote the best interests of the Province." From the beginning he gave vent to that anxiety in a bruising fashion. In June 1818, in a minor way, he helped set the stage for the charge of seditious libel against the Scottish agitator Robert Gourlay*. Later that month he confronted Gourlay in the streets of Kingston brandishing a whip, which he used to good effect on the unarmed Scot. Arrested and subsequently released, he had given Kingstonians a visible demonstration of where he stood politically. A now prominent local, Hagerman was elected to the House of Assembly for the riding of Kingston on 26 and 27 June 1820. He defeated, by 119 votes to 94, George Herchmer Markland*, a pupil of Strachan's, a friend of Robinson and John Macaulay, and the son of leading Kingstonian Thomas MARKLAND.

Hagerman entered the eighth parliament (1821–24) with a reputation outside Kingston at odds with his beliefs. A surprised Robinson at York admitted to Macaulay in February 1821 that he had been "grievously mistaken" about Hagerman: "He is any thing but a Democrat. Indeed his conduct is manly, correct & sensible & shews in every thing that kind of independence most rarely met with which determines him to follow the right side of a question tho' it may appear unpopular – his speeches gain him great credit." Such a misapprehension by Robinson, who had known Hagerman since 1810, worked with him (albeit briefly) during the war, and cooperated with him in the charge against Gourlay, may reflect a more widespread confusion about political stances. Mackenzie, after all, initially believed Jonas Jones to be a member of the opposition in the same parliament. Whatever the nature of the misunderstanding, it was quickly rectified. By mid February Hagerman and Robinson were working together and taking the lead on administration measures. The end of session won Hagerman strong praise from the attorney general, who wrote to John Macaulay: "Our friend Hagerman is a sterling good fellow, free from prejudices, and with every bias on the right side. . . . His talents & information can not well be spared."

In his political views Hagerman was "illiberal," to use the word Robinson would attach to himself in 1828 (the word "conservative" had not yet entered the political lexicon of Upper Canadians). He was also, to adopt another of Robinson's phrases, a "wellwisher of *Church & State*." In 1821 he supported William Warren BALDWIN's defence of aristocracy and primogeniture against an intestate estate bill sponsored by Barnabas Bidwell* and David McGregor Rogers*. To vote for the measure would, Hagerman argued, "be departing from every thing venerable, noble, and honorable; . . . Democracy was, like a serpent, twisting round us by degrees, it should be crushed in the first instance, for if the bill passed, it would not leave them the British Constitution but a mere shadow." For Hagerman, the essence of the constitution was monarchy and executive prerogative. That same year he opposed a bill repealing the civil list since "it was necessary that the Executive government should have a fund of this description at their disposal; it is the case in all governments except those that are purely democratical. . . . Monarchy should be supported, and if you infringe a hair's breadth, you endanger the whole fabric." He was also a leading participant in the debate over Barnabas and Marshall Spring* Bidwell's eligibility to sit as members, the opening shot in the war known as the alien question.

At another level, Hagerman proved a good constituency man, working on and proposing a number of measures of local concern. His major role in this regard was to second John Macaulay's leadership of Kingston's pro-union forces when the question of a union with Lower Canada arose in 1822. The separation of the old province of Quebec in 1791, he maintained, had "most unnaturally rent asunder . . . subjects of the same great and glorious empire, whose interests nature has made inseparable, and whose strength and improvement depends solely and entirely on their being united by concurrence of habits and sentiments, and a right understanding of their common interest." Macaulay argued the case for union on financial and economic grounds; Hagerman agreed with his views but concentrated on political and constitutional matters, which were the leading concerns of anti-unionists such as Baldwin. Hagerman, an ardent defender of the Constitutional Act of 1791, which had given Upper Canada its constitution, was as concerned as Baldwin not to jeopardize any of its essential parts. He favoured union as a means of overwhelming at an early stage Lower Canadian oppositionists whose advocacy of the assembly's powers at the expense of the Legislative Council's threatened "that balance between absolute monarchy and democracy, which so beautifully distinguished the British Constitution." What happened in the lower province would affect Upper Canada sooner or later, Hagerman argued. Thus, Upper Canadians should shun the role of "indifferent observers" or risk "losing the constitution under which they live." Though popular with Kingston's mercantile community, Hagerman's advocacy of union was insufficient to guarantee his re-election in 1824.

In fact, in a two-way race – a third candidate, Thomas DALTON, a local brewer and banker, withdrew – Hagerman was defeated, polling a mere 11 votes short of his opponent's total. Dalton took credit for Hagerman's loss, but the explanation is more complex. As S. F. Wise has argued, Hagerman may have been hurt by his injudicious remarks in the dispute over the "pretended" Bank of Upper Canada at Kingston. Hagerman had been an early director and shareholder, as was Dalton; at the time of the bank's collapse in 1822 he was its solicitor and shortly thereafter he became chairman of the board of directors to oversee its dissolution. In March 1823 parliament declared the bank illegal, made the directors liable for its debts, and set up a commission consisting of John Macaulay, George Markland, and John KIRBY to handle the institution's affairs. The commissioners' report, tabled the following year, was unfavourable to the bank's administrators. Hagerman attacked the report, defending the directors with the exception of Dalton. Dalton responded with a masterpiece of vitriol condemning as spurious Hagerman's criticism of the commissioners and accusing him of being in league with them to destroy his reputation. Since as early as January 1823 Hagerman's own reputation had been undermined by "reports and insinuations" that his conduct as chairman was not in the best interests of the bank, Dalton's squib identifying him with the agents of the York élite may well have raised the ire of those who suffered by the bank's failure and thus influenced the outcome of the election.

Hagerman's defeat may also have had to do with his bumptious manner, which carried over into every aspect of his career. At a social gathering in York on 30 Dec. 1823 Hagerman, in the presence of Lieutenant Governor Maitland, Chief Justice William Dummer Powell*, and Mr Justice William Campbell, insinuated, as Campbell related the incident to Maitland's secretary, Major George HILLIER, that judges were "in the habit of deciding otherwise than according to the laws we are appointed to administer." An annoyed Campbell was left with the option of passing over the incident "in silence as an instance of rudeness and ill manners unworthy of serious notice, or of adopting such measures as I may conceive best adapted to the support of my judicial character, and to the proper notice of personal insult." Early that year Hillier had been "very much distressed" by a report of a "flagrant breach of decorum" on Hagerman's part towards Robert BARRIE, commissioner of the Kingston dockyard. Strachan informed Macaulay of the "many rumours" surrounding this affair and of Hagerman's "recent argument" with Thomas Markland. Yet there was more. Strachan had been told that Hagerman wished to be solicitor for the bank commissioners who were investigating the bank of which he was already the solicitor – "an indelicacy," Strachan sighed, "which I would have considered incredible."

If Hagerman could give offence, with such apparent ease, to men of his own rank and station, he could prove unbearable to others. As collector, he enforced customs regulations with exactitude. He had, for instance, invaded Carleton Island, N.Y., in 1821 to seize a depot of tea and tobacco kept there by Anthony MANAHAN, whom he dismissed as a smuggler and a "Yankee Merchant." He even suggested to Hillier that he should be allowed occasional recourse to a military force to assist him. Early in July 1824 one Elijah Lyons was accidentally shot by a student in Hagerman's law office who was aiding him in this instance in his customs duties. Two months later 31 Kingstonians complained to Maitland of Hagerman's "proceedings and conduct." When "in the hands of a passionate, vindictive, ambitious, or speculating person" the enormous powers of the collectorship were, the petitioners wailed, "dangerous to the rights and property of individuals, the usual course of business, and the public peace."

Having been forced out of political life temporarily, Hagerman returned to his legal practice and his various endeavours. He bought, sold, and let properties throughout the Midland District and beyond it. He served as an agent for a number of proprietors and sometimes acquired lots in partnership with others. He was vice-president of the Kingston Savings Bank in 1822 and a director of the Cataraqui Bridge Company four years later. The failure of the "pretended" bank had cost him dearly, £1,200 plus contingencies by his reckoning, and by 1825 he had "to save money." He declined the offer of a District Court judgeship in October of that year because "I cannot afford to give up any portion of my practice in the Kings Bench, which I have reason to think wd. be materially affected by discontinuing my acceptance of suits in the inferior court." He was, however, willing to take an out-of-district judgeship and on 14 June 1826 Hillier notified him of his appointment to the Johnstown District.

Hagerman was a skilled lawyer who had, with Bartholomew Crannell Beardsley*, defended John Norton* of the charge of murder in 1823. He won further notoriety for himself in the fall of 1826 by defending the young bucks who had destroyed Mackenzie's printing-office and press. Although his law office was "lucrative" in the 1820s, Hagerman was tiring of it, and his professional weariness coincided with his reservations about town life. In 1827 he purchased a country property, living with his family in a "small, but comfortable stone cottage" until a "more spacious Mansion" was completed. He had "no intention" of returning to Kingston: "I have been living long enough in a style of expense, agreeable (to be sure) to my own taste, but which with reference to the claims of my little ones, it is not prudent I should continue."

In that year he was looking for advancement. He sought, he told Hillier, "preferment *in my profession*" but not "in any other department." He hoped that if an opportunity arose "during the *present administration*" he would not be disappointed. Early the next year he memorialized Maitland for elevation to the Court of King's Bench – Campbell was in England seeking a pension on which to retire and judge D'Arcy Boulton* was ailing and close to retirement. At that time the administration of justice was swirling in a storm of controversy [*see* William Warren Baldwin], the result of William FORSYTH's petition to the assembly in January 1828 complaining of Maitland's high-handed treatment of him. The political skies darkened further with the dismissal of Mr Justice John Walpole Willis* in June 1828 and no doubt became even more threatening with Hagerman's unexpected nomination to the bench as Willis's successor that same month. Hagerman was simply too much the partisan for his appointment to restore to the Maitland administration any of the goodwill it had lost on such issues as political reform, the clergy reserves, the administration of justice, and the alien question. There was one boon for the opposition in Hagerman's nomination: he was unable to contest the general election held that summer.

Having been allowed sufficient time to wind up his affairs in Kingston and move to York to take up his unconfirmed appointment, Hagerman went on circuit in August 1828. He reported to Hillier from Brockville that "I have so far had no very unpleasant duty to perform, nothing has occurred worthy of particular note." Matters quickly changed when, in Hamilton on 5 September, he presided at the trial of Michael Vincent, charged with murdering his wife. Casting aside the tradition that a judge should serve as the accused's counsel, not his prosecutor, Hagerman advised the petit jury that "the deceased had been murdered by the prisoner; and he had no difficulty in saying such was his opinion." Over the objections of John Rolph*, who was acting for the defence, the jury retired and found Vincent guilty. Hagerman sentenced him to execution and dissection, and three days later he was hanged in a badly botched manner. Bartemas Ferguson*, editor of the *Niagara Herald*, found Hagerman's charge "remarkable" and wondered whether it had given "an undue bias to the jury." Francis Collins* of the *Canadian Freeman* saw in Hagerman's action an extraordinary departure, yet another instance of irregularity in the administration of justice. In his view Hagerman was an incompetent whose only qualification for the bench was sycophancy. Although the feeling was by no means universal, it was shared by many among the administration's opponents. After the ninth parliament opened in January 1829, Hagerman was, as Robert Stanton* observed, "every day called Judge Kit and has every odious invective brought against him." By July rumours abounded that his appointment would not be confirmed. They proved true. Robinson replaced Campbell on the bench and James Buchanan Macaulay replaced Hagerman. The new lieutenant governor, Sir John Colborne*, reported to the colonial secretary that Hagerman thought himself "ill used."

But there were compensations. Since his arrival in August 1828 Colborne had shunned Maitland's key advisers, Robinson and Strachan, and Hagerman stepped alone into the limelight of gubernatorial favour, becoming for a time the conduit for privileged information. To make up for the loss of his judgeship he was appointed solicitor general on 13 July 1829. His prestige was enhanced the following year by his election victory over Donald Bethune* in Kingston. He was re-elected in 1834, handily beating William John O'GRADY. By this time Kingston had become Hagerman's private bastion; he was elected by acclamation in 1836.

With Robinson on the bench government management of the assembly in the eleventh parliament (1831–34) fell to Hagerman and Attorney General Henry John Boulton* – with disastrous results. The latter was an inept dandy, the former was unequal to the task. Hagerman's strength was his dogged commitment to the administration and to his own principles of church and state. His talent was a natural eloquence invigorated by the passion of the moment. The *Kingston Chronicle* caught him in full swing during an 1826 trial, and the editor's conclusion was apt: "We have heard those who could, perhaps, reason more closely than Mr. Hagerman but very few indeed whose eloquence . . . is more powerful." He was, as Thomas David Morrison* would characterize him in

1836, "the Thunderer of Kingston," a man given to "violent expressions of opinion." Yet in debate, discourse, or conversation, once excited or engaged, Hagerman usually did more harm than good to the causes he so forcefully espoused. The most glaring example was his role, with Boulton, in the repeated expulsions of William Lyon Mackenzie from the assembly. When word of their actions reached Lord Goderich, the colonial secretary, both law officers were dismissed in March 1833. Colborne protested, however, and Hagerman, now a widower, set off for England to appeal. He returned the following year with a reinstatement from the new colonial secretary, Lord Stanley.

He also returned with a new wife. According to George Markland, "The match was not approved of in a certain quarter of the country – *they* said openly that nothing had ever occurred which caused so much annoyance – *The* Miss Merry and Kit Hagerman oh it was horrible they said." Perhaps it was her attractions that made politics and his official duties irksome to Hagerman. Or perhaps it was a desire for change such as had overtaken him in the mid 1820s. Whatever it was, Robert Stanton noted in 1835 Hagerman's inability to put his imprint on the twelfth parliament and his more frequent absences from the house. He was, however, there, and on the defensive, in 1835 when he unsuccessfully opposed M. S. Bidwell's election as speaker, and when the house reduced his salary as solicitor general from £600 to £375.

That year, moreover, he was embroiled in a defence of the Church of England and the clergy reserves following upon Colborne's endowment of 44 Anglican rectories in December, a political error of enormous proportions. For Hagerman, a self-declared "High Church & King's man" who had equated dissent with "infidelity," the established church was a key bulwark against immorality, equality, and a godless democracy. He was a devout member of his own congregation, St George's in Kingston, and in 1825 had been a member, with John Macaulay and Stanton, of a committee that wrote an arrogant defence of the Anglicans' exclusive jurisdiction over the town's lower burial-ground. When John Barclay* penned a claim for the equal rights of the Church of Scotland, Hagerman, as Robinson revealed, was one of the three anonymous authors who replied. In 1821 he had naturally assumed a direct connection between Robert Nichol*'s remark in the assembly that there was no established church in Upper Canada and the desecration of the Anglican church in York later in the evening. Given his convictions, it is not surprising to find him leaping to Colborne's defence in the matter of the Anglican rectories. The lieutenant governor's blunder was, however, only compounded by Hagerman's thoughtless affronts to virtually every other denomination.

Hagerman's efforts in 1836 to stem the political fury aroused in the assembly by Lieutenant Governor Francis Bond Head*'s confrontation with the Executive Council [*see* Robert Baldwin*; Peter Perry*] were futile. He made up his mind "to retire into private life." His parliamentary and official duties kept him from his private office "longer than is convenient, to say nothing of the great draw back upon my domestic comfort." There had been rumours in October 1834 of his possible re-elevation to the bench. Change did come but it was not what he wanted. On 22 March 1837 he succeeded Robert Sympson Jameson* as attorney general; Hagerman's law partner since 1835, William Henry Draper*, took over the solicitor generalship. Colonial Secretary Lord Glenelg, however, refused to approve Hagerman's appointment. He had no reservations about Hagerman's "private character and public merit" but professed grave doubts about the compatibility of his religious opinions with those of the government. At issue were Hagerman's denigrating remarks about the Church of Scotland in the assembly on 9 February. The congregation of St Andrew's Church in Kingston (Barclay's old church) had forwarded to the Colonial Office a resolution condemning Hagerman's "grossly incorrect statements and intemperate language." Head explained to Glenelg in September that Hagerman's speech had been "purposely and mischievously made as offensive as possible to the Scotch" by Mackenzie in his newspaper. Combined with Hagerman's personal assurances as to what had been said, Head's defence persuaded Glenelg to order Hagerman's warrant in November.

The outbreak of rebellion in December 1837 (Hagerman had noted on 30 November "the general quiet and contentment that prevails") brought – or necessitated – renewed commitment to public life. He was preoccupied through 1838 and 1839 with administrative details and judicial questions relating to the handling of rebels and Patriots. Although he was the father-in-law of Head's secretary, John Joseph*, the connection availed him little more than ready access to the lieutenant governor. Robinson was Head's key adviser, and two recent recruits to the administration, John Macaulay and Robert Baldwin Sullivan*, were the rising stars. Hagerman could not match their abilities in administrative work, analysis, or policy. Head's terse notations about the men on his executive capture Hagerman perfectly: "Able speaker loyal constitutionalist but I have no very high opinion of his judgement. Sound, honest." Neither Hagerman's standing as a courtier nor the cast of characters in government changed greatly when Sir George Arthur succeeded Head in March 1838. Arthur considered him "an honest straight forward Person – Sees matters rightly, and will speak with energy – but, then, He is not a hard Worker!" Arthur was aghast at Hagerman's reaction to the arrival of the report of Lord Durham [LAMBTON]: "He read the Report, and then went out to a party to Dinner! – Whereas He should have sent an excuse, & at once have set down & commented upon it, & without loss of time brought it under the notice of the House."

The question of a union of Upper and Lower Canada had been a topic of growing concern through the second half of the 1830s and Hagerman's stand is of interest. In February 1838 he indicated in debate that he would support union only if there were sufficient safeguards to ensure English-Protestant supremacy. Confronted by the union bill of 1839 he damned it as "republican in its tendency" and urged strengthening the "Monarchical principle." But when the bill came to a vote in the assembly on 19 Dec. 1839, Hagerman, brave declarations of opposition to the contrary, supported the union. The swaggering attorney general had in fact wilted under pressure from Governor Charles Edward Poulett THOMSON. On 24 November Thomson, in private conversation with Arthur and John Macaulay, had wondered why "officers appeared to act as if they regarded not the will of the Government in any matter of public policy." The governor's first impulse was to dismiss his recalcitrant law officer but he decided against it on the advice of Arthur. After a frank discussion with Thomson on 7 December, Hagerman emerged with his bold opposition to union intact. Five days later he declared in the assembly that administrators could not be coerced into supporting it. He was, however, crumbling rapidly. In the assembly on the 19th he explained that since the union resolutions were before the house "by command of the Sovereign," "if the vote in favour . . . was persisted in, he would vote for them." John Macaulay informed a correspondent that he was disturbed to "see Hagerman's friends set up a comparison between his conduct & mine upon the Union Question – I would be sorry to set up so high as he did & after all break down." "You will soon hear," he added, "that he has retired . . . to a Puisne Judgeship." And indeed, with Levius Peters SHERWOOD's retirement, Hagerman joined Robinson, J. B. Macaulay, MacLean, and Jones on the bench, the appointment taking place on 15 Feb. 1840. His former partner Draper succeeded him as attorney general.

Upon his elevation Hagerman turned over his law practice to James McGill Strachan*. He had hoped for an immediate leave but was obliged to wait until late August 1840 before sailing to England with his wife; they returned in July 1841. Compared to the demands of his previous life, the routines of the court must have seemed somewhat dull. Between March 1840 and October 1846 he travelled the circuit to various assizes on ten occasions, holding court almost 50 times. He also had the regular sittings of Queen's Bench *en banc*. His career as a judge awaits further study but one possible contribution should be noted. On 15 April 1840 he presided at the trial in Sandwich (Windsor) of Jacob Briggs, a black man charged with the rape of an eight-year-old white girl. The legal definition of rape required proof of both penetration and emission, and Hagerman so instructed the jury. Despite contradictory evidence – medical testimony for the defence held "it would have been impossible for a full grown man, particularly a Negro to have entered the body" of a young girl – the jury found Briggs guilty, and Hagerman sentenced him to execution. Reporting on the case to the Executive Council, Hagerman overlooked the necessity of proving emission and concentrated on the question of penetration, coming to the conclusion, "most consistent with Law and reason," that to convict for rape it was not necessary to prove that the hymen had been ruptured. After consulting with his colleague J. B. Macaulay, Hagerman decided that there was no legal objection to the jury's verdict. The councillors agreed but commuted the sentence to transportation. The following year the statute on rape was revised and the technicality with respect to emission abandoned, a move hailed by feminist historians as a major turning-point in the law. Although evidence of a direct connection between Hagerman's report and the 1841 law is lacking, it seems reasonable to conclude that it had some impact upon law officers as indicating the views of the judiciary.

Political power was gone for Hagerman in the 1840s. Chastened by his brush with Thomson, he had assured Arthur in August 1840 of his resolve "not to mix myself with party strife or discussion in any way." The following year, from London, Arthur reported to Thomson, now Lord Sydenham, that he had seen Hagerman at a party and that he "talked a great deal as he always does but he was subdued in all his remarks." In 1842, however, Hagerman did not hesitate to urge John Solomon CARTWRIGHT "on *no account whatever* to associate yourself in the Govt with abettors of treason – or the apologists of traitors."

In his private life Hagerman was shaken by the death of his second wife in 1842, but his grief was allayed by his faith in the providential origins of all change. In 1823 he had offered his sympathy to John Macaulay on the death of a younger brother. "We cannot," he wrote, "expect to pass through this life without afflictions, and when Providence dispenses them we may be benefited by reflecting that by being good and virtuous we shall *avert* the *remorse* which attaches to those who are compelled to regard them as the punishments due to vice." He himself had been fortified by his convictions over the course of many family bereavements. Of his daughter Anne Elizabeth Joseph's death in 1838, he notified an acquaintance that "it has pleased God to take this Child from me."

Hagerman was married for a third time in 1846.

Caroline Tysen was an English lady like his second wife. That year he was planning to retire to England when he took ill. His will, signed in a barely legible scrawl and noteworthy for the omission of any mention of religion, stipulated various bequests, the most important of which went to his two surviving daughters. He made provision for his son Frank, presumably a feckless youth who had been a disappointment to him, with the caveat that the executors pay the yearly amount only if they "shall consider that it is right and proper . . . having a due regard to the manner in which he shall conduct himself." On 18 March 1847 Larratt William Violett Smith, a young lawyer, wrote: "Poor Judge Hagerman is still lingering on, so reduced that he may be said to be dying. His worthless son staggers drunk to his bedside in the daytime, whilst his nights are spent in the most abandoned company." Hagerman died two months later; shortly afterwards his wife returned to England.

Hagerman had been useful to successive administrators from Maitland to Arthur. He enjoyed his greatest intimacy with Colborne, who would, however, in time seek out Robinson as a confidant. Hagerman was, perhaps, especially in the late 1830s, a convenient symbol of the uncompromising courtier in what was then known as the "family compact" – certainly Francis Hincks*'s *Examiner* portrayed him as such – but he lacked the talents and intellect which made Robinson, Strachan, Macaulay, and Jones more important. His forte was sound and fury and more often than not it got him into trouble.

ROBERT L. FRASER

Christopher Alexander Hagerman is the author of *Letter of Mr. Attorney General to the editor on the subject of Mr. Bidwell's departure from this province* . . . (Toronto, 1838). A speech he delivered in the assembly was published in *Speeches of Dr. John Rolph, and Christop'r A. Hagerman, esq., his majesty's solicitor general, on the bill for appropriating the proceeds of the clergy reserves to the purposes of general education* . . . (Toronto, 1837). His "Journal of events in the War of 1812" for 1813–14 is held at the MTRL.

AO, MS 4; MS 35; MS 78; MS 186 (mfm.); MU 1376; MU 1838, no.537; MU 2319; MU 2818; RG 22, ser.155; ser.159, Nicholas Hagerman, Daniel Hagerman. Law Soc. of U.C. (Toronto), Minutes. MTRL, William Allan papers. PAC, MG 24, A40; RG 1, E3; L3; RG 5, A1; RG 7, G1. PRO, CO 42. *Arthur papers* (Sanderson). [Thomas Dalton], *"By the words of thy own mouth will I condemn thee"; to Christopher Alexander Hagerman, esq.* ([Kingston, Ont.?, 1824]; copy at MTRL). *Doc. hist. of campaign upon Niagara frontier* (Cruikshank), vols.1–2, 6, 8–9. Charles Durand, *Reminiscences of Charles Durand of Toronto, barrister* (Toronto, 1897). [Charles Grant, 1st Baron] Glenelg, *Lord Glenelg's despatches to Sir F. B. Head, bart., during his administration of the government of Upper Canada* . . . (London, 1839). F. B. Head, *A narrative, with notes by William Lyon Mackenzie*, ed. and intro. S. F. Wise (Toronto and Montreal, 1969). "Journals of Legislative Assembly of U.C.," AO *Report*, 1914. *Select British docs. of War of 1812* (Wood). "A register of baptisms for the township of Fredericksburgh . . . ," comp. John Langhorn, *OH*, 1 (1899): 34, 38. [L. W. V.] Smith, *Young Mr Smith in Upper Canada*, ed. M. L. Smith (Toronto, 1980). U.C., House of Assembly, *Journal*, 1832–40.

British Colonist, 1838–39. *Canadian Freeman*, 1828. *Chronicle & Gazette*, 1833–45. *Examiner* (Toronto), 1838–40. *Kingston Chronicle*, 1819–33. *Kingston Gazette*, 1815. *Niagara Herald* (Niagara [Niagara-on-the-Lake, Ont.]), 1828. *Patriot* (Toronto), 1835–36. *Royal Standard* (Toronto), 1836–37. *U.E. Loyalist*, 1826. *Weekly Register*, 1823. *York Weekly Post*, 1821. *Death notices of Ont.* (Reid). *DHB* (biog. of Michael Vincent). Reid, *Loyalists in Ont.* C. B. Backhouse, "Nineteenth-century Canadian rape law, 1800–92," *Essays in the history of Canadian law*, ed. D. H. Flaherty (2v., Toronto, 1981–83), 2: 200–47. D. R. Beer, *Sir Allan Napier MacNab* (Hamilton, Ont., 1984). William Canniff, *History of the settlement of Upper Canada (Ontario), with special reference to the Bay Quinte* (Toronto, 1869; repr. Belleville, Ont., 1971). Darroch Milani, *Robert Gourlay, gadfly*. R. L. Fraser, "Like Eden in her summer dress: gentry, economy, and society: Upper Canada, 1812–1840" (PHD thesis, Univ. of Toronto, 1979). W. S. Herrington, *History of the county of Lennox and Addington* (Toronto, 1913; repr. Belleville, 1972). Lindsey, *Life and times of Mackenzie*. *Robertson's landmarks of Toronto*, 1: 274. S. F. Wise, "The rise of Christopher Hagerman," *Historic Kingston*, no.14 (1966): 12–23; "Tory factionalism: Kingston elections and Upper Canadian politics, 1820–1836," *OH*, 57 (1965): 205–25.

HALE, JOHN, office holder, militia officer, politician, JP, and seigneur; b. 1765 in England, eldest son of Colonel John Hale and Mary Chaloner; d. 24 Dec. 1838 at Quebec.

John Hale belonged to a very old family from the north of England. His father, a close friend of Major-General James Wolfe*, commanded the 47th Foot at Quebec in 1759. It was he whom Wolfe, as he was dying, chose to bear the news of the taking of Quebec to London. Hale seemed destined to follow in his father's footsteps. He joined the marines on 2 Dec. 1776 and became a lieutenant in the 2nd Foot on 12 May 1779. In 1793 he was put on half pay as a captain, and in the years following he accompanied Prince Edward* Augustus to Halifax as his aide-de-camp and military secretary. Back in England early in 1798, Hale married Elizabeth Frances Amherst* in London on 3 April 1799. They were to have four daughters and eight sons, including Edward* and Jeffery*.

Hale returned to Quebec in June 1799 as deputy paymaster general of the British troops stationed in the Canadas. In 1807 he succeeded Thomas Aston Coffin* as inspector general of public accounts. He also received a number of commissions. In 1800 he was named to the commission for the management of the Jesuit estates. Along with John Mure* and François Bellet*, in 1811 he was appointed commissioner for obtaining plans for a parliament building. Governor Sir George Prevost* made him a justice of the peace for the districts of Quebec, Trois-Rivières, and Montreal in 1813. In 1818 Hale was named to a committee to assist sick and destitute strangers. He was a member of the Legislative Council from 3 Dec. 1808 to 27 March 1838, and served as speaker three times – 23 Feb. 1814 to 16 Jan. 1815; 21 Feb. 1815 to 21 Jan. 1816; and 7 Feb. 1817 to 10 March 1823. He sat on the Executive Council from 28 Dec. 1820 until his death. At the request of Governor Lord Dalhousie [RAMSAY], he was also on a three-member committee charged in 1823 with examining the state of the public coffers under Receiver General John CALDWELL. When Caldwell was found guilty of misappropriating funds, Hale was appointed to replace him on 25 November, and he remained receiver general until his death. Like his predecessor, he was unable to avoid criticism from the Patriote party, which accused him of authorizing expenditures without consulting the assembly.

The Hales, who came from wealthy families, owned properties in England as well as in Upper and Lower Canada. In July 1799 Hale bought several pieces of land and a house on Rue Saint-Louis at Quebec. He sold the residence at a substantial profit on 3 June 1815, and then on 5 March 1818 paid £4,210 for three other lots and a two-storey stone house on Rue des Carrières. On 27 Sept. 1819 he bought the seigneury of Sainte-Anne-De La Pérade from Marie-Anne Tarieu de Lanaudière. Hale, who conducted himself as a good seigneur with his *censitaires*, did not hesitate to demand his due, and he had two attorneys working closely with him to manage affairs in his absence. He added to his already considerable fortune by acting as attorney or financial backer for certain tradesmen from Quebec and the region, among them William Bacheler Coltman*, George Waters ALLSOPP, John Cannon*, Chief Justice John Elmsley*'s widow, and the minister and managers of St Andrew's Church.

From May 1805 till March 1812 Hale was colonel of the 3rd Battalion of the town's militia. In 1813 he took on for some weeks the duties of treasurer of the Quebec office of the Loyal and Patriotic Society of the Province of Lower Canada, which had been founded to assist wounded militiamen. He was president of the Quebec Savings Bank from 1821 to 1823, and then vice-president from 1823 to 1826. He also served as vice-president of the Trois-Rivières agricultural society around 1823. Every winter Hale and his family would return from the manor-house of Sainte-Anne-De La Pérade to Quebec, where he and his wife joined in the social life of the capital. He belonged to the Literary and Historical Society of Quebec and the Quebec Emigrant Society in 1821–22, and was a trustee of the Musée Chasseur at Quebec in 1829 [*see* Pierre CHASSEUR].

His family's reputation and his loyalty to the government combined to bring John Hale positions of trust which he filled honourably throughout his career.

CHRISTINE VEILLEUX

John Hale is the author of "Observations upon crickets in Canada," Literary and Hist. Soc. of Quebec, *Trans.*, 1 (1824–29): 254–55.

ANQ-Q, CE1-61, 27 déc. 1838; CN1-26, 1801; CN1-49, 1818–38; CN1-116, 1836–38; CN1-208, 1830–38; CN1-230, 1800–25; CN1-256, 1799; CN1-262, 1805–19; P1000-48-931. PAC, MG 23, GII, 18. *Docs. relating to constitutional hist., 1819–28* (Doughty and Story). *Quebec Gazette*, 30 May, 6 June 1805; 23 May 1811; 1 April 1813; 26 Dec. 1838. F.-J. Audet, "Les législateurs du Bas-Canada." *Cyclopædia of Canadian biog.* (Rose and Charlesworth). Desjardins, *Guide parl.* Literary and Hist. Soc. of Quebec, *Index of the lectures, papers and historical documents . . . , 1829 to 1891*, comp. F. C. Würtele and J. C. Strachan (Quebec, 1927). *Officers of British forces in Canada* (Irving). "Papiers d'État – Bas-Canada," PAC *Rapport*, 1891: 1–206; 1893: 1–123. *Quebec almanac.* P.-G. Roy, *Inv. concessions.* Turcotte, *Le Conseil législatif.* R. C. Dalton, *The Jesuits' estates question, 1760–1888: a study of the background for the agitation of 1889* (Toronto, 1968). "La famille Hale," *BRH*, 38 (1932): 750–51.

HAMEL, ANDRÉ-RÉMI, lawyer, office holder, and author; b. 22 Oct. 1788 at Quebec, son of Charles Hamel, a tinsmith, and Marie Bedouin; d. 24 March 1840 in Leeds, Lower Canada.

André-Rémi Hamel did his classical studies at the Petit Séminaire de Québec in the period 1804–12. In 1813 he began articling under Quebec lawyer Louis Plamondon*. He was called to the bar on 20 April 1818 and went into practice at Quebec. There, on 23 June of the following year, he married Marie-Adélaïde Roy, an aunt of Pierre-Joseph-Olivier Chauveau*. Among those he later took in as articling students were Chauveau and René-Édouard Caron*, who became respectively premier and lieutenant governor of Quebec.

Although he had little interest in politics, in December 1827 Hamel, along with Amable BERTHELOT, Hector-Simon HUOT, Louis Lagueux*, and John NEILSON, joined a 35-member committee headed by Joseph-Rémi VALLIÈRES de Saint-Réal and appointed at a meeting of voters from the town of Quebec. The committee was established to draw up and submit to the king and the British parliament a petition listing grievances about the composition of the Legislative Council and its subordination to the executive authority, the exorbitant expenditures resulting from sinecures, the ineffectiveness of assembly grants in furthering education, the allocation of public revenues without the assembly's prior consent, the mismanagement of public lands, and the attempts by the British parliament to change the constitution without the knowledge of the province's residents.

This petition, as well as another more vehement one sent by a committee from the Montreal region, was submitted to London. A House of Commons committee studied the questions raised and published a report acknowledging the validity of the Canadians' grievances. Its recommendations were not acted upon, however, and most of the complaints set out in 1828 were reiterated in the famous 92 Resolutions of 1834 [*see* Elzéar BÉDARD].

In 1831, while still in practice, Hamel published, under the pseudonym Un Ami de l'Ordre, *La question des fabriques*, which had first appeared as extracts in the *Quebec Gazette* a few months earlier at the time the assembly was studying a bill introduced by Louis Bourdages* to permit the presence of property owners at the election of churchwardens and the rendering of accounts by the *fabriques*. The assembly consulted numerous parish priests and, with one or two exceptions, the clergy as a whole was opposed to the bill. In his pamphlet Hamel cited various conciliar laws, edicts, and canons in support of those who were against the proposal. His argument was based on the fact that the assets and income of a *fabrique*, consisting of free gifts, pew rentals, and fees for services, belonged exclusively to the church. Since administration of private assets did not come under the state, there was no requirement for churchwardens to be elected democratically or for accounts to be rendered in public. After making some amendments, the assembly adopted the bill, but it was rejected by the Legislative Council.

On 11 July 1832 Hamel was appointed advocate general of Lower Canada, replacing George Vanfelson* who had resigned. He acquired a certain reputation while holding this office. On 18 Feb. 1834 Hamel was summoned before the assembly because, in his capacity as advocate general and without the authorization of the house, he had given the governor, Lord Aylmer [WHITWORTH-AYLMER], a legal opinion on the by-election of December 1833 in Stanstead riding. Hamel had confirmed the returning officer's decision to declare Wright Chamberlin elected, even though Marcus Child* had apparently received 70 votes more. The house considered his giving an opinion in this matter an infringement of its rights and privileges and the speaker, Louis-Joseph Papineau*, publicly reprimanded Hamel. It is important to bear in mind that the rebuke was delivered at the time when the assembly was debating the 92 Resolutions, which included a denunciation of direct interference by the governor and legislative councillors in the election of the people's representatives and particularly in the choice of returning officers. In the event, the next day the assembly declared Child officially elected.

Le Canadien on 21 Feb. 1834 none the less stressed the courageous action taken by Hamel, who had chosen to appear before the assembly and face up to his responsibilities. Six days later the members of the Montreal bar met to protest the reprimand. They regarded this incident as a direct attack on the independence of the bar, which was necessary for the protection of the individual and the defence of citizens' rights. Historian Robert Christie* considered that Hamel's opinion "was in accordance with the law, and no doubt conscientious."

On 2 May 1839 Hamel was named a commissioner of the Court of Requests in the district of Quebec, and on 14 May he was made a QC. He discharged his duties until he succumbed to a stroke in Leeds, near Quebec, on 24 March 1840, at 51 years of age. His remains were taken to Quebec and buried three days later in the crypt of Notre-Dame cathedral. In its obituary the *Quebec Gazette* on 28 March paid homage to Hamel: "Gifted with outstanding talents that were constantly and almost exclusively used in the study of law, Mr Hamel was one of the most distinguished lawyers in [his province]: his activity and his zeal, which led him to observe scrupulously all the requirements of a legal system reputed to be unworkable, made him, during the short space of time that he administered justice, an exemplary magistrate."

CLAUDE VACHON

André-Rémi Hamel is the author of *La question des fabriques* (Québec, 1831), published under the pseudonym Un Ami de l'Ordre.

ANQ-Q, CE1-1, 23 oct. 1788, 23 juin 1819, 27 mars 1840. ASQ, Fichier des anciens. PAC, MG 30, D1, 15: 14–16; RG 4, B8: 7048–51; RG 68, General index, 1651–1841. *Le Canadien*, 19, 21, 24 févr. 1834. *La Gazette de Québec*, 19–20 févr. 1834, 28 mars 1840. F.-J. Audet, "Commissions d'avocats," *BRH*, 39: 581; "Conseils du roi," *BRH*, 41 (1935): 609–10; "Conseils du roi dans le Bas-Canada," *BRH*, 31 (1925): 57; "Procureurs généraux de la province de Québec (1764–1791)," *BRH*, 39 (1933): 276–77. Philéas Gagnon, *Essai de bibliographie canadienne . . .* (2v., Québec et Montréal, 1895–1913; réimpr. Dubuque, Iowa, [1962]). H. J. Morgan, *Bibliotheca Canadensis*; *Sketches of celebrated Canadians*, 472. P.-G. Roy, *Les avocats de la région de Québec*; *Fils de Québec*, 3: 42–43; *Les juges de la prov. de Québec*. Tanguay, *Dictionnaire*, 4: 451–52. Bernard Vinet, *Pseudonymes québécois* (Québec, 1974), 244. Buchanan, *Bench and bar of L.C.*, 55, 89–90. Chapais, *Cours d'hist. du Canada*, 3: 187–202; 4: 16–25. N.-E. Dionne, *Les trois comédies du "statu quo," 1834* (Québec, 1909), 40–56. Edmond Lareau, *Histoire de la littérature canadienne* (Montréal, 1874). J.-E. Roy, *Hist. de Lauzon*, 5: 285–341. Paul Bernier, "Le droit paroissial avant et depuis Mignault," *La Rev. du notariat* (Québec), 46 (1943–44): 175–99. "Les disparus; l'honorable André-Rémi Hamel," *BRH*, 31 (1925): 548. "Le docteur John Buchanan," *BRH*, 17 (1911): 102.

HAMILTON, ALEXANDER, businessman, militia

officer, JP, office holder, and judge; b. 3 July 1790 in Queenston (Ont.), son of Robert Hamilton* and Catherine Robertson, *née* Askin; m. 25 Jan. 1816 Hannah Owen Jarvis, daughter of William Jarvis*, in Niagara (Niagara-on-the-Lake), Upper Canada, and they had eight daughters and three sons; d. 19 Feb. 1839 in Queenston.

Alexander Hamilton attended school at Queenston and Niagara and was taken to Scotland in 1795 for further education. On his return, he worked for a short period in his father's business, but he had only a desultory exposure to it before Robert Hamilton's death in 1809. His father left the stock and facilities of his major enterprises of retailing, forwarding, and portaging around Niagara Falls to him and his brother GEORGE. As a result of changing economic circumstances in Upper Canada, these enterprises were already showing signs of decline at the time of Hamilton's death. Because of the brothers' inexperience and a complex will which virtually froze the assets of their father's estate until a stepbrother, John*, had reached the age of majority in 1823, George and Alexander quickly ran down the once highly successful business. In 1811 they further complicated their situation by renting, along with their uncle Charles Askin, saw- and grist-mills in Canboro Township from Benjamin Canby. The following year Alexander and Charles purchased the operation, agreeing to pay £22,000 for it. With the outbreak of war, Hamilton abandoned all attempts to revive his father's enterprises.

Hamilton saw extensive service in the War of 1812, particularly with small raiding and reconnoitring parties. He had become a captain under Major Thomas MERRITT in the Niagara Light Dragoons on 1 May 1812 and later served under William Hamilton Merritt* in that unit and in the Provincial Light Dragoons. He was specifically mentioned by Major-General Roger Hale Sheaffe* in dispatches concerning the battle of Queenston Heights and was present at the retreat from Fort George (Niagara-on-the-Lake) in 1813 as well as at many of the other major engagements on the Niagara peninsula.

Hamilton emerged from the war burdened with the debts built up by him and his brothers before the war. He placed himself further in debt by borrowing almost £1,000 from his father's estate and sinking it into an attempt to revitalize his milling concern at Canboro. Despite his attempts, the business collapsed in 1817 and he and Charles Askin were reduced to trying to sell their Canboro holdings in an attempt to meet its debts. For a time, however, Hamilton's fortunes appeared to turn. In the winter of 1817–18 he was approached by William Smith (evidently a former member of a Detroit fur-trading concern), who had been offered a contract for the portaging of the North West Company's goods at Niagara. The Montreal firms of the NWC were willing to lend money to Hamilton and Smith towards the purchase of facilities. These were expensive, however, and competition stiff, with three companies vying in the small and fragmented portaging trade at Niagara. Collapse for Hamilton and Smith came in 1821, when the NWC amalgamated with the Hudson's Bay Company and ceased to use the lower Great Lakes route for shipments. Hamilton and Smith found themselves not only without trade but saddled with debts for the facilities they had purchased.

These debts exhausted what remained of Hamilton's share of his father's estate. He had already run through the monetary portion of it. To meet his part of the debts of Hamilton and Smith, he was forced to sign over his share of the lands so that by 1828 his patrimony was depleted.

After the War of 1812, Hamilton's interests had turned increasingly from business to patronage, and he systematically applied for major posts in the Niagara District as they became vacant. In 1817 he received his first commission as a justice of the peace. His search for office was undoubtedly aided by the fact that, although he sympathized with the agitation stirred up by Robert Gourlay*, in its early stages, he was not vociferously pro-Gourlay, in contrast to several of his brothers. The prestige of his family name and continuing contacts were also important to Hamilton in gaining office. His correspondence indicates that he relied upon the intervention of his brother-in-law, Samuel Peters Jarvis*, and the Reverend John Strachan*. The latter had had a long association with the Hamilton family – it was Robert Hamilton who had arranged that he be brought from Scotland as a tutor for Richard Cartwright*'s children – and he accepted a position as an executor of Hamilton's estate. Strachan's admiration for Alexander's "amiable manners and gentlemanly conduct" obviously served the younger Hamilton well. Among the more important positions he held, for various periods between 1821 and 1839, were postmaster and deputy collector of customs at Queenston, surrogate court judge, and sheriff of the Niagara District. By 1833 his fortunes were sufficiently restored to allow him to begin construction at Queenston of a mansion, Willowbank, which still stands.

Hamilton was a pillar of his community and was involved in many of Queenston's interests: he acted, for example, as an early chairman of the Erie and Ontario Railroad Company and was a commissioner of the Niagara River Suspension Bridge Company. Both enterprises were essentially projects by which interests on the Niagara River, led by Queenston, attempted to compete with the Welland Canal and restore a flow of trade to the river-front.

In December 1837 Hamilton embarked with a body of volunteers to help in the defence of Toronto and was part of the force which met William Lyon Mackenzie*'s rebels. As sheriff of the Niagara District, Hamilton was charged by the provincial government with gathering information on seditious persons in that region, a task in which he was aided by such magistrates as George Rykert* of St Catharines. Hamilton took part in guarding the Niagara frontier and conducted an investigation of the Short Hills raid [*see* Linus Wilson Miller*]. When the executioner failed to appear to carry out the sentence of death on James Morreau, one of the leaders of the raid, Hamilton performed it himself on 30 July 1838, having arranged, as an "act of kindness," that Morreau drop 18 feet before the rope snapped his neck. He was later complimented by the government for the "cool and firm manner" in which the execution was performed.

BRUCE G. WILSON

AO, MU 1726. DPL, Burton Hist. Coll., John Askin papers, Charles Askin ledger, 1813–15; G. Hamilton to C. Askin, 11 Dec. 1817. MTRL, Alexander Wood papers, John Strachan to Wood, 13 June 1806. PAC, MG 19, A3, 19: 623–44, 6265–68, 6277; 38: 304–6; MG 24, D45, Alexander Hamilton to James Hamilton, 28 June 1821; I26, 1–2, 4, 6, 10–15, 64–65; RG 5, A1: 35123, 109369–74, 109742–45, 109931–32, 110292–94, 110419–24; RG 68, General index, 1651–1841: 428, 539, 668. *Doc. hist. of campaign upon Niagara frontier* (Cruikshank), 4: 72; 5: 138–39; 6: 178–81, 209. "Early records of St. Mark's and St. Andrew's churches, Niagara," comp. Janet Carnochan, *OH*, 3 (1901): 38, 43, 48–49, 60, 75. *John Askin papers* (Quaife), 1: 539. "The Niagara frontier in 1837–38; papers from the Hamilton correspondence in the Canadian Archives . . . ," ed. A. H. U. Colquhoun, Niagara Hist. Soc., [*Pub.*], no.29 (1916). "Reminiscences of American occupation of Niagara from 27th May to 10th Dec. 1813," Niagara Hist. Soc., [*Pub.*], no.11 (n.d.): 27–28. *St. Catharines Journal*, 21 Feb. 1839. Chadwick, *Ontarian families*, 1: 146. Read, *Rising in western U.C.*, 150. B. G. Wilson, *Enterprises of Robert Hamilton*.

HAMILTON, Sir CHARLES, naval officer and governor of Newfoundland; b. 25 May 1767, elder son of Sir John Hamilton and Cassandra Agnes Chamberlayne; m. 19 April 1803 Henrietta Martha Drummond, and they had one son; d. 14 Sept. 1849 in Iping, England.

Charles Hamilton was bred to the navy. His maternal grandfather had been an admiral and his father was a captain who earned a baronetcy for his work in the defence of Quebec in 1775–76. Charles went to sea in the summer of 1776 as a captain's servant on his father's ship, the *Hector*. From 1777 to 1779 he attended the Royal Naval Academy at Portsmouth and then rejoined the *Hector* as a midshipman. Between 1780 and 1810 he served in the East and West Indies, the North Sea, the Mediterranean, and off the coast of Africa, rising to become a rear-admiral and commander-in-chief on the Thames on 31 July 1810. He was promoted vice-admiral of the blue on 4 June 1814. On 25 April 1818 he became naval commander-in-chief of Newfoundland and Labrador and on 9 May was appointed governor. He arrived on 19 July, relieving acting administrator Captain John Bowker.

The policy of appointing admirals as governors has been criticized by historians of Newfoundland, who have echoed contemporary complaints that these men were, as a petition from the inhabitants of St John's stated, "educated from their youth in a system of their own" and thus were unfit for "the exercise of that discrimination and patience so essential in the administration" of colonies. In Hamilton's case the criticism was only partly valid. He was not without civil experience, having served as an MP for various constituencies in the south of England and in Ireland for about 13 years between 1790 and 1812, although he was on active service for most of that time. He could also claim to be "not altogether ignorant of the history of early colonization, having passed a great portion of my life in the Plantations."

Unfortunately for Hamilton, Newfoundland's institutions had not kept pace with the times, and his instructions were virtually identical to those given to the 18th-century governors. Hamilton was deeply conservative and he did value Newfoundland as "a good Nursery for seamen," but he also acknowledged that it could not remain simply "a station for the seasonal fishery." One sign that the Colonial Office had also arrived at this conclusion was that Hamilton was expected to establish a year-round residence and he was the first governor to be accompanied by his wife.

Horrified by the lack of public buildings and the narrow streets and crowded wooden houses of St John's, Hamilton built a court-house, began work on a jail, and sought to impose a building code on the town, particularly after it was again devastated by fires in 1818 and 1819. He also supported the construction of churches by the Church of England, although he refused to expand the public education system and in 1823 protested when the Colonial Office gave a grant to the Newfoundland School Society, composed mainly of dissenters and low-church Anglicans. But most of Hamilton's efforts at civic improvement came to little, either for lack of funds or because he could not enforce his regulations. Even after he received more extensive legal authority from parliament in 1820, he found it difficult to effect reforms: "No endeavours of mine or powers I possessed could induce the inhabitants to adopt more cleanly habits." None the less the Hamiltons actively participated in the social life of the capital. Lady Hamilton, "the kind and constant friend of the Widow and the Orphan," was a talented artist who left for posterity a portrait of the Beothuk Demasduwit*.

Ironically Hamilton inadvertently accelerated the destruction of the Beothuks. In his eagerness to "extend to that miserable people the blessings of Civilization," he authorized John Peyton's ill-considered expedition in 1818. Although its main purpose was to establish friendly contacts, the mission resulted in the death of two Indians and the capture of Desmasduwit. Hamilton ordered an investigation but turned it into what was later termed a "cover-up." He was also responsible for the equally unsuccessful expedition of Commander David BUCHAN in 1819–20. He did provide assistance to Shawnadithit* when she gave herself up to William Cull* in 1823.

Hamilton was unable to diversify Newfoundland's economy. Having been instructed to promote agriculture, he soon reported that the soil was "so much worse than I had envisioned" that it was only suitable for "Grass & Potatoes." Although he favoured small grants for fishermen, he did little to encourage such grants, and he dismissed proposals for roads into the interior as unnecessary because the island was inevitably dependent on the fisheries. The collapse of the cod market after the Napoleonic Wars led Hamilton to place greater emphasis on the rapidly expanding seal fishery and to encourage the whale and Labrador salmon fisheries. Because of the depressed economy, large numbers of destitute people had flooded into St John's. Hamilton's solution was to match funds raised by private subscription for the relief of the poor, while deporting as many of them as possible to the British North American colonies or the mother country. In 1822 he provided approximately £370 for relief rations in St John's but gave more than £468 towards removing paupers from the island. Hamilton was primarily concerned with increasing government revenues, but his powers were hampered by the depression and by the legal decisions of Chief Justice Francis FORBES, including his declaring invalid the governors' proclamations, which traditionally had been assumed to have the force of law.

Forbes's decisions, combined with the growing outcry against the practice of appointing naval officers as surrogate judges, led the Colonial Office to revamp the legal system. Hamilton returned to London on 18 Oct. 1822 to assist in the process. However, the juridicial provisions of the 1823 Newfoundland bill owed more to Forbes and the legal adviser at the Colonial Office, James Stephen, than it did to Hamilton. With great reluctance Hamilton went back to the island in July 1823 to assess public opinion and to complete his accounts. He left again in November, returning to his family home at Iping. Although he continued to draw half pay until 5 July 1824 and was occasionally consulted by the Colonial Office, he never again held an appointment. On 22 July 1830 he became an admiral and on 19 Jan. 1833 was made a KCB. He had succeeded to the baronetcy on his father's death in 1784.

When defending his administration, the latter part of which had been marked by political discord, Hamilton claimed in 1824 that "if the system required alteration it was no fault of mine." Yet he cannot be absolved of all responsibility. His opposition to the proposed incorporation of St John's was short-sighted and he stubbornly defended the surrogate system – partly because it justified a larger naval establishment – and delayed its inevitable abolition. Indeed, he probably accelerated the demand for reform by over-reacting to the least sign of opposition. His prolonged dispute with William Dawe, the only trained lawyer on the island, was particularly damaging. Hamilton dismissed him from his position as notary in 1818 and later fined him for contempt when Dawe legitimately challenged the authority of a court of oyer and terminer established and presided over by Hamilton. Dawe's heated attacks on the governor led the English reformer Joseph Hume to demand an examination of Hamilton's accounts in 1823. Although Stephen's investigation uncovered that Hamilton, with a salary and a vice-admiral's pay and allowances, had been selling surplus coal purchased for Government House, it largely exonerated him of wrongdoing.

Hamilton never understood the strength of the pressure for change because he had little respect for those pushing for reform, a group he referred to as "adventurers without principle (or property . . .)" and "a few troublesome persons." Thus it is hardly surprising that the last of the admiral-governors, even though a resident, did little to redeem the reputation of that office.

PHILLIP BUCKNER

PRO, CO 194/61–72; CO 195/7. G.B., Parl., *The parliamentary debates* (London), [2nd] ser., 5 (1821): 1015–17; 8 (1823): 702–4; 9 (1823): 245–55. *DNB*. Marshall, *Royal naval biog*. W. R. O'Byrne, *A naval biographical dictionary: comprising the life and service of every living officer in Her Majesty's navy . . .* (London, 1849). C. H. Currey, *Sir Francis Forbes: the first chief justice of the Supreme Court of New South Wales* (Sydney, Australia, 1968). M. A. Lewis, *A social history of the navy, 1793–1815* (London, 1960). A. H. McLintock, *The establishment of constitutional government in Newfoundland, 1783–1832: a study of retarded colonisation* (London and Toronto, 1941). W. S. MacNutt, *The Atlantic provinces: the emergence of colonial society, 1712–1857* (Toronto, 1965). Paul O'Neill, *The story of St. John's, Newfoundland* (2v., Erin, Ont., 1975–76). Prowse, *Hist. of Nfld.* (1896). F. W. Rowe, *Extinction: the Beothuks of Newfoundland* (Toronto, 1977). Marjorie Smith, "Newfoundland, 1815–1840: a study of a merchantocracy" (MA thesis, Memorial Univ. of Nfld., St John's, 1968).

HAMILTON, GEORGE, businessman, militia officer, office holder, and politician; b. October 1788 in Queenston (Ont.), son of Robert Hamilton* and Catherine Robertson, *née* Askin; m. 2 Aug. 1811, in York (Toronto), Maria (Mary) Lavinia Jarvis, daughter of William Jarvis* and Hannah PETERS, and they had three sons and five daughters; d. 20 Feb. 1836 at his residence in Hamilton, Upper Canada.

George Hamilton received some schooling locally before his father escorted him to Scotland in 1795 for further education. After their father's death in 1809, George and his brother ALEXANDER inherited his various enterprises. Between 1809 and 1812 they mismanaged business affairs and clashed with their brothers and also with their influential kin who were trustees of the estate. During the War of 1812 George, who had received a commission in the militia in 1808, held the rank of captain in Thomas MERRITT's Niagara Light Dragoons. He took part in the capture of Detroit and the battle of Queenston Heights in 1812 and the battle of Lundy's Lane in 1814.

The disruption of trade and immigration that accompanied the war exacerbated a decline in the Hamiltons' business that had been evident even at the time of Robert Hamilton's death. When peace was restored George set out to re-establish himself. He shifted his interest to the Head of the Lake (the vicinity of present-day Hamilton Harbour). In July 1815 he purchased 257 acres in Barton Township from James Durand* for £1,750. Within a year he reached an agreement with a neighbouring landowner Nathaniel Hughson to develop a town site there. They empowered Durand, the local assemblyman, to act as their agent in the sale of town lots. This initiative coincided with the government's decision in 1816 to erect a new district in the area and to designate Hamilton's site its capital. The political and business dealings behind the selection of the site are obscure. They had, no doubt, something to do with Durand's influence in the House of Assembly and Hamilton's connections. To accommodate a court-house and jail, the central public buildings in a district capital, Hamilton ceded two blocks of land, of two acres each, to the crown. The town site itself, modelled on the popular grid pattern of most North American frontier towns, was carved into readily surveyed parcels. In 1828–29, when the original lots had been sold, Hamilton would add more. By the 1830s the village of Hamilton (incorporated in 1833) contained rivals who would defeat George's bid to locate the market on his lands; instead he was forced to settle for a more modest hay market.

George Hamilton was drawn into politics through his association with Robert Gourlay* in the late 1810s. He may have become involved in the agitation partly because of a personal setback with a milling venture on the Grand River; the operation seems to have failed by 1819. It is possible that the regional grievances of the Niagara peninsula, especially the unsettled claims for war losses (Hamilton's among them), contributed to his dissatisfaction, and his Presbyterian background perhaps played a role as well. Moreover, he undoubtedly perceived the clergy and crown reserves as impediments to settlement and therefore to the advancement of his own interest. In 1818 he and William Johnson KERR carried Gourlayite resolutions to Lieutenant Governor Sir Peregrine Maitland*, who refused to receive them. Hamilton and Kerr reacted by running, successfully, for the assembly in the election of 1820. Hamilton was one of the representatives for the riding of Wentworth in the eighth (1821–24), ninth (1825–28), and tenth (1829–30) parliaments. These years coincided with the rise of the village of Hamilton and mark the zenith of George Hamilton's influence and fortunes.

From his initial appearance in the assembly in February 1821 until March 1828, Hamilton aligned himself with reformers. At first, he worked closely with John Willson*, his fellow member from Wentworth. Following Willson's election as speaker in 1825, Hamilton associated with John Rolph*. Resentful of the Maitland administration's treatment of Gourlayites such as Richard BEASLEY, he constantly needled Attorney General John Beverley Robinson*. Reform positions drew his support: he favoured the seating of Barnabas Bidwell*, criticized the state of public accounts, and advocated the assertion of the assembly's prerogatives. He complained about retrenchment which, he believed, threatened internal development. Rank and hierarchy were little appreciated by this merchant of Presbyterian background. He naturally opposed the various measures and practices which gave the Church of England its favoured status; indeed, his religious views were particularly liberal.

The tie between a moderate reformer such as Hamilton and commercial interest was evident in his impatience with the slow rate of settlement and the depressed state of public works. A series of resolutions in 1823, moved by William Warren BALDWIN and seconded by Hamilton, criticized the lack of immigrants, proposed the elimination of the reserves, urged the location of new settlers close to roads and mills, and recommended the granting of entire townships to men of capital able to develop mills and forges. With his mercantile background, Hamilton was wary of taxes on trade and opposed duties on salt and whisky (to finance the Welland Canal). He maintained that the more orderly keeping of public accounts could ensure the financing of improvements, presumably by reducing the fees paid to the colony's officials. As late as March 1829, he returned to the topic of immigration and, with Willson, introduced a bill to encourage it.

During the 1820s, George sponsored several measures of express benefit to the village of Hamilton. Beginning in 1823, he pressed the government to cut a canal linking Lake Ontario with Burlington Bay (Hamilton Harbour). Once the work was underway, problems between the canal's commissioners and their contractor, James Gordon Strobridge*, took some of the lustre off an important local improvement despite its successful completion. From 1825 to 1827, Hamilton worked to secure public funding for a new court-house and jail at Hamilton, an undertaking which stirred up resentment from rival communities [*see* Peter Desjardins*] and brought critical petitions against it. George was forced to defend Hamilton's status as capital of the Gore District. In March 1828 he moved assembly acceptance of a petition requesting a grant of £2,000 for work on the stalled Desjardins Canal project, but reformers Peter Perry* and Marshall Spring Bidwell* moved, successfully, to postpone a decision.

In 1829 Hamilton was badly squeezed between his constituency and the reformers by the "Hamilton Outrage" – the hanging in effigy of the lieutenant governor over his refusal to release imprisoned journalist Francis Collins* [*see* Strobridge]. As events got out of hand, Allan Napier MacNab*, a Hamilton lawyer, was jailed for contempt of the assembly. He had refused to testify before a house committee examining the outrage. George tried to chart a moderate course, but more often than not, this tack placed him and Willson at odds with other reformers eager to pursue the issue for all it was worth. Another local affair which caused him similar problems was a complaint by George Rolph (John's brother), clerk of the peace, against Gore District magistrates for wrongful dismissal. Because it reflected critically upon Hamilton's associates among the Wentworth gentry, he refused to support it. He recoiled from a partisan exploitation of reform issues embarrassing to the Gore District and his own political survival, but, in spite of the charge by some historians that such trimming indicated a pro-government stance, Hamilton's fundamental inclinations were reform-oriented. In March 1829, at the same time as the events surrounding the outrage were unfolding, Hamilton voted for resolutions designed to assert the assembly's claim to control over finances whereas Willson voted against them.

Controversy over his role as a town-site promoter and failure to campaign aggressively cost Hamilton his seat in the election of 1830. He finished last in a four-way fight: Willson topped the polls and MacNab edged out Durand. MacNab was a political newcomer who had advanced himself swiftly because of his role in the outrage and his support for the interests of Hamilton and Dundas. Concurrent with MacNab's rapid rise was Hamilton's embarrassment over a shortfall in his accounts as district treasurer. Although he made up the deficiency personally, his stature may have been damaged by its disclosure and the outlay of funds may have hampered his ability to finance his re-election. He remained in public life but without a platform. He could scarcely dispute the affable and younger MacNab's pursuit of improvements to local transportation and he had found, as a result of his loss in the 1830 election, that he could not associate with radical reformism. Indeed, in 1831 he spoke against William Lyon Mackenzie* at a local political meeting. The following year he chaired a hastily organized board of health formed to handle the cholera epidemic. In 1834 he stood, unsuccessfully, against MacNab for the newly established seat for Hamilton. Still a relatively esteemed member of the Burlington Bay gentry, Hamilton had, none the less, become unelectable.

George Hamilton took up politics to enhance his personal fortune and to shape society in ways conducive to commercial success. In his espousal of causes and principles harmonious with commerce and land speculation he was no different from the "family compact." Yet his adherence to reform principles is a reminder that the colonial élite of which he was part was not at one on political matters; consideration of the province's future invited conflict over the proper social ends of policy and over the correct management of resources to achieve those ends. Hamilton combined support for the crown with advocacy of a broadly latitudinarian constitution dominated by the assembly. This combination would be, in effect, the basis for the political accord reached in the 1840s and 1850s. Along with other moderates of the 1820s, the privileged North American Scot had hit upon the formula of increased immigration, religious toleration, improvements to transportation, and a collaboration of business and government that has often flourished since as policy in Canadian politics.

JOHN C. WEAVER

AO, RG 1, A-I-6: 4820–21, 8728–31; RG 22, ser.155. PAC, MG 24, D45, 7, Thomas Clarke to James Hamilton, 10 Oct. 1821; RG 5, A1: 22753–55. Private arch., Miss Ann MacIntosh Duff (Toronto), Family geneal. docs. Wentworth Land Registry Office (Hamilton, Ont.), Barton Township, deeds, vol.A (1816–29) (mfm. at AO). U.C., House of Assembly, *Journal*, 1821–30; 1826–27, app.R. *Kingston Chronicle*, 15 Dec. 1826, 16 Feb. 1827. *Upper Canada Herald*, 1, 15, 29 March, 24 May 1825. Armstrong, *Handbook of Upper Canadian chronology* (1985). *DHB*. D. R. Beer, *Sir Allan Napier MacNab* (Hamilton, 1984). Darroch Milani, *Robert Gourlay, gadfly*. J. C. Weaver, *Hamilton: an illustrated history* (Toronto, 1982), 16–17. B. G. Wilson, *Enterprises of Robert Hamilton*.

HAMILTON, GEORGE, businessman, office holder, militia officer, JP, and judge; b. 13 April 1781 in Hamwood (Republic of Ireland), third son of Charles Hamilton, businessman, and Elizabeth Chetwood; d.

7 Jan. 1839 at Hawkesbury, Upper Canada, and was buried near St Andrews (Saint-André-Est, Que.).

George Hamilton's family was of Lowland Scots origin but had taken up estates in Ireland. In the early 19th century, operating largely out of Liverpool, it was involved in the Baltic timber and Madeira wine trades, no doubt among others. Probably in 1804, but certainly by June 1806, George had arrived at Quebec to establish a branch of the family operations. In 1808 he was selling Madeira wines received via Liverpool, and by May 1809 he had taken his brother William into partnership. Until at least 1811 the firm of George and William Hamilton operated as "Auctioneers & Brokers," selling everything from nails to silk parasols in its rooms in Upper Town.

After 1807 the Liverpool Hamiltons were briefly cut off from their Baltic timber supplies by Napoleon's continental blockade. Lured by lucrative British Admiralty contracts for naval stores, they followed the example set early in the decade by Henry USBORNE and transferred at least part of their timber operations to the Canadas, where the Admiralty generated war business worth £2,500,000 in 1809 alone. On 31 Aug. 1809 George and William Hamilton took a 21-year lease on a lot and beach at the mouth of the Rivière Chaudière in Lower Canada from the seigneur of Lauzon, Henry Caldwell*. The firm immediately announced its readiness to receive rafts of timber and staves at "New Liverpool Cove." In addition to exporting timber, in part in ships they had built at New Liverpool, the Hamiltons sold it at Quebec to the growing shipbuilding industry. In March and April 1810 their firm became the representative on the St Lawrence of the underwriters of London, Liverpool, Dundee, and Aberdeen; as such it was empowered to take charge of distressed or wrecked vessels not represented by an authorized insurance agent in Lower Canada.

In 1809 two up-country lumberers, Thomas Mears and David Pattee*, had contracted to supply timber to the Hamiltons. To finance operations Mears and Pattee received advances against delivery. They became unable to fulfil their obligations, however, and by October 1811 the Hamiltons had seized their only tangible asset, a deal mill at Hawkesbury. William moved to Hawkesbury to take charge of the mill and of the lumbering operations, which were carried out largely along the Rideau River. Shortly after he took over, a fire wiped out the mill and its stock of wood, but, deciding to exploit a recent doubling of the British duty on Baltic timber, the Hamiltons rebuilt on an expanded scale despite disruption of the export trade caused by the War of 1812. Remaining at Quebec, George was responsible for negotiating timber sales and securing Admiralty contracts; during the summer of 1813 he disposed of more than 300,000 cubic feet of timber, staves, and deals on the Quebec market. From May to December 1815 the Hamiltons operated with a third partner, George Davies, as "Hamilton's and Davies." In March 1816 New Liverpool Cove, which by then included a house, wharf, building slips, workshop, forge, "steam house," warehouse, and workmen's lodgings, was put up for sale or let from 1 May. However, the Hamiltons carried on as George and William Hamilton until the end of 1816, when the company was dissolved following William's retirement.

Backed by the prestige of the Liverpool firm, George had been welcomed quickly into upper-class Quebec society. By early 1807 he was already among the 21 leading merchants and office holders of conservative convictions who constituted the exclusive Barons' Club; others were Caldwell, Herman Witsius RYLAND, George HERIOT, and Thomas Dunn*. From 1807 to 1815 Hamilton was successively treasurer and steward of the Quebec Races which, through meets, sought to improve the quality of horses in the colony as well as to provide entertainment; he either bred or imported horses for sale. During the War of 1812 he was a lieutenant in Quebec's 3rd Militia Battalion, and then aide-major and finally major under Caldwell in the 2nd Lotbinière battalion. In 1814 he received a commission of the peace for Quebec. On 18 March 1816, at 34, he married before the Anglican bishop of Quebec, Jacob Mountain*, Susannah Christiana Craigie, 17-year-old daughter of the late executive councillor John Craigie*; they would have at least seven, and possibly ten, children.

The newly-weds were soon transported from the gaity of Quebec society to the sombre bush of the Ottawa valley. On William's retirement George was joined in the business by his brothers Robert and John. Robert managed marketing in Liverpool while John moved in at New Liverpool; George took his experience to Hawkesbury. The mill-site, at the head of the Long Sault Rapids, was ideal. It was within easy reach of the timber stands on the Ottawa River and its tributaries. The rapids provided ample power and an obstacle to the rafting of timber to market at Quebec; lumberers unwilling to break up and then rebuild their rafts sold them to Hamilton. Finally, the Ottawa valley was opening up, and settlers were happy to sell logs from their lands in return for merchandise from the store that Hamilton had the astuteness to build. Unlike other up-country lumberers, Hamilton, as part of an integrated company, could avoid the costs and delays occasioned by middlemen at Quebec and in England. The Hawkesbury operation grew; by 1818 it employed 80 men, a large number for the time, and in 1822 it reportedly ran 40 saws.

To achieve these results Hamilton had to adapt to conditions governing the timber trade in the valley: he employed both strong-arm tactics and political pressure, no doubt exploiting his contacts at Quebec. His position and basis of power in valley society were established between 1816 and 1823. In March 1816 he was appointed a justice of the peace and a judge of the newly created Ottawa District Court of Upper Canada; in August 1818 he was named with George Garden* and Joseph PAPINEAU a commissioner for the improvement of water communications between Lower and Upper Canada on the St Lawrence and Ottawa rivers; in April 1822 he was made, with Joel Stone*, a commissioner in the Ottawa District under the Alien Act; in June he received a commission of *dedimus potestatem* and became lieutenant-colonel of the Prescott Reserve Militia of Upper Canada; and by January 1823 he was one of three school commissioners for the Ottawa District.

Hamilton had sought to use his position to promote social order and prosperity in the valley, in part through the creation of large, stable lumbering enterprises, of which his would be one. His model of local leadership was the English squire, but he found himself surrounded at Hawkesbury by an American community which, in addition to supplying strong competition in business, was to his mind the source of seditious democratic ideas in the region. Among its leaders were Mears and Pattee, whom Hamilton had put out of business only temporarily. Mears, who was competing successfully with Hamilton for timber, was the district sheriff; Pattee was a justice of the peace and a judge of the Surrogate Court. Made vulnerable by the expense of rebuilding the mill after the fire of 1812, which had been of suspicious origins, Hamilton indulged in violent means to meet competition from Mears.

Conflict between the Hamilton and Mears factions intensified from 1819 when the executive government of Lower Canada, pressed for revenues as a result of a long-standing conflict with the House of Assembly [*see* George RAMSAY], began to enforce crown timber rights more stringently. The timber industry in the valley had been stimulated in the early years by cutting on crown lands under Admiralty contract, the timber there being reserved exclusively for naval stores. Following the war the trade had shifted to supplying domestic needs in the colonies and Britain. In the wilderness, far from the eyes of government officials, the reservation of timber on crown lands for naval purposes went largely ignored. Some timber, known to have been taken by trespass, had been seized, but the trade had become so important to the colonial economy that enforcement of crown rights had been half-hearted. From 1819, however, rafts were seized more frequently; they were then sold, usually back to their original owners, and the proceeds deposited in the crown revenues. In order to compete Hamilton had engaged in illegal cutting on crown lands, and he feared denunciation by Mears.

The Upper Canadian elections of 1820 pitted the Hamilton and Mears factions against each other in the united counties of Prescott and Russell. The contest, dirty and violent, ultimately ended with the House of Assembly declaring Pattee the victor over William Hamilton, returned from England apparently to represent the firm's interests politically. Efforts by George Hamilton to besmirch Pattee with an old charge of forgery and counterfeiting had failed, and rejection of the charge by the Executive Council of Upper Canada constituted a chastening rebuff to Hamilton. Moreover, since 1819 he had been obliged to reduce his illegal cutting on crown lands lest he be arraigned in his own court.

Hamilton's misfortunes were not at an end. The brothers' precarious finances were dealt a stunning blow when the British wood market took a severe downturn in 1821. Their operations were financed through a firm called Robert Hamilton, Brothers and Company, the contact with Liverpool bankers being provided by Robert. He, however, fell deeply into debt to Gillespie, Moffatt and Company of Montreal [*see* George Moffatt*], to which he was obliged to give a lien on the Hawkesbury works, and his death the following year probably impaired the brothers' ability to finance their debts and operations. In March 1823 New Liverpool Cove (three houses, more than 450 acres of land, 11 acres of beaches, as well as wharfs and other buildings) and the Hawkesbury installations (200 acres of land, two sawmills and a grist-mill, three barns, a forge, a bake-house, stores, and houses for the workmen) were advertised for sale on 1 November. In May the assets of the Hamiltons' firm were assigned to its creditors, represented by the merchants Henry McKenzie* and George AULDJO of Montreal and Mathew BELL of Quebec. A reorganization, probably to obtain financing, had brought a new partner to Quebec, Abraham Gibson – the firm becoming Hamilton and Gibson – and apparently sent John to Liverpool. This partnership ended in July, but a loan was found in Britain at the eleventh hour and sale of the Hamiltons' business narrowly avoided. Still, it would seem, misfortune dogged George Hamilton; within a short space of time in 1822–23, according to the Reverend Joseph Abbott*, not only did John die but George's house at Hawkesbury, with all its contents, burned to the ground, and while he and his family were descending the Ottawa to Montreal their canoe overturned in rapids and his three young children drowned.

Strong-willed and resilient, Hamilton set about rebuilding his business. Reconstruction was hampered by legal complications over John's estate. Yet, thanks to a recovery of the timber market, Hamilton was able to expand; by 1825 the number of his employees, reduced to 50 or 60 in 1822, had risen to 200. The settlement of John's estate permitted Hamilton to reorganize on solid ground, and in 1830 he took into partnership a trusted employee and veteran of battles with the Mears faction, Charles Adamson Low. Together they built a business that by 1835 was marketing annually some 11,500,000 board feet of pine from three locations and was valued at £66,000. This expansion made the firm of Hamilton and Low one of the three largest deal manufacturers in the Canadas, and its mills rivalled those of the Montmorency and Etchemin rivers near Quebec [*see* Henry Caldwell; Peter Patterson*], producing nearly one-half of the deals exported from the Ottawa valley.

No longer with his back to the wall after 1823, Hamilton reassessed the conduct of the timber trade and the conditions governing it. While maintaining his strategy of promoting social order and large companies, he adjusted his tactics. He now eschewed violence as contributing to instability in the trade – already high because of constantly fluctuating market conditions – and ultimately to the bankruptcy of legitimate lumberers. Thus he was shocked at the implication of his fellow lumberers in the Shiner riots of the 1830s [*see* Peter Aylen*], although, imbued as he was with the Scots-Irish disdain for his fellow countrymen, he had no other objection to this ethnic conflict between Irish Catholic and Canadian labourers.

Hamilton turned increasingly to his influence in government to promote his ends, but he seems to have preferred not to sit in the legislature of either Upper or Lower Canada. Most notably he sought to regularize the harvesting of timber on crown lands. Though he had felt obliged to participate in illegal cutting, he had never accepted the situation. That the very basis of the industry resided in an unlawful activity, he perceived, resulted in instability. The illegal cutting encouraged small entrepreneurs to undertake operations at will, thus contributing to reckless overproduction and breeding violence as producers rushed to cut the best timber; although hardly a forest conservationist, unlike most of his contemporaries Hamilton sensed the limits of the Ottawa valley forest and the necessity for administering it carefully. Finally, enforcement of crown timber rights from 1819, if more stringent, was nevertheless capricious, and the uncertainty it bred had a deleterious effect on the trade in general. With other large operators, therefore, Hamilton urged the governments of Upper and Lower Canada to make a satisfactory provision for pursuit of the trade. Either crown timber lands must be alienated to private ownership or licences given for cutting on them. There was general agreement among lumberers that the latter system would be preferable since it would permit operators of all sizes to function without immobilizing capital in land purchases. Hamilton foresaw that it would enable big firms to obtain licences on large areas, or limits, which could then be used as collateral for borrowing in Montreal, Quebec, and Britain. Furthermore, the grouping of several limits would permit integrated operations such as his own to work more efficiently.

The executive governments of Upper and Lower Canada, motivated by the lure of stable revenues from licences, responded favourably. In 1826 regulations were introduced that permitted the cutting of timber on crown lands by licence in return for fees determined by auction [*see* Charles SHIRREFF]. Surveyors general of woods were appointed: John Davidson, a former business agent of Hamilton, for Lower Canada in 1826 and Peter ROBINSON for Upper Canada in 1827. In 1828 Hamilton himself was made a collector of fees on the Rivière Rouge, Lower Canada, where he obtained licences on much of the timber land. However, the new system, and subsequent modifications to it, was geared more to generating revenues for the colonial executives than to providing a framework for cutting on crown lands. Hamilton became a prominent critic of it, arguing that it permitted men of no means to enter the trade, and thereby destroyed the market, the quality of the product, and the stability of revenues for legitimate lumberers. He proposed regulations of his own, which included a down payment on fees in order to discourage speculation on cutting privileges and to put the trade into the "Hands of Capitalists." About 1832, with the support of Charles Shirreff, crown timber agent at Bytown (Ottawa), Hamilton persuaded Lord Aylmer [WHITWORTH-AYLMER], governor of Lower Canada, to adopt his system. It was followed in a slightly modified form in Upper Canada.

Having won a political victory at Quebec for large firms, Hamilton then led them in a struggle with small operators for control of the limits themselves. The principal battlefield was the Gatineau valley. The largest tributary of the Ottawa below the Chaudière Falls, the Rivière Gatineau had become the centre of the timber industry in the Ottawa system by the late 1820s. To control the Gatineau an association of large limit-holders, which included Peter Aylen, Philemon Wright and Sons, and Hamilton and Low, was formed around 1830 to obtain cutting rights and improve transportation on the river; it succeeded on both counts, and by late 1832 had expended £2,000 on improvements. During the winter of 1831–32 the associates discovered that a number of small operators such as Nicholas Sparks*, non-members of the association, were cutting along the river without licence but with the complicity of Shirreff. Complaints to the Crown Lands Department of Lower Canada and to the crown having produced no results, Hamilton appealed to other Lower Canadian officials, with whom he had cultivated excellent relations. With the aid of John Davidson, who had become assistant to the commissioner of crown lands in Lower Canada, Hamilton drafted a petition to Aylmer requesting reservation of the Gatineau limits to the associates on fair and rational terms. Private lobbying produced results: in

November 1832 an order in council granted to them what became known as the Gatineau privilege. It gave the associated firms, except Hamilton and Low, the exclusive right for two years to take out red pine timber to a limit of 2,000 pieces a year and permitted Hamilton and Low to cut a maximum of 12,000 saw-logs. Nomination of Hamilton as superintendent of the river was withdrawn after vociferous complaints by Shirreff that it eroded his rights.

The Gatineau privilege produced an immediate uproar in Bytown and the lower Ottawa valley; amid rumours of imminent violence on the Gatineau, a commission of inquiry was appointed. It endorsed the Gatineau privilege, reproducing from Hamilton's petition to Aylmer the arguments in favour of large firms and invoking the associates' investments in improvements as justifications. Despite disputes among the associates, which degenerated into violence in 1841, the privilege would be renewed repeatedly until 1843, and Hamilton and Low was even able to obtain a similar arrangement for itself on the Rouge.

Protected through the Gatineau and Rouge privileges from the competition of numerous small entrepreneurs, and owning privately timber tracts in Plantagenet, Clarence, and Cumberland townships in Upper Canada, Hamilton and Low continued to expand rapidly its production of deals and timber; by 1839 the firm was employing "several hundred" men a year. Hamilton remained an active proponent of big enterprise, political leadership oriented to economic development, and firm social controls in the Ottawa valley. An avid follower of political events in both British North America and the mother country, he was, like his colleagues in the trade, a constant exponent of toryism and the needs of the empire. The rebellions of 1837–38 offered him the opportunity to rally his militia companies in support of British authority. However, a trip made in bitter weather in early December 1838 to review a reserve company at Plantagenet resulted in a severe cold, to which he succumbed in January 1839. He bequeathed the business to his sons Robert and George, who, later joined by their brother John*, carried it on.

With Philemon WRIGHT, who died just six months after him, George Hamilton was among the first of the great timber barons who played an important part in the public life of British North America in the 19th century. At his worst he was headstrong and opinionated, an inveterate tory of undemocratic principles and élitist sensibilities, prepared even to overstep the law in order to get his way. At his best he brought to the crude and brutal frontier that was the Ottawa valley in the early years of the timber trade a rare politeness of manners and generosity of spirit. Significantly, Hamilton was a gifted businessman and lobbyist. He bent his energy, determination, and influence to building an important firm in a fundamental sector of the colonial economy and to bringing a modicum of stability to a trade plagued by the fluctuating markets and the repeated spates of oversupply that generate the boom-and-bust syndrome of staple-producing colonies. Perhaps inevitably, however, he came to equate the welfare of his own firm with the well-being of the timber trade generally.

ROBERT PETER GILLIS

[The author wishes to thank S. J. Gillis who made available the results of her research on the lumber trade, without which this biography could not have been written. R.P.G.]

ANQ-Q, CE1-61, 18 mars 1816; CN1-262, 31 août 1809; E21/1863, 1870, 1873. AO, MU 1199, letter-book no.2; RG 22, ser.155. AUM, P 58, U, George Hamilton to James Stuart, 5 Feb. 1813; Hamilton to William Johnson, 23 May 1814; George and William Hamilton to Michael O'Sullivan, n.d. PAC, MG 24, D7; RG 1, E3, 61: 49, 53–63; RG 5, A1: 23247–48, 25157–59, 39235–38, 68315–18; RG 9, I, B5, 6; RG 68, General index, 1651–1841: 70, 139, 194, 212, 299, 345, 426, 445, 637. L.C., Legislative Council, *Journals*, 1836, app.C. *Bytown Gazette, and Ottawa and Rideau Advertiser*, 16 Jan. 1839. *Quebec Gazette*, 17 May 1804; 29 May 1806; 20 May, 2 July 1807; 7 July, 8, 15 Sept. 1808; 18 May, 10, 31 Aug., 23 Nov. 1809; 10, 17 May, 14, 21 June, 12 July, 9, 16, 23 Aug., 6 Sept., 18 Oct., 22 Nov. 1810; 3 Jan., 28 March, 25 April, 16 May, 11 July, 10 Oct. 1811; 23, 30 April 1812; 17, 24 June 1813; 27 April 1815; 18 April, 16 May 1816; 4, 16 Jan. 1817; 2 Sept. 1822; 31 July, 4, 18 Sept., 6 Nov. 1823. Armstrong, *Handbook of Upper Canadian chronology* (1967). H. J. Morgan, *Sketches of celebrated Canadians*. *Officers of British forces in Canada* (Irving). *Quebec almanac*, 1815: 85. M. S. Cross, "The dark druidical groves: the lumber community and the commercial frontier in British North America, to 1854" (PHD thesis, Univ. of Toronto, 1968). S. J. Gillis, *The timber trade in the Ottawa valley, 1806–54* (Parks Canada, National Parks and Hist. Sites Branch, *Manuscript report*, no.153, Ottawa, 1975). W. D. Lighthall, "English settlement in Quebec," *Canada and its provinces; a history of the Canadian people and their institutions . . .* , ed. Adam Shortt and A. G. Doughty (23v., Toronto, 1913–17), 15: 160–61. A. R. M. Lower, "Lumbering in eastern Canada: a study in economic and social history" (PHD thesis, Harvard Univ., Cambridge, Mass., 1928); *The North American assault on the Canadian forest* (New York, 1938; repr. 1968). Ignotus [Thomas Chapais], "Le club des Barons," *BRH*, 4 (1898): 251–52.

HANINGTON, WILLIAM, businessman, JP, and office holder; b. *c.* 1759 in England; m. 1792 Mary Derby, daughter of the loyalist Benjamin Derby (Darby), in St Eleanors, St John's (Prince Edward) Island, and they had five sons and seven daughters; d. 14 Sept. 1838 in Shediac Cape, N.B.

William Hanington was one of the first English settlers in southeastern New Brunswick, where he established himself on Shediac Bay. A dynamic businessman with interests in many areas, he was an important figure locally, since for nearly 40 years he controlled economic development in the region and held all the main public offices.

Almost nothing is known of Hanington's early days in England. Before arriving in New Brunswick he is supposed to have been a fish merchant in London, like his father. In 1784 he paid £500 sterling for 5,000 acres that had originally been granted by Michael Francklin*, lieutenant governor of Nova Scotia, to Captain Joseph Williams and others in 1768. This land was located in the large region the Acadians called Gédaïc, where a number of Acadian families were already living. In 1785 Hanington took possession of his property, which included the area later known as Shediac Cape and Gilberts Corner. Some Acadian squatters probably moved off towards what would become Grande-Digue, but others are believed to have become farmers on Hanington's lands.

Hanington was above all a businessman, and was involved in a wide variety of enterprises; before long he was recognized as the most influential man in his community and had acquired great prestige extending beyond Shediac Bay, with its economic centre at Shediac Cape. Hanington's commercial interests included the fur trade, fishing, lumbering, shipbuilding, agriculture, importing, wholesaling and retailing, and land speculation. His eldest son, William, followed in his footsteps, becoming a lumbering entrepreneur, mill owner, and landowner in the Cocagne region.

Hanington occupied a number of different governmental posts and few aspects of the economic and social life of the Shediac region escaped his influence, since for many years he was the only person holding office in the vicinity. He became a justice of the peace around 1805 and retained this office for more than a quarter of a century. Some five years later he was appointed tax collector at Shediac, a position involving many tasks and more extensive duties than that of customs officer: he issued licences to pedlars, inspected ships and assured himself of the sailors' health, and collected the tax based on tonnage that was earmarked for a fund in aid of sick and disabled sailors. For several years he was also inspector of highways and bridges, responsible for maintaining the roads running from Shediac to the villages of Dorchester and Petitcodiac (Dieppe) and for distributing the funds allocated by government for materials and labour. He did not retire from his public offices until he was well advanced in years, around 1833. Hanington encouraged settlement and acted on several occasions in favour of petitioners from the region, supporting their requests for land. In 1814, for example, he intervened with Surveyor General George Sproule* to prevent the granting to others of the lowlands on which some Acadians around Barachois were settled.

In 1825 Hanington was by far the largest landowner in the Shediac Bay area; his holdings were valued at more than £4,000, in a community where properties were worth £300 on average. Almost all large-scale shipping activities were conducted on his lands, where wharfs, warehouses, stores, and a shipbuilding yard had been erected. At his death in 1838, he had about 7,500 acres, situated in the immediate region of Shediac Cape but also at Grande-Digue, Tidiche (Dupuis Corner), Wellington, Bouctouche (Buctouche), Cocagne, Shemogue, and Sussex. He owned mills, lent money, and held several mortgages on land around Shediac Cape, Cocagne, and Bas-Cap-Pelé, as well as notes signed by borrowers from Bouctouche to Cap Tourmentin (Cape Tormentine); the Catholic missionary Antoine GAGNON of Grande-Digue owed him £54 borrowed in 1833 for a period of ten years. Some debts could be repaid in kind, such as agricultural products, wood, or fish.

Hanington's situation in Westmorland County helped propel some members of his family on to the political scene. His third son, Daniel, who was a farmer and mill owner, became a justice of the peace and a commanding officer in the militia. He was first elected to the House of Assembly in 1834, became a member of the Executive Council, and was later called to the Legislative Council. His son, Daniel Lionel*, was premier of New Brunswick in 1882 and 1883.

Tradition has it that William Hanington was the founder of what became the town of Shediac. It would be more accurate to say that he was the earliest and principal promoter of economic activity in the Shediac region, and the person behind the founding of the Anglican parish of St Martin's-in-the-Woods at Shediac Cape, of which he was one of the first churchwardens. English and loyalist families clustered around him and formed the nucleus of the anglophone governing class in the region.

JEAN-ROCH CYR

Centre d'études acadiennes, univ. de Moncton (Moncton, N.-B.), A1-4-4; A3-1-8 (copies). Mount Allison Univ. Arch. (Sackville, N.B.), Parks Canada Webster Chignecto coll., 7001-70 (William Milne papers), William Hanington, account of men belonging to the brigantine *St. Nicholas of Aberdeen*, 18 June 1812; 7001-205 (Shediac papers), D. L. Hanington, "Shediac" (1904); William Hanington, memorial to Thomas Carleton, 23 Jan. 1789 (copy); 7001-226 (Westmorland County, justices of the peace), item 2; 7001-261 (Westmorland County, land grants), no.2393; 7001-345 (William Hanington, "Daybook No.4, commenced May 21st, 1827"). N.B. Museum, J. C. Webster papers, indenture, 9 Oct. 1784 (copy). PANB, MC 1156, X: 65–68; RG 3, RS538, I1, resignation of Hanington *et al.*, *c.* 1831–32; P1: 4; RS561, A1, 15 March 1816; RG 4, RS24, account of duties collected at Shediac, 1810–33; S36-P22, S36-R8.28–29, S40-P10, S40-R31.19, S41-R9.31, S43-R12.11; RG 7, RS74, A, 1838, William Hanington; 1849, William Hanington; RG 10, RS108, William Hanington Sr and Jr, 24 June 1810; William Hanington Jr, 1818; John

Hanington *et al.*, 1824; RS663A, William Hanington, 14 July 1818; 1819; William Hanington Jr, 1818. St Martin's (Anglican) Church (Shediac), St Martin's-in-the-Woods, vestry records (mfm. at PANB). *Royal Gazette* (Saint John, N.B.; Fredericton), 1785–1838. Marilyn Bateman Dumaresq, *Hanington family tree* ([rev. ed., Wabush, Nfld.], 1980). A. W. Crouch, *Some descendants of Joseph Crouch of Lambourne, Berkshire, William Hanington of London, England, Capt. Archibald MacLean of New Brunswick and related families* (Nashville, Tenn., 1971). F. C. Bell, *A history of old Shediac, New Brunswick* (Moncton, 1937). F. R. K. Sayer, *A history of Shediac Cape* (mimeograph, [Moncton], 1966; copy at N.B. Museum). J. C. Webster, *A history of Shediac, New Brunswick* ([Shediac], 1928). Clément Cormier, "Petite chronologie de Shédiac," Soc. hist. acadienne, *Cahiers* (Moncton), 3 (1968–71): 237–50.

HARMON, DANIEL WILLIAMS, fur trader and diarist; b. 19 Feb. 1778 in Bennington, Vt, fourth son of Daniel Harmon and Lucretia Dewey; d. 23 April 1843 in Sault-au-Récollet (Montreal North), Lower Canada.

At the time of his birth Daniel Williams Harmon's parents kept an inn at Bennington; later, in 1796, the family moved to Vergennes, Vt. The elder Harmons were fervent members of the Congregational Church, and much of their piety would cling to Harmon through his years in the fur trade. Yet, as a young man, he found the puritanical atmosphere of his home too stifling and in 1799 he made his way to Montreal, where he became a clerk to the fur brokers McTavish, Frobisher and Company [*see* Simon McTavish*]. In 1799 or early 1800 he was engaged as a clerk by the North West Company at £20 a year; upon leaving for the northwest on 29 April 1800 he began the journal in which, for 19 years, he kept a record not only of the daily life of a fur trader but also of his moral struggles in a libertarian and often libertine environment.

Harmon was posted first to Fort Alexandria (near Fort Pelly, Sask.), where he stayed for five years. In February 1805 the post had dependent on it, he noted with characteristic precision, upwards of 70 people who required at least 450 pounds of buffalo meat daily. He also observed in his journal for 1803 the violence that had emerged in the trade rivalry between the NWC and the New North West Company (sometimes called the XY Company). "This jarring of interests, keep up continual misunderstandings, and occasions frequent broils between the contending parties. . . . Here a Murderer escapes the Gallows, as there are no human laws that can reach or have any effect on the People of this Country." In February 1805 he heard with satisfaction that the strife had ended as a result of the union of the NWC and the XY Company. In subsequent years he would carefully avoid involvement in the even more violent confrontations between the Nor'Westers and the men of the Hudson's Bay Company.

Later in 1805 Harmon was transferred to South Branch House (near Batoche, Sask.), where he stayed until 1807. It was there that he married according to the custom of the country. Already, at Fort Alexandria, he had been approached by Cree chiefs offering their young daughters, and he had undergone inner struggles in which an inherited puritanism had triumphed over his natural inclinations. "Thanks be to God alone," he noted on 11 Aug. 1802, "if I have not been brought into a snare laid no doubt by the Devil himself." At South Branch the temptation was greater, for the girl, 14-year-old Lizette Duval, was an attractive Métis, the daughter of a Canadian voyageur and a Snare Indian, and he felt the loneliness of "all gentlemen who remain, for any length of time, in this part of the world. . . . If we can live in harmony together, my intention is to keep her as long as I remain in this uncivilized part of the world, but when I return to my native land shall endeavour to place her into the hands of some good honest Man, with whom she can pass the remainder of her Days in this Country."

Harmon's relationship with his Métis wife, who was later baptized as Elizabeth but whom he referred to in his journal only as "my woman" or "the mother of my children," turned out to be exemplary. She accompanied him from South Branch in 1806 to Cumberland House (Sask.) and later to Sturgeon Lake in the Nipigon department, and then on to the Athabasca department – Harmon arrived at Fort Chipewyan (Alta) on 7 Sept. 1808. They later moved to Fort Dunvegan, in the Peace River country, remaining there until 1810. They then crossed the Rocky Mountains to New Caledonia (B.C.), recently opened to the fur trade by another Vermonter, Simon Fraser*, and under the charge of John STUART.

For the next nine years Harmon remained in this country, serving mainly at Fort St James on Stuart Lake, with periods at Fort Fraser. It was a life of varied activity. Harmon estimated that trading for furs occupied only a fifth of his time. He paid much attention to making New Caledonia's forts self-sufficient in food by accumulating large stocks of dried salmon (sometimes there were 25,000 fish in his warehouse) and pioneering agriculture in the region, where the short, hot summer with long days was excellent for growing vegetables. As well, he carefully observed and recorded the life of the Carrier Indians among whom he worked. He taught his wife and their daughters English, and sent their sons home to Vermont for schooling; their family was large, and accounts of its size vary from 10 to 14, of whom some at least died young. In 1818 he was made a wintering partner in the NWC. The following year he left New Caledonia for Lower Canada.

By now his eldest son was dead and the loss had profoundly affected his attitude toward his wife, whom he decided he could not abandon after all. "How could I spend my days in the civilized world, and leave my beloved children in the wilderness? The thought has in it the bitterness of death. How could I tear them from a mother's love, and leave her to mourn over their absence, to the day of her death?" With his wife and children he arrived at Fort William (Thunder Bay, Ont.) on 18 Aug. 1819. On that day he ended his diary. Harmon and his country wife, who were formally married later, travelled to Montreal and then on to Vergennes, Vt, pausing in Burlington for Harmon to make arrangements for the publication of his journal, which appeared in 1820. By that time he had returned to the fur trade and was in charge of the post at Rainy Lake (near Fort Francis, Ont.).

When the NWC was absorbed by the HBC in 1821 he became a chief trader under an arrangement whereby he would resign immediately but retain his share for seven years. He subsequently returned to his native state, but, like many fur traders, did not prosper once he had left the northwest. With his brother Calvin he set up a store and sawmill, around which they developed a small settlement, Harmonsville (Coventry.) Daniel did badly and, probably during the winter of 1842–43, left to rent a farm at Sault-au-Récollet near Montreal. There he succeeded no better than at Harmonsville; he died almost in poverty on 23 April 1843, survived by his wife and six children and leaving an estate worth less than £100.

Daniel Williams Harmon was not one of the great names in fur-trading history. He served mostly in subordinate positions and carried out no explorations. His fame rests solely but solidly on his *Journal*, which is not only a fine descriptive narrative of life in the trade during the early years of the 19th century, but also a moving account of moral dilemmas confronted and resolved.

GEORGE WOODCOCK

Daniel Williams Harmon's journal, heavily edited and rewritten for publication by the Reverend Daniel Haskel of Burlington, Vt., appeared as *A journal of voyages and travels in the interiour of North America, between the 47th and 58th degrees of north latitude, extending from Montreal nearly to the Pacific Ocean, a distance of about 5,000 miles, including an account of the principal occurrences, during a residence of nineteen years, in different parts of the country . . .* (Andover, Mass., 1820; repr. New York, 1922). Harmon's original diary is no longer extant, but a manuscript copy of it (perhaps in Harmon's own hand) made in 1816 and sent to his relatives in Vermont is preserved in the Univ. of Iowa Libraries, Special Coll. and MSS (Iowa City); a photocopy is available at the PAC. This manuscript, entitled "Copy of a Journal or Narrative of the most material circumstances occured to and some thoughts and reflections . . . during the space of sixteen years while in the North West or Indian Country," was used in the preparation of a new edition, *Sixteen years in the Indian country: the journal of Daniel Williams Harmon, 1800–1816*, edited and with an introduction by William Kaye Lamb (Toronto, 1957). This edition also includes, from the 1820 version, Harmon's journal entries for 1816–19.

There is a portrait of Harmon in the Bennington Museum (Bennington, Vt.); it is reproduced in both editions of his journal and in John Spargo, *Two Bennington-born explorers and makers of modern Canada* ([Bradford, Vt.], 1950).

Docs. relating to NWC (Wallace). Brown, *Strangers in blood*. Marcel Giraud, *The Métis in the Canadian west*, trans. George Woodcock (2v., Edmonton, 1986). Innis, *Fur trade in Canada* (1930). Morton, *Hist. of Canadian west* (Thomas; 1973). Van Kirk, *"Many tender ties"*. M. [E.] Wilkins Campbell, *The North West Company* (Toronto, 1957); *The Saskatchewan . . .* (New York, 1950). J. H. Archer, "Tales of western travellers: Daniel Williams Harmon," *Saskatchewan Hist.* (Saskatoon), 4 (1951): 62–67.

HART, EZEKIEL (Ezechiel), businessman, seigneur, militia officer, JP, and politician; b. 15 May 1770 in Trois-Rivières, Que., second son of Aaron Hart* and Dorothea Judah; d. there 16 Sept. 1843.

Like his brothers Moses*, Benjamin*, and Alexander (Asher), Ezekiel Hart obtained part of his education in the United States. In 1792 Aaron Hart brought Ezekiel into his store on Rue du Platon in Trois-Rivières and involved him in his fur-trade activities. The following year Ezekiel was in New York and lived for a while at the home of Ephraim Hart and his wife Frances Noah. There he met Mrs Hart's niece, Frances Lazarus, and in February 1794 they were married. He also looked after family affairs and settled the estate of his uncle Henry Hart, who had been a merchant in Albany, N.Y.

On 2 Dec. 1796 Hart and his brothers Moses and Benjamin went into partnership "to build a Brew and Malt House for the purpose of carrying on the business of brewing Ale or Beer . . . and likewise to erect a manufactory of Pot and perlash . . . and also a Bake House for the Baking of Bread and Biscuit" in Trois-Rivières. By the terms of the agreement the three were to hold equal shares in the firm, which would operate under the name of M. and E. Hart Company and would have the financial backing of their father. The written consent of all the partners was necessary to change the agreement, which was for a six-year period. On 20 March 1797 Ezekiel Hart bought a piece of land on Rue Haut-Boc on which "hops for brewing were cultivated and flourished." Lots near the St Lawrence were also purchased, and on 7 November the firm hired mason Dominique Gougé to build the brewery "from this date to the 30th day of next April for two shillings, Halifax currency, per day." Gougé also contracted "to work at night when necessary without other recompense."

The various buildings projected were soon finished, with the apparent exception of the bakehouse – at least, there is now no trace of it. Production of beer and potash reached quite high levels. On 26 March 1800 the company hired Baptiste Dubois of Bécancour "to start at the end of next April and continue until all the ash has been used up." The terms of the contract were clear: Dubois "guarantees to make good potash. . . . The aforementioned M., E., and B. Hart promise to pay the said Baptiste Dubois eighteen Spanish dollars a month, and, if they are not satisfied with him at any time, to pay him and dismiss him."

When Ezekiel Hart withdrew from the M. and E. Hart Company, it owned several lots on which were "a stone brewery and a potashery, with all the pumps, vats, barrels, three potash boilers, and a copper boiler of about 120 gallons capacity." Near by stood a malt-house, and beyond it was the lot on Rue Haut-Boc "with a frontage of sixty feet and a depth of one hundred and sixteen . . . planted in hops." Ezekiel sold everything to Moses for £338 6*s.* 8*d.*, at a date unknown but apparently soon after Aaron Hart's death in 1800. Subsequently Ezekiel followed in the footsteps of his father, who was in every respect his model. He went into the import and export trade, kept a general store, never let a good business deal pass, and acquired property. Besides inheriting the seigneury of Bécancour, he bought a great deal of land, mainly at Trois-Rivières and Cap-de-la-Madeleine.

At this period, however, Hart shared with Moses and Benjamin a passion for politics. A document held at the American Jewish Historical Society Archives in Waltham, Mass., gives the results, in order, of an election in which Louis-Charles Foucher, John Lees*, Pierre Vézina, and a man named Hart were candidates. The names of the 138 voters and their votes are listed on four pages. In fact, on 6 Aug. 1804 Foucher and Lees were elected to the House of Assembly for Trois-Rivières, which at that time was entitled to two members. The other candidates are not known, but it is clear the document refers to this election. Which Hart was involved – Moses or Ezekiel? Moses, who was on the voters' list, voted for only one candidate – Hart, of course. His future wife, Mary McCarthy, who owned property and therefore had the right to vote, voted for Foucher and Hart. Alexander and Benjamin voted for Lees and Hart. As Foucher, Lees, and Vézina are not on the voters' list, and neither is Ezekiel, it may be inferred that it was he who was the candidate. The inference is substantiated by an address "to the Worthy and Independent Electors of the Town of Three-Rivers," dated 22 June 1804 and bearing Ezekiel Hart's name, which is also held at Waltham. "My interest is connected with yours," the candidate declared, promising to carry out the duties of the office sought after "to the utmost of my abilities and that of the interest of this my *native Place*."

Hart's victory in the 1807 by-election in Trois-Rivières precipitated an important political episode and controversy that would cause much ink to flow and give rise to many interpretations. In the contest, held to replace Lees who had died that year, four candidates took to the hustings: Mathew BELL, Thomas COFFIN, Pierre Vézina, and Ezekiel Hart. Historian Benjamin Sulte* relates that "judge Foucher, assemblyman, started off the affair with a rather long speech entirely partial to Coffin." At the first show of hands Vézina had the fewest votes and immediately withdrew in favour of Coffin. Hart none the less took the lead, with 59 of 116 votes. Coffin, with 41, and Bell, with 16, in turn withdrew before the day was ended. It was Saturday, 11 April 1807. Hart, the successful candidate, was asked by the returning officer to sign certain documents but in great embarrassment, again according to Sulte, he requested that the signing be delayed until the Sabbath was over. When pressed, he simply signed Ezekiel Hart, 1807, disregarding the formula "in the year of our Lord."

As the session at Quebec was coming to an end, Hart had to wait until a new one began on 29 Jan. 1808 before he could be sworn in. Foucher and Hart, who had been opponents in Trois-Rivières riding, now found themselves together at Quebec, and both were in serious difficulties. They were regarded as politicians favouring the English party, and their right to sit in the assembly was contested by the members of the Canadian party, who were anxious to secure a stable majority for themselves in the house. Since most of them could not afford a prolonged stay at Quebec, with neither salary nor living expenses being supplied, they decided to expel from the assembly two vulnerable members of the opposing party: the judge, who in their opinion could not both pass laws and see to their enforcement, and the Jew, who had not been able to take the prescribed oath. Consequently, Hart could not "attend, sit, or vote." He was excluded from the assembly by a resolution. Contrary to the claim often advanced, the Canadians and the English-speaking members did not vote *en bloc* on the question. Attorney General Jonathan SEWELL, for example, voted in favour of Hart's expulsion. Paradoxically, Hart, who had been elected by a riding with largely Canadian and Catholic voters, was expelled by an assembly controlled by a majority that was also Canadian and Catholic. "I rather suspect," traveller John Lambert* commented, that "they [the Canadians] wished to keep the majority on their side, and if possible, to get a French, instead of an English member in the House."

The resolution mentioned that Hart was of the Jewish religion and that he had "taken the Oath in the manner customary only for persons of that persuasion." Hart had in fact put his hand on his head and substituted the word Jewish for Christian. In the debate it was emphasized that a Jew does not believe in the New Testament, which is an integral part of the Bible. In short, Hart had taken an oath that was being disputed as invalid. This reason, which some thought a pretext, was used to justify his expulsion. He protested, in vain, and had to return home. In any event, the session was coming to an end. Four years having passed since the last general election, Governor Sir James Henry Craig* dissolved the house on 27 April 1808.

In these elections Hart again received the 59 votes he got in the previous one. Judge Foucher, whose presence in the house had stirred up another lively debate, was fourth with 32. Joseph Badeaux* obtained one more vote than Pierre Vézina. This time Hart took the oath "in the Christian manner." Nevertheless the debate resumed when the legislature opened on 10 April 1809 and went on longer. On 19 April, after several votes, the assembly resolved that Hart was the same person who had already been expelled "as he professes the Jewish religion." The debate became more complicated. In the end, he was denied the right to sit and to vote because of his religion. Faced with conflicting opinions, Craig turned to London on 5 June. On 7 September the colonial secretary, Lord Castlereagh, confirmed that a Jew could not sit in the assembly. But Craig, who was determined to bring the Canadian members to heel, had dissolved the house on 15 May and announced new general elections. What would Hart do?

Some historians have claimed that Hart again stood as a candidate. A Mr Hart did indeed come in fourth, with 32 votes – Moses Hart, according to the *Quebec Gazette* of 2 Nov. 1809. As for Ezekiel, judging from available documents he was turning his attention resolutely to his business affairs at that time. It would be up to his sons to continue the political struggle. Samuel Becancour, Aaron Ezekiel*, and Adolphus Mordecai* Hart would have a strong influence on the 1831–32 legislation that gave Jews in Lower Canada full recognition of their rights as citizens.

Ezekiel Hart was admitted into the militia in June 1803 and served as a lieutenant in the 8th Battalion of Trois-Rivières militia, which was placed under Lieutenant-Colonel Charles-Michel d'Irumberry* de Salaberry in 1812. He may or may not have been at the battle of Châteauguay, since about that time he was posted to a unit that did not take part in the engagement, the 1st Battalion of Trois-Rivières militia, in which he became a captain in 1816. On 16 May 1830 he was promoted colonel of the 1st Battalion of Saint-Maurice militia.

When Hart died in 1843, he was accorded an impressive funeral. The stores in Trois-Rivières closed, and the 81st Foot paid him final honours. He was buried in the second Jewish cemetery in Trois-Rivières, which was on a lot that he himself had given for it. Hart is believed to have had 10 children. At the time he dictated his last will on 20 June 1839, his wife had been dead for 18 years, and he left his possessions to Samuel Becancour, Aaron Ezekiel, Ira Craig, Adolphus Mordecai, Esther Eliza, Harriet, and Caroline Athalia. On 30 Nov. 1843 notaries Laurent-David Craig and Joseph-Michel Badeaux set about inventorying the estates of Hart and his wife. It took them nearly three months to go through the belongings in the house and the store on Rue du Platon. Hart had been rich. He had lived in an enormous, comfortable, and well-furnished house with 16 rooms.

Craig and Badeaux took more than three days to make a partial list of the books in Hart's library. Often they merely marked down a batch of old books. Yet their inventory of books, valued at £80, ran to 17 pages and listed dictionaries, including a Hebrew-Latin one, a world history in 23 volumes, the *Encyclopædia Britannica* in 17 volumes, works on law, medicine, geography, and history, among them a history of the Jews in two volumes, the laws of Moses, a German Bible, an annotated history of the Old Testament, travel accounts, and, of course, treatises on brewing beer alongside classics such as *Don Quixote* and the *Thousand and one nights*.

Ezekiel Hart had undoubtedly been a remarkable person for his time and place. Like his father, he had maintained good relations with his associates, but he mixed more easily with the upper class. Famous travellers stayed in his home. Ezekiel had also been a good husband and father. In addition to large holdings in real estate, he had given his children a refined and careful upbringing that would be passed on to his descendants.

DENIS VAUGEOIS

[The basic sources for this biography are the Hart papers at ASTR (0009), the Hart family papers at the American Jewish Hist. Soc. Arch. in Waltham, Mass., and the Hart family papers at the McCord Museum (M21359). The Château Ramezay (Montreal) owns an oil portrait of Ezekiel Hart.

The inventory of the joint estate of Ezekiel Hart and Frances Lazarus is nearly 200 pages long, about one-quarter of it being a list of household goods. The original is at the archives in Waltham; a copy is in the minute-book of notary Laurent-David Craig (ANQ-MBF, CN1-19, 30 nov. 1843). Historian and archivist David Rome supervised the compilation of an important set of documents relating in particular to the political ventures of the Harts; this extensive work was published as "On the early Harts," *Canadian Jewish Arch.* (Montreal), 15–18 (1980).

Several historians have taken an interest in Ezekiel Hart's career as a member of the assembly, including Jean-Pierre Wallot in *Un Québec qui bougeait*, 149–53, 163–64, and in "Les Canadiens français et les Juifs (1808–1809): l'affaire Hart," *Juifs et Canadiens*, Naïm Kattam, édit. (Montréal, 1967), 113–21; and Benjamin Sulte in "Les miettes de l'histoire," *Rev. canadienne* (Montréal), 7 (1870): 426–43, and in *Mélanges historiques . . .* , Gérard Malchelosse, édit. (21v., Montréal, 1918–34), 19: 47–56.

The following works are also useful: John Lambert, *Travels through Lower Canada, and the United States of*

North America, in the years 1806, 1807, and 1808 . . . (3v., London, 1810); Frederic Gaffen, "The sons of Aaron Hart" (MA thesis, Univ. of Ottawa, 1969); Denis Vaugeois, "Bécancour et les Hart," *Le Mauricien médical* (Trois-Rivières, Qué.), 4 (1964): 65–71. D.V.]

HASKINS, JAMES, teacher, doctor, and poet; b. between 1802 and 1805 in Dublin, son of Charles Haskins, a merchant, and —— Kelly; m. 10 March 1835 Mary Ann Everitt of Kingston Township, Upper Canada, and they had one child; d. 10 Oct. 1845 at Frankford, Upper Canada.

James Haskins was of a moderately wealthy background, his father being a merchant and supplier of clothing to the British army. At the age of 17 James entered Trinity College, Dublin, from which he graduated with an AB in 1824. Instead of entering his father's business, he followed his inclinations and his love of classical literature and taught in various locations in Ireland and England. This career permitted extensive travel in Ireland and on the Continent.

Haskins returned to Trinity College to study surgery and to take an MB in 1833. Shortly thereafter, accompanied by his sister and an aunt, he immigrated to Upper Canada. He arrived in Belleville in July 1834 and on 13 August obtained a certificate to practise medicine. His own comments indicate that he did practise in Belleville, although there is not much information available about his movements from 1834 to 1836. On 10 March 1835 he married 15-year-old Mary Ann Everitt. A Hastings County historian, Gerald E. Boyce, reports Haskins opening a "classical" school in 1836 and applying, unsuccessfully, that September for the post of master of a proposed district grammar school. Haskins may well have taught at a Belleville seminary for girls taken over by his sister in 1834. By 16 June 1837 he was advertising in the Kingston *Chronicle & Gazette* that he was opening a medical practice at "Yarker's Mills" in Loughborough Township on the River Trent, citing his accreditation and good references and noting his earlier success as a doctor. Haskins was very happy there and wrote much poetry. But the happiness did not last. Mary Ann died giving birth to a daughter and Haskins, in his grief, moved to Frankford. There he lived in relative obscurity, practising medicine and writing the majority of his poems, finding outlets for some of them in the *Literary Garland* and the *Church*.

It is concerning this segment of his life that the two main sources of information about his character and early death particularly clash. The first, a poem by Susanna Moodie [Strickland*], with accompanying comments, was first published in the *Literary Garland* in 1846. She makes Haskins a "Neglected son of Genius," unable to cope with an anti-intellectual society and driven by it to a reclusive life and alcoholism. She perpetrates the story that Haskins and another doctor "entered into a compact to drink until they both died." The story serves Moodie's purposes, which are to indicate the terrible abuse of alcohol in the colonies and the antagonism and suspicion with which the arts were regarded. Her observations on Haskins are, however, supported by William Hutton*, who noted in March 1844 that Haskins "drinks hard." The second source, an introductory memoir by his friend Henry Baldwin, appeared in the posthumous collection of Haskins's *Poetical works* in 1848. Baldwin, who visited Haskins often at Frankford, protects the doctor's reputation, mentioning nothing of a drinking problem but viewing him as one who chose solitude because of his grief and his deeply religious nature. He indicates that Haskins exhausted his health by the strenuousness of his service as a doctor in the area and by a too intense devotion to his poetry and his intellectual pursuits. He also observes that Haskins suffered frequent attacks of ague and had a susceptibility to diseases of the chest; his comments suggest that Haskins may have died of tuberculosis.

Perhaps the truth lies somewhere between the two views. Haskins's poetry would indicate that he was a very religious and a contemplative person, stressing as it does the illusory nature of earthly bliss and the general unworthiness of man. His longest work, "The Cross," written after the death of his wife, is a religious epic, his version of paradise lost and found, written in Spenserian stanzas; it often reflects his personal afflictions and a sense of his own personal unworthiness. Several other poems are elegiac in nature and clearly show how keenly he felt the loss of his wife.

In his poetry Haskins was more interested in the symbolic use of nature than in specific and local characteristics. His dominant images are of storm, wind, and darkness, representing man's condition and urging him toward the peace and love of Christ. He is more akin to Blake or Shelley in his poetic texture than to Wordsworth.

There are some specific personal digressions, however, and in "The Mediterranean Sea," which appeared in the *Literary Garland* early in 1846, he indicates that his life as a doctor in Canada was not easy: he faced many demands for service in severe weather when travel was difficult, often with little or no remuneration. Yet, trying as his situation was, he indicates that he could not live "in crowded city-pent / Like eagle in its cage," but would roam "E'en as the wind, / Walking upon the mountain." Unappreciated he may have been, but his was a chosen rather than an imposed solitude.

In Canadian literary history Haskins has been, like so many other minor poets, neglected. His fate until now has been to serve as an analogue for Susanna Moodie's own sense of being on the fringes of literary culture. And yet in his time he served other purposes, both in revealing his own nourishment by the great English Romantic poets and by the classical writers and in professing a conservative reaction to progress, materialism, and other earthly snares. He must have appealed to many people, as he did to Baldwin, as a man of learning and strong religious conviction.

CARL BALLSTADT

James Haskins's published works include "The Mediterranean Sea; a poem," *Literary Garland*, new ser., 4 (1846): 13–16, 73–76, and *The poetical works of James Haskins . . .* , ed. Henry Baldwin (Hartford, Conn., 1848), both issued after his death.

PAC, RG 5, B9, 63: 624. [Susanna Strickland] Moodie, "Sonnet to the memory of Dr. James Haskins," *Literary Garland*, new ser., 4: 76. *Chronicle & Gazette*, 29 April, 16 June 1837; 22 Oct. 1845. *Church*, 1838. *Death notices of Ont.* (Reid). *An index to the "Literary Garland" (Montreal, 1838–1851)*, comp. Mary Markham Brown (Toronto, 1962). G. E. Boyce, *Hutton of Hastings: the life and letters of William Hutton, 1801–61* (Belleville, Ont., 1972). Walter Lewis and Lynne Turner, *By bridge and mill: a history of the village of Frankford* (Kingston, Ont., 1979).

HASSALL, THOMAS, Chipewyan interpreter, guide, Methodist lay preacher, and teacher; b. *c.* 1811; m. 13 Feb. 1841 Elizabeth ——, and they had a number of children; d. 11 Sept. 1844.

In 1823, at Fort Churchill (Churchill, Man.), the Reverend John WEST persuaded the subject's father, a hunter, to send the boy to the Red River settlement (Man.) to be educated by David Thomas JONES at the Anglican mission. He attended the mission school for eight years; on 24 June 1827 he was baptized by Jones and named after Thomas Hassall of Lampeter, Wales, who had recommended Jones for a missionary posting. In 1831 young Thomas entered the service of the Hudson's Bay Company.

Two years later he was engaged as interpreter for the Arctic expedition of Commander George Back*. Hassall travelled with the expedition as far as Lake Athabasca, where Back reported that "being unaccustomed to speak his native tongue, he was not altogether adapted for the first introduction of a party amongst the Indians." Hassall remained at Fort Resolution (N.W.T.) and Fort Reliance and rejoined the expedition in the spring of 1834 for its return to Norway House (Man.).

Hassall remained with the HBC until the coming of Methodist missionaries to the northwest in 1840. Robert Terrill Rundle* arrived at Norway House in June of that year and James EVANS followed in August. Hassall immediately associated himself with the new mission. On 20 August he was chosen to be a witness at the marriage of Benjamin and Margaret Sinclair, and in September 1841 the Hassalls' daughter, Margaret, was baptized by Evans at Cumberland House (Sask.). Evans made Hassall the interpreter and schoolmaster at Norway House, and as a result of his care the school was "in a prosperous state," Evans reported to the London Missionary Society in July 1844. "He is indeed an indefatigable and useful auxiliary to the Missionary, and deserves my highest commendation. His qualifications, piety, and unremitting labours and anxiety to promote the interests of the cause of God, and to instruct the natives, together with the fact that he speaks English well, French tolerably well, Cree fluently, and Chippewayan, (not Ojibaway, but an entirely different language,) to which nation he belongs, and amongst whom he has been already very useful, – have induced me to grant him a licence as a Local Preacher in this Territory." Although it was not uncommon for natives to be made class leaders, few were licensed by the Methodists as lay preachers, in part because of a shortage of funds to pay them. Hassall was the only one so named in the northwest at the time; Henry Bird Steinhauer* and Benjamin Sinclair were licensed later.

On 1 Aug. 1844 Evans, Hassall, and three others left Norway House in an urgent effort to reach the Athabasca country before a Roman Catholic priest, Jean-Baptiste Thibault*, disturbed the loyalties Evans had established among the Indians. On 11 September, when they were within three days of Île-à-la-Crosse (Sask.), Evans was preparing to shoot some ducks from their canoe. "The piece went off and Alas! lodged its contents under poor Thomas' left shoulder. He looked around, sunk down, and was no more."

GERALD M. HUTCHINSON

PABC, Add. MSS 635. PAM, HBCA, D.5/12; E.4/1a: f.64. SOAS, Methodist Missionary Soc. Arch., Wesleyan Methodist Missionary Soc., corr., North America, Hudson's Bay territories, William Mason to secretaries, 20 Aug. 1844. UWOL, Regional Coll., James Evans papers, box 4734, items 115, 189–91, 213. George Back, *Narrative of the Arctic land expedition to the mouth of the Great Fish River, and along the shores of the Arctic Ocean in the years 1833, 1834, and 1835* (London, 1836), 56, 89, 281, 465. James Evans, "Extract of a letter from the Rev. James Evans, general superintendent of the Wesleyan missions in the Hudson's-Bay territories, dated July, 1844," *Wesleyan-Methodist Magazine*, 68 (1845): 414. R. T. Rundle, *The Rundle journals, 1840–1848*, intro. and notes G. M. Hutchinson, ed. H. A. Dempsey (Calgary, 1977). Boon, *Anglican Church*. G. [M.] Hutchinson, "British Methodists and the Hudson's Bay Company, 1840–1854," *Prairie spirit: perspectives on the heritage of the United Church of Canada in the west*, ed. D. L. Butcher *et al.* (Winnipeg, 1985), 28–43. Nan Shipley, *The James Evans story* (Toronto, 1966).

HEAD, SAMUEL, doctor, merchant, JP, office holder, and judge; b. *c.* 1773 in Halifax, son of Michael Head; m. twice; he and his first wife had one child; m. secondly 2 Jan. 1817 Sophia Augusta Eagleson, daughter of the Reverend John Eagleson*, in Liverpool, N.S., and they had probably four children; d. 16 Nov. 1837 in Halifax.

The son of a surgeon, Samuel Head received his own medical training in England and in 1803 became a member of the Royal College of Surgeons of London. He started a practice in surgery and medicine in Halifax about 1804 and ran a pharmacy which had been established by his father around 1790. Because of the relatively large number of doctors in Halifax, it was difficult to set up a medical practice there. Head's pharmacy was thus a key element in his career and he operated it until he died. Before he had taken it over, the pharmacy had been for some time the only one in town, and it remained an important source in the colony for medicine, medical supplies and equipment, and such items as herbs, perfumes, and dyes. This trade was particularly lucrative during the war with France. After 1812, when war broke out with the United States, there was an increased demand for medical supplies aboard vessels as well as at the naval hospital in Halifax and the prisoner of war hospital on Melville Island.

By 1814 Head felt sufficiently secure financially to open a private 40–50 bed hospital on Water Street for travellers and sick and injured seamen. The cost of renovating the building proved to be high and Head turned to the House of Assembly for a grant. The application was unsuccessful, partly because the government had no interest in establishing marine hospitals such as existed in Great Britain and the United States. Furthermore, the government was convinced that public health care was fully provided by the asylum for the poor. The hospital never met Head's ambitions and, though it seems to have had enough patients to remain open until his death, played no apparent role in the development of medical practice in the town.

Head's interest in providing better medical facilities in Halifax extended to a concern about the competence of medical practitioners. Over the years a number of people in the town claimed to have had medical training. In 1819 Head, along with other British-trained physicians, called for the licensing of doctors in order to eliminate "medical quacks." Since this campaign threatened to affect those with unorthodox medical views, some politicians saw the doctors' proposal as self-serving, and it was not until 1828 that the legislature agreed to establish a simple method of registration for doctors.

Head's concern for the quality of medical treatment and his attempts to establish a hospital reflected his belief in the importance of public duty. Caring about the condition of the poor, he chaired the committee of charity of the Charitable Irish Society from 1819 to 1834. As well, he was a founder in 1820 of the Halifax Poor Man's Friend Society, and he remained active in this organization until it was disbanded in 1827. His sense of duty found yet another outlet after his appointment as a justice of the peace in 1810.

Public awareness of health issues began to increase in the 1820s, especially after a serious epidemic of typhus and smallpox in 1827. Responsibility for providing health care to the less fortunate lay with the commissioners of the poor, but during the epidemic they had seen their prime duty to be towards the inmates of the asylum for the poor. Head and other justices attempted to have the magistrates assume responsibility for dealing with any future epidemic. These efforts were successful to the point that on the appearance of smallpox in 1831 the magistrates ordered a vaccination of children of the poor. When the disease continued to spread, the magistrates, with the government's support, undertook to open a lazaret on Melville Island, which was operated by Head, John Stirling, and Matthias Francis Hoffmann*. However, such activities did not deal with the broader question of furnishing medical aid to the poor. This issue was raised by a group of doctors, aided by the grand jury of Halifax County, who wished to make the hospital in the asylum for the poor accessible not only to the indigent but also to the working poor, thereby extending the potential clientele of the doctors. To this end they urged the magistrates to break the hold of the commissioners of the poor over the hospital. Although professing sympathy with the aims of the agitators, the magistrates refused to confront the commissioners on the issue. In this instance, Head preferred to remain silent rather than engage in public criticism of fellow officials and the doctor of the asylum, William Bruce ALMON.

In 1832 the agitation over the asylum hospital was only a small part of the concern over health-related issues as the public authorities, led by Lieutenant Governor Sir Peregrine Maitland*, prepared to cope with a possible cholera epidemic. One new piece of provincial legislation in 1832 established a central board of health, which was to deal with an actual outbreak of disease, and another established local bodies of health wardens which were charged to enforce measures designed to prevent an epidemic. Head's most immediate involvement in the campaign to deal with a possible outbreak of cholera was as a health warden for St John's Ward in Halifax.

Nova Scotia escaped without an epidemic of cholera in 1832, but the magistrates nevertheless became the objects of popular wrath because it was their duty to raise taxes to finance sanitation projects. Indeed, criticism of local policies generally extended to them regardless of whether or not they were to blame. This tendency was especially evident during the cholera epidemic which did come in 1834. In that year Lieutenant Governor Sir Colin CAMPBELL forced local health boards to make all the decisions concerning the epidemic. Head was fully occupied by his duties as a health warden, but during the fall he had to bear the attacks on the magistrates which culminated in letters published in the *Novascotian, or Colonial Herald* by Joseph Howe*. These attacks were partly the result of the fear and frustration created by the epidemic. In another, more basic, sense the epidemic merely crystallized a resentment against the magistrates which had been developing for some years.

Head was not prepared to compromise with his critics. He had taken his duties seriously, his record of attendance in the sessions was good, and his dedication had been recognized in 1831 by his appointment to the Inferior Court of Common Pleas. Nor was he prepared to accept any public criticism of other magistrates. In fact, he shared the view that, since the magistrates were appointed by the executive, they were responsible only to it and should be shielded from unwarranted attacks. Head was thus one of the magistrates who urged the government to prosecute Howe for criminal libel. He received a shock when Howe was unexpectedly acquitted and perhaps a worse one when a committee appointed by the provincial government reported that the magistrates had not carried out their duties responsibly. Unlike some of his fellow magistrates who withdrew from public affairs after these attacks, Head continued to serve and in 1835 was appointed to the central board of health.

In 1837 Head died of typhus fever. His widow soon discovered that the estate was in poor condition. Although his debts could have been cleared by the sale of some large tracts of land, because Head had died intestate it was not until 1841 that the administrators of the estate were able to settle the accounts.

K. G. Pryke

PANS, RG 1, 214½ (transcripts); RG 25, C, 5; RG 34-312, P, 10. Royal College of Surgeons of England (London), Membership records, 1803–26. N.S., House of Assembly, *Journal and proc.*, 1814–35. *Acadian Recorder*, 1804–37, esp. 18 Jan. 1817, 18 Nov. 1837. *Nova-Scotia Royal Gazette*, 1804–37. J. M. Beck, *Joseph Howe* (2v., Kingston, Ont., and Montreal, 1982), 1. Geoffrey Bilson, *A darkened house: cholera in nineteenth-century Canada* (Toronto, 1980). G. E. Hart, "The Halifax Poor Man's Friend Society, 1820–27; an early social experiment," *CHR*, 34 (1953): 109–23.

HEARN. *See* Herron

HECK, SAMUEL, Methodist preacher and farmer; b. 28 July 1771 in Camden Township, N.Y., son of Paul Heck and Barbara Ruckle*; m. *c.* 1797 Lois Wright, and they had eight children; d. 18 Aug. 1841 at his home in Augusta Township, Upper Canada.

Paul and Barbara Heck were members of a group known as Palatines who migrated from Ireland to New York in 1760. In Ireland many had become followers of John Wesley, and in North America the Hecks, and particularly Barbara, took an active part in the formation of the first Methodist society in New York City. Subsequently, they and other Palatine families moved to Camden Township, near modern Bennington, Vt, and established a Methodist community there. With the American Revolutionary War the Hecks became loyalist refugees and in 1785 they settled in Township No.7 (Augusta), in what would soon become Upper Canada.

Once more, the Hecks and other Palatine Methodists kindled the flame of Methodist teaching, and their settlement became one of the two centres of a Methodist community in Upper Canada which began to take shape in 1790. Samuel Heck was converted and, anxious "to tell to all around, What a dear Saviour he had found," he was licensed as an exhorter, probably in 1797. In 1803 he was made a local preacher, that is, someone authorized to conduct services in the absence of the itinerant, or travelling preacher, and to assist the latter at camp meetings and on other occasions; his licence would be renewed shortly before his death. In conformity with the practice of the Methodist Episcopal Church in the United States, to which the Methodist societies in Upper Canada belonged, Heck was ordained deacon in 1817 and elder in 1828. In the latter capacity he had authority to administer the sacraments, but was not expected or empowered to participate in the itinerant ministry.

Throughout his life Heck farmed in Augusta where he offered hospitality to a long succession of travelling preachers in his comfortable home. For many years he was secretary of the Augusta Circuit Quarterly Meeting and he preached regularly. In 1817 he was one of the trustees in Augusta who assumed responsibility for building a new meeting-house. That year he signed a letter to the British Conference protesting the intrusion of Wesleyan Methodist missionaries into the Upper Canadian circuits. However, he did not join those local preachers who left the Canada Conference after its union in 1833 with the British Conference, a merger that gave rise to a new Methodist episcopal church in Upper Canada.

Regrettably, Heck's letters have not survived. If he wrote his sermons, which is unlikely, they too have disappeared. He was evidently a kindly, humble, and unpretentious man who was greatly respected and admired. It was said that "all the Christian graces shone very brightly in the life and character of our departed father, but no one more clearly than the grace of patience." He "was emphatically a man of peace," who was saddened by the divisions in Canadian Methodism and particularly by the break between the Canadian and British conferences in 1840.

Samuel Heck was one of a select company of local leaders whose regular preaching over many years, faithful commitment to Methodist teaching, and willingness to sustain their church helped to lay strong foundations for the community in Upper Canada. During the frequent absences of the itinerant ministers, they maintained continuity in teaching and discipline and provided much of the material support required for the institutional growth of Methodism. They endeavoured with considerable success to secure acceptance of an evangelical faith, to uphold a high standard of individual morality, to perpetuate Upper Canada's distinctive mixture of British and North American values, and to persuade their brethren that Christianity should transcend national boundaries.

G. S. French

SOAS, Methodist Missionary Soc. Arch., Wesleyan Methodist Missionary Soc., corr., Canadas, no.222 (petition, Bay Quinty Circuit, 4 Feb. 1817) (mfm. at UCC-C). UCC-C, "A collection of documents relating to the Hecks, Emburys, and other clans," comp. Eula [Carscallen] Lapp (copies); Methodist Church, Augusta District, minutes of district meetings, 1834–44. *Christian Guardian*, 20 Oct. 1841. J. [S.] Carroll, *Case and his cotemporaries* . . . (5v., Toronto, 1867–77), 4: 350. Eula Carscallen Lapp, *To their heirs forever* (Belleville, Ont., 1977).

HENEY, HUGUES, lawyer, militia officer, JP, politician, and office holder; b. 9 Sept. 1789 in Montreal, son of Hugue Heney, a merchant, and Thérèse Fortier; m. there 14 Oct. 1817 Marie-Léocadie Foucher, daughter of judge Louis-Charles Foucher, and they had seven children; d. 13 Jan. 1844 in Trois-Rivières, Lower Canada.

Hugues Heney did his classical studies at the Collège Saint-Raphaël in Montreal from 1798 till 1806. On completing them, he articled with Joseph Bédard, a Montreal lawyer, for five years. Called to the bar on 19 Dec. 1811, he entered the profession in Montreal and soon built up a large practice. In the War of 1812 he held the rank of lieutenant in the 2nd Militia Battalion of Montreal. On 16 Oct. 1813 he was transferred to Montreal's 3rd Militia Battalion, of which he became adjutant. He served in this capacity for the rest of the war.

Heney was appointed justice of the peace for the district of Trois-Rivières on 8 July 1815 and for the district of Montreal on 21 May 1818. Two years later he was elected for Montreal East to the House of Assembly of Lower Canada. He represented this riding until 1832. A friend of Louis-Joseph Papineau*, he belonged to the Canadian party and shared in its struggles against the government of the province. At a protest meeting in Montreal on 7 Oct. 1822 he was named to a committee of 18 leading inhabitants of the town and its environs that was set up to fight a plan to unite Lower and Upper Canada [*see* Denis-Benjamin Viger*].

In 1827 Heney, along with Papineau and six other assemblymen, signed a declaration condemning the decision of Governor Lord Dalhousie [Ramsay] to prorogue the assembly and rejecting the accusations he had levelled against it. That year the governor had revoked the commissions of Heney and other militia officers who were friends of Papineau. Dalhousie's successor, Sir James Kempt* was, however, to reinstate Heney, who later attained the rank of lieutenant-colonel. In February 1828 Heney, Papineau, and 15 others signed the instructions given by a Montreal committee to Denis-Benjamin Viger, John Neilson, and Austin Cuvillier, the three men delegated to go to England and lay the Canadians' grievances about the political situation in Lower Canada before the British authorities. Heney was appointed commissioner for the building and repair of churches on 20 July 1830, and visitor of the schools in Champlain and Saint-Maurice counties on 18 June 1831.

In December 1831 Heney differed with Papineau and most of the Patriote assemblymen on a much discussed bill dealing with *fabriques* [*see* Louis Bourdages*]. He voted against the bill at the second reading and abstained from voting at the third reading. He resigned his seat on 28 Feb. 1832 and on 1 March was named clerk of the House of Assembly. On 26 July he became commissioner for the erection of new parishes and on 27 October commissioner for the subdivision of old ones. He was appointed *grand voyer* (chief road commissioner) for the district of Trois-Rivières on 7 December. In November the governor, Lord Aylmer [Whitworth-Aylmer], had offered Heney a seat on the Executive Council. Papineau had already refused this office and had asked the Patriotes to decline any similar offer. None the less Dominique Mondelet* accepted appointment that month, and for doing so he was considered a traitor by the members of the Patriote party. Heney in turn accepted Aylmer's invitation, and on 28 Jan. 1833 he was named to the Executive Council.

In 1835 Heney indicated to John Neilson, a former Patriote who had been sent to England by Papineau's opponents to convey the grievances of the British merchants and the moderate assemblymen, that he fully supported the mission. He added his opinion that "there are abuses . . . in all human institutions . . . that it is permissible to correct them and eliminate them using all decent and loyal means short of a call to sedition and revolt; that the house must be repaired and not overturned . . . that the elective principle, though good in itself, turns vicious indeed when it is exploited for purposes inspired by national hatreds, religious controversies, or other interested motives." These remarks, meant as unfavourable allusions to the

Patriote party, show how far Heney had by then moved from his former associates. On 5 Nov. 1836 he was appointed commissioner for the summary trial of small causes at Saint-François-du-Lac.

At the time of the 1837 rebellion Heney had a hand in preparing the Executive Council's recommendations concerning the insurrection. On 21 Dec. 1837 he was also appointed commissioner for administering the oath of allegiance. His collaboration with the authorities caused him to be severely criticized by the Patriote leaders, who accused him of having repudiated all his former principles.

When the Act of Union came into force on 10 Feb. 1841, Heney lost his seat on the Executive Council. He was not appointed to the new one formed three days later by Governor Lord Sydenham [THOMSON]. He lost his position as *grand voyer* that year when the office was abolished. In 1842, however, he was appointed commissioner to revise the statutes and ordinances of Lower Canada, along with Alexander Buchanan* and Gustavus William Wicksteed. They had not yet accomplished this task when Heney died, at the age of 54, in Trois-Rivières on 13 Jan. 1844.

JACQUES L'HEUREUX

Hugues Heney is the author of *Commentaire ou observations sur l'acte de la 31e année du règne de George III, chap. 31, communément appelé Acte constitutionnel du Haut et du Bas-Canada* (Montréal, 1832). The minutes Heney kept can be found in P.-G. Roy, *Inventaire des procès-verbaux des grands voyers conservés aux Archives de la province de Québec* (6v., Beauceville, Qué., 1923–32), 3: 224–38.

ANQ-M, CE1-51, 9 sept. 1789, 14 oct. 1817. ANQ-MBF, CE1-48, 17 janv. 1844. PAC, MG 24, B1, 6: 53; 8: 344; B2: 1339, 1538, 1586, 2857; MG 30, D1, 15: 409–23; RG 4, B8: 6753–61; RG 7, G1, 24: 644; 26: 19; 35: 279; RG 68, General index, 1651–1841; 1841–67. *Docs. relating to constitutional hist., 1819–28* (Doughty and Story). L.C., House of Assembly, *Journals*, 1830–32. *L'Aurore des Canadas*, 16 janv. 1844. *Le Canadien*, 19 janv. 1844. *Quebec Gazette*, 9 Jan. 1812; 28 May 1818; 7 June 1819; 20 March, 20, 24 April, 3 July, 21 Aug., 11 Dec. 1820; 26 July 1821; 5 Dec. 1822; 2 April 1827. F.-J. Audet, *Les députés de Montréal*, 17, 92–94, 153; "Les législateurs du Bas-Canada." F.-M. Bibaud, *Le panthéon canadien* (A. et V. Bibaud; 1891), 116–17. Desjardins, *Guide parl.* H. J. Morgan, *Bibliotheca Canadensis. Officers of British forces in Canada* (Irving). *Quebec almanac*, 1810–23. Tanguay, *Dictionnaire*, 4: 80. Wallace, *Macmillan dict.* Michel Bibaud, *Histoire du Canada et des Canadiens, sous la domination anglaise* [1760–1830] (Montréal, 1844; réimpr. East Ardsley, Angl., et New York, 1968), 235, 282. Chapais, *Cours d'hist. du Canada*, 3: 122–23; 4: 113–14. Maurault, *Le collège de Montréal* (Dansereau; 1967). Ouellet, *Bas-Canada*, 317, 321, 344, 404, 413. J.-E. Roy, *L'ancien Barreau au Canada* (Montréal, 1897), 77. Rumilly, *Papineau et son temps*, 1: 103, 113, 242, 244, 261. *Les ursulines des Trois-Rivières depuis leur établissement jusqu'à nos jours* (4v., Trois-Rivières, Qué., 1888–1911), 4: 73. F.-J. Audet, "En marge d'un centenaire: citoyen distingué, il rendit à son pays d'éminents services; c'est le souvenir qu'a laissé à ses concitoyens l'honorable Hugues Heney, jurisconsulte distingué," *La Presse*, 16 sept. 1933: 30; "Grands-voyers du district de Trois-Rivières," *BRH*, 10 (1904): 228. Gérard Malchelosse, "La famille Heney," *BRH*, 49 (1943): 361–63. P.-G. Roy, "Les grands voyers de 1667 à 1842," *BRH*, 37 (1931): 456; "Les grands voyers de la Nouvelle-France et leurs successeurs," *Cahiers des Dix*, 8 (1943): 232–33.

HENRY, EDME (Edmund), notary, politician, militia officer, land agent, businessman, and office holder; b. 15 Nov. 1760 in Longueuil (Que.), son of Edme Henry, surgeon-major in the Régiment Royal Roussillon, and Geneviève Fournier; m. first Eunice Parker; m. secondly 9 Oct. 1828 Marie-Clotilde Girardin in La Prairie; d. there 14 Sept. 1841 and was buried in the crypt of the parish church.

After the Seven Years' War, Edme Henry's father settled on Saint-Pierre and Miquelon, leaving his wife and family in Montreal. Henry attended the Collège Saint-Raphaël from 1772 to 1778 and studied law for three years under Simon Sanguinet*. Commissioned a notary on 2 July 1783, he began practice in Montreal. His career was interrupted between 1787 and 1793 when family matters took him to Saint-Pierre and Miquelon. After the islands were captured by British forces under James Ogilvie* in 1793, Henry pleaded his status as a British subject and was allowed to return to Lower Canada with his family and possessions.

After being re-established in his commission on 17 Feb. 1794, Henry resumed his practice, settling in La Prairie, where he quickly rose to local prominence. He was elected to the House of Assembly for Huntingdon County in 1810. He held the seat until 1814, but attended few of the sessions. In response to a private solicitation of his opinion by the governor-in-chief, Sir George Prevost*, on the reasons for the Canadians' alienation from the administration, Henry replied that jealousy over patronage was a major source of discontent, and that those who were dissatisfied had in turn created doubts in the mind of the clergy as to the government's plans. The two groups therefore acted in concert to oppose the administration's projects. Henry proposed as solutions a greater decentralization, and especially an attempt by the government to gain more support in the countryside, among the common people rather than the élite.

Henry's absence from the assembly was due in part to his military commitments. A major in the Beauharnois battalion of militia since 15 May 1812, he fought at the battle of Châteauguay in October 1813 [*see* Charles-Michel d'Irumberry* de Salaberry] and commanded the Boucherville battalion of militia after Lieutenant-Colonel Charles William Grant was made prisoner by the Americans in December. On 2 July

1822 he was promoted lieutenant-colonel in the 2nd Battalion of Huntingdon militia. His services were rewarded on 27 July 1825 by a grant of 1,000 acres in Kilkenny Township.

Henry's period of greatest activity as a notary was between 1794 and 1814 when he drew up a total of 4,352 acts. From 1800 to 1804 his nephew Louis Barbeau studied under him, and after Barbeau was commissioned in 1804, they worked as partners. Henry's early clients had included the seigneur Gabriel Christie*. In 1803, after Christie's son Napier Christie Burton had succeeded to his father's estate, Henry, together with Samuel Potts, was given power of attorney to collect the debts due to it. In 1815, when it was clear that Christie Burton would not be returning to Lower Canada, Henry was appointed his land agent, a position he retained until the seigneur's death on 2 Jan. 1835. On 15 Jan. 1821 Henry was made crown agent for the seigneury of Prairie-de-la-Madeleine. Although he kept his commission as a notary until 1831, his activities as land agent took up much of his time, and after 1815 he notarized only 20 acts.

Henry's role as a land agent contributed to his influence in the La Prairie region, as did his marriage in 1828 to Marie-Clotilde Girardin, widow of prominent local merchant Jean-Baptiste Raymond*. He became one of the largest proprietors in La Prairie, using his position as agent to acquire land for himself and to favour family and friends with advantageous grants. His own property included a steam-powered grist-mill, perhaps located on the seigneurial reserve at Napierville which he claimed as his own, a mill site in Stanbridge Township, 60 houses in Sherrington Township, a large stone house in La Prairie, and over 2,500 acres in various parts of the province, including the grant in Kilkenny Township.

Not surprisingly, the development of roads and projects such as the Chambly Canal received Henry's support. He was twice made a commissioner of roads and bridges, on 28 May 1829 to open a road between Dorchester (Saint-Jean-sur-Richelieu) and La Prairie and on 1 June 1830 to supervise the macadamization of roads in La Prairie. In the Christie seigneuries he was responsible for the survey of a main road cutting diagonally through Bleury and Sabrevois.

As Christie Burton's agent, Henry established the villages of Christieville (Iberville), Napierville, and Henryville in 1815. He had the remaining land in the seigneuries surveyed, granted some of it, and leased out the reserved mill sites to interested merchants and sawyers. The *censitaires* complained that he sold ungranted lands instead of conceding them freely. Henry does not appear to have kept accurate records during his administration, and his practice of giving receipts on "scraps of paper" which were easily lost meant that some *censitaires* would later claim that they had been forced to pay more arrears than they owed. As long as Henry was agent, however, complaints were muted. Robert Hoyle*, member of the assembly for L'Acadie, preferred to keep his position on seigneurial tenure quiet, saying, "I should regret, to provoke or offend Mr Henry the agent, unnecessarily, by saying much publickly." Henry's administration ended in 1835, but as executor of Christie Burton's will he remained responsible for the collection of arrears in rent. He arranged for these to be sold, at a heavily discounted rate, to his wife's grandson, Montreal lawyer Alfred Pinsoneault, son of Paul-Théophile Pinsonaut*. The push to collect these arrears and their transformation into interest-bearing obligations added to resentment of seigneurial tenure in Christie Burton's seigneuries and contributed to social tension, especially in Léry and Bleury; both seigneuries were heavily implicated in the rebellions of 1837–38.

Not all of Henry's activities were related to land development and promotion. He was also an owner, with his stepdaughter's husband, Joseph Masson, and others, of the steamboat *Edmund Henry*. In 1837 he founded Henry's Bank at La Prairie, with a branch in Montreal. That summer, when his cashier (general manager) "decamped with the ready cash," $130,000, he was forced into bankruptcy, but he was eventually able to pay all claims, several properties he had previously owned having mortgages in favour of the bank. It seems unlikely that his personal fortune recovered from this blow. In 1840 his wife filed a suit against him, probably to protect her own property rights; his land in Kilkenny, the house in La Prairie, and a mill site in Napierville were sold by the sheriff. Henry died the following year leaving her all of his remaining possessions. Since he had waived the necessity of an inventory, the size of his estate at that time is unknown. Henry's influence and social position in the La Prairie region had clearly been much greater than the value of his estate in 1841 might have indicated. Through his profession and his personal ties he had occupied a key position in the social network of the area.

Françoise Noël

Edme Henry's minute-book, with instruments for the period 1783 to 1831, is at ANQ-M, CN1-200.

ANQ-M, CE1-2, 9 oct. 1828; CE1-12, 20 janv. 1760; CM1, 1/8, 14 janv. 1842; CN1-107; CN1-134, 8 oct. 1828; CN1-233; CN1-299; CN4-20. PAC, MG 8, F99; MG 19, A2, ser.3, 183; MG 24, B141, 20 Dec. 1832; MG 30, D1, 15: 426–44; RG 1, L3[L]: 18706–23, 43541–53, 51572–82, 73487–97, 83161–80, 97121–30; RG 4, B8: 127–29, 268–75, 546–51, 10445. Can., Prov. of, Legislative Assembly, *App. to the journals*, 1843, app.F. *Quebec Gazette*, 2 May 1838. *Officers of British forces in Canada* (Irving). Françoise Noël, "Gabriel Christie's seigneuries: settlement and seigneurial administration in the upper Richelieu valley,

1764–1854" (PHD thesis, McGill Univ., Montreal, 1985). F.-J. Audet, "Edme Henry," *BRH*, 33 (1927): 150–54. C. S. Howard, "Canadian banks and bank-notes: a record," *Canadian Banker* (Toronto), 57 (1950), no.1: 30–67.

HERBERT, SARAH, author, publisher, and educator; b. October 1824 in Ireland, daughter of Nicholas Michael Herbert and Ann Bates; d. 22 Dec. 1846 in Halifax.

Sarah Herbert seems to have begun her life in Nova Scotia rather dramatically, since she was probably one of the two "infants" wrecked with her parents and other relatives on the *Nassau*, a passenger ship that broke up off Sable Island on 13 May 1826 en route from Ireland to Quebec. Her 23-year-old mother and several other relatives subsequently died of typhus when transported to Halifax, but by 1827 Sarah's father seems to have sufficiently recovered from the ordeal to establish himself in the city as a shoemaker. He married Catherine Eagan in Halifax on 3 Sept. 1828, and their daughter Mary Eliza* was born the following year.

Throughout their lives, Sarah and Mary Eliza were to be spoken of as literary sisters and collaborators. Their father's fortunes improved in the world as he moved from being a shoemaker and cordwainer to being a manufacturer of blacking and of chest-expanding braces. An 1871 obituary identifies him as the son of the Reverend Nicholas M. Herbert of Tipperary and therefore a close relation of the Earl of Dysart and other members of the Irish gentry. This relationship with a distinguished family may partly explain the interest of the Herbert sisters in heroines of refined sensibility, although both clearly wrote to satisfy society's taste for popular romance. Their father's strong Wesleyan and temperance interests were also to find reflection in their fiction and poetry, but this background tended to manifest itself in the writing of Sarah more pronouncedly than in the work of Mary Eliza. By her late teens, Sarah was submitting religious prose and poetry to Maritime journals such as the *Olive Branch*, the *Morning Herald, and Commercial Advertiser*, and the *Novascotian*, all of Halifax, and the *Amaranth* and the *British North American Wesleyan Methodist Magazine* of Saint John, N.B.

In September 1843 Herbert's serial "Agnes Maitland" won a fiction contest sponsored by the *Olive Branch*. Like her "History of a Halifax belle," also published in the *Olive Branch*, "Agnes Maitland" was an undramatic and sentimental novella advocating temperance and moral and religious principles. It subsequently appeared in pamphlet form and was one means by which Herbert was brought into prominence in the affairs of the *Olive Branch*. By 19 April 1844 she had become sole editor and proprietor of the paper, and she reinforced the literary and temperance direction of the journal with the publishing of American writing by Harriet Elizabeth Beecher Stowe and Catherine Maria Sedgwick and regional work by John McPHERSON and herself. However, the paper unexpectedly collapsed in July 1845, possibly because of Herbert's declining health. Her poem "Presentiments, New Year's Day, 1846" indicates that she knew herself to be fatally ill, and a year later, on 21 Dec. 1846, she died of consumption.

In addition to her writing and editing, Herbert was active in the educational and church affairs of Halifax. In the early 1840s she operated a school which emphasized students' "moral culture" as well as their "intellectual advancement," and she promised in her teaching "to continually illustrate theory by reference to example and experiment." Her endeavours as Sunday school teacher, tract distributor, and secretary of the Halifax Female Temperance Society were acknowledged in a funeral sermon, "On the death of the much lamented Sarah Herbert," preached at the Wesleyan Methodist chapel in January 1847 and printed in the *Halifax Morning Post*. Here, as in subsequent descriptions of Herbert's life, her virtue and her early death created a romantic aura around her memory. Two essays published in the *Provincial: or Halifax Monthly Magazine* in 1852 stressed her piety and poetic sensibility, and as late as 1876 Andrew Shiels*'s *The preface; a poem of the period* paid lengthy tribute to her talents:

Upon her pages, pleasing and polite,
She marvels as the multitudes delight, . . .
Whilst she, – ah! yes, the Mayflower's grow
 and fade
Upon the grave where Sarah Herbert's laid.

In spite of the sentimental feeling which grew up around Sarah Herbert, it is clear that her youthful talents never had an opportunity to develop as did those of her sister. Mary Eliza's fiction reveals her ability to develop comic confrontation and shows an understanding of society's expectations of women in the 19th century. Sarah's work, on the other hand, rarely transcends the sentimental pieties and moral tone inspired by her religious and temperance background. However, as an early female editor and publisher in British North America, and as a supporter of literary endeavour in Nova Scotia in the 1840s, she made a modest contribution to the province's evolving literary culture.

GWENDOLYN DAVIES

[The author wishes to acknowledge the assistance of Terrence M. Punch in directing her to the obituary of the Reverend Nicholas M. Herbert, *Acadian Recorder*, 5 Dec. 1871. G.D.]

Sarah Herbert's novella "Agnes Maitland" appeared in the *Olive Branch* (Halifax) from 13 Oct. to 17 Nov. 1843 and subsequently as a pamphlet entitled *Agnes Maitland, a temperance tale* (Halifax, n.d.), no copies of which have been located. "The history of a Halifax belle" was serialized in the *Olive Branch* from 5 Jan. to 2 Feb. 1844. A collection of Sarah's poems was published posthumously along with those of Mary Eliza in *The Æolian harp; or, miscellaneous poems* (Halifax, 1857).

PAC, MG 24, C4. PANS, Churches, Brunswick Street United (Halifax), Methodist reg. of baptisms, nos.21, 133, 263, 358, 569; reg. of marriages, 1828–29, no.14 (mfm.); MG 5, Halifax County, Camp Hill Cemetery, Halifax, reg. of burials, 1844–69 (mfm.). *Acadian Recorder*, 15 July 1826. *Free Press* (Halifax), 1 Aug. 1826. *Halifax Morning Post & Parliamentary Reporter*, 5 Jan. 1847. *Novascotian*, 13 July, 3 Aug. 1826; 28 Dec. 1846. *Nova-Scotia Royal Gazette*, 31 May, 14 June 1826. *Olive Branch*, 7 Jan. 1843–4 July 1845 (esp. 16 June, 8 Sept. 1843, 19 April 1844–4 July 1845). *Burke's landed gentry* (1875), 1: 615–16. R. J. Long, *Nova Scotia authors and their work: a bibliography of the province* (East Orange, N.J., 1918). H. J. Morgan, *Bibliotheca Canadensis*. *The Oxford companion to Canadian literature*, ed. William Toye (Toronto, 1983). Tratt, *Survey of N.S. newspapers*. Albyn [Andrew Shiels], *The preface; a poem of the period* (Halifax, 1876). Gwendolyn Davies, "A literary study of selected periodicals from Maritime Canada, 1789–1872" (PHD thesis, York Univ., Toronto, 1980). J. S. Thompson, "Introductory memoir," John McPherson, *Poems, descriptive and moral . . .* (Halifax, 1862), ix–xix. *Acadian Recorder*, 17 July 1872. "Half hours with our poets . . . ," *Provincial: or Halifax Monthly Magazine*, 1 (1852): 273–76. D. C. Harvey, "Newspapers of Nova Scotia, 1840–1867," *CHR*, 26 (1945): 294. M. E. Herbert, "More of Sarah Herbert," *Provincial: or Halifax Monthly Magazine*, 1: 347–52.

HERIOT, FREDERICK GEORGE, army and militia officer, landowner, JP, office holder, and politician; b. 11 Jan. 1786, baptized at home on 14 January, and presented in the Anglican church in St Helier, Jersey, on 11 August, third son of Roger Heriot, an army surgeon, and Anne Susanne Nugent; d. unmarried 30 Dec. 1843 in Drummondville, Lower Canada, where he was buried on 1 Jan. 1844.

Frederick George Heriot was a descendant on his father's side of an old and quite prominent Scottish family, the Heriots of Trabroun. On his mother's side he was related to the ancient Irish aristocracy through the Nugents of Westmeath. He has often been confused with his cousin George HERIOT, the deputy postmaster general of Lower Canada from 1800 to 1816.

In the summer of 1801 Heriot, then 15, went into the army as an ensign in the 49th Foot. The following year he arrived in Lower Canada under Lieutenant-Colonel Isaac Brock*'s command, and subsequently his advance was rapid; promoted captain in 1808, he was appointed brigade major, under Major-General Francis de Rottenburg*, in 1811. For some years he lived at Quebec, where garrison life was considered pleasant; in his spare time he turned to horse-racing, with some success.

After the United States declared war on 18 June 1812 Heriot was posted on 26 March 1813 to the Voltigeurs Canadiens as acting major under Lieutenant-Colonel Charles-Michel d'Irumberry* de Salaberry; he would become brevet major on 10 June. On 1 April he set off from the camp at Saint-Philippe-de-Laprairie for Upper Canada at the head of four companies of Voltigeurs and on 13 April he reached Kingston. With his men he shared in the changing fortunes of the British army. After the raid on Sackets Harbor, N.Y., on 28–29 May [*see* Sir James Lucas Yeo*], he was mentioned in dispatches. The risk of invasion increased, and on 26 Oct. 1813 the battle of Châteauguay against the advancing Americans immortalized Salaberry and his Voltigeurs. Heriot and three of his companies were then at Prescott, but they left around 6 November to pursue other American forces moving down the St Lawrence towards Montreal. The battle of Crysler's Farm took place on 11 November [*see* Joseph Wanton Morrison*]. Heriot narrowly escaped capture by dint of his skill as a horseman; his conduct earned him another mention in dispatches and a gold medal. The corps of Voltigeurs was subsequently increased and reorganized in Lower Canada; Salaberry, who was thinking of relinquishing the command, offered Heriot the opportunity to purchase it. Heriot, with the backing of Sir George Prevost*, took over as commanding officer on 11 April 1814 and held the rank of militia lieutenant-colonel until the end of hostilities. Once the war was over, the Voltigeurs were disbanded, on 1 March 1815. Heriot himself was given the option of resuming his previous rank in the 49th Foot, with the prospect of a prompt return to England and a slim chance of promotion in peacetime. For this 29-year-old officer an unexpected career was to open up, however.

While the British government was developing a new colonization policy, the Lower Canadian House of Assembly recommended that lands not yet granted be given to disbanded soldiers. A semi-military settlement thus came into being in the valley of the Rivière Saint-François, and on 1 May 1815 Heriot was appointed to administer it, with the assistance of Pierre-Amable Boucher de Boucherville and several officers from various regiments. The post assured him an income of £300 and £100 for travelling expenses, exclusive of his half pay. He set to work immediately, inspected the area, and on 8 June asked for a grant of 1,200 acres in Grantham and Wickham townships on which to build a village. That summer saw the birth of Drummondville, and its beginnings seemed promising in the opinion of Administrator Sir Gordon Drummond*, who visited the settlement in the autumn. By 1816 houses, a hospital, school, and barracks were being laid out; a post office had already been built. Heriot had prepared a spacious home, Comfort Cottage, some distance away on a hillside, and was having his farm cleared and mills built. But there were serious set-backs: crop failure in 1815 and 1816; desertions; a reduction in military aid and a threat to shut down the operation in 1819; an epidemic in 1820; and in 1826 a fire that devastated the countryside and the village, with only Heriot's house and the two chapels spared. Despite the many disasters, through untiring efforts Heriot managed to maintain the small community, which was totally dependent upon him. He served, in fact, at one and the same time as justice of the peace, trustee and visitor of schools, and commissioner for the building of roads; he was attentive to his fellow citizens' needs and came to their aid. By donating lots he ensured that there would be a Catholic mission and a Church of England parish. He would have liked to dedicate both to St George, but even at the risk of offending him, the Catholic bishop, Joseph-Octave Plessis*, chose the name of Saint-Frédéric for the mission.

The first land grants Heriot had himself received amounted to little more than 600 acres. He considered that his devotion to duty and his service record entitled him to something more and let it be known through numerous petitions. Some of his requests were granted, and he increased his holdings through numerous purchases, with the result that the investigators appointed by Lord Durham [LAMBTON] affirmed in 1838 that he owned 12,000 acres and classified him among the land-grabbers. However, they failed to point out that he was one of six major landowners who lived on their lands, that he was actively engaged in agricultural improvement and stock raising, and that he claimed to have helped develop 40,000 acres.

When Buckingham riding was split in 1829, Heriot was easily elected to the House of Assembly for the new riding of Drummond on 7 November, his opponent having himself voted for him. He was re-elected by acclamation in 1830 and on 31 Jan. 1833 resigned his seat. Assiduous in carrying out his duties, he had taken a particular interest in the means of communication within the colony. In April 1840 he was called to serve on the Special Council but took part in only one session.

Meanwhile Heriot's record of service had earned him a CB in 1822 and the title of aide-de-camp to the governor in 1826. He reached the rank of colonel on 22 July 1830 and was promoted major-general on 23 Nov. 1841. During the 1837 rebellion he had been entrusted with the military organization of the Eastern Townships, and in December of that year he had gone around the Saint-François region to recruit and organize volunteers.

During a trip to England and Scotland in 1840 Heriot re-established links with his family; two of his cousins were in the entourage of the Duke of Wellington, who was his host. In Lower Canada another cousin, Robert Nugent Watts, who was elected to the Legislative Assembly for Drummond on 15 March 1841, had taken up residence in his house; Heriot made over a large part of his belongings to him in 1842. Heriot by then was seriously ill and he died on 30 Dec. 1843, just before his 58th birthday. The local people, both Catholic and Protestant, gave him a moving funeral on 1 Jan. 1844, with the bells of both churches tolling together.

Frederick George Heriot was much regretted by those who had known him; he was praised for his courtesy, tolerance, charitable spirit, devotion to duty, and generous hospitality. He was an unassuming man who liked to see himself as an ordinary farmer, although in fortune and style of living he resembled the English gentry which was considered a desirable source of settlers for the Canadas. A warm-hearted man with a sense of duty, he had lived up to his family's motto: *Fortem posce animum* (Be of brave heart).

MARIE-PAULE R. LABRÈQUE

[Although Frederick George Heriot always signed Heriot, his name appears with other spellings, and in Drummondville (Que.) it is written with an accent (Hériot). Joseph-Charles Saint-Amant supposedly had access to original materials but he used Herriot in his *L'Avenir, townships de Durham et de Wickham, notes historiques et traditionnelles . . .* (Arthabaska, Qué., 1896), an error he corrected in *Un coin des Cantons de l'Est; histoire de l'envahissement pacifique mais irrésistible d'une race* (Drummondville, 1932). Almost all references to Heriot contain errors, such as confusing him with his cousin, stating that he was born in 1766, or maintaining that he arrived in Drummondville in 1816 instead of 1815 (as in Wallace, *Macmillan dict.*, and Michelle Guitard, *Histoire sociale des miliciens de la bataille de la Châteauguay* (Ottawa, 1983)).

Heriot left no instructions in his will about his papers and they have disappeared. It is therefore hard to come to any conclusions about his education (it was very good judging from his correspondence), his personal relationships, or his political opinions. Only an article written by a relative, J. C. A. Heriot, "Major General, the Hon. Frederick George Heriot, CB," *Canadian Antiquarian and Numismatic Journal*, 3rd ser., 8 (1911): 49–75, provides information about Heriot's family and about the man himself. J.-A. Saint-Germain, *dit* frère Côme, *Regards sur les commencements de Drummondville* (Drummondville, 1978), a revised version of a manuscript prepared in 1965, was the first to use modern methods in assessing archival records, and his is the best study available. Michelle Guitard and Christian Rioux, both formerly with Parks Canada, provided the author with useful information on military history.

A portrait of Heriot by Samuel Hawksett is held at the Château Ramezay in Montreal, and the McCord Museum has another, by an unknown artist, formerly attributed to his cousin George Heriot, which appears to be a better likeness. A copy of an unsigned portrait is included in C. P. de Volpi and P. H. Scowen, *The Eastern Townships, a pictorial record; historical prints and illustrations of the Eastern Townships of the province of Quebec, Canada* (Montreal, 1962), and as frontispiece to the article by J. C. A. Heriot. M.-P.R.L.]

AAC-Q, 50, 99. AAQ, 210 A, IV–XII; 69 CD, X: 177–79. ANQ-MBF, CN1-21, 11 avril 1844. ANQ-Q, E17; E21; P-289/1, 3: 43. Arch. de l'évêché de Nicolet (Nicolet, Qué.), Cartable Saint-Frédric. Bureau d'enregistrement, Drummond (Drummondville), Reg. A, 1, nos.1, 503. PAC, MG 11, [CO 42] Q, 132: 74, 81; 137: 165; 161: 132; 163: 253; 178: 131; 216: 209; RG 1, L3[L]: 51639; RG 4, A1, index; RG 8, I (C ser.), 202: 134; 622: 124; 625: 79; 683: 138; 1170: 128–29; 1173: 149a; 1203½B-41: 39; 1224: 77–78; 1227: 137; 1706: 32; RG 31, C1, 1825, 1831, Grantham. Private arch., Lucille Richard Pépin (Drummondville), corr., 1963. "Anticipation de la guerre de 1812," PAC *Rapport*, 1896: 71. St George's (Anglican) Church (Drummondville), Reg. of burials, 1 Jan. 1844. Joseph Bouchette, *Topographical map of the province of Lower Canada . . .* (London, 1815; repr. Montreal, 1980). Elmer Cushing, *An appeal addressed to a candid public; and to the feelings of those whose upright sentiments and discerning minds, enable them to 'weigh it in the balance of the sanctuary'* . . . (Stanstead, Que., 1826). [J. G. Lambton, 1st] Earl of Durham, *Report on the affairs of British North America, from the Earl of Durham . . .* ([London, 1839]). L.C., House of Assembly, *Journaux*, 14 mars 1815: 365; 1830–32; 31 janv. 1833: 363; Special Council, *Journals*, 20 April, November 1840. *Select British docs. of War of 1812* (Wood). Henry Taylor, *Journal of a tour from Montreal, thro' Berthier and Sorel, to the Eastern Townships of Granby, Stanstead, Compton, Sherbrooke, Melbourne, &c., &c., to Port St. Francis* (Quebec, 1840), 74. [Frederic] Tolfrey, *Tolfrey, un aristocrate au Bas-Canada*, introd. de P.-L. Martin, trad. (Montréal, 1979), 69. Jacques Viger, "Lettres de Jacques Viger à Madame Viger, 1813," *Rev. canadienne*, 59 (janvier–juin 1914): 213–19, 306–13. *British Colonist and St. Francis Gazette* (Stanstead), 13, 27 July, 3 Aug. 1826. *La Minerve*, 9 janv. 1844. *Missiskoui Standard* (Frelighsburg, Que.), 24 Nov., 5, 12, 19 Dec. 1837. *Montreal Gazette*, 14 Nov. 1829; 7 Nov., 7 Dec. 1837; 21 April 1840. *Montreal Herald*, 26 June 1826. *Quebec Gazette*, 1808–44, esp. 8, 15 June 1809; 12 July 1810; 10 Oct. 1816; 6 May 1822; 28 June, 3 July 1826; 5 Jan. 1844. *Quebec Mercury*, 13, 29 Aug. 1816; 27 June 1826; 4 Jan. 1844. *Sherbrooke Gazette and Townships Advertiser* (Sherbrooke, Que.), 28 Dec. 1837. *Le Spectateur canadien* (Montréal), 14 oct., 9 déc. 1816; 24 févr. 1817.

F.-J. Audet, "Les législateurs du Bas-Canada." G. R. Balleine, *A biographical dictionary of Jersey* (London and New York, [1948]). F.-M. Bibaud, *Le panthéon canadien* (A. et V. Bibaud; 1891), 117. Joseph Bouchette, *The British dominions in North America; or a topographical description of the provinces of Lower and Upper Canada . . .* (2v., London, 1832); *Topographical description of L.C.; A topographical dictionary of the province of Lower Canada* (London, 1832). Caron, "Inv. de la corr. de Mgr Plessis," ANQ *Rapport*, 1928–29: 191, 193. *The encyclopedia of Canada*, ed. W. S. Wallace (6v., Toronto, [1948]), 3. F. A. Evans, *The emigrant's directory and guide to obtain lands and effect settlement in the Canadas* (London and Edinburgh, 1833). *Inventory of the military documents in the Canadian archives*, comp. E. A. Cruikshank (Ottawa, 1910). Langelier, *Liste des terrains concédés*, 401. Le Jeune, *Dictionnaire*. Hormisdas Magnan, *Dictionnaire historique et géographique des paroisses, missions et municipalités de la province de Québec* (Arthabaska, Qué., 1925). *The makers of Canada; index and dictionary of Canadian history*, ed. L. J. Burpee and A. G. Doughty (Toronto, 1911). Roger Milton, *The English ceremonial book . . .* (New York, 1972). H. J. Morgan, *Sketches of celebrated Canadians*, 314. *Officers of British forces in Canada* (Irving), 105, 107, 109. P.-G. Roy, *Les noms géographiques de la province de Québec* (Lévis, Qué., 1906). *The service of British regiments in Canada and North America . . .*, comp. C. H. Stewart (Ottawa, 1962), 223. "State papers – L.C.," PAC *Report*, 1896: 74–75, 80–81, 90–91. H. G. Todd, *Armory and lineages of Canada* (Yonkers, N.Y., 1919), 82–85.

L.-P. Audet, *Le système scolaire*, vols.3–4. Mark Bence-Jones and Hugh Montgomery-Massingberd, *The British aristocracy* (London, 1979), 148–49. Raoul Blanchard, *Le centre du Canada français, 'Province de Québec'* (Montréal, 1947). R. G. Boulianne, "The Royal Institution for the Advancement of Learning: the correspondence, 1820–1829; a historical and analytical study" (PHD thesis, McGill Univ., Montreal, 1970). F. W. Campbell, *Canada post offices, 1755–1895* (Boston, Mass., 1972), 45. Ivanhoë Caron, *La colonisation de la province de Québec* (2v., Québec, 1923–27), 2. T.-M. Charland, *Histoire des Abénakis d'Odanak (1675–1937)* (Montréal, 1964). Ernestine Charland-Rajotte, *Drummondville, 150 ans de vie quotidienne au cœur du Québec* (Drummondville, 1972). Christie, *Hist. of L.C.* (1848–55), vols.2–3. L.-P. Demers, *Sherbrooke, découvertes, légendes, documents, nos rues et leurs symboles* ([Sherbrooke, 1969]). Douville, *Hist. du collège-séminaire de Nicolet*, vol.1. *Drummondville: a short story* (Drummondville, 1983). [Matilda] Edgar, *General Brock* (Toronto, 1904). G. [E.] Finley, *George Heriot, painter of the Canadas* (Kingston, Ont., 1978); *George Heriot, postmaster-painter of the Canadas* (Toronto, 1983). Rodolphe Fournier, *Lieux et monuments historiques des Cantons de l'Est et des Bois-Francs* (Montréal, 1978). Gates, *Land policies of U.C.*, 86. Albert Gravel, *Pages d'histoire régionale* (24 cahiers, Sherbrooke, 1960–67), nos.1, 3, 17. Gwyn Harries-Jenkins, *The army in Victorian society* (London and Toronto, 1977). J. M. Hitsman, *The incredible War of 1812; a military history* (Toronto, 1965), 159–74. Claudette Lacelle, *The British garrison in Quebec City as described in newspapers from 1764 to 1840* (Ottawa, 1979). Jules Martel, "Histoire du système routier des Cantons de l'Est avant 1855" (thèse de MA, univ. d'Ottawa, 1960). Jean Mercier, *L'Estrie* (Sherbrooke, 1964). A. W. Mountain, *A memoir of George Jehoshaphat Mountain, D.D., D.C., C.L., late bishop of Quebec . . .* (London and Montreal, 1866). Maryse Perrault Gilbert, *Jacques Adhémar, premier marchand canadien-français de Drummondville (1815–1822) . . .* (Drummondville, 1981), 42. G. F. G. Stanley, *The War of 1812: land operations* ([Toronto], 1983). *The storied province of Quebec; past and present*, ed. William Wood *et al.* (5v., Toronto, 1931–32), 2. Sulte, *Hist. de la milice*. F. M. L.

Thompson, *English landed society in the nineteenth century* (Toronto, 1963). R. L. Way, "The day of Crysler's Farm," *The defended border: Upper Canada and the War of 1812 . . .* , ed. Morris Zaslow and W. B. Turner (Toronto, 1964).

Ivanhoë Caron, "La colonisation du Canada sous le Régime anglais (1815–1822)," Qué., Bureau des statistiques, *Annuaire statistique* (Québec), 8 (1921): 503–59. "Centenaire de Drummondville: manifestations à jamais mémorables," *La Presse*, 2 juill. 1915: 1. M. S. Cross, "The age of gentility: the formation of an aristocracy in the Ottawa valley," CHA *Hist. Papers,* 1967: 105–17. "La joie règne à Drummondville," *La Presse*, 1er juill. 1915: 5. J. H. Lambert, "The Reverend Samuel Simpson Wood, BA, MA: a forgotten notable, and the early Anglican Church in Canada," Canadian Church Hist. Soc., *Journal* (Glen Williams, Ont.), 16 (1974): 2–22. Gérard Malchelosse, "Deux régiments suisses au Canada," *Cahiers des Dix,* 2 (1937): 261–96. Jules Martel, "Les troubles de 1837–1838 dans la région de Sherbrooke," *La Rev. de l'univ. de Sherbrooke* (Sherbrooke), 5 (1964–65): 39–58. Louis Martin, "Le ministère de Jean Raimbault," *Les Cahiers nicolétains* (Nicolet), 4 (1982): 39–75. Paul Mayrand, "Histoire de Drummondville," *Rev. Panorama* (Nicolet), 1956–62. *Montreal Daily Star*, 2 July 1915. Maurice O'Bready, "La colonie de George Frederick Heriot," *La Rev. de l'univ. de Sherbrooke,* 5: 221–28. *La Parole* (Drummondville), 23 juin 1955. N. D. Pilchard, "The parish of Drummondville," *Quebec Diocesan Gazette* (Quebec), 3 (1945), nos.1–2. J.-O. Prince, "Notes sur les registres de Drummondville," *Le Journal des Trois-Rivières* (Trois-Rivières, Qué.), 10 nov. 1865: 2; 14 nov. 1865: 3; 21 nov. 1865: 2–3; 1er déc. 1865: 2–3; 5 déc. 1865: 2; 22 déc. 1865: 2. J.-C. Saint-Amant, "L'honorable Frédéric-George Herriot," *BRH*, 8 (1902): 171–74. "Saint-Frédéric de Drummondville," *BRH*, 5 (1899): 227. [J.-A.] Saint-Germain, dit frère Côme, "Propos sur les Voltigeurs," *La Parole*, 11 juill. 1973: 59. James Stokesbury, "Reposing especial trust," *British Heritage* (Harrisburg, Pa.), 2 (1981), no.4: 22–31.

HERIOT, GEORGE, office holder, landscape artist, and author; b. 1759 in Haddington, Scotland, eldest of four children of John Heriot, sheriff clerk of Haddington, and Marjory Heriot; d. unmarried 22 July 1839 in London.

As a member of the Scottish minor gentry, George Heriot received a sound classical education. He appears to have initially attended the Duns Academy and the grammar school at Coldstream. Subsequently he studied at the Royal High School, Edinburgh, from 1769 to 1774, under two eminent classical masters, Luke Fraser and Alexander Adam.

Between 1774 and 1777 Heriot seems to have resided in Edinburgh, where he most likely received instruction in drawing and painting. He was befriended by that Scottish Maecenas, Sir James Grant, who encouraged him to pursue a career in art. In 1777 Heriot left for London planning to take up this vocation, but for some inscrutable reason did not; instead he sailed to the West Indies. During four years there he made many notes and sketches of the life and landscape of the islands and composed a poem based on his experiences. *A descriptive poem, written in the West Indies* was published on his return to Britain in 1781.

Back in Britain, Heriot enrolled as an officer cadet at the Royal Military Academy, Woolwich (London), where he was given instruction by the academy's chief drawing master, the eminent topographical artist Paul Sandby. Officer cadets were trained in landscape drawing, valuable in the field for the planning and execution of strategy and for the recording of troop movements and deployment. It was perhaps also under the tutelage of Sandby that Heriot was introduced to the concept of the Picturesque, that connoisseurship of scenery wherein nature is examined in terms of art. The essential characteristics of the Picturesque in nature as in painting are irregularity of form and balanced compositions. Subjects chosen to convey these characteristics are often localized and rural; the style is present in Heriot's water-colours and sketches of the mid to late 1780s and in a series of etched picturesque views of the Channel Islands which he published in 1789–90. Indeed, evidence of the Picturesque was to survive in Heriot's art until the end of his career.

By about 1783 Heriot was no longer formally associated with the Royal Military Academy, although he continued to live and work in Woolwich, as a civilian clerk attached to the Board of Ordnance, and to make sketches there as well as in the Channel Islands and locations in southern England. In 1792 he was posted to Quebec and promoted clerk of the cheque in the Ordnance department. Heriot was to remain in Lower Canada until 1816, except, apparently, for two periods of absence, in 1796–97 and in 1806. His first years at Quebec are not well documented. Sketches record visits in and about Quebec and Montreal, perhaps on Ordnance business. In November 1792 he published a sketch of Jersey in the *Quebec Magazine* and the following year he prepared a view of Quebec, perhaps also intended for publication. When he returned to Britain in 1796 he resided in London, travelled to the south coast, and made at least one sketching foray into Wales. From the autumn until Christmas he was enrolled at the University of Edinburgh. He then returned to London. A water-colour prepared from his sketches of Wales and two Canadian views were accepted by the Royal Academy of Arts for exhibition in the spring. Heriot probably sailed for Lower Canada soon afterwards, taking notes and making sketches on the voyage.

The impact of his visit to Britain was considerable. While there he had been stimulated by the art he had seen and by his success as an artist. He returned with a fresh enthusiasm for the Canadas; he began to read about their past and to make elaborate notes and numerous sketches of the places he visited and the peoples he encountered. His sojourn abroad had affected his artistic vision of the Canadas; his drawings and water-colours assumed a new confidence and his landscape forms developed a new strength and grandeur. In London he had probably studied the simply handled and remarkably strong water-colours of younger British artists such as Thomas Girtin, Joseph Mallord William Turner, and John Varley. Either in Britain or in Lower Canada he had also become familiar with Lieutenant George Bulteel Fisher*'s *Six views of North America* . . . (London, 1796). He was influenced by this work, especially by Fisher's use of the Picturesque in depicting Canadian landscape.

The visit to Britain apparently benefited Heriot still further. In 1797, through the influence of his brother John, a prominent Tory newspaper editor there, he added to his post as clerk of the cheque the more senior position of assistant storekeeper general, under John Craigie*. Two years later, on learning that Heriot held both offices and received two salaries, the commander-in-chief of the forces in British North America, Prince Edward* Augustus, removed him from the senior post. While in Britain, however, Heriot had met, again through his brother's connections, Prime Minister William Pitt, and in 1799 Pitt recommended him for the position of deputy postmaster general of British North America when it became vacant on the removal of Hugh Finlay*. Heriot was appointed on 18 Oct. 1799.

The office of deputy postmaster general, which Heriot assumed at Quebec the following April, at first seemed well suited to his talents. In his Ordnance post, which he did not relinquish, he had proved himself a capable administrator; now he worked hard to establish the mails on a better footing. His predecessor had begun twice-weekly service between Montreal and Quebec, but east and west of those centres, on poor roads which passed through sparsely settled countryside, service was much slower. Heriot embarked on an ambitious program of improving the mails between Quebec and Halifax, as well as through Upper Canada. His initial enthusiasm was dampened by the inflexibility of postal regulations and by the lack of interest and understanding of the postmaster general in London, to whom he was directly responsible. Regulations required that any postal service be self-supporting, that expenses incurred in expanding or improving a service be justified by a corresponding increase in revenue, and that all profits be forwarded to the postmaster general in London. Thus, Heriot's scheme of using excess revenue from the more populated parts of Upper Canada to finance improvements in service to the isolated but rapidly expanding southwestern section of the province was blocked by his superiors in London. He did, however, receive aid from the lieutenant governor, Peter Hunter*, who was anxious to improve communications within the province. To put into effect his proposals for more frequent service, he made in 1801 the first of several trips to Niagara (Niagara-on-the-Lake). His plans were not entirely successful, but by 1805 he had managed to increase winter service to Niagara from one delivery during the entire season to one delivery per month, and additional couriers were placed on the Montreal–Kingston route.

His posts in the Ordnance and the Post Office brought him into contact with the military and administrative élite of Lower Canada. He was probably a friend of Lieutenant-Colonel John Nairne*, whose seigneury at Murray Bay he had visited as early as 1798, and he was on close terms with his cousin Frederick George HERIOT, a British army officer. In 1807, at least, he was a member of Quebec's exclusive Barons' Club, composed of prominent administrators and merchants such as Herman Witsius RYLAND and George HAMILTON.

Heriot's first years as deputy postmaster general were difficult ones, but he found solace in writing. As a result of his interest in Lower Canada's past, he published in London in 1804 *The history of Canada, from its first discovery*. Based largely on *Histoire et description générale de la Nouvelle France* . . . (3v., Paris, 1744) by Pierre-François-Xavier de Charlevoix*, the work was one of the first histories of Lower Canada published in English. Like Charlevoix's work, it ended in 1731. Although he had envisaged more than one volume, Heriot never published a second.

Heriot seems to have enjoyed his travelling. Improvement of postal facilities took him on frequent journeys between Quebec and Montreal and in 1807 he visited New Brunswick and Nova Scotia. That trip resulted in a warm and lasting friendship with judge Edward Winslow*. His travels provided him with the opportunity to make notes and sketches of the country and of the inhabitants he met. So rich a collection of material, both notes and sketches, did he amass that he decided to write a book about his journeys illustrated with his own views and figure studies. In 1807 in London he published his well-known *Travels through the Canadas*. The first part of the book is largely a topographical description of the towns and settlements he had visited or read about, from Newfoundland to Lake Superior, with particular attention paid to picturesque geographical features, especially Niagara Falls which "surpass in sublimity every description . . . the powers of language can afford." The second half, highly derivative, describes the manners and customs of various Indian nations. Yet *Travels* is significant within the Canadian context. It is one of the earliest books to describe the Canadian landscape largely from the point of view of the Picturesque.

Although his writing and sketching provided him with pleasant relaxation, Heriot had been constantly plagued by problems with the post caused by a growing population. Not only did mail regulations frustrate his plans for improving deliveries and opening new routes, but he had difficulties with the administration at Quebec. He lacked tact and diplomacy, was strong-willed, and displayed an exaggerated sense of self-importance. The combination proved to be unfortunate: his attempts to gain the cooperation of the colonial government often ended in failure. Late in 1801, within days of Finlay's death, Heriot wrote to Sir Robert Shore MILNES, lieutenant governor of Lower Canada, requesting two posts held by his predecessor. Heriot probably considered them not only his due, but necessary for the smooth functioning of the postal system. A seat on the Legislative Council would lend him the government's ear, and the appointment as superintendent of post houses would enable him to control the transportation and lodging on which the postal couriers were dependent. He obtained neither. Milnes defended his choice of Gabriel-Elzéar Taschereau* as superintendent to the colonial secretary and added criticisms concerning Heriot's character and lack of qualifications. Relations between Heriot and the lieutenant governor began to deteriorate. In 1805 Heriot was asked by Milnes to accept, after hours, dispatches for delivery to a ship anchored in the Quebec harbour; he refused. When Milnes sent a stinging rebuke, Heriot wrote back in a less than conciliatory tone: "I consider the sending [of] papers to me without any written request . . . as highly disrespectful, and that I am by no means officially obliged to cause any Letters or dispatches to be sent on board of Vessels." Outbursts of this sort created resentment among colonial officialdom that increased as the years passed and resulted in complaints being lodged against Heriot in London.

In 1806 Heriot returned to Britain, probably on family business. The next year, back in Quebec, he faced mounting criticism from the business community in the colonies concerning the slowness of the mails. Problems escalated during the War of 1812. The colonial administration began to make demands on him and his service which he felt were excessive and in certain cases unjustified. In 1813 he wrote to the postmaster general complaining that the governor, Sir George Prevost*, was meddling: "He has made it a practice to interfere with the Post Office, as if that Department were solely under his Controul." Prevost's conduct was "unlike any that I have ever before experienced." Attending this difficulty was Heriot's increased responsibility, which did not diminish with the ending of hostilities. As a result, he found fewer opportunities for "cultivating society." In 1815 he wrote to the postmaster general of the growing burden of work associated with his established duties and the addition of new responsibilities, which now included the superintendence of postmasters and couriers, the examination of the various post office accounts, the writing of the controllers' sheets (originals and duplicates), and the payment of employees. His request for a raise in salary was refused; word had reached London concerning the difficulties which Heriot was causing the colonial administration.

Heriot's request for an increased salary had likely also been prompted by the fact that he had lost his Ordnance post as clerk of survey, to which he had been promoted in 1804. In 1813 a member of the Board of Ordnance with whom he had quarrelled earlier took his revenge. He ordered Heriot to Kingston, knowing that his responsibilities as deputy postmaster general necessitated his presence at Quebec. When Heriot refused to take up the Kingston post he was suspended from the service.

In 1815, after a visit to New York and Washington to discuss the restoration of postal deliveries from Britain through the United States, Heriot began to contemplate resignation. The decision was precipitated by the harassment of Sir Gordon Drummond*, administrator of Lower Canada, who in a letter to Heriot at the end of October insisted that he immediately carry out some postal reforms. Heriot replied but he did not answer Drummond's lengthy questions. Drummond sent a fiery missive to London complaining of the deputy postmaster's unconscionable behaviour. Although Heriot considered travelling to England to explain his administrative problems to the postmaster general, in January 1816 he decided instead to resign. The following summer he sailed from Quebec for England, knowing that he had seen the Canadas for the last time. After his return to Britain, Heriot made frequent trips abroad – visiting France, Italy, Austria, Spain, and Germany. In 1824 he published two numbers of an illustrated travel book. Entitled *A picturesque tour made in the years 1817 and 1820, through the Pyrenean Mountains*, it was to be his last work. He continued to travel and to sketch – indeed, almost until the last year of his life. He died in London in July 1839, the cause of death being indicated as "decay of nature."

Two other British topographical artists working in Canada whose backgrounds were similar to Heriot's were Thomas Davies* and James Pattison COCKBURN. Their landscape water-colours of Canada, like those by Heriot, were painted mainly in leisure hours and were kept as attractive reminders of the places they had visited. Cockburn enjoyed recording the urban scene; Davies, like Heriot, showed a preference for the countryside and outlying settlements, although both were attracted to the grandeur of Canada's rivers and forests.

Heriot's significance is threefold: as an energetic office holder, as a writer, and most important, as an artist. As deputy postmaster general he began an ambitious program of improving deliveries and increasing postal stations from Halifax to Sandwich (Windsor). His attempts to create a better service were a mixed success. Postal regulations fettered him and attempts to gain the cooperation of the colonial administration often failed, largely owing to his abrasive personality. As a writer, he made a contribution to the early travel literature of Canada. As a colonial landscape artist, he is more significant. His water-colours and drawings (which received no serious attention until the beginning of the 20th century) are supremely attractive works of art, often felicitously coloured and sometimes quite precisely detailed. As unconscious social documents they are invaluable. They provide eloquent witness to a life and landscape long since gone. On another level of significance they mirror the culture and skill often associated with those many-selved individuals whom 18th-century Britain cultivated and from whom the colonial service and settlements greatly benefited.

GERALD E. FINLEY

A detailed list of George Heriot's water-colours, oil paintings, sketch-books, and engravings can be found in a biography of him by G. [E.] Finley, *George Heriot, postmaster-painter of the Canadas* (Toronto, 1983). Heriot is the author of *A descriptive poem, written in the West Indies* (London, 1781); *The history of Canada, from its first discovery, comprehending an account of the original establishment of the colony of Louisiana* (London, 1804); *Travels through the Canadas* ... (London, 1807; repr. with intro. Toronto, 1971); and *A picturesque tour made in the years 1817 and 1820, through the Pyrenean Mountains, Auvergne, the departments of High and Low Alps, and in part of Spain* (London, 1824), of which only two parts were published.

GRO (London), Death certificate, George Heriot, 22 July 1839. Library of Congress, MS Division (Washington), Caldwell Woodruff, "Family of Heriot of Castlemains, Dirleton, Haddington, Scotland . . ." (typescript, Baltimore, Md., 1918). PAC, RG 8, I (C ser.), 284, 1219. PRO, CO 42/121, 42/128, 42/140, 42/144, 42/146, 42/163. Univ. of Edinburgh Library, Special Coll. Dept., Matriculation records. *Edinburgh Rev.* (Edinburgh and London), 12 (1808–9): 212–25. G. E. Finley, *George Heriot* (Ottawa, 1979); *George Heriot, painter of the Canadas* (Kingston, Ont., 1978). William Smith, *The history of the Post Office in British North America, 1639–1870* (Cambridge, Eng., 1920; repr. New York, 1973). Jean Bruchési, "George Heriot, peintre, historien et maître de poste," *Cahiers des Dix*, 10 (1945): 190–205. J. C. A. Heriot, "George Heriot," *Canadian Antiquarian and Numismatic Journal*, 3rd ser., 7 (1910): 101–5.

HERRON (Hearn), WILLIAM, Roman Catholic priest; b. 11 Jan. 1784 in St Bridget of Killaly, probably near Blackwater (Republic of Ireland), son of Martin Herron and Mary Herron; d. early October 1838 in Placentia, Nfld.

William Herron came to the Newfoundland mission from Ireland in the spring of 1811 as a candidate for the priesthood. Almost immediately, the vicar apostolic, Patrick Lambert*, whose practice it was to send clerical students for training in Lower Canada, assigned Herron to the Séminaire de Nicolet. Faced with a shortage of priests, Lambert sought to have him return to Newfoundland as early as September 1813, but Herron was judged not yet sufficiently advanced in his studies. His ordination to the priesthood took place in the chapel of the Ursuline convent in Quebec on 21 Aug. 1814. He was the second priest ordained for the Newfoundland vicariate.

The bishop of Quebec, Joseph-Octave Plessis*, was eager to have Herron serve among the Irish in his own diocese and in February 1816 proposed exchanging him for Father Alexander Fitzgerald, a Dominican priest then in Newfoundland but destined for Quebec. Lambert was absent from Newfoundland at the time, but the request was turned down by Thomas Anthony Ewer*, his vicar general. Despite this refusal, Herron appears to have remained in Quebec for some time after his ordination.

Herron's first known appointment in Newfoundland was as curate to Ewer in Harbour Grace from February 1817 to October 1818. It is probable that he went directly from there to the district of Placentia, where he served for the remainder of his life. Although technically curate to the parish priest of Placentia, Andrew V. Cleary, Herron appears to have been primarily responsible for the Catholics scattered throughout the outports of Placentia Bay and along the south and west coasts. One of Herron's first accomplishments was the building of a chapel at Burin in 1819. Remarkable for the method of its construction, this chapel had been prefabricated by a Nova Scotia carpenter and shipped to Newfoundland for assembly. Thereafter, Herron made his residence in Burin, although officially he remained curate of Placentia.

In the first years of his priesthood, Herron was, according to Lambert's successor, Thomas Scallan*, "indefatigable and zealous, an excellent missionary." Stories are told of his constant journeys by sea and land, and of his frequent camping in makeshift tilts in the woods. Although Herron's pastoral charge encompassed a vast expanse of coastline, he appears to have visited even far-flung places regularly. His marriage returns for October 1826, for example, show marriages celebrated from Little Placentia (Argentia) to Burgeo. Among Herron's pastoral responsibilities was that of caring for the spiritual needs of the

Micmacs at St George's Bay on the west coast. Despite the distance involved, Herron apparently gave them regular attention. Indeed, his labours among the Indians of Newfoundland earned him the title "apostle to the Micmac Indians."

In this connection Herron is sometimes credited with being the first white man to have traversed the interior of Newfoundland, a recognition which is usually given to William Eppes Cormack* for his journey in 1822. Herron is said to have made a similar journey in 1820, proceeding from St John's to Notre Dame Bay by sea and crossing overland on foot to the west coast, a walk of some 200 miles. Like Cormack, he is supposed to have been accompanied by a single Indian guide. However, the earliest documentary reference to Herron's trip seems to be in a missionary report on the west coast prepared by Mgr Thomas Sears in 1877. The only known reference by Herron himself concerning travel to St George's Bay speaks of voyaging by sea.

Herron had an interest in church affairs in Nova Scotia and Lower Canada not uncommon among the Newfoundland clergy under Lambert and Scallan, and indicative of the closer ecclesiastical relationship which existed between Newfoundland and the mainland prior to the episcopate of Michael Anthony FLEMING. From 1822 to 1824 Herron carried on a correspondence with Plessis in which he offered to obtain Newfoundland and Irish candidates for the priesthood to serve in the Quebec diocese. Herron also pointed out the danger of proselytism in the case of Catholic youth attending a free school recently established in Halifax, a jurisdiction without a bishop at the time.

Herron seems to have remained at Burin until after the death in 1829 of Father Cleary, when he succeeded to the office of parish priest of Placentia. However, by 1830, Herron's powers were failing. Fleming described him still as "indefatigable" but noted that he lacked prudence. Later the bishop said that Herron already had been afflicted by a mental illness. This condition allowed him to fulfil his duties only rarely, and for several years he had to be assisted by a curate, Edmond Doyle. In 1833 Burin became a separate parish, and in 1835 Father Pelagius Nowlan took effective control of the Placentia area. Herron's death came three years later.

Unfortunately, few details of Herron's missionary activities appear to have survived. Even by the standards common among Newfoundland clergymen of that day, however, his efforts in caring effectively for so large a territory for over ten years were nothing short of heroic. There can be little doubt that his zeal and activity contributed to his untimely illness and death.

RAYMOND J. LAHEY

AAQ, 12 A, H; 210 A, VIII; 30 CN. Arch. of the Archdiocese of St John's, Return of marriages, 1825–27. Archivio della Propaganda Fide (Rome), Scritture riferite nei Congressi, America settentrionale, 2 (1792–1830). Cathedral of the Immaculate Conception (Harbour Grace, Nfld.), Reg. of baptisms. PRO, CO 194/61, 194/64, 194/66, 194/70. M. [A.] Fleming, *Relazione della missione cattolica in Terranuova nell'America settentrionale . . .* (Rome, 1837). *Newfoundlander*, 20 Aug. 1829, 18 Oct. 1838. M. F. Howley, *Ecclesiastical history of Newfoundland* (Boston, 1888; repr. Belleville, Ont., 1979). Prowse, *Hist. of Nfld.* (1895). Thomas Sears, *Report of the missions, Prefecture Apostolic, western Newfoundland*, [ed. M. Brosnan], ([Corner Brook, Nfld., 1943]). J. A. O'Reilly, "Priests and prelates of the past (a few of many incidents)," *Nfld. Quarterly*, 2 (1902–3), no.4: 10–11. Kevin Whelan, "County Wexford priests in Newfoundland," *Past* (Wexford, Republic of Ire.), 1985: 55–67.

HEUSTIS (Huestis), DANIEL D., Patriot filibuster and author; b. 1806 in Coventry, Vt, son of Simon Heustis; d. after 1846.

The son of a farmer "in moderate circumstances," Daniel D. Heustis was one of ten children who were educated, he later recalled in his autobiographical *Narrative*, "as well as their limited means would allow." The family was staunchly Presbyterian and republican; though he would claim at his trial in 1838 that he had "no religion," as a youth he adopted his father's republican views. "For the blessings of liberty and republican government," he wrote, "I was early taught to cherish a lively gratitude. Tyranny and oppression, of every kind, I was led to abhor and detest." At age 10 he moved with his family to Westmoreland, N.H., and in his early manhood he was employed by a farmer near Roxbury (Boston), Mass., and then by a storekeeper there. In 1834 Heustis settled in Watertown, N.Y., where he worked in an uncle's "boating business" before joining a firm of morocco dressers as a sales and purchasing agent in 1835. Two years later he went into partnership with a cousin, butchering as well as trading in groceries and West Indian goods. At his trial the following year he described himself as a butcher; he was unmarried at the time and appears to have remained so.

It was during his commercial travels between 1835 and 1837 that he became familiar with the deep discontents that stirred many people in both Upper and Lower Canada. The outbreak of rebellion in the lower province in 1837 [*see* Wolfred Nelson*] induced him to "embark in the attempt to liberate the people of Canada from the thraldom of British tyranny." It was not, however, until after William Lyon Mackenzie*'s defeat north of Toronto and escape to the United States that Heustis decided, at Watertown on 10 Jan. 1838, to give up business and devote himself entirely to "the cause of Canadian liberty." He made for Rochester, where he encountered John Rolph*, Donald M'Leod*, and Silas Fletcher, all Upper Canadian fugitives, who sent him on with three cannon to Buffalo, the Patriot headquarters [*see* Thomas Jefferson Sutherland*]. There Heustis met Mackenzie and received a captain's commission in the Patriot army. Returning to Watertown with Mackenzie, he was later arrested for violating American neutrality laws – part of the official American reaction to William Johnston*'s abortive Hickory Island raid – but was soon discharged.

That spring he was enrolled, along with 1,900 others, as a member of the Hunters' Lodge at Watertown, then a hotbed of Patriot activity. Several weeks later he was one of the 50 men from Watertown who joined a larger force at Youngstown, N.Y., for the purpose of rescuing the Patriots captured after the Short Hills raid in June and jailed at Niagara (Niagara-on-the-Lake). The removal of the prisoners, including Jacob R. BEAMER, Samuel Chandler*, and Linus Wilson Miller*, to Fort Henry at Kingston, however, caused the raiders to disband. Heustis next joined the force which left Sackets Harbor on 11 November to invade Upper Canada. Under the leadership of Nils von SCHOULTZ, he participated two days later in the battle of Windmill Point, near Prescott on the St Lawrence River. Of the 186 men in the invading force, 177 were killed or taken prisoner [*see* Plomer Young*; James PHILIPS].

Heustis, as one of the prisoners, was brought to Fort Henry to be tried before a court martial in December 1838. According to a dispatch later sent by Lieutenant Governor Sir George Arthur* to Lord Normanby at the Colonial Office, "persons of higher influence" entered a plea on Heustis's behalf on the grounds that his "station in society (appeared) to have been rather above that of the generality of the brigands." The plea, however, was rejected. He was found guilty of "piratical invasion" and on 17 December was sentenced to death. "We were in the hands of the Robespierres of Canada," he dramatically recalled, "and the guillotine was in readiness to despatch its victims." Heustis's first appeal to Arthur for clemency, prepared in his cell late that month and conspicuously absent from his *Narrative*, was followed by petitions from residents and officials in the Watertown area, all affirming that Heustis had been misled in his Patriot actions. In April 1839, by which time ten of the Patriots involved in the Prescott action had been hanged, Heustis pleaded convincingly that he had been deceived by "evil and designing men in his Country and by Refugees and Rebels from this province to join in the late unwarrantable attack." As a result of the appeals on his behalf, he was considered for a pardon by the Executive Council, though he was still regarded by one government official as "one of the most active & influential of the Brigands." In the end, 60 of those not executed, including Heustis, had their sentences commuted to transportation for life to the British colony of Van Diemen's Land (Tasmania).

While in jail in Fort Henry, the prisoners, almost all Americans, had been visited by Arthur, whom Heustis later described as a "short, stout-built man" with "a tyrannical look about him." Soon after, wrote Heustis, the Americans celebrated the "ever glorious Fourth of July . . . as well as circumstances would permit. Out of several pocket handkerchiefs a flag was manufactured, as nearly resembling the 'star-spangled banner' as we could conveniently make it. . . . We had faced the enemy, as did the heroes of Bunker Hill, . . . and we saw no cause for self-reproach."

In September 1839 the prisoners were taken to Quebec, where they were joined by 18 Patriots captured in western Upper Canada (including Elijah Crocker WOODMAN), 58 Lower Canadians, and 5 other criminals. All were put aboard the transport *Buffalo*, which sailed on 27 September and reached Hobart Town (Hobart) on 12 Feb. 1840. After some days in dock, where the prisoners were addressed by Lieutenant Governor Sir John FRANKLIN, the Lower Canadians sailed on to Sydney and the Upper Canadians and Americans were taken to Sandy Bay road station, a few miles along the coast from Hobart Town. They were put to work on the roads. According to Heustis, the variety and quality of their food never changed: "one pound and five ounces of coarse bread, . . . three fourths of a pound of fresh meat, half a pound of potatoes, and half an ounce of salt, with two ounces of flour for skilly in the morning, and the same at night. This was the daily ration for each man, without variation, from one end of the year to another." From a pint of the broth made from boiling the meat, "it was frequently no difficult matter to scrape off a spoonful of maggots."

After four months at Sandy Bay road station the prisoners were divided up; some, including Heustis, were sent to Lovely Banks station, then to Green Ponds station, and later to Bridgewater (east of Hobart Town), where they worked on a causeway. From there Heustis and others went on to Jericho and Jerusalem, in the southern midlands of the island. "On their journey they passed through Jericho and crossed the River Jordan," he commented sourly, "and at Jerusalem they 'fell among thieves.' There were no Samaritans in that region." He was moved next to Browns River station, near the coast, where they found the "conveniences for flogging . . . in a high state of perfection," though, he recorded, no American was ever flogged during his stay on the island.

On 16 Feb. 1842, after the normal two-year probation period had expired, Heustis and his fellow prisoners were granted tickets of leave, which allowed them to move freely within a designated area. Heustis was assigned to Campbell Town, in the midlands, where he earned good wages cradling wheat. The next year he had a visit from his brother. Heustis was recruited that year to hunt bush-rangers (escaped convicts), but did not have much success. He was none the less commended for his good "conduct" and, when free pardons began to be distributed in 1844, he was among the first to receive one, at Hobart Town. In January 1845 he joined 25 other former prisoners in signing on as replacements for an indifferent crew on the whaler *Steiglitz*, bound for New Zealand and northwestern America. The group left the ship and broke up at Honolulu, in the Sandwich (Hawaiian) Islands.

After various adventures and delays in California and Chile, Heustis eventually arrived in Boston on 25 June 1846 on the *Edward Everett*. He went on to Watertown to face a tumultuous reception from his family and friends, who "fired cannon and called out a band of music." Shortly after, he paid a visit to the battlefield near Prescott; he noted later that he would "leave the reader to imagine the feelings with which I trod again that field of deadly strife." In 1847 Heustis's *Narrative* was published in Boston. Described by the historian Edwin Clarence Guillet* as "the most scholarly of the Patriot narratives," it reveals the fine edge to which Heustis's Patriot resentments had been honed during his years in penal servitude. He rejoiced that the régime of Sir George Arthur had passed. *The emigrant*, a recent publication of Arthur's predecessor, Sir Francis Bond Head*, he dismissed as "the wail of a lickspittle of an aristocracy, who finds himself and his immediate friends kicked out of power . . . by the very men, to obtain whose countenance they shed patriot blood like water, and doomed scores of American citizens to the horrid life of penal colonists." Above all, he bitterly lamented that "the Canadian people, in whose behalf we fought, were less true and faithful to the cause of liberty than our revolutionary sires." At this point, in 1847, Heustis's account ends, and with it such knowledge as we have of his life and adventures.

GEORGE RUDÉ

Daniel D. Heustis's autobiography, *A narrative of the adventures and sufferings of Captain Daniel D. Heustis and his companions, in Canada and Van Dieman's Land, during a long captivity; with travels in California, and voyages at sea*, was published in Boston in 1847.

Arch. Office of Tasmania (Hobart, Australia), CON 31/22; CON 60/1. PAC, RG 5, A1: 117005, 117011, 117049–51, 120741–55. Guillet, *Lives and times of Patriots*. M. G. Milne, "North American political prisoners: the rebellions of 1837–8 in Upper and Lower Canada, and the transportation of American, French-Canadian and Anglo-Canadian prisoners to Van Diemen's Land and New South Wales" (BA thesis, Univ. of Tasmania, Hobart, 1965).

HILL, JOHN, businessman and JP; baptized 7 April 1754 in Topsham, England, son of Samuel Hill and Elizabeth Summerhill; m. there 19 April 1775 Margaret Ferguson, a widow, and they had at least three sons; d. 28 March 1841 in Exmouth, England, at age 87.

Little is known of John Hill's background or early life. He apprenticed as an anchor-smith in his native Devon and by 1775 was in partnership with one David Sweetland, expanding into general commercial activity, buying and selling vessels, and transporting coal and iron. His first appearance in the North American trade was recorded in 1783, when he was listed as owner of the ships *Diana* and *Peggy*, both bound for Newfoundland with the cessation of hostilities. Although still in partnership with Sweetland, Hill had by this time moved to London (Eastcheap and later Rotherhithe), and by 1786 he was in business on his own as John Hill and Company. He soon became one of the major fishing merchants in the Ferryland district of Newfoundland, employing inshore fishermen, running one of the banking vessels in the area, and supplying sealers. He employed first John Barry and then John Baker as agents, but after 1797 he used John Rowe.

During the American Revolutionary War Hill had also become involved with St John's (Prince Edward) Island, initially in partnership with Edward Lewis, MP, one of the original proprietors of the Island. By 1779 Hill had become a joint proprietor with Lewis of Lot 5, and the two began settling Lewis Town (Alberton South) on that lot in June 1788 by sending a master shipbuilder and several agents there. Hill also became involved in a commercial venture in Charlottetown and on the eastern end of the Island with merchants John Cambridge* and William Bowley. He first visited his North American operations in 1790, noting with pride the successful construction in that year on the Island of the schooner *Industry*, 41 tons, the earliest of many vessels he built there. The partnership with Cambridge and Bowley projected a large-scale triangular trade with the West Indies and Newfoundland in fish and timber, but soon ran afoul of the Byzantine politics on St John's Island. Several of the partners' vessels, including the *Industry*, were seized by zealous customs officials for alleged trading infractions, and Hill became convinced when he visited Charlottetown in the summer of 1790 that the administration of Lieutenant Governor Edmund Fanning* was as hostile to development by proprietors as Walter Patterson*'s had been. Hill returned to London to lead their opposition to the Fanning régime, and supported a petition calling for a remission of quitrent arrearages and a reduction of payments, along with an offer to use the money saved to convey "useful subjects" to the Island.

Before a full audience of proprietors in London on 27 Jan. 1791, Hill brought a draft address to the proprietors and merchants of London complaining of the actions of Fanning's government. He spoke to the draft heatedly and at length. The result was a memorial of 19 June complaining against "almost all the officers of Government on that Island who by a Combination amongst themselves and their gross Misconduct of the Government have greatly retarded the Settlement obstructed and oppressed the commerce and discouraged the Fisheries of your Majesty's said Island." This "combination" was allegedly led by Fanning, Chief Justice Peter Stewart*, Attorney General Joseph Aplin*, and the collector of customs, William Townshend*. Hill was one of six proprietors, including Cambridge, to allow his name to stand on the complaint; the remaining proprietors dissociated themselves from it. Since all the complainants were known allies of the discredited Walter Patterson, the complaint was politically linked with the former administration. It proved impossible to document conspiracy or to find independent witnesses to attest to the memorial's list of petty harassments and favouritism, and the administration of the Island was fully exonerated from all charges by the Privy Council in 1792.

The clumsy and premature attack freed Fanning's government from subsequent and more easily substantiated charges of maladministration. The attack had other implications as well. The officials who had been charged sued Cambridge successfully for malicious prosecution in the Island's Supreme Court, and Cambridge in turn sued Hill and Bowley for shares of the damages assessed. Initially unable to find a lawyer not involved in the affair, Hill lost his case and Cambridge ended up with his Island assets. Captain John MacDonald* of Glenaladale, a resident proprietor, reopened the case on Hill's behalf in 1794, but the jury cast aside his new evidence and English legal opinions. Hill and Bowley appealed to the king in council, eventually overturning the judgements early in the next century. Hill maintained that he did not oppose the right of the complainants to sue, but did object to the case being heard in an Island court presided over by one of the complainants, Peter Stewart. To absentee proprietor James William Montgomery he added, none "who values his Character or Property will adventure amongst such unprincipled people, they have ruined every man who has hitherto attempted to Carry on business there." Most proprietors, including Montgomery, refused to support Hill or to join his continued criticisms of the Fanning government, preferring to deal with it as best they could.

Hill returned to the attack in 1801 with a lengthy exposé of the Island submitted to the Colonial Office, obviously written with the assistance of MacDonald, whose prose style and nose for malicious gossip are evident on every page of the portraits of leading Islanders which comprise a large portion of the text. It was scornful of the character of virtually every member of the administration and legislature. One legislator was described as "so Addicted to drinking that when he gets a Cask of Spirits to his House, he lies drunk in his Bed until the Cask is exhausted and he leaves his Wife and Children to plough and work in the Fields," and another as "presented by the Grand Jury for incestuous intercourse with his Daughter in law." A leading official was said to "set all decencys at defiance, by resisting the payment of the Surgeon's Bill for curing him and his wife of a Complaint he had communicated to her." Despite the venom of the portraits, they generally ring true when compared with other evidence.

Given his understandably cynical attitude to Prince Edward Island it was hardly surprising that Hill turned his attention for the first years of the 19th century back to Newfoundland. In 1800 he was operating one banking vessel, two shallops, and one three-hand skiff, and was employing 18 fishermen and 7 shoremen. He had a number of vessels crossing the Atlantic (including the *John MacDonald* and later the *Lord Selkirk*) and continued sealing ventures as well. He kept out of the island's politics, allowing his agents to manage his affairs. Although like most fishing merchants he was constantly in the courts, he seems to have run into serious financial trouble there only around 1810, when his brig *Devonshire*, loaded with fish and oil, struck ice and was lost at sea. Hill had already gone into bankruptcy in England in 1807, but not until 1810 did he begin selling off his assets in the Newfoundland trade. By 1815 John Hill and Company was completely insolvent and, despite high cod prices, a forced sale of its assets brought credits of only seven shillings in the pound.

Hill had returned to Prince Edward Island in 1806, having won his Privy Council case around then. In that year he had a vessel built on the Island for the Newfoundland trade (the ill-fated *Devonshire*) and resumed business at Cascumpec. In 1810 he sought a blacksmith and cooper for the Island. He had begun corresponding in 1806 with lawyer James Bardin Palmer*, who served briefly as his agent and who later insisted that Hill's openly expressed political views and aims dismayed him. Hill ultimately became one of the principal critics of Palmer, and gathered much of the evidence which the British government used to relieve Palmer of his offices in 1812. By 1814 he was fully back into the tangled politics of the Island, and was one of the major signatories to a proprietors' petition calling for an end to the restriction on the original grants to settlement by foreign Protestants. The petition also insisted that attempts to force some proprietors to improve their property should not prevent others from "vesting their capital on the improvement of their lands. It is necessary that property should not only be secure but should be universally felt to be secure."

Hill also opened a correspondence in 1814 with the recently arrived lieutenant governor, Charles Douglass Smith*, who appeared to concur with many of his strictures and criticisms of Island administration. Proprietors like Lord Selkirk [Douglas*] and Sir James Montgomery took Hill seriously. By the end of the Napoleonic Wars Hill was sole proprietor of lots 2 and 4–6, and held half of Lot 7, all on the underdeveloped western end of the Island. Despite his mercantile activity he was not an active improver, although he was prepared to rent land for 999 years to tenants while reserving timber, water, and trade rights and allowing the tenants rights only to the land itself. He apparently expected great deference from his tenants, most of whom were engaged in timbering operations, and one later observer recalled, "I distinctly remember that in his presence heads were uncovered, and every possible respect shown him."

While Palmer was in England in 1813 to clear his name after he had been dismissed from public office, he was contacted by Hill's creditors concerning the fraudulent concealment of assets by Hill at the time he went bankrupt in 1807. When Palmer returned to the Island and attempted to prove the allegations, Hill, in alarm, joined Attorney General William Johnston* to bring eight charges of professional and political misconduct against him. In the hearing at the Court of Chancery in 1816 Palmer denied that he had used "malicious artifice" to injure Hill's character, but admitted that "he did zealously endeavour to expose and fairly substantiate facts relative to the said Hill's bankruptcy" on the Island, including the result of a court action brought in England by Hill against William Spraggon (an Island timber merchant with whom Hill had had dealings) for "calling him a fraudulent bankrupt under which the jury gave one shilling damages." As the Palmer affair suggests, Hill had continued to operate on Prince Edward Island as if the 1807 bankruptcy had never occurred, although he advertised his Island lands for sale in Newfoundland and London as "John Hill insolvent." In 1818 the Lewis Town business of William Maddox Hill and Company (which Hill carried on in partnership with his son) was reorganized as John Hill and Son, and in London as Hill and Son.

Hill constantly travelled between the Island and London on his vessels. Despite an irregular residency he was appointed a justice of the peace in 1820. Disaster struck later that year. John Hill and Son's stores in Lewis Town were broken into and robbed, the thieves setting fire to the warehouse to cover their tracks. The losses were reported to exceed £8,000. Although he was not initially suspected, one of Hill's own employees, a recent immigrant from England named James Christie, was soon arrested as an accomplice in the crime. Christie confessed, absolving his family from involvement and blaming his actions on "the powerful temptation of the devil." He was quickly tried, convicted, and executed in March 1821, the case being front-page news in the local papers for weeks. But punishing the perpetrator did little for Hill's financial situation. John Hill and Son did not long survive the fire; the partnership was dissolved in July 1821 and was replaced by a firm conducted by William Maddox Hill and Samuel Smith Hill under the name Hill Brothers.

John Hill appears to have retired from active business in 1821, although he continued to travel between England and the Island. He spent the remaining years of a long life in Devon staying one step ahead of his creditors and attempting to salvage some of his Island property from the bankruptcy of 1807. Despite his insolvency he was involved in proprietorial politics until 1835, when he leased his lands to Thomas Burnard Chanter*. With John Stewart* he helped to lead the campaign in Britain for the dismissal of Lieutenant Governor Smith in 1824 and participated in the one against the Land Assessment Act of 1833, which heavily taxed Island lands and provided for forfeiture and sale of lots if assessments were not honoured [*see* Sir Aretas William Young*]. Hill and other proprietors insisted that the tax was an escheat in disguise, passed by an assembly where low property qualifications denied proprietors and their agents a proper voice. In a private letter to the colonial secretary, Hill commented that this "British constitution in miniature is the damnd'st bore upon earth." It was his valedictory pronouncement upon an island in which he had been embroiled for half a century.

Hill's career is illuminating in two respects. It indicates some of the obstacles to success with which transatlantic merchants had to deal, explaining why few of them survived with their fortunes intact. It also suggests the importance of close mercantile links, hitherto largely unrecognized, between Prince Edward Island and Newfoundland in the late 18th and early 19th centuries.

J. M. BUMSTED

Church of Jesus Christ of Latter-Day Saints, Geneal. Soc. (Salt Lake City, Utah), International geneal. index, Topsham, Devon, Eng., reg. of baptisms, 5 July 1748, 7 April 1754; reg. of marriages, 20 Jan. 1745, 19 April 1775. GRO (London), Death certificate, John Hill, 28 March 1841. Hunt, Roope & Co. (London), Robert Newman & Co., letter-books, November 1793. PAC, MG 23, E5, 2. PANL, GN 5/1, Ferryland, 25 Sept. 1786, 24 Nov. 1791, 8 Nov. 1794. PAPEI, Acc. 2702, Smith–Alley coll., "Minutes of the Proceedings of the Proprietors of St. John's Island, June 17, 1790–January 27, 1791"; Acc. 2810/171; Acc. 2849/143, 2849/158; RG 6, Court of Chancery, box 1, "Report of Committee of Council for Hearing Appeals from Plantations on Petition of William Bowley to Privy Council, heard 6 March 1799." P.E.I. Museum, File information concerning John Hill. PRO, CO 226/16: 151, 364; 226/17: 213 *et seq.*;

226/30: 177–86; 226/50: 222–32, 249 (mfm. at PAPEI); CO 231/2, 29 June 1808. SRO, GD293/2/78/25–27. G.B., Privy Council, *Report of the right honourable the lords of the committee of his majesty's most honourable Privy Council, of certain complaints against Lieutenant Governor Fanning, and other officers of his majesty's government in the Island of St. John* ([London, 1792]). *Colonial Herald, and Prince Edward Island Advertiser* (Charlottetown), 8 May 1841. *Newfoundland Mercantile Journal*, 3 July 1818. *Prince Edward Island Gazette*, 8 May 1818; 22 May, 7, 25 Nov. 1820; 20 Jan., 16, 31 March, 23 July 1821. *Royal Gazette and Newfoundland Advertiser*, May, July 1810; December 1815. *Sherborne Mercury or the Weekly Magazine* (Sherborne, Eng.), 10 Feb. 1783. *Trewman's Exeter Flying-Post, or Plymouth and Cornish Advertiser* (Exeter, Eng.), 20 June, 16 Sept. 1775; 14 March, 16 May 1777; 27 Aug. 1779. *The register of shipping* (London), 1800–10. *Canada's smallest province: a history of P.E.I.*, ed. F. W. P. Bolger ([Charlottetown, 1973]). Basil Greenhill and Ann Giffard, *Westcountrymen in Prince Edward's Isle: a fragment of the great migration* (Newton Abbot, Eng., and [Toronto], 1967; repr. Toronto and Buffalo, N.Y., 1975). Esther Moore, "A study of the settlement of Ferryland" (undergraduate research paper, Memorial Univ. of Nfld., St John's, 1972; copy at MHA), 16. *Pioneer* (Alberton, P.E.I.), 7 Feb. 1877.

HILLIER, GEORGE, army officer and office holder; b. in Devizes, England; m. 31 Jan. 1820 in York (Toronto) Caroline Ann Givins, daughter of James GIVINS, and they had at least one child, a son; d. 22 Dec. 1840 in Fort William, Calcutta, India.

George Hillier began his career in the British army on 23 March 1809, when he was appointed an ensign in the 29th Foot. Promoted lieutenant on 10 May 1811, he was with his regiment in Spain at the bloody battle of Albuera that year. He was one of the lucky few who escaped unscathed. The shattered 29th returned to England in November; Hillier, however, remained behind as one of three officers of the regiment attached to the Portuguese army. On 1 July 1813 he became a captain and joined the 74th Foot, with which he saw further action in the Peninsular War. Sent to Flanders, he fought with his unit at the battle of Waterloo in 1815 and received the Waterloo medal. He was advanced to brevet major on 21 June 1817. At some point while in Europe he served with Peregrine Maitland*. The two men became friends, and when Maitland, now Sir Peregrine, was appointed lieutenant governor of Upper Canada, Hillier took up duties as his civil secretary.

Hillier arrived in York with Maitland and his entourage in August 1818. The running of the gubernatorial office was an administrative task which encompassed every matter that landed on the lieutenant governor's desk. Hillier's position entailed no formal power but offered great possibilities for wielding influence. Depending upon a number of circumstances – ability, force of personality, intimacy with the lieutenant governor, and mastery of detail, to name a few – there was room for a civil secretary to be a real force on the Upper Canadian scene. Over the course of the province's colonial history, most secretaries, for whatever reason, were content to act as head clerks. Few made of themselves what would now be considered a chief executive assistant. John Macaulay* did (and possibly his successor Samuel Bealey Harrison* as well) during Sir George Arthur*'s administration from 1838 to 1841. But Macaulay and Harrison served only briefly. Hillier held his position for ten years, the entire duration of Maitland's lieutenant governorship. And no one, before or after, exploited the intrinsic potential of the office as he did.

Some power devolved upon him naturally. Maitland was an aloof individual and, although a few Upper Canadians such as John Beverley Robinson* and John Strachan* became favourites and were probably as close to the lieutenant governor as it was possible for them to be, only Hillier was an intimate. Access to Maitland's confidence was the more difficult because of the long periods he spent at his preferred residence, Stamford Park, near Niagara Falls, which often made direct communication with him impossible. By reason both of his friendship with Maitland and of his office, Hillier was the gatekeeper to the lieutenant governor's court. But he was not just the only conduit of information to and from the gubernatorial office; he was also Maitland's chief counsellor. His position was the more important because Maitland, in spite of his personal and physical remoteness, exercised his full authority over every detail of his administration. Hillier was responsible for coordinating the activities of the lieutenant governor's principal advisers, Robinson, Strachan, and Macaulay, and for arranging the implementation of policy. As the administration was drawn further into controversy during the 1820s, on such issues as the alien question, the clergy reserves, and the partiality of justice, Hillier, like Robinson and Strachan, became more deeply involved in the fundamental workings of Maitland's court. A letter written in 1828 to the colonial secretary complained of the "Military and Clericle Domination" gripping the province and cited the treatment meted out to those unwilling "to act in Compleat Subservience to Major Hillier Dr Strachan and Attorney General Robinson." Francis Collins*, an uncompromising opponent of Maitland's administration, suggested in 1828 just how far Hillier was associated with the government. In his newspaper, the *Canadian Freeman*, Collins alleged that during the July election contest in York between Robinson and Thomas David Morrison*, Robinson was "so far pressed" to ensure his victory that "Major Hillier, his Excellency's private secretary . . . and a mere sojourner here, was bro't down to the poll and voted as a tenant! Is not this most shameful?"

Hillier's greatest contributions to shaping events in the colony would almost certainly have been his private, and unrecorded, conversations with Maitland. He was on friendly terms with Robinson, Macaulay, Christopher Alexander HAGERMAN, and (to a lesser extent) Strachan, and it is evident from the tone of their letters to him that he could be relied upon to influence Maitland and, moreover, that his influence was crucial. In 1822 he intervened with the lieutenant governor to ensure that Strachan, then engaged in a dispute with Chief Justice William Dummer Powell*, would receive a favourable report at the Colonial Office. Robinson worked successfully through Hillier in 1824 to secure approval from Maitland for Strachan's proposed trip to England that year. Two years later Robinson arranged for Hillier to smooth over with his superior any problems associated with Peter ROBINSON's immigrants. Hillier's recommendation was crucial in Macaulay's acquisition of government printing contracts, and he undoubtedly helped Hagerman obtain his district judgeship in 1826. He was not, however, uncritical of his friends. In 1823 he had not hesitated to indicate to Macaulay his distress over Hagerman's reported treatment of Robert BARRIE, the commissioner of the Kingston dockyard.

Robinson occasionally wrote casual letters or notes to Hillier, as did Hagerman, but they had to be careful not to overstep the bounds. Replying to a letter from Hillier relating developments in the alien question in 1826, Hagerman excused his familiarity: "I should write in a more guarded, and (certainly) less free style. To you I write, as I would speak to you, I express my opinions ardently but I hope not presumptuously." Letters could and did contain a mixture of official matters, political developments, and private news. A proud father, Hillier had related to Hagerman in December 1826 that his son was "getting on well with his teething."

So close was Hillier's relationship with Maitland that he spoke *ex cathedra* for him on a range of issues. He had no compunction about instructing Macaulay on the topics to be discussed in the *Kingston Chronicle*. "You would do well to remark," he wrote in 1821, ". . . that the Atty Genl. [Robinson] voted *for* the bill for preserving the independency of the Commons." "I shall give you all the information I can from time to time in this loose way," he continued; Macaulay was left to "dish up for the public according to your own taste." On a subsequent occasion he mentioned "another little history I would like you to give to the public in your own Words."

Hillier consulted widely on matters of patronage and sought information from different sources on a host of topics, all for Maitland's judgement. Maitland was scrupulous about his royal prerogative of extending mercy to convicted felons. In each instance Hillier dutifully gathered the necessary documents, occasionally having to harass recalcitrant judges to comply, and placed them before the lieutenant governor who scrawled his decision on them, leaving it for Hillier to ensure that the matter was attended to.

Although Maitland and Hillier relied on a number of Upper Canadian advisers and were prepared to promote their interests on occasion, they were by no means ciphers. One incident in 1828 indicates the extent to which the lieutenant governor, with Hillier, exercised his own judgement. With Hagerman's temporary elevation to the bench, his position as collector of customs at Kingston became open. Macaulay had long coveted it and used every means available to him to get it. He was anxious about how to proceed with Hillier since a friend of the major's, James Sampson*, was also an applicant for the job. Hillier was reassuring: "With regard to your delicacy towards myself, (which I feel & appreciate) of addressing your application in an official form as knowing that Sampson, another candidate, was a particular friend of mine, allow me to observe that I have always, regarded yourself in that light also." Neither Sampson nor Macaulay got the collectorship. Strachan was appalled and told Hillier that the rejection of Macaulay was "a matter of astonishment to all the Friends of Govt." As Strachan related the episode to Macaulay, Hillier just "shrugged & acknowleged your claims." "Nothing could be worse in taste and heart," Strachan concluded, "than Sir P. or rather Perhaps Col Hilliers conduct for the last year in the way of appointment." Maitland's isolation from his Upper Canadian advisers toward the end of his governorship may in part explain his imprudent decision not to proceed against William FORSYTH of Niagara Falls through the courts.

When Maitland left Upper Canada in November 1828, Hillier went with him. He had been appointed deputy quartermaster general in Jamaica, with the rank of brevet lieutenant-colonel, on 24 July 1828. Four years later he obtained a majority in the 62nd Foot and joined it in Bangalore, India. In 1834 the regiment moved to Burma, where Hillier became acting commanding officer; he served in this capacity until 1835, when he became junior lieutenant-colonel of the unit. In that year, as a temporary brigadier, he had command of Moulmein and the surrounding province. Ill health forced him in 1839 to recuperate in Calcutta, where he returned, again because of sickness, the following year and died of apoplexy.

An Anglican and a freemason, Hillier had lived in a picturesque cottage in York, once owned by Peter Russell*. Though he had been among the most powerful men in Upper Canada's history, the death of the major-domo of the Maitland administration received only passing notice there.

ROBERT L. FRASER

[I should like to thank Stuart R. J. Sutherland for sharing with me his knowledge of military sources. R.L.F.]

The bulk of correspondence in the Upper Canada sundries (PAC, RG 5, A1) for Maitland's governorship consists of letters to and from Hillier. For the most part, this material is formal in nature. The political and, to a degree, the personal sides of the man are revealed in his correspondence with John Macaulay (AO, MS 78). Other references may be found in the John Beverley Robinson papers (AO, MS 4), the Strachan papers (AO, MS 35), the Colonial Office correspondence (PRO, CO 42), and the *Canadian Freeman*, 17 July 1828. The works listed below are also useful.

Annual reg. (London), 1841: 210. *United Service Journal* (London), 1841, pt.I: 575. Charles Dalton, *The Waterloo roll call; with biographical notes and anecdotes* (2nd ed., London, 1904; repr. 1971). *Death notices of Ont.* (Reid). G.B., WO, *Army list*, 1809–41. H. [E. E.] Everard, *History of Thos. Farrington's regiment, subsequently designated the 29th (Worcestershire) Foot, 1694 to 1891* (Worcester, Eng., 1891). N. C. E. Kenrick, *The story of the Wiltshire Regiment (Duke of Edinburgh's), the 62nd and 99th Foot (1756–1959)* . . . (Aldershot, Eng., 1963). *Robertson's landmarks of Toronto*, 1: 303; 3: 419. Scadding, *Toronto of old* (Armstrong; 1966).

HINDENLANG (Hindelang), CHARLES (sometimes known as **Lamartine** and as **Saint-Martin**), Patriote; b. 29 March 1810 in Paris; d. 15 Feb. 1839 in Montreal.

Charles Hindenlang, whose family were Parisian merchants of Swiss Protestant descent, enlisted in the French army in 1830, at the time of the July revolution. He became an officer, by slow degrees moving through the lower ranks. In the autumn of 1838 he was in New York, where a French businessman by the name of Bonnefoux (Bonnafoux) recruited him for the Patriote army in Lower Canada and introduced him to Ludger Duvernay*. He took up service at the same time as another French officer, Philippe Touvrey, and two Polish officers, Oklomsky and Szesdrakowski. They were sent to Rouses Point, N.Y., where Théophile Dufort received them before sending them across the border with Robert Nelson*.

On the night of 3–4 Nov. 1838 they reached Napierville in Lower Canada. Cyrille-Hector-Octave CÔTÉ hailed Nelson as "president of the provisional government" and introduced Hindenlang as "Brigadier-General Saint-Martin." Hindenlang was to teach tactical manœuvres to the Patriotes assembled at Napierville. But time was short. After the uprisings at Beauharnois, La Prairie, and Caughnawaga (Kahnawake) failed, Lieutenant General Sir John Colborne* decided to march towards the American border with 5,000 men. Nelson, along with Hindenlang and 600 men, hastily departed for Odelltown, a strategic point near the frontier. On 8 November they were at Lacolle and by the next morning at Odelltown, where some loyal volunteers had barricaded themselves in the church. Without even one cannon, indeed almost without arms, the Patriotes could not lay siege to the church for long and had to beat a retreat late in the afternoon. Arriving back in Napierville, they received the order to scatter. Hindenlang went off with 14 men, but he was exhausted and wound up alone with Adolphe Dugas, a young medical student. Before he could cross the border he was taken prisoner. When the British found out his identity, they sent him to Montreal, where he was put in jail on 14 November.

During the next three months Hindenlang adopted an ambiguous, even contradictory stance. When he arrived in Montreal he signed a long "declaration" stating that he had been misled by rebel leaders and harshly denouncing Nelson in particular, whom he called a rogue, coward, and traitor. He ended his confession by offering to serve the right cause to make amends for his brief aberration. This document, surprisingly, was made public in *L'Ami du peuple, de l'ordre et des lois* on 17 Nov. 1838, as were two letters from Hindenlang, one to his companion Touvrey and the other to a friend by the name of Henri, both thus appearing in print before the two could have received them. Hindenlang repeated to Touvrey the accusations he had levelled against Nelson, and he even spoke of magnanimity on the part of the British. Hindenlang had signed his confession at the request and in the presence of Pierre-Édouard Leclère*, a well-known justice of the peace. Touvrey, however, denied in the New York paper *L'Estafette* Hindenlang's claim that he had come to New York to deal with family business. According to Touvrey, he had decided to come and fight for liberty as soon as news of the insurrection in the autumn of 1837 reached Paris. It may well be asked how the confession had been forced out of Hindenlang. Côté was to assert in the *North American* (Swanton, Vt) on 30 Oct. 1839 that Leclère had written a portion of it, in particular the paragraph concerning the offer to collaborate.

On 22 Jan. 1839 Hindenlang came before a court martial, with Irish lawyer Lewis Thomas Drummond* in attendance. Among the prosecution's nine witnesses were four Canadians; one, the curé of Saint-Cyprien parish at Napierville, Noël-Laurent AMIOT, stated that Hindenlang had called the Canadians cowards after the battle of Odelltown. The young Frenchman was found guilty on four counts, but the judges gave him two days to prepare his defence. On 24 January he presented two legal arguments for having the trial declared invalid: the writ summoning him before the court had incorrectly spelled his name Hindelang, and he could be tried only by his peers – a jury – since he was in a country under English criminal law. The two legal points were rejected. He then made a speech, saying that his sole mistake was to have been unsuccessful, but he refrained this time from denouncing the Patriote leaders. He was sentenced to death. Two days later he wrote a long letter to

Governor Colborne, reminding him that some British subjects in Spain had done the same thing as he had, and that when they were captured, they had been considered prisoners of war and were not executed as rebels. In this letter he again excoriated Nelson for his conduct.

News that executions were imminent reached the Montreal jail on 12 February, and the list of the five condemned men was known the following day. At 9:00 A.M. on 15 February, Hindenlang mounted the scaffold bravely, attended by Dr John Bethune*, rector of Christ Church, Montreal. He made a short speech and cried "Vive la liberté!" From 6:00 A.M. he had been making copies of his speech for other prisoners to transcribe and pass around. Historian Mason Wade claims that Hindenlang was executed because he "refused to save his neck by turning state's evidence." This is quite conceivable, but there is no way of knowing whether he had indeed come to fight to freedom or to set up his father's business. In the event it is his courageous death alongside Chevalier de LORIMIER, Amable Daunais, François Nicolas, and Pierre-Rémi Narbonne that has been remembered.

Hindenlang's activity in Lower Canada raises the question of the role played by France and the French in the rebellions of 1837–38. It is certain that the French government never took any part, from near or from afar, in the insurrections. The French ambassador to Washington, Édouard de Pontois, followed events closely, as was his duty. In the summer of 1837 he came to the valley of the St Lawrence, taking care to meet the civil authorities. He also attended a Patriote meeting at Saint-Constant, near La Prairie, and even had a meal with Louis-Joseph Papineau*. After Hindenlang's capture he requested his British counterpart in Washington, Henry Stephen Fox, to ask Colborne to treat Hindenlang humanely. A few other natives of France in Lower Canada came out personally for or against the rebellion, most of them being sympathetic to the Patriotes. Among the latter were businessmen Victor Bréchon and Bonnefoux, actor Firmin Prud'homme, Joseph Lettoré, and others. On the English party's side were the superior of the Séminaire de Saint-Sulpice in Montreal, Joseph-Vincent Quiblier*, and journalists Alfred-Xavier Rambau* and Hyacinthe-Poirier Leblanc* de Marconnay.

The story of Charles Hindenlang in Lower Canada has a final episode. According to parish priest Étienne Chartier*, Papineau wanted to take legal action against Colborne when he learned that "le Vieux Brulôt" was returning to England. He reached an agreement with the former agent in England of the Lower Canadian assembly, John Arthur Roebuck*, to institute criminal proceedings for murder in the Court of King's Bench. Guillaume Lévesque*, a young Montrealer who had shared Hindenlang's cell, and Hindenlang's own brother thought of instituting a civil action. According to Chartier, having got wind of the matter the British cabinet informed Queen Victoria and she hastened to raise Colborne to the peerage. This, to all intents and purposes, put him beyond reach of the law. Roebuck and Papineau had to give up the idea of taking legal action against Lord Seaton.

CLAUDE GALARNEAU

ANQ-M, P1000-3-298. ANQ-Q, E17/31, nos.2331–450; E17/37, nos.2941–3040; E17/51, nos.4101–52; P-68, nos. 3–4; P1000-49-976; P1000-65-1291. AUM, P 58, U, Hindenlang to L. T. Drummond, 9, 13 Feb. 1839. PAC, MG 24, B2, 3: 3346–49, 3567–69; B143; MG 30, D56, 18: 16–17. "Confession de Charles Hindenlang (d'abord connu sous le nom de Lamartine)," *BRH*, 42 (1936): 622–28. "Papiers Duvernay," *Canadian Antiquarian and Numismatic Journal*, 3rd ser., 5: 182–84; 7: 77–86. F.-X. Prieur, *Notes d'un condamné politique de 1838* (Montréal, 1884; réimpr. 1974). *Report of state trials*, 2: 5–35. *L'Ami du peuple, de l'ordre et des lois* (Montréal), 17 nov. 1838; 9, 16 févr. 1839. *North American*, 30 Oct. 1839. *Le Patriote canadien* (Burlington, Vt.), 4 déc. 1839. *Le Populaire*, 10 juill. 1837. Caron, "Papiers Duvernay," ANQ *Rapport*, 1926–27: 145–258. *Le répertoire national* (Huston; 1893), 2: 190. Christie, *Hist. of L.C.* (1866), 5: 250–56. David, *Patriotes*, 171–237. Jean Ménard, *Xavier Marmier et le Canada, avec des documents inédits: relations franco-canadiennes au XIXe siècle* (Québec, 1967), 179–88. Mason Wade, *Les Canadiens français, de 1760 à nos jours*, Adrien Venne et Francis Dufau-Labeyrie, trad. (2e éd., 2v., Ottawa, 1966), 1: 215–17. L.-O. David, "Les hommes de 37–38: Charles Hindenlang," *L'Opinion publique*, 5 févr. 1880: 61–62. Ægidius Fauteux, "Les carnets d'un curieux: Charles Hindenlang ou le Lafayette malheureux du Canada," *La Patrie*, 2 juin 1934: 40–41, 43. Robert La Roque de Roquebrune, "M. de Pontois et la rébellion des Canadiens français en 1837–1838," *Nova Francia* (Paris), 3 (1927–28): 238–49, 273–78, 362–71; 4 (1929): 3–32, 79–100, 293–310.

HOLBROOK (Holbroke), JAMES, schoolmaster; b. *c.* 1793, almost certainly in England; d. 25 April 1846 in Fredericton.

James Holbrook emigrated from England to New Brunswick "in the prime of life." He was residing in Sackville at the time he was offered the appointment as master of the English school of the College of New Brunswick in Fredericton. The college council had approached him on the strong recommendation of William Botsford*, speaker of the House of Assembly and a resident of the Sackville area. Holbrook accepted the offer on 22 March 1822 at a salary of £100 per annum, together with all the tuition money. Tuition was fixed at £4 per annum but was subject to reduction in particular cases at the discretion of the council, which also reserved the right of admitting gratis the children of those wholly unable to pay. The council, estimating that the position would be worth £200 in all, believed nevertheless that the number of pupils would depend upon the application and ability of the master. In his acceptance Holbrook undertook to repair to Fredericton as soon as his "little pecuniary affairs" had been arranged.

The College of New Brunswick was at that moment in its history undergoing a significant change. Steps towards its founding as an academy of liberal arts and sciences had been taken in 1785, and teaching on the primary to secondary school levels had begun in about 1787. The institution's charter as the College of New Brunswick, with the style and privileges of a university, had been granted in 1800, but university work was just beginning in 1822, when James Somerville* obtained permission to teach courses towards a degree. All three levels of education were conducted in the same building until university classes were transferred to a new structure, opened in 1829 with a royal charter as King's College.

On his arrival in Fredericton, Holbrook was given his own schoolroom, for which he had to provide fuel. The English school, to which he was assigned, had to be conducted on the monitorial system, in which Holbrook was apparently well versed. His work and that of George McCawley* of the grammar, or classical, school – which ran parallel to the English school – were considered so successful that on 28 Dec. 1822 the college council deemed it proper to take public notice of their diligence. Their labours had resulted in a great improvement in their respective scholars. To encourage the students the council resolved to distribute appropriate rewards to deserving scholars at the half-yearly examinations. On 27 March 1824 Holbrook and McCawley had £25 added to their salaries, a sum which was to be continued as long as the legislature provided an additional grant to the college of £75 per annum.

It is clear that Holbrook was, soon after his arrival, accepted as a member of the social and official élite of the diminutive capital. Having built the first house on the hill to the south of Fredericton, on the property known as Frogmore, Holbrook married on 22 Oct. 1828 Grace Hailes, daughter of the late Lieutenant-Colonel Harris William Hailes, who had served as administrator of the province in 1816–17. One of their three daughters was to marry the Reverend Charles G. Coster, son of George Coster*, archdeacon of New Brunswick and titular president of King's College. Holbrook's property was later purchased by James Carter*, chief justice of the province, whose third wife was Charles Coster's sister. Another of Coster's sisters married James Robb*, first professor of chemistry and natural history in the college. Holbrook's family connections illustrate the close relationships that existed among the leading members of Fredericton society in these years.

James Holbrook continued a most successful teacher in the collegiate school, as the preparatory school was called after 1828, until his death in Fredericton at the age of 53. That he was universally well liked may be surmised from the fact that a headstone was placed over his grave in the Old Burying Ground by his former pupils.

ALFRED G. BAILEY

UNBL, MG H9, L. M. Beckwith Maxwell, "The Fredericton High School, the oldest English grammar school in Canada" (typescript, 1944); UA, "Minute-book of the governors and trustees of the College of New Brunswick," 107–10, 113–15. *Royal Gazette* (Fredericton), 28 Oct. 1828. Hill, *Old Burying Ground*. L. M. Beckwith Maxwell, *An outline of the history of central New Brunswick to the time of confederation* (Sackville, N.B., 1937; repr. Fredericton, 1984).

HOLLAND, JOHN FREDERICK, surveyor, army and naval officer, landowner, JP, office holder, politician, and militia officer; b. probably during the winter of 1764–65 at Observation (Holland) Cove, St John's (Prince Edward) Island, natural first child of Samuel Johannes Holland* and Marie-Joseph Rollet; m. by 1790 Mary Emily Tissable, and they had three sons and three daughters; d. 17 Dec. 1845 in Charlottetown.

The circumstances of John Frederick Holland's upbringing and early career were dictated by the movements of his father, surveyor general of the province of Quebec and the Northern District of North America, 1764–1801. Samuel preferred to have his family close by, and it was during his survey of St John's Island that John was born. The peripatetic Holland household was the only school known to "St. Johns Jack": he learned the French language from his mother, Latin besides; and from his father he assimilated the practical skills of army and survey life. With the commencement of the American revolution and Samuel's escape from Perth Amboy, N.J., to England, John saw the family through a brief imprisonment and eventual evacuation. His charges safe, in 1777 John joined the British navy as a midshipman, and in 1779 was on the *Nautilus* when it accompanied Sir George Collier*'s squadron to relieve Fort George (Castine, Maine). That year he was commissioned an ensign in the King's Royal Regiment of New York, a unit raised by Sir John Johnson*. Promoted lieutenant in 1781, he was only 19 when he left the army in 1783.

Peace did not inhibit John's rambling ambitions. With his father now returned to normal duties at Quebec, and with his godfather, Frederick Haldimand*, ensconced as governor there, John obtained a position as an assistant engineer on the team surveying locations for loyalist settlements west of the Ottawa River, and over the winter of 1783–84 he laid out a town site at Cataraqui (Kingston, Ont.). In 1786 he was set to work surveying the boundary between Quebec and New Brunswick.

Samuel Holland's fond hope had been that his eldest son would succeed him as surveyor general, and he sent John to England in 1789 to seek approval for their joint commission. Instead, on the recommendation of Sir Joseph Banks*, early in 1790 John was appointed to investigate the rumour of a navigable water-way west of Great Slave Lake which might lead to the Pacific Ocean. Holland's travels had at some point taken him to Lake Superior, and his skills as a surveyor also made him a likely candidate to establish an overland route. The Nootka Sound controversy [*see* George Vancouver*] delayed Holland's departure, and by the time he reached Quebec in the autumn of 1790 news of Alexander Mackenzie*'s discovery that this water-way led to the Arctic Ocean rendered the mission unnecessary.

By this time, like his father and brother Frederick Braham, John had married a French Canadian Roman Catholic, but his career had not been such as to instil domestic habits. He was drawn, rather, to boisterous masculine society in camp and town, and his rude manner began to threaten his career. Initially favoured by the patronage of his father and godfather, Holland was subsequently protected by Prince Edward* Augustus (later the Duke of Kent and Strathearn), who had a high regard for the services of Samuel and his family. Prince Edward commissioned John a lieutenant in his regiment in 1794, and posted him to assist in the construction of the citadel at Halifax. He also consented to be godfather to at least one of John's children. Regrettably, not even Prince Edward could save Holland from himself. Certain unspecified indiscretions at his new post led to his being dispatched in 1798 to Charlottetown as acting town major, assistant engineer, and barrack master. He went on half pay the following year. With the departure of the Duke of Kent from North America in 1800 and the death of his father in 1801, Holland's prospects collapsed: his post as assistant engineer was abolished in 1802; he was replaced as acting town major by 1805; and he lost his position as barrack master in 1817.

Holland fell back on the Island property he had inherited from his father, consisting of the eastern half of Lot 28, to which his mother and a sister moved. But John preferred to hold court in Charlottetown, where he was a renowned "Buffo" at many public dinners. Justice of the peace from 1802 and high sheriff in 1809–10, Holland had a reputation for irregularities, including fraud and complicity in a duel. In 1812, "when his wife and family were in an absolute state of distress," he allegedly "brought a woman from Halifax and lived in notorious intimacy with her in Charlottetown." One of his sons "asked the Chief Justice leave to shoot her"; no reply has been recorded.

Holland's political activities were just as effervescent as his social life. First elected to the House of Assembly in 1803, he soon found common cause with another recent arrival, James Bardin Palmer*. Both men employed opposition tactics in order to secure recognition and preferment from the entrenched élite. They were elected for Charlottetown in 1806 and, when the new house met, Palmer nominated Holland as speaker, only to see him lose to Robert Hodgson*. The two allies fell out later that same year when Palmer was appointed adjutant general of militia, a position coveted by Holland, who had to settle for the office of clerk of ordnance stores. Thus, when Palmer became closely connected with a new political faction known as the Loyal Electors, Holland joined their opponents, the "old party." In order to thwart the ambitions of Palmer and his associates, Holland in 1810 ensured the invalidation of the victories of two Loyal Electors in by-elections held under his supervision as high sheriff. At the general election two years later Holland attempted to use his influence over the Charlottetown garrison to carry the royalty, but lost the ensuing riot as well as his seat.

He had also joined a campaign in 1811 to paint the Loyal Electors as a secret club of Jacobins intent on usurping the legitimate government. Although the Electors specifically denied Holland's "most wanton unprovoked and ignorant" accusations, his and like insinuations were accepted in London. In October 1812 Lieutenant Governor Joseph Frederick Wallet DesBarres*, who had supported the Loyal Electors, received notice of his recall: William Townshend* was appointed administrator; Palmer was immediately dismissed from his various offices; and before the year was out Holland was adjutant general of militia. At an unspecified date he attained the militia rank of colonel.

The new lieutenant governor, Charles Douglass Smith*, was quickly convinced of the seditious intent of the Loyal Electors. By default he was drawn towards the "cabal," as the "old party" was called by its enemies, and specifically to Holland, recommended to him by none other than the Duke of Kent. Indeed, with the Loyal Electors in disgrace and the leaders of the "cabal" deceased, aged, or ill, Holland unexpectedly emerged as a "Major domo" among Island politicians. He was appointed to the Council on 3 Jan. 1815 and acted as collector of customs, controller, and naval officer. Between Smith and Holland there was something of a meeting of minds: both were military men by temperament as well as vocation, and when Smith decided in October 1815 to stiffen the enforcement of militia laws he had Holland's full support. Within a month this program had resulted in a near mutiny, and Smith credited his adjutant general of militia with quelling the disturbance.

In the aftermath of the militia incident Holland wrote two important letters to Smith detailing the moribund state of the "cabal" and raising the spectre of a resurgent Loyal Electors. Holland anticipated being called upon to act as Smith's confidant and adviser, but he had misread his man. Smith, like Holland, had a will of his own, and he chose to build his own party of compliant functionaries, including three of his sons and two sons-in-law. Holland was among many Islanders upset at being isolated from power, and by 1818 he and Attorney General William Johnston* had deserted Smith. Thereafter, under the guidance of John Stewart*, Holland helped to fashion a new oppositional alliance. Smith responded by removing Holland and Johnston from Council on 4 Jan. 1819, hinting darkly at a secret conspiracy centred on the masonic lodge in Charlottetown, of which Holland was a member from 1810 to 1827. In fact, with the notable exception of Palmer, who once again bucked a trend and shifted his support to Smith, the lieutenant governor came to be opposed by almost every faction on the Island as well as by the proprietors in London, and in 1824 he was replaced by John READY.

Holland did not reap any reward from the change in government: he did not stand again for the assembly, he was not invited back into the Council, and he did not receive any new administrative post. The neglect of Holland was, apart from his reputation for personal instability, due to his rigorous enforcement of the unpopular militia law even after Smith had dropped him from the Council. When the new assembly met in 1825 it demanded a reorganization of the militia. It also investigated Holland's expenses as adjutant general and as a justice of the peace. Holland survived this inquisition but found the duties of adjutant general greatly reduced under Ready. When the militia act was amended in 1833 Holland was dropped from his post in favour of an old Smith protégé, Ambrose Lane*. After two futile atempts to be re-elected to the assembly in 1834, Holland withdrew from active political life.

The assembly's crack-down on Holland's expenses took its financial toll. In December 1826 he had begun renting his Charlottetown home, Holland Grove, as a gubernatorial residence. The following July he sold his interest in his late father's farm near Quebec, and in April 1835 he and the other heirs sold 29 200-acre lots in Kingsey Township in Lower Canada. Holland's eldest son, Samuel John, who had been wounded in 1813 at the battle of Crysler's Farm, died in England in 1822, and in July 1831 he also lost his long-suffering wife. He resigned as a justice of the peace on 25 June 1841.

Holland's career was colourful rather than distinguished. His early years read like a novel by G. A. Henty: a life of stirring boyhood adventure, against a backdrop of great events, culminating in recognition by eminent patrons. Holland proved to be temperamentally ill equipped to deal with middle age and the mundane affairs of peace-time. The fact that he was for a time in the front rank of politicians on Prince Edward Island says more about the quality of the local élite than it does about Holland's abilities. As Island society grew and matured his rambunctious character was increasingly out of place. It was typical of the man that when he ran in 1830, at age 66, for the position of churchwarden at St Paul's Church in Charlottetown, he was elected "amidst much clamour, and the conflict, not of tongues alone, but of blows."

M. BROOK TAYLOR

[Researchers have not been able to confirm the date of John Frederick Holland's birth given in Willis Chipman, "The life and times of Major Samuel Holland, surveyor-general, 1764–1801," *OH*, 21 (1924): 11–90. This article, citing unspecified family records, advances the date 27 Oct. 1764. M.B.T.]

ANQ-Q, CN1-284, 14 oct. 1800 (copy at P.E.I. Museum). BL, Add. MSS 21728: 252–62; 21730: 17–19; 21737, pt.I: 281–82; 21745, pt.I: 42; 21784, pt.II: 34–37; 21877: 157–61 (copies at PAC). PAPEI, Acc. 2541/127; Acc. 2825/59–60; Acc. 2849/3; 2849/6: 103; 2849/10; 2849/39; 2849/124–25; 2849/135; Acc. 2881/46, "The Scool Room"; RG 1, commission books, 13 Oct. 1806, 11 May 1810; RG 16, land registry records, conveyance reg., liber 6: ff.36, 41, 45; liber 7: f.84; liber 13: f.347. P.E.I. Museum, File information on Holland family. PRO, CO 226/19; 226/20: 17, 85; 226/21: 70, 95, 112, 115; 226/26: 11, 60; 226/27: 25, 82–88; 226/28: 3–6, 20–22, 26; 226/29: 67–77; 226/30: 7, 116, 131–39; 226/31: 12–33, 72–77; 226/32: 43; 226/35: 3–5, 15, 71, 166–67; 226/36: 52–53; 226/37: 109–10. Royal Arch., Windsor Castle (Windsor, Eng.), Add. 7/72–7/414 (mfm. at Can., Parks Canada, Halifax Defence Complex, Halifax). St Paul's Anglican Church (Charlottetown), Reg. of baptisms, marriages, and burials, esp. 23 Dec. 1799 (mfm. at PAPEI). Supreme Court of P.E.I. (Charlottetown), Estates Division, liber 4: f.229 (will of J. F. Holland) (mfm. at PAPEI). [Thomas Douglas, 5th Earl of] Selkirk, *Lord Selkirk's diary, 1803–1804; a journal of his travels in British North America and the northeastern United States*, ed. P. C. T. White (Toronto, 1958; repr. New York, 1969). "North-western explorations," PAC *Report*, 1889: 29–38. *Islander*, 20 Dec. 1845. *Prince Edward Island Gazette*, 16 Feb. 1818. *Prince Edward Island Register*, 6 Sept., 11 Oct. 1823; 18 Sept. 1824; 8 Jan., 5, 17 Feb., 18, 31 March, 15 April, 13 Sept. 1825; 26 Sept. 1826; 1 May, 3 July 1827; 12 July, 19 Aug. 1828; 13 April 1830. *Royal Gazette* (Charlottetown), 19 July 1831; 4, 7 Feb., 17 April, 30 Oct. 1832; 2, 9 April, 14 May 1833; 7 Jan., 4, 11, 18 Feb., 4 March, 14, 28 Oct., 16 Dec. 1834; 20 Jan. 1835; 31 July 1838; 29 June 1841; 23 Dec. 1845. *Weekly Recorder of Prince Edward Island* (Charlottetown), 9 Feb., 31 Aug. 1811. G.B., WO, *Army list*, 1796–1818. *N.S. vital statistics, 1813–22* (Punch), no.2697. Morton, *Hist. of Canadian west* (Thomas; 1973), 401–2, 410, 412. I. L. Rogers, *Charlottetown: the life in its buildings* (Charlottetown, 1983). D. W. Thomson, *Men and meridians: the history of surveying and mapping in Canada* (3v., Ottawa, 1966–69), 1: 222. Glyndwr Williams, *The British search for the northwest passage in the eighteenth century* (London and Toronto, 1962), esp. 250–52.

HOMER, JOHN, ship's captain, merchant, politician, and author; b. 3 Sept. 1781 in Barrington, N.S., son of Joseph Homer and Mary Atwood; m. first 1812 Elizabeth B. White, and they had three sons; m. secondly 21 July 1823 Nancy Crocker, a widow, in Halifax, and they had two sons and two daughters; d. 3 March 1836 in Halifax.

John Homer's grandfather was a Boston merchant who established himself in Barrington at the beginning of the American revolution. His father, Joseph, was for more than 20 years clerk and bookkeeper to John Sargent*, another Barrington merchant. Like many other boys living on the coast of Nova Scotia, John went to sea. When he was 17 he took up residence in the United States and "to answer Commercial purposes became a Citizen of that Country." In 1814, because of the war between Britain and the United States, he took the oath of allegiance to George III, erected a house in Barrington, and moved his family there.

After the end of the war in 1815 Homer and other Nova Scotians carried cargoes of fish to the West Indies, invested the proceeds in produce, sailed to the United States, where they purchased flour and breadstuffs, and then returned home. When Nova Scotia–registered vessels were banned from American ports in September 1818, Homer "went in vessels belonging to Boston, ostensibly as pilot, but in reality as master." In five years he made about 50 voyages, carrying from "three to thirty thousand dollars" each time to pay for flour and other goods in the United States. He also traded to Holland, Denmark, Norway, and Sweden.

On 6 July 1826 Homer was elected to the House of Assembly from Barrington Township. There were no organized political parties when Homer sat in the assembly, but he was generally in the minority when votes were taken. For instance, in 1829 he was one of only 10 members who voted to rescind the resolution to imprison assemblyman John Alexander Barry*, and in 1834 he was among the minority who voted for an elected Council. In the latter year, during the debate on the size of the civil list, Homer stated that "it had been published that he said he would vote against every thing – he would vote against every thing that was wrong, and he would certainly vote against making any additions to the Civil List whatever." "Was it consistent with justice and human rights," he asked, "that any one man should receive 69 times as much in a public office as a labouring man could earn?"

Homer was most active in the fisheries committee, where he served from 1827 to 1835. The high cost of outfitting fishing expeditions was a constant complaint and, as member for a township where almost the entire male population was employed in the fishery, shipping, or shipbuilding, Homer advocated that the provincial government pay generous bounties on salt, fish, and the tonnage of vessels. He and other representatives from fishing regions were able to have bills passed for that purpose, only to see them defeated in the Council, which was more interested in exports than in the fishery. In 1828, however, a compromise was reached when the legislature appropriated £15,000 to pay bounties on dried codfish of a merchantable quality for export and on every ton of registered shipping owned in Nova Scotia and employed in the bank, sea, or Labrador fishery.

In 1833 the fisheries committee recommended that £12,000 be set aside to aid the fisheries for three more years, but the report was not adopted. The following year masters of vessels in the Labrador fishery from Barrington asked for a bounty "to encourage our Fishermen to make their voyages from their own homes in our own vessels" rather than in American ones. As chairman of the fisheries committee, Homer pointed out that the American government paid a bounty of four dollars per ton and noted that many fishermen from Barrington and Argyle were working on vessels owned in Eastport, Maine. He asked that a tonnage bounty be paid to offset the American one, and also requested that a bounty be paid to those who took "mackerel with the hook, between Cape Sable and Cape Canso." The assembly agreed to grant a tonnage bounty for three years, but the bill was rejected by the Council, and aid to the mackerel fishery was not approved in the assembly.

Homer was not only involved in political efforts on behalf of the fishery. The Halifax and Barrington Fishing Association was founded by him and operated for several years with three vessels. Although the schooner *Betsey*'s voyages made some profit, there were unexpectedly large losses in the business as a whole. At a meeting of the shareholders in Halifax in February 1835, Homer declared that the association was "a ruinous concern," and the shareholders resolved to sell the vessels and any other property at public auction.

Homer represented a constituency where the fishing interest was paramount, but he was "a warm friend to the agricultural interest," served on the agricultural committee of the assembly from 1829 to 1835, and was president of the Barrington Agricultural Society, founded in 1831. In 1834 he published in Halifax *A brief sketch of the present state of the province of Nova-Scotia, with a project offered for its relief.* In it he urged the protection of Nova Scotian farmers by means similar to the corn laws of England: a ban on the importation of American flour, government aid to encourage oat and flour mills, and a central granary at Halifax where local flour could be inspected, packed, and distributed. These measures would, he claimed, also be of tremendous assistance to the fishermen because they would stop "the constant drain upon our specie to purchase flour and meal from the United States."

Homer died of pulmonary disease while the legislature was in session, and the Council and assembly prorogued to attend his funeral on 5 March 1836. His tombstone in St Paul's cemetery declares that as an assemblyman he had "honestly and Steadely Advocated the rights of the people." The *Acadian Recorder* paid tribute to his "frank sincerity of character [and] unvarying independence of conduct," while Alexander Lawson* of the *Yarmouth Herald and Western Advertiser* stated that "his abilities were always assiduously and earnestly directed to what he conceived to be objects of advantage to his native land."

In his will, Homer left half his estate to his sons by his first marriage and half to his wife. Unfortunately, he died insolvent, with debts totalling £1,238. The inventory of the estate indicates that Homer possessed more lavish furnishings than were usually associated with a fisherman or trader, for there was a considerable amount of mahogany furniture, china, glass, silver, and books, among the last being works by Adam Smith, Joseph Addison, and Sir Walter Scott. His widow was allowed to keep some furniture and utensils necessary for herself and her four young children, but the rest was sold.

PHYLLIS R. BLAKELEY

PANS, MG 3, 1873; RG 1, 227, docs.20–21; RG 5, P, 42, 1834; 121–22; RG 14, 58, no.61. St Paul's Anglican Church (Halifax), Reg. of marriages, 21 July 1823; reg. of burials, 5 March 1836 (mfm. at PANS). "Barrington, Nova Scotia, vital records," ed. A. A. Doane, *Mayflower Descendants* (Boston), 8 (1906): 140. N.S., House of Assembly, *Journal and proc.*, 1826–36. *Acadian Recorder*, 11 Nov. 1820, 7 Feb. 1835, 5 March 1836. *Novascotian, or Colonial Herald*, 11 March, 1, 29 April, 17 June 1830; 8, 16 Feb., 29 March 1832; 27 Feb., 10, 17, 24 April, 4, 11, 25 Dec. 1834; 3 March 1836. *Yarmouth Herald and Western Advertiser* (Yarmouth, N.S.), 12, 18 March 1836. *Directory of N.S. MLAs*. Edwin Crowell, *A history of Barrington Township and vicinity . . . 1604–1870* (Yarmouth, [1923]; repr. Belleville, Ont., 1973), 293, 298–99, 311, 418–20, 492–93. A. A. Lomas, "The industrial development of Nova Scotia, 1830–1854" (MA thesis, Dalhousie Univ., Halifax, 1950), c.4. W. G. Crowell, "John Homer, M.L.A., of Barrington," N.S. Hist. Soc., *Coll.*, 32 (1959): 31–54.

HONEY, JOHN BURROWS. *See* BURROWS, JOHN

HORNE, ROBERT CHARLES, army and militia officer, surgeon, printer, publisher, JP, office holder, and bank teller; m. secondly 10 May 1815 Isabella Leah Gamble, and they had three sons, two of whom survived childhood; d. 26 Oct. 1845 in Toronto.

Robert Charles Horne was born in England around 1780; by the time he came to the Canadas several months before the outbreak of the War of 1812, he was a member of the Royal College of Surgeons of London, was married, and had a daughter. At the beginning of the war he applied for the post of assistant surgeon to the Glengarry Light Infantry Fencibles. The appointment was confirmed on 29 Oct. 1812 and he joined his regiment at Fort George (Niagara-on-the-Lake), Upper Canada, early in 1813. When American forces captured Fort George that May, Horne lost all his baggage. He served later at Kingston, where in May 1814 his wife died and where one year later he married a sister of William* and John William* Gamble. On 25 Aug. 1816, while he was stationed at York (Toronto), his regiment was disbanded and he went on half pay. In 1822 he was appointed surgeon to the Regiment of North York militia; three years later he was raised to full pay as a staff surgeon for the army medical establishment in Upper Canada but, declining to serve, he was struck off the army list on 25 Dec. 1826.

When he was reduced to half pay in 1816, Horne immediately began his career as a printer and publisher. That December he printed the constitution of the Bible and Common Prayer Book Society of Upper Canada, of which he had been a founding member in York on the 3rd of that month. Soon after his first booklet was printed, Horne also became king's printer and the proprietor of the official provincial newspaper, the *York Gazette*, which had fallen on hard times. Its press had been damaged or destroyed when the Americans captured York in 1813, and the two publishers who preceded him had served short and ineffective terms. Horne was soon requesting that the government purchase a modern press and adequate supplies of type and that it permit him to raise his fees, which the Executive Council allowed with some qualifications. He also changed the name of the newspaper to the *Upper Canada Gazette*.

Horne's ready conversion from the army to the printing press, and his apparent success at publishing, suggest some prior experience, perhaps in England, but no evidence has been found to support this speculation. During his years as king's printer he published several books and pamphlets, including Charles FOTHERGILL's reply to Robert Gourlay*'s attack in 1818 on Lieutenant Governor Sir Peregrine Maitland*. The following year he began printing John Strachan*'s journal, the *Christian Recorder*. His tenure was not, however, without unhappy incidents. In 1818 he was called before the bar of the house to explain "acknowledging himself the author" in an advertisement for the provincial statutes in the *Gazette* on 19 March. Horne attended, admitted his guilt, and apologized. About 1820, he hired Francis Collins*, a printer, and early in 1821 deputed him to report the House of Assembly debates for the *Gazette*. The government disagreed with an apparent slanting of these reports and on 9 Feb. 1821 summoned Horne again to the bar of the house, where apparently he excused himself on the grounds that he had not reported the debates himself. He escaped with only a sharp reprimand after making humble apology. Soon after, Maitland refused to allow Horne to publish reports of the debates in the *Gazette*. On 1 March Horne began the *York Weekly Post*, an adjunct to the *Gazette* which he used to report the debates. Late that year Horne resigned his position as king's printer, describing himself as being "disgusted with a situation always peculiarly anxious and disagreeable." On 1 Jan. 1822 he was succeeded by Charles Fothergill; Collins, who applied for the post, was snubbed.

During these post-war years, Horne had been active in other matters. In 1817 he was involved in a minor capacity in the preliminaries to the unfortunate duel between John Ridout and Samuel Peters Jarvis*, being one of those who separated the two men during their fisticuffs in the street at York. In addition to his work with the Bible society, Horne was appointed secretary of the Society of Friends to Strangers in Distress when that group was created at York in October 1817. In February 1821 he was secretary to the Agricultural Society of Upper Canada, and for more than 15 years, beginning on 3 June 1822, he served as a justice of the peace for the Home District.

When Horne left the publishing business in 1822, he became chief teller to the newly founded Bank of Upper Canada. He had no obvious qualifications for the post but he apparently gave satisfaction since he continued in it for the remainder of his life. It is at least possible that an initial assistance to him was the fact that his wife and the wife of William Allan*, president of the bank, were sisters; Horne had also been an incorporator of the new bank. Little is known of Horne's activities with the bank, whose chief and most visible officer was Thomas Gibbs Ridout*, the cashier. But as a conservative individual he would have been comfortable in this "family compact"-controlled environment. His conservative stance is easily proven by his inclusion in the long list of those attacked by William Lyon Mackenzie*.

Horne seems not to have practised medicine after 1816, but on 7 April 1823 he was named a member of the Medical Board of Upper Canada, on which he played an active role for almost two decades. He also served as treasurer of the College of Physicians and Surgeons of Upper Canada during its existence from May 1839 to January 1841. Mackenzie had scourged the board in 1824, warning would-be applicants that they would have "to encounter the *jaw bone* of a Sampson [James Sampson*], the *quantum suff.* of a Horne, and the Slipslopic *queries* of that modern Hippocrates, Doctor Judge Clerk Powell [Grant Powell]."

Even more indicative of Mackenzie's antipathy for Horne was the arson committed personally by the former on Horne's home during the rebellion of 1837. Horne, an active and resolute tory, had purportedly refused Mackenzie some of the services of the Bank of Upper Canada and had expressed contempt for him. On 5 Dec. 1837 Mackenzie interrupted his march to Toronto to go to Horne's home on Yonge Street just north of Bloor; he entered uninvited, abused those who were there, and set fire to the house with his own hands. Mrs Horne had to flee with her children through the snow and, according to author William Canniff*, thereby contracted a condition that affected her health permanently. Historian John Charles Dent* has suggested that Mackenzie was deranged at the time. Certainly the act seems to have helped to turn against him many who previously had been uncertain in their allegiance. On 23 Feb. 1839 a special commission recommended that Horne be reimbursed £2,127 18*s*. 9*d*. for his losses.

Horne's last public act that has come to light took the form of a long letter written on 26 June 1841 to the mayor of Toronto, George Monro*, concerning "the Mayor's recent Proclamation on the subject of nuisances." In it, Horne suggested remedies for some "nuisances" – tanneries in populous areas; dirty, cluttered, poorly maintained streets; soapsuds thrown into the street that "accumulate in pools, deepened by the feet of cattle and the wallowing of pigs, and become exceedingly offensive." To the end, the man remained the doctor, and sought to improve public health.

Charles G. Roland

AO, MS 78, John Strachan to Macaulay, 25 Feb. 1819; RG 22, ser.305. CTA, RG 1, B, R. C. Horne to Mayor [George Monro], 26 June 1841 (mfm. at AO). PAC, RG 1, E3, 10: 99–114; 60: 240–50; RG 5, A1: 10565–66; RG 8, I (C ser.), 84: 209; 289: 52–53; 1168: 99; 1169: 106. *Colonial Advocate*, 18, 27 May 1824. *Upper Canada Gazette*, December 1816–December 1821. *York Weekly Post*, 22 Feb.–26 Dec. 1821. William Johnston, *Roll of commissioned officers in the medical service of the British army . . .* (Aberdeen, Scot., 1917). William Kingsford, *The early bibliography of the province of Ontario . . .* (Toronto and Montreal, 1892). Canniff, *Medical profession in U.C.* J. C. Dent, *The story of the Upper Canadian rebellion; largely derived from original sources and documents* (2v., Toronto, 1885). E. C. Guillet, "Pioneer banking in Ontario: the Bank of Upper Canada, 1822–1866," *Canadian Paper Money Journal* (Toronto), 14 (1978): 9–18.

HOWARD, PETER, farmer, businessman, politician, JP, office holder, and doctor; b. *c.* 1771 in the American colonies, probably New York, fourth son of

Matthew Howard; m. first Sarah Munsel (Munsall), and they had three sons and two daughters; m. secondly 17 Oct. 1833 Margaret Seaman, a widow, and they had no children; d. 24 Nov. 1843 in Brockville, Upper Canada.

Peter Howard's father was a farmer living in Pittstown, N.Y., when the American revolution broke out. Taking up arms with the British in 1777, he served with several loyalist corps, was employed as a spy, and was captured several times. After the war he settled in western Quebec with his family. In 1791 Peter petitioned the government for land as the son of a loyalist and was granted 200 acres. He owned property in several townships in the newly formed province of Upper Canada but made his residence in Elizabethtown Township, where his father and other family members lived. A comfortable farmer, by 1804 he had 85 acres cultivated, 400 uncultivated, several animals, and a still. He also, for a time, had an inn. In 1802 his name had been removed from the United Empire Loyalist list as a result of Lieutenant Governor Peter Hunter*'s administrative reforms aimed at reducing the numbers eligible for free land grants. How Howard reacted is not known, but loyalists generally were outraged at what seemed to be a violation of the king's intention.

Howard contested the riding of Leeds in 1804 and easily topped the poll, drawing support from a cross-section of local society, including Joel Stone*, Levius Peters SHERWOOD, and Peet SELEE. During the fourth parliament (1805–8) the opposition in the assembly gained in strength; Howard's association with it, however, came later and gradually. He seconded Ebenezer Washburn*'s District School Bill in 1805. The following year he introduced and supported the petition headed by William Buell* to move the district jail and court-house to the site of present-day Brockville. He also seconded another Washburn initiative, to form a board to regulate medical practitioners in the province. His modest prominence yielded modest rewards, including an appointment to the local magistracy in 1806. He worked conscientiously on behalf of his constituents to settle matters concerning land title and, with the assemblyman for neighbouring Grenville, Samuel Sherwood, pressed the government for proper surveys of the back townships in Leeds County.

There was, in short, nothing to hint at Howard's participation in one of the most dramatic parliamentary moments in Upper Canada before the War of 1812. On 5 March 1808 Howard, Thomas Dorland*, and David McGregor Rogers* retired from the house, depriving it temporarily of a quorum. They objected to the proposed amendment removing the statutory time limit on the District School Act of 1807. The uproar was triggered by Sherwood's successful attempt to change the standing orders to accommodate a third reading of the amendment that day. The threesome had as little use for the procedure, which they considered unparliamentary, as for its intent. Lieutenant Governor Francis Gore* was outraged, stripping Howard and Dorland of their offices but meeting with less success in handling Rogers. In a letter to Charles JONES of Elizabethtown (Brockville), Sherwood damned Howard for allowing "his perverse & obstinate disposition to govern him & lead him into an act the most violent & disorderly that can be" and closed by urging Jones to ensure that "this matter . . . be painted in true colours to the People of Your County."

The general election in May provided an occasion for judging the popularity of Howard's action. He was re-elected in a bitterly fought contest which revealed his strong egalitarian impulses. Neither Dorland nor Rogers had much use for the aristocratic emphasis of the British constitution; Howard had none, and in fact evinced little sympathy for monopolies of any sort. He responded to the "fiery darts of falsehood," explaining to his constituents that the loss of office had been "nothing unexpected, for we had our choice, to stay and wrong our people, or Come away and lose our offices, and for my own part I did not engage to legislate to Gratify the Governor, But to support your rights." An anonymous campaign document, by either Howard or one of his supporters, put the matter in a broader context. In dispute was the preponderance of "Law characters" in the house and their tendency to "Enact Such Laws As would best Suit themselves." Howard was portrayed as a constituency man, and "above all . . . the POOR MANS FRIEND." The conspiracy of lawyers would increase taxes for their own benefit and permit the seizure of land in payment of debt, which would allow the country to be "Parceled out into Lordships and the Common people reduced To Slavery!" The writer exhorted farmers to elect their own kind and "Guard against the Combinations of the great . . . it is natural for them to oppress the Poor."

The fifth parliament (1809–12) became increasingly polarized. Howard moved steadily closer to the opposition led by Joseph Willcocks*. In 1810, for instance, he voted with the minority against condemning John Mills JACKSON's pamphlet as seditious libel. His own initiatives were as varied as they were distinctive: his continuing concern with regulating the medical profession, his attempt to prevent irregularities at elections, his bill to provide relief for the poor, and his bill "to prevent all Plays of interludes, Puppet Shows, Rope Dancers, or Stage Plays from performing in this Province for hire or gain." By 1811 his voting pattern was identical with those of the most radical members of the opposition coterie, Willcocks, John Willson*, and Benajah Mallory*. During the 1812 session, while supporting the general thrust of revisions to the Militia Act, he apparently cast the deciding vote – in his capacity as chairman of the whole – against an amendment requiring all militiamen to abjure any loyalty to the United States. He also introduced, as William Lyon Mackenzie* would note in 1833, the first petition for a secret ballot.

Howard contested the general election in June 1812 but was defeated by L. P. Sherwood, helped by Charles Jones's smear campaign against him. Four years later Howard won his seat back. During the seventh parliament (1817–20), he was less prominent (missing the 1819 session altogether). Many opposition issues still received his support but on one key issue he was willing to circumscribe civil rights. Mackenzie, in his 1828 survey of the province's political past, noted Howard's support of the infamous "Gagging Bill" of 1818, which was used against Robert Gourlay*. During the debate, Howard called Gourlay a "great seducer, [who] could persuade the people to any thing. . . . [Howard] had stated to the people they had no grievances." He ran again in 1820 and 1824, but without success. Yet he never lost his taste for politics. In 1830 he chaired a meeting held in Brockville to support the candidacies of his son Matthew Munsel and William Buell* Jr. He was involved in similar electoral meetings in 1834 and 1836; moreover, in the later year he was elected president of the Johnstown District Reformers' Society. By that point he had come to represent the area's reform tradition. Andrew Norton Buell* had intervened personally for Mackenzie in 1836 to reclaim from Howard some personal notes of the Toronto newspaperman. Howard was not forthcoming and, as Buell wrote to Mackenzie, "The Dr. is rather dilatory . . . & it would be very unpleasant to me to press him about the matter, as he is an old friend & his family & extensive Connections are generally reformers and it might . . . be injurious to the Cause of reform were I to do so."

After the war Howard had served as a road commissioner. In 1819 he moved from Elizabethtown to mills he had acquired in Yonge Township. Active as a doctor since before the war, he was examined by the Medical Board of Upper Canada in July 1828 and licensed to practise medicine on 5 Feb. 1830. When he took up residence in Brockville in 1833, the *Brockville Recorder* noted "his long practice and acquaintance with the diseases incident to this community."

ROBERT L. FRASER

AO, MS 516, A. N. Buell to W. L. Mackenzie, 21 Jan. 1836; MS 520; MS 537; MU 275; RG 1, A-I-6; RG 21, United Counties of Leeds and Grenville, census records. BL, Add. MSS 21826–28 (copies at PAC). PAC, MG 24, B7; RG 1, E3; E14; L3; RG 5, A1; B9; RG 68, General index, 1651–1841. PRO, AO 12 (mfm. at PAC). QUA, 3077. "Journals of Legislative Assembly of U.C.," AO *Report*, 1909, 1911, 1913–14. *Loyalist settlements, 1783–1789: new evidence of Canadian loyalist claims*, comp. W. B. Antliff (Toronto, 1985), 105. W. L. Mackenzie, *The legislative black list, of Upper Canada; or official corruption and hypocrisy unmasked* (York [Toronto], 1828). "Political state of U.C.," PAC *Report*, 1892: 32–135. U.C., House of Assembly, *Journal*, 1831: 34, 36, 38. "Upper Canada land book C, 29th June, 1796, to 4th July, 1796; 1st July, 1797, to 20th December, 1797" and "Upper Canada land book D, 22nd December, 1797, to 13th July, 1798," AO *Report*, 1931. *Brockville Recorder*, 1833–36. *Colonial Advocate*, 1824, 1833. *Kingston Chronicle*, 1819–20. *Kingston Gazette*, 1816–18. *York Gazette*, 1808. *Death notices of Ont.* (Reid). *Marriage bonds of Ont.* (T. B. Wilson). Reid, *Loyalists in Ont.* T. W. H. Leavitt, *History of Leeds and Grenville, Ontario, from 1749 to 1879* . . . (Brockville, Ont., 1879; repr. Belleville, Ont., 1972). Patterson, "Studies in elections in U.C.," c.3.

HOYLES, NEWMAN WRIGHT, ship's captain, businessman, politician, office holder, and JP; b. 30 Aug. 1777 in Dartmouth, England, second son of William Hoyles, doctor, and Anne Wright; m. there in 1801 Lucretia Brown, and they had three sons and six daughters; d. 29 Feb. 1840 in St John's.

Born in a south Devon seaport traditionally associated with the Newfoundland migratory fishery, Newman Wright Hoyles went to sea at 15. Captain of a brig at 21, he sailed the North Atlantic trading routes, calling at West Indian, European, and Newfoundland ports. By 1806 he had formed a mercantile partnership with Thomas Follett, member of a long-established Newfoundland firm of Devonshire origin. Hoyles's marriage in 1801 to the daughter of the doctor attached to the military garrison at Placentia, Nfld, strengthened his ties to the island. He became a permanent resident of St John's no later than 1810, when he was one of 36 merchants and planters who met to determine the price of fish and cod oil for the season. In 1812 he became the agent of the Marine Insurance Society, established by the merchants of St John's; by 1815 he was conducting his own insurance brokerage and within a year was the appointed agent of Lloyd's of London.

A new partnership, which had been formed in 1813 with Hugh William Brown, a London merchant, insurance broker, and probably a brother-in-law, enabled Hoyles to survive the post-1815 depression in the fish trade. With branches at Port de Grave and Trepassey and fishing stations on the Labrador coast, Brown, Hoyles and Company became a leading mercantile firm, owning sea-going vessels, importing goods, and exporting fish.

In 1813, and possibly earlier, Hoyles had been elected to the committee of the Society of Merchants, a body which, in the absence of any locally constituted authority, played a large part in town government. Hoyles became a member of the lighthouse, powder-magazine, and pilotage committees. As the prime mover in framing regulations for the employment of harbour pilots, Hoyles earned the disapproval of Governor John Thomas Duckworth* for not obtaining his prior sanction. In 1819 Hoyles, declaring his support for the incorporation of St John's, referred to the disrepute into which pilotage had fallen because no municipal authority existed to enforce regulations. Indeed all other municipal concerns, including the police, the fire companies, and the hospital, had suffered the same fate, he said. At a town meeting which he chaired later in 1819, he presented the unanimous decision of the grand jury, of which he was foreman, that authority to establish a civil police, provide for the poor, and regulate fire companies, pilotage, and the hospital, lighthouse, and powder-magazine should be vested in a committee chosen at a town meeting and authorized to levy property taxes. Hoyles was on a committee elected to frame a bill of corporation, but contention over property assessments prevented its submission to the governor.

In 1823 Hoyles was elected vice-president of the St John's Chamber of Commerce, the executive body of the newly established Commercial Society. Alongside William CARSON and Patrick MORRIS, he also served as treasurer of the "Committee of Inhabitants" delegated to consider the bill recently introduced into the British parliament for the reorganization of Newfoundland's courts. The committee, resolved to see the appointment of a local legislature to superintend expenditure of public revenue, prepared its own outline of a bill. In 1824 the British judicature act, which also provided a charter of incorporation for St John's but fell far short of the committee's expectations, was passed. Hoyles's support of reform was undoubtedly given some credibility by his social prominence. At various times between 1819 and 1824 he served as treasurer of the St John's Library Society, a steward of St John's Charity School, an Anglican churchwarden, captain of the fire company he established in 1824, chairman of the committee for poor relief and of the Marine Insurance Association, and foreman of the grand jury. Recognizing his importance, Governor Thomas John Cochrane* appointed Hoyles in 1825 an aide-de-camp with the rank of lieutenant-colonel. At the same time, with reservations to cover the conflict of interest which could result from his business pursuits, the governor recommended him, without success, for a position on Council.

In 1827 Hoyles, as president of the Chamber of Commerce, forwarded a petition to London protesting the extension of import duties. The next year he was one of those who requested a public meeting for the purpose of petitioning parliament not to impose further import duties but to grant a local legislature. Speaking at the meeting and referring to Patrick Morris as "the O'Connell of Newfoundland" and to William Carson, who also spoke, as a "still greater patriot," Hoyles foresaw no financial difficulties for a colonial legislature. When representative government was granted in 1832, Hoyles, who had divested himself of his mercantile interests, sat in the assembly for Fortune Bay and was appointed colonial treasurer in December of that year.

Hoyles, who had nominated Carson at the hustings in 1832, was a supporter of reform but reform concerned chiefly with local grievances and the enactment of municipal regulations. He introduced bills to regulate the storage of gunpowder, fire companies, pilotage, and the spread of infectious diseases; to open a fire-break; to provide relief for disabled seamen and fishermen; and to establish hospitals. His intention in 1833 to introduce a bill for the incorporation of St John's was not realized. The financial difficulties of the assembly were manifold, aggravated by developing party strife. Hoyles as colonial treasurer incurred the wrath of the assembly, the reformers in particular, by the payment in November 1834 of £853 6*s.* 11*d.* on the unconstitutional warrant of Governor Cochrane, and he did not sit in the assembly after 1836. He continued as colonial treasurer until his death. Between 1838 and 1840 he served on the board of health, the board of commissioners for pilotage, and as a justice of the peace and cashier of the Savings Bank. His son Hugh William* was to serve as Newfoundland's first native-born premier (1861–65) and as chief justice (1865–80).

PAMELA BRUCE

Cathedral of St John the Baptist (Anglican) (St John's), Reg. of baptisms and burials. Devon Record Office (Exeter, Eng.), 2537 A (St Petrox, Dartmouth), reg. of baptisms and marriages; 2992 A (St Saviour, Dartmouth), reg. of baptisms. MHA, Hoyles name file. PANL, GN 2/1/A, May, 9 Oct. 1822; 19 Oct. 1825. Private arch., N. J. S. Hoyles (Grand Bend, Ont.), "The house of Hoyles," comp. H. L. and N. W. Hoyles (1913). PRO, BT 98/6–9. Nfld., House of Assembly, *Journal*, 1833–35. *Newfoundland Mercantile Journal*, 1819–20, 1824. *Public Ledger*, 1810, 1824, 1827–29. *Royal Gazette and Newfoundland Advertiser*, 1810–13, 1815–16, 1828, 1832–34, 1840. Gunn, *Political hist. of Nfld.* Leslie Harris, "The first nine years of representative government in Newfoundland" (MA thesis, Memorial Univ. of Nfld., St John's, 1959). A. H. McLintock, *The establishment of constitutional government in Newfoundland, 1783–1832: a study of retarded colonisation* (London and Toronto, 1941). Prowse, *Hist. of Nfld.* (1895). Keith Matthews, "The class of '32: St. John's reformers on the eve of representative government," *Acadiensis* (Fredericton), 6 (1976–77), no.2: 80–94. *Royal Gazette and Newfoundland Advertiser*, 10 Sept. 1907.

HUBERT, LOUIS-ÉDOUARD, merchant, politician, and militia officer; b. 15 Feb. 1766 in Montreal, son of Pierre Hubert and Marie-Josephte Chartier; d. 9 Nov. 1842 in Saint-Denis on the Richelieu, Lower

Canada, and was buried in the crypt of the parish church.

Louis-Édouard Hubert was a descendant of a respected family of Parisian magistrates that had come to New France around 1665 and that gave Quebec its ninth bishop, Jean-François Hubert*. His father engaged in shipbuilding in Montreal and was a foreman and inspector of timber under the French régime. He was still a foreman and inspector in 1775 when the Americans took Montreal, drove him from his house, and forced him into hiding for several months.

Louis-Édouard studied in Montreal and at the Petit Séminaire de Québec. He then settled at Saint-Denis on the Richelieu, a country town, set in the prosperous seigneury of the same name, which was experiencing rapid growth in trade and commerce; parish priest François Cherrier* even saw it as the future seat of a bishopric. On 22 Nov. 1796, at Saint-Antoine-de-la-rivière-Chambly (Saint-Antoine-sur-Richelieu), Hubert married Cécile Cartier, daughter of the wealthy merchant Jacques Cartier* and subsequently aunt of Sir George-Étienne Cartier*. Through her mother, Cécile was a cousin of Bishop Joseph-Octave Plessis*. The couple were to have a large family, of whom three daughters and four sons are known.

Hubert soon became a leading local figure. He bought properties and ran a large business in the parish, which was renowned for wheat production. On 5 July 1800 he was elected for Richelieu to the House of Assembly and he sat, with no great regularity, until 1804; he did not seek re-election. At the opening of the first session of this third parliament he had agreed to serve on a committee to set up free schools, yet he was not in attendance when the bill was introduced. During his entire term he voted on only eight occasions, supporting both the Canadian and the English parties. At this time he was experiencing the effects of an economic slump and his business was deteriorating. In June 1804 several creditors obtained an attachment against a number of his properties. He retrieved the situation, however, and when Sir James Henry Craig* visited Saint-Denis in 1810, Hubert could stable the horses of the governor and his entourage with no difficulty.

During the War of 1812 against the United States, Hubert took an active part in the defence of his country. By 15 Sept. 1812 he had been commissioned lieutenant and quartermaster of the 2nd Select Embodied Militia Battalion of Lower Canada and by 7 October he had reported to the camp at La Prairie. He accompanied the troops on manœuvres that took them as far as Lacolle, marching in all weathers and sleeping on the ground – rough exercise for a man of nearly 50. Except for a stint in Chambly he seems to have spent the rest of the war at La Prairie.

Hubert resigned his commission on 24 May 1814 and resumed his commercial and agricultural activities. He took an interest in his children's education, sending two of his sons to the Collège de Saint-Hyacinthe and a daughter to the Ursuline convent in Trois-Rivières. He also settled the large estate his father-in-law had left. By a proclamation of the Prince Regent, Hubert was entitled as a militia officer to 500 acres in the Eastern Townships; he applied and on 24 July 1823 secured a certificate for lots in Upton Township. Although he took all kinds of steps and even incurred the expense of surveyor's fees, he never succeeded in obtaining them. Incensed at learning that these lots had been granted to the Martignys in spite of his efforts, he accused that family of collusion with the surveyor general. He pressed his claims until 1837 and was offered land in various townships, but got no concrete results. His services to the crown were no more recognized than those rendered in 1775 by his father, in whose name he had submitted a similar fruitless request.

At the time of the rebellions in 1837–38 Hubert did not support the Patriotes. His home was ransacked none the less by British troops after the battle of Saint-Denis. Two of his sons were at Saint-Eustache with Patriote Jean-Olivier Chénier, and he went through an anxious period after they were taken into custody at Saint-Antoine-sur-Richelieu, where they had gone into hiding. They were held from 6 Jan. 1838 until July, when they were released – in at least one case on £2,000 bail. In 1840 a committee of the Special Council recommended that Hubert be paid nearly £115 in compensation for the damages he had suffered, but nothing was done on his behalf at the time and the whole matter caused a great stir for a decade.

Louis-Édouard died at 76 years of age, leaving his wife and a number of descendants. Rue Saint-Hubert in Saint-Denis on the Richelieu is a reminder of the family who once lived there and of its head, Louis-Édouard, a highly regarded member of a bourgeoisie still not well known that, through social, economic, and political activity, had a considerable influence on the community at large.

Marie-Paule R. LaBrèque

A portrait of Louis-Édouard Hubert wearing his red militia coat was painted by his friend the notary Jean-Joseph Girouard* at Laprairie during the War of 1812.

ANQ-M, CE1-3, 22 nov. 1796; CE1-51, 16 févr. 1766; CE2-12, 12 nov. 1842. ANQ-Q, E21. Arch. de la Soc. d'hist. régionale de Saint-Hyacinthe (Saint-Hyacinthe, Qué.), Fg-12; Notes de Claire Lachance. ASSH, A, Fg-3; Fg-41; Fg-46. PAC, RG 1, L3[L]: 108; RG 4, A1, index; RG 31, C1, 1825, 1831, Saint-Denis (Richelieu). *The Elgin–Grey papers, 1846–1852*, ed. A. G. Doughty (4v., Ottawa, 1937), 4. L.C., House of Assembly, *Journals*, 1801–4; Special Council, *Journals*, 1840. *Quebec Gazette*, 9 July 1800, 14 June 1804, 8 Oct. 1812, 18 July 1839. F.-J. Audet, "Les législateurs du Bas-Canada." F.-J. Audet et Fabre Surveyer, *Les députés au premier Parl. du Bas-Canada*.

J. D. Borthwick, *Montreal, its history, to which is added biographical sketches, with photographs, of many of its principal citizens* (Montreal, 1875). Bouchette, *Topographical description of L.C.* Langelier, *Liste des terrains concédés*, 415–19, 636, 1482. Le Jeune, *Dictionnaire*, vol.1. Hormisdas Magnan, *Dictionnaire historique et géographique des paroisses, missions et municipalités de la province de Québec* (Arthabaska, Qué., 1925). *Mariages de St-Antoine-sur-Richelieu (1741–1965)*, Irénée Jetté et Benoît Pontbriand, compil. (Québec, 1966). *Officers of British forces in Canada* (Irving). J.-B.-A. Allaire, *Histoire de la paroisse de Saint-Denis-sur-Richelieu (Canada)* (Saint-Hyacinthe, 1905). Francine Bouchard *et al.*, *La vallée du Richelieu: introduction à l'histoire et au patrimoine* (Québec, 1981). Chapais, *Cours d'hist. du Canada*, vol.2. Ouellet, *Bas-Canada*. J.-B. Richard, *Les églises de la paroisse de Saint-Denis-sur-Richelieu* ([Saint-Hyacinthe], 1939); *Les événements de 1837 à Saint-Denis-sur-Richelieu* ([Saint-Hyacinthe], 1938). Sulte, *Hist. de la milice*. Alastair Sweeny, *George-Étienne Cartier: a biography* (Toronto, 1976). B. J. Young, *George-Étienne Cartier, Montreal bourgeois* (Kingston, Ont., and Montreal, 1981). J. [E.] Hare, "L'Assemblée législative du Bas-Canada, 1792–1814: députation et polarisation politique," *RHAF*, 27 (1973–74): 361–95.

HUDON, HYACINTHE, Roman Catholic priest and vicar general; b. 28 Nov. 1792 in Rivière-Ouelle, Lower Canada, son of Jérémie Hudon and Marie Bergereau; d. 12 Aug. 1847 in Montreal.

Having been a brilliant student in classical and theological studies at the Petit Séminaire and then the Grand Séminaire de Québec, Hyacinthe Hudon was ordained priest by the bishop of Quebec, Joseph-Octave Plessis*, at Nicolet on 9 March 1817. Within a few days he was named assistant priest of Saint-Denis parish, at Saint-Denis on the Richelieu. He was assigned to the mission church in the parish of Saint-Thomas (at Montmagny) in August, and then became assistant priest at the cathedral of Notre-Dame at Quebec in October. On 19 Oct. 1818 he was appointed to the chapel in the *faubourg* Saint-Roch, where he was also to ensure that the Collège de Saint-Roch and the schools founded by Plessis operated smoothly.

In 1822 Hudon replaced Rémi Gaulin* at the Arichat mission in Nova Scotia. He returned to Lower Canada four years later, and Bishop Bernard-Claude Panet* put him in charge of the parish of Sainte-Madeleine at Rigaud and of the mission in the seigneury of Petite-Nation. On 16 Feb. 1832 he was made curé of Sainte-Famille at Boucherville. During his eight years there, he saw to the completion and decoration of the church, which had been built in 1801. In this connection, François-Maximilien Bibaud* observed that Hudon "dreamed of attracting Italian artists to Canada and improving [the] churches, from which he wanted to remove many bad pictures that were not true adornments."

In 1835 Hudon strongly supported the creation of an episcopal see in Montreal. In October he sent the archbishop of Quebec, Joseph SIGNAY, a petition to Pope Gregory XVI from the Montreal clergy in favour of a separate bishopric. When faced with Signay's refusal to forward it to Rome before obtaining London's assent, he undertook, with the help of the superior of the Séminaire de Saint-Sulpice in Montreal, Joseph-Vincent Quiblier*, to have the priests in the district sign a copy, which was dispatched to the authorities in Rome on 21 November. Rome replied favourably in 1836 and the district was made a diocese. Jean-Jacques LARTIGUE, the archbishop of Quebec's auxiliary in Montreal, became its first bishop. He took possession of his see on 8 September of that year. In November he proposed the names of Hudon, Ignace Bourget*, and François-Xavier Demers to the Sacred Congregation of Propaganda for the office of coadjutor; Bourget was then appointed.

At the time of the 1837 rebellion in Lower Canada, Hudon was censured by the Patriotes, who would not forgive his appeals for moderation and who, wrongly, accused him of being the enemy of his own parishioners and of informing on them. They went so far as to sentence him to death. Hudon had, however, not been afraid to make common cause with his fellow priests in the Richelieu valley, who were disturbed by Lartigue's pastoral letter of 24 Oct. 1837 condemning the actions of the Patriote leaders. They had earnestly begged the bishop to intervene with the British authorities on behalf of the Canadians. In November 1837 Hudon had even been entrusted by Lartigue with obtaining clerical support for a petition asking the British authorities to take the needs of the colony into consideration.

In September 1840 the new bishop of Montreal, Bourget, summoned Hudon to his side and on 21 Jan. 1841 named him a canon of the chapter of Notre-Dame church. On 29 April Hudon became vicar general, and from 3 May till 23 September he and his colleague Antoine Manseau* managed the diocese while the bishop was in Europe.

Hudon, who was concerned about the school question in Lower Canada, protested energetically to the governor, Lord Sydenham [THOMSON], against the education bill presented in the Legislative Assembly in July 1841. In May 1842 he was named to the Montreal board of examiners for licensing teachers. Hudon was delegated by Bourget to go to Kingston, Upper Canada, in October 1843 to explain to the assembly the views and desires of the Catholic bishops concerning the Jesuit estates and the founding of a Catholic university at Quebec.

In December 1843 Bourget sent Hudon to Rome to facilitate the appointment of Jean-Charles Prince* as his coadjutor and to work for the creation of an ecclesiastical province, in accordance with the wish expressed by eight bishops in their petition to the pope in June. On 31 Oct. 1844 Hudon returned to Montreal with a papal brief establishing the first ecclesiastical province in Canada and with the metropolitan's pall, which he formally handed over to Signay on 24 November.

In 1843 Hyacinthe Hudon was the first Canadian to become an honorary canon of Chartres in France. In April 1844 he was elected dean of the chapter of Montreal. He died, a victim of his devotion, on 12 Aug. 1847 while organizing help for Irish immigrants stricken with typhus. Canon Alexis-Frédéric Truteau* was chosen to succeed him as vicar general.

GILLES CHAUSSÉ

ACAM, 901.117. ANQ-M, CE1-51, 13 août 1847. ANQ-Q, CE3-1, 28 nov. 1792. Arch. de la Compagnie de Jésus, prov. du Canada français (Saint-Jérôme, Qué.), A-3-3. [Ignace Bourget], *Mémoires pour servir à l'histoire du chapitre de la cathédrale de S. Jacques de Montréal* (Montréal, 1882). Allaire, *Dictionnaire*. F.-M. Bibaud, *Dict. hist.*; *Le panthéon canadien* (A. et V. Bibaud; 1891). Caron, "Inv. de la corr. de Mgr Panet," ANQ *Rapport*, 1933–34: 256, 293, 310, 336; 1935–36: 229; "Inv. de la corr. de Mgr Plessis," 1932–33: 100, 121–22, 140, 190; "Inv. de la corr. de Mgr Signay," 1936–37: 303, 317. Desrosiers, "Inv. de la corr. de Mgr Bourget," ANQ *Rapport*, 1946–47: 147–48, 152, 164; 1948–49: 429, 444, 456, 472; "Inv. de la corr. de Mgr Lartigue," 1941–42: 492; 1943–44: 306–7, 324–25. [L.-A. Huguet-Latour], *Annuaire de Ville-Marie, origine, utilité et progrès des institutions catholiques de Montréal* . . . (2v., Montréal, 1863–82). Chaussé, *Jean-Jacques Lartigue*. Lemieux, *L'établissement de la première prov. eccl.*

HUESTIS. *See* HEUSTIS

HUMBERT, STEPHEN, baker, merchant, politician, militia officer, office holder, Methodist lay leader, singing teacher, author, and musician; b. 1766 or 1767 in New Jersey, son of Stephen Humbert and Elizabeth —; m. first Martha —, and they had at least two sons and three daughters; m. secondly 25 Oct. 1818, in Boston, Mary Adams, *née* Wyer, and they had at least three daughters, one of whom died in infancy; d. 16 Jan. 1849 in Saint John, N.B.

Stephen Humbert spent the revolutionary years working in New York with his father, a baker, before his loyalist family immigrated to Parrtown (Saint John) in 1783. He continued working in his father's trade, but soon developed diverse commercial and personal interests. Humbert's business expanded to include shipping and general merchandising. He also built a book and music shop on the lower floor of his home, located on the South Market Wharf in Saint John.

Humbert sat as alderman on the Saint John Common Council for some years in the period 1812–22. He also served as a member of the New Brunswick House of Assembly for the city of Saint John from 1809 to 1820, when he was defeated in his bid for re-election by Hugh JOHNSTON. In that year he became preventive officer, charged with breaking up the illegal plaster of Paris trade between New Brunswick and the United States; his son John served as his deputy. Stephen had perhaps been prepared for the dangerous duties of this position by his service in the militia. He had been appointed a captain in the Saint John County regiment in 1805 and had served throughout the War of 1812 and beyond. Defeated when he again stood for the assembly in 1827, Humbert protested to the house, alleging undue election, but later withdrew his petition against the successful candidate, Robert Parker*. In the general election of 1830 he was returned for Saint John County and City, and he served to 1834, losing in the election that year. John Humbert sat in the house as member for Kings County from 1827 to 1834.

A Methodist, Stephen Humbert took an active part in the organization of the first Methodist society in Saint John, founded in 1791. By his own account he preached for several years as a lay leader in the Saint John chapel and periodically carried full responsibility for the congregation in the absence of an ordained minister. He worked closely with the Nova Scotian Methodist leader William Black*, with Abraham John Bishop, the first Methodist exhorter to be stationed in Saint John, and with James Man*, who served for a time on the Saint John circuit. Humbert's *Rise and progress of Methodism, in the province of New Brunswick*, printed in 1836 by Lewis W. Durant and Company of Saint John, describes the establishment of the Methodists there between 1791 and 1805. The book documents the turnover from North American to British Methodist authority and the tensions that accompanied this change. To his bitter dismay Humbert lost his leadership role in the Saint John chapel to Joshua MARSDEN, a missionary sent out to the Maritime colonies by the British Wesleyan Conference in 1800. For a time Humbert preached in nearby Carleton. About 1805, at the request of its members, he resumed preaching in the Saint John chapel, in the absence of Marsden's successor, William Bennett*, another British Methodist. Since his differences with the British Methodists could not be resolved, however, he eventually set himself up in opposition to the main chapel, conducting his services in a room that had been offered to him. When mediation by William Black failed, Humbert appears to have severed his connection with the Saint John chapel.

Humbert is perhaps best known as a singing-school leader, a composer, and the compiler of the first English tune-book published in Canada. In October 1796 he advertised the opening of a singing school in a large upper room on King Street. There he taught singing techniques and the rudiments of music theory, working primarily with a repertoire of sacred vocal music drawn from New England tune-books. Singing schools had been popular in the American colonies since the 1720s, providing recreation as well as instruction. Often conducted by itinerant singing masters, such schools would last from six to eight weeks, classes being held three evenings per week, and would conclude with a formal concert to display the participants' new vocal skills. Saint John was fortunate to have had a resident singing master.

To meet the needs of his singing-school classes Humbert compiled his own tune-book, which he had printed in New England in 1801. That November he advertised "THE *union, harmony, or British America's* SACRED VOCAL MUSIC" as ready for sale in Saint John, Fredericton, Annapolis Royal, and Halifax (where Thomas Daniel Cowdell* acted as his agent). The volume contained an introduction on the principles of vocal music and a collection of anthems, hymn tunes, and texts selected by Humbert from the New England tune-books available to him. According to his advertisements, the 1801 edition contained a number of original tunes by the compiler. The second edition, printed late in 1816 or early in 1817 by C. Norris and Company of Exeter, N.H., was "much improved and enlarged." It included a comprehensive "Introduction to the Grounds of Musick," with vocal exercises, borrowed verbatim from the 1817 edition of *The village harmony, or youth's assistant to sacred musick* . . . , a popular New Hampshire tune-book, as well as a large complement of British tunes and anthems and a number of original tunes. Some of Humbert's own works bore distinctive titles, such as "St. John," "Gagetown," "Sussex Vale," "Halifax," "Carleton Side," and "Frederickton." The texts were set in three or four parts with the tune placed in the tenor voice according to contemporary custom. *Union harmony* was intended for use primarily as a singing-school textbook, but Humbert ambitiously hoped that it might also serve as an anthem- and hymn-book. Indeed, he may have increased the number of British tunes in the second edition to make the work more suitable for use in British Methodist and Anglican church services. The volume was reissued with additional new materials in 1831 and 1840. Humbert appears to have continued conducting periodic singing schools in Saint John until at least 1840 when he founded a sacred music society.

Humbert's "Singing School" song describes a typical singing school of his day. Written in the fuguing style, a music idiom popular among North American composers in the 18th century, its staggered musical entries were designed to show off each vocal section of the newly trained choir.

'Tis pleasing to my pensive mind,
To recollect the hours,
When socially we all combin'd,
To exert our vocal powers.

Oft we beguil'd the winter eve,
Forgot the chilling storm,
The charms of music to receive,
The sacred notes perform.

MARGARET FILSHIE LEASK

No copy of the 1801 edition of Humbert's tune-book has been found. The second edition is entitled *Union harmony: or British America's sacred vocal musick, from the most approved English and American composers, with some original musick on special occasions, to which is prefixed a concise introduction* (Saint John, N.B., 1816). Information about its contents presented in this biography is based on Nicholas Temperley, "Stephen Humbert's *Union harmony*, 1816," *'Sing out the Glad News': hymn tunes in Canada*, ed. John Beckwith (Toronto, 1987), and on Temperley's hymn-tune indexing project at the Univ. of Ill. (Urbana-Champaign), in preparation. For the publication history of *Union harmony*, including locations of copies, see Barclay McMillan, "Tune-book imprints in Canada to 1867: a descriptive bibliography," Biblio. Soc. of Canada, *Papers* (Toronto), 16 (1977): 31–57. The full title of Humbert's history of Methodism in Saint John is *The rise and progress of Methodism, in the province of New Brunswick, from its commencement until about the year 1805* (Saint John, 1836).

National Gallery of Canada (Ottawa), J. R. Harper papers, J. R. Harper, "Spring tide: an enquiry into the lives, labours, loves and manners of early New Brunswickers." PANB, MC 1156, VII (copy at N.B. Museum). Saint John Regional Library, "Biographical data relating to New Brunswick families, especially of loyalist descent," comp. D. R. Jack (4v., typescript), 2: 129. *New-Brunswick Courier*, 20 Jan. 1849. *New-Brunswick Royal Gazette* (Saint John; Fredericton), 1 Sept., 3 Nov. 1801; 12 Oct. 1816. *St. John Gazette, and Weekly Advertiser* (Saint John), 4 Nov. 1796. *Encyclopedia Canadiana*. *Encyclopedia of music in Canada*, ed. Helmut Kallmann *et al.* (Toronto, 1981), 438, 837–38. W. G. MacFarlane, *New Brunswick bibliography: the books and writers of the province* (Saint John, 1895). *N.B. vital statistics* [1754–1852] (Johnson *et al.*). PANB, "A new calendar of the papers of the House of Assembly of New Brunswick," comp. R. P. Nason *et al.* (3v., typescript, Fredericton, 1975–77). Clifford Ford, *Canada's music: an historical survey* (Agincourt [Toronto], 1982), 29–30. Helmut Kallmann, *A history of music in Canada, 1534–1914* (Toronto and London, 1960). MacNutt, *New Brunswick*.

HUNT, JAMES, sail-maker, office holder, businessman, and politician; b. 9 Sept. 1779 in Dartmouth, England, son of Thomas Hunt; m. April 1817 Mary Sloat Garland, probably in Kingsbridge, Devon, and they had at least one son and two daughters; d. 1 April 1847 at Quebec.

James Hunt arrived at Quebec from Dartmouth in June 1803 and immediately set up as a sail-maker in a rented shop near the Landing Place, or Cul-de-Sac, in Lower Town. Since shipbuilding was only just becoming an important activity, he initially encountered little competition. In July 1804 he was appointed a constable for Lower Town, perhaps an indication that he was physically imposing. He was probably the "Mr Hunt" who provided sails for the naval sloop *Wolfe*, built at Kingston, Upper Canada, during the War of 1812. In 1815 he acquired a shop of his own at the Landing Place, and in 1818 he purchased a second, on Rue Saint-Pierre, and took four apprentices in "the Art and Mystery of a Sail Maker."

Hunt was a "distant" relative of the second partner in Newman, Hunt and Company of London, the cornerstone of a remarkably old and established complex of firms of Dartmouth origin. It operated in England, Ireland, Portugal, Spain, North and South America, and eastern Africa, and was particularly important in the Newfoundland trade. Judging Hunt to be "a very respectable character," Newman, Hunt decided about 1820 to employ him on "all occasions" that business took them to Quebec. Having previously viewed the Quebec wine trade as too competitive, the firm now began to ship its well-known port to him annually. The partners initially complained that their middle-aged novice misunderstood or "passed by our instructions as though they had not existed" and that he did not have the "mode of doing business . . . Customary with regular Mercantile Houses," but Hunt proved adaptable, and Newman, Hunt's port was soon standard in the messes of the big Quebec garrison. Often on Hunt's advice, Newman, Hunt gradually added to its shipments Mediterranean products, Madeira and cognac, Caribbean rum, molasses and sugar, Newcastle coal, and Swedish iron, as well as copper and lead. In return Hunt exported lumber products and provisions, especially flour and "Canada Pork," but at little profit to Newman, Hunt; Lower Canadian shingles were "not liked" by the firm's Newfoundland branch, the unseasoned staves were considered "very Sappy" compared to the American product for the casks of its Oporto operation in Portugal, and the flour was sometimes "sour" and sold "very badly."

Hunt seems to have received and sold shipments, at least until 1835, at Rayner's Wharf near Rue du Cul-de-Sac. In 1826 he purchased dock facilities on the Rivière Saint-Charles off Rue Saint-Paul, but he rented them out. In 1837–38 he acquired Hunt's Wharf, formerly owned by his brother Thomas (after whom it was probably named), a leading Quebec architect and builder. Considered the third most valuable wharf in town, its "several spacious Warehouses" and counting-houses were leased to substantial merchants and to the St Lawrence Steamboat Company. Hunt's shops and wharfs formed the nuclei of concentrations of property he acquired gradually. In the 1820s he bought several lots, often adjoining, on Rue du Cul-de-Sac, Rue Saint-Pierre, and Rue Sous-le-Fort, and others on Rue Saint-Paul (owned jointly with William Henderson, a pioneer in insurance at Quebec), on Rue du Sault-au-Matelot, and near the Marché Saint-Paul. Along with Hunt's Wharf he acquired a block of properties stretching from it to Rue Saint-Pierre, another block in Upper Town facing the glacis of the Citadel, and "Competence Farm" on the Saint-Charles. He also became the owner of scattered lots in the *faubourgs* Saint-Jean and Saint-Roch and along the St Lawrence on Rue Champlain, as well as of a farm and sawmill in Stoneham Township, north of Quebec. A number of these properties, fitted up as shops, inns, or other commercial establishments, brought good rents. He also had several vaults, in which he and his lessees stored wines. His prominence as a businessman from the 1820s is reflected in his position as a director of the Quebec Fire Office, the Quebec Fire Assurance Company, and the Quebec Bank and as a stockholder in the City Bank (of Montreal), the Bank of British North America, the Welland Canal Company, the Company of Proprietors of the Chambly Canal, the Quebec and Halifax Steam Navigation Company, and other concerns. In 1840 he was appointed a city councillor.

Wealthy and healthy at 60, Hunt began to reduce his pace. In 1840 he gave to a long-time employee, William Hunt, half ownership and the management of his sail-making firm which, thenceforth as James Hunt and Company, continued to operate at the original two locations. Four years later he handed over the trading firm to a son-in-law, Weston Hunt, who moved its headquarters to Hunt's Wharf. After 40 years in the crowded, noisy Landing Place, James Hunt moved to the quiet and comfort of one of his houses opposite the Citadel, filling it with good furniture and many books; four vehicles occupied part of the stables. At his death in 1847 Hunt was still receiving rents from his properties, was owed £5,000 by his sail-making firm, and held debts totalling nearly £26,000 from leaders in many fields of business in the city, including William Price*, a timber merchant, John William Woolsey*, a businessman, and the hardware merchant François-Xavier Méthot*, as well as from John Saxton Campbell*, a former shipbuilder there. The Hunt family continued to prosper after James's death, and in the 1880s was reputed to be among Quebec's largest holders of real estate.

A. J. H. RICHARDSON

ANQ-Q, CE1-61, 3 avril 1847; CN1-16, 20 janv. 1815; CN1-49, 9 nov. 1818, 19 avril 1819, 7 mai 1840; CN1-67, 7 mai 1840; CN1-116, 30 mars 1821, 22 avril 1829; CN1-188, 19 févr. 1827; CN1-197, 27 oct. 1819; 1er juill., 20–21 nov. 1820; 1er févr., 20 mars, 1er août, 1er sept., 29 oct., 19 nov. 1821; 9 juill. 1822; 25 juin 1823; 20 janv., 1er juin 1825; 11 janv., 10 févr., 25 mars, 7 nov. 1826; 27 févr., 9 mars, 24 avril, 11 juill., 2 oct., 29 déc. 1827; 7 janv., 7 avril 1828; 2, 4 févr., 26 mai, 17 juin, 7 sept. 1829; 9 mars 1830; 13, 17 mai, 31 août 1831; 3, 24 sept., 31 oct., 13 déc. 1832; 9 mars 1833; 10 mars 1834; 17 janv., 22 mai, 22 août 1835; 25, 30 avril, 19, 21 mai 1838; 28 avril 1841; 24 mars, 30 avril, 5 juin, 12 juill., 13 août 1842; 31 oct. 1844; 28 févr., 12 mars, 22 déc. 1845; 18 févr., 31 juill. 1846; 28–29 janv., 11, 18–19 févr., 4 mars, 19 avril 1847. Hunt, Roope & Co. (London), Newman, Hunt & Co., records (mfm. at PAC). Mount Hermon Cemetery (Sillery, Que.), James Hunt's tombstone. PAC, MG 24, D48; National Map Coll., H2/340-Québec 1835, 1845; H3/340-Québec 1829, 1830; H3/350-Québec [1836]. "Les dénombrements de Québec" (Plessis), ANQ *Rapport*, 1948–49: 186. *Recensement de Québec, 1818* (Provost). *Quebec Gazette*, 16 June, 7 July 1803; 16 Aug. 1804; 15 June 1815; 31 Oct. 1816; 8 Jan. 1818; 18 Feb., 6 May, 14 June, 29 Nov. 1819; 24 Feb., 15, 22 June, 21 Aug. 1820; 25 Jan., 5 July, 15 Oct. 1821; 25 July, 24, 31 Oct. 1822; 9 June 1823; 16 Feb. 1824; 17 Feb., 17 March, 19 May, 13 Oct., 14 Nov. 1825; 16 March, 15 June 1826; 15 Feb., 16 Aug. 1827; 17 Jan., 17 April 1828; 17 Jan., 19 Feb., 14 May 1829; 17 June 1830; 20 Feb., 16 April, 14 Sept., 15 Oct. 1832; 13 Feb., 12 Aug., 14 Oct. 1833; 10 Jan., 19 March, 18 April, 13 June, 22 Oct. 1834; 13 March, 15 July, 12 Aug., 14 Sept. 1835; 17 Feb., 19 July 1836; 15 Feb., 17 April 1837; 23 June 1838; 17 April, 15 Sept. 1839. *Quebec Mercury*, 1 March 1831; 12 Feb., 1 March 1842. *Quebec almanac*, 1823: 117; 1828: 121–23; 1833: 147–48, 152, 154; 1838: 158, 160, 166; 1841: 41, 176. *Quebec directory*, 1844–45, 1847–48, 1852, 1857, 1860–61, 1865–68, 1877, 1887–88. Christina Cameron et Jean Trudel, *Québec au temps de James Patterson Cockburn* (Québec, 1976), 43, 53. *Quebec Morning Chronicle*, 22 Sept. 1882. F. C. Würtele, "The English cathedral of Quebec," Literary and Hist. Soc. of Quebec, *Trans.*, new ser., 20 (1891): 63–132.

HUNTER, CHARLES, lawyer and journalist; b. 4 Sept. 1808 at Quebec, son of Charles Hunter, a merchant-cooper, and Elizabeth Tough; d. 31 July 1839 in Rimouski, Lower Canada.

Charles Hunter articled at Quebec with Joseph-Rémi VALLIÈRES de Saint-Réal and Charles Panet and was called to the bar on 11 June 1833. On 4 June 1837 he went to a meeting held in the Marché Saint-Paul at Quebec to protest Lord John Russell's resolutions [*see* Denis-Benjamin Viger*]. At that gathering he spoke, along with such other Patriotes as Augustin-Norbert Morin*, Charles Drolet*, Louis-Théodore Besserer*, and Jean Blanchet*, in defence of the principles in the 92 Resolutions, which laid out the House of Assembly's main grievances and demands.

Hunter then joined his friend Robert-Shore-Milnes Bouchette* in founding the Patriote newspaper the *Liberal/Le Libéral*, which was first issued at Quebec on 17 June 1837. Bouchette was responsible for editing the French part and Hunter the English. The paper claimed it existed primarily to serve democracy. For the editors there was no contradiction between the extension of the elective principle and a healthy colonial administration. Free institutions should ensure the country's prosperity and thereby help increase the wealth of the British empire. Hyacinthe-Poirier Leblanc* de Marconnay, editor of *Le Populaire* (Montréal), accused the *Liberal* of being a branch of Montreal's *Vindicator and Canadian Advertiser*. Hunter and Bouchette rejected this charge, while admitting that they defended the same principles.

In August the *Liberal* expanded to four issues weekly, two in each language. But as the result of a blunder on Hunter's part the English edition ceased publication on 28 October. An article of his, published on Wednesday 18 October, drew down upon him the wrath of the curé of Notre-Dame in Quebec, Charles-François Baillargeon*, the following Sunday. Hunter had denounced the attitude taken by some of the clergy on political questions. He claimed that the judges, magistrates, and ecclesiastical hierarchy were convinced they had supreme authority in the province and that in exhorting the faithful not to concern themselves with the questions of the day the priests, Baillargeon among them, were encouraging the population to submit passively to the established authorities.

Hunter retracted his statements on 25 October, but unfortunately he could not make amends for his error. He declared that he had never intended to attack the doctrine of the Roman Catholic Church, whose great principles he acknowledged, Protestant though he was. Priests doubtless received their authority in religious matters from God, but as an enlightened man he insisted upon taking account of events, since failure to take a position in politics in that period of crisis was thoroughly undesirable. On 28 October the *Liberal* announced that it was going to stop publishing.

The days of the paper's French edition were also numbered. Although its directors and shareholders, among them Pierre CHASSEUR, Joseph Légaré*, and Morin, disowned Hunter's article, their political activities made them suspect. They were arrested at the beginning of November, and on the 14th were obliged to withdraw from the enterprise. The Comité Permanent de Québec, a body formed in September which Hunter had joined, attributed the persecution of the Patriotes to Robert Symes, deputy chief of the Quebec police. Political unrest had defeated *Le Libéral*, which ceased publication on 20 Nov. 1837.

Warrants of arrest had been issued against Bouchette and Hunter for high treason, but Hunter, who apparently was luckier than his associate, managed not to get caught in the period before an amnesty was declared. He was imprisoned in March 1839 on the suspicion of having helped the American Patriots Edward Alexander Theller* and William Wallin Dodge flee Quebec after their escape from the citadel in the autumn of 1838.

The official list of political prisoners that was sent to London on 23 April 1839 indicated that Charles Hunter's case was being studied, and mentioned that he had been joint editor with Bouchette of a seditious newspaper. He was released on 29 April without being formally charged. He did not enjoy his freedom for long, however. Having gone to Rimouski to argue a case, he caught a chill, apparently, and died there on 31 July.

GINETTE BERNATCHEZ

ANQ-Q, CE1-66, 25 sept. 1808. PAC, MG 30, D1, 16: 238–40. *Le Libéral* (Québec), 17 juin–20 nov. 1837. Fauteux, *Patriotes*, 271. P.-G. Roy, *Les avocats de la région de Québec*, 224; *Les petites choses de notre histoire* (7 sér., Lévis, Qué., 1919–44), 7: 216–17.

HUNTER, Sir MARTIN, army officer and colonial administrator; b. 7 Sept. 1757 in Medomsley, England, son of Cuthbert Hunter and Anne Nixon; m. 13 Sept. 1797 Jean Dickson, and they had seven sons and four daughters; d. 9 Dec. 1846 at Antons Hill, the Scottish estate inherited by his wife.

Martin Hunter received his early schooling at Allendale on his father's estate and in Newcastle upon Tyne. Commissioned an ensign in the 52nd Foot in 1771, he was sent to live with Lieutenant-General John Clavering in Hampshire, where he attended school at Bishop's Waltham. Two years later, small for his 16 years, he joined his regiment at Quebec and in 1774 went with it to Boston.

On 19 April 1775 Hunter was at Lexington when the firing began that precipitated war between the British and Americans. Few soldiers can have seen so much action over the next three years. On 17 June he was at Bunker Hill; not yet 18, he became a lieutenant on the following day. After the evacuation of Boston in March 1776, he spent some time in Halifax and then went to New York. Subsequently he served mainly with the light infantry. He was present on 27 Aug. 1776 when the Americans were driven from Brooklyn, and then took part in the attack on Fort Washington and the pursuit to the Delaware. The following year, on 11 September, he participated in the battle of Brandywine, Pa, and ten days thereafter was wounded in the side during a surprise bayonet attack on the Americans at Paoli. At Germantown in early October the light infantry suffered such severe losses that, a short time later, Hunter was promoted captain at the early age of 20. In the autumn of 1778, after the retreat from Philadelphia to New York, he returned to England. At that time the 52nd had been 16 years in North America and had lost more officers and men killed and wounded in the Revolutionary War than any other regiment in the army.

In 1783 Hunter left Britain for ten years' service in India. He participated in a number of engagements in the Mysore War, including the decisive night attack in February 1792 on Tipu Sahib's entrenched camp under the walls of Seringapatam, when he commanded the 52nd and was credited with keeping the commander-in-chief, Lord Cornwallis, from being taken prisoner. In one of the charges of the 52nd, he was severely wounded.

Hunter had already received his majority in the 91st Foot before this battle and after his return to England he was promoted lieutenant-colonel on 19 July 1794. He subsequently rose steadily through the ranks. Early in 1797, having transferred to the 60th Foot, he commanded a brigade at the capture of Trinidad and the siege of Puerto Rico. Shortly after his marriage in 1797 he joined the 48th Foot and went with it to Gibraltar. In 1800 he commanded that regiment at the siege of Malta. He was again in the West Indies in 1801 but returned to England early the following year when Martinique was restored to France by the Treaty of Amiens.

As a reward for his distinguished service, Hunter was chosen in June 1803 to be colonel of the New Brunswick Fencibles, one of four infantry regiments to be raised for service in North America, but not elsewhere. In respect of pay, clothing, arms, and accoutrements, these units were to be on the same footing as regiments of the line; a colonel who brought his regiment up to strength could expect the handsome emoluments received by commanders of regular regiments. Hunter arrived in New Brunswick in the autumn and immediately organized a vigorous recruiting campaign to attract scarce North American manpower. He was particularly successful in Lower Canada, which provided more men than the Maritime provinces did. Substantial numbers were also obtained in Scotland. In October 1805 the regiment, then nearly 600 strong, passed inspection and was placed on the establishment effective from 25 June. Five years later it was granted the status of a line regiment, becoming the 104th Foot. Under that name, after a famous winter march to Quebec, it would serve with distinction in Upper Canada in 1813 and 1814. Hunter remained the regiment's colonel until it was disbanded in May 1817, and its success was largely due to his equable personality, his initiative in attracting competent officers and obtaining men, and his devotion and common sense in handling day-to-day affairs.

Militarily, New Brunswick was a district in the Nova Scotian command, which in turn was a district in the North American command. As the senior active officer in the province, Hunter became commanding officer of the forces there on the departure of Lieutenant Governor Thomas Carleton* in October 1803, and also second in command of the Nova Scotia district. Promoted major-general in 1805, he took over the command in Halifax on the death of Lieutenant-General William Gardiner in 1806, and held it until the arrival of Sir George Prevost* two years later. The same year he again assumed command in Halifax, while Prevost was in the West Indies, returning to New Brunswick in April 1809. In August 1811 he was back in Halifax, Prevost having gone to Quebec as commander of the forces in North America. He remained there until Sir John Coape Sherbrooke* assumed the position of lieutenant governor and commander-in-chief of the Nova Scotia district on 16 October.

When, late in 1807, the attitude of the American government led the British to expect a declaration of war, a large part of the militia of Nova Scotia and New Brunswick was called out at Hunter's request. At the end of March 1808 he reported to the War Office that, according to the best information he could get, "war with Great Britain is predetermined by [Thomas] Jefferson and his party who are completely under French influence and only want a favorable opportunity to commence hostilities." He therefore felt obliged to keep the militia under arms until the arrival of Prevost with reinforcements in April brought an end to the emergency. In the summer Prevost issued instructions to Hunter "calculated to prevent any act which could carry the construction of hostility." In particular, care was to be taken not to interfere with the Americans in their possession of Moose Island in Passamaquoddy Bay, a convenient base for New England traders willing to defy their own government's ban on commerce with British possessions. Faced with the Napoleonic blockade Britain was in urgent need of the American products that could be re-exported from her colonies.

In civil affairs New Brunswick had been administered since 1803 by a succession of temporary appointees. The separation of the civil authority and the military command that had occurred on Lieutenant Governor Carleton's departure was, however, ended by an instruction issued on 28 Jan. 1808. Hunter, or in his absence the officer commanding the forces, was placed first on the list of councillors. He was sworn in as president of the Council on 24 May 1808, displacing Edward Winslow*, and from then until June 1812 he was lieutenant governor in all but name, except for the two interludes in Halifax. Although in 1811 the Council asked the colonial secretary to make Hunter lieutenant governor, he was denied the security and prestige of the office because of the British government's inability or unwillingness to provide a pension for Carleton, who retained the position until his death in 1817.

Hunter's political task was an easy one. By 1808 partisanship in the assembly created few difficulties. Sessions of the legislature dealt only with routine matters or with questions relating to defence. The one exception was an act of 1810 that extended voting rights to Roman Catholics by substituting a declaration of loyalty for the severely Protestant oath laid down in 1791. It is unlikely Hunter played any significant role in initiating the change, though he almost certainly gave it strong support, for in so far as he showed any party sympathies his inclination was whiggish.

When Hunter arrived in New Brunswick in 1803 the economy was in the doldrums. When he departed in 1812 it was flourishing, transformed by a series of measures adopted by the British government that led to a much more profitable fishery and to a revival of the building of ships for long-distance trade. However, the most fundamental change in the economy resulted from Britain's efforts to assure a supply of timber for the fleet and for the home market. A crisis had arisen in 1807 as a result of the American embargo and the virtual exclusion of British timber buyers from the Baltic following the treaty between France and Russia. To encourage colonial exports, duties were placed on Baltic timber that were to remain in force until two years after the war with France ended. British North American timber merchants were quick to respond to this golden opportunity. With its abundant rivers and convenient harbours, New Brunswick was able to increase its production rapidly and between 1807 and 1810 exports trebled. In 1810 Hunter found it necessary to make a strong representation to the Colonial Office on the need for more strict control of timber cutting, but it was several years before action was taken.

In the session of 1812 the assembly made £10,000 available to the government for the defence of the province. This gesture would seem to have been a mark of Hunter's popularity, since the annual revenue in 1811 had been only about half that amount. Hunter was not to have an opportunity to spend it, for on 15 June he was replaced by George Stracey Smyth*. His promotion to lieutenant-general on 1 January had given him a rank too high for his command, but he had no political friends in high places to find him another. Though he lived a further 34 years, he was employed only in honorary positions. He became a full general in 1825, and was awarded a GCH in 1832 and a GCMG in 1837.

In 1804 Mrs Hunter had joined her husband in Fredericton, then a village of about 120 houses. She was young, lively, intelligent, and happy, fond of dancing and parties but with a dignity and graciousness that was appreciated by those who valued decorum in the president's wife, the first lady of provincial society. As the seat of government and headquarters of the regiment, Fredericton took on the character of an English county town during the Hunter years, and members of the leading loyalist families, mixing in the company of British officers, had their gentility revitalized. Hunter himself was a handsome man, athletic both in build and in inclination. While in the Maritimes he made some remarkable journeys for a man his age, travelling overland from Halifax to Saint John on one occasion, to see for himself if the route was feasible in case troops had to be moved that way. He seems to have been successful in earning the approval of both superiors and subordinates, though Edward Winslow questioned his knowledge of civil matters, referring to him as "wonderfully out of his element in a Chancery Court, or Land Office." Seventeen years after his death an old friend wrote of him as "the most *un*selfish person I have ever known" and evoked "his high sense of honor, his scrupulous integrity . . . , his modesty which 'never boasted of itself', his habitual gentleness of manner, [and] his feeling kindness and consideration for all around him."

D. M. YOUNG

PAC, MG 30, D1, 16: 237–54. PANB, RG 1, RS330, A6a; RS333, A3–A5; RG 2, RS6, A. PRO, CO 188/15–18; CO 189/11; CO 324/67. UNBL, MG H11. *The journal of Gen. Sir Martin Hunter, G.C.M.G., C.H., and some letters of his wife, Lady Hunter . . .*, ed. Anne Hunter and Elizabeth Bell (Edinburgh, 1894; typescript at Saint John Regional Library, Saint John, N.B.). N.B., House of Assembly, *Journal*, 1808–12; Legislative Council, *Journal* [1786–1830], vol.1, 1808–12. *Winslow papers* (Raymond). *Royal Gazette* (Saint John), 1808–12. *DNB*. G.B., WO, *Army list*, 1771–1837. PANB, "A new calendar of the papers of the House of Assembly of New Brunswick," comp. R. P. Nason *et al.* (3v., typescript, Fredericton, 1975–77), 1. D. R. Facey-Crowther, "The New Brunswick militia: 1784–1871" (MA thesis, Univ. of N.B., Fredericton, 1965). Hannay, *Hist. of N.B.* Lawrence, *Judges of N.B.* (Stockton and Raymond). MacNutt, *New Brunswick*. W. A. Squires, *The 104th Regiment of Foot (the New Brunswick Regiment), 1803–1817* (Fredericton, 1962).

HUOT, HECTOR-SIMON, lawyer, politician, and office holder; b. 16 Jan. 1803 at Quebec, son of François Huot*, a merchant and politician, and Françoise Villers; d. there 25 June 1846.

After studying at the Petit Séminaire de Québec, Hector-Simon Huot articled with his brother-in-law, Louis Lagueux*, and was called to the bar on 2 May 1825. He then practised at Quebec, where he quickly made a name for himself as a lawyer. From 26 Oct. 1830 till 27 March 1838, along with François-Xavier Larue*, he represented Portneuf in the Lower Canadian House of Assembly. Huot came from the merchant class and was familiar with the thinking of the French *philosophes* (his library had some 70 works by Rousseau, Montesquieu, and Voltaire), and he soon joined the ranks of the moderate young Patriotes from the Quebec region. In 1830 Huot, along with Étienne Parent*, René-Édouard Caron*, Elzéar BÉDARD, and Jean-Baptiste Fréchette, raised the funds to relaunch *Le Canadien* in order to have a vehicle for the group's ideas. From 1831 to 1842 the editor was Parent, whose moderating influence encouraged the young assemblymen from the region to advocate non-violent action in the cause of constitutional reform. This attitude inevitably ran counter to the views of the radical wing from the Montreal district led by Louis-Joseph Papineau*. Like most of the members from Quebec, Huot signed the 92 Resolutions in 1834 [*see* Elzéar Bédard]. The rivalry between the two groups grew steadily, however. In 1835, therefore, when the possibility of sending an agent to England to defend the assembly's views was under consideration, the Quebec Patriotes hastily proposed Papineau so that they could take advantage of his absence. But on 9 April he wrote Huot a long letter declining this honour and display of confidence being shown him and pointing out the inexpediency of sending a delegation to London. From then on the split between the two camps seemed final. After the rebellion of 1837–38 Huot left politics but none the less continued to take an interest in public affairs. In 1840 he was active in the campaign against the planned union of Upper and Lower Canada.

Huot left his mark primarily in the field of education. In January 1831 the assembly set up a permanent committee of 11, Huot among them, to study the whole question. Huot was named its chairman in 1835, and on 25 Jan. 1836 he had the privilege of introducing the first bill to set up normal schools in Lower Canada. It was anticipated that five would be opened, three at Quebec, Montreal, and Trois-Rivières to be run by religious communities and the other two at Quebec and Montreal to be administered by laity. Huot was appointed secretary of the committee to establish the school run by laity at Quebec. It encountered a scarcity of resources and competent teachers as well as strong Protestant reaction against a predominance of Catholics in the administration, and the Quebec normal school apparently never opened. Huot also worked alongside Joseph-François PERRAULT as secretary of the Education Society of the District of Quebec. He was its president for a number of years, according to an obituary in the *Quebec Gazette* of 26 June 1846.

In June 1840 Huot also became secretary of the library of the Quebec bar. On 15 August he was elected to the municipal council of Quebec but upon being appointed registrar of Berthier County on 7 Jan. 1842 he resigned. On 14 Feb. 1843 he was hired by the office of the provincial secretary as clerk. He left this post in April of the following year to assume the duties of protonotary of the district of Quebec.

On 16 Feb. 1830, at Quebec, Hector-Simon Huot had married Josephte Clouet, daughter of a Beauport farmer. She was a cousin of Étienne Parent and a niece of Michel CLOUET. The Huots had one daughter. Mme Huot died at Quebec on 10 March 1846, just three months before her husband. Their remains lie in the crypt of Notre-Dame cathedral in Quebec.

CHRISTINE VEILLEUX

ANQ-Q, CE1-1, 16 janv. 1803, 16 févr. 1830, 30 juin 1846; CN1-147, 15 févr. 1830; CN1-197, 1er mai 1820; CN1-255, 4 juill. 1846; P1000-51-1006. ASQ, Fichier des anciens.

L.C., House of Assembly, *Journals*, 1831–36, 1844–46. L.-J. Papineau, "Lettre de L.-J. Papineau à Hector-S. Huot," *BRH*, 38 (1932): 282–93. *Quebec Gazette*, 4 Nov. 1830; 11 March, 26 June 1846. F.-J. Audet, "Commissions d'avocats," *BRH*, 39: 583. Beaulieu et Hamelin, *La presse québécoise*, vol.1. Desjardins, *Guide parl.*, 129, 151. "Protonotaires du district de Québec," *BRH*, 10 (1904): 117. P.-G. Roy, *Les avocats de la région de Québec*, 224. L.-P. Audet, *Le système scolaire*, vols.5–6. Buchanan, *Bench and bar of L.C.*, 102, 114. J.-C. Falardeau, *Étienne Parent, 1802–1874* (Montréal, 1975). J.-J. Jolois, *Joseph-François Perreault (1753–1844) et les origines de l'enseignement laïque au Bas-Canada* (Montréal, 1969). Labarrère-Paulé, *Les instituteurs laïques*. P.-G. Roy, *Toutes petites choses du Régime anglais* (2 sér., Québec, 1946). Benjamin Sulte, *Mélanges historiques . . .*, Gérard Malchelosse, édit. (21v., Montréal, 1918–34), 14. F.-J. Audet, "François Huot," *BRH*, 37 (1931): 695–702. Fernand Ouellet, "Papineau et la rivalité Québec–Montréal (1820–1840)," *RHAF*, 13 (1959–60): 311–27.

HUOT, MARIE-FRANÇOISE, named **Sainte-Gertrude**, sister of the Congregation of Notre-Dame, teacher, and superior of the community (superior general); b. 10 Oct. 1795 in L'Ange-Gardien, Lower Canada, daughter of Pierre-Michel Huot and Marie-Françoise Huot; d. 8 Nov. 1850 in Montreal.

Marie-Françoise Huot spent some time at the boarding-school run by the Congregation of Notre-Dame in Sainte-Famille on Île d'Orléans. In 1815, at the age of 19 years and 9 months, she entered the noviciate in Montreal. She took the habit on 26 June 1816, receiving the name Sainte-Gertrude, and then on 10 July 1817 made her vows. Subsequently she taught in various missions: Saint-Laurent on the island of Montreal, Saint-François (at Saint-François-Montmagny), Lower Town Quebec, Sainte-Marie-de-la-Nouvelle-Beauce (Sainte-Marie), Saint-Denis on the Richelieu, Terrebonne, and Berthier, as well as at the boarding-school of the mother house in Montreal. She was back in Lower Town when she was chosen to be assistant superior of the community in 1839. The next year she was elected superior, but only held the office for three years, being forced by illness to insist upon being relieved of it. She did, however, remain assistant to the superior, Marie-Catherine Huot*, named Sainte-Madeleine, until 1848. She then entered the infirmary, where she died of cancer two years later.

Sister Sainte-Gertrude's superiorship came at the time when Ignace Bourget* assumed authority as bishop of the diocese of Montreal. The Congregation of Notre-Dame was affected in both its internal life and its external development by the zeal and the authoritarian style of Bourget, who declared himself "the principal pastor in the community." On 30 April 1843, following a visitation during which he brought together all the sisters of the mother house and the missions, he issued a pastoral letter about their affairs. In it he dealt with many articles of the rule, from the religious training of novices to the wearing of "cotton and flannel bonnets, as well as linen ones," and the employment of "dark-coloured handkerchiefs if [the sisters] use tobacco."

Several amendments to the rule affected the teaching provided by the sisters. Bourget decreed, for example, that lay women teachers could be appointed to assist them in schools in the suburbs, especially for teaching English. He also ordered them to exchange their traditional method of instruction for that of the Frères de la Doctrine Chrétienne, and to admit into the missions as day pupils "young girls whose parents might be too poor to pay for their board at the convent." The sisters accepted such changes reluctantly, and Sister Sainte-Gertrude spoke for them to the bishop, who, fearing "the serious inconveniences that occur, in religious communities as elsewhere, when the authorities are turned with the wind like a weathercock," insisted on having the final word.

Under Sister Sainte-Gertrude's superiorship, the Congregation of Notre-Dame decided in 1841 to move its Quebec mission to a site near the church of Notre-Dame-des-Victoires in Saint-Roch parish, in accordance with a wish expressed by Bishop Joseph-Octave Plessis* before his death. The community also founded a convent in the parish of Saint-Joseph, at Les Cèdres, which became its fifteenth mission in the countryside, despite the fact that there were only about 80 sisters all told.

Until that time they had had establishments only in the dioceses of Quebec and Montreal, and in French-speaking environments, even though they gave a class in English for the boarders and day boarders in Montreal. Late in 1841, yielding to pressure from Rémi Gaulin*, bishop of Kingston, and Bourget, they founded their Kingston mission. Three of the sisters who had volunteered for it were chosen and approved by Bourget. In Montreal the *Mélanges religieux* of 3 December commented upon the Kingston foundation: "It is time for the daughters of the admirable Marguerite [Bourgeoys*, named du Saint-Sacrement], to go and carry the spirit and the virtues of their founder elsewhere." It was the Congregation of Notre-Dame's first mission in the modern sense of the term. Speaking about it the sisters admitted "that on seeing their premises . . . they began to envy Mother Bourgeoys's stable." On 9 Jan. 1842 Abbé Jean-Charles Prince* wrote to the superior, "The work of founding your institute in Kingston seems to me important enough to be of interest later for the ecclesiastical and religious history of Canada." While the boarding- and day-schools were being organized in Kingston, the sisters had agreed to set up a mission at Red River (Man.), where in Bishop Joseph-Norbert Provencher*'s view the Hudson's Bay Company wanted Canadian priests and nuns rather than French missionaries. But the bishop of Quebec had already made arrangements with the Sisters of Charity of the Hôpital Général of Montreal [*see* Marie-Louise Valade*, named Mother Valade], and the Congregation of Notre-Dame "received a polite refusal until further notice."

The life of the Congregation of Notre-Dame under Sister Sainte-Gertrude makes patent the community's subordination to ecclesiastical authority. It thus contradicts the school of historiography which contends that the nuns were self-governing women and "the first feminists" in Canadian and Quebec history. Having taken the vow to renounce personal independence, these women showed no desire for collective independence. By conviction and by obedience they were clearly submissive to the hierarchical church.

ANDRÉE DÉSILETS

ACAM, RLB, IV–VI. ANQ-Q, CE1-3, 11 oct. 1795. Arch. de la Congrégation de Notre-Dame (Montréal), Reg. des baptêmes et sépultures. [D.-A. Lemire-Marsolais, dite Sainte-Henriette, et] Thérèse Lambert, dite Sainte-Marie-Médiatrice, *Histoire de la Congrégation de Notre-Dame* (11v. en 13 parus, Montréal, 1941–), 8: 177; 9: 234–41. Pouliot, *Mgr Bourget et son temps*, vol.3.

I

INGLIS, JOHN, Church of England bishop; b. 9 Dec. 1777 in New York City, son of the Reverend Charles Inglis* and Margaret Crooke; m. 31 Aug. 1802 Elizabeth Cochran (Cochrane) in Windsor, N.S., and they had eight children; d. 27 Oct. 1850 in London.

After the British evacuation of New York in 1783, John Inglis accompanied his father and two sisters to England. He returned to North America in 1787, on Charles Inglis's appointment as the first bishop of Nova Scotia. An only son, Inglis enjoyed the doting attention of his widowed father, who always entertained nepotic ambitions for him. He received his education in Windsor: he was the first registrant at the academy established there in 1788 [*see* William Cochran*] and subsequently studied for five and a half years at King's College, where he pursued "with distinguished success, a course of liberal instruction, as well in Classical learning, as in Philosophy, both Natural and Moral." In 1798 he became his father's private secretary and two years later made his first extended trip to England. He was especially charged with purchasing books for King's College library and furthering his father's plans for securing financial support for new missions. He also sought to improve his own prospects through contacts with bishops and aristocrats. The archbishop of Canterbury was sufficiently impressed to recommend him for an Oxford MA in 1801.

On his return John was ordained by his father as deacon on 13 Dec. 1801 and priest on 27 June 1802. He was appointed missionary to Aylesford, formerly part of John Wiswall*'s mission, which was near Clermont, the Inglises' Annapolis valley estate. At the same time the bishop arranged for John's appointment as his official secretary and as his ecclesiastical commissary, a modest equivalent to an archdeacon. He continued in these offices until 1816, returning to England in 1806–7, 1812–13, and 1816 on behalf of the colonial church and his own career. His talents were widely acknowledged but his lack of seniority, to say nothing of his familial relationship to the bishop, spoiled his chances of becoming suffragan in 1812 when his father was largely incapacitated by a stroke, and bishop in 1816 on his father's death. Instead he succeeded to the rectorship of St Paul's Church, Halifax, on Robert Stanser*'s elevation to the bishopric. There he acquired a reputation as a devoted pastor and captivating preacher. He was known to all social classes, being a faithful visitor to the poor of the parish and an erudite chaplain to the House of Assembly.

As "confidential adviser" of his father and "efficient substitute" for Stanser, who returned permanently to England in late 1817, Inglis supervised the diocese during the quarter-century preceding his own installation as third bishop in 1825. One of his main preoccupations was King's College. Shortly after his first journey to England on behalf of the college in 1800, the institution was chartered and endowed. Although Inglis agreed with his father that the college's principal function was that of a theological seminary, one of the objects of his visit to England in 1806–7 was to promote a revision of the statutes in order to open it to non-Anglicans. He was successful: the statutes were amended so that subscription to the Thirty-nine Articles was made a condition for the award of degrees but not for entry to the college. He also persuaded the Society for the Propagation of the Gospel to establish scholarships at King's for the sons of missionaries.

The financial and administrative misfortunes of the college during the 1810s became a cause of great concern to Inglis. At the same time the church's monopoly of higher education seemed to be threatened by the Presbyterians' fledgling Pictou Academy [*see* Thomas MCCULLOCH] and by what Inglis called the "quite needless and romantic" interdenominational college in Halifax conceived by Lieutenant Governor Lord Dalhousie [Ramsay]. After his appointment to the board of governors of King's in 1821, Inglis was charged with another major campaign for scholarships, chairs, and capital costs – "a begging scheme," according to Lieutenant Governor Sir James Kempt* – which he conducted by circular letter in England. Its failure led to the first of many attempts to unite King's and Dalhousie College. Inglis supported the union but it failed to impress the archbishop of Canterbury, who as patron had the final word on any matter relating to King's.

While Inglis was campaigning for King's, the students, including those destined for the church, were being educated in what one observer described as a "nursery of Fanaticism." Evangelical and Calvinistic influences within the church generally were to plague Inglis's whole career. Both Calvinism and tractarianism in moderation were acceptable to him as a churchman; his objections were more political than doctrinal. He believed that if the church was to retain its pre-eminent position in the diocese in terms of rights and privileges, it must present a united front to its critics. There was no room for party within it, since, as he frequently claimed, "if our little number is divided our usefulness will be woefully abridged." He also maintained that "a good son or daughter of the Church will readily obey every direction which has been enjoined by her authority," whether or not "there was sufficient reason for such direction." Distrustful of his own judgement, as he confessed in 1830, he found it easy to determine the official church line: what the English bishops collectively approved or disapproved became his standard too. As a result, he viewed suspiciously the evangelical societies associated with Exeter Hall in London. When the English hierarchy condemned the non-sectarian schools of the British and Foreign School Society and promoted instead schools organized by the National Society for the Education of the Poor in the Principles of the Established Church, Inglis responded by introducing a National school into St Paul's parish in 1816 to compete with the Royal Acadian school, founded three years earlier by Walter Bromley. Inglis's refusal to cooperate with other Protestants, to say nothing of his failure to work with more broadminded churchmen in educational and charitable enterprises, created an unfavourable public impression at the very time that Anglican privileges were beginning to arouse resentment among rival denominations and leading colonial reformers. Undaunted, Inglis also openly opposed the British and Foreign Bible Society as a competitor of the Society for Promoting Christian Knowledge. He fostered local committees of the SPCK in order to counteract the impact of the Bible Society's literature.

His exclusivist position alienated those Anglican colleagues who were low church and to some extent ecumenically inclined, especially those who had been exposed to evangelical influences during their clerical training at King's. Before 1825, however, the greater danger to the church seemed to come from without rather than from within. As he would do for the best part of 50 years, Inglis fought a rearguard action to preserve the privileges of the minority church establishment from the "tyranny of majorities." At stake was the church's monopoly of certain civil rights and state funds available for religious and educational purposes.

In the area of civil rights, one of the most hotly contested issues was the Church of England's claim to have an exclusive right to marry by licence. Inglis rejected any compromise. When St Matthew's Church in Halifax requested the right for its clergyman, he allowed that this was an exceptional case because St Matthew's belonged to the respectable, government-supported Church of Scotland. But "if the well marked line between the Established Church and any one body of Dissenters is once transgressed, it will be utterly impossible to find another equally plain between that one description of Dissenters and *all the rest*." In 1819 the tory government in Britain agreed with Inglis and disallowed the colonial legislation which would have given dissenting clergymen the right to perform marriages by licence between members of their own congregations according to their own rites. Only in 1832 was the matter resolved in their favour.

Inglis also opposed Roman Catholic emancipation from civil disabilities. In the celebrated case of Laurence Kavanagh* in 1822, he objected to the admission of a Roman Catholic to the assembly because of what he considered the unenlightened, illiberal principles of Catholicism. Like most Protestants of his day, he thought Catholicism regressive, complaining that "we have daily experience of the support of the most extravagant and preposterous doctrines of Popery among us, by fictitious miracles, which are as boldly asserted and as readily believed as in the darkest ages." Towards the end of his life Inglis looked askance when St Mary's College was launched in 1841 and a local Catholic hierarchy was recognized by government in 1849.

As an establishmentarian he even fought against the legal incorporation of dissenting and Catholic congregations, something which other churchmen, including his brother-in-law, Brenton Halliburton*, a member of the Council, were prepared to facilitate. As for the church's financial privileges, Inglis sought to prevent non-Anglicans being accorded a right to share in the proceeds from glebe and school lands which had been reserved on the creation of the townships and augmented in 1813 by the addition of dean and chapter lands for the support of the bishop. As an estate-owner in the Annapolis valley, he knew enough about land values to appreciate that the revenue from the grants was prospective rather than immediate. He therefore felt that they must be preserved intact for the future funding of the church. In the period before reformers insisted on the assembly's right to control crown lands, Inglis suggested that disguising church land as crown land might protect the church from the opprobrium of dissenters until there was enough income to excite public concern. With regard to the even more contentious issue of school lands, a test case occurred at Newport in 1821 when the school trustees, who had been accustomed to divide the proceeds among all the schoolteachers in the township, were requested to give them exclusively to the newly appointed SPG teacher. This matter remained unresolved for six years, by which time dissenters' rights were accorded some small recognition, through continued representation on the board of trustees, in what was otherwise an Anglican victory.

Despite his unflinching establishmentarianism, Inglis commanded wide respect during his years as rector of St Paul's. All that changed in 1825; the popularity he had built up within the church evaporated when he was elevated to the bishopric of Nova Scotia on Stanser's retirement. Having secured his succession in England in 1824, which was formalized by a consecration on 27 March 1825, he arranged for his replacement at St Paul's. Without consulting the congregation, who had always claimed the right to choose their own rector, he recommended to the crown the transfer of Robert Willis* from Saint John to Halifax, ostensibly on the ground that he was the most senior clergyman in the diocese. Inglis quite deliberately overlooked his own curate, the evangelically minded John Thomas Twining*, who emerged as the people's choice. As a result, Willis was locked out of the church and a large portion of the congregation seceded, first under Twining's tutelage but ultimately to gravitate to St George's Church, the Anglican alternative in Halifax, the Baptist church of the Reverend John BURTON, or the Methodist church. Chancery proceedings instituted to regain episcopal control of St Paul's Church were abandoned only after Inglis arrived back in the diocese on 8 Nov. 1825. Twining was blacklisted and prevented from obtaining any further position for which the bishop's recommendation was necessary.

Inglis assumed the supervision of a diocese which included Nova Scotia, New Brunswick, Prince Edward Island, Newfoundland, and Bermuda. Within five years, during which he made regular episcopal tours, he realized that the task was beyond the capabilities of one man. Though aided by four archdeacons – Willis in Nova Scotia and Prince Edward Island, George Best* in New Brunswick, George Coster* in Newfoundland, and Aubrey George Spencer* in Bermuda – he worked for the subdivision of the diocese. This was achieved with the appointment of Spencer as bishop of Newfoundland and Bermuda in 1839 and John Medley* as bishop of Fredericton in 1845. Louis Charles Jenkins was appointed ecclesiastical commissary for Prince Edward Island in 1842.

Inglis's frequent visitation tours, which occupied most of the summer and autumn each year he was in Nova Scotia (he was in Britain in 1831 and again in 1837–40), were designed to inspire colonial churchmen, confirm adherents, consecrate churches and cemeteries, ordain clergy, and keep an eye on missionaries and teachers. He was also appointed to the council in each jurisdiction and was assiduous about consulting with the governors and leading citizens. No part of the diocese was neglected though he considered his two lengthy episcopal tours in Newfoundland and three in Bermuda totally inadequate. He particularly prided himself on the number of first visits to new communities that he was able to include each year.

For a man who was much closer in temperament to an English aristocrat than to a colonial pioneer – he was described as "the most polished gentleman of his time" next to King George IV – the episcopal tours must have been a humbling experience. The visitations brought out an uncharacteristic degree of tolerance and flexibility in his nature. Appreciating the need for the church to accommodate itself to local customs and conditions, he condoned lay baptism and lay preaching in communities without clergymen. Moved by the mixture of poverty and industry, ignorance and piety he found in small communities and outports, he bent the rules to consecrate unfinished churches in missions where the people had done their best and he preached in the shells of buildings, in barns, in dissenting chapels, in schoolrooms, and on the decks of vessels.

What little Inglis was able to do to alleviate the spiritual and educational destitution he witnessed on his travels was hampered by diminishing financial resources and inadequate human resources. The colonial church entered its most severe crisis in the 1830s. The financial foundations began to crumble, not so much because of attacks by dissenters but because of the marked change in British colonial policy when the economy-minded and broad-church whigs came into office. Under threat of the withdrawal by 1835 of parliamentary aid to the church directly and, through the SPG, indirectly, Inglis succeeded in guaranteeing the salaries of those clergymen already employed but for the future he had to look to colonial sources to supplement and ultimately replace government grants and SPG donations. Yet funding by the SPG remained the major source of both salaries and grants for church building during his episcopate. Unable to rely on the local governments, and in any case suspicious of the dissenters therein, Inglis still despaired of the lack of productivity of a land endowment, though he devoted gallons of ink to the discussion of the Church of England's rights to glebe and school lands. Privately he advocated a general church tax, the proceeds of which might be allocated according to the denominational preferences of the taxpayers, but he knew that the only real option was voluntary contributions by the individual congregations. To this end, in 1836 the bishop proposed the establishment of the Diocesan Church Society, which soon spawned district branches throughout the diocese. The Church Society took over the SPCK's function of distributing religious literature, encouraged spiritual instruction in destitute communities through the appointment of visiting missionaries, contributed to the church-building funds of poor settlements, provided help to theological students, and worked for the maintenance of a church school in each mission.

Meanwhile King's College continued to be a source of worry to Inglis. The college had finally been opened, without restrictions, to dissenters in 1829 but a second attempt to unite it with Dalhousie had again been thwarted by the archbishop of Canterbury. Much to Inglis's chagrin, several of the *ex officio* positions on the board of governors of King's had by the 1830s gone to dissenters, and King's College, Fredericton, became a potential source of rivalry when it opened in 1829. With the proliferation of denominational colleges through the 1830s, Inglis decided in 1841 that "this playing at Universities is rather contemptible" and that the division of funds from the legislature into so many small portions was wasteful. At least one good result would accrue: "We shall be left in peace at Windsor." The peace lasted only a few years. By the mid 1840s the SPG had to cut back on salaries and support for King's College. Confronted with the additional likelihood of a reduced annual government grant to King's, the ailing Inglis sent one of his clergymen to England on the college's behalf in 1847 but it was an unsuccessful pilgrimage for funds.

In 1846, 26 of the 37 resident clergymen who congregated in Halifax for a visitation had been educated at King's, evidence of its critical role as the handmaid of the church. Despite the manifest shortage of clergy, Inglis would ordain only those approved by the SPG or graduates of King's College, and his refusal of men sent out from Britain by other Anglican societies exposed him to criticism. Although many of the missionaries saw long service, Inglis also had to deal with periodic thinning of their ranks through forced resignations on account of poor physical or mental health, intemperate habits, misdemeanours, or revelations of immorality such as fornication, homosexuality, and uncanonical marriages.

By the 1840s Inglis's failure to halt both the erosion of Anglican privileges and the general tendency among Protestants towards cooperation on a whole range of religious and moral issues refocused his attention on rifts within his own church. One such conflict occurred over the Colonial Church Society, the evangelical Anglican organization which was designed to provide missionaries, catechists, and teachers for destitute British immigrants and which favoured a broad, cooperative approach with non-Anglicans. Originating in Western Australia in 1835, this British society turned to the diocese of Nova Scotia in 1839 while Inglis was in England and in the following decade extended its aid to 30 communities in the province. Because the society was unsanctioned by the Anglican hierarchy and duplicated the work of the SPG, flagging though that had become, Inglis refused to approve it and indeed went out of his way to undermine its efforts, especially after he had failed in 1841 to bring it under local episcopal control. His principal objection to the CCS was its independence of the SPG but he also worried that it might undermine the local initiatives he was trying to foster through the Diocesan Church Society.

Inglis lost his battle against the CCS chiefly because it received the backing of prominent clerics and laymen. The leading supporter among the clergy was Robert Fitzgerald Uniacke*, rector of St George's, Halifax. He was joined by Twining, the perennial evangelical thorn in the bishop's side, William Cogswell, the curate at St Paul's, and Jenkins, the senior clergyman in Prince Edward Island. When John Medley became bishop of Fredericton in 1845, the CCS enjoyed his sympathetic cooperation. The lieutenant governors of the Maritime colonies also patronized it, leaving Inglis peculiarly isolated on this issue.

Preoccupied by diocesan matters Inglis kept his absences from home to a minimum and only his last visit to England, in 1850, was made on his own behalf. Nevertheless, given his metropolitan connections and social preferences it is fitting that Inglis should have died in England while seeking medical treatment. It is also fitting that his remains should have received a humble burial – he was interred in the family vault of Sir Rupert Dennis George, former provincial secretary of Nova Scotia, in St Mary's churchyard, Battersea (London) – because he, like his father before him, did not concern himself about such things as an impressive cathedral or expensive monuments. The Inglis family never returned to Nova Scotia except for the eldest, mentally unstable son, Charles, a physician. His will bequeathed the family estates to King's College and St Mary's Church, Aylesford, but it was successfully contested on the ground of his insanity.

The positive aspect of John Inglis's personal legacy was a greatly expanded church, adjusting itself to local circumstances and learning by necessity to rely on its own resources. Despite Inglis's exertions, however, it was a church much diminished in its official status and social influence. His death marked the disestablishment of the Church of England in Nova Scotia: his successor as bishop, Hibbert Binney*, received neither a British salary nor a seat on the Legislative Council, and King's College lost its preferential grant. The loss of Anglican privileges was attributable not only to the democratization of colonial institutions and the gradual withdrawal of British support, but also to the suspicion and hostility that Inglis had aroused both at home and in England. His refusal to promote interdenominational cooperation, his failure to heal the breaches within colonial Anglicanism, and his preference for a heavy-handed episcopal approach made him, in the end, something of an anachronism in colonial society of the liberal reform era.

JUDITH FINGARD

Two collections of John Inglis's papers have come down to us through his descendants. Microfilm copies of a collection which belonged to the late Sir John Inglis, a great-grandson of the bishop, are available in PANS, Biog., John Inglis letters, and in PAC, MG 23, C6, ser.4. A separate collection remains in the possession of Colonel John Inglis of Hope Bowdler, Eng., a great-great-grandson.

Inglis is the author of the following works: *A sermon preached in the parish church of St. Paul, at Halifax, on Sunday the 11th of June, 1815, after the funeral of Mrs. Mary Stanser . . .* (Halifax, 1815); *A charge delivered to the clergy of his diocese, by John . . . bishop of Nova Scotia, at Halifax, in August, 1830; at Bermudas, in May, 1830, and at Fredericton, New Brunswick, in August, 1831* (London, 1831); *A sermon preached in the cathedral church of St. Paul, on Thursday, June 11, MDCCCXXXI, at the yearly meeting of the children of the charity schools in and about the cities of London and Westminster* (n.p., n.d.); *Sermon preached in the parish church of St. Paul, at Halifax; on behalf of the Incorporated Society for the Propagation of the Gospel in Foreign Parts, on the 19th February, 1832 . . .* (Halifax, 1832); *The judgment seat of Christ; a sermon, preached on board his majesty's ship, "President," in the harbour of Halifax, on Sunday, the 1st of November, 1835 . . .* (Halifax, [1835?]); *Memoranda respecting King's College, at Windsor, in Nova Scotia . . . by one of the alumni* (Halifax, 1836); *The claim of the Society for the Propagation of the Gospel, upon all members of the church; a sermon* (London, 1840); *Journal of the visitation of the diocese of Nova Scotia, in New Brunswick, in the autumn of 1840, by the right rev. the lord bishop of Nova Scotia . . .* (London, 1841); *A journal of visitation in Nova Scotia, Cape Breton, and along the eastern shore of New Brunswick, by the lord bishop of Nova Scotia, in the summer and autumn of 1843* (3rd ed., London, 1846); and *A journal of visitation through the south-western portions of his diocese, by the lord bishop of Nova Scotia . . .* [1844–45] (2 pts., London, 1846–47).

NLS, Dept. of MSS, MSS 2265–505, 2568–608, 3022. PRO, CO 217/98–99, 217/102, 217/140–47, 217/151–55, 217/158–59, 217/161, 217/163, 217/165, 217/167–68, 217/171–73, 217/176, 217/178–81, 217/184–85, 217/194, 217/202; CO 218/30. RHL, USPG Arch., C/CAN/NS, 9–11; Dr Bray's Associates, minute-books, 1835–45; journal of SPG, 28–46. Univ. of King's College Library (Halifax), Univ. of King's College, Board of Governors, minutes and proc., 1787–1851; corr. relating to King's College. J. C. Cochran, *A sermon in reference to the death of the Right Rev. John Inglis, bishop of Nova Scotia* (Halifax, 1850). Colonial Church and School Soc., *Annual report* (London), 1841–51. Diocesan Church Soc. of N.S., Executive Committee, *Report* (Halifax), 1839–50; *Report of proc.* (Halifax), 1839–50. Halifax Assoc. in Aid of the Colonial Church Soc., *Annual report* (Halifax), 1848–51; *Formation and proceedings* (Halifax, 1847). *Christian Messenger*, 29 Nov. 1850. *Church Times* (Halifax), 1848–51. *Colonial Churchman* (Lunenburg, N.S.), 1836–40. *Morning News* (Saint John, N.B.), 15 Nov. 1850. Susan Buggey, "Churchmen and dissenters: religious toleration in Nova Scotia, 1758–1835" (MA thesis, Dalhousie Univ., Halifax, 1981). A. W. H. Eaton, *The Church of England in Nova Scotia and the tory clergy of the revolution* (New York, 1891); *The history of Kings County, Nova Scotia . . .* (Salem, Mass., 1910; repr. Belleville, Ont., 1972). Judith Fingard, "The Church of England in British North America, 1787–1825" (PHD thesis, Univ. of London, 1970). H. Y. Hind, *The University of King's College, Windsor, Nova Scotia, 1790–1890* (New York, 1890). C. H. Mockridge, *The bishops of the Church of England in Canada and Newfoundland . . .* (Toronto, 1896). H. A. Seegmiller, "The Colonial and Continental Church Society in eastern Canada" (DD thesis, prepared Windsor, N.S., 1966, for ACC, General Synod, Huron College, London, Ont., 1968). F. W. Vroom, *King's College: a chronicle, 1789–1939; collections and recollections* (Halifax, 1941). Peter Burroughs, "Lord Howick and colonial church establishment," *Journal of Ecclesiastical Hist.* (Cambridge, Eng.), 25 (1974): 381–405; "The search for economy: imperial administration of Nova Scotia," *CHR*, 49 (1968): 24–43.

IRWIN, THOMAS, teacher, surveyor, philologist, and author; d. 1847 near Naufrage, P.E.I.

It is not known when Thomas Irwin emigrated from his native Ireland to Prince Edward Island, or how he earned his living there before receiving licences to teach (1830) and to practise surveying (1835). He was an accomplished student of languages and at some point obtained a manuscript copy of a Micmac grammar prepared by Father Pierre Maillard* a century earlier. While learning their language Irwin came to identify with the plight of the Micmacs. Born a Catholic, he had grown up speaking Irish and was early forced to learn English, the language of the Protestant despoilers of his homeland. He saw the Micmacs as a people similarly oppressed, evicted from their lands and threatened with the loss of their identity. They were suffering what he had suffered, and he swore to devote his life to helping them.

Irwin first enters the historical record in 1829, at which point he was living at Rollo Bay. That year he sent a copy of "the principles of the Mickmack language," a work he had compiled, to the editor of the Halifax *Free Press* to print as space allowed. He also offered to publish a book in Micmac containing morning and evening devotions and a catechism. Nothing came of either project. The Micmacs, Irwin argued, were a superior people, for their language demonstrated mental faculties of the highest order. Capable of an almost infinite variety of expression, the language had "all the *mellifluous softness of the Italian – the solemn and majestic gravity of the Spanish, joined to the copiousness of both, and a more philosophical and beautiful construction than either*." By June 1830 a grammar he had prepared of the Micmac language was ready for the press. Consisting of nearly 300 pages, the work, Irwin announced, would be published and sold for a dollar a copy when sufficient subscribers were found.

Perhaps to encourage subscriptions, Irwin printed from June to December eight extracts of his grammar in James Douglas Haszard*'s *Prince Edward Island Register* and its successor, the *Royal Gazette*. There, and two years later in Joseph Howe*'s *Novascotian, or Colonial Herald*, he condemned the conduct of whites who, from Cape Horn to Greenland, branded natives as cruel and faithless even while stealing their lands and driving them to extinction. He called for the formation of "Philo-Indian societies" that would win the confidence of the local Indians and teach them how to farm. This appeal fell flat, as did his plans for the grammar. Despite strenuous efforts to promote the book, not enough subscribers came forward to make publication possible.

In April 1831 Irwin tried another tack. He petitioned the House of Assembly on behalf of the Indians, asking that they be given education and land where they could settle and learn agriculture; a committee was struck to consider ways of helping them. In the mean time, Irwin contested a by-election in Kings County that July but lost to William Cooper*. When the next session opened in January 1832 Louis Francis Algimou and four other chiefs presented a petition, drafted by Irwin, asking for land and "books to show our children good things." The assembly looked briefly at the possibility of buying land and voted £50 to the Board of Education to provide books of elementary instruction in the Micmac language. Irwin claimed to have just such a work "in process," based on a standard spelling book of the day but including some of the devotional texts that had been translated into Micmac by the Catholic missionaries of the previous century. Ignoring Irwin, the board announced that it could find no elementary book in the Micmac tongue and voted not to claim the grant. In 1834 he again stood for election in Kings County and was defeated.

In February 1840 Irwin made another approach to the assembly, petitioning to have his elementary textbook put into print. A committee considered his manuscript and expressed concern about its accuracy because there was no one qualified to assess it. It recommended instead that no more than £50 be placed at the disposal of the lieutenant governor, Sir Charles Augustus FitzRoy*, to pay schoolmasters to teach the Micmacs in English. Three years later Irwin tried for the last time, offering to donate a year of his time to instruct the Micmacs in their own tongue from his elementary school book, if the assembly would pay to print it. The whole assembly debated this petition on 20 March 1843 and the majority took the view that the Indians should learn English. However, since there were more Micmacs in Nova Scotia than in Prince Edward Island, the house offered to pay Irwin's expenses if he wanted to peddle his book in Halifax.

Irwin could no longer contain his anger and on 1 April 1843 published a furious letter in the *Colonial Herald, and Prince Edward Island Advertiser*. "This country is the rightful inheritance of the Indians; it has been wrested from them by the hand of power, and no equivalent has been given them." Now the "spirit of English domination" demanded that even their language be destroyed. The "domineering Saxons" had murdered "the Welsh bards," plundered "the records of Scotland," and had lately made an effort in Canada "to obliterate the French." Never, if he could help it, would the mellifluous language of the Micmacs be supplanted by the "mongrel medley" of the Saxons. He also took the House of Assembly's advice and wrote again to Joseph Howe for support. Now that he was Nova Scotia's commissioner of Indian affairs Howe too thought that the Micmacs should learn English, and the correspondence ceased in June 1843. There is no evidence that Irwin was aware of the work then being done for Indians in New Brunswick by Moses Henry Perley* or that he tried to enlist his support.

Irwin's career as a champion of the Micmacs was one of unrelieved failure. For almost 20 years he was the only white person in Prince Edward Island to demonstrate publicly any sympathy for the Indians. His Catholic religion ensured a partisan reception for any of his proposals, and the Catholic clergy failed to support him. Yet his enthusiasms were not entirely wasted. The Reverend Silas Tertius Rand*, a Baptist, arrived in Charlottetown in the summer of 1846 and went on to form the Micmac Missionary Society on the lines Irwin had once proposed. Rand also became a world-renowned authority on Micmac language and oral history, and he acknowledged that he owed his start to the fragmentary grammar Irwin had once published in the *Register* and in the *Royal Gazette*.

In 1830 Irwin had written in the *Royal Gazette*, "I

conclude I have 50 years yet to live (accidents by sea and land excepted)"; just such a mishap claimed him some 17 years later. He was last seen alive at Big Pond on 14 Feb. 1847 while on a journey eastwards along the shore from Naufrage. Nearly a month later his body was discovered on the sea ice some distance from the shore. An inquest established that he had strayed from the path, "and the weather being then very inclement, had perished from cold – Verdict accordingly." For at least the last ten years of his life he had resided at St Peters; he left no relatives on the Island.

L. F. S. UPTON

None of Thomas Irwin's manuscripts appear to have survived. Sixty-five manuscript pages of his elementary textbook and 124 pages of his grammar were auctioned in Paris in 1884 when the French scholar Alphonse-Louis Pinart sold the collection described in *Catalogue des livres rares et précieux, manuscrits et imprimés, principalement sur l'Amérique et sur les langues du monde entier* . . . (Paris, 1883); their present whereabouts are unknown.

PANS, RG 1, 432: 159–61, 178–79, 188–94, 216–21. P.E.I. Museum, File information concerning Thomas Irwin. Supreme Court of P.E.I. (Charlottetown), Estates Division, papers of administration for Thomas Irwin estate. P.E.I., House of Assembly, *Journal*, 8–9 April 1831; 4, 7 Jan. 1832; 19 Feb. 1840; 20 March 1843. *Colonial Herald, and Prince Edward Island Advertiser* (Charlottetown), 29 Feb., 11 April 1840; 18 Feb., 4, 25 March, 1 April 1843. *Islander*, 26 March 1847. *Novascotian, or Colonial Herald*, 29 Aug., 5 Sept. 1832. *Prince Edward Island Register*, 2 Feb., 27 April, 4–18 May, June, 13, 27 July, 3–17 Aug. 1830. *Royal Gazette* (Charlottetown), 24–31 Aug., 14, 28 Sept., October, 2 Nov., 7 Dec. 1830; 31 Jan., 7 Feb. 1832; 15 Oct. 1833; 25 Nov., 2, 23 Dec. 1834; 13 Jan., 24 Feb. 1835; 28 March, 4 April 1843; 23 March 1847. *P.E.I. calendar*, 1837–47. Upton, *Micmacs and colonists*. J. B. [James Bambrick], "Days of Bishop McEachern, 1790–1836," *Prince Edward Island Magazine* (Charlottetown), 3 (1901–2): 151. L. F. S. Upton, "Indians and Islanders: the Micmacs in colonial Prince Edward Island," *Acadiensis* (Fredericton), 6 (1976– 77), no.1: 21–42; "Thomas Irwin: champion of the Micmacs," *Island Magazine* (Charlottetown), no.3 (fall–winter 1977): 13–16.

J

JACKSON, JOHN MILLS, author, merchant, and JP; b. *c.* 1764 on St Christopher (Saint Kitts-Nevis), son of Josiah Jackson, a doctor, and Elizabeth Gerrald; m., with at least two sons and four daughters; d. 1836 in England.

After receiving a BA from Balliol College, Oxford, in 1783, John Mills Jackson resided on St Vincent, where he owned property. He claimed to have lost a "considerable" portion of it during the Carib uprising of 1795. Four years later he became aide-de-camp to the island's commander-in-chief. At some point thereafter he returned to England (possibly to Wiltshire), but he left in 1805 to visit Lower Canada. There he possessed, "by right of inheritance, a claim to a large and very valuable tract of land." He also had an interest in Upper Canada and, prior to leaving England, he purchased land there.

Jackson arrived at York (Toronto) in August 1806 and on 21 September he petitioned the Executive Council for land, intending to become "a permanent Settler." Surveyor General Charles Burton WYATT described him as "a gentleman of respectability." Jackson associated with Robert THORPE, Wyatt, Joseph Willcocks*, and William Weekes*, all of whom were now actively opposed to the province's executive. Their agitation reached a fever pitch during the campaign, beginning in October, that led up to the by-election in December to replace Weekes in the House of Assembly for the riding of Durham, York East, and Simcoe. Thorpe campaigned successfully for the seat and Jackson's support for him brought the Oxford graduate into the circle of opposition.

In one notable incident, on 27 November during a dinner at Jackson's home, liquor had flowed and convivial talk had turned to politics. Willcocks blasted Lieutenant Governor Francis Gore* and when others objected, Jackson, certain guests alleged, labelled the lieutenant governor a "damned Rascal" surrounded by "that damned Scotch faction" – an allusion to advisers such as John McGill* and Thomas Scott*. Jackson went so far as to say that the Executive Council and Gore's predecessor, Peter Hunter*, "had plundered the Country." A few outraged guests left to Jackson's parting shot, "Damn the Governor and the Government: push about the bottle." In the event, depositions detailing what was described as seditious talk were taken and sent to Gore, who was capable of punitive action. Thorpe and Wyatt were eventually suspended from office while Willcocks was dismissed. But Jackson's case was different. He was too well connectted – his younger brother was a British MP. Solicitor General D'Arcy Boulton* considered Jackson liable for prosecution but, since Jackson was about to return to England, Gore directed him to forget the matter.

By early summer 1807 Jackson was back in England and on 5 September he wrote to Colonial Secretary Lord Castlereagh "relating a few of those grievances" which he had found in Upper Canada. Gore had feared such an eventuality and later explained to his superiors that Jackson's "hostility . . . arose from his being refused a quantity of Land, on account of his improper conduct." In fact, it had been on 24 Jan. 1807, four months after Jackson's application, that Gore first notified the colonial secretary that Jackson might apply for land. When Jackson left, the council rejected his petition because he was absent from the province.

Jackson's letter to Castlereagh was a dress rehearsal for a more extended treatment. His pamphlet, *A view of the political situation of the province of Upper Canada*, published in London in 1809, explained how the most "loyal, attached, and determined people" had become so "aggrieved, enslaved, and irritated" that they were on the verge of revolt. He catalogued "impolitic and tyrannical proceedings" and, citing as an example the extravagant sums spent on Alexander Grant*'s useless Provincial Marine, pointed to the "ruinous expenditure and mismanagement of the public money" that had characterized Upper Canadian government since Hunter. The grievances of the Six Nations Indians [*see* Thayendanegea*] and of military and loyalist claimants for free land were trotted out as examples of the frustration of imperial policy by local officialdom. The administration of justice was singled out for partiality. Finally, Thorpe, Wyatt, and Willcocks were identified as upholders of the constitution and martyrs in the cause of liberty. Yet there was nothing radical about Jackson's tract; rather it was an appeal to imperial authorities to right colonial wrongs lest Great Britain's ability to withstand Napoleonic despotism be hobbled.

In England the pamphlet stirred not the slightest fuss. The Earl of Moira recommended it to the Prince Regent as "really an interesting work." But in Upper Canada conventional counter-revolutionary minds understood Jackson's opposition to the executive as insurrectionary. The reaction of William Dummer Powell* was typical: the pamphlet was the work of a man with only passing acquaintance of the colony, whose "Channel of Information was a wretched faction of disappointed Mal contents." Gore, who thought Thorpe to be the real author, refuted it point by point in a letter to his superiors. A public response came in 1810 from Richard Cartwright* of Kingston, whose *Letters, from an American loyalist* was predictable in its condemnation. In an episode later seized upon by William Lyon Mackenzie*, Crowell Willson and James McNabb* brought before the assembly in March 1810 a motion condemning Jackson's screed as "a false, scandalous and seditious libel . . . tending to alienate the affections of the people . . . and to excite them to insurrection." The resolution passed, as did an address approving Gore's administration and damning Jackson's work, against the opposition of John Willson*, Willcocks, David McGregor Rogers*, and Peter HOWARD. Nothing, however, came of such denunciations.

Jackson returned to the province about May 1810 and by 30 May 1811 he had opened a general store at Springfield Park, his estate three miles north of York on Yonge Street. His sons later joined him in the business. There had been rumours late in 1811 of his intention to run in the next general election. In 1816 he stood, unsuccessfully, for the riding of York East. The following year he sold the business, or his share of it at least. Anxious to relocate within the province, Jackson petitioned the council without success for a grant in late 1818. The council referred the matter to Sir Peregrine Maitland* on the ground that Jackson had "associated and identified himself with a faction . . . whose conduct led to their suspension and removal from Office." Jackson had, in fact, continued to associate with Gore's adversaries, underwriting the cost of Thorpe's libel case against Gore in 1817–18. The petition was referred to the colonial secretary, who agreed not to interfere on Jackson's behalf. Jackson was outraged and took the opportunity to vindicate his supposedly notorious actions. In a letter to Major George HILLIER on 29 Dec. 1818 he denied the existence of a faction and outlined "the Violence" of Gore's conduct, which had resulted in two successful libel suits (Thorpe's and Wyatt's) against the former lieutenant governor. He was merely a legitimate claimant for land whose "aim was peaceably to induce His Majesty's ministers to investigate, and rectify those discontents then existing . . . and which I am confident will cease under the prudent and wise Government of Sir Peregrine Maitland."

Jackson had never been a radical and subsequent events reveal his political opinions to have been as respectable as he was. In 1828, having sold his Springfield Park estate and some other lands in 1819, he bought property and settled in Georgina Township on Lake Simcoe where a daughter and her husband already lived. All his daughters married well. One had wed a nephew of the Earl of Westmorland, another married Augustus Warren Baldwin*. Jackson, who was a shareholder in the steamer *Simcoe*, built at Holland Landing, signed the usual sort of loyal addresses, including one in 1832 which condemned "the attempts of turbulent, disaffected, and interested individuals" to attack Sir John Colborne*'s administration. He also was one of the seven members of the Georgina Club, the intent of which was expressed in the couplet: "For in this Club each member tries / To d—n McKenzie, and his Lies." Small wonder he was made a justice of the peace in 1833. Two years later he was urging Anglican authorities to erect a church in Georgina because Sundays had become "a holiday in which an opportunity is taken to commit much excess of debauchery amongst the low classes of Society." Jackson died in 1836 while on a trip to England.

What has been designated as radicalism in Jackson was really best interpreted by Robert Gourlay* when he wrote of the oppositionists of the first Gore administration: there was "never any disagreement about the principles of government. The sole cause of discontent arose from the abuses of executive power." Within the spectrum of 18th-century politics, Jackson's opinions were both whig and traditional.

ROBERT L. FRASER

[Neither the Wiltshire indexes to wills, 1830–50, nor the indexes to English wills, 1837–46, provide any information about the date and place of Jackson's death, the only source for which is *Robertson's landmarks of Toronto*, 2: 705–6. R.L.F.]

The full title of John Mills Jackson's pamphlet, issued at London in 1809, is *A view of the political situation of the province of Upper Canada, in North America; in which her physical capacity is stated; the means of diminishing her burden, encreasing her value, and securing her connection to Great Britain, are fully considered.*

AO, MS 88; MS 537; MU 1365, Lake Simcoe South Shore Hist. Soc., "Georgina, history of a township" (portfolio of loose printed sheets, n.p., 1972); RG 22, ser.131. MTRL, James Givins papers; W. D. Powell papers. PAC, RG 1, L3; RG 5, A1; RG 68, General index, 1651–1841. PRO, CO 42/362; 42/365. York North Land Registry Office (Newmarket, Ont.), Abstract index to deeds, Georgina Township (mfm. at AO). *The correspondence of George, Prince of Wales, 1770–1812*, ed. Arthur Aspinall (8v., London, 1963–71), 6: 399, 409. "Journals of Legislative Assembly of U.C.," AO *Report*, 1911. "Minutes of the Court of General Quarter Sessions of the Peace for the Home District, 13th March, 1800, to 28th December, 1811," AO *Report*, 1932. *Statistical account of U.C.* (Gourlay), vol.2. *Town of York, 1793–1815* (Firth). *York, Upper Canada: minutes of town meetings and lists of inhabitants, 1797–1823*, ed. Christine Mosser (Toronto, 1984). *Canadian Freeman*, 1832–34. *Gleaner, and Niagara Newspaper*, 1819. *Upper Canada Gazette*, 1817–19. *York Gazette*, 1811. *Alumni Oxonienses; the members of the University of Oxford, 1715–1886 . . .* , comp. Joseph Foster (4v., Oxford and London, 1888), 2: 736. Creighton, *Empire of St. Lawrence*. Gates, *Land policies of U.C.* J. E. Middleton and Fred Landon, *The province of Ontario: a history, 1615–1927* (5v., Toronto, [1927–28]), 1: 148–52. Scadding, *Toronto of old* (Armstrong; 1966). W. N. T. Wylie, "Instruments of commerce and authority: the civil courts in Upper Canada, 1789–1812," *Essays in the history of Canadian law*, ed. D. H. Flaherty (2v., Toronto, 1981–83), 2: 3–48. G. C. Patterson, "Land settlement in Upper Canada, 1783–1840," AO *Report*, 1920. W. R. Riddell, "The legislature of Upper Canada and contempt: drastic methods of early provincial parliaments with critics," *OH*, 22 (1925): 186–201.

JACKSON, RICHARD. *See* RICHARDS, JACKSON JOHN

JACKSON, Sir RICHARD DOWNES, army officer and colonial administrator; b. 1777, probably in Petersfield, England, son of Christopher Jackson; d. 9 June 1845 in Montreal.

Richard Downes Jackson entered the British army on 9 July 1794 as an ensign in the Coldstream Foot Guards. He served in Ireland during the rebellion of 1798, in Germany in 1798 and 1805, and at the assault on Copenhagen in 1807. In March 1810 he joined the army of Arthur Wellesley, later Duke of Wellington, at the siege of Cadiz and at Barrosa, where he fought with distinction. He remained in the Iberian peninsula as assistant quartermaster general from 1811 to 1814, was promoted colonel in 1814, and was knighted on 12 April 1815.

Jackson was appointed colonel of the Royal Staff Corps and deputy quartermaster general in 1820. A major-general by 1825, he became honorary colonel of the 81st Foot in 1829. His first major command was the northern military district of England during the 1830s. There, in the unruly period of anti-poor-law agitation and Chartism, his qualities of balanced judgement and common sense won wide respect. Worried by the inadequacy of the resources at his disposal, he emphasized the importance of good organization and quick movement of troops to meet the threat of civil unrest. He became a lieutenant-general in June 1838.

The following year Jackson was appointed commander-in-chief of the forces in British North America to replace Sir John Colborne*. Although his nomination took effect on 16 Sept. 1839, he reached Quebec only on 17 October, in the ship that also carried the new governor-in-chief, Charles Edward Poulett THOMSON. Within days of his arrival Jackson set out on an inspection of the Richelieu valley, a likely invasion route, and he immediately began to campaign for improved frontier defences. His initial appreciations, noting "the present unsettled state of our affairs" with a powerful and expansive United States, made a strong case for more men and better communications but laid greatest stress on fortifications – "bulwarks" against increased American power.

Jackson's requests, however, were modest and his bureaucratic victories were correspondingly small. Characteristically, he saw the other point of view and could sympathize with London's drive for economy. With the signature of the Webster–Ashburton Treaty in August 1842, Anglo-American tensions eased considerably. Jackson, who had seen regular army strength in British North America climb to over 12,000 men in early 1842, now acquiesced in substantial reductions to his forces.

There is no evidence that Jackson's concern for the frontier continued into his later years in the Canadas. The sending of his aide-de-camp and nephew by marriage, Henry James Warre, and Lieutenant Mervin Vavasour* to carry out reconnaissance in the Oregon country in 1845–46 was authorized by London. The initiative for the survey of the St Lawrence and the

Great Lakes in 1845 under Captain Edward Boxer* had also come from the home government, not Jackson.

In the Canadas memory of the rebellions of 1837–38 remained fresh, and fear of insurrection was still vivid. There were frequent requests for troops in aid of the civil power. Jackson voted in the elections for the Legislative Assembly in 1844, an exceptional action for a British commander in a colonial garrison, probably out of a desire to show solidarity with the voices of reason and loyalism.

Jackson served three stints as temporary head of government. In Thomson's absence, he was twice administrator of Lower Canada, from 18 Nov. 1839 to 19 Feb. 1840 and from 8 to 31 July 1840. Then, from 24 Sept. 1841, shortly after Thomson's death, until Sir Charles BAGOT assumed office on 12 Jan. 1842, he was administrator of the united province of Canada.

Charles Dickens was Jackson's guest in Montreal near the end of the celebrated author's first trip to North America in 1844. Dickens, a frustrated actor, presented an evening of theatricals to the garrison, rejoicing in the "iron despotism" with which he dominated the proceedings as both actor and stage manager. It was perhaps this behaviour that led him to conclude, as he left for home two months later, that "Sir Richard . . . has blotted me out of the Calendar of his affections altogether I know."

In stark contrast to Dickens, Jackson was thoroughly unostentatious. "My chief," wrote Warre, "was a man of very simple habits and a perfect gentleman used to travel in an ordinary tweed suit rather loosely made." He enjoyed the solitude of his country retreat in William Henry (Sorel), where he could rest and hunt. By 1845, tired of his long absence from England and from his daughters (his wife had died some years before), he asked to be recalled. Just as his replacement, Charles Murray Cathcart*, was arriving, an apparently healthy Jackson was struck down by apoplexy in the heat of early summer. He was buried in William Henry where he had asked, only weeks before, to be laid to rest if he should die in Canada.

NORMAN HILLMER and O. A. COOKE

PAC, MG 24, A17, ser.I, 2; ser.II, 6; F71, 1, 28; MG 30, D1, 16: 358–71; RG 8, I (C ser.), 60, 174–76, 282, 305, 675, 750, 769, 827, 916, 960, 1036–37, 1194B. PRO, WO 1/536–41, 1/552–53 (mfm. at PAC). Charles Dickens, *The letters of Charles Dickens*, ed. Madeleine House *et al.* (3v. to date, Oxford, 1965–), 3. *Gentleman's Magazine*, July–December 1845: 309. *Montreal Gazette*, 12 June 1845. *Quebec Gazette*, 11 June 1845. G.B., WO, *Army list*, 1795–1840. *Hart's army list*, 1840–45. Kenneth Bourne, *Britain and the balance of power in North America, 1815–1908* (Berkeley, Calif., 1967). J. M. S. Careless, *The union of the Canadas: the growth of Canadian institutions, 1841–1857* (Toronto, 1967). G.B., Army, *The record of the Coldstream Guards*, ed. R. J. Marker *et al.* (3 pts. in 1v., London, 1950). J. M. Hitsman, *Safeguarding Canada, 1763–1871* (Toronto, 1968). Edgar Johnson, *Charles Dickens, his tragedy and triumph* (New York, 1952). Elinor Kyte Senior, *British regulars in Montreal: an imperial garrison, 1832–1854* (Montreal, 1981). [Daniel] MacKinnon, *Origin and services of the Coldstream Guards* (2v., London, 1833), 2. F. C. Mather, *Public order in the age of the Chartists* (New York, 1967).

JANSON. *See* FORBIN-JANSON

JARVIS, HANNAH. *See* PETERS

JEFFERY, THOMAS NICKLESON, office holder, politician, and colonial administrator; b. 1782 in England, eldest son of John Jeffery and Elizabeth —— of Poole, Dorset; m. 3 May 1805 Martha Maria Uniacke, daughter of Richard John Uniacke* Sr, in Halifax, and they had four sons and one daughter; d. there 21 Oct. 1847.

Thomas Nickleson Jeffery began his career in 1798 as an audit clerk in London, and through the influence of William Pitt he was appointed collector of customs at Halifax while still a minor. On 13 Sept. 1803 he received his commission and officially assumed his duties. The salary was small but the fees lucrative, and the latter were found very burdensome by merchants, particularly those engaged in the coasting trade. In 1820 a committee of the House of Assembly claimed that "many evils, and violations of Law, do exist in the Halifax Department of the Custom-House." The evidence supporting the charges was suspect; one important witness had previously been dismissed from the customs service by Jeffery because of fraud. Jeffery was quite correct when he told Lieutenant Governor Sir James Kempt* that "it is the establishment and not the officers that is the object aimed at." As part of the reform of the trade laws in 1825, fees were abolished, but the assembly always considered Jeffery's new salary of £2,000 to be too high.

Appointed to the Council on 8 Aug. 1810, Jeffery loyally supported the high-church tory views of his father-in-law, Richard John Uniacke. As administrator of the province from 9 Oct. 1832 to 2 July 1834, after the departure of Lieutenant Governor Sir Peregrine Maitland*, he performed his duties to the approbation of Joseph Howe*, who wrote in the *Novascotian, or Colonial Herald* that "Mr. Jeffery's administration has been highly acceptable to all classes," and praised his desire "on all occasions . . . to preserve the peace and promote the welfare of the country." Jeffery also received a highly complimentary address signed by 700 citizens. Perhaps Howe would have praised Jeffery less had he known that Jeffery in his correspondence with the Colonial Office had opposed both the separation of the Council into legislative and executive bodies and the union of King's and Dalhousie colleges. On the former matter, he gave somewhat spurious reasons for his opposition, claiming that "no change would stop dissatisfaction, or silence complaint among those who are already discontented" and that "just discontent" over the precedence of councillors would arise. When the Council was separated in January 1838 Jeffery became a member of the Executive Council. He resigned with four others on 1 Oct. 1840 to allow Lieutenant Governor Lord Falkland [Cary*] to include the leaders of the reform party.

In 1815 Jeffery had been made responsible for the care of the blacks sent to Nova Scotia after the War of 1812. A depot was established on Melville Island and he seems to have carried out his duties with compassion and efficiency. He settled some of the families on his lands near the Shubenacadie River. His salary for this duty was about £1,500 and probably helped finance the building of his Georgian summer residence of Lakelands, 30 miles from Halifax on the Windsor road. Here he engaged in gentlemanly farming; in 1833 the ornithologist John James Audubon found "his house . . . large, good looking, and the grounds . . . in fine order."

Jeffery from all accounts was of a generous disposition, giving his time and money for the encouragement of public improvements. He was apparently "charitable to profusion," perhaps more than was wise, since on his death his wife was left with "wholly insufficient" means to sustain her position in society. Lieutenant Governor Sir John Harvey* unsuccessfully tried to secure her a pension. Collectors of customs were never popular in Nova Scotia but over 40 years Jeffery performed to the general satisfaction of both his fellow Nova Scotians and his superiors. The respect in which he was held was demonstrated at his funeral, the reporter for the *Acadian Recorder* commenting that "there was a larger concourse than we ever remember to have seen at any funeral at Halifax." Even in outports such as Pictou, flags flew at half-mast.

B. C. CUTHBERTSON

PANS, MG 1, 1489; RG 1, 53–54, 112, 119, 214–14½, 229, 420. PRO, CO 217/86, 217/96, 217/139, 217/143, 217/149, 217/155–56; CO 218/31. N.S., House of Assembly, *Journal and proc.*, 1820–21. *Acadian Recorder*, 30 Oct. 1847. *Novascotian, or Colonial Herald*, 3 July 1834. Cuthbertson, *Old attorney general*. Marion Gilroy, "Customs fees in Nova Scotia," *CHR*, 17 (1936): 9–22; "The imperial customs establishment in Nova Scotia, 1825–1855," *CHR*, 19 (1938): 277–91.

JENKINS, WILLIAM, Presbyterian clergyman; b. 26 Sept. 1779 in Kirriemuir, Scotland; m. Jane Forrest in Scotland; m. secondly Mary Hatfield Stockton in the United States, and they likely had nine children; d. 25 Sept. 1843 in Richmond Hill, Upper Canada.

As a young man William Jenkins intended to enter the ministry of the Associate Synod of the Secession Church in Scotland, and he attended the University of Edinburgh, though without graduating. He emigrated to the United States about 1800 and continued his theological studies, proving himself an outstanding Greek and Hebrew scholar. He also studied several local Indian languages. In 1807 the Associate Reformed Presbytery of Saratoga licensed him to preach and, presumably soon after, ordained him when he was called as a missionary to a group of Oneidas at Oneida Castle, N.Y. He had apparently served the group previously as a student missionary with the help of an interpreter.

Owing to some difficulty with the Northern Missionary Society, Jenkins moved to Upper Canada in 1817, and he bought a farm in Markham Township. In 1819 he joined the Presbytery of the Canadas, an independent Canadian body organized the year before by Robert Easton* and others. Raised in the Secession Church, Jenkins was a committed voluntarist who felt that taking government money was "in some measure a silent approbation of" the union of church and state that was "the cause of many wars, persecutions and unjust measures" throughout Christendom. In 1834 he withdrew from the United Synod of Upper Canada (the successor in the province to the Presbytery of the Canadas) because it accepted such funds. He was admitted in 1837 to the Missionary Presbytery of the Canadas in connection with the United Associate Synod of the Secession Church in Scotland, which had been organized three years before by William Proudfoot* and other Secession Church missionaries and was thoroughly voluntarist.

On arriving in Upper Canada, Jenkins had started a congregation in Mount Pleasant (Richmond Hill), the site of his home church, and others in neighbouring townships. Moreover, in the course of his ministry he visited as far afield as Peterborough, the Bay of Quinte, and the Grand River. His marriage register records 852 weddings performed by him in various places. Despite his strenuous efforts, a report on his congregations by Proudfoot and the Reverend Thomas Christie in 1835 observed that "all the churches under Mr. Jenkins are in a languid state, owing, in part, to the scantiness and desultory nature of the supply he can give them."

Jenkins was noted for his honesty, charity, moral rigidity, and radical politics. A friend and admirer of William Lyon Mackenzie*, Jenkins along with William Warren BALDWIN, Robert Baldwin*, Egerton Ryerson*, Jesse Ketchum*, and others founded a committee in December 1830 to promote religious equality in Upper Canada. Their petition, forwarded to the imperial government in 1831 on behalf of the "Friends of Religious Liberty" demanded the removal of clergymen from political positions, the institution of equal rights for clergy of all denominations, the modification of the King's College charter, and the secularization of the clergy reserves. Jenkins was subjected to both verbal and physical attacks by supporters of the "family compact" and in 1832 his horse died after being brutally mutilated by persons unknown. "Do they think to intimidate me from duty by such treatment?" he wrote to the *Christian Guardian*. "I would even rather die myself, doing my duty, than live by neglecting it." Jenkins's son, James Mairs Jenkins, was charged with participating in the rebellion of 1837 but escaped to the United States. William's letters to his exiled son are a commentary on events in Upper Canada after the uprising. "This is a wretched country," he exclaimed in 1839. "When shall justice among men be attended to?"

During the last three years of his life Jenkins suffered from an illness that gradually restricted his travelling and lost him some of his congregations, but he continued preaching until two weeks before his death on 25 Sept. 1843. During his lifetime his colourful personality had made him the object of several perhaps apocryphal stories. He reportedly woke a man snoring during church service by hitting him on the head with a Bible and announcing, "If you'll not hear the word of God, then feel it!" When teased about his shabby coat by Archdeacon John Strachan*, he supposedly retorted, "Ah, weel, Jock, I hae na turned it yet."

JOHN S. MOIR

Some of William Jenkins's correspondence has survived in private hands and is the basis of Mariel Jenkins, "Grace seasoned with salt: a profile of Reverend William Jenkins, 1779–1843," *OH*, 51 (1959): 95–104. Short biographies are available in "Memoir of the late Rev. Wm. Jenkins, minister of the United Secession Congregation, Richmond Hill," *Presbyterian Magazine* (London, [Ont.]), 1 (1843): 277–79; in "Sketches from the life of the Rev. William Jenkins, late of Richmond Hill," *Canadian United Presbyterian Magazine* (Toronto), 4 (1857): 321–24; 5 (1858): 136–38; and in "Rev. William Jenkins of Richmond Hill," ed. A. J. Clark, *OH*, 27 (1931): 15–76, which also reproduces Jenkins's marriage register. The UCC-C and the Presbyterian Church in Canada Arch. (Toronto) contain some scattered information, including copies of Jenkins's letters to his son James.

JOHN (Gohn), NOEL, Micmac chief; fl. 1821–41 in New Brunswick.

An Indian reserve at Buctouche, N.B., was authorized by the province on 1 Nov. 1810; it lay on the north side of the Buctouche River and was 3,500 acres in extent. The Buctouche Indians were closely connected to those of the Richibucto River, and all met at Richibucto Island (Indian Island) each 26 July for the St Ann's Day festivities.

Parts of the reserve were laid out in 100-acre lots to be held for a term of years by individual Indians. Noel John was one of these by 1821. He was a man of some education, for on 20 July of that year he wrote in his own hand to Provincial Secretary William Franklin ODELL that "some of the Frenchmen" were trying to take over Cocagne Island, the only place where his band could cut hay. To oblige the Indians to give up the island, he explained, would be to force them to give up farming. He evidently met with some success, for the Indians were able to continue using part of the island.

John was not averse to losing some of the reserve lands; he sold a mill site on the river in 1832 and confirmed the transaction in a petition that he signed as chief, making Xs for 14 members of his band. But when a small portion was sold off in 1837 at the high price of 10*s*. an acre, and more in 1839 at 3*s*., the proceeds went into the casual revenues of the province instead of benefiting the Indians.

Moses Henry Perley*, New Brunswick's commissioner of Indian affairs, who undertook an extensive investigation into the condition of the province's Indians in 1841, expressed a high regard for Noel John. He was, said Perley, "well informed as to Indian affairs [and] very intelligent," a man who "possesses much influence with the Indians" of the Buctouche–Richibucto area and who deserved the medal that had been promised to him. Such medals were of considerable importance as marks of official approval and as badges of rank that were passed on from chief to chief. With suitable ceremony, Perley presented one to John in October 1841.

Perley asked John to accompany him as interpreter on the second stage of his investigations, a journey which would take him to northern New Brunswick. John, he wrote, had "a perfect knowledge of the dialects spoken on the Coast." After such a mark of official esteem, John presumably agreed.

Chief John was the only member of the Buctouche band to live in a house, and he also owned some property. The rest lived in wigwams on the reserve. Perley reported it to be one of the more successful settlements. The population stood at 93, of whom 51 were children, a good ratio not always found. The Indians relied largely on fishing and fowling, but had cleared a hundred acres of land, raised a little wheat and had harvested 660 barrels of potatoes in the previous year. There were also five white squatters on the land. Attrition of the reserve continued, and by the time of confederation it was reduced to slightly over 2,700 acres.

L. F. S. UPTON

N.B. Museum, W. F. Ganong papers, box 38, item 3, Sydenham to Sir John Harvey, 10 Dec. 1840; items 17–18, M. H. Perley to Alfred Reade, 9–10 Aug. 1841. PAC, RG 10, CII, 469, Harvey to Thomson, 16 June 1840. PANB, RG 2, RS7, 26: 68; RS8, Indians, 1/1, John Noel to W. F. Odell,

20 July 1821. PRO, CO 188/106: 206–33. UNBL, MG H54, Peter and Albert Smith, petition to Sir Archibald Campbell, 10 April 1832; Noel John, certificate, 14 Aug. 1832. N.B., House of Assembly, *Journal*, 1838: 188; 1842, app.: civ–cv, cxxvii–cxxviii. *Source materials relating to N.B. Indian* (Hamilton and Spray). Upton, *Micmacs and colonists*.

JOHNSTON, ELIZABETH. *See* LICHTENSTEIN

JOHNSTON, HUGH, businessman, politician, and JP; b. 3 April 1790 at Grimross Neck, near Gagetown, N.B., fifth son of Hugh Johnston* and Ann Gilzean; m. first 15 June 1822, in Lincoln, Elizabeth Murray Bliss, daughter of John Murray Bliss*; m. secondly 30 April 1828, in Saint John, Harriet Maria Millidge, daughter of Thomas MILLIDGE; d. 13 April 1850 at Roseneath, his estate in Queens County.

Hugh Johnston was the son of a Scottish merchant who had arrived in Saint John shortly after the loyalist migration. His father's firm, Hugh Johnston and Company, would become one of the largest merchant houses in New Brunswick, with extensive connections in both the West Indies and the United Kingdom. Following a local education, young Johnston served for a period in his father's company before entering into a partnership with Robert William Crookshank. The firm prospered. By 1826 Crookshank and Johnston possessed assets to the value of more than £50,000, including four vessels, three Saint John mercantile properties, a variety of mortgages and book accounts, and the personal notes of virtually every major merchant in the city. That same year, at the age of 36, Johnston decided to retire from business and devote himself to public life. This decision followed the death of his first wife. It paralleled that of another second-generation business leader, Charles Simonds*, with whom Johnston's subsequent career was to be intimately involved and whose niece he was to marry.

Johnston received £25,000 as his share of Crookshank and Johnston. That sum together with the assets acquired through other business activities gave him a total capital in excess of £40,000 in May 1826. The funds were invested in a number of speculative and revenue-yielding ventures in New Brunswick. Three years later Johnston acquired a seventh of his father's estate. In 1839 his New Brunswick investments totalled £37,000 and yielded a guaranteed income of £1,200. In a good year, however, capital gains on real estate and bank stock might double that income. The course of Johnston's investments between his retirement from business in 1826 and his death in 1850 reflected changing economic trends in the colony. Nearly 80 per cent of his 1826 portfolio consisted of mortgages and notes of hand, the largest note being that for £15,000 owed by his former partner at 6 per cent. As Crookshank's debt was gradually met over the course of the next decade, Johnston transferred the funds into real estate. By 1835, at the height of the settlement process in the province, more than half of Johnston's capital was invested in land. After 1836 he acquired a penchant for bank stocks and municipal bonds, his new investment policy reflecting a growing interest in financial institutions. He served as a director of both the Bank of New Brunswick and the New Brunswick Marine Assurance Company in the 1830s and 1840s. In the early 1830s he was also a director of the New Brunswick Mining Company.

In 1830 Johnston replaced his father as a magistrate of the city and county of Saint John, an office he held until his death. His most important work in public life, however, was at the provincial level. He had succeeded his father as a member of the House of Assembly in 1820, representing Saint John City. Re-elected in 1827, he apparently did not stand in the 1830 contest. In 1834 he won a Queens County seat when a former member, Charles Harrison, threw his support behind him. This electoral success was not surprising. The Johnston family had a close and long-standing connection with the central Saint John River valley and Hugh Johnston was one of the largest landowners in Queens and Sunbury counties.

At the first session of the assembly in 1835 Johnston was nominated for the speakership, perhaps the most influential political office in the province apart from that of lieutenant governor. He declined the nomination, which eventually went to Simonds. During the political crisis of 1835–37 Johnston strongly supported Simonds and the populists, who argued that control of the crown lands and their revenues should be removed from Thomas Baillie*, the commissioner, and the Executive Council, and vested instead in the House of Assembly. The strength of his influence in the assembly was revealed in 1837 when, in response to the demands of the reformers in the assembly, Sir John Harvey* reorganized the Executive Council to include two assembly members. Simonds and Johnston were sworn into office on 15 August, becoming the first assemblymen to sit on the Executive Council. For the next four years they represented the reformers in opposition to the "official party," which was composed of Baillie and representatives of a number of traditional office-holding families. Simonds and Johnston had the advantage of the lieutenant governor's ear and his sympathy, and they pressed their advantage in an effort to reduce Harvey's support for the office holders.

Johnston remained a consistent reformer throughout his tenure of office on the Executive Council. He was one of six New Brunswick delegates who in 1838 proceeded to Quebec in an attempt to persuade Lord Durham [LAMBTON] not to resign the governorship. His reputation as a reformer, however, brought about his electoral defeat. Although he did not support the policies of Harvey's successor, Sir William George MacBean Colebrooke*, who was attempting to introduce efficient centralized government and municipal corporations into New Brunswick, he fell victim to the popular reaction against the lieutenant governor's proposed reforms. In the bitterly contested elections of 1842–43 he was rejected in rural Queens and resigned from the Executive Council. Stung by the loss of popular support, Colebrooke reorganized his government in an effort to recognize the conservative element that now dominated the assembly. Johnston was nevertheless appointed to the new Executive Council, and then called to the Legislative Council in order to provide grounds for his inclusion. He remained in the government until early 1845, when, after the death of William Franklin ODELL, Colebrooke named his son-in-law Alfred Reade as provincial secretary. Johnston was one of four members of the Executive Council who resigned in protest at this arbitrary and seemingly self-serving act. The political crisis was resolved only by the intervention of the colonial secretary, who disallowed the appointment and commanded Colebrooke to restore a more popularly based government. Colebrooke invited Johnston, Edward Barron Chandler*, and Robert Leonard Hazen* to rejoin the government, but they would do so only if the "Canadian system" were introduced in New Brunswick. Colebrooke capitulated in January 1846 and Johnston returned to the government. He remained in office until after Colebrooke's departure but offered his resignation on the arrival of Sir Edmund Walker Head* in 1848.

Johnston retired to his estate of Roseneath, where he died in 1850 at the age of 60. He had been a leading member of the Church of Scotland. He was survived by his wife, two sons, and five daughters. After providing his wife with a life annuity of £300 and a gift of his town and country homes, his will divided the remainder of his estate in roughly equal shares among his seven children.

T. W. ACHESON

N.B. Museum, Hugh Johnston account-books, I: 5–10, 166–69, 222–25. PANB, MC 1156, IV: 67. *New-Brunswick Courier*, 20 Dec. 1834, 24 Jan. 1835, 19 Aug. 1837, 6 Oct. 1838, 13 April 1850. MacNutt, *New Brunswick*.

JOHNSTON, JAMES, businessman, journalist, and politician; b. in Ireland; d. 16 June 1849 in Bytown (Ottawa).

James Johnston immigrated to the Canadas in 1815 and in May 1827 leased property in Bytown. During the next two decades he was at the centre of a series of local conflicts which reveal the ethnic and religious tensions in the young town. Although originally a blacksmith by trade, Johnston functioned in Bytown as a general merchant and an auctioneer. He also developed considerable property holdings in both the town and the surrounding townships.

From his first years in Bytown, Johnston demonstrated a pugnacious and mercurial nature which, coupled with a biting, satirical tongue, would win him large numbers of ardent supporters as well as many bitter enemies. In May 1831, during events displaying the animosity between civilians and the military, Johnston and Alexander James CHRISTIE "jostled and threatened" Joseph N. Hagerman, solicitor for the military authorities operating the Rideau Canal, who was in court defending a group of soldiers. If such action indicated agreement between Johnston and Christie, it soon passed, for in early 1834 the little Irish auctioneer complained to Lieutenant Governor Sir John Colborne* that "all my Scotch enemy" had gathered together with "the well known Doctor Christie" in order to attack him. Johnston argued that Scottish magistrates displayed an ethnic bias – a complaint echoed a few years later by the only local Irish magistrate, Daniel O'Connor. Johnston, however, had also been complaining about O'Connor. An Orangeman, he argued that O'Connor, a Roman Catholic, used his powers only to punish enemies. In July 1835 O'Connor countered by arguing that "neither friend nor foe can escape" Johnston's accusations and that he was motivated by jealousy. Shortly afterwards, in late October, unknown enemies burned down Johnston's house.

Only a few months later Johnston embarked on a short-lived newspaper career. Commencing on 24 Feb. 1836, his paper, the *Bytown Independent, and Farmer's Advocate*, lasted only two issues, but those issues clearly revealed the editor's personality and concerns. He promised to advance the interests of "every true Briton – IRISHMEN and their descendants first on the list" and refused to "pledge himself to please either Whig or Tory." Nevertheless, Johnston, at this point identified as a reformer, was critical of Colborne, was savage in attacking Solicitor General Christopher Alexander HAGERMAN, and widely cited Marshall Spring Bidwell*. In some articles he stopped only just short of slander. After two issues he sold his press to Christie, who subsequently published the *Bytown Gazette, and Ottawa and Rideau Advertiser*.

Not surprisingly Johnston's aggressive behaviour angered some, and in early 1837 he was subject to a series of brutal attacks. On 2 January, at a meeting to elect the Nepean Township Council, Johnston and several others were badly beaten. The riot, provoked by Peter Aylen* but fuelled by religious antagonism, marked a break in Aylen's relationship with Johnston, who had worked politically with Aylen and was then one of his sureties. Johnston's home was attacked on 9 March by a group of Aylen's followers (Shiners) who believed that he was aiding in an attempt to have Aylen arrested. Only a few weeks later, on 25 March, three lumbermen, presumably acting for Aylen, attempted to kill Johnston when he crossed Sappers' Bridge. Johnston was badly but not fatally injured and his assailants were subsequently sentenced to three years in the penitentiary.

Johnston's political career was equally stormy. In 1834 and 1836 he ran for a provincial seat as a reformer in Carleton County. Defeated at both elections by John Bower Lewis and Edward Malloch, Johnston claimed election fraud each time but his protests were dismissed. Feelings between Johnston and Malloch remained sufficiently bitter that during a session of the Court of Queen's Bench in April 1840 the two men began to quarrel and then "flew at each other like cats, shedding blood and tearing coats without mercy."

Johnston was finally elected for Carleton in March 1841, after withdrawing from the Bytown election in favour of Stewart Derbishire*. Johnston's campaign focused on the abuses committed by the late assembly and on the need for independent politicians. He promised never to become "the cringing sycophant of the Government nor the people," and he emphasized the various ways in which government policy had unfairly hurt the lumber industry. The Protestant Johnston was proposed by the Catholic O'Connor, and, at a time when national and religious biases were alarmingly high, the Carleton election passed quietly.

During his years in parliament, Johnston worked to advance Ottawa valley interests and to promote Bytown as the future site of government. Although he spoke perhaps too often, he was an efficient debater and, according to Derbishire, had "more business knowledge and power of *hitting* hard and in the *right places* than ¾ of the House." Increasingly, however, Johnston's political behaviour reflected his Orange lodge attachment. In late 1843 he opposed a bill to ban secret societies, which caused another break with O'Connor. The split, however, did not prevent Johnston from being easily re-elected in 1844.

Although Johnston had begun his political career as a reformer, by the 1840s he was voting as an independent moderate conservative. A close friend and drinking companion of fellow member William DUNLOP, Johnston also consistently opposed responsible government, because he felt it threatened the integrity of independent legislators. On 14 May 1846, less than three months after Dunlop had submitted his resignation from the assembly to become superintendent of the Lachine Canal, Johnston also resigned, claiming that "the ingratitude and never-ceasing coercion of Ministers were too much for me." The Toronto *Examiner*'s correspondent, however, believed "Poor Johnston is altogether lost in the house; he does not often exhibit, his drunken companion Dunlop being absent." Nevertheless, Johnston ran in the resulting by-election the following month, losing to George Lyon*. He campaigned, again unsuccessfully, in December 1847, when he was once more the target of an assault, this time by two ruffians on Barrack Hill.

During the last years of Johnston's life, his personal fortunes suffered, probably as a result of his drinking. At his death, he was survived by his wife, Jane, and the total value of his estate had shrunk to a little less than £700. Despite the conflict and controversy associated with Johnston and the dissipation of his final years, he remained a popular figure in Bytown. Even with only a few hours' warning before his funeral, "the largest [assemblage] we have ever seen in Bytown," wrote the *Packet*, an opponent of the deceased, "accompanied the remains of Mr. Johnston to the grave – a sufficient evidence, if any were wanting, of the wide spread reputation he enjoyed."

RICHARD REID

AO, MU 1858, no.2366½; MU 1860, no.2526; RG 22, ser.155. PAC, MG 24, I9, 4: 1100–1, 1212–13, 1281; MG 29, B15, 48, William Bell notebooks, book 8, April 1840; MG 30, E78, 1, Daniel O'Connor to Sir John Colborne, 13 July 1835; O'Connor to ——, 4 Dec. 1844; RG 5, A1: 75052–54, 95252, 96076–79. *Bathurst Courier and Ottawa General Advertiser* (Perth, [Ont.]), 17 Oct. 1834; 2 Oct. 1835; 8 July, 9 Sept. 1836; 17 Aug. 1838; 13 March 1840; 26 March 1841. *British Whig*, 17 June, 8 July 1834; 2 April, 2 Oct. 1835; 22 March 1837. *Bytown Gazette, and Ottawa and Rideau Advertiser*, 30 June 1836, 27 Sept. 1837. *Bytown Independent, and Farmer's Advocate* (Bytown [Ottawa]), 24 Feb., 10 March 1836. *Chronicle & Gazette*, 18 Jan. 1845. *Kingston Chronicle*, 28 April 1832. *Packet* (Bytown), 27 Nov., 11 Dec. 1847; 24 June 1849. *Illustrated historical atlas of the county of Carleton (including city of Ottawa), Ont.* (Toronto, 1879; repr. Port Elgin, Ont., 1971). M. S. Cross, "The dark druidical groves: the lumber community and the commercial frontier in British North America, to 1854" (PHD thesis, Univ. of Toronto, 1968), 376, 423, 452–53, 458–59.

JOLIETTE, BARTHÉLEMY, militia officer, notary, politician, seigneur, businessman, and JP; b. 9 Sept. 1789 in Saint-Thomas parish (Montmagny), Que., son of Antoine Jolliet (Joliette), a notary, and Catherine Faribault; m. 27 Sept. 1813 Charlotte Lanaudière (Tarieu Taillant de Lanaudière) at Lavaltrie, Lower Canada, and they had one child, Charles Barthélemy, who died in 1820 at five years of age; d. 21 June 1850 in Industrie (Joliette), Lower Canada.

Barthélemy Joliette belonged through his father to the family of explorer Louis Jolliet* and through his mother to the Faribaults of L'Assomption. His father died a few years after Barthélemy's birth, in 1791. His mother then returned to live in the Montreal region, and on 23 Sept. 1799 she married François Pétrimoulx. Young Barthélemy attended the village school in L'Assomption and in 1804 was sent to learn the profession of notary in the office of his maternal uncle Joseph-Édouard Faribault*. He could not have had a better teacher. Faribault was not only a prosperous and respected notary but the prototype of the notary-businessman. In fact, he managed properties for various people and looked after several sawmills and flour-mills in the region. On 3 Oct. 1810 Joliette received his notary's commission: he could then stand on his own feet.

Joliette's career can be divided into three major periods. During the first, from 1810 to 1822, he practised his profession and emerged as one of the local élite. The second period, which extended from 1822 to 1832, was marked by his activities as a seigneur and entrepreneur. The last, from 1832 to 1850, corresponded to his activities as a businessman and politician.

Joliette's later success may overshadow his notarial career. He was in practice only from 1810 to 1824, but during his busy years he drew up more than 300 deeds annually, and, after 1815, often more than 350. Consequently he could count on a large and regular income. In 1812 he was able to buy a well-situated house in the small market town of L'Assomption and have it altered to suit his needs. At that time L'Assomption served a rapidly growing rural area as a centre for services. Furthermore, Joliette had an excellent reputation and people came from the neighbouring parishes to consult him. According to his first biographer, Joseph Bonin, he was recognized for his skill in sorting out complicated matters.

Joliette made a good match in 1813 when he married Charlotte Lanaudière. She was the daughter of Charles-Gaspard Tarieu Taillant de Lanaudière and Suzanne-Antoinette Margane de Lavaltrie, and brought as her dowry an undivided quarter of the seigneury of Lavaltrie as well as other properties of lesser importance. For the moment these holdings were not any use to the young couple because the donor, Charlotte's maternal grandmother, had reserved the usufruct for herself until her death, which occurred in 1815. After that the Joliettes let Charlotte's mother have their share of the income from the seigneury.

During these years Joliette gradually became a leading member of the community. He had been a militia officer since 1808, was posted as a captain to the Lavaltrie battalion of militia in 1812, and took part in the War of 1812. He became major in the battalion in 1814. He also ventured into politics, but his earliest attempts were unsuccessful. He ran in Leinster in 1814 but was beaten by Jacques Trullier*, *dit* Lacombe. He contested the outcome successfully, but lost decisively in the new election that was ordered. In 1820 he was once more a candidate in the riding and was finally elected, but the session was prorogued a short time later and he did not run in the elections that followed. In another connection, Joliette was chosen as commissioner for rebuilding the parish church in 1819. Thus by the beginning of 1820s he was clearly well established in the region's élite; connected with distinguished families, engaged personally in economic development as either an owner or an administrator, he received certain posts and was prominent professionally.

The year 1822 was an important one in Joliette's career, for his mother-in-law's death freed up the Tarieu Taillant de Lanaudière estate. The children, Pierre-Paul, Charlotte, and Marie-Antoinette, became its owners. The eldest, Pierre-Paul, was entitled to 50 per cent of the rights, and the two sisters to 25 per cent each. Charlotte, who had already received her share as a dowry, waived her rights. The assets consisted mainly of the seigneury of Lavaltrie and the first concessions of Kildare Township, which bordered on it. To that were added a few rights to the seigneuries of Petit-Longueuil and Saint-Vallier. Joliette soon gave up his notarial practice in favour of a new career as a seigneur and entrepreneur. It was a completely new orientation for him.

Joliette was, of course, only indirectly a seigneur, since in reality his wife held title to the property. He meant nevertheless to be treated as such, and it is his name that appears on the various leases that the seigneurs of Lavaltrie granted. On the whole, Joliette had no difficulty obtaining recognition of himself as a seigneur, except at the church; he demanded seigneurial privileges there, but they were refused him by Bishop Jean-Jacques LARTIGUE in 1826. He dominated the coseigneurs, however. Even though the principal heir, Pierre-Paul Tarieu Taillant de Lanaudière, held half the rights on the seigneury, he seems not to have been interested in the day-by-day running of affairs, which he gladly left to his brother-in-law. The other Lanaudière sister was married to a doctor, Peter Charles Loedel, who participated in Joliette's undertakings. Joliette had in his favour his background as a notary and the experience he had gained with his uncle, who had administered the seigneury of Lavaltrie from 1812 to 1822. He held another winning card. Having let his mother-in-law receive all the income from the seigneury after 1815, he had her sign an acknowledgement of debt in 1820. Thus when his wife refused the legacy, they became the estate's creditors. Joliette's fundamental role in affairs was confirmed by a private contract signed in 1825.

From the outset the seigneurs proceeded to develop Lavaltrie in three important ways: tightening up management, exploiting the forest resources, and creating the village of Industrie. In 1822, 370 of the *censitaires* were in debt to the seigneurs for about 80,000 *livres*; within three years virtually the entire sum had been paid back, and it seems clear that arrears were less tolerated. More attention was being paid to management. The *censitaires* were urged to pay their debts, and some did so by supplying labour or even sawlogs for the mill. As for the obstinate, 19 of them had to face lawsuits. The new seigneurs also kept a jealous eye on their right of banality: for example, in 1825 they required the parish priest, Joseph-Marie Bellenger*, to remind his flock of their obligation to take their wheat to the seigneurial mill. The priest informed the bishop fully of the harshness of Joliette's management.

The project that really gave new impetus to the seigneury, however, was lumbering. Lavaltrie still had a few pieces of land that had not been distributed for settlement, but, more important, not all its territory was occupied, some still being in standing timber. Consequently a new seigneurial domain was formed by taking back five properties along the Rivière L'Assomption. They had a remarkable pine forest that was logged for the Quebec market. Joliette probably wanted to maximize his profits by sawing the wood into planks of standard dimensions for export to Great Britain instead of selling it as squared timber. To do that, he had to put up a sawmill capable of handling the wood and to ensure that he had adequate means for transporting his planks to Quebec. In December 1822 contracts were signed for the construction of an imposing three-storey stone mill measuring 115 feet by 50. This building was intended to be a multi-purpose one: it was also to serve as a flour-mill and it contained a shingle-mill and carding and fulling machines. The first logs went through in the spring of 1824. As for transportation, the planks were moved on sleighs to bypass the rapids on the river and then were taken on rafts as far as the St Lawrence, where they were loaded on ships for Quebec.

Once the new domain had been cleared, in the autumn of 1826, the lumbering operation came to belong solely to Joliette and Peter Charles Loedel; Pierre-Paul Tarieu Taillant de Lanaudière seems to have been excluded. The partners, seeking a regular supply of wood, reached agreements with the neighbouring seigneurs to log their lands. At that time the seigneuries on the back concession such as Ramezay and Ailleboust, which adjoined Lavaltrie, were just beginning to be settled. The first time the planks were sold at Quebec, Joliette went down there expressly for the purpose; later he proceeded through contracts that included advances on consignment, as in 1827 when he did business with William Price*.

Development of a village constituted the third component of the profit-making plan. The building of a large mill was the starting point for the population centre to be created. The advantages were numerous. The village-type lots offered an opportunity for the seigneurs to make additional profits, particularly through the workings of the *lods et ventes*. In addition, by attracting to the site the surplus population from neighbouring parishes they could be assured of a sufficiently large reservoir of labour, which could in turn attract or facilitate other investments. The village of Industrie offered people of the region job possibilities that did not exist elsewhere.

The first building sites were granted in November 1824, and in 1826 Joliette and Loedel decided to put up residences, imposing for the time and place, that they called their manor-houses. The little village gradually expanded under the stimulus of various new services. For example, around 1825 a former clerk in Joliette's office, Jean-Olivier Leblanc, came to set up as a notary at Industrie; from then on it was no longer necessary to go to Berthier-en-Haut (Berthierville) or L'Assomption to have deeds drawn up, and the residents of surrounding parishes acquired the habit of coming to the village. In 1826 Joliette was appointed justice of the peace and could settle small causes in his region. He was promoted lieutenant-colonel of the 2nd Battalion of Warwick militia in 1827. Three years later he was also elected to the House of Assembly for L'Assomption, a treasured proof of the esteem in which he was held. He retained his seat until 1832, when he was called to the Legislative Council. The village, however, was not successful in obtaining a church, for the bishop would not allow it. Yet a recognition of suzerainty and census in 1829 shows that Industrie already counted 35 houses and 29 other buildings of various sorts, whereas the village of Saint-Paul, about a mile away, had only a score. Industrie was demonstrating its success, to which an article published in Michel Bibaud*'s *La Bibliothèque canadienne* in 1829 testified. This progress was not achieved without a certain rivalry, as the bishop's resistance shows, for the village's growth took place to the detriment of Saint-Paul and also of the concessions opened up in the other seigneuries.

The year 1832 marked a new stage in Joliette's career. On top of his appointment to the Legislative Council, an effect of which was to establish his prestige, came the death of his brother-in-law Pierre-Paul, which strengthened his authority. As guardian of the latter's children, he was thenceforth in control of 75 per cent of the seigneurial rights. He would now endeavour to consolidate his enterprises.

Management of the seigneury seemed to be going smoothly, and Joliette's only new initiative was to have the land roll redone in 1833. Wood monopolized his energies. He increased production capacity around 1837 by having a second sawmill built not far from the first; that year he interested a newcomer, merchant Edward Scallon*, in his undertakings. The search for raw material was forcing his employees farther and farther up the rivers. In the 1840s, for example, he received permission to cut timber along the Rivière L'Assomption over a distance of 26 miles from the mouth and for 10 miles on each side of the river and its tributaries. He conducted his logging operations in two ways, by organizing the camps himself or subcontracting. In 1835, for example, he contracted with a farmer in Kildare Township for delivery of 5,000 pine logs; a few months later the farmer shared out the cutting to other farmers, keeping a substantial quantity of logs for his own camp.

The selling of planks was still done at Quebec, and, from 1839 to 1846, through the agency of Ryan Brothers and Company. The Ryans advanced Joliette money and undertook in turn to sell his production for a five per cent commission. This system, advantageous for an entrepreneur who lacked capital, could not, however, withstand a series of price drops on the Quebec market, because the supplier then became indebted to the merchant and piled up deficits. And indeed, in the late 1840s the lumber trade was encountering difficulties.

In order to stimulate the village's growth, Joliette tried new investments. In 1839 he had a distillery built, rapidly making ownership of it over to his partner Scallon. He is also supposed to have had other plans, such as one for a glass factory, but his main achievement, at the end of the 1840s, was unquestionably his railway. In the hope of solving once and for all the problem of transportation for his lumber and also of giving Industrie direct access to the St Lawrence, Joliette envisioned a line 12 miles or so long that would link his village with that of Lanoraie. In February 1847 Joliette, Loedel, Scallon, and Gaspard Tarieu de Lanaudière (Joliette's nephew) applied for incorporation. Late in the year the shares in the new firm, named the Compagnie du Chemin à Rails du Saint-Laurent et du Village d'Industrie, were offered for sale in the region. Work began on the embankments in 1848 and the line, finished in 1850, was inaugurated with great ceremony on 1 May. The rolling-stock, which was second-hand, had been bought from the Champlain and St Lawrence Railroad.

Along with these contributions to the economic development of the village Joliette succeeded in realizing two other projects, one for a church and the other for a college. In 1841 the bishop of Montreal, Ignace Bourget*, finally gave permission to build a chapel. Joliette was not satisfied; in 1842 he began to construct a church, largely at his own expense, and the following year he obtained canonical erection of a new parish. His village now provided the essential services. Three years later Joliette had a college built that was handed over in 1847 to the care of the Clerics of St Viator, who had recently arrived from France [*see* Étienne Champagneur*].

Joliette's interest in education was not new. He had already concerned himself with the primary schools at L'Assomption in 1825 and 1831. He wanted the Collège de Joliette, however, to offer a training different from that given in the classical colleges, which he criticized for teaching only Latin and not giving young people an adequate education. In fact, he was not keen on the teaching of Latin, favouring English and mathematics. Clearly he wanted his college to give courses oriented towards the business professions, and he appears to have convinced the Clerics of St Viator of the soundness of his ideas.

These investments had important repercussions on the development of Industrie, which began to look more and more like a real urban centre. While recognizing the merits of its patron, the parish priest, Antoine Manseau*, was not deceived about the general purpose of these investments by Joliette, who was determined to retain ownership of the church and college. A man of dictatorial nature, he conducted himself as the master of his domain and was bent on retaining control of all his people.

Joliette's political career was uneventful. Having served as a legislative councillor since 1832, he became a member of the Special Council following suspension of the constitution in February 1838. At the time of the rebellion in 1837 he remained a firm loyalist, refusing to support Louis-Joseph Papineau*'s party and actively opposing any attempt at agitation in his region. In December 1837 he presided over an assembly of the magistrates and militia officers of the region that reaffirmed its loyalty to the government. Later he acted directly as justice of the peace and signed at least one arrest warrant, in January 1838. Joliette seems to have been absent from the Special Council for the vote on union of Upper and Lower Canada in 1839. After the union was proclaimed, he was appointed to the new legislative council on 9 June 1841. That year he supported an amendment expressing doubts about the legality of the union. Apparently he did his work seriously, piloting petitions or carefully preparing addresses for the council as a whole.

In 1850 Joliette, who was ill, gave in to the chiding of Father Manseau and the Clerics of St Viator: he turned over ownership of the church and college with the adjoining lands to the parish priest and the Clerics respectively. Before he died he had the chance to see his railroad, which he called his last work, in service.

Barthélemy Joliette had wielded enormous influence which extended well beyond the village he had founded. Testimonies to his renown are not lacking. For his Rivardville in the novel *Jean Rivard, économiste* (1864), Antoine Gérin-Lajoie* took his inspiration especially from Joliette's creation of Industrie. As early as 1874 a biography of Joliette was published. During the first half of the 19th century he had indeed been an important player in the growth and development of the Lower Canadian economy. He had known how to seize the possibilities offered by the seigneury, the *censitaires*, and the economic situation in order to carry out his plans. For any discussion of urbanization, industrialization, the transition from feudalism to capitalism, or the evolution of the seigneurial régime, his story is interesting and exemplary.

JEAN-CLAUDE ROBERT

Barthélemy Joliette's minute-book for the period 1810–48 is at ANQ-M, CN5-24. It contains 3,030 instruments, 2,997 of which date from before October 1824. The most important archival sources for studying his career are the collections of the Soc. hist. de Joliette (Joliette, Qué.) and the minute-book of notary J.-O. Leblanc at ANQ-M, CN5-25.

ANQ-M, CE5-6, 27 sept. 1813; CE5-13, 23 sept. 1799; CE5-14, 9 sept. 1814, 16 juill. 1820; CE5-24, 25 juin 1850. ANQ-Q, CE2-7, 9 sept. 1789. PAC, MG 24, L3; MG 30, D1. *La Bibliothèque canadienne* (Montréal), 9 (1829). *L'Avenir* (Montréal), 9 août 1850. *L'Encyclopédie canadienne* (Montréal), 1842–43. *Le Populaire*, 11 déc. 1837. Caron, "Inv. des doc. relatifs aux événements de 1837 et 1838," ANQ *Rapport*, 1925–26: 145–329. Desjardins, *Guide parl.* Hélène Lafortune et Normand Robert, *Inventaire des minutes notariales de Barthélemy Joliette, 1810–1848 . . .* (Montréal, 1980). *Mariages du comté de Berthier (du début des paroisses à 1960 inclusivement)*, Lucien Rivest, compil. (4v., Montréal, 1966). Turcotte, *Le Conseil législatif*.

Hector Berthelot, *Montréal, le bon vieux temps*, É.-Z. Massicotte, compil. (2e éd., 2v. en 1, Montréal, 1924). [Joseph Bonin], *Biographies de l'honorable Barthelemi Joliette et de M. le grand vicaire A. Manseau* (Montréal, 1874). Antoine Gérin-Lajoie, *Jean Rivard, économiste; pour faire suite à Jean Rivard le défricheur* (4e éd., Montréal, 1925). Michelle Guitard, *Histoire sociale des miliciens de la bataille de la Châteauguay* (Ottawa, 1983). L.-P. Hébert, *Le Québec de 1850 en lettres détachées* (Québec, 1985). Hélène Lafortune, "La situation de la profession notariale à L'Assomption entre 1800 et 1850" (thèse de MA, univ. de Montréal, 1981). J.-B. Meilleur, *Mémorial de l'éducation du Bas-Canada* (Montréal, 1860). Monet, *Last cannon shot*. J.-C. Robert, "L'activité économique de Barthélemy Joliette et la fondation du village d'Industrie (Joliette), 1822–1850" (thèse de MA, univ. de Montréal, 1971). Christian Roy, *Histoire de L'Assomption* (L'Assomption, Qué., 1967). J.-E. Roy, *Hist. du notariat*. Rumilly, *Papineau et son temps*. L.-P. Turcotte, *Le Canada sous l'Union, 1841–1867* (2v., Québec, 1871–72). R. R. Brown, "The St. Lawrence and Industrie Village Railway," Railway and Locomotive Hist. Soc., *Bull.* (Boston), 70 (August 1947): 39–43. J.-H. Charland, "Joliette, P.Q., Canada," *Rev. canadienne*, 23 (1887): 328–38. "Le fondateur de Joliette," *BRH*, 43 (1937): 223. Ernest Gagnon, "Les frères de Louis Jolliet," *BRH*, 8 (1902): 313. J.-C. Robert, "Un seigneur entrepreneur, Barthélemy Joliette, et la fondation du village d'Industrie (Joliette), 1822–1850," *RHAF*, 26 (1972–73): 375–95. David Schulze, "Rural manufacture in Lower Canada: understanding seigneurial privilege and the transition in the countryside," *Alternate Routes* (Ottawa), 7 (1984): 134–67.

JONES, AUGUSTUS, surveyor, land speculator, farmer, and militia officer; b. 1757 or 1758 in the Hudson River valley, N.Y., son of Ebenezar Jones; d. 16 Nov. 1836 near Paris, Upper Canada.

Augustus Jones's grandfather immigrated from Wales to North America before the American revolution. The family settled on the Hudson River, probably in Dutchess County, N.Y., and then in the vicinity of Newburgh, where Augustus, who had trained as a surveyor in New York City, figured in land transfers in 1783–84. Accompanied or followed by his father and several of his brothers and sisters, he later moved to the new loyalist settlements on the Niagara peninsula, locating initially in Saltfleet Township. On 9 June 1787 he presented to the commanding officer at Fort Niagara (near Youngstown, N.Y.), Major Archibald Campbell, an introductory letter from Cadwallader Colden, son of a former lieutenant governor of New York and a prominent loyalist. The letter, Augustus later recollected, attested to his "good moral, and loyal character" and to his surveying abilities. Sworn in as a crown surveyor on the 11th, he began working with various survey parties. In January 1788 the commanding officer of the upper posts, Captain Jonas Watson, made him an assistant to Philip Frey, the deputy surveyor for the Nassau District. Jones served as acting deputy surveyor from November of the following year to early in 1791, when, on instruction from Deputy Surveyor General John Collins* at Quebec, he officially replaced Frey, who had left the province.

The ambitious Jones intended to build up large personal landholdings in Upper Canada similar to those of the great New York landholders such as the Coldens. Through the system of petition and grant, he acquired extensive lands in Saltfleet and Barton townships during the 1790s, in addition to town lots in Newark (Niagara-on-the-Lake) and York (Toronto). In 1797 and 1805 he received from the Mohawk war chief Joseph Brant [Thayendanegea*], reputedly in payment for surveys on the Grand River, two leases of land there which together comprised roughly ten square miles. In 1801 Jones unsuccessfully attempted to secure from the government an even larger tract in return for constructing a road from York to the Head of the Lake (the vicinity of present-day Hamilton Harbour).

The energetic surveyor had an extraordinary capacity for work. During the 1790s, he recalled in 1832, he "surveyed the greater part of the Townships from Fort Erie to the head of Lake Ontario," the lands along the Grand River, "the course of the north shore of Lake Ontario, from Toronto to the river Trent," town plots for Niagara (Niagara-on-the-Lake) and York, Dundas Street linking Lake Ontario and the Detroit frontier, and Yonge Street connecting lakes Ontario and Simcoe. The work of the early surveyors was difficult and dangerous. Often Jones surveyed in the midst of winter, for, when the ground was hard and the leaves were gone, it was easier to see through the dense forest. Clearly he was a vigorous man with an iron constitution, as agile on snowshoes (with a pack on his back) as in a loaded birchbark canoe. In summer he frequently contracted ague or malarial fever. Once, his horse threw him, the fall fracturing his breastbone. During the summer of 1794 he and his men killed 700 rattlesnakes at the Head of the Lake. But nothing deterred him. In the opinion of R. Louis Gentilcore, a historical geographer, between 1787 and 1795 "no other surveyor in Upper Canada surveyed and subdivided so much important land."

Employing Indians in his survey parties, Jones came to know both the Mohawk and the Mississauga Ojibwa peoples, whose languages he learned. A number of Indians came to trust him. When the Ojibwas momentarily contemplated rebellion against the British in 1797 after a Queen's Ranger had murdered Wabakinine*, head chief of the Mississaugas at the western end of Lake Ontario, they made Jones a party to their plans, asking if he would join them. Instead, he immediately notified the province's administrator, Peter Russell*, of the situation. Joseph Brant employed him on many surveys on the Grand River. The two men, who lived at opposite ends of Burlington Beach, became close friends. In addition to leasing him land on the Grand, Brant made Jones his agent on occasion, in land purchases among other matters, and named him one of his executors. A number of the Iroquois who opposed Brant's policy of leasing out their reserve lands to whites refused to accept the validity of Brant's two leases to Jones.

Jones established family ties with both the Mohawks and the Mississaugas. On 27 April 1798 the surveyor, then in his early 40s, married Sarah Tekarihogen (Tekerehogen), 18-year-old daughter of Tekarihogen*, a Mohawk chief. Eventually eight children were born to them. Simultaneously, at least in the early years of this marriage, Jones maintained a previous relationship with a young Mississauga woman, Tuhbenahneequay (Sarah Henry), the daughter of Wahbanosay, a Mississauga chief. Together they had at least two sons, Thayendanegea [JOHN] born in 1798 and named after Brant, and Kahkewaquonaby [Peter*], born in 1802.

Jones's full-time work for the government ceased for unknown reasons in 1800. Possibly he decided to retire to his farm in Saltfleet Township and to undertake less strenuous work than surveying. Perhaps the Executive Council let him go: it may have feared his close ties with Brant, who, as the leading native spokesman in Upper Canada, had frequently clashed with the authorities. Possibly doubts about his family's alleged loyalty in the American revolution had reached government circles at this time. Definitely one of his brothers-in-law, James Gage, had fought for the Americans. Also, it appears from a pension application submitted to the American government in 1855 by the widow of his brother Ebenezar that Ebenezar had served with the American forces. Certainly the violent tone in which Lieutenant Governor Sir Francis Bond Head* referred in 1836 to Augustus as "an American surveyor" who "in open adultery had children by several Indian squaws" infers that the government doubted his family's loyalist status; it definitely questioned his morality.

After his departure from government service in 1800, Jones farmed for some 17 years with Ebenezar and their nephew James Gage* as his immediate neighbours. The retired surveyor became a prominent settler in the area, serving as a militia captain from 1794 to 1811. Around 1801 Augustus and Sarah Jones joined the Methodist Episcopal Church. The Reverend Nathan Bangs* remembered Jones's Mohawk wife as "a very amiable and interesting woman." Sarah, another contemporary reported, "though retaining Indian costume presided at the table with a taste equal to a refined lady's." At the same time she imparted much of her Indian way of life to her children, teaching her daughter Catharine about herbs and their proper uses. In his *Life and journals*, Peter, who with his brother John had been raised by their natural mother, wrote that his father endeavoured "to instill moral principles into the minds of his children" and tried, with limited success, to prevent them from working or hunting on the Sabbath.

In 1817 Jones and his family, including Peter, left Saltfleet for the Mohawk Village (Brantford) and his wife's people on the Grand River. Personal financial loss, and perhaps the prejudice of white neighbours against his Indian family, best explain his decision. During the War of 1812 damage worth more than £250 had been done to his farm. On 27 May 1815 arsonists burned his barn. For several years Jones farmed on the plains bordering on the Grand, and then, in his 70s, he moved north to Cold Springs, his tract of 1,200 acres on Dundas Street, east of Paris. He supported his family by farming and by selling off portions of his vast estates. Energetic to the end, he died in 1836 before he could erect the mill he intended to build at his constantly bubbling spring. To complement the mill, the old surveyor had planned to lay out the land around it in town lots.

No actual physical description of Jones has survived. One quickly acquires a sharp image of him, however, from reading his survey diaries and personal correspondence. A physically strong and ambitious man, whose wives and best friends were Indians, he lived in two worlds simultaneously and, particularly in his first years in Upper Canada, served as a bridge between them.

DONALD B. SMITH

AO, MU 4756, no.6 (photocopy); RG 1, A-I-1, 32: 1, 25; A-I-6: 2723–24, 2729–32; C-I-9, 2: 57; CB-1, boxes 29, 40. PAC, RG 1, L3, 260: J20/15; 261a: J22/1, 3; RG 10, D3, 103–4, 108. PRO, CO 42/439: 271. Victoria Univ. Library (Toronto), Peter Jones coll., Eliza[beth Field] Jones Carey papers, diary, 26 Aug., 13 Sept. 1834. Nathan Bangs, *An authentic history of the missions under the care of the Missionary Society of the Methodist Episcopal Church* (New York, 1832), 183. *Corr. of Hon. Peter Russell* (Cruikshank and Hunter), 1: 50; 2: 261. *Corr. of Lieut. Governor Simcoe* (Cruikshank), 1: 24. "District of Nassau: minutes and correspondence of the land board," AO *Report*, 1905: 300, 303, 309, 319–20, 327. *John Askin papers* (Quaife), 2: 311, 320, 325. Peter Jones, *Life and journals of Kah-ke-wa-quo-nā-by (Rev. Peter Jones), Wesleyan missionary*, [ed. Elizabeth Field and Enoch Wood] (Toronto, 1860). "Records of Niagara, 1805–1811," ed. E. A. Cruikshank, Niagara Hist. Soc., [*Pub.*], no.42 (1931): 117. *Valley of Six Nations* (Johnston). *Upper Canada Gazette*, 10 July 1794, 22 July 1815, 3 June 1824. *DHB*. M. F. Campbell, *A mountain and a city: the story of Hamilton* (Toronto and Montreal, 1966), 22. Johnston, *Head of the Lake* (1958). "Augustus Jones," Assoc. of Ont. Land Surveyors, *Annual report* (Toronto), 1923: 112–21. Elizabeth [Field] Carey, "Mrs. Sarah Jones, Mohawk," *Christian Guardian*, 13 March 1861. Grant Karcich, "Augustus Jones, Upper Canada public land surveyor," *Families* (Toronto), 22 (1983): 321–26.

JONES, CHARLES, businessman, office holder, politician, and militia officer; b. 28 Feb. 1781, second son of Ephraim Jones* and Charlotte Coursol (Coursolles); m. first 8 June 1807 Mary Stuart, daughter of John Stuart*, in Kingston, Upper Canada, and they had three sons; m. secondly 1820 Florella Smith, with whom he had three sons and two daughters; d. 21 Aug. 1840 in Brockville, Upper Canada.

Charles Jones was a member of one of the first loyalist families to settle in the upper St Lawrence valley, in Township No.7 (Augusta, Ont.) in 1784. For an aspiring family, satisfactory education was to be had only in Great Britain or the United States, and it was to the latter that his parents sent young Charles in the 1790s. Returning in 1800, he became clerk of the Johnstown District Court, a post arranged by Solomon Jones*, scion of another establishment family of no relation. Charles and his brothers, William, JONAS, and Alpheus, were to vie with that family for tory favours and, indeed, in late 1808 or early 1809 Solomon's son replaced Charles. As clerk of the court, and as district treasurer from 1803 to 1814, Charles's duties carried him throughout the counties of Leeds and Grenville, and he acquired a familiarity with the potential of the region which no doubt was helpful in his many subsequent land transactions there.

About 1802 Jones settled in Elizabethtown Township, most likely at the site of Elizabethtown (Brockville) on the St Lawrence River, and by 1803 he had opened the town's first general store. He may have been set up by his father, a merchant, but thereafter Charles's orders for imports were generally handled by Parker, Gerrard, Ogilvy and Company of Montreal. In 1805 Jones bought 300 acres of riverfront property adjacent to land owned by William Buell*, thus bringing him face to face with another of the region's founding families. In a lifelong rivalry for local prominence, Jones, an Anglican, was the conservative tory, while Buell, who became a Presbyterian, represented the liberal strain. They agreed on the value of education, hard work, parliamentary democracy, and the rule of law, and were even prepared to act cooperatively when it appeared in their interests to do so. A mutual undertaking which paid handsome dividends to both families began in 1808, when Jones contracted to build a new district court-house and jail at Elizabethtown and agreed to organize the public subscription for its construction. Buell donated the land. Completion of the structure in 1811 assured their village's ascendancy over Johnstown, the old administrative centre. The new town-site grew rapidly, and the names of both Buell and Jones were suggested for it. The standoff between Williamstown and Charlestown was resolved by the death of Major-General Sir Isaac Brock* in the War of 1812, which allowed each contestant to display his pride in the British connection and agree upon the use of the revered general's name. The rivalry was intense, but gentlemanly.

Charles Jones held lots and rental properties in Brockville, as well as rural lands, including millsites, throughout Leeds and the Rideau area. His father owned some 11,000 acres at the time of his death in 1812, some of which might have been part of the 5,200 acres held by Charles in Elizabethtown Township in 1815. Jones was constantly buying and selling lots. To contemporaries such as Joel Stone*, he seemed to display a degree of greed and insensitivity which, if real, would blemish a generally upstanding character. The proportion of his land which was cleared for farming rose from 5 per cent in 1805 to about 25 per cent in 1840. This rate matched province-wide averages, although Jones achieved it largely by selling off undeveloped land. He had an acute business sense and should be remembered as a developer and opportunist, not an absentee landlord. The philanthropic side of his land interests is evident in his gifts of land in Brockville for an Episcopal church (1812), school (1819), Presbyterian church (1825), and market square (1833). In his will he left land for present-day Victoria Park, and offered more for a military academy, streets, and other public uses.

Jones's most valuable rural land was that purchased in 1809 in Yonge Township, west of Brockville, where William Buell had mills. A saw- and flour-milling complex, Yonge Mills had been constructed by Jones before 1806 and by 1828 flour-milling had become his principal enterprise. In 1830–31 he used the property to secure mortgages totalling more than £11,500 from Peter McGill* and George Moffatt* of Montreal. Milling- and shipping-books and more than 600 letters show that about a quarter of the milling was custom work for farmers throughout Leeds, and that the rest was performed for larger, merchant accounts. Yonge Mills was a moderately large operation for its day, producing some 12,000 barrels of flour annually for the export trade. This output amounted to about 10 per cent of all flour passing down the St Lawrence valley in the late 1830s. Jones was away from Brockville for weeks at a time, buying wheat and arranging milling contracts from Prince Edward County around the shore of Lake Ontario to the Niagara peninsula and, by 1840, in Ohio. His cousins Henry and Sidney Jones of Brockville shipped for him, and the Quebec firm of Tremain and Moir was his main agent at Quebec and Montreal for customers downstream or overseas. It was a tightly knit business involving kinship ties and loyalty to old associates.

Jones believed that industry would not take hold in the Canadas and that the future lay in agriculture, an opinion shared by William Buell* Jr as editor of the *Brockville Recorder*. To be marketable, Jones maintained, Canadian flour had to be of unsurpassed quality, and he did not permit his brand to be affixed to an inferior product. He employed American craftsmen and machinery where Canada's were inadequate. Greater efficiency was achieved at Yonge Mills after 1835 through diversification: distilling whiskey, using the mills' by-products to raise hogs, and starting a cooperage.

The existing accounts for Jones's Brockville store cease in 1830, but correspondence regarding merchandise indicates that he was still in retailing through the 1830s. At various times during that decade he owned shares in banks, in the Cataraqui Bridge Company, in the Inland Forwarding and Insurance Company, and in the schooner *Trafalgar* and steamboat *Brockville*. As well, Jones was interested in the development of a copper mine in Bastard Township and an ironworks at Furnace Falls (Lyndhurst) [*see* Abel Stevens*]. The town of Woodstock, Upper Canada, and his nephew by marriage, Allan Napier MacNab*, asked him for loans. All these ventures, like his lands, Jones dealt with decisively. For instance, in 1835 he abandoned his interest in the forwarding and insurance company as a sign of his displeasure at the move of its head office from Brockville to the rival village of Prescott.

The public career of Jones paralleled his rise in business. Appointed a militia captain in the War of 1812, he was briefly held prisoner by the Americans. In 1819 he was made president of the newly founded Johnstown District Agricultural Society. The following year Attorney General John Beverley Robinson* appointed him a commissioner under the alien act of 1814, with powers to confiscate land improperly held. He was commissioned as a magistrate in July 1822 but refused the office, claiming he did not have the time because of his "different avocations." From 1822 until his death Jones was colonel of the 2nd Regiment of Leeds militia, and took an active role in improving the distribution of weapons and in training and defence. He served, as well, with John Macaulay* and others on the provincial commission for internal navigation which, in 1823, reported on Samuel Clowes's survey of a proposed canal route from Lake Ontario to the Ottawa River, through the Rideau region well known to Jones.

In 1816 Jones had contested the single seat for Leeds in the House of Assembly. He had been particularly incensed at the imposition of martial law during the war, and his long and tedious campaign speeches stoutly defended British parliamentary tradition. Defeated by Peter HOWARD, he tried again in 1821 and was successful, holding one of the two Leeds seats until 1828. He resigned his seat that year in response to attacks on a position he took in the assembly on the raising of import duties for educational purposes. Perhaps because of his friendships with Robinson and John Strachan*, he was immediately appointed to the Legislative Council, where he sat through the final years of his life.

Throughout the 1830s the Jones family was prominent in Brockville affairs. Appointed to the local board of health in 1835, Charles served as president of the Brockville Constitutional Society in 1836 and of the board of police the following year. In 1836–37 political expediency brought Charles and Jonas together with Ogle Robert Gowan*, the organizer of Orangeism in Upper Canada and a Brockville resident. Gowan used his alliance with the Joneses and other members of the tory establishment to give visibility to himself and his causes. Charles had economic interests in the regions settled by Gowan's Irish followers and the alliance prevented the balance of political power from swinging to the Buells. In January 1838, however, Jones broke with Gowan over his wish to establish an Irish brigade in the Leeds militia. Jones opposed such efforts to "excite national distinctions," as the Orange leader had also done during the recent rebellion, and in May he withdrew his subscription to Gowan's *Statesman* because of the "incendiary tendency" of its editorials. The Joneses never regained their political primacy and in July 1839 an anonymous Orangeman, writing in the *Brockville Recorder*, claimed that the district's "family compact" had been "annihilated."

The fortunes of Charles Jones turned sadly downward in the last three years of his life. The buoyant economy had broken in the spring of 1837, and the wheat crop was of poor quality. He had trouble collecting and discharging debts, and was involved in a dispute over the *Trafalgar*. The political unrest of December 1837 and the militia's call-to-arms six months later, to guard against possible invasion by Patriot forces based in the United States, were disturbing to such defenders of the rule of law as Jones, who also feared for his mills. Exiled rebels even threatened his life. Differences with his son Frederick, a student at Yale College, disturbed Jones, and another son, Stuart, died in 1839. He travelled to England for the summer of 1839 in an effort to restore his declining health, but he weakened further the following spring and died in August 1840 of unrecorded causes.

Jones died as compact toryism was decaying, a misfit in the era of union politics and administrative reform. Furthermore, rapidly rising immigration, the accelerating pace of land clearance, and massive growth in the quantities of grain and other cargoes involved in the Great Lakes trade, all combined to overwhelm the ingrown community in which Jones had led a sheltered, almost blissful life.

THOMAS F. McILWRAITH

AO, MS 520, John Elmsley to Solomon Jones, 26 Feb. 1800; MU 3155–88; RG 21, United Counties of Leeds and Grenville, Elizabethtown Township, assessment rolls, 1800–5; RG 22, ser.155. Leeds Land Registry Office (Brockville, Ont.), Abstract index to deeds, Elizabethtown Township, concession 1, lots 10–11; Yonge Township, concession 1, lot 8 (mfm. at AO). PAC, MG 24, B7; RG 5, A1: 28896–97, 29818–21, 29925–27, 33631–48, 37267–326, 103404–9, 115971–72, 116012–14, 117198–205; RG 68, General index, 1651–1841: 447, 670. *Arthur papers* (Sanderson). *The parish register of Kingston, Upper Canada, 1785–1811*, ed. A. H. Young (Kingston, Ont., 1921). *Chronicle & Gazette*, 24 May 1834; 15 June 1835; 26 March, 11 May 1836; 4, 19 Jan. 1837; 22 Aug., 25 Nov. 1840. *Kingston Chronicle*, 28 May 1819; 17 Jan. 1823; 2, 9, 23 Feb., 16, 30 March, 6 April 1827. Chadwick, *Ontarian families*, 1: 173–75. D. H. Akenson, *The Irish in Ontario: a study in rural history* (Kingston and Montreal, 1984). Ian MacPherson, *Matters of loyalty: the Buells of Brockville, 1830–1850* (Belleville, Ont., 1981). R. W. Widdis, "A perspective on land tenure in Upper Canada: a study of Elizabethtown Township, 1790–1840" (MA thesis, McMaster Univ., Hamilton, Ont., 1977). W. H. Cole, "The local history of the town of Brockville," *OH*, 12 (1914): 33–41. E. M. Richards [McGaughey], "The Joneses of Brockville and the family compact," *OH*, 60 (1968): 169–84.

JONES, DAVID THOMAS, Church of England missionary, politician, and teacher; b. *c.* 1796, probably in Wales; m. May 1829 Mary Lloyd, and they had six children; d. 26 Oct. 1844 in Llangoedmor, Wales.

David Thomas Jones "was brought up to farming" but in 1820, after two years of study at Lampeter seminary in Wales, he was accepted by the Church Missionary Society as a missionary candidate. He was ordained deacon in December 1822 and was priested in April 1823. That summer he sailed on the Hudson's Bay Company's ship *Prince of Wales* to relieve for a year John WEST, the Anglican missionary and HBC chaplain at the Red River settlement (Man.).

West's schemes of "establishing schools and missionaries all over the country" were considered by George Simpson*, governor of the HBC's Northern Department, to be unacceptable to the company and of no benefit to the Indian or the mixed-blood. In 1823 Simpson wrote to company director Andrew Colvile in London opposing West's return, but he praised Jones, "who will be a great acquisition to us." Jones subsequently succeeded West in the charge of the first Protestant mission in the northwest and in the chaplaincy. During the summer of 1824 he built a second church, Middle Church (St Paul's), a few miles downstream from the original mission at Upper Church (St John's), and started a day-school at Middle Church.

Jones and his co-worker, the Reverend William Cockran*, who joined him in 1825, were both low church and eventually modified their liturgy to attract Red River's Presbyterian, Gaelic-speaking settlers. One of them, Alexander Ross*, later described Jones as a "fine and eloquent preacher; tender-hearted, kind, and liberal to a fault. . . . he was all but idolized." Cockran, however, became critical of Jones's social prestige and regarded him as lacking interest in the Indians. They agreed nevertheless in being unsympathetic to many local customs; in July 1824 Jones had deplored as sacrilege West's practice of baptizing, without religious preparation, the Indian or mixed-blood wives of traders before their marriages.

In 1828 Jones took a leave of absence from Red River. While in England he informed the Church Missionary Society's committee in February 1829, "It is generally considered that the sphere of our influence is not to extend beyond the boundaries of the Colony." He returned in the fall with his bride to resume his clerical and teaching duties. Mary Jones soon established a close relationship with Simpson's wife, Frances Ramsay Simpson*. In 1832, encouraged by George Simpson, Jones proposed a boarding-school or seminary at Upper Church "for the moral improvement, religious instruction, and general education of Boys; the sons of Gentlemen belonging to the Fur Trade." This establishment, which became known as the Red River Academy, the first English-speaking high school in the northwest, was privately financed by Jones but was dependent on Simpson and the HBC's Northern Council for students and patronage. Construction of the academy's buildings, begun in October 1832, was completed the following summer. As well, a female seminary was set up within the academy. In August 1832 Jones had asked the Church Missionary Society to find a "Governess . . . of matured Christian experience" and a "Tutor . . . practically acquainted with Land Surveying." Mrs Mary Lowman and John MACALLUM arrived in the fall of 1833 to fill these positions.

At the same time that the academy was founded, Jones replaced West's log mission-house at Upper Church by a stone church, which became part of Bishop David Anderson*'s cathedral in 1861. Joined to this stone church were a day-school and a Sunday school, both conducted by Peter Garrioch. The Indian school founded by West and continued by Jones was moved to Lower Church (St Andrew's) at Grand Rapids and placed under Cockran's guidance.

Despite a deepening rift between Cockran and Jones, the academy, which Simpson described as "an honour & credit to the country," flourished, having 14 pupils in 1833, 40 a year later, and 23 boys and 24 girls in 1835. Nearly all the students, many of mixed blood, were the children of HBC officers, including James Bird*, George Simpson, and the father of Alexander Kennedy Isbister*. By February 1835 Jones had been appointed to the Council of Assiniboia. When his wife died on 14 Oct. 1836, after childbirth, he was shattered: "The Superintendence of the Seminaries I am rendered totally unfit for." In August 1838 he left for England, with his family. He served at Lampeter as curate and as professor of Welsh at St David's College and, from March 1843 until his death in 1844, as rector at Llangoedmor. The HBC had purchased the Red River Academy from him and later sold the buildings to his successor, John Macallum.

S. M. JOHNSON and T. F. BREDIN

National Library of Wales (Aberystwyth), Llangoedmor parish, reg. of burials, 30 Oct. 1844. PAC, MG 19, E1, ser.1: 7825, 8011 (mfm. at PAM). Univ. of Birmingham Library, Special Coll. (Birmingham, Eng.), Church Missionary Soc. Arch., C, C.1/O, journal of D. T. Jones (mfm. at PAM). *Haul* (Llandovery, Wales), 9 (1844): 398. Alexander Ross, *The Red River settlement: its rise, progress and present state; with some account of the native races and its general history, to the present day* (London, 1856; repr. Edmonton, 1972). Boon, *Anglican Church*. D. T. W. Price, *A history of Saint David's University College, Lampeter* (1v. to date, Cardiff, 1977–). Van Kirk, *"Many tender ties"*. J. H. Archer, "The Anglican Church and the Indian in the northwest," Canadian Church Hist. Soc., *Journal* (Toronto), 28 (1986): 19–30. J. E. Foster, "Program for the Red River Mission: the Anglican clergy, 1820–1826," *Social Hist.* (Ottawa), no.4 (November 1969): 49–75. A. N. Thompson, "The wife of the missionary," Canadian Church Hist. Soc., *Journal*, 15 (1973): 35–44.

JONES, JOHN (Thayendanegea, Tyantenagen), surveyor, schoolmaster, Methodist exhorter, translator, and Mississauga Ojibwa chief; b. 10 July 1798 at the Humber River, Upper Canada, son of Augustus JONES and Tuhbenahneequay (Sarah Henry), the daughter of a Mississauga chief; d. 4 May 1847 in London, Upper Canada.

When John Jones was born, Joseph Brant [Thayendanegea*], his father's close friend, gave him his own Mohawk name. Young Thayendanegea and his brother Kahkewaquonaby [Peter Jones*] were raised at the western end of Lake Ontario among their mother's people. She taught them the religion of her ancestors and the skills of a successful hunter. Their father, whose legal wife was a Mohawk woman, lived near by and took an interest in the welfare of his Mississauga sons. In 1805 he secured for them from some Mississaugas two tracts of land at the Credit River, each two square miles in area. The boys saw him in the summer months when their mother's band camped in the still-forested section of his large farm. During a visit in 1809 William Case*, a Methodist preacher, baptized John. Later, probably after the War of 1812, his father sent him to a local school. In 1817 John and Peter accompanied their father and stepmother to their new farm on the Grand River. Six years later John was studying his father's profession, surveying, in Hamilton.

After Peter converted to Methodism in 1823, John immediately became his greatest ally in spreading the Gospel among the Mississaugas. He taught at the Indian mission school, first at Davisville (near Brantford) [*see* Tehowagherengaraghkwen*] and then at the Credit Mission (Mississauga). John WEST, an Anglican clergyman, visited his classroom in July 1826 and reported, "He appeared every way qualified as a schoolmaster, and under the lively influence of Christian principles, was devoted to his work."

In late 1823 Jones had married Kayatontye, or Christiana Brant, the granddaughter of Joseph. She contributed a great deal to village life. Trained in the white woman's "housekeeping," she taught these skills to the Mississauga women, then valiantly trying to adjust to living year round in log cabins rather than in wigwams. An excellent singer, she also instructed them in singing. In the 1830s a series of tragedies struck the family. Disease carried away Christiana and four of the children. The only surviving child drowned in the Credit River. Around 1830 Jones became consumptive and was obliged to resign from the Credit Mission school, although he continued to teach Sunday school.

In 1835, after his recovery, Jones married Mary Holtby, the daughter of an English-born Methodist preacher who lived just north of the mission. The band welcomed the young woman, giving her an Indian name, Pamekezhegooqua. One of the four children born of this marriage, Alfred Augustus Jones (Misquahke), later taught at the mission school and served as superintendent of the New Credit Sunday School for 35 years.

At the Credit Mission, John Jones loyally supported his brother Peter and his uncle Joseph Sawyer [Nawahjegezhegwabe*], both chiefs of the band. He taught farming techniques to his people and was secretary treasurer of a company that was established in 1834 to operate wharfs and warehouses at the mouth of the Credit River and that was partly owned by the band. He acted as a Methodist exhorter and helped put the Scriptures into Ojibwa, translating with Peter's help the Gospel of St John. About 1840 John himself became one of the band's three chiefs, and in 1845 he served as the secretary of the Grand Council of Ojibwas at Saugeen (Saugeen Indian Reserve). Peter Jones provided his industrious brother's best epitaph when he wrote a few months after John's death, "His loss to me and to the Tribe will never be replaced."

DONALD B. SMITH

A letter from John Jones to the editor of the *Christian Guardian*, dated 16 Aug. 1845, was published in the issue of 27 August under the title "The Indians of Canada West." His translation of *The Gospel according to St. John*, edited by Peter Jones, appeared in London in 1831.

UCC-C, Credit Mission, record-book. [Elizabeth Field Jones], *Memoir of Elizabeth Jones, a little Indian girl, who lived at River-Credit Mission, Upper Canada* (New York, 1847). Peter Jones, *Life and journals of Kah-ke-wa-quonā-by (Rev. Peter Jones), Wesleyan missionary*, [ed. Elizabeth Field and Enoch Wood] (Toronto, 1860). Benjamin Slight, *Indian researches; or, facts concerning the North American Indians . . .* (Montreal, 1844). John West, *The substance of a journal during a residence at the Red River colony, British North America: and frequent excursions among the north west American Indians . . .* (2nd ed., London, 1827), 292. *Christian Guardian*, 6 Nov. 1833, 19 May 1847, 12 Jan. 1848. Betty Clarkson, *Credit valley gateway; the story of Port Credit* ([Port Credit (Mississauga, Ont.)], 1967).

JONES, JONAS, lawyer, militia officer, politician, judge, office holder, farmer, businessman, and JP; b. 19 May 1791 in Augusta Township (Ont.), third son of Ephraim Jones* and Charlotte Coursol (Coursolles); m. 10 Aug. 1817 Mary Elizabeth Ford in York (Toronto), and they had 11 sons (3 of whom died in infancy) and 3 daughters; d. 30 July 1848 in Toronto.

Jonas Jones was raised in an atmosphere of privilege. His father was a loyalist who had risen in wealth and influence after settling in Augusta Township. Young Jonas was educated, as were many children of the province's early élite, at John Strachan*'s grammar school in Cornwall. There he formed friendships with other pupils such as John Beverley Robinson*, John Macaulay*, George Herchmer Markland*, and Archibald McLean*. In 1808 Jonas embarked on a career in law as a student in Levius Peters SHERWOOD's office at Elizabethtown (Brockville).

After their school days in Cornwall, the coterie of friends corresponded regularly for a time. But gradually the glow of those years faded as differences in personality and deportment became more apparent. In Robinson's opinion Markland was too effeminate, McLean's personal appearance left much to be desired, and Jones's single-minded sexual interests were (though Robinson himself was no prig) inappropriate to a gentleman. In May 1809 Robinson wrote to Macaulay that Jones's frequent letters "often . . . to be sure do not afford much mental food for he talks of nothing but what he calls '*pieces*.'" The randy young squire from Elizabethtown pursued this topic to a point that made Robinson terminate their correspondence the following year.

The death of his father in 1812 did not affect Jones's career. He was left approximately 900 acres of land, £200 to purchase law books, and a sum for "reasonable expences, till he shall be admitted to the bar." The War of 1812 intervened in his career but did not deter his professional advancement. Jones enlisted as a lieutenant in the 1st Leeds Militia and saw action under George Richard John Macdonell* at Ogdensburg, N.Y., on 22 Feb. 1813. By the conclusion of hostilities Jones was a captain commanding a flank company. He was admitted to the bar in 1815 and set up a practice in Brockville.

Jones took easily to politics. His family, along with the Sherwoods and the Buells, dominated Brockville, the district town. With his strong regional base he was elected in 1816 in the riding of Grenville to the seventh parliament (1817–20), and was re-elected in 1820 to the eighth (1821–24) and in 1824 to the ninth (1825–28). From the political standpoint of the late 1820s and early 1830s, it was easy for oppositionists such as William Lyon Mackenzie* to lump Jones with Robinson, Macaulay, and Christopher Alexander HAGERMAN as if their political opinions were identical. In 1824, however, Mackenzie believed Jones to be an opponent of the administration of Lieutenant Governor Sir Peregrine Maitland*. Jones was certainly never as unabashed a supporter of the executive as Robinson and Hagerman, and, in fact, moved closer to a ministerialist position only during the turmoil of the ninth parliament. In the previous two parliaments he was an independent. Yet disagreement with the pre-eminent courtiers was a matter of emphasis rather than fundamentals. Jones had, for instance, played a part in the opposition to Robert Gourlay* in 1818. At a meeting held by Gourlay in Augusta Township on 27 May Jones attempted to dissuade "the people . . . from falling into his delusive schemes." Moreover, at Gourlay's trial for libel on 31 August Jones acted as the prosecutor. To him, Gourlay's activity was illegitimate for it seemed to call the nature of government into question.

Jones's criticisms in the seventh and eighth parliaments concerned measures which would, he thought, threaten the balance of the British constitution. In 1817 he questioned Robert Nichol*'s legislation of the previous year which had provided the executive with a perpetual annual grant of £2,500. During the parliamentary session of 1821–22 he initiated a bill to repeal this grant against the opposition of Attorney General Robinson and Hagerman. In his view, it was a matter of constitutional principle that "all grants to his Majesty's government should be annual, and not permanent." It was, he thought, "an injustice to the country at large to put the privilege of disposing of the public money out of their [the assembly's] own hands" and he read from Sir William Blackstone to support his point. Jones, in a speech which later caused Mackenzie to suppose him a radical, was astonished that Hagerman appeared willing to surrender not only the "privileges of the house, but the liberties of his constituents, and of the whole country" to the executive. He supported royalty, he exclaimed to applause which "shook the building to its very base," "but not by *slavish* obsequiousness." The assembly's power was "the constitutional check of the democratic upon the other branches of the Legislature," and Jones wanted it "inviolable." The same constitutional concern led to his opposition to the proposed union of the Canadas in 1822. At a Brockville meeting chaired by Sherwood on 19 November, Jonas and his brother CHARLES were among those objecting to various clauses of the imperial bill for union. Most objectionable were provisions calculated to reduce the prerogatives of the assembly and increase those of the executive. Jones had already written to Macaulay, the chief advocate of the union in Upper Canada: "You are a Staunch Gov't man. I am as much disposed to support the Govt in what I consider right as you or any other man can be; but I will never consent to yield the privileges of the people and sacrifice all to the Influence of the Crown."

Jones showed his independence on other issues. Although an Anglican, he was a moderate with respect to the Church of England's privileges. On several occasions he supported bills which would have liberalized the province's restrictive marriage law. In 1821 he seconded William Warren BALDWIN's bill to repeal the Sedition Act of 1804, which had made possible Gourlay's banishment. The act had few defenders, among them Robinson and Hagerman. Jones supported his profession in defending the Law Society Bill of 1821, which his brother, then MHA for Leeds, attacked on the grounds that "to give this power to such a society was dangerous." Furthermore, Jonas was capable of supporting initiatives on non-political issues made by political opponents. In 1825 he supported Marshall Spring Bidwell*'s bill to abolish the statutory provision for punishing women by whipping.

In his early parliamentary career Jones approached the 18th-century English tradition of a country opposition on such matters as executive power, protection of individual liberty, and the rights of the assembly. Here there was little difference between him and Baldwin or, after 1816, Nichol. But on a range of issues crucial to provincial economic development, Jones moved close to the court tradition best articulated by Robinson and Hagerman. They emphasized a strong government (albeit, in contrast to Jones, one dominated by the executive) and a positive role for the state in matters such as finance and economic development, particularly the building of large public works. Improvements to navigation had been a favourite and early topic of Nichol's, but the first substantive attempt to direct the house's attention to it was by Jones. On 23 Feb. 1818 he moved that the house take "into consideration the expediency of improving the Navigation of the River St. Lawrence." The occasion marked the public beginning of his longstanding interest in canals and economic improvement. He was named chairman for the assembly's representation on a joint parliamentary committee. Its report, tabled on 26 February, claimed improvement of the St Lawrence to be of the "very first importance" to Upper and Lower Canada. By 11 March the assembly and Legislative Council had agreed to a joint address urging President Samuel Smith* to raise navigation with the governor-in-chief, Sir John Coape Sherbrooke*. The address led to the appointment of commissioners from both provinces [*see* George Garden*], who adopted, in August 1818, six resolutions favouring improvement. In October Jones brought the commissioners' report before another joint parliamentary committee, which supported its thrust but concluded that provincial financial resources were inadequate to the task.

The assembly slowly adopted an expanded role in the planning of large public works, especially canals, through the 1820s. The principals in determining strategy were Nichol, Macaulay, and Robinson. Jones, whose family had firm roots in the Laurentian trading system (Charles owned mills and a store), played an important role as an assemblyman in assisting Robinson's initiatives. In January 1826, for example, he seconded a bill introduced by the attorney general authorizing the government to borrow £50,000 on debenture to be loaned to the privately owned Welland Canal Company [*see* William Hamilton Merritt*]. Such loans were anathema to oppositionists such as Bidwell and John Rolph*. Jones's support, however, was not unqualified. During a debate early in 1827 he flatly opposed another loan to the company "unless . . . the resources of the Country would authorise it, independent of the necessary sums for other public works." Jones feared undue concentration of resources upon the Welland Canal at the expense of canals along the St Lawrence, which he considered to have priority. With Charles Jones, Robinson, and McLean, among others, he was a member of the joint parliamentary committee struck in January 1827 to study improvement of the St Lawrence. It reported, later in the month, that the proposed canal should be undertaken as a "public measure" and be able to accommodate navigation by schooners, the largest lake-travelling vessels, but no action was taken.

Jones's early reputation for political independence had crumbled by the late 1820s. More important, and perhaps related, the base of his political success was weakening. In 1827 Mackenzie described the two Jones brothers as ministerialists, supporters of the tainted Maitland administration. To the diminutive Scot, they were "the bullies of parliament: Noisy, ill-bred, and quarrelsome from disposition, they are rendered much more so by the indulgence of the assembly." As the general election of 1828 approached, the rumour was, Mackenzie reported, that they would maintain their political hegemony "chiefly thro' IRISH influence." But it was not to be. Charles was appointed to the Legislative Council and, running in Leeds, Jonas finished a poor third behind John Kilborn and William Buell* Jr. Three years later a return to the assembly was thwarted by Hiram Norton in a by-election in Grenville.

Several circumstances contributed to Jones's defeats. Factionalism was rife within the local élite and, though suited to the rough-and-tumble of politics, Jones suffered the consequence of those divisions. Moreover, his appearance of independence had suffered. During the Maitland administration he had acquired a plurality of offices: notary for the Johnstown District (1818), trustee of the district board of education, judge of the Bathurst District Court and Surrogate Court (both 1822), judge of the Surrogate Court for the Johnstown District (1824), and judge of the Johnstown District Court (1828). He had also been appointed colonel of the 3rd Regiment of Leeds militia in 1822. He had become, to a growing opposition, a symbol of the favouritism which seemed to mark Maitland's governorship. Thirdly, the old loyalist townships fronting on the St Lawrence, whose interests were represented by men such as Jones, faced a challenge from the back townships and the Irish who settled there. And, on one particular issue, the alien question, Jones was vulnerable. He had played a leading role during the seventh parliament (1821–24) in unseating Barnabas Bidwell* and then in the attempt to expel his son Marshall Spring. But the alien question, as it unfolded during the 1820s, had potential repercussions for Irish immigrants as well as Americans. Jones introduced in 1826 the petition of Joseph K. Hartwell, a local Orangeman, and others of the Johnstown District to be naturalized under a private member's bill if a public act was not forthcoming. Jones supported their petition and, according to Robert Stanton*, "this staggered a good many." Jones expended much time in the spring of 1827 clarifying his support for the government-sponsored Naturalization Bill. In characteristic fashion he quoted from Blackstone as an authority validating his stand. Mackenzie certainly thought the Irish would support Jones in the election of 1828 and perhaps they did. Their presence had made an impact by 1826, and within a few years, under the leadership of Ogle Robert Gowan*, they became a force to be reckoned with by Jones and others.

On the domestic front Jones enjoyed a growing family – between 1818 and 1840 his wife gave birth to 14 children – and affluence. His legal practice flourished. He had become a bencher of the Law Society of Upper Canada in 1820 and was recognized as a leading member of the bar. He enjoyed the benefits of his judgeships. Major George HILLIER, Maitland's secretary, conferred with him on patronage within the district, and on occasion Jones undertook legal work for the government at various assizes. He sought other offices. In 1828 he applied, unsuccessfully, for the collectorship of customs at Kingston, which Hagerman had vacated upon his temporary elevation to the Court of King's Bench. Jones, in fact, had been Maitland's first choice for this judgeship but he had been dissuaded by Strachan, who argued "that the Province would not bear two Brothers in Law on the Bench." (Judge L. P. Sherwood had married Jones's sister.) It was Jones's "misfortune," Strachan wrote to Macaulay, "to be one of a connexion which engrosses so many offices he suffers from it." Any suffering was mitigated by Jones's prosperity. In addition to the land he had inherited, he himself received several grants from the crown as the son of a loyalist and as a militia officer during the war. To these lots he added many acquired by purchase, thus becoming one of the leading landowners in the Johnstown District. When the construction of the Rideau Canal opened up new areas for settlement, Jones could offer for sale in 1829 more than 60 lots scattered across four districts.

A gentleman farmer well known as a "spirited Agriculturalist," Jones oversaw a thriving farm near Brockville. He specialized in breeding livestock, particularly sheep. In 1830 he purchased pure-bred animals from Commodore Robert BARRIE of the Kingston dockyard. Five years later his sheep won prizes in competition at local fairs; in 1837 he was offering brood-mares, colts, draught-horses, oxen, and sheep for sale. As well, Jones had business interests. With his brother Charles he owned mills at Furnace Falls (Lyndhurst). In January 1837 they offered to sell their site there as well as the Beverly Copper Mine to two Americans. In the 1830s Jonas had badgered the president of the Bank of Upper Canada, William Allan*, to open a branch in Brockville but Allan was, he wrote to Macaulay in June 1830, "not in favour ... *at Present*." Undeterred, Jones chaired a meeting at Brockville in August calling upon the legislature to charter a local bank. In 1833 a branch of the Bank of Upper Canada was established and Jones was appointed a director of it. That same year he became a director of the Saint Lawrence Inland Marine Assurance Company and in 1834 he was made its president.

Jones's continued interest in navigation on the St Lawrence became a preoccupation during the 1830s. At the opening of the second session of the tenth parliament in 1830 Lieutenant Governor Sir John Colborne* drew the notice of the legislature to the great river. Within a short time an act was passed providing for three commissioners to determine the best mode of improving navigation. Chaired by Jones, the commission estimated costs for the appropriate canals. An act establishing another commission for the improvement of the St Lawrence was passed in 1833. Jones was appointed its president, and John Macaulay and Philip VanKoughnet* were among its members. The commission first met on 19 Feb. 1833, whereupon Jones and two other commissioners travelled to New York, Pennsylvania, and New Jersey to gather information and confer with American engineers. Jones tabled the commission's report in December. On the basis of a survey by Benjamin Wright, the dean of American canal-builders, it "safely" estimated that £350,000 would provide obstacle-free navigation for steamboats from Lake Ontario to Montreal. The commissioners urged borrowing the entire sum even without the co-operation of Lower Canada since Upper Canada "could not possibly incur any risk of financial embarrassment." Jones had attempted to raise a loan of £70,000 while in the United States but failed. As a result of the commission's recommendations the 1833 act was repealed and a new one was passed in 1834. The following year parliament approved a bill to appropriate £400,000 for building the St Lawrence canals and refinancing the public debt. No single piece of legislation in provincial history furnishes such tangible evidence of the Upper Canadian faith in canals and economic development, and Jones had been one of the faith's first prophets. In 1834, under his presidency, work had begun on the first project, the Cornwall Canal, and within two years plans were under way to extend work to other sections of the St Lawrence.

Politically, developments in the early 1830s had been less edifying. The bruising and at times violent entry of Gowan and his Orangemen into politics brought about a major realignment of political power in the Johnstown District. In 1833 Jones and Henry Sherwood* were elected to represent the East Ward on Brockville's Board of Police, and Jones became its president. The contest had been a bitter struggle with the Orangemen. Further acrimony resulted from the disruption of a board meeting presided over by Jones in October. The culprit was James Gray, a disgruntled political rival of Jones's and a friend of Gowan's. On 9 Jan. 1834 the barn, stables, and sheds of Jones's farm were burnt. Gray was charged, convicted of arson, and imprisoned without benefit of bail. His wife and friends, including Gowan, petitioned on his behalf, complaining of Jones's "unbounded influence ... over the Sheriff, and the great Majority of the Magistrates." The following month Gowan found even more reason to complain. He had arrived back in Brockville from a trip to find his nephew in jail. Unable to secure his release, Gowan was on the verge of going to York when, he wrote, Jones procured a "Warrant against me, for a conspiracy to injure his character, founded upon the Affadavit of a Girl of ill fame, and the inmate ... of a Bagnio in this town." He was astounded that his bail was set at £400 and that he would be tried before Jones and other magistrates, "the majority highly excited against me, and having Mr Jonas Jones, as my Judge and Accuser." Tension between the camps of Jones and Gowan heightened during the election of 1834, in which Jones supported reformers William Buell Jr and Matthew Munsel Howard. Jones and his followers were apparently duped by Gowan, who topped the polls in Leeds with a fellow tory, Attorney General Robert Sympson Jameson*. In one fracas of an election marred by Orange violence Jones was roughed up while trying to restore order. His last electoral triumph – he failed to win the tory nomination over Richard Duncan Fraser* for the spring by-election in Leeds in April 1836 – came in Grenville in the general election later that year. By an uneasy anti-reform truce with the Orangemen, Jones and Gowan defeated Buell and Howard.

Jones was nevertheless tiring of politics. In the first session of the thirteenth parliament (1836–40) he showed little of the relish of his early days as a parliamentarian. He was, with Archibald McLean and Allan Napier MacNab*, a candidate for the speakership. McLean would win but the prospect of Jones as speaker dismayed W. W. Baldwin, who thought he would "probably offend half his side of the house – his rough and confident manner is often provoking." On one notable occasion in February 1837 Jones supported Hagerman's unrepentant defence of the Anglican rectories recently established by Colborne. His most important contribution came as chairman of the house committee on finance. It was examining the provincial debt, which had reached almost £600,000, most of it for public works and especially St Lawrence navigation and the Welland Canal. Yet, with financial crisis looming [*see* John Henry Dunn*], Jones remained convinced that the works would be "a productive source of revenue." Moreover, they were essential to the prosperity of "a new Country like Canada, with a limited revenue," and could "only be constructed upon the credit of the Province."

When the opportunity arose to leave politics, his law practice, and Brockville, Jones seized it. On 23 March 1837 Lieutenant Governor Sir Francis Bond Head* appointed him and McLean to fill two openings on the Court of King's Bench. Jones quickly resigned his other judgeships. He attempted to give up the presidency of the St Lawrence commission but Head prevailed upon him to wait and Jones did not relinquish it until the following year. He was succeeded by John McDonald* amidst financial difficulties resulting from the depression of 1837 and disruptions caused by the rebellion. Jones suggested to Head that he and McLean should receive registrarships of counties as a means of vacating their seats in the assembly; otherwise, he wrote on 29 May 1837, "I am apprehensive that some embarrassment and difficulty may be produced." Head agreed and Jones was appointed registrar for Dundas County, from which office he resigned on 14 June.

Jones had barely settled into the routine of his judicial activities when rebellion broke out in December. He was immediately appointed one of Head's aides-de-camp and commanded a small picquet; he was the first man to enter Montgomery's Tavern after the rebels had been routed. The aftermath of the rebellion and the subsequent border raids increased the work of the judges for a short period. Jones with Robinson recommended in May 1838 that executions be kept to a minimum and banishment, "an appalling punishment," be reserved for but a few. He repeated this advice to Lieutenant Governor Sir George Arthur* in December after the capture of numerous prisoners at the battle of Windmill Point [*see* Nils von SCHOULTZ]. The object of the death penalty was "to hold out an example of terror and by that means to prevent as far as possible" repetition of the offence. Thus, "judicious selection" rather than "the great number of executions" was desirable as "frequent exhibitions of the last pangs of expiring nature have a tendency to counteract the end of punishment." Jones handled several treason cases with little of the sympathy he often evinced for criminals. The jury's verdict of guilt for Jacob R. BEAMER he considered "fully warranted." At Benjamin Wait*'s trial, the jury recommended mercy, prompting Jones to demand it produce the grounds on which the recommendation was based, but it could not.

Like most Upper Canadian superior court judges, Jones had little use for men who abused women. When John Solomon CARTWRIGHT forwarded a petition in favour of the convicted rapist William BRASS, Jones reported to John Joseph*, Head's secretary: "I consider the case a very aggravated one and unattended with a single palliating circumstance." In October 1839 he took no notice of petitions from the chiefs of the Six Nations attacking the credibility and character of a young Indian woman who had been raped by Noah Powlis, a Mohawk. Between November 1839 and July 1840, Jones used every judicial means possible to obtain a free pardon for Grace Smith, a young black girl convicted of arson. When his own recommendation failed to convince an Executive Council anxious to make an example, he consulted his brother judges and delivered their opinion that "the Judgment of death . . . in this case is erronious." This time the council concurred. In October 1840 he urged Arthur not to consider a pardon for Eliza Mott who had been convicted with her ten-year-old daughter of stealing. He had sentenced the girl, "apparently very intelligent and . . . an interesting child," to a mere week in jail in the hope that, "if she is provided for, away from her mother she may yet become a good Member of Society, with her, it is not to be expected."

Politically, Jones got on well with Head, who later described him as "the most calm fearless man it had ever been my fortune to be acquainted with," but his influence on the administration was negligible, even though reform-oriented men such as James Buchanan, the British consul in New York, considered him one of the major figures in the "family compact." Jones did replace Robinson as temporary speaker of the Legislative Council in 1839 after Robinson went on leave, but he resigned the position in June 1840 upon the chief justice's return. Arthur had apparently expected much of Jones as speaker and was disappointed. When MacNab sought the position early in 1841, Arthur wrote to Governor Sydenham [THOMSON]: "His connexion Mr Justice Jones with five times the natural Talent, and with rather superior *legal* acquirements, was quite unequal to it."

From his appointment in 1837 almost to his death in 1848, Jones sat on the King's Bench with some of his oldest friends (Robinson, McLean, and Hagerman). His death was unexpected. He left his chambers feeling drowsy and at Robinson's suggestion decided to take a walk before dinner. He collapsed in a building he owned and was found hours later (a child had reported that judge Jones was lying there drunk), completely paralysed on the right side and unable to talk. He died on 30 July and was buried before many of his family had arrived. His will was unusual – he left everything to his wife. An obituary noted that his "keen talents . . . as a debater, together with his sterling consistency, did much to stem the torrent of republicanism in the stormy days of Mackenzie's career." Robert Baldwin* wrote to Robinson: "I ever admired the vigor and industry with which he applied himself to the administration of justice And the real kindness of heart which notwithstanding an abruptness of manner which occasionally startled even those who knew him well and was often misunderstood by those who had not that advantage, I think eminently distinguished him."

Hagerman had died the previous year. It seemed as if an age was passing. Worn out by decades of political battle, the youthful friends had left the fray one by one. By the time of the declaration of union on 10 Feb. 1841, the political views which they represented were in eclipse. A generation of native-born political leaders was quickly, and for the most part quietly, passing from the scene. John Macaulay was disturbed by these deaths and wrote to Robinson in a long lament for the age of gentlemen: "Poor Christopher & Jonas! the former, liked by me, notwithstanding some feelings of which the world sometimes spoke too severely – more distinguished as a barrister than as judge – the other, an old & valued friend whose sudden loss I can hardly get over."

ROBERT L. FRASER

AO, MS 4; MS 12; MS 35; MS 78; MU 1054; MU 1856, no.2179; RG 22, ser.155, Ephraim Jones (1812); Jonas Jones (1848). MTRL, William Allan papers; Robert Baldwin papers. PAC, MG 24, B7; RG 1, E3; L3; RG 5, A1; RG 43, CV, 1. PRO, CO 42. *Arthur papers* (Sanderson). "Journals of Legislative Assembly of U.C.," AO *Report*, 1913–14. W. L. Mackenzie, *The legislative black list, of Upper Canada; or official corruption and hypocrisy unmasked* (York [Toronto], 1828). "Parish register of Brockville and vicinity, 1814–1830," ed. H. R. Morgan, *OH*, 38 (1946): 77–108. U.C., House of Assembly, *Journal*, 1825–28, 1836–37. *Brockville Gazette* (Brockville, [Ont.]), 1828–32. *Brockville Recorder*, 1830–36. *Chronicle & Gazette*, 1833–45. *Colonial Advocate*, 1825–34. *Correspondent and Advocate* (Toronto), 1836. *Examiner* (Toronto), 1848. *Kingston Chronicle*, 1819–33. *Kingston Gazette*, 1817–18. *U.E. Loyalist*, 1827. Chadwick, *Ontarian families*. *Death notices of Ont.* (Reid). *Marriage bonds of Ont.* (T. B. Wilson). Reid, *Loyalists in Ont.* D. H. Akenson, *The Irish in Ontario; a study in rural history* (Kingston, Ont., and Montreal, 1984). R. L. Fraser, "Like Eden in her summer dress: gentry, economy, and society: Upper Canada, 1812–1840" (PHD thesis, Univ. of Toronto, 1979). Patterson, "Studies in elections in U.C." E. M. Richards [McGaughey], "The Joneses of Brockville and the family compact," *OH*, 60 (1968): 169–84.

JUCHEREAU DUCHESNAY, MICHEL-LOUIS, army and militia officer, seigneur, JP, and office holder; b. 14 Dec. 1785 in Beauport, Que., son of Antoine Juchereau* Duchesnay and Catherine Le Comte Dupré; m. there 3 Nov. 1808 Charlotte-Hermine-Louise-Catherine d'Irumberry de Salaberry, and they had six sons and five daughters; d. 17 Aug. 1838 in Petite-Rivière-Saint-Charles, Lower Canada, and was buried two days later under the seigneurial pew in the parish chapel at Sainte-Catherine.

Michel-Louis Juchereau Duchesnay came from one of the richest families of the seigneurial aristocracy in the Quebec region. He was the third and last child born of the second marriage of the seigneur of Beauport, who also owned several other seigneuries. Michel-Louis spent his childhood in wealth and comfort. In 1794 his mother left the manor-house after being accused of adultery. Michel-Louis, who was put in the custody of his father, was sent as a boarder to the Petit Séminaire de Québec.

Like his brother Jean-Baptiste*, Duchesnay chose a military career, and in 1805 they were both commissioned as ensigns in the 60th Foot. The two young men served in England and reached the rank of lieutenant in the regiment in January 1806. Duchesnay quit the British army and left England a year and a half later. He returned to Lower Canada to take possession of the legacy left by his father at his death on 15 Dec. 1806. Although he was hoping to inherit a sizeable fortune, he had been left only the use of the seigneuries of Gaudarville and Fossambault. He was none the less able to make a good match, marrying a daughter of Ignace-Michel-Louis-Antoine d'Irumberry* de Salaberry. Salaberry, who owned part of the fief of Beauport and was an influential figure in Quebec society, was pleased with the marriage, which extended the network of his relations and brought his daughter substantial benefits from the fortune of Catherine Le Comte Dupré, her mother-in-law. In 1811 Catherine lent the young couple £700 to purchase some land at Petite-Rivière-Saint-Charles, where they settled.

During the War of 1812 Duchesnay served as a captain in the Voltigeurs Canadiens under his brother-in-law Charles-Michel d'Irumberry* de Salaberry. He distinguished himself in the battle of Châteauguay on 26 Oct. 1813, as did his brother Jean-Baptiste. Early in the following year he left his regiment in order to pay more attention to his family and his properties. But he continued to serve in the militia as major of the Lotbinière battalion, to which he was posted in 1815. Duchesnay devoted himself to managing the affairs of his mother, who was investing in landed property or in *rentes constituées* (secured annuities) and bonds. He also attended to development of the seigneuries of Gaudarville and Fossambault, increasing their value through land grants and repairs to the seigneurial buildings.

Duchesnay was able to use his position in society and his network of family connections to secure government patronage. Thus in 1815 he received a commission as justice of the peace for the district of Quebec that was periodically renewed and was chosen commissioner for the improvement of internal communications in the Quebec region. He also was given a commission of the peace for the district of Gaspé in 1819 and 1824, serving as a commissioner, along with George Waters ALLSOPP, Robert Christie*, and Jean-

Thomas Taschereau*, to determine the claims of holders of land in the district of Gaspé, settle land disputes, and inquire into the needs of those living in the Gaspé peninsula. The investigators made three visits to the Gaspé and submitted at least one report before their term of office expired in April 1825. In 1820 Duchesnay, like his half-brother Antoine-Louis*, was appointed commissioner for the building of churches and presbyteries in the district of Quebec and the government renewed his commission in 1830. In 1827 he replaced Taschereau, a connection by marriage, as deputy adjutant general of the Lower Canadian militia. The following year he was called upon to serve as superintendent of Indian affairs at Quebec.

Duchesnay inherited the entire estate (both real property and movables) of his mother when she died on 14 Nov. 1836. He was therefore able to live comfortably until his death two years later. A widower for many years, Duchesnay left seven children, who shared their father's estate. The eldest, Édouard-Louis-Antoine-Alphonse, received the best portion, inheriting the seigneuries of Gaudarville and Fossambault.

CÉLINE CYR

ANQ-Q, CE1-5, 15 mars 1786, 3 nov. 1808; CE1-39, 20 août 1838; CN1-147, 9 mai 1808, 13 juin 1815; CN1-178, 4 sept. 1823; CN1-230, 22 déc. 1806, 27 mars 1811, 14 févr. 1812, 24 juin 1815. PAC, MG 24, G45; RG 68, General index, 1651–1841. Le Jeune, *Dictionnaire*. *Officers of British forces in Canada* (Irving). Gilles Paquet et J.-P. Wallot, *Patronage et pouvoir dans le Bas-Canada (1794–1812); un essai d'économie historique* (Montréal, 1973). P.-G. Roy, *La famille Juchereau Duchesnay* (Lévis, Qué., 1903); *La famille Le Compte Dupré* (Lévis, 1941). Céline Cyr, "Portrait de femme: Catherine Dupré, indépendante et rebelle," *Cap-aux-Diamants* (Québec), 2 (1986–87), no.1: 15–18.

K

KALLIOU. *See* CALLIHOO

KEMBLE, WILLIAM, army officer, office holder, printer, editor, and JP; b. 1781 in Clapham (London); m. Rebecca Franks, and they had two sons who died in infancy and a daughter; d. 5 March 1845 at Quebec.

William Kemble, who came from an important merchant family in London, received an education in the classics and left to settle in the Canadas in 1802. He first lived in Upper Canada, where he became acquainted with Lieutenant Governor Francis Gore*, and then in 1807 took up residence at Quebec. He joined the British army, becoming an ensign in the Royal Newfoundland Regiment on 26 April 1810 and a lieutenant in the Glengarry Light Infantry Fencibles on 6 Feb. 1812. On 12 July 1812 he was appointed assistant military secretary to Governor Sir George Prevost* at Quebec, a post he retained until he rejoined his regiment in July 1813. In April or May 1814 he was attached to the Volunteer Incorporated Militia Battalion of Upper Canada, in which he served as paymaster. On 25 July he took part in the battle against the Americans at Lundy's Lane. He was put on half pay in June 1816 and remained on it until 1826.

In May 1813 Kemble and his family had moved into the second floor of master carpenter Jean-Baptiste Bédard*'s house at the corner of Rue Saint-Joachim and Rue Saint-François (Rue d'Youville), in the *faubourg* Saint-Jean at Quebec. When the war with the United States ended, he received various military and civilian posts. In 1816 he was appointed king's printer for Upper Canada and moved to York (Toronto). Writing on 20 August, he appealed to John NEILSON, the king's printer for Lower Canada, to supply him with coats of arms and a schedule of rates. But in 1817 he had to hand his job over to printer Robert Charles HORNE.

Kemble returned to Quebec and in 1823 became editor of the *Quebec Mercury* [*see* Thomas Cary* Jr]. Three years later his brother Francis, a merchant in London, gave him the financial help that enabled him to invest in the New Printing Office, which published the paper. On 5 Dec. 1826 he thus became a partner of Pierre-Édouard Desbarats* and Thomas Cary Jr in the concern. Shortly before, on 2 November, he had again been appointed king's printer, this time for Lower Canada, conjointly with John Charlton FISHER. In 1826 Kemble was also made a justice of the peace for the district of Quebec, and his commission was renewed two years later.

Kemble failed to comply with certain agreements between himself and his brother, and on 15 Dec. 1828 Francis made lawyer Robert Christie* and Quebec merchant William Stevenson his proxies for the purpose of cancelling his loan. On 6 Aug. 1829 he did an about-face and, according to the notarized deed, as a "good brother" lent the necessary money to William's wife Rebecca; she, along with Cary Jr and Josette Voyer, the widow of Desbarats, then became owners of the New Printing Office.

Kemble, who retained his place as associate king's printer until 1841, nevertheless kept a connection with the New Printing Office and continued as editor of the *Quebec Mercury* until 1842. He was renowned as a newspaperman. It was said that his memory and his knowledge of historical facts were remarkable, and he was induced to contribute to several periodicals, including the prestigious *Simmond's Colonial Magazine and Foreign Miscellany* of London.

Kemble took an active part in social life at Quebec. On 16 Oct. 1835, for example, with some fellow citizens of British origin who met at the Albion Hotel on the Côte du Palais, he helped found the St George's Society of Quebec. Its first secretary, he subsequently became vice-president and president. According to one biographer he always gave generously to charitable appeals.

Kemble had lost his wife on 28 March 1839, and on 5 March 1845 he died at his residence on Rue des Grisons. His funeral was held in the Anglican Cathedral of the Holy Trinity at Quebec. Carrying their banner, the members of the St George's Society led the impressive procession. Among those who signed the burial certificate was Kemble's long-time colleague, John Charlton Fisher. The *Quebec Mercury* paid tribute to its former editor, stressing his quick-wittedness and his talents as a communicator.

JEAN-MARIE LEBEL

ANQ-Q, CE1-61, 30 mars 1839, 8 mars 1845; CN1-81, 15 juill. 1825, 2 févr. 1829, 23 juin 1831; CN1-188, 30 juill. 1824; 20 juin, 10 juill. 1826; 31 juill. 1827; 14 janv. 1831; CN1-230, 1er févr. 1813; CN1-253, 12 nov. 1823, 5 déc. 1826, 19 juin 1827, 6 août 1829. AVQ, V, B, 1826–30. PAC, MG 24, B1, 169. *Quebec Mercury*, 8 March 1845. Beaulieu et Hamelin, *La presse québécoise*. H. J. Morgan, *Sketches of celebrated Canadians*. *Officers of British forces in Canada* (Irving). George Gale, *Quebec twixt old and new* (Quebec, 1915), 239. J. A. Macdonell, *Sketches illustrating the early settlement and history of Glengarry in Canada, relating principally to the Revolutionary War of 1775–83, the War of 1812–14 and the rebellion of 1837–8 . . .* (Montreal, 1893), 183. Claude Galarneau, "Les métiers du livre à Québec (1764–1859)," *Cahiers des Dix*, 43 (1983): 150, 159. "L'imprimeur du roi William Kemble," *BRH*, 42 (1936): 361.

KENDALL, EDWARD NICHOLAS, naval officer, Arctic explorer, hydrographer, and author; b. October 1800, probably in England, eldest of four children of Edward Kendall and M. C. Hicks; m. May 1832 Mary Anne Kay, and they had four children; d. 12 Feb. 1845 in Southampton, England, and was buried at Carisbrooke, Isle of Wight.

The son of a naval captain, Edward Nicholas Kendall was a member of an old Cornish family, the Kendalls of Pelyn, near Lostwithiel. He was educated at the Royal Naval College, Portsmouth, and entered the Royal Navy on 26 Oct. 1814. He served as a midshipman on a number of ships, one of which, the *Erne*, was wrecked off the Cape Verde Islands in 1819. In the struggle to save the vessel's stores, he received injuries from which, by his own account, he never fully recovered. Other early experiences included surveying in the North Sea for three years, in consequence of which he was selected to act as assistant surveyor on George Francis Lyon's Arctic expedition of 1824. The expedition, which was to cross the Melville Peninsula (N.W.T.) and explore part of the north coast of North America, failed to penetrate through Roes Welcome Sound and returned home. Lyon reported favourably on Kendall's work, and Kendall was again selected for Arctic service, with John FRANKLIN, who set out overland for the Mackenzie River in 1825 to explore the north coast westwards and eastwards from the Mackenzie delta. Kendall served as assistant surveyor on the eastern branch of the expedition under Dr John Richardson* in 1826; they successfully charted the coast from the delta to the Coppermine River. The expedition returned to England in 1827, and on 30 April of that year Kendall was commissioned lieutenant. Evidently both Franklin and Richardson had held him in high regard throughout the expedition. After their return Franklin was moved to write to Kendall's mother praising her son's "talent, enterprize and unwearied zeal," adding that "the amiableness and piety of his mind, his goodness of disposition and his ever cheerful temper induced and strengthened that esteem and regard that we shall ever entertain for him."

In 1828 Kendall joined the *Chanticleer* for a scientific voyage to the South Atlantic and, particularly, to the South Shetland Islands region of the Antarctic. Again his main duty was surveying. After most of the expedition's work was complete, Kendall left the *Chanticleer* at St Helena early in 1830, and was transferred to the *Hecla* to continue a survey of the west coast of Africa that had been interrupted by the death from disease of many of the ship's officers and crew. That survey, once resumed, was cut short by the defectiveness of the *Hecla*, which arrived back in England later in 1830.

After his return Kendall was sent, under the direction of the Colonial Office, on a confidential mission to determine by astronomical observation disputed points on the boundary between New Brunswick and Maine [*see* Sir Howard Douglas*]. He conducted other surveys in New Brunswick during that mission, and upon his arrival home in 1831 he was engaged in the compilation of a map of the province. Colonial Secretary Lord Goderich recommended Kendall for promotion after that service, Kendall petitioned the king to the same purpose, and a hearty commendation to the Admiralty from Franklin followed. All these requests went unheeded and Kendall remained a lieutenant; he apparently did not see active service again. In 1832 he married a niece of Franklin, who was delighted by the match.

About 1833 Kendall became involved in the New Brunswick and Nova Scotia Land Company, formed to promote the development by immigrants of a tract purchased from the government in New Brunswick [*see* Thomas Baillie*]. As the company's commissioner at Fredericton, he issued a report to the directors on the general condition of the colony in 1835, but nothing is known of his further involvement with the company. While in Fredericton the Kendalls became close friends of James Robb* and his family.

By March 1838 Kendall had returned to Britain, where he pursued his interest in steam transportation, becoming superintendent of the West India Mail Steam Navigation Company. About 1843 he joined the Peninsular and Oriental Steam Packet Company and at the time of his death was its superintendent in Southampton. In 1855 a son, Franklin Richardson, joined the company.

CLIVE HOLLAND

Edward Nicholas Kendall is the author of "Observations on the velocity of sound at different temperatures," in John Franklin, *Narrative of a second expedition to the shores of the polar sea, in the years 1825, 1826, and 1827 . . .* (London, 1828; repr. Edmonton, 1971), app.IV; "Account of the Island of Deception, one of the New Shetland Isles," Royal Geographical Soc. of London, *Journal*, 1 (1830–31), no.4: 62–66; *Reports nos.1 & 2 on the state and condition of the province of New Brunswick: with some observations on the company's tract; laid before the court of directors of the New Brunswick and Nova Scotia Land Company . . .* (London, 1836); and *Remarks on steam communication between England and Australasia; as combined with a system of weekly communication between the colonies of Australasia* (Southampton, Eng., 1842).

Kendall's account of his journey from Fort Franklin to York Factory in 1826–27 as a member of the second Franklin expedition remains in manuscript among his papers in the Royal Geographical Soc. Arch. (London). A microfilm copy of the journal is available at the Glenbow-Alberta Institute Arch. (Calgary). Among the maps produced by Kendall are those listed in *Maps and plans in the Public Record Office* (3v. to date, London, 1967–), 2, nos.632, 1052–53, 1394, 4174. His topographic sketches are noted in Harper, *Early painters and engravers*.

Isle of Wight County Record Office (Newport, Eng.), Reg. of births, marriages, and burials, 15 Feb. 1845. NMM, P&O/100, F. R. Kendall file. N.B. Museum, J. C. Webster papers, packet 137, prospectus, New Brunswick and Nova Scotia Land Company, 28 Feb. 1833. Scott Polar Research Institute (Cambridge, Eng.), MS 248/310; 248/432/1–3; MS 696. *The letters of James and Ellen Robb: portrait of a Fredericton family in early Victorian times*, ed. A. G. Bailey (Fredericton, 1983). Ramsay, *Dalhousie journals* (Whitelaw), vol.3. *Memoirs of hydrography, including brief biographies of the principal officers who have served in H.M. Naval Surveying Service between the years 1750 and 1885*, comp. L. S. Dawson (2v., Eastbourne, Eng., [1883]–85; repr. in 1v., London, 1969), 1: 105.

KERR, JAMES (until at least 1806 he signed **Ker**), lawyer, judge, and politician; b. 23 Aug. 1765 in Leith, Scotland, third son of Robert Kerr and Jean Murray; d. 5 May 1846 at Quebec.

James Kerr, the son of a prominent merchant in Leith, received his early education at a local grammar school. On 1 Sept. 1785 he was admitted to the Inner Temple, London. While pursuing his legal studies there he enrolled at the University of Glasgow, but he did not graduate. He was called to the bar, and in 1793 was practising on the London and Middlesex circuits. By the following year he was married. He and his wife, Margaret, would have at least seven children, two of whom would die in infancy.

To improve his prospects, Kerr immigrated to Lower Canada, and on 10 Aug. 1794 he received his commission as a lawyer. By 1795 or 1796 he was sufficiently well established to bring out his wife and children. On the voyage to England a French vessel captured his ship and he was taken prisoner. Soon exchanged, he rejoined his family and brought them to Lower Canada in 1797. In France he had acquired knowledge which was, in his own words, "deemed important." As a reward for transmitting it to the British government he was appointed on 19 Aug. 1797 judge of the Vice-Admiralty Court of Lower Canada.

Kerr's nomination permitted him to continue his legal practice. One of his most controversial cases was a defence of Clark Bentom*, charged in 1803 with illegally exercising the office of a minister. In reply to an inflammatory pamphlet written by Bentom, accusing Kerr of having deserted and betrayed him, Kerr published a vigorous rebuttal of Bentom's "ill founded and malevolent censure." On 1 July 1809, giving up his practice, Kerr was named a puisne judge of the Court of King's Bench for the district of Quebec. He was appointed to the Executive Council on 8 Jan. 1812 and became, *ex officio*, a member of the Court of Appeals. During the absence of Chief Justice Jonathan SEWELL from 1814 to 1816, Kerr presided over the Quebec Court of King's Bench as senior judge and was president of the Court of Appeals.

By 1816 Kerr was living in a "neat," well-furnished home, having a coach-house and stables for eight horses, in the *faubourg* Saint-Jean. The property demonstrated Kerr's interest in horticulture since it contained a garden sown "with every vegetable suitable to the climate," as well as gooseberry and currant bushes, vines, asparagus beds, and 90 fruit trees. After his wife's death in 1816, he put his home up for rent or sale and left for Britain on personal business. He remarried in Scotland some time before his return in 1819, but his wife, Isabella, who was 25 years his junior, died at Quebec in 1821, leaving him with at least an infant son.

From 1819 to 1827 Kerr was among four executive councillors auditing the public accounts. Appointed to the Legislative Council on 21 Nov. 1823, he served occasionally as speaker during Sewell's absences, particularly in 1827. Highly conscious of his status as a judge and office holder, Kerr seems to have spent beyond his means in order to maintain his position in society. In 1824 his debts totalled £3,227 16*s*. and his salaries of £1,333 were attached for the benefit of his creditors. One of their trustees, Mathew BELL, cautioned Governor Lord Dalhousie [RAMSAY] in 1825 that Kerr was "agreeable in society" but was not respected; "irregular in money transactions," he was "indebted to his tradesmen & always in distress." Despite an income of £1,400, plus fees, he was occasionally prosecuted in court for non-payment of debts.

In part as a result of his financial difficulties, from 1828 Kerr was embroiled in a series of disputes concerning his conduct, salary, and fees. Although characterized by a contemporary as "a thorough gentleman of the old school," he was inclined to outbursts of temper, even in court. That year Bartholomew Conrad Augustus Gugy*, a proctor in the Vice-Admiralty Court whom Kerr had suspended for contempt of court, presented to the House of Assembly what Louis-Joseph Papineau* described as "the most acrimonious petition I have ever seen." A committee was struck to examine Gugy's 51 accusations; its work would drag on for several years. Meanwhile, in December 1828, the Committee of Trade at Quebec protested the rate and structure of Kerr's fees as judge of the Vice-Admiralty Court, and even argued that by an ordinance of 1780 his salary had been set in lieu of them. At the same time the assembly voted Kerr's salary on the condition that he not receive fees. In response to the assembly's action Kerr argued that it created a dangerous precedent; the assembly could attach numerous conditions to its voting of the civil list, thus encroaching on the privileges of the Executive and the Legislative councils and creating a "French democracy." However, Sir James Kempt*, who had succeeded Dalhousie in the administration of Lower Canada, ordered Kerr to forego fees if he wished to retain his salary, and Kempt's decision was supported in 1831 by Colonial Secretary Lord Goderich.

Kerr's many difficulties induced him to support whole-heartedly a collective effort by the Lower Canadian bench, launched in 1824, to obtain independence for the judiciary from the legislative and executive branches of government. Under Sewell's leadership the judges sought guaranteed salaries and pensions in order to free themselves from dependence on the assembly, and commissions during good behaviour in order to render them autonomous of the royal pleasure. On the other hand, like all the judges, Kerr opposed the assembly's efforts to ensure the independence of the judiciary from the councils by removing judges from seats on those bodies. He feared that such action would limit the royal prerogative of appointment and deprive the councils of valuable members. He was also concerned, however, about the further loss of income that he would suffer. Thus, in 1831, when asked by the governor, Lord Aylmer [WHITWORTH-AYLMER], to resign from the Executive Council and to refrain from attending the Legislative Council, he complied but requested 6,000 acres of land for himself and 1,200 for each of his children as compensation. The request was refused.

Early in 1832 the assembly demanded Kerr's suspension from his judgeships on the basis of several of Gugy's charges. In particular, Kerr was accused of lacking knowledge of Lower Canadian law, "acting partially and unjustly," displaying "a want of Temper and Courtesy," not paying attention during hearings, rendering contradictory judgements, and illegally reversing his decisions. The assembly also argued that Kerr's two judgeships were incompatible. Aylmer refused to suspend Kerr, and Goderich dismissed the charges since Kerr had been given no opportunity to defend himself. None the less Kerr left for England in 1833 to vindicate his character and to present various claims to the Colonial Office and the Admiralty.

Kerr had long been demanding compensation for revenue lost after the Admiralty's prize court had been removed from Quebec to Halifax in 1801. The Admiralty insisted that he first pay £1,190 in droits which he had retained since 1816. In England that year, Kerr had deposited the money with his agent but had then been forced to draw on it to pay his passage back to Lower Canada. Obliged to settle with the Admiralty in 1834, Kerr was forced to borrow since the assembly in recent years had often refused to vote the civil list and the judges were owed substantial arrears in salary. To his dismay, not only was his claim to £4,088 for the loss of prize fees refused, but on 24 Sept. 1834 he was dismissed as judge of the Vice-Admiralty Court for having "Kept back a Sum of money belonging to the Public on Excuses not strictly correct." Kerr had barely begun to prepare a protest when he learned that his resignation as judge of the Court of King's Bench was required because of his dismissal from his other judgeship. Kerr's protests to the Admiralty, the Colonial Office, and friends such as Dalhousie, largely on the grounds of long and loyal service and of expenses necessary to the maintenance of his social position, were to no avail. He stalled for time in hopes of being able to negotiate a pension or obtain more favourable treatment under a new government. He then refused to resign, arguing that to do so would constitute admission of guilt, and he was eventually dismissed. After his return to Lower Canada in 1836 he disputed with the Colonial Office the termination dates of his commissions and claimed £1,200 in arrears of salary. He published a petition to the House of Commons for redress but obtained nothing.

By January 1837 Kerr had suffered "an attack of paralysis of the head." Unable to speak, he lived in retirement until his death, apparently with reduced means since he was supported by his children. A devout member of the Church of England, he sought comfort in daily readings of the Bible. To the end Kerr viewed himself as a sacrificial victim offered by the British government to appease a factious assembly, whose enmity he had aroused by his loyal defence of the royal prerogative. He was probably no less competent than many of his colleagues, but his indebtedness and continual grasping for fees and emoluments ultimately led to his downfall.

PAULETTE M. CHIASSON

James Kerr is the author of *Letter to Mr. Clark Bentom* ([Quebec, 1804]) and *Petition of James Kerr, esq., to the Honorable the House of Commons* (Quebec, 1836). An oil portrait of Kerr is at PAC, Picture Division.

ANQ-Q, CE1-61, 12 juin 1816, 11 févr. 1821, 8 mai 1846; CN1-253, 23 août 1824; P1000-55-1054; Z300076 (microfiche), James Kerr et famille. Church of Jesus Christ of Latter-Day Saints, Geneal. Soc. (Salt Lake City, Utah), International geneal. index. Inner Temple Library (London), Admission records. PAC, MG 24, B167; RG 4, B8: 6325–27 (mfm. at ANQ-Q); RG 68, General index, 1651–1841. PRO, CO 42/223; 42/230; 42/236–38; 42/240–41; 42/244; 42/253; 42/255; 42/260; 42/277 (mfm. at ANQ-Q). *Docs. relating to constitutional hist., 1819–28* (Doughty and Story), 238–39. L.C., House of Assembly, *Journals*, 1835–36, app.V; Legislative Council, *Journals*, 1823–31. Ramsay, *Dalhousie journals* (Whitelaw). *Quebec Gazette*, 24 Aug., 5 Oct., 14 Dec. 1815; 1 Feb., 13 June 1816; 23 Oct. 1820; 26 Nov. 1821; 1 Jan. 1824; 11 May 1846. *Quebec Mercury*, 9 Feb. 1832. *Browne's general law list, being an alphabetical register of the names and residences of all the judges, serjeants, counsellors ... attornies* (12v., London, [1777–97]), 1793. Hare et Wallot, *Les imprimés dans le Bas-Canada. The matriculation albums of the University of Glasgow from 1728 to 1858*, comp. W. I. Addison (Glasgow, Scot., 1913). H. J. Morgan, *Sketches of celebrated Canadians*. P.-G. Roy, *Les juges de la prov. de Québec*. Buchanan, *Bench and bar of L.C.* Rumilly, *Papineau et son temps*.

KERR, WILLIAM JOHNSON, Indian Department officer, JP, and politician; b. 1787, son of Robert Kerr* and Elizabeth Johnson; m. Elizabeth Brant, daughter of Joseph Brant [Thayendanegea*], and they had four sons and one daughter; d. 23 April 1845 at Wellington Square (Burlington), Upper Canada.

A grandson of Sir William Johnson* and Mary Brant [Koñwatsiˀtsiaiéñni*], William Johnson Kerr gained prominence during the War of 1812 as an officer in the Indian Department. At the battle of Queenston Heights in October 1812 he, John Brant [Tekarihogen*], and John Norton* led the Six Nations forces that helped push back the invading Americans. In November, along with Norton and Major James GIVINS, Kerr was with the Indians at Fort Erie, where they helped stem an American attack. When Indian forces defeated the Americans at Beaver Dams (Thorold) in June 1813, he and Brant were at the head of a hundred warriors from the Grand River who fought alongside Dominique Ducharme* and a large party of Six Nations Indians from Lower Canada. In September a small detachment of warriors under the direction of Kerr and William Claus* was given special thanks by Major-General Francis de Rottenburg* for their "gallant and spirited conduct" in a recent action. Later in the war (possibly at the battle of Lundy's Lane), Kerr was captured and he spent some time at Cheshire, Mass., as a prisoner of war. Fellow captive William Hamilton Merritt* described him as "a very fine young man, tall and handsome."

Kerr's appointment in 1817 to the magistracy of the Niagara District reflected his position as a junior member of the local élite, and like others of that élite he took part in the reform agitation associated with Robert Gourlay*. He was one of the residents of Louth Township who on 20 April 1818 met and approved an address by Gourlay, and he was designated clerk of the meeting. When representatives from various townships in the district met at St Catharines on 4 May, Kerr was elected secretary. Regional delegates met at York (Toronto) on 6 July, and Kerr became a member of the executive committee of the York convention. He and George HAMILTON met with Lieutenant Governor Sir Peregrine Maitland* to discuss grievances, but Maitland rejected the convention's petition as unconstitutional. Strong action by the government against Gourlay, and against convention chairman Richard BEASLEY as well, seems to have made Kerr and others tread cautiously. There was, however, enough sympathy among the electorate to see Kerr gain the seat for 2nd Lincoln when voting for the House of Assembly took place in July 1820.

Kerr's activities on behalf of reform, whatever their motivation, do not seem to have done him any long-term harm. In 1827 he received a commission of the peace for the Gore District, and as early as 1828 he was superintendent of the Burlington Bay Canal, a government-financed project the construction of which, begun by James Gordon Strobridge*, was still going on. By this time Kerr was probably one of Allan Napier MacNab*'s followers. Certainly, by March 1832, when at a raucous political meeting in Hamilton William Lyon Mackenzie* was roughed up, Kerr was one of the tory crowd. He grabbed the diminutive Scot and pulled him down from a table on which he had jumped to speak. Later in the evening Kerr organized some local thugs to thrash Mackenzie. He was prosecuted and fined for his part in the assault.

Kerr's family connections and his role in the War of

1812 had likely always given him a certain amount of influence with the Six Nations. Following the death in 1832 of John Brant, the head chief of the Confederacy, Kerr's influence undoubtedly increased. It was the right of his mother-in-law, Catharine Brant [OHTOWAˀKÉHSON], to name Brant's successor, and she chose her infant grandson, the Kerrs' son William Simcoe Kerr. When Absalom Shade* was promoting the Grand River Navigation Company in the early 1830s, Kerr was one of the people he called on to persuade the Indians to purchase shares. At the time of the rebellion of 1837, about 100 warriors volunteered to serve under Kerr against the rebels. Someone had convinced them that if the supporters of Mackenzie and Charles Duncombe* gained power the Grand River lands would be confiscated. Although Kerr cannot be identified as the source of this rumour, he claimed to believe in its truth. During the summer of 1838 he and some Six Nations volunteers were involved in capturing the Short Hills raiders [*see* Jacob R. BEAMER].

Kerr was considered for appointment to the Legislative Council in 1838, but his name was dropped from the final list. At the time of his death he was living in the house that Joseph Brant had built at Wellington Square. His wife survived him by only two days.

IN COLLABORATION

PAC, RG 68, General index, 1651–1841. *Arthur papers* (Sanderson). *Rebellion of 1837* (Read and Stagg). *Select British docs. of War of 1812* (Wood). *Valley of Six Nations* (Johnston). *Death notices of Ont.* (Reid). D. R. Beer, *Sir Allan Napier MacNab* (Hamilton, Ont., 1984). C. M. Johnston, *Brant County: a history, 1784–1945* (Toronto, 1967), 21–22, 40; *Head of the Lake* (1958). E. A. Cruikshank, "Post-war discontent at Niagara in 1818," *OH*, 29 (1933): 14–46. G. J. Smith, "Capt. Joseph Brant's status as a chief, and some of his descendants," *OH*, 12 (1914): 89–101.

KETCHUM, SENECA, tanner, Anglican lay preacher, and philanthropist; b. 17 Aug. 1772 at Spencertown, N.Y., eldest son of Jesse Ketchum and Mary (Mollie) Robbins; m. Ann Mercer, daughter of Thomas Mercer, a pioneer settler in York Township; they had no children; d. 2 June 1850 in York Mills (Toronto).

Following a common pattern of the period, several members of the Ketchum family in succession settled in Upper Canada. Seneca Ketchum is said to have arrived in Kingston in 1792 and spent several years there. His uncle Joseph obtained a land grant in Scarborough Township in 1795. Seneca may have moved with him and can have reached York (Toronto) no later than 1797, when he and his younger brother Jesse* were listed as inhabitants of Yonge Street. Ketchum quickly entered with zest into the life of his adopted community, becoming briefly secretary of Rawdon Masonic Lodge in that year. He began to buy up land, his holdings eventually embracing what are now the Bedford Park and Teddington Park areas of north Toronto, and he established a tanning and shoemaking business that also involved much general trade. Other members of his family, including his father, joined him in 1802.

Whether through the burden of settling the family or – according to one story – an unsuccessful drawing of lots with Jesse for the hand of their attractive young housekeeper, Ann Love, Ketchum suffered a mental breakdown in 1803. Despite this setback, he was active before long in the educational and religious affairs of the community. A devout Anglican, he helped to purchase a site for St John's Church, York Mills, and contributed much of the labour for the erection of the first building in 1817. He soon extended the range of his activities, organizing Sunday school classes and conducting informal services in outlying settlements.

In 1820 Ketchum secured a land grant in Mono Township, near the present Orangeville, and over the years he added considerably to his holdings there. He was still living on Yonge St in 1830, when he signed a petition to incorporate a turnpike company, and in 1831 was still buying land there. In 1835, however, Anglican missionary Adam Elliot* found him at Mono, noting that he had already "formed several Sunday Schools, and instructed above a hundred persons in the Church catechism." In his new home, indeed, Ketchum soon outdid his previous efforts in church extension. In 1837 he built a log church on his own land that was the precursor of St Mark's, Orangeville, and local tradition credits him with the foundation of at least half a dozen Anglican churches in the area. He also made several large gifts of land to the church, for purposes ranging from the support of theological students to the foundation of a "Sailors' Home."

Unhappily Ketchum's zeal eventually led him into conflict with church authorities. During his last few years he pressed so vigorously the claims of his neighbourhood to be the residence of a permanent minister that Bishop John Strachan* had to warn others against his exuberance. Having given so much to the church, Ketchum bitterly accused Strachan of ingratitude. In the midst of the controversy he died while staying with his nephew by marriage, Presbyterian clergyman James Harris, and was buried with Anglican rites at St John's on 4 June 1850.

Ketchum seems never to have recovered completely from the effects of his early mental illness, being described after his death by Archdeacon Alexander Neil Bethune* as "an earnest-minded but not very sane individual." No one ever doubted his loyalty to the church, his special concern for young people, or his generosity to his neighbours, however, and his ecumenical spirit was demonstrated by his willingness to operate an undenominational Sunday school out of a Methodist meeting house or to use a Presbyterian catechism where it seemed appropriate. "Very few had as much of the milk of the human kindness as he had, and few had less tears shed over his grave," was the pithy if ungrammatical comment of his nephew Jesse Ketchum, who proceeded to contest his will.

JOHN WEBSTER GRANT

Seneca Ketchum's contributions are recognized by a memorial window at St John's, York Mills (Toronto), and a plaque at St Mark's (Orangeville, Ont.). Both churches acknowledge him as their chief founder. A portrait of him is held by St John's.

ACC, Diocese of Toronto Arch., R. W. Allen papers, 34, R. W. Allen, "Notes on the county of Simcoe" (typescript, 1945); Church Soc. of the Diocese of Toronto, land reg., 1802–59. AO, Land record index, Joseph Ketchum, Seneca Ketchum; MS 35, letter-book, 1844–49; MU 597, no.17. MTRL, E. J. Hathaway papers. PAC, RG 1, E3, 100: 153–63. St John's, York Mills, Indentures, 1817; Reg. of baptisms, marriages, and burials. UCC-C, Perkins Bull coll. *The Stewart missions; a series of letters and journals, calculated to exhibit to British Christians, the spiritual destitution of the emigrants settled in the remote parts of Upper Canada . . .* , ed. W. J. D. Waddilove (London, 1838), 37, 94. *York, Upper Canada: minutes of town meetings and lists of inhabitants, 1797–1823*, ed. Christine Mosser (Toronto, 1984). *Christian Guardian*, 14 April 1841. *Globe*, 4 June 1850. Helen Ketchum, "A resume of the ancestry of Seneca Ketchum and his brother Jesse Ketchum II . . ." (typescript, 1959; copy at St John's). *Marriage bonds of Ont.* (T. B. Wilson). W. P. Bull, *From Strachan to Owen: how the Church of England was planted and tended in British North America* (Toronto, 1937). M. A. Graham, *150 years at St. John's, York Mills* (Toronto, 1966). E. J. Hathaway, *Jesse Ketchum and his times . . .* (Toronto, 1929).

KIMBER, RENÉ, merchant, office holder, JP, and militia officer; b. 1 Sept. 1762 at Quebec, son of Joseph-Antoine Jékimbert (Kimber), who had served in the colonial regulars, and Geneviève Allard; d. 12 Nov. 1841 in Trois-Rivières, Lower Canada.

In 1780, at 18 years of age, René Kimber was working as a clerk for Louis Germain, a Quebec merchant. Whether by ambition or by chance his course was set quite early, since at the time of his marriage on 19 May 1785 he was described as a merchant. The fact that he promised his wife, Marie-Josette Robitaille, a jointure of 1,000 *livres* seems to indicate that his business was flourishing. They were to have 17 children, but only 3 outlived him. In 1789 he rented one part of the second storey of a building he owned on Rue Saint-Joseph in Upper Town to John Krepper, a merchant furrier, and the other part to notary Joseph-Bernard Planté*. Kimber had a store on the ground floor and lived in the building himself until 1792. What happened in the next three years is not clear. In the 1795 census he is given as living at 16 Rue de la Fabrique and is listed simply as a clerk with C. C. Hall and Company. Had his business failed? If so, he must have made a quick recovery, since in 1798 he is identified in the census as a merchant residing at 17 Rue de la Fabrique.

It is not known when Kimber decided to move to Trois-Rivières and go into business there, but on 25 July 1799 he signed an address from the citizens of the town to Governor Robert Prescott*. Kimber soon became "one of the important figures in Trois-Rivières." In 1809 he formed a partnership with Pierre Bruneau*, a Quebec merchant, in this way maintaining a link with businessmen in his home town; the partnership ended in 1812. He was supplied by fellow merchant Moses Hart*, who advanced him goods for his store in Trois-Rivières. In 1827 Kimber's business career earned him the position of warden of the House of Industry there.

Kimber had been appointed inspector of the local Fire Society in 1799. He was commissioned a justice of the peace for the district of Trois-Rivières in 1811, and in this capacity supervised the construction of the House of Correction in 1813–14. In 1819 he became a captain in the Trois-Rivières battalion of militia. His son, René-Joseph, was then a supernumerary officer in that battalion, having served in the 4th Select Embodied Militia Battalion of Lower Canada.

Kimber was also involved in matters of social concern within his community. From 1803 until at least 1832 he served as commissioner for the relief of the insane and foundlings in his district. He was also a commissioner on the Trois-Rivières Board of Health in 1832 and a commissioner for the building of churches and presbyteries from 1832 to 1839. He was on the board of the Trois-Rivières House of Correction for the period 1812–35, serving as its treasurer from 1816 to 1829. In 1818 he was elected a churchwarden in the parish of Immaculée-Conception in Trois-Rivières, and he was also to become chairman of the public trustees of the municipality of Trois-Rivières.

René Kimber carved a remarkable place for himself in Trois-Rivières society early in the 19th century. His will and the inventory of his property after his death show that he was a philanthropist concerned with the well-being of his fellow citizens. For example, he took care to donate a sum to the Séminaire de Nicolet for the "education of young people." In spite of all his other preoccupations, he evidently managed to increase his wealth, since he was able to leave his two daughters a great many properties. Kimber's death was noted with regret. The *Quebec Gazette* of 15 Nov. 1841 eulogized him, observing that "he was a good citizen, an exemplary father of a family, and universally beloved and respected."

JOHANNE NOËL and RENALD LESSARD

ANQ-MBF, CE1-48, 17 nov. 1841; CN1-6, 26 mars 1800, 10 févr. 1809; CN1-47, 15 oct. 1818; 16 sept., 10 déc. 1841. ANQ-Q, CE1-1, 2 sept. 1762, 19 mai 1785; CN1-205, 17 mai 1785; CN1-230, 6 juill. 1789. ASQ, Séminaire, 16, no.30. ASTR, 0009 (copie aux ANQ-Q). PAC, MG 30, D1, 16: 774–76; RG 4, A1: 40635–36, 40937, 41070; RG 68, General index, 1651–1841. "Les dénombrements de Québec" (Plessis), ANQ *Rapport*, 1948–49: 11, 65, 114. L.C., House of Assembly, *Journals*, 1818–32. *Quebec Gazette*, 26 Dec. 1811, 22 Sept. 1814, 15 Nov. 1841. *Quebec almanac*, 1813. P.-G. Roy, *Fils de Québec*, 2: 127–28. *Les ursulines des Trois-Rivières depuis leur établissement jusqu'à nos jours* (4v., Trois-Rivières, Qué., 1888–1911), 2: 400. "La famille Jékimbert ou Kimber," *BRH*, 21 (1915): 201–5. Benjamin Sulte, "Kimber," *Le Trifluvien* (Trois-Rivières), 4 déc. 1906: 6.

KIRBY, ANN (Macaulay), mother and businesswoman; baptized 11 Nov. 1770 in Knaresborough, England, daughter of John Kirby and Ann ——; m. 13 Feb. 1791 Robert Macaulay* in Crown Point, N.Y., and they had three sons; d. 20 Jan. 1850 in Kingston, Upper Canada.

In 1774 Ann Kirby's parents brought her and her brothers William and JOHN from Yorkshire to New York. There, at Crown Point, she met and in 1791 married the loyalist merchant Robert Macaulay, a business associate of her brother John. They went to live in Kingston. In 1800, at the age of 30, Ann was left a widow and from this time until her death she assumed the responsibility for raising her family and took part in running the family business and holdings. Marriage to Robert Macaulay had provided her with a position of some influence in the tory village of Kingston and a network of friends and relatives for support. None the less, being left on the Upper Canadian frontier with three young sons must have been a daunting experience.

Ann Macaulay considered that her first duty was to care for and support her family. To her, as to many of her world in Upper Canada, education was the key to advancement and happiness. In 1803 she sent her eldest sons, John* aged 11 and William* aged 9 (Robert started some time later), to Cornwall to be educated under John Strachan* and she subsequently made arrangements for them to learn French and to receive professional training. Recognizing that girls too needed formal education, she would repeatedly recommend in 1839–40 that her eldest granddaughter be sent to school. Ann maintained a lifelong interest in the progress of all her sons, encouraging them to be "diligent and sensible" in their endeavours. Her frequent correspondence with each of them helped to cement strong bonds of affection and respect.

An astute woman who was undoubtedly familiar with her husband's business interests, Ann Macaulay oversaw his estate. With her brother John as partner, she was involved until 1817 in John Kirby and Company, the firm created from the Macaulay holdings. After its dissolution, she maintained an interest in her own considerable investments. Though her brother and later her son John handled the actual running of her business affairs, she was consulted and gave advice. She also kept up with personal and social commitments to friends and the community. She was an active member of the local Anglican church, St George's, and after the War of 1812 she joined a number of influential Kingston women in various philanthropic endeavours. In 1817 she was a subscriber to the Kingston Auxiliary Bible and Common Prayer Book Society and during the 1820s served as a director and manager of the Female Benevolent Society, which operated a small hospital. Morever, Ann Macaulay could always be counted on to support such worthy causes as the relief of fire victims in New Brunswick's Miramichi valley in 1825 and of cholera victims in Kingston, the newly established Queen's College, the Cataraqui Bridge Company, and the building fund for a monument to Sir Isaac Brock*.

Yet, throughout her life, family came first. She kept house for her son John until his marriage in 1833. For a short time after this she lived alone in her new stone house, Knaresborough Cottage, but returned to the Macaulay residence when John moved to Toronto to manage his political affairs. And when his wife died in 1846, Ann, at the age of 76, assumed maternal responsibility for the care in Kingston of John's four children. She died there four years later. As a woman in Upper Canada in the first half of the 19th century, Ann Macaulay undoubtedly subscribed to the cult of true womanhood so assiduously embraced by the colonial élite – the belief that a woman's proper sphere of influence was in the home as wife and mother. Though clearly a strong, capable businesswoman and active member of her community, she saw her primary role as that of a mother, and it was one she fulfilled conscientiously and well.

JANE ERRINGTON

AO, MS 78. Parish arch., Knaresborough (Knaresborough, Eng.), Reg. of baptisms, 11 Nov. 1770. *The parish register of Kingston, Upper Canada, 1785–1811*, ed. A. H. Young (Kingston, Ont., 1921). *Chronicle & Gazette*, 28 March 1840. *Kingston Chronicle*, 8 Dec. 1820, 6 June 1822, 11 Aug. 1826, 4 May 1827. *Kingston Gazette*, 22 March, 12 April 1817. *Upper Canada Gazette*, 15 Dec. 1825. Margaret [Sharp] Angus, "The Macaulay family of Kingston," *Historic Kingston*, no.5 (1955–56): 3–12.

KIRBY, JOHN, businessman, militia officer, office holder, JP, and politician; b. 1772 in Knaresborough, England, son of John Kirby and Ann ——; m. first Mary Nixon, *née* Macaulay; m. secondly 28 Feb. 1822 Cecilia Bethune (d. 1842), daughter of John Bethune* and widow of Walter Butler Wilkinson; he had no children; d. 19 Dec. 1846 in Kingston, Upper Canada.

John Kirby came to North America from Yorkshire with his parents in 1774 and settled with them on a farm near Fort Ticonderoga (near Ticonderoga, N.Y.). His father joined the British quartermaster general's department two years later at St Johns (Saint-Jean-sur-Richelieu), Que., where he located with his family after the American revolution. Though John Sr's name was expunged from the United Empire Loyalist list in 1798 by Upper Canada's Executive Council, on the grounds that it had been improperly inserted, he had apparently "shared in the troubles to which all loyalists were exposed." For John Jr the resulting family sympathies, contacts he made during the 1780s, and the opportunity to better his lot undoubtedly prompted him to move to Kingston, the small, tightly knit loyalist settlement where he gradually established himself as a merchant.

Kirby was introduced into the community and its commerce by Robert Macaulay*, who married his sister ANN in 1791. John may have worked as an agent in New York for the firm of Macaulay and Markland prior to its dissolution in 1792 or 1793. Kirby, who claimed to have taken up residence in Kingston in 1796, continued in the business with Macaulay until the latter's untimely death in 1800. John and Ann then assumed joint control of the diversified business, forming John Kirby and Company, which lasted until 1817. In addition to running its storage, wharfage, and commission business, John exported flour and other local produce on his own account and imported goods from the United States for sale in Kingston. And, perhaps because of a shortage of capital, he entered into other partnerships to finance specific projects, including (with Captain Henry Murney) the importing of tobacco and gin, and (with Thomas Clark*) the trans-shipment of goods at Queenston.

By the early 1820s, it seems, Kirby was financially secure and confident enough to conduct alone his general forwarding and merchandising business, together with other diverse interests. He was an agent for various business figures, including in 1823 Henry Atkinson, the Royal Navy's timber contractor at Quebec, and in 1826 Allan Macpherson of Napanee. Kirby engaged in extensive land speculation, and frequently lent money to associates. After the War of 1812 he had expanded his activities to include part-ownership in two steamships on Lake Ontario, the *Frontenac*, launched in 1816 [*see* James McKenzie*], and the *St George*, launched in 1834. As well, in 1826 he was one of the founding subscribers of the Cataraqui Bridge Company, an interest he maintained for the next ten years, serving first as a director and then as president.

By the mid 1820s Kirby's growing reputation as one of Kingston's most successful and respected businessmen was augmented by his participation in community projects undertaken to promote the economic development and prosperity of the area. Initially it was undoubtedly self-interest that prompted him to enter loose associations with other businessmen for such purposes. In 1813, for example, he was one of those who formed the Kingston Association, which attempted to regulate business by agreeing to "issue and accept bills for the convenience of making change." Six years later, he joined a group that wanted to regulate the fraudulent valuation of the halfpence of various currencies then in circulation by accepting only the British halfpenny. Kirby's interest in monetary matters also led him into an increasing involvement with banking institutions in the colony. By July 1817 he had become a trustee of the Bank of Upper Canada at Kingston, which was awaiting royal assent for a charter. The next year a private bank of the same name (later known as the "pretended" Bank of Upper Canada) was established, but Kirby's involvement in this institution is uncertain [*see* Thomas DALTON]. In February 1819 he was selected to sit on a committee established to investigate the feasibility of introducing a savings bank in Kingston, and in 1822, when such a bank was established, he was elected one of its vice presidents. After the "pretended" Bank of Upper Canada had been outflanked by the Bank of Upper Canada at York (Toronto), he seems to have moved quickly to support the latter. In 1823 his expertise and involvement were put to use by the provincial government, which appointed Kirby, his nephew John Macaulay* (the York bank's Kingston agent), and George Herchmer Markland* as commissioners to investigate and settle the affairs of the pretended bank. In 1830 Kirby became a director of the Bank of Upper Canada and ten years later was made a director of the Commercial Bank of the Midland District.

In the 1820s he had also been active in efforts to promote the union of the Canadas, a cause fervently advocated by John Macaulay, and to coordinate Kingston's business affairs more closely with those of Montreal. His own business concerns, together with his commitment to community development, led him to help organize the St Lawrence Association in 1824 to encourage the improvement of navigation on the St Lawrence. In addition, he supported in 1835 the proposed construction of a canal from Loughborough Lake to Kingston and in 1836 plans to improve the Welland Canal. In the latter year he represented landowners in the arbitration on drowned lands along the Rideau Canal. The economic advancement of Kingston, he clearly realized, depended on the development of the colony as a whole, and he did all in his power to enhance both.

Business was not his only, or perhaps even his primary, concern. Like others of his generation and class, he believed that he had a responsibility to serve the community at large. Shortly after his arrival in Kingston he began an active and long connection with the Church of England. In 1802 and again in 1810 he served as a warden at St George's Church. In the 1820s, as his wealth and prominence grew, Kirby became a principal subscriber to the building fund for a new church and, along with Thomas MARKLAND, Peter Smith*, Christopher Alexander HAGERMAN, and others, he was appointed to the committee to oversee the project. In 1842 he was a founding member of the Midland District Society, established to promote religion in the area, and throughout his residency in Kingston, it appears, Kirby was one of those who ensured that the local Anglican minister had an adequate income. His formal participation in church affairs was supplemented, particularly after 1815, by a growing commitment to the various social reform organizations beginning to appear in Upper Canada. In keeping with his belief that adherence to the dictates of God and to organized religion was essential to social order and public virtue, he helped found the Kingston Auxiliary Bible and Common Prayer Book Society in 1817, and served as its treasurer until 1827. He was vice-president of the Society for Promoting Christian Knowledge during much of that period, a member and president of the St George's Society in the 1830s, and in the following decade a founder and vice-president of the Association to Promote Christian Knowledge and for the Propagation of the Gospel among Destitute Settlers.

Kirby obviously realized, however, that religious instruction alone was not enough to ensure order and prosperity. Education was also essential. Thus he supported the building of a local school in 1815, subscribed to the newly established Queen's College in 1840, and served as treasurer of the Midland District School Society between 1842 and 1844. In 1811 he had joined other concerned citizens in underwriting financially the shaky *Kingston Gazette* [*see* Stephen Miles*], and in the 1810s he conscientiously donated time and money to the local library, as he did later to the Kingston Mechanics' Institute. As well, he was a founding member of the local agricultural society in 1819 and throughout the 1820s served as a manager for the Kingston Assembly, which organized lectures, dances, and other events.

After 1815, however, it had become evident to Kirby and other prominent townspeople that churches and schools alone could do little to alleviate the problems created by the flood of immigrants into Kingston. Often destitute, diseased, and disillusioned, many were ill prepared to start life in the New World. Christian duty and public order demanded that something be done, and Kirby and other community leaders rose to the occasion. In 1817 he became a founding member of the Kingston Compassionate Society, which he served as treasurer. Two years later, he joined the Committee on the Means of Supporting Paupers in Kingston and in 1820 made a considerable donation to the Kingston Benevolent Society. His continuing concern prompted him in 1832 to stand as president of the Emigrant Society of Kingston. During the 1820s and 1830s, Kirby also gave his whole-hearted support to his wife's activities in the Female Benevolent Society, and frequently added to its coffers. It was not just residents of Kingston who benefited from his philanthropy. When fire wreaked havoc in New Brunswick's Miramichi valley in 1825, he organized and chaired the local meeting to collect subscriptions. And while in the Legislative Council (1831–41), he was instrumental in directing government funds to hospitals and private charities throughout the colony.

Perhaps one of the most significant and, for Kirby, most satisfying achievements was his work to gain adequate health care for those in the Kingston area. His interest began in 1809, when he added his name to a petition to the government requesting land for a hospital. Ten years later he subscribed to a hospital building fund. It was not until 1832, however, when a cholera epidemic threatened local residents, that Kirby became directly involved. As chairman of the newly formed Kingston board of health, he put considerable time and effort into organizing and implementing measures, such as the regulation of local sanitation, intended to arrest the disease. In addition, Kirby and his committee established a cholera hospital and provided facilities for quarantining prospective victims, most of whom were recently arrived immigrants. When cholera struck again in 1835, 1836, and 1837, he again chaired the board of health and directed its activities.

Kirby was known in Kingston for far more than his business interests and philanthropic endeavours, however. A political conservative throughout his life, he was an ardent supporter of the province's tory administration. Upper Canadians had a duty, he believed, to support the government and the crown. Accepting the need for order and stability in society, he believed that some men, like himself, were by virtue of their wealth, rank, and ability called to lead. Prompted by this conviction, he was a member of the local militia, rising in 1838 to the rank of lieutenant-colonel and becoming a year later commanding officer of the 1st Regiment of Frontenac militia.

Much of Kirby's political career, and his influence, resided within the confines of eastern Upper Canada. In 1813 he was appointed road-master for Kingston and the surrounding township; five years later he was commissioned as a magistrate for the Midland District, a position he held until his death. He was appointed returning officer for Frontenac in 1816 and eight years later became commissioner for elections. Though politics was never a central part of his life,

Kirby's beliefs and business and personal connections with such prominent families as the Marklands, Macaulays, and Herchmers made him a member of Kingston's influential tory élite. In the complex factionalism which characterized Kingston's tories, he sided with John Macaulay and George Herchmer Markland and by the late 1820s his reliability as a tory was apparent. Not only had he publicly repudiated radical politics and the activities of Robert Gourlay* in 1819, but he had signed frequent petitions supporting the lieutenant governor and the colonial administration. In 1824 he was a principal subscriber to the fund established to erect a monument to Sir Isaac Brock*, who had become an increasingly important symbol, to the province's tories, of Upper Canadian and not just British courage and loyalty. Subscribing to the fund was not only a social action but an almost obligatory demonstration of loyalty.

Such good public service and Kirby's growing prominence were recognized in 1831 by his appointment to the Legislative Council. Throughout the next ten years, he travelled to York to take part in colonial policy making. Though he apparently cut back his business activities – he leased his wharf and store to George Wheatley Yarker in 1833 – he remained particularly interested in the economic development of the colony, giving considerable attention to proposed banking legislation and supporting measures to improve colonial transportation and communication. But Kirby never forgot his responsibilities to his town. In the mid 1830s he was instrumental in obtaining a government grant for a new hospital there and he supported, without success, a motion to establish a provincial quarantine station in the area.

Kirby's sympathy toward the provincial administration became clearly evident in 1837–38 when, in his view, political unrest threatened to destroy those political and social institutions he had spent much of his life defending. During the rebellion he joined many others in expressing his concern for the security of the colony, and a year later was pleased to be a member of the militia court martial convened at Fort Henry to try Nils von SCHOULTZ and other Patriots captured near Prescott. The aftermath of the rebellion and the report subsequently presented by Lord Durham [LAMBTON] dismayed Kirby, however, who, despite his earlier support of commercial union with Lower Canada, was apprehensive in 1839 about Durham's proposal for the union of the provinces. In correspondence with John Macaulay he questioned the plan, as did other extreme conservatives, and reacted fearfully to the possible use of French in parliament and the courts. The one consolation, to Kirby, was that Kingston was to be the new capital.

Kirby's concern about union and the new government and his own deteriorating health undoubtedly contributed to his failure to be reappointed to the Legislative Council in 1841. Yet it seems that he did not regret his permanent return to Kingston and private life. During the last years of his life, Kirby, in semi-retirement, was once again able to devote his attention to those concerns that most interested him. Between 1841 and 1845 he served as an associate judge in the Midland District Assizes. In 1844 he apparently headed the petition inviting John A. Macdonald* to run in Kingston in the provincial election that fall. As the grand old man of Kingston, president of the St George's Society, and commanding officer of the local militia, Kirby became involved in ceremonial duties, and he resumed his participation in local church and school affairs. For perhaps the first time in his life, he now had time to travel with family and friends. Having no children of his own, he had taken a keen interest in the concerns of his nephews, John, William*, and Robert Macaulay. He and John, through common business and political interests, had become particularly close, and this relationship, and that with his sister Ann, seemed to become even closer in the 1840s.

At the time of his death in December 1846, Kirby was, as the editor of the *Argus* commented, "one of a class which we regret to say is speedily passing away from amongst us." The people of Kingston remembered him as an astute businessman, "successful in mercantile pursuits," who was always "hospitable and unostentatious . . . freely bestowing his substance and his sympathy where the call of benevolence or charity invited his attention." John Kirby had been, in all senses, a tory gentleman. In his long life he achieved personal wealth and influence. As one of the early settlers in Upper Canada, he had watched and materially contributed to its establishment and growth. He had also proven himself to be a staunch advocate of the loyalist ideal and, by example, had supported the conservative ideals of service and stewardship. Indeed, Kirby was one of the generation that had been instrumental in the establishment of Upper Canada as a British and conservative society.

JANE ERRINGTON

AO, MS 78; RG 22, ser.155. PAC, RG 1, L3, 268: K3/7; 270: K8/1, 24; 271: K11/33; 271a: K13/14; RG 5, A1; B25, 4, 4 July 1824; RG 16, A1, 133, files for 1806–10, 1815; 134, file for 1820; 135, files for 1823–24; RG 68, General index, 1651–1841: 432, 670. QUA, 2199c, letter-books, Richard Cartwright to Peter Hunter, 31 March 1801; 2244, minutes, 1842–44; 2254. *Kingston before War of 1812* (Preston). *The parish register of Kingston, Upper Canada, 1785–1811*, ed. A. H. Young (Kingston, Ont., 1921). U.C., Legislative Council, *Journal*, 1832, 1836–37. *Argus; a Commercial, Agricultural, Political, and Literary Journal* (Kingston), 22 Dec. 1846. *Chronicle & Gazette*, 1833–46. *Kingston Chronicle*, 1819–33. *Kingston Gazette*, 1811–18. *Upper Canada Herald*, 15 March, 22 Nov. 1825; 13 Nov. 1830. *Heritage Kingston*, ed. J. D. Stewart and I. E. Wilson

(Kingston, 1973). K. M. Bindon, "Kingston: a social history, 1785–1830" (PHD thesis, Queen's Univ., Kingston, 1979), 438–42. Margaret [Sharp] Angus, "The Macaulay family of Kingston," *Historic Kingston*, no.5 (1955–56): 3–12. H. P. Gundy, "The Honourable John Kirby of Kingston," *Douglas Library Notes* (Kingston), 9 (1960), no.1: 2–4.

KIROUET. *See* QUIROUET

KITTSON, WILLIAM, militia officer and fur trader; b. *c.* 1792 in Lower Canada; d. 25 Dec. 1841 at Fort Vancouver (Vancouver, Wash.).

William Kittson was the adopted son of George Kittson of William Henry (Sorel), Lower Canada. He served during the War of 1812 with the Voltigeurs Canadiens, becoming a second lieutenant in February 1815 and going on half pay in July. In 1817 he joined the North West Company as an apprentice clerk and was sent to the Columbia department. Two years later he was at Fort Nez Percés (Walla Walla, Wash.) with Alexander Ross*, who later related how Kittson had received his initiation into the country when he was sent with supplies for the trapping expedition of Donald McKenzie* in the Snake River country. Kittson was over-confident and trusting as to the ways of the natives; as a result, all of the party's horses were stolen and Kittson and his companions had to complete their journey on foot. They wintered with the expedition at Day's Defile (Little Lost River, Idaho) in 1819–20. From 1820 to 1821 he was at Spokane House (near Spokane, Wash.) and, following the amalgamation of the NWC and the Hudson's Bay Company in 1821 [*see* Simon MCGILLIVRAY], he was retained by the HBC.

In 1824–25 Kittson was second in command of the Snake country expedition under Peter Skene Ogden*. Kittson's journal from 20 Dec. 1824 to 26 Aug. 1825 and his map of the area both help to verify the travels of the Ogden party. He proved equal to the demands of the expedition and his previous experience with the NWC stood him in good stead. Ogden had trouble with his men, most of whom were freemen and proved unreliable, but Kittson supported him in his dealings with them and with the American traders they met. Kittson would "face anything in the shape of danger," Governor George Simpson* noted in 1825. As well, he spoke Kootenay and other Indian languages and had become a good man of business.

From 1826 to 1829 he was in charge of Kootenae House near Windermere Lake (B.C.) and in 1830–31 he was at Flathead Post (Mont.). In 1831 he returned to Kootenae House, remaining in charge there for three years. He appears to have discharged these assignments well, drawing a favourable description from Simpson in his "Character book" of 1832: "A sharp, dapper, short tempered, self sufficient petulant little fellow of very limited Education, but exceedingly active and ambitious to signalize himself. . . . Conducts the business of his Post very well."

In 1834 Kittson was entrusted with the management of trade, farming, and stock raising at Fort Nisqually (near Tacoma, Wash.). The fur returns there had been declining, a circumstance which Kittson ascribed to disease among the Indians. Under his adept management, returns began to improve and the farming operation was successful, though the soil was not entirely suitable for the cultivation of crops. In 1839 Kittson treated a small field with manure and took off 250 bushels of wheat as a result. He remained in charge until October 1840, when he was obliged to go to Fort Vancouver on account of ill health which had plagued him since the previous spring. He declined steadily and died on 25 Dec. 1841. Kittson had had a country wife, a Walla Walla woman. He later married Helen, the daughter of Finan McDonald, another fur trader, and they had three sons and one daughter, who were named as beneficiaries in his will.

ERIC J. HOLMGREN

The account William Kittson wrote of the Snake country expedition has been published as "William Kittson's journal covering Peter Skene Ogden's 1824–1825 Snake country expedition," ed. D. E. Miller, *Utah Hist. Quarterly* (Salt Lake City), 22 (1954): 125–42.

HBRS, 3 (Fleming); 4 (Rich); 13 (Rich and Johnson); 28 (Williams). Alexander Ross, *The fur traders of the far west*, ed. K. A. Spaulding (Norman, Okla., 1956). *Select British docs. of War of 1812* (Wood), 2: 372. George Simpson, "Character book," *HBRS*, 30 (Williams); *Fur trade and empire: George Simpson's journal . . . 1824–25*, ed. and intro. Frederick Merk (rev. ed., Cambridge, Mass., 1968). *Officers of British forces in Canada* (Irving), 107, 109. Wallace, *Macmillan dict.* Rich, *Hist. of HBC* (1960), vol.3. Van Kirk, *"Many tender ties"*.

KOHLMEISTER, BENJAMIN GOTTLIEB, Moravian missionary and translator; b. 6 Feb. 1756 in Reisen (Rydzna, Poland); m. 1793 Anna Elizabeth Reimann in Labrador, and they had four children; d. 3 June 1844 in Neusalz (Nowa Sól, Poland).

Like many Moravian missionaries, Benjamin Gottlieb Kohlmeister came of relatively humble stock. His father was a baker, and Benjamin's childhood was characterized by a series of moves made to try to improve the family's economic circumstances. As a result, he received little formal education. In Warsaw, soon after the death of his father, Kohlmeister was apprenticed to a cabinet-maker. When he completed his training in 1775, he wandered from town to town for some years. Already an enthusiastic Christian, Kohlmeister made contact with a Moravian congregation at Dresden (German Democratic Republic). Impressed and attracted by the sect, he went on to its headquarters at Herrnhut, where he was in due course accepted as a member of the congregation.

Kohlmeister subsequently worked at the Moravian settlement of Christiansfeld, Denmark, until 1790. That year he was called to mission service in Labrador, and began a 12-year residence at Okak, the most northerly of the three stations then operated by the Moravians [*see* Jens Haven*]. Intelligent, adaptable, and apparently well liked, Kohlmeister first took charge of the school, which enabled him to learn Inuktitut quickly. Later he supervised the trade with the Inuit. He also acted as a doctor. Kohlmeister was moved in 1802 to Hopedale, where he presided over a religious revival unprecedented since the Moravians' settlement in Labrador in 1771. A sermon preached at the end of December 1803 sparked a general awakening which spread to Nain and Okak. It was a turning-point for the mission since it led to the firm establishment of a Moravian theocracy in northern Labrador.

In 1806 Kohlmeister returned to Europe on leave. Detained there because of wartime travel restrictions, he was able to discuss with the mission board the question of expanding the work of the Labrador mission. A significant number of Inuit from Ungava (Que.) and Hudson Strait had visited the Moravian settlements, and the missionaries thought the bulk of the Inuit might live in that direction. Kohlmeister was instructed to lead an expedition into the area and prepare a report. He spent the winter of 1810–11 at Okak, and the following June began his journey, accompanied by another missionary, George Kmoch, and 15 Inuit. They sailed north in a shallop to Cape Chidley and then south down the east side of Ungava Bay. Naming the George River after George III the missionaries went on as far as the Koksoak River, which they ascended to the present site of Fort Chimo. At both places they identified suitable locations for mission stations.

Kohlmeister returned to Okak in October, impressed by what he had seen and in favour of an Ungava settlement. Though he was supported by both the mission board and the missionaries, no such settlement was built. The continuance of the war and heavy expenses led to postponements and second thoughts. By 1814 the Moravians were debating whether to persist with the Ungava project or to build a fourth station north of Okak. The second alternative was eventually chosen, the deciding factor being the opposition of the Hudson's Bay Company to the first. It objected to any trading by the mission within its territory, yet the Moravians insisted that a station had to help pay for its support. Soon after the Moravians' exchanges with the HBC, the company began the exploration and exploitation of the peninsula.

In 1818 Kohlmeister was appointed general superintendent of the mission and moved to its headquarters at Nain. He left Labrador 6 years later and spent the last 20 years of his life at Herrnhut and Neusalz, as active in church affairs as his age and health permitted. A simple and pious man, Kohlmeister was nevertheless clever, curious, and versatile. He read widely to make up for his lack of education, and became an accomplished amateur botanist as well as a good linguist – he was one of the translators of the New Testament into the Labrador Inuktitut dialect. In all, as one obituarist put it, he was "a favourable specimen of the genuine Moravian missionary."

JAMES K. HILLER

Benjamin Gottlieb Kohlmeister and George Kmoch published an account of their 1812 journey to Ungava Bay as *Journal of a voyage from Okkak, on the coast of Labrador, to Ungava Bay, westward of Cape Chudleigh; undertaken to explore the coast, and visit the Esquimaux in that unknown region* (London, 1814). Among Kohlmeister's religious works is *Tamedsa Johannesib aglangit, økautsiñik Tussarnertuñik, Jesuse Kristusemik, Gudim Erngninganik*, a translation of the Gospel of John into the Labrador Inuktitut dialect; several others with which he was involved are cited in J. C. Pilling, *Bibliography of the Eskimo language* (Washington, 1887); repr. as J. C. Pilling, *Bibliographies of the languages of the North American Indians* (9 pts. in 3 vols., New York, 1973), vol.1, pt.1.

Moravian Church in G.B. and Ire. Library (London), Soc. for the Furtherance of the Gospel, minutes, 15 March, 25 Oct. 1813; 9 May, 19 Dec. 1814; 8 May, 10 Nov. 1815; 17 May, 16 Dec. 1816; 6 April 1818 (mfm. at Memorial Univ. of Nfld. Library, St John's). *HBRS*, 24 (Davies and Johnson), xxxvi–xxxviii. *Memoir of Br. Benj. Gottlieb Kohlmeister, missionary among the Esquimaux in Labrador* . . . (London, 1845). Alan Cooke, "The Ungava venture of the Hudson's Bay Company, 1830–1843" (PHD thesis, Univ. of Cambridge, Cambridge, Eng., 1970), 12. J. K. Hiller, "The foundation and the early years of the Moravian mission in Labrador, 1752–1805" (MA thesis, Memorial Univ. of Nfld., [1967]), 222–25.

?KWAH (Quâs), Carrier chief; b. *c.* 1755 on what is now Stuart Lake, B.C., son of Tsalekulhyé and a woman from Nat-len (Fraser Lake); d. 1840 at Fort St James, New Caledonia.

Legend has it that ?Kwah and his brother Œhulhtzœn (Hoolson) gained fame by avenging the murder of their father, who was killed by another Carrier group about 1780. The story is likely well founded, for inter-village conflicts among the Carriers, especially over women and gambling matters, were common. At some point ?Kwah became a nobleman. Since the tribe practised matrilineal succession, it would have been from a deceased male relative on his mother's side, likely his uncle, that he gained this status. Upper Carrier villages ranged from about 40 to 120 persons and each had a chief and one or two nobles. By 1806, when the North West Company built Fort St James on the east end of Stuart Lake, ?Kwah was living near by with his four wives and was considered by the Carriers to be the village chief. In accordance with custom, he maintained his status by periodically giving inter-village feasts. One of his official responsibilities was to act as arbitrator in feuds between villages.

The earliest firsthand account of ʔKwah, given by NWC trader Daniel Williams HARMON, dates from 1811. In a business dispute with the trader, ʔKwah asserted that the only difference between them was that Harmon could read and write. "You send a great way off for goods, and you are rich and want for nothing," the chief remarked. "But do not I manage my affairs as well as you do yours? When did you ever hear that Quâs was in danger of starving? . . . I never want for any thing, and my family is always well clothed." As their confrontation grew more heated, Harmon became convinced that ʔKwah was trying to intimidate him, and he beat the chief with a measuring-stick. A short time later ʔKwah feasted Harmon and apologized for his behaviour, but this was not the last time that he tested the traders. Although ʔKwah often angered them, and they him, he worked hard to ensure that both they and his own family were well provided with food, especially salmon from the weir which he toiled to keep in repair. ʔKwah "is the only Indian who can and Will give fish, and on whom we Must depend in a great Measure," wrote trader James McDougall. Being a noble, ʔKwah inherited the right to certain beaver lands. Assisted by his sons and sons-in-law he was, like his fellow nobles, a chief supplier of beaver and other furs to Fort St James.

Perhaps best remembered by whites was ʔKwah's role in saving the life of James Douglas*, at the time a Hudson's Bay Company employee in charge at the post. The incident stemmed from the murder by two Carriers in 1823 of two HBC employees belonging to Fort George (Prince George) over a sexual liaison. The traders requested that the Indians kill the two murderers, and ʔKwah was suspected of dissuading them from doing so. Several years later one of the culprits visited ʔKwah's village. He hid in ʔKwah's house, the chief being away, but was killed by Douglas and other HCB men when discovered. After ʔKwah returned, he and the other villagers stormed the post demanding an explanation. While ʔKwah's nephew held a sword at Douglas's breast, the chief requested that no blood be shed. Gifts were thrown by the women of the post, and the Indians went home, compensation for the death having been received. Despite the mob frenzy, ʔKwah had maintained his composure, probably realizing that to harm the traders would eventually bring retribution.

ʔKwah died during the summer of 1840 and that November a funeral feast was held in his honour. Unlike his ancestors, he was buried instead of being cremated. At his death he was perhaps the most important Indian in New Caledonia, from both the traders' and the Carriers' perspective. The whites had dubbed him king of the Carriers. His third son, who succeeded ʔKwah's brother as chief despite the matrilineal tradition, became known as the Prince. ʔKwah left 16 children and numerous grandchildren. When missionaries began baptizing Indians in the area during the middle of the 19th century, the family was given the surname Prince.

CHARLES A. BISHOP

PAM, HBCA, B.119/a/1; B.188/a/1–19; B.188/b/1–6; B.188/e/1–5 (mfm. at PAC). D. W. Harmon, *Sixteen years in the Indian country: the journal of Daniel Williams Harmon, 1800–1816*, ed. W. K. Lamb (Toronto, 1957). C. A. Bishop, "Kwah: a Carrier chief," *Old trails and new directions: papers of the third North American Fur Trade Conference*, ed. C. M. Judd and A. J. Ray (Toronto, 1980), 191–204. A.-G. Morice, *The history of the northern interior of British Columbia, formerly New Caledonia, 1600 to 1880* (Toronto, 1904). W. P. Johnston, "Chief Kwah's revenge," *Beaver*, outfit 274 (September 1943): 22–23.

L

LAFFERTY. *See* LEFFERTY

LA FRAMBOISE, MARGUERITE-MAGDELAINE. *See* MARCOT

LALAWETHIKA. *See* TENSKWATAWA

LAMARTINE, CHARLES HINDENLANG, known as. *See* HINDENLANG

LAMB, HENRY, farmer and businessman; b. probably in Pennsylvania; m. and had four sons and a daughter; d. 22 Jan. 1841 in Beverly Township, Upper Canada.

Of Scots descent, Henry Lamb was considered a loyalist by historian Robert Kirkland Kernighan, although what part, if any, he played in the American revolution is not known. According to Richard BEASLEY, a Barton Township magistrate, he came to Upper Canada in 1799 and settled at the head of Lake Ontario. In June 1803 he applied for a land grant but this was denied the following year because he had gone back to the United States during the winter. After his return to Upper Canada he lived in Beverly and

Flamborough townships and in the Grand River area. Lamb seems to have bought land, cleared and improved it, and then sold it to settlers with sufficient cash to pay for his effort. He thus accumulated capital, and by 1821 he had settled permanently in Beverly.

Lamb's land was located on the edge of a large swamp along the road from Shade's Mills (Cambridge) to Dundas. The Beverly Swamp was a fearsome place, complete with unfriendly Indians, wolves, and quicksand, but Lamb nevertheless opened a tavern near by. His success was considerable. In 1821–22 he built his great house, a two-storey timber structure measuring 20 by 40 feet and enclosed by a stockade, within which he kept cows and pigs. By 1825 he had built a sawmill and had become the wealthiest landowner in Beverly, a position he maintained until his death.

Lamb was clearly a promoter. In 1829 he wrote to Peter ROBINSON, the commissioner of crown lands, to ask for a contract to cut a road from Guelph to the proposed Waterloo turnpike in Beverly and thus shorten the route between Shade's Mills and Guelph by 11 miles. Though he did not get the contract (a road had already been cut, Robinson explained), he continued to write to the colonial government. He stressed the fact that he had encouraged a better class of settlers to come to Beverly and asked for support in the form of information on crown and clergy reserves that might become available.

In the early 1830s he attempted his largest promotion, a planned community, to be called Romulus, centred on his land in concession 6 in Beverly, at a site west of the present village of Rockton. Romulus was to have Anglican and Roman Catholic cathedrals. Free land and building materials were to be available for any other denomination. A market-square, cricket-ground, and race-track were also planned and the town would boast a theatre, concert-hall, and ballroom. Lamb advertised in English newspapers for artisans and tradesmen, promising free housing, firewood, and no municipal taxation for 25 years. Part of his promotional material was a map which showed the settlement at the centre of the civilized world. Romulus, however, was a complete failure. Only two settlers arrived, both in 1834, one to start a store and the other to farm. None of the public buildings was ever built. Nevertheless, for local residents, Henry Lamb was Mayor Lamb, a recognized leader in the area. His sawmill and tavern seem to have continued successfully, and in 1837 he established a grist-mill. A year later, by which time he had accumulated 1,250 acres in Beverly, he sported the only "pleasure wagon" there.

Lamb was a man of some mystery to his contemporaries. His wife claimed aristocratic lineage in France. He was reputed to have had a secret room in his tavern where gentlemanly strangers met in masonic rituals. Now he is viewed as an Upper Canadian enthusiast who saw opportunity in the soil of Beverly Township and who tried to create a city in the New World. A pragmatist he nevertheless was. His only known comment on life, made after fighting off an attack by Indians, has come down through the folklore of Beverly: "A man might as well lose his life as his pork."

PHILIP CREIGHTON

AO, RG 1, A-I-6: 7662–65; C-IV, Beverly Township, concession 5, lot 12; RG 21, Wentworth County, Beverly Township, assessment rolls, 1821–34, 1837–39; RG 22, ser.204, reg.F (1840–43): 149–52. PAC, RG 1, L1, 26: 32; L3, 286: L9/1. Wentworth Land Registry Office (Hamilton, Ont.), Abstract index to deeds, Beverly Township (mfm. at AO). "Index to *The pioneers of Beverly* by John A. Cornell," comp. Faye West (typescript, Edmonton, 1980; photocopy at AO). J. A. Cornell, *The pioneers of Beverly; series of sketches* . . . (Dundas, Ont., 1889; repr. [Galt (Cambridge), Ont., 1967]). Johnston, *Head of the Lake* (1958). The Khan [R. K. Kernighan], "A city that was not built" and "Legends of Romulus," *Pen and pencil sketches of Wentworth landmarks* . . . (Hamilton, 1897), 118–20, 121–23. M. F. Campbell, "Romulus recalled: wolves integral part of Beverly's history," *Hamilton Spectator*, 7 Dec. 1954: 25. "Mouldering ruins only vestige of Beverly dream city . . . ," *Hamilton Spectator*, 15 July 1946. Passerby, "Here and there in Wentworth," *Hamilton Spectator*, 28 Aug. 1933: 18.

LAMBTON, JOHN GEORGE, 1st Earl of Durham, colonial administrator; b. 12 April 1792 in London, eldest son of William Henry Lambton and Lady Anne Barbara Frances Villiers, daughter of George Villiers, 4th Earl of Jersey; m. first 1 Jan. 1812 Harriet Cholmondeley at Gretna Green, Scotland, and they had three daughters; m. secondly 9 Dec. 1816 Lady Louisa Elizabeth Grey, and they had two sons and three daughters; d. 28 July 1840 in Cowes, Isle of Wight, England.

John George Lambton came from a family that had lived in the valley of the Wear in the north of England since at least the 12th century. The feudal lord Robert de Lambton (d. 1350) is the most distant ancestor who can be documented. Through marriages nearly always based on family interests and social affinities, the Lambtons had in time become connected with the greatest English families and were distantly related to the royal family. In this privileged milieu, the traditions of military and political service were firmly rooted. Thus, William Henry Lambton, like his father before him, had been elected to the House of Commons for Durham City, which he represented from 1787 till 1797.

The Lambtons derived much of their income from coal-mines on their lands. Around 1812 mining earned them about £80,000 annually, and Lord Durham was said to have had 2,400 miners in his employ by 1833. Consequently the family maintained numerous and varied relations with the mercantile and industrial bourgeoisie. And even if Durham naturally had an unqualified attachment to his aristocratic heritage, it did not prevent him from celebrating in his own way the rise of the middle class or establishing relations with both his own and other local workers that were quite unusual among the well-to-do. Radical tendencies were not new in his family: his father had acquired a reputation as a revolutionary by helping to found the Society of the Friends of the People in 1792 and the society had delegated him to present a petition to parliament strongly urging reform of the House of Commons.

Young John had little time, however, to be influenced by his father, who died of tuberculosis at 33 in 1797 when the boy was but 5 years old. His mother soon married Charles William Wyndham and does not seem to have had any desire to look after her children. Thus John and his brother William Henry went to live with a family friend, Dr Thomas Beddoes, a scientist whose radical ideas were well known. The boys remained with him until John was 13. A hypersensitive youngster in delicate health, he suffered enormously from the loss of his father and the attitude of his mother, according to historian Chester William New.

After studying under tutors, Lambton in 1805 enrolled in Eton College, where he spent four years. Surprisingly, in view of his health, instead of going to university he immediately chose a military career, joining the 10th Hussars as a cornet in 1809. He took an equally unpredictable step on 1 Jan. 1812 when he eloped to Gretna Green with Harriet Cholmondeley, marrying her against the wishes of his guardians. Matters evidently were soon straightened out, since within a few weeks the couple agreed to go through the ceremony again. The marriage lasted only three years, for Harriet died of tuberculosis in 1815. Overwhelmed by the tragedy, Lambton considered giving up the new career he had embarked upon with his election to the House of Commons for Durham County in September 1813. He retained his seat until 1828, however.

Lambton is said to have been a man of a little more than medium height, elegant in his bearing. Like most of his class he adored horse-racing, hunting, and fishing, but he was fonder than usual of the arts, history, and politics. If his numerous detractors are to be believed, he surpassed his peers in arrogance, vanity, and love of show. Yet none of his adversaries dared question his exceptional independence of mind, courage, frankness, or sincerity. When Sir Henry Thomas Liddell withdrew his political backing from Lambton, reproaching him for a reform zeal he implied was revolutionary, he experienced these qualities. Lambton retorted bluntly, "I beg to say that I feel gratitude for your frankness, compassion for your fears, little dread of your opposition and no want of your support." Lambton had what was needed for a career as a political reformer, and some thought he might before long become the leader of a reinvigorated Whig party. His health and many other factors kept him from sharing these views.

Lambton was beyond doubt a true reformer. New quite accurately describes him as a radical Whig and a moderate Radical. It was in this spirit that he supported the great reform measures of his time: dissenters' rights, emancipation of Catholics, free trade, universal education, and the founding of mechanics' institutes and the University of London. Early in his political career Lambton concentrated on parliamentary reform. Although historians differ in their assessment of his contribution to the debates, he admittedly holds a privileged place, along with Lord Grey, Lord John Russell, and Lord Brougham, in the history of the Reform Act of 1832.

Since Lambton did not raise the issue of electoral reform openly until 1819, it is hard to say what his aims were when he went into politics as a Whig. Presumably he soon became aware of the faulty nature of the British electoral system. Certainly he had been struck by the fact that boroughs were over-represented as compared with the counties, and he also knew that the system favoured the gentry and aristocracy to the virtual exclusion of the middle class and the masses. On 17 April 1821 he introduced a bill to abolish rotten boroughs and extend the vote that foreshadowed the 1832 legislation. Fierce Tory opposition and Whig doubts helped defeat it, however. While not entirely shutting out the working class, in running up the flag for reform Lambton was in fact inviting his compatriots to let the upper and middle classes, along with some popular elements, share power. Though not yet prepared to advocate universal suffrage, he favoured the secret ballot and supported the idea that parliamentary elections should be more frequent.

Lambton had understood the decisive role that the middle classes played in building up industrial and urban England. He spoke of it with enthusiasm and acknowledged that they had superior wealth and equal competence, talent, and grasp of politics. In his eyes, these factors justified their demands to share by right in political power. His attitude earned him the sympathy, confidence, and support of the moderate middle-class radicals, who were attempting to shape public opinion through newspapers and political associations and thus were in constant contact with popular elements alive to the idea of reform.

Consequently Lambton was both a disturbing and an indispensable figure for the Whig aristocrats. This idealistic nobleman – he was created Baron Durham on 29 Jan. 1828 – urged them unceasingly to go farther than they wanted. On the other hand, especially during the repeated crises in the period 1830–32, while pressing them to go as far as they had to, he proved a dependable intermediary between them, the middle classes, and the people. It is not surprising that when the Whigs came to power in 1830 under Lord Grey, his father-in-law, Durham was made chairman of a committee to prepare a bill on parliamentary reform. During this time of great turbulence, the outcome of which was uncertain until the very end came on 7 June 1832, Durham played a role that left in no doubt the depth of his commitment. He was never tempted to see the passage of the bill as the final stage of parliamentary reform. Neither the bourgeoisie nor the masses really got what they wanted, or all they wanted, from the act of 1832. The responsibility for this result rested not only with the aristocracy, but also with middle-class fear of the masses and, it must be added, with similar fears among some in the upper ranks of the working class.

The period from the Reform Act until his appointment as ambassador to Russia in 1835 was one of the most difficult in Durham's life and career. Honours came his way: he was raised to the rank of Viscount Lambton and Earl of Durham on 23 March 1833. He was, however, overwhelmed by an almost unbroken series of family misfortunes affecting him in body and spirit. His eldest son, Charles William, died at age 13 on 24 Dec. 1831, and his mother the following year. Then in the space of four years he lost all the remaining children of his first marriage. This was also the time when he broke with companions of long standing. His split with Lord Brougham was an important public event, but his permanent retirement from the cabinet in 1833 as a result of repeated disagreements with Lord Grey on matters relating to reform clearly marked the beginning of his isolation.

Although Durham was frequently mentioned after 1830 as the future leader of the Whigs, his chances of obtaining the post seem to have grown increasingly slim. It was not entirely by chance that, with his chiefs' encouragement, his career took a new turn towards foreign affairs, particularly after 1832. He was involved in the achievement of independence by Belgium and Greece and in the accession of Prince Leopold to the throne of Belgium, and then was entrusted in July 1832 with a mission to the tsar. When Lord Melbourne became prime minister in 1835, he promptly named Durham ambassador to Russia. There he had the orders of St Andrew, Alexander Nevsky, St Anne, and the White Eagle conferred on him. Two years later he returned to England and was awarded the Order of the Bath.

Durham had barely got settled in England when on 22 July 1837 Melbourne proposed that he undertake another mission abroad, to the Canadas, where a crisis generally thought insoluble was growing worse. Durham categorically refused. In December, however, after rebellion had broken out in both Upper and Lower Canada, Melbourne made a fresh attempt, promising him virtually dictatorial powers as governor-in-chief of the British North American colonies and high commissioner. Durham let himself be persuaded.

From the moment he accepted the appointment on 15 Jan. 1838 until his departure for the Canadas on 24 April Durham was far from idle. In addition to familiarizing himself with Colonial Office files and having discussions with those of its staff best acquainted with developments in the colonies, he was in direct contact with men involved in Canadian affairs in various capacities such as George Moffatt*, William Badgley*, Louis-Hippolyte La Fontaine*, Edward Ellice*, and John Arthur Roebuck*. He also proceeded to choose his own aides, who included Charles BULLER, Edward Gibbon Wakefield*, and Thomas Edward Michell Turton.

On 27 May 1838 the *Hastings* cast anchor at Quebec. Two days later Durham landed and quickly made a proclamation promising to show an open mind and to treat everyone fairly. On 1 June he dissolved the Special Council which upon the suspension of the constitution on 10 February had been made responsible, along with the Executive Council, for settling urgent matters. On 2 June he appointed his own Executive Council, from which members of the earlier body were excluded. Buller, Turton, Colonel George Couper, Randolph Isham Routh*, and Dominick Daly* were named to it. On 28 June he formed a new Special Council, which included Vice-Admiral Sir Charles Paget, Sir James Macdonell*, Lieutenant-Colonel Charles Grey, Buller, and Couper.

Of all the problems the new governor had to resolve without delay, none was more urgent and delicate than the fate of the Lower Canadian political prisoners. Administrator Sir John Colborne* had already released 326 of them, but 161 remained in jail awaiting trial. Durham quickly realized that if he followed the expeditious method adopted by the lieutenant governor of Upper Canada, Sir George Arthur*, who had had some prisoners executed, he risked making the situation irremediable. On the other hand he had no doubt that any approach necessitating a jury would be hazardous, for given the state of mind prevalent in the province, it would be impossible to find an impartial one. To be lenient while cognizant of the seriousness of the acts committed, Durham felt obliged to resort to a strategy which would only succeed if his agents could bring the principal prisoners around to admitting their guilt. On 26 June eight of them including Rodolphe DES RIVIÈRES, Siméon Marchesseault*, and Wolfred Nelson* signed such an acknowledgement. Two days later Durham made public his decision to order the eight transported to Bermuda and to prohibit 16 other prominent Patriotes who had found refuge in the United States – Louis-Joseph Papineau*, Cyrille-

Hector-Octave Côté, and Édouard-Étienne Rodier among them – from returning to Lower Canada on pain of death. The other prisoners, except those who had participated in the execution of Joseph Armand, *dit* Chartrand, and Lieutenant George Weir, were given amnesty.

The wisdom of Durham's solution was recognized by the people of Lower Canada and initially by the Whigs themselves, including even those hostile to him. A change was in the wind, however, from the day Lord Brougham began to denounce certain aspects of Durham's decisions as illegal, in particular the fact that he had sent men accused but not tried into exile in a colony over which he had no jurisdiction, and that he had also pronounced the sentence of death on fugitives. Durham quickly lost the support of his own party and its leader, Melbourne, who backed repudiation of the decree of 28 June. Durham did not learn of this situation until 19 September, when he read about it in a New York newspaper. He believed that for reasons having nothing to do with his mission he had been betrayed by the party leaders. His resignation was inevitable and irreversible. On 9 Oct. 1838, he made public the documents concerning his repudiation and announced officially that he was resigning and returning to England. On 1 November he sailed on the *Inconstant*, reaching Plymouth on 26 November and London on 7 December.

The gesture did not, however, mean that his mission was over. In the early weeks of his stay in the Canadas he had set up an extremely busy schedule of work. In addition to a heavy agenda of social gatherings, it called for frequent meetings with leading figures in colonial society, travel in the Canadas, and above all the establishment of commissions to inquire into such matters as settlement, immigration, education, municipal institutions, commutation of the seigneurial régime on the island of Montreal, registry offices, police, and the judicial system. In the period from 18 June to 25 August six of these working groups had been created and had immediately turned to their tasks.

The commissions worked so well that by the time Durham left he had a fairly clear idea of what his report would contain. All that remained was to write it, a task that took until late January 1839. The proofs were submitted to cabinet on 31 January, four days before the report was presented to the Colonial Office. In the interval, by some unknown means, the London *Times* began publishing excerpts from the document, so that the British public knew its essential elements before it was officially laid before parliament on 11 February.

When Durham had left on his Canadian mission, he had felt that his task would not be complicated. He thought he might discover in North America, and Lower Canada in particular, the sort of conflicts so common in Europe, such as the one in which he had been involved in England at the time he had committed himself to parliamentary reform. He expected that the crisis would have readily discernible outward manifestations, and without doubt it would be so essentially political, and secondarily social, that reform of the constitution would suffice to cure it. After his arrival in the colony, Durham reached the conclusion that from the perspective of a need for reform, the solution available within the framework of British institutions implied the introduction of responsible government as a key measure. In the course of a visit he paid to Upper Canada, Robert* and William Warren Baldwin indeed drew his attention to this idea, which they considered of the greatest importance.

On the extension of ministerial responsibility to the colonies Durham took a position similar to the one he had adopted on parliamentary reform. He believed that in granting responsible government to the colonies, far from inciting them to become independent, the British government would not only put an end to sterile struggles and violence but would also confirm certain enduring links between Britain and her dependencies. "I admit," he wrote, "that the system which I propose would, in fact, place the internal government of the colony in the hands of the colonists themselves. . . . The constitution of the form of government, – the regulation of foreign relations, and of trade with the mother country, the other British Colonies, and foreign nations, – and the disposal of the public lands, are the only points on which the mother country requires a control."

If Durham had believed the crisis he had to resolve could be reduced to a class struggle or a conflict between the executive power and the people's assembly, he would have felt free to write a report centred merely upon the benefits of responsible government for the six colonies. But, having come to the conclusion that in Lower Canada the conflict depicted as a class struggle was really a racial one, he was convinced he had to go beyond such recommendations. A closer examination of the tenor of his discussion of the Lower Canadian situation forces the realization that his conclusions derived less from ethnic considerations than from his liberalism and his great sympathy for the historical role of the middle class. On finding the institutions of the *ancien régime* functioning among the French Canadians as they had formerly in France, he may have tended as a good liberal simply to heap upon these people the scorn he felt for absolutist and feudal France. Unlike most other contemporary societies, that of French Canada did not have the strong middle class Durham saw as essential. In his view, that class had played a predominant role in the French revolution and the industrial revolution in England and had given the development of the United

States its progressive stamp. He attributed the peasant nature of French Canadian society to its absence. "The mass of the community exhibited in the New World the characteristics of the peasantry of Europe," he wrote. He noted there were elements in both the French-speaking and the English-speaking populations which, if brought together, could have constituted a solid middle class. However, in his discussion of the conduct of French Canadians in the professions, he characterized them not as agents for social progress but as the prime defenders of the old order against the new forces, even though they had regularly used the language of liberalism and democracy. He did succeed in discovering genuine forces for development in the English-speaking milieu. It was among the merchants, who were obliged to seek support from governors and the imperial authorities to protect themselves, that the reform measures most likely to ensure economic progress and social change had been taking shape. They were prevented from acting, he said, by a conflict so deep that it permeated the entire life of the colony. "I expected to find a contest between a government and a people: I found two nations warring in the bosom of a single state: I found a struggle, not of principles, but of races; and I perceived that it would be idle to attempt any amelioration of laws or institutions, until we could first succeed in terminating the deadly animosity that now separates the inhabitants of Lower Canada into the hostile divisions of French and English."

Durham had not intended to build his analysis around the concept of race, an approach that, had he been aware of it, he himself would have found offensive. But his reactions to the national conflicts dividing society in Lower Canada were so strong that in his report he reduced virtually everything to race. From this perspective, the situation seemed to him so irremediable and French Canadian society so incurably ossified that he ended up recommending such an unrealistic and illiberal solution as the assimilation of French Canadians to a culture he judged superior. Certainly it was his great concern with the ethnic question that prompted him to reject federation in favour of legislative union of Upper and Lower Canada, although this recommendation was accompanied by a firm proposal for responsible government. For assimilation to be realized, however, Durham was counting essentially on demographic forces which, he was certain, would work for the English-speaking population, rather than on straightforward legal and institutional constraints.

The question of union, like that of colonial autonomy, had been in the air for three decades. Since 1810 the English-speaking merchants of Montreal and Quebec had been calling for union of the Canadas under one government. After the failure of the Union Bill of 1822, the merchants had asked that Montreal be annexed to Upper Canada, without, however, giving up their basic demand. In his report Durham had sought to recommend solutions to the whole problem of the Canadas, which had been perturbing colonial societies for so long and was reverberating in London. Yet neither the idea of responsible government nor that of a legislative union as he had defined it was accepted by the imperial government. Provided as it was with clauses concerning equal representation, the Union Act of 1840 did not respect the priority of principles set forth by Durham. It is none the less true that the debate in which he had engaged, examining the main points more thoroughly than anyone else before or after him, would not come to an end either in 1841 with the union of Upper and Lower Canada or even in 1848 with the attainment of responsible government.

Since childhood Durham had constantly been threatened with tuberculosis. His father, his first wife, and four of his children had been carried off by it. Throughout his life he was forced to cease his activities at certain times because of illness. Regularly, and sometimes for rather long periods, he was obliged to perform his duties while enduring great suffering. His delicate health grew worse long before the end of his stay in the Canadas. Upon his return to England, once his report had been made public, he was again urged to reduce the pace of his work, although his responsibilities within organizations set up to colonize New Zealand were not absorbing his time to any great extent. Except for the rare social engagement when he found a chance to make peace with former colleagues and friends, including Brougham and Melbourne, from February 1840 on he kept more and more to his residence at Cowes, where he died on 28 July. His second wife and four of their children survived him.

FERNAND OUELLET

John George Lambton's *Report on the affairs of British North America, from the Earl of Durham . . .* was issued by parliament in 1839 as G.B., Parl., Command paper, 1839, 17, no.3, and also as a separate publication ([London, 1839]). It has been republished as *Lord Durham's report on the affairs of British North America,* ed. C. P. Lucas (3v., Oxford, 1912; repr. New York, 1970), and as *Lord Durham's report,* ed. G. M. Craig (Toronto, 1963). There is a French translation: *Rapport de Durham*, M.-P. Hamel, trad. et édit. (Montréal, 1948).

[Charles] Grey, *Crisis in the Canadas: 1838–1839; the Grey journals and letters*, ed. William Ormsby (Toronto, 1964). [L. E. Grey, Countess of] Durham, *Letters and diaries of Lady Durham*, ed. Patricia Godsell (Ottawa, 1979). *Burke's peerage* (1970). Fauteux, *Patriotes*. Wallace, *Macmillan dict*. John Benson, *British coalminers in the nineteenth century: a social history* (Dublin and New York, 1980). Michael Brock, *The great Reform Act* (London, 1973). Buckner, *Transition to responsible government*. *The colonial reformers and Canada, 1830–1849*, ed. Peter

Burroughs (Toronto, 1969). Leonard Cooper, *Radical Jack; the life of John George Lambton, first Earl of Durham, 1792–1840* (London, 1959). Richard Fynes, *The miners of Northumberland and Durham* (Wakefield, Eng., 1971). E. J. Hobsbawm, *Labouring men; studies in the history of labour* (London, 1975). Mark Hovell, *The Chartist movement* (Manchester, Eng., 1963). Ged Martin, *The Durham report and British policy: a critical essay* (Cambridge, Eng., 1972). C. W. New, *Lord Durham; a biography of John George Lambton, first Earl of Durham* (Oxford, 1929). Ouellet, *Bas-Canada*; *Hist. économique*. Harold Perkin, *The origins of modern English society, 1780–1880* (London, 1972). *Pressure from without in early Victorian England*, ed. Patricia Hollis (London, 1974). Taft Manning, *Revolt of French Canada*. E. P. Thompson, *The making of the English working class* (London, 1963). Roger Viau, *Lord Durham* (Montréal, 1962).

LANCASTER, JOSEPH, educator; b. 25 Nov. 1778 in Southwark (London), son of Richard Lancaster, a sieve maker, and Sarah Foulkes; m. first 5 June 1804 Elizabeth Bonner, and they had one daughter; m. secondly 1825 Mary Robinson; d. 23 Oct. 1838 in New York.

Joseph Lancaster obtained a relatively modest education. He learned to read at two dame-schools and to enjoy military discipline at a school run by a former army officer. Following a religious experience, he ran away from home at age 14 "to teach . . . poor blacks the word of God" but, out of funds, he had to enlist in the navy at Bristol and only secured his discharge through the intervention of friends. In 1798, after having twice served as a teacher's assistant, he brought a few poor neighbouring children into his father's home to teach them to read. In 1801 he moved to a larger room on the Borough Road in Southwark over which was inscribed: "All who will may send their children and have them educated freely, and those who do not wish to have education for nothing may pay for it if they please." Unable to pay assistants, Lancaster designated the older scholars as monitors to teach the younger pupils in small classes. These monitors were in turn supervised by a head monitor. The use of monitors was not new, but Lancaster developed an elaborate system of mutual instruction involving them in the maintenance of discipline by punishment (cages and pillories) and reward (rank badges, orders of merit, and prizes), as is described in his *Improvements in education, as it respects the industrious classes of the community* (London, 1803). He offered a limited fare of reading, writing, and arithmetic, but was opposed to the inclusion of more subjects only because of the expense. In fact he encouraged the most promising scholars by selecting and training them to become future teachers who would propagate his system.

Lancaster's teaching and promotion of his system won the attention of the dukes of Bedford and Sussex and Lord Somerville, as well as the patronage of George III. But in 1808 his financial improvidence led his friends Joseph Fox, a Baptist, and William Allen, a Quaker, to establish the Royal Lancasterian Society in order to administer donations and maintain the model school. Labelled the "Goliath of Schismatics" in 1805 by one of his opponents, Mrs Sarah Trimmer, Lancaster, himself a Quaker, incurred the wrath of the established church because of his belief that public schools should not be controlled by, or serve, any denomination. To represent the interests of the Anglican Tories and to rival the Royal Lancasterian Society, which was supported by nonconformists and liberal reformers, the National Society for Promoting the Education of the Poor in the Principles of the Established Church was established in 1811, based on Andrew Bell's monitorial system. Echoes of the controversy had been heard in the Canadas in the opinions of schoolteacher and Anglican minister John Strachan*, who in 1809 credited Bell with the "discovery" of monitorial schools and dismissed Lancaster's plan.

As outlined in his *Report of J. Lancaster's progress from the year 1798*, published in 1811, Lancaster's extensive travels and lectures throughout the British Isles had served to implement on a large scale his inexpensive, practical method of instruction for the poor. Visits to the Borough Road school by supporters showed that it had attracted attention from as far away as the United States and Venezuela. But because of Lancaster's lack of business sense, arrogance, and quarrels with his friends, the committee of managers of the Royal Lancasterian Society began to exert more control over the finances and administration of the society and in 1814 Lancaster was demoted from his position as promoter of the society to the salaried post of superintendent. Even the name of the society was changed, to the British and Foreign School Society. Later that year, after a scandal allegedly involving the flogging of monitors for amusement, he resigned. He was disowned by the Society of Friends for financial irresponsibility. In addition, the failure of his private school in Tooting (London) left him bankrupt. These vagaries are recorded in his *Oppression and persecution; or a narrative of a variety of singular facts that have occurred in the rise, progress and promulgation of the Royal Lancasterian system of education*, published in Bristol in 1816.

Although Lancaster was experiencing professional difficulties in England, his non-denominational monitorial system was being well received in the United States and in British North America. The London committee of the British and Foreign School Society was promoting his system in the Canadas. The Reverend Thaddeus Osgood* established a school at Quebec in 1814, and another in Kingston three years later. It may have been his use of the monitorial system at Quebec that led the House of Assembly's committee on education to comment favourably in a report of 1815 on the cheapness and efficiency of Lancaster's method of teaching; an extract from *Improvements* was annexed to the report and a bilingual edition of the book was published in Montreal that year. The next year a motion for a grant to set up other schools based on his plan was lost by only four votes. Opposition by Anglican and Catholic clergy to Osgood's school at Quebec eventually led to its closure. It was quickly replaced by other monitorial schools: those of the British and Canadian School Society, modelled on the British and Foreign School Society, those established by Joseph-François PERRAULT, and the National schools at Quebec and Montreal. Their attendance of 300–400 students per school eventually attracted grants from the assembly, £200 in 1823, £1,650 in 1825, and more in subsequent years. Other schools were encouraged to introduce the monitorial method by a grant of £100; for example the school at Trois-Rivières received one "provided that the system of mutual instruction be adopted therein, and that Children having a Certificate of poverty from the Trustees, be therein admitted *gratis*." During 1813–14 Walter BROMLEY had established in Halifax the Royal Acadian School, based on the principles of the British and Foreign School Society. In the same decade auxiliaries of the British and Foreign Bible Society, which supplied cheap editions of the Scriptures for students to learn to read in monitorial day- and Sunday schools, proliferated in the colonies: Nova Scotia (1810), Lower Canada (1812), Upper Canada (1816), Prince Edward Island (1817), New Brunswick (1819), and the Red River colony (1820).

Some time during the early 1820s ill health forced Lancaster to move from the United States, where he had settled in 1818, to the warmer climate of Venezuela. There he accumulated only debts and bitterness because of the broken promises of assistance from the country's president, Simón Bolívar. Meanwhile his system continued to be lauded in the Canadas by Louis-Joseph Papineau*, speaker of the House of Assembly, Perrault, and others. In 1828, a year after his return to New York, he travelled to Quebec, where he lectured, visited schools, and considered the prospects. Sir James Kempt* extended his patronage by subscribing £100 for a proposed journal of education. Lancaster settled in Montreal in September 1829. The following month he began to teach children "either deficient in their alphabet, or unable to spell correctly a few words of two or three letters." Within a month some of the children were able to read "readily or fluently in 'various parts' and 'copius passages' of the New Testament." Subsequently he opened a school at his residence on Rue Saint-Jacques, financed in part by the sale of a number of valuable engravings and maintained by the labour of his daughter and stepchildren. Beginning with 30 students, the attendance rose to 58 after he moved to more commodious quarters on Rue du Canal. His pupils' fees of £10 per quarter, which less than half of them paid, were supplemented by grants from the assembly: £100, doubled to £200 on a motion by Papineau in 1830, £200 in 1831, and in 1832 £100 plus £5 for each of up to 10 students whom he instructed in the teaching and managing of a school. School visitors Jacob De Witt* and Louis-Michel Viger* reported to the assembly in 1832 their approval of the "great progress" and order they had found. Austin CUVILLIER, another visitor, viewed Lancaster's efforts differently, commenting that "respectable persons whose children have been at Mr. Lancaster's School . . . complain that their children do not make more progress at his School than at the ordinary Schools, and that the prices are higher than at other Schools."

Initially Lancaster had planned to remain in or near Montreal. He had set up a printing-press and in October 1830 launched the *Gazette of Education and Friend of Man*. In the only issue published there was more self-promotion than there were essays on education. Lancaster petitioned William IV in 1831 for a grant of 100 acres in nearby La Prairie "for the purpose of founding a seminary there and making a home where I may live and die," but his request was refused. The following year he delivered a tirade against the governor-in-chief, Lord Aylmer [WHITWORTH-AYLMER], because the Board of Health had seized, for cholera patients, a shed which Lancaster had helped erect for the reception of poor Irish immigrants. That year, in a close by-election opposing Stanley Bagg and Daniel Tracey*, he voted for Bagg, the father of one of his pupils, despite the dissuasions of his supporters in the assembly, De Witt and Papineau. When his grant was not renewed, he was unable to continue with only his pupils' fees. Although he planned to reopen his institution after soliciting funds, he soon returned to the United States. Through the support of a few gentlemen in England he received an annuity. During his final months, he rekindled an interest in training monitors in England, but died in New York having been trampled by a runaway horse.

HEATHER LYSONS-BALCON

Most of Joseph Lancaster's published works are listed in the *National union catalog*.

L.C., House of Assembly, *Journals*, 22 March 1815; 16 Feb. 1816; 17 March 1830; 1831–32, app.Ii, 1st report. *Canadian Courant and Montreal Advertiser*, 16 Dec. 1829. *Quebec Gazette*, 30 March 1815. Beaulieu et Hamelin, *La presse québécoise*, vol.1. *DNB*. William Corston, *A brief sketch of the life of Joseph Lancaster; including the introduction of his system of education* (London, [1840]). Mora Dickson, *Teacher extraordinary, Joseph Lancaster,*

1778–1838 (Sussex, Eng., 1986). David Salmon, *Joseph Lancaster* (London, 1904). G. W. Spragge, "Monitorial schools in the Canadas, 1810–1845" (D.PAED. thesis, Univ. of Toronto, 1935). Judith Fingard, "'Grapes in the wilderness': the Bible Society in British North America in the early nineteenth century," *SH*, 5 (1972): 5–31. G. W. Spragge, "Joseph Lancaster in Montreal," *CHR*, 22 (1941): 35–41.

LANGFORD, JAMES J. (or **James I.**), jeweller and silversmith; b. in or about 1815; the son, probably adopted, of John and Grace Langford; m. 12 Oct. 1843 Jane Grant in Halifax, and they had no surviving children; d. there 6 Feb. 1847.

The evidence of James J. Langford's family background is contradictory. Grace Langford's second husband, the silversmith Peter Nordbeck*, claimed in a petition to the Halifax County Court of Probate that Grace was the mother of James Langford, but she could not have been the natural mother. Aged 31 at his death, James must have been born in 1815 or early 1816. There is, however, no record of the birth of James Langford at that time; moreover, another son of John and Grace Langford, William Payne, was born on 1 Sept. 1815. It seems likely, then, that James was adopted.

John Langford, a goldsmith and jeweller, had come to Halifax from London shortly before September 1809. Through him James may have been heir to a rich family tradition of metal work in England. Two Langfords had been pewterers there in the late 1670s, as was Thomas Langford of London in 1751 and afterwards. During the period 1719–57 John Langford, also of London, was active in the same craft, and a second John Langford was working in pewter in 1780; both used symbols that included a forearm holding a hammer over a small horizontal barrel. In addition to these five pewterers, John Langford and Thomas Langford were active as silversmiths in England in the decade 1766–76. The relationship, if any, of these craftsmen to each other and to James Langford and his father is unclear. That James's symbol was a bent arm holding a hammer raised in a position to strike may suggest a connection.

James Langford became closely associated with other silversmiths in Halifax. His father had been a partner of Lewis (Ludovic) Hulsman from 1809 to at least 1811, and James grew up on Granville Street, where the silversmiths Richard Upham MARSTERS, Gustave La Baume, Peter Nordbeck, and Henry Mignowitz were working. Nordbeck, who became his stepfather in 1833, was later the most successful Nova Scotian silversmith of his time. James Langford may have apprenticed with either Nordbeck or Mignowitz, who had been partners at least twice between 1824 and 1831. When, on 14 July 1838, he announced that he had commenced business, he described himself as a "Working Gold & Silversmith, Jeweller, &c" and gave his address as "adjoining Mr. Mignowitz's stone building."

Langford acquired considerable public patronage as a silversmith. Within two years he was advertising hollow-ware, and several of his chalices have survived, including one that he made with Nordbeck. Chalices by local silversmiths are relatively scarce, perhaps because in largely Protestant Nova Scotia religious commissions were less important than they were in, for example, Lower Canada. A commemorative tankard of Langford's was presented in July 1841 to the secretary of the Halifax Agricultural Society. As early as April 1840 Langford had taken Franz F. Meyer as his assistant and on 1 Nov. 1841 they became partners. In addition to making gold- and silver-ware they imported "jewelry, Plated Ware and fancy Goods in General." The partnership, like many others between Halifax silversmiths, did not last long, and after 15 months it was dissolved. From then until his death in 1847 Langford seems to have devoted his energy to his work in silver. His newspaper advertisements stressed the variety of his flatware and serving pieces and noted that he made them in all patterns.

Langford died without a will. Nordbeck and Jane Langford then petitioned the Court of Probate to appoint as administrators of his estate Jane's father, Daniel Grant, and Nordbeck himself, both of whom were creditors of Langford. The appointment was co-guaranteed by Alexander Troup and Charles D. Witham, both silversmiths and jewellers. Langford's most valuable asset was his business, and it was quickly sold to William James Veith and George Witham. They used his symbol of the raised bent arm holding a hammer and in describing their services they mentioned the same products and the same patterns that Langford had offered. After the dissolution of their partnership two years later, Veith carried on alone until 1860.

Langford's career was short; nevertheless, a relatively large quantity of his silver still exists. His best pieces, such as the sugar tongs in the Public Archives of Nova Scotia, are effortless and confident. A set of six knives in the Henry Birks Collection at the National Gallery of Canada is remarkable both for the delicacy of the leafy pattern engraved at the base of the blades and for their rarity, since knives are virtually unknown in Canadian silver. Langford's ideas and designs were innovative and experimental, and as a result his surviving work is surprisingly diverse. His early death left the Halifax silversmithing community without one of its most energetic, capable, and promising members.

BRIAN D. MURPHY

The main surviving examples of James Langford's work as a silversmith are in the Henry Birks Coll. of Silver at the National Gallery of Canada (Ottawa) and, to a lesser extent, at the N.S. Museum (Halifax). In addition, the following institutions each possess one of his spoons: the Montreal Museum of Fine Arts, the McCord Museum, and the Royal Ont. Museum, Sigmund Samuel Canadiana Building (Toronto).

Halifax County Court of Probate (Halifax), Estate papers, no.205 (James J. Langford) (mfm. at PANS). PANS, RG 35A, 1–3. St Paul's Anglican Church (Halifax), Reg. of baptisms. *Acadian Recorder*, 14 Sept. 1833; 14 July 1838; 8 Feb. 1840; 6 Nov. 1841; 5 July 1845; 6 Feb., 27 March, 17, 24 April, 1, 8 May 1847. *Halifax Morning Post & Parliamentary Reporter*, 4 Nov. 1841; 25, 27, 29 Jan., 1, 3 Feb. 1842. *Novascotian*, 12 Sept. 1833; 9, 16 April, 9 July 1840; 1 Sept. 1842; 30 Jan., 20, 27 Feb. 1843; 8 Feb. 1847. *Times* (Halifax), 27 July 1841, 17 Oct. 1843. H. H. Cotterell, *Old pewter, its makers and marks in England, Scotland, and Ireland* . . . (London, 1929; repub. 1963). C. J. Jackson, *English goldsmiths and their marks* . . . (2nd ed., London, 1921; repr. New York, 1964). J. E. Langdon, *Canadian silversmiths, 1700–1900* (Toronto, 1966). D. C. Mackay, *Silversmiths and related craftsmen of the Atlantic provinces* (Halifax, 1973). Harry Piers and D. C. Mackay, *Master goldsmiths and silversmiths of Nova Scotia and their marks*, ed. U. B. Thomson and A. M. Strachan (Halifax, 1948). D. [C.] Mackay, "Goldsmiths and silversmiths," *Canadian Antiques Collector* (Toronto), 7 (1972), no.1: 22–26.

LANGLEY. *See* LONGLEY

LANGUEDOC, FRANÇOIS (baptized **François de Borgias**), businessman, politician, office holder, seigneur, JP, and militia officer; b. 11 Oct. 1790 at Quebec, son of Jacques Languedoc and Angélique Samson; m. there 15 Feb. 1813 Anna Maria Philipps, and they had eight children; d. 23 Sept. 1840 in Saint-Édouard, near Napierville, Lower Canada.

As a child François Languedoc lived in Lower Town Quebec, on Rue Notre-Dame, among merchants like his father. In 1812 he bought a sixth of the shares in John White and Company, which had been running a ships' chandlery since 1810. The partnership agreement, registered before a notary on 13 Aug. 1813, was to last for four years, but the company was dissolved on 1 Jan. 1814. Languedoc and White kept the enterprise in operation on their own, under the same name.

Like most merchants of the period, Languedoc and White diversified their activity. They obtained contracts to supply and transport goods for the army or the government and ran public auctions. In 1816 they formed partnerships with John CALDWELL and John Goudie*, amongst others, to operate a ferry between Quebec and Pointe-Lévy (Lauzon and Lévis) and to run a steamboat linking Quebec and Montreal; Languedoc was secretary-treasurer of both companies. Along with White, he was among the first promoters of the Chambly canal. In addition he took part in the meetings that led to the founding of the Bank of Quebec in 1818.

Well known in his milieu for his business activities and his participation in various organizations, Languedoc was elected to the House of Assembly for Lower Town Quebec in 1816, winning by 17 votes over Pierre Bruneau*. His interest in business matters did not slacken; on more than one occasion during his term, which ended on 9 Feb. 1820, he brought forward or supported petitions from the Quebec merchants. In 1817 he was appointed commissioner for the improvement of the internal communications of Quebec County.

The early 1820s were a difficult period for Languedoc, since "through commercial misfortunes" he was no longer able to meet his obligations. One by one he ceded his properties at Quebec, including his house on Rue du Sault-au-Matelot, or put them up for sale. In 1821 the partnership with White was broken off; Languedoc was apportioned the company's goods, but also its debts. He remained in business more or less successfully until 1824 and then went to live permanently on Saint-Georges seigneury, southeast of Montreal.

Languedoc had bought this 12,000-acre property in Sherrington Township in 1817. From 21 June 1823 he held the land officially *en franc-alleu noble*. As soon as his status as seigneur was confirmed, he turned in earnest, and with success, to putting the management of Saint-Georges in order. He had a land roll prepared, which listed 239 *censitaires*, built a seigneurial manor-house at Saint-Édouard, and purchased a sawmill on the west bank of the Rivière de la Tortue and put up a grist-mill there. He maintained the rates of *cens et rentes* in effect prior to 1823 but instituted a sale price of from 10 to 20 shillings per *arpent*, and he encouraged people to settle the arrears in their yearly payments.

In 1830 Languedoc went back into politics. He was elected for L'Acadie by acclamation, along with Robert Hoyle*, but he took little part in the debates, crucial though they were if only because of the notorious question of supplies. Often absent because of illness, he was, however, in the house when the 92 Resolutions were brought in and he stood opposed to them [*see* Elzéar BÉDARD]. He ran again in the elections held in the autumn of 1834 but was defeated by Cyrille-Hector-Octave CÔTÉ, a supporter of Louis-Joseph Papineau*.

Languedoc also held several public offices: commissioner for the summary trial of small causes from 1828 till 1832, justice of the peace from 1830, and commissioner empowered in 1837 to receive the oath of allegiance. He was an officer in the 2nd Battalion of Quebec's militia until 1824; in 1830 he joined the 3rd Battalion of Huntingdon militia with the rank of lieutenant-colonel. Languedoc's actions as a magistrate left deep-seated grudges, notably in Patriote Pierre-Rémi Narbonne, whom he arrested on 7 Nov.

1837. Once released, Narbonne had those he recruited for the Association des Frères-Chasseurs solemnly swear that they would slit Languedoc's throat.

François Languedoc escaped such a fate. Nor was he murdered in the doorway of his manor-house, as Joseph-Edmond Roy* claimed. He was in fact carried off by illness a few weeks before his fiftieth birthday. By the terms of his will his estate was divided equally among his surviving children, his wife having died in 1836. The heirs continued to manage the seigneury and draw income from the properties their father had bought in various townships.

ANDRÉE HÉROUX

ANQ-M, CE1-54, 25 août 1827, 18 mai 1832; CE4-4, 31 juill., 18 août, 4 nov. 1836; 25 sept. 1840; CN1-327, 21 janv., 13 avril, 15 juill. 1825; CN4-10, 22 déc. 1835; 2, 20 févr., 2 août 1837; 18 juill. 1839; 2 janv., 4 sept., 13, 26–27 nov., 1er, 4, 7 déc. 1840; M-7, 13 nov. 1840. ANQ-Q, CE1-1, 12 oct. 1790, 15 févr. 1813, 21 janv. 1815, 25 août 1817, 16 août 1819, 20 sept. 1820, 8 déc. 1821, 14 juill. 1824; CE1-2, 18 oct. 1821; CN1-49, 22 mars 1817, 14 avril 1818, 1er févr. 1826; CN1-116, 15 août 1816; 20 janv., 3 févr. 1832; 21 juill. 1835; CN1-171, 13 août 1813; CN1-208, 3 févr. 1832; CN1-230, 26 avril, 20 juin, 29 déc. 1817; 18 juill. 1823; CN1-253, 12, 15 janv., 22 févr., 27 mai 1814; CN1-262, 14 févr. 1813; 5 août 1815; 5 sept. 1816; 6 déc. 1817; 13–27 juin, 6 août 1818; 22 janv., 3 mars, 16 sept. 1819; 24 févr., 5–6, 8, 10, 12–13, 15–24, 26, 28, 31 mars, 1er–3, 5–10, 12, 15–16, 18–23, 28 avril, 1er, 10, 15, 20–21, 24, 28–29 mai, 10–11, 15, 24–25, 30 juin, 1er, 7, 15 juill., 31 août, 14, 20 sept., 9, 14, 26, 28 oct., 4, 9 nov., 15, 23, 28, 29 déc. 1820; 11, 13 janv. 1825; 5 juill., 27 oct. 1827; 26 mai 1830; 26 mai 1834; E17/37, no.3033; T11-1/425, no.536; 1/426, no.537; T11-301/3558, 1820, 1: 239; 301/3563, 1822, 1: 303–5; 301/3564, 1823, 1: 278; 301/3567, 1824, 1: 418. PAC, RG 31, C1, 1825, Sherrington Township (mfm. at ANQ); 1831, Saint-Édouard; RG 68, General index, 1651–1841. "Les dénombrements de Québec" (Plessis), ANQ *Rapport*, 1948–49: 82, 131, 181. L.C., House of Assembly, *Journaux*, 1817: 41, 71, 75, 119, 121, 143, 163, 275, 345, 381, 415, 445, 481, 503, 609, 611, 799; 1818: 39, 47, 64, 72–73, 82, 104, 119, 121, 147, 149, 155–56, 158–59, 174, 182, 193, 195, 198, 202, 213, 217, app.1; 1819: 19, 27–28, 30, 34–35, 49, 51, 59–60, 69, 72, 80, 93, 110, 120, 192, 207, 215, 218–19, 224; 1820, app.G; 1821–22: 162; 1823: 225; 1831: 36, 176, 181, 326; 1832: 37, 256, 283, 289, 311–12, 327, 367, 369; 1832–33: 102, 305, 352, 547; 1834: 266, 310, 337, 353, 382, 386, 465, 474; *Statuts*, 1818, c.18: 101–57; 1823, c.14: 307–15. *Recensement de Québec, 1818* (Provost), 202. *Le Canadien*, 10 nov., 3 déc. 1834. *Montreal Gazette*, 19 Oct. 1830, 11 Nov. 1834. *Quebec Gazette*, 10 May 1810; 23 Jan. 1812; 22 April, 30 Dec. 1813; 3 March 1814; 19 Oct. 1815; 14, 28 March, 4, 11 April, 16 May, 19 Dec. 1816; 13 March, 3 April, 1 May, 11, 18 Sept., 13 Nov. 1817; 12 Feb., 26 March, 14 May, 11 June, 19 Oct. 1818; 11–12 Jan., 2 Feb., 4, 25 March, 19, 21 April, 7 June, 23 Aug., 14 Oct. 1819; 27 March, 15 June, 17 Aug., 21 Sept., 12 Oct., 23 Nov. 1820; 3, 17 May, 17 June 1821; 17 June, 5, 12 Dec. 1822; 10 Feb., 21 April, 9 June, 7 Aug., 9 Oct., 6, 17 Nov. 1823; 17 May 1824; 25 Sept. 1840. Bouchette, *Topographical description of L.C.* Caron, "Inv. de la corr. de Mgr Panet," ANQ *Rapport*, 1933–34: 277–78; 1934–35: 339; 1935–36: 169; "Inv. des doc. relatifs aux événements de 1837 et 1838," 1925–26: 272. Desjardins, *Guide parl.* Desrosiers, "Inv. de la corr. de Mgr Lartigue," ANQ *Rapport*, 1942–43: 8, 52, 61, 63, 67; 1943–44: 258. Fauteux, *Patriotes*, 331–33. Langelier, *Liste des terrains concédés*, 1543, 1559, 1580, 1584–86. *Quebec almanac*, 1813: 80; 1814: 76, 81; 1815: 81; 1816: 75; 1817: 42, 66, 77; 1818: 42, 51, 69, 83; 1819: 83, 138; 1820: 81; 1821: 85; 1822: 89; 1823: 53, 91; 1824: 93; 1825: 95; 1829: 62; 1830: 50, 68; 1831: 42, 68, 71, 179; 1832: 49, 69, 73; 1833: 41, 69, 73, 219; 1834: 44, 72, 249; 1835: 68; 1837: 72; 1838: 47, 58; 1839: 46, 57, 238; 1840: 43, 59; 1841: 45. P.-G. Roy, *Inv. concessions*, 5: 106–7. Raymonde [Landry] Gauthier, *Les manoirs du Québec* (Montréal, 1976), 86–87. Roy, *Hist. de Lauzon*, 4: 100. Robert Sellar, *The history of the county of Huntingdon and of the seigniories of Chateauguay and Beauharnois from their first settlement to the year 1838* (Huntingdon, Que., 1888), 493. "François Languedoc," *BRH*, 60 (1954): 49. "François Languedoc était-il notaire?" *BRH*, 58 (1952): 150–51. J. P. Heisler, "Les canaux du Canada," *Canadian Hist. Sites*, no.8 (1973): 96. É.-Z. Massicotte, "Louis Roy, dit Portelance, député de Montréal de 1804 à 1820," *BRH*, 32 (1926): 169. P.-G. Roy, "Les concessions en fief et seigneurie sous le Régime anglais," *BRH*, 34 (1928): 321–25.

LARTIGUE, JEAN-JACQUES, Roman Catholic priest, Sulpician, and bishop; b. 20 June 1777 in Montreal, son of Jacques Larthigue, a surgeon, and Marie-Charlotte Cherrier; d. there 19 April 1840.

An only son, Jean-Jacques Lartigue belonged to a noted Montreal family. Shortly before 1757 his father, who was from Miradoux, France, had accompanied regular troops to New France as a surgeon. His mother, who came from Longueuil, was the daughter of François-Pierre Cherrier*, a merchant and notary at Longueuil and then at Saint-Denis on the Richelieu. By 1784 Lartigue was enrolled in the preparatory class at the Collège Saint-Raphaël (from 1806 the Petit Séminaire de Montréal), where he proved studious and brilliant. Upon completing the final two years of the classical program (Philosophy), he began in September 1793 to attend the English school run by the Sulpicians, and he then articled for three years with Montreal lawyers Louis-Charles Foucher and Joseph Bédard. With his cousin Denis-Benjamin Viger*, Lartigue developed an abiding interest in Lower Canadian politics, following the example of his uncles Joseph PAPINEAU, Denis Viger*, and Benjamin-Hyacinthe-Martin Cherrier, who were members of the House of Assembly.

In 1797 Lartigue made a decision that marked a turning-point in his life. Before being called to the bar he gave up this promising career in favour of the priesthood. "A chance and quite insignificant incident . . . an unpleasantness he experienced," according to Bishop Charles La Rocque*, seems to have prompted his sudden decision. On 23 Sept. 1797 the bishop of Quebec, Pierre Denaut*, conferred the tonsure and minor orders upon him in the parish church of Montreal. Lartigue spent the next two years teaching at the Collège Saint-Raphaël, as was the custom at the time, while pursuing his theological studies under the Sulpicians. In September 1798 he signed a public instrument recording his irrevocable decision to enter holy orders. The bishop, in the church of Longueuil, made him a subdeacon on 30 Sept. 1798 and a deacon on 28 Oct. 1799. Denaut then appointed him his secretary, to replace Augustin Chaboillez* who had been named to the parish of Sault-au-Récollet (Montreal North).

Lartigue was ordained to the priesthood on 21 Sept. 1800 at Saint-Denis on the Richelieu, in the presence of his uncle François Cherrier*, who was the local curé, his mother, and numerous other relatives. Despite his delicate health, he showed himself full of energy in adding to his responsibilities the duties of assistant priest at Longueuil, where the bishop continued to be curé. As secretary Lartigue carried out several important tasks, reshaping the Quebec ritual for instance, and he often accompanied Denaut on pastoral visits. The most arduous of these visits was made in 1803 to the Maritimes, in the far reaches of the diocese where no bishop had gone for 117 years. Exhausted and seriously ill, Lartigue almost died at Miramichi, N.B. He also was actively engaged in the administration of the diocese. In the absence of coadjutor Joseph-Octave Plessis*, who lived at Quebec, he proved a judicious adviser at a time when the Canadian church was under heavy attack from Lieutenant Governor Sir Robert Shore MILNES and his close associates Jonathan SEWELL, Herman Witsius RYLAND, and Jacob Mountain*.

Bishop Denaut's death on 17 Jan. 1806 enabled Lartigue to realize a long-cherished dream of becoming a Sulpician. The prospect of a "calmer, more solitary, more contemplative life" and a more intensely intellectual one appealed to him. On 22 Feb. 1806 he left the presbytery in Longueuil and rejoined his former teachers, having been admitted as a member of the community a week before. He was the first Canadian to be received into the Séminaire de Saint-Sulpice since the coming in 1793 of the French Sulpician *emigrés*.

On his arrival at the seminary Lartigue was attached to ministry in the parish, being responsible for one of its four sections. He also became in turn bursar and archivist and devoted himself to various intellectual activities, such as drawing up "schedules of ceremonies" for the parish and preparing a French edition of the New Testament. The latter project, valued by Plessis, now bishop of Quebec, because of his concern about the expansion of Protestant organizations in the province, would occupy much of Lartigue's time, especially in 1818–19, when for several months he gave it priority.

In 1806 Plessis had enlisted Lartigue to refute Attorney General Sewell's argument in the legal proceedings that curé Joseph-Laurent Bertrand* had instituted against his parishioner Pierre Lavergne, a dispute that involved the legality of the creation of new parishes. In July 1812 the superior of the Séminaire de Saint-Sulpice, Jean-Henry-Auguste Roux*, entrusted Lartigue with the delicate task of securing obedience from the inhabitants of the Pointe-Claire and Lachine regions who had demonstrated violently against conscription. Three years later Plessis invited him to write a new catechism, but he did not feel qualified to do so. On six occasions between 1814 and 1819 he accompanied Bishop Bernard-Claude Panet*, the coadjutor, on his pastoral visits in the Montreal region.

No mission, however, would be as important as the one to the British government that Lartigue undertook in 1819 at Roux's request. The title-deeds held by the Séminaire de Saint-Sulpice to the seigneuries of Île-de-Montréal, Lac-des-Deux-Montagnes, and Saint-Sulpice had long been contested by both the civil authorities and some well-known jurists. In the spring of 1819 the matter had been brought up again in the Legislative Council. There was more real prospect than ever that Saint-Sulpice would be despoiled of its property. Concerned that the governor, the Duke of Richmond [Lennox*], had serious doubts about the legality of the seminary's title-deeds, Roux decided to take the case to the British authorities in London. The timing was especially appropriate since Plessis was preparing to go there to ask for letters patent for the Séminaire de Nicolet and obtain permission to divide his diocese, which was much too large. The presence of Plessis was sure to facilitate the task of Saint-Sulpice's emissary. The superior chose Lartigue as being particularly qualified for the mission because of his knowledge of the law and mastery of English. On 3 July 1819 he sailed on the *George Symes* with Plessis and his secretary Pierre-Flavien Turgeon*.

Lartigue arrived in London on 14 August and with the help of Plessis immediately addressed himself to pleading the seminary's case. He met with indifference from officials and repeated rebuffs from Colonial Secretary Lord Bathurst, who, besides being prejudiced against him, was waiting for a report from the officers of the crown before reaching a decision. Lartigue's approaches to the former governor-in-chief of British North America, Sir John Coape Sherbrooke*, the vicar apostolic in London, William Poynter, the French ambassador to Great Britain, the Marquis de Latour-Maubourg, and some eminent London lawyers produced no results. During his stay in Paris from 23 October till 29 November he also failed to persuade the French authorities to intervene with the British government. When he left London on 6 June 1820 to return to Montreal, the seminary's case was really no further ahead. Yet his presence had not been vain. The British authorities had given up for the time being the idea of seizing the property of Saint-Sulpice. Lartigue could not know that he had indeed prepared the ground for the accord that would be reached 20 years later to the advantage of the seminary.

When he went to London to defend the seminary's interests, Lartigue was entirely unaware of Plessis's intentions for him. Having failed to secure permission to divide the diocese of Quebec, Plessis had obtained the government's agreement to recognize four auxiliary bishops as his representatives in Upper Canada, the northwest, the Maritimes, and the district of Montreal. On 17 Sept. 1819 Lartigue learned that the archbishop had him in mind for the Montreal post. Although reluctant at first to accede to Plessis's wishes, he finally replied affirmatively, but on condition that his superiors assented. Antoine de Pouget Duclaux, superior general of Saint-Sulpice in Paris, left the decision to Lartigue's immediate superior, Roux, who gave an evasive reply in December 1819. Lartigue's fears were confirmed: Roux apparently would consent to his becoming a bishop if he left the seminary. In March 1820 Lartigue received apostolic letters naming him bishop of Telmessus in Lycia, as well as auxiliary and suffragan to Plessis. For Lartigue, who was obliged by papal order to accept the office a short time later, a new life was beginning. He would no longer be a Sulpician, but auxiliary bishop in Montreal. Jean-Baptiste THAVENET had perhaps been a better prophet than he realized when he observed not long before: "One more word about the episcopate being offered you. It reminds me of the regional bishops of Rome in the 5th century: you would be bishop, not of Montreal but in Montreal. You would be the bishop's vicar there, and the vicar general would no longer be anything, etc. And if you were not a member of the seminary (as would inevitably happen), what a sad existence for you!"

Lartigue was consecrated bishop on 21 Jan. 1821 in the church of Notre-Dame in Montreal. He became responsible for the largest district in Lower Canada. Bounded on the northeast by the Trois-Rivières region, on the south by Vermont and New York, and on the southwest by Upper Canada, the district of Montreal had nearly 200,000 inhabitants, 170,000 of them Catholics spread out over 72 parishes and missions. Almost nine-tenths of Montreal's 18,767 inhabitants belonged to the Roman Catholic Church. There were many religious establishments and they were thriving. Besides the Séminaire de Saint-Sulpice and the church of Notre-Dame, the town had the Petit Séminaire, the Recollet chapel, and the chapel of Notre-Dame-de-Bonsecours, a convent for girls run by the Sisters of the Congregation of Notre-Dame, and two hospitals, the Hôtel-Dieu and the Hôpital Général.

Several important tasks awaited the new bishop. The theological and spiritual training of the clergy was distinctly inadequate at the time, a situation Lartigue wanted to remedy quickly. In 1825 he established at the recently opened bishop's palace a theological school, the Séminaire Saint-Jacques, which under the direction of his secretary and right-hand man, Ignace Bourget*, quickly became a nursery of ultramontanism. Papal infallibility would be taught there 40 years before a Vatican council proclaimed the dogma. At a period when there were violent clashes between gallicans and ultramontanes in France, Lartigue regarded the church as a body with a strongly hierarchical organization untouched by democratic concepts of power and subject in all things to papal authority. The absolute primacy of the sovereign pontiff was the key element in this definition. "Pastor to the pastors" and endowed with infallibility quite apart from the bishops' assent, the pope by divine right had "pastoral jurisdiction over all the bishops in the world," whom he could move or remove as he wished.

This concept of the church and this love for the person of its head came to Lartigue partly from his respect for Hugues-Félicité-Robert de La Mennais, whose *Essai sur l'indifférence en matière de religion* (Paris, 1817) he had eagerly read at the time of his trip to Europe. From 1820 Lartigue had assiduously absorbed the writings of Joseph de Maistre, Philippe-Olympe Gerbet, and La Mennais, which he received regularly through Parisian bookseller Martin Bossange. As a subscriber to several Lamennaisian periodicals, including *Le Drapeau blanc*, *Le Mémorial catholique*, and *L'Avenir*, he developed an unbounded admiration for La Mennais, as a "superior writer and thorough papist" who made people "love religion and its visible head on earth." Sick at heart, he would learn of the denunciation and then of the condemnation by Pope Gregory XVI's encyclicals in 1832 and 1834 of the man whose system of philosophy and, even more, whose ultramontanism he would never repudiate.

To Lartigue the task of ensuring greater cohesion and stability in the Canadian church seemed just as important. Consequently he worked to get improvement of the legislation concerning civil recognition of the parishes and the right of religious corporations and communities to own and acquire landed property. In addition he fully supported Plessis's plan to regroup all the dioceses in British North America. After the bishop's death, Lartigue took the initiative himself, with the result that the plan was carried out in 1844, when the ecclesiastical province of Quebec was established as the first one in Canada.

Imbued with the idea of the supremacy of the

church over secular society, Lartigue was no less concerned with the development of the Christian faith and understanding of the Catholics in his diocese. He demanded their absolute obedience to the rules of conduct laid down by the bishops and counted on their action to preserve the prerogatives of the church and ensure its influence upon society. To achieve these ends he wanted to set up a religious press run by the episcopal authorities to "shape and control public opinion" and direct it to the benefit of the church. His successor, Bishop Bourget, would achieve this aim in 1841 with the publication in Montreal of *Mélanges religieux* [*see* Jean-Charles Prince*].

The same concern led Lartigue to take a keen interest in education. He maintained that teaching was essentially a responsibility of the church, not the state, and he advocated a school system independent of the Royal Institution for the Advancement of Learning [*see* Joseph Langley Mills*] but connected with the parishes; in 1824, at the time the *fabrique* schools act was passed, he expressed a wish that the clergy take as much advantage of the legislation as possible. It authorized parish priests and churchwardens to acquire funds and to devote part of the income of the *fabriques* to establishing elementary schools. Lartigue had not waited to set an example. Upon taking up residence in the new bishop's palace he had opened a free school which by 1826 had nearly 80 boys and girls. A short time later he established a second school in a house bought for the purpose; he entrusted its management to the Association des Dames Bienveillantes de Saint-Jacques, an organization founded in July 1828 to educate girls from poor families. He showed constant solicitude for the Collège de Saint-Hyacinthe [*see* Antoine Girouard*], which was under his jurisdiction from 1824 and which, under the direction of Jean-Charles Prince, became in effect a "Lamennaisian college."

Lartigue was also involved in social concerns. In 1827 he strongly encouraged the founding of the Association des Dames de la Charité, a lay benevolent society to help the poor in Montreal [*see* Marie-Amable Foretier*]. When in the summer of 1832 a terrible cholera epidemic struck the town, he supported the association's plan to open an orphanage for the children of immigrants, mostly Irish, who had died of the disease. Lartigue was the spiritual adviser of Émilie Tavernier*, one of the most active members of the association, and it was at his suggestion that she had founded a refuge for frail or sick elderly women in 1830. In addition, Lartigue and the Canadian Sulpician Nicolas Dufresne* had helped Agathe-Henriette Huguet, *dit* Latour, in 1829 to establish the Charitable Institution for Female Penitents.

Yet these achievements came in the course of a particularly agitated episcopate, one that was marked by incessant struggle, either with the Séminaire de Saint-Sulpice in Montreal, or the British authorities, or the new secular Canadian leaders. In 1837 Lartigue recalled his years as bishop with resentment: his life had been "strewn with the vicissitudes of temporal affairs, and almost equally composed of happy events and adversities." Many a time he begged Bishop Plessis and his successors to "withdraw [him] at last from this wretched life," offering his resignation on several occasions to the authorities in Rome.

The first 15 years of Lartigue's episcopate were marked by a confrontation with the Séminaire de Saint-Sulpice. It began with the bishop's decision in January 1821 to reside in Montreal rather than in a parish on the south shore of the St Lawrence, as it is thought that Roux wished. Roux was firmly convinced that in deciding "to raise one of their colleagues to the episcopacy" Plessis had sought to "introduce a Canadian bishop into the seminary" to diminish the influence of the French Sulpicians and bring the institution under his control. This conviction explains Lartigue's exclusion from the seminary in February 1821, when he was forced to seek shelter at the Hôtel-Dieu of Montreal, as well as the astonishing removal of the episcopal throne from the parish church of Notre-Dame by the churchwardens in July during Lartigue's absence. It also explains their decision in September 1822 to build a new church [*see* James O'Donnell*], probably to thwart Lartigue's plan in building the church of Saint-Jacques.

It was inevitable that there would be conflict between the auxiliary bishop and the Sulpicians, who since their arrival in 1657 had always exercised a strong hold on Montreal. Lartigue had thought that by taking care to consult his Sulpician superiors and by insisting upon an order from the pope to accept episcopal office, he would overcome his colleagues' reservations. In reality, Roux did not want a Canadian bishop in Montreal, even a Sulpician one, lest the exclusively French character of the seminary be changed; rarely does decolonization proceed smoothly.

Lartigue consequently rebuked the Sulpicians for trying in both Rome and London to ensure that they could recruit men of French origin, denounced the policy of discrimination against the Canadian Sulpicians within the community, and in 1833 energetically opposed the seminary's efforts to get a French Sulpician appointed apostolic prefect in Montreal. Lartigue did not believe in "a devious policy [designed] to handle every question gently" which "ended up spoiling everything." Had he received more support from Plessis he would surely have reminded the Sulpicians more vigorously that they could not constitute a church within the church and would have dealt more severely with recalcitrant parish priests such as Augustin Chaboillez, Jean-Baptiste Saint-Germain*, and François-Xavier PIGEON who were partisans of Saint-Sulpice.

In 1835, however, a *rapprochement* between Lartigue and the seminary began. By August Lartigue was ready to choose a successor for himself who would be "acceptable to Saint-Sulpice." Indeed, the illness and sudden death in May of Pierre-Antoine Tabeau*, who was to have succeeded him, had given him much cause for reflection. The celebration on 24 Sept. 1835 of French Sulpician Jacques-Guillaume ROQUE's jubilee in the priesthood, which took place in the bishop's presence, sealed this reconciliation. From then on the greatest harmony reigned. In December 1836 Lartigue wrote to the superior, Joseph-Vincent Quiblier*, with obvious joy: "I can assure you that I have gladly forgotten all that has happened over fifteen years, and think only of cherishing and favouring your house." The following year the superior general of Saint-Sulpice in Paris, Antoine Garnier, entrusted the seminary to the bishop's protection and benevolent attention.

Among the aims that were pursued unflaggingly by Lartigue during his episcopate the complete independence of the church must receive the greatest emphasis. Maintaining that the Canadian church was independent of the political authority and refusing to be regarded "simply as a tool in the hands of the executive," he energetically opposed the British authorities, who had no need to subjugate the church or dictate a line of conduct to religious leaders. Unlike bishops Plessis, Panet, and Joseph SIGNAY, who thought that the liberty of the church depended upon their obedience to Britain's instructions, Lartigue had realized that, in a country where representative institutions existed, the church did not have to seek the protection of politicians; it enjoyed an autonomous power by virtue of the authority it exercised over the faithful, who were also electors. Eager for the freedom of action enjoyed by Bishop Benoît-Joseph Flaget, his colleague in Bardstown, Ky, Lartigue knew that with a touchy and disputatious Protestant government the only policy to pursue was that of the *fait accompli*. He adopted it at the time the diocese of Montreal was created when, in Marcel Trudel's words, he had "the courage to make the first gesture of absolute independence." He insisted to Bishop Joseph-Norbert Provencher*, a colleague from the northwest visiting Rome in October 1835, that the authorities in Rome should attach no importance "to the British government's consent to or approval of such an arrangement," and in November, without the knowledge of Governor Lord Gosford [ACHESON], he sent to the pope the Montreal clergy's request for an episcopal see at Montreal.

This bold policy bore fruit. On 13 May 1836 Pope Gregory XVI signed the bull creating the new diocese of Montreal and the brief appointing Lartigue to it. As Lartigue had foreseen, when London found itself faced with the *fait accompli*, it accepted the new bishop, the colonial secretary giving his consent on 26 May. The bishop of Montreal took possession of his see on 8 September amid general enthusiasm. A short time later Lartigue made a second gesture that was no less decisive: he handled the matter of his coadjutor with Rome without prior discussion with the governor, indeed, without even a mention of it. A new era had dawned in the relations between the Canadian church and the state. The British authorities would intervene less and less in the internal affairs of the church, the appointment of bishops, and the establishment of new dioceses. The bishop of Montreal had shown his colleagues and successors the way. This major step forward would be confirmed in 1849 under responsible government, when the church would become independent of the state.

Another matter brought Lartigue into conflict with the leaders in the House of Assembly, in particular his cousin Louis-Joseph Papineau*. When in 1791 parliamentary institutions had been put into place in Lower Canada, the new spokesmen for the Canadian community soon aroused the distrust of the ecclesiastical authorities. The latter did not easily accept being supplanted by leaders who, if not hostile to the church, were at least not much inclined to accept their instructions. Nevertheless, although their official policy was one of non-intervention, the representatives of the church unquestionably supported the Canadians' cause. For his part Lartigue, who was deeply affected by the injustices inflicted upon his compatriots, always displayed a keen interest in the struggles of the political leaders and the aims they pursued. His correspondence with his cousin Denis-Benjamin Viger, Papineau's right-hand man, furnishes eloquent proof of this interest, particularly in 1822, when a bill to unite the two Canadas was presented to the British parliament, and in 1828, at the time of a mission to London by Viger, Austin CUVILLIER, and John NEILSON. In 1827 he justified the non-interventionist policy of the clergy that he had consistently advocated: "It is important for [the Canadians] that at this juncture we not pique the government, which in reacting might unwittingly do religion much harm . . . ; moreover, without our creating a disturbance the government in England will know of our true feelings and will discern what we are thinking despite our silence if it sees the masses, upon whom we have a great influence, as it knows, complaining with virtually one voice against the administration."

From 1829, however, relations between the Patriote party and the bishops deteriorated rapidly. Taking issue with the aims pursued by the leaders of the assembly, particularly in the schools act of 1829 and the 1831 bill on *fabriques* [*see* Louis Bourdages*], in which could be sensed the influence of 18th-century French deistic liberalism and a strong democratic tendency, Lartigue led a counter-offensive; it would defeat the liberals' attempts to limit the influence of the church upon the people and to define Canadian society in terms other than its religious affiliation. Worried by the rise of an increasingly aggressive and demanding Canadian nationalism and by the clearly revolutionary tone of the radical political leaders, who scarcely inspired confidence in him, in the end he utterly opposed them. He noticed with alarm that the movement to emancipate the Canadians was going ahead without the church, indeed was proceeding against it, and that the small degree of freedom the Canadian church had managed to obtain was threatened by both the British government and the Canadian politicians themselves. The test of strength between the two forces came in 1837. On 24 October, in a pastoral letter to his diocese, the bishop of Montreal condemned the action of the Patriote leaders, basing his argument on a biblical doctrine that legitimate civil authorities held power from God. At the same time, along with the moderate wing of the Patriote party he cast serious doubt on the wisdom and validity of the radicals' policy, which he considered as imprudent as it was harmful. The divorce between church and assembly first evident six years earlier was complete.

Events vindicated Lartigue. After suffering defeat at Saint-Charles-sur-Richelieu and then at Saint-Eustache, the Patriotes lost faith in their leaders, particularly when they were abandoned by several. Despite the unfavourable reactions at first provoked by his intervention, even within a section of the clergy, Lartigue soon appeared as a true leader, independent, lucid, anxious to merit his compatriots' confidence and capable of proposing to them a more realistic program than that of the Patriote leaders. Two developments convinced the Canadians of the selflessness of Lartigue and their other religious leaders, who had rallied around him. On 9 Nov. 1837, at the request of the parish priests from the Richelieu valley, he endorsed a petition for the rights of Canadians that all the priests in Lower Canada signed. As well, he and his coadjutor brought support to the unfortunate victims who were filling the prisons, particularly after the abortive uprising on the night of 3–4 Nov. 1838. Meanwhile, late in January 1838 Lartigue had interceded with Lord Gosford to get the government in London to agree not to alter the constitution of Lower Canada or impose union of the two Canadas, as the faction supporting union from 1822 ardently desired. When in the spring of 1839 word came of the recommendations in the report by Lord Durham [LAMBTON], which were designed to "anglify" and "decatholicize" the Canadians by a legislative union and a system of non-denominational schools, Lartigue encouraged his clergy to sign a new petition to the queen, the House of Lords, and the Commons in order to oppose the plan.

At this decisive moment in the history of French Canada, when the Canadians found themselves abandoned, even misled by their political leaders, the religious leaders had stepped in and put themselves at the service of the nation. The Canadian church thereupon regained the authority it had exercised over the Canadian collectivity before the introduction of parliamentary institutions. Thenceforth it constituted a political force with which the new Canadian leaders, more moderate and more reasonable, would have to reckon.

Lartigue, who had been ill for a number of years, died on 19 April 1840. The press, *Le Canadien* in particular, unanimously stressed the greatness of his episcopate. More than 10,000 people attended his funeral in the church of Notre-Dame on 22 April. As many more were present the next day in the cathedral of Saint-Jacques to hear Bishop Bourget pay him a final tribute. With the death of the first bishop of Montreal the Catholic and ultramontane reaction, of which he had been the chief architect, was irretrievably under way. Bourget, his successor, who had been steered in this direction by a preparation spanning 16 years as a secretary and 3 years as a bishop with Lartigue, would continue his work.

GILLES CHAUSSÉ and LUCIEN LEMIEUX

Detailed bibliographies for Jean-Jacques Lartigue and the period 1777–1840 may be found in Chaussé, *Jean-Jacques Lartigue*, and Lemieux, *L'établissement de la première prov. eccl*.

AAQ, 1 CB, VI–VIII; 26 CP, I–VII. ACAM, 255.109; 295.101, .103; 465.101; 583.000; 780.034; 901.012–18, .021–25, .028–29, .033, .037, .039, .041, .047, .050, .136–37, .150; RLL, I–III. Arch. de la Compagnie de Jésus, prov. du Canada français (Saint-Jérôme, Qué.), 2196, 3182–83. Arch. du séminaire de Saint-Sulpice (Paris), Fonds canadien, dossiers 22, 27–29, 52, 55, 59, 63, 67, 73–76, 79–89, 94, 98–99. ASQ, Fonds Viger–Verreau, sér.O, 0128. ASSM, 1bis; 21; 24, B; 27. PAC, MG 24, B2, 1, 2, 16–21; B6, 1–12; B46; J15. Allaire, *Dictionnaire*. F.-M. Bibaud, *Dict. hist.*; *Le panthéon canadien* (A. et V. Bibaud; 1891). Desrosiers, "Inv. de la corr. de Mgr Lartigue," ANQ *Rapport*, 1941–42, 1942–43, 1943–44, 1944–45, 1945–46. G.-É. Giguère, "La restauration de la Compagnie de Jésus au Canada, 1839–1857" (thèse de PHD, 2v., univ. de Montréal, 1965). J.-P. Langlois, "L'ecclésiologie mise en œuvre par Mgr Lartigue (relations église-état) durant les troubles de 1837–1838" (thèse de LL, univ. de Montréal, 1976). Anne McDermaid, "Bishop Lartigue and the first rebellion in the Montreal area" (MA thesis, Carleton Univ., Ottawa, 1967). Yvette Majerus, "L'éducation dans le diocèse de Montréal d'après la correspondance de ses deux premiers évêques, Mgr J.-J. Lartigue et Mgr I. Bourget, de 1820 à 1967" (thèse de PHD, McGill Univ., Montréal, 1971). Léon Pouliot, *Mgr Bourget et son temps*, vol.1; *Trois grands artisans du diocèse de Montréal* (Montréal, 1936). L.-P. Tardif, "Le nationalisme religieux de Mgr Lartigue" (thèse de LL, univ. Laval, Québec, 1956). É.-J.[-A.] Auclair,

"Le premier évêque de Montréal, Mgr Lartigue," CCHA *Rapport*, 12 (1944–45): 111–19. François Beaudin, "L'influence de La Mennais sur Mgr Lartigue, premier évêque de Montréal," *RHAF*, 25 (1971–72): 225–37. J.-H. Charland, "Mgr Jean-Jacques Lartigue, 1er évêque de Montréal (1777–1840)," *Rev. canadienne*, 23 (1887): 579–82.

LAWRENCE, ALEXANDER, cabinet-maker, upholsterer, and musician; b. 8 April 1788 in Methlick, Scotland; m. first Mary Wilson in Scotland, and they had four sons and two daughters; m. secondly 6 June 1833 Margaret Barr in Saint John, N.B., and they had two sons and three daughters; d. 28 Oct. 1843 in Saint John, although his residence was a farm at Norton.

Alexander Lawrence emigrated from Aberdeen, Scotland, in 1817, arriving in Saint John on the ship *Protector*. He began his business of cabinet-maker and upholsterer on King Street in August that year. In May 1819 he formed a co-partnership with Robert Sheed, which lasted until June 1821. During this period, Lawrence took the oath of freeman of Saint John on 21 Jan. 1820. His shop, which he had moved a number of times in 1817–19, was situated on Germain Street from May 1820 until April 1827, when he relocated on King Street, next to the Masonic Hall; there he remained until his retirement.

Lawrence had come out to Saint John in the company of the Reverend Dr George Burns, a minister for the city's new Presbyterian kirk, St Andrew's. The church gave Lawrence an opportunity to be involved in music and he became the first precentor of the kirk. Presumably he served in this capacity until he remarried; he then attended Trinity Anglican Church. Soon after his arrival from Scotland, he had advertised that he would give lessons in sacred vocal music, both in a weekly class as well as privately. His interest in music is further demonstrated by his involvement in the Sacred Music Society. He was instrumental in its formation in 1837 and served as its president until his death.

A freemason, Lawrence was active in St John's Lodge No.29 of Saint John. He was entered in April 1818, raised in June 1818, and in due course advanced to the degrees of fellow of the craft and master mason. On 17 Jan. 1820, the royal arch degrees were conferred upon him in the Carleton chapter. He served as senior warden in 1827 and 1828, and as worshipful master the following year. A delegate to the meeting which formed the Grand Lodge of Free and Accepted Masons of New Brunswick in 1829, he was elected senior grand deacon for 1830 in that body. In April 1830, his brethren in the St John Lodge presented him with an address engrossed on parchment in recognition of his important services. Lawrence was active in the formation of the Saint John Mechanics' Institute in 1838. He served as a director from 1838 to 1841 and as vice-president in 1842.

In September 1842, Lawrence announced that he was retiring from business around the first of the year, at which time his sons Joseph Wilson* and George Hunter would take over his cabinet-making shop. They carried it on into the latter part of the 19th century. Lawrence retired to a farm in Norton and died within a year.

T. G. DILWORTH

City of Saint John, N.B., City Clerk's Office, Common Council, minutes, V: 111 (mfm. at PANB). N.B. Museum, St Andrew's (Presbyterian) Church (Saint John), reg. of baptisms, 1817–35; reg. of marriages, 1817–31 (typescript); Trinity (Anglican) Church (Saint John), reg. of baptisms, 1835–60, nos.250, 666; vestry minutes, 28 March 1842 (typescript). PANB, RG 7, RS71, 1843, Alexander Lawrence. *City Gazette* (Saint John), 17 Sept., 17 Dec. 1817; 28 April, 5 May 1819; 10 May 1820; 13 June 1821; 13 June 1833. *Herald* (Saint John), 10 April 1839. *Morning News* (Saint John), 15 April 1840, 30 Oct. 1843. *New-Brunswick Courier*, 6 Sept. 1817, 2 June 1827, 31 March 1832, 8 June 1833, 17 April 1841. *Weekly Chronicle* (Saint John), 6 April, 3 Aug., 7 Dec. 1838; 16 Aug. 1839; 7 Aug., 2 Oct. 1840; 14 Aug. 1841; 15 April, 12 Aug., 23 Sept. 1842; 3 Nov. 1843. *Weekly Observer* (Saint John), 3 April 1832. W. F. Bunting, *History of St. John's Lodge, F. & A.M. of Saint John, New Brunswick . . .* (Saint John, 1895). E. P. Costello, "A report on the Saint John Mechanics' Institute, 1838–1890" (MA thesis, Univ. of N.B., Fredericton, 1974), 37.

LAWSON, WILLIAM, businessman, office holder, JP, and politician; baptized 14 March 1772 in Halifax, son of John Lawson and Sarah Shatford; m. there 26 Nov. 1793 his stepsister Elizabeth Handyside, and they had 14 children; d. there 29 Aug. 1848.

William Lawson was a member of a prominent Halifax family which had come from Boston in 1750. His father was a leading merchant in the town, and the family's connections certainly aided William throughout his career. By 1800 William had established himself in business with Charles Ramage Prescott*. The firm of Prescott and Lawson traded with the West Indies, the Canadas, Spain, and Portugal, and in 1809 the two men took Joseph Allison into partnership. Prescott, Lawson and Company was dissolved by mutual consent in December 1811, but Lawson continued in business, importing naval stores and provisions from the United States during the War of 1812. With William Bruce ALMON and Lewis Johnston he was a principal of the Halifax Sugar Refinery Company, which developed during the 1820s but suffered losses when a trade act of 1830 opened the British West Indies to American merchants.

Early in his career Lawson became involved in politics. He served as a member of the House of Assembly for Halifax County from 1806 to 1836, and in January 1838 he was appointed a member of the Legislative Council, on which he sat until the session of 1845. Joseph Howe* stated in 1837 that Lawson, "though wealthy and fairly entitled to the notice of the Government," had never been made a member of the old Council because "he was too plain spoken and would not bend to the views of that body." Certainly Lawson was reported to be outspoken and forthright. In 1812 he uttered "divers words, reflecting upon [Lewis Morris WILKINS] in his character of Speaker, and upon the House," and was forced to apologize for them.

Lawson also took part in the administration of Halifax. He was commissioned a justice of the peace in 1816, 1819, and 1845, and in December 1828 he sat on the committee for the supervision of public buildings. More important, he served as treasurer for the town and county of Halifax between 1835 and 1838, commissioner of the revenue commission from 1816 to 1845, and a commissioner for the poor in 1835. The appointment as treasurer was in part responsible for Lawson's defeat in the election of 1836, since the nomination was made by the Council at a time when that body's decisions were increasingly unpopular. An avid farmer, Lawson served as treasurer of the Central Board of Agriculture for a year until supplanted by John YOUNG in December 1819. Lawson remained a member of the board's managing committee, and he was critical of Young for accepting a salary and for mistakes in the handling of funds allotted to the board.

Throughout the late 1820s Lawson and other merchants pressed for the establishment of a public bank to break the monopoly held by the privately owned Halifax Banking Company, founded in 1825 [*see* Henry Hezekiah Cogswell*]. Early in 1832 a public meeting in Halifax passed resolutions calling for a public bank, and soon afterwards Lawson introduced a bill in the assembly to charter a bank. Attempts before 1825 to start public banks had foundered mainly on the opposition of country members, who were averse to the moneyed interests of Halifax and feared that a chartered public bank would have a permanent monopoly. However, the supporters of a public bank, who included William Blowers Bliss* and James Boyle Uniacke*, argued that its charter would not be exclusive and stated that "a dozen more might be given." There were political overtones to the debate. Five councillors were among the owners of the Halifax Banking Company, and proponents of the public bank drew to their side members who may not have approved of the plan but who were opposed to the Council.

Although the assembly favoured the establishment of a public bank, there was concern about the responsibility of those who would become its directors, and the charter which went to the Council contained stringent safeguards, such as a clause which required shareholders to be liable for twice the amount of their holdings in case of insolvency. This clause was an innovation in British North America, and came at a time when most banks limited liability to the value of a shareholder's stock. Predictably, the Council amended the charter in order to place more restrictions on the operations of the bank. After some wrangling between assembly and Council the charter passed on 31 March with additional safeguards, more in total than applied anywhere else in British North America. Among the directors of the Bank of Nova Scotia, as it became, were a high proportion of assemblymen, Lawson, Bliss, and Uniacke all joining the board. Lawson was elected president, and the original stock list was headed by a subscription of £1,000 for 20 shares in his name, possibly paid for with funds inherited from his father.

Political factors caused antagonism between the Bank of Nova Scotia and the Halifax Banking Company, but a controversy over the redemption of bank notes dominated the first two years of their coexistence. By its charter the Bank of Nova Scotia had to redeem its notes in specie, and when it requested that the Halifax Banking Company redeem Bank of Nova Scotia notes in specie it was refused. The impact of the disagreement began to be felt adversely in the province, and early in 1833 steps were taken in the assembly to resolve the issue. On 20 April a bill passed which permitted the Bank of Nova Scotia to redeem its notes in provincial treasury paper, thus placing it on an equal footing with the Halifax Banking Company. By 1834, in the face of economic depression in the province, rivalry had given way to cooperation as the two banks began to evolve a system for the exchange of cheques and notes.

During the formative years of the Bank of Nova Scotia, Lawson was the most influential person in the institution. Overcoming the opposition of the Halifax Banking Company required firmness and determination, qualities which are evinced in his correspondence. He was threatened by his rivals in ways other than competition, such as in 1832 when Cogswell, in his capacity as president of the Halifax Board of Health, ordered the first quarters chosen by the bank made into a hospital for cholera victims. The bank grew steadily during Lawson's tenure as president, but his own business declined, largely because of American competition. This situation no doubt contributed to his decision in March 1837 to resign as president. In a tribute to his leadership his fellow directors expressed their "thanks for the unwearied attention bestowed on the Institution." Thereafter Lawson confined himself largely to his official duties. His house at the corner of Hollis and Salter streets, built by Malachy Salter* about 1760, was sold by his heirs in 1856 to John Esson*.

JANE HOLLINGWORTH NOKES

Bank of Nova Scotia Arch. (Toronto), Fine Art Coll., portrait of William Lawson; RG 1, ser.1, unit 1 (President's letter-book, 1832–40); unit 3 (Directors' minute-book, 1832–75); ser.2, unit 1 (Annual report, 1832); ser.5, unit 1 (Charter, 1832); RG 18 (Capital stock); RG 49 (Photo coll.); Secondary source file, material on William Lawson. Halifax County Court of Probate (Halifax), Estate papers, no.300 (mfm. at PANS). PANS, MG 100, 174, no.18; RG 5, P, 121. *Novascotian, or Colonial Herald*, 1835–36. *Directory of N.S. MLAs*. [T. B. Akins], *History of Halifax City* (Halifax, 1895; repr. Belleville, Ont., 1973). *History of the Bank of Nova Scotia, 1832–1900; together with copies of annual statements* ([Toronto, 1900]). *History of the Bank of Nova Scotia, 1832–1932* ([Toronto, 1932]). Joseph Schull and J. D. Gibson, *The Scotiabank story: a history of the Bank of Nova Scotia, 1832–1932* (Toronto, 1982).

LEAVITT, THOMAS, businessman; b. *c.* 1795 in Saint John, N.B., son of Jonathan Leavitt and Hephzibah Peabody; m. there 26 July 1822 Mary Ann Ketchum; d. there 24 Oct. 1850.

Thomas Leavitt was the son and grandson of pre-loyalist settlers in the Saint John River valley. His father had come to Portland Point (Saint John) in 1762 with James Simonds* and had served as ship's captain and pilot for the firm of Simonds, Hazen, and White prior to the American revolution. His maternal grandfather, Captain Francis Peabody, had been a founder and leader of the Maugerville settlement [*see* Israel Perley*]. Peabody's other daughters had married James Simonds and James White; thus Thomas Leavitt was born into a wide and influential family network. Jonathan Leavitt prospered as a shipowner and mariner in the new loyalist city of Saint John and at his death in 1811 left a considerable estate to his eight sons and two daughters. Thomas Leavitt's share of this patrimony was a half-interest in the family home, ownership of four choice lots in Saint John, and a seventh part of a large landholding on the Miramichi River.

In 1817 Leavitt was admitted as a merchant freeman of the city of Saint John and from that time until his death played an active and influential role in the business life of New Brunswick. Like most early leading merchants he acquired a perpetual lease to one of the water lots on the harbour. This property permitted him to maintain his own wharf, offered a centre for his commercial activities, and provided him with a modest regular income from wharfage fees. At the height of his career, in the 1830s and 1840s, he was to serve as agent both for the Liverpool Association of Underwriters and for a number of New York marine insurance companies. In 1835 he would be made United States consul for Saint John.

Leavitt's growing business interests led him to a concern for the financial structures of the province. He was too young in 1820 to participate in the formation of the Bank of New Brunswick, but like many ambitious young merchants he pressed for a rapid expansion of capital through the formation of new banking institutions. His activity here, which began in 1824, eventually took him to the presidency of the City Bank in 1837. Following its absorption by the Bank of New Brunswick in 1839, Leavitt became president of that institution. He also associated with two marine insurance companies in Saint John.

Leavitt spoke out strongly on most issues of concern to the Saint John merchant community. He opposed the Debtors Bill of 1822, which would have lessened the penalties against absconding debtors, pushed for legislation to punish those guilty of taking timber from the rivers and streams of the province, opposed the practice of allowing certain licensed merchants to import American goods directly and dispose of them at public auctions, and argued in 1831 for the payment of provincial bounties on every ton of shipping built and fitted out in New Brunswick. He was an active member of the Saint John Chamber of Commerce.

Leavitt was a freemason and Church of Scotland Presbyterian. An active layman in St Andrew's Church, he participated in 1832 in the struggle of the church trustees to wrest control of finances from the elders. He was part of a large group of city Presbyterians who challenged the Church of England's monopoly of education in the province in the 1830s, demanding the appointment of non-episcopalians to the Madras School Board and to the council of King's College.

Leavitt died at Saint John on 24 Oct. 1850 at the age of 55; he was survived by four sons and three daughters.

T. W. ACHESON

PANB, RG 4, RS24, S33-P11; RG 7, RS71, 1811, Jonathan Leavitt. *A schedule of the real estate belonging to the mayor, aldermen and commonalty of the city of Saint John . . . January, 1842* (Saint John, N.B., 1849; copy at PANB). *New-Brunswick Courier*, 28 March, 14 Nov. 1835; 1 April, 13 May 1837; 11 May 1839; 1 Jan. 1842; 26 Oct. 1850. *Morning News* (Saint John), 25 Oct. 1850.

LE BRETON, JOHN, army officer, farmer, mill-owner, and JP; b. c. 1779 on Jersey; m. 18 Nov. 1828 Susan (Susannah) George; they had no known children; d. 24 Feb. 1848 in Toronto.

John Le Breton's parents appear to have been John Le Breton, a ship's captain in the Newfoundland trade, and his wife Jane; they evidently brought John to Newfoundland as an infant. Entering the Royal Newfoundland Fencible Regiment as an ensign in 1795, he became a lieutenant in 1798 and in 1807 obtained a permanent army lieutenancy in the unit's successor, the Royal Newfoundland Regiment. In 1808, while serving at Quebec, he requested a posting either to an armed vessel on the St Lawrence River or as adjutant of a militia battalion in Upper Canada; in support of the former he cited his fluency in French and his experience in command of a cutter off Newfoundland. The following year he became deputy assistant quartermaster general at Quebec, a temporary staff appointment he held until March 1812. Between April and October he acted as adjutant of the Voltigeurs Canadiens; in November he returned to the Royal Newfoundland Regiment, serving as an assistant engineer.

An aggressive officer whose ambition outreached his achievements, Le Breton nevertheless participated with distinction in nine actions during the War of 1812. In October 1813 he was sent to Detroit under truce by Major-General Henry Procter* to request the humane treatment of prisoners taken by the Americans at Moraviantown and the restoration of their private property. Secretly he was to assess the Americans' strength at Detroit and on Lake Erie. In December Commodore Sir James Lucas Yeo* described him as a "very clear headed intelligent Officer." Le Breton returned to the quartermaster general's department in February 1814 and remained with it until mid 1815. During that period he pressed unsuccessfully for authorization to raise and command an Upper Canadian "Corps of Rangers." He was severely wounded and disabled at Lundy's Lane in July 1814. Between July 1815 and April 1816 he was on leave in England and in the Canadas. Promoted captain in the 60th Foot in March 1816, he went on half pay later that month.

In March 1815 Le Breton had petitioned for land in Upper Canada. Four years later his grant was located in Nepean Township in the Ottawa River valley, where he settled and later erected mills. His holding, which he called Britannia and which was later known as Le Breton Flats, was near the Chaudière Falls property of Robert Randal*, part of which Le Breton tried to buy or lease. By May 1819 he had built a storehouse there. The key to the property's importance was its location – at Richmond Landing, the main transit depot for the military settlements of Perth and Richmond. In December 1820 Le Breton bought the Randal property for £449 at a sheriff's sale in Brockville. Though legally transacted, the purchase became part of Randal's litany of political grievances, and immediately established Le Breton before many as an obstreperous opportunist. Governor Lord Dalhousie [RAMSAY] accused him of acting on privileged information, reputedly overheard at a dinner in Richmond the preceding August, about the government's intention to develop a new depot at Richmond Landing. A number of the district's compact of half-pay officers and gentlemen later supported Le Breton by testifying that no such news had been discussed at the dinner. Le Breton repeatedly refused to relinquish the landing to the government for less than £3,000 despite the direct involvement of an offended Dalhousie who questioned the legality of his purchase and loathed the characteristic aggressiveness of his resistance. His title survived a court challenge by the crown in 1828, following which he began to subdivide the property, now adjacent to the newly established settlement of Bytown (Ottawa) and the Rideau Canal.

Le Breton's modest accomplishments as a settler are overwhelmed in the historical record by a series of disputes which preoccupied him for almost two decades and create the impression of an embittered veteran in an almost constant state of grievance. First appointed as a magistrate for the Montreal District in 1821, he petitioned Lieutenant Governor Sir Peregrine Maitland* unsuccessfully in 1822 to have his name reinstated on a list of magistrates for Upper Canada from which it had been inexplicably struck. His action was motivated in part by his need for income (he claimed to have invested more than £2,000 in his settlement) and partly by rampant lawlessness in Nepean. In 1820 he had protested to Maitland's secretary, Major George HILLIER, the theft of timber from his land. In 1823–24 he was assaulted by timbermen, whom he viewed as plunderers and thugs, some of whom, including Philemon WRIGHT, had again stolen timber. Solicitor General Henry John Boulton* contended in 1824 that the timbermen accused by Le Breton that year had had a contract with him and that any dispute should be resolved in court, a course that Le Breton, who often pressed charges of trespass, declined to follow, possibly because of the cost and uncertain outcome. In 1825 he realized some additional income by commuting his half pay, and finally, in 1830 and again in 1838, he was commissioned a magistrate for the Bathurst District.

Between 1827 and 1839 Le Breton was embroiled with Lieutenant-Colonel John BY, other military authorities, and provincial law officers over his claims for losses resulting from the construction of the Rideau Canal and related works. The running controversy centred on timber allegedly taken from his property and on the Royal Engineers' construction of a dam and deepening of a channel for floating timber past the Chaudière Falls as part of the developments near the canal's entrance. Situated adjacent to Le Breton's property, these works prevented him from erecting his own dam and ruined the mill-site. This dispute with the authorities, which may rank next to that involving Nicholas Sparks* as the longest and most complicated to arise from the canal's construction, illustrates Le Breton's painful inability to negotiate productively. He refused to accept either By's offer of compensation or adjudication by jury, and though one senior military officer supported his claims, the contestants could not agree on an arrangement for arbitration. Eventually, both the Colonial

Office and the Upper Canadian administration of Sir George Arthur* despaired of ever settling with Le Breton. At this point the civil courts became his only recourse; he evidently took no legal action, perhaps because of the probable expense and likely futility.

In the midst of this tribulation Le Breton married in Quebec, and continued to visit there periodically. In early 1832 he tried to build a bridge from ice, utilizing the studies he had made before the War of 1812 of ice movements on the St Lawrence. His main occupation, however, remained farming at Britannia (in 1842, for instance, he occupied 660 acres, of which 60 were improved). He supplemented his income by selling land. His last sale of Chaudière land took place in 1837, though his interest in development there continued; in 1840 he and John George Howard* corresponded about the latter's plans for a bridge in the area. Le Breton's wife died in July 1847 and he subsequently moved to Toronto, where he passed away the following winter. A large memorial stone was erected at his grave in St James' Cemetery by his five nieces, who lived in Toronto and to whom he had left his estate.

DAVID ROBERTS

[Although John Le Breton was born in Jersey, an extensive search by the Soc. jersiaise (St Helier, Jersey) in 1979–81 failed to locate any certain reference to his baptism. More recent research indicates that he may have been baptized in Newfoundland, possibly in the Anglican parish of Conception Bay (Harbour Grace). D.R.]

AO, MS 516, Charles Waters to Mackenzie, 21, 28 July 1835; MU 1915, envelope for 1823; RG 1, A-I-6, 7, 24; RG 22, ser.155; ser.224, reg.A, John Le Breton, Susan Le Breton. MHA, Le Breton name file. MTRL, J. G. Howard papers, journals, 27–28 April, 4 May 1840. Ottawa-Carleton Land Registry Office (Ottawa), Nepean Township, abstract index to deeds; deeds, nos.3859–60. PAC, MG 24, A12, 4, 14, 20 (transcripts); RG 1, E3, 46: 198–215; L3, 286: L10/33; 289: L13/72; 292: L17/15; 305a: L leases/94; RG 5, A1; RG 8, I (C ser.); RG 31, C1, 1842, Nepean Township; RG 68, General index, 1651–1841: 354, 358, 471, 484. Private arch., David Roberts (Toronto), A. J. H. Richardson, "Settlements at 'Richmond Landing,' Ottawa" (copy); S. R. J. Sutherland, "Le Breton" (typescript). PRO, CO 42/362, 42/411, 42/463; WO 27/89, 15 Oct. 1805; 27/91, 7 April 1807; 27/99, 4 June 1810; 27/103, 14 June 1811. St James' Cemetery and Crematorium (Toronto), Record of burials, 26 Feb. 1848; tombstone, lot 1, section U. *Select British docs. of War of 1812* (Wood), 3: 33, 35–36. *British Colonist*, 25 Feb. 1848. *Packet* (Bytown [Ottawa]), 24 July 1847. *Marriage notices of Ont.* (Reid). *Officers of British forces in Canada* (Irving), 6, 8, 105. H. P. Hill, *Robert Randall and the Le Breton Flats: an account of the early legal and political controversies respecting the ownership of a large portion of the present city of Ottawa* (Ottawa, 1919). R. [F.] Legget, *Ottawa waterway: gateway to a continent* (Toronto and Buffalo, N.Y., 1975). G. W. L. Nicholson, *The fighting Newfoundlander: a history of the Royal Newfoundland Regiment* (St John's, [1964?]). P.-G. Roy, *Toutes petites choses du Régime anglais* (2 sér., Québec, 1946), 1: 269–70. H. [J. W.] Walker and Olive [Moffat] Walker, *Carleton saga* (Ottawa, 1968).

LEFEBVRE DE BELLEFEUILLE, LOUIS-CHARLES (also called **Charles** or **Charles-Louis**), Sulpician and missionary; b. 12 Jan. 1795 in Saint-Eustache, Lower Canada, younger son of Antoine Lefebvre de Bellefeuille, seigneur of Cournoyer, and Louise-Angélique Lambert Dumont, daughter of Eustache-Louis Lambert Dumont, seigneur of Mille-Îles; d. 25 Oct. 1838 in Montreal.

Louis-Charles Lefebvre de Bellefeuille was a descendant of two great Canadian families that had distinguished themselves during the French régime. From 1807 to 1815 he pursued the classical program of studies at the Petit Séminaire de Montréal, as did most of his brothers. His principal teachers were Antoine-Jacques Houdet* and Claude Rivière. Upon completion of the final two years (Philosophy), he began his theological education with Jacques-Guillaume ROQUE, the director of the Petit Séminaire. He was also a regent at that time.

As his studies progressed, Lefebvre de Bellefeuille took the various steps leading to the priesthood. He was ordained priest by Joseph-Octave Plessis* in Montreal on 5 June 1819. Although he had already spent a period of time at the Lac-des-Deux-Montagnes (Oka) mission to learn the Algonkin language, he was named assistant priest in the Montreal parish of Notre-Dame that year. He was admitted as a member of the community of Saint-Sulpice in Montreal on 31 Jan. 1821. His duties included performing baptisms, attending burials, and drawing up the appropriate religious and civil records. As well, he visited the sick and the poor of the *faubourgs* Saint-Joseph, Saint-Antoine, and Sainte-Anne. From time to time he also taught the catechism in the chapel of Notre-Dame-de-Bonsecours and served as confessor to the sisters of the Congregation of Notre-Dame. He preached five or six times a year, at Sunday mass or during the solemn novena of St Francis Xavier, a devotion then performed by many.

Attracted to the Lac-des-Deux-Montagnes mission by fellow Sulpician Anthelme Malard, Lefebvre de Bellefeuille stayed there once more from 1824 to 1826, and after further pastoral training at Montreal in 1826 and 1827, he was named superior in 1828. The mission had three sites and some 900 people: the village itself, which had a few whites but mostly Indian inhabitants, an Iroquois village, and an Algonkin village. The seminary had never, from the beginning of the mission in 1721, granted any land to the Indians. It received the usufruct of a reasonable part of the domain reserved for the Indians' use. After the conquest this arrangement gave rise to complaints, originally from the Iroquois in particular, and later it created difficulties between the Sulpicians and all the groups in the mission. Lefebvre de Bellefeuille was confronted with a number of claims in July 1828. The Algonkins sent the secretary of the Indian Department, Duncan Campbell Napier*, a memorial laying out 11 grievances, ranging from the priest's refusal to help the Indians with alms to accusations of ill treatment of a poor widow. On 1 August he refuted these allegations, and the Algonkin council apologized to him.

In October 1834 Lefebvre de Bellefeuille returned to Montreal and resumed his duties as assistant priest. During the summers of 1836, 1837, and 1838 Bishop Jean-Jacques LARTIGUE sent him to open missions to the Indians in the northwest of Lower Canada. He had been chosen because of his knowledge of Algonkin, and in 1836 with Jean-Baptiste Dupuy* he went by canoe to Fort Timiskaming (near Ville-Marie), where he spent 13 days. He returned after performing 142 baptisms and 4 marriages. The following year he left Montreal alone, spent two weeks with his converts of the previous year at Fort Timiskaming, and then travelled to Lake Abitibi for a first visit of 9 days. But he ran short of provisions and had to turn around. On his way back he stopped at several posts that he had visited the year before. In all, he performed 190 baptisms and 21 marriages. His biggest mission, however, was to take place in 1838. He covered 1,500 miles, visiting Fort Timiskaming and Lake Abitibi again before continuing on to Grand Lac Victoria. As he was suffering from great fatigue, he returned in haste to Montreal. It appears that he performed 550 baptisms in the course of these three trips. In so doing he opened up northwestern Lower Canada to the Roman Catholic faith.

Exhausted by his missionary activity, Lefebvre de Bellefeuille, whose health had always been delicate, died of typhoid fever on 25 Oct. 1838. Two days later Bishop Ignace Bourget* officiated at his burial, which took place in the crypt of Notre-Dame in Montreal. An Oblate missionary, Nicolas Laverlochère, later wrote of him: "The first missionary to these parts had to have a unique ability to win people's hearts. Although it is now seven years since God recalled him, his name is still blessed by all who knew him, whatever their race or religion."

BRUNO HAREL

Louis-Charles Lefebvre de Bellefeuille is the author of "Relation d'une mission faite à l'été de 1837, le long de la rivière de l'Outawa jusqu'au lac de Témiskaming, et au-dela jusqu'au lac d'Abbitibbi dans le district de Monseigneur de Juliopolis" and "Précis de la relation de la troisième mission de Mr Bellefeuille à Temiskaming, Abbitibbi et Grand Lac," both published in Assoc. de la Propagation de la Foi, *Rapport* (Montréal), 2 (1840): 17–88.

AAQ, 12 A, H: ff.124, 227–28; 303 CD, II, no.61. ACAM, 901.137. ANQ-M, CE1-51, 27 oct. 1838; CE6-11, 12 janv. 1795; CN6-2, 16 mai 1818. Arch. du collège de Montréal, Cahiers de la congrégation, 1766–78; Livres de comptes de la congrégation; Palmarès, 1808, 1810, 1812–13; Reg. des élections; Reg. des réceptions, 5 févr. 1809. ASSM, 8, A; 24, F. J.-B. Dupuy, "Journal d'un voyage fait à Témiskaming en 1836," Assoc. de la Propagation de la Foi, *Rapport*, 1 (1839): 24–53. Allaire, *Dictionnaire*. Joseph Bouchette, *A topographical dictionary of the province of Lower Canada* (London, 1832). [J.-]H. Gauthier, *Sulpitiana* ([2e éd.], Montréal, 1926). Tanguay, *Répertoire* (1893). Louis Bertrand, *Bibliothèque sulpicienne ou histoire littéraire de la Compagnie de Saint-Sulpice* (3v., Paris, 1900), 2: 118. [François Daniel], *Histoire des grandes familles françaises du Canada ou aperçu sur le chevalier Benoist et quelques familles contemporaines* (Montréal, 1867), 481. Alexis De Barbezieux, *Histoire de la province ecclésiastique d'Ottawa et de la colonisation dans la vallée de l'Ottawa* (4v., Ottawa, 1897), 1: 186–91. Donat Martineau, *Le fort Temiskaming* (2e éd., Rouyn, Qué., 1969), 62–65. Maurault, *Le collège de Montréal* (Dansereau; 1967). Sœur Paul-Émile [Louise Guay], *La baie James, 300 ans d'histoire militaire, économique, missionnaire* (Ottawa, 1952), 76–77. Yvon Charron, "Monsieur Charles de Bellefeuille, missionnaire de l'Outawais (1836–38)," *RHAF*, 5 (1951–52): 193–226. J.-A. Cuoq, "Anotc kekon," RSC *Trans.*, 1st ser., 11 (1893), sect.I: 137–79. J.-B. Harel, "Louis-Charles Lefebvre de Bellefeuille, prêtre de Saint-Sulpice, 1795–1838," CCHA *Sessions d'études*, 49 (1982): 7–24. A. C. de L. Macdonald, "Notes sur la famille Lambert du Mont" and "La famille Le Febvre de Bellefeuille," *Rev. canadienne*, 19 (1883): 633–40, 739–47; 20 (1884): 168–76, 235–47, 291–302. Olivier Maurault, "Les vicissitudes d'une mission sauvage," *Rev. trimestrielle canadienne*, 16 (1930): 121–49. "Le premier évangélisateur de l'Abitibi," Soc. de géographie de Québec, *Bull.* (Québec), 13 (1919): 309–10.

LEFFERTY (Lafferty), JOHN JOHNSTON (Johnson), doctor and politician; b. *c.* 1777 in the American colonies, probably in New Jersey; m. 17 Aug. 1800 Mary Johnson, and they had four sons and three daughters; d. 26 Oct. 1842 in Drummondville, Upper Canada.

John Johnston Lefferty seems to have been the son of Bryan Lefferty, a lawyer and judge of Somerset County, N.J., who was connected to the family of Sir William Johnson*. John Johnston came to Upper Canada in 1797, settling in the Niagara peninsula where he practised medicine. The following year his godfather, Sir John Johnson*, wrote to William Claus* from Lachine asking to find out "in What Manner I can Serve him [Lefferty]. . . . If he will send me a list of Medicines Suitable for his practice, I will send it home, and get it out for him." During the War of 1812 Lefferty served as assistant surgeon of militia; he lost his home at Lundy's Lane (Niagara Falls) when it was burnt by American troops.

In 1818 he was a co-owner of an apothecary shop in St Catharines. Lefferty rose to prominence when he was elected for the 2nd and 3rd riding of Lincoln to serve in the ninth parliament (1825–28). He emerged as a notable critic of Sir Peregrine Maitland*'s administration and, as he put it, said "a great deal about the office-holders during the discussion of the alien question and the Welland canal, but not upon other questions." On one occasion during the alien debate, Speaker John Willson* had to call him to order for abusing Attorney General John Beverley Robinson*. On a subsequent occasion Lefferty declared: "The Proclamation of the ever to be lamented [Sir Isaac Brock*] had declared all those to be subjects who remained in the country at the time of the late war, and who had nobly defended the Province and fought for their king." Lefferty added that "he would rather suffer his arm to rot from his shoulder than consent to call himself an Alien." John Clark, a fellow member from Lincoln, attributed the measure of independence assumed by the house to the efforts of men such as John Rolph*, Marshall Spring Bidwell*, and "the learned and all Eloquent Doctor from Lundy's Lane – an honor to his constituents."

Yet, as Lefferty himself noted, his attacks on the administration were largely confined to two issues. On a number of political points, he sharply disagreed with other critics of the executive. He did not object to the custom of sheriffs' selecting grand jurors, a stance which earned him a sharp attack from Peter Perry*. He supported the marriage bill of 1826 which allowed Methodists and other denominations the right to perform marriages; however, the next year he would denounce an apparently similar measure. He repeatedly clashed with Perry, Rolph, and Bidwell over their opposition to tough legislation for handling the problem of absconding debtors. His concern in this instance may have reflected his own experience as a doctor. He called Perry's bill to introduce statute labour for absentee landowners "perfectly absurd," since £4,000 worth of wild lands would oblige an owner to provide 160 days of labour. Furthermore, as Lefferty gained parliamentary experience, he came to consider as wasted effort time spent on popular bills which, to his mind, would only be rejected by the Legislative Council. Despite these problems with his fellow critics of the Maitland régime, Lefferty joined in the opposition's furore over the dismissal in 1828 of judge John Walpole Willis*.

Prior to the election of 1824, William Lyon Mackenzie* had alleged, correctly, that Lefferty had been among the first to support, and the first to repudiate, Robert Gourlay*. And later, no doubt with Lefferty's independent political behaviour in mind, Mackenzie labelled him an "eccentric legislator." The tag, however, did not hurt and in the election of 1828 he was returned for 3rd Lincoln, placing a strong second among the four members elected. During a debate in the tenth parliament (1829–30), James Hunter SAMSON accused Lefferty of changing his position: once "abusing the office-holders in York . . . he now comes forward to defend them." Lefferty explained that the province "now . . . had another head of the government, and he was pleased with him." Sir John Colborne* had, he thought, done "more for the province for the short period of his residence than any Governor that preceded him."

Lefferty's most notable parliamentary initiative came at the close of his career. Early in 1830 he introduced a bill empowering magistrates to enforce observance of the Sabbath. He denounced such varied activities as shooting and skating on the Lord's Day, adding: "It was a common thing, too, for persons to leave their work, and assemble at grog-shops on Saturday night and drink and carouse until the next night, and thus, not only disregard the Sabbath, but render themselves unfit to attend to business on Monday, or perhaps through the week. In this way, it was an injury, not only to the morals, but also to the industry of the country." In the course of debate he went even further than the intention of his bill, observing that he thought "people ought to be obliged to attend public worship somewhere on the Sabbath." This statement provoked a strong reaction not only from fellow legislators but also from at least one newspaper and its correspondents.

In the 1830 election William Crooks was returned with Bartholomew Crannell Beardsley* for the 2nd and 3rd riding of Lincoln. Lefferty may not have run. In the general election four years later sheriff Alexander HAMILTON, the returning officer, declared him elected by one vote. His opponent, David Thorburn, appealed this ruling to the new assembly, dominated by critics of the provincial administration, and a committee directed Hamilton to alter his report – which he did under protest. Allan Napier MacNab*, a staunch supporter of the executive, led the fight against adoption of the committee's report in the house. But the assembly, in a vote clearly divided on party lines, supported Thorburn. Small wonder a historian reviewing the incident saw Lefferty as one of the "stalwarts" of the "ruling caste."

Lefferty was a noted figure in the Niagara area. In 1810 his spirited exertions saved a man from being carried over the falls. An admirer of good horses, he was renowned for his "*standing* song, 'Twelve bottles more;' and an everlasting anecdote." His home at Lundy's Lane, prior to its destruction by fire in the 1820s, contained a host of "rare and curious things, animate and inanimate," including an assortment of animals, Indian bones and crockery, dinosaur and animal bones, military paraphernalia, rare books, skates, a hornets' nest, "an *electrifying* machine," assembly journals, alien question resolutions, pharmacopoeias, carefully filed copies of the *Colonial Advocate* ("a remarkable and convincing instance of . . . wisdom and good sense," Mackenzie thought), and "3569 *doctor's phials*, bottles and jars filled with fluids, unguents, and powders of various kinds."

A genial legislator of independent mind, he was, perhaps, best captured in the surprisingly warm words of a political opponent, Robert Stanton*, who in 1826 described him thus: "a broad goodnatured face full of fun and mirth, and after all a great deal of the milk of human kindness lies in his disposition – in the house he rattles away laughing all the time, and the only reason he is heard is because his voice is at the top of the House – and he is not improperly and facetiously called the representative of the Falls of Niagara."

PETER A. RUSSELL

AO, MS 74, John Clark to William Chisholm, 26 Jan. 1826; MS 78, Robert Stanton to John Macaulay, 29 Jan. 1826, 6 Feb. 1835. MTRL, W. W. Baldwin papers, B. C. Beardsley to Baldwin, 1 Aug. 1828. John Clark, "Memoirs of Colonel John Clark, of Port Dalhousie, C.W.," *OH*, 7 (1906): 157–93. *Canadian Freeman*, 1 Dec. 1825. *Christian Guardian*, 12 Dec. 1829, 27 Nov. 1830. *Colonial Advocate*, 8 July 1824, 29 Dec. 1825, 4 Jan. 1827, 1 Feb. 1828. *Kingston Chronicle*, 4 Jan. 1826, 9 Feb. 1827. *Patriot* (Toronto), 3, 6, 19 Feb. 1835. *Upper Canada Herald*, 9, 16 Jan. 1827; 12 Feb., 18 March 1828; 20, 27 Jan., 10 Feb., 17 March 1830. Armstrong, *Handbook of Upper Canadian chronology* (1967). "1828 Upper Canada election results table," comp. R. S. Sorrell, *OH*, 63 (1971): 67–69. Canniff, *Medical profession in U.C.* Ernest Green, "John DeCou, pioneer," *OH*, 22 (1925): 92–116.

LEITH, JAMES, fur trader; b. 1777 in Glenkindie, Scotland, and baptized 3 August in the parish of Strathdon, son of Alexander Leith and Mary Elizabeth Gordon; d. 19 June 1838 in Torquay, England.

James Leith's family was wealthy and well connected. James probably came to Lower Canada in 1794 in company with George Leith, a Detroit merchant who was involved in 1798 in the formation of the New North West Company (sometimes called the XY Company). By 1 Dec. 1799 James was one of its wintering partners, and by 1801 he was on the Peace River (Alta/B.C.). He remained a partner after the firm's merger with the North West Company in 1804.

Leith spent much of his NWC career east of Fort William (Thunder Bay, Ont.), wintering at "Folle Avoine" (1806–7), Michipicoten (1807–10), and Monontagué and Lake Nipigon (1812–15). West of Lake Superior, he spent one winter at Red River (1811–12) and three at Rainy Lake (1810–11 and 1815–17). Leith and John Haldane* split the NWC's council in 1815 by their hostility toward the company's Montreal agents. The following year Leith became embroiled in the troubles between Lord Selkirk [Douglas*] and the NWC. He was one of the 11 partners who accompanied former partner Archibald Norman McLeod to Red River to retaliate for Colin ROBERTSON's seizure of Nor'wester Duncan CAMERON, and to distribute presents to the Métis who had taken part in the killing of HBC territorial governor Robert Semple* and others at Seven Oaks (Winnipeg). In 1817 Leith was again sent to Red River to help the special commissioners William Bacheler Coltman* and John FLETCHER reconcile the factions there as the Colonial Office had demanded.

In October 1818 Leith was in York (Toronto) for the trials of two participants in the Seven Oaks incident [*see* Douglas], and in the autumn of 1819 he assisted McLeod's efforts in Lower Canada to secure speedy trials of various Nor'Westers or the dismissal of charges being pressed by Selkirk against them. Leith himself was named in some indictments, but he was one of the least belligerent partners. The NWC's council chose him in 1820 to take charge of the Athabasca River department; he made his headquarters on the Peace River, which then enjoyed an unusually quiet winter.

Leith benefited from the merger of the NWC and the Hudson's Bay Company in 1821, becoming a chief factor. His non-partisanship in the struggle with the HBC had annoyed some NWC colleagues without earning him friends in the opposite camp. But Colin Robertson, speaking in 1822 of Leith's resistance to "undue influence," now summed him up well: "This gentleman, though not possessed of bright parts, has strong natural acquirements, good sound sense, and highly honourable principles." He returned to the Athabasca country for one season (1821–22). The rest of his career, to 1829, was passed in charge of Cumberland House district (Sask.), where he had few important duties except to assist the transports of other districts in summer.

Granted furlough in 1829 and 1830, he sailed for London on 15 Sept. 1829 and retired officially on 31 May 1831. The previous year he had transferred Colquoich, the thousand-acre estate which had been settled on him, to his elder brother, Sir Alexander Leith. James took lodgings at Torquay, but kept in touch with former fur-trade colleagues, including Chief Factor John STUART. The two toured the Continent together in 1836–37.

An aloof and colourless individual, Leith did nothing remarkable during his lifetime, but he is remembered for a charity set up after his death. He left half of his estate in trust for "establishing propagating and extending the Christian protestant Religion in, & amongst the native aboriginal Indians in . . . the Hudson's Bay Territory." His interest in religion and the Indians is on record from the early 1820s. He canvassed for the Rupert's Land Bible Society, and his views in 1823 on the Indians of the Cumberland House district were enlightened for the time: "Their ideas on many points of what the civilized world terms honourable conduct will not bear to be strictly examined into, entirely from circumstances and their situation in life and not to defaults in the gifts of nature." No reliable source has been found for a tradition that Leith, who may have married according to the custom of the country, established the trust because Indians had killed his wife and children at The Pas (Man.). Some such event may have occurred before 1805, but a tale told to John Henry Lefroy* in 1843 at The Pas, evidently by Henry Budd*, is the source of all published accounts of Leith's "noble revenge."

Leith's trust was to be administered by his brother William Hay and, *ex officio*, the Anglican dean of Westminster, the bishop of London, and the governor and deputy governor of the HBC. Two trustees declined to act; this refusal and family protests threw the estate into the Court of Chancery. About £15,000 was released in 1848 to endow the Anglican diocese of Rupert's Land [*see* David Anderson*] and a year later the HBC pledged an annual grant of £300 to launch the charity properly. Appropriately, a portrait of Leith hangs at Bishopscourt in Winnipeg.

PHILIP GOLDRING

An undated oil portrait of James Leith, owned by the ACC, Diocese of Rupert's Land (Winnipeg), is located at the PAM.

PAC, MG 19, A35, 7, pt.IV: 31–41; E1, ser.1: 2761–62, 3962–64, 3984–85; E2, item 95, Ready to McLeod and Leith, 5 Oct. 1819; MG 24, A2: 913–17; L3: 25629–43; RG 4, B46: 1442–46, 1458–68. PAM, HBCA, A.36/8: ff.225–28 (copy); A.38/27–30; B.39/e/4; B.49/a/42–44; B.49/e/3; C.1/916. UTFL, MS coll. 31, box 24, notes on James Leith. Ross Cox, *The Columbia River: or, scenes and adventures during a residence of six years on the western side of the Rocky Mountains . . .*, ed. E. I. and J. R. Stewart (Norman, Okla., 1957). *Docs. relating to NWC* (Wallace). G.B., Parl., House of Commons paper, 1819, 18, no.584: 195–97, 200, *Papers relating to the Red River settlement*. John Halkett, *Statement respecting the Earl of Selkirk's settlement upon the Red River . . .* ([enlarged ed.], London, 1817; repr. [Toronto, 1970]), app.EE. *HBRS*, 2 (Rich and Fleming); 3 (Fleming). *Quebec Gazette*, 3 July 1794. R. A. Pendergast, "The XY Company, 1798 to 1804" (PHD thesis, Univ. of Ottawa, 1957), 64. J. N. Wallace, *The wintering partners on Peace River from the earliest records to the union in 1821; with a summary of the Dunvegan journal, 1806* (Ottawa, 1929). [H.] B. Willson, *The life of Lord Strathcona & Mount Royal, G.C.M.G., G.C.V.O. (1820–1914)* (London and Toronto, 1915). E. R. Bagley, "James Leith takes his revenge," *Beaver*, outfit 274 (June 1943): 36–37.

LEMAIRE, MARIE-MARGUERITE, superior of the Sisters of Charity of the Hôpital Général in Montreal; b. 14 May 1769 in Lac-des-Deux-Montagnes (Oka), Que., daughter of Ignace Lemaire, a merchant, and Marie-Louise Castonguay; d. 12 April 1838 in Montreal.

Marie-Marguerite Lemaire showed ability as a student when she attended a school run by the Congregation of Notre-Dame. Her studies completed, she helped her father in his business and her mother with the housework. She read in her spare time, mainly the lives of the saints. As gifted as she was serious, she longed for the religious life. When she was 16, she sought admission to the Hôtel-Dieu of Montreal, but she was rejected because of a slight infirmity that made her limp. She then applied to the Hôpital Général of Montreal and was accepted because of her many talents. She entered the convent on 21 Nov. 1785 and took perpetual vows on 24 Jan. 1788.

Sister Lemaire was driven by an extraordinary passion for work. Having devoted herself to humble tasks for about ten years, she was named bursar of the community in 1798. In this capacity she managed the seigneury of Châteauguay and Île Saint-Bernard, both owned by the Hôpital Général. She drew up the land roll of the seigneury herself and hired a surveyor to determine its boundaries officially. She also had to stand up to the Indians of nearby Caughnawaga (Kahnawake), who were trying to take over Île Saint-Bernard. She even defied them by pulling out the crops they had sown, and they decided to beat a retreat. Another threat came from the seigneur of Beauharnois, who wanted to have his agent take possession of the Îles de la Paix (which were part of the seigneury of Châteauguay) and had some of the trees cut down. The matter was taken to the courts, which decided in her favour; the community received damages for the losses suffered.

When the Lachine canal was being built, Sister Lemaire was vigilant and firm. Learning that the engineers were determined to encroach upon the community's lands at Pointe-Saint-Charles (Montreal), she went to the work sites and protested energetically. The offenders acknowledged that the nuns were within their rights.

In addition to being enterprising and determined, Sister Lemaire was recognized for her kindness. During the War of 1812, for example, her efforts in nursing a British soldier to recovery brought his enthusiastic gratitude. Another time she bravely went to the rescue of some travellers in peril on ice-floes in the St Lawrence, and she offered them hospitality in the manor-house of Châteauguay.

On 20 July 1821, three days after the death of the superior, Thérèse-Geneviève Coutlée*, Sister Lemaire was elected as her successor. Contrary to custom she retained the office of bursar. Like her predecessors she applied herself to recovering the annuities that the community held in France. She succeeded in this endeavour through the help of Sulpician Jean-Baptiste THAVENET. Mother Lemaire used these funds to enlarge the Hôpital Général, supervising the work herself. In addition she had extensive improvements made to the seigneury of Châteauguay. In 1823 she agreed to shelter 40 Irish orphan girls at the request of the Sulpicians, who undertook to pay for part of their keep. During her tenure as superior the community received Scottish and Irish women into its ranks.

On 3 Sept. 1833 Marie-Marguerite Lemaire resigned as superior because of ill health, and Marguerite BEAUBIEN replaced her. She spent the last five years of her life in the hospital's infirmary, where she died on 12 April 1838. She is remembered as an intrepid woman, attentive to the nuns' living conditions and filled with compassion for the poor. She had contributed greatly to improving the material circumstances of the community.

HUGUETTE LAPOINTE-ROY

Arch. des Sœurs Grises (Montréal), Dossier de sœur M.-M. Lemaire, corr.; hist. personnelle, doc.3, 5, 7–8; post mortem, doc.2; Reg. des baptêmes et sépultures de l'Hôpital Général de Montréal. [Albina Fauteux et Clémentine Drouin], *L'Hôpital Général des Sœurs de la charité (Sœurs Grises) depuis sa fondation jusqu'à nos jours* (3v. parus, Montréal, 1916–).

LE MOYNE DE LONGUEUIL, MARIE-CHARLES-JOSEPH, Baronne de LONGUEUIL (Grant), seigneur and philanthropist; b. 21 March 1756 in Montreal, daughter of Charles-Jacques Le Moyne de Longueuil, Baron de Longueuil, and Marie-Anne-Catherine Fleury Deschambault; d. there 17 Feb. 1841 and was buried six days later at Longueuil, Lower Canada.

The posthumous daughter of the third baron, who was listed as missing after the battle of Lac Saint-Sacrement (Lake George, N.Y.), Marie-Charles-Joseph Le Moyne de Longueuil was the twin sister of Marie-Catherine-Joseph, who died when only a few months old. As a young child she lived with her mother at the Hôpital Général in Montreal. Her grandfather, Joseph Fleury* Deschambault, acted as her guardian and attended to her interests.

Shortly after her father's death, Paul-Joseph Le Moyne* de Longueuil, brother of Charles*, the second baron, had claimed that the title was his, since he was the last male descendant of the first baron. The matter was taken before the most eminent jurists in Paris. Between 1771 and 1776 they delivered three opinions, all favourable to Marie-Charles-Joseph, to whom the title of fourth baroness of Longueuil fell by right. She spent the years 1774–77 in France with her mother to lay claim to a pension for the services rendered by her father and her brothers and the losses suffered by her family during the Seven Years' War. For a time she received 300 *livres* per annum.

On 7 May 1781, after her return to the province of Quebec, Marie-Charles-Joseph married David Alexander Grant, a captain in the 84th Foot and nephew of William Grant*, who had married her mother 11 years earlier. Doubtless because of her husband's military duties, she first lived at Quebec, where she gave birth to three sons, the eldest of whom, Charles William, would be the fifth baron of Longueuil. Then the family settled down in the manor-house on Île Sainte-Hélène, near Montreal. In 1791 William Grant gave the couple the barony of Longueuil and the banal rights on Île Sainte-Hélène. That year their daughter Marie-Élisabeth, who would later become the seigneur of Pierreville and Belœil, was born.

On 20 March 1806 Mme Grant was widowed. The inventory of the joint estate shows that the family's fortune was based on real property: the barony of Longueuil, the seigneuries of Belœil and Pierreville, 36,400 acres in Upton, Roxton, Barford, and Hereford townships in Lower Canada, and half of Wolfe Island, near Kingston in Upper Canada (another 26,000 acres). A short time later she had to fight several legal actions brought by *censitaires* in the barony because her husband had sold, rather than granted, woodlands, an action contravening the regulations governing seigneurial property.

By 1819 Mme Grant was settled in Montreal, on Rue Sainte-Marie (Rue Notre-Dame). She also owned a residence on Rue Charlotte in Longueuil. In 1823 she contributed to Longueuil's economic boom by having a steam-mill built for carding and milling. In 1829 she handed over half of the barony of Longueuil to Charles William, in return for his oath of fealty and homage. With the population of the village of Longueuil increasing rapidly, she had part of the domain divided into lots in 1835 and got a street plan drawn up by surveyor Joseph Weilbrenner.

Mme Grant was known as a pious and charitable woman. In 1809 she ceded part of the site of the old fort in Longueuil, which was falling into ruin, for a new church to be built. Three years later she granted the parish priest, Augustin Chaboillez*, some land near the church on which he had a spacious house built for himself, and in 1815 she let him have another property behind the church to enlarge the cemetery. In 1821 she subscribed to the Quebec Emigrants' Society. At that time the barony of Longueuil was expanding towards the village of Dorchester, which would later become the town of Saint-Jean (Saint-Jean-sur-Richelieu). Mme Grant gave a piece of land for another church to be built [*see* Gabriel Marchand*] in 1826. The next year she agreed to become president of the Association des Dames de la Charité, an organization founded by Angélique Blondeau, the widow of Gabriel Cotté*. At the time of the terrible cholera epidemic in 1832, a group of pious ladies inspired by Mme Cotté set up the Orphelinat Catholique de Montréal, an orphanage of which Mme Grant was also named president. She held both offices until her death.

Marie-Charles-Joseph was the last legal French descendant of the Le Moyne de Longueuil family in Canada. As had her mother, by her marriage she enabled the new masters of Lower Canada to make their way into the ranks of the Canadian nobility. With her death the barony of Longueuil passed permanently into the hands of the new British "aristocracy." The abolition of the seigneurial system was at hand.

LOUIS LEMOINE

A portrait of Marie-Charles-Joseph Le Moyne de Longueuil is reproduced on page 24 of the work by Marie-Claire Daveluy cited below.

ANQ-M, CE1-12, 23 févr. 1841; CE1-51, 21 mars 1756; CN-174, 31 mai–16 oct. 1806. ANQ-Q, CE1-61, 7 mai 1781; CN1-25, 5 mai 1781. Arch. du diocèse de Saint-Jean-de-Québec (Longueuil, Qué.), 7A/49, 67; 12A/25; 14A/19, 28. Arch. nationales (Paris), Fonds des Colonies, B, 149: ff.369, 432½; 161: f.76. ASN, AP-G, L.-É. Bois, G, 12: 222. ASQ, Fonds Viger–Verreau, sér.O, 0176: 3–5, 22–39; 0178: 14–18. BVM-G, Fonds baronnie de Longueuil, pièces 1–508. PAC, MG 24, L3. "Les Grant de Longueuil," J.-J. Lefebvre, édit., ANQ *Rapport*, 1953–55: 123–84. *Quebec Gazette*, 26 Nov. 1821, 15 July 1822. F.-J. Audet et Fabre Surveyer, *Les députés au premier Parl. du Bas-Canada*, 239–40. F.-M. Bibaud, *Le panthéon canadien* (A. et V. Bibaud; 1891). *Montreal directory*, 1819–20. P.-G. Roy, *Inv. concessions*, 2: 64; 4: 82, 84. Auguste Achintre et J.-A. Crevier, *L'île Sainte-Hélène: passé, présent et avenir; géologie, paléontologie, flore et faune* (Montréal, 1876), 10–12. M.-C. Daveluy, *L'Orphelinat catholique de Montréal (1832–1932)* (Montréal, 1933), 303–4. Alexandre Jodoin et J.-L. Vincent, *Histoire de Longueuil et de la famille de Longueuil* . . . (Montréal, 1889). Robert Rumilly, *Histoire de Longueuil* (Longueuil, 1974). T. Beauchesne, "Les barons de Longueuil," *Nova Francia* (Paris), 4 (1929): 311–15, 362–67. Odette Lebrun, "Épouses des LeMoyne: les baronnes de Longueuil," Soc. d'hist. de Longueuil, *Cahier* (Longueuil), 2 (1973): 3–10.

LE PRÊTRE, JOHN McDONELL, known as. *See* McDONELL

LEPROHON, JOSEPH-ONÉSIME, Roman Catholic priest, teacher, and school administrator; b. 16 Feb. 1789 in Montreal, eldest son of Jean-Philippe Leprohon, a merchant, and Marguerite Parent; d. 19 May 1844 in Nicolet, Lower Canada.

When he was seven, Joseph-Onésime Leprohon was deeply upset by his mother's death. His father sent him to the Collège Saint-Raphaël (the Petit Séminaire de Montréal from 1806), where he did his classical studies, despite delicate health, and stood out because of his concern for others. In 1809 he entered holy orders and was immediately sent to the Séminaire de Nicolet as a regent and teacher of the second-, third-, and sixth-year classes (Syntax, Method, and Rhetoric). He took great interest in the pupils and easily won their respect and affection. Having continued with his theological studies at the same time, he was ordained priest on 6 Feb. 1814. He served first as assistant priest in the parish of Saint-Joseph at Deschambault, and was then moved to the parish of Saint-Mathieu at Belœil; in 1816 he became director of the Séminaire de Nicolet.

At the time of his arrival the seminary was in a precarious state as a result of five years of financial difficulties and painful conflict between the superior, Jean RAIMBAULT, and the preceding director, Paul-Loup Archambault*. Thus the bishop of Quebec, Joseph-Octave Plessis*, had sought an educator who was capable of taking the seminary in hand. Leprohon quickly proved the very man for the situation. At the beginning, however, he noted certain "prejudices" held against him by the superior, the teachers, and the pupils; for some years there was also friction with his family – "ill-arranged matters related to my father and my brothers" – as well as reproaches from his father for having left his parish charge, "where he saw me as his consolation and perhaps as his support." To his father, and his bishop (in whom he confided), Leprohon pointed out his affection for the establishment "to which I have sacrificed all my personal interests."

The substantial work that Leprohon put in helped him to come through these difficulties. Moreover, like his predecessors, he lent a hand to the parish priest of Nicolet, Jean Raimbault. He was spiritual director for 175 to 200 penitents and helped Raimbault to the best of his ability: "For high masses, baptisms, burials, visiting the sick at night, and sermons, I do what I can to comply with his wishes, because these functions do not keep me so far removed from the community." In addition he was the spiritual director of the clergy at the school and professor of theology until almost the end of his term of office. He also helped manage the seminary, particularly before the office of bursar was created. Hence he travelled about the Quebec region in 1825 to raise funds for building the new seminary and he often had a say in the work, which went on for almost ten years.

Leprohon made his mark initially as director. As the person responsible for securing respect for the regulations from teachers and pupils, he demanded attention to duty and maintained strict control. He was insistent that the bishops of Quebec make explicit certain points that were not entirely clear; in particular he tried to get the date of the summer holidays moved forward, but without success. Although outwardly austere, Leprohon proved kind, fatherly, and affectionate to everyone, and on occasion he unhesitatingly sided with his young protégés. In 1836, for example, on the strength of some boys' complaints, he asked Bishop Joseph SIGNAY to advise the bursar to see that the pupils were well fed. He also endeavoured to provide more varied leisure activities for them. He encouraged them to grow flowers for the altar, and, according to

Abbé Louis-Édouard Bois*, "he worked to such good purpose that first he got a small garden for all the boys, then a small flowerbed in the garden for each of them, then finally yearly prizes for the most devoted, the most constant, the most hard-working." He also installed a carpentry shop out of which came some notable articles, such as a lattice-work pyramid and columns crowned with a globe made in 1836 by the future bishop of Trois-Rivières, Louis-François Laflèche*.

Leprohon devoted equal time to his duties as prefect of studies. Here too he had to innovate and deal with chronic shortages. To get the most from a largely untrained teaching body that was continually being replaced, he endeavoured to provide textbooks and teaching material – in 1836, for example, he had the archbishop of Quebec buy instruments used for physics, which Abbé John Holmes* brought back from Europe. Leprohon enriched the library, supervising the lending of books himself. He visited classes regularly and gave assignments which he corrected, and he organized sessions in his room at which historical works were read. Attaching special importance to competition and the awards made to the best pupils, he kept mark books and prize lists, compiled honour books in which were transcribed the best pieces of work, and arranged for public examinations and ceremonial prize days. It was also during his tenure as director that professors of theology and philosophy were recruited. Through these manifold efforts the Séminaire de Nicolet was able to come close to the standards of the Petit Séminaire de Québec and the Petit Séminaire de Montréal. But the double task of being director and prefect of studies became a handicap. Towards the end of the 1830s Leprohon was widely regarded as out of date, and his teaching methods were considered old-fashioned and inadequate. But he was so much part of the establishment and his devotion had been so complete that no one dared ask him to leave "his" seminary.

Raimbault's death in 1841 provided a solution. It had long been anticipated that Leprohon would succeed to the parish charge of Nicolet, and it was offered to him; a logical promotion, the post did not take him away from his life-work. He accepted the appointment, though he was full of nostalgia for the seminary. According to Charles Harper*, for several weeks he was unable "to make up his mind to move into the presbytery . . . he is bored there, dislikes it there, and does nothing but talk of the seminary." Little by little he got caught up in his new post, and he became a good parish priest, taking his predecessor as his example. But early in May 1844 he caught pneumonia, and on the 19th he died, at age 55.

Joseph-Onésime Leprohon typifies the administrators who shaped Quebec's classical colleges and indelibly marked generations of boys who became its professional men and priests. Joseph-Guillaume Barthe* has well described the role he played: "This martyr to duty, this model of devotion, whose name not one of those who came under his *motherly* thumb (fatherly would not be tender enough) pronounces without emotion or without being transported. On earth, he was nothing but an instrument unknown outside but venerated as a saint inside this establishment, where he brought up three generations of men . . . all of whom were proud to own that they were his disciples." Only one reproach can be made: he himself destroyed some of his papers and, further, stipulated in his will that "all the papers, letters, manuscripts, and writings in his possession on the day and at the hour of his death" be burned.

NIVE VOISINE

The ASN holds notes of various courses given by Joseph-Onésime Leprohon which were taken down by his students: AP-G, "Traité abrégé de mythologie" (1809); "De la versification latine" (1810); "Cours de philosophie et physique" (*c.* 1810); "Epitome rhetorices" (1821); "Rhetorica" (n.d.).

AAQ, 515 CD. ANQ-M, CE1-51, 16 févr. 1789. ANQ-MBF, CE1-13, 21 mai 1844. ASN, AO, Séminaire, cahiers de comptes de bibliothèque, J.-O. Leprohon, 1833–36; fonds Leprohon, I, 44; lettres des directeurs et autres à l'évêque de Québec, II–III. Barthe, *Souvenirs d'un demi-siècle*. [L.-É. Bois], *Notice sur M. Jos O. Leprohon, archiprêtre, directeur du collège de Nicolet* . . . (Québec, 1870). Douville, *Hist. du collège-séminaire de Nicolet*. Claude Lessard, *Le séminaire de Nicolet, 1803–1969* (Trois-Rivières, Qué., 1980).

LÉRY, CHARLES-ÉTIENNE CHAUSSEGROS DE. *See* CHAUSSEGROS

LÉTOURNEAU, JEAN-CHARLES, notary, office holder, and politician; b. 28 Nov. 1775 in Saint-Pierre-de-la-Rivière-du-Sud, Que., son of Joseph-Marie Létourneau and Marie-Françoise Cloutier; d. 21 April 1838 in the parish of Saint-Thomas (at Montmagny), Lower Canada.

Although he came from a humble family with little education, Jean-Charles Létourneau did classical studies at the Petit Séminaire de Québec, where he was a day-pupil from 1789 to 1792. His teachers said at the time that he was an intelligent, gifted, but unruly student. Subsequently he articled with notaries Roger Lelièvre and then Nicolas-Gaspard BOISSEAU. He was licensed to practise as a notary public on 18 July 1803 and settled in Saint-Thomas.

On 24 Nov. 1806, in the parish church of Saint-Thomas, Létourneau married Catherine Boisseau, daughter of his former employer and of Catherine Gaspé, whose father was Ignace-Philippe Aubert* de Gaspé. Even though no children were born to them and there was a great difference in their ages, they apparently led a happy life until Catherine died on 13 Feb. 1833.

A man with a sharp eye, slim and carefully dressed, Létourneau proved to be witty, learned, and patriotic. After a stormy youth, in which he claimed to take his inspiration from Voltaire, and in spite of his ardent nationalism, he reputedly sobered down with age, ardour giving way to "more reasonable and more moderate" sentiments.

In 1826 Létourneau began to take on civic responsibilities. On 8 May he became a commissioner for repairing the schoolhouse in Saint-Thomas, a duty shared with his brother-in-law Ignace-Gaspard Boisseau, among others. Then on 29 May 1829 he was appointed commissioner to open roads in the parish of Saint-Thomas, and on 12 May 1831 he became commissioner for conducting the census in L'Islet County.

A great admirer of Louis-Joseph Papineau*, Létourneau took an interest in politics and sought election in the riding of Devon on 25 Aug. 1827. He was successful and replaced Joseph-François Couillard-Després in the House of Assembly, where he sat along with Jean-Baptiste Fortin. Enjoying the broad confidence of his constituents, he was returned in the new riding of L'Islet in 1830 and 1834, and retained his seat until the constitution was suspended in February 1838. Since he was a disciple of Papineau, it was not surprising that in 1834 he voted for the 92 Resolutions and opposed the amendments put forward by John NEILSON. Létourneau was then at the height of his popularity. Later, Flavien-Édouard Casault, in a history of Saint-Thomas published in 1906, called him "a remarkable man." Just after his death Edmund Bailey O'Callaghan* would say that he was "a good democrat, and an honest Canadian, felt for his Country like a man, and defended her as a Representative, honestly and steadily."

"After a long and painful illness," Létourneau died on 21 April 1838, leaving the people of Montmagny and L'Islet to mourn a "good relative, sincere friend, [and] devoted citizen." His impressive funeral cost £25, a huge sum at the time for this sort of ceremony in the country. He was buried in the crypt of the parish church of Saint-Thomas.

Through unremitting work, attention to detail, and exceptional knowledge of the law, Jean-Charles Létourneau had been able to amass a tidy fortune. In particular he owned a remarkable library of rare books. It was housed in an attractive and well-furnished home that gave proof of his good taste. Létourneau bequeathed the books to his neighbour and great friend Étienne-Paschal Taché*.

NELSON MICHAUD

Jean-Charles Létourneau's minute-book, containing instruments for the period 23 July 1803–6 March 1838, is at ANQ-Q, CN2-26.

ANQ-Q, CE2-6, 29 nov. 1775; CE2-7, 24 nov. 1806, 13 févr. 1833, 21 avril 1838; CN2-7, 1787–89. ASQ, Séminaire, 103, nos.29c, 31–32. PAC, MG 24, B2: 1989–91, 2294–97, 2911–12; RG 4, A1, 241, 358; B8: 485–89; B72, 25–26. *Quebec Gazette*, 21 July 1803, 11 Jan. 1810, 19 Feb. 1833. F.-J. Audet, "Les législateurs du Bas-Canada." Desjardins, *Guide parl.* F.-É. Casault, *Notes historiques sur la paroisse de Saint-Thomas de Montmagny* (Québec, 1906). Jacques Castonguay, *La seigneurie de Philippe Aubert de Gaspé, Saint-Jean-Port-Joli* (Montréal, 1977). Chapais, *Cours d'hist. du Canada*, vol.4. Gérard Ouellet, *Ma paroisse: Saint-Jean Port-Joly* (Québec, 1946). P.-G. Roy, *La famille Aubert de Gaspé* (Lévis, Qué., 1907). "Cinq belles figures de Montmagny," *Québec-Hist.* (Montmagny, Qué.), 2 (1972), no.1: 65.

LE VASSEUR BORGIA, JOSEPH (he signed **LeVasseur Borgia**), lawyer, newspaper proprietor, militia officer, and politician; b. 6 Jan. 1773 at Quebec, son of Louis Le Vasseur Borgia, a blacksmith, and Marie-Anne Trudel; d. there 28 June 1839.

François-Maximilien Bibaud* asserts in *Le panthéon canadien* that the Borgia family of Quebec was Italian in origin, and Benjamin Sulte* and other historians also make this claim. In fact, Joseph Le Vasseur Borgia's ancestors were all of French descent, and his grandfather was the first Le Vasseur to have Borgia added to his surname.

Joseph Le Vasseur Borgia spent his early childhood in the *faubourg* Saint-Jean at Quebec. He was seven when his famiy moved into Upper Town to Rue Sainte-Famille near the Petit Séminaire. From 1786 till 1792 he did his classical studies in this institution. Accused of attending a theatrical performance, he was expelled at the end of April 1790, but was re-admitted the following year, this time as a boarder. On 30 April 1792, in a public session at the Petit Séminaire, he was one of five students who defended propositions in mathematics, ballistics, astronomy, and physics before an audience of dignitaries including Prince Edward* Augustus.

Le Vasseur Borgia subsequently articled as a lawyer and on 18 July 1800 was licensed to practise. He opened an office at Quebec and over the years he became famous for plain but solid speeches. When someone mentioned his lack of eloquence to Sir James Henry Craig*, who had heard him argue in court, the governor retorted: "That is true, but I think there are few lawyers in this colony who have as profound a knowledge of Roman law." Le Vasseur Borgia defended a great many people, and he also found himself up on charges in court on a number of occasions. He had many disputes with protonotary Joseph-François PERRAULT. Relations between the two became more acrimonious in 1805 when Perrault sued him for outstanding fees. They confronted each other in cases several times more between then and 1825.

From the outset of his legal career Le Vasseur Borgia was attracted to politics. On 10 Oct. 1805 he announced his candidature in the by-election that had been called following the death of William Grant*, who had represented Upper Town Quebec in the House of Assembly. Le Vasseur Borgia and Perrault ran against each other and by splitting the French-speaking vote helped ensure the election of John Blackwood*, the English-speaking candidate. Although somewhat chagrined, Le Vasseur Borgia was nevertheless determined to try his luck again at the first opportunity. He put an announcement in the *Quebec Gazette* of 19 December: "The support I have received . . . notwithstanding the combined efforts of certain public caballers, is . . . a testimony of the public esteem." On 18 June 1808 he was elected member for Cornwallis, whose interests he upheld in the house from then until 1820, and again from 1824 to 1830, when his political career came to an end.

In 1806 Le Vasseur Borgia had joined Pierre-Stanislas Bédard*, Jean-Thomas Taschereau*, François Blanchet*, and others in founding *Le Canadien*, a newspaper championing the interests of the French-speaking professional class. Angered by their support for this publication, which he considered "libellous and seditious," Craig dismissed Le Vasseur Borgia and other proprietors of *Le Canadien* from their posts as militia officers on 14 June 1808. In March 1810 he had the paper's presses seized and threw Bédard, Taschereau, Blanchet, and printer Charles Lefrançois* into jail. Despite assertions to the contrary by some writers, Le Vasseur Borgia managed to escape the governor's wrath and was not imprisoned. His reputation as an eminent lawyer and his moderate political stance are thought to have been instrumental in saving him from the fate of the newspaper's other principals.

In 1812 the new governor, Sir George Prevost*, courted the leaders of the Canadian party in order to secure their support and loyalty in the war against the United States. Thus, Le Vasseur Borgia got his militia officer's commission back and was promoted captain in Quebec's 1st Militia Battalion. There was soon dissension in the battalion when Le Vasseur Borgia again clashed with Perrault. He was placed under arrest and brought before a court martial on 9 November and 9 December 1812, accused of conduct "subversive of good order and military discipline in having refused obedience to the orders of Lieut.-Colonel Perrault, his Commanding Officer." In the end he was acquitted. The prospect of having to fight against the American invaders held little appeal for Le Vasseur Borgia. Moreover, according to historian François-Xavier Garneau*, he had attended a secret meeting held at Quebec to discuss taking a neutral stand in this conflict, which some Canadians saw as concerning only England and the United States.

Late in 1812 Le Vasseur Borgia was back in his familiar place in the House of Assembly. Although he was never a great orator, he participated diligently in the work of the house and served on numerous committees. Often taken aback by the violence of the debates in the assembly, he had presented a motion on 9 Feb. 1811 to the effect that "to interrupt a member whether by striking with his fist, or in swearing, is a breach of the privileges of this House." Only once in the course of his long parliamentary career did he lose his temper. On 10 March 1819 he turned on Samuel Sherwood, insulted him, "made threatening grimaces at him," and pursued him across the house, according to a witness, Philippe Panet*. His conduct gave rise to vehement debate that lasted nearly eight hours. Denis-Benjamin Viger* went so far as to demand that Le Vasseur Borgia be imprisoned. But in the end the assembly agreed to put him in the custody of the sergeant-at-arms.

At the time of the incident, the house was studying the administration of justice, a matter of deep concern to Le Vasseur Borgia. In the house on 6 March 1815 he had argued with conviction in favour of the adoption in Lower Canada of British civil law and the repeal of the Coutume de Paris, customary law, and the edicts, decrees, ordinances, and declarations in use since the time of New France. His long practice as a lawyer had often shown him the difficulty of "finding one's way in this inextricable maze." Philippe-Joseph Aubert* de Gaspé used to relate that one day Le Vasseur Borgia, realizing he had lost 20 years of his life studying legal tomes, concluded he had better trust his judgement and in times of difficulty fall back on chance with dice and a dice-box.

As a member initially of the Canadian party, Le Vasseur Borgia abided by the opinions and decisions of his colleagues. In the 1820s, however, he gradually moved away from Louis-Joseph Papineau* and his supporters. On 8 Jan. 1825, in the voting for speaker, he backed Joseph-Rémi VALLIÈRES de Saint-Réal rather than Papineau. Le Vasseur Borgia retired from the parliamentary scene in 1830, the year that Cornwallis was split into the ridings of Kamouraska and Rimouski, and he was not involved in the discussions and meetings preceding the rebellions of 1837–38. At the end of June 1838 he went to present his respects to Governor Lord Durham [LAMBTON], who had recently arrived in the colony.

A highly cultured man, over the years La Vasseur Borgia had built up an impressive library, with textbooks on law and jurisprudence alongside many other volumes, including works on history, mythology, philosophy, astronomy, and chemistry. His diary reveals his passion for history. Notes from research on the Le Vasseur Borgia family and the French monarchy are mingled with detailed enumerations of the bishops of Quebec and the governors of the colony under the French and British régimes. At his retirement Le Vasseur Borgia calculated that between 1831 and 1836 he had devoted four months and ten days to putting his personal papers and his "case papers" in order.

Le Vasseur Borgia's final years were saddened by poverty and by the death of his son Narcisse-Charles, who had begun articling under his direction in 1825 and had been licensed to practise law on 27 Feb. 1830. Narcisse-Charles was said to have inherited his father's talents as a lawyer. But he was in frail health, and on 5 Nov. 1834, at the age of 30, he died. Le Vasseur Borgia, without means, had to rely on the generosity of some Quebec lawyers, who organized a subscription to defray the costs of his son's funeral. In neglecting his law practice to devote himself to his political career, he had soon run into financial difficulties, and in 1817 he had had to part with his library.

Joseph Le Vasseur Borgia died on 28 June 1839, after "an illness of several weeks" according to *Le Canadien*, and was buried in the Cimetière des Picotés. For 17 years he had been the senior member of the bar in the district of Quebec. Aubert de Gaspé remembered him as a man who was "unbiased, generous, and of remarkable delicacy in his sentiments." A lawyer to be reckoned with and a respected politician, he had compensated for his lack of eloquence by the quality of his arguments. "He was a wise man," said Bibaud. Although his was a less prominent role than that of the Bédards, Vigers, and Papineaus of his time, he was one of the most frequently consulted and most influential politicians in Lower Canada from the founding of *Le Canadien* in 1806 until his departure from politics in 1830.

JEAN-MARIE LEBEL

ANQ-Q, CE1-1, 6 janv. 1773, 10 nov. 1834, 2 juill. 1839; CN1-230, 28 mai 1811; 8 avril 1813; 20 avril 1815; 27 juill. 1816; 26 févr., 7 nov. 1825; CN1-253, 23 avril 1829. ASQ, C 36: Fichier des anciens; 102; MSS, 193; Polygraphie, XIX, no.41; Séminaire, 73, nos.1g–1h. PAC, MG 11, [CO 42] Q, 107. P.[-J.] Aubert de Gaspé, *Mémoires* (Ottawa, 1866; réimpr. Montréal, 1971). "Les dénombrements de Québec" (Plessis), ANQ *Rapport*, 1948–49: 9, 59, 109, 172. L.C., House of Assembly, *Journals*, 1809–19, 1825–30. *Recensement de Québec, 1818* (Provost), 266. *Le Canadien*, 1er juill. 1839. *Quebec Gazette*, 31 July 1800; 10 Oct., 19 Dec. 1805; 12 May, 16 June 1808; 20 April, 12 Oct., 9, 30 Nov. 1809; 1, 8 March, 26 April, 3 May 1810; 4 June, 1 Oct., 19 Nov., 24 Dec. 1812; 18, 25 April 1816; 26 March 1818. F.-M. Bibaud, *Le panthéon canadien* (A. et V. Bibaud; 1891), 32. Hare et Wallot, *Les imprimés dans le Bas-Canada*, 90, 139, 234, 237, 315–16. Le Jeune, *Dictionnaire*, 2: 147. *Officers of British forces in Canada* (Irving), 141. P.-G. Roy, *Les avocats de la région de Québec*, 52; *Fils de Québec*, 2: 164–66. Wallace, *Macmillan dict*. T.-P. Bédard, *Histoire de cinquante ans (1791–1841), annales parlementaires et politiques du Bas-Canada, depuis la Constitution jusqu'à l'Union* (Québec, 1869), 65, 100, 104, 111, 120, 135, 162. Chapais, *Cours d'hist. du Canada*, 2: 180, 192, 206; 3: 8, 13, 24, 188. Ouellet, *Bas-Canada*, 164, 301. Gilles Paquet et J.-P. Wallot, *Patronage et pouvoir dans le Bas-Canada (1794–1812); un essai d'économie historique* (Montréal, 1973), 120. P.-G. Roy, *À travers les mémoires de Philippe Aubert de Gaspé* (Montréal, 1943). Rumilly, *Papineau et son temps*, 1: 37, 42–43, 64, 76, 152, 174. Benjamin Sulte, *Histoire des Canadiens-français, 1608–1880 . . .* (8v., Montréal, 1882–84), 8: 66, 73, 76–77, 79. Taft Manning, *Revolt of French Canada*, 56, 98. Wallot, *Un Québec qui bougeait*, 79, 126, 150, 164. F.-J. Audet, "Joseph LeVasseur-Borgia," RSC *Trans.*, 3rd ser., 19 (1925), sect.I: 65–78. P.-B. Casgrain, "Le moulin à vent et la maison de Borgia lors de la bataille des plaines d'Abraham," *BRH*, 6 (1900): 37–41. J. [E.] Hare, "L'Assemblée législative du Bas-Canada, 1792–1814: députation et polarisation politique," *RHAF*, 27 (1973–74): 361–95. "Le jeune avocat LeVasseur Borgia," *BRH*, 42 (1936): 96–97.

LEYS, JOHN, marine engineer; b. *c.* 1791 in Aberdeen, Scotland; d. 8 April 1846 in St Croix (Virgin Islands).

John Leys may have been the John Lees of Nineveh, England, who in 1812 signed articles of employment for five years with the Birmingham engineering firm of Boulton and Watt. Lees was to work in the "business of Filing, Turning, & Fitting wrought, and Cast Iron Goods for the Manufactory of Steam Engines and other purposes." For this work he was to be paid 19*s*. weekly for the first half of the term and 20*s*. weekly for the balance.

In the spring of 1816 Gillespie, Gerrard and Company of London [*see* Samuel Gerrard*], acting as agents for the owners of the *Frontenac* (a paddle-wheel vessel then under construction at Bath, Upper Canada), ordered a steam-engine from Boulton and Watt. The London firm also requested that a competent engineer be sent to assemble, install, and operate it. Leys offered to go for two years at £160 a year. This sum was considered high but, when no one else offered to go, he was engaged. By the time these arrangements had been concluded, the 56-horsepower engine had already been shipped to Liverpool. Leys had to rush off quickly. He did, however, manage to arrange for some of his salary to be sent to his mother in Aberdeen.

The account in the *Kingston Gazette* of the launch of the *Frontenac* in September 1816 sparked predictions that it would be "finished and ready for use in a few weeks." It was not, the delay being caused, in part, by wrangles over the engine with customs officials at Quebec which began in December. Not until the following May did the steamship sail across Kingston harbour, damaging the machinery of one of its paddle-wheels in the process. Although the *Frontenac* was the first steamboat to be launched on the Great Lakes, the subsequent delay had allowed the

American vessel *Ontario* to make the first voyage under steam. Much of the delay may be ascribed to problems with the Boulton and Watt engine.

Once the *Frontenac* went into operation, relations between Leys and its captain, James McKenzie*, were far from smooth, as later attested by Henry Scadding*: "At the outset of steam navigation, men competent to superintend the working of the machinery were . . . not numerous, and Captains were obliged in some degree to humour their chief engineer when they had secured the services of one. Capt. McKenzie . . . was somewhat tyrannized over by Mr. Leys, who was a Scot, not very tractable; and the *Frontenac*'s movements, times of sailing, and so on, were very much governed by a will in the hold, independent of that of the ostensible Commander." Despite such friction, Leys and McKenzie both enjoyed salaries which John Spread Baldwin, a York (Toronto) merchant, described in 1817 as "immense."

A brief partnership of uncertain nature with his brother Francis in Pickering Township broke up in the spring of 1827, when John (or Jock as he was familiarly known) returned to the lake as engineer of Captain Hugh Richardson*'s *Canada*. According to Scadding, Leys "was long well known in York." One of those who claimed him as a "good friend" was William Lyon Mackenzie*. In August 1827 he noted in his *Colonial Advocate* Leys's departure for Montreal to get a new paddle-wheel shaft for the *Canada*. Five years later Leys supported Mackenzie in his bid for re-election to the House of Assembly.

Beyond his experience in the Canadas, Leys's career as a marine engineer is still a mystery. It is relatively easy to identify steamboat captains but the rest of the crew lived in obscurity. The *Toronto directory* for 1837 describes him simply as an "Engineer," living on Lot (Queen) Street. He must have accumulated some wealth; in the same year he was a minor shareholder in the British America Fire and Life Assurance Company. When he died in St Croix in 1846, he was said in an obituary to have gone there for his health. He had left more than £600 and an annuity to his mother and sisters in Scotland, and had instructed his executors to convert the balance of his assets into cash, to be invested in mortgages, real estate, and the erection of buildings for rent. The resulting income was to go to his brother William and his children so long as they maintained the properties and the insurance on them.

WALTER LEWIS

AO, RG 22, ser.155. Birmingham Public Libraries (Birmingham, Eng.), Boulton and Watt coll., articles of agreement concerning employment of John Lees with M. R. Boulton and James Watt Jr, 26 May 1812; letter-book 40, Boulton and Watt to Gillespie, Gerrard and Company, 21, 23, 30 May, 3, 10 June 1816. UTFL, MS coll., Western Assurance Company papers, vol.100 (British American Assurance Company, day-book, 1837–41). *Town of York, 1815–34* (Firth), 39–40. *Colonial Advocate*, 2 Aug. 1827, 9 Feb. 1832. *Kingston Gazette*, 14 Sept. 1816, 24 May 1817. *Upper Canada Gazette*, 21 April 1827. *Death notices of Ont.* (Reid). *Toronto directory*, 1837. Scadding, *Toronto of old* (1873), 556.

LICHTENSTEIN, ELIZABETH (Johnston), author; b. 28 May 1764 in Little Ogeechee, Ga, only child of John G. Lightenstone and Catherine Delegal; m. 21 Nov. 1779 William Martin Johnston in Savannah, Ga, and they had ten children, only three of whom survived her; d. 24 Sept. 1848 in Halifax.

Elizabeth Lichtenstein's father, a native of Cronstadt (Kronstadt, U.S.S.R.), immigrated to Georgia some time in the mid 18th century, and anglicized his surname to Lightenstone. He served Governor Sir James Wright in several capacities and during the American Revolutionary War was a guide and adviser to the Georgia Light Dragoons. Because of her father's frequent absences from home, Elizabeth was largely brought up by her mother and, on her death, by a great-aunt, both of whom apparently stimulated her interest in reading and writing. In 1776 her father left for Nova Scotia. The 12-year-old Elizabeth successfully presented to the board of commissioners in Savannah a petition, drawn up by her grandfather, asking for possession of her father's estate, which was in danger of being confiscated because of his loyalist activities.

In 1779 Elizabeth married William Martin Johnston, a captain in the New York Volunteers, and shortly afterwards she moved with him to New York. They later returned to Savannah, and then early in 1782 went to Charleston, S.C. When that town was evacuated by the British in December, she and her children went to St Augustine (Fla). In the one and a half years they spent there she enjoyed the best health of her life, as she later commented. After the Floridas were ceded to Spain in 1784, the entire family sailed for Scotland where William completed the medical studies that the war had interrupted. In 1785 he began to practise in Kingston, Jamaica, where his family joined him the next year. Until 1806 Elizabeth and the children often returned to Great Britain, for reasons of health. Late that year they went to Nova Scotia. On their arrival, they learned that William had died of dropsy. Elizabeth had to return to Jamaica to settle her husband's estate, but was back in Nova Scotia by 1810. She first took up residence in Annapolis Royal near her father and daughter, Elizabeth Wildman, who had married Thomas Ritchie* in 1807, and later moved to Halifax.

In Nova Scotia Elizabeth had a relatively stable life. Although she frequently travelled between Annapolis and Halifax to visit friends and family, she only once left the colony. In 1824 she went to England to have cataract surgery. Twelve years later, at the age of 72, she wrote her memoirs, largely for the sake of her grandchildren. *Recollections of a Georgia loyalist* has significance because its author had experienced the disruptions of the loyalist migrations and belonged to an important colonial family. She died in Halifax on 24 Sept. 1848 and was buried at Camp Hill Cemetery.

From *Recollections* emerges Elizabeth's deep religious faith, which had a puritanical tone. She was convinced that all the bitter sorrows of her life were punishment for her sins. The memoirs are largely an account of the personal problems of the author and her family, with much attention to illness and little interest in the ideology or military events of the American revolution, although she briefly mentions hardships of loyalists in Savannah and the turning against her father which showed "the violence with which civil wars are entered upon." Elizabeth seems to have accepted that a woman's place was in the home, and it is evident that despite her being well read and well educated for her day, her life revolved around her immediate household.

Elizabeth's children married into some of the most prominent families in Nova Scotia, such as the Ritchies, the Almons, and the Pryors. One of her sons, James William Johnston*, became the leader of the Conservative party in the colony, and another, John, was a member of the House of Assembly.

JULIE MORRIS and WENDY L. THORPE

Elizabeth Lichtenstein Johnston's *Recollections of a Georgia loyalist* was edited by Arthur Wentworth Hamilton Eaton* and published in New York and London in 1901.

Halifax County Court of Probate (Halifax), Estate papers, no.292 (Elizabeth Lichtenstein Johnston) (mfm. at PANS). PRO, AO 12/4–5, 12/59, 12/99, 12/109, 12/125–28 (mfm. at PAC); AO 13, bundle 36 (mfm. at PANS). *Church Times* (Halifax), 29 Sept. 1848. W. H. Siebert, "The legacy of the American revolution to the British West Indies and Bahamas . . . ," Ohio State Univ., *Bull.* (Columbus), 17 (1913), no.27.

LILLY, GEORGE, auctioneer, notary, militia officer, lawyer, office holder, and judge; b. in the early 1770s in the Thirteen Colonies, possibly in Boston; m. 25 Jan. 1800 Mary Ann Roberts in St John's, and they had at least seven children; d. 10 Sept. 1846 in St John's.

George Lilly was probably the son of loyalist William Lilly, a Harbour Grace magistrate. By his own account he came to Newfoundland "at a very early period of my life with my Father who left America in consequence of the revolution." He apprenticed as a clerk with the St John's merchant Nathaniel Philips, and by 1810–11 had established himself as a notary public and auctioneer. During the War of 1812 he helped to raise and equip a militia, serving himself as adjutant and captain. In Newfoundland's economic crisis of 1815–19, Lilly's services as auctioneer and conveyancer were much in demand; but his premises were destroyed in the St John's fire of 21 Nov. 1817, and he subsequently endured financial losses when rents fell on property he had acquired on long-term lease from the government. It appears that he was not successful in business.

Gradually Lilly focused his attention on the practice of law. He had no professional education in that area, but in the absence of properly trained lawyers, early judges in Newfoundland permitted unqualified attorneys to plead before the courts. In 1826 Lilly was formally enrolled as a barrister. He would be remembered by reformers as attorney for the plaintiffs in the suits by Philip Butler and James Lundrigan* in the Supreme Court in 1820 against David BUCHAN and John Leigh*, the surrogate judges who had ordered the two fishermen whipped. In both cases, the jurors found for the defendants. Lilly in the 1820s was not averse to being associated with the cause of reform. His name appears, for example, among the early signatures on the petition to the king provoked by the Butler–Lundrigan incidents, and he also supported later calls for the granting of a legislature. In the 1832 election for the first house of assembly, however, he endorsed fellow lawyer William Bickford Row*, an indication that Lilly saw himself as allied with establishment interests. When Governor Sir Thomas John Cochrane* in 1834 named Lilly as acting clerk of the House of Assembly, reformer William CARSON opposed the appointment. In 1835 Lilly signed a public address supporting one of the reformers' most prominent opponents, Chief Justice Henry John Boulton*.

Cochrane appointed Lilly acting assistant judge in the Supreme Court in September 1834. He would serve in this capacity until 1845 when, on the death of Edward Brabazon BRENTON, he was at last given a permanent appointment. Lilly advanced his claims for an assistant judgeship on a number of occasions after 1834, but his capacities were not highly regarded, and he was not as well connected as other aspirants. He was, Governor Henry Prescott* noted, "the only Barrister to whom the half salary allotted to an acting officer was an inducement to accept it."

It was while he was acting as assistant judge that Lilly played an important part in a confrontation that helped to undermine representative government in Newfoundland, and he showed considerable courage and, perhaps, intelligence in the affair. On 9 Aug. 1838 he was applied to for a writ of habeas corpus by Bryan Robinson*, solicitor for Edward Kielley*, a respected surgeon being held in custody on a warrant issued by William Carson in his capacity as speaker of the assembly. Kielley had allegedly committed a breach of the assembly's privileges. Lilly granted the writ, returnable on the following morning, and was in chambers on 10 August when Kielley was duly brought before him. After listening to Robinson's arguments, and without then considering whether the assembly had the right to commit for contempt, Lilly decided that the warrant was void. He later stated as his reason that it did not "disclose a sufficient ground of commitment."

On the following day, the sergeant-at-arms of the assembly, Thomas Beck, accompanied by five or six of the house's "Doorkeepers and Messengers" as assistants, entered the judges' chambers and tried to arrest Lilly, acting on another warrant of the speaker. Lilly told Beck that he did not recognize either his authority or that of the assembly. If the arrest were to proceed, he added, "it must be by force." Beck and his assistants thereupon seized him, "some by the collar, others by the arms and some pushed me from behind, and so dragged and forced me with great violence" downstairs to the speaker's room – the House of Assembly being in the same building. There he was incarcerated. Soon afterwards, accompanied by a "great crowd of men and boys," who had presumably gathered to witness that extraordinary phenomenon, the arrest of a judge, he was taken to Beck's home where he was held for two days. On 13 August he was released as a consequence of the prorogation of the legislature by Governor Prescott.

On the same day he was discharged, Lilly delivered his judgement on the imprisonment of Kielley. In a cogent and lengthy argument, he denied Carson's claim that the assembly possessed analogous powers to those of the House of Commons. Moreover the power claimed in this instance was unnecessary. While members of the house were "particularly entitled, to protection in the due performance of their functions," the laws of the land were "equally open to them as to every other lawfully constituted body." Lilly's arguments were presented again as a dissenting opinion in December 1838 when, in *Kielley* v. *Carson*, the Supreme Court ruled in favour of the assembly; but in January 1843, the judicial committee of the Privy Council in London in effect sided with Lilly and rejected the claims of the house. How far Lilly himself was responsible for the learned judgement he presented is not clear. Success has many fathers, and subsequently both Robinson and Edward Mortimer Archibald*, chief clerk and registrar of the Supreme Court, took credit for the arguments. Archibald said he "prepared the judgment" in its entirety, and Prescott seemed to confirm this in an official dispatch to London.

Lilly's career afterwards as judge was pursued chiefly in the humbler duties of the northern circuit. They involved, according to his own statement in 1845, experiencing the "dangers incident to a sea voyage at a stormy part of the year, . . . from the Effects of which I have been no slight sufferer." He said he had tried some 2,000 cases, not one of which had been appealed. In 1845 Governor Sir John Harvey* remarked of his career as a circuit judge that Lilly's "mild and conciliating manners, have rendered him a great favorite with the Inhabitants of the Out Harbours."

PATRICK O'FLAHERTY

Cathedral of St John the Baptist (Anglican) (St John's), Reg. of baptisms, marriages, and burials (mfm. at PANL). Law Soc. of Nfld. (St John's), Barristers' roll. MHA, George Lilly name file; William Lilly name file. PANL, GN 2/1/A, 20–22, 34, 39; GN 2/2, January–April 1835: 273; July–December 1838: 179–236; GN 5/2/A/1, 8–9 Nov. 1820. PRO, CO 194/64–126; CO 199/20–42 (copies at PANL). Supreme Court of Nfld. (St John's), Solicitors' roll. Nfld., House of Assembly, *Journal*, 1834–35. *Newfoundlander*, 16 Aug. 1838. *Newfoundland Mercantile Journal*, 1816–19, esp. 11 Dec. 1816, 16 Jan. 1818. *Newfoundland Patriot*, 1838. *Public Ledger*, 1838. *Royal Gazette and Newfoundland Advertiser*, 25 Nov. 1817, 16 June 1835. E. J. Archibald, *Life and letters of Sir Edward Mortimer Archibald* . . . (Toronto, 1924). Prowse, *Hist. of Nfld.* (1895).

LLOYD, JESSE, businessman, office holder, rebel, and farmer; b. 11 Jan. 1786 in Springfield Township, Pa, third son of William Lloyd and Susannah Heacock; m., reportedly in 1813, Phoebe Crossley, and they had at least ten children; d. 27 Sept. 1838 in Tippecanoe County, Ind.

There is some evidence to suggest that William Lloyd and his family arrived at Niagara (near Youngstown, N.Y.) in 1788 but soon returned to the United States. They probably immigrated to Upper Canada at about the same time as their youngest son, Jesse, who arrived early in 1808. Family members settled in King and Whitchurch townships, with Jesse renting a clergy reserve lot in the latter. Descended from a long line of Quakers, he joined the Yonge Street Meeting of the Society of Friends in 1814, but did not take an active role in the meeting. By renting a clergy reserve, he was violating one of the rules of the meeting, which opposed state-supported churches. He did, however, refuse to send his team of horses for use during the War of 1812, when ordered to do so, because of his Quaker beliefs.

In 1824 Lloyd bought a lot in Tecumseth Township on which he is reported to have built a sawmill. By 1828 he had turned his attentions to King Township, where his father had a sawmill and served as a township officer. Over the next five years Jesse leased, bought, or tried to buy several lots, mainly clergy reserves in the northwest part of King. On 60 acres of one lot he constructed mills, which he soon sold, and set aside numerous town-lots which he also sold, thus creating the village of Lloydtown. By the mid 1830s this had become one of the largest and most prosperous communities north of York (Toronto). Lloyd himself built a substantial brick house near the village. His success, however, did have a price. In 1836 his eye for good property involved him in a dispute with an "impoverished" widow over a clergy reserve lot, and he lost money when the Executive Council ruled against him. Five years earlier his membership in the Yonge Street Meeting had been cancelled because of non-attendance. This action appears to have ended his involvement with the Quakers, although he and his wife continued to dress in the simple garments of the members of that faith.

Political activities had increasingly occupied Lloyd's time. Between 1829 and 1836 he held elected office in King every year but one, serving as an overseer of highways or poundkeeper or township commissioner. He also became involved in provincial politics. In 1834 he was elected to a convention to choose reform candidates for the upcoming general election. Exactly when and where Lloyd had met and become a supporter of William Lyon Mackenzie* is not known, but it probably occurred during the latter's electoral campaigns of the early 1830s. Mackenzie was familiar with Lloydtown as early as 1831, and Lloyd, a leading voice in the area, was definitely a close friend and partisan of the reform leader by the mid 1830s.

In 1837 reformers, disillusioned with the actions of Lieutenant Governor Sir Francis Bond Head*, instigated under the impetus of the Toronto group the formation of political unions to voice the desire for reform. Lloyd was active in the King society and in forming societies in neighbouring townships. He appears to have been involved from the beginning once Mackenzie had decided there had to be a rebellion. When John Rolph* needed evidence, in October 1837, that Lower Canadian reformers were prepared to rebel, Lloyd was dispatched to Montreal to secure proof. The letter he brought back from Thomas Storrow Brown* did not contain the needed statement but Mackenzie read between the lines, insisting that there was a hidden message of rebellion. Since Lloyd made no denial, it would appear that he was cooperating with Mackenzie in his plan to push their supporters into rebellion by misinforming them.

Mackenzie met in mid November with several leading men from the Home District to convince them that there was support for an uprising and that a demonstration of forceful resolve was all that was needed to change the government. Lloyd was there, presumably supporting Mackenzie's claims. He also helped to raise and lead a large contingent from the Lloydtown area, which became known as a hot-bed for rebellious activity. This group was said to be the best trained and most determined of the rebels who gathered at Montgomery's Tavern north of Toronto.

Following their defeat on 7 December, Lloyd fled to the United States. A government notice offering £500 for his capture described him as having "long straight hair rather thin and turning gray – stoops very much in his gait, has scarcely any teeth left – one remarkably prominent, which is much observed when he speaks, very round-shouldered, and speaks with a strong Yankee accent, height about five feet ten or eleven inches; generally dresses in a drab or brown homespun clothing." Lloyd's name was so well recognized that Mackenzie used it when he drew up a list of "Provisional Government" officials on Navy Island later in December. Lloyd, however, took little or no part in events along the border. In 1838 he went to live in Indiana, where in the fall he caught a fever and died. Although he had been successful in developing Lloydtown, his estate was modest, consisting mainly of livestock, and the farm itself was only partially paid for. Since Lloyd had been an absconding rebel, his wife had to petition for the right to pay off the remainder owed so that she could retain it.

RONALD J. STAGG

[The author wishes to thank R. Douglas Lloyd for providing additional genealogical information.

The most obvious source of information on the life of Jesse Lloyd, *The bridging of three centuries: the life and times of Pheobe Crossley Lloyd – the girl bride of a rebel of 1837* ([Schomberg, Ont., 1951]; copy at AO), a pamphlet published from material gathered by Jesse M. Walton and E. Gladstone Lloyd, is perhaps also the poorest since it is filled with misinformation. Other readily available sources which are better but contain contradictions include: John Barnett, "Silas Fletcher, instigator of the Upper Canadian rebellion," *OH*, 41 (1949): 7–35; M. E. Garbutt, "King Township, York County, 1800–1867: a historical sketch," *OH*, 52 (1960): 85–97; an undated newspaper clipping, probably from the *Banner* (Aurora, Ont.), entitled "The village of Lloydtown . . ." in the York County hist. scrapbook (AO, MU 2601, no.45, 1: 131–33); and the notes on Lloyd in the C. R. Dent coll. (AO, MU 837).

Much of the story of Lloyd's life is drawn from fragments in various document collections. His estate is itemized in his will, AO, RG 22, ser.155. Land dealings can be found in PAC, RG 1, L1, 37: 514; L3, 148: Canada Company, p.17a; 273A: K16/45, K17/18; 305: L leases, 1799–1819/18; and 305A: L leases, 1801–36/111. Further land records are available in AO, RG 1, C-IV, King Township; Simcoe Land Registry Office (Barrie, Ont.), Abstract index to deeds, Tecumseth Township (mfm. at AO); and York North Land Registry Office (Newmarket, Ont.), Abstract index to deeds, King Township (mfm. at AO). For Lloyd's service as a municipal officer see AO, RG 21, York County, King Township, municipal minute-books, 1809–44 (mfm.). His involvement with the Quakers is recorded in Pickering College Library (Newmarket), Friends Coll., B-2-83-84, C-3-97, C-3-100. References to Lloyd and Lloydtown by William Lyon Mackenzie appear in the *Colonial Advocate*, 11 Aug. 1831.

Lloyd's participation in reform activities can be studied in the Dent coll. at the AO and in the *Constitution* of 9 Aug. 1837. His activities in 1837 are summarized in *Rebellion of 1837* (Read and Stagg). A physical description of him at this time is given in the *Upper Canada Herald*, 12 Dec. 1837. The difficulties over his estate are discussed in PAC, RG 1, L3, 296: L22/21. Information on family members appears in William Lloyd's will, AO, RG 22, ser.305. R.J.S.]

LONGLEY (Langley), GEORGE, businessman, farmer, office holder, politician, and JP; baptized 22 April 1787 in Newbiggin, east of Penrith, England, third son of William Langley, tailor, and Sarah Scott; m. 18 Feb. 1824 Ruth Wells, and they had three sons, one of whom died in infancy, and one daughter; d. at sea en route from Quebec to London, and was buried 13 Aug. 1842 in the parish of Milton-next-Gravesend, England.

Emigrating to Quebec about 1812, George Longley entered the timber trade there and in 1815 became by provincial appointment a master culler and measurer, who could be engaged by timber merchants. He likely worked for one of the large timber-trading partnerships until about 1823 when he formed his own company, Longley and Dyke, with Joseph Dyke, a former principal clerk in the firm of Peter Patterson*. At their yard near Wolfe's Cove (Anse au Foulon) they assembled cargoes of timber for export and also did some shipbuilding.

During the 1820s the focus of Longley's interest broadened and changed. In February 1822 he had purchased a parcel of good farmland on the St Lawrence River in Augusta Township at Pointe au Baril, adjacent to the site where within a few months Ziba and Jehiel Phillips would establish the village of Maitland. Two years later he married a daughter of local businessman William Wells and by 1826, when he settled in Maitland, Longley had doubled his holdings to more than 460 acres and had acquired a controlling interest in a water-powered grist-mill in the area. He remained in partnership with Joseph Dyke until that December, after which he appears to have been interested in the timber trade at Quebec only as an occasional supplier. As late as 1833 he was petitioning against the timber tolls charged on the Rideau Canal.

Grist-milling for export was attractive in Upper Canada during the 1820s because of the completion of the Lachine and Welland canals, the opening up of rich wheat-growing lands around the lower Great Lakes, and the extension of British trade preferences to Canadian wheat and flour in 1825–27. Moreover, in contrast to ports located on the lakes, Maitland had advantages that could be reflected in the final cost of flour milled there. It could be loaded directly onto river-boats for the trip to Montreal, while flour produced elsewhere often had to be carried by lake-boats to the St Lawrence and then trans-shipped to vessels better suited to traversing rapids and canals. Longley soon recognized the limited capacity of the water-mill, and in 1827–28 he built a 90-foot stone windmill on Pointe au Baril. In about 1837, when the shortcomings of the windmill became apparent, it was enlarged and altered to become one of the earliest steam-powered mills in the province. After this time it could produce up to 150 barrels of flour a day and about 20 men were employed at peak periods. Among other benefits, the expansion enabled Longley to grind large volumes of wheat for such customers as John McDonald*, a major mill-owner at Gananoque.

Longley's enterprise was also evident elsewhere in Maitland. In late 1827 or early 1828 he opened a merchant's shop, which stocked a great variety of cloths, and he was postmaster from 1836 until his death. His farm was best known for its livestock, particularly sheep and cattle, which were sold and bred regularly to improve blood-lines in the interests of better animal husbandry. Near the mill and the farm he built for himself in 1828 an "elegant and commodious" stone villa which survives as one of the best examples of 19th-century domestic architecture in the province. Longley led the efforts that resulted in the construction in 1826–27 of St James (Anglican) Church, Maitland. He was instrumental as well in the establishment in 1833 of the Maitland Academy, a private school which closed about a year later.

Beyond the bounds of the village, Longley had limited but important interests. In 1828 he was swept into the House of Assembly for the riding of Grenville as a reformer, although he evidently admired the liberal policies of the British tory statesman George Canning. Longley seldom spoke in the house, but he was a conscientious member, giving particular support to a bill providing grants for agricultural societies and serving on the select committee on the Welland Canal Company. When the death of George IV brought about an unexpected dissolution and a general election in 1830, he was a candidate again but was defeated.

His public life thereafter was restricted largely to those interests with which he had been associated in the assembly. He was chosen the first president of the Grenville County Agricultural Society when it was formed in 1830. That year he was appointed to the committee formed in Brockville to improve navigation on the St Lawrence and from 1833 until his death he was a commissioner of the St Lawrence canals [*see* Jonas JONES]. In 1833 he received his first commission as a justice of the peace. During the 1830s he was a director of the Saint Lawrence Inland Marine Assurance Company and of the Brockville board of the Commercial Bank of the Midland District. Longley died in 1842 en route to England seeking a cure for ill health.

STEPHEN OTTO

ACC, Diocese of Ont. Arch. (Kingston), St James Anglican Church (Maitland, Ont.), subscription list, April 1825. ANQ-Q, CN1-49, 6 oct. 1823; CN1-197, 17 sept. 1824. AO, MU 842, J. G. Malloch, diary, 31–33, 41, 79; MU 1760, George Longley to C. & J. McDonald, 24 Feb., 2, 19, 27 March, 4, 9 April, 20 June, 11, 19 Aug., 15, 21 Sept., 1 Oct. 1840; RG 21, United Counties of Leeds and Grenville, Augusta Township, assessment rolls, 1822–50; RG 22, ser.155. Cumbria Record Office (Carlisle, Eng.), Reg. of baptisms, marriages, and burials for the parish of Newbiggin, 22 April 1787. Grenville Land Registry Office (Prescott, Ont.), Abstract index to deeds, Augusta Township, concession 1, lots 27, 30–32. PAC, MG 24, I110, W. F. Wallace to his uncles in England, 2 July 1827 (photocopy); RG 5, A1: 65069–73, 69516–18; B9, 16: 1036; RG 68, General index, 1651–1841: 174, 176, 479, 492, 509, 517. QUA, 2239, box 13, folder 132, list of persons employed at mill (n.d.); MC, Wells family papers, Ruth Longley to W. B. Wells, 7 Oct. 1826, 9 March 1830, 21 Jan. 1833. Can., Prov. of, Legislative Assembly, *App. to the journals*, 1846, 1: app.F, no.16. L.C., *Statutes*, 1808, c.27. U.C., House of Assembly, *App. to the journal*, 1833–34: 69–79.

Brockville Gazette (Brockville, [Ont.]), 29 Jan., 19 Feb., 11 June 1830; 4 Jan. 1831. *Brockville Recorder*, 18 May, 16 Nov. 1830; 11 April 1833; 7 Dec. 1837; 23 May 1839; 20 July, 14 Dec. 1843; 29 Jan. 1852; 5 July 1855. *Chronicle & Gazette*, 23 Aug. 1828; 27 Nov. 1830; 29 June 1833; 6 June 1835; 26 March 1836; 21 June 1837; 18 May 1839; 19 Feb., 3 Dec. 1842; 19 April, 22 Nov. 1843; 20 Nov. 1847. *Colonial Advocate*, 12 May 1831. *Montreal Gazette*, 4 Aug. 1828, 1 Nov. 1830. *Montreal Transcript*, 17 Sept. 1842. *Quebec Gazette*, 13 July 1815, 7 July 1823. *Upper Canada Gazette*, 13 Jan. 1827. *Quebec almanac*, 1816–19. *Quebec directory*, 1822. W. H. Smith, *Smith's Canadian gazetteer; comprising statistical and general information respecting all parts of the upper province, or Canada West . . .* (Toronto, 1846; repr. 1970). T. W. H. Leavitt, *History of Leeds and Grenville, Ontario, from 1749 to 1879 . . .* (Brockville, 1879; repr. Belleville, Ont., 1972), 75–76.

LONGUEUIL, MARIE-CHARLES-JOSEPH LE MOYNE DE LONGUEUIL, Baronne de. *See* LE MOYNE

LONGWORTH, FRANCIS, tanner, politician, office holder, JP, and militia officer; b. 1766 in County Westmeath (Republic of Ireland), son of Francis Longworth and Mary Fitzgerald; m. 29 March 1797 Agnes Auld in Charlottetown, and they had 13 children, including Francis* and John*; d. there 27 Feb. 1843.

Born into an Anglican, Anglo-Irish family, Francis Longworth immigrated to St John's (Prince Edward) Island around 1791. He was a tanner by trade, but by no means a simple tradesman: he had financial substance, education, and social weight. Within a decade of his arrival he had built a tannery and collected the lands necessary for an exemplary farm in Charlottetown Royalty. An established businessman and a vestryman for St Paul's Church, Longworth by the turn of the century was already a member of the small Charlottetown élite.

Longworth made his only foray into the political arena in 1803, winning a by-election for a Georgetown seat in the House of Assembly, which he held until 1806. It appears that he supported Robert Hodgson*'s escheat faction. Longworth did not find his true role in public life until February 1814 when Lieutenant Governor Charles Douglass Smith* appointed him a justice of the peace. Smith found him a congenial magistrate and named him high sheriff three times. Longworth reciprocated by supporting Smith and his political ally of the 1820s, James Bardin Palmer*.

Smith made many enemies: he alienated absentee proprietors by attempting to escheat their lands, and worried the local élite by refusing to place himself in their hands. Not surprisingly he was charged with personal aggrandizement and corruption by the powerful forces he had offended. Longworth, as a Smith appointee and voluble Palmer supporter, could not escape the censure which befell Smith's few allies upon the lieutenant governor's dismissal in 1824. In 1825 the assembly accused Longworth of "irregular practices" as a justice of the peace, charges never substantiated.

Chastened but not repentant, Longworth was almost alone in his willingness to defend Smith's record. He believed that the economy with which Smith had run the Island's affairs compared favourably with the deficits of his successor, John READY. Longworth took some satisfaction in pointing out how the assemblymen who had charged Smith with corruption had squandered the budgetary surplus he had left behind, and were now forced to impose new taxes, "taking care not to forget themselves" in the distribution of revenues raised thereby.

As time passed, with animosities of the Smith era fading, and the ranks of surviving early settlers thinning, Longworth came to be regarded as a grand old man of a bygone era. Patriarch of a large family, he watched his offspring take up important posts on the Island. He himself continued as a justice of the peace and magistrate, and was once more appointed high sheriff in 1835. An active member of the Central Agricultural Society, he had helped to create the Benevolent Irish Society in 1825, and was its president from 1828. In 1839 he retired from the militia as a lieutenant-colonel. Longworth died after a long illness, and was mourned as "a man of sterling worth, honor and integrity," with any resonance of past controversies appropriately muted.

M. BROOK TAYLOR

PAPEI, Acc. 2849/119; RG 1, commission books, 1 Feb. 1814, 2 May 1815, 29 May 1835; RG 16, land registry records, conveyance reg., liber 9: ff.73, 99. P.E.I. Museum, File information concerning Francis Longworth. PRO, CO 226/19; 226/20: 81; 226/32: 268; 226/36: 28. St Paul's Anglican Church (Charlottetown), Reg. of baptisms, marriages, and burials; Vestry minutes, 1798–99 (mfm. at PAPEI). Supreme Court of P.E.I. (Charlottetown), Estates Division, liber 4: f.134 (will of Francis Longworth) (mfm. at PAPEI). *Prince Edward Island Gazette*, 20 Dec. 1817. *Prince Edward Island Register*, 5 Feb., 31 March 1825; 19 June 1827; 18 March 1828; 3 Nov. 1829. *Royal Gazette* (Charlottetown), 26 Feb., 19, 26 March, 26 Nov. 1833; 28 Oct. 1834; 25 June 1839; 28 Feb. 1843.

LORIMIER, CHEVALIER DE (baptized **François-Marie-Thomas**, he later received the given name Chevalier, apparently from his uncle and godfather François-Chevalier de Lorimier; generally referred to as François-Marie-Thomas-Chevalier de Lorimier, he always signed Chevalier de Lorimier), notary and Patriote; b. 27 Dec. 1803 in Saint-Cuthbert, Lower Canada, third of the ten children of Guillaume-Verneuil de Lorimier, a farmer, and Marguerite-Adélaïde Perrault; d. 15 Feb. 1839 in Montreal.

Chevalier de Lorimier was a descendant of an old family of French nobility which had remained in New France after the conquest and whose decline led its members to seek integration into the rising Canadian bourgeoisie in the 19th century. It is not known when his parents came to live in Montreal, but it is certain that in 1813 young Chevalier began his classical studies at the Petit Séminaire de Montréal. At the time he finished these in 1820, he evidently had not yet chosen a profession, since he did not begin articling under Pierre Ritchot, a Montreal notary, until three years later. During his period of training he became friends with his employer.

In his political testament Lorimier noted that he had become active in politics as early as 1821 or 1822, when he was 17 or 18 years old. An idealist enamoured of liberty and drawn from the outset to the national cause, he was one of a group of young men who early became involved in the struggles that Louis-Joseph Papineau* and his supporters were waging against the governor, Lord Dalhousie [RAMSAY], and the Executive and Legislative councils of Lower Canada. Lorimier in all likelihood participated in the vast campaign organized in 1822 to protest against the plan to unite Lower and Upper Canada [*see* Denis-Benjamin Viger*]. In December 1827, when the conflict between the governor and the House of Assembly had entered an extremely tense phase, he signed a petition from the inhabitants of Montreal County to King George IV that among other things condemned the "arbitrary and despotic" conduct of Dalhousie and asked for his recall, denounced the pluralism engaged in by a small group of privileged individuals, and requested an enlarged number of seats in the assembly proportional to the increased population of Lower Canada.

Lorimier was commissioned to practise as a notary on 25 Aug. 1829 and drew up his first instrument on 6 September. A fortnight later he set up his office in a house in the *faubourg* Saint-Antoine, probably not far from the home in which his parents had resided since at least 1819. Subsequently he went into partnership with Ritchot, and when Ritchot died in 1831, he drew up the inventory of his assets as a mark of gratitude and friendship. On 10 Jan. 1832, in Montreal, he married Henriette Cadieux, eldest daughter of the late Jean-Marie Cadieux, a notary. He then went to live on Rue Saint-Jacques, in a house his wife had inherited at her father's death, and he also moved his office there. The couple were to have five children, but two of their daughters and their only son died in infancy. Through intelligence, transparent integrity, and devotion to work, Lorimier built up a good practice. His minute-book discloses that his clients in the main were members of the liberal professions, small merchants, craftsmen, and Canadian farmers from the town and island of Montreal; in particular he drew up a great many contracts for Gabriel Franchère*, the American Fur Company's principal agent in Montreal, during the period from 1832 to 1837.

By his activity as a notary and his enthusiasm for politics Lorimier soon became an influential member of the professional middle class of Montreal and a figure close to the Patriote leaders. During the 1832 by-election to the assembly for Montreal West he was one of the keenest supporters of Daniel Tracey*, the publisher of the Montreal *Vindicator and Canadian Advertiser*, who had been imprisoned for libelling the Legislative Council, and he was largely instrumental in securing him the seat. However, on 21 May during a riot at the end of the polling in which three Canadians died, Lorimier narrowly escaped injury when a shot fired by a soldier of the 15th Foot broke the handle of his umbrella. He took an energetic part in the Patriote party's campaign in the 1834 general election, supporting the candidates who were in favour of the 92 Resolutions. Two years later he eagerly contributed to the subscription launched by Édouard-Raymond Fabre* to compensate the publisher of *La Minerve*, Ludger Duvernay*, for his imprisonment on a charge of contempt of court.

Like most of Papineau's supporters, Lorimier was strongly opposed to the British parliament's adoption in March 1837 of Lord John Russell's resolutions, which flatly rejected the Patriote party's demands for reforms and confirmed the hold of the provincial executive on the public moneys of Lower Canada. Thus he threw himself into the resistance movement organized by the Patriote leaders in April. He was present at nearly all the large protest meetings in the

Montreal region in the period preceding the rebellion. On 15 May he was appointed secretary for the Montreal County meeting held at Saint-Laurent on the island of Montreal. At this gathering a body to focus resistance, the Comité Central et Permanent du District de Montréal, was set up and Lorimier and George-Étienne Cartier* were elected co-secretaries. The committee was to meet weekly in Fabre's bookshop on Rue Saint-Vincent, and its task would be "to attend to the political interests of this county" and "to correspond with the other counties" in order to coordinate resistance. On 29 June Lorimier also acted as secretary for the city of Montreal meeting that solemnly protested against the implementation of the Russell resolutions, "which annihilate the constitutional rights in the Province." He made a point of honour of attending, along with many prominent Montreal Patriotes, the Assemblée des Six Comtés held on 23 October in Saint-Charles-sur-Richelieu. He went as well to the meeting of the Fils de la Liberté in Montreal on 6 November, only to be shot in the thigh during a clash between this society and the Doric Club which deteriorated into a ransacking of the *Vindicator*'s offices.

On 14 or 15 Nov. 1837, before warrants for the arrest of the Patriote leaders were issued by the governor, Lord Gosford [ACHESON], Lorimier fled Montreal hurriedly, leaving behind his wife, children, possessions, and practice, and headed for the county of Deux-Montagnes. Arriving there on 15 November, he was soon appointed captain in the local militia battalion and was ordered to put himself under the command of Jean-Olivier CHÉNIER at Saint-Eustache. During the month that followed he played an important role alongside Chénier and Amury GIROD in preparing for armed struggle in the region. He was at the battle of Saint-Eustache on 14 December. Realizing the futility of the efforts to repel Sir John Colborne*'s forces, which were superior in number, he advised Chénier and his followers to lay down their arms, but in vain. At the height of the fighting he escaped, while there was still time, to the neighbouring village of Saint-Benoît (Mirabel). From there he went to Trois-Rivières with a few companions, crossed the St Lawrence, and finally reached the United States by way of the Eastern Townships.

After his arrival Lorimier stayed in Montpelier, Vt, for a time and then moved on to Middlebury, where a group of Patriotes had arranged to meet in order to discuss the possibility of a new uprising. Among those present on 2 Jan. 1838 were Lorimier, Papineau, Robert Nelson*, Edmund Bailey O'Callaghan*, Cyrille-Hector-Octave CÔTÉ, Édouard-Élisée Malhiot*, Édouard-Étienne RODIER, the curé Étienne Chartier*, and Lucien GAGNON. Undoubtedly Papineau's temporizing and hesitant approach at this meeting disappointed Lorimier. A week later he was present at a meeting in Swanton. It was probably then that he came around to the views held by Nelson and Côté and to their plans for setting in motion an invasion of Lower Canada. After Nelson took command of the Patriote army and began preparing for the invasion, Lorimier went to join him at Plattsburgh, N.Y. On 28 February he was serving as a captain in the army that crossed the border. When Nelson read the proclamation of the independence of Lower Canada, Lorimier was at his side. Poor organization and planning and intelligence leaks doomed the expedition. Lorimier sought refuge in the United States, where he was imprisoned, along with others, for violating American neutrality. He was quickly acquitted by a jury sympathetic to the Patriote cause.

In the first months of exile Lorimier had a difficult time. To all intents and purposes he had given up his profession and consequently had no work or income. He was also without news of his family and worried about having left them in Montreal without means of subsistence. But rather than let himself be discouraged by his personal problems and by the set-back in February 1838, he decided to devote himself to reorganizing the rebel movement. By March Lorimier in all probability was helping to set up the Association des Frères-Chasseurs, which he undoubtedly lost no time joining. As Nelson and his colleagues saw it, the purpose of this secret, paramilitary society was to support the Patriote army by initiating an uprising inside Lower Canada once an offensive had been launched from the American border. In May Lorimier's wife, Henriette, came to join him in Plattsburgh, where she lived with him until August. It can be assumed that her visit caused Lorimier to vacillate painfully between his obligations to his family and his commitment to revolution. He nevertheless returned to Lower Canada several times that summer to recruit members for the society and make preparations for the uprising in the counties of Deux-Montagnes and Beauharnois. On the strength of promises from Nelson and Côté, he assured those joining the society that an army enjoying the blessing of the American government would come to their support and provide the weapons and ammunition they needed. In July, having returned to Plattsburgh from one of these trips, he confided in a letter to a friend the deep feelings stirring in him just months before the new insurrection: "I am ever ready to *spill my blood* on the soil which gave me birth, in order to upset the infamous British Government – top, branches, roots, and all."

It is difficult to determine exactly what role Lorimier played when the second uprising began on the night of 3–4 Nov. 1838. Laurent-Olivier David* says only that Lorimier was at Beauharnois when the Patriotes there seized Edward Ellice*'s seigneurial manor-house and went on board the steamship *Henry Brougham* to inspect it. The author of the account of

Lorimier published in the Swanton *North American* on 15 May 1839 and another biographer, Hector Fabre*, state that Lorimier had the rank of brigadier-general in the Patriote army at the time these events took place. François-Xavier Prieur, a merchant at Saint-Timothée who was one of the leaders of the uprising at Beauharnois, noted that until that night "de Lorimier had taken no active part in the movement, at least as far as I know." What is certain is that once the Patriotes from Beauharnois had completed their mission, they waited in vain for Nelson's orders.

On 7 November Lorimier and Prieur set out from Beauharnois with 200 men to reinforce the Patriotes at Camp Baker, in Sainte-Martine, who were facing the approach of an infantry regiment. Another leader of the uprising, Jean-Baptiste-Henri BRIEN, a doctor at Sainte-Martine, disclosed in a declaration made to the authorities two days after he was imprisoned on 18 November that Lorimier had come "to encourage the people to remain firm" and not to give up the fight. On 9 November after the Patriotes at Camp Baker had beaten off an attack by a detachment of the 71st Foot, Lorimier strongly condemned their commanding officer James Perrigo, a merchant at Sainte-Martine, for dissuading his companions from pursuing the soldiers as they fled. A few hours after the fighting ended the Patriotes from Beauharnois received news of Nelson's defeat at Odelltown. They dispersed the next day, before two militia battalions from Upper Canada arrived. Those of them who were the most gravely compromised attempted under Lorimier's leadership to seek refuge in the United States, but Lorimier himself, caught in the crossfire of a corps of volunteers, lost his way in the dark and was arrested near the border on the morning of 12 November. He was taken on foot to the jail in Napierville, and on 22 or 23 November was removed to Montreal Prison.

On 11 Jan. 1839 Lorimier, along with 11 companions, appeared before a court martial presided over by Major-General John Clitherow*. Shortly after the court opened, Perrigo was excluded from the trial. The accused were represented by lawyers Lewis Thomas Drummond* and Aaron Philip Hart, who were allowed to prepare only written pleas for their clients. Having consulted with them, Lorimier made an initial protest challenging the jurisdiction of the court martial and demanded a trial before a civil court. His demand was dismissed. The trial was conducted in an atmosphere of violence. Lorimier defended himself tenaciously in a hall filled with officials eager for blood. He proceeded to cross-examine the witnesses, led them to contradict themselves, and disputed all the evidence brought against him. It was so much wasted effort. Unbeknown to Lorimier, Brien, who was terrified at the prospect of mounting the scaffold, had already signed a declaration informing in particular against his companion in return for the authorities' promise that he would be treated leniently. This confession proved more damaging to Lorimier than any of the testimony given by witnesses. Having failed to capture the principal leaders of the rebellion, the authorities fell back on the one they considered the most prominent of the Beauharnois rebels. Charles Dewey Day*, the deputy judge advocate, specifically attacked Lorimier, depicting him in his address to the court as an extremely dangerous criminal who had fomented the rebellion and deserved to die on the gallows. At the end of the trial on 21 January, the accused were all found guilty of high treason; Lorimier alone was not recommended to the executive for clemency.

Drummond and Hart took repeated steps with Governor Colborne and the members of the Special Council to save Lorimier's life, but in vain. On 9 Feb. 1839 they made their final move, asking for a writ of prohibition. Unfortunately, the Court of King's Bench rejected the request. On 14 February Henriette de Lorimier sent a letter to Colborne begging him to reprieve her husband, whose execution had been decreed the day before. Colborne did not even deign to reply to her petition.

On 15 Feb. 1839, at 9:00 A.M., Lorimier mounted the steps of the scaffold with a firm tread, in company with Charles HINDENLANG, Amable Daunais, François Nicolas, and Pierre-Rémi Narbonne. On the eve of his execution he had written his political testament, in which he expressed the hope that his country would one day be liberated from British domination. He concluded it with moving and pathetic words: "As for you, my compatriots – may my execution and that of my companions on the scaffold be of use to you. May they show you what you must expect from the British government. I have only a few hours to live, but I wanted to divide this precious time between my religious duties and the duty [I owe] to my countrymen. For them do I die on the gibbet the infamous death of the murderer; for them do I part from my young children, [and] from my wife, who have only my industry for their support; and for them do I die exclaiming – 'Long live Liberty! Long live Independence!' " Lorimier's body was buried in the former Catholic cemetery of Montreal, where Dominion Square is today. His wife, unable to pay the debts that he had contracted, was obliged to renounce his estate. Lorimier's remains are believed to have been exhumed in 1858 and in all probability were placed beneath the memorial in Notre-Dame-des-Neiges cemetery dedicated to the victims of 1837–38.

In 1883 journalist Laurent-Olivier David got up a public subscription to assist Henriette de Lorimier and her two daughters, who were living in poverty at L'Assomption. With the help of Honoré Beaugrand*, publisher of *La Patrie*, and writer Louis-Honoré Fréchette*, he collected $1,300; $1,000 went to

Lorimier's widow by way of reparations from the nation. That year the Montreal city council in a fitting reversal passed a resolution changing the name of Avenue Colborne to Avenue de Lorimier. According to the *North American*, Lorimier was of roughly medium height and had a dark complexion and black hair and eyes. In an article on him in the 10 March 1881 issue of *L'Opinion publique*, David described him as having an "oval-shaped" face, regular features, a high forehead, and a "gentle and intelligent countenance." "One thought on sight," David concluded, "of a good-hearted, imaginative man with a refined intellect."

That a figure such as Chevalier de Lorimier has been presented in very different ways in historical works is hardly surprising. There is one point, however, on which historians and his biographers are in agreement: the sincerity of his convictions. Historian Pascal Potvin, though he condemned the blindness of some of the leaders in the 1838 rebellion, was forced to recognize this quality in Lorimier. The author of the *North American* biography and David maintained that Lorimier was one of the Patriotes who believed most strongly that the rebellion would succeed. True to himself, he had carried out the mission that had been entrusted to him: the Beauharnois Patriotes had fulfilled their part in the planned invasion, and they had then formed one of the last groups of insurgents to resist the British army. Lorimier's only errors were probably to have trusted too much in Nelson and Côté for the preparation and progress of the uprising – but could he have done otherwise under the circumstances? – and to have believed in the Americans' promise of support. His greatest merit was to have taken to the limit his political ideal and his revolutionary commitment, at the cost of his own life. Lorimier has won his place in history as a great Patriote and as a martyr to the cause of independence for Lower Canada.

MICHEL DE LORIMIER

Chevalier de Lorimier's minute-book, containing notarized instruments for the years 1829–38, is at ANQ-M, CN1-122. Originals and copies of some interesting correspondence with his wife, relatives, and friends, which he wrote mostly during the time he spent in the Montreal jail, are located in various archives, including the following: ANQ-M, P-224/1, no.78; ANQ-Q, E17/37, no.2972; P1000-8-124; P1000-49-976; P1000-66-1317; P1000-87-1806; ASQ, Fonds Viger–Verreau, carton 67, no.6; ASTR, 0032 (coll. Montarville Boucher de la Bruère), papiers Wolfred Nelson; BVM-G, MSS, Lorimier à [L.-A.] Robitaille, 12 févr. 1839; and David MacDonald Stewart Museum (Montreal), Lady La Fontaine album, Lorimier à [Lady La Fontaine (Adèle Berthelot)], 15 févr. 1839. The declaration of political principles which Lorimier wrote on the eve of his execution is at ANQ-Q, E17/37, no.2971 (copies in P1000-49-976 and P1000-66-1317).

Lorimier's correspondence has been reproduced in newspapers and other publications. The *North American*, a paper put out by sympathizers to the Patriote cause, published most of his letters on 15 May, 7 Aug., 6 Nov. 1839 and 22 Jan., 24 June, 25 July 1840 (the issue of 22 Jan. 1840 contains a letter which is particularly illuminating about his state of mind while he was planning the second insurrection of July 1838). In addition, Ludger Duvernay's *Le Patriote canadien* (Burlington, Vt.), a paper for Patriotes who had sought refuge in the United States, printed a few items in its issue of 13 Nov. 1839. Less than ten years later, author James Huston* included all of Lorimier's letters in *Le répertoire national* (1848–50), 2: 97–108. Toward the end of the 19th century Laurent-Olivier David also published the entire correspondence in "Les hommes de 37–38: de Lorimier," *L'Opinion publique*, 10 févr. 1881: 61–62; 3 mars 1881: 97; 10 mars 1881: 109–10; this article was reprinted in his *Patriotes*, 237–63. Some correspondence has been published in the 20th century: "Testament politique de Chevalier de Lorimier (14 février 1839)" and "Lettre du patriote Chevalier de Lorimier à sa femme (15 février 1839)," ANQ *Rapport*, 1924–25: 1, 32; "Lettre de Chevalier de Lorimier à Pierre Beaudry (14 février 1839)," ANQ *Rapport*, 1926–27: 145; and "Lettre du Chevalier de Lorimier au baron de Fratelin (15 février 1839)," *BRH*, 47 (1941): 20.

A pencil sketch of Lorimier, attributed to Jean-Joseph Girouard*, is found in the Lady La Fontaine album, David MacDonald Stewart Museum.

ANQ-M, CC1, 23 avril 1839; CE1-51, 10 janv. 1832; CE5-19, 27 déc. 1803; CN1-32, 10–13 mai, 20 juin 1839; CN1-270, 3 sept. 1823, 9 janv. 1832. ANQ-Q, E17/6, no.7; E17/14, no.793; E17/27, nos.2027–30; E17/28, nos.2031, 2047, 2051, 2058–60, 2062–63, 2075; E17/37, nos.2968, 2973; E17/39, no.3116; P-68/3, no.313; P-68/4, no.429; P-68/5, no.559; P-92. Arch. de la ville de Montréal, Doc. administratifs, procès-verbaux du conseil municipal, 27 juin 1883. BVM-G, Fonds Ægidius Fauteux, notes compilées par Ægidius Fauteux sur les patriotes de 1837–38 dont les noms commencent par la lettre L, carton 6. David MacDonald Stewart Museum, Pétition, janvier 1828. PAC, MG 24, A2, 50; A27, 34; B2, 17–21; B39; RG 4, B8: 2908–18; B20, 28: 11218–19, 11256–59, 11297–300; RG 31, C1, 1825, 1831, Montreal. [Henriette Cadieux], "Lettre de la veuve du patriote de Lorimier au baron Fratelin," *BRH*, 46 (1940): 372–73. "Un document inédit sur les événements assez obscurs de l'insurrection de 1837–38," [F.-L.-G.] Baby, édit., *Canadian Antiquarian and Numismatic Journal*, 3rd ser., 5 (1908): 3–31. Amury Girod, "Journal kept by the late Amury Girod, translated from the German and the Italian," PAC *Report*, 1923: 370–80. "Papiers Duvernay," *Canadian Antiquarian and Numismatic Journal*, 3rd ser., 6: 6–7, 9–10; 7: 20–23, 25–26, 184–85. L.-J.-A. Papineau, *Journal d'un Fils de la liberté*. F.-X. Prieur, *Notes d'un condamné politique de 1838* (Montréal, 1884; réimpr. 1974), 89–139. *Rapport du comité choisi sur le gouvernement civil du Canada* (Québec, 1829), 351–53. *Report of state trials*, 1: 293–376; 2: 141–286, 548–61. *Le Canadien*, 15 nov. 1839. *La Minerve*, 13, 20 déc. 1827; 10, 28 janv. 1828; 21 sept. 1829; 11, 15, 18 mai, 29 juin 1837. *Montreal Gazette*, 22 Jan., 19 Oct. 1839. *North American*, 22 May, 4, 11, 18 Dec. 1839.

Appleton's cyclopædia of American biography, ed. J. G. Wilson and John Fiske (7v., New York, 1888–1901), 4:

26–27. Fauteux, *Patriotes*, 19–20, 65–74, 141–42. J.-J. Lefebvre, *Le Canada, l'Amérique: géographie, histoire* (éd. rév., Montréal, 1968), 175. Le Jeune, *Dictionnaire*, 2: 168–69. *Montreal directory*, 1819. *Quebec almanac*, 1830–38. Wallace, *Macmillan dict.* J. D. Borthwick, *History of the Montreal prison from A.D. 1784 to A.D. 1886 . . .* (Montreal, 1886), 40, 43–44, 51–52, 90–96. L.-N. Carrier, *Les événements de 1837–38* (2e éd., Beauceville, Qué., 1914). Chapais, *Cours d'hist. du Canada*, 3: 189–91. Christie, *Hist. of L.C.* (1866). David, *Patriotes*, 171–72, 277–86. Émile Dubois, *Le feu de la Rivière-du-Chêne; étude historique sur le mouvement insurrectionnel de 1837 au nord de Montréal* (Saint-Jérôme, Qué., 1937), 122, 177–78. Hector Fabre, *Esquisse biographique sur Chevalier de Lorimier* (Montréal, 1856). Émile Falardeau, *Prieur, l'idéaliste* (Montréal, 1944). Filteau, *Hist. des patriotes* (1975), 117, 207–8, 274–76, 301–6, 358–63, 371, 401–22, 435–39. [C.-A.-M. Globensky], *La rébellion de 1837 à Saint-Eustache avec un exposé préliminaire de la situation politique du Bas-Canada depuis la cession* (Québec, 1883; réimpr. Montréal, 1974). Augustin Leduc, *Beauharnois, paroisse Saint-Clément, 1819–1919; histoire religieuse, histoire civile; fêtes du centenaire* (Ottawa, 1920), 175–78. Michel de Lorimier, "Chevalier de Lorimier, notaire et patriote montréalais de 1837–1838" (thèse de MA, univ. du Québec, Montréal, 1975). É.-Z. Massicotte, *Faits curieux de l'histoire de Montréal* (2e éd., Montréal, 1924), 86–98. Maurault, *Le collège de Montréal* (Dansereau; 1967). Ouellet, *Bas-Canada*. J.-E. Roy, *Hist. du notariat*, 2: 453; 3: 7, 9–17. P.-G. Roy, *Toutes petites choses du Régime anglais* (2 sér., Québec, 1946), 2: 33–36. Rumilly, *Papineau et son temps*. Robert Sellar, *The history of the county of Huntingdon and of the seigniories of Chateauguay and Beauharnois from their first settlement to the year 1838* (Huntingdon, Que., 1888), 505–43. André Vachon, *Histoire du notariat canadien, 1621–1960* (Québec, 1962). Mason Wade, *Les Canadiens français, de 1760 à nos jours*, Adrien Venne et Francis Dufau-Labeyrie, trad. (2e éd., 2v., Ottawa, 1966), 1: 342.

Ivanhoë Caron, "Une société secrète dans le Bas-Canada en 1838: l'Association des Frères Chasseurs," RSC *Trans.*, 3rd ser., 20 (1926), sect.I: 17–34. L.-O. David, "Les hommes de 37–38: de Lorimier," *L'Opinion publique*, 24 mars 1881: 133–34; 7 avril 1881: 157–58; 14 avril 1881: 169–70; 21 avril 1881: 181. "De Lorimier," *L'Opinion publique*, 28 juin 1883: 301. L.-A. Fortier, "Correspondance: victimes de 37–38," *La Tribune* (Montréal), 24 mars 1883: 2. J.-J. Lefebvre, "Jean-Marie Cadieux, notaire, 1805, et sa descendance," *La Rev. du notariat* (Outremont, Qué.), 69 (1966–67): 122–32, 196–202. É.-Z. Massicotte, "La famille de Lorimier: notes généalogiques et historiques," *BRH*, 21 (1915): 10–16, 33–45. Victor Morin, "Clubs et sociétés notoires d'autrefois," *Cahiers des Dix*, 15 (1950): 185–218; "La 'République canadienne' de 1838," *RHAF*, 2 (1948–49): 483–512. Pascal Potvin, "Les patriotes de 1837–1838: essai de synthèse historique," *Le Canada français* (Québec), 2e sér., 25 (1937–38): 667–90, 779–93. Marcelle Reeves-Morache, "La Canadienne pendant les troubles de 1837–1838," *RHAF*, 5 (1951–52): 99–117. "La veuve de Lorimier," *L'Opinion publique*, 19 juill. 1883: 340. "La veuve du patriote de Lorimier," *BRH*, 32 (1926): 330.

LORIMIER, JEAN-BAPTISTE DE (known as **Jean-Baptiste, Chevalier de Lorimier**), interpreter, office holder, and JP; baptized 5 May 1786 in Caughnawaga (Kahnawake), Que., second son of Claude-Nicolas-Guillaume de Lorimier* and Louise Schuyler; m. 26 Nov. 1827 Marguerite Rousseau in Saint-Régis (Akwesasne); d. 4 Oct. 1845 in Montreal.

Jean-Baptiste de Lorimier was descended from a distinguished Canadian family with a long tradition of military service. The Patriote Chevalier de LORIMIER belonged to another branch of the same family. Jean-Baptiste's father, resident agent of the Indian Department in Caughnawaga since 1775, was probably instrumental in obtaining for his son a departmental post as an interpreter there in May 1810. His mother, Louise Schuyler, was an Iroquois from Caughnawaga, and so his ties with the community were close. Lorimier was subsequently appointed interpreter and lieutenant at Lac-des-Deux-Montagnes (Oka) effective 26 Sept. 1812. He was promoted captain and resident agent at Saint-Régis on 11 May 1813. Just over two weeks later he was one of the Indian Department officers ordered to the Niagara frontier with a detachment of warriors from Lower Canada for service in the conflict with the Americans.

Arriving in the Niagara peninsula early in June, Lorimier and about 300 Indians under the overall command of his brother-in-law Captain Dominique Ducharme* joined a group of some 100 Mohawks from the Grand River led by Captain William Johnson KERR. They played the major role in the defeat of Lieutenant-Colonel Charles Boerstler's expedition near Beaver Dams (Thorold) on 24 June [*see* James FitzGibbon*]. Lorimier commanded the Indians from Saint-Régis during this engagement.

Lorimier remained in the Niagara area for the next two months, as the Americans, operating from the captured Fort George (Niagara-on-the-Lake), continued to clash with British troops and Canadian militiamen. On 17 August American soldiers, accompanied by a few Iroquois from New York, overwhelmed a small picket-guard he commanded. Seriously wounded, he spent the remainder of 1813 as a prisoner of war. By the time he was exchanged at the beginning of 1814, his treatment at the hands of his captors had become the subject of some controversy between the British and American commands. Major-General Francis de Rottenburg* had referred in a dispatch of 8 Sept. 1813 to the "ignominious treatment inflicted upon Capt Lorimier." Lorimier's wounds and imprisonment were to affect his health for the rest of his life.

On 8 Aug. 1814 Lorimier was made captain in the newly established Embodied Indian Warriors, of which his father was deputy superintendent. He spent the remainder of that year in the canoe guards which protected the flotillas travelling to British posts on the upper Great Lakes, his knowledge of various Indian dialects making him especially useful. At the end of the war he returned to his duties at Saint-Régis, where in June 1815 he sat on a commission investigating the community's grievances concerning property disputes on the reserves and their charges that they had been cheated by local whites.

The following year Lorimier was seconded for service in the expedition to the Red River led by Lord Selkirk [Douglas*]. He was present when Selkirk captured the North West Company's Fort William (Thunder Bay, Ont.) in August 1816. Sent east with some of the NWC partners who were to face trial in Upper Canada, he narrowly escaped drowning when a sudden storm on Lake Superior overturned his canoe, killing Kenneth MacKenzie* and eight others. On 18 July 1817 he and Métis interpreter Louis Nolin were two of the six witnesses at the signing of a treaty at the Red River settlement (Man.) between Selkirk and five Cree and Saulteaux chiefs, including Peguis*. Selkirk thought highly of Lorimier and in the spring of 1818 recommended him to escort Roman Catholic missionaries Joseph-Norbert Provencher* and Sévère Dumoulin* to the settlement. Provencher described his escort as a "gay, pleasant, polite and honest man." Sir John Johnson*, superintendent general of the Indian Department, noted that Lorimier's experience made him well suited for the task and arranged for his duties in the department to be temporarily assumed by others.

Lorimier became involved in the escalating conflict between the NWC and the Hudson's Bay Company. In July 1817 government officials inquired into whether he had acted improperly during the Selkirk expedition. Although Lorimier denied any direct association with either of the companies, in March 1819 he was indicted with several others on charges that they had conspired to ruin the NWC's Indian trade. No doubt inspired by the bitterness created at the time of Selkirk's expedition, these charges were apparently dropped. They had no effect on Lorimier's subsequent career. He continued in his Indian Department post until his retirement in 1832. He had been made a justice of the peace for the district of Montreal in October 1821.

Jean-Baptiste de Lorimier spent the last part of his life quietly and respectably. He left an estate evaluated at approximately 6,000 *livres*. His career was not a spectacular one, but it was significant. He was representative of a group of Canadians of mixed-blood ancestry who ably served the Indian Department in a variety of capacities in the late 18th and early 19th centuries. His personal courage and linguistic versatility led to a career of some distinction, even though his initial postings were clearly obtained through family influence.

DOUGLAS LEIGHTON

ANQ-M, CE1-25, 5 mai 1786; CE1-51, 26 nov. 1827, 7 oct. 1845. PAC, RG 8, I (C ser.), 230, 256–58, 363, 679, 688B, 692, 1168, 1170–71, 1203½A, 1218, 1224; RG 10, A3, 488–91, 497; A6, 627, 633. *Documents relating to northwest missions, 1815–1827*, ed. G. L. Nute (St Paul, Minn., 1942). Alexander Morris, *The treaties of Canada with the Indians of Manitoba and the North-West Territories, including the negotiations on which they were based, and other information relating thereto* (Toronto, 1880; repr. 1971). *Quebec Gazette*, 11 March 1819, 25 Oct. 1821. Morice, *Dict. hist. des Canadiens et des Métis*. *Officers of British forces in Canada* (Irving). E. J. Devine, *Historic Caughnawaga* (Montreal, 1922). Rich, *Fur trade* (1967). Sulte, *Hist. de la milice*. É.-Z. Massicotte, "La famille de Lorimier: notes généalogiques et historiques," *BRH*, 21 (1915): 10–16, 33–45.

LORING, ROBERT ROBERTS, army officer; baptized 27 Sept. 1789 in Englefield, England, youngest of five sons of Joshua Loring and Elizabeth Lloyd; grandson of Joshua Loring*; m. 3 Feb. 1814 Mary Ann Campbell, daughter of William Campbell*, in York (Toronto), Upper Canada, and they had two sons and three daughters; m. secondly 19 July 1828 Ann Smith in Overton (North Yorkshire), England, and they had two sons and two daughters; d. 1 April 1848 in Toronto.

Robert Roberts Loring joined the 49th Foot as an ensign on 15 Dec. 1804, and the following July arrived at Quebec to join the regiment, which had been in the Canadas since 1802. On 3 Sept. 1806 he was promoted lieutenant. Early in his career Loring demonstrated an affinity for staff work. Roger Hale Sheaffe*, then a lieutenant-colonel, claimed to have noticed him as an ensign, and when Lieutenant-General Gordon Drummond* assumed command of the forces in the Canadas in 1811, he was impressed with how Loring was "performing the duties of Adjutant" in the 49th and added him to his staff. Loring accompanied Drummond to Britain in October 1811, but the outbreak of war with the United States in 1812 convinced the young officer that his duty lay in North America, and he returned to Lower Canada that autumn.

On 26 June 1812 Loring had become a captain in the 104th Foot and on 29 Oct. 1812 he was appointed aide-de-camp to Sheaffe, the new administrator of Upper Canada. Many of Loring's responsibilities in this position were routine, but with the increasing intensity of the war and Sheaffe's attention to defensive preparations they assumed more pressing urgency. One concern which Sheaffe inherited from Sir Isaac Brock* was the loyalty of the population, and the alien boards set up by the new administrator in Niagara (Niagara-on-the-Lake), York, and Kingston provided considerable work for his aide-de-camp.

Loring's first action was during the American attack on York in April 1813. At one point Sheaffe and Loring were between the enemy and the retreating

British. When the magazine of Fort York exploded Loring suffered "a severe contusion," an injury which resulted in the partial disabling of his right arm. Sheaffe returned to England in November, and when in December 1813 Drummond arrived to assume command of the forces in Upper Canada, he appointed Loring to his staff, first as aide-de-camp and later as civil secretary. Loring gradually assumed ever larger responsibilities, becoming in practice Drummond's personal secretary.

In December 1813 Loring was with Drummond at the capture of Fort Niagara (near Youngstown), N.Y., and on 25 July 1814 he was promoted brevet major. Before he learned of his advancement, however, he was captured in the battle of Lundy's Lane, and he spent the remainder of the conflict in Cheshire, Mass. One of his fellow captives was the young William Hamilton Merritt*. Merritt's account of his not unpleasant imprisonment includes several mentions of his friend Loring, whom he described as "Clever in the cabinet, cool and determined in the field."

Following his repatriation, Loring arrived at Quebec with Drummond on 3 April 1815. A week later he was officially appointed the latter's private secretary, a post he filled until Drummond returned to England in May 1816. Loring resumed his military career by joining the 104th and on 17 Aug. 1816 was appointed brigade-major, at Kingston, but he held the job only until 24 June 1817, one month after being placed on half pay. Loring remained in Upper Canada, and on the death of the provincial secretary, William Jarvis*, offered himself without success for the position. In September 1818 he was living in Kingston, where he owned a town lot, but it is not clear what he did to support himself and his family until 9 Dec. 1819, when he transferred to a captaincy in the 76th Foot.

On 20 June 1820 Loring was made assistant military secretary to the new commander-in-chief in British North America, Lord Dalhousie [RAMSAY], and a year later he became a brigade-major. He was involved in various organizations at Quebec such as the Agriculture Society and the Quebec Emigrants' Society, but this was not a happy time for Loring: a daughter died in 1820 and another daughter and his wife in 1822.

In October 1821 Loring was invited to assist Lieutenant-Colonel John Harvey* in the deputy adjutant general's department, and he moved to Montreal as superintendent of the quartermaster general's department. From September 1825 he acted as assistant adjutant general at York in the absence of Lieutenant-Colonel Colley Lyons Lucas FOSTER. Placed on half pay on 20 March 1827, he left for England on leave that summer. Soon after his return in September 1828 he was notified that he had been appointed an inspecting field officer of militia in Nova Scotia with the rank of lieutenant-colonel. Loring arrived there in the spring of 1829 and remained for eight years performing routine administrative tasks until early 1837, when the House of Assembly repealed the grant to the inspecting field officers. On 1 Jan. 1838 he was appointed to be "Employed on a Particular Service" in the Canadas. Again placed on half pay on 29 October, in November 1839 he was permitted to sell his commission. He appears to have lived off the proceeds at his Toronto home until his death.

Robert Roberts Loring was the quintessential staff officer, a quality which was recognized early and utilized by a number of commanders. His name appears in a huge volume of correspondence, but almost all the documents reflect his work, and his personal life remains largely hidden. He did have one serious personal problem, however, which arose directly from his staff position. In 1814 Drummond granted him 700 acres in Lincoln County, Upper Canada. These lands had previously been granted to two different persons, but when it was discovered that one of the lots included a salt spring, the original grantees were induced to locate elsewhere. A complicated series of mistakes allowed two other families to settle on the land. When Loring received the lots, it was charged that he was taking advantage of his position on Drummond's staff. He refused to give them up, paying one of the settlers for his improvements but wrangling for years with the other. Local residents and government officials in Toronto and London had strong feelings about the issue. Many sided with Loring, but he was left with a clouded reputation because others could never accept that he had not used his connections for personal gain.

CARL CHRISTIE

PAC, MG 11, [CO 42] Q, 133, 255, 320–26, 330; MG 24, K2; RG 8, I (C ser.), 2–4, 51, 122, 126, 170, 192, 203, 234–35, 240, 273, 280, 605, 747, 900, 973, 1176–77, 1181–82, 1186, 1188, 1203½P. *Doc. hist. of campaign upon Niagara frontier* (Cruikshank). *Select British docs. of War of 1812* (Wood). *Quebec Gazette*, 11 July 1805; 6 April 1815; 25 May 1815–29 Feb. 1816; 4 Dec. 1817; 19 March, 31 Aug. 1818; 9 Aug., 26 Nov. 1821; 15 July 1822. G.B., WO, *Army list*, 1805–40. W. R. O'Byrne, *A naval biographical dictionary: comprising the life and service of every living officer in Her Majesty's navy . . .* (London, 1849). C. W. Humphries, "The capture of York," *The defended border: Upper Canada and the War of 1812 . . .*, ed. Morris Zaslow and W. B. Turner (Toronto, 1964), 251–70. G. F. G. Stanley, *The War of 1812: land operations* ([Toronto], 1983).

LOUNT, SAMUEL, blacksmith, surveyor's assistant, businessman, politician, and rebel; b. 24 Sept. 1791 in Catawissa, Pa, eldest son of Gabriel Lount and Philadelphia Hughes; m. 1815 Elizabeth Soules, and they had seven children; hanged 12 April 1838 in Toronto.

Samuel Lount first came to Upper Canada when his father brought the family to Whitchurch Township in 1811, but he returned to Pennsylvania on business and spent the duration of the War of 1812 in the United States. Returning to Whitchurch in 1815, for the next three years Lount studied blacksmithing and he became an excellent craftsman. In the fall of 1818 he moved to Newmarket, where he kept a tavern for two years. During that time Lount, who was a skilled woodsman, assisted his brother George in the surveying of West Gwillimbury, Tecumseth, and Innisfil townships. He also explored the Nottawasaga River for the government in preparation for settlement.

Lount next lived in Whitchurch for about a year and a half, and then moved to the Holland Landing area. He was primarily a blacksmith, helping to build the first steamboat on Lake Simcoe, the *Sir John Colborne*, but he also kept a store in partnership with George for several years, and during the last two years of his life he was a farmer. An extremely generous man, Lount was sought out by many who immigrated to the Lake Simcoe region. He provided advice and assistance without thought of compensation and became one of the most highly respected settlers in the area. This stature led to offers of public office and requests that he become a candidate for the House of Assembly, but Lount preferred to remain in the background. He turned down the position of registrar of lands for Simcoe County in favour of George, and when asked to run for the assembly in 1828 he declined and supported John Cawthra.

In 1834 Lount was persuaded to run for Simcoe County and was successful. With his strong concern for his fellow man, he gravitated to the reformers, and he became a friend and ally of William Lyon Mackenzie*. In the election of 1836 Lount was defeated by William Benjamin Robinson*, who was assisted by what the reformers felt were corrupt practices on the part of the provincial executive, and he became disillusioned with normal political processes. He thus participated in the political union movement of the summer and fall of 1837 which was designed to pressure the British government to effect reforms. In the fall Lount was one of the small number of locally prominent men whom Mackenzie approached with a scheme to replace the provincial government with one responsive to the needs of the people.

Lount eagerly agreed to the plan, which involved a march on Toronto on 7 December, because he was assured by Mackenzie that it could be accomplished without bloodshed and would have the approval of prominent supporters of the government. He used his popularity in the area south of Lake Simcoe to influence many others to join the march. When a message from Dr John Rolph* urged that the uprising be advanced to 4 December to forestall rumoured preparations by the government, Lount led one of the first parties to reach Montgomery's Tavern, north of Toronto, the headquarters selected by Mackenzie.

Lount was at the centre of activity until the rebellion failed on the 7th. However, the deaths of a rebel and a loyalist on the first night gave him strong misgivings about the venture. Despite Mackenzie's opposition, he attempted to get medical aid for the dying loyalist, Colonel Robert Moodie. On 5 December, Lount and David Gibson* stopped Mackenzie from burning Sheriff William Botsford Jarvis*'s house as he had burned the home of Dr Robert Charles HORNE.

When loyalist forces dispersed the rebels on 7 December, Lount tried to flee to the United States. He and another man attempted to row across Lake Erie but were blown back and arrested as possible smugglers. Accused of treason, Lount pleaded guilty and petitioned for mercy. Despite supporting petitions bearing thousands of signatures, Lieutenant Governor Sir George Arthur* and the Executive Council decided that some examples had to be made and condemned him to death. Lount and Peter MATTHEWS were executed on 12 April 1838 in the courtyard of the Toronto jail. The government then confiscated Lount's small amount of property.

RONALD J. STAGG

[One of the best sources of information on Lount's life is a letter written by his wife Elizabeth. This appears in the Mackenzie–Lindsey papers, Mackenzie corr., at AO, MS 516; it is to William Lyon Mackenzie and is dated 12 April 1850, from Pontiac, Mich. Another excellent source is A. F. Hunter, *A history of Simcoe County* (2v., Barrie, Ont., 1909; repr. 2v. in 1, 1948). A small amount of biographical detail is also to be found in George Lount's petition to the Executive Council, dated 2 Jan. 1840, in PAC, RG 1, E3, 46, file 38. Lount's version of his role in the rebellion is contained in his petition in PAC, RG 5, A1: 107033–38, and his statement in RG 5, C1, 9, file 1209. For a broader discussion of Lount's role and additional sources, see R. J. Stagg, "The Yonge Street rebellion of 1837: an examination of the social background and a re-assessment of the events" (PHD thesis, Univ. of Toronto, 1976). R.J.S.]

LUGGER, ROBERT, Church of England clergyman and educator; b. 11 Feb. 1793 in Plymouth Dock (Plymouth), England, son of Joseph Lugger and his wife Elizabeth; d. 28 June 1837 in Plymouth.

The son of a gentleman, Robert Lugger received a grammar school education and was prepared for a professional career. That career was deferred, however, by a stint in the Royal Artillery during the Napoleonic Wars, one which carried over into the post-war period when he was assigned in 1817 to fortification projects in Barbados. But clearly he also found time to pursue his long-held plan to become a teacher. Backed by the Church Missionary Society, he organized what he called a "National Negro School" on the island in 1818 and endeavoured, through the use of the innovative Bell system of monitorial instruction, to deal with the circumstances of a slave society. The experience convinced him that "*education alone will never do*, unless the ground be broken up and the *good seed* sown at the *same time*." His subsequent missionary career in Upper Canada would be fully committed to a merger of the tutorial and the spiritual.

Following a medical discharge from the army and his return to England in 1819, he matriculated at St Catharine's College, Cambridge, was ordained in 1823, and received his degree the following year. At the college he appears to have befriended a brother of Sir Peregrine Maitland*, the lieutenant governor of Upper Canada. Sir Peregrine was known to take a keen interest in the welfare of its Indian inhabitants and this connection, combined with the influence at Cambridge of the evangelical movement, may well have shaped Lugger's course as a missionary and inspired his later comment that he would be willing to collaborate with missionaries of other persuasions.

The occasion presented itself in 1827 when he was interviewed and accepted by the New England Company to serve as its first resident missionary among the Six Nations in the Grand River valley of Upper Canada. The company, a lay organization formed in the 17th century to minister to New England's Indians, had been forced to shift its labours to New Brunswick after the American revolution. But difficulties there with "wandering" Micmacs and Malecites made the sedentary Iroquois community on the Grand a more tempting field. Of the six nations, the Mohawks held out the most promise. For some years they had been calling for a resident Anglican missionary and repeatedly complained of the failure of the Society for the Propagation of the Gospel, hitherto the principal missionary agency at work among them, to meet their needs on a regular basis. They had had to get by with visits from clergymen at Niagara (Niagara-on-the-Lake) or Ancaster [*see* Ralph Leeming*] and services conducted by catechists such as Henry Aaron Hill [Kenwendeshon*]. Lugger was the person selected by the New England Company on 15 June 1827 to put things right.

Lugger's knowledge of the Iroquois came from extensive reading and from conversations with William Wilberforce, the abolitionist, who had informed him of the educational work at Grand River of John Norton*. Like Norton and like the Moravians, who worked among the Delawares at New Fairfield (Moraviantown) [*see* Christian Frederick DENKE], Lugger planned to combine conventional religious instruction with training in the mechanical arts. He was also anxious to follow the Bell system and he had every expectation of "getting the Mohawk School as forward as possible in order to send out teachers to other parts."

The community that greeted Lugger in 1827, made up of some 2,200 Iroquois, including roughly 600 Mohawks, had for years been unflatteringly described by overseas visitors who did not share an earlier generation's fascination with the "simple nobility" of the Indian. But for Lugger, the incurably optimistic missionary-teacher, there were encouraging signs. For one thing, John Brant [Tekarihogen*], the well-regarded son of Joseph [Thayendanegea*], had tried to keep alive the cultural initiatives that his father had launched at the Grand River. He had, for example, seen to the completion of two schools near the Mohawk chapel. After his arrival Lugger collaborated for a time with John Brant, notably in the compilation of a Mohawk grammar.

Although he was greeted warmly by the Mohawks, Lugger fared less well among those Senecas, Cayugas, and Delawares who embraced the teachings of Skanyadariyoh (Handsome Lake), the Seneca prophet who had sparked a dramatic revival of traditional Iroquois religious practices at the turn of the century and who had scorned the Indians' adoption of white ways. All the same, Lugger enjoyed some success among the Onondagas, Oneidas, and Tuscaroras; the Tuscaroras indeed requested and received a missionary of their own, the Reverend Abram Nelles*, who served as Lugger's assistant.

More troublesome than Handsome Lake's legacy was the competition Lugger faced from the Methodists' ambitious presence in the valley. Their successes among the Iroquois [*see* Tehowagherengaraghkwen*] probably eroded Lugger's aim to work closely with other missionaries and fostered in him the high church tendencies that a visiting Presbyterian clergyman, William Proudfoot*, observed. There was also a falling out with John Brant in 1831 over the competing claims of Methodism and the Church of England in the valley. Brant and his followers among the Upper Mohawks sided with the Methodists while the Lower Mohawks (the two groups were named after their original villages in the Mohawk valley) clung to Lugger. Brant also accused the missionary of trying to undermine his authority by dismissing a teacher whom he favoured. All of this was accompanied by the criticism some chiefs levelled against the instruction offered in the mission's schools for the way it was weakening such traditional pursuits as hunting and fishing.

In spite of controversy Lugger persevered with what became in 1831 the show-piece of his mission – his long-sought-after school of industry for teaching skills to the Indians, known after 1850 as the Mohawk Institute. In spite of Indian scepticism and hostility, classes were organized to teach spinning and weaving to the girls and carpentry, tailoring, and farming to the boys. Then, to reinforce the institution as an educational centre, he converted it into a boarding-school in 1836, even though some officials warned that the concept was totally alien to the Indian. The venture survived and in recent times has been transformed into a thriving cultural centre for Woodland Indians.

Its founder, however, did not live to see the fruition of his show-piece. Barely months after the boarding-school opened, an ailing Lugger returned to England, where he died. On the eve of his departure a delegation of Mohawks and Oneidas had returned him their "sincere thanks . . . for all the good things you have done . . . as well as for our temporal as our Eternal interests." Both Lugger and his wife were complimented on their efforts to protect the Indians from the worst effects of the white man's world and to bring to them not only the Word of God, but medicines and emotional comfort when they had fallen ill.

Although missionary activity has come to be denigrated as the spiritual component of an aggressive imperialism that paid scant heed to non-European cultures, Lugger's career from "palm" to "pine" could be perceived as having played a part in cushioning the impact of a dynamic civilization upon ones much less so, and as having applied ameliorative educational formulas then flourishing in the imperial metropolis to an island in the Caribbean and a frontier in Upper Canada.

CHARLES M. JOHNSTON

AO, MS 35, unbound papers, extract from letter by T. G. Anderson to Mr Partlock, 6 Nov. 1826; John Strachan, draft of letter to Church Missionary Soc., 27 Feb. 1827. BL, Add. MSS 21882: 106. Devon Record Office, West Devon Area (Plymouth, Eng.), 166/8 (Stoke Damerel), reg. of baptisms, 19 July 1794. Guildhall Library (London), MSS 7913/2: 166, 171, 175; 7920/2: 75–76, 82, 244–45, 262, 265–67, 273–74; 7920/3: 69, 95; 7923: 148–50, 159; 7956, 24 Feb. 1806, 17 Jan. 1815 (New England Company papers). RHL, USPG Arch., journals of SPG, 39: 235, 239. Six Nations Indian Office Arch. (Brantford, Ont.), Chisholm file, accounts and letters; Council letter-book, 1832–37; Six Nations *vs*. New England Company; Statistical report, 1827. G.B., Parl., House of Commons paper, 1836, 7, no.538: 1–853, *Report from the select committee on aborigines (British settlements)* . . . , 49, 635. John Howison, *Sketches of Upper Canada, domestic, local, and characteristic* . . . (Edinburgh and London, 1821; repr. Toronto, 1970). John Norton, *The journal of Major John Norton, 1816*, ed. C. F. Klinck and J. J. Talman (Toronto, 1970). *Valley of Six Nations* (Johnston). John West, *A journal of a mission to the Indians of the British provinces, of New Brunswick, and Nova Scotia, and the Mohawks, on the Ouse, or Grand River, Upper Canada* (London, 1827). *Alumni Cantabrigienses* . . . , comp. John and J. A. Venn (2 pts. in 10v., Cambridge, Eng., 1922–54). S. D. Clark, *Church and sect in Canada* (Toronto, 1948). Elizabeth Graham, *Medicine man to missionary: missionaries as agents of change among the Indians of southern Ontario, 1784–1867* (Toronto, 1975). C. M. Johnston, "To the Mohawk Station: the making of a New England Company missionary – the Rev. Robert Lugger," *Extending the rafters: interdisciplinary approaches to Iroquoian studies*, ed. M. K. Foster *et al.* (Albany, N.Y., 1984), 65–80. J. W. Lydekker, *The faithful Mohawks* (Cambridge, 1938). Robert Potts, *Liber Cantabrigiensis* . . . (Cambridge and London, 1855). Annemarie Shimony, *Conservatism among the Iroquois at the Six Nations Reserve* (New Haven, Conn., 1961). Isabel Thompson Kelsay, *Joseph Brant, 1743–1807: man of two worlds* (Syracuse, N.Y., 1984). J. D. Wilson, "'No blanket to be worn in school': the education of Indians in early nineteenth-century Ontario," *SH*, 7 (1974): 293–305.

LUSHER, ROBERT LANGHAM, Methodist minister, author, and newspaper editor; b. *c.* 1787 in London; m. Esther ——, and they had at least one son and two daughters; d. 10 July 1849 in Montreal.

Robert Langham Lusher was attracted to the Methodist movement as a young man. In 1817, having been accepted as a probationer for the ministry, he was appointed by the British Wesleyan Conference to overseas missionary work. Lusher's first assignment was Montreal, where he arrived with his young family late in 1817. Except for a year in Quebec, from 1817 until the summer of 1822 he served the Montreal circuit; while there he was received into full connection by the British conference in 1821.

At Lusher's arrival in Montreal, the town's Methodists numbered probably fewer than 100 and were largely loyalists of the mercantile and artisan classes. They were divided in their allegiance to American or British church authorities, but by 1820 had united under the British Wesleyan Conference. Lusher's style of preaching soon began to make Methodism respectable in Montreal, overcoming the prevailing prejudice against Methodist preachers as what a letter in the *Montreal Gazette* termed "strolling enthusiasts." He was able to obtain civil registers for baptisms, marriages, and burials and the Montreal Methodist society increased in numbers and affluence so that a larger chapel was soon required. The Methodist Chapel, as it was called, was completed in 1821. Under Lusher's leadership Methodists co-operated with other denominations in establishing several religious and benevolent institutions such as the Montreal General Hospital and the Emigrant Society of Montreal. He was, however, disappointed by one development within his own denomination: the agreement of 1820 between British and American Methodist authorities [*see* Henry Ryan*] which left Upper Canada under the influence of the American preachers, many of whom, he believed, held the "[British] constitution and Government in the utmost contempt."

In 1822 Lusher was appointed to Halifax and in 1825 to Liverpool, N.S. On both circuits he travelled to isolated settlements along the southern shore. He returned to England in 1827 and served in Oldham, Halifax, Manchester, and Bath. At the request of the

Montreal Methodist society, in 1838 he was once again assigned to the Montreal circuit by the Wesleyan Missionary Committee of the British conference and at the same time was appointed to preside over the Lower Canada District, a post he held for a year.

Relations between the British Wesleyan Conference, responsible for Lower Canada, and the Canada Conference, presiding in Upper Canada, were greatly strained. One of the chief points at issue was the policy of the *Christian Guardian*, edited by Egerton Ryerson*, who did not hesitate to criticize government policy on the disposition of the clergy reserves. In a letter to fellow minister Robert Alder*, Lusher perhaps reflected a typically British attitude in his horror of the *Christian Guardian*'s "inflammatory character . . . calculated to promote dissatisfaction and disaffection to the Government" as well as its "anti-Wesleyan position in reference to the Church of England and its union with the state." In August 1840, immediately after the British Wesleyan Conference had officially broken its link with the Canada Conference (Lower Canada remaining as it had been, a district in direct connection with the British conference), a new church paper, the *Wesleyan*, appeared. It was published twice monthly in Montreal with Lusher as its first editor. The aim of the *Wesleyan* was to disseminate British Methodist news and opinion throughout the Canadas, no doubt as an antidote to the influence of the *Christian Guardian*. After a year Lusher gave up the editorship and in 1842 moved to Trois-Rivières. The paper resumed publication in Toronto.

Lusher's later years were clouded by ill health. After serving the Trois-Rivières circuit for less than two years, he retired in 1843 to live in Montreal among the members of his former congregation, who greatly revered him. Robert Langham Lusher's contribution to the social and religious life of British North America was conservative rather than creative or original. In upholding a British attitude of uncritical deference to authority he perhaps failed to appreciate the need of the colonial church to shape its witness within its own social context.

NATHAN H. MAIR

Robert Langham Lusher is the author of *The last journey: a funeral address, delivered . . . July 8, 1838, occasioned by the death of the late Rev. John Barry . . .* (Montreal, 1838); *The laws of Wesleyan Methodism epitomized and arranged . . .* (Manchester, Eng., 1834); *Recollections of the outlines of a sermon, delivered . . . April 3, 1825, on occasion of the death of Mrs. Eunice Waterman . . .* (Halifax, 1827); and *A sermon, preached at the Wesleyan Chapel, Quebec, Sunday, March 26th, 1820, occasioned by the death of his late majesty George the Third* (Montreal, 1820). He was the editor for the first volume of the *Wesleyan*, which was published at Montreal from 6 Aug. 1840 to 8 July 1841.

St James United Church (Montreal), Memorial letter-book, 17 Jan. 1842. SOAS, Methodist Missionary Soc. Arch., Wesleyan Methodist Missionary Soc., corr., North America (mfm. at UCC, Maritime Conference Arch., Halifax). UCC, Montreal-Ottawa Conference Arch. (Montreal), 7/StJ/1/1; Montreal Presbytery, St James Street Methodist Chapel (Montreal), reg. *Wesleyan* (Toronto), 2 (1841–42)–3 (1842–43). Wesleyan Methodist Church, *Minutes of the conferences* (London), 11 (1848–51). Wesleyan Methodist Church in Canada, *The minutes of the annual conferences . . . from 1824 to 1845 . . .* (Toronto, 1846). *Wesleyan-Methodist Magazine*, 41 (1818)–43 (1820); 48 (1825)–49 (1826); 54 (1831). *Canada Temperance Advocate* (Montreal), February–March 1840. *Canadian Courant and Montreal Advertiser*, 23, 30 Jan., 6 Feb., 18 Dec. 1819; 5 June 1821. *Christian Guardian*, 25 July 1849. *Montreal Gazette*, 28 Nov. 1808. *Montreal Herald*, 11 Oct. 1817–20 March 1819; 18 Dec. 1819; 17, 24 Feb. 1821; 26 Jan. 1822. *Montreal Transcript*, 21 Oct. 1837; 2 Jan., 31 May, 14 June 1838; 8 Aug. 1840; 10 July 1849. Borthwick, *Hist. and biog. gazetteer*. G. H. Cornish, *Cyclopædia of Methodism in Canada, containing historical, educational, and statistical information . . .* (2v., Toronto and Halifax, 1881–1903). E. A. Betts, *Bishop Black and his preachers* (2nd ed., Sackville, N.B., 1976). J. [S.] Carroll, *Case and his cotemporaries . . .* (5v., Toronto, 1867–77). G. E. Jacques, *Chronicles of the St-James St. Methodist Church, Montreal, from the first rise of Methodism in Montreal to the laying of the corner-stone of the new church on St. Catherine Street* (Toronto, 1888). N. H. Mair, *The people of St James, Montreal, 1803–1984* ([Montreal, 1984]). J. H. Turner, *Halifax books and authors . . .* (Brighouse, Eng., 1906).

LYMBURNER, ADAM, merchant, militia officer, colonial agent, and politician; b. 1745 or 1746 in Kilmarnock, Scotland; d. unmarried 10 Jan. 1836 in London.

Adam Lymburner came to Quebec to take over the business of his brother John, who had disappeared at sea in 1772. John had arrived in the new British colony by 1761 as a result of mercantile associations with Brook Watson* and Robert Hunter, the latter a London merchant with connections among Ayrshire-men in the Quebec trade. He had built up operations that included sealing, whaling, and salmon fishing from posts on the remote Labrador coast. Established at Quebec, Adam immediately engaged in the triangular fishing trade. Typical was an arrangement in 1773–74 whereby Hunter purchased a ship for George Cartwright*, a Labrador merchant, who dispatched it to Cadiz, Spain, for wine that Lymburner would market at Quebec, where the ship took on, for Cartwright's post at Charles Harbour, bread and other supplies generally "cheaper . . . than in England."

During the American invasion of Quebec in 1775, Lymburner served in the British militia, rising to the rank of second lieutenant. In October, with other officers, he "insisted" that Governor Guy Carleton* compel resident Americans either to leave the city or to take up arms in its defence. By early December, however, Lymburner had resigned from the militia;

historian François-Xavier Garneau* has caustically asserted that he fled to Charlesbourg, but his reasons for resigning and his whereabouts that winter remain obscure. On 31 December his house on Rue du Sault-au-Matelot, in Lower Town Quebec, was the scene of vicious combat.

At the end of 1775 Lymburner's commercial interests extended from Britain well into the Canadian interior. He owned one of the 11 vessels then engaged in the Quebec trade (3 were owned by Hunter) and was involved in the fur trade from Montreal. In 1776 he provided security on the licence of a Montreal fur trader supplied by Hunter, and two years later he hired a clerk for Jean-Étienne Waddens*, who was also supplied by Hunter and was connected to John McKindlay*, an Ayrshire "relation" of Lymburner. In 1787 Lymburner was the Quebec agent for Richard Dobie*, another fur trader.

Although Lymburner's fishing posts were hit hard by an American privateer in 1779 and "fail'd" in 1782, they remained the central element in his import-export business. By 1783, in association with William Grant* and Thomas Dunn*, Lymburner and his brother Mathew dominated sealing along the Labrador–Gulf of St Lawrence coast. The return of peace that year increased competition for fishing locations, and Quebec's merchants, led by the Lymburners and Grant's nephew David Alexander Grant, pressed for official action against intrusions by American vessels, a concern that lasted until at least 1785.

About 1781 Lymburner had brought his brother and John Crawford, their nephew, into his business as clerks. Strictly trained by Adam, who intended eventually to return to Britain, Mathew became his junior partner and with Crawford carried on operations (mainly the fisheries) from about 1786 or 1787, functioning in a commercial chain that included Hunter in London and McKindlay and William Parker, another Ayrshireman, in Montreal. Mathew's involvement allowed Adam to travel, mostly through the United States, and to throw himself into the province's constitutional debates, for which he had exceptional social and political "abilities," as remarked in the diaries of aspiring merchants Joseph Hadfield and Robert Hunter Jr in 1785. Constantly polite, and hospitable despite chronic asthma, Lymburner possessed a "usage du monde," as Hunter put it, that stood him in good stead with most of Quebec's "first characters," British and Canadian. In June Hunter was impressed by Lymburner's account of a recent American tour, including a visit with George Washington, and struck as well by Lymburner's "fine head of hair instead of a wig he used to wear."

On constitutional matters Lymburner shared the radical concerns of such merchants as George Allsopp* and William Grant. During an unruly debate in the Legislative Council in April 1784 over the introduction of habeas corpus, Lymburner was among a small group of men who clamoured for admission to the council chamber. In November he signed a petition for a representative assembly which quickly became the basis of sustained agitation for reform. To an investigation in 1787 into the administration of justice [*see* Sir James Monk*] he recounted his losses as a result of appearances in the Court of Common Pleas; judge Adam Mabane* described him with disdain as "one of those subjects who left the province in November 1775." Following on the investigation he was sent by Canadian and British committees to London to press the petition of 1784 and repeal of the Quebec Act, judicial reform, and the institution of English commercial law. Seen by Carleton, now Lord Dorchester, as a "decent sensible man" with "no hostile intentions to administration," and equipped with instructions from the committees, he arrived in London in December 1787.

Lymburner lobbied persistently to have the constitutional issue brought before parliament. Acting with a group of influential merchants, notably Hunter Sr and Watson, he marshalled and drafted documentation (including a pamphlet in 1788), challenged contrary positions, and spoke eloquently before the bar of the House of Commons. Faced by ministers concerned with European and broader imperial questions and with such domestic issues as the trial of Warren Hastings for corruption and cruelty in India and George III's bouts of presumed insanity, Lymburner lamented the lack of interest demonstrated by British politicians in Canadian affairs. His argumentation, often bordering on blatant propaganda, stirred up the parliamentary opposition, however. "Mr [William] Pitt was as roughly handled and closely pinned down as ever he was in that House," Lymburner reported to the British committee at Quebec in May 1788. "I have . . . ," he claimed with some exaggeration, "opened the eyes of ministry with regard to our Province."

Lymburner's efforts to maintain a close correspondence with the committees in the colony were made difficult in 1788 by their inability to agree on instructions to him. To its support of the program of 1784 the Canadian committee added a request for the restoration of the province's general laws as they had existed at the time of the conquest. As well, it demanded that the Roman Catholic Church be released from the "King's Supremacy" (as imposed by the Quebec Act) and that the properties of Quebec's religious communities be confirmed. Alarmed by these instructions, Quebec's attorney general, James Monk, considered naïve Lymburner's supposed belief that commercial interests could ensure a British majority in an assembly. He advised Watson to keep a cautionary hand on the zealous agent, whose commercial association with many Canadians, he told former attorney general Francis Maseres*, probably biased his representations. Lymburner, however, needed no control; he prudently submerged the Canadian demands and the differences in his instructions.

More problematic for Lymburner was the division of the province, a key part of the closely kept constitutional plan devised by Home Secretary William Wyndham Grenville in 1789. Lymburner strenuously opposed partition, preferring instead coexistence of the sort displayed by Scotland and England. During the spring of 1790 he vainly tried, through MPs Thomas Powys and Charles James Fox, to discover the full details of Grenville's plan. The following year he lobbied futilely with Grenville, his successor Henry Dundas, and former under-secretary Evan Nepean, pressing his original demands. On 23 March 1791 he appealed impassionately at the bar of the Commons for a "united Province," asserting that two governments would create debilitating expense and that the proposed provinces were linked geographically and economically. He added, prophetically, that since the only ocean ports would be in the lower province the colonies would become enmeshed in fiscal dispute. Claiming to represent both Canadian and British colonists, he played down the fact that the British would politically be in a minority in the new lower province by concentrating on past grievances: "the exhausted and impoverished State" of the province, arbitrary government, and legal and judicial uncertainty. His plea against division falling on deaf ears, he later shifted his attention to representation in the assembly of the lower province. With typical initiative, he submitted a plan to Dundas calling for Montreal and Quebec to have seven members each, a proposal Dundas dismissed outright. Nevertheless the Constitutional Act of 1791 contained some of the reforms that Lymburner had urged on behalf of the British and Canadian committees.

Lymburner's efforts did not go unrecognized. On 16 Sept. 1791, while still in England, he was appointed to Lower Canada's Executive Council. Three months later Quebec's merchants gathered at the Merchant's Coffee House to pass a resolution of thanks. The following year he was posted as a candidate for Lower Town Quebec in the new province's first general election, but he was defeated in absentia. Though he would later claim credit for the introduction of a representative assembly, in the early 1790s it was his reservations about the constitution that claimed attention in the Canadas. In 1794 a disheartened Upper Canadian loyalist, Richard Cartwright*, wrote to Isaac Todd* that "experience has almost made me a convert to Mr. Lymburner's opinion . . . that the country would be found unequal to support the expence of two Governments."

Lymburner remained in England after 1791 with a "Complaint of an Asthmatic Nature – for which he was informed the severe cold of the winters in Canada was extremely . . . pernicious." While recovering there, he took every opportunity to tender to government his views on Lower Canadian affairs. His paper on the Anglo-American tensions of 1793, which typically had no evident effect, did illustrate his grasp of the complex relationship between commerce and transatlantic diplomacy. In 1799 he returned to Quebec. Having ignored a warning from Dorchester in 1794 to attend the Executive Council or resign, he attempted to take his place in July but on a unanimous motion was ignominiously barred for non-attendance. His petitions to Britain in protest proved fruitless.

Despite his absences in England, Lymburner had remained lucratively involved in the Labrador fisheries. In 1795 he sold his commercial properties in Lower Town Quebec to his brother, who would continue in the salmon and seal trades until about 1823. Vigorously managed by Mathew, the Labrador posts were operated under two main companies: Lymburner and Crawford, until after the latter's death in 1803, and the New Labrador Company from 1808. Adam, in addition to registering several vessels with his brother and William Grant, helped finance and supply Mathew's activities, in part from Joseph Hadfield in Britain; however, the full extent of Adam's concern remains unclear.

In 1807 Lymburner returned permanently to London, but his interest in Lower Canadian affairs remained undiminished. He corresponded over the next 16 years with Roman Catholic bishop Joseph-Octave Plessis*, who respected his advice on church-state relations and praised him as "a friend of the Catholics, although Protestant." Plessis, however, almost certainly did not share his friend's view of the Roman Catholic and Anglican churches as "fellow labourers in different parts of the same vineyard." Lymburner's letters display his propensity to flatter and charm, and the bishop probably exaggerated his influence with British politicians despite Lymburner's confession in 1810 that since his return he had been avoiding them. At the same time Lymburner's separation from Lower Canada made it difficult for him to comprehend the "acrimonious" state of politics there during the governorship of Sir James Henry Craig*. In 1814 he deplored the fact that the Canadas did not maintain authorized agents in London to inform ministers of affairs as did most colonial assemblies.

The 1820s were for Lymburner years of continued, almost nostalgic, interest in Lower Canada and of severe rheumatism, which he linked to his inactivity during winters there. Drawing upon his substantial wealth, he toured Europe in 1822, only to be shocked at how deep the seeds "sown by the french revolution" had put down roots. His spirits revived later that year when Plessis invited him to oppose an imperial bill for uniting the Canadas, which had originated among the lower province's civil servants and British merchants. Now viewing the Constitutional Act of 1791 with a sense of personal achievement, he favoured preservation of Lower Canada's distinctive interests. Effort on his part was unnecessary – fortunately, for he was confined to his home. He advised Louis-Joseph Papineau* and John NEILSON, sent in 1823 to oppose the union, that the bill generated little interest at Westminster. "The Delegates will experience some of the difficulties I had to encounter 33 or 34 years ago to get the present constitution for the province," he wrote to Plessis. "No cause of any importance can be supported here without great exertion of body and mind, because the people here feel little interest in the affairs of distant colonies. . . . The great object is to instruct the speakers fully on the facts of the case. . . . But my time of activity is past. It is a new scene for M[rss] Papineau and Neilson."

Lymburner died on 10 Jan. 1836, at about age 91, and at his request was buried in St George's Church, Bloomsbury (London), alongside Alexander Auldjo*, a long-time friend from colonial days. Lymburner bequeathed sums and annuities totalling £88,150 to numerous nieces and nephews, their children, the children of friends, and others. Properties in Kilmarnock, including those inherited from his father, were left to a grandnephew there.

DAVID ROBERTS

[Adam Lymburner is the author of a pamphlet printed in London in 1788, no copy of which has been positively identified. This item is possibly *A review of the government and grievances of the province of Quebec, since the conquest of it by the British arms . . .*, which is generally attributed to Francis Maseres, but reflects Lymburner's style and specific interests. He is also the author of *Paper read at the bar of the House of Commons, by Mr. Lymburner, agent for the subscribers to the petitions from the province of Quebec, bearing date the 24th of November 1784 . . .* (Quebec, 1791). There is a portrait of Lymburner at the MTRL. D.R.]

ANQ-Q, CN1-230, 7 août 1795, 4 nov. 1796, 10 oct. 1804; CN1-262, 26 nov. 1799, 26 févr. 1803, 3 janv. 1806; P-313, 2, George Allsopp to A. M. Allsopp, 4 Nov. 1799, 6 June 1801. ASQ, Polygraphie, XXXVII, no.12. AUM, P 58, U, Lymburner à Jacques Perrault, 25–26 mars 1790; 5 janv., 12 juill. 1791. BL, Add. MSS 21759: 116–19; 21867: 145. Greater London Record Office (London), P82/GEO1/59, 72. McGill Univ. Libraries, Dept. of Rare Books and Special Coll., MS coll., CH293.S253. PAC, MG 19, A2, ser.3, 2: 23, 97, 104–5; 20: 2755; MG 23, A2, 10: 61–73, 98–100; GII, 19, vol.2: 66–93; GIII, 1, vol.1: 150–77; MG 24, L3: 28443–53 (copies); RG 4, A1: 7103–4; A3, 1; RG 42, E1, 1381–82. Private arch., David Roberts (Toronto), A. J. H. Richardson, "Adam Lymburner, etc." PRO, CO 5/147: 13–15 (copies at PAC); CO 42/1, 42/5, 42/25, 42/34, 42/48, 42/51–52, 42/59, 42/61, 42/63, 42/65–66, 42/72, 42/87–88, 42/93, 42/104, 42/107, 42/113–15, 42/120; PROB 11/1856: 11292–94. William L. Clements Library, Univ. of Mich. (Ann Arbor), Melville papers, Lymburner to Henry Dundas, 18 Sept. 1793.

[George] Cartwright, *Captain Cartwright and his Labrador journal*, intro. W. T. Grenfell, ed. C. W. Townshend (Boston, 1911), 148, 170. *Corr. of Lieut. Governor Simcoe* (Cruikshank), vol.1. *Docs. relating to constitutional hist., 1759–91* (Shortt and Doughty; 1918), 742–54, 1029. G.B., Parl., *The parliamentary history of England . . . to the year 1803 . . .* (London), 27 (1788–89): 506–33; Privy Council, Judicial Committee, *In the matter of the boundary between the Dominion of Canada and the colony of Newfoundland in the Labrador peninsula, joint appendix* (12v., London, 1927), 7: 3466–78, 3484, 3492, 3531–32. Joseph Hadfield, *An Englishman in America, 1785, being the diary of Joseph Hadfield*, ed. D. S. Robertson (Toronto, 1933). Robert Hunter, *Quebec to Carolina in 1785–1786; being the travel diary and observations of Robert Hunter, Jr., a young merchant of London*, ed. L. B. Wright and Marion Tinling (San Marino, Calif., 1943), 20. James Jeffry, "Journal kept in Quebec in 1775 by James Jeffry," ed. William Smith, Essex Institute, *Hist. Coll.* (Salem, Mass.), 50 (1914): 125, 141. "Journal of the principal occurrences during the siege of Quebec by the American revolutionists under generals Montgomery and Arnold in 1775–76," ed. W. T. P. Short, *Blockade of Quebec in 1775–1776 by the American revolutionists (les Bastonnais)*, ed. F. C. Würtele (Quebec, 1906; repr. Port Washington, N.Y., and London, 1970), 55–101. "Orderly book begun by Captain Anthony Vialar of the British militia . . . ," ed. F. C. Würtele, Literary and Hist. Soc. of Quebec, *Hist. docs.* (Quebec), 7th ser. (1905): 155–265. Simeon Perkins, *The diary of Simeon Perkins, 1797–1803*, ed. C. B. Fergusson (Toronto, 1967). William Smith, *The diary and selected papers of Chief Justice William Smith, 1784–1793*, ed. L. F. S. Upton (2v., Toronto, 1963–65). *Quebec Gazette*, 1764–1823. *Quebec Herald and Universal Miscellany*, 15 Dec. 1788, 16 Nov. 1789. Caron, "Inv. de la corr. de Mgr Plessis," ANQ *Rapport*, 1927–28, 1928–29, 1932–33.

Marie Tremaine, *A bibliography of Canadian imprints, 1751–1800* (Toronto, 1952), 333–34, 361. E. T. D. Chambers, *The fisheries of the province of Quebec, part I: historical introduction* (Quebec, 1912). Christie, *Hist. of L.C.* (1866), 1: 74–115. John Ehrman, *The younger Pitt: the years of acclaim* (New York, 1964). F.-X. Garneau, *Histoire du Canada depuis sa découverte jusqu'à nos jours*, Alfred Garneau, édit. (4e éd., 4v., Montréal, 1882–83), 2: 453; 3: 71–72, 240, 244. H. A. Innis, *The cod fisheries; the history of an international economy* (rev. ed., Toronto, 1954). H. M. Neatby, *The administration of justice under the Quebec Act* (London and Minneapolis, Minn., [1937]); *Quebec: the revolutionary age, 1760–1791* (Toronto, 1966). *The Scots abroad: labour, capital, enterprise, 1750–1914*, ed. R. A. Cage (London, 1985). Pierre Tousignant, "La genèse et l'avènement de la constitution de 1791" (thèse de PHD, univ. de Montréal, 1971). "L'honorable Adam Lymburner," *BRH*, 37 (1931): 556–58. Gérard Malchelosse, "Une seigneurie fantôme: Saint-Paul du Labrador," *Cahiers des Dix*, 10 (1945): 293–328. W. H. Whiteley, "Newfoundland, Quebec, and the Labrador merchants, 1783–1809," *Nfld. Quarterly*, 73 (1977), no.4: 18–26.

M

MACALLUM, JOHN, teacher, Church of England minister, office holder, and politician; b. 1806 in Fortrose, Scotland; m. February 1836 Elizabeth Charles in the Red River settlement (Man.), and they had two daughters; d. there 3 Oct. 1849.

John Macallum attended King's College, Aberdeen, from 1820 to 1824 and received an MA from this institution in April 1832. In September 1833, at the age of 27 and with some experience as a schoolmaster, he arrived at Red River. Hired at a salary of £100 per annum, he was to teach at the academy established by the Reverend David Thomas JONES for "the sons of Gentlemen belonging to the Fur Trade." He was initially unimpressed with the calibre of his students. Soon after his arrival he noted in a letter to James Hargrave*, the Hudson's Bay Company's chief officer at York Factory, that "the juvenile mind here is in a melancholy state of vacancy . . . with none of that mass of general information which an English child, properly educated, has accumulated by the time he has reached the fourth year." Macallum was determined to make improvements in the education of these youngsters.

In 1835 the governess of the Red River Academy, Mrs Mary Lowman, retired to marry Chief Factor James Bird*, and Macallum assumed responsibility for both female and male students. He apparently achieved some positive results with the girls, for many parents, including John Dugald Cameron*, were pleased that their daughters were finally learning something other than sewing and cooking. In 1836 he married one of his students, a mixed-blood daughter of Chief Factor John Charles. Two years later Macallum's sister, Margaret, married his wife's father; the resulting relationships of Charles and Macallum caused a stir among the refined ladies of the settlement.

Macallum succeeded Jones as headmaster of the academy in 1837. Initially he leased the buildings from the HBC, which owned the property, but in 1841 he purchased the school for £350. Throughout his tenure he enjoyed the support of the HBC's governor, George Simpson*, and the Council of the Northern Department, which granted him £100 annually to keep the academy running efficiently.

Under Macallum's guidance it maintained a high level of excellence. During his tenure courses were offered in Greek, Latin, geography, Bible study, history, algebra, writing, and elocution. In 1840 he happily assured Hargrave that "the schools are well supported, & supply us with as much work as we can all execute." Two years later he noted that his students' "progress is pleasing, their deportment correct, and their docility, attention, & application highly commendable." One of them, the Reverend Benjamin McKenzie, grandson of Roderick McKenzie*, recalled in 1928 that Macallum "prepared a goodly number of postmasters, clerks and future chief traders and chief factors" for the HBC and was a "conscientious and faithful worker" who "perhaps over-estimated the use of the rod." The letters of Letitia Hargrave [Mactavish*] also suggest that he was a strict disciplinarian, with a strong sense of morality. Indeed, she observed critically in 1843, if Indian or mixed-blood mothers were not formally married he refused to allow them to visit their children, a policy she viewed as "fearfully cruel for the poor unfortunate mothers did not know that there was any distinction." Macallum, however, was unaffected by criticism and the HBC's executive did not seem much concerned.

In June 1844 he was ordained priest by Bishop George Jehoshaphat Mountain*, who was visiting the settlement. He was assigned to St John's parish there, and in March 1845 was made assistant chaplain to the HBC. Macallum nevertheless continued to devote himself to the students at the academy. "He thought the Academy his work, for that he lived," David Anderson*, the first bishop of Rupert's Land, reported in 1850. As a leading resident of the region, Macallum had been appointed in March 1836 to the colony's pioneer government, the Council of Assiniboia. He served as its clerk in 1839, was a member of its committee of economy in 1845, and acted as Red River's coroner from 1839 to 1849.

Macallum suffered an attack of jaundice during the summer of 1849 and never recovered, dying on 3 October. His wife and daughters left Red River the following year to live with her father, who had settled in Edinburgh in 1845. She was so distraught over the death of her husband that she attempted suicide in 1852 and was placed in an asylum for a year. In his will, John Macallum had stipulated that Bishop Anderson should be offered the Red River Academy. He accepted and paid £300 for it. Excellence in education was thus to continue at Red River.

ALLAN LEVINE

PABC, Add. MSS 635, folder 93, Ross to Macallum, 15 March 1848 (photocopy). PAC, MG 19, A21, ser.1, 3, 5–6, 8–9, 11, 15–16, 22, 24. PAM, HBCA, B.135/c/2: f.96; B.239/k/2: ff.158, 169, 173, 184, 189d, 196, 199, 207, 210, 219d, 225, 232d, 233, 236; D.4/23: ff.60d–61; D.4/58: f.162; D.5/4: ff.370–71; D.5/23: ff.357–57d; D.5/26: ff.160, 558–58d, 698–98d; MG 2, C23, no.96. *Canadian north-west* (Oliver), 1: 63, 85, 275–78, 283–84, 317–27, 355. Hargrave, *Hargrave corr.* (Glazebrook). Letitia [Mactavish] Hargrave, *The letters of Letitia Hargrave*, ed. Margaret Arnett MacLeod (Toronto, 1947). Boon, *Anglican Church*. T. F. Bredin, "The Red River Academy," *Beaver*, outfit 305 (winter 1974): 10–17. "Living pupil of 92 recalls

Red River academy of 40's: Rev. Benjamin McKenzie . . . describes Red River settlement school attended by H.B. officers' sons 85 years ago," *Manitoba Free Press* (Winnipeg), 3 March 1928: 9.

MACAULAY, ANN. *See* KIRBY

McCONVILLE, JOHN, schoolteacher; b. *c.* 1793 in Newry (Northern Ireland), son of Meredith McConville and Mary McCardle; m. 7 Jan. 1832 Mary Magdalen Mackie in Berthier-en-Haut (Berthierville), Lower Canada, and they had three daughters and three sons, two of whom, Joseph Norbet Alfred and Arthur, became lawyers; d. 10 Sept. 1849 in Industrie (Joliette), Lower Canada.

Nothing is known of John McConville's life before he came to Lower Canada. At the time he left his native land early in the second decade of the 19th century, he firmly intended to take up a teaching career in the colony. His progress in the profession is rather difficult to follow, but he is known to have been a schoolmaster first in Montreal, then at Vaudreuil, and finally at Berthier-en-Haut, where he settled.

McConville was involved in teaching during the period when the Royal Institution for the Advancement of Learning [*see* Joseph Langley Mills*] was drawing scathing criticism from the Catholic clergy, particularly because of its enforcement of regulations about the hiring of teachers – an enforcement that varied according to the differing interpretations placed on these rules by politicians and churchmen. The Royal Institution in principle appointed teachers able to teach in French to places where the majority of the population was French Canadian, and English-speaking teachers to predominantly English-speaking areas. However, some school inspectors, known as visitors, did not hesitate to turn away candidates on religious grounds.

McConville was one of those rejected. Having learned that Augustus Wolff was giving up teaching, on 22 Sept. 1823 he applied from Vaudreuil, where he was living, for a post as schoolmaster at Berthier-en-Haut. Legislative councillor James Cuthbert, a visitor for the Royal Institution, supported his request. McConville had actually taught Cuthbert's children for seven years. Nevertheless John Campbell Driscoll, the Anglican minister, who replied to McConville, turned him down, citing the regulations, which he seemed to take pleasure in muddling. In his letter of 10 Oct. 1823 he explained that "the Royal Institution requires *Protestant* Masters, able to *teach* and speak the French Language for the *Government* Schools of which Berthier is one." McConville, who was Catholic and was able to teach in French, did in fact meet the hiring requirements. But he did not get a teaching position at Berthier-en-Haut until 1833. He ended his career at the Académie de Berthier [*see* Louis-Marie-Raphaël Barbier*].

In 1836 there were serious discussions in educational circles about establishing normal schools, to train teachers for their profession. When the plan finally took shape, Abbé John Holmes*, from the Petit Séminaire de Québec, was appointed to find people qualified to teach in these schools. On 27 April McConville, who was eager to obtain one of the posts, wrote to Edmund Bailey O'Callaghan*, a trustee of the Montreal normal school. In his letter he mentioned the various teaching positions he had held during his 20-year career and stressed his professional abilities, which included an aptitude for teaching, in both customary languages, history, arithmetic, writing, geography, "the use of the globes," book-keeping, geometry, trigonometry, algebra, surveying, and navigation. Holmes chose to look abroad and sought to engage experienced teachers from the United States, France, and England by contract. McConville was not hired for the normal schools.

Despite his qualifications McConville was not able to achieve fully his professional ambitions. Nevertheless in his long career he demonstrated competence as a schoolmaster.

MARÎSE THIVIERGE

AAQ, 60 CN, A: 36, 42. ANQ-M, CE5-1, 7 janv. 1832; CE5-40, 12 sept. 1849. ASQ, Fonds Viger–Verreau, boîte 15, liasse 1, no.13; Polygraphie, XLII: 18. L.C., House of Assembly, *Journals*, 1831–32, app.II; 1835–36, app.OO. L.-P. Audet, *Le système scolaire*, vols.4, 6.

McCORMICK, WILLIAM, politician, militia officer, businessman, office holder, JP, and author; b. 30 May 1784, probably in the Ohio country, eldest child of Alexander McCormick and Elizabeth Turner; m. 29 Jan. 1809 Mary Cornwall in Colchester Township, Upper Canada, and they had 13 children, one of whom died in infancy; d. 18 Feb. 1840 on Pelee Island, Upper Canada.

During the American Revolutionary War, William McCormick's father, a fur trader in the Ohio country, served with Captain Henry Bird's expedition against Kentucky and also with Captain William Caldwell* of Butler's Rangers. After the war he appears in records as a resident of Detroit but he also operated a trading post at the rapids of the Miamis River (Maumee, Ohio). When his post was destroyed during the battle of Fallen Timbers [*see* Michikinakoua*] in August 1794, he moved to Upper Canada, settling first in Malden Township and then in Colchester Township. As the eldest son William became responsible for the family at his father's death in 1803. Six years later he strengthened his position in the county by marrying a daughter of John Cornwall, loyalist, prominent landowner, and former member of the House of Assembly. McCormick's own political ambitions soon flourished and in May 1812 he was elected to the assembly for Essex County. He was re-elected in 1816 and again in 1820. As an assemblyman, he tried unsuccessfully for some time to have the county seat moved from Sandwich (Windsor) to Amherstburg.

During the War of 1812 McCormick had seen action with the 1st Essex Militia, initially as a lieutenant and then as a captain; he was present at the attacks in 1813 on Frenchtown (Monroe, Mich.) and on Fort Meigs (near Perrysburg), Ohio. His service in the war ended with his capture in late 1813 or January 1814. After the return of peace, McCormick secured a contract to supply pork to Fort Malden (Amherstburg). To carry it out, he leased Pelee Island from Alexander McKee and, with a partner, raised several hundred pigs there. Another of his enterprises was a general store in Colchester which was in operation by at least 1821. He also enjoyed success in acquiring offices. In 1815 he was appointed the deputy collector of customs at Amherstburg, in 1816 a magistrate, and in 1821 the deputy postmaster in Colchester. As well, he remained active in the militia and in 1816 was appointed to the Board of Militia Pensions for the Western District. In 1820, along with the Reverend Richard Pollard*, McCormick was instrumental in the building of Christ Church in Colchester.

McCormick's financial position improved markedly around 1819 as a result of an inheritance of some £10,000 from an Irish uncle. He used his new source of wealth to add to the land which he had already acquired. In addition to Pelee Island, the lease of which he bought in 1823, he made large property investments on the mainland; from 1820 to 1824 he purchased 1,290 acres and held a mortgage on over 700 more. After 1825, however, he began to sell more land than he purchased – mainly to finance activities on the island – and at his death he held less than 300 acres on the mainland. His land speculation was profitable: in the period from 1820 to 1839 he realized £2,770 from land which had cost him roughly £900.

To settle the estate of his Irish uncle McCormick was required to travel to England and Ireland in 1823. While in London, as part of a campaign to promote agriculture in the Western District, he sent a memorial to the House of Commons advocating an imperial preference on tobacco, a crop in which some Upper Canadian landowners saw considerable potential and on which McCormick relied for his cash income. To attract settlers to the district, he prepared a sketch of the area and distributed it in Ireland; this account remains the most extended contemporary discussion of conditions in the Western District. He returned to Upper Canada in 1825.

When McCormick had leased Pelee Island in 1815, title was in doubt because the Indian title had never been extinguished. Both his lease from McKee and his subsequent purchase of the lease, therefore, were of dubious legality. That said, McCormick was fully convinced that he was the rightful lessee, and from the mid 1820s he made the island the focus of his activities. He helped promote the construction of a lighthouse in 1833; the following April he was appointed lighthouse-keeper, and in the summer he moved his family to the island. In the mid 1830s he entered into an agreement with a contractor from Ohio to erect a sawmill which would produce cedar ties for a railway under construction in that state. He also obtained a contract to supply cedar posts for Fort Malden. This appropriation for his own use of the island's red cedar created animosity. One person complained to the government that McCormick was acting illegally since the island still belonged to the crown, but the commissioner of crown lands decided in McCormick's favour. The issue of title, however, remained unsettled until 1866, when the government issued an order-in-council confirming title in the McCormicks.

McCormick's life was seriously disrupted in February 1838 when a group of Patriots crossed the ice from Ohio and occupied the island. He and his family fled to the mainland and a detachment of British troops forced the invaders to withdraw. Two years later McCormick died on Pelee Island. By his will he attempted an equitable division of the island among his family. He also stipulated that none of his children, or their heirs, was to dispose of any land until at least the third generation "unless it be to a coheir and of the name of McCormick." His wishes were soon contravened by his eldest son, who appropriated much of the valuable timber land for himself and who sold land to people from Ohio.

K. G. Pryke

William McCormick's account of the Western District, prepared in 1824 for distribution in Ireland, is preserved in AO, Hiram Walker Hist. Museum coll., 20-135 (G. F. Macdonald papers). It has been published as *A sketch of the Western District of Upper Canada, being the southern extremity of that interesting province*, ed. R. A. Douglas (Windsor, Ont., 1980).

AO, Hiram Walker Hist. Museum coll., 20-148; Land record index; RG 1, A-I-6: 13710–11. DPL, Burton Hist. Coll., William McCormick papers. PAC, MG 19, A3; RG 1, L3, 307A: Mc20/147; 337: M11/50; 338: M11/254; 341: M12/203, 241; 377: M misc. 3, 1802–65/3; RG 5, A1; RG 8, I (C ser.), 1219; RG 9, I, B1. Joseph Delafield, *The unfortified boundary: a diary of the first survey of the Canadian boundary line from St. Regis to the Lake of the Woods . . .*, ed. Robert McElroy and Thomas Riggs (New York, 1943). *John Askin papers* (Quaife), vol.1. F. C. Hamil, *The valley of the lower Thames, 1640 to 1850* (Toronto, 1951; repr. Toronto and Buffalo, N.Y., 1973). Marion McCormick Hooper, *Pelee Island, then and now* ([Scudder, Ont., 1967?]). K. M. J. McKenna, "The impact of the Upper Canadian rebellion on life in Essex County, Ontario, 1837–42" (Parks Canada, National Hist. Parks and Sites Branch, *Microfiche report ser.*, no.187, Ottawa, 1985). G. E. Reaman, *A history of agriculture in Ontario* (2v., [Toronto, 1970]). Thaddeus Smith, *Point au Pelee*

Island: a historical sketch of and an account of the McCormick family, who were the first white owners on the island (Amherstburg, Ont., 1899).

McCULLOCH, THOMAS, Presbyterian minister, educator, office holder, JP, author, and naturalist; b. 1776 in Fereneze, near Paisley, Scotland, second son of six children of Michael McCulloch and Elizabeth Neilson; m. 27 July 1799 Isabella Walker, and they had nine children; d. 9 Sept. 1843 in Halifax.

Thomas McCulloch was a product of 18th-century industrialization and the Scottish Enlightenment. Paisley, a centre of the textile trade, was prosperous, and its prosperity extended to the artisan class of the region, to which Thomas's father, a master blockmaker for the printing of cloth, belonged. Thomas grew up amid the intellectual ferment of the Enlightenment's scientific and philosophical innovation. He graduated in logic from the University of Glasgow in 1792. With a skill for classical languages, he taught Hebrew as a student and upon graduation pursued the study of languages along with his interests in church history and the British constitution. He also undertook the study of medicine but did not complete the course. Instead, Thomas attended the theological hall of the General Associate Synod in Whitburn (Lothian). Here were trained the ministers of the Secession Church, so called because of its origin in Ebenezer Erskine's separation from the Church of Scotland in 1733.

Licensed by the Presbytery of Kilmarnock, McCulloch was called in 1799 to Stewarton, southwest of Glasgow, where he was ordained. Six weeks later he married the daughter of the Reverend David Walker, minister of the Old Light burgher congregation of nearby Pollokshaws (Glasgow). He sought demission from Stewarton four years later, a move subsequently attributed by his son to lack of financial support. Shortly thereafter he applied to the General Associate Synod for assignment to North America and was appointed to Prince Edward Island.

McCulloch's education and early years instilled a committed Calvinism, a philosophical liberalism, and an intellectual appetite which found expression in his subsequent teaching, writing, and political vision. Family piety and filial duty apparently drove him to seek a missionary field. He himself admitted that it took several years before he could persuade himself that his situation was preferable to that of his brethren at home.

McCulloch arrived in Pictou, N.S., with his family in November 1803. Warned against attempting to cross the Northumberland Strait so late in the year, he wintered in Pictou. Tradition has it that two townsmen, seeing the globes depicting the physical and celestial worlds which McCulloch had brought with him, determined to keep him there. In June 1804 he was inducted into the "Harbour" church, later the Prince Street Church. Like his colleagues James Drummond MacGregor* and Duncan Ross*, McCulloch made journeys to communities unsupplied with Presbyterian ministers, including Halifax. He was popular in the capital, and in 1807 he received a call to settle there. The Associate Presbytery of Pictou determined that the church's interests were better served by his remaining in Pictou. McCulloch returned to the Halifax congregation briefly in 1817 to mediate a dispute with their minister; his address, published as *Words of peace . . .* , admonished against the evil fruits of contention and the congregation's neglect of "that progress in godliness" which was their duty as Christians and Presbyterians. In 1824 he resigned his Pictou ministry in order to devote himself exclusively to educational matters.

Within two years of his arrival in Pictou McCulloch had initiated the activity that would become his life's dedicated, and at times obsessive, goal. In 1803 King's College at Windsor, the province's sole institution of higher learning, had effectively excluded dissenters, who formed 80 per cent of the province's population, from its facilities and honours. Educated in the Scottish universities where students of all denominations were accommodated, McCulloch abhorred this religious exclusiveness. He held, moreover, that a liberal education, which could be obtained only in universities, was essential for the training of preachers. Recognizing the great lack of Presbyterian ministers and the realism of MacGregor's belief that Nova Scotia would never be adequately served by relying upon ministers formed in Scotland, McCulloch developed a concept for training a Nova Scotian ministry. The first practical step, taken in 1806, was the initiation of a school in his house, where boys were taught the branches of learning beyond those of the common schools; by 1807 a subscription of £1,150 had been pledged towards a college. Unable at the outset to obtain government assistance, McCulloch's school operated by local subscription until the provincial grammar school act of 1811 gave it official aid. When the log schoolhouse he had built on his property burned in 1814, he had 30–40 students. His appeal to the lieutenant governor for aid in rebuilding garnered £100 from public funds.

In 1809 hostile locals had taken the occasion of Lieutenant Governor Sir George Prevost*'s visit to Pictou to implant suspicions in the official mind about McCulloch's loyalty. A threatening letter followed, advising him to leave the country. McCulloch's stalwart defence of his loyalty and the testimonies of well-placed friends disarmed the allegation, and he served in 1810 as district treasurer and from at least 1810 to 1815 as a justice of the peace. One of those upon whom McCulloch had called for defence against the allegation was Bishop Charles Inglis*. In 1803, amid the tensions of the Napoleonic Wars, the bishop's charge to his clergy had cast aspersions on the loyalty of Roman Catholics in the province. A warm response from Edmund Burke*, the Catholic vicar general, provoked a political and theological controversy in which McCulloch, applying his scholarship, entered the lists as Protestant champion. In *Popery condemned . . .* (1808), dedicated to Inglis, and *Popery again condemned . . .* (1810), McCulloch illustrated from the Scriptures and teachings of the Christian church the theological justification of Protestantism and the misrepresentations of the papal church. His focus transformed the controversy from a largely political struggle into a primarily religious one. McCulloch's efforts were so acceptable to the Anglican leadership that an informal approach was made to him through William Cochran*, vice-president of King's College, to join the Anglican communion and the college staff. With some surprise its spokesmen learned that McCulloch's Presbyterianism prevented him from subscribing to the Church of England's Thirty-Nine Articles, as such an appointment required. The decision bound McCulloch more firmly to his conviction that an institution of higher education open to the dissenting denominations had to be established in Nova Scotia.

The introduction of an interdenominational form of the monitorial school system in Nova Scotia in 1813–14 again called McCulloch's pen into action. The first school for children of the lower classes to operate in Halifax since the 1780s, Walter BROMLEY's Royal Acadian School sparked controversy between Anglican establishmentarians such as Richard John Uniacke* and Alexander CROKE, who believed education should teach children to become members of the established church, and nonconformists such as McCulloch, who regarded the churchmen's proposals for conformity as infringing on the legal right to dissent. McCulloch argued that where each denomination lacked the wealth and influence to maintain its own institution, all communions could reap the benefits of a Christian education for their children by cooperating in an interdenominational Protestant association to support a single institution. A sermon of February 1814, *The prosperity of the church in troublous times . . .*, lauded the hand of Providence in the emergence of interdenominational cooperation through societies devoted to promoting religious objectives. Though McCulloch did not serve on the boards of such institutions as the Royal Acadian Society and the British and Foreign Bible Society, by his pithy defence of their principles through extensive newspaper correspondence he defined the parameters of Nova Scotia's practical religious toleration.

In 1815 the Presbyterians, led by McCulloch, initiated the legislative process to establish an interdenominational institution of higher learning at Pictou. Their chief motive was to provide the requisite classical training for theological candidates. The public agenda, however, emphasized the non-sectarianism of the institution because the Presbyterians needed the support of Methodists, Baptists, and liberal Anglicans to achieve success. The low-key approach to the legislature made no mention of granting degrees, teaching theology, or financial assistance but asked only for an academy. In the religiously diverse assembly, the academy bill passed without a division. In the Anglican-dominated Council, Brenton Halliburton* agreed to further an explicitly Presbyterian academy. The act of incorporation as passed in 1816 placed no denominational restrictions on students but required an oath of adherence from trustees and teachers to the established churches of England or Scotland. In the view of the promoters, this imposition of a denominational board of trustees was a temporary expedient. The act reflected assemblyman Edward Mortimer*'s political astuteness and his ability to persuade the mercurial McCulloch of the advantages of responding to political reality.

With McCulloch as principal, Pictou Academy began classes in May 1818. His address at the opening of its building later that year, published as *The nature and uses of a liberal education illustrated . . .*, expounded his convictions. A liberal education included both the traditional classical education and the sciences (philosophy, mathematics, and the physical sciences) in order that men could know and understand the world in which they lived. It taught them not only facts but also a system of principles for classifying them, as well as the skills and inclination to continue acquiring knowledge. "A liberal education is valuable," McCulloch argued, "not so much on account of the information which a young man picks up in college as for the habits of abstraction and generalization which he imperceptibly contracts in the course of his studies." He pressed in the *Acadian Recorder* of Halifax early in 1818 for "an open and general seminary for the higher branches of learning," and he warned of the dangers of a system which forced many inhabitants to seek their education in foreign places, especially the United States, because of the denominationally exclusive nature of higher education at home. McCulloch believed as strongly as any Anglican establishmentarian that education must imbue Christian principles in its students. The object of education was "the improvement of man in intelligence and moral principle, as the subsequent basis of his happiness." To this end education should also set before youth models of good and useful precepts. McCulloch was insistent, however, that all should be educated without regard to distinctive religious beliefs.

As an instructor of young men preparing to enter the professions and the Presbyterian ministry, McCulloch was driven by the scope and depth of his own intelligence. He epitomized the fusion of education and religion which characterized Scottish social philosophy of his age. Scientific technique was the handmaid of religious enquiry: "a public instructor in the church . . . must be a man of knowledge and also possess a facility of communicating knowledge" so that the order of the church would be upheld. In a country where educational facilities were minimal, McCulloch recognized, education might come from private study as well as from seminary instruction, but he saw his role as dedicated to eliminating such necessity as the sole option for dissenting clergymen. Through correspondence with the Reverend Edward Manning*, McCulloch sought common ground on education between Presbyterians and Baptists in an attempt to attract Baptist support for his seminary.

In addition to McCulloch's philosophy of education and his personal dedication, what distinguished his institution was his incorporation of scientific instruction into the curriculum. He instilled in his students a scientific curiosity and a sense of the moral worth of science. As early as 1820 he had acquired from Scotland used chemical apparatus and, beginning in 1827, had also given public lectures on the fundamental principles of chemistry. Accompanied by experiments, these lectures significantly enhanced his personal popularity and renown. They reached a climax in 1830 when, according to McCulloch, public lectures in Halifax did "more good to the Academy and its interests than anything that had previously happened." His collecting of regional insects and birds also strengthened the scientific image of the academy. In 1822, partly in recognition of a collection of Nova Scotian insects donated to the University of Glasgow, he was awarded a DD from that institution. At the same time, assisted by his lifelong friend the Reverend James Mitchell of Glasgow, he negotiated LLDs for the academy's two staunchest political friends, Samuel George William ARCHIBALD and Simon Bradstreet Robie*, and James MacGregor was also awarded a DD. The following year, when forwarding a collection of insects to the University of Edinburgh, he sought degrees for Halliburton, judge James Stewart, and Chief Justice Sampson Salter BLOWERS. Contrasting at that time his institution with the government-favoured college at Windsor, McCulloch was careful to draw attention to his courses in mathematics, natural philosophy, and the physical sciences, which were absent at King's College.

The initial opponents of Pictou Academy were members of the Halifax tory establishment, dominated by the Church of England. Their spokesmen in Council, Uniacke and his son-in-law Thomas Nickleson JEFFERY, made an intransigent stand against the academy. Convinced that higher education in the hands of the established church alone could implant in society's future leadership principles of social order and of the British constitution, they rejected McCulloch's conviction that a liberal education on a non-sectarian basis would provide for the most reliable development of responsible citizens. The Reverend John INGLIS, the staunchest defender of the Anglican monopoly on higher education, was the most persistent advocate of their perception that Pictou Academy was "likely to rise or decay as the college at Windsor [was] depressed or advanced." Equally antagonistic was the provincial treasurer, Michael Wallace*, whose animosity towards the district of Pictou dated from his political defeat there in 1799. Moreover, certain councillors had financial reasons for wishing to contain the ambitions of commercial Pictou.

In 1818 a controversy over the dissenters' claim to the use of marriage licences gave McCulloch an issue around which to rally dissenting interests. When Inglis, as Anglican commissary, refused to issue licences to dissenters, McCulloch engineered a petition to the legislature, signed by various dissenting ministers, which sought recognition of their right to marry by licence. McCulloch was also an active protagonist of the issue in the local press. In a pungent letter to the *Acadian Recorder* bearing his familiar pseudonym Investigator, he laid out the bases of the dissenting argument. For him, however, the marriage licence dispute was "a trial of strength" designed "for the purpose of attaching the methodist and baptist clergy to our seminary" and an opportunity to embarrass the Anglican church and challenge Inglis. In 1821, after the Colonial Office had disallowed a bill permitting dissenting ministers to marry by licence, McCulloch's interest in the question waned, for he had by then discovered that "[Methodist and Baptist] good will would not extend beyond professions." He was content that the issue "is hanging over the head of the church and can be renewed at any time." His interest revived in 1825 when the licence question became one of four issues upon which he led the Presbyterian Church of Nova Scotia in seeking formation of an interdenominational board which would coordinate dissenting action. In the late 1820s the licence question again became an issue around which McCulloch worked to rally common action on behalf of dissenters in the legislature as a way of gaining support for his academy.

Under Mortimer's guidance, the academy had obtained a £400 grant from the legislature in 1819, but its supporters failed again to procure a non-denominational board of trustees. Nevertheless, both Baptists and Methodists gave McCulloch warm testimonials when he made a tour to Boston, New York, and the Canadas that year. Moreover, Mortimer and Robie sought an American DD for McCulloch in recognition of his theological accomplishments and his articulate defence of dissenting interests. Their efforts failed but the following year McCulloch was awarded a DD by Union College in Schenectady, N.Y.

Mortimer's death late in 1819 had left effective leadership of the academy in McCulloch's hands. It was he, for example, who suggested in 1821 that the bill to grant the academy's charter be linked with that for Dalhousie College to achieve acceptance in the Council and the Colonial Office. Political leadership on the academy question passed to the skilful Archibald, who, with the assistance of George Smith of Pictou and Charles Rufus FAIRBANKS in the assembly and Robie and Halliburton in the Council, shepherded the academy's interests annually through the legislature. McCulloch was actively involved in the applications. He appeared as a witness before the assembly and Council, and his prolific promotional correspondence on education was supported by the timely production of diverse petitions. By 1821 he was complaining that he had come to Halifax so often to further the academy "that I am ashamed to show my nose in town when the House is sitting." As well, his anonymous and increasingly popular letters in the *Acadian Recorder* at this time satirizing the follies of Nova Scotian society might well have made him shy of too much publicity in Halifax. In their own way, they reinforced the social and religious principles underlying McCulloch's vision of the academy. Its supporters failed to obtain a non-denominational board of trustees, degree-granting status, or a permanent operating grant, but an annual subvention demonstrated the academy's political success for almost a decade. By 1825 it was widely recognized for the quality of its instruction, the commitment of its principal, and its acceptance among dissenters in meeting their needs for higher education.

In seeking degree-granting status for the academy, McCulloch and his colleagues had been stymied in 1817 when Lord Dalhousie [RAMSAY] had initiated a third institution of higher learning, to be situated in Halifax. Although he approved of the academy, Dalhousie was insistent that it was equivalent to a Scottish academy and that it would never obtain his support in aspiring to a higher status, which he foresaw as belonging to his own college. McCulloch's efforts to persuade him to place his college under the control of the Presbyterian Church of Nova Scotia, rather than pursue an alliance with King's College, faltered on Dalhousie's committed establishmentarianism and his ambitions to rise in the imperial administration. The failure in 1823–25 of his successor, Sir James Kempt*, to unite King's and Dalhousie colleges in Halifax in an interdenominational university reduced the threat to McCulloch's aspirations for degree-granting status for his academy. Unable, however, to obtain the power of accreditation in Nova Scotia, in 1825 he sent the first three graduates of his divinity program to Scotland, where they passed the qualifying examinations for the University of Glasgow with praise.

The creation of the Presbyterian Church of Nova Scotia in 1817 had been the result of action by the Presbyterian ministers outside Halifax, mainly Secessionists. McCulloch helped to develop the terms of union, and he was the author of the synod's first report. He was active in synod committees, and in 1821 he served as moderator. Appointed the synod's professor of divinity that year, he led the church in petitioning for government funding of a theological chair at the academy. Despite rejection of this request, McCulloch for the rest of his life taught the theological courses usual for degrees in divinity in Scotland, the synod paying him a nominal annual sum. He might complain of personal jealousies and lack of ardour within the synod, but by 1825 the Presbyterian Church of Nova Scotia looked upon the province, particularly the eastern portion, as its domain, and McCulloch was its undisputed leader.

While McCulloch and other preachers of the Secession Church were dedicating their substantial energies to the development of Presbyterianism in Nova Scotia over more than 20 years, the Church of Scotland had remained unorganized and its ministers isolated. Until the arrival of the Reverend Donald Allan FRASER at Pictou in 1817, there were no Church of Scotland ministers in eastern Nova Scotia. By 1824 Fraser was joined at Pictou by the Reverend Kenneth John MacKenzie, who came as the representative of the church's missionary wing, the Glasgow Colonial Society. Had the promise of society missionaries not seemed to McCulloch to threaten the field to which he intended to send divinity graduates of Pictou Academy, the number of Scottish settlers in eastern Nova Scotia might have absorbed all the ministers that both churches could provide. Likewise, had the Secessionists and Kirkmen not found themselves competing for the same region in the presence of two such ambitious, stubborn, and volatile personalities as MacKenzie and McCulloch, they might have complemented each other rather than conflicted.

Initiation of Glasgow Colonial Society activities in Nova Scotia coincided with McCulloch's long-anticipated tour to Scotland, by which he hoped to solidify the position of his church and to advance the interests of the academy. Armed with testimonials from the Methodists, the Baptists, the province's barristers and attorneys, and leading members of the assembly, he set off in July 1825. Soon after his arrival, his stormy meeting with the secretary of the Glasgow Colonial Society, the Reverend Robert Burns*, alienated the Church of Scotland from McCulloch's cause. McCulloch argued vehemently that, rather than funding Scottish ministers to settle in Nova Scotia, the society would better fulfil its aims by aiding locally trained clergymen, familiar with the country, in their first years with a congregation. His strongly worded *Memorial*, published in July 1826, charged the society with a deliberate intent to counteract the work of the Presbyterian Church of Nova Scotia.

The *Memorial* provoked a vituperative press controversy in Scotland over the objectives and operations of the society that continued until 1828 through Burns's *Supplement*, McCulloch's *Review of the "Supplement"*, and Burns's reply. The formation by McCulloch's Scottish Secessionist friends late in 1826 of the Glasgow Society for Promoting the Interests of Religion and Liberal Education among the Settlers of the North American Provinces in order to aid the Presbyterian Church of Nova Scotia and Pictou Academy heightened the denominational animosity in Scotland. Moreover, McCulloch was severely frustrated by the meagre results of his fund-raising efforts on behalf of the academy. As he complained to MacGregor, "I have tried many a trade but begging is the worst." A severe financial depression in Scotland and his rancorous relations with the Glasgow Colonial Society deprived him of the success Inglis had achieved in England for King's College a year earlier.

The controversy over the Glasgow Colonial Society did not remain a solely Scottish struggle. Both MacKenzie and the Kirk spokesman in Halifax, the Reverend John Martin, forwarded their comments on McCulloch's *Memorial* to Burns. As early as September 1826, letters in the *Acadian Recorder* extended the controversy to Nova Scotia. By the end of the year, the newspaper polemics had fixed its centre firmly in Pictou. Although McCulloch did not return to Nova Scotia until December 1826, he and MacKenzie were seen throughout as the dispute's principals in the province. Their debate began the next spring when McCulloch published in the Halifax newspapers an extended response to Burns's *Supplement*. Maintaining the separation between Kirkmen and Secessionists that existed in Scotland but which was much less noticeable in Nova Scotia, the Church of Scotland ministers found themselves and their fledgling missionary society under McCulloch's virulent attack. Fulfilment of his aspirations, they saw, would deny them not only their assumed role as the representatives of Presbyterianism in a British colony but also any place in the missionary field in Nova Scotia. In Michael Wallace the Kirkmen found a sympathetic respondent who linked their discontent with opposition to the academy in the Council.

MacKenzie and Fraser, the Kirk spokesmen, based their opposition to the academy on three points. First, although authorized as a Scottish-style academy serving Presbyterian needs, the academy was clearly operated as an interdenominational college. Claiming to represent the majority of Scottish settlers in eastern Nova Scotia, who had had a Kirk affiliation when they emigrated, the Kirkmen argued that the region needed the elementary branches of learning which had been excluded from the academy. Secondly, by fulfilling in practice the principal purpose for which Dalhousie College, with its Kirk affiliation, had been founded, Pictou Academy conferred upon the Presbyterian Church of Nova Scotia a status which the Church of Scotland both lacked and assumed to be its right. Thirdly, Kirk hostility was directed against the theological instruction provided to candidates for ministry in the Presbyterian Church of Nova Scotia. The trustees of the academy always insisted that any denomination wishing to have its divinity candidates instructed there could make arrangements similar to McCulloch's, but so long as the Kirk refused to accept the validity of a native ministry there could be no common ground on this point. Unwilling to submit to McCulloch's iron dictatorship among the trustees, MacKenzie and his colleagues found themselves unable to alter management of the academy except by public confrontation.

It has been argued by Dr William B. Hamilton that between 1820 and 1825 McCulloch and Pictou Academy were becoming "synonymous with the battle for political and educational reform" and that by the end of this period "narrow denominational questions had been transformed into a constitutional issue of wide significance." During these years Pictou Academy did emerge as a significant issue of contention between the assembly, dominated by dissenting interests and rural members, and the Council, representing establishmentarian and Haligonian interests. By 1825, despite persistent opposition from Wallace, Uniacke, and Jeffery, the legislative bounty to the academy, in nearly annual grants of £400, totalled £2,600. McCulloch was satisfied that his institution would eventually "creep into the civil list" with a permanent annual grant like that given King's College. A strong push in 1825 by the assembly nevertheless failed to obtain implementation of the academy's three persistent requests – college status, a non-sectarian board of trustees, and a permanent annual grant. Moreover, that year a change of membership in Council altered the balance in favour of the academy's opponents. The changes included the appointment of John Inglis, recently named bishop of Nova Scotia. McCulloch blamed Inglis and his "spiderweb tactics" for the shift of balance, but in fact Inglis did not possess the influence in Council attributed to him. His persevering defence of church interests, however, melded comfortably with the defence of the church establishment by other councillors, and McCulloch was unable to recognize the crucial distinction between Inglis's influence and the opposition to Pictou and its economic aspirations by councillors such as Enos Collins* and Charles Ramage Prescott*. As a result, dissenting promoters of Pictou Academy often focused simplistically upon Inglis's vote in explaining their rejection.

Attempts to reach a compromise between the

Kirkmen and the Presbyterian Church of Nova Scotia and between the assembly and the Council continued to characterize the Pictou Academy question between 1826 and 1831. McCulloch became increasingly convinced that compromise would destroy the institution. A decade of promoting and protecting the academy had led him to a practical social liberalism which embraced tenets of civil and religious liberty incompatible with the strongly conservative philosophy dominant in Council. Pictou Academy became not an educational institution responsive to the needs of the province but McCulloch's divine mission in the service of ecumenical Christianity. His total commitment to the institution's promotion and defence lay at the root of the inflexibility that dominated the dispute in the late 1820s. By the end of 1826 McCulloch saw himself in the martyr's role, "marked out as a scapegoat to bear the sins of the people." Embittered by the animosity of the Glasgow Colonial Society and disillusioned by what he perceived to be lukewarm brethren in Scotland, McCulloch attacked the proposed bill which would have given the academy a permanent annual grant because it attached government officials to the institution's board of trustees.

The trustees' "New Year's Resolutions" of 1827, vaunting the institution and restating its objectives unflinchingly, were their response to McCulloch's sense of crisis. Although the principal admitted that the resolutions were "all flummery," their strident citing of natural rights and the academy's right to equal legislative treatment with King's College elicited "much raging of enemies" and "too great falling off of friends," among them Brenton Halliburton. The failure of the trustees' heavy-handed approach was evident in the absence of a Pictou Academy bill in 1827. Despite such warnings of the danger of their course, the trustees, led by McCulloch, pursued it unrelentingly. That year, in the *Colonial Patriot* of Pictou [*see* Jotham BLANCHARD], the academy's supporters established a radical voice informed of and responsive to reform currents in the Canadas. Although McCulloch publicly denied any direct involvement in the journal, he was widely assumed to be the master-mind behind it, and by 1829 he was openly a contributor. In providing a voice of civil and religious liberty in Nova Scotia, the *Colonial Patriot* reflected and strongly advocated the philosophical position of which Pictou Academy was more and more a symbol.

Increased politicization of the trustees' demands from 1827 exacerbated the religious tensions that the Glasgow Colonial Society controversy and the "New Year's Resolutions" had provoked. The Church of Scotland's objections to the academy were annually laid before the legislature in petitions from 1828 to 1832. Their convenient arguments, numerous signatures, and regional origin gave substance to the academy's opponents in Council. By the spring of 1828, when addressing the constitutional issues which the conflict over the academy had raised, Halliburton noted correctly that the controversy "had been inflamed into a religious struggle for political domination . . . : Are the Dissenters, or the Kirk of Scotland, to have the religious and political sway throughout the Eastern section of Nova Scotia?" Nevertheless, the conflict had also become linked to an issue which dominated the province: had the Council the constitutional right to reject money bills initiated, and repeatedly sustained, by the assembly? Between 1825 and 1830 the Council rejected no fewer than seven bills for the financial support of the institution.

In McCulloch's eyes, "The Academy is the only thing in the British provinces which prevents the [bishop] from having the education of the whole under his and the church's management and they are employing every means within doors and out of doors fair or foul to put us down." With the legislative grant withdrawn after 1828, McCulloch was forced to direct additional energy towards encouraging donations from Scotland and greater efforts among supporters in Nova Scotia, by whom societies were formed in 1829. The annual organization of legislative petitions from diverse congregations and denominations was also essential to offset the activities of the Kirkmen. By the spring of 1829, McCulloch, disillusioned and despairing, concluded that "there is no safety for our Academy but getting the province into a flame." A "summer's roasting" of Council in the *Patriot* led him to believe that the journal would "either obtain for [the academy] a permanence directly or by revolutionizing the Council terminate in the same end." As these activities focused on the government, they were perceived by the institution's opponents less as a defence of the institution than as a deliberate disturbance of the orderliness and peaceful harmony of the province.

Encouraged by the opposition to the academy in Council, the Church of Scotland clergy held adamantly to the claim that they represented order and loyalty to government and that their position concerning the academy expressed local needs. As a denomination, the Kirk was considerably strengthened in the late 1820s, and in 1831 the founding of the Pictou *Observer and Eastern Advertiser* with MacKenzie as editor gave Kirkmen a voice through which to express and consolidate their position. In the election of 1830 they were initiated into electoral politics. Although the candidates they supported were defeated, the strength of their showing in the district of Pictou gave credence to their claims of popular support. Moreover, by adhering in 1831 to the position that the conflict was a religious one between Presbyterians, they undermined the Secessionist argument that the academy's cause represented the flourishing of legitimate reformist sentiments and the championing of religious liberty similar to challenges in Britain and Upper Canada.

The continuous stalemate over the academy issue in the province encouraged lobbyists of the opposing parties to present their positions to the Colonial Office in 1831. McCulloch wrote the trustees' petition, which Blanchard presented. The political skills of Archibald, the trustees' president, and of Halliburton, who wrote a lengthy critique of the trustees' petition, led Colonial Secretary Lord Goderich to accept from Blanchard's and Halliburton's exposition a familiar analysis that assigned a political reason to colonial woes. In July 1831 Goderich instructed Lieutenant Governor Sir Peregrine Maitland* that "a Bill should be passed which might give to the Academical Institution at Pictou . . . permanent pecuniary assistance from the Public Revenues." In response Maitland advised that it was "between the members of the Kirk of Scotland and . . . Seceders from the Kirk, that the contention really exist[ed]," rather than solely "between the Council, or the Established Church, or both, and the supporters of the Institution." Goderich acknowledged that in such a religious confrontation between two parties reported nearly equal in numbers, a grant to one would settle nothing. He therefore instructed Maitland to take no initiative other than "endeavouring to reunite the contending parties and of encoraging both branches of the Legislature . . . to settle the question by some amicable adjustment of the Law."

Unable to settle the academy dispute in an amicable manner, government effectively stepped aside. Late in 1831 Maitland made efforts to conciliate McCulloch and MacKenzie, but they foundered on the former's adamancy. However, fear of imperial displeasure and the more conciliatory attitude of moderate members appointed in the early 1830s gave Council renewed incentive to seek a settlement of the question of which all parties were weary. The resulting act of 1832 was a compromise on all sides. The lower branches were to be taught at the academy, and the higher branches were to continue. An annual grant of £400 for ten years was to be allocated primarily to salaries for McCulloch (£250) and the master of the lower branches (£100). Of the thirteen trustees, seven were to remain. Maitland, adhering to his conviction that both parties must be accommodated, appointed representatives of the Church of Scotland to four of the six seats to be filled. By internalizing the dispute within the board of trustees, Maitland undoubtedly hoped to see it resolved in the operation of the institution. The antagonism between McCulloch and MacKenzie made this expectation unrealistic.

The restructuring of Pictou Academy by the legislation of 1832 marked the beginning of a critical stage in McCulloch's career. Up to that point he could claim effective control of the institution. With four of his opponents named to the board of trustees, however, he realized that his personal power had been markedly diminished. As early as 1833 wrangling and insult characterized the board's meetings, and McCulloch, though legislated to it, had ceased to participate. Amid growing economic recession, pecuniary and public support for the academy fell away. McCulloch repeatedly complained of the failure of the Kirk representatives to deliver the financial aid they had promised upon appointment to the board of trustees, and he remained subject to their virulent personal attacks. Moreover, in 1831 A Presbyterian, writing in the *Acadian Recorder*, had accused McCulloch of redirecting to the academy funds raised in Scotland to relieve the sufferers of the devastating Miramichi fire of 1825. Although the charges had been refuted, they were republished in pamphlet form in 1833, denied in Scottish attestations published in the *Acadian Recorder* in 1834, and renewed in the Pictou *Observer* in 1835.

In January 1835, advising Lieutenant Governor Sir Colin CAMPBELL that Pictou Academy could no longer be kept in useful operation, McCulloch applied for "some other way beneficial to the Province" in which he might "derive a subsistence from the education of youth"; a year later he repeated his request to the assembly. His despondency derived not only from the adversarial environment of the academy but also from the deaths of two of his children in 1834 and 1835. Surrounded at various times by his mother, sister, brothers, nephew, wife, and nine children, McCulloch had always depended upon his close-knit and like-minded family for support.

Renewed negotiations for uniting King's and Dalhousie colleges were taking place in 1835–36, and McCulloch's friends were eager to see him appointed to Dalhousie. McCulloch reluctantly agreed, but cited to Mitchell only the negative factors of Halifax, specifically its corrupt urban environment and its predominant Anglicanism. In 1836 McCulloch submitted his resignation as the synod's professor of divinity. He later claimed that he did so because he perceived dissatisfaction with his continuance and not because the synod had failed to endow the appointment as undertaken in 1832. He was persuaded to resume the position a year later and continued in it until his death. By the fall of 1837, after legislation to restore Pictou Academy to its original intent had failed to pass, McCulloch was so distressed by its condition that he seriously contemplated retiring to Britain.

The negotiations for one provincial university having collapsed, in the 1838 legislative session Archibald and his son Charles Dickson* coordinated a successful effort to release McCulloch from Pictou and open the doors of Dalhousie College. Apparently focused on Pictou Academy, the bill translated McCulloch, with £200 of the government grant, to the

Halifax college. Debate on the bill replayed the struggle of a decade earlier. Vocal Kirk opposition included Fraser's testimony before the legislature and personal attacks on McCulloch, especially the reprinting of A Presbyterian's pamphlet. Others of the academy's old opponents, the Halifax merchants and the Anglicans, also opposed the bill, for they saw higher education thereby slipping from their hands. Dissenters of various denominations and Roman Catholics supported it for its potential in leading to an institution of higher learning without denominational restrictions.

McCulloch was appointed president of Dalhousie College at a meeting of its board of governors on 6 Aug. 1838 and was its first president to assume office. Also appointed professor of logic, rhetoric, and moral philosophy, he resigned from Pictou Academy in September and moved to the capital. In addition to the regular program, McCulloch taught an evening session in logic and composition for "young gentlemen." Recognizing the irony of his appointment after 30 years of struggle against the Halifax-based establishment, he summed up: "God has given me to possess the gate of my enemies." He saw himself at last as "head of the education of the province."

The same meeting of the governors determined that Dalhousie's intention in founding a college was to create a Church of Scotland–affiliated centre and that its professors, excluding McCulloch, must be adherents to the Kirk. As a result the Reverend Alexander Romans, Kirk minister at Dartmouth, was appointed professor of classics in place of Edmund Albern Crawley*, pastor of the Granville Street Baptist Church and a recognized scholar to whom appointment had been informally promised to obtain Baptist support for the legislation appointing McCulloch. Incensed by his rejection, Crawley persuaded the Nova Scotia Baptist Education Society in November to establish a college in association with Horton Academy. As McCulloch was not seen to be involved in or supportive of the governors' decision, his good relationship with the Baptist clergy was not seriously impaired. The following year, when the pulpit of the Granville Street Baptist Church was vacant on account of Crawley's move to the new college at Wolfville, McCulloch provided supply preaching to the congregation, from which they derived "comfort and satisfaction."

McCulloch's Halifax years were not prosperous ones. It was understood as a term of his nomination that he would refrain from involvement in political or related matters outside his office. Although Kirkmen continued to attack his appointment after it had taken effect, McCulloch reported to Mitchell in May 1839: "I meddle with nobody and nobody now ventures to meddle with me." In spite of the recognition accorded to his intellect, his scholarship, and his skills as a teacher, he did not enjoy the confidence of the college's board of governors in the institution's direction, financial management, or aspirations. Efforts were made to reverse the imposed sectarian affiliation. One proposal, which McCulloch advocated, was to return the college to its founder's non-denominational intent and another, which he opposed, was to introduce a Roman Catholic to the faculty. Neither effort succeeded.

In other spheres, McCulloch was active in re-establishing a congregation in Halifax in affiliation with the Presbyterian Church of Nova Scotia. He was horrified by an embryonic *rapprochement* between Kirk and Secession interests in both Scotland and the province, which he blamed on British-educated ministers who did not understand the needs or the deep-seated animosities in the local situation. McCulloch also saw in the proposals a disregard of "scriptural purity," and he looked to his former students in the synod to support his adamant opposition to the gestures of such clergy as the Reverend John Sprott* and the Reverend Thomas Trotter* in exploring a possible union of Presbyterians in Nova Scotia.

During the years of religious and educational controversy leading to McCulloch's appointment to Dalhousie College, one of the advantages he had maintained over his adversaries had been his considerable skill as a writer of sermons, theological arguments, political observations, and satire. Halifax was to afford him more time for such endeavours, but without the catalyst of battle, McCulloch seems to have turned to the pen less frequently in the years after 1838. None the less, his image was firmly fixed in the popular imagination because of his authorship of a series of 16 satirical letters which he had begun to publish anonymously in the *Acadian Recorder* on 22 Dec. 1821. Purportedly the chronicles of an unidentified Nova Scotian township, the letters not only satirized the indolence, restlessness, and get-rich-quick mentality of rural dwellers and townsfolk but also revealed the limitations of McCulloch's self-righteous and pawky narrator, Mephibosheth Stepsure. Obviously intended as a satiric norm at the beginning of the sketches, the lame Stepsure had become as covetous of social recognition as his neighbours by the end of the first series of letters on 11 May 1822. Thus, his signature "Gent." at the end of the last letter signified not only a climax to the double-edged satire but also a process of character revelation in the letters that carried them beyond the merely episodic form of most belletristic newspaper epistles to the beginnings of more unified fiction. In this sense, the first series of Stepsure letters remains more structurally satisfying than do the original Sam Slick sketches by Thomas Chandler Haliburton* in 1835 or *Sunshine sketches of a little town* by Stephen Butler Leacock* in 1912, although all three works effectively utilize the conventions of newspaper sketch writing for comic effect.

From the beginning, the Stepsure letters were enormously popular, evoking laughter, as one correspondent described them, until "the rafters o' the house fairly shook wi' the clamer and the din." Under the guise of Stepsure's busybodyish, concerned letters to "you Halifax gentry," McCulloch created a collection of typecast ne'er-do-wells who forsook the values of the land for the riches and social mobility associated with merchandising, shipbuilding, timbering, and trade. With names like Mr Tipple, Jack Scorem, Shadrach Howl, and Miss Sippit, they assumed comic proportions, their characters revealed in passages of lively slapstick or by Mephibosheth's dry wit. Thus, Mr Gypsum was not "by any means a professed drunkard," the stranger in town "died, because he could not live any longer," and Stepsure's neighbours "are never in a hurry, except when they are farming, going from home, or getting out of church." The passages on the Whinges' hostelry are typical in revealing the wasted opportunities of the townsfolk, for not only were mice, frogs, and hair ingredients of the soup, but guests also found that "they were not without bedfellows." Such humour has been cited by Northrop Frye as "quiet, observant," and "deeply conservative in a human sense," based not on "wisecracks" but on "a vision of society." For this reason, Frye sees McCulloch as "the founder of genuine Canadian humour," a humour based on an understanding of cultural context and on the distinction between what is past and what is permanent. Stepsure's concern with gadding about, the insubstantiality of charismatic religions, and the destruction wrought by an over-abundance of alcohol in his society illustrates the social and moral sensibility underlying the comedy: "I was neither a great man nor a great man's son: I was Mephibosheth Stepsure, whose highest ambition was to be a plain, decent farmer."

The message in the letters could not have been more timely. During his tenure as lieutenant governor from 1816 to 1820, Dalhousie had expressed concern about the wasted farming opportunities in the province and had supported John YOUNG's polished letters in the *Acadian Recorder* advocating improved agricultural practices. Between 1828 and 1831 Joseph Howe* was to explore the same theme in his "Western rambles" and "Eastern rambles" in the *Novascotian, or Colonial Herald*, but neither he nor the other advocates of an agricultural economy gave life to their message as forcibly and as colourfully as did McCulloch's Stepsure. With a hoe in one hand and a Bible in the other, Stepsure preached the virtues of living frugally, educating the mind, serving the community, and honouring the family. His endorsement of hard work and his conviction that "time is money" sounded a note not dissimiliar to that of Benjamin Franklin's Poor Richard, but the Christian morality underlying Stepsure's social vision made McCulloch's narrator appear more community-oriented than Franklin's. Both authors were masters of dry understatement and both had a keen eye for human idiosyncracy, but the punctuation of Stepsure's deliberate and prosy style with slapstick, archly worded earthiness, throw-away lines, and mock literalness created a tone quite different from the laconic philosophizing of Franklin's better known persona. Moreover, while McCulloch could frame an axiom as adeptly as could Franklin or Haliburton ("He who spends his wages before they are due, is always behind with his payments"), he went beyond them in exploring the psychology leading to his neighbours' downfall. Whereas the effect of the Sam Slick sketches was to dazzle the reader by their exuberance of language and audacity of characterization, the effect of the Stepsure letters was to provide thoughtful, if predictable, reasons for Nova Scotians' decline and fall. That they struck some chord is illustrated not only in McCulloch's inability to find unthumbed copies to send home to friends in Scotland, but also in the comment of the *Acadian Recorder* on the day the first series concluded: "They have painted with such inimitable truth the thoughtless, luxurious, and extravagant habits of our population; that we see ourselves as in a mirror, reflected back in them. . . . The correction of these follies must be the first step in the augmentation of the provincial capital; and the severe satires, which are directed against them in the letters of our correspondent, cannot fail to produce a certain effect." As McCulloch explained in a letter to James Mitchell of Glasgow in November 1822, "No writing [in] these provinces ever occasioned so much talk. Almost every one who read them was angry in his turn and by and by laughed at his neighbour. One of the Judges told me that he believed our Governor had them by heart."

Even before he had experienced the success of the Stepsure letters, McCulloch had the intention of reaching "at least the twentieth letter" and of "then adding notes and illustrations and sending the whole home as a sample of the way in which we get on in the western world." At the conclusion of the first 16 letters in 1822, he recopied and polished them, framed them with a comic dialect letter to Scotland from Stepsure's Covenanting friend, Alexander Scantocreesh, and entitled them "The chronicles of our town, or, a peep at America." In November 1822 he sent the manuscript to Mitchell with instructions to take the anonymous letters to a bookseller who "might sometime or other consent to publish them as a sketch of American manners." In the mean time, on 4 Jan. 1823, McCulloch began to publish a new series of Stepsure letters in the *Acadian Recorder*, in which he developed a sustained moral tale of a young Scots immigrant to Nova Scotia named William. This series differed from the first in a number of ways, for it included another letter writer (Scantocreesh), it elaborated one long tale instead of a number of short ones, and it presented a central narrator of known character (Stepsure). The result was essentially non-dramatic, although the appearance of certain letters by Censor in the *Acadian Recorder* between 21 Dec. 1822 and 25 Jan. 1823 acted as a catalyst for the continuation of the series. The mysterious Censor charged that "Stepsure is constantly wading in a dung-pit, bespattered with dirt and all the marks of vulgarity." The mock pain of Stepsure's response in the fourth letter and his mock-heroic parody in the sixth illustrate the stylistic strengths of which McCulloch was capable. By the end of the sixth letter on 29 March 1823, McCulloch seems to have realized that he had diffused the focus of his original plan and had in fact created a novella. At this point he contemplated sending "William" to the editor of the *Edinburgh Christian Instructor and Colonial Religious Register*. However, it did not appear in the journal, and McCulloch yoked it to "Melville," a second immigrant story, and took them both with him to Scotland when he went there in 1825.

Neither his abortive attempts at fund raising nor his controversy with the Glasgow Colonial Society allowed McCulloch much time for literary pursuits while in Scotland, but he was none the less able to shepherd two publications through the press. In January 1826 Oliphant's brought out "William" and "Melville" under the general title *Colonial gleanings*, and in June McCulloch supervised the publication of his *Memorial*, the rebuttal to Robert Burns and the Glasgow Colonial Society. Each of these works was reminiscent of the Stepsure letters in its observations on the quality of frontier life and the flexibility of social distinctions in Nova Scotia, but "William" and "Melville" offered a far more sombre treatment of McCulloch's themes than had the Stepsure letters. The two tales were favourably reviewed in the *Edinburgh Theological Magazine* of February 1826, and extracts from "Melville" were reprinted in the *Novascotian* later than year. "William" was now integrated thematically and stylistically with "Melville." Both young men grow up in the same area outside Glasgow, seek their fortunes in Nova Scotia, and lose everything they covet when they ignore examples of Christian lives. As contemporary in their own way as the Stepsure series in exposing the temptations facing young immigrants in Halifax and the countryside, the tales showed a new dimension of McCulloch's literary sensibility. References to the history of the Covenanters in the west of Scotland and to the persecution of William's great-grandfather by Melville's tend to unify the novellas, but they also reveal the historical avenue that McCulloch was beginning to explore in his fiction. The product of a Covenanting area of Scotland, McCulloch also had an anti-burgher's identification with the Covenanting tradition. His introduction of this theme into "Melville" was therefore a natural development of his personal and theological background, but it was given a particularly Nova Scotian cast by his inclusion of the Reverend James MacGregor as a character. MacGregor appeared in "Melville" as a sterling exemplar of the Christian piety and service that also inform McCulloch's historical Covenanting characters. MacGregor's presence also helped to consolidate the increasingly religious tone of McCulloch's fiction, for in his lengthy sermon to Melville there was an elaboration of the Calvinist vision which formed the moral underpinnings of such earlier characters as Scantocreesh and the biblically named Mephibosheth Stepsure.

By 16 Jan. 1828, when he had been back in Nova Scotia for little more than a year, McCulloch told Mitchell that he was engrossed in writing another novel, three volumes in length and concerned with "popery and the progress of Lollardism in the west of Scotland not forgetting a due quantity of witches kelpies and other gods whom our fathers worshipped." Set in McCulloch's boyhood haunts during the reign of James III, "Auld Eppie's tales" was framed by a modern narrator returning home after years of wandering to discover: "Where many a generation with few wants and as few comforts, dozed away life in tranquil indolence, cotton mills, and bleachfields, and printfields, cover the face of the earth; and that ancient and contented race, who knew no toil nor travail beyond sacraments and fairs, have wasted away before an intruding horde of eager faced, bustling beings, whose cravings for wealth, nothing but the philosopher's stone can appease." The note of rapid social change sounded in this passage was one already introduced into Scottish writing by Sir Walter Scott and John GALT. Like them, McCulloch attempted to counterpoint against these modern intrusions a Scotland of oral tales, unsullied beauty, and traditional folkways. There was nothing nostalgic about McCulloch's novel, however, for in the corrupted relationships of the pre-Reformation church with the common people he revealed the roots which had led to the Reformation and, in a sense, to the rise of the Covenanters in Scotland. While "Auld Eppie's tales" was not a Covenanting novel in the true sense, it none the less revealed in the indomitability and enduring humour of everyday folk such as Jock of Killoch and Clunk the spirit of the Scottish people that would later infuse a movement like the Covenanters'. With its use of Scots for everyday speech, its theme of local witchcraft, its integration of a traditional Lowlands tower into the story, its folk image of Auld Eppie, and its tales of early Scotland, "Auld Eppie's tales" contained many of the local elements that had made Scott and Galt popular novelists in Scotland. Although McCulloch was anxious that the novel "amuse," he saw it as a serious contribution to the historical and religious sensibility of Scottish readers.

Between 29 June and 29 Dec. 1828 McCulloch sent sections of "Auld Eppie" to Mitchell with strict instructions that his identity be kept a secret. Explaining that he had written the novel partly in reaction to Scott's interpretation of "our ancestors" in *Tales of my landlord*, McCulloch also revealed that he needed money if he were not "to turn my hand to planting potatoes or something else that will keep the teeth of my family apart." Thus he was particularly anxious about the publisher to whom the novel was to be submitted, suggesting that it might be given to William Blackwood, who had bestowed a gift of books on Pictou Academy in 1826 and who had been "kind" to him when he had been in Scotland. McCulloch was therefore doubly devastated when Blackwood rejected not only "Auld Eppie's tales" but also "The chronicles of our town," which had lain dormant in Scotland since 1822. Praising the "Chronicles" for their "picturesque sketches of life and manners" and for their "rich humour," Blackwood argued that the refined taste of the time would reject any contemporary writing that had "the pungency and originality of Swift." Declaring that he himself was not one of "those squeamish folks of the present generation," Blackwood none the less felt he had to reject both works for the broadness of their humour, claiming that "penetrating as it were into Scott's field, a work of this kind requires to be done with exquisite skill, and to be as free as possible from anything which ordinary readers would be apt to object to as coarse." To palliate McCulloch, whose talents he professed to admire very highly, Blackwood offered him the opportunity of rewriting some of the Stepsure letters for his magazine. He was to address them specifically to a Scottish audience and to make no reference to their having been published previously in "any of the Canadian Papers." Blackwood also invited McCulloch to submit other contributions to *Blackwood's Edinburgh Magazine*, offering him 8 to 10 guineas a page for anything accepted.

Stung to the quick by Blackwood's assessment, McCulloch angrily instructed Mitchell to retrieve his manuscripts, writing that "dirty as Bl. thinks my novels I judge them purity itself compared with his magazine and it would be a subject of serious consideration with me whether I ought to write for a publication whose tendency is so irreligious." That the "Chronicles" did make reference to breaking wind and emptying chamber-pots was undeniable, but such features enlivened the slapstick which a satirical Club sketch recalled so nostalgically when it discussed the Stepsure letters in the *Novascotian* on 15 May 1828: "Did you ever read his Mephiboschetch, that set the hale kintra laughin' for months at his odd stories about gable ends and cabbage?" However, McCulloch's submissions to Blackwood's had come at a time when there was an increasing shift toward gentility in the British press. Galt had already encountered similar difficulties with the serialization of "The last of the lairds" in *Blackwood's* in 1826, and his novel was subsequently considerably bowdlerized by the publisher while he was in Upper Canada. McCulloch would never afford Blackwood this opportunity, reiterating to Mitchell between 1829 and 1833 his desire to retrieve his manuscripts from Blackwood and indicating that any new novels would be submitted elsewhere.

In a letter to Mitchell in December 1833, McCulloch asked him to obtain Oliphant's rate for a novel of approximately 400 pages on the "Days of the Covenant." As with an unpublished story on James MacGregor, a major portion of this manuscript survives in the McCulloch papers at the Public Archives of Nova Scotia. Set in 1669 in the decade before the murder of Archbishop James Sharp, the manuscript confirms how preoccupied McCulloch was with celebrating the religious courage of the Covenanters. Filled with many of the same supernatural, folkloric, and romantic elements as "Auld Eppie's tales," the "Days of the Covenant" is like "Auld Eppie" and the Stepsure letters in revealing that McCulloch's strengths lay in the characterization of ordinary folk rather than in the portrayal of lairds, abbots, and other figures of public consequence.

In July 1834 McCulloch indicated to Mitchell that his improved financial situation and his failure to please the public had decided him against trying to publish any more manuscripts in Scotland. He occasionally submitted light passages to Nova Scotian newspapers, however, and there is evidence that he was the Timothy Ticklemup who wrote on Parson Drone for the *Acadian Recorder* on 6 April 1833 and the Mr C. Currycomber who wrote for the *Morning Herald, and Commercial Advertiser* (Halifax) in 1841. In 1839 Mitchell had unsuccessfully sought a publisher for a theological manuscript, possibly "Calvinism: the doctrine of the scriptures," and he concluded it was better suited to the American situation and market than to the Scottish. It was eventually published in Glasgow in 1846. In 1841 McCulloch was working on another manuscript on the divinity of Christ, which appears never to have been published. He made no effort to publish any of his fiction locally even after he had directed Mitchell to retrieve the manuscripts. It was not until 1862 that a book-length edition of the first 16 Stepsure letters, based on those in the *Acadian Recorder*, was to appear.

McCulloch's other interests remained strong in his final years. Not least of these was his preoccupation with natural history. Beginning after the opening of Pictou Academy with an interest in insects and, after his 1825–26 visit to Britain, extending it to birds,

McCulloch made the study of natural history both an avocation and a teaching tool throughout his Pictou years. His gifts of insects to the universities of Glasgow and Edinburgh, his acceptance into the Wernerian Society of Edinburgh in 1823, his contributions to private collectors, and his plant exchanges with the Scottish naturalist Patrick Neill also brought recognition to his work. By 1828 he had opened a natural history museum in the west room of the academy, filling it with "birds, four footed beasts, and creeping things." John James Audubon was much impressed by the collection when he visited Pictou in 1833, taking away gifts of birds, shells, and minerals. Audubon's visit initiated years of collaboration with Thomas McCulloch Jr, later professor of natural philosophy at Dalhousie, and resulted in the younger McCulloch's sending samples of Nova Scotian bird life to Audubon in New York. Lack of provincial support for his endeavours led to the senior McCulloch's sounding out the British Museum's interest in the collection in 1834. When it decided against buying the Pictou Museum, Thomas McCulloch Jr transported the collection to Britain and sold sections to individual collectors such as the Earl of Derby. Its equal had never before left North America, McCulloch ruefully wrote to Mitchell, but, undaunted by the loss, he and his son began a second major collection when McCulloch moved to Halifax. His last years were spent scouring the province for specimens and included a collecting trip to Sable Island in company with one of his former students, Adams George Archibald*. In the 1820s McCulloch had written to Mitchell about returning from his insect collecting "stung in every accessible part and as itchy as any poor Scotchman can be." His letters to Mitchell in 1841 reveal that he was as dedicated as ever in his pursuit of specimens, some of which survive in a small collection at Dalhousie University. These two faithful correspondents were reunited once more before McCulloch's death when he returned to Scotland in 1842. Here he again met old colleagues, one of whom was to recall McCulloch's weeping profusely in his pew as memories were stirred, coming up to the pulpit, and giving "my people a most interesting and animated address, descriptive of Nova Scotia."

McCulloch was driven by his intellect, his Calvinist faith, his philosophical liberalism, and his enormous energy. His early theological works acquired for him an intellectual standing in the province, and his newspaper and pamphlet polemics subsequently kept him in the public eye. The powerful logic and clarity of his arguments lent strength to his consistent exposition of the necessity for fair treatment of dissenters in a province which gave legal recognition to dissent. As the Stepsure letters demonstrate, he could use satire, as well as scholarship and logical argument, to show his vision of Nova Scotian society. His Scottish education and his commitment to the Secession branch of Presbyterianism shaped his perspective of that society. From his strong Calvinist faith came a determination to "fill these provinces with a race of evangelical preachers." His fundamental secular belief lay in the capacity of a liberal education to build a Christian nation of informed, responsible citizens. When his idealism was thwarted by political reality, he turned his powers to the emerging reform cause in Nova Scotia, linking it to similar movements in Britain and the Canadas. Nevertheless, although an intellectual framework was being defined, no political party was established to implement reform in Nova Scotia until Joseph Howe took up the cause. McCulloch's intellect and his energy made him impatient with those whose dedication did not equal his own and with the adherence of those not his intellectual equals to positions he had shown to be illogical. His confidence in the justice of his own positions made him confrontational rather than co-operative, and his sense of his own integrity kept him from compromise. He thus attracted ardent admirers and intense friendships, but also passionate enemies. When his path crossed those of other ambitious, aggressive men such as Inglis and MacKenzie, there was no common ground. McCulloch's ultimate impact was made through his students – lawyers, businessmen, scholars, clergymen, missionaries, educators, and scientists – whose abilities and visions he shaped, and through his contribution to Canadian literature.

SUSAN BUGGEY and GWENDOLYN DAVIES

[The single most important collection of material written by Thomas McCulloch is that of his papers in PANS, MG 1, 550–58. It includes his lengthy and detailed correspondence with James Mitchell and Mitchell's son James, drafts of documents and local correspondence, notes of his scientific lectures, and his theological and literary papers. The last include manuscripts of the first 16 of the Stepsure letters, incomplete manuscripts of "William," "Auld Eppie's tales," and "Days of the Covenant," stories on "Morton" and James MacGregor, and assorted fragments. S.B. and G.D.]

McCulloch's religious publications include *Popery condemned by Scripture and the fathers: being a refutation of the principal popish doctrines and assertions* . . . (Edinburgh, 1808); *Popery again condemned . . . : being a reply to a part of the popish doctrines and assertions contained in the remarks on the refutation, and in the review of Dr. Cochran's letters, by the Rev. Edmund Burke* . . . (Edinburgh, 1810); *The prosperity of the church in troublous times* . . . (Halifax, 1814), republished *with introductory remarks by Rev. Robert Grant* (New Glasgow, N.S., 1882); *Words of peace: being an address, delivered to the congregation of Halifax . . . in consequence of some congregational disputes* . . . (Halifax, 1817); *The report of a committee, appointed by the synod of the Presbyterian Church of Nova-Scotia, to prepare a statement of means for promoting religion in the church* . . . (Halifax, 1818); *A lecture, delivered at the opening of the first theological class in the Pictou academical institution . . .* (Glasgow, 1821); *A memorial from the committee of missions of the Presbyterian Church of Nova Scotia, to the Glasgow Society for Promoting the Religious Interests of the Scottish Settlers in British North America . . .* (Edinburgh, 1826); *A review of the "Supplement to the first annual report of the Society . . ."; in a series of letters to the Rev. Robert Burns . . .* (Glasgow, 1828); and *Calvinism, the doctrine of the Scriptures . . .*, which was issued posthumously (Glasgow, [1846]). In addition McCulloch is identified in a manuscript dedication as a member of the committee responsible for a pamphlet entitled *The subjects and mode of baptism ascertained from Scripture, being a conversation between a private Christian and a minister . . . ; by a committee of the Associate Presbytery of Pictou* (Edinburgh, 1810), a copy of which is in the Univ. of Edinburgh Library. His 1818 lecture on education appeared as *The nature and uses of a liberal education illustrated; being a lecture, delivered at the opening of the building, erected for the accommodation of the classes of the Pictou academical institution* (Halifax, 1819).

McCulloch's published literary works are *Colonial gleanings: William and Melville* (Edinburgh, 1826) and the Stepsure letters. The latter did not appear in novel form until 1862, when Hugh William Blackadar* printed an anonymous Halifax edition entitled *The letters of Mephibosheth Stepsure* (the imprint date of 1860 on the title page is an error). A modern edition, with an introduction by Northrop Frye and notes by John Allan Irving and Douglas G. Lochhead, has been published under McCulloch's name as *The Stepsure letters* ([Toronto], 1960), and a new edition with an introduction by Gwendolyn Davies is currently being prepared by the Centre for Editing Early Canadian Texts at Carleton Univ. (Ottawa).

Atlantic Baptist Hist. Coll., Acadia Univ. (Wolfville, N.S.), Edward Manning, corr., vol.1; Thomas McCulloch letters, 1821–25. Dalhousie Univ. Arch. (Halifax), DAL, MS 2-40 (Thomas McCulloch papers); MS 2-41 (J. J. Audubon letters). NLS, Dept. of MSS, MS 7638: 83–84. PANS, MG 1, 165; 793, nos.27, 39, 44–45, 68–69; 1845, folder 2, no.23; MG 100, 181, nos.22–23; Places, Pictou, Pictou Academy papers, including minute-books, 1806–46 (mfm.); RG 1, 225, docs.58–60; 227, doc.89; 248, doc.181; 282, docs.129–45; 439, no.89. PRO, CO 217/152–54; CO 218/29–30. UCC, Maritime Conference Arch. (Halifax), Family and individual papers, box 22, envelopes 82–82g (Thomas McCulloch papers), esp. envelopes 82 (Pictou Academy and other institutions, 1823–74), 82f (corr., 1807–43); Presbyterian Church of N.S. (United Secession), minutes of the synod, 1 (1817–42)–2 (1842–60). UCC-C, Glasgow Colonial Soc., corr., I (1821–28)–VI (1836–38), corr. for 1824–36 (mfm. at PAC). [Robert Burns], *Supplement to the first annual report of the Society in Glasgow for Promoting the Religious Interests of Scottish Settlers in North America . . .* (Glasgow, 1826). *Acadian Recorder*, 1813–30. *Colonial Patriot*, 1827–30. *Free Press* (Halifax), 1817–28. *Novascotian, or Colonial Herald*, September–November 1838. *The Oxford companion to Canadian literature*, ed. William Toye (Toronto, 1983), 480–81. Wallace, *Macmillan dict.*

Susan Buggey, "Churchmen and dissenters: religious toleration in Nova Scotia, 1758–1835" (MA thesis, Dalhousie Univ., Halifax, 1981). V. L. O. Chittick, *Thomas Chandler Haliburton ("Sam Slick"): a study in provincial toryism* (New York, 1924; repr. 1966), 378–79. Gwendolyn Davies, "'A Past of Orchards': rural changes in Maritime literature before confederation," *The red jeep and other landscapes: a collection in honour of Douglas Lochhead*, ed. Peter Thomas (Fredericton, 1987). W. B. Hamilton, "Education, politics and reform in Nova Scotia, 1800–1848" (PHD thesis, Univ. of Western Ont., London, 1970); "Thomas McCulloch, advocate of non-sectarian education," *Profiles of Canadian educators*, ed. R. S. Patterson *et al.* ([Toronto], 1974), 21–37. D. C. Harvey, *An introduction to the history of Dalhousie University* (Halifax, 1938). *Literary history of Canada: Canadian literature in English*, ed. C. F. Klinck *et al.* (2nd ed., 3v., Toronto and Buffalo, N.Y., 1976), 1: 107–8. William McCulloch, *The life of Thomas McCulloch, by his son*, [ed. I. W. and J. W. McCulloch] ([Truro, N.S., 1920]). B. F. MacDonald, "Intellectual forces in Pictou, 1803–1843" (MA thesis, Univ. of N.B., Fredericton, 1977). S. G. McMullin, "Thomas McCulloch: the evolution of a liberal mind" (PHD thesis, Dalhousie Univ., 1975). J. S. Martell, "Origins of self-government in Nova Scotia, 1815–1836" (PHD thesis, Univ. of London, 1935). George Patterson, *A history of the county of Pictou, Nova Scotia* (Montreal, 1877; repr. Belleville, Ont., 1972). J. [E.] Tulloch, "Conservative opinion in Nova Scotia during an age of revolution, 1789–1815" (MA thesis, Dalhousie Univ., 1972). Marjory Whitelaw, *Thomas McCulloch: his life and times* (Halifax, 1985). D. C. Harvey, "Dr. Thomas McCulloch and liberal education," *Dalhousie Rev.*, 23 (1943–44): 352–62. Robin Mathews, "*The Stepsure letters*: puritanism and the novel of the land," *Studies in Canadian Literature* (Fredericton), 7 (1982): 128–38. Gene Morison, "The brandy election of 1830," N.S. Hist. Soc., *Coll.*, 30 (1954): 151–83. Beverly Rasporich, "The New Eden dream: the source of Canadian humour: McCulloch, Haliburton, and Leacock," *Studies in Canadian Literature*, 7: 227–40. H. L. Scammell, "Why did Thomas McCulloch come to Dalhousie?" N.S. Hist. Soc., *Coll.*, 31 (1957): 64–72. Vincent Sharman, "Thomas McCulloch's Stepsure: the relentless Presbyterian," *Dalhousie Rev.*, 52 (1972–73): 618–25. Donald Stephens, "Past or permanent," *Canadian Literature* (Vancouver), no.10 (autumn 1961): 83–84. Marjory Whitelaw, "Thomas McCulloch," *Canadian Literature*, nos.68–69 (spring–summer 1976): 138–47. B. A. Wood, "The significance of Calvinism in the educational vision of Thomas McCulloch," *Vitæ Scholasticæ* ([Ames, Iowa]), 4 (1985), nos.1–2: 15–30; "Thomas McCulloch's use of science in promoting a liberal education," *Acadiensis* (Fredericton), 17 (1987–88), no.1: 56–73.

MACDONALD, JOHN SMALL, businessman, politician, militia officer, JP, and office holder; b. *c.* 1791 on Saint John's (Prince Edward) Island, son of John MacDonald of West River and Margaret MacDonald of Glenaladale; m. at St Andrews, P.E.I., Isabella McDonald, daughter of Donald and Catherina McDonald, and they had at least seven girls and one boy who survived infancy; d. 20 Jan. 1849 in Charlottetown at age 58.

John Small Macdonald was, judging by his correspondence, well educated. He was a farmer and proprietor, and he lived most of his adult life near the West River in Queens County. His mother was sister to Captain John MacDonald* of Glenaladale, a major figure among Highland Scots on the Island. Along with Captain John's son Donald*, John Small retained to some extent the prestige and responsibility of a Highland laird. The anomaly of this conceit in an increasingly democratic era made Macdonald's political career a particularly interesting one.

When the political disabilities he and others suffered as Roman Catholics were removed in 1830, Macdonald that year contested and won a seat in the House of Assembly for Queens County. The enfranchisement of Catholics coincided with, and indeed may have fostered, pressure for a court of escheat to confiscate land holdings deemed in default of the terms of the original grants made in 1767. The practical result of escheat would have been the redistribution of land owned by large, mostly absentee, proprietors to tenant farmers. This issue immediately placed Macdonald in a dilemma. A large proportion of tenants were Catholic Highland Scots, many of whom were his constituents, and to all of whom he appears to have felt some responsibility. Conversely, he was himself a proprietor, albeit neither a large nor an absentee one, and was necessarily concerned by a movement which placed property rights in jeopardy.

Macdonald's response was to push for almost any expedient short of a full escheat that would allay tenant agitation. Thus, while opposing the radicalism of the escheat leader, William Cooper*, Macdonald was willing to countenance such reforms as quadrennial elections, colonial responsibility for the civil list, and even a limited confiscation of lands held by grossly delinquent proprietors. This position was sufficiently acceptable that Macdonald won re-election not only in 1834, but also in the face of the Escheat party's great victory in 1838. Given the defeat of other moderates that year, Macdonald's position as a spokesman for the Catholic Highland Scots must have been crucial in tipping the balance in his favour.

As the escheat movement dissipated in the 1840s Macdonald's political difficulties eased, and he was routinely returned to the assembly until his retirement in 1846. In 1839 he was appointed to the Executive Council by Lieutenant Governor Sir Charles Augustus FitzRoy*, and this post he held until his death. Never a major force in either body, Macdonald did interest himself in obtaining public funds for the temperance society and for Thomas Irwin's book of elementary instruction in the Micmac language. His last major recorded speech was on the Bible question in 1845; his sage advice was that the less said on the topic the better.

A trustee of St Andrew's College in St Andrews, and then of the Central Academy in Charlottetown, Macdonald was a member and president of the Highland Society and of the Central Agricultural Society. He also served as a captain of militia. From 1825 until his death he was a justice of the peace, and he was appointed high sheriff of Queens County in 1839.

An interesting correspondence took place between Macdonald and John Barelli and Company of London from 1843 to 1848. In common with many Island landowners Macdonald tried his hand at shipbuilding, and he used Barelli as an agent to sell both ship and cargo. Their exchange of letters charts the frustrations of a small shipbuilder dependent on local subcontractors and foreign agents. When Macdonald sent Barelli his barque *Friendship* its sale was long delayed, and accomplished only at a reduced price. According to Barelli, the barque was so badly built that claims from the new owners would more than wipe out any profits. The ship's low quality gave Macdonald's next vessels such a poor reputation that they could only be sold at a loss. This experience apparently stalled Macdonald's career as a shipbuilder. He died some £4,000 in debt. It can only be surmised how many other small operations came to a similar end.

In 1841 the assembly had referred to Macdonald as a member of the "family compact." Even if his cousin was a large proprietor, the label understates the importance of Macdonald's consciousness of his ethnic and religious heritage and distorts his political record.

M. Brook Taylor

PAPEI, RG 1, commission books. P.E.I. Museum, File information concerning J. S. Macdonald. Private arch., Jean and Colin MacDonald (St Peters, P.E.I.), MacDonald family papers, docs.75–184 (copies at PAPEI). Supreme Court of P.E.I. (Charlottetown), Estates Division, papers of administration for J. S. Macdonald estate. P.E.I., House of Assembly, *Journal*, 3, 11 Feb., 6 April 1831; 26 Jan. 1835; 22 Jan. 1839; 1841: 151; 24 Jan. 1843. *Examiner* (Charlottetown), 22 Jan. 1849. *Prince Edward Island Register*, 27 Oct. 1825, 27 Nov. 1827. *Royal Gazette* (Charlottetown), 14 Sept. 1830; 24 Jan. 1832; 29 Jan., 5, 26 Feb., 19 March, 26 Nov. 1833; 1 April, 9, 23 Dec. 1834; 24, 27 Feb., 31 March 1835; 26 April, 7 June, 20 Sept. 1836; 9 Oct., 27 Nov. 1838; 12 Feb., 12 March, 7 May, 23 July 1839; 16 Feb., 20 April 1841; 19 July 1842; 28 March, 25 April, 9 May, 13 June, 11 July, 3 Oct., 26 Dec. 1843; 30 Jan. 1844; 15 April 1845; 9 April 1846; 23 Jan. 1849. *Canada's smallest province: a history of P.E.I.*, ed. F. W. P. Bolger ([Charlottetown, 1973]). MacKinnon, *Government of P.E.I.*, 53. *Herald* (Charlottetown), 17 Oct. 1888. J. F. Snell, "Sir William Macdonald and his kin," *Dalhousie Rev.*, 23 (1943–44): 321.

MacDONALD, WILLIAM PETER, Roman Catholic priest, journalist, and author; b. 25 March 1771 in the parish of Eberlow, Banffshire, Scotland, son of Thomas MacDonald and Ann Watt; d. 2 April 1847 in Toronto.

William Peter MacDonald studied at the seminary of Douai, France, and at the Royal Scots College in Valladolid, Spain, where he was ordained to the priesthood on 24 Sept. 1796. After teaching for two years at the seminary in Aquhorthies, Scotland, he was employed from 1798 to 1810 in the Catholic ministry in his native land. In 1810 he participated in the expedition to liberate the deposed Ferdinand VII of Spain, held prisoner by Napoleon, and two years later he was appointed chaplain of the Baron de Roll's regiment of infantry. For some time before his return to Scotland in 1814 he served as chaplain to the British embassy in Madrid. He continued to work in the Scottish missions until Bishop Alexander McDonell of Kingston, Upper Canada, invited him to his diocese in 1826. Having responded favourably to this overture, MacDonald was assigned to St Raphaels parish in Glengarry County, where he ministered from December 1826 to 1829 and became first rector of Iona College. Shortly after his arrival, he was promoted vicar general of the diocese of Kingston. The Canadian clergy was impressed with Bishop McDonell's new recruit, a man who had already published a book of poetry dedicated to Edward* Augustus, the Duke of Kent.

MacDonald was to serve as pastor of a number of Upper Canadian parishes: Kingston 1829–34, Toronto 1834–35, Bytown (Ottawa) 1835–36, Brockville 1836–38, Hamilton 1838–46, and Toronto 1846–47. He wrote two more works during these years, one a polemical anti-Protestant tract, the other a pamphlet refuting arguments made by the Anglican archdeacon of Toronto, John Strachan*, on the occasion of the conversion to Roman Catholicism of John Elmsley*. He also compiled a collection of hymns which remained unpublished. Upon being transferred to Hamilton late in 1838, he immediately undertook the construction of a stone church, completed in the autumn of 1839, and a stone rectory, which was finished shortly afterwards.

MacDonald never got along well with his ecclesiastical superiors. Mutual suspicion, even contempt, seems to have been the prevailing mood. After arriving in Bytown in the autumn of 1835, he proceeded to make arrangements with the Catholics of Hull and Templeton, in the diocese of Montreal, to serve their religious needs in return for their contributing to the support of the two priests in Bytown. Bishop Jean-Jacques Lartigue of Montreal was not consulted and was consequently miffed. The year before, when Bishop McDonell had appointed MacDonald to Toronto, coadjutor bishop Rémi Gaulin* commented that given his poor qualities as a parish administrator, MacDonald was a most unfortunate choice, particularly in the light of the strong feeling in Toronto against the Scots. For his part, MacDonald was regularly critical of his bishops and his fellow clergymen.

On 22 Oct. 1830 appeared the first issue of the *Catholic*, a weekly newspaper established by MacDonald and printed in Kingston by Thomas Dalton. The title page explains the paper's *raison d'être*: "an exposition of the Catholic doctrine, designed to repel the calumnies and misrepresentations, which though so often refuted, have been constantly reiterated in the sectarian papers in these provinces." A spirited, and sometimes acrimonious, debate was thus initiated between the *Catholic*, Egerton Ryerson*'s *Christian Guardian*, Adam Hood Burwell's *Christian Sentinel*, and other newspapers. The last issue of volume I of the *Catholic* appeared on 14 Oct. 1831. The author/publisher then discontinued the paper, alleging overwork and some criticism. Ten years later, however, MacDonald resurrected the periodical. It continued until May 1844, when it was sold. From 1841 through 1844, MacDonald frequently complained of the lack of financial support for his paper from various churchmen. "All is dead in our Diocese," he commented.

Following the erection of the diocese of Toronto on 17 Dec. 1841, its first bishop, Michael Power, appointed MacDonald his vicar general (10 May 1842). MacDonald was the promoter of the first Toronto synod, held in early October 1842. In March 1844, however, Power dismissed MacDonald as vicar general for disciplinary reasons, although he kept him as pastor of Hamilton. The bishop's main complaint was that, contrary to the regulations of the synod, MacDonald did not wear his soutane on the streets of Hamilton.

Within two years MacDonald had not only been reinstated as vicar general but, along with Father John James Hay, had also been chosen by Power to administer the diocese of Toronto during the bishop's six-month journey to Europe. In December 1846 MacDonald left Hamilton, where he had been replaced by Edward John Gordon*, to reside in the newly completed bishop's palace in Toronto. He died there on 2 April 1847, his remains being buried in the unfinished St Michael's Cathedral.

Robert Choquette

William Peter MacDonald's volume of poetry dedicated to the Duke of Kent was published in London in 1818 as *The moneiad: or, the power of money*. His anti-Protestant tract appeared under the title *The Protestant, or negative faith refuted, and the Catholic, or affirmative faith demonstrated from Scripture* (Kingston, [Ont.], 1836). The Arch. of the Roman Catholic Archdiocese of Toronto holds a bound volume of his manuscript hymns entitled "Hymns translated from the latin Originals; With Others; and Occasional Poems on Sacred Subjects, composed by the Rev[d]. W[m]. MacDonald, Vicar General, U.C." at M (Macdonell papers), AE22.01. MacDonald is also the author of *Remarks on Doctor Strachan's pamphlet against the Catholic doctrine of the real presence of Christ's body and blood in the Eucharist* . . . (Kingston, 1834).

ACAM, 255.102, 834-5. Arch. of the Archdiocese of Kingston, AI (Alexander MacDonell papers, corr.), 1C24-9, 2C3-32, 2C4; BI (Remigius Gaulin papers, corr.), 1C15-1, -3, -5; CI (Patrick Phelan papers, corr.), 2C21. Arch. of the Roman Catholic Archdiocese of Toronto, LB 02 (Michael Power, letter-book, 1842–65): 130–32, 145–47, 260–61; M (Macdonell papers), AE01.01–2, .04; AE02.01; AE16.01; AE19.03; CA17.01, .03, .09. Michael Power, *Constitutiones diocesanæ in synodo Torontina prima latæ et promulgatæ* (Toronto, 1842). *Catholic, a Religious Weekly Periodical* (Kingston; Hamilton, [Ont.]), 1830–31, 1841–44. Robert Choquette, *L'Église catholique dans l'Ontario français du dix-neuvième siècle* (Ottawa, 1984). S. D. Gill, "'The sword in the Bishop's hand': Father William Peter MacDonald, a Scottish defender of the Catholic faith in Upper Canada," *Study Sessions*, 50 (1983): 437–52.

McDONELL, ALEXANDER (from 1838 he signed **Macdonell**), Roman Catholic priest and bishop, office holder, and politician; b. 17 July 1762 in Glengarry, Scotland; d. 14 Jan. 1840 in Dumfries, Scotland.

Alexander McDonell, to whom Thomas D'Arcy McGee* would refer as the "greatest Tory in Canada," belonged to a Highland clan which had supported Prince Charles, the Young Pretender, in 1745, and had suffered the consequences of his failure. Despite harsh government measures to repress Highland culture after the rebellion, the Macdonells and many other Jacobites were quick to enter British military service when the occasion offered. Perhaps their attitude showed simply an acceptance of the inevitable or, more likely, it reflected the conviction of the Catholic clergy that only loyal submission would bring relief. Because of the penal laws the young Alexander McDonell, as other Catholics, received only a sketchy education at home and had to go abroad for formal religious training. After entering the Scots College in Paris, he went on to the Royal Scots College at Valladolid, Spain, in 1778 to complete his studies for the priesthood. Moulded by the theology and morality taught there at the time, McDonell emerged strictly orthodox and deeply conservative. On 16 Feb. 1787 he was ordained and he returned to the Highlands as a missionary priest that year. A huge man who would always have a problem with his weight, Big Sandy or Mr Alistair as he was known served first in Badenoch and then in Lochaber, ministering to his flock of Gaelic-speaking crofters.

But the clan system, with its reciprocal rights and obligations, was collapsing. McDonell sought employment for his parishioners in Glasgow and succeeded in placing them in the expanding cotton industry. Early in 1792 it was decided that he should be given charge of the Glasgow mission. Economic respite for the Highlanders was short-lived, since the outbreak of war with revolutionary France in 1793 disrupted trade with Europe and they were once again in desperate straits.

Some time that year, Father McDonell made contact with the young and Protestant clan chieftain, Alexander Ranaldson Macdonell of Glengarry, to whom he swiftly attached himself. Either singly or together, they concocted a scheme of offering the unemployed Highlanders to the British government as a fencible regiment, willing to serve outside England or Scotland, unlike the other fencibles who claimed to be home defence units. After a trip to London to seek acceptance of the plan, McDonell returned briefly to Glasgow and the displeasure of his bishop, who was distressed by the priest's neglect of his mission. Although appearing contrite, McDonell was determined to follow Glengarry, perhaps aspiring to bring him back to the Catholic fold, more likely hoping to find some alternative employment for his people.

In any event, the offer of service was accepted by the British government. The Glengarry Fencibles were embodied with Glengarry as colonel; Alexander McDonell was appointed chaplain on 14 Aug. 1794, the first Catholic chaplain in the British army since the Reformation. The regiment went to Guernsey in 1795, to remain in relative idleness guarding against a French invasion which never came. When rebellion broke out in Ireland in 1798, the fencibles were hastily transferred there. During the four years that his regiment served in Ireland, McDonell lost few opportunities to reinforce the reputation of the Catholic Highlanders for devoted loyalty. He was determined to make himself as useful as possible to the British authorities, never questioning the extent to which influence and patronage affected the success of people or policies.

The brief Peace of Amiens in 1802 brought the disbanding of many non-regular regiments and McDonell's people were once again without support. Even worse, McDonell himself was betrayed by Glengarry, being unfairly left responsible for the chieftain's debts, and had to endure the humiliation of a stay in prison. Prospects in Scotland were still gloomy after his release in January 1803, and he resolved to persuade the government to acknowledge the regiment's service by making grants of land in Upper Canada to its former members. His conservative sympathies would have made the United States an unacceptable refuge and he resisted proposals that he lead his flock to the Caribbean. The positive inducement which drew him to Upper Canada was that many Glengarry Macdonells who had fought as loyalists in the American revolution had relocated in the eastern end of this remote province, where a county had been named Glengarry. Moreover the military service of McDonell's group had earned them influential friends such as Lieutenant Governor Peter Hunter*, who had been their commander in Ireland and who had said he would welcome them to Upper Canada.

McDonell left Scotland in early September 1804. He was on his way to a province where Catholics were few and where he would be the only priest. On his way through Lower Canada he called on the coadjutor bishop, Joseph-Octave Plessis*, and on 1 Nov. 1804 received ecclesiastical jurisdiction from the bishop, Pierre Denaut*. Plessis, who succeeded Denaut early in 1806, was the only member of the French Canadian hierarchy with whom McDonell ever developed a warm relationship. The two became firm friends and Plessis saw in McDonell a useful ally in his plan to divide the enormous diocese of Quebec, which included all of British North America. As a first step, he appointed McDonell his vicar general and informed him privately that he would be named bishop of Upper Canada, *in partibus*, as soon as the division took place.

Meanwhile McDonell had established himself at St Raphaels, in Glengarry County, but his field of action was all of the province. He worked to secure the promised land grants for the former fencibles, saw to it that friends and relatives received appointment as surveyors and sheriffs, and acquired sites in Kingston and York (Toronto) for future churches. His own salary was paid in Montreal by the governor-in-chief, an arrangement McDonell believed implied official recognition, besides making him somewhat independent of the local government at York. He immediately began a long campaign to have the government of Upper Canada provide salaries for Catholic priests and teachers. In his view there were many advantages to such an arrangement, both for the church and for the authorities. Dependence on government, he argued, would ensure steady loyalty, and the state in return would be committed to the continuing support of the church. In addition, the Catholic clergy, freed of reliance upon their congregations for maintenance, could exercise a greater influence over them. Although the early response to this scheme was encouraging, a number of years would pass before it was achieved, and part of the cost would be a rupture with John Strachan*, the leading figure of the Church of England in the province.

In the mean time, the deterioration of relations between Britain and the United States presented McDonell with a challenge rife with opportunity and eventually brought him to provincial prominence. In 1807 he had urged that the Glengarry men be enrolled in the militia and Colonel Isaac Brock*, for one, familiar with the priest's past military exertions, was enthusiastic. Governor Sir James Henry Craig* decided, however, that McDonell's enthusiasm was greater than his ability to raise a regiment, and the proposal was shelved. Just prior to war's outbreak, Brock was administrator of Upper Canada and commander of the forces there. He welcomed a hurried visit by McDonell to York and quickly approved the raising of a Glengarry regiment, happy to have men of proven loyalty amid a population he viewed with considerable suspicion. Governor Sir George Prevost* agreed and, without waiting for the assent of the home authorities, on 24 March 1812 ordered formation of the regiment. Father McDonell, of course, was chaplain.

But there were other ways in which the priest would serve. He took an active and effective role in the provincial election of 1812, made more exciting by the dangers of war. Glengarry was no problem. It was not only solidly tory, but solidly Macdonell. According to writer John Graham Harkness, the clan "seems to have had a monopoly of Parliamentary honours . . . of the members elected to the Assembly . . . from 1792 to 1840, all [but two] were connected by blood or marriage with the Macdonells." With Glengarry well in hand, Father McDonell, at the urging of the future chief justice, Archibald McLean*, intervened in Stormont and Russell in support of John Beikie, the government candidate, who succeeded in turning out the incumbent, Abraham Marsh, a sharp critic of the administration. McDonell's timely message to the Catholic community contributed to the desired result.

Altogether, McDonell's fortunes prospered during the war. Brock's most acute strategic problem was his line of communications to Lower Canada and its vulnerability to American attack along the waterways. With the approval of Prevost, in 1813 McDonell was appointed commissioner to oversee the cutting of a road to link the two provinces. Such recognition greatly enhanced his prestige, not least on account of the substantial patronage he thus acquired for the Eastern District. The Glengarry Light Infantry Fencibles acquitted themselves admirably in the war and writer William Foster Coffin* would later liken McDonell to "a medieval churchman, half bishop, half baron, [who] fought and prayed, with equal zeal, by the side of men he had come to regard as his hereditary followers." His salary was doubled and he won the warm support of the new administrator of Upper Canada, Gordon Drummond*, in his renewed attempt to get Catholic priests on the government payroll. The loyal support of the war effort by Upper Canadian Catholics, McDonell argued to Prevost, made clear the beneficial effect that would flow from firm and steady leadership.

McDonell was soon to have the opportunity to make his case at a higher level. In June 1816 Plessis joined him in Kingston to consecrate the first Catholic church there and begin McDonell's long association with what would become his episcopal see. Plessis had decided that the aftermath of the war provided the opportune time to forward his plan for dividing the diocese of Quebec, and McDonell was to be his chosen instrument. This role would require a journey to London and allow McDonell to seek the approval and the intervention of the British authorities in support of government salaries for Catholic priests and teachers in Upper Canada. He set off from Halifax in the autumn of 1816 on his twofold mission.

Upon his arrival in London, McDonell began a virtual year-long siege of the Colonial Office. Lord Bathurst, the colonial secretary, seemed willing enough to satisfy Plessis's wishes but, as McDonell well knew, the matter would have to be handled very delicately. He proposed to Bathurst that the diocese be divided into vicariates apostolic rather than independent sees, which would have carried territorial designations and alarmed the Church of England. Taking a curiously gallican line, he argued that since the vicars apostolic would owe their positions and thus their loyalty to the British government, imperial interests would be as well served as the administrative convenience of the Catholic Church in British North America. The colonial secretary was apparently convinced. London informed the Vatican that it would favour such a division of Quebec and recommended those whom it considered suitable as vicars apostolic – names which McDonell had provided and which included his own.

McDonell also sought to persuade Bathurst that government support for Catholic teachers and priests would further the interests of the state. Immigration to Upper Canada quickened after the war and he proposed a seminary to train a Catholic élite which would guard the faithful against the infection of democratic influences from the United States. Such an élite would also assume positions of responsibility in the local government. It was not at all lost on McDonell that John Strachan, recently appointed executive councillor, was introducing his former pupils into important offices; he did not wish the Catholics to be left behind. After much hesitation on Bathurst's part and importuning on McDonell's, the colonial secretary partially met the request. On 12 May 1817 he approved the salaries but directed that they be paid out of Upper Canadian revenues. McDonell would have greatly preferred to have them paid from London and thus be independent of the provincial government, but he had to be content with this limited success.

If not a triumph for McDonell, the journey had clearly been useful, and he returned to Upper Canada late in the autumn of 1817. Some time would pass before his negotiations concerning the division of the diocese bore fruit. It was only in January 1819 that the Vatican made him and Angus Bernard MacEachern* vicars apostolic and titular bishops subordinate to Plessis, who was named archbishop. Plessis had not been consulted and for various reasons was not pleased with the arrangement. As a result the briefs were never executed. New ones were issued in February 1820 and McDonell was made titular bishop of Rhesæna, suffragan, and episcopal vicar general. On 31 Dec. 1820 he was consecrated at Quebec in the chapel of the Ursuline convent.

Meanwhile the rumour that McDonell was to be made bishop and government salaries paid to Catholic priests and teachers had been received with indignation by John Strachan. Jealous of the position of the Church of England and anxious about his own prospects for a mitre, Strachan, as McDonell correctly surmised, used his influence to block the appropriation of the salaries from government revenues. It would be several years before Bathurst's promise would be redeemed. McDonell had also had to contend with that recurring upset of colonial political life, the appointment of a new lieutenant governor. Francis Gore* was succeeded in 1818 by Sir Peregrine Maitland*, who for ten years was the focus of power relationships in Upper Canada and exercised a determining influence in the complex patronage network which sustained the governing élite. The political arm of this élite was led by Strachan and John Beverley Robinson*, who acquired much control over the lieutenant governor. It was during Maitland's term of office that this "family compact" reached its zenith. They were never to have the same position with his successors.

McDonell's demonstrated loyalty, conservative ideology, and power over the people of his district made him of considerable utility to the government. Although he could never be of the family compact, given their determined support of the Church of England as the established church, he was certainly with them in their stout resistance to republican and levelling influences. He equally shared their attachment to Britain, but like Strachan, he was never an uncritical colonial. To the extent that McDonell buttressed the local government and its conservative policies, he was accorded a share in the patronage system, consulted by officials in matters of concern to him, and assured full consideration of his opinions on public affairs. In a real sense, he was an associate member of the governing élite and by the end of the 1820s was perceived by radical critics of the government as a pillar of its support.

In bringing himself to Maitland's attention, McDonell relied on the useful web of Scottish sympathies in the Canadas. He secured a charter from the Highland Society of London and, in concert with many of the partners and senior officials of the North West Company, formed the Highland Society of Canada. He successfully induced Maitland to accept election as its first president and modestly assumed the office of vice-president himself. His intimacy with the Nor'Westers was due not only to romantic sentiment for the Highlands. They contributed to his building campaigns and covered his bank loans. McDonell, in return, persuaded Plessis to delay the introduction of more missionaries to Red River because a successful colony there would threaten the NWC's activities. Only after the company's merger with the Hudson's Bay Company in 1821 was McDonell at all encouraging in his advice to Plessis about western expansion of the church.

Maitland saw in McDonell a useful ally and, in recognition of his acceptability, he was named to the land board of the Eastern District, made a member of a committee investigating the purchase of Indian lands, and appointed one of the commissioners to end the long dispute over the boundary of Upper and Lower Canada. Thus encouraged, McDonell prevailed on Maitland to intervene in the matter of the promised salaries. He now strengthened his argument by pointing to the growing influx of Irish Catholics, whose "turbulent disposition and want of control" would require careful handling by additional priests and teachers, preferably from Ireland. Maitland acceded to the request; but although McDonell was gratified that the 1823 appropriations included the long-delayed salaries, he was determined to visit England to collect the arrears he felt were owed by the colonial secretary.

There were other issues as well that McDonell's presence in London might forward. Plessis still hoped that the division of the diocese of Quebec would be complete; that is, that McDonell and his fellow vicars general MacEachern, Jean-Jacques LARTIGUE, and Joseph-Norbert Provencher* would be made bishops-in-ordinary with their own diocesan sees and suffragan to himself as metropolitan. The colonial secretary had been reluctant to accept the implications of four more independent Roman Catholic bishops in British North America. With the powerful support of Governor Lord Dalhousie [RAMSAY], Plessis and McDonell judged the time appropriate for a personal and private approach to Bathurst.

In addition, McDonell had been taking a hand in the intensifying political debate in 1821–22 over the proposal for a union of Upper and Lower Canada. Claiming that the Eastern District of the upper province was stoutly opposed to such a union, he joined Strachan and Robinson in arguing that all of Upper Canada would be irreparably injured. Louis-Joseph Papineau* tried to recruit McDonell as part of a Lower Canadian delegation bound for London to protest. McDonell declined on the ground that he would not be able to proceed to Britain until the spring of 1823. He did write flattering letters of introduction for Papineau, although he soon changed his opinion. But his concern about the impact of any union upon French Canadians was patent. They must not be provoked into disaffection, he wrote in January 1823 to his old friend Lord Sidmouth. "Both the Canadas are filling fast with Scotch Radicals, Irish rebels and American Republicans." A combination of these elements could well end the connection with Britain. Though written partly for effect, the letter reveals that his concerns were broader than the interests of Upper Canada alone.

McDonell left Upper Canada in the spring; his journey was to keep him away for over two years but would see the accomplishment of most of his objectives. After fortuitously meeting John Beverley Robinson in London and being reassured that the bruited union was a dead issue, he made a brief visit to the Highlands. He took the occasion to cultivate John GALT, a founder of the Canada Company. In return for much useful information on land matters in Upper Canada, including the most recent report of the Crown Lands Department, McDonell received some stock in the new company and, later on, a beautiful church site in its chief town of Guelph. Upon his return to London, his personal business with the Colonial Office drew his immediate attention. Somewhat to his surprise, Lord Bathurst capitulated readily in the matter of the arrears, and the Treasury, through the timely intervention of the bishop's cousin Charles Grant, the future Baron Glenelg and colonial secretary, agreed to a payment of £3,400 in full settlement. McDonell's high standing with the Colonial Office was further witnessed when Bathurst increased his salary to £400, a reward endorsed by Maitland, Dalhousie, and even John Strachan.

The erection of separate dioceses in British North America took considerably more time. Bathurst had given up his former opposition, partly at Dalhousie's urging. Despite Bathurst's willingness, however, McDonell finally had to travel to Rome in the spring of 1825 to assure the Vatican that the creation of new Roman Catholic jurisdictions in a non-Catholic land would not cause an unfavourable reaction and, indeed, had the approval of the British government. Formal presentations to the assembled cardinals and the tedious wait for the lumbering Vatican bureaucracy to produce results were eventually followed by papal sanction of three new dioceses, Kingston (1826), Charlottetown (1829), and Nova Scotia (1842).

It was August of 1825 when McDonell returned to London to share his achievement with the colonial secretary. But it became evident that Bathurst was now much preoccupied with the effect of increasing immigration to British North America by the Irish and, in particular, the dangerous prospect that they might coordinate activities with Daniel O'Connell in the United Kingdom. The bishop seized the occasion to seek more funding for Irish priests who could exercise a firm control over their restless flocks. It was a foretaste of the years of anxiety McDonell would be caused by events in the Irish Catholic community of Upper Canada. Soon after his arrival home in the autumn of 1825, he accompanied Maitland on a tour through the recently settled Irish districts in the Ottawa valley and enlisted his support. Although the lieutenant governor was sympathetic, he promised no funds and McDonell eventually received £750 annually from Bathurst. The colonial secretary diverted the funds from the proceeds of the Canada Company to provide salaries for additional Irish priests.

Early in 1826 Upper Canada became the diocese of Kingston and McDonell its bishop (he often used the form Regiopolis). The announcement of his appointment drew the somewhat petulant envy of Strachan, but did not prevent McDonell's active collaboration with the governing élite in the provincial election of 1828. He even attempted, though unsuccessfully, to induce Attorney General Robinson to stand for election in Glengarry. The riding was safe enough, although to McDonell's dismay the Catholics were unable to agree on a candidate and a Presbyterian supporter of the government was returned. More appalling, however, was the fact that the new House of Assembly contained a majority of critics and opponents of the executive, marked, if not led, by the increasing radicalism of William Lyon Mackenzie*.

Equally disconcerting that eventful year was the prospect of a new lieutenant governor. Maitland's replacement, Sir John Colborne*, was an unknown quantity. The bishop would soon be seeking his aid to help him channel the Irish Catholic immigrants into respectable paths. And among those recent immigrants was a priest named William John O'Grady, whose erratic career would challenge the bishop's influence over his flock and drag him more deeply into the politics of Upper Canada.

McDonell welcomed O'Grady at first, convinced as he was that Irish priests were best suited to Irish Catholic congregations. In January 1829 he gave O'Grady the important, and visible, charge at the provincial capital, since the Catholics in York were overwhelmingly Irish. O'Grady was also entrusted by the bishop to act as intermediary with Lieutenant Governor Colborne. McDonell was pleased enough with his performance to give O'Grady the power of vicar general early in 1830. But disturbing rumours began to circulate in York that O'Grady was neglecting his pastoral obligations, that he was too familiar with a local woman, and, worst of all, that he was meddling in reform politics and was increasingly identified with Mackenzie. In the summer of 1832 McDonell determined to end such scandal by transferring O'Grady to Brockville. When O'Grady refused, the bishop felt that he had no alternative but to suspend him from the priesthood.

O'Grady appealed to Colborne in January 1833 to intervene on his behalf, and the whole affair became distressingly public as Mackenzie's *Colonial Advocate* supported O'Grady and the bishop's authority was warmly endorsed by the *Canadian Freeman*, edited by Francis Collins*, and Thomas Dalton's *Patriot and Farmer's Monitor*. The public was treated to almost weekly instalments of the controversy in the press. It was a painful and difficult episode for McDonell, not least because he had had such hopes for O'Grady. In the bishop's view, the reputation of the Catholic population for loyalty and respectability was at stake and hence the future of the church in Upper Canada. It was not so much that O'Grady was meddling in politics that exercised McDonell, but that he was doing so in the wrong cause. The bishop would never concede that supporting the government was anything but one's proper duty. Yet he could hardly denounce O'Grady for his political activity without being accused of hypocrisy. The rebellious priest had therefore to be censured on ecclesiastical grounds of insubordination to his religious superior.

Colborne was not impressed by O'Grady's tortured argument that jurisdiction over the church had passed from France to Britain with the conquest, thus giving the lieutenant governor, as the representative of the crown, the right to intervene in the quarrel. After consulting his law officers, Colborne simply passed the matter on to the colonial secretary, who supported the bishop's authority as well. After an unsuccessful visit to Rome, O'Grady abandoned his challenge and in January 1834 returned to Upper Canada where, as a journalistic ally of Mackenzie, he continued to bedevil the bishop. While McDonell considered himself vindicated, he was deeply scarred by the dispute. He would never again give his trust so fully to another newcomer, and his ecclesiastical authority was exercised far more closely over his clergy thenceforward. Nor would he retreat from open political activity since the reputation of the Catholics of Upper Canada for loyalty had to be redeemed.

His own public position was secure. He was a sincere admirer of Colborne and, for his part, Colborne welcomed McDonell's support. One of his first objectives in Upper Canada had been to broaden representation in the Legislative Council and the bishop was one of the first appointees recommended to the Colonial Office. The mandamus summoning him to the council was dated 13 Sept. 1830, but because of illness he was not sworn in until 21 Nov. 1831. Although he attended only infrequently, McDonell saw his appointment both as a personal honour and as recognition of the just place of Catholics in the public life of the province. All churches, he hoped, would now be placed on an equal footing, and by churches he meant the churches of England, Scotland, and Rome, since all others were merely sects. Colborne, and also the new governor, Sir James Kempt*, were quite open to him in matters of patronage, providing land for new churches and salaries for additional priests to attend the steady stream of Irish Catholic immigrants.

McDonell continued to engage in partisan political activities, and was therefore among the targets of Mackenzie's frequent diatribes against the provincial executive. After successive expulsions from the assembly, Mackenzie carried his cause to the Colonial Office in the summer of 1832. His wide-ranging strictures included a direct attack on the presence of Strachan and McDonell in the Legislative Council. The response of Colonial Secretary Lord Goderich, a long letter of 8 Nov. 1832 to Colborne which became widely known as the Goderich memorandum, caused a sensation. Although Goderich discounted Mackenzie's more inflammatory accusations, the colonial secretary apparently concluded that much was awry in the distant colony. He informed Colborne, *inter alia*, that he had little sympathy with the continuing presence of McDonell and Strachan in the Legislative Council. In February 1833 the tories passed a stinging rebuke in the council, denouncing Mackenzie, rejecting Goderich's ill-informed intervention, and warmly defending the two clergymen. The independence of the upper house must be maintained, they countered, if its essential role as balance-wheel of the constitution was to be protected. The connection with Britain would only be threatened by such wrong-headed meddling by Colonial Office officials acting on such wicked and malicious testimony as that of Mackenzie. Goderich was shortly replaced by Lord Stanley and the issue subsided, but it made clear that Upper Canadian tories were anything but submissive colonials. In a letter to Sir James Kempt, McDonell drove home the point. The allegiance of Upper Canadians was fragile and could be disrupted as well by the reluctance of the home government to sustain the local executive as by the machinations of the unprincipled Mackenzie, he wrote.

Throughout 1833, the bishop remained at York to re-establish harmony in the distracted congregation and to exploit his friendship with Colborne. But he was now 71 and eager to set up permanent residence in Kingston. He wished also to be free of the routine administration of the diocese. He had begun the laborious process of persuading Quebec, London, and the Vatican to approve the appointment of an acceptable coadjutor. Such was his standing with the authorities, both political and ecclesiastic, that in the end matters went surprisingly swiftly. He avoided potential quarrels between the Scots and Irish in his flock by selecting a priest from Lower Canada, Rémi Gaulin*, who spoke English. It was a happy choice and McDonell could confidently turn over the running of the diocese to his new coadjutor. There would, however, be little leisure and no withdrawal from the public eye. The election of 1834 threw the province once again into political turmoil.

Perhaps it was complacency, but the tories put little effort into the campaign and failed utterly to recognize the rising tide of unrest that swept the reformers into a majority in the assembly. Bishop McDonell took no part in the election in Kingston where Christopher Alexander HAGERMAN easily turned back the challenge of O'Grady. Elsewhere in the province, including the Eastern District, tory candidates were overwhelmed. In Glengarry, Alexander McMartin*, the tory stalwart, was defeated by the bishop's radical cousin, Alexander Chisholm. It was hardly McDonell's fault. Nevertheless, it was clear that even the Highlanders were susceptible to reform agitation and could not be taken for granted. The election produced a fractious assembly with a disunited reform majority, mostly moderates, but with a determined band of radicals led by Mackenzie. McDonell and the tories would pay a high price for their neglect.

The bishop and his colleague in the Legislative Council, Archdeacon John Strachan, were favourite targets of the radicals in the assembly and the experience drew the two churchmen closer together. McDonell even supported Strachan's continuing crusade for a mitre. He wrote to his cousin Lord Glenelg, who was now colonial secretary, advocating the promotion. Strachan was touched by McDonell's support and, although unsuccessful at the time, he soon became bishop of Toronto. The two would have need of each other in the future as Mackenzie continued his attacks. Having persuaded the assembly in 1835 to create a special committee to investigate the grievances of the province, with himself as chairman, Mackenzie devoted a surprising amount of time to harassing Strachan and McDonell. Much of his evidence came from private letters of McDonell to O'Grady when the latter was still acting as vicar general. Few of the moderate reformers took the former priest seriously, but McDonell was greatly embarrassed by the affair.

Misreading the special committee's report as the considered opinion of the assembly, the Colonial Office concluded that matters in Upper Canada were at a sorry pass and decided to replace Colborne as lieutenant governor. McDonell rose to his defence and in a bitter letter to his cousin the colonial secretary in December 1835, denounced Mackenzie and his wicked fulminations. Mackenzie, meanwhile, had launched an inquiry into the funds that the bishop received from the Canada Company and demanded an accounting. McDonell flatly refused and was supported by Glenelg.

Shortly after his arrival in January 1836, the new lieutenant governor, Sir Francis Bond Head*, received a petition from the assembly which demanded, among other things, that McDonell and Strachan be compelled to resign from the Legislative Council. When asked by Head for his comments on the petition, McDonell stoutly refused to give up his post. He had no intention of showing "so much imbecility in my latter days, as to relinquish a mark of honour conferred upon me by my Sovereign to gratify the vindictive malice of a few unprincipled radicals." He defended Strachan as well, claiming that "I never saw him engaged in any political discussion of any kind"! "Politics" were only indulged in by opponents of the government. Both Head and Glenelg were apparently satisfied by the response.

In any case, the dispute was soon lost sight of as relations between the assembly and Head collapsed completely. In the summer of 1836 the province was plunged into its most violent election campaign ever. McDonell gave his complete attention to the Eastern District. The issue was clear – defence of the constitution against disloyalty. The bishop issued an address "to the Catholic and Protestant Freeholders of the Counties of Stormont and Glengarry." Accusing the radicals of attempting to sever the connection with Britain and preventing necessary expenditures on roads, canals, and other improvements, he went on to defend Sir Francis as a true reformer. Even the Orange order hailed his performance, cancelling its traditional parade at the capital on 12 July and toasting the bishop's patriotism. Supporters of the government took 10 of the 11 seats in the district. McDonell and the tories seemed well satisfied with the result, but the electoral defeat would soon drive Mackenzie to more desperate measures.

The bishop used his considerable credit with Head and the executive to secure a bill of incorporation for a seminary early in 1837. He was well aware, however, that the struggling Catholics of Upper Canada were in no position to finance it. He faced the prospect of another journey to Britain to seek funds for an adequate endowment. But he was soon caught up in local events. The Catholic hierarchy still sought the creation of a separate ecclesiastical province in British North America, which would involve the tricky problem of getting the British government to recognize the Catholic bishop of Quebec as metropolitan without provoking anxiety in the Church of England. The Lower Canadian bishops again turned to McDonell for help and he made an extended visit to Montreal and Quebec in the summer of 1837. He persuaded the governor, Lord Gosford [ACHESON], to support the initiative in London, but the matter added yet another reason for McDonell to travel to Britain.

He returned to Kingston in the early autumn of 1837 to make preparations for the journey and found the upper province in a state of great excitement. With many of the moderate reform leaders, such as Robert Baldwin* and Marshall Spring Bidwell*, withdrawn from active politics, Mackenzie was lashing out randomly at all his many antagonists. Perhaps equally important, the tories had lost confidence in Head, whose ideas on economic development, especially banking, ran counter to their own. Despite McDonell's implacable opposition to Mackenzie, the bishop was not blind to the political resentment against oligarchic control. In a letter to Lord Durham [LAMBTON] after the rebellion, he condemned the radicals but could not refrain from pointing out that many Upper Canadians were angered at seeing "a certain party in and about Toronto assume too much power and exercise what they think too much influence . . . so much so that there is hardly a situation of trust or emolument but what is engaged by themselves and their friends." When the vexed question of the clergy reserves and the pretensions of the Church of England are added, McDonell was not far from the position of the moderate reformers. But on the question of rebellion, there could be no intermediate position.

During the border excitements of 1838, McDonell fretted about the unreliability of much of the population of the province, saw military ineptitude everywhere, and drew on his past exploits to urge the formation of fencible regiments to defend Upper Canada. As the emergency receded, the bishop turned to the familiar problem of accommodating himself to a new lieutenant governor. He headed an impressive list of local notables who welcomed Sir George Arthur* to Kingston. The two would get on famously. He also made an urgent plea to Lord Durham to resolve the question of the clergy reserves, which the bishop argued was the single most distracting issue in the province. Durham included McDonell's letter in his *Report* as evidence for his blistering attack on the reserves. When the rebellion erupted again in Lower Canada after Durham's departure, McDonell even volunteered, "old and stiff as I am," to take the field at the head of his clansmen. Arthur declined his offer politely but followed his recommendations for appointments. The bishop's most effective action was a well-circulated address to the inhabitants of Glengarry in which he rallied support for the government. With Arthur's encouragement, he also published a similar address to the Irish Catholics of the province.

In the new year, 1839, the threat of invasion receded, and the politically active turned to the debate over Durham's recommendation for a "responsible" executive. McDonell took no part in the discussions. He was finally preparing for his much delayed return to England and Scotland to raise funds for his seminary, Regiopolis College, the cornerstone for which he hopefully laid in June. Sir George Arthur was as encouraging as possible, even proposing to name the bishop an official emigration agent of the province and defray his expenses. McDonell sailed from Montreal on 20 June 1839.

After 40-odd years, the bishop was well known to Colonial Office officials. But in truth, there was little he could accomplish in seeking to persuade them that he and his church were entitled to a share in the clergy reserves. At that moment, the energetic Charles

Edward Poulett THOMSON, who would be appointed governor in September, was preparing a scheme for their distribution. So while McDonell received a friendly and sympathetic welcome, his task was impossible. He would have to rely on whatever private funds he could raise for his seminary. He attempted, as well, to meet his obligations to Sir George Arthur. In early October he travelled to Scotland and then Ireland, hoping to induce the local bishops to support his emigration schemes. Pneumonia laid him low in Dublin and, after an apparent recovery, he returned to Scotland. But at Dumfries, on 14 Jan. 1840, he weakened and died.

McDonell's death coincided almost exactly with the end of the separate existence of Upper Canada. So also would pass from the philosophy of toryism there the values he saw as essential to true liberty – order, stability, deference. His profound social and political conservatism would become as irrelevant as the oligarchy with whom he had quarrelled, cooperated, and struggled to make Upper Canada a British haven for Scots and Irish Catholics.

J. E. REA

This work has been drawn almost exclusively from primary sources.

AO, MS 4; MS 35 (mfm. at PAC); MS 78; MS 498; MU 1147; MU 1966–73; MU 3389–90 (photocopies at PAC). Arch. of the Archdiocese of Kingston (Kingston, Ont.), A (Alexander MacDonell papers). Arch. of the Roman Catholic Archdiocese of Toronto, M (Macdonell papers). Archivio della Propaganda Fide (Rome). PAC, MG 19, A35; MG 24, A27; A40; J1; J13, Alexander McDonell, "The Glengarry Highlanders" (transcript); RG 1, E3; RG 5, A1; C2; RG 7, G1; RG 8, I (C ser.). PRO, CO 42. Scottish Catholic Arch. (Edinburgh), Blairs letters; Preshome letters. SRO, GD45 (mfm. at PAC). *Arthur papers* (Sanderson). U.C., House of Assembly, *Journals*; Legislative Council, *Journals*. *Canadian Freeman*. *Chronicle & Gazette*. *Colonial Advocate*. *Kingston Chronicle*. *Kingston Gazette*. *Patriot* (Toronto). Caron, "Inv. de la corr. de Mgr Plessis," ANQ *Rapport*, 1927–28, 1928–29, 1932–33. Desrosiers, "Inv. de la corr. de Mgr Lartigue," ANQ *Rapport*, 1941–42, 1942–43, 1943–44, 1944–45, 1945–46. Craig, *Upper Canada*. J. G. Harkness, *Stormont, Dundas and Glengarry: a history, 1784–1943* (Oshawa, Ont., 1946). Lemieux, *L'établissement de la première prov. eccl.* H. J. Somers, *The life and times of the Hon. and Rt. Rev. Alexander Macdonell . . .* (Washington, 1931). Maurice Taylor, *The Scots College in Spain* (Valladolid, Spain, 1971). K. M. Toomey, *Alexander Macdonell, the Scottish years: 1762–1804* (Toronto, 1985).

MACDONELL, ALEXANDER, Roman Catholic priest; b. 1782 in Knockfin (near Kiltarlity), Scotland, son of Hugh MacDonell and Mary Chisholm; d. 19 Sept. 1841 in Indian Point (Inverness County), N.S.

Alexander MacDonell did his theological studies at the College of Killechiarain in Lismore, Scotland, from 1803 to 1808. Both he and Colin P. GRANT, another Highland Catholic missionary who served in Nova Scotia, were ordained by Bishop John Chisholm on Easter Sunday, 17 April 1808. Following ordination he was appointed to a mission at Kintail, Scotland, where he remained until poor health forced him to relinquish his charge in 1811. That same autumn he went to Nova Scotia; it is not known whether anyone asked him to come or whether he simply decided to immigrate on his own accord.

Shortly after his arrival MacDonell began serving as an assistant to the Reverend Alexander MacDonald in the parish of Arisaig. His first months in the province were fatiguing; Gaelic-speaking missionaries such as MacDonell were few in number, and he was forced to cover an extensive territory on foot, on horseback, or by boat. Apart from Arisaig, he ministered for a while to Antigonish, and he also covered the western section of Cape Breton. Throughout this period he suffered from poor health, and on a pastoral visit in 1811 Bishop Joseph-Octave Plessis* found him to be sickly. During this same visit Plessis suggested to MacDonell that he should undertake further study in order to compensate for deficiencies in his theological training, but because of his enormous work-load MacDonell was not able to follow this suggestion until 1815, when it was arranged that he study under the Reverend François Lejamtel* in Arichat, N.S. He stayed there for four months, returning to Arisaig in November.

MacDonell's responsibilities were dramatically increased by the death of his pastor, Alexander MacDonald, in April 1816. For the next two years he continued to serve Arisaig and did missionary work in Cape Breton; as well, from October 1816 to September 1817 he attended to the spiritual needs of the people in Antigonish, replacing the Reverend Rémi Gaulin*. His flock in Arisaig were apparently satisfied with his pastoral efforts, since they petitioned Bishop Plessis to allow him to remain there. Although MacDonell did not originate this petition, Vicar General Edmund Burke* of Nova Scotia assumed that he had and showed his annoyance by suggesting to Plessis that it might be better for MacDonell to work in Cape Breton or return to Scotland. Plessis officially appointed MacDonell to Cape Breton on 15 April 1818.

Upon arrival in Cape Breton, MacDonell is said to have lived with a cousin in Indian Point. Selecting the Judique district as his base, he ministered – despite his continuing bad health – to all of the Highland Catholics in what is now Inverness County. In Cape Breton in the early 1820s there were seven Scottish Catholic settlements and only MacDonell and the Reverend William Fraser* to serve them. Vicar General Angus Bernard MacEachern* of Prince Edward Island, who had responsibility for Cape Breton at this time, met MacDonell on his first pastoral visit there in 1823; he stated that the priest would need assistance in order to cover his extensive mission, since "he is too heavy for snow shoes, and no horse can carry him through deep snow." On another occasion MacEachern expressed the belief that MacDonell was simply too slow to cover his territory satisfactorily. The corpulent MacDonell may have been slow in his movements but he was certainly effective: he assisted in having a number of churches erected, became involved in educational matters, and had some influence in provincial politics. Moreover, along with MacEachern, Grant, and Fraser, he must be given some credit for maintaining the strength of Roman Catholicism in northeastern Nova Scotia.

Worn out by missionary labours, MacDonell died in Indian Point on 19 Sept. 1841; at the time of his death he was the longest-serving priest in what is now the diocese of Antigonish. Buried in the old cemetery by Father Vincent de Paul [Jacques Merle*], his remains were later transferred to the new one in 1894. Strong and favourable memories of MacDonell remain in the Judique area. Among his ecclesiastical colleagues in Nova Scotia, Burke apparently had little use for him, referring to his "very limited ability." Fraser, however, was more impressed. In 1828, by now vicar apostolic of Nova Scotia, Fraser noted that MacDonell "is an elephant in bulk and, like the elephant, good natured. He wants activity, but that cannot be expected; in other respects exemplary."

R. A. MacLean

AAQ, 210 A, VIII: 301; IX: 354; 310 CN, I: 92; 312 CN, IV: 3, 122, 125 (copies at Arch. of the Diocese of Antigonish, N.S.). Arch. of Scots College (Pontifical) (Rome), Vicars Apostolic, 12, A. B. MacEachern to Angus MacDonald, 10 Aug. 1830 (copy at Arch. of the Diocese of Antigonish). Arch. of the Diocese of Antigonish, Files of the diocesan historian, A. A. Johnston, manuscript sketches, no.97 (Alexander MacDonell). PANS, RG 14, 39, 1841, nos.60, 64. [H.-R. Casgrain], *Mémoire sur les missions de la Nouvelle-Écosse, du Cap-Breton et de l'île du Prince-Édouard de 1760 à 1820 . . . réponse aux "Memoirs of Bishop Burke" par Mgr O'Brien* . . . (Québec, 1895). J.-O. Plessis, "Journal de deux voyages apostoliques dans le golfe Saint-Laurent et les provinces d'en bas, en 1811 et 1812 . . . ," *Le Foyer canadien* (Québec), 3 (1865): 73, 105; *Journal des visites pastorales de 1815 et 1816, par Monseigneur Joseph-Octave Plessis, évêque de Québec*, Henri Têtu, édit. (Québec, 1903), 61. Caron, "Inv. de la corr. de Mgr Plessis," ANQ *Rapport*, 1927–28, 1928–29, 1932–33. *Mabou pioneers* . . . , ed. A. D. MacDonald and Reginald Rankin (2v., [Mabou, N.S., 1952?]–77). Tanguay, *Répertoire* (1893). A. A. Johnston, *A history of the Catholic Church in eastern Nova Scotia* (2v., Antigonish, 1960–71). J. L. MacDougall, *History of Inverness County, Nova Scotia* ([Truro, N.S., 1922]; repr. Belleville, Ont., 1976). J. C. Macmillan, *The early history of the Catholic Church in Prince Edward Island* (Quebec, 1905). Cornelius O'Brien, *Memoirs of Rt. Rev. Edmund Burke, bishop of Zion, first vicar apostolic of Nova Scotia* (Ottawa, 1894). [Sagart Arisaig (Ronald MacGillivray)], *History of Antigonish*, ed. R. A. MacLean (2v., [Antigonish], 1976).

McDONELL, JOHN, known as **Le Prêtre** (beginning in the 1830s he signed **Macdonell**), militia officer, fur trader, businessman, judge, office holder, and politician; b. 30 Nov. 1768 in Scotland, son of John McDonell of Scothouse; d. 17 April 1850 in Pointe-Fortune, Upper Canada.

John McDonell was born into a distinguished Catholic family with a long military tradition, the Macdonells of Scothouse (Scotus) in the Isle of Skye. His father, known as "Spanish" John because of his service in the Spanish forces during the war against the Austrians in the 1740s, had been a supporter of the Stuart cause before immigrating to the New World in 1773. That year, with his family and about 600 members of the Macdonell clan of Glengarry, he moved to the Mohawk valley of New York. During the American Revolutionary War, Spanish John and his elder son, Miles Macdonell* (the first governor of Assiniboia, 1811–15), joined the loyalist forces. Young John saw some military service after 1788, when he was gazetted an ensign in the Cornwall and Osnabruck battalion of militia. By that time the family had moved to the province of Quebec and were settled near present-day Cornwall.

By May 1793 John had entered the service of the North West Company as a clerk, and he was sent west to the Qu'Appelle valley. He rose rapidly, becoming a wintering partner about 1796. Three years later he was in charge of the Upper Red River department, where he remained until 1809, when he was given charge of the Athabasca department. While in the northwest he earned the nickname Le Prêtre, apparently because of his piety and insistence that his men observe the feasts of the Roman Catholic Church.

By the early summer of 1812 McDonell was preparing to leave the northwest on rotation to Montreal. In a letter to his brother Miles in July he expressed his uncertainty about whether he would return to the interior; he did, in fact, retire from the NWC that year. Upon reaching Fort William (Thunder Bay, Ont.) in July, he learned that war had broken out with the United States and he decided to join other fur traders in a proposed attack on the American garrison at Mackinac Island (Mich.). The expedition was successful [*see* Charles Roberts*] but McDonell and his friends arrived too late to participate. In October he was commissioned captain in the Corps of Canadian Voyageurs and, after only three weeks of service, was taken prisoner at the battle of Saint-Régis. In April 1813 he was established in the lower Ottawa valley, where he purchased 1,000 acres of land in Hawkesbury Township and near Pointe-Fortune, which lay on the provincial boundary. It is not clear when he actually settled there – he may have remained in the Canadas through at least part of 1814, but he later recalled being in the interior that year. There is also evidence which suggests that in 1814 McDonell was considering retiring in the Red River settlement (Man.), where the Earl of Selkirk [Douglas*] had offered to grant him a township of 10,000 acres.

Apparently McDonell decided not to accept this offer because by about 1817 he had established himself on the Upper Canadian side of Pointe-Fortune, where he built a large house, Poplar Villa, and started farming. To this home he brought his Métis wife, Magdeleine Poitras, whom he had married according to the custom of the country some time before 1797. In June 1812, when he was on his way back from the interior, he had written to Miles that she had been with him for 18 years since coming "under my protection" in her 12th year. Always conscious of his duty, he had no intention of following the practice adopted by many other fur traders of leaving their country wives behind when they retired in the east, a custom McDonell found "cruel." Instead, he had determined to take Magdeleine with him and to provide his children with a "common education so that they may work their way thro' life in some honest calling." Three children had already been sent east to be educated and the remaining three had accompanied John and their mother to the Canadas in 1813. Prior to his departure on the Mackinac expedition the previous year, McDonell had drawn up a will dividing his property equally among the children and providing for an annuity of £50 for Magdeleine. Yet he may never have taken proper steps to ensure their rights to his property. Although a marriage contract had been drawn up on 13 April 1813, just before he purchased the land at Pointe-Fortune, there was evidently no marriage. On 24 April 1853, three years after McDonell's death, Magdeleine went through an act of posthumous marriage to ensure that she and her children would be his legal heirs. They had had four sons and two daughters.

After settling in Pointe-Fortune McDonell became the leading businessman in the area. He ran a general store in the village, and by 1819 had established himself as an early member of the network of forwarders who kept freight moving on the Ottawa to and from Montreal. He was associated in this activity with the firms of Grant and Duff, and Whiting and Crane, both of which carried on business on the St Lawrence as well as the Ottawa. Between Pointe-Fortune and Hull he worked with Thomas Mears of Hawkesbury Mills and with Philemon WRIGHT of Hull. About 1819 he invested in a steamboat, but it was doomed to failure because, Miles told John in October 1819, the vessel (then at Lachine) drew too much water.

A tall man (at least six feet three inches in height) who occasionally dressed in full Highland garb, McDonell was active in public affairs. In 1816 he was appointed a judge of the Ottawa District Court, a post he held for nine years, and he served as a district roads commissioner. From 1817 to 1820 he represented Prescott in the Upper Canadian House of Assembly. In 1822 he was made colonel in the Prescott Reserve Militia.

Despite his successes in the business world and in public life, McDonell never enjoyed financial security or stability. Undoubtedly, he lost from his investment in the steamboat. He gave lavishly to churches, schools, and his family. Bishop Alexander McDONELL of Kingston regularly called upon him for donations. As well, Miles Macdonell, who was always in need of money, drew regularly on his brother's account with the NWC. It was John who paid most of the expenses for the costly schooling of Miles's daughters in Montreal and who cared for Miles when his health failed after his return from the interior. An additional cause of his financial distress may have been Poplar Villa itself. In 1820 Governor Lord Dalhousie [RAMSAY] described McDonell as a man who had made his fortune with the NWC but who "like a fool . . . has spent his all in a big house, which he said he can't now afford to furnish." Because of this distress McDonell took out numerous mortgages against his property. By 1830 his financial needs were so pressing that Miles's son Donald Æneas MacDonell* felt it necessary to sign over his own claims to moneys owed his father by the Selkirk estate in order to try to relieve his uncle's indebtedness. The Selkirk moneys could not be collected, however, and in 1842 John McDonell was forced to list his house and property for sale. Somehow, he managed to avoid selling his home, and he died there eight years later. He was buried across the river in St Andrews (Saint-André-Est, Que.).

HERBERT J. MAYS

John McDonell's diaries have been published as "Mr John McDonnell: some account of the Red River (about 1797), with extracts from his journal," *Les bourgeois de la Compagnie du Nord-Ouest* (Masson), 1: 265–95, and "The diary of John Macdonell," *Five fur traders of the northwest . . .*, ed. C. M. Gates ([2nd ed.], St Paul, Minn., 1965), 61–119.

AO, MU 1780, A-1-1–A-4. Ont. Heritage Foundation, Property Restoration Unit (Toronto), T. A. Reitz, "Macdonell House, Pointe Fortune, Ontario" (archaeological research report, 1981). PAC, MG 19, E1; E4; MG 25, 62: 653–58. "Journals of Legislative Assembly of U.C.," AO *Report*, 1912: 369. Ramsay, *Dalhousie journals* (Whitelaw), 2: 33–34. Chadwick, *Ontarian families*. *Legislators and legislatures of Ont.* (Forman), 1: 43. Reid, *Loyalists in Ont.*, 196. Brown, *Strangers in blood*. J. M. Gray, *Lord Selkirk of Red River* (Toronto, 1963). Ruth McKenzie, "The John Macdonell House, 'Poplar Villa,' Point Fortune, Ontario" (typescript, Environment Canada – Parks, agenda report, no.1969-10, 1969; copy at Can., Parks Canada, Hist. Sites and Monuments Board Secretariat, Ottawa). Morton, *Hist. of Canadian west* (1939). Rich, *Fur trade* (1967). Van Kirk, *"Many tender ties"*. M. [E.] Wilkins Campbell, *The North West Company* (Toronto, 1957). J. G. Harkness, "Miles Macdonell," *OH*, 40 (1948): 77–83. A.-G. Morice, "A Canadian pioneer: Spanish John" and "Sidelights on the careers of Miles Macdonell and his brothers," *CHR*, 10 (1929): 212–35 and 308–32.

McDONELL (Collachie), ALEXANDER, army and militia officer, office holder, politician, and land agent; b. 16 April 1762 in Fort Augustus, Scotland, second son of Allan McDonell of Collachie and Helen MacNab; brother of Angus*; m. early 1805 Anne Smith, sister of Samuel Smith*, in York (Toronto), Upper Canada, and they had five sons, including Allan Macdonell*, and two daughters; d. 18 March 1842 in Toronto.

Like other tacksmen families in the Highlands of Scotland, especially those of Roman Catholic persuasion, the McDonells of Collachie were by the 1770s under extreme economic pressure from their clan chieftain, and decided to emigrate to North America. Accompanied by other families of MacDonalds and MacDonells, they arrived in New York in 1773, settling under the auspices of Sir William Johnson* in the heart of the Mohawk valley. When the American revolution broke out, Allan McDonell joined his kinsmen in supporting the crown, and he was imprisoned by the rebels in 1776. He remained in custody until 1779, when he escaped to the province of Quebec and became a loyalist pensioner. His son Alexander enlisted in 1776 as a volunteer in the 1st battalion of the Royal Highland Emigrants, serving in the campaigns in the middle states and in the occupation of Philadelphia. With the evacuation of that city he made his way to Quebec and received a lieutenant's commission in Butler's Rangers, leading several raiding parties down the Mohawk valley in the last years of the war. As a half-pay officer Alexander joined his family in Quebec and accompanied them to Kingston in 1790. A wartime friendship with John Graves Simcoe* brought Alexander to Upper Canadian prominence in 1792 when Simcoe appointed him sheriff of the Home District; he transferred his residence to York in 1797. In 1793 he organized and accompanied an expedition under Simcoe to Lake Simcoe and Georgian Bay, his fluency in French, English, Gaelic, and Indian languages proving useful on this as on other occasions throughout his career.

The favour which had been shown to McDonell in Upper Canada survived Simcoe's departure in 1796, and in 1800 he was elected to the House of Assembly for Glengarry and Prescott; he would sit off and on in the house for over 20 years. Glengarry undoubtedly chose him to represent the Highland community because of his family connections and his residence at York. In the 1804 session he seconded an unsuccessful motion to change the name of York to Toronto, and he failed also to get majority support for a bill requiring schools in each district in the province. A surviving fragment of McDonell's diary for 1799 indicates that he was an active member of the small bachelor élite in the tiny capital of York, dining in the mess, drinking tea and wine in great quantities, and playing whist in the evening. Early in 1800 he served as second to John Small* in the notorious duel in which Attorney General John White* was fatally wounded; a few years earlier he had himself been challenged to a duel by William Jarvis*.

In 1804 McDonell was appointed agent of the Earl of Selkirk [Douglas*] in Upper Canada. Selkirk had met McDonell late in 1803 on his whirlwind tour of North America and had been impressed with him. The earl was always partial to Highland Catholics as subalterns, and McDonell's political and social connections made him a particularly attractive choice to supervise Selkirk's proposed settlement and private estate near Lake St Clair. Lieutenant Governor Peter Hunter* tried to warn Selkirk of McDonell's weaknesses, but the advice went unheeded. Unfortunately, neither Baldoon, as the settlement became known, nor McDonell's stewardship of it was successful. Selkirk and his agent had failed to appreciate the expense and difficulty of establishing a settlement in a wilderness area remote from communication and trade routes. Selkirk wanted his Highland settlers isolated from assimilating influences, and he was quite correct that the site he had selected was ideal for raising sheep, particularly because of adjacent marshlands. But the marshes bred malarial mosquitoes and the location was exposed to possible American depredations in time of war.

What Selkirk needed, even before the death in September 1804 of his resident manager, William Burn*, was a dependable supervisor on the spot. McDonell, indeed, had agreed in June 1804 to move to nearby Sandwich (Windsor) and devote his full attention to Selkirk's affairs. Required by Selkirk to surrender all offices, McDonell understood, his employer noted, "that in accepting my agency he would take to it as his permanent employment & that he relinquished every idea of applying personally or by friends for Govt. promotion." Such commitments were soon forgotten. McDonell's political obligations – he was speaker of the assembly from 1805 to 1807 – and his continued ambition for office combined with his marriage in 1805 to anchor him firmly at York, and he spent increasingly less time at the troubled settlement.

Instead of a resident man of business, McDonell soon became an absentee paymaster, unable to control either expenditures or the restive Highlanders who had arrived at Baldoon in 1804. Although gaps in the accounts and the problems of currency conversion make it impossible to ascertain precisely how much Baldoon cost Selkirk, the figure was in excess of £10,000 sterling – and in the end he would have little to show for the outlay but thousands of acres of wilderness. In fairness to McDonell, it should be stated that he repeatedly warned Selkirk of the difficulties of the site and of the undertaking, but he also ignored specific instructions from his employer to remove the settlers to safer ground after the first malaria epidemic. A series of resident managers proved incapable of dealing with Baldoon's many problems, even though Dr John Sims may have done a better job from 1807 to 1809 than McDonell allowed.

As early as 1807 McDonell suggested to Selkirk that he would like to be relieved of his agency if a better appointment such as the provincial receiver generalship became available. Selkirk replied, "It has appeared to me for some time past that your avocations are now so multiple that it is impossible for you to devote your individual attention to my affairs as constant residence at Baldoon would require a sacrifice of other objects more important to yourself." But better jobs did not come along, and McDonell found his agency more attractive just as Selkirk, appalled at the bills he was receiving, both for their magnitude and for the sloppiness of the accounting system, was moving to replace him. Over the years McDonell had repeatedly ignored Selkirk's instructions and orders, as well as the pleas from Sims to provide a safer refuge for the nearly 1,000 breeding sheep on Selkirk's home farm in the event of an American war. In the first days of conflict, Sims predicted, "some party on the other side will endeavour to obtain possession of the sheep at Baldoon," a prescient anticipation of exactly what would finally destroy Selkirk's venture in 1812. Selkirk in effect replaced McDonell with Thomas Clark* of Sandwich in 1809, but the damage had been done. Clark reported after examining the accounts that there was no fraud, only lack of proper attention to the business.

Unlike fellow agent James Williams* on Prince Edward Island, McDonell did obey Selkirk's summons to England to report in detail on his stewardship and accounts, departing Upper Canada on 29 June 1811 and returning in 1812 just in time to be appointed deputy paymaster general of the militia with the rank of colonel. He was captured by the Americans at Niagara (Niagara-on-the-Lake) in May 1813 and was incarcerated in the same prison in Lancaster, Pa, which a generation earlier had contained his father. Although he appears to have returned to York on parole by early 1814, he was not formally exchanged and able to resume his military duties until 25 May 1814. The loss of income was a serious blow.

Following the close of the war, McDonell in July 1815 accepted the superintendency of the Perth settlement, a belated attempt by the British government to populate Upper Canada with potential soldiers by encouraging emigration from Scotland. He was extremely popular with the emigrants, perhaps because the largesse he showed was backed by government credit and because he resided in the settlement, however briefly. After settling the Perth people in the summer of 1816, McDonell was appointed assistant secretary of the Indian Department in Upper Canada and took up temporary residence at Niagara, where he complained constantly of the costs and disadvantages of living away from York. By 1818 he was building a substantial residence in York which was a social centre of the town for many years. The income to support this establishment and a large family came from his army pension, offices, and 10,000 acres of prime land he had acquired in the province, but he was perennially short of money and worried about his financial situation. Eventual appointment as inspector of licences for the Home District, a post he held from 1828 to 1841, was particularly lucrative and welcome. He was named to the Legislative Council in January 1831 and served faithfully until the council was abolished in February 1841, an unreconstructed member of the "family compact," Roman Catholic branch. In 1835 he was made a director of the Bank of Upper Canada.

Alexander McDonell was one of the most prominent members of his religious persuasion in York from his first residence there, and he was a lay leader of Catholics throughout most of his long life. A close friend of his namesake Bishop Alexander McDONELL, he assisted in the erection of St Paul's Church in York in 1821, having from 1806 been one of the lay trustees of the Catholic church lot in the town. He served as treasurer of St Paul's congregation in 1830, and he supported McDonell when the bishop suspended the Reverend William John O'GRADY for resisting church authority. He also led York Catholics in periodic expressions of support for the government against the reformers in the 1830s, and was one of those who made possible the special position and privileges enjoyed by Catholics in an ostensibly Protestant province.

McDonell's career spanned the transition from loyalism to "family compact" in Upper Canada, and while offering some substantiation for those who would link the two, it also reminds us that neither was the monopoly of those who supported the Church of England. Like many of his kinsmen in North America, he was equally at home in the drawing-room or the wilderness, and throughout his life he lived in accordance with his mother's early injunction "never to forget that all the blood in his veins was of a Highland gentleman." Honour was of great importance to Alexander McDonell, and although some might occasionally question his judgement, none ever doubted his integrity.

J. M. BUMSTED

Two short journals kept by Alexander McDonell (Collachie) have been published: his "Diary of Gov. Simcoe's journey from Humber Bay to Matchetache Bay, 1793" is in Canadian Institute, *Trans.* (Toronto), ser.4, 1 (1889–90): 128–39, and a fragment from a diary of 1799 appears as "A journal by Sheriff Alexander Macdonell . . ." in J. E. Middleton and Fred Landon, *The province of Ontario: a history, 1615–1927* (5v., Toronto, [1927–28]), 2: 1246–50.

Arch. of the Roman Catholic Archdiocese of Toronto, M (Macdonell papers), AB35, esp. 35.08. PAC, MG 19, E1, ser.1: 14540–55, 14601–4, 14843–45; MG 24, I8, 1–36. *Corr. of Lieut. Governor Simcoe* (Cruikshank), 4: 10–11. [Thomas Douglas, 5th Earl of] Selkirk, *Lord Selkirk's diary, 1803–1804; a journal of his travels in British North America and the northeastern United States*, ed. P. C. T. White (Toronto, 1958; repr. New York, 1969), 147, 326, 341. *Examiner* (Toronto), 23 March 1842. Chadwick, *Ontarian families*, 1: 10–14. [A. J. Dooner, named] Brother Alfred, *Catholic pioneers in Upper Canada* (Toronto, 1947), 4, 7–9, 21–23, 25–31. I. C. C. Graham, *Colonists from Scotland: emigration to North America, 1707–1783* (Ithaca, N.Y., 1956; repr. Port Washington, N.Y., and London, 1972), 81 *et seq.* Norman Macdonald, *Canada, 1763–1841, immigration and settlement; the administration of the imperial land regulations* (London and Toronto, 1939), 240–45. J. A. Macdonell, *Sketches illustrating the early settlement and history of Glengarry in Canada, relating principally to the Revolutionary War of 1775–83, the War of 1812–14 and the rebellion of 1837–8 . . .* (Montreal, 1893). A. E. D. MacKenzie, *Baldoon: Lord Selkirk's settlement in Upper Canada*, ed. George Kerr (London, Ont., 1978). Hazel [Chisholm] Mathews, *The mark of honour* (Toronto, 1965), 37–40. W. L. Scott, "The Macdonells of Leek, Collachie and Aberchalder," CCHA *Report*, 2 (1934–35): 22–32.

McDOUALL, ROBERT, army officer; b. March 1774 in Stranraer, Scotland, second son of John McDouall, a magistrate of the town; d. there unmarried 15 Nov. 1848.

Robert McDouall received a tolerable education in Scotland and England before being placed in a business establishment in London. His father and uncle hoped that he would become a merchant, but the young man was attracted to a military career. With his father's reluctant approval he purchased an ensigncy in the 49th Foot on 29 Oct. 1797 and a lieutenancy in the 8th Foot three days later. McDouall took part in the British expedition to Egypt in 1801, and he was promoted captain on 24 Oct. 1804. He saw service during the Copenhagen expedition of 1807 and at Martinique in 1809 before coming to Lower Canada with his battalion in May 1810. Soon after the outbreak of war with the United States in the summer of 1812, McDouall was appointed an aide-de-camp to Governor Sir George Prevost*. He was with Prevost at the attack on Sackets Harbor, N.Y., in May 1813, and was then sent to the Niagara peninsula with instructions for Brigadier-General John VINCENT. McDouall later claimed to have suggested the attack at Stoney Creek on 6 June, in which he took part. Promoted major in the Glengarry Light Infantry Fencibles on 24 June, he was sent home with dispatches and was made brevet lieutenant-colonel on 29 July. He came back to the Canadas before the end of 1813.

McDouall's connection with Prevost was undoubtedly responsible for his selection late that year as commandant of Michilimackinac (Mackinac Island, Mich.), which since its capture from the Americans in July 1812 [*see* Charles Roberts*] had been the key British military and fur-trade post in the northwest. Being "fully sensible to the chances of enemy attack," he had detailed conversations with Prevost about the reinforcement of the post and conducted a correspondence with William McGillivray* of the North West Company to obtain advice about local conditions. Under his leadership an expedition bringing reinforcements and much-needed supplies reached Michilimackinac on 18 May 1814 after a difficult journey via York (Toronto), Lake Simcoe, and Nottawasaga Bay.

Late the next month McDouall received news that the Americans had taken Prairie du Chien (Wis.), a strategic post on the Upper Mississippi. He at once realized that if the enemy were not removed "there was an end to our connextion with the Indians . . . tribe after tribe would be gained over or subdued, & thus would be destroyed the only barrier which protects the Great trading establishments of the North West & the Hudsons Bay Companys." He at once sent a force under William McKay* "to dislodge the American Gen[l] from his new conquest," and Prairie du Chien was retaken on 20 July.

The dispatch of McKay's expedition had reduced the garrison of Michilimackinac, a cause for concern in light of intelligence that the Americans were planning an attempt to recapture the island. Over the summer the defences were strengthened, but McDouall's numbers were still much smaller than the 1,000 troops in four warships which appeared off Michilimackinac on 26 July. When the enemy landed on 4 August, McDouall moved to meet them with 140 soldiers and several hundred Indians. As the opposing forces were skirmishing McDouall received a false report that American troops were in his rear, and he began a retreat in which most of the Indians joined. Left behind was a band of Menominees, who "commenced a spirited attack" upon the enemy. The Americans, after losing "their second in Command [and] several other officers" in a short time, retired "in the utmost haste & confusion" to their boats, McDouall noted.

Although Michilimackinac was not attacked for the duration of the war, the Americans destroyed the British base at Nottawasaga Bay and stationed two vessels near Michilimackinac to prevent supplies from reaching the garrison. Rations were short when Lieutenant Miller Worsley* of the Royal Navy arrived on 30 August with supplies. With McDouall's approval, he carried out an attack which captured the American vessels and ensured British control of the northwest during the conflict.

In the spring of 1815 McDouall learned that peace had been signed and that "the mutual restoration of all Forts" had been ordered. He was "penetrated with grief at the restoration of this fine island, a fortress built by Nature for herself," and lamented that "our negociators as usual, have been egregiously duped . . . they have shewn themselves profoundly ignorant of the concerns of this part of the Empire." As preparation for the restoration of Michilimackinac, which occurred on 18 July 1815, the British had established a base on nearby Drummond Island (Mich.), and McDouall was commandant there until the reduction of the garrison in June 1816. Before leaving for Scotland the same year, he asked McKay to sit for a portrait, as it was his intention "to embellish [his] retreat" with paintings of his wartime friends.

McDouall spent the remainder of his life at Stranraer. Although eager to return to active duty, he was not employed again, being promoted colonel in July 1830 and major-general in November 1841. In February 1817 he had been appointed a companion of the Order of the Bath for his efforts at Michilimackinac. Later in life McDouall was much influenced by the teachings of the Free Church of Scotland, and he gave generously of his time and money to its works, contributing to the libraries of the church's colleges in Edinburgh and Toronto. A solid, dedicated, and astute officer, Robert McDouall was representative of the British military and naval personnel who served with courage and quiet distinction in British North America during the War of 1812 while their confrères were enjoying the limelight cast by the Napoleonic battles of Salamanca and Vitoria.

ROBERT S. ALLEN

AO, MS 35. DPL, Burton Hist. Coll., Robert McDouall, orderly book, Drummond Island, 1815. PAC, MG 19, E5; RG 8, I (C ser.), 685, 688, 1219. Andrew Bulger, *An autobiographical sketch of the services of the late Captain Andrew Bulger of the Royal Newfoundland Fencible Regiment* (Bangalore, India, 1865). "Major-General M'Douall, C.B.," Free Church of Scotland, Pub. Committee, *Monthly-Ser. of Tracts* (Edinburgh), no.58 (July 1849). G.B., WO, *Army list*, 1798–1848/49. *Officers of British forces in Canada* (Irving). B. L. Dunnigan, "The British army at Mackinac, 1812–1815," Mackinac Island State Park Commission, *Reports in Mackinac Hist. and Archaeology* (Mackinac Island, Mich.), no.7 (1980). A. R. Gilpin, *The War of 1812 in the old northwest* (Toronto and East Lansing, Mich., 1958). R. S. Allen, "The British Indian Department and the frontier in North America, 1755–1830," *Canadian Hist. Sites*, no.14 (1975): 5–125. B. L. Dunnigan, "The battle of Mackinac Island," *Mich. Hist.* (Lansing), 59 (1975): 239–54.

McDOWALL, ROBERT, clergyman of the Reformed Protestant Dutch and Presbyterian churches; b. 25 July 1768 in Ballston Spa, N.Y., the son of John McDowall, an officer in the British army, and a Miss Graham; m. December 1800 Hannah Washburn, daughter of Ebenezer Washburn*, and they had one daughter and three sons; d. 3 Aug. 1841 in Fredericksburgh Township, Upper Canada.

Robert McDowall's parents married at Dumfries, Scotland, and settled in the colony of New York shortly before his birth. Early in 1790 Robert was licensed to preach by the Classis of Albany, the local organization of the Reformed Protestant Dutch Church, and was sent to Upper Canada as a missionary. The reasons for this trip are uncertain, but after McDowall's death it was claimed that he had been invited by loyalist leader Peter Van Alstine, who had come from the region of Albany.

After visiting loyalist settlements on the north shore of the St Lawrence River and Lake Ontario and gathering several "congregations" during the summer of 1790, McDowall was asked by those in Ernestown, Fredericksburgh, and Adolphustown townships to become their permanent minister. He decided, however, to obtain a formal education before accepting their call. He attended Williams College at Williamstown, Mass., completed his education at Union College in Schenectady, N.Y., and was ordained in 1797 by the Classis of Albany. Despite petitions for ministers from Presbyterians in the Bay of Quinte region to churches in Scotland and the United States, no clergy had arrived by the time McDowall returned to his early mission field in 1798 as official representative of the Classis of Albany.

McDowall preached briefly at Elizabethtown (Brockville) but refused an invitation to stay there. He moved westward to settle at what is now Sandhurst, in Fredericksburgh Township, where he opened his first church on 6 July 1798. From this base McDowall itinerated over the hundred-mile stretch from Meyers' Creek (Belleville) to Elizabethtown. He also visited the York (Toronto) region, and a contemporary source asserts that he once journeyed as far west as Sandwich (Windsor). It was his custom to herald his arrival in an isolated settlement by blowing a moose horn. He was noted as a strong sabbatarian, and as a strict Calvinist who, in 1804, engaged in a day-long debate on predestination with Samuel Coate, a Methodist itinerant. He also debated episcopal ordination that year with John Langhorn*, the local Anglican clergyman.

Within a year of his arrival in Upper Canada McDowall had six organized and one unorganized mission districts with about 425 families. Encouraged by his success, the Classis of Albany sent five other missionaries on tours of the province. In 1806 McDowall reported that he had three formed congregations in the Bay of Quinte area and that although he preached six to nine times per week he could visit his whole mission only once every three to six weeks. Missionaries from other churches were visiting the area and, he warned, unless the people "have immediate assistance, they will be rent into so many sects that they will be unable to support a minister of any denomination." The classis continued to send missionaries, at least 18 by 1818; McDowall, however, remained its only settled minister-missionary in Upper Canada. By 1810 he had founded 14 churches between York and Elizabethtown, but prospects for consolidation of his efforts by the church were destroyed by the anti-Americanism engendered during the War of 1812. In 1819 the whole mission enterprise in Upper Canada was abandoned, but McDowall had already joined the indigenous Presbytery of the Canadas when it was formed a year earlier [*see* Robert Easton*].

In 1819 this presbytery was reorganized as a three-presbytery synod and McDowall was elected its first moderator. The synod, however, proved ineffective and was dissolved into two independent presbyteries, for Upper and Lower Canada, in 1825, just as the Church of Scotland's mission auxiliary, the Glasgow Colonial Society, was organized to send its clergy to British North America. By claiming religious, political, and social superiority over other Presbyterians the Church of Scotland disrupted many local congregations, and at last, in 1832, the provincial presbytery proposed a union with that church. As senior member of the local Presbyterian clergy, McDowall was drawn into the negotiations, only to discover that his American background made him ignorant of Scottish Presbyterian traditions. He withdrew from the talks but did, along with most local Presbyterians, join the Church of Scotland synod which had been organized in 1831.

McDowall had been on the committee that set up the Ernestown Academy in 1811 [*see* William Fairfield*] and he was a trustee of the school that opened in the front concession of Fredericksburgh in 1817. In the early 1830s he was involved in an abortive attempt to establish a Presbyterian seminary near Picton, and reputedly he was also involved in the early stages of the creation of Queen's University. In his later years he spent considerable time farming. An active member of the Midland District Agricultural Society, he won its prize for the best farm in the district in 1835.

McDowall was buried at the site of his first church. An obituary remarked that "as a Preacher, Mr. McDowal excelled in doctrinal exposition – he stated his sentiments with great clearness, singular vivacity of style and manner, and with powerful application to men's consciences and hearts." The record of his 40-year ministry is evidence both of the extent of his travels and of the scarcity of clergy: his baptismal register (of which one-third has been lost) lists 1,638 christenings in 24 different townships and it is estimated that he performed some 1,300 marriages. The centenary of his settling in Upper Canada was celebrated at Sandhurst in 1898 with religious services, and with speeches by such prominent figures as principal George Monro Grant* of Queen's University and Lieutenant Governor Sir Oliver Mowat*, who had been baptized by McDowall 77 years earlier.

JOHN S. MOIR

[Robert McDowall is the author of an early Upper Canadian pamphlet, *A sermon on the nature of justification through the imputed righteousness of the Redeemer* (York [Toronto], 1805), and a collection of sermons, *Discourses, on the sovereign and universal agency of God, in nature and grace* (Albany, N.Y., 1806). Most of his personal papers were destroyed by fire in 1876. A manuscript volume containing the surviving portion of his baptismal and marriage registers is preserved along with a few other items in the McDowall papers, QUA, 2189; extracts from this volume were published as "Rev. Robert McDowall's register," ed. T. W. Casey, *OH*, 1 (1899): 70–108.

In the absence of extensive documentary remains it is impossible to verify much of the legend surrounding Robert McDowall. Accounts of his mission work are in the Reformed Protestant Dutch Church in North America, General Synod, *Acts and proc.* (New York), 1 (1771–1812): 307–10, 350–57. Biographical references can be found in the *Kingston Gazette*, 21 Oct. 1817; *Chronicle & Gazette*, 25 Aug. 1841; William Canniff, *History of the settlement of Upper Canada (Ontario), with special reference to the Bay Quinte* (Toronto, 1869; repr. Belleville, Ont., 1971); Gregg, *Hist. of Presbyterian Church* (1885); R. J. McDowall, "Items of Presbyterian history," *Canada Presbyterian* (Toronto), new ser., 1 (1877–78): 804 (a letter from one of McDowall's grandsons); J. S. Moir, "Robert McDowall and the Dutch Reformed Church mission to Canada, 1790–1817," *Halve Maen* (New York), 53 (1978), no.2: 3–4, 14–16; and the same author's "Robert McDowall, pioneer Dutch Reformed Church missionary in Upper Canada," *Presbyterian Hist.* (Hamilton, Ont.), 23 (1979), no.1: 1–4; no.2: 1–4; 24 (1980), no.1: 1–4. J.S.M.]

MACFARLANE, JAMES, businessman, printer, editor, office holder, JP, and militia officer; b. in Scotland; m. 26 April 1834 Isura Carrington in Oswego, N.Y., and they had two sons; d. there 29 July 1847.

James Macfarlane came to Kingston, Upper Canada, from Scotland shortly after the War of 1812, apparently as an assisted settler. In November 1824 he purchased the *Kingston Chronicle*, a leading tory paper since its establishment by John Macaulay* and Alexander Pringle five years earlier. Macfarlane announced his intention to carry on its tradition.

Brought up "under the British Constitution," he was determined to be "guided by adherence to its principals"; for the next 23 years he championed the colonial executive and defended its policies.

Newspaper publishing was not lucrative and Macfarlane's circulation was limited. Like many of his contemporaries, he diversified his activities. In August 1828 he started the *Brockville Gazette*. He ensured that its content and politics reflected tory policies, leaving the actual editing to another; the following year he sold the paper to his editor and a Kingston associate. A steadier and more important supplement to his income came from job printing, bookselling and bookbinding, and the sale of stationery. For a time he was also the local agent for the *Encyclopedia Americana*. He printed several books and at least twice (in 1834 and 1836) compiled an almanac. His most ambitious project, however, was the compilation and printing of *The statutes of the province of Upper Canada . . .* (1831). Originally, he had attempted the project on his own, but he was obliged to join forces with Hugh Christopher Thomson*, another well-known local printer, to finish it.

Despite a fire in 1833, Macfarlane prospered and became increasingly involved in other commercial projects. From 1826 to 1835 he was the Kingston agent for the Alliance British and Foreign Life and Fire Assurance Company of London. In 1830, under the name of James Macfarlane and Company, he began to import garden supplies including flowers, ornamental trees, and seeds. Periodically, he speculated in land. In 1837 he transferred the bindery part of his business to a Montreal firm. His major commitment remained the *Chronicle*, which was the basis of his growing involvement in community affairs and gave him a voice in political matters.

His interest in community affairs had begun shortly after he took charge of the paper. He provided publicity for organizations such as the Dorcas Society and the Female Benevolent Society and he willingly allowed his office to be used by a number of societies and institutions as a depository for contributions. He also frequently gave of his time and money to worthy causes promoting education and poor relief. And, as might be expected, he supported various local commercial organizations and projects. Finally, he was a member of the Presbyterian church, the St Andrew's Society, and the Celtic Sons of Upper Canada.

It is, perhaps, not surprising that town leaders such as Macaulay, John KIRBY, and Allan MacLean provided public endorsements for Macfarlane's seed business, or that he received a number of influential appointments. In 1832 he was chosen to sit on the committee responsible for examining the district treasurer's report and also became a member of the Board of Health. The following year he became a commissioner of the Court of Requests. Respectability and growing influence brought more onerous positions. In 1836 and again the next year he oversaw the Board of Health's responses to the problem of cholera. He was appointed a JP in 1834 and held the position until his sudden death in 1847.

As editor of the *Chronicle* Macfarlane frequently proclaimed his loyalty to king, country, and constitution. He supported the executive's policies on such matters as trade with the United States and banking legislation, and he defended its handling of the alien question [*see* Sir Peregrine Maitland*]. He was appalled by the activities of William Lyon Mackenzie* and the increasingly radical agitation often associated with him. An officer in the militia since 1824, he was a member of the court martial held at Fort Henry in 1838 to try the prisoners taken at the Patriot attack on Prescott [*see* Nils von SCHOULTZ].

Personally and professionally, Macfarlane had come a long way since his arrival in Kingston and his success had rested on a number of factors. He had sustained a strong personal commitment to his community and to a tory view of its needs; he had also supported local philanthropic endeavours, commercial projects, and cultural organizations. These beliefs and involvements, undoubtedly sincere, were also good for business. Once he was accepted by the local élite, his success was ensured and his influence certain.

JANE ERRINGTON

British Whig, 6 April 1847. *Brockville Gazette, and General Advertiser* (Brockville, [Ont.]), 1828–29. *Chronicle & Gazette*, 1833–47. *Chronicle and News*, 1847–49. *Kingston Chronicle*, 1819–33. *Upper Canada Gazette*, 12 April 1825. *Upper Canada Herald*, 22 Nov. 1825. E. J. Errington, "The 'Eagle,' the 'Lion,' and Upper Canada: the colonial elites' view of the United States and Great Britain, 1784–1828" (PHD thesis, Queen's Univ., Kingston, Ont., 1984). H. P. Gundy, *Early printers and printing in the Canadas* (2nd ed., Toronto, 1964).

MACGHILLEATHAIN, IAIN (John MacLean), Gaelic poet; b. 8 Jan. 1787 in Caolas, on the island of Tiree, Scotland, third son of Allan MacLean and Margaret MacFadyen; m. 19 July 1808 Isabella Black in Glasgow, and they had four sons and two daughters; d. 26 Jan. 1848 in Addington Forks, N.S.

John MacLean, who was referred to in Scotland as Iain MacAilein (John, son of Allan) and Am Bàrd Thighearna Chola (Bard of the Laird of Coll), would be known in Nova Scotia as Am Bàrd MacGhillEathain (Bard MacLean). He was probably the last of the traditional bards, whose duty it was to record in verse the important events in the life of the clan chief and his family. According to the standards of his time, he was well educated, being literate in both Gaelic and English. At the age of 16 he was bound as an apprentice to a shoemaker on the island of Tiree. After completing his apprenticeship three years later, he worked in Glasgow as a journeyman for about a year and subsequently returned to Tiree to practise his trade. In 1810 he was drafted into the Argyll militia. Military life did not agree with him, however, and a substitute was secured upon a payment of £40; his discharge is dated 17 Jan. 1811. He then went back to Tiree where, in addition to shoemaking, he was a merchant on a small scale.

MacLean had begun composing poetry when quite young, and after returning to Tiree in 1811 he spent much of his free time collecting Gaelic songs in the Highlands. In 1818 he published in Edinburgh a collection of poetry called *Orain nuadh Ghaedhlach, le Iain Mac Illeain, ann an Eilean Tirreadh* . . . (New Gaelic songs by John MacLean in the island of Tiree). Dedicated to Alexander MacLean, Laird of Coll, this book contains 22 poems by John MacLean and 34 by other major Gaelic poets. Included are songs by Alexander Mackinnon and Mary Macleod that cannot be found elsewhere.

Not long after the appearance of this volume, MacLean decided to emigrate to Nova Scotia. His motives are uncertain. He was not a victim of the Highland clearances and he undoubtedly enjoyed the prosperity and social honours that would have accrued to the Laird of Coll's bard. Yet a hint is given in one of his poems that he had offended his own chief by praising another too highly, and a reprimand could have sparked a desire for artistic independence. He may also have been attracted by the offers and promises of emigration agents, who travelled through the Highlands describing British North America as a land of opportunity.

Having made up his mind to emigrate, against considerable opposition from his friends, MacLean financed the passage for himself and his family by using his newly printed book as security. The MacLean family sailed from Tobermory in August 1819 on the ship *Economy*, arriving in Pictou, N.S., about 1 October. They stayed in Pictou for a week or so and then went by boat to Merigomish. The next spring MacLean cleared some of the trees from the lot he had acquired and planted potatoes. In the summer he built a small log house which he called Baile-Chnoic (Hill Farm); it was while living in this house that he composed his famous song *Oran do America* (Song to America), better known as *A' choille ghruamach* (The gloomy forest). In 1829 the poet and his son cleared land near James River and built a home there. Two years later the family moved to what is now known as Glen Bard, in Antigonish County.

Apart from his spiritual songs, MacLean's poetry may be divided into two categories: those poems which were composed in the style of the 18th-century panegyric poets, consisting for the most part of eulogy and elegy, and those which are in the style of "village verse." Most of his poems of Scottish provenance are of the former type; his Nova Scotia poems, inspired by local events such as an election, a wedding, a Highland ball, or even a watch raffle, are of the latter. *A' choille ghruamach* strikes a chord that will later resonate in the poetry of another Gaelic bard in Nova Scotia, John MacDonald [Iain MacDhòmhnaill 'Ic Iain*]. In it MacLean complains bitterly of life in the New World, particularly of the loneliness and back-breaking toil, extremes of heat and cold, plagues of insects, and wild animals. Much of his invective is directed against those agents who lured so many Scots to North America with their fabulous stories of wealth and freedom. The poem was sent to Tiree, where it caused his friends much distress; the Laird of Coll offered him free land for life if he returned, but he refused. MacLean's graphic description of pioneer life in the New World is said to have kept many people from emigrating. In his own case, however, initial discontent with his situation evaporated as his circumstances improved in the course of the 1820s. Apparently well liked by his neighbours, MacLean was a good friend of the Reverend Colin P. GRANT, the Roman Catholic priest at Arisaig. He also was a fervent admirer of the Reverend James Drummond MacGregor* of Pictou. After the disruption of the Church of Scotland in 1843, MacLean joined Nova Scotia's Free Church.

Gaelic scholar Alexander Maclean Sinclair*, a grandson, described MacLean this way: "Nature gave the poet a mind of great capacity; but evidently it did not intend that he should become a wealthy man. He never attended regularly to his work; his mind was not upon it. Poetry occupied his thoughts when pegging sole-leather in Scotland, and cutting down trees in America; it took complete possession of him. . . . He was clannish, and took pleasure in visiting his friends and acquaintances." Another writer, dubbing MacLean an "enthusiastic Highlander," said that he was "about five feet and nine inches in height, stout and well-built. He had dark hair and grey eyes, and a broad and massive forehead. His voice was soft and musical, and he was a good singer."

MAUREEN LONERGAN WILLIAMS

Many of John MacLean's compositions are included in the MacLean MSS at PANS, MG 15, G, 2, no.2, a copy of which is available in the Special Coll. Dept., St Francis Xavier Univ. Library, Antigonish, N.S. Others may be found in *The MacLean songster; clarsach na coille: a collection of Gaelic poetry*, comp. A. M. Sinclair, ed. Hector MacDougall (2nd ed., Glasgow, 1928), and in *Dain spioradail le Iain Mac-Gilleain maille ri beagan de laoidhean Mhic Griogair, nach robh gus a so air an clo-bhualadh*, [ed. A. M. Sinclair] (Edinburgh, 1880), which in addition to spiritual songs by MacLean contains a few hymns, previously unpublished, by James Drummond MacGregor. A translation of *A' choille ghruamach* by Watson Kirkconnell* is given in "John MacLean's 'Gloomy Forest,'" *Dalhousie Rev.*, 28 (1948–49): 158–62; the Gaelic text is in *The MacLean songster*. Translations of two additional songs appear, along with the Gaelic texts and a short biography of MacLean, in *The emigrant experience: songs of Highland emigrants in North America*, ed. and trans. Margaret MacDonell (Toronto and Buffalo, N.Y., 1982), 68–79. English translations of MacLean's Nova Scotia songs are provided in Maureen Lonergan [Williams], "The Canadian songs of John MacLean" (MA thesis, Univ. of Glasgow, 1977).

Alexander Mackenzie, *The history of the Highland clearances* (2nd ed., Glasgow, 1914). Derick Thomson, *An introduction to Gaelic poetry* (London, 1974). *Casket* (Antigonish), 6, 13 July 1961; 11 Jan. 1962. *Chronicle-Herald* (Halifax), 10 July 1961: 5. *Post* (Sydney, N.S.), 23 April 1921. D. M. Sinclair, "John Maclean: a centenary," *Dalhousie Rev.*, 28: 258–65.

McGILLIVRAY, SIMON, businessman; b. *c.* 1783 or more likely in 1785 in Dunlichty parish, Inverness-shire, Scotland, son of Donald McGillivray and Anne McTavish; m. 23 Nov. 1837 Ann Easthope, and they had two daughters, one born posthumously; d. 9 June 1840 in Blackheath (London), England.

Simon McGillivray, the son of a poor tenant farmer on the Clovendale estate, benefited like his older brothers William* and Duncan* from the help of his maternal uncle, Simon McTavish*, who saw to his education. Because he had a lame foot, instead of coming to the Canadas and being put through the same kind of apprenticeship in the fur trade as his two brothers, Simon McGillivray worked for McTavish, Fraser and Company of London. This enterprise, which had been founded by McTavish to maximize the North West Company's profits, supplied the Montreal firm with trade goods, obtained credit for it, looked after shipments, and sold the pelts at the best price on the London market. When his uncle died in 1804 McGillivray inherited £500.

The following year he became a partner in McTavish, Fraser and Company, which assigned him one of the nine shares, and then in 1808 granted him another. In 1811 he was made a partner of McTavish, McGillivrays and Company (formerly McTavish, Frobisher and Company). The firm already held four of the nine shares of McTavish, Fraser and Company and by this move increased its holdings in the enterprise to two-thirds. McGillivray had visited Montreal at the time of his uncle's death. Over the following years he quickly gained experience in the firm's affairs, being involved in its ordinary transactions, in negotiations to obtain a charter for the NWC, and in William McGillivray's efforts to gain some control of HBC assets. When Lord Selkirk [Douglas*] turned the last-mentioned endeavour to his advantage and announced his firm intention of setting up a colony on the banks of the Red River, Simon was put in charge of a press campaign in England against him, but to no avail. He told the NWC winterers that Selkirk "*must be driven to abandon* [his plan], for his success would strike at the very existence of our trade." In 1814, when McTavish, McGillivrays and Company was being reorganized, Simon came to Montreal and put in an appearance with his three shares as heir presumptive of his brother William, who with him was the only legitimate representative of the NWC in England. His authority in McTavish, Fraser and Company, where he worked daily, had grown steadily, whereas that of his cousin John Fraser, its financial expert in McTavish's time, had gradually decreased. Since September 1808 the London firm had no longer had any outsiders in its ranks.

It was while working largely from London, and within the context of McTavish, Fraser and Company affairs, that McGillivray became involved in the emerging and deepening crisis in the NWC, without understanding its importance for a long time. But, as the struggle against Selkirk and the HBC became more intense and profits continued to fall, it became impossible not to sense that matters were at a delicate pass. In October 1820 William McGillivray finally realized how serious the situation was. From then on Simon took the leading role: the solution he devised, with Edward Ellice*'s help, was to merge the two giant fur companies. He later wrote, "In the month of December 1820, *I* opened a negotiation with the Hudson's-Bay Company, for a general arrangement upon a *new basis*; which, with the co-operation of my friend Mr. Ellice, was in three months concluded." In January 1821 Colin ROBERTSON, speaking of the two men engaged in the discussions in the name of the NWC, remarked: "I like Simon much better than his friend the Member of Parliament; there is a sort of highland pride and frankness about the little fellow that I don't dislike." The merger of the two rivals was effected late in March. On 27 May Simon was in Montreal, working to get the agreements accepted. On 12 June he and William left Montreal to meet the NWC partners at Fort William (Thunder Bay, Ont.). On 21 July, his mission accomplished, he departed for Hudson Bay. On 12 July Robertson had written: "Simon McGillivray has carried everything without even the semblance of opposition. The first day he opened the business, the second the Deed and Release was signed, and the third all was peace and harmony." Despite an appearance of balance within the new organization and the presence on the joint committee of William and Simon McGillivray, the situation steadily deteriorated. The agreement establishing McTavish, McGillivrays and Company came to an end in 1822; it was succeeded that year by McGillivrays, Thain and Company, but both companies finally went bankrupt in 1825.

Simon McGillivray's role in these developments is

probably open to question. It is certain, however, that one of the main beneficiaries of them was Ellice. Since the period of the American revolution, the Ellice family had been more interested in the fur trade in the southwest, but it probably had ambitions to gain control of the riches in the northwest. It would not be surprising if the outcome of the crisis in part stemmed from a long and patient pursuit by the family to ensure its supremacy in the fur-trade economy.

Simon McGillivray's career was by no means over. In 1829 he was chosen by the United Mexican Mining Association of London to help reorganize the administration of the company's silver mines. On his return from Mexico, he became one of the owners of the *Morning Chronicle and London Advertiser* in 1835. In 1837 he married the eldest daughter of his partner John Easthope. He died in 1840. A mason, at his death he was still provincial grand master of Upper Canada, an office he had held since 1822.

FERNAND OUELLET

Les bourgeois de la Compagnie du Nord-Ouest (Masson). *Docs. relating to NWC* (Wallace). Innis, *Fur trade in Canada* (1962). E. A. Mitchell, *Fort Timiskaming and the fur trade* (Toronto and Buffalo, N.Y., 1977). Rich, *Fur trade* (1967). J. R. Robertson, *The history of freemasonry in Canada from its introduction in 1749 . . .* (2v., Toronto, 1899). M. [E.] Wilkins Campbell, *McGillivray, lord of the northwest* (Toronto, 1962); *Northwest to the sea; a biography of William McGillivray* (Toronto and Vancouver, 1975). Wallace McLeod, "Simon McGillivray (ca 1785–1840)," *Ars Quatuor Coronatorum* (Margate, Eng.), 96 (1983): 1–35.

McGRAY, ASA, wheelwright, Baptist minister, and farmer; b. 18 Sept. 1780 in North Yarmouth (Maine), son of William McGray; m. 7 March 1801 Susanna Stoddard in Durham (Maine), and they had at least five boys and two girls; d. 28 Dec. 1843 in Centreville, N.S.

Asa McGray, the son of a tavern-keeper in Durham and a wheelwright by trade, was converted to Methodism there in 1805 and baptized by immersion. He began preaching in 1813. Increasingly attracted to the Free Will Baptist movement, however, he was ordained in Fairfax (Albion) by the Fairfax Baptist Church on 26 Sept. 1814. After preaching for two years he moved to Windsor, N.S., one of many Free Will advocates drawn to the colony from the District of Maine. There he supported himself as a wheelwright and preached on occasion.

In 1820 or 1821 McGray moved to Centreville on Cape Sable Island, where there may have been a Baptist church operating on the Calvinist model. On 22 March 1821, assisted by another minister, Thomas Crowell, he organized, perhaps from the earlier church, the first Free Will Baptist Church in Nova Scotia. This group differed from the Regular Baptists of the colony primarily in its rejection of Calvinism and the espousal of open communion. Its members were determined, as recorded in the church minutes, to have the "Scriptures of Truth as our only and all-sufficient rule of faith and practice." In these and other matters they were still strongly influenced by the legacy of Henry Alline* and the Great Awakening. With little competition, McGray's church grew rapidly, fuelled by periodic revivals.

McGray was instrumental in the establishment of other Free Will Baptist churches in surrounding communities on the island and in ordaining candidates to serve them. In 1834 these churches were formed into a quarterly meeting, or conference, a loose organization of independent churches. On 17 June 1837 a partial union was effected between the Free Will Baptists and the Free Christian Baptists, a similar group under the leadership of the Reverend Joseph Norton. Disagreements between Norton and McGray led in 1839 to the embittered withdrawal of McGray and most members of his church. They assumed their former name and in 1840 allied themselves with the Farmington Quarterly Meeting, in Maine. It was not until 1867 that the Free Christian and Free Will Baptist bodies in Nova Scotia were reunited as the Free Baptist Conference. In 1906 this body merged with the Calvinist Baptists to form the United Baptist Convention of the Maritime Provinces.

McGray served his church and community selflessly, helping to build bridges and schools. He often acted as doctor, and his wife as midwife. In 1827 he established the first Sunday school on the island. Following the tradition of his church, he received no payment for his pastoral services and even provided the first meeting-place at his own expense by enlarging and remodelling his home. His livelihood derived from farming, supplemented with occasional offerings made by members of the congregation. It was not until 1838 that the church agreed to contribute towards his support.

The dispute with Norton was but one of many deep divisions in the Baptist movement that marked McGray's final years, as evangelicals in Nova Scotia attempted to make choices from what was at times a bewildering array of contending factions. McGray's free-will doctrines and emphasis on open communion would eventually play an important role in shaping Maritime Baptist views. Ironically, it took a preacher from Maine to reintroduce and uphold in Nova Scotia the legacy of Henry Alline at a time when most of Alline's disciples, including Edward Manning* and Joseph DIMOCK, were moving down other, more "orthodox," paths.

BARRY M. MOODY

Atlantic Baptist Hist. Coll., Acadia Univ. (Wolfville, N.S.),

Centreville, Shelburne County, N.S., United Baptist Church records, records of Cape Sable Island Free Baptist Church; Edward Manning, journals. *A treatise on the faith of the Free Baptists of Nova Scotia* (n.p., n.d.; copy at Atlantic Baptist Hist. Coll.). *Christian Messenger*, 25 Aug. 1837. S. B. Attwood, *The length and breadth of Maine* (Orono, Maine, 1973). *Free Baptist cyclopædia*, ed. G. A. Burgess and J. T. Ward (Chicago, 1889). Bill, *Fifty years with Baptist ministers*. Edwin Crowell, *A history of Barrington Township and vicinity . . . 1604–1870* (Yarmouth, N.S., [1923]; repr. Belleville, Ont., 1973), 253–56, 519–20. Levy, *Baptists of Maritime prov*. Saunders, *Hist. of Baptists*. I. D. Stewart, *The history of the Freewill Baptists for half a century* (Dover, [N.H.], 1862).

McINTOSH, JOHN, farmer; b. 15 Aug. 1777 in New York, son of Alexander McIntosh and Juliet ——; m. Hannah Doran (Dorin), and they had six sons and five daughters; d. between 19 Sept. 1845 and 10 Jan. 1846 near McIntosh's Corners (Dundela), Upper Canada.

John McIntosh has been linked in Canadian legend with an apple, one of Ontario's, if not Canada's, agricultural successes in the 20th century. He is said to be the originator of the apple which bears his name. But the success story really belongs to the apple, with which McIntosh had not much more than a chance encounter. Neither the myth associated with him nor the reality comes even remotely close to the remarkable story of the American figure John Chapman, popularly known as Johnny Appleseed.

John's father was a Scottish immigrant who settled near Harpersfield, N.Y., in 1773 and was a loyalist during the American revolution. According to one account John came to Upper Canada in 1796, another places the date of his arrival at 1801, and yet a third claims he immigrated at age 18. Perhaps the first two versions come together in a chronology suggested by one writer, that he immigrated in 1796 and married in 1801. He apparently bought land in the St Lawrence valley, in Matilda Township, where on 8 March 1813 he purchased the west half of lot 9, concession 5.

McIntosh farmed this property until his death. It was there that either he or his son Allan (as some accounts have it) discovered in the bush and transplanted the seedling apple trees now known as the McIntosh. There is no documentary evidence that conclusively establishes either the father or the son as the discoverer of the seedlings, which probably derived from the Fameuse (Snow) apple. A strong oral and recorded tradition credits Allan with the appreciation of the apple, its eventual propagation, and the establishment of a nursery later in the century. This assumption seems reasonable.

The apple's qualities only began to be recognized in the late 19th and early 20th centuries. It had not been popular with farmers and as late as 1876 it was not included on the long list of varieties displayed at the international exhibition in Philadelphia by Ontario's fruit growers. In a paper read before the annual meeting of the Ontario Fruit Growers' Association in 1891, a New Yorker lauded the apple, which was "becoming a great favorite and sells in our city markets as a fancy fruit stand apple." But as late as 1905 one farmer urged upon the association the need for farmers to seek "something better" than the Mac and two other popular apples. The Mac's popularizer was William Tyrrell Macoun*, dominion horticulturist, whose work at the Central Experimental Farm in Ottawa affirmed the apple's outstanding suitability for the Canadian climate and the increasingly important urban markets. He had long considered it as requiring "no words of praise, it is one of the finest appearing and best dessert apples grown." The fruit-experiment stations established by the federal government published short lists of desirable apples and long lists of undesirable ones. The Mac was consistently on the former. It was large, sweet, attractive, and a "regular bearer," and its only flaws, susceptibility to spot and easy bruising, could be overcome by chemical spraying and proper packaging. In 1907 Macoun reported that "it is only during the past ten or fifteen years that the fruit has become widely known. So great is the popularity . . . at present that the nurserymen cannot meet the demand for trees."

In 1909 the president of the fruit growers' association, Ernest D'Israeli Smith*, noted that of late years "orchardists have gone into the growing of apples on an extensive scale, directly for commercial purposes." A huge number of species were then grown by Ontario's farmers, and Macoun had long urged specialization and reduction in response to markets and for economy of production. The Mac was one of his choices and by the first decade of the 20th century resistance to it was eroding. The association's historical committee passed a resolution in 1909 setting aside $50 to erect a memorial on the spot where the first seedling had been planted "over a century ago." The date was unlikely but that did not matter. "This variety has taken its place as the highest type of dessert fruit" and has "shown its adaptability to a wide range of territory." In 1912 a monument was erected on the McIntosh farm "by popular subscription."

As Harold Jones, a nurseryman in Maitland, Ont., put it in 1905, the best types of apple had "originated largely from chance seedlings. McIntosh Red was of this description but it was one of a million." It is perhaps unfortunate that Macoun used the word originator to describe John McIntosh's connection to the apple. He was sensible enough to credit propagation of the apple to Allan McIntosh. The apple's fame would probably have come as an enormous surprise to John, an illiterate and pious Methodist farmer who had the good fortune to own the land on which the "one of a million" tree was found. He died at his home in Matilda Township, possibly in late September 1845.

ROBERT L. FRASER

AO, RG 22, ser.194, reg.D (1842–60): 29–31. Dundas Land Registry Office (Morrisburg, Ont.), Abstract index to deeds, Matilda Township, 1: 145, 184 (mfm. at AO). Reid, *Loyalists in Ont.*, 93. J. S. Carter, *The story of Dundas . . .* (Iroquois, Ont., 1905; repr. Belleville, Ont., 1973), 243, 394, 433. J. G. Harkness, *Stormont, Dundas and Glengarry: a history, 1784–1945* (Oshawa, Ont., 1946). M. E. [Hillman] Waterston, *Pioneers in agriculture: Massey, McIntosh, Saunders* (Toronto, 1957). Ont., Dept. of Agriculture, *Fruit growing opportunities in Ontario, Canada* ([Toronto, 1908]); *The fruits of Ontario, 1906* (Toronto, 1907); Dept. of Commissioner of Agriculture and Public Works, *Report of the commissioner of Agriculture on the products, manufactures, etc., of Ontario, exhibited at the International Exhibition, Philadelphia, 1876* (Toronto, 1877). *Canadian Horticulturist* (Grimsby, Ont.), 22 (1899): 396–97, 506; 23 (1900): 24, 45–46. Fruit Growers' Assoc. of Ont., *Annual report* (Toronto), 1873, 1876, 1881, 1883, 1885, 1889, 1891–92, 1894–95, 1900, 1903, 1905–6, 1909. L. A. Morse, "The biggest Mac of all: the MacIntosh – solid, reliable, luscious and our own," *Leisure Ways* (Toronto), 4 (September 1985): 12–17. Ont., Dept. of Agriculture, *Annual report of the fruit experiment stations of Ontario, under the joint control of the Ontario Agricultural College, Guelph, and the Fruit Growers' Association of Ontario* (Toronto), 1903; 1907: 12–13; Fruit Branch, *Report* (Toronto), 1910.

McKENZIE, JAMES, fur trader, JP, and businessman; b. *c.* 1777 near Inverness, Scotland, son of Alexander Mackenzie and his wife Catherine; d. 18 July 1849 at Quebec.

In 1795 James McKenzie began a seven-year apprenticeship with the North West Company under his brother RODERICK in the Athabasca department. The journals he kept at Fort Chipewyan (Alta) in 1799–1800 illuminate the harshness of life in the fur trade; they also reveal his contempt for Canadians, Indians, and the NWC alike. "Bound to forward his company's interest," he physically abused the "Potties" (members) of the New North West Company (sometimes called the XY Company), sold Indian women to *engagés*, provided Indians with bad tobacco and watered-down rum, gave credits to hunters indebted to the XY Company, and, once, rewarded rather than punished a hunter responsible for an *engagé*'s death – all, he cynically confessed, for more beaver and thus more "hard cash" for the NWC's shareholders.

Promoted partner in 1802, he was reassigned to the Athabasca country, then being infiltrated by the Hudson's Bay Company. According to Peter Fidler*, who headed its campaign, McKenzie constructed a "watch house" near the HBC's post and ordered the destruction of the company's property; he debauched Indians, plundered furs, and "ill-used" Indians and HBC servants for trading with each other. Such "harsh and Barbarous usages," Fidler reported, ultimately provoked some Chipewyans into killing six NWC "bullies." After the amalgamation of the two North West companies in 1804, which brought Samuel BLACK into the fray for the NWC in the Athabasca, McKenzie's harassment intensified and in 1806 the HBC withdrew from the area.

That year the NWC appointed McKenzie to the king's posts and Mingan, starting in 1807 after his rotation at Montreal. In January 1807, while in Montreal, he joined the Beaver Club. Illness delayed him at Quebec until 1808, when he toured his new domain by canoe. Journeying up the Rivière Saguenay, across Lac Saint-Jean, and along the Rivière Chamouchouane to Fort Ashuapmouchouan (on Lac Chigoubiche), he then traversed the Labrador coast to Musquaro, where he met Naskapi Indians, whom he found to be "naturally timid," "treacherous," "indolent," and "thieves." Normally wintering at Tadoussac, he also assumed the duties of the NWC's agency at Quebec, which took him occasionally to Montreal. This arrangement facilitated visits to his brothers Roderick and Henry*, and to his two mixed-blood sons (he had had a country wife) at nearby Terrebonne, where he bought a house in 1811. He was there in 1815 aiding John McDonald* of Garth to "dispossess" some 400 HBC voyageurs of a local tavern. In a list of NWC partners prepared at about this time for Lord Selkirk [Douglas*], McKenzie was described as an "Indolent and Easy" trader.

About 1818 he apparently left the NWC to become an independent merchant at Tadoussac and Quebec. He was first commissioned as a justice of the peace in 1821, when he may have settled permanently at Quebec. His new situation and the depressing effect of the HBC–NWC merger on his finances did little to alter some of the cynical opinions he had formed as a Nor'Wester; he testified in 1823 to a legislative committee on crown lands that the king's posts Indians were "stupid" and "suspicious," whereas to another witness, François Verrault, they were "mild, charitable and hospitable."

On 10 Feb. 1825 McKenzie married Ellen Fitzsimons, the under-aged daughter of the late Captain Thomas Fitzsimons. The obligations imposed on James by their contract – mainly the setting up of a life annuity for Ellen – undoubtedly contributed to his eager acceptance of the HBC agency at Quebec in 1827. By 1840 the company's lease of the king's posts and its timber operations on the Saguenay, initiated in the 1830s by William CONNOLLY, were being opposed by Quebec merchants. Despite McKenzie's defence of the company, a firm headed by William Price* acquired a three-year timber licence, following which the area was opened up to unlicensed lumbermen. Chastised by Governor Sir George Simpson* in 1843 for accepting shares in James Gibb*'s sawmill company at Portneuf, McKenzie justified his action by citing his growing family's financial needs.

Straitened circumstances plagued him to the end. Though he had granted mortgages to his wife to establish her annuity, she found it necessary to petition Simpson, in vain, for a pension following his death in July 1849. McKenzie, Simpson claimed two months later, had been a "mercantile agent," not a "commissioned officer"; moreover, he had left a "considerable deficit in the Cash." Ellen McKenzie died the following year, survived by four of their seven children.

JEAN MORRISON

[The author wishes to acknowledge the kind assistance of Henri McKenzie Masson of Outremont, Que. J.M.]

James McKenzie's Athabasca journal and his account of the king's posts are in McGill Univ. Libraries, Dept. of Rare Books and Special Coll., MS coll., CH173.S155 and CH177.S159 respectively. They have been published with certain deletions and revisions as James McKenzie, "Extracts from his journal, 1799–1800, Athabasca District" and "The king's posts and journal of a canoe jaunt through the king's domain, 1808; the Saguenay and the Labrador coast" in *Les bourgeois de la Compagnie du Nord-Ouest* (Masson), 2: 369–99 and 401–54. Masson's edition of the 1808 journal was reproduced under the title "Yesterday: a canoe jaunt through the king's domain in 1808," alongside J. A. Burgesse's description of the region in 1948, "Today: from Quebec to the Saguenay and Lake St. John in 1948," under the collective heading "The king's domain, today and yesterday" in the *Beaver*, outfit 279 (June 1948), 32–38.

ANQ-M, CN1-29, 6 juin 1795. ANQ-Q, CN1-197, 18 mars 1848, 20 févr. 1849; CN1-253, 5 févr. 1825; Z300076 (microfiche), James Mackenzie et famille. PAC, MG 19, B1, 1: 22; B3: 7, 9 (transcript); E1, ser.1: 187, 8430–31 (transcripts). PAM, HBCA, A.44/8: f.101; A.44/9: f.53; B.170/c/1: ff.23–39; D.4/40: f.9; D.5/2: ff.115–19, 183–85, 339, 345, 363, 378–79; D.5/22: ff.166–67. Presbyterian Church in Canada Arch. (Toronto), St Gabriel Street Church (Montreal), reg. of baptisms, marriages, and burials (mfm. at AO). *Les bourgeois de la Compagnie du Nord-Ouest* (Masson), 1: 56. *Docs. relating to NWC* (Wallace). Hargrave, *Hargrave corr.* (Glazebrook). L.C., House of Assembly, *Journals*, 1824, app.R. *Morning Chronicle* (Quebec), 20 July 1849. *Quebec Gazette*, 3 Dec. 1818, 5 July 1821. J. G. MacGregor, *Peter Fidler: Canada's forgotten surveyor, 1769–1822* (Toronto and Montreal, 1966). C. W. Mackenzie, *Donald Mackenzie: "king of the northwest"* . . . (Los Angeles, 1937). R. S. Allen, "Peter Fidler and Nottingham House, Lake Athabasca, 1802–1806," *Hist. and Archaeology* (Ottawa), 69 (1983): 283–347. Karlis Karklins, "Nottingham House: the Hudson's Bay Company in Athabasca, 1802–1806," *Hist. and Archaeology*, 69: 3–281.

MACKENZIE, RODERICK (although the name is frequently written **McKenzie**, he signed Mackenzie), fur trader, militia officer, office holder, JP, author, and politician; b. *c.* 1761 near Inverness, Scotland, eldest son of Alexander Mackenzie and Catherine ——; m. *c.* 1788 *à la façon du pays* an Indian woman, and they had three children; m. 24 April 1803 Rachel Chaboillez, daughter of Charles-Jean-Baptiste Chaboillez*, and they had at least two sons and three daughters who survived infancy; d. 15 Aug. 1844 in Terrebonne, Lower Canada.

Roderick Mackenzie was the most prominent of several men of that name who were involved in the fur trade. He was a first cousin of the explorer Sir Alexander Mackenzie*, and three of his brothers, Donald*, JAMES, and Henry*, were fur traders, as were his father-in-law, his brother-in-law Charles Chaboillez*, and his relative by marriage Simon McTavish*.

Roderick arrived in the province of Quebec in 1784 – presumably because of his ties with his cousin, since by 1785 he was employed as a clerk and Alexander's assistant in Gregory, MacLeod and Company [*see* John Gregory*; Normand MacLeod*]. The firm, which had earlier concentrated on the trade in the Detroit region, had turned its attention to the northwest in the winter of 1783–84, but it could not match the resources of its well-established rival, the North West Company. Mackenzie, who was sent to Snake (Pinehouse) Lake (Sask.) for the winter of 1786–87, brought word to Grand Portage (near Grand Portage, Minn.) in the summer that the intense rivalry had led to the murder of John Ross, a wintering partner in Gregory, MacLeod. At McTavish's invitation, Gregory, MacLeod joined the NWC later that year, ending the friction.

By 1787 Mackenzie had decided to leave the fur trade, apparently feeling that his position as clerk, which gave him no share in profits, was akin to slavery. Alexander dissuaded him and the following year Roderick joined his cousin in the Athabasca department. He was sent to establish Fort Chipewyan (Alta) at the southwestern end of Lake Athabasca and was left in charge of the fort, which became the company's headquarters in the region, during Alexander's absences in 1789, 1791–92, and 1792–93. From 1794 Alexander ceased to be a wintering partner and Roderick succeeded him as head of the department. The following year Roderick became a partner in the NWC. During his return from a furlough spent in the east in 1798–99, he rediscovered an old canoe route that had been used by the French; the discovery allowed the NWC to shift its trans-shipment base from Grand Portage, which had become American territory, to Kaministiquia (Thunder Bay, Ont.).

By the end of the century Roderick had spent almost 15 years in the northwest and his ultimate desire was to return to the comforts of civilization. By all accounts he was a tough and resourceful man, but he had been in the shadow of Alexander, who had a reputation for driving men hard. Yet Roderick and Alexander were close friends until 1799. Roderick was not a party to the quarrel between Alexander and McTavish which contributed to his cousin's departure in that year from McTavish, Frobisher and Company, the dominant firm in the NWC coalition. In Roderick's words, "The absence of Mr. MacKenzie from the concern created a vacancy and . . . application was made to me to supply his place which I accepted though with great reluctance." The reluctance was no doubt in anticipation of Alexander's displeasure and indeed he did not write to Roderick until 1805.

In November 1800 Roderick Mackenzie became a partner in a reorganized McTavish, Frobisher with McTavish, Gregory, William* and Duncan* McGillivray, and William Hallowell. He agreed to spend one last winter, 1800–1, in the west and then he settled in Terrebonne. After he ceased to be a wintering partner, he was required to surrender one of his two NWC shares. He gave up the other in 1805 as part of the reorganization occasioned by the NWC's absorption of the New North West Company (sometimes called the XY Company). On 1 Dec. 1806 McTavish, Frobisher was reconstituted as McTavish, McGillivrays and Company with the McGillivrays, William Hallowell and his brother James, Angus Shaw*, and Mackenzie as partners. Mackenzie's participation in the firm's affairs started to wane, although he continued to attend the NWC meetings at Fort William (Thunder Bay) until 1808. By 1813 he was over 50 and he elected not to renew his place in the partnership. His one-fifteenth share was bought out by his partners for £10,000, payable in annual instalments. Perhaps as early as 1805 and at least during 1812–13 he was a partner with his brother Henry, the Hallowells, and other prominent fur traders in Mackenzie, Oldham and Company, a firm connected with the trade. He retained a financial tie with McTavish, McGillivrays and when it went bankrupt in 1825 he sued the partners, including his brother Henry, winning a judgement of £7,308 plus interest three years later. He was unable to collect and in 1832 sold his claim to Samuel Gerrard* for £6,500.

During his career Mackenzie displayed literary interests that are at odds with the usual image of a fur trader. He apparently had books sent to him on a regular basis, and according to one source he established a library for NWC employees in the Athabasca. Once settled in Terrebonne, he spent considerable energy collecting material on the fur trade, the Indians, and the natural history of the west. In 1806 he had a 60-page questionnaire prepared for distribution to fur traders. Printing delays forced him to send a one-page circular instead. Many of the materials he collected were published by his grandson-in-law Louis-François-Rodrigue Masson* in *Les bourgeois de la Compagnie du Nord-Ouest*. Mackenzie himself has been credited with the authorship of the history of the fur trade that appears as the introduction to his cousin's *Voyages from Montreal* and of "A brief account of the fur trade to the northwest country . . . ," published anonymously in the *Canadian Review* of 1824. A member of the Literary and Historical Society of Quebec and the American Antiquarian Society, he was also a fellow of the Royal Society of Northern Antiquaries at Copenhagen.

In 1814 Mackenzie purchased the seigneury of Terrebonne from the McTavish estate, agreeing to pay £8,000 plus £1,200 per year until the total, £28,000, had been attained. He planned to continue McTavish's commercial development of the property and wrote of raising the annual revenue from £1,000 to £3,000. He never became a seigneur, however, and had to leave the property in 1824 after a court action, initiated by McTavish's widow, cancelled his purchase because the executors had exceeded their authority in making the sale. He nevertheless continued to live in Terrebonne.

Mackenzie received a number of appointments typical of a man of his station. In 1812 he was commissioned a lieutenant-colonel in the Terrebonne militia. From 1804 to 1816 he was a justice of the peace for the Indian Territory and from 1821 to 1839 he was a justice for the districts of Montreal, Quebec, Trois-Rivières, Gaspé, and Saint-François. He was appointed a commissioner of roads and bridges for the county of Effingham in 1817 and it was probably in this capacity that two years later he promoted improvements to the Rivière des Prairies so as to facilitate the passage of timber rafts. He also served as a commissioner for the erection of free schools in Terrebonne–Effingham in 1809, and on a commission to study the best means of building a bridge between Montreal and the mainland in 1832.

Mackenzie's most significant appointment was to the Legislative Council of Lower Canada on 10 May 1817. The appointment, which he held until March 1838, was a measure of his standing since fellow members were among the most prominent men of their time. He was very active on the council in the 1820s and was on good terms with the governor-in-chief, Lord Dalhousie [RAMSAY]. His political views were representative of the opinions of the Montreal merchant community. He was an ardent supporter of the union of the Canadas proposed in 1822 and resolutely opposed to the views of the Patriote majority in the House of Assembly.

Little is known of the Indian family Mackenzie left behind in the northwest. His daughter Nancy* married fur trader John George MCTAVISH *à la façon du pays* and another daughter, Louisa, married Angus Bethune*, a chief factor in the Hudson's Bay Company. Mackenzie formally married a Roman Catholic according to Anglican rite but gave money to, and had one of his sons of the marriage baptized at, the Presbyterian St Gabriel Street Church in Montreal. Of the children born to him and his second wife, Alexander became an officer in the British army, Charles Roderick took up law, and his daughters married prominent businessmen or lawyers.

Roderick Mackenzie was a solid member of the second rank of Montreal fur traders. Always a follower rather than a leader, he chose semi-retirement after his fur-trading days rather than active participation in mercantile life. He continued to identify with and promote the interests of Montreal's merchant community until failing health in the 1830s removed him from public life.

PETER DESLAURIERS

Roderick Mackenzie is probably the author of the introduction to Alexander Mackenzie's *Voyages from Montreal, on the river St. Laurence, through the continent of North America, to the Frozen and Pacific oceans; in the years, 1789 and 1793; with a preliminary account of the rise, progress, and present state of the fur trade of that country*, [ed. William Combe] (London, 1801) and of "A brief account of the fur trade to the northwest country, carried on from Lower Canada, and of the various agreements and arrangements under which it was conducted," *Canadian Rev. and Literary and Hist. Journal* (Montreal), no.1 (July 1824): 154–57.

ANQ-M, CE1-63, 24 avril 1803. McGill Univ. Libraries, Dept. of Rare Books and Special Coll., MS coll., CH21.S57, CH23.S59, CH27.S63, CH149.S19, CH171.S153, CH175.S175. PAC, MG 24, L3: 9550–58, 26406–9, 26713–20; RG 68, General index, 1651–1841. *Les bourgeois de la Compagnie du Nord-Ouest* (Masson). *Docs. relating to NWC* (Wallace). Alexander Mackenzie, *The journals and letters of Sir Alexander Mackenzie*, ed. W. K. Lamb (Toronto, 1970). *Montreal Transcript*, 20 Aug. 1844. F.-J. Audet, "Les législateurs du Bas-Canada." P.-G. Roy, *Inv. concessions*. Turcotte, *Le Conseil législatif*. Campbell, *Hist. of Scotch Presbyterian Church*. Henri Masson, *Joseph Masson, dernier seigneur de Terrebonne, 1791–1847* (Montréal, 1972). W. S. Wallace, *The pedlars from Quebec and other papers on the Nor'Westers* (Toronto, 1954).

MACKINTOSH, WILLIAM, fur trader; b. *c.* 1784; d. 16 Feb. 1842 in Lachine, Lower Canada.

William MacKintosh's birthplace and parentage remain obscure. He joined the North West Company as a clerk about 1802 and was posted to Lesser Slave Lake (Alta) for the winter of 1803–4. In 1805 he replaced John Clarke* on the Peace River, which probably remained his wintering ground until 1819. MacKintosh played a vital role in opposing the Hudson's Bay Company's invasion of the Athabasca country, the Nor'Westers' most profitable department. Clarke, who joined the HBC in 1815, established Fort Wedderburn on Lake Athabasca that year but, being short of provisions, he planned to winter his party near MacKintosh's post, Fort Vermilion (near Fort Vermilion, Alta), where game was usually more plentiful.

MacKintosh shattered this opposition. Provisions were scarce and he "used all his influence, and some force" to prevent Clarke from encountering Indians or trading with them. Nor'Wester Willard Ferdinand Wentzel, writing from Fort Chipewyan, expressed "exultation" at the result: "No less than 15 men, 1 clerk with a woman and child died of starvation going up Peace River." Three of these deaths had occurred during the winter while the HBC party waited for MacKintosh's terms. Every HBC post had to surrender trade goods to its NWC neighbour in exchange for provisions to survive the winter. MacKintosh was rewarded when the NWC made him a partner on 22 July 1816. His role was never forgotten by the HBC; Nicholas Garry* summed him up as "the man who arranged the starving of Mr. Clarke's Men in Athapascow." According to HBC officer Colin ROBERTSON in 1819, "the whole of his conduct during the present contest, was marked by the most deliberate and wanton acts of cruelty towards the Company's servants."

After the 1815–16 season the HBC sent stronger parties to the Athabasca country. In 1818 Clarke surprised Fort Vermilion, and held MacKintosh briefly. Wentzel reported the encounter as an NWC victory, but historian Edwin Ernest Rich has determined that Clarke retrieved from Fort Vermilion goods which MacKintosh had seized earlier. By the spring of 1819 the prestige of the Nor'Westers on the Peace River had sharply declined.

Late in June the NWC suffered a further blow, at Grand Rapids (Man.), when HBC Governor William WILLIAMS intercepted and arrested MacKintosh, Benjamin Joseph Frobisher*, Angus Shaw*, John George MCTAVISH, and other Nor'Westers on their way to council at Fort William (Thunder Bay, Ont.). At the time of his capture on the 23rd, MacKintosh was suffering from diarrhoea, which "required his frequent retirement" to the woods. There he built a raft and escaped, leaving suicide notes to discourage pursuit. Of the four partners captured at Grand Rapids, only MacKintosh was available for service in 1819–20. The NWC sent him back to the Peace River, but to Fort Dunvegan rather than Fort Vermilion. Near Frog Portage (near Pelican Lake, Sask.) in the autumn of 1819 he was again seized but senior HBC officers let him go. In January Robertson reported with satisfaction that MacKintosh had sent away most of the families at his post and was living there with his wife, short of provisions. Some time before 1820 he had married according to the custom of the country Sarah Gladu, daughter of a Métis freeman on the Peace River.

At the union of the HBC and the NWC in 1821, the deed poll named MacKintosh a chief trader, and provided for his promotion to chief factor, which occurred in 1823. The amalgamation brought him once again into contact with Clarke. After travelling together one day, probably in the winter of 1821–22, they ended a dispute by exchanging pistol shots across a camp-fire.

MacKintosh held no important commands under the HBC. In 1822 the Council of the Northern Department sent him back to Fort Dunvegan, where his nominal control of all Peace River business was resisted by his subordinates and by Edward Smith, the chief factor in charge of the whole Athabasca district. During MacKintosh's tenure at Fort Dunvegan, an epidemic carried off a quarter of the natives trading at the post, and because of his intention to move Fort St John (near Fort St John, B.C.), he may have been partly responsible for the bad relations with the Beaver Indians who traded there, which led to the murder of five employees.

In 1824 MacKintosh was assigned to serve with Clarke at Lesser Slave Lake. Governor George Simpson* feigned surprise when the two quarrelled, and the following year he had Council move MacKintosh to become the sole officer in the Nelson River district, which had been virtually stripped of fur-bearing and game animals. A colleague reported to Simpson in 1825 that he thought MacKintosh so much under his wife's control that the HBC's interest suffered in his district. In the summer of 1829 MacKintosh took charge of Cumberland House (Sask.), a quiet post astride the route to the districts farther north and west. Following his transfer back to Fort Dunvegan in 1832, his health began to fail. He was given sick leave in 1834–35, and after two years on furlough he resigned on 1 June 1837. MacKintosh was at the Red River settlement (Man.) on 28 June 1836 when the Reverend David Thomas JONES formalized his country marriage. He later moved to Lachine, where he died on 16 Feb. 1842 "after a short illness." His elder son, William, died nine days later. The bulk of MacKintosh's property went to his surviving son, with £1,000 going to his unmarried daughter and £100 to each of his three married ones.

MacKintosh was so closely linked to violent and controversial events that a balanced evaluation of his career is hard to achieve. John Tod*, writing long afterwards, added an attempt to poison James Murray Yale* to the list of MacKintosh's crimes, and described "his ever shifting countenance & restless black eye" that suggested "nature had designed him the harbinger of plots, treasons, & strategems." The desperate partisanship which sustained him on the Peace River was wasted and frustrated after the coalition of 1821. If he is to be remembered, it must be as a fitting adversary for John Clarke. The two were, to rely again on Tod, "close neighbours, & in fact always considered as forming part of the advance guard of the two opposing bodies, who had kept the country in a state of civil war so long."

PHILIP GOLDRING

ANQ-M, CE1-80, 1842. PAC, MG 19, A38; B1, 3: 55. PAM, HBCA, A.33/4: ff.191–97; B.39/b/2: 33–40, 44–47, 52, 60; B.141/e/2: ff.1–2d; B.239/k/1–2; D.5/7: f.273d; E.4/1b; E.11/1: f.170d. UTFL, MS coll. 31, box 25, file 7. *Les bourgeois de la Compagnie du Nord-Ouest* (Masson), 1: 117, 123. *Docs. relating to NWC* (Wallace). *HBRS*, 1 (Rich); 2 (Rich and Fleming); 3 (Fleming); 30 (Williams). George Simpson, *Fur trade and empire: George Simpson's journal . . . 1824–25*, ed. and intro. Frederick Merk (Cambridge, Mass., 1931). *Montreal Gazette*, 17 Feb. 1842. Rich, *Fur trade* (1967). J. N. Wallace, *The wintering partners on Peace River from the earliest records to the union in 1821; with a summary of the Dunvegan journal, 1806* (Ottawa, 1929).

McLAREN, NEIL, fur trader, merchant, and farmer; b. 1766 at Loch Earn, Scotland, son of Donald McLaren; d. 25 Sept. 1844 in Port-au-Persil, Lower Canada.

Neil McLaren belonged to the ancient Clan McLaren (MacLabhrainn), of Loch Earn, in Perthshire. In 1791 he immigrated to Lower Canada. On arriving at Quebec he was hired for a three-year period by Lymburner and Crawford, a company engaged in the seal and salmon fisheries in Labrador [*see* Adam LYMBURNER]. He entered the service of the North West Company around 1795 and in July 1799 was working as a clerk in the Tadoussac trading-post, at the mouth of the Saguenay.

In April 1800 McLaren was sent 90 miles up the Saguenay to Chicoutimi; this post, which was then the terminus for navigation on the river, served three others inland: Pointe-Bleue, on Lac Saint-Jean, Ashuapmouchouan, on the Rivière Ashuapmouchouan, and the post on Lac Mistassini, which was still farther away. McLaren ran the trading and social activities of this large factory until October 1805.

While he was at Chicoutimi McLaren kept a journal that sheds much light on daily life in the establishment. A man of order, discipline, and exceptional perseverance, every day he recorded in a big exercise book the temperature and the direction of the winds; he mentioned the visitors passing through, Indians as well as others; he described the work done by the men to maintain the buildings, the labours of the different seasons, the care of the garden and of domestic animals, not forgetting, of course, the hunt, which was carried on in autumn and winter. No detail escaped his keen eye. His particular concern was the meticulous attention required in preparing the goods to be sent to the inland posts. Everything was checked and weighed; choosing the Indians who were to transport these valuable goods was no haphazard affair. When the crews returned, he sorted out the furs they brought back and tied them up into bales ready for dispatch by the next ship chartered by the company.

On 4 Oct. 1805 Jean-Baptiste Taché was named to head the Chicoutimi post, and a few days later McLaren was transferred to Musquaro, at the mouth of the Rivière Romaine on the north shore of the St Lawrence. McLaren ceased keeping his journal on 26 November, an apparent indication that he was leaving this post for good. He has been traced to La Malbaie, where he was game-warden. It was there that in 1806 or 1807 he married Margaret Hewit, daughter of John Hewit, the manager of the seigneury of Murray Bay, which belonged to Christiana Emery, John Nairne*'s widow. Thanks to good relations between his father-in-law and the seigneur, McLaren received a grant *en censive* of two pieces of land in the Port-au-Persil concession, a few miles downstream from La Malbaie; he settled there with his family around 1815.

McLaren then devoted himself to agriculture, but engaged in the lumber business from time to time. In 1836, for example, he acted as official agent for Peter McLeod*, a lumberman who left his mark on the Saguenay region. That year the Hudson's Bay Company received a three-year permit to cut wood on the territory of the king's posts in Lower Canada. The HBC immediately entrusted McLeod with organizing lumbering operations around the Rivière Noire, near Saint-Siméon in the Charlevoix region. Responsibility for looking after McLeod's interests fell to McLaren.

When the HBC's cutting permit was sold to the Société des Entrepreneurs des Pinières du Saguenay in 1837 [*see* Alexis Tremblay*, *dit* Picoté], Neil McLaren went back to Port-au-Persil, where he busied himself developing his land and raising his family of four boys and five girls. He died in a mishap there, at the age of 78, on 25 Sept. 1844. His body rests in a burial vault at Port-au-Persil, close to his home, the cradle of the McLaren family in Canada.

JEAN-PAUL SIMARD

Neil McLaren's "Post journal kept at Chicoutimi, 1800–1805" is at PAC, MG 19, D5.

ANQ-Q, CN1-197, 16 oct. 1837; CN4-9, 3 janv., 19 avril, 22 oct. 1836; 9, 19 oct. 1837. ANQ-SLSJ, P-2, dossier 66, pièces 1–3, 6, 10, 23, 25–27. *Cadastres abrégés des seigneuries du district de Québec* . . . (2v., Québec, 1863). Lorenzo Angers, *Chicoutimi, poste de traite, 1676–1852* (Montréal, 1971). J.-P. Simard, "Biographie de Thomas Simard," *Saguenayensia* (Chicoutimi, Qué.), 20 (1978): 4–6.

MACLEAN, JOHN. *See* MACGHILLEATHAIN, IAIN

McLEOD, ALEXANDER RODERICK, fur trader and explorer; b. *c.* 1782 in the province of Quebec; d. 11 June 1840 in Lower Canada.

Alexander Roderick McLeod joined the North West Company in 1802, and served on the Peace River (Alta/B.C.) and in the Athabasca country; his journal for the summer of 1806 was written at Fort Dunvegan. Historian James Nevin Wallace has described him as a powerfully built man who played a "secondary role" in the rivalry with the Hudson's Bay Company. At the coalition of the two companies in 1821, McLeod was appointed a chief trader in the HBC's Athabasca district, and entered a new and controversial phase in his fur-trading career. As early as the 1822–23 season, he was criticized for his "preposterous and galling use of authority" in the Mackenzie River district, and his posting south to the Columbia district in 1825 was the prelude to a series of dramatic incidents in the Oregon country, where rival British and American traders had equal rights.

While Peter Skene Ogden* was opening up the Snake River country in the interior for the HBC, McLeod was entrusted with a series of flanking expeditions south from Fort Vancouver (Vancouver, Wash.), along the Oregon coast. In this way Chief Factor John McLoughlin* hoped to scour the region for furs and to discover whether the river, called the Buenaventura, rumoured to flow from the Rocky Mountains into the Pacific, somewhere between the Columbia River and San Francisco Bay, existed. Given the difficulties of the drainage system of the Snake country and the Great Basin, such a river, if navigable, would have been of considerable commercial value. It did not exist but hopes were pinned for a time on the Sacramento River. McLeod, who was later described by Governor George Simpson* as an overbearing figure who was nevertheless an "excellent shot, skilful Canoe Man and a tolerably good Indian Trader," was not quite the man for this search. After reaching the Columbia in the fall of 1825, he set out in May 1826 with his own brigade on a summer trapping expedition towards the Umpqua River (Oreg.). It was characteristic of much that was to come that he turned back short of his destination, though he picked up from the Indians reports of a "great river" south of the Umpqua. In September 1826 he left Fort Vancouver with instructions from McLoughlin "to hunt and explore" in that area. He travelled past the Umpqua to the Tootenez (Rogue) River, but found it unimpressive and partly blocked at its mouth by a sand-bar. He arrived back at Fort Vancouver in March 1827.

In 1827–28 McLeod wintered on the Umpqua, finding few furs, and in the summer of 1828 he commanded a punitive expedition against the Klallam Indians of Hood Canal (Wash.), who had killed five HBC men. The death of more than 20 Indians was to call down on McLeod severe censure from the company's London committee, but to McLoughlin the expedition had been "most judiciously conducted."

On his return McLeod was given a more ambitious task.

Hopes of finding a large navigable river to the south persisted, and new information about the region had reached Fort Vancouver after the killing of the party of American trader Jedediah Strong Smith in July 1828. McLeod was dispatched two months later to retrieve Smith's goods and, using the trader's map of the trail from San Francisco Bay, to head the HBC's penetration into Mexican California. The first part of the task was skilfully accomplished without bloodshed, but McLeod then left his men on the Umpqua, contrary to orders, while he returned to Fort Vancouver "for instructions" and, some said, for Christmas and to see his family. Sent back to his brigade in January, he continued south and, fighting off Indians, reached the Sacramento valley in April; but as he moved back north, away from the area of Mexican influence, his party was caught by winter in the mountains of northern California. McLeod lost his horses, cached his furs (which were to be ruined by melting snow), and, leaving his men on the Umpqua, arrived at Fort Vancouver in February 1830.

His conduct was widely regarded as incompetent and irresponsible; some, including his friend John STUART and, perhaps more surprisingly, George Simpson, found reasons for his behaviour in his broken health. McLeod himself wrote of the difficulties of crossing rugged terrain and dealing with unenthusiastic men. But in March the London committee, castigating him as "extremely deficient in energy and zeal," denied him the chief factorship he expected, and had him posted to the Mackenzie district the following year. His "Southern" expeditions, though they never produced large returns of fur, did serve significantly in maintaining the HBC's presence in the Oregon country.

The eventful years of McLeod's career were over. As he journeyed from Fort Simpson (N.W.T.) in 1833 to the Canadas to recover his health, he received a letter from George Simpson, who believed McLeod "would have made an excellent *Guide*," promising him his support for a chief factorship if he agreed to serve on George Back*'s Arctic expedition. This he did, faithfully, until 1835, accompanied by his Indian wife and three children. Although, by arrangement, he did not accompany Back down the Great Fish (Back) River to the Arctic Ocean, he hunted, fished, and established camps for the party. His reward came when he was made a chief factor in 1836. His last years in the northwest were spent at Great Slave Lake (1835–37) and Fort Dunvegan (1837–39).

McLeod died in June 1840 while on furlough. He left in his will "some small property" and about £5,000 to the mixed-blood woman he had married according to the custom of the country in his NWC days, and to their seven surviving children, including Sarah* and Alexander Roderick Jr, who had participated in James DICKSON's short-lived army of liberation. McLeod considered their mother to be his "legitimate wife" (contrary to the attitude of many fur traders in country marriages) and in 1841 the Doctors' Commons in England declared their marriage legally valid.

GLYNDWR WILLIAMS

PAM, HBCA, A.6/22: f.60; A.36/10: ff.9–18; B.39/b/2: 86; D.4/22: f.40d; D.4/123: ff.58–66. George Back, *Narrative of the Arctic land expedition to the mouth of the Great Fish River, and along the shores of the Arctic Ocean in the years 1833, 1834, and 1835* (London, 1836). *HBRS*, 3 (Fleming); 4 (Rich); 23 (Davies and Johnson); 30 (Williams). *The Hudson's Bay Company's first fur brigade to the Sacramento valley: Alexander McLeod's 1829 hunt*, ed. D. B. Nunis (Sacramento, Calif., 1968). Brown, *Strangers in blood*. R. H. Dillon, *Siskiyou trail: the Hudson's Bay Company route to California* (New York, [1975]), 163–64, 177. Van Kirk, *"Many tender ties"*. J. N. Wallace, *The wintering partners on Peace River from the earliest records to the union in 1821; with a summary of the Dunvegan journal, 1806* (Ottawa, 1929), 78, 122–34.

McLEOD, JOHN, fur trader; b. 1788 in Stornoway, Scotland; d. 24 July 1849 in Montreal.

John McLeod entered the Hudson's Bay Company in Scotland as a writer (clerk) in 1811, the early part of his career being very much connected with the fledgling Red River colony (Man.) founded by Lord Selkirk [Douglas*]. He helped to recruit men in the Hebrides before sailing in July as part of the advance party for the settlement. Forced to winter at York Factory (Man.), McLeod, travelling with Governor Miles Macdonell*, did not reach Red River until the summer of 1812. For the next few years he was active in establishing posts in the southern part of present-day Manitoba, including Turtle River (1812–13) and Portage la Prairie (1813–14), but he spent every summer at the slowly growing colony. Having been given charge of the HBC's operations at Red River in 1814–15, he tried to defend the colony from attack by Nor'Westers and Métis in June 1815. Although it was virtually disbanded, he and three others stayed, salvaging what they could. Later that summer, McLeod strengthened the company's fort at Point Douglas (Winnipeg) and worked with Colin ROBERTSON to re-establish the settlement. Then, after wintering at a post several hundred miles to the west, McLeod went to the HBC establishment at Pembina (N.Dak.), where he assisted in a raid on the North West Company's post led by Robert Semple*, the new governor of the Red River colony. McLeod did not witness the further destruction of the Red River settlement in June 1816, however, because he was conducting several Nor'Westers prisoner to Norway House (Man.).

In 1816–17 he was given charge of the English River district, at Île-à-la Crosse (Sask.). There he met such strong opposition from the Nor'Westers, led by Samuel BLACK, that by April he was forced to seek refuge at Fort Carlton. Later that season McLeod was arrested by the Nor'Westers for his participation in the confiscation of their property at Pembina. He went to Montreal in the summer of 1817 to stand trial and help defend Lord Selkirk's interests. The case against him being dismissed, McLeod returned to Red River in 1818 in charge of a large brigade, which included a group of French Canadian settlers and the first Roman Catholic missionaries, Sévère Dumoulin* and Joseph-Norbert Provencher*. The ensuing season he was again given charge of the English River district. In the spring of 1819, during a visit to Fort Carlton, he married *à la façon du pays* Charlotte, a daughter of HBC officer John Peter Pruden* and his native wife. McLeod remained in the English River district for several more years, spending a number of winters at Buffalo Lake (Peter Pond Lake, Sask.). He acquitted himself well, being described by Colin Robertson in 1819 as "a brave interested little fellow." With the union of the HBC and NWC in 1821, he was given the rank of chief trader in the new concern.

McLeod spent the next season at Green Lake, south of Île-à-la-Crosse, where his first son, Malcolm, was born. In the fall of 1822 he took his wife and two small children across the Rocky Mountains, having been given charge of the Thompson River district, with headquarters at Thompson's River Post (Kamloops, B.C.). He contributed to the HBC's opening up of the lower Fraser, journeying to the river's mouth in 1823, but his overall management of the district did not impress Governor George Simpson*, who visited the Pacific slope in 1824–25. He found McLeod wasteful, intimidated by the Indians, and preoccupied with family concerns, and he engineered the trader's removal from the region. Although given a furlough in 1825, McLeod appears to have spent it in the Indian country and did not leave for the east until early in 1826, most of his family having been sent ahead with the fall brigade under Chief Factor James McMillan*. After struggling through deep snows in the Rockies, McLeod and young Malcolm were surprised to find the rest of the family at Jasper House (Alta). They had spent the winter snowed in near the Yellowhead Pass, where in February Charlotte had given birth to a second daughter.

In the summer of 1826 McLeod took charge of Norway House and oversaw the substantial rebuilding of this post. The Anglican missionary David Thomas JONES performed a church marriage there for the McLeods in August 1828. McLeod, who showed considerable concern for the education and welfare of his family, took his two eldest sons to school in Scotland when on furlough in 1830–31. Upon his return he found himself relegated to the comparatively unimportant charge of the Saint-Maurice River district in Lower Canada, with headquarters at Weymontachingue. It is obvious from Simpson's entry in his "Character book" during this period that in the governor's opinion McLeod remained a mediocre officer, "well meaning" but "quite a clown in address" and so confused and deficient in talent that he "should consider himself fortunate in his present situation which is more valuable than a man of his abilities could reasonably aspire to in any other part of the World." Nevertheless, McLeod appears to have managed the trade of the district well, in spite of the encroachments of petty traders. He remained in this charge for the rest of his career, feeling increasingly ill used at the company's continual denial of a chief factorship. McLeod believed that he deserved such a promotion and needed it because of the expenses he incurred in educating his children. His wife and five minor children (they had three sons and six daughters in all) were left in straitened circumstances when he died suddenly of cholera in 1849, apparently while still in the HBC's service. Malcolm McLeod, who became a lawyer in Montreal, always felt that his father deserved more recognition for the role he had played in the early history of western Canada. He carefully preserved his father's papers, which contain an extensive correspondence with fellow traders in Rupert's Land.

SYLVIA VAN KIRK

A volume of extracts from John McLeod's journal, 1811–16, describing the journey from Stornoway and the establishment of the Red River settlement, was compiled and annotated by his son Malcolm. The manuscript is in the John MacLeod papers, PAM, MG 1, D5, and has been published as "Diary, etc., of chief trader, John MacLeod, Senior, of Hudson's Bay Company, Red River settlement, 1811," ed. H. G. Gunn, N.Dak., State Hist. Soc., *Coll.* (Bismarck), 2 (1908): 115–34. McLeod's original journal has not been located, but an electrostatic copy of it is in his papers at the PAM.

ANQ-M, CE1-130, 25 juill. 1849. PABC, Add. MSS 635, box 4, folder 116, John McLeod to Donald Ross, 1 March 1848; 1249, box 2, folders 7, 13, 15; E/E/M22, Malcolm McLeod, Life of John McLeod Sr. PAC, MG 19, A23. PAM, HBCA, A.10/27: 513–13d; D.5/10–42. Univ. of Birmingham Library, Special Coll. (Birmingham, Eng.), Church Missionary Soc. Arch., C, C.1/0, letters and journals of William Cockran. *HBRS*, 1 (Rich); 2 (Rich and Fleming); 30 (Williams). Ranald MacDonald, *Ranald MacDonald, the narrative of his early life on the Columbia under the Hudson's Bay Company's regime . . .* , ed. W. S. Lewis and Naojiro Murakami (Spokane, Wash., 1923), 100, note 89. George Simpson, *Fur trade and empire: George Simpson's journal . . .* , ed. and intro. Frederick Merk (rev. ed., Cambridge, Mass., 1968). [H. G. Gunn], "The MacLeod manuscript," N.Dak., State Hist. Soc., *Coll.*, 2: 106–14.

McLEOD, JOHN M., fur trader and explorer; b.

1795 in the parish of Lochs, Isle of Lewis, Scotland, son of Kenneth MacLeod, jackman; fl. 1816–42.

John M. McLeod arrived in Montreal in March 1816, having signed a six-year contract with the North West Company. He first served as a clerk on the Churchill River and was probably the one who hailed Governor George Simpson* of the Hudson's Bay Company at Grand Rapids (Man.) in June 1821 with news of their companies' coalition. Joining the HBC, McLeod was appointed clerk at Île-à-la-Crosse (Sask.). Frequently referred to in company records as John McLeod Jr, to distinguish him from Chief Trader John McLeod, he was transferred in 1822 to the Athabasca district and accompanied Simpson that autumn from York Factory (Man.) to Fort Chipewyan (Alta). The governor appraised him as a "decent young man but not such a sharp fellow as I took him for, he is thoughtless and requires to be kept at a distance which is done." By the time they had reached Fort Chipewyan in late December, Simpson had to surrender him unexpectedly to the needs of the Mackenzie River district. He then recommended McLeod to Chief Trader Alexander Roderick McLeod in January as a "young Gentleman of much promise . . . and I am much mistaken if he does not turn out a valuable acquisition to your staff."

McLeod arrived in the district in March 1823 and would remain there for 12 years, excelling in "voyages of discovery." Simpson had specified that its trade be expanded westward and that Indian tribes be contacted to check the flow of furs to the Russians on the northwest Pacific coast. McLeod spent the summers of 1823 and 1824 exploring nine mountain ranges adjacent to the South Nahanni River (N.W.T.). He encountered the Nahanis, agreed on a rendezvous with them, and was praised for his "indefatigable exertions" in this initiative. McLeod served primarily at Fort Simpson (N.W.T.) until 1832, often as sole manager and with the full confidence of the frequently absent chief factor, Edward Smith. In the summer of 1831 he set out to find the source of the Liard River's west branch (Dease River, B.C.), note a possible location for a post, and identify the source of any river running to the coast. On this successful journey he covered about 500 miles and met for the first time five Indian tribes.

That summer Simpson decided to transfer McLeod to the king's posts in the Montreal department because of his "steady habits of business and correct conduct." Although displeased, McLeod dutifully left with the spring express in 1832. Simpson described him then in his famous "Character book" as an "active well behaved Man of tolerable Education. Speaks Cree, understands a little Chipewyan is an excellent Trader and has of late been employed on Severe exploring Service." Edward Smith and Alexander Roderick McLeod interceded on his behalf and persuaded Simpson to order him back to "where he can be more useful at present than any where else."

By the summer of 1833 McLeod had returned to the Mackenzie River district and was assigned to move Fort Halkett to a new location (near Coal River, B.C.), on the west branch of the Liard. From that post in 1834, the year in which he was promoted chief trader, he undertook a more difficult expedition up the west branch, covering 311 miles of "hitherto unknown country" to Dease Lake. From there he travelled to the Stikine River, where he found evidence of trading by coastal Indians. However, Simpson had decided that exploration in this region should cease because it was too expensive and too slow. Furthermore, he instructed the district to reduce its employees. Stationed at Rivière-au-Liard (Fort Liard, N.W.T.) in 1835, McLeod did not expect to be transferred but in June he left for the Columbia district.

John McLoughlin*, the chief factor at Fort Vancouver (Vancouver, Wash.), chose McLeod in 1836 to lead a trading outfit southwest into the Snake River country and to head the delicate operation of meeting American traders there in order to sell them HBC supplies. He was treated "coolly" by them, but achieved "every object" McLoughlin had in mind, particularly the maintenance of the HBC's control of trade, and was sent back to the American rendezvous, near Green River (Wyo.), in 1837. The following year he boarded the HBC schooner *Cadboro* to search for the company's trappers lost near the Sacramento River valley (Calif.); assisted by the Russians at Bodega Bay and Mexican officials, he found them. While at Bodega Bay, he informally discussed with the Russian American Company's chief manager, Ivan Antonovich Kupreianov, the affairs of their two companies.

McLeod had no permanent position in the Columbia district and he left on furlough in 1840. He took a leave of absence the following year, retired from HBC service in 1842 at 47 years of age, and appears to have returned to Great Britain. McLeod's 26 years as a fur trader were highlighted by his zeal and success in exploring the territory adjacent to the Liard River and its tributaries. Mount McLeod, west of Dease Lake, was named after him.

S. M. Johnson

PAM, HBCA, B.39/b/6: 44, 62; B.85/a/4; B.85/a/6: ff.1–10; B.200/a/2: ff.1–12; B.200/a/5: ff.62–75; B.200/a/14: ff.2–17; B.200/b/7: 1–2, 13–15, 21, 26–27, 49; B.200/d/51: f.45; B.200/e/1: f.6; B.200/e/3: ff.2–3; B.200/e/5: f.1; B.200/e/10: f.3; B.200/e/11: 1–3; B.200/e/17: ff.6–7; B.239/g/1: f.63; B.239/g/2: f.8; B.239/g/3: f.11; B.239/g/69: f.28; B.239/k; B.239/x/5a: f.732; D.4/2: ff.19–20; D.4/20: ff.15–16; D.4/21: f.50; D.4/98: f.39; D.4/117: f.55; D.4/127: ff.50, 81; F.5/3, no.55. *Canadian north-west* (Oliver), 1: 660; 2: 799, 816. *HBRS*, 1 (Rich); 3 (Fleming); 4 (Rich); 6 (Rich); 30 (Williams). Morton, *Hist. of Canadian west* (1939). R. M. Patterson, "The Nahany lands; J. M.

McLeod's exploration in 1823 and 1824 of the South Nahanni River country," *Beaver*, outfit 292 (summer 1961): 40–47.

McLOUGHLIN, MARIE-LOUISE, named **de Saint-Henri**, Ursuline, teacher, and superior; b. 28 Aug. 1780 in Rivière-du-Loup, Que., daughter of John McLoughlin and Angélique Fraser; sister of John McLoughlin*; d. 4 July 1846 at Quebec.

Marie-Louise McLoughlin, the daughter of fervent Catholics, enjoyed a peaceful, happy childhood. When she was six, she made her first visit to her maternal grandfather, Malcolm Fraser*, the seigneur of Mount Murray. Delighted with her sweet manner, Fraser insisted on keeping her with him. He sent her to the best Protestant schools at Quebec and gave her every opportunity to broaden her knowledge and develop her talents.

When she was 15, Marie-Louise expressed a desire to attend the Ursulines' boarding-school at Quebec, with the approval of her parents and her maternal grandmother, who was a Catholic herself. Her grandfather consented reluctantly, making it clear that he would go to the length of disinheriting Marie-Louise and her family if she were to adhere to Catholicism. To his great displeasure, during her first year at the school in 1795–96, she obtained religious instruction from Abbé Philippe-Jean-Louis Desjardins*, then chaplain of the Ursulines and the Hôtel-Dieu of Quebec. She made her profession of faith and took her first communion when she was 16. Then, braving her grandfather's retaliation, she entered the noviciate on 21 Nov. 1798 with the agreement of her family, who accepted the material consequences of this act. The following year, on the day she donned the habit, she took the name de Saint-Henri, and the officiating priest confirmed her. She made her vows on 18 Feb. 1800.

Marie-Louise de Saint-Henri, who was a fine English teacher, also learned to teach science under the aegis of Abbé Desjardins. She understood better than others the necessity of carefully preparing the young nuns who were planning to teach. As novice mistress from 16 Dec. 1811 to 15 May 1814, she arranged for them to be freed from various domestic tasks in order to be able to give them a better training through prayer, study, and reflection for their tasks as educators. Her enthusiasm worked wonders.

Marie-Louise de Saint-Henri held in turn the highest administrative posts in the convent, serving as bursar (15 May 1814 to 20 April 1818, 27 April 1824 to 26 April 1830, and 25 April 1836 to 24 April 1839), superior (20 April 1818 to 27 April 1824 and 26 April 1830 to 25 April 1836), and assistant superior (24 April 1839 to 25 April 1842). In these various capacities she directed the substantial advances in education made at the Ursuline school during the early decades of the 19th century. Possessing a remarkable sense of organization, she managed to stabilize the convent's finances, which had been in a precarious state since the conquest. From 1837 until her death she was helped in this task by Thomas Maguire*, the community's chaplain. In particular she undertook to put up an apartment building for rental purposes, had two apartments built for families of modest means, and put an addition on the chapel.

In the classroom the best teachers gave lessons to both the Ursulines and the pupils. The records list Frederick GLACKEMEYER and Stephen Codman for music, and James BOWMAN, who did Marie-Louise de Saint-Henri's portrait, for painting. A steady stream of teaching materials was sent to her from Europe by her brother Dr David McLoughlin. In 1844, at the request of Archbishop Pierre-Flavien Turgeon* of Quebec, she agreed to undertake, with the help of Maguire, the drafting of the "Règlement des élèves du pensionnat des Dames Ursulines de Québec," a rule designed to systematize existing practices in her teaching establishment, which was the largest in the colony. New ideas which Maguire had picked up during a stay in Europe were included in it. From then on teaching was to be based on such principles as the placement of pupils of similar ability in the same class and an increased emphasis on understanding rather than on memorization.

Marie-Louise de Saint-Henri's zeal and high spirits suggested that she still had many years ahead of her when suddenly, at the age of 65, she passed away. She had held the office of zelatrice to the superior since 25 April 1842. A capable but also kindhearted woman, she had never forgotten the members of her family, and her many letters show how deeply she had shared in their worries and in their difficulties with their children's education. She was mourned by her family and the community, and the friends of the convent eulogized her, paying tribute to her appreciation of culture, her business sense, and her rare qualities of heart.

SUZANNE PRINCE

ANQ-Q, CE3-3, 10 sept. 1780. Arch. du monastère des ursulines (Québec), Actes de professions et de sépultures, 1; Actes des assemblées capitulaires, 1; Annales, I: 397, 455–56, 462; II: 102, 113–14; Livre contenant les actes des assemblées capitulaires, 1802–42; Reg. des professions religieuses et des décès, 1778–1882. B. B. Barker, *The McLoughlin empire and its rulers . . .* (Glendale, Calif., 1959). Burke, *Les ursulines de Québec*, 3: 249, 397; 4: 455, 592. *Glimpses of the monastery: scenes from the history of the Ursulines of Quebec during two hundred years, 1639–1839* (2nd ed., Quebec, 1897). P.-G. Roy, *À travers l'histoire des ursulines de Québec* (Lévis, Qué., 1939).

McMAHON, JOHN BAPTIST, Roman Catholic priest; b. April 1796 in the diocese of Kilmore

(Republic of Ireland), son of Michael McMahon and Mary Malone; d. after 1840, probably in the United States.

John Baptist McMahon, who had been an officer in the British army, came to Lower Canada in 1821 bearing a testimonial from the bishop of Kilmore. In September of that year Bishop Jean-Jacques LARTIGUE selected him to teach English at the Collège de Saint-Hyacinthe. There McMahon was able to study theology and learn French. After his ordination to the priesthood in Montreal on 18 Sept. 1824, he was sent to Chambly and then to Saint-Eustache. In September 1825 he became chaplain of the church of Saint-Jacques in Montreal. McMahon remained to a degree independent of the archbishop of Quebec, Joseph-Octave Plessis*, and of his auxiliary in Montreal, Lartigue: he did not take an oath to stay in the colony and he provided for his own living, securing ordination through "a patrimony fixed on the seigneury of Monsieur Dessaules [Jean Dessaulles*], of Maska, and on another [property] in the town of Quebec." Consequently he claimed in 1828 "to be lending himself" to the bishop of Quebec for the Percé and Douglastown missions, and six years later in a spirit of sacrifice he accepted the cure of souls in Sherbrooke.

In 1834, then, McMahon became the first resident priest of the new parish of Saint-Colomban (Saint-Michel), an area for which the Drummondville mission had taken responsibility since 1816. With 280 families numbering 1,124 persons, it covered an immense territory, 90 miles by 70, and a complete pastoral visit entailed a 400-mile trip and 11 days on horseback.

Demanding in size, the Sherbrooke mission had a diversity of population that made it still more difficult. Three ethnic groups lived side by side: the British, American loyalists, and the Canadians. Among these groups at least three classes of citizens had appeared: a wealthy aristocracy of Protestant clergy and members of the legal profession; a bourgeoisie of property owners, primarily British; and a proletariat of craftsmen, day labourers, servants, and squatters, of American or Canadian descent. McMahon's parishioners were by no means generous and he often complained of their apathy towards religion. "It is sinful for a young priest to spend his best years . . . among the indifferent," he said in a letter of 28 March 1835 to the archbishop of Quebec, Joseph SIGNAY. The ethnic multiplicity meant variety in religion, and the Catholic priest was in contact with Anglican, Methodist, Presbyterian, and Universalist ministers who, while they adopted a conciliatory attitude in their personal relations, denounced papistry and sometimes harboured a certain jealousy towards Catholicism.

It was probably this political and religious situation that prompted McMahon to take a strong stand against the Patriotes in 1837 and 1838. In proclaiming his loyalty to the crown he hoped to win the confidence of the region's British residents. He published a long article condemning the rebellion in the *Sherbrooke Gazette and Townships Advertiser* of 16 Nov. 1837. Then, during the octave of Christmas he delivered three hour-long sermons on the duty to obey constituted authority. He also called a meeting at Tingwick and had some Canadians and Irish sign a proclamation of submission. His zeal was judged ill-timed and brought him a severe reprimand from Archbishop Signay.

The population's diversity may also explain the accusations against McMahon which were communicated to Signay in the spring and summer of 1839. He was accused of being drunk, of being vicious towards non-Catholics, particularly Methodists, and of engaging in immoral conduct. A canonical investigation conducted early in October by vicar general Thomas Cooke*, the parish priest of Trois-Rivières, and Hubert Robson, the curé of Drummondville, was unable to establish that he was guilty. Nevertheless, taking into account the harm done to McMahon's reputation and the requests he had made in 1835, 1837, and 1838 for an exeat, Signay agreed early in 1840 to let him leave his charge.

McMahon was replaced by Peter Henry Harkin, who until then had been assistant priest of the parish of Saint-Roch at Quebec. In March 1840 Cooke advised Harkin about the attitude he should adopt towards McMahon, admonishing the new incumbent "to see him only rarely and at his home in order to avoid scandal [and] to urge him to go and offer his services elsewhere." Cooke was in fact afraid that he might soon see "this poor priest wandering about the country despite his *Exeat*." But McMahon chose to go to the United States, where no further trace of him has been found.

ANDRÉE DÉSILETS

John Baptist McMahon is the author of *Dialogue between a young gentleman and a divine* (Quebec, 1833).

AAQ, 2 CB, XI: 8; 320 CN, VII: 194. *Annuaire du séminaire Saint-Charles-Borromée, Sherbrooke, affilié à l'université Laval en 1878, année académique 1916–1917* (Sherbrooke, Qué., 1917). Desrosiers, "Inv. de la corr. de Mgr Lartigue," ANQ *Rapport*, 1941–42. C.-P. Choquette, *Histoire du séminaire de Saint-Hyacinthe depuis sa fondation jusqu'à nos jours* (2v., Montréal, 1911–12), 1. Albert Gravel, *Messire Jean-Baptiste McMahon, premier curé-missionnaire de Sherbrooke, 1834–1840* (Sherbrooke, 1960). Maurice O'Bready, *De Ktiné à Sherbrooke; esquisse historique de Sherbrooke: des origines à 1954* (Sherbrooke, 1973). Léonidas Adam, "L'histoire religieuse des Cantons de l'Est," *Rev. canadienne*, 89 (janvier–juin 1921): 19–34. É.-J.[-A.] Auclair, "La pénétration catholique et française dans les Cantons de l'Est," Semaines sociales du Canada, *Compte rendu des cours et conférences* (Montréal), 5 (1924): 360–73. J. I. Little, "Missionary priests in Quebec's Eastern Townships: the years of hardship and discontent, 1825–1853," CCHA *Study sessions*, 45 (1978): 21–35. Gladys

Mullins, "English-speaking priests who evangelized the Eastern Townships," CCHA *Report*, 7 (1939–40): 50–52.

MACNIDER, ADAM LYMBURNER, businessman, militia officer, office holder, and JP; b. 10 Sept. 1778 at Quebec; m. 19 Sept. 1812 Rosina Aird in Montreal, and they had six children; d. 19 Nov. 1840 either in Métis (Métis-sur-Mer, Que.) or on the seigneury of Mitis, and was buried in Côte Sainte-Catherine (Outremont, Que.).

Born into a merchant family of Quebec, Adam Lymburner Macnider was named after a prominent businessman, Adam LYMBURNER. The boy's uncles John and Mathew Macnider were Quebec merchants, and his aunt Margaret Macnider was married first to James Johnston*, yet another Quebec merchant. Macnider began business in Montreal some time before 1810, probably as a representative of the family's commercial interests; in September 1811 he was operating under his own name as an auctioneer and broker. By May 1812 he had entered into a partnership with an old family friend, Samuel Southby Bridge, as Macnider and Bridge, commission merchants and auctioneers. This partnership was dissolved early in 1814. Shortly thereafter Macnider formed a similar association with his brother-in-law, John Aird, which traded in property, liquor, dry goods, and groceries. Macnider also established a partnership with James Scott; they did a large mercantile trade on commission, which in 1824 included 2,000 volumes of "scarce and valuable books."

By 1825 Macnider was operating under three names, A. L. Macnider and Company, Macnider, Aird and Company, and Macnider and Scott, and was probably among the city's most important commission merchants and auctioneers. He owned two vessels, the brig *Hibernia* and the schooner *Concordia*, and during the 1825 shipping season he and Scott were the largest importers in Montreal, receiving 26 separate consignments. They imported textiles, haberdashery, earthenware, coal, and steel from Liverpool, London, Belfast, Greenock (Scotland), and Leith and exported wood, wheat, and potash.

Although large, the firm of Macnider and Scott was unable to withstand the trade crisis of 1825–26 [*see* George Garden*]. In the latter year Macnider's house and store were auctioned by the sheriff for the substantial sum of £3,850. The following year the company declared bankruptcy, unable to meet debts totalling £34,617, of which £22,547 was due to firms in Britain. Macnider and Scott held credits to the amount of £27,931, but some £13,764 was considered bad or doubtful. In addition the company had lost £3,225 on a shipment of wheat, £2,500 on a consignment of potash, and, largely as a result of the failure of Maitland, Garden, and Auldjo [*see* George AULDJO], £3,000 on bills of exchange. Macnider, however, was not broken. By August 1828 he was again in business under his own name, selling on consignment or by auction everything from coal bricks to Dutch dolls. In fact, he seems to have made a remarkable recovery, and during another crisis, in 1836, he was a major creditor; that year he inherited £500 from the estate of Adam Lymburner.

Macnider's business interests were not confined to the wholesale trade. In 1819 he was a director of the Montreal Savings Bank and the Montreal agent for the Quebec Fire Assurance Company. He was an incorporator of the Bank of Canada in 1822 and later became a director. A member of the Scotch Presbyterian Church (later known as St Gabriel Street Church), he served on the congregation's temporal committee in 1816–17, and was its president in 1824 and its vice-president in 1825. In 1817 he joined a special committee to raise financial support for the Reverend Henry Esson*, the learned young clergyman who had recently been selected for the charge, and the following year he was the congregation's treasurer. Later he would support the Esson side in an unseemly dispute with a faction backing the Reverend Edward BLACK over the incumbency and over possession of the church. In 1820 he was commissioned an ensign in Montreal's 1st Militia Battalion, which grouped many leading British businessmen. By 1828 he had been promoted captain, and during the rebellions of 1837–38 he served with that rank in the 3rd battalion of Montreal Loyal Volunteers. In 1821 he helped establish the Montreal General Hospital on Rue Dorchester and in 1828 he became one of its governors. He was appointed a warden of Trinity House in 1822, and from 1824 to 1827 he served as a grand juror. He subsequently received a number of other appointments: justice of the peace in 1830, commissioner on the Montreal Board of Health during the cholera epidemic of 1832, presiding officer in the *faubourg* Saint-Antoine for the election of town councillors in 1833, and deputy master of Trinity House in 1834.

In June 1839 Macnider was named a commissioner for the repair of the Métis, or Mitis, road. By then he was living on the seigneury of Mitis, which two of his sons had inherited from John Macnider. He died there or in the village of Métis in November 1840. Both Macnider's business career, marked by its family ties as well as by its diversity, adversity, and recovery, and his participation in the civil and religious life of his community were typical of a man of his class and time.

CARMAN MILLER

ANQ-M, CE1-126, 19 sept. 1812, 2 déc. 1840. ANQ-Q, CN1-284, 23 août 1800. McCord Museum, M13630. Montreal Business Hist. Group, Commercial lists, 17, 23 May, 22 July 1825; Cross-reference, protests, Macnider, Aird, Wythe, 7 April 1820; Macnider and Scott to John Moir and

Company, 23 Jan. 1827. PAC, RG 5, A1: 81369–2013; RG 68, General index, 1651–1841. L.C., House of Assembly, *Report of the special committee, to whom was referred that part of his excellency's speech which referred to the organization of the militia* (Quebec, 1829); *Reports and evidence of the special committee . . . to whom were referred the petition of the inhabitants of the county of York, that of the inhabitants of the city of Montreal, and other petitions praying the redress of grievances* (n.p., 1829); *Statutes*, 1821–22, c.27. *Canadian Courant and Montreal Advertiser*, 16 March, 27 April, 18 May, 1 June 1812; 23 Jan., 27 Feb. 1813; 25 June 1814; 6 April 1816. *Montreal Gazette*, 16 Sept., 18, 25 Nov. 1811; 25 May, 21 Sept., 12 Oct. 1812; 26 April, 3 May 1814; 4 March 1816; 25 Jan. 1827; 3, 6, 10 Nov. 1828; 28 May, 13 Aug., 26, 29 Oct. 1829; 22 Feb., 1 March 1830. *Quebec Gazette*, 14 Sept. 1815; 22 May, 14 Aug., 16 Oct. 1817; 26 Oct., 23 Nov. 1820; 24 May 1821; 1 April 1830. Borthwick, *Hist. and biog. gazetteer*, 55. *Montreal directory*, 1819. Campbell, *Hist. of Scotch Presbyterian Church*. Elinor Kyte Senior, *Redcoats and Patriotes: the rebellions in Lower Canada, 1837–38* (Stittsville, Ont., 1985), 214. J.-C. Lamothe, *Histoire de la corporation de la cité de Montréal depuis son origine jusqu'à nos jours . . .* (Montréal, 1903). Henri Masson, *Joseph Masson, dernier seigneur de Terrebonne, 1791–1847* (Montréal, 1972). Robert Sweeny, "Internal dynamics and the international cycle: questions of the transition in Montreal, 1821–1828" (PHD thesis, McGill Univ., Montreal, 1985); *Protesting history: 4 papers* (Montreal, 1984). F.-J. Audet et Édouard Fabre Surveyer, "Matthew McNider," *La Presse*, 13 août 1927: 41.

McPHERSON, JOHN, schoolteacher and poet; b. 4 Feb. 1817 in Liverpool, N.S., son of James McPherson; d. 26 July 1845 in North Brookfield, N.S.

John McPherson spent his first 17 years in Liverpool, where he obtained most of his formal schooling. He then went to live with his uncle, Donald McPherson, at North Brookfield in the northern part of Queens County, and there came under the influence of Angus Morrison Gidney*, a young schoolteacher at nearby Pleasant River. Gidney inspired a love of poetry in McPherson and encouraged his writing. Subsequently, as a Halifax newspaper editor, Gidney helped McPherson get his poetry published and brought his verse to the attention of literary-minded people in the capital. Of these, John Sparrow Thompson* and Sarah HERBERT became the most influential in McPherson's brief literary career.

As a young man, McPherson had a great deal of trouble deciding what to do with his life. Between 1835 and 1840 he pursued a variety of jobs. He worked briefly in Halifax as a clerk, and then sailed to the West Indies in search of opportunity. However, he soon returned home and began to train as a carpenter. At the same time he became increasingly involved in writing poetry. From 1838 to 1840 his verses appeared frequently in Halifax newspapers, particularly the *Novascotian* and the *Haligonian*, and in the *Colonial Pearl*, a local literary periodical.

The year 1841 seemed to be a turning-point in McPherson's life. He began work as a schoolteacher at Kempt, near North Brookfield, a job more compatible with his literary interests. He was there for two years, and during that time, on 12 Dec. 1841, he married his cousin Irene, Donald McPherson's daughter. He was also gaining a reputation as a poet of considerable promise and was developing a poetic style more distinctly his own. He taught briefly at Maitland Bridge in Annapolis County, but soon returned to North Brookfield. It had become increasingly apparent that his teacher's salary was not sufficient to support a wife and new baby girl, nor did earnings from his writings meet expectations. In the midst of his despair over deepening poverty, his health, always delicate, began to fail. None the less, he managed to sustain a high level of poetic activity. From 1841 to 1844 he continued to publish often in Halifax newspapers and in Sarah Herbert's journal, the *Olive Branch*. In 1843 John Henry Crosskill* published McPherson's temperance poem *The praise of water*, the only booklet of his verse to appear during his lifetime.

By 1843 his health would not allow him to work steadily and his economic circumstances were becoming desperate. Friends in Halifax, including an anonymous contributor later identified as William Young*, an MHA, helped by collecting money that permitted him to purchase land and commence building a small cottage. Relieved of the burden of providing accommodation for his family, McPherson hoped to support them through his writings. But by the time they moved into the home in December 1844, McPherson's health was very poor and the cottage, unfinished because the funds raised had been insufficient, was not really ready for winter habitation. On 1 May 1845 he had to be moved into his uncle's home at North Brookfield; there he died on 26 July in his 29th year, leaving his wife and two children.

Like poet Grizelda Elizabeth Cottnam Tonge* in the generation before him, McPherson by his early death had a special place created for him in the hearts of those committed to establishing a native literary tradition. The harshness of his circumstances and the fatal delicacy of his health seemed to symbolize the difficulties and sacrifices involved in nurturing Nova Scotia's cultural development in the early 19th century. The apparent expendability of local literary activity was further demonstrated by the fact that McPherson's poetry was not collected and published in book form until 1862, 17 years after his death. It was Thompson who finally brought together a selection of McPherson's poetic remains.

Because of Thompson's efforts, McPherson, unlike Tonge, survives as more than a romantic literary myth. He speaks for himself through a sizeable body of verse. Unfortunately, Thompson's collection does not readily reveal McPherson's strengths as a poet. In his choice and arrangement of the poems Thompson generally fails to distinguish between conventional treatments of aspects of morality and religion and McPherson's more perceptive poetic statements rising from his innate sensitivity to the nature of his own life and his experience of the natural world around him. At his best, McPherson projects a vision of individual consciousness in harmony with a particular set of natural circumstances. For example, in his poem "Scenes," he writes:

I love at night's mysterious hour,
To muse beside the solemn sea,
And feel its strange mysterious power,
And mark its waves, the wild the free,
While hallowed visions sway the soul
Resigned to thought's sublime control.

But this harmony, while idyllic and pictured as a release from daily cares, is usually haunted by an awareness of the passing or dying of all things. Thus there is often an element of nostalgia, a Celtic melancholy which significantly colours the tone and mood of the poetry. This effect is most evident in such poems as "The may-flower," "Autumnal musings," "Dying in spring," and "The beautiful is fading." In expressing his feelings for the beautiful yet transitory character of mortal existence, McPherson frequently turns to flower imagery.

McPherson was buried on a hill near North Brookfield, on the eastern side of the old Annapolis Road overlooking Tupper Lake. His wife put up a simple headstone. In 1906 the grave was moved to the cemetery of the North Brookfield Baptist Church.

THOMAS B. VINCENT

John McPherson's poetry was first published at various times during the period 1835–45 in a number of Maritime newspapers, including the *Amaranth* (Saint John, N.B.), the *Yarmouth Herald and Western Advertiser* (Yarmouth, N.S.), and, in Halifax, the *Christian Messenger*, *Colonial Pearl*, *Haligonian and General Advertiser*, *Novascotian*, *Olive Branch*, and *Temperance Recorder*. His temperance composition *The praise of water; a prize poem* appeared in Halifax in 1843. J. S. Thompson brought out a selection of his works under the title *Poems, descriptive and moral . . .* (Halifax, 1862), and prefaced it with an "Introductory memoir."

PAC, MG 24, C4. PANS, MG 1, 848, no.15. *Acadian Recorder*, 2 Aug. 1845. *Novascotian*, 30 Dec. 1841. R. J. Long, *Nova Scotia authors and their work: a bibliography of the province* (East Orange, N.J., 1918), 161. J. F. More, *The history of Queens County, N.S.* (Halifax, 1873; repr. Belleville, Ont., 1972), 196–200. "Half hours with our poets . . . ," *Provincial: or Halifax Monthly Magazine*, 1 (1852): 83. D. C. Harvey, "The centenary of John McPherson," *Dalhousie Rev.*, 25 (1945–46): 343–53. R. R. McLeod, "Notes historical and otherwise of the Northern District of Queens County," N.S. Hist. Soc., *Coll.*, 16 (1912): 117. "More of John McPherson," *Provincial: or Halifax Monthly Magazine*, 1: 167–72.

McTAVISH (Mactavish), JOHN GEORGE, fur trader; b. *c.* 1778, probably in Dunardary, Argyll, Scotland, son of Lachlan Mactavish, Chief of Clan Tavish; d. 20 July 1847 in Lac-des-Deux-Montagnes (Oka), Lower Canada.

The second son of the impoverished last chief of Clan Tavish, John George Mactavish was recruited into the service of the North West Company in 1798 by his illustrious distant relative Simon McTavish*, whose spelling of the family name he adopted. A well-educated young man, he apparently spent his first years clerking at the company's headquarters in Montreal, although he did attend the summer rendezvous at Grand Portage (near Grand Portage, Minn.) in 1802. As Montreal offered little adventure, in 1803 he was excited to be part of the NWC expedition which attempted to challenge the Hudson's Bay Company's monopoly directly by building posts on James Bay [*see* Simon McTavish]. Arriving at Charlton Island (N.W.T.) by sea from Quebec in early September, he was given charge of the warehouse erected there, Fort St Andrews, but he frequently travelled to the post built on Hayes Island (Ont.) near Moose Factory. Relations with the HBC people were cordial enough that McTavish took for a country wife Charlotte, a daughter of John Thomas*, the HBC's chief at Moose Factory, and his native wife. By the fall of 1806, however, the Nor'Westers had decided to abandon their enterprise at James Bay and McTavish returned to Quebec, leaving a distressed Charlotte behind.

Subsequently, McTavish was posted to the interior, wintering at Fort Dunvegan on the Peace River in 1808–9. References to his attendance at meetings of the Beaver Club indicate that he was in Montreal in 1810–11, but later in 1811 he was part of the brigade under John McDonald* of Garth which crossed the Rocky Mountains to supply David Thompson* on the upper Columbia River. McTavish wintered at Spokane House (near Spokane, Wash.) and accompanied Thompson back to Fort William (Thunder Bay, Ont.) in 1812. McTavish was then to play an important role in the NWC's successful challenge to the Pacific Fur Company on the coast. He and his brigade reached the American company's Fort Astoria (Astoria, Oreg.) in April 1813 to await the arrival of an NWC supply ship, but when it failed to appear they returned to the Spokane posts for the summer, being provisioned by the Astorians. McTavish and an enlarged flotilla returned to Astoria in the fall with the news that Britain and the United States were at war and that ships were being sent to capture the American post. McTavish forthwith entered into negotiations with the

Pacific Fur Company to sell its assets to the NWC, the deal being completed on 16 October. Although he was to be criticized for having accepted unfavourable terms, his actions were supported by William McGillivray*, the head of the NWC. He had been made a partner earlier that year. It was probably during this period that McTavish took as his second mixed-blood country wife, Nancy McKenzie*, who had been entrusted by her father, former Nor'Wester Roderick MACKENZIE, to the guardianship of trader John STUART of New Caledonia (B.C.).

For McTavish, the 1813–14 season was a troublesome one at Astoria, now called Fort George; there were conflicts over management and trouble with the Indians. In the spring of 1814 he led an armed expedition up the Columbia to retaliate against the tribe that had attacked and pillaged two NWC canoes at the Cascades (near Cascade Locks, Oreg.). He appears to have been on furlough the next year, but spent the 1815–16 season again in the Columbia department.

McTavish was apparently east of the Rockies from the 1816–17 season on, and became embroiled in the final stages of the conflict with the HBC. In 1818 he was sent to winter in the Athabasca country: on coming out the next summer he was one of the partners captured by the HBC governor, William WILLIAMS, at Grand Rapids (Man.). He was transported to York Factory and sent to England for trial, but when these proceedings came to nothing, he left for North America in March 1820 aboard the *James Munroe*. At Montreal he was instructed to proceed post-haste into the interior to retaliate, and he was in charge of the party that arrested Colin ROBERTSON in June at Grand Rapids. In the last season before the coalition of the two companies, McTavish was given charge of Fort William.

At the union in 1821 he was made a chief factor, and it is a mark of his influence and the esteem in which he was held that he was placed in charge of York Factory, now the main depot for the HBC's Northern Department. Governor George Simpson*, who had taken a liking to him even though they had been trade rivals when they first met aboard the *James Munroe*, had high praise for his business skills and his efficient management at York. In 1824 McTavish was named to preside at Council in the event of Simpson's absence. During the 1820s McTavish's family was growing apace: he and Nancy McKenzie, whom fur trade society regarded as Madam McTavish, had at least five daughters.

On 22 Feb. 1830, however, when on furlough in Scotland, McTavish married Catherine A. Turner of Turner Hall, Aberdeenshire, thus taking the unprecedented step of casting aside his mixed-blood wife without first making provision for her. Simpson, who supported him in this action, did likewise two days later. The McTavishes returned to North America with the Simpsons later that year, travelling with them by canoe from Montreal to Michipicoten (Michipicoten River, Ont.), where McTavish branched off to take his bride to his new posting at Moose Factory, headquarters of the Southern Department. Although he had been well liked for his kind and generous nature, his cruel abandonment of his native family led to severe attacks upon his character, particularly by John Stuart and Donald McKenzie*, which hurt him deeply. Simpson, as his remarkably detailed and intimate correspondence with McTavish reveals, staunchly defended him and arranged for Nancy McTavish to be married off. In spite of this loyalty, the governor did confide in his "Character book" of 1832 that he was concerned about McTavish's extravagant living habits and signs of intemperance.

By the early 1830s McTavish had become so corpulent that a friend declared he had never seen "such a stout man." Because of his health, McTavish was given a furlough in 1835–36 and was then transferred to the comfortable post of Lake of Two Mountains near Montreal. In 1837 he purchased the farm given up by the company at Lac des Chats (near Quyon), Lower Canada. He was grief-stricken by the death of his wife in October 1841; she had brought him much happiness and two more daughters. Finding life unbearable as a widower, he married in March 1843 a woman much his junior, Elizabeth (Eppie) Cameron, a niece of Chief Factor Angus Cameron*. This union produced another pair of daughters.

After a career of almost 50 years in the fur trade, McTavish died following a short illness in 1847. In his will he divided his estate, which was valued at approximately £6,000, between the daughters of his marriage to Catherine Turner and his current wife and family.

SYLVIA VAN KIRK

A letter by John George McTavish was published under the title "The Nor'Westers invade the Bay," ed. W. S. Wallace, *Beaver*, outfit 277 (March 1947): 33–34.

ANQ-M, CE1-63, 11 oct. 1841; CM1, 1/12, 20 juill. 1847 (will of J. G. McTavish) (copy at PAM, HBCA). PAC, MG 19, A21, ser.1. PAM, HBCA, B.4/b/1: f.15; B.135/a/91–94; B.135/c/2; D.4; D.5; E.4/1a: 39, 44d, 61d; E.24/4; F.3/2; J. G. McTavish file. Gabriel Franchère, *Journal of a voyage on the north west coast of North America during the years 1811, 1812, 1813, and 1814*, trans. W. T. Lamb, ed. and intro. W. K. Lamb (Toronto, 1969). *HBRS*, 1 (Rich); 10 (Rich); 30 (Williams). Letitia [Mactavish] Hargrave, *The letters of Letitia Hargrave*, ed. Margaret Arnett MacLeod (Toronto, 1947). Van Kirk, *"Many tender ties"*.

MALIE, JOSEPH (he also signed **Malli** and **Mally** and was sometimes called **Tkobeitch**), Micmac chief; fl. 1841–46.

According to band tradition, Joseph came to the Restigouche Indian Reserve from Nova Scotia. His nickname, Tkobeitch, is derived from *tgôpetj*, the Micmac word for twin, and the designation Malie is the name of his twin sister, Marie, added to his own for further identification. Descendants use Malley or Molley as a family name.

Joseph Malie was the principal in the "three chiefs mission" that visited London early in 1842 seeking assistance for the Restigouche Micmacs. He was accompanied by Pierre Basquet* and François Labauve. The delegation had two main grievances to present: the whites' practice of netting all the salmon entering the Restigouche River, thus destroying the spawning run, and a dispute over land boundaries going back over 50 years. An erroneous survey by William Vondenvelden* in 1787 – a committee of the Executive Council later implied that the error was deliberate – had given part of the Indians' lands to whites. A protest to the Lower Canadian government by chief Francis CONDO had led to the retrieval of some of the land in 1824, but the Micmacs wanted full satisfaction of their claim. In 1838 they petitioned Lord Durham [LAMBTON], and the problem was referred to a committee of the Executive Council and thence to John Wilkie, a clerk of the peace at New Carlisle, Lower Canada, for investigation. Wilkie reported in June 1840 that part of the land was the object of litigation between two whites and he advised that if the government wanted to purchase land from the settlers to give back to the Indians it should wait until the lawsuit had been concluded. Their patience wearing thin, the Micmacs told their troubles to Captain Henry Dunn O'Halloran, a sympathetic British army officer stationed in New Brunswick, who visited the reserve in 1841. O'Halloran encouraged them to take their problems direct to London and gave Joseph Malie a letter of introduction to the colonial secretary, Lord Stanley.

The Indian delegation left Dalhousie, N.B., in November 1841 and had an interview with Stanley at the Colonial Office in January. Malie was the spokesman. He informed Stanley that new laws were needed to protect the salmon fishery and money had to be raised to finish a church being built. The members of the delegation brought with them a gift for Queen Victoria which she accepted "with satisfaction" (though not in person), expressing "a warm interest" in their condition and ordering medals for each of them. In a series of interviews outside the Colonial Office, Malie poured out the story of the lands that had been filched from his people. They had once had a written deed for their lands but the priest had lost it, whites had moved in, and "there seems to be a Right and Wrong with the White men which Indians cannot comprehend." He specified the presents he wanted, a wide range of goods from blankets to iron ploughs, and, finally, asked to be granted a strip of land for himself freehold.

Stanley maintained that all these grievances were the proper concern of the authorities in the colonies. He arranged for the swift return of the Indians aboard the *Warspite*, sailing for New York in February. There the British consul booked their passage to Saint John, where they arrived on 22 April 1842. Stanley went so far as to outline the Indians' complaints to Governor Sir Charles BAGOT and ordered inquiries into the fishery laws and the land claims. Meanwhile, the Micmacs lost no time in petitioning the Canadian legislature against the fishing methods of the whites, and Joseph Malie's name headed the list of those who signed the protest.

Malie was evidently a strong personality. He was active at Restigouche as late as 1846, when the local missionary called him his "right arm." Generations later it was said on the reserve, "There has been no chief since Joseph Malli."

L. F. S. UPTON

PAC, RG 10, CII, 469–70. Can., Prov. of, Legislative Assembly, *App. to the journals*, 1847, 1: app.T, no.96. *Source materials relating to N.B. Indian* (Hamilton and Spray), 110–13. *New-Brunswick Courier*, 23 April 1842. Upton, *Micmacs and colonists*. Père Pacifique [de Valigny] [H.-J.-L. Buisson], "Ristigouche, métropole des Micmacs, théâtre du 'dernier effort de la France au Canada,'" Soc. de géographie de Québec, *Bull.* (Québec), 20 (1926): 171–85.

MANAHAN, ANTHONY, businessman, JP, militia officer, politician, and office holder; b. *c.* 1794 in Mount Bellew, County Galway (Republic of Ireland); m. Sarah Phebe Nugent (d. 1847), and they had at least three daughters, one of whom died in infancy; d. 21 Jan. 1849 in Kingston, Upper Canada.

The names of Anthony Manahan's parents and his early circumstances are unknown, but it is evident that he came of a respectable Roman Catholic background and received a basic education. About 1808 he and a brother emigrated to Trinidad. There, by his own account, he "filled a public situation of trust" and gained the confidence and friendship of Governor Sir Ralph James Woodford. As well, he married a daughter of John Nugent, a member of the island's Council. For unknown reasons he left Trinidad in 1820 and went to Kingston, where he became a merchant and formed Anthony Manahan and Company, apparently in cooperation with a relative, Patrick Manahan of New York.

In 1824 Anthony Manahan, Peter McGill*, and Robert Hayes became assignees of the Marmora Iron Works, in Hastings County. Since its initial development in 1820 under Charles Hayes, an Irish businessman, the works had been plagued with problems, including the lack of a good transportation system between Marmora Township and the Bay of Quinte. McGill bought the works in 1825 and the following year chose Manahan to manage it, probably because most of the workers were Irish Catholics and because Manahan too had invested in the venture. He was unable, however, to make it show a profit; in October 1831 he left the works and returned to Kingston, having lost "several thousand pounds." He went back into business there as a merchant and commission agent, "with doubtful prospects of success," and began trying, without immediate result, to get a government job in addition to the magistracy he had received in 1829.

Though living in Kingston, Manahan continued to have a strong interest in the affairs of Hastings County. In December 1831 he headed a petition from inhabitants of the region asking for improvements in the road to the ironworks. Appointed major of the 2nd Regiment of Hastings militia in 1826 and colonel in 1830, he went on active service with the regiment in 1837, supervising the transfer of arms from Kingston to Belleville. In 1836, proclaiming "undeviating constitutional principles" and opposition to "ultraism of any kind," he had been elected to one of the two seats for Hastings in the House of Assembly. There, in 1836–37, he advocated government support for the creation of a Trent River canal system, which would afford easier access to the "abandoned" Marmora Iron Works. In 1837 Manahan, George Neville Ridley, and Isaac Fraser formed a commission to report on the feasibility of moving the provincial penitentiary from Kingston to Marmora. The majority report, signed by Manahan and Ridley, recommended the transfer and recommended as well the use of cheap convict labour at the works, but the proposals were never acted upon.

Manahan also took up the cause of his fellow Irish Catholics in Upper Canada. In 1838 he submitted a memorial to Lord Durham [LAMBTON] alleging systematic discrimination against Irish Catholics by the Upper Canadian élite. He asked for justice to "my fellow Catholics, not one of whom," he claimed, held "any office of profit or emolument" in the province. On several other occasions he was quick to react, publicly and in private correspondence with government officials, to anti-Catholic attacks or to specific cases of discrimination. He expected that his actions would make him "a host of enemies in the notorious Family Compact," and to some extent they did. In February 1838 John Macaulay*, reacting to Manahan's complaints about both the compact and an appointment to the Midland District Grammar School, wrote to his mother: "I suppose he wanted a Catholic appointed – nothing but supremacy will satisfy such people." At the time Manahan was himself in the government's employ. From 1837 to 1844 he was crown lands agent for the Midland and Prince Edward districts and in 1838–40, and possibly earlier, he was employed by the chief emigration agent to supervise the settlement of immigrants in the Kingston area.

In 1841 Manahan was elected to the Legislative Assembly for Kingston. Though a conservative and moderate adherent of Lord Sydenham [THOMSON], he maintained a correspondence with Robert Baldwin*, the solicitor general and reform leader, whose electoral campaign in Hastings he supported. He resigned his seat on 18 June 1841, three days after the opening of parliament, in order to create an opening for Sydenham's provincial secretary, Samuel Bealey Harrison*. Manahan was rewarded the same day by being appointed collector of customs for Toronto.

He seemed at last to have gained a position that promised security, but in fact his financial troubles persisted. In an attempt to improve operations in the collector's office he spent public money freely on rent, furnishings, supplies, and additional employees. All of these expenditures the government refused to sanction since, as the inspector general's office repeatedly pointed out to him, there was no provision for them under the law. On 5 April 1843 Manahan resigned in favour of his son-in-law William Moore Kelly, who had been doing the work of the office for some time. When Manahan's accounts were audited he was informed that he owed the government more than £400 because of unauthorized expenditures and overcharges on commission. The assistant commissioner of crown lands, Tancrède Bouthillier, and the chief emigration agent for Upper Canada, Anthony Bewden Hawke*, reported that he was also in arrears to their offices, where he had made "sundry claims" either not authorized or unsupported by vouchers despite his having been told often about "the proper mode of accounting for public money." He returned to Kingston later in 1843. His property was sold in 1844 and 1845 to pay his debts to the government.

In the election of 1844 Manahan ran again for Kingston but was defeated by John A. Macdonald*. Though the *Kingston Herald* described Manahan as the "most liberal" of the two, it did not name him among the reformers running in local ridings. His apparent political shift in the early 1840s is difficult to explain; possibly it derived in part from his becoming disillusioned by the provincial élite's mistreatment of Irish Catholics. His last years were spent in a vain attempt to regain some measure of solvency. In 1846 he renewed a petition to the government, which he had been submitting periodically over many years, to be compensated in the amount of £2,530 for the loss in 1821 of a shipment of tea and tobacco wrongly seized at Carleton Island, N.Y., by the then collector of customs at Kingston, Christopher Alexander HAGERMAN. The Executive Council refused his request. In 1847 Manahan applied for the position of police magistrate of Kingston on the grounds that he had been a justice of the peace since 1829 and that he had the support of the Kingston City Council. His letter of application to the provincial secretary was "put by." Two years later Manahan died at the age of 55.

J. K. JOHNSON

AO, MS 78, John Macaulay to Ann Macaulay, 8 Feb. 1838. Hastings Land Registry Office (Belleville, Ont.), Abstract index to deeds, Marmora Township, concession 4, lot 8 (mfm. at AO). MTRL, Robert Baldwin papers, A57, nos.45–46. PAC, MG 24, D16, 115: 74820; MG 26, A, 2a, 543: 257107; RG 1, E3, 52: 303–18; L1, 32: 411; RG 4, A1, 542: 67; RG 5, A1: 64912, 125019–67; C1, 9, file 1176; 79, file 30549; 112, files 6178, 6187; 133, file 8112; 191, files 15171, 16535, 16605; RG 9, I, B5, 3, 6; RG 68, General index, 1651–1841: 467. *Arthur papers* (Sanderson), 3: 493. F. H. Baddeley, "An essay on the localities of metallic minerals in the Canadas, with some notices of their geological associations and situation, &c.," Literary and Hist. Soc. of Quebec, *Trans.*, 2 (1830–31): 357. *Debates of the Legislative Assembly of United Canada* (Abbott Gibbs *et al.*), 1: 69, 187, 818, 838–39, 901, 1003. [J. G. Lambton, 1st] Earl of Durham, *Report on the affairs of British North America, from the Earl of Durham . . .* ([London, 1839]), app.A, no.7. U.C., House of Assembly, *App. to the journal*, 1839–40, 1, pt.II: 2; *Journal*, 1826–27, app., no.12; 1829: 57; 1831, app.: 210; 1832–33, app.: 19. *British Whig*, 23 March, 7 April 1838. *Chronicle & Gazette*, 1834–44. *Daily British Whig*, 23 Jan. 1849. *Globe*, 27 Jan. 1849. *Kingston Chronicle*, 7 March 1823, 14 Jan. 1832. *Kingston Herald*, 1 Oct. 1844. *Patriot* (Toronto), 2 Aug. 1836. *Upper Canada Herald*, 24 Feb. 1826. *Death notices of Ont.* (Reid), 131, 303, 342. *Marriage notices of Ont.* (Reid). *Ont. marriage notices* (T. B. Wilson), 65. G. E. Boyce, *Historic Hastings* (Belleville, 1967). Gertrude Carmichael, *The history of the West Indian islands of Trinidad and Tobago, 1498–1910* (London, 1961), 383. N. F. Davin, *The Irishman in Canada* (London and Toronto, 1877), 366. Ont., Bureau of Mines, *Report* (Toronto), 1892: 15–16.

MARANDA, JEAN-BAPTISTE, Roman Catholic priest and vicar general; b. 10 Feb. 1803 in Saint-Laurent, Île d'Orléans, Lower Canada, son of Charles Maranda and Marie-Angèle Beaudoin; d. 10 March 1850 in Arichat, N.S.

Jean-Baptiste Maranda studied from 1814 to 1822 at the Petit Séminaire de Québec and from 1823 to 1827 was a student and teacher at the Grand Séminaire. Following ordination on 10 Dec. 1826, he asked the archbishop of Quebec, Bernard-Claude Panet*, to give him a posting near the sea for the sake of his health. Panet agreed, and on 21 Sept. 1827 assigned him to Arichat, on Cape Breton Island. He arrived on 12 October and began to assist the Reverend Jean-Baptiste Potvin, another native of Lower Canada, in ministering to the area's mixed population of Acadians, Micmacs, English, Irish, and Scots. Not caring to travel because of his fragile constitution, Maranda served mainly in and around Arichat while Potvin attended to the more distant missions. Maranda found the people poor but friendly, and noted that most of the conversation revolved around the fishing industry. During his first winter he studied English and, he reported, ate a lot of fish; perhaps because his health had deteriorated he also expressed a desire to return to Quebec. This wish was granted, and he left in July 1828.

Appointed assistant at Saint-Gervais, near his place of birth, he remained there until late December, when Panet allowed him to take sick leave at Saint-Jean, Île d'Orléans. From April to September 1829 he was administrator at Saint-Jean and was then appointed pastor at another parish on the island, Saint-François. For four years beginning in September 1831 he was parish priest at Château-Richer, east of Quebec, with responsibility as well in 1831–32 for L'Ange-Gardien. Although plagued by poor health throughout his career, by September 1835 Maranda was well enough to accept another appointment to Arichat, this time as pastor.

Maranda arrived at Arichat on 24 September. Glad to be back, he was soon involved in building a new church, Notre-Dame, and in serving his flock of 2,300. He was now fluent in English and his correspondence reveals that he was satisfied with his work among both French- and English-speaking parishioners. Moreover, his relationship with Bishop William Fraser*, vicar apostolic of Nova Scotia, was very good. He spoke of having peace, despite privations, in Arichat – perhaps a reference to the rebellions of 1837–38 in Lower Canada.

The first mass in his new church was offered in October 1837. Unfortunately, 13 months later a fire destroyed the presbytery and the parish registers. Although a new presbytery was completed around June 1840, Maranda, perhaps discouraged by that loss, or by a return of ill health, or by troubles with his Irish Catholic parishioners, asked to be replaced. The archbishop of Quebec, Joseph SIGNAY, complied on 21 August by assigning Louis-Alexis Bourret, not yet three years ordained, to succeed him. When Maranda and another Nova Scotia missionary, the Reverend John Quinan, met Bourret in Arichat at the end of the month, they agreed that he was not healthy enough to do the job. Bourret consented to become Maranda's assistant if Signay would allow Maranda to remain. Maranda went to Quebec to try to persuade Signay to accept this plan, but was unsuccessful. He was assigned instead to La Malbaie, Lower Canada. Signay, however, in response to additional pleas by Maranda, Bourret, and Fraser, wrote to Bourret on 23 Oct. 1840 ordering him to Quebec and stating that Maranda would stay in Arichat. Shortly after Maranda resumed his work there in November, he received from Signay an unsought exeat cutting him off from his native diocese. Fraser responded by promptly and gladly incorporating him into his own vicariate apostolic.

When Fraser was made bishop of Arichat on 20 July 1845, the church there became a cathedral and Maranda, as pastor, became its first rector. At the same time, if Maranda's obituary is to be believed, Fraser appointed him vicar general. Despite his chronic poor health, Maranda continued his excellent work in the Arichat area, particularly among the Acadians and Micmacs. Fraser valued his services, for Maranda was one of a number of French-speaking missionaries who, along with their Gaelic-speaking colleagues, made the Roman Catholic church a powerful institution in eastern Nova Scotia. He was buried at Arichat in March 1850, and was succeeded by Étienne Chartier*.

R. A. MACLEAN

AAQ, 312 CN, VI–VII (copies at Arch. of the Diocese of Antigonish, N.S.). Arch. of the Diocese of Antigonish, Files of the diocesan historian. Allaire, *Dictionnaire*. Caron, "Inv. de la corr. de Mgr Panet," ANQ *Rapport*, 1933–34: esp. 322. Tanguay, *Répertoire* (1893). A. A. Johnston, *A history of the Catholic Church in eastern Nova Scotia* (2v., Antigonish, 1960–71).

MARCOT, MARGUERITE-MAGDELAINE (La Framboise), fur trader; b. February 1780, daughter of Jean-Baptiste Marcot and Marie Neskech; d. 4 April 1846 on Mackinac Island, Mich.

Marguerite-Magdelaine Marcot's father was a fur trader in the upper Great Lakes country from the 1740s, and her mother was the daughter of an Ottawa chief. Where Magdelaine was born is uncertain, though in June 1780 the family was residing at Fort St Joseph (Niles, Mich.). The American revolution forced them to move to British-held Mackinac Island. Magdelaine was only three when her father was killed and her mother returned to her native village near the mouth of the Grand River (Mich.). The family was devoutly Roman Catholic and on 1 Aug. 1786 Magdelaine was baptized at Michilimackinac (Mackinac Island) by a visiting priest. When she was about 14 she married by the custom of the country Joseph La Framboise, a trader. On 11 July 1804 they solemnized their marriage before a missionary at Michilimackinac.

Magdelaine's family ties and her participation in his business helped Joseph and they became prosperous. Their trade centred on the Grand River though Joseph apparently had connections with both Montreal and Milwaukee (Wis.). Magdelaine, who became known as Mme La Framboise, a designation that was to remain with her for life, was with him in the autumn of 1806 when an enraged Indian killed him as he knelt in prayer at their camp on Lake Michigan. His murderer was later brought to her for vengeance. Instead, she forgave him. Having accumulated the winter's furs, she returned undaunted to Michilimackinac and then pressed on to Montreal. There she worked with her husband's relatives to settle his estate. She subsequently became one of the leading traders in the Upper Lakes region.

Mme La Framboise held a prominent place in society at Michilimackinac. She was away in 1816 when her daughter, Josette, who had been educated in Montreal, married in a civil ceremony American army captain Benjamin Kendrick Pierce, the commandant of Fort Michilimackinac. When she returned, a second lavish ceremony and party were held in the home of her close friend Elizabeth, also an Ottawa and a trader, and the wife of David Mitchell*. Mme La Framboise wore full Indian dress, her regular attire. Pierce, whose brother later became president of the United States, built a fine home for his mother-in-law and family which still stands.

By this time Madame was considering giving up the Indian trade. The American Fur Company's powers were growing and she had resisted as an independent trader; in 1818 her refusal to follow the AFC's practice of restricting the trade of liquor to the Indians drew harsh complaints from Ramsay Crooks*, an AFC agent. She finally joined the company later in 1818, a move which took her enterprises as far afield as the Big Sioux River (S.Dak./Iowa) in the competition with the Columbia Fur Company and other interests. In 1822 she gave up business and sold her trading post on the Grand River. The Indians in that area expressed their love for her by presenting her with a section of land the following year.

Now retired and wealthy, she devoted herself to the education of young people and to her church. When the Reverend William Ferry came to Michilimackinac in 1823 to begin a school for Indian children, she opened her home to him even though he was a Protestant. Later a Catholic school operating in her home served as a rival to his enterprises. She took in many children and hired teachers to train and catechize them. In the process, she learned to read and write in both French and English. When, in 1827, Ste Anne's Church was moved, she donated a lot for its new location.

During the 1830s and 1840s Mme La Framboise's door was frequently opened to passing notables. Among others, Alexis de Tocqueville and Sarah Margaret Fuller, the American woman of letters, stopped to call and were amazed at this remarkable person. She was described by Juliette Augusta Kinzie as "a woman of a vast deal of energy and enterprise – of a tall and commanding figure, and most dignified deportment." As Mme La Framboise grew old her health failed, but she still travelled frequently to Montreal to visit her son, Joseph, who had become a merchant. Mackinac Island remained her home, however, and it was there that she died on 4 April 1846.

DAVID A. ARMOUR

Arch. paroissiales, Sainte-Anne-de-Michillimakinac (Mackinac Island, Mich.), Financial record-book, 1828–38; Liber defunctorum missionis S. Anna, Mackinac, 1825–26; 1844–91: 89; Reg. des baptêmes, 1823–89. Bayliss Public Library (Sault Ste Marie, Mich.), Port Mackinac, records, 19 June [1811 or 1819]. DPL, Burton Hist. Coll., American Fur Company, ledger, 5 Nov. 1804, 25 May 1805; James Henry, Mackinac Store journal, 1802–4; Claude Laframboise to John Kinzie, 11 June 1807; George Schindler to Solomon Sibley, 9 July 1807. Mackinac County Courthouse (St Ignace, Mich.), Reg. of the post of Michilimackinac, 99–100. Mich., Dept. of Natural Resources, Lands Division (Lansing), Private claims, nos.710–11. National Arch. (Washington), RG 75, Records of the Office of the Secretary of War relating to Indian affairs, letters received, abstract of licences to trade in Indian country, 1 Sept. 1821–31 Aug. 1822. Wis., State Hist. Soc., H. S. Baird papers. *American Missionary Reg.* (New York), 5 (1824), no.3: 89–90. *Mich. Pioneer Coll.*, 10 (1886): 405–7, 599; 11 (1887): 193, 350; 13 (1888): 58; 17 (1890): 325–26. H. R. Schoolcraft, *Personal memoirs of a residence of thirty years with the Indian tribes on the American frontiers, with brief notices of passing events, facts and opinions, A.D. 1812 to A.D. 1842* (Philadelphia, 1851; repr. New York, 1975), 478, 569. Wis., State Hist. Soc., *Coll.*, 9 (1882): 144; 11 (1888): 164, 373–74, 376; 12 (1892): 162–63; 14 (1898): 36–47; 18 (1908): 484–85, 507–9; 19 (1910): 44, 59, 65, 77, 86, 109, 133, 140, 146, 150. "Calendar of the American Fur Company's papers, part II: 1841–1849," American Hist. Assoc., *Annual report* (Washington), 1944, 3: 1599, 1638. L. H. Burbey, *Our worthy commander; the life and times of Benjamin K. Pierce* (Fort Pierce, Fla., 1976), 21–32. G. S. Hubbard, *The autobiography of Gurdon Saltonstall Hubbard: Pa-pa-ma-ta-be, "the swift walker"*, intro. C. M. McIlvaine (Chicago, 1911), 22–23, 133. I. A. Johnson, *The Michigan fur trade* (Lansing, 1919), 129–33. D. [S.] Lavender, *The fist in the wilderness* (Garden City, N.Y., 1964), 264–65, 288. [J. A. Magill] Mrs J. H. Kinzie, *Wau-bun, the "early day" in the northwest . . .*, ed. and intro. Louise Phelps Kellogg (Menasha, Wis., 1948). P. C. Phillips, *The fur trade* (2v., Norman, Okla., 1961), 2: 368, 378. M. M. Quaife, *Lake Michigan* (New York, 1944), 201–3, 207. E. O. Wood, *Historic Mackinac; the historical, picturesque and legendary features of the Mackinac country . . .* (2v., New York, 1918), 2: 125–33. M. E. Evans, "The missing footnote or, the curé who wasn't there," American Catholic Hist. Soc. of Philadelphia, *Records*, 84 (1973): 199. J. E. McDowell, "Madame La Framboise," *Mich. Hist.* (Lansing), 56 (1972): 271–86; "Therese Schindler of Mackinac: upward mobility in the Great Lakes fur trade," *Wis. Magazine of Hist.* (Madison), 61 (1977–78): 125–43. *Mich. Hist. Magazine* (Lansing), 10 (1926): 639–41; 11 (1927): 311, 490–92; 12 (1928): 154–56, 615; 13 (1929): 143–46. V. L. Moore, "A Pocahontas of Michigan," *Mich. Hist. Magazine*, 15 (1931): 71–79.

MARIE-ESTHER DE SAINT-JOSEPH. *See* CHALOUX

MARIE-LOUISE DE SAINT-HENRI. *See* MCLOUGHLIN

MARIE-ROSE, EULALIE DUROCHER, named Mother. *See* DUROCHER

MARKLAND, THOMAS, businessman, militia officer, JP, and office holder; b. 1757 in the American colonies; m. 8 June 1787 Catherine Herchmer (Herkimer), and they had a son, George Herchmer Markland*; d. 31 Jan. 1840 in Kingston, Upper Canada.

Before the American revolution Thomas Markland was a large landowner in the Mohawk valley of New York. A declared loyalist, he moved in 1784 to Cataraqui (Kingston) where, in recognition of his commitment to the royalist cause, he received 24 lots, some of which he held jointly with other loyalists. Markland had, it seems, little interest in farming and kept the land as an investment, selling much of it at a profit over the next ten years. By 1788 he had entered into a lucrative partnership with another loyalist, Robert Macaulay*. The two men trans-shipped goods, opened a small retail store, and took on agency work for the congregation of St George's Church and prominent individuals such as Sir John Johnson*. During the last years of the partnership, which was dissolved in 1792 or 1793, Markland apparently assumed increasing responsibility for the day to day operations. On his own, he exported flour and pork to Lower Canada and imported goods from the United States; he may also have had a small retail business. By 1800 he was one of Kingston's principal merchants, second only to Richard Cartwright* in the quantity of goods handled, and by the War of 1812 he had become one of the major landowners in the area. Although mercantile pursuits and land speculation together formed the basis of Markland's considerable wealth, his primary interest was the market-place.

In addition to his mercantile prominence, Markland was considered a gentleman of property and standing. His partnership with Macaulay and his marriage drew him into close personal association with two old and respected families in Kingston. Actively involved in the affairs of St George's Church, in 1789 he was one of the vestrymen who petitioned the government for land on which to erect a building, and the following year he donated money to the building fund. He rented a pew and assumed various duties: vestryman (1792), warden (1803 and 1805), and member of the committee to find a replacement for the Reverend John Stuart* (1811). The militia provided another outlet for his energies. He had enrolled in the local unit by 1791 and quickly rose to the rank of captain, a position he held in the flank company of the 1st Frontenac Militia throughout the War of 1812. He was promoted lieutenant-colonel in 1816 and colonel five years later, a rank he held until his retirement in 1839.

During the 1790s he had also begun to take a role in local affairs: he became a justice of the peace in 1794;

he served in the Court of Requests; and he was a member of the committee commissioned to oversee the building of a jail. In 1796 he was appointed treasurer of the Midland District, a position he held until 1837. In 1800 he became a commissioner for determining the loyalty of prospective subjects and taking the mandatory oath of allegiance required of all new settlers. Four years later he received the appointment of commissioner for taking affidavits. At the end of the War of 1812, Markland, now 58 and one of the few original loyalists active in Kingston, was still a recognized business and social leader, who went on to acquire even more offices.

Markland continued to run his mercantile enterprises and took an increasingly active part in various organizations promoting local development. Of primary concern to Kingston merchants was the lack of banks. Markland had in August 1813 been a notable omission from the group of merchants involved with the Kingston Association, which had agreed to issue bills in exchange for specie [*see* Joseph Forsyth*]. In fact, he had considered it an attempt "to injure his credit." The background of this dispute is a mystery, and the acrimony surrounding it had been forgotten when in 1817 Markland became a trustee of a commercial bank proposed for Kingston, the Bank of Upper Canada. For at least three years (1818–21), he was the local agent for the Bank of Montreal [*see* John Gray*]. In 1819 Markland and several other merchants investigated the feasibility of a savings bank, which was established in 1822. He joined John Macaulay* and John Kirby in supporting the chartered Bank of Upper Canada at York (Toronto) over the "pretended" Bank of Upper Canada of Kingston [*see* Thomas Dalton]. In 1830 he supported the formation of the Commercial Bank of the Midland District (located in Kingston) and he served as a director in 1832.

Markland's concern for economic development was not restricted to financial institutions. He advocated the union of the Canadas in 1822, and again in 1838, as essential for commercial prosperity. In 1824 he became a member of the St Lawrence Association which had been organized to promote improving the navigability of the river. Privately, and as a justice of the peace and district treasurer, he encouraged whatever means were at hand to improve local transportation: bridges, canals, and ferries. Moreover, although not personally interested in matters such as the most efficient and productive use of land, in 1819 he had been instrumental in the formation of an agricultural society and he willingly held the post of vice-president for two years.

As a 19th-century conservative, Markland, like many others of his type, believed he had a responsibility to serve, a responsibility he continued to respect after the war. His connection with the Anglican church and church-related activities increased. Among other things, he was one of the men chosen by St George's in 1823 to oversee the building fund and subsequent erection of a new church. In 1835 he was appointed to a provincial committee investigating the use of the clergy reserves. A founding member of the Kingston Auxiliary Bible and Common Prayer Book Society, he was its president from 1819 to 1822. Throughout the 1830s he was a subscriber to, and vice-president of, the local branch of the Society for Promoting Christian Knowledge and president of the Kingston Auxiliary of the British and Foreign Bible Society. He also assisted other denominations. He publicly supported the building of a Presbyterian church and in 1817 he contributed to a British Wesleyan chapel in Kingston. That same year he subscribed to the British Methodist Society and in 1832 he donated money to the Wesleyan Methodist Auxiliary Missionary Society.

Until his death, Markland played a leading role in numerous educational and social institutions. His involvement with education began in 1815 when he became a trustee of the Midland District School Society; he continued to support the organization for the next 20 years and was its president in 1832. In addition he was a benefactor of the Lancasterian school [*see* Joseph Lancaster], supported the establishment of Union Sunday schools, subscribed to Queen's College in 1840, and served for a short time as manager of the local library. He was a founding member of a number of organizations in which he held office and to which he subscribed annually: the Kingston Compassionate Society, the Society to Provide Relief for Widows, the Emigrant Society, and the Men's Auxiliary of the Society for Promoting Education and Industry among the Indians and the Destitute. And it was Markland who in 1819 chaired meetings held in Kingston and Bath to establish relief for the poor. The same year Markland and others also took direct action to build a hospital in Kingston and he was both a shareholder and one of the trustees appointed to oversee the project. He served as president of the local temperance society in 1832.

Thomas Markland was perhaps the most influential member of the local "family compact." A firm supporter of the executive during the debates centring on Robert Gourlay* and the disturbances of 1837, he had, however, little direct contact with York officialdom. Connections with York he seems to have left to his son who, by virtue of age, personal contacts, and political beliefs, fitted into the society of the post-war capital where he had some impact on broad colonial policies. Several years before his death, Markland resigned his post as treasurer of the Midland District. "This gentleman," as the Kingston *Chronicle & Gazette* extolled him, "is one of the oldest and most respected inhabitants." The editors thanked him "for his long, zealous and efficient service as a public man."

JANE ERRINGTON

ACC, Diocese of Ont. Arch. (Kingston), St George's Cathedral (Kingston), minute-books for St George's Church, vols.I–II. AO, RG 40, D-1, box 4. PAC, RG 16, A1, 133, files for 1805–9, 1815. QUA, 2244. "District of Mecklenburg (Kingston): Court of Common Pleas," AO *Report*, 1917: 190–353. *Kingston before the War of 1812: a collection of documents*, ed. R. A. Preston (Toronto, 1959). *The parish register of Kingston, Upper Canada, 1784–1811*, ed. A. H. Young (Kingston, 1921). *Chronicle & Gazette*, 1833–43. *Kingston Chronicle*, 1819–33. *Kingston Gazette*, 1814–18. *Officers of British forces in Canada* (Irving). Reid, *Loyalists in Ont.* K. M. Bindon, "Kingston: a social history, 1785–1830" (PHD thesis, Queen's Univ., Kingston, 1979). William Canniff, *History of the settlement of Upper Canada (Ontario), with special reference to the Bay Quinte* (Toronto, 1869; repr. Belleville, Ont., 1971). E. J. Errington, "The 'Eagle,' the 'Lion,' and Upper Canada: the colonial elites' view of the United States and Great Britain, 1784–1828" (PHD thesis, Queen's Univ., 1984). Patterson, "Studies in elections in U.C." H. P. Gundy, "The Honourable John Kirby of Kingston," *Douglas Library Notes* (Kingston), 9 (1960), no.1: 2–4. W. D. Reid, "Johan Jost Herkimer, U.E., and his family," *OH*, 31 (1936): 215–27. S. F. Wise, "Tory factionalism: Kingston elections and Upper Canadian politics, 1820–1836," *OH*, 57 (1965): 205–25.

MARQUIS, PIERRE CANAC, *dit*. *See* CANAC

MARRYAT, FREDERICK, author; b. 10 July 1792 in London, second of 15 children of Joseph Marryat and Charlotte Von Geyer; m. 21 Jan. 1819 Catherine Shairp, and they had 11 children, 8 of whom survived infancy; d. 9 Aug. 1848 in Langham, Norfolk, England.

Frederick Marryat, "a model young scamp" at Mr Freeman's Academy in Ponders End (London), ran away twice with the intention of going to sea. His determination led his father, an influential businessman and later a Tory member of parliament, to get the boy a berth in September 1806 as a volunteer on the naval frigate *Impérieuse*. After service in various ships that saw more action than most, Marryat passed for lieutenant in October 1812. Promotion was delayed until 26 December because he had not been christened "according to the rules of the Established Church of England."

Between 1813 and 1815 Marryat demonstrated the first signs of haemoptysis, the expectoration of blood from the lungs or bronchi, possibly caused by an unsuccessful attempt to save a seaman who had fallen overboard. His bravery and humanity were recorded in a series of certificates dating from this period, and brought him a medal from the Royal Humane Society. In 1815 Marryat was promoted commander. He commanded the *Beaver* sloop in 1820–21 and was one of three officers to sketch Napoleon on his deathbed at St Helena on 5 May 1821. Four days later he took to England the dispatches reporting Napoleon's death, and until going on half pay in February 1822, he was employed in the prevention of smuggling in the English Channel. In 1823 he sailed for Burma, where he distinguished himself by adapting a small steam vessel for naval operations. On 14 April 1825 he was confirmed in the rank of post captain. He returned to England in January 1826, paid off his ship, and on 26 Dec. 1826 was made a CB for his services in Burma. He had one more sea command, the frigate *Ariadne*, from November 1828 to November 1830, protecting British subjects in the Azores during a struggle for the Portuguese throne.

Marryat then took up the career as a writer that he had been flirting with for a number of years. In 1817 he had published *A code of signals for the use of vessels employed in the merchant service* (London), which remained in official use until 1857. In 1819 he was made a fellow of the Royal Society in recognition of this work as well as for his skill at caricature and his knowledge of science. He would also receive the cross of the French Legion of Honour in 1833 for his services to navigation. His second work, which appeared in 1822, dealt with suggestions for the abolition of impressment. In 1829 in London he published his first, largely autobiographical, novel, *The naval officer; or, scenes and adventures in the life of Frank Mildmay*. He became editor of the *Metropolitan Magazine* (London) in 1831 and its proprietor from 1832 to 1836. By 1836 he had published eight more novels, including *Mr. Midshipman Easy*, one of his best-known works. His vivid narrations of adventures, written with zest and humour, together with his talent for characterization, brought him immediate popular and financial success.

Volatile, even unstable, Marryat became progressively more estranged from his wife. On 3 April 1837 he left for America, ostensibly "to examine what were the effects of a democratic form of government and climate upon a people which, with all its foreign admixture, may still be considered as English," but also with a view to taking action to protect his copyright from pirated American editions of his books and to escape from his marital problems. (He would draw up a formal instrument of separation in 1838.) Most of his time in North America was spent in the United States, but on hearing of the rebellions in Upper and Lower Canada he considered it his "duty as an officer to come up and offer my services as a volunteer." In mid December 1837 he marched north from Montreal with the forces led by Major-General Sir John Colborne* and Lieutenant-Colonel George Augustus Wetherall*. He took part in the battles at Saint-Eustache and Saint-Benoît (Mirabel) against the

Patriotes led by Jean-Olivier CHÉNIER and Amury GIROD. On 18 December he wrote to his mother, "It has been a sad scene of sacrilege, murder, burning, and destroying. All the fights have been in the churches, and they are now burnt to the ground and strewed with the wasted bodies of the insurgents. War is bad enough, but civil war is dreadful. Thank God it is all over." Several months after the battles, at a St George's Day dinner in Toronto, he proposed the health of Andrew Drew* for his efforts in cutting out the Patriot vessel *Caroline* in December 1837. Consequently, when he returned to the United States he had to brave the wrath of the American mob. He was burned in effigy in the towns he visited, but he weathered the storm with humour and even enhanced his popularity before leaving for England on 20 Nov. 1838.

Marryat's brief and meteoric passage through the Canadas gave him a smattering of knowledge of the region, which is reflected in *A diary in America* and other books. *A diary*, written after his return to England, was widely circulated. It contains vivid descriptions of the events at Saint-Eustache and Saint-Benoît and is one of the few accounts of the rebellion in Lower Canada written from a British point of view. Marryat is highly critical of the Canadians, believing that the chief cause of the rebellion in Lower Canada was Britain's "continual yielding to French clamour and misrepresentation." He advocates total assimilation as the solution to the colony's problems. "If . . . we put the claims of British loyalty against the treason of the French – the English energy, activity, and capital, in opposition to the supineness, ignorance, and incapacity of the French population, – it is evident, that not only in justice and gratitude, but with a due regard to our own interests, the French Canadians must now be *wholly deprived* of any share of that power which they have abused, and that confidence of which they have proved themselves unworthy." He writes favourably of Upper Canada, which offered to British immigrants the advantages of a temperate climate, fertile soil, and abundant natural resources. Addressing his remarks mainly to a British audience, he argues that the chief benefit of the colonies to Britain is as a bulwark against American expansionism. Of his other works, *The settlers in Canada . . .*, published in 1844 "for young people," is said to have been based on the Lovekin family, Irish gentry who came to Clarke Township, Upper Canada, in 1796, and there is a dubious suggestion that Dick Short, one of the characters in *Snarleyyow; or, the dog fiend* (London, 1837), was modelled on a Peterborough man.

On his return from North America Marryat ran short of money, in spite of a generous legacy and the profits from his numerous works. He moved to a property in the country near Langham in 1843 and lived on the proceeds of the children's books to which he now devoted most of his energy. He died there in 1848.

A British naval historian summed Marryat up best: "energetic beyond the ordinary, gifted in diverse ways, never common-place, uncertain in temper and behaviour, and, like many other men and women, tending to overvalue the past as it receded." Described by one admirer from Upper Canada as "a man, a gentleman and a person of force and humour," he shared the values of thousands of British middle and upper class settlers of the 19th century in North America.

W. A. B. DOUGLAS

Frederick Marryat is the author of *A diary in America, with remarks on its institutions* (3v., London, 1839) and other works listed in the *National union catalog*.

NMM, MRY/6, 11; C. G. Pitcairn-Jones, notes on sea officers. Trent Univ. Arch. (Peterborough, Ont.), B-69-001 (Marryat papers). *DNB*. G.B., Admiralty, *The commissioned sea officers of the Royal Navy, 1660–1815*, [ed. D. B. Smith *et al.*] (3v., n.p., [1954]). Marshall, *Royal naval biog.*, vol.3, pt.I: 260. David Hannay, *Life of Frederick Marryat* (London and New York, 1889; repr. New York, 1973). M.-P. Gautier, *Captain Frederick Marryat; l'homme et l'œuvre* (Montréal, 1973). Robina and K. M. Lizars, *Humours of '37, grave, gay and grim: rebellion times in the Canadas* (Toronto, 1897). Christopher Lloyd, *Captain Marryat and the old navy* (London and New York, 1939). Florence Marryat, *Life and letters of Captain Marryat* (2v., London, 1872). Oliver Warner, *Captain Marryat, a rediscovery* (London, 1953).

MARSDEN, JOSHUA, Wesleyan Methodist minister and author; b. 21 Dec. 1777 in Warrington (Cheshire), England; m. 1804 Mary Seabury in Halifax, and they had at least eight children, five of whom died in infancy; d. 11 Aug. 1837 in Hoxton (London).

Joshua Marsden was the offspring of a "respectable" and prosperous family which was reduced to modest circumstances by their father's feckless conduct. As a result he received only a common-school education. Subsequently, he must have read widely, for his published writings are literate and scholarly. In common with many others who became evangelical preachers, he was convinced, in retrospect, that he had been an exceptionally dissolute youth, who fought with other boys, deceived his parents, was "shockingly disobedient" to his mother, played cards, danced, "got intoxicated with spirituous liquors," and "was proficient in singing profane songs." On occasion, however, he "would weep" over his "own wickedness," and conclude that his "heart had in it the seeds of universal sin."

In 1796 Marsden enlisted in the navy, partly to escape the religious entreaties and reproofs of his mother. In this "shocking seminary for vice" he witnessed "profaneness in all its diabolical characters." Fortunately, perhaps, his ship was wrecked in December 1796 off Alderney. Returning penniless to England and fearful of the press-gangs, he joined the crew of a merchant ship. Once again he narrowly escaped death, and when the ship docked he stole away and returned home, fully cured of his interest in life on the sea. Having taken refuge in the country to escape the attention of the press-gangs, he was invited to Methodist services. The sermons jarred his conscience, but as yet "the idea of true piety in its self-denying and pleasure-hating austerity was by no means pleasing" to him. Frequently beset with fear that he was damned, tempted by his corrupt nature, comforted by John Wesley's sermon on justification by faith, he sometimes rolled on the floor "in an agony of distress." On Whit Sunday 1798, inspired by the preaching of George Marsden, he saw "the dark clouds of unbelief" vanish from his mind, and he "felt power to lay hold on Christ by faith." "God's love became the ruling principle, God's word the standard, and his glory the end of [his] actions."

As a new convert with "an ardent love for souls," Marsden was persuaded to preach, and he was soon enrolled as a local preacher on the Bolton circuit of the British Methodist Conference. At this point, the Methodist connection, animated by the zeal of the Reverend Thomas Coke, was beginning to establish overseas missions, and Marsden decided to become an itinerant and a missionary. Thus when William Black* came to England in 1799 seeking ministerial recruits to replace the preachers from the American Methodist Episcopal Church who had helped him to build the Methodist societies in the Maritime provinces of British North America, Marsden offered to become a missionary to Nova Scotia. At the conference session of 1800, Marsden, William Bennett*, and two others were appointed to work with Black under Coke's general direction. They arrived in Halifax on 4 October, and Marsden was stationed on the Cumberland circuit, the area in which Black had begun his mission to Nova Scotia.

Marsden remained on the Cumberland circuit until 1802 and was stationed subsequently at Annapolis Royal, Halifax, Liverpool, and Saint John, N.B. In June 1802 he was ordained by Bishop Francis Asbury at the conference held in New York, and in 1804 he was admitted to full connection in the British conference. Four years later the indefatigable Coke prevailed on Marsden to take an appointment in Bermuda, an inhospitable colony which had imprisoned its first Methodist missionary. He arrived in Bermuda in early May 1808, having again narrowly escaped shipwreck, feeling "pensive and dejected . . . the only consolation I had was in God and my bible."

Once more Providence proved to be on Marsden's side. In the slavery-dominated Bermudian society he affirmed by example his belief that the blacks were human beings, supervised the building of a chapel in which integrated services were held, opened a Sunday school in which blacks learned to read, and managed to quell the opposition of the government and the white community. When he came to Bermuda he was considered "an imposter, an enthusiast, or something worse"; when he left in 1812, there were 136 members in the Methodist society.

Marsden's arrival in New York coincided with the outbreak of the War of 1812. Unable to go overland with his family to British North America or to sail to England, he was interned, in effect, in the United States. Asbury, however, gave him a temporary circuit appointment under the supervision of Freeborn Garrettson*, who earlier had helped to found the Methodist community in the Maritime provinces. In contrast to many of his countrymen, Marsden admired the United States, a country with "scarcely any relics of that once overgrown superstition, popery. In the soil of true freedom, such a baneful moral nightshade, must always be stunted for want of moisture." He participated in several camp meetings, "those stupendous means of grace," where he was "carried along as by the force of a delightful torrent." The experience led him to conclude that God had put "his broad signet upon these ordinances of the forest world."

On 23 Oct. 1814 Marsden sailed at last for England. He never left the soil of his birth again. He was stationed on various circuits in England, beginning with Plymouth Dock (Plymouth) in 1815. In 1836, in failing health, he became a supernumerary on the First London circuit. Marsden preached for the last time on 30 July 1837 in the famous City Road chapel on Isaiah 40: 5–8, stressing the importance of early dedication to God.

Joshua Marsden was not an outstanding preacher and he never attained prominence in the conference. Although he was evidently esteemed in the circuits on which he served and earned the respect of Asbury, he was not a charismatic figure. Unlike Black and Garrettson, he did not spark a series of revivals; rather he described his role as

A rural bishop, he will often preach,
Beneath the spreading oak or towering beech;
In sylvan scenes, proclaim the saving word,
The wood his chapel, skies his sounding board;
Or to each log-hut, in the forest maze,
This woodland priest the light of life conveys. . . .

Marsden was friendly with socially prominent men such as Lieutenant-Colonel Samuel Vetch Bayard and Simeon Perkins*; and he galvanized the Methodists of Saint John, many of whom were poor or indifferent, to construct a new chapel, in whose building he took an active part. To the Methodists of Nova Scotia and

New Brunswick he was an exemplar of a simple, unadorned Methodism, in which the essential identity of the English connection and the societies in British North America, and of English and British North American culture, was never questioned.

Unlike many of his brethren, Marsden was a prolific writer. His autobiography, *Grace displayed*, his *Narrative of a mission*, and his numerous poems have few literary pretensions, but they provide fascinating insights into his daily routine, his moods, and his inner spiritual life.

Whenever possible, Marsden "divided the day into regular parts," rising habitually at four each morning. The hours from four until eight were for meditation and writing, the rest of the morning for pastoral visits, the afternoon for reading and holding class meetings, and the evening for conducting services. The bitter winters in North America were a severe trial; his Madeira became syrup; he warmed himself with glasses of gin; and on his travels he encased himself in a veritable mountain of clothing – to no avail. New Brunswick, he noted, was "far more cold than Nova Scotia; (than which no region needs be much more severe)." He commented frankly on "the map of his own miseries," the product, he believed, of his sustained inability to resist temptation and his interest in "curious and pleasing books and studies." He was consoled and sustained by his profound belief in Providence, "the glory and inheritance of every faithful Christian missionary." He admitted that many thought it presumptuous "to suppose that the great God will arrest the course of the elements at the request of a poor worm." Nevertheless, he was convinced that God gave particular answers to his prayers, rescuing him from perils at sea and intervening decisively at every crisis in his life. For him:

> God is ever near at hand,
> Golden shield from danger;
> Near the Niger or the Nile,
> Or where forests bound thee,
> On creation's furthest isle,
> Mercy's smiles surround thee!

In August 1837, after a brief illness, he is said to have "closed his eyes and without a struggle died to live."

G. S. French

Joshua Marsden's writings include his autobiography, *Grace displayed: an interesting narrative of the life, conversion, Christian experience, ministry, and missionary labours of Joshua Marsden . . .* (New York, 1813; 2nd ed., 1814), and *The narrative of a mission to Nova Scotia, New Brunswick, and the Somers Islands; with a tour to Lake Ontario . . .* (Plymouth-Dock [Plymouth], Eng., 1816; repr. New York, 1966; 2nd ed., London, 1827). The second editions of both works were consulted in the preparation of this biography. Additional publications by Marsden, including several volumes of poetry, are listed in the *National union catalog* and the *British Library general catalogue*. An engraved portrait of Marsden appears in the second edition of *Grace displayed*.

SOAS, Methodist Missionary Soc. Arch., Wesleyan Methodist Missionary Soc., corr., North America (mfm. at UCC-C). Wesleyan Methodist Church, *Minutes of the conferences* (London), 2 (1799–1807)–8 (1836–39). G. G. Findlay and W. W. Holdsworth, *History of the Wesleyan Methodist Missionary Society* (5v., London, 1921–24), 1. G. [S.] French, *Parsons & politics: the rôle of the Wesleyan Methodists in Upper Canada and the Maritimes from 1780 to 1855* (Toronto, 1962). Smith, *Hist. of Methodist Church*.

MARSHALL, JOSEPH, JP, judge, militia officer, politician, and farmer; b. *c.* 1755 in Glenkeen (Northern Ireland), fourth child of Joseph Marshall and Mary (Hagan?); m. Margaret ––, probably in Georgia before 1783, and they had three sons; d. 3 June 1847 at his home in Guysborough, N.S.

Joseph Marshall was a boy of 13 in 1769 when his family immigrated to Georgia. They settled on the Ogeechee River, west of Savannah. Family tradition recounts that the Marshalls moved to British-controlled territory in West Florida at the outbreak of the American revolution. Along with several of his brothers, Marshall joined the loyalist forces, and in April 1779 he was appointed lieutenant-colonel of a Georgia militia regiment. In May 1780 he was commissioned captain in the Carolina King's Rangers, a loyalist corps raised in the Floridas but composed principally of Georgians. The Rangers fought through the bitter southern campaign and were finally withdrawn to St Augustine (Fla), the last British foothold in the south. Most of the corps, as well as veterans of two other Carolina regiments, were evacuated with their families to Halifax in October 1783. They were disbanded there early in November and, despite the onset of winter, were then transported along the eastern shore to Country Harbour, where the loyalist township of Stormont was surveyed the following spring.

The inhospitable, although scenic, terrain of Country Harbour presented formidable difficulties for the new settlers, and within a few years many had left in search of brighter economic prospects elsewhere. Although Marshall had been granted 1,100 acres of land at Country Harbour, he too moved, to the more sheltered shores of Chedabucto Bay. He purchased land on the east side of Guysborough Harbour early in 1795 and developed a substantial property, called Glenkeen after his birthplace.

Marshall played a prominent role in the Guysborough area throughout his long life. He was appointed a justice of the peace in May 1784 and served as a judge of the Inferior Court of Common Pleas from 1799 until the court's abolition in 1841. One of the most senior loyalist officers to settle in Guysborough, he was commissioned a major in the Sydney County militia in 1794, although he does not appear to have served, possibly being disgruntled at the appointment of the less experienced but more influential Thomas CUTLER as lieutenant-colonel. In 1808, when the county regiment was divided in two, Marshall was appointed lieutenant-colonel of the 10th (Dorchester) Battalion with Cutler's son, Robert Molleson, becoming lieutenant-colonel of the 19th (Guysborough) Battalion.

Marshall also represented Sydney County in the House of Assembly for two terms, the first of three generations of his family to serve in the legislature. He was elected in February 1800, too late to attend the first meeting, but he took his seat at the spring session of 1801. Despite the problems of travelling from one of the most isolated areas of Nova Scotia, Marshall was in regular attendance through the heated debates of the eighth assembly. He served on a number of committees, principally those dealing with road appropriations, and usually voted with William Cottnam Tonge*'s "country party." Re-elected in 1806, Marshall again was usually found among Tonge's supporters. He endorsed, for example, Tonge's attempt to eliminate complimentary references from the assembly's address to the retiring lieutenant governor Sir John Wentworth*.

Marshall did not attend the 1811 legislative session and planned to retire in favour of his son John George* when an election was called that autumn. The younger Marshall and another new candidate, John Ballaine, were to stand unopposed but at the last moment one of the former members, John Cunningham, decided to run. Joseph Marshall, Cunningham, and Ballaine then met and agreed that in order to avoid the expense of a contested election the two previous members would be acclaimed. However, John George, who had not been at the meeting and was irritated at its outcome, determined to stand. His father then willingly withdrew to help with the younger man's ultimately successful campaign in the contested election that ensued.

Unlike many Guysborough residents, Marshall was primarily a farmer, and he served on the first executive of the Guysborough and Manchester Farmer Society in 1819. He exemplified the many loyalists of middle rank who became community leaders in their new homes, and indeed as a southerner he is more representative of Nova Scotia loyalists than traditionally has been acknowledged, since analysis of their origins indicates that as many as 30 per cent were from the southern colonies. One of the founders of what is now Guysborough County, Marshall was the progenitor of a family of prosperous farmers and merchants whose tradition of public service culminated in the career of his great-grandson Sir John George Bourinot*.

JUDITH TULLOCH

PANS, Biog., W. M. Marshall, scrapbook (mfm.); MG 100, 186, nos.17–19; RG 1, 169, 171–73. Harriet Cunningham Hart, *History of the county of Guysborough* (Belleville, Ont., 1975). A. C. Jost, *Guysborough sketches and essays* (Guysborough, N.S., 1950).

MARSTERS, RICHARD UPHAM, clock- and watchmaker, jeweller, silversmith, and inventor; b. 1787 in Onslow, N.S., son of Nathaniel Marsters and Mary Upham; m. 7 March 1819, in Halifax, Ann McKay, widow of a Scottish merchant, and they had at least one daughter; d. 25 Jan. 1845 in Falmouth, N.S.

According to a genealogical record compiled by William Marsters Brown, a cousin of Richard Upham Marsters, the Marsters family were English Jews who emigrated to Massachusetts. Richard's paternal grandparents left Salem, Mass., to settle in Falmouth soon after 1760. The family was probably related to that of William Marsters, clock- and watchmakers of Holborn, London, who removed to St John's in 1787 and thence to the United States in 1818. Through the marriage of his father's sister Deborah, Marsters was cousin not only to William Marsters Brown but to Michael Septimus Brown*, the noted silversmith.

At the age of 14 Marsters was apprenticed to David Page, a silversmith and watchmaker of Onslow, N.S. By 31 May 1817 he had opened a business in Halifax as a clock- and watchmaker, offering as well the repair of jewellery and of compasses and quadrants. He noted that he had had "many years of practical knowledge in the line of his profession." This experience had likely been acquired in Falmouth, for there is some evidence to suggest that after completing his apprenticeship he had moved to his grandfather's home. An advertisement of October 1819 promoted his regular services and also informed fellow watchmakers that "any kind of Watch Wheels will be made and gilded agreeably to order, upon short notice." That year he engraved a silver medal, now in the Wolfville Historical Society Museum, for presentation by the Central Board of Agriculture. Soon afterwards he produced for the 1st Regiment of Halifax militia a splendidly inscribed gold medal which was awarded on 20 June 1820 as a prize for accuracy in shooting; this piece is now in the Nova Scotia Museum.

Marsters was an inventor of note, described by historian Beamish Murdoch* as "of great scientific genius." In April 1819 he announced that he had invented, for the use of steamboats and floating mills, a "Water or Propelling Wheel" that was to function completely underwater. "By this construction," he maintained, "the largest Ship may be navigated over the roughest seas . . . [and mills] may be built in any harbour or bay where there is the smallest current without assistance of any kind of dam." Seven years later, on 16 February, Marsters petitioned the House of Assembly for help in purchasing a transit instrument to aid in improving chronometers, and that April he was granted £98 by the legislature. In his advertisements as a watch- and clockmaker in the *Halifax Journal* through February 1828 he noted that he had set up "a temporary observatory" which enabled him "to rate all time-pieces with great exactness." On 22 Aug. 1831 his announcement in the same newspaper included testimonials from the master and lieutenant of the government brig *Chebucto* affirming the accuracy, on voyages to Bermuda from 1825 to 1830, of a small chronometer made by Marsters. His was reportedly the first chronometer to be manufactured in North America.

Marsters had visited Great Britain in the 1820s and in 1832 he was living in New York. By 1838 he was resident in Windsor, N.S. An estrangement from his wife occurred around this time and in June 1838 he published a notice disclaiming responsibility for her debts. Nothing is known about the last seven years of his life. By his will, dated 9 Dec. 1844, he left his entire estate to his daughter Ruth; his executors were unable to locate her, however, and "could not say if she were living or dead."

DONALD C. MACKAY

PANS, MG 1, 160A; 1642, nos.89–133, 187; RG 1, 443, no.8; 449, no.158; RG 36, 57, no.1503, esp. item 1. *Acadian Recorder*, 31 May, 16 Oct. 1817. *Halifax Journal*, February 1828, 22 Aug. 1831, 19 Dec. 1832. *Novascotian, or Colonial Herald*, 14 June 1838. *Times* (Halifax), 11 Feb. 1845. D. C. Mackay, *Silversmiths and related craftsmen of the Atlantic provinces* (Halifax, 1973). Brooks Palmer, *The book of American clocks* (New York, 1950). Murdoch, *Hist. of N.S.*, 3: 548. R. C. Brooks, "Nautical instrument-makers in Atlantic Canada," *Nova Scotia Hist. Rev.* (Halifax), 6 (1986), no.2: 45–48.

MARTIN, JOHN WILLS, merchant, JP, office holder, and politician; b. in England, likely in Dorset; m. first 1 April 1827 Phoebe Cooper; m. secondly 24 Jan. 1839 Martha Taylor; d. after 1843.

Born probably in the early 1790s, John Wills Martin arrived in St John's from Poole, Dorset, in 1816. Little is known of his early years in Newfoundland, but in 1821 he was employed as a clerk at Trinity by George Garland and Sons of Poole [*see* George Garland*]; six years later he was posted to Twillingate. By 1828 he was the agent for the principal mercantile establishment at St Mary's, Slade, Elson and Company, another Poole firm. Philip Henry Gosse* was a clerk in the company and his son's biography of him records that there was "nothing genial" about Martin; "consequential and bumptious in his deportment, he enjoyed wielding his rod of authority."

In 1830 Martin was appointed a justice of the peace for the southern district. Shortly thereafter he became a member of the board of education and in 1834 was appointed a commissioner of roads for the district. By September 1830 authorities in the outports had received instructions from the central reform committee at St John's to ascertain how the inhabitants felt about a local legislature, a goal long sought by such reformers as William CARSON and Patrick MORRIS. Martin chaired the public meeting at St Mary's, gave the main address in which he proudly announced his full conversion to the idea of representative government, and compiled the resolutions for submission to the central reform committee.

In 1832 Martin was elected as one of the two members for Placentia–St Mary's in the first House of Assembly. The legislative process was characterized by discord, primarily between the elected house and the appointed Council [*see* Sir Thomas John Cochrane*], and by a kindling of religious animosities which ushered in a troubled period in the history of the colony. His participation in debate showed Martin had signs of promise as a practical legislator, though his speeches reflect an ostentatious and verbose manner. For reasons which may have stemmed from his arbitrary and calculating character, he also emerged as a vehement opponent of the reformers, especially Carson, whom he regarded as "his most deadly enemy."

Martin introduced bills to regulate the police force on the island, to establish light-houses along its treacherous coasts, and to initiate courts of general sessions of the peace. He opposed remuneration for elected members and, with Charles Cozens, a member for Conception Bay, the idea that bankruptcy should render a member ineligible to sit. Martin weathered a bitter altercation relating to his own eligibility, since as a mercantile agent he did not technically occupy his own premises. He fiercely defended the independence of members without appeal to their constituents. As well he supported a bill to increase the number of members in the assembly. With Patrick Kough*, he played a leading role in defeating Carson's efforts to create a municipal government in St John's. In 1834, as a member of the assembly, he was appointed a governor of the newly formed Savings Bank at St John's.

The bumptious side of Martin's nature was reflected in a celebrated incident at St Mary's in 1834–35. He, his two clerks, and a servant were the only Protestants in this Roman Catholic community of about 500. According to the report which Martin filed later, the local priest, James W. Duffy*, applied to Martin for a specific piece of land on which to erect a church. Refused the site, the priest and his flock forcibly took possession of it and began building. Martin, about to leave to attend the assembly in St

John's, charged his clerks not to have any dealings with the priest. When Duffy was refused a gallon of brandy, Martin alleged, he led his flock in January 1835 in the burning of a fish-flake erected by Martin on formerly common property which gave access to Duffy's church. Proceedings were instigated against the priest and nine others. All charges were dropped in May 1837 after it was discovered that Martin had both exaggerated and misrepresented the situation. During this dispute Martin had in 1835 arbitrarily dismissed the local constable, William Burke, a Roman Catholic. Five years earlier, Martin had dismissed another constable, Thomas Christopher, but as a result of an investigation had been ordered to reinstate him and explain his actions.

Martin did not run again for election after he had finished his term in the assembly in 1836, at which time he was transferred to Carbonear to head a larger branch of Slade, Elson and Company. That year he was appointed a justice of the peace for the northern district. On 30 April 1838 the company's branch operations in Newfoundland were declared insolvent by the northern circuit court and Martin became one of the three provisional trustees of the estate. Later in the year he was appointed by the regular trustees as their agent in liquidating the business. When the enterprise was offered for sale on 1 May 1839 it was advertised as "one of the most complete mercantile establishments in Nfld." Dividends were paid to its creditors from 1839 to 1847, though Martin had left Carbonear during the early 1840s.

In 1843 he was appointed a justice of the peace for Fogo. The fact that this was a junior appointment in the most law-abiding district of Newfoundland indicates that it was probably a stipendiary position and that he had abandoned his commercial career. His name does not appear in the appointment lists issued by the governor's office for 1849. It appears likely that he returned to England since no record of his death can be found in Newfoundland.

CALVIN D. EVANS

MHA, Martin name file. PRO, CO 194/94. *Dr William Carson, the great Newfoundland reformer: his life, letters and speeches; raw material for a biography*, comp. J. R. Smallwood (St John's, 1978), 81. Nfld., House of Assembly, *Journal*, 1833–36. *Newfoundlander*, 26 Jan. 1832; 7 March 1833; 8, 27 Feb., 17 March, 10 July, 16 Oct. 1834. *Public Ledger*, 26 June 1827; 17 Sept. 1830; 13 Jan. 1832; 11, 15 Jan. 1833; 7–14 Feb., 4, 18 April 1834; 3 March 1835; 1 Jan., 12 April, 17, 27 May, 13, 16 Dec. 1836. *Royal Gazette and Newfoundland Advertiser*, 29 Oct. 1816; 11, 29 Jan., 27 Nov. 1832; 4–25 Feb., 18, 25 March, 1–22 April, 17 June, 8, 29 July, 21 Oct. 1834; 2 June 1835; 13, 27 Dec. 1836; 8 May, 18 Sept., 13 Nov., 4 Dec. 1838; 7 May, 24 Sept., 17 Dec. 1839; 14 July 1840; 29 Aug. 1843; 14 Dec. 1847. *Times and General Commercial Gazette* (St John's), 6, 20 Jan. 1836; 13 Feb. 1839. E. [W.] Gosse, *The life of Philip Henry Gosse, F.R.S.* (London, 1890), 62. Gunn, *Political hist. of Nfld.* Joseph Hatton and Moses Harvey, *Newfoundland, the oldest British colony; its history, its present condition, and its prospects in the future* (London, 1883), 101–9. M. F. Howley, *Ecclesiastical history of Newfoundland* (Boston, 1888; repr. Belleville, Ont., 1979), 325–38. Prowse, *Hist. of Nfld.* (1895), 427–39, 664.

MARTINET, *dit* **Bonami, LOUIS**, friar, Recollet, and schoolteacher; b. 5 Dec. 1764 in Montreal, son of Henri Martinet, a soldier, and Marie-Joseph Descaris; d. 9 Aug. 1848 at Quebec.

Louis Martinet, *dit* Bonami, lived in the Recollet convent in Montreal for several years before he took the habit of the community on 6 June 1785. It is not known where he did his noviciate, but he made his vows at the friary in Quebec on 14 June 1786, and on 26 December he received the sacrament of confirmation from the coadjutor, Bishop Jean-François Hubert*.

The future of the Recollet community had been clouded after the conquest. In October 1763 Governor James Murray* received instructions concerning the colony's religious orders. He was to do everything he could to prevent the Recollets and Jesuits from recruiting new members. In the period 1784–94 the Recollets admitted at least ten members, taking advantage of the degree of toleration shown by the governors, but they conferred the priesthood on none. Although they were not expelled from their house, it was used also as a prison and a repository for the official archives of the government; as well, they shared their church with Protestants, probably from 1762.

The event that brought the end of the community in Lower Canada must have been witnessed by Brother Louis. On 6 Sept. 1796 fire destroyed the Recollets' church and convent. Philippe-Joseph Aubert* de Gaspé relates that for some days the poor Recollets were to be seen wandering about near the ruins. On 14 September Bishop Hubert secularized the Quebec Recollets who had made their profession after 1784. They would no longer live in community but as far as possible had to respect the vows they had pronounced at their profession. A short time later the superior, Father Félix Berey Des Essarts, and the 15 brothers dispersed [*see* Louis Demers*; Pierre-Jacques Bossu*, *dit* Lyonnais].

Louis Martinet, *dit* Bonami, who continued to be called Brother Louis, took up residence in the *faubourg* Saint-Roch at Quebec and became a schoolteacher. In the autumn of 1806 Bishop Joseph-Octave Plessis* made him bursar of the Séminaire de Nicolet. Its superior, Jean RAIMBAULT, was not pleased with his services. Brother Louis is supposed to have been inattentive and somewhat apathetic in performing his duties. He returned to Quebec in 1807 to resume his teaching post. François-Xavier Garneau*, Stanislas Drapeau*, and Antoine Plamondon* were among his pupils. For many years after his retirement around 1830 he made consecrated wafers for a number of parishes in the Quebec region.

Brother Louis owned large pieces of property in the *faubourg* Saint-Roch, including some granted him by the nuns of the Hôpital Général. He was a syndic at the time the first church of Saint-Roch was built and in 1826 he signed a petition for the founding of the parish of that name.

Around 1846 Louis de Gonzague Baillairgé* discovered in the attic of Brother Louis's dwelling a banner he claimed was the Carillon flag. Brother Louis had recovered it at the time of the fire in the Recollets' church, where it supposedly had been deposited by Father Berey Des Essarts on his return from the French victory at Carillon (near Ticonderoga, N.Y.) in 1758 [*see* Louis-Joseph de Montcalm*]. The flag, now held at the Petit Séminaire de Québec, was venerated as a relic in the latter half of the 19th century, being taken out only on special occasions. Octave Crémazie* made it the subject of one of his most famous poems. In 1915 Ernest Gagnon*, writing under the pseudonym Pierre Sailly, revealed that it was a religious banner and not a flag. Its presence at the battle of Carillon remains unsubstantiated.

Brother Louis, who had continued to wear the garb of the Recollets, became an almost legendary figure at Quebec as a representative of the era of New France. Abbé Charles Trudelle remembered vividly this man with the tanned complexion and quick, dark eyes who, leaning on his cane, went regularly to the seminary. Brother Louis was stricken with paralysis in the autumn of 1845. The last surviving Recollet at Quebec, he died on 9 Aug. 1848 and was buried in the church of Saint-Roch. It was not until the beginning of the 20th century that the Friars Minor, by then called Franciscans, would be back in the city.

JEAN-MARIE LEBEL

ANQ-M, CE1-51, 5 déc. 1764. ANQ-Q, CE1-22, 12 août 1848; CN1-212, 15 sept. 1827; 2 mai 1829; 3 avril, 15 juin 1832; CN1-213, 20 juill. 1843; 20 janv. 1844; 15, 23 mai, 8 août 1846; 14, 21–22 août, 1er sept. 1848; CN1-230, 3 mai 1805, 6 nov. 1806, 21 août 1813, 15 mai 1815. Arch. des franciscains (Montréal), Dossier Louis Martinet, dit Bonami. ASQ, Polygraphie, XXXI: 1–2. P.[-J.] Aubert de Gaspé, *Mémoires* (Ottawa, 1866; réimpr. Montréal, 1971). *Mandements, lettres pastorales et circulaires des évêques de Québec*, Henri Têtu et C.-O. Gagnon, édit. (18v. parus, Québec, 1887–), 2: 499–500. *Le Journal de Québec*, 10 août 1848. Caron, "Inv. de la corr. de Mgr Panet," ANQ *Rapport*, 1934–35: 358; "Inv. de la corr. de Mgr Plessis," 1927–28: 246; 1932–33: 77. Jacques Archambault et Eugénie Lévesque, *Le drapeau québécois* (Québec, 1974). Douville, *Hist. du collège-séminaire de Nicolet*, 1: 30, 34, 38–39; 2: 3*. J.-C. Gamache, *Histoire de Saint-Roch de Québec et de ses institutions, 1829–1929* (Québec, 1929), 39–40, 263. O.-M. Jouve, *Les frères mineurs à Québec, 1615–1905* (Québec, 1905). J. M. LeMoine, *L'album du touriste . . .* (2e éd., Québec, 1872), 40–41. J.-B. Meilleur, *Mémorial de l'éducation du Bas-Canada* (2e éd., Québec, 1876). Morisset, *Peintres et tableaux*, 2: 75–76, 117. Marcel Trudel, *L'Église canadienne sous le Régime militaire, 1759–1764* (2v., Québec, 1956–57), 2. Charles Trudelle, *Le frère Louis* (Lévis, Qué., 1898). *L'Abeille* (Québec), 24 févr. 1881. "Le frère Louis," *BRH*, 7 (1901): 206. Lormière, "Le frère Louis," *BRH*, 7: 267. Nicolet, "Le frère Louis," *BRH*, 4 (1898): 125. Pierre Sailly [Ernest Gagnon], "Le prétendu drapeau de Carillon," *Rev. canadienne*, 69 (juillet–décembre 1915): 304–9.

MASSON, JOSEPH, businessman, militia officer, seigneur, politician, and judge; b. 5 Jan. 1791 in Saint-Eustache, Que., son of Antoine Masson, a carpenter, and Suzanne Pfeiffer (Payfer); d. 15 May 1847 in Terrebonne, Lower Canada, was buried three days later in the old church of Terrebonne, and was reinterred on 20 March 1880 in the present one, in the Masson family vault.

Joseph Masson's forebear Gilles Masson was born in Poitou, France, in the 1630s, according to historical accounts. Reportedly he came to New France some time after 1663 and married Marie-Jeanne Gauthier in 1668, by which time he was living on the fief of La Poterie as a *censitaire*. It is possible that he and some of his descendants took part seasonally in the fur trade, but the family was traditionally engaged in farming. After some unsettled and uncertain years, he finally took up residence in 1691 at Sainte-Anne-de-la-Pérade (La Pérade), near Trois-Rivières, where he died in either 1715 (according to Cyprien Tanguay*) or 1716 (according to Henri Masson). Joseph Masson the businessman was a descendant of Gilles Masson's third son, Joseph.

Although Antoine Masson was illiterate, Joseph attended school. An only son, he had three sisters of whom Catherine alone outlived him. He was placed as an apprentice in the establishment of Duncan McGillis, a British businessman, at Saint-Benoît (Mirabel), where he began as a clerk in 1807. His contract stipulated that he was to serve his employer for two years in return for board, lodging, light, heat, and laundry; he was to be paid £36, one half at the end of a year and the other at the end of his contract. The terms store clerk and apprentice merchant were then almost synonymous. Consequently, during apprenticeship the clerk was initiated into all phases of commercial activity. Joseph probably had more than his turn at the counter, but he took the opportunity to learn how to keep the books, collect accounts, and speak English. He also familiarized himself with the manufacture and sale of potash, an activity he was to engage in for a great part of his life. The pot- and pearl ash business, which along with the lumber trade was expanding at the beginning of the 19th century, played a significant role in the economy of parishes and regions where the land was just beginning to be cleared. Once he had fulfilled his obligations to McGillis, Masson went to Montreal and found a job with a Mrs McNider, who was also in the retail trade.

Shortly after arriving in the town, Masson became acquainted with Scottish merchant Hugh Robertson, and their meeting marked the start of his career as a businessman. Indeed, in May 1812 Hugh Robertson told William, his brother and partner in Glasgow, about having just hired "a very canny lad who is going to work for me as a crier." Having had some difficulties at the start of his career, Hugh Robertson had come to Lower Canada in 1810 at the age of 33 as representative of Hugh Robertson and Company, a Glasgow firm exporting mainly woollens and other textiles in exchange for potash, wheat, and lumber of various sorts. For several years the firm seemed beset by adversity. In 1814 it was put into bankruptcy. Masson's fate hung on that of the firm – at one point he was dismissed, then he was rehired. What his ambitions were at the time is not known, but much later, when he had become successful, he remarked: "Mr Robertson has but one charge against me which is my ambition to do too much business and as he says [my] wishes to make too much *money*. but [I] always told him I would make all my Hay while the Sun was shining and why take twenty years to make a fortune if [one] can be made in five *without any risks*." Masson's career was to unfold principally within the Robertson brothers' firm.

Once in operation again, the company reorganized. To safeguard itself from reverses of fortune, it founded two firms, W. Robertson and Company in Glasgow and Hugh Robertson and Company in Montreal. As Hugh Robertson had great difficulty adapting to the Canadian climate and hoped to return for good to Britain as soon as possible, he made attractive offers to Masson, to whom he was considering entrusting management of the Montreal firm. Masson refused to join as a salaried employee and insisted on the status of partner. He was allotted an eighth of the profits in what now became Robertson, Masson and Company; the Scottish house remained entirely under the Robertson brothers.

Even before his partnership agreement with the Robertsons went into effect on 1 May 1815, Masson was sent to Britain to do the spring purchasing with William Robertson. It was something he would do so often for the rest of his life, at times every year, that he never ceased learning about the Canadian and British markets. Hugh made a revealing remark to his brother about their young Canadian partner in 1814, when he was still unfamiliar with conditions in the British market: "I am quite confident that with his experience of local market needs his expenditures will be warranted by the good selection he will make there." Choosing goods that would sell well in Lower and even Upper Canada and importing them in sufficient quantities would always be Masson's chief concerns; he often differed with Hugh Robertson, who feared they might buy too much. In 1821, when Robertson was back in Scotland, Masson reassured him: "But let the shipments be ever so large, there is not a House here that has a better chance then we have if even so good, as we have the first call of the whole of most Respectable Marchants . . . and there is no House that can undersell us. . . . At all times I recommand you to send a proportion of every articles we order if possible." As he observed to Robertson: "The care one brings to business is half the battle, and very often lack of information can work against our interests."

When Robertson left for Scotland aboard the *Montréal* on 15 Aug. 1815, not long after the partnership came into effect, Masson was given charge of the Canadian firm in Montreal. His increased responsibilities and the efficient manner in which he carried them out made a reallocation of the company's profits and losses necessary. On 31 March 1818 a new partnership agreement increased his share of profits in the Montreal firm to a third. Masson also had the use of Robertson's house in Montreal for nothing. In June 1819, after William Robertson's death, Masson was authorized to take 50 per cent of the profits.

Up till that time Masson's successes had been uninterrupted and fairly rapid, although not startlingly so. Without investing any capital at the beginning, he had managed to amass substantial sums and to acquire a great deal of experience in business. On 6 April 1818, in La Prairie, he had married 19-year-old Marie-Geneviève-Sophie Raymond, the daughter of Jean-Baptiste Raymond*, who was a businessman in the village. The son of a fur trader, Raymond traded in grain and potash, as did Masson, and he had represented Huntingdon in the Lower Canadian House of Assembly from 1800 to 1808.

By the early 1820s Masson's career was well launched, and from then on he would devote his energies to expanding his enterprises, regardless even of his partner's exhortations to prudence and moderation. In 1843 Masson wrote to Robertson: "You ought to have known that all my ambition and fealings [were] for the interest and honor of my *Firms*, as I have all along determined to beat every house around me and bring *them down* which is all in the way of trade, and in which I have not failed yet." These remarks reveal the unusually intense motives that swayed him. They also draw attention to the extraordinary effort put forth by a man utterly sure of being master of his fate, who confessed, "As I had a great deal of confidence in myself, and always knew what I could do for the business . . . the whole of my time & mind was with the business night & day and all the business was done by myself (as I was always at my post) therefore I was quite master of what could be done and this is now proven by the result of our *success*."

The fortune Masson built up over the years was based first of all on his import-export business, which gradually grew and became diversified. In 1830 this firm consisted of three companies, W. and H. Robertson and Company in Glasgow, run by Hugh Robertson; Robertson, Masson, LaRocque and Company in Montreal, run by Masson, François-Antoine La Rocque*, and Struthers Strang; and Masson, LaRocque, Strang and Company at Quebec, managed by John Strang. Naturally, then and for a long time afterwards, Hugh Robertson and Masson held more than 80 per cent of the capital of all three. In 1833 the total investment amounted to £80,200 and the value of the goods imported rose to about £100,000. In 1827 the sales in Great Britain of potash alone were worth £31,678. Masson unquestionably had gone further than other Canadian businessmen in establishing contacts with the British market, but he was by no means the only one doing so. La Rocque and Charles Langevin, to mention just two of the people he worked with, were part of this small but visible group.

Masson's involvement in the import-export business was to lead him to take an interest in the shipping trade that was not then common among Canadian businessmen. In 1825, having given serious thought to getting a ship built to carry Robertson, Masson and Company's products, he decided to buy a brand-new 290-ton vessel which he named the *Sophie*, after his wife. He had originally envisaged providing 50 per cent of the capital for this venture, but decided to take in a larger number of shareholders and in the end held only 12½ per cent. In 1830 he purchased the *Artemis* in the name of Robertson, Masson, LaRocque and Company, and in 1832 he added the *Robertson* to the list of sailing ships. It was not until 1836 that he bought a share in a steamship, the *Edmund Henry*. These initiatives illustrate the process of diversification in his enterprises.

It is not surprising that Masson was interested in improving the means of inland communication in Lower Canada. In 1821 he joined a group of businessmen in asking the assembly to incorporate a company to build a canal from Lac des Deux Montagnes to Lachine and from there to the Courant Sainte-Marie at Montreal. Along with Horatio Gates*, Daniel Arnoldi, and a number of other entrepreneurs, he made a fresh attempt in 1831, still with the idea of incorporating a canal company. Plans for building railways also interested him up to a point. In 1831 he signed a petition to get a railway built from La Prairie to Lake Champlain using wooden rails – indeed he was one of the first to put his name to the document, along with John Molson* and Peter McGill*. The following year he was an incorporator of the Company of Proprietors of the Champlain and St Lawrence Railroad, and in 1846 he was offered an interest in it.

Masson seems to have paid attention to all the money-making prospects in Lower Canada. In 1836, for example, British businessman Robert Armstrong obtained a charter from the assembly for a company to provide Montreal with gas lighting for 21 years. This firm, the Montreal Gas Light Company, built a gasworks and appointed Albert Furniss manager. John Strang and Hugh Robertson bought about a hundred shares in it and soon were urging Masson to follow suit. By 1840 Furniss, Robertson, Strang, and Masson were its sole shareholders, Furniss holding half the shares; the following year, however, Masson acquired another 25. In 1842 he himself owned more than a third of the shares in the company, which the city of Montreal sought to buy in 1845 for £25,000. But he had a broader interest in this sort of undertaking. At Quebec he and John Strang in 1842 founded the Quebec Gas, Light and Water Company, capitalized at £15,000. He and Furniss had also undertaken in 1841 to set up the City of Toronto Gas Light and Water Company. By 1842 he had invested £24,250 of the £40,000 put into it. Three years later he sold his shares to Furniss.

A merchant of Masson's calibre, bent on outclassing his competitors, was bound to move into banking, which already wielded considerable power and influence in the province through its stranglehold on credit. By 1824 he had bought a few shares in the Bank of Montreal, and he kept adding more until 1830, when he had 21. Naturally Hugh Robertson encouraged him while reiterating the need for prudence. In 1826 Masson was even elected a director of the bank. On being re-elected unanimously, he wrote to Robertson, probably to counteract his prejudices against risky ventures: "I send you this list [of shareholders with voting rights] to show some of your freinds how we stand here, in fact we are now considered to be the first House here." In 1830 he acquired another 31 shares, paying £91 5*s.* apiece. He then told his partner that he had not embarked on this course with the idea of making money, that is to say, as a speculation, but "merely to show off and it had Just the effect that I expected, that is of rising our credit [at] the Bank as well as out of the Bank with out limits. . . . If our name is on it, it will pass." Masson consequently put a lot of pressure on his Scottish partner to make systematic use of bank credit in order to increase their annual purchases from £40,000 to £80,000 at favourable rates. Clearly, for Masson a bank was not primarily a safe place for the savings of private individuals or firms, but rather a credit organization. In 1834 he was elected vice-president of the board of the Bank of Montreal. He is also believed to have done business with the City Bank in Montreal, the Gore Bank, and the Commercial Bank of the Midland District.

Although he had entered the business world without capital, Masson gradually succeeded in asserting his authority within an enterprise that operated in both Lower Canada and Scotland. It was only after Robertson, who had first been his patron and then for more than 30 years his partner, retired that he freed himself from him. Masson's unfailing loyalty had been coupled with an apparently well-founded feeling that he was more creative and productive and had been to some degree exploited. This aspect of his personality fitted well with his need to dominate. In 1847 he finally attained the eminence in his enterprises that should long since have been his, given his talent and his passion for work. At that time the Montreal firm took the name Joseph Masson, Sons and Company, while the one in Quebec bore the name Masson, Langevin, Sons and Company and the one in Glasgow Masson, Sons and Company. Only then could Masson determine the volume of purchases made by his Canadian firms in Great Britain and make use at his own discretion of the facilities for credit accorded him by the local banks.

His success would not have been so complete if Masson had not added landed property to his fortune. He had, of course, bought numerous lots in Montreal, but these could not truly complement his social prominence. From the time his success was becoming manifest, Masson began to cast his eye on seigneuries for sale. In 1832 he offered £25,150 for Terrebonne, which was being sold at auction. It had been acquired by Simon McTavish* for £25,000, sold to Roderick MACKENZIE for £3,000 more in 1814, and then recovered in 1824 by McTavish's widow, Marie-Marguerite, and her second husband, William Smith Plenderleath, through a judicial decision. There is no doubt that the purchase gratified Masson's aristocratic inclinations, which did not, however, keep him from getting all he could from an investment that some years brought him more than £3,000.

Around 1842 Masson may well have been worth about £200,000. It was only to be expected that, as a prominent entrepreneur with extensive property, he had been promoted militia captain in 1823, appointed to the Montreal Committee of Trade in 1824, elected first churchwarden of Notre-Dame parish in Montreal in 1828, raised to the Legislative Council in 1834, appointed justice of the special sessions of the peace held in Montreal in 1836, and then elected municipal alderman there in 1843. His career followed the pattern common at his level of society in Lower Canada as elsewhere. He was the major Canadian businessman of the period 1830–40. It was he who had the greatest success in gaining access to the suppliers in Great Britain, just as he was one of the few to have done business as far away as Toronto. His success proves that the obstacles ordinarily cited to account for the poor performance of Canadians in the economic field – favouritism, trouble obtaining credit, difficulty in establishing contacts in Britain and business connections in Upper Canada – were not as significant as is claimed, nor was any supposed incapacity due to ethnic origin. The essential obstacles lay in the social structures that determined certain choices.

Masson never tried to play the role of leader of a Canadian capitalist bourgeoisie engaging in economic activity within a francophone market. His colleagues and competitors came from both ethnic groups. His dealings with Charles Langevin, Charles Humberston, a commercial agent in Liverpool, the Strang brothers (John, Struthers, and Andrew), and his hired clerks, and above all his relations with Hugh and William Robertson, provide the proof. His relationship with François-Antoine La Rocque is further evidence: La Rocque had also been in the wholesale trade, but like the Langevin brothers, Charles and Jean, he encountered serious financial difficulties. When Masson wanted to open his firm at Quebec in 1828, he thought of bringing La Rocque into business with him. In 1830 La Rocque officially became his partner, in theory with a capital of £4,000 and with four shares. Not only did La Rocque not cover the amount of his investment, but he was soon negotiating with a group of Canadian businessmen, including Pierre-Louis Le Tourneux (Letourneux), Léonard Bouthillier, and Jean-Dominique Bernard, which proposed to set up a company with a capital of £100,000 and the goal of assuring the Canadians' success over the foreigners who were growing rich at the expense of the French-speaking populace. Masson was invited to join, but evidently he had no intention of being part of this group, which in fact was directed against him. The firm of LaRocque, Bernard et Compagnie, also called the Great Concern, was founded in 1832, but it did not survive the economic crisis of 1837. In May 1838 it went into bankruptcy. Masson was not, however, insensible to feelings of ethnic solidarity: his affinities with the cultural milieu from which he came were genuine; they remained, however, subordinate to economic communities of interest. That is why Masson was never a Patriote: politically his support went to those defending the interests of the British mercantile group, although this stance did not preclude a certain prudence on his part at times.

Joseph Masson was no doubt one of the most important Canadian businessmen in Lower Canada in the 19th century. He and his wife Marie-Geneviève-Sophie had 12 children, 5 girls and 7 boys, but 4 died before the age of three. The others married into bourgeois and seigneurial families: the McKenzies, Globenskys, Bossanges, Dumas, Burroughses, Wilsons, and Desjardins.

FERNAND OUELLET

ANQ-M, CE1-2, 6 avril 1818; CE6-11, 5 janv. 1791; CE6-24, 18 mai 1847, 20 mars 1880. ASQ, Fonds Viger–Verreau, sér.O, 021. PAC, MG 30, D1, 20: 432–33; RG 68, General index, 1651–1841; 1841–67. Can., Prov. of, *Statutes*, 1841, c.65; 1842, c.23. L.C., *Statutes*, 1831–32, c.58. *La Minerve*, 17 mai 1847. F.-J. Audet, "Les législateurs du Bas-Canada." Borthwick, *Hist. and biog. gazetteer*. *Montreal directory*, 1819, 1842–47. *Quebec almanac*, 1819–41. Tanguay, *Dictionnaire*, 5: 561. Turcotte, *Le Conseil législatif*. Hector Berthelot, *Montréal, le bon vieux temps*, É.-Z. Massicotte, compil. (2e éd., 2v. en 1, Montréal, 1924), 1: 20–22. Denison, *La première banque au Canada*, 2: 419. C.-A. Gareau, *Aperçu historique de Terrebonne; 200e anniversaire de fondation et congrès eucharistique* (Terrebonne, Qué., 1927). J.-P. Hardy et D.-T. Ruddel, *Les apprentis artisans à Québec, 1660–1815* (Montréal, 1977). *Histoire de la corporation de la cité de Montréal depuis son origine jusqu'à nos jours . . .* , J.-C. Lamothe *et al.*, édit. (Montréal, 1903). Henri Masson, *Joseph Masson, dernier seigneur de Terrebonne, 1791–1847* (Montréal, 1972). Raymond Masson, *Généalogie des familles de Terrebonne* (4v., Montréal, 1930–31), 3: 1700–12. Monet, *La première révolution tranquille*. Ouellet, *Bas-Canada*; *Hist. économique*. P.-G. Roy, *Les petites choses de notre histoire* (7 sér., Lévis, Qué., 1919–44), 5: 249–51; *Vieux manoirs, vieilles maisons* (Québec, 1927), 40–42. Léon Trépanier, *On veut savoir* (4v., Montréal, 1960–62), 3: 96–97. Tulchinsky, *River barons*. É.-J.[-A.] Auclair, "Terrebonne, les Masson, leur château," RSC *Trans.*, 3rd ser., 38 (1944), sect.I: 1–14. F.-J. Audet, "En marge d'un centenaire: la belle carrière de l'hon. Joseph Masson . . . ," *La Presse*, 18 nov. 1933: 47; "1842," *Cahiers des Dix*, 7 (1942): 215–54. Georges Bhérer, "Le 'Château Masson,'" *L'Action catholique, suppl. illustré* (Québec), 17 oct. 1943: 6, 11. Léo Boismenu, "Les étapes d'un manoir canadien: le 'Château Masson,'" *Rev. trimestrielle canadienne*, 10 (1924): 297–309. "Le fief et la seigneurie de Terrebonne," *BRH*, 36 (1930): 385–90. J.-J. Lefebvre, "Jean-Moïse Raymond (1787–1843), premier député de Laprairie (1824–1838), natif du comté," *BRH*, 60 (1954): 109–20. Wilfrid Le Maistre de Lottinville, "Le collège Masson de Terrebonne," *BRH*, 53 (1947): 249–52. "Le manoir seigneurial de Terrebonne," *BRH*, 30 (1924): 409. Henri Masson, "Gilles Masson (1630–1716), 'faux seigneur de la côte et seigneurie de Saint-Pierre,'" SGCF *Mémoires*, 17 (1966): 162–67.

MATTHEWS, PETER, militiaman, farmer, and rebel; b. 1789 or 1790 in the Bay of Quinte region (Ont.), son of Thomas Elmes Matthews and Mary Ruttan (Rutan, Rattan); m. in the early 1830s Hannah Major, and they had eight children; hanged 12 April 1838 in Toronto.

The early years of Peter Matthews's life are obscure. His mother was from a loyalist family and his father was probably a loyalist. It is difficult to determine where his family lived because records are incomplete and Peter's father was rather careless about patenting his lands. Thomas Matthews apparently was granted land in Marysburgh Township and then in Sidney Township. About 1799 the family moved to Pickering Township, where Thomas obtained 350 acres and Mary 200 acres.

In Pickering the Matthews family was quite public-spirited, contributing to the building of a school and working to improve the major road in the area, the Brock Road. Thomas was active as a local official, and he and two or three sons served in the militia during the War of 1812, Peter being a sergeant. Peter pledged a donation to the Methodist college to be built at Cobourg, but died before it could be honoured.

It was this desire to serve others that apparently caused Peter's death. The family was unhappy with the services provided to the rural inhabitants by the government at Toronto. Although not as prominent a public figure as his father had been, Matthews was involved in local reform politics in a small way and was drawn into the events preceding the rebellion of 1837. He was active in the political union movement of the summer and fall of that year, which was designed to pressure the British government to grant reforms, and he was evidently persuaded by some of his neighbours, most notably the Baptist minister George Barclay*, to take part in the uprising planned by William Lyon Mackenzie*. A much liked and a prosperous man who had a successful farm and the proceeds from the sale of his father's land in Sidney, Matthews was a logical choice to lead the men from Pickering and nearby townships who joined the rebellion.

Matthews's party of about 50 left Pickering on 5 December and arrived at Montgomery's Tavern on Yonge Street north of Toronto the next day. On the morning of the 7th, Matthews and about 60 men were sent by Mackenzie to the bridge across the Don River east of the city. There they were to create a diversion which Mackenzie hoped would prevent government forces from attacking Montgomery's until the reinforcements he was expecting had arrived there. Matthews's party killed one man and set the bridge and some houses on fire before being driven off by loyalist forces. The rebellion failed that day and Matthews fled, but he was captured in a farmhouse in York Township. He pleaded guilty to a charge of treason and petitioned for mercy. Although evidence about his role was contradictory, the Executive Council decided that he had been a leading figure in the uprising and held him responsible for the fires and the death at the bridge. Despite appeals for clemency signed by thousands, Matthews was executed with Samuel LOUNT on 12 April 1838. His property was seized by the crown, but in 1848, after pardons had been extended to most of the rebels, it was returned to the family.

RONALD J. STAGG

[Thomas Elmes Matthews appears on some early lists of loyalists, but not on others; see, for example, BL, Add. MSS 21827–28 (mfm. at PAC), and AO, RG 1, A-IV, 80. His claim to be a loyalist, his probable location, and some information about his family are contained in AO, RG 1, A-I-6: 1766–67; C-I-3, 14, 18; C-I-4, 40; Hastings Land Registry Office (Belleville, Ont.), Abstract index to deeds, Sidney Township (mfm. at AO); and PAC, RG 1, L3, 376: M misc. 1, 1789–1803/25; 379A: M leases/180; 380: M leases/261. There is information on the Matthews–Ruttan connection in "Ruttan of Canada: research outline for five generations," comp. J. R. Meachem (mimeograph, West Palm Beach, Fla., 1974; copy at AO), and information on Mary Ruttan's loyalist background in AO, MU 1130, no.27 ("A part of the family of Ruttan," family tree, comp. H. N. Ruttan, Toronto, 1975), and MU 2383–84. The story of the Matthews family in Pickering is told, with some inaccuracies and contradictions, in W. A. McKay, *The Pickering story* ([Brougham, Ont.], 1961). Peter Matthews's role in the uprising and some personal details appear in PAC, RG 5, A1: 99017–18, 99030–32, 104969–89; and RG 1, E3, 33: 61–63; 45: 34–42; 50: 44–47. The fate of the Matthews property is dealt with in AO, MS 88, Robert Baldwin *et al.*, opinion book, 226. R.J.S.]

MAUSE. *See* MEUSE

MEAGHER, THOMAS, tailor, office holder, and businessman; b. *c.* 1764 in County Tipperary (Republic of Ireland); m. Mary Crotty, a widow, and they had three sons; d. 26 Jan. 1837 in Waterford (Republic of Ireland).

Thomas Meagher, likely the son of a farmer, settled in St John's during the early 1780s. He became apprenticed to an immigrant Irish tailor, whose widow he was to marry. In the late 18th century, with the growth of a permanent population, tailoring like other trades was emerging in Newfoundland, and many who took it up were Irish. Nothing is known about how Meagher was to organize his craft or about its scale, but evidence suggests that between 1800 and 1807 he used British cloth suppliers and had a largely Irish Catholic clientele.

Meagher gradually accumulated enough capital to enter the retail and wholesale trade, and about 1811 he gave up his tailoring business. He was a member of the St John's Society of Merchants in 1807 and a shipowner the following year. By then he was investing in the local land market, as was typical of the rising Irish in the town, and had leased an interest in a large waterfront property to two Tipperary merchants. In 1809 he had interests in two harbourfront premises which were insured for £2,500. He also held a large field southwest of Fort Townshend and a town garden. Two years later he rented two more lots, formerly fishing ships' rooms, from the government for £120 annually. Most of these and the other properties he was to acquire were sublet to Irish shopkeepers and artisans, providing Meagher with capital to expand his mercantile enterprises.

By 1808 Meagher had bought the *Mary*, which he replaced the following year with the *Triton*; in the fall of 1809 he shipped more than 1,350 quintals of cod and other products to Waterford. On the return voyage the *Triton* carried provisions and 62 passengers, an example of the trade that formed the core of his operations for more than a decade. His trading routes quickly expanded to include other ports in North America. It was a propitious time to invest: the demand for cod in southern Europe was growing and profits from the passenger and supply trades were considerable.

Each fall Meagher dispatched orders for supplies and instructions for passengers in the subsequent season and sent local bills of exchange, usually drawn by Newfoundland-based agents or partners of British or Irish houses. Through the winter, Richard Fogarty, Meagher's principal agent in Waterford, disposed of produce Meagher had shipped in the fall, notably cod and cod oil, and also lumber and occasionally re-exports such as sugar. He assembled supplies for Newfoundland from local artisans and merchants. Meagher did not restrict his transatlantic supply base to Waterford – he received regular shipments from England, in particular Liverpool, where in 1813 he registered his third brig, the *Beresford*, to replace the *Triton*, and engaged the firm of Ryan and Sons as agents [*see* Henry Shea*]. Diversification of import products was one of the keys to commercial success in the Newfoundland supply trade, and Meagher offered a comprehensive range of commodities from food and drink to clothes and feather beds. On 1 Jan. 1816 he formally admitted two of his sons, Thomas and Henry, as partners at a time when several St John's firms were collapsing because of the recession in the fisheries. In fact, Meagher was even expanding his operations from Harbour Grace to Burin.

In 1818 Meagher moved to Waterford to supervise his trade and fulfilled the dream of almost every Irish merchant by purchasing a Georgian villa outside the town. He left Thomas Jr in charge of the St John's business with a new partner, Thomas Beck, but by 1820 both Thomas and Henry had joined him in Waterford. With the establishment of a mercantile base in Ireland, Thomas Meagher, Sons and Company could conduct its Newfoundland trade more effectively, but just when the Meaghers seemed poised to expand their business, they decided to abandon it. In June 1820 they tried, unsuccessfully, to sell the *Beresford*. That August they signed an agreement dissolving the partnership with Beck and in December they announced they were withdrawing from St

John's. Yet 1821 was one of their busiest years. The *Beresford* continued to sail and the Meaghers bought the *Betty and Nancy*, already engaged in the Waterford–St John's trade, from Beck who remained their agent. A year later, with Beck, they registered a shallop in St John's, likely to replace a schooner they had lost on the French Shore.

The firm had, nevertheless, also suffered set-backs. A fire in July 1819 destroyed the main waterfront premises in St John's and, although Meagher and Sons immediately began to rebuild, the effort was likely a drain on resources when considerable capital was being committed to the Waterford enterprise. That December the company advertised the property for sale. Meagher and Sons lost or sold at least four vessels between 1820 and 1823 and was not recorded subsequently as a shipowner, yet in 1824 it was listed among the few Waterford houses specializing in the Newfoundland trade. However, the city's trade with Newfoundland was collapsing, and in 1825 the firm leased most of its premises in Waterford to other merchants. Only one further transaction of the company involving Newfoundland is recorded.

Meagher's commercial success in St John's was based in part on the accumulation of properties which he then sublet. He followed a similar strategy in Waterford where he gradually acquired much of the extensive holdings of the Quans, a mercantile family related to him through marriage. Meagher sold his country estate in 1829 and moved into Waterford, where he and his wife lived with their son Thomas. Retired from active trade, and widowed in 1832, Meagher made a will leaving all his property to Thomas in trust for Thomas's children. He died in 1837.

Meagher's progression from apprentice tailor to successful merchant was a major accomplishment and gained him respect from all denominations. In St John's he was one of the few Catholic Irish elected to a committee of the Benevolent Irish Society, which had been established in 1806, and he served as treasurer from 1814 until his departure from Newfoundland. In 1812 Meagher provided "a very liberal gift of books" to the newly established Sunday school in the town and he was president of the parish committee appointed to organize the construction of a house for the Catholic clergy. The Meagher company ranked with merchant James MacBraire* in assisting the St John's poor in 1817 during the recession. Moreover, because of Meagher's long residence in Newfoundland and consequent knowledge of its economic and cultural character, he frequently acted as a juror or arbiter in disputes over payment for goods and services, infringements of shipping regulations, transfers of property, and cases involving theft, assault, and murder. In 1811 he was appointed to the grand jury, one of only a dozen Irishmen to be so honoured, and he also served as a fire warden, special constable, and member of the hospital committee. Meagher and his wife forged close links with the emerging middle-class Irish community, particularly the tailor-traders and the Tipperary merchant families. He was, for example, godfather to the eldest child of Patrick MORRIS and to the daughter of Henry Shea.

A loyal and impartial public servant, Meagher was rarely involved in politics. He had joined the general protest in 1811 over the government's decision to allow the ships' rooms in St John's to be leased and in 1813 was on the jury that acquitted the tailor John Ryan in a controversial suit brought by the government. Meagher had quit Newfoundland before the growth of political protest in the 1820s, and in Waterford he left politics to his son Thomas, who was to be elected the first Catholic mayor of the city in two centuries and later served in the House of Commons. The most famous member of the Meagher dynasty was a grandson, Thomas Francis, known as Meagher of the Sword. A lawyer and gifted orator, he departed from his family's position of support for Daniel O'Connell and became a leader of the Young Ireland movement; he was exiled and eventually became temporary governor of the Montana Territory in the United States.

JOHN MANNION

Basilica of St John the Baptist (Roman Catholic) (St John's), St John's parish, reg. of baptisms, 1803–17; reg. of marriages, 21 Nov. 1807, 13 Feb. 1809, 24 Oct. 1814 (mfm. at PANL). PANL, GN 2/1/A, 10: 66; 19: 120; 20: 117; 21: 157; GN 5/2/A/1, 1804, 1806–9, 1811–16, 1820–21, 1826; GN 16/1, reg. of rents: 2; P1/5, 18 Dec. 1809, 12 Oct. 1811; P3/B/14, letter-book, 1811–13 (photocopies); P7/A/18, letter-book and ledger, 12 March, 6 May 1814; 17 Aug. 1817; 9, 30 May 1818. Phoenix Assurance Company Ltd. (London), Jenkin Jones, report to Matthew Wilson on St John's, 6 June 1809 (photocopy at PANL). PRO, BT 107, 1820: 31, 84: 1822: 27 (copies at MHA). Registry of Deeds (Dublin), Deeds, 737: 579; 801: 227; 803: 424, 426; 876: 399, 401. "Extracts from the census of the city of Waterford, 1821," comp. E. W. Kelly, ed. Kathleen Kelly, *Irish Genealogist* (London), 4 (1968–79): 23. *Lloyd's List* (London), 1810, 1817. *Morning Post, and Shipping Gazette* (St John's), 22 Nov. 1849. *Newfoundland Mercantile Journal*, 23 May 1817–2 July 1821. *Public Ledger*, 16 May 1817. *Ramsey's Waterford Chronicle* (Waterford, [Republic of Ire.]), 4 April 1811–18 April 1822. *Royal Gazette and Newfoundland Advertiser*, 11 June 1810–8 Dec. 1817; 1 May 1832. *Waterford Mirror*, 24 April 1810, June 1819, 30 March 1825, 27 March 1830, 26 Jan. 1837. *The register of shipping* (London), 1808, 1818, 1820. Michael Cavanagh, *Memoirs of Gen. Thomas Francis Meagher . . .* (Worcester, Mass., 1892). *Centenary volume, Benevolent Irish Society of St. John's, Newfoundland, 1806–1906* (Cork, [Republic of Ire., 1906?]). M. F. Howley, "How Meagher became a millionaire; a true story of old St. John's," *Nfld. Quarterly*, 4 (1904), no.3: 2–3.

MENZIES, ARCHIBALD, naval officer, surgeon, botanist, and artist; b. in Weem, Scotland, and baptized 15 March 1754, son of James Menzies and his wife Ann; m. Janet ——; they had no children; d. 15 Feb. 1842 in Notting Hill (London), England.

After receiving at the Weem parish school a basic education, of the sort which so often gave Scots gardeners an advantage over their less educated English counterparts, young Archibald Menzies worked as a gardener for Sir Robert Menzies of Menzies, the clan chief, who was keenly interested in new plants. Archibald's four brothers were also gardeners. One, William, moved to Edinburgh to work in the botanical garden established by Professor John Hope in 1763 and Archibald followed him there. Hope, noting his intelligence, encouraged him to study at the University of Edinburgh, where between 1771 and 1780 he attended classes in medicine, surgery, chemistry, and botany. In 1778 Menzies toured the western Highlands to collect rare plants for two London physicians. After studying at Edinburgh he became assistant to a surgeon in Caernarvon, Wales; in 1782 he joined the Royal Navy as an assistant surgeon. He served that year at the battle of the Saints, in the West Indies, and in 1784 was posted to Halifax, N.S. He collected botanical specimens there and sent seeds for the Royal Botanic Gardens, Kew (London), to Sir Joseph Banks*, then Britain's most influential patron of science. On his return to England in 1786 he studied in Banks's rich library and herbarium. His Nova Scotian collections included lichens and seaweeds, one of which was to be illustrated in Dawson Turner's botanical history, *Fuci* (1809), and he saw plants raised from his Nova Scotian seeds at Kew.

On Banks's recommendation, Menzies was appointed surgeon to the *Prince of Wales*, commanded by James Colnett* on a fur-trading venture to the Pacific coast of North America and to China. It sailed in October 1786 and the following year reached Nootka Sound (B.C.), where Menzies spent a month collecting specimens. The *Prince of Wales* returned to England in 1789. Again on Banks's recommendation, he was appointed naturalist in 1790 to the *Discovery*, under Commander George Vancouver*, who was under instructions to take over from Spanish officers the property at Nootka claimed by Britain and to survey the northwest coast. The *Discovery* and its companion ship, the *Chatham*, left England in 1791. In 1792, and again in 1794, Vancouver was at the Sandwich (Hawaiian) Islands; when David Douglas* visited in 1834 he found that the Hawaiians remembered Menzies as the "red-faced man who cut off the limbs of men and gathered grass." In 1792 at Nootka, while Juan Francisco de la Bodega* y Quadra and Vancouver negotiated the property transfer, Menzies made further botanical collections.

Vancouver surveyed the coast south from Cook Inlet (Alas.) in 1794 before beginning the long voyage home. Whenever possible Menzies collected material. At Santiago (Chile) seeds served for dessert by the governor caught his attention. He pocketed some, planted them aboard the *Discovery*, and thus introduced the monkey puzzle tree, a Chilean pine, into British gardens. The *Discovery* reached England in October 1795. Relations between Menzies and Vancouver, now a sick, irascible man, had become strained. Menzies had had to take on the duties of the ship's surgeon, as well as preserve the plants destined for Kew. The destruction of a number of them during a rainstorm caused a quarrel which led Vancouver to recommend a court-martial for Menzies, but Menzies later apologized and Vancouver withdrew his charges.

Menzies served in the Royal Navy, mostly in the West Indies, until 1802, when he was forced by asthma to resign. Thereafter he practised medicine in London, busy with patients and much esteemed by naturalists, particularly for his knowledge of mosses and ferns. In 1799 he had received an MD from King's College, Aberdeen. He retired in 1826 and died in 1842 at the age of 88. His portrait by Eden Upton Eddis hangs at Burlington House, London, in the rooms of the Linnean Society, to which he had been elected in 1790.

Menzies's contribution to science by publication was small. However, between 1783 and 1795 he gathered at least 400 species new to science, a number of them from the western coast of North America, especially Vancouver Island. Through his collections in an area botanically so little known, he added much to the pool of information. His specimens, along with those collected by John Scouler, John Richardson*, Thomas Drummond,* and David Douglas, were of great value to the noted botanist Sir William Jackson Hooker for his *Flora Boreali-Americana* (2v., London, 1840), and Hooker named *Silene menziesii* in his honour. Menzies was a skilled botanical artist; Hooker published several of his accurate and sensitive drawings of plants. His other discoveries included the madroño (*Arbutus menziesii*), one of the most beautiful of Canadian trees, and the Douglas fir (*Pseudotsuga menziesii*), popularly named for David Douglas and one of the tallest trees in the country. Western species of delphinium, ribes, and spiræa, among other plants, likewise bear the botanical epithet *menziesii*. Other species named for him grow in Hawaii, New Zealand, and Australia. A number of place names in present-day British Columbia, notably Menzies Bay and Mount Menzies, commemorate him. His private herbarium is in the Royal Botanical Garden, Edinburgh, and there are numerous specimens collected by him in the herbaria of the British Museum (Natural History), London, and the Royal Botanic Gardens, Kew.

WILLIAM T. STEARN

Of Archibald Menzies's small body of published research, only one report pertains to Canada: "A description of the anatomy of the sea otter, from a dissection made November 15th, 1795," written jointly with Everard Home and published in the Royal Soc. of London, *Philosophical Trans.*, 86 (1796): 385–94. Several other scientific papers are mentioned in his *DNB* biography. Menzies kept extensive journals during the voyage of the *Discovery*, portions of which have been published as *Hawaii Nei 128 years ago*, [ed. W. F. Wilson] (Honolulu, 1920); *Menzies' journal of Vancouver's voyage, April to October, 1792*, ed. C. F. Newcombe and John Forsyth (Victoria, 1923); "Archibald Menzies' journal of the Vancouver expedition: extracts covering the visit to California," ed. Alice Eastwood, Calif. Hist. Soc., *Quarterly* (San Francisco), 2 (1924): 265–340; and "Le *Discovery* à Rapa et à Tahiti, 1791–1792; journal d'Archibald Menzies," ed. Dorothy Shineberg, Soc. d'études océaniennes (Polynésie Orientale), *Bull.* (Papeete, Tahiti), 18 (1981): 789–826.

GRO (Edinburgh), Weem, reg. of births and baptisms, 15 March 1754. Univ. of Aberdeen Library, MS and Arch. Sect. (Aberdeen, Scot.), King's College and Univ., record of MD degree, 22 July 1799. Univ. of Edinburgh Library, Special Coll. Dept., Medical matriculation index, 1771–80. "Archibald Menzies," Linnean Soc. of London, *Proc.*, 1 (1842): 139–41. *The Banks letters: a calendar of the manuscript correspondence of Sir Joseph Banks* . . . , ed. W. R. Dawson (London, 1958). *Gentleman's Magazine*, January–June 1842: 668–69. George Vancouver, *A voyage of discovery to the North Pacific Ocean and round the world, 1791–1795*, ed. W. K. Lamb (4v., London, 1984). *Dictionary of British and Irish botanists and horticulturists, including plant collectors and botanical artists*, comp. Ray Desmond, intro. W. T. Stearn (London, 1977). G. [S.] Godwin, *Vancouver; a life, 1757–1798* (London, 1930; repr. New York, 1931). F. R. S. Balfour, "Archibald Menzies, 1754–1842, botanist, zoologist, medico and explorer," Linnean Soc. of London, *Proc.*, 156 (1943–44): 170–83. D. J. Galloway and E. W. Groves, "Archibald Menzies, MD, FLS (1754–1842), aspects of his life, travels and collections," *Arch. of Natural Hist.* (London), 14 (October 1987): 3–43. W. L. Jepson, "The botanical explorers of California, 6: Archibald Menzies," *Madroño* (San Francisco and Oakland, Calif.), 1 (1929): 262–66. J. J. Keevil, "Archibald Menzies, 1754–1842," *Bull. of the Hist. of Medicine* (Baltimore, Md.), 22 (1948): 796–811.

MENZIES, GEORGE, printer, newspaperman, and poet; b. 1796 or 1797 in Kincardine, Scotland; m. 13 Feb. 1841 Harriet Burton; d. 4 March 1847 in Woodstock, Upper Canada.

On 3 April 1846 and on many occasions thereafter the *Woodstock Herald, and Brock District General Advertiser*, edited by George Menzies, carried a notice of the planned publication of his "Poetical Scraps," "the scatterings of nearly thirty years' intercourse with the Press, having occasionally found their way into some of the most distinguished periodicals in both hemispheres." Menzies intended to publish the book on subscription, the most common way for poets to proceed at the time, but it did not appear. Instead his widow, who carried on with the paper, succeeded in publishing the volume in 1850 as *The posthumous works of the late George Menzies*. These "Poetical Scraps" have the air of being a personal record and, therefore, provide a glimpse into the religious life, the loyalties, and the frame of mind of a Scottish emigrant of humble origins who by his own desire and tenacity carved a niche for himself as a moderate voice in the provincial press of Upper Canada.

According to Menzies's obituary in the *Herald*, he trained as a gardener in his native Scotland and served his apprenticeship in the area of Brechin, but upon completing his training he indulged his love of history and literature by travelling through the country visiting the sites of battles and places referred to in song and story. Menzies "cultivated" his mind to the extent that he became qualified to teach and served for several years as a schoolmaster in Scotland. In 1833 he emigrated to Upper Canada, probably for the common reason of anticipated opportunity to better his condition although several of the poems dwell on a disappointment in love, apparently around his 30th year, and others acknowledge an attraction to "sublime" sites such as Niagara Falls.

Indeed, it appears that Menzies was immediately drawn to the Niagara area and he maintained a lifelong fascination with the falls, which he expressed in his writing and in collecting both whimsical and serious literary curiosities about them. In 1846 he published these in a slim volume, *Album of the Table Rock*, which also included his own guide to points of interest for tourists. Ten years earlier Menzies had served his apprenticeship as a newspaperman and printer in the Niagara area, with the *St. Catharines Journal*. Thereafter he joined the *Niagara Reporter* and in September 1837, with John Simpson*, he founded the *Niagara Chronicle*. Menzies left the *Chronicle* some time in 1839 and may have worked briefly with Thomas DALTON on the Toronto *Patriot*. In July 1840, in partnership with Alexander Hay, he launched the *Woodstock Herald, and Brock District General Advertiser*, of which he was the editor. Hay left the *Herald* in October 1846 and Menzies carried on alone until his death early the next year.

The motto of the *Herald* was "British Connection, With Responsible Government," clearly reflecting the moderate outlook of its editor. When in November 1846 Menzies was charged by a correspondent with being a fence-straddler, he replied it was indeed so, but the fence he straddled was the British constitution; from that fence, he said, he was able to look down on the antagonistic flocks. This had always been his position, and he reminded his readers of his original prospectus, which had asserted his intent to be non-partisan, "conservative but not bigoted – liberal but not levelling." His wish was to preserve the British constitution as the basis of government in the Canadas, but to acknowledge that "new circumstances may render necessary a new system of tactics." Such an outlook naturally made him an opponent of the radicalism of William Lyon Mackenzie* and a supporter of responsible government, which in 1846 he urged the new governor-in-chief, Lord Elgin [Bruce*], to move toward with understanding and swift decision.

Menzies's general philosophic outlook was that of a dour Scottish Presbyterian. Perhaps his attitude, especially in his later years, was chastened by his apparently frequent illness, although his poetry and his editorial observations indicate a life of hard work as well as a religious conviction that life is a trial and an illusion that must be endured, the only relief being that "safe harbour on the shores of some world in which there is no time at all." Even when his writing diverges from such themes, the issues and tones are still serious and sombre. There is a good deal of nostalgia for his native land with its personal associations, picturesque beauty, and tradition of minstrelsy. His favourite poet, not surprisingly, was Burns, whose work he sometimes emulated, but he indicates that he had studied the classics and was fond of reading the British poets of his time.

Nostalgia was not constant. In fact the *Herald* reveals quite a different facet to Menzies's personality, for it was his custom frequently to replace the political editorial with a folksy column of sardonic humour entitled "Extracts from an unpublished dictionary." Each column is comprised of an alphabetical list, one word for each letter, with definitions calculated to ridicule the follies and pretensions of individuals and institutions. Eloquence, for example, is "the power of employing many words of equivocal, or no, meaning, generally used in parliaments and pulpits." In such columns as well as in his other journalistic and poetic pursuits Menzies evinced a basically sceptical view of human activities and sought to be the "guardian of existing good."

CARL BALLSTADT

The main collection of Menzies's poetry, *The posthumous works of the late George Menzies, being a collection of poems, sonnets, &c., &c., written at various times when the author was connected with the provincial press*, was published by his widow in Woodstock, [Ont.], in 1850; an edition also appeared in Aberdeen, Scot., in 1854. Menzies himself edited and published *Album of the Table Rock, Niagara Falls, C.W., and sketches of the falls, &c.* (Niagara [Niagara-on-the-Lake, Ont.], 1846).

Chatham Gleaner of News, Literature & General Intelligence (Chatham, [Ont.]), 16 March 1847. *St. Catharines Journal*, 11 March 1847. *Woodstock Herald, and Brock District General Advertiser*, July 1840–March 1847. J. J. Talman, "Three Scottish-Canadian newspaper editor poets," *CHR*, 28 (1947): 166–77.

MERRITT, NEHEMIAH, businessman and JP; b. 1 Dec. 1770 in Rye, N.Y., fifth son of Thomas Merritt and Amy Purdy; m. 29 Jan. 1802 Isabella Milby of Shelburne, N.S.; d. 25 May 1842 in Saint John, N.B.

The Merritt family were loyalists of modest circumstances who left Westchester County, N.Y., following the American revolution. Young Nehemiah went to Parrtown (Saint John) in 1783 with his parents and adult brothers. By the time he reached his mid 20s himself several members of his family had left the city, notably his brother THOMAS.

Merritt began his career as a fisherman and was admitted a freeman fisherman of the city of Saint John in 1795. He gradually moved from the retailing of fish to the function of general merchant, working for a time in partnership with Gregory VanHorne. By middle age he had been admitted to the inner circle of the city's merchant élite. He owned his own wharf in Saint John Harbour – and was one of the first merchants permitted to extend his wharf past the low-water line – participated in the marine carrying trades and in the purchase and sale of ships, and in 1820 was among the 20 men who successfully petitioned for the creation of the Bank of New Brunswick. Merritt shared in the expanding timber trade of the 1820s and 1830s. By 1837 his was one of the principal private accounts handled by the bank. Four years later his firm was operating four vessels totalling nearly 1,600 tons, and the editor of the *Morning News*, George Edward Fenety*, included it in a list of companies involved in the processing of timber at Carleton (Saint John). In addition Merritt served as a director of the Bank of New Brunswick, the New Brunswick Fire Insurance Company, the New Brunswick Mining Company, and the Saint John Mechanics' Whale Fishing Company and acted as president of the Saint John Marine Insurance Company. At the time of his death he was reputed to be the wealthiest man in Saint John.

Despite the influential role that Merritt played in the business community, he always remained on the margin in terms of social recognition of his prominence. As late as 1829 he served as a grand juror, a position usually reserved for lesser merchants on the rise and for respectable master tradesmen. He was appointed a port warden of Saint John that year but was denied the coveted honour of being named a magistrate of the county and city of Saint John until 1834. He was 64 years old before he attained this sign of gentility.

Merritt remained active well into old age. In 1835 he was part of the consortium that proposed to build a bridge over the Saint John River near the Reversing Falls. Five years later he was one of a group of merchants who participated in the tariff debate on the side of local flour millers. He died at his residence in

Saint John on 25 May 1842. A freemason, he had been a member of the Church of England.

Apart from the considerable investment he had in his firm, Merritt left an estate valued at more than £40,000. He had invested heavily in city bonds and by 1842 had been the city's largest private creditor, holding more than £8,000 of the civic debt. Most of the remainder of his estate was invested in real estate. He owned 12 lots and houses in Saint John and 17 acres of prime development land around the city, another 1,100 acres in the Saint John River valley, 800 acres in Nova Scotia, more than 3,300 acres in Northumberland and Norfolk counties, Upper Canada, three New York City houses, and farms at Niagara Falls, N.Y., and Pembroke, Maine. His will provided a life interest in the family home and £300 a year to his widow. The remainder of the estate was divided in roughly equal proportions among three sons and a daughter.

T. W. Acheson

N.B. Museum, Bank of New Brunswick, ledger, 1837–38; Saint John, "Register of voters," 1785–1860. PANB, RG 2, RS8, magistrates, Saint John, 1834; RG 4, RS24, S45-P54, S53-P142; RG 7, RS71, B6: 131–43. N.B., House of Assembly, *Journal*, 1842, app.: cclvii–cclxxii. *A schedule of the real estate belonging to the mayor, aldermen and commonalty of the city of Saint John . . . January, 1842* (Saint John, N.B., 1849; copy at PANB). *Morning News* (Saint John), 28 April 1841. *New-Brunswick Courier*, 18 March 1815; 8 April 1820; 14 March, 6 June 1829; 28 May 1842. W. F. Bunting, *History of St. John's Lodge, F. & A. M. of Saint John, New Brunswick, together with sketches of all masonic bodies in New Brunswick from A.D. 1784 to A.D. 1894* (Saint John, 1895).

MERRITT, THOMAS, army and militia officer and office holder; b. 28 Oct. 1759 in Bedford, N.Y., son of Thomas Merritt and Amy Purdy; brother of Nehemiah; m. 27 July 1781 Mary Hamilton in Charleston, S.C., and they had one son and five daughters; d. 12 May 1842 in St Catharines, Upper Canada.

In his memoirs, Thomas Merritt stated that he was "educated at Harwood [Harvard?] College for a Physician." When the American Revolutionary War broke out his father remained loyal to the crown and moved his family to New York City. On 1 May 1778, perhaps through the influence of his father, Merritt obtained a cornetcy in Emmerich's Chasseurs, subsequently transferring to the Queen's Rangers under John Graves Simcoe*. Merritt spent the war fighting in the southern colonies, and Simcoe was impressed with the young officer. On one occasion Merritt was captured and crammed "with about Twenty others . . . in a small nasty dark place, made of logs, called a Bull pen." He immediately organized his fellow prisoners, led them in a successful escape, and brought the party 50 miles to British-controlled territory. Offered a lieutenancy in another corps as a reward, Merritt declined, to Simcoe's great relief.

In 1782 Merritt and his bride followed the British army to New York. The next year they accompanied the Queen's Rangers and most of the Merritt family to New Brunswick, where Merritt tried to live the life of a retired officer after he was placed on half pay in October. In March 1790 the couple appears to have been in Bedford, N.Y. Merritt was soon tempted to join his old commander in Upper Canada. He travelled in 1794 to Newark (Niagara-on-the-Lake), where Simcoe "gave him so great encouragement" that he brought his family and settled on Twelve Mile Creek, near present-day St Catharines.

The Merritts seem to have adapted to the routine of pioneer life and became pillars of the community on the Niagara peninsula. Simcoe assigned Merritt 2,000 acres in the western part of the province and made grants to all his children, and in 1798 Merritt successfully petitioned for two town lots in Newark. Late that year he received the appointment of deputy surveyor of the king's woods, and on 5 Oct. 1803 he became sheriff of the Niagara District. Merritt's prominence was also reflected by his presence on the executive of the local agricultural society. Despite evidence that he was never a good farmer or businessman, he and his family appear to have lived comfortably.

With the outbreak of war between Britain and the United States in 1812, Merritt was appointed major commandant of a troop of militia cavalry named the Niagara Light Dragoons. During the battle of Queenston Heights, Merritt appears to have served Major-General Roger Hale Sheaffe* well after the death of Sir Isaac Brock*. He later accepted part of the blame for the lack of preparedness on the heights, telling a family friend that no sentry had been posted because "they thought the Devil himself could not get up there." Three days after the battle Merritt was a pallbearer at Brock's funeral.

From that point Merritt, while retaining nominal command of the dragoons, increasingly left active command to his son, William Hamilton*. He was ill in October 1813 and unable to retreat with the British army from Four Mile Creek to Burlington Heights (Hamilton) [*see* John Vincent]. As a result, he was taken prisoner to Fort George, near Niagara (Niagara-on-the-Lake), by the traitor Joseph Willcocks* and held for a short time. It is not clear whether his house was burned when Niagara was destroyed by the Americans in December, but he did suffer some damages. In July 1814 Merritt had to oversee the executions of convicted traitors ordered by the "Bloody Assize" [*see* Jacob Overholser*]. His son felt that this experience affected him profoundly and perhaps caused him to retire prematurely from official duties. Nevertheless, Merritt remained sheriff until January 1820.

In the years following the war Merritt's shortcomings as a farmer appear to have got him into some difficulty, and it was only through his son's financial acumen that his affairs were put on a solid footing. By the 1820s Merritt was in retirement, but he continued to be amused by the "daily routine of life" and "a choice selection of friends." He "spends his time at the corner or spreading the news," wrote his daughter-in-law. Merritt took particular pleasure in parties. On the occasion of his 76th birthday a family friend commented that he "got through dinner about 6 in the evening danced and played cards till 10 next day." At his burial another friend remarked that "there was a Grate many People more than I evere See at any Funeral before."

Thomas Merritt is a good example of an Upper Canadian loyalist from a reasonably prosperous background who, thanks to his connections and perseverance, attained a position of some prominence in his new land. His experiences as a young subaltern hardly fitted him for the offices to which he was appointed, but in his old age he was one of the most popular citizens in St Catharines.

CARL CHRISTIE

AO, MS 74. PAC, MG 24, E1; K2. *Doc. hist. of campaign upon Niagara frontier* (Cruikshank). G.B., WO, *Army list*. *Officers of British forces in Canada* (Irving). C. J. Ingles, *The Queen's Rangers in the Revolutionary War*, ed. H. M. Jackson (n.p., 1956).

METCALFE, CHARLES THEOPHILUS, 1st Baron METCALFE, colonial administrator; b. 30 Jan. 1785 in Calcutta, second son of Major Thomas Theophilus Metcalfe and Susanna Selina Sophia Debonnaire, widow of John Smith; d. 5 Sept. 1846 at Malshangar, near Basingstoke, England.

Charles Theophilus Metcalfe came to the Canadas at the end of a long career in colonial administration. Of old Yorkshire and Irish stock, he was inordinately proud of his father, who had acquired a substantial fortune as agent for military stores in the East India Company at Calcutta. A few months after Metcalfe's birth, the family returned to England, where Major Metcalfe was elected a director of the company (1789) and a member of parliament (1796). He was created baronet in 1802. Metcalfe's mother was the daughter of a South African colonist. Reserved, strong willed, and ambitious for her children, she doted on Metcalfe's elder brother, Theophilus John.

Metcalfe's education began at an undistinguished preparatory school in Bromley, Kent. In 1796 he went to Eton College. Although totally uninterested in sports and overshadowed by the talented Theophilus John, he was profoundly happy there. He read Gibbon, Ariosto, Voltaire, and Rousseau for leisure, in a training that was self-consciously directed at future greatness. In frequent conflicts with Theophilus and in occasional disputes with college masters, he developed the habit, which he called "holding out," of persisting doggedly in a crisis until he had won or irretrievably lost.

Reluctantly leaving Eton in March 1800 and abandoning the prospect of further education at Oxford or Cambridge, Metcalfe took up the Bengal writership his father had obtained for him in the East India Company. He was by then 16, short in stature, and very plain in looks; his considerable intelligence was matched by a warm, equable disposition, deep attachment to his family, and the fortunate capacity to keep the cares of the day separate from the other compartments of his life. An Anglican, he was already sincerely religious.

Metcalfe arrived in India near the start of one of the last spurts in the expansion that, between 1757 and 1818, would establish Britain as the dominant power on the Indian subcontinent. Although ill adapted to conquest – he rode poorly and disliked hunting and shooting – he established his military credentials at the storming of Dig in 1804 as a volunteer in the advance guard of Lord Lake. In general, however, he stuck to "the political line." His first major assignment, in 1808–9, was a mission to Ranjit Singh, the great Sikh maharajah of the Punjab, with whom by hard bargaining and threats he concluded a treaty that somewhat unjustifiably established his reputation as a skilled negotiator. Between 1811 and 1818, and again from 1825 to 1827, he was the resident at Delhi, a key post on the frontier of British India, where he was the *de facto* ruler, largely independent of the British government at Calcutta and yet the centre of a web of imperial diplomacy stretching into Nepal and the states of central Asia.

As British rule moved into a phase dominated by consolidation and reform, Metcalfe made a corresponding transition, becoming in 1827 a member of the Supreme Council of India. His position as the second most important figure in the administration was recognized by his appointment as provisional governor general in December 1833, a rank which he held until 1838. On 20 March 1835 he became acting governor general after Lord William Cavendish Bentinck retired because of ill health. But disappointment, undiminished by the receipt of a GCB on 14 March 1836, followed. The non-confirmation by the whig government of his appointment as governor general was the first of several slights, as he perceived them to be. Rather than sacrifice dignity or principle, he resigned from the East India Company on 1 Jan. 1838. Although he had never married, he had fathered three Eurasian sons during his years in India.

Back in England after 37 years, the bearer of a high reputation, a personal fortune of £100,000, and a baronetcy (since the death of Theophilus John on 14 Aug. 1822), Metcalfe hankered for the large responsibilities and heavy work-load of the past. He accepted the governorship of Jamaica and during his tenure, from 26 Sept. 1839 to 21 May 1842, succeeded in surmounting, at least temporarily, the major crisis in relations between the intransigent plantocracy and the newly liberated black population that had been the reason for his appointment. In consequence, he was recognized as a great conciliator, and it was probably this factor, together with belief in his "superior powers of Government," that led Lord Stanley, colonial secretary in the conservative administration of Sir Robert Peel, to offer Metcalfe the post of governor-in-chief of the province of Canada. The offer was accepted on 19 Jan. 1843.

Like Jamaica, the Canadas were thought to be in crisis. In September 1842 Metcalfe's predecessor, Sir Charles BAGOT, had overcome a political deadlock by calling the Lower Canadian and Upper Canadian reformers under Louis-Hippolyte La Fontaine* and Robert Baldwin* to his Executive Council. This "great measure," as Bagot termed it, compromised two major aspects of imperial policy, anglicization of the Canadians and maintenance of the method of governing used by Lord Sydenham [THOMSON], the latter involving rule by the governor with the support of a non-party executive and a non-party majority in the House of Assembly. While accepting Bagot's assurances that he had averted recognition of responsible government in the extreme or party form advocated by Baldwin, the British government deeply regretted his action, and it chose Metcalfe in the hope that, without repudiating the "great measure," he might, in some vaguely defined way, return the implementation of British policy in the colony to a firm footing.

Assuming office on 30 March 1843, Metcalfe soon reached an unusual assessment of the colonial situation. On the one hand, he concluded that the Canadians had been justifiably aggrieved at their exclusion from office and that Bagot's remedying of this evil was the chief of the "very beneficial effects" of his administration. On the other hand, it was clear to him that the events of September 1842 and the fatal illness that afflicted Bagot from late in that year had convinced all parties in Canada that responsible government had been introduced in a more extreme form than Bagot had conceded. The members of the Executive Council were considered to be ministers and to constitute a cabinet. That "cabinet" was now dominated by one party, almost all its members acknowledging the leadership of La Fontaine and Baldwin and conceiving, as Metcalfe saw it, that their interest lay in strengthening their support largely through the distribution of patronage. In short, the constitutional position had already passed beyond that he had been sent to remedy.

Temperament, training, and his instructions prevented Metcalfe from accepting this situation. He meant to be the effective head of the administration, consulting the council whenever law, usage, or the public good required but taking ultimate responsibility himself. He intended to conciliate all parties, and viewed patronage as an essential instrument to that end. He would be neither "a nullity" nor "a tool in the hands of party." More clearly even than Baldwin, he understood that this plan of administration was consistent with responsible government as interpreted by his predecessors Lord Durham [LAMBTON], Sydenham, and Bagot, and that it differed fundamentally from the party government to which La Fontaine in particular was now wedded. The great difficulty was not that Metcalfe regarded Sydenham's method of governing as ill adapted to colonial circumstances, which he did, but rather that sustaining it imposed on him the necessity of maintaining a majority in the Legislative Assembly, which, in the event of a clash with La Fontaine and Baldwin, would be extremely difficult. By 10 May Metcalfe considered such a clash inevitable.

Metcalfe tried to ensure that, when the conflict occurred, it took place on an issue and in circumstances of his own choosing. Yet he also sought to avert it. The ministers too were anxious for harmony. Initially, therefore, Metcalfe's relations with them were cordial, and even later he agreed with them on many issues. At its first meeting the Executive Council presented him with three urgent problems; he strongly supported its recommendations. He reported to Stanley that the council's choice, Montreal, was "decidedly the fittest place" to be capital of the union, and he appealed to the home government to announce this decision as its own, in an effort to minimize opposition in Upper Canada. Similarly, Metcalfe urged the imperial authorities to grant a general amnesty for all offences except murder committed during the rebellions of 1837–38. Finally, he asked Stanley that he be permitted, despite instructions to the contrary, to announce at the opening of the legislature that, if an adequate civil list was granted by the assembly, the British government would repeal that part of the act of union which compelled the province, irrespective of its wishes, to provide the stipulated funds.

In supporting these steps Metcalfe was concerned to reduce the high level of party spirit which had made a deep impression on him at his arrival. He also showed much political realism, contending, for example, that the whole province was opposed to the civil list clause. His arguments revealed a rejection of the policy of forced anglicization. Metcalfe declared that "if the French Canadians are to be ruled to their satisfaction, and who could desire to rule them otherwise? every attempt to metamorphose them systematically into English must be abandoned." Thus, Kingston was precluded from being the provincial capital because it was "a foreign land" to the Canadians. He also urged that the act of union be amended to give French and English equal status in the legislature. Opposition to anglicization naturally improved Metcalfe's standing with the French bloc in the assembly, but it also reflected deeply held beliefs which had originated in his early education and had shown themselves in his Indian policy.

Unfortunately for Metcalfe, Stanley and Peel were already heavily committed against the measures he advocated, and, although Stanley in particular felt that he was yielding in a way he would to few governors, the British administration either rejected the recommendations or hedged its approval with so many conditions that the governor felt unable to act. He set out determinedly to change or circumvent the British response. On Stanley's ruling that the council must take the political consequences of its decision concerning the seat of government, he could do nothing. But his dispatches were to keep hammering away at the civil list issue, and he soon achieved the practical, if not the political, effect of a general amnesty partly by pardoning individuals within his jurisdiction almost willy-nilly.

The intransigence of the imperial government reduced Metcalfe's standing in the eyes of the councillors and raised doubts about his good faith. But his relationship with them was already deteriorating. From the start he waged a daily struggle to maintain what he believed was the due authority of his office. As early as April 1843 clashes occurred over appointments. Metcalfe failed to understand the thorough use tories had previously made of patronage for party purposes; his ideal was a non-partisan bureaucracy where selection rested on fitness for office rather than political affiliation. There were also clashes over policy. When the governor pardoned three leading Upper Canadian rebels, La Fontaine demanded equal treatment for three of his compatriots, including the exiled leader Louis-Joseph Papineau*. Although Metcalfe recognized the strength of this claim, he resisted until La Fontaine reached the point of resignation, probably feeling that the Colonial Office would reject the concession unless he could show that there was no alternative. Another source of conflict was the violent tory Orange order [*see* Ogle Robert Gowan*], which the reformers sought to proscribe in ways Metcalfe thought counter-productive and an infringement of civil liberties. He rapidly developed an extreme aversion to La Fontaine, whom he regarded as dictatorial. While the reformers slightingly referred to him as "Old Square Toes," "le grand Mogul," and, later, "Charles the Simple," his dispatches contemptuously described them as "the Democratic Party."

Rupture finally came when each side found the existing relationship intolerable. Before the parliamentary session began on 28 Sept. 1843 Metcalfe resolutely refused to dismiss the tory Robert Sympson Jameson* from the speakership of the Legislative Council because he regarded the executive's request that he do so as purely a reflection of party animosity. When Jameson resigned of his own volition, the governor demonstrated his independence by entering into his own negotiations to fill the vacancy. After the session opened the ministers' parliamentary proceedings led Metcalfe to conclude that on the civil list question he had been the victim "from first to last" of "a premeditated breach of confidence, such as will for ever preclude me from again seeking any confidential communication from them." Moreover, the councillors, without first informing him, announced an important change of policy, making the chairmanship of the Board of Works held by Hamilton Hartley Killaly* a non-political rather than an Executive Council position, while Metcalfe reserved the Secret Societies Bill for royal assent without previously informing La Fontaine. The governor and his ministers were also in dispute over charges made against the provincial secretary, Dominick Daly*. Finally, on 24 Nov. 1843, after Metcalfe had named a tory, Francis Powell, clerk of the peace for the Dalhousie District, La Fontaine and Baldwin formally demanded that the governor not make any appointment without first taking their advice and that he then make it in a manner "not prejudicial" to their "influence." Two days of fruitless discussions ensued, during which the executive councillors contended that this principle was essential to the operation of responsible government, while the governor claimed that it would result in the virtual surrender of the prerogative of the crown. On 26 November all the councillors except Daly resigned. Five days later, after debate in the Legislative Assembly, the ex-ministers were overwhelmingly supported by 46 votes to 23. The assembly was prorogued on 9 December.

On 9 Oct. 1843 Metcalfe had written, "I can see nothing but embarrassment and convulsion as the probable consequences of [the ministers'] dismissal." Nevertheless, he had managed to break with them on the issue and in the way he wished; now, after the ministers' resignations, he was determined not to yield. His aim was to form an administration of moderate conservatives, moderate reformers, and Canadians, and if, at its recall, the assembly failed to support the new body, to hold a general election.

The key to Metcalfe's plan was the large, compact phalanx of Canadian members in the assembly. Astutely realizing that as a group they were committed to national survival rather than responsible government, Metcalfe had already taken steps to elevate the ageing Denis-Benjamin Viger* as a rival to La

Fontaine. Now he called Viger to the council, hoping, though without much conviction, that his high prestige and extensive connections, particularly with the still-powerful Papineau family, might win for him a substantial body of Canadian support. On 12 Dec. 1843 Viger took office and shortly thereafter set off to gather followers in Lower Canada.

The conservatives were already strongly behind the governor. Some initially regretted his stand on responsible government, others, Metcalfe realized, would not necessarily be more amenable than La Fontaine and Baldwin to his notions of the relationship between the governor and his council. But Metcalfe had a profound sympathy with them, believing they comprised the bulk of the province's loyal citizens. Sir Allan Napier MacNab*, their leader in the assembly, had, by the violence of his resistance to the former administration, rendered himself ineligible for the council. John Solomon CARTWRIGHT, MacNab's lieutenant, was prevented by ill health and his wife's opposition from accepting Metcalfe's offer. So William Henry Draper*, a moderate conservative, came reluctantly out of political retirement. He entered the council on the same day as Viger and, like Viger, held no portfolio.

Metcalfe's efforts to attract support from moderate reformers were directed largely towards Samuel Bealey Harrison* and William Hamilton Merritt*, but eventually both declined the offer to join the council. For many months the outcome of the crisis remained uncertain. While negotiations continued, public opinion waxed and waned, and a struggle went on to influence it. Metcalfe was agreeably surprised by the spontaneous outburst of loyal feeling in Upper Canada that followed the ministers' resignations, a development greatly assisted by the powerful, polemical rhetoric with which he replied to popular addresses on the subject. Edward Gibbon Wakefield*, Isaac Buchanan*, and Egerton Ryerson*, three influential moderates, were early won over. They were active in support of the government, and published letters or pamphlets which appear to have had significant impact. A by-election for the riding of London and municipal elections in Toronto in January 1844 turned out favourably for pro-government candidates. On the other hand, the delay in completing the Executive Council hurt the governor's cause, the extreme reformers in the west of the province organized effectively, and Baldwin remained confident of popular support.

French Canada was crucial, and there, despite repeated assurances from Viger that he was on the brink of success, no large body of supporters was won. Metcalfe did what he could, securing pardons for Canadians transported after the rebellion, confirming Montreal as the seat of government, and even recommending payment of arrears of salary as speaker of the Lower Canadian assembly to Papineau. "The pardons of their Countrymen . . . as well as the whole conduct of the Government towards them during my administration ought to have given me some influence among them," Metcalfe declared, but he added significantly, "I see no symptoms of any such effect." In April a "readiness to oppose the British Government" showed itself in a Montreal by-election, which was won by La Fontaine's candidate, Lewis Thomas Drummond*, over the pro-government businessman William Molson*. Although Metcalfe regarded the result as determined solely by the outrageous violence of Irish labourers brought in from the Lachine Canal, he confessed that it had dismayed his Lower Canadian supporters "to a degree that I could not have supposed possible from such a cause." His advisers began to urge an immediate dissolution, but the governor, "holding out" as had been his wont, refused to play his last card prematurely. He approached Canadian politicians independently of both Viger and La Fontaine. Still the habit of unity and the powerful organization of the French leader held firm; Augustin-Norbert Morin*, Côme-Séraphin Cherrier*, Frédéric-Auguste Quesnel*, and René-Édouard Caron* refused office, and only four Canadian members of the assembly could be reckoned as willing even to support the administration. By 28 July 1844 the negotiations with the Canadians had virtually ended.

The formation of the Executive Council was now rapidly completed. It proved to be a satisfactory but undistinguished body. Denis-Benjamin Papineau* accepted the commissionership of crown lands. The attorney generalship east was finally occupied by James Smith*, a Montreal lawyer bearing the twin disadvantages of British origin and lack of a parliamentary seat. Viger became president of the council and Daly remained provincial secretary. There were thus four Lower Canadians out of a complement of six. Draper was appointed attorney general west and was government leader; William Morris*, a moderate conservative and influential lay leader of the Church of Scotland, became receiver general. The post of inspector general was left temporarily vacant after four Upper Canadian reformers declined it. Henry Sherwood*, a Toronto tory moving erratically from exclusive to moderate views, became solicitor general west outside the council. The appointments made, Metcalfe changed his mind about meeting the existing parliament and on 23 September called a general election.

The campaign was short and heated. Metcalfe himself entered the struggle, playing on the theme of loyalty with great skill. Though local issues were important in many contests, the determining factors seem to have been the responsiveness particularly of the immigrant population in Upper Canada to Metcalfe's appeals and the unpopularity there of the reformers' measures. Economic prosperity may also have aided the conservatives and certainly helped to prevent the considerable violence and disorder that accompanied polling from degenerating into worse. In Lower Canada contests were generally quieter because more one-sided. Metcalfe's men won eight seats in the tory Eastern Townships and picked up Montreal itself. But in general La Fontaine's machine worked with brilliant efficiency to capture approximately 29 of the 42 Lower Canadian seats. In Upper Canada the government won all but a dozen of the seats. In total, the new Executive Council had a small but workable majority.

The outcome was a triumph for Metcalfe, and it was recognized as such not only in Canada but also in London. Throughout his long, difficult struggle with La Fontaine and Baldwin, Metcalfe had been strongly supported by the British government. Queen Victoria as well as Peel and Stanley seem early to have accepted the inevitability of a clash between the governor and his council, and they demurred only at the concessions Metcalfe wanted to make in order to avoid or postpone it. The very day La Fontaine and Baldwin resigned, Metcalfe received a private letter from Stanley which warned, "On one point I am sure it is necessary that you should be firm – I mean in the disposal of Patronage." Now their gratitude and admiration were boundless. On 1 Dec. 1844 Peel wrote to Metcalfe informing him of Her Majesty's intention of conferring a barony on him. Hé was created Baron Metcalfe the following month.

Metcalfe's triumph was won at great personal and political cost, however. Some years before leaving India, he had contracted a small cancer on his right cheek. Untreated, it worsened. When it eventually was treated, the applications proved debilitating. For a time after 1842 there was some remission, yet gradually the tumour spread. In April 1844 an alarmed Stanley sent out a physician, George Pollock, with detailed instructions from leading London specialists, but during Pollock's application of caustic chloride of zinc Metcalfe's health deteriorated. He lost the sight of his right eye; his left eye was also weakened. He bore the affliction uncomplainingly. Well aware of the impact his untimely retirement would have on the political situation, he did his work as best he could in a darkened room with the help of readers and writers. This extraordinary fortitude gained him much sympathy; it was a factor in both the general election and the bestowal of the barony.

The political cost lay in the fact that Metcalfe had set out to be a governor above party and had been compelled to enter the realm of party conflict. This contradiction would have been less evident had his new Executive Council held a less dubious claim to being non-party. But Metcalfe's administration, apart from the apolitical Daly, consisted of conservatives supplemented by two Canadians, and after the general election these two could muster but one follower in the assembly. Although the electoral balance had probably been determined mainly by moderate reformers who voted for government candidates, no reformer joined the Executive Council before or after the election. (The vacant position of inspector general was filled by a tory, William Benjamin Robinson*.) Furthermore, because of his illness Metcalfe relied increasingly not only on his civil secretary, James Macaulay Higginson*, but also on his ministers, particularly Draper, whom he considered the ablest man of business in the province. Inevitably power passed from the governor to the council, so that by late 1845 the relationship was almost exactly the one he had set out to reverse, except, of course, that the party in office was, in Metcalfe's view, a party of genuine loyalty to Britain.

It was enough, and there were compensations. By the end of his term the imperial government had capitulated on the general amnesty, the civil list, and the language question. The last was an especially significant concession, for it indicated the abandonment of forced anglicization as an element of British policy; it was granted only in recognition of the severe pressure Metcalfe was under to maintain the reputations of Viger and Denis-Benjamin Papineau and to add, if possible, to their following. In Upper Canada the government ran into trouble because its supporters had no common policy and their ostensible leader, Draper, totally lacked political influence. The parliamentary session of 1844–45 thus ended with the government being forced by its own high-church wing to withdraw its main measure, a bill to establish a "University of Upper Canada," in which Metcalfe had taken a personal interest. But most government business got through the assembly with majorities of between three and six votes. Though discontent continued among its Upper Canadian supporters, Metcalfe's experiment seemed, in the latter part of 1845, to be not without hope of being sustained.

Metcalfe stuck to his post, keen to forward the work he had begun, keen, too, to show loyalty to those who had supported him. But in October a sudden deterioration in his health left him unable to perform adequately the duties of his office. With the permission of the Colonial Office and the assurance from his councillors that he could do no more for the Canadas, he resigned. Charles Murray, Earl Cathcart*, took over as administrator. On 26 November Metcalfe left for England, virtually blind, barely able to eat or speak, and with a gaping hole in his cheek. He died a little over nine months later.

During the first half of the 19th century the British presence in India was dominated by a small group of "glorious sahibs." Metcalfe was the most complex and arguably the greatest of them. Certainly he was conservative there: his strong sense of historical continuity and his typically 18th-century toleration for other cultures made him a stout opponent of attempts to anglicize Indian society. But he was also extraordinarily progressive, particularly concerning criminal punishment and slavery at Delhi. Furthermore, he showed a remarkable determination to pursue honest, efficient government, even at the expense of particular British interests and, if necessary, his own career.

One might question the frequent statement that Metcalfe's experience in India unfitted him for the task of administering the Canadas, a colony of white settlers with an advanced representative system of government. His attitude to colonial responsible government was identical in theory with, and more realistic in practice than, that of Stanley and Peel; he was as politically successful as Sydenham, the great politician among the Canadian governors of this period, under more difficult circumstances; and, though his views became less favourable towards the Canadians in the last year of his governorship, he was as sympathetic to their aspirations as any imperial representative of the era. The relationship between Metcalfe's different careers is complex and difficult to trace because, despite the views many historians hold of his Canadian viceroyalty, he was a flexible administrator. Throughout, however, there was a common core of ideas, a consistent although developing character, and above all a constant dramatic purpose. In the Canadas, full of Byronic despair, the failing hero flung himself against the ineluctable forces of history, acting out to the last the epic in which, while still a schoolboy, he had cast himself a paladin.

Although the limited success Metcalfe won on the Canadian constitutional question did not last, his administration was of considerable significance in Canadian history. As James Maurice Stockford Careless has pointed out, Metcalfe clarified the concept of responsible government and inadvertently contributed to the full implementation of the La Fontaine–Baldwin version of it by failing to produce a viable alternative. Resolving the short-term crisis of 1843–44, he provided a valuable breathing space in which the imperial government was able to adjust to the new reality of Canadian affairs. Thus he helped to ensure that, when responsible government came fully into operation in 1848, it did so peacefully. The historian William George Ormsby has pointed to Metcalfe's more positive and deliberate contributions to Canada's development, in particular his part in bringing about the abandonment of anglicization as a major element in British policy. Finally, Metcalfe had a notable impact on Canadian conservatism, reconciling it to responsible government of whatever form. But his emphasis on loyalty to Britain as the litmus test of colonial politicians and his belief that, despite responsible government, Britain must retain significant power in the internal affairs of Canada strengthened elements in conservative thought that were to be central to their outraged response to the Rebellion Losses Bill of 1849.

DONALD R. BEER

Charles Theophilus Metcalfe is the author of "On the best means of acquiring a knowledge of the manners and customs of the natives of India," *Essays by the students of the College of Fort William in Bengal* . . . (3v., Calcutta, 1802–4). He also wrote a number of political essays, but only one, *Friendly advice to conservatives* (n.p., 1838), no copy of which has been located, appears to have been published; "Friendly advice to the working classes," published as an appendix to *Selections from the papers of Lord Metcalfe; late governor-general of India, governor of Jamaica, and governor-general of Canada*, ed. J. W. Kaye (London, 1855), is said to contain opinions similar to those expressed in that essay. The *British Library general catalogue* lists addresses delivered by and presented to Metcalfe in Jamaica and Canada.

AO, MS 35; MU 1147. Cornwall Record Office (Truro, Eng.), DD.HL(2)318–61, DD.HL(2)469. MTRL, Robert Baldwin papers. PAC, MG 11, [CO 42] Q, 505–27; MG 24, A15 (mfm.), A33, B2, B6, B8, B14, E1; RG 7, G1; G3, 1–2, 8; G14, 10–17; G17A, 2–3; G17C. PRO, CO 537, 141–43 (mfm. at PAC). *Debates of the Legislative Assembly of United Canada* (Abbott Gibbs *et al.*). Francis Hincks, *Reminiscences of his public life* (Montreal, 1884). J. W. Kaye, *The life and correspondence of Charles, Lord Metcalfe* . . . (2v., London, 1854). Egerton Ryerson, *Sir Charles Metcalfe defended against the attacks of his late counsellors* (Toronto, 1844); *"The story of my life" . . . (being reminiscences of sixty years' public service in Canada.)*, ed. J. G. Hodgins (Toronto, 1883). E. G. Wakefield, *A view of Sir Charles Metcalfe's government, by a member of the provincial government* (London, 1844). *DHB* (biog. of Sir Allan Napier MacNab). J. M. S. Careless, *The union of the Canadas: the growth of Canadian institutions, 1841–1857* (Toronto, 1967). Michael Edwardes, *Glorious Sahibs; the romantic as empire-builder, 1799–1838* (New York, 1969). George Metcalfe, "William Henry Draper," *The pre-confederation premiers: Ontario government leaders, 1841–1867*, ed. J. M. S. Careless (Toronto, 1980), 32–88. Monet, *Last cannon shot*. W. P. Morrell, *British colonial policy in the age of Peel and Russell* (London, 1930). W. [G.] Ormsby, *The emergence of the federal concept in Canada, 1839–1845* (Toronto, 1969). D. N. Panigrahi, *Charles Metcalfe in India: ideas & administration, 1806–1835* (Delhi, 1968). Gilles Pesant, "L'affrontement des deux nationalismes sous Metcalfe, 1843–1845" (thèse de MA, univ. de Montréal, 1973). Eric Stokes, *The English utilitarians and India* (Oxford, 1959). E. [J.] Thompson, *The life of Charles, Lord Metcalfe* (London, 1937). Philip Woodruff [Philip Mason], *The men who ruled India* (London, 1953; repr. 1971).

MEUSE (Mius, Mause, Muse), ANDREW JAMES, Micmac chief; fl. 1821–50 in Nova Scotia.

In January 1821 Andrew James Meuse, speaking on behalf of the "Division of the Micmac Nation residing near the Gut of Annapolis Royal," petitioned the Nova Scotia House of Assembly against passage of a bill that would outlaw shooting porpoises in the bay. He argued that the killing of porpoises, which were one of the Indians' principal resources, was a "natural right" that did no harm to the whites. He made an impressive appearance at the bar of the house. Years later, he was reported to have said: "I see among [the members] but one face that I know, and that man is trying to take away from the Indian the source of his livelihood." He talked at length of the wrongs suffered by his people and made an eloquent statement of their cause. The bill, which had already passed two readings, was thereupon voted down.

The Halifax philanthropist Walter BROMLEY first met Meuse, "the man who nobly pleaded his peoples cause," in September 1822. Meuse asked him to apply to the government on behalf of the band for a 1,000-acre grant contiguous to their encampment at the Annapolis Basin. In 1825 the two men went to England together. It was reported that Meuse hoped to solicit permanent grants of land for the Indians so that they could become farmers. According to an anecdote published five years later by Thomas IRWIN of Charlottetown, Meuse had applied to Lieutenant Governor Sir James Kempt* for land at Bear River, near the Annapolis Basin, and was told that he might have it but would receive no grant lest he transfer it to the whites. Kempt, however, gave his word that the Indians would not be disturbed in their possession of the site. Indignant, Meuse replied: "Before the arrival of Europeans in our country, my forefathers were the rightful lords of this country, and I, their son, must supplicate, in the most humble manner, a foreign Governor for a morsel whereon to build a wigwam; and yet I am refused!" Knowing what his people had suffered, what faith could he put in the word of a governor? "No; I will go to England and petition the King – from him alone I hope for redress." Whether or not he petitioned the king while he was in London, he did meet some of the leading Quaker philanthropists of the day and opened a correspondence with them. He did not succeed in obtaining a freehold grant, but 1,000 acres were set aside on Bear River at the request of Abbé Jean-Mandé SIGOGNE and judge Peleg Wiswall of Digby. Meuse was to be the man in charge of the experimental settlement.

Land was surveyed in 1827 and divided into 30-acre lots. A family that cultivated its land for three consecutive years was to be confirmed in possession of it, but was still not to be given a freehold grant; a family that neglected its holding for three years would forfeit it to another Indian cultivator. The first people moved to Bear River in 1828. The provincial government provided some supplies and the distant Quakers gave financial support.

On 12 Feb. 1828 a petition in the name of Andrew Meuse, chief of the Indians of the Western District, had been presented at the bar of the assembly by Charles Glode.* The petitioner prayed "for the suppression of the selling of Strong Liquors to Indians in the Province." The appeal eventually led to the passage of an ineffective law that left banning the sale of liquor to the discretion of local magistrates. In the *Novascotian, or Colonial Herald* Joseph Howe* editorialized on the virtues of natives such as Glode and Meuse.

The prospects looked fair. By 1831 there were 17 families, 69 people, living at Bear River; they had cleared land and brought in good crops of potatoes. Meuse successfully petitioned the assembly for help to construct a road and £100 to build a chapel. He paid a second visit to London in 1831–32, spending much of his time in the company of famous philanthropists: Elizabeth Fry gave him a portrait of herself that he later hung in his living-room. He was presented to the king and queen, who gave him a medallion.

From the first, Abbé Sigogne had been afraid that Quaker support for the settlement might in some way damage the Indians' Catholic faith. Even before Meuse's second visit to England, he was complaining that the chief had become indifferent to religion and was a bad influence on his people. Worse was to come, for at some time after his return Meuse took to drink; he pawned the royal medal and Sigogne had to redeem it. As a result of such misconduct, Meuse was displaced as chief and Jack Glode elected in his stead. In 1834, a visitor to Bear River complained that the Indians had "literally thrown away" their advantages: their clearings overgrown, they themselves feasted and frolicked until starvation forced them to beg.

Despite these set-backs, Meuse remained the leading personality at Bear River. He apparently climbed back into Sigogne's good graces, for the abbé gave him a letter of introduction when he went to Yarmouth in 1835 to raise £25 for the chapel. He is also known to have visited the United States on fund-raising drives, possibly in 1836. But the settlement continued to falter and by 1841 it was reportedly down to seven families.

Two Indians visited Joseph Howe in Halifax in November 1841. One of them was undoubtedly Meuse, who had known Howe for a number of years. Howe could not but be impressed with Meuse: here was a man who had been to London and "talks familiarly of Mr. Gurney, Mrs. Fry, and other distinguished Philanthropists." The two visitors convinced Howe that he had to think of the Indians, not in the whites' terms of townships and counties, but as bands under distinct district chiefs. They urged that each chief be given a plan and a clear description of the lands set aside as reserves within his jurisdiction, and each be responsible for parcelling out land among his people. Building on the model of early Bear River, they stressed the need for provincial assistance with tools, seed, and stock for each group, and the desirability of a house for the chief, a chapel, and possibly a school. Howe hurried to incorporate these ideas with his own in a letter to Lieutenant Governor Lord Falkland [Cary*], thus paving his way to becoming Nova Scotia's first Indian commissioner.

Howe, in his new official capacity, visited Bear River in 1842 and found a location with good soil and ready access to the porpoise and herring fishery of the Gut. There were "boundless hunting grounds" close by, and the Indians could earn cash by the sale of cordwood at neighbouring Bear River village. Meuse, despite his "infatuation," was still the leading man. The tales of desolation had been exaggerated. Most of the Indians had taken the pledge of temperance and Howe was optimistic that the reserve could become a centre for the "civilization" of the Micmacs. He identified 14 families, some 65 people, and 4 of those families already lived in comfortable frame-houses. If only Meuse were a sober man! He "would be invaluable as an Agent of the Government, and a guide and exemplar of his own people."

Disaster struck the community in the mid 1840s. The potatoes rotted in the ground, the fishery failed, and sickness caused many deaths [*see* Gabriel ANTHONY]. Meuse was one of those stricken, but he survived. Bear River recovered slowly. Meuse was among the ten chiefs who paraded through Halifax in February 1849 carrying a petition that called for aid to resume farming after the blight. The last reference to him came in July 1850, when the Baptist missionary Silas Tertius Rand* visited the Annapolis Basin. Rand was reading from the Bible when Meuse "told me in good English not to say anything against their religion." Rand concluded his discourse with a tale of war against the Mohawks long ago. Sigogne would have approved of Meuse at the last.

Andrew Meuse had married Magdalen Tony, and they had four boys and two girls. Louis Noel accompanied his father on the second visit to London. Five of the children were sent to school and became literate in the English language.

L. F. S. UPTON

Arch. of the Archdiocese of Halifax, Edmund Burke papers, [J.-M. Sigogne] to Joseph Bond, [1835]. N.B. Museum, J. C. Webster papers, packet 31, [Walter Bromley], "Report of the state of the Indians in New Brunswick under the patronage of the New England Company, 14th August 1822." PANS, MG 1, 979, folder 8, Bowman to Peleg Wiswall, 10 Oct. 1828; J.-M. Sigogne to Wiswall, 29 March 1831; list of Indians, January 1832; MG 15, B, 3, no.104; RG 1, 430, nos.21–22; 431, no.22; 432: 1–6, 111–14; RG 5, P, 2. PRO, CO 217/178: 89–101. Micmac Missionary Soc., *Annual report of the committee* (Halifax), 1850. N.S., House of Assembly, *Journal and proc.*, 1821: 30–31, 36, 77–78; 1828: 208; 1830: 578, 584, 701, 705; Legislative Council, *Journal and proc.*, 1843, app.7: 22. *Acadian Recorder*, 29 March 1834. *Halifax Journal*, 27 Dec. 1824. *Halifax Morning Post & Parliamentary Reporter*, 1 Feb. 1842. *Novascotian, or Colonial Herald*, 13 Aug. 1830. *Prince Edward Island Register*, 29 June 1830. *Times and Courier* (Halifax), 27 Feb. 1849. Murdoch, *Hist. of N.S.*, 1: 168–71. Upton, *Micmacs and colonists*. Judith Fingard, "English humanitarianism and the colonial mind: Walter Bromley in Nova Scotia, 1813–25," *CHR*, 54 (1973): 123–51.

MILES, FREDERICK WILLIAM, Baptist minister and educator; b. *c.* 1806 in Maugerville, N.B., elder son of Elijah Miles* and his second wife, Elizabeth Harding; m. first 29 Oct. 1832 Charlotte Mears in Boston, and they had a daughter who died young; m. secondly Eliza Billings, *née* Moore, of London, and they had one daughter; d. 2 Feb. 1842 in Fredericton.

Elijah Miles was an adherent of the Church of England, but his second wife was a nonconformist, which might account for their two sons eventually espousing the Baptist faith. Frederick William Miles was educated at King's College in Windsor, N.S., graduating on 17 June 1824, and while there came under the influence of the Reverend David Nutter, a prominent Baptist preacher in the area. Miles was baptized into the Germain Street Baptist Church at Saint John in 1828 and on 7 September of that year was ordained its minister. During his two years as pastor, he received 50 members into the church.

In 1830 Miles left Saint John to study at the theological seminary in Newton, Mass., where he probably met his first wife, a native of Boston. He returned briefly to serve at his first charge before being called in 1833 or 1834 to the Fredericton Baptist Church. Miles's arrival in the New Brunswick capital coincided with a growing attack on the privileges of the Church of England, especially in education. In 1833 the established church dominated state-supported schools and its interests were staunchly protected by members of the Legislative Council, which in contrast to the elected House of Assembly was composed of crown appointees.

Miles and William Boyd Kinnear*, a Fredericton lawyer and MHA, are credited with first suggesting a Baptist seminary for New Brunswick. Their proposal was discussed and accepted at the annual meeting of the New Brunswick Baptist Association held in St George in July 1833, and both were included on a seven-member committee requested to draft a prospectus. In September a public meeting in Saint John formed the New-Brunswick Baptist Education Society and elected the Reverend Joseph Crandall* president and John McNeil WILMOT vice-president. The society chose Fredericton as the site for the seminary and upon completion of a building in December 1835 appointed Miles first principal. Charlotte Miles was placed in charge of the female students. Women were admitted on an equal basis with men, and "in this respect," according to scholar George Edward Levy, "the Baptist Seminary at Fredericton pioneered for all Canada." Admission was open to every denomination and no religious tests were required. In fact, non-Baptists formed the majority of the 70 pupils in the first class.

"The granting of provincial aid to this school seems to have set a kind of precedent for legislative aid to denominational schools other than Anglican," to cite a modern authority. In 1835 the assembly approved a grant of £500 for the seminary, but the Legislative Council withheld its approval, even though the petition for assistance was supported by "about six hundred respectable individuals belonging to the several religious denominations in this province." This pattern would be repeated a number of times in the next few years. A later petition had as many as 2,000 names. Finally, in 1840, a grant of £500 was approved, and by the mid 1840s the seminary was receiving an annual subvention.

A total of 109 male and 94 female students had entered the seminary by July 1838. Mrs Miles had died in December 1837 and the next year poor health forced her husband to give up his position temporarily to the Reverend Charles Tupper*, father of Sir Charles*. Miles was sent to England to try to recover his health and to find financial support for the school. Besides a special donation for a library, he collected £415. He also married Mrs Billings, a widow with a small son. Unfortunately, his health failed to improve sufficiently and he had to resign the principalship six months after his return in October 1839. Miles continued to work for the New-Brunswick Baptist Education Society until his death at the age of 36 in February 1842.

RICHARD WILBUR

N.B., House of Assembly, *Journal*, 1842–46; Legislative Council, *Journal*, 1842–46. *Columbian Centinel* (Boston), 31 Oct. 1832. *Royal Gazette* (Fredericton), 15 April 1840. I. L. Hill, *Old Burying Ground*; *Some loyalists and others* (Fredericton, 1976). Newton Theological Institution, *Historical catalogue* (12th ed., Newton Centre, Mass., 1925). Bill, *Fifty years with Baptist ministers*. H. G. Davis, *The history of the Brunswick Street United Baptist Church . . .* ([Fredericton, 1964]). Levy, *Baptists of Maritime prov.* K. F. C. MacNaughton, *The development of the theory and practice of education in New Brunswick, 1784–1900: a study in historical background*, ed. A. G. Bailey (Fredericton, 1947). Saunders, *Hist. of Baptists*. A. A. Trites, "The New Brunswick Baptist Seminary, 1833–1895," *Repent and believe: the Baptist experience in Maritime Canada*, ed. B. M. Moody (Hantsport, N.S., 1980), 103–23.

MILLAR, JAMES, businessman, militia officer, JP, and office holder; b. *c.* 1782 in Riccarton, Scotland; m. 27 Feb. 1838 Eleanor Catherine Gibb, youngest daughter of Benaiah Gibb*, in Montreal; d. there 27 July 1838.

By 1807 James Millar was established in a merchant partnership in Montreal with Alexander Parlane under the name of Millar, Parlane and Company. Since Millar was only 25 at the time, he must have come from a prosperous family. Millar, Parlane was an importer and wholesaler of fine cloth and fancy goods. By 1816 the firm was regarded as one of the most substantial importers in Montreal. Its success is a measure of the prosperity of the town's bourgeoisie since its merchant-tailor customers, including Gibb and Company, operated by Benaiah Gibb until 1815, clothed Montreal's economic and political élite. Like other firms, Millar, Parlane grew and diversified in step with the economies of Upper and Lower Canada. It was, by 1818, an active exporter of wood, flour, and ashes and its imports became more varied. By 1820 Parlane had taken up residence in Liverpool, where he acted for the firm until its dissolution in 1824.

Millar and another partner in Millar, Parlane, William Edmonstone, immediately formed a new association, which continued to operate under the old name until 1835, when it became Millar, Edmonstone and Company. In 1831 Hugh Allan* joined the firm as a commission agent, and in 1835 he became a partner. By 1837 the company was one of the three largest general importers in Montreal, receiving 12 vessels that year. Millar may have been a shipowner, but neither of his firms was until Millar, Edmonstone acquired the 214-ton barque *Thistle* in 1836. Thereafter, under Allan's influence, the firm rapidly evolved into a shipping company.

Like many merchants of his day Millar was involved in banking. From June to November 1825 he served on the board of the Bank of Montreal. He supported George Moffatt* and the younger directors in their successful struggle over loan policies with the president, Samuel Gerrard*. Millar was also associated with Moffatt in 1831, when they and Benjamin Hart* were trustees of the bankrupt estate of John Spragg, a partner in Spragg and Hutchinson. Millar was nominated a provisional director of the Montreal branch of the Bank of British North America in 1836. He may also have served as a director of the Montreal Savings Bank and of the Montreal Insurance Company.

A significant member of the Montreal business community, Millar received a variety of appointments honorific and useful, the latter indicating his interests and the needs of the business community. In common with many of his fellow merchants, he served as a justice of the peace, from 1821 to 1837; in 1820 he became an ensign and the following year a lieutenant in Montreal's 1st Militia Battalion. He fulfilled civic responsibilities by sitting on the board of the Montreal General Hospital, acting as a warden of the House of

Industry from 1827, and presiding over the municipal election in Sainte-Marie Ward, Montreal, in 1833. He served the business community on a committee formed in 1821 "to seek relief Measures for the agriculture and trade of the country" [*see* John Richardson*], on the Board of Cullers from 1823, and on a committee to select the site of a new custom-house in 1834. From 1831 he acted as a commissioner of roads and bridges in Wickham and Grantham townships, where he owned land.

One of the second generation of post-conquest Montreal merchants, Millar had had no connection with the fur trade; rather, his companies' success was based on new staple trades and the growing demand for consumer goods in Upper and Lower Canada. About 1866 Jedediah Hubbell Dorwin*, recalling the firm of Millar, Parlane from the days of his youth, compared it to Montreal's largest retail establishments in the 1860s, "the Benjamins and the Mussens or the later Morgans." Though prosperous, Millar was, however, in the second rank of merchants of his day, and did not have the economic or political prominence of a George Moffatt or a Peter McGill*.

PETER DESLAURIERS

[The subject of this biography should not be confused with his fellow citizens James Millar, an English freeholder, and James Morton Millar, a Scottish Presbyterian merchant who married the sister of the subject's wife, Eleanor Catherine Gibb. The author would like to thank Paulette M. Chiasson of the *DBC/DCB* for her assistance. P.D.]

McCord Museum, J. H. Dorwin, "Antiquarian autographs," 18; M21411, nos.260, 489. PAC, MG 24, D84: 21–22, 27–48; MG 30, D1, 21: 683; RG 68, General index, 1651–1841. *Montreal Gazette*, 1 March, 28 July 1838. *Quebec Gazette*, 27 Nov. 1817; 24 May, 27 Aug. 1821; 3 May 1824. Campbell, *Hist. of Scotch Presbyterian Church*. Denison, *Canada's first bank*. Tulchinsky, *River barons*.

MILLIDGE, THOMAS, businessman, politician, JP, and judge; b. 12 Aug. 1776 in New Jersey, son of Thomas Millidge* and Mercy Berker (Barker); m. 10 Sept. 1801 Sarah Simonds, and they had 12 children; d. 21 Aug. 1838 in Saint John, N.B.

Thomas Millidge was seven years old when he arrived in Nova Scotia with his parents as part of the 1783 loyalist migrations. His father, a major in the New Jersey Volunteers, became a deputy surveyor of Nova Scotia, served in the House of Assembly, and was active as a magistrate and a colonel in the militia. He thus provided an enviable model for his son.

As a young man Thomas Millidge moved across the Bay of Fundy to Saint John and established himself as a shipbuilder on the Kennebecasis River. The site of his operations eventually became known as Millidgeville and would be amalgamated with the city of Saint John in 1889. In 1801 Millidge married Sarah Simonds, daughter of James Simonds*, a founding member of the pre-loyalist Saint John firm of Simonds, Hazen, and White. Eight of their twelve children survived to adulthood; of these, seven married into prominent loyalist and pre-loyalist families, thereby helping to sustain the élite, Anglican and largely loyalist, in 19th-century New Brunswick.

In September 1816 Millidge successfully stood for election to the House of Assembly in the constituency of Saint John County and City. That year New Brunswick had experienced a crop failure which temporarily crippled an agricultural industry already more than subordinate to lumbering and shipbuilding as the perceived and real source of wealth. Millidge sat on the assembly committee that investigated the immediate damage inflicted by this crisis as well as the long-range implications for provincial development. The committee addressed the first problem by recommending that financial outlays be made "to provide for the relief of the poor and for the necessities of the province." Even more important, Millidge and his assembly colleagues introduced a bill to encourage the development of agriculture. Millidge retained his seat in the election of October 1819.

Over the years Millidge became a prominent merchant and head of an important shipowning family. During the 1820s he had several vessels, at least two of them constructed for him by John Haws*; in his shipbuilding activities he was in partnership with Simeon Lee Lugrin, also a loyalist descendant. As did others of his generation, Millidge experienced the risks endemic in the world of water transport, especially as it pertained to the rocky coves along the Bay of Fundy. His father had survived a shipwreck off Musquash Cove (Musquash Harbour) in 1787. Years later, in 1836, a whale-ship Millidge had built, the *Thomas Millidge*, was wrecked near the same cove a few miles outside Saint John.

Millidge actively participated in many spheres of urban and business life. He was a member of Saint John's first social club, the Subscription Room at the Exchange Coffee House, itself the site of numerous meetings held to assess means of strengthening and advancing the city's commercial life. Population growth and commercial expansion led in 1819 to the founding, by Millidge and others, of the Saint John Chamber of Commerce. These advances also spurred the creation in 1820 of British North America's first chartered bank, the Bank of New Brunswick; Millidge sat on its prestigious board, which also included such important businessmen as John Robinson*, William Black*, and Nehemiah MERRITT. By this time, in his mid forties, Millidge was at the apex of his career, prominent as a merchant, shipbuilder, assemblyman, and magistrate for Saint John County. Subsequently he became president of the Chamber of Commerce (1828) and a founding director of the New Brunswick

Fire Insurance Company (1831) and the Saint John Water Company (1832).

Thomas Millidge was a member of the Church of England. He died in 1838 and was buried in Fernhill Cemetery, Saint John. His son Thomas Edward guided the family's business interests through the economic transformation of the mid and late 19th century, a period in which the city's commercial decline contrasted sharply with the hope of his grandfather's and the promise of his father's generation.

ELIZABETH W. MCGAHAN

PANB, MC 1156 (copy at N.B. Museum). N.B., House of Assembly, *Journal*, 1817, 1831. *Royal Gazette* (Fredericton), 27 April 1831. *Elections in N.B. Millidge ancestors*, comp. E. de B. [Millidge] Crossman (Winnipeg, 1980). *N.B. vital statistics, 1784–1815* (Johnson *et al.*). Esther Clark Wright, *The loyalists of New Brunswick* (Fredericton, 1955; repr. Hantsport, N.S., 1981); *Saint John ships and their builders* (Wolfville, N.S., [1975]). I. L. Hill, *Some loyalists and others* (rev. ed., Fredericton, 1977). *Historical essays on the Atlantic provinces*, ed. G. A. Rawlyk (Toronto, 1967; repr. 1971). D. R. Jack, *Centennial prize essay on the history of the city and county of St. John* (Saint John, N.B., 1883), 114. Graeme Wynn, *Timber colony: a historical geography of early nineteenth century New Brunswick* (Toronto and Buffalo, N.Y., 1981). T. W. Acheson, "The great merchant and economic development in St. John, 1820–1850," *Acadiensis* (Fredericton), 8 (1978–79), no.2: 3–27. J. R. Armstrong, "The Exchange Coffee House and St. John's first club," N.B. Hist. Soc., *Coll.*, 3 (1907–14), no.7: 60–78. "Board of Trade; the first St. John Chamber of Commerce: a sketch of the institution from its earliest days down to the present time," *Daily Sun* (Saint John), 3 April 1889: 14.

MILNES, Sir ROBERT SHORE, colonial administrator; b. *c.* 1754 in England, eldest son of John Milnes, of Wakefield, a magistrate and deputy lieutenant of the West Riding of Yorkshire, and Mary Shore, originally of Sheffield; m. 12 or 13 Nov. 1785 Charlotte Frances Bentinck, great-granddaughter of William Bentinck, 1st Earl of Portland, and they had three sons and two daughters; d. 2 Dec. 1837 in Tunbridge Wells (Royal Tunbridge Wells), England.

Historical works have in general subscribed to the assessment that his contemporary, historian Robert Christie*, made of Robert Shore Milnes: a well-meaning administrator but not an able one, too easily influenced and lacking in self-confidence. This judgement, however, does not stand up to an examination of the man, his ideas, and his role.

After a military career in the Royal Horse Guards, Milnes left the army in 1788 with the rank of captain. Seven years later he was governor of Martinique. On 4 Nov. 1797 he was appointed lieutenant governor of Lower Canada, and on 15 June 1799, at 53 years of age, he was sworn in; on 30 July 1799 he replaced Governor Robert Prescott* as administrator of the province. A baronetcy was conferred on him on 21 March 1801. Milnes left for England on 5 Aug. 1805 but remained administrator until 12 Aug. 1805 and lieutenant governor until 29 Nov. 1808. Thomas Dunn* assumed his duties as administrator until Governor Sir James Henry Craig* arrived in October 1807.

Milnes had replaced Prescott, who was recalled because of the violent quarrelling between two British factions in the Executive Council over land grants in the townships. This conflict had paralysed the British party (also called the English or government party) since 1797. Moreover, the constitution of 1791 having in the event ensured that the Canadians would dominate the House of Assembly and the British both Legislative and Executive councils, an open confrontation between the Canadian party and the British party was inevitable. Internationally the climate of war lent itself to intrigues and unrest, even in Lower Canada. At the same time increasing integration of the colonial economy into the Atlantic one was transforming the socio-economic face of Lower Canada. The colony would be ready to exploit the massive opening up of imperial markets to Canadian timber, a sudden and important development in 1807.

Early in his administration Milnes achieved at first try what no British governor had accomplished until then without resort to force: the call-up of an eighth of the militia of Montreal and the surrounding region in 1801 to fend off a possible American invasion. Even at Trois-Rivières volunteers came pouring in. Long before Craig's term, Milnes was in communication with spies who reported to him from the United States. And he could take pride in being able to send generous sums raised by subscription to defray the mother country's expenditures for war. As for the remaining problems, he tackled them in a comprehensive and coherent manner, except perhaps for costly infrastructures (canals, for example) which the debt-ridden colonial legislature and the British government put off till later.

On 1 Nov. 1800 Milnes sent the home secretary, the Duke of Portland, a long dispatch identifying the obstacles to the growth of British settlement in Lower Canada and suggesting various measures to deal with them. In his opinion, although the 1791 constitution was based on unassailable fundamental principles, it would bear fruit only if the government had a strong and dynamic aristocracy to rely on as a counterweight to the humble folk who elected the assembly. Unfortunately, the colony, unlike England, had no such landed aristocracy, because the seigneurial régime levelled social classes and impoverished the seigneurs. Furthermore, the Roman Catholic Church was beyond state control and consequently the constitution and royal instructions were not applicable to it. The disbanding of the militia after the conquest had undermined another means of government influence. Finally, parliamentary government had added to the difficulties because the popular assembly debated government measures. The lieutenant governor's correspondence makes it clear that in his view the Canadians remained French and were not moving any closer to the British.

To deal with these serious problems, Milnes considered it necessary to foster the rise of a powerful and rich aristocracy that would influence both the voters and the assembly, a body regrettably composed of easily swayed ignoramuses. Only an aristocracy could offset the popular element, on which the executive had no check. Various concrete measures could set the desired change in motion: getting British people to settle the townships quickly; bringing the Catholic clergy under the authority of the crown; making use of a then submissive clergy and the captains of a reorganized militia for political or even electoral ends to secure a majority in the assembly favourable to the government; increasing civil expenditures and patronage, since Canadian seigneurs sought positions just as did the British; maintaining the imperial government's assistance with the expenses of civil government, assistance soon made up for by the income from crown lands in the townships; and lastly, encouraging education.

Milnes's opinions were based on personal observation and on the views of a set of British advisers who included the Anglican bishop Jacob Mountain*, the attorney general Jonathan SEWELL, the civil secretary Herman Witsius RYLAND, and the merchants John Richardson* and John Young*, the latter a member of the Executive Council. All were convinced that the ultimate solution lay in assimilating the Canadians. More than 40 years after the events of 1760, through their writings and their initiatives in the Executive and Legislative councils, and even in the assembly, this group tried to implement an overall plan for the creation and development of a British and Protestant society, which they considered the normal consequence of the conquest. But, unlike Craig, Milnes never threw himself into the fray. He thus retained full liberty of action, while at the same time supporting the British party discreetly and effectively. In contrast with what would happen in the period 1807–11, the party did not question the 1791 constitution.

Milnes's viewpoint was in large measure shared by the Duke of Portland. Portland admitted that little could be done for the seigneurs – patronage was too important for the British and it occasioned too much quarrelling. He approved the idea of "prudently" subjecting the Catholic Church to the royal prerogative, even if it meant giving the bishop a generous allowance, and he was in favour of a thorough reorganization of the militia. According to the home secretary, British settlement would in time inevitably reduce the "ascendancy" of the old subjects, the Canadians.

Milnes unfolded his plan of action on all fronts. For instance, despite his numerous arguments with William Osgoode*, the independent-minded chief justice who was kept out of this scheming, he broke a deadlock in the Executive Council so that between 1799 and 1809 it distributed more than 1,400,000 acres among some 60 senior officials, rich merchants, and other large landowners, through the system of township leaders and associates [*see* Samuel Gale*]. Paradoxically this land speculation would in fact slow down British settlement, though accelerating it was the lieutenant governor's primary aim. In 1822 Milnes himself was the beneficiary of a grant of 50,465 acres in Stanstead, Compton, and Barnston townships.

Following repeated complaints in the 1790s from the Canadians, particularly in the assembly, about the seizure by the crown of the Jesuit estates and the plan to give some of these lands to Jeffery, Lord Amherst*, as a reward for his military services, Milnes, with the backing of Sewell and Solicitor General Louis-Charles Foucher as well as of the Executive Council, took up an idea put forward by Mountain in 1799: using part of the estates to finance a public school system in which English would be taught free of charge to the Canadians, among whom it was making little headway. For him as for Mountain, it was their ignorance of English that was dividing the population into "two separate people, those who by their situation, their common interests, and their equal participation of the same laws and the same form of government should naturally form but one."

In pursuit of this plan the Royal Institution for the Advancement of Learning [*see* Joseph Langley Mills*] was established in 1801 by an act that managed to pass in the assembly because of absenteeism among members of the Canadian party (several of the votes were close, for example 8 to 7, 11 to 10). In practice the statute conferred absolute control of public education in Lower Canada upon the civil administrator and his minions. A few Canadian "placemen" had backed the British majority in the assembly on certain points. Admittedly the basic intentions of the authors of the statute were apparent only in the confidential dispatches of the lieutenant governor, who considered the Royal Institution a temporary step and who would submit a plan in 1803 to use the income from crown lands to finance colleges and even a university. It was not until 1824 that the British authorities, at home and in the colony, accepted – if with bad grace – the creation of a parallel public school system under the control of Canadians.

Following a scenario conceived by Sewell, Milnes sought to abolish the seigneurial régime by degrees. He proposed to have the colonial legislature pass a law that would require payment of arrears on seigneurial dues accumulated in the crown seigneuries (essentially the towns of Quebec and Trois-Rivières) since the conquest. There would be a general outcry, he thought, and it would thus be necessary to change the system of tenure in those seigneuries, an example that little by little would be followed throughout the province. The aim of this measure was to attract British settlers into the seigneurial area, mingle British and Canadians, and assimilate the latter. The assembly, however, amended the 1801 act to such an extent that the hoped-for commotion never occurred.

As for the Catholic Church, the state lost no opportunity to interfere in its internal administration, for instance, with complaints about parish priests, requests for information, particularly from the Sulpicians, and a refusal to grant the *fabrique* of Notre-Dame in Montreal permission to hold property in mortmain. Sewell even proposed an overall plan to Milnes which would make the Catholic Church subject to the royal prerogative and undermine its internal and external influence alike: "patronage" – the appointment of parish priests – would be entrusted to the government and the bishop was to be brought into the councils and consequently into politics. Sewell suggested other methods, such as isolating the clergy by excluding foreign priests, and obliging the bishops to reside at Quebec, which would mean their having to live in a style befitting their social rank.

The Anglican bishop also pressed Milnes. In 1803, 1804, and on various occasions later Mountain waxed indignant at what he perceived to be the wide powers, the autonomy, the wealth, honours, and privileges enjoyed by "the Church of Rome." He demanded vigorous measures to subordinate it and to establish the Church of England more firmly. He hoped, however, that as the townships were settled, "at no very distant period, the Protestants in this Province will outnumber the Papists." This sentiment was shared by Ryland, who expressed his disgust regarding the papists and demanded the submission of the "superintendent" of the Church of Rome to the royal prerogative. However, in the troubled international context, London considered it ill advised to provoke a religious war.

In the law courts Attorney General Sewell intervened in the name of the state to deny the legal existence of the Catholic bishop and of the parishes created after the conquest. In 1805 he conducted strenous negotiations about this matter with the coadjutor, Bishop Joseph-Octave Plessis*, who was representing Bishop Pierre Denaut*. Attracted by the apparent moderation of Milnes, Denaut petitioned the king for civil recognition of his title as Catholic bishop of Quebec. Milnes was secretly congratulating himself on his victory and was already calculating the income to be drawn from the Sulpician estates. He could not know that after his departure from the colony, Denaut would die and the administrator Thomas Dunn would proceed in all haste to swear in an episcopal successor, without waiting for instructions from London.

Where civil jurisdiction was concerned Milnes and London disregarded the minority opinion of the Canadian judges and decreed that English law applied in matters of inheritance and dower for lands held in free and common socage. As another element of his strategy the lieutenant governor persuaded the assembly in 1803 to pass an act reorganizing the militia.

Milnes also intervened to encourage prestigious British figures to run in the 1804 elections in order to get more of their number into the assembly. Similarly he secretly solicited petitions to get separate electoral ridings for the townships and thus bring an additional "10 or 12 British members" into the assembly.

These plans for assimilation and for putting things in order inevitably created a stir, even though they were often fairly moderate and long-term initiatives, compared with the more radical projects and more clear-cut opinions of the British party. It quarrelled regularly in the assembly with the Canadian party about a host of questions. In 1800 the two groups confronted each other over the Jesuit estates, the qualifications of assemblymen, the quorum, and civil law. In 1801 the issues were the abolition of seigneurial tenure, the Royal Institution, and the use of French civil law which in Sewell's view made it impossible to create an effective aristocracy since it prevented social inequalities. The assembly did, however, agree to extend trial by jury to the entire civil field through a bill that, ironically, was amended drastically by the Legislative Council, which for once had a majority of Canadians. In 1802 there were clashes over paying the expenses of assembly members from ridings at a distance from Quebec in order to reduce absenteeism (the bill was defeated). The disputes in 1803 were over the plan to form companies of volunteers, and the demands of the townships for such things as registry offices, roads, new ridings, a court of common pleas, or a census. In 1804 the issues were the use of patronage, and establishment of the Presbyterian Church in the townships (one of the votes of 8 to 8 was decided by the speaker). In 1805 they were in conflict over the proposals for the abolition of seigneurial tenure and of lineal repurchase, printing in French of a table of contents for the *Lex parliamentaria*, and the house translator's salary; at the same time an all-British committee of the Executive Council was proposing that the lieutenant governor ask London directly for the creation of new ridings and circuit courts, the construction of highways, and the establishing of registry offices, the Church of England, and the militia in the townships.

The general election in 1800, like that of 1804, was hotly disputed, with much brawling, lampooning, and insults. In 1804 as a result of the quality of the candidates and the exceptional efforts of the British their numbers in the assembly increased from 14 to 17. In 1805 the quarrels and passions intensified. The British party realized it was fated to remain a minority in the assembly, even though it was the dominant force in the councils. It suffered a severe set-back when the majority imposed a tax on trade rather than on land in order to build new prisons in the towns [*see* Ignace-Michel-Louis-Antoine d'Irumberry* de Salaberry]. In the colony and in London its petitions met with a certain indifference from the authorities, who were more responsive to the interests of landowners and aware of the urgent need for putting up these buildings.

The British party's newspaper, the *Quebec Mercury*, was launched at the beginning of January 1805 [*see* Thomas Cary*], and it quickly mounted frontal attacks on the Canadians' nationality, customs, laws, and religion; it assumed an increasingly violent tone and ultimately demanded that Lower Canada be transformed into what it ought to have been: a British colony. The violence of this quarrel, which had, however, broken out after numerous altercations, has led to the mistaken belief that the "race war" began in 1805. The refusal of Milnes to intervene publicly in politics meant that the debates were carried at a pitch different from that under Craig, who presented himself as the head of the British party, now become a party of officialdom. Undeniably, however, in Milnes's administration the climate was deteriorating and collaboration of the two parties on social and economic questions (public works, social measures, public finances), which had thus far been possible, would become increasingly rare and difficult in the years to come.

Milnes was a sociable man, interested in arts and letters, and he enjoyed receptions which Lady Milnes, reputed to be beautiful and charming, graced by her presence. He apparently had an active family life. Skilled at maintaining ambiguity, he forged links with some of the Canadians, even though he was secretely advocating their assimilation. In support of the community, he was a member of the Fire Society and contributed to a fund in aid of the victims of the conflagration at Quebec in 1804.

Milnes left for England on 5 Aug. 1805, after receiving addresses of thanks and good wishes. From time to time he was to be consulted on Canadian affairs, but he would play no decisive role, probably because of the direct and committed style of his successor, Craig. In 1809, 1810, and 1811 Craig would simply make the same overall assessment as Milnes, but he would recommend different means to arrive at the same ends. Certainly Milnes had not displayed the same vigour in acting. There is no doubt whatsoever about the lucidity of his reasoning, and in other circumstances his program might have had a better chance of success.

JEAN-PIERRE WALLOT

Materials from a number of manuscript and record groups at the PAC were consulted, including MG 17, A7-2; MG 23, GII, 10; MG 24, B1; B3; L3; RG 7, G1; G2; G15C; RG 8, I (C ser.); RG 14, A1; A3. Useful for the period 1797–1805 were RG 4, A1; A2; for 1797–1808, MG 11, [CO 42] Q; RG 1, E1; L1; L3[L]; and for 1799–1805, MG 5, B2 (transcripts); RG 9, I, A1; RG 10.

AAQ, 210 A, 1797–1808. ACC-Q, 72–77, 86–88. Univ. de Montréal, Service des bibliothèques, coll. spéciales, coll. Melzack. *Docs. relating to constitutional hist., 1791–1818* (Doughty and McArthur). *Gentleman's Magazine*, 1785, January–June 1838. L.C., House of Assembly, *Journals*, 1793–1809. *Mandements, lettres pastorales et circulaires des évêques de Québec*, Henri Têtu et C.-O. Gagnon, édit. (18v. parus, Québec, 1887–). *British American Register* (Quebec), 1802–3. *Le Canadien*, 1806–8. *Montreal Gazette*, 1797–1808. *Quebec Gazette*, 1797–1808. *Quebec Mercury*, 1805–8. *Burke's peerage* (1890), 1114–16. Caron, "Inv. de la corr. de Mgr Denaut," ANQ *Rapport*, 1931–32; "Inv. de la corr. de Mgr Hubert et de Mgr Bailly de Messein," 1930–31; "Inv. de la corr. de Mgr Panet," 1933–34; "Inv. de la corr. de Mgr Plessis," 1927–28, 1928–29, 1932–33. H. J. Morgan, *Sketches of celebrated Canadians*, 134. L.-P. Audet, *Le système scolaire*, vol.3. Christie, *Hist. of L.C.* (1848–55), vols.1, 6. Ouellet, *Bas-Canada*. Taft Manning, *Revolt of French Canada*. J.-P. Wallot, *Intrigues françaises et américaines au Canada, 1800–1802* (Montréal, 1965); *Un Québec qui bougeait*.

MIUS. *See* MEUSE

MOLSON, JOHN (John Molson Sr), businessman, landowner, militia officer, and politician; b. 28 Dec. 1763 in Moulton, Lincolnshire, England, son of John Molson and Mary Elsdale; m. 7 April 1801 Sarah Insley Vaughan in Montreal, and they had three children; d. 11 Jan. 1836 in Boucherville, Lower Canada.

Having lost his father by the time he was six and his mother when he was eight, John Molson was put under the guardianship of his maternal grandfather, Samuel Elsdale. Early in July 1782, at the age of 18, he emigrated to Montreal, and immediately became involved in various commercial endeavours with family friends who had arrived at the same time as he. He went into the meat business with the two James Pells, father and son, who were both butchers, and then he joined in a brewing enterprise which Thomas Loid (Loyd) set up that year at the foot of the Courant Sainte-Marie in the *faubourg* Québec.

Coming as he did from the English gentry, Molson naturally wanted to own a farm. During his first year in the colony he bought 160 hectares of land in

Caldwell's Manor, south of Montreal. He parted with it in the spring of 1786, when he began to run the brewery. He had sued Loid for repayment of a debt in the summer of 1784, and as Loid had formally admitted the justice of the case, the buildings had been seized and put up for auction. At an initial sale on 22 October there had been no offers, but at the second, held on 5 Jan. 1785, eight days after Molson had attained his majority, he was the only bidder. He put James Pell Sr in charge of the brewery and on 2 June sailed for England from New York. He could now settle his business affairs himself.

In England, Molson bought some equipment for the brewery. Returning to Montreal on 31 May 1786, he took over management of the operation. He oversaw the enlargement of the plant and began to buy grain for the coming season of malting and brewing. His first purchase, on 28 July, was an exciting event for him, as the entry in the little notebook he kept for his expenditures shows: "28th, Bo[t] 8 bush[s] of Barley to Malt first this Season, Commencement on the Grand Stage of the World." Rarely does the spirit of enterprise find such clear expression but, as a letter from Molson to his business agent in England indicated, it also spurred the Lower Canadians: "People here are more of an enterprising spirit than at home, as it is in a great measure owing to that restlessness that induces them to quit their native shore."

During the next 20 years Molson dedicated himself to his business. He invested in it all the funds at his disposal in order to enlarge his facilities and production. It is estimated that he received about £10,000 sterling from a succession of inherited properties, including the family home, Snake Hall, which was sold on 11 June 1789. Molson had turned away from the import-export business in 1788 because the risks were too great and the profits too slow; he also foresaw that the large-scale fur trade would run into increasing difficulties. He therefore did not seek to diversify his activities during this period. In 1806 he considered opening a brewery in York (Toronto) and was warmly encouraged to do so by his correspondent D'Arcy Boulton*, who also hailed from Moulton, but nothing came of the idea.

Molson preferred to reinvest continually in his Montreal establishment and for that purpose went occasionally to England, as in 1795 and 1797, to buy equipment. The young immigrant had decided to put his money into a sector which was at the forefront of technological innovation in that country during the late 18th century. The influx of loyalists to the colony, and then the first arrivals of British immigrants, opened a market for him and soon there was a demand even from French Canadians, who had not previously been inclined to drink beer. As there was not much barley being produced in the Canadas, Molson induced farmers to grow it by initially supplying them with seed, to be paid back in kind at the rate of two bushels for one.

After his return from England in 1786, Molson had begun living with Sarah Insley Vaughan, who was four years older than he. They remained together and had three children: John*, born in 1787, Thomas*, born in 1791, and William*, born in 1793. They were married on 7 April 1801 at Christ Church in Montreal; according to the declaration they made in the marriage contract drawn up that day by notary Jonathan Abraham Gray, they wanted to acknowledge their mutual affection and legitimize their three children. Sarah signed the contract and the church register with a cross.

Not much is known about how well the young entrepreneur fitted into Montreal business circles, then dominated by the big fur merchants, most of them Scottish. From June to December 1791 and from June 1795 to June 1796 he is known to have held the masonic office of worshipful master of St Paul's Lodge, which indicates that he had a connection with a social group who recognized him. Molson had been married in the Church of England because at the time it was the only Protestant denomination legally permitted to keep registers of births, marriages, and deaths. But as early as 1792 he had contributed financially to the building of the Scotch Presbyterian Church, later known as St Gabriel Street Church [*see* Duncan Fisher*], and he remained an active member until at least 1815. In this way, he associated with the community of important Scottish merchants in Montreal.

During the first decade of the 19th century, conditions arising from the Napoleonic Wars were transforming the economy of the St Lawrence valley and giving it new life: the fur trade economy was gradually replaced by the lumber economy, at a time when agriculture was expanding, particularly in Upper Canada. Steam, the new source of energy, led to technological innovations, and after a great deal of experimenting and testing, ships could be propelled with it, for a time at least, on inland water-ways. In 1807 Robert Fulton began to sail the *Clermont* on the Hudson; in 1808 some businessmen from Burlington, Vt, commissioned brothers John and James Winans of that town to build a steamboat for the run along Lake Champlain and the Rivière Richelieu to Dorchester (Saint-Jean-sur-Richelieu); in June 1809 the *Vermont* went into service.

By a notarized contract on 5 June, Molson became the third member and financial backer of a partnership founded by John Jackson, "mechanic," and John Bruce, "shipbuilder," who were building a steamboat to carry passengers between Montreal and Quebec. The most surprising technical aspect of this undertaking was the construction of the engine at George Platt's foundry in Montreal. On 1 Nov. 1809 the

Accommodation left Montreal at two o'clock in the afternoon; it reached Quebec 66 hours later, on Saturday, 4 November, at eight in the morning, after 30 hours at anchor in the shallows of Lac Saint-Pierre; the return trip to Montreal up the St Lawrence took seven days. The vessel had regular sailings from June to October 1810, the engine having been made more powerful during the winter. The partnership ended with Molson buying the shares of Bruce and Jackson, who said they could no longer take the substantial losses being incurred. In the mean time, on 7 Sept. 1810, Fulton had proposed to Molson the joining of their two enterprises; the terms of the proposal did not seem sufficently advantageous to Molson, who took no action. Late in October he left Montreal for England to order a steam-engine for the next ship, the *Swiftsure*, from the firm of Boulton and Watt. The vessel was under construction in Hart Logan's shipyard on Rue Monarque in Montreal from August 1811 and it was launched on 20 Aug. 1812.

To diversify his interests Molson had again chosen a sector in which the most recent technological advances had occurred. The brewery had been expanding since 1786, bringing him ever increasing profits, and hence he was able to assume the losses experienced with the *Accommodation*. He did try to obtain a measure of protection by asking the House of Assembly on 6 Feb. 1811 for a monopoly of steam navigation on the St Lawrence between Montreal and Quebec. His request was put forward by Joseph PAPINEAU and Denis-Benjamin Viger* and granted by the assembly, but was rejected by the Legislative Council. With the outbreak of the War of 1812, however, circumstances would prove extraordinarily favourable to shipping on the St Lawrence. Molson offered his ship to the army for the duration of hostilities, but met with a refusal. The military none the less had to use it occasionally on a commercial basis for transporting troops and their supplies. Molson took part in the war as a lieutenant in the 5th Battalion of Select Embodied Militia. Promoted captain on 25 March 1813, he resigned his commission on 25 November.

Early in 1814 another steam-engine was ordered in England. The *Malsham* (an archaic form of the name Molson), which was built in Logan's shipyard as well, was launched in September and went into service immediately. The *Lady Sherbrooke* was added in 1816 and the *New Swiftsure* in 1817. With the end of the war between France and Britain and the economic depression of 1815, British immigrants began to arrive at Quebec in growing numbers and to seek transportation up the St Lawrence, towards the Great Lakes, and on the Richelieu and the Ottawa. In 1815 Molson purchased a wharf with all its facilities at Près-de-Ville in Quebec from Robert Christie* and Monique-Olivier Doucet; in 1819 he also bought a house at 16 Rue Saint-Pierre. On 16 Feb. 1816 he had obtained from the Executive Council a 50-year lease on a waterfront lot at Montreal with a renewal option, and he proceeded to put up a wharf. It was located in front of a property he had purchased from Sir John Johnson* on 16 Dec. 1815, on which stood a private residence at the corner of Rue Saint-Paul and Rue Bonsecours; in 1816 Molson added two wings to the building and turned it into the Mansion House Hotel. A wharf at William Henry (Sorel) apparently fitted into this network as did the sizeable commercial activity to obtain on contract the wood for steam, which was to be delivered to the various wharfs up and down the St Lawrence where the ships called. By about 1809, Molson had introduced his sons, John, Thomas, and William, to the manufacturing aspects of his enterprises. On 1 Dec. 1816 he formed the first of a long series of partnerships with them under the name John Molson and Sons [*see* John Molson Jr]. Having transferred greater responsibilities in his enterprises to his sons, Molson could become active in politics. In March 1816 he was elected to the House of Assembly for Montreal East. Politics were closely interwoven with the fundamental interests of the merchants in Lower Canada. Molson did not attend the 1817 session; he was probably not even in the colony. The 1818 session having begun on 7 January, he presented himself on 2 February to be sworn in and take his seat. In the 1819 session, which was prorogued on 24 April, he participated from the opening till about 20 March. He did not run in the 1820 election.

Molson was an active member of the assembly. All the important issues attracted his attention: trade, public finances, banks and currency, inland shipping, education and health, municipal by-laws, fire protection, regulations for public houses and inns, the House of Industry (of which he was a trustee in 1819, according to Thomas Doige's directory), and the Montreal Library. Two questions concerned him more directly, the Lachine Canal and the Montreal General Hospital. From 1815 to 1821 he took part in the debate over the construction of the canal, speaking out for a private undertaking and a route that favoured his shipping interests. In January 1819, with the support of the merchants, he presented a petition to the assembly for the establishment of a public hospital in Montreal [*see* William Caldwell*]. The petition was not accepted by the house because of a procedural error that was declared on 18 March; Molson was still in attendance on 19 and 20 March, but did not appear again. The Montreal General Hospital was founded that same year as a private institution, and the four Molsons contributed to the subscription launched in 1820 to buy a lot on Dorchester Street and put up the building.

Even when not in the assembly, Molson continued to follow events closely. In 1822 the presentation to the House of Commons in London of a plan for the union of Upper and Lower Canada caused a political stir in the colony. In Montreal some eminent businessmen, Molson among them, formed a committee in support of the bill which held a public meeting and collected 1,452 signatures.

The description that Hector Berthelot* gave of Molson in the Montreal newspaper *La Patrie* in 1885 has often been repeated; on the basis of old people's recollections going back as far as 1820, he portrayed Molson in blue tuque, wooden shoes, and homespun. His final paragraph, however, has not always been noted: "After he closed his brewery at night, he took off his rustic garb, donned black evening dress and a white waistcoat, and sported a pince-nez on a long ribbon. When he was dressed grandly, Mr Molson behaved like a steamboat owner." But probably also not kept in mind is Édouard-Zotique Massicotte*'s caution in his introduction to the 1916 edition of Berthelot's articles that during his lifetime the writer was considered less a historian than a humorist.

At the time Molson was transferring managerial responsibilities in the shipping firm to his eldest son, some financial groups in Montreal (in particular the brothers John* and Thomas Torrance and Horatio Gates*) and at Quebec (John Goudie*, Noah Freer, and James McDouall, among others) were beginning to compete fiercely on the St Lawrence, launching various steamboats. The competition led to overinvestment, and then to consolidation of the firms. On 27 April 1822 the St Lawrence Steamboat Company [*see* William Molson] was created, with assets including six ships, three belonging to the Molsons; its management was handed over to John Molson and Sons, which held 26 of the 44 shares. Rivalry with the Torrances continued for some time, but it was finally resolved by cartel agreements on services, prices, and even co-ownership of certain ships.

Meanwhile the Mansion House Hotel had burned down on 16 March 1821; rebuilt in 1824, the year in which Molson acceded to the rank of worshipful sword bearer in the Provincial Grand Lodge of Lower Canada, it was renamed the Masonic Hall Hotel. Molson became provincial grand master for the district of Montreal and William Henry in 1826. At the end of December 1833, finding himself in opposition to his council on a matter of principle, he resigned. Upon the death of John Richardson* in 1831, the chairmanship of the Montreal General Hospital fell to Molson. When the cornerstone of the part to be named the Richardson Wing was laid, Molson officiated as provincial grand master in a ceremony at which masonic honours were rendered.

In the early 1820s, as the shipping assets had been removed from John Molson and Sons and placed in the St Lawrence Steamboat Company, the family firm had to be reorganized. In addition, Thomas Molson had decided to settle in Kingston, Upper Canada, and his departure entailed another large withdrawal of assets from the firm. An agreement establishing a new John Molson and Sons was made in 1824, to take effect retroactively from 1 Dec. 1823, the date on which the accounts of the former company had been stopped. William Molson took over management of the brewery from Thomas.

In 1825 Molson Sr gave up his residence in the *faubourg* Québec of Montreal and moved to Belmont Hall, a magnificent house at the corner of Sherbrooke and Saint-Laurent. For some time he had owned Île Saint-Jean and Île Sainte-Marguerite, which form part of the Îles de Boucherville. It was to these islands that his ships returned in the autumn for their winter berths and on them Molson established an estate to which he could withdraw now and then. There he kept a sheep-breeding establishment large enough that the sales of meat to butchers and wool to wholesale merchants appeared in the company accounts. On 10 March 1825 the Theatre Royal company was formed [*see* Frederick BROWN]. The principal shareholder, Molson received 44 shares worth £25 each in return for a property he transferred to it on Rue Saint-Paul.

Although during his term as an assemblyman Molson had taken an interest in the founding of the Bank of Montreal [*see* John Richardson], he had made no financial commitments. He had offered to put up the bank building on one of his properties, but the board of directors had unanimously turned down his proposal and had decided on 10 Oct. 1817 that the bank would buy a lot and erect a building itself. John Molson Jr was elected to the board of directors in 1824. In the crisis that split the board in 1826 [*see* Frederick William Ermatinger*] and put Richardson's group in the minority, Ermatinger gave up his place so that Molson Sr could become president. A short time later John Jr resigned to enable Ermatinger to regain his seat. During the elder Molson's term of office, which lasted until 1830, the bank had to deal with the liquidation of major fur-trading houses that declared bankruptcy, in particular Maitland, Garden, and Auldjo and the firms linked with the brothers William* and SIMON McGillivray. It was Simon who had recommended that Molson be named to succeed William as provincial grand master for the district of Montreal and William Henry, notifying him by a letter sent from London in 1826.

In 1828 John Molson and Sons had its responsibilities narrowed; as the agent of the St Lawrence Steamboat Company it was concerned only with shipping. A new partnership was formed under the name of John and William Molson, bringing together the two Johns and William. John Jr withdrew in April 1829, however, and the association was dissolved; on 30 June a new John and William Molson was founded, which included only Molson Sr and William. On 1 May John Jr had set up Molson, Davies and Company with the brothers George and George Crew Davies; as for William, he went into partnership on 1 May 1830 with his brother-in-law John Thompson Badgley to create Molson and Badgley. Molson Sr acted as financial backer and stood surety for both undertakings. In the mid 1820s, with a workshop attached to the brewery on Rue Sainte-Marie as a basis, Molson had established St Mary's Foundry, handing it over to William's management. In 1831, on the eve of the opening of navigation on the Rideau Canal, Molson Sr joined with Peter McGill*, Horatio Gates, and others in forming the Ottawa and Rideau Forwarding Company.

Once more in the early 1830s an important new field for investment was being opened up by technological innovation: the railway. On 14 Nov. 1831, after an earlier petition had been rejected, a group of 74 Montreal businessmen, including Molson, asked the assembly for incorporation as the Company of Proprietors of the Champlain and St Lawrence Railroad; they planned to build the very first railway in either Upper or Lower Canada, from La Prairie to Dorchester [*see* John Molson Jr]. Molson Sr bought 180 shares in the company, thus becoming the largest shareholder, but he was not named to its initial board of directors, which was formed on 12 Jan. 1835.

It was clear that by now Molson was interested only in investing: "I have retired from any active part in business for some years past," he wrote to the London bankers Thomas Wilson and Company in 1830. He had run in the 1827 elections in Montreal East but had been defeated. However, Lord Aylmer [WHITWORTH-AYLMER] called him to the Legislative Council in January 1832, along with Peter McGill. The previous year, upon the death of the man generally considered the dean of the Montreal business community, John Richardson, George Moffatt* had been appointed. The three men focused to such an extent on the same questions and causes that one can truly speak of the Molson–McGill–Moffatt trio. Together they sat on most of the committees for public investment, taxation, and monetary, banking, and financial matters. Their shared opinions and interests were patent in the dissent they voiced in February 1833 on the question of sharing with Upper Canada the customs duties collected at Quebec. They took the opportunity to ask that the counties of Montreal and Vaudreuil be detached from the lower province and annexed to the upper one. Like McGill and Moffatt, Molson belonged to the Constitutional Association of Montreal, even though he was less active in it than his eldest son. During his four years as a legislative councillor, he was even more assiduous than he had been as an assemblyman 15 years before; on 23 Dec. 1835, less than three weeks before his death, he was still taking part in council.

Towards the end of his life, he became interested in the organization of a Unitarian congregation in Montreal, which among its supporters had a great many merchants of New England origin. In 1832 he was one of a group that purchased a lot for which a chapel was planned, but the initiative was set aside for a while when the pastor died.

In 1833 William Molson added a large distillery to the brewery. The following year Thomas left Kingston to rejoin his brother in Montreal. Through a new partnership contract with their father, signed on 21 Feb. 1835 but retroactive to 30 June 1834, they formed John Molson and Company [*see* William Molson]; once more John Jr did not join the firm.

Molson had lost his wife on 18 March 1829, and in his seventy-second year he was stricken with an illness that swiftly brought about his own death, on 11 Jan. 1836, at his estate on Île Sainte-Marguerite. The newspapers carried quite detailed eulogies, but *La Minerve* mentioned one of his qualities in a somewhat veiled fashion: "Mr Molson belonged to that small number of Europeans who, coming to settle in Canada, reject all national distinctions; just as he had started his fortune with those born in this land, so he always had a large number of Canadians in his employ, whose loyalty must have helped to ensure his considerable profits." The funeral took place at Christ Church in Montreal on 14 January, and he was buried in the old cemetery of the *faubourg* Saint-Laurent. Later his remains were transported with his wife's to Mount Royal Cemetery, to rest in the impressive mausoleum that their sons put up in 1860. The day after his funeral the board of the Bank of Montreal decided that the directors would go into mourning for 30 days.

Minutes before his death Molson had dictated his last wishes to notary Henry Griffin, in the presence of Dr Robert Nelson* and Frederick Gundlack. He required his sons to do what they had been incapable of doing during his lifetime: work together in the same enterprises. Each of them, as both residuary legatee and executor of the will, was part owner of the others' businesses or benefited from the income that these brought in, and each was accountable to his brothers. As the will included some ambiguous parts on which even the notary and the two witnesses could not agree, the brothers instituted legal proceedings against one another, with John on one side and Thomas and William together on the other. At the end of five years they wearied of these disputes and by a strange twist asked the two people whom their father had named in his will to be executors along with them, Peter McGill and George Moffatt (who had both withdrawn), to serve as arbitrators and set the conditions for the division of the assets and income, defining reciprocal rights and obligations. Not until 1843, seven years after their father's death, did the three brothers truly come to respect his last wishes.

A portrait of John Molson is in the family's possession. In a will made on 30 Jan. 1830 he had stipulated: "It is my will that my portrait painted in oil shall be the property of such of my sons and their heirs as shall own the said brewery after my decease." Perhaps he was seeking to tell posterity which of his numerous enterprises he considered to be the most important; it was the one that had marked his "Commencement on the Grand Stage of the World."

ALFRED DUBUC

[John Molson Sr figures quite prominently in each of the three published works on the Molson family. B. K. Sandwell, *The Molson family, etc.* (Montreal, 1933), is a serious endeavour, although occasionally too laudatory, which deals almost exclusively with John Molson Sr and his three sons. The work is useful for studying the genealogy of the family. Merrill Denison, *The barley and the stream: the Molson story; a footnote to Canadian history* (Toronto, 1955), is a more thorough investigation of the history of the whole family, but too many statements (including dates) are open to question and are not supported (and in some instances are contradicted) by primary sources. S. E. Woods, *The Molson saga* (Garden City, N.Y., 1983), has been severely criticized by reviewers, and the author's goal of presenting the inside story of the Molsons has elicited little interest.

Papers relating to the Molsons are to be found principally at PAC, MG 28, III57; vols.1, 10–11, 13, 19, 21, 27–30, 33, and 35 were used in the preparation of this biography. The records of the Montreal Board of Trade (mfm. at PAC, MG 28, III44) and the journal of Jedediah Hubbell Dorwin* (PAC, MG 24, D12) contain references to John Molson. Other materials concerning him are held at the McGill Univ. Libraries, Dept. of Rare Books and Special Coll., CH16.S52, CH330.S290; McCord Museum, M19110, M19113–15, M19117, M19124, and M21228; and ANQ-M, in the minute-books of notaries Isaac Jones Gibb (CN1-175), Jonathan Abraham Gray (CN1-185), and Henry Griffin (CN1-187); Musée du château Ramezay, docs.520 and 523; Bank of Montreal Arch., Court Committee of Directors, minute-books, 1817–36. A.D.]

By-laws of St. Paul's Lodge, no.514 ... (Montreal, 1844). *Docs. relating to constitutional hist., 1791–1818* (Doughty and McArthur); *1819–28* (Doughty and Story). *History and by-laws of Saint Paul's Lodge, no.374* ... (Montreal, 1876; 2nd ed., Montreal, 1895). L.C., House of Assembly, *Journals*, 1816–20; Legislative Council, *Journals*, 1832–36; *Statutes*, 1792–1836. *Select documents in Canadian economic history*, ed. H. A. Innis and A. R. M. Lower (2v., Toronto, 1929–33), 2: 140–41, 199–200, 295. "Union proposée entre le Haut et le Bas-Canada," PAC *Rapport*, 1897: 33–38. *L'Ami du peuple, de l'ordre et des lois*, 13 janv. 1836. *La Minerve*, 14 janv. 1836. *Montreal Gazette*, 12, 16 Jan. 1836. *Morning Courier* (Montreal), 14, 21 Jan. 1836. *Quebec Gazette*, 15 Jan. 1836. F.-J. Audet, *Les députés de Montréal*, 88–91. Borthwick, *Hist. and biog. gazetteer*, 34–35, 37–38, 44, 50–51, 53. Joseph Bouchette, *The British dominions in North America; or a topographical description of the provinces of Lower and Upper Canada* ... (2v., London, 1832), 1: 431; *Description topographique du Bas-Canada*, 489–90. Desjardins, *Guide parl. Montreal directory*, 1820: 20–21, 23, 26, 30, 108.

F. D. Adams, *A history of Christ Church Cathedral, Montreal* (Montreal, 1941). W. H. Atherton, *History of the harbour front of Montreal since its discovery by Jacques Cartier in 1535* ... ([Montreal, 1935]), 3–4; *Montreal, 1535–1914* (3v., Montreal and Vancouver, 1914), 2: 138, 271, 275–79, 283, 435, 527, 556, 575–76, 607–8. Hector Berthelot, *Montréal, le bon vieux temps*, É.-Z. Massicotte, compil. (2v. en 1, Montréal, 1916), 1: 23–25; 2: 11, 18, 53. Campbell, *Hist. of Scotch Presbyterian Church*, 82–83, 121–24. Christie, *Hist. of L.C.* (1848–55). François Cinq-Mars, *L'avènement du premier chemin de fer au Canada: St-Jean–Laprairie, 1836* (Saint-Jean-sur-Richelieu, Qué., 1986), 47–53, 80–86, 91–97, 109–11. G. E. Cone, "Studies in the development of transportation in the Champlain valley to 1876" (MA thesis, Univ. of Vt., Burlington, 1945). J. I. Cooper, *History of St George's Lodge, 1829–1954* (Montreal, 1954). Creighton, *Empire of St. Lawrence*. Denison, *La première banque au Canada*, 1: 219–74. Franklin Graham, *Histrionic Montreal; annals of the Montreal stage with biographical and critical notices of the plays and players of a century* (2nd ed., Montreal, 1902; repr. New York and London, 1969). J. H. Graham, *Outlines of the history of freemasonry in the province of Quebec* (Montreal, 1892), 168, 170–73, 182. *Hochelaga depicta* ..., ed. Newton Bosworth (Montreal, 1839; repr. Toronto, 1974). H. E. MacDermot, *A history of the Montreal General Hospital* (Montreal, 1950), 4: 2, 4, 12, 34, 41–42, 110. Peter Mathias, *The brewing industry in England, 1700–1830* (Cambridge, Eng., 1959). A. J. B. Milbourne, *Freemasonry in the province of Quebec, 1759–1959* (n.p., 1960), 72, 75–76, 78–80, 82. Ouellet, *Bas-Canada*; *Hist. économique*. S. B. Ryerson, *Unequal union: roots of crisis in the Canadas, 1815–1873* (2nd ed., Toronto, 1973). Alfred Sandham, *Ville-Marie, or, sketches of Montreal, past and present* (Montreal, 1870), 91–93. Maurice Séguin, *La "nation canadienne" et l'agriculture (1760–1850): essai d'histoire économique* (Trois-Rivières, Qué., 1970). Taft Manning, *Revolt of French Canada*. G. J. J. Tulchinsky, "The construction of the first Lachine Canal, 1815–1826" (MA thesis, McGill Univ., Montreal, 1960); *River barons*, 14, 25, 51, 111, 213–14, 216–17. G. H. Wilson, "The application of steam to St Lawrence valley navigation, 1809–1840" (MA thesis, McGill Univ., 1961). Owen Klein, "The opening of Montreal's Theatre Royal, 1825," *Theatre Hist. in Canada* (Toronto and Kingston, Ont.), 1 (1980): 24–38.

MONDELET, JEAN-MARIE, notary, JP, office holder, politician, and militia officer; b. *c.* 1771, or possibly 29 April 1773 and baptized François in Saint-Charles-sur-Richelieu, Que.; son of Dominique Mondelet* and Marie-Françoise Hains; d. 15 June 1843 in Trois-Rivières, Lower Canada.

Jean-Marie Mondelet, the only surviving child of 12 or 13, began his classical studies in the Collège Saint-Raphaël, Montreal, in 1781 and completed them in the Petit Séminaire de Québec from 1788 to 1790. His mother being unable to bear his continued absence, Mondelet sacrificed his dream of studying law in order to return to the Richelieu valley. He articled with notary Jean-Baptiste Grisé of Chambly and, after receiving his commission on 24 Sept. 1794, opened a practice in Saint-Marc, where his parents lived. He quickly took two students of the profession, Étienne Ranvoyzé* and Paul-Théophile Pinsonaut*, and from 1799 he was for a while in partnership with Ranvoyzé. By the time he married Charlotte Boucher de Grosbois in Boucherville on 29 Jan. 1798 he had acquired a modest but respectable fortune and social position as a rural member of the Canadian professional bourgeoisie. Contracted with provision for a community of property, according to French law, the marriage settlement included a dower of £150 and was witnessed on Mondelet's behalf by a cousin, Joseph Ainsse, son of fur trader Joseph-Louis*, and by Gabriel Franchère, a merchant and father of Gabriel*, a future fur trader. The couple would have three children. On 1 June 1798 Mondelet was named a justice of the peace for the Montreal district; over the years his commission would be renewed and extended to include the districts of Trois-Rivières (1811), Quebec (1815), and Saint-François (1821) in Lower Canada and even of Johnstown in Upper Canada (1815).

An ambitious man, Mondelet wanted to be in Montreal, and in 1801 he asked an intimate friend, Ignace-Michel-Louis-Antoine d'Irumberry* de Salaberry, to procure for him the post of police inspector or that of clerk of the land roll. He was still in Saint-Marc in May 1802, but soon after, at the request of several public men of Montreal, he moved there (taking his mother), and before long had built up an extensive practice. In 1804, with businessman John Richardson*, he was elected to the House of Assembly for Montreal West; four years later he and Solicitor General James Stuart* were returned without opposition for Montreal East. Mondelet was relatively faithful in attendance and active on committees, manifesting a particular interest in prison reform and reinforcement of the notarial profession, the reputation of which had become tarnished since the conquest. In 1808 he introduced a bill to establish qualifications for those aspiring to become notaries and, incidentally, to encourage secondary studies by reducing the period of articling for college graduates. The bill passed the assembly after heated discussion but died in the Legislative Council.

Mondelet mostly supported the nationalist Canadian party, which dominated the assembly, voting with it on 17 of 26 occasions from 1805 to 1808 and on 4 of 6 occasions in 1808–9. He moved in the social circle surrounding the Papineau–Viger family, which was influential in the party, until late 1808 at least. However, in January 1809, as tensions increased between the assembly and Governor Sir James Henry Craig*, an observer remarked to Jacques Viger* that Mondelet "feared . . . you were pushing matters a little too far" and was becoming critical of *Le Canadien*, the party's newspaper, for its attacks on the administration. When, that fall, Mondelet again ran in Montreal East, the Canadian party put up the popular Joseph PAPINEAU, forcing him to desist; switching to Montreal West, he was handily defeated by Denis-Benjamin Viger*. "I succumbed under the accusation of being too devoted to the interests of the government," Mondelet wrote to a friend. "I have lived and I will die devoted to the government." In the spring of 1810, after Craig had seized *Le Canadien* and imprisoned those chiefly responsible for it, Mondelet was narrowly defeated in Montreal West, 287 to 281, by Joseph Papineau, who undercut him tactically at the last minute by loudly proclaiming his own loyalty and his support for Craig.

Mondelet's wife had died in 1802. On 29 Dec. 1811, as if in defiance of the nationalists, he married Juliana Walker, widow of Anglican priest James Sutherland Rudd, after having signed a marriage contract that renounced any community of property. Two of the witnesses were Louis Chaboillez* and Michel-Eustache-Gaspard-Alain Chartier* de Lotbinière, whose politics were no doubt closer to Mondelet's own. The couple would have three children. Since his arrival in Montreal, Mondelet had begun accumulating government appointments. Named a commissioner for the Lachine turnpike in 1805, he had been appointed a commissioner to remove the fortifications of Montreal in 1807, when he was also a trustee for the construction of a market-house. After his electoral defeat of 1809 the appointments increased rapidly in number. Three were of particular importance: in February 1810 he was made joint president with Thomas McCord* of the Montreal Court of Quarter Sessions, an influential post in municipal affairs and the administration of justice; in December 1811 he became a police magistrate; and in August 1812 he was appointed coroner for Montreal.

Following the outbreak of the War of 1812 Mondelet was commissioned a major in the militia. In 1813 he sat on a board chaired by James McGill* which suggested means of reinforcing the sedentary militia. That June, Hugues HENEY, a nationalist, reported to Jacques Viger that the "quasi General Mondelet" and Louis-Joseph de Fleury Deschambault had tried in vain to raise a 7th battalion of militia "as a proof of their loyalty and their sincere desire . . . to obtain a position." In fact, Fleury Deschambault incorporated a battalion of sedentary militia, which became known as the 7th Select Embodied Militia Battalion, with himself as the colonel and Mondelet as major. On its disbandment in November 1813 Mondelet transferred to the Pointe-Claire battalion of militia, of which he became lieutenant-colonel in April 1814; he would be named its commander in 1820.

As his militia duties lessened at the end of and after the war, Mondelet accepted new civil appointments, such as those of commissioner for the building of churches and parsonages (1814), commissioner for the improvement of internal communications in the county of Montreal (1817), commissioner for repairing jails and court-houses (1818), and warden of the House of Industry (1818). He had some non-governmental social interests. He was a promoter of the Company of Proprietors of the Montreal Library, founded in 1819 to manage a library established about 1796 by the Montreal Library Association, and in 1821 he subscribed to the Quebec Emigrants' Society. In general, however, his energies were consumed by his private and public careers, which occasionally mingled. In June 1821 he was commissioned a king's notary, an appointment that brought a significant increase of business in his already thriving practice since it authorized him to execute notarial business of the government and the army; in particular he drew up all the land concessions in the crown seigneury of Sorel and all the acts relative to its seigneurial land roll, which he was commissioned in 1822 to establish. In September 1821, possibly to accommodate the increase, he formed an association with Paul-Édouard Daveluy of Varennes, near Montreal, and they operated from an office conveniently located next door to that of the sheriff.

By 1822 Mondelet seems to have effected a certain reconciliation with the Canadian party, principally it would seem through Jacques Viger. He shared that party's fear of a proposed union of the Canadas [*see* John Richardson], although he considered the rise of the union project "a little our own fault." At the same time he was among a group that urged construction of a cathedral church for Bishop Jean-Jacques LARTIGUE of Montreal, a cousin of Louis-Joseph Papineau* and Denis-Benjamin Viger, both of whom supported Lartigue in a struggle with the predominantly French Séminaire de Saint-Sulpice for the spiritual hegemony of Montreal. Later Mondelet was a fund-raiser for the cathedral, which the Sulpicians attempted to oppose by planning a vast new parish church of Notre-Dame. His removal in 1824 as police magistrate and joint president of the Court of Quarter Sessions seems to have been the result of numerous complaints against the organization of the police rather than a political reprimand for his support of nationalist causes, since the politically unimpeachable McCord suffered the same fate. Yet, under the highly suspicious Governor Lord Dalhousie [RAMSAY], Mondelet's increasing identification with the Canadian party, no doubt reinforced by the more radical views of his sons Dominique* and Charles-Elzéar*, rendered vulnerable his position as a favourite of the administration. In March 1824 Mondelet was discharged from his commission to draw up the land roll of the seigneury of Sorel, and in 1827 he lost the position of king's notary. When, in November 1827, Dalhousie deprived his sons of their militia commissions, Mondelet resigned his own.

Mondelet remained a moderate nationalist, nevertheless. He admired the zeal of Denis-Benjamin Viger and in February 1831 found Papineau "more commendable than ever." On the other hand, he praised to Jacques Viger the prudence of Dalhousie's successor, Sir James Kempt*. By 1830 he had recovered his militia commission, which he retained until 1839 at least, and in May 1832 he was appointed to the newly formed Montreal Board of Health, established when a cholera epidemic of massive proportions struck Lower Canada [*see* Matthew WHITWORTH-AYLMER]. After Kempt's departure, however, in an atmosphere of rising political tension between the colonial administration and the Patriote party (as the Canadian party had come to be known) moderate political ground increasingly became a no man's land, under attack from both sides. Radical nationalists even viewed the failure of the government and the boards of health to contain the cholera epidemic as an underhand attempt to reduce the Canadian population. Once again drawing back from confrontation, Mondelet became identified by nationalists with the British administration.

The dangers inherent in holding the middle ground in Lower Canadian politics were revealed forcefully to Mondelet following a by-election in Montreal West on 21 May 1832 during which British troops killed three Canadians [*see* Daniel Tracey*]. Mondelet arrived at the scene immediately after the shooting to begin the coroner's inquest. At the request of several Patriotes, Papineau quickly descended on him. "[I] saved him from making a number of stupid mistakes; he committed a thousand others knowingly and voluntarily," Papineau told John NEILSON at Quebec. A few days later a coroner's jury voted nine to three for the arrest of two British officers, but, feeling that the law required unanimity, Mondelet adjourned the inquest to the August criminal assizes. Only under pressure from an aggressive Papineau did he finally order the arrest of the officers, who were later released on bail. The English party protested that Mondelet had accepted a packed jury, "almost all readers of *La Minerve*," the newspaper of the Patriote party, and that Papineau had constantly intervened to direct Mondelet's conduct of the inquest. As well, one of the officers charged that Mondelet had refused to allow consideration of the context of the shootings, and in July the colonial secretary, Lord Goderich, deemed it "most unfortunate that the Coroner's jury were allowed to separate without giving a [unanimous] verdict." The officers were acquitted at the criminal assizes, and while their conduct was being formally approved by the king at the end of the year Mondelet was being grilled by a committee of inquiry of the assembly, which was dominated by the Patriote party. Jacques Viger found that Mondelet "offers elegant sentences, many compliments, sweet sayings, risky assertions on points of law, but especially far too much reticence" (due to a "faulty memory") and added that "his testimony will not do him honour, and . . . could do him much harm." After one grilling, remarked Viger, "he dined . . . at the Château," the governor's residence.

By 1834 Mondelet's sons were also under strong attack from the Patriote party, for accepting government offices. The following year Mondelet conducted an inquest into the death by starvation or by freezing of an inmate of the Montreal prison and only reluctantly signed the jury's verdict of negligence on the part of the disreputable warden and other prison officials. Mondelet himself blamed the horrible conditions in the prison, and was said to have remarked that the death resulted from inaction on prison reform by a legislature preoccupied with political problems. Incensed, the assembly, in a procedure long since denounced by former civil secretary Herman Witsius RYLAND and others in the English party, inquired into Mondelet's conduct and, without hearing the accused, published a report in June 1836 charging him with breach of its privileges. Its demand that Mondelet be fired as coroner was rejected by Governor Lord Gosford [ACHESON]. Meanwhile, Mondelet, who was especially attached to the position of coroner, had pleaded with the assembly, almost abjectly, to be heard and spared. A new prison was built in 1837 but, as the Patriote rebels of 1837–38 learned, conditions within it were hardly better than those Mondelet had denounced in the old one.

Mondelet's private life had been tinged with the tragedies typical of his time: not only had his first wife died at a young age, but half of his children did not survive infancy, and his beloved mother expired in his house in 1813. Mondelet himself long suffered from extreme rheumatism and from injuries sustained in a buggy accident. He grew deaf and blind and had an agonizing asthmatic condition. He ceased practising as a notary in June 1842 after drawing up act no.7,041; two years earlier he had been given the honour of recording the installation in the cathedral of Montreal of Lartigue's successor, Ignace Bourget*. Mondelet died in 1843 at Trois-Rivières, aged about 72 years.

Independent and outspoken, Jean-Marie Mondelet had been an extremely competent, conscientious, and ambitious office holder, whose career and political fortunes had been blown about in the brisk and then violent political cross-winds of early 19th-century Lower Canada. He had tried to hold a moderate nationalist position, but he became conservative whenever nationalist views and actions turned radical. His political commitment was peripheral to his interest in public service, however, and as coroner in particular he had been able to combine his legal talents with his administrative ability and find an outlet for his boundless energy.

In collaboration with ELIZABETH ABBOTT-NAMPHY and MARGARET MACKINNON

ANQ-MBF, CE1-48, 19 juin 1843. ASQ, Fonds Viger-Verreau, sér.O, 0139: 130–31, 239–43, 245–48; 0141: 193–95; 0143: 239; 0144: 6, 17–18, 21, 157–59, 167–69; 0145: 57–59, 63; 0146: 168, 326–28; 0147: 19–21, 95–100, 202–3 (mfm. at PAC). AUM, P 58, U, corr. de J.-M. Mondelet, 1811, 1827–39. PAC, MG 30, D1, 21: 740–807; RG 68, General index, 1651–1841. Univ. of B.C. Library, Special Coll. Division (Vancouver), Michaud coll., box 2, file 2. L.C., House of Assembly, *Journals*, 1805–9, 1835–37. J.-M. Mondelet, "Lettre de M. J.-M. Mondelet à l'honorable M. Louis de Salaberry," *BRH*, 33 (1927): 249–50. *Le Canadien*, 9 oct. 1809. *La Minerve*, 19 juin 1843. *Montreal Gazette*, 19 June 1843. *Quebec Gazette*, 25 April 1799; 27 Dec. 1804; 7 Aug. 1806; 19 Feb., 23 April, 7 July 1807; 3, 17 March, 26 May 1808; 20, 27 April, 4, 11 May, 15 June, 16 Nov., 14 Dec. 1809; 15 Feb., 12 April, 22 Nov. 1810; 15 Aug., 26 Dec. 1811; 10 Sept. 1812; 6 April 1815; 5 June, 18 Sept. 1817; 18, 28 May, 27 Aug. 1818; 7 June, 28 Oct. 1819; 28 Feb., 20 April, 26 Oct., 27 Nov. 1820; 20 Aug., 4 Oct., 19, 26 Nov. 1821; 24 May 1824. F.-J. Audet, *Les députés de Montréal*. Desrosiers, "Inv. de la corr. de Mgr Bourget," ANQ *Rapport*, 1946–47: 85; "Inv. de la corr. de Mgr Lartigue," 1941–42: 385, 396. P.-G. Roy, *Les juges de la prov. de Québec*.

J. D. Borthwick, *History of the Montreal prison from A.D. 1784 to A.D. 1886* . . . (Montreal, 1886), 11. France Galarneau, "L'élection pour le Quartier-Ouest de Montréal en 1832: analyse politico-sociale" (thèse de MA, univ. de Montréal, 1977), 126–30, 133, 139, 146. Maurault, *Le collège de Montréal* (Dansereau; 1967). Ouellet, *Bas-Canada*. J.-E. Roy, *Hist. du notariat*, 2: 229, 275. Rumilly, *Hist. de Montréal*, vol.2; *Papineau et son temps*. Taft Manning, *Revolt of French Canada*, 380–81. André Vachon, *Histoire du notariat canadien, 1621–1960* (Québec, 1962), 88. F.-J. Audet, "Les Mondelet," *Cahiers des Dix*, 3 (1938): 191–216; "Pierre-Édouard Leclère (1798–1866)," 8 (1943): 109–40. "Biographie du juge Mondelet," *L'Opinion publique*, 19 déc. 1872: 601–4. J. E. Hare, "L'Assemblée législative du Bas-Canada, 1792–1814: députation et polarisation politique," *RHAF*, 27 (1973–74): 361–95. Fernand Lefebvre, "La vie à la prison de Montréal au XIXe siècle," *RHAF*, 7 (1953–54): 524–37. Gérard Malchelosse, "Généalogie de la famille Mondelet," *BRH*, 51 (1945): 51–60. Victor Morin, "Clubs et sociétés notoires d'autrefois," *Cahiers des Dix*, 14 (1949): 187–222.

MONK, MARIA, author; b. 27 June 1816 in Dorchester (Saint-Jean-sur-Richelieu), Lower Canada, daughter of William Monk and Isabella Mills; d. in the summer of 1849 at New York.

Maria Monk was a difficult child. According to her mother, when she was about seven she stuck a slate-pencil into her ear, an accident that caused permanent brain damage. At an early age she began to show signs of dissolute conduct and to engage in prostitution. In November 1834 her mother had her confined in the Charitable Institution for Female Penitents, a home established and run by Agathe-Henriette Huguet, *dit* Latour. But far from improving, Maria's behaviour led to her expulsion in March 1835; she was pregnant by then.

Maria ran off to the United States. There she found herself at the centre of an anti-Catholic nativistic controversy that had reached a peak when a mob set fire to the Ursuline convent in Charlestown (Boston) on 11 Aug. 1834. In October 1835 a New York newspaper published a statement by Maria describing her life as a nun at the Hôtel-Dieu of Montreal. She claimed that on the order of the superior and of the auxiliary bishop, Jean-Jacques LARTIGUE, she had had to kill a companion who refused to submit to the revolting demands of the priests. The article announced the forthcoming publication of a "complete and detailed account" of the scenes at the Hôtel-Dieu.

In January 1836 the *Awful disclosures of Maria Monk*, a work that she was supposed to have written, came out in New York. In it were described the infamous things she claimed to have suffered as a Catholic nun. On 13 Feb. 1836 Alfred-Xavier Rambau*, editor of the Montreal paper *L'Ami du peuple, de l'ordre et des lois*, noted the recent publication of the volume, which he termed "as dull as [it is] untruthful." It related that Maria Monk had been given a Protestant upbringing, but that upon her conversion to Catholicism she had entered the convent of the Hôtel-Dieu of Montreal. After she had taken her vows, the superior told her to "obey the priests in all things," and this, she discovered "to her utter astonishment and horror," meant "to live in the practice of criminal intercourse with them." The priests could reach the nuns' quarters by an underground passage connecting the convent with the Séminaire de Saint-Sulpice, and the children born from these unholy unions were immediately baptized and strangled. She was supposed to have been present at the murder of a nun who was resisting the priests' advances and at the strangling of two babies after their baptism and to have found the place in the basement of the Hôtel-Dieu where the bodies were buried, as well as the tunnel communicating with the seminary.

According to her account Maria was soon pregnant by Abbé Patrick Phelan*. Unable to contemplate the cruel fate that would be inflicted upon her child, however, she had fled the convent. The first edition of the work ended with this episode. A new one published within the year contained other details. It disclosed that the fleeing nun realized it would be difficult for her to leave Montreal without being intercepted. In a fit of despair she resolved to drown herself, but two workmen persuaded her that she must go on living in order to expose the turpitudes of "popery." She then reached New York, where, alone and friendless, she was again tempted to put an end to her days by fasting. Fortunately some kind souls took her to a refuge, where she recounted her adventures to a Protestant minister. He was so impressed that he exhorted Maria to relate the facts, so they might be publicized. The book ended with a report of her trip to Montreal with the Reverend William K. Hoyt to confirm her revelations.

The immediate success of the publication brought out the truth about the real authors of this fabrication, for there was soon a dispute over the division of the profits. Evidence in court revealed that Hoyt, a determined foe of Catholicism, had helped Maria in her flight to the United States, and that the *Awful disclosures* had been written from Maria's oral account by the Reverend John Jay Slocum, a Presbyterian minister, with the assistance of Hoyt, the Reverend George Bourne, and others, who had pocketed most of the profits from this best-seller.

In the autumn of 1836 another fugitive, Sister St Frances Patrick, who said that she too came from the Hôtel-Dieu, turned up in New York at just the right moment to substantiate these sensational revelations. She had been a nun at the same time as Maria and claimed to be able to corroborate each of her assertions. The two appeared at a public meeting and, after embracing effusively, conversed for some time about their stay together at the Hôtel-Dieu.

The controversy split people into supporters and opponents of Maria Monk. To get at the truth, it was essential that an inquiry be held on the spot. On 15 Oct. 1836 *L'Ami du peuple* noted that the American journalist William Leete Stone had gone to Montreal and had obtained permission to inspect the Hôtel-Dieu thoroughly with Maria Monk's book in hand. At the end of his inspection, according to the paper, he acknowledged: "After 10 minutes the imposture had become as plain as day. I now declare more openly and boldly than *ever that neither Maria Monk nor Francis Partridge have ever set foot in the convent of the Hôtel Dieu*." Stone published the results of his investigation in his newspaper and later in a pamphlet.

Stone's refutation was the most telling blow dealt Maria Monk's tales in the United States. In Lower Canada attention had also been given to proving the falsity of her vile claims. John Jones and Pierre-Édouard Leclère*, proprietors and editors of *L'Ami du peuple*, took the initiative. It fell to them, as allies of the Sulpicians, to defend the seminary against her atrocious calumnies. Consequently, on 21 Aug. 1836 Bishop Lartigue could write to a resident of Mascouche to dissuade him from preparing a pamphlet against her abominable book because a refutation was being printed in New York, to be published, as well, in Glasgow and Dublin. In Lartigue's opinion an additional work "would accord too much importance to such a wretched and absurd story that induces Presbyterians and Methodists in the United States to swallow all these absurdities as honey." The refutation to which he was referring was the slim volume in which Jones and Leclère had collected a number of declarations and depositions made under oath that demolished Maria's inventions.

Slocum, whose involvement was made explicit by their rebuttal, reacted quickly by publishing a pamphlet in his protégée's name early in 1837. On 22 January Lartigue informed Archbishop Joseph SIGNAY of Quebec that "Maria Monk has given the public a new pamphlet in which she spews forth more horrible stuff than ever against the clergy of this country, in which she is stupid enough to say that, on orders, she herself poisoned one of the nuns of the Hôtel-Dieu of Montreal when she was her companion." The bishop wondered whether it might be possible to get the governor of New York to extradite her so that she could be tried for her calumnies and libels, because many people in the United States apparently still believed the infamous tales she was telling.

But on the other side of the border Maria's popularity was beginning to wane, and many Protestant publications were of the opinion that the matter was all a fraud. In August 1837 she disappeared from New York. Turning up in Philadelphia, she claimed that she had been kidnapped by some Catholic priests who wanted to put an end to her revelations about the convents. Her wild nonsense did not prevent some people from believing the tales in a final publication attributed to her in 1837: *Further disclosures by Maria Monk, concerning the Hotel Dieu nunnery of Montreal*. It claimed that nuns from the United States and Canada were going to Île des Sœurs, near Montreal, to give birth to illegitimate children. On 18 March and 24 April 1837 Lartigue confided to the vicar general of New York that through Stone he had given a Protestant organization in New York permission to visit the Hôtel-Dieu again, and even Île des Sœurs, a step being called for by a New York newspaper.

The result of this investigation was probably conclusive, for the Monk affair then went into a decided decline. In 1838 Maria had a child by an unknown father, this time without attributing the paternity to a priest. Shortly afterwards she married, but through her habitual drunkenness and debauchery she squandered her husband's savings, and he soon left her. In 1849 she was arrested in a house of ill repute for having stolen money from the man she was entertaining, and she was incarcerated in a New York prison. Half mad, she died there in the summer of 1849.

Maria Monk remains the sad heroine of a volume that American historian Ray Allen Billington says was "important as sensational propaganda against Catholicism." According to his estimate, 300,000 copies of *Awful disclosures* were sold before the Civil War.

PHILIPPE SYLVAIN

Maria Monk is assumed to be the author of *Awful disclosures of Maria Monk, as exhibited in a narrative of her sufferings during a residence of five years as a novice, and two years as a black nun, in the Hotel Dieu nunnery at Montreal . . .* (New York, 1836), which went through numerous editions and translations, as well as of *Further disclosures by Maria Monk, concerning the Hotel Dieu nunnery of Montreal; also, her visit to Nuns' Island, and disclosures concerning the secret retreat* (Boston, 1837).

ANQ-M, CE4-17, 23 juill. 1816. *Affidavit of Madame D. C. McDonnell (matron of the Montreal Magdalen Asylum)* (n.p., 1836). [John Jones and P.-É. Leclère], *Awful exposure of the atrocious plot formed by certain individuals against the clergy and nuns of Lower Canada through the intervention of Maria Monk . . .* (New York, 1836). J. J. Slocum, *Furthur disclosures by Maria Monk, concerning the Hotel Dieu nunnery of Montreal . . .* (New York, 1837). W. L. Stone, *Maria Monk and the nunnery of the Hotel Dieu; being an account of a visit to the convents of Montreal, and refutation of the "Awful disclosures" . . .* (New York, 1836). Desrosiers, "Inv. de la corr. de Mgr Lartigue," ANQ *Rapport*, 1944–45: 195, 198, 230, 236, 239. R. A. Billington, *The Protestant crusade, 1800–1860; a study of the origins of American nativism* (New York, 1938), 99–109. Gustavus Myers, *History of bigotry in the United States* (New York, 1943), 154–60. R. A. Billington, "Maria Monk and her influence," *Catholic Hist. Rev.* (Washington), 22 (1936–37): 283–96. Bernard Dufebvre [Émile Castonguay], "Le 'roman' de Maria Monk," *Rev. de l'univ. Laval* (Québec), 8 (1953–54): 569–80. Philippe Sylvain, "L'affaire Maria Monk," *Cahiers des Dix*, 43 (1983): 167–84.

MONVIEL (Monteil, Montviel), FRANÇOIS VASSAL DE. *See* VASSAL

MORRIS, PATRICK, merchant, shipowner, farmer, author, politician, and office holder; b. probably *c.* 1789 in Waterford (Republic of Ireland); m. 26 April 1814 Mary Foley in Harbour Grace, Nfld, and they had one daughter; m. secondly 1830 Frances Bullen in Cork (Republic of Ireland), and they had four sons and two daughters; d. 22 Aug. 1849 in St John's.

Patrick Morris came to St John's around 1804 to work as a clerk for Luke Maddock, a Waterford merchant and possibly a relative, who had settled there a quarter-century before. Like that of most Irish-Newfoundland merchants Morris's social background remains obscure, but it was modest and he brought little or no capital from his homeland. Maddock typified the expanding Irish trading community in late 18th-century St John's. His business was small, focusing on the importation of provisions from Waterford and manufactures from Liverpool, largely in English vessels. His clientele were Irish Catholic planters, artisans, and servants in the town and nearby outports. Maddock also operated a shop and tavern in the centre of town, sublet tenements to fellow immigrants, and ran a farm. Within the relatively short span of six or seven years Morris had apparently accumulated enough expertise, capital, and connections to launch an independent trade. He leased premises on the waterfront in 1810 and quickly organized a business modelled on that of his former employer, whose demise shortly afterwards probably left Morris with an established clientele.

Morris entered mercantile trade on the crest of a boom in the cod economy. Supplies and wages were high but so were profits. Passengers from Ireland, the main overseas source of seasonal labour, increased in concert with the volume of supplies. St John's, moreover, controlled much of this inflated traffic. By the time Morris entered mercantile trade, four-fifths of all shipping to the island docked there. From its inception his trade centred on the importation of passengers and provisions from his native Waterford and the return of cargoes of cod and oil. For his vessels Morris initially relied largely on shipowners from Teignmouth, in England, but he purchased a brig in the fall of 1814, another in 1819, and two more deep-sea vessels by 1825. His pattern of trading was typical of Irish merchants resident in St John's at this time. Waterford was the focal point of transatlantic trade, but it gradually faded as a profitable source of supplies. Morris then sent his ships to Cork and Liverpool, and after 1825 to Hamburg (Federal Republic of Germany) and Danzig (Gdańsk, Poland) where, he reported, prices for foodstuffs were only half those in British ports.

Morris did not restrict himself to the fishery. St John's, built almost entirely of wood, was expanding and there was a boom in construction, particularly following the fires of 1816 and 1817. He imported timber from St Andrews and Miramichi, in New Brunswick, and later sent his ships to these ports and Quebec to carry it direct to Waterford. There he loaded his vessels with brick, limestone, and slate for St John's. He also imported a wide range of household goods, mainly from Liverpool, and coal from Sydney, N.S., and British ports.

St John's was not only the primary centre for the redistribution of imported supplies and passengers but also the hub of the island's export trade. Commerce with the outharbours was based on credit and barter; merchants advanced supplies to planters in the spring in exchange for a pledge of fish and oil in the fall. Morris announced as early as 1812 that he would follow this arrangement. His trading territory outside St John's was primarily the shore south of the town, by now heavily Irish, and the populous Conception Bay. At the latter place he established an informal partnership with a fellow Waterford merchant, Thomas Foley of Harbour Grace, whose daughter he married in 1814. By the mid 1820s Morris had five coasting schooners, reserved largely for outharbour trade. In winter these were usually sent sealing, an industry he believed had considerable potential. In 1832, for example, he dispatched six schooners, averaging 75 tons, with 132 sealers to the ice. These men, almost all Irish, paid Morris 30 shillings each for a berth and were given supplies and half the catch. His captains were paid £5 a month plus a bonus for every pelt. At the peak Morris shipped over 10,000 sealskins to the London market in one season. He also operated a schooner fishery at a room he held in Labrador. Every May he sent a ship, usually one back from sealing, with a crew of six men and supplies to fish in this remote harbour. Once dried, the fish was taken to St John's and the schooner then returned for a second cargo.

Morris used kin extensively on both sides of the Atlantic to help coordinate his trade. One brother, James, and their brother-in-law Robert Kent formed a partnership in Waterford in 1813 to supply passengers and provisions and to handle imports of cod and oil. Another brother, Simon, a trader in Waterford, came to St John's in 1828 to work with Patrick along with two sons of James Morris and four sons of Robert Kent. Simon's son Edward* arrived in 1832. James Kent became Morris's partner in 1828 but later returned to Waterford as partner with his brother John Kent*, who established in St John's an independent trade identical to that of Morris, his uncle.

With his intimate Waterford connections and his knowledge of the local labour market in St John's and its hinterland, Morris was in a good position to prosecute the passenger trade. Prior to his purchase of a ship he had acted as a migration agent for Irish merchants. He charged a five per cent commission for collecting passage money and remitting it to Ireland. By 1815, the peak year of Irish migration to St John's, he was carrying people out and home on his own ship. He also acted as agent for two other vessels with passengers from Waterford and advertised these vessels as taking freight and passengers to Halifax and Miramichi. In September he served notice to all who had come out that spring "to pay their passage money on or before November 10 or their bail notes will be sent back to Waterford for collection." For a time he was the leading merchant in the passenger trade. Virtually every year between 1815 and 1835 advertisements appeared in the St John's or Waterford papers announcing the departure of his ships. By 1819, having moved into the timber trade, he took emigrants direct from Waterford to Saint John, Miramichi, and Quebec.

Morris built up his business at a time when many established houses in St John's were giving up because of the economic recession that followed the Napoleonic Wars. He was one of several young merchants or traders who moved in to fill the vacuum. By 1820, his trade firmly established, he was determined to protect and enhance it. He tended to lay the blame for Newfoundland's woes on the government. France and the United States had been granted generous concessions in Newfoundland waters after the war. By 1822 they accounted for two-thirds of the fishery. During the war Newfoundlanders had conducted a profitable inshore fishery in areas abandoned by the French, especially in the north, but their expansion had been blocked with the return of the French. Unlike France, Britain offered few financial incentives to the fishermen and even imposed duties on breadstuffs from the United States. Morris accepted the view that the fishery was the key to Newfoundland's economic growth, but he also argued all his life that the colony could not prosper without the development of a local agriculture. He accused the large merchant houses of deliberately misleading government regarding the unsuitability of Newfoundland for commercial farming in order to protect their import trade in food. Morris maintained that food prices were too high, a serious handicap to the growth of a profitable planter fishery. A reduction in the cost of cod production through the development of a local food supply would benefit both fisherman and exporting merchant.

Morris was willing to put his theories to the test. In 1823 he acquired a farm just outside the town and by 1836 had 40 acres "in a high state of cultivation" with extensive outbuildings and a handsome cottage, his family residence. He leased a second farm of 50 acres near by to an Irish tenant. Morris viewed the growth of farming as an Irish phenomenon, occurring mainly in those areas with which he was most familiar through trade. As a leading importer of Irish servant labour, the president of the Benevolent Irish Society and the Agricultural Society, and from 1836 to 1840 a member of the House of Assembly he was in a pivotal position to promote farm settlement.

Morris, however, greatly exaggerated the prospects for farming and the government's resistance to it. Long before he settled in St John's the government had responded to the problems of a precarious food supply by granting small plots to the military and civilians for subsistence cultivation. Senior military personnel were awarded large grants for commercial farms. Indeed one of these, given to Captain Thomas Skinner* in 1792, was the farm acquired by Morris in 1823. Regulations regarding squatting were relaxed during the war and civilians secured grants to commence commercial farming. All these advances were important, according to Morris, in warding off poverty during the post-war recession and he cited them as precedents when he began his campaign to promote agriculture after 1820. Twenty years of agitation brought some progress. Governor Thomas John Cochrane*, who shared his enthusiasm to a degree, introduced a road-building program and set an example by developing a farm of his own. A few merchants followed suit but most were sceptical, dismissing Morris's views on agriculture as "visionary and utopian." By 1840, however, Morris could point to 300 commercial farms established in the environs of St John's alone, and to expanding pockets of agriculture in other parts of the island.

The political struggle to win government support for local agriculture was part of a broad movement for general reform. Between 1800 and 1820 Newfoundland was transformed from a predominantly transient fishing society to a largely permanent community. But its governance remained outmoded, with institutions fashioned for a migratory fishery. One example was the judicial system, which Morris deemed absurd. Civil cases continued to be adjudicated by surrogates, many of them still drawn from the navy patrolling the coast each summer. Although they were appointed by the governor many were, in the opinion of Morris and the reformers, unqualified and unfit to serve as judges. They were seen as successors to the "illiterate admirals" who, hand in glove with the West Country merchants, had for centuries held the fishermen in servitude.

Two cases of rough justice meted out by surrogates finally brought Patrick Morris on to the public stage. They concerned a pair of fishermen in Conception Bay, James Lundrigan* and Philip Butler, who were unable to erase their debts and in July 1820 were flogged for resisting the confiscation of their properties. With the support of the reformers the two men sued the surrogates involved, Commander David Buchan and the Reverend John Leigh*, but the charges were dismissed. A meeting, chaired by Morris, was held in St John's to protest what he called "flagrant acts of cruelty and injustice." Those attending agreed to pay the fishermen's court expenses and provide for their families through the winter. They agreed also to pursue every legal and constitutional means to have the laws that permitted the appointment of such surrogates repealed. In November 1820, at a second public meeting, a committee of inhabitants with Morris at its head was appointed for this purpose, and a memorial signed by 180 residents was drawn up for presentation to Governor Sir Charles Hamilton. Apart from the Conception Bay incident, examples of the surrogates' incompetency were cited and other grievances outlined, including an unjust tax on fishing boats, the delay in providing an act to guide rebuilding in St John's after the fires, and the lack of a local legislature.

Some of the seeds of the liberal reform party that came to dominate much of the political life of Newfoundland for a generation are discernible in this protest. Eight of the thirteen members of the committee were Irish, most remained politically active, and some, such as Patrick Doyle* and Thomas Beck, were involved with Morris in party politics for a lifetime. Eighty per cent of those signing the memorial were Irish and included almost all the merchants and traders and many of the shopkeepers, publicans, and leading artisans of that nationality then resident in the town. The reformers were ignored by the British merchants who dominated the commerce of St John's. But Morris had the support of some liberal Protestants such as his close friend Robert Roberts Wakeham, and the most important member on the committee was the Scottish doctor William CARSON. For almost a decade Carson had been involved in agitation for reform and he was Morris's mentor. Indeed most of the grievances and possible solutions articulated by Patrick Morris through the 1820s had already been publicized by Carson.

Although numerically dominated by the Irish, the movement for reform precipitated by the surrogates had neither an ethnic nor a sectarian character. The four constables delegated to eject the fishermen were Irish and Lundrigan's trial was conducted in an Irish planter's home at Port de Grave. The sheriff, surrogates, judge, and jury were all Protestants, but there is no reference to this fact nor is there any explicit demand for Catholic rights in Morris's copious writings on disadvantaged Newfoundland through the 1820s. He was motivated primarily by a deeply held conviction that the judiciary was despotic. Even before Carson arrived in St John's in 1808 Morris had deprecated the local magistrates and justices in private correspondence.

Governor Hamilton forwarded the inhabitants' memorial to the Colonial Office even though he opposed it, and it was presented to the House of Commons. The response from London was inchoate, but this was the first time in three decades that Newfoundland's institutions had been debated in parliament, and the reformers responded by preparing a more comprehensive submission in 1822. Very much the product of Morris and Carson, it included a summary of the problems besetting the British fishery, an argument for agricultural development to ward off poverty and stem the tide of migration to the United States, and a call for institutional reform. In November 1823 Morris presided over what he described as "the most numerous and most respectable meeting ever held in St. John's," to consider the details of a British bill "on the better administration of justice in Newfoundland." London's ideas were largely rejected and a list of specific demands submitted. They included the introduction of qualified judges, a police force, a constitutional authority to direct local expenditure, and the removal of all restrictions on agriculture. The 1820 committee was expanded to include 14 new members, all British and some from respectable merchant houses. Their sudden interest was a response to the threat that an appointed council might be created to govern St John's. Morris, who was going to Waterford for the winter, was persuaded to go on to London and help their barrister "urge the reasonableness" of the petition. He arrived in March 1824 and over the next two months frequently saw Robert John Wilmot-Horton of the Colonial Office, with whom he had heated debate over the committee's proposals. He also met members presenting and supporting the bill in both houses of parliament. To bolster Newfoundland's case and stave off "the most vile conspiracy" of some conservative cod merchants Morris completed and published his first pamphlet while in London, addressed to the secretary of state for the colonies.

The efforts of the reformers were finally rewarded with the judicature act of 1824. It was something of a landmark in Newfoundland legislation, belated recognition by government that the island was a settled colony and that the migratory fishery was over. The surrogate system was replaced by circuit courts with qualified judges; the Supreme Court was revised and enlarged; and a civil governor with rights to grant crown land for agriculture was appointed. Under Carson's tutorship Morris had orchestrated the inhabitants' agitation, so influential in fostering the act, and had personally helped shape the character of the legislation. It remained his proudest achievement in public life. In a vote of thanks Carson lauded "the zeal of assiduity of Mr. Morris, the personal sacrifices he made" on behalf of the inhabitants.

The act did little, however, to ameliorate the plight of Newfoundlanders and the reformers decided to push for representative government. It had been listed as a desideratum in their submissions but had not been elaborated. Morris, fresh from his London experience, urged caution, compromise, and the need for unity of purpose. Like everybody else he was vague on the form a locally constituted authority should take. The act of 1824 provided a charter of incorporation for St John's with powers to frame by-laws and levy rates by assessment. The threat of taxes split the reformers. Morris recommended that the assessment include proprietors and a tax be levied on the rental value of properties. He further proposed that the municipal council be elective, that all candidates have estates valued at £100 or more, and that the franchise be awarded to men with properties worth £10 freehold or £20 leasehold. Although a number of the town's resident British merchants with substantial property had joined the reform committee in 1823, some of these led the opposition to the proposed mode of assessment. They claimed they were willing to pay their way but not in the manner Morris proposed. Despite Morris's covert assurances to Chief Justice Richard Alexander Tucker* that he could resolve the differences within the committee the attempt to incorporate collapsed, a warning of things to come. Governor Cochrane concluded that elections were unwise and the idea of incorporation was abandoned.

The reformers refocused on the campaign for a local legislature. When in London Morris had requested "some constitutional form of government to foster the internal resources of the country." He countered arguments that the island could not afford it by citing colonial revenue statistics over the previous decade. But London ignored the committee's vague representations for a legislature, offering instead precisely what they had urged Morris to protest in 1824, an appointed council. Morris perceived the need of a more developed case for constitutional government and prepared a pamphlet, *Arguments to prove the policy and necessity of granting to Newfoundland a constitutional government* (London, 1828). He conceded that a local assembly would be dominated by merchants but maintained that they would be Newfoundland residents committed to an integrated agricultural and maritime economy beneficial to all classes.

It is impossible to measure what impact this pamphlet and others, with their fuzzy suggestions, sometimes preposterous statistics, and sanguine notions of Newfoundland development, had on London. Certainly Morris was becoming a familiar figure there. He had been the only Irish merchant recommended by Cochrane to sit on a proposed council in 1825, and when submitting another Morris memorial on the Irish to the Colonial Office in 1828 the governor noted that he was "a very respectable merchant and an influential person among the Roman Catholics of Newfoundland." While visiting London in 1827 Morris had defended in print the state of Newfoundland society, religion, morals, and education recently impugned by the bishop of Chester. He was back in the spring of 1828 to attend a House of Commons debate on the Passenger Acts, and he presented a memorial on the subject to the colonial secretary based on his personal experience. By now his position as a leader among the reformers had been considerably diminished, however. He had moved to Waterford in 1826 and did not return to St John's for five years. He was succeeded as principal Irish spokesman for reform there by his nephew John Kent. In Ireland Morris stepped on to a larger stage, transferring his expertise and reforming zeal to the struggle for Catholic emancipation and repeal of the union with Britain, although he maintained his political links with Newfoundland. Early in 1831, for example, he organized a petition of Waterford merchants for representative government in Newfoundland and was active on his return to St John's that summer in the final push towards this goal. He was there when news of its achievement trickled through but he departed for Ireland in the summer of 1832 prior to the start of the election campaign. Six weeks later the ethnoreligious harmony that had characterized the reform movement through the 1820s, and for which the conciliatory Morris was given much credit by both Protestant merchants and administrators, was shattered. John Kent declared his candidacy for St John's district and was quickly embroiled in an overtly sectarian battle for power.

Although there was always an undertow of ethnic tension in St John's, Patrick Morris had scrupulously avoided exploiting it for political advancement. He had arrived in the town near the end of Bishop James Louis O'Donel*'s tenure there. O'Donel was a close friend of Luke Maddock and the young Morris was no doubt impressed by the loyalty of the principal Irish inhabitants to their spiritual leader and by the accord that prevailed between the Catholic Irish and the other inhabitants. In his pamphlets and in his speeches in Ireland on Catholic emancipation Morris stressed the importance of religious harmony, citing examples such as that of Bishop Thomas Scallan*, who organized Irish volunteer labour to help build an Anglican church in St John's. The priests in Newfoundland were, in his view, "pious, learned and liberal." As in Ireland they were supported not by government but by the congregation, a fact of which Morris was especially proud. Morris also vaunted the "religious, moral and peaceable" character of the immigrant Irish. Many were destitute, yet they were orderly and peaceful. This conduct he attributed in part to the aid extended by established residents, both Catholic and Protestant. The Irish, he said, soon forsook homeland feuds and prejudices and were absorbed by a society free of sectarian hostility. But Morris informed the governor that their quiescence should not be mistaken for apathy or indifference to their lot. Though loyal "they labour under many and great grievances and are in a far worse situation than persons professing the same religion in the neighbouring Colonies." They were denied, for example, the right to practise law because of the qualification oaths included in the act of 1824, to become magistrates, or to hold other official positions. Their silence was "entirely occasioned" by the desire of Bishop Scallan and "the most influential members of his body to preserve the harmony which so happily exists amongst all denominations." Cochrane concurred, noting somewhat prophetically to the Colonial Office that it was a harmony "still in the power of any designing or even ill-judging individual to endanger."

In Ireland after 1826 Morris incorporated Newfoundland into the struggle for Catholic emancipation, presenting a donation to the cause on behalf of Newfoundlanders. He was a popular speaker and quickly advanced to a position of prominence in the movement. When emancipation was finally granted in 1829 Newfoundland's conservative attorney general,

James Simms*, attempted to block its extension to the island on constitutional grounds. A petition was drawn up in St John's and sent to Morris with instructions to transmit it to Daniel O'Connell and the Marquis of Lansdowne for presentation to both houses of parliament. Morris concluded, correctly, that this action was unnecessary. Governor Cochrane had already contacted the Colonial Office for advice and the issue was speedily resolved. But the view of some Catholics in St John's that Morris's procedure was high-handed was an early sign of opposition within the Catholic community.

Morris returned to live permanently in St John's in 1833. During his short absence the political scene had been transformed. A "popular" Irish faction emerged during the elections of 1832, led by the militant new bishop, Michael Anthony FLEMING, his priests, and some of the reformers, particularly Carson, Kent, and Doyle. They challenged the local bastions of Protestant privilege and were also at odds with more moderate, largely middle-class elements in the Catholic community. Morris was a moderate, even if six years in Ireland had probably hardened his stance on Catholic rights, but he had close personal and kinship ties with the leadership of the new "democratic" party. Doyle was probably his uncle by marriage, Kent was his nephew and protégé, and Carson was his mentor. The conservative opposition claimed that Morris had opposed Fleming's appointment as bishop because of the latter's hard line and that relations between them were strained. Unless he had altered his views dramatically Morris was bound to have reservations about some aspects of the bishop's policy but loyalty to the church, political instinct, and intimate family ties ensured his support. Fleming's sister was a close friend of Morris's daughter, was godmother to his eldest son, and married John Kent early in 1834. Fleming, moreover, had heaped praise on Morris as president of the Benevolent Irish Society and was chairman of a committee honouring him prior to his departure for Ireland in 1832. And Morris was upset by criticism from a section of the Irish community over his handling of the petition on emancipation.

Shortly after his arrival back in Newfoundland Morris cancelled his subscription to the St John's *Times and General Commercial Gazette*. Its editor, John Williams McCoubrey*, a Waterford Presbyterian, had insulted Fleming and one of his priests, the fiery Edward Troy*. Two weeks later five priests recruited by Fleming in Ireland arrived on one of Morris's ships and the bishop himself, with Sister Mary Bernard Kirwan* and three other nuns, docked at Morris's wharf the following day. An address of welcome was delivered by Patrick Doyle, chairman of the Catholic committee of inhabitants, before a large, enthusiastic crowd and Carson provided his carriage to take the nuns to the episcopal residence. All the elements of the new party had been assembled for public display.

A by-election of December 1833 reinforced the divisions within the Irish community. Carson, the reform candidate, was opposed by Tipperary merchant Timothy Hogan, an ally of Morris in the reform movement through the 1820s but a supporter of the moderate Catholic candidate against Kent and Carson in 1832. Morris helped organize Carson's campaign. The battle for Irish support was bitter, with allegations that the clergy threatened to deny the sacraments to any Catholic who even traded with, let alone voted for, Hogan. He withdrew and later left the island, as did a number of his leading Irish supporters. Henry David Winton*, editor of the *Public Ledger*, denounced the Fleming faction and troops were called in to disperse an angry crowd assembled before his house. At a public meeting the reform leaders, including Morris, accused the governor of reverting to despotic tactics to suppress civil liberties.

Relations also worsened with the arrival in November 1833 of a new chief justice, Henry John Boulton*. Highly conservative, Boulton was determined to concentrate power in the hands of the colonial administration and the Protestant merchant class. He introduced various legal changes that provoked Morris and the reformers, but by far the most offensive to Morris personally was what he called an attempt "to sweep away every vestige of the laws that for centuries had regulated the trade and fisheries of the Island." The judicature act of 1824 had confirmed an ancient custom giving servants prior rights to fish and oil for their wages in the event of a planter's insolvency, and current suppliers prior claims over past creditors. Bolstered by mercantile support, Boulton arbitrarily set aside these and other rights and customs of the fishery. Morris claimed that as a merchant he could save £1,000 to £1,500 a year under the new credit arrangements "though my business was very much contracted." Enraged by Boulton's despotism and hostility to Irish Catholic aspirations, the reformers were determined to remove him. Morris searched the records of the Colonial Office to demonstrate the antiquity and pervasiveness of servants' liens and the custom of current supply. Rooted in the law of bottomry, they had long been adapted by both French and English to the cod fishery. Merchants, planters, and servants were intimately bound, Morris argued, by ties of credit based on trust. A planter was more an agent than a debtor of the merchant; each spring he proceeded to a distant harbour with the merchant's property and with servants bound to him and the merchant both. All parties were protected by the law of current supply. Boulton was profoundly ignorant of the subtleties of this system and of the distress and chaos he had caused amongst the fishermen by altering it. In 1838, Morris, by then a member of the assembly, would be part of a three-man delegation to London that at least secured Boulton's removal from the bench.

By the late 1830s the trade from Waterford in passengers and provisions was greatly reduced and Morris withdrew from it. He became increasingly involved in local politics as a champion of reform, forging strong links with the immigrant Irish in St John's, particularly the more recent arrivals. They served as a public pressure group to help wring concessions from a recalcitrant administration. When in 1835 Boulton jailed Robert John Parsons*, editor of the *Newfoundland Patriot*, for contempt of court, Morris and Carson formed the Constitutional Society to obtain his release. All but 2 of the 13 members on the committee were Irish and among these were Morris, Doyle, Morris's brother and nephew, and two other relatives. A petition was framed and dispatched to London with 5,000 signatures. It was the most impressive display of signed support for any Newfoundland cause to that time. Further pressure was brought to bear by a large crowd assembled outside the jail, some threatening violence. The Colonial Office ordered that Parsons be released, an event celebrated by a festive march of some 200 supporters led by Morris and the committee. Petitions, speeches, and colourful marches, sanctioned by the Catholic Church, had become standard tactics amongst the reformers but Morris insisted on constitutional protest, discouraged sectarianism, and opposed violence.

By 1835 the last major migration of the Irish to St John's had virtually run its course. The town was now dominated by immigrants, and they formed the backbone of Morris's support. His long involvement in the passenger trade and as a merchant supplier meant he was at least known to most of them and as a fellow-immigrant from the southeast he shared cultural traditions. Morris cemented these ties through his activities with institutions and committees catering to the immigrants. As well as being president of the Benevolent Irish Society, he was president of the Committee for the Relief of Distress, member of the Board of Directors for the Relief of Disabled Seamen and Fishermen, and vice-president of the St John's Association of Fishermen and Shoremen. It came as no surprise that Morris, Kent, and Carson swept St John's in the general elections of 1836 and 1837. The campaign in St John's had been marred by sectarian tension, intimidation, and the threat of violence. Following a particularly provocative march of some 300 through the streets of the town, Morris and his clique, including several priests, were charged with unlawful assembly. The charges were later dismissed by a Protestant jury.

Nine of the fifteen seats in the second House of Assembly were held by Catholics, and a tenth reformer, Carson, was elected speaker. Morris quickly emerged as an especially active member. He flooded the house with petitions signed by hundreds of his constituents for roads, bridges, land grants, public wharfs, and other improvements. He requested money for minor officials such as constables, some retired, others in distress. A considerable minority of the petitioners were poor Protestants, a group Morris had pledged to represent in his election campaign. He chaired committees examining the state of fishing, farming, and the administration of justice and wrote reports on these subjects which were printed by the house. As a delegate in London in 1838 – his first time there as a politician – Morris pressed for some of his favourite causes: the removal of restrictions on agriculture, a less expensive policy of crown land grants under the control of the assembly, money for roads and bridges, bounties for the fishery, concurrent rights on the French Shore, and a legislative branch in Council elected by the assembly or the amalgamation of both houses. As in the past, however, most of these requests were denied or deferred.

In Newfoundland the Protestant Council and merchants were strongly opposed to the assembly and resisted reform. They regarded the liberal politicians as factious demagogues ruled by a power-hungry and militant clergy, "ignorant, besotted Catholics from the southwest of Ireland . . . so bound by the magic spell of Popery they are quite incapable of properly exercising political power." Morris was eloquent in the assembly's defence. He dismissed charges of disloyalty, lawlessness, danger to property, and Catholic supremacy, and defended stoutly the accomplishments of the second assembly, particularly its record of road construction, repeal of acts imposing taxes on the importation of vital fresh food, and fiscal responsibility. Much more would have been achieved, he maintained, had it not been for the trenchant opposition of Council. Although Governor Henry Prescott* had his reservations about the reformers he agreed with the last point. In an attempt to improve the disposition of Council he suggested the appointment of two members from the House of Assembly, Morris and Doyle. The Colonial Office expressed concern, however, over the precise role such members would play in communications between the governor and the house, and the appointments were not made.

Early in 1840 Morris finally secured his reward for two decades of public service: the office of colonial treasurer, which carried with it a salary of £400 a year, the highest in government, and a seat in Council. The appointment drew a flood of comment from the local press. McCoubrey denounced it in the *Times*, as did Winton in the *Public Ledger*. Parsons of the liberal *Patriot* praised Morris for his perseverance, firmness, integrity, and judgement, but pointed out that he would have to vacate his seat in the assembly. This Morris refused to do, causing a split in the reform ranks. Led by a jealous Carson, who ridiculed Morris in the *Newfoundlander*, the lower house expelled the new colonial treasurer.

The rift widened with the subsequent by-election in May 1840: James Douglas*, a liberal Scottish merchant and close ally of Morris, was nominated by him and received virtually unanimous support from the reformers. But a week before the election Bishop Fleming persuaded Laurence O'Brien*, a protégé and cousin of Morris and now a merchant, to run. Disillusioned with the political process, the Protestant merchants did not even name a candidate so the election developed mainly as a contest between the reform factions within the Irish community. Douglas retained the support of Morris, Doyle, and many moderate, respectable Catholics, despite Fleming's alleged assertion that a vote for O'Brien was a vote for the church. O'Brien won narrowly after a turbulent campaign.

The strong support for Douglas was hailed by both the liberal and the conservative press as a sign that the hegemony over political life of the Catholic Church, with its largely Irish immigrant following, could be broken. During the election some native residents, representing a group now rapidly expanding in the town, established a society to work for orderly progress through unity. It was interdenominational and was supported by Morris and Doyle, a native. This stance isolated them further from the rest of the family, who supported Fleming and his faction. The Fleming group sensed a new party that would eventually displace them. The bishop had agreed to act as a security for Morris as colonial treasurer but now changed his mind, claiming the construction of the cathedral had drained his financial resources. Morris infuriated him with a public statement in the *Patriot* that this claim was not true. O'Brien replaced Morris as president of the Benevolent Irish Society and the *Patriot*, with which Morris was associated, was replaced by a new journal, the *Newfoundland Vindicator*, as printer for the house. But when in 1841 Morris was accused of speculating with treasury funds the family quickly closed ranks and the *Vindicator* sprang to his defence. Cash advances had been deposited quarterly in the local bank of which Morris was governor and cashier and his nephew and former mercantile agent, Edward Morris, was manager. While Morris took a short leave of absence that summer, the acting treasurer refused to follow this practice, placing the funds instead in the commissariat. He argued that the bank was really a trading company and the money was unsafe there. A meeting between Carson, Kent, Doyle, and the governor resolved the issue in Morris's favour but his management of the treasury surfaced later as a major controversy.

Morris availed himself fully of his seat on Council to press for reform. He continued to present petitions from artisans, fishermen, and farmers and also introduced bills submitted by his political allies in the lower house. Despite his long speeches and even another pamphlet, Council was generally unbending. Not all of Morris's positions were popular. He supported a militia bill despite 8,000 signatures opposing it and sided with government in directing substantial funds for fire victims toward reconstruction of the Anglican church and the custom-house, court-house, and jail. But he was also active in collecting funds for the relief of famine victims in his homeland.

On 20 Aug. 1849 Patrick Morris made his will, leaving £1,500 to one of his daughters and his estate, valued at £2,000, to his wife and her remaining children. He died two days later at his country residence just north of St John's. On that day the colonial secretary instructed the attorney general to arrange an audit of Morris's accounts as treasurer. He also directed Edward Morris and the treasurer's clerk to assist with the audit. Two weeks later the auditors reported some £6,600 missing. A detailed examination of the accounts back to 1840 followed. Most of the revenue Morris had received – £450,000 in eight years – had been deposited in the savings bank but he did not keep a regular record of withdrawals. The clerk was dismissed but Governor John Gaspard Le Marchant* reported that the fraud could not be traced because "the affairs of the deceased . . . have been left in a very confused and embarrassed state." A writ of extent was issued in September against the Morris estate. His personal effects, including all household furniture, plate, a library of 600 volumes, all crops, livestock, and farm implements, were advertised for sale. No one bid against Mrs Morris for possession of the household goods but the auction realized only £674, a ruinous amount according to the family. Despite a widespread belief that Morris was above suspicion and the deficit was due to sloppy bookkeeping, the governor had little alternative but to move against his sureties and the estate. He bluntly informed the assembly that Morris was a defaulter and in private correspondence to the Colonial Office referred to "the ingenuity with which he managed to conceal his frauds." The family protested but his name was never cleared. A compromise settlement on the deficit was finally reached whereby James William Tobin*, a leading merchant, member of Council, and brother-in-law of Mrs Morris, agreed to pay £4,000 to the government in six annual instalments, free of interest charges. Mrs Morris was allowed £150 a year from the estate. She and her five children departed for Ireland, renting the cottage and farm to Patrick's brother Simon and his son Edward. Following the bankruptcy of Tobin, Patrick Morris's eldest son returned to St John's to negotiate a final settlement with the government.

Throughout his long political career Morris championed the rights of the poor and disadvantaged. But like all successful merchants he developed and maintained a strong sense of social class. His second wife was the daughter of a well-to-do doctor in Cork. Morris could be patronizing about "the lower orders," especially the propertyless poor of St John's. He was much more concerned with the political advancement of the Catholic middle class. He was untroubled by criticism that a Newfoundland house of assembly would be the preserve of the merchants, arguing that it was very much in the mercantile interest to support all classes. In Ireland he had the opportunity to indulge in bourgeois display. He invited, for example, 250 "ladies and gentlemen of the first rank and respectability in Cork City" to a "sumptuous dinner" and dance aboard one of his new vessels on the king's birthday in 1829. Shortly afterwards he acquired a handsome villa with 100 acres downstream from Waterford.

Morris also made use of institutions such as the Benevolent Irish Society to promote his ambitions and promulgate his views. An original member in 1806, he joined Doyle on a committee in 1815 and was entrusted with the management of the society's property and finances. By 1823 over £7,000 had been collected locally, a sign of growing Irish responsibility which Morris was proud to report to the governor. He succeeded as president, likely in 1824, and held this office for most of the remainder of his life. Like his predecessor, James MacBraire*, Morris was a popular president, treading his way delicately, if not always successfully, through the thicket of conflicts that beset the Irish community, and the society. He was also a generous donor.

Restless energy, driving ambition, and business acumen enabled Morris to overcome ordinary origins and succeed in an intensely competitive world dominated by Protestant British merchants. This goal could not have been achieved alone. He began in an ethnically focused trade under the tutelage of friends and kin from home. Eventually he became the head of a political and commercial clan probably unprecedented amongst the immigrant Irish in British North America. A dozen of his kinsmen were merchants and agents in St John's alone. Six had been elected to the House of Assembly by 1842; five were appointed to Council, virtually the only Catholics to be so honoured up to 1858, and two became presidents of that body. They dominated the presidency of the Benevolent Irish Society for close to half a century. John Kent was elected speaker in the assembly, then prime minister. The temperamental Morris fought publicly with most of this clan but they invariably rallied to his cause in a crisis. More important, they provided a network within the Irish community in St John's and the Avalon peninsula that lay at the base of Morris's mercantile and political enterprise.

For close to 30 years Patrick Morris was acknowledged as the leading Irish layman in what had become a major centre of Irish settlement. Parsons wrote in the *Patriot*, "He was held in high esteem by persons of all classes, creeds and diversities of political opinion." Even an old political foe, McCoubrey of the *Times*, lauded his honesty, sincerity, and compassion. As his funeral passed the Anglican church, the bell sounded its tribute to a long-respected friend.

JOHN MANNION

Patrick Morris's publications include *Observations on the government, trade, fisheries and agriculture of Newfoundland . . . by an inhabitant of the colony* (London, 1824); *Remarks on the state of society, religion, morals, and education at Newfoundland . . .* (London, 1827); *Arguments to prove the policy and necessity of granting to Newfoundland a constitutional government . . .* (London, 1828); *Six letters intended to prove that the repeal of the Act of Union and the establishment of a local legislature in Ireland, are necessary to cement the connection with Great Britain* (Waterford, [Republic of Ire.], 1831); and "Memorial of Patrick Morris, esq., to the Right Honourable Lord Glenelg, her majesty's principal secretary of state for the colonies," published in Nfld., House of Assembly, *Journal*, 1838 (2nd session), app.: 87–105. Several additional pamphlets by Morris are listed in *Bibliography of Newfoundland*, comp. A. C. O'Dea, ed. Anne Alexander (2v., Toronto, 1986).

Cathedral of the Immaculate Conception (Harbour Grace, Nfld.), Reg. of marriages, 26 April 1814. PANL, GN 2/1, 47: 365–66, 372, 375; GN 2/2, 1826, 1832; GN 5/2. PRO, CO 194/68, 194/76–77, 194/133, 194/137. Nfld., House of Assembly, *Journal*, 1837, app.: 225–28. *Lloyd's List* (London). *Newfoundlander*, esp. 23 Aug. 1849. *Newfoundland Mercantile Journal*. *Newfoundland Patriot*. *Newfoundland Vindicator* (St John's). *Patriot & Terra Nova Herald*, esp. 25 Aug. 1849. *Public Ledger*. *Royal Gazette and Newfoundland Advertiser*. *Times and General Commercial Gazette* (St John's). *Waterford Mirror* (Waterford). *The register of shipping* (London). Gunn, *Political hist. of Nfld.* John Mannion, "Patrick Morris and Newfoundland Irish immigration," *Talamh an Eisc: Canadian and Irish essays*, ed. C. J. Byrne and M. [R.] Harry (Halifax, 1986), 180–202.

MORTIMER, GEORGE, Church of England clergyman; b. 20 May 1784 in England, son of Harvey Walklate Mortimer, a gunmaker on Fleet Street, London; m. 21 Feb. 1812 Mary Barford; d. 15 June 1844 in Thornhill, Upper Canada.

George Mortimer's mother died while he was a baby, and he was placed in the care of a relative in Birmingham, where a long illness left him deformed. After his father remarried in 1787, he returned home and was privately educated. For seven years, beginning in 1798, he apprenticed at Mr Otridge's bookstore in the Strand. He became a spiritual disciple of philanthropist Joseph Butterworth, a seller of law books at whose house William Wilberforce and others of the "Clapham sect" gathered.

While preparing for college, Mortimer studied the church fathers, whose writings would inspire the Oxford movement, and at the same time widened his acquaintance with evangelical leaders. A sensitive young man, he was often moved to tears by his reading of Christian authors. After graduating in 1811 from Queen's College, Cambridge, he worked in a Shropshire parish. Though his bishop regarded this earnest young evangelical with some suspicion, he ordained him to a curacy there in May 1811. Mortimer later served at Bristol and in Somerset.

Discouraged by political and economic circumstances in England and convinced that clergymen who were "the unbeneficed-unpatronized heads of large families must . . . sooner or later decamp," Mortimer left for Upper Canada in 1832. He was offered the parish of Thornhill, where two years earlier a frame church had been erected on land donated by Benjamin THORNE and others. Bishop Charles James STEWART assured him of an income of £100 from the clergy reserves, and the parish promised to pay a further £40–50 and supply a home at a moderate rent. Especially at first Mortimer was distressed by his situation. His house was small and he believed the reserves provided people with an excuse to neglect his needs. Since he had a private income, however, he did not suffer. Indeed he identified politically with "the more loyal and opulent" class and was able to devote a tithe to the poor and to other benevolent causes. When in 1836, his spirits worsened by bad health, he prepared to move, his parishioners begged him to stay. He decided to build a substantial house at his own expense, and his health improved.

The rebellion of 1837 was an uneasy period for Mortimer. As the recipient in 1836 of one of the 44 rectories granted by Sir John Colborne*, he feared himself a target for the rebel parties that passed his door on the way to Toronto in December 1837 [*see* William Lyon Mackenzie*]. Though he was spared, he buried one victim, Colonel Robert Moodie, in the churchyard, surrounded by mourners armed with swords and fowling pieces. The demonstration was, he remarked, "altogether uncalled for."

As time passed, Mortimer felt his circumstances improved. The church building was enlarged in 1840, and in 1841 he was able to write, "In England all was struggling and difficulty, and no possibility of settling my family; while here, I am enabled to call every reasonable comfort around me." His custom was to spend most of the day in his study, and to devote two or three hours to driving about the parish. He visited each family, including Roman Catholics and dissenters. Though he did not regard episcopacy as essential to a church and was friendly towards dissenters, he did warn them against the sin of schism. He delivered a similar admonition to his own parishioners when he suspected they were neglecting his evening services to attend Methodist meetings. He established a Sunday school and a temperance society, but not all his initiatives were successful. Weekday meetings along Methodist lines were discontinued because of people's reluctance to discuss religion. Only a dozen people availed themselves of the books in the village's Library of Useful Knowledge, to which he had contributed.

Although Mortimer felt his first responsibility was to prepare his flock for heaven, he was conscious of his own "latent infidelity, as to the reality of the coming world." While preaching on the afterlife, on the evening of 10 Oct. 1841, he suffered a nervous attack from which he never fully recovered. Care of the parish was entrusted to his curate, the Reverend Adam Townley, and the rector undertook less demanding work at the German Mills, some four miles distant. He resumed charge of the parish in 1843. On 15 June 1844, having learned that his bookseller in Toronto had received a new shipment, he set out for the city. He was thrown from his carriage and died of his injuries.

Mortimer was a man to whom family relationships mattered deeply. He had great affection and respect for his stepmother and formed a close attachment to his brother Thomas and sister Mary, with whom he corresponded throughout his life. His views on matrimony reflect the growing emphasis in his time on the importance of love and companionship to marriage. Before his wedding with Mary Barford, his "dearest friend," he made himself a series of resolutions, promising to avoid "*pettishness*," "*pertinacity*," and "*self-will*," and to "cultivate a *tender* and *affectionate* manner . . . sharing every *domestic* and *maternal* anxiety." He vowed that he would "consult her in everything . . . give her the freest access to all my papers, letters, &c." and "commit to her entire management all my money concerns." "As to the arrangement of *domestic concerns*," he wrote, he would "interfere as little as need be." Their relationship indeed turned out well. When his sister was about to be married he wished her the same happiness that he enjoyed. He was the father of three sons and three daughters, in whom he took much pride. His decision to emigrate for their sake was probably sound. By 1844 Arthur was already a rector, and Herbert became president of the Toronto Stock Exchange.

RICHARD E. RUGGLE

[George Mortimer directed his papers to be destroyed after his death and the vestry minutes of Holy Trinity Church (Thornhill, [Ont.]) for this period were lost in a fire. The church register which he used survives and is in the ACC, Diocese of Toronto Arch. R.E.R.]

AO, MS 35, letter-books, 1839–43, John Strachan, circular to Mortimer *et al.*, 10 June 1840; corr. to Mortimer, 13 April 1840, 5 April 1841, 10 March 1843; 1839–66 ("to societies"), letter concerning memorials of Deacon and Mortimer, 19 April 1842; 1844–49, corr. to Dr O'Brien, 7 Dec. 1846; unbound papers, letters missive authorizing the bishop of Quebec to institute the Rev. Geo. Mortimer to the parsonage at Thornhill, 16 Jan. 1836; MS 199, M. S. [Gapper] O'Brien, journals, 11 Feb. 1834. *The life and letters of the Rev. George Mortimer . . .*, ed. John Armstrong (London, 1847).

MOSCHELL, JOHANN ADAM (until around 1820 he signed **Moschel**), German Reformed minister; b. 3 Nov. 1795 in Mannheim (Federal Republic of Germany), natural son of Johann Friedrich Moschel and Maria Elisabetha Windenheimer; m. 20 April 1820 Mary Ann James in Lunenburg, N.S., and they adopted at least one child, a girl; d. 26 Jan. 1849 in Hohensachsen near Heidelberg, Grand Duchy of Baden (Federal Republic of Germany).

Johann Adam Moschell originated from the capital of the Palatinate, where a strong Calvinist tradition had prevailed since the Reformation. The secondary education he acquired in his home town indicates a middle-class background. His stepfather was a quartermaster in the Bavarian army when Moschell began to study philosophy and theology at Rupert Charles University of Heidelberg in 1813. After graduation two years later, he served for about a year as an auxiliary preacher of the Reformed Church in nearby Laufen and Gallenweiler. It is not known when or where he was ordained. Upon his return to Mannheim a suggestion that he go to Nova Scotia reached him. The German Reformed Church at Lunenburg, St Andrew's, needed an assistant for the Reverend Bruin Romkes Comingo*, and the Lutheran pastor in that community, the Reverend Ferdinand Conrad Temme, agreed to help a sister congregation by issuing a call to the university at Heidelberg.

Moschell set out on 17 Oct. 1817 and arrived in Nova Scotia on 21 February. When Comingo died in January 1820, Moschell was on his own. During the initial years he was apparently quite eager to fulfil his duties. The German language was used in preaching, and the Heidelberg Catechism, introduced before Moschell's arrival, figured in religious instruction. Serving the extensive parish required much dedication. It comprised some 2,000 souls scattered over 750 square miles, forcing Moschell to travel 1,500 miles each year. One telling example of his activity was the building and dedication in 1828 of a new church which cost £1,200 and could seat between 800 and 900 people. His marriage to Mary Ann James of his parish tied him further to his congregation.

Problems arose during the later years of his ministry in Lunenburg. One observer, the Reverend George Patterson*, remarked in the 1880s that Moschell's "conduct unfortunately exhibited scenes over which charity must throw a vail." According to this source the congregation's well-being began to suffer from some lack of guidance, but no details are provided. Moschell, at any rate, considered a return to Germany, and when a new post was promised him in Baden he left Lunenburg in 1837. On his departure he recommended that the congregation join the Synod of Nova Scotia in connection with the Church of Scotland, in order to ensure development in the future. His advice was followed, although it meant the abandonment of services and instruction conducted in German. The merger does not appear to have caused undue hardships to the parish. He was succeeded by the Reverend Donald Allan FRASER.

Moschell arrived in Mannheim on 31 Aug. 1837. After a short stay in Wieblingen, near Heidelberg, he served as minister in the nearby communities of Plankstadt and Edingen from April 1838 to April 1840, and then at Hohensachsen until his death in 1849. His wife returned to Nova Scotia the same year.

Moschell left a distinct mark in Nova Scotia. The first duly educated and ordained minister of his church in the province, he was responsible for the acceptance of his congregation into a church with a similar confession. This development guaranteed the religious integrity of an ethnically distinguished community while facilitating its integration into Nova Scotian society.

U. SAUTTER

Evangelische Kirchengemeindeamt (Mannheim, Federal Republic of Germany), Taufbuch, 1764–94. Evangelische Pfarramt (Hohensachsen, Federal Republic of Germany), Beerdigungsbuch, 1811–69; Kirchenbuch, 1840–49. PANS, MG 1, 742, no.6. St Andrew's Presbyterian Church (Lunenburg, N.S.), Dutch Reformed Church records, J. A. Moschell, *Curriculum vitae*; photographic portrait. Synod of Nova Scotia in connection with the Church of Scotland, *Minutes* (Halifax), 1837: 48–57. *N.S. vital statistics, 1813–22* (Punch), no.1945. M. B. DesBrisay, *History of the county of Lunenburg* (2nd ed., Toronto, 1895; repr. Belleville, Ont., 1980), 91–92. J. A. Flett, *The story of St. Andrew's Presbyterian Church, Lunenburg, N.S.* (n.p., 1970), 13–14, 134–35. Gregg, *Hist. of Presbyterian Church* (1885). Udo Sautter, "Ein Deutscher Geistlicher in Neuschottland: Johann Adam Moschell (1795–1849)," *German-Canadian Yearbook* (Toronto), 1 (1973): 153–59.

MUIRHEAD. *See* DUVERNET

MUNRO, HUGH, businessman, JP, judge, politician, office holder, farmer, and agriculturalist; b. *c.* 1764 in Ross-shire, Scotland; m. Martha —; father of three sons and three daughters; d. 25 Sept. 1846 in Bathurst, N.B.

Hugh Munro received his early education in Scotland and immigrated with his parents to New York in 1774. Nine years later he went with other loyalists to Quebec, and when Gaspé was opened to loyalist settlement in 1784 he moved to New Carlisle; he was described at this time as a lumberman. In 1792 he was appointed a judge of the Inferior Court of Common Pleas, only to be removed in 1794 when the judicial district of Gaspé was reorganized. He then crossed the Baie des Chaleurs and settled near St Peters (Bathurst), N.B., where he began operations as a merchant and shipper of fish.

Munro soon expanded his activities into lumbering. In 1818 he claimed his was "the first and most ancient establishment" in the timber trade of Nepisiguit Bay; that year he cut about 5,000 tons of timber and had many people employed in the woods. He also built ships but records of this activity are sparse. One vessel constructed in 1818 was valued with its cargo at approximately £2,000. For many years Munro was to dominate the commercial life of St Peters. He was a friend and associate of Robert Ferguson* of Restigouche and did business as well with Gilmour, Rankin and Company of Miramichi [*see* Alexander Rankin*].

In 1807 Munro was appointed a justice of the peace and judge of the Inferior Court of Common Pleas for Northumberland County. He entered politics in 1819 as a candidate for one of the two county seats in the House of Assembly; defeated, he lodged a protest claiming that the sheriff had shown favouritism to his opponent. He was successful in the election of the following year, and was to hold his seat until 1827, when Northumberland County was divided and the county of Gloucester created. That year, as the most influential settler in the new shire, he was appointed justice of the peace, judge of the Inferior Court of Common Pleas, registrar of wills and deeds, and trustee of the grammar school. He was also elected the county's first representative in the assembly.

Munro had a keen interest in agriculture. At his residence, Somerset Vale, he had what was described as "a skillfully disposed and well cultivated farm, which like an *Oasis*, smiles upon the wilderness, from which years of unremitting industry have reclaimed it." In 1825 he was a member of the committee appointed by the assembly to consider ways of improving agriculture and promoting immigration; it recommended the creation of the New-Brunswick Agricultural and Emigrant Society. Active in this association until it ceased to exist, Munro sat on its central committee from 1828 to 1830. He was also the organizer and first president of the Gloucester County society, formed in 1828.

Over the years Munro became unpopular for a number of reasons. He was thought to acquire property by claiming that others had not fulfilled the conditions of their grants and, after the land was escheated, using his influence in Fredericton to have it regranted to himself. Accused of tyranny in his dealings with Acadians, he reportedly imprisoned a man for no reason on one occasion and then assaulted him before his release. He was also said to have withheld from his constituents money that had been authorized by the assembly for work on the roads and for bounties on grain, on the grounds that they would spend the money unwisely and in any case ought not to receive the bounties, which he, their representative, had voted against in the house.

In the election of 1830 Munro's political dominance in Gloucester County was challenged by William End*. End claimed that Munro held power through the support of the local magistrates, who were corrupt and owed their appointments to his influence. Promising to end despotism, End gained the backing of Acadian and Irish voters and was able to defeat Munro. At about the same time Munro's commercial power was threatened by the expansion into the Nepisiguit area of other entrepreneurs, notably Joseph Cunard*. Munro was among the lumbermen of the region who protested against the huge timber reserves granted to Cunard by the commissioner of crown lands, Thomas Baillie*. Cunard was to lose his reserves, but he continued to expand his activities and local lumbermen were no longer able to control the region.

On several occasions Munro tried to get compensation from the government for the office he had lost when the district of Gaspé had been reorganized in 1794. When he made a last attempt, in 1840, Lieutenant Governor Sir John Harvey* claimed he was "too old for office" and, though "very worthy and respectable, not sufficient indigent to make any relief acceptable (which can be offered to gentlemen)." Munro lived out his last years quietly on his farm, where he died in 1846.

W. A. SPRAY

N.B. Museum, W. F. Ganong papers, box 32, memorial of Hugh Munro, 25 Feb. 1840; Hugh Munro, letter-book; SB 2, F1, no.11 (E. B. Biggar, "Bathurst, its first settlers and their many and strange adventures," paper read before the N.B. Hist. Soc., 1894) (typescript); J. C. Webster papers, packet 1, Sir Howard Douglas, letter-book, Douglas to Lord Dalhousie, 7 May 1827. PAC, MG 24, A17, ser.I, 1: ff.185–86; L6, 3, N.B. Agricultural and Emigrant Soc., minute-book no.1 (1825–30). PANB, MC 1156, IX: 64; RG 3, RS538, B5: 26, 38, 80, 106; RG 4, RS24, S28-P28; RG 7, RS64, A, 1846, Hugh Monro; RG 10, RS108, Hugh Munro, 1805, 1807, 1820, 1828. PRO, CO 188/41: 144–49; CO 189/13: 29–30, 421–23, 521–22. Robert Cooney, *A compendious history of the northern part of the province of New Brunswick and of the district of Gaspé, in Lower Canada* (Halifax, 1832; repub. Chatham, N.B., 1896), 195. *Gleaner* (Miramichi [Chatham]), 21 Sept. 1830; 24 Jan. 1843; 24 Jan., 3 Oct. 1846. *Mercury*, 29 May, 26 June 1827; 19 Feb. 1828. *New-Brunswick Royal Gazette*, 7 March 1820. M. M. Hunter, *Pioneer settlers of the Bay Chaleur in the nineteenth and twentieth centuries* (Bathurst, N.B., 1978), 13, 17. MacNutt, *New Brunswick*. Graeme Wynn, "The assault on the New Brunswick forest, 1780–1850" (PHD thesis, Univ. of Toronto, 1974), 5–6, 43–44, 97–100,

220, 224–25, 271, 286. Observer [E. S. Carter], "Linking the past with the present," *Telegraph-Journal* (Saint John, N.B.), 10 April 1930.

MURRAY, ANNE (Powell), gentlewoman and author; b. 26 April 1755 in Wells, Norfolk, England, daughter of Dr John Murray and Mary Boyles; m. 3 Oct. 1775 William Dummer Powell*, and they had nine children of whom two survived her; d. 10 March 1849 in Toronto.

Anne Murray's father was a Scottish physician who moved to England and in 1768 began to practise in Norwich. When his sister Elizabeth visited him the following year, he was struggling to support a large family. Elizabeth Murray had immigrated to North America in 1739 with her brother James and had become a successful shopkeeper in Boston. Her second husband, a wealthy Boston distiller, had recently died. Rich and childless, Elizabeth offered to take responsibility for Dr Murray's three eldest children, John, Mary, and Anne. John and Mary were sent to Boston, and when Elizabeth returned to America in 1771, she took Anne with her.

Anne had been educated in Fakenham and at Mrs Palmer's boarding-school in Norwich, but her aunt thought that this only prepared girls for "the gay seens of life." An unusual woman for her time, she believed in the importance of practical business training, and she established Mary and Anne in a millinery shop in Boston. Mary looked after the shop and accounts while Anne, according to her aunt, was "very induserous at her needle." When Mary returned to England in 1774, a homesick Anne became the shop's manager, a position for which she was totally unfitted. She was miserably aware of a milliner's low social status, and this "loss of Caste" remained a bitter memory all her life; as an old woman she recalled the "irreparable humiliation" of these years.

Despite her feelings of inferiority, Anne Murray moved freely in Boston mercantile society, where she met William Dummer Powell, the son of a prominent merchant. William and Anne reached a secret understanding by the time that William's loyalist activities made it advisable for him to leave America. Anne's aunt reluctantly approved their marriage in 1775, but her parents' permission was not obtained. William did not even ask his father, because, as he later wrote, "there was little probability of consent." They were married immediately before sailing to England; this was called an elopement in Boston, and by William himself.

The young couple lived in Norfolk and London while William studied law. In 1779 he went to Quebec, leaving his wife and three sons at Norwich; the following year Anne joined him in Montreal, where he had established his practice. She moved frequently in the next 18 years, following the vagaries of her husband's career and ambitions. She lived in Montreal (1780–83), Boston (1783–84), North Yarmouth, Mass. (1784–85), Montreal (1785–89), Detroit (1789–91), England (1791–93), Detroit (1793–94), and Newark, later Niagara-on-the-Lake (1794–98). Finally the Powells moved to York (Toronto), where Anne spent more than 50 years.

During her travels Mrs Powell became preoccupied with the importance of social status and strict decorum, despite (or perhaps because of) her milliner's past and the impropriety of her marriage. As the capital of Upper Canada, York had from the beginning pretensions beyond its size and a fixed social hierarchy. When Mrs Powell arrived, her husband was a judge, so that her social position was high. Gradually the "vast propriety," which Thomas Aston Coffin* had ascribed to her, and her inflexible morals made her the town's social arbiter. In 1807–8, for instance, she successfully challenged Lieutenant Governor Francis Gore* himself when he tried to rehabilitate an outcast, Mrs John Small, publicly accused of adultery. In an age when social status had a strong influence on opportunity and success, Mrs Powell's power was very real.

Like society, government was "aristocratical" to Mrs Powell; she equated political opposition with low origins and unseemly behaviour. In her early years in Upper Canada she had thought of herself as an American, but the War of 1812 made her vehemently British. She abhorred those who opposed the government, from Robert THORPE, "an object of contempt & disgust," to the "Arch fiend" William Lyon Mackenzie*. Robert Baldwin* was "a good moral character, but a decided Radical"; his cousin Robert Baldwin Sullivan*, on the other hand, was "of low origin and . . . profligate habits." As with other high tories, her post-rebellion villains were the governors-in-chief themselves – "the false traitor Lord Durham [LAMBTON]" and "the *little* great Man," Lord Sydenham [THOMSON], with his "meanness and tyranny." The "Arch enemy," however, was John Strachan*, whom she blamed for all her husband's misfortunes in Upper Canada.

When Powell became chief justice in 1816 his wife's position was enhanced, but her social supremacy did not survive the scandal associated with her daughter Anne*. In her girlhood Anne Powell was much admired. With her mother's approval she was courted by a "wealthy young Merchant Miller," but after "a long & earnest suit" Anne rejected him. Mrs Powell herself rejected another suitor, "that animal St. George [Laurent Quetton* St George]," probably because of his profligacy. After an abortive romantic involvement with John Beverley Robinson*, Anne's behaviour became more and more eccentric. She had many violent altercations with her mother, often over the control of Mrs Powell's two granddaughters who lived with them. By 1820 Mrs Powell was convinced of her daughter's insanity, and wanted to establish her somewhere away from home, "but I have every reason to think she will not separate herself quietly from the family, and the Idea of compulsion sickens me." In 1822 Anne fled her parents' house in pursuit of Robinson and his wife, and died in a shipwreck off Ireland. The facts, rumours, and innuendoes of the tragedy brought disgrace to the family, and Mrs Powell withdrew from society.

In 1825, when her husband's political difficulties ended his judicial and administrative career, the Powells wanted to leave the colonies. Mrs Powell joined her husband in England in 1826, not intending to return. She had become embroiled in controversy with some of her family over a legacy from her aunt Elizabeth, and an indiscreet letter she wrote to Upper Canada created a lasting breach with most of her English relatives. Because of their "ebullitions of malevolence," the Powells came back to York in 1829, where they lived quietly while Powell's mental powers declined. After his death in 1834, Mrs Powell remained in her old home with her unmarried daughter Elizabeth. Deaf and crippled with rheumatism, she rarely went out, but various other members of her family lived with her for extended periods. She was still concerned with charitable activities and with the welfare of her descendants, although she was increasingly out of touch with their world.

In her old age, Mrs Powell faced "unalterable infamy and disgrace" within her own family. One of her granddaughters, Elizabeth Van Rensselaer Powell (Mrs John Stuart) was divorced for adultery – the first divorce in Upper Canada. In the necessary preliminary to parliamentary divorce, her husband sued her lover, Lieutenant John Grogan, and in November 1839 was awarded more than £600 damages and costs. Grogan was thus forced to sell his commission. The divorce bill was passed by the Upper Canadian legislature in February 1840, shortly before Mrs Stuart gave birth to "another victim to her depravity," but was reserved for royal assent. When it became law in June 1841, the lovers married immediately and left the province, returning the following year. Mrs Powell's sympathies were entirely with the deserted husband and children; she never forgave her "wicked" granddaughter, and was furious when the Grogans attempted to re-enter society in Kingston.

Throughout her long life, Mrs Powell was an inveterate writer of letters. More than 700 of them have survived. The early ones were to friends near Boston, but the bulk of her correspondence was with her brother George, of New York, and her husband, who was frequently absent on circuit and on trips to England. She wrote frankly about every detail of her life, family, and community. Never lukewarm in her opinions or their expression, she described such things as the seven-foot geraniums flanking the piano in her drawing-room, the totally unexpected birth of a baby to an unmarried servant in her employers' bed, the excitement of enemy invasion in 1813 and armed rebellion in 1837, and the "system of wrong and Robbery" embodied in the 1839 Clergy Reserves bill. Although she was an outstanding woman in early Toronto, she is equally important as a recorder of life among the élite of Upper Canada.

EDITH G. FIRTH

A portion of Anne Powell's voluminous correspondence has been published under the title "Letters of Mrs. Wm. Dummer Powell, 1807–1821," ed. Janet Carnochan, Niagara Hist. Soc., [*Pub.*], no.14 ([1906]): 1–40.

AO, MS 537; MS 787; MU 843. Library of Congress, MS Division (Washington), Christian Barnes, letters. Mass. Hist. Soc. (Boston), Paul Revere papers; J. M. Robbins papers. MTRL, S. P. Jarvis papers; W. D. Powell papers. PAC, MG 23, HI, 4; 8. Private arch., K. M. J. McKenna (Kingston, Ont.), Research files and draft PHD thesis (Queen's Univ., Kingston, in preparation). James Murray, *Letters of James Murray, loyalist*, ed. Nina Moore Tiffany, assisted by S. I. Lesley (Boston, 1901). *Town of York, 1793–1815* (Firth); *1815–34* (Firth). *York, Upper Canada: minutes of town meetings and lists of inhabitants, 1797–1823*, ed. Christine Mosser (Toronto, 1984). N. F. Cott, *The bonds of womanhood: "woman's sphere" in New England, 1780–1835* (New Haven, Conn., 1977). K. M. J. McKenna, "Anne Powell and the early York elite," *"None was ever better . . .": the loyalist settlement of Ontario; proceedings of the annual meeting of the Ontario Historical Society, Cornwall, June 1984*, ed. S. F. Wise *et al.* (Cornwall, Ont., 1984), 31–43; "Options for élite women in early Upper Canada: the case of the Powell family" (paper presented to the CHA annual meeting, Winnipeg, 1986). M. B. Norton, "A cherished spirit of independence: the life of an eighteenth-century Boston businesswoman," C. R. Berkin and M. B. Norton, *Women of America: a history* (Boston, 1979), 48–67. W. R. Riddell, *The life of William Dummer Powell, first judge at Detroit and fifth chief justice of Upper Canada* (Lansing, Mich., 1924). R. J. Burns, "God's chosen people: the origins of Toronto society, 1793–1818," CHA *Hist. papers*, 1973: 213–28. W. R. Riddell, "The first Upper Canada divorce," *Bench and Bar* (Montreal), 2 (1932), no.3: 8, 10.

MURRAY, Sir GEORGE, army officer and colonial administrator; b. 6 Feb. 1772 in Ochtertyre, near Crieff, Scotland, son of Sir William Murray and Lady Augusta Mackenzie, daughter of the 3rd Earl of Cromarty; m. 28 April 1825 Lady Louisa Erskine; before their marriage they had one daughter; d. 28 July 1846 in London.

George Murray was educated at the High School of Edinburgh and the University of Edinburgh. On 12 March 1789 he received a commission in the 71st Foot, on 5 June he transferred to the 34th Foot, and on 7 July 1790 he purchased an ensigncy in the 3rd Foot

Guards, becoming a captain on 16 Jan. 1794. During 1793 and 1794 he saw action in the Low Countries. On 5 Aug. 1799 he was made a lieutenant-colonel and joined the quartermaster general's department. Between 1799 and 1806 he served in several minor campaigns, and in 1807 during the expedition to Copenhagen he worked closely with Major-General Sir Arthur Wellesley, the future Duke of Wellington. In 1808 Murray became quartermaster general of the army in Portugal and on 9 March 1809 was promoted colonel. During the Peninsular War his tactical arrangements made a substantial contribution to Wellington's victories; on 4 June 1811 he was made a brigadier-general and on 2 December he was given the local rank of major-general. For the critical role he played in organizing Wellington's advance through Portugal and Spain in 1812–13 he was awarded a Portuguese knighthood and on 27 Sept. 1813 was invested with the Order of the Bath.

In December 1814 Murray accepted a posting to British North America and, after a hazardous journey by sled from Halifax, arrived in Quebec on 2 March 1815. After notifying Governor Sir George Prevost* of his dismissal and while awaiting the arrival of Prevost's successor, Sir Gordon Drummond*, Murray busied himself by preparing a study of the defences of the Canadian colonies. On 4 April Drummond appointed him commander of the forces and provisional lieutenant governor of Upper Canada. Murray assumed office on 25 April but was still awaiting instructions when he learned of the renewal of hostilities in Europe. At the end of May he left to rejoin Wellington but much to his chagrin missed the battle of Waterloo; he was made chief of staff of the army of occupation, and lived in splendour in Paris and Cambrai. He became, next to Wellington, the most decorated man in the British army. At this time he formed an attachment to Lady Louisa Erskine, the wife of Lieutenant-General Sir James Erskine of Torriehouse, with whom he lived continuously from 1820 and whom he married in 1825 after her husband's death. The relationship was to cost him dearly socially and to hinder his political advancement. In November 1818 the allied army disbanded and Murray was appointed governor of the Royal Military College on 18 Aug. 1819. In March 1824 he was elected to parliament and on 6 March was selected by Wellington to be lieutenant-general of the Board of Ordnance. From 1825 he commanded the forces in Ireland until on 25 May 1828 he became colonial secretary in the Wellington government.

Although Murray had limited political experience, he was considered a "good man of business" and his appointment was popular among the British North American governors, many of whom had served with him in the Napoleonic Wars. Sir James Kempt* predicted Murray would make "a *Capital Colonial Secretary*" and expected to see him "cutting a figure in Parliament." The appointment was also warmly received by colonial tories – such as John Strachan* – who had met Murray during his fleeting visit to Canada and who inundated him with advice. Both groups were doomed to disappointment. Murray was a conservative but one of a comparatively liberal bent who proclaimed himself "no enemy to that kind of reform which can be interpreted into a gradual, and cautious adoption of our Political system to the alterations of circumstances which time brings with it." He was determined to discover "the views taken by opposite parties" in the colonies and to give the assemblies a "fair share of power." Unfortunately Murray's good intentions were not matched by his performance. He was not a good speaker and did not cut a figure in the House of Commons. Moreover, Murray found his work as secretary onerous and he exercised only a perfunctory control over business; in the words of a subordinate these were "years of torpor" at the Colonial Office. Nor did he represent his department effectively in Cabinet, where he was "overawed" by Wellington.

In 1828 when the House of Commons select committee on Canada recommended substantial reforms in the administration of the Canadas, Murray vacillated. Although he wished to end the prolonged dispute with the Lower Canadian assembly over the civil list, his indecision allowed that body to seize the initiative and left the governor, Kempt, in an untenable position. Murray also wished to settle the long-standing debate over the distribution of the clergy reserves in Upper Canada but, even though he rejected the "Exclusive Principle," he was determined to give "peculiar encouragement" to the established churches of England and Scotland and he could not decide how to reconcile these objectives. By 1830 Wellington was under great pressure to transfer him to a less important post. When he left office that November he had, in fact, resolved few of the issues in dispute between the Canadian reformers and the British government and his departure was little regretted throughout British North America, even by those officials, such as Sir John Colborne*, whom he had appointed.

Murray lost his parliamentary seat in 1832 but regained it in 1834. He served as master general of the Ordnance, with a seat in the Cabinet, in Sir Robert Peel's ministry (1834–35). He lost his seat again in 1835 and was defeated in 1837, 1839, and 1841, although he again served as master general of the Ordnance, this time without a seat in the Cabinet, from 1841 until 1846. On 27 May 1825 he had become a lieutenant-general; he rose to the rank of general on 23 Nov. 1841. Murray's military reputation is secure, although overshadowed by Wellington's, but he was one of the weakest secretaries of state in the first half of the 19th century and, though alone among them he had visited the British North American colonies, his impact there was slight.

PHILLIP BUCKNER

[The papers of General Sir George Murray are found in NLS, Dept. of MSS, Adv. MSS 46.1.1–46.10.2. There is only one dispatch from Murray while he was in Upper Canada (PRO, CO 42/356: 61–63); however, the files for all the British North American colonies between 1828 and 1830 contain many items directed to him as well as a much smaller number of his responses. There are a number of letters between Murray and the Duke of Wellington in *Despatches, correspondence, and memoranda of Field Marshal Arthur, Duke of Wellington, K.G.*, ed. [A. R. Wellesley, 2nd] Duke of Wellington (8v., London, 1867–80), and frequent references to Murray in the Dalhousie papers at the SRO, esp. GD45/3/27B: 159, 201, 215. [Edward Law, 1st Earl of] Ellenborough, *A political diary, 1828–30*, ed. [R. C. E. Abbot, 3rd Baron] Colchester (2v., London, 1881), [Harriet Fane] Arbuthnot, *The journal of Mrs. Arbuthnot, 1820–1832*, ed. Francis Bamford and [Gerald Wellesley, 7th] Duke of Wellington (2v., London, 1950), and Sir Henry Taylor, *Autobiography of Henry Taylor, 1800–1875* (2v., London, 1885) are also useful. Murray's military career is examined definitively in S. P. G. Ward, "General Sir George Murray," Soc. for Army Hist. Research, *Journal* (London), 58 (1980): 191–208. Murray's report on Upper Canada has been reproduced in G. S. Graham, "Views of General Murray on the defence of Upper Canada, 1815," *CHR*, 34 (1955): 158–65. His career at the Colonial Office is assessed in D. M. Young, *The Colonial Office in the early nineteenth century* ([London], 1961) and my own *Transition to responsible government*. P.B.]

MUSE. *See* MEUSE

N

NAFZIGER, CHRISTIAN, colonizer; b. 1776 in Bavaria (Federal Republic of Germany); m. Maria —–, and they had three sons and two daughters; d. 13 April 1836 in Wilmot Township, Upper Canada.

The Nafzigers were members of the Amish Mennonite faith, which had its roots in the Anabaptist or radical wing of the Reformation. The Amish, generally considered the most traditional of the different Mennonite groups, took their name from Jacob Ammann, a Swiss Mennonite bishop under whose leadership they became a distinct group around 1700.

In late 1821 Christian Nafziger, a peasant farmer from near Munich, left his family in Bavaria and travelled to Amsterdam. With the help of Mennonite friends in Holland he set sail for Philadelphia in December 1821. Apparently blown off course, his ship reached New Orleans the following March. Travelling by river-boat up the Mississippi to Cincinnati, he made his way to Pennsylvania, the home of a considerable colony of Mennonites. With land there becoming expensive, his friends suggested that he try the Canadas, where cheaper land was presumably available.

Having been supplied with additional funds and a means of conveyance, Nafziger arrived in Upper Canada in August 1822. With the assistance of a few Mennonites in Waterloo County, led by Jacob Erb, application was made to Lieutenant Governor Sir Peregrine Maitland* at York (Toronto) for land in Lincoln County for approximately 70 Amish families. On 4 September the Executive Council approved the request in principle. Nafziger immediately returned to Europe via New York and London, where he supposedly had an audience with King George IV to confirm the grant.

In early 1824, in response to a petition submitted by Erb on Nafziger's behalf, land was set aside for the new immigrants in present-day Wilmot Township and was surveyed by John GOESSMAN. The "German Block," as it became known, consisted of 200-acre lots along either side of three parallel roads running west of the main Mennonite settlement. Each family was to receive 50 acres of free land, provided a house was built and land cleared for a roadway fronting the property. The remaining 150 acres of each lot could be purchased later.

The Amish began arriving in 1824. Nafziger did not return until 1826, when he took up residence on lot 6, north of Bleam's Road. He had brought his wife and children with him. Also accompanying him on the voyage was Bishop Peter Nafziger, who would serve as bishop (elder) of the Amish congregation, the first in Canada, until his emigration to Ohio in 1831.

In 1828 the 150-acre sections of the block were transferred to King's College, the provincially supported university, which set a high price on the land. Christian Nafziger and the German settlers subsequently complained to the commissioner of crown lands, Peter ROBINSON, who in January 1830 instructed the surveyor Samuel Street Wilmot to inspect the block and report on land values and the number of inhabitants entitled to consideration. The following month Wilmot reported that 55 "very industrious and peaceable Dutch settlers" from Germany and Pennsylvania had cleared 1,197 acres. He recommended that the 150-sections should be sold at reasonable prices to the original settlers who had fulfilled the conditions of their grants and that speculators should be compelled to give up their land within the settlement. Confusion evidently remained, for in 1832 the issue of the deed to

Nafziger's 150-acre section was complicated by the college's title.

Little is known of Nafziger's personal life or character. He was, it is clear, a rather adventurous person, willing to risk leaving his family, indebting himself, and launching on a dangerous journey. Although interested in bettering his lot, he included other members of his faith in his intent. His action opened to others of his native land the door to the possibility of a better life in the New World.

The wave of Amish immigration set off by Nafziger's explorations was not long contained in the "German Block" but spilt over into Perth, Oxford, and Huron counties. Nor were the new German immigrants all Amish. Roman Catholics and Lutherans hailing from the same areas of Europe as the Amish soon followed them to Upper Canada. Although these early settlers differed in their religious beliefs, they had much in common culturally, and their descendants have lived and worked side by side for generations.

ORLAND GINGERICH

AO, RG 1, A-I-6: 9505–6; C-IV, Wilmot Township, lot 5, North Erb Street. PAC, RG 1, E2, 20; L3, 208a: G15/42; 209: G16/8. *Canada Museum, und Allgemeine Zeitung* (Berlin [Kitchener, Ont.]), 28 April, 5 May 1836. L. J. Burkholder, *A brief history of the Mennonites in Ontario . . .* ([Toronto], 1935). Orland Gingerich, *The Amish of Canada* (Waterloo, Ont., 1972). B. M. Dunham, "Mid-European backgrounds of Waterloo County," *OH*, 37 (1945): 59–70.

NAU, LOUIS, Roman Catholic priest; b. 15 Sept. 1799 in Lanoraie, Lower Canada, and baptized the next day in the parish of Sainte-Geneviève-de-Berthier (at Berthierville), son of Charles Nau, a farmer, and Louise Pagé; d. in or after 1843.

The Naus, who were in humble circumstances but not poor, lived in the southernmost part of the seigneury of La Noraye, which in 1802 was annexed to the new parish of Sainte-Élisabeth, in the diocese of Joliette. They were held to be deeply religious; introducing their children early to prayer and to regular participation in confession and the Eucharist, they hoped to have a priest in the family. Young Louis was probably the son who showed the greatest inclination, but as there was no school in the parish before 1810, he was unable to complete elementary studies until he was 18. Thus it was only in 1817 that his parents, with the blessing of their curé, Joseph-Benjamin Keller, could send him to the Petit Séminaire de Montréal.

Nau's stay in the institution left its mark on him. In this milieu of Sulpician priests he no doubt was nurtured on monarchist and gallican traditions. In 1821, moreover, he witnessed the struggles of his teachers against Jean-Jacques LARTIGUE, the auxiliary bishop in Montreal. They not only refused to recognize the bishop's authority, but also maintained that the proposed establishment of a new diocese in Montreal was contrary to canon law. The mood of independence prevailing at the time in the Petit Séminaire de Montréal certainly fostered in Nau a tendency to be disputatious.

Upon completing classical studies in 1825 Nau chose to enter the priesthood, and in the autumn he went to the Grand Séminaire de Montréal. No sooner had he settled in than he was entrusted with teaching at the Séminaire de Saint-Hyacinthe. On 26 Feb. 1826 Lartigue tonsured him there. The following year Nau began theological studies at the Grand Séminaire de Québec, and on 25 March 1829 he was ordained priest by Bernard-Claude Panet*, archbishop of Quebec.

When he left the Grand Séminaire, Nau was considered a reliable man wholly respectful of the rules of his calling. The first known observation about him, made at the time of his ordination, is unequivocal: he was said to be pious, zealous, obedient to his superiors, and ready to serve the cause of religion, to which he was deeply attached. Panet also considered him a likely candidate, devoted to doing good and endowed with deep faith. At that time his superiors were unaware of the other side of his personality. Nau also turned out to be stubborn and self-willed, devoid of tact or moderation and barely able to endure contradiction.

Nau was named assistant priest at Saint-Jacques-de-l'Achigan (Saint-Jacques) in September 1829. He turned the local curé, Jean-Romuald Paré, against him in less than three months. Judging the two men temperamentally incompatible, Panet moved Nau to another parish, making him assistant priest at Maskinongé early in 1830. Once again the local curé, Louis Marcoux, was soon complaining of his behaviour. Informed of this new problem in January 1831, Lartigue showed that he nevertheless had confidence in Nau by finding him a post as assistant priest at Saint-Benoît (Mirabel). In October he made him assistant priest at Saint-Hyacinthe; however, the bishop left him there just a few months, because he had long wanted to make him a rural curé.

On 27 Feb. 1832 Nau officially became curé of the parish of Sainte-Madeleine (at Rigaud). Only a month after he had taken up his charge the churchwardens were accusing him of being arrogant and of seeking to manage on his own the assets belonging to the *fabrique*. The dispute became acrimonious and spread through the parish when Nau threatened in 1833 to take legal action against those parishioners who did not pay the fees for the rites of the church. At the end of the year petitions demanding his immediate recall were sent to the bishop in Montreal. In addition, some of Nau's flock subjected him to a charivari and hanged him in effigy outside his presbytery. Anxious to avoid the worst, Lartigue called upon Nau to leave. In January 1834, after repeated entreaties from Joseph SIGNAY, the archbishop of Quebec, he sent Nau to Saint-Jean-Baptiste-de-Rouville. Headstrong and unbending, Nau paid no attention to the bishop's orders and did not move to his new parish until five months later. This initial act of defiance set Lartigue against Nau, whom he considered a perpetual nuisance. Nor would the priest make any gesture of submission to his bishop.

But it was the conflict he was to experience at Saint-Jean-Baptiste-de-Rouville that would launch Nau into an unprecedented struggle against Lartigue and make him an outcast as a priest. He was no sooner installed in his parish than his authority was contested by his churchwardens. During the first two years of his ministry he was accused, among other things, of insulting the local seigneur, Jean-Baptiste-René Hertel* de Rouville, and of attacking several people in the parish from the pulpit. His quarrel with the seigneur even brought him a severe warning from the bishop. In such an atmosphere relations with his flock could only deteriorate quickly. Once more petitions were sent to the bishop of Montreal, in 1836 in particular, and once more Nau was hanged in effigy. Angry and tired of these quarrels, Lartigue reacted swiftly. In August he ordered Nau to Saint-Valentin, where he had just appointed him parish priest. But Nau was determined not to leave his charge, and he took formal possession of it in the presence of a notary; at the end of September Lartigue therefore appointed Pierre Lafrance as curé of Saint-Jean-Baptiste-de-Rouville, without bothering to find out if Nau had left. These incidents made Nau feel persecuted, but convinced the bishop that he was dealing with a rebellious spirit. From then on both men refused to make any concessions whatsoever.

In the parish events happened quickly. On 24 October Lafrance ordered Nau to leave the presbytery, where he had barricaded himself, but to no avail. Ten days later, at the bishop's palace in Montreal, Nau appeared before an ecclesiastical court which confirmed Lartigue's decision to suspend him from priestly office. Despite this condemnation he reinstalled himself in the presbytery, more determined than ever to carry on with his duties and to hand nothing over to Lafrance. Saint-Jean-Baptiste-de-Rouville witnessed an unprecedented confrontation as two sides formed to defend their conflicting interests. The affair got into the newspapers and soon was creating a stir in clergy and lay circles. Early in 1837 some supporters of Lartigue and Lafrance decided to take the presbytery by storm. Armed with stakes and sticks, they succeeded in evicting Nau, who managed somehow to hide in the home of one of his friends in the parish.

In these circumstances Nau saw but one way to fight Lartigue and Lafrance: recourse to the civil courts. By lending his written support to the Patriote cause, he succeeded in winning the favour of lawyers Louis-Hippolyte La Fontaine* and Amable BERTHELOT, who agreed to take up his cause. In February 1837 they brought two actions in the Court of King's Bench, one for £2,000 against Bishop Lartigue for having suspended Nau from priestly office, the other, for £600, against Pierre Lafrance for having usurped the duties of parish priest at Saint-Jean-Baptiste-de-Rouville. Several months later La Fontaine brought new support to the rebellious curé by publishing in Montreal the pamphlet *Notes sur l'inamovibilité des curés dans le Bas-Canada*. When informed of this development, Lartigue promptly wrote and published, also in 1837, *Mémoire sur l'amovibilité des curés en Canada*. The legal case then became increasingly a pretext for confrontations between the Patriote party and the ecclesiastical authorities.

A year later the three judges, James Reid, George Pyke*, and Jean-Roch Rolland*, delivered their judgement. Considering Nau to have neither title to nor possession of the parish charge, they rejected his demands and ordered him to pay court costs. Despite this stinging set-back Nau was not one to feel disheartened: in 1839 he declared himself ready to continue the fight and appeal the judgement. But, ruined financially, he had to renounce the idea of any new recourse to justice, not least because he had been abandoned by the Patriote leaders, possibly as a result of the affidavits he had given against certain parishioners in 1838 and 1839.

From that time the struggle continued in the religious sphere. Early in 1842 one of Nau's friends, notary Charles Têtu of Saint-Jean-Baptiste-de-Rouville, published *Analyse et observations sur les droits relatifs aux évêques de Québec et de Montréal, et au clergé du Canada*. Imbued with gallican ideas, Têtu maintained that bishops had no right of control over parish charges and ecclesiastical benefices. Although not officially the author, Nau had clearly had a hand in writing the text. In February and March of the same year he wrote articles in the newspapers, reflecting on traditional gallican doctrines and openly supporting Têtu's pamphlet. He thought that in this way he could provoke a useful debate among his ecclesiastical colleagues on the question of the irremovability of parish priests and the exercise of authority within the church. He probably was also hoping to intensify the discontent that for two decades had been stirring up the lower clergy against certain forms of episcopal authority that were too absolute. This hope, however, proved vain. Isolated, dishonoured, forever a marked man, Nau had no choice but to submit or go into exile. It is not known if he then thought of abandoning the priesthood. It is questionable, however, whether such a step could have been taken or even contemplated at the time. Social pressure, accepted ways of thought, and legal structures combined to prevent a priest from moving in this direction. It seems, however, that an understanding was reached during the summer of 1842 between Ignace Bourget*, the new bishop of Montreal, and the restive priest. After the two had a discussion, Nau reputedly agreed to put his submission to his superiors down on paper, and in return the bishop of Montreal supposedly offered him a large parish charge. But the agreement was short-lived. In 1843 Nau decided to go into exile in the United States, and no one heard of him again.

A sad destiny, Nau's. He was a secondary figure rejected by most of his fellows, and his life in a way illustrates the fate awaiting those who refused to submit to ecclesiastical authority. Nevertheless, he had hastened his own ruin by spurning compromise with his superiors.

RICHARD CHABOT

[The note-book recording the deliberations of the *fabrique* of Saint-Jean-Baptiste-de-Rouville parish for 1798–1840, which is in the possession of that parish, includes a scathing attack dated 3 July 1834 by Abbé Louis Nau on his churchwardens, in particular for the way they were administering the *fabrique*'s property. R.C.]

AAQ, 210 A, XIV: 324, 328; XVI: 236. ACAM, 420.095; RLL, VI: 19, 107, 236. ANQ-M, CE5-1, 16 sept. 1799; CN6-4, 27 oct. 1836. ANQ-Q, E17/45, nos.1676, 3601, 3603a. Arch. de la chancellerie de l'évêché de Saint-Hyacinthe (Saint-Hyacinthe, Qué.), XVII.C.41, 17 nov. 1837–17 nov. 1839. [The file for Saint-Jean-Baptiste-de-Rouville for 1836 and part of 1837 has inexplicably disappeared and could not be consulted. R.C.] Arch. de la chancellerie de l'évêché de Valleyfield (Valleyfield, Qué.), Sainte-Madeleine (Rigaud), corr., 20 mai 1832, 4 janv. 1834. Arch. de l'évêché de Joliette (Joliette, Qué.), Cartable Saint-Roch-de-l'Achigan, 3 nov. 1829, 18 févr. 1830. ASSH, A, Fg-41, 2.1.30–32, 35–36. L.-H. La Fontaine, *Notes sur l'inamovibilité des curés dans le Bas-Canada* (Montréal, 1837). [J.-J. Lartigue], *Mémoire sur l'amovibilité des curés en Canada* (Montréal, 1837). Charles Têtu, *Analyse et observations sur les droits relatifs aux évêques de Québec et de Montréal, et au clergé du Canada* (Montréal, 1842). *L'Aurore des Canadas*, 11 févr., 4 mars 1842. *Le Canadien*, 18, 21 nov. 1836. *La Minerve*, 24 nov. 1836. J.-J. Lefebvre, "Le curé Louis Nau (fl. 1799–1843)," CCHA *Rapport*, 24 (1956–57): 65–90. Honorius Provost, "Le régime des cures au Canada français: l'inamovibilité," CCHA *Rapport*, 22 (1954–55): 85–103.

NEILSON, JOHN, publisher, printer, bookseller, politician, farmer, and militia officer; b. 17 July 1776 at Dornald, in the parish of Balmaghie, Scotland, son of William Neilson and Isabel Brown; d. 1 Feb. 1848 in Cap-Rouge, Lower Canada.

In 1791 John Neilson joined his elder brother Samuel* at Quebec to help him run the publishing firm of Brown and Gilmore, a legacy of their uncle William Brown*, who had died in 1789. By 1792 Samuel was already expressing his pleasure at the "essential service" John was rendering him. As a result of Samuel's untimely death on 12 Jan. 1793, John inherited the business but was a ward of the Reverend Alexander Spark* until he attained his majority in 1796. His younger brother William came from Scotland to join him in September 1795 but went back home in 1797 or 1798. In 1794, suddenly and without explanation, John had run off to New York, to the annoyance of Mr Spark, who reproved him. "I have been guilty of a piece of folly," said Neilson contritely. "You must make allowance for youth." And he had speedily returned.

On 6 Jan. 1797 at Trois-Rivières, in the presence of Anglican minister David-François de Montmollin* and in all likelihood of a Catholic priest as well, Neilson married Marie-Ursule Hubert, a niece of Jean-François Hubert*, the Catholic bishop of Quebec. They signed a marriage contract that day before Trois-Rivières notary Antoine-Isidore Badeaux. In it they agreed to have community of property, administered according to the Coutume de Paris. When Neilson announced this decision to his mother in August, he explained that he appreciated his wife's great merits, but, further, he had wished to symbolize his permanent establishment in Canada and to help lessen the baneful prejudices with which Canadians and British immigrants regarded each other. For her part, his mother regularly advised him to persevere himself and raise his children in the religion of his ancestors, Presbyterianism. At least 10 children were born – Isabel, SAMUEL, Mary, Elizabeth, William, Margaret, Janet, Agnes Janet, Francis, and John – some of whom died in infancy. The boys were brought up in the Presbyterian faith, the girls in the Catholic. Neilson remained deeply attached to his church, which he served in various capacities at Quebec, and he would be commemorated by a plaque in St Andrew's Church; but he had a pew in the Catholic parish of Quebec which he paid for on a regular basis.

From his earliest days in business, young John showed sure judgement, tact, and ability. He would use just enough threats or flattery to obtain payment of the numerous debts owed his firm or to gain customers. He had to be unusually zealous in his work: the printing-shop, newspaper, and bookshop were highly profitable, provided he kept a meticulous record of all the little accounts that accumulated and collected them systematically, even if doing so meant regular recourse to the law courts, despite his distaste for this process. His account-books were detailed to an extent seldom seen. He even kept a note of time lost, in hours and minutes.

Neilson was primarily a printer, publisher, and bookseller, "the largest consumer of paper in this country," according to his rival James BROWN of Montreal. In 1800 he secretly purchased a controlling interest in the business of his main Quebec competitor, Pierre-Édouard Desbarats*. The establishment of this near-monopoly was accompanied by efforts to expand his productive capacity. In 1795 he had purchased type in England for printing hymn-books. He took steps to procure a new press in the United States in 1801 and to bring in apprentices from Scotland or the United States – young Canadians apparently would not do.

The income of Neilson's printing-shop came mainly from government contracts for proclamations, statutes, the assembly journals, and so on, from private contracts for countless forms, posters, business cards, and similar items, and from the publication of the largest weekly newspaper in the two Canadas, the *Quebec Gazette*/*La Gazette de Québec*, which had been in existence since 1764. Aside from single copies sold, from the 1790s and until about 1806 there were some 500 subscribers a year. Around 1809–10 there were nearly 900 and in the period 1810–20, more than 1,000; half were French-speaking. From 1800 to 1820 the paper devoted about 54 per cent of its space to advertising, 21 to international news and travel accounts, 8 to military questions affecting the colony, 5 to social problems, 7 to politics, 3 to economic matters, 1 to cultural affairs, and less than 1 to religious concerns. Neilson did publish newspapers of a more literary and entertaining nature, such as *Le Magasin de Québec* (1792–94), the *British American Register* (1803), and the *Canadian Visitor* (1815), but they were unsuccessful. The population proved too small and too ill informed to support publications of this kind. As well, Neilson exchanged newspapers with numerous English, American, and French publishers and acted as their subscription agent.

Besides the printing-shop and the newspaper, Neilson owned the principal bookshop in the Canadas until the 1820s. There, of course, he sold all kinds of office supplies, paper, and notebooks; on occasion he also bound books for his customers. He supplied other printers and booksellers in both Lower and Upper Canada with stock-in-trade that he imported or went in person to get from specialized firms in the United States or Great Britain. He acquired foreign books in the same way and even tried to get works from France, although he at times took advantage of auctions of private libraries. He supplied the major public libraries in the colony, including that of the House of Assembly. Having a large printing-shop, he was able to turn out a good number of volumes himself – basically religious works and textbooks that were not available otherwise in wartime, political pamphlets, and technical books for the local market. At regular intervals he published catalogues of books for sale and he advertised his list in the *Quebec Gazette*. His shops dominated publishing in Quebec and printed 50 to 60 per cent of the approximately 800 works produced in Lower Canada between 1800 and 1820.

As a printer and publisher specializing in religious works and school texts, Neilson sold catechisms, song-books, alphabet primers, and devotional volumes. Of some 42,120 books in French purchased at his bookshop between 1792 and 1812, 70 per cent dealt with religion, 21 per cent with school subjects. As for books in English, which Neilson could import and consequently did not have to publish, 38 per cent were school texts, 20 per cent religious works. If religious and school books are deducted, the volume of annual sales drops by about 3,000 to 185 titles in English and 205 in French on average. These included writings of the Enlightenment and the thinkers who marked Western society at the time: Montesquieu, Diderot, Voltaire, Condorcet, Pufendorf, Helvétius, Rousseau, Bernardin de Saint-Pierre, Linnaeus, Condillac, Adam Smith, Malthus, Ricardo, Blackstone, Burke, Bentham, Dodsley, among others, not to mention the classical authors such as those of the 17th century. There were also volumes dealing with the practice of law, medicine, surveying, and the notarial profession. Neilson sold more French titles, but carried a broader range of English ones. However, in 1815, after the wars ended, the variety of works in French increased notably. The French-speaking customers, who formed half or a little more than half of his clientele, came from the ranks of the clergy, liberal professions, small businessmen, and seigneurs; the English-speaking purchasers were garrison officers, senior office holders, merchants, members of the liberal professions, and craftsmen.

An educated man whose intellectual horizons were never narrow, Neilson was perfectly at ease in English and French, travelled extensively, and broadened his culture. He maintained a voluminous correspondence with numerous literary and political figures in the colony, among them Joseph Quesnel*, Ross Cuthbert*, Pierre-Stanislas Bédard*, Louis-Joseph Papineau*, and Justin McCarthy. Another correspondent, Abbé Jean-Baptiste BOUCHER, pardoned Neilson's printing errors in return for being given bound copies of his own *Recueil de cantiques à l'usage des missions, des retraites et des catéchismes* (1795).

Having entered the assembly in 1818, Neilson decided on 29 April 1822 to hand his firm over to his eldest son, Samuel, who received a two-thirds interest, and a partner, William Cowan, who received one-third; under the government of Dalhousie [RAMSAY] political tensions were increasing, and John did not want to find himself in any conflict of interest or to harm a business he had so firmly established. Nevertheless Dalhousie withdrew the post of king's printer from Samuel and gave it to John Charlton FISHER in October 1823. John continued to take an interest in the firm, but from a distance. In May 1836 Samuel, who was gravely ill, made the business over to his brother William and in July he gave his father power of attorney to settle his affairs. These seem to have been profitable despite the political difficulties. As late as 1848, when an attempt was made to appraise Samuel's estate, the stocks in the printing-shop and the book-store alone were valued at £2,717 7*s.* 7*d.*

On occasion Neilson wrote poems, sometimes in French, one of them about death. In 1795 he bought the shares of the Théâtre Canadien. He belonged to the Quebec Library from 1799 to 1824 and the Quebec Exchange and Reading Room in 1822 and 1827, being its president in 1831. In 1842 he was named an associate member of the Literary and Historical Society of Quebec. He was keenly interested in educational matters. For example, he gave books and money to schoolmasters such as Louis Labadie* at Berthier-en-Haut (Berthierville), Louis Vincent and his Huron school at Jeune-Lorette (Wendake), and Antoine Côté in the parish of Saint-Thomas (at Montmagny). In 1816 he was president of the subscribers to the Quebec Free School [*see* Thaddeus Osgood*]. When he was in London the following year, he complained to the Foreign School Society of the difficulties that the House of Assembly was encountering in its efforts to develop a school system under the control of churchwardens or ministers and priests of the various churches. In 1821 he was a member of the committee to encourage and promote education in rural parishes. He also took an interest in education for the working classes, particularly with regard to agriculture. Nor was it by chance that he was constantly re-elected president of the Mechanics' Institute of Quebec, serving for the years 1834–43 and possibly even earlier. In addition he was visitor (inspector) of the colony's schools in 1831 and trustee of the Royal Institution for the Advancement of Learning [*see* Joseph Langley Mills*] in 1838 and 1839 at least.

Over and above his chief business and his commitment to cultural concerns, Neilson was active in a variety of fields, some remunerative, others humanitarian in nature. For example, from 1816 he settled immigrants at Valcartier. By 1828 he reputedly had attracted 500 people there and a similar number to the adjoining regions, in all some 1,000 Scots and Irish, as well as a number of English and Americans. It is not surprising, then, that he had become a member of the Quebec Emigrants' Society by 1819. He established immigrants on adjacent properties that he obtained mainly from the Jesuit estates, to the great displeasure of Herman Witsius RYLAND, who served on the commission that managed the estates for the crown and who detested his political orientation. In 1816 and 1818 for example, Neilson and Andrew STUART acquired 54 grants, each 3 *arpents* by 30. As early as 1802 he had bought land at Cap-Rouge, and he added another property in 1815 consisting of four irregularly shaped lots, purchased for £55, on which he took up permanent residence. Neilson also had a farm there and a sugar bush at Sainte-Anne-de-la-Pérade (La Pérade), which were worked by tenants. In the course of business he bought and sold a large number of holdings, which were mainly located in the Quebec region. In 1832 he owned 39 properties (some rented out) at Valcartier, Cap-Rouge, Cap-Saint-Ignace, and Sainte-Anne-de-la-Pérade, as well as 5 houses, 6 pieces of land in Stanbridge, 1,200 acres in Aston, 1,200 in Barford, and lands worth £700 in Upper Canada. He had also invested capital in a mill at Valcartier. In 1830 he was endeavouring to sell some holdings in Tingwick.

This interest in agriculture and settlement was also attested by his participation in the Agriculture Society in the district of Quebec, of which he was vice-president beginning in 1819, if not sooner, and president from 1826 till at least 1832. He appeared before the assembly committee examining the state of agriculture in the province during the 1823 session and spoke about what he had observed, particularly during his rounds in a great many parishes in the summers of 1819 and 1820. He himself experimented with new farming techniques. In 1818 he received several prizes for inventing a seeder, for ploughing the straightest furrow in a competition, and for having introduced a new plough.

Neilson was a shareholder and client of the Bank of Quebec and a shareholder in the Quebec Baking Society. He also lent money at interest, to consolidate debts or supply cash to various people in need of it. He extended easy credit to his customers and buyers, while, however, setting fixed, regular payment dates. The inventory of the Neilsons' community of property, made almost 20 years after John's death, still listed £30,143 6*s.* 8*d.* in debts owing to it and £692 in personal estate, against only £25 in liabilities. Credit, along with land holdings, constituted the basis of Neilson's fortune after he retired from business. There was still considerable landed property in the estate even in 1867: the Hubert fief (2 leagues by 2 leagues), a house, 34 lots, 8 farms in the seigneurial area and 9 in Stoneham, Barford, and Simpson townships.

Gradually Neilson moved into politics, and his first steps in this direction were orthodox. During the troubles in 1794 he signed a declaration of loyalty to the crown, and in 1799 he signed the address of good wishes to Governor Robert Prescott* on his departure. His newspaper rarely published anything audacious. In 1810, when people were being imprisoned under the régime of Governor Sir James Henry Craig*, the *Quebec Gazette* urged respect for the constitution and loyalty. Even under Dalhousie, Neilson became a lieutenant in the Quebec militia in 1824.

Neilson has been called a moderate liberal or a

moderate reformer. His even, patient temperament, untroubled by quick anger, his admiration for British institutions, which was accompanied by a certain attraction to American municipal institutions, his pursuit of a balance of powers: all these naturally drew him towards men such as Pierre-Stanislas Bédard, the leader of the Canadian party until 1811. Neilson was convinced of the need to do away with the abuses that had crept into the application of the 1791 constitution. Sympathetic to French Canadians and their institutions, in particular the seigneurial régime, and critical of the financial irresponsibility displayed by a clique of uncontrolled officials holding too many posts, he was drawn to Louis-Joseph Papineau, who gained ascendancy over the Canadian party in the period 1818–22. The fact was that Papineau himself proclaimed the benefits of monarchy and fought against the abuses of executive authority in the colony.

Neilson was elected for Quebec in 1818 under the banner of the Canadian party. In a way he constituted a moral security essential to this party, which was too closely identified with the French Canadians. He complemented Papineau by exhorting him frequently to have patience and perseverance – qualities Papineau admitted he did not possess. It is not surprising, therefore, that the two were sent as delegates to London early in 1823 with the petitions from Lower Canada against the union bill that had been laid before the House of Commons in 1822. They met the under-secretary of state for the colonies, Robert John Wilmot-Horton, Sir James McIntosh, Lord Bathurst, and others. In his personal notes, which are not dated, Neilson argued that it would not be useful to increase the property qualification for voting and stressed that a change in land tenure, made possible under a statute passed in London in 1822, could not come about unless the consent of the *censitaires* was secured and their right to take up land at no expense to themselves was assured. In the House of Assembly at the time of the 1823 hearings on the state of agriculture, he spoke in favour of the seigneurial régime and the right of *censitaires* to obtain land without payment. And around 1825–26 he advised the governor that application of the legislation permitting commutation of seigneurial tenure into freehold, which had been passed by the British parliament in 1822 and 1825, should be accompanied by crown intervention to ensure that the right of the *censitaires* to land at no cost was upheld.

In the assembly Neilson became involved in everything related to education, agriculture, and township development. Although he at times dissociated himself from Papineau's position, on the whole he supported the Canadian party, especially on the question of control of supply. In January 1828 he again went to London, with Denis-Benjamin Viger* and Austin CUVILLIER, to present the assembly's complaints against Dalhousie's administration to the British parliamentarians. Neilson appeared before a House of Commons committee early in June and laid out the matters on which he had strong views. He urged the necessity of handing over to the assembly control of all revenue collected by the province – a recommendation which the committee adopted in part, although it advised permanent appropriation of salaries for the governor, legislative councillors, and judges. As well, Neilson called for an annual vote of supply, item by item, and he denounced the making of expenditures not authorized by the assembly. He condemned the excessively close ties between the Legislative and Executive councils and the governor, which had resulted in the paralysis of the legislature. The behaviour of the Dalhousie administration he characterized as abusive and highhanded. In his view a reasonable agreement between the assembly and London on the question of supply could be reached if the rights of the house were recognized. With regard to land matters, he criticized the imperial parliament's interference in Lower Canada's internal affairs – the legislation of 1822 and 1825 permitting the commutation of seigneurial tenure – and he warned there would be a risk of fraud if registry offices were set up since the Canadians were unfamiliar with such institutions. He pointed out the pernicious consequences of having too many absentee landowners in the townships, and he noted the Canadians' preference for Canadian laws and seigneurial tenure providing easy access to free land, unless the assembly's measures to correct abuses in the system were blocked by the Legislative Council. Reform of that council was required, he stated, and might best be achieved if the crown appointed persons of means who were independent of the executive. He also defended the Catholic Church.

On 29 March 1830 Papineau thanked Neilson publicly for his services – the report of the commons committee had recognized in part the legitimacy of the complaints of the Patriote party (as the Canadian party had been called since 1826). Neilson drew up a series of proposals conceived in a spirit of conciliation. But times had changed. Already a deep split was developing between him and Papineau, who would soon move from the cordial correspondence of the 1820s to public insults. In a letter to Neilson in August 1832, Papineau let slip the phrase "our detestable constitution." Neilson, however, set great store by the constitution, by the links with Great Britain and the benefits that the colony derived from them – indeed by a whole series of institutions that could not be accommodated within the increasingly republican line being taken by the party's radical wing. Neilson, having always preached the righting of abuses, the preservation of institutions, harmony, tolerance, and respect for the colony's various ethnic backgrounds and religions, was disturbed by an emerging anticlericalism and nationalism in the party which he thought went too far. He railed against the assembly's failure to take any real advantage of the compromises suggested by London, and he feared the economic consequences that might ensue from the radicalizing of a large group within the Patriote party. He also rejected the idea of an elected legislative council, which was incompatible with the British constitution.

The break, already evident in 1831–32, was consummated in 1834 with the assembly's adoption of the 92 Resolutions [*see* Elzéar BÉDARD], whose violent tone and extreme nature were repugnant to a level-headed man such as Neilson. Watching helplessly the radicalization that followed the bloody by-election in Montreal in 1832 [*see* Daniel Tracey*], he asked how a responsible government, as Papineau conceived it, could be demanded when Papineau could not govern himself. In his view the Patriote party stance threatened mercantile and industrial interests, which in turn ensured the prosperity of farmers. Until 1831, he thought, the assembly had been on the defensive. But since the concessions made by the British government it had become "the assailant" and intended to wring from the crown rights that were incompatible with the constitution and monarchical institutions. Blinded by the ambition of a few individuals thirsting for power, who exploited national differences and jealousies, it had blocked supply, threatened rebellion, and neglected the wishes of the people. In March 1833 he stated in the *Quebec Gazette* that the constitution had first been betrayed by the governor and Legislative Council, and was now being betrayed by the assembly.

Some historians are of the opinion that Neilson lacked flexibility and consequently was unable to gather allies and act as a counterbalance to Papineau. Be that as it may, the radical group called him a traitor, and in the 1834 elections he was defeated in the constituency he had represented for more than 15 years. He then helped found constitutional associations in the colony. In 1835 he was commissioned to go to London, accompanied by William WALKER, and express the viewpoint of the moderate English-speaking merchants. What he was again seeking was the righting of abuses, but without sedition or revolt. He vainly tried to avert the rebellions.

Neilson became a member of the Special Council on 2 April 1838 and served on it till 1840, except for the brief period under the administration of Lord Durham [LAMBTON] when it was reconstituted. Faithful to his convictions, he fought against union of the two Canadas, a stand that earned him popular support and election to the assembly of the united Canadas in 1841. In 1844 the assembly named him speaker, but on 25 November of that year he was given a seat on the Legislative Council, which he retained for the rest of his life.

Along with business and politics, Neilson was active in various associations. For example, he was a member of the Quebec Fire Society from 1797, becoming its president in 1810. In 1809 he was elected vice-president of the Quebec Benevolent Society and then president, an office he held again in 1812 and 1817. In 1837 he was president of the St Andrew's Society of Quebec. He served as a commissioner to examine the prison system and as a trustee for demolishing the market house in Upper Town Quebec in 1815 and 1821. He was a justice of the peace continuously from 1815 (his mandate was last renewed on 23 Nov. 1838), and in 1845 he was appointed a commissioner of the Beauport asylum. Furthermore, his stature and probity made him an ideal person to be given powers of attorney for fellow merchants or to serve as guardian for minors. As he explained to people who sought his help, "Although my mission simply relates to the political concerns of the country, I shall always be happy to contribute every thing in my power to whatever may appear to be conducive to the general welfare."

At his death on 1 Feb. 1848 Neilson left a sizeable fortune (20 years later it exceeded £30,000, real estate not included), and a reputation for integrity and good judgement. He had brought his children up with affection but also with discipline – their numerous letters vainly requesting money are proof of that; he did, however, make sure they were established. The arrangements made in his will and that of his wife are indicative of the man. The usufruct of everything in the community of property was left to the survivor and the heirs were forbidden to contest legally the division made, on pain of being disinherited *ipso facto*. Shortly after his death, his son William paid £145 for a monument to be erected in the cemetery of the Presbyterian church in Valcartier, at the head of the grave.

Intelligence, culture, hard work, perseverance, moderation, firmness, and patience, these were some of the qualities that enabled John Neilson to pursue an uncommon career. Much has been made of his sense of thrift; his generosity, though not always disinterested, has perhaps been forgotten. For example, in 1804 he contributed to a subscription for victims of the Quebec fire and again in 1818 to one for the poor in the district of Quebec. In business or family matters he had extensive dealings with notaries, avoided lawyers and judges if possible, and preferred arbitration, settlement out of court, or a warning. With too many preoccupations, he at times neglected his own civic duties, among them keeping up the roads. In essence, Neilson seems to have been one of the earliest exemplars of the "Canadian" in the modern sense: bilingual, connected with people of various origins, optimistic about the country's future. His relative failure and his inability to create solid and lasting links for himself in the French Canadian milieu, whether business or political, are proof that the undertaking is difficult in any period.

Sonia Chassé, Rita Girard-Wallot, and Jean-Pierre Wallot

John Neilson's papers are located at the ANQ-M in P-1000-3-360; at the ANQ-Q in its collections of the Neilson family (P-193) and of the Neilson printing firm (P-192); and at the PAC in MG 24, B1, which covers the period 1764–1850. There are also items in other collections at the ANQ-Q, including those of Ludger Duvernay* (P-68), the Papineau family (P-417), and the Napoléon Bourassa family (P-418).

ANQ-MBF, CN1-4, 6 janv. 1797. ANQ-Q, CN1-16, 24 déc. 1806; 9 sept., 23 déc. 1809; 11, 17 sept., 13, 18, 21, 26 oct., 2 nov., 14–15 déc. 1813; 8, 14–15, 18, 21–22 janv., 15–16 juill., 27 oct. 1814; 31 oct., 26 nov. 1815; 26 janv., 19 févr., 12 juin, 25 juill. 1816; 26 nov., 24, 27 déc. 1817; 5 mai, 27 juill. 1818; 28 mars, 15 avril 1820; 4 mars 1822; 18 juill. 1823; 11 avril, 20 mai 1826; CN1-26, 30 juill. 1800; 16 mai 1815; 24 mai 1816; 27 août, 8 sept. 1818; 1er oct. 1823; CN1-33, 23 oct. 1866–20 mars 1867; CN1-49, 15 janv. 1833; CN1-66, 19 oct. 1860, 30 déc. 1865; CN1-116, 11 août 1819; 6 févr. 1821; 14 avril 1828; 27 mai, 5 juin, 19 juill., 18 oct. 1830; 26 janv. 1831; 13 août, 7 nov. 1832; 9 avril 1833; 2 mars, 1er avril, 17 oct. 1835; 22 avril, 7, 31 mai, 11 juill. 1836; 4, 26 avril, 20, 22 juill., 19 oct. 1837; 21 mars, 14 avril, 11, 21–22 sept., 12 oct. 1838; 30 avril, 22, 27 mai, 22 août 1839; 25 mai 1841; 9 juin, 1er août, 31 déc. 1843; 19 janv., 12 avril, 3, 23 mai 1844; 14 févr., 2 avril, 5, 28 sept. 1846; 23 avril 1847; 5 janv. 1848; CN1-208, 14 oct. 1824; 7 juin 1825; 10 juin 1826; 28 avril, 2 mai 1827; 4 oct. 1828; 17 déc. 1829; 27 oct. 1830; 18 oct. 1832; 19 juin, 20 oct. 1833; 17–18 nov. 1845; CN1-213, 28 juill., 21 déc. 1846; 19, 27 oct., 24 déc. 1847; 18, 25 févr., 23 mars, 8, 15 avril, 8–31 mai, 14, 24 juill., 11, 22–23 sept. 1848; 23 avril, 19 mai 1849; CN1-228, 11 avril 1826, 2 févr. 1828, 15 nov. 1831, 18 sept. 1833; CN1-230, 1er juin 1802; 22 mars, 24 oct. 1803; 13, 29 mars, 13 nov. 1804; 23 mai 1806; 28 juin 1813; 28 mai 1814; 27 mai, 14 sept. 1815; 29 juill. 1816; 31 juill., 29 août, 23 sept., 3 déc. 1817; 21 mars 1818; 6 oct. 1821; 30 oct. 1822; 13 janv., 13 sept. 1823; 9 mars, 10 juin, 2 nov. 1824; 6 juill. 1825; CN1-261, 13 oct. 1828; CN1-262, 23 mai 1800, 3 nov. 1809, 21 oct. 1811, 21 janv. 1812; CN1-267, 28 avril 1819; 23, 27 sept., 16 oct. 1823; 3 févr. 1824; 10 janv. 1825; 27 févr. 1826; 17 sept. 1829; 14, 16 avril 1832; 21 nov., 24 déc. 1833; 5 mars 1836; T-11/1, no.5118 (1799); no.5330 (1801); no.5440 (1802); no.6113 (1807); no.526 (1817); no.1191 (1824–25); no.11 (1827); no.756 (1829); no.744 (1830); no.763 (1830–32); no.598 (1837); no.1861 (1847); no.1868 (1847). PAC, MG 11, [CO 42] Q, 193–241; MG 55; RG 68, General index, 1651–1841; 1841–67. Univ. de Montréal, Service des bibliothèques, coll. spéciales, coll. Melzack, H. W. Ryland à John Ready, 5 oct. 1819. Univ. of B.C. Library, Special Coll. Division (Vancouver), Ryland papers.

L.C., House of Assembly, *Journals*, 1818–37; 1828–29, app.HH. Alexis de Tocqueville, *Tocqueville au Bas-Canada*, Jacques Vallée, édit. (Montréal, 1973). *Quebec Gazette*, 1790–1848. *DNB*. Hare et Wallot, *Les imprimés dans le Bas-Canada*. Le Jeune, *Dictionnaire*, 2: 336. J. [E.] Hare et J.-P. Wallot, "Les imprimés au Québec (1760–1820)," *L'imprimé au Québec: aspects historiques (18e–20e siècles)*, sous la direction d'Yvan Lamonde (Québec, 1983), 78–125; "Le livre au Québec et la librairie Neilson au tournant du XIXe siècle," *Livre et culture au Québec (1800–1850)*, sous la direction de Claude Galarneau et Maurice Lemire (Québec, 1988), 93–112. Ouellet, *Bas-Canada*. Taft Manning, *Revolt of French Canada*. Claude Galarneau, "Les métiers du livre à Québec (1764–1859)," *Cahiers des Dix*, 43 (1983): 143–65. J.-P. Wallot, "Frontière ou fragment du système atlantique: des idées étrangères dans l'identité bas-canadienne au début du XIXe siècle," CHA *Hist. Papers*, 1983: 1–29.

NEILSON, SAMUEL, printer, journalist, and publisher; b. 8 Feb. 1800 at Quebec, eldest son of John Neilson and Marie-Ursule Hubert; m. first 14 June 1831 Margaret McSkimming at Quebec; m. secondly 28 May 1835 Catherine James in New York; d. there 17 June 1837.

Samuel Neilson attended Daniel Wilkie*'s grammar school at Quebec and received a sound education there. His father removed him in order to have him finish his studies in Scotland, and in July 1816 the two sailed for Europe. After a short stay in Paris, Samuel settled in Glasgow, where he registered in a college on Richmond Street run by Dr William Chrystal. He spent three years there, studying Greek, Latin, philosophy, mathematics, and science. In the summer holidays he took special courses in bookkeeping, drawing, architecture, botany, and French. He also passed pleasant weeks at Gatehouse-of-Fleet with his paternal grandmother, his uncle William, and his aunts Isabel and Janet. Upon completing his studies in rhetoric and the two philosophy classes, he was awarded an MA in 1819.

Neilson returned to Quebec that summer and immediately went to work for his father, who was proprietor of the *Quebec Gazette* and of the biggest shop for printing, bookbinding, books, and office supplies in Lower Canada and who also held the office of king's printer. He had been elected member of the House of Assembly for Quebec in 1818, and there was some concern that difficulties, if not a conflict of interest, might arise from his holding the two offices at once. To avoid such a situation, he handed his printing enterprise over on 29 April 1822 to a company formed by his son Samuel and William Cowan. The partners received respectively two-thirds and one-third of the business.

The plan to unite Upper and Lower Canada was at the heart of political debate in the summer of 1822, and John Neilson sided wholeheartedly with the Canadian party. Governor Lord Dalhousie [Ramsay] was displeased, and offered John Charlton Fisher the position of publisher of the *Quebec Gazette*. Because Fisher was unable to come to an agreement with Samuel Neilson, the governor decided to strip Samuel of the commission as king's printer that he had granted him. On 22 Oct. 1823 he conferred it on Fisher, who also received authorization to bring out the *Quebec Gazette, published by authority*.

In January 1828 John Neilson went to London with Denis-Benjamin Viger* and Austin CUVILLIER to put the Canadian case against Dalhousie's maladministration. Dalhousie lost all sense of proportion and abused his prerogatives by taking severe measures against some justices of the peace and militia officers, and by arresting journalists for venturing to publish accounts of the mass meetings then being held. As a result Samuel was arrested four times, charged with libel, and released on bail. These difficulties occurred during his father's absence, but he did not lose his calm and maintained a dignified tone in his articles in the *Quebec Gazette*. Dalhousie was recalled in 1828, and Sir James Kempt*, who succeeded him, dropped the charges.

Founded in 1764 by William Brown* and Thomas Gilmore*, the *Quebec Gazette* had always been bilingual and since 1818 had appeared twice a week. In May 1831 Jean-Baptiste Fréchette and Étienne Parent* resumed publication of *Le Canadien* and a year later they turned it into a thrice-weekly paper. Doubtless spurred by the success of his competitors, Neilson altered his newspaper in April 1832, publishing two editions three times a week, one in English and the other in French. The change amounted to producing a daily paper and imposed an almost superhuman task upon Neilson. Some time later a calamitous cholera epidemic struck the town of Quebec, claiming thousands of victims. Those who could, left for the countryside, and John Neilson retired with his family to their farm at Cap-Rouge. But Samuel remained at the head of the paper, never absent for even a day from the shop on Rue de la Montagne (Côte de la Montagne), imperturbable, and temperate in the pages of the *Gazette* as well as in the short notes he penned to his father. One can readily imagine how overworked he was during this period.

In 1833 Samuel returned to the British Isles. He spent several months resting in Ireland, went to Scotland, and got as far as London. From there he wrote to tell his father that he intended taking up residence in Europe. He returned to Quebec, however, and did not end his partnership with William Cowan until 30 April 1836. On 31 May he turned the business over to his brother William, and in July he made his father his attorney. He was ill, and after he had consulted Quebec physicians Thomas FARGUES and James Douglas*, he left for Europe in July, stopping at Saratoga Springs and New York to seek the opinion of other doctors. In November 1836 he sailed for Madeira and the Mediterranean, where he spent the winter. He was back in New York on 16 June 1837 and died of tuberculosis the following day in the quarantine station of that city.

Samuel Neilson's destiny was tragic. The favourite son of his father, whose intelligence and good sense he had inherited, he was utterly devoted to his work and was still making plans in the autumn of 1836 for improving the newspaper and printing-shop. A keen observer of men and politics, he was also a talented writer and possessed real aptitude for drawing and painting, as his unpublished accounts of trips to the Saguenay and Madeira demonstrate. He was a reserved man and seems to have been an enigma to his close relatives. For example, none of his family is listed in the entry for his first marriage in the register of St Andrew's Church. His wife died a year or two later, and his second marriage took place in New York in 1835. Samuel Neilson was one of the most gifted young men of his generation. His untimely death together with his father's dominating personality kept him from fulfilling his early promise.

CLAUDE GALARNEAU

Samuel Neilson's unpublished narratives of his voyages, which he wrote on his return from the Saguenay and from Madeira, are at PAC, MG 24, B1, 19: 4 and 42: 2157–348 respectively. The PAC also holds important materials on Neilson and his family in the same collection: MG 24, B1, 19: 8; 24: 585; 36: 242–572; 38: 1038–45; 40: 1452–87; 42: 1736–2038.

ANQ-Q, CE1-66, 16 févr. 1800, 14 juin 1831; CN1-116, 29 avril 1822; 22 avril, 7, 31 mai, 11 juill. 1836. F.-X. Garneau, *Voyage en Angleterre et en France dans les années 1831, 1832 et 1833* (Québec, 1855), 236–37. *Le Canadien*, juin 1837. *La Minerve*, juin 1837. *Quebec Gazette*, April–May 1822, April–September 1832, April–May 1836, June–August 1837. *Quebec Mercury*, June 1837. Beaulieu et Hamelin, *La presse québécoise*. F.-J. Audet, "John Neilson," RSC *Trans.*, 3rd ser., 22 (1928), sect.I: 81–97. Ignotus [Thomas Chapais], "Le monument Wolfe et Montcalm à Québec," *BRH*, 5 (1899): 305–9. *Quebec Chronicle-Telegraph*, 21 June 1939.

NELLES (Nellis), ROBERT, businessman, office holder, JP, politician, and militia officer; b. 6 Oct. 1761 in Tryon County, N.Y., eldest son of Hendrick William Nelles (Nellis); m. first 1788 Elizabeth Moore (d. 1813), and they had five sons and three daughters; m. secondly 1814 Maria Jane Waddell, the widow of Samuel Bingle, and they had two sons and four daughters; d. 27 July 1842 in Grimsby, Upper Canada.

According to family tradition, Robert Nelles was descended from a Huguenot family that was driven from France to the Palatinate (Federal Republic of Germany) following the revocation of the Edict of Nantes in 1685. In 1709 they were uprooted once again by a French invasion and found temporary asylum in England. From there they were bundled off, along with 4,000 Palatinate refugees, to populate the colony of New York. War followed them. William Nelles (Nellis), Robert's grandfather, was pressed into taking part in an attack on New France within a year of his arrival in 1710. In 1759–60 Hendrick William Nelles, Robert's father, served in Sir William Johnson*'s Indian Department, with which he saw action during the Seven Years' War.

Friendship with the Indians had helped rebuild the family fortunes in New York, as it would later in Upper Canada. Abandoned by their British sponsors and denied title to their lands, the Palatinate immigrants had moved inland in the 1720s to settle among the Indians of the Mohawk valley. During the 1750s and 1760s Hendrick Nelles's cousin George Klock was surrounded in controversy because of his method of obtaining land from the Mohawks at Canajoharie (near Little Falls, N.Y.). Klock apparently got the Indians drunk, bartered their clothes off their backs, and then tricked them into signing deeds to vast tracts of land for a pittance. Although it seems that Nelles was not involved in such deals, he certainly did acquire a great deal of land. When old associations called him back to the Indian Department in 1777 (or revolutionary tensions drove him back), he left behind property that he later valued at £3,760, not counting stock and equipment.

After 1777 the Indian Department strategy was simply to destroy the settlements in the interior of New York that supplied the Continental Army. Captain Nelles (he anglicized his name to Henry at this time) accompanied Indians on many savage raids back into his own Mohawk valley, sacking homesteads, burning crops, and killing and scalping settlers. Through his intervention the Old Palatine Church, which his family had helped build, and the Nelles homestead were spared destruction. On one of these murderous missions in 1780 Nelles "recovered" his teenage son Robert, who joined him at Fort Niagara (near Youngstown, N.Y.) as a lieutenant in the Indian Department. Robert proved as energetic and resourceful at frontier terrorism as his father, leading raids in 1781 and 1782 with a cool fury. He returned in modest triumph from the 1782 campaign with "a parcel of negroes & wenches" in tow, for which he found a ready market in Niagara. At the end of the war, both Robert and his father were released from the Indian Department, but were retained on half pay.

Understandably, neither father nor son returned after the war to the district that they had razed. Instead, they followed their Indian clients to the Grand River valley, where they settled and did a little fur trading. In February 1787 Joseph Brant [Thayendanegea*] arranged for some 4,254 acres on the Grand River to be deeded to Henry Nelles and his sons Robert and Warner "to be possessed by them and their posterity." By the time of Henry Nelles's death in 1791, five of his sons were settled in Upper Canada. The Nelleses received other land grants for military service, loyalism, and compensation for lost property, and by 1800 they collectively owned 7,300 acres, most of it in the Niagara District, making them the sixth largest landholders on the peninsula.

Robert decided to develop more than 600 acres on Forty Mile Creek. There, on the site of present-day Grimsby, he built mills and a store, and commenced a grand stone mansion, The Manor, which still survives. In the 1790s he supplied hardware, household goods, textiles, and provisions to the small settlement. After 1800 he forwarded whiskey, grain, and flour from his mill to W. and J. Crooks at Niagara (Niagara-on-the-Lake) [*see* James Crooks*]. Joseph Brant sought his help both in supplying the Six Nations settlements and in the education of his own sons. Robert was also briefly pressed into service again as an Indian agent in 1797, delivering trade goods to the Mississauga Ojibwas under the terms of their recently concluded treaty. Thus Robert Nelles launched his own family from the elevated position accorded by landed wealth, a commercial income, and his continuing half pay.

Being a local notable in a deferential society, Nelles held various offices, such as town warden and justice of the peace, and was inevitably drawn into provincial politics. In the 1800 general election he headed the poll in the two-member riding of York West, 1st Lincoln, and Haldimand and he served in the House of Assembly until 1808, usually voting with the government majority. He seems to have devoted himself to local appropriations and regularizing the title to family land on the Grand River. While he was away at York (Toronto), his brothers, and later his eldest son, Henry, looked after the store and mills, and his wife, Elizabeth, tended a growing family that eventually numbered eight children.

War threatened life and property again in 1812 and Nelles, his brothers, and his son responded to the call to arms. Robert reported for duty as a captain in the 4th Lincoln Militia in 1812 but did not see much action during the next two years. The inhabitants of the Niagara District, many with loyalties cruelly divided by the war, seemed to prefer being spectators. The local militia remained inactive, undermanned and demoralized, especially after the American occupation in 1813. This state of affairs led to a general shake-up of command in the Lincoln militia in 1814 during which Nelles was promoted lieutenant-colonel of the 4th regiment. He quickly brought it up to strength with threats of fines and courts martial. Robert and his family fought in several battles, most notably at Lundy's Lane, where his son was captured and his brother wounded.

After the war he remarried and briefly returned to public life. In February 1814 he had been elected to the assembly for 1st Lincoln and Haldimand to replace the expelled Joseph Willcocks*. He held the seat until 1820; while he attended parliament, his son Henry managed the family mills. This separation has bequeathed to us a rare collection of touching love-letters between husband and wife. Robert Nelles (over the years the spelling gradually regularized to Nelles) was enormously proud of his military record and continued to take a great deal of interest in militia affairs. In 1822 he was rewarded with a promotion to colonel of his regiment. He scandalized and angered his neighbours with the unblushing favouritism of his appointments. For 20 or more years most of the officers in his regiment were members of the Nelles family. This situation aroused jealousy and resentment not only in the county but also within the Nelles family. In 1822 Robert promoted his son-in-law, but his brother William claimed seniority and marred the annual militia parade by beating his rival with a stick.

Robert Nelles's sons were all well educated by the standards of the day. They received an elementary education in a school their father had established at the Forty (Grimsby), and some of them were sent to York to continue their training in the care of the Ridouts and John Strachan*. Although raised a Lutheran in the German-speaking Palatinate community in New York, Robert helped build and became a pillar of the Anglican church in Grimsby. His son Abram* became a noted Church of England missionary to the Six Nations Indians. This appointment served to mark the great change that had taken place over the generations in the relative fortunes of the Nelles family and their Indian neighbours. Abram, a professional man from a well-off family, ministered to the poor and confined population of a reservation, descendants of the warriors his father and grandfather had fought alongside in three wars, whose friendship had so generously endowed the family with land.

H. V. NELLES

AO, MS 118; MS 502; MS 503; MU 3296. BL, Add. MSS 21661–892 (mfm. at PAC). HPL, File information on Robert Nelles. PAC, MG 19, F1; F2; F6; MG 24, D108; RG 9, I, B1; B4; B5; RG 10, A1; RG 19, E5(b), 4447. *The papers of Sir William Johnson*, ed. James Sullivan *et al.* (14v., Albany, N.Y., 1921–65). U.C., House of Assembly, *Journal*, 1800–10, 1816–20. *Valley of Six Nations* (Johnston). D. C. Nellis, [*Nellis family album*] (Topeka, Kans., 1888; copy in possession of H. V. Nelles). William Gillard and Thomas Tooke, *The Niagara escarpment: from Tobermory to Niagara Falls* (Toronto and Buffalo, N.Y., 1975), 100, 104. Barbara Graymont, *The Iroquois in the American revolution* (Syracuse, N.Y., 1972). [L. D. MacWethy and] Milo Nellis, *The old Palatine church, together with a description of the Gen. John Cochran house, also articles on the early Klock and Nellis pioneers* ([3rd ed.], St Johnsville, N.Y., 1930). Milo Nellis, *The Mohawk Dutch and the Palatines; their background and their influence in the development of the United States of America* (St Johnsville, [1951]). B. G. Wilson, *Enterprises of Robert Hamilton*. E. A. Brooks, "The story of William Sampson, first rector of Grimsby, 1817–1822," *Wentworth Bygones* (Hamilton, Ont.), no.11 (1975): 28. "The coming of the loyalists, 1783–1787" and "Fifty years of municipal government, 1790–1840," comp. R. J. Powell, *Annals of the Forty* ([Grimsby, Ont.]), no.1 (1950): 4–7, 32–35, 88, and no.2 (1951): 12. H. V. Nelles, "Loyalism and local power: the district of Niagara, 1792–1837," *OH*, 58 (1966): 99–114. J. G. Rossie, "The Northern Indian Department and the American revolution," *Niagara Frontier* (Buffalo), 20 (1973): 52–65.

NEWBIGGING, JAMES, businessman, JP, militia officer, and politician; b. 1805 or 1806, probably in Scotland; m. 26 Jan. 1834 Anne Louise Hagerman, niece of Christopher Alexander HAGERMAN, in York (Toronto), Upper Canada, and they had at least two sons; d. 9 Feb. 1838 in Toronto.

James Newbigging received his early Canadian mercantile training as a clerk in the firm of Gillespie, Moffatt and Company in Montreal. In 1829 he moved to York, where he bought a store on the market square. The following year he entered into a partnership with Alexander Murray, formerly a clerk in William Proudfoot*'s wholesale-retail store in York. Murray, Newbigging and Company was also a wholesale-retail business, selling a general line of groceries, dry goods, and spirits. As well, the company bought a wharf and storehouse, from William COOPER in 1830, and acted as commission agents. The development of the wholesale trade in York, by the firms of Newbigging, Proudfoot, Joseph Davis Ridout*, and others, prompted the York *Courier of Upper Canada* to proclaim in 1832 that "Country Merchants need no longer think of incurring the loss of time and expense of going to Montreal, since every article of Merchandise can be obtained in York, in equal abundance and variety, and upon Montreal terms."

Murray, Newbigging and Company quickly prospered, benefiting initially from the financial backing of a silent partner, Dr George Gillespie Crawford, who had inherited wealth from his father. Crawford suffered "great financial loss," however, and in 1834 his affairs were turned over to two trustees, John Strachan* and Robert Baldwin*. Despite the importance of his initial investment, Murray, Newbigging seems to have been largely unaffected by his problems.

By 1832 the firm had added to its other interests a wagon-and-boat freight service, which operated on a thrice-weekly basis between Toronto, Newmarket, Holland Landing, and The Narrows (Orillia). This sideline was carried on, in collaboration with a succession of out-of-town partners including Charles Scadding of Newmarket (brother of Henry*), until at least 1838.

Newbigging, though still a young man when he set up in York, soon gained a reputation for energy and competence in commercial affairs and rapidly engaged in business activities well beyond those of his own firm. He was one of the directors of the York branch of the Commercial Bank of the Midland District when it opened in 1832. Murray, Newbigging and Company became the agent for the Phoenix Assurance Company of London in 1833, and in 1834 Newbigging was a director of the newly formed British America Fire and Life Assurance Company of Toronto, the first local insurance firm. He was a member of a provisional committee created to conduct the affairs of the Toronto branch of the Bank of British North America when it was established in 1837. During the economic crisis of 1836–37, which produced a severe scarcity of specie in Upper Canada, he was among a small group of Toronto businessmen called upon to testify before a select committee of the House of Assembly on the monetary system in the province. In June 1837 he argued, without success, that the assembly should issue and sell interest-bearing bills both to the public and to the banks, which could then resume financing business activity and thus stimulate the employment of "thousands of labourers now nearly starving."

During the 1830s Newbigging was also deeply involved in the first attempt to build a railway linking Toronto with Georgian Bay. At a public meeting in Toronto on 26 July 1834, he was elected secretary and treasurer of the committee set up to advance the scheme. He was largely responsible for supervising the work of the surveyors of the proposed routes; as treasurer he collected subscriptions and kept the books at his Toronto store. The railway was incorporated in 1836 as the City of Toronto and Lake Huron Rail Road Company, with Newbigging as a director, secretary, and treasurer. He was one of its largest shareholders and most enthusiastic promoters, arguing that it would provide a valuable connection with the American midwest. Despite his energetic, possibly over-optimistic, promotion, the railway company failed to attract sufficient capital to permit construction.

Newbigging did not confine his organizing abilities to business concerns. He was one of the founders in 1833 of the Commercial News Room and in 1837 of the Upper Canada Club (Toronto Club), of which he was a manager and treasurer. A Presbyterian, he was a trustee and secretary of St Andrews Church and a manager of the local St Andrew's Society. He was appointed a justice of the peace for the Home District in September 1837, became a captain in the Toronto City Guards in December, and the following month was elected as an alderman for St David's Ward. His death at the age of 32, the result of "over fatigue . . . after the late rebellion," according to his wife, cut short an active and promising career. He may have left his wife little in the way of liquid assets. Destitute in 1844, she claimed that prior to his death he had purchased loyalist land rights to about 8,000 acres of land but that she had received only 3,000, which turned out to be "worthless."

J. K. JOHNSON

PAC, RG 5, A1: 100580–83; RG 9, I, B5, 8; RG 68, General index, 1651–1841: 508. *Town of York, 1815–34* (Firth). U.C., House of Assembly, *App. to the journal*, 1837, app., "Report of the select committee, to which was referred the subject of the monetary system of the province," 4–6. *Colonial Advocate*, 23 April, 3 Dec. 1829; 11 March, 13 May, 1 July, 1 Sept. 1830; 6 March 1834. *Courier of Upper Canada* (York [Toronto]), 4 Aug., 29 Sept. 1832. *Patriot* (Toronto), 1 Aug., 17 Nov. 1834; 21 Feb., 21 April 1837; 13 Feb. 1838. *Upper Canada Gazette*, 19 Nov. 1835, 7 Feb. 1839. *Marriage notices of Ont.* (Reid). *Toronto directory*, 1833–34, 1837. F. H. Armstrong, "Toronto in transition: the emergence of a city, 1828–1838" (PHD thesis, Univ. of Toronto, 1965). Canniff, *Medical profession in U.C.*, 316–17. F. H. Armstrong, "Toronto's first railway venture, 1834–1838," *OH*, 58 (1966): 21–41.

NISBET, THOMAS, cabinet-maker, upholsterer, militia officer, and businessman; b. *c.* 1777 in Duns, Scotland; m. 28 March 1803 Margaret Graham in Glasgow, and they had three sons and four daughters; d. 28 Dec. 1850 in Saint John, N.B.

Thomas Nisbet immigrated to New Brunswick in 1812 after being trained as a cabinet-maker under his father and working for a period in Glasgow. He set up business as a cabinet-maker and upholsterer on Prince William Street in Saint John. Although he was to occupy several different locations, his residence and business would remain on that street. He took the oath of freeman of the city of Saint John as a cabinet-maker in 1814.

Shortly afterwards, Nisbet imported from Jamaica a large quantity of mahogany; he was the first cabinet-maker in Saint John to import his own supply of this wood. Subsequently, he often advertised mahogany for sale at his ware-room. He worked primarily in mahogany and birch, but occasionally used maple, pine, and rosewood. His furniture falls within the Hepplewhite, Sheraton, Classical Revival, Regency, and American Empire styles and incorporates designs that were current in Great Britain and the United States.

Nisbet supplied furniture to cities other than Saint John. For example, he shipped a load of furniture to Fredericton in 1817 and again in 1830, in addition to having an agent there for a time. He employed numerous journeymen cabinet-makers, apprentices, turners, and carvers in his business. His was the first cabinet shop in Saint John to advertise the sale of piece-work to other cabinet-makers for use on their furniture. Nisbet's ware-room advertisements reveal that, in addition to his own productions, he sold imported items such as tea-caddies and portable writing-desks as well as curtain pins, picture-frame mouldings, brass stair-rods, and other fixtures for appointing the home. About 1822, he expanded his importing activities by joining with James Stewart to form James Stewart and Company. The firm dealt in British and East Indian goods, which were sold at its store on St John Street. The partnership was terminated in May 1828.

In April 1824, fire destroyed a portion of Saint John, and the principal sufferers were Nehemiah MERRITT, Noah Disbrow*, Thomas Adams, and Nisbet, with combined losses of £20,000. The *New-Brunswick Courier* stated that "the two latter, who are very industrious mechanics, deserve our deepest sympathy." Nisbet lost a property he had recently purchased and fitted up consisting of a dwelling-house and ware-room, as well as buildings in the rear, including workshops and stables. He subsequently ran an advertisement asking for early payment by those indebted to him, but there is no evidence that he was forced to mortgage or sell property to begin operating again. Within a week, he had resumed business in the premises he had vacated on purchasing his new property. By April 1825, he had erected on the site of the fire a brick building for his home, ware-room, and workshops.

Nisbet's output was greatest in the 1820s, judging by the quantity of advertising he did to sell furniture and to hire journeymen cabinet-makers. His capabilities, reputation, and business acumen are illustrated by the work he did for the province. When the arrival of Lieutenant Governor Sir Howard Douglas* was imminent in 1824, the House of Assembly allotted £750 for suitable furniture to decorate the public rooms of Government House in Fredericton and also made available funds for fixing up the residential portion of the building. Nisbet was involved in some of the repairs to Government House and received more than £170 for the work. Originally, the new furniture for the public rooms was to be obtained from England through John Bainbridge and Henry Bliss*, the provincial agents in London. In the end, however, Nisbet provided furniture valued in excess of £880 while Bainbridge and Bliss furnished items worth nearly £424. The nature of the repairs and of the furnishings Nisbet supplied is not known.

In September 1825, Government House caught fire, and the whole building with the exception of the northwest wing burned. The furniture was saved, but Nisbet subsequently provided a number of unspecified articles for the public rooms as well as furniture for the Council Chamber. About the same time he was also paid as agent in the acquisition of a residence for the lieutenant governor in Saint John.

In 1834, Thomas Nisbet Jr became a co-partner in his father's business, which was then styled Thomas Nisbet and Son. The firm's advertising was much reduced in the 1830s and 1840s, possibly the result of Nisbet Sr's interest in other areas. In 1840 and 1841, however, the company fitted up and furnished the new Executive Council chamber at a cost in excess of £740. When Thomas Jr died in 1845 at the age of 35, Nisbet placed a public notice in the newspapers calling for the settling of debts to and claims against both the firm and his son's estate. In the same advertisement, he stated that he had on hand an extensive assortment of superior new furniture. Nisbet did not dissolve Thomas Nisbet and Son until he assigned all his stock of furniture, materials, and tools to another son, Robert, in 1848. The business was carried on by Robert Nisbet until 1856.

After 1834, Nisbet had become heavily involved in two companies, the Saint John Mechanics' Whale Fishing Company and the Saint John Hotel Company. Charles Coles Stewart, the pioneer of the whale-fishing industry in Saint John, had fitted out the city's first whaler, the *James Stewart*, in 1833. It returned with a full cargo of oil and whalebone in April 1835. Inspired by this success, an organizing committee including Nisbet and John Haws* and 130 other mechanics and tradesmen from Saint John petitioned the House of Assembly that year to incorporate a whaling company. The legislature passed the act in June 1835, and by August all 5,000 shares at £10 each had been subscribed. Nisbet was elected to the first board of directors and then president, an office he held until his death.

Between May 1836, when its first whaler, the *Mechanic*, was launched, and November 1848, when the last whaler was sold, the company owned five ships which made a total of eleven whaling cruises. With the introduction of petroleum and the subsequent decline in demand for whale oil, the company began to consider closing down in late 1845. The remaining four ships were sold over the next few years, property was let and sold, and in 1850 the House of Assembly was petitioned to enact a bill authorizing the winding up of the company's affairs, which it did. The company had apparently been successful since it paid regular dividends from 1841 to 1854, reaching as high as 20 per cent in one year.

The act incorporating the Saint John Hotel Company was passed in 1835. With Moses Henry Perley* and others, Nisbet was elected to the first board of directors; he subsequently served as president from 1837 to 1849. The hotel opened to the public in November 1837 in the Masonic Hall, which had been renovated and furnished. It was always leased to various hotel-keepers so that the company did not operate the hotel on a day-to-day basis. During Nisbet's presidency, the company declared biannual dividends from May 1842.

In addition to his business involvements, Thomas Nisbet was an elder and trustee of St Andrew's

Presbyterian Church, was active in the St Andrew's and Highland societies, and was a freemason. He was also involved in the Saint John militia, from which he retired with the rank of captain in August 1834.

Thomas Nisbet was prominent in both the public and the commercial life of Saint John, but it is as a cabinet-maker that he is remembered today. He ran a well-managed and productive furniture business employing stylish designs, excellent materials, and good workmanship. That he had superior ability is illustrated by the labelled pieces which have survived. Among the more important of these are a sofa-table, writing-sewing stand, and sofa at the Royal Ontario Museum in Toronto, card-tables and a writing stand at the New Brunswick Museum in Saint John, a chest of drawers at the Beaverbrook Art Gallery and a chair and drop-leaf table at the York-Sunbury Historical Society Museum, both in Fredericton, and a card-table and desk at Kings Landing Historical Settlement, near Fredericton.

T. G. DILWORTH

City of Saint John, N.B., City Clerk's Office, Common Council, minutes, IV: 68 (mfm. at PANB). N.B. Museum, Church of England burial ground, Westmorland Road (Saint John), records (mfm.); Nesbitt family, CB DOC (typescript); Ward family papers, packet 7, no.8. PANB, RG 4, RS24, S33-Z1.2, S34-R6.3, S35-R3.33, S37-Z11.5, S45-P84, S46-P1, S57-P67, S63-P328; RG 10, RS108, Thomas Nisbet, 1820. N.B., House of Assembly, *Journal*, 1826–27. *City Gazette* (Saint John), 1812–41, esp. 10 April 1813; 14 July 1819; 16 Feb. 1820; 6 June 1821; 22 May, 13 June, 21 Nov. 1822; 24 July 1823; 15 April, 24 June, 2 Sept. 1824; 13 May 1837. *Herald* (Saint John), 18 Aug. 1841. *Morning News* (Saint John), 16 Aug. 1841. *New-Brunswick Courier*, 1812–50, esp. 28 Jan., 6 March 1815; 12 Oct. 1816; 9 June 1821; 10 April 1824; 24 Sept. 1825; 29 March 1828; 2, 30 Aug. 1834; 4 April, 12 Sept. 1835; 28 May 1836; 10 June, 18 Nov. 1837; 14 May 1842; 8 Feb., 1 March, 11 Oct. 1845; 2 Sept., 18 Nov. 1848; 12 May 1849; 2 Nov. 1850; also 11 Oct. 1856. *Royal Gazette* (Saint John; Fredericton), 1812–50, esp. 2, 16 March 1815; 29 July 1817; 13 April 1824; 20 Sept. 1825; 23 June 1830. *Star* (Saint John), 18 June 1822; 26 April, 31 May 1825. *Weekly Observer* (Saint John), 19 Aug. 1834, 11 Aug. 1835. W. F. Bunting, *History of St. John's Lodge, F. & A.M. of Saint John, New Brunswick . . .* (Saint John, 1895), 346–47, 368–69, 397–98. C. H. Foss and Richard Vroom, *Cabinetmakers of the eastern seaboard: a study of early Canadian furniture* (Toronto, 1977). D. R. Jack, *History of Saint Andrew's Church, Saint John, N.B.* (Saint John, 1913). H. G. Ryder, *Antique furniture by New Brunswick craftsmen* (Toronto, 1965).

O

ODELIN, JACQUES, Roman Catholic priest and polemicist; b. 5 Aug. 1789 in Saint-Constant, Que., son of Jacques Odelin and Marie-Angélique Lavigne; d. 9 June 1841 in Saint-Hilaire (Mont-Saint-Hilaire), Lower Canada.

Little is known of Jacques Odelin's life before he entered the Collège Saint-Raphaël in Montreal in 1801. Sulpician Antoine-Jacques Houdet* taught philosophy there, emphasizing the importance in logic of searching for criteria of truth. Houdet in Montreal and Abbé Jérôme Demers* at the Séminaire de Québec were the great figures in science and philosophy at the time in Lower Canada. Odelin left the college in 1811 and, choosing the priesthood, went to do theology at the Séminaire de Nicolet. He studied under either a professor or the superior, Jean RAIMBAULT, and also taught the fifth-year class (Belles-Lettres) in 1811–12, the two-year Philosophy program in 1812–13, the sixth year (Rhetoric) in 1813–14, and Philosophy again in 1814–16, probably using the notes he had taken in Houdet's courses.

Upon being ordained by Bishop Joseph-Octave Plessis* on 4 Feb. 1816, Odelin quit teaching to become assistant priest, first at Sainte-Marguerite-de-Blairfindie (L'Acadie) from 17 February to 18 Sept. 1816, and then in the Montreal parish of Saint-Laurent from September 1816 till September 1817. He was chaplain of the Hôpital Général of Quebec, with responsibility for mission work at Notre-Dame in Quebec and Sainte-Foy, from September 1817 till October 1819. Then Odelin received his first parish charge, at Saint-Grégoire (Bécancour), where he served until September 1821. He found that the parishioners showed some "indifference" to religion. The combined effect of "impertinent remarks" from churchwardens and others, difficulty in collecting the tithe, and a lawsuit to re-establish his authority led him to tell his bishop, in a mood reminiscent of Hugues-Félicité-Robert de La Mennais, that he was "convinced the spiritual ministry is inseparably linked to the temporal." In this region near Nicolet, where Odelin had already spent five years as a theological student, he discovered the "little France" around Lac Saint-Pierre whose moving spirits were French priests driven out by the revolution. In particular, Abbé Jacques-Ladislas-Joseph de Calonne* brought La Mennais to the attention of Canadians in 1819 as the author of the *Essai sur l'indifférence en matière de* *religion* (Paris, 1817), a work which he introduced in Lower Canada and which was of great interest to the Sulpician Jean-Jacques LARTIGUE.

Odelin's difficulties continued with his appointment in September 1821 as parish priest of Saint-Ours-du-Saint-Esprit (Saint-Esprit), where he would remain until 1827. In September 1825 and again in 1826 some prominent parishioners sent a petition to Lartigue about the scandal caused by their priest's fondness for the bottle and for "the fair sex." Odelin, a disputatious man, tackled these accusations from the pulpit and even considered launching a civil action against his accusers. Archbishop Plessis contemplated keeping him in office, but after an inquiry by vicar general François-Joseph Deguise, the curé of Varennes, he demanded Odelin's resignation and suspended his powers as parish priest for nearly five years, from February 1827 to October 1831. In February 1828 Odelin was still in his parish, living by himself. The following year he was at Detroit, having left "without permission or exeat," but he came back in August 1830. Bishop Lartigue and Archbishop Bernard-Claude Panet* then agreed to punish him, sending him to live with Jean-Baptiste Bélanger, the curé at Belœil, from August 1830 till October 1831 and imposing a "rule of life" upon him that required study of dogmatics and moral theology and of carefully chosen religious and devotional works suitable for clergy, as well as vigilance with regard to strong drink and "members of the other sex."

Upon being granted absolution, Odelin was named parish priest at Saint-Hilaire in October 1831 "to reward" the parishioners for their zeal in finally agreeing to "build a fine church" and ensure an additional tithe for a curé. Odelin continued none the less to experience other vexations in these years, with the rise of liberalism, indifference to religion, Protestant proselytizing in the region, crises in farming, and cholera epidemics. The parishioners rejected the assessment of tithes and neglected to pay them. For Odelin temporal matters were not easy: besides attending to maintenance and repair of the church and moving the cemetery, to survive he had to cultivate and enclose his garden, keep some beehives and a few animals (though without a stable or cowshed), and sell on the local market the apples he sometimes received in lieu of tithes.

It was against this background that a controversy broke out, this time of a philosophical nature, in which Odelin earned the title of "Canadian metaphysician." Censured by Lartigue in matters of discipline, Odelin took occasion to question the orthodoxy of the bishop, who was a disciple of La Mennais. On 12 and 13 Aug. 1833, during the annual year-end exercises at the Séminaire de Saint-Hyacinthe, the students publicly defended La Mennais's "theory" concerning common sense as the source of certainty. Odelin, who was attending the exercises, considered the matter so "strange" that he immediately proceeded to refute the pupils. He was arguing so vigorously that their philosophy professor, Joseph-Sabin Raymond*, had to come to their rescue in a long oratorical match that forced the cancellation of other parts of the program. Not satisfied with the answers given him, Odelin renewed the debate in *L'Ami du peuple, de l'ordre et des lois*, a Montreal newspaper, and in *L'Écho du pays*, of Saint-Charles (Saint-Charles-sur-Richelieu). In 1833 and 1834 he signed some 30 articles, using first the anagram Dionel and later his own name. As followers of La Mennais, Jean-Charles Prince* and above all Joseph-Sabin Raymond replied, publishing some 50 responses opposing his views.

In condemning the adoption "too hastily and without prior examination" of a doctrine "as new as [it is] dazzling, as unsound as inadmissible in its consequences," Odelin became, as one commentator has observed, "the first in Canada to perceive the subtle poison concealed in the overrated Lamennais's writings." Since Leo XII had approved La Mennais's doctrine of common sense and Gregory XVI had rejected the political ideas implicit in it, people in Lower Canada were wondering how one could accept an author's philosophy but not his political thinking. Odelin claimed it was impossible in this case, since there was a link between the philosophical doctrine and the political concepts. For Odelin, La Mennais's mistaken political notions stemmed from an erroneous conception of the common sense that he set up as the sole criterion of certainty, with the authority of revelation being relegated to the background. Odelin much preferred the position taken by Descartes, who in this matter affirmed the inviolable privilege of authority while upholding the sacred rights of reason.

The debate on common sense was in reality a debate on what, in systems of philosophy, could be advanced as orthodox doctrine. It was on this argument that the polemic ended, when on 15 July 1834 Gregory XVI condemned in *Singulari nos* the *Paroles d'un croyant* and consequently all of La Mennais. Although subsequent events did not confirm Odelin's thesis about the orthodoxy of Cartesianism – the official and universal philosophy of the church was proclaimed in 1879 to be that of Thomas Aquinas – the condemnation of La Mennais's philosophical ideas in general assured him victory over the teachers at the Séminaire de Saint-Hyacinthe. They complied, Abbé Prince publicly, with Lartigue's ban on teaching "anything from La Mennais's books, systems, or doctrine"; the bishop did not even want his name "or his authority to be mentioned in any way in teaching."

Politically, Odelin seems as a priest to have been loyal to the established authority. At the time of the rebellions in 1837–38 he took to heart Lartigue's recommendation to summon people to go back home and publicly demonstrate loyalty to the government. A nationalist in his own way, on 25 Feb. 1840 he signed a petition from the clergy of the diocese of Montreal against legislative union of Upper and Lower Canada.

A few months before he died Odelin published four new articles under the title "Pensées théologico-philosophiques." In these he discussed the authenticity of the Scriptures and examined in outline both man as a moral being and man seen through his intellectual faculties. Linking philosophical and theological contemplation, reason and revelation, Odelin showed that man participates in the Trinity through his senses and his intellect. For, he said, "if the properties of the increate and creative being as well as man's properties" are analysed "clearly and concisely," then "*trinity* and *generation in unity* will be perceived everywhere." The life of this contentious man ended, then, on a relatively serene note. His final article appeared alongside the funeral announcement noting his sudden, unexpected death, which occurred on 9 June 1841. The parish priest of Saint-Hilaire was buried in his church two days later.

YVAN LAMONDE and LOUISE MARCIL-LACOSTE

Correspondence concerning Jacques Odelin is held in the archives of the various dioceses in which he served (Quebec, Montreal, Joliette, Nicolet, and Saint-Hyacinthe), in either the file on the particular parish or that on Odelin himself. His correspondence with Bishop Plessis may be followed in Caron, "Inv. de la corr. de Mgr Plessis," ANQ *Rapport*, 1927–28, 1928–29, 1932–33; with Bishop Joseph SIGNAY in Caron, "Inv. de la corr. de Mgr Signay," ANQ *Rapport*, 1936–37, 1937–38, 1938–39; and with Bishop Lartigue in Desrosiers, "Inv. de la corr. de Mgr Lartigue," ANQ *Rapport*, 1941–42, 1942–43, 1943–44, 1944–45, 1945–46.

The polemical debate between Odelin and professors of the Séminaire de Saint-Hyacinthe is to be found largely in *L'Écho du pays* (Saint-Charles[-sur-Richelieu], Qué.) and *L'Ami du peuple, de l'ordre et des lois*, from 15 Aug. 1833 to 25 Sept. 1834. There is only one other piece known to have been written by Odelin: "Pensées théologico-philosophiques," in *Mélanges religieux*, 23 April, 14 May, 4, 11 June 1841.

ANQ-M, CE1-18, 6 août 1789; CE2-16, 11 juin 1841. Allaire, *Dictionnaire*. F.-M. Bibaud, *Le panthéon canadien* (A. et V. Bibaud; 1891). Gilles Chaussé, "Un évêque menaisien au Canada: Monseigneur Jean-Jacques Lartigue," *Les ultramontains canadiens-français*, sous la direction de Nive Voisine et Jean Hamelin (Montréal, 1985), 105–20. C.-P. Choquette, *Histoire du séminaire de Saint-Hyacinthe depuis sa fondation jusqu'à nos jours* (2v., Montréal, 1911–12), 1: 162–63. Douville, *Hist. du collège-séminaire de Nicolet*. Yvan Lamonde, *La philosophie et son enseignement au Québec (1665–1920)* (Montréal, 1980), 83–89, 96–105. Louise Marcil-Lacoste, "Sens commun et philosophie québécoise: trois exemples," *Philosophie au Québec*, Claude Panaccio et P.-A. Quintin, édit. (Montréal, 1976), 73–112. Maurault, *Le collège de Montréal* (Dansereau; 1967). Armand Cardinal, "Messire Jacques Odelin (1831–1841), premier curé résident à Saint-Hilaire," Soc. d'hist. de Belœil–Mont-Saint-Hilaire, *Cahiers* (Belœil, Qué.), 5 (juin 1981): 3–17. Émile Chartier, "L'abbé Jacques Odelin ou Audelin, dit Jolibois (5 août 1789–9 juin 1841)," *Rev. canadienne*, 72 (janvier–juin 1917): 27–37. Yvan Lamonde, "Classes sociales, classes scolaires: une polémique sur l'éducation en 1819–1820," CCHA *Sessions d'études*, 41 (1974): 43–59.

ODELL, WILLIAM FRANKLIN, office holder, notary, lawyer, surveyor, and politician; b. 19 Oct. 1774 in Burlington, N.J., only son of the Reverend Jonathan Odell*, loyalist poet and scholar, and Anne De Cou; m. 31 Dec. 1808 Elizabeth Newall (Newell), granddaughter of Dr Samuel Cooke, first Anglican rector of Fredericton, and they had four sons and four daughters who survived infancy; d. 25 Dec. 1844 in Fredericton.

William Franklin Odell was born into the circle of British North American office holders and named after his father's patron, William Franklin, the last royal governor of New Jersey. In 1784, when William was ten, his father became provincial secretary of the new province of New Brunswick where, according to historian William Stewart MacNutt*, he "spent a quarter of a century in sustaining the larger part of the business of government and finished his life as a poor man." No doubt it was the state of Jonathan's purse that kept William from having a university education and, in turn, it was the family's access to the small fruits of patronage that opened the way to a career in government service. On 16 March 1793, at age 18, he was appointed deputy clerk of the pleas of the Supreme Court, acting for the clerk, Colin Campbell; holders of this clerkship did not require legal training. He succeeded to the office on 19 July 1796 and became a pluralist, for the first time, on 2 Feb. 1802 when he received the additional appointment of clerk of the Legislative Council. He began reading law with Ward Chipman* in Saint John some time in the late 1790s and was named a notary public in 1802, admitted as an attorney in 1804, and called to the bar in 1806. His responsibilities in the Supreme Court were extended in November 1804: he became clerk of the crown with duties relating to the criminal jurisdiction of the court.

By 1807 Jonathan Odell was 70 years old and unable to keep up with his work, but he could not afford to retire because there was no provision for pensions in the colonial service. At the risk of jeopardizing his own career William, as a dutiful son, had increasingly to assume the daily burdens of the provincial secretary's office, with little apparent prospect of long-term gain, for the Colonial Office looked upon the proposal that he succeed his father as "objectionable on general principles." He was rescued from this invidious position through the intervention of Major-General Martin HUNTER, the administrator of New Brunswick, who had both affection and genuine admiration for the Odell family. Hunter asked that William be appointed provincial secretary "as a personal favor" to himself, as well as in recognition of William's qualifications and the faithful service of Jonathan. He took over the duties officially in 1812, received his commission as secretary, registrar, and clerk of the Council on 31 March 1815, and was sworn in as a member of the Council on 3 April 1815.

Odell was not sedentary and office bound. He enjoyed the outdoors, and from time to time as a young man acted as a deputy surveyor for the government; he surveyed the lands of the Miramichi Indians in 1808 [*see* John Julien*]. In 1818 he replaced Joseph BOUCHETTE as principal surveyor for the British in the determination of the boundary with the United States under article 5 of the Treaty of Ghent (1814). For more than three years he worked with and under the direction of his friends Ward Chipman Sr and Ward Chipman* Jr who, as joint agents on behalf of the government, were attempting to bolster the British claim to the upper Saint John valley by locating topographic features south of the Aroostook valley that could be plausibly represented as fulfilling the definition of the "North-west Angle of Nova Scotia" laid down in the Treaty of Paris (1783). In the summers of 1818, 1819, and 1820 Odell led survey parties comprised of around 25 men each year and employing more than a dozen canoes. In 1821 he prepared a report with a plan that showed a range of hills extending southwestward from the Saint John River at Mars Hill. The Americans protested that this map was inaccurate, and were particularly offended by the omission of the greater part of the chain of highlands near the St Lawrence on which they founded their claim. Odell, in turn, denied that there was a continuous chain of highlands, basing his assertion on the field-work in the area of Johann Ludwig TIARKS and others. The negotiations collapsed shortly afterwards, but over the next two decades there were several occasions on which Odell's knowledge of the ground was of value to the provincial authorities in dealing with tensions on the frontier.

By inheritance and training a "King's man," Odell was on intimate terms with most of the colony's administrators, the notable exceptions being George Stracey Smyth* and then Sir John Harvey*. With both men he was compromised by factional politics, in which intimate associates of his, first Ward Chipman Sr and later Thomas Baillie*, were at the centre of opposition to the administration. In 1819, during Smyth's term, Chief Justice Jonathan Bliss* deprived Odell of his post as clerk of the pleas and appointed his own son, Henry Bliss*, to the office, a move that is unlikely to have taken place without the connivance of the lieutenant governor. Odell was on excellent terms with Sir Howard Douglas*, who dominated the political scene from 1824 to 1829, but after Douglas departed he was drawn into a struggle for power on the side of Thomas Baillie, the commissioner of crown lands, at the centre of a group that later became known as the "official party." Their leading opponent was Charles Simonds*, whose supporters had a strong sense of being New Brunswickers and favoured the exercise of power by the assembly. The "officials," less narrowly provincial in outlook, emphasized the authority of the royal prerogative and the principle of strong executive government. The alliance between Odell and Baillie was cemented at the personal level by the marriage of Baillie, a widower, to Odell's daughter Elizabeth in 1832.

Next to the lieutenant governor the holders of the most powerful offices in the colony, Odell and Baillie aroused jealousy and hostility, particularly in 1832–33 when the old council was replaced by separate legislative and executive bodies and, as a result of their influence at the Colonial Office, they were appointed as the senior members of the new five-man executive. Robert Gowan* portrayed them in the *New-Brunswick Courier* as two rascally domestics, Wily Oh'Deil and Tommy, attempting to wrest control of "the Estate" from the well-meaning but innocent Scottish squire (the ineffectual lieutenant governor, Sir Archibald CAMPBELL). To counter the influence of the *Courier*, Odell and Baillie promoted the *Morning Chronicle*, a newspaper that first appeared in 1836, "too late," according to MacNutt, "to turn public opinion to the support of its sponsors."

In 1837 the Colonial Office transferred control of the crown lands to the assembly, appointed a new lieutenant governor, Sir John Harvey, and put New Brunswick into the forefront of constitutional experiment by authorizing changes in the Executive Council to bring it into accord with the assembly. In return the assembly guaranteed to provide for the salaries of Odell and the other holders of patent offices. Odell and Baillie had constitutional scruples about Harvey's calling of the legislature into session shortly after his arrival, and joined their fellow holders of imperial offices, the attorney general, Charles Jeffery PETERS, and the solicitor general, George Frederick Street*, in failing to show the customary courtesy of attending the lieutenant governor in state on the day he opened the legislature. Nevertheless, the Colonial Office refused to accept Odell's resignation from the Executive Council in 1837 when Baillie and Street were replaced by Simonds and Hugh JOHNSTON, politicians who had the confidence of the assembly. His local knowledge was regarded as indispensable. For the next four years he had to work with a lieutenant governor and councillors whose liberal views were repugnant to him. In these years he was once again involved in crises arising from the Maine boundary question; its settlement by the Webster–Ashburton Treaty of 1842 brought relief from the added duties which had devolved upon his office, though otherwise it seems to have provided him with little satisfaction. His service on the Executive Council came to an end after the elections of 1842–43 when Lieutenant Governor William MacBean George Colebrooke* reorganized that body.

Odell's decline into old age was troubled by family concerns. The turn of the wheel of political fortune frustrated the career of his eldest son, William Hunter*. In 1837 members of the bar objected to and prevented his becoming clerk of the crown. Odell did designate him officially as his deputy in the office of provincial secretary on 18 Aug. 1838, but this appointment made the situation the more embarrassing in 1840 when the young man created a scandal by rash public behaviour. Baillie's bankruptcy in 1839 also affected Odell, for it took away the property of his daughter Elizabeth and that of her children. Odell died on Christmas Day, 1844.

The Odell name is synonymous with bureaucracy, learning, and gentility in early New Brunswick. William spent his working life producing and directing the flow of parchment and paper through which the government maintained its structure and exercised its authority. Between them Jonathan and William held the office of provincial secretary for 60 years. During the greater part of that period, they were the most intimate counsellors of the lieutenant governors and administrators, were consulted on almost all business, produced the individual instruments appointing members of the Council, county clerks, justices of the peace, sheriffs, militia officers, and other provincial officials, carried on correspondence with local authorities in the name of the lieutenant governor and council, kept the records of council, participated in the process of authorizing and issuing land grants, and carried out special tasks, such as the taking of the census [*see* Henry George CLOPPER], assigned from time to time by the legislature. Even the matriculation of students at the College of New Brunswick (later King's College), Fredericton, required the issuing of a mandamus.

As a result of the economic prosperity which began at about the time he succeeded his father, William enjoyed an income from fees, most of it derived from crown lands grants and licences, that enabled him to live comfortably and to employ an adequate staff to carry out the business of the secretary's office. He also held many minor posts, some for income, some out of a sense of civic responsibility, and others, perhaps, for administrative convenience: paymaster of militia (1813), member of the board of the College of New Brunswick and of the council of King's College, secretary to the commissioners of quitrents (1832), fireward in Fredericton (1823), road commissioner, and clerk of the crown in Chancery (1839). His name keeps recurring in the records as a member of committees assigned to perform practical tasks in fields as far apart as building and banking.

Throughout his life William Franklin Odell enjoyed the support of a close-knit family that attempted to uphold genteel cosmopolitan Anglicanism in a colonial backwater. It seems fitting that New Brunswick continues to be reminded of this outdoorsman-courtier-bureaucrat through the existence of Odell Park and Game Refuge in the heart of Fredericton, once William's farm, a 300-acre property in much of which the natural forest is preserved.

D. M. YOUNG

N.B. Museum, N.B. Hist. Soc. papers, packet 5, no. 1; Odell family papers, packets 18–19; packet 20, items 9, 31; packets 21–25. PAC, MG 23, D1, ser. 1, 53; 54: esp. 649–55, 665–70; 60; MG 24, A3, Vaughan to Douglas, 6 Oct. 1827. PANB, RG 1, RS336, A2, Smyth to Bathurst, 17 April 1815. PRO, CO 188/17: ff.22–23, 38–39; 188/29: ff.297–98v; CO 189/11: 313; Goulburn to Odell, 26 Feb. 1818. *Royal Gazette* (Saint John, N.B.; Fredericton), 9 Jan. 1809, 11 Jan. 1813, 7 Jan. 1823, 22 March 1843, 1 Jan. 1845. Hill, *Old Burying Ground*. Lawrence, *Judges of N.B.* (Stockton and Raymond). MacNutt, *New Brunswick*. W. F. Ganong, "A monograph of the evolution of the boundaries of the province of New Brunswick," RSC *Trans.*, 2nd ser., 7 (1901), sect. II: 139–449. W. D. Hamilton, "Indian lands in New Brunswick: the case of the Little South West Reserve," *Acadiensis* (Fredericton), 13 (1983–84), no. 2: 3–28.

O'GRADY (Grady), STANDISH, farmer and poet; b. probably in 1789 or 1790 in County Limerick (Republic of Ireland), son of Standish Grady; m. Margaret Thompson, also of southern Ireland, and they had at least three children; fl. 1807–45.

Standish O'Grady's life in Ireland cannot be determined precisely; what information is known comes largely from his own writings and is occasionally contradictory. In addition, the existence of several contemporaries with the same name has led to some confusion. It appears that O'Grady entered Trinity College, Dublin, on 3 Feb. 1807 at age 17; he received his BA in 1810. On 3 Oct. 1813 he was ordained deacon of the Church of Ireland and on 24 July 1814 he was priested in the diocese of Limerick. He was collated priest of Tullybracky in this diocese on 16 Sept. 1817; before that he had been curate of Cullen in the diocese of Emly. From 1820 until his immigration to Lower Canada in 1836, he may have been rector of Kilnasoolagh and several other parishes in the diocese of Killaloe. His decision to emigrate was at least partly precipitated by the "tithe wars" that beset the Church of Ireland in the 1820s and 1830s and that left many clergymen without pay and, in his own words, in "the most abject state of distress." O'Grady became "[disgusted] with the government, and unable to exist at home, . . . sailed for America, with a small competency." A revenue of £382, owed to him since the early 1830s, was never paid.

O'Grady and his wife sailed from Waterford in early April 1836 and arrived in Quebec on 22 May. By August they were living on a farm near William Henry (Sorel); they remained in the area until at least 1842. A son was born in June 1836 but died the following January. Another was born in September 1837 and a daughter in March 1839. A young and an increasing family was only one of the many problems faced by O'Grady in his new home. Unaccustomed to hard physical work, unprepared for the severity of the Lower Canadian winter, and unable to cultivate a soil that was "a perfect compilation of sand not worth the labouring," he did not succeed as a farmer. One winter "a Canadian stud horse with one miserable cow were the only remnants of [his] stock which survived." His difficulties were exacerbated by the unrest resulting from the rebellions of 1837–38; unsympathetic to republicanism, he called Louis-Joseph Papineau* a coward who fled while "the bold, intrepid peasants" bled for his cause. In the end, poor health finally forced him to try to change his circumstances. O'Grady provides these details about his life as a Lower Canadian farmer in the lines and notes of his poem *The emigrant*.

In the summer of 1841 O'Grady visited Montreal to sell subscriptions to "a poetical composition." The editors of the *Literary Garland*, "favoured with glimpses at a few pages of this work," reported in their issue of August 1841 that it bore "the character of an epic poem, enriched with a considerable store of notes, of a laughter-inspiring nature, and occasionally sparkling with wit and genius." The lines they had read were "very beautiful," and the "respectable names" on the subscription list, together "with the highly flattering notes addressed to the author," afforded further evidence "that the work [was] of no inconsiderable merit." *The emigrant, a poem, in four cantos* was printed and published in Montreal by John Lovell* in 1841, although it was probably not distributed until early in the next year. On 20 Jan. 1842 the *Montreal Transcript* contained a long, mostly favourable review, and the following week it reprinted a short, enthusiastic notice from the *Montreal Messenger*.

The emigrant contains the first canto only of the title poem, along with copious notes and 13 short lyrics. In the preface O'Grady emphasizes that he is not "an enemy to emigration," but recommends Upper Canada rather than Lower Canada with its "excessive" cold and "too long" winters. He promises to tell more in his "next Canto" about Upper Canada, "by far a more desirable emporium for our redundant population." The first canto deals with several subjects, including the troubled state of "proud Erin," emigration, the climate of Lower Canada, the customs of the Canadians, and the political strife in the Canadas. These subjects are given an emotional force by being linked to and interwoven with the poet's own story and that of the fictional Alfred and Sylvia, young lovers who flee Ireland, elope to Lower Canada, and fail as miserably there as the poet himself. The canto, written in rhymed couplets, ends optimistically with the arrival of "rude spring" and "cheering hopes" because "mighty Wolfe [James Wolfe*] in Colborne [John Colborne*] still survives." Yet the discontinuous way in which the canto's various subjects are presented reveals the sense of displacement and despair felt by O'Grady as he composed "this first volume" and dedicated it to "Nobody."

Shortly after the publication of *The emigrant*, the O'Gradys left William Henry. In March 1843 the *Transcript* reported that O'Grady was a member of a committee of Irishmen from Montreal who went to Lachine in an attempt to quell riots that had broken out between feuding Irish labourers from Cork and Connaught, who had gone on strike to protest low wages during the construction of the Lachine Canal. He "mainly contributed to the success of the mission, by bringing several hundreds of the Corkonians to the spot, where a reconciliation was effected. He received the warm applause of his countrymen." By late 1845 "poor old O'Grady," apparently living somewhere in Upper Canada, was a "distressing case," according to the *British Canadian, and Canada West Commercial and General Advertiser*. Although "descended . . . from a highly respectable Irish Protestant family," he now had "the chill hand of poverty pressing heavily upon him," and "his grey hairs" were "descending in sorrow to the grave." O'Grady was "silent" about his "wants," so the newspaper was publishing "this brief notice – wholly unknown to him" – to ask for charity on his behalf. O'Grady could "be heard of" at the office of the *British Canadian*. As a result of this notice, the *Montreal Gazette* offered to receive "contributions" on O'Grady's behalf. The *Examiner*, however, was incensed by the request for charity and hinted, somewhat obscurely, that O'Grady's life had been one of "dissipation."

Nothing further is known about O'Grady. Most likely he died somewhere in Upper Canada. His monument is *The emigrant*, incomplete and disjointed, but still frequently anthologized and quoted. In its mixture of hope and despair, alienation and accommodation, it is a fitting memorial both to O'Grady and to the thousands of other Irish emigrants – Protestant and Roman Catholic – who, driven from their native land, arrived in North America in the middle decades of the 19th century.

MARY JANE EDWARDS

Standish O'Grady's death date has not been located despite extensive research in Ontario and Quebec. He is the author of *The emigrant, a poem, in four cantos* (Montreal, 1841), parts of which have been included in a number of anthologies, among them *The Oxford book of Canadian verse, in English and French*, ed. and intro. A. J. M. Smith (Toronto and New York, 1960) and *The new Oxford book of Canadian verse in English* (Toronto, 1982).

ANQ-M, CE3-1, 20 août 1836; 27 janv., 9 oct. 1837; 2 avril 1839 (mfm. at PAC). Representative Church Body Library (Dublin), MS 61. "Our table," *Literary Garland*, 3 (1840–41): 432. *Examiner* (Toronto), 19 Nov. 1845, which quotes the *British Canadian, and Canada West Commercial and General Advertiser* (Toronto). *Montreal Gazette*, 19 Nov. 1845. *Montreal Transcript*, 20, 27 Jan. 1842; 11 March 1843. *Quebec Gazette*, 23 May 1836. *Alumni Dublinenses . . .* , ed. G. D. Burtchaell and T. U. Sadleir (Dublin, 1924). *The Oxford companion to Canadian literature*, ed. William Toye (Toronto, 1983). D. H. Akenson, *The Church of Ireland, ecclesiastical reform and revolution, 1800–1885* (New Haven, Conn., and London, 1971). L. [M.] Lande, *Old lamps aglow; an appreciation of early Canadian poetry* (Montreal, 1957). *Literary history of Canada: Canadian literature in English*, ed. C. F. Klinck *et al.* (2nd ed., 3v., Toronto and Buffalo, N.Y., 1976), 1: 149–50. M. L. MacDonald, "Literature and society in the Canadas, 1830–1850" (PHD thesis, Carleton Univ., Ottawa, 1984). H. C. Pentland, "The Lachine strike of 1843," *CHR*, 29 (1948): 255–77.

O'GRADY, WILLIAM JOHN, Roman Catholic priest and journalist; b. in Ireland; d. about 18 Aug. 1840 in Pickering, Upper Canada.

There was nothing ordinary about William John O'Grady – not his abilities, not his personality, and certainly not his career. According to his own testimony, he was ordained a priest around 1816 and later served as secretary to the bishop of Cork – a position from which he may have been dismissed, if a statement by his *bête noire*, Bishop Alexander McDONELL, is to be believed. Some time in the late 1820s he and his brother John became attached to disbanded British troops who, under the command of Connell James Baldwin* and with William O'Grady serving as chaplain, emigrated to Brazil. What happened once they arrived is uncertain. One report maintains that efforts to enlist them in the Brazilian army provoked a mutiny; another says that they revolted when the authorities conscripted them to clear land. In later years McDonell was to claim that the enraged troops had turned on the O'Gradys, forcing them to flee Brazil. According to John O'Grady, however, the British ambassador requested him to organize an emigration of the British troops, who were in a "deplorable state." He complied and persuaded them to settle in Upper Canada. Five hundred men sailed from Rio de Janeiro on 26 July 1828.

Curiously, William O'Grady had arrived in Upper Canada by June. He immediately presented himself to McDonell in Glengarry and, before the astonished bishop could digest his testimonials, departed abruptly. He made his way to York, where he began acting as an assistant to the bishop's nephew Angus MacDonell, pastor of St Paul's. McDonell, eager to enlist Irish priests to serve the burgeoning Irish population, agreed to O'Grady's repeated requests that the church be turned over to him. The appointment, however, was not made official until January 1829, a delay that caused O'Grady some annoyance.

Once in charge of the church, O'Grady showed himself to be a man of considerable intelligence and charm who mingled easily with the grandees of York, including Lieutenant Governor Sir John Colborne*. He also proved to be an extraordinarily able and energetic priest, brimming with schemes for the advancement of Catholicism. His missionary travels took him to several townships in the vicinity of York. He constantly petitioned the government for land on which to build churches; he supervised the raising of funds for a parochial school in York and later oversaw its construction; he lobbied for financial assistance for the building of a convent; he suggested clerical conferences to control the "waywardness & impetuosity" of some priests. McDonell regarded O'Grady as a godsend and in January 1830 vested him with the "power and control" of a vicar general. O'Grady claimed not to wish an official appointment to this post, and indeed it was never made.

A turning-point in O'Grady's career came in 1830–31, when he had to deal with a messy controversy in the parishes of Sandwich (Windsor) and Amherstburg. Affairs in these parishes had been chaotic since the late 1820s, largely because of the inability of the two incumbents, Louis-Joseph Fluet of Amherstburg and Joseph Crevier, *dit* Bellerive, of Sandwich, to agree on the site of a proposed convent. Compounding the problem was the hostility of many residents, particularly French-speakers, towards the powerful Baby family. This hostility – rooted in resentment of the Babys' influence and also in ethnic prejudice against the non-French "compact" of which the Babys were conspicuous members – received concrete expression in the provincial election of October 1830, when Crevier and Fluet criticized François Baby*, a local candidate. Defeated, an enraged Baby fired off letters to O'Grady and McDonell demanding that the two priests be removed.

McDonell apparently instructed O'Grady to conduct an investigation. Upon arrival in the area, O'Grady found an appalling state of affairs – serious irregularities in Crevier's financial management of his parish, neglect of pastoral duties by both priests, and improprieties in their personal lives: in the case of Crevier, a "slovenly & almost filthy appearance even at the altar," and in Fluet's, sexual relations with a woman (whom he later married). O'Grady seems to have persuaded the priests to mend their ways, even to cease their quarrelling over the convent. By the time he returned to York, however, the situation had deteriorated.

In February 1831 O'Grady, once more on his bishop's instructions, returned to Sandwich. This time he set aside the carrot for the stick, placing the Sandwich church under interdict and ordering Crevier's transfer as well as suspending Fluet. The priests organized a public meeting in the Sandwich church, during which Crevier was reported to have denounced McDonell and Fluet to have boasted that he "did not care one fig for Bishop or Priest or even for the Pope & that it was the duty of the people to lock the Church doors & not Suffer themselves to be dictated to by Scotch and Irish Strangers." After petitions and counter-petitions, McDonell ordered O'Grady to reinstate Fluet and to allow Crevier to remain in Sandwich, at least until "legal proofs of his misconduct" could be obtained. This action, he explained to O'Grady, did not reflect any disapproval of his conduct; on the contrary, it was prompted by the intervention of Colborne and Archbishop Bernard-Claude Panet* of Quebec. O'Grady was unmollified. All along he had emphasized to McDonell that if "two Selfish Stiffnecked Priests" were allowed to insult the "Episcopal dignity," there would be "an end to all order & Subordination" in the diocese. Now his advice had been ignored and, even worse, his authority had been publicly undercut. Humiliated, O'Grady complained that McDonell's action had placed him in a "very awkward dilemma" and "all the discredit" would "fall upon me." Although willing to "sacrifice my own judgment," he warned McDonell that "Episcopal authority" had suffered a mortal blow. He then made it clear to his bishop that, if Crevier's faction again caused trouble, he would not intervene.

It would be going too far to say that the Sandwich affair was the root cause of O'Grady's eventual split with McDonell. What does seem likely, however, is that it so poisoned their relationship that, when it became necessary for the bishop to discipline O'Grady himself, the latter was hardly in a frame of mind to turn the other cheek. The events that led to their confrontation can be traced easily enough. Although O'Grady had initially won McDonell's respect for his work at St Paul's, he had also made enemies. In March 1829 attacks on his personal character were launched by Mrs Irma Boulton and St Paul's churchwarden William Bergin. By September 1830 O'Grady's relations with his churchwardens were barely civil, and by December 1831 some unidentified priests were charging that he had misappropriated church funds. The following year he was further accused of neglect of his pastoral obligations, association with radical reformers such as William Lyon Mackenzie*, and a disreputable personal life (both Irma Boulton and Francis Collins*, editor of the *Canadian Freeman*, claimed that he was sexually involved with a woman). That July McDonell presided over an investigation into O'Grady's conduct. The result was O'Grady's exoneration, but McDonell decided that it would be best to transfer him to the more tranquil setting of Prescott and Brockville. In a remarkable reversal for a priest who not long before had urged his bishop to uphold episcopal authority, O'Grady refused to leave York, replaced the hostile churchwardens with his own supporters, and locked the doors of St Paul's.

McDonell's first steps were to suspend O'Grady from the priesthood and to place St Paul's under interdict. He also instituted a legal action to regain possession of the church building, a suit that, after an initial defeat on a technicality, would be upheld in late 1833. O'Grady played a waiting game until October 1832 when he suggested to McDonell that their dispute be arbitrated by the Sulpicians in Montreal. This olive branch, however, was coupled with violent abuse of the bishop. In an astonishing letter he asked McDonell, "What in the name of common sense infatuates you? . . . Cannot all the experience of your long life teach you a lesson of usefulness. . . . But it is too late for you to make a beginning, and instead of learning how to live, it behoves you rather to study how to die." There was much more in the same vein, including an accusation that McDonell had misappropriated church funds.

For a time in the fall of 1832, following the intervention of James Baby* and John Strachan*, it appeared that peace might be achieved; however, their efforts foundered on O'Grady's stubbornness. Towards the end of that year, in association with James King, he established a newspaper, the *Canadian Correspondent*, in which he was to heap more abuse on McDonell and to take up the politics of radical reform. In January 1833, after McDonell had officially dismissed him from the priesthood, O'Grady turned to the lieutenant governor, presenting a petition which advanced the novel argument that McDonell could not turn him out of his parish because, after the Treaty of Paris in 1763, control over Catholic priests had been invested in the British crown. Attorney General Henry John Boulton* and Solicitor General Christopher Alexander HAGERMAN both wrote reports dismissing the priest's case. McDonell also rejected O'Grady's arguments, and Colborne took no action on the petition.

In May 1833 McDonell excommunicated O'Grady and his supporters; the latter promptly drew up a petition calling for an investigation into the bishop's financial management of the diocese. This memorial suffered the same fate as O'Grady's. Sent to Colborne, it was passed to McDonell for his comments and came to nothing. In August O'Grady left for Rome to appeal to the pope. McDonell, however, undercut his mission by writing beforehand to his friends in Rome, one of whom, Cardinal Thomas Weld, gave O'Grady a frosty welcome, advising him to return and submit to his bishop. Unable to meet with other Vatican officials, O'Grady made his way to London, where he petitioned the king, and then back to Upper Canada, arriving in January 1834. That March he sent a petition to the Colonial Office, again defending his conduct and accusing McDonell of peculation. He also, bizarrely enough, suggested to McDonell the importance of resolving their dispute. McDonell responded curtly, demanding O'Grady's complete submission and a full retraction of his "errors and falsehoods." It was the last communication between the two men. When the Colonial Office rejected his petition, O'Grady gave up his battle for St Paul's and turned his attention to his newspaper.

In O'Grady's case, the fight with the bishop had little to do with principle and everything to do with personality. Immensely proud, nursing a grudge over the Crevier–Fluet affair, O'Grady lashed out at McDonell because the bishop seemed intent on humiliating him. To the bishop, O'Grady had been a priest whom he had trusted and relied upon. His betrayal hurt McDonell deeply, and he retaliated with the fury that was so much a part of his Highland temperament. Yet there was more to his reaction than simple anger. In McDonell's mind, the structure of the church was a mirror image of the structure of society. By challenging episcopal authority, therefore, O'Grady was challenging the ideas and assumptions that were integral to McDonell's vision of a stable, hierarchical social order. To make matters worse, O'Grady's disobedience, as well as his radical politics, threatened what McDonell hoped to achieve in the political arena. The bishop had always made it one of his central goals to convince the civil authorities that his flock were law-abiding, orderly, and loyal to the crown. O'Grady's antics seemed to make a mockery of his efforts, and for this reason too McDonell moved quickly, and furiously, against him.

O'Grady may have been the prickliest thorn in McDonell's side, but he was not the only one. Besides Crevier, Fluet, and O'Grady himself, there were several other priests in the 1830s who were either rebellious, incompetent, or both, and the strain of dealing with them took a toll on the elderly bishop, who became increasingly cantankerous and suspicious. Yet, if O'Grady was not alone in his insubordination, he was not just another troublemaker. For one thing, the magnitude of the scandal he inflicted on the church had no parallel – not even Fluet and Crevier came close to embarrassing McDonell to the extent that O'Grady did. Further, like Fluet and Crevier but unlike the other clerical bad apples, O'Grady enjoyed considerable popular sympathy. Some of his supporters were Protestant liberals delighted to have found a stick with which to beat McDonell; the most notable was Mackenzie, but there were others too – Protestants were well represented at a pro-O'Grady meeting held at St Paul's in April 1833. He also had many supporters in the Catholic community. A band of followers in St Paul's backed him every step of the way, and on two separate occasions, in February and June 1833, York Catholics drew up petitions in his favour, the second of which bore no fewer than 840 signatures. McDonell dismissed these petitions as fraudulent, and it is quite probable that some of the signatories were Protestants and that others affixed their names without knowing what was at issue. Still, it stretches the imagination to believe that all, or even a majority, of the signatures were bogus. And in any case, what is important is not that O'Grady may have exaggerated his Catholic support but that, given his flagrant disobedience of church authority, he had any at all.

Determining why O'Grady enjoyed Catholic backing is not an easy task. It does seem clear that his popularity and the Irish presence in York were intertwined. By the early 1830s York had become the home of a sizeable Irish Catholic population, a population that would continue to grow rapidly during the rest of the decade. This community, united by its history, poverty, and lack of political power, was doggedly ethnocentric and, in keeping with its traditions, reformist in politics. Not surprisingly, McDonell always had his opponents among York Catholics, both as a Scot and as a pillar of the ruling oligarchy. His unpopularity was perhaps one of the reasons why St Paul's – a parish dominated by lower-class Irish – was so fractious, not only during O'Grady's tenure but also before and after it; other reasons appear to have been the marked division in the parish between Irish and non-Irish, and the presence in it of middle-class Irish Catholics such as King who played an important role in mobilizing discontent. McDonell's difficulties in bringing the parish into line were the greater because O'Grady was a brilliant demagogue who was able to tap his Irish parishioners' dislike of their bishop and turn it to his own purposes.

Any exploration of O'Grady's social and political views must rely heavily on the pages of the *Correspondent*, one of the most radical newspapers of the pre-confederation era. From the founding of this paper in late 1832 until August 1833, King was nominally its proprietor and editor, but there is little doubt that O'Grady was the real force. During O'Grady's subsequent absence in Europe, King assumed sole responsibility, and the results showed in the increasingly tame, even bland, editorial columns. Whatever King's status during the six months after his partner's return in January 1834, O'Grady was clearly in charge again, setting the editorial tone in feisty and passionately radical pronouncements. In July King severed ties with the *Correspondent*; its proprietor was now listed as John Reynolds, but O'Grady remained its real master. In November, it merged with Mackenzie's *Colonial Advocate* and was renamed the *Correspondent and Advocate*. O'Grady continued as editor until the paper's collapse on the eve of the rebellion.

The *Correspondent* – like the two other major Irish Catholic newspapers of the pre-confederation period, Collins's *Canadian Freeman* and Charles Donlevy*'s *Toronto Mirror* – was a profoundly Irish paper, its patriotism being reflected in attacks on Britain and in demands for the repeal of the union of 1800. In addressing the Irish question, however, the *Correspondent*, like the *Freeman* and the *Mirror*, was careful to state its preference for Daniel O'Connell's peaceful agitation over attempts at armed insurrection. The radical nature of O'Grady's vision became more apparent when the paper reflected on social and economic issues in Upper Canada, or on the grander problem of the structure of human society. His social and political philosophy – like the man himself – was remarkably complex, drawing its inspiration from a variety of traditions including Enlightenment rationalism, the radical whiggery of the 18th century, American Jacksonianism, and the revolutionary thought of the early 19th century. Combined, these traditions created a bubbling cauldron of liberal ideas that set O'Grady and McDonell poles apart. The same ideas also isolated him from his fellow reformers, who, Mackenzie being a notable exception, subscribed to many of the social and political values of their tory opponents. In O'Grady, as in Mackenzie, a highly visible strain of democratic egalitarianism gave his politics a cutting, revolutionary edge.

O'Grady's radicalism can be seen in any of his editorials in the *Correspondent*, which abounded with attacks on monopolies, corporations, and the principle of state aid to religion, whatever its denominational stripe. The *Correspondent* also took a great interest in the revolutionary spirit then ridding Europe of the "rubbish of ages"; it repeatedly proclaimed that government derived its authority from the people and existed only to promote their happiness; it constantly expressed its concern for the plight of the poor and railed against their oppressors. The democratic egalitarianism that inspired the paper was occasionally evident in calm, closely reasoned editorials such as the one explaining that the "legitimate object of good government is to prevent as far as possible the extremes of wealth and poverty, and diffuse equally, through all classes, the bounties of nature." More typically, it was expressed in angry denunciations of Upper Canada's "gentlefolk," that "aristocracy of pensions – placemen, pimps, panders and expectants." An editorial of 1834 asserted that "those silken creatures and their families" should "earn their bread like other people, by honest industry."

Throughout the 1830s, the *Correspondent* displayed an unwavering commitment to Upper Canadian reform. It lavished praise on a select group of heroes, prominent among whom were Marshall Spring Bidwell* and Mackenzie, and it hurled invective at every tory in sight; the paper's victims included O'Grady's one-time friend, Colborne, now a "corrupt and deceitful imbecile," and John Beverley Robinson*, "who, secreted in the back ground of intrigue and deception, directs every movement of his knavish satellites." In the *Correspondent* O'Grady advanced prescriptions for Upper Canada's well-being. Most were conventional: "cheap and economical" government, promotion of railways and canals, and responsible government. Yet the *Correspondent* did separate itself from the crowd. Reflecting its egalitarian values, it called for a tax on the wealthy and denounced the property qualification for voters as an example of "old feudal abominations." It also took a particularly rigorous stance on the issue of responsible government. When Robert Baldwin*, John Rolph*, and John Henry Dunn* were appointed to the Executive Council in February 1836, the *Correspondent* warned that "the people, never will repose confidence in an Executive Council composed of such discordant and irreconcileable materials as Tories and Reformers equally divided." For O'Grady, clearly, what was needed was a reform council that reflected the political will of the reform-dominated assembly.

O'Grady, largely because of his association with the *Correspondent*, was a key figure in the reform movement of the 1830s. In the provincial election of 1834 he ran unsuccessfully against Hagerman in Kingston. By the end of the year he was a member of the Constitutional Reform Society and sat on the executive of the Canadian Alliance Society. In the spring of 1835 he appeared before Mackenzie's select committee on grievances and late the same year he travelled with Mackenzie to Lower Canada to meet leading reformers there. During 1836 he played an important role at two reform meetings in Toronto, in June and October. At the second he was one of the reformers given the crucial task of overseeing the creation of political unions throughout the province. By early 1837 he was on the executive of the Constitutional Reform Society and was active as well in the Toronto Political Union. At a meeting of the latter in April 1837, he introduced a resolution, which was carried, advocating a reform convention for the purpose of sending delegates to London. Another of his resolutions, which also passed, proposed a petition to the king "on the deplorable state of the Province, and the reckless legislation of the present unconstitutional house of Assembly."

For unknown reasons, in November 1837 O'Grady sold the *Correspondent*'s press and type to Charles FOTHERGILL in exchange for land in Pickering Township and cash; after the sale, two issues of the paper were published in combination with Mackenzie's *Constitution*, but it then collapsed completely. Over the next few months O'Grady vanishes from view. Probably living in Pickering Township, he does not appear to have taken any part in the rebellion, and, more surprising, in the midst of the Patriot raids the following year he seems to have provided the government with military intelligence. From the evidence – a single letter from Robert Baldwin Sullivan* to Lieutenant Governor Sir George Arthur* – it is not clear whether O'Grady was acting as a government spy or whether his supplying of information was merely the result of a careless tongue. If he was, in fact, betraying Mackenzie and his old radical friends, his volte-face would have been yet another example of the abrupt transitions that had characterized his life.

Whatever O'Grady was doing in his last years, it appears that he remained committed to the cause of reform, if not to sedition. In March 1838 John Ryerson* reported meeting him in the home of Thomas David Morrison*. According to Ryerson, O'Grady was uncowed by recent events and still thought that the dream of a reformed Upper Canada was attainable. Yet if the New Jerusalem was within reach, he would let others bring it about. From 1838 on he seems to have lived an uneventful life in Pickering Township. A coroner's inquest concluded that his death there in 1840 was a "visitation of God."

CURTIS FAHEY

AO, MS 709; RG 1, C-IV, Pickering Township, concession 1, lot 15, esp. 339–42. Arch. of the Roman Catholic Archdiocese of Toronto, M (Macdonell papers) (mfm. at AO). Durham Land Registry Office (Whitby, Ont.), [Ontario County], South Pickering Township, abstract index to deeds, vol.A (1795–1955): 19, 58–59, 140 (mfm. at AO). PAC, RG 1, L3, 393A: O15/27, O16/12; RG 5, A1: 52643–44, 66839–44, 69249–54, 69541–50, 71951–88, 73285–86, 76980–81, 77152–53, 91128. PRO, CO 42/418: 385–94. *Arthur papers* (Sanderson). *Town of York, 1815–34* (Firth). U.C., House of Assembly, *Journal*, 1835: 22–23, 26–31, 37–38. *Canadian Correspondent* (York [Toronto]; Toronto), 1833–34. *Canadian Freeman*, 1828–33. *Cobourg Star*, 27 Aug. 1840. *Colonial Advocate*, 1833. *Correspondent and Advocate* (Toronto), 1834–37. *Examiner* (Toronto), 19 Aug. 1840. *Patriot and Farmer's Monitor*, 1833. *Toronto Patriot*, 21 Aug. 1840. W. P. Bull, *From Macdonell to McGuigan: the history of the growth of the Roman Catholic Church in Upper Canada* (Toronto, 1939). J. E. Rea, *Bishop Alexander Macdonell and the politics of Upper Canada* (Toronto, 1974). C. B. Sissons, *Egerton Ryerson: his life and letters* (2v., Toronto, 1937–47), 1. *The story of St. Paul's parish, Toronto . . .*, ed. Edward Kelly ([Toronto], 1922).

OHTOWA?KÉHSON (Ahdohwahgeseon, Adonwentishon, Catharine, Catharine Brant), head woman of the turtle clan of the Mohawks; b. *c.* 1759 on the Mohawk River (N.Y.); d. 23 or 24 Nov. 1837 near Brantford, Upper Canada.

Catharine was the daughter of a Mohawk woman of noble birth who was probably head woman of the clan in her own time. Her grandmother was Sarah, the wife of Karaghtadie*, who likewise was probably head woman. The position was an important one. With it went authority to appoint or depose the Tekarihogen, the leading sachem of the Six Nations Confederacy, although actual exercise of that authority involved much councilling among all classes of the Mohawks. Catharine's father was Indian agent George Croghan, but she grew up in a thoroughly Mohawk environment and throughout her life preferred Indian ways. She understood English but declined to speak it, even in later years. On at least one occasion she wrote her name, spelling it Katerin, but she also signed by mark.

By 1779, during the American revolution, Catharine was living at British-held Fort Niagara (near Youngstown, N.Y.), to which many loyalist Indians had fled. There she married the twice-widowed Joseph Brant [Thayendanegea*], first in the Indian manner and later, in the winter of 1779–80, according to English law. American captives reported that Brant (whose previous marriages had been before clergymen) observed a wedding conducted by John Butler* in his capacity as magistrate and immediately insisted that Butler perform the same ceremony for Catharine and himself.

The Brants moved to the Grand River (Ont.) in the spring of 1785, the year after Governor Frederick Haldimand* gave to those Six Nations Indians who did not wish to live in the United States a great tract of land from the mouth to the source of that river. Here, in the best house in the Mohawk village, the couple entertained numerous guests. Patrick Campbell*, a Scottish traveller, visited them in February 1792. He described Catharine as tall, black-eyed, and handsome; richly dressed, she completely outshone two pretty young white ladies who were present. The Brants had several children by this date, and seven in all were born to them.

Aristocratic Catharine had much influence among the Six Nations. Her views carried weight with Henry Tekarihogen*, her elder half-brother (or possibly cousin), whom she or her mother had appointed head sachem some time before 1787. Her opinions would have counted with the women of the tribe especially, and they were a political force to be reckoned with. In 1793, when Lieutenant Governor John Graves Simcoe* of Upper Canada refused to give the Six Nations an unrestricted deed to the Haldimand grant so that they could sell land, Joseph Brant was extremely displeased. There followed a great tumult on the Grand River; the women met in council and charged their warriors to defend their land. It is impossible not to see Catharine's hand in this incident and in another one a few years later, in May 1802, when the women of the tribe apologized to Brant for their part in dissensions that had almost brought about his assassination.

Dissensions continuing, the Brants soon removed to what is now Burlington, at the head of Lake Ontario, where in a white neighbourhood Joseph had built a substantial house, sometimes called a mansion, on a property of about 700 acres. Joseph aspired to a genteel English way of life. Catharine evidently did not care. Although the family had servants, she did not hesitate, when she needed water, to send her little son John [Tekarihogen*] to fetch it, and she was known to set her white cat on the corner of the table during dinner and pour it a saucer of milk. Sophia Pooley, *née* Burthen, a slave of the Brants when she was young, recalled being beaten by Catharine, "who would tell me in Indian to do things and then hit me with any thing that came to hand, because I did not understand her." After an incident in which she had cut the girl's face with a knife, Joseph punished his wife "as if she had been a child" on his return home.

After her husband's death in 1807, Catharine returned to the old home on the Grand River. For many years a Brant party and an anti-Brant party survived among the Indians there. Henry Tekarihogen, and no doubt Catharine, too, tried to carry on Brant's political and economic policies. They long persisted in claiming for the Indians the lands along the upper reaches of the river (denied through a defect in the grant) and in trying to get an unrestricted deed. On Henry's death in 1830, or perhaps shortly before when he became totally blind, Catharine named her able son John as the new Tekarihogen. Following John's death from cholera on 27 Aug. 1832, she named the infant son of her daughter Elizabeth as head sachem.

Catharine was an industrious housewife, an earnest Christian. It is reported that in later years she could be seen every Sunday at the Mohawk chapel "dressed in a black velvet skirt, black silk over-dress, a black cloth blanket and black velvet cap with a fur band." Reflecting perhaps on the strange events of her own life, she often told her children that none can know what the future holds. She died exactly 30 years after her husband.

ISABEL T. KELSAY

AO, MS 148, sect.I, Brant family; RG 22, ser.204, will of Catharine Brant, proved 27 April 1839. PAC, MG 11, [CO 42] Q, 312-1: 18–19. Wis., State Hist. Soc., Draper MSS, 13F25, 13F31, 13F58, 13F94, 14F63, 21F16. James Buchanan, *Sketches of the history, manners, and customs of the North American Indians with a plan for their melioration* (2v., New York, 1824), 2: 36. Patrick Campbell, *Travels in the interior inhabited parts of North America in the years 1791 and 1792 . . .* (Edinburgh, [1793]), 190–91. W. W. Campbell, *Annals of Tryon County; or, the border warfare of New York, during the revolution* (New York, 1831), app., 16–17. *Corr. of Lieut. Governor Simcoe* (Cruikshank), 2: 115. [Thomas Douglas, 5th Earl of] Selkirk, *Lord Selkirk's diary, 1803–1804; a journal of his travels in British North America and the northeastern United States*, ed. P. C. T. White (Toronto, 1958; repr. New York, 1969), 161. *The refugee: a north-side view of slavery*, comp. Benjamin Drew, intro. T. G. Edelstein (Reading, Mass., 1969), 135–37. *Valley of Six Nations* (Johnston), 297. W. L. Stone, *Life of Joseph Brant – Thayendanegea* (New York, 1838), 2: 463, 500, 535, 537. Isabel Thompson Kelsay, *Joseph Brant, 1743–1807, man of two worlds* (Syracuse, N.Y., 1984). A. I. G. Gilkison, "Reminiscences of earlier years in Brant," *OH*, 12 (1914): 81–88.

O'SULLIVAN, MICHAEL, lawyer, militia officer, politician, JP, office holder, and judge; baptized 4 May 1784 in Clonmel (Republic of Ireland), son of John O'Sullivan and Eleonora O'Donel; d. 7 March 1839 in Montreal.

Related to the élite in Tipperary County (Republic of Ireland), Michael O'Sullivan was brought to Montreal at a young age and in 1799 enrolled in the Sulpician Collège Saint-Raphaël. Seven years later he graduated at the top of a class that had included at least three budding nationalists, Hugues HENEY, Jean-Moïse RAYMOND, and André Jobin*. In December 1805 O'Sullivan had begun articling with the brilliant young Montreal lawyer Denis-Benjamin Viger*. Perhaps to broaden his knowledge of English law and improve his prospects in private practice, he left Viger in March 1808 to finish his studies under the influential Stephen Sewell*. On 6 April 1811 he was commissioned a lawyer.

O'Sullivan's contacts in college and with Viger seem to have inspired him, about 1806, to write articles for *Le Canadien*, the mouthpiece of the nationalist Canadian party. His marriage on 1 June 1809 to Cécile Berthelet, daughter of the businessman Pierre Berthelet* and Marguerite Viger, had strengthened his ties with the Canadian bourgeoisie in Montreal; among the witnesses were Louis GUY, Pierre-Dominique DEBARTZCH, and the lawyer Benjamin Beaubien, along with Sewell and Dr George Selby*. Unfortunately, Cécile died in 1811. The following year O'Sullivan was commissioned a lieutenant and adjutant in the Beauharnois battalion of militia. He was aide-de-camp to Lieutenant-Colonel Charles-Michel d'Irumberry* de Salaberry at the battle of Châteauguay in 1813 and was cited in dispatches for bravery. O'Sullivan published an account of the battle in the *Montreal Gazette* of 9 Nov. 1813 in order to ensure to Salaberry "the justice that belongs to you" at a time when several, including Lieutenant-Colonel George Richard John Macdonell*, were claiming credit for the victory. O'Sullivan asserted that, with few exceptions, "the 300 men engaged together with their brave commander, were all Canadians," and exhorted, "Let this be told wherever mention is made of the battle of Châteauguay, and prejudice must hide its head." O'Sullivan's account became the cornerstone of all subsequent French Canadian interpretations of the battle.

Meanwhile, O'Sullivan had developed an important practice in Montreal and had acquired a reputation as an outstanding legal authority. William WALKER as well as Charles-Elzéar* and Dominique* Mondelet articled under him, and in 1818 he was associate counsel with his friend James Stuart* and with Samuel Gale* for Lord Selkirk [Douglas*], who had been charged with offences at Fort William (Thunder Bay, Ont.). James Charles Grant became O'Sullivan's law partner about 1822, and their firm maintained a prominent role in Montreal's legal community until Grant's death in 1836.

As a bright and well-connected lawyer with a reputation for bravery, O'Sullivan seemingly had had no trouble being elected to the House of Assembly for Huntingdon County in 1814. In the assembly he was a close associate of Stuart and focused his attention on judicial and administrative measures. His politics were reformist, but he appears not to have taken a prominent role in the numerous battles between the assembly and the colonial administration that marked the period, and he attended fewer than one-half of the sessions during his ten years in the house. However, his outspoken opposition to government support for a non-denominational hospital in Montreal – which he feared would attract patients from the Catholic Hôtel-Dieu – led him into a duel with a principal promoter of the project, Dr William Caldwell*. Wounded twice, O'Sullivan thereafter endured frequent bouts of agonizing pain and walked with a pronounced limp because one of the bullets had lodged against his spine and could not be removed. He resigned his seat in 1824 and was replaced by former classmate Jean-Moïse Raymond. Possibly he had begun to distance himself from the nationalism of the Canadian party, which dominated the house. As late as about 1822 he had hosted a gastronomic dinner for which Jacques Viger* had composed a patriotic song, but in January 1823 Hugues Heney accused him of seeking a "pointless quarrel" with Denis-Benjamin Viger over a judicial bill.

O'Sullivan's continuing close relations with his erstwhile mentors, the Sulpicians, whom he frequently advised on legal matters, would not have endeared him to the Canadian party after 1820. The following year the consecration of a Canadian, Jean-Jacques LARTIGUE, as auxiliary and suffragan bishop in Montreal of Joseph-Octave Plessis*, archbishop of Quebec, was perceived by the predominantly French Sulpicians as a threat to their spiritual domination of Montreal. Under Jean-Henry-Auguste Roux* they intrigued in the colony, in London, and in Rome to undermine Lartigue's authority and to force him to take up residence outside the town; meanwhile Plessis persuaded leaders of the Canadian party, principally Lartigue's cousins Denis-Benjamin Viger and Louis-Joseph Papineau*, to come to the suffragan's assistance. O'Sullivan supported the Sulpicians and provided advice on canon and civil law to Augustin Chaboillez*, a Canadian priest sympathetic to them, who in 1823–24 publicly contested the legality of Lartigue's appointment. In the same period O'Sullivan may have been influential in having a relation, James O'Donnell*, named architect for a large, new Notre-Dame church, built in part to forestall construction of a cathedral for Lartigue. In 1824 O'Sullivan toured England, France, and Italy, ostensibly on vacation, but in fact partly to lobby on behalf of the Sulpicians; his movements were closely followed by friends of Lartigue and Plessis. Although his efforts were ultimately unsuccessful, they probably contributed to rendering Lartigue's position uncomfortable for many years.

O'Sullivan's profile in the colony and in his profession rose steadily. He had been appointed major in the Beauharnois battalion of militia in 1821 (before transferring to Montreal's 1st Militia Battalion in 1830), and in 1832 was named a commissioner for the civil erection of parishes. Elected president of the Advocates' Library and Law Institute of Montreal in 1831 and 1832, he began giving courses in law, as did Sewell, Viger, and other eminent lawyers; in December 1831 he delivered public lectures on the history of Roman law down to Justinian I. In 1829 he had been appointed a commissioner for receiving evidence and in 1831 was made a king's counsel and a justice of the peace. Following the promotion of Charles Richard Ogden* to attorney general, O'Sullivan was appointed solicitor general in April 1833 by Lord Aylmer [WHITWORTH-AYLMER], on the basis of his past legal performances and his standing "in Public Estimation in this Province for probity, Professional ability & sound constitutional principles in politics."

O'Sullivan now moved in different social circles. On 17 May 1831 he had married Jeanne-Marie-Catherine Bruyères, widow of Dr David Thomas Kennelly and granddaughter of John Bruyères*, former seigneur and governor's secretary; the witnesses included Toussaint POTHIER, legislative councillor, and Charles William Grant, Baron de Longueuil and legislative councillor, as well as O'Sullivan's old friend Dr Selby and, surprisingly, Joseph PAPINEAU. O'Sullivan also professed different politics: his reformism had entirely given way to toryism. In 1835 Louis-Joseph Papineau felt that the political crisis in Lower Canada would be resolved if Aylmer could find the courage to mortify certain office holders, "but," he wrote to his wife, "the policy of O'Sullivan will prevail, that of temporizing . . . *then will the great débâcle come at last, which it would have been so easy to prevent.*" When the colony did explode into rebellion in 1837–38, O'Sullivan proved his worth as an efficient solicitor general. He was rewarded on 25 Oct. 1838 with the post of chief justice of the Court of King's Bench, Montreal district, but his tenure was cut short by his death on 7 March 1839, after only one term.

Despite substantial revenues from a flourishing legal practice and his judicial offices, O'Sullivan had accumulated significant debts, some dating back to 1815. He did not believe that he would leave an extensive estate, and it is doubtful that even the liquidation of his holdings, including four properties in Montreal and an extensive library, was sufficient to pay off his debts. His premature and debt-ridden end notwithstanding, O'Sullivan had made himself a leading member of the legal profession in Lower Canada. A man with undoubted abilities and with personal connections to the principal political, clerical, and social figures in 19th-century Montreal, he must be seen as a major Catholic figure of his time.

ALAN DEVER

ANQ-M, CE1-51, 1er mai 1809, 12 juin 1811, 17 mai 1831, 11 mars 1839, 20 juill. 1849; CN1-28, 8 oct. 1823; CN1-126, 7 déc. 1815; CN1-134, 1824–35; CN1-187, 31 mai 1824; CN1-192, 1834; CN1-194, 28 avril 1809; CN1-224, 12 avril, 15 mai 1839; 1840; CN1-305, 1825; CN1-396, 15 mai, 16 août, 19 nov. 1839. ANQ-Q, P1000-43-833. ASTR, 0419. PAC, MG 11, [CO 42] Q, 206: 213–14; MG 24, B2: 2072; MG 30, D1, 23; RG 4, B8: 6688–702, 10468; RG 68, General index, 1651–1841. L.C., House of Assembly, *Journals*, 1814–37. L.-J. Papineau, "Correspondance" (Ouellet), ANQ *Rapport*, 1953–55: 376. *L'Aurore des Canadas*, 8, 12 mars 1839. *Le Canadien*, 11 mars 1839. *Montreal Gazette*, 1 May 1809, 9 Nov. 1813, 7 March 1839. *Quebec Gazette*, 11 April 1811, 11 April 1816, 23 March 1818, 6 April 1820, 7 June 1821. Caron, "Inv. de la corr. de Mgr Panet," ANQ *Rapport*, 1935–36: 256–57; "Inv. de la corr. de Mgr Plessis," 1928–29: 192, 198–99; "Inv. des doc. relatifs aux événements de 1837 et 1838," 1925–26: 161, 204, 273. Louise Dechêne, "Inventaire des documents relatifs à l'histoire du Canada conservés dans les archives de la Compagnie de Saint-Sulpice à Paris," ANQ *Rapport*, 1969: 211, 226. Desrosiers, "Inv. de la corr. de Mgr Lartigue," ANQ *Rapport*, 1941–42: 439, 453, 458; 1942–43: 153, 155. Le Jeune, *Dictionnaire*. Ouellet, "Inv. de la saberdache," ANQ *Rapport*, 1955–57: 121. *Quebec almanac*, 1813–32. Wallace, *Macmillan dict.*

F.-J. Audet, *Les juges en chef de la province de Québec, 1764–1924* (Québec, 1927). Buchanan, *Bench and bar of L.C.* E. A. Collard, *Montreal: the days that are no more* (Toronto, 1976), 203–8. Michelle Guitard, "Les miliciens de la bataille de Châteauguay" (thèse de MA, univ. d'Ottawa, 1980). Lemieux, *L'établissement de la première prov. eccl.* Maurault, *Le collège de Montréal* (Dansereau; 1967); *La paroisse: hist. de Notre-Dame de Montréal* (1929). Camille Roy, *Nos origines littéraires* (Québec, 1909). J.-J. Lefebvre, "Quelques officiers de 1812," RSC *Trans.*, 4th ser., 4 (1966), sect.I: 69–136. Maréchal Nantel, "L'étude du droit et le Barreau," *Cahiers des Dix*, 14 (1949): 14. Benjamin Sulte, "Qui commandait à Châteauguay?" *BRH*, 1 (1895): 97–98.

P

PAINCHAUD, CHARLES-FRANÇOIS, Roman Catholic priest, missionary, and educator; b. 9 Sept. 1782 on Île aux Grues, Que., eldest son of François Painchaud, a seaman, and Angélique Drouin; d. 9 Feb. 1838 in Sainte-Anne-de-la-Pocatière (La Pocatière), Lower Canada.

Charles-François Painchaud was still quite young when his parents went to live at Quebec, on Rue Saint-Vallier in the *faubourg* Saint-Roch. His father, who had some education, taught him to read. Around 1792, because his talents were noticed by Joseph-Octave Plessis*, the parish priest of Notre-Dame, Charles-François entered the Petit Séminaire de Québec. When he was 15, and half-way through his classical studies, he lost his father; Plessis then entrusted him to the care of the parish priest of L'Ange-Gardien, Jean RAIMBAULT. Painchaud worked at his courses in the presbytery up to the final two years of the classical program (Philosophy), which he began at the Séminaire de Québec in 1799. While doing his theological studies he tutored the children of Lieutenant Governor Sir Robert Shore MILNES.

Ordained to the priesthood on 21 Sept. 1805, Painchaud became assistant priest at the Quebec cathedral for a few months, and then accepted the Baie des Chaleurs mission. One of his younger brothers, Alexis*, used to accompany him on his pastoral rounds there. Once his first three years were finished, he asked to be brought back, but in vain; he was to remain in the mission from 1806 to 1814. Using bold methods not precluding force, he led a crusade against alcoholism. For a long time his was the only ministry to the white population of the Gaspé peninsula. As parish priest at Carleton he served the faithful from Percé to Restigouche. Mission life marked him profoundly, and when he was appointed parish priest at Sainte-Anne-de-la-Pocatière in 1814 he seemed unable to adapt. After a year he asked to be moved to another region, either Montreal or Trois-Rivières, for reasons of conscience. The bishop turned a deaf ear, and Painchaud was to retain his charge until his death.

When Painchaud arrived, the parish had nearly 2,500 people. Though smaller than the parish of Rivière-Ouelle, it none the less constituted a rather heavy ministry for a curé with no assistant priest. It is difficult to give an idea of the sort of relations that Painchaud had with his parishioners, but he was probably more paternalistic than authoritarian. He was, after all, reputed to be a healer. His knowledge of folk and conventional medicine was often put to the test: people came from all over to consult him. As a result, in 1834 he advised his fellow priests in neighbouring parishes that from then on he would treat only sick people who presented a certificate attesting their inability to pay a doctor.

Painchaud's administrative responsibilities seemed to worry him. For one thing, the churchwarden in charge did not present his accounts on the dates specified. The archbishop's ordinances on the matter appear to have been followed in a rather desultory fashion, since on his pastoral visit in the summer of 1833 Joseph SIGNAY demanded that the accounts for 1832 be rendered. In 1813 Plessis had decided to set uniform fees for masses and other religious services. *Fabriques* and the parish priests, who shared these sources of revenue, were directly affected by this reform, and Painchaud accepted the new rates policy with great reluctance. Another administrative question about the parish priest's income and duties was raised in 1825. Painchaud was lumping together fees for low masses in order to sing high masses. He got himself out of difficulty with the archbishop by explaining that there was not enough time to celebrate all the masses and he had acted as he did only after giving his parishioners to understand that high masses sung for several intentions at once were better. Although he was apparently pleasant with his parishioners, he often vexed the episcopal authorities. For example, he wanted to compete with, if not supplant, the Société Ecclésiastique Saint-Michel, a diocesan mutual aid society that Plessis had helped found in 1799. He failed himself to get enough adherents and did not succeed in weakening it. Being used to quibbling with his superiors, Painchaud had gained a sense of how to take the initiative, riposte, and negotiate; he was thus able to overcome the archbishop's opposition to the plan of founding a classical college that he had cherished since at least 1820.

Painchaud launched the project at a difficult point in the mid 1820s. The Séminaire de Nicolet was under construction, and this limited the possibilities of financial assistance from the clergy. A succession of bad crops, which were particularly disastrous in the Côte-du-Sud region, left local farmers largely unable to support their curé's plan. It was hard to see how one could send a son to the college and especially meet the cost of his board when there was not enough for basic necessities. In the short term, rivalry from the neighbouring parishes was the most difficult obstacle, but it actually furnished a good opportunity to carry out the project.

Early in 1823 the assistant priest at Kamouraska, Jean-Baptiste Morin, presented a plan for a college to the archbishop. Plessis responded by enumerating the difficulties facing the undertaking. He did not oppose the plan, but expressed the view that it was necessary to collect funds, to put off execution to a later date, and to engage in discussion with the leading citizens in the surrounding localities. Things dragged on, partly because Morin did not inspire confidence and indeed was shocking people by his brazenly debauched conduct. Apart from the regions that were thinly populated or were poorly evangelized, Kamouraska may well have been one of the parishes in the east of the province where looseness of morals and indifference to religion were causing the archbishop the greatest concern. On the other hand, in the mid 1820s it had twice the population of Sainte-Anne-de-la-Pocatière. Rivière-Ouelle, which was itself entertaining vague notions of founding an institution for secondary education, was, with 3,500 inhabitants, also larger than Sainte-Anne-de-la-Pocatière, but Kamouraska nevertheless was best situated to serve Kamouraska County.

In the winter of 1826–27, with the parish priest's cooperation, leading figures of Kamouraska again promoted the idea of a college. While seeking Archbishop Bernard-Claude Panet*'s approval, they turned to the House of Assembly of Lower Canada for tangible support. The Kamouraska plan envisaged a secular undertaking supported by the state. Painchaud's views were more consonant with the educational philosophy of the clergy and the episcopal authorities. A letter from Panet dated 27 Jan. 1827 spurred him on: "I shall always be inclined to prefer the parish where such a building has been started, as long as no recourse to the legislature is needed." Though aware that the episcopate seemed to prefer Painchaud's initiative, the Kamouraska promoters refused to admit defeat. They maintained a veritable lobby at the assembly until that body decided early in 1829 to reject their request, specifically to avoid harming the college that was being built in the neighbouring parish. At Sainte-Anne-de-la-Pocatière the contract for a three-storey building had actually been let in March 1827, and construction was well on the way to completion. The autumn of 1829 had been set for the opening.

Once the college had been built with corvées and donated materials, Painchaud's troubles were still not over. He needed teachers. Panet, faced with the priest's plan, had authorized it partly because he feared a secular college would be put up within a few miles of the parish, but he said repeatedly that Painchaud had assured him he did not need clerics. At Quebec it was not yet thought that in the coming years the Collège de Sainte-Anne-de-la-Pocatière would be able to offer a complete classical program rivalling those of the Séminaire de Nicolet or the Séminaire de Québec. And there was the further question of whether regents at Sainte-Anne-de-la-Pocatière would be able to pursue their theological studies from the first stages with little or no supervision. When all these considerations had been carefully weighed, it was judged that laity from the Séminaire de Québec who were nearing the end of their studies could go to teach in the new establishment. Consequently there was no need for theological students as instructors. Painchaud, however, was not short of arguments for having a priest appointed as director or theology students selected as teachers. He negotiated with the archbishop, emphasizing that his founding of the institution had made it possible, among other things, to keep a secular college from being created. In the autumn of 1829 he presented Panet with a *fait accompli* – the building was finished – and an ultimatum: he would be supplied with ordinands, under Panet's authority, to serve as teachers or he would hand the college over to the archbishop. Acknowledging what human resources were available, and agreeing to be served after the older colleges, Painchaud succeeded in getting a staff of clergy. His only grounds for complaint would be the quality of the people he was given.

Painchaud was exasperated when he realized that at Quebec the clergy of the seminary and the archbishop's staff seemed disinclined to permit his institution to offer a complete course of study. Why would schoolboys from the Côte-du-Sud not come to do their two years of Philosophy at the seminary? In the mid 1830s Painchaud, backed by the local parish priests, refused to let the Collège de Sainte-Anne-de-la-Pocatière become a branch establishment to "knock the rough edges" off young farm boys for the Séminaire de Québec. In his eyes everything seemed to be conspiring to ruin his establishment. As if that were not enough, the director himself, Alexis Mailloux*, who had come to the college in 1834 on the express condition that Painchaud be kept out of academic and disciplinary matters, apparently was adopting the views of those who wanted to restrict the course of study. In the end, Painchaud succeeded in getting a complete course of study and adequate staff. In the year of his death the college accommodated some 100 pupils, entrusted to the care of seven teachers, and was administered by three priests.

The financial history of the institution in Painchaud's time reveals the precarious nature of a venture that endured despite an almost incredible lack of resources. Government alone could make up the operating deficits and, on occasion, deal with purchases of equipment. At the time Painchaud's college opened, the establishments at Chambly and Saint-Hyacinthe were getting government subsidies. In 1831 he obtained an initial grant of £500. In subsequent years he regularly received several hundred pounds which, added to what he got in tithes, more or less sufficed to provide for the pupils and for the staff, who received a salary commensurate with that of assistant priests. To obtain favours from the keepers of the public purse Painchaud again showed himself an expert negotiator. When he asked Louis-Joseph Papineau* for £1,000 in 1836, he told him how important his political support was, indicating that without it the college might well be reduced to a normal school. He then spiced his request with a profession of a "liberal" faith, which he contrasted with the ideology of the "extremist ecclesiastical partisans of the English party" at Quebec. Meanwhile the archbishop's staff was becoming worried about the fact that when the college had been turned over to its corporation some time between 1835 and 1837, Painchaud had endowed it with a domain including some seigneurial property burdened with heavy charges. At the founding of the institution, the seigneur of La Pocatière had waived the seigneurial dues normally collected on landed property alienated in mortmain. But the fief had subsequently been sold and the new owner, Amable Dionne*, was not bound to the previous remission. Payment of the seigneurial dues was to compromise the financial well-being of the college seriously for a long time after its founder's death in 1838, and the fears of the archdiocese were thus borne out.

Meanwhile, resources that were more or less unexpected appeased the creditors. In 1837 the college was bequeathed part of the estate of Quebec merchant Augustin Wexler. Several months after Painchaud's death parish priest Louis-Marie CADIEUX also died, having disposed of his estate beforehand in favour of either the Collège de Nicolet or the Collège de Sainte-Anne-de-la-Pocatière. The latter benefited in the end, but there is every reason to think no great sum was involved. It was the death in 1839 of the parish priest of Saint-Roch-des-Aulnaies, Louis Brodeur, that put the college on its feet for a time, since his estate brought it about £2,000. This bequest made up for that from Painchaud himself, whose will put the corporation, his residuary legatee, under various obligations, adding to the burden of a corporate debt estimated in 1838 to be about £1,000. In accordance with the terms of the founder's will, the institution had to pay his mother £25 a year for life, furnish the keep of a woman who had been a donor, distribute small sums to relatives and servants amounting in all to £40, and provide a boy who had been adopted by Painchaud with his keep and education. Although reluctant at first to recommend that the estate be accepted, Archbishop Signay thought that the college had a moral obligation to the founder and that a refusal would be considered most improper.

Those who had to deal with Charles-François Painchaud in the last ten years of his life found him particularly irascible. Of a nervous temperament, he tended to be disagreeable when encountering setbacks, and he was subject to periodic attacks of melancholy. One day, after reading *Le génie du christianisme*, he wrote to Chateaubriand that he had been spellbound: "I devour your works, their melancholy is killing me, all the while they delight me; it is ecstasy." Hypersensitive, with little inclination for the discipline and bookkeeping essential to the survival of his work, Painchaud was finally kept away from the institution by the austere Alexis Mailloux and others like him. A man of dreams and creative imagination, Painchaud had been propelled into action in unfavourable economic times. He was to die worn out by conflicts, feeling he had reaped ingratitude for his pains as provider, a role he had retained to the end by using what he received in tithes to keep the boarders.

SERGE GAGNON

AAQ, 210 A. ANQ-Q, CE2-1, 7 nov. 1782; CE2-7, 14 févr. 1838. Arch. de l'évêché de Sainte-Anne-de-la-Pocatière (La Pocatière, Qué.), Sainte-Anne-de-la-Pocatière; Collège de Sainte-Anne-de-la-Pocatière; Fonds Painchaud; Reg. de copies de lettres et autres doc. reçus ou envoyés. ASN, AP-G, L.-É. Bois, S, XI. Charles Bacon, *Éloge de messire C. F. Painchaud, fondateur du collège de Sainte-Anne* (La Pocatière, 1863). Barthe, *Souvenirs d'un demi-siècle*, 96–101. N.-E. Dionne, *Vie de C.-F. Painchaud* (Québec, 1894). Gérard Ouellet, *Histoire de Sainte-Anne-de-la-Pocatière, 1672–1972* (La Pocatière, 1973). Horace Têtu, *Souvenirs inédits sur l'abbé Painchaud, ancien curé de Ste-Anne-de-la-Pocatière* (Québec, 1894).

PAMBRUN, PIERRE-CHRYSOLOGUE, militia officer and fur trader; b. 19 Dec. 1792 in L'Islet, Lower Canada, son of André-Dominique Pambrun and Angélique Hiraque; m. 1821 Catherine Umfreville, a mixed-blood daughter of Thomas Umfreville, at Cumberland House (Sask.) *à la façon du pays*, and then in a formal manner on 8 Dec. 1838 at Fort Vancouver (Vancouver, Wash.); they had nine children; d. 15 May 1841 at Fort Walla Walla (Walla Walla, Wash.).

Pierre-Chrysologue Pambrun first chose a military career, "the most honourable state in which a virtuous and courageous young man can acquire distinction and make a future for himself," according to his father, a militia officer. With the outbreak of the War of 1812 Pambrun enlisted in the Voltigeurs Canadiens, a unit under Charles-Michel d'Irumberry* de Salaberry. He was promoted corporal in January 1813 and sergeant the following month. Acting on his father's counsel and making up for lack of education with courage, he distinguished himself in October at the battle of Châteauguay, and thus earned promotion to the rank of second lieutenant in 1814. He saw his hopes for a military career dashed, however, when instead of being integrated into the regular army the Voltigeurs were demobilized.

In April 1815 Pambrum entered the service of the Hudson's Bay Company as a clerk. Determined to regain from the North West Company the trade of the northwest, the company was conducting a recruiting campaign among Canadian voyageurs. Pambrun left for the Red River in May with the brigade under Colin ROBERTSON and was first assigned to Pembina (N.Dak.). Early in 1816 he accompanied Governor Robert Semple* on his tour of the company posts on the Red and Assiniboine rivers. On 12 April he was sent to Fort Qu'Appelle (Sask.) to get supplies for the settlers that Lord Selkirk [Douglas*] had sent out, and early in May he set out on the return journey with James Sutherland's 22 men in five canoes laden with 600 bags of pemmican and 22 bales of furs. On 12 May, as the brigade was approaching rough rapids, it was attacked by some 49 Nor'Westers under Cuthbert Grant* and others. Pambrun was taken prisoner and had to follow his captors from Fort Qu'Appelle, which they left at the end of May, to Fort Douglas (Winnipeg). He witnessed the sacking of Brandon House and the destruction at Fort Douglas; he also learned of the massacre at La Grenouillère (Seven Oaks) and of Semple's death. Taken to Fort William (Thunder Bay, Ont.), the NWC headquarters, he was released in August at the demand of Lord Selkirk, who had just arrived. In March 1818 the NWC brought charges against him for thefts said to have been committed at Red River during the winter of 1816–17. He spent the next years as a witness for the HBC, a process that took him to York (Toronto), Montreal, and in 1819 London. An account of the events he had lived through was published there in a collection of narratives relating to the conflict that also contained the testimonies of John Pritchard* and Frederick Damien Heurter.

Back at Hudson Bay in 1820, Pambrun served as a clerk in the Saskatchewan district until 1825. In 1820–21 he was at Cumberland House. The following winter he was at York Factory (Man.), where he was put in charge of the fishing operations at Rock Depot. Between July 1822 and April 1823 he supervised the men in the expedition sent to build a post on the Bow River. From this post he went to Edmonton House (Edmonton), and in September 1823 he was still there. He then spent the winter on the Smoky River.

From 1825 to 1831 Pambrun worked as a clerk in the district of New Caledonia (B.C.), mainly at Fort Kilmars (near Babine), where he arrived in June 1825. During the summer of 1826 he accompanied James

Douglas* and Francis Ermatinger on a thousand-mile trip as far as Fort Vancouver, the new supply centre for the district, and returned to Stuart Lake for the winter of 1826–27. Chief Factor William CONNOLLY subsequently gave him responsibility for Fort Kilmars (1827–29, 1830–31), as well as for Fort Alexandria (Alexandria) (1829–30). After being refused a leave in 1829 to go and settle some personal matters in Montreal, Pambrum was granted one in 1831; he travelled by way of Norway House (Man.) and York Factory.

Pambrun resumed his service in 1832, in the Columbia district. John McLoughlin* made him clerk in charge of Fort Walla Walla, an important post and one of the most dangerous because of the "numerous daring and warlike tribes" living near by. Despite some difficulties in 1835–36 and 1840, Pambrun acquired great influence over them. He even taught them some of the rudiments of Catholicism, thus preparing the way for abbés François-Norbert Blanchet and Modeste Demers*, who worked in the region from 1838.

Pambrun saw the Americans arrive in the Oregon country. In 1837 George Simpson* reprimanded him for having sold tobacco and trade goods to Captain Benjamin-Louis-Eulalie de Bonneville "at Freemens prices," an action contrary to the company's interests. The many American visitors and settlers who passed through Fort Walla Walla mentioned Pambrun's great hospitality. He always maintained the best of relations with the Presbyterian minister Marcus Whitman and his wife.

Despite his requests for promotion, Pambrun did not become a chief trader until 1839, after 24 years of service. He was one of the few French Canadians to reach such a senior rank in the HBC. Simpson had no very good opinion of him, judging by a note in his "Character book" in 1832: "An active, steady dapper little fellow, is anxious to be useful but is wanting in judgement and deficient in Education: Full of 'pluck', has a very good opinion of himself and is quite a 'Petit Maitre'. Does not manage the business of his Post well owing more to a want of discretion & foresight than to indifference or inattention." Other testimonials, while mentioning his lack of education, stress his leadership qualities, his daring, and his perseverance, traits which had made him the choice to lead men on dangerous expeditions and had ensured his success at Fort Walla Walla. At the time of his death McLoughlin observed: "The Company loses an excellent officer and a most able manager of the place under his charge."

Pambrun died at Fort Walla Walla on 15 May 1841 after falling off his horse. He was buried at the fort, but in 1844 his remains were taken to Fort Vancouver, where they were interred in consecrated ground on 9 March.

GRATIEN ALLAIRE

PAM, HBCA, A.1/61: f.87; A.34/1: ff.61–62; A.36/11: ff.92–101; P. C. Pambrun file. UTFL, MS coll. 30, J. N. Wallace, "Encyclopedia of the fur trade, biographical & geographical." *Catholic Church records of the Pacific northwest; Vancouver, volumes I and II, and Stellamaris mission*, trans. M. de L. W. Warner, ed. H. D. Munnick (St Paul, Oreg., [1972]). *HBRS*, 4 (Rich); 18 (Rich and Johnson); 30 (Williams). John McLoughlin, *Letters of Dr. John McLoughlin, written at Fort Vancouver, 1829–1832*, ed. B. B. Barker (Portland, Oreg., [1948]). *Narratives of John Pritchard, Pierre Chrysologue Pambrun, and Frederick Damien Heurter, respecting the aggressions of the North-West Company, against the Earl of Selkirk's settlement upon Red River* (London, 1819). Morice, *Dict. hist. des Canadiens et des Métis*. Benoît Brouillette, *La pénétration du continent américain par les Canadiens français, 1763–1846 . . .* (Montréal, 1939). George Bryce, *The remarkable history of the Hudson's Bay Company including that of the French traders of north-western Canada and of the North-West, XY, and Astor Fur companies . . .* (London, 1900). C. M. Drury, *Marcus and Narcissa Whitman, and the opening of the old Oregon* (2v., Glendale, Calif., 1973). Michelle Guitard, *Histoire sociale des miliciens de la bataille de la Châteauguay* (Ottawa, 1983). K. L. Holmes, "Pierre Chrysologue Pambrun," *The mountain men and the fur trade of the far west . . .* , ed. L. R. Hafen (10v., Glendale, 1965–72), 3: 239–47. Washington Irving, *The adventures of Captain Bonneville* (New York, 1904). A. D. Pambrun, *Sixty years on the frontier in the Pacific northwest* (Fairfield, Wash., 1978), 9–11, 143–50. Joseph Tassé, *Les Canadiens de l'Ouest* (2v., Montréal, 1878), 2: 299–320.

PANET, BONAVENTURE, merchant, politician, militia officer, office holder, and JP; b. 27 July 1765 in Montreal, son of Pierre Panet* and Marie-Anne Trefflé, *dit* Rottot; d. 12 March 1846 in L'Assomption, Lower Canada.

Bonaventure Panet came from a family of 17 children, the first 6 of whom died in infancy, and his chief claim to distinction was to have been a member of the first legislature of Lower Canada. At the time of election for Leinster on 11 June 1792 he was already well known in L'Assomption. He had established himself there as a merchant a few years after the period 1775–82, which he had spent at the Collège Saint-Raphaël in Montreal. Like most rural ridings, Leinster had two members, and another merchant from L'Assomption, François-Antoine Larocque, was also elected.

Scarcely a month later Larocque and Panet petitioned for 1,200 acres apiece to the north of the seigneury of Saint-Sulpice. They were doubtless disappointed that the land committee of the Executive Council granted them only 200 acres each, in Rawdon Township. The decision about the remainder was postponed until a surveyor's report had been submitted. Eight years later, on 28 March 1800, Panet made a new request for 1,200 acres, but it was turned down.

At the opening of the first session of the House of Assembly on 17 Dec. 1792, Panet took part in the noted debate on the choice of a speaker, which saw the first clash between French- and English-speaking members. He helped elect Jean-Antoine Panet*, a cousin, to the office, whereas his brother Pierre-Louis* voted against him. Panet was manifestly on familiar ground, indeed at home, in the assembly, where in addition to his brother and his cousin he found himself in company with his wife's brother-in-law Pierre Marcoux* (the husband of Marie-Anne Dunière), his cousin by marriage Pierre Guerout*, and his father-in-law Louis Dunière*. Panet had married his cousin Marguerite Dunière, daughter of Louis Dunière and Élisabeth Trefflé, *dit* Rottot, on 18 Nov. 1786. Surprisingly, the ceremony had been performed by Anglican minister David-François de Montmollin*. Then on 6 April 1787 the couple had had their union blessed by a Catholic priest in the cathedral of Notre-Dame at Quebec.

Panet was re-elected in 1796 and sat in the assembly until 4 June 1800. His political career subsequently suffered an eclipse, and he did not become member for Leinster again until 1809. This time he sat for only a short while, since Governor Sir James Henry Craig* dissolved the legislature on 1 March 1810.

From 1806 till 1834 Panet lived at Lachenaie, where he served as vendue master and auctioneer. During the War of 1812 he was active in the Blainville battalion of militia as captain and adjutant; he was promoted major on 1 Jan. 1818. That he was well known is evident from the numerous commissions he received. On 16 May 1817 he was named commissioner for the improvement of internal communications for Leinster County. On 28 June 1821 he became commissioner for the trial of small causes. That day he was also made justice of the peace for the district of Montreal, an appointment renewed in 1826 and 1828. Then on 22 June 1825 he was named census commissioner in Leinster riding. Panet was honoured at the Saint Jean-Baptiste day celebrations of 24 June 1834. The 16th toast at the fête paid him tribute, as one of the surviving members of the first assembly, noting that "having served his country in the house and in the field, [he] is devoting his final years to cultivating the soil that nourishes him."

Panet came back to live the last 12 or so years of his life at L'Assomption and he died there on 12 March 1846. At the time of his death he was a widower. He and his wife had had a son and three daughters, but only one daughter outlived him.

ROGER BARRETTE

ANQ-M, CE1-51, 27 juill. 1765; CE5-14, 15 mars 1846. ANQ-Q, CE1-1, 6 avril 1787; CE1-61, 18 nov. 1786. *La Minerve*, 16 mars 1846. *Quebec Gazette*, 31 May, 21 June, 20 Dec. 1792; 4 May, 19 Oct., 9 Nov. 1809; 22 May 1817; 23 April 1818; 20 April 1820. F.-J. Audet et Fabre Surveyer, *Les députés au premier Parl. du Bas-Canada*. Desjardins, *Guide parl*. Marcel Fournier, *Rawdon: 175 ans d'histoire* (Joliette, Qué., 1974). Christian Roy, *Histoire de L'Assomption* (L'Assomption, Qué., 1967). P.-G. Roy, *La famille Panet* (Lévis, Qué., 1906). F.-J. Audet et Édouard Fabre Surveyer, "Bonaventure Panet," *La Presse*, 17 sept. 1927: 61, 76. P.-G. Roy, "Le premier Parlement canadien," *BRH*, 1 (1895): 122.

PAPINEAU, JOSEPH, surveyor, notary, seigneurial agent, politician, and seigneur; b. 16 Oct. 1752 in Montreal, son of Joseph Papineau and Marie-Josephte Beaudry; d. there 8 July 1841.

Joseph Papineau's grandfather, Samuel Papineau*, *dit* Montigny, settled in New France in the late 17th century; after a military career he took up farming not far from Montreal. Joseph's father was also a farmer, but after several set-backs became a cooper, practising his craft in Montreal under difficult conditions. Brought up in modest circumstances where life was harsh and money hard to come by, young Joseph resolved to prove his worth, to become rich and powerful. This desire to succeed explains the determination with which he worked and his withdrawn and studious existence. His humble birth weighed heavily on his pride and youthful ambition. It is no exaggeration to say that his uncommon will-power gave the Papineau line its impetus and its character.

Papineau's father wanted him to follow in his footsteps and become a craftsman or a farmer, but when in 1758 the Sulpicians built a primary school, another direction opened up for him. At the end of his elementary studies in 1765, Papineau continued his education under Jean-Baptiste Curatteau*, the parish priest of Longue-Pointe (Montreal). His intelligence did not go unnoticed by the kindly and solicitous Curatteau, who, anticipating a bright future for him, persuaded his parents to send him to the Petit Séminaire de Québec in the autumn of 1767 so that he could complete his classical studies.

At Quebec, Papineau's enthusiasm never flagged. He took prize after prize and his incredible capacity for work won the admiration of his teachers and schoolmates. His successes brought him into close contact with the priests at the seminary; already they were keeping an eye on him as a brilliant young man who was serious, introverted, and yet highly gifted for philosophical speculation and mathematics. Papineau's development proceeded without break or crisis, and he presumably remained deeply marked by the religious and moral climate at the seminary. In that context his teachers surely would have had no difficulty in making him aware of the divine right of kings and the social values of the *ancien régime*.

Having no financial resources, Papineau went home in June 1771 after his studies finished. He found himself faced with a limited choice of careers: medicine, law, or surveying. In September he began to train as a surveyor with Jean De Lisle*, who also practised as a notary. Profiting from De Lisle's scientific erudition and extensive knowledge of geometry, he soon qualified himself. He received his surveyor's commission on 20 July 1773 and worked full time until 1775. His entry into the professional bourgeoisie signified that the Papineau family was beginning its rise.

As a surveyor Papineau revealed an unusual mind of a systematic bent. Equally demanding of himself as he was of others, he detested superficial, careless work, and he did not hesitate to redo whatever seemed imperfect to him. His professional qualities rapidly attracted the attention of the Sulpicians, who owned several seigneuries in the Montreal region. For two years Papineau was employed exclusively by them. He surveyed the boundaries of their seigneuries, making a number of plans, and checked the limits of various *censives* (seigneurial areas). The close relations he established with this important religious community enabled him to apply his knowledge of seigneurial matters and the seigneurial system and to build up a large practice around Montreal. Hardworking and thrifty, he had already bought some lots and buildings in the town itself.

Papineau was not satisfied, however. Surveying was time-consuming and entailed lengthy, difficult trips. The profession of notary had long attracted him and seemed more suited to his tastes and temperament. When French civil law gained recognition through the Quebec Act of 1774, Papineau was fully aware of the prospects in notarial work. He bound himself to article with De Lisle for five years beginning in 1775, although he did not abandon his activities as a surveyor. At the outbreak of war with the Americans in 1776, he interrupted his studies and devoted himself to the colony's defence. Given the task of carrying military dispatches to Governor Guy Carleton*, he showed himself worthy of trust and an ardent supporter of the monarchy and aristocratic values. He probably hoped to benefit from patronage in the near future but, despite his loyalty, he did not obtain any surveying contracts from the government and had to work almost exclusively for seigneurs and private individuals.

Papineau's career was, however, furthered by his marriage on 23 Aug. 1779 with Rosalie, daughter of François-Pierre Cherrier*. A former merchant who had become one of the most prominent notaries in the Richelieu region and a wealthy man, Cherrier had already acquired surgeon Jacques Larthigue and merchant Denis Viger* as sons-in-law. Papineau was thus entering a prosperous and influential family. His wife's dowry is evidence of the importance of this alliance and of the economic benefits Papineau derived from it.

On 18 July 1780 Papineau received a commission authorizing him to practise as notary throughout the province. Evidently he had substantial savings at his disposal, since shortly after his marriage he had bought his father's house and transformed it into a luxurious two-storey stone dwelling. Opening an office in it, he drew up his first deed on 5 Aug. 1780, the prelude to an exceptionally long and profitable career of more than 60 years which would see him prepare in excess of 5,000 instruments. His clients were drawn from an immense area that included Montreal and its suburbs, as well as the seigneuries of Saint-Hyacinthe, Île-Jésus, Saint-Sulpice, Mille-Îles, Lac-des-Deux-Montagnes, and Petite-Nation, and those along the Richelieu; they also came from all classes of society. His practice was divided into two distinct periods: a busy one from 1781 to 1803, and a quieter one from 1804 to 1841.

From the start Papineau served the Sulpicians of the Collège Saint-Raphaël (also called the Collège de Montréal) and a number of their *censitaires*, who consulted him about land sales and confirmation of title-deeds. His clientele grew rapidly, and he dealt increasingly with craftsmen in the town and farmers round about. From 1781 to 1788 he drew up an average of 147 acts annually. His office served as an observation post and provided an effective way of building up a network of influence.

This side of his professional activities led Papineau to an interest in public affairs. In November 1784 he joined the Canadian reform committee, which included both English- and French-speaking bourgeois members. He himself was instrumental in bringing together the Montreal and Quebec reform movements by helping to prepare a petition of 24 Nov. 1784, which was designed to gain the sympathy of the imperial authorities for the idea of instituting a house of assembly. Although Papineau had been educated within the framework of monarchical institutions and was attached to the values of the *ancien régime*, in this political debate he unhesitatingly sided with the bourgeoisie. He probably saw an assembly as the best means of protecting the rights of the French-speaking community. In addition, he likely wanted to maintain relations with the small, privileged group of Montreal merchants, whether French- or English-speaking. From 1787 his urban practice was growing and included merchants, builders, and land speculators.

In 1788, on behalf of the Séminaire de Québec, Papineau managed the seigneury of Île-Jésus and also that of Petite-Nation, which was not yet being developed. In the same year, the Sulpicians entrusted a number of administrative duties in their seigneuries to him. His efficiency guaranteed him these posts until early in the 19th century. It was as manager of the seigneury of Île-Jésus that Papineau distinguished himself particularly. Initially he was given considerable freedom of action by the seminary's bursar, who lived at Quebec, and in practice he assumed charge of development. He made the land grants, received fixed dues, kept an eye on property transfers so as to collect the *lods et ventes*, sold the wheat that was taken in as rent and as miller's fees, saw that the mills operated properly and were maintained. In addition to running the seigneury well, he radically changed its management. On the one hand he sought to rationalize production, for example by building a second mill in 1804 at his own expense to serve the *censitaires* better and sell wheat at Montreal and Quebec; on the other hand he worked to achieve a firmer control, for instance by increasing rents and re-instituting all the other seigneurial rights.

From his role as the agent of religious communities which were powers in the field of real estate, Papineau acquired economic advantages and means of influence. He also used his situation to broaden his scope as a notary and perfect his knowledge of seigneurial matters. As a result, in the period 1789–1803 his clientele increased by more than 40 per cent in the seigneuries of Île-Jésus, Lac-des-Deux-Montagnes, and Saint-Sulpice. Naturally he profited from the privileged means of gathering information that were provided by his multiple functions. As a notary, surveyor, and seigneurial agent who kept in constant touch with influential landowners and merchants and was in a position to interact with the seigneurial gentry, the clergy, and the bourgeoisie, Papineau was better situated than others to benefit from the seigneurial régime and its mode of operation. In the late 18th century, when there was a sizeable increase in the number of *censitaires* and the real estate market was flourishing, he was well placed to conduct numerous property transactions in both town and country.

At the outset, the sums Papineau invested were relatively small (less than 2,000 *livres* before 1788), but his later efforts were impressive. Between 1788 and 1803 he made land purchases worth more than 50,000 *livres*. He thus gained possession of an estate that was his pride and joy: a few lots and houses in Montreal itself, several parcels of land in the *faubourg* Sainte-Marie, and a group of properties in Saint-Martin (Laval). More than 3,000 *livres* was put out in interest-bearing loans. Despite the scale of his business dealings, Papineau continued lending small sums to farmers, craftsmen, and labourers.

While engaged in these varied occupations, Papineau was also following political life closely. The advent in 1791 of a constitutional régime with a house of assembly prompted him to enter politics. To learn how the new system worked he had to be initiated into a whole set of concepts and procedures. His interest aroused by the theorists of parliamentary government, he acquired a knowledge of English writers such as John Locke and Sir William Blackstone, whom he read and commented upon in minute detail. With great enthusiasm, he studied Burlamaqui's volume on natural law and the works of a good many French *philosophes*, in particular Bonnot de Mably, Bernardin de Saint-Pierre, Montesquieu, Voltaire, and Rousseau. Papineau discovered the idea of the sovereignty of the people and quickly came to admire British institutions. However, democracy found no favour in his eyes, and still less republicanism. Having broken with the absolutist tradition and become imbued with a certain liberalism, he remained a moderate monarchist. For him, the ideal political model was to be found in the British constitutional monarchy, which had maintained a balance between aristocratic and bourgeois values while avoiding the extreme radicalism and excessive liberty of revolutionary France. Again, reading the 18th-century *philosophes* led Papineau to distance himself from religious observances, despite the remorse that he felt with regard to his mother and his wife, who were both devout. Although he was no longer drawn to religion, he did not give up Catholicism until the 1810s, and he would return to it at the end of his life.

Papineau had a significant though unspectacular career in politics. He easily gained election to the House of Assembly for Montreal riding in 1792 through the backing of various Canadian and British merchants. In 1796 he won by acclamation in Montreal East. To have more time for his personal affairs he planned not to run in the July 1800 elections. But the voters would not hear of it and Papineau was again returned for Montreal, against his will. Political life left him dissatisfied – he saw it as a duty. Absorbed in his professional career, he was often absent from the assembly. In 1801, for example, he took no part in the debate on the creation of the Royal Institution for the Advancement of Learning [*see* Joseph Langley Mills*]. However, he knew how to intervene at the right moment. For instance, in 1793, at the time of the debate on the language to be used in legislation and in the deliberations of the assembly – where only a third of the members were English-speaking – Papineau fought with all his might against a motion that its proceedings be recorded in English alone. Thanks to his efforts and those of others, the house decided to have proceedings recorded in either French or English, according to whether they concerned French civil law or English criminal law. On less important matters he split his votes between the British and the Canadian groups. Clearly in this period Papineau was gathering a working knowledge of the parliamentary system and did not yet fully identify himself as an opponent of the English-speaking bourgeoisie.

Since he had acquired some part of the seigneury of Petite-Nation from the Séminaire de Québec in 1801 in lieu of fees, and the rest by purchase two years later, Papineau felt less and less interested in sitting in the assembly and did not run in the 1804 election. His departure from the political scene came at a time when the French-speaking professional bourgeoisie was becoming aware of belonging to a Canadian nation and eager to impose its views and its political leadership. A merciless struggle had begun between the Canadian party and the English-speaking merchants and officials who were challenging traditional institutions and using political machinery in order to make themselves the dominant class. This competition to control political institutions made it impossible for the assembly to function properly.

It was in this heady atmosphere that Papineau returned to active politics late in 1809 at the request of certain voters in Montreal East. Although he disapproved of the tack taken by some members from the Quebec region, he was determined to find a solution to the political crisis that was perturbing the assembly. In 1810 the imprisonment of Pierre-Stanislas Bédard*, leader of the Canadian party, made his task even more difficult. The French-speaking members demanded Bédard's release, so that he could take his seat in the house again. Papineau, with the backing of his son Louis-Joseph*, who had also been elected in 1809, demanded an inquiry into Governor Sir James Henry Craig*'s principal actions. Not satisfied with the answers he received, he pleaded Bédard's case with Craig, but in vain.

Nevertheless the threat of war with the United States and the arrival of a new governor known for his conciliatory views, Sir George Prevost*, had the effect of clearing the political atmosphere. The end of the parliamentary crisis hastened the end of Bédard's leadership and opened the way for the ambitious Louis-Joseph Papineau. He was elected speaker of the house in 1815 and, with his father's blessing, asserted himself more and more as the new leader of the Canadians. He was the designated heir, the bearer of the family's hopes in the political arena. At the same period another son, Denis-Benjamin*, was managing the seigneury of Petite-Nation and André-Augustin was a notary and merchant in Saint-Hyacinthe, where their sister Marie-Rosalie, who would marry the seigneur Jean Dessaulles* in 1816, was living. Toussaint-Victor was studying at the Petit Séminaire de Montréal and intended to enter the priesthood. The family's rise in society was more and more a collective endeavour to which its members contributed according to their talents. In the momentum the strong carried along the weak, and all profited from their father's success and his many connections. Papineau was close enough to his children to receive their confidences, but reserved enough to prevent rivalries and extremes of enthusiasm. Aware of his responsibilities, he had ensured the future of his descendants, who would become increasingly clannish. His financial success and his influence had determined the image of a family that would leave its mark on the social and political destiny of Lower Canada and Quebec for more than a century.

In 1814, when his electoral mandate came to an end, Papineau retired for good from the political scene and concentrated on administering Petite-Nation. There were already some 30 settlers living on it, and two mills had been built along the river of that name. A precise and meticulous man, Papineau had had a number of pieces of land surveyed and a plan made of the territory that was occupied. For several years the seigneurial forest had been exploited to keep a sizeable lumber business supplied. Upholding the seigneur's rights remained his main concern, however. The drafting of contracts for land grants, the updating of charges payable when property changed hands, and the regular collection of seigneurial dues were designed to obtain the maximum from the *censitaires* and to ensure sound management of the property. From the outset Papineau's main aims were to establish his rights firmly and to lay the bases for an efficient administration, in order to make himself an all-powerful seigneur. Since he derived his income from rents, he was in the clearly defined class situation of a man appropriating part of the product of the peasants' work through the system of seigneurial servitude. He was still putting money into land and he became a major speculator in the *faubourg* Sainte-Marie and at Saint-Martin. His method of building up his immense fortune, essentially in land, was a traditional one. In the end, his actions had enabled him to realize his aristocratic aspirations.

Papineau sold Petite-Nation to his son Louis-Joseph in 1817 for £500 and then devoted himself to his profession. He continued none the less to play a certain role in the seigneury's management, lavishing advice in his letters to Denis-Benjamin, who had remained in charge of development. Being 65, he also reduced his dealings in real estate and began to liquidate his assets. Papineau remained active professionally, however; in the last 24 years of his life he drew up at least 1,000 instruments. Considered to have reached the top in the notarial profession, he was increasingly drawn into complicated cases concerning tangled estates that belonged to families of the bourgeoisie and the seigneurial gentry. If a matter seemed involved, his judgement and discernment were called upon. He continued to work as a surveyor, laying out several roads and surveying several seigneuries in the district of Montreal.

Papineau also followed political events closely. The radicalization of the French-speaking assemblymen in the 1830s worried him. He did not approve of the stands taken by his son, who talked of democracy, a republican constitution, the sovereignty of the people, emancipation of the state, an educational system in the hands of the laity, and the separation of church and state. An admirer of British institutions, Papineau maintained his faith in the imperial government and became a supporter of constitutional reform, for in his view it was the English-speaking minority that threatened the survival of the French-speaking community. During the 1837–38 rebellions, despite his being Louis-Joseph's father, he was not disturbed by the British authorities. In 1838, when he was 86, he went to Saratoga (Schuylerville), N.Y., where his son had taken refuge after the defeat of 1837. He advised him to sell Petite-Nation quickly lest the government confiscate his property.

In his old age Papineau, who had already provided for all his children, was not without resources. The money owed him, 2,281 *livres*, was a substantial but fairly usual sum for the end of a career. His personal and real property was valued at £1,796. In his library there were more than 200 volumes on diverse subjects: tomes on English and French law stood side by side with the complete works of Rousseau, Raynal, and Voltaire, and books on herbal medicine, forging and milling, the perfect merchant, and mathematical puzzles.

With his health undermined by a serious illness, borne without complaint, and his spirit burdened by the painful events of 1837–38, Papineau turned to religion. Shortly before his death on 8 July 1841 he met Ignace Bourget*, the bishop of Montreal, and returned to Catholicism.

Joseph Papineau represented the first generation of a family typical of certain contemporary élite groups in its rise in society, its wealth, and the thrust of its political activity and choices. Through his qualities and personal gifts, his connections and the backing they brought him, he gave the impetus to its social ascendancy and laid the foundations of its fortune. His dazzling career and his manifold occupations, however, make it difficult to categorize him. By his culture Papineau was a man of the early 19th century, responsive to aspects of the Enlightenment and living in an intellectual and political atmosphere that was eroding the old structures. On the other hand, as the owner of a seigneury, and a defender of seigneurial rights and a type of management traditional among the seigneurial gentry, he also belonged to the past. He stood at a crossroads in this changing colonial society.

RICHARD CHABOT

The reports of surveys by Joseph Papineau, written between 1773 and 1775, are at ANQ-M, CA1-71, and his minute-book, containing 5,564 instruments passed between 1780 and 1841, is at ANQ-M, CN1-313.

ANQ-M, CE1-51, 16 oct. 1752, 8 juill. 1841; CE2-12, 23 août 1779; CN1-16, 18–19, 22 sept. 1800; 22 mai 1809; 18 août 1813; 26 oct. 1814; 7 mars, 5 avril, 24 juill. 1815; CN1-74, 23 juill. 1798; CN1-108, 15 sept. 1748, 16 juill. 1753; CN1-128, 7 oct. 1796; CN1-134, 8, 29 juill. 1822; 7 janv., 24, 28 oct. 1825; CN1-158, 18 oct. 1777, 13 avril 1779; CN1-194, 23 nov. 1801; 12 janv., 23 déc. 1803; 13 sept. 1804; 1er juin 1805; 4 août 1806; 30 oct. 1807; 3 mars, 17 oct. 1808; 15, 18, 24 févr., 8, 21 mars, 6, 14, 17 avril, 17 juin, 19 août 1809; 24 avril, 10, 29 mai, 7, 30 juin, 18, 20 oct., 5 déc. 1810; 3 avril, 7 juill., 18 août, 15 oct. 1811; 16 juill. 1814; 7 août 1815; 1er, 12 févr. 1816; 7 juill., 18 nov. 1817; 17 oct. 1818; CN1-310, 25 déc. 1841; CN1-317, 10 oct. 1818; CN1-385, 12–13 nov. 1829; 18 sept., 4, 9, 20 oct., 15 nov. 1830; 5 avril 1831; 16 avril, 25 mai 1832; 13 janv. 1835; 19 janv. 1838; 22 nov. 1839; 2 juill. 1840. ASQ, C 36; C 37; Polygraphie, VI, no.18; XXVII, no.76; S, 2–3; Séminaire, 40, nos.22, 22B–D, 22F–P; 82, nos.2–3, 6, 13, 13C, 16C, 16E–F, 16H–M; 120, nos.401, 407–9, 426; 121, nos.395–96, 398–402; 122, nos.73, 76, 139–41, 192, 500; SME, 17 mars, 21 avril 1788; 21 avril 1793; 26 mars 1794; 22 oct., 9 déc. 1798; 4 mai 1801; 27 juin 1802. ASSM, 8, A, carton 28; 9. PAC, MG 24, B2: 6–25, 78–81, 86–89, 178–81, 212–14, 239, 280–83, 288–90, 293–94, 303–5, 328–31, 433–37, 506–13, 528–31, 550–53, 558–61, 945–47, 1065–68, 1190–93, 1354–57, 1369–72, 1381–82, 1435–38, 1553–56, 1610–13, 1774–77, 2009–16, 2018–21, 2041–44, 2054–57, 2066–69, 3018–20, 3050–57, 3073–79, 3084–86, 3091–94, 3115–22, 3145–48, 3157–60, 3165–68, 3183–90, 3194–97, 3345–48, 3371–74, 3395–400, 3413–16, 3465–68, 3503–6, 3519–21, 3548–51, 3576–79, 5305–9, 5329–31, 5340–42, 5369, 5486, 5840–43, 6821–24; L3, 37, 24 April 1783; 39, 13 Sept. 1796; 44, 9 June 1787; 48, 26 Nov. 1787; MG 30, D1, 23: 775–819; RG 1, E3, 101: 55–58; RG 4, B8: 98–99; RG 68, General index, 1651–1841. Joseph Papineau, "Correspondance de Joseph Papineau (1793–1840)," Fernand Ouellet, édit., ANQ *Rapport*, 1951–53: 160–300. L.-O. David, *Biographies et portraits* (Montréal, 1876), 1–19. Desjardins, *Guide parl.* Claude Baribeau, *La seigneurie de la Petite-Nation, 1801–1854; le rôle économique et social du seigneur* (Hull, Qué., 1983), 21–27, 61–73, 81–83. L.-O. David, *Les deux Papineau* (Montréal, 1896), 5–43. Gérard Parizeau, *La société canadienne-française au XIXe siècle: essais sur le milieu* (Montréal, 1975), 383–413. Rumilly, *Papineau et son temps.* [R.] C. Harris, "Of poverty and helplessness in Petite-Nation," *CHR*, 52 (1971): 23–50. Fernand Ouellet, "Joseph Papineau et le Régime parlementaire (1791)," *BRH*, 61 (1955): 71–77. D.-B. Papineau, "Samuel Papineau," *BRH*, 39 (1933): 331–39.

PAQUIN, JACQUES, Roman Catholic priest and author; b. 9 Sept. 1791 in Deschambault, Lower Canada, son of Paul Paquin, a farmer, and Marguerite Marcot; d. 7 Dec. 1847 in Saint-Eustache, Lower Canada.

Jacques Paquin spent his childhood in a family of well-to-do farmers. His father served as the sacristan at the local church, and his mother was noted for her piety and charity. As a boy he probably identified with his parents and even then showed signs of an ardent spirit and a burning faith. He received his early education at the Latin school held in the presbytery by the parish priest Charles-Denis Dénéchaud. His precocious intelligence attracted the kindly attentions of Dénéchaud, who was already fostering his aspirations to a priestly vocation.

In 1805 Paquin made his desire to become a priest

known to his parents, and, far from standing in his way, they sent him to study at the Petit Séminaire de Québec. It was probably the appointment of his uncle, Abbé Jean-Baptiste Paquin, as director of the Séminaire de Nicolet in October 1808 that prompted him to enrol in this institution, where he finished his classical studies in 1813. That year Bishop Joseph-Octave Plessis* of Quebec named him to the Odanak mission and the parish of Saint-François-du-Lac as assistant to the priest, François Ciquard*. While pursuing theology on his own, Paquin began learning the Abenaki language. Of a generous and enthusiastic nature, he took the trouble to teach young Indians to read and write. After he had spent several months studying theology at the Grand Séminaire de Québec, Plessis conferred the priesthood upon him on 24 Sept. 1814 and named him assistant priest of the parish of Sainte-Anne at Varennes. The following summer he replaced the curé of Saint-Antoine-de-Padoue at Baie-du-Febvre (Baieville), Charles-Vincent FOURNIER, who was to accompany Plessis on a pastoral visit.

In September 1815 Plessis named Paquin to a parish he knew well, Saint-François-du-Lac, and to its mission of Odanak. Paquin, who had an exceptional capacity for work, devoted a great deal of time to his parish. But he neglected ministry to the Abenakis, who complained of his frequent absence from the mission. He even caused himself difficulties with them by speaking in strong terms, rarely using moderation and finesse. In truth, he was no longer happy at this place, and in 1817 he expressed a desire to be relieved of his post. Four years later Plessis responded to his wish and put him in charge of the parish of Saint-Eustache.

From the very first, Paquin involved himself in its administration. He was anxious to set its finances in order and make improvements to the church. In 1823, for example, he had one of the church towers taken down and requested that it be replaced by a portal and two towers topped by steeples with double open belfries. As for financial arrangements, he required his churchwardens to submit their accounts regularly. He was attentive in spiritual matters too, making himself available at any time for confession, baptism, or visits to the sick. He taught catechism to the children, devoted himself to the poor, and added splendour to church ceremonies. He also kept a close watch on his own interests. In 1829, for example, when the tithe received in grain decreased, he demanded that it also be paid in potatoes. He stuck to his own view with the same stubbornness in defending the parish boundaries.

Under Paquin's guidance parochial administration became more efficient and spiritual life more intense. In the eyes of Bishop Jean-Jacques LARTIGUE, the archbishop of Quebec's auxiliary in Montreal, Paquin was proving a conscientious pastor with the ardour of faith and the soul of a true priest. Consequently he proposed him for the post of archpriest of the Lac-des-Deux-Montagnes region. Paquin's parishioners, on the other hand, had mixed feelings about his conduct. Admittedly he was devoted, zealous, and assiduous, dividing his efforts between church and presbytery, but at the same time his strictness in moral matters, his tendency to domineer, and his ideological intransigence were not appreciated.

Certainly Paquin kept clear of the liberal and lay movement in his parish. In 1825 he refused to allow some of the parishioners to interfere in school issues, and he persuaded most of the people to build a school which would be administered by the *fabrique* and be under his control. But after passage in 1829 of the bill encouraging the establishment of schools that would be run by trustees, Paquin felt more and more threatened by certain liberals in his parish who wanted to set up schools that would foster national feeling. To counter this movement, he succeeded, with difficulty, in getting himself elected a trustee. In 1830 he undertook to build a convent. He aimed, then, at having a supervisory control of primary education in the parish.

When in 1831 he had to come to terms with the *fabriques* act designed to limit the influence of curés in parochial administration [*see* Louis Bourdages*], Paquin adopted an equally firm policy. He never allowed his parishioners to meddle in the affairs of the *fabrique*. Realizing that the church was in danger, he brought together some local priests to take concerted action against liberal French Canadian laymen, and he proposed founding a church newspaper as a means of such action. Determined and influential, Paquin even wanted Bishop Lartigue to call a general assembly of the clergy at Montreal or Trois-Rivières to consider ways of combatting the influence of the liberals.

Paquin also opposed the stirrings of nationalism. He felt threatened by the liberals' protest, fearing the loss of his privileges. Out of concern for law and order, he refused to associate with a movement that professed belief in the sovereignty of the people and ultimately planned to overthrow the government. Beginning in 1830 he frequently denounced the Patriote organizations in his parish as bent on making trouble. After the 1834 elections he declined to celebrate a thanksgiving mass to mark the Patriotes' victory. In 1837 he adopted an even firmer attitude towards the Patriote movement. Like a number of his colleagues in the Montreal region, he opposed armed revolt and rejected anything but a return to the values of the *ancien régime*. His attitudes are revealed in his strong opposition to the circulation of a work by Hugues-Félicité-Robert de La Mennais, *Paroles d'un croyant*, published in Paris in 1834.

Following Lartigue's instructions, Paquin fearlessly read the bishop's pastoral letter of 24 Oct. 1837 from the pulpit, despite intimation of reprisals from the Patriotes in his parish. A few days before the battle at Saint-Eustache on 14 December, the Patriote leaders in Deux-Montagnes County, Amury GIROD and Jean-Olivier CHÉNIER, met with him at the presbytery and tried in vain to persuade him to change sides. He remained hostile to the rebellion, threats of death and imprisonment notwithstanding. On the eve of the battle he fled with the assistant priest François-Xavier Desève to his farm near by. In 1838, after the pillage and destruction of Saint-Eustache, he published a *Journal historique des événemens arrivés à Saint-Eustache*, in which he pointed out that few of his parishioners had taken part in the rebellion and that most of its leaders lived outside the parish. He hoped in this way to obtain compensation from the government in order to rebuild his church, which had been destroyed in the battle.

After the failure of the uprisings of 1837 and 1838, Paquin divided his time between study and administration. He owned three pieces of land, one of them a meadow. He had a large enough income from what he sold or from the rental of his acreage to live comfortably, to complete several changes making his presbytery more attractive, and to improve his farm. On occasion he lent grain or money to parishioners. In April 1841, however, Bishop Ignace Bourget* was forced to admonish him severely for neglecting the cemetery and the ruins of the former church, for letting the choirboys play, laugh, and jostle during services, and for preaching too infrequently. Bourget asked him to fulfil his duty to his parish, which, he said, "has already been sufficiently afflicted in the temporal realm without suffering spiritual affliction." That year Paquin rebuilt the convent, which had burned down during the battle, and he also planned to invite the Congregation of Notre-Dame to supply teachers.

In 1843 Bourget gave Paquin permission to pursue his research for a history of the church by making a tour of the dioceses of Montreal and Quebec. He had begun this project around 1830 as a testimony to the church's great works and a reply to those challenging it. In 1846 he was expecting to publish the result of his efforts. A year later he put a prospectus in *Mélanges religieux* announcing the imminent publication of his book, but it never saw the light of day. Paquin died on 7 December of that year, after an acutely painful illness.

RICHARD CHABOT

Jacques Paquin is the author of the pamphlet *Journal historique des événemens arrivés à Saint-Eustache, pendant la rébellion du comté du lac des Deux Montagnes, depuis les soulèvemens commencés à la fin de novembre, jusqu'au moment où la tranquillité fut parfaitement rétablie* (Montréal, 1838) and of the manuscript "Mémoire sur l'Église du Canada," at PAC, MG 24, J15.

ACAM, 420.051; 901.021, 831-9; RLB, I: 119, 153; II: 373, 662; III: 615–16; IV: 22, 68; RLL, I: 151; II: 75, 151, 224, 292; III: 12, 124, 153; IV: 19, 33, 396; V: 221; VI: 106, 137, 254, 268; VII: 52, 291, 332, 402, 628. ANQ-M, CE6-11, 13 déc. 1847; CN1-271, 10 déc. 1843; 8 juill., 9 déc. 1846; CN1-326, 22 sept. 1823. ANQ-Q, CE1-25, 9 sept. 1791. AP, Saint-Eustache, Cahiers des recettes et dépenses de la fabrique, 1802–62. Arch. de l'évêché de Nicolet (Nicolet, Qué.), Cartable Saint-François-du-Lac, I, 1813–21. Arch. du diocèse de Saint-Jean-de-Québec (Longueuil, Qué.), 6A/52. ASN, AP-G, L.-É. Bois, G, 1: 428–30; 3: 121, 158; 10: 62. T.-M. Charland, *Histoire des Abénakis d'Odanak (1675–1937)* (Montréal, 1964); *Histoire de Saint-François-du-Lac* (Ottawa, 1942); "Les 'Mémoires sur l'Église du Canada' de l'abbé Jacques Paquin," CCHA *Rapport*, 2 (1934–35): 51–64. C.-H. Grignon, "La vie et l'œuvre du curé Paquin," *Cahiers d'hist. de Deux-Montagnes* (Saint-Eustache, Qué.), été 1978: 61–82. L.-J. Rodrigue, "Messire Jacques Paquin, curé de Saint-Eustache de la Rivière-du-Chêne (1821–1847)," CCHA *Rapport*, 31 (1964): 73–83.

PARENT, LOUIS-FRANÇOIS, Roman Catholic priest; b. 4 March 1778 at Quebec, son of Charles Parent and Charlotte-Cécile Rouillard; d. 1 June 1850 in Repentigny, Lower Canada.

The son of a baker in Upper Town Quebec, Louis-François Parent studied at the Petit Séminaire de Québec from 1789 to 1798. He then taught there while pursuing theology at the Grand Séminaire. He was not as gifted as his fellow-student Joseph SIGNAY, the future archbishop of Quebec. Parent was ordained on 19 Dec. 1801, and gained his early pastoral experience as curate in the parishes of Notre-Dame-de-Liesse at Rivière-Ouelle (1801–2), Saint-Joseph in the Beauce (1802–3), Immaculée-Conception at Trois-Rivières (1803–5), and Sainte-Famille at Boucherville (1805–6). Afterwards he was sent to Acadia, where he ministered for three years to the missions of Richibouctou (Richibucto-Village), Bouctouche (Bouctouche), and Gédaïc (Grande-Digue) in New Brunswick. His pastoral decisions there gave evidence of considerable discernment. He seems, however, to have suffered from being the only priest amongst a docile and faithful people scattered along the coast. He expressed the desire to be recalled. Consequently, in the autumn of 1809 Bishop Joseph-Octave Plessis* of Quebec named him curé of the parish of Saint-Henri-de-Mascouche (at Mascouche).

Parent at this time began to lend money at the legal interest rate of six per cent repayable in the form of life annuities. But his conduct in the end displeased the majority of his parishioners, who in the summer of 1831 presented a petition to obtain his resignation. The archbishop of Quebec, Bernard-Claude Panet*, probably convinced that the parishioners' allegations were valid, asked Parent to resign, but prohibited him from collecting during his retirement the one-third of the annual tithes from his former parish to which he would normally have been entitled. His savings, said the archbishop, ensured him a decent livelihood. Parent was slow in leaving the parish. Panet had to threaten a public inquiry into his conduct, even though he was not anxious to hold one. Parent clung to his parish charge, and in November the archbishop was forced to strip him of his priestly powers.

In September 1832, probably through his former classmate Bishop Signay, Parent secured the post of curé in the parish of Purification-de-la-Bienheureuse-Vierge-Marie at Repentigny. Three years later Signay conferred the title of archpriest upon him. But Parent's relations with his parishioners once more deteriorated. On 19 Sept. 1837 some 50 of them humbly addressed a petition to Bishop Jean-Jacques LARTIGUE of Montreal denouncing his priest's conduct on 14 counts. They accused him of simony, repeated lapses from his pastoral duties, and discrimination against certain parishioners. Parent told Lartigue that the document came from a coterie motivated by political aims, but he could find only one witness, the chief cantor, to refute the accusations.

Lartigue had more pressing worries in the autumn of 1837 and wanted to hush the matter up. But he was aware of Parent's stinginess and knew that this failing made him unbearable. The next spring he invited him either to leave his post and retire or to undergo a public inquiry into the complaints against him. Parent rejected both solutions. He even considered that he owned his parish charge. Archbishop Signay succeeded in getting a promise from him to retire voluntarily to Trois-Rivières the next year, but Parent failed to do so. In the summer of 1839 Parent provoked a fresh outcry among his parishioners when he manœuvred a minority of his churchwardens into letting work proceed on the building of a new church tower and on repairs to the windows, which were considered ill-timed.

Spiritual and religious life in Repentigny, while evincing no exceptional fervour, does not seem to have suffered much from these tensions: 80 per cent of the people took Easter communion in 1838 and 88 per cent in 1841. But complaints concerning Parent's avarice and unavailability continued to reach the new bishop of Montreal, Ignace Bourget*, who called upon him to resign in April 1845. Once more Parent promised to do so the following year. Faced with this delaying tactic, Bourget came to investigate, and on 5 September he relieved Parent of his parish charge. During the time he had been in office, the thrifty old priest had let the buildings in his care deteriorate completely, and he had contrived to obtain wood and material by schemes that his neighbour and successor, François Labelle, considered dubious.

Parent's death, which occurred at Repentigny on 1 June 1850, gave rise to a noted controversy. In his will he left a net estate of nearly £20,000, and he named Archbishop Signay his residuary legatee. The Séminaire de Nicolet was to receive a perpetual annuity of £198. Parent left nothing to the diocese of Montreal, although he had been in charge of two quite lucrative parishes in it. The episcopal corporation of Quebec inherited about £11,000, which brought a yearly income of £591. The Montreal clergy consequently began to grumble about the unfairness shown by the old man, who had hung on to his money to the very end and who now was enabling the diocese of Quebec to pay off the crushing debt incurred in putting up the new episcopal palace.

Many of Parent's relatives were patently disappointed at having been ignored. Young Quebec architect Joseph-Pierre-Michel Lecourt, the priest's nephew, even sent a petition to various important figures in London to get the episcopal corporation's legal right to receive estates revoked. This action, which was designed to bring pressure upon the archbishop of Quebec, created a certain stir in the newspapers in the spring of 1852. The *Montreal Witness* and the Toronto *Globe* supported Lecourt, claiming there had been undue pressure from the Catholic archbishop. In their comments on the matter other papers in Quebec and Montreal concluded that the terms of Parent's will ought to be respected.

Parent was thus unhappily famous after his death. For more than three decades he had used his savings and income to make money. He was probably one of the richest Catholic parish priests in the 19th century, but he was also one of the least edifying.

LOUIS ROUSSEAU

AAQ, 12 A, L: f.160; 210 A, XIV: 463; 40 CA, I: 21–25; 303 CD, I: 105; 516 CD, I: 22; 311 CN, V; 26 CP, VII: 73; Sér.E, III. ACAM, 350.102, 841-5; 355.104, 837-4, -5, -7, 839-1, -6, 845-2, 846-2, 850-6; RLB, I: 62–63; III: 533–34; IV: 30, 57. ANQ-M, CE5-16, 5 juin 1850. ANQ-Q, CE1-1, 5 mars 1778. *Mélanges religieux*, 2 avril 1852. Allaire, *Dictionnaire*, vol.1. Caron, "Inv. de la corr. de Mgr Panet," ANQ *Rapport*, 1935–36: 188, 194–95, 200, 217; "Inv. de la corr. de Mgr Plessis," 1932–33: 13, 32; "Inv. de la corr. de Mgr Signay," 1936–37: 329. Desrosiers, "Inv. de la corr. de Mgr Lartigue," ANQ *Rapport*, 1942–43: 118; 1945–46: 59, 76. P.-G. Roy, *Fils de Québec*, 2: 189–91. Douville, *Hist. du collège-séminaire de Nicolet*. Henri Têtu, *Histoire du palais épiscopal de Québec* (Québec, 1896), 177–79.

PAREPOINT. *See* PIERPOINT

PARKER, SNOW, mariner, businessman, politician, militia officer, judge, and JP; b. 16 May 1760 in Yarmouth, Mass., eldest child of Benjamin Parker and Mary Snow; m. 17 July 1780 Martha Knowles in Liverpool, N.S., and they had ten children; d. there 18 Sept. 1843.

Snow Parker's father, a mariner and fish merchant, came to Liverpool in the early years of the settlement. Though most if not all of his five sons also earned their living from the sea, it was Snow who laid the basis for a spectacularly successful career in trading, shipbuilding, and privateering which was to make him a wealthy man.

Parker came to manhood in the shadow of the American revolution, when rebel privateers cruised in Nova Scotian waters and sometimes raided coastal settlements. He was only 18 when the ship on which he was travelling from Halifax to Liverpool was intercepted by a privateer. Taken prisoner, he was carried to Port Mouton and then released after paying a ransom. This episode was recorded in the diary of a prominent Liverpool merchant and member of the House of Assembly, Simeon Perkins*, who from then until his diary stopped in April 1812 frequently recorded Parker's activities.

Parker began his business life as a coastal trader, often carrying freight for older, established merchants such as Perkins. In May 1783 Parker and his brother Benjamin purchased from the Liverpool merchant Benajah Collins his house, fish lots, stores, wharfs, and buildings for £550. The brothers then played a vigorous part in the salmon and mackerel fishery off Newfoundland, taking many hundreds of barrels and selling them not only to local merchants but also in American ports. Snow Parker made his start in the lucrative West Indies trade in September 1788 when he and co-owners Joseph Barss and Nathan Tupper launched the *Union*, a 100-ton brigantine of which he was also captain. Shipbuilding became an important part of his operations. By 1826, with the launching of the 450-ton *Mary Parker*, he was able to claim that he had built 46 vessels. These ships traded along Nova Scotia's coast, to American ports on the Atlantic and on the Gulf of Mexico, in the West Indies, and even to Europe. Others fished off Newfoundland.

It was those vessels which were built or sailed as privateers, however, that made Parker's fortune. The outbreak of war with France in 1793 and with the United States in 1812 had raised once again both the spectre of privateering and the prospect of making a great deal of money from financing privateers. Liverpool was the centre of privateering activity in Nova Scotia between 1793 and 1815, and Snow Parker was its leading exponent. He built, owned, financed, and acted as agent for several privateers, but did not sail them himself. The cargo of captured vessels could be speedily condemned in the Vice-Admiralty Court at Halifax, acquired cheaply at auction, and then retailed at a handsome profit. Moreover, the prizes themselves could be purchased, refitted, and then sent out as privateers or trading vessels.

Parker was an outstanding entrepreneur of the early 1800s, if only because of the number and variety of his activities. Unlike land-based merchants such as Perkins and Collins, whose merchandise he sometimes carried in his vessels, Parker was not simply a trader but also a master mariner. Like them, he was both a shipbuilder and – more important – a privateersman. In the heyday of privateering Parker was reputed to be the richest man in Liverpool. His fortune declined with the years, however, so that at the time of his death he was apparently worth no more than £1,500.

In June 1798 Parker had received his introduction to political life when he accompanied Perkins to an opening of the legislature and dined with Richard John Uniacke* who, as attorney general and advocate general of the Vice-Admiralty Court, was able to help those hoping to profit from privateering. When Perkins's successor as representative of Queens County, James Taylor, died in January 1801, Parker ran in the by-election held in March and won by acclamation. "Mr. Parker," wrote Perkins in his diary, "gave the Freeholders Plenty of wine & Spirits, with a Cold Collation. . . . The Business was very decently performed." Parker represented Queens County continuously for some 25 years, declining to stand only in 1826, when he was succeeded by John Barss*.

In May 1797 Parker had become a captain in the Queens County militia. He was commissioned judge of the Inferior Court of Common Pleas of Queens County in May 1810, and in June 1811 a trustee of the grammar school about to be erected in Liverpool. Parker also held six commissions as justice of the peace, the first granted in June 1810, the last in December 1841, when he was over 80.

J. B. CAHILL

PANS, Places, Liverpool, R. J. Long, "Annals of Liverpool and Queens County, 1760 to 1867" (mfm.); RG 1, 172: f.57; 173: ff.34, 40–41, 75; 175: f.204. Simeon Perkins, *The diary of Simeon Perkins . . .*, ed. H. A. Innis *et al.* (5v., Toronto, 1948–78). *Novascotian*, 16 Oct. 1843. *Epitaphs from the old cemeteries of Liverpool, Nova Scotia*, comp. Charles Warman (Boston, [1910]), 56–60. *Legislative Assembly of N.S.* (Elliott). *Liverpool privateering, 1756–1815*, comp. J. E. Mullins, ed. F. S. Morton (Liverpool, N.S., 1936), 25 *et seq.* J. F. More, *The history of Queens County, N.S.* (Halifax, 1873; repr. Belleville, Ont., 1972), 203.

PARKIN, EDWARD, priest of the Church of England, office holder, and teacher; b. 6 Feb. 1791 in Otley (West Yorkshire), England; m. 15 Sept. 1814 Sarah Cullen, and they had at least seven children; d. 30 Jan. 1844 in Fiddington (Market Lavington), England.

The son of a clergyman, Edward Parkin was ordained a deacon in the Church of England in May 1814 and a priest on 22 December. He taught school until a publication of the Society for the Propagation of the Gospel, outlining the spiritual needs of the colonies, induced him to apply for service in the Canadas. Accepted, he was sent to Quebec, where he arrived on 3 Sept. 1819 with his wife and two children.

On 8 October Parkin was licensed by Bishop Jacob Mountain* to minister at Chambly. The previous August a meeting of British residents there, guided by the Reverend Brooke Bridges Stevens*, had decided to build an Anglican church. Parkin and five lay leaders, notably Samuel Hatt, undertook the execution of the project. A contract was signed with François Valade in February 1820 for construction of a stone church with projecting chancel and graceful spire, and land for it was granted by the administrator of the colony, Sir Peregrine Maitland*. Parkin preached at the laying of the cornerstone on 11 May and barely six months later led the congregation in prayer at the first service in St Stephen's Church. The parish was erected civilly, with Parkin as rector, on 30 Sept. 1823. Parkin was also chaplain to the garrison at Fort Chambly and ministered to surrounding settlements. At Yamaska Mountain (Abbottsford) he encouraged the building of a church and served the congregation until the arrival of the missionary William Abbott in 1824.

Parkin had brought with him to Lower Canada a penchant for education, both general and religious. Either shortly before leaving England or soon after arriving at Chambly, he had had published in London *Ten sermons doctrinal and practical*; he wanted the profits, if any, to be applied to the construction of St Stephen's. He organized school classes in Yamaska Mountain and Rougemont as well as in South West River (Sainte-Brigide-d'Iberville) and Mount Johnston (Mont-Saint-Grégoire), where in 1824 he was appointed a commissioner for the erection of schools. He had begun a school in Chambly by 1821; by August 1826 he had a stone school house under construction there, and in October he was appointed a commissioner to oversee its erection. One year later some 40 children were attending classes in it under the aegis of the Royal Institution for the Advancement of Learning [*see* Joseph Langley Mills*]. In all, Parkin later estimated, he spent some £1,750 of his income on the construction of churches and schools in the colony. He also tutored; among his pupils were William King McCord* and sons of the prominent Montreal merchant George Moffatt* and of the hero of Châteauguay, Charles-Michel d'Irumberry* de Salaberry. By 1827 he was preparing two students for holy orders and apparently laying the basis for a seminary. However, Mountain's successor as bishop, Charles James STEWART, preferred to confide the seminary to a young Oxford graduate, Joseph Braithwaite.

To make way for Braithwaite, in the summer of 1828 Stewart removed Parkin to St Catharines, Upper Canada, where the people had long been requesting a missionary and where Parkin had visited in 1827. Within a year of his arrival, however, rocked by the death of a child and the effects of a fever that raged in the Niagara area, Parkin was obliged to accompany Stewart back to Lower Canada. To take the sea air he went along with Stewart in July and August 1829 on the bishop's pastoral visit of the Gaspé and on a social visit to Nova Scotia.

After their return to Lower Canada Stewart appointed Parkin to Sherbrooke and Lennoxville. Learning that an experienced teacher and Chambly parishioner, Mrs Mary Adelaide Tierney, was in financial distress with her large family, Parkin invited her in December to open a girls' school in Sherbrooke. That month, however, Stewart reported to the SPG that Parkin had become "deranged in his mind," and in March 1830 he resigned his charge and his position as missionary of the SPG. Early in April he announced the imminent publication of an essay on the Eastern Townships and an autobiography, but neither appeared. By the summer of 1830 he was able to be reappointed to Sherbrooke, but he again suffered fits of insanity and Stewart forced him to retire on 1 Oct. 1832.

After publishing his valedictory sermon in Montreal, Parkin took up teaching in Vermont. Unable to continue, he was obliged to leave his family there and return to England in 1833 to seek another posting or a pension. A petition to the government went unanswered, however, and in March 1834, embittered by his forced retirement and distressed by his mounting debts, Parkin pleaded with Colonial Secretary Edward George Geoffrey Smith Stanley for a rapid response, invoking his "mind naturally sensitive, and certainly *not strengthened* by the unutterable tortures to which it has been subjected for the last *four years* by the measures pursued towards me by my late Diocesan." Thanks to a recommendation from the SPG, he was finally awarded a pension of £100, and in 1836 he served for a time as a curate in Wiltshire. That April, with growing political conflict in Lower Canada preoccupying the Colonial Office, Parkin offered an unsolicited plan of "pacification" of the colony to a successor of Stanley, Lord Glenelg. It proposed concession to the House of Assembly of all but the territorial revenues of the crown (combined, if necessary, with reinforcement of troops in the colony), eventual exclusion of the French language from the legislature and the judiciary, massive government-sponsored immigration from Britain to the Eastern Townships, and commutation into freehold of lands held in seigneurial tenure. All were measures that had been suggested by others. Parkin was more original, at least for an Anglican, in proposing that the Jesuit estates fund be used exclusively to establish a college under the patronage of the governor and the co-presidency of the Roman Catholic and Anglican bishops, the moderator of the Church of Scotland, and the colonial head of the Wesleyan Methodist Church. Each of the four denominations represented would have its theological department, but otherwise teaching would be non-sectarian.

Meanwhile, Parkin's family had returned to England, but in 1837 his wife left him. He spent most of his time thereafter in mental institutions; at his death in 1844 he was residing in the Fiddington asylum. A son, John Buckworth Parkin*, became a noted criminal lawyer at Quebec and another, Edward Cullen, an SPG missionary in the diocese of Quebec from 1845 to 1890. The graceful church erected at Chambly, now designated an historical monument, still serves for worship and bears witness to the efforts of Edward Parkin and his people.

T. A. Ramsey

Edward Parkin is the author of *Ten sermons doctrinal and practical* (London, n.d.) and *Importance and responsibility of the Christian ministry* . . . (Montreal, 1832).

ACC, Diocese of Montreal Arch., Edward Parkin papers. ACC-Q, 104. McGill Univ. Arch., RG 4, Edward Parkin corr., 1824–28. PAC, RG 68, General index, 1651–1841: 264, 266, 312. PRO, CO 42/255: 249–54; 42/266: 427–28 (mfm. at ANQ-Q). RHL, USPG Arch., C/CAN/Que., folders 373, 474, 501; journal of SPG, 32–36, 38–40, 42–43. St Stephen's (Anglican) Church (Chambly, Que.), Minutes, 1819–47; Reg. of baptisms, marriages, and burials. *Montreal Gazette*, 8 April 1830. A. R. Kelley, "The Quebec Diocesan Archives: a description of the collection of historical records of the Church of England in the diocese of Quebec," ANQ *Rapport*, 1946–47: 189, 195, 267. R. G. Boulianne, "The Royal Institution for the Advancement of Learning: the correspondence, 1820–1829; a historical and analytical study" (PHD thesis, McGill Univ., Montreal, 1970), 448–58. C. P. C. Downman, *A concise chronological and factual history of St. Stephen's Anglican Church, Chambly, Que.: its 150th anniversary, 1820–1970* ([Montreal, 1970]). T. R. Millman, *The life of the Right Reverend, the Honourable Charles James Stewart, D.D., Oxon., second Anglican bishop of Quebec* (London, Ont., 1953); "Edward Parkin, first S.P.G. missionary at Chambly, 1819–1828," *Montreal Churchman* (Granby, Que.), 27 (1939), no.6: 16–17; no.7: 7, 19.

PAUL, LOUIS-BENJAMIN PEMINUIT. *See* Peminuit

PAUL, SAMUEL. *See* Peminuit Paul, Louis-Benjamin

PAWPINE. *See* Pierpoint

PAZHEKEZHIKQUASHKUM. *See* Bauzhigeezhig-waeshikum

PEABODY, FRANCIS, mariner, businessman, JP, and judge; b. 9 Nov. 1760 in Boxford, Mass., son of Captain Francis Peabody and Mary Brown; m. first a Miss Perley; m. secondly 1 Sept. 1808 Lydia Brooker, a widow, in Portland (Saint John), N.B.; there were no children by either marriage; d. 4 July 1841 in Chatham, N.B.

Francis Peabody grew up in Maugerville (N.B.), a settlement his father had helped found in 1762. He was involved as a youth in trade on the Saint John River, possibly in association with the firm of Simonds, Hazen, and White, two of his sisters having married James Simonds* and James White. In 1785 Peabody and Jonathan Leavitt owned a 16-ton schooner and were trading along the coast. Peabody lived in Saint John for a number of years; in the voters list for 1795 he is described as a mariner.

One of the places where Peabody traded was the Miramichi River. In 1799 he was given a licence to sell liquor there. According to local tradition, he sailed up the river with a cargo of goods from Halifax and moored his schooner to a large spruce tree, from which Chatham was to derive its first name, The Spruce. At that time there were no more than ten settlers in the immediate area. Peabody traded from his ship for salmon, shad, and alewives, which he sold in Halifax. In 1801 he bought a lot at The Spruce from one of the early settlers. Around this property developed a town that Peabody named Chatham. He continued his coastal trading for several years and then in 1804 took up residence at Chatham, where he opened a store. At that time he was in partnership with Jonathan, Daniel, and Francis Leavitt of Saint John. In 1807 Peabody was appointed a justice of the peace and judge of the Inferior Court of Common Pleas for Northumberland County.

Peabody's association with the Leavitts came to an end in 1810 and in the same year he entered into a partnership with his nephews Richard and Edward Simonds. In addition to property, their company owned a store in Chatham and a sawmill on the Sabbies River. The mill was sold to one of Peabody's grand-nephews, Stephen Peabody, in 1823, and at about the same time the partnership was dissolved. Some time before 1820 Peabody had also formed an association with Isaac Paley, a merchant from England who had married one of his nieces. Paley was his partner in the construction of at least one of the five vessels he is known to have built between 1816 and 1829. These vessels registered 1,594 tons and were valued at £15,940. One was destroyed in the Miramichi fire of 1825. The partnership with Paley was dissolved in October 1829 and Peabody then carried on business alone. His shipyard was bought in 1832 by Joseph Russell* and later passed into the hands of Joseph Cunard*.

Over the years Peabody acquired a number of stores, including a large stone one built in 1838. He also owned deal wharfs and timber booms as well as large blocks of property all along the river; he was continually issuing mortgages and through them he acquired much of his land. He was well known for his fair prices and honest treatment of customers. A contributor to the Chatham *Gleaner*, in a sketch published after Peabody's death, referred to him as "by far the most extensive and respectable merchant on the banks of the Miramichi." He was characterized as "cheerful, modest, and unassuming in his disposition . . . simple and unaffected in his manners; simple in his mode of life and altogether free from ostentation and pride." He was also noted for his hospitality. Henry Bliss*, who braved the almost non-existent roads to reach Chatham from Fredericton in 1819, claimed that one of Peabody's dinners made amends for all the hardships of the journey. A Presbyterian who contributed to the construction of St Andrew's Church in Chatham, Peabody also helped build St Paul's Anglican Church in Bushville. He never entered politics but he was a supporter of Joseph Cunard.

Peabody served on the relief committee set up to aid sufferers from the Miramichi fire and he was noted for his interest in the welfare and prosperity of the community. In 1833 he was appointed a member of the first board of health for Northumberland County. He was so popular in Chatham that in 1837, for his 77th birthday, his friends commissioned the Boston artist Albert Gallatin Hoit to paint his portrait. On his death, as a mark of respect, the *Gleaner* appeared edged in black and in its obituary notice Peabody was referred to as "the Father of the Settlement."

W. A. SPRAY

N.B. Museum, Peabody family, CB DOC. Northumberland Land Registry Office (Newcastle, N.B.), Registry books (mfm. at PANB). PANB, RG 3, RS538, B5: 38, 48; RG 18, RS153, I71, 1 Sept. 1808. UNBL, MG 3, H11, Henry Bliss to Simcoe Saunders, 22 Nov. 1819. Robert Cooney, *A compendious history of the northern part of the province of New Brunswick and of the district of Gaspé, in Lower Canada* (Halifax, 1832; repub. Chatham, N.B., 1896), 96. *Gleaner* (Miramichi [Chatham]), 6 Oct. 1829, 4 Oct. 1836, 3 Aug. 1837, 28 Aug. 1838, 6 July 1841, 17 Nov. 1843. *Mercury*, 20 June 1826, 2 Oct. 1827. *A genealogy of the Peabody family . . .*, comp. C. M. Endicott, ed. W. S. Peabody (Boston, 1867). *Vital records of Boxford, Massachusetts, to the end of the year 1849* (Topsfield, Mass., 1905). Esther Clark Wright, *The Miramichi: a study of the New Brunswick river and of the people who settled along it* (Sackville, N.B., 1944), 44–45. J. A. Fraser, *By favourable winds: a history of Chatham, New Brunswick* ([Chatham], 1975), 19–24. W. R. Godfrey, *History of Chatham* (Chatham, [1962]), 12–16, 18. Louise Manny, *Ships of Miramichi: a history of shipbuilding on the Miramichi River, New Brunswick, Canada, 1773–1919* (Saint John, N.B., 1960), 13–16, 19. J. McG. Baxter, "Francis Peabody, the founder of Chatham," Miramichi Natural Hist. Assoc., *Proc.* (Chatham), no.6 (1911): 35–54.

PECHEGECHEQUISTQUM. *See* BAUZHI-GEEZHIG-WAESHIKUM

PEMINUIT (Pominouet) PAUL, LOUIS-BENJAMIN (also called **Paussamigh Pemmeenauweet** and **Samuel Paul**), Micmac chief; b. 1755, probably in Nova Scotia, son of Paul Peminuit; m. Madeleine ——; d. 1843 in Nova Scotia.

Following the death of his father, Louis-Benjamin Peminuit Paul was chosen as chief at the Shubenacadie Indian Reserve (No.14) in April 1814. He and three of his brothers, Jean-Lucien, Pierre, and François, thereupon petitioned Lieutenant Governor Sir John Coape Sherbrooke* for confirmation of the appointment. In doing so they acted on the advice of Abbé Jean-Mandé SIGOGNE, who drafted the document and who had them express to King George III "the same loyalty and allegiance which they formerly kept to, and had for, the French Kings." They took the opportunity to request the help of the newly formed "Indian Society" (Walter BROMLEY's North American Indian Institution) to provide them with land and farm tools. The 120 men of Shubenacadie, they concluded, wanted good land for settlement, not a tract "back in the woods."

Sherbrooke replied with a commission under the sign manual, dated 28 April 1814, confirming Louis-Benjamin, not merely as chief of Shubenacadie, but as chief "of the Micmac Tribe of Indians this Province." The commission enjoined him to keep his tribe "Loyal, Industrious and Sober, and to render them good Subjects and Christians." They in turn were required to obey him as their chief. He was given a silver medal emblematic of his authority, and this was duly passed on to his successors. The wording of the commission later led to disputes with the Cape Breton Micmacs, who had been outside the jurisdiction of Nova Scotia in 1814 and had their own chiefs.

On 15 July 1815 Peminuit Paul presented himself at the head of a group of Indians to Joseph-Octave Plessis*, bishop of Quebec, who was visiting Halifax. His tales of suffering were so harrowing that they drew tears from the prelate. Plessis spoke to Sherbrooke about the meeting and was assured that the government would do everything it could to help these poor people.

The community at Shubenacadie survived but did not flourish, and Peminuit Paul eventually decided to seek legislative help to improve conditions. In March 1829 he petitioned the House of Assembly for the passage of a law that would ban the sale of alcohol to Indians. He also requested that "a number of the most active Indian Boys" be taught to read and write. The result of this initiative was a law that left it to the discretion of local magistrates to ban sales of liquor – which they never did – and provided free instruction for Indians at publicly supported schools – which some thenceforth attended.

The winter of 1830–31 was a starving time. Conscious that his people looked to him for protection and were "in a manner dependent on him for support," Peminuit Paul petitioned the assembly in January 1831. Through the Reverend William Morris, he described the cold and the hunger; the game that once supported life had been driven off by the white settlers. It was as difficult for the Indians to learn farming as it would be for whites to learn Indian ways and, for want of anything better, his people depended on the sale of their artifacts for survival. But the winter was so harsh, and fuel so scarce around Halifax, that they could not get into town to sell their goods. The only hope lay in immediate aid. The appeal was met out of the £100 budgeted annually for Indian relief.

The last of Peminuit Paul's petitions was undoubtedly dictated by him, for it has none of the conventional English phrasing of the earlier ones. Speaking to Queen Victoria courteously and as an equal, he explained: "I cannot cross the great Lake to talk to you for my Canoe is too small, and I am old and weak. I cannot look upon you for my eyes not see so far. You cannot hear my voice across the Great Waters. I therefore send this Wampum and Paper talk to tell the Queen I am in trouble. My people are in trouble . . . No Hunting Grounds – No Beaver – no Otter . . . poor for ever . . . All these Woods once ours . . . White Man has taken all that was ours . . . Let us not perish."

This petition was received at the Colonial Office in London on 25 Jan. 1841. Five days later a dispatch was on its way to Nova Scotia's new lieutenant governor, Lord Falkland [Cary*]. Her Majesty was deeply interested in the appeal, but the colonial secretary had no advice to offer because there was nothing on file. There was to be a full-scale inquiry and report on the condition of the Indians and Lord Falkland was to give the matter his immediate attention.

The inquiry was held, the report made, legislation enacted, and an Indian commissioner, Joseph Howe*, appointed. The flurry of activity that Peminuit Paul had sparked made little difference to the lives of the Indians. Blind and bedridden, he died in 1843. He was succeeded by his brother François; his son Jacques-Pierre Peminuit* Paul became chief in the mid 1850s on François's retirement.

L. F. S. Upton

[Special thanks are owed to Ruth Holmes Whitehead of the N.S. Museum (Halifax) for her assistance with Micmac names. L.F.S.U.]

Guildhall Library (London), mss 7956 (New England Company papers) (mfm. at PAC). N.S. Museum, Acc. 08.10; Acc. 31.24; mss, Piers papers, X (archaeology & ethnology), "Micmac genealogies and biographical material, uncatalogued notes." PANS, RG 1, 9, docs.1815, 1820 (transcripts); 430, doc.176. PRO, CO 217/177: 128–29; 217/179: 406–8. N.S., House of Assembly, *Journal and proc.*, 1829: 424; 1844, app.50: 127; Legislative Council, *Journal and proc.*, 1843, app.7: 23. J.-O. Plessis, *Journal des visites pastorales de 1815 et 1816, par Monseigneur Joseph-Octave Plessis, évêque de Québec*, Henri Têtu, édit. (Québec, 1903), 76. Ruth Holmes Whitehead, *The Micmac ethnology collection of the Nova Scotia Museum* (N.S. Museum, *Curatorial report*, no.25, 1974). Upton, *Micmacs and colonists*.

PÉPIN, JOSEPH, joiner, wood-carver, and militia officer; baptized 19 Nov. 1770 in Sault-au-Récollet (Montreal North), Que., son of Jean-Baptiste Pépin and Madeleine Lebeau; m. 14 Feb. 1803 Charlotte Stubinger in Boucherville, Lower Canada, and they had at least 17 children; d. 18 Aug. 1842 in Saint-Vincent-de-Paul (Laval), Lower Canada.

Joseph Pépin, a remarkable craftsman, practised at the time when parishioners in the Montreal region were decorating churches built since the early 18th century, and he profited from this favourable situation. He had been trained by Philippe Liébert* and settled in Saint-Vincent-de-Paul quite early, certainly before 1792. Louis Quévillon* was already there, and after his death in 1823 Pépin would carry on his work along with René Beauvais, *dit* Saint-James, and Paul Rollin*.

Under the French régime, meagre resources hindered large-scale projects, but by the late 18th century the syndics responsible for having church interiors finished were in a position to place orders. The ornamentation could include vaults and woodwork in the chancel and nave, major furnishings such as tabernacles and pulpits, and minor pieces such as crucifixes and candlesticks. Pépin and his team were able to meet all these needs. As master he took on numerous apprentices, some of whom (for example, Louis-Thomas Berlinguet) would later continue his work. He also gave employment to five of his sons as well as to children of the Pépin family living at Longue-Pointe (Montreal).

Between 1806 and 1812 the atelier, which employed numerous people, executed carvings for the churches in Saint-Jacques-de-l'Achigan (Saint-Jacques), Belœil, Saint-Roch-de-l'Achigan, Montreal, Saint-Ours, Saint-Jean-Baptiste-de-Rouville, Soulanges (Les Cèdres), and Chambly. Pépin took on alone the orders that came to his shop. On 3 Feb. 1815, however, he went into partnership with Quévillon, Saint-James, and Rollin "to carry out all the works of the said profession of wood-carving." The partners undertook to collaborate and to divide the tasks as fairly as possible. They agreed to finish on their own account the projects they had begun before the firm was created. The partnership does not seem to have brought the results anticipated, since it was dissolved in January 1817.

Thus in 1819 Pépin continued his work in the

church at Chambly in association with his long-time companions, Quévillon, Rollin, and Saint-James, but now without legal obligations, even though the sums involved were rather large. The church at Saint-Charles-sur-Richelieu kept him busy in 1820, as did the one at Rigaud in 1823 and at Saint-Benoît (Mirabel) in 1824. His sons had already taken over, however, and from then on entered into contracts in their own interests.

Pépin kept his workshop in Saint-Vincent-de-Paul while serving as captain, and later major, in the Île-Jésus battalion of militia (which in 1828 became the 3rd Battalion of Effingham militia). His seniority in the militia gave him a certain authority in the community. In 1837 he was involved in the rebellion along with his son Zéphyrin, a notary at Sainte-Scholastique (Mirabel) since 1826; on 30 November he was charged with high treason and put in jail. But he was released on 11 December and returned to his wood-carving. He made his will on 22 Nov. 1841 and died on 18 August of the following year.

Pépin's work was closely related to that of Quévillon, Saint-James, and Rollin. It incorporated neo-classical elements into models clearly taken from the French 18th century, which the wood-carvers were skilled in arranging to suit the church buildings and the tastes of parish priests and *fabriques*. The quality of his production and its influence on the first half of the 19th century put Joseph Pépin among the outstanding carvers of the Montreal region.

RAYMONDE GAUTHIER

ANQ-M, CE1-22, 14 févr. 1803; CE1-59, 19 nov. 1770, 20 août 1842; CN1-3, 4 oct. 1815; CN1-16, 11 juin 1803, 8 févr. 1821; CN1-43, 22 févr. 1812, 7 juill. 1815, 15 févr. 1819; CN1-68, 1er avril 1815, 23 mai 1826; CN1-80, 8 août 1825; CN1-96, 14 oct. 1805; 3 avril 1806; 26 févr. 1808; 16 juin 1810; 31 déc. 1811; 13, 19 févr., 13 juill. 1812; 23 janv. 1814; 28 janv., 4 oct. 1815; 25 janv., 28 mai 1817; 28 mars 1818; 16 mars 1819; 22 janv., 27 nov. 1820; 26 janv., 10 sept., 23 nov. 1821; 29 mars, 12 avril, 12 sept. 1822; 22 janv., 8 mai, 29 oct. 1824; 26 janv., 26 mars, 5 avril 1825; 12 juill. 1826; 28 févr. 1827; 17 mars, 1er août 1828; 23 avril 1832; 24 mars, 19 déc. 1834; 13 janv., 26 févr., 19 sept. 1836; 29 mai 1837; 1er août 1838; 15 févr., 22 nov. 1841; 3 déc. 1845; CN1-167, 7 janv. 1794, 13 févr. 1803; CN1-173, 25 mai, 26 juin 1830; 14 sept. 1831; 31 janv. 1833; CN1-179, 26 janv. 1824; CN1-334, 3 févr. 1815; CN5-8, 28 juill. 1816; CN5-13, 29 janv. 1825; CN6-3, 29 juill. 1792, 16 janv. 1793. MAC-CD, Fonds Morisset, 2, dossier Joseph Pépin. [F.-X. Chagnon], *Annales religieuses et historiques de la paroisse de St-Jacques le Majeur . . .* (Montréal, 1872), 22. Maurault, *La paroisse: hist. de Notre-Dame de Montréal* (1957), 21. Émile Vaillancourt, *Une maîtrise d'art en Canada (1800–1823)* (Montréal, 1920), 66–67.

PERRAULT, JEAN-BAPTISTE, fur trader, schoolmaster, and author; b. 10 March 1761 in Trois-Rivières, Que., son of Jean-Baptiste Perrault, a merchant, and Marie Lemaître; d. 12 Nov. 1844 in Sault Ste Marie, Upper Canada.

Jean-Baptiste Perrault came from a family that had quickly carved out an enviable place for itself in Canadian society. Among his uncles were Jacques*, known as Perrault *l'aîné*, an important Quebec merchant, and Joseph-François, vicar general, and among his cousins JOSEPH-FRANÇOIS, "the father of education for the Canadian people," Jacques-Nicolas*, a merchant and later seigneur, and Olivier*, a judge and legislative councillor. When his studies at the Petit Séminaire de Québec were ended, young Perrault turned to trade and travel. He spent the winter of 1783–84 as a clerk at Cahokia (Ill.) with a fur trader who was a friend of his father. Returning to Michilimackinac (Mackinac Island, Mich.) in the spring of 1784, he was hired to winter in the upper Mississippi district, an annual pattern repeated until 1805.

In these years Perrault was active in the Lake Superior region and particularly in the area from the Chippewa River (Wis.) upstream to the numerous lakes forming the headwaters of the Mississippi. He worked at first for the General Company of Lake Superior and the South [*see* John Sayer*; Étienne-Charles Campion*]. When it was dissolved around 1787, Perrault, with his experience in the "Indian trade," embarked upon a career as an independent trader. In 1793 he entered the service of the North West Company. First he was commissioned to build Fort St Louis (Superior, Wis.), also called Fort Fond-du-Lac. The following year he was sent to put up a fort at Upper Red Cedar Lake (Cass Lake, Minn.) and take charge of it. From 1799 till 1805 Perrault was responsible for a post at the Pic River on the north shore of Lake Superior.

During this period and afterwards the NWC was expanding in an endeavour to tighten its grip on the whole fur trade. Its thrust did not proceed smoothly. There was some irony in the fact that the most persistent opposition originated in its own ranks, from dissidents who formed the New North West Company (sometimes called the XY Company). Later Perrault related amusing anecdotes but also episodes of cruelty in this struggle, of which he himself would be a victim in 1811 in the Pic River region. Hence he expressed this severe judgement: "It must be said that the NW[t] was then legislator and king, killed, hanged, stole, and violated, etc. The extent of their crimes was close to the limit."

In 1805 Perrault returned to Lower Canada. He spent the year with his sick father at Rivière-du-Loup (Louiseville), joining his Indian wife and three children whom he had sent there two years before "to have them come into Christian civilization." He seemed to anticipate being back for good. As his contract with the NWC did not expire until 1808, however, he resumed his life as a wintering clerk. He went into the upper Saint-Maurice region in 1806–7 and spent the following winter at the post on the Rivière Agatinung (Gatineau). From then on his existence became more unpredictable than ever. For two years he was a schoolmaster at Saint-François-de-Sales (Odanak). In 1810 he set out on the expedition sent by John Jacob Astor which reached the Columbia River overland [*see* Alexander MacKay*], but he left the party at Michilimackinac. By a series of adventures he finally reached James Bay and he did not return to Lower Canada until two years later. During the War of 1812 he was at Kingston, Upper Canada, and then the NWC hired him as a master carpenter at Sault Ste Marie. Finally, in 1817 the Hudson's Bay Company put him in charge of the Michipicoten post (Michipicoten River). Two factors seem to have been primarily responsible for his uncertain situation: the difficulties in constantly moving a steadily growing family and the gradual disappearance of the allowances and privileges given clerks for the moves and upkeep of their families. In 1821 the merger of the two rival fur companies brought the permanent suspension of these privileges. Perrault realized that an era had come to an end and that there was no longer any room for him. He retired and took up residence at Sault Ste Marie.

At the prompting of ethnologist Henry Rowe Schoolcraft, who correctly saw in him an educated man of "great urbanity" with "a very retentive memory," Perrault decided when he was about 70 to recount his life as a "voyageur." In his narrative he remained so discreet about his private life that it cannot even be determined with certainty how many children he had. On the other hand he gave a detailed chronicle of a period in the history of the fur trade, identifying hundreds of people who took part as well as the routes, and describing the customs of this venturesome breed, the hazards of the profession, and the methods of barter. The abundance of precise information and the strictly chronological order show that Perrault had kept a careful record of his comings and goings and of the events he witnessed. The text is accompanied by 11 maps which delineate Perrault's routes in such an illuminating manner that, according to geographer Benoît Brouillette, the work is "even more valuable for the explorations than for the fur trade." Perrault's account is indeed of unquestionable importance to geographers and historians because of the wealth of material it contains.

LOUIS-PHILIPPE CORMIER

Jean-Baptiste Perrault's narrative, "Relation des traverses et des avantures d'un marchant voyageur dans les terrytoires sauvages de l'Amérique septentrionale, parti de Montréal le 28e de mai 1783," is in the H. R. Schoolcraft papers at the Library of Congress (Washington) and has been published as *Jean-Baptiste Perrault, marchand voyageur parti de Montréal le 28e de mai 1783*, L.-P. Cormier, édit. (Montréal, 1978). A few pages were translated by Schoolcraft and given the title "Indian life in the north-western regions of the United States, in 1783 . . ." for his *Historical and statistical information, respecting the history, condition and prospects of the Indian tribes of the United States* . . . (6v., Philadelphia, 1851–57; repr. New York, 1969), 3: 353–59. A translation of the full text appears in *Mich. Pioneer Coll.*, ed. J. S. Fox, 37 (1909–10): 508–619.

ANQ-MBF, CE1-48, 10 mars 1761. ASQ, Fichier des anciens. PAC, RG 68, General index, 1651–1841. *Les bourgeois de la Compagnie du Nord-Ouest* (Masson), 2: 165. *Docs. relating to NWC* (Wallace), 492. Wis., State Hist. Soc., *Coll.*, 10 (1888): 502; 18 (1908): 439, 441; 19 (1910): 173–74; 20 (1911): 397, 403, 430, 454. Morice, *Dict. hist. des Canadiens et des Métis*, 227. C. N. Bell, *The earliest fur traders on the upper Red River and Red Lake, Minn., 1783–1910* (Winnipeg, 1928), 16. Benoît Brouillette, *La pénétration du continent américain par les Canadiens français, 1763–1846* . . . (Montréal, 1939), 136–42. P.-B. Casgrain, *La vie de Joseph-François Perrault, surnommé le père de l'éducation du peuple canadien* (Québec, 1898), 17, 22–24, 147. Joseph Tassé, *Les Canadiens de l'Ouest* (2v., Montréal, 1878), 1: 337, 340.

PERRAULT, JOSEPH-FRANÇOIS, businessman, educator, writer, office holder, politician, journalist, and philanthropist; b. 2 June 1753 at Quebec, son of Louis Perrault and Josephte Baby; m. 7 Jan. 1783 Ursule Macarty in Montreal, and they had 12 children; d. 5 April 1844 at Quebec.

Joseph-François Perrault came from a family of merchants. His father and both his grandfathers, François Perrault* and Raymond Baby, engaged in the fur trade, as did a good many of his uncles, including François Baby* and Jacques Baby*, *dit* Dupéront. The only one of them not in trade, Canon Joseph-François Perrault, was his godfather. The end of the French régime proved a difficult time for his family. His father and several of his uncles fled to Trois-Rivières during the siege of Quebec in 1759. There, three years later, Joseph-François lost his mother, who left eight children, the eldest not yet 11. His father returned to Quebec in 1763 and went to France to see about furs he had sent to La Rochelle; he placed the children in the care of his brother Jacques Perrault*, known as Perrault *l'aîné*, and sister-in-law Charlotte Boucher de Boucherville. The children were sent as boarders to the Ursulines and the seminary in Quebec, and thus received the upbringing and education characteristic of these institutions. Joseph-François began his studies at the Petit Séminaire on 11 Oct. 1765. He definitely spent six years there, since he was in Rhetoric in 1770–71, and he probably did the first half of the two-year Philosophy program. But Joson, as he was called, did not have time to complete his schooling. His father, who had decided to settle in Louisiana, sent for his children. Joseph-François left

Quebec by ship on 24 June 1772 with two of his brothers and his three sisters. After a voyage dogged by mishap, they reached New Orleans in January 1773. They were initiated into a new society and were rather shocked by its exotic manners. Joseph-François thought that the children of the Creole families were dissolute, ignorant, and lazy, but that the French were educated and well bred. To pass the time he worked without pay for a New Orleans merchant from Bordeaux, France.

Because Louis Perrault had been detained by his business at St Louis, Mo., he had not been able to greet his children upon their arrival. When in the spring of 1773 he asked Joseph-François to join him, the young man travelled up the Mississippi with Pierre de RASTEL de Rocheblave's father, Philippe-François. On reaching St Louis he set to work with extraordinary energy, running the business in his father's absence, learning Spanish, and even acting as French secretary to the governor of Spanish Louisiana. He became attached to this far-away corner of the world and got to know the Indians and the merchants, Canadian, French, British, and American.

Political events were to change the course of Perrault's life. When the American revolution reached the settled part of the Mississippi country, Canadians there were torn between the two warring sides. In 1779 Perrault set off for Virginia, by way of the Mississippi and the Ohio, to collect the money that American officer George Rogers Clark owed his father; he was never to see his father again. Perrault's flotilla was attacked on 4 October by Indians allied with the British. He was captured and then taken to Detroit, where he arrived on 3 Nov. 1779. After a trip marked by suffering and privation, his survival hinging on his good physical condition and luck, he was welcomed by his uncle Baby, *dit* Dupéront. While waiting for permission to return to St Louis, he spent several months recovering his health. True to character, he found ways to occupy himself, teaching his cousins and studying bookkeeping from works in his uncle's library. He left Detroit in May 1780 and reached Montreal early in the summer. Then in July he went to Quebec, where he passed some weeks with his Perrault and Baby uncles and aunts. Setting off again on 30 August, he stayed in Montreal for a while and was back in Detroit by autumn. Because it was too dangerous to travel to St Louis, he again accepted the hospitality of Baby, *dit* Dupéront, and resumed his work as tutor for the winter. In 1781 Baby made him his agent in Montreal and lent him £750 to go into business for himself. It was in Montreal that, after being romantically involved with a Mlle Gamelin and making plans for marriage with Marie-Appolline Bailly de Messein (who later became the wife of Eustache-Ignace Trottier* Desrivières Beaubien), Joseph-François on 7 Jan. 1783 married his cousin Ursule Macarty. He had met Ursule, the daughter of a fur trader, in the Illinois country. At the time of the marriage she was 16 and he 29. Four months later his father died. He went to Virginia the following year to try once more to recover the money advanced to Clark, but in vain.

Returning to Montreal, Perrault gave his attention to his retail business, but as the competition was too intense, he had to give it up in 1787. He then taught bookkeeping, translated legal works, and prepared factums for private individuals; he also went into the theatrical business with Louis DULONGPRÉ and Pierre-Amable De Bonne*. In 1790 he started articling with lawyer Pierre Mézières while continuing with the numerous activities that enabled him to support his family. From time to time he wrote to Quebec, soliciting a position from the governor. In 1794, at the end of his resources and, with the death of Mézières, unable to complete his articling after five years, he presented a petition to the House of Assembly for permission to practise law none the less. A bill to this effect was brought in but did not pass. In 1795, however, through the good offices of his friend judge De Bonne, Perrault was appointed clerk of the peace and protonotary at the Court of King's Bench at Quebec. A new life lay before him.

Now settled at Quebec, Perrault distinguished himself by his zeal and his capacity for work. Soon he added to his two offices the post of keeper of the registers of baptisms, marriages, and burials for the district of Quebec. In July 1796 he was elected to the House of Assembly for Huntingdon. But he was seldom in the house, most of his time being devoted to his numerous administrative tasks. Things seemed to be going well for Perrault – he had bought a property called the Asile Champêtre on the north side of the Chemin Saint-Louis. Then on 23 April 1800 he suffered the loss of his wife.

Perrault was re-elected to the assembly that year, and this time he took an active part in its affairs. In 1801 he introduced an education bill to counter the one to establish the Royal Institution for the Advancement of Learning then under discussion. His bill was defeated, and the house resumed debating the bill on the Royal Institution, which it passed. Perrault worked on seven committees in 1801; one of these prepared an initial plan for houses of correction in the various districts, and he collaborated on a second plan the following year. Even though he distinguished himself in the assembly, he was defeated in the 1804 elections. Since the government had not implemented the committee's recommendations concerning houses of correction, Perrault took the matter up again and proposed a plan for a reformatory that would also engage in farming for the inmates' subsistence. In 1807 he took part in a violent controversy with Pierre-Stanislas Bédard* in the *Quebec Gazette*. It was ostensibly about the appointing of militia officers, but actually stemmed from the fact that Perrault was sympathetic to the colony's British administration and Bédard was opposed to it. In 1808 Perrault again ran in Huntingdon, with no greater success. This time he had to face the opposition of *Le Canadien*, which called him a "dangerous individual for the government and the Canadians" and a "tool" of De Bonne. Perrault went so far as to participate in demonstrations in the streets of Quebec and to fight with the supporters of Jean-Antoine Panet*, who in the end won the seat. He met with defeat again in the 1810 elections, this time in Quebec County. In expressing thanks to his supporters, he denounced "the *congreganists, sacristans, and beadles* of the ROMAN CATHOLIC CHURCHES," who, he said, had voted against him, whereas "the members and servants of the Protestant churches" had supported him.

In 1816 at the annual meeting of a voluntary organization supporting free schools, part of a movement which had begun in London and at Quebec in 1814, Perrault was elected to the executive committee. He refused the office, while promising the committee his financial and personal aid. In 1808 he had been admitted to the Literary Society of Quebec, along with his eldest son, Joseph-François-Xavier. He had also joined the freemasons, although just when is not known. In 1812 he was elected grand junior warden of the Provincial Grand Lodge of Lower Canada; six years later he became grand senior warden, and in 1820 provincial deputy grand master. In 1816, with notary Michel Berthelot and Joseph Leblond, he had founded a lodge at Quebec, the Frères Canadiens, with himself as master. In 1822 he was listed as a "past grand officer."

All the efforts Perrault had made in the field of education since 1801 were suddenly to bear fruit. In 1821, for example, the Education Society of the District of Quebec was founded by a group he organized and he was elected president. This society was created to secure free education for the town's destitute children, reportedly nearly a thousand in number. Lord Dalhousie [RAMSAY], Bishop Joseph-Octave Plessis*, the clergy, and many other Quebec leaders had lent him their support. A public subscription was organized and the directors of the association asked the House of Assembly for a grant, which it continued to accord until 1846. The school opened with 90 children, and by 1833 it had 415 Canadian and Irish girls and boys. In 1823 Perrault founded and served on the board of another association for poor children, the British and Canadian School Society of the District of Quebec, which made no provision for instruction in religion other than readings from the Bible on Saturdays. The school opened on Rue des Glacis, in the *faubourg* Saint-Jean, but was later moved to the *faubourg* Saint-Roch. In 1837 it was reported to have taken in since its inception 2,360 children of both sexes and trained 46 school teachers competent to teach using the system developed by Joseph LANCASTER, of which Perrault had become a most enthusastic proponent. In organizing free schools for poor children he had used this monitorial system of teaching.

Perrault's leadership in the two educational associations from September 1823 must have created difficulties for him with both French- and English-speaking colleagues. And he had against him Bishop Jean-Jacques LARTIGUE, who liked neither the Royal Institution, nor the school of the British and Canadian Society – the "Bible school," as he called it – nor Lancaster's system. Perrault quit the Education Society of the District of Quebec in 1825, and three years later handed in his resignation to the other society as well. He then advanced another educational plan. In 1829 he built a school for boys in the *faubourg* Saint-Louis. It was blessed on 29 April 1830 and opened its doors to 229 children, 169 being Canadian and 60 Irish. Next he built a school for girls near by. The primary course depended upon monitorial instruction, with two teachers in each school, a man and a woman, who were helped by senior students of both sexes. In addition Perrault wanted to give children in his establishments practical training: for the boys this meant farming, for the girls lessons in spinning, weaving, and knitting. He had even considered developing a normal school in the two institutions, and he offered religious instruction only to those who requested it. In 1832 he founded a practical school of agriculture, located on the Rivière Saint-Charles, and entrusted its administration to Amury GIROD. He wanted to add a normal school to it, but had to close the establishment after a year since the cost was far beyond his means. In the same period he developed what amounted to a plan for organizing a school system for Lower Canada, which he published in the *Quebec Gazette* on 3 Oct. 1833. This system roused all right-thinking people against him, with Bishop Lartigue at their head, since he was preaching free, compulsory schooling for all. In April 1836, after a bill to set up normal schools at Quebec and Montreal was passed, Perrault offered his services to the management committee of the École Normale de Québec, but his offer was not taken up. The following year he had to close his two schools in the *faubourg* Saint-Louis, since he no longer had the means to keep them open and the assembly had terminated its grants to him.

An enigmatic person, Perrault. He had had his share of personal trials, but he was an exemplary father and grandfather and a citizen who could be counted upon, one who could never refuse a request and gave his friends his money and his help. In his private life Perrault was kind and affectionate, but he had acquired an odd life-style. Rising at 4 or 5 A.M., depending on the season, he would write for three or four hours before leaving for the court-house, where his punctuality was proverbial. As protonotary, he had developed orderly work habits that lawyers had to follow to the letter. He apparently reserved for the court-house his moodiness and his at times somewhat violent manner of speaking; at other times he could engage in repartee full of finesse and humour. He would go home at noon to eat and devoted his afternoons and evenings to personal affairs, visiting the schools, drafting texts, receiving friends, and going to bed invariably at 9 o'clock.

Having been appointed to public office through the help of his friend De Bonne, who was outspoken in his support of the English party, Perrault in some ways was captive to circumstance, and from 1795 he sided with that party. In the autumn of 1806 he, De Bonne, and Jacques Labrie* established *Le Courier de Québec*, a bi-weekly newspaper bitterly opposed to the Canadian party and its paper *Le Canadien*. Perrault contributed to *Le Courier de Québec* until it ceased publication in December 1808. When *Le Vrai Canadien* was founded at Quebec in 1810, Perrault participated in it. This extremely pro-government paper lasted one year. But in the 1830s Perrault seems to have been on the side of the moderates, even proposing reforms in a pamphlet entitled *Moyens de conserver nos institutions, notre langue et nos lois*, published at Quebec in 1832. He did not, however, countenance taking up arms.

Grandfather Perrault, as he was already being called around 1820, was one of the leading citizens at Quebec. He was a practising Catholic who neglected none of his duties as a Christian and saw to it that his family circle followed his example. At the same time, in his school plans and projects he was an avowed advocate of non-sectarianism. His contribution in money and personal efforts to the cause of education between 1820 and 1837 shows that he was a philanthropist in the true sense of the word in his time. This philanthropy was assuredly inspired by love for his country, but also by the ideal he had conceived of bringing together the major groups developing in Lower Canada: Canadians, English, Scots, and Irish, Catholics and Protestants. His membership in freemasonry, which none of his biographers mention, could explain his zeal in promoting education of the poor. Recognized as the father of education for the Canadian people, a title bestowed upon him in the *Journal de Québec*'s obituary, he has also been associated with the origins of secular education by biographer Jean-Jacques Jolois. Jolois goes on to say that Perrault did not belong to his time. But even if he was not understood or accepted by his contemporaries, he was one of the most active participants in the public, political, social, and educational life of Lower Canada. He remained extraordinarily active until the day before his death, on 5 April 1844 in his sleep.

CLAUDE GALARNEAU

[There are Joseph-François Perrault papers at ANQ-Q, P1000-79-1623; the collection consists of letters received by Perrault in the autumn of 1833.

In addition to his activities as office holder, politician, and educator, Perrault engaged in writing in the years from 1789 to 1839, producing some 30 published items, exclusive of articles in Quebec newspapers, and nine unpublished works. Ten of his published books and five of those in manuscript are longer than 100 pages. His production is essentially of a pedagogical nature, consisting of translations, compilations, and abridgements of works published in Europe. Detailed lists of Perrault's publications may be found in Réginald Hamel *et al.*, *Dictionnaire pratique des auteurs québécois* (Montréal, 1976), and Jean-Jacques Jolois, *J.-F. Perrault (1753–1844) et les origines de l'enseignement laïque au Bas-Canada* (Montréal, 1969). C.G.]

ANQ-M, CE1-51, 7 janv. 1783. ANQ-Q, CE1-1, 2 juin 1753, 8 avril 1844. ASQ, Fichier des anciens; MSS, 104–10. L.C., House of Assembly, *Journaux*, 1793–94: 225–27, 293; 1795: 186, 218–20; 1801: 280. "Quatre lettres inédites de Joseph-François Perrault," L.-P. Cormier, édit., *Rev. de l'univ. Laval* (Québec), 17 (1962–63): 508–19. *Le Canadien*, mai–juin 1808. *Le Journal de Québec*, 9, 11 avril 1844. *Quebec Gazette*, 14 May 1795; 16 Oct. 1806; 10, 17, 24 Sept., 1 Oct. 1807; 7 July 1808. Hare et Wallot, *Les imprimés dans le Bas-Canada*. L.-P. Audet, *Le système scolaire*, 3: 57–61; 5: 79–80; 6: 194–236. Prosper Bender, *Old and new Canada, 1753–1844: historic scenes and social pictures or the life of Joseph-François Perrault* (Montreal, 1882). P.-B. Casgrain, *La vie de Joseph-François Perrault, surnommé le père de l'éducation du peuple canadien* (Québec, 1898). M.-A. Perron, *Un grand éducateur agricole: Édouard-A. Barnard, 1835–1898; essai historique sur l'agriculture de 1760 à 1900* ([Montréal], 1955). J.-E. Boucher, "The father of Canadian education, J.-F.-X. Perrault, deputy gd. master Lower Canada G.L.; a talk before the Masonic Study Club," *Masonic Light* (Huntingdon, Que.), 3 (1949): 76–84, 105–6. P.-B. Casgrain, "Joseph-François Perrault," *BRH*, 5 (1899): 175–76; "Nos institutions, notre langue et nos lois," *BRH*, 4 (1898): 181–82. Marine Leland, "Joseph-François Perrault: années de jeunesse, 1753–1783," *Rev. de l'univ. Laval*, 13 (1958–59): 107–15, 212–25, 417–28, 529–34, 630–39, 689–99, 804–20.

PETERS, CHARLES JEFFERY, lawyer, office holder, judge, and politician; b. 8 Oct. 1773 in Hempstead, N.Y., second son of James Peters and Margaret Lester; m. first 23 Nov. 1797 Elizabeth Baker in Upper Canada, and they had 12 children; m. secondly 19 Nov. 1823 Marianne Elizabeth Forbes in Saint John, N.B., and they had nine children; d. 3 Feb. 1848 at Salamanca Cottage, just outside Fredericton.

Originally named Jeffery in honour of Sir Jeffery Amherst*, Peters was renamed Charles Jeffery after the death of his younger brother Charles in 1775. In 1783 he accompanied his father, a central figure among the loyalist élite and one of the signers of the famous "petition of the 55" [*see* Abijah Willard*], on the spring fleet to Nova Scotia, arriving at Parrtown (Saint John) in May.

The Peters family would remain influential for several generations. James, the father, was appointed a justice of the peace and judge of the Inferior Court of Common Pleas for Queens County soon after his arrival there and later became lieutenant-colonel in the Queens County militia. He was elected to the House of Assembly in 1792 and remained a member until he retired in 1816. Among Charles Jeffery's brothers, Thomas Horsfield served as the Probate Court judge for Northumberland County from 1825 to 1851 and as a member of the Legislative Council from 1845 until his death in 1860. Harry, a member of the assembly from 1816 to 1828, sat on the Executive Council from 1828 to 1832 and on the Legislative Council from 1828 to 1843. William Tyng became the clerk of the Legislative Council in 1833 and Benjamin Lester* the police magistrate for Saint John in 1849. Sister Sarah married Thomas Wetmore*, the attorney general from 1809 to 1828. A nephew, James Horsfield Peters*, became a justice of the Supreme Court of Prince Edward Island and married the eldest daughter of Sir Samuel Cunard*; a niece, Mary, married Joseph Cunard* (Samuel's brother), successively a member of the assembly, the Legislative Council, and the Executive Council; another nephew, Benjamin Lester Peters, was both common clerk and police magistrate for the city of Saint John, as well as a judge of the County Court for the city and county of Saint John; finally, a cousin, William Peters, served as a justice of the peace and, in the 1820s, as a member of the House of Assembly.

Charles began the study of law in the office of Ward Chipman* Sr in 1791, despite the latter's pessimistic view of the possibilities of a legal career in New Brunswick. Chipman later recalled admonishing James Peters "that the business of the law was at so a low an ebb in this and the neighbouring provinces that it might be a long time before your son would be able to maintain himself by this profession." Charles was admitted as an attorney in 1794 and, at his father's request, began his practice in the province. Because Chipman's warning was accurate, however, he soon left for the Canadas, where in 1796 he was given a licence to practise in Upper Canada by Lieutenant Governor John Graves Simcoe*. His father then had to contend with Chipman's request for the delayed payment for his son's education.

After a brief time practising law in Kingston, Charles returned to Saint John, and on 9 Jan. 1799 he became common clerk of the city, an office that also made him clerk of the sessions, county clerk, and clerk of the Inferior Court of Common Pleas. (When he resigned this commission on 3 June 1825 he was replaced by a nephew, James Peters.) In 1799 as well Edward Winslow*, the surrogate general, appointed him deputy surrogate and judge of probate for Saint John County. He assumed these duties on 5 October and held the positions until 1827, when he took a leave of absence during his tenure as solicitor general; a permanent replacement was appointed in 1828. Peters also held two other offices concurrently: judge of the City Court and keeper of the records of the city and county of Saint John. On 8 Feb. 1808 he became judge of the Vice-Admiralty Court.

Peters's private practice in Saint John increased substantially when his chief rivals, Chipman and Jonathan Bliss*, were raised to the bench in 1809 and he became the senior practising lawyer in the province. He was said to have had for many years the most lucrative practice of any member of the bar, and he built "a very handsome stone residence" in the city. But not all of his cases were of the type to yield substantial rewards. In 1810 he unsuccessfully defended the Reverend James Innis, a Baptist minister charged with breaking the marriage laws of the province, and shortly thereafter he was the legal counsel of Henry More Smith, the jail-breaker immortalized in Walter BATES's *The mysterious stranger* . . . (New Haven, Conn., 1817).

Peters was made king's counsel on 24 May 1823 and on 25 March 1825 he replaced Ward Chipman* Jr as solicitor general. On 7 Sept. 1828 he was appointed by Lieutenant Governor Sir Howard Douglas*, who described him as "a Gentleman of talent, integrity and great legal knowledge," to succeed his brother-in-law Thomas Wetmore as attorney general; Robert Parker* then became solicitor general. The position of attorney general required Peters's almost constant employment on government business and he was forced to relocate in Fredericton. He was thus obliged to surrender his judicial posts and also the bulk of his private practice since Fredericton was "an Inland retired village" and offered fewer opportunities. But it was undoubtedly a sacrifice worth making, for the office of attorney general, though it carried a permanent salary of only £150, involved substantial fees which normally swelled the emoluments to over £1,000 per annum, "a sum barely sufficient," Peters nevertheless claimed, "to maintain and support a Family in decency and comfort."

Yet the position turned out to be less lucrative than Peters had hoped. One major source of fees was taken from him in 1828 when the commissioner for crown lands, Thomas Baillie*, decided to place in the hands of the advocate general, George Frederick Street*, prosecutions against those who cut timber illegally. Moreover, Peters's predecessor as attorney general had been given large advances for work that Peters was left to perform and for which he could not gain payment since Wetmore had died insolvent. Finally, during the restructuring of the land-granting system in 1827–31, the primary responsibility for preparing land grants was transferred from the attorney general to the commissioner of crown lands, and Peters's fees were commuted in 1830 for £400. Protesting that the amount was too small, he petitioned London, vainly, for compensation.

Despite his complaints Peters remained one of the highest-paid civil servants in the colony, with a salary at least as large as that of any of the puisne judges, and he had probably developed a substantial private practice. In 1834, on the death of John Saunders*, he applied for the post of chief justice but contrary to the "usual routine" of advancement he was passed over for Ward Chipman Jr, who had better contacts in London. Moreover, he was not offered – apparently because it was assumed he would not accept – the less-well-paid vacancy on the bench created by Chipman's promotion. On 22 Oct. 1834 he chaired the meeting held by the bar to protest the appointment to this judgeship of James Carter*, a British lawyer, although out of solicitude for Carter's position he declined to sign the petition drafted at the meeting. During the next few years, as the revenues of the land-granting department and Peters's responsibilities increased, he continued to appeal against the sum he had been given as compensation, claiming that the loss of fees had cost him £700 per annum. Yet in 1845 he declined to apply for the vacancy on the bench created by the resignation of William Botsford*, likely because of his advanced age, although perhaps also from financial considerations.

Peters's primary responsibility as attorney general was to represent the crown's interest before the courts and to initiate public prosecutions. Partly because of the fees involved, for many years he conducted virtually all of the government prosecutions in the colony. Occasionally these cases brought him to public attention, particularly in 1828 and again in 1831 when he took charge of prosecuting American trespassers in the disputed territory of Madawaska. Throughout his term he was involved in the problems surrounding the gradual transfer of control over the provincial lands and forests from the lieutenant governor to the assembly, rendering opinions on the legality of ownership of lands granted prior to 1784 and on Thomas Baillie's actions. As the attorney general, he was the head of the bar and attended meetings of its members; he was active in the Law Society of New Brunswick, founded in 1825, and participated in its reorganization as the Barristers' Society in 1844. But he does not seem to have been particularly eminent at the bar. Few students-at-law came into his offices, and those who did appear to have studied with his partner and son-in-law, Abraham K. Smedus Wetmore; indeed, only one student – William Boyd Kinnear* – is known to have read law with him. Nor was he invited to serve on any of the legal commissions appointed while he was attorney general.

Not surprisingly, Peters was largely conservative in his outlook. In 1800, for example, he was one of the lawyers who sprang to the defence of slavery [*see* Caleb Jones*]. He appears to have been a moderate in his religious views, believing that the Church of England, which he supported, should not rely on the government or on any form of "extrinsic aid." But in politics he strongly championed the royal prerogative. In 1833 he defended the right of Lieutenant Governor Sir Archibald CAMPBELL to proceed with the collection of quitrents even when Chief Justice Saunders denied their legality. A few months later Campbell recommended his appointment to the Legislative Council, but although Campbell subsequently described him as "a most zealous and efficient officer," Peters was not among the small clique upon whom the lieutenant governor relied for advice. Nor did he play a prominent part in the deliberations of the council. In 1837 he was appalled, like most of the permanent civil servants, by the decision to surrender the crown revenues to the assembly, but he did not attempt to obstruct the implementation of the new policy. He thus retained the good will of Lieutenant Governor Sir John Harvey*, who supported Peters's claim for compensation when the assembly discontinued in 1837 the £100 voted annually to the attorney general as a kind of retainer. In fact, it was because Peters never sought the influence exercised by such politically active attorneys general as Upper Canada's John Beverley Robinson* that he was able to hold on to his office during the turbulent political changes of the 1830s and 1840s. He was the last person in New Brunswick to hold the position of attorney general for life. In 1846, during the lieutenant governorship of Sir William MacBean George Colebrooke*, he was appointed to the Executive Council.

Whether Peters could have retained the attorney generalship on a non-political basis during the transition to responsible government is questionable, but it was a challenge he did not have to face since he died on 3 Feb. 1848 "after a short but severe illness." He was survived by 14 of his 21 children, to whom he left 22 city lots (some with buildings) in Fredericton and Saint John, rented at an annual income of £553, 30 unrented city lots, and one farm near Fredericton. Between 1848 and 1860 the executors of his estate paid out £7,131 2*s.* 6*d.*, and when the estate was finally settled in 1878 an additional $5,989.74 was disbursed. He thus bequeathed a substantial legacy.

PHILLIP BUCKNER and BURTON GLENDENNING

There are occasional references to Peters in the Colonial

Office records, esp. PRO, CO 188/37: 140; 188/41: 250–52; 188/43: 257–58; 188/45: 153–59; 188/46: 9–11, 38–39; 188/49: 328–31; 188/52: 93–98, 381–82; 188/59: 298–99, 301–11; in the appointments books at the PANB, esp. RG 3, RS538, B5 and I1; in the Winslow papers, UNBL, MG H2, 9: 115; and in the Harvey papers, PAC, MG 24, A17, ser.II, 4: 1161–62. There is a small collection of Peters family papers at the N.B. Museum and useful genealogical information in *A Peters lineage: five generations of the descendants of Dr. Charles Peters, of Hempstead*, comp. M. B. Flint ([Poughkeepsie, N.Y., 1896]); Observer [E. S. Carter], "Linking the past with the present," *Telegraph-Journal* (Saint John, N.B.), 30 Sept.–23 Oct. 1931; and the *New-Brunswick Royal Gazette*, 2 Dec. 1823. The only secondary source of any importance is Lawrence, *Judges of N.B.* (Stockton and Raymond).

PETERS, HANNAH (Jarvis), gentlewoman and author; b. 2 Jan. 1763 in Hebron (Marlborough), Conn., only surviving child of the Reverend Samuel Andrew Peters and his first wife, Hannah Owen; m. 12 Dec. 1785 William Jarvis* in London, and they had seven children; d. 20 Sept. 1845 in Queenston, Upper Canada.

Hannah Peters's father was the Church of England minister in Hebron; her mother died when she was two. Hannah was sent to school in Boston, where she remained when her father's strong tory views forced him to flee to England in 1774. She later joined him in Pimlico, then an undeveloped suburb of London; he claimed that she had been educated "in England, France and Germany." After her marriage to William Jarvis, another loyalist exile, the young couple lived with Peters in Pimlico, where their three eldest children were born. On John Graves Simcoe*'s recommendation, Jarvis was appointed provincial secretary and registrar of Upper Canada, and in April 1792 the Jarvis family sailed for Canada. Her husband reported that "Mrs. Jarvis leaves England in great spirits."

After a stormy voyage on which Hannah Jarvis showed "invincible courage," and a short time in Kingston, the family arrived in Newark (Niagara-on-the-Lake) in September 1792. Jarvis bought a log hut and immediately began to build an addition, a matter of some urgency because his wife was pregnant. "I make no doubt I shall do very well," she wrote when her only son, aged five, died of diphtheria; Samuel Peters Jarvis* was born less than a month later. Two more children were born in Newark, and another after the family moved to the new capital, York (Toronto), in 1798.

Society there was small and insular, but still had dissension within it between those from Britain and those from the United States. Both Hannah Jarvis and Anne Powell [MURRAY] deeply resented the bias against the Americans, including loyalists, shown by the British families. From the first, Hannah detested "the old Rogue" (Peter Russell*) and "the little stuttering Vixon" (Elizabeth Posthuma Simcoe [GWILLIM]). She hated Mrs Simcoe for her wealth, and what she thought was parsimony, conceit, selfishness, and undue influence, especially over Lieutenant Governor Simcoe. "Money is a god *many* worship." Robert Hamilton* and his family were the Jarvises' closest friends.

Samuel Peters's first letter to his daughter in Upper Canada urged the couple to live in harmony with all men, and with economy, but unhappily they did neither. Amid acrimonious wrangling, Jarvis lost much of his income in 1795 when the fees on land patents were redistributed among colonial officials. Like Mrs Simcoe and Mrs Powell (but with less justification) Hannah Jarvis had utter confidence in her husband's ability, so much so that she regarded those who criticized or harassed him as bitter enemies. Worse than Hannah's vehement partisanship, however, was the Jarvises' total inability to practise economy. Even before they moved to York, they were noted for ostentation and "unbounded extravagance." Attempts at retrenchment were made; in 1801, for example, Hannah Jarvis wrote, "I have turned tailoress for my family, not even the Secretary excepted." Such efforts were not enough, nor did the grant of £1,000 in 1815 as compensation for Jarvis's earlier loss of fees solve their financial difficulties. Finally, in October 1816, Jarvis, with his wife's consent, transferred all his property and debts to his son, Samuel Peters Jarvis.

William Jarvis died less than a year later. Stoically his wife attended his funeral alone; Samuel was in jail charged with murder in a fatal duel, and her other children did not receive word in time. Hannah Jarvis was now completely dependent upon her son, except for a government pension of $100 a year and her loyalist grant of 1,200 acres of wild lands which produced taxes but no income. For a time she remained in her old home, now belonging to Samuel, but in May 1819 she left York to spend the rest of her life in lengthy visits to her daughters in Hamilton, Niagara, Queenston, and Newmarket. She received the rent of the house in York for several years, and was thus able to send some money to her father, now living in penury in New York. In 1825, when Samuel as his father's heir received £1,000 further compensation for lost fees and was building himself a large house, he sold 400 acres of his mother's land, with her consent, to pay his builder.

By the 1830s Hannah Jarvis was living most of the time with her daughter Hannah Owen (the wife of Alexander HAMILTON) in Queenston, helping her cope with a big house and frequent pregnancies. She was there in 1839 when Hamilton died, leaving his pregnant wife and nine children penniless. "You are all God's children now," Hamilton said. The household's sole income was Hannah Jarvis's tiny pension. Hannah Hamilton took in sewing, earning 2*s.* 6*d.* a shirt, while her mother, now in her late 70s, looked after the house and young children, assisted by her older granddaughters, and did all the work in the poultry yard and vegetable garden except the spring digging. Hannah Jarvis, who had once had eight servants and slaves, now spent her days washing, ironing, scrubbing, cleaning, mending, and cooking. She who had once owned the first carriage in Upper Canada now travelled in a borrowed lumber wagon. "Strangers have . . . come foreward and placed coverings on their Backs." There was often no money in the house, and sometimes no food.

Throughout it all, "the Old Lady," as her grandchildren called her, maintained her customary energy, fortitude, and cheerfulness. In 1815 a niece had described her as "the most active Woman that I ever saw . . . it is surprising to see her fly about the House as she does"; in her old age she was "as active as ever." Close to death from an incurable stomach tumour, she dreamt of thieves among the turkeys – and finished knitting garters for the entire Hamilton brood.

In her early days, Hannah Jarvis wrote long letters to her father and her half-brother, William Birdseye Peters*, with detailed descriptions of her life in the upper echelons of society, as well as bitter invective against those she disliked. In her declining years she kept a diary notable for its pathetic record of toil and hardship. Many Upper Canadians, of course, spent their entire lives in such drudgery, but Hannah Jarvis was a gentlewoman in a classed society. Through the imprudence of her husband and son-in-law, and the insensibility of her son, she became almost destitute. It was Hannah Jarvis's misfortune that she had more energy and sense of responsibility than any of the men whose duty it was to protect her.

EDITH G. FIRTH

Some of Hannah and William Jarvis's correspondence has been published as "Letters from the secretary of Upper Canada and Mrs. Jarvis, to her father, the Rev. Samuel Peters, D.D.," ed. A. H. Young, Women's Canadian Hist. Soc. of Toronto, *Trans.*, no.23 (1922–23): 11–63.

AO, MS 787; MU 2316. MTRL, [E. Æ. Jarvis], "History of the Jarvis family" (typescript, [190?]); S. P. Jarvis papers; William Jarvis papers. PAC, MG 23, HI, 3. Univ. of Guelph Library, Arch. and Special Coll. (Guelph, Ont.), J. MacI. Duff coll., Samuel Peters papers. Samuel Peters, "'Bishop' Peters," ed. A. H. Young, *OH*, 27 (1931): 583–623; *A history of the Rev. Hugh Peters, A.M.* . . . (New York, 1807). *Town of York, 1792–1815* (Firth). *York, Upper Canada: minutes of town meetings and lists of inhabitants, 1797–1823*, ed. Christine Mosser (Toronto, 1984). *The Jarvis family; or, the descendants of the first settlers of the name in Massachusetts and Long Island, and those who have more recently settled in other parts of the United States and British America*, comp. G. A. Jarvis *et al.* (Hartford, Conn., 1879). W. B. Sprague, *Annals of the American pulpit* . . . (9v., New York, 1857–59). A. S. Thompson, *Jarvis Street: a story of triumph and tragedy* (Toronto, 1980).

PFOZER, JOHANN GEORG. *See* POZER, GEORGE

PHILIPS, HENRY (Heinrich) JOSEPH, piano manufacturer; b. 7 Sept. 1811 in Hattersheim (Federal Republic of Germany), son of Henricus Philippus Philips and Catharina Glöckner; m. 17 May 1835 Louisa Carolina Schmidt in Hamburg (Federal Republic of Germany); fl. 1845–50 in Nova Scotia.

Henry Joseph Philips had apparently learned the cabinet-making trade before his arrival in Hamburg around 1830. From 1830 to 1835 he worked with a Mr Wagner crafting musical instruments. On 3 April 1835 Philips was admitted as a citizen of the city. In the Hamburg directory of 1842 he was listed as the successor to a Mr J. A. M. Schrader at a pianoforte factory, and in 1845–46 he appears as a piano manufacturer.

In 1845 Philips came to Nova Scotia with pianos to sell and was so successful that he decided to open a factory in Halifax. Sir John Harvey*, the lieutenant governor, purchased a piano from him – one which is reputed to have been the first piano manufactured not only in the colony but also in what was to become Canada. About two years later Philips formed a partnership with a John B. Philips, possibly his brother; John had come to Halifax about 1845. In October 1847 H. and J. Philips of Barrington Street was advertising "Home Manufactured PIANO FORTES" and requesting the ladies and gentlemen of Halifax to "call and examine our new Iron framed grand square SEVEN OCTAVE double Action" pianos. The partners stated that they had made their instruments expressly for the Nova Scotia climate and claimed that their "correctness and fullness of tone is not to be surpassed by any foreign production."

The partnership was dissolved on 1 Aug. 1848 and Henry Joseph Philips continued the Piano Forte Manufactory at the same location, setting up later on Granville Street. In October he advertised that he had just built several new instruments "with all the LATEST IMPROVEMENTS and in the NEWEST FASHION . . . [which] can be sold at a LOWER PRICE than any imported Pianos of the same size and pattern." He continued to promote his instruments in the Halifax newspapers throughout 1849 and 1850, after which time all trace of him is lost. John B. Philips remained in Halifax manufacturing pianos until he sold his establishment on 29 July 1859 and apparently left the colony. In 1857 he had advertised himself as the inventor of the "Patent Iron Piano Forte" and listed eight instruments in walnut, mahogany, and rosewood with prices from £35 to £100.

According to historian Harry Piers, "all parts of their pianos, except the imported keys and actions, were made here by Henry J. Philips; H. & J. Philips, and finally J. B. Philips, from about 1846 to 1859." As well as being the first people to manufacture pianos in British North America, the Philipses encouraged the emigration from Europe of craftsmen who continued their trade in Nova Scotia for the next several decades.

PHYLLIS R. BLAKELEY

PANS, RG 32, 157, 2 Sept. 1847. Staatsarchiv Hamburg (Hamburg, Federal Republic of Germany), Bürgerbuch von 1835, no.191; Hamburger Adressbücher, 1839–46; Hochzeitenbuch der Wedde II von 1835, no.263. N.S., Provincial Museum and Science Library, *Report* (Halifax), 1936–37: 29–30. *Morning Courier* (Halifax), 5 Oct. 1847; 6 June, 22, 25 July, 8 Aug., 3, 24 Oct., 30 Dec. 1848. *Morning Journal and Commercial Advertiser* (Halifax), 26 Sept. 1859. *Times and Courier* (Halifax), 18 Jan. 1849. *Cunnabell's N.-S. almanac*, 1857: 94; 1858: 84. *Halifax and its business: containing historical sketch, and description of the city and its institutions* . . . (Halifax, 1876), 96–97. G. E. G. MacLaren, *Antique furniture by Nova Scotian craftsmen*, advisory ed. P. R. Blakeley (Toronto, 1961), 90–95.

PHILIPS, JAMES, businessman and Patriot; b. *c.* 1800 probably in Yonge Township, Upper Canada; m. 19 March 1823 Salome Brown, and they had two daughters; d. 13 Nov. 1838 at the battle of Windmill Point, near Prescott, Upper Canada.

The early life of James Philips is cloaked in obscurity. Although he was a native Canadian, his birthplace can only be deduced from circumstantial evidence; he may have been the son of Philip Philips, an American Baptist who had located in Yonge. In 1825 James settled on a farm occupying the site of present-day Philipsville, in Leeds County. In addition to developing his farm, he opened a store and a tavern within a few years, and entered into an agreement with James and Jonah Brown which permitted them to build saw- and grist-mills on his property. Together with a tannery and a potashery, constructed later, these improvements made Philips's farm the focus of a village, which was later named in his honour.

Philips became involved in politics at least as early as 1831. A reformer, he circulated petitions, served on committees, and demonstrated his interest in other minor ways. Such casual involvement, however, soon became difficult in a county which experienced turmoil and violence unparalleled in Upper Canada. Local politics, already marked by a bitter tory-reform split, were enlivened further by the Orange order, which, under the aggressive leadership of Ogle Robert Gowan*, succeeded in organizing recent immigrants from Ireland and in transferring the turbulence of Irish politics to Leeds. Gowan and other Orangemen used their influence and tactics of intimidation on the side of the tories. The resulting violence drew Philips into an increasingly active and conspicuous role in the reform movement.

During the campaign leading up to the general election of October 1834, he was a township delegate to the nomination meeting for the county and served on a committee formed to draft an address to the voters on behalf of the reform candidates, William Buell* and Matthew Munsel Howard. Violence and intimidation reached such levels during the polling that the House of Assembly overturned the election of the "Constitutional" candidates, Gowan and Robert Sympson Jameson*, on the grounds that freedom of election had not existed. A by-election was held the following March but again violence erupted at the poll and the re-election of Gowan and Jameson was quashed. This by-election was of special significance for Philips, for the county's single poll was located at Beverly (Delta), not far from his home. On 3 March some of the voters, including a number of Orangemen, stopped near his tavern. A dispute between the reform and tory factions quickly escalated into an attack on the tavern and on Philips's home. One of the Orangemen was killed and a charge of murder was brought against Philips. He was acquitted in September but the reformers pointed to the accusation and trial as an example of the extremes to which Gowan and his supporters would go to ruin an opponent.

The prominence into which Philips was catapulted by the trial added greatly to his stature within the reform movement. Proposed in January 1836 as a candidate for the next election, he lost the nomination to Buell and Howard, who were returned in a by-election in March. He assisted in organizing the reformers of the region into local committees of vigilance and management and on 11 July he was elected a vice-president of the newly formed Johnstown District Reformers' Society. The constitution which he and its other members drew up called for the introduction in Upper Canada of "responsibility in the Administration of Government," vote by ballot, and "the modification of the Legislative Council so as to ensure its sympathy with the wishes of the people." However, the return of Gowan and Jonas JONES in the general election earlier that month had effectively checked the exertions of the area's reformers, including Philips. He seems to have turned his attention more to his business affairs. In May 1837, for example, he was promoting a scheme to improve the navigation of Whitefish (Morton) Creek from Beverly to the Rideau Canal.

After William Lyon Mackenzie*'s uprising failed in 1837, Philips and several other prominent local reformers departed for the United States. He joined the Hunters' Lodge, a secret organization formed in the United States professedly to free the Canadas from British domination. Philips was accused of taking part in the Hunters' raid on Hickory Island in the St

Lawrence River, but this claim was not substantiated. In early July 1838 Philips, allegedly heavily armed, made a scouting expedition through the townships along the Rideau. Later that year, on 11 November, he was a member of the Patriot army of Hunters that invaded Upper Canada near Prescott [*see* Nils von SCHOULTZ]. Two days later Philips was killed in repelling an attack by British soldiers and militiamen under Colonel Plomer Young*.

HARRY PIETERSMA

AO, RG 1, A-II-5, 3 (report book, 1811–24); C-IV, Bastard Township; RG 21, United Counties of Leeds and Grenville, Bastard Township, census and assessment rolls, 1826–37; RG 22, ser.12, tavern licences; ser.176, 2, James Philips, 1842; RG 53, ser.2, 2: ff.129–32. PAC, RG 1, L3, 410A: P22/29; 412: P3/2. QUA, 2247, letter-book 1, Benjamin Tett to Major Young, 8 July 1838. "A record of marriages solemnized by William Smart, minister of the Presbyterian congregation, Brockville, Elizabethtown, Upper Canada," ed. H. S. Seaman, *OH*, 5 (1904): 195. *Brockville Recorder*, 13 Oct. 1831; 31 Jan., 21 Feb., 14, 21 March, 4, 11 April, 19 Dec. 1834; 2 Jan., 6, 13 March, 11, 18 Sept., 25 Dec. 1835; 5 Feb., 15 March, 8, 15 April, 6 May, 17 June, 1, 22 July 1836; 20 June 1837; 14 June, 15 Nov. 1838. *Chronicle & Gazette*, 5 Dec. 1838. *Statesman* (Brockville, [Ont.]), 24 Feb., 7, 14 July 1838. D. H. Akenson, *The Irish in Ontario: a study in rural history* (Kingston, Ont., and Montreal, 1984). Ian MacPherson, *Matters of loyalty: the Buells of Brockville, 1830–1850* (Belleville, Ont., 1981). Patterson, "Studies in elections in U.C.," 210.

PICKARD, HANNAH MAYNARD. *See* THOMPSON

PIENOVI (Pianovi), ANGELO (Angello or **Angel**, the latter his apparent preference, at least *c.* 1833; sometimes called **M. Angelo**), painter and decorator; b. *c.* 1773 in Genoa (Italy); d. 17 Nov. 1845 in Montreal.

Angelo Pienovi is said to have received his training as an artist at the "Academy of Rome," but nothing is known of his career in Europe. His presence in North America is mentioned for the first time in 1811, at New York, when he painted a drop-curtain with views of the city for a theatre.

Pienovi came to Montreal in 1828 at the time construction of the new church of Notre-Dame was being completed. In September 1827 its architect, James O'Donnell*, had contacted the *fabrique*'s agent in New York, where he had previously practised, in order to find a painter for the decoration and finishing of the church interior. As Pienovi declared himself available, the agent had a contract drawn up in late April 1828 stipulating that the artist undertook to "paint adorn and ornament in fresco and oil or either . . . in such manner and after such drawings, patterns, descriptions and directions as may be furnished and given to him" by the *fabrique*. That body was to supply him with certain "very simple" colours, "principally yellow ochre, indigo, umber, lime." A friend of the *fabrique* who also knew Pienovi had sent a warning to Montreal about the artist's character, noting that he was "a person of great talents and excellent taste but I believe is rather dissipated." Thus the contract specified the penalties he would suffer if he failed to do the work, notably a daily fine double his fees.

At the very beginning these fears proved well founded, for Pienovi, who would later be called a "scoundrel," lingered in New York for four days, squandering two-thirds of his travel allowance. He does not seem to have incurred his employers' censure, however. The indications are that he respected the terms of his contract in executing large decorative works inside the new building, which was scheduled to be consecrated in the third week of October 1828, and also that the results were sufficiently pleasing to earn him at least one other contract of the same sort.

In 1832 Pienovi again emerges from the shadows. Towards the end of October he finished decorating the "portal vaulting" of Notre-Dame, a lesser piece of work that has disappeared. At the same time he put up scaffolding to do fresco work in the new church of the Sisters of Charity of the Hôpital Général in Montreal, a task that occupied him for 11 months.

In September and October 1833, when that project was coming to an end, Pienovi inserted an advertisement in *La Minerve*; referring to his experience in decorating churches, he sought "work, along his line . . . : churches, architectural commissions, salons, landscapes, ornamentation, in fresco, oil, or tempera." He was then living "at the hay market," not far from Notre-Dame, and was about 60 years of age. Despite what seems to have been a new start, no trace has been found of Pienovi until 1841, when he did the decoration on the "transparent screen of the great window" in Notre-Dame, a piece that must be considered minor. Then, after a short interval during which he was not heard from and was said to have "wandered" about western Canada, Pienovi died in Montreal in 1845, at the recorded age of 72.

Pienovi's career was unusual. An Italian decorator who by all accounts brought a thoroughly European craftsmanship to North America, he ended up working within the framework of a neo-Gothic form of architecture, a source of innovation in French Canada, under an Irish Protestant architect who had laboured for 12 years in the United States. At the time, reaction to Pienovi's decorative work in Notre-Dame was generally negative. Seeing the lack of finish and the meagreness of the decoration, one critic spoke of a "smear of colours . . . without poetry and without taste," while another accused the artist of having caused the death of O'Donnell, who, he said, "died of a broken heart, disgusted at the bad taste which had spoiled his handiwork."

Unfortunately the traces of Pienovi's brush disappeared in 1876 under the decorations of a Frenchman named Cleff. Nevertheless, in his defence it must be remembered that the role he had played in decorating the vaulting was determined by budgetary constraints which forced him to resort to expedients, and also by his obligation to respect the precise directions in the architect's drawings. For example, to replace the ribbing initially intended by O'Donnell, Pienovi had to paint the "hollow" vaulting in black and projecting sections in grey. These colours probably also had to compensate for the excess light from the great window, which had been given plain glass because there was not enough money to put in stained glass.

As for the decoration of the pillars, here again Pienovi had to conceal a noticeable defect, the excessive width of the nave, which Napoléon Bourassa* later called "an ugly amphitheatre for a hippodrome." The paint he applied made the vertical elements stand out more independently and in this way reinforced the sense of height. Pienovi probably had given decorative motifs to these painted surfaces, adopting a style of Gothic inspiration, as the terms "medley of colours" and "spotted" used by some critics suggest. After all, it seems unthinkable that O'Donnell had had Pienovi come from New York simply to cover up extensive surfaces in monochrome.

It would be the task of Victor Bourgeau* to finish Notre-Dame's interior. Around 1830 an Italian painter he had met, Pienovi according to some, introduced him to Giacomo da Vignola's treatise, as a result of which Bourgeau was inspired to try his hand at wood-carving. Angelo Pienovi could thus be credited with an unexpected influence that would lead to the completion of what he had only been able to sketch in roughly under O'Donnell's direction as a makeshift dictated by financial exigencies.

DAVID KAREL

ANQ-M, CE1-51, 17 nov. 1845. AP, Notre-Dame de Montréal, boîte 23, chemise 34, brouillon d'une lettre de la fabrique à James O'Donnell, 16 mai 1828; Cahiers des délibérations de la fabrique, 28 sept. 1828; Fichier, 20 ou 28 sept. 1827, 20 juin 1828; Lettre de John Power à F.-A. Larocque, 14 mai 1828; Lettre de Lewis Willcocks à F.-A. Larocque, 30 avril 1828; Livres de comptes, 26 oct. 1832: 194; 4 nov. 1841: 359. Arch. des Sœurs Grises (Montréal), Livres de comptes, septembre 1832: 102; septembre 1833: 114. MAC-CD, Fonds Morisset, 1, Montréal, île de Montréal, église Notre-Dame; 2, dossier Angelo Pienovi. E. T. Coke, *A subaltern's furlough . . .* (London, 1833), 335. *La Minerve*, 9 sept.–3 oct. 1833; 24 nov. 1845. G. C. Groce and D. H. Wallace, *The New-York Historical Society's dictionary of artists in America, 1564–1860* (New Haven, Conn., and London, 1957; repr. 1964). Harper, *Early painters and engravers*. Maurault, *La paroisse: hist. de Notre-Dame de Montréal* (1957), 63. Morisset, *La peinture traditionnelle*, 134. F. [K. B. S.] Toker, *The Church of Notre-Dame in Montreal; an architectural history* (Montreal and London, Ont., 1970), 23, 36, 61, 66, 92.

PIERPOINT (Parepoint, Pawpine), RICHARD, also known as **Captain Dick** and **Black Dick**, soldier, militiaman, labourer, and farmer; b. *c.* 1744 in Bondu (Senegal); d. before 27 Sept. 1838 near Fergus, Upper Canada.

Whether slaves or free men, blacks in early Upper Canada were obscured in the historical record by the persistence of slavery and by their lack of political clout, small numbers, and illiteracy. Occasionally the life of an individual is illuminated by an extraordinary event, such as a criminal act [*see* Jack York*], but for most blacks historical evidence is fragmentary. This is the case for Richard Pierpoint.

Pierpoint's fascinating odyssey began in West Africa, where about 1760 he "was made a Prisoner and Sold as a Slave." Shipped to the American colonies, he became the slave of a British officer. During the American revolution he took the opportunity offered to slaves of enlisting in the British forces and gaining their freedom. Although by 1779 it was rare for blacks to serve in the northern British armies, much less the loyalist provincial corps, Pierpoint was a pioneer in John Butler*'s rangers. By 1780 he was stationed with them in the Niagara region of Quebec. On 20 July 1784 his name appeared among those of disbanded rangers on a list of persons intending to settle in that area. Blacks were entitled to the same proportion of land as their fellow loyalists and about 1788 Pierpoint, under his more common name of Captain Dick or Black Dick, was granted 200 acres of land on Twelve Mile Creek, in what later became Grantham Township. He received his patents for the land on 10 March 1804, only to sell his lots on 11 Nov. 1806, one going to the dominant figure in the region, Robert Hamilton*.

On 29 June 1794 Pierpoint had been one of 19 signatories to a petition of "Free Negroes" to Lieutenant Governor John Graves Simcoe*. This brief document provides a rare glimpse into black settlement. The group consisted of veterans of the "late War," and "others who were born free with a few who have come, into Canada since the peace." Apparently landless and socially isolated for the most part, they were "desirous of settling adjacent to each other in order that they may be enabled to give assistance (in work) to those amongst them who may most want it." They urged Simcoe "to allow them a Tract of Country to settle on, separate from the white settlers." The petition was quickly scotched on 8 July by a committee of the Executive Council. Its minute-book suggests the petition's emphasis on land separate from whites as the most likely explanation.

Between 1806 and the War of 1812 Pierpoint probably resided in Grantham Township, earning his living as a labourer. War once again provided him with an opportunity for change and he "proposed to raise a Corps of Men of Colour on the Niagara Frontier." His offer was turned down but a small black corps was raised locally by Robert Runchey in October 1812. The old ranger volunteered immediately, serving as a private from 1 Sept. 1812 to 24 March 1815. The Coloured or Black Corps, as it was sometimes called, varied between 27 and 30 men, excluding sergeants and officers. It saw action at the battle of Queenston Heights on 13 Oct. 1812 and was involved in heavy fighting during the siege of Fort George (Niagara-on-the-Lake) on 27 May 1813. The corps remained with Brigadier-General John VINCENT's army on the retreat west to the head of Burlington Bay (Hamilton Harbour) and then followed it east again after the battle of Stoney Creek on 6 June 1813. For the remainder of the war the blacks were used for labour or garrison duty, stationed either at Fort Mississauga (Niagara-on-the-Lake) or Fort George and possibly seeing action at Lundy's Lane on 25 July 1814. When the corps was disbanded in 1815 Pierpoint returned to the life of a labourer in the Grantham area.

On 21 July 1821 Pierpoint, then a resident of Niagara (Niagara-on-the-Lake), petitioned Lieutenant Governor Sir Peregrine Maitland* for aid since he was finding it "difficult to obtain a livelihood by his labor" and was "above all things desirous to return to his native country." His wish to return to the West African settlement he had left in the hold of a slave-ship some 60 years earlier was not realized. Instead the old soldier received a location ticket for 100 acres of land in unsettled Garafraxa Township on the Grand River, near present-day Fergus. Most of the grants here were to military claimants, including two other members of the Coloured Corps, Robert Jupiter and John Vanpatten. Of the three, only the aged Pierpoint took up his land, becoming one of the area's earliest settlers. In May 1825 he completed the settlement duties – clearing and fencing five acres and erecting a house.

On 28 Jan. 1828 Captain Dick made out his will, witnessed by sons of two former officers in Butler's Rangers. The lone black in a settlement of whites, he had "no heirs nor relations." He left his farm and a claim to one of his former lots in Grantham to a resident of Halton County, Lemuel Brown. Unfortunately Pierpoint had given the wrong concession number for the Grantham property and the Surveyor General's Office reported the claim unsubstantiated. Pierpoint's will was proved on 27 Sept. 1838. He had probably died that year or in late 1837 – an old African brought by the slave trade to the frontier of settlement in a land he never took for his own.

ROBERT L. FRASER

AO, RG 1, A-I-2, 30: 427; C-I-3, 132: 76; C-IV, Garafraxa Township, concession 1; Grantham Township, concession 6, lots 13–14; concession 8, lot 13; RG 22, ser.235, will of Richard Pawpine, 1838. BL, Add. MSS 21828: 38 (copy at PAC). Niagara North Land Registry Office (St Catharines, Ont.), Abstract index to deeds, Grantham Township, 1: ff.87, 131 (mfm. at AO). PAC, MG 9, D4, 9: 187 (transcript); RG 1, L1, 19: 195; L3, 196: F misc., 1788–95/68; L7, 52a; RG 5, A1: 26441–44; RG 8, I (C ser.), 688E: 113, 115; 1701: 208. St Catharines Public Library, Corps of Colour, nominal return, 15 March 1819. Wellington South Land Registry Office (Guelph, Ont.), Abstract index to deeds, West Garafraxa Township, 5 (mfm. at AO). "District of Nassau: minutes and correspondence of the land board," AO *Report*, 1905: 340. *Doc. hist. of campaign upon Niagara frontier* (Cruikshank), 1: 51; 4: 161, 170; 5: 221, 271; 6: 73, 331; 7: 51. "Settlements and surveys," PAC *Report*, 1891, note A: 4. *St. Catharines Journal*, 24 May, 12 June 1856. *The centennial of the settlement of Upper Canada by United Empire Loyalists, 1784–1884* . . . (Toronto, 1885). G. E. French, *Men of colour: an historical account of the black settlement on Wilberforce Street and in Oro Township, Simcoe County, Ontario, 1819–1949* (Stroud, Ont., 1978). J. N. Jackson, *St. Catharines, Ontario; its early years* (Belleville, Ont., 1976). Benjamin Quarles, *The negro in the American revolution* (Chapel Hill, N.C., 1961). E. [A.] Cruikshank, "The battle of Fort George," Niagara Hist. Soc., [*Pub.*], no.12 (1904): 21, 29, 34. W. R. Riddell, "Some references to negroes in Upper Canada," *OH*, 19 (1922): 144–46.

PIGEON, FRANÇOIS-XAVIER (baptized **François**), Roman Catholic priest, teacher, author, school administrator, publisher, and journalist; b. 9 Nov. 1778 in Sault-au-Récollet (Montreal North), Que., sixth child of Barthelemy Pigeon, a carpenter, and Marie Delorme, a linen maid; d. 8 Oct. 1838 in La Prairie, Lower Canada.

François-Xavier Pigeon came from a family of humble artisans who were striving to move upwards from the place they shared with day-labourers and farmhands in the lower ranks of late-18th-century rural society. Education for their children represented a way to rise. In these circumstances Pigeon's parents were counting heavily on him, for he showed himself to be an unusually gifted child. He quickly learned that life was difficult and money hard to come by; as a result he developed a taste for diligence and success and a desire for respectability. In 1785 Pigeon began attending the school in Sault-au-Récollet run by the parish priest, Jean-Marie Fortin. Six years later he started Latin with the new priest, Louis-Amable Prevost.

In 1792 Pigeon entered the Collège Saint-Raphaël in Montreal. He soon displayed an aptitude for study and the life of the mind. His scholarly successes drew him closer to his teachers, who took notice of his brilliance. At the completion of his classical studies, they considered him a young man of superior intelligence, profound faith, and unassailable moral character. His future as a priest looked bright. For his part, Pigeon was much attached to the college, which was known for its gallican and monarchist ideas. He apparently had not revealed all sides of his personality, however; though admittedly fervent, devoted, zealous, and enthusiastic, he was also devious, acrimonious, turbulent, and independent.

Pigeon began studying theology at the Grand Séminaire de Québec in 1800. He did not add greatly to his theological knowledge there because he spent most of his time supervising studies and lecturing at the Petit Séminaire. He continued to show an intellectual bent; he worked extremely hard, being keen on reading and passionately fond of philosophy. His superiors predicted an outstanding future for him in teaching.

In January 1803 Pigeon was ordained priest by Bishop Pierre Denaut* of Quebec and was immediately appointed professor of philosophy at the Petit Séminaire, which was undertaking certain educational reforms at that time. A year later Pigeon published a work considered to be the first geography textbook in what is now Canada, *Géographie à l'usage des écoliers du petit séminaire de Québec*. He was making his mark as a thinker at this institution, inspiring and giving leadership to pedagogical activity from both intellectual and practical points of view. He was appointed director of the Petit Séminaire in 1804. In his new office he was generally recognized and respected, but at the same time he met with some mistrust because of his inflexibility; he even set several teachers against him because of his free and outspoken style of discussion.

Bishop Denaut named Pigeon director of the students and professor of theology at the Grand Séminaire in 1805. Ardent and so impetuous as to take ill-considered action at times, Pigeon soon aroused distrust and suspicion. More and more Denaut feared this priest who found compromise repugnant and always wanted to assert his own ideas. It was evident that Pigeon was no longer wanted at the Séminaire de Québec.

Joseph-Octave Plessis*, Denaut's successor, decided to bring him into line and sent him as curate to the parish of Sainte-Rose (at Laval) in 1806, and then to Notre-Dame-de-Saint-Hyacinthe (Notre-Dame-du-Rosaire) the following year. In a better frame of mind by then, Pigeon was named curé of the parish of Saints-Anges at Lachine late in 1808. There he maintained good relations with his bishop and his parishioners; he was active, set up a school, had an addition put on the presbytery, and encouraged the most visible forms of public worship.

In 1810 Bishop Plessis put Pigeon in charge of Saint-Philippe-de-Laprairie. From the outset, Pigeon was concerned to restore order in the parish. Full of a sense of responsibility towards parishioners, he exercised authority firmly and showed little tolerance for misdemeanours, demanding absolute respect for Christian morality; he fought against cohabitation, more or less accepted marriage of close relatives, and insisted on the annual observance of Easter duties by everyone. At the same time he favoured more frequent attendance at the sacraments and encouraged processions, which for him were tangible signs of religious vitality in the parish. He also replaced the novena with the forty hours' devotion, which he thought more likely to bring his flock back to Christian piety. Thus he made himself known during his first dozen years as a pastor who demanded much of his parishioners. He was one of the few priests held up by Plessis as an example.

Jean-Jacques LARTIGUE's appointment as the archbishop of Quebec's auxiliary in Montreal in 1820 thrust Pigeon into the limelight. Like the Sulpicians, who did not appreciate the extension of episcopal authority on Montreal Island, Pigeon and a few dissatisfied priests were not pleased with the arrival of a new bishop who would interfere with routine matters in their parishes. A quarrel over the establishment of the diocese of Montreal thus surfaced and created a situation encouraging the expression of disagreement within the lower ranks of French Canadian clergy.

Pigeon became a leader in this movement of protest. In 1821 he ventured to differ with Lartigue about the division of his parish. A year later he categorically refused to read from the pulpit the bishop's decree on the question. He set up a Latin school without consulting Lartigue and made plans to build an art school. He also took Lartigue's appointment as an occasion for open display of gallican ideas. His gallicanism was in essence ecclesiastical, deriving from opposition to the advent of a bishop in the district of Montreal. To achieve his ends Pigeon was not afraid to engage in controversy: he wrote pamphlets asserting his claims and composed long lists of complaints full of biting sarcasm. In 1822 he sent Plessis a memorandum that was highly abusive of Lartigue. Cantankerous and provocative, he did not shrink from confrontation with his bishop; he even had his letters delivered to Lartigue by a bailiff.

Pigeon and the parish priest of Longueuil, Augustin Chaboillez*, wrote pamphlet after pamphlet, and article after article for newspapers, and they directed and coordinated the overall strategy of the protest movement. In 1823 they declared bluntly that the pope could not raise Montreal to an episcopal district without the consent of the clergy and the faithful. That year Chaboillez published a pamphlet entitled *Questions sur le gouvernement ecclésiastique du district de Montréal*. In 1824 Pigeon set up a printing-shop to carry on the fight with the bishop and keep both priests and people better informed. Some 15 pamphlets were printed, dealing with church doctrine on morality, ecclesiastical discipline, the sacraments, the lives of the saints, liturgy, and prayer. Pigeon undertook to publish his correspondence with Lartigue and Plessis, accompanied by quotations from gallican authors, in two pamphlets.

In 1826 Pigeon brought out a weekly newspaper, *La Gazette de Saint-Philippe*. It was the second church newspaper in the Canadas and he was its editor. The paper consisted of one or two articles of apologetics, a column of religious news, and correspondence from readers. His goal was to arouse both ordinary Catholics and his fellow clergy, who knew little about their rights within the church. The newspaper soon ran into resistance from Lartigue. Late in 1826 *La Gazette de Saint-Philippe* ceased publication, since most of the priests in the district of Montreal had shown little interest in it and had quickly come around to Lartigue's viewpoint.

A year later Pigeon gave up and submitted unreservedly to the bishop. In an about-face, he attacked the liberal movement within the Patriote party, and he increased his contacts with Lartigue, as if eager to admit that the bishop was right about liberalism. From 1830 the two had more numerous and thoughtful exchanges of views. Assured of Pigeon's subservient and even sympathetic silence, Lartigue could henceforth act with complete peace of mind. In 1835 Pigeon unhesitatingly signed a petition exhorting the Holy See to allow the district of Montreal to be raised to an episcopal see.

Having been reconciled with his bishop, Pigeon was content at the end of his life to perform the rites, administer the sacraments, and run his parish in a suitable manner. Freed of all his difficulties, he led a peaceful existence of prayer, reading, and visiting the priests in the neighbouring parishes. On occasion he even received them in his house, which was built of stone and surrrounded by a huge garden. With the 1,000 *minots* of wheat from the tithe, he had an income large enough to live comfortably, buy some land, and help his nephew enter holy orders. Pigeon also owned an impressive library, which consisted not only of books used in his ministry but also of works that defended the moral and philosophical doctrines of the church.

During the rebellions of 1837–38 Pigeon adopted Lartigue's stance and used all the means at his disposal to keep his parishioners from taking part in armed revolt. If he read Lartigue's pastoral letter of 24 Oct. 1837 from the pulpit with some hesitation, it was because he feared reprisals from the Patriotes in his parish. Physically exhausted by then, he passed away on 8 Oct. 1838.

François-Xavier Pigeon belonged to the intellectual and social élite among the clergy. Around 1820 this minority was giving close attention to the great doctrinal alternatives current among priests and laity. Some of the group championed gallicanism, others adhered to the school of Hugues-Félicité-Robert de La Mennais, and a few even spread a certain liberalism. Yet these priests were no match for a church that was strongly hierarchical and was dominated by an ultramontane Catholicism emphasizing Providence. Moreover, no common action or ideology linked them. These factors probably explain why Pigeon soon rallied to his superiors. At the time of the rebellions of 1837–38 the entire body of French Canadian clergy would blindly follow the directives of the ecclesiastical authorities, oppose armed revolt, and zealously defend the ideals of a society harking back to the *ancien régime*.

RICHARD CHABOT

François-Xavier Pigeon is the author of *Géographie à l'usage des écoliers du petit séminaire de Québec* (Québec, 1804), *Réponse à M. Deshons Montbrun, adressée aux bons et honnêtes habitans de la campagne* (Montréal, 1818), and *Rapports entre le curé de St. Philippe et Monseigneur de Québec* (s.l., 1826).

AAQ, 210 A, XII: 521; XIII: 75, 242, 372. ACAM, RLL, I: 66; II: 26, 82, 98, 100, 140, 261, 268, 279, 338; III: 53, 129, 134, 265; IV: 37, 88, 99, 160, 267, 346. ANQ-M, CE1-4, 9 nov. 1778; CE1-54, 11 oct. 1838; CN1-233, 23 déc. 1826; CN1-245, 16 mars 1837; CN4-33, 27 avril 1832; 23 avril, 14 août 1838. AP, Saint-Philippe (Laprairie), Cahier des recettes et dépenses de la fabrique, 1810–38; Saints-Anges (Lachine), Cahier des recettes et dépenses de la fabrique, 1809. Arch. du diocèse de Saint-Jean-de-Québec (Longueuil, Qué.), 9A/12–105. ASN, AP-G, L.-É. Bois, G, 10: 131. ASQ, Grand livre, 12F, 58; Lettres, T, 79, 111–12, 124; MSS, 433: 7, 27, 141, 153; 437: 375–76; Séminaire, 120, no.296A. *Le séminaire de Québec: documents et biographies*, Honorius Provost, édit. (Québec, 1964). C.-P. Beaubien, *Le Sault-au-Récollet, ses rapports avec les premiers temps de la colonie; mission-paroisse* (Montréal, 1898). Maurault, *Le collège de Montréal* (Dansereau; 1967). J.-J. Lefebvre, "Saint-Constant–Saint-Philippe de Laprairie, 1744–1946; la vie religieuse," CCHA *Rapport*, 13 (1945–46): 125–58.

PLENDERLEATH, WILLIAM. *See* CHRISTIE, WILLIAM PLENDERLEATH

POMINOUET. *See* PEMINUIT PAUL

PORTELANCE, LOUIS ROY. *See* ROY

PORTEOUS, ANDREW, merchant, militia officer, office holder, and JP; b. c. 1780, possibly in Montreal, son of John Porteous, merchant, and Josepha Carqueville; m. Anne Mompesson, and they had at least three children; d. 16 Dec. 1849 in Toronto.

Andrew Porteous was already in business in Montreal at age 17 and may have been in association with his brother William by 1807 when they were owed £1,500 by Dominique Rousseau*. Subsequently Porteous was a partner in the firms of Porteous and Hancox and Company of Montreal and Cringan, Porteous and Company of Quebec, both of which traded in dry goods, spirits, wine, gunpowder, wax, and glass. In June 1817 he was able to buy a large lot and stone house in the *faubourg* Sainte-Marie. The same year he purchased a pew in the gallery of the Scotch Presbyterian Church (later known as St Gabriel Street Church), and by 1820 he was a member of the church's temporal committee. The following year he was made a captain in Montreal's 1st Militia Battalion, which he had joined as an ensign in 1811.

Porteous's prosperity had become more apparent than real, however, following a series of reverses. His partnerships had been dissolved in October 1817, his store on Rue Saint-Paul had been robbed of more than £200 in cash and merchandise in December, and in March 1819 his property in the *faubourg* Sainte-Marie was announced for sale at a sheriff's auction. As well, by late 1826 he was burdened with the responsibility for seven orphaned children of two brothers. In January 1827, supported by a large number of prominent Montrealers, he petitioned Governor Lord Dalhousie [RAMSAY] for assistance in the form of a government appointment. A year and a half later, on 1 July 1828, Porteous was made postmaster of Montreal.

The upheaval in Porteous's career was soon followed by one in his religious life. Unable to continue financial support to its two ministers, Henry Esson* and Edward BLACK, the St Gabriel Street congregation divided violently over which one should remain [*see* William Caldwell*]; Porteous supported Black, a burly evangelical. When arbitrators decided in 1832 in favour of Esson, Porteous joined Black's new congregation, which opened St Paul's Church in 1834, and subsequently became a prominent member of it.

Although Porteous still experienced financial difficulties in the early 1830s, he was apparently out of debt by March 1835, and in November he was granted about 100 acres of land in Shefford Township. His improved circumstances owed much to an income from all sources in the Montreal post office of £754, of which £200 nevertheless went to pay his three assistants and to purchase stationery and supplies. He was not enchanted with conditions of work, however. In late 1834 he induced the merchants of Montreal to petition for an increase in his salary (which was £346), and in January 1835 he remonstrated with deputy postmaster general, Thomas Allen Stayner*, upon the "insufficiency and unsafe state of the present Post Office." With a tailor's shop and a dry-goods store below it, a printing-office on one side, and a boarding-house on the other, he feared "the danger to which the Post Office, with its valuable contents, is hourly exposed to from fire." He also complained that to reach him the public had to climb an unlit flight of stairs and then make their way across a small lobby half-filled with firewood. Porteous's complaints may have gone unnoticed, since the Post Office Department was considered by the British government rather as a source of revenue than as a service to the public; a similar complaint had been lodged by the town's merchants more than 15 years earlier. In September 1840, "feeling the infirmities of age growing upon him and being convinced that he is unequal to . . . the heavy and constantly increasing duties of his Office," Porteous resigned in favour of a nephew, James Porteous, who supported him from the salary of the position.

Porteous moved to Upper Canada, and in April 1846 he was given a commission of the peace for the Newcastle District. Toward the end of his life he lived with a daughter and son-in-law in Toronto. He died there in December 1849, aged 69, "by the bursting of one of the great arteries of the heart," and was interred the following spring.

MYRON MOMRYK

PAC, MG 17, A7-2-3, 13; MG 24, L3: 30618; MG 25, 321; MG 44, L, 4: 444; 9: 308 (copies); RG 1, L3[L]: 65065, 77970; RG 4, A1, 247: 63; RG 9, I, A5, 4: 74; RG 68, General index, 1841–67. L.C., House of Assembly, *Journals*, 1835–36, app.GG. *Canadian Courant and Montreal Advertiser*, 26 Aug., 22 Oct. 1814; 18 March, 2 Sept., 14 Oct. 1815. *Globe*, 20 Dec. 1849. *Montreal Witness, Weekly Review and Family Newspaper*, 31 Dec. 1849. *Quebec Gazette*, 13 Nov. 1817; 1 Jan. 1818; 18 March 1819; 24 May, 13 Sept. 1821; 25 July 1822; 9 Jan. 1823. *Montreal directory*, 1819. *Officers of British forces in Canada* (Irving). Campbell, *Hist. of Scotch Presbyterian Church*. F.-J. Audet, "Andrew Porteous," *BRH*, 42 (1936): 712–13.

POST, JORDAN, watchmaker, businessman, and office holder; b. 6 March 1767 in Hebron, Conn., one of eight children of Jordan Post and Abigail Loomis; m. 3 Feb. 1807 Melinda Woodruff, and they had three sons and four daughters; d. 8 May 1845 in Scarborough Township, Upper Canada.

At the age of 21 Jordan Post left home to learn the trade of watch- and clock-maker. About the turn of the century his father, brothers, and sisters decided to immigrate to Upper Canada. At least one brother had taken up land in Pickering Township in 1798 and several family members settled in Trafalgar Township. Post Jr, as he became known, brought his trade to York (Toronto) in 1802.

As York's first watchmaker, Post had a thriving business. His father, who arrived in the village about 1808, apparently did well as a bakery owner. The younger Post received a 200-acre grant in 1804 in Hungerford, an undeveloped township, and over the next 30 years he acquired considerable additional property. He shrewdly invested in land in the western section of York and in rural land slightly to the west of the town itself, in what would become the centre of present-day Toronto. From his sales of properties, which began in the 1820s and continued until his death, he made a substantial profit, far more than he could make at his trade. He also acquired a large property in Scarborough Township (lots 5 and 6 in concession 1), part of a lot in Markham Township, and four lots in undeveloped townships.

Aside from his trade and successful dealings in land, Post had other business interests. In 1813, with William Allan*, Alexander Wood, and others, he was a founder of the York Association, which issued "Bills for the convenience of making change" in business dealings, there being a shortage of specie in Upper Canada. For a brief time during the War of 1812, when business was poor, he kept a tavern. He did not, however, devote all his energies to making money. Like his father, he was a town officer, serving as a pathmaster in 1810 and 1819. His sense of civic duty also led him to set aside two parts of his town land, on Yonge and George streets, for market sites. Although neither market was ever developed, Post at least attempted to provide the citizens of York with something more than lots for sale.

Post also made contributions in the fields of education and religion. In 1820 he subscribed to the setting up of Thomas Appleton*'s common school in York and the following year became one of its trustees. Also in 1820 he pledged lumber worth £100 (Halifax currency), to be delivered within four years, for the building of a secessionist Presbyterian church.

In late 1833 or early 1834, at an age when many men contemplated slowing the pace of their lives, Post suddenly moved to his land in Scarborough to begin a new career. A sawmill was constructed on Highland Creek, which ran through his property, and his shipment of lumber to ports around Lake Ontario soon became a prosperous business. In addition, he kept a store. Post died in Scarborough in 1845. Henry Scadding* was later to describe him as a "tall New Englander of grave address . . . [who] always wore spectacles. From the formal cut of his apparel and hair he was, quite erroneously, sometimes supposed to be of the Mennonite or Quaker persuasion." Although he is remembered chiefly as Toronto's first watchmaker, in reality he was a prominent businessman and one of the city's most successful early speculators.

Ronald J. Stagg

[The author wishes to thank Mr William Daniels of Toronto, who provided information and constructive criticism. The Reverend C. Glenn Lucas, archivist-historian of the UCC-C, was also of assistance by providing documents relating to the Methodist church built on Post's King Street property. R.J.S.]

AO, RG 22, ser.155. Conn. State Library (Hartford), Indexes, Barbour coll. PAC, RG 1, L1, 24: 8; 31: 449; 32: 421; L3, 401: P5/48, P7/2; 406: P15/59; RG 5, A1: 47568–71, 114832–34. Toronto Land Registry Offices, Abstract index to deeds, City of Toronto; Scarborough Township, concession 1, lots 5–6 (mfm. at AO). York North Land Registry Office (Newmarket, Ont.), Abstract index to deeds, Markham Township (mfm. at AO). "Marriage licenses issued at Toronto, 1806–1809," *Ontario Reg.* (Madison, N.J.), 2 (1969): 225. "Minutes of the Court of General Quarter Sessions of the Peace for the Home District, 13th March, 1800, to 28th December, 1811," AO *Report*, 1932: 171, 178. *Town of York, 1793–1815* (Firth); *1815–34* (Firth). "Wesleyan Cemetery, Highland Creek, Scarborough," comp. W. D. Reid, *Ontario Reg.* (Lambertville, N.J.), 6 (1982): 141. *York, Upper Canada: minutes of town meetings and lists of inhabitants, 1797–1823*, ed. Christine Mosser (Toronto, 1984). *Death notices from "The Christian Guardian," 1836–1850*, comp. D. A. McKenzie (Lambertville, 1982). *A history of Scarborough*, ed. R. R. Bonis ([2nd ed.], Scarborough [Toronto], 1968). Hazel [Chisholm] Mathews, *Oakville and the Sixteen: the history of an Ontario port* (Toronto, 1953; repr. 1971). *Robertson's landmarks of Toronto*, vols.1–3, 6. Scadding, *Toronto of old* (Armstrong; 1966). *The township of Scarboro, 1796–1896*, ed. David Boyle (Toronto, 1896). L. B. Jackes, "Jordan Post's original hotel," *Globe and Mail* (Toronto), 20 April 1954: 6.

POTHIER, TOUSSAINT (baptized **Jean-Baptiste**), businessman, militia officer, seigneur, politician, and office holder; b. 16 May 1771 in Montreal, son of Louis-Toussaint Pothier and Louise Courraud Lacoste; d. there 22 Oct. 1845.

Toussaint Pothier was a descendant of Étienne Potier, *dit* Laverdure, who came from Charenton, on the outskirts of Paris. The son of a prosperous merchant who had helped found the North West Company, he went into the fur trade early. As an agent of the Michilimackinac Company, which was created in 1806, he, along with Josiah Bleakley*, George Gillespie, and others, signed an agreement with the NWC that year which divided trading territories between the two enterprises. Because of ruthless competition, however, in 1810 the Michilimackinac Company sold its interests to Forsyth, Richardson and Company and McTavish, McGillivrays and Company, both Montreal firms associated with the NWC. The following year these two companies joined John Jacob Astor in forming the South West Fur Company, and Pothier was involved in the new organization. Over the years he became a wealthy man. A plan of Montreal published by the surveyor general, Joseph Bouchette, in 1815 shows that several properties in the centre of town belonged to him, including an immense piece of land along what is now Rue Craig, where a huge military riding-school was built. Pothier also owned the seigneuries of Lanaudière (sometimes called Lac-Maskinongé) and Carufel, which he had bought on 17 March 1814. He carried out various large-scale improvements that made them extremely valuable, and he even considered building a manor-house on the Rivière Maskinongé.

Pothier often travelled to the Great Lakes on business. In July 1812, during the war against the United States, he participated in the taking of Michilimackinac (Mackinac Island, Mich.), with a force of British troops, Indians, and some Canadian voyageurs whom he had recruited himself from the ranks of the NWC [*see* Charles Roberts*]. The fall of this important American trading-post was the prelude to the capture of Detroit by Major-General Isaac Brock* on 16 Aug. 1812.

On 10 Jan. 1820, when he was already 49, Pothier married Anne-Françoise Bruyeres, the under-age daughter of the late Ralph Henry Bruyeres*. They had a daughter, Jessé-Louise (Jessy Louise), who was born on 19 May 1824 and was married to the queen's printer George-Paschal Desbarats* on 1 Oct. 1849. On the recommendation of Governor Lord Dalhousie [RAMSAY] Pothier was appointed to the Legislative Council of Lower Canada on 22 July 1824, and he remained a member until 1838. In April of the latter year, at the request of the administrator, Sir John Colborne*, he accepted a place on the Special Council. That body was dissolved by Governor Lord Durham [LAMBTON] on 1 June. In November, after Durham's departure, Pothier was appointed by Colborne to the Executive Council, as well as to the Special Council that approved the proposals of Governor Lord Sydenham [THOMSON] for union of the two Canadas. Indeed he served as president of the Special Council from November 1838 to November 1839. He relinquished all political responsibilities for good in February 1841.

Pothier held several other important offices. He served as commissioner for the improvement of the port of Montreal, member of a commission created in 1821 to oversee construction of the Lachine Canal [*see* François Desrivières*], commissioner for exploring the country between the Saint-Maurice and Ottawa rivers, and arbitrator in the division of customs revenues between Upper and Lower Canada. In 1827 he helped found the Natural History Society of Montreal, to which he made generous gifts for several years. On 21 Sept. 1839 he became sheriff of the judicial district of Montreal, but for reasons unknown he was replaced by an English-speaking sheriff five days later.

Pothier was Peter McGill*'s partner in the Company of Proprietors of the Champlain and St Lawrence Railroad, a firm that built the first railway in Upper and Lower Canada. Running from La Prairie to Saint-Jean (Saint-Jean-sur-Richelieu), it went into service on 21 July 1836. In addition, since 1815 he had been administering the extensive estate of his friend Pierre Foretier*. In 1816 he had had to sue the heirs, among whom was Marie-Amable Foretier*, the wife of Denis-Benjamin Viger*, to force them to return to the corpus of the estate assets they had misappropriated. This lawsuit, a landmark in judicial annals, lasted more than 25 years, wending its way through the various levels of the court system. It was complicated in 1841 by Pothier's bankruptcy, apparently the result of unfortunate dealings in stocks and shares of companies engaged in the fur business. Pothier died four years later.

Over time Toussaint Pothier became a controversial figure. During years of ethnic and social disturbances, his presence on government bodies, and in particular on the Special Council where there were but a handful of Canadians among an overwhelming majority of British members, had made him suspect; for some it even clearly identified him as a turncoat. Historian Gérard Filteau calls him a traitor to his compatriots. On the other hand, for Francis-Joseph Audet*, Pothier "showed himself an experienced statesman, an honest and true patriot" in the report on the political situation that he wrote in 1829 at the request of the colony's administrator, Sir James Kempt*; in Audet's opinion, Pothier "upheld the cause of his compatriots, who were, he said, His Majesty's best subjects."

PHILIPPE POTHIER

ANQ-M, CE1-51, 28 avril 1767, 16 mai 1771, 10 janv. 1820, 21 mai 1824, 25 oct. 1845, 1er oct. 1849. ASSH, A, Fg-5, "Brochures judiciaires." PAC, MG 24, C7; RG 68, General index, 1651–1841. *John Askin papers* (Quaife), 2: 37. L.-J. Papineau, "Correspondance" (Ouellet), ANQ *Rapport*, 1953–55: 278, 283, 307. Toussaint Pothier, "Mémoire de l'honorable Toussaint Pothier," PAC *Rapport*, 1913: 92–103. *Select British docs. of War of 1812* (Wood), 1: 397, 429–30, 448–52. Wis., State Hist. Soc., *Coll.*, 11 (1888); 19 (1910). *Montreal Gazette*, 21 April 1808. *Quebec Gazette*, 23 Dec. 1813, 16 Sept. 1816. F.-J. Audet, "Les législateurs du Bas-Canada"; "Shérifs de Montréal," *BRH*, 8 (1902): 200. Caron, "Papiers Duvernay," ANQ *Rapport*, 1926–27: 240, 243. Desjardins, *Guide parl. The encyclopedia of Canada*, ed. W. S. Wallace (6v., Toronto, [1948]), 5: 146. *The fur trade in Minnesota; an introductory guide to manuscript sources*, comp. B. M. White (St Paul, Minn., 1977), 16, 27. É.-Z. Massicotte, "Répertoire des engagements pour l'Ouest conservés dans les Archives judiciaires de Montréal . . . [1620–1821]," ANQ *Rapport*, 1944–45: 424; 1945–46: 227, 238–39, 319. *Officers of British forces in Canada* (Irving), 166–69. Ouellet, "Inv. de la saberdache," ANQ *Rapport*, 1955–57: 123, 125, 161. P.-G. Roy, *Inv. concessions*, 3: 269. Tanguay, *Dictionnaire*, 6: 421–22. Turcotte, *Le Conseil législatif*. K. W. Porter, *John Jacob Astor, business man* (2v., Cambridge, Mass., 1931; repr. New York, 1966). Rumilly, *Hist. de Montréal*, 2: 242. Joseph Tassé, *Les Canadiens de l'Ouest* (2v., Montréal, 1878), 1: 148.

F.-J. Audet, "À propos d'un centenaire: un des pionniers pour l'amélioration du port," *La Presse*, 24 juin 1933: 49; "John Bruyères," *BRH*, 31 (1925): 343. J.-J. Lefebvre, "La vie sociale du grand Papineau," *RHAF*, 11 (1957–58): 479.

Richard Lessard, "La seigneurie de Lanaudière ou du Lac Maskinongé" and "Notes sur la seigneurie de Carufel," *BRH*, 33 (1927): 219–20 and 359–60. Frère Marcel-Joseph, "Les Canadiens veulent conserver le régime seigneurial," *RHAF*, 7 (1953–54): 378, 383. É.-Z. Massicotte, "Le bourgeois Pierre Fortier," *BRH*, 47 (1941): 179; "L'honorable Toussaint Pothier," 26 (1920): 223–24; "Les mutations d'un coin de rue," 45 (1939): 271–74; "Les shérifs de Montréal (1763–1923)," 29 (1923): 110. "Les morts de 1839," *BRH*, 32 (1926): 21. Fernand Ouellet, "Toussaint Pothier et le problème des classes sociales (1829)," *BRH*, 61 (1955): 147–59.

POWELL, ANNE. *See* MURRAY

POWELL, GRANT, physician, surgeon, militia officer, office holder, JP, and judge; baptized 30 May 1779 in Norwich, England, third son of William Dummer Powell* and Anne MURRAY; m. 1 May 1805 Elizabeth Bleeker (Bleecker) of Albany, N.Y., and they had four sons and six daughters; d. 10 June 1838 in Toronto.

Grant Powell was educated in England and apprenticed to a surgeon in Norwich. At the end of his term, an aunt wrote in 1799, he "did not sufficiently understand his profession to be of any essential service" to his master and he was £80 in debt. This pattern of professional and financial incompetence was to mark his career. Family connections failed to get him a post with the British army and his father, a judge in Upper Canada, could find him nothing in the Canadas. Grant moved to the United States and tried to establish himself in a number of places before settling into a medical practice in Stillwater, N.Y., by April 1803. It was not a success and he sank deeply into debt. When he was 30, his mother noted that "he is now the only son who calls for advice or assistance." His wife's family refused to help him and his father again failed in efforts to find him a place. Plans to move to Albany and to York (Toronto), Upper Canada, fell through.

In 1810 he abandoned his practice and moved to Montreal, where the death of a local doctor (probably Charles Blake*) soon made an opening for him. Full of hope, and promising prudence, he began to practise and in March 1812 was appointed a medical examiner for the district of Montreal. On the outbreak of war in June, he left Montreal and later that summer, probably on the recommendation of Major-General Isaac Brock*, was appointed acting surgeon to the Provincial Marine at York. During the first American capture of York, in April 1813, his house was plundered and during the second, in July, he and John Strachan* acted as civilian spokesmen for the beleaguered town, from which the British had retreated. Powell remained acting surgeon throughout the winter but lost his post in the spring when, as a result of the Provincial Marine's displacement by the Royal Navy, British medical officers arrived in Upper Canada. He served for the rest of the war as a surgeon in the Volunteer Incorporated Militia Battalion.

During the war his father was at last able to help him, securing for him in May 1813 an appointment as clerk of the House of Assembly, at an annual salary of £250. Powell also obtained positions on the bench: in April 1813 he had become official principal (judge) of the Court of Probate, in 1814 he was appointed a justice of the peace, and in 1818 he was made a district court judge. Over time he served on a number of boards, commissions, councils, and societies. By February 1818, according to his mother, he had "declined" practising medicine but maintained a connection with the profession as a member of the Medical Board of Upper Canada (1819–38) and the York hospital board (1821), and as a health officer for York and vicinity (1832–33). Powell's interests were primarily official and political. In 1827 he left his post in the assembly to become clerk of the Legislative Council, an office he retained until his death. A tory, he supported the election in 1828 of John Beverley Robinson* and the candidacy in January 1830 of Sheriff William Botsford Jarvis*, who had married his niece.

As he reached the age of 40 in 1819, he seemed at last to be settled and he was optimistic about the future. A growing family nevertheless strained his resources and he never did learn to manage what money he had. In 1826 he suffered a heavy blow when the assembly refused to raise his salary. His father, who feared that he had "borrowed a loaf from the oven," noted then that the payment of arrears on his half pay as a militia surgeon would come as a "sensible relief." Powell continued to depend on his father, drawing in advance on his inheritance and looking to him for help for his children. It was, perhaps, a sense of failure and the constant worry about money which made him, in his 50s, a man of "intolerable, sarcastic, supercilious manners," his mother informed her brother. Powell grew prickly and very conscious of his position; in 1837 he resigned from King's College Council when he found his name listed below those of newly appointed members. At that time, too, he spoke critically of Lieutenant Governor Sir Francis Bond Head*, which action, his mother later wrote, "exposed him to neglect and incivility." His death left his family in financial difficulties. His son William Dummer, supported by Chief Justice John Beverley Robinson, petitioned for the appointment as clerk of the Legislative Council and his widow asked for a pension, but neither request succeeded.

GEOFFREY BILSON

Academy of Medicine (Toronto), MS 137 (Proceedings of the Medical Board of Upper Canada, 1819–48). AO, MU 1532;

MU 1537; RG 22, ser.94, 2: 208; ser.155. MTRL, W. D. Powell papers. Norfolk Record Office (Norwich, Eng.), Archdeacon's transcript for Norwich, St Clements, reg. of baptisms, 30 May 1779. PAC, RG 4, B28, 47: 272–75; RG 5, A1: 19098–100, 70543, 108854–55; C1, 2, file 291; 6, file 603; RG 8, I (C ser.), 84: 221–22, 228–29, 248–49; 1168: 292; 1717: 65; RG 19, E5(a), 3745, claim 335; RG 68, General index, 1651–1841: 64, 74, 182, 219. *Arthur papers* (Sanderson), 1: 195–96. [Anne Murray] Powell, "Letters of Mrs. Wm. Dummer Powell, 1807–1821," ed. Janet Carnochan, Niagara Hist. Soc., [*Pub.*], no.14 ([1906]): 1–40. *Select British docs. of War of 1812* (Wood), 1: 397; 2: 190–93. *Town of York, 1815–34* (Firth). U.C., House of Assembly, *App. to the journal*, 1839, 2, pt.II: 844. *Patriot* (Toronto), 12 June 1838. Armstrong, *Handbook of Upper Canadian chronology* (1967). Chadwick, *Ontarian families*, 1: 32–34. *Toronto directory*, 1833–34, 1837. R. J. Burns, "The first elite of Toronto: an examination of the genesis, consolidation and duration of power in an emerging colonial society" (PHD thesis, Univ. of Western Ont., London, 1974). Canniff, *Medical profession in U.C.*, 559–62. W. G. Cosbie, *The Toronto General Hospital, 1819–1965: a chronicle* (Toronto, 1975). *A history of Upper Canada College, 1829–1892; with contributions by old Upper Canada College boys, lists of head-boys, exhibitioners, university scholars and medallists, and a roll of the school*, comp. George Dickson and G. M. Adam (Toronto, 1893), 52. W. R. Riddell, *The life of William Dummer Powell, first judge at Detroit and fifth chief justice of Upper Canada* (Lansing, Mich., 1924). *Robertson's landmarks of Toronto*, 1: 188–89, 193; 3: 288. Scadding, *Toronto of old* (Armstrong; 1966). F. N. Walker, *Sketches of old Toronto* (Toronto, 1965).

POWER, MICHAEL, Roman Catholic priest and bishop; b. 17 Oct. 1804 in Halifax, second child and eldest son of William Power, a sea captain, and Mary Roach; d. 1 Oct. 1847 in Toronto.

Michael Power's parents had both immigrated to Nova Scotia from Ireland and settled in Halifax, where they married. On the advice of Edmund Burke*, the bishop of Quebec's vicar general in Nova Scotia, their son Michael prepared for the priesthood. After studies in Montreal and Quebec, he was ordained in Montreal on 17 Aug. 1827 by Bishop John Dubois of New York. Power was then appointed missionary at Drummondville (1827–31) and subsequently served as pastor at Montebello in the Ottawa valley (1831–33), at Sainte-Martine, near Valleyfield (Salaberry-de-Valleyfield) (1833–39), and at La Prairie (1839–42). During the last posting he was also vicar general of the diocese of Montreal. While he was at Montebello, his bishop, Jean-Jacques LARTIGUE of Montreal, acting on the request of Bishop Alexander MCDONELL of Kingston, entrusted him with the nearby Catholic missions on both sides of the Ottawa River, including the Upper Canadian missions of Plantagenet, Hawkesbury, and Pointe-à-l'Orignal. Much to McDonell's regret, however, Power refused to attend the south side of the river.

In the spring of 1841, McDonell's successor, Rémi Gaulin*, began to seek some assistance in the ecclesiastical government of his vast diocese, which covered all of Upper Canada. He wanted a division of the diocese, whether by the appointment of an auxiliary bishop or by an absolute division, or at the very least the selection of a coadjutor bishop. Noting in a letter to Bishop Ignace Bourget* of Montreal that the province would become more and more Irish, he suggested that Michael Power be appointed to the new bishopric: "This gentleman is sufficiently Irish to be well thought of here and sufficiently Canadian to live up to all we might expect of him." Power would, he believed, be perfectly acceptable to both Rome and London as well. Archbishop Joseph SIGNAY of Quebec and Bishop Pierre-Flavien Turgeon*, his coadjutor, immediately issued a letter certifying to the 36-year-old Power's good character and worthiness for the episcopate and recommending him to the Holy See. In May 1841, accompanied by Father Power and Father Joseph-Octave Paré*, Bishop Bourget travelled to Europe, where the proposed division of the diocese was favourably received by both the pope and the Colonial Office.

On 17 Dec. 1841 the new diocese, covering the western half of Upper Canada, was erected and Power chosen as its first bishop. He was left free to select his episcopal city and to recommend the exact border between his diocese and Gaulin's. The papal bulls of the bishop-elect arrived in March 1842. Subsequently Rome agreed to his choice of Toronto as his see and to the proposed line of demarcation between the two dioceses. On 8 May 1842 Power was consecrated in the parish church at La Prairie by Bishop Gaulin assisted by bishops Bourget and Turgeon. He arrived in Toronto on 25 June to be formally installed in his new diocese the next day.

In 1842 the diocese of Toronto included some 50,000 faithful; in the city of Toronto there were 3,000 Catholics in a total population of about 13,000. The diocese was served by 19 priests, 16 of whom attended its first synod, held in October 1842. Four of the clergy were French Canadian, among them Jean-Baptiste Proulx* at Manitoulin Island, while most of the others were of Irish or of Scots extraction, including vicars general William Peter MACDONALD at Hamilton and Angus MacDonell at Sandwich (Windsor). The first synod adopted a series of regulations of a disciplinary nature designed to establish the new diocese and its parishes on a firm footing. Pastors were not to wander outside of their assigned territories, confessional boxes were to be provided in churches, private confessions were forbidden except for the deaf or sick, no fees were allowed for the administration of sacraments, baptismal fonts were to be erected and baptismal registers kept, private baptisms were forbidden in most instances, and the consent of parents was required for baptisms of children except where a child was in danger of death. No marriages would be allowed in private homes and immigrants wishing to marry were to be thoroughly investigated. Pastors must reside in their parishes and the permission of the bishop would be required for an absence of one week or more. Clerics were to be very careful in their dealings with women and must always dress appropriately. The Roman missal and breviary were to be used in the diocese, Butler's catechism being the standard text in English-speaking missions and the Quebec catechism in French-speaking missions. As of 1 Jan. 1843 priests were to hold duplicate ledgers for baptisms, confirmations, marriages, and burials.

Power had wasted no time in providing his new diocese with dynamic leadership. In August and September 1842, shortly after his arrival in Toronto, he had undertaken his first pastoral visitation, to Penetanguishene and Manitoulin Island, and to the western part of the diocese in Amherstburg, Sandwich, and Tilbury. During the course of his episcopate he had to cope with several unworthy clerics and did not hesitate to threaten and apply harsh punishment. One of his important achievements was the foundation of St Michael's Cathedral in Toronto. Construction began in April 1845 according to plans by William Thomas*. Although Power lived to see the completion of the nearby bishop's palace, which was blessed on 7 Dec. 1846, the cathedral was not dedicated until 29 Sept. 1848, nearly a year after his death.

While pastor of La Prairie, Power had been instrumental in establishing the Society of Jesus in his parish, an order that was only then returning to Canada [*see* Clément Boulanger*]. In the autumn of 1842 he asked the general of the Jesuits for men to assume direction of the Indian missions in the western and northern parts of his diocese. When the priests Pierre Point and Jean-Pierre Choné finally arrived in July 1843, they went immediately with their superior, Jean-Pierre CHAZELLE, to the parish of L'Assomption at Sandwich, which was to serve for some years as the order's base of operations in the diocese. The Jesuits remained based at Sandwich, while developing their missions, until 1859; they left when Bishop Pierre-Adolphe Pinsoneault* of London made Sandwich his episcopal see.

By 1847 there were 25 priests in the diocese of Toronto; of the 10 who were French-speaking, 7 were Jesuits. The numbers were not adequate to the need, however, and in January 1847 Power left on a six-month visit to Europe, seeking to recruit additional priests and also to raise money for his cathedral. While in Ireland he arranged for the Loretto sisters to establish a mission in Toronto [*see* Ellen Dease*, named Mother Teresa]. He also witnessed the famine that was driving unprecedented numbers of Irish to emigrate. More than 90,000 landed at Quebec in 1847. Typhus was rife among them and spread to the Canadian towns that welcomed them, including Toronto. Power contracted the disease while calling on some of the victims and succumbed to it on 1 Oct. 1847. He was 42 years of age.

Though his episcopate was short, the first bishop of Toronto had through his energetic administration laid the foundations for a flourishing diocese. It is fitting that his effigy, sculpted by John COCHRANE, should adorn the main entrance to St Michael's palace in Toronto. He was eventually succeeded in 1850 by Armand-François-Marie de Charbonnel*.

ROBERT CHOQUETTE

Michael Power, *Constitutiones diocesanæ in synodo Torontina prima latæ et promulgatæ* (Toronto, 1842).

ACAM, 255.102, 833-4, -7, 841-3, 842-4, -5; 255.104, 841-1, 843-6, -8, 847-3. Arch. of the Roman Catholic Archdiocese of Toronto, LB 02 (Michael Power, letterbook, 1842–65), Power to Angus MacDonell, 18 April 1843; Power, circular letter to clergy, 25 Aug. 1845. Gérard Brassard, *Armorial des évêques du Canada . . .* (Montréal, 1940). Robert Choquette, *L'Église catholique dans l'Ontario français du dix-neuvième siècle* (Ottawa, 1984). *Jubilee volume, 1842–1892: the archdiocese of Toronto and Archbishop Walsh*, [ed. J. R. Teefy] (Toronto, 1892), 107–40.

POZER, GEORGE (at birth he was named **Johann Georg Pfozer**; he signed **Georg Pfozer** but in official records was called George Pozer), merchant, landowner, and JP; b. 21 Nov. 1752 in Wilstedt (Federal Republic of Germany); m. 11 Jan. 1776 Magdalen Sneider in Schoharie, N.Y., and they had six children; d. 16 June 1848 at Quebec.

At the age of 21, George Pozer, who came from a humble family and had almost no education, left the village where he was born and went to North America. By 1773 he was living at Schoharie, near Albany, but some three years later the military situation prompted his departure for New York. There he engaged in the bakery and grocery business, profiting from supply contracts with the British army. In his old age Pozer often recalled this period of his life, the real or imaginary risks that he said he had run, the Yankees' brutality, and his meeting with a compatriot, businessman John Jacob Astor, who would remain for him the symbol of success. In the autumn of 1783 he left with his wife and two sons for England, along with the troops and other loyal subjects forced to evacuate the city. From this decade of experience he took with him £838 in savings and a certificate of good character and faithful services.

After a short stay in Wilstedt and some time in London concluding arrangements with his correspondents, he sailed for Quebec in the spring of 1785. He settled in the town, and through endeavours that started with his first grocery store and extended to real estate operations, with money lending and discounting in between, Pozer succeeded in building a fortune over 30 years. Then, having outlived his ambitions, he had another 30 years to consolidate it. When he died, the balance sheet of all the years spent patiently accumulating wealth showed approximately: furniture and cash, £529; securities, £12,000; debts owing him, £15,029; town properties estimated on the basis of rental value, about £60,000; three seigneuries, and 6,800 hectares held in free and common socage. There is no way to assess the value of his rural properties. In any event it was a large, and highly visible, fortune, and no less visible was its owner, who still, in the mid 19th century, wore breeches, stockings with buckled shoes, a blue frock-coat, and a tricorn hat. While his heirs grew impatient and his tenants continued to bring him their quarterly rent or beg for more time, the old German, who was said to be a millionaire, became a familiar figure to passers-by. They would see him on the doorstep of his house on Rue Saint-Jean taking the air and greeting with pleasure those who stopped to chat.

His fortune had begun with trade, but nothing set Pozer apart from the many other merchants who were both importers and retailers yet were just moderately successful. He got his goods from Hardess Mantz and Company in London – glassware, crockery, wine, tea, and other groceries, which were transported by English shipowner John Brown. These imports were worth between £200 and £500 annually. Pozer retailed the merchandise himself, along with local produce. From 1806 to 1826 he sent sawn timber to Brown on a commission basis, one cargo a year, rarely more. From time to time he had contracts to supply the Quebec garrison, but he was not one of the principal purveyors.

To throw light on the shadowy area separating these modest commercial endeavours from the process of making a spectacular fortune it would be necessary to analyse another set of practices basic to most of his initial accumulation of wealth: financial trading through discounting and lending. Few traces remain of this business activity. Pozer reportedly profited from army bills, which the government made legal tender during the War of 1812, but this would have been only one operation among many. He discounted notes and bills of exchange on a regular basis and made short- or medium-term loans at the current six per cent rate. His clients were mainly merchants and businessmen, and with them the loan was generally made by private note. Consequently it is not possible to reconstitute these transactions by referring to obligations signed before a notary or debts recorded in the inventory of his estate, which were mostly arrears in rents and annuities, along with a few large debts that were long outstanding and probably not recoverable. During the period when Pozer was active, money-lending was for him an operation separate from his mercantile business and involving a diversified clientele, among whom were enough small borrowers that it is clear anyone could turn to him. A letter from one Charles Laparé, written in English, is proof: "Having made up my mind to Commence business in the Blacksmith line, but not having the Means, I have to solicit from you for the term of two years by paying interest the Sum of thirty pounds Currency. Reference can be made to Mr Rivrain as to my caracter and conduct he having known me for some time. I have the honor to be yours most obedient humble servant."

In 1793, eight years after arriving at Quebec, Pozer bought a house on Rue Saint-Jean into which he moved his grocery store and his family. This purchase marked the beginning of his investments in town property, and in the next 20 years he purchased 17 more buildings. Seven of them brought in a good return: an inn on Rue Buade (1794), a bakery on Rue de la Fabrique (1800), the Freemasons' Hall (1804), an inn on Rue des Jardins, the Belfast Coffee House and the London Coffee House in Lower Town (1808–9), and another large property on Rue Saint-Jean (1811). These investments absorbed the profits from trade and money-lending as they came in, and if at the beginning some purchases exceeded his liquid assets, rental payments soon were added to the other income so the momentum was kept up until 1814. After that, Pozer's ventures in the seigneury of Aubert-Gayon (Aubert-Gallion) and problems in his family temporarily diverted his attention from the real estate market. In 1824, when he was 72, he started attending public auctions again and gradually added to his holdings 16 more properties as well as 165 *rentes constituées* (secured annuities) in the *faubourg* Saint-Roch (1825). Certain acquisitions in this period were dictated by circumstance. In addition to four attachments of debtors' real property, Pozer filed a claim in the bankruptcy of Colin McCallum, the husband of one of his granddaughters, to whom he had lent £15,000, probably because they were family members. Through this claim he came into possession of St Andrew's Wharf in 1839.

Managing all these properties was expensive. At least two notaries worked alternately as Pozer's agents, receiving fees and a commission on each contract, but he was still able to keep a close eye on income, as well as on expenditures for the inevitable major repairs to these old houses. The handsome portfolio in bank and government securities that he built up from 1837 corresponded to a re-directing of his investments.

When he died, Pozer owned three seigneuries, including Saint-Normand in the Montreal area, which he had purchased in 1845 as a step in recovering

McCallum's debt. The other two, which were located in Nouvelle-Beauce, represented real estate operations that had an important place in his career. He expected much from them and spared no pains to ensure that they met his expectations. In 1807 he paid £550 for Aubert-Gayon, 9,666 hectares of land difficult to reach and virtually uninhabited. To develop it and doubtless also to impress the colonial authorities, Pozer conceived a plan for a model settlement. In Wilstedt and its environs he recruited some 40 peasants, who landed at Quebec with their families in October 1817. His goal was to get them to grow hemp on his seigneury, since the cultivation of this crop was being promoted by the government. He had heavy expenses, because he was obliged to support all these people until the first harvest, at least. The following year he proudly sent to England a large quantity of hemp prepared by the best techniques used in the Rhineland. But it did not sell well, and since he was not given the promised export subsidy, the experiment was a failure. Furthermore, the Germans, who were inexperienced at clearing land and unprepared for the isolation and harshness of the region, left Aubert-Gayon without repaying the money advanced to them. From then on the seigneury would develop at a snail's pace. Pozer counted more on the timber reserve than on settlement, which distance and the burden of dues did nothing to encourage. His son William, who settled on the seigneury around 1829 and who scratched out a mediocre living from it, was tempted to think that he had been disinherited when he received it as his share of Pozer's estate, along with the 6,800 hectares in the adjoining township of Shenley. But these properties would be extremely valuable in the second half of the century.

The development of Saint-Étienne, a fief of 8,900 hectares purchased for £1,700 in 1829, was a different matter. Being closer to markets and better suited to farming, it quickly attracted settlers from the neighbouring seigneuries of Lauzon and Sainte-Marie. The dues on it would always be modest but, when collected from some 200 *censitaires* and added to the income from the mills and sawmills, they were an attractive revenue in relation to the small investment, even after arrears were taken into account. Eventually Pozer entrusted management of Saint-Étienne to his grandson, George Pozer, but until he was over 80 he regularly went down to the Beauce to look into his affairs and shake up his relatives, to whom he had given jobs here and there in his mills and on his lands and from whom he demanded unflagging zeal in return.

Pozer's family and community life can be followed through the court action to have his will set aside, which was unsuccessful. Ninety-seven people were called to give evidence on the old man's conduct and opinions. He had been accustomed to speak readily of his family, but with great bitterness. While still young, the sons had been brought into his business, and were then encouraged to stand on their own feet, with financial backing. Jacob, the eldest, was the only one to make his mark but he was foolhardy, in the eyes of his father, who congratulated himself on not having backed him unreservedly. Jacob died at 45, preceded by George, who was only 25, and followed by John, who died at 35 and who, like his brothers, left nothing but debts. Pozer then had only William to count on. Although William had long been a disappointment, their relations improved when he agreed to settle at Aubert-Gayon. Pozer's two daughters married late in life and against his wishes. Elizabeth became the wife of a small merchant, John Southeron, who made her unhappy and earned her father's lasting hatred. Hannah ran off with a newly landed carpenter whom Pozer took into his service two years later when the wretched couple came to beg his forgiveness. He was deeply affected by his wife's death in 1826 – it was the final blow in this series of bereavements and vexations. Subsequently he lived with Hannah, by then widowed and for ever devoted to him, and with the son born of her brief marriage, George Alford. He also took responsibility for his other grandchildren, orphans without means of support; he imposed a harsh discipline upon them that included going to work at a very early age rather than continuing in school, for which he had little use. George Pozer, the first-born of all these offspring, was the only one to enjoy an unexpected indulgence. He received secondary education but wasted his life; his grandfather, immensely hurt, nevertheless bequeathed him the undivided usufruct from Saint-Étienne. As they grew up, the others escaped from Pozer's authority but remained near by, hoping for a fair share in the inheritance. They received quite small legacies or nothing at all. Except for properties in the country, Pozer left his fortune, both personal and real, to George Alford, who had grown up at his side and whose devotion and docility never flagged.

Pozer had at first hoped for social recognition commensurate with his loyalty to the crown, his success, and his efforts to become integrated into the British and Anglican society with which he brushed shoulders. It was refused him. He was shut out of the system of promotions and favours that normally rewarded even minimal success in the business world. For example it was only after ten years of negotiations that the government agreed to let him keep the land in Shenley as part of an exchange. A commission as justice of the peace, received when he was 70, could not obliterate past disappointments or make him forget that in the eyes of polite society he was just that fellow Pozer, the miser, the usurer. He had led a simple and well-ordered existence – perhaps the eccentricities he affected in his old age were a way of provoking those who had always kept him at a distance. His quarrel with the municipality about porches and steps is an example. In 1842 Pozer refused to comply with the regulation obliging owners to remove at their own expense those encroaching upon the sidewalks. Having lost in court, sooner than pay the costs he let furniture be seized, whereupon he gave a banquet for the whole neighbourhood.

By his way of life especially, George Pozer, an uneducated man of the people, who was too rich and a foreigner to boot, set himself apart from the bourgeoisie which for these reasons had forced him to remain on the fringes. Rejecting the privacy that goes with wealth, Pozer created around him the sociability of the village. People had only to open the door, which had no knocker, to be welcomed as friends. Those who all day long trooped into the ground-floor room were craftsmen and small businessmen with the same social background as his. Among them was a group of fellow Germans, and Pozer was never so happy as when he could speak his own language and reminisce about his native land.

LOUISE DECHÊNE

Because he was the owner of numerous buildings at Quebec and a money-lender, and because he received annual payments secured on 165 plots in the *faubourg* Saint-Roch, George Pozer is mentioned every year in a great many notarial acts held at the ANQ-Q. The other party to the contract sometimes chose the notary, and so a few of these transactions are in the records of Jean Bélanger (CN1-16), Archibald Campbell* (CN1-49), John Greaves Clapham (CN1-67), Pierre-Louis Deschenaux* (CN1-83), Edward Glackmeyer (CN1-116), Roger Lelièvre (CN1-178), Louis Panet (CN1-208), and Joseph-Bernard Planté* (CN1-230), but most of the contracts were signed before Pozer's own notary. Jacques VOYER acted in that capacity from 1803 to 1842, and there are 167 acts under Pozer's name in his minute-book (CN1-285). From 1842 John Childs dealt with Pozer's affairs, drawing up 217 instruments for him and for his heirs (CN1-64). Acts relating to his estate are in Child's minute-book and include wills dated 27 Oct. and 15 Nov. 1847 and 29 April 1848, the deeds of gifts to George Alford dated 17, 28 July, 5 Oct. 1846 and 4 March, 18 Sept. 1847, and the inventory begun on 6 July 1848 after Pozer's death.

ANQ-Q, P-240, 2; 45; 52; T6-1/44. AVQ, VII, E, 1; VIII. McCord Museum, M21968, corr., invoices, and copy of proceedings to set aside a will, Court of Queen's Bench, no.2150, 30 April 1849, Alford *vs* Southeron. PAC, RG 1, L3[L]: 2464–73, 78339–83. *Cadastres abrégés des seigneuries du district de Montréal* . . . (3v., Québec, 1863). *Cadastres abrégés des seigneuries du district de Québec* . . . (2v., Québec, 1863). "Les dénombrements de Québec" (Plessis), ANQ *Rapport*, 1948–49: 1–250. *Rapport des commissaires nommés pour s'enquérir de l'état des lois et autres circonstances qui se rattachent à la tenure seigneuriale dans le Bas-Canada, et appendice* (Montréal, 1844), 163, 177, 291–92. *Recensement de Québec, 1818* (Provost). *Morning Chronicle* (Quebec), 19 June 1848. *Quebec Gazette*, 16 Oct. 1817, 1 Aug. 1825, 17 June 1848. *Quebec almanac*, 1822–41. Philippe Angers, *Les seigneurs et premiers censitaires de St-Georges-Beauce et la famille Pozer* (Beauceville, Qué., 1927). George Gale, *Historic tales of old Quebec* (Quebec, 1923). J. M. LeMoine, *Picturesque Quebec: a sequel to "Quebec past and present"* (Montreal, 1882), 156, 236. Honorius Provost, *Sainte-Marie de la Nouvelle-Beauce; histoire civile* (Québec, 1970). J.-E. Roy, *Hist. de Lauzon*. Robert Vézina et Philippe Angers, *Histoire de Saint-Georges de Beauce* (Beauceville, 1935). Philippe Angers, "Le docteur William-Ernest Munkel," *BRH*, 33 (1927): 350–51. Louise Dechêne, "La rente du faubourg Saint-Roch à Québec, 1750–1850," *RHAF*, 34 (1980–81): 569–96. "Les disparus," *BRH*, 35 (1929): 539. "Le millionnaire Jean-George Pozer," *BRH*, 42 (1936): 358–59.

PRING, DANIEL, naval officer; b. *c.* 1788 at Ivedon Penn, near Honiton, England; m. 27 Aug. 1810 Anne ——; they apparently had no children; d. 29 Nov. 1846 in Kingston Harbour, Jamaica.

Daniel Pring entered the Royal Navy as a midshipman on 13 Feb. 1800, and after exceptional performance as a midshipman, master's mate, and acting lieutenant he was given command in January 1808 of the 12-gun schooner *Paz*, captured the year before in an attack on Montevideo (Uruguay). Confirmed in rank on 12 May 1808, Pring had a highly successful commission with this vessel, in European waters and on the North American station. In September 1811 he joined the *Africa* (64 guns), flagship of Rear-Admiral Herbert Sawyer at Halifax. Twelve months later he went to Sir John Borlase Warren*'s flagship, the *San Domingo* (74 guns), and on 5 March 1813 he was sent, with Lieutenant Robert Heriot BARCLAY and several other officers, to command vessels on the lakes of Canada.

On 5 May Pring took charge of the *Royal George* (22 guns) on Lake Ontario, but when Captain Sir James Lucas Yeo*, the new senior naval officer in the Canadas, arrived ten days later he gave Pring the *Wolfe* (20 guns). On 17 July Yeo selected him to organize the dockyard and naval establishment at Île aux Noix, in the Rivière Richelieu, and to assume command on Lake Champlain. Pring was confirmed in the rank of commander on 13 Nov. 1813.

Yeo's choice was a fortunate one; Pring's energetic and imaginative support of the army resulted in a series of raids and defensive measures that kept American forces off balance for the better part of a year. Pring was instrumental in the destruction of naval and military installations at Plattsburgh, N.Y., in August 1813 and at Cumberland Head, N.Y., in December. In January 1814 he supervised the construction of gunboats at Coteau-du-Lac to defend Montreal against possible attack from the west, and on 30 March he gave supporting fire from sloops and gunboats to help defend the blockhouse in the Rivière Lacolle.

Pring could not, with the forces at his disposal,

prevent the buildup on Lake Champlain of a strong and efficient American naval force under an exceptional officer, Thomas Macdonough, and on his recommendation two new vessels, the 16-gun brig *Linnet* and the 37-gun ship *Confiance*, were constructed. In September 1814 Yeo's new second in command, Captain George Downie, took over *Confiance* and the squadron on Lake Champlain.

Preparations for a British offensive on the western shore of Lake Champlain were then in their final stages. The *Confiance* was not ready when the army under Sir George Prevost* began its advance, so on 3 September Pring sailed in *Linnet*, accompanied by 11 gunboats, to protect the army's left flank. Five days later he was joined by the *Confiance*, still short of equipment, and the sloops *Chubb* and *Finch*. At dawn on 11 September – the men of the *Confiance* "unacquainted with each other and with their Officers, . . . in a Ship which had been sixteen days before, on the Stocks" – Downie led his flotilla into action. The vessels sighted the American ships and gunboats anchored in Plattsburgh Bay at seven and began firing at eight. By a quarter to eleven Downie had been killed, *Confiance* had struck her colours, and Pring had surrendered the remaining vessels to Macdonough.

This defeat was the subject of intense mutual recrimination between the army and the navy, but Pring and several other officers were judged by a naval court martial to have "conducted themselves with great Zeal Bravery and Ability." Promoted post-captain on 19 Sept. 1815, in June 1816 he received an appointment to command the naval establishment on Lake Erie at the mouth of the Grand River. Retrenchment brought this appointment to an end before the summer of 1817 was out, and Pring went on half pay for nearly 20 years. On 1 Dec. 1836 he received command of the *Inconstant* (36 guns); in 1838 he brought Lord Durham [LAMBTON] home from Quebec in this vessel. On 28 July 1841 he took charge of the *Thunderer* (84 guns). That ship paid off in December 1843, and Pring was placed on half pay until 16 Sept. 1845, when he was given the *Imaum* (76 guns), with the rank of commodore, and became senior naval officer at Jamaica. Late in 1846 yellow fever spread among the ships at Jamaica, and he may well have been a victim of this epidemic.

Neither Pring nor his contemporaries were forthcoming about his private affairs. He spent his first years, and his years on half pay, at his home in Devon, Ivedon Penn. When he died he left a considerable amount of land to his widow and other property to a close friend in Tavistock. There is no known portrait of Pring and no memorial. The fact remains that he played an indispensable part in protecting the Montreal frontier during the War of 1812.

W. A. B. DOUGLAS

[Secondary sources make few references to Pring; he played a marginal role in the War of 1812, in spite of the responsibility that was thrust upon him. To place his activities in context, standard histories of the War of 1812 should be consulted. The best bibliography is *Free trade and sailors' rights: a bibliography of the War of 1812*, comp. J. C. Fredriksen (Westport, Conn., and London, 1985). [E. B. Brenton], *Some account of the public life of the late Lieutenant-General Sir George Prevost, bart., particularly of his services in the Canadas* . . . (London, 1823), contests statements about the defeat at Plattsburgh made at Pring's court martial but has little bearing on Pring himself, since it was Downie who was the object of controversy. A. T. Mahan, *Sea power in its relations to the War of 1812* (2v., Boston, 1919), has yet to be superseded. Theodore Roosevelt, *The naval war of 1812; or, the history of the United States Navy during the last war with Great Britain; to which is appended an account of the battle of New Orleans* (2v., Philadelphia, 1902), is still quite durable. W.A.B.D.]

NMM, C. G. Pitcairn-Jones, notes on sea officers. PAC, RG 8, I (C ser.), 166, 230, 273, 679–83, 694, 730–32, 1203, 1219–21. PRO, ADM 1/2346–52 (mfm. at PAC); ADM 23/106; ADM 50/227; PROB 11/205. *Select British docs. of War of 1812* (Wood). G.B., Admiralty, *The commissioned sea officers of the Royal Navy, 1660–1815*, [ed. D. B. Smith *et al.*] (3v., n.p., [1954]). Marshall, *Royal naval biog.* [Dwells entirely on Pring's service on Lake Champlain. W.A.B.D.] W. R. O'Byrne, *A naval biographical dictionary: comprising the life and services of every living officer in her majesty's navy* . . . (London, 1849).

PROPHET. *See* TENSKWATAWA

PROULX (Proust, Prou), LOUIS, farmer, businessman, seigneur, and politician; b. 29 Oct. 1751 in Nicolet (Que.), son of Jean-Baptiste Proulx, a farmer, and Marie-Magdeleine Pinard; d. there 3 March 1838.

Louis Proulx belonged to a farming family that had established itself in the Trois-Rivières district during the early days of French settlement. Since 1725 his father had lived at Nicolet, where, having bought more than 480 *arpents* of land, he engaged in activities related to agriculture. In all likelihood Louis settled down early in life on one of the family properties to farm.

In 1779 Proulx hired a skipper to carry wheat to Quebec on the *Saint-Pierre*, which he owned, and he called himself a merchant, a designation implying a social rank above that of his family. At the time he was speculating principally in grain, his most important concern, and cattle. He would buy wheat from farmers in Nicolet and through a well-organized transportation network sell it to various Quebec merchants, who dealt with him direct. He traded cattle for the most part locally, leasing much of his livestock to farmers in his parish. Proulx was also interested in buying land, albeit on a modest scale. In addition, he made loans in grain and small sums of money to the farmers around Nicolet. By exploiting the forests on his farm he was able to market firewood in Trois-Rivières. In the 1780s he became an important merchant in his community and by developing various local initiatives to the full he established a base for the accumulation of capital.

On 18 Jan. 1784, at the age of 32, Proulx married Marie-Anne Brassard, the daughter of a wealthy farmer from Nicolet. This advantageous match assisted him in maintaining his social status and enhancing his popularity with local farmers. From that time his activities became regional in scope and he concentrated avidly on acquiring more land through clever and persistent scheming. Sometimes he took direct steps, buying a lot and then renting or selling it at a profit. But he also seems to have proceeded indirectly. He would engage in such transactions as lending money or grain and setting up *rentes constituées*, a type of annuity which was a loan under the legal guise of a contract, and then wait until the farmers were so heavily in debt that selling their land for a pittance was their only option. There was seldom a year that he did not manage to take possession of a property in his own parish or neighbouring ones through a type of sale known as *à réméré*, which allowed for repurchase by the vendor within a set period and which was, in fact, a disguise for borrowing. Between 1784 and 1798 he indeed obtained from vendors unable to buy back their land nearly 50 lots which he later sold at top price. Proulx adopted, then, a capitalistic approach to property, which to him was not only a sure and stable element, but also a source of financial gain. His constant concern was to keep his holdings in line with currency fluctuations and potential profits.

A shrewd merchant, Proulx made an effort to diversify his investments, as he had done at the beginning of his career. Even though he had put a good part of his liquid assets into landed property, he continued to speculate in commodities such as wheat and cattle. He handled the building and repairing of local churches as a contractor. By the late 18th century Proulx was a powerful and indeed pre-eminent merchant who became increasingly active on the regional level.

In 1798 the curé of Nicolet, Louis-Marie Brassard*, conscious of his parishioner's influence and prestige, named him head churchwarden. Six years later Proulx was elected to the House of Assembly for Buckingham, which he represented until 1808. His importance can, moreover, be gauged by the fact that on 23 Jan. 1810 his only daughter, Marie-Anne, married François Legendre of Gentilly (Bécancour), a surveyor who also represented Buckingham in the assembly and whose late father had been a major landowner – altogether an ideal marriage for both families.

After 1800 Proulx concentrated on acquiring seigneuries. An excellent occasion had arisen in 1796 when seigneur Dominique Debartzch's widow, Marie-Josephte, had taken the initiative in selling him a large part of La Lussodière, a rich seigneury upstream from Nicolet. In 1812 Proulx set out to purchase as much of the adjoining seigneury of Saint-François as he could. He bought the share of co-seigneur François-Xavier Crevier on 23 July, and that of Crevier's brother Joseph-Antoine a week later. In February 1817 he persuaded his own brother Joseph to cede him the seigneurial rights he had acquired from his wife, Geneviève Crevier Descheneaux. Finally, that year he bought the shares and portions belonging to Joseph Mercure.

Proulx, however, was not satisfied merely to have the title of seigneur. His properties were enterprises to be made as profitable as possible. Precise and meticulous, he first put the registers of seigneurial dues into order. In 1818 he had his territory mapped by his son-in-law. Then he listed the full names of the tenants in a large register, and recorded the details about each parcel of land, including area, location relative to neighbouring parcels, dues, and the principal changes in ownership since the original leases had been granted. In this way he acquired a thorough knowledge not only of his domains and what they produced, but also of the income from them and the attached seigneurial rights.

In January 1828 Proulx, who was 76, resigned himself to handing all his property over to Legendre by a deed of gift. He seemed to feel that not being able to leave his estate to a son bearing his name was a shameful misfortune. In his final years he was content to live quite simply. Nicolet was truly an ideal retreat, allowing him to observe the work on the land and cultivate his garden at leisure. He passed away quietly on 3 March 1838, and he was buried two days later in the parish church, a mark of his distinction.

Doubtless the earliest of his farming family to liberate himself from working the land, Louis Proulx is an excellent example of those who managed to rise in society and build up an impressive fortune. His achievement needs to be seen especially within the framework of a colony which after the conquest experienced an unprecedented growth in population and new access to British markets. His exemplary success confirms the dynamic and extensive commercial activity of rural Lower Canada in the late 18th and early 19th centuries.

RICHARD CHABOT

ANQ-M, CN3-78, 12 févr. 1817; CN3-88, 23 sept. 1796. ANQ-MBF, CE1-13, 30 oct. 1751, 18 janv. 1784, 23 janv. 1810, 4 mars 1838; CN1-4, 15 mars 1792; 8 janv., 19 févr., 4, 15 mars 1796; 1er févr., 24 mai, 28 juill., 8 sept., 18 nov. 1797; 23 mars, 23 avril 1798; 8 févr. 1799; CN1-5, 31 juill. 1779; 17 juin 1780; 23 juill. 1781; 16 févr., 6 août 1782; 17 janv., 16 juill. 1783; 16 mars 1784; 27 mars, 25 juill., 2 août 1786; 13 janv. 1787; 21 mars 1788; 15 févr., 16 août 1790;

31 mai 1791; 29 mai 1792; 11 juin 1793; 27 févr., 23 mai 1794; 1er avril, 27 mai, 24 nov. 1795; 7–9, 11 janv. 1796; 27 janv. 1797; CN1-6, 31 juill. 1812; CN1-31, 25 févr. 1803; 23 mars, 20 août 1812; 7 janv. 1828; CN1-35, 8 févr. 1817; CN1-79, 23 mars 1807. AP, La Nativité-de-Notre-Dame (Bécancour), Cahiers des recettes et dépenses de la fabrique, 1764–85, 1786–1832; Saint-Antoine-de-Padoue (Baieville), Cahiers des recettes et dépenses de la fabrique, 1735–1818; Saint-Édouard (Bécancour), Cahiers des recettes et dépenses de la fabrique, 1784–1930; Saint-Jean-Baptiste (Nicolet), Cahiers des recettes et dépenses de la fabrique, 1734–1822. ASN, AP-G, J.-B. Lozeau, 1–3; M.-G. Proulx, reg. des généalogies, 300–6; succession, 2, no.6. F.-J. Audet, "Les législateurs du Bas-Canada." F.-J. Audet et Fabre Surveyer, *Les députés de Saint-Maurice et de Buckinghamshire*, 69–74. Desjardins, *Guide parl.*, 125. P.-G. Roy, *Inv. concessions*, 3: 72, 75–76; 5: 114, 119–20. Bellemare, *Hist. de Nicolet*, 86. T.-M. Charland, *Histoire de Saint-François-du-Lac* (Ottawa, 1942), 94–96, 220, 264. J.-P. Wallot, "La querelle des prisons (Bas-Canada, 1805–1807)," *RHAF*, 14 (1960–61): 262, 265.

PURDY, WILLIAM, miller; b. 2 Aug. 1769 in Westchester, N.Y., son of Jesse Purdy; m. first Elizabeth Brundage; m. secondly Hulda Yates; m. thirdly Sabia Wilcox; d. 22 Jan. 1847 in Bath, Upper Canada.

William Purdy's father, a loyalist, served in Emmerich's Chasseurs during the American Revolutionary War. In 1787 William moved to St Johns (Saint-Jean-sur-Richelieu), Que., and two years later to the newly formed loyalist settlements on the upper St Lawrence. He received a land grant there in Yonge Township. In 1816 Purdy moved to Vaughan Township, where he purchased the mills of John Lyons. The destruction by fire of a new flour-mill in 1828 may have been a deciding factor in Purdy's sale of the entire property, located north of York (Toronto), to Benjamin THORNE and William Parsons.

In December 1829 Purdy petitioned for a new mill-site. The following year he was granted 400 acres in Ops Township in the Newcastle District on the condition that he build a dam and saw- and grist-mills there. Despite difficulties with spring floods and fever, he had made good progress by September 1830. He had planted part of the five or six acres he had cleared and, at the site of present-day Lindsay, had "quarried out of a Rock on the Bank of the [Scugog] River, a place sufficient to set my saw Mill and for the [flume], and have erected a good and Substantial frame, with a good Solid frame of Dam." James Grant Chewett*, of the Surveyor General's Office, thought Purdy "should receive all possible encouragement." When John Langton* stayed overnight at Purdy's in October 1833, he noted that the mills had what he imagined to be "the largest mill-dam in the world." That same month Purdy petitioned for the patents on his land, asking also that existing and future deeds on lots already overflowed by the mill-pond should carry reservations protecting him "in the right of keeping the water at its present height" and from lawsuits for damages. This petition was granted by the Executive Council on 9 May 1834.

Purdy's dam had a dramatic impact upon the area. Once a meandering stream, the Scugog became navigable for more than 30 miles as water overflowed 1,050 acres along its course, converting a marshy, tamarack forest into Lake Scugog. Many welcomed good mills and a navigable stream in an area lacking both, but there was concern that no effort had been made to calculate the effect of the dam, and many lost land or mill privileges because of the drowning.

In 1835 a parliamentary committee appointed Nicol Hugh BAIRD, an engineer, to report on the impact of the dam and the probable effect of its removal. Baird believed that improved navigation was an asset to the area and would tie into government efforts to create a main canal linking Simcoe and Rice lakes, but maintained that a dam with a 5-foot lift, instead of 12, would be sufficient. This structure would reduce both the size of the flooded area and the stretch of navigable waters, but would still allow ample power for Purdy's mills, which, he claimed, could be more efficient. Baird appeared confident that a road or railway would be built linking Windsor Harbour (Whitby) and Lake Scugog, that the Trent canal (not completed until 1905) would be developed, and that boats would never require more depth. The government accepted his major recommendation that it build its own dam, with a 5-foot lift, below Purdy's. However, it provided no incentive for Purdy to remove his.

Purdy supported a petition of 1836 for the construction of the proposed Trent canal and a road from Windsor Harbour. His main concern, however, was the issue of indemnification. He had hoped to be protected from lawsuits, particularly by those owners whose patents were issued before 1834, but he received little government support. In January 1837 Purdy again petitioned the government for flooding rights on the lands overflowed as a result of his dam. Alexander McDonell*, who was in charge of settlement in the area, confirmed that Purdy had been assigned the mill-site because of his knowledge of mills in similar situations and admitted that the mills were "in every respect adequate to the demand of the surrounding Country." He nevertheless denied "Knowledge of any promise of indemnification" for the flooding of any lands patented before or after 1834.

The divisiveness caused by Purdy's mills became evident in the aftermath of the rebellion of 1837–38. A false rumour circulated in the Peterborough area that William Lyon Mackenzie* was hiding in the mills. Purdy, who apparently had spoken out against the "family compact," was arrested on 13 Dec. 1837 and taken to the district jail in Cobourg. Along with the 11 others arrested from the Newcastle District, including John Gilchrist*, he was discharged without trial. In the summer of 1838 armed settlers attacked his dam, which they believed was the source of an outbreak of fever and ague.

The provincial Board of Works had nearly completed its dam before settling with Purdy and his sons the terms for removing theirs. In December 1843 they were granted £400 plus "the use of all surplus water that would not be needed for navigation" in exchange for relinquishing damage claims and keeping the new dam (completed by the summer of 1844) in repair. Responsibility for the new dam and management of the mills fell upon two of his eleven children, his sons Hazzard Wilcox and Jesse Thomas, for William had transferred most of his claim to them in 1836 and had no remaining interest after February 1839. In 1838 he and Jesse moved to Bath, where William spent his last nine years peaceably as a farmer. Jesse inherited the farm in 1847 and sold it to Hazzard in 1850. Both later moved to Meaford, Upper Canada, and then to North Dakota.

The controversy over the dam remained long after the Purdys had left. William Purdy, in tune with the spirit of material development characteristic of the age and of millers at all times, was frustrated. He had improved navigation and provided adequate mills for an area that otherwise had limited potential. Yet, even though he was probably a reformer, the reformers treated his dam and mill as examples of the excesses of the government, and the government provided only guarded support, choosing to believe that Purdy's difficulties were the result of his building his dam too high.

ELWOOD H. JONES

AO, RG 1, A-I-6: 8289; A-II-2, 1: 209. Bath United Church (Bath, Ont.), Cemetery records. Ont., Ministry of Citizenship and Culture, Heritage Administration Branch (Toronto), Hist. sect. research files, Victoria RF.1. PAC, RG 1, L1, 35: 404; L3, 402: P8/64; 404a: P12/146; 408: P18/107; 418: P misc., 1775–95/182; RG 5, A1: 55219–21, 55319–25, 60463–68; RG 68, General index, 1841–67: 42. Victoria Land Registry Office (Lindsay, Ont.), Deeds, Ops Township, nos.542, 568, 744, 3067–68, 4212 (mfm. at AO). Can., Prov. of, Legislative Assembly, *App. to the journals*, 1843, app.Q, schedule AA; 1845, app.AA. John Langton, *Early days in Upper Canada: letters of John Langton from the backwoods of Upper Canada and the Audit Office of the Province of Canada*, ed. W. A. Langton (Toronto, 1926). U.C., House of Assembly, *App. to the journal*, 1835, no.99; 1836, no.13; 1837–38: 386–87; 1839, 2, pt.I: 156; *Journal*, 1835: 32, 40, 195, 218, 398–400; 1836–37: 154, 161. *The valley of the Trent*, ed. and intro. E. C. Guillet (Toronto, 1957). *British Whig*, 4 Nov. 1834. *Christian Guardian*, 7 April, 12 May 1847. *Chronicle & Gazette*, 27 Dec. 1834. *Cobourg Star*, 20 Dec. 1837. "Purdy family history," comp. Kaireen Morrison (typescript, 1982; copy in possession of Elwood Jones, Peterborough, Ont.). *"Bless these walls": Lindsay's heritage*, ed. Moti Tahiliani (Lindsay, 1982). *History of Toronto and county of York, Ontario* ... (2v., Toronto, 1885), 2: 127. L. A. Johnson, *History of the county of Ontario, 1615–1875* (Whitby, Ont., 1973). Watson Kirkconnell, *County of Victoria centennial history* (2nd ed., Lindsay, 1967), 31–32, 94–95. Lindsey, *Life and times of Mackenzie*, 2: 376. John Squair, *The townships of Darlington and Clarke, including Bowmanville and Newcastle, province of Ontario, Canada* (Toronto, 1927). F. G. Weir, *Scugog and its environs* (Port Perry, Ont., 1927).

PURVIS, NANCY, merchant and schoolteacher; b. *c.* 1790; d. 9 April 1839 in Bridgetown, N.S.

Nothing is known about the place of Nancy Purvis's birth, the names of her parents, or her childhood. At some point she married James Purvis, a customs employee in Halifax, whose origins are also unknown. He died intestate on 15 April 1830 at the age of 57, leaving Nancy with three daughters under age. In June, undoubtedly because of the financial hardships imposed by her husband's death, she began a millinery and haberdashery business from her residence opposite Government House. This venture evidently was short-lived, since it was not advertised after September. The next year, a notice appeared in the *Novascotian, or Colonial Herald* in which Mrs Purvis announced that with the assistance of her daughters she proposed to open a school for young ladies in Halifax "on the following Terms, viz: For Reading, Writing, Arithmetic, Grammar, Geography, plain and Fancy Needle work 30s. per Quarter. Young Children, who may require to be taught only Reading and plain Work, 20s. French and Music, if required, by competent Masters, on the usual terms." Whether the proposed school was successful or not is uncertain, since the notice ran until January 1832. By 1834 Mrs Purvis and her daughters had changed residence and had embarked once more upon an educational program for young women. The daughters stated in the *Novascotian* of 18 September that their school was now open for the reception of pupils, "to whose minds and manners the most scrupulous attention will be paid." No further mention was made of this institution, and it is not known if the school was a new one or a continuation of the previous one.

By 1836 Mrs Purvis and her daughters had moved to Bridgetown. There they apparently began operation of a ladies' seminary, whose initial establishment was said to have been due largely to the enterprise of John Quirk*, a local hotel-keeper, and other concerned citizens who wished to give their daughters more advantages in education. The school is believed to have been situated in a house built by the Reverend William ELDER, across the street from the public school or academy. One of the Purvis daughters in fact taught at the academy, commencing on 11 May 1836 "at ten shillings per quarter" and continuing at least until 1840.

The "Purvis School," as it was often called, was said to have been a model of its kind, and served the need for more advanced education of women in the Bridgetown area. The institution was apparently discontinued after three years, however, at the death of Mrs Purvis on 9 April 1839. It was undoubtedly its closing and the region's generally inadequate educational facilities that prompted Bridgetown residents to petition the House of Assembly in 1840 for a grant towards the establishment of an academy or superior school for the higher branches of education. The petition noted that the inhabitants were unable from their own resources either to secure or to continue the services of individuals "deemed efficient to teach these branches."

Nancy Purvis and her daughters provided educational opportunities of a sort in an age when the needs of young women and girls were very much neglected. From the 18th century to the middle part of the 19th, schools for girls of the upper and middle classes tended, like theirs, to be private boarding-schools in homes and residences. Large centres of population such as Halifax featured numerous and often sporadic endeavours of this kind by individuals (frequently widows and their daughters) [*see* Ann Cuthbert Rae*]. In general the curriculum of these schools emphasized drawing-room accomplishments and social etiquette rather than academic subjects. The aim, as one contemporary schoolmistress put it, was "to form the manners of the ladies . . . , that they may become the graceful and elegant insignia of opulent and well disciplined minds."

Other schoolteachers of the 1830s made a greater contribution to the education of young women in Nova Scotia, but Nancy Purvis and her daughters are of note because their lives reflected the enterprise of women forced to support themselves financially upon the deaths of husbands or fathers. Not all women of this age were uninvolved in business or, as Alexis de Tocqueville believed, were confined to the "narrow circle of domestic concerns and tasks."

WENDY L. THORPE and JULIE MORRIS

Halifax County Court of Probate (Halifax), Estate papers, P94 (James Purvis) (mfm. at PANS). PANS, MG 4, 2, reg. of burials in Bridgetown and Wilmot: 4 (typescript); RG 1, 449: 15. *Novascotian, or Colonial Herald*, 1830–39. Elizabeth Ruggles Coward, *Bridgetown, Nova Scotia: its history to 1900* ([Bridgetown], 1955).

PUSHEE, NATHAN, farmer, miller, and militia officer; b. October 1758 in Lunenburg, Mass., eldest child of Nathan Pushee and Elizabeth Priest; m. 20 April 1787 Jane Porter, *née* Brown, and they had nine children; d. 31 Oct. 1838 in Newport, N.S.

At the outbreak of the American revolution in April 1775 Nathan Pushee enlisted as a private in Gardner's Massachusetts Battalion and took part in the battle of Bunker Hill. In March 1776 he was transferred to the Life Guard protecting General George Washington, serving with it until the end of the year. The following January Pushee re-enlisted in the 3rd Continental Light Dragoons, and was promoted trumpet-major. With this unit he was engaged in the battles of Brandywine, Paoli, Germantown, and Monmouth. In September 1778 Pushee was at Old Tappan, N.J., when the dragoons were surprised at night by British forces, and was one of the few who escaped. Re-enlisting again in December 1779, Pushee became trumpet-major in Washington's Light Dragoons (into which his former regiment was incorporated) and moved to the southern theatre. The commander of the regiment was William Washington, a kinsman of George Washington, and this circumstance accounts for the false tradition that Pushee was George Washington's trumpet-major. On 14 April 1780 Pushee was among the victims of another successful surprise attack by the British when he was captured in the engagement of Moncks Corner.

Taken to Charleston, S.C., Pushee and more than 500 comrades faced almost certain death from disease and poor food in British prisons, and in order to escape this fate they agreed to enlist in the British army provided they did not have to fight their fellow Americans. Pushee joined the Duke of Cumberland's Regiment, a provincial unit, and was sent to Jamaica, where he became a sergeant in Captain Gideon White*'s company. At the end of the war those who had served in British regiments could not return to the United States because they were excluded from the terms of amnesty. The commander of Pushee's regiment, Lord Charles Greville Montagu, arranged for those men who wished land to be taken to Nova Scotia, and they arrived in December 1783. In the spring of 1784 they went to Chedabucto Bay, where the following year Pushee received 200 acres in Manchester Township.

Pushee and some fellow soldiers did not remain in the area long, since they wanted to find more fertile lands closer to the water. They went to Antigonish Harbour, where disbanded soldiers under Lieutenant-Colonel Timothy Hierlihy had already settled at Town Point. The attempt to establish a village at Town Point failed, and Pushee moved to the rich intervale lands on the south side of the West River, on what became St Andrew's Street in the town of Antigonish. The Napoleonic Wars brought a demand for timber in Britain, and Antigonish flourished because it was at the junction of two rivers down which timber could be floated. Pushee erected a sawmill, and sold it in 1818 to his son Henry and John G. Peabody. Considered by some as the founder of Antigonish, in the census of

1827 he was listed as a farmer with 35 acres under cultivation, 18 horned cattle, 30 sheep, and 6 pigs. Pushee served as an officer in the local militia and as a school trustee, and was one of the founders of the Dorchester Presbyterian church.

In 1838 a more lenient act of the American Congress and newspaper publicity about a fellow soldier suggested to Pushee that he apply for a pension as an American soldier. In his application from Boston, dated 6 October, he ignored his time in the British army and said only that he was taken prisoner at Moncks Corner and escaped after 11 months' captivity. On the 12th he was paid $1,056 in back pension and shortly thereafter left for Nova Scotia, where he visited old friends at Newport. There the excitement and strain of travel brought on a fatal heart attack.

PHYLLIS R. BLAKELEY

Antigonish County Court of Probate (Antigonish, N.S.), Estate papers, A69 (will of Nathan Pushee) (mfm. at PANS). Antigonish County Registry of Deeds (Antigonish), Deeds, vols.½, 1–3 (mfm. at PANS). National Arch. (Washington), RG 15, W 13835 (Nathan Pushee). New England Historic Geneal. Soc. Library (Boston), W. P. Greenlaw, "Descendants of Gabriel Pouchi or Pushee." PANS, MG 12, Misc., 6, no.76; RG 14, 3, nos.6, 16, 63. A. C. Jost, *Guysborough sketches and essays* (Guysborough, N.S., 1950), 117–23, 279–81. [Sagart Arisaig (Ronald MacGillivray)], *History of Antigonish*, ed. R. A. MacLean (2v., [Antigonish], 1976). D. G. Whidden, *The history of the town of Antigonish* (Wolfville, N.S., 1934), 39–46.

PUTNAM, WILLIAM, businessman, militia officer, and Patriot; b. *c.* 1794 in Pennsylvania, eldest son of Seth Putnam; m. Eleanor Dygart, and they had seven children; d. 4 Dec. 1838 in Windsor, Upper Canada.

About 1795 Seth Putnam, who had sided with the rebels in the American revolution, settled in Upper Canada, just east of present-day London. His wife and eldest son, William, followed him in 1797. In several ways young William proved to be a loyal, successful colonist, fighting in the War of 1812, building a saw- and grist-mill, and later establishing a distillery and running a tavern. He acquired substantial properties, some of which he farmed. In fact, he was a pillar of his community: he held township office, twice acted as foreman of the London District's grand jury, rose to the rank of captain and was appointed adjutant in the local militia, and became grand master of a masonic lodge.

Despite his successes, William harboured grievances against the government. He felt that his father had never been adequately paid for extensive road work he had undertaken and that he himself had been given less land than he deserved for his war services. He must also have been upset by the government's refusal to sell him a lot he had mistakenly occupied, on which he had cleared 25 acres. Perhaps such grievances helped incline him to the reform side of politics. Certainly, he was there by 1837 when the agitation preceding the rebellion was at its height. That fall the reformers of Dorchester Township named him a delegate to the grand provincial convention planned by William Lyon Mackenzie*. In early December he chaired a meeting in Delaware Township to establish a political union. On 8 December, after the outbreak of the rebellion, he attended a gathering in London where reformers discussed what their reaction to it should be. Essentially, they decided to do nothing. On the 16th, when all knew that the rebellion had been crushed, he and others met in Delaware and decided to importune the local Indians not to take up arms against the reformers.

Soon, Putnam was arrested for his activities and taken to London. The magistrates there heard incriminating, but only circumstantial, evidence against him, including his own foolish denial that he had attended the London meeting of 8 December. They refused his request for bail. The grand jury later indicted him on a charge of treason for his participation in an alleged conspiracy hatched at London. He was released on 2 May. Unfortunately, he could not return to his farm; while he was in jail, its buildings had been burnt to the ground, reputedly by "a political incendiary."

A personal friend, Mahlon BURWELL, apparently warned Putnam he was to be rearrested. He fled to Detroit where he joined the Patriots, Upper Canadian refugees and their American allies who were bent on "revolutionizing" the Canadas. In late June he was back in the province. The details of what ensued are uncertain, but, clearly, he shot and killed a Captain William Kerry (Cary), who was apparently trying to arrest him, in Dawn Township, close to the St Clair frontier. He fled again to Detroit, where his family joined him in exile.

By the end of November Putnam, now a "general" with the Patriots, was helping plan an invasion of Upper Canada. Having mustered fewer than 200 men, the leader of the proposed expedition, General L. V. Bierce, wished to abort it, but Putnam insisted that it proceed. On the early morning of 4 December he and others led a small force across the Detroit River to Windsor. The Patriots set fire to the local militia barracks, killing some militiamen and capturing others. Then they burnt the steamer *Thames* and killed and mutilated surgeon John James Hume. The Patriot leaders divided their men into two main groups and, as militiamen under Colonel John Prince* rushed in from Sandwich (Windsor), Putnam placed his force in an orchard. His men, under heavy fire, soon broke and ran. Putnam, who had vainly tried to stem their flight, fled in turn, only to be shot down. The raid, and Putnam's life, was at an end.

Putnam paid a heavy price for his part in the troubles of 1837–38. Many who knew him well regretted his fate. For example, John Talbot*, former editor of the St Thomas *Liberal*, who had fled the province in December 1837 to escape arrest, deplored Putnam's part in the Windsor raid, but wrote, "I am sorry for poor Putnam – he was honest and sincere." On balance, Putnam deserved pity. He had not plotted rebellion in December 1837 but had been jailed nevertheless. This and other persecutions, real or imagined, drove him to his doom at Windsor.

COLIN READ

PAC, RG 5, A1: esp. 85600–1, 106669–86, 106820, 112787–96; B36, 1–2. Jedediah Hunt, *An adventure on a frozen lake: a tale of the Canadian rebellion of 1837–8* (Cincinnati, Ohio, 1853), 4–7, 28. Robert Marsh, *Seven years of my life, or narrative of a Patriot exile; who together with eighty-two American citizens were illegally tried for rebellion in Upper Canada in 1838, and transported to Van Dieman's Land* . . . (Buffalo, N.Y., 1848), 20–25. *Rebellion of 1837* (Read and Stagg). Guillet, *Lives and times of Patriots*. Read, *Rising in western U.C.* J. M. Gray, "The life and death of 'General' William Putnam," *OH*, 46 (1954): 3–20. "The Windsor raid of 4 Dec., 1838," *Putnam Leaflets* (Danvers, Mass.), 3 (1899), no.2: 41–65. [This useful piece largely consists of a manuscript about Putnam prepared by his son Warner Herkimer. C.R.]

Q

QUÂS. *See* ʔKWAH

QUESNEL, JULES-MAURICE (baptized **Julien-Maurice**), fur trader, militia officer, businessman, office holder, JP, and politician; b. 25 Oct. 1786 in Montreal, fourth child and second son of Joseph Quesnel* and Marie-Josephte Deslandes; d. there 20 May 1842.

The son of a cultivated merchant, Jules-Maurice Quesnel, like his older brother, Frédéric-Auguste*, was educated by the Sulpicians at the Collège Saint-Raphaël in Montreal, but he was a student there for only two years (1797–99). By 1804 he was a clerk for the North West Company at Fort des Prairies, or Fort Augustus (Edmonton). In the winter of 1805, as an assistant to David Thompson*, he freighted goods into the Rocky Mountains in preparation for an expedition westward. He was at Rocky Mountain House (Alta) in October 1806 and the following month conducted an exploratory expedition into the mountains. In the late summer of 1807 he was sent to New Caledonia (B.C.) with supplies and instructions for Simon Fraser* to follow the Columbia River to its mouth. He accompanied Fraser on his perilous voyage in 1808 down what turned out to be the Fraser River, not the Columbia, and back. The first major tributary they reached was named the Quesnel; later the lake it drains and the town which developed at the confluence of the Fraser and Quesnel rivers would be named for him as well.

Quesnel stayed in New Caledonia until 1811. He wrote forlornly in 1809 to a friend, Joseph-Maurice Lamothe*, "My interests obliging me to remain in the North for a long time . . . , despite the little hope there is for a young man at present in this country I am resolved to continue to its term the career that I had the misfortune to undertake." Isolation, a steady diet of dried salmon, and poor trade led him to characterize New Caledonia as a place where "there is nothing to be had but misery and boredom." The strongest men were reduced to near incapacity for work after only three years, he claimed, and "although I am of an excellent temperament, I perceive that my health is already declining."

In the summer of 1811 Quesnel left the NWC and returned east. He was commissioned an ensign in Montreal's 2nd Militia Battalion on 2 April 1812 and promoted lieutenant on 14 July. He may have fought in the War of 1812, but if so he did not let his participation interfere with the development of his commercial interests. By 1813 he was resident in Kingston, Upper Canada, and engaged in trade there, and by 1814 he had settled in York (Toronto), where he was warned by his brother about the dangers of speculating in rum on his own account. From 1815 until 1818 Quesnel spent time in both York and Montreal, but after his marriage to Josette Cotté on 10 June 1816, in Montreal, he apparently wanted to settle in that town, and by 1818 he seems to have done so. His wife was a daughter of the late fur-trade merchant Gabriel Cotté* and a sister-in-law of former fur trader François-Antoine La Rocque*; the couple probably did not have children.

In the spring of 1815 Quesnel and John Spread Baldwin, a brother of WILLIAM WARREN, had joined in partnership with Laurent Quetton* St George, by whose firm, Quetton St George and Company, Quesnel had previously been employed. St George left that year for his native France and did not return until 1819, leaving the business in the hands of Quesnel and Baldwin. Quetton St George and Company was a small firm by Montreal standards though substantial for Upper Canada. In Montreal, Quesnel purchased wholesale from the city's importers a wide array of foodstuffs, drinks, and merchandise; as well he sold Upper Canadian produce, particularly flour and potash, on behalf of a store in York operated by Baldwin and another in Niagara (Niagara-on-the-Lake). The extension of credit was a necessary operation, and by 1819 the firm was owed £18,000–£19,000, largely by farmers, a sum greater than its net worth.

In May 1820 Quesnel and Baldwin bought out St George for four annual payments of £1,000 plus interest at six per cent. Baldwin tried to assert primacy and at one point backed out of the new partnership. He soon conceded, however, and the reorganized firm was known as Quesnel and Baldwin. It carried on the wide variety of commercial and financial activities conducted by its predecessor, possibly dealing at times direct with British firms and adding timber to its exports. The economic context was difficult, and in August 1821 Quesnel was elected to an 11-man committee of Montreal merchants which was to press the British government to admit Upper and Lower Canadian grain and flour without restriction into the British market. Flour was the firm's main export, but fluctuating prices on the English market frequently caused the company losses; the mark-up on imports provided more reliable profits. Quesnel and Baldwin prospered enough to allow the partners to pay debts amounting to several thousand pounds by 1825. However, the firm showed little growth, the volume of trade remaining relatively constant; for example the company appears to have shipped regularly 1,000–1,500 barrels of flour and 75–125 barrels of ashes per annum to Montreal. In April 1825 its net worth was £15,200, of which £10,642 was in debts, and in 1832 that worth was evaluated at only £19,134, including £9,215 in debts. From 1820 to 1832 the company provided Quesnel with an average income of £693 a year.

Quesnel and Baldwin also engaged in ancillary activities. Both partners were shareholders in the Company of Proprietors of the Lachine Canal and in the Bank of Upper Canada. They declined having an agency for the Bank of Canada, however, because Baldwin feared the bank would harm their reputation. The firm owned a share in a steamboat on the Kingston–York route and took a one-tenth share in a 120-ton steamboat launched at York in 1825 for the York–Queenston run.

The partnership agreement forming Quesnel and Baldwin expired in 1832 and was not renewed. Quesnel seems to have retired from active business and lived comfortably thenceforth as a *rentier*. He was, however, involved in the operations of the port of Montreal and concerned with navigation on the St Lawrence. From 1830 to 1839 he was a warden of Trinity House, Montreal, a government-appointed body which controlled pilots, pilotage fees, lighthouses, and navigation markings on the river; in 1839 he became deputy master, and he served until 1842. At the same time, from 1830 to 1836 he was on the harbour commission with George Moffatt*, a sometime business associate, during a period when merchants were pushing for greater expenditures on port improvements; several Canadian merchants served on that body in the 1830s and 1840s. In 1832 he lobbied his brother Frédéric-Auguste, who was a member of the House of Assembly, on behalf of St Lawrence steamboat operators and Montreal merchants. Four years later he succeeded George AULDJO as chairman of the Montreal Committee of Trade; Austin CUVILLIER replaced him in 1837.

In the 1830s promotion of port development meant taking a stand on some of the great political issues of the day, and Quesnel's sympathies lay primarily with the English party, of which the Montreal merchant community was a major element. Early in his term on the harbour commission Quesnel had briefly resigned in protest against the assembly's refusal to vote money for port improvements, believing that his presence on the commission was among the reasons inciting the Patriote majority to deny funding. As the positions of the English and Patriote parties grew more polarized in the early 1830s, Quesnel joined concerned merchants, British and Canadian, including Cuvillier, Joseph MASSON, and Horatio Gates*, in calling for retention of the constitutional *status quo*. Having been appointed a justice of the peace in 1830, he was among a number of Canadian magistrates, including Pierre de RASTEL de Rocheblave, Louis GUY, and Pierre-Édouard Leclère*, who in November 1837 warned the Canadians that those "who push you to excess" would abandon them and that they should follow those "who call you to peace." In January 1838 along with Cuvillier, Rastel de Rocheblave, and other moderates, he formed the Association Loyale Canadienne du District de Montréal to oppose the resort to arms. His appointment to the Special Council in April 1838 and his reappointment in November for the life of that body indicate his standing with the government, and his willingness to serve is eloquent testimony to his views. He, seigneur James Cuthbert, and John NEILSON were the only members to vote against the union of the Canadas, pressed on the council by Governor Lord Sydenham [THOMSON]; however, in accepting an appointment to the Legislative Council in 1841, he indicated his reconciliation to union and his pro-imperial sentiments.

Since his return to Montreal Quesnel had accumulated various honours and appointments. He had been promoted captain in the 2nd Battalion of militia in 1825, and he remained willing to serve until at least 1830. A warden of the House of Industry in 1829, he was appointed a commissioner for the relief of destitute emigrants in 1835 and a commissioner of foundlings and indigent sick in 1841. He accepted an appointment from Bishop Jean-Jacques LARTIGUE in 1838 to act as a lay administrator of the revenues of the Association for the Propagation of the Faith. He was an appointed city councillor from 1840 until his death in 1842. His burial in the parish church of Notre-Dame was witnessed by his old friend La Rocque and by judge Jean-Roch Rolland*.

Jules-Maurice Quesnel's business activities paralleled those of many of his Scottish merchant contemporaries and, like them, he developed an attachment to the British empire and its institutions. It was clear to him and to Canadian colleagues that the imperial connection was essential to their prosperity. He therefore rejected as political folly the radical notions of petit bourgeois Patriote leaders as he did the more extreme political proposals of British tory merchants.

PETER DESLAURIERS

The author wishes to thank Paulette M. Chiasson of the *DBC/DCB* for her assistance.

ANQ-M, CE1-51, 25 oct. 1786, 10 juin 1816, 23 mai 1842. ANQ-Q, P-222. BVM-G, Fonds Jules Quesnel. PAC, MG 19, A12, 4; A16; MG 24, L3: 10792, 11009–13; MG 30, D1, 31: 358; MG 55/24, no.152; RG 68, General index, 1651–1841; 1841–67. *Les bourgeois de la Compagnie du Nord-Ouest* (Masson), 1: 397. Simon Fraser, *The letters and journals of Simon Fraser, 1806–1808*, ed. W. K. Lamb (Toronto, 1960). *New light on the early history of the greater northwest: the manuscript journals of Alexander Henry . . . and of David Thompson . . .*, ed. Elliott Coues (3v., New York, 1897; repr. 3v. in 2, Minneapolis, Minn., [1965]). David Thompson, *David Thompson's narrative of his explorations in western America, 1784–1812*, ed. J. B. Tyrrell (Toronto, 1916): xlix. *Quebec Gazette*, 27 Aug. 1821, 4 Sept. 1823. William Notman and [J.] F. Taylor, *Portraits of British Americans, with biographical sketches* (3v., Montreal, 1865–68). Turcotte, *Le Conseil législatif*. Chaussé, *Jean-Jacques Lartigue*, 219. E. A. Collard, *The Montreal Board of Trade, 1822–1972: a story* ([Montreal], 1972), 53. Robert Rumilly, *La Compagnie du Nord-Ouest, une épopée montréalaise* (2v., Montréal, 1980); *Hist. de Montréal*, 2: 192; *Papineau et son temps*. J.-J. Lefebvre, "Les députés de Chambly, 1792–1967," *BRH*, 70 (1968): 3–20. É.-Z. Massicotte, "La famille du poète Quesnel," *BRH*, 23 (1917): 339–42.

QUIROUET (Quirouët, Quirouêt, Kirouet), FRANÇOIS (baptized **Pierre-François**), merchant, militia officer, auctioneer, JP, office holder, and politician; b. 28 Feb. 1776 at Quebec, son of François Quirouet and Marie-Anne Hil (Isle); d. 27 Sept. 1844 in Saint-Gervais, Lower Canada.

Nothing has been discovered of the early part of François Quirouet's life. Since he had the same given name as his father and grandfather, he probably came from a family that valued tradition. When he married Catherine MacKenzie, daughter of a Quebec cooper, on 10 June 1799, he called himself a merchant.

From 1805 until 1811 Quirouet acted as adjutant for the parish of Sainte-Anne, at Sainte-Anne-de-la-Pocatière (La Pocatière), in the Kamouraska battalion of militia, from 1810 the Rivière-Ouelle battalion. The following year he was a lieutenant in the 2nd Battalion of Quebec's militia. He was promoted captain in that unit in 1821 and eventually reached the rank of lieutenant-colonel. His militia duties, which reflected his growing prestige, remained of minor importance in his career, however.

Besides being a merchant, in 1811 Quirouet had an auctioneer's licence, which was renewed in 1816. He owned two houses at Quebec, his residence at the corner of Rue Sainte-Anne and Rue du Trésor and his business premises at 11 Rue du Sault-au-Matelot. He rented part of the latter building to his friend Martin CHINIC, and he, his brother Olivier Quirouet, and Chinic carried on a flourishing enterprise, Quirouet, Chinic et Compagnie, there. Specializing in importing, auctioneering, and commission work, Quirouet amassed a tidy fortune in the course of the first three decades of the 19th century and became a respected member of the Quebec financial world. On 7 May 1818 he was elected vice-president of the Quebec Benevolent Society, which he had joined in 1807. This mutual aid society lent money, gave its members financial and moral support in times of illness, and paid for their funerals. On 6 May 1819 Quirouet succeeded John NEILSON as its president and he retained the office until 1829, except during 1822. As a director of the Bank of Montreal's Quebec branch in 1820 and 1821 [*see* Daniel Sutherland*], he also helped establish the banking system at Quebec. When the Quebec Savings Bank opened on 26 March 1821, he assumed the vice-presidency and held it for eight years.

Quirouet also played an important role in the life of the town. In 1819 he became president of the Quebec Fire Society for a year. From 1821 to 1827 he was a member of the Education Society of the District of Quebec. As a justice of the peace he took an active part in local government from 1 Aug. 1821 till 3 July 1826. In this capacity he approved numerous plans for laying down mains and for draining, macadamizing, extending, and repairing streets in the wards of Upper and Lower Town as well as in the *faubourgs* Saint-Jean and Saint-Roch. After 1828 he was less involved in Quebec's social life. Having given up his building on Rue du Sault-au-Matelot and then his residence in Upper Town, he moved to Saint-Gervais on the south shore. In the 1831 census he was listed as a "bourgeois" in that locality and described as owning about 787 *arpents* of land on which he grew oats, potatoes, and peas. He was also justice of the peace in Saint-Gervais and commissioner for the summary trial of small causes in the seigneury of Livaudière.

Quirouet returned frequently to Quebec, however, to carry out his duties as a member of parliament, since on 11 April 1820 the voters of Orléans had chosen him as their sole representative to the House of Assembly. He was re-elected three times, and then from 1830 to 1833 represented the riding along with Jean-Baptiste Cazeau. In his early days in the assembly, Quirouet brought forward a bill for the construction of a road from Saint-François to Saint-Jean on Île d'Orléans, but it was rejected by the Legislative Council. On 26 Dec. 1820 he introduced a measure dealing with the maintenance of order in churches, this time meeting with success; the act was renewed in 1823. During the same session, on 16 Jan. 1821, he moved first reading of a bill to incorporate the Quebec Fire Assurance Company, but in the end it was denied royal assent. In January 1822 he informed the house that during a meeting of the Legislative Council John Richardson* had claimed there was a secret committee of the assembly deliberating the recall of Governor Lord Dalhousie [Ramsay]. The house reacted swiftly. After an inquiry confirmed Quirouet's statement, the assembly requested the governor to dismiss Richardson from council. Dalhousie refused, alleging that the resolution touched upon freedom of debate and was couched in terms unbefitting a legislative body. In 1823 Quirouet managed to have an act passed to authorize the construction of treadmills for the use of houses of correction. That year he attempted to get the town of Quebec incorporated, but the measure was rejected by the Legislative Council. On 21 May 1826 he brought forward his final bill, which dealt with repairing the Quebec jail. He subsequently worked mostly on assembly committees, in particular those on banking (1826), public accounts (1831), and trade and commerce (1831–32). On 25 Oct. 1833 he was called to the Legislative Council, being sworn in on 9 Jan. 1834. He remained on it until the constitution was suspended.

François Quirouet had an unusual career for a Canadian in the first half of the 19th century, but it typified several interests in play at Quebec at the time. After making a fortune in the import trade, he became an influential figure in the financial élite. An assemblyman for nearly 14 years, he opposed the union bill of 1822 [*see* Denis-Benjamin Viger*], supported Louis-Joseph Papineau*, and fought against voting supplies *en bloc* [*see* Sir Francis Nathaniel Burton*]. In 1833, however, he apparently dissociated himself from the radicals and refused to back the resolutions denying the constitutional utility of the Legislative Council. He was appointed to the council that year and, unlike his colleague Viger, he never dissented from its decisions. On the outbreak of the rebellion, he was made a commissioner for administering the oath of allegiance. When he died at the age of 68 years and 7 months, all the leading citizens of the Bellechasse region attended his funeral; he was buried in the nave of the church of Saint-Gervais.

François Drouin

ANQ-Q, CE1-1, 29 févr. 1776, 10 juin 1799; CE2-17, 30 sept. 1844. AVQ, I, 1, juillet 1814–juin 1823; V, B, juin 1823–mai 1833; VII, E, 1. PAC, RG 31, C1, 1825, Haute-Ville de Québec; 1831, Saint-Gervais; RG 68, General index, 1651–1841. L.C., House of Assembly, *Journals*, 1820–33; Legislative Council, *Journals*, 1834–37. Quebec Benevolent Soc., *Rules of the Quebec Benevolent Society* . . . (Quebec, 1819). *Recensement de Québec, 1818* (Provost). F.-J. Audet, "Les législateurs du Bas-Canada." Desjardins, *Guide parl.* J.-J. Lefebvre, *Le Canada, l'Amérique: géographie, histoire* (éd. rév., Montréal, 1968). *Quebec almanac*, 1806–41. *Quebec directory*, 1822, 1826. Turcotte, *Le Conseil législatif*.

R

RADCLIFF (Radcliffe), THOMAS, militia officer, JP, and politician; b. 17 April 1794 in Castlecoote (Republic of Ireland), eldest son of Thomas Radcliff and Elizabeth Mitchell; m. Sarah Ann Armstrong, and they had five sons and three daughters; d. 6 June 1841 at Amherst Island, Upper Canada.

The Radcliffs were a prominent Irish Anglican family. Thomas Radcliff Sr was chaplain to Ireland's lord lieutenant as well as subdean and prebendary of St Patrick's Cathedral in Dublin. Young Thomas Radcliff was educated at Trinity College. He was not, however, attracted to the church, as several of his brothers were, but to the military. A giant of a man – most sources put him at 6 ft 5 in. and 210 pounds – he joined the 27th Foot in 1811 as an ensign, becoming a lieutenant two years later.

During the Peninsular War Radcliff fought in many battles; in 1814 he was transferred to British North America where he saw action at Plattsburgh. Returning to Europe, he missed the battle at Waterloo but did participate in the triumphal march into Paris. In 1816 he went on half pay, taking up a position at the Richmond Penitentiary in Ireland where his father was chaplain. In 1832 Thomas, who had sold his half pay, his brother William, and their two families left an increasingly turbulent Ireland for Upper Canada's Adelaide Township, west of London.

Adelaide grew quickly, as Thomas and William

pointed out in their contributions to *Authentic letters from Upper Canada . . .* , published by their father in 1833. In his letters Thomas outlined the various methods his "choppers" and others used to clear the land of trees. He also described the religious state of the colony, decrying the lack of Anglican clerics and indicating that those it had were often "*Drones*." He was impressed with life in Upper Canada, claiming that "there are no people who live so luxuriously as the yeomen" and that "a single grievance does not really exist" in the colony. Such conclusions endeared him to officialdom and doubtless helped to convince Lieutenant Governor Sir Francis Bond Head* that Radcliff was both "intelligent and respectable."

As early as 31 May 1833 Radcliff was made a magistrate. He also received a militia commission, becoming colonel of his regiment in 1837. When rebellion broke out that year, he assumed command of the militia guarding the district jail and was one of the magistrates at London examining persons charged with treason. On 1 Jan. 1838 he was put in command of the Detroit frontier, then menaced by the Patriots – Canadian refugees and their American sympathizers. Arriving on the frontier, Radcliff found provisions and *matériel* in short supply and the militia "in a cruel state of disorganization." Fortunately the enemy were little better prepared. On 9 January the schooner *Anne*, which had been firing upon Fort Malden at Amherstburg, ran aground. Radcliff ordered some of his men to wade out and board her. They did so, capturing "all descriptions of useful equipments" and 21 Patriots. The commander of the vessel, Edward Alexander Theller*, later observed that Radcliff had ordered the prisoners be treated humanely. An attempt in early February to have the House of Assembly grant Radcliff a sword for his services proved abortive, but he was to receive other rewards. Much to the chagrin of certain militia officers about London who regarded him as a "fawning sycophant," he was commissioned lieutenant-colonel of the 11th Provisional Battalion on 9 Nov. 1838. Then on 27 Feb. 1839 he was appointed a legislative councillor.

After the revolt Radcliff moved to Port Credit. He became collector of customs at Toronto, but before he could assume his duties he died at Amherst Island while rowing a boat. The crown granted his widow £150 in recognition of his many services; none the less she and her family faced an uncertain economic future, for Radcliff had not died a wealthy man.

COLIN READ

AO, MU 2366. MTRL, James Hamilton papers. *Arthur papers* (Sanderson), vol.1. *Authentic letters from Upper Canada . . .*, ed. Thomas Radcliff, intro. J. J. Talman (Toronto, 1953). *Cyclopædia of Canadian biog.* (Rose and Charlesworth). C. O. [Z.] Ermatinger, *The Talbot regime; or the first half century of the Talbot settlement* (St Thomas, Ont., 1904). R. B. Ross, "The Patriot war," *Mich. Pioneer Coll.*, 21 (1892): 509–609.

RAIMBAULT, JEAN, Roman Catholic priest, professor, and school administrator; b. 3 Feb. 1770 in Orléans, France, son of Étienne Raimbault, a merchant, and Françoise Doucet; d. 16 Feb. 1841 in Nicolet, Lower Canada.

The youngest in a family of four, Jean Raimbault did his classical studies at the Collège Royal d'Orléans, and in 1787 he enrolled at the Séminaire d'Orléans, which at that time was run by the Sulpicians. A student of "brilliant mind" and "irreproachable conduct," according to the superior, he was tonsured on 29 May 1789. Rather than take the oath of loyalty to the Civil Constitution of the Clergy that was imposed by the decree of 1790, he left the seminary and made his living as a tutor until he was conscripted on 6 Oct. 1793. In December, while his regiment was stationed on the Belgian frontier, he deserted and took shelter at the Maison du Refuge de Forest, a seminary founded in Brussels by French bishops in exile. He was assisted in getting from there to London, where he was welcomed by Jean-François de La Marche, bishop of Saint-Pol-de-Léon in France, who obtained help for him. Knowing it would be some time before he could return to France, he decided to emigrate to Lower Canada. Through François-Emmanuel Bourret, the former director of the Séminaire d'Orléans who had been charged by Bishop Jean-François Hubert* with paying the passage of a dozen priests to Quebec, he sailed from Portsmouth, England, on 1 June 1795 and arrived on 6 July.

Pierre Denaut*, the coadjutor to the bishop of Quebec, received Raimbault when he landed, took him to Longueuil, and on 26 July conferred the priesthood on him. Raimbault was entrusted with the teaching of philosophy and sciences at the Petit Séminaire de Québec. Forced by ill health to give up this work in 1797, Raimbault was then named assistant priest at Château-Richer. In October Denaut, who had become bishop of Quebec, appointed him to the parish charge of L'Ange-Gardien. Besides attending to pastoral duties, Raimbault taught school in the presbytery, a task that undermined his constitution over the years. In September 1805 Denaut made him curé at Pointe-aux-Trembles (Montreal), in the hope he would be able to recover his health there.

Raimbault was 35 by this time. He was a priest of the *ancien régime*, frugal, benevolent, hostile to any form of liberalism, touchy on matters of precedence, and ill disposed to delegating his authority. He was seen as "a man of morals, letters, and taste." Bishop Joseph-Octave Plessis*, who held him in high esteem, thought him the man to take charge of Saint-Jean-Baptiste parish in Nicolet and keep an eye on the development of the seminary he had just established there.

Without much enthusiasm Raimbault accepted this charge and in the autumn of 1806 moved into his new presbytery, a well-built but plain dwelling with a room used as a parish hall. There he was to lead a routine existence until his death. A housekeeper took care of the domestic tasks, and a hired man worked the patch of land belonging to the *fabrique* and looked after the barn and stable. For his part, Raimbault dedicated himself entirely to his priestly calling, keeping his distance, however, from the seigneurs, the local bourgeoisie, and the Canadian curés in the diocese. During his time in office, Nicolet experienced rapid development. The parish had 1,200 communicants in 1810, and 2,500 in 1836. The growth in population, together with the way in which people were scattered about the seigneury of Nicolet, made his task heavier as the years went by.

Raimbault was, then, increasingly busy, with the liturgical offices, the sacraments, record-keeping for the *fabrique*, and such charitable works as the care of the sick and needy. He was zealous in carrying out his duties. He distributed part of his tithes among the poor, lent money interest-free to parishioners in difficulties, and took pains to develop a feeling for liturgy among his parishioners. In 1817 he used his own funds to buy some paintings from the collection of Louis-Joseph DESJARDINS, *dit* Desplantes, in order to create an uplifting atmosphere in his church. He kept a close eye on the conduct of his people and the doings of the Protestants.

Raimbault's reputation as a pastor soon spread beyond the limits of the parish. In 1825 Plessis named him archpriest, an office empowering him to give advice to his colleagues, grant dispensations, and accord absolution in cases of reserved sin. More than once Plessis entrusted him with special missions related to the erection of new parishes or sought his counsel on legislative measures and amendments to ecclesiastical discipline. Raimbault was also chaplain to the Ursulines of Trois-Rivières and for several years was responsible for the Drummondville mission. From 1830 the expansion of the elementary school system added to his tasks. He was both trustee and visitor, and thus had control of the choice of school-mistresses, curricula, and discipline. Despite all this activity, he had some free time, which he used for corresponding with his family and reading religious books, periodicals, and newspapers. He also liked visiting fellow *émigré* priests who had charge of a group of parishes near Trois-Rivières – an area referred to as "little France." He devoted the rest of his time to the seminary, of which he was the superior.

Plessis thought the task of the superior was to guarantee the reputation of the seminary "by his gifts, his knowledge, and his virtue" and to supervise its development. In reality, this rather vague mandate allowed Raimbault to give free rein to his authoritarian and centralizing temperament. He was soon interfering in every aspect of administration. He busied himself with the enlargement of the premises (1806–9), the nature of the teaching, and even the admission and intellectual progress of the students. Clashes between the superior and successive directors of the establishment, such as Paul-Loup Archambault*, occurred frequently. Raimbault complained that the seminary priests gave him too little help in his parish ministry and did not always keep him informed of what was going on in the seminary; for their part, directors accused him of exceeding his mandate. In 1816 Plessis endeavoured to put the seminary on a firmer footing. He named Joseph-Onésime LEPROHON director and started the process of incorporation that would culminate in 1821. It was a chance to clarify roles. The bishop retained control of the seminary. He drew up the instructions for the director and the bursar as well as regulations for the pupils, reserving for himself, however, the right to authorize plans for expansion. The superior was to attend to construction on the site itself and to supervise the intellectual, spiritual, and material life of the institution. The director was to deal with enforcement of the regulations, curriculum matters, and the purchase of school equipment: like the bursar, he had to report to the superior. For 25 years the seminary was run by Raimbault and Leprohon. In the period 1825–30 they erected a new, three-storey building with a dormer roof, using plans drawn up by Jérôme Demers*. They then turned their attention to ensuring the quality of teaching staff and to instilling the spirit needed to prepare an élite body of clergy and laity for the service of the church.

Jean Raimbault died on 16 Feb. 1841. He would be remembered as a zealous pastor and devoted educator. To his friend Leprohon, who assumed his parish charge, he bequeathed all his possessions, to be used for the benefit of young men attending the seminary.

IN COLLABORATION

The factual information for this biography was provided by Louis Martin, "Jean Raimbault, curé à Nicolet de 1806 à 1841" (thèse de MA, univ. de Montréal, 1977).

AAQ, 210 A, II–IV, X–XVII. ANQ-MBF, CE1-13, 19 févr. 1841. AP, Saint-Jean-Baptiste (Nicolet), Livres des délibérations de la fabrique, 1734–1822; Livres de comptes, 1734–1822. Arch. de l'évêché de Nicolet (Nicolet, Qué.), Cartable Saint-Jean-Baptiste de Nicolet, corr. Jean Raimbault. ASN, AO, Polygraphie, I–IV. Bellemare, *Hist. de Nicolet*. [L.-É. Bois], *Étude biographique sur M. Jean Raimbault, archiprêtre, curé de Nicolet, etc.* (Québec, 1869). Douville, *Hist. du collège-séminaire de Nicolet*. Claude Lessard, "L'histoire de l'éducation au séminaire de Nicolet, 1803–1863" (thèse de D.E.S., univ. Laval, Québec, 1963).

RAMSAY, GEORGE, 9th Earl of DALHOUSIE, army officer and colonial administrator; b. 22 Oct. 1770 at Dalhousie Castle, Scotland, eldest son of George Ramsay, 8th Earl of Dalhousie, and Elizabeth Glene; m. 14 May 1805 Christian Broun, and they had three sons; d. 21 March 1838 at Dalhousie Castle.

George Ramsay received his primary education from his mother and later attended the Royal High School, Edinburgh, and the University of Edinburgh. Following his father's death in November 1787, he felt obliged, perhaps for financial reasons, to pursue a military career and in July 1788 purchased a cornetcy in the 3rd Dragoons. Promoted captain in January 1791 on raising his own independent company, he later joined the 2nd battalion, 1st Foot, then in Gibraltar. In June 1792 he became major of the 2nd Foot by purchase, and in December 1794 he advanced to lieutenant-colonel. He led its 2nd battalion in the West Indies from 1795 and in December was wounded during an unsuccessful attack against a French party on Martinique. Stationed in Ireland during the rebellion of 1798, he took part the following year in an expedition to Helder (Netherlands), and received the brevet rank of colonel in January 1800. After service at Belle-Île-en-Mer, France, and Minorca, he commanded assaults on the forts at Abukir and Rosetta (Rashīd), Egypt, in 1801. He was back in Gibraltar in 1802 before taking up the duties of brigadier-general on the staff in Scotland the following year, when he managed some time at home for agricultural improvements on his estate.

Promoted major-general in April 1808, Dalhousie participated in the ill-fated expedition to Walcheren (Netherlands), and in August 1809 he became colonel of the 6th Garrison Battalion. In the autumn of 1812 he was appointed commander of the 7th Division under the Marquess of Wellington on the Iberian peninsula with the local rank of lieutenant-general; he received the full rank in June 1813. He took part in actions at Vitoria, Spain, in the Pyrenees, and at Toulouse, France. In May 1813 he became colonel of the 26th Foot, and he remained so the rest of his life. Although he was probably not among Wellington's better commanders, being often slow-moving and pedantic, he received several honours, including the thanks of both houses of parliament for his services, a KB in 1813, and a GCB in 1815 when he was also created Baron Dalhousie in the peerage of the United Kingdom. Since 1796 he had been a representative peer of Scotland in the House of Lords. He would be promoted general in July 1830.

Like many of Wellington's Peninsular officers after the war, Dalhousie embarked on a career as a colonial administrator. In the spring of 1816 he solicited appointment as lieutenant governor of Nova Scotia in succession to Sir John Coape Sherbrooke*. His motives were to follow Sherbrooke as commander-in-chief in the Canadas and to relieve "financial concerns" resulting from heavy building expenses on his estate incurred "in these times of general distress." Appointed in July, he arrived in Halifax on 24 October, bringing to his new position at age 46 an intelligent and well-stocked mind, an exacting sense of duty, a readiness to command and an expectation of being obeyed, a cold, aloof manner with a touch of aristocratic hauteur, and a prickly personality reinforced by a dour Scottish Presbyterianism. Conscientious to a fault and full of curiosity, he at once familiarized himself with the province. With an appreciative eye for rugged scenery and an insatiable interest in agricultural improvement, he adopted the habit of making frequent tours of the countryside, confiding his impressions to the pages of a journal. To record provincial life more graphically he took with him an official draftsman, John Elliott Woolford*, whose artistic production, along with that of others, he patronized.

Dalhousie's attention was immediately drawn to the plight of poor settlers and immigrants, then arriving in increasing numbers. Refugee blacks sent from the United States during the War of 1812 posed an urgent problem. To avert starvation among them Dalhousie renewed an issue of government rations until June 1817, hoping that, if then settled on land and given seeds and implements, the refugees might subsist by their own efforts. With the British government urging economy, Dalhousie halved the number of recipients in the summer of 1817 by restricting rations to families who had cleared land and to the aged and infirm. He acknowledged, however, that most of the refugees would long require support, which neither the legislature nor the inhabitants were keen to provide. "Slaves by habit & education, no longer working under the dread of the lash," he commented despairingly, "their idea of freedom is idleness and they are therefore quite incapable of Industry." There was talk of repatriating them to the United States or of sending them to join former Nova Scotian blacks in Sierra Leone; they refused to go to the West Indies lest they be returned to slavery.

Dalhousie regarded the destitute condition of the Micmac Indians in much the same light. Critical of their apparent indolence, he was willing to grant lands to be held in trust for those who "shew disposition to settle & plant potatoes." He endorsed the humanitarian endeavours of Roman Catholic priests and of social activists such as Walter BROMLEY, while opposing attempts by Bromley and others to meddle with the customs and Catholicism of the Micmacs as "improper" and tending "to defeat the object of settling them."

British immigrants, too, experienced difficulties establishing themselves, and Dalhousie stressed the long-term advantages of providing initial government aid in rations, tools, and seeds. The obstacles immigrants faced in obtaining land soon convinced him that the substantial fees charged for processing titles, the deficiencies of surveys, the frauds of land-jobbers, and the tracts of unimproved land in private ownership all required attention. The prospect of settling on their own smallholdings no doubt attracted immigrants, but Dalhousie preferred the notion of conveying extensive areas to wealthier proprietors who would then grant long leases to new settlers. As things stood, "every man . . . is laird here, & the classes . . . known in England as Tenantry & peasantry do not exist in these Provinces & probably will not be formed untill a full stop is put to the System of granting lands" and public sale introduced.

Dalhousie was keen to promote improved methods of farming. He established fruitful relations with John YOUNG, a fellow Scot and a Halifax merchant, whose celebrated *Letters of Agricola* . . . , first published from 1818 to 1821, were later dedicated to him. He prompted a reluctant legislature to spend money on importing seeds and superior breeds of stock from Britain and was patron and president of the Central Board of Agriculture, formed at Halifax. For a time local societies, with annual shows and prizes, were all the rage, but such fashionable enthusiasm proved transitory, and Dalhousie remarked: "There is an obstinacy, an aversion to improvement that may be led but will not be driven in this new world; a slowness that is sickening to a man of the other Hemisphere, who has seen the rapidity with which art & science is bursting upon the intellects of the nations of Europe, & who feels the desire to open the eyes & the energies of men here as there – but it won't move out of its own pace, & will require the patience of more than one man's life to do what seems to me within the accomplishment of a very few years."

Dalhousie believed the provincial government might accelerate development by constructing roads that would open up the colony to settlement, commerce, and the readier exchange of information as well as possibly serve a military purpose. Typical of this design was a project in which disbanded soldiers were located along a new cross-country road from Annapolis Royal to the South Shore. A long-mooted reunification of Cape Breton with the mainland colony was again actively considered on the ground that it would bring the people and coal mines of the island back into the mainstream of provincial development. Government action could achieve only limited effects, however, even in this country "capable of great improvement," and Dalhousie was quick to applaud individual habits of industry and sobriety or to criticize laziness and improvidence in the lower class whenever he saw evidence of them during his travels.

Given his aristocratic background, Dalhousie was most comfortable in the company of the civil and military élite of Halifax, some of whom Lady Dalhousie mischievously satirized in delightful portraits. As ready to embrace dissenters as Anglicans, he undoubtedly preferred councillors to assemblymen, and discriminated between "the most respectable men – disposed to support the Government from Loyalty and right principles" and the "double faced Halifax Politicians, or Country Colonels, more addicted to Rum and preaching than to promote the welfare of the State." His attitude towards colonial merchants was more ambivalent, unless they happened to be fellow Scots, but he actively supported petitions to the British government concerning the terms of the Anglo-American commercial agreement of 1818. Congressional restrictions on access to American ports by foreign shipping threatened Nova Scotia's prosperous carrying trade as well as the import of necessary supplies from New England. Dalhousie therefore welcomed Britain's designation of Halifax as a free port, which might preserve its role as an entrepôt for British manufactures to be sent to the United States and American produce destined for the West Indies. He believed it to be "the only measure which can reanimate the industry & the spirit of the Merchants, at present failing & dejected." Dalhousie also shared Nova Scotian anxieties about the readmission of Americans to the fisheries, and he disliked the prospect of their establishing thereby closer commercial and possibly political relations with the provincial outports.

With his Scottish educational background and enthusiasm for improvement, Dalhousie deplored the sorry state of higher learning in Nova Scotia. King's College, Windsor, inconveniently located 40 miles from the bustling capital, languished from a lack of funds, a dilapidated building, and "violent open war" between its president, Charles Porter*, and its vice-president, William Cochran*. More fatally in Dalhousie's view, it served the needs only of members of the Church of England and was therefore unsuited to a community three-quarters of whom were dissenters. To break the Anglican monopoly and rescue education from the competition of denominations [*see* Thomas MCCULLOCH], Dalhousie conceived the idea of a college open to youth of all religions and every class of society. Obtaining advice from Principal George Husband Baird of the University of Edinburgh, Dalhousie envisaged a school modelled on that institution, with professors lecturing on classics, mathematics, and eventually moral and natural philosophy. A site was chosen on the Grand Parade in Halifax and the venture launched through appropriation of customs duties levied in 1814–15 at occupied Castine (Maine). On 22 May 1820, after agreeing with genuine reluctance that the college be named in his honour, Dalhousie laid the cornerstone with full masonic and military honours. The difficulties of finding money to complete the edifice, obtaining a royal charter of incorporation, and appointing the first instructors would fall to his friend and successor Sir James Kempt*. Dalhousie himself could do little more than watch helplessly from a distance as the premature, under-subscribed, and as yet lifeless enterprise hung fire amidst the indifference of the legislature and the anxious aversion of high-churchmen, led by the Reverend John INGLIS, whom Dalhousie later described as a "Hypocritical Jesuit."

For all his criticism of Anglican exclusiveness, Dalhousie was not always sympathetic towards the claims of dissenters. Responding to a flood of petitions, the provincial legislature in 1819 passed a controversial bill extending to ministers of all denominations the right of Anglican clergy to marry by government licence. Dalhousie reserved the bill for imperial decision. He found customary practices objectionable in two particular regards; he disliked having to sign blank forms, in quires at a time, and he considered dangerous the practice whereby Anglican clergymen, in return for a fee, redirected licences to dissenting ministers, so that they could then perform the ceremonies according to their own rites. If the system was to be reformed Dalhousie wanted the privilege to marry by licence restricted, and certainly not extended beyond the Church of Scotland; ample security existed for the sound principles and character of the clergy of the two established churches, he believed, but none for the homely preachers patronized by dissenting congregations.

If Dalhousie found himself at odds with the House of Assembly over marriage licences, reform of the provincial militia constituted a more serious bone of contention. Concerned about the defenceless state of the colony, with its dilapidated barracks and fortifications and a force of British troops hardly sufficient to fulfil ordinary garrison duties in Halifax, Dalhousie placed great store by an efficient militia. From 1818 two successive assemblies refused to entertain his proposals for reorganization and inspection of the militia, since they were likely to involve increased expenditure. The issue brought to a head growing friction between the lieutenant governor and the assembly over control of provincial finances, and in 1820 it ruptured hitherto cordial relations between them. At the end of the session of 1820, as Dalhousie was preparing to take over the governorship at Quebec, he belatedly discovered that the assembly had omitted to make financial provision for inspection of the militia – an underhand trick, he felt, characteristic of a growing petulance on its part as revealed in a recent fondness for secretive, irregular proceedings, "a sort of jealousy of the Council, & an inclination to refuse intercourse with the Executive Government during the Session." Dalhousie also regarded the assembly's action as a personal insult to the king's representative. "I am disappointed & vexed," he recorded, "that a very few cunning Yankees . . . should have outwitted, & defeated me." In a fit of pique, he refused the star and sword valued at 1,000 guineas voted him by the assembly as a parting token of esteem and, blaming the speaker, Simon Bradstreet Robie*, declared that he would not again have accepted the mercurial, disputatious, "sneaking little lawyer" in that responsible position. It was perhaps as well for political harmony in Nova Scotia, and for Dalhousie's peace of mind, that he was about to hand over his duties to the more pliable Kempt.

From the beginning Dalhousie had considered his appointment as an essential apprenticeship for "the high and important command in Canada." He had had what he regarded as a tacit understanding with Earl Bathurst, the colonial secretary, that he would succeed Sherbrooke, who openly endorsed his candidature after suffering a paralytic stroke early in 1818. Dalhousie had, therefore, been hurt and angered when he learned that the Duke of Richmond [Lennox*], Bathurst's impecunious brother-in-law, had been given the coveted command. He had met Richmond in the course of an extensive tour of the Canadas in the summer of 1819 and told the governor that he intended to resign that autumn. Then, in September, he heard of the duke's death from hydrophobia. Refraining this time from requesting the vacancy, Dalhousie waited to see whether he would be going to Quebec or retiring to Scotland. Meanwhile, he pondered the challenge of Lower Canada, "a country where violent party feelings have long separated the two distinct Classes of the King's subjects – the English and the French." In that command, he thought, "I must stand the cast of the die, prospering, do honour to myself, or failing, I must lose the little share of my Country's praise which I have already received." In November he learned the bittersweet news of his appointment on 12 April 1820 as governor-in-chief of British North America.

Taking with him good memories and genuinely fond farewells from friends and councillors, Dalhousie departed from Halifax on 7 June 1820 and arrived at Quebec on the 19th. The capital had a certain scenic grandeur as befitted a viceregal city, but the streets were "narrow & filthy – the people noisy & vociferous . . . [with] monks & friars at every turn." He was appalled by his official quarters, the Château Saint-Louis. Successive governors had passed on their tattered furniture at exorbitant valuation, producing a "Harlequin dress of apartments, in which every succeeding generation had paid for the rags of the preceding, & casting out the worst, had put in a little new to mend its own comfort." Confronted with an outlay of £5,000 before he had touched a shilling of his salary, Dalhousie bemoaned that he could not afford "that sort of furniture which ought to be in the public residence of the Governor General of His Majesty's American dominions."

With a general election in progress and no need to summon the legislature for several months, Dalhousie was able to spend a quiet summer acquainting himself with Lower Canada, its people, and their affairs. He would make it an annual pleasure to undertake extended excursions through the Canadas and would as often as possible escape to the governor's house at William Henry (Sorel) for he grew increasingly to detest Quebec. From the outset he was determined to maintain his custom of confining official business to three days a week, reserving the others for private avocations, personal correspondence, and reading. Unfortunately, the cramped accommodation of the cottage at William Henry precluded his offering spare beds to friends and entertaining guests to dinner, and over the next few years he vainly tried to persuade British authorities to build a house for the commander of the forces at this key military location more suited to his dignity. His failure pointed up British indifference to the governor's status, a "very bad policy," he grumbled, in a province where "much of the mischief arises from the really *state of contempt* to which the king's representative is lowered, without a house to live in respectably, or any patronage to distinguish merit, or public service."

As in Nova Scotia, Dalhousie embarked on agricultural enterprise. In 1821 he purchased 50 acres adjoining the property at William Henry for £400. By 1823 he had 41 acres in clover, 200 sheep, and 6 cows and had drained a further 20 acres of swamp, which were then sown with oats and grass. In 1821 he leased 50 acres at Wolfesfield, on the outskirts of Quebec. More ambitiously, the same year he rented a 250-acre establishment at Beauport from the commissioners for the Jesuit estates in order "to establish a farm for future Governors as an appendage to the Chateau, & which may prove not only an example to [the] public, but useful to the family"; however, bad management and "heavy expence" forced him to give up this venture within a year. He and his wife also began a botanical garden, and plants were assiduously exchanged with Dalhousie Castle.

The Dalhousies actively patronized social and cultural institutions that might arouse in Canada the 'march of mind' then evident in Britain. The governor supported the Quebec Bible Society and the British and Canadian School Society of Montreal [*see* William Lunn*], donated books and money to village libraries, presented beavers and bears to a zoological society (and sent a collection of stuffed Canadian birds to the college museum in Edinburgh). To preserve the voluminous records relating to the early history of Indian tribes gathered by the Jesuits and other religious bodies, and to stimulate research and inquiry, Dalhousie was instrumental in forming the Literary and Historical Society of Quebec in 1824. Since "in England these societies lead to every improvement, amusing, instructive, moral & Religious," he mused, "in Canada they will & must first lead to harmony in private life; the use of books will put down that narrow minded tyranny of the Catholic Priesthood; will open new views, and new sentiments more suited to the present state of the civilised world." He subscribed £100 a year to the society for fear "that if not pushed with spirit now in the outset, . . . it may droop & die as almost all foreign, or European plants do in the Province at the present day." Books, instruments, and a cabinet of mineralogical specimens were ordered from London. Attendance at meetings remained thin, however. "We make miserably slow progress," he bemoaned in 1827; "want of talent, education, and liberal feeling in this Catholic country are sad checks upon any attempt like this." That year Lady Dalhousie presented a paper on Canadian plants to the society. Apart from indulging her interests in the sciences, exceptional in a woman of her time, she enthusiastically fulfilled the more conventional role of the governor's wife, that of patroness of literature and the arts. In 1824 the writer Julia Catherine Beckwith* had dedicated her novel, *St Ursula's convent . . .* , to the governor's wife.

That first carefree summer of 1820 Dalhousie undertook, mainly for military purposes, a visit of settlements in eastern Upper Canada, the Ottawa valley, and southwestern Lower Canada. The following year, with Woolford, he toured as far as Lake Superior. His intention of presenting his credentials as governor of Upper Canada to the Legislative Council was abandoned in order not to ruffle the feathers of the sensitive lieutenant governor, Sir Peregrine Maitland*. Nevertheless Dalhousie was determined that "the Governor in Chief ought to take an active part in the administration of all the several Governments committed to his care . . . to a degree that shall not affect the local powers of the Lt Governors, but require them to communicate with me confidentially on public measures, & on the state of the Provinces generally."

Dalhousie's tours of inspection reinforced his view that local and British funds could usefully be devoted to developing land and water communications in the Canadas in order to strengthen military defence and to open up areas for settlement. Particularly needed were trunk roads to link Montreal with Bytown (Ottawa) and the Eastern Townships and local roads to service settlements springing up in the western districts. Like other military men, Dalhousie was an enthusiastic advocate of canal building, particularly of the Ottawa–Rideau system. The possibility of cost-sharing with the Lower Canadian legislature was freely mentioned, and by 1825, after a military commission under Sir James Carmichael SMYTH had reported expansively on the requirements and expense of Canadian defence, the Board of Ordnance was committed to executing and financing the Rideau canal. In 1826 and 1827 Dalhousie visited the site of Lieutenant-Colonel John BY's grandiose scheme, which was to cost the British taxpayer dearly. Dalhousie was impressed as well with the importance as a public work of the Lachine Canal [*see* John Richardson*], which he visited in May 1826, and regretted that the Canadians showed no more interest in it than in the splendid new Notre-Dame church then being built in Montreal [*see* James O'Donnell*]. "The conclusion must be," he felt, "that there is no natural disposition to public improvement – they would go on to the end of time, indolent, unambitious, contented, & unenterprising."

Dalhousie stressed to British authorities that canal building would also offer ready employment to the immigrants then arriving massively at Quebec, two-thirds of whom were being drawn into the United States instead of reinforcing the scanty population of the Canadas. He was profoundly concerned at the way in which Americans were locating themselves in the western frontier districts, placing themselves "between us & the only remaining warrior tribes in that district, to cut off our alliance & influence with them." A loyal population had to be encouraged to people the western regions and efforts made to form among them an effective, well-disposed militia. On the other hand, he decided that the expensive practice of building military settlements might be discontinued because of the influx of British immigrants.

In the early 1820s some 10,000 migrants were arriving each year at Quebec, many of them destitute Irish who placed severe strains on the charity and good will of the colonists, the provincial legislature and British government being reluctant to spend public money on unwelcome paupers. Dalhousie, too, expressed unease at the invasion of needy, turbulent Irish, and he strongly opposed the schemes of assisted emigration sanctioned by the Colonial Office in 1823 and 1825. The settlers brought out by Peter ROBINSON, he claimed, were inadequately superintended, and their locations in Upper Canada were remote and too close to the American border. Public money should be used, he argued, not to bring out Britons, who were in any case paying their own passages in their thousands, but to prepare sites for settlement. He came increasingly to regard the Baie des Chaleurs region of the Gaspé as a better location for immigrants, since it was accessible by ship, easily supplied, and presented individuals with no distracting alternatives to work or starvation.

At a time of extensive immigration, Dalhousie's attention was drawn to the evils of land administration in the Canadas even more compellingly than it had been in Nova Scotia. Thousands of acres held by absentees remained in their wild state, and the crown needed the power to escheat all uncultivated grants. Settlement and communications were also impeded by the "altogether unwise, impolitic and mischievous" plan of setting aside crown and clergy reserves as a landed endowment, which had so far yielded negligible revenue. No one would lease such land while he might obtain his own smallholding. Equally objectionable was the Anglican monopoly of the clergy reserves, the exclusion of the established church in Scotland from a share of landed endowments being a sore point with the Presbyterian governor. He contended that the inequity, having "created a great deal of heart burning & uncharitable feeling" between Anglican and Presbyterian clergy, "must be removed or the irritated feelings of the present day will grow into rooted discontent, and . . . end in disloyalty." For both the crown and the clergy reserves Dalhousie favoured sales instead of grants or leases. Not averse to the operations of large-scale proprietors, he nevertheless opposed the resort to monopolistic, speculative land companies such as the Canada Company [*see* John GALT] and the Lower Canada Land Company [*see* William Bowman FELTON] as a means of accelerating settlement, which was a necessarily slow process.

In addition to increasing control by government over land granting, Dalhousie intended to strengthen the forces of law and order. "This Country is grown too large for the old established regulations," he told Kempt. "Those that 50 years ago sufficed for the whole Province are now called for in every County. The Circuit, the Grand Jury, & the Q. Sessions [Court of Quarter Sessions] in *districts* are not now sufficient; the immense population requires increased number of Magistrates, more jails, & more frequent exercise of the Laws than was necessary in times gone by."

To maintain political tranquillity Dalhousie resolved to pursue a course above the partisan squabbles that had disfigured Lower Canada's recent history. "It seems . . . as if popularity had been the sole object of . . . all the Governors in Canada – & to it there were only two paths – the French or the English – Catholic or Protestant – & each succeeding chief followed in regular opposition to . . . his Predecessor – there is no steadiness nor prudence . . . & the mischief was increased by frequent change of Governors." Dalhousie determined to remain beholden to no one, steering wide of the "political managements which . . . have led Govt to be itself the cause of the troubles." This was no mean task in a divided community led by politicians scrambling for favours with a "ravenous appetite." Being a stranger to everyone, he resolved to hold himself "most cautiously guarded against the advice of those in power because they are most likely to be warped and influenced by former discussions." In consequence he was obliged to rely for political counsel and administrative assistance on humdrum officials who carried little weight. His civil secretary from 1822, Andrew William COCHRAN, for example, had many admirable qualities as an assistant and confidant but few political contacts of value outside the circle of British officials. Choice and circumstance therefore threw Dalhousie on his own resources; it was a lonely and vulnerable position.

Dalhousie also intended initially to show due regard for the Canadians. He was spontaneously drawn to the habitants, whom he perceived as submissive and respectful with their "civil & even polished manners." They may have reminded him of the Highland crofters, just as the Canadian seigneurs passably resembled Scottish lairds. "If there is trouble & discontent to be found [among the Canadians]," he thought, "it is among the lawyers, & in troubled waters these have ever delighted." Even so, it was "only justice to the sons of the old Canadian families that the road of honour should be laid open to them in every branch of the Public Service." Ultimately, loyalty would be secured through the deprecation of all distinction, religious and ethnic, and the granting of office or favour "only by the test of abilities, or of conduct." In line with this approach, Dalhousie in December 1820 appointed the speaker of the assembly, Louis-Joseph Papineau*, to the Executive Council. Not that Dalhousie liked Papineau, whom he considered rather "an ill tempered, cross, tho' clever barrister, [who] scarcely knows the rules of good Society." Nor did he intend "to flatter, or to coax" the assembly. Rather he wanted the public to "know that I am acting a frank, fair, and candid part with them, free from intrigue and free from guile," and hoped "to push every public man to do his duty in his station & to draw towards unanimity & cordial cooperation in the public affairs."

In his dealings with the Canadians in the assembly, Dalhousie's impartiality and forbearance were soon placed under severe strain. His best intentions were offset by two fatal disabilities: an exotic political conservatism and a tetchy temperament. Reading British history, he identified with the early Stuart kings and their defence of the royal prerogative against parliamentary encroachment, an episode which he thought "peculiarly applicable to my present situation" but which did not provide him with a sound guide for managing a colonial assembly bent on enlarging its power at the expense of the governor and councils. Dalhousie conceived of the prerogative as a constructive form of authority and believed that "the King's Representative in these Provinces must be the guide and helmsman in all public measures that affect the public interests generally." The role of the assembly was distinctly subordinate, and its duty was to accept direction by the executive. In the inevitable disputes that arose with the assembly, Dalhousie reacted with acute sensitivity for his authority and dignity as the representative of the sovereign and instinctively personalized every attack or reverse. Lacking pliability and a sense of proportion, he allowed trivial incidents to become inflated into major constitutional issues. Like all embattled imperial administrators, then and since, he rationalized initiatives, criticisms, and resistance on the part of the assembly as the conduct of a few ambitious agitators, unrepresentative of responsible opinion in the community, but exercising a temporary influence over an ignorant, deluded populace.

This ambivalent view of the Canadians as both contented subjects and turbulent politicians was reflected in Dalhousie's attitude towards the Roman Catholic Church in Lower Canada. He recognized that the Catholic religion might act as a conservative, stabilizing force in society and as a defence against American influence, if not as a positive inculcator of loyalty to the British connection. He thought every encouragement should be given the church in promoting education among Canadian youth. For this purpose he strongly but vainly urged on the colonial secretary the advantage of transferring superintendence of Catholic schools from the Protestant-dominated board of the Royal Institution for the Advancement of Learning to a parallel Catholic corporation [*see* Joseph Langley Mills*]. Dalhousie's championship of the educational and pastoral activities of the Catholic clergy might have secured him an invaluable source of support, but his Presbyterian upbringing disinclined him to embrace a relaxed attitude towards the Catholic Church. He was invariably suspicious of the priest who dabbled in politics.

Dalhousie's suspicions extended to the archbishop of Quebec, Joseph-Octave Plessis*, who might have brought him the backing of Canadian moderates had the governor worked for an understanding with that influential prelate as two recent predecessors, Sir George Prevost* and Sherbrooke, had profitably done. From the outset, however, Dalhousie condemned their administrations as excessively pro-Canadian and examples of partisanship to be avoided. As well, despite sharing with Plessis certain views on education, Dalhousie was uneasy about the archbishop's authority and prestige and feared the growth of an overweening sacerdotal power in the province. Dalhousie was also puzzled – and then, probably under the influence of Herman Witsius RYLAND and Andrew William Cochran, angered – by Plessis's independent conduct as a member of the Legislative Council. He increasingly regarded Plessis as a moving spirit of the Canadian party in the assembly, a disturber of harmony in the legislature, a "deep & designing Hypocrite." So powerful was the archbishop's hold over Catholic assemblymen, parish priests, and ordinary electors, he believed, that it undermined freedom of debate and the working of the constitution. The governor was no better pleased with the "mischievous machinations" of Jean-Jacques LAR-

TIGUE, a cousin of Papineau and his ally Denis-Benjamin Viger* and suffragan bishop at Montreal of the bishop of Quebec. He therefore came to urge on Bathurst that the crown reassert its authority over the church, and he even claimed that the most respectable priests – by whom he meant particularly François-Xavier PIGEON and Augustin Chaboillez* – wanted the government to do so.

As his relations with the assembly and the clergy deteriorated in the 1820s, Dalhousie evinced a more hostile view of Canadian Catholics. It was not long before his growing distrust of the Canadians undermined his intention of bringing them into the colonial administration. He contended that his efforts to do so were frustrated because too few Canadian aspirants measured up to his demanding standards of ability and conduct.

Yet Dalhousie had approached his first session of the provincial legislature in 1820–21 with considerable optimism. Finance seemed likely to be the only contentious topic and that ought at once to be settled by an intimation from the British government that the disposal of crown and of provincial revenues must be kept distinct. For years the assembly had been trying to extend its power at the expense of the executive, in part by asserting a right to control the appropriation of all revenues. In 1818 Sherbrooke had engineered a compromise that might have provided a fruitful precedent. However, his successor, Richmond, adopted a hard line, recommending to Bathurst that no bill providing for the civil list should be approved unless the total sum requested was voted unconditionally and permanently, advice that was accepted and repeated for Dalhousie's guidance.

This resolute approach harmonized with Dalhousie's personal inclinations. In 1820–21 he requested the legislature to pass a supply bill for the lifetime of the king, immediately provoking a confrontation between the two houses. Under the prompting of the leader of the Montreal merchants, John Richardson, the Legislative Council, not content with throwing out the bill, adopted a series of resolutions that became part of the standing rules of the upper house. Contravening English constitutional practice, and in a language insulting to the lower house, the council asserted its control over the form and procedure for future money bills. Dalhousie thought the council had adopted an unexpectedly bold stand against "a violent attempt [by the assembly] to dictate in all measures of Government" and instinctively sided with it. In the session of 1821–22 Dalhousie repeated his request for a permanent civil list, but the assembly refused to pass any appropriation bill until the council withdrew its offending resolutions. When there seemed a possibility that the council might concede, the governor, suspecting Plessis's influence, showed no compunction about threatening the dismissal of wavering officials on the council, a tactic, he complacently noted, that "had the best effects." Dalhousie believed that the assemblymen had fatally overreached themselves and would be disowned by their constituents once the deadlock had produced a suspension of provincial services. As well, the authorities in London would now see the representatives in their true colours. He determined to lie on his oars and wait for salvation from a bill introduced into the imperial parliament in June 1822 which proposed to reunite the Canadas and thereby create a majority of English-speaking members in the new legislature. "I rejoice in this glimpse of Sunshine on the Province," he told Cochran, even though he had not been consulted on the bill, for under the existing constitution he found himself "a Cypher in the high station." His hopes were disappointed; criticism in the House of Commons induced ministers to withdraw the bill in July.

In 1823, with Papineau absent in London to counter reintroduction of the union bill and a more compliant speaker, Joseph-Rémi VALLIÈRES de Saint-Réal, in the chair, Canadian leaders accepted a temporary, partial accommodation on supplies. Indeed the assembly appropriated funds for local purposes with a liberality that clashed with Dalhousie's attempts to slash government spending in response to the earlier financial deadlock. Through economy, he thought, his financial means could be made adequate to all reasonable demands, once confusion in the public accounts had been sorted out. He had not anticipated, however, the discovery that year of the defalcation of Receiver General John CALDWELL, to the amount of some £96,000, as a result of mercantile speculation with public funds. This revelation, besmirching Dalhousie's administration, elicited his severest censure. In the session of 1824 the assembly investigated the Caldwell affair and called on "British justice & generosity to repay the deficit to the Province," Caldwell being an imperial officer and the audit of his accounts a British responsibility. At the same time the assembly reiterated a catalogue of ill usage by the mother country that signalled a return to its recalcitrance. It refused to vote the supplies, and Dalhousie lamented the evident weakness of the government in the house, where there were no forceful spokesmen to present or defend the administration's point of view or to act as a channel of communication between executive and assembly. Closing a barren session, the governor privately hoped that "the good sense of the country" would disown its factious representatives at the next election, by which time parliament might have decisively intervened with a new plan of union.

Dalhousie's thoughts turned to an impending leave of absence in Britain and longer-term prospects. From his earliest days at Quebec he had been subject to periodic bouts of homesickness and grumbling about his predicament. At the end of 1821 he had reflected gloomily: "I am fretful & tired of this . . . unprofitable waste of my life here. I would willingly resign my command . . . could I do so with honour. But can I throw up my task merely because it was plaguy & troublesome, & difficult? . . . Could I avow myself unequal to a post into which I had in a manner forced myself? Could I confess myself to my Sovereign an officer unworthy of his notice, by want of firmness & perseverance? Happen what may, I never can disgrace myself so deeply."

Nevertheless, personal concerns could not be entirely dismissed. In 1821 Dalhousie grew increasingly alarmed at discrepancies appearing in the financial accounts submitted by his agents in Scotland. As well, during the summer of 1822 he suffered a recurrence of an inflammation of the eyes and blurred vision that he had first experienced on the eve of his departure from Nova Scotia. Confined to a darkened room for much of the time at William Henry, he received little relief from either leeches or medication. In 1823 he obtained permission to take leave, but, postponing his departure, that summer paid an official visit to Nova Scotia. Entertained royally by old friends and admirers, the recipient of flattering addresses, Dalhousie was happily in his element, considering his treatment "the reward of service." Finally, on 6 June 1824 he left Quebec for Britain, uncertain whether he would be returning.

The journey was undertaken in part to enlighten the Colonial Office about Lower Canadian difficulties; the results proved disastrous for Dalhousie, personally and politically. The shrewd, urbane, easy-going Bathurst found the governor a high-minded, dour, boring Scot, and was careful not to invite him to his country house in Gloucestershire as he did many other visitors from the Canadas. Dalhousie himself noted, "I never approached him on the affairs of Canada, but he heard me with impatience, and appeared delighted when I rose to take my leave." Dalhousie retired to his Scottish castle to settle private affairs, leaving Cochran in London to discuss official business for him.

On his departure from Quebec Dalhousie had left in charge Lieutenant Governor Sir Francis Nathaniel Burton*, advising Burton to postpone until his return the summoning of the new assembly, to be elected in the summer of 1824, unless the lieutenant governor was prepared to undertake the disagreeable task of rejecting Papineau as speaker. However, counselled by Herman Witsius Ryland, who nursed a grudge against Dalhousie, Burton soon saw the credit he might reap by resolving the financial deadlock with a daring initiative. Convening the legislature in 1825, he persuaded the assembly to vote the supplies for one year without raising awkward issues of principle and then, chiefly through the influence of Ryland and Plessis, obtained approval of the bill in the Legislative Council. When Dalhousie heard of Burton's coup, triumphantly reported to the Colonial Office, he protested that the arrangement implicitly conceded the assembly's pretensions to appropriate crown revenues. His arguments convinced Bathurst, who in June 1825 censured Burton for having disobeyed instructions on financial affairs given in 1820–21. Dalhousie arrived back at Quebec in mid September, confident that his stand on the financial dispute had the backing of his superiors, and Burton left for London.

Dalhousie's equanimity was soon shattered. Burton having made a convincing defence of his action, the colonial secretary lifted the censure, and Burton breezily informed Papineau and friends that Dalhousie had lost the confidence of his superiors. A furious Dalhousie dismissed as "a schoolboy's excuse" Burton's plea that he had been ignorant of the instructions of 1820–21 because Dalhousie had taken them to England. "The substance was well known to him in his residence, & confidential intercourse with me for two years on the most intimate & friendly terms," Dalhousie contended. Now, he complained, Bathurst's withdrawal of the reprimand disarmed him of the authority necessary to refuse a bill similar to Burton's.

Taking advantage of a private visit to England in 1826–27 of Chief Justice Jonathan SEWELL, Dalhousie sought to persuade the colonial secretary of the necessity for his decisive intervention and for parliamentary amendment of the provincial constitution to rescue the authority of the crown's representative in the colony. However, Sewell weakened Dalhousie's position by agreeing with Burton that the supply bill of 1825 had not infringed the executive's right to dispose of the revenues under its control, and the English law officers reached the same conclusion. The under-secretary, Robert John Wilmot-Horton, unkindly blamed Dalhousie and Cochran for having misled the Colonial Office in the matter.

Borne down by these trials, Dalhousie again considered relinquishing his thankless post. But so long as he remained in harness, he was determined to uphold the prerogatives of the crown against the demands of the assembly. Papineau and Viger evinced politeness and cordiality, but soon they revived claims to financial control, being unwilling to surrender the gains made in 1825. Since Dalhousie refused to accept another bill in that form, no supplies were voted. With "all the polite & fawning manners," he wrote, the assemblymen had proved themselves "detestable dissemblers." "They are truly in character Frenchmen – there is not a spark in them of British honour, or honesty, Loyalty or Patriotism – a half dozen of democratic attorneys lead by the nose a set of senseless ignorant fools, who not knowing to read, cannot know the Constitution nor the Laws of their Country – they are . . . incapable of the great trust devolved upon them." Only one conclusion was possible: "The Country is unfit for such an Institution as a Parliament in the present state of society & advancement"; to have granted it was like "the folly of giving a lace veil to a Monkey or a Bear to play with."

The governor contemplated dissolving the legislature, but Sewell and John Richardson, who, along with businessman Mathew BELL, were his closest advisers, dissuaded him from resorting to a futile but irritating election. Confronted by the problem of meeting essential expenditures with inadequate crown revenues, Dalhousie looked to London. Although the Colonial Office was not prepared to restructure the constitution, it did support his policy of preserving the financial independence of the provincial executive by refusing to surrender crown revenues except in return for a permanent civil list. In consequence Dalhousie was authorized to deposit in the military chest, ostensibly for security, surplus funds accumulating from provincial acts, which the legislature had the right to control, and to "borrow" from them to pay the expenses of government.

Dalhousie's flagging spirits were momentarily revived in the summer of 1826 by a visit to Nova Scotia, where "Champaign in rivers flowed around" in "one continued scene of riot & amusement." After a more sober tour of New Brunswick and the Gaspé, he inspected the site of the Rideau canal in Upper Canada. The Lower Canadian legislature reconvened in January 1827; when in March the assembly rejected his request for supplies, Dalhousie abruptly prorogued the session, and then later dissolved the legislature, "with the chief view of rejecting Papineau as Speaker in future." The governor may also have hoped that sufficient British or moderate members would be elected to offer leadership in the house to those who wished to change sides. That objective required a more interventionist role in politics by the agents of government, and despite professions of calm impartiality in dispatches sent home, Dalhousie launched into the election campaign with vigour and ruthlessness. Being resident at William Henry, he openly backed the candidate there, Attorney General James Stuart*, berating the local priest, Jean-Baptiste Kelly*, for stirring up hostility to the government. In Montreal and Quebec opponents were struck off the lists of magistrates. Throughout the province a purge of militia officers was conducted on the grounds that officers had refused to attend summer musters, had exhibited a spirit of disobedience to orders, thinking that the assembly's failure to renew the existing militia bill meant that no militia law was in operation, or had abused the government at public meetings [*see* Nicolas-Eustache Lambert* Dumont]. Such naked resort to intimidation exacerbated hostility in the country parishes, and by this masterpiece of miscalculation Dalhousie produced an assembly in which the number of his supporters was even more meagre. He continued to blame a knot of agitators led by Papineau and backed by a few newspapers in Quebec and Montreal. Behind them lay "the deep & cunning intrigue of the Clergy . . . , and all ascribe . . . to them chiefly, the astonishing & otherwise unaccountable influence of Papineau's faction." Thus, by self-deception or wishful thinking, Dalhousie could reassure officials in London that "really the tranquillity & contented happiness of the people in Lower Canada is almost Proverbial . . . *there is no foundation whatever* for . . . Reports of 'trouble in Canada.'"

Consoling himself with the thought that he had always followed faithfully Bathurst's instructions of 1820–21, Dalhousie believed that on the results of the coming session "the minister must judge whether to put a new hand here." He had in fact already informally requested leave to attend to private affairs in Britain, having received in October 1826 the dreaded news of the bankruptcy of his trusted regimental agent. He estimated that his loss would be from £10,000 to £12,000. Six months later he learned that he might obtain a military command in India. While he was waiting for leave the Colonial Office authorized him to request a permanent civil list of a reduced amount, but he feared that a reduction would unduly cramp the activities of government. Such a surrender would be objectionable "were I not flapping my wings & ready for a start," he confided to Kempt. "I will not remain to concede one hair's breadth of what I have hitherto maintained."

The assembly met in November 1827 and Papineau was duly elected speaker. In a final dramatic gesture and assertion of the royal prerogative, Dalhousie commanded the house to make another choice. When Papineau's selection was confirmed and resolutions passed to the effect that "the King's approval was mere form, empty words, not at all necessary," Dalhousie prorogued the session. He justified his action to the colonial secretary by arguing that he could not acknowledge as speaker someone intimately connected with seditious newspapers and "notoriously opposed to justice, impartiality, and moderation in that chair, and publickly engaged to use the whole weight of his influence against the views of Govt for an accomodation." For Dalhousie, Papineau personified the evil forces against which the governor had to struggle. The finances were no longer, if they ever had been, the real subject of controversy. "His object is Power – his spurring motive, personal & vindictive animosity to me 'the Governor' – arrogant, head-strong & self willed." Dalhousie hoped that the constitution of 1791 would be suspended, since "instead of uniting the Canadian and British subjects in mutual friendship, and social habits; instead of uniting them in admiration of the principles of the Constitution which had been given them – [it] has had exactly a contrary effect; . . . a Canadian hates his British neighbour, as a Briton hates a Frenchman, by an inborn impulse." "The Canadians have succeded," he added, "in obtaining a majority of votes in the House of Commons of this Province – a jealousy & hatred of the superior education, & superior industry of his British neighbour have led him to believe, that if he loses that majority, he loses also, liberty, laws, religion, property, and language, every thing that is valuable on earth." The other major cause of the province's ills, Dalhousie maintained, was the persistent indifference and neglect of the Colonial Office. "Greater confidence in the Governor of the Province, would immediately smooth, unite, and put an end to all the workings of a few seditious demagogues," he reflected.

Dalhousie's rejection of Papineau created consternation in London, where ministerial confidence in the governor had been steadily waning. The new colonial secretary, William Huskisson, decided that no settlement seemed likely in Lower Canada while Dalhousie remained. Perhaps through his Scottish patron, Lord Melville, first lord of the Admiralty and formerly president of the India Board of Control, Dalhousie was appointed commander-in-chief of the army in India. His request for leave of absence was refused, however, and he was advised early in 1828 to set out for India as soon as possible, without tarrying in Britain to explain his conduct. Dalhousie considered his appointment the summit of his ambition and "the highest mark of approbation the King could convey of my conduct here." Still, because his administration might be attacked, he wanted an unequivocal declaration of approval from the colonial secretary. Indeed, the leaders of the Patriote party had been busy with addresses and petitions of grievance, employing, Dalhousie charged, secrecy, "cunning care," and scare tactics to collect signatures and crosses on blank rolls of parchment from deluded Canadian peasants. To ensure that his views were heard in London, he briefed Scottish relatives and acquaintances and sent Samuel Gale*, a Montreal lawyer, armed with addresses from the "loyal, respectable, and well-informed" members of the community, particularly from the Eastern Townships, whose interests Gale also represented. Gale had neither contacts nor familiarity with England, he recognized, but "well received he must be, because he is in every thing gentlemanlike."

Dalhousie did not anticipate personal difficulties from an investigation of Lower Canadian questions by ministers and parliament. In fact, he welcomed it as a preliminary to corrective legislation. At first private letters from Britain suggested that his conduct was generally approved. In May 1828 Huskisson defended his administration in the Commons and advocated amendment of the act of 1791. Between May and July a select committee heard evidence from interested parties [*see* Denis-Benjamin Viger]. Then, however, absenteeism on the part of government members enabled opposition MPs to carry the committee's report, which was sympathetic to the grievances of the assembly and critical of Dalhousie. The report had been influenced by the arrival in London, after the committee had closed its inquiry, of a petition, with 87,000 signatures, protesting against Dalhousie's purge of the militia and the magistracy. The allegations were recorded in a postscript to the report, without comment, but even Huskisson censured the dismissals.

Immediately before leaving the colony, Dalhousie presided at a ceremony for placing the top stone on a monument to James Wolfe* and Louis-Joseph de Montcalm*, Marquis de Montcalm. Erected in a prominent position near the Château Saint-Louis, overlooking the river, this memorial, which Dalhousie considered "Wolfe's monument," had been an enthusiasm of the earl's, completed with his own subscription to compensate for Canadian indifference. The ceremony clearly assumed a personal importance in the same way that laying the foundation stone of Dalhousie College had done on his departure from Nova Scotia. "I am vain enough," he recorded, "to think it in some respects, a monument to my own name, at the last hour of my Administration of the Government in this Country." The following day, 9 Sept. 1828, Kempt was sworn into office as his successor, and Dalhousie departed with "all the pomp, power & parade which belonged to me as the Representative of my Sovereign."

In England Dalhousie read the evidence and report of the select committee with "utter astonishment." He took particular exception to the concluding paragraphs of the report as condemning him unheard. Further, he encountered a patent lack of sympathy on the part of the new colonial secretary, Sir George MURRAY, a fellow Wellingtonian officer from whom he had expected better. Murray held out no hope of either an official investigation or a public vindication. Rather, he urged a dignified silence. Privately (but not officially), however, he agreed to Dalhousie's having printed and circulated among friends copies of his observations on the petitions and evidence placed before the committee. Dalhousie accordingly confined his efforts to sending copies to Cochran for distribution among close acquaintainces in Lower Canada. From a Murray "cold & insensible," there could be no appeal to Wellington as prime minister. "I might as well appeal to a stone wall," Dalhousie thought, since Wellington would be a thousand times more frigid and indifferent than Murray to anyone who was not of a "courting character." Dalhousie thus left for India in July 1829 without obtaining the vindication he had sought.

In India the perceived injustice of his treatment continued to rankle, and Dalhousie seems to have decided that redress lay in stating his case to the king.

However, with the demise of George IV and the advent of a Whig ministry in 1830, his last hopes must have faded. His mood was not improved by India's heat, which he found oppressive. He may have suffered a stroke in March 1830, but he was well enough to tour Burma the following year, and he derived some relief from residence in the cooler hill-station of Simla. However, with his health palpably unequal to his onerous responsibilities, he resigned his command and returned to Britain in April 1832. Six months later he suffered a fainting fit, and the following February a further attack rendered him a "couch invalid," unable to see or write for several months. For a year or more he lived abroad – Nice and Strasbourg (France) and Wiesbaden (Federal Republic of Germany) – returning to his beloved Dalhousie Castle in 1834. There he spent his final years in pain and decrepitude and ultimately in blindness and senility. He died on 21 March 1838; a former sparring-partner, Bishop John Inglis, responding to an invitation to dine, attended the funeral instead and represented all those colonists who remembered the governor with affection or dislike. Dalhousie's beloved "Lady D" died less than a year after her husband, on 22 Jan. 1839. As the wife of a civil administrator, she had accompanied him everywhere, sharing his interests and pains, and like him she had carried out her official duties conscientiously, with dignity and charm.

The geologist John Jeremiah Bigsby* portrayed Dalhousie as "a quiet, studious, domestic man, faithful to his word, and kind, but rather dry," adding that "he spoke and acted by measure, as if he were in an enemy's land." An anonymous Lower Canadian critic described him less sympathetically as "a short, thick set, bowleg man . . . often called the Scotch ploughman," avaricious – "indeed saving was his chief object" – and extremely vain, "passionate & tyrannical or kind as the moment directed," given to blaming his subordinates for his difficulties, a man who "tried and parted in anger with all parties." "Ill luck hung over him," this observer concluded. Despite the differences, both portraits – Bigsby's through the suggestion of assailed loneliness – indicate that Dalhousie was not well suited by temperament to govern an obstreperous colony enjoying representative institutions with their accompanying clash of opinions and warring factions. Another contemporary, the author John Richardson*, later asserted that Dalhousie had not possessed the "quickness and pliability of mind . . . in all the degree necessary to the Governor of so turbulent a country" that was enjoyed by a successor, Lord Sydenham [THOMSON]. Although no dullard, being a man of intellectual curiosity, wide reading and interests, and sensitivity to the beauties of nature, Dalhousie as a civil administrator manifested the tendencies to plodding and pedantry that had characterized his style as a military commander.

Dalhousie was accustomed to a hierarchical society, Scottish and military, in which he ordered and others obeyed. He had no patience with those who showed disrespect, challenged authority, or, in the case of the lower class, had ideas above their station. Much of this behaviour in Lower Canadians he considered a result of their "total neglect of education." In Dalhousie's world, rulers exercised paternal authority for the welfare of the people and gave disinterested public service in the British aristocratic tradition. It was as an essential part of his public duty that he unremittingly championed improvement, both economic and intellectual. This concern was a hallmark of his Scottish educational and cultural background and of a Scottish society in which leadership and example afforded the key to social progress.

Nova Scotia was sufficiently élitist and deferential to permit Dalhousie to act out his perceived role as a benevolent father-figure at a time when popular discontent had not yet assumed an overtly political form. At Quebec, he was made conscious of the governor's lack of power, resources, and patronage. Unable himself to advance the public good by purposeful action, Dalhousie came to condemn the constitutional structure as wholly unsuited to the colony's needs and character. "The Govt altogether is the worst piece of machinery I ever handled, and the British Constitution might have been given with equal propriety to Cats & dogs, as to the discordant Protestant & Catholic population of this Country," he complained. His ingrained aversion to Catholics and to the Canadians, inculcated by his sturdy Presbyterianism and years of fighting France, no doubt heightened and coloured his animosity towards political opponents in Lower Canada.

Dalhousie, however, would likely have reacted in a similar fashion to criticism or challenge in any colony where dissension was rife. He lacked philosophical detachment. His responses were shaped more decisively by temperament than by conservative political principles. Perhaps insecure in the face of opposition by more sagacious politicians than himself, he became paranoiac in his detection of intrigue. Criticism was taken as personal affront. Set-backs obsessed him. With a brooding, even morbid, cast of mind which his deep religious convictions cultivated as well as assuaged, he easily became prey to melancholy reflection. Under such dispositions he entertained agonizingly ambivalent feelings about his career of public service. Despite possessing few compelling qualifications, he had been ambitious to reach the highest commands and thus gain honour and repute as well as financial security. But he remained painfully aware of the sacrifices that this career had exacted in terms of peace of mind, home life, private avocations, and friendships, and he perpetually evinced a nostalgic longing for his native Scotland. The circumstances of his departure from Lower Canada, however, implanted a sense of injustice and ingratitude that rankled for the rest of his life. For all Dalhousie's achievements as a colonial governor, the man and his destiny were not happily matched.

PETER BURROUGHS

George Ramsay, 9th Earl of Dalhousie, is the co-author, probably with his civil secretary Andrew William Cochran, of *Observations on the petitions of grievance addressed to the imperial parliament from the districts of Quebec, Montreal, and Three-Rivers* (Quebec, 1828). His journals are at SRO, GD45 (mfm. at PAC); they have been published in part as *The Dalhousie journals*, ed. Marjory Whitelaw (3v., [Ottawa], 1978–82). There are portraits of Dalhousie at the National Gallery of Scotland (Edinburgh) and Dalhousie Univ. (Halifax), and a silhouette is at the PAC. Drawings and paintings John Elliott Woolford did for Dalhousie and caricatures painted by Lady Dalhousie form part of a sizeable collection of drawings, water-colours, engravings, maps, plans, and other documents assembled by Dalhousie. This material was brought back to Canada from Scotland in the 1980s and distributed among five institutions: the N.S. Museum (Halifax), Dalhousie Univ., the PANB, the National Gallery of Canada (Ottawa), and the PAC. Further details are provided in Marie Elwood, "The study and repatriation of the Lord Dalhousie Collection," *Archivaria* (Ottawa), no.24 (summer 1987): 108–16.

GRO (Edinburgh), Cokpen, reg. of births and baptisms, 18 Nov. 1770; reg. of deaths, 21 March 1838. PAC, MG 23, GII, 10; MG 24, A64, B1, B2, B3, B6, B16. PANS, MG 1, 253; RG 1, 63, 111–12, 288–89. PRO, CO 42/185–216; CO 43/25–27; CO 217/98–139; CO 218/29; CO 323/147–57; CO 324/73–90. J. J. Bigsby, *The shoe and canoe, or pictures of travel in the Canadas, illustrative of their scenery and of colonial life; with facts and opinions on emigration, state policy, and other points of public interest . . .* (2v., London, 1850), 1: 27. Robert Christie, *Memoirs of the administration of the government of Lower Canada, by the Right Honorable the Earl of Dalhousie, G.C.B., comprehending a period of eight years, vizt: – from June, 1820 till September, 1828* (Quebec, 1829). G.B., Parl., *Hansard's parliamentary debates* (London), 3rd ser., 19 (1828): 300–44; House of Commons paper, 1828, 7, no.569, *Report from the select committee on the civil government of Canada* (repr. Quebec, 1829). L.C., House of Assembly, *Journals*, 1820–28. John MacGregor, *British America* (2v., Edinburgh and London, 1832), 2: 54–56. N.S., House of Assembly, *Journal and proc.*, 1816–20. [John] Richardson, *Eight years in Canada; embracing a review of the administrations of lords Durham and Sydenham, Sir Chas. Bagot, and Lord Metcalfe, and including numerous interesting letters from Lord Durham, Mr. Chas. Buller and other well-known public characters* (Montreal, 1847), 187. G.B., WO, *Army list*, 1787–1838. H. J. Morgan, *Sketches of celebrated Canadians*, 248–51. *The Scots peerage, founded on Wood's edition of Sir Robert Douglas's peerage of Scotland . . .*, ed. J. B. Paul (9v., Edinburgh, 1904–14). Wallace, *Macmillan dict.* Susan Buggey, "Churchmen and dissenters: religious toleration in Nova Scotia, 1758–1835" (MA thesis, Dalhousie Univ., 1981). Christie, *Hist. of L.C.* (1848–55), vols.2–3. Judith Fingard, "The Church of England in British North America, 1787–1825" (PHD thesis, Univ. of London, 1970). K. E. Killam, "Lord Dalhousie's administration in Nova Scotia" (MA thesis, Univ. of Toronto, 1931). Lambert, "Joseph-Octave Plessis." William Lee-Warner, *The life of the Marquis of Dalhousie* (2v., London, 1904), 1. Helen Taft Manning, "The civil list of Lower Canada," *CHR*, 24 (1943): 24–47; *Revolt of French Canada*.

RANDAL, STEPHEN, teacher, office holder, and journalist; b. 1 Jan. 1804, probably in Danby, Vt, son of Benjamin Randal and Roxana Case; m. 1828 Lamira Juliana Munson in Saint-Armand, Lower Canada, and they had at least two daughters; d. 27 April 1841 in Stanstead, Lower Canada.

During Stephen Randal's childhood, his parents moved across the Vermont border to Saint-Armand, where he came to the notice of Anglican missionary Charles James STEWART, becoming his protégé after the death of the senior Randal in 1811. Stephen's education, provided and directed by Stewart, was intended to prepare him for holy orders. After preliminary studies in Saint-Armand, in 1819 he entered the grammar school (from 1821 the Royal Grammar School) in Montreal. He studied there, under Alexander SKAKEL, until 1824. Because Randal did not feel a call to the ministry, Stewart arranged for him to take charge of the grammar school to be opened at St Thomas, Upper Canada, in the Talbot settlement in 1825. At the school (later named the Talbot Seminary) Randal acquired his first experience teaching classical languages; he later wrote that Colonel Thomas Talbot*, the founder of the settlement, had been "very kind" to him.

In 1827 Randal applied for the position of headmaster at the Gore District Grammar School in Hamilton. The trustees disagreed over the choice from among the three applicants, one of whom was John Rae*, and the matter was settled in Randal's favour by John Strachan* in his capacity as president of the Board for the General Superintendence of Education. Although a later biographer, Mabel Grace Burkholder, found Randal "fond of the classics and weak in mathematics," reports indicate that he was a successful teacher. Burkholder provides a rendition of one of Randal's reports: "Boys 41, girls 24; 16 in Latin, 4 in French, 7 in mathematics; English grammar, geography and astronomy 10; arithmetic 25; writing 40. To six pupils education was given gratis." Early in the 1830s Randal proposed an "evening school" for adults (to be started if he received 12 applications) but the pioneering move in adult education never materialized.

Randal was also involved in various other aspects of life in Hamilton. In 1833, the year of the town's incorporation, he served as town clerk and for a few months that year he was secretary of the newly formed board of police. An inseparable friend of George HAMILTON, the founder of the town, Randal, aided by his wife and sister, gave frequent parties for the young people of Hamilton's prominent families. In 1835 he was a charter member of Christ's Church, the town's first Anglican church.

Late in 1831 Randal, having decided to combine publishing and teaching, issued a prospectus for a semi-monthly literary paper, the *Voyageur*, "devoted one half to native literary productions and the remainder to good foreign selections." It is uncertain exactly when it began or how long Randal published it (it had ceased by 1836); a contemporary, Charles Morrison Durand, blamed its demise on "it being too refined for the times." Late in 1833 or early in 1834 Randal resigned from his teaching position to edit the radical newspaper the *Hamilton Free Press*, founded by William Smith. Again it is uncertain exactly how long he edited this paper but by 1836 he claimed to have been "riddled by the shot of both [political] parties. Unacquainted with the management of a printing establishment, I was cheated, bamboozled and ruined."

After trying unsuccessfully to support his family by running a private school, he sent his wife and family back to her father to allow himself "a year to wander." However, "surprised at the result of the elections (1836)," which saw the bulk of the reformers defeated [*see* Sir Francis Bond Head*], he returned to Upper Canada "determined to spend the remainder of the year in getting better acquainted with the real sentiments of the people." He travelled throughout the province "sometimes as a political lecturer, sometimes as an editor," and he again published a short-lived literary journal, *Randal's Magazine*, in Hallowell (Picton).

When the Upper Canadian rebellion broke out in December 1837, he returned to his family in Lower Canada and took a teaching position at the Frost Village Academy, receiving the meagre salary of £40. Less than four years later he died in straitened circumstances at the age of 37.

Stephen Randal was described by a contemporary as "a very odd but gifted young man." According to Durand, "he prided himself on walking and looking like Lord Byron, in whose day he lived. He and Byron had club feet and curly hair and a look of genius." Perhaps it was Randal's personality, as well as his political and educational views and teaching ability, that has caused him to be remembered in spite of his many failures and his short life.

KATHARINE GREENFIELD

HPL, Board of Police, minutes, 16 March, 17 Aug. 1833; Scrapbooks, H. F. Gardiner, 216: 90 (Charles Durand, letter to the editor, *Herald* (Hamilton, Ont.), written 16 Aug. 1900); C. R. McCullough, "Famous people, landmarks, and events." *Documentary history of education in Upper Canada from the passing of the Constitutional Act of 1791 to the close of Rev. Dr. Ryerson's administration of the Education Department in 1876*, ed. J. G. Hodgins (28v., Toronto, 1894–1910). *DHB*. R. W. James, *John Rae, political economist; an account of his life and a compilation of his main writings* (2v., Toronto, 1965). Johnston, *Head of the Lake* (1967). Mabel Burkholder, "New light on Hamilton's first school teacher," *Hamilton Spectator*, 7 Nov. 1942. "Evening 'Times' ready to move to new quarters; Hamilton journalism from small beginnings up to the present . . . 1831 to 1888," *Evening Times* (Hamilton), 3 April 1888.

RANKIN, WILLIAM, printer and newspaperman; d. October 1837 in Demerara (Guyana).

Nothing is known of William Rankin before his appearance in Prince Edward Island in the early 1830s. He was likely a kinsman of Coun Douly Rankin*, a prominent Islander and an opponent of the colony's administration; it is probably significant that Coun Douly's son George spent 30 years in Demerara, where William would die. William first enters the historical record on 8 July 1835 when he testified at a trial in Charlottetown involving John Henry WHITE, a printer and publisher. William stated that he had been a printer about eight years, that he had worked for White from December 1833 to the following July, and that he had then gone to work for James Douglas Haszard*, another newspaperman. On 2 Feb. 1836 William announced in Haszard's *Royal Gazette* plans to publish in Charlottetown a weekly newspaper on "liberal and patriotic principles." He produced the first issue of the *Prince Edward Island Times* on 26 March 1836, in his printing shop. His opening editorial observed that such a paper "has been long and loudly called for, and we trust it will not be unkindly received by those whose voices brought it into existence." The real question, as he would subsequently discover, was not whether he was well received by friends, but how he would be treated by the other side.

Despite initial problems caused by the failure of all his type to arrive, Rankin's paper was professionally laid out and edited, demonstrating his considerable experience at the task. From the outset he made its political emphasis clear by closely aligning it with Coun Douly Rankin and the Escheat party. He attacked the Council and its supporters in the House of Assembly, who opposed escheat, as a "baseless Fabric of Tyranny." The paper called for "Reform and Liberty," advocating such measures as the establishment of a literary society, a mechanics' institute, and a newspaper reading-room in Charlottetown. It reprinted material from reform newspapers in Nova Scotia and the Canadas in an obvious effort to relate the escheat movement to other political stirrings in British North America.

Beginning with the second issue, the *Times* carried a column of Gaelic verse as a regular feature. Most of its local material consisted of provocative letters to the editor from pseudonymous correspondents, although one on 10 May 1836 criticizing the agent of the 6th Earl of Selkirk, William Douse*, for exploiting tenants appeared over Coun Douly Rankin's initials. The *Times* was highly critical of the *Royal Gazette*, with which it traded invective personal and political over that spring and summer. The comments of Veritas about the administration's paper were typical of the tone of the exchange: "The habits of the caterpillar and the reptile were still conspicuous on its pages; and its principles were redolent of the muck-worm, *it smelled of the dirt*." Rankin complained in June that the post office was arresting the progress of copies of his paper to outlying subscribers, and the "whole Tribe of proprietary agents," which the *Times* openly attacked, was obviously restive over the paper's editorial opinions and exposés.

The last available copy of the *Times* is dated 9 Aug. 1836, and is undoubtedly its final issue. The *Royal Gazette* explained the cessation when it reported laconically on 13 September that a case for an assault on William Rankin, *The King* v. *Douse*, had been dismissed in magistrate's court because of the non-appearance of the complainant. Rankin had apparently already departed from the Island, and he died of yellow fever in the Caribbean a year later. Prince Edward Island was not ready in 1836 to support and tolerate a newspaper as blatantly political and outspoken as the *Times*, and William Rankin was clearly a victim of intimidation by those he had publicly criticized in its pages.

J. M. BUMSTED

P.E.I. Museum, File information concerning William Rankin. *Report of the trial held at Charlotte-town, Prince Edward Island, July 8th, 1835 . . .* (n.p., n.d.; copy at PANS), 4–5. *Prince Edward Island Times* (Charlottetown), 26 March–9 Aug. 1836 (copy at PAPEI). *Royal Gazette* (Charlottetown), 2 Feb., 19 April, 13 Sept. 1836. W. L. Cotton, "The press in Prince Edward Island," *Past and present of Prince Edward Island . . .*, ed. D. A. MacKinnon and A. B. Warburton (Charlottetown, [1906]), 113–20.

RASTEL DE ROCHEBLAVE, PIERRE DE, fur trader, businessman, militia officer, JP, politician, and office holder; b. 9 March 1773 in Kaskaskia (Ill.), son of Philippe-François de Rastel de Rocheblave and Marie-Michelle Dufresne; m. 9 Feb. 1819 Anne-Elmire Bouthillier in Montreal, and they had nine children; d. 5 Oct. 1840 in Coteau-Saint-Louis on Montreal Island.

Philippe-François de Rastel de Rocheblave, sometimes called the Chevalier de Rocheblave, came to New France during the Seven Years' War and seems to have fought in the Ohio region. He was at Fort Chartres (near Prairie du Rocher, Ill.) in 1760, and in the following years he established himself at Kaskaskia as an officer in the colonial regular troops. Around 1765 he moved from Kaskaskia, which had passed into British hands, to Ste Genevieve (Mo.) on the west bank of the Mississippi in territory that France had ceded to Spain. There he took command of the Illinois country for the Spaniards. After quarrelling with the Spanish governor in New Orleans, he recrossed the Mississippi around 1773 or 1774 and settled once more at Kaskaskia, where he soon became the commandant, this time in the service of the British. In July 1778 he was taken prisoner by American troops under George Rogers Clark and sent to Virginia. Evidently having escaped, in the spring of 1780 he reached New York, which was still in British hands. Shortly after the war ended, he settled with his family in Montreal, and from 1789 they lived at Varennes. Rocheblave took an interest for a time in the fur business, and from 1792 until his death on 22 April 1802 he served as member for Surrey in the Lower Canadian House of Assembly. In May 1801 he was appointed clerk of the land roll.

Pierre de Rastel de Rocheblave himself also went into the fur trade. In 1786 he seems to have been looking after his father's interests at Detroit. The Chevalier de Rocheblave bought goods in Montreal and sent them to Detroit, and was doing business with Étienne-Charles Campion*, Richard Dobie*, James Fraser, and Jean-Baptiste Barthe, John Askin*'s brother-in-law and agent, among others. Subsequently Pierre worked as a clerk in Detroit for "Messrs Grant, Alexr Mackenzie [Alexander McKenzie*], and Mcdonell [possibly John McDonald* of Garth]." From December 1797 to May 1798 he was in Montreal, where, probably using money he had saved in the preceding decade, he hired 12 voyageurs to go to Michilimackinac (Mackinac Island, Mich.) and the Mississippi region.

Rocheblave was a founder of the New North West Company, also called the XY Company [*see* John Ogilvy*]. Established on 20 Oct. 1798, the firm was intended to compete with the NWC, which dominated the fur trade in the northwest. One of the six wintering partners, he was put in charge of the Athabasca department. The fierce competition between the two rivals sometimes degenerated into acts of violence. In 1803 Rocheblave himself was indirectly involved in one of them. His clerk, Joseph-Maurice Lamothe*, killed James King, the clerk working for Nor'Wester John McDonald of Garth. McDonald, who recorded the event in his diary, did not hold it against Rocheblave, however, and even called him "a gentleman."

When the XY Company merged with the NWC on 5 Nov. 1804, Rocheblave was the only Canadian other than Charles Chaboillez* to be made a proprietor in the reorganized NWC. He was put in charge of the Red River department, a post he held until 1807. At the annual meeting that year he was given responsibility for the Athabasca department, and then in the summer of 1810 for the Pic department on Lake Superior. The following winter he ordered his clerk to starve out independent trader Jean-Baptiste PERRAULT and his two *engagés*, who had established themselves on the Pic River. Perrault had to turn to Rocheblave for food in February 1811, and Rocheblave took advantage of his predicament to get his trade goods for a pittance.

An incident that occurred during the annual meeting of the NWC's agents and winterers at Fort William (Thunder Bay, Ont.) in the summer of 1811 demonstrates the influence Rocheblave had acquired. On 28 January William McGillivray*, John Richardson*, and John Jacob Astor had reached an agreement in New York to set up the South West Fur Company. By its terms the shares of the new firm were to be divided among Astor himself and the two Montreal firms of McTavish, McGillivrays and Company and Forsyth, Richardson and Company. The NWC was to hand over its trading posts on American territory to the South West Fur Company. This arrangement required the approval of the members of the NWC and when McGillivray submitted the terms to the meeting in July, several winterers strongly objected to them. After much discussion McGillivray finally brought the dissenters round by proposing Rocheblave as manager of the new company.

War between the United States and Great Britain apparently kept the South West Fur Company's plans in abeyance, however, and enabled the NWC to consolidate its hold on the fur trade in American territory. Rocheblave himself scarcely had time to assume his duties, for on 2 Oct. 1812 he became captain in the Corps of Canadian Voyageurs recruited from the NWC. After the unit was disbanded, he served on the staff of the sedentary militia of Lower Canada with the rank of major in the "Indian and conquered countries," according to his commission, dated 1 Sept. 1814.

In the post-war years Rocheblave played an increasingly important role in the fur business. On 6 Feb. 1815 he entered into partnership with Forsyth, Richardson and Company, McTavish, McGillivrays and Company, and the NWC to form a commercial enterprise for an eight-year period. In this new and unnamed organization each of the three participating firms held nine shares and Rocheblave three. He was to receive an annual salary of £500. In return, the agreement stipulated: "He is to make the necessary preparations for the annual Outfits, to hire and engage the men, provide boats and canoes, provisions &c bale up and transport the Goods, and generally do every thing that is termed *Making the Outfits*; He is to manage and settle the business of the Concern at Michilimakinac, or wherever else it may be found convenient to transact the affairs of the Concern, assort, and bale the Furs for shipping, and deliver each Fall in due season a correct Memorandum of goods for this trade for the ensuing year."

Within months Forsyth, Richardson and Company, McTavish, McGillivrays and Company, and Rocheblave reached a new agreement with Astor to carry on the fur trade in American territory jointly for a five-year period. The agreement was, however, terminated before it expired. In April 1816 Congress passed an act restricting fur-trade licences on United States territory to citizens of that country, and Astor bought out the interests of his Canadian partners the following year. In the mean time on 24 April 1817 Rocheblave had succeeded Kenneth MacKenzie* as the NWC agent for Sir Alexander Mackenzie and Company. This new appointment brought him an annual salary of £400 and one per cent of the firm's profits. Around the same time he was given joint responsibility for the voyageurs' fund with Thomas Thain*.

Since he was in charge of organizing the western fur trade for the Canadian firms, Rocheblave was inevitably affected by the conflict surrounding the early days of the Red River settlement (Man.). When Lord Selkirk [Douglas*] seized Fort William in August 1816, he ousted Rocheblave and the other NWC partners there. Rocheblave assisted William McGillivray in the expedition that recaptured the fort in the spring of 1817. A year later he was called to testify at the trial of Colin ROBERTSON and others accused of having destroyed the NWC's Fort Gibraltar (Winnipeg) in the spring of 1816; all were acquitted.

Early in 1818 Rocheblave looked after transportation for two of the first Catholic priests in the west. In February, Bishop Joseph-Octave Plessis* had given Abbé Pierre-Antoine Tabeau* the task of making preparations for the westward journey of four missionaries, abbés Joseph-Norbert Provencher*, Sévère Dumoulin*, and Joseph Crevier, *dit* Bellerive, and seminarist William Edge. To preserve the missionaries' independence Tabeau proposed that the NWC and the HBC each supply transportation for two of them. Lord Selkirk objected to hiring several of the men whom Tabeau suggested, but Rocheblave let him choose the voyageurs, and he personally took Tabeau as far as Fort William. He also provided the missionaries with letters of recommendation to the NWC posts and took it upon himself to forward their mail to Montreal, to the great satisfaction of the church authorities.

In July 1821, when Nicholas Garry* went to Fort William to settle the details of the NWC's merger with the HBC, Rocheblave, who was present, was given the responsibility for drawing up the inventory of the NWC assets. He seems to have devoted some years to the task; in September 1822, for example, he went with John Stewart to Tadoussac, in Lower Canada, for this purpose.

Two months later, in Montreal, McGillivrays, Thain and Company was formed to liquidate the affairs of McTavish, McGillivrays and Company and to serve as agent for the HBC, looking after its interests in the Montreal district. But in August 1825 Thomas Thain, who was in charge of the firm's business at Montreal, collapsed under the burden and returned to Great Britain. Simon McGILLIVRAY entrusted management of the HBC interests to Rocheblave in February 1826. He did not have this responsibility for long, however. In a letter to the company's directors in London dated 14 June Governor George Simpson* noted: "De Rocheblave has acted very efficiently and properly during his interim management of the Company's affairs here at Montreal. His duties are now finished." Rocheblave did act as the HBC agent in Trois-Rivières in 1826 and 1827 before retiring permanently from the fur business, in which he had worked for nearly four decades.

Though he was in his mid fifties, Rocheblave did not have the temperament to remain idle. For a decade he had been channelling his money into the purchase of land, acquiring part of Coteau-Saint-Louis in particular. He had settled there in 1819 with his young wife on a property previously owned by Joseph Frobisher*. As the years went by, Rocheblave bought 12 or more pieces of land in the seigneuries of Châteauguay and La Salle, which he rented out along with other properties and shops in Montreal. Moreover he acquired 1,000 acres in Bristol Township on the Ottawa River. He became a partner in the Montreal firm of LaRocque, Bernard et Compagnie, which was in business from 1832 to 1838. With three other Canadians, his father-in-law Jean Bouthillier, François-Antoine La Rocque*, and Joseph MASSON, he promoted the construction of the first railway in the Canadas, the Champlain and St Lawrence Railroad.

Despite his numerous activities Rocheblave went into politics. His father and brother had been assemblymen, and from 1824 till 1827 he himself held the seat for Montreal West. On 9 Jan. 1832 he was called to the Legislative Council, and when it was replaced by the Special Council in 1838, he became a member of that body, on which he remained until his death. Being of a rather conciliatory disposition, he always maintained a moderate attitude in political matters, during a troubled period when radical stances were common. In the assembly he had sometimes voted with the Patriote bloc, at other times with the government's supporters, a pattern that did not, however, prevent Louis-Joseph Papineau* from showing confidence in him. Later, even though he was at times shocked by the behaviour of the governor, in particular that of Lord Aylmer [WHITWORTH-AYLMER], Rocheblave did not take a more radical position. In November 1837, along with 11 other Canadian magistrates, he signed an address to the inhabitants of the district of Montreal urging them to abstain from violence. The following January, as president of the Association Loyale Canadienne du District de Montréal, which was circulating a petition against the plan to unite Upper and Lower Canada, he signed a declaration stating the organization's views. This conciliatory attitude unfortunately displeased certain Patriotes, including Louis-Victor Sicotte*, who in a letter to Ludger Duvernay* said Rocheblave was incompetent and called him a pygmy. Yet in December 1838 Rocheblave was among those testifying before a court martial in favour of Guillaume Lévesque*, a young Patriote who narrowly escaped being hanged.

Rocheblave took on various public responsibilities in addition to his business and political activities. He was churchwarden of the Montreal parish of Notre-Dame (1817), justice of the peace for the district of Montreal (1821), juror in the Court of Oyer and Terminer (1823), treasurer of the committee for building the new church of Notre-Dame (1824), commissioner for the exploration of the territory between the Rivière Saint-Maurice and the Ottawa (1829), member of the grand jury of the Court of King's Bench and commissioner of roads (1829), commissioner for the relief of the insane and foundlings, for the supervision of the building of the Lachine Canal, and for building a new prison in the district of Montreal (1830), commissioner to draw the boundary between Lower and Upper Canada (1831), commissioner for rebuilding government property located in Montreal (1832), commissioner for the civil erection of parishes for several years (from 1832), and commissioner to erect a jail and court-house in Missisquoi County (1834). In 1836, after Montreal's charter had expired, Rocheblave was appointed to the Court of Special Sessions of the Peace created to run municipal affairs. The following year he was made a commissioner to administer the oath of allegiance.

To maintain that Rocheblave reached the top of his economic and political world solely because of his social origins would be injudicious. Certainly, his father had been a governor in the colonial administration, but in a region of minor importance; the elder Rocheblave had also been a member of the House of Assembly, but at a time when the post did not necessarily confer a privileged rank; he tried his hand at the fur business just when Pierre was starting out, but he did not make a fortune in it, quite the reverse. Pierre de Rastel de Rocheblave seems to have owed his rise in society rather to his personality, which was marked by determination and a conciliatory way of dealing with people. Most statements by his contemporaries confirm this view. Only the eldest of Rocheblave's children benefited from his success, the others having died young. In the fashionable circles of Montreal at the end of the 19th century his daughter Louise-Elmire had a salon that for many years drew distinguished visitors to enjoy "magnificent dinners that went on for hours." She died unmarried on 9 Aug. 1914 in Montreal, and with her the Canadian branch of the Rastel de Rocheblaves disappeared.

PIERRE DUFOUR and MARC OUELLET

[Pierre de Rastel de Rocheblave's papers were lost when the house his widow occupied was destroyed by fire in 1860. That the materials illustrating Rocheblave's activities are widely scattered and consequently difficult to piece together is no doubt part of the reason he does not occupy a place in Canadian historiography commensurate with his importance. P.D. and M.O.]

ANQ-M, CE1-51, 15 janv. 1820; 26 juin, 11 juill. 1821; 1er nov. 1822; 9 sept. 1824; 10 déc. 1826; 14 fév. 1830; 7 juin, 10 juill. 1832; 27 déc. 1834; 30 avril 1835; 3 janv. 1838; 8 oct. 1840; 22 mars 1844; 2 mai 1846; CN1-28, 7 déc. 1820; CN1-134, 2 mai 1816; 8–9 avril 1817; 17 mars 1819; 3, 7 oct., 29 déc. 1820; 9 févr., 3 mai 1821; 7 janv., 27 avril 1822; 5 août 1823; 30 oct. 1826; 12 juin 1827; 18 janv., 1er mars, 11 avril, 24, 31 mai, 16 juill. 1828; 24 févr., 1er oct. 1829; 23 oct. 1830; 12 janv., 13, 31 mai, 20 juill., 6 août 1831; 19 sept., 27 déc. 1832; 22 juill. 1833; 10 juin 1835; 23 nov. 1836; 12 oct., 10 nov. 1837; 25, 31 janv., 5 févr., 30 mai, 13 oct. 1838; 19 janv., 20 avril 1839; CN1-167, 23 juin, 28 sept. 1802; 24, 29 mars 1813; CN1-192, 1er août 1835, 29 avril 1836, 9 avril 1839; CN1-194, 6 févr. 1819, 9 nov. 1831; CN1-216, 6, 26 mars, 5 juill. 1838; CN1-224, 23 sept. 1836; 12 oct. 1840; 18 juin, 29 juill. 1841; 12 juill. 1842; 19 sept. 1844; 2 avril 1845; CN1-269, 12 juin 1813; CN1-320, 20 mai 1835; CN1-396, 3 févr. 1836, 30 nov. 1838. ANQ-Q, P-362/1. ASQ, Fonds Viger–Verreau, sér.O, 049, no.15; 0521. AUM, P 58. PAC, MG 8, G14; MG 19, B3; National Map Coll., H1/300, 1831. PAM, HBCA, D.4; E.20/1: f.212. T.-R.-V. Boucher de Boucherville, "Journal de M. Thomas Verchères de Boucherville . . . ," *Canadian Antiquarian and Numismatic Journal*, 3rd ser., 3 (1901). *Les bourgeois de la Compagnie du Nord-Ouest* (Masson). Gabriel Franchère, *Journal of a voyage on the north west coast of North America during the years 1811, 1812, 1813, and 1814*, trans. W. T. Lamb, intro. W. K. Lamb (Toronto, 1969). D. W. Harmon, *Sixteen years in the Indian country: the journal of Daniel Williams Harmon, 1800–1816*, ed. W. K. Lamb (Toronto, 1957). *HBRS*, 2 (Rich and Fleming); 3 (Fleming). Robert La Roque de Roquebrune, *Testament de mon enfance* (2e éd., Montréal, 1958). L.C., House of Assembly, *Journals*, 1828–29, app.; 1830, app. Alexander Mackenzie, *The journals and letters of Sir Alexander Mackenzie*, ed. W. K. Lamb (Toronto, 1970). *New light on the early history of the greater northwest: the manuscript journals of Alexander Henry . . . and of David Thompson . . .* , ed. Elliott Coues (3v., New York, 1897; repr. 3v. in 2, Minneapolis, Minn., [1965]). "Papiers Duvernay," *Canadian Antiquarian and Numismatic Journal*, 3rd ser., 6 (1909): 87–90. L.-J. Papineau, "Correspondance" (Ouellet), ANQ *Rapport*, 1953–55: 185–442. J.-B. Perrault, *Jean-Baptiste Perrault, marchand voyageur parti de Montréal le 28e de mai 1783*, L.-P. Cormier, édit. (Montréal, 1978). *Thunder Bay district, 1821–1892: a collection of documents*, ed. and intro. [M.] E. Arthur (Toronto, 1973). Wis., State Hist. Soc., *Coll.*, 3 (1857); 18 (1908); 19 (1910). *Montreal Gazette*, 6 Oct. 1840. *Quebec Gazette*, 25 Oct. 1821, 12 Sept. 1822, 26 May 1823, 7 Oct. 1840. *Quebec Mercury*, 16 Dec. 1805.

F.-J. Audet, *Les députés de Montréal*. Caron, "Inv. de la corr. de Mgr Panet," ANQ *Rapport*, 1935–36: 157–272; "Inv. de la corr. de Mgr Plessis," 1927–28: 215–316; 1928–29: 87–208; "Inv. de la corr. de Mgr Signay," 1936–37: 123–330. Béatrice Chassé, "Répertoire de la collection Couillard–Després," ANQ *Rapport*, 1972: 31–81. Louise Dechêne, "Inventaire des documents relatifs à l'histoire du Canada conservés dans les archives de la Compagnie de Saint-Sulpice à Paris," ANQ *Rapport*, 1969: 147–288. Desjardins, *Guide parl.* Desrosiers, "Inv. de la corr. de Mgr Bourget," ANQ *Rapport*, 1945–46: 135–224; "Inv. de la corr. de Mgr Lartigue," 1942–43: 1–174; 1944–45: 175–266. *The founder of our monetary system, John Law, Compagnie des Indes & the early economy of North America: a second bibliography*, comp. L. M. Lande (Montreal, 1984). Philéas Gagnon, *Essai de bibliographie canadienne . . .* (2v., Québec et Montréal, 1895–1913; réimpr. Dubuque, Iowa, [1962]), 2. É.-Z. Massicotte, "Répertoire des engagements pour l'Ouest conservés dans les Archives judiciaires de Montréal . . . [1620–1821]," ANQ *Rapport*, 1942–43: 261–397; 1943–44: 335–444; 1944–45: 309–401. *Officers of British forces in Canada* (Irving). *Quebec almanac*, 1815–16. Monique Signori-Laforest, *Inventaire analytique des Archives du diocèse de Saint-Jean, 1688–1900* (Québec, 1976). Turcotte, *Le Conseil législatif*.

Norman Anick, *The fur trade in eastern Canada until 1870* (Parks Canada, National Hist. Parks and Sites Branch, *Manuscript report*, no.207, Ottawa, 1976). Brown, *Strangers in blood*. Denison, *Canada's first bank*. W. T. Easterbrook and H. G. J. Aitken, *Canadian economic history* (Toronto, 1967), 176–77. R. D. Elmes, "Some determinants of voting blocs in the assembly of Lower Canada, 1820–1837" (MA thesis, Carleton Univ., Ottawa, 1972). G. P. de T. Glazebrook, *A history of transportation in Canada* (Toronto, 1938; repr. in 2v., New York, 1969), 1: 43. *Hochelaga depicta . . .* , ed. Newton Bosworth (Montreal, 1839; repr. Toronto, 1974). Innis, *Fur trade in Canada* (1962). J.-C. Lamothe, *Histoire de la corporation de la cité de Montréal depuis son origine jusqu'à nos jours . . .* (Montréal, 1903). Lemieux, *L'établissement de la première prov. eccl.* B. C. Payette, *The northwest* (Montreal, 1964). R. A. Pendergast, "The XY Company, 1798 to 1804" (PHD thesis, Univ. of Ottawa, 1957). Linda Price, *Introduction to the social history of Scots in Quebec (1780–1840)* (Ottawa, 1981). Robert Rumilly, *La Compagnie du Nord-Ouest, une épopée montréalaise* (2v., Montréal, 1980); *Hist. de Montréal*; *Papineau et son temps*. Léo Traversy, *La paroisse de Saint-Damase, co. Saint-Hyacinthe* (s.l., 1964). Tulchinsky, *River barons*. M. [E.] Wilkins Campbell, *The North West Company* ([rev. ed., Toronto, 1973]). Marthe Faribault-Beauregard, "L'honorable François Lévesque, son neveu Pierre Guérout, et leurs descendants," SGCF *Mémoires*, 8 (1957): 13–30. É.-Z. Massicotte, "Quelques rues et faubourgs du vieux Montréal," *Cahiers des Dix*, 1 (1936): 105–56. "Nécrologie: madame de Rocheblave," *La Patrie*, 18 déc. 1886: 4. Guy Pinard, "Montréal, son histoire et son architecture: la prison du Pied-du-Courant," *La Presse*, 30 nov. 1986: A8; "Le club des ingénieurs," 21 sept. 1986: 28, 53. Albert Tessier, "Encore le Saint-Maurice," *Cahiers des Dix*, 5 (1940): 145–76.

RAYMOND, JEAN-MOÏSE (Jean-Moyse), merchant, manufacturer, militia officer, politician, JP, and office holder; b. 5 Jan. 1787 in La Tortue (Saint-Mathieu), Que., son of Jean-Baptiste Raymond* and Marie-Clotilde Girardin; d. 8 Feb. 1843 in Saint-Jacques-de-l'Achigan (Saint-Jacques), Lower Canada, and was buried in L'Assomption.

Jean-Moïse Raymond grew up in La Tortue and around the turn of the century moved with his family to La Prairie..He attended the Collège Saint-Raphaël in Montreal from 1798 to 1805, and some time before 1810 he became a partner in his father's mercantile business. On 20 Nov. 1810 he married 16-year-old Archange Denaut, daughter of a La Prairie merchant, and through the marriage he strengthened his business connections and social ties in the community. Tragedy soon struck: their only child, a daughter, died in 1812 at age three months and was followed to the grave by Archange herself in January 1813.

On 7 Oct. 1813 Raymond was appointed a major commanding two companies of the Boucherville battalion of militia, which were held in reserve at the battle of Châteauguay later that month. The following year, back in La Prairie, he received from his father a commercial establishment opposite the parish church as an advance on his inheritance. The only surviving son, Jean-Moïse was heavily involved in the land transactions of his crippled and chronically ill father and in the growing business of Jean-Baptiste Raymond et Fils, which conducted the processing of potash, sawmilling, and the sale of household and manufactured goods to local farmers in return for wheat. His second marriage, on 5 June 1815 to 18-year-old Angélique (Marie des Anges) Leroux d'Esneval, was as advantageous as the first; her father was Laurent Leroux*, a merchant of L'Assomption and an increasingly prominent local official. They would have 13 children, 9 of whom survived to adulthood.

Well connected and prosperous, Raymond, like his father, took an interest in politics. In 1822 he was active in a movement, organized in part by the Canadian party under Louis-Joseph Papineau*, to abort a projected union of the Canadas. Two years later he was elected to the Lower Canadian House of Assembly for Huntingdon County, which his father had represented from 1800 to 1808. From 1830 to 1838 Jean-Moïse held Laprairie County, which had been created from Huntingdon in 1829. A conscientious back-bencher, in regular attendance (thanks to his prosperity in business) at a time when absenteeism was high, he was active in standing and select committees on trade. He was a faithful supporter of Papineau and voted with the Patriote party (formerly the Canadian party) on major issues leading up to, and including, the 92 Resolutions in 1834. He was not a radical, however, and he scandalized more extreme Patriotes in 1832 when he subscribed to a new conservative newspaper, *L'Ami du peuple, de l'ordre et des lois* (Montréal), controlled by the Sulpicians [*see* Alfred-Xavier Rambau*]. Although a member of the legislature from one of the province's more volatile areas, Raymond seems not to have participated in any of the inflammatory local meetings held by the Patriotes in the autumn of 1837, and he probably discouraged violence. In 1830 he had been given a commission of the peace for the district of Montreal and in 1831 had been appointed a school inspector for Laprairie County.

Raymond had taken over the family firm on his father's death in 1825, and he maintained it in La Prairie until the end of the 1830s. However, poor harvests due to disease, tight credit, and the destruction consequent on the rebellions of 1837–38 brought heavy losses; in 1839 he liquidated the business and moved his family to L'Assomption, where he had obtained land from Leroux. The same year he opened a whisky distillery, probably at Saint-Jacques-de-l'Achigan. Credit still being tight, he had trouble meeting his bills; a brother-in-law, Joseph MASSON, protested non-payment of promissory notes in 1839 and 1840 and refused him any further advances. The following year Raymond was returned by acclamation for Leinster County in the first elections held under the new union constitution [*see* Charles Edward Poulett THOMSON]. With Austin CUVILLIER, John NEILSON, Augustin-Norbert Morin*, Frédéric-Auguste Quesnel*, and Denis-Benjamin Viger* among others, he consistently denounced the union. In January 1842, however, perhaps for financial reasons, he resigned to accept the remunerated post of registrar of Leinster County.

A little more than a year after his appointment Raymond died following a "short but violent illness," and was buried in the parish church of L'Assomption. Over time his mother's remarriage and the marriages of some of his sisters had connected him with a number of leading figures in the La Prairie region and elsewhere in the colony, including Masson, Edme HENRY, Paul-Théophile Pinsonaut*, a notary and businessman, Pierre-Joseph Godefroy de Tonnancour, a lawyer and assemblyman for Trois-Rivières, and John William McCallum, a lawyer and major in the militia. Raymond's life, in its remarkable continuity with that of his father, exhibits many of the characteristics of the Lower Canadian local and regional élite. Through their careers and marriages Raymond's children maintained and even reinforced the family's social position: two sons became merchants and another a lawyer; of his daughters, one married a notary and another the lawyer Magloire Lanctôt*, while a third became a nun in the Hôtel-Dieu in Montreal.

ALAN DEVER

ANQ-M, CE1-2, 20 nov. 1810; CE1-54, 5 janv. 1787; CE5-14, 5 juin 1815, 11 févr. 1843; CN1-32, 1837–40; CN1-134, 1828–40; CN1-199, 1832; CN1-299, 1836; CN1-380, 1840; CN1-394, 1833–36. Can., Prov. of, Legislative Assembly, *App. to the journals*, 1843, app.F. *Debates of the Legislative Assembly of United Canada* (Abbott Gibbs *et al.*), vols.1–2. L.C., House of Assembly, *Journals*, 1825–37. *L'Aurore des Canadas*, 16 févr. 1843. *La Minerve*, 13 févr. 1843. F.-J. Audet, "Les législateurs du Bas-Canada." Caron, "Papiers Duvernay," ANQ *Rapport*, 1926–27: 145–258. Desjardins, *Guide parl. Inventaire des actes notariés du village de Laprairie, 1670–1860*, Michel Aubin, compil. (s.l., 1975). *Mariages de Laprairie (Notre-Dame-de-la-Prairie-de-la-Madeleine), 1670–1968*, Irenée Jeté et Benoît Pontbriand, compil. (Québec, 1970). *Mariages du comté de L'Assomption (du début des paroisses à 1960 inclusivement)* (3v., Montréal, 1962). *Quebec almanac*, 1814–25. P. G. Cornell, *The alignment of political groups in Canada, 1841–1867* (Toronto, 1962), 5. Henri Masson, *Joseph Masson, dernier seigneur de Terrebonne, 1791–1847* (Montréal, 1972). Benjamin Sulte, *La bataille de Châteauguay* (Québec, 1899). J.-J. Lefebvre, "Jean-Baptiste Raymond (1757–1825), député de Huntingdon (Laprairie), 1800–1808," *BRH*, 58 (1952): 59–72; "Jean-Moïse Raymond (1787–1843), premier député de Laprairie (1824–1838), natif du comté," *BRH*, 60 (1954): 109–20.

READY, JOHN, office holder, army officer, politician, and colonial administrator; b. *c.* 1777; m. first 18 June 1804 Susanna Bromley in East Grinstead, England, and they had two sons and two daughters; m. secondly 13 Dec. 1836 Sarah Tobin, daughter of Sir John Tobin, in Malew, Isle of Man, and they had one son and one daughter; d. 10 July 1845 in Castletown, Isle of Man.

Nothing is known of John Ready before he entered the British army as an ensign on 6 Jan. 1796 at age 19. By 1813 he had risen to the rank of lieutenant-colonel without purchasing any commissions. It is possible that he advanced his military career through distinguished service, although his subsequent appointments in the colonial administration lend credence to the supposition that he had influential friends. Unsubstantiated family lore has it that the Duke of Wellington stood as godfather to one of Ready's children. When his battalion was disbanded in 1815 Ready was placed on the Irish half-pay list, and he joined the staff of the Duke of Richmond [Lennox*], lord lieutenant of Ireland, as his secretary. When Richmond was named governor-in-chief of British North America in May 1818 Ready became his military secretary and, shortly after their arrival at Quebec in July, his civil secretary. Ready was appointed commissioner for the management of the Jesuit estates (1818), to the committee charged with overseeing construction of the Lachine Canal (1819) [*see* François Desrivières*], and, after the death of Richmond in August 1819, curator of his estate.

Richmond's successor, the Earl of Dalhousie [RAMSAY], had met Ready during a visit to Quebec in 1819 and had recorded a favourable impression of him in his private journal. When Dalhousie arrived at Quebec the following year he retained him as civil secretary, subsequently naming him aide-de-camp, acting provincial secretary, and a member of the Executive Council. After beginning to work with Ready he revised his opinion. He recorded in his journal the dissatisfaction occasioned by Ready's holding so many offices, and Ready's apparent difficulty in discharging his duties. He also complained that Ready was ignorant of business procedures and law, and could not speak French. However, there is evidence that Ready was on friendly terms with John NEILSON and Louis-Joseph Papineau*, leaders in the House of Assembly's opposition to Dalhousie, and was sympathetic to their political stance. It is possible that this friendship influenced Dalhousie's antipathy to Ready as much as any perceived incompetence. Whatever the reason, Dalhousie determined early in 1822 to remove Ready who, when approached for his resignation on 29 January, asked that it should appear to have come from him, as a wish to return with his family to England. By November 1822 Ready had settled his affairs and sailed for England. He was replaced as civil secretary by Andrew William COCHRAN.

In April 1824 Ready was appointed lieutenant governor of Prince Edward Island, but his departure was delayed by the ill health of his wife, whom he was obliged to leave behind in Brighton. Favourable reports of Ready's previous public service had preceded him, and a large crowd, happy that the unpopular Charles Douglass Smith* was being replaced, gave Ready a boisterous reception as he disembarked at Charlottetown on 21 Oct. 1824.

Ready soon dissolved the House of Assembly, which had not sat since 1820, and called an election. The new legislature convened on 14 Jan. 1825. In his opening address Ready indicated that the main reason for summoning the legislators was to renew or to revise acts which had expired or were about to expire, and he suggested that the session deal only with essential measures. The assembly promised to refrain from presenting "any matter which we may conceive either of doubt or difficulty." Before the session closed on 24 March, the speaker, John Stewart*, stated that the revenue or supply bill, legislation initiated by the assembly to raise money for the government's use, had been passed because of the assembly's confidence in Ready, but cautioned that "the Colony looks forward with much anxiety, to the period, when your Excellency will feel yourself at liberty to give your assent to an annual Act, for appropriating the whole produce of the Revenue." The *Novascotian, or Colonial Herald* (Halifax) observed that "the main object to which the wishes of the House are bent and which the people will never rest satisfied till they accomplish is the repeal of a permanent revenue act which rendered the late Governor independent of the House."

At issue were two acts, passed in 1785 and 1795, which imposed duties on distilled and brewed liquor. The funds thus raised were referred to as the permanent revenue, control of which was vested in the lieutenant governor and the Council. When these laws were enacted the Island's population was small, and the little revenue derived from them barely met the expenses of government. However, by Ready's time the population was much larger, and the permanent revenue had increased until it amounted to almost two-thirds of total revenue. Ready wrote to Colonial Secretary Lord Bathurst to present the assembly's suggestion for a change in the legislation. Bathurst made it clear that Ready could use all of the income for the benefit of the colony but that there was to be no change in the law. Armed with that reply, Ready summoned the legislature on 12 Oct. 1825 for a short session prior to his planned departure for England. The assembly had been notified of Bathurst's decision but Stewart, at the close of the session, tenaciously raised the question once again. He suggested that the assembly's initial confidence in Ready had been justified by his management of the public expenditures to date, and that as long as he was administering them the assembly would not be apprehensive. He reminded the house that Ready would not always be with them, and, because the permanent revenue had been wasted or misused during previous administrations, the assembly was still interested in gaining control of it.

The assembly, to exert pressure in this matter, then decided that if it was not to have control of the permanent revenue, it would prevent the Council from interfering in the disposition of the remaining one-third of the Island's revenue, which was under the assembly's control. Accordingly, it declined to give the Council the opportunity to deliberate separately on each item in the appropriations bill, in which the assembly specified how the revenue was to be used. The Council reluctantly passed the bill but sent a resolution to the assembly which stated that in future it would refuse to assent to any appropriations bill unless each item had been "previously submitted by the House of Assembly in separate resolutions . . . and shall have severally received their assent." Debate on the issue then came to a temporary halt. Ready prorogued the legislature on 27 Oct. 1825 and sailed for England on 10 December to attend to family affairs, his wife having died there in March. George WRIGHT administered the colony in his absence.

While in England, Ready, along with Stewart, who was also on a visit, and C. D. Smith, the former lieutenant governor, was interviewed by a committee of the House of Commons on the subject of immigration to the British North American colonies, and he was presented at court. He returned to Prince Edward Island on 10 Dec. 1826, bringing his two daughters, one of whom survived only a few months. In the spring word was received that his elder son had died in January in England.

The session of the legislature which opened on 20 March 1827 presented the assembly with its first opportunity of responding to the Council's resolution of October 1825, and it lost no time informing the Council that supply bills originated with the assembly and were not to be altered by the Council. At the end of the session the assembly included an appropriation clause as part of each revenue bill so that the Council would be forced to "take all or reject all." The Council passed some of the bills and rejected others, leaving a shortfall of revenue. The legislature was prorogued on 7 May 1827 without a supply bill having been passed.

Ready, when he wrote to Bathurst for instructions, indicated that his sympathies were with the assembly which, he said, was adhering to "invariable usage . . . from the time of the first Session to the present." He further suggested that, although it was accepted practice in Nova Scotia, where the councillors were able and respected, to allow them "a voice in the Appropriation," he had a much lower opinion of the ability and integrity of the Island's councillors and doubted the wisdom of giving them "the right to interfere in the appropriation of what additional Revenue may be raised, (particularly as the whole of the permanent Revenue is at the disposal of the Governor and Council alone.)"

In reply, William Huskisson, the new colonial secretary, indicated his support for the assembly's position and his regret that the Council "have thought fit now, for the first time, to act upon a claim of at least doubtful right." However, in a private letter to Ready, Huskisson suggested that as a matter of courtesy the assembly might allow the Council to deliberate on the separate items in the appropriations bill as was the custom in Nova Scotia. Ready was left to his own resources and at the opening of the legislature on 20 March 1828 he could only appeal to both bodies to reconcile their differences for the good of the colony. Nevertheless, the assembly stood firm in its refusal to concede to the Council but did submit the appropriations bill separately from the revenue bills. Since the Council was not permitted to alter any of the revenue bills to which it objected, it refused to pass the appropriations bill. The session then came to an end on 5 May.

Ready wrote to Huskisson on 27 May suggesting that no solution to the impasse could be expected without changes in the Council. He admitted that the assembly was not entirely blameless and recommended that either the Council or the assembly, or both, be dismissed. In Britain there had been another cabinet change, and Ready's letter was answered on 3 July by the second under-secretary of the Colonial Office, Robert William Hay, who suggested that giving in to the assembly would lead to "very great inconvenience." Hay probably felt that the assembly's stand was to be discouraged lest it prompt similar claims in neighbouring colonies. He went on to say that the Council could not be dismissed because its members had been appointed by the king for life. Ready responded in September that it was the considered opinion on the Island that since members of the Council had been appointed by lieutenant governors they could be removed by a lieutenant governor.

Still the Colonial Office refused to sanction wholesale dissolution of the Council but agreed, at Ready's suggestion, to remove one of the antagonists, Samuel George William ARCHIBALD, the chief justice and president of Council, and replace him with Edward James Jarvis*, who was sworn into office on 30 Aug. 1828. By rewarding those on Council who cooperated and by getting rid of Archibald, Ready achieved a realignment which made the Council more amenable to compromise. The appropriations bill for 1829 was passed, and harmonious relations were restored between the two bodies for the remainder of Ready's term.

The quitrents levied by the British government continued to be of prime concern during this period as during previous administrations. Ready dutifully forwarded petitions for their remission but succeeded only in obtaining leave to use the derived income for the welfare of the Island.

In June 1830 Ready learned that his term of office was to expire shortly, and news of his departure became generally known by April 1831. The assembly, concerned that his successor might not be as prudent in disbursing the permanent revenue, determined in May to petition the king to repeal the permanent revenue acts. It also approved spending £400 for the purchase of plate as a parting gift to Ready in gratitude for his benevolent administration. When word was received in August that Ready's successor, Sir Murray Maxwell, had died before leaving Britain, a petition was circulated requesting that Ready be permitted to remain. Before the petition could be forwarded the announcement arrived that Aretas William Young* had been appointed in Maxwell's place, and Ready prepared to leave.

During Ready's years on the Island there was no resolution to the problem of the quitrents or the permanent revenue acts. However, in three key areas directly affecting the daily life of the average settler there were dramatic improvements for which Ready was largely responsible: agriculture, road building, and education. He had promoted an agricultural society which continued for many years to support and encourage the farmer. He had imported at his own expense valuable pedigree livestock which gradually improved the local stocks. His promotion of road-building projects resulted in "mere bridle paths" being converted into good roads; the outcome was an extensive network which greatly facilitated inland communication. He supported the assembly's interest in extending educational opportunities until there was a schoolhouse in almost every community. Probably most appreciated was his allocation of a large part of the permanent revenue to finance these projects.

For months prior to Ready's departure on 10 Oct. 1831, the pages of Charlottetown's *Royal Gazette* contained tributes to his administration and to him. The editor, James Douglas Haszard*, observed that "perhaps no public officer ever retired from so elevated a station, more unfeignedly and generally regretted."

In 1832 Ready was appointed lieutenant governor of the Isle of Man, and was sworn in at Castletown on 11 December. An address of welcome mentioned the favourable reports that had preceded him. In November 1841 he was promoted major-general. For the last nine months of his life Ready was seriously ill and unable to attend to his public duties. Two medications were prescribed: morphine, and atropine for external use. On 10 July 1845 he was given atropine internally, and he died within hours. A coroner's inquest determined that the poisoning was accidental. Ready was buried with full military honours at Malew on 17 July. His obituary in the *Manx Sun* stated that he had been highly esteemed there as a just administrator who had remained impartial and aloof from party factions, and as a gentleman who was unfailingly generous, kind, and courteous.

ELINOR VASS

[The historical record is silent on the identity of Ready's parents and the place and date of his birth. The usual sources for such information are so unyielding that a professional searcher engaged by the author remarked: "I get the impression that this man did not want any record kept of his background." An item in Ready's army records (PRO, WO 25/772: 94), using data supplied by the subject, suggests a birth date of *c.* 1777, and is in contrast with his obituary in the *Manx Sun* (see below) which places the event some five years earlier. The entry in Lord Dalhousie's diary for 11 May 1828 records his belief that Ready, who "was supposed to be a natural brother of Earl Bathurst," was more probably his son. Simple arithmetic renders the latter highly unlikely

(Bathurst was ten years old in 1772), and the fact that Dalhousie made a similar comment about Sir John Harvey* in the same entry invites scepticism. E.V.]

Church of Jesus Christ of Latter-Day Saints, Geneal. Soc. (Salt Lake City, Utah), International geneal. index. PAC, MG 24, B1, 5: 98–101. PRO, CO 226/42: 7, 41, 315, 363, 569; 226/43: 12; 226/44: 98–99, 103, 197; 226/45: 47, 53, 71–72, 118, 188–89, 191, 205, 301–2, 371, 431; 226/46: 253; 226/47: 145; 226/48: 241; CO 227/7: 237, 257–58, 261, 302 (mfm. at PAPEI); WO 42/39: 66. West Sussex Record Office (Chichester, Eng.), East Grinstead, reg. of marriages, 18 June 1804. *Annual reg.* (London), 1845: 288. P.E.I., *Acts of the General Assembly . . . , 1773–1834* (Charlottetown, 1834), 90, 222; House of Assembly, *Journal*, 27 Oct. 1825, 27 May 1827, 10 May 1831; Legislative Council, *Journal*, 20–21 March 1827, 2 May 1828, March–April 1829. Ramsay, *Dalhousie journals* (Whitelaw), 1: 153, 173; 2: 26, 29, 62, 113–15, 118–23, 132–33, 141, 186; 3. *Manx Sun* (Douglas, Isle of Man), 18 Dec. 1832; 2 Sept. 1836; 12, 19 July 1845. *Montreal Gazette*, 17 Nov. 1818. *Novascotian, or Colonial Herald*, 11 May 1825, 8 June 1826. *Prince Edward Island Register*, 24 July, 28 Aug., 23 Oct., 13 Nov. 1824; 20 Jan., 31 March, 11, 20 May, 20 Oct., 8 Nov., 20 Dec. 1825; 12 Dec. 1826; 13 Feb., 27 March, 1, 8 May, 6 Nov. 1827; 25 March, 6 May, 28 Oct. 1828; 31 March, 9 May 1829. *Quebec Gazette*, 30 July, 3 Aug. 1818; 5 Aug. 1819; 27 June 1820; 4 Jan. 1821. *Royal Gazette* (Charlottetown), 11 Jan., 19 April, 16, 23 Aug., 6 Sept., 11 Oct. 1831 (copies available at PAPEI). Desjardins, *Guide parl.* Elinor Vass, "The agricultural societies of Prince Edward Island," *Island Magazine* (Charlottetown), no.7 (fall–winter 1979): 31–37.

REIFFENSTEIN, JOHN CHRISTOPHER (he also signed **John Christoph** or **Jean Christoph Reiffenstein**), army and militia officer and businessman; b. *c.* 1779; m. 14 June 1806 Miriam Carr in Halifax, and they had three children; d. 7 March 1840 in New York City.

According to historian Benjamin Sulte*, John Christopher Reiffenstein came from a branch of the princely German family of Thurn und Taxis. Nothing is known of his childhood or youth. He went into the British army in 1795, and on 22 May 1804 was commissioned an ensign in the 98th Foot and appointed adjutant. In 1805 he went overseas with his regiment, first to Bermuda and then to Nova Scotia. In 1807 he left that province for Quebec. Early in 1808 he gave up his commission in the 98th Foot, and on 30 June he became quartermaster of the Royal Newfoundland Regiment. He resigned at the end of 1811 after a court martial found that he had made the men in his regiment pay twice as much for some pieces of their kit as the price asked elsewhere, and also that he had lost or destroyed all the official receipts for his various transactions.

Having abandoned his army career, Reiffenstein joined the militia. On 13 June 1812 he was made staff adjutant under Lieutenant-Colonel Augustus Warburton. War with the United States took the two men to the La Prairie region, where they remained from January to March 1813, to Amherstburg in Upper Canada in April, and to Detroit and Sandwich (Windsor, Ont.) from May to September. On 5 October Reiffenstein participated in the battle of Moraviantown, which saw Warburton taken prisoner and the great Indian leader Tecumseh* killed. He himself left before the outcome was decided. Alarmed by what seemed an impending American victory he went to Burlington Heights (Hamilton), and told Colonel Robert Young that Major-General Henry Procter*'s force had been defeated. Young immediately informed Major-General John VINCENT, who was near Fort George (Niagara-on-the-Lake). Vincent ordered his men to withdraw. Meanwhile Reiffenstein made his way to York (Toronto), and then to Kingston. There he reported to Major-General Francis de Rottenburg* and his colleague Duncan Darroch that Procter's force had been taken prisoner by an American army of 8,000 which was advancing rapidly towards Burlington Heights. This story was not true. Some time later Reiffenstein got back to Quebec, and from there, probably before 25 October, he was sent to Montreal. The false rumours of which he was the author had spread panic throughout Upper Canada, and Rottenburg held him responsible for Vincent's hasty retreat, which had seriously weakened the British military position in the Niagara peninsula. Reiffenstein was made adjutant of the 1st Select Embodied Militia Battalion of Lower Canada on 21 November, but his appointment as staff adjutant was taken from him the following 29 January, in all likelihood as a result of the efforts of Procter and Rottenburg. He seems to have served as adjutant until the end of the war.

Returning to civilian life, Reiffenstein embarked upon a business career in Lower Canada. He settled at Quebec and went into partnership with James Robinson, of London, under the name of Reiffenstein and Company. In 1814 he went to England, and in January of the following year put his first advertisement in the *Quebec Gazette*. He was initially established on Rue Saint-Pierre, but on 1 May 1816 he moved his business to Rue du Sault-au-Matelot and also changed partners, Quebec merchant William Phillips replacing Robinson. Their firm was dissolved on 1 May 1817 and he resumed his association with Robinson. Reiffenstein and Company remained in business until April 1820, when the partnership was terminated. Reiffenstein continued on alone, until his son John Edward came to help him around 1830.

For a quarter of a century, Reiffenstein was an important auctioneer and prosperous merchant. His army service, it seems, had given him a good idea of what to sell. He started out liquidating war surplus items, including 800 pairs of Russia duck trousers and 700 knapsacks. He often went to England and France, and to Germany where his two sisters and brother John Christian, a wine merchant, lived. Reiffenstein made at least six trips between 1814 and 1833, buying large quantities of fabrics and clothes, furniture and hardware, tea, coffee, and wine, pictures, prints, and books. Among his customers were the Séminaire de Québec and painter Joseph Légaré*, who bought about 40 pictures from him in 1823. Prior to 1825 Reiffenstein several times announced in the *Quebec Gazette* the arrival of consignments of 3,000–5,000 volumes, many of them written in French. He also dealt in church ornaments and sacred vessels, which brought him the custom of the clergy and the *fabriques*. He was the owner of the *Highland Lad*, a brig built at Quebec by John Goudie*, which he used for transatlantic shipments.

Reiffenstein, who owned a large lot in the *faubourg* Saint-Jean, sought to aid the poor by subscribing to the Quebec Fire Society and the Quebec Emigrants' Society, and also to the Waterloo fund, which had been set up to help the families of men who were killed or wounded in the great battle. He does not seem to have been tempted to venture into politics, but in a letter he wrote to John NEILSON from Paris in August 1833 he revealed his keen admiration for the 1830 revolution in France.

CLAUDE GALARNEAU

[The author wishes to thank Stuart R. J. Sutherland of Toronto for information he provided relating to the military career of John Christopher Reiffenstein. C.G.]

ANQ-M, CN1-116, 12 déc. 1817; CN1-208, 17 juin 1829; P1000-3-360. ANQ-Q, CE1-61, 2 avril 1809, 5 oct. 1855; CN1-49, 14 sept. 1812, 21 juin 1813, 6 nov. 1815. ASQ, Séminaire, 126, nos.272–75. PAC, MG 24, B1, 189: 4392; RG 8, I (C ser.), 226: 62–63; 678: 164–65; 680: 169, 216–19, 242–46, 259–60, 269–72, 290–94, 319–21; 1168: 68–72; 1203½J: 18, 218. PRO, WO 17/1509, 17/1517; WO 27/99. *Quebec Gazette*, 1815–40. G.B., WO, *Army list*, 1810. Raymond Gingras, *Liste annotée de patronymes d'origine allemande au Québec et notes diverses* (s.l., 1975). *N.S. vital statistics, 1769–1812* (Punch). *Officers of British forces in Canada* (Irving). Réjean Lemoine, "Le marché du livre à Québec, 1764–1839" (thèse de MA, univ. Laval, Québec, 1981). J. R. Porter, "Un peintre et collectionneur québécois engagé dans son milieu: Joseph Légaré (1795–1855)" (thèse de PHD, univ. de Montréal, 1981). "Le sieur Reiffenstein," *BRH*, 45 (1939): 62–63. Benjamin Sulte, "Reiffenstein," *Le Monde illustré* (Montréal), 28 juin 1890: 131.

RIALL, Sir PHINEAS, army officer; b. 15 Dec. 1775 in Ireland, probably in Clonmel (Republic of Ireland), third son of Phineas Riall of Clonmel and Catherine Caldwell; m. 18 Dec. 1819 Elizabeth Scarlett in Borgue, Scotland; d. 10 Nov. 1850 in Paris.

Phineas Riall entered the army as an ensign in the 92nd Foot on 31 Jan. 1794, gained a lieutenancy in March and a captaincy on 31 May, and became major in the 128th Foot on 8 December. After this rapid rise in seniority Riall served with the 128th until he was reduced with it in 1797. He remained on half pay for seven years, becoming a brevet lieutenant-colonel barely two weeks after his 24th birthday. On 21 April 1804 Riall transferred to a majority in the 15th Foot, and with it he saw his first active service and combat. He appears to have been with the 15th when it sailed for the West Indies in 1805, and he was certainly there by 1809, when he commanded a brigade in the attack on Martinique. Riall was also in charge of a brigade at the capture of Guadeloupe, and he was commended in dispatches. Following this flurry of activity, he returned to England in July 1810.

On 25 July Riall was promoted brevet colonel by seniority, and he transferred to the 69th Foot as a lieutenant-colonel on 27 December. He was promoted major-general on 4 June 1813, again by seniority, and on 10 August he was posted to the Canadas along with Lieutenant-General Gordon Drummond*. The Duke of York, commander-in-chief of the British army, referred to Riall as "an active and intelligent young man," and there is no doubt that Drummond and he represented welcome reinforcements to Lieutenant-General Sir George Prevost*, commander-in-chief in British North America, who had had difficulties with some of his subordinates.

Upon arrival at Quebec in November, Riall was sent to command in the Montreal region. Soon afterwards he accompanied Drummond to Upper Canada, where the latter took over as commander of the forces and administrator. Drummond was determined to attack the American forces on the Niagara frontier, and on 18 December he mounted an expedition against Fort Niagara (near Youngstown), N.Y. As soon as the assault force reached the American side of the Niagara River on the morning of the 19th, Riall crossed the river at Lewiston with 500 regulars and a similar number of Indians. Riall's force had originally been intended to act as a reserve to the attackers of Fort Niagara, but because it fell so quickly he was able to act elsewhere. Encountering virtually no opposition, he entered Lewiston and captured a quantity of ammunition and supplies. As the Americans retreated, Riall moved through Youngstown and a Tuscarora Indian village, leaving behind charred ruins, as the Americans had at Niagara (Niagara-on-the-Lake) earlier in the month. All parts of Riall's force committed depredations, but the Indians were particularly cruel and killed several civilians. It is unfortunate that the operation got out of hand, because in other respects it was highly successful. Riall advanced past Fort Schlosser and Manchester (Niagara Falls), both of which were razed, as far as Tonawanda Creek, less than ten miles from Buffalo, before returning to Queenston via Lewiston.

Though a vast array of stores and many soldiers had been captured, Drummond was not satisfied. He wanted to ensure that any threat on the Niagara frontier was eliminated for a considerable time, and on 29 December he instructed Riall to cross the Niagara again, this time to disperse the increasing American forces and raze the villages of Buffalo and Black Rock (Buffalo) "in order to deprive the enemy of the cover which these places afford." Provisions and flour were to be brought back, and any stores incapable of being moved were to be destroyed. Most important, Riall was to burn three American naval vessels on shore near Buffalo Creek. Drummond issued strict instructions against looting and intoxication in order to avoid the excesses of Lewiston.

Except for some minor problems, the operation went off almost exactly as planned. During the night of 30 December, Riall landed above Niagara Falls with a force composed mainly of regulars but including some militia and Indians. After repulsing American attacks on their initial position, the British pushed on at dawn against a strong resistance. When they persisted in their attack the defenders broke and ran, leaving behind stores and ordnance. Buffalo was taken, the vessels were burned, and, as Riall reported, "considerable quantities of clothing, spirits and flour" were set on fire. Buffalo and Black Rock, both of which had been evacuated, were then also burned. Riall now dispatched a force which destroyed "the remaining cover of the enemy on this frontier" towards Fort Niagara. Within a period of about three weeks the situation on the Niagara frontier had completely changed. It is not clear, however, to what extent the credit for the British successes should be divided between Drummond, who took the responsibility for the offensive and made the plans, and Riall, who led two of the key operations.

Following the campaign, Drummond went to York (Toronto), leaving Riall in command on the frontier. Things were quiet, and much of Riall's energy in the first months of 1814 was applied to attempts to improve the commissariat arrangements. On 10 June he reported that all was calm, but by the 23rd he informed Drummond about enemy movements that indicated they would attack "at no great distance of time."

Riall did not have long to wait. On the morning of 3 July he learned that an American force had landed near Fort Erie, and he immediately rode to Chippawa, ordering reinforcements to follow. Fort Erie surrendered after a token resistance and the American force of about 4,000 men advanced towards Chippawa. Late in the afternoon of 4 July, the American brigadier-general Winfield Scott, commanding the advance guard, could see Riall's troops across the Chippewa (Welland) River, and he pulled back a couple of miles for the night. The next day both armies wanted to attack. Riall had been reinforced and, because of his belief in the inferiority of American troops, he was prepared to pit his estimated 1,500 men against Scott's 2,000. At about 5:00 P.M. he came out from behind his works to give battle.

Riall quickly learned that the enemy had used the last few months well. Scott's disciplined and well-trained force inflicted heavy casualties on his own in a classic European-style battle. Riall has been criticized for failing to coordinate the components of his force, but not for a lack of courage. He led from the front. As casualties mounted, however, and it became clear that the Americans could not be bested, he retreated across the Chippawa. He had lost over 400 in killed, wounded, and missing; the American total was lower by about 100. Two days later he had to retreat all the way to Fort George (Niagara-on-the-Lake) to avoid being encircled by the advancing Americans.

The British admitted defeat, but none of their leaders was prepared to concede the campaign. Reinforcements flocked to Riall at Fort George, and Drummond himself headed for the Niagara peninsula. The Americans had followed Riall to the vicinity of Fort George, but after waiting in vain for their navy to cooperate in assaults on forts George and Niagara, they retired towards Chippawa. Riall had busied himself in preparing his forces for the battle which was inevitable, and when the Americans withdrew he pushed forward about 1,000 regulars, who assumed a strong defensive position at Lundy's Lane near Niagara Falls. Drummond had ordered him to follow and harass the enemy but not to attack or act precipitately. Consequently, when Scott moved against the position at Lundy's Lane on 25 July, Riall started to withdraw. Fortunately, Drummond arrived with reinforcements and countermanded Riall's order. In the battle which ensued Riall was severely wounded in the arm and captured early on, and he could hardly take much credit for the victory.

Riall spent the rest of the summer and most of the fall in congenial captivity in the United States. A fellow prisoner, the young militia officer William Hamilton Merritt*, described him as "very brave, near sighted, rather short, but stout." Efforts were made to exchange Riall, but without any success until November. Before he sailed for England on parole in December 1814 he visited other prisoners, giving the impression of a caring commander.

No mention can be found of Riall for over a year after his return to England, presumably because he was waiting for his wound to heal. He surfaces on 18 Feb. 1816 when he was appointed governor of Grenada, a post he held until 1823. On 27 May 1835 Riall was promoted lieutenant-general, and in 1831 he was made a knight commander of the Royal Hanoverian Order. Two years after this honour he was knighted. On 20 May 1835 Sir Phineas was appointed colonel of the 74th Foot, and on 24 April 1846 he was transferred to his old regiment, the 15th Foot. He had been promoted general on 23 Nov. 1841.

Phineas Riall appears to have been an example of a young man from a family of means who owed his early advances in the army to the purchase of commissions. When called upon to command troops in battle he acquitted himself with some distinction and earned further promotion, as well as awards and commendations, by merit. During his short stay in North America he played a significant part in the war on the Niagara frontier.

CARL CHRISTIE

PAC, RG 8, I (C ser.), 230: 17; 388: 146–51; 389: 174; 681: 38, 240, 249–51, 267, 319; 682: 2, 5; 683: 19–20, 96, 171–74, 183–85, 192, 230, 306; 684: 14–17, 51, 57, 65, 84, 116, 124, 126, 129, 134, 169, 177, 179, 198, 202, 237; 685: 271; 686: 8; 688E: 150; 692: 172; 693: 146, 193; 694: 6, 49–50; 1171: 105; 1172: 70a; 1203½K: 88; 1203½L: 78; 1219: 134, 176, 180–82, 230, 245, 260, 266; 1221: 106, 211, 235–36; 1222: 4, 13, 132, 165; 1227: 7, 46, 91. *Doc. hist. of campaign upon Niagara frontier* (Cruikshank). *Gentleman's Magazine*, January–June 1851: 202. *Select British docs. of War of 1812* (Wood). *Quebec Gazette*, 4 Nov. 1813. *DNB*. G.B., WO, *Army list*, 1800–36. *Hart's army list*, 1841–42, 1847. *Officers of British forces in Canada* (Irving). Gilbert Auchinleck, *A history of the war between Great Britain and the United States of America, during the years 1812, 1813, and 1814* (Toronto, 1855; repr. London and Toronto, 1972). J. W. Fortescue, *A history of the British army* (13v. in 14, London, 1899–1930), 7: 12–17; 9: 346–49; 10: 106. D. E. Graves, "Joseph Willcocks and the Canadian Volunteers: an account of political disaffection in Upper Canada during the War of 1812" (MA thesis, Carleton Univ., Ottawa, 1982). J. M. Hitsman, *The incredible War of 1812: a military history* (Toronto, 1965). G. F. G. Stanley, *The War of 1812: land operations* ([Toronto], 1983).

RICHARDS, JACKSON JOHN (also known as **Jean Richard** and **Richard Jackson**), Methodist minister and Sulpician; b. 21 Feb. 1787 in Alexandria, Va, son of Thomas Richards and his wife Anna; d. 23 July 1847 in Montreal.

Jackson John Richards came from a Protestant family with at least three children. Very early his father destined him for the ministry, and to that end entrusted him to a Presbyterian clergyman who taught him the rudiments of Latin and Greek. Little is known of Richards's life until 1807, when he became a Methodist itinerant and set out for the Canadas. After a stay in Buffalo, N.Y., and a visit to Niagara Falls, he reached York (Toronto), where he preached to Methodist congregations and Indians.

Richards arrived in Montreal on 19 Aug. 1807, having come by boat from Kingston. Shortly afterwards he contacted Sulpicians Jean-Henry-Auguste Roux*, Candide-Michel Le Saulnier*, Jean-Jacques LARTIGUE, and Simon Boussin. It seems that he wanted to convert the priests of the Séminaire de Saint-Sulpice, but things worked out differently. On 31 October, in the presence of notary Thomas Barron and Denis-Benjamin Viger*, Richards formally abjured Protestantism. From 1807 till 1809 he furthered his education at the Petit Séminaire de Montréal, and, since he wished to become a priest, he began theological studies while serving as a regent in the college.

Having received permission to ordain Richards from John Carroll, the bishop of Baltimore, Bishop Joseph-Octave Plessis* conferred the priesthood on him at Notre-Dame church in Montreal on 25 July 1813. Richards left the Petit Séminaire de Montréal in 1815 to embark upon what was to be a long and fruitful parish ministry. He served principally at the chapel of Notre-Dame-de-Bonsecours in Montreal, where he gathered the town's English-speaking Catholics, most of whom came from Ireland.

Richards was admitted to the Sulpician community as a member on 17 Feb. 1817 and became assistant to the bursar in 1821. He rapidly won the confidence of Roux, the superior. In the 1820s the seminary was deeply divided on the questions of its property and the authority over the institution of archbishops Plessis and Bernard-Claude Panet* of Quebec and Bishop Lartigue, their auxiliary in Montreal. Richards shared the opinion of the majority, who came from France, and the bishops' letters clearly show their opposition to his influence and ideas. Richards accompanied Roux to Europe in June 1826 and stayed there until August 1828. He acted as Roux's interpreter in the political and ecclesiastical circles of London. In particular, the superior was negotiating a settlement of the question of Saint-Sulpice's property, but the Canadian bishops and priests did not accept his solution. The Sulpicians were, in fact, ready to cede some of their seigneurial rights in return for a fixed, perpetual annuity.

On his return to Montreal, Richards resumed his ministry and his administrative duties. In September 1829 the exasperation of the archbishop of Quebec reached a peak when Roux named Richards acting curé of Notre-Dame during Le Saulnier's illness. Panet challenged the practice followed by Sulpician superiors of appointing parish priests by virtue of their office, without seeking canonical confirmation from episcopal authority. In addition, like Lartigue, Panet considered Richards a foreigner who did not have sufficient knowledge of French. The following December, in the face of the two bishops' repeated protests, Roux appointed Claude Fay curé of Notre-Dame in place of Richards, without, however, seeking episcopal confirmation.

In 1831 Richards, who had been naturalized the previous year, officially became the priest in charge of

English-speaking Catholics, who now held their own services in the chapel of the Recollet friary. He continued his ministry to the Irish until the end of his life. In 1833 he added the duties of bursar to the Séminaire de Saint-Sulpice, assuming responsibility for ensuring good administration and the physical well-being of those living there.

Contemporary correspondence indicates that Jackson John Richards had a most beneficial influence on the priests and faithful in Lower Canada and the United States. He was asked for advice and sometimes for material help. In 1847 a typhus epidemic broke out among the Irish immigrants. Those stricken were herded into lazarets at Pointe-Saint-Charles (Montreal). Richards was unsparing in his aid. He caught the disease himself and died on 23 July. Jean-Charles Prince*, the coadjutor bishop of Montreal, buried him in Notre-Dame church the following day.

BRUNO HAREL

ACAM, 465.101, 818-1, 829-1, -2, -3. ANQ-M, CE1-51, 24 juill. 1847. Arch. du séminaire de Saint-Sulpice (Paris), Fonds canadien, MSS 1230. Arch. of the U.S. Province of the Sulpician Order, St Mary's Seminary and Univ. (Baltimore, Md.), Obituary notes, vol.1. ASSM, 11, B, no.25; 21; 24, B; E. *Mélanges religieux*, 30 juill. 1849. Desrosiers, "Inv. de la corr. de Mgr Lartigue," ANQ *Rapport*, 1941–42; 1942–43; 1943–44. Louis Bertrand, *Bibliothèque sulpicienne ou histoire littéraire de la Compagnie de Saint-Sulpice* (3v., Paris, 1900), 2: 582. Chaussé, *Jean-Jacques Lartigue*. *Golden jubilee of the reverend fathers Dowd and Toupin . . .* , ed. J. J. Curran (Montreal, 1887). J.-M. Leleu, *Histoire de Notre-Dame de Bon-Secours à Montréal* (Montréal, 1900). Lemieux, *L'établissement de la première prov. eccl.* J. R. Danaher, "The Reverend Richard Jackson, missionary to the Sulpicians," CCHA *Report*, 11 (1943–44): 49–54.

RICHARDSON, SAMUEL, surveyor and office holder; b. 1795 or 1796 in Pembrokeshire, Wales; m. Prudence Caldwell; d. 2 March 1843 in Oro Township, Upper Canada.

Samuel Richardson came to Upper Canada in July 1819 and received his licence as a land surveyor on 10 March 1821. That summer he worked for a short time as a supernumerary clerk at Sherbrooke, the naval depot situated where the Grand River empties into Lake Erie, and later served on a schooner, *Confiance*, based at Grand River, while engaged in a survey of the boundary line between Upper Canada and the United States.

On 6 November, Commodore Robert BARRIE named Richardson storeporter in the naval establishment at Penetanguishene, a position he held until discharged in June 1834, after the breakup of the establishment. During this period he also made a number of surveys, and was referred to by William CHEWETT as "a deputy surveyor belonging to the Naval Department at Penetanguishene." In June 1829 he was ordered to discover "the most eligible mill site in the vicinity of Penetanguishene, for the use of the Establishment," and from June to September he laid out 20 lots on the west side of Penetanguishene harbour.

The naval establishment at Penetanguishene shared with traders and settlers the problem of transporting goods from Lake Ontario to Georgian Bay. From early days a well-travelled route had existed from York (Toronto) to Lake Simcoe, but there was no short, easy route from there to Penetanguishene. In April 1830 Richardson surveyed a line suitable for a road from Matchedash Bay by Coldwater River to Bristol Channel (now Lake Couchiching) which was used extensively for many years.

A major expedition was organized in 1835 to explore the country north from Mara Township to Lake Nipissing and so to establish the continuation of the division line between the Home and Newcastle districts. It was led by Lieutenant John Carthew of the Royal Navy, with Captain Frederick Henry Baddeley*, a Royal Engineer, as geologist and Richardson and William Hawkins as surveyors. The party worked from July to November, by which time the new line stretched about 78 miles from the northwest corner of Mara to a point probably in the present township of Chapman. The extensive reports of Carthew, Baddeley, and Hawkins were printed in an appendix to the journal of the House of Assembly, but Richardson's report, which covered only technical details, was not included.

The west side of the Narrows (Orillia) between lakes Simcoe and Couchiching was a strategic point for access to Georgian Bay and to the undeveloped lands to the north. When the Ojibwa Indians in this area, under Chief Musquakie*, moved north to Rama Township in 1839, the territory became available for white settlement. Richardson then received instructions to lay out a town plot on lots 7 and 8, concession 5, township of South Orillia, site of the present city of Orillia. In 1841 he conducted surveys in Eldon Township, and from August to November 1842 he surveyed a number of lots in Barrie.

Some time after the naval establishment at Penetanguishene had been broken up, Richardson had moved to Oro Township. In the summer of 1841 he was appointed treasurer of Simcoe County (after 11 Jan. 1843 Simcoe District); on several occasions he served as a boundary commissioner for the Home District. Richardson took no active part in provincial politics and, shortly before his death, was referred to as a "Soft Tory" in a letter from Benjamin Walker Smith, newly appointed sheriff of the Simcoe District, to Robert Baldwin*. Richardson died on 2 March 1843, survived by his wife, two sons, and a daughter.

FLORENCE B. MURRAY

AO, Land record index; MU 2114, 1861, no.15; RG 1, A-I-6: 17534–36, 17584–86; CB-1, boxes 9, 22–23, 29, 31. MTRL, Robert Baldwin papers, A65, no.93a; A71, no.57. Ont., Ministry of Natural Resources, Survey Records Office (Toronto), Instructions for crown surveys (mfm. at AO). PAC, MG 24, F66, 3; RG 5, A1: 53115–30; RG 8, III, A, 34. PRO, ADM 42/2199, 42/2202; ADM 106/2002. Simcoe County Arch. (Minesing, Ont.), File information concerning Samuel Richardson. *Minutes of the Simcoe District Municipal Council, 1843–1847* (Barrie, Ont., 1895), 4, 40, 69, 122, 153, 162, 164–65, 197. *Muskoka and Haliburton, 1615–1875: a collection of documents*, ed. F. B. Murray ([Toronto], 1963), xlix–l, 72–82. U.C., House of Assembly, *App. to the journal*, 1836–37, no.37. A. F. Hunter, *A history of Simcoe County* (2v., Barrie, 1909; repr. 2v. in 1, 1948), 1: 41, 45, 260; 2: 127–30, 161, 269, 300.

ROBERTSON, COLIN, fur trader, merchant, and politician; b. 27 July 1783 in Perth, Scotland, son of William Robertson, weaver, and Catherine Sharp; m. *c.* 1820 Theresa Chalifoux, and they had seven children; d. 4 Feb. 1842 in Montreal.

Colin Robertson was born into a hand-weaving family before the trade collapsed from the competition of factories. In his boyhood there seemed enough future in his father's craft for him to become an apprentice weaver. Hudson's Bay Company governor George Simpson*, who came to dislike him intensely, asserted in his "Character book" of 1832 that Robertson was "too lazy to live by his Loom"; he conjured up the image of a youth who spent his time reading novels and "became Sentimental and fancied himself the hero of every tale of Romance that passed through his hands." Whether or not, as Simpson claimed, Robertson "ran away from his master," it is certain that he did not finish his apprenticeship, abandoning hand-weaving and finding his way to New York, where he worked in a grocery store. There, Simpson stated, Robertson "had not sufficient steadiness to retain his Situation." On the other hand, it seems evident that Robertson at this time gained enough experience in salesmanship to make him feel competent in later years to set up as a wholesale merchant in the intervals of his involvement in the fur trade.

There is no definite information about when Robertson came to the Canadas, but he entered the service of the North West Company as an apprentice clerk before the end of 1803. Two years later an HBC trader, William Linklater, reported that Robertson, with two NWC employees, caught up with him at Otter Portage (Sask.) and "means to keep us company until we arrive at Isle a la Crosse [Sask.]." Clearly Robertson had been deputed to travel close to HBC men on the Saskatchewan River and prevent their trading with the Indians.

In 1809 Robertson left the service of the NWC, partly, it appears, because of slowness in promotion after the Nor'Westers had absorbed the partners of the New North West Company (sometimes called the XY Company), and partly because of his difficulty in working with the irascible John McDonald* of Garth, with whom he once fought a duel. Contrary to Simpson's belief that he was dismissed, the NWC's letter to Robertson on his departure makes it clear that he was retiring from a post in which he had served with loyalty and competence. Still, he was already in touch with the HBC Chief Factor William Auld*, whom he had visited at Cumberland House (Sask.) in 1809 before retiring and who was convinced of the need for vigorous opposition to the NWC. During that visit, an understanding seems to have been reached, since, when Robertson sailed to England, he paid his fare with a loan from Auld, who also gave him an introduction to the London committee of the HBC.

On reaching London, Robertson found the HBC in a state of flux and re-organization. Lord Selkirk [Douglas*] and Andrew Wedderburn had become powerful shareholders and were changing the company in ways that made inevitable a more aggressive policy towards its trading rivals. Robertson immediately put forward a proposal that the company should turn to the attack by pushing its trade into the Athabasca country, then dominated by the Nor'Westers, and that it should do so by using Canadian voyageurs, recruited in Montreal and experienced in travelling and trading in the Indian country. He suggested the establishment of an agency in Montreal to organize such an expedition, and hoped to be placed in charge. The London committee was attracted by Robertson's plan but did not find it immediately expedient, and on 21 Feb. 1810 rejected it, while offering Robertson employment. He wished, however, to join the company on his own terms, and left London for Liverpool, where he and his brother Samuel set up as general merchants and ships' chandlers. In 1812 he went into a partnership with Thomas Marsh of Liverpool that was to last for about five years.

Although Robertson seemed to be planning a future outside the fur trade, he followed the rapid turn of events in the northwest; Selkirk's establishment of the Red River colony (Man.) in 1812 across the Nor'Westers' main trade routes had made a confrontation between the two companies unavoidable. When Robertson was summoned to London for a meeting with Wedderburn early in 1814, he went with a revised plan for the attack on the Athabasca country, which he submitted on 15 March. Having conserved its resources through retrenchment, the committee was now prepared for the expansion on which the company's survival depended. As a feint, Joseph Howse* would be sent with a strong force to re-establish the fort at Île-à-la-Crosse, but the real expedition would be under Robertson. To compensate him for possible losses owing to his absence from business in Liverpool, the committee agreed that Marsh and Robertson should supply the HBC with any woollen or cotton goods it needed.

On 22 May Robertson sailed from Liverpool. The ship went in slow convoy for protection against French warships and privateers and was several times delayed by storms, so that he did not reach Quebec until 27 Sept. 1814. He hurried to Montreal and, posing as an agent of Selkirk selling land in the Red River colony, began to make arrangements for the first HBC expedition supplied from Montreal. He had missed a season, and it was not until 17 May 1815 that he eventually set out for the interior with 16 canoes, 160 voyageurs, and 3 former Nor'Westers he had persuaded to accompany him: John Clarke*, François Decoigne*, and Robert Logan*.

Robertson was, on the whole, well fitted for the enterprise. He knew the country for which he was bound; he also knew both the methods of the Nor'-Westers and the personalities of the men with whom he would be contending. He was a braggart, but an audacious one: his favourite maxim was "When you are among wolves, howl!" A striking man, six feet tall, with a long aquiline nose, a crest of undisciplined red hair, and a fondness for quoting Shakespeare and drinking Madeira, he was generous, flamboyant, extravagant, and he cultivated these qualities when he was among the voyageurs on whom his success depended. "Glittering Pomposity," he once remarked, "has an amazing effect on the Freemen, Metiss and Indians." But he was genuinely courageous, willing to take risks, and aware of the advantage to be gained from anticipating his opponents. The same qualities tended at times to make him blind to danger, and he sometimes underestimated his enemies, but the fact that his Athabasca plan on the whole turned out so successfully and heralded the end of the NWC as an independent organization, suggests that he was far from the "frothy trifling conceited man" sketched by Simpson.

Even before Robertson got as far as Red River he found that the antagonism of the Nor'Westers towards Selkirk's colony had peaked in open violence. Miles Macdonell*, first governor of Assiniboia, had been arrested by the Nor'Westers and transported to Lower Canada. The settlement had been burnt down, and Robertson met some of the dispossessed settlers on their way to the Great Lakes. He took them back with him, and at the request of James Bird* and Thomas Thomas* agreed to re-establish the colony, while on 4 Aug. 1815 his expedition was sent on to the Athabasca country under John Clarke. On 15 October Robertson seized the NWC's Fort Gibraltar (Winnipeg), and, upon extracting from Duncan CAMERON a promise that NWC depredations would cease, returned it to him. Robertson then rebuilt the HBC's Fort Douglas (Winnipeg), which the rival traders had destroyed. He spent the winter on Red River, dealing forcibly with renewed threats from his opponents, and in March 1816 he again seized Fort Gibraltar. Despite such aggressive initiatives, Robertson's relations with Robert Semple*, who had arrived in November 1815 as the new governor of Assiniboia, deteriorated badly. Semple's concerns lay in provisioning the colony while Robertson was determined to blockade the rivers and prevent the Métis from supplying pemmican to the NWC brigades going west. Thoroughly upset, he left Red River on 11 June 1816, intending to return to England and his foundering business.

Robertson reached York Factory (Man.) early in July and, while awaiting a ship there, heard two pieces of news which suggested that his plans had come to nothing. As soon as he had left Fort Douglas, the Nor'-Westers had stepped up their provocations against the Selkirk settlers, and on 19 June, at Seven Oaks (Winnipeg), Semple and about 20 of his men had been killed. Meanwhile, harassed by the Nor'Westers, Clarke's expedition had ended in starvation and failure, and Clarke himself had been arrested by Samuel BLACK.

Robertson finally sailed for England on 6 October, but his ship was held in the ice of Hudson Bay and he wintered at Eastmain Factory (Eastmain, Que.) and Moose Factory (Ont.) until breakup. By March 1817 he had learned that he would be arraigned at Montreal on charges brought against him by the NWC for his seizure of Fort Gibraltar. He arrived at Montreal in August, resolved to clear his name, but within months he had also become deeply involved in planning his next assault on the Athabasca country. By refusing to accept bail and insisting on going to prison, he gained a trial in the spring of 1818 and was acquitted. He was thus freed for the Athabasca counter-attack which – considering the discontent among the wintering partners of the NWC – he believed might break its spirit. His English business had drifted into bankruptcy in his absence, but Selkirk agreed to guarantee it, and in the summer Robertson set out from Montreal with 10 canoes, 10 officers, and 100 voyageurs.

As he moved into the interior of Rupert's Land, the survivors of Clarke's ill-fated expedition joined him, so that by the time he left Lake Winnipeg he had 27 canoes and 190 men, including the liberated Clarke. Arrested by the persistent Samuel Black in October on charges of attempted murder and imprisoned in Fort Chipewyan (Alta), Robertson contrived to smuggle out messages to his men which encouraged them to resist the Nor'Westers. Then, in June 1819, when he was being taken out of the Athabasca country as a prisoner, he escaped at Cumberland House and returned to lead the HBC's expedition into the interior later that year. He wintered at St Mary's Fort (near Peace River, Alta). On his way out in the summer of 1820 he was ambushed and re-arrested by the Nor'-

Westers at Grand Rapids (Man.) and taken to Lower Canada. He escaped at Hull, and went south into the United States.

From New York Robertson returned to England. But Selkirk, who had guaranteed his business, had died in April 1820 and he had to flee to France to avoid imprisonment for debt. By August 1821 he had settled with his creditors for two shillings on the pound, and was free but, as so often in his life, penniless. He returned to Lower Canada via the United States. Robertson was still a legal fugitive but, of greater consequence, from about 1819 he had lost the support of the London committee. As a result he was not directly involved in the negotiations that led to the union of the HBC and the NWC in 1821 [*see* Simon McGILLIVRAY]. Indeed, he had resisted the coalition, arguing that the HBC had been at the point of taking control in the Athabasca country. Still, there is little doubt that his determined assaults on the Athabasca between 1816 and 1820 were major factors in breaking down the opposition of the Nor'Westers to union.

Robertson was appointed a chief factor in the reorganized company in 1821 and was put in charge of Norway House (Man.). At this time he and Simpson – both of them energetic and audacious men – were in good accord. Although noting that as a "man of business he does not shine," Simpson wrote in 1822 that Robertson "is a pleasant Gentlemanly Fellow and has none of those narrow constricted illiberal ideas which so much characterises the Gentry of Rupert's Land." But over the next decade Simpson developed the animus that is evident in his "Character book." One can surmise that much of the reason for this change of attitude lay in the fact that the very characteristics which made Robertson invaluable as an aggressive leader in the conflict with the Nor'Westers made him seem bombastic and ineffectual in the routine work of the HBC after 1821, when, without rivals, it had no further need for men of dramatic action. Trade was now largely a matter of bargaining and accountancy, and Robertson had no flair for either.

He moved on from one post to another, mostly according to Simpson's whims, and after 1821 received no promotion. In 1822 he was sent to Fort Edmonton (Edmonton), back to Norway House the following year, and in 1824 to Fort Churchill (Churchill, Man.). In 1825 he went to England to arrange the education of his eldest son, Colin. (He was a good husband and father, and treated his Métis wife with a consideration that coarser men, like Simpson, mocked.) On returning to North America he went to Fort Churchill until 1826, then to Island Lake and Oxford House, and in 1830 to Fort Pelly (Sask.).

In 1831 there was a major quarrel between Robertson and Simpson, whose racial prejudices were offended when Robertson brought his wife to Red River and tried to introduce her into what passed for society in that little settlement. Robertson now decided to retire, and made plans to sail for England and try to persuade the committee to let him retain his share as a wintering partner. But in 1832, before he could depart, he had what seems to have been a stroke, which paralysed his left side and from which he never completely recovered. For the next five years he was officially and unofficially on leave, not resuming work until 1837, when he was posted to New Brunswick House (on Brunswick Lake, Ont.).

Robertson retired officially in 1840, after the HBC had agreed to buy out his share. So extravagant had he remained in his style of living that the sale barely paid off the mortgage on his Montreal house. He was glad to accept a pension of £100 a year from the committee, though he spent many times that amount in borrowed money to get elected in 1841 as member of the Legislative Assembly for Deux-Montagnes. He did not live long to enjoy his political office. On 3 Feb. 1842 he was thrown from his sleigh, and the next day he died.

For a few years before 1821 Robertson had been an influential figure, helping materially to change the nature of the fur trade and the history of Canada, for no other individual did more to bring the NWC to an end. But after 1821 he became a cipher in the enlarged company he had helped to create. During the last decade of his life he was in obvious mental as well as physical decline, clinging in memory to his long-past feats as compensation for the frustrations of his later years.

GEORGE WOODCOCK

GRO (Edinburgh), Perth, reg. of births and baptisms, 27 July 1783. PAC, MG 19, E1. PAM, HBCA, A.34/2; E.10; F.1–F.7. *HBRS*, 1 (Rich); 2 (Rich and Fleming). *Papers relating to the Red River settlement* . . . ([London, 1819?]). G. C. Davidson, *The North West Company* (Berkeley, Calif., 1918; repr. New York, 1967). J. M. Gray, *Lord Selkirk of Red River* (Toronto, 1963). Innis, *Fur trade in Canada* (1930). Morton, *Hist. of Canadian west* (Thomas; 1973). Rich, *Hist. of HBC* (1958–59), vol.2. M. [E.] Wilkins Campbell, *The North West Company* (Toronto, 1957).

ROBERTSON, WILLIAM, military surgeon, physician, office holder, JP, and educator; b. 15 March 1784 at Kindrochit, his father's estate near Blair Atholl, Scotland, second son of James Robertson and Jean Stewart; m. 21 Jan. 1806 Elizabeth Amelia Campbell in Sydney (N.S.), and they had 12 children; d. 18 July 1844 in Montreal.

The son of a Scottish laird, William Robertson received his early schooling in Scotland and was appointed ensign in the 73rd Foot at age 13. The following year, as an officer, he saw action during the

Irish rebellion. Between 1802 and 1805 he studied medicine at the University of Edinburgh, attending three sessions, but he did not graduate. He acquired a degree much later, in 1832 – *honoris causa* from the University of Vermont.

Following his studies in Edinburgh, Robertson accepted the post of ship's surgeon for a voyage to New York and New Orleans. On 9 July 1805 he was appointed hospital mate for the army medical department in British North America. Late in 1805, when he was on his way to join the hospital staff, his ship was wrecked off the coast of Cape Breton and he narrowly escaped drowning. He found refuge in the home of William Campbell*, attorney general of Cape Breton. There he met Campbell's daughter, whom he later married.

Robertson became an assistant surgeon in the 49th Foot on 23 Oct. 1806 and served in this capacity for more than six years. On 29 July 1813 he was promoted surgeon in the 41st Foot. He saw action in the War of 1812, accompanying his regiment to the Niagara frontier and assisting in December 1813 at the storming of Fort Niagara (near Youngstown), N.Y. In 1815 he was placed on half pay in Montreal as a medical practitioner. The following year he was commissioned a medical examiner for the district of Montreal, a nomination he would receive several times between 1816 and 1839.

When the Montreal General Hospital opened its doors in 1819, Robertson was the senior member of its medical staff. Not long afterwards he, the Reverend John Bethune*, Alexander SKAKEL, and others were appointed commissioners to oversee the construction of a new building on Rue Dorchester, completed in 1822. The first recorded operation in the new hospital, an amputation of the leg at the thigh, was performed by Robertson. In 1823 the medical officers of the hospital – Robertson, John STEPHENSON, William Caldwell*, and Andrew Fernando Holmes* – set up a school known as the Montreal Medical Institution. Robertson was its head and its instructor in midwifery and diseases of women and children. In 1829 the institution became the medical faculty of McGill College, and Robertson was appointed professor of midwifery and diseases of women and children, and official head of the faculty. (The title of dean was not used during his lifetime.) On the death of Caldwell in 1833 Robertson succeeded to the professorship of the theory and practice of medicine, a post he held until his retirement in 1842.

In 1818 Robertson was appointed a magistrate or justice of the peace. These officers were responsible for civic government in Montreal and, in particular, for keeping the peace during elections. On 21 May 1832, during a by-election in Montreal West contested by Daniel Tracey* and Stanley Bagg, fighting broke out at Place d'Armes, near the poll. Robertson, one of the two magistrates on duty at the poll, read the riot act. As the "riot" became more serious, troops fired into the crowd, killing three persons. Robertson was later accused of having ordered the soldiers to shoot. Although he was officially exonerated of any criminal act by the grand jury of Montreal, many, including Louis-Joseph Papineau*, continued to regard him as having abused his powers and thus of having been responsible for the "murder" of the three. Papineau's accusations provoked Robertson to challenge him to a duel, which Papineau refused on the grounds that he was condemning Robertson for public, not private, acts. The bitterness remained and Robertson was no doubt an unpopular figure in some quarters. However, he must have enjoyed the confidence of many. In 1833, when government by city council replaced rule by justices, he served as a presiding officer at the first municipal elections. From 1836 to 1840 rule by justices was briefly reintroduced and he was again appointed a magistrate. Robertson was named to the first Board of Health in Montreal, established in 1832 to deal with an anticipated outbreak of cholera. Seven years later he was made a commissioner to provide a temporary asylum for the insane.

Illness forced Robertson's retirement from all active work in 1842 and two years later he died. A memorial tablet was erected in the Montreal General Hospital and is still on display there. In 1894 his portrait, by an unidentified artist, was presented to the medical faculty by his family and descendants. It was destroyed by fire in 1907 but, using a photograph as a model, Robert Harris* painted another, which now hangs in the McIntyre Medical Sciences Building of McGill University.

E. H. BENSLEY

ANQ-M, CE1-130, 22 juill. 1844. GRO (Edinburgh), Blair Atholl, reg. of births and baptisms, 15 March 1784. McGill Univ. Arch., RG 38, c.1, minute-book, 1823–33. PAC, RG 8, I (C ser.), 221; RG 68, General index, 1651–1841. Univ. of Edinburgh Library, Special Coll. Dept., Medical matriculation index, 1802–5. "The late Dr. Robertson," *Montreal Medical Gazette*, 1 (1844–45), no.5: 146–47. *Vindicator and Canadian Advertiser*, 9 Dec. 1834. *Commissioned officers in the medical services of the British army, 1660–1960*, comp. Alfred Peterkin *et al.* (2v., London, 1968). Abbott, *Hist. of medicine*. W. H. Atherton, *Montreal, 1535–1914* (3v., Montreal and Vancouver, 1914). Campbell, *Hist. of Scotch Presbyterian Church*. Ægidius Fauteux, *Le duel au Canada* (Montréal, 1934). S. B. Frost, *McGill University: for the advancement of learning* (2v., Montreal, 1980–84). R. P. Howard, *A sketch of the late G. W. Campbell . . . being the introductory address of the fiftieth session of the medical faculty of McGill University* (Montreal, 1882). H. E. MacDermot, *A history of the Montreal General Hospital* (Montreal, 1950). Taft Manning, *Revolt of French Canada*. M. E. [S.] Abbott, "Early American medical schools: the faculty of medicine of McGill University," *Surgery, Gynecology and Obstetrics*

(Chicago), 60 (1935): 242–53; "An historical sketch of the medical faculty of McGill University," *Montreal Medical Journal*, 31 (1902): 561–672. F.-J. Audet, "Des hommes d'action à la tête de Montréal il y a 100 ans," *La Presse*, 4 nov. 1933: 30. E. H. Bensley, "William Robertson, M.D., first official head of the McGill medical faculty," *Montreal General Hospital News*, 17 (1978), no.2: 9–10. E. A. Collard, "The man who hoaxed Sir John A. Macdonald," *Gazette* (Montreal), 13 Oct. 1984: B2. R. W. Quinn, "The four founders," *McGill Medical Undergraduate Journal* (Montreal), 5 (May 1936): 5–11. R. F. Ruttan, "Dr. William Robertson," *McGill Univ. Magazine* (Montreal), 1 (1902): 178–79. "Sixty-first convocation of the medical faculty of McGill University," *Montreal Medical Journal*, 22 (1894): 775–89. B. R. Tunis, "Medical licensing in Lower Canada: the dispute over Canada's first medical degree," *CHR*, 55 (1974): 489–504.

ROBICHAUX, VÉNÉRANDE, businesswoman; b. 1 March 1753 in Annapolis Royal, N.S., daughter of Louis Robichaux*, a merchant, and Jeanne Bourgeois; d. 22 Nov. 1839 at Quebec and was buried three days later in Sainte-Anne's chapel in the cathedral of Notre-Dame.

Although he was on good terms with the British government of Nova Scotia, Vénérande Robichaux's father was no more able than his Acadian compatriots to escape deportation in 1755 [*see* Charles Lawrence*]. He did manage, however, to get sent with his family to Boston, where he had friends in mercantile and business circles. After three months the Robichauxs were moved by the Massachusetts government to the adjacent town of Cambridge. They apparently wanted to stay there permanently since in 1766 they let pass the opportunity to return to Nova Scotia with most of their companions in exile. In 1775, however, under the stress of the American revolution they decided to make their way back and to settle at Quebec. Vénérande's parents could not endure further moves because of their advanced age, and she, the youngest of the family, became and remained their support until the end, her father dying on 20 Dec. 1780 and her mother on 18 March 1790. Two of her brothers had died shortly after their arrival.

Vénérande's brother Otho* followed in his father's footsteps and went into trade. He had gone with his brothers Frédéric and Florent to the Miramichi region, in what was shortly to become New Brunswick, and there in 1781 he had bought the business and property of Pierre Loubert (Loubère), the husband of one of his cousins. Otho relied on Vénérande to dispose of his goods and do his purchasing. The products he sold in the market-places at Quebec included oysters, salmon, tallow, feathers, maple sugar, furs, cranberries, and boxes of birchbark decorated by the Micmacs with porcupine quills. In return Vénérande sent him sheets, linen, blankets, flour, spinning-wheels, carding-combs, and medicaments.

During her stay in Cambridge Vénérande had become proficient in English. Her father had also taught her to read and write French and had seen that she acquired some general knowledge, as her correspondence demonstrates. About 15 letters that she wrote between 1781 and 1831 to Otho, his son Louis, and her relatives Michel Allain and Édouard (Nede) LeBlanc, all of Neguac, have been preserved by the Robichauds in that locality.

At Quebec Vénérande lived for a long time with her cousin Marie-Vénérande Pelerin, wife of gold- and silversmith François Ranvoyzé*. Among the visitors she received were family friends from Boston, and English residents of Miramichi and Restigouche who sometimes acted as couriers for her. The missionaries of the Baie des Chaleurs region, such as René-Pierre Joyer, Louis-Joseph DESJARDINS, *dit* Desplantes, and Thomas Cooke*, invariably went to see her when passing through Quebec. Acadians from the bay who were engaged in coastal trading up to Quebec – among others Jean-Baptiste Robichaux (the son of another deportee, Jean-Baptiste Robichaux*) – also paid her regular visits. On one occasion she noted her pleasure at receiving the Ganishes and Pominvilles, two Micmac families from Miramichi who brought her the local news. She was well informed about social, political, and military life at Quebec and frequently told her correspondents about it. While maintaining good relations with the British, she remained attached to her "beloved Acadia," and kept telling herself that one day "the English perhaps will pay for the suffering they have caused us."

Despite her complaints and worries, Vénérande Robichaux had a moderately comfortable existence, as the inventory of her assets reveals; she made her nephew Édouard LeBlanc, of Neguac, her residuary legatee.

DONAT ROBICHAUD

ANQ-Q, CE1-1, 25 nov. 1839; CN1-212, no.8310. Arch. de l'évêché de Bathurst (Bathurst, N.-B.), Papiers Robichaud. Centre d'études acadiennes, univ. de Moncton (Moncton, N.-B.), Fonds Placide Gaudet, 1.31-13A. "Les dénombrements de Québec" (Plessis), ANQ *Rapport*, 1948–49: 20. Placide Gaudet, "Acadian genealogy and notes," PAC *Report*, 1905, 2, pt.III. Donat Robichaud, *Les Robichaud: histoire et généalogie* (Bathurst, [1967]). Pierre Belliveau, *French neutrals in Massachusetts . . .* (Boston, 1972).

ROBINSON, PETER, office holder, businessman, fur trader, militia officer, politician, and JP; b. 1785 in New Brunswick, eldest son of Christopher Robinson* and Esther Sayre; brother of John Beverley* and William Benjamin*; he had at least a son and two daughters; d. 8 July 1838 in Toronto.

Peter Robinson spent his childhood on the move. He was in New Brunswick for three years, in Lower

Canada for four, and in Kingston, Upper Canada, for six before his family settled in York (Toronto) in 1798, the year his father died. As a loyalist and surveyor general of woods and forests, Christopher Robinson left his wife and six children an established place in York society. Unfortunately, he left little means to sustain it, and in 1800, at 15, Peter was given a position as clerk of the Home District Court of Requests.

Esther Robinson's second marriage, in 1802 to Elisha Beman*, a York merchant and land speculator who soon settled at the site of Newmarket, introduced Peter to a different way of life and to the business career he would follow until 1822. In 1812 Robinson, who had moved to Newmarket, acquired a mill there, the first of the several he and his brothers bought or built for lease, and in 1814 he began buying lots north of the village. Over the next 18 years he acquired eight lots on Yonge Street, including the site of the village of Holland Landing, which developed around a mill built by Robinson. He invested in numerous other enterprises: an inn, a schooner on Lake Simcoe, a distillery, and farms, but his greatest personal involvement was as a fur trader employing agents in the back country and as a merchant supplying the trade. Although the portion of this trade falling to Yonge Street traders was small, Robinson shared in the temporary prosperity brought by the War of 1812 to the Lake Simcoe route to the upper Great Lakes. By the mid 1820s Robinson Brothers was active on the French River. In total, Peter's various enterprises yielded him a comfortable income which by 1824 exceeded his personal needs.

At the start of the war, Robinson had raised a rifle company, attached to the 1st York Militia. This company, made up of experienced woodsmen, travelled overland to join in Major-General Isaac Brock*'s successful attack on Detroit in August 1812. Robinson was one of 13 captains in York when that town surrendered to the Americans in April 1813. The following year he put his backwoods knowledge to use again in helping Fort Michilimackinac maintain communications with York during the American blockade of Mackinac Island (Mich.).

Robinson opened two apparently short-lived stores in York, one in partnership with his brother-in-law D'Arcy Boulton Jr in 1810, the other in 1820. After his election to the House of Assembly for York East in 1816 and, with William Warren BALDWIN, for York and Simcoe in 1820, he spent more of each year in York. A staunch government supporter, he chaired a committee on St Lawrence River navigation and reported on the repair and construction of the parliament buildings. In 1818 he received his first commission of the peace for the Home District. Five years later he became a director of the newly formed Bank of Upper Canada.

The three Robinson brothers took a close interest in one another's welfare and participated in joint investments; Peter and William were associated in business. Over the years John, who had a home, a family, and a prominent position in government, increasingly assumed the role of head of the family, although Peter rarely went so far as to take the good advice he frequently offered. Peter was able to offer John money in the event that he decided to try to establish himself in England, but it was John who obtained for Peter the interview that led to a new career.

In 1822, with John and his wife, Peter went to England for the first time, as a tourist. Early the following year John introduced him as an expert on backwoods settlement to his friend Robert John Wilmot-Horton, the new under-secretary of state for the colonies. An enthusiastic Malthusian, Wilmot-Horton had a scheme to bring peace and prosperity to Ireland through the sponsored emigration of thousands of dispossessed tenant farmers whose continued presence blocked agricultural improvement. He had obtained the government's consent to a small-scale, experimental scheme for sending emigrants to Upper Canada, and he found his superintendent in Peter Robinson.

Wilmot-Horton deliberately introduced his scheme in the Blackwater River valley of County Cork, a region where there was no tradition of emigration and where the Insurrection Act was in force. He sent Robinson there in the spring of three successive years. If nothing else, Robinson proved for Wilmot-Horton what a single personable interviewer with a few key introductions could accomplish. On his first visit to the Blackwater valley, Robinson found that there were many who were willing to equate assisted immigration with transportation. Two years later, the would-be immigrants needed sponsorship even to get on a list. Robinson was besieged by applicants at every town and wrote in terms of 50,000 vying for 2,000 places. At the completion of the difficult task of selection in 1825, he was satisfied that his candidates were "a better description of people than those taken out in [18]23 altho' they are wretchedly poor" – poverty being one of Wilmot-Horton's firm pre-conditions. In 1823 Robinson sailed from Cork with 568 individuals, bound for the military and Lanark settlements in the Bathurst District of Upper Canada. A second immigration was postponed in 1824, but in 1825 Robinson took 2,024 immigrants to the Newcastle District.

In the context of his circle at York, Peter appeared unusually tolerant of his Roman Catholic charges, in striking contrast to his brother John. The members of Lieutenant Governor Sir Peregrine Maitland*'s administration supported the settlements for Peter's sake and because of Wilmot-Horton's interest and instructions, but they held to the belief that Irish Roman Catholics were the least desirable of British settlers.

Robinson's 1823 immigrants were therefore watched with nervous anticipation. Although a few failed to adjust to settlement among Irish and Scots Protestants, as a group they were involved in only one incident, in May 1824, serious enough to attract more than local attention. Colonel James FitzGibbon* went to mediate and the government continued its support, but Robinson's 1825 settlers were to be located off by themselves.

The one-time parliamentary grants for the larger and more ambitious immigration of 1825 produced difficulty for Robinson's management of the operation. The grants were made late in the spring, so late that he arrived in Upper Canada after the settlers. It had been impossible to make the advance preparations which might have cut costs. Hindsight suggested that a depot should have been established, and the work of opening a settlement begun, during the previous winter, the customary season for transporting bulk supplies by sleigh and chopping a first clearing. There had been no funds and no authority for this work. For the same reason, the ships' surgeons who conducted the immigrants up the St Lawrence had to make do with existing facilities. Robinson's organization was greatly criticized for holding the immigrants in an improvised tent city at Kingston until his arrival in August, but this action had been taken on Maitland's orders. Once at Kingston, Robinson moved his settlers forward to the Newcastle District and onto the lots he chose for them with an energy and resourcefulness that showed him at his best.

In 1823 William Marshall, his second in command, had criticized his indulgence. In 1825 Robinson declared that he intended to be stricter at Scott's Mills, the depot for the distribution of supplies. In fact, order within the settlement depended on good will and on his personal authority over the immigrants, and he continued to seek to "gain them by kindness." George Hume Reade, their doctor in 1825 and a more sympathetic observer than Marshall, singled out for particular praise Robinson's "kind manner" and "upright principle" in his handling of "the lower class of the Irish." Robinson liked his job and had no doubt in 1824 that he preferred working with Wilmot-Horton to the possibility held out by John GALT of superintending the sale of the crown lands of Upper Canada in the future Canada Company.

In the sparsely settled townships of the Newcastle District to the north of Rice Lake, the 1825 immigrants were certain of a welcome from the inhabitants and of a good choice of crown land. But they faced a long, difficult journey in an unusually hot summer. The heat aggravated both the fever and ague contracted locally and the endemic illnesses that the immigrants brought with them. Robinson himself developed a fever from which he "never perfectly recovered," and most of his assistants were also sick over the course of the summer and fall. At Scott's Mills a town-site was surveyed by Richard Birdsall* in 1825 and named for Robinson. The community which grew up around the depot contained grist- and sawmills built with government funds and became the hub of a rudimentary road system. Many Upper Canadians would have spent the money differently, but most could agree that the Peterborough immigration had successfully pioneered a new region. Robinson is still best remembered as the founder of Peterborough.

Robinson had left the 1823 immigrants as soon as they were located. He stayed with the 1825 settlers until March 1826, when he completed a personal inspection of all lots and a report of improvements. In all, he had located just under 2,000 immigrants in nine townships in the Newcastle District. Not all locations had been taken up and some remained temporarily vacant as families regrouped to begin work on a single lot, but still the totals of land cleared and of produce raised, which Robinson sent off to Wilmot-Horton, were signs of a flourishing settlement. Robinson's stock was high in the Colonial Office when he returned to England in 1826 and 1827 to give evidence to two select committees on emigration called at Wilmot-Horton's instigation.

Wilmot-Horton's scheme, in its Irish formulation, proved too expensive to win the sponsorship of government or landlord. Although he recognized his failure in Britain, he sought to provide for the continuation of some elements of his scheme in Upper Canada after his resignation in January 1828. Before he left office, he had Robinson appointed, in July 1827, commissioner of crown lands (Upper Canada's first) and surveyor general of woods. The Crown Lands Department was created to oversee the implementation of a new policy for the sale of crown properties, including disposal by auction and payment by instalment which, Wilmot-Horton believed, would allow indigent immigrants to acquire land. In November Robinson took on the added duty of commissioner for the clergy reserves. These appointments gave him a place he had not had before in the inner circle of government, first as a member of the Executive Council and in 1829 on the Legislative Council. The only significant public revenues Robinson collected as surveyor of woods were timber duties in the Ottawa valley, which were handled by a clerk and by agents [*see* Charles SHIRREFF]. Most of his time was devoted to administering the sale of crown and clergy reserves and, to a degree that could not have been predicted from his instructions, assisting immigrant settlers.

Although he was never one of the principal players in the controversy surrounding the clergy reserves, Robinson, as commissioner, determined the spirit in which the imperial Clergy Reserves Sales Act of 1827 would be implemented. This act allowed the alienation of up to one-quarter of the reserves at a specified annual rate and most of this land was either sold or leased by the time Robinson left office in 1836. Clergy lots could be paid for in easy instalments over a number of years, terms reminiscent of those proposed in Wilmot-Horton's emigration committees. Robinson was generous in his interpretation of the rules, particularly in allowing conversion from lease to freehold. His system was open to abuse, but it put ownership within the reach of many settlers, and enabled others, including a number of those who had come with him in 1823 and 1825, to provide for their children close to home.

Robinson's tenure in the Crown Lands Department was shaped by a dramatic rise in immigration from the British Isles which peaked in 1832, the year of a cholera epidemic. Contemporary statistics for emigration to British North America are understated and unreliable, but they reflect reality. Figures of 12,000–13,000 for 1826–29 rose through 30,000 in 1830 to 58,000 in 1831 and 66,000 a year later, dropping to 28,000 in 1833. Each year a proportion of the immigrants arriving in Upper Canada failed to fit into the province's economy. They could not find work and lacked the capital to establish themselves by their own efforts. Lieutenant Governor Sir John Colborne*, who replaced Maitland in 1828, turned to Robinson to use his expertise and the resources of his department to provide for indigent immigrants. In addition to agents responsible for a port, road project, or settlement, Robinson employed others on a casual basis as particular needs arose. Agents in the lake ports directed needy immigrants to their colleagues inland who, at specified places, offered work, usually the opening of roads, and 50-acre lots on extended terms.

The program got off to a modest start in 1829 in Ops Township, in the Newcastle District, and expanded rapidly in 1831–32. The Ops experiment was supervised by Alexander McDonell*, Robinson's most active assistant in his 1825 settlement, who had been rewarded with a crown lands agency in 1827. His accounts for "subsisting, locating and employing" immigrants in the Peterborough area between May 1831 and April 1833 indicate settlement in 11 townships. Advertisements in 1832 directed indigent settlers also to John McNaughton in the Bathurst District for crown lands in Ross, Pembroke, and Westmeath townships, and to Wellesley Richey in the Home District for land in Sunnidale, Oro, Medonte, and Orillia. In the Western District, Roswell Mount* assisted settlers in Adelaide and Warwick.

All Robinson's agents had wide spending powers. The instructions of Colonial Secretary Lord Goderich to Colborne stressed self-help – employment for the immigrants rather than the direct aid which Wilmot-Horton had given. Recent immigrants had not proved efficient at clearing and chopping, however, and Robinson and his agents were caught between these orders and the pressing needs of families who were in their care because they had no other recourse. Much depended on the experience and discretion of the agents, for Robinson issued orders requiring prior approval of new expenses only in May 1833.

The severest test came in summer 1832 when Upper Canada's first cholera victims were identified. Colborne based his strategy on the belief that the greatest danger lay in allowing large numbers of immigrants to congregate in temporary quarters. Top priority in 1832 went to moving immigrants out of York and the other towns along their route. Robinson's network held up under this pressure despite the difficulties caused by fear of infection. Charges for transportation rose and in some communities all doors were closed to strangers. Yet even Roswell Mount, at the distant end of the chain, got his people placed and in some shape for winter. The epidemic did not lead to civil disorder and families did not starve in the new settlements. In midsummer 1832 Robinson began to see what the cost of this achievement would be. His policy, as in the 1820s, was always to get immigrants settled and to worry about accounts only after the end of the short season in which they could be located successfully. His effort indeed proved so costly that it destroyed his operation rather than brought it credit. Robinson was sick in August and Colborne involved himself increasingly in ordering retrenchments. As winter arrived, with more and larger bills, it became clear that some agents, Mount being the most notorious, had lost control of their spending. After Colborne had added related expenses, such as grants for district hospitals, the total he reported to Colonial Secretary Stanley in September 1833 was £13,286, more than twice the £5,000 allocated for immigrant needs in 1832–33. Colborne defended himself stoutly, but Wilmot-Horton's successors in the Colonial Office were unsympathetic to assisting settlement and they now sought to end the practice.

1833 was a bad year for Robinson. His health, delicate and uncertain since 1831, if not 1825, now clearly reduced his capacity for public and private business. Pleading the demands of his offices, he had procrastinated for years in drawing up his final account as Wilmot-Horton's superintendent. British Treasury officials lost patience in 1833 and stopped his salary until in 1834 he closed the account by paying £1,968 17*s.* sterling into the military chest. Imperial land policy was again under review, and on 1 July 1834 responsibility for a less ambitious immigration establishment was transferred to Anthony Bewden Hawke*, who thus became Upper Canada's chief immigration agent. Robinson seems thereafter to have concentrated his remaining energy on his work within the Executive Council, notably the land claims that made up the bulk of its business.

In 1836 Robinson participated as a councillor in two events that led to major controversies. Just before he left Upper Canada in January, Colborne had endowed 44 Anglican rectories with land, an action that infuriated the reformers. It was Robinson and two fellow councillors, Joseph Wells* and George Herchmer Markland*, who had approved the patents. In March, Robinson was one of the expanded council of six members who resigned to protest Lieutenant Governor Sir Francis Bond Head*'s treatment of the council. Although Robinson was the presiding member, it is unlikely that he had the health or ambition to do more than follow advice, either in resigning (at the urging of Robert Baldwin* and John Rolph*) or in offering, with Wells, Markland, and John Henry Dunn*, to withdraw his resignation. Head refused the offer. Robinson was still on a bad footing with the lieutenant governor when a paralytic attack on 23 June left him "deprived of the use of his left side." Seeing no prospect of Robinson's recovery, Head demanded his early resignation from the Crown Lands Department and, in order for its business to continue, offered the position to Robert Baldwin Sullivan*. Robinson closed his books as commissioner for crown lands and for clergy reserves on 1 August but seems to have continued as nominal surveyor general of woods until 9 May 1837.

Robinson wrote his will that month on the realistic assumption that most of the land he had acquired privately would have to be sold to cover his accounts. A list of his lands in 1837 recorded more than 7,592 acres and a couple of additional properties in Toronto. Printed family records say that Peter died unmarried, but two children, Isabella and Frederick, were his main concern in his will. After his death in July 1838, John Beverley Robinson supervised an arrangement whereby Isabella moved to Whitchurch Township to board on the farm her father had given her, with Frederick joining her in the school holidays.

John was also left to settle Peter's account with the government. In 1835 William Lyon Mackenzie* in the seventh, and final, report of his assembly committee on grievances had objected to shortcomings in the accounts submitted by Robinson and his agents. In 1840 one of the committees of Lieutenant Governor Sir George Arthur*'s commission on public departments looked at the books on which these accounts were based. The committee, chaired by William Allan*, recommended a complete review and restructuring of an accounting system which was both confused and inadequate. The problem was not limited to crown lands and was rooted in the failure of the Upper Canadian government to match a great increase in its business with the new accounting methods developed in the mercantile community. Even so, Robinson's "almost unconquerable repugnance" to return to old accounts must have contributed to laxity in the office and, while his personal honesty was not in question, his reputation as an administrator suffered. His executors were forced to make payments from his private funds, but in December 1840 John Beverley Robinson was able to inform Arthur "that there now remains *no balance against my brother on any account whatever*."

The plans for immigration which Wilmot-Horton introduced would have been dangerously theoretical without Peter Robinson. He provided the local knowledge and practical good sense missing from many 19th-century colonization schemes. Robinson also brought an unusual amount of first-hand experience to the job of commissioner of crown lands. So long as the emphasis was on opening the province by making land available to actual settlers, his priorities were right. Once attention shifted to the administration of his office, he appeared old-fashioned. As John Beverley Robinson feared, Peter's lack-lustre performance in York overshadowed his achievements. Robinson is remembered for Peterborough, but not for his sustained interest in promoting the settlement which helped to shape many other parts of the province.

WENDY CAMERON

AO, MS 4; MS 524; RG 1, A-I-4, 2; A-I-6, 7–11; RG 22, ser.155. Derby Central Library (Derby, Eng.), Catton Coll., Sir R. J. Wilmot-Horton papers. PAC, RG 5, A1, 59–75, 137–60; RG 68, General index, 1651–1841: 430, 670. PRO, CO 42/415–16 (mfm. at AO); CO 384/12–13 (mfm. at PAC). G.B., Parl., House of Commons paper, 1826, 4, no.404: 1–381, *Report from the select committee on emigration from the United Kingdom*; 1826–27, 5, no.550: 225–882, *Third report from the select committee on emigration from the United Kingdom, 1827*. *Town of York, 1793–1815* (Firth); *1815–34* (Firth). *The valley of the Trent*, ed. and intro. E. C. Guillet (Toronto, 1957). R. J. Wilmot-Horton, *Ireland and Canada; supported by local evidence* (London, 1839). D. H. Akenson, *The Irish in Ontario: a study in rural history* (Kingston, Ont., and Montreal, 1984). Wendy [Stevenson] Cameron, "Wilmot Horton's experimental emigrations to Upper Canada: his management of the emigrations and his evaluation of the prospects and progress of his settlers" (B.LITT. thesis, Univ. of Oxford, 1972). H. I. Cowan, *British emigration to British North America; the first hundred years* (rev. ed., Toronto, 1961). Gates, *Land policies of U.C.* H. J. M. Johnston, *British emigration policy, 1815–1830: "shovelling out paupers"* (Oxford, 1972). E. A. Mitchell, *Fort Timiskaming and the fur trade* (Toronto and Buffalo, N.Y., 1977). C. W. Robinson, *Life of Sir John Beverley Robinson, bart., C.B., D.C.L., chief-justice of Upper Canada* (Edinburgh and London, 1904). W. R. Smith, "The early development of three Upper Canadian towns," York Univ., Dept. of Geography, *Discussion paper* (Toronto), no.16 (1977). [Ethel Willson Trewhella *et al.*], *History of the town of Newmarket* (n.p., [1968?]). Alan Wilson, *The clergy reserves of Upper Canada: a Canadian mortmain* (Toronto, 1968). Wendy [Stevenson] Cameron, "Selecting Peter Robinson's Irish emigrants," *SH*,

9 (1976): 29–46. J. B. Gilchrist, forthcoming article, *Families* (Toronto).

ROCHEBLAVE, PIERRE DE RASTEL DE. *See* RASTEL

RODIER, ÉDOUARD-ÉTIENNE (baptized **Étienne-Édouard**), lawyer, politician, and Patriote; b. 26 Dec. 1804 in Montreal, son of Barthélemy Rodier and Marie-Louise Giroux; d. there 5 Feb. 1840.

Édouard-Étienne Rodier's family belonged to the urban petite bourgeoisie; industrious and frugal, it nevertheless lacked wealth and education. His father had been a voyageur and had made a little money in the fur trade. After 1800 he had launched into the retail trade, setting up a dry goods and fur store in the *faubourg* Saint-Joseph of Montreal. Édouard-Étienne's childhood was thus spent in the world of small business, at the mercy of creditors and risky commercial ventures. Like his father, he had only his own resources to count on. If he wanted to improve his status in society, education was the sole means of advancement.

In 1812 Rodier entered the Petit Séminaire de Montréal. After completing the elementary classes there, he began classical studies in 1814. He was a serious pupil who paid close attention to his Sulpician teachers. Nothing at this period suggested that he would become an impassioned spokesman for the independence of Lower Canada and a new, genuinely liberal, social order.

When his classical studies were ended, Rodier was uncertain what career to take up. He first contemplated entering holy orders, but finally chose the legal profession since it would allow him to participate in public life, which interested him intensely. In July 1822 he began articling with lawyer Hippolyte Saint-Georges Dupré in Montreal. Four months later he entered the employ of Dominique-Benjamin Rollin, a renowned lawyer. He remained with Rollin for five years, until his studies were finished, and he distinguished himself by his enthusiasm for hard work and his broadmindedness.

On 7 Jan. 1826 in Montreal Rodier married Julie-Victoire Dumont, daughter of a small cooper. The details in the marriage contract about the young woman's dowry and the material guarantees agreed to by Rodier confirm that the couple's financial situation was precarious. Rodier even had to work in his father's shop to make ends meet. When he finally received his commission as a lawyer on 28 May 1827, he decided to practise in Montreal. An excellent conversationalist whose oratorical gifts were already acknowledged, he extended his influence among the most reputable members of the liberal professions through a network of connections and solid friendships. Thus he soon built up a large practice. From 1827 to 1831 he handled some 60 lawsuits and took more than 40 cases before the courts. A new life was beginning for him as a brilliant young lawyer, recognized and accepted within his profession. This dazzling situation was saddened, however, by his wife's death on 14 June 1829.

Rodier's professional successes did not, however, lead him to neglect public affairs. In the years from 1827 to 1830 he openly supported Louis-Joseph Papineau*'s attempt to establish his authority and unify the Patriote party, which had been known as the Canadian party until 1826. A new partisan newspaper, *La Minerve*, defended the policies advocated by Papineau. Rodier was sympathetic to these new directions and joined the organization. Along with Louis-Hippolyte La Fontaine*, Augustin-Norbert Morin*, Charles-Ovide Perrault, Jean-Olivier CHÉNIER, Clément-Charles Sabrevois* de Bleury, Wolfred* and Robert* Nelson, and Cyrille-Hector-Octave CÔTÉ, he represented a new generation and a radical element within the party.

Rodier belonged to various study groups that met in Édouard-Raymond Fabre*'s bookstore and in the printing-shop belonging to Ludger Duvernay*, who became a close friend. In the 1830s these groups were in a state of intellectual ferment. Some of their members were full of admiration for the July revolution in France and for American political institutions; they read and quoted the 18th-century *philosophes*, attacked the abuses of the colonial régime, and denounced the constitutional impasse in which Lower Canada found itself. Rodier was clearly responsive to these influences.

Rodier's political and professional career was furthered by a second marriage in 1831. On 6 June he married Élise Beaupré, eldest daughter of Benjamin Beaupré, one of the leading merchants in L'Assomption. The income she brought made it possible for Rodier to live more comfortably and gave him greater freedom to pursue a political career. He was able to give up his law office in Montreal and move to L'Assomption, where he launched into politics. Elected to the House of Assembly for that riding after Barthélemy JOLIETTE had resigned his seat, he remained a member from 30 July 1832 until 27 March 1838.

In the course of the summer of 1832 Rodier saw both his father and his mother-in-law, Julie Mercier Beaupré, die of cholera. Fearing for his own life, he drew up a will. In it, the usual religious invocations were replaced by patriotic allusions.

In January 1833, when the session resumed, Rodier drew the attention of his colleagues by coming out in favour of making the Legislative Council elective, a proposal Papineau was championing enthusiastically. His stands in the house that year brought him into contact with the most important Patriotes of his time. A fiery and exceptionally eloquent speaker, he rapidly became a voice for the party's message.

Beginning in 1834 Rodier committed himself wholly to political action, deserting his law office more and more. In 1833–34, for example, he took only one case into court, and a minor one at that. When the 92 Resolutions were put forward, Rodier participated in all the activities and meetings. In April 1834 he challenged his best friend, Pierre-Édouard Leclère*, an acknowledged member of the English party, to a duel. Fortunately the two fired without hitting each other. Three years later, on the eve of the rebellion, Rodier was involved in another duel that ended in about the same way. On 24 June 1834 in Montreal he made a speech at the first Saint-Jean-Baptiste banquet [*see* Jean-François-Marie-Joseph MacDonell*]. He was extremely active in the elections held that autumn. Everywhere he went he enthralled the voters, and he was easily returned in his own riding. The eloquent orator of the assembly was now a popular speaker as well.

In 1835 Rodier attracted notice by his closing speech at the Saint-Jean-Baptiste banquet in Montreal. It revealed his opposition to the official position of the Catholic Church on civil authority and also reiterated his faith in the people as the natural and legitimate source of all power. Rodier was thus increasingly coming to represent the minority active within the Patriote party that wanted to change the political institutions of the colony and overturn the social structure. He proposed that a republic be set up and the seigneurial régime be abolished; he was also opposed to trade with the United Kingdom, dominated as it was by British merchants. He urged the creation of a national economy centred on the rise of small independent producers and local industries. In August 1837, to set an example for his compatriots, he showed up in the assembly dressed in homespun.

It is certain that at the time of the 1837 rebellion Rodier helped develop the Patriotes' strategy and that he was intimately involved in the events. Although he disagreed with Papineau about maintaining the seigneurial régime, he apparently accepted the stands he took on the question of French Canadian nationhood. In May he addressed the voters in Richelieu riding. A month later he was invited to speak at Longueuil. Late in July he delivered a speech at Varennes. On 23 October, to the Assemblée des Six Comtés held at Saint-Charles-sur-Richelieu, he openly preached armed revolt. He did not confine himself merely to stirring up the crowd. Along with Thomas Storrow Brown* and André Ouimet* he was a leader of the Fils de la Liberté, a revolutionary organization founded on 5 September that brought together a number of students and young professionals in Montreal. On 6 November a riot involving the Doric Club, whose members were young English-speaking Montrealers, and the Fils de la Liberté broke out. Rodier took an active part in the bloody clash. A few days later, on 16 November, warrants were issued for his arrest and that of 25 other Patriotes. Knowing that he was being hunted, Rodier hastily took the road to Napierville, where Côté was waiting for him.

The two men came to an immediate understanding. While Papineau and Dr Edmund Bailey O'Callaghan* headed for Saint-Denis on the Richelieu, Côté, Rodier, Duvernay, Lucien GAGNON, and several others planned an attack on Saint-Jean (Saint-Jean-sur-Richelieu) at the end of November. When they heard that British military forces had arrived in the area, Rodier and his companions dropped the scheme and decided to go to Swanton, Vt, to reorganize. On 6 December Rodier, as an officer of a small Patriote battalion, took part in an ill-fated expedition to Moore's Corner (Saint-Armand-Station); he was wounded there and was taken to Swanton.

During a meeting in Middlebury, Vt, on 2 Jan. 1838, at which the possibility of another insurrection was discussed, Rodier violently attacked Papineau for being opposed to abolition of the seigneurial régime. Even apart from this speech the deep disagreement between the two men had become evident, and the following months would simply confirm it. Rodier reproached Papineau for his inactivity and strengthened his own authority and his hold on the fugitives. Along with Côté and Robert Nelson he became a leader in the 1838 revolutionary movement. He was a major participant in preparations for the invasion of February 1838 and in the drafting of the proclamation of independence issued that month [*see* Robert Nelson].

In March 1838 Rodier moved to Burlington, Vt. After the failure of the February invasion, he had become increasingly anxious. Intrigues, suspicions, and underhand tricks multiplied inside the revolutionary organization. Even though he spent most of his time trying to rally his companions to a common cause, the movement was exhausting itself in internal fighting. Relations between Rodier and Côté were no longer good. As summer wore on a break between the two became imminent.

Rodier was not at the end of his troubles. For eight months he had been suffering from uncertainty. At Burlington he had no money, no profession, no job. To meet his needs he even had to work as a waiter in an inn. He saw little of his wife and had no news of his children. On 28 Oct. 1838, when his wife came for him, Rodier left his companions without a moment's hesitation. He had been excluded from the amnesty proclaimed by Lord Durham [LAMBTON] on 28 June, but when London repudiated the governor's decree, Rodier could return to Lower Canada. He posted a bond for £3,000 and went to L'Assomption.

Rodier intended to devote himself thenceforth solely to his profession. He sought to become a model husband and the fondest of fathers, and to lead a quiet life. In the eyes of his former Patriote friends he was a pariah, a coward, a traitor indeed, and on 28 Nov. 1838 he published a letter in *Le Canadien* to reply to the calumnies being heaped upon him.

Édouard-Étienne Rodier died on 5 Feb. 1840 in Montreal at 35 years of age, his health undermined by over-exertion and failure. In an article of 12 February in the *North American*, a newspaper published in Swanton, Côté revenged himself on Rodier by calling him a turncoat.

RICHARD CHABOT

AC, Montréal, Cour du banc du roi, 1822–37; Beauharnois (Valleyfield), minutiers, Godefroy Chagnon, 21 mai, 4 nov. 1838. ANQ-M, CE1-51, 7 janv. 1800, 26 déc. 1804, 7 janv. 1826, 7 févr. 1840; CE5-14, 6 juin 1831; CN1-28, 27 sept. 1817; 18 juin 1819; 29 sept. 1821; 16 juill., 23 oct. 1822; CN5-3, 22 mars 1834, 22 mai 1838; CN5-8, 19 oct. 1838. ASQ, Fonds Viger–Verreau, carton 22, nos.68–69. ASSH, A, Fg-4, dossier 16. BVM-G, Fonds Ægidius Fauteux, étude biographique sur É.-É. Rodier par Ægidius Fauteux accompagnée de notes, références, copies de documents, coupures, etc. concernant ce patriote; notes compilées par Ægidius Fauteux sur les patriotes de 1837–38 dont les noms commencent par les lettres R et S, carton 9. PAC, MG 24, B2: 1690–93, 1900–3, 1989–91, 2847–52, 2951–54, 2961–64, 2983–86, 2999–3002, 3012–15, 3031–34, 3046–49, 3097–99, 4103–6, 6090–97; MG 30, D1, 5; 26: 529–35; RG 4, B8: 8206–9. *L'Ami du peuple, de l'ordre et des lois*, 26 avril 1834. *Le Canadien*, 4 mars, 29 avril, 3 juill. 1835; 28 nov. 1838. *La Minerve*, 1er mai 1834. *Montreal Gazette*, 21 Aug. 1832. *North American*, 12 Feb. 1840. *Quebec Gazette*, 28 June 1832. Caron, "Papiers Duvernay," ANQ *Rapport*, 1926–27: 162–63, 169–70, 177, 181, 191, 193. Ægidius Fauteux, *Patriotes*; *Le duel au Canada* (Montréal, 1934), 124–35, 219–25. Maurice Grenier, "La chambre d'Assemblée du Bas-Canada, 1815–1837" (thèse de MA, univ. de Montréal, 1966), 93. Robert Rumilly, *Histoire de la Société Saint-Jean-Baptiste de Montréal: des patriotes au fleurdelisé, 1834–1948* (Montréal, 1975), 19, 24–25, 30, 34–35; *Hist. de Montréal*, 2: 199–201, 203, 208–10, 226, 228, 230, 238, 244; *Papineau et son temps*. L.-O. David, "Édouard Rodier," *La Presse*, 18 juin 1921: 18. Ægidius Fauteux, "L'histoire d'Édouard Rodier, le lion de L'Assomption," *Le Devoir* (Montréal), 5 janv. 1938: 7.

ROQUE, JACQUES-GUILLAUME, Sulpician, school administrator, and vicar general; b. 24 Jan. 1761 in Belmont, France, son of Guillaume Roque and Catherine Durand; d. 3 May 1840 in Montreal and was buried two days later in the crypt of the church of Notre-Dame.

In 1777 Jacques-Guillaume Roque entered the Séminaire de Saint-Charles in Toulouse, where he did all his theological studies. Subsequently he obtained a doctorate in canon law from the Université de Toulouse. After being ordained priest on 24 Sept. 1785, he asked to be admitted to the community of the Society of Saint-Sulpice as a member. He spent a year in Paris doing the solitude (noviciate) and was then sent to teach theology in the Séminaire d'Angers, becoming its director in 1789. He was already known as a man "of great merit, respected and loved by all." Two years later he refused to take the oath of loyalty to the Civil Constitution of the Clergy. Imprisoned on 17 June 1792, he was sentenced to transportation to French Guiana. He succeeded in escaping, however, and reached Spain on 12 September. The bishop of Orense received him warmly and put him in charge of teaching theology to the clerics in the diocese.

Roque decided to come to Lower Canada in 1796. Upon his arrival at the Séminaire de Saint-Sulpice in Montreal on 24 October, he was given pastoral duties in the parish of Notre-Dame, and he was also named director of the nuns of the Hôtel-Dieu. In 1806 he became vicar general, an office he retained until his death. In October 1806 he replaced Sulpician Jean-Baptiste-Jacques Chicoisneau* as director of the Petit Séminaire de Montréal, which had been entirely rebuilt after a fire three years earlier. He remained in this post until 1828 and was responsible for drawing up several customaries as well as various regulations for the establishment. In addition, along with his colleagues Antoine-Jacques Houdet* and Claude Rivière, he prepared a French grammar and a Latin one.

On 21 Jan. 1821 Roque assisted Archbishop Joseph-Octave Plessis* of Quebec at the consecration of Sulpician Jean-Jacques LARTIGUE, who had been named auxiliary bishop in the district of Montreal. This appointment gave rise to a serious conflict between Lartigue and his former colleagues in the Society of Saint-Sulpice. Since he held Lartigue in high esteem, Roque adopted a neutral and prudent attitude. He had previously directed Lartigue in his theological studies and had always been generous in giving him judicious advice. At the request of his superior, Jean-Henry-August Roux*, he recorded his comments for a memorial prepared by Jean-Charles Bédard*, a Canadian Sulpician who had taken a stand against the seminary's efforts to block the installation of Lartigue.

In October 1828 Roque became chaplain to the nuns of the Congregation of Notre-Dame. Two years later, when Roux was overwhelmed by illness and infirmities, Archbishop Bernard-Claude Panet* of Quebec asked Roque to take on the duties of superior temporarily. The celebration of Roque's golden jubilee in the priesthood on 24 Sept. 1835 would seal the reconciliation between Lartigue and the seminary that had begun in the spring. The 8,000 faithful present in Notre-Dame were deeply moved by Roque, who during the mass offered in the presence of about 100 priests came forward "to cast himself at the bishop's knees to renew the vows of his priesthood." According to Father Léon Pouliot, at this moment there was truly "the union of minds and spirits, long lost, always awaited, finally found again." Joseph-Vincent Quiblier*, superior of the Séminaire de Saint-Sulpice, provides confirmation: "None of us had seen anything greater, or more touching. Everyone, without exception, was ecstatic with admiration and joy. . . . The pope will be pleased to learn how this matter has turned out. . . . I regret none of the small sacrifices that this reconciliation has cost me. . . . People say that the bishop of Telmesse and the superior of the seminary are now at one."

Jacques-Guillaume Roque died on 3 May 1840. On the eve of his death Bishop Lartigue had come to see him and asked him to remember "himself and his diocese" in prayers. After Roque's death his former pupils decided to wear mourning for a month. They all recognized his great saintliness and several of them, including Lartigue, sought a piece of his cassock or a lock of hair. On 2 Feb. 1856 a young man from Montreal declared that he had been miraculously cured by a relic containing some of Roque's hair.

GILLES CHAUSSÉ

ACAM, 465.101, 901.025, 901.137. AD, Aveyron (Rodez), État civil, Belmont, 25 janv. 1761. ANQ-M, CE1-51, 5 mai 1840. Arch. du séminaire de Saint-Sulpice (Paris), Circulaires des supérieurs, I, Garnier Mollevault, 14 juin 1840; Fonds canadien, dossiers 73, 98–99, 111–14. ASSM, 1 bis, tiroir 4; 11, tiroir 47; 13, tiroir 50; 24, B; 27, tiroirs 93, 96; 49, tiroir 169. *Mélanges religieux*, 7 mai 1841. Allaire, *Dictionnaire*. F.-M. Bibaud, *Dict. hist.*; *Le panthéon canadien* (A. et V. Bibaud; 1891). [J.-]H. Gauthier, *Sulpitiana* ([2e éd.], Montréal, 1926). Louis Bertrand, *Bibliothèque sulpicienne ou histoire littéraire de la Compagnie de Saint-Sulpice* (3v., Paris, 1900), 2: 120–21. Chaussé, *Jean-Jacques Lartigue*. Dionne, *Les ecclésiastiques et les royalistes français*.

ROY, THOMAS, surveyor, engineer, author, and geologist; d. 28 July 1842 in Toronto.

It seems probable that Thomas Roy was born in the Miramichi valley in northern New Brunswick, a son of Scottish settlers. An 1810 report by one Thomas Roy, a surveyor of woods at St Peter's (Bathurst), N.B., bears a striking resemblance in its style and handwriting to reports prepared by the subject of this biography.

Roy arrived in Toronto in July 1834 and soon secured work inspecting the harbour. In September he was engaged as surveyor for Upper Canada's first railway project, the Simcoe and Ontario. Although he surveyed most of the route from Holland Landing to Toronto, financial difficulties postponed construction and resulted in his resignation in March 1836. In subsequent letters to William Henry Draper* (MHA for Toronto) and the city's council, Roy criticized the adoption of a new route, to Lake Huron, which bypassed Lake Simcoe and much of the hinterland north of Toronto.

In March 1835 he had applied for appointment as city engineer to report, with an engineer named by the lieutenant governor, on the state of the harbour. He won the position, and in his examination of the harbour was accompanied by Captain Richard Henry BONNYCASTLE (probably the government's appointee) and a "Mr. Call" (possibly James CULL). Roy was subsequently retained by the city to work on such projects as paving, drainage, and street lines. In its obituary, the Toronto *Examiner* said that he had "planned and carried into execution the various public improvements which have raised this city to its present state of prosperity."

Roy's sound knowledge of engineering, along with an indication of his road and sewer work, is demonstrated in his *Remarks on the principles and practice of road-making, as applicable to Canada*, published in Toronto in 1841 and a truly remarkable work. Many of his observations, notably on drainage, have relevance today. He was critical, as were other engineers, of the costly decision to rebuild Yonge Street in a straight line. He was aware, too, of the problems with planked-road construction, then widely used in the Canadas, and hoped that the "present mania for plank roads may be arrested before it produces so much evil." He even suggested educational standards for those responsible for road design and construction. Roy supported the contention of Cull, Bonnycastle, and others that macadamization would prove less expensive than planking; in 1842 he prepared an estimate for macadamizing part of Bay Street in Toronto. But like Cull, he failed to comprehend that the province could not yet afford a system of macadamized roads.

Concurrent with Roy's work as an engineer were his pioneering geological studies. His railway survey had apparently introduced him to the succession of ridges north of Toronto, formed as the prehistoric shores of the predecessors of Lake Ontario. In addition to describing the ridges in lectures to the mechanics' institute in Toronto, he prepared a paper on them for the Geological Society of London. Presented on his behalf by Charles Lyell, a noted British geologist, the paper was discussed at meetings of the society on 22 March and 5 April 1837. According to the printed summary of the paper, it described the successive stages of the Great Lakes and included calculations of the rate and manner in which they drained to present-day levels. Roy's insightful study provided a benchmark for later Canadian geologists, including Arthur Philemon Coleman*.

Roy corresponded not only with Lyell but also with James Hall, of the geological survey of New York. His surviving letters to Hall, between 1838 and 1842, display his wide knowledge of the geology of British North America and the adjacent parts of the United States; as well, they reveal an acquaintance with England from travelling there. A geological map prepared by him consisted of a cross-section of the country from the "coal field of Pennsylvania through the Niagara District and the Home District to the Granite Rocks beyond Lake Simcoe." The map achieved some fame in Roy's lifetime and was known both to Lyell and to William Edmond Logan* who saw it in a legislative library. The work was apparently destroyed in one of the fires which plagued the early legislative buildings of Canada.

When Lyell first visited North America, Roy arranged the brief Canadian part of his trip in the spring of 1842. He met Lyell at Niagara Falls and later took him on a tour of the ridges north of Toronto. Lyell acknowledged Roy's help in his *Travels in North America*, but it was left to Bonnycastle, in *Canada and the Canadians, in 1846*, to pay due tribute to him: Roy was a "person little appreciated and less understood by the great ones of the earth at Toronto [unquestionably a reference to Logan and his colleagues], and no one has done him even a shadow of justice, but Mr. Lyell, who, having no colonial dependence, had no fears in so doing." Thomas Roy died on 28 July 1842; although he had married, it is uncertain whether he had any children.

ROBERT F. LEGGET

Thomas Roy's article "On the ancient state of the North American continent" appeared in the Geological Soc. of London, *Proc.*, 2 (1833–38): 537–38.

AO, RG 1, A-I-6: 17241–44. CTA, RG 1, B, 1835, 1837, 1841–42. R. H. Bonnycastle, *Canada and the Canadians, in 1846* (2v., London, 1846), 1: 186–87. Charles Lyell, *Travels in North America, in the years 1841–42; with geological observations on the United States, Canada, and Nova Scotia* (2v., New York, 1845), 2: 85. *British Colonist*, 10 Aug. 1842. *Examiner* (Toronto), 17 Aug. 1842. *Toronto directory*, 1837. F. H. Armstrong, "Toronto's first railway venture, 1834–1838," *OH*, 58 (1966): 21–41. A. P. Coleman, "The Iroquois Beach," Canadian Institute, *Trans.* (Toronto), ser.4, 6 (1898–99): 29–44. M. S. Cross, "The stormy history of the York roads, 1833–1865," *OH*, 54 (1962): 1–24. [G. R. Gilbert], ["Old shore lines in the Ontario basin"], Canadian Institute, *Proc.* (Toronto), ser.3, 6 (1887–88): 2–4. R. F. Legget, "An early treatise on road making; Thomas Roy – an unsung hero of early Canadian engineering," "Thomas Roy: an early builder of Toronto," and "Railway survey conflicts cause 'mystery' engineer to resign," *Canadian Consulting Engineer* (Don Mills [Toronto]), 15 (1973), no.11: 36, 38; no.12: 48–49; 21 (1979), no.2: 44–47.

ROY-AUDY, JEAN-BAPTISTE, woodworker and painter; b. 15 Nov. 1778 at Quebec, son of Jean-Baptiste Roy-Audy, a woodworker, and Marguerite Gauvreau; d. probably around the beginning of 1848 in or near Trois-Rivières, Lower Canada.

Jean-Baptiste Roy-Audy was baptized in the cathedral of Notre-Dame at Quebec the day after he was born. Less than a year later his mother died, and he spent his childhood with his father in their house on Rue Saint-Georges (Rue Hébert) and with his uncle Pierre Audy. After some elementary studies he went into his father's shop, where he did the accounting while learning to work with wood. In the course of his apprenticeship he took drawing lessons from François Baillairgé*. There were ties of friendship linking the two families; in 1811 François and Pierre-Florent* Baillairgé would witness his father's death certificate.

By 1800 Roy-Audy had become a skilled worker whose reputation extended beyond his Quebec clientele. That year he built an organ case for the *fabrique* of Notre-Dame in Montreal. In March 1802 he opened a woodworking shop in his father's house and there he also painted some signs and did some lettering. On 27 July he married Julie Vézina, and they took up residence on Rue Saint-Georges, where they lived until 1808.

Roy-Audy was branching out in his professional occupations. In 1807 he offered his services as woodworker, cabinet-maker, and wheelwright, advising that he could paint, varnish, and add coats of arms to carriages he built. When contracting a promissory note in 1809 he termed himself a painter. Professional artists of the period usually called themselves "historical and portrait painters," and Roy-Audy can hardly be said to have such a career at this time. But it becomes increasingly evident that he was progressing from simple carpentry to delicate and precise work. By 1818 he had abandoned his labour as a craftsman to launch into an artistic career. There were several factors behind the change: the sale of his assets at auction in 1816 because of financial difficulties, the arrival in 1817 of Philippe-Jean-Louis Desjardins*'s collection of paintings, which would serve as models and as objects for restoration, the beginnings of a market for paintings, and his own artistic talents.

Settling at Saint-Augustin-de-Desmaures, west of Quebec, for the years 1818–24, Roy-Audy finished his training by copying pictures. He did only a few portraits, those of Abbé François-Joseph Deguise (around 1821), Maximilien Globensky* and his wife (1823), and the former governor, the late Sir George Prevost* (1824), amongst them. He concentrated on religious paintings for the churches in Saint-Augustin-de-Desmaures, Varennes, Boucherville (1814–24), Longueuil (1820–22), Rivière-du-Loup (Louiseville) (1820), Deschambault (1820–21), Lotbinière (1820–23), and Saint-Roch-de-l'Achigan (1822).

In 1824 Roy-Audy returned to Quebec. Although

he advertised in the newspapers, his business was poor. By 1828 he was back in his refuge at Saint-Augustin-de-Desmaures, and then he went to Montreal. In 1831 he did two paintings for the church at Longueuil. It was during this period that Roy-Audy really began producing portraits, with one of himself and another of archpriest R. Fréchette in 1826. In response to market demand he copied those of famous men and did original paintings. His best-known works include portraits of future bishop Rémi Gaulin* (1831), Abbé Jacques-Guillaume ROQUE (1836?), and future archbishop François-Norbert Blanchet (1838). The last portraits bearing his signature that have been found date from 1838.

Roy-Audy's subsequent life and career are shrouded in mystery. He seems to have died around the beginning of 1848 leaving no traces. At that time academic art was invading Lower Canada, and self-taught painters such as Roy-Audy had fallen almost wholly out of favour with the public, despite the vigour of their artistic expression.

Jean-Baptiste Roy-Audy's art was above all naïve, and therein lies its interest. The artist did not master all the techniques of painting, such as perspective, anatomy, foreshortening, and composition. Some of these technical problems obviously diminished when he was doing copies, which constitute the greater part of his religious production. But in portraiture he had to rely solely on his own talent. His instinct as a naïve painter led him to search for the spirit of his subjects and, guided by his elementary sense as a craftsman, he was able, despite his limited technical means, to seize their underlying personality with considerable success.

MICHEL CAUCHON

ANQ-Q, CE1-1, 16 nov. 1778, 15 juill. 1779, 25 juill. 1802, 9 janv. 1811; CN1-16, 21 févr. 1809; CN1-253, 1er août 1824. AP, Notre-Dame de Montréal, boîte 1800, 1.5–6; Saint-Antoine (Longueuil), livres de comptes, 2: f.57. Arch. du monastère des ursulines (Québec), Fonds L.-J. Desjardins. MAC-CD, Fonds Morisset, 2, dossiers François Baillairgé, J.-B. Roy-Audy. *Quebec Gazette*, 25 March 1802; 14 May, 4 June 1807; 25 April 1816. Michel Cauchon, *Jean-Baptiste Roy-Audy, 1778–c.1848* (Québec, 1971).

ROY PORTELANCE, LOUIS (he also signed **Roi**, **Roy**, and **Roi Portelance**), merchant, politician, and militia officer; b. 16 Oct. 1764 in Saint-Joachim parish (at Pointe-Claire), Que., son of Joseph Roy, *dit* Portelance, and Catherine Mallet; d. 2 March 1838 in Kamouraska, Lower Canada.

Louis Roy Portelance was the son of a farm labourer from Lachine on Montreal Island who had married a young widow from Pointe-Claire. He studied at the Collège Saint-Raphaël in Montreal from 1778 till 1784, and subsequently signed up as a voyageur in the fur trade. When on 7 Sept. 1791 he married his first cousin Marie-Josephte Périnault at Notre-Dame church in Montreal, he was 26 and a resident of that town. The bride, aged 31, already had three sons from her marriage to Jacques Varin*, *dit* La Pistole, a Montreal silversmith who had died in January of that year; the eldest, Jacques, then almost 14, attended the wedding. On 2 May 1792 Roy Portelance became the father of a daughter, Sophie, the only one of his children who would reach adulthood, and it was she who on 10 Jan. 1814 married Montreal merchant Frederick Glackmeyer, son of Quebec musician Frederick GLACKEMEYER.

Roy Portelance became a lumber merchant shortly after his marriage. He set up in business on Rue du Saint-Sacrement, between Rue Saint-Éloy (Saint-Éloi) and Rue Saint-Nicolas, on lots he had purchased when the property in the dissolved communal estate of his wife and her first husband was sold. He also purchased an orchard in the *faubourg* Saint-Antoine and bought his father's land at Lachine in return for a life annuity paid to his parents. Subsequently he acquired two more properties in town, one on Rue du Saint-Sacrement, the other on Rue Saint-Pierre, which he rented to merchants and schoolmasters.

Roy Portelance's main commercial outlet was the Montreal market. No trace of transactions for exporting lumber has been found in the notarized deeds. He profited from Montreal's growth in population at the turn of the century, supplying boards and planks to numerous woodworkers, carpenters, and entrepreneurs in the town and its suburbs. Among his customers was a major building contractor, Charles-Simon DELORME. Roy Portelance obtained part of his wood from his brother Jacques, who owned a sawmill at Saint-Régis and every spring sent him some cribs (small rafts made of tree trunks, boards, and planks), each worth nearly 1,000 *livres*.

By now quite prosperous, Roy Portelance was one of the local élite in the early years of the 19th century. Respected by his fellow citizens, he sat in the House of Assembly for Montreal from 1804 till 1815, and then for Montreal East from 1816 till 1820. In the 1804 elections he obtained 1,183 votes, the other candidates, Benjamin Joseph Frobisher* and Denis-Benjamin Viger*, receiving respectively only 769 and 445. During the War of 1812, like a number of the assemblymen, he served as an officer in the militia of his riding. He received a captain's commission in Montreal's 2nd Militia Battalion on 3 April 1812 and later he was promoted major and lieutenant-colonel.

On 4 Sept. 1809 Roy Portelance, who had been widowed on 6 Jan. 1808, was married again at Quebec, to which town his parliamentary duties took him. His marriage in the cathedral of Notre-Dame to Louise Languedoc, daughter of a Quebec merchant and sister of François LANGUEDOC, was solemnized by his stepson Jacques Varin, then parish priest in Terrebonne. Three children born to the couple would reach adulthood. Mme Roy Portelance died in 1818 at 33, following childbirth.

As an assemblyman Roy Portelance worked on various committees. He was a member, for example, of committees on the regulation of the export trade in lumber, the establishment of a new market-place in Montreal, the construction of a bridge from Île Jésus to Montreal Island, and the preservation of the orchards in Notre-Dame parish in Montreal. In voting, he sided with the Canadian party on most issues. For example, he supported the resolutions to finance prisons through customs duties in 1805 [*see* Ignace-Michel-Louis-Antoine d'Irumberry* de Salaberry] and to render judges ineligible to sit in the assembly in 1808 [*see* Sir James Henry Craig*; Pierre-Amable De Bonne*]. In the 1830s advanced age prevented him from being active in political matters. He remained sympathetic to Louis-Joseph Papineau*'s cause, however. When the radicals succeeded in expelling Dominique Mondelet* from the house because he had accepted appointment to the Executive Council, Roy Portelance was urged to stand for election in Montreal. But nothing came of the idea, since Governor Lord Aylmer [WHITWORTH-AYLMER] refused to consider Mondelet's seat vacant. On 15 May 1837 Roy Portelance agreed to preside at a meeting of the residents of Montreal County to protest the British government's coercive measures [*see* Chevalier de LORIMIER].

Roy Portelance had probably quit the lumber business some time in the 1820s, content to live on his income. On 12 Feb. 1835, however, he joined some merchants loyal to the Patriote party in forming the partnership of Viger, De Witt et Compagnie, which would also be known as the Banque du Peuple [*see* Louis-Michel Viger*; Jacob De Witt*]. In the autumn of 1837 Roy Portelance left Montreal and went to live with Jacques Varin, who was now the parish priest of Saint-Louis at Kamouraska. He died there suddenly on 2 March 1838, aged 73, and was buried in the parish church on 5 March in the presence of politicians Jean-Baptiste Taché, Joseph Robitaille, and Amable Dionne*.

Louis Roy Portelance seems to have been quite an important Montreal merchant in the early 19th century. Esteemed by his fellow citizens, he adopted the ideas of reform held by many in the French Canadian bourgeoisie of the time. His political activity remained limited, however, probably because of his advanced age when the crisis of the 1830s reached its dénouement.

LISE ST-GEORGES

ANQ-M, CE1-2, 13 juill. 1840; CE1-37, 17 oct. 1764; CE1-51, 7 sept. 1791, 2 mai 1792, 14 sept. 1794, 29 juill. 1797, 7 janv. 1808, 10 janv. 1814, 9 juill. 1818, 29 sept. 1829, 7 août 1832, 21 janv. 1834, 17 sept. 1838; CN1-74, 30 août, 25 sept. 1798; CN1-134, 1824–35; CN1-194, 25 oct. 1808; CN1-202, 17 oct. 1760; CN1-270, 1824–35; CN1-305, 1824–35; CN1-313, 7 mars 1809; CN1-320, 1824–35. ANQ-Q, CE1-1, 4 sept. 1809; CE3-3, 5 mars 1838; CN1-230, 3 sept. 1809. PAC, MG 24, B2: 1607–9. *La Minerve*, 18 févr. 1835; 8, 18 mai 1837. Allaire, *Dictionnaire*, 530. F.-J. Audet, *Les députés de Montréal*, 360–63; "Les législateurs du Bas-Canada." Caron, "Inv. de la corr. de Mgr Hubert et de Mgr Bailly de Messein," ANQ *Rapport*, 1930–31: 250. Desjardins, *Guide parl.*, 133–34. Archange Godbout, "Nos ancêtres au XVIIe siècle," ANQ *Rapport*, 1951–53: 481. *Officers of British forces in Canada* (Irving), 167. Léon Pouliot, "Inventaire analytique de la correspondance de Mgr Ignace Bourget pour l'année 1846," ANQ *Rapport*, 1965: 103. Turcotte, *Le Conseil législatif*, 240. R. S. Greenfield, "La Banque du peuple, 1835–1871, and its failure, 1895" (MA thesis, McGill Univ., Montreal, 1968). Rumilly, *Hist. de Montréal*, 2: 116. Sulte, *Hist. de la milice*, 28. J. [E.] Hare, "L'Assemblée législative du Bas-Canada, 1792–1814: députation et polarisation politique," *RHAF*, 27 (1973–74): 379–80. J.-J. Lefebvre, "La vie sociale du grand Papineau," *RHAF*, 11 (1957–58): 479. É.-Z. Massicotte, "Louis Roy, dit Portelance, député de Montréal de 1804 à 1820," *BRH*, 32 (1926): 169. P.-G. Roy, "La famille Glackemeyer," *BRH*, 22 (1916): 202–3. J.-P. Wallot, "La querelle des prisons (Bas-Canada, 1805–1807)," *RHAF*, 14 (1960–61): 69–70, 262, 265, 267–68.

RYAN, JOHN, printer, newspaperman, office holder, and merchant; b. probably on 7 Oct. 1761 in Newport, R.I.; m. 25 June 1780 Amelia Mott, daughter of John Mott of Long Island, N.Y., and they had eight children; d. 30 Sept. 1847 in St John's.

From his youth, as he would later declare, John Ryan "religiously adhered to his Allegiance" to the British crown. At Newport in the late 1770s he was apprenticed to the loyalist printer John Howe*. Ryan's activities during the American Revolutionary War are obscure, but on the evacuation of Rhode Island in 1779 he accompanied the British army to New York and remained there until 1783. In August 1783 he was co-editor with William Lewis* of the *New-York Mercury; or, General Advertiser*. Ryan arrived on the Saint John River about 17 October as a member of a refugee militia company of loyalists, of which Lewis was captain. With him were his wife, one child, and a servant. He received jointly with Lewis a grant of land in the settlement of Parrtown at the mouth of the river. (In 1785 Parrtown and Carleton were united under the name Saint John.)

It was in Carleton, on or about 18 Dec. 1783, that Lewis and Ryan published the first number of the *Royal St. John's Gazette, and Nova-Scotia Intelligencer*, the earliest newspaper in what is now New Brunswick. The paper quickly began exposing the favouritism and incompetence displayed in the distribution of land to loyalists, and fell into official disfavour. In March 1784 the two printers were indicted by a grand jury for libel. It is possible that the paper's fiery rhetoric was supplied mainly by Lewis, since Ryan gave little indication in his subsequent career of an inclination to criticize officials or governments. He did, however, sign the "Huggeford Petition" of 24 Dec. 1784, an elaborate statement of loyalist grievances addressed to Governor Thomas Carleton*.

For nearly two years Lewis and Ryan had the only newspaper and printing-press in the community. In October 1785 Christopher Sower*, another loyalist and the newly appointed king's printer, began the *Royal Gazette and the New-Brunswick Advertiser*, thus forcing Lewis and Ryan to drop "Royal" from the name of their paper. The loss of official printing to their rival at the *Royal Gazette* may have had the effect of sharpening the anti-government tendency of Lewis's and Ryan's paper, and in May 1786 the two printers found themselves once again charged with libel, this time before the Supreme Court of New Brunswick. They were convicted and fined. Earlier in 1786 the partnership between Lewis and Ryan had been dissolved, and the business was left in Ryan's hands. He remained as publisher of what was now the *St. John Gazette, and Weekly Advertiser* until 1799, when he replaced Sower as king's printer and acquired the *Royal Gazette*. Ryan sold the *St. John Gazette* to his brother-in-law, Jacob S. Mott*.

In 1806 Ryan went to Newfoundland, leaving the *Royal Gazette* in the hands of his partner William Durant, who had been his apprentice. On 22 September he was given permission by Governor Sir Erasmus Gower* to establish a printing-office and weekly newspaper in St John's. (Two weeks earlier Gower had authorized Walter Charles Davids, a visiting actor, to set up a printing-office, but Davids had not done so.) Ryan was recommended to the governor by the magistrates and merchants of St John's as "a person of good and respectable character." In a move that showed the extent of the governor's arbitrary power in Newfoundland, Gower imposed the condition that Ryan give bond in the Court of Sessions for £200, "with good securities, that previously to the printing of each number of the said Paper, he shall submit the perusal of the proposed contents thereof, to the Magistrates . . . and not insert in the said Paper any matter which, in their opinion or the opinion of the Governor for the time being, may tend to disturb the peace of His Majesty's Subjects." Governor John Holloway*, a year later, further specified that Ryan "not suffer to be inserted in his paper any Paragraph or Extracts from other papers, which indicated any thing inflammatory against the Government of Great Britain, or its dependencies, or any paragraph which may tend to sow dissention among the inhabitants of this Island, and never to give, or suffer any opinion to be given upon the policy of other Nations." Under these restrictions the press, albeit a fettered one, was inaugurated in Newfoundland. The first number of the *Royal Gazette and Newfoundland Advertiser* was published by Ryan and his son Michael on or about 27 Aug. 1807. It displayed the royal coat of arms on the mast-head and its motto was: "Fear God: Honor the King." In the prospectus "John Ryan & Son" promised that their paper would never "offend the Ear of delicacy or distress the heart of Sensibility; its columns will never be occupied by party controversy." Ryan by 1810 was styling himself "Printer to the King's Most Excellent Majesty," though there was no official appointment as king's printer and no salary.

The *Royal Gazette* was a single sheet, folded to form four pages. The paper appeared every Thursday until 1816, when it moved to Tuesday to gain an advantage over a competitor. On occasion there were "Extraordinary" issues on days other than the normal one, and supplements. A carrier delivered the paper around St John's. Circulation was modest. Its contents were notices and proclamations from government offices, mercantile advertisements, "intelligence" reprinted from British and foreign papers, parliamentary and congressional proceedings, and local news. Rudimentary illustrations occasionally were provided in advertisements. The back page sometimes featured a "Poet's corner" and entertainment such as anecdotes and short essays. Perhaps not surprisingly in view of Holloway's strictures, there was virtually no editorial comment in the paper's early years. It tended to be a dry assemblage of advertisements and notices, reflecting a milieu more concerned with merchandise and shipping than with politics. Nevertheless, the appearance of a newspaper in St John's was of great importance, since it provided an organ for public debate – though it was admittedly little used for this purpose – and alerted the city's emerging middle class to developments in neighbouring colonies. It was readily apparent from the *Royal Gazette* how far Newfoundland lagged behind the Canadas, Nova Scotia, New Brunswick, and even Prince Edward Island in terms of the progress of representative institutions. Once the paper appeared, agitation for a legislature, and for other reforms, was sure to follow.

In addition to issuing the *Royal Gazette*, Ryan's office supplied the other printing needs of the local merchants and government. He printed government proclamations, for example, and maintained a stock of insurance policies, indentures, bills of lading, bills of exchange, mates' and carpenters' protections, shipping papers, and similar forms for the trade. Undoubtedly most of these came from his own press. As early as 1807 he printed two pamphlets for the Benevolent Irish Society in St John's, but he undertook little in this line. He also functioned as a stationer, selling a great variety of imported writing paper, message- and visiting-cards, ledgers, journals, calendars, almanacs, prayer-, hymn-, and school-books, quills and portable pens, ink, slates, and much more. In addition, he sometimes offered for sale items such as shingles, pork, chocolate, chairs, and lumber. Though a printer, Ryan apparently kept an alert eye on the general requirements of the market-place.

The period 1807–14 was marked by expansion in the Newfoundland economy, and Ryan seems to have prospered. The "most sedulous attention to his duty as Editor," he observed in his sober way in 1813, "has been rewarded by a steady encouragement." In October 1809 he was given permission by Holloway to build a printing-office and stationer's shop. The following year his son Michael, who had founded unsuccessful newspapers in Saint John and Fredericton prior to coming to Newfoundland, and who by 1810 was no longer connected with the *Royal Gazette*, requested permission to start a second paper in St John's. It was to be called the "Commercial Register." The request, which was turned down by Governor Sir John Thomas Duckworth*, was probably a sign that Ryan was encouraging his offspring to enter a promising local trade. Duckworth's rejection drove Michael Ryan to Barbados. By 1813 Alexander Haire and Robert Lee had, with the permission of Governor Sir Richard Goodwin Keats*, established a second press in the city and were printing materials such as shipping papers and handbills. In October they made a formal request to issue a newspaper the following spring; Keats refused to grant it. On hearing of their application, Ryan had requested either that no second paper be allowed or, if it were, that his son Lewis Kelly Ryan be given authorization to operate it.

Early in 1814 the crown lawyers in London made a key decision on freedom of expression in Newfoundland. They advised that the governor did not have the power to restrain a person from setting up a printing-press or newspaper. On or about 2 Sept. 1815 Haire and Lee began publishing the *Newfoundland Mercantile Journal*, a twice-weekly newspaper that in fact represents the beginning of a free press in Newfoundland. Writing in its columns, reformer William Carson soon pointed out that the *Royal Gazette* was not free; subjects such as "magisterial delinquency, or clerical imposition" could not be taken up in Ryan's paper. Lewis Kelly Ryan replied that in editing the *Royal Gazette* his father "never considered himself bound by any other restriction, than what *his own* prudence might suggest, and his *situation* as Printer to his Majesty imposed upon him." But in fact John Ryan himself once complained, in 1813, that the "restrictions and regulations" under which he conducted the paper were such as to deprive him of "the multiplied benefits of a free press." The fact that the *Royal Gazette* continued, after restrictions on the press were lifted in 1814, to be in essence the mouthpiece of the government shows, however, that Ryan was also well aware of the advantages of close ties to the ruling establishment. On the appearance of the *Mercantile Journal* and other papers, Ryan none the less had to share government business with his rivals.

In February 1814 Ryan announced that he was leaving Newfoundland for New Brunswick, and from March 10 of that year until 13 Jan. 1818 the *Royal Gazette* was printed and published by Lewis Kelly Ryan for his father. John Ryan apparently went to the neighbouring colony to close out his concerns there. In 1814 and 1815 he was in Saint John calling in debts and advertising the dissolution of his partnership with Durant. He may well have had arrangements to conclude with other firms. How soon he returned to Newfoundland is unclear. Perhaps he came back on learning of the disastrous fire in St John's on 12 Feb. 1816, in which his printing-office was "wholly destroyed"; or after the fire of 7 Nov. 1817, in which the "major part" of his establishment was once again burnt. (The offices of the *Royal Gazette* would be wholly or partially consumed by fire on five occasions between 1816 and 1846.) Shortly after John Ryan resumed the editorship of the paper, Lewis Kelly Ryan began publishing the *Newfoundland Sentinel, and General Commercial Register*, the earliest journal in Newfoundland to be dedicated to reform. The paper, the first number of which appeared on or about 4 July 1818, survives in only one issue. Reformer Robert John Parsons* would later describe it as "a Journal bold, daring, and formidable to misgovernment." It lasted until 1822 and was published out of the *Royal Gazette* office.

There is a gap in the file of the *Royal Gazette* between 1818 and 1828, though occasional numbers survive. By the latter date, the state of local journalism had considerably altered. The *Mercantile Journal* as well as the *Sentinel* had disappeared, to be replaced by the *Public Ledger*, which dates from 1820, and the *Newfoundlander*, which commenced 4 July 1827. A newspaper had appeared also in Conception Bay, the *Harbor Grace and Carbonear Weekly Journal, and General Advertiser for Conception Bay*, which published its first number at Harbour Grace on 6 Aug. 1828. (A second Conception Bay paper came out in 1829.) As journalism became more lively and competitive in Newfoundland, the role of Ryan's paper as the dull, official gazetteer, staying aloof from the clamour of partisan and sectarian debate, choosing rather "to record than to advise," became more pronounced. But there were signs even from the mid 1820s that the advance of reform did not meet with his approval. These signs culminated in a highly unusual editorial on 28 Sept. 1830, in which Ryan (if indeed it was Ryan – John Collier Withers had by this date a large role in conducting the paper) came out against a legislature for Newfoundland. The colony, it was stated, "has not yet attained sufficient ripeness to legislate for itself." In response to those who pointed to the advantages the neighbouring colonies had received from a representative government, the editor, who seemed to know whereof he wrote, noted that "not a word had been said of the bickerings, the heart-burnings, the rancorous feelings of ill-will, which has marked the frequent struggles of the different branches of the Legislatures, and of the parties to which they gave rise." He was able to show how little had been accomplished by the legislature in Prince Edward Island, despite that colony's manifest advantages. And he pointed to the powerlessness of any local body to effect a change in such critical matters as the French and American fishing rights on the Newfoundland coast. The editorial contains perhaps the most cogent series of arguments presented at the time against representative government. The day was, of course, long past when such arguments could be effective, and liberal opinion had given up taking the *Royal Gazette*'s "balderdash" seriously.

Ryan's family life was marked by tragedy. Two of his sons, Michael and Lewis Kelly, perished at sea, in separate incidents in the 1820s, on their way to the West Indies. Lewis Kelly's sudden departure from St John's in 1821 was made, it seems, to avoid a court appearance in which he was to face a criminal charge for libel. A third son, who gave "essential service" in the printing-office, died at 17 of injuries sustained in coasting down a hill, and a fourth died while on a visit to his brother Michael in Barbados. In May 1832 Ryan's wife Amelia died. Before the year was out Ryan had formed a partnership with his employee John Collier Withers to continue the publication of the *Royal Gazette*. It is apparent that Ryan's active participation in the printing business had ended by 1832. Writing in 1847, Withers noted that he had, jointly with Ryan, "held the appointment of Queen's Printer for the last 15 years, – during which period, (the infirmities of advanced age having prevented Mr. Ryan from assisting therein in any manner) the duties of the office have solely devolved upon me." Ryan died in 1847 "after a protracted and painful illness."

John Ryan was one of Canada's pioneering printers and newspaper proprietors. He has been credited with establishing an "independent tradition" in New Brunswick journalism; and in Newfoundland his *Royal Gazette* brought to the attention of a remote and backward colony developments in the great world beyond its headlands. At his death he was described, not without reason, as "the father of the Press in British North America."

PATRICK O'FLAHERTY

[The most important sources of information about John Ryan are his own newspapers, especially the *Royal Gazette and Newfoundland Advertiser*. The file of this paper, which began in 1807, is incomplete: the available years, up to Ryan's death, are 1810–18 (with a large gap in the year 1816) and 1828–47. The *Newfoundland Mercantile Journal* for 1816–27, and other newspapers such as the *Public Ledger* and the *Newfoundland Patriot*, provide additional information. Ryan's New Brunswick career and his activities as a printer prior to coming to that colony have not been studied. However, the following are important secondary sources: D. G. Bell, *Early loyalist Saint John: the origin of New Brunswick politics, 1783–1786* (Fredericton, 1983); J. R. Harper, *Historical directory of New Brunswick newspapers and periodicals* (Fredericton, 1961); and T. M. Barnes, *Loyalist newspapers of the American revolution, 1763–1783: a bibliography* (Worcester, Mass., 1974). P.O'F.]

Cathedral of St John the Baptist (Anglican) (St John's), Reg. of baptisms, marriages, and burials (mfm. at PANL). PANB, MC 1316, J. R. Harper, "Christopher Sower, 1754–1799"; RG 5, RS42. PANL, GN 2/1/A, 1806–47; GN 2/2, 1826–47. PRO, CO 194/45–127. Saint John Regional Library (Saint John, N.B.), "Ward scrapbook of early printers and newspapers of New Brunswick," vol.3 (mfm. at PANB). J. R. Harper, "Christopher Sower, king's printer and loyalist," N.B. Hist. Soc., *Coll.*, no.14 (1955): 67–109.

RYLAND, HERMAN WITSIUS, office holder and JP; b. *c.* 1759, probably in Northampton or Warwick, Warwickshire, England, second son of John Collett Ryland and Elizabeth Frith; d. 20 July 1838 in Beauport, Lower Canada.

Herman Witsius Ryland no doubt received his early education from his father, a Baptist minister and teacher who later became a prominent educator. Young Ryland subsequently trained for the army and was appointed assistant deputy paymaster general to the British forces in North America. He arrived at New York in the fall of 1781 during the American Revolutionary War and was detached to the captured British troops in Lancaster, Pa. He fulfilled his duties competently and at the end of the war returned to England with the commander-in-chief, Sir Guy Carleton*.

Apparently discharged, Ryland spent nearly a decade in search of another position until Carleton, now Lord Dorchester and governor of Lower Canada, chose him as his civil secretary in 1793; he arrived at Quebec with Dorchester on 24 September. His duties included the issuing of letters patent and commissions and the maintenance of the governor's correspondence. Britain being at war with France, he also kept copies of all documents relating to French intrigues in Lower Canada. The post was, as he claimed, "of as great a Trust as any in the colony." With a salary of £200, he was able to bring to Quebec his fiancée of 10 years, an Englishwoman named Charlotte Warwick, whom he married about 26 Dec. 1794. They would have nine children, of whom only four would survive Ryland.

When Dorchester returned to England in 1796,

Ryland was pressed to remain as secretary to the new governor, Robert Prescott*. As an inducement, he was made clerk of the Executive Council in succession to Jenkin Williams* with a salary of £100 and income from fees. In this position he registered orders-in-council, wrote warrants for payment of expenses, filed petitions, and prepared the public accounts. He quickly impressed the governor. A dispute arose between the two over a private matter, however, and Ryland resigned as secretary in May 1798, took leave of absence as clerk of the Executive Council, and, with his family, left for England in June to search for "a more eligible Provision." His ship was captured by French revolutionary privateers, some of whom were taken prisoner when it was recaptured by a British vessel. In England Ryland successfully urged humane treatment for them and their exchange for British prisoners John Black* and Henry Cull*.

Supplied with information by Quebec merchant John Young*, Ryland worked in London for the recall of Prescott, who was engaged in an embarrassing public squabble with members of the Executive Council over the administration of crown lands. Ryland believed his actions effective, and indeed in 1799 Prescott was replaced in the administration of the colony by Lieutenant Governor Robert Shore MILNES. The colonial secretary, Lord Portland, urged Ryland to return to Quebec as Milnes's civil secretary, using for persuasion the promise of an income of £1,000 per annum, to be attained in several steps. As a start Ryland's salary as clerk of the Executive Council was raised to £400.

Ryland arrived back at Quebec in early July 1799 and immediately established the most cordial professional and personal relations with Milnes. As well, he re-established his excellent rapport with Anglican bishop Jacob Mountain*, the two men sharing certain preoccupations in religious matters. For Ryland, as for most public men of the time, religion had important political ramifications. "In a political point of view it is immaterial whether the mass of the People be Protestants or Papists, provided the Crown is in full possession of the Patronage of the Church," he believed, "but a House of Assembly composed of Men differing in Religion language and manners from those of the Parent State is the most powerful engine of mischief that can be devised in a conquered Province . . . unless counterbalanced by an adequate influence and authority on the part of the Crown." Ryland was not, however, indifferent to Catholicism, "a religion which sinks and debases the human mind." Indeed he established as a personal objective "gradually to undermine the authority and influence of the Roman Catholic Priest." He therefore urged Mountain to insist that the government place the Church of England on a prestigious basis in order to give the bishop weight "in the eyes of French Canadians who are accustomed to see . . . shew and splendour." (Privately, however, this Baptist by birth and upbringing envisaged for the "Protestant Church establishment . . . as much *splendour* and as little *power* as possible.") Meanwhile, he felt, priests should be licensed; this done, "the King's Supremacy would be established, the authority of the Pope would be abolished, the country would become Protestant."

To reduce Roman Catholic clerical influence, Ryland promoted state-controlled education, and he supported the establishment of the Royal Institution for the Advancement of Learning [*see* Joseph Langley Mills*]. He advocated founding a college at or near Quebec, "under the eye of Government," in which the classical subjects, but not theology, would be taught. The educational system would be financed by the consolidated revenues from the Jesuit estates, already in government hands, and the Sulpician estates, the appropriation of which, on "generous" terms to the clergy, was "pregnant with . . . extensive Consequences." In July 1805 many of Ryland's views, shared by Mountain and Attorney General Jonathan SEWELL, found their way into a dispatch by Milnes to the colonial secretary, Lord Camden, on the political state of the colony.

With the assistance of Milnes and Lord Spencer, Ryland gradually obtained fulfilment of Portland's salary commitment to him. In 1802 Milnes appointed him clerk of the crown in chancery to succeed Hugh Finlay* at a salary of £100, and in 1804 he was awarded a pension of £300 per annum. Milnes departed the following year, taking with him a petition to the king from Roman Catholic bishop Pierre Denaut* requesting legal recognition of the bishop of Quebec. The petition represented a tactical victory for the colony's English party, of which Ryland had become a leading figure, it being presumed that the petition would be granted only in return for concessions, notably the licensing of priests. Denaut died in January 1806, and Ryland saw in the acceptance of a successor and the appointment of a new coadjutor splendid opportunities for the government to pressure the hierarchy into making concessions. Despite strong protests on Ryland's part, however, the administrator of the colony, Thomas Dunn*, allowed the oaths of office to be taken by Joseph-Octave Plessis* as bishop, and by Bernard-Claude Panet* as coadjutor, without conditions. Ryland had come to see Plessis as a man of dangerous stature, diplomatic abilities, and independence of mind, while Panet was the brother of Jean-Antoine Panet*, speaker of the House of Assembly and a leader of the Canadian party. The coadjutor's appointment, Ryland feared, would increase Plessis's influence in the assembly and give the Canadian party, through the speaker, "the whole patronage of the Romish Church . . . and the prodigious influence attending it."

The assembly had only recently become an object of concern for Ryland, who, until the revolutionary scare of the mid 1790s [*see* Robert Prescott], had held moderately liberal political views. He rightly saw that body as attempting to assume unilaterally the privileges enjoyed by the British House of Commons. The most disquieting of these, Ryland felt, was "the high and dangerous Power of arrest, Fine and Imprisonment," which was used against newspaper editors Thomas Cary* and Edward Edwards* and Montreal businessman Isaac Todd* in 1805 for publicly criticizing the assembly. "Seeing myself, as I fear, for Ever cut off from my native Country, and my Children, in all probability destined to grow up Strangers to the happy land of their Forefathers," Ryland wrote to Lord Spencer in August 1806, "I cannot but anxiously wish that every wise and eligible Means may be adopted for binding this distant Colony as long as possible to the Parent State, for uniting their Interests by assimilating their Religion, Manners and Government, and for rendering this Scion as like as possible to the original Stock." Thus, although his views were diametrically opposed to those of the Canadian nationalists, he was motivated by the same considerations that preoccupied them: Lower Canada had become his home, and he wished to feel secure in the possession of it for himself and his descendants.

Ryland approved, therefore, of the union of the civil and military command of the colony under Lieutenant-General Sir James Henry Craig* in 1807. With the assistance of Mountain and Dunn, Ryland quickly ensured his continuance in the post of civil secretary under Craig, and there immediately sprang up between the two men an exceptional bond of friendship and a perfect meeting of minds on political matters. Ryland urged on Craig the need to reinforce, by the appointment of worthy Britons (as opposed to Canadian- or American-born colonists), both the Legislative Council, which he considered the first line of defence against assaults by the assembly on the royal prerogative, and the colonial judiciary. Having Craig's entire confidence, Ryland coordinated intelligence operations as war with the United States became imminent, receiving reports from secret agents John Henry* (mainly to Montreal businessman John Richardson*) and Daniel Sullivan, an American under-secretary.

After March 1810, when Craig found himself facing a full-blown crisis in his relations with the assembly, he turned to Ryland to justify in England the repressive measures he had taken and to obtain acceptance there for a wide range of proposals designed to increase executive influence and the British presence in the colony. In late July Ryland arrived in England with 16 dispatches for the colonial secretary, Lord Liverpool. After learning that the ministry was weak and that it feared offending the Canadian majority, he set himself to gauging "the particular sentiments and relative strength of the parties in and out of power" and to arranging lobbies by influential British merchants trading to the Canadas. His energetic and resourceful efforts notwithstanding, the mission bogged down as the British government became paralysed with its own concerns. Liverpool refused to risk the House of Commons on any of Craig's proposals requiring legislative action, such as reunion of the Canadas.

In 1811 Ryland began to push for two measures that required only a ministerial directive to the governor, namely the appropriation of the Sulpician estates and government appointment to Roman Catholic cures. By dint of "a reasonable share of impudence and perseverence," he succeeded in early April in having the two points referred to the law officers of the crown. Three months later they responded: the crown had the right to take both actions. Their opinion, however, was strongly qualified; a "sort of possessory title" had been for so long left to the church, they asserted, that only by "compromise or amicable arrangement" should the crown attempt to recover its rights.

This opinion Ryland transmitted to Sir George Prevost*, who succeeded to the administration of Lower Canada in September 1811 and who had agreed, under pressure from Liverpool, to retain Ryland's services as civil secretary. Despite a lengthy stay in England, Ryland had decided that, given his age and large family, he must return to the colony: the very number of his positions there precluded all idea of exchanging to advantage. Indeed, Craig had added to them. In January 1811 the governor had appointed him treasurer of the Jesuit estates commission at £150 per annum and in June he became secretary; Ryland had been a commissioner (an unremunerated post) since 1807. In addition, Craig had strongly urged Liverpool to name Ryland to the Legislative Council. The appointment, made in December 1811 without Prevost's knowledge, had been sought by Ryland for a number of years, in part to stiffen the council's resistance to the encroachments of the assembly, and in part as a precaution against loss of the civil secretaryship.

By "the very cold reception" his communications met with from Prevost, Ryland suspected long before he arrived back at Quebec in June 1812 that his position as secretary was threatened. He was already depressed by the failure of a mission that had cost him £1,900, and he now discovered that he had been effectually displaced by the interim secretary, Edward Brabazon BRENTON, and Brenton's assistant, Andrew William COCHRAN. The house allotted to him as secretary had been emptied of his belongings and given to Brenton, and his pew in the Cathedral of the Holy Trinity had been transferred to officers of the garrison. In the governor's office, Cochran remarked, Ryland became "a mere cypher . . . and after having been so long Prime Minister the change . . . [was] extremely galling." Prevost was publicly humiliating him, Ryland speculated, "to mark as decidedly as possible . . . [the governor's] determination to deviate in everything from the system of his predecessor." Not one to suffer insult meekly, Ryland refused to be pushed out of the secretaryship until, in April 1813, Prevost agreed to increase his salary and allowances as clerk of the Executive Council, enabling him to maintain his income and save face.

Prevost's "deviation" from Craig's system consisted in winning the support of the leaders of the Canadian party – notably Louis-Joseph Papineau* – and of Plessis and the Catholic clergy. On the other hand he ignored the English party, not even consulting Ryland about his mission. For Ryland, Prevost's policies merely encouraged the assembly to pursue its efforts to acquire all the powers exercised by the House of Commons. Seeking to base in theory his objection to the assembly's attempts, Ryland argued that the privileges of the Commons were not all applicable in the colony because they arose from immemorial usage in a specifically British context, that is, they were established by British common law. There might be "a Common Law with regard to the privileges of Provincial Legislatures" to be ascertained "from the practice in our former North American Provinces," but, if additional privileges were required by the provincial legislatures, "they ought to be established by . . . Statute." Curiously, Ryland's insistence on formal legislation had a Gallic flavour that contrasted with the quintessentially British approach of the Canadian party, which was attempting to proceed by informal precedent. The idea of a colonial common law never caught on among thinkers of the English party, probably because the American colonies, having revolted, constituted a reference of doubtful value, but the concept of the British constitution as the unexportable product, in its purest form, of a specific historical context was gaining popularity, as Robert-Anne d'Estimauville* was to show later. Ryland also opposed Prevost's courting of Plessis, who was "a tyrant to his clergy (though but the son of a blacksmith) and who in point of duplicity, bigotry and ambition has . . . never been surpassed!" Neither did Ryland, in common with the English party, approve Prevost's strictly defensive strategy in the War of 1812. "Surely it will sooner or later be found out," he reflected in May 1813, "that the wisest means of obtaining peace is to render war as distressing as possible to your enemy." It seems almost certain, therefore, that Ryland was among a small group of legislative and executive councillors, including Mountain, Young, and Pierre-Amable De Bonne*, that conspired in 1814 to have the governor recalled.

Since Ryland could no longer influence executive policy as civil secretary, the Legislative Council became his principal forum. From 1814 to 1831 he would attend nearly 80 per cent of its meetings, an exceptional record. Very quickly he became an acknowledged expert on procedures and privileges, and a watchdog of the council's interests *vis-à-vis* the assembly. This role made him a prime target at a time when, under the influence of James Stuart*, the assembly was pursuing a strategy of impeaching leading office holders opposed to its objectives, beginning with chief justices James Monk* and Sewell. In early 1815 it succeeded in trapping Ryland in a conflict of roles involving two of his offices. Summoned as clerk of the crown in chancery to explain to a committee of the assembly a technical irregularity in an election writ, Ryland was, as a legislative councillor, unable to do so without authorization from the council, which was adjourned. Ever resourceful, Ryland had Prevost replace his commission as clerk with a joint commission naming himself and one Thomas Douglas, whom he delegated to appear on his behalf. The assembly was ultimately constrained to admit defeat, but Ryland did not escape unscathed. A motion in the assembly to consider "the gross Faults and Neglects, and Malversations in Office" of which Ryland was accused in the committee's report was reprinted in the press. From this notoriety, Ryland complained to a confidant, Provincial Secretary Thomas Amyot, he had "no hope of redress . . . in the public opinion," since members of the assembly "may publish what Libels they please without fear of the Pillory!" Prevost urged the Colonial Office to replace Ryland as clerk of the crown in chancery, but the governor himself was recalled, to Ryland's unalloyed delight, before any action was taken.

Prevost's successor, Sir Gordon Drummond*, was more receptive to Ryland's opinions; indeed, he employed only Ryland to present his messages to the Legislative Council. Drummond's administration was too short to be influential, however, and that of his successor, Sir John Coape Sherbrooke*, marked a return to Prevost's policies and "the tyranny of the most oppressive . . . democracy that ever existed." "Arrests and Commitments, terror and dilapidation, accusations and impeachments are the order of the day," Ryland wrote to Amyot in February 1817. "The Press is brought into compleat subjugation to the Assembly. . . . Persons accused by this Body have no tribunal to appeal to within the Province."

It was in part to obviate this difficulty and in part to insure a more satisfactory handling of impeachments than had existed that in 1817 the Prince Regent conferred on the Legislative Council authority to adjudicate the impeachment of judge Louis-Charles Foucher on accusations brought forth by Austin

CUVILLIER. Ryland, sensing an undermining of the royal prerogative and fearing that office holders would be left at the mercy of the legislature, argued ingeniously to Sherbrooke that the council could judge only the accusations and not the accused, in the manner of a grand jury, and that the crown alone could pronounce and execute the sentence. Ryland's position was also dictated by his concern for an apparent weakening of the Legislative Council after additions had been made to it by Prevost and Sherbrooke. "It may be argued," he wrote to Amyot, "that as you have a *Mob* in the Lower House, you ought also to have one in the upper to contend with them." But it was less the number than the type of members that concerned him, and he complained in Februry 1818 that the council had been "new modelled" by the introduction of Plessis the previous year. In 1819 his efforts to have removed from a bill authorizing construction of the Lachine Canal a clause which protected the Sulpician estates as private property was voted down in council; however, Ryland eventually succeeded, with the complicity of Sherbrooke's successor, the Duke of Richmond [Lennox*], in reviving efforts to have the estates appropriated by the government [*see* Jean-Henry-Auguste Roux*].

Richmond's premature death in August 1819 constituted a blow to Ryland's political policies and to his ambitions to place his maturing sons in provincial offices. Richmond's successor, Lord Dalhousie [RAMSAY], initially proposed to bring "the general business [of government] under my own hands with the aid of old Mr Ryland . . . who tells me that he did all the business himself & only referred the matter of form to be executed in Council"; indeed, in March 1821 Dalhousie assured Ryland that he and Sewell were the only ones from whom "advice and confidential Council" were solicited. However, Dalhousie disliked "the grasping at places" of which Ryland was an eminent practitioner, and he had Ryland's eldest son, William Deane, removed as Amyot's deputy at Quebec and recommended Ryland's own removal as clerk of the crown in chancery. In addition he planned to replace by a single commissioner the entire Jesuit estates commission, on which Ryland, as commissioner, secretary, and treasurer, exercised influence politically and administratively.

When Dalhousie returned to England on leave in 1824, therefore, Ryland was disposed to promote the administration of his interim replacement, Lieutenant Governor Sir Francis Nathaniel Burton*, in hopes that the arrangement would be made permanent. The major political problem in the colony being the struggle for control of government finances, Ryland pointed out to Burton that he could gain much credit were he to resolve the problem and would lose nothing should he fail in the attempt. Ryland even outlined the strategy Burton should employ to get an acceptable supply bill through the assembly, and once that had been accomplished he ensured the bill's passage through council by forging a temporary alliance with Plessis to defeat Richardson, the leader of the English party there. He then collaborated closely in Burton's defence when Dalhousie charged that the supply bill had sold out the independence of the colonial executive. Ryland, in fact, was probably Burton's closest adviser, privy to dispatches, consulted on delicate matters, and asked to draft public statements and replies to important correspondence. In accepting this role he adopted a language hitherto anathema to him. In reply to Dalhousie, Ryland assured Burton that he had been right in "pursuing a conciliatory course which was calculated to bring [the assembly], *by degrees*, to a constitutional and liberal mode of proceeding with respect to supplies."

The return of a rancorous Dalhousie in 1825 and the departure of Burton under censure marked Ryland's political eclipse. Dalhousie announced in April 1826 the abolition of the Jesuit estates commission and in June had Ryland's salary as clerk of the crown in chancery stopped. The beleaguered office holder complained bitterly of this treatment to a trusted friend, Sir James Kempt*, lieutenant governor of Nova Scotia, whom he kept informed of political developments in Lower Canada. When Kempt replaced Dalhousie in 1828, Ryland urged him to have passed a supply bill similar to Burton's in order to break a deadlock between the assembly and the executive that was costing office holders dearly in unpaid salaries. Kempt did so the following year, and Ryland combined with Sewell to squeeze the bill through the Legislative Council.

Kempt's successors, lords Aylmer [WHITWORTH-AYLMER] and Gosford [ACHESON], consulted Ryland more on administrative than on political matters, profiting from his vast experience in procedure. However, they accepted courteously his political advice, the copies of his London correspondence of 1810–12, and several memoranda on political issues which it had been the lot of every governor since Craig to receive. Under Aylmer, Ryland's conciliatory tack on government finances ended abruptly when the assembly refused to respond favourably to the Revenue Act of 1831, by which control of all colonial revenues was given unconditionally to the assembly in hopes that it would vote a civil list of some £6,000. The executive thus found itself without revenues to pay even the limited number of salaries and pensions it had maintained in recent years when no supplies were passed. Thenceforth, rather than seek an accommodation with the assembly, Ryland urged repeal or amendment of the act, a recommendation that the Gosford commission would make in 1836. Like many in the English party, Ryland also favoured union of the Canadas, an idea he had promoted consistently since

1810 at least. He remained a stalwart defender of the Legislative Council, but, consistent with his earlier opposition to the assembly's actions in similar cases, he vainly opposed imprisonment by the council of newspaper editors Daniel Tracey* and Ludger Duvernay* for having published articles "libellous" of it. He also increasingly acted in that house as the regional representative from Quebec, introducing and defending petitions for improvement of the town's roads, bridges, and markets.

Kempt, Aylmer, and Gosford all promoted, with suitable restraint given the financial restrictions imposed on the colonial executive, Ryland's claims to compensation for the loss of positions, salaries, and pensions that he had suffered both under Dalhousie and through the assembly's refusal to vote supplies. In November 1830 he was awarded 2,205 acres of land in Chester and Tingwick townships, but he had no success in efforts to obtain advances on his back-pay or appointments for his sons. Having been scrupulously honest as an administrator of public funds in all his offices, he spent his last years under increasingly severe financial restraint. His only other known property was a "small Estate" at Beauport, acquired in 1805 and added to substantially in 1813. Joseph BOUCHETTE noted that its "two handsome stone dwelling-houses with gardens and summer-houses, surrounded by a wall" attracted much attention because of "the rich prospect they command over the basin of Quebec." A veritable symbol of British dominance by its wall and commanding position, this summer retreat and experimental farm developed into Ryland's permanent residence from 1817. Fluent in French, entertaining excellent personal relations with the habitants, and being prominent in government, he was called on occasionally by local residents to defend their interests against the bureaucracry, a role which eminently suited his combative nature.

Ryland's health gave out about 1834. On 18 June 1838 he requested leave of Governor Lord Durham [LAMBTON] to retire as clerk of the Executive Council in favour of his son George Herman, his assistant for 17 years. He died a month later, probably not knowing that after so many previous failures to place his sons, this last effort would succeed.

The real Herman Witsius Ryland has been distorted by a century and a half of hostile historiography. Not given to introspection and self-questioning, he can be perceived only through the tone of his writings and glimpses provided by contemporaries. Plessis said that he was "an astute diplomat and good enough when one knew how to approach him," but also that he was "not a man one could pump." Mathew BELL described him in 1825 as "a bullying old servant of the Public." Ryland enjoyed solitude, family life, and the quiet of the country, yet was comfortable with the highest imperial officials in London. He was a man of passionate nature; in 1821 Kempt remarked to him that "[your] inevitable *Sanguin temperament* Still leads you to indulge in excesses of various Kinds; you continue to *love a Man* . . . With all your heart and Soul, or to hold him and all that he does in utter aversion." His friends lauded his discretion, loyalty, and generosity; his enemies reproached his secretiveness, "duplicity," and pettiness. His only humour was biting sarcasm. He had a surprising number of intimate friends: Mountain, Young, Milnes, Craig, Amyot, Burton, Kempt, François Baby*, and Sir George Pownall*. Almost all were British-born; Ryland looked down on colonials, Canadian and American, including Sewell.

As a Georgian office holder Ryland was typical in his insatiable hunger for posts and pensions for himself and his sons; he was less so, perhaps, in his scrupulous honesty and evident competence. The assembly's attacks on his administration were shots in the dark and, though often investigated, he was never impeached; it was his political views and influence that attracted its fire. He was a colonial tory, suspicious of democracy, popular politicians, and colonial ways, a defender of aristocracy and the royal prerogative, nostalgic for the mother country. The nature of his posts, especially those of civil secretary, clerk of the Executive Council, and legislative councillor, and the nature of Lower Canadian government, particularly the brevity of tenure in the highest office, made a man of Ryland's experience and forcefulness highly, if discreetly, influential; he was an *éminence grise*. In politics he could be diplomatic and manœuvre with the best; he was patient and persevering. His intensity and tenacity matched that of the leaders of the Canadian party and sprang from a similar source; unlike British administrators and many office holders and merchants, but like the Canadians themselves, Ryland knew that he and his posterity were in Lower Canada to stay, and that their future depended on what became of the colony. Whereas the Canadian nationalists saw Lower Canada as an offshoot of French culture, Ryland saw it as an outpost of Britain. He shared the "garrison mentality" – as historian Frank Murray Greenwood aptly describes it – of most British occupants of the colony, yet he did not live behind defensive walls in isolation from the habitants; in Beauport he was aware of and involved with their social and economic concerns. He probably assessed correctly a lack of militancy in the habitants around Quebec, but he surely underestimated the intensity of dislike for foreign dominance to which nationalists could appeal. The roots of the rebellions of 1837–38, which he had anxiously foreseen, were more profound than he perceived, and for that reason the policies he advocated played a major role in bringing them about.

JAMES H. LAMBERT

[The author wishes to thank Jacqueline Roy for her assistance in analysing the personality of Herman Witsius Ryland. A portrait of Ryland is held at the PAC. J.H.L.]

ACC-Q, 73, no.180; 74, nos.7, 9; 75, nos.84–85; 76, nos.1, 7, 10, 16–17, 20, 32, 87; 77, nos.43, 67, 84, 88, 105; 78, nos.47, 52; 81, no.70. ANQ-Q, CE1-61, 22 juill. 1838; CN1-230, 5 nov. 1813; CN1-262, 26 juill. 1805; E21/73–75; P-192/2, no.121; P1000-90-1863. Antiquarian and Numismatic Soc. of Montreal, H. W. Ryland, 1789–1833 (mfm. at PAC). ASQ, Fonds Viger–Verreau, sér.O, 0147: 143. ASTR, 0461. McGill Univ. Libraries, Dept. of Rare Books and Special Coll., MS coll., CH10.S46. PAC, MG 23, GII, 10: 7918–19; MG 24, A2: 2347–49; A40: 1898–99; B2: 465, 573, 588, 1399, 5389–90; B3; B16: 160–61; MG 30, D1, 27: 66–105; MG 53, nos.199, 215; RG 1, L3[L]: 83, 2244, 2468, 83566; RG 4, A1: 22477, 30073, 41072–79; 141: H. Dunn to J. Taylor, 3 Feb. 1815; A2, 35, S. Walcott to H. W. Ryland, 13 Sept. 1847; RG 8, I (C ser.), 673: 158. PRO, CO 42/107–11, 42/113, 42/115, 42/124, 42/126, 42/142–44, 42/148, 42/150, 42/157, 42/162, 42/184, 42/186, 42/203–4, 42/209, 42/211–12, 42/214, 42/225, 42/230, 42/233, 42/238, 42/240, 42/244, 42/252, 42/263, 42/266, 42/271, 42/277, 42/280 (mfm. at ANQ, PAC). QUA, MC, Thomas Amyot to H. W. Ryland, 1811–35; Nathaniel Atcheson to H. W. Ryland, 3 Sept. 1810. Univ. de Montréal, Service des bibliothèques, coll. spéciales, coll. Melzack. Univ. of B.C. Library, Special Coll. Division (Vancouer), Ryland papers.

"Les dénombrements de Québec" (Plessis), ANQ *Rapport*, 1948–49. [E. P. Gwillim] Simcoe, *The diary of Mrs. John Graves Simcoe . . .*, ed. J. R. Robertson (Toronto, 1911; repr. [1973]). L.C., Legislative Council, *Journaux*, 1795–1813: 5, 106–9; 1814: 9, 30, 35, 37, 76, 81, 92, 111; 1815: 10–11, 15–16, 18, 22, 24, 28, 31, 36–37, 55, 58, 74, 77, 104, 107–9, 118; 1816: 6, 9, 13–15, 19, 29–30, 40; 1817: 8, 16, 27–29, 158; 1818: 12, 20, 58, 66, 136; 1819: 18, 59, 130–31; 1820: 14, 22; 1820–21: 10, 31, 43; 1821–22: 10–11; 1823: 14, 18, 28, 91, 104–5; 1824: 13, 202–3; 1825: 13, 35, 62; 1826: 13, 19, 21, 33, 47, 75, 187; 1828–29: 18, 37, 39, 41, 50, 53–54, 59, 83; 1830: 12, 29; 1831: 52, 63, 81, 83, 125–26, 153–54, 194–95, 220; 1831–32: 15, 18–19, 48, 52, 109–13, 132, 136; 1832–33: 28, 68, 89, 252–54; 1834: 13–14, 147–52; 1836: app.F. William Smith, *The diary and selected papers of Chief Justice William Smith, 1784–1793*, ed. L. F. S. Upton (2v., Toronto, 1963–65). *Quebec Gazette*, 30 June 1796; 24 May 1798; 11 July 1799; 18 Feb. 1802; 8 May 1806; 23 April, 22 Oct. 1807; 1, 15 April 1813; 30 March 1815; 21 June 1819; 6 Jan. 1820; 27 Jan., 25, 29 Dec. 1823. *Quebec Mercury*, 13 Feb. 1821. Bouchette, *Topographical description of L.C. DNB*. Christie, *Hist. of L.C.* (1866), vol.6. R. C. Dalton, *The Jesuits' estates question, 1760–1888: a study of the background for the agitation of 1889* (Toronto, 1968). Claude Galarneau, *La France devant l'opinion canadienne (1760–1815)* (Québec et Paris, 1970). Lambert, "Joseph-Octave Plessis." T. R. Millman, *Jacob Mountain, first lord bishop of Quebec; a study in church and state, 1793–1825* (Toronto, 1947). J.-C. Nadon, "Herman Witsius Ryland et les intérêts britanniques dans le Bas-Canada" (thèse de MA, univ. d'Ottawa, 1967). Taft Manning, *Revolt of French Canada*. Wallot, *Un Québec qui bougeait*. F.-J. Audet, "Herman-Witsius Ryland," RSC *Trans.*, 3rd ser., 23 (1929), sect.i: 47–56. Ignotus [Thomas Chapais], "Le club des Barons," *BRH*, 4 (1898): 251–52. Frère Marcel-Joseph, "Les Canadiens veulent conserver le régime seigneurial," *RHAF*, 7 (1953–54): 387–89. P.-G. Roy, "Les ponts de la rivière Saint-Charles," *BRH*, 46 (1940): 86–92.

S

SAGAUNASH. *See* CALDWELL, BILLY

SAINTE-GERTRUDE, MARIE-FRANÇOISE HUOT, named. *See* HUOT

SAINT-JAMES, RENÉ BEAUVAIS, *dit. See* BEAUVAIS

SAINT-MARTIN, CHARLES HINDENLANG, known as. *See* HINDENLANG

SAINT-RÉAL, JOSEPH-RÉMI VALLIÈRES DE. *See* VALLIÈRES

SAMSON, JAMES HUNTER, lawyer, politician, and office holder; b. *c.* 1800 in Ireland, son of James Samson, who later became an officer in the British army; m. 4 March 1828 Alicia Fenton Russell, niece and ward of Sir John Harvey*, in London, and they had no issue; d. 26 March 1836 in Belleville, Upper Canada.

James Hunter Samson probably came to the Canadas in 1813, when his father's regiment, the 70th Foot, began its tour of duty there. At the age of 16 he sought, unsuccessfully, an ensigncy in the 70th. Studying at York (Toronto) in 1818, he became the close friend of Robert Baldwin*. In 1819, as a law student in Christopher Alexander HAGERMAN's Kingston office, he began a regular correspondence with Baldwin. His letters show Samson as articulate, sensitive, fond of poetry, hard-working, and ambitious, but also insecure, subject to fits of depression, and extremely jealous of anyone who threatened to come between himself and Baldwin.

After Samson was called to the bar in November 1823, he became the first resident lawyer at Belleville. Life was not easy in this lumbering, farming, trading community of fewer than 500 people. He claimed "many battles and storms" with one judge and he was financially embarrassed on occasion. He came, however, to enjoy a reputation as a "Barrister of no ordinary talent" and was recognized by the Law Society of Upper Canada, which elected him a bencher in 1835. Samson championed the cause of the fledgling Church of Scotland congregation at Belleville, serving as a trustee, writing letters to the press and various officials, and putting up the first minister after his arrival from Scotland. When cholera threatened in 1832, he donated funds to help build Belleville's first hospital, personally supervising its hasty construction within a fortnight. He also served as a member of the local board of health and was a member of the village council.

From 1828 until his death he represented the riding of Hastings in the House of Assembly. Initially, he claimed to be a moderate, supporting the "principles of Whiggism"; however, in 1829 during the assembly's first session Samson revealed his true colours. After attempting, unsuccessfully, to delete comments that were highly critical of the executive branch of government from the reply to the speech from the throne, he was the lone member to vote against the reply. His military background, allegiance to Hagerman (regarded by historians as a pillar of the "family compact"), aristocratic connections through marriage, and basic distrust of republicanism probably explain this vote.

Samson's subsequent voting pattern led William Lyon Mackenzie* to call him "a selfish illiberal creature" and place him prominently on his "Black List" for 1830. Stung by this attack, Samson played a leading role in the libel and breach of privilege charges against Mackenzie in December 1831. He described articles in the *Colonial Advocate* as "gross, scandalous, and malicious libels – intended and calculated to bring this House and the Government of this Province into contempt." The assembly declared Mackenzie guilty of the libel and also approved Samson's resolution that Mackenzie's defence tactics made him "guilty of a high breach of the privilege of this house." Samson then won support for his motions expelling Mackenzie from the house and calling for a new election.

When Mackenzie's supporters touched off a series of protest rallies, Samson appeared at the Belleville meeting to expose the "falsehood, absurdity and inconsistency" of Mackenzie's position. His own resolution of loyalty recognized that Upper Canada's institutions were imperfect, but it maintained "we have less cause of complaint, than any people on earth; and the means of redress are in our own power."

From 1832 to 1835 Samson played a modest role in the assembly. He chaired several committees, including the 1832 select committee on grievances that dealt with civil rights and favoured the creation of additional banks in the province. He also spoke out on the need for improving navigation of the St Lawrence. In 1836 his health and state of mind became topics for local editorial comment when he was unable to attend the house. His father's death in 1832 had been a serious blow and political differences with Baldwin had diminished this once vital friendship he had clung to. Samson sought solace in alcohol, which contributed to his death in March 1836, aged 36.

GERALD E. BOYCE

AO, MU 2008, no.21; RG 22, ser.155. Lennox and Addington County Museum (Napanee, Ont.), Lennox and Addington Hist. Soc. Coll., Benson family papers. MTRL, Robert Baldwin papers, esp. A69: 19–76. PAC, MG 24, C12; RG 8, I (C ser.), 6: 967. U.C., House of Assembly, *Journal*, 1825–36. *British Whig*, 1834–36. *Chronicle & Gazette*, 1833–36. *Colonial Advocate*, 1828–34. *Kingston Chronicle*, 1820–33. G.B., WO, *Army list*, 1810–33. *The service of British regiments in Canada and North America . . .*, comp. C. H. Stewart (Ottawa, 1962). R. M. and Joyce Baldwin, *The Baldwins and the great experiment* (Don Mills [Toronto], 1969). G. E. Boyce, *Historic Hastings* (Belleville, Ont., 1967); *Hutton of Hastings: the life and letters of William Hutton, 1801–61* (Belleville, 1972).

SATTIN, ANTOINE, Sulpician and teacher; b. 18 Feb. 1767 in Lyons, France, son of Joseph Satin and Pierrette Ocard; d. 23 June 1836 in Montreal.

Antoine Sattin entered the Séminaire Saint-Irénée in Lyons on 1 Nov. 1788. During the revolutionary turmoil in this city, Sattin, who was then a subdeacon, signed a public protest against an address that was published in *Le Courrier de Lyon* of 23 July 1790 and was believed to have been written by seminarists dissatisfied with the strict régime in the institution. Sattin is thought to have been ordained on 19 March 1791. He joined the Sulpicians and did his solitude (noviciate) in Paris. Like many priests who refused to take the oath of loyalty to the Civil Constitution of the Clergy, he went into exile in Switzerland; once there, he expressed a determination to go to Lower Canada. He was in the group of 11 Sulpicians who landed at Montreal on 12 Sept. 1794 [*see* Jean-Henry-Auguste Roux*].

Admitted to the community of the Séminaire de Saint-Sulpice as a member on 29 September, Sattin was subsequently assigned to the ministry in Notre-Dame parish. He also celebrated mass in the chapel of Notre-Dame-de-Bonsecours. In 1801 he was appointed to the Collège Saint-Raphaël (from 1806 the Petit Séminaire de Montréal), where he taught Latin and French.

Sattin gave up this post to become chaplain of the nuns of the Hôtel-Dieu of Montreal in 1813. In 1815 he assisted Sulpician Jean-Baptiste-Jacques Chicoisneau*, who held the same office at the Hôpital

Général, and three years later he replaced him. From then on Sattin devoted himself to the poor, the sick, and the old. He proved a valued counsellor. His beneficial influence on novices, professed nuns, and other sisters encouraged them to greater zeal, and his judicious remarks and advice helped the community carry out the plans of their founder, Mme d'Youville [Dufrost*].

Among Sattin's interests were the practical aspects of life at the hospital, such as the quality of the food, the fire-fighting equipment, new buildings, and repairs. The sisters' journal describes him as a skilful engineer. He drew the plans for renovations to the hospital and chapel in 1832 and for a Way of the Cross in 1834. He further served the community by writing a biography of Mme d'Youville from testimonies such as that of Mother Thérèse-Geneviève Coutlée*.

In July 1825 Sattin became the director of the Confrérie de la Sainte-Famille, which brought devout women together every second Tuesday to pray and listen to sermons by the chaplain. The women combined mutual aid with prayer and took a particular interest in those members who needed encouragement or material and moral support. The group, which numbered 60 in 1825, each year acquired 7 or 8 new members who had to go through four months of probation before being admitted. In 1833 there were more than 100 in the sisterhood. The following year one of Sattin's colleagues, Jean-Baptiste Roupe*, replaced him as director.

Sattin was a member of the general council of the Séminaire de Saint-Sulpice from 25 Jan. 1821 and from 2 Sept. 1829 of the small council which it appointed to assist the superior in routine matters. Consequently he was closely involved in events that put the seminary in turmoil. Tension initially arose from conflict between the Canadians and the Sulpicians who had come from France; the Canadians felt threatened, even overwhelmed, by their French colleagues, who held all the positions of prestige and power in the establishment. The appointment in 1820 of Jean-Jacques LARTIGUE, a Canadian Sulpician, as bishop of Telmessus and the archbishop of Quebec's auxiliary in Montreal caused a stir in the seminary [*see* Jean-Charles Bédard*] and also among the secular clergy [*see* Augustin Chaboillez*; François-Xavier PIGEON]. A voyage to Europe made by the superior, Jean-Henry-Auguste Roux, in 1826 to address the question of the Sulpicians' seigneurial rights heightened the dissension. Sattin sided wholeheartedly with the French members of the community, for he deeply feared the Canadians' influence.

In his ministry to the poor at the Hôpital Général Sattin, whose health was deteriorating, had the help of Sulpician Sauveur-Romain Larré from November 1835. He suffered a paralytic stroke on 1 June 1836 and died on 23 June. The superior of Saint-Sulpice, Joseph-Vincent Quiblier*, wrote at the time: "His prudence was exceptional, and his piety of the most gentle kind. Everywhere he went he succeeded in winning young people's affection and in inspiring them with a love of piety and hard work."

BRUNO HAREL

Antoine Sattin is the author of "Vie de madame Youville, fondatrice et première supérieure des Sœurs de la Charité de l'Hôpital Général de Montréal, communément nommées Sœurs Grises, dédiée à cette même communauté" (1828), which is at the Arch. des Sœurs Grises (Montréal) and has been published in ANQ *Rapport*, 1928–29: 387–436. A portrait of Sattin which has been attributed to Louis-Chrétien de Heer* is at the mother-house of the Sœurs Grises de Montréal.

ANQ-M, CE1-51, 25 juin 1836. Arch. du séminaire de Saint-Sulpice (Paris), Fonds canadien, dossier 76. Arch. des Sœurs Grises (Montréal), Ancien journal, I–III; Dossier Antoine Sattin. Arch. municipales, Lyon (France), État civil, Saint-Nizier, 19 févr. 1767. ASSM, 16; 17; 21; 24, B, 5–6; 25, dossier 2; 32. [L.-A. Huguet-Latour], *Annuaire de Ville-Marie, origine, utilité et progrès des institutions catholiques de Montréal* . . . (2v., Montréal, 1863–82). Louis Bertrand, *Bibliothèque sulpicienne ou histoire littéraire de la Compagnie de Saint-Sulpice* (3v., Paris, 1900), 2: 117. Dionne, *Les ecclésiastiques et les royalistes français*. Robert Lahaise, *Les édifices conventuels du Vieux Montréal: aspects ethno-historiques* (Montréal, 1980), 496–501. Gérard Morisset, *L'architecture en Nouvelle-France* (Québec, 1949).

SAUVAGEAU (Savageau), CHARLES (Michel-Charles), musician, conductor, teacher, composer, author, and music dealer; b. probably in October 1807 at Quebec, son of Michel Sauvageau and Marie-Angélique Corbin; m. there 20 April 1830 Marie-Angélique Lévêque, and they had at least 12 children, most of whom died in infancy; d. there 16 June 1849 and was buried 19 June in the Cimetière Saint-Louis.

Charles Sauvageau was born of Michel Sauvageau's first marriage, which took place in 1799 at Quebec; after the death of his wife, Michel married Marie-Anne Atkin, the widow of Pierre Racine, in 1827. Charles probably spent his infancy and childhood at Quebec, where his father was a notary. Nothing is known of the formative period of his life other than that in 1820 he studied for a year at the Petit Séminaire de Québec. Contemporaries attributed his superior musicianship to "constant application and innate talent, for he was self-taught," as a journalist with *L'Abeille* observed.

One of the first times that Sauvageau was referred to as a musician was in 1832, perhaps because he was hired as music teacher for a group of at least 12 boys who had been recruited that winter by John Chrisostomus Brauneis* "with the aim of qualifying them to be musicians in the military band of the Quebec artillery." The following year Sauvageau announced on 15 November that a "Quadrille Band" was being established. In 1834 and 1835, according to notices in the *Quebec Mercury*, it was assimilated into the Band of the Quebec Militia Artillery. Sauvageau became more closely linked with this group of 18 performers for, if Philéas Gagnon* is right, he took over conducting it in 1836. His close relations seem to have been maintained, since in 1847 the band of the Canadian militia apparently was still supplying the personnel for the Bande de la Société Saint-Jean-Baptiste, of which Sauvageau had been conductor since 1842. In the absence of written records, nothing is known about the members of "Mr C. Sauvageau's regular orchestra," which played during the interludes in the amateur musical evening at the École des Glacis on 25 June 1840. The Quebec Philharmonic Union, which he conducted in 1848 and 1849, is, however, known to have consisted of amateurs.

Sauvageau not only served as a conductor but also performed in public with equal success as a violinist, from at least 1833, in musical and dramatic evenings usually organized by himself. The editor of *Le Fantasque*, his brother-in-law Napoléon Aubin*, noted in 1842 that these came to resemble "what might almost be called family parties." He demonstrated his virtuosity by playing variations, imitations on the violin of different instruments, and themes with variations on a single string. The few pieces he composed and published between 1840 and 1844 give only a hint of his talents as a composer and virtuoso.

In the course of his career Sauvageau also devoted himself zealously to teaching music. In 1840 he dedicated to his pupils the two waltzes that were his earliest compositions. His plans to open an academy of music for amateurs in 1841 having fallen through, he apparently gave private lessons before being hired by the Petit Séminaire de Québec as a music teacher for the period 1846–49. According to *L'Abeille* he was "the first Canadian artist at Quebec to teach music in all its branches," in particular singing and stringed instruments such as the violin and guitar. In 1841 he stimulated a spirit of competition in his young pupils by instituting musical evenings in the town which were hailed as a novelty. Like his contemporary and rival Théodore-Frédéric Molt*, Sauvageau wrote a work on theory, published by Aubin, that was directed at a broad audience – his pupils, school principals, and the general public. The manual's title, *Notions élémentaires de musique, tirées des meilleurs auteurs*, contents, and price were all changed substantially between the initial offer for its sale by public subscription in February 1844 and the announcement of its publication in May 1845. For his pupils and the public Sauvageau kept a shop in his home. An advertisement that he put in *Le Castor* in May 1845 indicated that he "continues to take it upon himself to supply orchestras with the requisites. His store carries new music, ruled paper, all kinds of instruments, strings, etc.; he will also sell on commission valuable instruments and in general everything relating to his art." Sauvageau's success as a teacher is clear from the accounts of the musical evenings presented by his pupils, and even more from the exceptional accomplishments of his eldest son Flavien. At age 10 Flavien had already played the violin in public, accompanied by his father on the cello, but he met a tragic death at 15 in the fire at the Théâtre Saint-Louis on 12 June 1846. Quebec musician Joseph Lyonnais, a maker of stringed instruments, is also said to have been taught by Sauvageau.

That Charles Sauvageau's accomplishments in the course of a life that was full but not long – he died "aged 41 years and 8 months" – were modest does not diminish the place he holds as a musician in the history of Quebec culture in the second quarter of the 19th century. He in fact carried out a program that had been outlined by the intellectuals of the time, among them Napoléon Aubin. Aubin, who was truly his mentor, at every turn singled out the social significance of Sauvageau's many-sided activities. In 1841 he suggested in various articles that Sauvageau "form a public class at Quebec for teaching popular song," an idea the musician quickly took up. He countered the view of those tempted to compare Sauvageau with a foreign violinist named Nagel, who stayed at Quebec in 1842, and made an analysis at that time of "Mr Sauvageau's efforts to introduce, cultivate and bring to fruition, particularly among his working-class compatriots, a taste for an art that seeks its adepts and finds its leading lights in all ranks . . . , an art that releases the rich man from his idleness and the poor man from his work." In the three marches composed by Sauvageau he found "the cheerful, pastoral, naïve style that characterizes Canadian music," and he believed that these airs should therefore be handed down to posterity along with other, older ones. Moving from words to action, Aubin put his press at Sauvageau's service. Sauvageau's musical career unfolded, in this early period of Canadian nationalism, under a political banner which had some success. In August 1844 when *Le Ménestrel* invited the Quebec "dilettanti" to attend one of his concerts, it noted: "Their presence in large numbers will demonstrate the popularity that our national musician so rightly enjoys."

LUCIEN POIRIER

In the years 1840–44 Charles Sauvageau wrote music for voice, violin, piano, and guitar, and compiled *Notions élémentaires de musique, tirées des meilleurs auteurs et mises en ordre par Charles Sauvageau* (Québec, 1844), a "work dedicated especially to his students." His published pieces include a piano accompaniment for Aubin's *Le dépit amoureux*, which appears in *L'Album artistique et lyrique* (Québec), no.1 (1840); *Deux valses*, for piano, announced in *Le Fantasque* (Québec), 27 avril 1840 and published in the *Literary Garland*, 3 (1840–41): 476–77, in an arrangement by W. H. Warren of Montreal; and the music for *Chant canadien* (Québec, 1843), with words by François-Réal Angers*, and for *Trois marches canadiennes: marche de Josephte, marche de Jean-Baptiste, marche de Pierrot* (Québec, 1843). He also published the following pieces in 1844 in the music section of *Ménestrel* (Québec), vol.1: *Chant national . . .* , with words by François-Magloire Derome*; *Valse du ménestrel*; *Solo de violon composé sur le motif d' "Auld Robin Gray"*; *Gallopade du ménestrel* for the piano; arrangements of Pierre Petitclair*'s *Valse de Sophie* and *Valse de Caroline* for the piano; and *Valse* for the guitar. The *Chant national* also appears in *L'Artisan* (Québec), 9 juill. 1844. No text of the variations on *Long, long, ago* that he wrote and played on 20 Feb. 1849, survives. Only *Chant canadien* was particularly successful, being reprinted in various works including the *Journal de l'Instruction publique* (Québec et Montréal), 3 (1859): 109–11 (under the name "Chant national"); *Le Soleil* (Québec), 5 oct. 1901: 6; the 3rd edition of *Chansonnier des colléges mis en musique* (Québec, 1860), 15–17; *La lyre canadienne . . .* (Québec, 1847), 84, and (4e éd., 1886), 52 (with the annotation "music by N. Aubin"); and *La nouvelle lyre canadienne . . .* (nouv. éd., Montréal, [1895]), 58 (without any mention of the composer).

ANQ-Q, CE1-1, 12 mai 1804, 5 mars 1831, 1832–49, 14 juin 1846, 19 juin 1849; CE1-22, 20 avril 1830; CE1-93, 24 avril 1827; P-239/93. ASQ, C 38; C 43; Fichier des anciens; MSS, 433: 201; Séminaire, 218, no.7. *L'Abeille* (Québec), 21 juin 1849. *L'Artisan*, 7, 17, 21 nov. 1842; 9 juill., 20 août, 3 sept. 1844. *Le Canadien*, 25 févr. 1832; 30 juill., 29 oct. 1841; 24, 27 juin, 7 nov. 1842; 3, 5, 7, 10 juill., 1er sept. 1843; 23 sept. 1844; 18 juill., 25 août 1845. *Le Castor* (Québec), 29 févr., 19, 27 août 1844; 5 mai 1845. *Le Fantasque*, 27 oct. 1838; 16 mars, 27 avril, 11 mai, 22 juin, 6 juill. 1840; 2 août 1841; 19 nov. 1842; 3 juill., 3 août 1843. *Le Journal de Québec*, 25 juin, 8 juill., 5 oct. 1843; 24, 26 sept. 1844. *Morning Chronicle* (Quebec), 14 Jan., 7, 28 Feb., 3 March 1848; 16 Jan. 1849. *Quebec Gazette*, 10, 12 July 1843. *Quebec Mercury*, 19 Nov., 24 Dec. 1833; 27 Dec. 1834; 17 Nov. 1835; 15 Feb., 21 March, 23 Sept. 1844; 19 April 1845; 2 March 1848; 11, 16 Jan., 8, 13, 17, 24 Feb. 1849. *Almanach ecclésiastique et civil de Québec, pour 1846 . . .* (Québec, 1845), 66. *Almanach métropolitain de Québec, pour 1849 . . .* (Québec, 1848), 26. *Catalogue of Canadian composers*, ed. Helmut Kallmann (2nd ed., Toronto, 1952; repr. St Clair Shores, Mich., 1972), 211. *Chansons sur textes français II*, Lucien Poirier, édit. (Ottawa, 1987), 32, 98. *Dictionnaire biographique des musiciens canadiens* (2e éd., Lachine, Qué., 1935), 272–74. *Encyclopedia of music in Canada*, ed. Helmut Kallmann *et al.* (Toronto, 1981). Philéas Gagnon, *Essai de bibliographie canadienne . . .* (2v., Québec et Montréal, 1895–1913; réimpr. Dubuque, Iowa, [1962]), 1: 449. A.-G. Lyonnais, *Généalogie de la famille Lyonnais en Canada* (Ottawa, 1901), 49. J.-G. Sauvageau, *Dictionnaire généalogique des familles Sauvageau au Canada et aux États-Unis, 1669–1969* ([Québec, 1978]), 89, 96.

Willy Amtmann, *La musique au Québec, 1600–1875*, Michelle Pharand, trad. (Montréal, 1976), 383–85. Maria Calderisi, *Music publishing in the Canadas, 1800–1867* (Ottawa, 1981), 15, 22, 28, 37, 63. H.-J.-J.-B. Chouinard, *Fête nationale des Canadiens français célébrée à Québec en 1880: histoire, discours, rapport . . .* (4v., Québec, 1881–1903), 1: 570, 624; 4: 307–8, 311, 504, 513, 515, 521–22. Vivianne Émond, "'Musique et musiciens à Québec: souvenirs d'un amateur' de Nazaire LeVasseur (1848–1927): étude critique" (thèse de M.MUS., univ. Laval, Québec, 1986), 45–52, 59–61. Clifford Ford, *Canada's music: an historical survey* (Agincourt [Toronto], 1982), 38–39. Claire Grégoire-Reid, "Les manuels de théorie musicale publiés au Québec entre 1811 et 1911" (thèse de M.MUS., univ. Laval, 1987), 15, 72, 79–80, 122, 153–55. Helmut Kallmann, *A history of music in Canada, 1534–1914* (Toronto and London, 1960), 71, 78–79, 82, 114, 188. T. J. McGee, *The music of Canada* (New York and London, 1985), 54. France Malouin-Gélinas, "La vie musicale à Québec de 1840 à 1845, telle que décrite par les journaux et revues de l'époque" (thèse de MA, univ. de Montréal, 1975), 21, 28, 37–39, 52–53, 81, 84–85, 94, 111, 113, 123, 170–71, 175, 178, 182, 186, 189–90, 193–94, 197–200, 206, 209. Raymond Vézina, "La Société Sainte-Cécile," Marc Lebel *et al.*, *Aspects de l'enseignement au petit séminaire de Québec (1765–1945)* (Québec, 1968), 160, 191. Nazaire LeVasseur, "Musique et musiciens à Québec: souvenirs d'un amateur," *La Musique* (Québec), 1 (1919): 76, 86–87, 100–1. France Malouin-Gélinas, "La vie musicale à Québec, 1840–45," *Les Cahiers canadiens de musique* (Montréal), 7 (1973): 9–22. P.-G. Roy, "L'Hôtel Union ou Saint-George, à Québec" and "À propos de musique: la première fanfare québécoise," *BRH*, 43 (1937): 12–14 and 353–56 respectively; "Le Théâtre Saint-Louis, à Québec," 42 (1936): 186. Lucien Serre, "L'ancêtre des Sauvageau," *BRH*, 34 (1928): 23.

SAYER, PIERRE-GUILLAUME, fur trader; b. *c.* 1796, son of John Sayer*, fur trader, and his country wife, Obemau-unoqua (Nancy?); d. after May 1849.

The place and date of Pierre-Guillaume Sayer's birth are uncertain, but, as he was thought to be 53 years old in 1849 and his father traded primarily in the Fond du Lac district south and west of Lake Superior between 1793 and 1805, it may have occurred in that region about 1796. In 1805 the elder Sayer moved to Lower Canada; Pierre-Guillaume, in the way usual for children of country marriages, was left with his mother's people and was assimilated to the Métis. He learned to speak French and became, in time, a Roman Catholic. In 1824 he settled at Grantown (St François Xavier, Man.) on the Assiniboine River [*see* Cuthbert Grant*; Joseph-Norbert Provencher*]. There, in 1835, he married Josette, elder daughter of fur trader Alexander Frobisher; they were to have at least one son. Confusion of first names in the Red River censuses makes it difficult to locate precise information on Sayer, but it appears that he farmed in a small way. Presumably he also went on the annual buffalo hunt with the Grantown party.

Sayer's significance derives from his trial in the

General Quarterly Court of Assiniboia on 17 May 1849. The free trade in furs, practised in the Red River valley since 1821, had greatly increased with the opportunity from 1843 to sell at Pembina (N.Dak.) to Norman Wolfred Kittson*, who was in direct competition with the Hudson's Bay Company. Sayer was arrested for illegally trading in furs, and was brought before the court by Chief Factor John Ballenden* in a case designed to test the legality of the monopoly claimed by the HBC. Sayer's counsel was James Sinclair*, a representative of the free traders of Red River; the two were backed by Louis Riel* Sr, who, with the Reverend George-Antoine Bellecourt*, had organized the Métis to protest against both the monopoly and the inadequate representation of the Métis on the Council of Assiniboia. Presided over by the judicial recorder, Adam Thom*, the trial was by jury and was conducted fairly. Sayer admitted to trafficking in furs, but claimed that he had been exchanging presents with relatives, an Indian manner of trading.

The jury returned a verdict of guilty but recommended mercy on the ground that Sayer had genuinely believed that the Métis were permitted to trade freely. Ballenden accepted the recommendation and Sayer was freed. Riel promptly asserted that the verdict was tantamount to a surrender of the HBC monopoly. This view was at once taken up by the Métis assembled outside the court-house, who cried "Le commerce est libre!" So it was to be: the HBC abandoned its efforts to maintain a monopoly and began aggressive competition with the free traders. Sayer's trial was thus a landmark in the history of the Canadian west.

The date and place of his death are unknown.

W. L. MORTON

Canadian north-west (Oliver), 1: 352. *Docs. relating to NWC* (Wallace). *HBRS*, 19 (Rich and Johnson). Alexander Ross, *The Red River settlement: its rise, progress and present state; with some account of the native races and its general history, to the present day* (London, 1856; repr. Edmonton, 1972), 371–79. Morice, *Dict. hist. des Canadiens et des Métis*. Gerald Friesen, *The Canadian Prairies: a history* (Toronto, 1984). Marcel Giraud, *The Métis in the Canadian west*, trans. George Woodcock (2v., Edmonton, 1986). Morton, *Hist. of Canadian west* (1939). G. F. G. Stanley, *Louis Riel* (Toronto and Montreal, 1963).

SAYRE, JAMES, businessman, office holder, and JP; b. 7 Sept. 1761 in Philadelphia, son of the Reverend John Sayre, a Church of England minister, and Mary Bowes; d. 22 March 1849 at Dorchester Island, N.B.

James Sayre, one of eight children who survived infancy, spent his early years moving from one Anglican mission to another in New England. The events following upon the Declaration of Independence in July 1776 restricted his formal education. His father was then serving as minister of the Society for the Propagation of the Gospel in Fairfield, Conn., a stronghold of toryism [*see* Daniel Morehouse*]. John Sayre made no secret of his sympathies for the crown and encouraged his children to carry provisions to jailed parishioners. Advertised as an enemy to the country, he was banished from Fairfield for about seven months, and after his return his movements were severely restricted.

On 8 July 1779 Major-General William Tryon and a body of British troops occupied Fairfield. Tryon's decision to burn the homes of pro-revolutionaries inadvertently resulted in the destruction of loyalist homes as well, including that of John Sayre. Destitute, Sayre, his wife, and their children fled to Flushing, N.Y.; by 1781 they had reached New York City. There Sayre joined forces with loyalists seeking refuge in the province of Nova Scotia. He was an agent and one of the famous 55 loyalists who in July 1783 petitioned the commander-in-chief in North America, Sir Guy Carleton*, for substantial land grants in their proposed new home [*see* Abijah Willard*]. Sayre received a grant in Parrtown (Saint John, N.B.), where he ministered to the loyalist arrivals. His son James, who had arrived in Parrtown with the "spring fleet" of 1783, obtained a grant in the vicinity of Gagetown. By 1784 John had moved on to Maugerville, dying there in August. His widow then sold her husband's lands to James.

On 17 March 1790, in Trinity Church, Saint John, James married Polly Smith, a loyalist from Rhode Island. She was a daughter of Dr Nathan Smith, a physician who would serve as MHA for Saint John City from 1795 to 1802. The couple were to have five sons and five daughters. They settled in Maugerville, where James had a general store and small milling business. He appears also to have had some business connections with William Pagan*, a noted loyalist merchant in Saint John. In 1803 the Sayre family moved to the busy shipbuilding and shipping harbour of Dorchester Island, close to Dorchester, the shiretown of Westmorland County. They were the first loyalists to settle this high-tide island. Sayre built a frame-house and slowly acquired land, but success in business eluded him. As his son William Pagan Sayre wrote in 1816, "My father has not been very fortunate in increasing his worldly estate. . . . Various heavy losses and disappointments in his mercantile line put him considerably aback." James had nevertheless quickly assumed a leading role in the community. In 1807 he was named a town and parish officer and a justice of the peace. Seven years later he became high sheriff, a post he held until 1826 when he was succeeded by his son William Pagan. From 1834 to 1849 he was harbour master and collector of customs for Dorchester.

At his death in March 1849 Sayre was buried in Dorchester Pioneer Cemetery beside his wife, who had predeceased him by 11 years. He had died intestate, leaving an estate valued at £455, a sum which may suggest that his fortunes in business had improved. Sayre's life was intimately interwoven with the loyalist presence in New Brunswick. A strong supporter of the crown, he had fled his homeland, married a loyalist, and settled permanently in the province. Several of his sons remained in Dorchester, married into loyalist families, and became active members of the community. Through his sister Esther, the wife of Christopher Robinson*, Sayre was connected with one of the most powerful loyalist families of Upper Canada.

DELLA M. M. STANLEY

PANB, RG 10, RS108, 1785, no.149; 1815, no.353; RG 18, RS159, A1. Saint John Regional Library (Saint John, N.B.), A18 (loyalist family papers index), no.32 (mfm. at PANB). St Paul's Anglican Church (Sackville, N.B.), Reg. of burials, 1849 (mfm. at PANB). Westmorland County Probate Office (Moncton, N.B.), Probate record book C: 181, 247. *Royal Gazette* (Saint John; Fredericton), 8 Nov. 1785, 27 July 1836, 19 Dec. 1838, 9 June 1841, 5 May 1843. T. M. Banta, *Sayre family; lineage of Thomas Sayre, a founder of Southampton* (New York, 1901). *N.-B. almanack*, 1829–49. Lorenzo Sabine, *Biographical sketches of loyalists of the American revolution* (2v., Boston, 1864; repr. Port Washington, N.Y., 1966). W. O. Raymond, "Pioneer missionaries of the church in New Brunswick . . . ," *Church Work* (Halifax), 9 Nov. 1911: 2.

SCHNEIDER, JOSEPH, settler and sawmill owner; b. 24 May 1772 in Lancaster County, Pa, son of Jacob B. Schneider and Maria Herschi; m. 21 Feb. 1798 Barbara Eby, sister of Benjamin Eby*, and they had seven children; d. 27 Oct. 1843 in Berlin (Kitchener), Upper Canada.

Joseph Schneider's father immigrated with his parents to Pennsylvania from the Palatinate (Federal Republic of Germany) in 1736. In 1806, three years after Jacob's death, two of his sons, Christian and Jacob, settled in block 2 (Waterloo Township), in the vicinity of present-day Kitchener. Joseph and a group of other Mennonites followed them, making the month-long journey in horse-drawn wagons. Schneider purchased and settled on lot 17 of the German Company Tract of block 2. It was the attraction of inexpensive land, as well as the desire to remain under British rule in the years after the American revolution, that brought many Mennonites to the area, among them Benjamin Eby and Samuel D. Betzner*. Geographical isolation allowed them to practise their religion and language freely, although at first it forced them to travel to such centres as Dundas for supplies and services.

Schneider was an active figure among the Mennonite settlers and, with Eby, is often regarded as a founder of Kitchener. He helped open the first local road, which ran from his farmstead to the Dundas road and was known as Schneider's road until the 1870s. In 1808–9 he and four other heads of families hired a teacher to open the first school in the area. He was involved four years later in the building of the first Mennonite meeting-house, headed by Eby; in 1834 Schneider participated in the construction of a new church. Perhaps as early as 1816 he had built a sawmill on what is still known as Schneider's Creek, and in the 1820s a blacksmith shop and tavern were erected by Phineas Varnum on land leased from Schneider. Together these enterprises formed the commercial nucleus of the developing village, known variously as Sand Hills, Ebytown, and, later, Berlin. In 1835 Schneider strongly supported the establishment of its first newspaper, Heinrich Wilhelm Peterson*'s *Canada Museum, und Allgemeine Zeitung*, of which he was a stockholder.

Schneider died on 27 Oct. 1843. Among the possessions he left to his family were traditional objects valued by Pennsylvania Germans, including a tall case clock, the works for which he had brought with him in 1807. The clock still stands in the house he built about 1820, Kitchener's oldest structure and now a museum. In other local collections are two family bibles: one, in the Mennonite Archives of Ontario, a rare edition published in Zurich in 1560 by Christoph Froschauer and brought to Upper Canada by Schneider; the other, in the possession of a descendant, printed in Lancaster County in 1805 and containing striking examples of *fraktur* (ornamental writing), executed by teacher-artist Jacob Schumacher in 1821.

Schneider's farming and milling operations were continued by his youngest son, Joseph E., who in 1849 had the family's history printed in Berlin in a small booklet, possibly the earliest published genealogy in Canada. In 1874 he was a charter member of the Reforming/Reformed Mennonites (later the Missionary Church).

E. REGINALD GOOD and PAUL TIESSEN

Toronto and York Land Registry Office (Toronto), "Old York County," deeds, 5, no.1839 (mfm. at AO). Waterloo South Land Registry Office (Kitchener, Ont.), Waterloo Township, abstract index to deeds, German Company Tract, lot 17 (mfm. at AO). E. E. Eby and J. B. Snyder, *A biographical history of early settlers and their descendants in Waterloo Township*, with *Supplement*, ed. E. D. Weber (Kitchener, 1971), 136. John English and Kenneth McLaughlin, *Kitchener: an illustrated history* (Waterloo, Ont., 1983). *Hannes Schneider and his wife Catharine Haus Schneider, their descendants and times, 1534–1939*, ed. J. M. Snyder (Kitchener, [1940]). *Herkommen und Geschlechts Register der Schneider Familie* (Berlin [Kitchener], 1849). P. G. Klassen, "A history of Mennonite education in Canada, 1786–1960" (D.ED. thesis, Univ. of Toronto,

1970), 73–74. W. V. Uttley, *A history of Kitchener, Ontario* (Kitchener, 1937; repr. [Waterloo, 1975]), 17. M. [H.] Snyder Sokvitne, "The Joseph Schneider house, 1820," Waterloo Hist. Soc., [*Annual report*] (Kitchener), 1966: 20–27. W. V. Uttley, "Joseph Schneider: founder of the city," Waterloo Hist. Soc., *Annual report* (Waterloo), 1929: 111–19. G. K. Waite, "Joseph Schneider sawmill operations, 1848–1859," Waterloo Hist. Soc., [*Annual report*], 1985: 57–65.

SCHOULTZ, NILS VON (baptized **Nils Gustaf Ulric**), Patriot; b. 6 or 7 Oct. 1807 in Kuopio (Finland), second surviving child of Nils Fredrik von Schoultz and Johanna Henrica Gripenberg; m. 20 March 1834 Ann Cordelia Campbell in Florence (Italy), and they had two daughters; hanged 8 Dec. 1838 in Fort Henry, near Kingston, Upper Canada.

Surely no more delightful or respected scoundrel ever set foot in Canada or left as much of an impression there in such a short time as Nils von Schoultz. The son of a middle-rank official, Nils was taken to Sweden with the rest of the family when the Russians overran the province of Finland in 1808. After his father's death in 1816, his mother took all but one child back to Finland, where her brother ran a school. Schoultz was educated there and, when the family returned to Sweden in 1821, at the military academy in Karlberg. The same year he entered the Royal Svea Artillery Regiment, and by 1825 he had become a warrant officer second class. He resigned his commission in November 1830, quite possibly after being asked to do so because of gambling debts, and worked for the army for a while.

In 1831 Schoultz began the semi-nomadic existence which was to characterize the remainder of his life. He went to Poland to fight against the Russians for Polish freedom. Captured, he escaped and made his way to France, where he joined the Foreign Legion, and he served in north Africa. The type of warfare was repugnant to him, and in 1832 he managed to leave the Legion. The next year he arrived in Florence to visit some members of his family. There he met and courted Ann Campbell, a young Scottish tourist. The newlyweds moved to Sweden in 1834, accompanied by Ann's mother and sister, and with the small part of his mother-in-law's estate that was immediately available to her Schoultz paid some of his debts and purchased a mill. However, he was without a continuing livelihood, and in addition to a wife, in-laws, and servants he soon had two young daughters to support. As a result he established a laboratory and began experimenting in the hope of discovering potentially valuable manufacturing processes.

In June 1836 Schoultz journeyed to England, both to find a buyer for a red dye he had invented and to obtain more of his mother-in-law's estate. The dye proved unstable and Schoultz, who had much energy and enthusiasm but less patience, apparently became discouraged. He accepted a fellow Swede's offer of passage to the United States in the hopes of becoming a success there. When he left England he told neither his wife nor his wife's relatives in London, who had been entertaining him.

It was as Nils Scholtewskii von Schoultz, a 39-year-old Pole, that Schoultz introduced himself in the United States. Upon his arrival at New York in August 1836, his entrepreneurial instincts directed him to the salt works at Salina (Syracuse) and Syracuse in upstate New York, where considerable profits were to be made by extracting salt from brine. Schoultz soon devised an improved process for obtaining the salt, had it tested, and travelled to the American salt-producing areas interesting manufacturers in his process before applying to have it patented. Everywhere his courtly and charming manner won him new friends and even financial supporters. He acquired property in Virginia, applied for American citizenship, and settled temporarily in Salina with a new friend, Warren Green, to await the granting of his patent. Some contemporary accounts suggest that he was courting a local woman, possibly Emeline Field, Green's niece. He wrote to his wife in June 1837 promising to send a large amount of money in the near future, but he had no further correspondence with Europe. These actions suggest that Schoultz was building a new life; however, his sudden death makes it impossible to establish his ultimate intentions.

Just as the Polish cause and life in the Foreign Legion had seemed romantic and heroic to Schoultz, so did the cause of the Canadian people in 1838. He was drawn into one of the Hunters' Lodges, secret societies formed in the northern states following the rebellions of 1837 for the purpose of freeing the Canadas from British rule. After recruiting in New York City in the fall of 1838, Schoultz agreed to take part in an attack planned against Prescott, Upper Canada. On 11 Nov. 1838 the steamboat *United States* left Sackets Harbor, N.Y., and then towed two schooners full of men down the St Lawrence towards Prescott. One of the schooners, carrying Schoultz and between 150 and 200 men, landed a short distance east of Prescott. However, mishaps and the fire of a British war steamer [*see* William Newton Fowell*] prevented the other vessels from reaching the Upper Canadian side. Schoultz had only a minor rank, but with the senior officers on American soil he was elected leader. Using a stone windmill and several stone houses, he organized a defence which held for five days against a large British force of militia and regulars commanded in succession by colonels Plomer Young* and Henry Dundas, and supported by three armed steamers under Captain Williams Sandom*. Contact with the American side brought word of reinforcements and later of rescue, but neither was forthcoming. On the 16th the invaders, who by then were reduced to firing bolts, door hinges, and nails, succumbed to a mass attack.

Schoultz and his surviving men were taken to Fort Henry, where a court martial began on 26 November. At the suggestion of some British officers, who were impressed by his manner and his military background, he employed a young Kingston lawyer, John A. Macdonald*, as his counsel. However, Schoultz's gallant nature worked against him. Despite Macdonald's advice, he insisted that although he had invaded Upper Canada in a complete misunderstanding of the inhabitants' desires he was still guilty of an attack and should pay for his crimes. Accordingly, he was condemned to hang, but since he was believed to have been a Polish officer it was decided to execute him at Fort Henry instead of at the district jail with the other nine condemned men from the Prescott invasion force. Sentence was carried out on 8 December.

To the end Schoultz remained a gallant romantic. His will divided the bulk of his estate, most of which was to come from the sale of the patent to his salt process. Some of the proceeds were to be used to support the widows of the four men killed on the British side during the battle and to assist the Roman Catholic Regiopolis College being built in Kingston. The remainder of his money was to be divided equally between his wife and his mother, Warren Green, and Green's sister. Of Green's share, $1,000 was to go to his niece. There is no evidence that money was ever received for the patent. In letters published after his death Schoultz asked the American people not to think of avenging him and acknowledged that the Canadians were not discontented. At the end of his hectic life he was 31 years old.

RONALD J. STAGG

[The only source for the European portion of Schoultz's life is a somewhat coy but solid biography: Ella Pipping, *Soldier of fortune: the story of a nineteenth century adventurer*, trans. Naomi Walford (Boston, 1971), originally published in Swedish as *En orons legionär: Nils Gustaf von Schoultz, 1807–1838* ([Helsinki, Finland, 1967]). Written by a descendant, this work is largely based on family papers. It is not quite as good on North American events but is easily supplemented from a variety of sources. Official accounts of events near Prescott and of Schoultz's trial are to be found in PAC, RG 1, E3, 3: 116–76, and PRO, CO 42/451: 553–61; 42/452: 115, 120–21, 321–23, 338–78. His will is reproduced in CO 42/462: 133–52. Accounts, often very different, of the battle of Windmill Point are given in various contemporary newspapers; see for example *Mackenzie's Gazette* (New York), 17, 24 Nov., 15, 22 Dec. 1838; the Kingston *Chronicle & Gazette*, 14 Nov.–29 Dec. 1838; the *Kingston Spectator*, 30 Nov., 7 Dec. 1838; 11 Jan. 1839; the *Upper Canada Herald*, 13, 20 Nov. 1838; 1 Jan. 1839; and the *Brockville Recorder*, 15 Nov., 13, 27 Dec. 1838. These newspapers also reproduce several letters by Schoultz and a bogus biography (often edited or altered) of the "Pole" Schoultz, originally published in the *Onondaga Standard* (Onondaga, [Ont.]). Much of the above material also appears in Guillet, *Lives and times of Patriots*; O. A. Kinchen, *The rise and fall of the Patriot Hunters* (New York, 1956); and S. S. Wright, *Narrative and recollections of Van Diemen's Land, during a three years' captivity of Stephen S. Wright . . .*, ed. Caleb Lyon (New York, 1844). R.J.S.]

SECORD, DAVID, businessman, JP, politician, and militia officer; b. August 1759 in New York City, son of James Secord and Madelaine Badeau; m. first Jessie Millard; m. secondly Catharine Smith; m. thirdly Mary Page, widow of a Mr Dunn; he had 14 children; d. 9 Aug. 1844 in St Davids, Upper Canada.

David Secord's family moved to Northumberland County in the Susquehanna valley of Pennsylvania in 1772. Five years later, during the American revolution, his father joined Butler's Rangers [*see* John Butler*] and led 54 of his neighbours and 3 of his sons, including David, to Niagara (near Youngstown, N.Y.). James subsequently joined the Indian Department and David served as a corporal in the rangers from April 1777 to their disbandment in June 1784. He was wounded in the thigh, according to one account, at the battle of Oriskany. Following the war he settled with his father near Queenston, on the Niagara peninsula. David was instrumental in developing the community of St Davids on Four Mile Creek, where he built a sawmill in 1791; a grist-mill had been erected on the creek by Peter Secord (possibly an uncle) in 1789 and David's brother James and his wife, Laura Ingersoll*, also settled there. By 1812 David owned three houses, a grist-mill, a blacksmith shop, a general store, and other property.

Secord also achieved a measure of official prominence: he was commissioned as a justice of the peace in 1796 and he represented 2nd Lincoln in the fifth parliament of Upper Canada (1809–12). He had been made a lieutenant of militia in 1788, a captain in 1794, and major in the 2nd Lincoln Militia in 1806. He claimed to have fought in every significant engagement in the Niagara District during the War of 1812 and he commanded his regiment at the battle of Lundy's Lane on 25 July 1814 [*see* Sir Gordon Drummond*]. His buildings at St Davids, which he later valued at £3,796, were destroyed by American troops that month.

After the war Secord sat in the House of Assembly for 3rd Lincoln in the seventh parliament (1817–20). At this time he was closely associated with the agitation for reform stirred up by Robert Gourlay*. In April 1818 Secord chaired a meeting of inhabitants of Niagara Township which approved Gourlay's third address and set up the mechanism for electing the representatives from other townships in the peninsula who were to petition the Prince Regent on the state of affairs in Upper Canada and to attend a provincial gathering. He attended the Upper Canadian Convention of Friends to Enquiry held at York (Toronto) in July. His support for Gourlay, however, probably did not indicate any deep-seated hostility to the government.

Secord received no payment on his war loss claims until 1837; in 1840 he was forced to petition for the interest, £1,296, due on his compensation. His war losses and his large family combined meant a rather indigent old age. He died in August 1844 and was buried in the Methodist cemetery at St Davids.

BRUCE G. WILSON

PAC, MG 11, [CO 42] Q, 427, pt.I: 3–16; RG 1, E3, 47: 3; L3, 448: S1/2; RG 19, E5(a), 3741, claim 50. *Doc. hist. of campaign upon Niagara frontier* (Cruikshank), 8: 72–73. *Principles and proceedings of the inhabitants of the district of Niagara, for addressing His Royal Highness the Prince Regent respecting claims of sufferers in war, lands to militiamen, and the general benefit of Upper Canada* (Niagara [Niagara-on-the-Lake, Ont.], 1818). [A substantial portion of this pamphlet is reproduced in *Statistical account of U.C.* (Gourlay; ed. Mealing; 1974).] Armstrong, *Handbook of Upper Canadian chronology* (1967). Chadwick, *Ontarian families*, 2: 84. *Death notices of Ont.* (Reid). "Loyalist and pioneer families of West Lincoln, 1783–1833," comp. R. J. Powell, *Annals of the Forty* (Grimsby, Ont.), no.8 (1957): 26. Reid, *Loyalists in Ont.*, 277. Darroch Milani, *Robert Gourlay, gadfly*, 177.

SÉGUIN, FRANÇOIS-HYACINTHE, notary and diarist; b. 17 Aug. 1787 in Terrebonne, Que., eldest son of François Séguin, a farmer, and Charlotte Clément; m. there first 8 July 1815 Marie-Josephte Augé, and they had one child; m. there secondly 18 June 1838 Geneviève-Luce Robitaille, a widow; d. 19 Aug. 1847 in his native town.

In 1801 François-Hyacinthe Séguin began articling with Joseph Turgeon, a notary at Terrebonne. He seems not to have remembered his seven-year apprenticeship with pleasure, since he described his master as a speculator, extortioner, and drunkard. He was commissioned notary on 15 Oct. 1808 and opened an office at Terrebonne, where he practised all his life.

Séguin would probably have been forgotten had he not left a diary full of observations and reflections on society in Lower Canada. Besides being an interesting chronicle of religious and social life at Terrebonne, the journal, which runs from 7 Feb. 1831 to 2 March 1834, contains one of the most vigorous and articulate testimonies extant on the Patriote movement and republican liberalism. Written in a nostalgic vein, it comments extensively on history and politics. Séguin also vents his feelings against society in acid sketches of his contemporaries and close relatives.

The diary shows that he read the newspapers avidly and was passionately interested in political events of the day. He reveals himself as deeply religious, obsessed with death, and much involved in his community. He was attentive to natural, meteorological, and astronomical phenomena, and enthusiastic about fishing. Highly critical of his profession, he questioned the relevance of the admission examination, calling it "a mockery rather than a serious inquiry" whence came additional ignorant promoters of chicanery. Taking an interest in the financial, constitutional, educational, and judicial problems of Lower Canada, he reflected upon questions such as the death penalty, and he professed an orthodox kind of rationality, denouncing intemperance, superstition, and charivaris.

Séguin was a reactionary conservative who feared the consequences of the French revolution and the spread of atheism. Devoted to order and profoundly anti-democratic, he maintained that the will of the people was but "a poor machine that lets itself be driven by those who have cajoled it the most or have been the most lavish with servility and flattery."

In parliamentary events, which he followed with interest, Séguin found much to ponder. He was conscious of living in a pre-revolutionary period and longed to return to quieter times when peace and contentment reigned in Lower Canada. He was ill disposed towards the press and political clubs and denounced the strategy used in the House of Assembly by the Patriotes, who sought to overturn everything without improving anything. Furthermore, he criticized the Constitutional Act of 1791 for creating turmoil in the country by introducing popular sovereignty.

Three events in the course of 1832 gave Séguin the chance to express his anti-Patriote convictions. In March he was present at the triumphal return to Montreal of Ludger Duvernay* and Daniel Tracey*, who had been imprisoned for seditious libel. He was shocked by this popular demonstration and thought that the authorities should have been more severe with these "two wretched newsmongers." The spring by-election in Montreal West that year led to a riot in May, during which the British army fired on the crowd and killed three French Canadians [*see* Daniel Tracey]. Séguin seized the occasion to denounce the trouble-makers and thunder against popular suffrage. He even thought that the Patriotes had fomented the disturbance for fear of losing the election. An attentive and discerning observer of the cholera epidemic and its victims, he followed newspaper accounts of the spread of the disease at Quebec and Montreal, and he kept an annotated record of the deaths. In his view it was a scourge sent by God to rid Lower Canada of the disturbances prevalent there. He described the consternation of the people, the helplessness and contradictory opinions of the doctors, and the renewed religious observance.

François-Hyacinthe Séguin died in Terrebonne on 19 Aug. 1847. His death passed virtually unnoticed by the Montreal press. Paternalistic, with a passion for stability and order, Séguin was ill at ease with the social and revolutionary ferment of his time. His diary seems the work of a dour man, full of resentment. His writings remain a vigorous plea for a Lower Canada submissive to king, God, and the age-old traditions of the *ancien régime*. In the face of a nationalist historiography that has consigned to oblivion the French-speaking defenders of the British régime, Séguin recalls to mind the deep divisions within Lower Canadian society.

RÉJEAN LEMOINE

François-Hyacinthe Séguin's minute-book, containing instruments for the period 1808–47, is at ANQ-M, CN6-27. His diary, which has never been published, is at PAC, MG 24, I109.

ANQ-M, CE6-24, 17 août 1787, 8 juill. 1815, 18 juin 1838, 23 août 1847. PAC, RG 68, General index, 1651–1841. *Montreal Gazette*, 25 Aug. 1847. *Quebec Gazette*, 20 Oct. 1808. Raymond Masson, *Généalogie des familles de Terrebonne* (4v., Montréal, 1930–31), 4: 2190–95.

SELEE (Seeley), PEET (Peer, Peter), artisan, businessman, and militiaman; b. 4 June 1766 in the American colonies, probably in Connecticut; m. first Rebecca Peet, and they had at least nine children; m. secondly 22 Jan. 1833 Hannah Whooley (Woolley), a widow, and they had no children; d. 25 Nov. 1844 in Elizabethtown Township, Upper Canada.

A trained blacksmith, Peet Selee reputedly emigrated from Connecticut "with a company bound for the Bay of Quinte." All that is certain about his movements, however, is that he settled in Yonge Township in 1789. Possibly he had been attracted there by a number of Connecticut Selees in the Johnstown District. He farmed and, as one of the area's earliest blacksmiths, he utilized the surrounding woods for charcoal, probably producing the simple iron implements needed by settlers. He apparently prospered and, according to an 1879 account, he participated in at least two partnerships: one with Caleb Seaman, another blacksmith; the other with Daniel Jones, an early Brockville mill proprietor. About 1805 Selee and others erected a sawmill on a creek near by in Elizabethtown Township. He then moved to the site, where he resumed forging and engaged apprentices.

During the War of 1812 Selee was in various local militia detachments. In 1821, however, his wartime loyalty – he had taken the oath of allegiance in 1801 – was questioned; it was alleged that he had conducted a clandestine ferry operation across the St Lawrence River and speculated in American land. One magistrate claimed in his defence that Selee had served during the war "without suspicion of aiding or assisting the enemy." The issue, however, did not die and four years later a legal suit was brought against him, unsuccessfully as it turned out, for the utterance of "seditious words."

Following the war Selee had expanded his enterprises, adding by 1818 a tavern, inn, and mercantile store to his milling and forging operations. To a limited extent he also speculated in unsettled lands in nearby townships. Although Selee worked as a blacksmith and miller until his death, after 1819 he gradually reduced his local landholdings. In 1825 he sold a major portion of them to his son Truman. By 1832 the tavern and store were closed but Selee continued to operate the sawmill, the site of which became the hamlet of Selee's Corners. Following his death his wife Hannah inherited most of his estate, including his prized blacksmith's tools.

DAVID ROBERTS

AO, MS 519, Thomas Smyth to Joel Stone, 14 Sept. 1821; RG 1, C-IV, Elizabethtown and Yonge townships; RG 21, United Counties of Leeds and Grenville, Elizabethtown Township, census and assessment records, 1797–1845; RG 22, ser.12, 1–8, esp. 4: 62–63; ser.17, box 3, road report no.19; ser.18, boxes 1, 6–7; box 10: 4. Leeds Land Registry Office (Brockville, Ont.), Abstract index to deeds, Elizabethtown Township, concession 4, lot 32; North Crosby Township, concession 2, lot 23; Deeds, Elizabethtown Township, concession 4, lot 35, no.T212 (will of Peet Selee, registered 26 May 1845); Will of Justus Seelye, registered 9 July 1831 (transcript). MTRL, D. W. Smith papers, A9: 239–42. PAC, RG 1, L3; RG 9, I, B7, 6. "District of Luneburg: Court of Common Pleas," AO *Report*, 1917. "Journals of Legislative Assembly of U.C.," AO *Report*, 1913. "A record of marriages solemnized by William Smart, minister of the Presbyterian congregation, Brockville, Elizabethtown, Upper Canada," ed. H. S. Seaman, *OH*, 5 (1904): 217. *Brockville Recorder*, 5 Dec. 1844. T. W. H. Leavitt, *History of Leeds and Grenville, Ontario, from 1749 to 1879* . . . (Brockville, 1879; repr. Belleville, Ont., 1972). "Memoirs," *New England Hist. and Geneal. Reg.* (Boston), 108 (1954): 311.

SEWELL (Sewall), JONATHAN, lawyer, musician, office holder, politician, author, and judge; baptized 6 June 1766 in Cambridge, Mass., son of Jonathan Sewall (Sewell) and Esther Quincy; d. 11 Nov. 1839 at Quebec.

Jonathan Sewell was born into a prominent and cultivated Massachusetts family and, with his younger brother, Stephen*, grew up on the love and encouragement of his parents. His loyalist father, attorney general of the colony, earned the enmity of American patriots, and on 1 Sept. 1774 a terrified eight-year-old Jonathan witnessed the sack by a patriot mob of the family mansion in Cambridge. Within a week the Sewalls moved to Boston; a year later they arrived in London. In 1778 the family settled in Bristol, where they adopted the English spelling of the family name, Sewell. Jonathan discovered a talent for the theatre, and his performance in a school play impressed the celebrated actress Sarah Siddons, who described him as "Dame Nature's chosen son." He had innate abilities in music and painting as well, and his father found that he had "impetuous and penetrating" powers of mind. Edward Winslow* later described him as "one of the finest lads I ever saw."

After briefly attending Brasenose College, Oxford, Jonathan left England in early 1785 under the care of Attorney General Jonathan Bliss* of New Brunswick to study law with an old family friend, Solicitor General Ward Chipman*. To improve his courtroom skills Sewell founded in Saint John the Forensick Society, a student club that debated moot points of law. He also got an apprenticeship in conservative politics as a campaigner for the government party, of which Chipman was a leader. In October 1787 he was appointed registrar of the Vice-Admiralty Court. The following May he was called to the bar, and he soon had a clientele. His family had been reunited in Saint John, but in the summer of 1789 he moved to Quebec, where there was greater scope for his abilities.

That October, thanks to strong recommendations from Chipman and judge Joshua Upham*, Sewell acquired his lawyer's commission. He quickly found that Scottish and Canadian barristers monopolized civil litigation, and he was contemplating a move to Montreal when, in October 1790, he was appointed attorney general of the province of Quebec *pro tempore*. The position eventually went to James Monk*, but, boosted by the temporary appointment, Sewell's private practice flourished. Its growth was also due to Sewell's rapid mastery of French civil law, with which he had been unfamiliar on his arrival.

Sewell's success partially reflected his acceptance by Quebec's British community. Its members embraced him even more readily after he became a protégé of Prince Edward* Augustus, who, impressed by Sewell's proficiency as a violinist, engaged him to lead an amateur orchestra in regular musical evenings. Sewell acquired the most recent works of European composers and for one concert composed new verses to "God save the King" which would create a sensation in 1800 when sung on a London stage by the actor Richard Brinsley Butler Sheridan after an attempted assassination of George III. Sewell's social relations were not only cultural; in September 1793 he had baptized "a natural child" named John St Alban Sewell.

Sewell shared the moderately liberal views of his social entourage. He promoted the efforts of Chief Justice William Smith* to establish a non-denominational university, opposed slavery, and was a firm believer in habeas corpus. Although a staunch defender of the royal prerogative, he supported a balanced constitution with an important role for an elected house of commons. He welcomed the granting of an assembly for Lower Canada by the Constitutional Act of 1791 (but regretted the division of the province) and in 1792 published *An abstract from precedents of proceedings in the British House of Commons* to guide the assembly's deliberations.

In 1793 Governor Lord Dorchester [Guy Carleton*] and Smith obtained Sewell's appointment as solicitor general and inspector of the king's domain. With Monk, Sewell analysed and worked to suppress a series of militia riots in 1794. Both men demonstrated a tendency, widespread among British inhabitants, to view the rioters as pawns of French revolutionary and American agents. After Monk's elevation to the bench in 1794 Sewell prosecuted the unfinished cases – demonstrating considerable leniency, in accordance with Dorchester's prudent policy of treating political offenders lightly. In 1795 Sewell took a leading role with Chief Justice William Osgoode* and Montreal lawyer Arthur Davidson* in successfully opposing legislation that would have opened the legal profession to unqualified persons. On 9 May 1795, thanks to Dorchester and Osgoode but over the opposition of Monk, who detected a serious rival in this "Going Man," Sewell was appointed attorney general and advocate general. He was named judge of the Vice-Admiralty Court in June 1796.

The office of the attorney general was an important one in the Lower Canadian administration. In addition to drafting government regulations and legal instruments, the attorney general prosecuted cases of all sorts, including those involving state security. With the aid of Montreal merchant and magistrate John Richardson*, among others, Sewell established an intelligence network that would function for more than a decade with relative effectiveness. When a series of riots broke out in 1796–97 over a new road act, Sewell reported to Governor Robert Prescott* that they were orchestrated by French emissaries who were seconded by demagogic politicians such as Joseph PAPINEAU and Jean-Antoine Panet*, both groups playing on "pretended grievances" and on the "profound Ignorance" that was "too surely the Characterisk of the Canadians." On Sewell's recommendation, arrests were made at Quebec and troops sent to Montreal to stiffen the resolve of timid magistrates. At Quebec 23 of the 24 persons indicted, and at Montreal 11 of the 13 tried, were convicted; the sentences were light but the conviction rate impressed.

Imbued with the loyalists' sense of the fragility of the social order and fearing that the colony was to be invaded by a French fleet, Sewell drafted what became the Better Preservation Act of 1797. It suspended habeas corpus, in some cases on mere suspicion of undefined "treasonable practices." In addition, this cleverly worded statute authorized imprisonment of assemblymen to permit the incarceration of the Panet–Papineau faction should the invasion materialize. In May 1797 the arrest of the American David McLane* for treason offered the possibility of making an example. Sewell prosecuted, and in the course of building up a strong case he was party to dubious transactions that compromised the justice of the proceedings. Following McLane's execution there were no more riots. Clearly mob action, and the fear that it might become organized and strengthened by a discontented militia, undermined Sewell's moderately liberal views.

Sewell's approach to ordinary criminal cases contrasted strikingly with his treatment of security issues. No blurring of the law to serve the royalist cause altered his respect for the rights of the accused or his belief that penal law must be interpreted restrictively; indeed, on more than one occasion he agonized over the fate of helpless individuals caught in the system. Of the nearly 400 indictments Sewell drafted between 1793 and 1802, only 170 were of Canadians and 43 of women.

Sewell spent much of his time writing an astonishing array of legal opinions for the government. Almost all are models of clarity, convincingly argued and well supported by authorities. Most display a concern to protect the rights of the crown; his insistence on support from legal authorities worked to the detriment of land claims by Indians who rarely had "any Title or any other evidence Whatever" sufficient to impress him.

Sewell was aware of the distinction between an opinion grounded in law and one based on policy preference, but in certain areas – and in none more frequently than ecclesiastical affairs – he crossed the line between the two. When dealing with the Church of England he normally confined himself to legal authorities and more than once, to the dismay of his intimate friend Anglican bishop Jacob Mountain*, they led him to "an Opinion which I adopt against my will." Although he considered that the Church of England in the colony lacked in law certain rights essential to its functioning (such as the legal existence of parishes), he did believe it to be an established church. In the case of the Roman Catholic Church, Sewell asserted that policy dictated the exercise of a royal supremacy he believed was sanctioned in law, and he argued that a supposed lack of legal recognition of the church by British law should be exploited to oblige it to accept royal supremacy. Initially convinced that the church was "merely tolerated," by 1801 he had come to fear "with too much certainty" that it had, in fact, been established by the Quebec Act of 1774. To Lieutenant Governor Sir Robert Shore MILNES he expressed the opinion that, given the independence of the church and the ignorance and superstition of the population, the influence exerted over the inhabitants by the clergy and the bishop was "immense" and "highly dangerous." However, he added, "to direct [the bishop] is to direct all," and since the root of the executive's problems in the colony was, he felt, a lack of sway over the people, the control of the church was the best means to obtain it. The government must therefore use its "right of nominating the Bishop, the Coadjutor and the Parish priest which it assumed by the conquest of Canada but has never yet exercised."

In the spring of 1805, encouraged by Milnes, Sewell engaged coadjutor bishop Joseph-Octave Plessis* in discussions designed to bring Bishop Pierre Denaut* to request legal recognition of his position and of his church in return for his own recognition of royal supremacy. Ultimately, Denaut's decision to petition the king for legal recognition of his office in the form of letters patent under conditions to be determined by the crown constituted a tactical victory for Sewell. When Denaut died in early 1806, Sewell, along with Civil Secretary Herman Witsius RYLAND, tried in vain to persuade the administrator of the colony, Thomas Dunn*, not to accept Plessis as bishop, or Bernard-Claude Panet* as his coadjutor, until the crown had replied to Denaut's petition. Despite recurrent reminders from Sewell, Mountain, and Ryland, the British government never responded.

Executive influence over the Canadian population could also be obtained, Sewell believed, through control of education, so, with Mountain and Milnes, he worked out the details of a scheme for government-financed and -directed elementary schools in the countryside staffed by loyal Canadian teachers who would instruct habitant children in the English language and the blessings of British rule. He drafted the government bill, which, amended by the assembly to impotence with respect to the education of Canadians, established the Royal Institution for the Advancement of Learning in 1801.

For Sewell, the anglicization of the population was essential if the colony was to be kept under British rule. This could be advanced more rapidly by encouraging massive immigration, particularly of Americans. Unfortunately, the seigneurial system discouraged immigration, and Sewell provided Milnes with opinions as to the legal means available to make the system so onerous that the population itself would be induced to seek conversion to freehold tenure.

The role of the attorney general being in part political, in 1796, shortly after his appointment, Sewell had obtained election to the assembly for William Henry (Sorel), one of two ridings in which British inhabitants constituted the majority. In the house he was often called on to draft bills, but with regard to government business he normally played a role secondary to that of leaders of the English party such as John Young* and Pierre-Amable De Bonne*. He supported the party, except on two controversial issues – the financing of prisons in 1805 [*see* Ignace-Michel-Louis-Antoine d'Irumberry* de Salaberry] and the expulsion of Ezekiel HART, a Jew – in which his legal opinions obliged him to break rank. He remained in the assembly until 1808.

Sewell continued in private practice while attorney general. His official function enabled him to transmit quickly to his clients the latest information on pending legislation; but he was aware of possible conflicts of interest, and on at least three occasions refused private business on that ground. By the early 19th century he probably had the foremost practice in the colony, his clients being largely prominent businessmen, office holders, and seigneurs. In the early 1800s he defended Young when Young was sued for debt by Catherine Le Comte Dupré; his successful plea that French law had been modified by practice since the conquest was interpreted by Canadian nationalists as an attack on the Canadians' legal tradition. Sewell took under his wing aspiring lawyers such as Edward Bowen*, James Stuart*, Jean-Thomas Taschereau*, and Philippe-Joseph Aubert* de Gaspé, instilling in them a great respect for the forms of the law.

According to Aubert de Gaspé, Sewell treated his clerks like his own children. On 24 Sept. 1796 he had married Henrietta Smith (familiarly known as Harriet), a daughter of the late chief justice and, at 20, "a woman of great beauty," in Aubert de Gaspé's estimation. The marriage was born out of love and would be lived in love. Of their 16 children the Sewells were fortunate to lose only four in infancy. Sewell was a highly attentive father; on one occasion, for example, he protested angrily when a son in school received corporal punishment, a means of discipline he abhorred. In 1805 Sewell moved his burgeoning family into a mansion he had had built just inside the Porte Saint-Louis. Valued at some £4,000, it helped to introduce into Quebec the Palladian architecture then popular in Britain and the United States. The Sewells entertained constantly at dinner parties and were highly prized guests in the best British and Canadian homes. Sewell was a member of the exclusive Barons' Club and was an active shareholder in the Union Company of Quebec, which in 1805 built the Union Hotel as a focal point of social life at Quebec. Sewell much preferred Quebec's high society to that of Montreal, which he found scandalous and frivolous. He particularly deplored the coldness shown to their wives by Montreal's businessmen, with "their male clubs, companies, & coffee houses." Trois-Rivières was a social "purgatory" and afforded him as attorney general "more occupation speaking comparatively than the whole district of Montreal."

On 22 Aug. 1808 Sewell was appointed chief justice of Lower Canada in succession to Henry Allcock*. It was a post he had been seeking since 1801 with the assistance of a battery of influential people. Immediately after taking office, he consulted with his colleagues on ways to systematize and streamline court procedures, and in 1809 he published orders and rules of practice for the Court of King's Bench at Quebec and for the Court of Appeals. Monk followed suit in Montreal two years later. Sewell attended to his judicial duties assiduously; from 1809 to 1823 he was present on 90 per cent of all court days during which he was in the colony. He was a highly competent criminal-law judge, fair except where the colony's security was concerned. His addresses to grand juries, often published, were model lectures on complex fields of law.

Sewell generally believed serious crime to be increasing among the Canadians and, like many of his judicial contemporaries, he maintained that it took root in immorality. Following late 18th-century orthodoxy, he considered that any fundamentally dishonest or immoral act was a misdemeanour, even though not covered by law. He constantly inveighed against taverns, gambling houses, and brothels – "public Seminaries of Depravity" – holding that they introduced misery and disease into the lives of the working classes, whose social utility was diminished in consequence. He was slightly in advance of his time in his concept of punishment. No adherent to the selective-terror school of theologian William Paley, he drew inspiration from Sir William Blackstone's Enlightenment-inspired attacks on what Blackstone called the "multitude of sanguinary laws." Sewell's sentences were designed to prevent crime rather than punish the guilty and he felt that it was the certainty, not the severity, of punishment that deterred crime. He was even known to spare penitent parties a record and imprisonment in the company of hardened criminals. He believed capital punishment necessary for violent or potentially violent crime but found it a terrible ordeal to pronounce. On occasion he stretched the evidence so as to invite acquittal for non-violent property crimes carrying the death sentence, and in some cases, including convictions for murder, he intervened to save a prisoner from the gallows. To the end Sewell would persist in efforts to lessen recourse to the death penalty through reduction in the number of crimes punishable by death and through transportation of felons; however, he was thwarted by the indifference of the assembly and the Colonial Office.

Compared to criminal cases, civil suits were a pleasure for Sewell. He had a tendency to favour the crown whenever the political interests of the government were deeply engaged, but if his judgements are not entirely impartial, they are remarkable for their clarity of expression, their search for general principle, and the depth of scholarship that underpins them. Sewell probably did more than anyone to professionalize the administration of civil justice prior to codification of civil law in 1866.

As chief justice, Sewell took a seat on the Executive Council in September 1808. For £100, the salary of an ordinary councillor, he presided over all committees of the whole, all committees on questions of state, the committee of public accounts until 1818, the land committee until 1828, and the Court of Appeals. The governor referred most matters to the council and generally accepted its advice; since often no more than six councillors were present and Sewell was by far the most faithful in attendance, he held great sway over the government. He was called to the Legislative Council in September 1808 and in January 1809 he became its speaker. Able, despite being speaker, to debate and vote (twice in the case of a tie) and again extremely faithful in attendance, he ultimately exercised an influence over it comparable to that of Louis-Joseph Papineau* in the assembly.

Sewell's roles made him easily the most powerful official in the colony after the governor. His influence was particularly evident during the administration of Sir James Henry Craig*. In 1809, as opposition to Craig's policies was expressed with ever-increasing virulence in *Le Canadien*, the newspaper of the Canadian party, Sewell, as chief justice, warned a grand jury that the "Liberty of the press," like all civil liberties, was subject to "the good of the community" and that "whensoever the press is prejudicial to the public weal It is abused." A year later he was among the executive councillors who advised Craig to seize *Le Canadien* and to detain Pierre-Stanislas Bédard* and others connected with it on suspicion of treasonable practices under the Better Preservation Act. Although politically involved in Bédard's arrest, he had no compunction about acting in his judicial role to preside over a court that rejected Bédard's application for habeas corpus. This kind of mixing of politics and judicial administration had been condemned as unconstitutional by the British parliament in 1806, and in Lower Canada it brought criticism from the bar. Confident in Sewell's control of the court system, Craig was able to intimidate a formerly fractious assembly.

In May 1810, at Craig's request, Sewell analysed the political ills of the colony. They arose, he believed, "1st From the French predilections in the great Mass of the Inhabitants, and 2^{ly} From want of Influence and power in the Executive Government." "The great links of connection between a Government and its subjects are religious, Laws and Language," he asserted. Those links did not exist in the colony. British and Canadians nurtured a "national antipathy," and since no "incorporation of two such Extremes can ever be effected," he concluded "the Province must be converted to an English Colony, or, it will ultimately be lost to England."

To achieve this objective, he again urged encouragement of large-scale American immigration, conversion from seigneurial to freehold tenure, and construction of Craig's Road to open up the Eastern Townships. Confiscation of the Sulpician estates would finance government-controlled education and a declaratory act of parliament would confirm royal supremacy over the Roman Catholic Church. Political reform was needed. Sewell recommended imposing a higher property qualification for voters and members of the assembly, convinced that a combination of British "industry and perseverence," Canadian "Idleness," and the manner of bequeathing property characteristic of each group would ensure to British colonists the bulk of landed property. To accelerate anglicization he recommended "an incorporate union of the Two Provinces of Upper and Lower Canada" which would leave each province its existing system of laws. Craig supported all of Sewell's proposals except union; later, however, he came to accept the idea of union.

Britain did not endorse Sewell's program. Craig's replacement, Sir George Prevost*, attempted to conciliate the Canadian party. The change was not to Sewell's liking, but following the advent of war with the United States he was agreeably surprised to find the Canadians evincing "universally a sincere and loyal desire to assist in every way for the defence of the Country," and he exercised a moderating influence within the English party. In July 1812 he made a major contribution to the war effort by proposing the army bills scheme, generally attributed to Young, who had, rather, recommended a provincial bank; Sewell's scheme, which was adopted, placed the issuing of currency in imperial military hands.

In January 1814 the relative political calm in the colony was shattered when the assembly attacked the rules of practice published by Sewell in 1809 and by Monk in 1811. Following the lead of Stuart, Sewell's former pupil, who for personal reasons had developed a "rancorous hatred" towards him and his brother Stephen, the assembly impeached Sewell and Monk, in part on the grounds that some of their rules constituted legislation and that the judges had thereby usurped the role of the assembly. More than three-quarters of the assembly's charges were political, however, Sewell being accused particularly of poisoning Craig against the Canadians, attempting "to extinguish all reasonable freedom of the Press," and promoting "American dominance." Sewell was soon in "a state of pitiable distress," noted Assistant Civil Secretary Andrew William COCHRAN; although he was "a man of great talent, his feelings are fine and his nerves weak." The other judges and the Executive Council quickly declared themselves included in the indictments relating to the rules of practice. Sewell and Monk were thrown together to prepare a defence with the assistance of Richardson. Sewell, it was decided, would defend their cause in London.

In early June 1814 the entire Sewell family left for England. At the Colonial Office Sewell quickly learned that the political charges against him would not even be considered: to heed them, Colonial Secretary Lord Bathurst claimed, "would be to admit that a councillor was responsible for the acts of a Governor [which is] contrary to every principle." The rules of practice were referred to the Privy Council for examination. In his defence Sewell asserted that the assembly's ultimate objective was the "revolutionary project" of "transferring the Executive Power and Prerogatives of the Crown, to the Legislative." The crown had therefore to rescue its judicial and administrative officers from dependence on the elected body. Sewell transformed his own defence into an attack on Prevost's conciliatory administration. In the end Prevost attributed his recall more to Sewell's efforts than to possible displeasure over his conduct of an attack on Plattsburgh, N.Y., in 1814. In June 1815 the Privy Council announced that none of the rules of practice was unconstitutional. In 1818 they would be reprinted without change.

Meanwhile, Sewell had turned to other matters. The War of 1812 had made colonial defence a primary concern in London. To address it, in November 1814 Sewell sent to Prince Edward Augustus, now the Duke of Kent, a plan for union of all the British North American colonies. The Canadians, he now realized, would fight the Americans as long as they could retain their language, laws, and religion under British rule. But effective resistance to the more powerful enemy could be achieved, he thought, only by the combined efforts of all the colonies. Initially, he envisaged a central executive and legislature, with each colony retaining a lieutenant governor and an executive council. Sewell's proposals sought to reinforce the crown and executive at the expense of the legislature and to free judicial and administrative officials from harassment by elected assemblies. No doubt criticism of the small place he left to the central legislature induced Sewell to modify his plan by adding provincial legislatures to handle strictly local matters. His scheme was then apparently published in 1814 as *A plan for the federal union of British provinces in North America*. It was a product of the New England loyalist mind; like a federal plan drafted by his father in 1784, and contrary to another proposed by his New Yorker father-in-law, it sought to achieve stability by excluding the masses from the political process rather than by admitting them into it.

Sewell arrived back at Quebec on 4 July 1816 to a rare salute from the fortress. With him he brought a highly flattering letter from Lord Bathurst instructing Governor Sir John Coape Sherbrooke* to promote Sewell's interests. Sherbrooke warned Bathurst that "an infatuated dislike amounting almost to detestation" of Sewell "pervades all classes," particularly the clergy. Thanks to the governor's skilful management, however, the assembly even voted Sewell a salary of £1,000 as speaker of the Legislative Council in return for the council's agreeing to make permanent Papineau's equivalent salary as speaker of the assembly.

Throughout his long involvement in public life Sewell had remained active socially. In December 1808 he had assumed the patronage of a literary society formed by Aubert de Gaspé and other young men of Quebec. He promoted the theatre and attempted in vain to persuade Plessis to lift his prohibition of it for Catholics. In October 1818 he was appointed to the board of the Royal Institution. A few months later he chaired a meeting of the managers of the Quebec Dispensary. Long a subscriber to the Agriculture Society, in 1819 he donated to it a fine imported cow and her bull calf.

Sewell's re-engagement in the maelstrom of Lower Canadian politics from 1816 did nothing for his health. In July 1820 an alarmed Governor Lord Dalhousie [RAMSAY], cognizant of "how large a space [Sewell] fills in the direction of public affairs," warned Bathurst that "a Complication of disorders, arising from intense study, and anxiety of mind appears to have broken his Constitution." Dalhousie developed an exceptional friendship and political relationship with his urbane, conservative, and well-informed chief justice. In November 1820 he told Bathurst that "as my Confidential adviser in the . . . administration of the Government, I turn to him on all occasions of difficulty." None the less, Sewell's unpopularity with the assembly induced Dalhousie to contemplate replacing him as speaker of the Legislative Council with Lieutenant Governor Sir Francis Nathaniel Burton* in order to improve the productivity of the legislature. The change was not made, however.

In the 1820s, as his numerous sons came of age, Sewell's nepotism gave the Canadian party new reasons to detest him and promoted in Dalhousie the only serious reservation he had about the chief justice. The governor was particularly upset in late 1822 when Sewell, in a politically reckless move, jumped at the position of sheriff of Quebec for his son William Smith. Predictably, the assembly attacked the appointment as prejudicial to the administration of justice. Nevertheless, only Dalhousie's firmness discouraged Sewell in 1826 from pursuing his strenuous efforts to have another son, Robert Shore Milnes, appointed protonotary for the district of Quebec.

It was as an office holder, in fact, that Sewell approached the issues of the day. With regard to financial matters, for example, he insisted that salaries be the priority item of payment on the civil list and, taking a line in opposition to his merchant colleagues in the English party, in 1821 he combatted, unsuccessfully, incorporation of the Quebec Fire Assurance Company, the Quebec Bank, and the Bank of Montreal. Again it was as an office holder that Sewell responded to a growing sentiment in the early 1820s, particularly among Montreal merchants, for a legislative union of the Canadas. He gave Dalhousie a copy of his plan of 1814 for federation, but the governor rejected it as according too much influence to the crown and executive and likely to provoke a furious reaction from the assembly. In any case Dalhousie too preferred a legislative union of the Canadas, and he supported just such a scheme in 1822. Sewell, however, warned the Colonial Office that the proposed plan was arousing hostility among the Canadians. Once more he put forward his project for federating all the colonies. Undersecretary Robert John Wilmot-Horton had Sewell's proposal published in 1824 along with one by the attorney general of Upper Canada, John Beverley Robinson*, under the title of *Plan for a general legislative union of the British provinces in North America*. Meanwhile, in early 1823, Sewell had urged Dalhousie not to allow a clause respecting religion to be included in any union bill, for fear of provoking the Canadians; rather, he suggested the negotiation of a "Concordat," on the basis of Denaut's petition, whenever a successor to Plessis had to be appointed.

Sewell's opposition to the proposed legislative union of the Canadas in 1822 was noticed in the assembly (he had engineered defeat of a motion for it in the Legislative Council), and at the end of the session of 1823 Dalhousie recorded that "the whole House of Assembly in body has dined at the private house of the Chief Justice"; only Papineau declined. Under the temporary administration of Burton in 1824–25 the political tensions that had characterized Dalhousie's administration decreased to such an extent that even Papineau was constrained to exchange invitations with Sewell. However, Burton's efforts to appease Canadian nationalists made the chief justice uneasy. In early 1825 Sewell suggested the rejection of Papineau as speaker of the assembly, but Burton refused. When Burton worked out a compromise supply bill with the house, Sewell abstained from voting on it in the Legislative Council; although he disliked the bill, he believed that it was politically and constitutionally acceptable and so strongly supported in council that a negative vote on his part would have been useless. Disenchanted, Dalhousie later accused him of "trimming and manoeuvring."

Sewell was more clearly conciliatory towards the Canadians while on the bench in the early 1820s. Before a grand jury in 1822 he applauded the growing acceptance of both French civil and English criminal law as "the triumph of good sense over national prejudice." When the post of advocate general came open in early 1823 he recommended that it be reserved for "a Canadian gentleman of the first standing at the Bar." Sewell's influence in improving the quality of the judiciary remained strong, but his presence in court declined for reasons of health. At the same time the judicial system was increasingly taxed. The number of causes handled by the provincial courts of King's Bench had swelled from 1,103 in 1808 to 3,409 in 1826. In 1828 Sewell warned Dalhousie that the courts had become overwhelmed.

The bench had other problems. The refusal of the assembly from the early 1820s to provide what the judges deemed reasonable pensions to Monk and Isaac Ogden spurred them, led by Sewell, to seek financial independence of that house. Appealing to the Colonial Office, they invoked the necessity for an independent judiciary and also requested appointment during good behaviour rather than royal pleasure. Sewell argued that the colonial judiciary had matured to such a point that the judges should be placed on the same footing as their British counterparts. The Colonial Office agreed to the change of tenure on condition that the assembly guarantee a satisfactory salary and pension. The assembly, on the other hand, demanded that the judges be excluded from the councils and sought to use the establishment of a fixed salary and pension as a springboard for its claim to control crown revenues. The independence of the judiciary, consequently, became one more issue of controversy in the 1820s and 1830s.

Sewell's place in the social and cultural life of Quebec continued to grow. In 1824 he was obliged to purchase the Union Hotel for £4,215 at a sheriff's auction in order to protect his large investment in it. Having no desire that he or his sons go into business, he leased the hotel. The same year he won the Royal Institution's prize for service to education, and in 1825–26 acted as president of the institution. At Dalhousie's urging, he and his brother-in-law, William SMITH, had been instrumental in founding the Literary and Historical Society of Quebec in 1824. Named a vice-president in March 1824, he gave the society's first paper in May, a study of French law before 1663 as it applied to the colony. He was president of the society in 1830 and 1831.

Sewell, whose wife was Presbyterian, supported St Andrew's Church financially, but was an active, devout Anglican. For many years he presided over the Quebec branch of the British and Foreign Bible Society, and he was a leading member of the Cathedral of the Holy Trinity. By 1824 the cathedral was too small and Sewell offered to build a chapel of ease on condition that he and his heirs could name the incumbent. Bishop Mountain accepted the offer and Sewell named as incumbent his son Edmund Willoughby. Sewell purchased a lot on Rue Saint-Stanislas and had the building, called Holy Trinity chapel, constructed on the model of Ranelagh Chapel in London. He spent more than £3,500 on the building which, opened in November 1825, could seat 800. Dalhousie pronounced it "neat," but found Edmund Willoughby "unfit & unqualified."

In June 1826 Sewell and his entire family became

extremely depressed by the death of a 12-year-old daughter. Leaving his three eldest boys to manage his affairs, he took his wife and other children to England and the Continent. The family arrived in London in early August, and three weeks later Sewell was received by Bathurst at his estate in Cirencester. Immediately afterwards the Sewells embarked for France and Belgium. In Calais Sewell was taken by the mayor for a Frenchman, and in Paris he bought 600 volumes of French law for the Advocates' Library at Quebec. By the end of September the family was back in London.

Sewell made frequent trips to Cirencester and spent many hours at the Colonial Office, being consulted on behalf of the Royal Institution, the provincial judges, and Dalhousie. Although he presented Dalhousie's views on Burton's supply bill, he admitted the bill's validity. He persuaded the Colonial Office to accede to the assembly's demand that Britain reimburse the colony for the defalcation of Receiver General John CALDWELL, but the Treasury refused to pay. He learned that the ministry would not consider major constitutional reforms as Dalhousie wished; however, he obtained authorization for the governor to borrow from unappropriated funds under the assembly's control to pay expenses, a major gain for the executive.

The Sewells returned to Quebec in late spring 1827. The rest had restored Sewell's combativeness. He virtually wrote the provocative speech with which Dalhousie opened the legislature in late 1827 and successfully advised the governor to take the momentous step of refusing the assembly's election of Papineau as its speaker. Not surprising, he was the subject of strong attacks in petitions drawn up in 1828 by Patriote constitutional committees. To a charge that the public had little confidence in the Court of King's Bench at Quebec, he replied that in 20 years only 153 of 4,000 decisions had been appealed and one-half of those solely to delay execution. Sewell's identification with Dalhousie extended to chairing a committee to erect a monument to James Wolfe* and Louis-Joseph de Montcalm*, which the governor viewed as a testimonial to his own administration.

Dalhousie was replaced at the head of the government in 1828 by Sir James Kempt*, who in March 1829 negotiated with the assembly a supply bill modelled on that passed by Burton in 1825. Sewell whole-heartedly backed the measure, even employing his double vote in the Legislative Council. Late in 1829 Papineau thought that "the chief justice would like to make peace in his old age." Indeed, when in 1830 it became clear that the Colonial Office accepted the exclusion of the judges from the Executive Council in partial fulfilment of a demand by the assembly that they be excluded from both councils, Sewell readily offered his resignation; it was accepted on 14 October. He remained speaker of the Legislative Council, but in a supposedly non-partisan advisory capacity.

Nevertheless, Sewell viewed Kempt's administration as fuelling "the ponderous Car of Democracy" at the expense of the royal prerogative. Increasingly he registered his dissent from conciliatory votes in the Legislative Council, and in 1834, after years of debate, that body finally deprived him of his double vote and left him only the right to break ties. In 1831, however, he had successfully rallied opposition there to the *fabriques* bill [*see* Louis Bourdages*]. Earlier that year, when the council, acting under doubtful legal authority, had arrested the Patriote editors Ludger Duvernay* and Daniel Tracey* for having published articles critical of it, Sewell had reprimanded the two men before sending them to jail. Subsequently the Quebec Court of King's Bench refused them a writ of habeas corpus. These incidents provoked public outrage. A crowd, singing "La Marseillaise" and "La Parisienne," marched to Sewell's mansion; recalling the mob of 1774, Sewell was frightened.

The hardening of Sewell's political views in the late 1820s and early 1830s was probably a reaction to the radicalization of the Patriote party and was reflected in an opinion expressed to Governor Lord Aylmer [WHITWORTH-AYLMER] in November 1834 that no more Canadians should be appointed to the bench. Aylmer heeded Sewell's advice, but his successor, Lord Gosford [ACHESON], did not. In the mean time, Sewell's tireless efforts on behalf of his sons – three Sewells were on the establishment of the Legislative Council in 1832 – were satirized in a popular Patriote song, "C'est la faute à Papineau." Sewell played only a minor role during and after the rebellions of 1837–38 because most of the disturbances occurred in the Montreal district. In court he articulated an extreme royalist interpretation of the law of treason, but he issued writs of habeas corpus, before that recourse was suspended, to a number of Quebec Patriotes, including politician Augustin-Norbert Morin* and the painter Joseph Légaré*. He was reappointed to the Executive Council by Governor Lord Durham [LAMBTON] in June 1838, but he remained only until Durham's departure in November. In his report Durham singled out Sewell's federal plan of 1814.

Meanwhile, in declining health, Sewell had resigned as chief justice on 20 Oct. 1838. He was replaced by Stuart. Sixty-two members of the bar underlined in an address the progress that their profession had made under Sewell's leadership. Indeed, Sewell's reputation as a judge and legal thinker had reached into the United States: he had been consulted in 1822 on the preparation of a penal code for Louisiana; eight years later he was elected to the prestigious American Philosophical Society; in 1832 Harvard University conferred on him an honorary LLD; in 1835 the Massachusetts Historical Society elected him a corresponding member; and about 1839 the *American Jurist and Law Magazine* (Boston) commented that Lower Canadian cases "derive their chief interest from the learned judgements of that enlightened and accomplished Jurist Chief Justice Sewell."

During the 1830s Sewell had continued to add threads to the cultural fabric of Quebec. In 1831–32, to save another substantial investment, he had purchased Nicolas-François Mailhot*'s Royal Circus and hotel. He transformed the circus into a theatre, employing local artists such as Légaré to do the decoration, and then leased it. Known as the Theatre Royal, it opened in February 1832 with a benefit play for the poor, Sewell himself apparently having written the welcome address, which underlined the moral and social vocation of the theatre. The venture did not thrive, but the successive lessees bore the brunt of the losses. Sewell also founded a quartet with himself and Archibald Campbell* as violinists, Louis-Édouard Glackmeyer* as flautist, and J. Harvicker as cellist; they gave concerts, cultivated a taste for classical music at Quebec, and formed a generation of amateur musicians. Finally, Sewell gave lodging in 1838 to the Italian miniaturist Gerome Fassio*, with whom he conversed in fluent Italian.

Sewell's family life had remained idyllic, occasionally burdened by his depressions, but more often lightened by his humour. In old age, as in youth, he wrote poems "For Mrs Sewell My own dear Jewell," and to the end he generously supported his children in financial or other difficulties.

Sewell died on 11 Nov. 1839 and was buried four days later from Holy Trinity cathedral; a monument depicting him, sculpted in London at a cost of £600, was erected by Harriet in Holy Trinity chapel. He died intestate, but Harriet was guaranteed one-third of the estate by her marriage contract; the remainder was divided equally among the ten surviving children and two orphaned grandchildren (counting as one). Sewell's mansion reflected not only the wealth of its former owner but also his views and tastes: a picture of Dalhousie graced a nursery wall, two violins lay in the study, the wine cellar was plentifully stocked, and the library boasted 1,476 volumes (of which 1,120 were on law, politics, or public administration). The estate also included 14 properties in Upper Town (almost all acquired in the 1830s), a country seat at Auvergne, land on the Rivière Saint-Charles, and large tracts of wild land, which Sewell had begun to settle, in Ham and Tingwick townships. With landed properties worth £20,692, bonds in England worth £16,020, a large deposit in the Quebec Bank, and accounts receivable, his estate had a value of £39,209 after deduction for bad debts.

Somewhat above the average height at five feet seven inches, handsome, intelligent, witty, and bilingual, Sewell was an attractive man. Aubert de Gaspé considered him "one of the most estimable men I ever knew." Unlike many of his contemporaries in the tight, personal world of Lower Canadian politics, he was not mean-minded. Although painfully sensitive to criticism, he could stand back philosophically and look at politics with humour. When his office as speaker of the Legislative Council was turned into an orderly room for a militia regiment, he wrote:

We know the Assembly was always in fact
A disorderly House to the Letter
And 'tis firmly established by many an act
That their Speakers own Room was no better.
The reverse in the Council, The whole world have seen
There order was ever in Bloom
And the Speaker's apartment, at all Times has been,
And still is, an orderly Room.

Order and the means of establishing it were the judicial and political objects of this loyalists' son, traumatized early in life by mob disorder and later profoundly troubled by the seeming bloody chaos of the French revolution. Sewell feared the potential tyranny of the people unrestrained by religion, education, and the ownership of property. Neither the French language nor the French law disturbed him, for he mastered both, and he was not a religious bigot; but the Canadians in their masses, in their presumed ignorance and malleability at the hands of demagogues or priests, frightened him in their potential for revolution or despotism.

His own family and the means of establishing it were scarcely less important in Sewell's mind. He was prepared to suffer terrible attacks to ensure the future of his sons in Lower Canada, and in this determination he represented a class of office holders who had decided to make the colony their country. A man of subtlety and suppleness – for which Ryland detested him – Sewell was less rigid in action, if not views, than many of his colleagues in the English party. At the same time he suspected conciliatory governors of wanting to buy peace and an honourable retirement to Britain or advancement at the expense of the British colonial population. Advocating a well-ordered administration of justice, oligarchic rule by British colonists, anglicization of the colony, and maintenance of the royal prerogative, Sewell attempted to erect the four walls of a fortress that he believed would protect the British community; he thus shared the "garrison mentality" of more rigid colleagues. In addition, through his participation in the founding of social organizations and in his efforts to foster a cultural life in the colony, Sewell helped to form a collective conscience in the colony's British population. Reinforced by immigration and economic growth after the War of 1812, they gradually moved out of their defensive shell and attempted to fashion a colonial society in their own image. This development, resisted by Canadian nationalists, may have been an important underlying factor leading to the rebellions of 1837–38.

F. MURRAY GREENWOOD and JAMES H. LAMBERT

A portrait of Jonathan Sewell hangs in the Canadian Senate; a copy of it is at PAC, C11156.

Jonathan Sewell is the author of *An abstract from precedents of proceedings in the British House of Commons* (Quebec, 1792); *Orders and rules of practice in the Court of King's Bench, for the district of Quebec, Lower Canada* (Quebec, 1809); *Rules and orders of practice in the provincial Court of Appeals* (Quebec, 1811; 2nd ed., 1818); *A plan for the federal union of British provinces in North America* (London, 1814); *An essay on the juridical history of France, so far as it relates to the law of the province of Lower-Canada . . .* (Quebec, 1824); and, with John Beverley Robinson, *Plan for a general legislative union of the British provinces in North America* (London, [1824]), repub. in *General union of the British provinces of North America* (London, 1824).

ACC-Q, 62, 123. ANQ-Q, CE1-61, 22 sept. 1793, 15 nov. 1839; CE1-66, 24 sept. 1796; CN1-27, 17 oct. 1832; CN1-80, 1er, 8 mai 1832; 12 févr., 3 mai 1842; 31 mai 1844; 7 avril 1847; CN1-138, 29 janv. 1840; CN1-208, 23 août 1824; 24 juin 1826; 10, 17 sept., 26 oct., 19 déc. 1831; 20 août 1832; CN1-256, 24 févr., 23 sept. 1796; 19 oct. 1797; CN1-262, 16 avril 1796; 16 févr. 1802; 22 août, 27 oct. 1803; P-319; P1000-90-1863; T11-1, reg. of the Court of King's Bench, 1808–30: 3545–87; T11-1/98 (1804), no. 5905; T11-1/2684, 3 oct. 1807; T13-1/408: 152, 223–24. McCord Museum, M21411. McGill Univ. Libraries, Dept. of Rare Books and Special Coll., MS coll., CH27.S63, A. W. Cochran to Roderick Mackenzie, 23 Feb. 1835; MS439. Mass. Hist. Soc. (Boston), Jonathan Sewall papers. PAC, MG 23, D1, ser.1, 3, 6; D2, 1, 5–7, 9; GII, 10; 14, ser.1, 2: 954–58; MG 24, A7; B1, 173: 5161–62; B2: 395, 538, 548, 572–73, 588–89, 604, 1194–95, 1345, 1779, 3003; B3, 3: 589, 654; 4: 81, 161, 209–10, 310–11, 527; B4, 2: 26–32; B10: 18–19; B16: 14, 422, 594, 654–55, 681–82, 766; D4: 49, 79; MG 30, D1, 27: 575–77; RG 1, E1, 33–40; L3L: 345, 2416, 4113, 86662–63, 86667; RG 4, A1, Sewell to John Ready, 23 Jan. 1822; Sewell to Charles Yorke, 19 Oct. 1830; B8: 6255–70; B20, 1–2; RG 7, G15C, 4; RG 8, I (C ser.), 246: 86; RG 68, General index, 1651–1841. PRO, CO 42/89–90, 42/97, 42/102, 42/104, 42/109, 42/114, 42/116–17, 42/119, 42/124, 42/127–28, 42/130–36, 42/138, 42/141, 42/143, 42/148, 42/156–57, 42/159, 42/161, 42/165–67, 42/170, 42/173, 42/175, 42/178, 42/180, 42/185–86, 42/191, 42/194, 42/196, 42/200, 42/203–4, 42/209, 42/211–12, 42/214, 42/216–17, 42/220, 42/222–25, 42/228, 42/230, 42/232, 42/235–36, 42/242–43, 42/252, 42/257, 42/262, 42/264, 42/271–73, 42/277–78. SRO, GD45/3 (mfm. at PAC). Univ. de Montréal, Service des bibliothèques, coll. spéciales, coll. Melzack.

P.[-J.] Aubert de Gaspé, *Mémoires* (Ottawa, 1866; réimpr. Montréal, 1971). *Church and state in Canada, 1627–1867: basic documents*, ed. J. S. Moir (Toronto, 1967). "Les dénombrements de Québec" (Plessis), ANQ *Rapport*, 1948–49: 72, 115, 173. "Desseins des républicains français sur le Canada," PAC *Rapport*, 1891: 57–85. *Docs. relating to constitutional hist., 1759–91* (Shortt and Doughty; 1918); *1791–1818* (Doughty and McArthur); *1819–28* (Doughty and Story). G.B., *Statutes*, 34 Geo. III, c.54. L.C., House of Assembly, *Journals*, 1797–1808, 1815–16; *Proceedings in the assembly of Lower Canada on the rules of practice of the courts of justice, and the impeachments of Jonathan Sewell and James Monk, esquires* (n.p., 1814); Legislative Council, *Journals*, 1795–1839; *Statutes*, 1797, c.6. Joseph Papineau, "Correspondance de Joseph Papineau (1793–1840)," Fernand Ouellet, édit., ANQ *Rapport*, 1951–53: 191. L.-J. Papineau, "Correspondance" (Ouellet), ANQ *Rapport*, 1953–55: 191–442. Ramsay, *Dalhousie journals* (Whitelaw), vols.2–3. *Reports of cases argued and determined in the courts of King's Bench and in the provincial Court of Appeals of Lower Canada, with a few of the more important cases in the Court of Vice Admiralty . . .*, comp. G. O. Stuart (Quebec, 1834). William Smith, *The diary and selected papers of Chief Justice William Smith, 1784–1793*, ed. L. F. S. Upton (2v., Toronto, 1963–65); "The London diary of William Smith, 1803–1804," ed. L. F. S. Upton, *CHR*, 47 (1965): 150. *Canadian Colonist and Commercial Advertiser* (Quebec), 18 Nov. 1839. *Le Canadien*, 4 juill. 1807. *Montreal Gazette*, 20 March 1797. *Quebec Gazette*, 4 Nov. 1790; 26 March, 25 June 1795; 6 Oct. 1796; 6 April 1797; 12 June 1800; 20 Aug. 1801; 27 Dec. 1804; 6 Feb. 1806; 12 Jan., 22 June 1809; 5 July 1810; 30 March, 15 April, 7 Dec. 1815; 29 Feb., 11 July 1816; 9 April, 10 Dec. 1818; 6 Sept., 18 Oct. 1819; 18 Jan. 1821; 23 Sept. 1822; 11 Dec. 1823; 6 Oct. 1825. *Quebec Mercury*, 15 March 1814, 19 March 1822, 2 Oct. 1824, 2 July 1839.

F.-J. Audet, *Les juges en chef de la province de Québec, 1764–1924* (Québec, 1927). Christina Cameron et Monique Trépanier, *Vieux Québec: son architecture intérieure* (Ottawa, 1986). Caron, "Inv. de la corr. de Mgr Panet," ANQ *Rapport*, 1933–34; "Inv. de la corr. de Mgr Plessis," ANQ *Rapport*, 1927–28; 1932–33; "Inv. des doc. relatifs aux événements de 1837 et 1838," ANQ *Rapport*, 1925–26: 323. *Encyclopedia of music in Canada*, ed. Helmut Kallmann *et al.* (Toronto, 1983). Fauteux, *Patriotes*, 172, 295. Hare et Wallot, *Les imprimés dans le Bas-Canada*. William Notman and [J.] F. Taylor, *Portraits of British Americans, with biographical sketches* (3v., Montreal, 1865–68). George Pyke, *Cases argued and determined in the Court of King's Bench for the district of Quebec in the province of Lower-Canada, in Hilary term, in the fiftieth year of the reign of George III* (Montreal, 1811). *Vital records of Cambridge, Massachusetts, to the year 1850*, comp. T. W. Baldwin (2v., Boston, 1914–15). C. [R.] Berkin, *Jonathan Sewall: odyssey of an American loyalist* (New York and London, 1974). Ginette Bernatchez, "La Société littéraire et historique de Québec (the Literary and Historical Society of Quebec), 1824–1890" (thèse de MA, univ. Laval, Québec, 1979), 136, 138. A. R. Beverley, *Trinity Church, Quebec, a historical sketch* (Quebec, 1911), 12. Buckner, *Transition to responsible government*. R. P. Burns, "The English viewpoint on the proposed union of 1822 to unite the provinces of Lower and Upper Canada" (MA thesis, Univ. of Ottawa, 1966). *The centenary volume of the Literary and Historical Society of Quebec, 1824–1924*, ed. Henry Ievers (Quebec,

1924). Christie, *Hist. of L.C.* (1848–55), 1: 322; 6. *Church directory and a brief historical sketch of Trinity Anglican Church, Quebec, P.Q.* ([Quebec], 1931). R. C. Dalton, *The Jesuits' estates question, 1760–1888: a study of the background for the agitation of 1889* (Toronto, 1968). H. L. Duff, *The Sewells in the New World* (Exeter, Eng., 1924). Mollie Gillen, *The prince and his lady: the love story of the Duke of Kent and Madame de St Laurent* (London, 1970; repr. Halifax, 1985). F. M. Greenwood, "The development of a garrison mentality among the English in Lower Canada, 1793–1811" (PHD thesis, Univ. of B.C., Vancouver, 1970). J. [E.] Hare *et al.*, *Histoire de la ville de Québec, 1608–1871* (Montréal, 1987), 207. Helmut Kallmann, *A history of music in Canada, 1534–1914* (Toronto and London, 1960). Lambert, "Joseph-Octave Plessis." J. W. Lawrence, *Footprints; or, incidents in early history of New Brunswick, 1783–1883* (Saint John, N.B., 1883), 14. J. M. LeMoine, *Monographies et esquisses* (Québec, 1885), 157, 160. MacNutt, *New Brunswick*. T. R. Millman, *Jacob Mountain, first lord bishop of Quebec; a study in church and state, 1793–1825* (Toronto, 1947). Rumilly, *Papineau et son temps*, vol.1. Taft Manning, *Revolt of French Canada*. J.-P. Wallot, *Intrigues françaises et américaines au Canada, 1800–1802* (Montréal, 1965); *Un Québec qui bougeait*.

J.-C. Bonenfant, "Les projets théoriques de fédéralisme canadien," *Cahiers des Dix*, 29 (1964): 73–74. Céline Cyr, "Portrait de femme: Catherine Dupré, indépendante et rebelle," *Cap-aux-Diamants* (Québec), 2 (1986–87), no.1: 15–18. J.-M. Fecteau, "Régulation sociale et répression de la déviance au Bas-Canada au tournant du 19e siècle (1791–1815)," *RHAF*, 38 (1984–85): 499–521. F. M. Greenwood, "L'insurrection appréhendée et l'administration de la justice au Canada: le point de vue d'un historien," *RHAF*, 34 (1980–81): 57–93. J. [E.] Hare, "L'Assemblée législative du Bas-Canada, 1792–1814: députation et polarisation politique," *RHAF*, 27 (1973–74): 375–76, 379. Frère Marcel-Joseph, "Les Canadiens veulent conserver le régime seigneurial," *RHAF*, 7 (1953–54): 45–63, 224–40. É.-Z. Massicotte, "Papineau et la chanson" and "Nouvelle version de la chanson *C'est la faute à Papineau*," *BRH*, 24 (1918): 8–9 and 375–78. André Morel, "Les crimes et les peines: évolution des mentalités au Québec au XIXe siècle," *Rev. de droit* (Sherbrooke, Qué.), 8 (1977–78): 385–96. W. H. Nelson, "The last hopes of the American loyalists," *CHR*, 32 (1951): 22–42. A. J. H. Richardson, "Guide to the architecturally and historically most significant buildings in the old city of Quebec with a biographical dictionary of architects and builders and illustrations," Assoc. for Preservation Technology, *Bull.* (Ottawa), 2 (1970), nos.3–4: 32–33. P.-G. Roy, "Le Cirque royal ou Théâtre royal (Royal Circus ou Royal Theatre)," *BRH*, 42 (1936): 641–66; "L'Hôtel Malhiot, rue Saint-Jean, à Québec," *BRH*, 42: 449–52; "L'Hotel Union ou Saint-George, à Québec," *BRH*, 43 (1937): 3–17; "Une maison historique du Vieux-Québec," *BRH*, 32 (1926): 703–4. Christine Veilleux, "Les Glackemeyer, deux générations de musiciens," *Cap-aux-Diamants*, 1 (1985), no.2: 31. J.-P. Wallot, "Plaintes contre l'administration de la justice (1807)," *RHAF*, 20 (1966–67): 30–31.

SHAW, EMILY ELIZABETH (Beavan), teacher and author; b. likely in Belfast, daughter of Samuel Shaw; fl. 1838–45.

Emily Elizabeth Shaw's father was a sea captain who in his brig *Amaryllis* made numerous voyages between Belfast and Saint John, N.B. Emily went to New Brunswick around 1836, in all probability to stay with relatives; her name appears in school records as a student and later as a teacher. On 19 June 1838 she married Frederick William Cadwallader Beavan, who is listed in the *New-Brunswick almanack* of that year as surgeon to the Queens County militia. He also appears in school records as a teacher. After marriage, the couple lived at English Settlement, near Long Creek, in Queens County.

While there, Mrs Beavan contributed six tales and four poems to Robert Shives*'s *Amaranth* (Saint John, 1841–43), the first magazine in New Brunswick to devote the bulk of its pages to literary materials. The value of her contributions is minimal. In poetry she was an enthusiastic follower of Felicia Dorothea Hemans, and in fiction her stories oscillated between the sensationalism of John Richardson*, the author of *Wacousta* (1832), and the florid sentimentality of her idol, Professor John Wilson ("Christopher North" of *Blackwood's Edinburgh Magazine*). In 1843 the Beavans left New Brunswick for Ireland, and in 1845 the firm of George Routledge in London published the book which is her sole claim to remembrance, *Sketches and tales illustrative of life in the backwoods of New Brunswick, North America, gleaned from actual observation and experience during a residence of seven years in that interesting colony*.

Intended as a handbook to give prospective settlers pertinent information with respect to the conditions and flavour of life in the settlements of early New Brunswick, *Sketches and tales* succeeds in that purpose far better than do its more widely acclaimed Nova Scotian and Upper Canadian counterparts, Thomas Chandler Haliburton*'s *The old judge* (1849) and Susanna Strickland* Moodie's *Roughing it in the bush* (1852). Not only is information presented more systematically and objectively in Mrs Beavan's book, but it covers a much wider range of settlement life, extending to such areas as education, religion, the details of farming and lumbering operations and the reasons why they are so conducted, the significance of the timber trade, the consequences of the imposition of copyright regulations in British North America, the effect of the frontier upon speech patterns and of the climate upon women's skins.

Nor is the book lacking in imagination. Mrs Beavan demonstrated a real talent in establishing an imaginative and novel framework in which to set her factual material, and the enthusiasm with which she describes nature, and men's and women's attempts to conquer or come to terms with it, must have been contagious to contemporary readers. She is weakest when she attempts to be literary. In such instances her lofty style is not supported by consistency of grammar, and her tales and sketches (with the single exception of a racy eyewitness account of the great fire on the Miramichi in 1825, related in excellent dialect) are poor examples of the genres from which they have been derived by imitation. For all that, *Sketches and tales* remains the best and liveliest account of life in the New Brunswick of the first half of the 19th century and as such is not only delightful in its own right but extremely useful to the student of history, education, agriculture, religion, and sociology as well.

FRED COGSWELL

Mrs Beavan's *Sketches and tales* was reprinted in St Stephen, N.B., in 1980.

UNBL, Marjorie Jardine Thompson, biog. notes on Mrs Beavan, 29 April 1975. *Early marriage records of New Brunswick: Saint John City and County from the British conquest to 1839*, ed. B. Wood-Holt (Saint John, 1986). *N.-B. almanack*, 1838. Jonas Howe, "The *Amaranth*," *Acadiensis* (Saint John), 2 (1902): 198–206.

SHAWNEE PROPHET. *See* TENSKWATAWA

SHEA, WILLIAM RICHARD, printer and newspaperman; b. 1813 in St John's, fourth son of Henry Shea* and Eleanor Ryan; d. there 17 March 1844.

William Richard Shea belonged to a prominent St John's family. His father was a merchant and one of the founders in 1806 of the Benevolent Irish Society. William must have gained a measure of importance at an early age for he is listed as a petty juror in 1833.

Having served his apprenticeship in the newspaper business under John Williams McCoubrey* of the St John's *Times and General Commercial Gazette*, William became the printer and publisher of the *Newfoundlander* in May 1837. This paper had been established in 1827 by his brother John. William may also have acted as editor at the beginning of his tenure but by November 1842 his brother Ambrose* occupied the position. The *Newfoundlander* engaged in a lively and continuing controversy with the other Newfoundland newspapers of the day, particularly the *Times* and Henry David Winton*'s *Public Ledger*. Shea, who vigorously defended the British Whigs, was especially critical of the Tories' proposed policies for Ireland. Yet he pleaded non-partisanship in politics.

The *Newfoundlander* supported the campaign through 1837–38 for the dismissal of Chief Justice Henry John Boulton*, who had been accused of being too severe in his judgements and of adhering too rigidly to the law. The celebrated case in 1838 of Dr Edward Kielley*, a government medical officer, implicated Shea as printer of the *Newfoundlander*. On 6 August an altercation had arisen in the streets between Kielley and John Kent*, reform member for St John's, in which Kielley was alleged to have threatened the member. Kent curiously appealed to the assembly for the settling of the affair and the arrest of Kielley was ordered by the speaker, William CARSON. The following day, 7 August, he appeared before the house. Kielley was subsequently returned to custody but acting assistant judge George LILLY released him on 10 August and declared that the assembly had acted beyond its legal powers. The *Newfoundlander* had published a report on Lilly's judgement and the house considered a motion that Shea should be brought before it to answer for gross violation of privileges. The exercise proved to be futile and Shea was not summoned to appear.

In 1841 the collector of customs, James Morton Spearman, brought a libel action against the *Newfoundlander* based on charges made by the paper in early 1840. The newspaper reported that Spearman had attempted to obtain for himself from the local branch of the Bank of British North America three per cent interest on the public monies of his department deposited there prior to making the quarterly payments to the colonial treasurer required by law. Spearman sought £1,000 in damages but in July 1842 the verdict was given in favour of the defendants. During the proceedings it was revealed that Spearman had indeed applied to the manager for this arrangement but had been refused.

Shea retained his position as printer and publisher of the newspaper until his death after a three-day illness. His brother Ambrose succeeded him. In 1846 another brother, Edward Dalton*, assumed control of the *Newfoundlander* and retained it until 1884.

CALVIN D. EVANS

Newfoundlander, 18 May 1837–25 April 1844. *Newfoundland Indicator* (St John's), 23 March 1844. *Patriot & Terra Nova Herald*, 20 March 1844. *Public Ledger*, 19 March 1844. *Royal Gazette and Newfoundland Advertiser*, 19 March 1844. *Star and Newfoundland Advocate* (St John's), 21 March 1844. *Times and General Commercial Gazette* (St John's), 20 March 1844. *A list of names of prominent people at the time Newfoundland was granted representative government: St John's, 1833* (St John's, 1971). *Newfoundland men; a collection of biographical sketches . . .*, ed. H. Y. Mott (Concord, N.H., 1894), 1. *Notable events in the history of Newfoundland; six thousand dates of historical and social happenings*, comp. [P. K.] Devine and [J.] O'Mara (St John's, 1900). *When was that?* (Mosdell), 117. P. K. Devine, *Ye olde St. John's, 1750–1936* (St John's, 1936), 16, 96–97, 110–11. Gunn, *Political hist. of Nfld.*, 52–61. Joseph Hatton and Moses Harvey, *Newfoundland, the oldest British colony; its history, its present condition, and its prospects in the future* (London, 1883), 87–91. Paul O'Neill, *The story of St. John's, Newfoundland* (2v., Erin, Ont., 1975–76), 104, 184, 400–1, 462, 464, 824, 831, 909, 918. Charles Pedley, *The history of Newfoundland from the earliest times to the year 1860* (London, 1863), 399–409. W. H. Hayward, "Sir Ambrose Shea, K.C.M.G. (1815–

1905), one of the fathers of confederation," *Atlantic Guardian* (Montreal), 6 (1949), no.2: 27–29.

SHEPARD, JOSEPH, farmer, militiaman, mill owner, office holder, and political organizer; b. probably 10 Aug. 1765 in New Hampshire; m. 11 April 1803 Catherine Fisher, and they had four sons and at least four daughters; d. 3 May 1837 in York Township, Upper Canada.

Born of Irish parents, Joseph Shepard chose to come to Upper Canada as a young man. Although the year of his arrival is unknown, he may have been the Joseph Shepard who applied for and received, but did not take up, a loyalist grant of land in Kingston in 1790. This possibility is consistent with the tradition that he was an Indian trader in the Bay of Quinte area before coming to the Home District. Shepard may have come to York (Toronto) as early as 1793, but the first record of his being there is his successful application for land near by early in 1796. A report of 1797 identifies him as living in Hope Township, and it may well be that he moved in and out of York before settling on his property in 1798.

The 200 acres Shepard acquired were on Yonge Street, some eight miles north of York, in the midst of the forest. Within a few years he also acquired the next lot. Later he acquired other land in the area and 100 acres in Tecumseth Township, the latter as a reward for his service in the War of 1812. As a private in the 3rd York Militia, he was at the battle of York in April 1813, suffering injuries in the explosion of the powder magazine serious enough to warrant a lifetime pension.

Shepard's original lots became a very profitable farm on which he built a sawmill and a grist-mill run by his sons. A man with a social conscience, he shared his success, giving the land and some money for the erection of an Anglican church, now known as St John's, York Mills. Also, between 1804 and 1823, he served three times as assessor for York Township and twice as poundkeeper and as overseer of highways and fences. In 1819 he and Jesse Ketchum* were selected by the town meeting to oversee the building of a bridge on Yonge Street.

Shepard's concern for his fellow citizens made him an early champion of reform, a political position unusual for supporters of the Church of England. For almost two decades before a reform movement emerged in the 1820s, he was one of the leading voices of reform in the Home District. In 1807 he served as the chairman of two meetings that supported judge Robert THORPE's campaign against the government. In June 1812, shortly before the beginning of the war, Shepard stood in York East and Simcoe for election to the assembly on a platform of no repeal of habeas corpus. Administrator Isaac Brock* wanted repeal to facilitate dealing with disloyal elements in the population but Shepard opposed giving such power to non-elected authorities. He was soundly defeated by the government candidate, Thomas Ridout*, because of a split in the anti-repeal vote.

When the Farmers' Storehouse Company was created in 1824 to store members' produce and to buy and sell for them, Shepard was a founding director, the company appealing to his populist democratic sympathies. In the late 1820s two issues occupied his attention, the alien question [*see* Sir Peregrine Maitland*] and the fate of judge John Walpole Willis*. Shepard was on the four-member "central committee of the inhabitants of Upper Canada" that in April 1827 sent Robert Randal* to England with petitions opposing the Naturalization Bill. In July 1828 he was one of 44 men who issued a notice calling for a public meeting to discuss grievances. The meeting, held in York on 5 July, passed resolutions, in the form of a petition, opposing the dismissal of Willis and calling for reforms.

That same year Shepard became involved with William Lyon Mackenzie*. Although he is reported to have been, like many reform-minded men, leery of Mackenzie's intemperate actions, he was persuaded to nominate Mackenzie in York County for election to the assembly. He continued to do so for the next five elections, until the riding was divided in 1833. In the general election the next year, with Mackenzie running in one of the new York ridings, Shepard was nominated for another, but he gracefully declined in favour of David Gibson*, a younger man.

Shepard died a few months before the rebellion of 1837. All four of his sons participated in the uprising and his farm was used as a staging area for those going south to John Montgomery*'s tavern. His wife assisted by tying strips of cloth around their arms to identify them as rebels. Joseph Shepard had worked to take political power away from the non-elected minority and it is not surprising that his family tried to follow the principles he had established.

RONALD J. STAGG

AO, Land record index; MS 451, York County, York Township, St John's Anglican Church cemetery, York Mills [Toronto]; RG 1, C-IV, York Township; RG 22, ser.305, 1837. PAC, RG 1, L3, 448A: S2/58; 450A: S3/232; 493A: S misc., 1788–95/89–90; RG 5, A1: 49388, 50743–46, 50763–64. PRO, CO 42/343: 200–1; 42/347: 60–61; 42/348: 148–63; 42/385: 51. *Town of York, 1793–1815* (Firth). *York, Upper Canada: minutes of town meetings and lists of inhabitants, 1797–1823*, ed. Christine Mosser (Toronto, 1984). *Canadian Freeman*, 13 Dec. 1827; 11, 24, 31 July 1828. *Constitution*, 10 May 1837. M. A. Graham, *150 years at St. John's, York Mills* (Toronto, 1966). P. W. Hart, *Pioneering in North York: a history of the borough* (Toronto, 1968). *Robertson's landmarks of Toronto*, vols.1–3.

SHERWOOD, LEVIUS PETERS, lawyer, office

holder, militia officer, politician, and judge; b. 12 Dec. 1777 in St Johns (Saint-Jean-sur-Richelieu), Que., second son of Justus Sherwood, a loyalist, and Sarah Bottum; m. 1804 Charlotte Jones, daughter of Ephraim Jones*, and they had four sons and three daughters; d. 19 May 1850 in Toronto.

Levius Peters Sherwood was educated in the law and called to the bar of Upper Canada in 1803. The following year he was appointed registrar for the counties of Grenville, Leeds, and Carleton and collector of customs, as well as inspector of flour, potash, and pearl ashes. On 16 March 1812 he was appointed surrogate treasurer of the Johnstown District. The coming of the War of 1812 served to increase his influence, both in the Johnstown District and beyond it. In March 1814 he was involved in the naming of magistrates for the district. On 24 May 1816, with the rank of lieutenant-colonel in the militia, he was appointed to examine applications for military pensions in the district.

Sherwood's public prominence continued to develop in post-war Upper Canada. In July 1818 he took part in the general conservative attack against Robert Gourlay*, who was gathering information about the province's condition. In October Sherwood was in York (Toronto) where he successfully defended two of Cuthbert Grant*'s party of Métis, Paul Brown and François-Firmin Boucher, against charges in connection with the murder of Robert Semple* during the troubles at Red River in 1816. Sherwood argued persuasively that the settlement there was little more than a camp of traders, by definition a rather wild group. His legal career continued to advance and in November 1820 William Dummer Powell* recommended successfully that he become a judge in the Johnstown District Court.

As his importance rose provincially, Sherwood maintained a strong influence in the district and in Brockville, where he had settled. In July 1822 he applied for membership on the district land board. He was active on the local board of education, and in April 1825 he was one of three churchwardens entrusted with land for the construction of St Peter's (Anglican) Church.

Sherwood entered provincial politics in the general election of 1812 when he defeated Peter HOWARD in the riding of Leeds. Sherwood took the riding again in 1820, leading the poll with 515 votes. By September 1821 he was serving as speaker of the House of Assembly, and the demands on his time were considerable, especially after the house was plunged into an extended controversy about Barnabas Bidwell*'s right to hold a seat. On at least two occasions Sherwood was compelled to ask for leaves of absence from his judicial duties in order to fulfill his political responsibilities.

The apogee of Sherwood's judicial career was his appointment to the Court of King's Bench in 1825. His priorities now shifted away from politics. In the years which followed, he found himself dealing with such varied cases as those of Dennis Russell, found guilty of rape in 1828, and Francis Collins*, a newspaper editor convicted of libel in the same year. A squabble with a fellow judge, John Walpole Willis*, in 1828 led to a strong defence of Sherwood by John Strachan*, who described him as "a most upright and religious man anxious to perform his duty."

Sherwood became increasingly unpopular in reform circles. In 1835 a rumour developed that he would shortly be retiring. Reluctant to see him on the civil list, the Canadian Alliance Society, a reform group, passed a series of resolutions condemning the suggestion that he should be pensioned off when he was clearly young enough to serve another 20 years. Nothing came of the rumour and Sherwood remained on the bench. Indeed his stature as a pillar of the establishment grew sufficiently that, on 17 Feb. 1838, a Kingston newspaper, the *British Whig*, specifically labelled him as a member of the "family compact."

In the immediate aftermath of the rebellion of 1837, Sherwood was prominent in the trials for treason which began at Toronto in March 1838. Late that year Lieutenant Governor Sir George Arthur* asked him what should be done with the prisoners taken during the failed invasion at Prescott in November [*see* Nils von SCHOULTZ]. Sherwood recommended that only the ringleaders should be hanged and that the others be committed to a penal colony for life. Execution, he argued, often excited pity in those who witnessed it, and thus undermined the lesson it was intended to teach.

Sherwood always kept an eye open for opportunities to deal in land. In 1820, in cooperation with Captain John LE BRETON, he had obtained a valuable lot near the Chaudière Falls on the Ottawa River; he later acquired more land there. By 1832 he was living in York near the foot of Yonge Street and had bought a lot adjacent to his residence which he was prepared to sell, at a high price. In 1840 he sought a lease for part of an island in the Ottawa River in order to erect a mill at the nearby falls.

Sherwood retired from the bench in 1840 although he continued to be vocal in conservative circles. In November 1842 he was a founding member of the Toronto Constitutional Society which had been formed in reaction to the policies of Governor Sir Charles BAGOT. In October 1843 Sherwood made it known that he supported a resolution William Henry Draper* had introduced in the assembly opposing the transfer of the seat of government from Kingston to Lower Canada. During this same period, he was appointed to the Legislative Council on 19 Aug. 1842 and the Executive Council on 1 Nov. 1843.

During the final years of his life he remained active both in his profession and in the religious and educational life of the community. In 1842 he had served as treasurer of the Law Society of Upper Canada. Two years later he expressed his willingness to return to the bench by sitting on the Court of Appeal. His devotion to the Church of England moved him in May 1842 to volunteer his services as a vice-president of the Church Society. Four years later, he was appointed, along with John Beverley Robinson*, to be treasurer of the Society for the Propagation of the Gospel. His contribution to education was as a member of the council of King's College in Toronto to which he was named on 27 Dec. 1841. For nearly half a century before his death in 1850 Levius Peters Sherwood, a man of devout conservative conscience, had served his community in many capacities.

IAN PEMBERTON

AO, MS 4, commission appointing J. B. Robinson and L. P. Sherwood as treasurers of the Soc. for the Propagation of the Gospel in Foreign Parts in Canada, 16 June 1846; MS 35, letter-book, 1827–39, Strachan to James Stephen, 11 April 1829; MS 51, George Bruce to Mackenzie, 30 Sept. 1830; Charles Waters to Mackenzie, 28 July 1835; MU 2106, 1832, no.14 (Robert Thompson to Peter Freeland, 15 Feb. 1832). PAC, RG 1, E3, 42: 233–39; 81: 9–10; L1, 39: 341–42; RG 5, A1: 7995–96, 9023–24, 24568–70, 26874–75, 29335–37, 30359–61, 30591–93, 32967–69, 33486–87, 49486–88, 49920–23, 52904–10; B5, 4: 265–66; 4a, Sherwood to J. M. Higginson, 11 July 1844; B7, 3; C2, 1: 391. "Parish register of Brockville and vicinity, 1814–1830," ed. H. R. Morgan, *OH*, 38 (1946): 77–108. *British Whig*, 23 Feb. 1835; 17 Feb., 23 March 1838. *Chronicle & Gazette*, 7 Feb. 1835; 17, 21 March 1838; 7 May, 30 July, 27 Aug., 12 Nov. 1842; 24 Oct. 1843. *Kingston Chronicle*, 21 July 1820. *Kingston Gazette*, 6 July 1816, 7 July 1818. *Marriage bonds of Ont.* (T. B. Wilson). D. B. Read, *The lives of the judges of Upper Canada and Ontario, from 1791 to the present time* (Toronto, 1888). Reid, *Loyalists in Ont.* Mary Beacock Fryer, *Buckskin pimpernel: the exploits of Justus Sherwood, loyalist spy* (Toronto and Charlottetown, 1981). H. M. Jackson, *Justus Sherwood: soldier, loyalist and negotiator* (n.p., 1958).

SHIRREFF, CHARLES, businessman, author, office holder, and JP; b. 26 July 1768 in Leith, Scotland, son of Robert Shirreff and Barbara Menzies; m. first 29 May 1793 Jane Wilson, and they had four sons and a daughter; m. secondly 14 Sept. 1808 Jane Coxon, with whom he had two sons and two daughters; d. 5 May 1847 in Bytown (Ottawa), Upper Canada.

Charles Shirreff came from a Scottish family of merchants and shipbuilders which had been involved in the Baltic timber trade. He left his business in Leith and immigrated to Upper Canada in 1817, settling near Smith's Creek (Port Hope) on Lake Ontario. Through connections with the provincial administration, he obtained a grant of 5,000 acres in the upper Ottawa River valley, to which he moved in 1818. Plunging into land promotion and the timber trade, he founded the settlement of Fitzroy Harbour, where he built a grist-mill in 1831. An early advocate of linking the Ottawa to either Lake Huron or Lake Simcoe by canal, that year he published his ideas in a pamphlet, *Thoughts on emigration and on the Canadas, as an opening for it*, which proposed bringing labourers to build public works, such as the Huron route, and then turning them to agricultural settlement. His plans largely came to nothing, however, and it was in the timber trade that he left his mark.

Shirreff was not himself a large operator but, cognizant of the problems created for the timber interests by illegal cutting, he became their leader in making representations to the Upper and Lower Canadian governments for the regulation of cutting on public lands. In 1826 a system had been introduced whereby the post of deputy surveyor general of woods was revived in each province to control the licensing of lumbermen, in part by limiting the size of timber berths. To collect dues, an agency was formed with an office at Bytown, concentrating on the Ottawa valley and responsible for both sides of the river and its tributaries above the Chaudière Falls, in addition to the Gatineau and Rideau rivers. Shirreff was offered the agency but deferred in favour of his son Robert, who assumed the position in 1826. Charles warned that two officers were necessary: one in Bytown to measure timber and take bonds, and one in Quebec to accept the payment of dues when the rafts were sold. The governments, however, believed that, no matter how impractical, the collection of dues should be at Bytown. Charles, without formal appointment, handled the business at Bytown from the start and Robert collected payments at Quebec.

Charles allied himself with the lumbermen in advocating the reform of this system and modifications to it. A new one, devised by George HAMILTON, a leading timber merchant, but proposed by Shirreff, was adopted in 1832. It permitted lumbermen to make an application to the commissioner of crown lands for limits, with a description of their boundaries and the quantity of timber they proposed to cut. The Bytown office would collect a down payment in the fall on the anticipated dues, with the balance being paid at Quebec in the spring. The new system favoured the industry since a lumberman could underestimate his expected cut and thus minimize the down payment at a time when he needed cash for the winter's operation.

But if Shirreff sided with Hamilton, he was not a cipher for such large operators. This was apparent in the difficulties over what became known as the Gatineau privilege. An association of lumbermen, including Peter Aylen* and the firm of Hamilton and Low, all of whom had legal limits on the Gatineau

River, had undertaken improvements there for driving purposes. They were angered in the winter of 1831–32 to find that a number of lumbermen were cutting illegally on the river. Further, Hamilton protested in March, Shirreff was encouraging others to take up berths there for the following year. Represented by Hamilton, the association requested in August 1832, and received from the Lower Canadian government three months later, a reservation of the Gatineau from the public sale of limits.

The creation of this monopoly caused an uproar in Bytown. Other lumbermen had started winter operations without proper licences, a practice which was condoned by the Bytown timber office. Shirreff complained vociferously in November, claiming that limits on the Gatineau, "a chief seat of the Timber trade," had been removed from public competition and therefore from his control. He urged Commissioner William Bowman FELTON to reverse the privilege in order to prevent the seizure of the property of the excluded lumbermen, "who will certainly not submit . . . without a struggle." Unfortunately for Shirreff, a commission of inquiry formed in January 1833 found in favour of leaving the privilege in place. Outmanœuvred politically, he found his authority undermined. Soon he was to find his reputation destroyed.

The cause was a scandal in the collection of dues. In 1830, after the departure of Robert Shirreff on an extended trip to the United States and England, Alexander Shirreff had come in to help his father at Bytown and an agreement had been reached with a firm at Quebec, Jones, Murray and Company, to handle the agency's business there. When this firm went bankrupt in 1833 it was revealed that Charles had been allowing the company to accept promissory notes rather than bonds as security for the timber dues it collected and that the provinces had lost approximately £3,600. Some historians have suggested that the Shirreffs deceived the governments and, perhaps, lined their pockets and those of local merchants with public funds. The charge of deceit, however, is difficult to comprehend. Charles testified in 1836 before a select committee in Upper Canada that the government had recognized, through correspondence, his informal role in the collection process. Equally as certain, government officials had been aware of the role played by Jones, Murray and Company since they had expressed concern over a private firm acting in the place of public appointees.

The nub of Shirreff's problems lay, perhaps, in relations with officials. He and Robert had never enjoyed good relations with Lower Canada's Crown Lands Department, especially with Felton, who was himself facing charges of fraud in land dealings. Completely exasperated by the Shirreffs over the Gatineau privilege and annoyed at Charles's practice of collecting dues on illegal timber rather than seizing it, he was determined to curb Charles's discretion in licensing. What the commissioner did not appreciate was that the government's unwillingness to finance accurate surveys made the boundaries of limits loose and trespass an easy misdemeanour. Finally, he had become convinced that collections should be made by a public official, but he apparently did not order Shirreff to cease employing Jones, Murray and Company. The problem was not that Charles had concealed his activities, but rather that they were so well known and were subjected to such criticism, especially by Felton, that a crisis had become a scandal.

As to the question of purloining funds, there is little evidence that this occurred. Shirreff, who had served as a magistrate since 1826, was not confronted during the investigation of 1836 with charges of fraud or corruption. There is no doubt that he did well out of the collectorship, doubling as a kind of agent for directing prospective settlers and for collecting slidages at Chats Falls, near Fitzroy Harbour. He had clearly been derelict, however, in not demanding that Jones, Murray and Company obtain proper securities for the dues collected. The recommendation of the select committee that securities be required in the future was the closest Shirreff came to censure. Yet the finding of incompetence was enough to ruin his authority as collector. He and Robert vacated the Bytown office in 1836, though there is no evidence to indicate whether this was a voluntary withdrawal or a dismissal. Their replacement, James Stevenson*, was considered to have more financial acumen than Charles Shirreff, but the eventual continuation of the system of making payments at Quebec confirmed its practicality.

Charles Shirreff turned to his other business and settlement enterprises. In 1837 he erected a sawmill at Fitzroy Harbour and by 1839 had opened a store. He died in Bytown in 1847.

ROBERT PETER GILLIS

Charles Shirreff is the author of two pamphlets, *A few reasons against any change in the system of our colonial lumber trade* and *Thoughts on emigration and on the Canadas, as an opening for it*, both published at Quebec in 1831.

ANQ-Q, E21/1877–78. AO, MU 3289. PAC, MG 11, [CO 42] Q, 338-1: 177, 179; 375-2: 350–60; RG 1, L1, 30: 441, 450; L3, 458: S11/237; 462: S13/146, 150, 156–57; 463: S14/80; RG 5, A1: 68315–18; RG 68, General index, 1651–1841: 457. U.C., House of Assembly, *App. to the journal*, 1836, app.54. *Packet* (Bytown [Ottawa]), 8 May 1847. *The Oxford companion to Canadian history and literature*, ed. Norah Story (Toronto, 1967), 609–10. Lucien Brault, *Ottawa old & new* (Ottawa, 1946). M. S. Cross, "The dark druidical groves: the lumber community and the commercial frontier in British North America, to 1854" (PHD thesis, Univ. of Toronto, 1968), 272–73. S. J. Gillis, *The timber trade in the Ottawa valley, 1806–54* (Parks Canada, National Parks and Hist. Sites Branch, *Manuscript report*, no.153, Ottawa, 1975). R. S. Lambert and Paul Pross, *Renewing nature's wealth; a centennial history of the public management of lands, forests & wildlife in Ontario, 1763–1967* ([Toronto], 1967), 41–42.

SIGNAY, JOSEPH (he signed **Signaÿ**, adding the accent still occasionally used at the time), Roman Catholic priest and archbishop; b. 8 Nov. 1778 at Quebec, son of François Signaÿ and Marguerite Vallée; d. there 3 Oct. 1850.

There were 11 children in the Signay family, but all except Joseph died before reaching adulthood, most of them in infancy. The ninth in the family, Joseph was raised by his mother, for his father, a seaman, was often away from home. He entered the Petit Séminaire de Québec in 1791 and proved a gifted and studious pupil. Six years later he went to the Grand Séminaire, where he studied until 1802. Although he taught at the Petit Séminaire while doing his theological studies, he none the less did extraordinarily well.

Signay was ordained priest by the bishop of Quebec, Pierre Denaut*, at Longueuil on 28 March 1802, and was named assistant priest at Chambly and then at Longueuil; he was made curé of Saint-Constant parish on 1 Oct. 1804. A year later he became the first parish priest of Sainte-Marie-de-Monnoir (Saint-Nom-de-Marie in Marieville), with responsibility for visiting and ministering to Catholics around Missisquoi Bay. During his nine years there he gained a reputation as an able administrator.

In the autumn of 1814 the parish priest of Quebec, André Doucet*, resigned, and rumour had it that Signay would be appointed to replace him. Signay himself was strongly opposed but, at the insistence of Bishop Joseph-Octave Plessis* of Quebec, on 19 November he officially took charge of the parish. Its finances and religious edifices were then in poor condition. True to his reputation, Signay soon set them in order. He never went beyond the parish but did cover it from one end to the other; he even conducted censuses in 1815 and 1818. He also took a great interest in the education of young children; according to his contemporaries he had a special gift for teaching them the shorter catechism.

When Plessis died on 4 Dec. 1825, Bernard-Claude Panet* succeeded him as archbishop and announced that he had chosen Signay as his coadjutor. Although the appointment was approved by Governor Lord Dalhousie [RAMSAY], ratification was slow in coming from Rome, because Panet had sent only Signay's name, rather than the three required; in addition, Bishop Jean-Jacques LARTIGUE, the archbishop of Quebec's auxiliary in Montreal, expressed some reticence when consulted. Panet succeeded in overcoming these obstacles, and the bulls were finally signed by Rome. On 20 May 1827, in the cathedral of Notre-Dame in Quebec, Signay was consecrated bishop *in partibus* of Fussola. He remained parish priest of Notre-Dame, nevertheless, until 1 Oct. 1831. On 13 Oct. 1832 Panet resigned and handed administration of the diocese over to his coadjutor. The authorities in Rome accepted his resignation. Panet died on 14 Feb. 1833, and two days later Signay became the third archbishop of Quebec.

Signay also had great difficulty in getting recognition for his chosen coadjutor, Pierre-Flavien Turgeon*, because of opposition from the Sulpicians and pettifogging from Rome. Backed by the majority of his clergy, Signay insisted on ratification of his choice and won. On 27 Jan. 1834 the Sacred Congregation of Propaganda assented, but requested that the archbishop of Quebec be told "the hasty and irregular nomination of the coadjutor has immensely displeased the Sacred Congregation" and "the normal procedure is to be firmly respected in future." Turgeon was consecrated bishop of Sidyma on 11 June 1834.

The victory was due largely to the work of the archbishop's procurator in Rome, Abbé Thomas Maguire*, who also helped get two other problems examined: the property of the Séminaire de Saint-Sulpice and the erection of the diocese of Montreal. The first problem had arisen many years before [*see* Jean-Henry-Auguste Roux*], but it became acute when in 1827–28 the Sulpicians indicated that they were ready to come to terms with the British government in the matter of their seigneurial rights. Alerted by newspaper accounts, both clergy and people voiced strong opposition, and Signay followed his predecessors' example in denouncing the idea. Maguire was consequently given the task of correcting the statements made in Rome by Sulpician Jean-Baptiste THAVENET and of requesting that the Sulpicians be strictly forbidden to negotiate with the government. The cardinals of Propaganda went only so far as to request in 1834 that nothing new be done and that they be consulted before any further attempt at negotiation. In fact the problem was resolved when the Sulpicians came to a meeting of minds with Lartigue about the creation of the diocese of Montreal.

Lartigue's appointment as auxiliary bishop in 1820 had greatly displeased his Sulpician colleagues, and he had become convinced that the difficulties would disappear if he were made bishop of Montreal and a diocese were erected. He had consequently put pressure on Plessis, Panet, and Signay to get a decision from Rome without waiting for London's assent. Like his predecessors, and despite repeated requests from his auxiliary, Signay pleaded instead for prudence and compromise, and long maintained that the British authorities' agreement was an essential preliminary. In February 1835, however, he resolved to write directly to Propaganda with the request for a diocese, but Rome was slow in replying. Relations between Lartigue and the Sulpicians improved, particularly on the occasion of the 50th anniversary of Sulpician Jacques-Guillaume ROQUE's ordination to the priesthood, on 24 Sept. 1835. The superior, Joseph-Vincent Quiblier*, even had the clergy sign a petition in favour of the erection of a diocese. When asked to transmit it to Rome Signay again delayed, to give himself time to sound out the civil authorities. On 24 December he finally gave in to Lartigue's entreaties. The petition, with clarification and support from Bishop Joseph-Norbert Provencher*, who was in Rome at the time, was examined by Propaganda in March 1836, but the bull erecting the diocese did not reach Montreal until 29 August.

These events revealed that the bishops of Quebec and Montreal already had differing perceptions of some problems; in the ensuing years the differences became more marked on the subject of relations between church and state, as well as on the governance of the Canadian church. Whereas Lartigue and his coadjutor Ignace Bourget*, as faithful ultramontanists, advocated a policy affirming the church's independence of the state, Signay, who was "purely and simply a man of the *status quo*" according to Father Jean-Baptiste Honorat*, preached respect for customs, prudence, and collaboration with the British authorities. He endeavoured to avoid all confrontation with the government and chose to shelve certain legitimate claims. The three bishops agreed, however, on one general principle: the clergy should be neutral in politics, except when religious interests were threatened.

The principle was particularly relevant at the time of the 1837–38 uprisings. Because the Quebec region remained relatively calm, Signay let events follow their course and did not intervene until after the first armed clashes had taken place. He asked the parish priests in the lower St Lawrence area to explain to their flocks that the troops arriving from the Maritimes were being called in not "for hostile purposes" but "to protect the inhabitants of the country and to maintain peace and order." On 11 Dec. 1837 he published a pastoral letter denouncing the insurrection as "a means . . . not only ineffectual, unwise, and fatal to those who make use of it, but also criminal in the eyes of God and our holy religion," and he warned his diocesans to watch for anything that might disturb the peace.

Signay's customary prudence was intensified in the late 1830s by the climate of insecurity and depression in Lower Canada. He was in favour of the Canadian clergy's address to the British parliament against the union of Upper and Lower Canada (it would eventually be forwarded in April 1840). But he also thought it useful in June 1838 to ask his priests to make known the views of the new governor, Lord Durham [LAMBTON], "either by having his proclamation read at the church door, or by any other means that prudence may suggest." In January 1840, however, he again urged his clergy to use their influence to secure signatures for a petition against the union; he and his coadjutor Turgeon talked with Governor Charles Edward Poulett THOMSON about the disastrous consequences of the imperial plan, and he congratulated Bourget on the firm language he had used with the governor.

From then on Signay left the initiative more and more to Bourget, the new bishop of Montreal, and sank into an "apathetic state" decried by a number of people. For example, when an education bill was introduced in 1841, he did not make known his reservations until after a violent denunciation of it had appeared in the *Mélanges religieux*, and some thought his remarks far too mild. He took the same attitude to the idea of setting up an ecclesiastical province, which had been entertained for a long time. Although Signay saw only the disadvantages and feared that it would be rejected by the imperial authorities, Bourget took up the matter with the Canadian bishops and presented the case to Rome. While awaiting a reply from Propaganda, he managed by his tenacity to calm the fears of Signay and his coadjutor and have them sign a petition to the Holy See in January 1843. In December Bourget sent Hyacinthe HUDON to Rome to further the cause, which was finally successful: in May 1844 the ecclesiastical province of Quebec was created.

A metropolitan against his will, Signay did everything he could to keep the promotion from taking effect. He was reluctant to receive the pallium and accepted it in November 1844 only on condition that "the *immediate* organization of the eccesiastical province not follow." Similarly he did not approve the holding of a provincial council. He said that in principle he was in favour of a gathering of this sort but wanted to delay calling it until the "relations desirable among those bishops who must take an active part in this work have been established beforehand." No such development occurred before his resignation, a step some people thought desirable in itself.

Bourget was one of those people. More and more irritated by Signay's failure to act and his never-ending objections to suggested changes and improvements – such as standardization of the liturgy and discipline, preparation of a new catechism, and establishment of a university – the bishop decided he would take advantage of a planned visit to Rome to call for his superior's resignation. He informed Signay of his intention in a letter of 25 Sept. 1846, which summed up the reasons that he proposed to lay before the pope: the archbishop's inertia as an administrator, the low level of respect and confidence he inspired, his inability to deal with important matters, and his lack of close relations with the suffragan bishops. Signay was deeply hurt by Bourget's frankness and did not realize that the bishop of Montreal was expressing sentiments widely shared. As far back as 1835 *Le Canadien* had denounced the archbishop's despotic rule. Vicar general Alexis Mailloux* was no less severe and wondered whether Signay had "the knowledge and the firmness combined with the independence from all human power that make a bishop what he must be." At "the wish" of the secretary of Propaganda, visiting French historian Abbé Charles-Étienne Brasseur* de Bourbourg also wrote an indictment denouncing Signay's extreme timidity, his stubborn and meddlesome disposition, and his inability "to take in the whole picture or enter into the details of orderly administration"; he furnished many examples of "the archbishop's incompetence," and of the savage opinions being circulated about him. This denunciation, kept secret at first, would appear almost word for word in Brasseur's *Histoire du Canada, de son Église et de ses missions*, which was published in 1852.

Although in large part justified, these accusations took little account of other, more positive, aspects. Timid as he was, Signay did defend his priests against the government, and with success. His contemporaries praised his zeal and his spirit of charity; when disasters struck the town of Quebec – two cholera epidemics and the burning of the *faubourgs* Saint-Roch and Saint-Jean – he was the first to organize relief and urge people to help others. He did not hesitate to make his financial contribution in these instances, as well as at the time the bishop's palace and the Séminaire de Nicolet were being built. He also took an interest in the missions and set up the Society for the Propagation of the Faith in 1836. His piety and his fondness for well-run ceremonies and for the liturgy in general were universally recognized.

Acquainted by Bourget with the situation in the archdiocese, the pope, not wanting to force Signay's resignation, thought a simple indication to the archbishop that he would be pleased to receive it would be sufficient. When in February 1847 Bourget informed Signay of the pope's attitude, the archbishop presented his own defence to the sovereign pontiff, saying at the same time that he was ready to resign. Rome did nothing. Dissatisfied, the bishop of Montreal threatened the archbishop with an accusation signed by the suffragan bishops. On 10 Nov. 1849 Signay handed administration of the archdiocese over to his coadjutor. Rome's acceptance of his retirement finally arrived in March 1850, when Signay's death was only a few months away. On 1 October he suffered a paralytic stroke, and two days later he died. In a detailed will he divided his property among various heirs, including the Séminaire de Nicolet, his servants, and the poor in the parish of Notre-Dame de Québec. His funeral occasioned the customary formalities, and Abbé Elzéar-Alexandre Taschereau* delivered the eulogy.

SONIA CHASSÉ

AAQ, 12 A, N: 192; 31-13A; 20 A, VI: 35, 38, 44, 52; VII: 1, 70; 1 CB, X: 175; XIII: 71, 75, 79, 81; XVI: 79; CD, Diocèse de Québec, I: 138, 163–64, 167, 180–81, 183, 194; VI: 161, 193; VII: 134; 515 CD, III: 149; IV: 20–21, 60; VI: 112, 224; 516 CD, I: 22, 70–70A, 73A, 77; 61 CD, Notre-Dame-de-Québec, I: 18, 57, 60–61, 63; 10 CM, IV: 189A, 209, 214; 11 CM, II: 141; 310 CN, I: 150; 60 CN, II: 26–30, 58, 61; IV: 135, 137; V: 126; VII: 31; 26 CP, III: 148; IV: 147; V: 165; VI: 230; IX: 41–42, 71–71A, 72; C: 91–92; H: 132; 30 CP, I: 3, 6–7; Sér.E, II: 24, 38; IV: 56. ACAM, 295.098–295.101. ANQ-Q, CE1-1, 9 nov. 1778, 7 oct. 1850. Archivio della Propaganda Fide (Rome), Acta, 1834, 194; Scritture riferite nei Congressi, America settentrionale, 5 (1842–48). ASN, Lettres des évêques, Signay à Harper, 1830–49; Signay à Raimbault, 1826–41. ASQ, Évêques, no.9, 30 nov. 1836; no.218, 2 mai 1841; Journal du séminaire, I, 10 sept. 1850; Lettres, W, 79; Y, 24, 26–27, 32; MSS, 885–88; MSS-M, 164, 208, 978; Polygraphie, XX: 15, 67; Séminaire, 38, no.35; 54, no.14; 75, nos.6–7, 11, 20, 22–23. *Mandements, lettres pastorales et circulaires des évêques de Québec*, Henri Têtu et C.-O. Gagnon, édit. (18v. parus, Québec, 1887–), 3. [E.-A. Taschereau], *Oraison funèbre et notice biographique de Sa Grâce l'illustrissime monseigneur Joseph Signay, premier archevêque de Québec* (Québec, 1850). J.-B.-A. Ferland, "Notice biographique sur Sa Grâce, monseigneur l'archevêque de Québec," *L'Ordre social* (Québec), 10 oct. 1850: 449–51. Caron, "Inv. de la corr. de Mgr Signay," ANQ *Rapport*, 1936–37; 1937–38; 1938–39. Henri Têtu, *Notices biographiques: les évêques de Québec* (Québec, 1889; réimpr. en 4v., Québec et Tours, France, 1930), 436–525. C.-É. Brasseur de Bourbourg, *Histoire du Canada, de son Église et de ses missions depuis la découverte de l'Amérique jusqu'à nos jours . . .* (Paris, 1852). Gaston Carrière, *Histoire documentaire de la Congrégation des missionnaires oblats de Marie-Immaculée dans l'Est du Canada* (12v., Ottawa, 1957–75), 2. Chaussé, *Jean-Jacques Lartigue*, 89–132. Jacques Grisé, *Les conciles provinciaux de Québec et l'Église canadienne (1851–1886)* (Montréal, 1979), 19–40. Lemieux, *L'établissement de la première prov. eccl.* Pouliot, *Mgr Bourget et son temps*, 2: 210–37. "Les frères et sœurs de Mgr Sinaï," *BRH*, 49 (1943): 122–23.

SIGOGNE, JEAN-MANDÉ, Roman Catholic priest and JP; b. 6 April 1763 in Beaulieu-lès-Loches, France, the eldest child of Mandé Sigogne and Marguerite Robert; d. 9 Nov. 1844 in Ste Marie (Church Point), N.S.

From his father, a cloth manufacturer, Jean-Mandé Sigogne inherited an uncommonly forceful character which, coupled with a moral rigorism, was the most striking characteristic of his pastoral career in Nova Scotia. The Sigognes encouraged learning for their children. Jean-Mandé, in particular, showed promise and eventually decided upon a vocation in the priesthood. At the Petit Séminaire de Tours he received the traditional classical education of pre-revolutionary France, mastering Greek, Latin, and Hebrew. He went on to firmly anti-Jansenist theological studies at the Grand Séminaire, and in 1787 he was ordained a priest for the diocese of Tours.

From this education Sigogne at age 24 emerged a

resolute gallican, and a man of refinement, sensibility, and substantial culture. During his years of formal study he had gathered an impressive personal library which included, along with ecclesiastical works, a good representation of reference books and dictionaries, secular history, Greek and Latin classics, and a number of French authors. A detailed inventory of 1792, the year in which the revolutionaries seized his belongings as state property, lists nearly 200 titles, and "a pile of book[s] in bad condition, heaped up in a large box, many volumes of no value, bound and unbound." Nor were the young abbé's cultural propensities limited to books: a smaller case contained "a number of unusual shell[s] and other items."

Sigogne was said to be small of stature "and in flesh, thin. His appearance was modest even to timidity." He was of frail health, "not strong in body." In Nova Scotia he complained variously of asthma, urinary disorders, and a "faint buzzing in the head." In 1808, in the aftermath of a severe illness, his hair rapidly turned grey.

Sigogne's only ecclesiastical appointment in France was as curate in Manthelan, a remote village some 12 miles west of Beaulieu-lès-Loches. He exercised this charge from 1787 to 1791. As early as April 1791 he rejected the Civil Constitution of the Clergy, but for a time his legal status remained ambiguous. He continued to function, perhaps semi-clandestinely, alongside the conforming curé for another seven months, during which he is described in municipal documents as "formerly curate." To his problems with the revolutionaries was added the hostility of his father, by now mayor of Beaulieu-lès-Loches, who turned him away from the family home because of his conservative politics.

Harassment of the refractory clergy turned to open persecution in late 1791. From November Sigogne carried on his ministry in secret. When *la patrie en danger* was declared in July 1792 the situation for the non-conforming clergy became untenable. In some accounts Sigogne is said to have barely escaped death. Whether on his own or aided by his father's influence, he contrived to leave France, as did the majority of the French clergy.

Sigogne made his way to England, where his presence is noted as early as 27 Aug. 1792. A month later he collected his first assistance from a recently formed committee of relief for the *émigré* clergy. Thereafter he may have found gainful employment as a wood-turner for several weeks. However, from January 1793 to June 1796 he collected his two guineas monthly from the committee; he had no other income. He may then have been engaged as a tutor in a noble house, or an Anglican private school, or both. In his latter years in England he lodged in Rotherhithe (London). There he gave French, Latin, Greek, and geography lessons, and sold devotional and stationery materials. During the time he spent in England, Sigogne achieved a thorough mastery of English.

In these years the lack of French-language priests in the Maritime colonies of British North America was an acute problem, and the *émigré* clergy in England therefore became a focus of interest. Since 1790 the Acadians of St Mary's Bay in the Clare district of Nova Scotia had become increasingly concerned about the inability of church authorities to meet their religious needs. The last French-language priests to minister to this area even on an occasional basis were Joseph-Mathurin Bourg* and Jean-Antoine Ledru*. After the latter's departure in 1788, the Acadians had to rely on English-speaking priests: William Phelan and Thomas Power paid occasional visits to St Mary's Bay, and Thomas Grace*, named Father James, was stationed there from 1790 to 1791. Petitions for a resident French-language priest from among the *émigré* clergy were earnestly seconded by James Jones*, the superior of missions in the Maritime colonies, and by Lieutenant Governor Sir John Wentworth*. Bishop Pierre Denaut* of Quebec and his coadjutor designate, Joseph-Octave Plessis*, had also pleaded the Acadians' cause in England. It was many years before they obtained satisfaction, however. Finally, in January 1799 an *émigré* priest in Boston forwarded 20 guineas in passage money to London, and that April the leader of the French clergy in England advised Denaut, "I have just procured from the government a passport for a kindly and worthy clergyman named M. Sigogne, who has departed to go and work under your orders."

After arriving at Halifax on 12 June, Sigogne spent a fortnight with Jones, his immediate superior. Then, having sworn allegiance to the crown, he sailed in a fishing vessel to the first of his two widely separated parishes, Ste Anne du Ruisseau in the Argyle district at the southwestern tip of the province. Three weeks later he proceeded some 50 miles north through the wilderness to his second parish, Ste Marie in the district of Clare. This mission was to be his headquarters for the rest of his life.

At least four times a year for the next two decades, and periodically after 1824, Sigogne was to undertake the onerous journey between Ste Marie and Ste Anne, travelling on horseback over unmade roads. From Ste Marie he would go to Ste Anne once in summer and once in winter, remaining each time two to three months in the lower parish. In response to sick calls he made many unscheduled journeys as well. The trip took three days, with overnight stops at Salmon River and Yarmouth. After the creation eventually of mission churches at West Pubnico in Argyle and Meteghan in Clare, Sigogne had to divide his activity four ways until 1819. That year a long-awaited second priest arrived to take charge of the Argyle mission. He was André Doucet*, who shortly founded a new mission at Bas-de-Tousquet (Wedgeport). After Doucet was forced by failing health to leave in 1824, Sigogne resumed his twice-yearly treks to Argyle until the arrival of a new priest in 1829. With the departure of the latter in 1833, the old abbé, now a septuagenarian, ministered to the lower missions until 1836, when a permanent pastor was finally found for Argyle. Apart from his constituted missions, Sigogne ministered as best he could to the isolated Catholics along the upper half of St Mary's Bay, from Sissiboo (Weymouth) to Digby, and to the Micmacs who arrived periodically at his residence in Ste Marie.

When Sigogne had first set foot among the Acadians of southwest Nova Scotia, he failed to find the idyllic, God-fearing communities which have often been portrayed in both history and folklore. Abject poverty, official neglect, and lack of stable pastoral care for a generation and a half after the expulsion of 1755 had caused indiscipline, ignorance, superstition, and moral laxity to flourish. Sigogne's impression of his new flock was anything but flattering. They were "a benighted people," he reported, "[steeped] in crass ignorance . . . , infected with ideas of equality [and] liberty, or rather licence and libertinism . . . and the most foolish [of them] is often the most stubbornly determined to set his wishes as the standard." Even occult practices, not unknown in Acadia, continued to thrive. As late as 1810, while Sigogne was absent from Argyle, a young maiden, "possessed by an evil spirit, sick with an unknown illness," was treated to a bizarre mixture of traditional prayer and a "recipe of old Acadia" involving 100 pins and 100 needles, a new knife, the heart of a black chicken, and the afflicted girl's urine, all boiled together in a newly made earthen pot.

Sigogne's rather bilious reaction to the Acadians, under the circumstances, is not surprising. He was particularly sensitive to their primitive republicanism, which reminded him of the moral chaos that had forced his exile from his own country. His revulsion echoed that expressed by royal officials, both French and English, as early as the second half of the 17th century. More recently, James Jones had warned that the missionary "will have to deal with people hard to lead; in regard to ecclesiastical regulations they are true Americans."

The abbé faced without delay the most urgent requirements of his far-flung missions: the resumption of the sacramental and liturgical life – hundreds of baptisms and the blessing of marriages, teaching the catechism, and the appointment of councils of elders whose purpose it was to "take a few salutary and needed measures for our spiritual and temporal benefit, and to maintain peace, justice, and unity amongst us, heeding religion, conscience and honour." The onerous material burden of erecting and financing adequate churches both at Ste Anne and at Ste Marie caused Sigogne the greatest and most sustained distress of his career. By 1800 natural population growth in the two districts had caused younger members to settle at increasing distances along the shore from the original centres where the churches stood. As settlement extended farther from Ste Anne and Ste Marie, religious obligations in the new villages became more and more difficult to fulfil. These geographic and demographic circumstances led to many years of dissension between priest and parishioners, and among the people of the different villages, on the issues of the location of new churches, the division of the original parishes, and the creation of new ones. Sigogne built new churches to replace inadequate ones at Ste Anne and Ste Marie (1809), and in ensuing years he constructed the first churches at Pubnico (1815) and Meteghan (1817). Following a disastrous fire in 1820, in which the villages of Ste Marie, Petit Ruisseau (Little Brook), and Grosses Coques were virtually wiped out, Sigogne built a new church and rectory at Ste Marie. Around 1831 he built the Micmac chapel at Bear River, and finally, in 1841, he erected his seventh church at Corberrie, the only one that remains to this day.

Marshalling the energies of his recalcitrant flock continued to be an ordeal long after the affairs of the churches had been resolved. To his death Sigogne found the Acadians "hard to satisfy and quarrelsome." He suffered incessant rebuffs, suits, and petitions, all of which he faithfully reported to his bishop. Plessis, who succeeded Denaut in 1806, clearly found all of this turbulence rather exceptional. "When will you be over the difficulties and the lawsuits?" he enquired in exasperation in 1817. "At your time of life one ages sufficiently without all those vexations."

The situation was not improved by Sigogne's forceful domination of virtually all matters pertaining to the temporality as well as the spirituality of his parishes. It is not surprising that successive bishops were obliged to confront him with what they felt was excessive rigour on his part, and to urge him towards moderation. Thus in 1800 Denaut, to whom Sigogne seemed "a bit odd in his behaviour," counselled leniency in the application of the church's teaching on such matters as usury, fasting, and abstinence. Yet Sigogne, even though he railed against what he called "follies, high jinks at all hours, and debauchery," imposed as harsh penances upon himself as he did upon others, and frequently requested that the bishop relax laws which he felt were too onerous for the faithful. For example, he sought consideration for those whose work obliged them to take their meals in Protestant households, and also requested the removal of eggs from the "flesh" category for purposes of abstinence.

The Acadians continued to resent the authoritarian ways of their pastor. They tested his patience with their quarrels about the proportion of support due from each village. Unfortunately for him, as long as such matters remained in dispute, no support was forthcoming. Thus he was frequently forced to beg from the pulpit for his subsistence. Despite his frail constitution, he was obliged to cut and transport his own firewood, and to maintain a vegetable garden in order to keep from starving. Privations such as these, and the hostility which caused them, took a severe emotional toll. Sigogne was frequently troubled by self-doubt, and regretted having offered himself for the New World at all. At times, in the throes of discouragement, he threatened to return to France, where the religious situation had become somewhat more stable. Alone in his backwater he was plagued by rejection and loneliness: he was driven to writing pathetic and petulant outbursts to his bishop, and to clerical friends who no longer troubled to answer his letters.

Sigogne's intellectual interests, his correspondence, his sermons, his friendships, and many impressions recorded by his contemporaries confirm that he was a man of refinement. His long career among unlettered Acadians did not diminish this quality. Captain William Scarth Moorsom*, travelling in Nova Scotia in the late 1820s, noted that Sigogne, "though buried in his retreat from all the thoughts and habits of the polished world, yet retains the urbanity of the old French School." He maintained his fluency in Hebrew and Greek by reading breviary passages in those languages. Joseph Howe* described him in the *Novascotian, or Colonial Herald* as deeply learned and of polished manners. Thomas Chandler Haliburton* found him "a man of strong natural understanding, well informed."

On at least one occasion Sigogne's intellectual preferences led to a strikingly unclerical outburst. The incident followed Plessis's pastoral visit of 1815, in the course of which he noted Sigogne's predilection for the gallican, or Parisian, breviary. After he returned to Quebec, the prelate wrote a firm reprimand and ordered Sigogne to use henceforth the repetitive and less lively but (in the diocese of Quebec) normative Roman version. Sigogne was so incensed that he threatened to abandon his mission on this issue alone. "I am more attached to my breviary," he wrote to Plessis, "than to the country, and . . . gold is worth more than old lead." The bishop allowed the matter to drop. When peninsular Nova Scotia became a vicariate apostolic under Edmund Burke* in 1817, his jurisdiction ceased.

Occasional impatience notwithstanding, Plessis was a source of much consolation for Sigogne. He never failed to praise, and even to marvel at, all that the abbé was able to accomplish in his difficult mission. Even after 1817 he invited Sigogne to continue writing as in the past. As a parting gesture in 1815, the bishop had honoured Sigogne by placing his new church at Meteghan under the patronage of Saint-Mandé (Saint Mandal). After the great Clare fire of 1820 Plessis strove, none too successfully as it turned out, to ease the Acadians' losses by gathering alms in Lower Canada on their behalf.

To this day the oral traditions of Argyle and Clare recall Sigogne's unyielding moral rigour. A large number of surviving sermons amply confirm this reputation. He used the threat of excommunication with singular results among a simple people who could not easily do without the consolations of religion. In this manner, though with much difficulty, Sigogne was able (at least during the months he was among them) to bring entire villages to their duty: to provide funds, labour, and materials to build their churches, to support their pastor, and generally to abide by the moral prescriptions of the faith.

The severest incident concerned an illicit marriage which, for reasons of consanguinity, Sigogne had refused to sanction in 1826. The young couple defied the pastor in his absence and were married before a Protestant clergyman. Sigogne, when he returned, took the matter vigorously in hand. He denounced the union as void and ordered the couple, and nine of their accessories, to withdraw from the church until they repented publicly and accepted an equally public penance. Within a fortnight the couple returned repentant, and heard their penance: for six years they were to advance no farther than the church entrance, and to wear white kerchiefs, so as to be recognized by all as fomenters of scandal. The matter was summarily concluded with the pastor extolling both the virtue of penance and penitents who accept its modalities with generosity. It was a dramatic stroke, fully in keeping with the abbé's reputation. Though it is unlikely that Sigogne held the parties to the full measure of the penance, there is no doubting its effectiveness in both the spiritual and the social lives of his parishioners.

Sigogne was more than a pastor of Acadian souls. His flock depended on him, as the only man among them both learned and fluent in English, to see to their temporal interests as well. With the aid of his friend judge Peleg Wiswall of Digby, Sigogne learned to draft deeds, wills, and other legal papers on behalf of his charges. He held these papers in a box in the rectory at Ste Marie. When his residence took fire during the 1820 conflagration and he tried to save these documents, he suffered severe burns that required more than a month of sustained medical care.

Some years after his arrival Sigogne's usefulness became known outside his districts: in 1806 he was appointed a justice of the peace, succeeding Amable Doucet*; Sigogne retained this post until at least 1841. He was of substantial service to the civil authority, which had hitherto paid slight attention to the legal requirements of the Acadians. Given his prominence in the eyes of the provincial authorities, Sigogne was also well suited to lead delegations to the seat of government in Halifax. In 1807 he successfully petitioned for new land grants at Salmon River to accommodate the growing population; years later he would be chiefly responsible for the first expansion of Acadian settlement away from the coastal area, at Concession and Corberrie, where he founded his last parish. As late as the year before his death, Sigogne appeared before Lieutenant Governor Lord Falkland [Cary*] on a public matter.

Sigogne considered ignorance to be the Acadians' most serious privation. His own considerable efforts to help them overcome this disadvantage failed; the parents were apathetic, the children indocile, and qualified teachers lacking. He persisted in berating his parishioners for their indifference to learning and their resultant inferiority in dealing with their English-speaking neighbours. Given that the Acadians lived for several decades after the dispersion on the very edge of starvation, it was not entirely fair of Sigogne to express himself so strongly and persistently on the matter of their ignorance.

He achieved a small measure of success by gathering under his roof at Ste Marie several promising young boys and dispensing to them what education he could. Frederick Armand Robicheau, the first Acadian member of the House of Assembly from St Mary's Bay, and other mid-century community leaders were the products of this system. Less than half a century after Sigogne's death the problem of Acadian education was addressed in a manner he undoubtedly would have approved: in 1890 a small classical college in the French tradition, the Collège Sainte-Anne, was founded at Ste Marie specifically as a memorial to Sigogne's efforts to free his flock from the bondage of illiteracy.

Another pastoral problem for Sigogne was the contempt in which persons of mixed Acadian and Micmac blood were held by the rest of the community. "It is the only area in which their rule of equality does not apply," he reported wryly. His interventions did not sit well with the rest of the population, and he soon decided to leave the solution of this problem to the passage of time and to intermarriage. More successful were Sigogne's pastoral endeavours on behalf of the Micmacs. They came from Bear River to Ste Marie each year on 26 July to celebrate their principal feast of St Anne. In order to minister to them adequately Sigogne set about learning their tongue, procuring Micmac manuscripts for the purpose at his own considerable expense in 1804. It was not long before he could boast of preaching in three languages on a Sunday. His chief concern for the Micmacs was the preservation of their faith [*see* Andrew James MEUSE], and he developed a fond attachment to them as a people. In the year of his death he wrote of them as "this forlorn people, whom I called my children." He regularly solicited assistance from the government on their behalf. Late in 1827 Sigogne and judge Wiswall were able to settle about 20 families on a small reserve at Bear River, where they pursued sedentary livelihoods. In 1828 Sigogne reported quarrels and discords among them, but the settlement endured. In 1831 a grant of £100 from the province allowed him to begin the chapel of St Francis Xavier.

It is one of the paradoxes of Sigogne's career that he was held in high esteem outside the French districts and bore his heaviest crosses in the Acadian community. He obviously enjoyed the society of those he hoped to influence on behalf of his flock. He regularly exchanged books, presents of apples and wine, and compliments with Wiswall. He nourished a high esteem for Haliburton, which the latter reciprocated, and maintained cordial relations with Joseph Howe, James Boyle Uniacke*, Laurence O'Connor Doyle*, and others. Haliburton, in return for the abbé's assistance in his election in 1826, championed such Sigogne-sponsored causes as education and roads and the abolition of the discriminatory oath imposed on Catholics by the Test Act of 1673. During the debate on the Catholic emancipation bill of 1826, which was introduced in the legislature by Richard John Uniacke*, Haliburton paid public tribute to Sigogne's character and to the exemplary loyalty and general orderliness which he inspired in his Acadian charges.

Sigogne elicited less enthusiastic regard from Edmund Burke, his ecclesiastical superior in Nova Scotia. The erratic Burke maintained a running feud with Sigogne. He found him stubborn and "of a somewhat irritable, not to say difficult disposition." This is precisely how many of the Acadians saw him, and Burke's opinion owed much to the petitions of complaint brought to him by Sigogne's enemies in Argyle and Clare. In 1815 Burke reported that although well bred, Sigogne was not very learned, an appraisal which contrasts strikingly with the other opinions we have of him.

In 1844 Sigogne entered the 82nd year of his life and the 46th of his Acadian ministry. He had not left Nova Scotia since his arrival in 1799; he had taken no leave, except for periodic journeys to the provincial capital at the head of some delegation or other. In his deeply spiritual way, he saw only supernatural reasons for the strength he mustered in the face of poor health and ill usage, and for the extraordinary exertions he managed in the pursuit of his apostolate. Towards the end of his life he wrote: "Divine providence to which I have sacrificed everything led me to find resources quite beyond my deserts and wholly sufficient." It is this conviction that explains his fortitude in the face of repeated temptations over the years to abandon the Acadians and return to France.

By 1835 the abbé's lifelong frailty had begun to turn

into paralysis. A description of the state of the Halifax diocese written in 1844, the last year of his life, reports that he required the support of two men to cross the yard from his rectory to his church. On 7 November, apparently while saying mass, Sigogne suffered a final stroke which completed his paralysis. He was carried to the rectory where he received the last rites, and was able to enjoy the consolation of a fellow priest by his side. At his own request he was taken back to the church sanctuary, where he expired at mid morning on the 9th. He was buried at Ste Marie. Nearly a half-century later, in 1892, his remains were moved across the highway to the centre of the greensward fronting the college recently inaugurated as his memorial. The monument erected on that occasion still stands. Sigogne was the most important figure in the survival of the French and Catholic traditions among the Acadians of southwest Nova Scotia, and he continues to be revered as such today in the districts of his apostolate.

BERNARD POTHIER

[Manuscript sources pertaining to Jean-Mandé Sigogne are scattered among many repositories in France, England, the Vatican, and Canada. French materials include AD, Indre-et-Loire (Tours), État civil, Beaulieu-lès-Loches, 1762–90; Manthelan, 1787–91; L^{v}642; Lz 698; Arch. municipales, Beaulieu-lès-Loches, Délibérations du Conseil municipal, 1780–97; and Arch. nationales (Paris), D XIX 21, dossier 338; 28, dossier 430. Important English sources are PRO, CO 217/67, 217/156; T 93/26: 1–8; 93/51, pts.1, 3; and Westminster Diocesan Arch., Archbishop's House (London), Non-British French clergy, no.37. Useful at the Vatican is Archivio della Propaganda Fide (Rome), Scritturi originali riferite nelle congregazioni generali, 965: f.760 (mfm. at PAC).

All sources documenting Sigogne's Nova Scotia career appear to be in Canada, and the most important of these are at the AAQ: 20 A, II; 210 A, III; 1 CB, VIII; 69 CD, V; 7 CM; 311 CN, VI; and especially (for Sigogne's own ecclesiastical correspondence is here) 312 CN, I, V, VII. The bulk of Sigogne's personal papers (the mass of letters he must have received from his ecclesiastical superiors and colleagues, his family in France, and his secular acquaintances) has been lost. Those that were in his possession at his death passed to his principal executor, Louis-Quentin Bourque. Some 40 years later these papers were acquired by Placide Gaudet*. They became the foundation of a series of articles by Gaudet entitled "L'abbé Jean-Mandé Sigogne" which appeared in the *Courrier des provinces maritimes* (Bathurst, N.-B.) from November to December 1885. Later, in 1908, Gaudet sold a portion of the papers to the PAC, where they now constitute the archives' collection of Sigogne documents (MG 23, C10). The balance remained with the bulk of Gaudet's papers and are today in the Centre d'études acadiennes, univ. de Moncton (Moncton, N.-B.), Fonds Placide Gaudet.

Further manuscript materials relating to Sigogne are available in various Canadian archives. Sources in the PANS include MG 1, 733A (typescript); 979, folders 1, 8; 1693, no.10; RG 1, 117; and RG 5, P, 69. This archives also has microfilm copies of the papers of Edmund Burke and William Walsh*, the originals of which are held at the Arch. of the Archdiocese of Halifax. The Arch. of the Diocese of Yarmouth (Yarmouth, N.S.) holds the following registers: District du Cap Sable, reg. des baptêmes, mariages et sépultures; Sainte-Anne-du-Ruisseau, reg. de la fabrique, 1799–1838; and Sainte-Marie, reg. de la fabrique. The Fonds Louis Surette at the same repository includes parish records and correspondence, both originals and typescript copies, and a further number of documents in Sigogne's hand, including his last will and testament. A few manuscript pieces are in the ASQ, Fonds Viger–Verreau, carton 7. A single Sigogne letter of 1842 is in the papers of William Fraser* at the Arch. of the Diocese of Antigonish (Antigonish, N.S.).

The following published works, arranged in chronological order of the events they describe, contain primary references to Sigogne: Dionne, *Les ecclésiastiques et les royalistes français*, 304–6, 438–39; "Visite pastorale de Mgr Denaut en Acadie en 1803," Henri Têtu, édit., *BRH*, 10 (1904): 289–90; J.-O. Plessis, *Journal des visites pastorales de 1815 et 1816, par Monseigneur Joseph-Octave Plessis, évêque de Québec*, Henri Têtu, édit. (Québec, 1903); Murdoch, *Hist. of N.S.*, 2: 571–78, 587–89; 3: 146–47; T. C. Haliburton, *An historical and statistical account of Nova-Scotia* (2v., Halifax, 1829; repr. Belleville, Ont., 1973), 2: 173; and W. S. Moorsom, *Letters from Nova Scotia, comprising sketches of a young country* (London, 1830), 256–58.

Newspapers which have published contemporary accounts or primary source documents include the *Novascotian*, 9 Oct. 1828, 23 Jan. 1840, 18 Nov. 1844; *Le Moniteur acadien* (Shédiac, N.-B.), 21 juin 1887; and *L'Évangéline* (Weymouth Bridge, N.-É.), 17 juill., 14 août 1889; 30 oct. 1890; avril, 1er, 26 nov. 1891; 12, 26 mai 1892; 18 févr., octobre–novembre 1897.

The first study of Sigogne, and the most intriguing because it is lost today, is a partial biography which appeared in one or more issues of a Paris religious paper in 1860, from the pen, it would seem, of Vicomte Joseph-Alexis Walsh. The title is "Vie de M^{r} l'abbé Sigogne Robert, missionnaire en Acadie (Nouvelle-Écosse)." The first extensive writing on Sigogne which has survived is Placide Gaudet's 1885 series of articles in the *Courrier des Provinces maritimes*, noted above. Gaudet's findings were in the main adopted by most of the writers who followed until the publication of G.-M. Oury's important article, "Les débuts du missionnaire Sigogne en Acadie," *Cahiers des Dix*, 40 (1975): 43–86. The most valuable of the early studies are: H.-R. Casgrain, *Un pèlerinage au pays d'Évangéline* (Québec, 1887); P.-F. Bourgeois, *Panégyrique de l'abbé Jean-Mandé Sigogne, missionnaire français à la baie Sainte-Marie, N.-Écosse, depuis 1799 jusqu'en 1844* . . . (Weymouth, N.-É., 1892); Alexandre Braud, "Les Acadiens de la baie Sainte-Marie," *Rev. du Saint-Cœur de Marie* (Abbeville, France), 1898: 90–93, 144–46, 173–76, 276–79, 336–39; 1900: 90–93, 122–24, 176–79, 214–18, 242–48, 309–15, 346–49; P.-M. Dagnaud, *Les Français du sud-ouest de la Nouvelle-Écosse* . . . (Besançon, France, 1905); G. [D.] McLeod Rogers, *Pioneer missionaries in the Atlantic provinces* (Toronto, [1930]); H. L. d'Entremont, "Father Jean Mandé Sigogne, 1799–1844," and L. L. Surette, "Notes on the life of Abbé Jean Mandé Sigogne," N.S. Hist. Soc., *Coll.*, 23 (1936): 103–15, and 25 (1942): 175–94. B.P.]

Allaire, *Dictionnaire*. Caron, "Inv. de la corr. de Mgr Denaut," ANQ *Rapport*, 1931–32; "Inv. de la corr. de Mgr Plessis," ANQ *Rapport*, 1927–28, 1928–29. [H.-R. Casgrain], *Mémoire sur les missions de la Nouvelle-Écosse, du cap Breton et de l'île du Prince-Édouard de 1760 à 1820 . . . réponse aux "Mémoirs of Bishop Burke" par Mgr O'Brien* . . . (Québec, 1895). Henry Faye, *La Révolution au jour le jour en Touraine (1789–1800)* (Angers, France, 1903 [i.e. 1906]). André Latreille, *L'Église catholique et la Révolution française* (2v., Paris, 1946–50), 1. A. Montoux, *La municipalité de Beaulieu-lès-Loches avant la Révolution, 1766–1789* (Loches, France, s.d.). A.-J. Savoie, "L'enseignement en Acadie de 1604 à 1970," *Les Acadiens des Maritimes: études thématiques*, Jean Daigle, édit. (Moncton, 1980), 419–66. Upton, *Micmacs and colonists*. Margery Weiner, *The French exiles, 1789–1815* (London, 1960). René Baudry, "Les pénitences publiques en Acadie," CCHA *Rapport*, 23 (1955–56): 117–23. Mary Liguori, "Haliburton and the Uniackes: Protestant champions of Catholic liberty (a study in Catholic emancipation in Nova Scotia)," CCHA *Report*, 20 (1953): 37–48. Soc. archéologique de Touraine, *Bull. trimestriel* (Tours), 27 (1943): 321. Mason Wade, "Relations between the French, Irish and Scottish clergy in the Maritime provinces, 1774–1836," CCHA *Study sessions*, 39 (1972): 9–33.

SIMCOE, ELIZABETH POSTHUMA. *See* GWILLIM

SIMONDS, RICHARD, businessman, politician, magistrate, and office holder; b. 24 April 1789 in Portland (Saint John), N.B., son of James Simonds* and Hannah Peabody; m. first 18 Aug. 1813 Ann Charters, and they had seven sons and one daughter; m. secondly 18 May 1829, in Annapolis Royal, N.S., Margaret Walker, widow of Lieutenant John Newton, RN; d. 2 May 1836 in Saint John.

Richard Simonds was born into one of the leading property-owning and business families in New Brunswick. After attending school in Portland, he further enhanced his prospects in life by entering into a partnership in 1810 with his maternal uncle, Francis PEABODY, a merchant and shipbuilder at Miramichi. From 1819 to 1824 he also carried on business separately as a merchant, providing supplies to farmer-lumbermen and in the process acquiring many titles to property and mortgages on farms. It was almost certainly due to the influence of his uncle, who had no children of his own, that Simonds was elected to the House of Assembly as one of the two members for Northumberland County at the general election of 1816, when he was only 27 years of age. But he appears to have acquired influence in his own right in that dynamic, tempestuous, and sprawling constituency, which at the time embraced more than a third of the province. He was re-elected in 1819, 1820, and 1827. He also served as a justice of the peace and justice of the Inferior Court of Commmon Pleas.

In the assembly he was joined in 1820 by his elder brother Charles*, who had been elected for Saint John County and City. The two brothers, whose political careers were to be closely intertwined, became the centre of a coterie of business connections, in-laws, and cousins who favoured a more open society. They were independent parliament men, following in the footsteps of their father, James, a member in the 1790s of the party around Amos Botsford* and James Glenie* that had asserted the powers of the assembly over the appropriation of revenue and had imposed restraints on the lieutenant governor and Council. In 1821 they voted in favour of a bill to enable dissenting clergymen to perform marriages; this was carried by a majority of two but was rejected by the Council. In 1825 the votes of the two brothers were critical in defeating a measure, strongly supported by Lieutenant Governor Sir Howard Douglas*, to make financial provision for circuit courts.

Early in 1824 Richard wound up his business affairs at Miramichi, having announced his intention to move to Saint John. This plan was likely associated with the management of his father's extensive and valuable properties, most of which he and Charles were to inherit as tenants in common in 1831. But it may have had a political as well as an economic purpose, for Richard did not settle in Saint John but in Fredericton, where he appears to have lived most of the time from 1825 to 1828.

In February 1828, at the first session of the new house following the general election of 1827, Richard Simonds was elected speaker. This was a coveted and prestigious position, for the assembly, following the traditions of the British House of Commons and the American colonial assemblies, accorded the speaker extensive authority over its proceedings. In December, after acting as speaker for only one session of the house, he resigned his seat on succeeding John Robinson* as provincial treasurer, an office that was in the gift of the lieutenant governor. His brother Charles was then unanimously elected speaker in his place.

There was at this time a convenient conjunction of the interests of the Simonds brothers and those of Lieutenant Governor Sir Howard Douglas. Douglas, an active and effective administrator, had been working since his arrival in 1824 to overcome the assembly's tradition of obstructing initiatives of the executive, using his social magnetism to cultivate close relations with the members. By 1828 he was well aware of the political advantages of working with the Simonds brothers and knew something of the administrative abilities of Richard, who before becoming speaker had been involved in several projects in which Douglas took a direct interest, notably serving as one of the commissioners for allocating the funds raised for the relief of victims of the Miramichi fire, as supervisor of the "great" road between Fredericton and Saint John by way of the Nerepis River, and as secretary of the New-Brunswick Agricultural and Emigrant Society. Richard also shared the lieutenant governor's interest in economic development and in the management of provincial funds. While he was speaker he held the position of paid secretary-treasurer of the agricultural and emigrant society, edited its report, and began to gather information for a report on the fisheries; he was also a member of the commission for the building of Government House.

The alliance with the Simonds brothers was not as productive as Douglas had hoped. In spite of their support he was unable to resolve imperial-provincial conflicts over the civil list, custom-house salaries, and the crown lands before leaving the province in March 1829, in part because of the dilatoriness of the British authorities and in part because the commissioner of crown lands, Thomas Baillie*, had too much influence at the Colonial Office. The one great issue that was resolved was that of assuring permanent financial provision for King's College, Fredericton, an issue which had arisen because the British government had included in the college charter illiberal provisions that were contrary to the spirit, though not to the letter, of the non-denominational terms the assembly had insisted upon in promising support in 1823. The Simonds brothers were Anglicans, but they were tolerant of other sects and rejected the principle of Anglican exclusiveness. It is therefore ironic that, in the face of the opposition of many of the assemblymen with whom they usually associated, they supported the passing of an act in 1829 which made possible the continuing existence of what was, in effect, a thoroughly Anglican institution. A member of the Council since January 1829, Richard Simonds was clearly a participant in, and a beneficiary of, the political alignment that saddled the province with a very unpopular college. He appears to have been completely overwhelmed by Douglas's personality at the time, expressing admiration for all of the lieutenant governor's actions in terms more suited to a courtier than an independent parliamentarian.

At the ensuing session of the legislature in 1830, when William Black* was administering the province, the assembly included in the revenue bill a provision giving jurisdiction in smuggling cases to the justices of the peace. This clause was designed to speed up the process of seizure of illegal imports and make revenue collecting more efficient, but it also had the effect of depriving the officers of the Supreme Court of emoluments. The Council refused to give its assent and the legislature was prorogued on 8 March without provision having been made for the revenue. Simonds, who had taken leave and gone to Saint John, returned hastily to Fredericton, where at another session of the legislature called for the purpose a few days later he was able to persuade the Council to agree to the bill.

In 1831, following the election called at the death of George IV, Charles Simonds was defeated in his bid to retain the speakership of the house. By then Thomas Baillie was assuming a dominating role on the political scene, able to get his way in the Council though not always in the assembly. After the old council was abolished in late 1832, Richard Simonds was called to the new Legislative Council, and during the remaining years of his life he was consistently to be found, along with George Shore* and William Black, voting in opposition to Baillie's policies.

Richard Simonds's entry into the office of treasurer in December 1828 had brought a higher level of activity and organization into that department. Since the office of provincial auditor was reorganized at about the same time, management of the funds at the disposal of the assembly became much more orderly. The treasurer was essentially an employee of the assembly, responsible for collecting the revenue, keeping the accounts, managing the funds, and paying out authorized sums under warrants from the lieutenant governor. Simonds moved to Saint John in order personally to carry out his duties as collector there, and in 1832 successfully resisted an order of Lieutenant Governor Sir Archibald CAMPBELL to move to Fredericton. He was responsible for supervising a staff of sub-collectors, one for each of the seaports and other points of entry in the province. As the chief financial officer of the legislature he was usually consulted regarding the incorporation of banks and insurance companies, and he helped in making arrangements for the placing of official funds and for the investment of company assets in the provincial debt. He remained treasurer until his death.

The Simonds brothers were the first speakers of the New Brunswick assembly to come from outside the circle of loyalist office holders. Their roots were firmly in business, though through their marriages and those of their sisters they came to have many connections with the social élite. Family background, personal interest, and wealth all contributed to their rise to positions of leadership. They seem always to have acted together in political matters, so that although Richard's career was in itself notable, in many ways it appears to be only a prelude to that of his elder brother, who was able to continue what they had started together.

Richard Simonds died at Saint John "after a short illness" at the age of 47.

D. M. YOUNG

N.B. Museum, Gilbert family records, vol.4; D. R. Jack papers, folder 1 (typescript); Richard Simonds, accountbook. Northumberland Land Registry Office (Newcastle, N.B.), Registry books, 1810–23, esp. 9: 54–60 (mfm. at

PANB). PAC, MG 11, [CO 188] New Brunswick A, 43: 142, 149–50; MG 23, D1, 5: 217–18; MG 24, A3, R. Simonds to Douglas, March 1829; L6, 1, material on Miramichi fire, 1825; 3, N.B. Agricultural and Emigrant Soc., minute-book, no.1 (1825–30). PANB, MC 1156; RG 4, RS24, esp. S36-M3.7, S37-Z11.1–6, S42-M3; RG 7, RS71, 1831, James Simonds. UNBL, MG H11. N.B., House of Assembly, *Journal*, 1816–32; Legislative Council, *Journal* [1786–1830], vol.2, 1829–30; 1831–36. *Mercury*, 23 Dec. 1828. *Royal Gazette* (Fredericton), 10 Feb. 1824, 22 April 1828, 11 May 1836. Hill, *Old Burying Ground*. F. A. Firth, "King's College, Fredericton, 1829–1859," *The University of New Brunswick memorial volume* . . . , ed. A. G. Bailey (Fredericton, 1950), 22–32. D. M. Young, "The politics of higher education in the Maritimes in the 1820's: the New Brunswick experience" (paper delivered at the Atlantic Studies Conference, Halifax, April 1980). J. McG. Baxter, "Francis Peabody, the founder of Chatham," Miramichi Natural Hist. Assoc., *Proc.* (Chatham, N.B.), no.6 (1911): 35–53.

SIMPSON, ALEXANDER, fur trader and author; b. 14 Jan. 1811 in Dingwall, Scotland; d. in or after 1845, probably in Scotland.

Alexander Simpson was the son of schoolmaster Alexander Simpson and his second wife, Mary Simpson. The younger generation of the Simpson family were all attracted to the fur trade. Alexander's brother Thomas served in the Hudson's Bay Company's Northern Department and their half-brother Æmilius* in the company's marine department. Their cousin George* (son of their mother's eldest brother) became governor of the company in North America in 1826. When George had visited the family in 1825, Alexander, in his own words, "was so lured by the highly coloured descriptions of adventure to be encountered, and wealth to be won," that he signed on with the HBC in 1827 and travelled overseas the following year.

His first assignment was as an apprentice clerk in the company's office at Lachine, Lower Canada, where in 1830 he was put in charge of accounting. George Simpson was pleased with his performance, finding him in 1832 "Well Educated, attentive to business . . . correct in conduct and private character," and of great potential utility to the company. As a lively young man, however, he frequently clashed with James Keith*, the superintendent at Lachine, and relations reached a breaking-point in 1834 in a dispute which apparently involved Alexander's having "looked tenderly on one of the Maid Servants." Keith decided to send him to Moose Factory (Ont.). He did not take kindly to the move, and persuaded Chief Factor John George McTavish to permit him to travel on a special express to Red River (Man.) so he could plead his case with George Simpson. The governor, though somewhat sympathetic to Alexander's plight, was annoyed at this waste of time and energy, and he ordered him to walk back to Moose "by way of a cooler" and to remain there as an accountant. Accordingly, in March 1835 Alexander returned to Moose, where he kept the books, performed other office duties, and occasionally filled private orders for merchandise wanted by officers and servants. It was hardly the life of adventure he had anticipated.

Finally, after four years, George Simpson assigned him to more lively tasks at Fort Vancouver (Vancouver, Wash.). The HBC had signed an agreement with the Russian American Company to divide the northwest coastal trade, and the London committee was developing plans to reorganize the company's Pacific operation. Stores were to be established in California and at the Sandwich (Hawaiian) Islands, and an endeavour called the Puget's Sound Agricultural Company was to produce wool, leather, tallow, and other products for the English and Pacific markets [*see* William Fraser Tolmie*]. Alexander was to assist Chief Factor John McLoughlin* with various aspects of these plans. In the fall of 1839 Simpson visited the Sandwich Islands to report on the prospects for business there; in 1840 he returned to Fort Vancouver via Monterey (Calif.) and San Francisco, where he purchased sheep for the agricultural company and scouted for information about resources, trade, and prices in California. McLoughlin was so pleased with his work that the young man was sent back to the Sandwich Islands to assist George Pelly in directing the HBC business at Honolulu. Two months after his arrival in January 1841, he was promoted chief trader.

Shortly after reaching the island of Hawaii, Simpson learned of the death of his brother Thomas, who had distinguished himself in Arctic exploration but had also become disliked for his petulant conduct and aversion to mixed-bloods. Alexander sailed to England to assist his bereaved family and to investigate the mysterious circumstances of Thomas's apparent murder or suicide. Upon returning to Hawaii in 1842, he discovered that Sir George was planning to transfer him to the Northern Department. Still distressed over his brother's death, Alexander was unwilling to move to a region with such unfortunate personal associations, and he told Sir George that he intended to resign after taking a leave of absence for the 1842–43 outfit. At first the elder Simpson was reluctant to agree to the resignation but Alexander soon became embroiled in an episode which made the governor reconsider.

Alexander was convinced that it would be in Great Britain's interest to annex the Sandwich Islands, but neither the HBC nor the British government was particularly receptive to the idea because of the potential for international conflict, given American and French interests in the Pacific. The British consul in Hawaii did take up the case and when he decided to go to England in September 1842 to press it, he appointed Simpson "acting consul." Simpson, by continuing to promote annexation, promptly became the centre of an international dispute which nearly burst into open battle, with British and American warships positioning themselves off Oahu. He finally left the islands in March 1843 after they had been occupied by the British, and the HBC was only too happy to recognize his resignation, effective 1 June.

Back in Scotland, he devoted his time to pressing several causes. In 1843 he published a book arguing the case for British annexation of the Sandwich Islands and edited Thomas's *Narrative of the discoveries on the north coast of America*. For two years he corresponded with the London committee, attempting to clear his brother's name and get a pension paid to his mother in light of Thomas's service. *The life and travels of Thomas Simpson, the Arctic discoverer*, which Simpson published in 1845 to gain public sympathy, remains an interesting account of northern exploration. Little is known of Alexander's later years. He apparently settled in Scotland, married, and died there, possibly in the early 1870s. According to retired fur trader Alexander Caulfield Anderson* in his 1878 manuscript "History of the northwest coast," Simpson had died "a few years ago."

KERRY ABEL

Alexander Simpson is the author of *The Sandwich Islands: progress of events since their discovery by Captain Cook; their occupation by Lord George Paulet; their value and importance* (London, 1843), *The life and travels of Thomas Simpson, the Arctic discoverer . . .* (London, 1845; repr. with intro. by John Gellner, Toronto, 1963), and *The Oregon territory; claims thereto of England and America considered; its conditions and prospects* (London, 1846).

Bancroft Library, Univ. of California (Berkeley), A. C. Anderson, "History of the northwest coast" (typescript at PABC). GRO (Edinburgh), Dingwall, reg. of births and baptisms, 26 Jan. 1811. PAM, HBCA, A.1/56; A.10/17–18; B.135/a/139–43; B.135/c/2; D.5/4–5, 7; Alexander Simpson file. Hargrave, *Hargrave corr.* (Glazebrook). *HBRS*, 6 (Rich); 19 (Rich and Johnson); 30 (Williams). Rich, *Hist. of HBC* (1958–59), vol.2.

SKAKEL, ALEXANDER, educator; b. 22 Jan. 1776 in Fochabers, Scotland, son of Alexander Skakel; m. first 7 Jan. 1808 Isabella Skakel, a cousin, in Montreal; m. there secondly 7 July 1823 Christian Dalrymple; he had at least one daughter, who died in infancy; d. 13 Aug. 1846 in Montreal.

Alexander Skakel entered King's College, Aberdeen, in 1789 and graduated MA five years later. He is said to have studied for the Presbyterian ministry, but he preferred to become a schoolmaster. In 1798 he went to Quebec, where he taught for a year. Invited to Montreal, he opened the Classical and Mathematical School there in 1799 and conducted it with considerable success. In 1811 some citizens collected £400 to equip his school handsomely with "philosophical apparatus" so that Skakel's teaching might include demonstrative experiments. From 1813 Skakel gave evening lectures to adults in his home.

In 1818 Skakel was engaged as master of the Grammar School in Montreal, and he brought with him his pupils and his scientific apparatus. Like a sister institution at Quebec [*see* Robert Raby Burrage*], this school had been founded in 1816 under the provincial Education Act of 1801; in 1821 both received the designation "Royal" when they came under the direction of the Royal Institution for the Advancement of Learning. Skakel's curriculum included, at the preparatory level, English, writing, arithmetic, and accounts, and at the advanced level, Latin, Greek, and natural philosophy, or science. Parents of means paid £8–£12 tuition per annum for their sons, no doubt partially subsidizing the free scholars (not necessarily paupers), of whom there were a maximum of 20 at a time until 1831. The majority Canadian party in the House of Assembly being hostile to the Royal Institution [*see* Joseph Langley Mills*], Skakel's salary of £200, paid from the Jesuit estates fund, was reduced to £100 from 1831 when that fund was surrendered to the provincial legislature. As well, Skakel was obliged to teach *gratis* a minimum of 20 pauper students. His grants were eventually suspended.

Skakel was active in Montreal intellectual circles, in which Scots were prominent. He was a friend of John Fleming* and of the Reverend James SOMERVILLE, whom he accompanied on scientific rambles, and undoubtedly was acquainted with their Quebec friend Daniel Wilkie*. From 1822 a former student, Andrew Fernando Holmes*, added chemistry lectures to Skakel's own evening conferences. An active member of the Natural History Society of Montreal, founded in 1827, Skakel was its president in 1835. About 1834 he was offered the post of professor of mathematics and natural philosophy at McGill College, but difficulties arising from the charter prevented the appointment's being made. He was awarded an honorary LLD by his alma mater in 1845.

Skakel also participated in social institutions of essentially Scottish foundation. One of 20 Scots who in 1807 established the Montreal Curling Club, the first such club in North America, he served as president in 1810 and 1821. At a meeting in April 1820 to raise funds for the recently founded Montreal General Hospital [*see* William Caldwell*], Skakel was elected to its committee of management, of which he was the chairman from 1822 to 1824. Secretary of the board of governors from 1823, he was made a governor for life in 1829.

At his death in 1846 Skakel left property valued at about £15,000 as an endowment for the hospital, subject to a life interest for his widow and brother and a constraint on the governors to provide yearly prizes of £10 for the Greek, Latin, and mathematics classes of the Royal Grammar School. His "philosophical and mathematical apparatus," improved by additions of his own worth £200, was left to McGill College. Inventoried in his will by categories – mechanics, hydrostatics, electricity, galvanism, magnetism, optics, and astronomy – the individual items included lenses, microscopes, telescopes, models of pumps, and "a large electrical machine complete."

A pioneer of British education in Montreal, Skakel had devoted 48 years to teaching in Lower Canada, 28 of them in the Royal Grammar School. Among his former pupils were Stephen RANDAL, Dr Archibald Hall*, the geologist and cartographer Sir William Edmond Logan*, Charles Richard Ogden*, attorney general of Lower Canada, and judge William Badgley*. Some success notwithstanding, Skakel's career in teaching had not been an easy one. He must have either lived frugally or enjoyed other sources of income, for the Royal Grammar School could not have enriched him greatly. Being under the Royal Institution, it was spurned by Canadian nationalist and Roman Catholic leaders, and since it was based on the classical curriculum of the English grammar schools, it was increasingly considered irrelevant by a British élite largely involved in business and commerce. In 1843 a group of Montreal merchants and professional men, wanting a school more in tune with 19th-century ideas in education, had established the High School of Montreal, patterned on that of Edinburgh. On Skakel's death this institution successfully petitioned to have his salary transferred to its master and absorbed the Royal Grammar School.

STANLEY B. FROST

ANQ-M, CE1-63, 7 juill. 1823, 16 août 1846; CE1-126, 7 janv. 1808. GRO (Edinburgh), Bellie, reg. of births and baptisms, 22 Jan. 1776. McGill Univ. Arch., MG 3080; RG 4, c.100–c.102; RG 96, c.1–c.3. Univ. of Aberdeen Library, MS and Arch. Sect. (Aberdeen, Scot.), King's College matriculation records and biog. data. L.-P. Audet, *Le système scolaire*, vols.3–4. R. G. Boulianne, "The Royal Institution for the Advancement of Learning: the correspondence, 1820–1829; a historical and analytical study" (PHD thesis, McGill Univ., Montreal, 1970). Campbell, *Hist. of Scotch Presbyterian Church*. E. I. Rexford *et al.*, *The history of the High School of Montreal* (Montreal, [1950]). M. E. [S.] Abbott, "An historical sketch of the medical faculty of McGill University," *Montreal Medical Journal*, 31 (1902): 561–672. John Calam, "The royal grammar schools," *Educational Record of the Prov. of Quebec* (Quebec), 79 (1963): 256–62.

SKERRY, JOHN, businessman, philanthropist, and office holder; b. 1763, probably in October, in Ballyhale (Republic of Ireland), eldest son of Luke Skerry and Mary Larissy; m. first Bridget Shea (d. *c.* 1803), and they had one son and one daughter; m. secondly 28 May 1807 Maria Meagher in Halifax, and they had one daughter; d. 1 Sept. 1838 in Dartmouth, N.S.

John Skerry's people were Roman Catholic tenant farmers. We know nothing of his life before he immigrated to Halifax in 1796 or 1797. Promptly after his arrival he was providing a ferry service between Halifax and Dartmouth, using two large scows to carry passengers, produce, and even animals. Each ferry, heavier than a long-boat, required a crew of two to operate its oars and a sail. In good weather the one-mile journey could be made in 30 to 40 minutes. There was no set schedule of departures. When enough fares had appeared, one of the crew would blow a conch-shell, cry "Over, over!" and set forth.

In 1807 Skerry expanded his operation by buying waterfront property in Dartmouth and erecting on it a hostelry, sometimes referred to as a hospital, and a wharf. At his inn Skerry kept a bar, rented accommodation to man and beast, and conducted what amounted to the town exchange. Passengers for the ferry put the fourpenny fee into a cask set out at the inn. Using these funds, Skerry lent money and bought real estate. On occasion, "Skipper Skerry" allowed the poor to take coins from his casks. That he was never robbed is likely explained by his reputation for honesty and charity.

The War of 1812 gave Skerry another opportunity to demonstrate his charity. Some 2,000 black slaves fled to Halifax from the Chesapeake Bay area, and they were assigned land at Preston, near Dartmouth. Having "traded slavery under the flag of liberty for freedom under the flag of empire," the refugees were in sore straits and needed help. Skerry responded by putting his inn at their disposal and storing their supplies. Between 1815 and 1818 he conveyed these newcomers, as well as the clergy and doctors who served them, back and forth on his ferries and made less than £100 for doing so.

It was around this time that Skerry began to experience competition from a new kind of ferry. In 1816 the Halifax Steam Boat Company started a service between Halifax and Dartmouth using a team-boat. This vessel, powered by a horse-driven paddle-wheel, was faster and more efficient than ferries that depended on sail and oar. Skerry and another operator protested to the House of Assembly concerning this threat to their livelihoods, but to no avail. Although he remained in business, Skerry foresaw that he could not prevail against "progress," and in 1822 he agreed to sell his operation to the new competitor and become a director of the company. The terms of the agreement were so favourable that he was able to retire.

Skerry remained active in educational, religious, and charitable endeavours. He was a Dartmouth school trustee in 1820–21, and he sought for several years to have a lot granted for a Catholic church there. Although in favour of the idea, the lieutenant governor, Lord Dalhousie [RAMSAY], felt the move was premature. Stating early in 1819 that he did not wish "to see at present any new establishment to take away from the highly respectable church" of Bishop Edmund Burke* in Halifax, he withheld his approval. In 1829 Skerry himself donated the required land. He had also been a member of the Charitable Irish Society from 1812, but resigned in 1832 when that society, for undisclosed motives, refused to give £10 towards the relief of workers building the Shubenacadie Canal [*see* Charles Rufus FAIRBANKS]. The skipper not only left the society, but gave the money out of his own pocket.

Skerry was not in tune with the reform movement of Laurence O'Connor Doyle* and Joseph Howe*, which arose in the 1830s. In 1836 he showed his support for the existing arrangements when he nominated a tory candidate for Halifax County. Skerry felt that progress could be made in ways other than by changing the political structure. In a letter to a nephew in Ireland he urged him to have his son educated. "Get your son to learn the grammar well," he wrote, "too much writing and figures is no good without the grammar. . . . In [case?] your son may arrive in America without learning or trade he is no use."

Skerry brought a number of his relatives out from Ireland and assisted them in becoming established in the New World, but he would have been distressed at their wrangling over his estate after he died. The litigation prevented the disbursal of his assets for over 15 years. In his will Skerry had asked for a plain and decent Christian burial devoid of ostentation, stating, "The cost of such useless trappings, I hope my dear wife will distribute amongst the poor for the good of my soul." An obituary summed up his career: "By the pursuit of a successful industry he acquired competence and wealth and the poor often found from his Hospital the comforts of a home."

TERRENCE M. PUNCH

Halifax County Court of Probate (Halifax), Estate papers, S73 (mfm. at PANS). Halifax County Registry of Deeds (Halifax), Deeds, 38: f.50 (mfm. at PANS). PANS, MG 9, no.42: 267; MG 15, 8–9; MG 20, 66; RG 5, P, 57; RG 36, chancery cases, no.1371. St Mary's Roman Catholic Basilica (Halifax), St Peter's Church [St Mary's Cathedral], reg. of marriages, 28 May 1807 (mfm. at PANS). *Novascotian, or Colonial Herald*, 6 Sept. 1838. [T. B. Akins], *History of Halifax City* (Halifax, 1895; repr. Belleville, Ont., 1973). M. J. Katzmann, Mrs William Lawson, *History of the townships of Dartmouth, Preston and Lawrencetown; Halifax County, N.S.*, ed. Harry Piers (Halifax, 1893; repr. Belleville, 1972). J. P. Martin, *The story of Dartmouth* (Dartmouth, N.S., 1957). J. M. and L. J. Payzant, *Like a weaver's shuttle: a history of the Halifax–Dartmouth ferries* (Halifax, 1979). T. M. Punch, *Some sons of Erin in Nova Scotia* (Halifax, 1980); "A note on John Skerry, a Kilkenny emigrant to Canada," *Irish Ancestor* ([Dublin]), 4 (1972): 86–89.

SMALL EYES. *See* ABISHABIS

SMITH (Smyth), Sir DAVID WILLIAM, army officer, office holder, and politician; b. 4 Sept. 1764 in Salisbury, England, only child of John Smith and Anne Waylen; m. first 1788 Anne O'Reilly, and they had eight children; m. secondly 1803 Mary Tyler, and they had one daughter; d. 9 May 1837 near Alnwick, England.

The son of a career soldier and educated under military tutors, David William Smith was commissioned an ensign in the 5th Foot (later the Northumberland Regiment) in 1779. He rejoined the regiment from marriage leave when it was posted to Detroit under his father's command in 1790. He held a series of regimental administrative posts there and, after the 5th was moved in June 1792, at Fort Niagara (near Youngstown, N.Y.). He also acted as clerk to the Hesse District land board from 26 Dec. 1791 to 7 June 1792.

The establishment of the new province of Upper Canada in 1791 did not provide any salary for a surveyor general, it being the view of the secretary of state, Henry Dundas, that the three assistant surveyors employed there could be directed by the surveyor general at Quebec, Samuel Johannes Holland*. The new lieutenant governor, John Graves Simcoe*, was supported by Holland's opinion in wanting a separate department for the upper province. Because of Smith's efficiency on the Hesse land board, and also because he thought the 5th the best-administered regiment in the province, Simcoe made him the unauthorized offer of a post as acting deputy surveyor general, without salary or fees until the appointment was approved. Smith accepted, and when he was at last confirmed as surveyor general of Upper Canada on 1 Jan. 1798 he received back salary not only from 28 Sept. 1792, the date of his commission from Simcoe, but also from 1 July 1792, when his service actually began. His claim for back fees was denied, but he was allowed a small commission on all fees paid through his office.

Financially, Smith made a good gamble by serving for over five years with no authorized salary. When he made up his final accounts for audit (to 30 June 1803), his own fees totalled £2,209 14*s*. 6*d*. sterling. The land regulations also allowed him and his family to accumulate more than 20,000 acres in 21 townships, 7,800 in Pickering. He was accused of using his office to pick the best land. "The lots marked D.W.S. are sure to be the choice spots," Lord Selkirk [Douglas*] wrote in 1803. Yet in moving to civil employment Smith was following his preference as well as his advantage. The 5th Foot was noted as a sociable regiment, and at Niagara the beauty and charm of his wife were admired; but he had no taste for the routine and society of garrison life. He was fashionably well mannered, yet by nature reserved, cautious, even suspicious. "I have no Cronys," he wrote to his Detroit friend John Askin* on 17 Jan. 1793. He articled in the law office of Attorney General John White* and was on the first list of licensed attorneys (7 July 1794), but he had no inclination to practise in the courts. He was promoted captain in 1795, but in the same year his father died and in the next his regiment was ordered to Quebec en route to England. As soon as his civil appointment was confirmed he resigned from the army.

Although their junior by more than a decade, Smith was with John McGill* and William Osgoode* the most trusted as well as the most energetic and capable of Simcoe's subordinates. It was his advice that determined the location of townships to be surveyed and opened to settlement. The "U.E. list" of loyalists exempted from land fees was his work; and when that exemption was at length sanctioned by the imperial government on 15 Dec. 1798 its extension to their children followed his proposals. The chequered plan of distributing reserves in townships, adopted on 15 Oct. 1792 and applied almost uniformly throughout the province, was his. It enlarged the area of the crown and clergy reserves from two-sevenths of land actually granted in each township to two-sevenths of the whole township, but it avoided surveying fractions of acres and he argued successfully against White that it met the Constitutional Act's requirement that clergy reserves be as nearly equal in value to one-seventh of granted land as circumstances would permit. He drafted the first plan for leasing crown reserves, as well as the one actually attempted in 1797. In both he was less concerned about revenue than about reconciling public opinion to the reserves' existence. The township surveys, conducted by 17 different deputies, were of varying quality, but they were systematically conceived and regularly executed.

Orderly surveys did not prevent endemic confusion in land granting. That arose in part from the ineffectiveness of some officials, particularly the provincial secretary, William Jarvis*, who was responsible for issuing title deeds. More fundamental was the inconsistency with which land policy was centrally administered. At first district land boards and then local magistrates could recommend grants, but from 20 July 1796 applications had to be made direct to the Executive Council, on which Smith sat from 2 March 1796. In abolishing the land boards the council reaffirmed the policy of making small grants to all respectable, law-abiding Christians capable of manual labour, but there were such varied expectations about the size of grants that the original plan of 200 acres for a single family, not 1,200 acres, had to be reiterated. Before joining the council Smith had begun an investigation of the grants of whole townships, which Simcoe had naïvely expected to produce organized settlement without fraud or speculation. Of 32 such grants Smith found only six with many actual settlers, and they had often simply moved from other locations in the province. Forfeitures of township grants, which began in May 1796, were difficult because no specific rules for settlement or improvement had been announced until 15 July 1794, and then only for lots along Yonge and Dundas streets.

Smith's relations with Peter Russell*, who was administrator of the province for the three years between Simcoe's departure in July 1796 and Peter Hunter*'s arrival in August 1799, were not cordial. His wife's illness (she died in 1798 when only 28) kept Smith aloof from the cliques being formed at Niagara and York (Toronto), although he was considered a social catch. He resented the grudging way in which Russell agreed that he could miss council meetings to attend her sick-bed. The two were nevertheless able to cooperate. The original "Yonge Street conditions" of settlement, gazetted on 15 July 1794, required only actual occupation and the erection of a house on every lot within a year of its location. They were increased in June 1798 to require that five acres be cleared and fenced, and by November 1802 had been extended to apply to most surveyed lands. The vexed question of officials' shares in land fees was settled, at least for the moment, by a new scale on 1 Oct. 1798; it almost doubled the patent fees, to £5 sterling on a 200-acre grant, but since half that sum was reserved to the crown the officials got less than before. A first attempt was also planned to sell rather than grant land. Smith estimated in 1798 that wild lands were worth from 6*d.* to 15*s.* an acre. When two townships were sold in 1800 they fetched only 9*d.* an acre, barely a third more than the fees on grants would have been.

Under Simcoe and Russell the fault in the land system most complained of was the delay in issuing final patents of ownership. Peter Hunter, zealous for quicker results, achieved a rush of patents in the six years before his death in August 1805 – over 7,000, a rate not matched until 1824. He did so, however, by effectively abandoning the settlement rules that Smith had laboured to apply. Insisting on them delayed fees as well as patents, so they had few defenders in the provincial administration. Smith obtained Chief Justice John Elmsley*'s opinion that ignoring them might be illegal, but when Henry Allcock* succeeded Elmsley Smith had no ally left. On 30 Dec. 1802 the Executive Council set a time limit of three days from its confirmation of a grant for the payment of fees, plus three weeks to take out a patent once it had been drawn up. All that remained of Smith's plan was a clause in the patent, with no provision for enforcement, requiring three years' residence.

More generally, too, Smith's influence on the council declined under Hunter, in spite of the fact that the lieutenant governor came to admire his efficient conduct of his office. "Six months of your labour," Hunter was reported as saying in 1803, "is of greater benefit to the Province than as many years of many others." Smith was not included in the committee to administer the government during Hunter's frequent absences at Quebec. He consoled himself with his fees, well aware as Attorney General Thomas Scott* reminded him that, when they had caught up on the backlog of patents, officials would have "killed the goose that produced the golden eggs."

For nearly all his time in Upper Canada Smith was also a member of the House of Assembly. He was first elected on 27 Aug. 1792 for Suffolk and Essex. Although unopposed, he spent more than £233 in treating the electors, whom he never got over calling "peasants." He was elected again in 1796 for the 3rd riding of Lincoln and yet again in 1800 for Norfolk, Oxford and Middlesex. By 1800 he had changed his electioneering tactics, giving away whisky rather than rum, beer, port, cheese, and roast oxen, but he continued to think of elections as popular festivals not closely related to issues of public policy. "The more broken heads and bloody noses there is, the more election-like," as he wrote to Askin. He found the first assembly to have "violent levelling Principles," although all but 3 of its 16 members were either active loyalists or British immigrants. The house agreed to his proposal for a land tax, which the Legislative Council rejected, but it would not accept his motion to have parish and town officers nominated by magistrates. He was convinced that there was a "country party" with republican sympathies and that a "court party" of gentry and officials was necessary to manage the assembly. He was speaker for all four sessions of the second assembly and for the first two sessions of the third, but the relative tranquillity of their debates owed less than he supposed to his management.

In July 1802 Smith left Upper Canada. Given leave because of recurrent bouts of fever, he had grown dissatisfied with his position at York. He had found friends there in Elmsley and Scott, but he still thought its society plebeian. And after ten years in the same office he looked to promotion as a welcome change from praise. On an earlier leave in 1799 he had undertaken a little self-advertisement, publishing a topographical description of the province and annotating for private distribution an English translation of a work by François-Alexandre-Frédéric de La Rochefoucauld*, *Voyage dans les États-Unis* . . . (8v., Paris, [1799]), to meet its criticisms of Simcoe's administration. He now took many of the papers of his office with him to England, perhaps with the idea of revising his topographical book, of which a second edition did appear in 1813. His hope was for a seat on the Legislative Council. Hunter wanted him back, describing his loss as "almost an irreparable one to the Province," but was unwilling to meet those terms. He was advised by Elmsley not to recommend the appointment: Smith's role in the forfeiture of township grants and in attempting to enforce settlement requirements had made him too unpopular with large landowners. Thus disappointed, and having remarried in England, Smith decided to stay there. On 12 May 1804 he gave notice of resigning all his Upper Canadian appointments. They included the lieutenancy of the county of York (held from 3 Dec. 1798), the command of its militia, and a list two pages long of minor offices and commissions.

Although Smith had prospered in Upper Canada, he was neither old enough nor well enough off to retire. With both Simcoe and Osgoode professing themselves unable to help, he had no patron in Whitehall. Even a clerkship of works for the Board of Ordnance was beyond his influence. All he could obtain was a pension on the Upper Canadian civil establishment. After nearly a year, however, he found a post, not in public life but as estate manager for one of the largest landowners in England, the Duke of Northumberland, who had been colonel of his old regiment. The returns from the piecemeal sale of his Upper Canadian lands were rather disappointing: about half of them, sold by 1833, brought little more than double his land fees. He had selected good land, but unlike John McGill and John Small* he had not concentrated on locations at York and could not watch the market closely. Still, he was able to buy a handsome property near Alnwick and to settle into a second career longer and happier than his first.

S. R. MEALING

[David William Smith issued *A short topographical description of his majesty's province of Upper Canada, in North America; to which is annexed a provincial gazetteer* (London, 1799) to accompany *A map of the province of Upper Canada, describing all the new settlements . . . from Quebec to Lake Huron*, which he compiled; the map appeared in London the following year. A second edition of the description and a new map were issued there in 1813, and the gazetteer portion alone, with a new appendix on Lower Canada, was published as *A gazetteer of the province of Upper Canada* . . . (New York, 1813). There is also an 1813 New York edition of the accompanying map.

Smith's replies to La Rochefoucauld appeared in the form of manuscript annotations in his copy of the 1799 Henry Neuman translation, *Travels through the United States of North America, the country of the Iroquois, and Upper Canada* . . . (2v., London, 1799), 1: 380–591 (the portion concerning Upper Canada), and in the form of "Notes upon Mr. de Liancourt's *Travels in Upper Canada*, by an Anglo-Canadian," appended to the same book. Both have been published as "La Rochefoucault-Liancourt's travels in Canada, 1795, with annotations and strictures by Sir David William Smith," ed. W. R. Riddell, AO *Report*, 1916.

Apart from three items – Riddell's introduction in the AO *Report*; "David William Smith: a supplementary note to the Canadian election of 1792," ed. C. C. James, RSC *Trans.*, 3rd ser., 7 (1913), sect.II: 57–66; and S. R. Mealing, "D. W. Smith's plan for granting land to loyalists' children," *OH*, 48 (1956): 133–37 – secondary accounts treat Smith only incidentally. The most useful is S. G. Roberts, "Imperial policy, provincial administration and defence in Upper Canada, 1796–1812" (D.PHIL. thesis, Univ. of Oxford, 1975). See also Gates, *Land policies of U.C.*, which does not entirely replace G. C. Patterson, "Land settlement in Upper Canada, 1783–1840," AO *Report*, 1920; A. F. McC. Madden, "The imperial machinery of the younger Pitt," *Essays in British history presented to Sir Keith Feiling*, ed. H. R. Trevor-Roper (London, 1964), 173–93; T. D. Regher, "Land ownership in Upper Canada, 1783–96: a background to the first table of fees," *OH*, 55 (1963): 35–48; and J. H. Richards, "Lands and policies: attitudes and controls in the alienation of lands in Ontario during the first century of settlement," *OH*, 50 (1958): 193–209.

Smith's life is best documented in his own papers and in his correspondence with John Askin, John Elmsley, and Thomas Scott, with scattered references in the papers of some other contemporaries. Relevant collections include the D. W. Smith papers and John Elmsley letter-book at the MTRL; the Peter Russell papers (MS 75) and Simcoe papers (MS 517) at the AO; and the John Askin papers (MG 19, A3) and Peter Hunter letter-books (MG 24, A6) at the PAC. There are helpful printed collections: *Corr. of Hon. Peter Russell* (Cruikshank); *Corr. of Lieut. Governor Simcoe* (Cruikshank); [E. P. Gwillim] Simcoe, *The diary of Mrs. John Graves Simcoe . . .*, ed. J. R. Robertson ([rev. ed.], Toronto, 1934); *John Askin papers* (Quaife); and *Town of York, 1793–1815* (Firth).

The most informative government departmental records are PRO, CO 42; the minutes of the Executive Council (PAC, RG 1, E1); and the audit of Smith's accounts (PRO, AO 1, bundle 316, no.5). The "Journals of Legislative Assembly of U.C." for 1792–94 and for 1798–1804 are printed in AO *Report*, 1909. Also printed are the "Grants of crown lands in Upper Canada . . . [1792–98]," AO *Report*, 1928–31, and the "Petitions for grants of land . . . [1792–99]," ed. E. A. Cruikshank, *OH*, 24 (1927): 17–144; 26 (1930): 97–378. S.R.M.]

SMITH, TITUS, farmer, surveyor, office holder, botanist, author, and journalist; b. 4 Sept. 1768 in Granby, Mass., eldest child of the Reverend Titus Smith and Damaris Nish; m. 4 Jan. 1803 Sarah Wisdom in Halifax, and they had five sons and nine daughters; d. 4 Jan. 1850 in Dutch Village (Halifax).

Titus Smith's father, a native of Massachusetts, was an itinerant minister, likely a Congregationalist, and an avid student of mathematics, theology, botany, chemistry, medicine, and languages. The younger Titus was educated first at home by his father and then at a private school in New Haven, Conn. A precocious student, at age four he was able to read with ease. As a younger brother, William, later recalled, "At seven he had made considerable proficiency in Latin, and at twelve could translate the most difficult Latin authors, and had also made good progress in the Greek." His interests and character were consistent with these attainments: "In early youth he evinced no desire to mingle in the amusements of children, but always sought the society of those from whom he could derive knowledge. His earliest desire appeared to be to perfect himself in the knowledge of languages such as Latin, Greek, German, and French." "I think," William observed, "it may with literal truth be said of him, that from two years of age he was never known to cry and seldom to laugh. I never saw him angry, and seldom much elated. With an even temperament he pursued whatever he undertook until it was accomplished."

In 1768 Titus's father became a convert to the teachings of the Reverend Robert Sandeman and was later ordained in his sect. When the American revolution broke out, Smith and other Sandemanians discovered that the sect's opposition to participation in violence or rebellion left its members vulnerable to the suspicion of rebels, who operated on the assumption that "he who is not for us is against us." The family took refuge on Long Island, N.Y., and in 1783 was evacuated to Halifax, where the Reverend Mr Smith responded to a call to preside over a church group. The family also farmed at Preston, near Dartmouth, and in 1796 moved to Dutch Village, west of Halifax.

Titus Smith Jr earned his living as a farmer and as an occasional land surveyor, a training he acquired in his twenties. On four occasions between 1808 and 1829 the provincial government appointed him an overseer of roads. The earliest mention of his interest in nature appears in the diary of Lieutenant John Clarkson [*see* David George*], who recorded on 12 Oct. 1791 that he had called upon "an honest gardener" who "is an excellent Botanist and lays out a part of his garden for experiments." Among these endeavours were attempts to acclimatize seeds to the Maritimes. Farmers and gardeners in Nova Scotia were then in the habit of using seeds imported from England. Smith observed that these seeds had a tendency to fail, and was successful in modifying them to local conditions.

Smith first came to public attention some ten years later when his breadth of knowledge and practical attainments secured him a commission from Lieutenant Governor Sir John Wentworth* to do an extensive survey of the province's interior. Nova Scotia's economic life then centred on the sea and the forest, and it was becoming evident that new settlers and new industries were needed. The province was little known, and the available information was both conflicting and unreliable. A 20th-century geographer, Andrew Hill Clark*, has stated that, although the suspicion was growing that most of the interior was a rocky, lake-strewn wilderness, "hope remained strong that large stretches of good land, and more certainly of good merchantable timber, might still be found." A particular need was to assess the colony's suitability for providing material important to the Royal Navy. A committee of the Council, appointed by Wentworth to consider the growing of hemp in Nova Scotia, reported that "Government should be put in possession of facts, and no longer rely on vague reports which, on one hand, have often depressed the worth of this country below its real value; – whilst others, especially the French writers, have given flattering descriptions above the truth." To that end the committee recommended that a survey be taken "of those inland parts which have been least visited or are entirely unknown, with the view of discovering those spots which are best adapted to the growth of Hemp, and the furnishing of other naval stores."

Wentworth, who had known the Smith family in New England before the revolution, issued instructions in May 1801 for Titus to "visit the most unfrequented parts, particularly the banks and borders of the different rivers, lakes, and swamps, and the richest uplands." He was to report on "the soil, the situation of the lands, and the species, quality and size of the timber; the quantity of each sort also, and the facility with which it can be removed to market." Smith set out that month on the first of three trips he would make into the interior between then and October 1802. He spent more than 150 days in the woods equipped with only his instructions, a compass, writing material, the best available map, "which was probably as much hindrance as help," and whatever he could wear and carry to sustain travel by foot over some of the roughest terrain on the continent.

Smith submitted the results of his explorations in the form of journals, ink drawings of plants, floral lists and descriptions, and a map, which remained the only general one of the province for some 30 years. His report provides a highly detailed account of Nova Scotia's forests, rivers, geological features, and wildlife. In addition to noting the growing scarcity of moose, caribou, and beaver ("I have not seen more than half a dozen inhabited Beaver houses in the whole course of my tour") and its effect on the native population ("the internal parts of the Province are but little frequented by the Indians in the Winter"), he listed most of the 33 species of forest trees native to the province's mainland, 50 shrubs, 20 species of grasses, sedges, and rushes, 20 other species in a catch-all category, and approximately 100 kinds of medicinal plants. Eville Gorham, an ecologist writing in 1955, states that Smith's journals reveal "insight into the pattern and process of vegetation development far in advance of his time," and that they "may well be the first major contribution to plant ecology in North America." Smith's exploration of the interior of Nova Scotia was the beginning of some five decades spent in the public eye dealing with botany, natural history, agriculture, and the correct use of natural resources at the time of the Industrial Revolution. When Halifax's Province House was completed in 1818, it was Smith who was asked to choose and plant the trees that would grace the square. Twenty years later, he was one of several expert witnesses invited to discuss conditions in Nova Scotia as part of the investigations of Lord Durham [LAMBTON]. During his visit to Quebec, the only time he left Nova Scotia as an adult, he gave testimony concerning geology, roads, land prices, the conditions and extent of cultivation county by county, and the province's potential for mineral production. These extensive comments were based on his journals which, he informed Durham's commission, "were written every night, while I was making those observations." In 1841, when the Central Board of Agriculture was founded in Halifax, the second such organization to bear that name, Smith became its secretary, a position he held until his death.

Smith often wrote and lectured on subjects relating to nature and how this resource ought to be used. In 1839 he encouraged Maria Frances Ann Morris*, a Halifax artist, in her wish to paint the province's flora, and wrote the descriptive texts to her *Wild flowers of Nova Scotia*. He was a regular contributor in the 1840s to several Nova Scotia newspapers, including Angus Morrison Gidney*'s *Yarmouth Herald* and Richard Nugent*'s *Colonial Farmer* (Halifax), which he edited. Characteristically, as reported by a son-in-law, "he was always beforehand with work. Up to the time of his death, and for years previously, he prepared a weekly article on agriculture for the *Acadian Recorder* of Halifax; and at the time of his decease he had several weeks' matter ready for the printer." He was a founder of the Halifax Mechanics' Institute and lectured before it on mineralogy, natural history, and painting. In 1833 he received a grant of £15 from the legislature to collect specimens of geology, botany, and mineralogy for the institute's museum.

Smith also possessed a reputation as a thinker. Called "the Rural Philosopher of the Dutch Village," a term that first appeared in Joseph Howe's* *Novascotian* in 1828, Smith espoused a "natural philosophy" that embraced three themes. First, he had a deep belief in God as a wise Providence. Secondly, he was persuaded that humanity had a duty to discover, use, and conserve nature's bounty. Finally, many progressive ideas embodied in the advance of industrialization were in his view out of rhythm with nature and therefore wrong.

In a lecture given in 1835 Smith spoke of the forests as "the garden of God," where nothing was superfluous or out of place. Smith placed God and nature together; the first concept expressed the personality of God, and the second the force of creation and preservation in the world. Life, Smith wrote, should accommodate itself to natural rhythms: "Whenever man neglects the dictates of nature, he is sure to be the sufferer." He was highly critical of the way in which European settlers, in contrast to the Indian inhabitants, squandered natural resources. Reasonable use, together with careful conservation, was Smith's message. An indication of his preparedness to seek the potential value in everything was his recommendation in the 1840s that Halifax use a series of lakes northeast of the city, called the Chain Lakes, as the source of its earliest supply of piped water. The 19th century's obsession with "progress" left Smith unimpressed. He criticized industrialization as being nothing more than a scheme to create great fortunes for capitalists while rendering the lives of the operatives unenviable. He believed that nature could provide for all if people were to husband resources and if surplus populations were to migrate to areas capable of carrying them.

Titus Smith died as a consequence of an attack of jaundice which struck in the autumn of 1849 and "which he tried to ward off by taking more than his usual exercise." His obituary in the *Acadian Recorder* stated: "Had circumstances placed him in a different sphere, we believe he possessed one of those giant intellects which is the production of an age, and capacitates its possessor to figure prominently in the world's history. But his was a different lot." Unlike John YOUNG or gentlemen farmers such as Bishop Charles Inglis*, Smith possessed a knowledge of agriculture in Nova Scotia that was empirically based and not the outcome of theoretical speculations founded on British or American conditions. He was a polymath and his concerns aroused in his countrymen more than a passing notice of nature and conservation. His broad interests permitted him to advise and assist his contemporaries in matters that included botany, biology, ecology, and agriculture. It appears that many people regarded him as an oracle. Through his studies and his travels Titus Smith probably knew his province better than anyone then alive. Indeed, it is doubtful whether Nova Scotians have seen his like since.

TERRENCE M. PUNCH

Titus Smith's journals are located at PANS, RG 1, 380–80A. Excerpts from them have been published in A. H. Clark, "Titus Smith, Junior, and the geography of Nova Scotia in 1801 and 1802," Assoc. of American Geographers, *Annals* (Washington), 44 (1954): 291–314; Eville Gorham, "Titus Smith, a pioneer of plant ecology in North America," *Ecology* (Durham, N.C.), 36 (1955): 116–23; Barbara Grantmyre, "Two peripatetic gentlemen," *Nova Scotia Hist. Quarterly* (Halifax), 6 (1976): 375–82; and Titus Smith, *A natural resources survey of Nova Scotia in 1801–1802* (Truro, N.S., 1955).

His testimony before Lord Durham's commission of inquiry was published in *Minutes of evidence taken under the direction of a general commission of enquiry, for crown lands and emigration* . . . (Quebec, 1839), Nova Scotia testimony, 18–25 [i.e. 29], where he is incorrectly identified as Silas Smith. The error was rectified when the information gathered by the commission was republished in *Report on the affairs of British North America, from the Earl of Durham* . . . ([London, 1839]); Smith's testimony appears in app.B: 134–40.

Smith is the author of "On the operations of *fungi* in disintegrating vegetable substances" and "A list of the principal indigenous plants of Nova Scotia," *Halifax Monthly Magazine*, 1 (1830–31): 339–42 and 342–45, and of *Lecture on mineralogy; delivered by Titus Smith, on March 5, 1834, before the Halifax Mechanics' Institute* (Halifax, 1834). Another lecture, read before the institute on 14 Jan. 1835, was published as "Natural history of Nova Scotia" in the *Times* (Halifax), 27 Jan. 1835: 29, and in the *Magazine of Natural Hist.* (London), 8 (1835): 641–62, under the title "Conclusions on the results on the vegetation of Nova Scotia, and on vegetation in general, and on man in general, of certain natural and artificial causes deemed to actuate and affect them." He also prepared the descriptive text for M. [F. A.] Morris, *Wild flowers of Nova Scotia . . . , accompanied by information on the history, properties, &c. of the subjects* (2 pts. in 1v., Halifax and London, 1840). His translation of two German legends appears as "Translations from the German," *Halifax Monthly Magazine*, 1: 389–91.

PANS, Map Coll., Nova Scotia general, "A map of Titus Smith's Track through the Interior of Nova Scotia"; RG 1, 411, [no.144]; RG 34-312, P, 8, 18 March 1816. John Clarkson, *Clarkson's mission to America, 1791–1792*, ed. and intro. C. B. Fergusson (Halifax, 1971). *Acadian Recorder*, 23 May 1829, 12 Jan. 1850. *Colonial Farmer* (Halifax). *Novascotian*, 3 July 1828, 7 Jan. 1850. *Nova-Scotia Royal Gazette*, 24 May 1808. *Encyclopedia Canadiana*. Sylvester Judd, *History of Hadley* . . . (Northampton, Mass., 1863). M. J. Katzmann, Mrs William Lawson, *History of the townships of Dartmouth, Preston and Lawrencetown; Halifax County, N.S.*, ed. Harry Piers (Halifax, 1893; repr. Belleville, Ont., 1972), 205–18. Harry Piers, *Titus Smith, "The Dutch Village Philosopher," pioneer naturalist of Nova Scotia, 1768–1850* (Halifax, 1938). S. B. Elliott, "Titus Smith – the Dutch Village Philosopher," *Education Nova Scotia* (Halifax), 4 (1974), no.16: 1–2. C. B. Fergusson, "Mechanics' institutes in Nova Scotia," PANS *Bull.* (Halifax), 14 (1960): 32, 35. J. S. Martell, "From Central Board to secretary of agriculture, 1826–1885," PANS *Bull.*, 2 (1939–41), no.3: 5. Harry Piers, "Artists in Nova Scotia," N.S. Hist. Soc., *Coll.*, 18 (1914): 139. T. M. Punch, "Maple sugar and cabbages: the 'philosophy' of the 'Dutch Village Philosopher,'" *Nova Scotia Hist. Quarterly*, 8 (1978): 19–38. William Smith, "Some account of the life of Titus Smith," Nova-Scotian Institute of Natural Science, *Trans.* (Halifax), 1 (1863–66), pt.4: 149–52. C. St C. Stayner, "The Sandemanian loyalists," N.S. Hist. Soc., *Coll.*, 29 (1951): 81–82, 104–5.

SMITH, WILLIAM, office holder, politician, and historian; b. 7 Feb. 1769 in New York, son of William Smith* and Janet Livingston; d. 17 Dec. 1847 at Quebec.

William Smith's father was a leading political figure in New York and in 1780, during the American revolution, he was appointed chief justice of the colony. When the British evacuated New York in late 1783 young William took ship for London, where he was joined by his father. The elder Smith had grave doubts about the boy's abilities but, as the only son, William received the best introduction to life that Smith could give him. He briefly attended a prestigious grammar school and, after abandoning it, was educated by a Swiss tutor. He became fluent in foreign languages, especially French, and developed a taste for Latin and the classics. Introduced by his father to the cultural life of the great city as well as to the labyrinthian politics of the British government and of the loyalist *émigrés*, William appears to have learned best that connections were the way to success, not a totally illegitimate conclusion in the closed world Smith Sr inhabited.

In 1786 William went to Quebec with his father, who had been appointed chief justice of the colony under the administration of Lord Dorchester [Carleton*]. Smith's efforts to found a university having failed, William's continuing preparation for life centred on practical training. He was given increasing responsibility for the vast family landholdings in New York and Vermont. In 1792 he petitioned for a land grant of 108 square miles on the Rivière Saint-François in Lower Canada. Through the influence of Smith, who was chairman of the colony's land committee, the petition was recommended, but ultimately the grant was never completed as a result first of bureaucratic complexities and then of political opposition [*see* Samuel Gale*]. In 1791 William had been commissioned an ensign in the Quebec Battalion of British Militia, and the following year, during the first elections held in Lower Canada, he ran for a seat in the House of Assembly but was soundly defeated. His father's friendship with Dorchester obtained his appointment on 15 Dec. 1792 as clerk of the Legislative Council, a post to which the assembly fixed a salary of £450 sterling in 1793.

On the death of his father late in 1793, William inherited three-elevenths of the Smith estate. The only male heir, he was nominally chief custodian of the family inheritance, but after 1796 the administration would be performed increasingly by his brother-in-law Jonathan SEWELL, who was more adept at such matters. On 6 April 1803 Smith was appointed master in Chancery for the province, mainly to run messages between the assembly and the Legislative Council; his chief recommendation for this unpaid position had been his innocuousness. But Smith had ambitions, and in 1803 he journeyed to England to try to obtain a salary for the post, to solicit further appointments – and to find a wife. Feeling himself "not sufficiently informed as to the advantages" of matrimony, he had long hesitated to marry. Necessity drove him to it, however. "Money is everything . . . ," he wrote to Sewell, "unless I marry a woman of fortune I shall be ruined." He found a suitable mate in Susanna Webber, a niece of the wealthy and influential merchant Sir Brook Watson*. Susanna had considerable "attractions," Smith informed Sewell in a letter which might have been written by Jane Austen. "She is pretty, not handsome, of a very good Family, with £200 a year *now* & one hundred more, at her mother's death – of a very amiable disposition, good Temper and good Sense – and what is better than all, will go to Canada, a country in the estimation of the women of this Country, the most barbarous and the most uncomfortable of the world." Smith also found a patron in the Duke of Kent [Edward* Augustus], who had much admired his mother during a stay in Lower Canada from 1791 to 1794; the duke assisted him in obtaining £81 sterling per annum as master in Chancery. Like his father in the early 1780s, Smith kept a diary of his sojourn in London.

Smith returned to Lower Canada with his bride in 1804. He worked on a history of the colony that he had apparently begun in 1800, perhaps in emulation of his father, who had published *The history of the province of New-York* . . . in 1757. John NEILSON furnished printing estimates in 1805 and 1809, but fearing the effect on his career of adverse public reaction, Smith dithered about publication. In 1810 he was given a commission of the peace, and two years later he began seeking appointment to the Executive Council; however, he received little encouragement from either friends or the government. Shortly before the War of 1812 he was promoted major in Quebec's 3rd Militia Battalion, but he did not see action. Realizing that his history might sell in the wake of the war, Smith had it printed by Neilson in 1815. That year a friend and an active supporter of his candidacy for executive councillor, Herman Witsius RYLAND, assured an English contact that the forthcoming work would force the crown to assert its rights *vis-à-vis* the assembly or to abandon them. He added that if the book had appeared under the "energetic" administration of Sir James Henry Craig* it might have facilitated acceptance by imperial authorities of that governor's draconian measures for extending the influence of the crown and reducing the power of the assembly. Since Craig's departure in 1811, however, the political tendency had been to conciliation rather than confrontation. Having second thoughts, Smith delayed publication of the history, ostensibly to correct errors and add material, and then left for England in the summer of 1815, possibly to promote claims to office. The decision to delay publication was perhaps wise; on his return from England he found a conciliatory governor, Sir John Coape Sherbrooke*, at the head of the administration. During Sherbrooke's tenure Smith was named a commissioner for the Jesuit estates in November 1816, appointed an honorary member of the Executive Council on 3 Feb. 1817, and promoted lieutenant-colonel commanding Quebec's 3rd Militia Battalion in May 1817. He was made a full member of the Executive Council, with voting rights, on 3 April 1823.

Smith did not lose interest in his "History," however, and in early 1823 he mentioned to Governor Lord Dalhousie [RAMSAY] his preoccupation with the deterioration and disappearance of historical sources in the colony. In April Dalhousie invited him along with Sewell and Joseph-Rémi VALLIÈRES de Saint-Réal to help form "a Society, not entirely 'Antiquarian' but Historical rather and Canadian," the principal objects of which would be "the early history of Canada, and particularly that which relates to the Indians," as well as the collection of "all books, papers, deeds or documents which are supposed to be still existing but neglected." The Literary and Historical Society of Quebec was founded the following year; Smith, however, seems to have played only a discreet role in its subsequent development. The time now seemed propitious for bringing out his history and, after protracted negotiations with Neilson over payment of printing costs since 1815, Smith released the *History of Canada* in two volumes in 1826.

The appearance of the *History* coincided with an increasingly determined effort on the part of the assembly, dominated by the nationalist Canadian party under Louis-Joseph Papineau*, to subject to its control the governor and the Executive and Legislative councils, led by Sewell and John Richardson* of the English party. In the mould of the English party, Smith had conceived the theme of his work to be "a Colony daily augmenting in Wealth, Prosperity and Happiness: now fortunately placed under the dominion of Great Britain and with a Constitution . . . which, . . . in assigning to its various branches, rights, peculiar to each, but necessary to the preservation of all, has been found in the harmony and co-operation of its powers . . . best adapted to the spirit and happiness of a Free People." Although Smith himself considered his book a "narrative" rather than a history, it did constitute an effort at analysis and synthesis; it was in any case a much more substantial work than its only predecessor in English, George HERIOT's *The history of Canada, from its first discovery . . .*, published in London in 1804. For the French régime, the subject of the first volume, Smith used a certain number of official and private manuscript sources, but his coverage and opinions were largely those of the *Histoire et description générale de la Nouvelle France . . .* (3v. and 6v., Paris, 1744) by Pierre-François-Xavier de Charlevoix* and of the "Histoire du Canada depuis l'année 1749 jusqu'à celle 176[0] . . ." by Louis-Léonard Aumasson* de Courville. He wrote of the earliest period of French settlement with relative impartiality, but as he brought his account down to the conquest he increasingly reflected views current in the English party; his treatment of church-state relations, for example, was heavily influenced by Sewell, who had long dealt with the subject. Perhaps in an effort to camouflage his *parti pris*, Smith made the second volume, which covers the period 1763 to 1791, little more than a compilation of documents; most of them were official in nature, but all were chosen to express his view that progress in the colony could be achieved only through the adoption of English law, land tenure, and education among other things.

Produced in an edition of 300 copies, the *History* sold only 68 in 1826 and 8 more in the three years following. Its sales reflected a certain disinterest in history which can also be seen in the disappointing reception given by the educated public to the Literary and Historical Society. The work did provoke a vigorous response by the priest Thomas Maguire* over its treatment of the Roman Catholic Church, but the leaders of the Canadian party opted to ignore it. It formed the basis for Joseph-François PERRAULT's treatment of the British régime in the *Abrégé de l'histoire du Canada . . .* (4v., Québec, 1832–36), a school textbook, and of the *Histoire du Canada, et des Canadiens, sous la domination anglaise* published in 1844 by the office holder Michel Bibaud*; neither work was influential. In 1826 as well Smith had edited for publication a continuation to 1762 of his father's history of New York.

The mild sensation in Smith's life produced by the publication of his *History* was followed by a return to tranquillity. In 1835, however, Governor Lord Gosford [ACHESON], who had been sent to the colony to quiet ever-intensifying discontent, one cause of which was plural and incompatible office holding, forced Smith to decide between the prestige of the executive councillor and the salary of the clerk of the Legislative Council. Smith chose the salary, but he was kept on as an executive councillor for political reasons until after the rebellion of 1837. Attempts to gain a knighthood were unsuccessful, and when the Canadas were unified in 1841 Smith was forced to retire from the clerkship on half salary as a pension; he was unable to persuade authorities to let a son replace him as clerk. He lived out his remaining years quietly in a summer house he had built at Cap-Rouge and in his substantial residence at Quebec, where he died on 17 Dec. 1847. He and his wife had had at least five children.

William Smith was a man of ordinary intellectual abilities who largely failed in his efforts to emulate a brilliant father. Indeed his father's domination of him had left him indecisive and lacking character; Dalhousie referred to him disdainfully as "Billy Smith." Without his father's breadth of vision, but trained to seek prestige and wealth, Smith became in Dalhousie's (albeit exaggerated) view "a mean self-interested adviser . . . [who] would do or say anything to please the reigning power." None the less, in his career Smith to some extent typified the influential anglophone oligarchy of office holders, and through his pioneering research and the publication of his *History* he promoted the preservation of historical documents and struggled to awaken in Lower Canada an interest in the study of the past.

J. M. BUMSTED

William Smith is the author of *History of Canada* . . . (2v., Quebec, 1815). The diary of his trip to London was published as "The London diary of William Smith, 1803–1804," ed. L. F. S. Upton, *CHR*, 47 (1966): 146–55. Smith edited a work by his father entitled *Continuation of "The history of the province of New-York," to the appointment of Governor Colden, in 1762* (New York, 1826).

ANQ-Q, CE1-61, 23 janv. 1815, 20 déc. 1847. New York Public Library, Rare Book and MSS Division (New York), William Smith papers. PAC, MG 23, GII, 10: 1658–61, 1673–76, 2412–15; MG 24, B1; RG 1, E1, 37: 124–25; 38: 429; L3[L]: 142; RG 4, A1: 40690; RG 68, General index, 1651–1841. PRO, CO 47/122. Univ. de Montréal, Service des bibliothèques, coll. spéciales, coll. Melzack, procuration, 5 juill. 1815; Ryland à Thomas Amyot, 20 août 1815; Ryland à sir John Coape Sherbrooke, 28 sept. 1816. Ramsay, *Dalhousie journals* (Whitelaw). William Smith, *The diary and selected papers of Chief Justice William Smith, 1784–1793*, ed. L. F. S. Upton (2v., Toronto, 1963–65). *Quebec Gazette*, 26 Oct. 1786; 24 May, 20 Nov. 1792; 25 April 1793; 1 Aug. 1816; 22 May 1817; 21 Nov. 1822; 11 Jan. 1827. Ginette Bernatchez, "La Société littéraire et historique de Québec (the Literary and Historical Society of Quebec), 1824–1890" (thèse de MA, univ. Laval, Québec, 1979), 134, 136. J. M. Bumsted, "William Smith Jr. and *The history of Canada*," *Loyalist historians*, ed. L. H. Leder (New York, 1971), 182–204. M. B. Taylor, "The writing of English-Canadian history in the nineteenth century" (PHD thesis, 2v., Univ. of Toronto, 1984), 136–45. L. F. S. Upton, *The loyal whig: William Smith of New York & Quebec* (Toronto, 1969). Ægidius Fauteux, "Le S . . . de C . . . enfin démasqué," *Cahiers des Dix*, 5 (1940): 231–92. Gustave Lanctot, "Les prédécesseurs de Garneau," *BRH*, 32 (1926): 533–34. "Le premier manuel d'histoire du Canada," *BRH*, 46 (1940): 288. P.-G. Roy, "William Smith, pluraliste renforcé," *BRH*, 44 (1938): 215–16.

SMYTH, Sir JAMES CARMICHAEL, army officer, military engineer, and author; b. 22 Feb. 1779 in London, eldest of five sons of James Carmichael Smyth and Mary Holyland; m. 28 May 1816 Harriet Morse, daughter of Robert Morse*, in London, and they had one son; d. 4 March 1838 in Georgetown (Guyana).

The father of James Carmichael Smyth, a doctor and author, sent his son to be educated at the Royal Military Academy in Woolwich (London). Smyth graduated in 1793, became a second lieutenant in the Royal Engineers in March 1795, and served as one of the chief engineering officers with the British forces in southern Africa between 1795 and 1808. During this period he also gained experience as a colonial official. In 1808 and 1809 he was in Spain with Sir John Moore's command, and between 1813 and 1815 he was one of the principal military engineers with the allied troops in the Low Countries, rising to the rank of brevet colonel by June 1815. At Waterloo he was on the Duke of Wellington's staff, and for his service he won the duke's approbation and sundry honours and decorations.

When Wellington took up the post of master general of the Board of Ordnance in 1818, in charge of fixed defences throughout the empire, Smyth became one of his principal executive officers. In 1823 Wellington sent Smyth, who had been created a baronet in August 1821, on tours of the defences and fortifications in the Low Countries and the British West Indies. The 1824 report on West Indian defence needs was the basis for all plans and works in the islands for the next generation. In 1825 Smyth, again on Wellington's instructions, performed the same service in British North America, and his report, dated 9 Sept. 1825, became the standard plan for fortifications until the mid 1840s. Smyth was promoted major-general in May 1825, and, after some engineering work in Ireland, in May 1829 he became governor of the Bahamas. In June 1833 he moved to the governorship of British Guiana (Guyana). There he helped to smooth out the problems associated with emancipation of the slaves, winning praise in the colony and London for his efforts. He died in this last office of a sudden illness. Between 1815 and 1831 Smyth had published eight volumes on military engineering, defence, and slavery.

The contributions Smyth made to the development of Canada stemmed from his 1825 report, in particular from his promotion of an existing scheme for a canal which would link the Ottawa River and Lake Ontario by the Rideau and Cataraqui river systems. Between April and October 1825 Smyth and two other engineers surveyed the entire frontier between British North America and the United States, travelling back and forth across the Atlantic. Their examination was rather too quick for complete efficiency. In his instructions, Wellington had emphasized the importance of a Rideau canal, and Smyth agreed that such a water-way was the most necessary component in the defence of the colonies. Seizing on some civilian estimates, he used these as a base for projecting a canal which would cost no more than £169,000. This figure was to prove inadequate in a number of ways, but its reasonable size was instrumental in winning Treasury approval. The Smyth commission judged that all the essential defence works for British North America would cost £1,646,218; this sum was too much for the Treasury. But Smyth and Wellington put priority on military canals, and were successful in obtaining funds for them. Without Smyth's efforts, the Rideau Canal would not have been built.

Wellington put Smyth in charge of the Rideau project in London, and Lieutenant-Colonel John BY was sent to do the building. Smyth worried that By had been rushed off without sufficiently specific instructions; when By submitted his first report in July 1826, these worries were substantiated. By complained that £169,000 was an inadequate amount, announced that he would build a system of canals that were over twice the intended width, and added that he was starting work which would cost more than £169,000. Smyth urged Wellington to restrain and discipline By and force him to conform to the original plans and costs. But the communications lag and the inertia within the Ordnance department were too great, and By succeeded in enlarging the project. Unfortunately, much of By's work was, from the defence point of view, futile, given restrictions on the size of military canals which were being built along the Ottawa River, and By and Canadian defence expenditures fell into deep disfavour in London during 1832 and 1833.

The other service to Canada rendered by Smyth was his book on the campaigns of the British army in North America, called *Precis of the wars in Canada, from 1755 to the Treaty of Ghent in 1814, with military and political reflections* (London, 1826). He focused on the 1813 and 1814 campaigns, which highlighted the dangers to military water communications along the American border. In other ways the *Precis* presented a short, orthodox assessment of the American wars.

G. K. RAUDZENS

Smyth's main Canadian activities are recorded in PRO, CO 42/205: 174; Wellington to Smyth, 11 April 1825; 193–200; WO 44/15: 297; 44/16: 24–25; 44/18: 65–67, 69–72; 44/19: 17–18; 44/24: 269–70; and SRO, GD45/3/390. His part in the Rideau Canal story is related in G. [K.] Raudzens, *The British Ordnance Department and Canada's canals, 1815–1855* (Waterloo, Ont., 1979), and his activities are mentioned in a number of other works relating to Canada's defences, notably in Kenneth Bourne, *Britain and the balance of power in North America, 1815–1908* (London, 1967). There is a four-column entry in the *DNB*.

SOMERVILLE, JAMES, teacher and Church of Scotland minister; b. 1 April 1775 in Tollcross, Scotland, only son of James Somerville, a merchant; d. 2 June 1837 in Montreal.

James Somerville received his degree in arts from the University of Glasgow at age 17. He completed a course in divinity in 1799 and was licensed to preach by the Relief Presbytery of Glasgow. Because there were few congregations within that presbytery, the need for new ministers was minimal. Somerville grew tired of waiting for a call and welcomed a position which came to him through a friend in Glasgow, that of educating the children of Scottish merchants living at Quebec. He arrived there on 3 June 1802 and quickly organized a school, offering "Reading, Writing, Arithmetic, English grammar, and the Latin and Greek languages." His teaching ability was appreciated by both his pupils and their parents.

Despite his background in the Relief Church, Somerville was well received by Alexander Spark*, a minister of the Church of Scotland and incumbent of the Presbyterian Scotch Church at Quebec, who must have been attracted by his personality and his ability in the pulpit. When the Reverend John Young* of the Scotch Presbyterian Church in Montreal, later known as the St Gabriel Street Church, was dismissed in 1802, Spark suggested Somerville as his successor.

Somerville preached in the Montreal pulpit in the autumn of 1802 and was invited to become the congregation's minister. His adherence to the Relief Church was not considered an impediment, the congregation requiring only that its minister be licensed by a presbytery in the British dominions. Although he accepted the charge, he returned to Quebec and taught until the end of the academic year. Meanwhile, Robert Forrest, an ordained minister also of Scottish extraction and education, preached in the Scotch Presbyterian Church while visiting Montreal in April 1803 and divided the congregation along socio-ethnic lines over the choice of a minister. The majority maintained the original call to Somerville; those who supported Forrest formed a separate Presbyterian congregation which shortly afterwards called Robert Easton* as its minister. On 18 Sept. 1803 Somerville was ordained by Spark, the Reverend John Bethune*, and Duncan Fisher*, a highly esteemed elder of the church; the three men had formed the Presbytery of Montreal, probably solely for the ordination.

Somerville, who was said to have been a little under middle stature and to have had "black and glossy [hair], with an easy curl," took a leading part in Montreal social circles. His was the first name on the roll of members of the Montreal Curling Club, begun in 1807, and in 1809 he established a literary society. He was a strong supporter of the Montreal General Hospital, founded in 1819, and, as an amateur naturalist, helped establish the Natural History Society of Montreal in 1827. A freemason, he was chaplain of the Provincial Grand Lodge of Lower Canada in 1829. It was not an easy life, however. His first wife, Marianne Veitch, a native of Edinburgh whom he had married at Quebec on 8 July 1805, died the following year leaving an infant daughter. On 4 April 1808 in Montreal he married Charlotte Blaney, who gave birth to a son in 1814; she died five years later. His son's death occurred late in 1832 and was followed within a few months by that of his daughter, who had been an invalid. Somerville's mental health seems to have been unsteady, and was probably worsened by these tragedies. To ease his load, Henry Esson* had been brought in as his colleague in 1817, but in the winter of 1822–23 Somerville retired from public duty with an allowance of £150 per year. He nevertheless remained the senior minister until his death in 1837, at which time he left most of his property to religious and benevolent institutions.

ELIZABETH ANN KERR MCDOUGALL

ANQ-M, CE1-63, 4 avril 1808; CE1-68, 5 juin 1837. ANQ-Q, CE1-66, 8 juill. 1805. UCC, Montreal–Ottawa Conference Arch. (Montreal), St Gabriel Street Church, parish records, box I. UCC-C, Biog. files. Borthwick, *Hist. and biog. gazetteer*. Campbell, *Hist. of Scotch Presbyterian Church*. [James Croil], *A historical and statistical report of the Presbyterian Church of Canada in connection with the Church of Scotland, for the year 1866* (Montreal, 1867). Gregg, *Hist. of Presbyterian Church* (1885). E. A. [Kerr] McDougall, "The Presbyterian Church in western Lower Canada, 1815–1842" (PHD thesis, McGill Univ., Montreal, 1969).

SOU-NEH-HOO-WAY (To-oo-troon-too-ra; baptized **Thomas Splitlog)**, Wyandot chief; d. in the spring of 1838 probably in Essex County, Upper Canada.

Sou-neh-hoo-way's boyhood or common name was To-oo-troon-too-ra which, translated as Splitlog, provides the appellation that is invariably used in documents. He was a younger brother of Roundhead [Stayeghtha*], a leader of the Wyandots from the Sandusky region of Ohio, and is sometimes confused with Tau-yau-ro-too-yau (Between the Logs), who was also from Sandusky and was the main adviser to Tarhe (Crane), principal chief of the American Wyandots.

With Roundhead, Splitlog opposed American expansion into the Ohio valley after the revolution and he fought at Fallen Timbers (near Waterville, Ohio) in 1794. Subsequently he, Roundhead, and their younger brother Warrow resettled with their families at Brownstown (near Trenton, Mich.), where they were drawn into the movement led by Tecumseh* and the Prophet [TENSKWATAWA]. On the outbreak of the War of 1812, Splitlog became one of the most active and steadfast of Britain's Indian allies. In September 1812 he served with Adam Charles Muir*'s force moving toward Fort Wayne (Ind.), and personally scouted entirely around the advancing American army. On 14 Nov. 1812, mounted on a white charger, he led an attack on enemy troops at the rapids of the Miamis (Maumee, Ohio), where American observers incorrectly reported him killed or seriously wounded. With Roundhead and Myeerah*, he was prominent in the defeat of the Kentucky militia at the battle of Frenchtown (Monroe, Mich.) on 22 Jan. 1813 and aided in capturing the American commander. He participated in the retreat of Henry Procter*'s troops up the Thames valley and fought at the battle of Moraviantown. In May 1814, joining the dissident Potawatomi chief Mkedepenase (Blackbird), he abandoned active operations in protest over the short rations allocated to their warriors. After a time, however, he returned to the field, and in early November he played a spirited part in the resistance made at the Grand River to a large American force under Brigadier-General Duncan McArthur that had advanced from Detroit. In February 1815 Lieutenant-Colonel Reginald James was counting on his assistance against a body of American infantry and cavalry said to be on the road to the village of Delaware.

After news of the Treaty of Ghent reached the colony, Splitlog and his followers settled in Essex County, on lands commonly known as the Huron Reserve. There he became recognized as the leader of a minority faction known as the Splitlog party. A full-blood, Catholic, traditional group opposed to the acculturated Methodist majority, the Splitlog party was adamantly against the surrender of parts of the reserve and the allocation of the remaining lands to individuals – the post-war panacea for "the Indian problem." Although Splitlog boycotted treaty councils and regularly protested to the Indian Department and the lieutenant governor, his objections were ignored and the government's negotiations were conducted with the Methodist group. In 1835 it was arranged that a portion of the reserve would be turned over to the crown and the remainder subdivided among band members. Splitlog's requests that the agreement be revoked were to no avail. None the less, because of his long and honourable service in war he was recognized as the most distinguished of the chiefs until his death in the spring of 1838. In 1843 many of the Methodist faction voluntarily joined the Ohio Wyandots and resettled in what is now eastern Kansas. The remainder of the band continued to dispose of its lands, until in 1892 the last pieces of the Huron Reserve were surrendered.

JAMES A. CLIFTON

PAC, RG 8, I (C ser.), 260: 306; 677: 97; 683: 218; 687: 114, 136; RG 10, A2, 29: 17347–49; A3, 489: 29582–84; A4, 60: 60711–13; 62: 61508–11. Wis., State Hist. Soc., Draper MSS, 11U97, 11U116. *Messages and letters of William Henry Harrison*, ed. Logan Esarey (2v., Indianapolis, Ind., 1922), 2: 220. *Mich. Pioneer Coll.*, 16 (1890): 50. *Weekly Reg.* (Baltimore, Md.), 3 (1812–13): 217. P. D. Clarke, *Origin and traditional history of the Wyandotts . . .* (Toronto, 1870).

SPRAGG, JOSEPH, educator; b. 28 March 1775 in Canterbury, England, possibly a son of Joseph Spragg and Frances ——; m. 18 Jan. 1802 Sarah Bitterman in

London, and they had three daughters and four sons; d. 17 Dec. 1848 in Toronto.

Joseph Spragg had become a schoolmaster by 1806, in which year he lived at New Cross (London). In 1819, possibly at the request of William Wilberforce, he entered the Central School of the National Society in London. Wilberforce recommended Spragg to Sir Peregrine Maitland*, lieutenant governor of Upper Canada, for the post of teacher at the school that Maitland intended to be the vanguard of a system of schools like those of the National Society in Britain, which functioned under the precepts of Andrew Bell's monitorial method. National schools had been set up in Lower Canada and the Maritimes [*see* Jacob Mountain*; George Stracey Smyth*]. These schools were similar in operation to the Lancasterian schools of the British and Foreign School Society in their utilization of older and brighter students as teaching monitors [*see* Joseph LANCASTER], but the essential difference was that the National Society, in using Bell's system, followed Church of England tenets. In his conviction that love of God and king should be the basic aim of colonial education, Maitland favoured such schools as a counterpoise to the non-denominational common schools that had been established in Upper Canada in 1816. Because of their frequent employment of American teachers and texts, he criticized them for "instilling principles into the pupil's mind unfriendly to our form of government."

One of Canada's first monitorial-school teachers, Spragg arrived in York (Toronto) in the summer of 1820 at the age of 45. The school in which he was to be set up already had an incumbent in common-school teacher Thomas Appleton*. He had to be removed but it required some tough talking by the Reverend John Strachan* as chairman of the district board of education before he agreed to resign. Critics of Maitland, such as reformer and school trustee Jesse Ketchum*, saw in these actions a deliberate attempt to replace the common school with what amounted to a church school. The trustees resigned along with Appleton and in their place Maitland appointed Attorney General John Beverley Robinson*, Surveyor General Thomas Ridout*, and Joseph Wells*. He then installed Spragg as the teacher of what became known as the Upper Canada Central School. Unfortunately for Maitland, Appleton refused to leave gracefully, and his case soon became a *cause célèbre*.

In September the Upper Canada Central School was opened for both boys and girls and, as in other schools in the National Society system, most were admitted free because their parents could not afford to pay fees. During the first year of operation, 158 children attended, the majority having had no previous instruction. Under Spragg's direction the monitorial system was applied, "by which those who teach and those who are taught are equally improved and benefitted." The government-sponsored school was patterned after the Central School in London, and it was intended that the York school would be a training-ground for teachers of similar schools throughout the colony – one in every town, according to Maitland. One scholar, George Warburton Spragge (Joseph's great-grandson), has estimated that at the most four or five schools were attempted; only the one at York survived for any length of time.

As a schoolmaster, Spragg had a mixed reputation. Even Wilberforce had admitted in 1820, "I cannot say that He has particularly fascinated me, tho' I have had very respectable recommendations of Him." Maitland, whose opinion may have been biased, spoke favourably in 1822 and again two years later of both Spragg and the school, but parental reports, presented in 1828 in the report of a select committee of the House of Assembly on a petition from Thomas Appleton, did not always agree. After Spragg had built a house on the western outskirts of York in 1824, he was frequently late for school and reports of his negligence increased. On one occasion in 1829 Lieutenant Governor Sir John Colborne*, visiting the school, found that Spragg had not arrived by 10 A.M. Colborne promptly suspended him for a time. Despite his spotty record, Spragg repeatedly appealed for more money and teaching assistance and sought personal promotion through new office. That he had a high opinion of himself is reflected in Henry Scadding*'s observation that, "though not in Holy Orders, his air and costume were those of the dignified clergyman." He did have some success in placing his three surviving sons in the 1820s: Joseph Bitterman and William Prosperous became clerks in the Surveyor General's Office and John Godfrey* was articled as a law student.

Spragg remained headmaster of the central school until his retirement in 1844, the year it closed its doors. By that time a church-run free school funded by the public treasury was an anomaly. Maitland's plan never materialized. Not only was the Bell system, with its Church of England bias, unacceptable to the majority of Upper Canadians, but the House of Assembly suspected that the National schools were intended to undermine the non-denominational common schools.

J. DONALD WILSON

[G. W. Spragge, "Monitorial schools in the Canadas, 1810–1845" (D.PAED. thesis, Univ. of Toronto, 1935), provides a full description of this system of education. The details of Maitland's plan to introduce National schools are discussed in my "Foreign and local influence on popular education in Upper Canada, 1815–1844" (PHD thesis, Univ. of Western Ont., London, 1970), 65–71. Conflicting views of the Appleton case are presented in G. W. Spragge, "The Upper Canada Central School," *OH*, 32 (1937): 171–91, and E. J.

Hathaway, "Early schools of Toronto," *OH*, 23 (1926): 322–27. J.D.W.]

National Soc. (Church of England) for Promoting Religious Education (London), Reg. of masters from the country, entry for J. Spragg. PAC, RG 1, L3, 463A: S14/160; RG 5, A1: 23980–83, 23987–95, 26393–95, 31899–901, 39075–77. PRO, CO 42/365: 328, 418, 420, 432–33; 42/366: 3 (mfm. at AO). St James' Cemetery and Crematorium (Toronto), Record of burials, 20 Dec. 1848; Tombstones, lot 29, sect.P. Trinity College Arch. (Toronto), G. W. Spragge papers, Spragg family genealogy. Univ. of Toronto Arch., A73-0015/001, extract of dispatch from Maitland to Bathurst, enclosed in Major Hillier to General Board of Education, 13 May 1823 (mfm. at AO). John Strachan, *The John Strachan letter book, 1812–1834*, ed. G. W. Spragge (Toronto, 1946), 212. U.C., House of Assembly, *Journal*, 1828, app., "Report on the petition of T. Appleton." U.C. Central School, *First annual report of the Upper Canada Central School, on the British National system of education* (York [Toronto], 1822), 7. *Globe*, 23 Dec. 1848. Scadding, *Toronto of old* (Armstrong; 1966).

SPROULE, ROBERT AUCHMUTY, water-colourist, miniaturist, and drawing-master; b. in Athlone (Republic of Ireland), second son of Thomas Sproule and Marianne Ardesoif; m. 8 Oct. 1831 Jane Hopper in Montreal, and they had two sons and four daughters; d. 1845 in March Township, Upper Canada.

Robert Auchmuty Sproule came to Lower Canada in 1826 and settled in Montreal. On 30 September he put an advertisement in the *Montreal Herald*, announcing himself as a miniaturist who had studied with "the best Masters in London and Dublin." In November 1829 he gave notice of his intention to bring out six views of Montreal, which did in fact appear the following year. Published by Adolphus Bourne*, they had been engraved on copperplate by William Satchwell Leney from Sproule's water-colours. The series marked the beginning of a fruitful collaboration between Bourne and Sproule that lasted until 1834 and led to the introduction of lithography into the colony. Bourne went to London lithographer Charles Joseph Hullmandel in 1832 for the printing of a group of works by Sproule, including four views of Quebec and a portrait of Louis-Joseph Papineau*. He returned to Montreal with a lithographic press and subsequently used it for Sproule's drawings. The results included the frontispiece for the *Montreal Museum or Journal of Literature and Arts* in December 1832, a portrait of Archbishop Bernard-Claude Panet*, one of St Francis Xavier, and a view of the steamer *Great Britain*, all three published in 1833, and a view of the church of Notre-Dame in Montreal printed in 1834. As well, Sproule transferred illustrations by Alexander Jamieson Russel and several others to stone for lithographing; they were printed by Bourne for *Hawkins's picture of Quebec; with historical recollections*, a work by Alfred Hawkins* that came out at Quebec in 1834.

In Montreal Sproule also taught drawing, a common practice among miniaturists of the period. His frequent moves with his family after 1834, however, suggest that it was not possible for him to make a living there. He can be followed through his children's births, rather than through his artistic activities, to Cornwall in Upper Canada around 1836, Williamstown around 1838, and finally the Bytown (Ottawa) region. In 1839 he was residing in Huntley, where his wife's family had lived since 1836; his father had also been living near by at Richmond since 1820. In 1840 Sproule and his wife received two acres of land in March Township from her brother, Albert Hopper. Sproule apparently kept a store at March Corners for a while, and later another one at Stittsville. In June 1844 he again advertised himself as a miniaturist and drawing-master, but this time in Bytown. When he died in November or December of the following year, he was reported to have been living in March Township.

Robert Auchmuty Sproule's name has lived on through his prints. The views of Montreal (copies of each edition and five of the original water-colours are held at the McCord Museum there) are said to make up the most handsome series published in Canada and to demonstrate the maturity achieved in pictorial printmaking during the first half of the 19th century. The other prints done by Sproule and Bourne were not always of the same quality as the Montreal and Quebec series, a quality attained partly through the collaboration of Leney, who was an excellent engraver, and Hullmandel. Except for one portrait of himself and another of his wife, Sproule's work as a miniaturist remains little known.

PIERRE B. LANDRY

[*Alumni Dublinenses* . . . , ed. G. D. Burtchaell and T. U. Sadleir (new ed., Dublin, 1935), 772, lists a Robert Sproule who was born *c.* 1799 and who studied at Trinity College; he is not the same person as the subject of this biography. P.B.L.]

ACC, Diocese of Ottawa Arch., Parish reg., 1838–69: 7, 47. ANQ-M, CE1-63, 8 oct. 1831. PAC, RG 31, C1, 1842, Goulbourn Township. *Bytown Gazette, and Ottawa and Rideau Advertiser*, 5 Dec. 1839, 4 June 1844, 17 April 1845. *Canadian Courant* (Montreal), 14 Nov. 1829; 8 Jan., 24 Sept. 1831; 16 June 1832. *Le Canadien*, 16 nov. 1832. *La Minerve*, 13 oct., 12 déc. 1831; 17, 21 mai, 18 juin 1832; 12, 19 août 1833. *Montreal Gazette*, 2 Nov. 1829, 27 June 1833, 8 May 1834, 8 Dec. 1845. *Montreal Herald*, 30 Sept. 1826. Mary Allodi, *Canadian watercolours and drawings in the Royal Ontario Museum* (2v., Toronto, 1974), 1, nos.727–30. Louis Carrier, *Catalogue of the Château de Ramezay, museum and portrait gallery* (Montreal, 1958), nos.722, 1589. *Catalogue of the Manoir Richelieu Collection of Canadiana*, comp. P. F. Godenrath (Montreal, 1930), nos.110–15. *A catalogue of the Sigmund Samuel Collection*, comp. C. W. Jefferys (Toronto, 1948), 74–76, 135. B. S. Elliott, "Arthur Hopper of Merivale, his children and grandchildren," *The Merivale cemeteries*, ed. J. [R.] Kennedy (Ottawa, [1981]). J. R. Harper, *Early painters and engravers*, 295; *Everyman's Canada; paintings and drawings from the McCord Museum of McGill University* (Ottawa, 1962), 41–43. "An index of miniaturists and silhouettists who worked in Montreal," comp. R. M. Rosenfeld, *Journal of Canadian Art Hist.* (Montreal), 5 (1980–81), no.2: 111–21. I. N. P. Stokes and D. C. Haskell, *American historical prints . . .* (New York, 1932; repr. Detroit, 1974). Wallace, *Macmillan dict.* J. C. Webster, *Catalogue of the John Clarence Webster Canadiana Collection, New Brunswick Museum* (3v., Saint John, N.B., 1949), 1, no.1308.

Mary Allodi, *Printmaking in Canada: the earliest views and portraits* (Toronto, 1980), 64–77, 84–89, 98–103, 126–27. C. P. de Volpi, *Québec, a pictorial record . . . , 1608–1875* (n.p., 1971), plates 75–78, 85–93. C. P. de Volpi and P. S. Winkworth, *Montréal, a pictorial record . . . , 1535–1885* (2v., Montreal, 1963). Alfred Hawkins, *Hawkins's picture of Quebec; with historical recollections* (Quebec, 1834). *Historical sketch of the county of Carleton* (Toronto, 1879; repr., intro. C. C. J. Bond, Belleville, Ont., 1971), 199. Yves Lacasse, "La recherche dans les musées: le cas du tableau-relief de la mort de saint François Xavier du Musée des beaux-arts de Montréal," *Questions d'art québécois*, J. R. Porter, directeur (Québec, 1987), 98. Morisset, *La peinture traditionnelle*, 77. J. W. Reps, *Views and viewmakers of urban America . . .* (Columbia, Mo., 1984). F. St G. Spendlove, *The face of early Canada: pictures of Canada which have helped to make history* (Toronto, 1958), 62–64. Claudine Villeneuve, "Les portraits de Louis-Joseph Papineau dans l'estampe de 1825 à 1845," *Questions d'art québécois*, 104–5, 116. Elizabeth Collard, "Nelson in old Montreal: a Coade memorial," *Country Life* (London), 146 (July–December 1969): 210. Peter Winkworth, "The pleasures of old Quebec," *Apollo* (London and New York), 103 (1976): 412–17.

STEPHENSON, JOHN, physician and educator; b. 12 Dec. 1796 in Montreal, youngest of five sons of John Stephenson, tobacconist, brewer, and merchant, and Martha Mair; m. there 26 July 1826 Isabella Torrance, and they had several children, of whom only one survived infancy; d. there 2 Feb. 1842.

John Stephenson attended school in his native town, notably at the Petit Séminaire de Montréal, and began his medical training with William ROBERTSON on 29 Dec. 1815, the apprenticeship fee being £50. In 1817 he enrolled at the University of Edinburgh, and he graduated in medicine in 1820. His thesis, entitled "De velosynthesi," describes one of the first successful repairs of a cleft palate, written by Stephenson not as the surgeon but as the patient. Although otherwise healthy, Stephenson had been born with an anomaly of his palate. After the operation, performed in Paris by Joseph-Philibert Roux in September 1819, his voice was more nearly normal and his problems in eating and drinking disappeared. That year he was made a member of the Royal College of Surgeons of London.

Stephenson returned to Montreal in 1820. He received his licence to practise in October 1821, his examiners being Daniel ARNOLDI and Robertson. Soon after, he and Andrew Fernando Holmes*, with whom he had studied in Scotland, joined the medical staff of the Montreal General Hospital; Stephenson lectured on anatomy and physiology at the hospital from 1822.

Along with Holmes and the other medical officers of the Montreal General Hospital, Robertson and William Caldwell*, Stephenson became convinced that formal instruction in medicine should be made available to Lower Canadian students. In November 1822 Stephenson and Holmes drew up a memorandum recommending the creation of a medical school. After it received the approval of their colleagues, the memorandum was sent to the governor-in-chief, Lord Dalhousie [RAMSAY]. It was accompanied by a letter suggesting that the medical examiners for the district of Montreal be the physicians of the hospital. Dalhousie approved of both plans. The hospital staff (which now included Henry-Pierre Loedel) was thus given the unusual prerogative of issuing licences to graduates from their own school. The arrangement was not looked upon with favour by some of the other physicians in Montreal [*see* Arnoldi]. Classes at the new school, called the Montreal Medical Institution, began in the autumn of 1823, and Stephenson was professor of anatomy, physiology, and surgery. He was also appointed secretary to the faculty, a position of considerable influence in the ensuing years. As teaching proceeded, the institution applied for a royal charter. Its request was refused because it had no affiliation with an educational establishment.

At this time, the bequest by James McGill* of money and property for the creation of a university or college in Montreal was in danger of being lost. A royal charter, obtained in 1821, would be rescinded if McGill College did not begin teaching. But that body had been unable to form a faculty in any discipline. The dilemma was resolved in 1829, when negotiations were concluded which permitted the Montreal Medical Institution to become the medical faculty of McGill College. Stephenson continued to teach anatomy, physiology, and surgery. His role in assuring the establishment of McGill was considered of prime importance by businessman Peter McGill*, who reputedly described Stephenson as "the man above all others to whom we owe McGill College." In 1831, for example, Stephenson forwarded a memorial to the governor, Lord Aylmer [WHITWORTH-AYLMER], petitioning on behalf of McGill College for the right to confer degrees. As Stephenson pointed out, McGill graduates acquired "Medical Honors" without difficulty from foreign countries; it was unfair that they had to travel outside Lower Canada to obtain them. Before degrees could be granted, however, the institution's statutes required royal approval. The statutes proposed by Stephenson were accepted with only slight alteration. McGill received the authority to confer degrees in medicine in July 1832. As registrar of the school, Stephenson had considerable influence until his death in 1842.

In 1820 or 1821 Stephenson had been appointed physician to the Sulpicians in Montreal and he maintained a busy general and surgical practice throughout his short career. He had the reputation of being well liked by his patients, although at least one of his students, Aaron Hart David, considered him not over courteous. Joseph Workman*, another student, did not share this opinion and soon after Stephenson's death wrote of his mentor in highly laudatory terms. Workman also wrote with approbation of Stephenson's method of treating uterine haemorrhage with large doses of a substance known as sugar of lead, "with unvarying success"; unfortunately, Workman's enthusiasm seems to have been misplaced.

A portrait of Stephenson was destroyed by fire in 1907 but, using a photograph, Andrew Dickson Patterson painted another in 1920 which now hangs in the McIntyre Medical Sciences Building of McGill University.

CHARLES G. ROLAND

John Stephenson's thesis was published as *De velosynthesi* (Edinburgh, 1820). A translation by W. W. Francis has appeared as "Repair of cleft palate by Philibert Roux in 1819: a translation of John Stephenson's *De velosynthesi*," intro. L. G. Stevenson, *Journal of the Hist. of Medicine and Allied Sciences* (New York), 18 (1963): 209–19.

ANQ-M, CE1-126, 10 janv. 1797, 26 juill. 1826; CE1-130, 5 févr. 1842. PAC, RG 4, A1; B28, 49: 858. *Toronto Patriot*, 15 Feb., 22 March 1842. *List of the graduates in medicine in the University of Edinburgh from MDCCV to MDCCCLXVI* (Edinburgh, 1867). Abbott, *Hist. of medicine*. J. J. Heagerty, *Four centuries of medical history in Canada and a sketch of the medical history of Newfoundland* (2v., Toronto, 1928). H. E. MacDermot, *A history of the Montreal General Hospital* (Montreal, 1950). M. E. [S.] Abbott, "An historical sketch of the medical faculty of McGill University," *Montreal Medical Journal*, 31 (1902): 561–672. A. H. David, "Reminiscences connected with the medical profession in Montreal during the last fifty years," *Canada Medical Record* (Montreal), 11 (1882): 1–8. B. R. Tunis, "Medical licensing in Lower Canada: the dispute over Canada's first medical degree," *CHR*, 55 (1974): 489–504. William Whiteford, "Reminiscences of Dr. John Stephenson, one of the founders of McGill medical faculty," *Canada Medical & Surgical Journal* (Montreal), 11 (1883): 728–31.

STEWART, CHARLES JAMES, clergyman of the Church of England, bishop, and politician; b. 13 or 16 April 1775 in London, third surviving son of John Stewart, 7th Earl of Galloway, and his second wife, Anne Dashwood; d. there unmarried 13 July 1837.

Charles James Stewart's early life was spent in Galloway House, Scotland, on his father's great but secluded estate. His tutor, the Reverend Eliezer Williams, is said to have recognized in him a "young man of the richest promise." In 1792 Charles matriculated to Corpus Christi College, Oxford, where he received a BA in 1795; he was granted an MA four years later by All Souls College.

Stewart was ordained to the diaconate of the Church of England in December 1798 and to the priesthood on 19 May 1799, both ceremonies being conducted in Oxford Cathedral. His decision to enter the ministry, and his orientation once in it, were no doubt influenced by Williams, son of a convert of the Methodist evangelical George Whitefield, and by his sister Catherine, Lady Graham, a friend of William Wilberforce and a disciple of Isaac Milner, two other eminent evangelicals. In June 1799 he was collated to the rectory of Orton Longueville (Orton), which he would retain until 1826.

Stewart had early contemplated missionary work overseas. In 1806, when the Anglican bishop of Quebec, Jacob Mountain*, was in England on furlough, Stewart's bishop, George Pretyman Tomline, recommended him. Mountain quickly appointed Stewart to the seigneury of Saint-Armand, Lower Canada, and even suggested that he succeed as bishop should Mountain obtain a much desired translation. Mountain failed to secure a new post, however, and it was simply as a missionary that Stewart arrived at Quebec on 27 Sept. 1807. "So unusual an undertaking in a man of family and independence," according to a sister of the bishop, "could not by the world in general be attributed to any but an enthusiast and a methodist." However, Stewart met several leaders of Quebec society, including President Thomas Dunn*, John HALE, Herman Witsius RYLAND, and Jonathan SEWELL, and laid all fears to rest. After proceeding to Montreal, where he was received by leading businessmen, such as William* and Duncan* McGillivray, Joseph Frobisher*, John Richardson*, James McGill*, and Isaac Todd*, he continued on to his mission.

Saint-Armand, on the Vermont border, was the seigneury of Thomas Dunn. A missionary of the Society for the Propagation of the Gospel, John Doty, had visited it as early as 1798, and from 1800 three others, James Marmaduke Tunstall, Robert Quirk Short*, and Charles Caleb COTTON, had served it while living in the western part at Philipsburg. Stewart, however, settled at Frelighsburg in the east. When Cotton opened a mission in adjacent Dunham Township in 1808, Stewart assumed charge of western Saint-Armand.

By 1809 Stewart had bought a log parsonage and built Trinity Church, Frelighsburg, the first regular place of Anglican worship in the Eastern Townships; he bore half the cost of constructing the church himself. His opening service attracted some 1,000 people from far and wide. Two years later he raised another church near Philipsburg, and at both points he brought together large regular congregations. News of his unusual success had quickly reached Quebec. In June 1809, Mountain's wife informed a friend: "He has quite changed the character of the people. . . . To all he extends his pastoral care in the most judicious and exemplary manner. I wish we had a 100 such clergymen. He is supposed to be a Calvinist but it is certainly an unjust accusation."

Stewart was continually on the move, and not only in Saint-Armand. Each year he journeyed to Montreal, sometimes more than once, conducting baptisms on the way, particularly at Caldwell's and Christie manors – also known as the seigneuries of Foucault and Noyan – where no resident missionary would be appointed until 1815. Neighbouring Shefford Township saw him from 1808 to 1810, and townships east of Saint-Armand in 1810 and 1813. He made frequent visits to Vermont, ministering to a congregation at Sheldon.

Stewart's pastoral work took many forms. To provide a focus for spiritual study during his absences he had a number of his sermons printed from 1810 to 1814, hundreds of copies of which were distributed freely. He evinced a keen interest in education and financially or morally supported the construction of several schools, subsequently paying the fees of many students. In 1812, although he entertained reservations about the judgement of the Congregational minister Thaddeus Osgood*, he helped him to raise money in England for an educational scheme, a humane society, and an asylum in the Canadas by providing him with introductions to influential friends. Mountain did not approve. During the War of 1812, when American troops twice entered Missisquoi Bay and foraged as far as Frelighsburg, Stewart remained with his flock, dispensing assistance to sufferers and arranging an exchange of local militiamen captured by the Americans in October 1813. In 1815, after seven years' intense labour and close observation of the townships, Stewart published *A short view of the present state of the Eastern Townships . . .*, intended to provide prospective immigrants with a concise description of the climate, topography, economy, and population of the region. In it he encouraged acceptance of American immigrants as "in many respects . . . the best settlers in a new country" and argued that the most effective means of acquiring their loyalty was to ensure their welfare and prosperity.

In August 1815, freed from his duties by the ordination and appointment as curate to Saint-Armand of James Reid, a local schoolmaster, Stewart returned to Britain on a visit. He expended much time and effort in raising, with Mountain's authorization, a fund of £2,500 for the building of churches in the Canadas. In 1816 Oxford conferred on him honorary degrees of BD and DD, and he arrived back in Lower Canada in November 1817. Finding Saint-Armand progressing favourably under Reid, he began a second pioneering effort at Hatley, some 50 miles to the east. In 1819 he opened a church, and a parsonage was nearing completion. As before, he journeyed through nearby townships, giving constant encouragement to church building, now facilitated by the fund he administered.

In 1819 Stewart was named travelling missionary by Mountain and the SPG to strengthen the church throughout the diocese. His appointment coincided with the beginning of heavy immigration to Upper Canada, which called for the kind of practical work he did. The laborious travelling increased. Leaving Hatley in January 1820, he made a grand tour of Upper Canada from Hawkesbury through Glengarry, Cornwall, Kingston, York (Toronto), and Niagara (Niagara-on-the-Lake) to Sandwich (Windsor). By the time he reached Hatley again in June 1820, he had covered nearly 2,000 miles. After a trip to England in 1820 he spent more than a year in 1821–22 journeying through the diocese. He was sent to England in March 1823 to defend Anglican claims to exclusive benefit from the clergy reserves, lands set aside to support a Protestant clergy. On this occasion Stewart also reopened his building fund, raising another £2,500, and sought government support of the Royal Institution for the Advancement of Learning [*see* Joseph Langley Mills*], of which he had recently been made a trustee. Soon after his return to Lower Canada, in November 1824, he again toured the townships, and he was travelling in Upper Canada when Mountain died in June 1825. Having remained the bishop's choice as a successor, he returned to England in July, and in November he received the appointment. He was consecrated in the chapel of Lambeth Palace on 1 Jan. 1826.

In his new role Stewart kept continually on the move. His vast diocese, which covered the populated area of the Canadas, included 50 parishes or missions, as many clergy, and 63 churches. From his arrival at Quebec in June 1826 until he visited England again in 1831, he journeyed to Upper Canada each year, conducted three complete visitations of that province, twice visited missions on the Ottawa River and in the Eastern Townships, and made the first Anglican episcopal tour of the Gaspé and the Baie des Chaleurs. In this first half of his episcopate he ordained 30 men, opened 17 new missions, and confirmed 3,800 persons. Beginning in 1830–31 he spent winters in York to enable him to pay closer attention to church affairs in the upper province, where thousands of immigrants were settling. His visitation of 1832 brought together many clergy at Montreal and at York despite a cholera epidemic. The following year he journeyed extensively eastward from York, and in 1834 he visited the Eastern Townships and Upper Canada.

Two major problems – the clergy reserves and a reduction in government grants to the SPG for payment of missionaries' salaries – plagued Stewart's episcopate but initiated the maturation of the colonial church. Challenges to exclusive Anglican control of the clergy reserves took two forms. The Church of Scotland claimed equal rights to proceeds from sale or rent of reserve lands, while other denominations, and even some Anglican laymen, rejected establishment and demanded secularization of the reserves in favour of public education. Stewart dutifully defended the Anglican position, but he was not a fighter and lacked political instincts. Although appointed to the legislative and executive councils of both colonies, he seems never to have attended meetings of either council in Upper Canada and to have appeared only irregularly in those of the lower colony. The pressure for secularization being greatest in Upper Canada, where the reserves were more extensive, it was the combative archdeacon of York, John Strachan*, who shouldered the brunt of the Anglican defence, but with an aggressiveness not always to Stewart's liking. Indeed Stewart, who preferred to live in peaceful coexistence with other denominations, made every effort not to intensify bitterness over the issue for fear that the church would become an object of general opprobrium and possibly from an understanding that privileges for any church were not acceptable to colonial society. The need to strengthen the church in the face of attacks, however, gave rise under Stewart to the founding in 1827 of a diocesan publication, the *Christian Sentinel and Anglo-Canadian Churchman's Magazine* (Montreal), edited for part of its short life by Brooke Bridges Stevens*.

The consequences of possible secularization of the clergy reserves were made more serious by a coincidental desire on the part of the British government to eliminate its grants to the SPG for the payment of missionaries' stipends. Since 1815 these grants had been the principal support of the church's work, enabling its missionaries to receive salaries averaging £200 per annum. Initially the government proposed to eliminate the grants by 1835 but, as a result of protests by Stewart and the SPG, ultimately clerical stipends suffered a reduction of some 15 per cent only. In Upper Canada income from the sale of clergy reserves replaced the grants from the SPG. Stewart had also to be concerned for his own stipend, amounting to £2,600 a year and a house allowance of £400. It and a number of other clerical salaries were paid from the army extraordinaries, a practice under attack by the increasingly strong movement in Britain for parliamentary reform. In the end the stipends were continued, but only for the lives of the incumbents.

Such threats to external sources of income had the effect of obliging the church to look within for funding, and in January 1834 Stewart issued the first call to Anglicans in the Canadas to support their clergy financially. Similarly, Stewart's episcopate witnessed the beginnings of a movement for self-government within the colonial church. In 1831 the Established Clergy Association of Lower Canada was formed in Montreal, and it was followed by similar bodies elsewhere. By 1836 pressure began building in favour of diocesan synods with lay participation, although the first would not be held until 1853. In these developments Stewart's role was not prominent, but in another, increasing lay participation in the church, he was a catalyst. With finances for clerical salaries restricted, and immigration increasing, Stewart supplemented the labours of the clergy by appointing catechists to act as lay readers. Initially sceptical, the SPG nevertheless funded the program, which became one of Stewart's most effective creations; indeed ten lay readers were subsequently ordained to the priesthood.

While contending with new developments Stewart did not lose sight of his traditional commitments to education and missions. At the time he became bishop Sunday schools were beginning to function successfully; National schools, in which the monitorial system was used and the church catechism taught [*see* Joseph SPRAGG], had been set up in Montreal, Quebec, and York; and in a number of Royal Institution schools church influence was strong. Stewart himself lent his support to a Sunday school society begun in 1830 by his replacement as travelling missionary, George Archbold. Although named the official visitor to King's College (University of Toronto) when it obtained its charter in 1827, Stewart largely left that institution to its founder, John Strachan. As *ex officio* principal of the Royal Institution from 1826, however, he was active in arduous efforts to set on foot McGill College in Montreal, the financial basis of which, a bequest to the Royal Institution from James McGill, was being contested in the courts by McGill's chief heirs, François* and James McGill Desrivières. On 24 June 1829 Stewart was able to deliver an address at the opening of the college, although its legal problems were far from over. A member of the governing body, he attended board meetings at Quebec until 1835. Stewart's most active contribution to education, however, stemmed from a desire to foster a native-born clergy. In 1828 he opened a seminary at Chambly, on the Rivière Richelieu, over which he placed a recent Oxford graduate, Joseph Braithwaite; 12 students were ordained before the school closed in 1838.

Stewart's other main preoccupation as bishop was missionary work. Although he had always favoured evangelization of the Indians, he was stimulated to action by Methodists in Upper Canada, among them

JOHN and Peter* Jones, and by Roman Catholics such as Joseph Marcoux* in Lower Canada. He did not begrudge them their success; rather he exhorted Anglicans to catch the Methodists' fervour and, in 1827, he asked Roman Catholic archbishop Bernard-Claude Panet* for a copy of Marcoux's Mohawk dictionary and grammar. In October 1830 he presided at the founding in York of a society for missionary work among Indians, which later that year broadened its scope to include destitute settlers; it operated for eight years. A similar society was formed at Quebec in 1835 and subsequently in Montreal.

To support missionary work, Stewart relied principally on the SPG, but he was obliged to appeal continually in the Canadas and in England for men and money. In 1834 he had circulated widely an *Address from the bishop of Quebec to the British public, in behalf of the Church of England in Canada*, making known the needs of his diocese. Inspired by it, the Reverend William James Darley Waddilove instituted the Upper Canadian Travelling Missionary Fund – or Stewart Missions – which in 13 years' existence supported at least 11 missionaries. Also as a result of the *Address*, the Upper Canada Clergy Society was founded in England in 1835–36 to supply and support missionaries from Britain. A lay effort, it initially encountered reticence on the part of Stewart, who had reservations about its Anglican commitment and relationship with the SPG, and then about the principle of having missionaries recruited by laymen; consequently it did not get into operation until 1837 and sent out or paid only some six missionaries before folding. Clerical recruitment, nevertheless, was another area in which Stewart achieved a measure of success; by 1837 his diocese counted 50 clergy in Upper Canada and 35 in Lower Canada. Growth did not match the rise in population, but it was respectable given the financial restrictions and political problems the bishop faced.

Stewart's unremitting labours resulted in his falling ill at Toronto in April 1835. Unsuccessful attempts to lighten the episcopal burden by dividing the diocese had been made periodically by Mountain and were repeated by Stewart in 1829 and 1831. Stewart's condition spurred another effort, and in 1835 he sent Archdeacon George Jehoshaphat Mountain* to England. Mountain succeeded in having created the position of suffragan bishop, with the title of bishop of Montreal but no salary; after much hesitation he consented to fill it and was consecrated in February 1836. On his return to Quebec he was commissioned by Stewart to administer the diocese from 17 September, and nine days later Stewart left for England. After slowly failing, he died in London in July 1837.

Having entered on his episcopate after almost 20 years' experience in colonial society, Charles James Stewart had approached his duties differently from his predecessor. Although prepared to receive the courtesies and accept the appointments due to his office, and ready to defend the privileges of the establishment, he subordinated such matters to the maintenance and extension of the church in colonial life, urging self-support and peaceful coexistence with other denominations in a pluralist society. Unmarried, enjoying a moderate private income in addition to a substantial salary, he was relieved of the financial and domestic concerns that were Mountain's lot and was thus able to travel extensively and spend freely on behalf of the church. He supported individual missionaries entirely, advanced funds to needy clergy and catechists, paid his own travel expenses and the salaries and expenses of his chaplains, subsidized the *Christian Sentinel and Anglo-Canadian Churchman's Magazine*, subscribed generously to societies for relief of the needy and to church building funds, and yet left a substantial estate to nieces and nephews and their families. Stewart's membership in a noble family gave him advantages in representing the needs of his diocese to the British government and people. Unlike the strapping but controversial Mountain, Stewart was somewhat ungainly in appearance and without pulpit gifts, but thanks to the simplicity of his disciplined life and to his humility, benevolence, and deep personal piety, he was almost universally liked and respected. The poet Adam Kidd* addressed him in a few artless stanzas as the "kindest, best of men." Even the critical Strachan paid a warm tribute to his departed diocesan in September 1837. A man of practical wisdom, unceasing activity, and religious zeal, Stewart left a record worthy of grateful remembrance.

THOMAS R. MILLMAN

An extensive list of Charles James Stewart's published works can be found in an appendix to T. R. Millman, *The life of the Right Reverend, the Honourable Charles James Stewart, D.D., Oxon., second Anglican bishop of Quebec* (London, Ont., 1953), which also includes a portrait of the bishop. One publication not cited in Millman's study is *A selection of psalms and hymns . . .* (Montreal, 1808).

ACC, Diocese of Montreal Arch., G. J. Mountain papers. ACC-Q, 29, 32, 40, 44, 46–71, 81, 91–96, 103–5, 107, 109–16, 118, 123, 129, 330–31. Bishop's Univ. Library (Lennoxville, Que.), C. J. Stewart to Lucius Doolittle, 1828–35. Holy Trinity (Anglican) Church (Frelighsburg, Que.), Docs. relating to the establishment of the mission at Saint-Armand. PAC, MG 23, GIII, 3; RG 4, A1; RG 7, G1. PRO, CO 42. RHL, USPG Arch., C/CAN/Que., 4: 370; C/CAN/Toronto, 4: 501; journal of SPG, 29–43. Ernest Hawkins, *Annals of the diocese of Quebec* (London, 1849); *Annals of the diocese of Toronto* (London, 1848). SPG, [*Annual report*] (London), 1808–12, 1814–15, 1818–19. *The Stewart missions; a series of letters and journals, calculated to exhibit to British Christians, the spiritual destitution of the emigrants settled in the remote parts of*

Upper Canada, to which is prefixed a brief memoir of . . . Chas. James Stewart, lord bishop of Quebec . . . , ed. W. J. D. Waddilove (London, 1838). Eliezer Williams, *The English works of the late Eliezer Williams, M.A., vicar of Lampeter . . . with a memoir of his life*, ed. S. G. A. Williams (n.p., 1840). *Christian Sentinel and Anglo-Canadian Churchman's Magazine* (Montreal), 1, 15 Oct., 12 Nov. 1830. *Church*, 30 March, 12 Oct., 9 Nov. 1839. *Missiskoui Standard* (Frelighsburg), 12 Sept. 1837. *Montreal Gazette*, 27 Aug. 1833. *Montreal Herald*, 19 Aug. 1815. *Quebec Gazette*, 1 Oct. 1807; 24 Aug., 21, 23 Sept. 1836. *Quebec Mercury*, 6 June 1826; 11 June, 17, 20, 22, 27 Sept., 11 Oct. 1836.

W. B. Heeney, *I walk with a bishop (Charles James Stewart)* (Toronto, 1939). *Lives of missionaries, North America: John Eliot, Bishop Chase, Bishop Seabury, Bishop Stewart, Rev. J. G. Mountain* (London, [1862]). T. R. Millman, *A brief account of the life of the Honourable and Right Reverend Charles James Stewart, D.D., second lord bishop of Quebec* (Edinburgh, 1948); *Jacob Mountain, first lord bishop of Quebec; a study in church and state, 1793–1825* (Toronto, 1947). G. H. Montgomery, *Missisquoi Bay (Philipsburg, Que.)* (Granby, Que., 1950). A. W. Mountain, *A memoir of George Jehoshaphat Mountain, D.D., D.C.L., late bishop of Quebec . . .* (London and Montreal, 1866). J. N. Norton, *Life of Bishop Stewart of Quebec* (New York, 1859). C. F. Pascoe, *Two hundred years of the S.P.G. . . .* (2v., London, 1901). Cyrus Thomas, *Contributions to the history of the Eastern Townships . . .* (Montreal, 1866). T. R. Millman, "Training of theological students in the old diocese of Quebec," "Joseph Braithwaite and the Bishop Stewart Theological Seminary," "The *Christian Sentinel* and its editors," "Home missions in the old diocese of Quebec," "The earliest collections of prayers printed in the Canadas for the use of members of the Church of England," and "Royal silver in the Church of England in Canada," *Montreal Churchman* (Granby), 27 (1939), no.4: 16–19; no.8: 20–22; no.12: 9–10; 28 (1940), no.9: 10–11; 31 (1943), no.10: 10–11; and 34 (1946), no.2: 3–4 respectively. "Philipsburg, St. Armand West" and [James Reid], "Frelighsburgh," *Church Chronicle for the Diocese of Montreal* (Montreal), 2 (1861–62): 167–73 and 153–57 respectively.

STEWART, THOMAS ALEXANDER, settler, JP, mill owner, and politician; b. 10 June 1786 in County Antrim (Northern Ireland), son of William Stewart; m. 17 Dec. 1816 Frances Browne*, and they had five daughters and six sons; d. 6 Sept. 1847 in Douro Township, Upper Canada.

Thomas Alexander Stewart was born and raised at Wilmont, the Stewart home near Belfast, in the comfortable circumstances of a landed family. In his youth he suffered an accident which left him permanently lame. He met Frances Browne at Wilmont in the summer of 1816 and they were married in Dublin six months later. For the next six years they lived in County Antrim, where Stewart was a partner in a textile firm. After it went bankrupt, he and Robert Reid, a brother-in-law and former partner, decided to emigrate to Upper Canada in search of a new life.

In June 1822 both families and their servants left Belfast for Quebec. Their careful planning was to ensure a welcome reception in Upper Canada. At York (Toronto) the following September, Stewart noted in a petition for land that he had been employed in the "Linen, Flour and cotton Business" and intended establishing himself as an "Agriculturist combined with any application of machinery he might find for his advantage." He was subsequently granted 1,200 acres in the unsettled township of Douro in the Newcastle District, about 30 miles north of the long-established front of settlement along Lake Ontario. In addition, he and Reid were empowered in April 1823 to supervise the development of a tract of 10,000 acres. They were unable to attract settlers, however, and released the land in 1825 for the use of the Irish immigrants brought in by Peter ROBINSON.

In the winter of 1822–23 the Stewarts thrust themselves into a harsh, backwoods environment which required all their fortitude to overcome. Unused to even simple household tasks, they were obliged to perform many jobs on their own, particularly after the unexpected departure of their servants. They faced extreme isolation and the slow development of the area was disheartening. Stewart considered moving to a cleared farm near Cobourg. He was further discomfited by the failure of his applications for employment by the Canada Company and for official positions, though in 1823 he did become a justice of the peace.

Stewart's fortunes were rescued by the rapid growth that occurred after 1825, when the Peterborough area was settled by Robinson's immigrants. Suddenly Stewart found several hundred people within a few miles of his farm. The stimulus provided by this colonization led to widespread progress in the area. He applied, unsuccessfully, in 1826 for permission to open a private land office in Peterborough. Stewart subsequently appears to have thrown himself into the role of community leader. He petitioned for local projects such as the bridging of the Otonabee River, the opening of the Trent water-way for navigation, and the creation of a new administrative district. In 1831 his farm was well established, with 54 acres cleared. Financial worries were still present, however, for no buyers appeared three years later when he advertised land for sale at $12 per acre. In 1834 his construction of a sawmill on the Otonabee, opposite his farm, and his contribution to the erection of St John's Church (Anglican) in Peterborough clearly reflected his interest in the community.

Stewart's conservative upbringing suited his appointment in 1833 to the Legislative Council, a post he held until the union of Upper and Lower Canada in 1841. He attended council sporadically, generally when matters pertaining to the Peterborough area were being discussed. His allegiance to the crown was evident from his role in mustering pro-government forces during the rebellion of 1837–38.

In his 50s, Stewart became increasingly interested in domestic affairs. He employed a manager on his farm in 1840, by which year 70 acres had been cleared. A new frame dwelling was occupied in late 1842, replacing, at last, the original log house. The Stewarts' large family must have been a source of considerable comfort to them, although the boys had been too young to be of much assistance during the critical years when the farm was being established. An inability to find cash may be reflected by Stewart's much delayed payment of fees, and the patenting of his original land, in 1843 – 21 years after settlement. His religious interests appear to have been strong and he drew great solace from reflection and prayer; he delighted in discussing such interests with his wife and with his sister who dwelt near by. Yet he was alert to more than merely local affairs. By 1847 he was assisting immigrants fleeing from the Irish famine.

In September of that year Stewart died of typhus. He was survived by his wife. Her letters home to Ireland, published in 1889, tell much of their Canadian experiences. Of the surviving ten children, several established themselves in the Peterborough community.

ALAN G. BRUNGER

Thomas Alexander Stewart is the author of a letter sent to Basil Hall and printed anonymously in Hall's *Travels in North America, in the years 1827 and 1828 . . .* (3v., Edinburgh, 1829), 1: 307–23. The letter is reprinted in *The valley of the Trent*, ed. and intro. E. C. Guillet (Toronto, 1957), 345–52. There is a portrait of Stewart in the Peterborough Centennial Museum and Arch. (Peterborough, Ont.).

AO, RG 1, A-I-6, 7, 14; RG 21, United Counties of Northumberland and Durham, Douro Township, assessment records, 1831, 1840 (mfm. at Trent Univ. Arch., Peterborough). PAC, RG 1, L3, 461: S13/106; RG 5, A1: 62903–5, 80133–36; RG 68, General index, 1651–1841: 452, 670. Peterborough Land Registry Office, Abstract index to deeds, Douro Township, concession 9, lots 3–4; concession 11, lots 1, 3; concession 12, lots 1–3; concession 13, lot 1 (mfm. at AO). Trent Univ. Arch., B-74-1005 (Frances [Browne] Stewart letters); B-74-1006 (Frances [Browne] Stewart coll.); B-78-008 (Frances [Browne] Stewart papers). Frances [Browne] Stewart, *Our forest home, being extracts from the correspondence of the late Frances Stewart*, ed. E. S. [Stewart] Dunlop (Toronto, 1889). A. G. Brunger, "Early settlement in contrasting areas of Peterborough County, Ontario," *Perspectives on landscape and settlement in nineteenth century Ontario*, ed. J. D. Wood (Toronto, 1975), 141–58. J. C. Lewis, "The letters of Frances Stewart," *Kawartha heritage: proceedings of the Kawartha Conference, 1981*, ed. A. O. C. and J. M. Cole (Peterborough, 1981), 83–92. *Through the years in Douro (Peterborough County – Canada), 1822–1967*, ed. J. A. Edmison (Peterborough, 1967).

STRANGE, JAMES CHARLES STUART, fur trader; b. 8 Aug. 1753 in Edinburgh, son of Robert Strange and Isabella Lumisden; m. first Margaret Durham; m. secondly 18 Dec. 1798 Anne Dundas, widow of Henry Drummond; d. 6 Oct. 1840 at Airth Castle, Scotland.

James Charles Stuart Strange, one of the earliest of the maritime fur traders on the northwest Pacific coast, was the son of Jacobite parents. His father, an engraver, fought under Prince Charles, the Young Pretender, and James was a godson of James, the Old Pretender. Robert Strange settled in London in 1750. James, along with his brother THOMAS ANDREW LUMISDEN, sought a career abroad. Both went to India and were successful in their respective fields: Thomas (who had served briefly as chief justice of Nova Scotia) became chief justice of the supreme court of Madras, and James a merchant in Madras with the East India Company and in private trade.

James was on leave in England when the account of Captain James Cook*'s third Pacific voyage was published in 1784 and, like a number of others, including the pioneer trader James Hanna*, he noted with great interest the suggestions made by Captain James King* on how to conduct a fur-trading expedition to the northwest coast. Strange sought the advice of Sir Joseph Banks* and, more important, secured the patronage in India of David Scott, a merchant in the China trade who wanted to loosen the East India Company's monopoly. Together, Strange and Scott planned an expedition. They privately purchased two ships and named them *Captain Cook* and *Experiment*. Both were well fitted out and the venture received some support from the East India Company in the form of a few troops commanded by Alexander Walker*. Strange was to go with the vessels as supercargo and would have overall direction of the enterprise. The expedition, which left India in late 1785, was supposed to serve the two British interests of commerce and exploration, but in the event it made little contribution to either.

Strange was too cautious and conservative to be successful as an explorer or a trader. The expense of fitting out the expedition had escalated to the point where only a major trading success could repay the investment. But the voyage was beset by misfortune from the beginning. Strange was unable to purchase goods along the Malabar coast for sale in China as he had planned, and not far out of Indian waters the *Experiment* was holed, necessitating a call at Batavia (Djakarta, Indonesia) for repairs. Many of the crew had already gone down with scurvy and Strange was ill prepared to deal with the scourge. The China leg of the outward journey was thus abandoned, but even so the expedition did not arrive on the northwest coast until 25 June 1786. It was already late in the season, but Strange anchored at Nootka Sound (B.C.) for a month to gather what sea-otter pelts he could. He conducted the trading negotiations himself and, like other traders, found that the Nootka Indians were shrewd bargainers. More interested in safety than profit, he kept the two vessels together rather than send them out separately to cover more ground. Leaving John Mackay* to establish a permanent shore-base, Strange departed from Nootka Sound in late July and headed north. He did not see anything of the mainland between the northern tip of Vancouver Island and Alaskan waters, and at Prince William Sound he was, once again, too late in the season to acquire many furs. So he set sail for China in mid September to sell what he had.

The expedition was a financial disaster. Strange sold his furs for about £5,600, which was not enough to cover the outlay. Nor had he contributed much to exploration and science. Apart from making some discoveries in the Queen Charlotte Strait area, he had added little to geographic knowledge of the northwest coast, and he was not particularly interested in the Indians, except as potential customers, so the account of the voyage by Walker contains much more ethnographic information than Strange provides in his journal.

Back in India Strange re-entered the Madras service, but left the East India Company in 1795. He returned to England where in May 1796 he became a member of parliament for the East Grinstead borough of Sussex. Two years later he married a daughter of Henry Dundas, secretary of state for war and the colonies and a former commissioner of the Board of Control for Indian affairs. Ruined by a bank failure in 1804, Strange returned to India to make another fortune before retiring in 1815 to Scotland, where he died in 1840.

ROBIN A. FISHER

Strange's account of his Pacific expedition was published as *James Strange's journal and narrative of the commercial expedition from Bombay to the north-west coast of America, together with a chart showing the tract of the expedition*, intro. A. V. Venkatarama Ayyar (Madras, India, 1928; repr. 1929). The PABC holds two transcripts based on different manuscript copies of Strange's "Narrative of a voyage to the North West Coast of America": one is a typescript, from a copy belonging to Strange's descendants (A/A/20/St8A), and the other a handwritten transcript of BL, India Office Library and Records [East India House Arch.], IOR, H/800: 1–145 (A/A/20/St8A2). Also at the PABC is an original manuscript by Strange of additions to Captain Cook's vocabulary of the Nootka Sound language, 1785–86 (F/8/St8).

BL, India Office Library and Records, IOR, E/4/316–17, 24; E/4/873: 1239; E/4/875: 333; H/494: 419–27; O/6/3: 577; P/240/62: 137; P/241/4: 124; P/241/5: 603; P/241/55: 1790 (copies at PABC). PABC, E/E/St8, extracts relating to Strange; M/St8. James Cook and James King, *A voyage to the Pacific Ocean* . . . (3v. and atlas, London, 1784), 3: 438–40. Alexander Walker, *An account of a voyage to the north west coast of America in 1785 & 1786*, ed. R. [A.] Fisher and J. M. Bumsted (Vancouver, 1982). R. [A.] Fisher, *Contact and conflict: Indian-European relations in British Columbia, 1774–1890* (Vancouver, 1977). B. M. Gough, *Distant dominion: Britain and the northwest coast of North America, 1579–1809* (Vancouver, 1980). David MacKay, *In the wake of Cook: exploration, science & empire, 1780–1801* (London, 1985).

STRANGE, Sir THOMAS ANDREW LUMISDEN, judge; b. 30 Nov. 1756 in England, probably in London, second son of Robert Strange, a prominent engraver, and Isabella Lumisden; brother of JAMES CHARLES STUART; m. first 28 Sept. 1797 Jane Anstruther in London; m. secondly 11 Oct. 1806 Louisa Burroughs, and they had a large family; d. 16 July 1841 in St Leonards (East Sussex), England.

Thomas Andrew Lumisden Strange entered Westminster School, London, in 1769 and Christ Church College at Oxford in 1774, graduating from the latter institution with a BA (1778) and an MA (1782). Admitted to Lincoln's Inn in 1776, he was called to the bar in November 1785 and four years later was appointed chief justice of Nova Scotia. Strange's appointment might be explained by his mother's friendship with Lord Mansfield, a former cabinet minister. The nomination came during a dispute between the Nova Scotia House of Assembly and the Council, in part involving charges of partiality against justices James Brenton* and Isaac Deschamps* of the Supreme Court who had presided in the absence of a chief justice.

Strange's main task on his arrival at Halifax in May 1790 was to conciliate the warring factions, which he found anxiously watching him. To that end he dined "with every one who invited me," including Jonathan Sterns, a lawyer whose suspension by Deschamps had been an early event in the so-called judges' affair. Strange reinstated Sterns and managed to establish friendly relations with Brenton and Deschamps, whom he found "very amiable, deserving persons and of great assistance to me." His tact, the passage of time, and the diversion created by the war with France in 1793 resolved the crisis.

For the most part, Strange's judicial duties had little to do with the dispute between assembly and Council. Most Supreme Court cases in the 1790s concerned the recovery of debts, which were usually small sums, although one case in 1790 involved a debt of more than £24,000 Halifax currency. Occasionally, however, cases with political overtones reached the court. In 1793 Solicitor General Richard John Uniacke* accused Francis Green*, son of a former treasurer of the colony, of libel in connection with an attempt by Uniacke and others to obtain some papers from Green. Strange found Green guilty and awarded Uniacke £500 in damages.

Although careful not to overlook his primary mission in Nova Scotia, Strange apparently also found time to use his influence as chief justice to oppose slavery. His successor, Sampson Salter BLOWERS, claimed that in cases involving runaway slaves Strange required "the fullest proof of the master's claim" and that since this was difficult to produce "it was found generally very easy to succeed in favour of the Negro." Blowers, as attorney general, and Strange frequently discussed how to proceed in such matters, and Strange decided to move slowly rather than "throw so much property as it is called into the air at once."

From the beginning many people in the colony liked Strange. Governor John Parr* expressed regret that Strange had not arrived earlier, and declared that the chief justice could have saved him much trouble and anxiety. Parr's successor, John Wentworth*, expressed satisfaction with Strange on numerous occasions. In 1793, for example, Wentworth reported that sessions of the Supreme Court had not been held in several counties that year, but said it was "notwithstanding the best diligence of our good Ch. Justice, who is indefatigable in his duty." When in 1794 Wentworth realized that Strange might be attracted to a post in another colony, he declared that it would be "the greatest misfortune to this province and to myself."

Bishop Charles Inglis* also spoke highly of Strange for his abilities as chief justice, his "life of strict probity & virtue," and his contribution as a member of the board of governors to the development of King's College. Strange apparently showed a much greater interest in the college than did some of his fellow governors. He visited it on several occasions, worked with Inglis on plans for new buildings, and gave £100 towards a college library. He was far more concerned by the possible cost of the college than Inglis was, but he hoped that it would become "the Centre of Learning to the King's Transatlantic Dominions."

Despite his evident popularity, Strange became unhappy in Nova Scotia. In 1794 he expressed dissatisfaction with Wentworth and "the Habits of his Family," an apparent reference at least in part to Wentworth's morals. He also alleged that Wentworth had not been open with him "in his views of Government." That year Strange sought the chief justiceship of Upper Canada, and expressed a desire to embrace "the first opportunity of quitting this place." In some measure, Strange wanted a move for financial reasons. His salary was to have been £1,000, with £200 to come from fees. But he discovered that the fees "consisted of small sums, to be received often from very indigent people, who could but ill afford to pay them," and he had found deriving any of his income from such a source disagreeable. From time to time Strange gave some of the £200 fee money for a law library, and then contributed to a collection of books "of a more popular Nature" for the town.

In 1795 Strange stopped seeking the appointment in Upper Canada and instead requested permission to tour the United States when the war with France ended. His desire to get away may have been strengthened by his feelings of loss after his close friend the Reverend Andrew Brown* departed for Scotland that year. On 25 July 1796 Strange himself left for England. Although he indicated that he was only going home for a visit, as he had in 1791, he was apparently not believed. In 1797 he informed Wentworth of his intention to resign. A year later he went to Madras (India) as recorder and president of its court. He was knighted on 14 March 1798, before his departure. In 1800 he became chief justice of the Madras supreme court, over which he presided until his return to England in 1817. He also wrote *Elements of Hindu law* (2v., London, 1825), for many years the definitive work on the subject.

As chief justice in Nova Scotia, Strange's achievement in keeping the peace and winning respect for the Supreme Court was no mean feat. Blowers's observation that Strange was "a most excellent theoretical lawyer," but had practised little and once made an error in a trespass case which he had had to point out, seems petty in view of the praise Strange received from many quarters.

DONALD F. CHARD

PANS, MG 1, 480 (transcripts), 1595–613; RG 39, HX, C, 1790 (A–K), 1792 (S–Z), 1793 (A–Z), 1794 (A–H). PRO, CO 217/36–37, 217/62–67 (mfm. at PANS). *Royal Gazette and the Nova-Scotia Advertiser*, 1790. *DNB*. Cuthbertson, *Old attorney general*. R. W. Winks, *The blacks in Canada: a history* (London and New Haven, Conn., 1971). Margaret Ells, "Nova Scotian 'Sparks of Liberty,'" *Dalhousie Rev.*, 16 (1936–37): 475–92. J. E. A. Macleod, "A forgotten chief justice of Nova Scotia," *Dalhousie Rev.*, 1 (1921–22): 308–13. T. W. Smith, "The slave in Canada," N.S. Hist. Soc., *Coll.*, 10 (1896–98): 1–161.

STREET, SAMUEL, businessman, JP, militia officer, and office holder; b. 14 March 1775 in Farmington, Conn., eldest son of Nehemiah Street and Thankful Moody; m. 5 Sept. 1811 Abigail Hyde Ransom, and they had one son and five daughters; d. 21 Aug. 1844 in Port Robinson, Upper Canada.

Samuel Street was a shrewd, well-located merchant who, by devoting himself to business, managed to become one of the wealthiest men in Upper Canada by the time of his death. In 1787 he had come to live with his uncle, Samuel Street*, at Chippawa (Ont.), after his father had been murdered at Cold Springs, N.Y. No doubt his uncle's membership in the Niagara peninsula's early mercantile community benefited the aspiration of Samuel Street Jr, as he became known, and ensured him a successful start in business along the Niagara River. He was entitled to 200 acres as the son of a loyalist, but a petition sent by his uncle in October 1796 secured for him an additional 400 acres, thus placing him on a "footing with others of his description." During this period he trained in his uncle's forwarding business at Niagara (Niagara-on-the-Lake). The first evidence of his own mercantile activity came in 1797, when he and Thomas Dickson*, either on their own or possibly on behalf of Thomas Clark*, received a shipment of skins, handkerchiefs, and gunpowder from Charles Wilson of Niagara Falls.

Street formed a partnership with Clark, an important merchant-forwarder at Queenston, by May 1798 but the association ended the following year. By 1803 Street was involved in milling operations at Niagara Falls. In August of that year he was clerk at the Bridgewater Mills at Chippawa, then operated as a leasehold by Robert Randal* and James Durand*; the following year Street and Durand formed a partnership. Its duration is uncertain but about 1808 or 1809 Street entered into a second association with Clark, creating a business concern which would become one of Upper Canada's largest and would last until the latter's death in 1835. Street's activities were so often those of Clark and Street that it is difficult to be sure when he is on his own. Even in personality the partners seem to be identical people whom the contemporary record rarely characterizes as individuals. From Street's correspondence it is evident that because of health problems (possibly arthritis), he rarely set foot beyond the Niagara Falls area, leaving Clark to travel about the province on business. The partnership initially revolved around two milling complexes: the Falls Mills, purchased by Clark in 1805 from John Burch and sold to Street two years later, and the nearby Bridgewater Mills. These were acquired from Durand in 1810, according to Clark, who secured the crown patent on the property in 1815. Randal contested Clark and Street's title to the property, but it was a futile effort, his claims quickly becoming enmeshed with a lengthy political assault upon the Niagara élite, including Street.

The location of the milling complexes, at the upper terminus of the Niagara portage road, was largely responsible for the success of Clark and Street in collecting wheat and flour from interior settlements. Flour processed at their mills was trans-shipped over the portage road to Queenston, and then shipped to Prescott for forwarding to Montreal and Quebec, where the Upper Canadian contribution to wheat and flour exports was rising sharply. In the absence of complete and consecutive account-books, it is difficult to estimate the long-term profitability of the firm's milling operations and flour sales. In 1808, 2,079 barrels of various grades of flour were sold at Quebec for approximately £4,400 to John Mure* and others. Clark's personal account-books for the period 1 January to 30 June 1810 record the firm's profit from flour sales at Montreal and Quebec as £11,461 15*s.* 6*d.* Both milling complexes, which Sir George Prevost* described in 1814 as the "most useful and valuable in the country," were burned by the Americans in July 1814. The firm's good fortune in having Clark appointed one of the commissioners for the assessment and payment of war losses in the Niagara District enabled it to recover much of its losses. Payment of most of the compensation on the Bridgewater property was delayed until 1833, however, as a result of actions taken by Robert Randal. Though only the Falls Mills were rebuilt (eventually to be turned into a woollen mill), Clark and Street nevertheless retained a monopoly on milling at Niagara Falls, according to former Niagara merchant James Crooks* in November 1814.

The success of the partners' mills provided them with a large source of capital which they utilized skilfully. With only a limited amount of capital available through loans from banking facilities, Street became one of the largest money-lenders and financiers in Upper Canada. The method by which money was lent, as well as the amount, varied from person to person. Borrowers ranged from William Haun, a Bertie Township farmer who asked for a loan of £25 in 1829 to purchase seed grain, to members of the important political, ecclesiastical, and commercial circles in Upper Canada. Attorneys general William Henry Draper* and Christopher Alexander HAGERMAN, legislative councillor Adam Fergusson*, London District treasurer John Harris, Joseph Bitterman Spragge of the Surveyor General's Office, Bishop John Strachan*, William Hamilton Merritt*, James Crooks, and Captain Hugh Richardson* were among those who owed Clark and Street anywhere from £100 to £15,000. Even at an interest of six per cent – the maximum allowed by British law – it is not surprising to see how the firm became wealthy. Moreover, Street had little sympathy for tardy debtors, who were dealt with strictly. John Callahan, a Welland Canal worker who owed Street but £6, was jailed for failure to repay. However, discretion was warranted with individuals such as John Strachan, who still owed money to Street's estate in 1862.

The profits made from milling and money-lending were further invested in stocks, debentures, transportation schemes, and land. By the 1820s Street's wealth began to show itself outwardly. On 22 Aug. 1824 he put up a £5,000 bond as security for Receiver General John Henry Dunn*. Next to the provincial government, Street was the largest stockholder in the Bank of Upper Canada in 1830 and probably the largest shareholder in the Gore Bank; as well, he held shares in the Bank of Montreal and a substantial number in the Commercial Bank of the Midland District. He possessed at least £3,500 worth of five-year provincial debentures, and owned debentures issued by both the Gore and the Wellington districts. In the business of transportation, he held at least £8,000 worth of Welland Canal Company stock, in addition to stock in the Erie and Ontario Railroad Company, Guelph and Dundas road, Stoney Creek and Hamilton road, Cobourg Harbour Company, Port Hope Harbour and Wharf Company, and Grand River Navigation Company. In 1844 the share of Street's estate which went to his son, Thomas Clark Street*, included stocks, bonds, debentures, and debts owed worth approximately £44,390. Street was a director in a number of the enterprises in which he held stock.

In building his portfolio, Street availed himself of the opportunities that were often drawn to his attention by people close to the source. Thus, in 1841, with the aid of William Hamilton Merritt, he was able to purchase a large number of shares in the Welland Canal Company that were to be redeemed for provincial debentures. The government's offer was a lucrative one, since the back-interest owing on the stocks was also to be credited in debentures once tolls collected on the canal surpassed £30,000. With Street's capital and Merritt's acquaintance with the stockholders, the two embarked on a purchasing spree. The success of the scheme rested on Merritt's buying stocks which could be got for less than their par value or on which a large amount of back-interest was owed. On paper, the debentures to be issued in exchange would represent a substantial gain over the initial outlay when the debentures were resold. The rate of interest to be given on the debentures was at first fixed at two per cent. However, when Merritt heard of impending legislation that would raise that amount to six per cent, he secretly advised Street to hold the debentures already purchased until the bill was passed, in 1843, and, in the mean time, to purchase all the stock he could. Street did not live to profit from this scheme, which is nevertheless a revealing example of how his fortune was amassed.

Few Upper Canadians could have matched the efforts of Thomas Clark and Samuel Street as land speculators. Street owned land, or had a mortgage on land, in virtually every district of the province. His methods of accumulating land again demonstrate his means of succeeding as a pioneer merchant. Farms were accumulated through default on mortgages, bonds, or promissory notes. Maintaining agents in areas such as the Grand River valley enabled him to purchase the best lots under the most favourable circumstances. Moreover, in land matters as in stocks and debentures Clark and Street utilized the efforts of informed people, among them John Harris, the London District treasurer. Clark and Street advanced Harris money for use by the London District for works such as the district jail and court-house in 1829. In return, Harris provided Clark and Street with favours regarding land they held or wanted to sell. Furthermore, he reported to them on tax-delinquent lands that would become available at sheriff's sales throughout the district. Clark and Street often sent agents, among them William and Walter Dickson, to buy such lands for them. The Dicksons would meet with Harris and travel to the sales, crediting purchases against the money the district owed Clark and Street. At tax sales in 1831 the firm purchased some 3,436 acres in the London District. In December 1839 Clark and Street deposited some £450 to meet the balance of purchases at tax sales, demonstrating that they could buy more than they lent.

A large speculator in loyalist land rights, Street was able to obtain locations with the help of John Radenhurst and Joseph Bitterman Spragge, clerks in the Surveyor General's Office. Both men were accused of suspicious practices involving the location and patenting of loyalist lands. Coincidentally Spragge was personally indebted to Street for £284, though there is no direct evidence of impropriety on Street's part. No doubt both clerks gave their full cooperation in any land dealings in which Street required assistance.

In a manner similar to their vigorous collection of money owed by debtors, Clark and Street were relentless in disputes over land they had purchased or sold. Their rate of success in suits involving land was high. Aside from their strong legal and political connections – they often consulted men of such stature as Attorney General Henry John Boulton* – they also took the trouble to appear in court or, if necessary, to pay the expenses of witnesses prepared to testify on their behalf.

It is difficult to estimate the total amount of land owned by Street. In 1832 a group of investors who included Clark and Street, William Allan*, and William FORSYTH purchased, along with 407 acres at Niagara Falls, the Pavilion Hotel, which was designed to become a model tourist resort known as "City of the Falls." The project eventually failed but the property was probably a profitable investment. Street acquired in 1832 a large number of town lots at Dunnville, at the junction with the Grand River of the feeder ditch to the Welland Canal. Added to his ownership of part of the hinterland of the Grand River, his directorship in the Grand River Navigation Company, and his substantial holding of Welland Canal stock, the Dunnville purchases neatly completed a monopoly in the development of that area. In 1839 he made one of his larger purchases, 14,777 acres in Sarnia Township. Five years later the share of his estate that went to his son included 15,680 acres throughout southwestern and central Upper Canada.

As a prominent member of the Upper Canadian financial community, Street was often solicited to act as an agent for various business concerns. Clark and Street acted in 1826 on behalf of Forsyth, Richardson and Company of Montreal in transactions involving Niagara merchants and millers. In the fall of 1836 Street was empowered to act for Robert Gillespie* in financial and land matters, subject to an agent's fee of 10 per cent at least in land dealings. Gillespie, a partner in a Montreal firm, was Thomas Clark's brother-in-law and owned significant tracts of land in the Western District. In estate matters Street was called upon to act as the executor for important Niagara figures, to settle accounts, and to disperse lands. Estates, as was the case with those of John and William Crooks, brothers of James, were frequently complicated and took a number of years to sort out. Often, in instances of prior involvement with the deceased, including the Crooks brothers, Street's participation in the settlement of their estates may well have been for reasons of self-interest.

Unlike his partner, Thomas Clark, who served as a legislative councillor, Street shied away from politics. He held local appointments not uncommon for a person of his stature – magistrate from 1796 and deputy-registrar – but seems to have stayed clear of direct political involvement. Street's magisterial opposition to Robert Gourlay*, however, led Gourlay to name him, a Connecticut native, as "heir direct of the blue-laws" ascribed to New Haven's Puritan government in the 17th century. As well, Gourlay assailed the "wretched dependence" of Clark and Street on government patronage, particularly under Francis Gore*. No doubt Street's time was consumed with business, but even there, as in the case of the dispute over the Bridgewater Mills, Clark and Street were the focus of reform ire.

Street seemed conscious of his standing in the Niagara community. At one time or another he was a secretary of the Niagara Bible Society, to which he supplied free bibles, a member of the Niagara Turf Club, a life member of the Niagara District Agricultural Society (on account of a "liberal donation"), and a member of the Canada Emigration Association. He also took an active role in military affairs, becoming a captain in the 3rd Lincoln Militia in September 1812, lieutenant-colonel in April 1822, and colonel in 1839.

Yet, no matter how deeply one explores Street's interests, it is difficult to escape the notion that his life focused on his business. His "incessant industry and attention to business" enabled him to become "the wealthiest individual in the Niagara District," according to his obituary in the *St. Catharines Journal*. It also noted that he had been in the "habit of exacting the last penny of interest," which does not seem as harsh a judgement of his character as that of a Thomas Lundy, who had accused Street in 1824 of selling flour to the Americans during their occupation of Fort George (Niagara-on-the-Lake) in 1813.

Street died at Port Robinson, on the Welland Canal, on 21 Aug. 1844. His fortune was left to his son, who managed to increase his share, and to his four surviving daughters, who married prominent personages, including Thomas Brock Fuller*, later the first Anglican bishop of Niagara, and Josiah Burr Plumb*, a future speaker of Canada's Senate.

BRUCE A. PARKER

AO, MS 500; RG 22, ser.155. MTRL, Samuel Street papers. Niagara Hist. Soc. Museum (Niagara-on-the-Lake, Ont.), H.VI.1 (mfm. at AO). Niagara South Land Registry Office (Welland, Ont.), Abstract index to deeds, Stamford Township, lot 174 (mfm. at AO). PAC, MG 24, B18, 13: 2319–21; D18; E1, 7; I26, 52; RG 1, E3, 108; L1, 20: 211–12; 28: 15–17, 121–62; L3, 448a: S2/70; 449: S2/202; 473: S21/107; RG 5, A1: 8938–45, 9889–90, 18532–33, 21450–52, 29634, 29678–79, 29715, 35561–62, 35924–27, 36249–52, 123939–40, 139227–29; RG 68, General index, 1651–1841: 402, 425. UWOL, Regional Coll., John Harris papers. *Doc. hist. of campaign upon Niagara frontier* (Cruikshank), 1: 177. "Early records of St. Mark's and St. Andrew's churches, Niagara," comp. Janet Carnochan, *OH*, 3 (1901): 37, 40. *Select British docs. of War of 1812* (Wood), 3: 147. *Statistical account of U.C.* (Gourlay; ed. Mealing; 1974). *British Colonist*, 8 Jan. 1847. *Canadian Emigrant, and Western District Commercial and General Advertiser* (Sandwich [Windsor, Ont.]), 3 Nov. 1835. *Colonial Advocate*, 10 June 1830, 3 March 1831. *Niagara Gleaner*, 23 April, 31 Dec. 1825; 27 Aug. 1827; 26 June 1830; 2 July 1831. *Niagara Spectator* (Niagara [Niagara-on-the-Lake]), 11 Dec. 1817. *St. Catharines Journal*, 3 Dec. 1840, 23 Aug. 1844. Chadwick, *Ontarian families*, 2: 175–76. *Death notices from "The Christian Guardian," 1836–1850*, comp. D. A. McKenzie (Lambertville, N.J., 1982). H. G. J. Aitken, *The Welland Canal Company: a study in Canadian enterprise* (Cambridge, Mass., 1954). R. C. Bond, *Peninsula village: the story of Chippawa* ([Chippawa, Ont., 1964]). E. A. Cruikshank, *A memoir of Colonel the Honourable James Kerby, his life in letters* (Welland, 1931), 13. William Kirby, *Annals of Niagara*, ed. Lorne Pierce (2nd ed., Toronto, 1927), 116. J. C. Morden, *Historic Niagara Falls; corroborated by information gleaned from various sources, with portraits and illustrations* (Niagara Falls, Ont., 1932). B. G. Wilson, *Enterprises of Robert Hamilton*. Ernest Green, "The Niagara Portage Road," *OH*, 23 (1926): 260–311; "Some graves on Lundy's Lane," Niagara Hist. Soc., [*Pub.*], no.22 (1911): 57–60.

STUART, ANDREW, lawyer, politician, office holder, and author; b. 25 Nov. 1785 in Cataraqui (Kingston, Ont.), fifth son of John Stuart*, a Church of England clergyman, and Jane Okill; m. first Marguerite Dumoulin, and they had two sons, one of them Andrew*; m. secondly Jane Smith, and they had three daughters and a son; d. 21 Feb. 1840 at Quebec.

The Stuarts, a large family, lived at Cataraqui from 1785 and had a place in the local élite through the influence of the Reverend Mr Stuart, rather than through their wealth. Andrew Stuart was privileged to have John Strachan* as a tutor for several years, and then went to Union College in Schenectady, N.Y. He studied law in Lower Canada and was called to the bar on 5 Nov. 1807. Like his brother James*, he went into practice.

Within a few years Stuart carved out an enviable place in the legal field, and despite stiff competition became one of the most sought-after and best-paid lawyers in the Quebec region. He was, in fact, involved in all the major cases. Early in his career, for example, he conducted a spirited defence of Pierre-Stanislas Bédard*, who had been imprisoned in March 1810 on the orders of Governor Sir James Henry Craig*. He did not, however, succeed in obtaining a writ of habeas corpus for him from the Court of King's Bench. Like François Blanchet* and Jean-Thomas Taschereau*, who were arrested at the same time, Bédard was involved in publishing *Le Canadien*. Stuart was chosen as counsel for the defence because he was on close terms with Bédard, who considered the Stuart brothers "friends of the Canadians." In addition, Stuart served as the lawyer for the Séminaire de Saint-Sulpice in Montreal, which had to defend the title to its assets against the crown's claims [*see* Jean-Henry-Auguste Roux*]. His clients also included Quebec financiers and wealthy merchants, in particular those who had founded the Quebec Bank in 1818 [*see* John William Woolsey*]. Stuart was legal adviser for the bank directors and on several occasions was able to get them out of difficulty. They certainly were not inexperienced in business, but they had every reason to congratulate themselves for having made an ally of such a renowned jurist.

Young lawyers found it interesting to be associated with Stuart. This was the experience of Henry Black*. Called to the bar in 1820, he practised in partnership with Stuart for a good many years. A number of young men who subsequently distinguished themselves articled with them. Joseph BOUCHETTE, a friend of Stuart's, entrusted his son Robert-Shore-Milnes* to him early in the 1820s, and William Locker Pickmore Felton*, later a Liberal-Conservative assemblyman, also articled in the office of Stuart and Black. It was to them that the Irish community of the town turned in 1831 when seeking to buy land on which to build a Catholic church for the English-speaking population [*see* John Cannon*].

In his *Souvenirs d'un demi-siècle* Joseph-Guillaume Barthe* tells of the trial of an Indian accused by the Hudson's Bay Company of murder and armed robbery. Andrew Stuart, with several colleagues, acted for the defence, James Stuart for the crown. The week-long trial gave the brothers a chance to exchange many arguments. The skirmishes between the two were not meant to amuse the spectators, but to some extent they were indeed part of a game. In another case, between Toussaint POTHIER and Marie-Amable Foretier*, Andrew had the opportunity to replace his brother; James apparently had had enough of confronting Joseph-Rémi VALLIÈRES de Saint-Réal, who was given to flamboyant courtroom speeches.

Stuart also expended considerable energy in the counterpart to his legal career, politics. He became involved at a time when the colony's political life was in process of transformation. He was first elected to the House of Assembly for Lower Town Quebec as a candidate of the Canadian party. He represented this riding from 13 May 1814 till 9 Feb. 1820, and then that of Upper Town from 25 July 1820 till 2 Sept. 1830. In its early years the Canadian party had a few English-speaking members, in particular John NEILSON and Andrew and James Stuart, for whom the rights of the assembly were of greater significance than the prerogatives of the crown. The two Stuarts came to have real influence on the party, whose leading members in the period before 1815 lived at Quebec. The colonial link and British institutions were not yet being challenged (as they would be around 1830), and it was the famous question of supply that became the Stuarts' favourite issue.

Andrew Stuart ran in Upper Town in the 1834 elections but was beaten. He had left the Canadian party a short time before to join the government camp. This change of direction can be attributed to his own intellectual consistency rather than to any struggle for influence within the Canadian party, which in 1826 had become the Patriote party. Louis-Joseph Papineau*, its leader, had hardened his stance and, although there were not many of them, the assemblymen who, like Stuart, were committed only to administrative reform chose to leave the party.

Subsequently Stuart proved a fierce adversary of Papineau. He sat once more for Upper Town Quebec from 26 March 1836 till 27 March 1838, replacing René-Édouard Caron*, who had resigned the seat. He came to support the planned union of Upper and Lower Canada, and as president of the Constitutional Association, which had in its ranks William Bristow*, Thomas Cushing Aylwin*, George Pemberton, and John Neilson, he went to England in 1838 to promote the scheme. On 25 October of that year he was appointed solicitor general of Lower Canada, an office he held until his death.

Stuart's talents as a jurist, combined with his political involvement, no doubt helped to open doors for him. He also acquired an undeniable distinction through frequenting the literary circles and learned societies of his time. With his brother James he belonged to the coterie of Louise-Amélie Panet, who held a salon in her manor-house at Sainte-Mélanie which they attended along with Jacques Viger*, Denis-Benjamin Viger*, and Louis-Joseph Papineau.

Stuart's interest in literature, history, and science led him to write several articles and works that show a detailed knowledge of the topics. Elected president of the Literary and Historical Society of Quebec in 1832, he gave a number of lectures before its members on subjects as varied as classical poetry and Roman history. In addition he produced several interesting essays that were published by the society.

On 23 Feb. 1828 Andrew and David Stuart had been appointed commissioners for exploring the tract of country known as the king's posts. Accompanied by geologist Frederick Henry Baddeley*, who was also a member of the Literary and Historical Society of Quebec, they visited that region, located north of the river and gulf of St Lawrence, and made a study of it. Their report, which Andrew wrote, was published by the society in 1831 under the title *Report of the commissioners for exploring the country lying between the rivers Saguenay, Saint Maurice and Saint Lawrence*. He contributed in a more tangible fashion to the development of the organization by helping it to obtain an initial government grant for the publication of its transactions. On several occasions he made personal donations to its library and museum.

Stuart also belonged to the Société pour l'Encouragement des Sciences et des Arts en Canada, of which he became vice-president. This association, which was founded at Quebec in 1827, pursued aims similar to those of the Literary and Historical Society. The most active members of one were often indeed leaders in the other. Sir James Kempt* finally intervened to encourage their amalgamation in 1829. Needless to say, these learned societies brought together the town's intellectual élite. At their meetings Andrew met his colleague Henry Black and his friends Joseph Bouchette and John Charlton FISHER. Stuart also contributed regularly to the *Star and Commercial Advertiser/L'Étoile et Journal de Commerce*, which was published at Quebec from 1827 till 1830. Then, with Fisher, he gathered together the information that was used by Alfred Hawkins* in writing *Hawkins's picture of Quebec; with historical recollections* (Quebec, 1834).

Andrew and James Stuart became well known in the field of law, where they excelled, although they did not acquire quite the same reputation. Both were renowned for their eloquence, but Andrew, it seems, showed more compassion in the practice of his profession, and his speeches in court more often contained pleas for leniency. A man of many and varied interests, he frequently won praise from his political adversaries, which, after all, is rather exceptional.

GINETTE BERNATCHEZ

Andrew Stuart wrote a number of articles for the Literary and Historical Society of Quebec. Appearing in its *Trans.*, 1 (1824–29): 52–61, 167–81, and 198–218 respectively are "Notes on the Saguenay country," "Of the ancient Etruscans, Tyrrhenians or Tuscans," and "Journey across the continent of North America by an Indian chief, about the middle of the last century, as taken from his own mouth, and reduced to writing by M. Le Page du Pratz"; and, in *Trans.*, 3 (1832–37): 261–70 and 365–86, "Canadian etymologies" and "Detached thoughts upon the history of civilization."

Stuart is also the author of *Notes upon the south western boundary line of the British provinces of Lower Canada and New Brunswick, and the United States of America* (Quebec, 1830); *Review of the proceedings of the legislature of Lower Canada in the session of 1831 . . .* (Montreal, 1832); *An account of the endowments for education in Lower Canada, and of the legislative and other public acts for the advancement thereof, from the cession of the country in 1763 to the present time* (London, 1838); *Succinct account of the treaties and negociations between Great Britain and the United States of America, relating to the boundary between the British possessions of Lower Canada and New Brunswick, in North America, and the United States of America* (London, 1838).

ANQ-Q, CE1-61, 24 févr. 1840; P-294. PAC, MG 24, B12; MG 30, D1, 28: 493–517; RG 68, General index, 1651–1841: 9, 199, 202, 214, 272, 661. *Docs. relating to constitutional hist., 1819–28* (Doughty and Story), 383. Literary and Hist. Soc. of Quebec, *Index of the lectures, papers and historical documents . . .*, comp. F. C. Würtele and J. C. Strachan (Quebec, 1927), v, vii, ix–x, xiv, xx, xxiv, xxviii, xl, xlii. P.-G. Roy, *Les avocats de la région de Québec*, 413–17. Barthe, *Souvenirs d'un demi-siècle* (1885), 292–98, 314–17. Ginette Bernatchez, "La Société littéraire et historique de Québec (the Literary and Historical Society of Quebec), 1824–1890" (thèse de MA, univ. Laval, Québec, 1979), 6, 67, 138. J. M. LeMoine, *Picturesque Quebec: a sequel to "Quebec past and present"* (Montreal, 1882); *Quebec past and present, a history of Quebec, 1608–1876* (Quebec, 1876), 276, 415. Marianna O'Gallagher, *Saint Patrick's, Quebec: the building of a church and of a parish, 1827 to 1833* (Quebec, 1981). Benjamin Sulte, *Histoire des Canadiens-français, 1608–1880 . . .* (8v., Montréal, 1882–84), 8. A. H. Young, *The Revd. John Stuart, D.D., U.E.L., of Kingston, U.C., and his family: a genealogical study* (Kingston, Ont., [1920]).

STUART, JOHN, fur trader and explorer; b. 12 Sept. 1780, probably at Leanchoil, near Nethy Bridge, Scotland, son of Donald Stuart and Janet Grant; d. 14 Jan. 1847 near Forres, Scotland.

After receiving some education, John Stuart joined the North West Company in 1796, perhaps under the auspices of Roderick MACKENZIE who had known him as a boy. Stuart was sent to Fort Chipewyan (Alta), and subsequently served at various posts in the Athabasca department. In 1805 he was assistant to Simon Fraser*, who had been charged with finding a supply route over the Rocky Mountains for the purpose of extending NWC operations into present-day British Columbia. That fall the two men established Rocky Mountain House (Alta) and the following year what would be called Fort St James (B.C.) on Stuart Lake. Because both Indians and traders were suffering from famine, Stuart was sent to explore a route to Nat-len (Fraser Lake), where provisions were reputed to be plentiful. On the strength of his report, Fraser built a post on that lake in 1806. Stuart spent the winter of 1806–7 on McLeod Lake at Fort McLeod, established in 1805.

With the arrival of extra men and supplies in the fall of 1807, preparations began for the descent of the river now known as the Fraser but then thought to be the Columbia. On 28 May 1808 Stuart, as second-in-command, left Fort George (Prince George) with Fraser and 22 men on the epic journey down the river. It was a harrowing experience requiring superhuman perseverance and skill in navigating the whirlpools, rapids, and perpendicular rock canyons. On 2 July they passed the site of New Westminster and came within sight of the Strait of Georgia. They returned upriver, arriving at Fort George on 6 August. The voyage was a disappointment, for the river was not a navigable supply route, nor was it the Columbia. Stuart had proven himself an invaluable lieutenant: he was a good judge of river navigation, kept the official log, took the meridian observations, and was fearless before the suspicious Indians, some of whom had never before seen white men.

Stuart returned to McLeod Lake and in 1809 was given charge of New Caledonia, the area west of the mountains. In 1813 he left Stuart Lake for the Columbia, searching for a supply route between New Caledonia and the Pacific coast. In October at Fort Astoria (Astoria, Oreg.), he was one of the signatories to the bill of sale of the Pacific Fur Company to the NWC. That year he became an NWC partner. Stuart returned to Fort St James in 1814, in which year trade goods were received from Fort George via the Fraser, Thompson, Okanagan, and Columbia rivers. This route, which enabled the posts in New Caledonia to receive their supplies by ship from England rather than overland from Montreal, does not appear to have been adopted permanently by the NWC.

From 1817 until 1820 Stuart seems to have been in charge of Pierre au Calumet (north of Fort McMurray, Alta). With other Nor'Westers he took part in the successful harassment of Hudson's Bay Company men, notably John Clarke*, who were trying to gain a toehold in the Athabasca country. By March 1821 he was back at Fort George, directing the establishment of Fort Alexandria (Alexandria, B.C.) that year.

After the amalgamation of the NWC and the HBC in 1821 Stuart was made a chief factor and remained in charge of New Caledonia until 1824. By that time he could "no longer engage in the trials and hardships" that had been almost natural to him, and he asked to be transferred. He prided himself on his understanding and treatment of the Indians and the murder by two Carriers in 1823 of two HBC employees at Fort George had profoundly affected him [*see* ʔKWAH]. He subsequently assumed charge of the Saskatchewan district (1824–26) and the Winnipeg district (1826–32). His appointment in 1832 to the Mackenzie River district, an unusual posting for an officer of his service and inclination, may have been a punitive act. In 1830 Stuart had grumbled about the business methods employed in New Caledonia by Chief Factor John McLoughlin* and he had criticized Governor George Simpson* and John George MCTAVISH for abandoning their country wives. Simpson's unnecessarily harsh description of Stuart in his "Character book" of 1832 was an about-face, for in 1828 he had referred to Stuart as "the Father . . . of New Caledonia; where for 20 years of his Life, he was doomed to all the misery and privation . . . who with a degree of exertion, of which few men were capable, overcame difficulties, to which the business of no other part of the country was exposed."

Stuart was granted a furlough in 1835, which was extended for health reasons until 1 June 1839, when he left the HBC's service. During that period, in 1838, he wrote to Simpson, Edward Ellice*, and Alexander Stewart, a long-time associate, recommending his nephew Donald Alexander Smith*, later Lord Strathcona, for employment in the HBC. Stuart retired to Forres, Scotland, and died near there at Springfield House in 1847. He had at least three children: a daughter, Isabel, born in 1802, whose mother is unknown, and two sons, Donald and John, by Catherine La Valle. In 1827 Stuart took another country wife, Mary Taylor. She joined him in Scotland in 1836 but because he withdrew his promise to marry her formally she returned to Rupert's Land in 1838. There was considerable litigation over Stuart's legacy to her, which Stuart's sisters managed to have reduced from £500 to £350.

Stuart was a man of courage, a good traveller and trader, and fair in his dealings with the Indians. He deserves to be remembered as an outstanding officer of the North West Company, and although he did not always agree with the management policies of the HBC he nevertheless served it well. Stuart Lake in British Columbia was named in his honour.

SHIRLEE ANNE SMITH

PAM, HBCA, A.1/60: 90; A.5/11: 160; A.10/7: f.306; A.44/3: 70; B.4/b/1: ff.9, 14d–15; B.39/a/10: ff.1d–5; B.188/a/1: ff.49–49d; B.188/b/1: f.43; B.200/a/15: ff.11d, 29d; B.239/k/1: ff.5d, 11d–12, 26, 43, 64d, 107d, 134d, 160d; B.239/k/2: 5, 31, 61; B.239/k/3: ff.43, 62d, 76d; C.1/834; D.4/116: ff.51d–53; D.5/31: f.482; E.24/1: ff. 14d–15, 31d; F.1/1: 271–72; John Stuart file. PRO, PROB 11/2138: ff.149–50. Simon Fraser, *The letters and journals of Simon Fraser, 1806–1808*, ed. W. K. Lamb (Toronto, 1960). Hargrave, *Hargrave corr.* (Glazebrook). D. W.

Harmon, *Sixteen years in the Indian country: the journal of Daniel Williams Harmon, 1800–1816*, ed. W. K. Lamb (Toronto, 1957). *HBRS*, 1 (Rich); 10 (Rich); 30 (Williams). G. C. Davidson, *The North West Company* (Berkeley, Calif., 1918; repr. New York, 1967). Rich, *Hist. of HBC* (1958–59), vol.2. Van Kirk, *"Many tender ties"*. J. N. Wallace, *The wintering partners on Peace River from the earliest records to the union in 1821; with a summary of the Dunvegan journal, 1806* (Ottawa, 1929). W. S. Wallace, "Strathspey in the Canadian fur-trade," *Essays in Canadian history presented to George MacKinnon Wrong for his eightieth birthday*, ed. Ralph Flenley (Toronto, 1939), 278–95. Corday MacKay, "With Fraser to the sea," *Beaver*, outfit 275 (December 1944): 3–7.

SWAYNE, HUGH, army officer and colonial administrator; eldest son of John Swayne, collector of excise at Cork (Republic of Ireland); d. 31 Oct. 1836 in Paris.

Hugh Swayne's military career began in April 1782, when he was appointed a second lieutenant in the Royal Irish Artillery. In August 1793 he rose to captain, and during 1797 and 1798 he served in Demerara and Berbice (Guyana). A lieutenant-colonel from 1 Sept. 1800, Swayne retired on full pay when the Royal Irish Artillery was amalgamated with the Royal Artillery early in 1801, and he became a brevet colonel in 1810. His reflections on the Napoleonic Wars spurred his interest in the planning of campaigns, which he dealt with in *A sketch of the etat major; or general staff of an army in the field* (London, 1810). The book reveals a practical turn of mind, and this characteristic likely influenced the British authorities to appoint Swayne on 26 Aug. 1812 as administrator of Cape Breton with the position of brigadier-general. On 4 June 1813 he was raised to major-general.

When Swayne arrived in Sydney on New Year's Day 1813 to take over from Nicholas Nepean*, he faced several problems. The most immediate was how to protect the island, whose defensive works had been described before the War of 1812 as "unworthy of Observation." In 1811 the garrison had been increased to 168 men and Nepean had made a few feeble moves to organize a militia. In the face of hostilities, however, these measures would be totally inadequate. The greatest danger was from the sea, but only two ships cruised the coasts. This weakness was revealed immediately after the outbreak of war when American privateers attacked fishing and trading vessels off Arichat, upsetting the commerce of that area and of the Strait of Canso.

Since Swayne could not count on help from Halifax, he took steps to lessen the colony's vulnerability. To ensure that the island could feed itself if cut off from outside supplies, in April 1813 he stopped the export of selected foodstuffs for six months. Later that year, as protection for the coal mines, he rebuilt a redoubt and barracks near them and had troops stationed there, to provide at least a show of strength in case of attack. Swayne also reorganized the militia, dividing the island into 20 districts, each with a captain and two lieutenants. He tried to choose as leaders men with previous military experience.

Another of Swayne's difficulties was with land. Freehold grants had been forbidden since 1789, and because many immigrants could not afford to lease they simply occupied untenanted sites. Moreover, since leasehold tenure was always uncertain, lessees often neglected to cultivate their land beyond the minimum required for survival. Swayne recognized the evils of this system and wanted grants reinstated, particularly because they were being made in Nova Scotia. Though the restraining order was rescinded only after Swayne's departure, the action was partly the result of his prodding.

Swayne had little understanding of and no patience with Cape Breton politics, which centred on the question of whether or not the colony should have a house of assembly. In the spring of 1812 Nepean had sided with the pro-assembly faction, headed by the attorney general, Richard Collier Bernard DesBarres Marshall Gibbons, and had dismissed from the Executive Council the chief justice, Archibald Charles Dodd*, who opposed an assembly. Nepean had agreed with Gibbons that in the absence of an assembly the collection of all taxes, and in particular the duty on imported rum, which was an important source of funds, should be stopped. This decision had left Cape Breton with practically no revenue.

Swayne had no appreciation of arguments that were depriving the colony of money during a war. He agreed with Dodd that its political problems were caused by a few vindictive individuals interested only in power, and in April 1813 he dissolved the council and reappointed such opponents of an assembly as Dodd and Richard Stout*. Swayne then canvassed the "leading inhabitants," as he termed them, and discovered that they were favourable to the rum tax. It was therefore reinstated, and when Gibbons protested he was pressured into resigning as attorney general. Undeterred, Gibbons began to question openly the legality of the tax. Swayne brought Richard John Uniacke* Jr from Halifax to serve as attorney general and began a prosecution of Gibbons, whom he saw as an enemy agent. Swayne's decisive actions and Gibbons's departure for England by March 1814 to seek reappointment put a temporary halt to political debate and allowed Swayne to spend the last year of his tenure concentrating on defence and the coal mines.

Under Swayne's predecessors the mines had usually been leased to private operators, who paid a royalty to the government on each ton of coal exported, but when Swayne arrived they were virtually abandoned because no lease had been negotiated. In order to keep prices down in the face of wartime inflation, late in 1813 Swayne had to accept a bid with a low royalty from Ritchie and Leaver, a firm which had operated the mines previously. Yet despite Swayne's efforts the Nova Scotia legislature complained of the high cost of Cape Breton coal and in 1815 petitioned successfully to be allowed to open mines in its own province. Swayne nevertheless carried on with Ritchie and Leaver, and Nova Scotia continued to purchase all the coal Cape Breton could ship.

By 1814 Swayne's efforts seemed to have been vindicated, and the Colonial Office was happy with his achievements. That year his health began to fail, and in July 1815 he requested a leave of absence, returning to England in September. Although Swayne does not seem to have been employed again, he was promoted lieutenant-general on 27 May 1825 by seniority. Apparently he never married.

At the end of Swayne's term, Cape Breton seemed poised for a period of growth. The militia was armed and organized, there was relative political tranquillity, and coal production was back on stream. Moreover, the colony was benefiting from the prosperity of the other Maritime colonies during the War of 1812 with the resulting increased demand for her coal, fish, and agricultural products. Although Swayne can hardly be credited with this particular development, his liberal attitude toward land grants, his reorganization of the militia, and the temporary political peace he achieved at least had provided a framework of stability.

R. J. Morgan

Hugh Swayne is the author of *A sketch of the etat major; or general staff of an army in the field, as applicable to the British service; illustrated by the practice in other countries* (London, 1810).

PAC, MG 11, [CO 217] Cape Breton A, 34; MG 24, A5; RG 8, I (C ser.), 229, 679, 722, 1706. PANS, MG 1, 262B. PRO, CO 217/132; CO 220/15; WO 1/96. Le Jeune, *Dictionnaire*. *The royal military calendar, or army service and commission book* . . . , ed. John Philippart (3rd ed., 5v., London, 1820), 3. W. S. MacNutt, *The Atlantic provinces: the emergence of colonial society, 1712–1857* (Toronto, 1965).

SWEETMAN, PIERCE, businessman and shipowner; b. 1761 or 1770 in the parish of Newbawn, County Wexford (Republic of Ireland), son of Roger Sweetman; m. 8 April 1791 Juliet Forstall in Waterford (Republic of Ireland), and they had two sons and three daughters; d. 17 April 1841 near Waterford.

Few Irish in Newfoundland could claim such a respectable lineage in the homeland or such reputable connections with the island prior to their arrival as Pierce Sweetman. He came from a prosperous farming family which had provided recruits to the upper echelons of the Roman Catholic Church, among them a bishop in Wexford. Richard Welsh, a native of nearby New Ross and one of Newfoundland's leading merchants in the 18th century, was likely his maternal grandfather. Following the death of Welsh and his son, Welsh's extensive capital, premises, and business at Placentia, Nfld, passed on to his three daughters and their children. The daughters had married William Saunders of Bideford, England, a former clerk and now managing agent in Placentia, Paul Farrell, a Waterford-based merchant already engaged in the Newfoundland trade, and probably Roger Sweetman. Using his English and Waterford connections, Saunders expanded this trade, particularly with southern Europe, and by 1786 was one of the leading shipowners resident in Newfoundland. In a letter that year to the king from Placentia, Prince William Henry noted that the firm had over £50,000 capital invested in the fishery.

Pierce Sweetman is first recorded at Placentia in 1785, when he was assistant agent to Thomas Saunders, a younger brother of William. Placentia was the principal harbour on the south coast of the island, and the fishery there was nearing its peak. Letter-books written at that place between 1788 and 1793 describe activities of the firm. After 1779 the Saunders family was based in Poole, Dorset, which was the pivot of the company's network, the port where the ships were owned and final decisions on their deployment made. Waterford supplied the salt provisions and the bulk of the migrant labour. In 1788 Pierce Sweetman spent the winter and spring there and in Poole helping assemble supplies and personnel. Arriving at Placentia in the fall, he assisted in the shipping of cod to the Iberian peninsula and supervised the departure for Waterford and Poole of vessels carrying cod oil and passengers. In December he sent out crews to cut wood. The company built its own ships, and during the winter Sweetman oversaw the construction of one deep-sea vessel and the beginning of another. Early in April 1789 he turned his attention to the fishing season. Although by this era the fishery at Placentia was prosecuted predominantly by resident planters and overwintering servants, a third of the labour still came from the British Isles. The firm preferred Irish labour, particularly ashore. Thomas Saunders believed that "for hard labour one Irish youngster is worth a dozen [English]." The fishery would peak in June with the arrival of millions of tiny caplin, which lured the cod inshore, but Sweetman had 19 shallops at sea by early May. Each boat had four or five men, and the crews were supervised by one of the company captains who had brought them out from Waterford. Another aspect of the company's operations was its backing of planters. Sweetman advanced them supplies in the spring on the promise of their cod and cod oil in the fall. Early in June 1789 he ordered the supplying of 25 planters once the caplin struck ashore.

The export of dried cod to the Iberian peninsula and Italy and to St John's for the West Indies was the key activity of the fishery. Considerable time and expertise was spent ensuring that the fish was properly culled and sorted to suit regional tastes abroad. "Sweetman has seen the whole of it shipped so it must be good," Thomas Saunders noted of one cargo in 1789. Almost every month from May to November one or more of the company's fleet departed from Placentia for southern Europe. Each captain was given written instructions to proceed to a particular port. European agents sold the cod, on company account, either in their home port or elsewhere depending on prices. Although Pierce Sweetman dealt with a dozen or more European agents, most shipments were consigned to a handful of houses with English or Irish connections. The close commercial and cultural ties between his homeland and Catholic Iberia facilitated the firm's trade. He himself sailed on one of the company vessels to Cadiz in 1789 to visit Waterford agents there and become more familiar with the conditions of Iberian trade.

The death of William Saunders in 1788 had implications for Pierce Sweetman's position within the company. Thomas Saunders became director and Sweetman was made a formal partner, the firm's name changing from William Saunders and Company to Saunders and Sweetman in 1789. Sweetman's marriage in 1791 to Juliet Forstall, the daughter of an influential large farmer near Waterford, confirmed him as a merchant of substance firmly entrenched in the upper levels of the town's Catholic middle class. Shortly afterwards, he became director of company operations in Waterford, replacing John Blackney, the second husband of one of Welsh's daughters.

The wars with France imposed new strains on the management of this transatlantic merchant fishery. At the outset, the trade prospered. Indeed, the year 1794 was the busiest in the century for the Waterford operations. But difficulties soon occurred. The price of foodstuffs rose, and fishermen and mariners became the targets of press-gangs. The flow of passengers from Waterford was reduced some years to a trickle, and people returning home in the fall attempted to avoid impressment by forcing captains to land in safer havens west of the port, thus disrupting the company's shipping. Moreover vessels were under threat from enemy ships, their flexibility was hampered by cumbersome convoys, and the traditional cod markets were insecure during the wars.

Pierce Sweetman moved to his native Newbawn in 1796, entrusting the diminished trade at Waterford to a relative and taking over one of his father's large farms. A few years later he installed his family in a fashionable villa on the banks of the Slaney, in Wexford, and resumed the role of a mobile merchant, travelling between Poole, Placentia, and Waterford to stimulate trade. He struggled to maintain a commerce with Spain, but disruptions there connected with the war resulted in a renewed concentration of shipping on Waterford, enhanced by a demand for cod to feed the rapidly increasing Irish poor. Pierce quitted Newfoundland permanently in 1803 and settled in Waterford. His brother Michael, who had married the only daughter and heir of Thomas Saunders, was left in charge at Placentia.

Following Thomas Saunders's death in 1808, the Sweetmans became the sole owners and Waterford the exclusive European base of the enterprise. Pierce Sweetman sent his son Roger F. to Placentia in 1813 to revitalize a languishing trade. Together they rebuilt the firm. Every spring Pierce shipped provisions, and often passengers, to Newfoundland. He was one of the few merchants in Ireland to continue in this migratory, transatlantic mode of trade, which by then had become archaic. Many of the indentured servants he sent out stayed on the island. Some settled in Placentia Bay and their numerous descendants are still there, the most striking consequence of an enduring mercantile enterprise. Few Irish merchants influenced migration and colonization overseas to this extent, and none is as clearly remembered for it in Irish Newfoundland folk tradition.

Pierce Sweetman differed from most other merchants in Ireland and even in the commerce between Ireland and Newfoundland by the degree of vertical integration in his trade. He dealt on company account, using his ships to collect supplies not only from Waterford but from English and Continental ports. He also persevered in a triangular trade that spanned the Atlantic. Although primarily a cod merchant, he did engage in ancillary activities, including the seal fishery, the transport of timber from Quebec to Waterford, and the shipping of goods from Waterford to England. Few firms endured as long as the Sweetmans in the volatile Newfoundland trade. Pierce's early success is clearly attributable to his middle-class background and impressive mercantile connections, rare among the hundred or more Catholic Irishmen who became cod merchants in the century after 1750. Management of an enterprise notorious for its unpredictability required a high degree of skill, and he succeeded throughout his career in maintaining a position as one of the most respectable merchants.

In Newbawn the Sweetman family had been a mainstay of the Catholic Church, and Pierce continued the tradition across the Atlantic. In 1785 Father Edmund Burke* came to Placentia to establish a Catholic chapel and parish, and he received timely support from Sweetman and from the Anglican William Saunders as well. In an increasingly Irish community such as Placentia, good relations with the established church and civil authorities were important to the success of a Catholic merchant. In 1786 Sweetman was the third largest donor to a fund for an Anglican church there. In that year also, he took the oath of allegiance from the new surrogate, Prince William Henry. Bishop Nicholas Sweetman of Wexford would not have approved. The kinship and partnership between the Catholic Sweetmans and the Anglican Saunderses, uncommon in Newfoundland mercantile tradition, did much to cultivate ethnic and religious rapport at Placentia. Indeed, in January 1829 the Sweetmans were singled out by Patrick MORRIS at a meeting of the Waterford Liberal Club attended by Daniel O'Connell for their contribution to religious harmony, a model for what could be achieved in Ireland between the two traditions.

On 5 April 1841 Sweetman made his will, dividing a considerable estate between his two daughters and surviving son, Roger F. He died two weeks later at Blenheim Lodge, on the banks of the Suir just outside Waterford, where he had lived with his family since 1810. "No man better sustained, in distant countries or at home, the character of British merchant," a local paper reported. "He was a deservedly adored husband, parent, friend, and a finished gentleman." His son continued the trade, first in Waterford, then in Placentia, until his death in 1862.

JOHN MANNION

Ballygunner cemetery (County Waterford, Republic of Ire.), Sweetman family plot. Clongeen, Faree, and Newbawn cemeteries (County Wexford, Republic of Ire.), Sweetman family headstones. Dorset Record Office (Dorchester, Eng.), D365, F10 (Benjamin Lester diary, 1796–1802), 6 July 1798. National Library of Ireland (Dublin), Dept. of MSS, Roman Catholic parish reg., Cathedral parish (Waterford), reg. of baptisms, marriages, and burials, 11 April 1775; St Patrick's (Waterford), reg. of marriages, 8 April 1791 (mfm. at MHA). Nfld. Public Library Services, Provincial Reference and Resource Library (St John's), Saunders and Sweetman, letter-book (copy at PANL). New Ross, Republic of Ire., Minutes of the corporation of Ross, 2 Oct. 1771. PANL, GN 2/1/A, 10: 197; GN 5/1, Placentia, 10 Sept., 27, 29 Oct. 1785; 20 July, 1, 22, 24 Aug., 4 Sept. 1786. Placentia cemetery (Placentia, Nfld.), Headstones of R. F. Sweetman, Ann [Welsh] Saunders, and Richard Welsh. PRO, CO 194/38, 194/40; PROB 11/965: ff.338–41 (Richard Welsh); 11/1165: ff.135–36 (William Saunders); 11/1510: ff.321–22 (Thomas Saunders). Registry of Deeds (Dublin), Deeds, items 9220, 44246, 49222, 59999, 207262, 350184, 389129, 460330, 497381, 574129, 576181, 583108, 596436, 663542, 665552, 689287, 735231. *Dublin Journal*, 8 Sept. 1767. *Finn's Leinster Journal* (Kilkenny, [Republic of Ire.]), 18 March, 15 April 1775. *Waterford Mail*, 21 April 1841. *Waterford Mirror*, 21 Jan. 1829.

SYDENHAM, CHARLES EDWARD POULETT THOMSON, 1st Baron. *See* THOMSON

T

TALBOT, EDWARD ALLEN, inventor, militia officer, JP, schoolmaster, author, and journalist; b. *c.* 1796 in Ireland, eldest child of Richard Talbot* and Lydia Baird; m. 11 May 1821 Phœbe Smith at Christ Church (Anglican), Montreal, and they had eight children; d. 6 Jan. 1839 in Lockport, N.Y.

Edward Allen Talbot had shown "unmistakable signs of inventive genius" as a child and had been educated with the intent of his entering and advancing in the British army, but the economic upheavals of the Napoleonic Wars and the disbanding of many regiments thereafter led the family to emigrate from Ireland in June 1818. Although Richard Talbot was the leader of a group of settlers who journeyed to Upper Canada on board the *Brunswick*, Edward had assumed a leadership role almost equal to that of his father's by the time their destination was reached.

Like his father and brother John*, Edward was totally unsuited for the life of a pioneering farmer, but in his case it was largely because of his scientific and literary interests. Thus, in the spring of 1820, the two brothers set out from the family homestead in London Township to return to Ireland. Stopping in Montreal, Edward renewed acquaintance with the family of Irishman Ralph Smith, stayed in that city for more than a year, and married Smith's eldest daughter.

Returning to London Township, probably in the summer of 1821, Talbot continued to work on the manuscript of a book that was to describe his travels to and in the Canadas. He also continued, like so many others of his day, to attempt to produce a device which could achieve perpetual motion. In August 1823 he set out for England by way of New York State, having purchased his parents' residence and the surrounding 100 acres, presumably as a means of providing for his own family should anything happen to him or to his father, who was then in poor health. It is believed that his visit to the United States was prompted by his attempts to achieve a perpetual motion device.

While in England, Edward was unsuccessful in his attempt to receive assistance from the Colonial Office to undertake an emigration scheme similar to that of his father's in 1818. He did succeed, however, in obtaining a favourable response from the colonial secretary, Lord Bathurst, to his father's petition for a redress of grievance "received at the hand of the Lieutenant Governor [Sir Peregrine Maitland*]" and in having his manuscript published. This two-volume work appeared during the summer of 1824, but at the Talbot family's own expense. *Five years' residence in the Canadas* reveals the author as a well-read and educated individual, rather conservative in outlook, and quite perceptive regarding life in the Canadas. His thesis is revealing in that he asserted the industrious poor who were willing to spend five or six years of hardship would be well rewarded, but there was little inducement for the gentleman. The work was a financial loss to the family since sales were limited and no royalties were received from the pirated translations which appeared soon after in France and Germany.

On 12 March 1824, while still in the British Isles, Talbot had been commissioned a captain in the 4th Regiment of Middlesex militia. He apparently returned to Upper Canada the following year and, as one of the most influential men in the northern portion of Middlesex County, he played an important role in the successful move to have the centre for the London District transferred from Vittoria in Norfolk County to the town plot of London. On 13 June 1829 he was commissioned a district magistrate. Ironically, London Township's only other magistrate was Ira Schofield, who, as major of the 4th Regiment, preferred five charges against Talbot that July. At a court martial in March 1830, Talbot brilliantly and successfully defended himself against all but one minor charge. He continued to serve as a militia captain and magistrate, and in January 1833 he chaired the Court of Quarter Sessions. In July 1834 he was one of the government appointees "to form and be a Board of Health for the Town of London"; fortunately the cholera epidemic of that year left London unscathed.

Following his return from the British Isles, Edward had expended much time, energy, and money both on his earlier scheme of perpetual motion and now on an improved steam-engine which could be used by vehicles on water, road, or rail. In July 1834 his plans for "Talbot's Atmospheric Propelling Engine" became the first invention patented by the government of Upper Canada. The invention, however, proved impractical because of its inventor's lack of both a basic knowledge of physics and sufficient funds. Two of Talbot's other schemes, namely, a railway line between the town of London and the head of Lake Ontario and a suspension bridge over the Niagara River, both presumably to be part of a line extending from Michigan to New York State, did see fruition, but not in his lifetime. Earlier, with his youngest brother, Freeman, Edward had "constructed a large strong wooden lathe" and produced all the heavy turning needed, especially for the stairs, in the construction of the court-house and jail at London during 1827–29 [see John Ewart*].

In 1831 Talbot joined forces with Robert Heron, a son of the editor of the Niagara *Gleaner*, to publish the London *Sun*. The first Upper Canadian newspaper printed west of Ancaster, the *Sun* appeared on 7 July and was issued sporadically until December 1833. Heron severed connections with the *Sun* late in 1832, as did his successor, William Conway Keele, a few months later; Talbot, although a supporter of the government, increasingly exhibited a more liberal political philosophy through his editorials. Talbot also used the newspaper to champion the construction of his envisioned railway line. He drew up the charter for the London and Gore Rail Road Company and his name headed the list of shareholders when the company was incorporated in March 1834.

It was apparently after the demise of the *Sun* that Talbot and his wife opened a school for a short period in London. Both proved to be excellent and well-educated teachers and attracted the children of some of the area's most prominent residents. Then, apparently after Edward's unsuccessful petition for the 500-acre grant of land to which he had originally been entitled, the family removed to Niagara (Niagara-on-the-Lake). There Talbot is said to have "conducted" a newspaper and pursued his theory of the invention of perpetual motion. By late 1835 his years of experiments, on which he had expended so much money and time to the exclusion of almost everything else, ended in failure. Suffering from acute alcoholism, he returned to London "a sickly-looking man, broken down in health and resources, with a very shabby appearance and a very large dependent family, very poor and poorly found," and again opened a school at his residence.

In the spring of 1836 a group of London-area moderates purchased the press of London's radical *Wesleyan Advocate*, which had been published from October 1835 to April 1836, and installed Talbot, an Anglican, as the editor of the *Freeman's Journal*. As with the *Sun*, he supported the government but advocated moderate reform. Despite his growing moderation he remained an enthusiastic supporter of the Orange order; indeed he was a member of the grand committee of the Grand Orange Lodge of British North America for the year 1835. All this changed during the elections in the summer of 1836.

The manipulations of Lieutenant Governor Sir Francis Bond Head* in the Middlesex riding as well as the London riots and their aftermath deeply wounded Talbot's sense of justice. Until the *Journal*'s demise that autumn, he used the paper to attack violently both Head and the Orange order. As a result, he was not recommissioned a justice of the peace in December 1836 and was stripped of his militia captaincy at about the same time. The removal from the magistracy was to weigh particularly heavily on him.

On the evening of 8 Dec. 1837 some of the reformers in Middlesex, genuinely fearing an assault on their property and lives by the local tories and Orangemen, met at Flannagan's Tavern in London to form a plan of defence. The meeting was chaired by William E. Niles* and both Edward and John Talbot attended. Although Edward had been confined to his room with dropsy for the previous eight months, he drafted the resolution of constitutional defence and acted as secretary of the meeting.

In early January 1838, on the day Edward and his family had intended to remove to Ypsilanti, Mich., where he expected to take on the editorship of a newspaper offered to him some six months earlier, he was arrested and his papers were searched. He was subsequently examined, bound over as a witness against London reformer Charles Latimer, and then released. Talbot publicly took leave of London on 13 May, stayed a short time in Detroit, and then removed to Ohio. By this time both his mind and his body were in an advanced state of deterioration. He took a dislike to the people and the climate of Ohio, and it was with relief that in July he accepted what was probably a pure act of charity on the part of the printer of the Lewiston *Telegraph*; he moved to Lewiston, N.Y., to co-edit that paper. Under Talbot's influence, the *Telegraph* dropped its support of the Patriots, but it soon fell "into a state of hopeless, drivelling somnolency," a by-product of Edward's diseased mind.

Just a few weeks before his death in January 1839, Talbot left the paper to seek medical assistance in nearby Lockport. His family, which had not accompanied him to the United States but had probably remained with his parents in London Township, was apparently notified of his imminent death. After sending his wife what little he still possessed, Edward voluntarily admitted himself to Lockport poor-house/hospital as an indigent. Subsequent to his death there, his remains were interred, undoubtedly in a pauper's grave, in the Cold Springs Cemetery.

Probably London's first mind of potential genius, Edward Allen Talbot was "an original thinker and a great projector of new schemes" who claimed a "high literary reputation" in both the Canadas and the British Isles and was "in every sense the gentleman." He had, however, no conception of the value of money and property, had been over impulsive, had consciously ruined his health, and for years had all but neglected his family.

DANIEL J. BROCK

Edward Allen Talbot's *Five years' residence in the Canadas: including a tour through the United States of America, in the year 1823* (2v., London, 1824) was reprinted in one volume in East Ardsley, Eng., and New York in 1968.

PAC, RG 9, I, B8, 1. Private arch., D. J. Brock (London, Ont.), F. C. Hamil to Fred Landon, 25 July 1961 (copy). *Christian Guardian*, 4 May 1836, 6 Feb. 1839. *Freeman's Advocate* (Lockport, N.Y.), 11 Jan. 1839. *Gazette* (London, [Ont.]), 27 July 1836, 2 March 1839. D. J. Brock, "Richard Talbot, the Tipperary Irish and the formative years of London Township, 1818–1826" (MA thesis, Univ. of Western Ont., London, 1969). F. T. Rosser, *London Township pioneers, including a few families from adjoining areas* (Belleville, Ont., 1975). D. J. Brock, "London's first newspaper: researcher discovers long-sought copy of *London Sun*," *London Free Press*, 3 July 1971: 8M. Fred Landon, "Some early newspapers and newspaper men of London," London and Middlesex Hist. Soc., *Trans.* (London), 12 (1927): 26–34.

TANNER, JOHN, hunter, guide, and narrator; b. *c.* 1780 along the Kentucky River, son of John Tanner; m. at least three times and had six or more children; d. in or after 1846.

John Tanner was the son of a former preacher from Virginia who had migrated to the Kentucky River country. After the boy's mother died, when he was two, the family moved to Elk Horn (Elkhorn City, Ky), and later to the confluence of the Ohio and Great Miami rivers, where the elder Tanner homesteaded. There, in 1789, John was kidnapped by Shawnees. Named Shaw-shaw-wa-ne-ba-se, meaning "falcon," he was later adopted by an Indian family. Shortly after his adoption he was sold to an old woman, Net-no-kwa, an Ottawa, and they moved first to Saginaw Bay (Mich.) and eventually, when Tanner was 13, to the Red River country (Man.), the home of Net-no-kwa's husband, a Saulteaux.

In his *Narrative* Tanner gives a vivid account of the process of adaptation he underwent in learning to live in a culture so remote from that in which he had been brought up. He realized that, as a child, he stood no chance of escaping from the Indians, and at the same time he was aware of how inadequate he was in the skills necessary for survival among the Saulteaux, a nomadic Ojibwa people who followed an ancient life-style as trappers and hunters in the northern woodlands, but who also on occasion pursued bison on the prairie. By the time Tanner joined them that life-style was changing through contact with white traders, the re-orientation of subsistence hunting towards fur gathering for profit, and the introduction of firearms and alcohol. But the basic structure of society was still largely unchanged, and Tanner observed and recollected it in vivid detail, so that his *Narrative* offers a remarkable account of the material culture of this people, though he had little to say about their spiritual life. The great shamanic society of the Midewiwin is never mentioned, though its ceremonials with their complex initiations were the most important events of the tribal year. Was Tanner, white by origin, excluded from initiation? Or did he feel bound by initiation to remain silent? His *Narrative* gives no answer.

Tanner's adoptive mother protected him from the brutal impatience of the Indian men, and eventually he became as skilled in trapping and hunting as his companions. For a long period he seems to have reconciled himself to Indian life. In his *Narrative* he contrasts the honesty of the Indians to the rapacity of the fur traders. He learned to speak the Indian languages and almost lost his own, to the point, he later remarked, where he "could not speak English so as to be at all understood."

He first married in 1800 in the non-committal Indian manner, and when his wife, Mis-kwa-bun-o-kwa, left him some seven years later, he yielded to community pressure and remarried about 1810. He soon found the demands of his second wife's family to be excessive. As a result, by 1812 he had begun to think of finding a way back to the life from which he had been snatched 20 years before. But the War of 1812 rendered travel impossible, and Tanner remained in the Red River country. When the settlers sent out by Lord Selkirk [Douglas*] arrived there in the summer of 1812, he hunted bison to give them winter food, and when Cuthbert Grant* of the North West Company tried to persuade the Indians to join him and his Métis followers in attacking the Hudson's Bay Company men, Tanner refused to be drawn in on either side. Yet, after Selkirk's men had captured Fort William (Thunder Bay, Ont.) in 1816, Tanner guided them from Lake of the Woods to Fort Douglas (Winnipeg) and helped them capture it from the Nor'Westers. After Selkirk arrived at Red River, he became interested in Tanner's history, gave him a small pension, and sent out a letter in an effort to establish communication with his family in Kentucky.

Without waiting for an answer, Tanner left Lake of the Woods in 1817 and, travelling via Detroit where his brother had gone to meet him, rejoined his relatives. Returning to Lake of the Woods about 1818 for his family, he persuaded his second wife and their three children to travel with him the following spring, but she stayed at Michilimackinac (Mackinac Island, Mich.) and one of the children died on the way back to Kentucky. It was 1819 by the time Tanner had finished this journey. He had long since been spoiled for the routine life of a farming community. In 1823 he returned to the northwest to claim his children by his previous marriage, catching up with his first wife at Rainy Lake (Ont.). She refused to surrender them, and persuaded an Indian to try to kill him by magic (shooting a bullet pierced by a deer sinew dyed green). Tanner survived under the care of Dr John McLoughlin*, but she vanished with the children.

Tanner made no further attempt to return to Kentucky. In 1824 he went to Michilimackinac where he worked as an interpreter for the American Indian agent and for 15 months as an employee of the American Fur Company. His second wife joined him temporarily but did not follow him when he moved in 1828 to Sault Ste Marie (Mich.), where he became an interpreter to the Indian agent there, Henry Rowe Schoolcraft. It was at about this time that Tanner met Edwin James, an American army surgeon, who patiently recorded his recollections and, along with a section of his own on Indian life and languages, had them published in New York in 1830. According to Schoolcraft, whose evidence may be biased, Tanner threatened James with violence for making him appear ridiculous, but in fact the *Narrative* seems to be an honestly rendered account of Tanner's immersion in an alien culture.

By the 1830s Tanner, whom Schoolcraft had dismissed in 1830, was once again experiencing a culture shock: having found it hard to change into an Indian boy at 9, he was now finding it just as difficult to fit into an American community. He appears to have become involved in the hostility between Schoolcraft and the Reverend Abel Bingham over the control of the mission school at Sault Ste Marie. Probably in the early 1840s he married, and lost, a white woman who could not accept his life-style. Tanner impressed the people of Sault Ste Marie as an increasingly suspicious and paranoid man, violent in temper, and contemptuous of the way Christians practised their beliefs. The mutual resentment between the community and Tanner broke out in 1846 when James Schoolcraft, Henry's brother, whom Tanner believed had defrauded him of money, was murdered. Tanner vanished at the same time, and immediately he was assumed to be guilty. He was never seen alive again, though a body found some years later in a bog near Sault Ste Marie was thought to be his; the identification was uncertain. So too was Tanner's guilt, for suspicion also rested on an army officer, Lieutenant Bryant Tilden, who is said to have made a deathbed confession, but the evidence on neither side was conclusive.

GEORGE WOODCOCK

John Tanner's reminiscences were published as *A narrative of the captivity and adventures of John Tanner, (U.S. interpreter at the Saut de Ste. Marie,) during thirty years residence among the Indians in the interior of North America*, ed. Edwin James (New York, 1830; repr., intro. N. M. Loomis, Minneapolis, Minn., 1956). The work was subsequently translated into French and German. Tanner's story was retold in an abridged version edited by James Macaulay, *Grey Hawk: life and adventures among the Red Indians* (London, 1883).

HBRS, 19 (Rich and Johnson). J. E. Bayliss *et al.*, *River of destiny, the Saint Marys* (Detroit, 1955). J. T. Fierst, "Return to 'civilization': John Tanner's troubled years at Sault Ste. Marie," *Minn. Hist.* (St Paul), 50 (1986): 23–36. G. L. Nute, "Border chieftain," *Beaver*, outfit 282 (March 1952): 35–39.

TAZEWELL, SAMUEL OLIVER, watchmaker, jeweller, piano tuner, and lithographer; fl. 1820–38.

Samuel Oliver Tazewell emigrated from England to Upper Canada some time before May 1820. His name appears in the *Kingston Chronicle* on 19 May 1820, when he announced that he had "commenced" business repairing watches and clocks. He stated that, "having had many years experience in London," he was "perfectly acquainted with the patent Lever, Horizontal and Duplex Scapements, Repeaters, &c &c." A year later in the same paper he advertised that he had opened a circulating library of "upwards of One Thousand Volumes of the most choice selected Novels, Plays, Voyages, Travels, &c. &c." In June 1825 he was one of the "friends of free discussion" who presented the *Upper Canada Herald*'s editor, Hugh Christopher Thomson*, with a silver cup engraved by Tazewell himself to mark their admiration for his "manly independence" in conducting the paper. Later that year Tazewell's name appears as a contributor to a relief fund for fire victims at Miramichi in New Brunswick. On 16 Oct. 1828 he announced in the *Canadian Freeman* his intention of opening on 1 November a jewellery store in York (Toronto), guaranteeing "the utmost satisfaction to all" because of his "experience of years in the city of London." But if he went to York, his stay was brief, for the following spring he was back in Kingston as a jeweller, specializing also in watch repairs, engraving, and piano tuning. In 1831 he added lithographic printing, after discovering a suitable Kingston limestone and building his own press, and thus became the first lithographer in Upper Canada.

At the request of Thomson, he wrote an article on the lithographic process for the *Herald* of 24 Nov. 1830 and nine months later he advertised his new press in the *Kingston Chronicle* as capable of reproducing "Maps, Plans, Views, Circulars, Music, Headings of Merchant Bills, and Steam Boat notices, with sketch of the Boat if required, Blank deeds and Memorials, Funeral Notices, embellished with suitable emblems, Bills of Exchange, &c. &c. &c. . . . Caricatures printed by the sketch being supplied." Some early samples of his art were presented to Lieutenant Governor Sir John Colborne* on 2 Aug. 1831, and by the end of the year Tazewell had completed a map of Kingston and one or two amusing cartoons.

In January 1832 Thomas DALTON, editor of the *Patriot and Farmer's Monitor*, expressed his admiration for Tazewell's discovery: "The fact is Tazewell, by research, / Has found out that the English Church, / Is built of *Lithographic Stone*; / And not the English Church alone, / But all stone houses in the Town." Another supporter was Captain Richard Henry BONNYCASTLE, who, in July 1833, reported Tazewell's discovery of Canadian lithographic stone in the *American Journal of Sciences and Arts*. The article was illustrated with drawings of the type of Canadian limestone used by Tazewell, who lithographed the drawings.

Late in 1832 Tazewell had moved his press to York in the expectation of obtaining government contracts from the newly appointed surveyor general, Samuel Proudfoot Hurd*. Although he obtained some work on a commission basis, he encountered relentless opposition from the senior draftsman, James Grant Chewett*, who saw his perquisites from expensive hand-drawn maps endangered by cheap lithographs. Moreover, because Chewett's father, WILLIAM, had recently been an unsuccessful candidate for the position of surveyor general, Chewett was determined to create difficulties for Hurd. He first refused to let any plans or maps go out of the office, and then complained that Tazewell's home-made press and Canadian stone were of inferior quality. Hurd countered by ordering a New York press and imported stones; Chewett then insisted they be used only by qualified draftsmen. Hurd temporized, allowing Tazewell to store the new press in his shop and to use it to complete orders on hand from the commissioner of crown lands. At this point, on 28 May 1834, Colborne intervened, ordering Hurd to have the press transferred to his department and instructing him not to employ Tazewell. Since none of the draftsmen were capable of operating the press, it fell into disuse. Tazewell was forced to take legal action to collect for work he had done, a suit settled out of court in 1835.

As an associate of the Society of Artists and Amateurs of Toronto, Tazewell was one of a dozen local artists (including Paul Kane*) who held a public exhibition of their work in 1834. His entries were "Six lithographs from Canadian stone" and three sketches of Niagara Falls. A son, listed in the catalogue as "Master Tazewell," was an honorary exhibitor, as was "Master Hurd," son of the surveyor general.

Denied any government contracts and prevented from using the New York press, on 9 Feb. 1835 Tazewell wrote an open letter accusing the government draftsmen of suppressing "this useful art of Lithography," and making it impossible for "the Person that brought forward the Art in this Province to gain a livelihood and to support his large Family." Colborne, however, declined to reinstate him, and by September 1835 he had moved to St Catharines and taken up his old trade of jeweller, watchmaker, and piano tuner. He continued to produce the occasional lithograph.

After Sir Francis Bond Head* succeeded Colborne, Tazewell addressed a petition to him on 10 March 1836 charging that he had been persecuted by Chewett, who had "blighted" his prospects as lithographer, to the injury not only of the petitioner but also of settlers who had been offered plans from the lithographic press "at the low price of a quarter of a dollar" but now had to pay 12*s.* 6*d.* for small township plans and "as high as ten Dollars for the larger." Head referred this petition to Chewett, who exonerated himself, vilified Tazewell, and stated that the press had been discontinued "owing to the expense attending the few copies wanted at any one time." No further action was taken.

At this point it becomes difficult to trace Tazewell's activities. On 27 Feb. 1837 his wife, Mary Ann, died in St Catharines. The following year an anonymous advertisement in the *St. Catharines Journal, and Welland Canal (Niagara District,) General Advertiser* solicited subscriptions of one dollar for a lithographic genealogical map of the "family compact," asking interested parties to forward their names to the "'*Artist of the Family Compact Map*', North American Hotel, Toronto." It is probable that this was Tazewell's final effort in Upper Canada and it seems likely that he left the province shortly thereafter. Almost a decade would pass before lithography was re-established in Upper Canada by Hugh Scobie*.

Samuel Oliver Tazewell's failure to obtain a government appointment is attributable mainly to bureaucratic obstruction. But he seems also to have antagonized even his well-wishers by his self-importance, his querulous temperament, impulsive behaviour, and lack of sound judgement.

H. P. GUNDY

No complete record of Samuel Oliver Tazewell's work exists. Most of his known pictorial prints are discussed and several of them are reproduced in Mary Allodi, *Printmaking in Canada: the earliest views and portraits* (Toronto, 1980). A copy of Tazewell's portrait of William DUNLOP (York [Toronto], *c.* 1833), previously only rumoured to exist, has recently been located in the UTFL. The MTRL possesses what is probably the only surviving copy of *An introduction to Greek declension & conjugation adapted to the abridgments of Matthiæ's grammar*, a school text lithographed by Tazewell for Upper Canada College at York in 1833. In addition, Tazewell is known to have printed more than 20 maps and town plans, copies of which are located in the National Map Coll. at the PAC, the Map Coll. at the AO (including a hand-coloured copy of the map of Kingston, [Ont.]), and the Royal Ont. Museum, Sigmund Samuel Canadiana Building (Toronto).

AO, MU 2106, 1835, no.5; RG 1, A-I-7, 9, file on maps (lithographing). PAC, RG 5, A1: 89128–34, 89741–51. R. H. Bonnycastle, "On the transition rocks of the Cataraqui," *American Journal of Sciences and Arts* (New Haven, Conn.), 24 (July 1833): 97–104. *Canadian Freeman*, 16 Oct. 1828. *Kingston Chronicle*, 19 May 1820; 18, 25 May 1821; 20 Aug., 5 Nov. 1831; 1 Jan. 1832. *Patriot and Farmer's Monitor*, 6 Oct., 7 Dec. 1832; 19 July, 9, 26 Nov. 1833. *St. Catharines Journal, and Welland Canal (Niagara District,) General Advertiser* (St Catharines, [Ont.]), 12 Nov. 1835, 9 March 1836, 2 March 1837, 20 Sept. 1838. *Upper Canada Herald*, 13 May 1823; 21 June, 22 Nov. 1825; 24 Nov. 1830. *Toronto directory*, 1833–34. H. P. Gundy, "Samuel Oliver Tazewell, first lithographer of Upper Canada," *Humanities Assoc. Rev.* (Kingston), 27 (1976): 466–83.

TEHOLAGWANEGEN (Tehoragwanegen, Tehora Kwanekeu). *See* WILLIAMS, THOMAS

TENSKWATAWA (Elskwatawa, first named **Lalawethika**, also known as the **Shawnee Prophet** and the **Prophet)**, Shawnee religious and political leader; b. probably in early 1775 in Old Piqua (near Springfield, Ohio), son of Puckeshinwa, a Shawnee warrior, and Methoataske, a woman of Creek descent; m. and had several children; d. November 1836 in what is now Kansas City, Kans.

Tenskwatawa's father was killed prior to his birth and the boy was abandoned by his mother, probably in 1779. As a child he was given the name of Lalawethika, meaning "rattle" or "noisemaker," which was indicative of his loud or boisterous personality, and he was raised by Tecumpease, an elder sister. His boyhood was overshadowed by two elder brothers, Chiksika and Tecumseh*, who were successful and admired by their peers. In contrast Lalawethika seems to have been an outcast, tolerated by his family but disliked by many members of the tribe. During his childhood he lost the sight of his right eye in an accident, and while an adolescent he became an alcoholic. As a young man he married, but failed to excel as a hunter or warrior. Although he did not participate in the Indian victories over Josiah Harmar and Arthur St Clair [*see* Michikinakoua*], he was present at the battle of Fallen Timbers and probably attended the Treaty of Greenville in 1795.

Following the treaty Lalawethika lived in western Ohio with a small band of Shawnees led by Tecumseh. In 1797 the band moved to eastern Indiana, where Lalawethika fell under the tutelage of Penagashea (Changing Feathers), an ageing medicine man. In 1804, upon the latter's death, he aspired to the status of shaman. Meanwhile, the Shawnees and other tribes were hard pressed to defend their traditional way of life against the advancing frontier. As the number of game animals dwindled and the fur trade declined, the Indians' economic base disintegrated. Many tribes were forced to make land cessions. Others suffered from alcoholism and disease, while traditional values among all the tribes seemed to be dissolving.

Although Lalawethika at first failed as a shaman, in the spring of 1805 he experienced a series of visions which changed his life. He claimed that during a trance he died and was carried to heaven where the Master of Life showed him both a paradise and a hell where unrepentant alcoholics like himself were subjected to fiery tortures. He renounced alcohol and declared that the Master of Life had chosen him to deliver the Indians from all their problems. He also declared that he would take a new name: Tenskwatawa, "the open door."

Tenskwatawa preached a doctrine which attempted to revitalize certain parts of traditional Indian culture and to modify others. He asked his followers to return to the communal life of their fathers. He also urged them to maintain good relationships with members of their families and their tribe. Above all, they should renounce alcohol and many other products of American culture. He informed his disciples that although the Master of Life had made the Indians, the British, the French, and the Spaniards, the Americans were the children of the Great Serpent, the evil power in the universe. The Indians were to avoid them. Indian women married to American men were to return to their tribes and the children of such unions were to remain with their fathers. Christian Indians were ordered to abandon their faith.

Instead, Tenskwatawa required his followers to pray to the Master of Life and provided them with "prayer sticks" inscribed with instructions for such petitions. He restored some traditional Shawnee dances and ceremonies, but forbad others and offered new rituals in their place. He ordered his followers to discard their personal medicine bags since these talismans no longer possessed any potency. If his disciples followed his instructions, game would return to the forests, and their dead friends and relatives would be brought to life. The Americans would be swept away (Tenskwatawa never provided an explicit description of this phenomenon) and the land would be restored to the Indians.

Tenskwatawa's teachings found a receptive audience among the tribes of Ohio and Indiana. During the summer of 1805 he established a new village near Greenville, in western Ohio. In the following months many Delawares in eastern Indiana were converted, and in March 1806 at Woapikamunk, a village on the White River, Tenskwatawa assisted the Delawares in assessing the guilt of some tribesmen accused of witchcraft. The Delawares eventually burned four of their kinsmen at the stake before the witch-hunt ceased. In May, Tenskwatawa conducted a similar purge among the Wyandots on the Sandusky River, but pro-American chiefs interceded to save the accused.

Alarmed by Tenskwatawa's growing ascendancy, William Henry Harrison, governor of Indiana Territory, attempted to discredit the Shawnee and wrote to the Delawares instructing them to ask Tenskwatawa to perform a miracle: "Ask of him to cause the sun to stand still – the moon to alter its course." On 16 June 1806 Tenskwatawa successfully predicted a near-total eclipse of the sun and his influence was markedly increased. During 1807 and 1808 Indians from many tribes travelled hundreds of miles to meet with him at Greenville. Kickapoos, Sauks and Foxes, Potawatomis, Ottawas, Menominees, and Winnebagos all journeyed to his village, and in the summer of 1808 so many Ojibwas were en route to Greenville that white traders found most of their villages on the southern shore of Lake Superior deserted. The influx alarmed American officials who sent several parties of agents to investigate the Prophet's movement, but he was able to convince them that his followers wished only to live in peace. The large numbers of Indians depleted his food supplies and American settlers in Ohio remained hostile to his movement. Hoping to relocate at a greater distance from the American frontier, where game was more plentiful, Tenskwatawa abandoned Greenville and in the spring of 1808 he established a new settlement, Prophetstown (Battle Ground, Ind.), at the mouth of the Tippecanoe River.

After this move Tenskwatawa developed ties with the British Indian Department. In June 1808 he sent Tecumseh to Amherstburg, Upper Canada, where he met with the deputy superintendent general of Indian affairs, William Claus*, and the lieutenant governor, Francis Gore*, asking for arms and provisions. To ease American suspicions, in August 1808 Tenskwatawa journeyed to Vincennes (Ind.), where he convinced Harrison that he was friendly to the United States and even persuaded him to provide food for his followers. But Tenskwatawa still could not feed all the Indians arriving at Prophetstown, and during the winter of 1808–9 many died. In the spring relations between Tenskwatawa's movement and the United States deteriorated as the Indians became alarmed over American attempts to purchase additional lands.

On 30 Sept. 1809 the Treaty of Fort Wayne, signed by representatives from the Miamis, Delawares, and Potawatomis, transferred over three million acres of Indian lands in Illinois and Indiana to the United States. It was a watershed in Tenskwatawa's career. Although he had opposed the agreement, he could not stop it, and many of his followers now rejected his religious leadership for the more political and military policies espoused by Tecumseh. Tenskwatawa continued to exert influence among the Indians at Prophetstown, but Tecumseh slowly eclipsed him. While Tenskwatawa remained on the Tippecanoe, Tecumseh travelled widely, using his brother's religious movement as the base for the political and military unification of all the tribes.

During the winter of 1810–11 the Prophet received several shipments of British provisions, and in the spring he met with a series of American emissaries sent by Harrison. Tenskwatawa treated them cordially, but in June 1811 he seized a shipment of American salt on the Wabash River. Later in the summer, when Tecumseh left Prophetstown to enlist the southern tribes, Tenskwatawa again remained behind, agreeing to protect the village but avoid a confrontation with Harrison. The governor then led an army of approximately 1,000 men against Prophetstown. They arrived at the Tippecanoe on 6 November and arranged to meet with Tenskwatawa on the following morning. Rather than surrender his village and supplies, Tenskwatawa decided to attack and he spent the night assuring his followers that his medicine would protect them from American bullets. Just before dawn on 7 November, about 700 Indians attacked the American camp while Tenskwatawa remained in the village praying for victory. After a three-hour battle the Indians withdrew and Tenskwatawa abandoned Prophetstown. Harrison claimed a victory, but both sides suffered similar casualties (60 to 70 killed).

The battle of Tippecanoe ended Tenskwatawa's claims of religious leadership, but he remained with Tecumseh, assisting in his brother's attempts to unify the tribes politically. A new village was built near the site of Prophetstown. Although the Shawnee brothers endeavoured to persuade the Americans that they would remain at peace, they strengthened their ties with the British. In June 1812 Tecumseh journeyed to Amherstburg while Tenskwatawa met with Indians who once again were arriving at their village. When news of the War of 1812 reached Indiana, Tenskwatawa went to Fort Wayne professing friendship to the United States, but after the fall of Detroit in August he urged the Indians in his village to attack Fort Harrison (Terre Haute, Ind.). The attack failed, and in December, after American military expeditions swept through the Wabash valley, Tenskwatawa fled to Upper Canada.

He did not remain there long. In the spring of 1813 he accompanied Tecumseh back to Indiana where they recruited warriors to assist the British in the defence of the Detroit region. They returned to Amherstburg on 16 April, and in May Tenskwatawa joined a large force of British and Canadian troops which besieged Fort Meigs (near Perrysburg, Ohio). Tenskwatawa took no part in the fighting, and following the siege he returned to Michigan where he spent the summer of 1813 at a small village on the Huron (Clinton) River. He did not participate in the British campaigns into Ohio in July and August, but he did meet with pro-American Wyandots at Brownstown (near Trenton, Mich.) where he opposed their efforts to detach the Indians from the British. In September he accompanied Major-General Henry Procter*'s forces as they abandoned Amherstburg and retreated east. On 5 Oct. 1813 Tenskwatawa was present at the battle of Moraviantown, but again took no part in the fighting and he accompanied Procter's party when it fled before the advancing Americans.

Following the battle Tenskwatawa spent the winter at the western end of Lake Ontario, attempting to reassert his leadership. He was supported by John Norton* of the Grand River Iroquois, and in the spring he and a small band of followers moved to the Grand River where Norton supplied them with food and other provisions. Although he was reluctant to assist the British in the further defence of Canada, in the summer he finally consented to lead a war party to the Niagara frontier. Yet he arrived on 6 July 1814, after the battle of Chippawa had ended, and his precipitate withdrawal on the following day resulted in a general Indian retreat that threatened the British position. He refused to participate in any further military actions, but he attended the conference at Burlington Heights (Hamilton) in April 1815 at which Indian agents announced that the war had ended.

In June 1815 Tenskwatawa and most of the other western tribesmen moved to the Amherstburg region in preparation for a return to the United States. He attended the conference at Spring Wells, near Detroit, in September at which the American representatives met with the exiles to negotiate the conditions for their return. At first he cooperated, but when he learned the Americans opposed his return to the Wabash valley, he became angry and went back to Amherstburg. In April 1816 he crossed over to Detroit where he met with Governor Lewis Cass, but was again denied permission to go back to the Tippecanoe. Meanwhile, most of the American Indians left for their former homes, and to encourage such an exodus, the British Indian Department reduced the rations of those exiles remaining in Upper Canada. By 1817 Tenskwatawa's followers numbered only about two dozen Shawnees, mainly relatives who relied upon him for their sustenance. Embittered, Tenskwatawa established a camp on Cedar Creek, in Essex County, where he lived for the next eight years, relying upon British rations but quarrelling with William Claus, John Askin Jr, and other Indian agents.

By 1824 the United States no longer considered the Prophet a threat and in July Cass invited him to return to Ohio and use his influence to persuade the Shawnees to remove west of the Mississippi. During the following summer Tenskwatawa led his handful of followers back to Wapakoneta, a Shawnee village in western Ohio, and in October 1826 he accompanied about 250 Shawnees who left Ohio for the west. After spending the winter of 1826–27 near Kaskaskia, Ill., in August 1827 they crossed the Mississippi and travelled as far as western Missouri. In the spring of 1828 they arrived at the Shawnee reservation in eastern Kansas. Tenskwatawa spent the remaining nine years of his life in relative obscurity, although he did pose for the artist George Catlin in 1832. He died in what is now Kansas City in November 1836.

During the War of 1812 and in the following decades most whites assumed that Tecumseh had dominated the Indian movement which emerged during the first decade of the century. His emphasis upon a centralized political leadership, although foreign to the tribesmen, seemed logical to them because it reflected their own political beliefs. Moreover, since Tecumseh seemed to epitomize the "noble savage," after his death white historians and writers enshrouded his life with apocrypha which made him a legendary figure. In contrast, Tenskwatawa usually has been portrayed as a religious charlatan who briefly ascended to a position of limited importance through his association with his brother. Yet Tenskwatawa initially dominated the Indian movement and his teachings were the magnet which drew the Indians together. During periods of social and economic deprivation Indian people often have turned to religious leaders for deliverance [*see* ABISHABIS] and Tenskwatawa's promises offered such a solution. The Indian coalescence remained a religious movement until 1810, when Tecumseh began to transform the Prophet's followers into a political and military confederacy. Since whites possessed little understanding of Indian religious beliefs, Tenskwatawa's teachings seemed strange and ellogical and they dismissed the Prophet as a bizarre religious figure of minor importance. Yet his faith seemed logical to people of his own culture. In the years between 1805 and 1810 Tenskwatawa was one of the most influential Indians in the Great Lakes region and he dominated the tribes' resistance to American expansion.

R. DAVID EDMUNDS

For a more complete listing of material relating to Tenskwatawa, the reader is referred to R. D. Edmunds, *The Shawnee Prophet* (Lincoln, Nebr., and London, 1983).

Tippecanoe County Hist. Assoc., County Museum (Lafayette, Ind.), George Winter papers. Wis., State Hist. Soc., Draper MSS, ser.T; 1YY–13YY. Benjamin Drake, *Life of Tecumseh and of his brother the Prophet; with a historical sketch of the Shawanoe Indians* (Cincinnati, Ohio, 1841; repr. New York, 1969). B. J. Lossing, *The pictorial field-book of the War of 1812 . . .* (New York, 1869). *Messages and letters of William Henry Harrison*, ed. Logan Esarey (2v., Indianapolis, Ind., 1922). "Shabonee's account of Tippecanoe," ed. J. W. Whickar, *Ind. Magazine of Hist.* (Bloomington), 17 (1921): 353–63. *The battle of Tippecanoe: conflict of cultures*, ed. Alameda McCollough (Lafayette, 1973). C. C. Trowbridge, *Shawanese traditions: C. C. Trowbridge's account*, ed. [W.] V. Kinietz and Erminie Wheeler-Voegelin (Ann Arbor, Mich., 1939).

THAVENET, JEAN-BAPTISTE, Sulpician; b. 2 Sept. 1763 in Bourges, France; d. 16 Dec. 1844 in Rome.

Jean-Baptiste Thavenet entered the Séminaire de Bourges in 1782 and was ordained priest in 1789. In May 1785 he had been admitted into the Society of Saint-Sulpice to do his solitude (noviciate) in Paris. In the course of the French revolution the Sulpicians, like many members of religious communities, experienced difficulties since they refused to take the oath of loyalty to the Civil Constitution of the Clergy. Non-juring priests had to go underground or into exile: Thavenet sought refuge in London. Facing an influx of French priests, the British government agreed to give a number of them permission to go to Lower Canada, temporarily changing the policy it had maintained since the conquest. On 4 June 1794 Thavenet, along with ten other Sulpicians, sailed from Portsmouth [*see* Jean-Henry-Auguste Roux*].

After an uneventful crossing the group reached Montreal on 12 September. The advent of these new members proved a stimulus to the community at the Séminaire de Saint-Sulpice, but it also created tensions that left their mark on Thavenet. The seminary was becoming Canadianized, since local candidates had been accepted to fill the vacancies and they were now in the majority. Some of them looked unfavourably upon the arrival in force of the Frenchmen. The French Sulpicians distrusted the Canadians and wanted to retain control of the seminary and to preserve links with the mother house in Paris. Such was the climate in which Thavenet started to work in Montreal.

By October 1794 Thavenet was teaching at the Collège Saint-Raphaël (which would become the Petit Séminaire de Montréal in 1806), but he did not get on well with its director, Jean-Baptiste Marchand*. In 1797 Bishop Pierre Denaut* of Quebec named him curate to assist François Cherrier* in the parish of Saint-Denis on the Richelieu. That same year he was assistant priest at Notre-Dame in Montreal. Then in 1800 he was sent as a missionary to Lac-des-Deux-Montagnes (Oka). There he learned enough Algonkin to translate works into that language and to prepare an Algonkin-French dictionary, which would remain in manuscript form. He began teaching again at the Petit Séminaire de Montréal in 1809 and in October 1815 he left for Paris.

Thavenet then embarked on a career in Europe as financial agent for several religious communities and lobbyist for the Séminaire de Saint-Sulpice of Montreal. His mission went through two phases: from 1815 to 1831 he worked in France and England, where he was preoccupied with matters related to the recovery of debts; from 1831 to 1844 he lived in Rome and kept the views of the Montreal Séminaire de Saint-Sulpice before the Curia. He took a vigorous part in the various episodes of the dispute between the bishops of Lower Canada and the Montreal Sulpicians, which regularly ended up in Rome [*see* Joseph-Vincent Quiblier*].

The religious communities in Lower Canada had some capital invested in France, particularly in annuities. During the revolution and the Napoleonic Wars not only did interest payments cease, but ownership of the annuities was called into question. After the Restoration the communities tried to recover their investments. Thavenet acted specifically for the Séminaire de Québec, the Ursulines, the Hôtel-Dieu of Montreal, the Congregation of Notre-Dame, and the Hôpital Général of Montreal. Obtaining payment of financial claims took prolonged efforts but was finally accomplished. It is calculated that the three women's communities of Montreal received 1,800,000 francs. According to historian Robert Lahaise, the infusion of capital signalled a new prosperity that resulted in a sudden upsurge of building by the Montreal communities and enabled them to modernize and enlarge their facilities. Thavenet's success even prompted some families to make use of his services. In 1826, for example, Barthélemy JOLIETTE and his brothers-in-law asked him to recover the estate left by a distant relative whose property had been sold as property of the nation.

Despite the positive results of his work and the devotion he had shown, Thavenet saw his administrative competence questioned. It was generally agreed that his bookkeeping was inadequate; Wilfrid-H. Paradis, who examined his files in Paris, considers them insufficently clear and precise. In addition Thavenet reputedly suffered from the bankruptcy of some of his agents and probably from their misappropriation of funds. In 1833–34 Abbé Thomas Maguire* spent several months with him trying unsuccessfully to make sense of his accounts; Maguire none the less thought that 150,000–160,000 francs had been lost through bankruptcies. When ordered by Archbishop Joseph SIGNAY of Quebec to render his accounts, Thavenet equivocated; he appeared unconvincing to the representatives whom Signay sent on several occasions, published a reply in 1836 to the objections of the committee examining his accounts, and seemed to believe that he was the victim of injustice and persecution because of his work with the authorities in Rome on behalf of the Séminaire de Saint-Sulpice in Montreal. Finally, in 1840 the archbishop withdrew his powers as agent, but his papers were not seized by the authorities in Rome until a few months before his death.

Thavenet had been instrumental in defending the seminary's interests. He quickly became its principal lobbyist and, being well placed in Rome, he proved a formidable adversary of its foes. During the first half of the 19th century the Sulpicians were confronted with two major problems. The first, which dated from the conquest, concerned the title to the seigneury of Île-de-Montréal: the Séminaire de Saint-Sulpice in Paris, which had been given the property, had made it over to the Montreal seminary in 1764, but the transfer had not been formally recognized by the government. This precarious situation rendered the Sulpicians cautious in managing their assets and encouraged them to remain loyal to the colonial authorities. Not until 1841 were their rights finally recognized. The second and much more complicated problem concerned the relations between the seminary and the ecclesiastical hierarchy of Lower Canada. The growth of the city and region of Montreal would lead to the creation of a new diocese in 1836 and a restructuring of authority within the church. Accustomed to being pre-eminent on the island and in the city, the Sulpicians were the losers from the start and did not look favourably on developments, particularly because they feared that a new bishop would covet their assets. This rivalry soon became linked with obvious friction between French and Canadians.

Thavenet was involved in all these problems. In 1819 he turned his attention to the rights of the Séminaire de Saint-Sulpice along with his colleague Jean-Jacques LARTIGUE, who had been sent to London. From 1821 relations between the seminary and the hierarchy deteriorated rapidly. Lartigue's elevation to the episcopacy, Bernard-Claude Panet*'s rejection of the proposed settlement of 1827 by which Saint-Sulpice would have exchanged its property for a government annuity [*see* Jean-Henry-Auguste Roux], the question of the episcopal authority to name the curé of Notre-Dame parish in Montreal, the archbishop of Quebec's refusal to allow the seminary to recruit priests in France, and the creation of a diocese in Montreal – all made it necessary for the Sulpicians to put their case in Rome. The indefatigable Thavenet served as spokesman for them there. He played a central role in the disputes, and in the opinion of those who have looked into the matter, he personally added fuel to the fire and kept dissension going through the stands he took, his voluminous correspondence, his reports (some anonymous), and his prejudices about Canadians. The fact that rivalry between the seminary and the bishop of Montreal continued long after his death, however, indicates that what was at issue went well beyond simple personality clashes: the institutional framework to be established for the Catholic population was at stake.

One last aspect of Thavenet's work must be stressed. He acted as agent of the Sulpicians and the religious communities in Montreal for the purchase of books, devotional objects, and accoutrements for use in religious rites.

Jean-Baptiste Thavenet's career illustrates well the relations that the Catholics in Lower Canada maintained with the outside world, in particular with the three key centres of London, Paris, and Rome. It also shows that in this area an individual might come to play a strategic role. Thavenet lived in Lower Canada only from 1794 to 1815 but he held an important place in its religious life.

JEAN-CLAUDE ROBERT

[The significance of Jean-Baptiste Thavenet's career is reflected in massive files at the ASSM (section 21, nos.17–18) and the Arch. du séminaire de Saint-Sulpice in Paris. The ACAM and the archives of almost all of the other religious communities which he served as agent also have correspondence files for him. W. H. Paradis, "Le nationalisme canadien dans le domaine religieux; l'affaire de l'abbé Thavenet," *RHAF*, 7 (1953–54): 465–82; 8 (1954–55):

3–24, provides a useful guide to the sources in Paris. Louis Rousseau, *La prédication à Montréal de 1800 à 1830: approche religiologique* (Montréal, 1976), describes the Séminaire de Saint-Sulpice at the beginning of the 19th century, and B. J. Young, *In its corporate capacity; the Seminary of Montreal as a business institution, 1816–1876* (Kingston, Ont., and Montreal, 1986), outlines its economic activities. The tensions that existed between Lartigue and the Sulpicians are examined in Chaussé, *Jean-Jacques Lartigue*. J.-C.R.]

J.-B. Thavenet is the author of *Résumé de la discussion des erreurs qui a cru voir dans mes comptes le comité qui a été chargé de les examiner* (Rome, 1836).

ANQ-M, CN1-295, 15 sept. 1826; CN5-25, 10 avril 1826. ASQ, Fonds Viger–Verreau, sér.O, 0141: 134. BVM-G, Coll. Gagnon, corr., J.-B. Thavenet à Morland and Co., 28 févr. 1831. Allaire, *Dictionnaire*. Dionne, *Les ecclésiastiques et les royalistes français*. [J.-]H. Gauthier, *Sulpitiana* ([2e éd.], Montréal, 1926). Robert Lahaise, *Les edifices conventuels du Vieux Montréal: aspects ethno-historiques* (Montréal, 1980). Pouliot, *Mgr Bourget et son temps*, vol.1. Rumilly, *Hist. de Montréal*, vol.2.

THAYENDANEGEA. *See* JONES, JOHN

THÉORAGWANEGON, THOMAS. *See* WILLIAMS, THOMAS

THOM, ALEXANDER, army officer, surgeon, mill owner, JP, judge, and politician; b. 26 Oct. 1775 in Scotland, probably in Aberdeen, son of Alexander Thom, farmer; m. first 5 Dec. 1811 Harriet E. Smythe (d. 1815) in Niagara (Niagara-on-the-Lake), Upper Canada, and they had children; m. secondly Eliza Montague (d. 1820); m. thirdly Betsy Smythe, and they had a son and two daughters; d. 26 Sept. 1845 in Perth, Upper Canada.

Alexander Thom graduated from King's College, Aberdeen, with an MA in 1791. On 25 Sept. 1795 he joined the 88th Foot as regimental mate, a post he assumed in the 35th Foot a year later. He became an assistant surgeon on 9 March 1797 and a surgeon on 30 Aug. 1799. In May 1803 he joined the 41st Foot, then stationed in Lower Canada, and served with it until he became a staff surgeon on 29 July 1813. His status is indicated by the fact that, in October 1812, he was a member of the official funeral cortège for Sir Isaac Brock* at Fort George (Niagara-on-the-Lake). Thom was one of those taken when the Americans captured Fort George in May 1813, and he remained in captivity until August. At that time he received permission from the Reverend John Strachan* to use his church at York (Toronto) for a hospital.

Towards the end of the war, the British government sought means to protect the Canadas' lines of communication against future invasion from the south. The St Lawrence River was patently unsafe, but Montreal and Kingston could be joined by a route along the Ottawa and Rideau rivers if this route could be settled. Thus, a scheme to promote such settlement by reliable British subjects, preferably with military experience, was born [*see* Sir Francis Cockburn*]. The first community was to be at Perth, and, as it was to be under the protection of the army during its formative years, the British government agreed to provide a surgeon for the settlers. Thom was recommended for this position on 15 Aug. 1815. That December he was apparently responsible for presenting to the provincial government a memorial on behalf of the first group of Scots settlers, who were reluctant to proceed to the Perth settlement because they understood that the land and climate there were unsatisfactory. By July 1816 he was at Perth on half pay. Retiring from this half-pay position on 15 Feb. 1817, he continued as the settlement's official doctor until military supervision ended in 1822.

Thom lived the remainder of his life at Perth, where he was a force in assuring the survival and growth of the town. In the early years his medical activities were often arduous; in September 1816, when the population was about 1,600, he requested additional medical men and urged that a hospital be built. At about this time he began to establish a business career that soon preoccupied him. He built a sawmill on the Tay River, which produced its first boards in July 1817, and soon after he built a grist-mill; in the opinion of William Bell*, the pioneer Presbyterian minister in Perth, Thom became so involved in these projects that he sometimes neglected his medical duties. In 1819 he was granted land in Perth and in the townships of Bathurst, Drummond, Sherbrooke, and Elmsley. Two years later he joined with other local citizens in petitioning for a market and fair. A magistrate from 1816, he was a member of the court of inquiry appointed by the military superintendent of the settlement, Cockburn, in 1819 that discovered the peculations of Joseph Daverne, the secretary-storekeeper for the Perth settlement. In 1824, with other magistrates, he faced the difficult task of controlling the "Ballyghiblin" riots in Ramsay Township [*see* James FitzGibbon*].

As Perth grew, Thom's influence lessened. A tory, he withdrew from the general election of 1824 in favour of fellow tory William Morris* but lost to him in 1834. Thom was elected in the Lanark by-election of February 1836 only to lose to Malcolm Cameron* and John Ambrose Hume Powell in July. According to William Bell, Thom was a decent man and the only doctor in Perth capable of rising above a concern for financial gain during the cholera epidemic of 1832. When the other medical men declined to form a board of health, Thom announced that he would serve alone, if necessary. The following year he fought a duel with Alexander McMillan "to decide an affair of honor." Shots were exchanged and, though Thom was slightly wounded, "the matter terminated amicably." Appointed a district court judge in 1835, he died in Perth ten years later.

CHARLES G. ROLAND

AO, Land record index; MS 552 (transcript). National Arch. (Washington), RG 98, 685. PAC, RG 5, A1: 13388–90; RG 8, I (C ser.), 291: 30; RG 68, General index, 1651–1841: 427, 537. Univ. of Aberdeen Library, MS and Arch. Sect. (Aberdeen, Scot.), Kings College and Univ., record of graduates, 30 March 1791. [L. W. V.] Smith, *Young Mr Smith in Upper Canada*, ed. M. L. Smith (Toronto, 1980). John Strachan, *John Strachan: documents and opinions; a selection*, ed. J. L. H. Henderson (Toronto and Montreal, 1969), 45. *Canadian Correspondent* (York [Toronto]), 26 Jan. 1833. *Globe*, 14 Oct. 1845. *Upper Canada Gazette*, 8 Dec. 1821. *Death notices of Ont.* (Reid), 13, 26, 179. *A dictionary of Scottish emigrants to Canada before confederation*, comp. Donald Whyte (Toronto, 1986), 413. William Johnston, *Roll of commissioned officers in the medical service of the British army . . .* (Aberdeen, 1917). *Legislators and legislatures of Ont.* (Forman), 1: 77. Canniff, *Medical profession in U.C.*, 650. Alexander Haydon, *Pioneer sketches in the district of Bathurst* (Toronto, 1925), 37–38, 48, 51, 147–48. J. S. McGill, *A pioneer history of the county of Lanark* (Toronto, 1968), 58. Isabel [Murphy] Skelton, *A man austere: William Bell, parson and pioneer* (Toronto, 1947), 113, 120, 124, 138–40, 263, 286.

THOMA. *See* TOMAH

THOMPSON, HANNAH MAYNARD (Pickard), novelist and housewife; b. 25 Nov. 1812 in Chester, Vt, the youngest of four children of Ebenezer Thompson and Hannah Maynard; m. 2 Oct. 1841 the Reverend Humphrey Pickard* in Boston, and they had two sons who died in early childhood; d. 11 March 1844 in Sackville, N.B.

When Hannah Maynard Thompson was about three years of age she moved with her family from Chester, Vt, to Concord, Mass., where she remained for ten years. It was here that she received her first instruction in Methodism, to which her parents were ardently committed. During her childhood years she became known for her art of story-telling and for her interest in "books, observation, conversation and reflection."

In the early spring of 1826, when Hannah was 13, Mr and Mrs Thompson moved to Wilbraham, Mass., to take charge of the Students' Boarding Hall associated with the Wesleyan Academy there. Hannah attended the academy, where, in addition to the regular subjects taught, she began a formal study of Methodism. Two years later her family moved to Boston; she joined them in 1829 and resided in the capital, except for an interval at Wilbraham, until her marriage in 1841.

In Boston, where she taught for a time, Hannah Thompson's interest in writing flourished. She wrote poetry, sketches (a favourite genre of the period), as well as prose fragments. Some of the sketches which are included in the *Memoir and writings of Mrs. Hannah Maynard Pickard* reveal her deep religious ardour and a growing appreciation of nature. "The little remembrancer," "Farewell of the closing year," "Beauty of contentment," "'Looking unto Jesus,'" and "The spider" are among the titles. The fragments, all of about one page, deal with such subjects as "Evening," "Man alone ungrateful," "The stormbird's flight," and "Prayer." In Boston she also wrote and published her most ambitious works of prose, *Procrastination; or, Maria Louisa Winslow* (1840) and *The widow's jewels; in two stories* (1844), both of which appeared anonymously as "By a lady."

Procrastination is a moral tale of 115 pages in which the certainty of the uncertainty of life and "the danger of delaying its highest interests" are the central themes. Maria, a "fashionably educated" 17-year-old who is fond of Boston's gay winter season, finds herself unable to learn from the religious experiences of others. Because of her predilection for new clothes, dancing, and fashionable parties, she fails, through delay, to bring happiness to Elizabeth, a sick friend. She becomes suddenly ill herself and dies, still a victim of her inability to "fix upon [her] thoughts the dangers of that evil most fatal to the soul – procrastination." The author asserts that the story is true and that only the names and dates have been changed. *The widow's jewels*, which appeared posthumously, is addressed to "little readers" and in its two stories, "Robert McCoy" and "Dennis Brooks," the author endeavours to bring home to new readers the fact that "there are gems of greater price" and these gems are the children of God.

In 1838 Hannah Thompson was invited to be preceptress in the Wilbraham academy. After some hesitation she accepted. According to her memorialist, "Her success was most signal and gratifying, and far greater than her modesty led her at any time to hope." Her work involved the supervision and instruction of over one hundred young women "of all moods and manners." It was at Wilbraham that she first met her future husband, Humphrey Pickard, then a student at Wesleyan University in Middletown, Conn. Hannah and Humphrey kept in touch by letter after his return to New Brunswick.

On 18 March 1841 Hannah's mother died. Following this loss, which affected her deeply as recorded in her letters to Pickard and in her journal, Hannah Thompson's life took on new dimensions. At the end of the spring term in 1841 she gave up her teaching position at the Wesleyan Academy and returned to Boston to keep house for her father. Her importance in the life of the academy was such that the principal travelled to Boston to urge her to return and delay her forthcoming marriage to Humphrey Pickard. She refused and the wedding took place in the Bromfield Street Church, Boston, on 2 Oct. 1841. Soon after, the couple left for Saint John, N.B.

On 7 Sept. 1842 the Pickards' first son, Edward Dwight, was born in Chelsea, Mass., where Hannah was visiting with relatives. She and the baby returned to Saint John on 29 October. Shortly afterwards, Mr Pickard was named principal of the Wesleyan Academy, newly built in Sackville [*see* Charles Frederick Allison*]. The Pickards moved there in January 1843. From then on Hannah's time was consumed with her new life in Sackville and all the demands implicit in the founding of an educational institution. She not only supported her husband's responsibilities as an administrator and a Methodist preacher, but also took charge of the domestic arrangements for the academy's students.

In 1844 the Pickards were expecting their second child. A boy, Charles Frederick Allison, was born on 19 February. He lived just a week. In less than a month, on 11 March, Hannah Pickard died at the age of 32. "Her sainted spirit is at rest," wrote the Reverend Samuel Dwight Rice*, agent of the academy. His was but one expression of the widespread grief felt by the Methodist community of which Hannah Pickard was a dedicated and well-loved member. Her elder child survived her by only two years.

DOUGLAS LOCHHEAD

An appreciation of Hannah Maynard Thompson by her brother-in-law, Edward Otheman, entitled *Memoir and writings of Mrs. Hannah Maynard Pickard; late wife of Rev. Humphrey Pickard, A.M., principal of the Wesleyan academy at Mount Allison, Sackville, N.B.*, was published in Boston in 1845. It contains much correspondence by Hannah and Humphrey Pickard and others, as well as poems, sketches, and fragments selected from Hannah's writings.

Cyclopædia of Canadian biog. (Rose and Charlesworth), 1: 140–42. *N.B. vital statistics, 1842–45* (Johnson). Watters, *Checklist of Canadian literature* (1972).

THOMPSON, TOLER (Tolar), agricultural improver; b. *c.* 1780 in Upper Sackville (N.B.), only child of John Thompson and Mary Toler, widow of John Grace; m. Alice Charters, and they had eight children; d. 23 June 1846, and was buried in Sackville Parish, N.B.

Toler Thompson is remembered in New Brunswick for his efforts to improve the Tantramar marshes in the Chignecto Isthmus. These marshes had been farmed to a limited extent by Acadians from the late 17th century until their expulsion from the region in 1755 [*see* Robert Monckton*]. Homesteads had been built on dry ground and some lower, flooded land had been made arable by means of dykes and arrangements of flap gates (*aboiteaux*). The gates were balanced to close under a seating head of tide and to open for the release of imponded fresh water when the tide dropped. The first English-speaking settlers, mainly from New England and later from Yorkshire, England [*see* Charles Dixon*], followed the same pattern of land use. To some extent, however, the region remained boggy into the 19th century. In 1816 the Methodist missionary Joshua MARSDEN noted that a journey to Tantramar involved "both trouble and fatigue, as the marsh was frequently overflowed . . . I was obliged on these occasions to have a guide, who rode with a long pole in his hand, which as the waters we rode through were muddy, he kept plunging to the bottom, a little ahead of his horse, to ascertain the direction of the creeks, and that we might not unawares plunge into any of them."

Of the second generation of marsh farmers, Thompson initiated valuable improvements in land use. These included definition of the topography, or the potential drainage pattern, of the marshes, excavation of drainage ditches (some of which served also as transportation canals), and construction of roads. He also developed a method of renewing the fertility of the marshlands which involved periodic flooding with silt-laden water from the Bay of Fundy. Upon precipitation of suspended solids and nutrients, the salt water was drained away. Residents of the Tantramar area still acknowledge indebtedness to Thompson for the creation of dry, wealth-producing pasture and crop land.

Details of Thompson's activities are scarce. When applying to Surveyor General George Sproule* for a grant of land in 1817, he indicated that he had undertaken to build a road from Great Bridge River to Point Midgic (Midgic) and had already spent £364 of his own money on it. In a supporting document William Botsford*, member of a prominent local family, described Thompson as "a person of enterprise and industry" who had been engaged for about three years in cutting a large ditch at the head of Sackville marsh "which has and will be attended with great public benefit, and has cost him much time and expense." That year Thompson obtained a government grant of £100 towards his road. In 1817–18 he was employed in cutting a canal from Mud Creek to Rush Lake, under the direction of the supervisors of the "great road" and the commissioners of sewers for the region; he was still trying to obtain full payment for his services in 1822. In 1821 he applied to the government for further assistance in constructing his road, on which he had spent another £136. He noted that his improvements enabled settlers to take up ungranted lands, facilitated the transport of timber and other materials, let in the tide "which overflows certain grounds, and the mud that is thereby left, will make good and beneficial Meadow Lands," and prevented the flooding that had previously damaged the main road to Halifax. The result of his petition is not known.

Popular tradition has it that Thompson was the grandson of the Irish peer John Toler, 1st Earl of Norbury. According to this account, which is somewhat confused and has many variations, Toler's daughter Mary eloped with John Grace, a groom or coachman in her father's employ, and came to the Chignecto area of Nova Scotia, where her husband drowned three years later. She then married John Thompson, a Yorkshireman, at Upper Sackville in New Brunswick. Attractive though the tradition is, it would seem to be without foundation since John Toler did not marry until 1778, about two years before Toler Thompson's birth.

R. J. CUNNINGHAM

[Family traditions concerning Toler Thompson were provided by Dr J. Toler Thompson of Moncton, N.B., in a series of interviews with the author. An undated notebook in Dr Thompson's possession, apparently compiled in the early years of the 20th century by another descendant, Cogswell A. Sharpe, supplied further details. R.J.C.]

PANB, RG 4, RS24, S29-P5, S30-P38. Westmorland Hist. Soc. (Dorchester, N.B.), Grave marker for Tolar Thompson. Joshua Marsden, *The narrative of a mission to Nova Scotia, New Brunswick, and the Somers Islands; with a tour to Lake Ontario* . . . (Plymouth Dock [Plymouth], Eng., 1816; repr. New York, 1966). W. C. Milner, *History of Sackville, New Brunswick* (Sackville, 1934); "Records of Chignecto," N.S. Hist. Soc., *Coll.*, 15 (1911): 74–75. C. W. Moffat, "Shall we establish an endowment to the memory of Tolar Thompson?" *Tribune-Post* (Sackville), 2 June 1947.

THOMSON, CHARLES EDWARD POULETT, 1st Baron SYDENHAM, colonial administrator; b. 13 Sept. 1799 at Waverley Abbey, England, third son and youngest of nine children of John Poulett Thomson and Charlotte Jacob; d. unmarried 19 Sept. 1841 in Kingston, Upper Canada.

Charles Edward Poulett Thomson's father was a partner in J. Thomson, T. Bonar and Company of London and St Petersburg (Leningrad, U.S.S.R.), for several generations a principal merchant house in the Russian-Baltic trade. After attending private schools until age 16, Thomson entered the family firm at St Petersburg. In 1817 he came home because of poor health and embarked on a prolonged tour of southern Europe. Following a stint in the firm's London office he returned to Russia in 1821 and over the next three years travelled extensively in eastern Europe. He established permanent residence in London in 1824 but frequently visited the Continent, especially Paris.

As "the youngest and prettiest child of the family," according to a brother, George Julius Poulett Scrope (Thomson), Thomson had been "the spoilt pet of all" and early evinced self-confidence and ambition. The diarist Charles Cavendish Fulke Greville described him as "the greatest coxcomb I ever saw, and the vainest dog." Certainly Thomson aped the manners of the aristocracy. His "love of great society" earned him the censure of his fellow merchants and members of his own family. Single, chiefly – his brother claimed – because he was in failing health and incessantly occupied, he was known as a sensualist. In the Canadas his establishment would, in the words of the author John Richardson*, "acknowledge . . . the sway of at least one mistress." Married or single, all women "excited his homage," but the "attentions" he devoted to a married woman in Toronto, Richardson recorded, "were so very marked, that the scandalous circles rang with them." He was also a gourmet who would try to introduce "French cookery" in the colonies.

Thomson was not content with the career marked out for him, and he was not a particularly successful businessman. In 1825 he was saved from disaster in a speculative venture only by the caution of an elder brother, Andrew Henry. Although fluent in French, German, Russian, and Italian, Thomson was barred from the foreign service, which was staffed by the great landed families. Nor was he sufficiently wealthy to buy his way into the aristocracy. Through his early support for parliamentary reform and liberal measures such as the ballot and the abolition of the corn laws, Thomson would reveal the resentment and frustration engendered by his uncertain status in the aristocratic society he frequented.

An early advocate of free trade, Thomson naturally became a friend of the Benthamites and was elected to the Political Economy Club. In 1825 Joseph Hume helped him secure the liberal nomination in Dover, and Jeremy Bentham canvassed for him during the election of May 1826. Thomson won, but only at great financial cost, and his election angered his family, who opposed his liberal views. In the House of Commons, according to one critic, Thomson was looked upon as a "bore"; his voice was "thin and effeminate" and his personal appearance "characteristic of a barber's apprentice." He rarely spoke on the "exciting party questions of the day," his brother Scrope noted, and his speeches on commercial matters were considered dogmatic. None the less, Thomson found an important aristocratic patron in John Charles Spencer, Viscount Althorp, who became chancellor of the Exchequer in the Whig administration formed in late 1830; he secured for Thomson the posts of vice-president of the Board of Trade and treasurer of the navy. Since Thomson's superior at the board, Lord Auckland, was a relative nonentity, Thomson conducted its business. Working closely with Althorp, he helped draft the abortive free trade budget of 1831, thus incurring the undying enmity of protectionists and completely alienating his family. His views were, however, popular with the manufacturing interests in the north of England; although returned for Dover in 1830, 1831, and 1832, he transferred to Manchester, where he was elected without campaigning in 1832 and re-elected in 1834 and 1837. From June until November 1834 and again in the Whig administration formed in April 1835, Thomson served as president of the Board of Trade, opening the department to free traders, making numerous minor reductions in customs regulations, and negotiating trade agreements with several European governments. Thomson expanded the responsibilities of the board and exercised a new control over private bills, especially railway and bank charters; when he sought to exert his authority to supervise colonial legislation, he plunged the Colonial Office into a bitter dispute with the Upper Canadian House of Assembly over currency and banking legislation.

In general, Thomson was not directly involved in formulating the cabinet's response to the political crisis in the Canadas. When news of the rebellions there reached London, he was, according to Lord Howick, "all for executions." Although once close to Lord Durham [LAMBTON], he was unsympathetic when Durham resigned after the cabinet failed to defend his ordinance exiling rebels to Bermuda; initially he apparently did not view the Durham report with much enthusiasm. In mid March 1839 he served on the cabinet committee that adopted a proposal for a federal union of the Canadas recommended by Edward Ellice*. After that scheme was abandoned, however, he voted with a slim majority in favour of a legislative union along the lines suggested by Durham.

Thomson became increasingly disillusioned with his position in the government, especially when passed over for the chancellorship of the Exchequer in early 1839. His chief complaint, however, was the cabinet's failure to adopt a major change in economic policy. The conventional Whig approach to finance had left the government virtually bankrupt, and Thomson knew that reforms were necessary. He also knew that he could not persuade the Commons to adopt them and consequently, when finally offered the Exchequer in the summer of 1839, he declined. On 6 September, over the opposition of timber merchants, he was commissioned governor-in-chief of British North America. The Canadian rebels, he predicted, "*can't* be more unreasonable than the ultras on both sides of the House of Commons." He insisted upon the unusually high salary of £7,000, an outfit of £3,000, and substantial casual expenses, and he received the pledge of a peerage if he was successful in his administration.

Before departing Thomson met with Durham and received his blessing. Thomson's primary goal was to get the support of the Canadians for a union acceptable to the British government, and to persuade them of the benefits of union he carried with him the promise of an imperial guarantee for a large loan. He landed at Quebec on 19 Oct. 1839 and took over the administration of Lower Canada from Sir John Colborne*. Thomson was aware that his appointment was viewed with dismay by colonial merchants. The *Pictou Observer* of Nova Scotia described him as a "selfish, prejudiced Russian timber merchant" and wished him "a good sousing in his favourite Baltic tar, with such a supply of feathers as may fortify him against the natural and political winter he has to encounter." Yet, after his first levee, on 21 October, Thomson claimed that his reception, even among the Quebec merchants, had been "certainly good."

On 23 October Thomson settled in Montreal and reported that, although the province was "quiet," only the power of the government kept French Canadians from "acts of insubordination." To discourage disaffection he refused to release from prison the Patriote leader Denis-Benjamin Viger* and had Augustin-Norbert Morin* arrested; he was, however, forced to release Morin because the original warrant for high treason lacked supporting testimony. On 11 November Thomson convened the Special Council, an appointed body of men of proven loyalty which had replaced the legislature after the rebellion of 1837. Only a rump of 15 members braved the snows to assemble in Montreal, and Thomson allowed them merely two days to debate the question of union. The terms he proposed were most unfair to Lower Canada – equal representation for the less populous Upper Canada, the charging of its higher debt against the united province, and a permanent civil list against which the Lower Canadian assembly had long fought – but only three members voted against them. Although Thomson reported that the matter of union was "over with," John NEILSON and others opposed to union raised petitions against it while the francophone press directly attacked "le poulet," as Thomson was called.

Inevitably, Thomson reacted angrily to such attacks. "If it were possible," he wrote in November 1839, "the best thing for Lower Canada would be a despotism for ten years more." Even before leaving Britain, according to the London *Colonial Gazette*, he had been "convinced by Lord Durham's Report, despatches, and *conversation*, that French ascendancy in Lower Canada is simply impossible" and had indicated that he would "uphold the principle of ascendancy for the majority with regard to all Canada." An admirer of France and French culture, Thomson was disturbed neither by the use of French, which he spoke fluently, nor by the efforts of French Canadians to preserve their heritage. However, like Durham, he believed in the innate superiority of British institutions and felt that they could be adopted by peoples with cultural traditions other than British.

Again like Durham, he thought that it was undesirable – and ultimately impossible – for French Canadians to isolate themselves in British North America; if they did, they would "grow up in their national prejudices and habits without any sympathy with their fellow Colonists." He was particularly scornful of the habitants – "a People not incapable of improvement, but still only to be very slowly & gradually improved in their Habits & Education." Although he blamed the Roman Catholic Church for keeping its faithful in ignorance and thus under its control, he was not anti-Catholic. He foresaw giving to that church a share of the proceeds from the clergy reserves, hitherto reserved to the Church of England, and upheld the claims of the Sulpicians to compensation for lost seigneurial rights; indeed, he admired the Sulpicians, most of whom were immigrants from France, finding in them a "reasoned, and, therefore, a steady attachment to . . . British rule, and a thorough contempt for those miserable antipathies of race which so universally prevail among the native Canadians."

In November Thomson departed for Toronto, where he assumed control of the government of Upper Canada on the 22nd. There was considerable hostility to union among officials in the colony, particularly those resident in Toronto, and when Thomson took the oaths of office, John Macaulay* noted, he was greeted with "an abortion of a cheer which was worse than silence." Thomson sought to dissipate opposition by meeting privately with members of the legislature, which was convened for 3 December. Within Upper Canada Durham's report had unleashed a broadly based campaign for reform, and Thomson correctly perceived that the "foolish cry for 'responsible Govt.'" had gained support because of Lieutenant Governor Sir George Arthur*'s "opposition to all reform and . . . his treating all those who opposed the official party as Democrats and Rebels." Thomson denounced "any scheme which would render the power of the Governor subordinate to that of a Council," but he had no objection to Durham's "practical views of Colonial Government" and promised to administer local matters "in accordance with the wishes of the Legislature." On this basis he secured the support of the reform minority in the assembly. To the conservative majority Thomson proffered assurance that union and the imperial guarantee of a loan would relieve the colony's financial embarrassments, and with Arthur's assistance he won over many moderates.

On 13 December Thomson's proposals were approved in the Legislative Council, 14 to 8, over the vehement opposition of Bishop John Strachan*. In the assembly Thomson had to work through Attorney General Christopher Alexander HAGERMAN, who initially opposed union, and Solicitor General William Henry Draper*, who did not like Thomson's terms. In the previous session the assembly had accepted union on condition that the seat of government be in Upper Canada, that Upper Canada receive more seats in the united legislature than Lower Canada, and that English be the only language of the legislature and courts. Although Thomson rejected conditions so "unjust and oppressive" to the French Canadians, union passed on 19 December. The conservatives continued their efforts to modify Thomson's terms. On 13 Jan. 1840 John Solomon CARTWRIGHT embodied their demands in an address that was carried 28 to 17, and Thomson reluctantly agreed that written records would be kept in English only, that there would be a property qualification for assemblymen, and that legislative councillors would be appointed for life. However, he refused to select Toronto as the seat of government, leaving the choice of a site "to be regulated by circumstances."

Thomson's commitment to integrating the French Canadians into the union had led him to seek for the minority "their fair share of the representation." The terms of union which he extracted from Upper Canada were the best he could get. The proscription of French in written documents was indefensible and ultimately unenforceable, and the equality of representation of the two Canadas was shortsighted, since Upper Canada was bound to grow more rapidly than Lower Canada. The decision to transfer the Upper Canadian debt to the United Province was also unfair, but Thomson correctly pointed out that the sums expended on "the great canals" were "of no less advantage to the Lower than to the Upper Province" and that the costs of completing the canal system would be "very trifling" in view of the long-term return on the investment.

On 23 Jan. 1840 Thomson submitted to Secretary of State Lord John Russell a draft bill apparently prepared with the assistance of Chief Justice James Stuart*. In general it sought to introduce union "with as little interference as possible" in existing institutions. It differed from a bill prepared by the Whig government the previous year, by leaving the structure of the Legislative Council unchanged, creating 76 single-member constituencies for the Legislative Assembly, imposing a £500 qualification for assemblymen, providing for publication of all records in English (although debates could be conducted in either language), and preserving the township form of municipal government in Upper Canada and extending it to Lower Canada. Thomson suggested that clauses dealing with the civil list be framed in London but insisted that it was unsafe "to leave the Government dependent on the Assembly."

A few days later Thomson also sent home his measure to deal with "the root of all the troubles" of Upper Canada, the clergy reserves [*see* John Strachan]. One-half of the income from the reserves was to be divided equally between the churches of England and Scotland and the other half distributed among the other denominations on the same basis. Strachan and the "family compact" tories, as well as doctrinaire reformers, opposed Thomson's bill, but an overwhelming majority in the assembly rallied to its support. In fact, as Thomson's civil secretary, Thomas William Clinton Murdoch, noted, the assembly "exhibited for the first time in Canada the working of a government majority on the same principles on which the parliamentary business had been conducted in the mother country." Although Thomson rejected the assembly's request to see any dispatches he had received on the subject of responsible government, he had, in Murdoch's view, "conceded the principle of responsibility as far as it had ever been demanded by the moderate reformers." Thomson strengthened his government by raising Hagerman to the bench, replacing him with Draper, and appointing Robert Baldwin* solicitor general. In early 1840 he wooed the large Canada Conference of the Methodist Episcopal Church by insisting that it, rather than the British Wesleyan Conference, receive government funds and by supporting Upper Canada Academy at Cobourg. He was rewarded with the consistent loyalty of Egerton Ryerson*'s *Christian Guardian* (Toronto), which Thomson described as "the only decent paper in both Canadas." On 10 Feb. 1840 Thomson prorogued the legislature and declared to Russell that if his union and clergy reserve bills – "the Reform Bill and Irish Church of Canada" – were accepted, "I will guarantee you Upper Canada."

Thomson was less optimistic about the prospect of reconciling French Canadians to union. On 18 February he left Toronto and in one of the most rapid journeys ever made by sleigh arrived in Montreal 36 hours later. He insisted that Lower Canada was quiet, that support for union was strong among moderates, and that Vital Têtu, a prominent merchant selected to carry anti-union petitions to London, was "a person of no importance"; yet privately he admitted to Russell that French Canadians would use representative institutions to resist any "practical measure of improvement." He therefore shoved through the Special Council a series of bills to facilitate union: they incorporated Quebec and Montreal, reorganized the judicial system, established a more efficient police force, and provided for the gradual extinction of seigneurial dues in Montreal.

Despite a "few inaccuracies" and an insufficient civil list, Thomson affirmed that the draft of the union bill which he received from Russell in May "will do." To ensure that French Canadian assemblymen imbibed "English Ideas" he chose Kingston as the capital of the united province, but to obtain French Canadian support he offered Louis-Hippolyte La Fontaine* the post of solicitor general, although La Fontaine declined the post. Having been pressured by Bishop Jean-Jacques LARTIGUE and the French Canadian élite of Montreal, Thomson released Denis-Benjamin Viger from prison in May, and in June he let lapse the suspension of habeas corpus by which means Viger had been held. When members of the English party protested compensation to the Séminaire de Saint-Sulpice for extinction of its seigneurial rights, Thomson denounced the "spirit of intolerance" shown by the British minority, and when he appointed the first corporations for Montreal and Quebec, he ensured that French Canadians were represented, albeit not equally, and selected René-Édouard Caron* as mayor of Quebec. The preference in patronage that he gave to the British of Lower Canada was in part forced on Thomson; he offered positions to French Canadians "whose loyalty is undoubted" and who accepted union as a *fait accompli*, such as Alexandre-Maurice Delisle* or Melchior-Alphonse de Salaberry*, but few would risk political stigma as *vendus*. Nevertheless, Thomson's efforts probably played a part in persuading moderate reformers such as La Fontaine to accept union and to work within the united legislature to achieve their goals.

To his "infinite annoyance," since he was overwhelmed with work and subject to recurring attacks of gout, with which he had been afflicted since age 30, Thomson was forced to depart on 3 July for Nova Scotia and mediate a dispute between Lieutenant Governor Sir Colin CAMPBELL, "playing the dunce at Halifax," and the House of Assembly. En route he spent two days in the Eastern Townships passing "under triumphal arches." He assumed control of the government of Nova Scotia on 9 July and recommended remodelling the Executive Council to include leading members from both sides in the assembly and compelling the chief government officials to sit in that house. Even Joseph Howe* proclaimed that Thomson was advising "exactly what the friends of what is called Responsible Government would have created." Indeed, Howe acknowledged that by including the leading public officers and heads of department in the council Thomson had made "an important refinement" to his own proposals. Ultimately Campbell's refusal to countenance Thomson's recommendations resulted in his replacement by Lord Falkland [Cary*].

In late July Thomson visited Prince Edward Island and met with Lieutenant Governor Sir Charles Augustus FitzRoy*. Soon after, he accompanied Lieutenant Governor Sir John Harvey* of New Brunswick on a whirlwind tour of Saint John and Fredericton and returned to Halifax full of praise for the "entire harmony" which Harvey, "the Pearl of Civil Governors" in his estimation, had established between the executive and the legislature. Later, however, he changed his view. Faced by acts of aggression from the United States, Thomson had pressured the British government into increasing substantially its garrisons in British North America and its expenditures on defensive works. In late 1840 Harvey's indecision about the use to be made of troops sent to his command, at his own request, infuriated the more bellicose governor-in-chief, who successfully recommended Harvey's dismissal. In April 1841 the governor insisted that the British government take an aggressive position with the United States, "whatever the consequences," in seeking the release of Alexander McLeod*, an Upper Canadian wrongly jailed in New York State for participation in the sinking of the rebel supply ship *Caroline* in December 1837. By stiffening the resolve of the British government, he contributed to the satisfactory negotiation of the Webster-Ashburton Treaty of 1842.

On 19 Aug. 1840 the governor had left Montreal for the Eastern Townships and Upper Canada, visiting more than 40 towns and selecting candidates for the forthcoming elections to the united parliament. During the trip he received a copy of the union act passed by the imperial parliament and discovered that, in order to secure the support of Sir Robert Peel and the Conservative opposition, Russell had omitted from the act arrangements for the creation of municipal institutions and had agreed to alter the distribution of seats in Lower Canada to inflate the number of English constituencies. He told Russell bitterly that he would deplore those concessions "to the end of my life" and considered resigning. He was mollified, however, when he learned of his elevation to the peerage as Baron Sydenham on 19 August, and he declared his intention to "stay and meet the first Parliament." He also learned that Russell had been compelled to modify his Clergy Reserves Act and allot to the Church of England what Sydenham believed was a "monstrous proportion" of the revenue derived from the reserves. None the less, after a personal appeal to the leadership of the Church of Scotland and to Egerton Ryerson, he remained confident of his ability to "beat both the Ultra Tories and the extreme Radicals" in Upper Canada in the forthcoming elections. He was less certain, however, of Lower Canada, where French Canadian leaders were determined to sabotage the union. Even after reshaping the electoral boundaries of Montreal and Quebec so that both would return representatives from the British commercial community, he predicted that the elections would be "bad" in the lower province, because French Canadians had "forgotten nothing and learnt nothing by the rebellion." Sydenham therefore used the Special Council to secure passage of 32 measures that he knew the French Canadians would oppose in the united legislature, including one establishing municipal institutions and another a system of land registration long demanded by the British minority.

Sydenham proclaimed the union on 10 Feb. 1841, the anniversary of the Treaty of Paris (1763) and of Queen Victoria's marriage (1840). He had visited Kingston in September 1840 to "patch up a place . . . to meet in the Spring" but, partly because of "a very distressing illness," was unable to move there until May 1841. His governmental tasks included completing arrangements with the British Treasury for a loan of £1,500,000 to pay off the accumulated debt of the Canadas and finish public works such as the Welland Canal. Even more time-consuming and laborious was the "entire reconstruction" of the administrative departments. Complaining of "the total want of system and power in the conduct of Government, and of the defective state of Departmental administration," Sydenham agreed with one of Durham's most important conclusions: the colonial government had to be reorganized to give the executive more effective control over the assembly. In line with recommendations by Durham and with principles, reflecting British practice, laid down by Russell, Sydenham argued that "the Offices of Govt [should be] arranged so as to ensure responsibility in those who are at their head and an efficient discharge of their duties to the Governor and the Public." Utilizing studies on Lower Canada commissioned by Durham, and on Upper Canada prepared by a royal commission established in 1839 by Arthur, he systematically erected a new departmental framework, reallocating functions among existing offices, particularly the Executive Council, the civil and provincial secretaries, the inspector general, and the receiver general, and creating new offices, such as the Crown Lands Department and the Board of Works. In July 1841 he announced the union perfected, with "Effective Departments for every branch of the public service." Since, on his insistence, the act of union had given to the executive the sole right to initiate money bills, the new system created a more centralized and efficient form of government, but it also made essential the command of a majority in the assembly.

For more than a year Sydenham had been preparing for what he described on 5 Feb. 1841 as the restoration to the people of control "over their own affairs, which is deemed the highest privilege of Britons." Elections were held in March and April. Sydenham carefully orchestrated the campaign, with the aid in Lower Canada of his military secretary, Major Thomas Edmund Campbell*, and assisted in Upper Canada by Murdoch, his other private secretary James Hopkirk, Draper, and Provincial Secretary Samuel Bealey Harrison*. He chose returning officers favourable to the government, issued land deeds to supporters and denied them to opponents, thus disenfranchising the latter, handed out promises of pensions and government patronage, browbeat recalcitrant officials into supporting the administration, and distributed polling-booths and troops where they would most benefit his sympathizers. In Upper Canada the collapse of the "family compact" party and the support of all reformers readily secured him a large majority. In Lower Canada, where the election was marked by considerable violence, he carried nearly one-half of the seats by appealing to the loyalty of the British minority, whose representation had been inflated by the act of union, and particularly by cultivating the business and Eastern Townships votes through attempts to repeal the imperial duty on grain and prohibit the entry into the Canadas of American produce. When accused by one Alexander Gillespie of interfering in the electoral process, Sydenham retorted: "If he means that I *personally* interfere he is quite misinformed, but the Govt. officials must try to get seats in Parliament . . . and they surely have a right to look after their elections."

The victory was extremely precarious since Sydenham led a hodgepodge of anglophones from various political backgrounds. About one-quarter of them were officials amenable to executive discipline, but, without independents such as Malcolm Cameron* or Isaac Buchanan*, Sydenham's administration could not retain the confidence of the House of Assembly. Moreover, a substantial proportion of members, many of whom had been selected as candidates by Sydenham personally, such as Stewart Derbishire* and Hamilton Hartley Killaly*, lacked political experience and had little influence in the legislature. Sydenham's support, therefore, fluctuated wildly during the first session, convened on 14 June 1841. His bill establishing a single bank of issue for the colony went down to defeat, but on almost every other matter he "came off triumphant." He embarked upon a general plan of public works, revised the local customs regulations, adjusted the currency, established elected municipal councils for Upper Canada, regulated the sale of wild lands, and created a system of common schools. Sydenham not only decided what measures to present to the legislature, but also, according to Murdoch, planned "the manner of introducing them, and the means of preventing or defeating opposition."

Sydenham's most serious adversaries were the radical reformers of Upper Canada, led initially by Robert Baldwin and Francis Hincks*. Although they had supported union, they were disillusioned by Sydenham's clergy reserves bill, which they considered a "poor return" for their support, and by Sir George Arthur's distribution of patronage. William Warren BALDWIN had quickly determined that Sydenham would be "one of the feeble and useless 'no party men'" and, since Sydenham had refused to head a unified reform movement, Hincks and Baldwin had sought to construct one in alliance with French Canadian reformers. On the eve of the meeting of the legislature Baldwin demanded that the Executive Council be reconstituted on a party basis, and Sydenham therefore dismissed him as solicitor general. During the session reformers repeatedly sought to embarrass the government, and on 3 September Baldwin tried to force a firm commitment from it to responsible government. Although Sydenham refused to bind himself to following the assembly's dictates on every issue and continued to play a major role in shaping the policies and personnel of the government, his ministers increasingly functioned like a cabinet (as Sydenham himself described them) and indicated to the assembly that they would resign if they lost the confidence of the house. Sydenham, too, was aware that he could not "continue the administration of public affairs with honour to himself, or advantage to the people," if his government was unable to retain that confidence.

Sydenham gave the impression that he expected his system to endure for at least a decade. In August 1841 he wrote to a brother that he would leave behind "a ministry with an avowed and recognized majority capable of doing what they think right, and not to be upset by my successor." In fact, his ministry was on the verge of disintegration by the end of the first session. Without virtually unanimous support from the British majority, it could not survive, but to maintain that support, noted Colborne, now Lord Seaton, Sydenham had to act "the part of a divided Tory in the Lower Province and of a Liberal in the Upper." As French Canadian opposition to the union diminished, the loose bonds of Sydenham's coalition disintegrated, and the more natural party loyalties among the British reasserted themselves. A perspicacious Seaton remarked that no governor could retain control "unless the machine is constantly worked by an Artist as clever and unscrupulous as the one that contrived to secure the majority of the first session." Sydenham did not live to see the collapse of his system. His health continued to deteriorate, and in July 1841 he submitted his resignation. He requested a GCB (civil division), which was awarded on 19 August. A few days after receiving news of the distinction and dissolving the legislature, Sydenham had a riding accident. A wound became infected, and on 19 September he died, in agony, of lockjaw. According to the Kingston *Chronicle & Gazette*, between 6,000 and 7,000 people "lined the road in dense masses" to witness his interment at St George's Church on 24 September. The anglophone newspapers praised Sydenham's "urbanity and condescension of manner," and Egerton Ryerson undoubtedly spoke for the majority in extolling "the noble mind which conceived those improvements and originated the institutions which will form a golden era in the annals of Canadian history." In private, "family compact" members such as John Beverley Robinson* denounced "that despicable Poulett Thomson" and predicted that "it will be long before the mischief can be remedied." The francophone press, remembering "his crimes," wasted little space lamenting the architect of what they saw as oppression.

Ryerson admitted that "the revolutions of time" were essential for "an adequate appreciation" of Sydenham's government. Yet Sydenham has remained controversial. In the early 20th century anglophone historians generally praised him. The revisionists have been less kind; Irving Martin Abella's Sydenham is "a ruthless Machiavellian, unprincipled and cunning, selfish and egotistic, autocratic, narrow-minded, and unbelievably vain." The best that even the most sympathetic French Canadian historian, Jacques Monet, can say about him is that he was "gouty, impatient, and on occasion, for long weeks at a time, bedridden." Undeniably, Sydenham found life in the colonies dull, and he had considerable disdain for those he had been sent to govern. When the Toronto *Herald* issued a sheet of doggerel criticizing him, he ordered "extra copies to be placed on his drawingroom tables for the amusement of New Year's callers, to whom he read them himself." Yet there is also abundant evidence of Sydenham's personal charm and his charisma in attracting support from such diverse personalities as Ryerson and Hincks. Despite frequent illnesses, he did not neglect official duties; he once wrote that he would frequently "breathe, eat, drink and sleep on nothing but government and politics," and he was responsible for more provincial legislation than any predecessor or successor. Many politically inspired measures – including the municipal incorporation acts, the Common School Act, and the language and judicial legislation – were subsequently amended substantially or repealed, but the administrative structure he created remained nearly intact during the union. As a former member of the British cabinet, Sydenham possessed unusual influence with imperial authorities. Thus he could force the Post Office Department to reduce postal rates considerably despite opposition from the deputy postmaster general, Thomas Allen Stayner*, and he repeatedly overrode efforts by the Treasury to reduce colonial expenditures. Although he believed that the imperial government must lay down the general principles regulating trade, he recognized "the great inconvenience" of its originating all changes and sought to give the local legislatures power to amend regulations. He was also fortunate in receiving the consistent support of Lord John Russell, who dominated the Colonial Office and the cabinet.

Most of Sydenham's contemporaries assumed that he introduced responsible government, and critics such as Seaton argued that he had made it "impossible to resist the demands" of a majority in the assembly. The first generation of historians of Canada, notably John Charles Dent* and Adam Shortt*, accepted that view, but more recently Kenneth N. Windsor, Donald Swainson, and Ged Martin, among others, have disagreed. The revisionist argument, however, places too much emphasis on the refusal by Russell and Sydenham to commit themselves to the principle of responsible government. The London *Colonial Gazette* pointed out in September 1839 that, "notwithstanding Lord John Russell's declaration against Responsible Government *by that name*, Mr. Thompson adopts the views of Lord Durham and accepts that the 'administration of local affairs [must be] in constant harmony with the opinion of the majority of the representative body.'" Sydenham did try to resist recognizing what he called the "absurd sense" of responsible government, as put forward by Robert Baldwin, according to which he must follow the advice of the majority on all matters, but then no governor prior to confederation could make such a commitment.

Revisionists also criticize Sydenham's intervention in the political process. His partisan use of the apparatus of state was, however, in line with British practice even in the post-reform era, although by acting as his own prime minister and party leader Sydenham involved the crown more directly than did the monarch in Britain or would Sydenham's successors. To some extent, as Murdoch had declared, government interference was an inevitable by-product of Sydenham's system of responsible government. So long as Sydenham worked through ministers responsible for his actions and supported by the assembly, nothing in his actions, however, was illegal, unconstitutional, or inconsistent with the basic principle of responsible government. And by the end of the session of 1841 that principle had become the established practice in the legislature of the United Province.

The charge that Sydenham wished to anglicize French Canadians is more accurate. He did treat them as a conquered race. Yet to condemn him for doing what he was sent to do is unreasonable. Certainly his objective was to make Lower Canada "essentially British, for unless that be done," he felt, "it will be impossible to cultivate it's natural resources, to improve the condition of it's inhabitants, or to secure its permanent connexion with the Mother Country." He thus encouraged immigration from Britain and sought to appease the Upper Canadians and the British minority in Lower Canada. The decision to establish the union had been taken by the British cabinet, and even with hindsight it is difficult to see any alternative method of restoring representative institutions to Lower Canada which would have been acceptable to the British inhabitants of both Canadas. In this sense, as Ged Martin has written, union was "dictated by the logic of events"; Sydenham considered "Anglification" an unavoidable consequence. Like most English liberals, he rejected notions of a multicultural society; as Janet Ajzenstat has argued, he believed that deep cultural cleavages prevent "the full realization of liberal rights" by leaving members of minority cultures vulnerable to exploitation.

Ultimately the union was not so disastrous to French Canada as its critics had predicted. French Canadians became a minority, but were numerous enough to defend their vital interests and secure enough to open a new era of collaboration with the anglophone majority. Without this imposed cooperation, confederation, which was not a feasible solution to the Canadian problem in the 1840s, might never have taken place. In this sense Sydenham deserves credit not only for preserving the British connection, which was the purpose of his mission, but also for laying the foundation of a more enduring and larger union. No governor had such a profound influence on the future development of the British North American colonies – not even Lord Durham.

PHILLIP BUCKNER

Some of Sydenham's correspondence has been published as *Letters from Lord Sydenham, governor-general of Canada, 1839–1841, to Lord John Russell*, ed. Paul Knaplund (London, 1931). A portrait of Sydenham appears as the frontispiece to *Memoir of the life of the Right Honourable Charles, Lord Sydenham, G.C.B., with a narrative of his administration in Canada*, ed. G. P. Scrope (London, 1843).

AO, MS 4; MS 35; MS 78. MTRL, Robert Baldwin papers. NLS, Dept. of MSS, MSS 15001–195. PAC, MG 24, A13, A17, A27, A30, A40, B29 (mfm. at PANS); RG 5, A1: 6510–7022; RG 7, G14, 5–6, 8; RG 68, General index, 1651–1841: 72. PRO, CO 42/296–300; 42/446–76; PRO 30/22/3E–4B. UCC-C, Egerton Ryerson papers. Univ. of Durham, Dept. of Palaeography and Diplomatic (Durham, Eng.), Earl Grey papers. *Arthur papers* (Sanderson). H. R. V. Fox, Baron Holland, *The Holland House diaries, 1831–1840*, ed. A. D. Kriegel (London, 1977). C. C. F. Greville, *The Greville memoirs: a journal of the reigns of King George IV and King William IV*, ed. Henry Reeve (8v., London, 1874–87). *Notices of the death of the late Lord Sydenham by the press of British North America . . .* (Toronto, 1841). [John] Richardson, *Eight years in Canada; embracing a review of the administrations of lords Durham and Sydenham, Sir Chas. Bagot and Lord Metcalfe, and including numerous interesting letters from Lord Durham, Mr. Chas. Buller and other well-known public characters* (Montreal, 1847). Samuel Thompson, *Reminiscences of a Canadian pioneer for the last fifty years: an autobiography* (Toronto, 1884; repub. Toronto and Montreal, 1968). *Three early nineteenth century diaries*, ed. Arthur Aspinall (London, 1952). *Colonial Gazette* (London), 18 Sept. 1839. *Novascotian, or Colonial Herald*, 24 Oct. 1839.

Janet Ajzenstat, "Liberalism and assimilation: Lord Durham reconsidered," *Political thought in Canada: contemporary perspectives*, comp. and ed. Stephen Brooks (Toronto, 1984), 239–57. Lucy Brown, *The Board of Trade and the free-trade movement, 1830–42* (Oxford, 1958). Buckner, *Transition to responsible government*. J. M. S. Careless, *The union of the Canadas: the growth of Canadian institutions, 1841–1857* (Toronto, 1967). Craig, *Upper Canada*. J. C. Dent, *The last forty years: the union of 1841 to confederation*, ed. D. [W.] Swainson (Toronto, 1972). S. E. Finer, "The transmission of Benthamite ideas, 1820–50," *Studies in the growth of nineteenth-century government*, ed. Gillian Sutherland (Totowa, N.J., 1972), 11–32. Norman Gash, *Reaction and reconstruction in English politics, 1832–52* (Oxford, 1965). J. E. Hodgetts, *Pioneer public service: an administrative history of the united Canadas, 1841–1867* (Toronto, 1955). O. A. Kinchen, *Lord Russell's Canadian policy, a study in British heritage and colonial freedom* (Lubbock, Tex., 1945). Ged Martin, *The Durham report and British policy: a critical essay* (Cambridge, Eng., 1972). Jacques Monet, *Last cannon shot*; "The personal and living bond, 1839–1849," *The shield of Achilles: aspects of Canada in the Victorian age*, ed. W. L. Morton (Toronto and Montreal, 1968), 62–93. W. [G.] Ormsby, *The emergence of the federal concept in Canada, 1839–1845* (Toronto, 1969). Adam Shortt, *Lord Sydenham* (Toronto, 1908). [G.] A. Wilson, *The clergy reserves of Upper Canada: a Canadian mortmain* (Toronto, 1968). K. N. Windsor, "Historical writing in Canada to 1920," *Literary History of Canada: Canadian literature in English*, ed. C. F. Klinck (Toronto, 1967), 231. I. M. Abella, "The 'Sydenham Election' of 1841," *CHR*, 47 (1966): 326–43. Ged Martin, "Confederation rejected: the British debate on Canada, 1837–1840," *Journal of Imperial and Commonwealth Hist.* (London), 11 (1982–83): 33–57.

THORNE, BENJAMIN, businessman, JP, office holder, and militia officer; b. 4 Jan. 1794 in Sherborne, Dorset, England, son of Benjamin Thorne and Heneritta ——; m. 3 Feb. 1831 Anna Maria Wilcocks in York (Toronto), and they had six sons and three daughters; d. 2 July 1848 in Thornhill, Upper Canada.

No man became a success in Upper Canada faster than Benjamin Thorne, few were more successful, and few fell faster or farther. In 1820 he and a brother-in-law, William Parsons, had come to Upper Canada to make their fortunes. Almost immediately Thorne bought property on Yonge Street north of York. Probably at about the same time, he and Parsons opened a store, run by Parsons, which was to form a focal point of the village (Thornhill) that Thorne helped to create during the 1820s and early 1830s. Within a few years he apparently leased all or part of the nearby milling complex of William PURDY, consisting of saw- and grist-mills and a tannery. By the time he bought the complex in 1829, after fire had destroyed the grist-mill, he had established a reputation as a skilled businessman.

In 1830 Thorne rebuilt and enlarged the mill complex. With a warehouse in Toronto, Thorne and Parsons became a large exporter of flour to England and an importer of metal, groceries, and dry goods. All buying and selling in England was handled by Thorne's brother, William, and William's company. To facilitate the forwarding of goods, Benjamin went into partnership in Montreal with Francis Harris Heward.

Thorne and Parsons continued to grow through the

1830s and into the 1840s. New managerial positions within the company were filled by relatives and by people brought out from Dorset. The firm eventually consisted of the two founders as well as Thorne's brother-in-law Horace S. L. Wilcocks and Henry Thompson, both of whom married daughters of Parsons. The company's rapid growth can be largely explained by the success of its flour-exporting business, a result in turn of the flour-mill's size, its location in a major wheat-growing district, and Thorne's ability to pay cash for wheat, a practice still not common in the colony. The cash came from various sources, including profits, his wife's family, and bank loans.

Thorne, a successful businessman, enjoyed good relations with banks throughout most of his career. Stock which he purchased in the Bank of Upper Canada allowed him to be elected a director, a position he held by June 1824 at the latest; he was subsequently elected for several one-year terms. In 1838 he became a director of the Toronto branch of the Commercial Bank of the Midland District. Finally, in 1842, he was appointed a director and president of the Toronto branch of the Bank of Montreal. When a committee of the House of Assembly had investigated the province's banking system in 1835, Thorne recommended that the Bank of Upper Canada open additional agencies and increase its capital stock so that it could provide more loans to help develop the province. Among those also testifying was William Lyon Mackenzie*, an ardent foe of monetary monopolies. It was neither the first time nor the last that Thorne and Mackenzie had public differences of opinion.

In 1830, although Thorne had no great interest in politics, he had been persuaded to run against Mackenzie in the provincial election of that year. To conservatives like Thorne, who failed to win a seat, Mackenzie's views represented disloyal American republicanism. In 1837, on the night of 4 December, a young man, Richard Frizzell, came to Thorne's house asking for assistance to reach Toronto and warn the authorities of Mackenzie's planned descent on the capital. Thorne, feeling that some of his mill employees were sympathizers, gave no aid for fear of retaliation against his property. However, with the defeat of Mackenzie's forces on the 7th, Thorne's conservative views prevailed.

Aside from the vexations caused by Mackenzie, life for Thorne was good during the 1830s. Much of Thornhill belonged to him; in 1829 he had had a post office established there and gave land for an Anglican church. There was even a society which imported books for its members, Thorne being the secretary. The small group that stood at the top of Thornhill's society also monopolized most of the government's appointments in the area. Thorne, for one, was first commissioned as a magistrate in 1833. As well, about 1837 he was appointed a trustee to finish the macadamization of Yonge Street begun by James CULL, and he was made a commissioner of the Home District Court of Requests during the same decade. Following the rebellion, he was commissioned captain in the 4th Regiment of North York militia.

The 1840s witnessed more growth in Thorne's enterprises. In 1843 he apparently leased the Red Mill at Holland Landing and turned it over to a partner, John Barwick. With this acquisition Thorne became probably the colony's largest producer of flour for export. A fourth company, B. Thorne and Company, was created to carry on much of the flour-exporting and metal-importing business.

In spite of friction between the partners, business continued to grow until 1846, when the repeal of the preferential British corn laws caused a huge drop in the demand for Upper Canadian flour. Thorne and his associates were caught with far too large a supply; early in 1847 Thorne and Barwick was dissolved. That year, however, renewed demand and an increase in the price paid for flour allowed Thorne to make up some of his losses. Despite a fall in price later in 1847, he confidently bought heavily for the next season, ignoring the misgivings of some of his associates. To back his purchases he borrowed against his personal wealth, estimated by him at more than £85,000. In 1848, a year of severe depression in Canada, the British market collapsed almost totally. The Bank of Upper Canada, which had backed Thorne in his expansion, called its loans and he was ruined. Ultimately his three companies and his personal holdings would be liquidated, but he did not live to see the final result. On the night of 1 July 1848 Thorne walked out behind his house and shot himself. He died a day later, having ended a brilliant career and lost a substantial fortune because of one bad business decision.

RONALD J. STAGG

AO, MS 94, William Pitt to John Norton, 16 June 1820; MU 2380, no.9; MU 2577, "An incident of the rebellion: something about the man who warned the people of Toronto of the advance of Mackenzie" (unidentified newspaper clipping, 1894); MU 4734, no.1; RG 22, ser.155. CTA, RG 1, B, Benjamin Thorne to A. T. McCord, 22 May 1841, 4 April 1842; report of committee on Market Block, 9 April, 20 Dec. 1842 (mfm. at AO). Dorset Record Office (Dorchester, Eng.), Sherborne Abbey, reg. of baptisms, 5 Feb. 1794. MTRL, B. Thorne & Co. papers. PAC, RG 1, L1, 36: 288; L3, 510: T leases/104; RG 5, A1: 23431–39, 35398, 89543, 93835–38, 96740–42, 108407; RG 68, General index, 1651–1841: 472, 507. York North Land Registry Office (Newmarket, Ont.), Abstract index to deeds, Markham Township; Vaughan Township (mfm. at AO). M. S. [Gapper] O'Brien, *The journals of Mary O'Brien, 1828–1838*, ed. Audrey Saunders Miller (Toronto, 1968). [L. W. V.] Smith, *Young Mr Smith in Upper Canada*, ed. M. L. Smith (Toronto, 1980). U.C., House of Assembly, *App. to the journal*, 1835, no.3. *British Colonist*, 14 Oct. 1844.

Colonial Advocate, 10 Feb. 1831. *Globe*, 5 July, 6 Dec. 1848. *Toronto Mirror*, 7 July 1848. *Commemorative biographical record of the county of York, Ontario . . .* (Toronto, 1907). *Toronto almanac*, 1839. D. M. FitzGerald, *Old time Thornhill* (n.p., 1970). D. M. FitzGerald *et al.*, *Thornhill, 1793–1963: the history of an Ontario village* (Thornhill, 1964). *History of Toronto and county of York, Ontario . . .* (2v., Toronto, 1885), 1: 122, 127. Audrey Saunders Miller, "Yonge Street politics, 1828 to 1832," *OH*, 62 (1970): 101–18.

THORPE, ROBERT, judge and politician; b. *c.* 1764 in Dublin, second son of Robert T. Thorp, a barrister, and Bonna Debrisay; m. with seven children; d. 11 May 1836 in London.

Robert Thorpe graduated with a BA in 1788 and an LLB in 1789 from Trinity College, Dublin. Some time previous to 1815 he appears to have been awarded an LLD. Admitted to the Irish bar in 1790, he entered the colonial service in 1801 when he was nominated chief justice of Prince Edward Island.

This colony was governed by the able, if somewhat venal, Edmund Fanning* who, through geniality, deft duplicity, and judicious inaction, had successfully steered his way between the demands of local factions and unpopular policies of the Colonial Office since 1786. Fanning was in collusion with the Island's landed proprietors, as Thorpe was not; moreover, the lieutenant governor's *laissez-faire* rule was antipathetic to the judge's rigidity of mind and probably stood as an obstacle to his ambition to make a name for himself in London. Something might be made of the colony, he once thought, "but the government must acquire vigour and respectability, the middle orders more sense and less sufficiency, and the lower classes must be less drunken and Idle before any good can be effected." Thorpe soon stirred up the attorney general, Peter Magowan*, to launch a number of prosecutions which seem to have been minor but irritating, and perhaps unjustified. Living on a salary in arrears, in a small house with a leaking roof, having a complaining wife and seven sickly children whom he despaired of educating, Thorpe was meanwhile "obliged at different times to quarrel with all orders through finding virtue in none." He came to loathe the colony. In hope of securing his salary, he sailed to England in 1804, carrying with him an unsolicited plan for uniting Prince Edward Island, Cape Breton, and Newfoundland to impress the colonial secretary. Off the coast of Ireland he was captured by the French and carried into Spain, from whence he contrived to escape.

In 1805 he was appointed puisne judge of the Court of King's Bench in Upper Canada. Arriving in York (Toronto) by 1 October, he found the reins of government in the hands of Alexander Grant*, the temporary replacement for Lieutenant Governor Peter Hunter*, who had died that August. Thorpe almost immediately fell in with a fellow Irishman, Executive Councillor Peter Russell*, who had expected to be made lieutenant governor himself, but never even regained the power and influence he had enjoyed before Hunter's arrival. Thorpe's opinions about Hunter, whom he never knew, almost certainly derived from the Russell circle, as did his hostility to Grant. "I expected that the avarice and imbecility of our [Upper Canadian] government would be highly injurious, but it has far surpassed my fears," Thorpe reported to the Colonial Office, and began to manœuvre to take the interim management of affairs into his own hands. Reasonably enough, he argued for establishing a court of chancery; and, harmlessly enough, he founded agricultural societies and tried to promote the building of roads by means of a lottery. But more important, he attempted to manage a political opposition of which he had a limited and distorted understanding. Grant held office until August 1806 when he was succeeded by the new lieutenant governor, Francis Gore*.

Political divisions in Upper Canada were essentially local in nature, having emerged within the districts either between justices of the peace representative of opposed sectional interests or, more commonly, between these appointed officials and their disappointed rivals for place who were beginning to oppose them from the hustings. Such divisions were often reinforced by further oppositions between long settled loyalists and newcomers from the American republic who were swamping them. At the ideological level politics were therefore characterized by the noisy opposition of a rhetoric of republicanism and one of loyalty to government established by law, a conflict made the more intense by threat of war with the United States. By 1806 a few spokesmen for the disaffected were being returned to the House of Assembly. But also at the capital were a number of persons who were at once alarmed by the threat of republicanism yet disaffected themselves from the Hunter government by reason of the "maladministration" and "unconstitutional" practices which they tended to assign as the causes of popular unrest. Among them were some Anglo-Irishmen – notably Russell's friends and Thorpe's crony the demagogic barrister William Weekes* – who, tending to understand local politics in terms of Irish analogies, became the judge's friends and advisers.

Thorpe's ideas derived from these people, from rhetoric and constitutional theory related to the paper independence enjoyed by Ireland prior to the union of 1800 and, more especially, from the ancient English law upon which that independence was theoretically based and upon which the judge was taken to be an authority. Loyalty to the crown would be maintained in Upper Canada, he argued, only if British subjects enjoyed certain rights to which they were entitled by law but which had been ignored during the Hunter régime. This enjoyment, it appeared, involved holding the executive responsible to the elected representatives of the people. Indeed, it is likely that Thorpe was the author of a tract in which it was contended that the "British Connection" might best be maintained if, after the model of the parliament at Westminster, executive authority were vested in a cabinet responsible, not to the governor, but to the local legislature. He expounded related doctrine both before the bar of the assembly and from the bench; and, during his victorious election campaign in 1807 to succeed Weekes in the assembly, these ideas informed his slogan: "The King, the People, the Law, Thorpe and the Constitution."

As a practical politician, Thorpe was foolish to a degree; but as a link between English and Irish constitutional concepts of the 17th and 18th centuries and certain notions later associated with the slogans "Responsible Government" and "Home Rule," he is a figure of some consequence in the history of ideas. His views and actions were incompatible, however, with what was then accepted imperial doctrine; and he was suspended from office by Gore in July 1807.

Despite his record as a trouble-maker, in 1808 Thorpe was appointed chief justice and judge of the Vice-Admiralty Court in Sierra Leone. He did not sail from England, however, until 1811 and he returned on leave in 1813. He then became involved in a dispute with the Colonial Office over £630 he was said to have owed to a surrogate who had acted for him in Sierra Leone during his absence. In March 1814 this sum was ordered paid out of his salary. In January 1815 he transmitted to the colonial secretary a number of charges against Charles William Maxwell, one-time governor of Sierra Leone, which also involved the probity of the African Institution, an organization set up by evangelical philanthropists to aid freed slaves. Lord Bathurst, the colonial secretary, was requested either to deal with these charges himself or to lay them before the prince regent in council. At the same time, Thorpe presented a memorial on his own behalf, praying for the return of the £630. Apparently scenting blackmail, Bathurst ordered him dismissed on the ground that, even if his charges were true, he had been derelict in his duty in not having brought them forward at an earlier date.

Up until 1828 Thorpe wrote many pamphlets in which he sought to bring his cause, and that of Sierra Leone, before parliament. In 1827 Joseph Hume appealed to Lord Goderich "as an act of humanity if not of justice" to do something for Dr Thorpe "to prevent him and his family from absolute starvation." At his death in 1836, however, former surveyor general Charles Burton WYATT reported to William Warren BALDWIN that Thorpe had left "an amiable family comfortably provided for."

G. H. PATTERSON

[Of Robert Thorpe's many pamphlets, just one treats his experience in Prince Edward Island and Upper Canada in any detail. What appears to be the only surviving copy of *Appendix to the case of Robert Thorpe, esq., L.L.D., elicited by a letter from Viscount Goderich, to Joseph Hume, esq., M.P.* (London, 1828) is in PRO, CO 267/88. A spate of articles related to Thorpe's pamphleteering appeared in the contemporary periodical press. There are also a number of references to him in G.B., Parl., *The parliamentary debates* (London), because, from time to time, he gave rise to questions and debate in the House of Commons. The most important source for Thorpe's career in Upper Canada is "Political state of U.C.," PAC *Report*, 1892: 32–135. Other material is found in the W. W. Baldwin papers at the MTRL and the Baldwin papers at AO, MS 88. His sojourns in Prince Edward Island and Sierra Leone are treated in the relevant volumes of PRO, CO 226 and CO 267 respectively.

The following secondary works are useful: S. D. Clark, *Movements of political protest in Canada, 1640–1840* (Toronto, 1959); Craig, *Upper Canada*; Creighton, *Empire of St. Lawrence*; R. B. McDowell, *Irish public opinion, 1750–1800* (London, 1944); William Renwick Riddell*'s piece on Thorpe in his *Upper Canada sketches: incidents in the early times of the province* (Toronto, 1922) and his "Scandalum Magnatum in Upper Canada," American Institute of Criminal Law and Criminology, *Journal* (Chicago), 4 (1913–14): 12–19. My own article, "Whiggery, nationality, and the Upper Canadian reform tradition," *CHR*, 56 (1975): 25–44, contains the supporting arguments for the interpretation of Thorpe presented here and makes the case that "An Upper Canada letter of 1829 on responsible government," ed. K. D. McRae, *CHR*, 31 (1950): 288–96, probably contains a fragment of an important Thorpe manuscript. It is worth noting that I have radically changed my thinking about the judge since I first dealt with him in my thesis, "Studies in elections in U.C." G.H.P.]

TIARKS, JOHANN LUDWIG (John Lewis), astronomer and surveyor; b. 10 May 1789 in Waddewarden (Federal Republic of Germany), son of the Reverend Johann Gerhard Tiarks and Christine Dorothea Ehrentraut; m. 1822 Auguste Antoinette Sophie Toel of Jever (Federal Republic of Germany), and of their several children one daughter survived to maturity; d. 1 May 1837 in Jever.

Johann Ludwig Tiarks received a doctorate in mathematics from the University of Göttingen in 1808 and took a position as a private tutor. In 1810 he had to flee to England to escape conscription in Napoleon's army. He soon became assistant librarian and factotum to Sir Joseph Banks* at the Royal Society in London. On Banks's recommendation, in 1817 he was appointed an astronomer for one of the commissions established under article 5 of the Treaty of Ghent (1814) to determine the boundary between eastern British North America and the United States. He acted for Joseph BOUCHETTE, who fell ill with "Lake Champlain fever" that year, and he remained with the survey after Bouchette was replaced as chief surveyor by William Franklin ODELL.

Tiarks arrived in September at Saint-Régis (Akwesasne), where the 45th parallel intersects with the St Lawrence, and there he began his astronomical observations. He was greatly impressed by the local Christian Mohawks and made friends with many in the village, as well as with their priest, Joseph Marcoux*. His journals and letters are full of comments about their way of life. "I have never been so touched as when I entered the church," he noted. "No one would believe how well mannered and with what discipline all the ceremonies of the Catholic church were observed by this wild nation. The women sat on one side, singing alternately each verse with the men, who sat on the other side." He grasped something of the matrilineal nature of Mohawk society and acquired some perception of the dominant role of women in the household. His enthusiasm for North America generally was reflected in his appreciation of the Indians. "There is something fascinating about them which gives the civilized person a feeling of freedom, health and renewed courage he cannot hold back," he wrote.

At the end of July 1818 Tiarks and his party left Saint-Régis and with the American surveying crew, headed by an old acquaintance from London, Ferdinand Rudolph Hassler, set out towards Lake Champlain. At the lake, which they reached before winter, both teams discovered independently that John Collins* and others had been incorrect in locating the position of the parallel there and that the million-dollar American fort at Rouses Point, N.Y., was actually in British territory. The American members of the boundary commission refused to acknowledge the findings, and the man who replaced Hassler as astronomer, Andrew Ellicott, was much less cooperative than his predecessor. He reportedly suggested to Tiarks that "we should not do our work so exactingly and forget about completing most of it." Feeling that his reputation was at stake, Tiarks refused to go along with the suggestion and was strongly supported by British Commissioner Thomas Henry Barclay*.

In 1819 Tiarks was working in the upper Connecticut River basin, where part of the boundary was intended to run. He spent time during the summer of 1820 mapping an area in what is now northwestern New Brunswick and nearby Quebec; in the fall he was again in the vicinity of the upper Connecticut. Disagreement between the British and American commissioners [*see* Ward Chipman*] soon brought his work in North America to a halt, however, and in 1821 he returned to Europe.

Tiarks came out to North America again in 1825 to determine the most northwesterly point of the Lake of the Woods, from which the international boundary was supposed to run due west to the Mississippi River. The following year he went back to London, where he remained until 1830 working on matters of concern to the boundary commission. The king of the Netherlands had been asked to arbitrate the boundary question, and in 1830 Tiarks was called to The Hague to explain certain points. After about a year he returned to Jever.

Tiarks had always hoped to be made a professor at a German university but no appointment was forthcoming. Nor did he live to see the signing of the Webster-Ashburton Treaty (1842) which settled the boundary controversy. In March 1837 he fell victim to a stroke, from which he failed to recover. A letter he wrote to his mother during his first winter in the Canadas shows almost a premonition of how his life was to unfold: "So lies our future in the dark, we flatter ourselves with hopes that will never be fulfilled, believe that we can do otherwise, but are the playthings of fate."

VINCENT O. ERICKSON

[Johann Ludwig Tiarks's papers were given by his great-grandsons Robert von Ranke Graves and Charles Patrick Ranke Graves to their Tiarks cousins in England, who deposited them in the family library at Foxbury. In 1972 Henry F. Tiarks presented the collection (with the exception of a few personal items and duplicate materials which remain in his possession at Foxbury) to the PAC, where it is now available at MG 24, H64, and constitutes the main primary source for this study. Tiarks left behind a wealth of unpublished materials, among them his journals and correspondence, reports, memoranda, and notes. The collection also includes five folio volumes, printed but not made available for circulation, of reports on the boundary commission, as well as copies of Tiarks's published scientific reports, which were exclusively on the subject of determining longitude and originally appeared between 1817 and 1829.

Other useful manuscript collections are the Thomas Barclay papers at the Maine Hist. Soc. Library (Portland) and the boundary commission records in the Chipman papers (PAC, MG 23, D1, ser.1, 31–60). Additional material on Tiarks in secondary sources is to be found in C. A. H. Franklin, *A short history of the family of Tiarks of Foxbury, Chislehurst, Co. Kent* (London, 1929); *Allgemeine deutsche Biographie* . . . (56v., Leipzig, [German Democratic Republic], 1875–1912), 39: 92–94; and *Oldenburger Sonntagsblatt* (Oldenburg, Lower Saxony, [Federal Republic of Germany]), 12 (1919), no.5. There are contemporary obituaries or obituary articles in the *Athenæum* (London), 1837: 366–67; *Oldenburgische Blätter* (Oldenburg), 28 Nov., 5 Dec. 1837; 16, 23 Oct. 1838; and the Astronomical Soc. of London, *Monthly Notices*, 4 (1836–39): 108–10. Robert von Ranke Graves in *Good-bye to all that; an autobiography* (London, 1929) and Alfred Perceval Graves in *To return to all that; an autobiography* (London, 1930) also provide information on Tiarks, but these must be read with caution.

For specific materials on the boundary question the reader is directed to S. F. Bemis, *A diplomatic history of the United States* (New York, 1936); A. B. Corey, *The crisis of 1830–1842 in Canadian-American relations* (New Haven, Conn., and Toronto, 1941); W. F. Ganong, "A monograph of the evolution of the boundaries of the province of New Brunswick," RSC *Trans.*, 2nd ser., 7 (1901), sect.II:

139–449; J. B. Moore, *History and digest of the international arbitrations to which the United States has been a party* . . . (6v., Washington, 1898), 1; and D. W. Thomson, *Men and meridians: the history of surveying and mapping in Canada* (3v., Ottawa, 1966–69). V.O.E.]

TIGER DUNLOP, WILLIAM DUNLOP, known as. *See* DUNLOP

TKOBEITCH. *See* MALIE, JOSEPH

TOBIN, JAMES, businessman, politician, office holder, and JP; baptized 19 April 1774 in Halifax, son of Michael Tobin and Catherine Hannah Murphy; m. there 25 Jan. 1800 Eleanor Lanigan, daughter of Patrick Lanigan from Callan (Republic of Ireland), and they had six children; d. 3 Nov. 1838 in Halifax.

The Tobins were a Roman Catholic Irish family who came to Halifax via Newfoundland early in the 1770s. Michael Tobin, a native of Waterford, was by trade a butcher. He rose to a modest competence as a victualler, supplying fish and meat to the government. After his death in 1804 his son James Tobin continued the business in partnership with a younger brother, Michael. The scale of their operations was limited at first, and it was not until late in the Napoleonic Wars that the family came into commercial prominence.

The Tobin brothers, in business as J. and M. Tobin, took advantage of the diversion of trade and other opportunities presented by the prolonged European war and the War of 1812. The value of goods imported by the company rose rapidly from about £800 (1810) to £19,183 (1814) and £60,797 (1816). In 1813 sale of cargo from prize vessels grossed £9,938. The firm traded in rum, molasses, and brown sugar with the West Indies, and imported wine and manufactured goods from overseas.

The profits of these activities were invested in mortgages, loans, and the provincial debt. In the period 1814–37 the Tobins granted 63 mortgages for amounts ranging between a few dozen and several hundred pounds apiece. Major note holders as well, the brothers held one-third of the provincial debt of Nova Scotia in 1818. By 1825 they had nearly £5,000 in provincial currency certificates, and in 1836 they were the province's largest creditors. Their investments were highly profitable: by 1829–30 the Tobins were collecting 18 per cent per annum on their large capital advances. They were also subscribers for shares in the Shubenacadie Canal project in 1829 [*see* Charles Rufus FAIRBANKS].

James Tobin invested £5,000 to become one of the eight founding partners of the Halifax Banking Company in September 1825. This venture returned annual dividends of up to 20 per cent and placed him in the inner circle of Halifax's commercial élite. Tobin's standing was recognized by his appointment to the Nova Scotia Council on 25 Jan. 1832 – he was the first Roman Catholic to achieve this elevation. He had been a commissioner of the court for the summary trial of actions in Halifax Township since 16 April 1817. Now he became not only a councillor, joining his banking partners Samuel Cunard*, Enos Collins*, and Henry Hezekiah Cogswell*, but also a commissioner and justice of the peace throughout the province. When the Council was divided into executive and legislative branches early in 1838, Tobin became a member of the Legislative Council.

Tobin's involvement in general community affairs, although relatively limited, reflected his Irish and Catholic origins. He joined the Charitable Irish Society on 17 May 1797 and on ten occasions served as a member of its committee of charity. At a time of considerable Irish immigration in the 1820s and 1830s this position was no sinecure. Michael Tobin rose to the chair of the society and succeeded his brother and business partner as a member of the Legislative Council. James Tobin was a warden of St Peter's Roman Catholic Church from 1800 until his death and in 1830 was a generous donor toward the completion of its successor, St Mary's Cathedral (St Mary's Basilica). In his will, Tobin left a substantial sum to the children of his daughter Eliza, wife of John James Sawyer, a Protestant. Those of the grandchildren who were Roman Catholic were to inherit their share of the bequest; those who were Protestant would simply enjoy a life interest. Though Tobin was a sincere Catholic, he was not a bigoted one. He supported Thomas MCCULLOCH's appointment as principal of Dalhousie College in 1838 by stating in council that if he had sons to educate he would place them under McCulloch's care.

Tobin in 1838 was the wealthiest Roman Catholic in the Maritimes, and one of the wealthiest men in Nova Scotia. At his death, his estate was valued at £50,360, investments and merchandise accounting for more than half of the total. Real estate and household effects were also of considerable worth. Tobin's personal effacement, cautious conservatism, and business acumen had gained him success and social standing. His influence on his co-religionists and fellow Irish had, however, been minimal once the Reform movement gained momentum in the 1830s; younger men such as Laurence O'Connor Doyle* began to express the liberal sentiments of the Irish constituency. Two of Tobin's sons achieved political prominence. Michael became a member of the Legislative Council and then of the Executive Council in Nova Scotia; James William* obtained the same positions in Newfoundland.

TERRENCE M. PUNCH

Halifax County Court of Probate (Halifax), Estate papers,

T40; Wills, 3: ff.284 *et seq.*; 5: ff.92–110 (mfm. at PANS). Halifax County Registry of Deeds (Halifax), Deeds, 41: f.42; 46: f.297; 47: f.298; 49: f.38; 53: f.472; 58: f.1; 63: f.75 (mfm. at PANS). PANS, MG 20, 65–66; RG 1, 195, 386; RG 31-104, 8–9. St Mary's Roman Catholic Basilica (Halifax), Account-book of St Peter's Church [St Mary's Cathedral], 1801–58 (mfm. at PANS). J. S. Martell, "A documentary study of provincial finance and currency, 1812–36," PANS *Bull.* (Halifax), 2 (1939–41), no.4. T. M. Punch, "Tobin genealogy," *Nova Scotia Hist. Quarterly* (Halifax), 5 (1975): 71–81.

TOLER, JOSEPH, gold- and silversmith, painter, and engraver; b. *c.* 1810 in Halifax, son of John George Toler; married; fl. 1831–42.

Joseph Toler's father was draftsman to the civil department of the Royal Engineers in Halifax and an amateur water-colourist. It is assumed that he instructed his son in the rudiments of painting but there is no record of Joseph's trade apprenticeship. By May 1831 Joseph was established in business as a gold- and silversmith with premises on Argyle Street in Halifax. A few examples of his work are preserved in the Nova Scotia Museum. Not all the pieces have his complete mark – J.T H with sovereign's head and lion passant – but the punches are highly distinctive.

Within a few years Toler seems to have abandoned silversmithing in favour of painting. An advertisement of 17 June 1834 in the Halifax *Times* announced that he had removed to Mrs Grover's Hotel and offered likenesses at 5*s.* coloured, 2*s.* 6*d.* bronze, and 1*s.* 3*d.* black. By 1837 he had set up in a studio on Hollis Street opposite St Matthew's Church and was also painting miniatures on ivory and cardboard. It was as a miniature painter that he advertised himself in the *New-Brunswick Courier* on 21 April 1838. Emphasizing that he would be in Saint John for a short time only, he offered miniatures on ivory at a price of from £1 and on board from 6*s.* 6*d.*; he had, he stated, "taken at Halifax alone more than one thousand." From Saint John he proceeded to Fredericton, where he advertised his services in the *Royal Gazette* on 20 July. He was back in Saint John the following year. Around March 1840 Toler became the drawing-master in the school opened in November 1839 by the Mechanics' Institute of Saint John. When the school year ended in the spring, an exhibition of his students' work was held. Noting that Toler had been in charge of the drawing classes for only about six weeks, the *Morning News* gave high praise to his efforts: "In this short time the dexterity acquired by all of his pupils, and the beauty and taste displayed in their drawings, prove at once his talents as a teacher, and his diligent exertion of them."

Toler's subsequent career is more obscure. On 16 March 1840 he had given notice in the *Morning News* that after 1 May he proposed to stop taking likenesses and return to metal work. Just six weeks later, however, he indicated his intention to open a school "in which the various branches of Drawing & Painting will be taught." Whether this establishment saw the light of day is not known. Among the services Toler offered in an announcement of 20 May, which ran until the end of the year, were gold and silver work, metal gilding, copperplate engraving and printing, wood cutting, and miniatures. In 1842 he advertised landscape and drawing classes. Nothing further is known of him, but it is thought that he may later have spent some time in Fredericton. Examples of his miniatures may be seen in the New Brunswick Museum.

D. C. Mackay and Stuart Smith

Acadian Recorder, 14 May 1831, 11 Feb. 1837. *Morning News* (Saint John, N.B.), 16 March, 27 April, 25 May 1840. *New-Brunswick Courier*, 21 April 1838; 13 April, 27 July 1839; 2 May 1840. *Royal Gazette* (Fredericton), 20 June 1838. *Times* (Halifax), 24 Nov. 1837. Harper, *Early painters and engravers*. D. C. Mackay, *Silversmiths and related craftsmen of the Atlantic provinces* (Halifax, 1973). G. [B.] MacBeath, "Artists in New Brunswick's past," *Arts in New Brunswick*, ed. R. A. Tweedie *et al.* (Fredericton, 1967), 121–48.

TOMAH (Thoma), FRANCIS (the name also appears as **Toma Francis**), Malecite chief; fl. 1813–50 in New Brunswick.

On 15 Oct. 1813 at Kingsclear, N.B., Francis Tomah was unanimously elected chief in the presence of New Brunswick's attorney general, Thomas Wetmore*. A commission for that office was issued to him the same day. He played a leading part in the negotiations begun in 1836 by the Penobscot tribe in the state of Maine. Angered by some fraudulent dealings on the part of their chiefs, the Penobscots applied to unite with the Malecite and Passamaquoddy tribes. An agreement was concluded that recognized the Malecites as the senior partners in the union, and the disgraced chiefs were replaced. The action left mischief behind it. Several Malecites were persuaded to petition the Maine House of Representatives in the winter of 1838, at the height of the "Aroostook war," stating that they had been expelled from New Brunswick and requesting support. Tomah hastened to assure Sir John Harvey*, lieutenant governor of the province, that the Malecites concerned – with the exception of one, a "worthless vagabond" – had been ignorant of what they were doing. Government could count on the Indians' support at all times.

Although their loyalty was unshaken, their faith in the government was sorely tried by the unchecked intrusions of white squatters on their reserves. When in the early 1840s the administration decided to regularize the squatters' position by leasing Indian land to them, and spoke in favour of locating the

Indians on individual holdings, Tomah presided over a full council at Kingsclear to protest. The Malecites, according to the resulting petition of 10 Jan. 1843, wanted to become farmers, adopt "settled habits," go to school, and "enjoy social blessings." They could achieve none of these goals while their lands were being daily plundered. They needed control of those lands, needed to hold them in common to avoid the disruptions that would flow from individual ownership; the council suggested that the whole tribe receive one grant to cover all the lands reserved to them in the Saint John River valley. The plea went unheeded. A petition of 1850, signed by Francis Tomah, complained of white encroachments on Indian lands in Carleton County.

Tomah was a well-known figure in Fredericton. Each New Year's Day the chief and his people paid their respects at the lieutenant governor's levee. The Indians would perform their dances and watch the strange quadrilles and waltzes of the whites. At one such reception, in 1841, Harvey presented the "respected old chief" with a silver medal on a blue ribbon.

L. F. S. UPTON

PANB, RG 2, RS8, Indians, 1/4, petition of Francis Toma, 10 Jan. 1843. UNBL, MG H54, Thomas Wetmore to Jonathan Odell, 15 Oct. 1813; commission to Toma Francis (copy). N.B., House of Assembly, *Journal*, 1850: 171. *Royal Gazette* (Fredericton), 17 July 1839, 6 Jan. 1841. W. O. Raymond, *The River St. John: its physical features, legends and history from 1604 to 1784* (Saint John, N.B., 1910), 469–71. L. F. S. Upton, "Indian affairs in colonial New Brunswick," *Acadiensis* (Fredericton), 3 (1973–74), no.2: 3–26.

TO-OO-TROON-TOO-RA. *See* SOU-NEH-HOO-WAY

TRIAUD, LOUIS-HUBERT (often corrupted to **Triand, Briand, Friand**, and even **Friend**), painter, painting- and drawing-master, and art restorer; b. 1790 in London of French parents; m. secondly 7 Jan. 1834 Élizabeth Pagé at Quebec; he had at least one daughter; d. there 14 Jan. 1836.

Louis-Hubert Triaud seems to have studied fine arts at the Royal Academy of Arts in London. On four occasions he exhibited works there, with a self-portrait in 1811 and with portraits of young women, two in 1818 and one in 1819. Triaud made his appearance at Quebec early in 1820. On 4 January an advertisement appeared in the *Quebec Mercury* announcing that he and Jean-Baptiste ROY-AUDY, as "portrait, miniature and historical Painters," will execute "any work in the above Mentioned Arts" and will teach "the Art of Drawing in all its branches, according to the method followed in the English and French Academies." The two painters worked in close collaboration and on at least one occasion signed the same work. But no grounds exist for believing that their association lasted beyond the first three months of 1820.

Triaud soon found a patron in Abbé Louis-Joseph DESJARDINS, *dit* Desplantes, who put in a good word for him with the Ursulines of Quebec in July. Triaud worked for them, doing his most famous picture, *La procession de la Fête-Dieu à Québec, en 1821*. Beginning in March 1821, he also taught the nuns' pupils for four months, giving three or four lessons weekly. According to one source the lessons were to include "sketching landscapes and painting in oils."

Triaud was helped in his painting career by his parents' friend Alexandre de Thémines, the bishop of Blois, France. From London Thémines wrote to Archbishop Joseph-Octave Plessis* at Quebec on 26 March 1821, describing the artist as "a young man of many talents, especially for painting." It may have been thanks to this intervention that in 1821 Triaud did a picture for the high altar in the church of Saint-André, near Kamouraska, portraying the martyrdom of the saint. As a result of several opportunities to demonstrate his competence, his reputation grew, and Abbé Desjardins did not hesitate to put his protégé's name forward when new commissions were being discussed. He even added that Triaud was capable of executing an excellent painting in three months.

Triaud also restored old works, notably alongside Antoine Plamondon* at Saint-Michel, near Quebec, in 1823. They were involved in "cleaning, repairing, and varnishing the four pictures in the nave of the church." This sort of task seems in some cases to have included attaching new canvas to the picture. Triaud "repaired" canvasses for the Ursulines the following year, and in 1825 he was again paid by the nuns for similar work.

The Hôtel-Dieu was another religious institution in the town of Quebec that took advantage of Triaud's talents, commissioning him in 1827 to paint the arms of the Duchesse d'Aiguillon, who had founded the hospital. A painting in its museum, *La vision de saint Antoine de Padoue*, dated 1830, bears Triaud's signature, but documentary evidence suggests that it is a restoration, since a work with this title had been exhibited from 1818 in the chapel and Triaud received payment in 1829 to restore a picture so titled.

In 1830 Triaud successfully tried his hand at what seems to have been a genre new to him. He painted some scenery representing Windsor Castle which was to be used in a production of Richard Brinsley Butler Sheridan's comedy *The rivals* at the Theatre Royal of Quebec. When the theatre was completely redone, he created a drop-scene for it, in 1832, with the help of J. F. Schinotti. Turning to ceremonial painting,

Triaud in 1833 executed a work for the Confrérie des Imprimeurs de Québec to celebrate the feast-day of St Augustine, their patron saint. It was a painting on satin of a printing-press resting on a globe, the entire composition suitably inscribed.

Nothing further is known of Triaud's professional activity, except for a few undated works. Mention should be made of a Baptism of Christ in the church at Rivière-Ouelle, a Madonna and Child at Sainte-Marie in Beauce, a portrait of Hector-Simon HUOT, and a self-portrait.

In 1835 Triaud's health was failing and he had a presentiment of his death. He passed away on 14 Jan. 1836, at the age of 46. Abbé Desjardins remembered him vividly and repeated Triaud's advice to those dealing with the problems encountered in restoring pictures. The formulas passed on by Desjardins were so detailed that one wonders if the painter left a written description of his methods. In any case, the void left by Triaud's death was felt particularly in the field of art restoration. "If Mr *Tri Tri* were alive," Abbé Desjardins wrote to the assistant superior of the Ursulines, Marie-Louise de Saint-Henri [MCLOUGHLIN], on 19 June 1840, "he would save you a great deal of trouble."

It is through the abbé's correspondence that glimpses can be caught of Triaud's personality. Desjardins called him "flighty" the first time he had occasion to mention him. Then in 1824, having enquired about his protégé's conduct, Desjardins expressed the fear that "he flits about," thinking it a pity that this talented man should be so irresponsible. Indeed, the painter's finances were then in such a disastrous state that Desjardins admitted he could do nothing further to save him from his creditors. During Triaud's death agony the abbé was astonished to see the mellowing of his character. He became "gentle as a *dove*, easier to attend to than a *nun*, and pious, almost like a hermit!"

Triaud was a figure of secondary importance in the artistic life of the capital during the second quarter of the 19th century, ranking behind Joseph Légaré*, Antoine Plamondon, and Jean-Baptiste Roy-Audy but superior to François Baillairgé* in painting. The relations between Triaud and Roy-Audy are far from clear, and were they better known, they might shed light on the question of the true paternity of certain works that are attributed to Roy-Audy. Furthermore, in the half-century between the return of Baillairgé from Paris in 1781 and that of Antoine Plamondon in 1830, Triaud was the only artist who could demonstrate to painters at Quebec, such as Légaré, artistic practices current overseas. Although he devoted little time to serious painting, Triaud had some such ambition, to judge by his 1820 advertisement. The records indicate clearly that he had taken the first steps in this direction.

Despite his love of art the flighty Louis-Hubert Triaud found living more difficult than painting, and he is still a shadowy figure. Were it not for his major work, *La procession de la Fête-Dieu*, he would be virtually unknown.

DAVID KAREL

[The author wishes to thank Michel Nadeau for making available research essential to the writing of this biography and John R. Porter for providing references to a number of articles in newspapers of the period. D.K.]

AAQ, 90 CM, Angleterre, II: 86. ANQ-Q, CE1-1, 16 janv. 1836; CE1-64, 7 janv. 1834. Arch. du monastère des ursulines (Québec), Fonds L.-J. Desjardins, II: 34, 64; III: 27, 89. MAC-CD, Fonds Morisset, 2, dossier L.-H. Triaud. *Le Canadien*, 20 janv. 1836. *Quebec Mercury*, 4 Jan. 1820, 20 Feb. 1830, 16 Feb. 1832, 29 Aug. 1833. Daphne Foskett, *A dictionary of British miniature painters* (2v., New York, 1972). Algernon Graves, *The Royal Academy of Arts . . .* (8v., London, 1905–6). Ulrich Thieme and Felix Becker, *Allgemeines Lexikon der bildenden Künstler von der Antike bis zur Gegenwart . . .* (37v., Leipzig, German Democratic Republic, 1907–50). Burke, *Les ursulines de Québec*, vol.4. B. S. Long, *British miniaturists* (London, 1928).

TROTTIER DES RIVIÈRES BEAUBIEN, MICHEL-RODOLPHE. *See* DES RIVIÈRES, RODOLPHE

TROYER, JOHN, farmer, businessman, medical practitioner, and exorcist; b. 3 Feb. 1753 in Brothers Valley, Somerset County, Pa, eldest son of David Michael Troyer and Magdalena Mast; m. Sophrona ——; d. 28 Feb. 1842 near Port Rowan, Upper Canada.

Of Rhineland ancestry and Tunker faith, John Troyer emigrated from Pennsylvania in 1789 with his wife, daughter, and son Michael. He later claimed to have "Suffered much by the Rebellious Americans, as they made no scruple to take all he had; and he came . . . to this Province in Order once more to enjoy Peace under His Majestys Good Laws." Troyer settled near Long Point on Lake Erie on a farm which is still known as Troyer's Flats. By 1797 he had a gristmill and a smithy, and he was in the process of building a 38-ton sloop, which he put up for sale the next year. Troyer, or Dr Troyer as he was usually called, was a figure well known in the area for his medical skills. Lacking any formal training, he practised blood-letting and gained fame for his herbal remedies.

Troyer's renown derives not from his exploits as an early settler but from his pre-eminence in the folklore of the region. Amelia Harris [Ryerse*], a former resident of Long Point, described him in her reminiscences as "a fine looking old man with a long flowing Beard. . . . He possessed a thorough knowledge of witches, their ways and doings, and the art of expelling them, and also the use of the Divining Rod with which he could not only find water, but could tell how far below the surface precious metals were concealed." Local tradition has it that Dr Troyer and his son would have discovered a famous treasure on the farm if, in their searching activities, their digging had not disturbed a phantom guardian of the treasure, a huge black dog who leapt out at them and drove them away. Also, a mischievous neighbour, Mrs Jennie Elizabeth McMichael, is said to have often teased Troyer with witchlike behaviour; she could always stop him from going on a hunting expedition – his marksmanship was famous – by laughing at him from behind bushes and then mysteriously crossing his path. Safely back in his house, Dr Troyer no doubt took comfort in the protective hex signs with which he surrounded himself as well as a witch trap that he set every night beside his bed. Even so, this trap had been no help when, as he averred, witches entered his bedroom one night, turned him into a horse, and rode him through the air across Lake Erie.

At Baldoon in the St Clair River country, and towards the end of 1829, the supreme test of Dr Troyer's skills in white magic began to develop. A certain farmer and fisherman, John T. McDonald, living on the banks of the Snye Carty, had built his house on a controversial site. BAUZHI-GEEZHIG-WAESHIKUM, the chief and medicine man at Walpole Island (Lambton County), claimed that McDonald had cut down a poplar grove haunted by a group of mamagwesewug (fairies), and so incurred mysterious and terrifying attacks on his house and farm; others maintained that McDonald's troubles began when he did not recognize the claims of an old woman who lived near by in the "long, low house." Some 20th-century commentators say that what happened in McDonald's house owed its occurrence to the presence in his family of a young orphan girl subject to seizures by a poltergeist. For three years, bullets with no apparent source whizzed through windows; other unexplained events took place – mysterious tramping sounds at night, the sudden and capricious levitation of heavy stones, dishes, firelogs, ladles, guns, and the house itself. Fires began to break out, a phantom dog appeared, domestic animals sickened and died, and crops failed.

Since no one in the Baldoon settlement seemed to be of any help, a Methodist minister advised McDonald to seek the aid of Dr Troyer. Both men made the journey to Long Point and when they stopped by the Thames River at night they were attacked by witches and other evil spirits whose cryings made rest impossible. At Long Point, Dr Troyer's daughter retired with her father's scrying stone which she consulted for long hours beneath his hat; both objects were famous for their powers of clairvoyant assistance. Exhausted by her experiences during her trance, she surprised McDonald by her minute knowledge of his predicament and his locale. She told him to make a silver bullet and shoot a strange goose that had lately wandered onto his property; on one of the bird's wings were some strange, black feathers. Back at Baldoon, McDonald followed her advice; when shot in the wing, the goose disappeared among the rushes to re-emerge in the "long, low house" as the old woman McDonald had quarrelled with, her arm newly broken. From that day on, the sufferings of the McDonald family ceased.

Although Dr Troyer's gentle and extraordinary personality never stopped attracting either strange events or their reportage, nothing else about his life is quite as memorable as his assistance in solving the Baldoon mystery. But almost as striking are the stories about his last days; just before his death he shot "a hawk, off-hand, from the peak of the barn roof." Thieves, it was reputed, came to rob his grave of magic talismans buried there; a great white bird drove them off. Despite the folkloric haze with which his figure is surrounded, perhaps we should not forget that John Troyer not only gave the Long Point marsh country its most legendary father figure but was the person who planted the first garden and the first orchard in Norfolk County and possessed its first medicine chest.

JAMES REANEY

Dr Troyer and the folklore surrounding him have found their way into Canadian theatre history in three short plays by Hilda Mary Hooke, "The witch-house at Baldoon," "Widows' scarlet," and "More things in heaven," in her *One act plays from Canadian history* (Toronto, 1942), 79–96, 97–116, and 117–30; and more recently in C. H. Gervais and James Reaney, *Baldoon* (Erin, Ont., 1976).

Church of Jesus Christ of Latter-Day Saints, Geneal. Soc. (Salt Lake City, Utah), International geneal. index. PAC, RG 1, L3, 495: T2/73; RG 5, A1: 56322–35. Private arch., James Reaney (London, Ont.), Corr. from Flora Aker, St Williams, Ont.; O. Morrow, Stirling, Ont.; R. G. T. Archibald, Unionville, Ont. UWOL, Regional Coll., J. A. Bannister papers. Peter Jones, *History of the Ojebway Indians; with especial reference to their conversion to Christianity . . .*, [ed. Elizabeth Field] (London, 1861). *Loyalist narratives from Upper Canada*, ed. J. J. Talman (Toronto, 1946). *Detroit Gazette*, 14 Nov. 1829. R. S. Lambert, *Exploring the supernatural: the weird in Canadian folklore* (Toronto, [1955]). N. T. McDonald, *The Baldoon mystery* (Wallaceburg, Ont., n.d.). E. A. Owen, *Pioneer sketches of Long Point settlement . . .* (Toronto, 1898; repr. Belleville, Ont., 1972). J. H. Coyne, "David Ramsay and Long Point in legend and history," RSC *Trans.*, 3rd ser., 13 (1919), sect.II: 111–26. George Laidler, "John Troyer of Long Point Bay, Lake Erie; an appraisal of associated fact and legend," *OH* (1947): 14–40.

TSAOUENHOHOUI. *See* VINCENT, NICOLAS

TYANTENAGEN. *See* JONES, JOHN

U

UNIACKE, NORMAN FITZGERALD, militia officer, lawyer, office holder, politician, judge, and JP; b. *c*. 1777, probably in Halifax, son of Richard John Uniacke* and Martha Maria Delesdernier; m. 23 Nov. 1829 Sophie Delesdernier in Vaudreuil, Lower Canada; d. 11 Dec. 1846 in Halifax.

The eldest son of Nova Scotia's attorney general, Norman Fitzgerald Uniacke was one of 12 children, several of whom were to become famous in the province. On 1 July 1796 he received a commission as a second lieutenant in the 2nd Halifax Militia Regiment. After being called to the Nova Scotia bar, he left for London in 1798 to finish his law studies and cultivate connections that would be useful in his career. Late in 1805 he entered Lincoln's Inn, the second Nova Scotian to be admitted to the English bar.

In 1807 Uniacke's father tried to have him appointed provincial secretary of Nova Scotia. The effort failed, but on 25 Aug. 1808 he was named by Lord Castlereagh to succeed the attorney general of Lower Canada, Jonathan SEWELL, who had become chief justice of the province. However, Governor Sir James Henry Craig*, who had not been informed of the appointment, issued a temporary commission to Edward Bowen* on 10 Sept. 1808. Bowen was obliged to resign, and Uniacke was able to take up his post officially on 20 June 1809.

Craig sought to get rid of the new attorney general. On 17 May 1810, through his secretary Herman Witsius RYLAND, he consulted the judges of the Court of King's Bench about Uniacke's competence. Sewell, Jenkin Williams*, Pierre-Amable De Bonne*, and James KERR replied that his acquaintance with criminal law was very superficial and his knowledge of civil law often inadequate; in addition, his French was extremely poor. The other judges, James Reid, James Monk*, Pierre-Louis Panet*, and Isaac Ogden, declared that they had had little or no opportunity to form an opinion. Craig suspended Uniacke on 31 May, granting him leave to go to England, and again gave a temporary commission to Bowen, recommending his appointment to Lord Liverpool. Bowen therefore held office in an acting capacity from 1810 to 1812. On 7 Feb. 1812 the new governor, Sir George Prevost*, sent Liverpool a petition from Bowen asking for the attorney generalship of Lower Canada, and he suggested that Uniacke receive a similar appointment for Upper Canada. But shortly afterwards Uniacke was reinstated, primarily through his father's influence.

Uniacke was elected to the House of Assembly for William Henry on 28 Aug. 1824. He remained a member only a short time, however, since on 1 Feb. 1825 Governor Lord Dalhousie [RAMSAY] persuaded him to accept appointment as a judge in the Court of King's Bench in the district of Montreal. On 24 May 1827 he was called to replace the judge in the district of Trois-Rivières, Pierre-Stanislas Bédard*, during the latter's absence. Uniacke received commissions as justice of the peace in different districts in the years between 1826 and 1833, and in the period 1827–33 he held commissions of oyer and terminer and general jail delivery. He retired in August 1834 and returned to Nova Scotia, where he was appointed to the Legislative Council in 1838.

The charge of incompetence brought against Uniacke was probably in large part justified. But the antipathy to him in the upper levels of government was also the result of various stands he took: he favoured civil recognition of Catholic parishes set up after the conquest, whereas their legal existence was contested, particularly by Sewell, because the Catholic bishop had never been officially recognized; furthermore, early in 1825 he supported Louis-Joseph Papineau* for the speakership of the House of Assembly, thus provoking the wrath of the English party. Such behaviour could only bring him animosity and resentment.

CHRISTINE VEILLEUX

PAC, RG 68, General index, 1651–1841. L.-J. Papineau, "Correspondance" (Ouellet), ANQ *Rapport*, 1953–55: 221. *Quebec Gazette*, 15 Sept. 1808, 22 June 1809, 4 June 1827, 21 Oct. 1830. F.-J. Audet, "Les législateurs du Bas-Canada"; "Procureurs généraux du Bas-Canada," *BRH*, 39 (1933): 276. Caron, "Inv. de la corr. de Mgr Plessis," ANQ *Rapport*, 1932–33: 208. Desjardins, *Guide parl. Directory of N.S. MLAs*. Lucien Lemieux, "Juges de la province du Bas-Canada de 1791 à 1840," *BRH*, 23 (1917): 88. Ouellet, "Inv. de la saberdache," ANQ *Rapport*, 1955–57: 131. "Papiers d'État – Bas-Canada," PAC *Rapport*, 1893: 16, 29, 32, 40–44, 49, 56, 62. P.-G. Roy, *Les juges de la prov. de Québec*. F.-J. Audet, *Les juges en chef de la province de Québec, 1764–1924* (Québec, 1927). Buchanan, *Bench and bar of L.C.*, 62–64. F.-X. Garneau, *Histoire du Canada depuis sa découverte jusqu'à nos jours*, Alfred Garneau, édit. (4e éd., 4v., Montréal, 1882–83), 3: 111, 211. F.-J. Audet, "Les juges de Trois-Rivières," *BRH*, 6 (1900): 246. N.-E. Dionne, "Le juge Bédard," *BRH*, 5 (1899): 250–52. Mary Liguori, "Haliburton and the Uniackes: Protestant champions of Catholic liberty (a study in Catholic emancipation in Nova Scotia)," CCHA *Report*, 20 (1953): 37–48. L. G. Power, "Richard John Uniacke: a sketch," N.S. Hist. Soc., *Coll.*, 9 (1895): 82–83.

USBORNE, HENRY, businessman and seigneur; b. *c*. 1780; d. 23 July 1840 in Ryde, Isle of Wight, England.

Henry Usborne was living in London by 1801 and was, in his own words, a "Large Manufacturer" in wood and a partner "in one of the principal Houses" carrying on trade with Russia via the Baltic Sea. The previous year the "Armed Neutrality" of Russia, Sweden, and Denmark, although temporary, had threatened Britain's timber supply and alerted Usborne's firm to the urgency of finding new sources of timber for Britain and the British navy, then at war with Napoleonic France. Early in 1801, therefore, Usborne moved to Quebec, probably the first important Baltic timber merchant to appear in the colony, and announced his "express purpose" of introducing a wood trade similar to that carried on with Russia.

In his first season Usborne purchased a large timber-storage area in Wolfe's Cove (Anse au Foulon) at Quebec and acquired timber lands and sawmills; on the Rivière Maskinongé alone he bought an eight-saw mill and 2,000 acres, and he also applied for a grant of 6,000–10,000 acres there. At the same time he prepared cargoes for 1802, when he would send home seven shiploads of pine; by 1803 he was filling 20 ships. In the latter year a "Mr. Osborne, an English Gentleman," built near Saint John, N.B., "a mill on the Russian plan . . . which works fifteen saws in a frame." This was perhaps the pioneer gang-saw in Canada, and Usborne's background suggests that he was the builder. In 1804 he purchased a further 2,500 acres of timber land on the Maskinongé. About that year Usborne began a steady program of shipbuilding, using master builders at Quebec such as John Goudie*. Between 1806 and 1809 he advertised space on at least eight different vessels sailing from Quebec, and in one month in 1809 no fewer than seven of his vessels arrived there in ballast, probably to load timber.

Lieutenant Governor Sir Robert Shore MILNES was struck by Usborne's commercial "Spirit" and noted that from the outset he had shipped "a much greater quantity [of wood] than has hitherto been exported from Canada in one Season." Milnes recommended Usborne warmly to Whitehall and stuck by him in 1803 when the shipwright officers of the dockyard at Chatham, England, decried his examples of Canadian oak as "unfit" for shipbuilding and repairs and suitable only for "inferior purposes." However, artificial shortages created by a "Timber Ring" of British merchants soon produced a market for Canadian wood, and Usborne's head start gave him great advantages. Yet, despite Milnes's support, another London firm, Scott, Idle and Company, obtained in 1804 the first Admiralty contract for Canadian masts, spars, and bowsprits. Three years later their Lower Canadian agents, John Mure* and James Hare Jolliffe, complained that Usborne was "attempting to throw every impediment" in the way of their fulfilling their engagement, was cutting illegally on crown lands (which were reserved to their exclusive use for supplying Admiralty needs), and was talking "of going next season still more extensively . . . into the mast and spar business." By 1809 Usborne's expansion had induced him to make heavy purchases of oak and pine on both sides of Lake Champlain.

Usborne apparently led a moderately active social life at Quebec. He was a committee member of the Quebec Fire Society, entered horses in the Quebec Races, and acted as a president of a "Country party" held at Sturch's Hotel in April 1808. His house was handsomely appointed, his cellars well stocked, and his stables filled. Among his possessions were "a Pipe of the Best Brazil Madeira that has been 7 years in Canada, . . . excellent fowling pieces, [and] a pair of Pocket Pistols"; by late 1808 he was parading around town in "a curricle built last Spring by one of the first Coach makers [in London], [with] a Harness Compleat of the latest Fashion." In 1803 a short-lived son had been born to Usborne and the illiterate wife of a sergeant stationed in the town.

By 1809 Usborne considered his Lower Canadian operations firmly established. That year he returned to London to direct operations there and formed a new partnership composed of himself, his brother Thomas, and Thomas Starling Benson. The Quebec firm was handed over to Peter Patterson*, who had been in Usborne's employ since 1805 at least. With James Dyke of Quebec and Richard Collins of Montreal as Lower Canadian associates and Usborne as his London partner, Patterson directed the firm of Patterson, Dyke and Company, which had its headquarters at Wolfe's Cove. Under Patterson's management the growth of Usborne's Lower Canadian operations accelerated, notably with the acquisition in 1811 from John Goudie and Henry Black of a large sawmill installation under construction at the Chute Montmorency near Quebec. With Usborne's capital and assistance Patterson subsequently expanded the size of the property by purchase and made the operation "probably as extensive as any in the world" in the opinion of a visiting American expert. The mills were among the most costly to have been built in the Canadas, largely because of the great zig-zag millrace, rock-cut and timber-lined, that fed them from above the falls; from the start they boasted several circular saws, apparently the first in Lower Canada. Patterson also expanded the firm's timber-cutting, shipbuilding, and maritime transport operations.

Meanwhile, in London, Usborne had wrested one-half of the Canadian mast, spar, and bowsprit contract from Scott, Idle and Company, possibly in 1812 but certainly by 1815. To reinforce communications the organization of 1809 was replaced in 1815 by a transatlantic interlocking firm, composed of the London partners and Patterson and Dyke, operating in London as Henry Usborne, Benson and Company and at Quebec as Peter Patterson and Company. By 1818 Henry Usborne, Benson and Company had obtained the entire Admiralty contract, which included much timber in addition to masts and spars; the firm continued to enjoy the monopoly until 1822. In 1820 Usborne testified before a committee of the British House of Commons that since 1801 his firm had invested some £40,000 in sawn-timber operations in the Canadas. By the 1820s it was also once again obtaining timber from Russia.

In 1823 Patterson and Thomas Usborne left the firm, Patterson taking over the Montmorency mills. Henry Usborne kept the Wolfe's Cove installation until 1831 when he sold it to Benson and an associate. He repurchased it in 1834 only to sell it again the following year to George William Usborne, said to be a brother but more likely a nephew. Henry's money may have been behind the firm of Atkinson, Usborne and Company, in which George William was a partner, and that of Longley and Dyke [*see* George LONGLEY]. Usborne also held lands in the Canadas, acquired for speculation or in satisfaction of debts. Some time after 1810 he had bought the 45,000-acre seigneury of Rivière-de-la-Madeleine, in the Gaspé, which was more useful for fishing than for lumbering. In the 1820s he was a director of the Canada Company, which, through the agency of John GALT, sponsored settlement on its vast holdings in Upper Canada, and he was a promoter of the abortive Lower Canada Land Company, which was to have been modelled on it [*see* William Bowman FELTON]. By 1835, however, he had sold out of the Canada Company, and he was not among the shareholders of the British American Land Company, which had replaced the Lower Canada Land Company.

In England Usborne enjoyed the easy social and public life of a rich merchant. By 1816, when he married Phœbe Ann Birch, a daughter of the member of parliament for Lancaster and sister of a baronet, he had a country seat in Norfolk called Heydon Hall which dated from the 16th century. In 1824 he was high sheriff of Suffolk and had possibly already transferred his seat to Branches Park in that county. Ten years later he was leasing a mansion on exclusive Portland Place in London; he filled it with "plate linen glass china books pictures prints [and] wines," and its stables contained several horses and carriages. By the time of Usborne's death in July 1840, apparently while he was on a visit to the resort of Ryde, Branches Park boasted "Gardens pleasure grounds Offices and buildings," and Usborne owned "farms Lands Tenements and Hereditaments" in Suffolk and Cambridge, and "Wharves and hereditaments in Canada." To his wife he bequeathed £500, the use of all his properties, and the residue of his estate, and to his surviving daughters, of whom there were at least two, he left trust funds of equal value to be established from the proceeds – which he estimated would be around £20,000 – of the sale of his properties.

A. J. H. RICHARDSON

ANQ-Q, CE1-61, 8 mai, 19 nov. 1803; CN1-16, 2, 13 nov., 4 déc. 1809; 25 févr. 1811; 10 janv., 12 déc. 1812; 20 sept. 1821; CN1-49, 23 mai 1835; 23 juill., 13 août 1836; 20, 26 oct. 1860; CN1-116, 23 janv. 1838; CN1-145, 27 juill., 4 sept. 1804; 13 nov. 1805; 16 sept. 1807; CN1-262, 30 sept., 15 oct. 1801; 21 oct. 1803; 20, 25 oct. 1804; 1er juin, 20 sept. 1805. Arch. judiciaires, Québec, Testament olographe de Peter Patterson, 17 juin 1851 (*see* P.-G. Roy, *Inv. testaments*, 3: 110). PAC, MG 24, B1, 189: 4038, 4042, 4044, 4046; D12, 1: 82; L3: 8808–26, 8898–903, 26392–403; MG 55/24, no.146; RG 1, L3L: 39870–910, 75303, 75799, 93429–57; RG 4, A1, Peter Patterson and Company to Sir Gordon Drummond, 27 Oct. 1815; William Price to Lord Aylmer, 8 Jan. 1831; B32, 1. PRO, CO 42/119: 191–94; 42/121: 121v; 42/123: 105; 42/135: 363–69; 42/140: 154; 42/180: 10, 722–24; 42/186: 16; 42/205: 364v, 369v; 42/248: 7. [Thomas Douglas, 5th Earl of] Selkirk, *Lord Selkirk's diary, 1803–1804; a journal of his travels in British North America and the northeastern United States*, ed. P. C. T. White (Toronto, 1958; repr. New York, 1969), 195. J. M. Duncan, *Travels through part of the United States and Canada in 1818 and 1819* (2v., Glasgow, 1823), 2: 198–201. G.B., Parl., House of Commons, *Report from the select committee on timber duties . . .* (London, 1835), 155; House of Commons paper, 1812, 3, no.210: 1–668, *Minutes of evidence, taken before the committee of the whole house . . . , relating to the orders of council*, 593, 601, 603, 613; House of Lords, *First report from the select committee . . . , appointed to inquire into the means of extending and securing the foreign trade of the country . . .* ([London, 1820]), 207–10. *Gentleman's Magazine*, July–December 1816: 273; July–December 1831: 464; July–December 1840: 442. Francis Hall, *Travels in Canada and the United States, in 1816 and 1817* (London, 1818), 72. Benjamin Silliman, *Remarks made on a short tour between Hartford and Quebec, in the autumn of 1819* (2nd ed., New Haven, Conn., 1824), 230–31, plate 8. *Winslow papers* (Raymond), 489. *Quebec Gazette*, 20 Aug. 1801; 15 July 1802; 13 Jan., 16 June 1803; 31 May, 7 June, 16 Aug. 1804; 16 May, 11 July 1805; 13, 15, 22 May, 13 Sept., 9, 22 Oct. 1806; 3 Sept. 1807; 31 March, 21 April, 5 May, 23 June, 8 Sept. 1808; 8 June, 6 July, 12, 19, 26 Oct. 1809; 12 April, 6 Dec. 1810; 5 Sept. 1811; 13 July, 10, 17 Dec. 1812; 29 April, 13 May, 16 July 1813; 5 Jan., 28 Sept. 1815; 21 March 1816; 21 Sept. 1818; 28 Jan., 13 May, 7 Oct. 1819; 18 July 1822; 7 July 1823; 1 Dec. 1847. Joseph Bouchette, *Topographical description of L.C.*, 425; *A topographical dictionary of the province of Lower Canada* (London, 1832) (entry on Beauport). *Burke's peerage* (1880), 115–16.

R. G. Albion, *Forest and sea power: the timber problem of the Royal Navy, 1652–1862* (Cambridge, Mass., 1926), 352–55. André Bernier, *Le Vieux-Sillery* ([Québec], 1977), 23. J. E. Defebaugh, *History of the lumber industry of America* (2v., Chicago, 1906–7), 1: 139–40. Povl Drachmann, *The industrial development and commercial policies of the three Scandinavian countries . . .* , ed. Harald Westergaard (Oxford, 1915), 12–13, 33–34, 84–85. S. J. Gillis, *The timber trade in the Ottawa valley, 1806–54* (Parks

Canada, National Parks and Hist. Sites Branch, *Manuscript report*, no.153, Ottawa, 1975). G. S. Graham, *Sea power and British North America, 1783–1820: a study in British colonial policy* (New York, 1968), 145–47. J. W. Hughson and C. C. J. Bond, *Hurling down the pine; the story of the Wright, Gilmour and Hughson families, timber and lumber manufacturers in the Hull and Ottawa region and on the Gatineau River, 1800–1920* (Old Chelsea, Que., 1964), 27, 29, 31. J. M. LeMoine, *Picturesque Quebec: a sequel to "Quebec past and present"* (Montreal, 1882), 156, 236. A. R. M. Lower, *Great Britain's woodyard: British America and the timber trade, 1763–1867* (Montreal and London, 1973), 46–47, 60, 144–45. MacNutt, *New Brunswick*, 152–53. Francis Parsons, *Six men of Yale* (Freeport, N.Y., 1971), 78–79. F. W. Wallace, *Wooden ships and iron men: the story of the square-rigged merchant marine of British North America, the ships, their builders and owners, and the men who sailed them* (Boston, 1937), 14. *The wood industries of Canada* (London, 1897). A. J. H. Richardson, "Indications for research in the history of wood-processing technology," Assoc. for Preservation Technology, *Bull.* (Ottawa), 6 (1974), no.3: 35–146.

V

VALENTINE, WILLIAM, painter, glazier, and daguerreotypist; b. 1798 in Whitehaven, England; m. 2 June 1822 Susannah Elizabeth Smith in Halifax, and they had two daughters; m. secondly 12 Dec. 1830 Sarah Ann Sellon in Halifax; d. there 26 Dec. 1849.

Nothing is known about William Valentine before he immigrated to Halifax in 1818. It has been suggested that he was a relative and pupil of Robert Field*, the most important painter in Nova Scotia at the beginning of the 19th century, but they apparently were never in the same place at the same time, and Joseph Howe*, who knew Valentine well, asserted that he was self-taught. On 23 Jan. 1819 Valentine first advertised himself as a teacher of drawing and on 6 March as a portrait and landscape painter. The "very liberal encouragement" he was experiencing evidently dwindled, perhaps because of the post-war economic depression in the province, and by August 1820 he had gone into partnership with his cousin James Bell in a "ship, sign, house and ornamental painting and glass firm." Valentine carried on as a painter and glazier on Stairs' Wharf after the partnership was dissolved in May 1824, and three years later he advertised his removal to a new shop just off Barrington Street.

Valentine's earliest paintings yet identified date from 1827. His main interest was in portraits, but he occasionally depicted historical subjects, such as *King John signing Magna Charta*, done about 1830 and now in the Nova Scotia College of Art and Design. He also ventured into classical themes, but these paintings have been lost. In December 1831 Valentine was an original member of the managing committee of the Halifax Mechanics' Institute, in which he retained a lifelong interest. The following year he presented to the institute a portrait of its first president, Dr William Grigor*, and he also finished a portrait of John Howe* for Howe's son Joseph. Despite his growing stature as an artist, Valentine had to leave Halifax to secure commissions. In August 1833 he advertised in the Charlottetown *Royal Gazette* as a portrait painter and miniaturist, and the next year he was in St John's in search of work. He seems to have had to revert to house painting when business was slack.

About 1836 Valentine travelled to England, where he studied the well-known painters of the day such as Sir Thomas Lawrence and made copies of their works. The experience had a noticeable effect on his painting, which improved markedly in tone and colour, and from the time he returned about March 1837 until 1844 he enjoyed his best success. His portraits from this period include those of Samuel George William ARCHIBALD, Thomas Chandler Haliburton*, Brenton Halliburton*, John YOUNG and his son William*, Peter Nordbeck*, John Sparrow Thompson*, Alexander Keith*, and well over 100 other eminent Nova Scotians and their wives. Valentine obtained the best of the local patronage, receiving virtually all his commissions from leading merchants and professionals.

In 1839 Valentine again travelled to Europe. That year the photographic process of Louis-Jacques-Mandé Daguerre was made public in France. Valentine reportedly claimed to have received instruction in daguerreotyping "at the very fountain-head in Paris," and it is possible he studied with Daguerre himself. The process evidently represented to Valentine a way of producing the cheap yet accurate portraits his clients demanded and a source of supplementary income. His earliest advertisement for daguerreotyping appeared in the Saint John *Morning News* on 15 Nov. 1841, and on 1 Jan. 1842 he announced in the Halifax *Times* that he was "prepared to execute Daguerreotype likenesses in a beautiful style" with the aid of a "first-rate apparatus" from the United States. Valentine also made visits to Charlottetown and St John's advertising the service. However, neither painting nor photography proved remunerative enough, and as late as 1848 he found it necessary to work as a house and sign painter.

Valentine's last known work is a portrait of Andrew MacKinlay*, president of the Mechanics' Institute, which was presented to that institution in October

1849. A few years before his death a fire in his studio destroyed many of his pictures and damaged his photographic apparatus, and this disaster is said to have hastened his end. It is not known how many portraits Valentine executed – the historian Harry Piers estimated between 125 and 150 – and there has never been a comprehensive exhibition of his work. However, after Field he was the most important portrait painter in early 19th-century Nova Scotia. An obituary in the *Novascotian* was written by Joseph Howe, who also composed a eulogy. Valentine is buried in Camp Hill Cemetery near his friend Peter Nordbeck.

D. C. MACKAY

Examples of William Valentine's work may be seen at the town hall in Liverpool, N.S., and in Halifax at the Atlantic School of Theology, the Law Courts of N.S., the N.S. College of Art and Design, the N.S. Museum, and the PANS. His oil self-portrait is in the PANS and has been reproduced (facing p.130) in the article by Harry Piers cited below.

Camp Hill Cemetery (Halifax), Gravestone inscription. PANS, RG 1, 448. Private arch., D. C. Mackay estate (Halifax), Harry Piers, two letters to L. A. Bowser concerning Valentine's painting *King John signing Magna Charta*, 30 Sept. 1929. *Catalogue of Mr. Eagar's exhibition of paintings* (Halifax, 1838). *Acadian Recorder*, 28 Jan. 1819. *Free Press* (Halifax), 8 Aug. 1820. *Royal Gazette* (Charlottetown), 6 Aug. 1833. *Times* (Halifax), 1 Jan. 1842. Harper, *Early painters and engravers*. National Gallery of Canada, *Catalogue of paintings and sculpture*, ed. R. H. Hubbard (3v., Ottawa and Toronto, 1957–60), 3. William Colgate, *Canadian art, its origins & development* (Toronto, 1943). Harper, *Painting in Canada* (1966). D. [C.] Mackay, "Artists and their pictures," *Canadian Antiques Collector* (Toronto), 7 (1972), no.1: 81–86. Harry Piers, "Artists in Nova Scotia," N.S. Hist. Soc., *Coll.*, 18 (1914): 101–65.

VALLIÈRES DE SAINT-RÉAL, JOSEPH-RÉMI (baptized Joseph-Rémi Vallières, he signed Vallieres de St Real), lawyer, militia officer, businessman, politician, judge, office holder, and JP; b. 1 Oct. 1787 in Carleton (Que.), fourth of eight children of Jean-Baptiste Vallières, blacksmith, and Marguerite Corneillier, *dit* Grandchamp; d. 17 Feb. 1847 in Montreal.

Joseph-Rémi Vallières was born into a family that had been settled in New France since at least 1670. His parents, after a stay in Carleton, on the Baie des Chaleurs, had moved to Quebec by 1792. Seven years later Joseph-Geneviève de Puisaye*, Comte de Puisaye, established a settlement of French refugee nobles at Windham, Upper Canada; soon finding that he lacked workers, Puisaye hired a number of Canadians, including Jean-Baptiste Vallières. Joseph-Rémi, then staying in Montreal, possibly for economic reasons, moved to Windham by June 1799. Vallières *père* died within a couple of years, however, leaving his widow destitute, and Joseph-Rémi was sent to Quebec to live with a maternal aunt and her cooper husband, Basile Amiot.

By mid 1803, therefore, although aged 15, Vallières had had little formal education, but thanks to a superior intelligence, voracious reading, much travelling, and prolonged contact with the cultivated population of Windham, he had independently acquired social graces and an astonishing range of knowledge. He was soon brought to the attention of the parish priest of Quebec, coadjutor bishop Joseph-Octave Plessis*, who took him into his residence and personally tutored him for 17 months. At the beginning of 1805 Vallières was enrolled in the Philosophy course at the Petit Séminaire de Québec. A classmate, Philippe-Joseph Aubert* de Gaspé, was dazzled by his intelligence and wit and charmed by his compassion. Aubert de Gaspé recounts that Vallières learned to speak Portuguese fluently in the space of three weeks in order to provide conversation for a lonely apprentice-clerk (his neighbour in Lower Town), brought from Lisbon by a business firm.

Vallières declined to study for the priesthood, bitterly disappointing Plessis. Determined to go into law, in the fall of 1806 he obtained from the parish priest of Carleton, Michel-Auguste Amiot, who was possibly a relative, the necessary certified copy of his baptismal record; either on his own initiative or at Vallières's request, Amiot added "de Saint-Réal" to the family name in the copy. From February 1807 to October 1808 and from the latter date to May 1812, Vallières studied successively with Charles Thomas, at Trois-Rivières, and Edward Bowen*, interim attorney general of Lower Canada, at Quebec. On 30 May 1812 he was commissioned a lawyer; Bowen, having recently been named a judge, left his current cases to his protégé.

Vallières had only begun to practise, however, when the War of 1812 broke out. In September he was commissioned a lieutenant in Quebec's 2nd Militia Battalion, and he did garrison duty until June 1813 at least. Meanwhile, at Quebec on 16 Nov. 1812, he married Louise Pezard de Champlain, daughter of Pierre-Melchior, "sieur de la Touche de Champlain, seigneur of Godefroy, Roctaillade, and other places." By September 1813 he was residing on one of the best streets in Quebec, called, ironically, Rue des Pauvres (Côte du Palais).

Vallières resumed the regular practice of his profession. On circuit, as at Quebec, he delighted in the exuberant company of his closest friends (and frequent opponents), Aubert de Gaspé, Louis Plamondon*, and Jacques Leblond; with Aubert de Gaspé and Plamondon he had been a member in 1809 of the short-lived Literary Society of Quebec. Of those Vallières represented in the Court of King's Bench at Quebec between 1815 and 1824, small retail merchants constituted 25–30 per cent, farmers 25–30, artisans 15, large merchants 10, professional men and government officials 10, and labourers 5. About 50 per cent of his clients were from Quebec and 45 per cent from rural parishes, particularly around Quebec, in the Beauce, and at Baie-Saint-Paul, La Malbaie, Sainte-Anne-de-La Pocatière (La Pocatière), and Kamouraska. Prominent clients included John White and Company [*see* François LANGUEDOC], the businessmen John Munn* and James McCallum*, the painter Jean-Baptiste ROY-AUDY, and Surveyor General Joseph BOUCHETTE; important British merchants in the colony generally placed their confidence in Andrew STUART. Archbishop Plessis, who had resigned himself to Vallières's independence of spirit, consulted him regularly after 1820, in particular on the erection of parishes and on legal aspects of the conflict opposing Plessis and Bishop Jean-Jacques LARTIGUE of Montreal to the Sulpicians and the priest Augustin Chaboillez*. Vallières trained a number of law students, among them Louis Lagueux* and a son of judge Olivier Perrault*. In 1822 Governor Lord Dalhousie [RAMSAY] considered Vallières and Plamondon "the first at the Quebec Bar in accomplishments & eloquence."

Most of Vallières's clients being of modest means, he was often obliged to give them credit, and he earned some income from interest. He also made small loans – rarely more than £25 – to farmers, retailers, and artisans, many of whom were clients. Some paid him back in land, and it was probably in this manner that he got into land speculation; outside Quebec many of his acquisitions were in parishes in which he had clients. Occasionally Vallières shared in the exploitation of land, as in the seigneury of Fossambault where he supplied lessees with livestock, seeds, and implements in return for the clearance and planting of bush sections or up to one-half of the harvest. He also obtained grants of rural land, bought interests in small seigneuries for resale, and purchased lands for speculation in the townships of Ham, Jersey, Ixworth, Windsor, and Horton.

Vallières dealt even more frequently in land at Quebec. He held lots and houses in Upper and Lower Town as well as in the parish of Sainte-Foy, but he was particularly active in the fastest growing parts of town, the *faubourgs* Saint-Roch and Saint-Jean. Although he even had a pew in the church of labouring-class Saint-Roch (in addition to one in the cathedral of Notre-Dame), he was most attracted to Saint-Jean, inhabited as it was by artisans and shopkeepers, people of his former social background and an important segment of his clientele. In September 1815 Vallières obtained from the Ursulines two vast grants of land in the *faubourg*, one on his own account and one in association with Aubert de Gaspé and Plamondon; he later bought out Plamondon and made other, minor, acquisitions. Between 1819 and 1827 he sold at least five large lots to speculators for a total of £2,623. Since most prospective grantees were artisans and shopkeepers, unable to purchase outright, Vallières usually ceded lots in return for the interest – generally between £2 and £5 annually – on a life annuity that constituted the price of the transaction and for the obligation by the grantee to build a house on the lot. From 1819 to 1828 he made at least 31 such grants for a total of £100 per annum in rents. In 1820 he became involved in running an inn in the *faubourg* after paying for the liquor permit of the penurious keeper.

Vallières had other sources of income. In 1819–20 he purchased three-quarters of the Pont Plessis, a toll-bridge over the Rivière Etchemin near Quebec. He was a substantial stockholder in the Quebec Fire Assurance Company by December 1819. In September 1822 he and the surveyor Patrick Henry Smith formed a copartnership for two years with the Montreal firm of MacPherson and Cuthbertson to produce timber and lumber for the booming Quebec market. He was a partner with François Languedoc and William Phillips in the King's Posts Company in 1823, and from 1826 to 1828 at least he rented out the Bécancour flour-mill in return for two-thirds to three-quarters of its flour production.

By 1819, despite an extravagant (some said dissipated) social life, Vallières had been able to purchase the home of Olivier Perrault, well situated on Rue Sainte-Anne at the Place d'Armes. The cost was a substantial £3,600, but Vallières was given 18 years to pay on the security of Pierre Casgrain*, seigneur of Rivière-Ouelle; in 1825 he made a large two-storey addition. The house was a manifestation of Vallières's social ascent, which his reconciliation with Plessis accelerated singularly. According to a contemporary, when the archbishop arrived back at Quebec in August 1820 from a trip to Europe Vallières was delegated to give the welcoming speech and, as a result, grew "by ten cubits in the eyes of the immense crowd that shook the heavens with its acclamations." That October Vallières was a subscriber to the Quebec Emigrants' Society, and the following year he was elected to the committee of the Education Society of the District of Quebec, headed by Joseph-François PERRAULT. He was a proprietor of the Bibliothèque de Québec in 1822, when it was liquidated.

In 1814 Vallières had been elected to the House of Assembly for Saint-Maurice. Defeated two years later, he was returned in March 1820 for Upper Town Quebec, which included the *faubourg* Saint-Jean, edging out the executive councillor William Bacheler Coltman* by four votes; he was elected again in July, without opposition, in the company of Andrew Stuart. Both in and out of the assembly Vallières made his mark as a moderate Quebec member of the nationalist

Canadian party. In 1822, for example, he was a leading figure at Quebec in a popular movement opposed to the projected union of Lower and Upper Canada, a union strongly favoured by Coltman. In January 1823 the virtual head of the Canadian party, Louis-Joseph Papineau*, was chosen as a delegate to London to oppose union, and Vallières, on a motion by the tory Charles Richard Ogden*, and strongly supported by the nationalist Louis Bourdages*, was elected to replace him as speaker of the assembly; previously, the house had rejected, among others, Papineau's choice, his cousin Denis-Benjamin Viger*. Although unanimous, Vallières's election signified that leadership of the party, which had shifted to Montreal after the retirement to a judgeship of Pierre-Stanislas Bédard*, had swung back to Quebec, whose deputies were generally more moderate.

No doubt sensing a potential improvement in the political climate, which had become increasingly tempestuous, Governor Lord Dalhousie courted Vallières in April 1823 by involving him in preparations for the creation of a provincial literary and historical society [*see* William SMITH]. However, at the founding meeting held at Quebec in January 1824, Vallières angered Dalhousie and Montrealer John Richardson* by persuading the gathering to adopt the name Literary and Historical Society of Quebec, rather than of Lower Canada, arguing, according to Dalhousie, that Quebec was "entitled to the distinction as the Capital, the residence of govt. & virtually implying the Province." Vallières was elected a vice-president of the society. Later in 1824 he accepted appointment as a trustee of the Royal Institution for the Advancement of Learning, even though it was opposed by Canadian nationalists and boycotted by Plessis as unfit to supervise the education of Catholic children [*see* Joseph Langley Mills*].

Dalhousie had noted in late 1823 the good-humoured, business-like atmosphere in the legislature with Vallières at the head of the assembly. Vallières even had the entire body to dinner so that, Dalhousie remarked, "the Speaker of the Commons entertained for the first time in Canada, King, Lords, & Commons in a body." The governor cautiously opened negotiations with Vallières to regulate the problem of supplies, which had long bedevilled the administration of the colony, but Papineau, who had arrived back in November and alone had refused Vallières's invitation to dinner, stiffened opposition in the house. After a procedural duel between Vallières and Papineau, a partial accommodation was reached; however, Dalhousie informed Colonial Secretary Lord Bathurst, "I can no longer entertain any hope that good sense and moderation will calm the irritation in the House of Assembly." Indeed, Papineau's return induced Vallières to reinforce his image as a nationalist. In February 1824 he strongly supported resolutions by Louis Bourdages condemning the Canada Trade Act, which had been passed by the British parliament in 1822 in place of an act of union; both men charged that parliament had interfered in the internal affairs of the colony through a clause encouraging conversion from seigneurial tenure to free and common socage. Papineau, who defended the act as a legitimate product of the supremacy of the imperial parliament, won the round, but Vallières triumphed in other battles during a sharp rivalry that persisted until Dalhousie prorogued the legislature in March 1824. The following month Vallières helped plan celebration of the king's birthday; yet in the winter of 1824–25 he complained strongly to visiting British MPs that Canadians were neglected in government appointments, which, he added, too often went to British dependants of the governor.

With Dalhousie in Britain, Lieutenant Governor Sir Francis Nathaniel Burton* called a new legislature, which met in January 1825. Despite a vigorous campaign in his favour by Bourdages and Joseph LE VASSEUR Borgia, Vallières lost the vote for the speakership, 32 to 12, to Papineau, who rallied the Montrealers and certain Quebec area representatives, including the influential John NEILSON. A rift appeared in the Canadian party as Vallières and Bourdages unsuccessfully contested in the assembly the election of some Papineau supporters, while Papineau reproached "the foolishness, the weakness, [and] the greed" of his Quebec opponents. Jean-Thomas Taschereau*, Andrew Stuart, and Vallières were "hand in glove," he grumbled in February 1826. "Never has the administration had in the house such an array of talent ready to undertake anything asked of it." Yet, while still attempting to effect a compromise on supplies, Vallières regularly stole Papineau's thunder with nationalist pronouncements on seigneurial tenure, introduction of English laws, and use of French in the administration of justice. In April 1826 a disconcerted Dalhousie wrote that "in this Session [Vallières] has shewn himself a straw blown by the wind, acting in direct contradiction of his line when Speaker in 1824." Later that year Viger remarked disapprovingly of Vallières that "the habits of the bar sometimes narrow ideas by concentrating them on questions of individual rights" as opposed to collective rights; he added that Vallières took positions on public affairs with the insouciance of a lawyer taking on a legal case. Yet Vallières took his nationalism seriously. In 1827, finding the Literary and Historical Society of Quebec dominated by British members, he joined Bouchette and others in founding the Société pour l'Encouragement des Sciences et des Arts en Canada [*see* Andrew Stuart].

In the elections of 1827 Vallières and Stuart defeated the Papineau candidates George Vanfelson* and Amable BERTHELOT in Upper Town, but Papineau supporters won almost everywhere else. Although in November Vallières was again advanced for the speakership, Papineau – proposed by Bourdages – won 39 to 5. When Dalhousie refused to accept Papineau as speaker, however, Vallières strongly denounced the action and asserted that the governor's approval was a mere formality. In the Montreal area the Patriote party (as the Canadian party was now known) hastily channelled popular indignation into a monster petition against Dalhousie's administration. At Quebec, a committee of 35 citizens, headed by Vallières, found the Montreal petition too radical and, to Papineau's disgust, carefully drafted another, which was both more complete in its coverage of controversial issues and more moderate in tone. For his part in the movement Vallières was stripped of his militia commission – he had risen to major – by an enraged Dalhousie, who would also have annulled his lawyer's licence had not cooler heads urged restraint. "Fickle as he is," Civil Secretary Andrew William COCHRAN told the governor, "he is the only man in the assembly who on a new election of a speaker would be chosen to replace Mr P." In November 1828, following Dalhousie's replacement by Sir James Kempt*, Vallières attempted to start off the legislative session on a cordial note; his flowery reply to the speech from the throne, however, was substantially amended by Papineau and his allies. A week later, when Papineau was delighted to see the house heating up against the administration, Vallières suddenly intervened. "Mr Vallières is always ready to mitigate the abuses that tend to uncover the faults of the administration," he complained to his wife, Julie Bruneau. "He is specious, he dragged along [François QUIROUET, Marc-Pascal de Sales* Laterrière, Louis Lagueux, Robert Christie*] and Ogden, who think like him, and all the rest of the house." Early in 1829 Julie warned her husband that most of the clergy found him too strident and, like Pierre-Flavien Turgeon*, preferred Vallières's more moderate nationalism.

Plessis's death in 1825 had not affected Vallières's position with the Quebec hierarchy. The new archbishop, Bernard-Claude Panet*, gave him a free rein on such issues as the establishment of a Roman Catholic Royal Institution for the Advancement of Learning [*see* Joseph Langley Mills] and the civil erection of parishes. Indeed, in February 1828 Panet proposed to Lartigue that they send Vallières to London with an address from the clergy opposing the sale of the Sulpician estates to the government. Lartigue, who had his own legal opinions on ecclesiastical matters and consulted, if anyone, his cousins Viger and Papineau, distrusted Vallières's independence of mind and insisted that a priest be sent instead.

By the late 1820s, Vallières had tired of his increasingly futile rivalry with Papineau; following the death of Olivier Perrault in March 1827 he had been "particularly urgent and busy," according to Dalhousie, in soliciting a judgeship. Possibly thanks to his election as speaker in 1823, Vallières's law practice had picked up considerably and he had taken into partnership 21-year-old Jean-François-Joseph Duval. He had acquired several important new clients, such as the businessmen James HUNT, John CALDWELL, John Cannon*, John Goudie*, Moses Hart*, and Samuel Gerrard*, several English firms, and the Union Company of Quebec, but most were occasional and the cream of the market still went to Andrew Stuart. In 1824, in 32 appearances in the Court of King's Bench, Vallières and Duval represented large businessmen 12 times; they appeared for farmers on 4 occasions only and not once for an artisan or a labourer. By October 1827 Duval had given way to Alexander Stewart Scott, who was also just beginning his career; the new association was only moderately active. Vallières had acquired an almost legendary reputation in judicial circles for spontaneous eloquence and brilliant argumentation, but also for erratic conduct. During one phase of a celebrated marathon case opposing Marie-Amable Foretier*, Viger's wife, and Toussaint POTHIER, Vallières, who represented Mme Viger, arrived in court one morning still swimming in the vapours of the previous night's potations. He mistakenly, but brilliantly, pleaded the case of his legal opposite, James Stuart*, before being placed on the right track by a bemused judge; he then demolished his own demonstrations with his accustomed flair and subsequently obtained judgement in his favour when Stuart and his assistants were unable to improve on them. Indeed, when facing Stuart, the only lawyer who intimidated him, he could become so nervous as to lose all consciousness of what he was saying and, being most eloquent when spontaneous, utterly rout his opponent. In the late 1820s he continued to train young men for the law, among them Charles HUNTER and Étienne Parent*.

When Pierre-Stanislas Bédard, provincial judge in Trois-Rivières, died in 1829, Vallières applied for his post. Kempt appointed him on 13 May, although it meant losing a voice for moderation in the assembly. According to Viger, competition had been stiff, but the nomination of Vallières "appears to give general satisfaction" as compensation for his persecution at Dalhousie's hands. "If there is not entire confidence in M. Vallières as a constitutional expert or legislator," remarked Viger (who also worried about indolence), "people have a just idea of the superiority of his understanding and of his knowledge in matters of civil jurisprudence." The *Quebec Gazette* applauded the appointment of a man "who has both the will and the capacity to administer justice according to the established laws of the country, without fear, affection or bias." In the subsequent by-election his protégé, Duval, defeated Papineau's candidate, Vanfelson.

In early February 1830 Vallières sold his home at Quebec to the lawyer and businessman Daniel McCallum for £2,000, but the entire sum went to the estate of Olivier Perrault. From 1829 to 1833 Vallières made his last 15 grants in the *faubourg* Saint-Jean and sold off land in the Eastern Townships and on the lower south shore of the St Lawrence. Possibly he made acquisitions around Trois-Rivières. His last personal tie to Quebec, his wife Louise, had died in April 1829 and a significantly broad mixture of mourners had attended the funeral, including James and Andrew Stuart, Solicitor General Ogden, Vanfelson, Le Vasseur Borgia, and Perrault. In Trois-Rivières Vallières struck up a relationship with the Jewess Esther Eliza Hart, daughter of EZEKIEL. A licence to marry was apparently obtained in Montreal in July 1831, but is unlikely to have been used. Esther was still alive when, on 26 April 1836, Vallières married the widow Jane Keirnan in the Catholic church at Trois-Rivières. He had had at least one son with Louise; he adopted several children while in Trois-Rivières and became a father figure for others, among them Joseph-Guillaume Barthe*, who idolized him. According to Barthe and to Barthe's contemporary Antoine Gérin-Lajoie*, as a judge Vallières found himself incapable of pronouncing the death sentence and went to any length to escape having to do so. In October 1830 he was given a commission of the peace for all of Lower Canada, and on 10 December his commission as provincial judge was replaced by another as resident judge of the Court of King's Bench in the Trois-Rivières district.

Trois-Rivières offered few outlets for a man of Vallières's social dispositions. He was the first president of the Société d'Éducation de Trois-Rivières, formed in 1830. He also took part in some political activities. In March 1830 he presided over a royalist dinner in honour of the local deputy, Ogden, and in the 1830s and early 1840s he and René-Joseph Kimber led a movement for revision of the lease to the Saint-Maurice ironworks, held by Mathew BELL, in order to open new lands for agriculture. After the uprising of 1837 Vallières granted a writ of habeas corpus to lawyer Édouard-Louis Pacaud* for the rebel André-Augustin Papineau, brother of Louis-Joseph. In June 1838 the new governor, Lord Durham [LAMBTON], who considered Vallières the premier Canadian legal mind, appointed him to the Executive Council to arbitrate between the judges from Quebec and those from Montreal when the council acted as the Court of Appeals.

Shortly before Durham's arrival, and again in early November 1838 after his departure, Administrator Sir John Colborne* suspended habeas corpus. In November judges Elzéar BÉDARD and Philippe Panet*, considering the action unconstitutional, granted a writ; they were suspended by Colborne, on 10 December. Four days earlier, but well aware of the risk he took, Vallières too had granted a writ, for a farmer from Rivière-du-Loup (Louiseville). When summoned to provide Colborne with the documents relative to his decision, Vallières complied, but he protested that an investigation by the executive would tend "to lessen the independence of the Bench." Nevertheless, supported by the Executive Council, the law officers, Ogden and Andrew Stuart, and the chief justices, James Stuart and Michael O'SULLIVAN, among others, Colborne suspended Vallières on 27 December. A few days later Barthe, having learned that he himself was to be arrested for having had published a poem that had been judged subversive, sought Vallières's advice; Vallières congratulated him on the publication, told him to receive his "baptism as a patriot and a political martyr," and gave him books to read in prison. Deprived of his salary, Vallières lived in financial embarrassment, but the chastisement did not deter him from signing a petition, in the spring of 1840, against a union that Britain was determined to impose on the Canadas through Governor Charles Edward Poulett THOMSON. With Papineau in exile, Canadian nationalists prepared to bring Vallières back into politics and propose him as speaker of the united assembly. However, on 8 August, Vallières, Bédard, and Panet were reinstated (with back-pay) by Thomson, who did not want political martyrs threatening the fragile union he was effecting.

On 1 June 1842 Sydenham's successor, Sir Charles BAGOT, named Vallières to succeed O'Sullivan as chief justice of the Court of King's Bench in the Montreal district; Vallières thus became the first Canadian to hold a chief justiceship. He stood, Bagot told Colonial Secretary Lord Stanley, "*consensu omnium* single and alone as the first lawyer in the country . . . equally versed in French and English laws and languages." The appointment effectively reduced the opposition to union; its leaders, Neilson and Viger, applauded unreservedly the elevation of "a man of genius who for 12 years shone under a bushel." However, according to Barthe, Vallières left Trois-Rivières a "shadow of himself" physically. He was subsequently so racked by leg pains that he often had to be carried to the bench, and he was even threatened by the ministry of William Henry Draper* with forced retirement as a result of frequent absences. Consequently, in July 1846 he rejected with disdain an offer of the presidency of the Executive Council made by the same government, which hoped by that means to undermine the Lower Canadian reform movement, led by Louis-Hippolyte La Fontaine*. At the end of the year Vallières was residing in Donegana's Hotel, a luxury establishment in the heart of Montreal. There he wrote his will, in a single sentence, leaving all his possessions "unto my beloved wife Mrs Jane Keirnan in full and unlimited property." He died the following

February. Antoine Gérin-Lajoie delivered a eulogy before the Institut Canadien of Montreal, a liberal intellectual body of which Vallières had been a member.

Aubert de Gaspé asserted that Vallières "was the most naturally talented man that Canada has ever produced," and this assessment has since been endorsed repeatedly. Vallières has inevitably been compared with Papineau by authors seeking to discover why he had been unable to lead the Canadian party on a more moderate course. Papineau's equal in intelligence and eloquence, a serious student all his life (he always had a book in his pocket), Vallières nevertheless enjoyed the good life too much to share Papineau's quasi-masochistic devotion to duty, public and private. As well Vallières was independent-minded; his lines of thought, resulting in part from a largely informal education, were too original and complex to excite a mass following and too flexible to attract party support at a time when political views were hardening into the opposing ideologies of liberal nationalism and colonial imperialism. He was thus ostracized by both sides in the late 1820s and throughout the 1830s. Only in the 1840s, when new patterns of thought and alliances emerged, did his originality become appreciated.

Vallières seems to have left no personal papers and consequently remains an enigma to historians, as he had been to his contemporaries. Laurent-Olivier David* wrote that his life "belongs to tradition rather than to history; there remains of him only the recollection of his abilities in the memory of those who knew him." Such a source must be employed with discretion, for Vallières amused himself by spinning tales of his mysterious past to such admirers as Aubert de Gaspé and Barthe, who faithfully consigned them to their memoirs. But if the 'facts' his contemporaries recount are often contradictory or patently incredible, the impressions of him formed by his friends – and grudgingly concurred in by his opponents – leave no doubt that Vallières de Saint-Réal was an extraordinary man.

JAMES H. LAMBERT in collaboration with
JACQUES MONET

There are hundreds of notarized instruments relating to Joseph-Rémi Vallières de Saint-Réal at the ANQ-Q in various minute-books: CN1-16, CN1-18, CN1-38, CN1-80, CN1-89, CN1-147, CN1-172, CN1-178, CN1-179, CN1-188, CN1-197, CN1-208, CN1-212, CN1-230, CN1-253, CN1-262, CN1-267, CN1-284, and CN1-285; these deeds are listed in ANQ-Q, P-239/99. A portrait of Vallières, executed by Théophile Hamel* from another, unknown portrait, is part of a collection depicting the speakers of the Legislative Assembly and the House of Commons in the Parliament Buildings at Ottawa; a photographic copy is at the PAC. Portraits of Vallières have been published in L.-O. David, "Galerie nationale: Joseph-Rémi Vallières," *L'Opinion publique*, 18 août 1870: 1–2, and P.-G. Roy, *Les juges de la prov. de Québec*.

ANQ-MBF, CE1-48, 26 avril 1836. ANQ-Q, CE1-1, 16 nov. 1812; T11-302/3550–79. AP, Saint-Joseph (Carleton), reg. des baptêmes, mariages et sépultures, 1er oct. 1787. ASQ, Fonds Viger–Verreau, sér.O, 0145: 4–7, 9–10, 12–14, 16–21; 0146: 296–98. AUM, P 58, U, Vallières de Saint-Réal à Samuel Gerrard, 20 nov. 1824; Vallières de Saint-Réal à A.-O. Tarieu de Lanaudière, 28 févr. 1820; Vallières de Saint-Réal à Marguerite Tarieu de Lanaudière, 31 oct., 9 nov. 1816; 8 août 1818; 4 janv. 1820; Vallières de Saint-Réal et John Cannon à George Ryland, 23 juill. 1825. PAC, RG 4, B8: 6793–809; RG 68, General index, 1651–1841. PRO, CO 42/281: 446–77 (mfm. at ANQ-Q). P.[-J.] Aubert de Gaspé, *Mémoires* (Ottawa, 1866), 258. Julie Bruneau, "Correspondance de Julie Bruneau (1823–1862)," Fernand Ouellet, édit., ANQ *Rapport*, 1957–59: 61. "Les dénombrements de Québec" (Plessis), ANQ *Rapport*, 1948–49. *Docs. relating to constitutional hist., 1819–28* (Doughty and Story), 212–13. Antoine Gérin-Lajoie, "Éloge de l'honorable Joseph Rémi Vallières de St Real, juge en chef du district de Montréal," *Album littéraire et musical de la Rev. canadienne* (Montréal), 1847: 86–90. L.-J. Papineau, "Correspondance" (Ouellet), ANQ *Rapport*, 1953–55: 213, 221, 228, 231, 233, 243, 251, 253. Ramsay, *Dalhousie journals* (Whitelaw). *La Minerve*, 22 févr. 1847. *Quebec Gazette*, 30 Oct. 1817; 5 March, 24 Aug. 1818; 15 May, 2 Dec. 1819; 9 March, 3, 6 July, 23 Oct. 1820; 10 May, 27 Aug., 20 Dec. 1821; 17 Oct. 1822; 16 Jan., 9 Oct., 13 Nov. 1823; 13 May 1824; 1 April 1830.

F.-J. Audet, *Les députés de Saint-Maurice (1808–1838) et de Champlain (1830–1838)* (Trois-Rivières, Qué., 1934); *Les juges en chef de la province de Québec, 1764–1924* (Québec, 1927). F.-M. Bibaud, *Le panthéon canadien* (A. et V. Bibaud; 1891). Caron, "Inv. de la corr. de Mgr Panet," ANQ *Rapport*, 1933–34: 321; "Inv. de la corr. de Mgr Plessis," 1928–29: 148, 177, 184; 1932–33: 195; "Inv. des doc. relatifs aux événements de 1837 et 1838," 1925–26: 398; "Papiers Duvernay," 1926–27: 227. Desjardins, *Guide parl.* Desrosiers, "Inv. de la corr. de Mgr Lartigue," ANQ *Rapport*, 1941–42: 431, 434. *Laurentiana parus avant 1821*, Milada Vlach, compil. (Montréal, 1976). H. J. Morgan, *Sketches of celebrated Canadians*. *Officers of British forces in Canada* (Irving). P.-G. Roy, *Les avocats de la région de Québec*. Barthe, *Souvenirs d'un demi-siècle*. T.-P. Bédard, *Histoire de cinquante ans (1791–1841), annales parlementaires et politiques du Bas-Canada, depuis la Constitution jusqu'à l'Union* (Québec, 1869), 283. Buchanan, *Bench and bar of L.C. The centenary volume of the Literary and Historical Society of Quebec, 1824–1924*, ed. Henry Ievers (Quebec, 1924). Christie, *Hist. of L.C.* (1848–55), 6: 396–405. J. C. Dent, *The last forty years: Canada since the union of 1841* (2v., Toronto, [1881]). Lemieux, *L'établissement de la première prov. eccl.* Monet, *Last cannon shot*. Ouellet, *Bas-Canada*. Rumilly, *Papineau et son temps*. Benjamin Sulte, *Mélanges historiques . . .*, Gérard Malchelosse, édit. (21v., Montréal, 1918–34), 19: 61–64, 84. F.-J. Audet, "Un juge en prison," *BRH*, 8 (1902): 113–16; "Vallières de Saint-Réal," *Cahiers des Dix*, 1 (1936): 202–12. L.-P. Desrosiers, "Montréal soulève la province," *Cahiers des Dix*, 8 (1943): 81. Raymond Douville, "La maison de Gannes," *Cahiers des Dix*, 21 (1956): 133–34. É.-Z. Massicotte, "Les mutations d'un coin de rue," *BRH*, 45 (1939): 271–74. Victor Morin, "Clubs et sociétés notoires d'autrefois," *Cahiers des Dix*, 14 (1949): 204. Fernand Ouellet, "Papineau et la rivalité Québec–Montréal (1820–1840)," *RHAF*, 13 (1959–60): 311–27. P.-G. Roy, "Les premières années de Vallière de Saint-Réal" and "Le nom Vallière de Saint-Réal était-il authentique?" *BRH*, 29 (1923): 129–33 and 161–68. Albert Tessier, "Une campagne antitrustarde il y a un siècle," *Cahiers des Dix*, 2 (1937): 199–206.

VAN EGMOND, ANTHONY JACOB WILLIAM GYSBERT (he signed **Anthonij J. W. G. Van Egmond**), settler and rebel; b. 10 March 1775 in Groesbeek, Netherlands; m. 1808 Marie Susanne Elizabeth Dietz in Mainz (Federal Republic of Germany), and they had five sons and three daughters; d. 5 Jan. 1838 in Toronto.

When settlers during the elections of 1835 in Upper Canada shouted that candidate Colonel Anthony Van Egmond had come from the Five Points slum of New York City, they were viciously wrong. But it must have come as a surprise to him that his claim to be descended from the counts Van Egmond of the Netherlands was considered false. Indeed it was. When he died on 5 Jan. 1838 the truth about his origins was hidden. A baptismal certificate, now in the hands of a descendant and never questioned, is actually the result of a deliberate attempt to conceal his original identity.

Van Egmond was born Antonij Jacobi Willem Gijben on 10 March 1775 at Groesbeek, Netherlands, the son of Johannes Arnoldus Gijben, *schout* (sheriff) of the region, and Maria Bloem, and he was baptized in the local Reformed church on the 12th. When the boy was 12 his father was found murdered, and in his 20s he became involved in criminal activity which forced him to flee to Germany. His offence must have been serious, for early in 1802 the superior court of his native province complained that repeated attempts to arrest him had failed and ordered that a determined effort be made to obtain his extradition to the Netherlands. Six months before the court's statements, someone identified as a "prominent business-man" in Emmerich (Federal Republic of Germany) had requested a copy of Gijben's baptismal certificate from the Groesbeek registers. It can be assumed that this document was used as the basis for the ingeniously contrived certificate hitherto accepted as genuine. Gijben's parents' names, his own name, and the names of some local residents are correctly given, but the claim made on the certificate to descent from the Van Egmond family was invented. The last count had died childless in 1707.

The whereabouts of Van Egmond, as he now became, are difficult to trace for the next several years. He may have joined the merchant marine in northern Germany; another document shows his membership in a masonic lodge in London. In 1808 he surfaces in Mainz, where he was apparently either a functionary in the legal system or an army officer. Van Egmond's life to 1819 is the subject of continuing research, but the information that has been found does not confirm the romantic stories told of him over the years. For example, he was not among the soldiers in Napoleon's march to Moscow. Neither was he wounded at Waterloo as an officer in the Dutch contingent; his name does not appear on the official list of casualties. It is more than likely that his army service, if any, was of extremely short duration. The most that can be verified is that Van Egmond was on the fringes of military activity, probably involved in merchandising, supplies, and transportation.

In 1819, with his wife and children, Van Egmond travelled via Amsterdam and Liverpool, England, to Philadelphia. Once there he continued to the area of Indiana, Pa, no doubt attracted by the possibility of purchasing land from the Holland Land Company. Van Egmond bought some land and settled there, but his life was anything but successful. Two sons and a daughter were added to the family, and although the older children were able to help out later, the success he sought stayed a respectable distance away from him. In 1826 his property was seized and sold at auction because taxes had not been paid.

The road from Pennsylvania to Upper Canada was well travelled about this time, and Van Egmond must have heard about the riches and fertile soil of the British province. Soon after his arrival in 1828 he acquired 200 acres in Oxford East Township. This purchase of Canada Company land brought him into contact with John GALT, the company's representative in Upper Canada. Galt saw in the newcomer a potentially useful person to help develop the Huron Tract, a million-acre triangle of company land bordering on Lake Huron. Not only could Van Egmond converse with the German-speaking settlers then immigrating to Upper Canada, but he also knew about working the land and about the movement of people and supplies. Furthermore, he was not unwilling to build roads in order to open up the bush.

Van Egmond's eminent suitability for his new role, his concern for the settlers, and his accomplishments give him a good claim to be considered a "father of the Huron Tract." By 1832 he and his sons had built the major part of the road from Waterloo to Goderich and part of the stretch between what is now Clinton and London. Along the former road he established inns which were managed by his son-in-law Andrew Helmer, Sebastian Fryfogel, and Andrew Seebach, and he himself took care of one near Clinton. There in 1829 he produced the first harvest of wheat in the Huron Tract, and to mark the occasion several officials of the Canada Company, including William DUNLOP, Samuel Strickland*, and Thomas Mercer Jones*, had dinner at his inn.

At the same time Van Egmond was becoming increasingly dissatisfied with the Canada Company. He apparently had lacked cash almost from the date of his arrival in Upper Canada, but the problem affected him in earnest when the company paid him for his services in the form of down payments on land. Moreover, although Van Egmond had access to several thousand acres, he was unable to make the further payments. He was also disappointed by the company's failure to attract settlers and to build public works in order to stimulate development. Van Egmond had acted as the representative in the tract for the *Colonial Advocate*, and he had corresponded with its former editor, William Lyon Mackenzie*. He wrote articles for the paper against the management of the Canada Company and even received the chance to appear before the select committee of the House of Assembly, chaired by Mackenzie, which in 1835 investigated grievances throughout the province. Van Egmond ran for the legislature in Huron County that year, but he was defeated by Robert Graham DUNLOP.

By the latter part of 1837 Mackenzie was making plans for an uprising in Upper Canada, and because he believed Van Egmond to have had considerable military experience he invited him to take command of the rebel forces. Although Van Egmond readily agreed, he arrived at the rendezvous at Montgomery's Tavern north of Toronto three days after the uprising had begun because Mackenzie had advanced the date from 7 December. He quickly became convinced that the rebel cause was hopeless but remained throughout the skirmish which took place on the 7th between the rebels and government forces. Once the rebels were defeated he attempted to escape, but was taken and jailed in Toronto. There he contracted a fatal illness, for whose treatment he was transferred to the Toronto General Hospital on 30 December. To the end he professed his innocence, but even his sons did not believe him. After his death most of his land was sold to pay his debts; his sons managed to retain enough to take up their father's plans, although without his political convictions. Naturalized in 1841 and 1842, they established successful enterprises in what later became the village of Egmondville.

Perhaps Robina and Kathleen Macfarlane* Lizars, in their reminiscences of the Canada Company, were correct in thinking that Van Egmond might have been spared for a longer life "had he not taken up misunderstood politics in a foreign land." But he had had the misfortune of becoming disenchanted with the Canada Company before many others.

W. J. VAN VEEN

[The above account is mainly based on original research done in Canada, the Netherlands, Germany, and Pennsylvania. In the Netherlands, the following materials at the Rijksarchief in Gelderland (Arnhem) proved useful: baptismal records in Inv. no.RBS 805; the three extradition-procedure papers in Inv. no.5018, 8 Jan. 1802; and the record of the Gijben murder case in Rechterlijk Archief Hoge Heerlijkheid Groesbeek, criminal cases, inv. no.6. The birth certificate of Van Egmond's eldest child is in the Staatsarchiv Mainz (Mainz, Federal Republic of Germany), GUI 1808, no.278 (9 April 1808).

The first and most thorough study of Van Egmond was made by Wilfrid Brenton Kerr, professor of history at the University of Buffalo, N.Y., and published in two sets of articles in the *Huron Expositor* (Seaforth, Ont.): "Colonel Anthony VanEgmond and the rebellion of 1837 in Huron County," 25 Sept.–11 Dec. 1931, and "The Canada Company and Anthony VanEgmond: the story of 1837 in Huron County," 16 Aug.–13 Sept. 1940. The first article also appeared in the *Signal* (Goderich, Ont.), 1 Oct.–24 Dec. 1931, and a copy of the latter is available as a series of unidentified scrapbook clippings at AO, MS 133. Kerr's work has not received the recognition it should. It apparently was his intention to write a full biography, but his death intervened and his notes have disappeared. Other original Van Egmond material appears in "Van Egmond's apology for his presence in Mackenzie's camp at Montgomery's," edited by Kerr, *OH*, 33 (1939): 99–103, and G. H. Needler, *Colonel Anthony Van Egmond: from Napoleon and Waterloo to Mackenzie and rebellion* (Toronto, 1956). The list of Dutch casualties at Waterloo appears in [François de Bas], *Prins Fredrik der Nederlanden en zijn tijd . . .* (4v. in 6, Schiedam, Netherlands, 1887–1913 [i.e., 1914]), 3: 1379–82. The Count Van Egmond data are found in A. W. E. Dek, *Genealogie der heren en graven Van Egmond* (2nd ed., Zaltbommel, Netherlands, 1970). Huron County is described in James Scott, *The settlement of Huron County* (Toronto, 1966), and in Robina and K. M. Lizars, *In the days of the Canada Company: the story of the settlement of the Huron Tract and a view of the social life of the period, 1825–1850* (Toronto, 1896; repr. Belleville, Ont., 1973); some material is found in [Samuel] Strickland, *Twenty-seven years in Canada West; or, the experience of an early settler*, ed. Agnes Strickland (2v., London, 1853; repr. Edmonton, 1970). I became acquainted with Van Egmond through Guillet, *Lives and times of Patriots*. W.J.V.V.]

VASSAL DE MONVIEL (Monteil, Montviel), FRANÇOIS (François-Xavier), militia and army officer, office holder, JP, and landowner; b. 4 Nov. 1759 in Boucherville (Que.), son of François-Germain Vassal de Monviel and Charlotte Boucher de La Perrière; m. there 18 Jan. 1796 Louise Perrault, daughter of the late Quebec merchant Jacques Perrault*, known as Perrault *l'aîné*, and they had at least one daughter, Charlotte, who married Louis-Aubert Thomas at Quebec on 4 Sept. 1821; d. 25 Oct. 1843 at Quebec.

François Vassal de Monviel's father, a career soldier, had come to the colony with the French regulars during the Seven Years' War and he died following the battle of Sainte-Foy in 1760. His widow established a new home for their son François when in November 1765 she married Pierre-René Boucher de

La Bruère, the future seigneur of Montarville, who belonged, as she did, to the Canadian nobility. In this social milieu, military pursuits were always encouraged. Boucher de La Bruère, who had been a soldier himself, must have approved when François participated in the British campaign against the rebelling Americans. For the young man this was the start of an active career in the militia and army.

Vassal de Monviel was just 17 when he joined the ranks of the Canadian auxiliary companies in 1776. The following year he took part as an ensign in the siege of Fort Stanwix (Rome, N.Y.). On active service until 1783, he travelled to France after the war to settle some family affairs. In 1787 his rank as a provincial ensign and his entitlement to half pay were recognized. He was granted 500 *arpents* of land near the seigneury of Beauharnois for his services. Some Canadians would have the good fortune to receive the backing of the colonial authorities in their requests for officer rank in the regular army. Vassal de Monviel was probably amongst them, since in 1796 he was said to be a lieutenant in the 7th Foot (Royal Fusiliers), a regiment on garrison duty in British North America from 1791 to 1802.

Vassal de Monviel was commissioned captain in the Royal Canadian Volunteer Regiment in 1797 and continued to serve in it until it was disbanded in 1802. In December 1807, while Sir James Henry Craig* was governor, he was appointed deputy adjutant general of the Lower Canadian militia. He reached the highest post in the militia, that of adjutant general, as successor to the ageing François Baby*, on 9 Oct. 1811. Made at a time when the United States was threatening the colony, this appointment was a recognition of Vassal de Monviel's extensive military experience. On occasion during the War of 1812 he was even called upon to carry out tasks generally entrusted to the adjutant general of the British forces in North America.

Among the militia officers Vassal de Monviel was certainly one of those most concerned with efficiency and most competent. In 1813 he presented a plan for a mass mobilization of the sedentary militia in the event of a large-scale American invasion. He put forward tactical considerations, in particular that Canadians should be used for guerrilla warfare, as well as practical suggestions, for example, that three brigades should be formed, each consisting of 5,088 men of the sedentary militia drawn from the various parts of the province. In October 11,295 militiamen from the Montreal region were conscripted as a result of a decision partly inspired by this plan. Vassal de Monviel also wanted officers' posts in the sedentary militia to be acquired by purchase; he thought such a measure would prevent them from being a haven for men eager to avoid active service.

After the War of 1812 Vassal de Monviel retained the office of adjutant general, and he held it until 1841, earning from £320 to £500 a year or sometimes even more. For his services during the conflict he also received 1,200 acres in Frampton Township, and in 1828 he obtained a further 1,200.

Apart from his military career Vassal de Monviel's public life was neither full nor exciting. In 1810 he tried unsuccessfully to win a seat in the Lower Canadian House of Assembly. He was transport commissioner for the district of Quebec, but only for a short period, from November 1812 to April 1813. He did, however, receive commissions as justice of the peace from 1813 to 1828, and in 1815 he was appointed commissioner to examine claims to compensation under the Militia Men Indemnification Act for injuries suffered in the War of 1812. From 1816 to 1830 he served as a commissioner for building churches and presbyteries. Furthermore, his popularity was such that he had the support of Quebec citizens when a subscription was organized to aid him after his house burned down in December 1824.

Vassal de Monviel seems to have done his work as adjutant general conscientiously; his personal testimony in December 1829 before the assembly committee examining the effects of reimposing a 1787 ordinance on the organization of the militia caused no stir, despite the Patriote party's open opposition to the measure. At the beginning of that year, however, he had provoked the wrath of the administrator Sir James Kempt*. Without submitting them to Kempt in advance, the adjutant general had printed and circulated the militia rolls, which were headed by the unfortunate list of the numerous dismissals ordered by Lord Dalhousie [RAMSAY].

Vassal de Monviel's extensive correspondence, undertaken in the course of his duties, leaves scant room for interpretation, since he revealed nothing of himself in it and simply performed with diligence his duty to transmit his superiors' orders. A man "of irreproachable character," in the opinion of *La Minerve*, he was able to carry out a delicate and important task, and at the same time to retain the confidence of both the authorities and his fellow citizens.

ROCH LEGAULT and LUC LÉPINE

ANQ-Q, P1000-102-2057. ASQ, Fonds Viger–Verreau, sér.O, 0144: 207–9. Bibliothèque nationale du Québec (Montréal), RES, AB, 43. PAC, MG 24, G5; RG 9, I, A1, 69: 18–19; 72: 104–6; A3, 3, 5; RG 68, General index, 1651–1841. L.C., House of Assembly, *Journals*, 1816–41; *Report of the special committee, to whom was referred that part of his excellency's speech which referred to the organization of the militia* (Quebec, 1829). "Nos miliciens de 1813," *BRH*, 2 (1896): 168. L.-J. Papineau, "Correspondance" (Ouellet), ANQ *Rapport*, 1953–55: 267–68, 352. *Recensement de Quebec, 1818* (Provost), 259. *La Minerve*,

2 nov. 1843. *Quebec Gazette*, 8 March 1810. Caron, "Inv. des docs. relatifs aux événements de 1837 et 1838," ANQ *Rapport*, 1925–26: 307, 310. *Historical record of the Seventh Regiment or the Royal Fusiliers . . .*, comp. Richard Cannon (London, 1847), 34–36. H. J. Morgan, *Sketches of celebrated Canadians*, 92–93. *Officers of British forces in Canada* (Irving), 100. Ouellet, "Inv. de la saberdache," ANQ *Rapport*, 1955–57: 115, 120, 123–24, 126, 128–30, 140, 143, 149–50, 153. *Quebec almanac*, 1795–1804. Michelle Guitard, *Histoire sociale des miliciens de la bataille de la Châteauguay* (Ottawa, 1983), 21. Roch Legault, "Les aléas d'une carrière militaire pour les membres de la petite noblesse seigneuriale canadienne, de la Révolution américaine à la guerre de 1812" (thèse de MA, univ. de Montréal, 1986). Luc Lépine, "La participation des Canadiens français à la guerre de 1812" (thèse de MA, univ. de Montréal, 1986). Sulte, *Hist. de la milice*, 19. Montarville Boucher de La Bruère, "Le 'Livre de raison' des seigneurs de Montarville," *Cahiers des Dix*, 4 (1939): 243–70. Philéas Gagnon, "Le Club des douze apôtres," *BRH*, 4 (1898): 90. P.-G. Roy, "Les officiers de Montcalm mariés au Canada," *BRH*, 50 (1944): 277–78. Régis Roy, "Vassal de Monviel," *BRH*, 23 (1917): 20. "Le 'Royal Canadien' ou 'Royal Canadian Volunteers,'" *BRH*, 7 (1901): 372. Benjamin Sulte, "Vassal de Monviel," *BRH*, 15 (1909): 317.

VIAU, PIERRE, Roman Catholic priest, educator, vicar general, and school administrator; b. 24 July 1784 in Saint-Constant, Que., and baptized at Saint-Philippe-de-Laprairie, Que., son of Pierre Viau, a farmer, and Marie-Josephte Barrette; d. 13 June 1849 in Montreal.

Pierre Viau received his classical education at the Collège Saint-Raphaël in Montreal from 1799 to 1806. When he decided to enter the priesthood in the autumn of 1806, he remained at the Petit Séminaire de Montréal, as the college was then called, and served as a regent. The following year he pursued his theological studies at the Séminaire de Nicolet, at the same time teaching the first-year class (Latin Elements) there; the director, Jean-Charles Bédard, considered him an excellent teacher for those beginning the classical program. Like most Catholic clergy in the colony at this time Viau completed his training for the priesthood at the Grand Séminaire de Québec. When he was admitted as a subdeacon, none of his relatives was in a position to secure for him the landed property required to become a priest; he gratefully turned to Claude Marotte, a farmer from Côte Sainte-Catherine at La Prairie. It was not uncommon for a benefactor to commit himself to mortgaging a lot or part of his farm in order to guarantee a future priest an annual allowance of 150 *livres* if need arose or until he was provided with an adequate benefice that would be equivalent. Such a title to property gave the bishop the assurance that "the cleric in holy orders would all his life have the resources necessary for a decent standard of living." Viau was ordained priest at Quebec on 3 Dec. 1809.

Having immediately been named assistant priest for the parish of Saint-Michel at Vaudreuil, and then in the autumn of 1810 for the cathedral of Notre-Dame at Quebec, Viau found himself with priests who gave him further pastoral training. After serving briefly in the parish of Sainte-Geneviève-de-Batiscan, near Trois-Rivières, in the spring of 1812 he was appointed priest of Saint-Ignace at Cap-Saint-Ignace, which included the Saint-Antoine mission on Île aux Grues. In the correspondence he carried on with the bishop of Quebec, Joseph-Octave Plessis*, Viau soon emerged as the epitome of the curé always anxious to delve into the imperatives of Catholic doctrine, especially in regard to ethics and canon law. His approach was rather casuistic, but his concern was intellectual.

All the same Viau was inclined to be strict in dealing with some matters: observance of Lent, pardon for fornicators, the wearing of cassock and surplice by those in the choir, swearing and uttering curses, participation in dances, embracing by fiancés. On the other hand Plessis, using his knowledge and his experience as a parish priest, found nuances and in certain cases weighed things in context while bringing out basic principles of Christian morality. His replies to Viau serve as illustration: children should obey their parents, rather than respect Lent against their parents' wishes; swearing was not a serious fault unless done in real anger; "twenty mortal sins of different sorts committed in a year are less embarrassing for a confessor than three or four relapses into the same mortal sin, because the second case shows a habit and the first does not"; but, taking into account numerous references to four of St Paul's epistles, all sexual relations outside lawful marriage were forbidden.

The concern for orthodoxy shown by Viau and the attention paid by Plessis to answering him carefully reveal an aspect of the pastoral duties of parish priest and bishop that is often unrecognized. Periodically – three or four times a year in Viau's case, though less frequently for some other curés – the bishop tried to further his priests' theological education and to help them acquire sound judgement for their ministry.

The training of Canadian priests at the beginning of the 19th century was indeed very limited. The first two years of study were often done in a classical college where they also served as the assigned teachers of a group of pupils. During the entire three-year program they had to master six volumes (3,600 pages) of the *Compendiosæ institutiones theologicæ*, published in Poitiers, France, in 1778. Anchored in faith from the start, the student learned to know God as the Trinity, in the Incarnation, and as a supernatural source of help, before he came to study human beings. They were perceived as sinners, able to renew contact with God through prayer and the sacraments. The two sources of revelation – Scripture and tradition – were treated in the final volume. It goes without saying that theological studies were quite hidebound. They provided precise knowledge about all religious matters, in a stereotyped pastoral perspective.

In Europe, as in Lower Canada, the training of ordinands was undertaken within a framework according prime importance to their spiritual and moral life. Viau was mindful of this emphasis when Bishop Plessis asked him in 1818 to become the director of the Grand Séminaire de Québec. "I sense that there is much to be gained in a seminary with respect to the ecclesiastical virtues. The example of the colleagues with whom one resides, the examples and lives of many young men, among whom are some full of ardour, are conducive in no small measure to virtue." Viau added a second reason for accepting this unexpected appointment: God's will was being revealed through that of his superiors.

Viau was probably not too disappointed with the two years he spent directing and teaching at the Grand Séminaire; for, having subsequently filled the parish charges of Saint-Nicolas, near Quebec, from 1820 to 1822, Sainte-Anne at Yamamiche from 1822 to 1825, and Saint-Pierre-du-Sud at Saint-Pierre-de-la-Rivière-du-Sud, which included the Saint-François mission (at Saint-François-Montmagny), in 1825 and 1826, he agreed to render a similar service in Bishop Jean-Jacques LARTIGUE's newly opened Séminaire Saint-Jacques in Montreal. But his assent to Lartigue came after some hesitation, reflection before God, and consultation with "respectable and sensible persons." Yet he added, "I do not much like the ministry, and since, nevertheless, I like to make myself useful, I accept gladly." He stated that his health did not allow him to fast at any time, and he recognized that "people have always reproached me with being too sedentary." In fact, this experience of seminary life did not last as long as the previous one. Lartigue quickly realized that Viau was having difficulty adapting to his work, and, moreover, that he displayed no particular talent. The charge of Notre-Dame-de-Liesse, at Rivière-Ouelle, had just come open with the departure of its curé, Bernard-Claude Panet*, to become archbishop of Quebec, following Plessis's recent death. Since Panet had sufficient confidence in Viau not only to name him to this charge but also to make him vicar general with responsibility for the entire lower St Lawrence region, Lartigue let him go after five months in office at the seminary.

Bishop Lartigue and Viau had still had time to appreciate each other, as their correspondence in the following decade unquestionably demonstrates. Viau sought Lartigue's opinion in certain areas where as vicar general he now exercised the ecclesiastical authority delegated by the bishop (permission to marry, reservation of sins, exemption from vows, interest rates on loans), and Lartigue made known to him his views on such matters as the bill concerning the *fabriques* [*see* Louis Bourdages*], his differences with the Sulpicians, the publication of an ecclesiastical newspaper, and of course, ultramontanism.

Viau at first endeavoured to moderate Lartigue's excessive enthusiasm for ultramontanism. In his view Alfonso Muzzarelli was "something of an advocate" for papal authority, Hugues-Félicité-Robert de La Mennais was unsatisfactory on the doctrine of the church in the early centuries, and Roberto Bellarmino lacked critical sense (on this matter he cited Nicolas Bergier and François-Xavier de Feller). He had further noted that Muzzarelli and La Mennais did not give the same account of the sixth canon of the Council of Nicaea and that Bellarmino, Muzzarelli, Charles-René Billuart, and Alfonso Maria de' Liguori held different views on the jurisdiction of bishops.

Lartigue was too firmly convinced of the value of ultramontanism to budge in the face of such questioning or shades of interpretation. "It would be a serious error," he stated, "to believe that the pope does not by divine right have pastoral jurisdiction over all the bishops in the world, and consequently that he cannot place them, move them, reinstate them, restrict or extend the limits of their jurisdiction." If few proofs could be found in the first three centuries of the church that the pope had nominated or confirmed bishops in their respective sees, it was because documents of the period had disappeared as a result of the persecutions, Lartigue went on. For his part he considered that the foundations on which La Mennais and Muzzarelli took their stand, even for the early centuries of the church, were solid. Moreover, Lartigue gave little credence to theologian Mathias Chardon's authority, especially because of his opinion on the supposedly priestly ordinations in the Church of England. Feller's opinion seemed risky to him, and Bergier's article on the bishops' jurisdiction insignificant. As for Muzzarelli, he sounded more like an Italian than an advocate. Viau acknowledged defeat: "I am willing to believe that I was wrong. Your range of knowledge is much broader than mine."

Nevertheless, Charles-François Baillargeon*, priest of the cathedral and later archbishop of Quebec, considered himself much less well informed than Viau, who as his curé at Cap-Saint-Ignace had shown him the way to the priesthood. Although, Baillargeon wrote to Viau, he had not gone through the theological writings as Viau had, analysed and collated their contents, or gone back to the sources, he shared his opinion about theologians: "I am completely convinced, as you are, that all their scholarship needs to be re-examined, that their way of dealing with the knowledge of God is generally imperfect, that by introducing bad philosophy into this sublime science or rather by wishing to base this divine science on a meagre philosophy [and] on a lot of subtleties, they have rendered religion very poor service; I say that they have destroyed the foundations of religion, forgetting that it is founded basically upon authority and substituting their own reasoning, their petty arguments." A gradual shift in the way of thinking of certain influential figures in the church of Lower Canada can be detected here. With the word "religion" being regularly used at the time for "church," the criterion of authority was coming to the fore in the church. The papacy and the ecclesiastical hierarchy were *ipso facto* being given enhanced importance.

The links between Viau and Baillargeon were close, especially after Baillargeon was able to rely on Viau to place six Irish children recently orphaned by cholera with families at Rivière-Ouelle. But by contrast they were strained between Viau and Panet's successor in the see of Quebec, Joseph SIGNAY. Signay encouraged his curé to study the Scriptures thoroughly and to develop refutations of bad books, but he could not see how all this work if put in print would really render service. Moreover, Signay considered him a complainer; since three-quarters of the priests suffered from rheumatism, how could physical disabilities be singled out in his case more than in that of the others? And what were the grounds for Viau's frequent demands to change his assistant priests? Where could the bishop find someone more perfect than the previous ones?

In this situation it is not surprising that Viau left the Quebec region in 1835 and went to Montreal to be closer to Lartigue. He took a rest at the Résidence Saint-Jacques, and then became the bishop's vicar general when the diocese of Montreal was established in 1836. That year there was no lack of work at the bishopric. Having been, in 1831, the first to advise Lartigue to appoint a coadjutor bishop, Viau now encouraged him to find a successor as soon as possible to his auxiliary, Pierre-Antoine Tabeau*, who had died the previous year without ever being consecrated bishop. It was in these circumstances that Ignace Bourget* was suggested as the best candidate, and Pope Gregory XVI gave his assent to the proposal.

In 1836 the act dealing with schools run by trustees, passed in 1829, was not renewed by the Legislative Council. Viau had long been aware of the government's legislative measures in the field of elementary education. Like many other parish priests, he had declined in 1822 the post of visitor for a school run by the Royal Institution for the Advancement of Learning which the government had offered him. The *fabrique* schools law which had been passed in 1824 had certainly been more consonant with his views. The year 1836 marked the end of competition between the schools run by trustees and those run by *fabriques*.

Viau took part, furthermore, in a meeting on 12 April 1836 called by mayor Jacques Viger* to consider the establishment in Montreal of the normal school provided for by a law passed on 21 March. At this meeting he was even elected on the first round of voting to the board of the École Normale de Montréal; he found himself working side by side with Louis-Joseph Papineau*, Viger, and Presbyterian clergyman Henry Esson*. Teaching began in the fall of 1837, and although rebellion broke out in November, the school was more or less successful. At this point Viau was named priest of the parish of Saint-Sulpice, near Montreal.

In light of all these developments, it is not surprising that in 1841 Viau gathered a group of priests in the presbytery at Repentigny to protest against the new school bill that had been introduced on 20 July and brought forward for second reading on 3 August. At the heart of the discussions was the place to be accorded in children's education to the various religious denominations. The Catholic clergy, for whom Viau was a spokesman, emphasized that the bishops had "by divine right the privilege of inspecting schools." After minor changes the bill, which sought to make broader provision for the establishment and upkeep of public schools, was enacted on 18 Sept. 1841 and went into force on 1 Jan. 1842. A system of elementary public schools was at last set up for the whole of the United Province of Canada. The principle of denominational schools was guaranteed within it, thanks in particular to the intervention of the Canadian Catholic clergy.

Three years later, at barely 60 years of age, Viau retired to the Hospice Saint-Joseph in Montreal. He died there on 13 June 1849 and was buried a few days later in the cathedral of Saint-Jacques. He had distributed his magnificent collection of books to various educational institutions during his lifetime.

Pierre Viau's personality was not necessarily an engaging one, at least on first meeting. His intellectual curiosity and the solitude he craved fostered his bent for research and his concern for truth and at the same time demonstrated them. His more or less frail state of health may have been an indication of great sensitivity, which might explain his difficulty in adapting to the practical side of pastoral ministry. In short, one may well ask whether he was not one of those perfectionists of exceptional intelligence who cannot be at ease in the world in which they live. Their aspirations greatly exceed what they can achieve.

LUCIEN LEMIEUX

AAQ, 12 A, F: ff.165, 187–88; G: ff.154, 172–73, 180; 210 A, VII: 452; VIII: 76–77, 171b, 506–7; IX: 340–44, 357–58; XVI: 161–63, 182–84, 293–95, 332–34; XVII: 84–87, 113–14; 61 CD, Saint-Nicolas, I: 35; 303 CD, I: 132. ACAM, 295.099, 827-5, 831-5, 832-4, 833-5-9, 834-2; 355.108, 837-1, 838-1–2, 839-1; 901.013, 829-1–2, 829-4, 829-6, 830-2, 831-5, 832-1-4, 833-2-3; 901.029, 833-1-3; 901.044, 826-1; RLB, II: 16, 21; RLL, IV: 134–43; V: 40–42, 44–45. ANQ-M, CE1-51, 13 juin 1849;

CE1-54, 24 juill. 1784. Arch. de l'évêché de Sainte-Anne-de-la-Pocatière (La Pocatière, Qué.), Saint-Ignace (Cap-Saint-Ignace), I: 76, 79, 94. Arch. de l'évêché de Trois-Rivières (Trois-Rivières, Qué.), D5, Viau à Plessis, 14 mars 1822; G5, Viau à Plessis, 1er août 1812. Adrien Cance, *Le code de droit canonique: commentaire succinct et pratique* (8e éd., 4v., Paris, 1949–52), 2: 428. J.-C. de La Poype de Vertrieu, *Compendiosæ institutiones theologicæ ad usum seminarii pictaviensis* . . . (6v., Poitiers, France, 1778). *Le séminaire de Québec: documents et biographies*, Honorius Provost, édit. (Québec, 1964). *Mélanges religieux*, 13 août 1841. *La Minerve*, 18 juin 1849. Allaire, *Dictionnaire.* Tanguay, *Répertoire* (1893). L.-P. Audet, *Histoire de l'enseignement au Québec* (2v., Montréal et Toronto, 1971), 2: 44–45. Chabot, *Le curé de campagne*, 59–60. [L.-]A. Desrosiers, *Les écoles normales primaires de la province de Québec et leurs œuvres complémentaires; récit des fêtes jubilaires de l'école normale Jacques-Cartier, 1857–1907* (Montréal, 1909), 55–56. Douville, *Hist. du collège-séminaire de Nicolet*, 1: 49. Labarrère-Paulé, *Les instituteurs laïques*, 60. Lemieux, *L'établissement de la première prov. eccl.*, 215, 300, 312, 322, 395. Maurault, *Le collège de Montréal* (Dansereau; 1967). Ouellet, *Bas-Canada*, 260–68. Pouliot, *Mgr Bourget et son temps*, 1: 124. J.-J. Lefebvre, "Saint-Constant–Saint-Philippe de Laprairie, 1744–1946; la vie religieuse," CCHA *Rapport*, 13 (1945–46): 125–58.

VINCENT, JOHN, army officer; b. 1764 in Ireland, the youngest of three sons of John Vincent and Catherine Love; d. unmarried 21 Jan. 1848 in London.

John Vincent entered the army as an ensign in the 66th Foot in July 1781 and was promoted lieutenant in August of the following year. On 15 Dec. 1783 he transferred to the 49th Foot, becoming a captain in October 1786. He served with this corps in the West Indies (he was present at the taking of Saint-Domingue (Haiti) in 1793), and also in the expeditions to north Holland in 1799 and to Copenhagen in 1801. Vincent had been promoted major in September 1795 and attained the brevet rank of lieutenant-colonel in January 1800.

In 1802 Vincent's regiment embarked for Lower Canada. The following year it moved to Upper Canada, where it spent the next nine years in garrison duty at York (Toronto) and Fort George (Niagara-on-the-Lake). The declaration of war between Britain and the United States in June 1812 found the British forces in Upper Canada in need of reinforcement, and by August Vincent had moved to strengthen Kingston with five companies of the 49th. With 31 years of service, he was considered a competent officer, albeit one with limited experience in combat. In November he had his first brush with the Americans when Commodore Isaac Chauncey chased the *Royal George* into Kingston Harbour. Vincent had been aware of the impending attack on the town, warned possibly by the volunteers who had flocked to Kingston to fight but whom Vincent could not supply with arms, not having sufficient in stock. Fortunately the attack was unsuccessful since shore artillery kept Chauncey at bay until the wind forced him to stand out. Vincent was commended by Lieutenant-General Sir George Prevost* for having inspired the defence of the town.

In February 1813 Prevost made Vincent brigadier-general and transferred him to the Niagara frontier to replace Major-General Sir Roger Hale Sheaffe*, who was ill. Vincent took over command of about 1,900 men: many of them, he informed Prevost in May, were unenthusiastic militiamen whose "desertion beyond all conception continues to mark their indifference." He apprised Prevost of the construction of American batteries opposite Fort George, his main garrison, which heralded a probable invasion. As part of his defensive preparations, he divided his force into three divisions: the right under Lieutenant-Colonel John Harvey*, the left under Lieutenant-Colonel Christopher Myers, and the centre under himself.

Late on 24 May, the American fleet began bombarding Fort George, supported by the newly constructed batteries across the Niagara River. On the 27th an American force of about 5,000 landed near by at Two Mile Creek. Aware of the limitations of his own force, Vincent ordered the fort evacuated, the guns spiked, and the ammunition destroyed. The British then retreated westward, taking up a defensive position along Burlington Heights (Hamilton). The Americans, who had successfully occupied the peninsula, sent a force of 3,500 infantry and 150 cavalry in pursuit of Vincent. On 4 June, while awaiting the Americans, he was promoted major-general.

The following day Harvey, who had made a reconnaissance of the American position at Stoney Creek, urged Vincent to make a forward movement against the enemy. Vincent agreed with his suggestion of a night attack to catch the enemy off guard, and in the early hours of 6 June Harvey, with about 700 regulars, fell upon the unsuspecting Americans. In less than three-quarters of an hour the British, despite heavy casualties, forced the Americans to abandon their positions, as well as their guns. Vincent, however, had not been in the battle. He had been thrown from his horse en route alone to the fight, got lost in the darkness, and found his way to the British lines only after the engagement was over, early on the morning of the 6th.

The American force retreated towards Forty Mile Creek, hoping to renew the attack after being resupplied. But on the 7th, Sir James Lucas Yeo*'s squadron successfully shelled the American encampment and either destroyed or captured 16 boatloads of supplies. The invaders pulled back to Fort George. Vincent followed with his force to Forty Mile Creek to support Yeo's actions and, Harvey wrote, "to give encouragement to the Militia and Yeomanry of the Country who are everywhere rising upon the fugitive

Americans, making them Prisoners & *withholding* all *Supplies*."

On the 23rd American major-general Henry Dearborn dispatched a force of some 570 men to attack Vincent's advance post, under Lieutenant James FitzGibbon*, near Beaver Dams (Thorold). While travelling to their destination the American force was ambushed by Indians on the morning of 24 June. After an exchange of fire which lasted little more than three hours, they surrendered to FitzGibbon, in effect ending the American threat on the Niagara frontier for the remainder of the year.

Vincent remained on the Niagara peninsula until news of the British defeat at the battle of Moraviantown on 5 October [*see* Henry Procter*] caused him to abandon his position at Forty Mile Creek for fear of an American advance from the west on the stores at Burlington Heights. The advance never materialized, and in December Lieutenant-General Gordon Drummond* sent Vincent to command at Kingston, replacing him on the Niagara frontier with Major-General Phineas RIALL. From Kingston Vincent moved in June 1814 to command the Montreal garrison until his departure for England on sick leave on 18 July.

In April Vincent had been given the sinecure of lieutenant governor of Dunbarton Castle, Scotland. Promoted lieutenant-general in May 1825 and general in November 1841, he became colonel of the 69th Foot in February 1836. In 1848 Vincent died in London at the age of 83.

OTTE A. ROSENKRANTZ

Annual reg. (London), 1848: 209. *Doc. hist. of campaign upon Niagara frontier* (Cruikshank). *Gentleman's Magazine*, January–June 1848: 542–43. *Select British docs. of War of 1812* (Wood). J. B. Burke, *Genealogical and heraldic history of the landed gentry of Ireland*, ed. L. G. Pine (4th ed., London, 1958). *Hart's army list*, 1846. *Officers of British forces in Canada* (Irving). "State papers – L.C.," PAC *Report*, 1893: 99–100. J. M. Hitsman, *The incredible War of 1812: a military history* (Toronto, 1965). J. K. Mahon, *The War of 1812* (Gainesville, Fla., 1972). Frederick Myatt, *The Royal Berkshire Regiment (the 49th/66th Regiment of Foot)* (London, 1968).

VINCENT, NICOLAS (baptized **Ignace-Nicolas**; called **Tsaouenhohoui**, "one who plunges things into the water," or "the hawk," the name of the hereditary civil chief of the Hurons of Jeune-Lorette), grand chief of the Hurons; b. 1769, probably 11 April, in Jeune-Lorette (Wendake), Que., son of Louis Vincent (Sawantanan) and Louise Martin (Thodatowan); m. there first 24 Nov. 1794 Véronique Petit-Étienne, a Huron, and they had nine children, one of whom, Christine, lived until 1903; m. there secondly 22 Jan. 1821 a Malecite named Madeleine, widow of Pierre-Jacques Thomas of Penobscot (Castine), Maine; d. 31 Oct. 1844 in Jeune-Lorette.

In 1699, without the knowledge of the Hurons, the French crown made over to the Jesuits the title to the seigneury of Sillery, which had been granted in 1651 to the Hurons and the other Christian Indians living there. Only after the suppression of the Society of Jesus by Pope Clement XIV in 1773 did the Hurons realize that they were no longer entitled to the dues derived from the working of their lands at Sillery. In 1791, alarmed and reduced to abject dependency, they initiated legal proceedings which were to extend over nearly half a century. In these proceedings the principal figure was Grand Chief Nicolas Vincent.

Their first petition seeking restitution of the seigneury of Sillery to the Huron nation was addressed to Governor Lord Dorchester [Carleton*] in 1791. They sent similar requests almost every year to each governor from Robert Prescott* to Lord Dalhousie [RAMSAY]. A typical petition, dated 13 Dec. 1823, reads: "The Petitioners conceive that the King of France could not validly give to the Jesuits that which he had already bestowed on the Indians. The Petitioners further represent that the other Indians of this country . . . are in the undisturbed possession of the Seigniories which the French Kings permitted them to retain in their own country. That the Petitioners alone, victims of the simplicity of their ancestors, and of the cupidity of the Jesuits, are divested of all, and reduced to utter poverty; even so that in a country of which their ancestors once were masters, they have lost all the right even of hunting, and dare no longer enter the forest, where they are daily expelled with violence by the proprietors, who consider them as malefactors, and treat them accordingly."

By 1824 all the Huron families despaired of getting any real attention paid to their difficulties and so entrusted their chiefs with the mission of travelling to England and making representations to King George IV on their behalf. On 15 November Nicolas Vincent, grand chief of the council of the Huron nation since 1810, along with André Romain (Tsohahissen) and Stanislas Koska (Aharathanha), council chiefs, and Michel Tsiewei (Téhatsiendahé), war chief, embarked on the brig *Indian*. In the first three months of 1825 "the four Canadian chiefs" had conversations with various members of parliament and, more important, they met with the colonial secretary, Lord Bathurst, who showed them great consideration and arranged for their living expenses to be paid by the government.

On 8 April 1825 the king received the four Huron chiefs, as their people had ardently hoped. The London *Times* reported the exchange between the Huron grand chief and the British sovereign in the course of this "ceremony." The audience began with George IV personally hanging around the necks of the four chiefs silver-gilt coronation medals bearing his likeness.

Grand Chief Vincent then made a speech in French to the sovereign that was an admirable and brief example of Indian rhetoric: "I was instructed not to speak in the royal presence unless in answer to your Majesty's questions; but my feelings overpower me; my heart is full; I am amazed at such unexpected grace and condescension, and cannot doubt that I shall be pardoned for expressing our gratitude. The sun is shedding its genial rays upon our heads. It reminds me of the Great Creator of the Universe – of him who can make alive and who can kill. Oh! may that gracious and beneficent Being, who promises to answer the fervent prayers of his people, bless abundantly your Majesty! May he grant you much bodily health; and, for the sake of your happy subjects, may he prolong your valuable life. It is not alone the four individuals who now stand before your Majesty who will retain to the end of their lives a sense of this kind and touching reception; the whole of the nation, whose representatives we are, will ever love and be devoted to you – their good and great father."

Speaking to Vincent and the other chiefs in French, George IV replied that he had always respected the fine people of the various tribes in his North American possessions and that he would take every occasion to enhance their well-being, ensure their happiness, and show himself to be truly a father. He then conversed with them in French and in the most gracious manner for more than a quarter of an hour.

The British press probably was not informed of the contents of the Hurons' petition, but reported that a promise had been made to the chiefs that territorial compensation would be granted to their nation if "certain lands" taken from them could not be given back. During the remaining four months of this venture in high diplomacy, which was of capital importance for all the Indian people, the Huron chiefs developed the strategies they would use to claim the return of their territory and consolidated their knowledge of the political workings of the British empire.

Assured of the sympathy and support of the highest imperial authorities, Vincent as chief made representations on several occasions to the Lower Canadian House of Assembly concerning his tribe's various grievances, particularly in the matter of hunting rights. In 1819 he officially addressed the assembly, the first Huron to do so. He spoke again quite often in the coming years, always in the Huron language, and his messages were translated by his older brother Louis Vincent (Sawantanan), who had his *baccalauréat*, or Michel Tsiewei. His statements, which were recorded in the minutes, show that he had an acute sense of responsibility, a shrewd mind, and a noble attachment to his people's traditional values.

In January 1829, at the request of the colony's government, which wanted to clarify the territorial boundaries of each of the seven Indian nations in Lower Canada, chief Vincent took on the task of making a reconnaissance of the traditional Huron lands and producing a map of them. The "Vincent" map matched the pictographic data on a wampum belt describing the territories; later that year chief Tsiewei explained the belt at Trois-Rivières in the presence of the chiefs of Indian nations concerned and the superintendent of Indian affairs at Quebec, Michel-Louis JUCHEREAU Duchesnay. The superintendent attested to the authenticity of the agreements, which were confirmed by the "truth" belts.

The final Huron chief to bear the name Tsaouenhohoui, Nicolas Vincent was one of the last hereditary chiefs, since the native system of choosing chiefs disappeared around the 1880s, after an elective method was instituted by the Canadian government. Chief Vincent died at 75 years of age and was buried on 2 Nov. 1844 in the Huron cemetery. On 5 November the *Quebec Mercury* observed: "The Grand Chief Nicholas Vincent . . . was the nephew of the late Grand Chief [José Vincent]. . . . The deceased was an eloquent orator in his native tongue, and particularly distinguished for his personal dignity and gracefulness of manner." Three portraits were painted of Vincent. The first was done by Joseph Hermeindel, an English artist and engraver, at the time of the Huron chiefs' stay in London in 1825, the second by the Huron artist Zacharie Vincent* around 1835, and the third by artist Henry Daniel Thielcke at Jeune-Lorette after the bestowal of an honorary chieftainship on an Englishman in 1838. All show the grand chief as a tall, alert man with fine features and a dignified air.

GEORGES E. SIOUI (ATSISTAHONRA)

ANQ-Q, CE1-28, 11 avril 1769, 22 janv. 1821, 2 nov. 1844. L.C., House of Assembly, *Journals*, February 1819, February 1824. *La Minerve*, 7 nov. 1844. *Quebec Mercury*, 5 Nov. 1844. *Times* (London), 12 April 1825. R. C. Dalton, *The Jesuits' estates question, 1760–1888: a study of the background for the agitation of 1889* (Toronto, 1968). "Les chefs hurons auprès de Georges IV," *BRH*, 11 (1905): 347–50. Victor Morin, "Les médailles décernées aux Indiens d'Amérique; étude historique et numismatique," RSC *Trans.*, 3rd ser., 9 (1915), sect.I: 310–11. "Mort de la plus vieille sauvagesse de Lorette," *Le Soleil* (Québec), 3 oct. 1903: 11.

VONDY, JOHN, doctor; b. *c.* 1820 in Miramichi, N.B., son of Thomas Vondy and Janet ——; d. 29 June 1847 on Middle Island, N.B.

John Vondy's father came to Miramichi in 1816 from the Isle of Man and operated a store in Chatham for many years. John was educated in Chatham and then went to England to complete his medical studies. On his return he apparently practised medicine in Woodstock for three or four years before setting up in Chatham, where he opened an office in a local hotel in April 1847.

At that time New Brunswick was experiencing the greatest influx of immigrants it had known since the 1830s. In 1847 thousands of refugees from the famine in Ireland were disgorged from foul-smelling, poorly equipped vessels at ports throughout the eastern United States and British North America; many of them carried diseases such as typhus. In New Brunswick, the majority of the immigrants arrived at Saint John and were quarantined at Partridge Island in hospital sheds and military tents. However, some ships turned up at Miramichi, where no adequate quarantine facilities existed. One of these was the barque *Looshtauk*, which arrived in the river on 2 June.

The *Looshtauk* had sailed from Liverpool, England, with 467 passengers; 117 had died of typhus on the passage and 100 others were ill when the ship reached Chatham on 4 June. The authorities were alarmed and unsure what to do with the sick. It was finally decided that temporary buildings would be erected on Middle Island, about two miles from Chatham, and, three days after their arrival, the immigrants were landed there. During the period of confusion another 40 had died. The port medical officers had done nothing to help the sick and they now refused to go to the island. The authorities had to find a doctor and Vondy volunteered his services.

Vondy went at once to the island and quickly discovered that its facilities were completely inadequate, with no shelter for many patients and no way of separating the sick from those free of disease. His own shelter was later described as "a piece of canvass and a buffalo skin." Requests to the local authorities for blankets, supplies, and additional buildings were generally ignored. Fresh food, when it was provided, could not be properly stored and the dysentery it caused killed some of those apparently recovering from the fever. With the arrival of two other ships, Vondy soon had over 300 patients. Because of the fear of the disease, however, it was difficult to find people to assist him and he had to make do with one man and a boy. He faced an almost impossible task and every day there were more deaths; 96 of the *Looshtauk* passengers died on the island.

Vondy was not permitted to leave the island for fear he would carry the infection with him. He worked long hours without adequate food or rest and eventually contracted the disease. Attempts were then made to get another doctor to go to the island. One refused to have anything to do with the immigrants. Finally Dr John Thomson* agreed to visit the island daily, but he would not stay there. Without proper care Vondy's condition worsened. His sister persuaded some friends to take her to the island, where she nursed her brother until he died on 29 June, at the age of 26. Three days later Dr James Patrick COLLINS, a volunteer assistant among the fever patients at Partridge Island, succumbed to the disease at an even younger age. Vondy's sister was placed in quarantine and was forced to remain 21 days on Middle Island amongst the sick and the dying. Her friends tried to rescue her but were caught by the armed guards who had been hired to patrol the island and prevent immigrants reaching the mainland.

All victims of the fever were buried on the island, but the authorities agreed to allow Vondy's body to be interred in St Paul's churchyard at Bushville. His remains were enclosed in a double, air-tight coffin and were brought to the town wharf in a boat, while all the ships in the harbour lowered their flags. Shortly after his death a fund was started for a memorial stone and a plaque. Like Dr Collins of Saint John, Vondy gave his life trying to help suffering immigrants at a time when many other doctors refused to tend them.

W. A. SPRAY

PANB, MC 216/11; RG 18, RS153, G3/5, 11 March, 3 July 1847, and n.d. G.B., Parl., Command paper, 1847, 47, [no.50]: 57, 138–39, *Papers relative to emigration to the British provinces in North America, and to the Australian colonies; part I: British provinces in North America. Gleaner* (Miramichi [Chatham, N.B.]), 6 April, 8 June–27 July, 24 Aug. 1847. Esther Clark Wright, *The Miramichi: a study of the New Brunswick river and of the people who settled along it* (Sackville, N.B., 1944), 52–54. J. A. Fraser, *By favourable winds: a history of Chatham, New Brunswick* ([Chatham], 1975), 69–70, 304. J. McG. Baxter, "Ship fever in 1847," Miramichi Natural Hist. Assoc., *Proc.* (Chatham), no.6 (1911): 7–15.

VOYER, JACQUES, notary, landowner, militia officer, office holder, and JP; b. 2 Jan. 1771 at Quebec, son of Charles Voyer, a notary, and Françoise-Charlotte Perrault; m. there 21 July 1800 Luce-Monique Pinguet; d. there 8 Jan. 1843.

Jacques Voyer was commissioned notary on 5 Feb. 1798 and set up an office in his home town. Prior to 1812 young Archibald Campbell* articled with him. Voyer took part in the defence of Lower Canada that year; having been made lieutenant-colonel of the Île d'Orléans battalion of militia on 5 April, he became a major in the 1st Select Embodied Militia Battalion of Lower Canada on 25 September, and was promoted lieutenant-colonel of the 4th battalion on 26 October. For some months he had acted as paymaster of the 1st battalion. Voyer seems to have distinguished himself during the war. It is evident that he gave it his complete attention, since there are no notarized deeds listed for 1814 and 1815 in the index of his notarial records. He put a notice in the *Quebec Gazette/La Gazette de Québec* on 25 May 1815 announcing his intention "to resume business as a notary public . . . on the Place du Marché [Place Notre-Dame] in Lower Town." At the same time he offered his services "to the public, and more particularly to the traders, merchants, and ship captains who before his departure for the frontier honoured him with their confidence." Among his regular clients was George POZER, whose appointed notary he was.

In 1806 Voyer had been a member of the company that had made a successful bid for Frampton Township. His brother-in-law Pierre-Édouard Desbarats* acted as township leader at the time. Among the other associates were George Pyke*, François VASSAL de Monviel, and William Berczy*. As a former militia officer, Voyer received 1,200 acres in the township in 1826. He obtained a further 1,072 acres in 1838. Considered to be a large landowner, he adopted the same methods of settlement as Desbarats and recruited settlers from among the large number of Irish who were arriving at the port of Quebec. Both men took care to choose robust and peaceable immigrants. The notice he published in the *Quebec Gazette* on 9 April 1827 was addressed to the settlers, mostly Irish, already living in the township. Voyer pointed out that he would grant them land "at the rate of 10 shillings in legal currency a year for 50 *arpents*, with no other charges whatsoever except for constructing and maintaining roads. They will have possession for three years without paying any rent."

Throughout his career Voyer was given various commissions that witness to his good name. On 24 May 1815, for example, he was appointed commissioner to examine claims to compensation under the Militia Men Indemnification Act for injuries suffered in the War of 1812. On 22 November he was named justice of the peace for the district of Quebec, an appointment renewed in 1821, 1828, 1833, 1836, and 1838. In the course of the last two years he was also a commissioner for building churches and presbyteries in that district. Voyer had always shown an interest in the field of education. In 1821 he had helped set up the Education Society of the District of Quebec, of which Joseph-François PERRAULT had been elected president. Voyer sat on the committee to draw up its by-laws along with Jérôme Demers*, Thomas Maguire*, Joseph SIGNAY, John NEILSON, and Joseph-Rémi VALLIÈRES de Saint-Réal, among others.

Jacques Voyer apparently had no children. In the handwritten will he made on 12 March 1823 he left all his property to his wife, enjoining her to pass the estate on to his nephews and nieces. He drew up his last notarized deed on 4 Aug. 1842 and died on 8 January of the following year. On 25 June 1845 Mme Voyer married Étienne Gauvin.

MADELEINE FERRON

Jacques Voyer's minute-book, containing instruments dated 9 Feb. 1798 to 4 Aug. 1842, is at ANQ-Q, CN1-285.

ANQ-Q, CE1-1, 2 janv. 1771, 21 juill. 1800, 11 janv. 1843. *Quebec Gazette*, 25 May 1815, 9 April 1827. F.-M. Bibaud, *Le panthéon canadien* (A. et V. Bibaud; 1891). Langelier, *Liste des terrains concédés*. *Officers of British forces in Canada* (Irving). J.-E. Roy, *Hist. de Lauzon*, 5: 86, 92; *Hist. du notariat*. P.-G. Roy, "Le notaire du roi Archibald Campbell," *BRH*, 32 (1926): 736–39.

W

WADE, ROBERT, farmer; b. *c.* 1777 in County Durham, England; m. *c.* 1802 Mary Hodgson, and they had four sons and eight daughters; d. 16 July 1849 in Hamilton Township, Upper Canada.

Robert Wade was born to a farming family involved in breeding pure-bred livestock. In 1819, with his wife and eight children, he immigrated to Upper Canada and purchased a 200-acre farm in Hamilton Township. One of the earliest improving farmers from England in the area, he was familiar with the latest British scientific principles of agriculture and was appalled by Upper Canadian farmers' lack of agricultural knowledge.

Improving farmers of the early 19th century in Upper Canada were primarily Lowland Scottish and English settlers who could afford either to buy farms and pay for clearing them or to purchase cleared farms. They brought with them an approach to farming influenced by the agricultural revolution in northwestern Europe and intended to maintain soil fertility. By mid century the Bay of Quinte region, the areas along Yonge Street and between Hamilton and Toronto, the London vicinity, and the Niagara peninsula had become known for their agricultural development. While these regions were being settled by various immigrant groups, British improving farmers such as Wade, though few in number, furnished according to historian Robert Leslie Jones "the leadership for the province, making a greater effort to keep abreast of the discoveries of their time in agricultural science."

Immediately upon settling, Wade began a systematic program of draining wet portions of his farm to improve his fields. His practice of thoroughly ploughing and harrowing the land before planting ensured far greater crop yields than were customary for the period. Fruit culture in the province was in its infancy at this time but Wade, recognizing its viability, recommended in 1820 that emigrants bring to Canada apple pips and various fruit-stones. As early as that year he planted fruit-trees on his farm, and by 1824 his apple orchard alone consisted of 100 trees.

Wade ran a prosperous mixed farm of crops and livestock. During a period when most farmers in Upper Canada were dependent on wheat, he concentrated on livestock and its improvement through breeding. In the early 1830s he began to purchase Durham ("Improved Shorthorn") cattle and Teeswater ("Improved Leicester") sheep from Britain and New York State. Shorthorns, a dual-purpose breed, were raised for both meat and milk. Wade turned his surplus of milk into profit when he established a small dairy on his farm to produce butter and cheese. His son Ralph won prizes for cheese at the Northumberland County agricultural fair as early as 1842 and a grandson, Henry, was later credited with bringing the factory method of making cheese from New York to central Upper Canada. Robert Wade was interested in Leicesters because they also served a dual purpose. Ralph won first prize for home-made wool cloth in the 1842 Northumberland fair and five years later Wade Leicesters, which took top prizes at the first provincial agricultural exhibition, were described as the best sheep for carcass weight and tallow yield ever killed in Toronto. Robert maintained a breeding program until the time of his retirement in 1848, and the work was continued by two of his sons, John and Ralph, and his grandson Henry, who were all well known in the pure-bred-stock business during the second half of the 19th century.

Inventions for the technological advance of agriculture were a family interest. Cultivating tools and harvesting machines were seen by Robert Wade as two of the greatest needs of farmers at the time. John reportedly invented a turnip-drill, a potato-washer, and a straw-elevator for a thresher, but he appears to have patented only one machine, a post-hole auger, and that in conjunction with John Helm of Port Hope, one of the province's first manufacturers of reapers. John Wade is also credited with importing, in 1844, the second reaping machine in the Newcastle District, perhaps even in Upper Canada.

To provide a forum for the discussion of agricultural topics, the Wades supported some of the earliest local and provincial agricultural associations. The Northumberland Agricultural Society, founded in 1828, faltered after a short time and was disbanded until 1836, when it was reorganized. At that time, it was decided to establish local committees of the county society and Robert Wade was named to represent Hamilton Township. The society sponsored biannual fairs, provided funds for prizes, and encouraged members to subscribe to farming journals and prepare papers on agricultural subjects for debate. Both Ralph and John Wade served extended terms as president of the society.

Robert Wade was a staunch Methodist, preferring at first to worship with a group of British immigrants of his faith rather than with the local American Methodist congregation. Following the erection of St Peter's Church (Anglican) in Cobourg during the 1840s, he joined that church. He died in 1849 and was buried in the family plot at St Peter's cemetery.

Wade did much to encourage the improvement of agriculture in Upper Canada during the first half of the 19th century. He was interested in both the theory and the practice of farming, making undeniable contributions in the areas of drainage, tillage, fruit culture, animal husbandry, dairying, use of machinery, and agricultural organization. His sons and grandsons followed his lead, many of them assuming leadership in the province's numerous agricultural associations.

SUSAN BENNETT

AO, MU 2388, ser.A-1–A-3; MU 2883; MU 3074 (photocopies). Edna Barrowclough, "The Wade letters (1819–67)," Cobourg and District Hist. Soc., *Hist. Rev.* (Cobourg, Ont.), 4 (1986). *British American Cultivator* (Toronto), new ser., 2 (1846): 399; 3 (1847): 138. *Canadian Agriculturist* (Toronto), 1849–63. *Cobourg Star*, 8 Sept. 1847; 15 March, 19 July, 2, 23 Aug., 11, 18 Oct. 1848; 18 July 1849. *Dominion short-horn herd book* (Ottawa), 1 (1886–87). R. L. Jones, *History of agriculture in Ontario, 1613–1880* (Toronto, 1946; repr. Toronto and Buffalo, N.Y., 1977). D. McL. Marshall, *Shorthorn cattle in Canada* (Guelph, Ont., 1932). Kenneth Kelly, "The transfer of British ideas on improved farming to Ontario during the first half of the nineteenth century," *OH*, 63 (1971): 103–11.

WALKER, WILLIAM, lawyer, militia officer, newspaper editor, and politician; b. 8 Aug. 1797, probably at Trois-Rivières, Lower Canada, son of William Walker, a merchant; d. 8 April 1844 in Montreal.

William Walker began legal studies in 1812, articling first with Michael O'SULLIVAN of Montreal and then with Charles Richard Ogden* of Trois-Rivières. Called to the bar of Lower Canada on 6 April 1819, he became "one of [its] most distinguished members," according to Montreal lawyer and author Arthur William Patrick Buchanan, as well as a linguist, scholar, and great orator. A man of small stature, he walked with a limp owing to a duel over "an affair of honour" with a fellow lawyer, Campbell Sweeney, in which his leg was shattered between the ankle and the knee. Walker was one of the original members of The Brothers In Law, a social organization for Montreal lawyers. He was also an ensign in the 6th Battalion of Montreal County militia and a member of St Paul's Church (Presbyterian).

Described by John Macaulay* as "a clever lawyer, who is said by some to have an eye to office," Walker came to public prominence in 1822–23 during the debate on the proposed union of the Canadas, a measure he advocated to improve commerce in the colonies. To expand Montreal's own commercial facilities, he and some of the town's most prominent businessmen lent money in 1831 for the New Market. Three years later he and John Donellan contested Montreal West on behalf of the merchant party against Louis-Joseph Papineau* and Robert Nelson*, a riotous election which his adversaries won by only 40 votes. Stung by the close defeat, Walker, Donellan, and their supporters met soon afterwards to protest alleged electoral irregularities and they formed a permanent pressure group, the Loyal and Constitutional Association. In April 1835 Walker was chosen by the Montreal branch of the association to accompany John NEILSON, the representative of the Quebec branch, to London, there to plead for reforms in the political system. During their discussions with the colonial secretary, Lord Glenelg, and the prime minister, Lord Melbourne, the delegates advised against an elected Legislative Council and called for legislation to facilitate commerce. Although Walker's instructions favoured union of the Canadas or the annexation of Montreal to Upper Canada, the Montreal committee had advised him not to press either, out of deference to the views of the Quebec association. In fact, he suggested neither, but put forward a third plan to place the St Lawrence in the hands of the imperial government to facilitate trade. Upon his return to Lower Canada, Walker visited Quebec in January 1836, together with James Holmes and Turton Penn, to plan a small meeting of both branches of the Constitutional Association. While there, he suggested a more ambitious scheme, an assembly of representatives of all the British North American colonies. Although there was no question of Walker's loyalties during the rebellions which followed, he served as lawyer for several Patriotes, including his old political rival Nelson, who in August 1838 was trying to negotiate a return to Lower Canada so as not to forfeit his bail.

An early advocate of responsible government, Walker became editor of the *Canada Times*, a reform newspaper founded in Montreal in 1840 by John James Williams. The paper is believed to have been established to combat the union of the Canadas, which Walker now opposed. He also became a bitter opponent of Lord Sydenham [THOMSON], and according to Macaulay, his editorial strictures upon the governor were "not less true than severe. – especially with respect to the appointments of mere adventurers to valuable offices." With his editorial duties and a demanding law practice, primarily in commercial law, Walker was "in the habit of dictating an editorial to one of his law students, and often concurrently dictated a legal opinion to another, advising a client or reading a book between the intervals."

In July 1842 Walker was elected to the Legislative Assembly for Rouville. He took his seat on 9 September, but within 10 days he received a leave of absence for the remainder of the session, perhaps because of illness. He resigned on 26 Aug. 1843 and died less than eight months later. As a reformer and follower of Francis Hincks*, and as a talented, articulate lawyer, well connected to Montreal's business community, Walker seemed destined to go far in the political world of the united Canadas. His death at 46 years ended what promised to be a distinguished public career.

CARMAN MILLER

William Walker is the author of *Mr. Walker's report of his proceedings in England, to the executive committee of the Montreal Constitutional Association* (Montreal, 1836). He should not be confused with the William Walker who was agent at Quebec for Forsyth, Richardson and Company and a member of the Special Council in 1838 and of the Legislative Council from 1842 until his death in 1863.

ANQ-M, CE1-130, 11 avril 1844. McCord Museum, M21413. PAC, RG 4, B8: 7061–71. *Arthur papers* (Sanderson), 3: 1945. Can., Prov. of, Legislative Assembly, *Journals*, 1842. *Montreal Gazette*, 5 July 1842, 9 April 1844. *Montreal Transcript*, 11 April 1844. *Pilot* (Montreal), 9 April 1844. *Quebec Gazette*, 14 April 1831. Beaulieu et Hamelin, *La presse québécoise*, vol.1. Desjardins, *Guide parl*. *Political appointments and elections in the Province of Canada from 1841 to 1865*, comp. J.-O. Coté (2nd ed., Ottawa, 1866). Buchanan, *Bench and bar of L.C.* Creighton, *Empire of St. Lawrence*. Ægidius Fauteux, *Le duel au Canada* (Montréal, 1934). Elinor Kyte Senior, *Redcoats and Patriotes: the rebellions in Lower Canada, 1837–38* (Stittsville, Ont., 1985). Ouellet, *Lower Canada*.

WARD, JOHN, businessman, militia officer, politician, and JP; b. 8 Nov. 1753 in Peekskill, N.Y., probably the son of Edmund Ward and Elizabeth Strange; m. 1777 Elizabeth Strange, and they had four sons and two daughters; d. 5 Aug. 1846 in Saint John, N.B.

During the American revolution John Ward fought on the side of the loyalists. Appointed an ensign in the Loyal American Regiment in 1776, he was promoted lieutenant on 7 Oct. 1777. When Major John André sailed aboard the *Vulture* in 1780 to meet with the American major-general Benedict Arnold*, who had been supplying information to the British, Ward commanded the escort troops, and after André had been arrested by a rebel patrol he took the general to safety. He also commanded the last provincial troops to leave New York for Parrtown (Saint John) in 1783. Owing to the lateness of the season, his men were forced to spend the winter there in tents. A son, John, was born into the Ward family that cold December.

Ward left Parrtown in 1784 to settle in the area that became known as Wards Creek. Finding it too far from the commercial centre of what had become the province of New Brunswick, he soon returned to Parrtown. The first of his mercantile ventures was a wholesale liquor business, the Saint John pioneer in the West Indies liquor trade that brought so much prosperity to the city. Located at South Market Wharf, in the heart of the city's commercial district, the firm soon expanded into general merchandise, to supply the needs of the ships that daily arrived at the Market Slip and the residents of the city who frequented the Market Square. Eventually, the company also moved into lumber milling and iron founding; one of its mills was situated at Point Wolfe, in present-day Fundy National Park.

On 21 Feb. 1812 Ward and five other businessmen successfully petitioned the House of Assembly for the exclusive right over ten years to operate steamboats between Saint John and the provincial capital of Fredericton. Their project was delayed because of war with the United States, but in 1816 the syndicate, now including Hugh Johnston*, succeeded in launching the *General Smyth*. The vessel sailed for the capital on 20 May, thus initiating the first steamer service on the Saint John. Subsequently, Ward was involved in other steamers that plied the river. In 1814 the firm of John Ward and Son (his eldest surviving son, Caleb, had joined the business) commissioned the first square-rigged vessel to be built at St Martins. Constructed under contract to James Moran, the 391-ton *Waterloo* was launched in 1815 and immediately set sail for Liverpool with a cargo of timber and staves. As an indication of his permanent interest in the shipbuilding area of St Martins, Ward had a house built in the region. In the 1830s and 1840s several of his firm's ships were constructed by François-Lambert Bourneuf* of Clare, N.S. Ward's company was evidently highly successful. It is believed that, at least for a short period around 1837, it controlled most of the property at South Market Wharf.

Ward was active in public life. In April 1799 he was elected an alderman for Saint John, a position he held until October 1809, when he won a seat in the provincial assembly for Saint John County and City. Returned to the house in 1816 and 1819, he sat until the dissolution of 1820; he then retired from politics. From 1827 to 1834 his son John would represent his father's old constituency. The House of Assembly *Journal* does not reveal that Ward Sr made any notable contributions to its proceedings. There is no doubt, however, that he used his position to further the goals of his firm. For example, on 9 June 1818 he was appointed one of the commissioners for laying out the road from Loch Lomond to Quaco Bay, the site of his shipbuilding activities. In 1818 as well he was made a justice of the peace, and he eventually became the senior magistrate of the city and county of Saint John. He also served for almost 40 years as a commissioner for the Bay of Fundy lighthouses. His firm not only provided building and operating materials for the lighthouses but also administered the tenders on lighthouse contracts.

Ward had retained his interest in military affairs after arriving in New Brunswick. On 4 May 1793 he had been one of the founding officers of Saint John's Loyal Company of Artillery, and on 12 Nov. 1806 he was promoted major. By August 1816 he had become commander of the 1st Battalion of the Saint John County militia. Later he commanded all the county militia, retiring on 23 June 1830.

Ward epitomized for his fellow citizens the traditional values of the loyalists. In recognition of his contributions to Saint John he was given the appellation "Father of the City," and during the 50th and 60th celebrations of the landing of the loyalists he was treated as the guest of honour. After his death in August 1846 the *New-Brunswick Courier* carried a poem dedicated to him: "Accept this tribute from a bard, / Who deems it justly due – / Peace to thy Ashes, Father WARD – / Hear Patriarch, adieu." Ward's personal drive and determination were no doubt missed in the firm he had established for it did not last into the 1860s. Moreover, the prophecy of a writer in 1846 that his name would "descend unsullied to posterity, and be held in reverence by future generations" did not come true – John Ward is all but forgotten in Saint John today.

HAROLD E. WRIGHT

City of Saint John, N.B., City Clerk's Office, Common Council, minutes, 1785–1846 (mfm. at Saint John Regional Library). N.B. Museum, A15 (John Ward); A141 (John Ward, account-book, 1785–89); Ward family papers, packet 20, items 135, 139; packet 29, items 12, 16, 21–29. PANB, MC 1156; RG 4, RS24, S21-P16. N.B., House of Assembly, *Journal*, 1809–20. *Winslow papers* (Raymond). *Morning News* (Saint John), 7 Aug. 1846. *New-Brunswick Courier*, 8, 29 Aug. 1846. J. B. M. Baxter, *Historical records of the New Brunswick Regiment, Canadian Artillery* (Saint John, 1896). A. G. Finley, "The Morans of St. Martins, N.B., 1850–1880: toward an understanding of family participation in maritime enterprise," *The enterprising Canadians: entrepreneurs and economic development in eastern Canada, 1820–1914*, ed. L. R. Fischer and E. W. Sager (St John's, 1979), 37–54. G. [B.] MacBeath and D. F. Taylor, *Steamboat days: an illustrated history of the steamboat era on the St. John River, 1816–1946* (St Stephen [-Milltown], N.B., 1982). Richard Rice, "The Wrights of Saint John: a study of shipbuilding and shipowning in the Maritimes, 1839–1855," *Canadian business history; selected studies, 1497–1971*, ed. D. S. Macmillan (Toronto, 1972), 317–37. T. W. Acheson, "The great merchant and economic development in St. John, 1820–1850," *Acadiensis* (Fredericton), 8 (1978–79), no.2: 3–27. J. R. Harper, "St. Martins' men build a ship in 1814," *American Neptune: a Quarterly Journal of Maritime Hist.* (Salem, Mass.), 21 (1966): 279–91.

WASHBURN, SIMON EBENEZER, militia officer, lawyer, office holder, and politician; b. probably 1794 in Fredericksburgh Township, Upper Canada, son of Ebenezer Washburn* and Sarah De Forest; m. 12 April 1821 Margaret FitzGibbon; d. 29 Sept. 1837 in Toronto.

The sixth of nine children in a prominent loyalist family, Simon Ebenezer Washburn attended the Kingston grammar school and then served in the militia in the War of 1812. He studied law under Dr William Warren BALDWIN in York (Toronto), was called to the bar of Upper Canada in January 1820, and practised in partnership with Baldwin until he established his own office in May 1825. He became a successful and highly respected lawyer. Among those who studied with him were William Hume Blake*, George Duggan*, and Joseph Curran Morrison*.

Washburn was clerk of the peace for the Home District from October 1828 until his death. As such, he administered the Court of Quarter Sessions and kept the court records; the fees he received averaged about £290 a year. He was also commissioned to administer oaths of various kinds, including the oath of allegiance. On 4 May 1829 Washburn became reporter to the Court of King's Bench, but he resigned six months later pleading the pressure of other business. He was a bencher of the Law Society of Upper Canada from 3 Nov. 1829 until his death. During the 1832 cholera epidemic he served on the York Board of Health.

Simon Washburn's name is connected with two Upper Canadian controversies. When, in June 1828, justice John Walpole Willis* cast doubt on the legality of the operations of the Court of King's Bench, Washburn joined William Warren Baldwin and his son Robert* in writing to request the opinion of justice Levius Peters SHERWOOD. Washburn pursued the matter no further and was not involved in the ensuing dispute. In a customs scandal of 1830 Washburn was criticized for delivering £75 to a customs officer for the release of some pork, allegedly smuggled by York merchant William Bergin. The payment had been arranged by Washburn's brother-in-law James FitzGibbon*, clerk of the House of Assembly, who was accused of bribery. Washburn, whose role was that of agent for FitzGibbon, emerged with his career undamaged.

In politics, Washburn had only minor success. He failed twice, in 1830 and 1832, to unseat William Lyon Mackenzie* as member of the assembly for York County, but he succeeded in 1837 in being elected alderman for St David's Ward in Toronto. He was active in the militia and in 1835 rose to be colonel of the 2nd Regiment of West York. As churchwarden of St James' Church, he assisted Archdeacon John Strachan* in the financial campaign to have a new stone church built in 1833.

Although Washburn was a conservative, Mackenzie observed in an obituary that "in some measure" he "took the liberal side in politics," a reference, presumably, to his association with the Baldwins in the Willis affair. Mackenzie noted also that as a lawyer Washburn had done some "very kind and generous" things, referring to his actions on behalf of blacks and others sentenced to flogging, execution, or lengthy imprisonment for relatively minor crimes. In such cases, he almost certainly provided free legal aid.

Simon Washburn was a generous and public-spirited man. He had a zest for life, exemplified by his love of skating, and was considered slightly eccentric for wearing a monocle.

RUTH MCKENZIE

AO, MS 35; MU 3054, "Data on United Empire Loyalists . . . ," comp. W. D. Reid (typescript, *c.* 1930); RG 22, ser.155; ser.159, 1801–58, R–Z, no.50. CTA, RG 1, B (mfm. at AO). Law Soc. of U.C. (Toronto), Minutes; Rolls. MTRL, William Allan papers. PAC, RG 1, E3, 95: 143; RG 5, A1: 7788, 7790–91, 24504–8, 37966–67, 41455–65, 46906–10, 50113–15, 52129–30, 54174–75, 61342–48, 61847, 62353–56, 65145–47, 65757–58, 65928–30, 98196–97; B9, 15: 636; RG 9, I, B3, 5; RG 68, 78: 385–86, 576; 79: 108; 127: 33–34. PRO, CO 47/144, 47/148–52 (mfm. at PAC). "A register of baptisms for the township of Fredericksburgh . . . ," comp. John Langhorn, *OH*, 1 (1899): 35, 38, 42, 47. *Canadian Freeman*, 15, 22, 29 July, 23 Sept. 1830. *Colonial Advocate*, 19 June, 2, 9 July 1828. *Constitution*, 4 Oct. 1837. *Upper Canada Gazette*, 12 May 1825. J. C. Dent, *The story of the Upper Canadian rebellion; largely derived from original sources and documents* (2v., Toronto, 1885), 1: 163–92. Lindsey, *Life and times of Mackenzie*, 1: 184–85, 241–42. W. R. Riddell, *The bar and the courts of the province of Upper Canada, or Ontario* (Toronto, 1928). *Robertson's landmarks of Toronto*, 1: 454–55. Scadding, *Toronto of old* (Armstrong; 1966).

WATTEVILLE, LOUIS DE (the name sometimes appears as **Abraham Ludwig Karl von Wattenwyl**), army officer; b. 1776 in Bern, Switzerland, and was baptized on 26 July of that year, son of David de Watteville and Magdalena (Élisabeth) Jenner, daughter of Abraham Jenner, bailiff of Grandson, Switzerland, from 1775 to 1780; m. 28 Sept. 1807 Sophie de Tavel at Wichtrach, in the canton of Bern, Switzerland, and they had nine children; d. 16 June 1836 in Rubigen, Switzerland.

Although he was a descendant of the Rubigen branch of the Wattenwyl family and was called Carl Ludwig von Wattenwyl in the registration of his death, Louis de Watteville used mainly French and signed the French form of his name. He began his military career in Europe, probably through the help of his father, an officer in the service of the Netherlands. He fought against France in a Swiss regiment serving the Netherlands in 1793 and 1794, and then in a Swiss corps of the Austrian army that was raised in March 1799 with British financial aid.

After the Treaty of Lunéville was signed by France and Austria on 9 Feb. 1801, Great Britain remained at war with France, and organized the various Swiss corps into a regiment that was posted to the Mediterranean theatre. On 1 May 1801 Watteville was made lieutenant-colonel of the new regiment, which was named after his uncle Frédéric de Watteville, its colonel and proprietor. There followed for Louis de Watteville a dozen years of service in various Mediterranean countries. With the regiment, he distinguished himself particularly in the battle of Maida, fought in the south of Italy on 4 July 1806, which led to a British rout of the French forces. For this brilliant action Watteville was decorated on 22 Feb. 1808 with the gold medal awarded to the commanders of the units present at the battle.

Watteville attained the rank of brevet colonel on 25 April 1810, and on 7 May 1812 he replaced his uncle as colonel and proprietor of De Watteville's Regiment. Although it was a Swiss unit in the service of Britain, it was largely made up of Germans, Italians, Poles, Hungarians, and Russians, with a handful of Greeks and Frenchmen. Roughly a fifth of its strength, including nearly all the officers, was Swiss.

Watteville was in Spain at Cadiz, where he had been since late in 1811, when the order came on 15 March 1813 to sail for the Canadas with his regiment. They were being sent as reinforcements for the small British garrison which had been resisting American attempts at invasion since the previous year, when the United States and Britain had gone to war. On 5 April Watteville, 41 officers, 1,414 men, 8 servants, 45 wives, and 38 children boarded six ships, which set sail the next day and reached Quebec on 4 June after calling in at Halifax.

Two days later Watteville and his unit continued on to Kingston, Upper Canada, where the regiment was posted. Watteville arrived on 29 June and immediately met Sir George Prevost*, governor general and commander-in-chief of the British forces in North America, himself an officer of Swiss descent. The two men got along well and Watteville's diary several times mentions "having dined at General Prévost's." For Prevost an experienced officer was an invaluable asset. Consequently on 5 July Colonel Watteville was named commandant of the Kingston garrison. The army staff in London seems to have shared his view, for on 11 August Watteville learned that he had been promoted major-general on 4 June, even though he had never been a brigadier-general. He had to abandon the scarlet coatee with black velvet facings and silver lace of his regiment and don the scarlet coat with dark blue facings and gold embroidery worn by general officers. In addition, although he was still proprietor of his regiment, he had to hand the command over to another officer.

No new instructions accompanied Watteville's promotion, and so he could not be employed as a major-general in the Canadas. As a result he spent August and September 1813 in Kingston impatiently waiting. Except for a mention in his diary on 12 September – the sole entry of its kind during his stay in the Canadas – that he had been "very ill all this last while," there was nothing to report. Having soon recovered, Watteville decided to go to England, sold his effects, and left Kingston on 12 October. Reaching Montreal on the 16th, he learned that on 29 July he had been designated by London to serve on the staff in North America. The general order announcing this news was finally published in Montreal on 17 October, as was Watteville's posting to the district of Montreal. He thus had command of the troops southwest of Montreal and on 19th October set up headquarters in the presbytery at Châteauguay.

There were rumours that the American army was assembling near the border. Watteville had only a handful of British regulars to count on. The troops at his disposal were mainly the Voltigeurs Canadiens and some battalions of the Select Embodied Militia of Lower Canada, the latter often made up of conscripts, under Lieutenant-Colonel Charles-Michel d'Irumberry* de Salaberry. After carrying out a reconnaissance on Watteville's orders, Salaberry reported to him on 22 October that the enemy was "in great strength": about 5,000 men, most of them regulars, the first units having crossed the border on the morning of 21 October.

From his advanced post Salaberry began to organize a defensive position. Watteville immediately assembled his troops to form a defence in echelon along the west bank of the Châteauguay and established himself "at the forks," where he received Prevost between 11 and noon on 26 Oct. 1813. At 1:00 P.M. the two officers set off on horseback for the advanced posts, but on the way they received news that those positions had been engaged with the enemy since 11 o'clock. Watteville immediately went on ahead. By the time he arrived, firing had already ceased and the battle of Châteauguay was over. The next day he forwarded Salaberry's report to Prevost, along with a letter of his own saying that the victory had to be attributed "both to the bravery of the troops and to the activity and good judgement exhibited by Lieutenant-Colonel de Salaberry in choosing and fortifying the position in the space of a few days" – high praise from an experienced officer.

Watteville was, however, taken to task by Major-General Richard Stovin and Colonel Edward Baynes for not having taken advantage of the victory to order that the Americans be pursued and harassed. After consulting Salaberry, he replied on 31 October, explaining in detail the "great danger" that a detachment sent in pursuit would have run. The American army, it is now known, withdrew in orderly fashion after the reverse suffered on 26 October. It would, in fact, have been extremely risky to attack a force that consisted mainly of regulars, who were more reliable than militiamen, and that was still well disciplined.

On 29 November Watteville returned to the presbytery at Châteauguay, where he was paying six dollars a week for lodgings. But on 28 December he left in a huff because he would not tolerate the parish priest's sending an "insolent" letter to his aide-de-camp. In the mean time he had been appointed to preside over a commission to examine claims for war damages, a delicate administrative task he carried out smoothly until the end of January 1814.

On 22 June Watteville was sent to Chambly to take command of a brigade of the Select Embodied Militia, and late in July he proceeded to the outposts at Lacolle, where Salaberry was established. The area was quiet except for occasional exchanges of fire between the Canadian and American scouts. But Watteville's respite was short-lived, since on 8 August he received a new appointment in Upper Canada. On his way there he dined in Montreal on 15 August with Prevost and several senior officers. At the camp of the British force besieging Fort Erie he met the officer in command of the troops in Upper Canada, Gordon Drummond*. When on 17 September the Americans attempted a sortie in the sector under Watteville a sharp battle ensued, but the British forces were well deployed, and the enemy finally had to withdraw. There were heavy losses – about 600 men on each side, according to Watteville. In his official report of 19 September Drummond praised Watteville's sound judgement and zeal. He was subsequently assigned to the advanced guard at Black Creek (Niagara Falls).

The war with the United States was, however, coming to an end. On 8 Oct. 1814 Watteville learned that his wife and children had arrived at Quebec, and on 25 October he requested two months' leave in Montreal, which was granted. He finally reached there on 20 December, rejoining his family "after an absence of more than two years," he noted with feeling in his diary – two long years, for he loved Sophie de Tavel deeply. Many times in his diary he mentions receiving letters from his wife or writing to her, and how much he hopes that she will come to Canada. For her part, Sophie was in love with her husband. She could have gone off to Switzerland, which had been liberated early in 1814, but she braved a difficult four-month voyage with her children in order to join him. Christmas of 1814 was undoubtedly a memorable one for them. On his leave, however, Watteville had to discharge the rather delicate, even painful, duty of sitting on the court martial convened in Montreal for the trial of Major-General Henry Procter*.

In February 1815 Watteville left for the Niagara peninsula, accompanied by his brother Rodolphe. They were dining with Drummond at York (Toronto) on 20 February when news came that Britain and the United States had signed the Treaty of Ghent on 24 December. The war was finally over.

Watteville remained in Upper Canada for the next year or so. He commanded the British troops in the Niagara region from his headquarters at Fort George (Niagara-on-the-Lake), and then in July 1815 he took up quarters at Kingston with his family. He was named commander-in-chief of the armed forces in Upper Canada on 7 October, but he wanted to retire from the service and was finally allowed to do so. On 27 July 1816 the Wattevilles left Kingston. They stayed in London from September 1816 to January 1817 and reached Bern on 18 January. Later they went to live in the château at Rubigen, where Watteville resided until his death in June 1836.

Louis de Watteville was level-headed, discreet, and efficient. Through his military experience and his love of order and work, he contributed to improving the quality of the British army staff in the Canadas during a critical period. His tactical arrangements, always made with great attention to detail, were the decisive factor at Châteauguay and Fort Erie. A demanding officer, he was fair and gave his subordinates the credit they merited. In that sense he was instrumental in raising Salaberry to the status of a military hero to the French Canadians. This reserved and methodical soldier was a patient and understanding man profoundly attached to his family. He no doubt had his faults, but history has forgotten them.

RENÉ CHARTRAND

[Two portraits of Louis de Watteville are known to exist, both in the hands of descendants at Bern, Switzerland. The first, a rather naïve work by an unknown artist showing him in the uniform of a major-general, seems to have been done in Canada, probably at Montreal, some time between 1813 and 1816, and is reproduced in P.-E. de Vallière, *Honneur et fidélité: histoire des Suisses au service étranger* (Lausanne, Suisse, 1940), 651. The second work, executed by a more skilled artist, also unknown, portrays Watteville in civilian clothes about 1820; it is included in E. H. Bovay, *Le Canada et les Suisses, 1604–1974* (Fribourg, Suisse, 1976), 25. Both portraits present him as a handsome, attractive man.

The principal source for this article is the four-volume journal Watteville kept from 1801 to 1826, which is with the Watteville family at the Château d'Au in the canton of Saint-Gall, Switzerland. A typescript is held by the Bibliothèque Militaire Fédérale at Bern (mfm. at PAC, MG 23, F96); volume 3, for the period 1 Oct. 1810–30 Sept. 1815, is particularly important. R.C.]

Arch. de l'État de Berne (Berne), Reg. des sépultures, 16 juin 1836. PAC, RG 8, I (C ser.), 229: 138; 233: 58, 77, 81; 680: 326, 331; 681: 100, 105, 130; 685: 164, 267; 686: 90,

93, 150, 168, 188, 200; 1170: 362; 1171: 117, 143, 291, 333; 1203½I: 46, 246; 1203½S: 86, 93; 1219: 125, 290, 293; 1221: 211. *Annual reg.* (London), 1815: 259–60. *Dictionnaire historique et biographique de la Suisse* (6v. et 1 suppl., Neuchâtel, Suisse, 1921–34), 4: 236–37. G.B., WO, *Army list*, 1803: 234; 1813: 448; 1816: 516. *Officers of British forces in Canada* (Irving), 9, 11. Ouellet, "Inv. de la saberdache," ANQ *Rapport*, 1955–57: 139. "Papiers d'État – Bas-Canada," PAC *Rapport*, 1896: 36, 38, 43. *The royal military calendar, or army service and commission book . . .*, ed. John Philippart (3rd ed., 5v., London, 1820), 3: 306–7. F.-M.-L.-R. Grouvel, *Les corps de troupe de l'émigration française, 1789–1815 . . .* (3v., Paris, 1957–64), 1: 329–34. C. T. Atkinson, "Foreign regiments in the British army, 1793–1802," Soc. for Army Hist. Research, *Journal* (London), 22 (1943–44): 13–14, 316–20. F.-J. Audet, "Abraham-Louis-Charles de Watteville," *BRH*, 32 (1926): 749–51. Gérard Malchelosse, "Deux régiments suisses au Canada," *Cahiers des Dix*, 2 (1937): 279–96.

WEDDERBURN, ALEXANDER, businessman, office holder, and author; b. *c.* 1796 in Aberdeen, Scotland; m. 15 Jan. 1823 in Saint John, N.B., Jane Heaviside, daughter of Thomas Heaviside, lumber merchant, and sister of Mary Heaviside*; they had one son and three daughters; d. 17 June 1843 in Saint John.

Not long after Waterloo, according to family legend, Alexander Wedderburn, a young naval officer, saw a girl board a packet for America. Finding her attractive, the story goes, he discovered her name and destination, followed her to Saint John in 1815, and subsequently married her. Wedderburn established himself as a wine merchant and land speculator there, acquiring several blocks of land in association with William* and Thomas Black, timber merchants and fellow Scots. In August 1829 he was appointed landing waiter and searcher of customs at St Andrews, probably through the influence of the Blacks, and in February 1831 he was given the same position in Saint John. In the 1820s he was the secretary of the Saint John Agricultural and Emigrant Society and was active in helping immigrants to get established. He claimed to have expended large sums of his own money in assisting them and both in 1827 and in 1828 he was given £100 by the House of Assembly as compensation. In 1829 he requested a grant of 12,000–14,000 acres of land as further compensation for his services. His request was supported by William Black, who was administering the government in the absence of Lieutenant Governor Sir Howard Douglas*, and the Colonial Office agreed to allow him 1,000 acres.

Because of the increase in the number of immigrants to New Brunswick after 1826, the Colonial Office decided to place an emigrant agent at Saint John, the first in the province; in July 1831 William Black appointed Wedderburn to the post at £300 a year, a very good salary for a minor government official. Wedderburn appears to have carried out his duties conscientiously for a number of years. With the decline of immigration in the early 1830s, however, he spent more and more of his time looking after his own business. As a result, he earned the displeasure of Douglas's successor, Sir Archibald CAMPBELL, who in 1834 reduced his salary to £100.

After the appointment of Sir John Harvey* to the lieutenant governorship in 1837, Wedderburn appealed to him to have his original salary restored. He claimed that he had been imprisoned for debts incurred since 1831 on behalf of immigrants and that he had not been compensated for his expenses. Harvey supported his application, saying that it would be better to abolish the office than to pay a salary inadequate for a gentleman in a full-time position. The Colonial Office, however, refused to interfere. In 1839 Wedderburn was upbraided by the home authorities for sending reports direct to Britain and was informed that in future he should submit them to the lieutenant governor. He also ran foul of Sir William MacBean George Colebrooke*, who had succeeded Harvey, and in 1842 he was ordered to confine himself to his responsibilities as emigrant agent and not to get involved in "extraneous duties." There are indications, too, that a fondness for drink had interfered with the conduct of his office. By 1843 Wedderburn was so sick that on 1 June Moses Henry Perley* was appointed to act for him temporarily. After he died later that month Perley took over the position.

In 1835 Wedderburn had had printed by Henry Chubb* in Saint John *Statistical and practical observations relative to the province of New-Brunswick, published for the information of emigrants*. In announcing its imminent appearance, a St Andrews newspaper commented on the author's "acknowledged talent" and his "indefatigable exertions to procure all the necessary authentic information."

W. A. SPRAY

N.B. Museum, Day family, CB DOC, information on Alexander Wedderburn; J. C. Webster papers, packet 1, Sir Howard Douglas, letter-book, Douglas to R. W. Hay, 18 Sept. 1829 (typescript). PANB, RG 1, RS345, A2: 85; RG 2, RS8, immigration, 1/1, Wedderburn to Sir John Harvey, 24 Jan. 1838; 1/4, undated information, collected 1841 for the commissioners of colonial lands and emigration; 6/2; RG 3, RS13, A3, W. F. Odell to Wedderburn; RS538, B5: 36, 39; RG 10, RS108, Alexander Wedderburn, 1820, 1825, 1830, 1835, 1840. PRO, CO 188/39: 441–42; 188/41: 198, 314–20; 188/50: 90–92; 188/60: 250–53; 188/62: 457–58; 188/67: 274. N.B., House of Assembly, *Journal*, 1827: 104; 1828: 120. *Gleaner* (Miramichi [Chatham, N.B.]), 25 Aug. 1835 (citing the St Andrews *Standard*). *Royal Gazette* (Fredericton), 23 Jan. 1823, 28 June 1843.

WENTWORTH, THOMAS HANFORD, painter,

daguerreotypist, and entrepreneur; b. 15 March 1781 in Norwalk, Conn.; d. 18 Dec. 1849 in Oswego, N.Y.

Thomas Hanford Wentworth was raised in Saint John, N.B., by an uncle but had returned to the United States by 1806. He may have visited England in 1805 and gone to Oswego from that trip, an hypothesis that would explain American scholarly opinion in the 1930s that he was an Englishman. On his arrival in Oswego he bought all the water-power sites in the area, and he seems also to have been involved in the freight and forwarding business. He was evidently prosperous: during the War of 1812 the Wentworth home was looted of its silver and of 20 roast ducks prepared for a dinner party.

Mantle Fielding's dictionary of American artists lists Wentworth as a painter of portraits in oils and miniature and an executor of profiles in pencil. It has been suggested that he produced over 3,000 pencil likenesses by 1824. This estimate is based on the fact that a series of six pencil sketches of the Pease family of Auburn, N.Y., is numbered consecutively from 3,225. Since these likenesses are dated between 1824 and 1826, and Wentworth was active until at least 1842, his total production must have been well over 3,000. Prolific as he may have been as a portraitist, Wentworth's American reputation is largely based on a series of 15 views of Niagara Falls, for which he did the drawings and prepared both lithographs and copperplate engravings. One set of three engravings was copyrighted on 4 June 1821.

Wentworth returned to Saint John in 1831 and established himself as a portraitist. "His manner," he announced on 12 December, "will be from PROFILE to PORTRAIT, in which is included Miniature on Paper or Ivory." He also advertised replicas of his Niagara Falls pictures and opened a subscription with the aim of engraving a view of Saint John that he had painted. His most popular print was issued in 1837 following a major fire in Saint John. His studio overlooked the main harbour area and Prince William Street, and he was able to describe the scene in considerable detail against a dramatic background of smoke and flame. Wentworth's activities in Saint John included the sale of cooking stoves, and one is left with the unproved but reasonable assumption that his return to the city was in part due to his uncle's business there.

Wentworth flourished in Saint John until 1842, advertising himself that year as a portrait painter and, ever the entrepreneur, as a taker of daguerreotypes. He had been instructed in the photographic technique by Hodgkinson and Butters, American daguerreotypists who visited Saint John in the summer of 1842. It is not known when Wentworth returned to Oswego. He died there in 1849 of paralysis. Married, he had had at least two sons, one of whom, William Henry, was also a portrait painter.

STUART SMITH

New-Brunswick Courier, 24 Dec. 1831, 14 June 1832, 29 March 1834, 28 Sept. 1842, 19 June 1847, 19 Jan. 1850. Mantle Fielding, *Dictionary of American painters, sculptors, and engravers; with an addendum containing additional material on the original entries*, comp. J. F. Carr (New York, 1965). Harper, *Early painters and engravers*; *Painting in Canada* (1966). *Antiques* (New York), 31 (January–June 1937): 10, 291; 32 (July–December 1937): 7–8; 33 (January–June 1938): 311. G. [B.] MacBeath, "Artists in New Brunswick's past," *Arts in New Brunswick*, ed. R. A. Tweedie *et al.* (Fredericton, 1967), 121–48.

WEST, JOHN, Church of England missionary, teacher, and author; b. November 1778 in Farnham, Surrey, England, and baptized 18 December, son of George West and Ann Knowles; m. 2 Oct. 1807 Harriet Atkinson in Wethersfield, England, and they had 12 children; d. 21 Dec. 1845 in Chettle, England.

As John West's father was an Anglican clergyman, the routine of the manse and the necessity of securing a gentlemanly calling probably influenced John's vocational choice and education. Repeating a pattern set by his elder brother, he became a deacon on 13 Dec. 1804, was ordained on 21 Sept. 1806, and graduated from St Edmund Hall, Oxford, with an MA on 8 June 1809. Following his ordination he was assigned curacies in Essex, where he formed an acquaintance with the Reverend Henry Budd, an evangelical rector. West did not obtain a permanent benefice until collated to the rectory of Chettle, in Dorset, early in 1820. By that time, however, it appears that the attitudes of the evangelical movement had become a matter of personal conviction with West and he had already offered to serve the Church Missionary Society in the field.

Benjamin Harrison, a director of the Hudson's Bay Company and a founding member of the CMS, appears to have been responsible for securing West's appointment as HBC chaplain in 1819. The company's London committee, anticipating that the trade war between the North West Company and the HBC would result in merger – it took place in 1821 – intended that surplus and retired servants from both companies, orphaned mixed-blood children, and others associated with the Protestant community in the west would have their spiritual requirements met in the Red River settlement (Man.), where schools, religious instruction, and pastoral care would be established by a chaplain in the company's employ. West's placement there also reflected the interest of Andrew Colvile and John Halkett*, executors of the estate of Lord Selkirk [Douglas*] and members of the London committee, in ensuring the progress of the settlement. As well, the committee believed that one of a number of missionary societies could be counted on for financial support if the mission were to include Indian children from the Red River region.

The first Protestant missionary to tour Rupert's

Land, West sailed for that territory on 27 May 1820 with George Harbidge, a school teacher, but left his wife and infant children behind, apparently with every intention of returning for them once a mission was firmly established. Emphasizing the evangelicals' goal of mission to non-Christian natives instead of his duties as HBC chaplain, West noted in his journal that his orders from the company were "to reside at the Red River Settlement, and under the incouragement and aid of the Church Missionary Society, . . . to seek the instruction and endeavour to meliorate the condition of the native Indians." Immediately after arriving at York Factory (Man.) in August, he visited Indian tents and observed a large number of orphaned mixed-blood and native children. He hastily drew up a plan calling for the care and education of indigent children at schools to be established in the Red River settlement. This plan he submitted to William WILLIAMS, resident governor of the HBC, for transfer to the London committee, but no action was taken. Convinced that his greatest opportunity for Christianizing lay in converting native children, West negotiated at York to have an Indian boy assigned to his care for his proposed Indian school in Red River. At Norway House he acquired another, a Swampy Cree orphan who was later christened Henry Budd*. West continued this practice throughout his stay in Rupert's Land [*see* Thomas HASSALL; Charles Pratt*] and, although the number of boys recruited remained small, he claimed to have established the practice whereby the "North American Indian of these regions would part with his children, to be educated in the white man's knowledge and religion."

Arriving at Red River in October 1820, West began a day-school a month later in a log cabin at Kildonan (Winnipeg) as a means of evangelizing the Indians of the region. The residents of nearby Red River began sending their children to the school, thereby shifting its emphasis toward satisfying the needs of the settlement's permanent community. West stressed "civilization" as well as Christianity with his students and began delineating a program of religious and practical instruction which included teaching domestic skills to girls and horticultural and cultivation skills to boys. He planned to duplicate this effort for Cree-speaking, mixed-blood children but failed to draw sufficient financial support.

West had begun his ministry in Red River at a critical time. The residual hatred and distrust resulting from a decade of violence in the fur trade had created an uneasiness in the heterogeneous settlement. The frustration caused by uncertain crops, the fear of attack by the Sioux or their interference with the buffalo staple, and the difficulty experienced in adjusting the social values of a fur trade society to those of a settled community found expression in a conflict between settlers and the HBC over the company's efforts to curtail illicit trade. In this conflict West was essentially neutral, but he was in a situation requiring resourcefulness and tact and was not flexible enough to adapt Church of England practices to suit his flock. Although attendance was steady at services, at a Sunday school established in Upper Fort Garry (Winnipeg) for the benefit of Indian wives and older children, and at the day-school, rapport between pastor and a variegated congregation was soon strained by his exclusiveness in administering communion and by his sermons. Nicholas Garry*, an HBC director, later noted that "West is not a good Preacher; he unfortunately attempts to preach extempore from Notes, for which he has not the Capacity, his discourses being unconnected and ill-delivered. He likewise Mistakes his Point, fancying that by touching severely and pointedly on the Weaknesses of People he will produce Repentance." However, even though evangelicals like West did not believe that in a society of sinners all temporal evils could be eliminated, they did insist that on deliberate moral wrongs, which clearly contravened God's law, no compromise was possible. West, for example, attacked marriage *à la façon du pays* as both immoral and socially destructive. To escape further rebuke, many of the company officers at the HBC's posts and principal settlers in Red River who had married in that fashion responded, sometimes reluctantly, by formalizing their vows.

A number of the groups in the settlement had particular difficulties in responding to West. The Presbyterian Scots, who had been promised a clergyman of their own by Lord Selkirk, were unhappy with his unbending use of Anglican liturgy. He was clearly not received as warmly as his successor, David Thomas JONES, who would successfully employ pastoral visits and accommodate the Presbyterians' biases. With the Swiss and De Meuron settlers West fared no better. At one point he offended everyone by refusing to baptize an illegitimate child. Except for several reportedly congenial visits with chief Peguis*, West largely ignored the Saulteaux residing at Netley Creek. He did, however, begin learning an unspecified Indian language while in the settlement. West did not interfere with the Roman Catholic missionaries, Sévère Dumoulin* and Thomas-Ferruce Picard* Destroismaisons, who reported his movements to their superiors, Joseph-Norbert Provencher* and Joseph-Octave Plessis*. His distribution of bibles in French and the news that he intended learning French from Destroismaisons excited fear that West might overstep the understood denominational boundaries in Red River, but nothing more came of his efforts.

West's uneven record in the Red River settlement reflected a focus on the Indian and a preoccupation with all of Rupert's Land rather than the settlement alone. To extend his ministry, he travelled by carriole to Brandon House and Fort Qu'Appelle (Sask.) in the early months of 1821, but his most extensive journeys were visits to York Factory during the summer months of 1821, 1822, and 1823. With the cooperation of Nicholas Garry, an auxiliary Bible society was formed at York in 1821, with the assembled officers of the company making a substantial subscription. The following year West was elated to learn that the CMS would bolster his mission efforts with money and by sending Elizabeth Bowden, a trained schoolmistress and George Harbidge's fiancée, to teach and supervise the Indian girls at Red River. When John Halkett, a company director, was in Red River to persuade near-mutinous settlers to remain, West accompanied him first to Pembina (N.Dak.) and subsequently to York, pressing upon a sympathetic ear the interests of the broad mission. While in York in 1822, West met the northern expedition of Captain John FRANKLIN, who had been exploring the Arctic since 1819 and who encouraged him to extend his missionary efforts north to the Inuit at Fort Churchill (Churchill). West went the following summer, travelling from York there and back on foot.

By 1822 the members of the council of the HBC's Northern Department were growing fearful that West's efforts to attract support for Indian schools from Red River to the Pacific and to draw natives into the Red River settlement would harm the fur trade. Governor George Simpson* reflected their view, objecting on practical grounds to problems of victualling permanent missions. West refused to compromise or appreciate that he required the support of the council as well as that of the London committee. He continued urging a strict observance of the Sabbath and attacking drunkenness. He allegedly threatened Simpson to get him to use his influence with the London committee to abolish the use of spirits, eliciting the governor's criticism that the chaplain was "inclined to deal too freely in politicks." With a trade in which spirits had important commercial, ceremonial, and therapeutic functions, such threats were not lightly dismissed. A planned appointment to the Council of Assiniboia was not confirmed before his residence in the settlement ended.

In June 1823 West left for England on what was to have been a temporary furlough, but his employment was terminated by the London committee early the following year. His position in Rupert's Land had been undermined as much by his activist nature and failure to conciliate as by the less than propitious circumstances he faced in the settlement and by the inchoate policy of the HBC on missions. The ill-defined nature of his terms of employment as chaplain and CMS missionary also contributed to his difficulties. Nevertheless, by emphasizing service to the Indians and to all of Rupert's Land, West began a practice of preparing native boys for Christian service and shaped the Anglican mission in the west for his successors, among them Jones, John MACALLUM, and William Cockran*.

West's *Journal*, published in 1824, recounted and publicized his mission experiences. A second edition issued in 1827 included an account of an investigative journey taken in 1825–26 for the British and Foreign Bible Society and the New England Company [*see* Oliver Arnold*; Molly Ann Gell*]. West's itinerary included stays in New York, Boston, and the company's mission on the Kennebecasis River in New Brunswick, and brief visits to Fredericton and Annapolis Royal, N.S. Critical of the poor moral example and rapacity of the whites in charge of company operations in New Brunswick and discouraged by the unshakeable Roman Catholicism of the Indians, West through his report was partly responsible for the decision to discontinue the operations of the company there in 1826. Journeying inland from Albany, N.Y., he observed the missionary efforts in Upper Canada of the Methodists and the Society for the Propagation of the Gospel and recommended to the New England Company that a resident Anglican missionary be placed among the Mohawks on the Grand River [*see* Robert LUGGER].

In England West continued to occupy the rectorship of Chettle, to which was added the parish of Farnham, Dorset, in 1834. He maintained a vigorous interest in missions in British North America and went to the Canadas in 1828 to assist in reviving interest in the British and Foreign Bible Society auxiliaries. West also devoted attention to the organization of agricultural workers emigrating to New South Wales (Australia), and was instrumental in establishing a National School in England. In 1834 he was appointed a domestic chaplain to Baron Duncannon, one of the authors of the Reform Bill of 1831. During the last years of his life he joined with other reform-minded clergymen and gentlemen in the establishment of a school near Chettle for the education and industrial training of gypsies. West died in December 1845 and was survived by four sons and two daughters.

RICHARD A. WILLIE

[The author would like to thank Mr Jack Bridcut of Farnham, Surrey, Eng., and Mr Ian H. S. Stratton of Salisbury, Eng., for their assistance. R.A.W.]

John West is the author of *The substance of a journal during a residence at the Red River colony, British North America; and frequent excursions among the north-west American Indians, in the years 1820, 1821, 1822, 1823* (London, 1824); the second edition (London, 1827) includes *A journal of a mission to the Indians of the British provinces, of New Brunswick, and Nova Scotia, and the Mohawks, on the Ouse, or Grand River, Upper Canada*, which was also issued separately the same year. His other publications include *A brief memoir of William B— . . . , with some remarks on the nature of true religion* (2nd ed., Blandford, Eng., 1839); and *Memoir of Mrs. John West, who died at Chettle, Dorset, March 23, 1839* (2nd ed., London, 1842), a fourth edition of which, published in London in 1866, includes a brief biographical notice of the author.

GRO (London), Death certificate, John West, 21 Dec. 1845. PAM, HBCA, A.1/52: ff.39–39d; A.5/6: 194; A.5/7: ff.128, 131d; p.236; A.10/2: ff.398–99, 404–5; B.235/a/5, 13 March 1823; D.4/3: ff.74–74d, 76d–77; D.4/8: f.15d; P337, files 4–8; P2543, esp. E. J. Lawson, "The unfulfilled: a study of John West, his family, friends and times, 1778–1845" (typescript). Surrey Record Office (Guildford, Eng.), Reg. of baptisms for the parish of Farnham, 18 Dec. 1778. Univ. of Birmingham Library, Special Coll. (Birmingham, Eng.), Church Missionary Soc. Arch., C, C.1/L.1, 1821–24; C.1/M.1, nos.3–5, 10–11, 13; C.1/O, corr. and journal of John West, 1822–23 (mfm. at PAC). *Canadian north-west* (Oliver), 1: 225, 638. Church Missionary Soc., *Proc. for Africa and the East* (London), 1819–24. *Documents relating to northwest missions, 1815–1827*, ed. G. L. Nute (St Paul, Minn., 1942). Nicholas Garry, "Diary of Nicholas Garry, deputy-governor of the Hudson's Bay Company from 1822–1835: a detailed narrative of his travels in the northwest territories of British North America in 1821 . . . ," ed. F. N. A. Garry, RSC *Trans.*, 2nd ser., 6 (1900), sect.II: 139–40, 157. *Gentleman's Magazine*, January–June 1839: 554; January–June 1846: 213–14. *HBRS*, 3 (Fleming). George Simpson, *Fur trade and empire: George Simpson's journal . . . 1824–25*, ed. and intro. Frederick Merk (Cambridge, Mass., 1931). Sarah Tucker, *The rainbow in the north: a short account of the first establishment of Christianity in Rupert's Land by the Church Missionary Society* (London, 1851).

Boon, *Anglican Church*. V. K. Fast, "The Protestant missionary and fur trade society: initial contact in the Hudson's Bay territory, 1820–1850" (PHD thesis, Univ. of Man., Winnipeg, 1984). J. E. Foster, "The Anglican clergy in the Red River settlement, 1820–1826" (MA thesis, Univ. of Alta., Edmonton, 1966). W. B. Heeney, *John West and his Red River mission* (Toronto, 1920). I. H. S. Stratton, "The work and ideas of John West, 1778–1845" (MA thesis, Univ. of Durham, Durham, Eng., 1977). A. N. Thompson, "The expansion of the Church of England in Rupert's Land from 1820 to 1839 under the Hudson's Bay Company and the Church Missionary Society" (PHD thesis, Univ. of Cambridge, Cambridge, Eng., 1962). J. H. Archer, "The Anglican Church and the Indian in the northwest," Canadian Church Hist. Soc., *Journal* (Toronto), 28 (1986): 19–30. V. [K.] Fast, "A research note on the journals of John West," Canadian Church Hist. Soc., *Journal* (Sudbury, Ont.), 21 (1979): 30–38. Judith Fingard, "'Grapes in the wilderness': the Bible Society in British North America in the early nineteenth century," *SH*, 5 (1972): 26–28; "The New England Company and the New Brunswick Indians, 1786–1826: a comment on the colonial perversion of British benevolence," *Acadiensis* (Fredericton), 1 (1971–72), no.2: 37–39. J. E. Foster, "Program for the Red River mission: the Anglican clergy, 1820–1826," *SH*, no.4 (November 1969): 49–75. C. J. Jaenen, "Foundations of dual education at Red River, 1811–1834," Man., Hist. and Scientific Soc., *Trans.* (Winnipeg), 3rd ser., 21 (1965): 35–68. J. J. Talman, "John West's visit to Ontario," *Canadian Churchman* (Toronto), 8 Aug. 1940: 452. A. N. Thompson, "John West: a study of the conflict between civilization and the fur trade," Canadian Church Hist. Soc., *Journal* (Sudbury), 12 (1970): 44–57.

WHITE, JOHN HENRY, printer, journalist, and businessman; b. *c.* 1797 near Birmingham, England; d. 28 July 1843 at Goose River, Lot 42, P.E.I.

Little documentation exists regarding John Henry White's early life. He learned the trade of bookbinder in Warwick, England, was listed as a printer and bookbinder in Boston by 1825, and took up residence in Halifax perhaps as early as the following year. A statement that he lived also in Saint John, N.B., cannot be verified. His move to Charlottetown in August 1829 may have been prompted by an advertisement placed a year earlier in Nova Scotia newspapers. The notice stated that a committee in Charlottetown, which included the politically ambitious James Bardin Palmer*, was anxious to establish a newspaper that would be "loyal, liberal, and impartial"; in fact, its purpose would be to express opinions not aired in James Douglas Haszard*'s *Prince Edward Island Register*.

Whatever motivated his move, it was Palmer who provided White with one of his first known printing contracts on the Island, an election broadsheet dated 7 Sept. 1830. More printing work followed. Around June 1832 he began printing the *Christian Visitor*, a religious newspaper, for an unidentified Anglican publisher. On 6 August, after overcoming delays in securing subscribers, he launched his own newspaper, the *British American*. In 1833 his tender to print a revised edition of the Island's statutes was accepted over Haszard's, and in subsequent years he printed the House of Assembly's *Journal* (1834, 1837, 1839) as well as a number of religious and educational tracts, including a pocket edition of the Psalms of David.

White's most noteworthy publishing achievement, however, was a stereotype edition of the Authorized Version of the Bible that he had begun printing in Halifax and continued when he moved to Charlottetown. Produced from plates likely acquired while he was in Boston, and in quarto, in his words "decidedly the best size for family use," his Bible was sold in two leather-bound parts complete with lithograph illustrations and a section for family records. This Bible, which White described as "the first work of magnitude printed in this or any of His Britannic Majesty's Possessions in North America," appears in fact to merit the distinction of being the first Authorized Version published in what is now Canada. His undertaking had potential for peril beyond the usual economic considerations in that the British crown held a monopoly on the printing of this translation. However, there is no evidence that his action landed him in trouble, or even that anyone noticed the transgression. He thus avoided the fate of the American Presbyterian minister in York (Toronto) whose attempt in 1827 to import copies of the Authorized Version that had been printed in the United States, also a transgression, was unmasked by William Lyon Mackenzie* that summer in his *Colonial Advocate* and in a broadside.

Spared controversy in publishing the Bible, White encountered it at almost every other turn in his printing career. The conservative views expressed in the *Christian Visitor* aroused heated responses in both the Island's *Royal Gazette* and the *Colonial Patriot* of Pictou, N.S. The latter, although noting that White only printed the paper, warned him not to become enmeshed in its management. White used his own *British American* to serve the political ambitions of his sponsors, Palmer and his group, by frequently criticizing the Island's ruling faction. The newspaper's bias made White many enemies. The commissioners appointed to superintend the printing of the revised statutes refused to accept his work when he submitted part of it for approval early in 1834, gave the job to Haszard, and later launched an action against White for breach of contract. White engaged William Young*, a lawyer from Halifax, to defend him. During the trial in July 1835 before Edward James Jarvis*, the chief justice, Young argued in part that the enmities aroused by the *British American* were primarily responsible for the suit. The jury decided for White, and in 1839 a committee of the House of Assembly ruled that he be reimbursed for the cost of defending himself.

The difficulties relating to White's association with the *British American*, whose last extant issue is 29 June 1833, limited the number of government contracts he was able to obtain, and he was compelled to turn to other pursuits. In August 1835 he launched a sloop, which he named the *Triumph* in reference to his victory the previous month. Unable to sell it at a profit as he had intended, he operated it himself. After discharging cargo at Goose River on 25 July 1843 the *Triumph* was driven ashore. Three days later, White, in an attempt to salvage rigging from the vessel, was killed when the mast fell upon him.

White's career demonstrates that life in a small colony for a printer with few government contracts was precarious. Despite his accomplishments, White's 14 years on Prince Edward Island were fraught with difficulties that were relieved only by his premature demise. He left no relatives on the Island.

MARIANNE G. MORROW and NICOLAS J. DE JONG

John Henry White's edition of *The Holy Bible, containing the Old and New testaments: translated out of the original tongues* . . . (3v. in 2) has been located in five collections: the American Bible Soc. Library (New York), Dalhousie Univ. Library, Special Coll. (Halifax), the Newberry Library (Chicago), the PAPEI, and Acadia Univ. Library, Rare Book Coll. (Wolfville, N.S.). All carry a Halifax imprint save for two of the three volumes at Acadia, which were printed in Charlottetown. No copy bears a date of publication. White's printing-press and copies of his Bible, along with its plates, were among the numerous items sold at the estate auction held shortly after his death; the fate of the plates is unknown. No copies of the *Christian Visitor* (Charlottetown) are extant, nor has its editor ever been identified. The only known run of the *British American* (Charlottetown), 6 Aug. 1832–29 June 1833, is at the PAPEI.

PAC, RG 42, E1, 1349. PAPEI, Acc. 2702/859; RG 3, petitions, 1836. St Paul's Anglican Church (Charlottetown), Reg. of burials, 30 July 1843 (mfm. at PAPEI). P.E.I., House of Assembly, *Journal*, 1836: 54. *Report of the trial held at Charlotte-town, Prince Edward Island, July 8th, 1835* . . . (n.p., n.d.; copy at PANS). *Colonial Herald, and Prince Edward Island Advertiser* (Charlottetown), 29 July 1843. *Colonial Patriot*, 18 April 1828; 1, 15 Sept., 6 Oct. 1832. *Islander*, 4 Aug., 1 Sept. 1843. *Phenix* (Charlottetown), 21 April 1828. *Royal Gazette* (Charlottetown), 17–24 July 1832, 1 Aug. 1843. *The Boston directory* (Boston), 1825, 1826. *The English Bible in America; a bibliography of editions of the Bible & the New Testament published in America, 1777–1957*, ed. M. T. Hills (New York, 1961; repr. 1962), xviii–xix, 86. M. G. Morrow, "John Henry White, the unknown printer," *Island Magazine* (Charlottetown), no.22 (fall–winter 1987): 29–30.

WHITWORTH-AYLMER, MATTHEW, 5th Baron AYLMER, army officer and colonial administrator; b. 24 May 1775, the eldest of five children of Henry Aylmer, 4th Baron Aylmer, and Catherine Whitworth; m. 28 July or 4 Aug. 1801 Louisa Anne Call, daughter of Sir John Call; they had no children; d. 23 Feb. 1850 in London.

Matthew Aylmer was only 10 when he succeeded his father in the ancient Irish barony of Aylmer and 12 when he entered the 49th Foot as an ensign. He became a lieutenant in 1791 and a captain in 1794. In 1798 he participated in an abortive British raid on Ostend (Belgium), was captured, and spent six months in a French prison. He won high praise from his commanding officer, Lieutenant-Colonel Isaac Brock*, for his role in the battle of Egmont-op-Zee (more properly Egmond aan Zee, Netherlands) in 1799. Two years later he rose to the rank of major in the 85th Foot, and in 1802 to lieutenant-colonel; however, he was then placed on half pay until June 1803 when he joined the Coldstream Foot Guards. On 25 July 1810 he became a colonel and an aide-de-camp to the king and on 4 June 1813 a major-general. He served as the assistant – and then from January 1812 as the deputy – adjutant general to Lord Wellington's army and commanded a brigade in several major battles of the Peninsular War, during which he was awarded the Military Cross with one clasp. He was given a KCB on 2 Jan. 1815 and knighted on 6 June. In 1814 he had been appointed adjutant general of the British forces in Ireland, where he remained until 1823. From 1823 to 1830 he was without employment and spent much of his time wandering across Switzerland and Italy. He was promoted lieutenant-general on 27 May 1825 and that year, upon the death of his uncle, the Earl of Whitworth, he changed his family name to Whitworth-Aylmer. He was made colonel of the 56th Foot in 1827 and transferred to the 18th Foot five years later.

Aylmer's enforced idleness ended when Sir James Kempt* resigned the administration of Lower Canada. In June 1830 the secretary of state for the colonies, Sir George MURRAY, who had also served with Wellington in the Peninsular War, offered the position to Aylmer. On 11 August Aylmer was appointed commander of the forces in North America, and on 13 October he landed at Quebec; he assumed control of the administration one week later. His commission as governor-in-chief was dated 24 Nov. 1830, but it was not formally registered at Quebec until 12 Feb. 1831. Aylmer had few obvious qualifications for his position; he had never served as a civil administrator, he had no political experience, and he came to Lower Canada, by his own admission, "a perfect stranger to all that relates to the country." Yet Murray's choice was based on more than friendship. Aylmer was one of the more distinguished and capable officers of his rank, he was a francophile, and, as Louis-Joseph Papineau* noted, he spoke French "with the greatest ease and elegance." Although leaning to the conservative side in British politics, he was not a partisan, and the reformers in the Canadas, reassured by their contacts in Britain, received him as "an able and clever man conciliatory in his disposition, liberal in his principles, and cincerely [*sic*] anxious to do good."

Recognizing his lack of knowledge, Aylmer none the less predicted that he would soon "be out of the *Awkward Squad*." He embarked on a series of tours which eventually took him to every part of Lower Canada, and he pronounced himself pleased with "the country, the people and the Climate." He and Lady Aylmer took their viceregal responsibilities seriously, contributing generously to a variety of causes, such as an emigrant fund, the Female Orphan Asylum, and the Quebec Driving Club (one of a number of organizations of which Lady Aylmer became patroness). They sought to foster the arts and culture, and attended many community activities, from ploughing matches to annual races in Trois-Rivières where Aylmer donated a silver cup to be awarded for a horse bred within the province. A wealthy man, Aylmer entertained frequently and lavishly at the Château Saint-Louis, the governor's residence; yet he avoided the error "into which most of our Governors have fallen . . . ," noted the Montreal reform newspaper, the *Vindicator and Canadian Advertiser*, "of attempting to impress on the minds of the 'natives' a something transatlantically superior pertaining to themselves." During a visit to the Indian reserve at Lac des Deux Montagnes he joined in the dancing when "obliged" to do so.

Aylmer wished particularly to convince French Canadians of his benevolence. Shortly after his arrival he donated money for a tablet over the spot "where lay the remains of brave Montcalm [Louis-Joseph de Montcalm*]." He disagreed vehemently with those who advocated a policy of assimilation, arguing that there were not British subjects "more loyal and true – than the People of Lower Canada" and that assimilation would weaken their loyalty and drive them into the arms of the United States. He defended the seigneurial system and sought permission to grant seigneurial lands under crown control to French Canadians who could not afford to purchase on freehold tenure. He exhibited a genuine desire to distribute government patronage with the utmost impartiality, reintegrating militia officers whom a predecessor, Lord Dalhousie [RAMSAY], had dismissed for opposition to the administration, increasing the number of French Canadians on the bench, ensuring a balance between francophones and anglophones on the commission of the peace, and making 8 of his first 14 appointees to the Legislative Council French Canadians. In 1831, to prove that he was "free of all party connections," he offered seats on the Executive Council to Patriote leaders Papineau and John NEILSON. Although both refused, Aylmer successively appointed the francophone reform members of the House of Assembly Philippe Panet*, Dominique Mondelet*, and Hugues HENEY. Undeniably, he did not go far enough; the Legislative and Executive councils and the high echelons of the civil service continued to be dominated by anglophones unsympathetic to the demands of the assembly. None the less, he went as far as, and at times farther than, his superiors in London wanted and, at least initially, he convinced Papineau that "he likes and desires the good of the province."

The legislature met for the first time under Aylmer in January 1831 when, labouring under "a severe indisposition," he delivered his speech from the throne "literally from my bed." Throughout the session he worked diligently to remedy the grievances of the assembly, many of which, he admitted, were "well founded." He introduced economies in the civil service, presented nearly all the executive documents requested by the assembly, protested to the British government delays in examining reserved colonial legislation, refused to bend regulations for interested parties, demanded more rigorous standards in accounting for public funds, launched an investigation of abuses in the land-grant system, and induced the judges (with the exception of Chief Justice Jonathan SEWELL) not to attend the Legislative Council while the Colonial Office deliberated on a long-standing demand for their exclusion from that body. In proroguing the legislature in March, he enquired for "any stray complaint" which the assembly had neglected.

Aylmer's most controversial effort to appease came after the assembly petitioned for the dismissal of Attorney General James Stuart*, an outspoken opponent of the Patriote party, at the end of the session. Under pressure from the assembly, in September Aylmer suspended Stuart pending adjudication of its charges in Britain. Reprimanded by the Colonial Office for suspending Stuart before he was given the opportunity to defend himself in the assembly, Aylmer rightly pointed out that not to have acted would have provoked "the utmost degree of ferment and agitation." In November 1832 the Colonial Office dismissed Stuart, who unsuccessfully challenged Aylmer to a duel. He was hailed as a martyr by those among the British minority in the colony who believed that Aylmer "dare not displease Mr. Citoyen Papineau by whom . . . he is held completely under cow." Aylmer's decision had enhanced his reputation with the reformers, however, and particularly with Papineau, who had earlier entertained the Aylmers at his country estate in June 1831. But though "on good (I may say cordial) terms" with Papineau, Aylmer was aware that a great gulf existed between them on a number of questions.

For more than a decade the main preoccupation of the assembly had been to obtain control of the provincial revenues, including those reserved to the crown by the Quebec Revenue Act of 1774 [*see* Sir Francis Nathaniel Burton*]. Murray's Whig successor at the Colonial Office, Lord Goderich, instructed Aylmer to submit a pared-down list of estimates to the assembly and to request a permanent civil list preparatory to a surrender of the crown revenues. The assembly paid little attention to Goderich's estimates and none to his request for a civil list, although it did vote supplies for one year. Ignoring Aylmer's advice to the contrary and influenced by his parliamentary under-secretary, Lord Howick, Goderich introduced a bill into parliament in the summer of 1831 surrendering the crown revenues unconditionally, and in September he ordered Aylmer to reconvene the legislature and again request a comparatively modest civil list. The assembly, however, refused salaries to several officials on Goderich's list and, when Aylmer foolishly tried to coerce it by hinting that he would reserve any bill deviating from Goderich's intentions, it refused permanent salaries to any officials. It seems unlikely that Goderich's proposals, which were rejected by 42 to 9, would have been accepted by the assembly even had Aylmer been more astute, and the disappointed governor closed the session in late February 1832, acknowledging that his friendly relations with the leaders of the Patriote party had been sorely strained.

In 1832 deterioration of those relations accelerated after three French-speaking Canadians were shot by British troops on 21 May during a turbulent by-election in Montreal [*see* Daniel Tracey*]. Aylmer's sympathies lay with the soldiers, and although he wrote to Papineau regretting the deaths, he refused to intervene in the subsequent judicial process, even when Papineau requested a military inquiry. He encouraged Solicitor General Charles Richard Ogden* to bring the case before a grand jury but later publicly praised the jury's exoneration of the military. Thereafter Papineau pointedly declined to attend receptions at the Château.

The anger of the Patriote party was fuelled by a cholera epidemic which in 1832 killed more than 7,000 people in the colony. Aylmer had prepared for the outbreak by persuading the legislature to establish a quarantine station at Grosse Île and a board of health at Quebec and to authorize such facilities elsewhere when necessary. Although Aylmer conscientiously enforced the quarantine regulations and issued money to the boards of health and the Montreal Emigrant Society, the measures proved wholly inadequate. Moreover, by insisting that only the law officers of the crown should prosecute he hindered the work of the boards, and by encouraging flight to reduce the incidence of cholera in the cities he contributed to the spread of the disease. Yet, on balance, he did not deserve the censure of the assembly, which also criticized him for issuing funds without its approval and for failing to control the influx of immigrants. In fact, Aylmer did wish to limit immigration and proposed to raise money by a tax on immigrants. When the assembly met in November 1832, it was in an angry mood; it declared Mondelet's seat vacant on his appointment to the Executive Council, passed a supply bill making no provision for a civil list, which the Legislative Council felt compelled to reject, and adopted an address, similar to one it had itself rejected in the previous session, demanding an elective legislative council.

To Aylmer these actions demonstrated intransigence, and he requested authorization from London to use the unappropriated funds surrendered to the legislature by Goderich's Revenue Act of 1831. Edward George Geoffrey Smith Stanley, later Lord Stanley, who replaced Goderich at the Colonial Office in April 1833, sympathized but would not act until the assembly had been given an opportunity to reconsider. Consequently, when Aylmer reconvened the legislature in January 1834 he virtually invited a confrontation. He refused to grant the assembly contingency funds of £7,000 and reserved 11 of the 12 bills passed by the legislature, disallowing the 12th. In return the assembly refused to vote supplies and passed 92 resolutions of grievance, including one demanding the governor's recall. Asserting that the resolutions were tantamount to a "Declaration of Independence," Aylmer sent to Stanley a draft bill restoring to the government control over the revenues surrendered to the assembly by Goderich's Revenue Act. Stanley was prepared to rescind Goderich's act, and he referred the 92 resolutions to a select committee of the House of Commons, which he assumed would exonerate Aylmer. But Stanley was replaced in June 1834 by Thomas Spring-Rice, an easy-going Irish Whig, who was determined to avoid confrontation. Spring-Rice persuaded the Commons committee to attribute the conflict in Lower Canada simply to "mutual misconceptions." After meeting with delegates from the assembly, he authorized Aylmer in September to borrow £31,000 from the military chest for unpaid salaries, assuming (erroneously) that the assembly would agree to repay the loan. Aylmer was dismayed by Spring-Rice's actions and by the failure of the select committee to vindicate his conduct.

Ironically, Aylmer had led the Colonial Office to adopt a more conciliatory policy by insisting that the radicals in the assembly were losing support. During the sessions of 1833 and 1834 a rift had developed within the Patriote party, and Aylmer sought to exploit it, in particular by cultivating the hierarchy of the Roman Catholic Church, which opposed the policies of the radicals. Although a devout member of the Church of England, Aylmer was unusually tolerant in his religious views, wishing, for example, to alter the oath taken by justices of the peace so that he could appoint Jewish magistrates [*see* Aaron Ezekiel Hart*]. He attended mass in the Roman Catholic cathedral as well as in his own, refused to go to the services of a local Anglican priest who had protested Aylmer's giving pecuniary aid to the Catholic Church, offered the Ursulines of Quebec refuge in the Château when a fire broke out in their convent, recommended that the Roman Catholic bishop be appointed to the Executive Council, and discouraged the Colonial Office from interfering with the Sulpician estates. In addition to cultivating the church, Aylmer deliberately chose his nominees for government posts from among the more conservative and "respectable" members of the Patriote party.

Aylmer's appointments, however, had the effect of weakening the moderates in the assembly, since appointees lost their seats. In any case Aylmer was himself an inadequate instrument for multiplying *vendus*. Progressively disenchanted with what he considered to be the ignorance and ingratitude of French Canadians, he had begun by September 1832 to argue that "British influence in Lower Canada . . . must ere long be paramount" and that French Canadians must "finally reconcile themselves to a fate which cannot be averted." In October he warned Sir John Colborne*, lieutenant governor of Upper Canada, that "when the king's Subjects are spoken of as Foreigners and the Canadians as a *Nation* held in subjection by another Nation, it becomes the constituted Authorities to be upon their Guard." By the spring of 1834 he was convinced that so long as the assembly was composed largely of French Canadians "the Constitution of the Province . . . will never work beneficially." After the passage of the 92 Resolutions his primary concern was to reconcile the American-born population in the Eastern Townships and the rapidly growing Irish communities in Montreal and Quebec by appointing representatives from both groups to positions of importance. In June 1835 he strongly endorsed the application of "an association of gentlemen" from the townships for permission to purchase a large quantity of land on terms similar to those given to the British American Land Company [*see* Sir Alexander Tilloch Galt*], despite vehement opposition from the assembly.

Gradually, in fact, Aylmer had come under the influence of the old official group. In April 1834 he appointed David CHISHOLME, one of Dalhousie's protégés, coroner of Trois-Rivières. When John FLETCHER was unable to accept a promotion on the bench suggested as recompense for "the persecution of the House of Assembly to which he has been exposed for a series of years," Aylmer recommended Samuel Gale*, who had acted as Dalhousie's agent in England in 1828 and served as counsel to the officers in command during the Montreal "massacre." This recommendation encountered strong opposition at the Colonial Office but was accepted under pressure from Aylmer on condition that the next vacancy would be given to a French Canadian.

Gale's appointment alienated many moderates on both sides. Aylmer added to his unpopularity by refusing money to Montreal during a second outbreak of cholera in 1834 and by retreating to the governor's cottage at William Henry (Sorel) during the height of the outbreak. Late that year the radicals won a sweeping victory at the polls, virtually eliminating the moderates from the assembly. Aylmer was not displeased with this result, arguing that it had "roused a feeling (hitherto dormant) in the British Population," which might, however, "lead to very serious results, unless prudently managed." He enthusiastically approved the formation of militant constitutional associations at Quebec and Montreal, and warned that the British minority were no longer prepared to accept domination by the assembly. He blamed the Patriote victory on "the Complacency with which the Canada Committee [of 1834] listened to sham Grievances" and predicted that the new assembly would be less reasonable than its predecessor. When the assembly met in February 1835, he made his prediction reality by refusing to issue money for the assembly's contingencies. In return the house again refused supplies and complained that Aylmer was prejudiced against French Canadians. On 18 March Aylmer prorogued the legislature and called upon Britain to find a solution to the constitutional and financial impasse.

The solution adopted by the Colonial Office was to replace Aylmer. Spring-Rice had begun to search for a successor in the autumn of 1834 and had promised Aylmer another government if he would resign. But Aylmer wanted exoneration, and he suggested sending a parliamentary commission to examine the assembly's charges. In April 1835 a three-man commission was appointed, but its head, Lord Gosford [ACHESON], would also become Aylmer's replacement. Aylmer bitterly resented his dismissal and was further antagonized when Gosford, who assumed control of the government on 24 Aug. 1835, dissociated himself from his predecessor. Aylmer's mood was not improved by a terrifying return voyage, described by Lady Aylmer in *Narrative of the passage of the "Pique" across the Atlantic* (London, 1837). Once in England, he attempted without success to obtain approval of his conduct by refusing appointment as commander of the forces in Ireland unless he got it. However, he did coerce the government into awarding him a GCB, on 10 Sept. 1836, and on 23 Nov. 1841 he became a general, but he never obtained an English peerage, to which he felt entitled, or another administrative post. On 23 Feb. 1850 he died in his London home of an aneurysm of the heart.

On leaving the colony Aylmer had expressed regret that his "anxious endeavours to promote the general welfare of Lower Canada, should have fallen (as they have) so far short" of his initial expectations and burst into tears when the small crowd which had gathered at the wharf cheered. In truth, Aylmer is a tragic figure. He was well meaning and as competent as most of the military men sent to govern British North America following the Napoleonic Wars. But Lower Canada required a governor with political skill, and as Aylmer had noted in October 1831, "I cannot look for advice, or support here, beyond the circle of my own family composed of Soldiers like myself; & on . . . [the other] side of the Water I am totally destitute of Political Connexions." Largely unprepared, he had found himself "called upon all at once to contend against those whose lives have been devoted to the Study of Law & Politics." The *Vindicator and Canadian Advertiser* declared that Aylmer had "earned a niche in Canadian History, alongside of the Craigs [Sir James Henry Craig*] and Dalhousies, and gained for himself the execration of half-a-million people"; the Whigs blamed him for the failure of their conciliatory policy; and historians sympathetic to them, such as Helen Taft Manning, have echoed this assessment. Yet, although Aylmer was guilty of serious errors of judgement, much of the criticism of him is unfair. Many of his blunders, as historian Fernand Ouellet notes, "were more or less provoked," and he never became as violently francophobic as Craig or Dalhousie, never lost his temper in public, never closed the doors of the Château to his opponents. He contributed to ethnic polarization in Lower Canada, but he was not responsible for it, nor could he, any more than Gosford, a civilian with considerable political experience, have prevented its development. Moreover, Aylmer was handicapped by the rapid changes of government in Britain during the early 1830s, serving under five secretaries whose views on Lower Canada differed sharply. Without "Political Connexions" in Britain, he was sacrificed to facilitate accommodation with the Lower Canadian assembly; the sacrifice, ironically, was in vain for by then the train of events leading to the rebellions of 1837–38 was probably irreversible.

PHILLIP BUCKNER

PAC, MG 24, A43; F66, 1; RG 1, E1, 40–41; RG 68, General index, 1651–1841: 72. PRO, CO 42/230–57; CO 43/28–30; CO 387/1–11. L. A. [Call Whitworth-Aylmer, Baroness] Aylmer, *Narrative of the passage of the "Pique" across the Atlantic* (London, 1837); "Recollections of Canada, 1831," ANQ *Rapport*, 1934–35: 279–318. L.C., House of Assembly, *Journals*, 1830–35. *Montreal Herald*, 8 Sept. 1832; 18, 23 Aug., 2 Oct. 1834; 8 Jan., 9 Feb. 1835. *Quebec Gazette*, 13, 17, 24 Jan., 19, 24 Feb., 5 March, 9, 21 April, 20 June, 29 Aug. 1834; 2 Jan., 23 Feb., 26 June, 10 Aug., 9, 16 Sept. 1835; 30 March 1850. *Times* (London), 26 Feb. 1850. *Vindicator and Canadian Advertiser* (Montreal), 19 Oct., 26, 30 Nov., 21, 24 Dec. 1830; 1 Feb., 24, 28 June, 1 July, 27 Dec. 1831; 3, 7 Feb., 2 March 1832; 21 March, 12 May, 23 June 1835. *Burke's peerage* (1890), 73. G.B., WO, *Army list*, 1788–1850. Geoffrey Bilson, *A darkened house: cholera in nineteenth-century Canada* (Toronto, 1980). Ouellet, *Lower Canada*. Rumilly, *Papineau et son temps*, vol.1. Taft Manning, *Revolt of French Canada*.

WHYTE, JAMES MATTHEW, businessman; b. *c.* 1788 in Scotland, son of James Whyte of Newmains, Lanarkshire; d. 9 June 1843 in Hamilton, Upper Canada.

Although James Matthew Whyte's family background and early experiences are obscure, he apparently was born into comfortable circumstances and his family claimed some connection to the Scottish gentry through marriage. After receiving what appears to have been a sound education, Whyte entered military service, becoming a lieutenant in the 1st Dragoon Guards in 1806 and a captain in 1812. He resigned his commission three years later, but, according to his tombstone, subsequently served as a lieutenant-colonel of the Surrey Regiment of Horse.

In 1811 Whyte had acquired a plantation in Jamaica. Located near the town of Morant Bay and named Cave Bottom, it was not a large plantation and in 1817 utilized the labour of only 12 slaves. However, he had taken it over at a propitious time: following the Napoleonic Wars demand increased for Jamaican sugar and coffee. Whyte appears to have prospered and to have achieved some prominence in colonial society, since he served as a justice of assize and on the island's Council. By the early 1830s the plantation economy was suffering from low prices, an over-population of slaves, and a growing sense of insecurity, heightened by the abolition movement in Great Britain and the slave rebellion of 1831. The outlawing of slavery in 1834 by the British parliament, with compensation to owners, afforded Whyte an opportunity to liquidate his assets and leave the colony.

Searching for new investment opportunities, he considered immigrating to the Canadas and in early 1834 departed Jamaica for Hamilton. He quickly became interested in the land market, receiving a patent on land in Cayuga Township in April. In January 1835 he sold the property to Allan Napier MacNab* for £500. Whyte became active, as well, in the promotion of Hamilton's two major commercial undertakings, the London and Gore Rail Road and the Gore Bank. The latter was his major business interest. Although not involved in the early promotion of the bank, which had been initiated in 1833 and was chartered two years later, he was instrumental in getting it off the ground. On 1 Sept. 1835 he chaired a meeting of promoters which arranged for the opening of stock subscription books and on 26 November, with Colin Campbell Ferrie*, he was given authority to apportion stock and make arrangements for the election of directors. Whyte purchased 40 shares, valued at £500, and commanded the confidence of enough shareholders to be elected to the first board of directors in February. Ferrie had also been elected and claimed the largest number of shareholders' votes, but the directors elected Whyte president in preference to him.

As president from 1836 to 1839, Whyte attended daily to the bank's affairs and his administration encouraged confidence among its correspondents. Close relations were established with the Bank of Upper Canada, which withdrew from Hamilton in April 1836 and sold all of the discounted notes in its office there to the Gore Bank. Whyte himself enjoyed the support by proxy of several Bank of Upper Canada shareholders who had also invested in the Gore Bank, and he continued to exercise a power of attorney in their behalf after he resigned the presidency. Likewise, in September 1839, the London banking firm of Reid, Irving and Company felt that its effectiveness as the Gore Bank's English correspondent rested on the firm's confidence in Whyte's direction.

Despite the efficacy of Whyte's presidency, shortly after the bank's incorporation conflict emerged among its directors. Initially, the local élite, which included MacNab, John Willson*, Absalom Shade*, and Whyte, controlled the board. Soon other directors, who were members of Hamilton's commercial community, including Ferrie, Edmund Ritchie, and John Young*, objected to MacNab's influence. He had sold land to the bank for its premises at prices many thought were inflated. As well, criticism of his conduct as the bank's solicitor in 1838 resulted in the transfer of this responsibility to his partner, John Ogilvie Hatt. But most objectionable to the commercial faction, suffering as it was from financial difficulties following the collapse of 1837, was the preference given by the bank to MacNab on accommodation. The bank, it was charged in 1839, had accepted inadequate security for his liabilities, reputed to exceed those of all of Hamilton's merchants combined. In response, the merchants, to maximize their voting power in the election of directors, attempted to have stock transferred among themselves and from out-of-province stockholders (who could not vote by proxy) to local supporters. The MacNab faction countered by challenging these share transfers in the Court of Chancery. Nevertheless, at the annual meeting of August 1839, the mercantile interests succeeded in electing a majority of sympathetic directors. Whyte, who had tried with some success to distance himself from MacNab, was re-elected president. But, faced with directors who opposed the policy exercised during his earlier tenure of office, he soon found himself in an untenable position and resigned from the board.

The mercantile group, with Ferrie now the bank's president, proved itself as guilty as the MacNab faction in monopolizing the bank's discounts of bills of exchange and promissory notes. In 1842 rumours were rampant in the press that the over-indebtedness of certain directors – Ferrie, Ritchie, and Richard Juson – threatened the bank. That year attempts were made on two fronts, as MacNab put it, to "capsize the needy crew" running it. Whyte and David Thompson were appointed to serve on a committee of shareholders to consider proposed revisions to the bank's charter. Contention then moved into the provincial legislature, where Thompson, the member for Haldimand, chaired a committee, on which MacNab also served, with the same purpose. In September 1842 the committee proposed an amendment to the charter, authored by MacNab, which would have prevented the bank from discounting any "paper bearing the signature or indorsement of the President, or of any Firm or Co-partnership of which he may be a member." Nothing, however, came of this challenge.

At his death in 1843 Whyte had attained a comfortable and highly respected position in Hamilton. He was well connected in London, England, and on occasion was able to provide MacNab, for example, with introductions to his acquaintances. Whyte's home, Barton Lodge, built in 1836 on the brow of the escarpment overlooking Hamilton, was one of the town's finest villas, and his library of more than 1,000 volumes must have been among the largest in the area. His estate was substantial. In a letter to his sister-in-law in 1827, Whyte, apart from calling himself an "inveterate snuff user," referred to his status as an "expatriated old Batchelor"; however, in his will he bequeathed property to his "reputed son," John Whyte of Jamaica. A Presbyterian, Whyte thought enough of the Reverend Alexander Gale* to leave him his silver plate. Besides his home, which was inherited by his brother, John Lionel, he owned real estate in Harwich Township and Picton, both in Upper Canada, and in Jamaica. He had £1,750 in Bank of Upper Canada stock and another £227 in unclaimed dividends. He maintained a cash credit in excess of £200 at the Gore Bank, but possessed only £100 in stock. He also held stock worth £320 in the British America Fire and Life Assurance Company and had lent more than £1,000 to various individuals.

Like other members of the gentry faced with few opportunities in Great Britain, Whyte had turned to the colonies. With capital brought from Jamaica, he was able to make substantial investments in the new financial institutions of Upper Canada and, thereby, to attain a prominence in finance and a standing in society which would not have been possible in the old country.

David G. Burley

AO, RG 1, C-IV, Cayuga Township, concession 1 (North Talbot Road), lots 3–6; RG 22, ser.155. Haldimand Land Registry Office (Cayuga, Ont.), Abstract index to deeds, North Cayuga Township, concession 1 (North Talbot Road), lots 3–6 (mfm. at AO). HPL, Clipping file, Hamilton biog. PAC, MG 24, D18. *Burke's landed gentry* (1914), 453. *DHB*. G.B., WO, *Army list*, 1808, 1813, 1815. D. R. Beer, *Sir Allan Napier MacNab* (Hamilton, Ont., 1984). Victor Ross and A. St L. Trigge, *A history of the Canadian Bank of Commerce, with an account of the other banks which now form part of its organization* (3v., Toronto, 1920–34), 1: 173, 177–80, 205–8, 214.

WILKINS, LEWIS MORRIS, lawyer, militia officer, office holder, politician, and judge; b. *c.* 1768 in Morrisania (New York City), N.Y., son of the Reverend Isaac Wilkins and Isabella Morris, sister of Lewis Morris, one of the signers of the American Declaration of Independence; m. 13 Aug. 1799 Sarah Creighton, daughter of John Creighton*, in Lunenburg, N.S., and they had seven children, including Lewis Morris* and Martin Isaac*; d. 3 Jan. 1848 at the family home in Windsor, N.S.

The father of Lewis Morris Wilkins was a New York loyalist who brought his family to Shelburne, N.S., in 1784. Details about the education of Lewis Morris are lacking. He may have studied law with his uncle Martin S., a Shelburne attorney, and he was admitted to the Nova Scotian bar about 1798. Commissioned lieutenant in the Lunenburg County militia on 6 July 1793, two years later he received a small grant in Lunenburg Township.

From 1798 to 1804 Wilkins served as sheriff of Halifax County. He then resigned and practised as a lawyer, appearing between 1804 and 1814 in a steadily increasing number of cases in the Halifax courts. He also had a large practice in Lunenburg County and in the district of Pictou, where his chief opponent was Samuel George William Archibald, and was an advocate in the Vice-Admiralty Court at Halifax. A student in his law office was John George Marshall*, who remembered Wilkins as "my kind and always firm and valuable friend."

Wilkins's political career began in 1799 with his election to the House of Assembly from Lunenburg Township, a district he represented for his entire career in the legislature. At the beginning of the 1806 session William Cottnam Tonge* was chosen speaker, but Lieutenant Governor Sir John Wentworth* was on bad terms with Tonge and rejected him. After debating Wentworth's action, unprecedented in Nova Scotia, for two days, the members elected Wilkins on 20 November. Wentworth approved of the less controversial Wilkins and after the session reported to Lord Castlereagh, the colonial secretary, that Wilkins had "performed the dutys of his situation during the Sessions with impartiality, diligence and decorum." Notwithstanding this praise, Wilkins collided with the lieutenant governor that session over an election in Annapolis Township which had been declared void by the assembly. Wentworth and the Council refused to issue new writs, claiming that the assembly had not the exclusive right to determine contested elections, and only after the English law officers had upheld the assembly's claim did Wentworth issue the writs to Wilkins.

The assembly was relatively peaceful for the next few years, but there were instances of discord. In 1809 Wilkins was prominent in opposing the decision of Administrator Alexander Croke to veto the appropriations bill, and in 1812 he led the assembly in condemning the Council's decision to modify a money bill. Besides acting as leader of the assembly, Wilkins corresponded with speakers in other colonies and with the agent of the assembly in London. He was also one of the commissioners for the expenditure in furnishing Government House and sat on the committee to plan the interior of Province House.

On 30 March 1816 Wilkins was elevated to the bench as third assistant judge in the Supreme Court, and he resigned from the assembly the following February. Soon after his appointment he moved to Windsor, where he became known for the lavish hospitality with which he welcomed visitors such as his intimate friend William Edward Parry*, the Arctic navigator, and Lieutenant Governor Lord Dalhousie [RAMSAY]. Whether because of the demands of Wilkins's social position or those of his large family, by the late 1820s his fellow judge James Stewart commented that Wilkins was "very poor." Stewart added that Wilkins was continually trying to have the judges' salaries increased, and that he disagreed with nearly everyone because his financial difficulties made him want to show his independence. He was certainly less than polite in the court-room. At the September sessions of 1829 in Pictou he was so rude to a plaintiff that he was rebuked by the latter's lawyer, James William Johnston*.

Wilkins's duties undoubtedly weighed on him. In 1816 the system of circuit courts hitherto in operation in certain counties was extended to the entire province. The journeys required of the two judges necessary to hold a court were long and arduous, and as Wilkins grew older he became less able to undertake them. No doubt for this reason, he tried for several years to have the law changed to allow one judge to hold court. When he succeeded in 1834 he rejoiced, since the younger judges would be able to perform the majority of the duties. In 1838 Wilkins was granted leave of absence to go to England for the recovery of his health. His "bodily infirmities" apparently prevented him from travelling on circuit again, although in 1839 and 1845 he attended court at Horton and Kentville respectively. On his death the barristers of the province eulogized him as "one of the most popular, eloquent and effective Advocates . . . distinguished . . . as the 'Poor man's Friend.'" His will left all his property to his wife and eldest son.

PHYLLIS R. BLAKELEY

PANS, MG 1, 979–80; RG 1, 303–5; RG 5, A, 6–22; R, 1; RG 39, HX, C, 78–88; J, 14–22, 102; KI, J, 5. N.S., House of Assembly, *Journal and proc.*, 1800–17, 1834–36. *Reports of cases, argued and determined in the Court of Vice-Admiralty, at Halifax, in Nova-Scotia, from . . . 1803, to the end of the year 1813 . . .*, comp. James Stewart (London, 1814). *Reports of cases argued and determined in the Supreme Court of Nova Scotia . . .*, comp. James Thomson (Halifax), 2, pt.I (1856). *Acadian Recorder*, 8 Jan. 1848. *Novascotian*, 10 Jan. 1848. *Royal Gazette and the Nova-Scotia Advertiser*, 20 Aug. 1799. *A calendar of official correspondence and legislative papers, Nova Scotia, 1802–15*, comp. Margaret Ells (Halifax, 1936). Beck, *Government of N.S.* Cuthbertson, *Old attorney general.* J. G. Marshall, *A brief history of public proceedings and events, legal, – parliamentary, – and miscellaneous, in the province of Nova Scotia, during the earliest years of the present century* (Halifax, [1878?]). Murdoch, *Hist. of N.S.*, vol.3. C. J. Townshend, *History of the Court of Chancery in Nova Scotia* (Toronto, 1900). Margaret Ells, "Governor Wentworth's patronage," N.S. Hist. Soc., *Coll.*, 25 (1942): 49–73.

WILLIAMS, THOMAS (also known as **Tehoragwanegen, Teholagwanegen, Tehora Kwanekeu,** and **Thomas Théoragwanegon**), Iroquois chief; b. *c.* 1758 in Caughnawaga (Kahnawake, Que.); d. there 16 Sept. 1848.

The grandson of Eunice Williams* and the great-grandson of the Reverend John Williams* of Deerfield, Mass., Thomas Williams was the son of Sarah Williams and a Caughnawaga man whose identity is unknown. Raised in the Catholic Indian community at Caughnawaga, perhaps by his maternal aunt, he spent hunting seasons in the area of Lac Saint-Sacrement (Lake George, N.Y.) and apparently enjoyed an unexceptional Indian boyhood. In the early 1770s he was recruited by Levi Frisbie, agent for Eleazar Wheelock, to attend Moor's Indian Charity School in Hanover, N.H. Williams accepted the invitation, but ill health, possibly smallpox, prevented his attendance.

Williams became a chief at Caughnawaga in 1777, and led some of the Indian allies of Major-General John Burgoyne* that year during the battles at Fort Ticonderoga (near Ticonderoga, N.Y.), Bennington, Vt, and Saratoga (Schuylerville, N.Y.). He was credited by his son and biographer Eleazer Williams* with having done so primarily to prevent "the effusion of [American] blood," but the claim is an unlikely one and it is impossible to detail his activities. According to the same source, the following year Williams joined an abortive raid into the Mohawk valley. In March 1780 he carried out a daring mission with Lieutenant Joseph Launière of the Indian Department. The members of the expedition made a brief attack on the American base at Machias (Maine) but gave up because of their small numbers and, after delivering dispatches to the British at Fort George (Castine), returned to Quebec. In May Williams reportedly accompanied Sir John Johnson*'s expedition against the Mohawk valley and was present at the attack on Colonel Frederick Visscher and his family. During this period he also participated in the raids led by Lieutenant Richard Houghton against American frontier settlements, including the attack of 16 Oct. 1780 on Royalton, Vt, which concluded his service to the British cause.

After the war Williams resumed seasonal activities in upstate New York and became acquainted with officials there. For several years, possibly as early as 1789 but certainly by 1793, he acted with Atiatoharongwen*, Ohnaweio (Good Stream), William Gray, and others as a deputy of the Seven Nations of Canada in their negotiations with the state of New York over land claims in the area of the Saint-Régis mission. The Seven Nations of Canada, as they called themselves, were Catholic mission Indians consisting of Iroquois from Caughnawaga and Saint-Régis (Akwesasne), Iroquois, Algonkins, and Nipissings from Lac-des-

Deux-Montagnes (Oka), Hurons from Jeune-Lorette (Wendake), and Abenakis from Saint-François-de-Sales (Odanak). They were both distinct and geographically separate from the Six Nations. Williams was a signatory to the treaty of 1796 which established the St Regis Reservation in New York State. The following year, according to his son, he was entrusted by the British authorities in Quebec with a secret reconnaissance mission to Lake Champlain. His success in this enterprise contributed to the defeat of the conspiracy said to have been promoted by David McLane*.

Following his grandmother Eunice's example, Williams periodically visited his New England relatives, and in 1800 he took two of his sons to Longmeadow, Mass., to be educated. In the spring of 1803 he was hired by McTavish, Frobisher and Company to serve in a fur-trade brigade leaving for Fort Moose (Moose Factory, Ont.). Williams thus joined the ranks of the Iroquois from Caughnawaga who accompanied traders west, reaching beyond the Red River to the Prairies and to the Rocky Mountains.

When the War of 1812 broke out, Williams was among the Indians who left Caughnawaga in 1813 to side with the Americans, accepting a standing invitation issued by President Thomas Jefferson. The American general Henry Dearborn attested to his influence in persuading many of the Indians of Lower Canada not to take up arms against the Americans, and recommended that Williams be compensated for his assistance. His military services during the war, which according to his son included action at the battle of Plattsburgh, were later formally acknowledged by the House of Representatives' committee on military affairs. He and his heirs petitioned for years and received occasional support from congressional committees, but there is no evidence that the American government ever awarded a pension in recognition of his services or compensation for his loss of property in Lower Canada, which was estimated at between $7,000 and $14,000. Williams's espousal of the American cause had made his return to Caughnawaga impracticable and by 1816 he had moved to the St Regis Reservation. There, he continued to represent his tribe in their dealings with the state of New York, acting as a deputy for negotiations in 1816, 1818, and 1824, and finally for the treaty of 1825, which further defined the reservation.

Williams had married Konwatewenteta (Konantewanteta), also known as Mary Ann Rice, on 7 Jan. 1779. The couple had 12 or 13 children between 1780 and 1807. Most of the information regarding Williams's career comes from his son Eleazer, who became a missionary among the Oneida and at Saint-Régis and who later capitalized on the absence of documentation recording his birth to pose as the "Lost Dauphin" of France. Information from Eleazer must be used warily and considered unreliable unless confirmed by other data.

It is not known when Williams returned to Caughnawaga, but certainly he had done so well before his death "in the 90th year of his age." His widow lived there until her own death on 1 May 1856, and his descendants continue to do so.

GEOFFREY E. BUERGER

ANQ-M, CN1-74, 25 avril 1803. BL, Add. MSS 21771, 21773, 21777, 21792–93, 21809–10 (mfm. at PAC). Mo. Hist. Soc. (St Louis), Eleazer Williams coll. Wis., State Hist. Soc., Eleazar Williams papers. *New England Hist. and Geneal. Reg.* (Boston), 3 (1849): 103. N.Y., Commissioners of Indian Affairs, *Proceedings of the Commissioners of Indian Affairs* . . . , intro. F. B. Hough (2v. in 1, Albany, N.Y., 1861). U.S., House of Representatives report, 31st Congress, 2nd session, no.89, 3 March 1851; 34th Congress, 3rd session, no.83, 16 Jan. 1857; 35th Congress, 1st session, no.303, 17 April 1858, and no.459, 29 May 1858; Senate report, 31st Congress, 2nd session, no.311, 20 Feb. 1851; 35th Congress, 1st session, no.86, 24 Feb. 1858. *Boston Daily Journal*, 17 Oct. 1848. *Handbook of American Indians north of Mexico*, ed. F. W. Hodge (2v., Washington, 1907–10), 2: 723–24. E. J. Devine, *Historic Caughnawaga* (Montreal, 1922). J. H. Hanson, *The lost prince: facts tending to prove the identity of Louis the Seventeenth, of France, and the Rev. Eleazar Williams, missionary among the Indians of North America* (New York, 1854). F. B. Hough, *A history of St. Lawrence and Franklin counties, New York, from the earliest times to the present time* (Albany, 1853). W. W. Wight, *Eleazer Williams – his forerunners, himself* (Milwaukee, Wis., 1896). Eleazer Williams, *Life of Te-ho-ra-gwa-ne-gen, alias Thomas Williams, a chief of the Caughnawaga tribe of Indians in Canada* (Albany, 1859).

WILLIAMS, WILLIAM, governor of the HBC; d. 14 Jan. 1837 in Brixton (London), England.

Before William Williams joined the Hudson's Bay Company he served in the East India Company, possibly as a ship's captain. In an affidavit in the East India's records a person with the same name declared that he had been born in Shirley (London) on 3 April 1771, and a William Williams is listed for voyages to India between 1788 and 1799. Whatever the details, there appears to be no doubt that our subject was a seafaring man; in the 1820s Captain John FRANKLIN called him an "expert sailor." Williams was engaged by the HBC as governor-in-chief of Rupert's Land on 20 May 1818 at a salary of £1,000 a year. He was described by the company as a man who had an "Enterprising and active mind & whose talents & habits of life are calculated to command obedience & to insure strict Discipline in all under his authority."

Williams arrived at York Factory (Man.) aboard the *Prince of Wales* in August 1818, and made his headquarters at Cumberland House (Sask.). He spent the winter writing letters of introduction to his officers and encouraging them in the various aspects of the trade. The Athabasca campaign, which pitted Colin ROBERTSON, John Clarke*, and other HBC men against the North West Company, was tactically important. The HBC had been driven from the area in 1815–16, but was now determined to succeed there. Nevertheless, the winter of 1818–19 was a trying one for the HBC men owing to the harassments of the NWC, which included the arrest of Robertson at Fort Wedderburn (Alta) by Samuel BLACK and Simon MCGILLIVRAY. Williams learned of this "illegal aggression" on 30 December, and decided to act. He arrived in the Red River settlement (Man.) in the spring of 1819 and collected a force of 30 men. In June, under his direction, a number of Nor'Westers were captured at Grand Rapids as they made their way to Fort William (Thunder Bay, Ont.). Williams executed bench warrants, which had been secured from Montreal, on bills of indictment found by a grand jury in Lower Canada against several Nor'Westers for murder, robbery, and burglary. He also issued his own warrants, as a magistrate of Rupert's Land, for the arrest of John George MCTAVISH, Angus Shaw*, and others for offences in Athabasca. In response the NWC had a bill of indictment preferred against Williams at Quebec for assault and false arrest. The warrant was not served but Williams escaped capture in the spring of 1820 only because he passed Grand Rapids the day before the Nor'Westers arrived.

Williams had exceeded his authority in issuing bench warrants for offences committed outside the HBC's chartered territory. In his defence it might be said that the unlawful arrest of Robertson was simply the latest unnecessary act in a long list of provocations. As well, there is sufficient evidence to support the company's statement in 1820 to Colonial Secretary Lord Bathurst that they had "in vain, laid before his Majesty's Government year after year undeniable proof of the most unlawful outrages committed by the North West Company" which had never been redressed.

Following the amalgamation of the two companies in 1821 Williams was appointed governor of the HBC's Southern Department [*see* Thomas Thomas*] at an annual salary of £1,200. This department comprised the territory to the east of Rainy Lake (Ont.), including Fort William, Moose Factory, and Eastmain Factory (Eastmain, Que.). The larger and more valuable Northern Department was given to George Simpson*, but Williams was to be the senior governor when both attended councils. These delicate appointments were arranged by Nicholas Garry*, who had been named in London to implement the merger of the companies and who thought it expedient that Williams be transferred from the Northern Department because he was a disruptive force. Williams was relieved to be offered the Southern Department, but why is open to conjecture. He may have considered that, though over-trapped, it would be easier to manage or, as he had a wife and daughter coming out from England (they arrived in 1822), he may have wanted to distance himself from his country wife Sally (daughter of Peter Fidler*) and their two children.

Williams spent the winter of 1821–22 at Cumberland House and arrived at Moose Factory on 10 July to take command of the Southern Department. The officers who formed its council, among them Thomas Vincent* and Angus Bethune*, were all veterans of the fur trade, and were reluctant to acknowledge, as the company's deputy governor and committee in London had lamely instructed, that "an efficient and oeconomical manner" of management had to be implemented. They attempted to overrule Williams's specific orders by writing directly to the governor and committee in London, whose ire they incurred by making recommendations in areas not within their jurisdiction. Williams had neither the knowledge of the fur trade nor the business ability to control these well-entrenched officers.

Given the nature of the two governors, friction between them was inevitable and disagreements soon arose over a number of issues, including the boundaries of their departments and methods of transport. Williams, who knew ships, contradicted Simpson on a number of matters involving coastal vessels at York and Moose factories. In his personal communications to the Southern Department Simpson was sarcastic, demeaning, and unhelpful. But Simpson, suave and diplomatic, had the complete confidence of Andrew Colvile, one of the most powerful members of the company's London committee, and easily outmatched the outspoken Williams.

At the request of the governor and committee Simpson travelled to London in the fall of 1825 for a "personal Conference . . . on many subjects connected with the interests and welfare of the Trade." They discussed in detail the business of the Southern Department, which had not been "conducted to our satisfaction." Simpson left London in February 1826 carrying the dispatch which recalled Williams to London since the company intended "to make considerable changes in the system of conducting the trade." Williams left Moose Factory on 9 Sept. 1826 with his family, which included a son born at Moose.

On his return to London Williams was released from the company and given a retirement allowance of £300 a year for six years. By August 1835 he was destitute owing to the financial failure of Rowland Stephenson, the firm in which he had invested his retirement allowance. He died at Brixton on 14 Jan. 1837.

Williams's appointment in 1818 appears to have been an act of desperation on the part of the HBC's governor and committee since his aggressive and outspoken manner, coupled with his lack of business experience, made him an unusual choice for governor-in-chief of Rupert's Land. The company, however, evidently realized that the passive measures practised by its officers could no longer prevail over the NWC. It then turned to a man of great personal courage who was determined to defend the rights of the company during a period when the officers in Rupert's Land were faring badly against the Nor'Westers. Like numerous fighting men before and after him, Williams was not suited for the rigorous, economic management which characterized the peaceful exercise of monopoly by the HBC after the termination of hostilities in 1821.

SHIRLEE ANNE SMITH

BL, India Office Library and Records [East India House Arch.], IOR, L/MAR/C/656: 207; L/MAR/C/657: 54, 209; L/MAR/C/669, no.293. PAC, MG 19, E1, ser.1: 8037–38 (mfm. at PAM). PAM, HBCA, A.1/51: f.114; A.1/52: f.107; A.1/53: f.39d; A.1/55: f.85; A.5/7: 51; A.5/8: 314; A.6/19: ff.64d, 90, 113; A.6/20: f.26; A.6/21: ff.38, 71d, 83; A.8/1: ff.83, 83d–84; pp.164, 170; A.10/3: f.369; A.10/4: f.25; B.22/a/21: f.47d; B.39/a/14: f.23; B.49/a/34: f.15; B.49/a/37: f.38; B.51/a/2: ff.4d, 5; B.135/k/1: 40–41; C.1/229: ff.5d, 42; C.1/787; C.1/788: ff.2d, 49; D.1/1; D.1/4: ff.26–30, 31–31d; D.1/7: ff.6d, 17, 17d, 18; D.1/c/1: ff.63–68. John Franklin, *Narrative of a journey to the shores of the polar sea in the years 1819, 20, 21 and 22 . . .* (2nd ed., 2v., London, 1824), 1: 100. Nicholas Garry, "Diary of Nicholas Garry, deputy-governor of the Hudson's Bay Company from 1822–1835: a detailed narrative of his travels in the northwest territories of British North America in 1821 . . . ," ed. F. N. A. Garry, RSC *Trans.*, 2nd ser., 6 (1900), sect.II: 155, 166. *HBRS*, 1 (Rich); 2 (Rich and Fleming); 3 (Fleming). Morton, *Hist. of Canadian west* (1939). Rich, *Hist. of HBC* (1960). Van Kirk, *"Many tender ties"*.

WILLOUGHBY, MARK, Church of England clergyman and educator; baptized 24 June 1796 in Chew Magna, England, son of William Hall Willoughby and Mary —; m. 10 Jan. 1844 Janet Scougall, widow of Robert Liston, in Montreal; they had no children; d. 15 July 1847 in Montreal.

Mark Willoughby was attracted to the Newfoundland Society for Educating the Poor, more commonly known as the Newfoundland School Society, from its beginnings in 1823. It was organized in England by a group of evangelical churchmen, led by Samuel Codner*, who were convinced that education linked with Christian truth based on Scripture was essential for settlers in the colonies. Assistant secretary of the society in 1823, Willoughby visited Newfoundland three years later and returned in 1829 as superintendent for the island. He held a Bible class in St John's in which one of his students was William Bennett Bond*, later primate of the Church of England in Canada. In 1832–33 he visited Lower Canada as the society's agent.

Willoughby was ordained a deacon in 1839 by Bishop Aubrey George Spencer* of Newfoundland, and shortly afterwards he moved to Lower Canada. He immediately accompanied Bishop George Jehoshaphat Mountain* on a tour of Mountain's large diocese of Quebec, in which the bishop promoted the extension of the school society's work. On 10 Feb. 1840 Mountain ordained Willoughby to the priesthood.

The new priest was soon assigned to Trinity Chapel in Montreal, then under construction to relieve the only Anglican parish of the city, Christ Church. The benefactor of the chapel, William Plenderleath CHRISTIE, had chosen Willoughby, and Mountain had accepted the nomination. The building, described by a contemporary as "a very elegant chapel" in the Gothic style, with a "chastely" interior, was consecrated, and Willoughby inducted as incumbent, on 20 May 1840. With the aid of two assistants, and thanks to a gift for administration and a manifest devotion to his vocation, Willoughby quickly won the trust and affection of his people; indeed, according to one member of his congregation, he was the best-loved clergyman in Montreal. The church soon boasted a number of prominent pew-holders, including Dr Andrew Fernando Holmes*, Samuel Gale*, Charles Dewey Day*, and Christopher Dunkin*, and it was attended by governors Sydenham [THOMSON], METCALFE (when he visited the city), and Cathcart*.

As a parish priest Willoughby continued to pursue his interest in education, and under his care the Trinity Chapel Sunday school became second to none in the diocese. In 1842 he was named to the board of examiners established under a recent provincial education act. As well, he maintained for some time his superintendency of the schools under the sponsorship of the Newfoundland School Society, and he claimed in 1845 to have established 70 such schools in the Diocese of Quebec.

In 1847, as ships docking at Montreal disembarked thousands of immigrants sick and dying of the dread typhus fever, Willoughby visited the sheds housing them to feed and to minister to the suffering. In July he contracted the disease and died, the first of five Anglican priests in the diocese who lost their lives in that service. During his illness the Sulpicians of the city sent frequently to enquire after him. Originally buried in the cemetery on Rue Dorchester, he was reinterred in Mount Royal Cemetery in 1871.

MARY NAYLOR

ANQ-M, CE1-84. PAC, RG 68, General index, 1841–67. *Berean* (Quebec), 7 Oct. 1847. Philip Carrington, *The Anglican Church in Canada; a history* (Toronto, 1963). *Jubilee history of Trinity Church, Montreal, 1840–1890*, comp. Henry Mott ([Montreal, 1890]). Brian Underwood, *Faith at the frontiers: Anglican evangelicals and their countrymen overseas (150 years of the Commonwealth and*

Continental Church Society) (London, 1974). T. R. Millman, "The church's ministry to sufferers from typhus fever in 1847," *Canadian Journal of Theology* (Toronto), 8 (1962): 126–36.

WILMOT, JOHN McNEIL, businessman, politician, JP, and judge; b. *c.* 1775 in Poughkeepsie, N.Y.; m. 27 Oct. 1808 Susanna (Susan) Harriet Wiggins in Saint John, N.B.; d. 7 Sept. 1847 in Lincoln, N.B.

The son of Lemuel Wilmot, a captain in the Loyal American Regiment, and Elizabeth Street, a sister of merchant Samuel Street*, John McNeil Wilmot was brought in 1783 to what became New Brunswick as part of the general loyalist migration. The elder Wilmot received land near Fredericton and here, on this loyalist frontier, his children were raised. Their experience produced in John and his brother William a curious amalgam of expectations as members of the élite and frontier rejection of the values which made that élite possible. Sons of a highly respected loyalist officer, they moved easily among the status-conscious first-generation loyalist patricians, married their daughters, and enjoyed the business advantages which membership in that group conferred. John married the eldest daughter of Samuel Wiggins, a prominent merchant; William married a daughter of Daniel Bliss, a member of the New Brunswick Council. Both men had grown up in rural central New Brunswick at precisely the time when Henry Alline*'s New Light tradition was being transformed into that most potent of Maritime frontier institutions, the Baptist movement. Among its early converts and strongest supporters were the Wilmot brothers. There was a price to be paid for this flouting of loyalist convention. While the Wilmots were always recognized as respectable, they were never acceptable to the tory inner circle which dominated the administrative structure of the province.

Like so many other ambitious young loyalists, John Wilmot abandoned the rural life as a young man and set out to seek his fortune in commerce. Operating first in Fredericton, possibly as agent for a Saint John house, he displayed considerable aptitude in his chosen calling. His success was capped in 1808 by his alliance through marriage with one of Saint John's leading merchant families. Within a few years he had established himself in the port city, where the firm of John M. Wilmot dealt in wholesale and retail dry goods. Wilmot's prominence in the business life of Saint John was demonstrated in 1813 when he obtained a perpetual lease to a South Market water lot. This lease permitted him to erect his own wharf in Saint John Harbour and to play an influential role in the conduct of the province's commerce.

In 1818 Wilmot obtained an auctioneer's licence and acted as agent for merchants outside New Brunswick in the disposal of their goods. The following year, in partnership with James Kirk, he formed John M. Wilmot and Company, a firm that became increasingly involved in the rapidly expanding timber trade. For the next 18 years Wilmot had an important part in that trade and was generally recognized as one of the principal merchants of the province. After 1830 he was joined in business by two sons; Robert Duncan* for several years acted as his father's agent in Liverpool, England. The timber trade was a profitable but exceedingly treacherous enterprise. Virtually all New Brunswick timber exports went to the United Kingdom and merchants' decisions on price and quantity had to be made a year in advance. The British market was, moreover, subject to periodic declines which could bankrupt any over-committed merchant. Wilmot was caught in just such a situation in 1837. The business survived the ordeal but by 1840 Wilmot appears to have withdrawn in favour of his son Robert Duncan.

Wilmot's business interests far transcended the activities of his own firm. He was an early leader of the Saint John business community, active in the promotion of the Chamber of Commerce and in other matters of common concern to the province's merchants. In 1812 he and several associates offered to build and operate a steamship that would provide a regular service between Saint John and Fredericton, in return for a government grant of a 20-year monopoly; their bid was unsuccessful [*see* John WARD]. Six years later, in an effort to break up the widespread illegal plaster of Paris trade between British and American territory, Wilmot and Lauchlan Donaldson chartered an armed schooner which they used to patrol the western Bay of Fundy.

In the early 1830s Wilmot became a leader in the fight for a second bank in Saint John, which would accommodate the growing timber trade. The Bank of New Brunswick, founded in 1820, was controlled by the loyalist administrative élite and a handful of leading merchants associated with them. By 1833 Wilmot was chairman of the committee which coordinated the campaign in the province and raised subscriptions for the bank throughout New Brunswick and in Boston, New York, and Philadelphia. With the assistance of a Saint John assemblyman, William Boyd Kinnear*, the committee twice succeeded in securing the passage of a bank bill in the House of Assembly only to have it defeated in the Legislative Council. The committee finally bypassed the legislature and on 16 Aug. 1834, with the assistance of Lieutenant Governor Sir Archibald CAMPBELL, secured incorporation of the Commercial Bank of New Brunswick through a royal charter. Wilmot served as a director of the new bank for most of the next decade.

Wilmot's other business activities included the New Brunswick Fire Insurance Company, of which he was successively promoter, director, and president in the 1830s, and the New Brunswick Mining Company, which he helped found and which sought to exploit the coal resources of the Grand Lake area of central New Brunswick.

Wilmot's public and religious concerns were as significant as his commercial and financial interests. Throughout his life he was one of the most influential Calvinist Baptist laymen and spokesmen in the province. The Maritime Baptist tradition was the archetypal frontier movement: it developed in hundreds of small rural communities and was transmitted to urban centres by the movement of migrants such as Wilmot and Amasa COY of Fredericton. Wilmot became a founder in 1810 of the Regular (Calvinist) Baptist church in Saint John and was active in efforts to organize a denomination in New Brunswick and ensure that it had equality with the Church of England. His major concern was to provide Baptist youth with an effective educational institution. In 1833 he and several other influential Calvinist Baptists founded the New-Brunswick Baptist Education Society. Joseph Crandall* served as president and Wilmot as vice-president of this agency, whose aim was to establish a Baptist seminary for the province. Opened in Fredericton in 1836 under the Reverend Frederick William MILES, the seminary encountered severe financial difficulties in its early years because the Legislative Council, after agreeing to an initial government grant, refused subsequent ones although assistance was provided to Church of England and Roman Catholic institutions.

Apart from his denominational concerns, Wilmot took a great interest in the ecumenical evangelical concerns of the 19th century. He was an officer of the interdenominational Saint John Sunday School Union Society, which developed in the early 1820s as a means through which basic literacy could be provided to the children of the poor. His major concern, however, was the New Brunswick auxiliary of the British and Foreign Bible Society, and he served as president of this influential organization for a number of years, finally retiring in 1839.

Wilmot also played an important role in public life. He was elected to the Saint John Common Council in 1815 and 1816 as alderman for Dukes Ward. The following year he was returned for Kings, and he served that ward from 1817 to 1821 and again from 1824 to 1828. As alderman he participated in the administration of the city, sat as a justice of the Inferior Court of Common Pleas, and served as a magistrate of the Saint John County sessions.

During much of this time Wilmot also served as a member of the House of Assembly for Saint John County and City. He was first returned in 1820 and sat until 1827. In 1833 Lieutenant Governor Sir Archibald Campbell appointed him to replace William Black* as mayor of the city. The following year he was removed from office, a certain sign that he had fallen into official disfavour. He had apparently made his radical views known. Later in 1834 he successfully contested the "crown lands" election [*see* Charles Simonds*] in his old constituency. His activities in the assembly were devoted to improving the navigation of the Saint John River and furthering the interests of the local business community and the Commercial Bank. He was re-elected in 1837 but did not re-offer in 1842.

In 1834 Wilmot had purchased the estate of Belmont, at Lincoln in Sunbury County, from the heirs of John Murray Bliss*, his brother William's brother-in-law. He died there on 7 Sept. 1847. "He was," said the *New-Brunswick Courier*, "an upright and consistent Christian, and . . . made the precepts of the Gospel the rule of his conduct." Despite his active public life his contributions to New Brunswick have been overshadowed by those of his son Robert Duncan and his nephew Lemuel Allan Wilmot*.

T. W. ACHESON

N.B. Museum, Ward family papers, packet 23, Wilmot to C. Ward, January 1836, 26 Jan. 1838. PANB, MC 1156, VII: 59; RG 4, RS24, S21-P12, S24-P43, S26-P19. *A schedule of the real estate belonging to the mayor, aldermen and commonalty of the city of Saint John . . . January, 1842* (Saint John, N.B., 1849; copy at PANB). *New-Brunswick Courier*, 11 April 1818; 4 June 1831; 8 Dec. 1832; 23 March, 6 April, 21 Sept. 1833; 15 Nov. 1834; 11 Sept. 1847. Lawrence, *Judges of N.B.* (Stockton and Raymond). A. R. M. Lower, *Great Britain's woodyard; British America and the timber trade, 1763–1867* (Montreal and London, 1973).

WINNIETT, JAMES, army officer, Indian Department official, office holder, and JP; b. *c.* 1777; d. 13 Aug. 1849 near Brantford, Upper Canada.

James Winniett was a career army officer who joined the 68th Foot in 1795 at the age of 18. He spent the next 34 years with the regiment, during which he was present at 13 Peninsular War engagements and rose to major. Sent to British North America at the end of the Napoleonic period, the 68th served in the garrison at Drummond Island (Mich.); Winniett was in charge of arrangements for the visit there by Governor Charles Lennox*, 4th Duke of Richmond and Lennox, in the summer of 1819. Later he was posted for various periods at Kingston, York (Toronto), and Quebec. By the late 1820s the regiment formed part of the Montreal garrison. Winniett sold his commission in August 1829 and moved to York County, Upper Canada. He applied for land in January 1830 and was given the first of several grants which by his death totalled 900 acres.

Settling near Brantford in 1830, Winniett spent the next two years as a middle-aged country squire. Like many other retired military men, he sought a government appointment; he had evidently been led to expect one through his contacts with the Upper Canadian administration. The sudden death in 1832 of John Brant [Tekarihogen*], superintendent of the Six Nations, provided a convenient opening. In November Lieutenant Governor Sir John Colborne* commissioned Winniett a superintendent in the Indian Department "to be stationed at the Grand River and to inspect occasionally the Indian Establishments in Upper Canada." He suggested that the position would not be an easy one. Factionalism among the Six Nations, mismanagement of Indian lands, and problems with white squatters were frustrating the government's hopes for quick results from the policy of assimilation. Winniett was ordered to evict squatters, to cooperate with missionaries, and to tighten up the superintendency's organization.

Land disputes were particularly acrimonious in the Grand River community because of the complexities arising from the original grant of 1784 and the subsequent sale or lease of large blocks by Joseph Brant [Thayendanegea*]. Squatters, who had no legal arrangements with anyone, were numerous. Timber thefts were common, and Winniett eventually sought extra help to minimize losses. Marcus Blair of Hamilton was made senior deputy surveyor of woods and forests on the Grand River, assisted by Charles Bain. Blair possessed an argumentative personality and was not entirely happy with departmental policies and the use of Indian constables. "I certainly can not by any means agree that any Indian should at his pleasure take my duty out of my hands," he complained to Winniett. The relationship between the two men was often tense.

In 1834 Winniett was president of the Grand River Navigation Company, a position which reflected the fact that the Six Nations owned 25 per cent of its shares. The investment decision, which had been made with the approval of Colborne and without the formal consent of the Indians, proved to be a great mistake, and one that Winniett's presence on the board of directors could not alleviate. The men who actually ran the company, William Hamilton Merritt* and David Thompson, managed the situation so that the Indians were obliged to sink more and more money into the scheme in order to save their original investment. Eventually they owned more than 80 per cent of the unprofitable enterprise. Winniett meanwhile had requested and received permission from the Indian Department to resign from the board.

Winniett's administrative performance as superintendent of the Six Nations was sometimes less than adequate. In 1836, for example, the schedules for annual Indian presents permitted the ordering of extra equipment. He failed to take advantage of this opportunity until reminded to do so by Chief Superintendent James GIVINS. At other times he misplaced departmental paperwork. Colborne had held out the possibility of Winniett's succeeding the elderly Givins but, unfortunately for Winniett, Colborne left office before the change could be made. His successor, Sir Francis Bond Head*, was aware of the situation; none the less he appointed Samuel Peters Jarvis* to the post in 1837. Indeed, when a general overhaul of government was planned in the late 1830s, Winniett was one of those officials slated for early retirement, probably because of his mediocre administrative abilities. This attempt to dismiss him embittered Winniett. Only a strong personal appeal – and the loyalty to the crown of the Six Nations during the troubles of 1837–38 – prevented his removal. When the royal commission of 1842–44 established by Governor Sir Charles BAGOT to investigate the Indian Department completed its work, Winniett was finally retired. David Thorburn of Queenston assumed some of his duties in mid 1844 and succeeded him as superintendent a year later.

Winniett continued to live in the Brantford area. He had acted as a collector of tolls on the Grand River and as a justice of the peace, and likely went on doing so after his retirement. His obituary in the *Hamilton Spectator, and Journal of Commerce* described him as a man "respected by all around him." Little is known of his family life. A daughter married Brantford doctor Robert Coucher. In his will Winniett left £200 for the education and support of Francis Alexander Atkins of Brantford Township, possibly an illegitimate son.

James Winniett's career was scarcely a remarkable one. He was typical of many retired military men who held minor offices in Upper Canada during the decades surrounding the political union of 1841. The course of his life does throw some light, however, on the difficulties of local Indian administration, on the nature of political patronage, and on the composition of local social élites in the period.

DOUGLAS LEIGHTON

AO, RG 1, A-VII; RG 22, ser.155. PAC, MG 9, D7, 40, vol.8, file 36; MG 24, A25, 2; RG 1, E3, 52, 102; L1, 33: 116; L3, 148: Canada Company, pp.32b–c, 41h; 531: W16/15; 541: W6/21; RG 5, B9, 1–2, 4, 71; RG 8, I (C ser.), 142, 363, 965; RG 10, A1, 121–22; A6, 718–19; B8, 628; CI, 6, vols.803, pts.I–II, 806. *Globe*, 21 Aug. 1849. *Hamilton Spectator, and Journal of Commerce* (Hamilton, [Ont.]), 22 Aug. 1849. J. D. Leighton, "The development of federal Indian policy in Canada, 1840–1849" (PHD thesis, Univ. of Western Ont., London, 1975). B. E. Hill, "The Grand River Navigation Company and the Six Nations Indians," *OH*, 63 (1971): 31–40.

WINNIETT, Sir WILLIAM ROBERT WOLSELEY, naval officer; b. 2 March 1793 in Annapolis Royal, N.S., third child of Sheriff William Winniett and Mary Totten; great-grandson of William Winniett*; m. 10 Aug. 1828 Augusta Julia Fenwick, daughter of Colonel William Fenwick of the Royal Engineers and god-daughter of the late Edward* Augustus, Duke of Kent, in Woolwich (London), England, and they had three sons and a daughter; d. 4 Dec. 1850 in Accra (Ghana) of "chronic dysentery."

William Robert Wolseley Winniett probably attended John McNamara's school at Annapolis Royal, and when he was 14 he entered the Royal Navy as a second class volunteer on the frigate *Cleopatra*, then at Halifax. The *Cleopatra* saw action against the French at Guadeloupe and Martinique in 1809, and assisted in the capture of the French frigate *Topaze* at the former place. On 20 Aug. 1811 Winniett, then a midshipman, was transferred to the *Africaine* and served for two years in the East Indies, being master's mate from June 1812 to October 1813. Thereafter he was on various ships in the waters off North America, Europe, and the West Indies until late 1818. On 24 December of that year he was assigned to the *Morgiana*, then on the African coastal patrol for the suppression of the slave trade. Promoted lieutenant on 29 Jan. 1821, Winniett remained on the African station, and on 17 March 1837 took command of the schooner *Viper*. The *Lightning*, which he commanded from 1 Jan. 1843, was one of the first steamers to be used as a warship by the Royal Navy. A commander from 5 Oct. 1843, on 24 Oct. 1845 Winniett became lieutenant governor of the Gold Coast (Ghana).

In 1843 the scattered British settlements of the Gold Coast had been united into a colony, which was placed under the jurisdiction of Sierra Leone. When Winniett arrived at Cape Coast Castle (Ghana) in April 1846 his main concerns were the protection of British traders and the slave trade. To the former end, in April 1847 he made a visit to the kingdom of Dahomey, the most powerful state in west Africa, and induced King Ghezo to sign a treaty of amity and commerce. The lieutenant govenor dispatched a further mission to the Dahomeyan capital of Abomey (Benin) in November 1848, but Ghezo refused to abolish the slave trade, which was highly profitable to his kingdom. Winniett was no less energetic on other fronts, and when in 1848 the king of Amanahia, a coastal state, murdered and harassed Europeans and Africans, Winniett persuaded other local rulers to join him in an expedition which captured and imprisoned the king. In September of the same year Winniett travelled to the kingdom of Ashanti, where he attempted to persuade King Kwaku Dua I to abolish human sacrifice. The journey marked the first visit of a British governor to the Ashanti capital of Kumasi (Ghana).

During 1849 Winniett was in England on leave, and on 29 June he was knighted "for important services performed by him in securing friendly treaties with several of the most powerful Sovereigns in Africa." In further recognition of his efforts, on 24 Jan. 1850 the Gold Coast settlements were made into an independent colony, with Winniett as the first governor. Winniett presided over the transfer of the Danish coastal forts to British control in March 1850, and later that year submitted a comprehensive and optimistic report on the progress of the colony, but he died in December, "sincerely regretted, no less by his countrymen and the [naval] profession at large, than by the tens of thousands of the black population" under his government. He was remembered in Nova Scotia as a successful naval officer and as "a colonist attaining one of the highest positions to which a British subject can aspire – not only that of Lieutenant-Governor, but of Governor-General."

PHYLLIS R. BLAKELEY

PRO, ADM 9/16/5732; ADM 196/6: 582. St Luke's (Anglican) Church (Annapolis Royal, N.S.), Reg. of baptisms, 1782–1817 (mfm. at PANS). *Acadian Recorder*, 4 Oct. 1828. *Novascotian*, 25 Feb. 1850, 31 March 1851. W. R. O'Byrne, *A naval biographical dictionary: comprising the life and services of every living officer in her majesty's navy* . . . (London, 1849), 1310. W. A. Calnek, *History of the county of Annapolis, including old Port Royal and Acadia* . . . , ed. A. W. Savary (Toronto, 1897; repr. Belleville, Ont., 1972). W. W. Claridge, *A history of the Gold Coast and Ashanti* . . . (2nd ed., 2v., London, 1964). G. W. Hill, *Nova Scotia and Nova Scotians* . . . (Halifax, 1858), 27–28. Christopher Lloyd, *The navy and the slave trade: the suppression of the African slave trade in the nineteenth century* (London, 1968). A. W. Savary, *Supplement to the "History of the county of Annapolis"* . . . (Toronto, 1913; repr. Belleville, 1973). D. C. Harvey, "Nova Scotia and the Canadian naval tradition," *CHR*, 23 (1942): 247–59.

WOLHAUPTER, JOHN, watchmaker, gold- and silversmith, and jeweller; b. *c.* 1771 in New York City, son of Gottfried Wolhaupter; d. 12 Jan. 1839 in Richmond Parish, N.B.

John Wolhaupter's father, who was from Bocken, near Schneeberg, in Saxony (German Democratic Republic), had settled in New York in or before 1759. John evidently apprenticed there and, to judge from existing bills and accounts, was established in business by 1790. That year he became a member of the Hiram Lodge of freemasons. In 1795 he married in New York Mary Payne Aycrigg, daughter of the late Dr John Hurst Aycrigg and of Rachael Lydekker, who had gone in 1785 to Saint John, N.B., with her second husband. Wolhaupter too had settled in Saint John some time before 1799. An advertisement in the *Royal Gazette* of 21 May 1799 states that "JOHN WOOLHAUPTER, CLOCK and WATCH-MAKER, . . . lately returned to this City from New-York . . . has taken a House in Germain-Street." "Lately returned" would seem significant since, when petitioning for land in 1820, Wolhaupter claimed that he had come to New Brunswick with the loyalists.

Wolhaupter was admitted a freeman of the city of Saint John in 1799. He continued his masonic activities and became treasurer of St John's Lodge No.29 when it was formed in 1802. On 28 May 1803, however, he announced in the *Saint John Gazette* that he intended "shortly to leave the Province for Some Months." In November he offered a house and lot adjoining his own for sale, but they had not been purchased by 2 Jan. 1804, when the advertisement ceased.

Wolhaupter apparently returned to New York, where he worked as a clockmaker, but by 25 May 1805 he was back in Saint John and had set up business on Prince William Street. Five years later, in July 1810, he announced the sale of some of his property and his intention to discontinue watchmaking and go into the jewellery line. Later that year he indicated that he would move to Fredericton and by 1813 he was established in the capital on Queen Street. In an advertisement of 12 May 1818 he offered at his premises the repair and cleaning of clocks and watches as well as the repair of gold-, silver-, and plate-ware. By this time his son Benjamin*, who was apprenticing with him, had taken a shop and the advertisement noted that "strict attention" would be paid to business at both places.

When he moved to a new shop on Camperdown Street in 1819, Wolhaupter announced his intention to carry on gold- and silversmithing. Yet he seems to have left the business in 1820, the year Benjamin completed his apprenticeship. At no time after 1821 is the older man mentioned in Benjamin's advertisements, nor is there any evidence of his continuing an independent trade. In 1826 he was granted land in Richmond Parish, near Woodstock. He did not move onto the property until 1831, and he died there eight years later. His wife followed him to the grave in 1842; they had had at least six children, four boys and two girls.

John Wolhaupter's career illustrates the disruption and redirection that many loyalist craftsmen endured. A few teaspoons (some of which may be seen in the York-Sunbury Historical Society Museum in Fredericton) have been identified as his work, but no clocks or watches and no jewels have, as yet, been identified. The clearest record of his life lies in a series of land purchases and sales, and one assumes that much of his capital was engendered on his repeated and extended trips to New York.

D. C. MACKAY and STUART SMITH

City of Saint John, N.B., City Clerk's Office, Common Council, minutes, 6 Nov. 1799. Saint John County Land Registry Office (Saint John), Record books, Cl: 116; Fl: 175; Hl: 4, 248 (mfm. at PANB). *Royal Gazette* (Saint John; Fredericton), 21 May 1799, 12 May 1818, 18 May 1819, 23 Jan. 1839. *Saint John Gazette*, 28 May, 5 Nov. 1803; 2 Jan. 1804; 27 May 1805. D. C. Mackay, *Silversmiths and related craftsmen of the Atlantic provinces* (Halifax, 1973). Brooks Palmer, *The book of American clocks* (New York, 1950). W. F. Bunting, *History of St. John's Lodge, F. & A.M. of Saint John, New Brunswick . . .* (Saint John, 1895).

WOOD, ALEXANDER, businessman, militia officer, JP, and office holder; b. 1772 and baptized 25 January in Fetteresso, near Stonehaven, Scotland, son of James Wood and Margaret Barclay; d. unmarried 11 Sept. 1844 at Woodcot in the parish of Fetteresso.

Alexander Wood came to Upper Canada as a young man, settling in Kingston about 1793 and investing £330 in the Kingston Brewery in partnership with Joseph Forsyth* and Alexander Aitken*. He moved to York (Toronto) in 1797 to establish himself as a merchant. He and William Allan* became partners; "neither advanced any money which brought us on a fair footing," but they built their shop on Allan's land. When the partnership was dissolved on 13 April 1801 its assets were divided with difficulty, so that neither partner wanted to renew their intercourse "by the exchange of a single word."

Wood immediately opened his own shop. Each autumn he ordered a wide assortment of goods from Glasgow or London, stressing quality and careful packing rather than price. Almost all his stock came from Britain except tea and tobacco, which, before the American Embargo Act was extended to inland waters in 1808, he bought in the United States through Robert Nichol*; small, immediate requirements were ordered from Montreal or New York. Wood was fortunate because his elder brother in Scotland, James, made up any deficit owing in Britain until full payment could be sent from Upper Canada. His customers included Lieutenant Governor Francis Gore*, a fair proportion of York's carriage trade, army officers, and the commissariat – none of whom paid as promptly as Wood wished. He also dealt with neighbourhood farmers, supplying their needs and exporting their flour. Fluctuations in the quantity and price of flour were frequent, but Wood prospered in this business. He was not so successful with potash or hemp, and made only one ill-fated sortie into the fur trade.

With William Allan and Laurent Quetton* St George, Wood was one of the leading merchants in York before the War of 1812. When he first arrived, it was little more than a clearing in the bush, far inferior to Kingston and the towns of the Niagara peninsula in commercial development, but it grew rapidly, stimulated by government money and the settlement of its hinterland. Wood belonged to the group of "scotch Pedlars" whose influence judge Robert THORPE so much deplored. "There is a chain of them linked from Halifax to Quebec, Montreal, Kingston, York, Niagara & so on to Detroit," he wrote in 1806. Wood carried on a regular correspondence with James

Irvine* (Quebec), James Dunlop* and James Leslie* (Montreal), Joseph Forsyth (Kingston), Robert Hamilton* and Thomas Clark* (Niagara peninsula), Robert Nichol (Fort Erie and Dover (Port Dover)), and other Scottish merchants, who gave and received assistance, and exchanged commercial and local news.

Wood was one of the few merchants accepted among York's élite. His closest friends were William Dummer Powell* and his family, with whom he was "a constant guest," and George Crookshank* and his family. A warm friendship was developing by correspondence with the Reverend John Strachan* in Cornwall. "Our sentiments agree almost upon everything," Strachan wrote in 1807. Wood was gazetted lieutenant in the York militia in 1798, appointed magistrate in 1800, and by 1805 was a commissioner for the Court of Requests, as well as being involved in every movement for community betterment or social enjoyment. His only problem was his health: he suffered, according to Dr Alexander THOM in 1806, from "a fullness of the Vessels of the Brain." Anne Powell [MURRAY] wrote that "his complaint . . . tho' not dangerous to his life is I fear to his intellects," and the Powells got medical advice for him in both New York and London.

In June 1810 Wood's world fell apart. Rumours spread throughout York that as a magistrate he had interviewed several young men individually, telling them that a Miss Bailey had accused them of rape. According to Wood, she had scratched her assailant's genitals; each of the accused, to prove his innocence, submitted to Wood's intimate physical examination. John Beverley Robinson* called Wood the "Inspector General of private Accounts . . . by which [name] he was occasionally insulted in the streets." St George's clerk reported that although Wood had received his shipment of British goods "no one goes near his shop." Judge Powell asked his friend about the story, and was horrified when Wood admitted its truth: "I have laid myself open to ridicule & malevolence, which I know not how to meet; that the thing will be made the subject of mirth and a handle to my enemies for a sneer I have every reason to expect." Powell replied that Wood's offence was more serious: his abuse of his position as magistrate made him liable to fine and imprisonment. The evidence was submitted to the public prosecutor, "but from its odious nature, investigation was smothered" on the understanding that Wood leave Upper Canada. On 17 Oct. 1810 he departed for Scotland, leaving his clerk in charge of his shop.

Despite the scandal, Wood returned to York on 25 Aug. 1812, just after the outbreak of war, and resumed all his previous occupations, including that of magistrate. He had lost the Powells' friendship, but the Crookshanks remained staunch friends and Strachan was now living in York – "Mr Wood commonly spends a couple of evenings and dines once with us during the Week," he wrote in 1816. As a merchant Wood struggled fairly successfully with the problems of wartime transportation and supply, but his commercial position is shown in the York garrison accounts, in which his sales are a poor third to those of St George and Allan. By 1815 he had virtually retired, although his shop was not formally closed until 1821.

In 1817 Wood inherited his family's estates and moved to Scotland, but in 1821 he returned to Upper Canada to settle his affairs. He would remain in York for 21 years, more involved with other people's concerns than his own. Since his first arrival in York, he had acted as an agent for absentee landowners and others with business in the capital, among them D'Arcy Boulton* Sr, James Macaulay*, Lord Selkirk [Douglas*], George Okill Stuart*, and the widow of Chief Justice John Elmsley*. Wood himself neither invested nor speculated in land, but he spent much time on land transactions and property management for friends and clients. Throughout his life in Upper Canada he was active as a director or executive member in many organizations, among them the Bank of Upper Canada, the Home District Agricultural Society, the St Andrew's Society, and the Toronto Library, and as the hard-working treasurer or secretary of others, including the Home District Savings Bank, the Loyal and Patriotic Society of Upper Canada, and the Society for the Relief of the Orphan, Widow, and Fatherless.

Wood's public service involved membership on several government commissions. In 1808, when he was appointed to the second Heir and Devisee Commission, he was the only commissioner who was neither an executive councillor nor a judge of the Court of King's Bench. Probably because of his frequent service as foreman of the Home District grand jury, he was appointed to commissions concerning the building of jails (1838) and a lunatic asylum (1839). He was a member of the special commission appointed in 1837 to examine persons arrested for high treason during the rebellion. On Strachan's recommendation he was appointed to the commission to investigate war claims in 1823, but Chief Justice Powell refused on moral grounds to swear him in. Wood promptly sued Powell for damages, and the whole story of the 1810 scandal was retold. Although Wood won £120 damages with costs, Powell refused to pay, and in 1831 he published a pamphlet about the case. After Powell's death, Wood visited his widow and forgave the debt. Mrs Powell, who usually reacted vehemently against anyone who had ever opposed her husband, wrote, "This liberal conduct reflects credit on our once zealous and sincere Friend."

In 1842 Wood visited Scotland intending to return

to Upper Canada, but he died there intestate in 1844. All his brothers and sisters had predeceased him, unmarried, including Thomas, who had come to York from Jamaica before 1810 and died in 1818. Because Canadian and Scottish laws of intestacy differed, it was necessary to establish Wood's place of residence. The case reached the Court of Session (Scotland's supreme court) in 1846 and the House of Lords two years later. In 1851 it was finally decided that Wood, despite his more than 45 years in Canada, had been a resident of Scotland, and by Scottish law his large estate passed to a first cousin once removed, "of whose existence he was most likely ignorant."

Alexander Wood had come to Upper Canada with a good education, some capital, and the financial backing of his brother in Scotland. He became a close friend of Powell and of Strachan, the two most influential men in the province in his time. As a merchant he generally avoided speculation or excessive risk, probably because of his innate conservatism and his feeling that his stay in Upper Canada was only temporary. By his business ability, the influence of his powerful friends, and the breadth and depth of his public service, he was able to avoid permanent stigma from the 1810 scandal. At his death the *British Colonist* called him one of Toronto's "most respected inhabitants."

EDITH G. FIRTH

AO, MS 6; MS 35; MS 88; MU 2828; MU 4742; RG 22, ser.94; RG 40, D-1. GRO (Edinburgh), Fetteresso, reg. of baptisms, marriages, and burials. MTRL, William Allan papers; Early Toronto papers, Board of Health papers, 20 June 1832; John McGill papers, B40: 42; W. D. Powell papers; Laurent Quetton de St George papers; Alexander Wood papers and letter-books. PAC, RG 5, A1. Royal Canadian Military Institute (Toronto), York garrison accounts. Can., Prov. of, *Statutes*, 1851, c.168. J. [M.] Lambert, "An American lady in old Toronto: the letters of Julia Lambert, 1821–1854," ed. S. A. Heward and W. S. Wallace, RSC *Trans.*, 3rd ser., 40 (1946), sect.II: 101–42. Loyal and Patriotic Soc. of U.C., *Explanation of the proceedings* (Toronto, 1841); *The report of the Loyal and Patriotic Society of Upper Canada; with an appendix, and a list of subscribers and benefactors* (Montreal, 1817). "Minutes of the Court of General Quarter Sessions of the Peace for the Home District, 13th March, 1800, to 28th December, 1811," AO *Report*, 1932. [W. D. Powell], *[A letter from W. D. Powell, chief justice, to Sir Peregrine Maitland, lieutenant-governor of Upper Canada, regarding the appointment of Alexander Wood as a commissioner for the investigation of claims . . .]* ([York (Toronto), 1831?]). John Strachan, *The John Strachan letter book, 1812–1834*, ed. G. W. Spragge (Toronto, 1946). *Town of York, 1793–1815* (Firth); *1815–34* (Firth). *York, Upper Canada: minutes of town meetings and lists of inhabitants, 1797–1823*, ed. Christine Mosser (Toronto, 1984).

British Colonist, 29 Oct., 1 Nov. 1844. *Church*, 1 Nov. 1844. *Examiner* (Toronto), 6 Nov. 1844. *Toronto Patriot*, 1 Nov. 1844. *Upper Canada Gazette*, 1797–1828. *Toronto directory*, 1833–34, 1837. *One hundred years of history, 1836–1936: St Andrew's Society, Toronto*, ed. John McLaverty (Toronto, 1936), 3–4, 87–88, 103. W. R. Riddell, *The life of William Dummer Powell, first judge at Detroit and fifth chief justice of Upper Canada* (Lansing, Mich., 1924). *Robertson's landmarks of Toronto*, esp. 2: 1007–21. Scadding, *Toronto of old* (1873). T. W. Acheson, "The nature and structure of York commerce in the 1820s," *CHR*, 50 (1969): 406–28. E. G. Firth, "Alexander Wood, merchant of York," *York Pioneer* (Toronto), 1958: 5–29. H. P. Gundy, "The family compact at work: the second Heir and Devisee Commission of Upper Canada, 1805–1841," *OH*, 66 (1974): 129–46. Douglas McCalla, "The 'loyalist' economy of Upper Canada, 1784–1806," *SH*, 16 (1983): 279–304.

WOOD, CHARLES, naval architect and shipbuilder; b. 27 March 1790 in Port Glasgow, Scotland, son of John Wood, a shipbuilder, and Elizabeth Household (Cameron); he did not marry but had a daughter; d. 27 May 1847 in Port Glasgow.

Charles Wood and his older brother John served in their father's shipyard. John Sr died shortly after laying the keel in 1811 for Henry Bell's pioneering steamer, the *Comet*, and his sons took over the yard and completed the vessel. They went on to earn an excellent reputation as designers and builders of 18 Clyde passenger steamboats and other craft. Among the vessels designed by Charles were a ceremonial barge for service on the Rhine, bought by the king of Denmark, and the steamer *James Watt* of 1820, whose lines revolutionized the shape of steamboat hulls.

In the early 1820s Charles found backers for a bold scheme to transport timber from Quebec to London in huge raft-ships able to accommodate extra-large sticks and the tallest pine masts, which were difficult, if not impossible, for ordinary ships to handle. Wood's vessels were to be built of square timber and serve only for one voyage, following which they would be broken up and their timber sold. Arriving at Quebec, Wood leased a large site at the westerly end of Île d'Orléans in August 1823 and set to work constructing his first vessel, the 3,690-ton *Columbus*; the largest merchantman previously built in the port was the 720-ton *Harrison* of 1811. Wood's extensive operation helped lift the shipbuilding industry out of a depression which had lasted since the War of 1812 and, according to the *Quebec Gazette*, through the existing demand for other construction work on ships, the "great number" of carpenters and labourers he employed "obtained high prices." The novel and immense project attracted considerable attention. Though it was recognized that Wood was a shipbuilder "of remarkable talents" and "intimate acquaintance with the scientific principles of the art," some believed that the *Columbus* would never float. However, with 4,000 tons of cargo on board it was safely launched on 28 July 1824. The river steamboats were on hand, and the St Lawrence was alive with an estimated 100 sailing craft. A crowd of 5,000, which had begun to gather the night before, watched as the vessel slid gently into the water to the strains of "God Save the King" played by regimental bands and to salvoes of cannon fire.

The *Columbus*, owned by a Scottish syndicate, was manned by a captain and 90-member crew that had been sent out from Scotland. Wood was aboard as, heavily laden, it weighed anchor on 5 September and was towed by the steamboat *Hercules* to Bic. Under sail, it ran aground at Betsiamites, and part of the cargo had to be sacrificed to get it off. Despite some loosening of its structure by the incident and notwithstanding bad weather, the *Columbus* reached London in late October, to a tremendous welcome. Though Wood had designed and built it to endure only one voyage, the *Columbus* was ordered by its owners to New Brunswick for a second cargo five months later, and it foundered in a gale – fortunately without loss of life.

Before leaving on the *Columbus*, Wood had laid the keel of a similar but even larger vessel, the 5,294-ton *Baron of Renfrew*. Launched with some difficulty in 1825, it crossed the Atlantic safely, only to be grounded by the pilots in the mouth of the Thames and eventually to break up on the French shore. Though much of the cargo was salvaged, the two losses made such rafts uninsurable and resulted in abandonment of the scheme.

From 1834 to 1836 Wood was in partnership with George Mills under the name Mills and Wood in Bowling, Scotland, on the north bank of the Clyde. In 1836 he took over the dockyard of James Lang at Dumbarton, where his production included the ship *Caledonia* for the Cunard Line. An intelligent, practical man, Wood went to London during the 1830s in a successful bid to get the tonnage laws changed so that they reflected the true capacity for carrying profitable cargo.

Wood kept abreast of political developments in Lower Canada, where conflict was building to an explosion. "The French Habitans . . . ," he wrote to Colonial Secretary Lord Glenelg in 1836, "were the most unsophisticated Moral people male and female I was ever among, and very much disposed to be contented." They should have been "most delicately attended to," he asserted, but in fact "the British are too apt to treat them as if they were actually black." He condemned the "mighty talkers" among the English party as "not less dangerous than M. Papineau [Louis-Joseph Papineau*] and the other French lawyers" who had mischievously excited discontent "against the energetic paternal government of Lord Dalhousie [Ramsay]." Affirming that virtually no rural Canadians spoke English but that "many a time they have called out to me for it," he believed that everyone should learn to speak it "perfectly." The Canadians "would not then be liable to be held down by the Saucy English, nor decoyed by the Cunning French," he argued. Since steam had made passage of the Atlantic "short and certain," Wood concluded that "Canada should be united to Great Britain and have Peers and Members of the British Parliament."

In the early 1840s Wood moved his shipyard to Castle Green in Dumbarton, but he was ruined by a bad contract on a vessel for the Royal Mail Company's West Indian Line. He then went to Amsterdam to advise builders, and returned to Port Glasgow in the 1840s to spend his remaining days at the home of his brother John.

John Scott Russell, one of Britain's foremost ship architects and engine designers of the 19th century, described Wood as "a genius in his way." According to Russell, the change in the tonnage laws was among "the greatest benefits conferred on Britain during [Wood's] lifetime," and one for which shipbuilders were "in great measure, and originally," indebted to him. Both Wood and his brother had been "distinguished by their eminent knowledge [and] . . . by the liberality with which they communicated that knowledge," even to their immediate business rivals. From these qualities Quebec shipbuilders undoubtedly profited during Charles Wood's presence among them.

Eileen Marcil

[The author wishes to thank Mrs May Scott of Bowling, Scotland, and Mr Michael Moss, archivist at the Univ. of Glasgow, for their assistance. E.M.]

Charles Wood is the author of *Ballast*, published in Glasgow in 1836.

ANQ-Q, CN1-197, 4 août 1823. GRO (Edinburgh), Port Glasgow, reg. of births and baptisms, 27 March 1790. Mitchell Library (Glasgow), J. C. Osborne, "John and Charles Wood: 18th century shipbuilders" (typescript). Private arch., Mrs May Scott (Bowling, Scot.), Wood family papers. Charles Wood, "Une lettre du constructeur Wood," *BRH*, 36 (1930): 543–44. *Quebec Gazette*, 29 July 1824. *Times* (London), 2 Nov. 1824, 1 June 1825. M. S. Cross, "The dark druidical groves: the lumber community and the commercial frontier in British North America, to 1854" (PHD thesis, Univ. of Toronto, 1968), 144–45. Paul Terrien, *Québec à l'âge de la voile* (Québec, 1984). J. S. Russell, "On the late Mr. John Wood and Mr. Charles Wood, naval architects, of Port Glasgow," Institution of Naval Architects, *Trans.* (London), 2 (1861): 141–48.

WOOD, ROBERT, timber culler, timber merchant, and shipowner; b. 10 Aug. 1792 at Quebec; m. there 4 Oct. 1817 Charlotte Gray, the daughter of a military clerk, and they had 11 children; d. 13 April 1847 in Savannah, Ga, and was buried at Quebec.

Although Robert Wood's origins have been obscured and romanticized by succeeding generations, there seems to be little doubt that he was the son of

Robert Wood, a servant who accompanied Prince Edward* Augustus to Quebec in August 1791. On 28 December of that year, at Quebec, Wood Sr married Marie Dupuis, *dit* Caton. The following year he was appointed doorkeeper of the Executive Council. At his death in November 1806 he was also a merchant. Later that month his widow appeared before the Court of King's Bench to request guardianship of the seven children born of their marriage, including the eldest, Robert.

In April 1812 Robert Wood was commissioned culler of timber, a position which indicated that he was already involved in the burgeoning timber industry in the port of Quebec. Three years later he was appointed master culler and measurer of masts and timber. Although Wood continued to hold the post of culler until 1837, he slowly began to expand his own operations. He took his brother George into partnership on 1 May 1818. The firm of Robert and George Wood, timber dealers and carpenters, supplied wood to such Quebec shipbuilders as John Munn*. Five years later, on 31 May 1823, having taken in William Petry as partner, the firm changed its name to Robert Wood and Company. Wood's timber cove was located at Anse Saint-Michel in Sillery.

The colonial timber trade of the early 19th century was characterized by cyclical fluctuations. Sharp rises in timber prices in 1824 and 1825 were accompanied by an increased demand for colonial shipping. In 1825 the *Charlotte and Maria* was built for Wood by Patrick Flemming and in 1826 two barques, the 403-ton *Georgiana* and the 391-ton *Corinthian*, were constructed for Wood's firm. By 1826, however, prices for timber and timber products had begun to drop sharply. In May Robert Wood and Company assigned the barques to Gillespie, Finlay and Company, which agreed to advance £1,500 for their completion and to sell them in England; after having recovered its loan and costs, it would pay a debt of £8,121 owed by Wood's firm to the Bank of Montreal and forward the balance, if any, to Wood. That autumn Wood's company went bankrupt, owing its creditors £17,579. The two barques, sold in 1827 and 1828, probably went at a substantial loss on the glutted market. Wood seems nevertheless to have made a rapid recovery. Despite only gradual improvement in the timber market after 1827, he had begun to build an imposing three-storey house at Anse Saint-Michel by the end of 1829.

Some time in or before 1847 Wood sailed to the West Indies in an attempt to restore his health; he died in Georgia on the return voyage to Quebec. He left an estate valued at approximately £54,152, as well as a three-storey house on Rue Sainte-Ursule and three lots in Acton Township. Among his belongings was a well-stocked library of historical, biographical, and poetical works.

It is not, however, for his role as a prosperous timber merchant that Robert Wood is remembered. He is better known as one of the children said to have been born to Prince Edward Augustus and Thérèse-Bernardine Montgenet*, known as Mme de Saint-Laurent. Family tradition states that he was given to the prince's former servant, to be raised as his son. That there is no record of Wood's birth or baptism in parish registers (the exact date is found in his mother's request for guardianship and on a memorial window placed in the Cathedral of the Holy Trinity, Quebec, by his children) was long considered an indication of royal descent and the absence piqued the curiosity of numerous historians. The information surrounding the family tradition of Wood's origins has been proved inaccurate and recent scholarship has established that no children were born of the 27-year relationship between the prince and his companion. When, how, and why Wood's parentage came to be the subject of such speculation remains a mystery.

In collaboration with MARIANNA O'GALLAGHER

ANQ-Q, CC1, 24 nov. 1806; CE1-61, 29 déc. 1791, 4 oct. 1817, 21 mai 1847; CN1-116, 22 févr. 1827, 29 déc. 1829, 7 oct. 1847; P-239; P1000-105-2105. PAC, RG 68, General index, 1651–1841. *Quebec Gazette*, 7 May 1818, 2 June 1823, 23 April 1847. *Quebec almanac*, 1794, 1830–38. Mollie Gillen, *The prince and his lady: the love story of the Duke of Kent and Madame de St Laurent* (London, 1970; repr. Halifax, 1985). A. R. M. Lower, *Great Britain's woodyard; British America and the timber trade, 1763–1867* (Montreal and London, 1973). Paul Terrien, *Québec à l'âge de la voile* (Québec, 1984).

WOODMAN, ELIJAH CROCKER, businessman and Patriot; b. 22 Sept. 1797 in Buxton (Maine), son of Edmund Woodman and Lydia Crocker; m. February 1819 Apphia Elden of Buxton, and they had three sons and four daughters; d. 13 June 1847 near the Juan Fernández Islands.

The son of sixth-generation Americans, Elijah Crocker Woodman worked as a farmer, lumberman, and stone mason before moving in 1830 to Upper Canada. He built a sawmill on Big Otter Creek near Dereham Forge (Tillsonburg), an area rich in timber. Two years later he was joined there by his wife and family, and by 1836 he had entered into partnership with Reuben W. Lamb. As a result of the economic depression of 1836, Woodman's timber business collapsed and he moved to London, Upper Canada. Possibly because of his business failure and his likely religious interests as a Universalist in social reform, he was drawn to radical developments in Upper Canadian politics.

Woodman took no part in William Lyon Mackenzie*'s abortive uprising near Toronto in December 1837 or in that led by Charles Duncombe* in the southwest part of the province. He did, however, on his own later admission, assist the rebels imprisoned at London by arranging witnesses for their trials and by attending to their needs in prison. Arrested in June 1838 on the charge of passing knives and files to them, he spent the summer in jail, evidently without being tried. After his release, by the end of August, he crossed over to the United States, where he became a member of the Hunters' Lodge, a combination of American and Canadian Patriots pledged to liberating Canada from British oppression.

In early December he accompanied the Patriot force which left Detroit on the *Champlain* to invade Upper Canada at Windsor. He claimed at his subsequent trial that the steamer was to have sailed to Black River, Mich., where he had business to transact, but that he was "forced off" with the invaders near Windsor. He apparently took some part in the ensuing skirmish [*see* John Prince*] but escaped. On 5 December he was arrested on the road to Chatham.

Woodman was taken to prison at London and was brought before judge advocate Henry Sherwood* at a court martial in January. Though he pleaded not guilty, he confided to his diary that he had prayed to be shot rather than hanged, for the sake of his family. He was convicted of "piratical invasion" and, after being sentenced to death, was ordered instead to be transported to Van Diemen's Land (Tasmania). In early April he and other prisoners were taken by wagon to Toronto, a trip he graphically described in his diary. Six weeks later they were moved to Fort Henry at Kingston. In September the group was shipped to Quebec, where prisoners from both Upper and Lower Canada were put aboard the transport *Buffalo*. To Woodman the four-month journey to Van Diemen's Land was uneventful and, on the whole, a welcome change from his prison experience of the past nine months.

On arriving at Hobart Town (Hobart) on 12 Feb. 1840, the Lower Canadian prisoners sailed on to Sydney; Woodman, Daniel D. HEUSTIS, and the other prisoners from Upper Canada were sent to the Sandy Bay road station, near Hobart Town, to work on the roads. Discipline, particularly in the first weeks, was extremely severe. Woodman, the least complaining of the Patriot diarists, found the system far more "rigid" than he had expected, yet his cheerfulness and fortitude were commended by a fellow diarist, Linus Wilson Miller*. Woodman was one of the group that was moved in June to Lovely Banks station, where conditions were even worse. It was there, after two years of penal servitude, that he received his ticket of leave and obtained employment as a carpenter and millwright at Mona Vale, the estate of William Kermode north of Hobart Town. In February 1844 Kermode supported Woodman's application for a conditional pardon. This was never granted, but on 23 July 1845 he received a free pardon, which allowed him to return home if he had the means to do so. But his health was bad, he was nearly 50 years of age, and he was almost destitute. Long a freemason, he received some financial support from the masonic lodge in Hobart Town. It was not until 2 March 1847 that, having found enough money for his homeward journey, he sailed in the *Young Eagle*, a whaler bound for the United States via Cape Horn. Stricken with tuberculosis, he weakened progressively during the journey and died off the Juan Fernández Islands on 13 June. He was buried at sea in sight of the South American coast two days later.

The *Young Eagle* was wrecked soon after, but a number of Woodman's diaries and papers were salvaged and returned, in due course, to his family near London. A daughter, Emeline, had married Elijah Leonard*; their son Frank Elton Leonard assembled these and other Woodman documents and had many copied.

GEORGE RUDÉ

Guillet, *Lives and times of Patriots*. Fred Landon, *An exile from Canada to Van Diemen's Land; being the story of Elijah Woodman, transported overseas for participation in the Upper Canada troubles of 1837–38* (Toronto, 1960). M. G. Milne, "North American political prisoners: the rebellions of 1837–8 in Upper and Lower Canada, and the transportation of American, French-Canadian and Anglo-Canadian prisoners to Van Diemen's Land and New South Wales" (BA thesis, Univ. of Tasmania, Hobart, Australia, 1965).

WRIGHT, GEORGE, office holder, businessman, militia officer, JP, judge, politician, and colonial administrator; b. 29 Dec. 1779 in Charlottetown, son of Thomas Wright* and Susanna Turner; d. there 13 March 1842.

George Wright's father, who became in 1773 the first surveyor general of St John's (Prince Edward) Island, founded one of its many office-holding families, and was most remembered by contemporaries for the number of his offspring. George worked for him for years as deputy surveyor. On 28 Dec. 1807 he married Phebe Cambridge, daughter of John Cambridge*, a prominent proprietor and merchant; the couple had six children. A younger brother Charles* subsequently married another Cambridge daughter, thus furthering the important alliance between the two families.

In 1808 George entered a partnership with Cambridge and his son Lemuel. It was dissolved in June 1813, and George was left in control of the firm's brewery and mills at Bird Island (Wrights) Creek, near Charlottetown. His business appears to have prospered.

In the mean time Wright had begun collecting

offices, appointments, and emoluments in typical Island fashion. He served as high sheriff in 1810–11. During the War of 1812 he was rapidly promoted from captain of militia to major to lieutenant-colonel. In January 1824 he became a JP with the rank of *custos rotulorum*, and an assistant judge of the Supreme Court in 1828. He was a prominent lay member of St Paul's parish in Charlottetown, a founder of the Central Agricultural Society (1827), and then its president (1830).

Wright had also been appointed to Council on 10 July 1813, just prior to the arrival of Lieutenant Governor Charles Douglass Smith*. In the early years of Smith's government Wright was regarded as an associate of James Bardin Palmer*, and his defiance of Smith in 1815 over a militia disturbance led to Smith's unsuccessful attempt to dismiss him from Council. Throughout the controversies involving Smith in the early 1820s Wright kept a low profile, frequently absent from Council for critical meetings but generally supportive of the administration. As senior member and president of Council, he found himself administering the colony from 10 Dec. 1825, the first of five times he served as its chief executive officer on an interim basis. This stewardship, during the absence of Smith's successor, John READY, in England, lasted exactly a year. In his role as administrator, Wright carried on routine business, chaired meetings of Council, sent reports to the Colonial Office, acknowledged dispatches, and forwarded petitions and other papers. One of his few decisive actions was the suspension of James Luttrell DesBarres as controller of customs for neglect of duty, complaints having been preferred by Lemuel Cambridge and other Island merchants.

On 12 Nov. 1827 the complex at Bird Island, consisting of a grist-mill, barley mill, sawmill, and distillery, all fitted with extensive machinery, was burnt to the ground by a fire which started in a drying kiln. Much of Charlottetown turned out to fight the fire or observe the spectacle; members of the Fire Engine Company were present in their "caps and tippets" but, unfortunately, without their fire engine; one from the garrison proved insufficient to stanch the flames. According to contemporary reports Wright suffered £1,500 worth of damage and was totally uninsured. Fortunately for George, his brother Charles, the surveyor general, died the following April and he assumed the office, the third member of his family to hold it. Although he remained in business of some sort, making several trips to Bristol, England, in the 1830s, he relied chiefly on his offices and lands to maintain his standard of living.

Wright served as administrator from 19 May 1834 to 29 Sept. 1834 while Lieutenant Governor Sir Aretas William Young* visited England, and again from 2 Dec. 1835 to 30 Aug. 1836 between Young's death and the arrival of Sir John Harvey*. On both occasions he appears to have carried out routine business but not to have taken many initiatives. By the 1830s the land question was in fierce agitation, with the establishment of the Escheat party led by William Cooper*, and remaining uncontroversial was not easy. In one of Wright's few recorded political statements he defended in 1837 an action he had taken as administrator in granting land in Georgetown Royalty, despite resolutions by local inhabitants and the House of Assembly, on the grounds that making grants was standard practice and no rights had been lost by the residents, since they had become enfranchised only after the grants had been made. On the other hand, he joined delegates from the Island in September 1838 in testifying before Lord Durham [LAMBTON] to the evils of the proprietorial system and the need for reform.

Wright served briefly as Island administrator in 1837 and 1841 before and after the tenure of Sir Charles Augustus FitzRoy*. Although it is true that special legislation was subsequently passed to confirm the actions he had taken in 1841, he had not been "without constitutional authority" as one scholar has insisted, since the precedent had long been established that the president of Council headed the administration in the absence of the lieutenant governor.

Hardly a major political figure on the Island, George Wright was an excellent exemplar of the prominence enjoyed by descendants of many of its early officers and of the perpetuation in certain positions of what amounted to hereditary claims (the day after Wright's death his son George* was provisionally appointed surveyor general). He also demonstrated, of course, both plural office holding and the close connection of Island officialdom with proprietorial and business interests. The wonder is that he emerged relatively unscathed from the political imbroglios of his time.

J. M. BUMSTED

PAC, MG 24, B133 (photocopies; copies at PAPEI). PAPEI, Acc. 2810/12; Acc. 3466, marriage licence, 26 Dec. 1807; RG 1, commission books, 72; RG 5, minutes, 10 July 1813, 6 Jan. 1824; petition, 1 July 1806. P.E.I. Museum, File information concerning George Wright. PRO, CO 226/43: 243–45 (mfm. at PAPEI). St Paul's Anglican Church (Charlottetown), Reg. of baptisms, marriages, and burials (mfm. at PAPEI). Lydia Cambridge Wright, "Lydia's perilous landing at St. George's Bay," ed. N. J. de Jong, *Island Magazine* (Charlottetown), no.11 (spring–summer 1982): 3. *Prince Edward Island Gazette*, 16 Aug. 1819, 17 Feb. 1820. *Prince Edward Island Register*, 20 Dec. 1825, 12 Dec. 1826, 13 Nov. 1827. *Royal Gazette* (Charlottetown), 15 March 1842. Duncan Campbell, *History of Prince Edward Island* (Charlottetown, 1875; repr. Belleville, Ont., 1972), 77. *Canada's smallest province: a history of P.E.I.*, ed. F. W. P. Bolger ([Charlottetown, 1973]). MacKinnon, *Government of P.E.I.*, 89. Elinor Vass, "The agricultural societies of Prince Edward Island," *Island Magazine*, no.7 (fall–winter 1979): 31–37.

WRIGHT, PHILEMON, colonizer, farmer, businessman, militia officer, JP, office holder, and politician; b. 3 Sept. 1760 in Woburn, Mass., son of Thomas Wright, a farmer, and Elizabeth Chandler; m. 1782 Abigail Wyman, and they had nine children; d. 3 June 1839 in Hull, Lower Canada.

Philemon Wright's forebear arrived about 1620 in what would become Salem, Mass., and succeeding generations of the family spent their lives at Woburn, where they were engaged mainly in farming. In 1744 Thomas Wright took as his first wife Patiance Richardson, who died four years later leaving him with two children. Philemon was born of his second marriage and was the fifth in a family of seven children. He was only 15 when he joined the rebels in the American War of Independence, and he apparently participated in the battle of Bunker Hill. Like the rest of his family he learned to farm, and around 1796 he owned three pieces of land. He had a few debts, doubtless some savings, and, in addition to his possessions, a strong desire to succeed.

Wright's contact with Jonathan Fassett of Bennington, Vt, might have resulted in a reversal of his plans to immigrate to Lower Canada, where the government was beginning to open lands beyond the seigneuries for settlement. On 12 Aug. 1796 Wright had bought half of Hull, Ripon, Grandison, and Harrington townships from Fassett for £600 sterling. He was unaware at the time that Fassett's land grant had been revoked by the government, but when he was informed he did not lose heart. On 17 April 1797 he petitioned for the grant of Hull Township, undertaking to proceed with a survey and to find associates and settlers. He initially tried to recruit men in Lower Canada, but population pressure there was still too slight to tempt employees – let alone settlers – to move somewhere as distant as the Ottawa region. He finally found his eight associates at Woburn and the surrounding area, choosing them from among and beyond his family and relatives. According to the common practice, the associates, who had received 1,200 acres of land, each handed 1,000 over to Wright. The final deed of grant was not signed until 3 Jan. 1806 and actually referred to less than a quarter of Hull Township, which contained 82,429 acres altogether.

On 20 March 1800, after taking the oath of loyalty along with the rest of his party, Wright reached the spot where the town of Wrightstown (Hull) would be built; with him were 37 men, 5 women, and 21 children, as well as 14 horses and 8 oxen. In addition to the associates and the 18 members of his immediate family there were about 10 labourers. When Wright took the first steps to settle Hull Township, he had a particular vision of the future. Agriculture not only was a traditionally valued activity in the milieu from which he came, but also seemed to fit with his concept of his own role in the building of a new society which would rest upon agriculture and landed property. Moreover, at the time he started his settlement, wheat was one of the two bases of Lower Canada's export trade, the other being furs. Lumbering still represented only a secondary element in the economy. Even after 1806, when the timber trade became the predominant commercial activity, Wright continued to preach the stabilizing virtues of agriculture in economic life. His view is understandable, since in a region as distant and isolated as Hull, farming proved indispensable for securing the inhabitants' subsistence at reasonable prices and even for lumbering operations and for the industries he dreamed of establishing.

Wright saw his ownership of a large amount of land as the essential condition for encouraging the growth of agricultural production and of other sectors. He did not intend to leave actual development of the region to others. He therefore constantly tried to increase his own domain, even if parts had to remain undeveloped for a while. By 1835 his family in various ways controlled 57,879 acres of Hull Township, 14,013 of which belonged to Wright himself, and he owned 22,965 acres in neighbouring townships. In thus accumulating real estate for himself, Wright sought neither the role of speculator nor the trappings of the gentry or nobility. Hence his hunger for land did not keep him from being quite liberal with fellow New Englanders who accompanied him or came to join him. Nor did it lead him to frustrate the hopes for land of the immigrants who arrived later in substantial numbers from Scotland and particularly from Ireland. In 1806 only 1,021 acres in Hull belonged to the settlers, whereas 12,190 acres were owned by the Wrights. In 1842, three years after Philemon's death, the family held 38,552 acres and the settlers 15,054.

The accusations of corruption levelled against Wright after his appointment as land agent in 1819 probably had some foundation but, contrary to the claims made, his actions did not stem from a desire to speculate. Wright's need for reserves of timber was proving to be substantial, but he also had to make land grants. To farm his own land, operate his lumber camps, transport his wood to Quebec, and run his mills, he required a sizeable pool of cheap seasonal labour. Many immigrants would be satisfied with renting on the concessions or taking up lots in the villages founded by the Wrights. Most of them, however, could not make a living or be persuaded to stay in Hull unless they had access to ownership of land; with land, it was still possible for them to enjoy a supplementary income unconnected with farming. Wright had 120 men working for him in 1817, whereas the other 68 families in the township hired only 15 labourers. Three years later the Wrights employed 164 men and 11 women. In addition they gave work to seven masons, six carpenters, four blacksmiths, two joiners, two tanners, a baker, a saddler, and two clerks. In 1820 more than half the adult male population of the township was in the pay of the Wrights.

Wright played a role of prime importance in the economic development upon which the very survival of his township depended. In his first year he cleared enough land to harvest a good crop of potatoes and wheat. At that time he lost 1,000 bushels of potatoes because of improper storage but, in compensation, his wheat yielded 40 bushels an acre. In this early stage of settlement, Wright could count on profits from his production of hemp, a crop that the British government subsidized for a number of years and that he had great success in growing. In 1808 his mills burned down, but he spared no expense in rebuilding them. In 1813 the wheat crop alone produced 3,000 bushels. Seven years later, 35,785 bushels were harvested on his farms, which were renowned in Lower Canada; grown less and less on his land from 1810, wheat made up only 13 per cent of the crop, whereas potatoes constituted 74.3 per cent. In 1823 this record, unsurpassed in the colony, was again exceeded: the grain crops from the Wright farms reached 71,630 bushels, a figure that then represented 50 to 60 per cent of the grain harvested in the township. In the course of the 1830s, however, production dropped considerably on the Wrights' land. Although soil depletion may have played a part in this set-back, other factors were at work. Not only were the sons less interested in agriculture than their father, but the inhabitants of the township and the Wrights cleared no new land for a score of years after 1831. This reverse must be linked as well with the rise in production costs due to the demand for labour to build the Rideau Canal and improve navigation on the Ottawa River between Hull and Montreal.

Wright had developed the agricultural base for lumbering after 1806 not only through producing oats, potatoes, and at certain times corn, but also through raising a great many cattle by the most advanced methods used in the United States and Great Britain. In 1814 the Wrights' herds numbered 295 animals, 45 per cent cattle and the rest horses, sheep, pigs, or goats. Ten years later there were 1,189 animals – 35 per cent of the township's total. Towards the end of the 1820s, however, the family withdrew rather quickly from this sector of activity, probably because they could not beat competition from outside or from the local inhabitants. In 1830 the number of animals in their herds had dropped by 50 per cent and constituted no more than 11.6 per cent of the total in the township.

Wright played such a central role in the economy of Hull Township that his participation in the import and retail trade, innkeeping, and light industry followed naturally. To this enterprising man, building grist, hemp, and carding mills or establishing a distillery, tannery, and shoemaker's shop seemed quite normal offshoots of extensive involvement in agricultural production, as did the founding of an agriculture society. Equipping smithies, a sawmill, and a potashery and constructing a huge store as well as the Columbia Hotel also formed part of a strategy to develop his economic force.

However Wright might extol in bucolic vein the benefits of agriculture, the basis of his unrivalled power was more and more to be found in lumbering. In 1806, when the timber business expanded in Lower Canada and the Maritimes as a result of the continental blockade, Wright observed, "It was time for me to look out for an export market to cover my imports." That was the year he had his first rafts of square timber floated down from Hull to the port of Quebec. To increase the efficiency of his ventures he founded the firm of Philemon Wright and Sons in 1814, with his sons Tiberius, Philemon, and Ruggles. During the 1820s he sent four or five rafts a year to Quebec, and in the next decade eight or nine. At the beginning he bought his wood primarily from settlers, but as marketable timber became scarcer on their lands he was forced to turn increasingly to his own camps for his supply. Obviously, everything related to the forest industry was of the greatest interest to the founder of Hull Township. Whether as an individual, a township leader, or a representative of the *grand voyer* (chief road commissioner) of the province, he assisted in developing the road systems in the township and even in the Ottawa region. To avoid waterfalls and rapids, which damaged his wood, Wright devised chutes later bought by the government. In 1819 he even built a steamship, the *Union of the Ottawa*, which was used for towing his rafts on the Ottawa River. Needless to say, this powerful man had frequent contacts, friendly or otherwise, with all the timber operators in the valley: the Hamiltons, Gilmours, Egans, Aumonds, Moores, McConnells, and many others. His influence and initiative were such that it is difficult to imagine even a secondary enterprise being established in the region at this period without his participation. He had founded a brickworks in 1814, and a cement factory shortly afterwards. Late in 1826 he became president of the new Hull Mining Company, which had been formed to work local iron ore deposits. Among its directors were John Mactaggart*, Alexander James CHRISTIE, Thomas McKay*, John Redpath*, and Robert Drummond*. Naturally, activity as feverish and extensive as Wright's did not produce all the results anticipated, and a good many of his ventures were short-lived. There were indeed moments, as in 1829 and just before his death, when Wright seemingly was on the verge of bankruptcy. None the less his accomplishments, lasting in many respects, show that economic development requires vigorous and imaginative leadership as well as favourable circumstances.

Wright's economic power was so far-reaching that it must be seen as permeating the entire lives of the township's inhabitants. For instance, when the government had to choose militia officers, it could not avoid turning to Wright, who was appointed captain in the Argenteuil battalion of militia in 1808. His sons Ruggles and Tiberius and his sons-in-law became officers in this unit around 1822. The same phenomenon occurred when the responsibilities of justice of the peace had to be entrusted to respectable persons in the township: in 1806 the governor appointed Wright. In 1821 it was the turn of Ruggles, and ten years later that of Tiberius and Wright's son-in-law Thomas Brigham. It is not surprising that in 1817 Wright became commissioner for the summary trial of small causes, an office assumed in 1835 by his nephew Charles Symmes and Brigham.

An analysis of the accumulation of power and influence by one man and one family in a new community would be incomplete if it took no account of social dimensions. Wright was also interested in education. It was through him that the Royal Institution for the Advancement of Learning was asked in 1808 to establish a school at Hull, a task entrusted to Robert Chambers. Chambers began teaching in a house built by Wright, but the unstable state of this fledgling rural community made things difficult for the schoolmaster. The venture was suspended four times before a fee-paying school was set up for some ten families in 1819. Although another Royal school was opened after 1820, instruction was not provided on a more regular basis until the following decade.

Although a believer, Wright was scarcely a religious person, yet he did not divorce himself completely from the various religious currents that circulated in Hull Township over the years. Baptists, Presbyterians, Congregationalists, Methodists, Anglicans, and Catholics were all present. First were the Congregationalists, a group to which Wright originally belonged but which was slow in getting organized to spread its message. Then came the Methodist preachers, who provided religious services irregularly from 1809 to 1823 to a population with few of their denomination. It was not until 1823 that six or seven citizens of Hull thought of founding a Methodist society. Wright, who was uneasy about the loose organization of the churches, would have been disposed to accept a resident minister of any faith. Although on occasion he spoke at Sunday religious meetings, he gradually came to favour the body that in his view better represented the spirit of the social class with which he was now associated, the Church of England. It was for this reason that Wright played such an important role in financial and other ways in the construction of the Anglican church at Wrightstown, which was completed in 1832. He distanced himself thereby from the religious affiliations of the less well-to-do, in particular the Irish and the French Canadians, whether Methodist or Catholic.

Few areas escaped the attentions of the leader of Hull Township. When prominent figures in the community were thinking of founding a masonic lodge in 1813, they hastened to suggest to Wright that he serve as master. To crown his achievements, Wright wanted to play a political role befitting his position and his rank in society. Accordingly he secured his election to the House of Assembly of Lower Canada for Ottawa riding in 1830. Having attended in the house quite regularly for four years, he decided not to seek re-election. He was never called to sit on the Legislative Council.

For 40 years Philemon Wright wielded a power close to absolute and universal in a region he had shaped to match his ideas and interests. He achieved this result because he had involved himself in every aspect of development in Hull Township; nothing of any importance had escaped his vigilance. The only people able in some degree to share his power were the members of his family. Ruggles was to take over from him; Philemon had died in 1821, and Tiberius and Christopher Columbus went to their graves soon after their father, in 1841 and 1843 respectively. Ruggles never played a role comparable to his father's, however. Two of Wright's daughters, Abigail (1796–1877), who married Thomas Brigham, and Christiana (1803–71), who married Jacob L. Morrison, survived him. The sole opposition to his authority came from Charles Symmes, the nephew who founded Aylmer. Symmes used the rivalries between the two communities to lead the struggle against the influence and power wielded by Wright on the local level and in the political sphere.

FERNAND OUELLET and BENOÎT THÉRIAULT

Philemon Wright is the author of "An account of the first settlement of the township of Hull, on the Ottawa River, L.C. . . . ," *Canadian Magazine and Literary Repository* (Montreal), 3 (July–December 1824): 234–46.

ANQ-O, M-122-9, 9 juin 1839; P-2. PAC, MG 24, D8, 6, 33, 112–13, 120, 124, 126, 129–30; RG 1, L3[L], 1–2, 7, 88, 208; RG 31, C1, 1825, 1842, 1851, Hull Township. L.C., House of Assembly, *Journals*, 1823–24, app.R. P. M. O. Evans, *The Wrights: a genealogical study of the first settlers in Canada's National Capital Region* (Ottawa, 1978). Lucien Brault, *Hull, 1800–1950* (Ottawa, 1950). E.-E. Cinq-Mars, *Hull, son origine, ses progrès, son avenir* (Hull, Qué., 1908). C. H. Craigie, "The influence of the timber trade and Philemon Wright on the social and economic development of Hull Township, 1800–1850" (MA thesis, Carleton Univ., Ottawa, 1969). Ouellet, *Hist. économique*. Léo Rossignol, "Histoire documentaire de Hull, 1792–

1900" (thèse de PHD, univ. d'Ottawa, 1941). B. S. Elliott, "'The famous township of Hull': image and aspirations of a pioneer Quebec community," *SH*, 12 (1979): 339–67.

WYATT, CHARLES BURTON, office holder; b. *c.* 1778 in London, son of James Wyatt, a renowned architect, and Rachel Lunn; m. 29 March 1805 Mary Rogers, and they had five children; divorced 1811 by Scottish decree on grounds of cruel conduct on his part; remarried; d. 4 Sept. 1840 in Barston, England.

Charles Burton Wyatt spent his childhood in London and at the country estate of his distinguished family. From 1799 to 1801 he served as a writer with the East India Company. In May 1804, partly through his father's influence, he was appointed surveyor general of Upper Canada, succeeding David William SMITH. His new position was worth £300 annually plus fees. The latter, however, had been diminished prior to his arrival with the suspension on 13 Jan. 1804 of the surveyor general's commission on surveys. Wyatt was already in financial difficulty and he feared that "my marriage without my father's consent, may be the means of depriving me of that ample supply of money, which, had the matter been otherwise I should have enjoyed on my arrival in America." None the less, his father financed his purchase of Smith's house in York (Toronto) for £750.

In November 1806 Wyatt complained to Colonial Secretary William Windham about the reduction in his fees. Within his own office, he accused William CHEWETT, the deputy surveyor general, of having made a poor survey of the tract purchased from the Mississaugas in 1805 [*see* Kineubenae*]. Moreover, he raised the ire of Lieutenant Governor Francis Gore* by bringing the issue before the House of Assembly rather than the executive. In September 1806 Wyatt's other assistant, clerk Thomas Gibbs Ridout*, had expressed dissatisfaction with his position. Wyatt first sought to replace him and ultimately, in defiance of Gore and the Executive Council, dismissed him on 31 December. Gore, on the advice of the council, ordered his reinstatement, but Wyatt refused, insisting "it is incompatible with my Commission, my own Security, and that of the Public." On 19 Jan. 1807 Wyatt was suspended by Gore and, in due course, was removed. He left the province early in February.

Wyatt's struggle with Gore involved a clash in interpretation of the prerogatives inherent in crown commissions. Wyatt believed there was a right vested in his commission which put him at liberty to conduct the affairs of his office without prior executive approval. Gore, the council, and Solicitor General D'Arcy Boulton* thought that his power was indeed restricted by his commission and that he could not replace clerks in his office who had been appointed by the crown or its representatives. The specific issue took on political interest since it was believed that Wyatt had dismissed Ridout for voting against Mr Justice Robert THORPE in the by-election to replace William Weekes*. Wyatt was properly identified with a number of the administration's strongest critics, including Thorpe and Joseph Willcocks*.

As surveyor general, Wyatt had also been directly involved with the legacy of protest arising from an attempt early in the decade by Lieutenant Governor Peter Hunter* to limit loyalist claims for land. Sympathizing with Hunter's critics, he believed that successive governors had overturned imperial policy. His own suspension was, he thought, a similar example of imperial policy being thwarted by local, and improper, action. Yet he had only "a sincere and zealous desire to the best of my judgment & ability to do the duties intrusted to me with fidelity benefit & honor to myself & my employers as well as the public."

Wyatt immediately returned to England to fight the suspension and to seek redress. His family had better connections than Gore and he expected, and got, its help in his complaint through official channels. The suspension had been based on the broad charge "of general opposition" and the specific one of having erased a name from a land location book in order to insert his own. The former proved too sweeping for him to handle. As for the latter, he had taken all the necessary steps to check the ownership of the lot and on this charge he was vindicated.

Describing himself as a victim of "colonial despotism" unable to obtain redress officially, Wyatt brought a law suit against Gore in England in June 1814. He charged that Gore had suspended him "maliciously, and without probable cause," had sent "false representations to the government," and had libelled him with claims of "disaffection . . . and general misconduct in his office." On 11 July 1816 the presiding judge ruled that Wyatt had not proved his case with respect to the suspension; however, he found Gore guilty of libel and awarded Wyatt damages of £300. Two years later Thorpe also won damages in a similar suit against Gore.

During the early 1830s Wyatt lived in pecuniary distress in Essex. He moved to Warwickshire in 1836, to live in retirement with his "amiable wife." He had long been troubled by a disease of the bladder and spent his final five months "in great pain." Historians have generally agreed that Wyatt was a man who overestimated both his influence and his security, and who misunderstood his position. Yet as historian Gerald Marquis Craig observes, "Perhaps his greatest offence had been his friendship with the malcontents, especially Thorpe." Other difficulties arose from Wyatt's concern that his department's practices with respect to both Indians and loyalists were at variance with imperial policy. In the final analysis, his political connections were not strong enough to sustain him on either side of the Atlantic.

ELWOOD H. JONES

AO, MS 88. MTRL, W. D. Powell papers; D. W. Smith papers. PAC, RG 1, E3, 93. PRO, CO 42/350. W. W. Baldwin, "A recovered letter: W. W. Baldwin to C. B. Wyatt, 6th April, 1813," ed. J. McE. Murray, *OH*, 35 (1943): 49–55. [Richard Cartwright], *Letters, from an American loyalist in Upper-Canada, to his friend in England; on a pamphlet published by John Mills Jackson, esquire: entitled, "A view of the province of Upper Canada"* (Halifax, [1810]). Joseph Farington, *The Farington diary*, ed. James Greig (8v., London, [1923–28]). Clement Gatley, *Gatley on libel and slander*, ed. R. [L.] McEwen and P. [S. C.] Lewis (7th ed., London, 1974). [J. M. Jackson], *A view of the political situation of the province of Upper Canada . . .* (London, 1809). "Political state of U.C.," PAC *Report*, 1892: 32–135. John Strachan, *The John Strachan letter book, 1812–1834*, ed. G. W. Spragge (Toronto, 1946). *Town of York, 1793–1815* (Firth). H. M. Colvin, *A biographical dictionary of English architects, 1660–1840* (2v., London, 1954). Antony Dale, *James Wyatt, architect, 1746–1813* (Oxford, 1956). Derek Linstrum, *Sir Jeffry Wyatville* (Oxford, 1972). H. H. Guest, "Upper Canada's first political party," *OH*, 54 (1962): 275–96. G. [H.] Patterson, "Whiggery, nationality, and the Upper Canadian reform tradition," *CHR*, 56 (1975): 25–44.

Y

YOUNG, JOHN, merchant, author, and politician; b. 1 Sept. 1773 in Falkirk, Scotland, son of William Young, a merchant, and Janet ——; m. Agnes Renny, and they had nine children, three of whom survived to adulthood; d. 6 Oct. 1837 in Halifax.

Around 1790 John Young entered the University of Glasgow, where he performed brilliantly in the theological course but did not graduate. Although he wished to study medicine, his father, who had hoped that he would become a Presbyterian minister, refused him further support. The young man then engaged in business at Falkirk and later at Glasgow, with no particular success.

It is likely that Young decided to emigrate to Nova Scotia because he was impressed with the commercial prosperity engendered by the War of 1812. On 30 April 1814 he arrived at Halifax with his wife and four sons, and immediately turned his attention to the disposal of a large stock of dry goods he had brought with him. Shortly thereafter he began a business under the name of John Young and Company. In September, British forces took Castine (Maine), and the customs office they established there allowed trade to be resumed between the Maritime provinces and New England. Seeing the opportunity, Young went to Castine, and during the eight months of British occupation he carried on "a thriving trade both legally and illegally." His son William*, who was barely 15, was his agent in Halifax, responsible for shipping the British goods imported by the firm to Castine, where Young was assisted by another son, 12-year-old George Renny*. The profits from Castine were used to develop the business at Halifax, but Young intimated to William that he would move to the United States if prospects were good. Indeed, just after the war William was his agent in New York for a brief period.

Young's correspondence during this period reveals a shrewd business mind preoccupied with success. His outlook is demonstrated in a letter to William, whom he advised to give the appearance of liberality, to be accurate in transactions, to study the characters of people in order to make the best bargains, and to "exercise a rigid economy." Young was pleased with his sons' developing commercial sense, and both continued in business for several years. Their letters show the family to be close-knit and affectionate.

The prosperity which the War of 1812 had brought to Nova Scotia evaporated soon after its end, plunging the province into depression. The distress experienced by farmers when the wartime demands of the military for beef, pork, and hay ceased was exacerbated by an unusually wet summer and a plague of field-mice in 1815 and by the famous "summerless year" of 1816. The government was obliged to import and distribute seeds. Although the harvest improved in 1817, agriculture remained in a low state the following year, the more so because of the long-standing belief that Nova Scotia was not good farming country. There were many, a contemporary writer claimed, who were convinced that the province "was only fit for pasturage, and would never repay the expense of regular cultivation."

The need to improve provincial agriculture impressed itself on Young. He had come to Nova Scotia with limited practical experience in farming through his work for Sir John Sinclair, a pioneer in Scottish agricultural reform, and he seems to have had a sound theoretical knowledge, apparently based on Sir Humphry Davy's *Elements of agricultural chemistry* (London, 1813) and Antoine-Laurent Lavoisier's *Traité élémentaire de chimie* (Paris, 1789). His comparison of the low state of farming in Nova Scotia with the excellence of Scottish agriculture, which one 20th-century commentator has described as "the most skilful . . . to be found anywhere" at the time, persuaded him to take action. He decided to make suggestions for improvement, and on 25 July 1818 he began a series of letters to the Halifax newspaper the *Acadian Recorder* under the pen-name of Agricola.

In his first letter Young suggested that local agricultural societies be formed. The next recommended the establishment of a central board of agriculture, to which the local societies should "look up, as the prime director of their movements, and as the focus of their converging influence and collected energy." He argued that agricultural societies had done much good elsewhere, and suggested that the proposed societies hold competitions in different categories of farming and award premiums. The fourth letter invited correspondence from "competent farmers," who were requested to sign their names, give the date and their place of residence, and describe the results of any experiments performed. In subsequent letters Young undertook a discussion of the factors affecting vegetation and tillage, beginning with observations on climate and soil and then reviewing agricultural machines, the clearing of land, and operations such as ploughing and harrowing. Throughout he suggested areas where Nova Scotia practices could be improved, particularly in farm equipment, the state of the land, summer fallow, and crop rotation. He intended to take up also livestock and miscellaneous topics, but by the time the letters stopped in the spring of 1821 even the section on vegetation and tillage had not been completed. A total of 64 letters was written, and 38 were collected in a book published in 1822.

It seems likely that the letters of Agricola were prompted not only by the state of agriculture but also by Young's hope of commercial advancement if with his efforts he obtained the patronage "of the classes of the metropolis who were regarded with respect." At all events, he evoked considerable enthusiasm. Hundreds responded to his request for letters, and by December 1818 agricultural societies had appeared in four counties. Moreover, Lieutenant Governor Lord Dalhousie [Ramsay], himself a keen farmer, praised his efforts. In correspondence with Agricola, whose identity was as yet unknown, Dalhousie urged him to call a meeting which would draw up a constitution for a provincial agricultural society. At a banquet of the North British Society on 30 Nov. 1818 he toasted Agricola and suggested that an agricultural society be formed in Halifax.

Dalhousie's interest proved decisive: a meeting was held on 15 December to organize a provincial agricultural society which would be a model for others to be formed and a source of information on farming. Many of the élite were among the 120 persons who became members; Dalhousie was named president and Agricola secretary. Young claimed that he was unprepared for the nomination, having "heard all the encomiums passed in the course of the discussion with the most immovable indifference. . . . But any tolerable judge of human nature might have discovered the unknown 'Agricola' in the involuntary heat and flush of his countenance at this appointment."

At the meeting plans were made to apply to the legislature for a constitution. In March 1819 Dalhousie approved a bill which incorporated the Central Board of Agriculture for seven years, and nine months later the legislature granted the constitution. The board's duties were to correspond with the county societies, publish useful information on farming, stimulate competition by offering premiums for improvements, and import and distribute livestock, implements, and seeds. In December Young, who had by then revealed his identity, was elected secretary and treasurer by acclamation.

The board began operation with high expectations, for besides the several hundred pounds raised by subscriptions to membership, it could draw on the £1,500 the legislature granted in 1819. Young hoped to meet expenses from these sources, and he wished to use £500 of the grant as prizes to individuals who demonstrated in competition that they had excelled in improving the quality of their livestock or produce. As secretary and treasurer, he received a salary of £250 a year, having argued that he had to neglect his own business for the work of the board. Not only did he handle all the board's correspondence and finances, but he was also responsible for ensuring that contests were held to judge vegetables, flax, seeds, and dairy products, that ploughing matches and livestock shows were in accordance with the board's regulations, and that premiums were awarded for growing cereals, clearing land, fallowing in summer, fertilizing, and erecting oatmeal mills. The meetings of the directors of the board also required preparation. Members sometimes brought new farm implements; discussions would be held as to their relative merits and a decision on their purchase made. The directors wisely devoted a small part of the board's private funds to the formation of a library of agricultural works.

By 1825, 30 local societies had been formed, 19 in the years 1818 to 1820. Their organization paralleled that of the board, each having a president, vice-president, and secretary, and they accepted the obligation to perform a certain number of experiments each year. Expenses were to be met through subscriptions, and initially the response was very good. Some assistance was granted by the board, such as the cost of maintaining purebred breeding stock over a period of time. Officials of the local societies corresponded regularly with Young and sometimes borrowed money from the board to buy new seed or implements.

Despite the promising beginning, interest in agricultural affairs slackened after 1820, although local societies were being formed as late as 1824. One indication of the decline came in November 1822, when it was moved at a board meeting that the implements of husbandry used as models should be sold. A few months later plans were under way to dispose of the stallion imported by the board. Membership in the board dropped steadily, from 235 in 1819 to 79 in 1824. The following year the House of Assembly refused to continue the annual grant to the board which it had made since 1819, and in 1826 it voted down a bill to renew the board's charter, ending government support of agriculture for the time being. Several local societies collapsed soon afterwards.

There were a number of reasons for the failure of the agriculture societies. One of the more important was Young's inability to carry out his duties as secretary and treasurer efficiently because of his involvement in other activities. His interest in agriculture had not prevented him from seeking to expand his commercial operations, his pious protestations to the contrary. Indeed, as is amply demonstrated in his papers, he had a deeper commitment to business than to agriculture. While working for the board he continued to import and sell dry goods, and he also traded in fish and lumber. Moreover, he tendered to supply manure to the Halifax garrison, and he held a contract for removing ashes from the barracks.

The criticisms that Young encountered as secretary and treasurer came partly as a result of delays in his responses to letters, but there were also occasional expressions of dissatisfaction with his methods of bookkeeping, with delays in the forwarding of supplies, and with a lack of information about competitions. In addition, Young too often failed in his responsibility to import and distribute seeds and livestock. Animals and fruit-trees were frequently dead on arrival at the local societies because Young had not arranged their transport with sufficient care. Seeds were sometimes shipped too late in the season and were not always in good condition. Inferior livestock might be substituted for a higher quality breed already paid for by the local societies. These derelictions of duty cost Young dearly, and during the final years of the board the farmers' attitude towards him was one of growing disappointment. Requests by local societies for an equal share of the government grant were refused by Young on the grounds that "the independent gentlemen and wealthy merchants" of Halifax were alone competent to handle those funds. Such patronizing only worsened the increasingly poor relationship between Young and the farming population, to whom he occasionally referred as "our Peasantry." It also gave credence to the charge that he was more interested in promoting himself with the élite of Halifax than in assisting the average farmer.

But Young also faced opposition within the board. He was under attack from colleagues such as William LAWSON for being both secretary and treasurer and for receiving a salary. The difficulties in acquiring suitable breeding stock and good seeds at reasonable prices and the delays in shipping and in the collection of accounts were all blamed on Young at one time or another. He was responsible for some of the problems, especially the late collection of accounts. There is little doubt, moreover, that he took personal advantage of his position. For example, in 1821 he sent his son William to Boston on behalf of the board to purchase livestock, and then as treasurer approved William's large bill for expenses. In 1819 he had purchased a farm near Halifax called Willow Park, and persuaded his fellow directors to make it the board's model farm. He was thus permitted to utilize the board's seeds, livestock, and implements and could cut his own costs. He also entered produce raised on the farm in competitions and won many prizes, some of which, however, he gave to the board.

The assumed superiority in Young's correspondence with societies was occasionally evident in his articles and added to his difficulties. A major criticism of his writing was that it was often arrogant and didactic. When establishing the rules for correspondents in the fourth Agricola letter, Young described them as constituting "the rampart in which Agricola has entrenched himself, that he may accomplish his scheme without disturbance, and be freed from the annoyance of doltish imbecillity." Although Young interpreted and explained sources well, his writings were aimed at the educated élite, and he did not express himself in a style the average farmer could follow easily. As a correspondent to the *Acadian Recorder* complained in 1823, "He never descends from his aerial heighth, but is always declaiming in the loftiest language of impassioned feeling." As a result some farmers lost interest in Young's ideas.

Nowhere was the effect of Young's personality better illustrated than in a controversy surrounding letters in the Halifax *Free Press*. Beginning in January 1819, a number of pseudonymous articles questioned some of Young's theories on agriculture. Young overreacted and, believing James Cuppaidge Cochran*, James William Johnston*, and others to be responsible, threatened to expose them as the force behind the *Free Press* unless they stopped their attacks. His critics responded with further articles, some of them particularly humorous, pointing out that Young's stately manner of expression, his intolerance of dissent, and the awarding of prizes were doing little to promote agriculture. Young's sensitivities were not soothed by his critics' indifference to his threats, and he was privately admonished by Cochran to "learn to bear with contradiction as wiser men have been obliged to do before you . . . let vanity no longer be the preponderating feeling of your character."

Despite the many attacks on Young, he had his share of supporters, who included Dalhousie, Lieutenant Governor Sir James Kempt*, judge William Hersey Otis Haliburton*, and a number of farmers throughout the province. Though Young undoubtedly deserved much of the criticism, it cannot be denied that he drew attention to the strengths and weaknesses of agriculture in Nova Scotia. By 1824 the local societies, while not having realized all of their initial ambitions, were certainly more conscious of the need for improvement in agricultural practices. Young's columns were not easily read by the average farmer, but correspondence from officers of local societies to Young indicates that they understood his articles and could transfer his knowledge to others. This dissemination of information is what Young hoped to accomplish, and although his writings did not yield the results desired or expected the experiment was certainly worthwhile. The information gathered at all levels was most impressive, and Young made it available to the public. More people were made conscious of the complexity of agriculture and became aware that it was not simply an occupation of the ignorant.

Agricola's writings appeared at a time when Nova Scotians were undergoing what has been described as "an intellectual awakening" and must be seen in that context. The Stepsure letters of Thomas McCulloch began appearing in the *Acadian Recorder* just as Young's were ending. In this series of satirical essays McCulloch used his main character, Mephibosheth Stepsure, to extol the virtues of pastoral life, hard work, and frugality, all of which, Young implied, were necessary for success.

The demise of the Central Board of Agriculture cannot be made solely the responsibility of Young, though his personality, other preoccupations, and reluctance to allow greater autonomy to the local societies all militated against success. Dalhousie's involvement was vital to the initial success of the project, for as long as he remained in Nova Scotia he displayed a keen interest in the board and faithfully attended its meetings. Had he remained after 1820 he might have prolonged its existence, but although his successor, Kempt, made his contribution, the first flush of enthusiasm cooled considerably without Dalhousie.

Between 1819 and 1826 the Central Board and local societies spent more than £7,000 of public money in addition to what they raised by their own efforts. Some £2,500 was distributed as premiums and prizes, £490 was given to the builders of oatmeal mills, £422 was spent on seeds, and £72 was voted for books on agriculture. The board, however, made mistakes. The import of seeds was discontinued in 1821 because of their poor quality and late arrival, as was the awarding of prizes for clearing the forest when it was realized that this work was proceeding too fast. There were also disagreements about the selection of breeding stock, and its import was stopped after 1821, as were the cattle shows held in different parts of the province. The most important objective of the Central Board was to make Nova Scotia self-sufficient in wheat. Too much emphasis was placed on this goal and it was never realized, perhaps because it was either premature or unrealistic.

From its inception the board had faced difficulties with numerous groups in the colony. Many farmers were unable to resist the pull of tradition. Consequently, they continued to bring land into production instead of working to increase soil productivity through the adoption of new methods of farming. Fishing communities, mainly in the western half of the province, questioned the annual grant to agriculture when their own industry did not receive anything comparable. Merchants were attracted to Young's articles when they first appeared because they desired an agricultural revival as a means of overcoming the existing economic depression. However, in 1818 legislative changes in Britain permitted the colonies to import American foodstuffs through designated free ports, of which Halifax was one. Nova Scotians no longer had to worry about prohibitions on American produce and hence did not feel the urgent necessity to increase agricultural production at home. Moreover, by 1825 it was evident that the British trend towards freer trade, as shown in the changes in the imperial trade regulations that year, would draw attention away from agriculture and towards trade and commerce.

Long before he completed the Agricola letters, Young had shown an interest in politics, and he had seriously considered standing for the assembly in 1820. In 1823 he ran unsuccessfully in Halifax Township. During this campaign, in which he was opposed by Charles Rufus Fairbanks, it was divulged that Young's son William, who was apprenticed to Fairbanks's law firm, had communicated the strategy of Fairbanks's campaign to his father. As a result Young had to use his influence with Chief Justice Sampson Salter Blowers and other judges to obtain William's release from his indenture.

Young entered the political arena again in 1824, this time in a by-election in Sydney County. Although he was victorious, soon after he took his seat on 15 Feb. 1825 petitions were forwarded to the house which contended that he was not a freeholder in the county and complained of election irregularities. An assembly committee declared the election invalid, but Young was returned in the subsequent vote, and he was allowed to take his seat on 1 Feb. 1826 without further difficulty. Nevertheless, his residence in Halifax caused dissatisfaction to many of his constituents, and as early as April 1826 Thomas Cutler of Guysborough warned him of potential trouble over this issue.

As an assemblyman Young did not hesitate to

express his opinion, and he usually gave a worthwhile exposition. A late 19th-century commentator felt that he sustained his positions with "clear and lucid oratory," and he would occasionally show a fine sense of humour. On the other hand, his discussions were longer than necessary and he was too insistent on giving the impression that he was standing on principle. One early subject of his attention was Pictou Academy. Although he supported the principle of a grant to the academy and was prepared to see it obtain the same aid as other institutions, he consistently opposed making the grant a permanent one. His opposition stemmed from the split between the Church of Scotland, to which he belonged, and the dissenting Presbyterians, one of whom was Pictou Academy's president, Thomas McCulloch. But he was mindful of the needs of his co-religionists as a whole, and in 1827 he spoke in favour of giving Presbyterian clergy full rights to perform marriages.

During the "Brandy Dispute" of 1830 [*see* Enos Collins*] Young upheld the rights of the assembly in its confrontation with the Council, arguing that his constituents and others would suffer unduly from the loss of tax revenue which the dispute might cause. He was returned in the election of that year, and during the sessions of the fourteenth assembly spoke out often. He was particularly active in scrutinizing expenditures, the more so where patronage might be involved. During the early 1830s the Shubenacadie Canal [*see* Charles Rufus Fairbanks], the salaries of custom-house officials, quitrents, banks, and currency drew his attention and comments. He also complained that Halifax received a disproportionately large share of the provincial revenue. In 1835 he advised where money could be saved through the abolition of unnecessary positions and spoke of retrenchment, pointing out that good business practices could make good sense in government.

Young followed his assembly speeches on retrenchment with 20 letters to the *Acadian Recorder* under the pseudonym of Joe Warner. In them he stated that the assembly needed members who sought reform and who would carry out the will of the people; his second purpose was to warn the public of the dangers of electing too many lawyers, whom he considered too self-serving to be effective members. He criticized harshly the manner in which public money was spent and stated that the waste of it by the house stemmed in part from the collaboration between certain assemblymen and the Council. His assault on the speaker of the assembly, Samuel George William ARCHIBALD, was especially virulent, since he accused him of using his position to advance his own interests. Some of the differences between the two men undoubtedly arose out of their opposing positions on Pictou Academy.

The election of 1836 was a difficult one for Young. His constituency of Sydney County had been divided that year, and he ran in the part which is now Antigonish County. The resentment against his non-residence surfaced once more, and at the end of the second day of polling he was a poor third of three candidates. That evening a delegation of his supporters visited Bishop William Fraser*, the Roman Catholic vicar apostolic of Nova Scotia, who lived in Antigonish, and suggested that he make his views on the election known. The following morning Fraser gave his support to Young, enabling the latter to salvage second place and one of the two seats. The reasons for Fraser's intervention are difficult to determine. It may be that he supported Young out of personal friendship and his appreciation of Young's efforts in 1830 to remove disabilities against Roman Catholics. Without Fraser's help, Young would certainly have lost.

When the new assembly convened on 31 Jan. 1837, Young was present. Although not in good health, he participated effectively in debate, opposing a bill to prevent the export of grain and potatoes, proposing a reduction in the salaries of the clerks of the house, and moving the appointment of a joint committee to examine public accounts. The major issue of the session centred on resolutions by the assembly condemning the Council for not allowing the public into its discussions when it acted in a legislative capacity. After the Council refused to consider the matter and implied that the assembly could be disciplined, Young introduced two resolutions designed to avoid a direct confrontation with the upper chamber such as had occurred in 1830. Joseph Howe* thought that Young's resolutions did not resolve the assembly's difficulties, and brought in 12 resolutions of his own which were both broader and more specific than Young's. Young supported the adoption of Howe's resolutions, but he may have regretted that Howe and not he reaped the glory of the moment.

By June 1837 Young's health had deteriorated to the point where most of his time was spent sitting in bed or an easy chair. He wrote to his son George Renny in August that he had improved, but he passed away at Willow Park on 6 October.

John Young in many respects epitomized the well-educated individual who arrived in the colonies and saw opportunities that others had overlooked or lacked the confidence to grasp. In his early advice to his sons he suggested that people were motivated by self-interest; such motivation often seemed to influence his own career in Nova Scotia. However, in reconciling his goals with the public interest he performed useful services for his adopted land.

R. A. MACLEAN

John Young published, under the pseudonym of Agricola, *The letters of Agricola on the principles of vegetation and tillage, written for Nova Scotia, and published first in the "Acadian Recorder" by John Young, secretary of the Provincial Agricultural Board* . . . (Halifax, 1822).

NLS, Dept. of MSS, MS 790. PANS, MG 1, 88–89, 554, 793; MG 2, 719–20, 726–32; RG 5, P, 1–3; RG 7, 2–3; RG 8, 1–2. *Catalogue of the Provincial Agricultural Library, with the rules and bye laws* (Halifax, 1825; copy at PANS). *Glimpses of Nova Scotia, 1807–24, as seen through the eyes of two Halifax merchants, a Wilmot clergyman and the clerk of the assembly of Nova Scotia*, ed. C. B. Fergusson (Halifax, 1957). T. C. Haliburton, *An historical and statistical account of Nova-Scotia* (2v., Halifax, 1829; repr. Belleville, Ont., 1973), 2. N.S., House of Assembly, *Journal and proc.*, 1825–37. William Young, "Journal of William Young, 1839," PANS, Board of Trustees, *Report* (Halifax), 1973, app.B. *Acadian Recorder*, 1818–23, 1836. *Colonial Patriot*, 1827–34. *Free Press* (Halifax), 1819–20, 1830. *Novascotian, or Colonial Herald*, 1825–37. *Directory of N.S. MLAs*. Beck, *Government of N.S.* Duncan Campbell, *Nova Scotia, in its historical, mercantile, and industrial relations* (Montreal, 1873). *Contributions toward the improvement of agriculture in Nova-Scotia; with practical hints on the management and improvement of live stock* . . . , comp. J. W. Dawson (2nd ed., Halifax, 1856). V. C. Fowke, *Canadian agricultural policy: the historical pattern* (Toronto, 1946; repr. 1978). A. C. Jost, *Guysborough sketches and essays* (Guysborough, N.S., 1950). Israel Longworth, *Life of S. G. W. Archibald* (Halifax, 1881). J. L. MacDougall, *History of Inverness County, Nova Scotia* ([Truro, N.S., 1922]; repr. Belleville, 1976). T. M. Punch, "The Halifax connection, 1749–1848: a century of oligarchy in Nova Scotia" (MA thesis, St Mary's Univ., Halifax, 1972). Howard Trueman, *Early agriculture in the Atlantic provinces* (Moncton, N.B., 1907). D. C. Harvey, "Pre-Agricola John Young, or a compact family in search of fortune," N.S. Hist. Soc., *Coll.*, 32 (1959): 125–59. J. S. Martell, "The achievements of Agricola and the agricultural societies, 1818–25" and "From Central Board to secretary of agriculture, 1826–1885," PANS *Bull.* (Halifax), 2 (1939–41), no.2 and no.3. J. L. Martin, "Farm life in western Nova Scotia prior to 1850," N.S. Hist. Soc., *Coll.*, 37 (1970): 67–84. Gene Morison, "The brandy election of 1830," N.S. Hist. Soc., *Coll.*, 30 (1954): 151–83. "The Young family," *Journal of Education* (Halifax), 4th ser., 8 (1937): 230–33.

GENERAL BIBLIOGRAPHY AND LIST OF ABBREVIATIONS

List of Abbreviations

AAQ Archives de l'archidiocèse de Québec
AC Archives civiles
ACAM Archives de la chancellerie de l'archevêché de Montréal
ACC Anglican Church of Canada
AD Archives départementales
ADB *Australian dictionary of biography*
ANQ Archives nationales du Québec
AO Archives of Ontario
AP Archives paroissiales
ASN Archives du séminaire de Nicolet
ASQ Archives du séminaire de Québec
ASSH Archives du séminaire de Saint-Hyacinthe
ASSM Archives du séminaire de Saint-Sulpice, Montréal
ASTR Archives du séminaire de Trois-Rivières
AUM Archives de l'université de Montréal
AVQ Archives de la ville de Québec
BL British Library
BRH *Le Bulletin des recherches historiques*
BVM-G Bibliothèque de la ville de Montréal, Salle Gagnon
CCHA Canadian Catholic Historical Association
CHA Canadian Historical Association
CHR *Canadian Historical Review*
CTA City of Toronto Archives
DAB *Dictionary of American biography*
DBF *Dictionnaire de biographie française*
DCB *Dictionary of Canadian biography*
DHB *Dictionary of Hamilton biography*
DNB *Dictionary of national biography*
DOLQ *Dictionnaire des œuvres littéraires du Québec*
DPL Detroit Public Library
GRO General Register Office
HBC Hudson's Bay Company
HBCA Hudson's Bay Company Archives
HBRS Hudson's Bay Record Society, *Publications*
HPL Hamilton Public Library
MAC-CD Ministère des Affaires culturelles, Centre de documentation
MHA Maritime History Archive
MTRL Metropolitan Toronto Reference Library
NLS National Library of Scotland
NMM National Maritime Museum
NWC North West Company
OH *Ontario History*
PABC Provincial Archives of British Columbia
PAC Public Archives of Canada/National Archives of Canada
PAM Provincial Archives of Manitoba
PANB Provincial Archives of New Brunswick
PANL Provincial Archives of Newfoundland and Labrador
PANS Public Archives of Nova Scotia
PAPEI Public Archives of Prince Edward Island
PRO Public Record Office
QUA Queen's University Archives
RHAF *Revue d'histoire de l'Amérique française*
RHL Rhodes House Library
RSC Royal Society of Canada
SGCF Société généalogique canadienne-française
SH *Social History*
SOAS School of Oriental and African Studies
SPG Society for the Propagation of the Gospel in Foreign Parts
SRO Scottish Record Office
UCC United Church of Canada
UNBL University of New Brunswick Library
UTFL University of Toronto, Thomas Fisher Rare Book Library
UWOL University of Western Ontario Library

General Bibliography

The General Bibliography is based on the sources most frequently cited in the individual bibliographies of volume VII. It should not be regarded as providing a complete list of background materials for the history of Canada in the 19th century.

Section I describes the principal archival sources and is arranged by country. Section II is divided into two parts: part A contains printed primary sources including documents published by the various colonial governments; part B provides a listing of the contemporary newspapers most frequently cited by contributors to the volume. Section III includes dictionaries, indexes, inventories, almanacs, and directories. Section IV contains secondary works of the 19th and 20th centuries, including a number of general histories and theses. Section V describes the principal journals and the publications of various societies consulted.

I. ARCHIVAL SOURCES

CANADA

ANGLICAN CHURCH OF CANADA, DIOCESE OF QUEBEC ARCHIVES, Lennoxville, Que. For a description of this archives, *see* A. R. Kelley, "The Quebec Diocesan Archives; a description of the collection of historical records of the Church of England in the diocese of Quebec," ANQ *Rapport*, 1946–47: 181–298, and [A.] M. Awcock, "Catalogue of the Quebec Diocesan Archives" (typescript, Shawinigan, Que., 1973; copy available at the archives).

Materials cited in volume VII include:

- 29: Letters patent appointing C. J. Stewart to be bishop of Quebec
- 32: Notarial certificate on consecration of C. J. Stewart as bishop
- 40: Appointments
- 44: Episcopal seals in wax
- 47–71: Parish reports, correspondence, and other material relating to the parishes
  - 50: Drummondville
  - 62: Quebec: Trinity
- 72–80: Correspondence of Jacob Mountain
- 81: Correspondence of Jacob Mountain, [C.] J. Stewart, and G. J. Mountain
- 82–102: Copies of letters and papers referring to diocese of Quebec
- 103–4: Letters from C. J. Stewart to J. Reid
- 105: Stewart letters
- 107–8: Correspondence between bishops of Quebec and SPG
- 109: Correspondence between bishops of Quebec and Society for the Promotion of Christian Knowledge
- 110: Clergy reserves and erection of parishes
- 111–13: Clergy reserves
- 114: Travelling missionaries
- 115: Stewart missions
- 116: Cathedral and parish of Quebec with institutions in Quebec
- 118: Education: McGill, Bishop's, Bishop's College School, etc.
- 123: Unbound manuscripts
- 129: Copies of correspondence of C. J. Stewart
- 330–31: Episcopate of C. J. Stewart

ARCHIVES CIVILES. *See* Québec, Ministère de la Justice

ARCHIVES DE LA CHANCELLERIE DE L'ARCHEVÊCHÉ DE MONTRÉAL. A detailed inventory of many of the registers and files in this depository can be found in *RHAF*, 19 (1965–66): 652–64; 20 (1966–67): 146–66, 324–41, 669–700; 24 (1970–71): 111–42.

The following materials are cited in volume VII:

Dossiers

- 255: Diocèses du Canada
  - .102: Kingston
  - .104: Toronto
  - .109: Saint-Boniface
- 295: Diocèses du Québec
  - .098–.101: Québec
  - .103: Saint-Hyacinthe
- 350: Paroisses
  - .102: Rapports pastoraux
- 355: Paroisses en particulier
  - .104: Purification-de-la-Bienheureuse-Vierge-Marie

.107: Saint-François d'Assise
.108: Saint-Sulpice
420: Prêtres en particulier
.051: Paquin, Jacques
.095: Lafrance, Pierre
465: Communautés d'hommes en particulier
.101: Compagnie de Saint-Sulpice
.103: Compagnie de Jésus
525: Communautés de femmes en particulier
.105: Sœurs des Saints-Noms de Jésus et de Marie
583: Lettres de laïques
.000: M
780: Associations et divers
.034: Journaux
901: Fonds Lartigue–Bourget
.012: G.-J. Brassier, vicaire général
.013: Notice biographique de Mgr Plessis; érection du diocèse de Montréal
.014: Mgr Lartigue: de Mgr de Philadelphie; de Mgr de New York; de Mgr de Bradstown; de Mgr Poynter
.015: Mgr Lartigue: contre l'admission des notables
.016: Mgr Lartigue: lettres personnelles
.017: Messieurs Maguire et Tabeau; division de Québec et biens de Saint-Sulpice; missions à Rome; projet de journal ecclésiastique
.018: Mgr Lartigue: gouvernement anglais et évêché de Montréal
.021: Question des notables; érection des paroisses; bills pour les communautés religieuses; éducation; écoles normales
.022: Mgr Lartigue: lettres de sa famille
.023: Mgr Lartigue: recensement; de D.-B. et Jacques Viger
.024: Mgr Lartigue: de François Bonin
.025: J.-G. Rocque et J.-V. Quiblier à Lartigue et Bourget
.028: Mgr Lartigue: de M. Montgolfier; de prêtres et d'amis; règlements divers; documents
.029: Lettres de Viau, Terrasse, Duclaux, Roux
.033: Mgr Lartigue: testament; M.-F.-J. Deguise: testament
.037: Mgr Lartigue: travaux
.039: Mgr Lartigue: sermons
.041: Mgr Lartigue: travaux d'Écriture sainte
.044: Diverses lettres à Mgr Bourget
.047: Mgr Lartigue: sermons
.050: J.-B. Thavenet à Lartigue
.055: Mgr Bourget: lettres personnelles et voyages à Rome (1846–47 et 1854–56)
.062: Lettres personnelles de Bourget
.117: M. H. Hudon à Bourget
.136: Notre-Dame: division de la paroisse
.137: Notre-Dame et Saint-Sulpice
.150: D.-B. Viger à Lartigue
RL: Registres de lettres
RLB: Registres des lettres de Mgr Bourget. An inventory of the correspondence of Mgr Ignace Bourget* from 1837 to 1843, compiled by L.-A. Desrosiers, has been published in ANQ *Rapport* [section III].
RLL: Registres des lettres de Mgr Lartigue. An inventory of the correspondence of Mgr Jean-Jacques LARTIGUE from 1819 to 1840, compiled by L.-A. Desrosiers, has been published in ANQ *Rapport* [section III].

ARCHIVES DE L'ARCHIDIOCÈSE DE QUÉBEC. A guide to the collection is available in CCHA *Rapport*, 2 (1934–35): 65–73.

The following were used in the preparation of volume VII:
A: Évêques et archevêques de Québec
12 A: Registres des insinuations ecclésiastiques
20 A: Lettres manuscrites des évêques de Québec
210 A: Registres des lettres expédiées. Inventories of the correspondence of a number of the bishops of Quebec, compiled by Ivanhoë Caron*, are available in ANQ *Rapport* [section III].
211 A: Registres des requêtes
31-13 A: Papiers personnels de Mgr Joseph Signay
C: Secrétairerie et chancellerie
CA: Statut du diocèse
40 CA: Corporations archiépiscopales
CB: Structures de direction
1 CB: Vicaires généraux
2 CB: Vicaires administrateurs et capitulaires
CD: Discipline diocésaine
303 CD: Titres cléricaux
515 CD: Séminaire de Nicolet
516 CD: Séminaire de Québec
61 CD: Paroisses
69 CD: Visites pastorales
Diocèse de Québec (being reclassified)
CM: Église universelle
10 CM: Correspondance de Rome
11 CM: Curie romaine-indults
7 CM: États-Unis
90 CM: Angleterre

CN: Église canadienne
30 CN: Terre-Neuve
310 CN: Île-du-Prince-Édouard
311 CN: Nouveau-Brunswick
312 CN: Nouvelle-Écosse
320 CN: Haut-Canada
60 CN: Gouvernement du Canada
CP: Église du Québec
26 CP: Diocèse de Montréal
30 CP: Diocèse de Saint-Hyacinthe
E: Administration temporelle

ARCHIVES DE LA VILLE DE QUÉBEC. A useful publication of this repository is *État sommaire des Archives de la ville de Québec* (Québec, 1977), edited by Murielle Doyle-Frenière.

Collections cited in volume VII include:
I: Juges de paix
1: Procès-verbaux des Sessions spéciales relatives aux chemins et ponts
V: Série chemins
B: Juges de paix
VII: Série finances
E: Bureau des cotiseurs
1: Rôles d'évaluation et d'imposition
VIII: Série marchés

ARCHIVES DE L'UNIVERSITÉ DE MONTRÉAL. The Service des archives de l'université de Montréal has prepared an important series of publications relating to its collections; a list of these can be found in *Bibliographie des publications du Service des archives* (5e éd., Montréal, 1987), edited by Denys Chouinard *et al.*

The following collection was cited in volume VII:
P 58: Collection Baby. The *Catalogue de la collection François-Louis-Georges Baby*, compiled by Camille Bertrand, with preface by Paul Baby and introduction by Lucien Campeau (2v., Montréal, 1971), provides useful information to researchers. Transcripts of the bulk of this collection, which is being classified at present, are available at PAC, MG 24, L3.
C: Colonisation
C2: Ventes et échanges
S: Papiers William Berczy
U: Correspondance générale

ARCHIVES DU SÉMINAIRE DE NICOLET, Nicolet, Qué. The repository is in the process of classifying its collections.

Materials cited in volume VII:
AO: Archives officielles
Polygraphie
Séminaire
Transfert du séminaire de Nicolet
AP: Archives privées
G: Grandes collections
L.-É. Bois
D: Documents historiques
G: Garde-notes
S: Succession/correspondance
J.-O. Leprohon
J.-B. Lozeau
M.-G. Proulx
Registre des généalogies
Succession/correspondance
Lettres des évêques
Seigneurie de Nicolet
Cahier du cens et rentes
Terrier

ARCHIVES DU SÉMINAIRE DE QUÉBEC.

Collections cited in volume VII:
C: Livres de comptes du séminaire
Collection Glackemeyer
Évêques
Fichier des anciens
Fonds Viger–Verreau
Boîtes: Papiers de H.-A.-J.-B. Verreau; Jacques Viger
Cartons: Papiers de H.-A.-J.-B. Verreau; Jacques Viger
Série O: Cahiers manuscrits
021: Élection du 25 avril et du . . . dans Montréal-Ouest
049: Album de 30 desseins par John Drake et de 2 par William Berczy
085: Extrait de décisions et remarques tirées de la Coutume de Paris
086: Journal des missions de 1811 et 1812 par Mgr Plessis
0128: Annales de l'Hôtel-Dieu de Montréal, 1734 à 1828
0139–52: Ma saberdache de Jacques Viger
0176: Baronnie de Longueuil, famille Lemoyne de Longueuil par Jacques Viger
0178: Les barons de Longueuil et la famille Lemoyne
0521: Livre de comptes de la Compagnie du Nord-Ouest
Journal du séminaire
Lettres
MSS: Cahiers manuscrits divers
12: Grand livre
104–10: J.-F. Perrault
141: N.-L. Amyot, Journal de voyage
193: Jos. Levasseur, Journal et notes
218–19: J.-F. Boucher, Lettres dogmatiques

281: J. Mannock, Manuel abrégé de controverse
433: A.-E. Gosselin, Officiers et professeurs du séminaire de Québec
436–37: A.-E Gosselin, Notices sur les prêtres du séminaire
885–88: Joseph Signaÿ, Recensement de la ville de Québec
MSS-M: Cahiers de cours manuscrits
103: Cours de rhétorique par François Leguerne
104: Cours de rhétorique par J.-M. Boissonnault
140: Félix Gatien, Cours d'arithmétique par Jean Raimbault
146: Cours de philosophie
153: Félix Gatien, Cours de philosophie par J.-B. Castanct
155: Félix Gatien, Cours de philosophie par J.-B. Castanet
164: Joseph Signaÿ, Cours de philosophie par Jérôme Demers
208: Joseph Signaÿ, Cours de théologie par P.-J. Bossu
978: Cours d'histoire ancienne par Joseph Signaÿ
Polygraphie: Affaires surtout extérieures
S: Seigneuries du séminaire
2: Terrier censier (Île-Jésus)
3: Censier (tome I) (Île-Jésus)
Séminaire: Affaires diverses
SME: Décisions du Conseil du séminaire

ARCHIVES DU SÉMINAIRE DE SAINT-HYACINTHE, Saint-Hyacinthe, Qué.

The following series were cited in volume VII:
Section A: Archives du séminaire
Fg-3: Raymond, J.-S.
Fg-4: Leclère, P.-É.
Fg-5: Morin, A.-N.
Fg-41: Saint-Pierre, P.-A.
Fg-46: Allaire, J.-B.-A.

ARCHIVES DU SÉMINAIRE DE SAINT-SULPICE, Montréal.

Sections cited in volume VII:
Section 1 bis: Démêlés relatifs aux biens
Section 8: Seigneuries, fiefs, arrière-fiefs et domaines
Section 11: Enseignement
Section 13: Communautés religieuses anciennes
Section 16: Émigration, immigration, colonisation
Section 17: Finance, banque, monnaie
Section 21: Correspondance générale
Section 24: Histoire, géographie et biographies
B: Biographies
E: Catalogues des prêtres de Saint-Sulpice
F: Cahiers Faillon
Section 25: Séminaire de Saint-Sulpice
Dossier 2: Emplois
Section 27: Séminaire, évêchés et paroisses
Section 32: Contrats de mariage, certificats
Section 49: Prédication et prônes

ARCHIVES DU SÉMINAIRE DE TROIS-RIVIÈRES, Trois-Rivières, Qué. A summary inventory of this repository was compiled by Yvon Thériault and published in ANQ *Rapport*, 1961–64: 67–134. The current classification system is given in *État général des fonds et collections conservés aux Archives du séminaire de Trois-Rivières* (Trois-Rivières, 1985), compiled by Denise Maltais *et al.*

Series cited in volume VII:
0009: Fonds Hart, famille
0032: Collection Montarville Boucher de la Bruère
0123: Fonds L.-M. Cadieux
0329: Fonds Thomas Coffin
0419: Fonds Michael O'Sullivan
0461: Fonds H. W. Ryland

ARCHIVES NATIONALES DU QUÉBEC. In 1980 the archives undertook the establishment of a new uniform classification for all of its regional centres. Inventories, catalogues, guides, conversion tables, and useful finding aids on microfiche are available in each repository.

CENTRE RÉGIONAL DE L'ESTRIE (ANQ-E), Sherbrooke

The following materials were cited in volume VII:
C: Pouvoir judiciaire, archives civiles
CE: État civil
1: Sherbrooke
41: Hatley Anglican Church
46: Protestant Episcopal mission at Sherbrooke and Lennoxville
2: Bedford
8: Sainte-Anne-de-la-Rochelle
38: Dunham Anglican Church
CN: Notaires
2: Bedford
21: Gale, Samuel
26: Lalanne, Léon
T: Justice
11: Cour supérieure
501: Saint-François

CENTRE RÉGIONAL DE MONTRÉAL (ANQ-M)

Collections cited in volume VII include:
C: Pouvoir judiciaire, archives civiles
CA: Arpenteurs
1: Montréal

71: Papineau, Joseph
CC: Tutelles et curatelles
1: Montréal
CE: État civil
1: Montréal
2: La-Nativité-de-la-Très-Sainte-Vierge (Laprairie)
3: Notre-Dame-de-la-Prairie-de-la-Madeleine
4: La Visitation (Sault-aux-Récollets)
5: Saint-Enfant-Jésus (Pointe-aux-Trembles)
10: Sainte-Anne (Varennes)
12: Saint-Antoine (Longueuil)
18: Saint-Constant
22: Sainte-Famille (Boucherville)
25: Saint-François-Xavier (Sault-Saint-Louis, Kanawake)
37: Saint-Joachim (Pointe-Claire)
51: Notre-Dame de Montréal
54: Saint-Philippe (Laprairie)
59: Saint-Vincent-de-Paul (Laval)
63: Christ Church Anglican (Montreal)
68: St George's Anglican Church (Montreal)
80: St Stephen's Anglican Church (Lachine)
84: Trinity Church (Montreal)
92: Evangelical Congregational Church (Montreal)
109: St James Street Methodist Church (Montreal)
124: St Andrew's Presbyterian Church (Lachine)
125: St Andrew's Presbyterian Church (Montreal)
126: St Gabriel's Presbyterian Church (Montreal)
130: St Paul's Presbyterian Church (Montreal)
132: Church of the Messiah (Montreal)
2: Saint-Hyacinthe
1: Saint-Hyacinthe-le-Confesseur (Saint-Hyacinthe)
10: Saint-Charles (Saint-Charles-sur-Richelieu)
12: Saint-Denis (Saint-Denis, sur le Richelieu)
16: Saint-Hilaire
3: Sorel
1: Christ Church (Sorel)
2: Saint-Antoine (Baie-du-Febvre)
6: Immaculée-Conception (Saint-Ours)
4: Saint-Jean
1: Sainte-Marguerite-de-Blairfindie (L'Acadie)
4: Saint-Édouard (Napierville)
6: Saint-Cyprien-de-Napierville
16: Saint-Valentin
17: Caldwell Anglican Church (Saint-Jean)
5: Joliette
1: Sainte-Geneviève-de-Berthier (Berthierville)
6: Saint-Antoine (Lavaltrie)
13: Saint-Sulpice
14: Saint-Pierre-du-Portage (L'Assomption)
16: Purification-de-Repentigny (Repentigny)
19: Saint-Cuthbert
24: Industrie (Joliette)
40: Saint-Paul (Joliette)
6: Saint-Jérôme
3: L'Annonciation (Oka)
9: Saint-Benoît (Mirabel)
11: Saint-Eustache
24: Saint-Louis (Terrebonne)
CM: Testaments
1: Montréal
CN: Notaires
1: Montréal
3: Adhémar, J.-B.
7: Arnoldi, G.-D.
14: Baret, M.-G.
16: Barron, Thomas
21: Cressé, L.-M.
28: Bédouin, Thomas
29: Beek, J. G.
32: Belle, Joseph
43: Boileau, René
68: Cadieux, J.-M.
69: Cadieux, G.-H.
74: Chaboillez, Louis
80: Charet, Michel
96: Constantin, J.-B.
107: Dandurand, R.-F.
108: Danré de Blanzy, L.-C.
110: Daveluy, P.-É.
116: Deguire, Charles
117: Deguire, J.-B.
121: De Lisle, J.-G.
122: Lorimier, Chevalier de
126: Desautels, Joseph
128: Desève, J.-B.
134: Doucet, N.-B.
135: Doucet, Théodore
158: Foucher, Antoine
167: Gauthier, J.-P.
173: Germain, Césaire
175: Gibb, I. J.

179: Girouard, J.-J.
184: Gray, E. W.
185: Gray, J. A.
187: Griffin, Henry
192: Guy, Étienne
194: Guy, Louis
199: Hébert, Médard
200: Henry, Edme
202: Hodiesne, Gervais
208: Hunter, J. S.
215: Jobin, André
216: Jobin, J.-H.
224: Lacombe, Patrice
233: Lanctôt, Pierre
243: Latour, Louis Huguet
245: Leblanc, F.-H.
255: Leguay, François (fils)
269: Lukin, Peter (père)
270: Lukin, Peter (fils)
271: Mackay, Stephen
273: Manthet, Nicolas
290: Mézières, Pierre
295: Mondelet, J.-M.
299: Moreau, L.-A.
305: O'Keefe, Richard
310: Papineau, A.-B.
313: Papineau, Joseph
317: Payment, Joseph
320: Peltier, Généreux
321: Pelton, T. J.
326: Pinet, Alexis
327: Pinsonnault, P.-P.
334: Prévost, Charles
353: Ross, William
375: Soupras, L.-J.
380: Terroux, C.-A.
383: Thibaudault, Louis
385: Truteau, Z.-J.
391: Vallée, Paul
394: Varin, J.-B.
396: Weekes, George
2: Saint-Hyacinthe
27: Dutalmé, P.-P.
79: Têtu, Charles
3: Sorel
78: Robin, Antoine (1805–53)
88: Robin, Antoine (1760–1808)
4: Saint-Jean
10: Brisset, Joseph
14: Decoigne, Louis
20: Gamelin, Pierre
24: Jobson, T.-R.
30: Lukin, J.-B.
33: Petrimoulx, F.-M.
5: Joliette
3: Archambault, Eugène
8: Bédard, Thomas
13: Charland, J.-B.-J.
24: Joliette, Barthélemy
25: Leblanc, J.-O.
6: Saint-Jérôme
2: Berthelot, J.-A.
3: Chatellier, Augustin
4: Coursolles, E.-G.
27: Séguin, F.-H.
M: Microfilms
7: Tutelles
P: Fonds et collections privées
26: Trudeau, Romuald
224: Fils de la liberté
P1000: Petits fonds
1-57: Bouchette, Joseph
3-298: Hindenlang, Charles
3-360: Neilson, collection
61-1240: Cardinal, J. N.

CENTRE RÉGIONAL DE LA MAURICIE–BOIS-FRANCS (ANQ-MBF), Trois-Rivières
The following were used in volume VII:
C: Pouvoir judiciaire, archives civiles
CE: État civil
1: Trois-Rivières
12: St Bartholemew's (Nicolet)
13: Saint-Jean-Baptiste (Nicolet)
48: Immaculée-Conception (Trois-Rivières)
50: St James Protestant Congregation Church (Trois-Rivières)
2: Arthabasca
6: Saint-Frédéric (Drummondville)
CN: Notaires
1: Trois-Rivières
4: Badeaux, A.-I.
5: Badeaux, J.-B.
6: Badeaux, Joseph
7: Badeaux, J.-M.
19: Craig, L.-D.
21: Cressé, L.-M.
31: Dumoulin, F.-L.
32: Dumoulin, J.-E.
35: Duvernay, J.-M. Crevier
47: Guillet, Valère
56: Leblanc, A.-Z.
62: Lemaître Lottinville, Flavien
79: Ranvoyzé, Étienne
91: Trudel, Augustin

CENTRE RÉGIONAL DE L'OUTAOUAIS (ANQ-O), Hull
Materials used in volume VII include:
M: Microfilms
122-9: Église anglicane St James (Hull)
P: Fonds et collections privées
2: Fonds Wright–Mackay

I. ARCHIVAL SOURCES

CENTRE D'ARCHIVES DE QUÉBEC (ANQ-Q)
C: Pouvoir judiciaire, archives civiles
 CC: Tutelles et curatelles
  1: Québec
 CE: État civil
  1: Québec
   1: Notre-Dame de Québec
   2: Notre-Dame-de-l'Annonciation (L'Ancienne-Lorette)
   3: L'Ange-Gardien
   4: Saint-Étienne (Beaumont)
   5: Notre-Dame de Miséricorde (Beauport)
   8: Sainte-Famille (Cap-Santé)
   11: Sainte-Famille (île d'Orléans)
   12: Saint-Pierre (île d'Orléans)
   22: Saint-Roch (Québec)
   25: Saint-Joseph (Deschambault)
   28: Saint-Ambroise (Loretteville)
   39: Sainte-Catherine
   61: Holy Trinity Cathedral (Quebec)
   64: St Paul's Chapel (Quebec)
   66: St Andrew's Presbyterian Church (Quebec)
   68: Wesleyan Methodist Church (Quebec)
   71: Garrison of Quebec Anglican Church (Quebec)
   75: Aubigny Anglican Church (Lévis)
   79: St Michael's Anglican Church (Sillery)
   93: Hôpital Général de Québec
  2: Montmagny
   1: Cap-Saint-Ignace
   2: Notre-Dame-de-l'Assomption (Berthier-en-Bas)
   6: Saint-Pierre-de-la-Rivière-du-Sud (Montmagny)
   7: Saint-Thomas-de-la-Pointe-à-la-Caille (Montmagny)
   17: Saint-Gervais
   18: Saint-Jean-Port-Joli
   25: Saint-Roch-des-Aulnaies
  3: Kamouraska
   1: Notre-Dame-de-Liesse (Rivière-Ouelle)
   3: Saint-Louis (Kamouraska)
   11: Saint-André (près de Kamouraska)
 CN: Notaires
  1: Québec
   16: Bélanger, Jean
   18: Belleau, R.-G.
   21: Bernard, Joseph
   25: Berthelot Dartigny, M.-A.
   26: Berthelot, Michel
   27: Besserer, L.-T.
   28: Bigué, Paul
   33: Bolduc, Henri
   38: Boudreault, Étienne
   49: Campbell, Archibald
   64: Childs, John
   66: Cinq-Mars, Charles
   67: Clapham, J. G.
   80: DeFoy, C.-M.
   81: De Léry, William
   83: Deschenaux, P.-L.
   89: Dugal, Charles
   104: Fraser, Alexander
   116: Glackmeyer, Edward
   138: Hunt, Joseph
   145: Jones, John
   147: Laforce, Pierre
   171: Lee, Thomas
   172: Lefebvre, F.-X.
   178: Lelièvre, Roger
   179: Lelièvre, Siméon
   188: Lindsay, E. B.
   197: McPherson, L. T.
   205: Panet, J.-A.
   208: Panet, Louis
   212: Parent, A.-Archange
   213: Parent, A.-Ambroise
   228: Planté, C.-D.
   230: Planté, J.-B.
   253: Scott, W. F.
   255: Sirois-Duplessis, A.-B.
   256: Stewart, Charles
   261: Tessier, Michel
   262: Têtu, Félix
   267: Vaillancourt, F.-X.
   284: Voyer, Charles
   285: Voyer, Jacques
  2: Montmagny
   6: Boisseau, I.-G.
   7: Boisseau, N.-G.
   12: Fraser, Simon
   21: Larue, Abraham
   24: Fournier, P.-C.
   26: Létourneau, J.-C.
   28: Michaud, Thadée
   34: Pelletier, S.-N.
   35: Piuze, Rémi
   48: Verreau, G.-A.
  3: Kamouraska
   7: Boisseau, N.-G.
   8: Bernier, Ignace
   11: Cazes, Louis
   17: Dionne, Augustin
  4: Saguenay
   9: Gauvreau, C.-H.
E: Pouvoir exécutif
  4: Secrétariat provincial
  17: Justice

6–52: Événements de 1837–38
18: Registraire
21: Terres et forêts
73–75: Biens des jésuites, administration
297: Demandes de terres des miliciens
356: Arpenteur général
1863, 1870, 1873, 1877–78: Administration des terres publiques
P: Fonds et collections privées
34: Chandler, famille
40: Chaussegros de Léry, famille
52: Couillard Després, Azarie
68: Duvernay, Ludger
69: Fabre, É.-R.
78: Fisher, J. C.
92: Girouard, J.-J.
98: Gugy, famille
144: Bédard, Elzéar
184: Banque de Québec
192: Neilson, famille
193: Neilson, imprimerie
222: Quesnel, Jules
239: Roy, P.-G.
240: Seigneuries
289: Salaberry, famille de
294: Stuart, famille
313: Allsopp, George
319: Sewell, famille
362: Rastel de Rocheblave, famille
365: Hart, famille
386: Chaussegros de Léry, famille
398: Baillairgé, François
409: Desrivières, famille
417: Papineau, famille
418: Bourassa, Napoléon, famille
600: Collection initiale
4: Cartes et plans
668: Richardson, A. J. H.
P1000: Petits fonds
2-26: Allsopp, G. W.
2-34: Amiot, Laurent
8-124: Beaudry, P.-J.
11-184: Berthelot, Amable
14-255: Bouchette, Joseph
43-833: O'Sullivan, Michael
48-931: Hale, famille
49-976: Hindenlang, Charles
51-1006: Huot, H.-S.
55-1054: Kerr, James
65-1291: Lévesque, Guillaume
66-1317: Lorimier, Chevalier de
79-1623: Perrault, J.-F.
87-1806: Robitaille, L.-A.
90-1863: Ryland, H. W.
102-2057: Vassal de Monviel, famille
105-2105: Wood, Robert

T: Pouvoir judiciaire
6-1: Cour de justice, Régime britannique
11-1: Cour supérieure
11-301: Cour supérieure, registre des jugements
11-302: Cour du banc du roi, registre des jugements
Z: Copies de documents conservés en dehors des ANQ
Q: Québec (en dehors des ANQ)
6: État civil, Catholiques
45: Saint-François-d'Assise (Beauceville)
300076: Index des baptêmes, mariages et sépultures des protestants de la région de Québec, *c.* 1790–1815

CENTRE RÉGIONAL SAGUENAY–LAC-SAINT-JEAN (ANQ-SLSJ), Chicoutimi

The following collection was used in volume VII:

P: Fonds et collections privées
2: Tremblay, Victor

ARCHIVES OF ONTARIO, Toronto. A *Guide to the holdings of the Archives of Ontario*, ed. B. L. Craig and R. W. Ramsey (2v., Toronto, 1985), is supplemented in the archives by unpublished finding aids, some of which are also available on microfiche.

Materials used in volume VII include:

Canada Company records
Hiram Walker Historical Museum collection
Land record index
Map Collection
MS: Microfilm Series
4: Robinson, Sir John Beverley
6: Crookshank–Lambert letters
12: Robinson, Peter
35: Strachan, John
74: Merritt, William Hamilton
75: Russell family
78: Macaulay family
88: Baldwin family
94: Norton, John
106: Chisholm family
107: Church records collection, St Andrew's Presbyterian Church (Williamstown, Ont.)
118: Nelles, William
148: Flamborough West manuscript collection
186: Cartwright family papers, John Solomon Cartwright and Robert Cartwright letters
198: Reive, W. G., collection
296: Jones, William
302: Bates family
393: Baird papers

451: Cemetery records collection
498: Baby, Jacques Duperon
500: Street, Samuel and Thomas
502: Nelles, Abraham
503: Nelles, Robert, papers
516: Mackenzie–Lindsey papers, Mackenzie correspondence
517: Simcoe, John Graves, papers, Canadian section
519: Stone, Joel
520: Jones, Solomon
524: Robinson, Peter
526: Berczy, William von Moll
537: Ridout papers
552: Bell, William
709: Macdonell, Alexander
787: Jarvis–Powell papers

MU: Manuscript Units
275: Blanchard, Harry D.
281: Bonnycastle, Richard H.
500–15: Cartwright family
572: Clark, Duncan
593–692: Commercial records collection
837: Dent, Charles R.
838–66: Diaries
875–77: Dickson, William
934–44: Douglas, H. Townley, collection
1054: Ford family
1057: Foster, Colley Lyons Lucas
1113–15: Galt, John
1116–39: Genealogies collection
1147: Gowan, James R. and Ogle
1197–284: Hamilton Brothers records and Hawkesbury Lumber Company records
1364–65: Henry, Margaret Dodds Snell, collection
1375–81: Hodgins, John George
1532–37: Jarvis–Powell papers
1726: Hamilton, Alexander
1760: McDonald, Colin and John
1780: Macdonell, John "Le Pretre"
1817–910: Mackenzie–Lindsey papers, Mackenzie newspaper clipping collection
1915–17: Mackenzie–Lindsey papers, Robert Randall records
1966–73: McMartin, Alexander
2005–12: Marriage records collection
2031–83: Military records collection
2095–147: Miscellaneous collection
2196–205: Northwest Company collection
2316: Peters, Samuel
2319–20: Pilkington estate papers
2366: Radcliffe family
2380: Rebellion of 1837
2383–84: Reid, William, collection
2388–89: Riddell family
2554–55: Rousseau family
2577: Rebellion of 1837–38 scrapbook
2601: Scrapbooks
2813–22: Small–Gowan papers
2828–31: Smith, Frederick Peter
2883: Steele, John
3054: United Empire Loyalist miscellaneous materials
3074–75: Wade family letters
3155–88: Yonge Mills records
3289: Shirreff, Charles, family
3296: Nelles, Henry William
4734: Thorne, Benjamin
4736–53: Jackes papers
4756: Miscellaneous records

RG 1: Ministry of Natural Resources
A: Office of surveyor general, commissioner of crown lands, and minister
I: Correspondence
1: Letters received, surveyor general
2: Surveyor general's letter-books
4: Commissioner's letter-books
6: Letters received, surveyor general and commissioner
7: Subject files
II: Reports and statements
1: Surveyor general's reports
2: Commissioner's reports
5: Heir and Devisee Commission reports
IV: Schedules and land rolls
VII: Miscellaneous records
B: Financial Services Branch
IV: Survey accounts
C: Lands Branch
I: Land grants
3: Fiats and warrants
4: Location
9: Miscellaneous records
IV: Township papers
CB: Surveys and Mapping Branch
1: Survey diaries and field notes

RG 4: Ministry of the Attorney General
32: Central registry, criminal and civil files

RG 8: Records of the provincial secretary
I-1: Main office
P: Pre-confederation correspondence

RG 21: Municipal records

RG 22: Court records
Court of General Quarter Sessions of the Peace
Brockville (Leeds and Grenville)
ser.12: Minutes
ser.17: Road and bridge records
ser.18: Tavern and shop licensing records

Toronto (York)
ser.94: Minutes
ser.96: Filings
Court of King's Bench
ser.125: Term-books
ser.131: Judgement docket-books
ser.138: Criminal filings
Court of Probate
ser.155: Estate files
Surrogate courts
Brockville (Leeds and Grenville)
ser.176: Registers
Cobourg (Northumberland and Durham)
ser.187: Registers
Cornwall (Stormont, Dundas, and Glengarry)
ser.194: Registers
Hamilton (Wentworth)
ser.204: Registers
ser.205: Estate files
Kingston (Frontenac)
ser.159: Estate files
Ottawa (Carleton)
ser.224: Registers
St Catharines (Niagara North)
ser.234: Registers
ser.235: Estate files
Toronto (York)
ser.302: Registers
ser.305: Estate files
RG 40: Heir and Devisee Commission
D: Claims case files
1: Second commission
RG 53: Recording Office
Records of land
ser.2: Index to land patents by district

ARCHIVES PAROISSIALES. The most noteworthy holdings of parish archives in Quebec are the registers of baptisms, marriages, and burials, copies of which are deposited at the Archives civiles of the judicial district in which the parish is located [*see* Québec, Ministère de la Justice]. Parish archives usually contain many other documents, including parish account-books, records of the *fabriques*, registers of parish confraternities, notebooks of sermons, and sometimes correspondence.

BIBLIOTHÈQUE DE LA VILLE DE MONTRÉAL, Salle Gagnon.

Series cited in volume VII:
Collection Gagnon
Fonds Ægidius Fauteux
Fonds baronnie de Longueuil
Fonds Jules Quesnel
MSS

CITY OF TORONTO ARCHIVES.

The following collection was used in volume VII:
RG 1: City Council
B: Papers

HAMILTON PUBLIC LIBRARY, Special Collections Department, Hamilton, Ont.

Archives files, clipping files, scrapbooks, and other materials were used in the preparation of volume VII.

MCCORD MUSEUM, Montreal. For information on this and other archival collections at McGill University, see *Guide to archival resources at McGill University*, ed. Marcel Caya *et al.* (3v., Montreal, 1985).

Series cited in volume VII:
M13630: Bridge, Samuel Southby
M19110, M19113–15: Molson, Thomas, diaries
M19117: Molson, Thomas, licence
M19124: Molson, Thomas, diary
M20483: Hale, Edward
M21228: Molson family
M21359: Hart family
M21411: McCord family
M21413: Brothers-in-Law Society of Montreal
M21585: Morris and Felton family
M21968: Pozer family

MCGILL UNIVERSITY ARCHIVES, Montreal. Information on the various collections is available in *Guide to archival resources at McGill University*, ed. Marcel Caya *et al.* (3v., Montreal, 1985).

Series cited in volume VII:
Private archives
MG 1007: McGill, James
MG 3080: Skakel, Alexander
Archival records of McGill University
RG 4: Secretariat of the Royal Institution for the Advancement of Learning and the Board of Governors
RG 38: Faculty of Medicine
RG 96: Montreal General Hospital

MCGILL UNIVERSITY LIBRARIES, DEPARTMENT OF RARE BOOKS AND SPECIAL COLLECTIONS, Montreal. For information on archival collections at McGill University, see *Guide to archival resources at McGill University*, ed. Marcel Caya *et al.* (3v., Montreal, 1985).

Collections cited in volume VII include:
CH10.S46: Ryland, H. W.
CH16.S52: Molson, William
CH21.S57: McKenzie, Roderick
CH23.S59: McKenzie, Roderick
CH27.S63: McKenzie, Roderick

CH149.S19: MacTavish, Frobisher & Co.; McTavish, McGillivrays & Co.
CH171.S153: McKenzie, Roderick
CH173.S155: MacKenzie, James
CH175.S175: McKenzie, Roderick
CH177.S159: MacKenzie, James
CH202.S180: Christie, A. J.
CH293.S253: Comité canadien
CH330.S290: Molson, William
MS430: Blackwood, Thomas
MS433: Frobisher, Joseph
MS435: McGill, James
MS439: de Léry Macdonald papers

MARITIME HISTORY ARCHIVE, Memorial University of Newfoundland, St John's. For information on the collections held at the archive see *Preliminary inventory of records held at the Maritime History Group*, comp. Roberta Thomas under the direction of Keith Matthews ([St John's, 1978]); *Check list of research studies pertaining to the history of Newfoundland in the archives of the Maritime History Group* (7th ed., [St John's], 1984); and *An index to the name files . . .*, comp. Gert Crosbie under the direction of Keith Matthews ([St John's], 1981). Various other indexes to individual collections at the archive are also available.

Materials cited in volume VII include items in the name file collection, consisting of some 20,000 files, arranged by surname, concerning anyone connected in any way with the Newfoundland trade or fisheries between 1640 and 1850. The files are compiled from a wide range of sources, and each entry includes a reference to the original source.

METROPOLITAN TORONTO REFERENCE LIBRARY. For information on the library's manuscript holdings, see *Guide to the manuscript collection in the Toronto Public Libraries* (Toronto, 1954).

Manuscripts consulted for volume VII include:
William Allan papers
Robert Baldwin papers
William Warren Baldwin papers
John Elmsley letter-book
James Givins papers
Samuel Peters Jarvis papers
William Dummer Powell papers
Laurent Quetton de St George papers
Peter Russell papers
Sir David William Smith papers
Alexander Wood papers

MINISTÈRE DES AFFAIRES CULTURELLES, CENTRE DE DOCUMENTATION. *See* Québec, Ministère des Affaires culturelles

NATIONAL ARCHIVES OF CANADA, Ottawa. The National Archives of Canada (referred to elsewhere in volume VII under its official name until 1987, Public Archives of Canada) has published guides to its holdings in the various divisions, including *General guide series 1983, Federal Archives Division*, comp. Terry Cook and Glenn T. Wright (1983), and *General guide series 1983, Manuscript Division*, comp. [E.] Grace [Maurice] Hyam and Jean-Marie LeBlanc (1984).

The following inventories to materials in the Manuscript Division and in the Government Archives Division (formerly the Federal Archives Division) which were used in the preparation of volume VII have been published:
General inventory, manuscripts, volume 1, MG 1–MG 10 (1971)
General inventory, manuscripts, volume 2, MG 11–MG 16 (1976)
General inventory, manuscripts, volume 3, MG 17–MG 21 (1974)
General inventory, manuscripts, volume 4, MG 22–MG 25 (1972)
General inventory, manuscripts, volume 5, MG 26–MG 27 (1972)
General inventory, manuscripts, volume 7, MG 29 (1975)
General inventory, manuscripts, volume 8, MG 30 (1977)
General inventory series, no.1: records relating to Indian affairs (RG 10), comp. Peter Gillis *et al.* (1975)
General inventory series, no.6: records of Statistics Canada (RG 31), comp. Sandra G. Wright and Thomas A. Hillman (1977)
General inventory series, no.8: records of the Department of Public Works (RG 11), comp. B. Hallett (1977)
General inventory series: records of the Department of Railways and Canals (RG 43), comp. Glenn T. Wright (1986)

An older series of inventories has been essentially superseded by unpublished inventories available at the National Archives of Canada, but the following are still of some limited use:
Record group 1, Executive Council, Canada, 1764–1867 (1953)
Record group 4, Civil and Provincial secretaries' offices, Canada East, 1760–1867; Record group 5, Civil and Provincial secretaries' offices, Canada West, 1788–1867 (1953)
Record group 7, Governor General's Office (1953)
Record group 8, British military and naval records (1954)
Record group 9, Department of Militia and Defence, 1776–1922 ([1957])

Also useful are *Census returns, 1666–1881, Public Archives of Canada* (1982) and *Checklist of parish registers, 1986* (4th ed., 1987). The holdings of the Cartographic and Architectural Archives Division (formerly the National Map Collection) are listed in *Catalogue of the National Map Collection, Public Archives of Canada, Ottawa, Ontario* (16v., Boston, 1976).

The National Archives of Canada publishes the *Union list of MSS* [*see* section III], which lists holdings of the Government Archives and Manuscript divisions. It has also issued a *Guide to Canadian photographic archives*, ed. Christopher Seifried (1984). Addenda to published inventories, unpublished inventories of manuscript and record groups, and finding aids to individual collections are available at the National Archives of Canada, which also makes available a large number of finding aids on microfiche.

The following collections were cited in volume VII:

MG 5: Ministère des Affaires étrangères, Paris
- B: Mémoires et documents
  - 2: Angleterre

MG 8: Documents relatifs à la Nouvelle-France et au Québec (XVIIe–XXe siècles)
- F: Documents relatifs aux seigneuries et autres lieux
  - 74: Saint-François du Lac
  - 99: McGinnis papers
- G: Archives paroissiales
  - 14: Illinois (église catholique)
  - 67: Shearith Israel congregation, Jewish, Montreal

MG 9: Provincial, local, and territorial records
- A: New Brunswick
  - 10: Reports on archives and local records
- D: Ontario
  - 4: Department of Lands and Forests
  - 7: Church records
    - 40: Ontario cemetery recordings

MG 11: Colonial Office, London
- [CO 42]. Q series. The Q transcripts were prepared by the PAC before the PRO reorganization of 1908–10 and include most of what is now in CO 42 up to the year 1841, plus material now found in CO 43, as well as items from other series. Most of the documents for the period covered by volume VII are calendared in PAC *Report*, 1890–93, 1896–1902, 1941–45.
- [CO 188]. New Brunswick A. Transcripts in the New Brunswick A series, a composite series prepared by the PAC, are virtually identical to the documents in CO 188 series for the period after 1802.
- [CO 217]. Nova Scotia A and Cape Breton A. From 1802 the transcripts in the Cape Breton A series cited in volume VII are from PRO, CO 217, and they have been calendared in PAC *Report*, 1895.

MG 17: Ecclesiastical archives
- A: Roman Catholic Church
  - 7-2: Séminaire de Saint-Sulpice, Montréal

MG 19: Fur trade and Indians
- A: Fur trade, general
  - 2: Ermatinger estate
  - 3: Askin family
  - 12: La Mothe, famille
  - 16: Quesnel, Jules-Maurice
  - 21: Hargrave family
  - 23: MacLeod, John
  - 35: McGillivray, Simon
  - 38: Newton, William Henry
- B: Fur trade, companies and associations
  - 1: North West Company
  - 3: Beaver Club
- D: Fur trade, post records and journals
  - 5: Fort Chicoutimi
- E: Red River settlement
  - 1: Selkirk, Thomas Douglas, 5th Earl of
  - 2: Red River settlement
  - 4: Macdonell, Miles
  - 5: Bulger, Andrew
- F: Indians
  - 1: Claus family
  - 2: Johnson family
  - 6: Brant family

MG 23: Late eighteenth-century papers
- A: British statesmen
  - 2: Chatham, William Pitt, 1st Earl of
- B: American revolution
  - 35: Berthelot, Amable
- C: Nova Scotia
  - 6: Inglis family
  - 10: Sigogne, Jean-Mandé
- D: New Brunswick
  - 1: Chipman, Ward, Sr and Jr
  - 2: Winslow, Edward
  - 9: New England Company
- E: Prince Edward Island
  - 5: Fanning, Edmund
- GI: Quebec and Lower Canada: government
  - 3: Chisholme, David
- GII: Quebec and Lower Canada: political figures
  - 10: Sewell, Jonathan, and family
  - 14: Smith, William
  - 18: Hale, John, and family
  - 19: Monk, James, and family
- GIII: Quebec and Lower Canada: merchants and settlers
  - 1: Allsopp, George, and family
  - 3: Ruiter (Ruyter) family
- GV: Quebec and Lower Canada: miscellaneous
  - 1: Boisseau, Nicolas-Gaspard

HI: Upper Canada: political figures
- 1: Simcoe, John Graves
- 3: Jarvis, William, and family
- 4: Powell, William Dummer, and family
- 5: White, John
- 8: Murray, George W.

HII: Upper Canada: merchants and settlers
- 6: Berczy, William von Moll

MG 24: Nineteenth-century pre-confederation papers

A: British officials and political figures
- 2: Ellice, Edward, and family
- 3: Douglas, Sir Howard, and family
- 5: Swayne, Hugh
- 6: Hunter, Peter
- 7: Milnes, Sir Robert Shore
- 12: Dalhousie, George Ramsay, 9th Earl of
- 13: Bagot, Sir Charles
- 15: Derby, Edward George Geoffrey Smith Stanley, 14th Earl of
- 17: Harvey, Sir John
- 19: Roebuck, John Arthur
- 21: Campbell, Sir Archibald
- 25: Head, Sir Francis Bond, and family
- 26: Buller, Charles
- 27: Durham, John George Lambton, 1st Earl of
- 30: Sydenham, Charles Edward Poulett Thomson, Baron
- 33: Metcalfe, Charles Theophilus Metcalfe, Baron
- 40: Colborne, Sir John, 1st Baron Seaton
- 43: Aylmer, Matthew Whitworth-Aylmer, 5th Baron, and family
- 64: Burton, Sir Francis Nathaniel

B: North American political figures and events
- 1: Neilson collection
- 2: Papineau, famille
- 3: Ryland, Herman Witsius, and family
- 4: Young family
- 6: Viger, Denis-Benjamin
- 7: Jones, Charles
- 8: Morris, William
- 10: Dunn, Thomas
- 11: Baldwin, William Warren and Robert
- 12: Stuart, Sir James
- 14: La Fontaine, Sir Louis-Hippolyte
- 16: Cochran, Andrew Wilson
- 18: Mackenzie, William Lyon
- 28: Kimber, Joseph-René
- 29: Howe, Joseph
- 34: Nelson, Wolfred
- 36: Walcott, Stephen
- 37: Perrault, Charles-Ovide et Louis
- 39: Brien, Jean-Baptiste-Henri
- 46: Cherrier, Côme-Séraphin
- 78: Gagnon, Lucien
- 126: Quesnel, Frédéric-Auguste
- 127: Fabre, Édouard-Raymond
- 130: Clark(e), Thomas, and family
- 133: Wright, Charles
- 141: Hoyle, Robert
- 143: Hindenlang, Charles
- 147: Caldwell, William
- 167: Kerr, James, and family

C: Correspondents of political figures
- 3: Duvernay, Ludger
- 4: Thompson, John Sparrow
- 7: Pothier, Jean-Baptiste-Toussaint
- 11: Brown, Thomas Storrow
- 12: Benson, Alicia
- 37: McMartin, Alexander

D: Industry, commerce, and finance
- 4: Goring, Francis
- 7: Hamilton, George
- 8: Wright, Philemon, and family
- 12: Dorwin, Jedediah Hubbell
- 16: Buchanan, Isaac, and family
- 18: Whyte, James Matthew
- 19: Ward papers
- 45: Hamilton, James
- 48: Hunt, James
- 61: Campbell, Archibald M.
- 84: Bayley, H. C.
- 99: Birnie, George and Alexander
- 108: Nelles, Robert

E: Transportation
- 1: Merritt papers

F: Military and naval figures
- 29: Communications and settlement
- 66: Barrie, Robert
- 71: Warre, Sir Henry James
- 73: Durnford, Elias Walker

G: Militia
- 5: Vassal de Monviel, François
- 45: Salaberry, famille de
- 46: Burwell, Mahlon, and family

H: Exploration, travel, and surveys
- 64: Tiarks, Johann Ludwig

I: Immigration, land, and settlement
- 4: Galt, John
- 8: Macdonell of Collachie family
- 9: Hill collection
- 26: Hamilton, Alexander
- 46: Canada Company
- 102: Christie, Alexander James, and family
- 109: Séguin, François-Hyacinthe
- 110: Fussey, William

J: Religious figures
- 1: Strachan, John
- 13: Macdonell, Alexander
- 15: Paquin, Jacques
- 40: Barnley, George

K: Education and cultural development
- 2: Coventry, George

13: Société d'éducation de la ville de Trois-Rivières
L: Miscellaneous
3: Baby collection
6: Delancey–Robinson collection
MG 25: Genealogy
62: Kipling collection
321: Porteous family
MG 26: Papers of the prime ministers
A: Macdonald, Sir John Alexander
MG 27: Political figures, 1867–1950
I: 1867–96
E: Members of the House of Commons and the Senate
30: Ferguson collection
MG 28: Records of post-confederation corporate bodies
III: Business establishments
18: Robin, Jones and Whitman Limited
44: Montreal Board of Trade
57: Molson archives
MG 29: Nineteenth-century post-confederation manuscripts
B: Scientific
15: Bell, Robert
D: Cultural
61: Morgan, Henry James
106: Woodburn, Alexander Smith
MG 30: Manuscripts of the first half of the twentieth century
C: Social
20: Gaudet, Placide
D: Cultural
1: Audet, Francis-Joseph
56: Leymarie, A.-Léo
E: Professional and public life
78: Willis–O'Connor family
MG 44: Great Britain, General Post Office
MG 53: Lawrence Montague Lande Collection
MG 55: Miscellaneous documents
RG 1: Executive Council: Quebec, Lower Canada, Upper Canada, Canada, 1764–1867
E: State records
1: Quebec, Lower Canada, Upper Canada, Canada: Executive Council, minute-books (on state matters)
2: Quebec, Lower Canada, Upper Canada, Canada: Executive Council, draft minutes and reports
3: Upper Canada: Executive Council, submissions on state matters
11: Oaths of allegiance and of office
14: Quebec, Lower Canada, Upper Canada, Canada: clerk of the Executive Council Office, records of the clerk
L: Land records
1: Quebec, Lower Canada, Upper Canada, Canada: Executive Council, minute-books (on land matters)
3: Upper Canada and Canada: Land Committee, petitions for land grants and leases
3L: Quebec and Lower Canada: Land Committee, land petitions and related records
6: Departmental records
B: Lower Canada, Upper Canada, Canada: surveyor general
7: Quebec, Lower Canada, Upper Canada, Canada: miscellaneous records
RG 4: Provincial and Civil secretaries' offices: Quebec, Lower Canada, Canada East
A1: Quebec and Lower Canada: S series (correspondence received)
A2: Lower Canada: civil secretary, draft correspondence
A3: Quebec and Lower Canada: civil secretary and clerk of the Executive Council, registers and day-books
B8: Quebec and Lower Canada: applications for commissions to act as notaries and advocates
B20: Quebec, Lower Canada, Canada East: applications for pardons or clemency
B28: Quebec, Lower Canada, Canada East: applications for licences, bonds, and certificates
B32: Quebec, Quebec: shipping returns for the port of
B37: Lower Canada and Canada East: rebellion records
B45: Lower Canada: declarations of aliens
B46: Lower Canada: commission of inquiry into the Red River disturbances
B53: Lower Canada and Canada East: commissions relating to seigneurial tenure
B58: Quebec, Lower Canada, Canada East: customs, records relating to
B72: Lower Canada and Canada East: clerk of the crown in chancery, election records
C: Provincial secretary's correspondence, 1841–67
2: Quebec, Lower Canada, Canada East: provincial secretary's letter-books
RG 5: Provincial and Civil secretaries' offices: Upper Canada, Canada West
A1: Upper Canada sundries: correspondence of the civil and provincial secretaries
B5: Upper Canada and Canada West: commissions and letters patent
B7: Upper Canada and Canada West: applications for appointments to public office
B9: Upper Canada and Canada West: bonds,

certificates, and applications for licences
B25: Upper Canada and Canada West: clerk of the crown in chancery, election records
B36: London District, U.C.: records relating to the treason hearings by the magistrates of the
B37: London District, U.C.: militia general courts martial
C: Canada West: Provincial Secretary's Office
1: Numbered correspondence files
2: Letter-books
RG 7: Canada: Governor General's Office
G1: Dispatches from the Colonial Office
G2: Dispatches from the Colonial Office
G3: Secret and confidential dispatches from the Colonial Office
G14: Miscellaneous records
G15C: Civil secretary's letter-books
G16C: Upper Canada: civil secretary's letter-books
G17A: Governor General's Office, governor general's internal letter-books, Canada
G17C: Governor General's Office, civil secretary's letter-books, Canada
RG 8: British military and naval records
I: C series (British military records)
II: Ordnance records
III: Admiralty records
IV: Vice-Admiralty Court records, Halifax
RG 9: Militia and defence
I: Pre-confederation records
A: Adjutant General's Office, Lower Canada
1: Correspondence
3: General orders
5: Registers of officers
B: Adjutant General's Office, Upper Canada
1: Correspondence
3: Militia: general orders
4: Pensions and land grants
5: Registers of officers
7: Nominal rolls and paylists
8: Special records
RG 10: Indian affairs
A: Administrative records of the imperial government
1: Records of the governor general and lieutenant governors
1–7: Upper Canada, civil control
120–23: Petitions
2: Records of the Superintendent's Office
26–46: Deputy Superintendent General's Office, correspondence
3: Records of the military
488–97: Military Secretary's Office, Montreal
4: Records of the Chief Superintendent's Office, Upper Canada
47–77: Correspondence
124–39, 739, 748, 751: Jarvis correspondence
498–509, 749: Letter-books
6: General office files
625–27: Miscellaneous files
629–48: Accounts
718–19: Macaulay report
B: Ministerial administration records
3: Central registry system
1855–3554: Red (Eastern) series
8: General headquarters administration records
628, 782: Governor General's Office
737, 766–68A: G. M. Matheson, notes and indices
10017–31: Blue books
C: Field Office records
I: Superintendency records
2: Western (Sarnia) Superintendency
569–71: Letter-books
6: Six Nations (Grand River) Superintendency
803–93: Correspondence
II: Agency records
469–70: New Brunswick northeast agency: general administration records
D: Indian land records
3: Six Nations (Grand River) Superintendency
103–13: Grand River claims
RG 11: Department of Public Works
A: Board of Works records
1: Official correspondence
40–77, 148: Correspondence in subject files
2: Registers and indexes
93–95: Subject registers
96–100: Registers of letters received
110: Register of appointments
3: Minutes, letter-books, and reports
112–15: Minutes of meetings
116–31: Letter-books
132: Letter-book of the secretary of the Board of Works
136–40: Reports
RG 14: Records of parliament, 1791–1867
A: Lower Canada
1: Legislative Council, minutes, addresses, and petitions
3: Legislative Assembly, journals
RG 16: Department of National Revenue
A: Customs, excise, and inland revenue
1: Correspondence and returns

RG 19: Department of Finance
E: Departmental correspondence
5(a): Board of claims for War of 1812 losses
5(b): Loyalist victualling list, Upper Canada
RG 30: Canadian National Railways
274–81: Montreal and Lachine Railroad
RG 31: Statistics Canada
C: Census field
1: Census returns
RG 37: National Archives of Canada
A: General correspondence, subject files
RG 42: Marine Branch
E: Ship registration
1: Shipping registers
RG 43: Department of Railways and Canals
C: Canal records
II: Trent Canal
1: Commission records
V: St Lawrence canals
1: Commission for Improving the Navigation on the River St Lawrence
RG 68: Registrar general

NEW BRUNSWICK MUSEUM, Saint John, N.B. For a description of its holdings *see* New Brunswick Museum, *Inventory of manuscripts, 1967* ([Saint John, 1967]).

The following are the principal collections used in volume VII:
Bank of New Brunswick, ledger, 1828–38
Files of miscellaneous original and photocopied documents relating to New Brunswick, designated A (original record books), CB DOC (vertical files), F (folders), and SB (scrapbooks)
William Francis Ganong papers
Jarvis family papers
New Brunswick Historical Society papers
Saint John, "A register of voters for the purposes of the elections of mayor, aldermen, councillors, and constables, of the city of Saint John: prepared from the records of the city freemen . . . ," 1785–1869
Ward family papers
John Clarence Webster papers

PRINCE EDWARD ISLAND MUSEUM AND HERITAGE FOUNDATION, Charlottetown. Various files were consulted in the preparation of volume VII for biographical and genealogical data on Island residents. In addition the following item was cited:
"Charlottetown manuscript" (n.d.)

PROVINCIAL ARCHIVES OF BRITISH COLUMBIA, Victoria. In 1975 the archives began a new cataloguing system for its manuscript holdings. Manuscripts catalogued since then have been assigned Additional manuscript (Add. MSS) numbers. Manuscripts catalogued under the old system are gradually being converted to the new one and given Add. MSS numbers.

Materials cited in volume VII include the following:
Add. MSS 345: Gertrude A. Rhodes papers, documents relating to the Red River settlement
Add. MSS 635: Donald Ross collection
Add. MSS 1249: Malcolm McLeod collection
E/E/St8: Louisa Mure, "Recollections of by-gone days" (1883)
M/St8: James Charles Stuart Strange, miscellaneous material

PROVINCIAL ARCHIVES OF MANITOBA, Winnipeg. For information on the collections see its *Preliminary inventory, 1955* (Winnipeg, [1955]).

The following materials were used in the preparation of volume VII:
MG 1: Indians, exploration and fur trade
D: Fur trade, individuals
5: MacLeod, John
MG 2: Red River settlement
C: Individuals and settlement
23: Logan, Robert
38: Garrioch, Peter
MG 7: Church records and religious figures
D: Roman Catholic
13: Belleau collection
P337: Archives of the Ecclesiastical Province of Rupert's Land
P2543: Lawson, Elsie J., collection
Hudson's Bay Company Archives. The PRO and the PAC hold microfilm copies of the archives' records for the years 1670 to 1870, and are acquiring the microfilm for the period 1871–1904 as it is produced. For more information concerning the copies held at the PAC and the finding aids available, see *General inventory, manuscripts, 3*. The articles by R. H. G. Leveson Gower, "The archives of the Hudson's Bay Company," *Beaver*, outfit 264 (December 1933): 40–42, 64, and Joan Craig, "Three hundred years of records," *Beaver*, outfit 301 (autumn 1970): 65–70, provide useful information to researchers. For series of HBCA documents published by the HBRS, *see* section II.
Section A: London office records
A.1/: London minute-books
A.5/: London correspondence books outward – general
A.6/: London correspondence books outward – HBC official
A.8/: London correspondence with her majesty's government
A.10/: London inward correspondence – general
A.12/: London inward correspondence from governors of HBC territories
A.30/: Lists of servants

A.31/: Lists of commissioned officers
A.32/: Servants' contracts
A.33/: Commissioned officers' indentures and agreements
A.34/: Servants' characters and staff records
A.36/: Officers' and servants' wills
A.38/: Legal cases
A.44/: Register book of wills and administrations of proprietors, etc.
Section B: North America trading post records
B.3/a: Albany journals
B.3/b: Albany correspondence books
B.4/b: Fort Alexander correspondence books
B.8/a: Fort Assiniboine journals
B.22/a: Brandon House journals
B.32/a: Chatham House journals
B.39/a: Fort Chipewyan journals
B.39/b: Fort Chipewyan correspondence books
B.39/e: Fort Chipewyan reports on districts
B.42/a: Fort Churchill journals
B.49/a: Cumberland House journals
B.49/e: Cumberland House reports on districts
B.51/a: Fort Dauphin journals
B.85/a: Fort Halkett journals
B.94/a: Jasper House journals
B.115/a: Lesser Slave Lake journals
B.119/a: McLeod Lake journals
B.135/a: Moose Factory journals
B.135/c: Moose Factory correspondence inward
B.135/k: Moose Factory minutes of council
B.141/a: Nelson House journals
B.141/e: Nelson House reports on districts
B.149/a: Nipigon House journals
B.159/a: Fort Pelly journals
B.170/c: Quebec correspondence inward
B.177/a: Red Lake journals
B.179/a: Reindeer Lake journals
B.188/a: Fort St James journals
B.188/b: Fort St James correspondence books
B.188/e: Fort St James reports on districts
B.198/a: Severn House journals
B.198/b: Severn House correspondence books
B.200/a: Fort Simpson journals
B.200/b: Fort Simpson correspondence books
B.200/d: Fort Simpson account-books
B.200/e: Fort Simpson reports on districts
B.235/a: Winnipeg journals
B.235/c: Winnipeg correspondence inward
B.235/d: Winnipeg account-books
B.239/a: York Factory journals
B.239/b: York Factory correspondence books
B.239/c: York Factory correspondence inward
B.239/d: York Factory account-books
B.239/g: York Factory abstracts of servants' accounts
B.239/k: York Factory minutes of council
B.239/x: York Factory servants' ledgers
B.239/z: York Factory miscellaneous items
Section C: Records of ships owned or chartered by the HBC
C.1: Ships' logs
Section D: Governors' papers
D.1/: William Williams
D.4/: George Simpson outward correspondence books
D.5/: George Simpson correspondence inward
Section E: Miscellaneous records
E.4/: Red River settlement, register of baptisms, marriages, and burials
E.5/: Red River settlement, census returns
E.6/: Red River settlement, land registers and records
E.8/: Red River settlement, papers relating to the disturbances
E.10/: Colin Robertson records
E.11/: Nicholas Garry records
E.20/: Papers relating to king's posts
E.24/: John Stuart records
Section F: Records of allied and subsidiary companies
F.1/: North West Company minute-books
F.2/: North West Company post journal
F.3/: North West Company correspondence
F.4/: North West Company account-books
F.5/: North West Company servants' contracts
F.6/: North West Company and North West Company Partners' Trust deeds and agreements
F.7/: North West Company and North West Company Partners' Trust legal opinions and legal cases

PROVINCIAL ARCHIVES OF NEW BRUNSWICK, Fredericton. For information on the manuscript holdings, *A guide to the manuscript collections in the Provincial Archives of New Brunswick*, comp. A. C. Rigby (Fredericton, 1977), is useful, although the classification system used when it was published has since been revised.

Materials used in the preparation of volume VII include:

MC 1: Family history collection
216: Kathleen Williston collection
239: Coy family papers
288: New Brunswick Barristers' Society collection
300: York-Sunbury Historical Society collection
1156: Graves papers
1316: John Russell Harper collection
RG 1: Records of the lieutenant governors and administrators
RS330: Thomas Carleton
RS333: Martin Hunter
RS336: George Stracey Smyth
RS345: William Colebrooke

RG 2: Records of the central executive
RS6: Minutes and orders-in-council of the Executive Council
RS7: Executive Council records, Ottawa series. An artificial series available on microfilm at the PANB and at PAC, MG 9, A1. An outline of the contents is available in PAC, *General inventory, manuscripts, 1*; the original documents are in the possession of the PANB but have been reorganized.
RS8: Executive Council records, New Brunswick series. An artificial series available on microfilm. The PANB holds the original documents but they have been extensively reorganized.
RG 3: Records of the provincial secretary
RS13: Departmental correspondence
RS266: Population returns and statistics, Saint John County
RS307: Administration of state oaths
RS538: Appointments and commissions
RS561: Administration of roads
RG 4: Records of the New Brunswick General Assembly
RS24: Legislative Assembly sessional records. The PANB has prepared a calendar for the years 1786 to 1832: "A new calendar of the papers of the House of Assembly of New Brunswick," comp. R. P. Nason *et al.* (3v., typescript, Fredericton, 1975–77).
RG 5: Records of the superior courts
RS42: Supreme Court records: original jurisdiction
RG 7: Records of the probate courts
RS64: Gloucester County
RS66: Kings County
RS69: Queens County
RS70: Restigouche County
RS71: Saint John County
RS74: Westmorland County
RS75: York County
RG 10: Records of the Department of Natural Resources
RS108: Land petitions
RS663: Timber and sawmill petitions
RG 11: Records of the Department of Education
RS657: College of New Brunswick
RG 18: Records of the Department of Municipal Affairs
RS153: Northumberland County Council records
RS157: Sunbury County Council records
RS159: Westmorland County Council records

PROVINCIAL ARCHIVES OF NEWFOUNDLAND AND LABRADOR, St John's. For information on the collections see *Preliminary inventory of the holdings . . .* and *Supplement . . .* (2 nos., St John's, 1970–74).

The following materials are cited in volume VII:
GN: Government records – Newfoundland
GN 2: Department of the Colonial Secretary
1: Letter-books, outgoing correspondence
2: Incoming correspondence
GN 5: Court records
1: Surrogate Court
2: Supreme Court
GN 16: Department of the surveyor general
1: Register of rents
P: Private records
P1: Governors' private papers
5: Duckworth papers
P3: Pre-1855 papers
B: Mercantile
14: Richard Fogarty collection, Waterford, [Republic of Ireland]
P7: Businesses
A: Fishing related
18: Ryan & Morris collection, Burin
P8: Benevolent organizations
A: Churches
11: Congregational Church

PUBLIC ARCHIVES OF NOVA SCOTIA, Halifax. For a description of the collections see *Inventory of manuscripts in the Public Archives of Nova Scotia* (Halifax, 1976).

Materials used in the preparation of volume VII include:
MG 1: Papers of families and individuals
11: William Bruce Almon diary
18–83: Mather Byles Almon business papers
88: Archibald family correspondence
89: Samuel G. W. Archibald correspondence
109–24: Winthrop P. Bell documents
160A: William M. Brown genealogy
165: John Cameron diary
181–218: Chipman family documents
253: Copy of thesis concerning Lord Dalhousie's administration in Canada
262B: Dodd family documents
334: Brenton Halliburton papers
479–80: Charles Inglis documents
550–58: Thomas McCulloch documents
733A: Isabella Owen, notes from scrapbooks
742–44: George Patterson documents
793: Simon B. Robie documents
817–63: Thomas B. Smith collection
947–62: White family documents
979–80: Peleg Wiswall documents
1489: T. N. Jeffery family documents

1595–613: Bliss family papers
1619–50: Charles St C. Stayner collection
1693: Haliburton family papers
1845: C. B. Fergusson papers

MG 2: Political papers
719–25: George Renny Young papers
726–30: John Young papers
731–82: William Young papers

MG 3: Business papers
154: Halifax Fire Insurance Company documents
306–17: Robert Thomson, Shelburne, business papers
1873: John and P. F. Homer, Barrington, account-book

MG 4: Churches and communities
2: St James' Anglican Church (Bridgetown), records

MG 5: Cemeteries

MG 9: Scrap-books

MG 12: Great Britain, army

MG 15: Ethnic collections
B: Indians
C: Negroes
G: Gaelic collection

MG 20: Societies and special collections
61–70: Charitable Irish Society, Halifax
180: Halifax Poor Man's Friend Society
670: Nova Scotia Historical Society MSS

MG 100: Documents, newspaper clippings, and miscellaneous items

RG 1: Bound volumes of Nova Scotia records for the period 1624–1867
5–11: Transcripts relating to the government at Annapolis Royal
29–185: Documents relating to the government of Nova Scotia: dispatches, letter-books, and commission books
186–214½H: Council, minutes
219–85: Miscellaneous documents
286–300: Legislative Council, selections from the files
301–14: Legislative Assembly, selections from the files
385–87: Correspondence between the governors of Nova Scotia and the British minister at Washington
410–17: Papers of the settlement of Halifax
419–22: Papers of negro and maroon immigrations and settlements
430–32: Indians
438–39: Schools and school lands
443–54: Census and poll tax
491–98: Records of proceedings of the Vice-Admiralty Court of Nova Scotia
525: Annotated copy of Murdoch, *Hist. of N.S.* [*see* section IV]

RG 2: Records of the governors' and lieutenant governors' offices

RG 4: Records of the Legislative Council of Nova Scotia
LC: Petitions, reports, resolutions, and miscellaneous papers

RG 5: Records of the Legislative Assembly of Nova Scotia
A: Assembly papers
P: Petitions
R: Reports and resolutions

RG 7: Records of the provincial secretary of Nova Scotia

RG 8: Records of the Central Board of Agriculture of Nova Scotia

RG 14: Education

RG 20: Lands and forests
A: Land grants and petitions
B: Cape Breton land papers
C: Crown lands

RG 25: Public health
C: Miscellaneous

RG 31: Treasury
102–20: Impost, excise, and revenue

RG 32: Vital statistics
132–69: Marriage bonds

RG 34: Court of General Sessions of the Peace
312: Halifax County
321: Shelburne County

RG 35A: Halifax city and county assessments
1–4: Halifax city assessments

RG 36: Court of Chancery

RG 39: Supreme Court
AP: Annapolis County
HX: Halifax County
KI: Kings County

RG 40: Court of Vice-Admiralty

PUBLIC ARCHIVES OF PRINCE EDWARD ISLAND, Charlottetown.

Materials used in the preparation of volume VII include:

Acc. 2541: Natural History Society for Prince Edward Island
2702: Smith–Alley collection
2810: Ira Brown papers
2825: T. E. MacNutt papers
2849: Palmer family papers
2881: Peake–Brecken collection
2918: Bell papers
3466: Prince Edward Island Heritage Foundation collection

RG 1: Lieutenant Governor

RG 3: House of Assembly

RG 5: Executive Council

RG 6: Courts

RG 16: Registry Office

QUÉBEC, MINISTÈRE DE LA JUSTICE. The Archives civiles and the Archives judiciaires du Québec, which are under the joint jurisdiction of the courts and the Ministère de la Justice, are now separate repositories as a result of the reclassification of the former Archives judiciaires. They are deposited at the court-houses in the administrative centres of the 34 judicial districts of Quebec. A list of the judicial districts can be found in *The Quebec legal directory*, ed. Andrée Frenette-Lecoq (Montreal, 1980).
ARCHIVES CIVILES. These archives retain documents for the last 100 years, including registers of births, marriages, and deaths, notaries' *minutiers* (minute-books), and records of surveyors active in the district. Earlier documents are held by the ANQ.

QUÉBEC, MINISTÈRE DES AFFAIRES CULTURELLES, CENTRE DE DOCUMENTATION, Québec. The Ministère des Affaires culturelles has consolidated into one documentation centre the collections of all its previously existing centres, including that of the Inventaire des biens culturels.

Series cited in volume VII:
Fonds Morisset
1: Inventaire de l'art et de l'architecture
2: Dossiers des artistes et artisans

QUEEN'S UNIVERSITY ARCHIVES, Kingston, Ont. For information on the collection see *A guide to the holdings of Queen's University Archives*, ed. Anne MacDermaid and G. F. Henderson (2nd ed., Kingston, 1986).

In addition to various MC (Manuscript collection) materials, the following numbered collections were used in the preparation of volume VII:
2189: Robert McDowall papers
2199a: John Solomon Cartwright papers
2199c: Richard Cartwright papers
2239–40: Jones family papers
2244: Midland District School Society records
2247: Tett family papers
2254: John Kirby papers
2256: John Macaulay papers
2263: Presbyterian Church of Canada records
2270: Kirkpatrick–Nickle legal collection, Auldjo family papers
2402: William Bell papers
3077: Joel Stone papers

UNITED CHURCH ARCHIVES. The present-day United Church Archives is a descendant of 19th- and 20th-century archival collections of various Canadian Methodist, Presbyterian, Congregational, and Evangelical/United Brethren in Christ bodies. The Central Archives of the United Church of Canada at Victoria University, Toronto, is national in scope. Material of local interest, including the official records of the conferences concerned, is housed in regional conference archives.
CENTRAL ARCHIVES, Toronto

Various materials were used in the preparation of volume VII, in particular the Egerton Ryerson papers.

UNIVERSITY OF NEW BRUNSWICK LIBRARY, Archives and Special Collections Department, Fredericton.

Materials used in volume VII include:
BC-MS: Beaverbrook collection
Sir Howard Douglas letter-books
MG H: Historical
H2: Winslow family papers
H9: Lilian Mary Beckwith Maxwell papers
H11: Saunders papers
H54: Indian affairs – New Brunswick
UA: University archives
"Minute-book of the governors and trustees of the College of New Brunswick," 1800–28

UNIVERSITY OF TORONTO, THOMAS FISHER RARE BOOK LIBRARY. For a description of holdings see *The Thomas Fisher Rare Book Library: a brief guide to the collections* (Toronto, 1982).

Materials used in volume VII include:
MS coll. 30: James Nevin Wallace, "Encyclopedia of the fur trade, biographical & geographical"
MS coll. 31: William Stewart Wallace collection
MS coll. 126: James Little Baillie papers
MS coll. 140: Charles Fothergill papers

UNIVERSITY OF WESTERN ONTARIO LIBRARY, Regional Collection, London, Ont. A description of the municipal record and personal manuscript collections is available on microfiche in *Regional Collection: the D. B. Weldon Library catalogue*, ed. S. L. Sykes (4 fiches, London, 1977).

Various personal manuscript collections proved useful in the preparation of volume VII, in particular the following:
James Evans papers

FRANCE

ARCHIVES DÉPARTEMENTALES. For a list of analytical inventories *see*: France, Direction des archives, *État des inventaires des archives nationales, départementales, communales et hospitalières au 1er janvier 1937* (Paris, 1938); *Supplément, 1937–1954* [by R.-H. Bautier] (Paris, 1955); and *Catalogue des inventaires, répertoires, guides de recherche et autres instruments de travail des archives départementales, communales et hospitalières . . . à la date du 31 décembre 1961* (Paris, 1962). For copies of documents held by the PAC see *General inventory, manuscripts, 1*: 87–99. There is a uniform system of classification for all departmental archives.

GREAT BRITAIN

BRITISH LIBRARY, Department of manuscripts, London. For a brief guide to catalogues and indexes of the manuscript collections, *see* M. A. E. Nickson, *The British Library: guide to the catalogues and indexes of the Department of Manuscripts* (2nd ed., London, 1982). The *Index of manuscripts in the British Library* (10v., Cambridge, Eng., 1984–86) provides person and place entries for all collections acquired up to 1950. For copies of documents from the British Library in the PAC see *General inventory, manuscripts, 3*.

The following collections were used in the preparation of volume VII:

Add. MSS 21661–892: Official correspondence and papers of Lieutenant Governor Sir Frederick Haldimand

India Office Library and Records. For information on this institution, which holds the archives of the East India Company and its successor, the India Office, *see* S. C. Sutton, *A guide to the India Office Library, with a note on the India Office Records* (London, 1967), and M. I. Moir, *A general guide to the India Office Records* (London, 1988). Under the jurisdiction of the Foreign and Commonwealth Office until 1982, it is now a department of the British Library's Humanities and Social Sciences Division.

India Office Records
- E: East India Company: General correspondence
  - E/4: Correspondence with India
- H: Home miscellaneous series
- L: Departmental records
  - L/MAR: Marine Department
- O: Biographical records
- P: Proceedings of the government of India and of the presidencies and provinces

GENERAL REGISTER OFFICE, London. Death records for various individuals were consulted in the preparation of volume VII.

GENERAL REGISTER OFFICE FOR SCOTLAND, Edinburgh. Information concerning the parish registers held by the GRO is available in *Detailed list of old parochial registers of Scotland* (Edinburgh, 1872). Registers of baptisms, marriages, and burials for several Scottish parishes were used in the preparation of volume VII.

NATIONAL LIBRARY OF SCOTLAND, Department of Manuscripts, Edinburgh. Information on the manuscript collections is available in *Catalogue of manuscripts acquired since 1925* (5v. to date [1–4, 6], Edinburgh, 1938–).

Materials used in the preparation of volume VII include:

Advocates' manuscripts
- Adv. MSS 46.1.1–46.10.2: Murray papers

Manuscripts
- MSS 789–802: Constable & Cadell letter- and business-books
- MSS 2264–505, 2568–608, 3022: Cochrane papers
- MSS 6660–7000: William Wilson & Son papers
- MSS 7638–58: United Presbyterian Church, letter-books
- MSS 9250–307: Dunlop papers
- MSS 15001–195: Ellice papers

NATIONAL MARITIME MUSEUM, London. For information on the manuscript collections see *Guide to the manuscripts in the National Maritime Museum*, ed. R. J. B. Knight (2v., London, 1977–80).

The following materials have been used in the preparation of volume VII:

Personal collections
- BIE: Barrie papers
- MRY: Marryat papers

C. G. Pitcairn-Jones, "The commissioned sea officers of the Royal Navy, 1660–1815"

Records of business and non-governmental organizations
- P&O, Personal histories

PUBLIC RECORD OFFICE, London. For an introduction to the holdings and arrangement of this archives see *Guide to the contents of the Public Record Office* (3v., London, 1963–68). For copies of PRO documents available at the PAC see *General inventory, manuscripts, 2*.

The following series were used in the preparation of volume VII:

Admiralty
- Accounting departments
  - ADM 42: Yard pay books
- Admiralty and Secretariat
  - ADM 1: Papers
  - ADM 9: Returns of officers' services
  - ADM 12: Indexes and compilations, series III
  - ADM 50: Admirals' journals
- Navy Board
  - ADM 106: Navy Board records
- Admiralty
  - ADM 196: Officers' service records, series III

Board of Trade
- Registrar general of shipping and seamen
  - BT 98: Agreements and crew lists, series I
  - BT 107: Ships' registers

Colonial Office. [*See* R. B. Pugh, *The records of the Colonial and Dominions offices* (London, 1964).]
- America and West Indies
  - CO 5: Original correspondence, etc.
- America, British North
  - CO 6: Original correspondence

Australia, South
CO 13: Original correspondence
CO 15: Sessional papers
Bermuda
CO 38: Entry books
Canada
CO 42: Original correspondence
CO 43: Entry books
CO 47: Miscellanea
Ceylon
CO 54: Original correspondence
Malta
CO 158: Original correspondence
New Brunswick
CO 188: Original correspondence
CO 189: Entry books
CO 193: Miscellanea
Newfoundland
CO 194: Original correspondence
CO 195: Entry books
CO 197: Sessional papers
CO 199: Miscellaneous
Nova Scotia and Cape Breton
CO 217: Original correspondence
CO 218: Entry books
CO 220: Sessional papers
Prince Edward Island
CO 226: Original correspondence
CO 227: Entry books
CO 231: Miscellanea
Sierra Leone
CO 267: Original correspondence
Colonies, General
CO 323: Original correspondence
CO 324: Entry books, series I
CO 325: Miscellanea
Emigration
CO 384: Original correspondence
Private collections
CO 387: Aylmer papers
Supplementary
CO 537: Correspondence
Exchequer and Audit Department
AO 1: Declared accounts (in rolls)
AO 12: Claims, American loyalists, series I
AO 13: Claims, American loyalists, series II
Home Office
Channel Islands, Scotland, Ireland, etc.
HO 102: Scotland, correspondence and papers
Prerogative Court of Canterbury
PROB 11: Registered copy wills
Public Record Office
Documents acquired by gift, deposit, or purchase
PRO 30/22: Russell papers
PRO 30/55: Carleton papers
Registrar General
RG 4/965: Authenticated register, Bow Meeting House (Presbyterian), Exeter
Treasury
Expired commissions, etc.
T 93: French Refugees Relief Committee
War Office
Correspondence
WO 1: In-letters
WO 43: Selected "Very Old Series" and "Old Series" papers
Returns
WO 17: Monthly returns
WO 25: Registers, various
WO 27: Inspection returns
WO 42: Certificates of birth, etc.
WO 76: Officers' services, records of
Ordnance Office
WO 44: In-letters
WO 55: Miscellanea
Judge Advocate General's Office
WO 85: Deputation books
Private collections
WO 211: Hart papers

RHODES HOUSE LIBRARY, University of Oxford. United Society for the Propagation of the Gospel Archives. In 1985 the society's archives were closed; its holdings are being transferred to Rhodes House Library. For information about materials relating to Canada, *see* William Westfall and Ian Pearson, "The archives of the United Society for the Propagation of the Gospel and Canadian history," Canadian Church Hist. Soc., *Journal* (Toronto), 25 (1983): 16–24.

Some materials, particularly in the C/CAN series, were reorganized and reclassified by the USPG after having been microfilmed by the PAC. As a result, references to microfilm copies of USPG records do not always correspond to those of the archives itself. For copies of USPG documents available at the PAC, see *General inventory, manuscripts, 3*.

The following collections were consulted:

C/CAN: Unbound letters from Canada, 1752–1860. Letters from the Nova Scotia, Quebec, and Toronto groupings were used.
Dr Bray's Associates, minute-books
Journal of proceedings of the Society for the Propagation of the Gospel. Comprises bound and indexed volumes of the proceedings of the general meetings held in London from 1701, and four appendices, A, B, C, D (1701–1860).

SCHOOL OF ORIENTAL AND AFRICAN STUDIES LIBRARY, University of London. The archival collections of several missionary societies are deposited in the library.

The following collections were used in the preparation of volume VII:
Council for World Mission Archives. The library has published a general guide to the collection: C. S. Craig, *The archives of the Council for World Mission (incorporating the London Missionary Society): an outline guide* (London, 1973).
London Missionary Society
Correspondence, North America
Methodist Missionary Society Archives. Canadian material was microfilmed by the PAC in 1955, when the originals were held by the Methodist Missionary Society; *see* PAC, *General inventory, manuscripts, 3*.
Wesleyan Methodist Missionary Society
Correspondence, North America

SCOTTISH RECORD OFFICE, Edinburgh. A comprehensive listing of materials relating to Canada is provided by the SRO's "List of Canadian documents" (typescript, 1977, with updates to 1983), available at major Canadian archives. An appendix records Canadian documents in private archives as surveyed by the National Register of Archives (Scotland).
The following are cited in volume VII:
CE: Customs and excise
CE60: Port Glasgow and Greenock
1: Collector of customs, letter-book
GD: Gifts and deposits
GD45: Dalhousie muniments
GD51: Melville Castle muniments
GD248: Seafield muniments
GD293: Montgomery of Stanhope estate papers in the muniments of Messrs Blackwood and Smith, W.S., Peebles

UNITED STATES

DETROIT PUBLIC LIBRARY, Burton Historical Collection.
Various materials were used in the preparation of volume VII, in particular the following:
John Askin papers

STATE HISTORICAL SOCIETY OF WISCONSIN, Madison. For information on the manuscript collection see *Guide to the manuscripts of the Wisconsin Historical Society*, ed. A. M. Smith (Madison, 1944), *Supplement number one*, ed. J. L. Harper and S. C. Smith (1957), and *Supplement number two*, ed. J. L. Harper (1966).
Various materials were used in the preparation of volume VII, in particular the Draper MSS, which are discussed at length in *Guide to the Draper manuscripts*, ed. J. L. Harper (1983).

II. PRINTED PRIMARY SOURCES

A. OFFICIAL PUBLICATIONS AND CONTEMPORARY WORKS

ARCHIVES NATIONALES DU QUÉBEC, Québec
PUBLICATIONS [*see also* section III]
Rapport. 54 vols. 1920/21–1976/77. There is an index to the contents of the first 42 volumes: *Table des matières des rapports des Archives du Québec, tomes 1 à 42 (1920–1964)* ([Québec], 1965).
ARCHIVES OF ONTARIO, Toronto
PUBLICATIONS
Report. 22 vols. 1903–33.
The Arthur papers; being the Canadian papers, mainly confidential, private, and demi-official of Sir George Arthur, K.C.H., last lieutenant-governor of Upper Canada, in the manuscript collection of the Toronto Public Libraries. Edited by Charles Rupert Sanderson. 3 vols. Toronto, 1957–59.
Les bourgeois de la Compagnie du Nord-Ouest: récits de voyages, lettres et rapports inédits relatifs au Nord-Ouest canadien. Louis-[François-]Rodrigue Masson, éditeur. 2 vols. Québec, 1889–90; réimprimé New York, 1960.
CANADA, PROVINCE OF
LEGISLATIVE ASSEMBLY/ASSEMBLÉE LÉGISLATIVE
Appendix to the . . . journals/Appendice . . . des journaux, 1841–59. See also *The Legislative Assembly of the Province of Canada: an index to journal appendices and sessional papers, 1841–1866*, comp. P. A. Damphouse (London, Ont., 1974).
Journals/Journaux, 1841–66.
LEGISLATIVE COUNCIL/CONSEIL LÉGISLATIF
Journals/Journaux, 1841–66.
Statutes/Statuts, 1841–66. English title varies: *Provincial statutes of Canada*, 1841–51; *Statutes of the Province of Canada*, 1852–66.
For further information on the English-language publications of the Province of Canada, *see* Bishop, *Pubs. of government of Prov. of Canada* [section III].
Canadian Antiquarian and Numismatic Journal. Montreal. Published by the Antiquarian and Numismatic Society of Montreal. [1st ser.], 1 (1872–73)–13 (1886); 2nd ser., 1 (1889–90)–3 (1893–94); 3rd ser., 1 (1898)–13 (1916); 4th ser., 1 (1930)–4 (1933). Not published 1884, 1887–88, 1891, 1895–97, 1900, 1903–7, and 1917–29.

The Canadian north-west, its early development and legislative records; minutes of the councils of the Red River colony and the Northern Department of Rupert's Land. Edited by Edmund Henry Oliver. (PAC publications, 9.) 2 vols. Ottawa, 1914–15.

CHAMPLAIN SOCIETY, Toronto

PUBLICATIONS

55 vols. to date, exclusive of the Hudson's Bay Company series [see *HBRS*], the Ontario series, and the unnumbered series. Issued only to elected members of the society who are limited in numbers.

13–15, 17: *Select British docs. of War of 1812* (Wood).

22: *Docs. relating to NWC* (Wallace).

24: Hargrave, *Hargrave corr.* (Glazebrook).

ONTARIO SERIES

13 vols. to date. Available for sale to the general public.

5: *Town of York, 1793–1815* (Firth).

7: *Valley of Six Nations* (Johnston).

8: *Town of York, 1815–34* (Firth).

12: *Rebellion of 1837* (Read and Stagg).

The correspondence of Lieut. Governor John Graves Simcoe, with allied documents relating to his administration of the government of Upper Canada. Edited by Ernest Alexander Cruikshank. (Ontario Historical Society publication.) 5 vols. Toronto, 1923–31.

The correspondence of the Honourable Peter Russell, with allied documents relating to his administration of the government of Upper Canada during the official term of Lieut.-Governor J. G. Simcoe, while on leave of absence. Edited by Ernest Alexander Cruikshank and Andrew Frederick Hunter. (Ontario Historical Society publication.) 3 vols. Toronto, 1932–36.

Debates of the Legislative Assembly of United Canada, 1841–1867. General editor, Elizabeth Abbott [Nish] Gibbs. 12 vols. in 28 to date. Montreal, 1970– .

"Les dénombrements de Québec faits en 1792, 1795, 1798 et 1805." Joseph-Octave Plessis, compilateur. ANQ *Rapport*, 1948–49: 1–250.

The documentary history of the campaign upon the Niagara frontier. . . . Edited by Ernest [Alexander] Cruikshank. (Lundy's Lane Historical Society publication.) 9 vols. Welland, Ont., [1896]–1908.

Documents relating to the constitutional history of Canada. . . . Edited by Adam Shortt *et al.* (PAC publication.) 3 vols. Ottawa, 1907–35.

[1]: *1759–1791*. Edited by Adam Shortt and Arthur George Doughty. 2nd edition. (PAC, Board of Historical Publications.) 2 parts. 1918.

[2]: *1791–1818*. Edited by Arthur George Doughty and Duncan A. McArthur.

[3]: *1819–1828*. Edited by Arthur George Doughty and Norah Story.

Documents relating to the North West Company. Edited by William Stewart Wallace. (Champlain Society publications, 22.) Toronto, 1934.

Gentleman's Magazine. London, 1731–1907.

HARGRAVE, [JAMES]. *The Hargrave correspondence, 1821–1843.* Edited with introduction and notes by George Parkin de Twenebrokes Glazebrook. (Champlain Society publications, 24.) Toronto, 1938.

HUDSON'S BAY RECORD SOCIETY, Winnipeg

PUBLICATIONS

33 vols. General editor for vols.1–22, Edwin Ernest Rich; vols.23–25, Kenneth Gordon Davies; vols.26–30, Glyndwr Williams; vols. 31–33, Hartwell Bowsfield. Vols.1–12 were issued in association with the Champlain Society [*q.v.*] and reprinted in 1968 in Nendeln, Liechtenstein; vol.13 was reprinted in Nendeln in 1979.

1: Simpson, George. *Journal of occurrences in the Athabasca Department by George Simpson, 1820 and 1821, and report.* Edited by Edwin Ernest Rich, with an introduction by Chester [Bailey] Martin. Toronto, 1938.

2: Robertson, Colin. *Colin Robertson's correspondence book, September 1817 to September 1822.* Edited with an introduction by Edwin Ernest Rich, assisted by Robert Harvey Fleming. Toronto, 1939.

3: *Minutes of Council, Northern Department of Rupert Land, 1821–31.* Edited by Robert Harvey Fleming, with an introduction by Harold Adams Innis. Toronto, 1940.

4: McLoughlin, John. *The letters of John McLoughlin from Fort Vancouver to the governor and committee, first series, 1825–38.* Edited by Edwin Ernest Rich, with an introduction by William Kaye Lamb. London, 1941.

6: McLoughlin, John. *The letters of John McLoughlin from Fort Vancouver to the governor and committee, second series, 1839–44.* Edited by Edwin Ernest Rich, with an introduction by William Kaye Lamb. London, 1943.

10: Simpson, George. *Part of dispatch from George Simpson, esqr, governor of Ruperts Land, to the governor & committee of the Hudson's Bay Company, London, March 1, 1829; continued and completed March 24 and June 5, 1829.* Edited by Edwin Ernest Rich, with an introduction by William Stewart Wallace. Toronto, 1947.

13: Ogden, Peter Skene. *Peter Skene Ogden's Snake country journals, 1824–25 and 1825–26.* Edited by Edwin Ernest Rich, assisted by Alice Margaret Johnson, with an introduction by Burt Brown Barker. London, 1950.

18: [Black, Samuel]. *A journal of a voyage from*

Rocky Mountain Portage in Peace River to the sources of Finlays Branch and North West Ward in summer 1824. Edited by Edwin Ernest Rich, assisted by Alice Margaret Johnson, with an introduction by R. M. Patterson. London, 1955.

19: Colvile, Eden. *London correspondence inward from Eden Colvile, 1849–1852*. Edited by Edwin Ernest Rich, assisted by Alice Margaret Johnson, with an introduction by William Lewis Morton. London, 1956.

21–22: Rich, *Hist. of HBC* [*see* section IV].

23: Ogden, Peter Skene. *Peter Skene Ogden's Snake country journal, 1826–27*. Edited by Kenneth Gordon Davies, assisted by Alice Margaret Johnson, with an introduction by Dorothy O. Johansen. London, 1961.

24: *Northern Quebec and Labrador journals and correspondence, 1819–35*. Edited by Kenneth Gordon Davies, assisted by Alice Margaret Johnson, with an introduction by Glyndwr Williams. London, 1963.

28: Ogden, Peter Skene. *Peter Skene Ogden's Snake country journals, 1827–28 and 1828–29*. Edited by Glyndwr Williams, with an introduction and notes by David Eugene Miller and David H. Miller. London, 1971.

29: Simpson, George. *London correspondence inward from Sir George Simpson, 1841–42*. Edited by Glyndwr Williams, with an introduction by John S. Galbraith. London, 1973.

30: *Hudson's Bay miscellany, 1670–1870*. Edited with introductions by Glyndwr Williams. Winnipeg, 1975.

The John Askin papers. Edited by Milo Milton Quaife. (DPL, Burton historical records, 1–2.) 2 vols. Detroit, 1928–31.

"The journals of the Legislative Assembly of Upper Canada . . . [1792–1824]." AO *Report*, 1909, 1911–14. The journals for part of 1794 and for 1795–97, 1809, 1813, and 1815 are missing.

LITERARY AND HISTORICAL SOCIETY OF QUEBEC/ SOCIÉTÉ LITTÉRAIRE ET HISTORIQUE DE QUÉBEC, Quebec

PUBLICATIONS

Transactions. [1st ser.], 1 (1824–29)–5 (1861–62); new ser., 1 (1862–63)–30 (1924).

Literary Garland. Montreal. [1st ser.], 1 (1838–39)–4 (1841–42); new ser., 1 (1842–43)–9 (1851). Subtitle varies. The Bibliographical Society of Canada has brought out *An index to the "Literary Garland" (Montreal, 1838–1851)*, comp. Mary Markham Brown (Toronto, 1962), and has published additions and corrections in M. L. MacDonald, "*An index to the 'Literary Garland'* updated," in its *Papers* (Toronto), 19 (1980): 79–83.

LOWER CANADA/BAS-CANADA

HOUSE OF ASSEMBLY/CHAMBRE D'ASSEMBLÉE

Journals/Journaux. Quebec, 1792/93–1837.

LEGISLATIVE COUNCIL/CONSEIL LÉGISLATIF

Journals/Journaux. Quebec, 1792/93–1837.

SPECIAL COUNCIL/CONSEIL SPÉCIAL

Journals/Journaux. Montreal, 1838–41.

Provincial statutes/Les statuts provinciaux. Quebec, 1792/93–1837.

For further information *see* Thériault, *Les pub. parl.* [section III].

Michigan Pioneer Collections. Lansing. 40 vols. 1874/76–1929. To avoid confusion the Michigan Historical Commission, Department of State, Lansing, has standardized the citation for these volumes, which were originally published by various historical agencies and under various titles. Volumes are traditionally cited by their spine dates.

NATIONAL ARCHIVES OF CANADA, Ottawa (officially known as the Public Archives of Canada until 1987)

BOARD OF HISTORICAL PUBLICATIONS

Docs. relating to constitutional hist., 1759–91 (Shortt and Doughty; 1918).

NUMBERED PUBLICATIONS [*see also* section III]

9: *Canadian north-west* (Oliver).

OTHER PUBLICATIONS [*see also* section III]

Docs. relating to constitutional hist., 1791–1818 (Doughty and McArthur).

Docs. relating to constitutional hist., 1819–28 (Doughty and Story).

Report/Rapport. 1881–19 . Annually, with some omissions, until 1952; irregularly thereafter. For indexes, *see* section III.

NEW BRUNSWICK

HOUSE OF ASSEMBLY

Journal. Saint John, 1786–1814; Fredericton, 1816– . Title varies: *Journal of the votes and proceedings*; *Journal and votes*; *Journals*.

LEGISLATIVE COUNCIL

Journal. Fredericton, 1831–92. The pre-1831 journals were published as *Journal of the Legislative Council of the province of New Brunswick . . .* [1786–1830] (2v., Fredericton, 1831).

NEW BRUNSWICK HISTORICAL SOCIETY, Saint John

PUBLICATIONS

Collections. 12 nos. in 4 vols. and 22 additional nos. to date. 1894/97– . Used primarily for the documents reproduced.

NEWFOUNDLAND

GENERAL ASSEMBLY

Journal. St John's, 1843–46. From 1842 to 1847 the House of Assembly and Legislative Council were amalgamated into the unicameral General Assembly. No assemblies took place in 1842 or 1847.

HOUSE OF ASSEMBLY

Journal. St John's, 1833–1933, except for the period from 1842 to 1847 when the house was replaced by the General Assembly.
NOVA SCOTIA
HOUSE OF ASSEMBLY
Journal and proceedings. Halifax, 1761– . Title varies; this title in effect from 1789.
LEGISLATIVE COUNCIL
Journal and proceedings. Halifax, 1836–1928.
ONTARIO HISTORICAL SOCIETY, Toronto
PUBLICATIONS
Corr. of Hon. Peter Russell (Cruikshank and Hunter).
Corr. of Lieut. Governor Simcoe (Cruikshank).
OH [*see* section v].
"Papiers de Ludger Duvernay." *Canadian Antiquarian and Numismatic Journal*, 3rd ser., 5 (1908): 167–200; 6 (1909): 1–33, 87–138, 151–86; 7 (1910): 17–48; 8 (1911): 21–43, 76–96.
PAPINEAU, LOUIS-JOSEPH. "Correspondance de Louis-Joseph Papineau . . . [1820–39]." Fernand Ouellet, éditeur. ANQ *Rapport*, 1953–55: 191–442.
PAPINEAU, [LOUIS-JOSEPH-]AMÉDÉE. *Journal d'un Fils de la liberté, réfugié aux États-Unis, par suite de l'insurrection canadienne, en 1837*. 2 vols. to date. Montréal, 1972– .
"Political state of Upper Canada in 1806–7." PAC *Report*, 1892: 32–135.
PRINCE EDWARD ISLAND
HOUSE OF ASSEMBLY
Journal. Charlottetown, 1788–1893, except for the years 1798–1805 when no journals were printed. Title varies.
LEGISLATIVE COUNCIL
Journal. Charlottetown, 1827–60.
PUBLIC ARCHIVES OF CANADA, Ottawa. *See* NATIONAL ARCHIVES OF CANADA
[RAMSAY, GEORGE, 9TH EARL OF] DALHOUSIE. *The Dalhousie journals*. Edited by Marjory Whitelaw. 3 vols. [Ottawa], 1978–82.
The rebellion of 1837 in Upper Canada: a collection of documents. Edited by Colin [Frederick] Read and Ronald John Stagg. (Champlain Society/Ontario Heritage Foundation publication, Ontario series, 12.) Toronto, 1985. [Trade edition.] [Ottawa], 1985.
Recensement de la ville de Québec en 1818 par le curé Joseph Signaÿ. Honorius Provost, éditeur. Québec, 1976.
Report of the state trials, before a general court martial held at Montreal in 1838–9: exhibiting a complete history of the late rebellion in Lower Canada. . . . 2 vols. Montreal, 1839.
Select British documents of the Canadian War of 1812. Edited with an introduction by William [Charles Henry] Wood. (Champlain Society publications, 13–15, 17.) 3 vols. in 4. Toronto, 1920–28; reprinted New York, 1968.
SIMPSON, GEORGE. "The 'Character book' of Governor George Simpson, 1832." In *HBRS*, 30 (Williams): 151–236.
Source materials relating to the New Brunswick Indian. Compiled by Willis D. Hamilton and William Arthur Spray. Fredericton, 1976. Another edition. 1977.
Statistical account of Upper Canada, compiled with a view to a grand system of emigration. Compiled by Robert [Fleming] Gourlay. 2 vols. London, 1822; reprinted East Ardsley, Eng., and New York, 1966. Abridged and with an introduction by Stanley Robert Mealing. 1 vol. Toronto, 1974.
The town of York, 1793–1815: a collection of documents of early Toronto. Edited by Edith Grace Firth. (Champlain Society publications, Ontario series, 5.) Toronto, 1962.
The town of York, 1815–1834: a further collection of documents of early Toronto. Edited by Edith Grace Firth. (Champlain Society publications, Ontario series, 8.) Toronto, 1966.
UPPER CANADA
HOUSE OF ASSEMBLY
Appendix to the journal, 1835–1839/40.
Journal, 1821, 1825–1839/40. For the period from 1792 to 1824, *see* "Journals of Legislative Assembly of U.C.," AO *Report*, 1909, 1911–14.
LEGISLATIVE COUNCIL
Journal, 1828–1839/40. The earlier journals are available in "The journals of the Legislative Council of Upper Canada . . . [1792–1824]," AO *Report*, 1910, 1915.
Statutes, 1793–1840.
The valley of the Six Nations; a collection of documents on the Indian lands of the Grand River. Edited by Charles Murray Johnston. (Champlain Society publications, Ontario series, 7.) Toronto, 1964.
Wesleyan-Methodist Magazine. London, 1778– . Title varies: *Arminian Magazine*, 1–20 (1797); *Methodist Magazine*, 21 (1798)–44 (1821), 150 (1927)– ; *Wesleyan-Methodist Magazine*, 45 (1822)–136 (1913); *Magazine of the Wesleyan-Methodist Church*, 137 (1914)–149 (1926).
Winslow papers, A.D. 1776–1826. Edited by William Odber Raymond. Saint John, N.B., 1901.
WISCONSIN, STATE HISTORICAL SOCIETY, Madison
PUBLICATIONS
Collections. 31 vols. 1854–1931.

B. NEWSPAPERS

The following newspapers were particularly useful in the preparation of volume VII. Numerous sources have been used to determine their various titles and their dates of publication. These include, for all areas of the country: Canadian Library Assoc., *Canadian newspapers on microfilm, catalogue* (2 pts. in 3, Ottawa, 1959–69), *Union list of Canadian newspapers held by Canadian libraries* (Ottawa, 1977), and for pre-1800 newspapers, Marie Tremaine, *A bibliography of Canadian imprints, 1751–1800* (Toronto, 1952); for New Brunswick: J. R. Harper, *Historical directory of New Brunswick newspapers and periodicals* (Fredericton, 1961); for Newfoundland: "Chronological list of Newfoundland newspapers in the public collections at the Gosling Memorial Library and Provincial Archives," comp. Ian McDonald (typescript; copy in Nfld. Public Library Services, Provincial Reference and Resource Library, St John's), and *Serials holdings in Newfoundland libraries* (13th ed., 4v., St John's, 1987); for Nova Scotia: D. C. Harvey, "Newspapers of Nova Scotia, 1840–1867," *CHR*, 26 (1945): 279–301, Tratt, *Survey of N.S. newspapers* [*see* section III], and *An historical directory of Nova Scotia newspapers and journals before confederation*, comp. T. B. Vincent (Kingston, Ont., 1977); for Ontario: *Catalogue of Canadian newspapers in the Douglas Library, Queen's University*, comp. L. C. Ellison *et al.* (Kingston, 1969), *Dict. of Toronto printers* (Hulse) [*see* section III], *Early Toronto newspapers* (Firth) [*see* section III], *Inventory of Ontario newspapers, 1793–1986*, comp. J. B. Gilchrist (Toronto, 1987), and W. S. Wallace, "The periodical literature of Upper Canada," *CHR*, 12 (1931): 4–22; for Prince Edward Island: PAPEI, "Checklist and historical directory of Prince Edward Island newspapers, 1787–1986," comp. Heather Boylan (typescript, Charlottetown, 1987); and for Quebec: Beaulieu et Hamelin, *La presse québécoise*, vols.1–2 [*see* section III]. Bishop, *Pubs. of governments of N.S., P.E.I., N.B.* [*see* section III], gives information on official government gazettes in the Maritime provinces.

Acadian Recorder. Halifax. 16 Jan. 1813–May 1930.

L'Ami du peuple, de l'ordre et des lois. Montréal. 21 July 1832 to at least 18 July 1840.

L'Aurore des Canadas. Montréal. 15 Jan. 1839–23 March 1849.

British Colonist. Toronto. 1 Feb. 1838–September 1859.

British Whig. Kingston, Ont. 8 Feb. 1834–29 Nov. 1926, under various titles, including: *British Whig* (to 16 Jan. 1835); *British Whig, and General Advertiser for the Midland District* (as of 20 Jan. 1835); and *British Whig, and General Advertiser for Canada West* (by the 1840s). A daily edition began on 1 Jan. 1849 under the title *Daily British Whig*. On 1 Dec. 1926, the paper merged with the *Daily Standard* to form the *Whig-Standard*, which continues to the present.

Brockville Recorder. Brockville, Ont. 16 Jan. 1821–22 Feb. 1957, under various titles; its full title until 15 July 1847 was *Brockville Recorder, and the Eastern, Johnstown, and Bathurst Districts Advertiser*; on 1 Sept. 1853 it became simply the *Brockville Recorder*.

Bytown Gazette, and Ottawa and Rideau Advertiser. Ottawa. 9 June 1836 to around 1861, under various titles.

Canadian Freeman. Toronto. From about June 1825 to August 1834.

Le Canadien. Québec; Montréal. Published at Quebec from 22 Nov. 1806 to 4 Dec. 1891, and then at Montreal until 11 Feb. 1893 and from 22 Dec. 1906 to 11 Dec. 1909.

Christian Guardian. Toronto. 21 Nov. 1829–3 June 1925. A general index is available at the UCC-C.

Christian Messenger. Halifax. 6 Jan. 1837 to the end of 1884; merged with the *Christian Visitor* (Saint John, N.B.) to form the Saint John *Messenger and Visitor*. Its full title was *Christian Messenger and Repository of Religious, Political, and General Intelligence for Nova Scotia and New Brunswick*.

Chronicle & Gazette. Kingston, [Ont.]. 29 June 1833 to around October 1847, when it became the *Chronicle and News*. Its full title was *Chronicle & Gazette, and Weekly Commercial Advertiser* (29 June 1833–3 Jan. 1835), and *Chronicle & Gazette, and Kingston Commercial Advertiser* (7 Jan. 1835–1847), except for a brief period in 1840 when the subtitle was dropped. The paper was a continuation of the *Kingston Gazette* (25 Sept. 1810–29 Dec. 1818) and the *Kingston Chronicle* (1 Jan. 1819–22 June 1833).

Chronicle and News. Kingston, Ont. See *Chronicle & Gazette*

Church. Cobourg, [Ont.]. 6 May 1837–27 June 1840 and 14 July 1843–3 July 1846. Toronto. 11 July 1840–30 June 1843 and 17 July 1846–26 July 1855. Hamilton. 3 Aug. 1855–25 July 1856.

Cobourg Star. Cobourg, Ont. 11 Jan. 1831 to the end of 1879; on 8 Jan. 1880 it merged with the *Sentinel* to form the *Sentinel-Star*, which continues to the present. Its full title was *Cobourg Star and Newcastle District Gazette* until 22 Sept. 1841 when the subtitle was dropped.

Colonial Advocate. Queenston, [Ont.]. 18 May–18 Nov. 1824. Continued at York [Toronto] until 30 Oct. 1834. Title varies: *Colonial Advocate and Journal of Agriculture, Manufactures and Commerce* (to 30 Sept. 1824); *Colonial Advocate* (7 Oct. 1824–28 Nov. 1833); *Advocate* (5 Dec. 1833–30 Oct. 1834). On 4 Nov. 1834 it merged with the *Canadian Correspondent* to form the

Correspondent and Advocate (November 1834–November 1837).

Colonial Patriot. Pictou, N.S. 7 Dec. 1827–20 May 1834. Its full title was *Colonial Patriot and Miscellaneous Selector* from 17 Dec. 1828 to 9 Dec. 1829.

Constitution. Toronto. 4 July 1836–6 Dec. 1837.

Daily British Whig. Kingston, Ont. See *British Whig*

Examiner. Charlottetown. 7 Aug. 1847 to at least 29 May 1922, under various titles.

Examiner. Toronto. 3 July 1838–29 Aug. 1855; absorbed by the *Globe*.

La Gazette de Québec. See *Quebec Gazette*

Gleaner. Miramichi [Chatham], N.B. 28 July 1829–17 April 1880. Subtitle varies. The paper superseded the Miramichi *Mercury* (*q.v.*).

Gleaner, and Niagara Newspaper. Niagara [Niagara-on-the-Lake, Ont.]. 4 Dec. 1817–1837. At some time between February and April 1830 it became the *Niagara Gleaner*.

Globe. Toronto. 5 March 1844–21 Nov. 1936. On 23 Nov. 1936 it merged with the *Daily Mail and Empire* to form the *Globe and Mail*, which continues to the present.

Halifax Morning Post, & Parliamentary Reporter. 1 Oct. 1840–30 June 1848. Subtitle varies.

Islander. Charlottetown. 2 Dec. 1842 to at least 26 Dec. 1873, under various titles; its full title until 31 Dec. 1852 was *Islander, or Prince Edward Weekly Intelligencer and Advertiser*.

Le Journal de Québec. Published from 1 Dec. 1842 to 1 Oct. 1889, with some changes in title. Replaced *La Gazette de Québec* (see *Quebec Gazette*) when it ceased publication in November 1842.

Kingston Chronicle. Kingston, [Ont.]. See *Chronicle & Gazette*

Kingston Gazette. Kingston, [Ont.]. See *Chronicle & Gazette*

Mélanges religieux. Montréal. Published from 14 Dec. 1840 to 6 July 1852 under various titles, including: *Prémices de mélanges religieux* (to 19 Jan. 1841); *Mélanges religieux* (20 Jan. 1841–October 1842); and *Mélanges religieux, scientifiques, politiques, et littéraires* (October 1842–August 1847).

Mercury. Miramichi [Chatham], N.B. 21 Feb. 1826–31 March 1829; superseded by the *Gleaner* (*q.v.*).

La Minerve. Montréal. Published from 9 Nov. 1826 to 27 May 1899 under various titles.

Montreal Gazette/La Gazette de Montréal. 25 Aug. 1785 to the present. A bilingual continuation of the *Gazette littéraire, pour la ville & district de Montréal* (1778–79). Since August 1822 it has appeared only in English, with several changes in title.

Montreal Herald. 19 Oct. 1811–18 Oct. 1957.

Montreal Transcript. 4 Oct. 1836 to around 1873, under various titles.

Morning Chronicle. Quebec. 18 May 1847–30 June 1925, under various titles. On 2 July 1925 it merged with the *Quebec Daily Telegraph* to form the *Chronicle-Telegraph*, which continues to the present.

Morning News. Saint John, N.B. 16 Sept. 1839–8 April 1884, under a variety of titles, of which *Morning News* was the most common. Its title to the end of March 1840 was *Commercial News and General Advertiser*.

New-Brunswick Courier. Saint John, N.B. 2 May 1811–1865.

New-Brunswick Royal Gazette. Saint John; Fredericton. See *Royal Gazette*

Newfoundlander. St John's. 1827 to the end of 1884.

Newfoundland Mercantile Journal. St John's. From about 2 Sept. 1815 to 1827; issues are available only from 1816.

Newfoundland Patriot. St John's. See *Patriot & Terra-Nova Herald*

Niagara Gleaner. See *Gleaner, and Niagara Newspaper*

North American. Swanton, Vt. 11 April 1839 to at least 12 Aug. 1841. The paper was a Patriot organ, "edited by Canadians and Americans" and dedicated to "Canadian Rights and Independence."

Novascotian, or Colonial Herald. Halifax. 29 Dec. 1824–1926; no issues after 25 Dec. 1925 are available. Its title was *Novascotian, or Colonial Herald* until 2 Jan. 1840 when it became simply the *Novascotian*.

Nova-Scotia Royal Gazette. Halifax. 3 Jan. 1801–9 Feb. 1843. The paper began as the *Halifax Gazette* on 23 March 1752 and continued under various titles, including *Royal Gazette and the Nova-Scotia Advertiser* (7 April 1789–30 Dec. 1800). On 16 Feb. 1843 it became the *Royal Gazette*, which continues to the present.

L'Opinion publique. Montréal. 1 Jan. 1870–27 Dec. 1883.

La Patrie. Montréal. 24 Feb. 1879–9 Jan. 1978.

Patriot. Kingston, [Ont.]. 12 Nov. 1829–23 Oct. 1832. Continued at York [Toronto], 7 Dec. 1832–November 1855. Title varies: *Patriot and Farmer's Monitor* (to 18 March 1834); *Patriot* (to the end of 1839); and *Toronto Patriot* (as of 3 Jan. 1840). The paper was absorbed by the *Leader* in 1855, except for a weekly edition which continued until October 1878.

Patriot and Farmer's Monitor. Kingston, [Ont.]; Toronto. See *Patriot*

Patriot & Terra-Nova Herald. St John's. July 1833–June 1890, under various titles; issues are available only from 1834. Its title to 6 July 1842 was *Newfoundland Patriot*.

Le Populaire. Montréal. 10 April 1837–3 Nov. 1838.

La Presse. Montréal. 20 Oct. 1884 to the present.

Prince Edward Island Gazette. Charlottetown. See *Royal Gazette*

Prince Edward Island Register. Charlottetown. See *Royal Gazette*

Public Ledger. St John's. From about 1820 to the end of 1882, under various titles; issues are available only from 1827. Its full title was *Public Ledger, and Newfoundland General Advertiser* to 17 July 1860 when the subtitle was dropped.

Quebec Gazette/La Gazette de Québec. 21 June 1764–30 Oct. 1874. Bilingual to 29 Oct. 1842, but with separate English and French editions appearing on alternate days from 2 May 1832; as of 1 Dec. 1842 the French edition was replaced by *Le Journal de Québec* (*q.v.*) and the paper appeared only in English.

Quebec Mercury. 5 Jan. 1805–17 Oct. 1903, under various titles.

Royal Gazette. Charlottetown. 24 Aug. 1830 to the present; official government gazette since July 1851. Its predecessors include: *Weekly Recorder of Prince Edward Island* (from 17 Sept. 1810 to at least 25 Nov. 1813); *Prince Edward Island Gazette* (from about January 1814 to at least 11 May 1822); and *Prince Edward Island Register* (from at least 26 July 1823 to 17 Aug. 1830).

Royal Gazette. Saint John, N.B. 11 Oct. 1785–February 1815. Continued at Fredericton, 10 March 1815 to the present. It began publication as the *Royal Gazette, and the New-Brunswick Advertiser*; since 1 Dec. 1802 it has been called simply the *Royal Gazette*, with the following exceptions: *Royal Gazette, and New-Brunswick Advertiser* (4 Jan. 1808–11 April 1814); *New-Brunswick Royal Gazette* (18 April 1814–12 May 1828).

Royal Gazette and Newfoundland Advertiser. St John's. 27 Aug. 1807–October 1924; superseded by the *Newfoundland Gazette*, the official government gazette which continues to the present.

Royal Gazette and the Nova-Scotia Advertiser. Halifax. See *Nova-Scotia Royal Gazette*

St. Catharines Journal. St Catharines, Ont. 15 Oct. 1835 until around 1917 or 1918. Issued under various titles, including: *St. Catharines Journal, and Welland Canal, Niagara District, General Advertiser* (to the end of 1843; from 15 Dec. 1836 on, *Niagara District* is enclosed in parenthesis); and *St. Catharines Journal* (as of 3 Jan. 1844). A continuation of the *Farmers' Journal and Welland Canal Advertiser* (1 Feb. 1826–20 Jan. 1834) and the *British American Journal* (28 Jan. 1834–24 Sept. 1835).

Times. Halifax. 3 June 1834–27 June 1848.

Times and General Commercial Gazette. St John's. 15 Aug. 1832–23 March 1895.

Toronto Patriot. See *Patriot*

U.E. Loyalist. York [Toronto]. See *Upper Canada Gazette*

Upper Canada Gazette. Newark, later Niagara [Niagara-on-the-Lake, Ont.]. 18 April 1793–25 Aug. 1798. Continued at York [Toronto] until some time in 1849; latest extant issue is 9 March 1848. Title varies: *Upper Canadian Gazette; or, American Oracle* (to 28 March 1807); *York Gazette* (15 April 1807 to the end of 1816); *Upper Canada Gazette* (from 2 Jan. 1817). Issued in two parts, 1821 to 1828, with official announcements appearing as *Upper Canada Gazette* and the newspaper portion under the following titles: *York Weekly Post* (22 Feb.–26 Dec. 1821); *Weekly Register* (18 April 1822 to at least the end of 1825); and *U.E. Loyalist* (3 June 1826–24 May 1828).

Upper Canada Herald. Kingston, [Ont.]. 9 March 1819 to at least 31 Jan. 1851, under various titles, including: *Upper Canada Herald* (to 19 July 1836); *Upper Canada Herald, a Political, Agricultural & Commercial Journal* (26 July 1836–9 Feb. 1841); and *Kingston Herald; a Canadian Journal, Political, Agricultural & Commercial* (as of 16 Feb. 1841).

Vindicator and Canadian Advertiser. Montreal. 12 Dec. 1828–7 Nov. 1837. Title varies: *Irish Vindicator, and Canada General Advertiser* (12 Dec. 1828–17 Feb. 1829); *Irish Vindicator, and Canada Advertiser* (20 Feb.–24 July 1829); *Vindicator and Canada Advertiser* (28 July 1829–1 July 1831); *Vindicator* (5 July 1831–October 1832); and *Vindicator and Canadian Advertiser* (October 1832–7 Nov. 1837).

Weekly Register. York [Toronto]. See *Upper Canada Gazette*

York Gazette. York [Toronto]. See *Upper Canada Gazette*

York Weekly Post. York [Toronto]. See *Upper Canada Gazette*

III. REFERENCE WORKS

ALLAIRE, JEAN-BAPTISTE-ARTHUR. *Dictionnaire biographique du clergé canadien-français*. 6 vols. Montréal et Saint-Hyacinthe, Qué., 1908–34.

[1]: *Les anciens*. Montréal, 1910.

[2]: *Les contemporains*. Saint-Hyacinthe, 1908.

[3]: [*Suppléments*.] 6 parts in 1 vol. Montréal, 1910–19.

[4]: *Le clergé canadien-français: revue mensuelle* ([Montréal]), 1 (1919–20). Only one volume of this journal was published.

[5]: *Compléments*. 6 parts in 1 vol. Montréal, 1928–32.

6: Untitled. Saint-Hyacinthe, 1934.

ALMANACS. The almanacs cited in vol. VII have been listed under this heading to facilitate their identification. Because titles within series vary and publishers often change, the almanacs have in the main been listed under a general title, with the specifics found on title pages following.

Almanach de Québec. See *Quebec almanac*

Belcher's farmer's almanack. Halifax, 1824–1930. Edited by Clement Horton Belcher from 1824 to 1870 when its publication was taken over by the firm of McAlpine and Barnes, later the McAlpine Publishing Company. From 1824 to 1831 its title was *The farmer's almanack* . . . ; in 1832 it became *Belcher's farmer's almanack* . . . , a title it retained with minor variations until its disappearance.

Cunnabell's Nova-Scotia almanac. Halifax, 1834–68. Published by Jacob Sparling Cunnabell, 1834–36; William Cunnabell, 1837–68. From 1834 to 1841 its title was the *Nova-Scotia almanack* . . . ; in 1842 it became *Cunnabell's Nova-Scotia almanac* . . . , and in 1851 *Cunnabell's Nova-Scotia almanac, and farmer's manual*. . . .

Halifax almanac. Halifax, 1790–?. Published until at least 1821. Its actual title was *An almanack . . . calculated for the meridian of Halifax, in Nova-Scotia*. . . . Publishers: John Howe, 1790–1815; David Howe, 1816; unknown, 1817–20; John Munro, 1821.

The merchants' and farmers' almanack. . . . Saint John, N.B., 1839–63. Published by William L. Avery. From 1839 to 1841 its title was *The merchants' and farmers' provincial almanac*. . . .

Montreal almanack, or Lower Canada register. . . . Montreal, 1829–31. Published by Robert Armour.

New-Brunswick almanack. Saint John, 1812–64. Published by Henry Chubb, and later by his firm. Its title varies; from 1812 to 1830 it was *An almanack*. . . .

The Nova-Scotia calender, or an almanack. . . . Halifax, 1769–1801. Published by Anthony Henry.

Prince Edward Island calendar. Charlottetown, 1836–73. Published by James Douglas Haszard, 1836–50; J. D. and George T. Haszard, 1851; unknown, 1852–54; G. T. Haszard, 1855, 1857–62; Haszard & Owen, 1856; unknown, 1863–64; Laird & Harvie, 1865–66; David Laird, 1867–73.

Quebec almanac/Almanach de Québec. Quebec, 1780–1841 (except for 1781, 1790, and 1793). Published by William Brown from 1780 to 1789, and continued by the Neilson family from 1791 until 1841. The spelling and language of the title vary, but from 1780 to 1789 it appeared solely in French as the *Almanach de Québec*, and from 1813 to 1841 it was published in English only as *The Quebec almanack; and British American royal kalendar*.

The Toronto almanac and royal calendar, of Upper Canada. . . . Toronto, 1839. Published by Charles Fothergill. *See also* next entry.

York almanac. Published at York [Toronto] from 1821 to 1826. The issues for 1821 and 1822 appeared as *The York almanac, and provincial calendar* . . . , [printed by Robert Charles Horne], and from 1823 to 1826 it was published by Charles Fothergill as *The York almanac and royal calendar, of Upper Canada*. . . . *See also* Fothergill's *Toronto almanac*, above.

ARCHIVES NATIONALES DU QUÉBEC, Québec PUBLICATIONS [*see also* section II]

P.-G. Roy, *Inv. concessions*.

——— *Les juges de la prov. de Québec*.

ARMSTRONG, FREDERICK HENRY. *Handbook of Upper Canadian chronology and territorial legislation*. (University of Western Ontario, Lawson Memorial Library publication.) London, 1967. Revised edition. Toronto and London, 1985.

AUDET, FRANCIS-JOSEPH. "Commissions d'avocats de la province de Québec, 1765 à 1849." *BRH*, 39 (1933): 577–96.

——— *Les députés de Montréal (ville et comtés), 1792–1867*. . . . Montréal, 1943.

——— "Les législateurs du Bas-Canada, 1760–1867." Manuscript held by the Morisset Library, University of Ottawa. 3 vols. 1940.

——— ET ÉDOUARD FABRE SURVEYER. *Les députés au premier Parlement du Bas-Canada, [1792–1796]*. . . . Montréal, 1946.

——— *Les députés de Saint-Maurice et de Buckinghamshire*. *See* FABRE SURVEYER

Australian dictionary of biography. Edited by Douglas Pike *et al*. 10 vols. to date. Melbourne, 1966– .

BEAULIEU, ANDRÉ, *et al*. *La presse québécoise, des origines à nos jours*. [2e édition.] 8 vols. to date [1764–1954]. Québec, 1973– . Vols. 1–2 [1764–1879] were prepared by André Beaulieu and Jean Hamelin. *Index cumulatifs (tomes I à VII) (1764–1944)*. 1987.

Belcher's farmer's almanack. See ALMANACS

BIBAUD, [FRANÇOIS-MAXIMILIEN]. *Dictionnaire historique des hommes illustres du Canada et de l'Amérique*. Montréal, 1857.

——— *Le panthéon canadien; choix de biographies*. Nouvelle édition. Revue, augmentée et complétée par Adèle et Victoria Bibaud. Montréal, 1891.

A bibliography of Canadiana, being items in the Public Library of Toronto, Canada, relating to the

early history and development of Canada. Edited by Frances Maria Staton and Marie Tremaine. Toronto, 1934; reprinted 1965. 2 supplements to date. 1959– .

1: Edited by Gertrude Mabel Boyle with Marjorie Maud Colbeck. 1959; reprinted 1969.

2: Edited by Sandra Alston with Karen Evans. 2 parts to date. 1985– .

BISHOP, OLGA BERNICE. *Publications of the government of the Province of Canada, 1841–1867*. (National Library of Canada publication.) Ottawa, 1963 [i.e. 1964].

——— *Publications of the governments of Nova Scotia, Prince Edward Island, New Brunswick, 1758–1952*. (National Library of Canada publication.) Ottawa, 1957.

BORTHWICK, JOHN DOUGLAS. *History and biographical gazetteer of Montreal to the year 1892*. Montreal, 1892.

BOUCHETTE, JOSEPH. *A topographical description of the province of Lower Canada, with remarks upon Upper Canada, and on the relative connexion of both provinces with the United States of America*. London, 1815; reprinted Saint-Lambert, Que., 1973. Published in French as *Description topographique de la province du Bas Canada . . .* (Londres, 1815; réimpr., J. E. Hare, édit., [Montréal, 1978]).

The British Library general catalogue of printed books to 1975. 360 vols. London, 1979–87.

BURKE, JOHN. *A genealogical and heraldic history of the commoners of Great Britain and Ireland, enjoying territorial possessions or high official rank; but uninvested with heritable honours*. 4 vols. London, 1833–37. *Burke's genealogical and heraldic history of the landed gentry*. 18th edition. Edited by Peter Townend. 3 vols. 1965–72.

——— *General and heraldic dictionary of the peerage and baronetage of the United Kingdom. . . .* London, 1826. *Burke's genealogical and heraldic history of the peerage, baronetage and knightage*. 105th edition. Edited by Peter Townend. 1970.

The Canadian biographical dictionary and portrait gallery of eminent and self-made men. 2 vols. Toronto, 1880–81.

The Canadian encyclopedia. Edited by James Harley Marsh. 3 vols. Edmonton, 1985.

CARON, IVANHOË. "Inventaire de la correspondance de Mgr Bernard-Claude Panet, archevêque de Québec." ANQ *Rapport*, 1933–34: 235–421; 1934–35: 321–420; 1935–36: 157–272.

——— "Inventaire de la correspondance de Mgr Jean-François Hubert, évêque de Québec, et de Mgr Charles-François Bailly de Messein, son coadjuteur." ANQ *Rapport*, 1930–31: 199–351.

——— "Inventaire de la correspondance de Mgr Joseph-Octave Plessis, archevêque de Québec, 1797 à [1825]." ANQ *Rapport*, 1927–28: 215–316; 1928–29: 89–208; 1932–33: 3–244.

——— "Inventaire de la correspondance de Mgr Pierre Denaut, évêque de Québec." ANQ *Rapport*, 1931–32: 129–242.

——— "Inventaire de la correspondance de Monseigneur Joseph Signay, archevêque de Québec – [1825–1840]." ANQ *Rapport*, 1936–37: 125–330; 1937–38: 23–146; 1938–39: 182–357.

——— "Inventaire des documents relatifs aux événements de 1837 et 1838, conservés aux Archives de la province de Québec." ANQ *Rapport*, 1925–26: 146–329.

——— "Papiers Duvernay conservés aux Archives de la province de Québec." ANQ *Rapport*, 1926–27: 147–252.

CHADWICK, EDWARD MARION. *Ontarian families: genealogies of United-Empire-Loyalist and other pioneer families of Upper Canada*. 2 vols. Toronto, 1894–98; reprinted 2 vols. in 1, Lambertville, N.J., [1970]. Vol.1 reprinted with an introduction by William Felix Edmund Morley, Belleville, Ont., 1972.

Cunnabell's Nova-Scotia almanac. See ALMANACS

A cyclopædia of Canadian biography. . . . Edited by George Maclean Rose and Hector [Willoughby] Charlesworth. 3 vols. Toronto, 1886–1919. Vols. 1–2 were edited by Rose, vol. 3 by Charlesworth. Subtitles and series titles vary.

Death notices of Ontario. Compiled by William D. Reid. Lambertville, N.J., 1980.

DESJARDINS, JOSEPH. *Guide parlementaire historique de la province de Québec, 1792 à 1902*. Québec, 1902.

DESROSIERS, LOUIS-ADÉLARD. "Correspondance de Mgr Ignace Bourget . . . [1837–1843]." ANQ *Rapport*, 1944–45: 137–224; 1946–47: 85–175; 1948–49: 347–477.

——— "Inventaire de la correspondance de Mgr J.-J. Lartigue." ANQ *Rapport*, 1941–42: 347–496; 1942–43: 3–174; 1943–44: 212–334; 1944–45: 175–266; 1945–46: 45–134.

Dictionary of American biography. Edited by Allen Johnson *et al*. 20 vols., index, and 2 supplements [to 1940]. New York, 1928–58; reprinted, 22 vols. in 11 and index, [1946?]–58. 5 additional supplements to date [to 1965]. Edited by Edward Topping James *et al*. 1973– . *Concise DAB*. 3rd edition. 1980.

Dictionary of Hamilton biography. Edited by Thomas Melville Bailey *et al*. 1 vol. to date [to 1875]. Hamilton, Ont., 1981– .

Dictionary of national biography. Edited by Leslie Stephen and Sidney Lee. 63 vols., 3 supplements, and index and epitome [to 1900]. London, 1885–1903; reissued without index, 22 vols., 1908–9. 7 additional supplements to date [to 1970]. Edited by

Sidney Lee *et al*. 1912– . *Concise DNB*. 2 vols. [1953]–61. *Corrections and additions to the "Dictionary of national biography"*. Boston, 1966.

A dictionary of Toronto printers, publishers, booksellers, and the allied trades, 1798–1900. Compiled by Elizabeth Hulse. Toronto, 1982.

Dictionnaire de biographie française. Jules Balteau *et al*., éditeurs. 16 vols. and 3 fascicules [fasc. 97–99] to date [A to Hautier]. Paris, 1933– .

Dictionnaire des œuvres littéraires du Québec. Maurice Lemire *et al*., éditeurs. 5 vols. Montréal, 1978–87.

DIRECTORIES. Issued initially as single works, these frequently became regular, usually annual, publications in the 19th century. Because titles within series vary greatly, and because editors or compilers frequently change, the directories used in the preparation of vol. VII have been grouped by region and under a general title. Details for the specific years cited are given below. For further information *see* Ryder, *Checklist of Canadian directories*, *infra*.

Montreal directory. Montreal. Issues cited in vol. VII are *An alphabetical list of the merchants, traders, and housekeepers, residing in Montreal . . .* , comp. Thomas Doige (1819; repr. 1899; 2nd ed., 1820); and *The Montreal directory . . .* , comp. R. W. S. Mackay (1842/43–47).

Quebec directory. Quebec. Used in vol. VII are *The directory for the city and suburbs of Quebec . . .* (1790) and *Number II of the directory . . .* (1791), comp. Hugh MacKay; *The Quebec directory . . .* , comp. T. H. Gleason (1822); John Smith (1826); and Alfred Hawkins (1844–45, 1847–48); *Mackay's Quebec directory . . .* , comp. R. W. S. Mackay (1848/49–52); *McLaughlin's Quebec directory . . .* , comp. Samuel McLaughlin (1857); *The Quebec directory . . .* , ed. G.-H. Cherrier (1860–61, 1865–66, 1867–68); *Cherrier's Quebec directory . . .* , comp. A.-B. Cherrier (1877); and *Cherrier's Quebec City directory . . . /Almanach des adresses Cherrier de la ville de Québec . . .* , comp. A.-B. Cherrier (1887–88).

Toronto directory. Toronto. Issues cited in vol. VII are *York commercial directory, street guide, and register, for 1833–4 . . .* , comp. George Walton ([1833]); and *The city of Toronto and the Home District commercial directory and register with almanack and calendar for 1837 . . .* , comp. George Walton (1837).

Directory of the members of the Legislative Assembly of Nova Scotia, 1758–1958. Introduction by Charles Bruce Fergusson. (PANS publications, Nova Scotia series, 2.) Halifax, 1958. See also *Legislative Assembly of N.S.* (Elliott).

Early Toronto newspapers, 1793–1867: a catalogue of newspapers published in the town of York and the city of Toronto from the beginning to confederation. Edited by Edith Grace Firth, with an introduction by Henry Cummings Campbell. Toronto, 1961.

Elections in New Brunswick, 1784–1984/Les élections au Nouveau-Brunswick, 1784–1984. (New Brunswick Legislative Library publication.) Fredericton, 1984.

Encyclopædia Britannica; a new survey of universal knowledge. [14th edition.] Edited by Warren E. Preece *et al*. 23 vols. and index. Chicago, 1966. *The new Encyclopædia Britannica*. 15th edition. 30 vols. 1977.

Encyclopedia Canadiana. Edited by John Everett Robbins *et al*. 10 vols. Ottawa, 1957–58. [Revised edition.] Edited by Kenneth H. Pearson *et al*. Toronto, 1975.

FABRE SURVEYER, ÉDOUARD, ET FRANCIS-JOSEPH AUDET. *Les députés de Saint-Maurice et de Buckinghamshire (1792 à 1808)*. Trois-Rivières, Qué., 1934.

FAUTEUX, ÆGIDIUS. *Patriotes de 1837–1838*. Montréal, 1950.

Grand Larousse encyclopédique. 10 vols. Paris, 1960–64. 2 suppléments. 1969–75. *Grand dictionnaire encyclopédique Larousse*. 10 vols. 1982–85.

GREAT BRITAIN, ADMIRALTY. *A list of the flag-officers of his majesty's fleet. . . .* London, 1777–1840.

——— *The navy list. . . .* London, 1815– .

GREAT BRITAIN, WAR OFFICE. *A list of the general and field-officers, as they rank in the army. . . .* London, 1754–1868. Cited in individual bibliographies under the title *Army list*. *See also* Hart, *The new annual army list*.

Guide to the reports of the Public Archives of Canada, 1872–1972. Compiled by Françoise Caron-Houle. (PAC publication.) Ottawa, 1975.

Halifax almanac. See ALMANACS

Handbook of North American Indians. Edited by William C. Sturtevant *et al*. (Smithsonian Institution publication.) 7 vols. to date [5–6, 8–11, 15]. Washington, 1978– .

HARE, JOHN [ELLIS], ET JEAN-PIERRE WALLOT. *Les imprimés dans le Bas-Canada, 1801–1840: bibliographie analytique*. Montréal, 1967. Only one volume, *1801–1810*, was published.

HARPER, JOHN RUSSELL. *Early painters and engravers in Canada*. [Toronto], 1970.

HART, HENRY GEORGE. *The new annual army list. . . .* London, 1840–1916. The title on the cover is *Hart's army list*. *See also* G.B., WO, *A list of the general and field-officers*.

HILL, ISABEL LOUISE. *The Old Burying Ground, Fredericton, N.B.* 2 vols. in 1. Fredericton, 1981.

Index to reports of Canadian archives from 1872 to 1908. (PAC publications, 1.) Ottawa, 1909.

[LANGELIER, JEAN-CHRYSOSTÔME.] *Liste des terrains concédés par la couronne dans la province de Québec, de 1763 au 31 décembre 1890*. Québec, 1891. Also published in English as *List of lands granted by the crown in the province of Quebec from 1763 to 31st December 1890* (1891).

LEBŒUF, JOSEPH-[AIMÉ-]ARTHUR. *Complément au dictionnaire généalogique Tanguay*. (SGCF publications, 2, 4, 6.) 3 sér. Montréal, 1957–64. *See also* Tanguay, *Dictionnaire*.

The Legislative Assembly of Nova Scotia, 1758–1983: a biographical directory. Edited by Shirley B. Elliott. [Halifax], 1984. A revised edition of *Directory of N.S. MLAs* [*see* above].

Legislators and legislatures of Ontario: a reference guide. Compiled by Debra Forman. (Ontario Legislative Library, Research and Information Services publication.) 3 vols. [1792–1984]. [Toronto, 1984].

LE JEUNE, LOUIS[-MARIE]. *Dictionnaire général de biographie, histoire, littérature, agriculture, commerce, industrie et des arts, sciences, mœurs, coutumes, institutions politiques et religieuses du Canada*. 2 vols. Ottawa, [1931].

Marriage bonds of Ontario, 1803–1834. Compiled by Thomas B. Wilson. Lambertville, N.J., 1985.

Marriage notices of Ontario. Compiled by William D. Reid [and edited by Thomas B. Wilson]. Lambertville, N.J., 1980. See also *Ont. marriage notices* (T. B. Wilson).

MARSHALL, JOHN. *Royal naval biography; or, memoirs of the services of all the flag-officers, superannuated rear-admirals, retired-captains, post-captains, and commanders, whose names appeared on the Admiralty list of sea officers at the commencement of the present year, or who have since been promoted. . . .* 4 vols. in 8 and 4 supplements. London, 1823–35.

Merchants' and farmers' almanack. See ALMANACS

Montreal almanack. See ALMANACS

Montreal directory. See DIRECTORIES

MORGAN, HENRY JAMES. *Bibliotheca Canadensis: or a manual of Canadian literature*. Ottawa, 1867; reprinted Detroit, 1968.

——— *Sketches of celebrated Canadians, and persons connected with Canada, from the earliest period in the history of the province down to the present time*. Quebec and London, 1862; reprinted Montreal, 1865.

MORICE, ADRIEN-GABRIEL. *Dictionnaire historique des Canadiens et des Métis français de l'ouest*. Kamloops, C.-B., 1908; Québec, 1908. 2e édition, augmentée d'un supplément. Québec, 1912.

NATIONAL ARCHIVES OF CANADA, Ottawa (officially known as the Public Archives of Canada until 1987)

NUMBERED PUBLICATIONS

1: *Index to reports of PAC*.

OTHER PUBLICATIONS [*see also* section II]

Guide to reports of PAC (Caron-Houle).

Inventories of holdings in the Manuscript Division [*see* section I].

Union list of MSS (Gordon *et al.*; Maurice Hyam).

Union list of MSS, supp. (Maurice Hyam *et al.*).

NATIONAL LIBRARY OF CANADA, Ottawa

PUBLICATIONS

Bishop, *Pubs. of government of Prov. of Canada*.

——— *Pubs. of governments of N.S., P.E.I., N.B.*

Ryder, *Checklist of Canadian directories*.

The national union catalog, pre-1956 imprints. . . . 754 vols. London and Chicago, 1968–81.

New-Brunswick almanack. See ALMANACS

New Brunswick vital statistics from newspapers. See *Vital statistics from New Brunswick newspapers*

Nova-Scotia calender. See ALMANACS

Nova Scotia vital statistics from newspapers. . . . Compiled by Terrence Michael Punch and Jean M. Holder. (Nova Scotia Genealogical Association publications, 1, 3, 5–6, 8, 10–11.) 7 vols. to date [1769–1847]. Halifax, 1978– . Vols. [1]: *1813–1822* and [3]: *1769–1812* were compiled by Punch, the remainder by Holder. Cover title as above, but title on title-page varies. Until 1986 the Nova Scotia Genealogical Association was a division of the Royal Nova Scotia Historical Society [*see* section V].

Officers of the British forces in Canada during the War of 1812–15. Compiled by Lukin Homfray Irving. (Canadian Military Institute publication.) [Welland, Ont.], 1908.

Ontario marriage notices. Compiled by Thomas B. Wilson. Lambertville, N.J., 1982. Supplements and complements *Marriage notices of Ont.* (Reid) [*see* above].

OUELLET, FERNAND. "Inventaire de la saberdache de Jacques Viger," ANQ *Rapport*, 1955–57: 39–176.

"Papiers d'État – Bas-Canada, [1791–1823]." PAC *Rapport*, 1891: 1–206; 1892: 155–293; 1893: 1–123; 1896: 1–256; 1897: 257–402. *See also* "State papers – L.C."

Place-names and places of Nova Scotia. Introduction by Charles Bruce Fergusson. (PANS publications, Nova Scotia series, 3.) Halifax, 1967; reprinted Belleville, Ont., 1976.

Places in Ontario: their name origins and history. Compiled by Nick and Helma Mika. 3 parts. Belleville, Ont., 1977–83.

Prince Edward Island calendar. See ALMANACS

PUBLIC ARCHIVES OF CANADA, Ottawa. *See* NATIONAL ARCHIVES OF CANADA

PUBLIC ARCHIVES OF NOVA SCOTIA, Halifax

NOVA SCOTIA SERIES

2: *Directory of N.S. MLAs*.

3: *Place-names of N.S.*

Quebec almanac. *See* ALMANACS

Quebec directory. See DIRECTORIES

RAYBURN, ALAN. *Geographical names of New Brunswick*. (Canadian Permanent Committee on Geographical Names, Toponymy study, 2.) Ottawa, 1975.

——— *Geographical names of Prince Edward Island*. (Canadian Permanent Committee on Geographical Names, Toponymy study, 1.) Ottawa, 1973.

REID, WILLIAM D. *The loyalists in Ontario: the sons and daughters of the American loyalists of Upper Canada*. Lambertville, N.J., 1973.

Le répertoire national, ou recueil de littérature canadienne. James Huston, compilateur. 4 vols. Montréal, 1848–50; réimprimé sous le titre de *Répertoire national*, Robert Melançon, édit., (1982). 2ᵉ édition. 1893.

ROY, PIERRE-GEORGES. *Les avocats de la région de Québec*. Lévis, Qué., 1936 [i.e. 1937].

——— *Fils de Québec*. 4 sér. Lévis, Qué., 1933.

——— *Inventaire des concessions en fief et seigneurie, fois et hommages et aveux et dénombrements, conservés aux Archives de la province de Québec*. (ANQ publication.) 6 vols. Beauceville, Qué., 1927–29.

——— *Les juges de la province de Québec*. (ANQ publication.) Québec, 1933.

RYDER, DOROTHY EDITH. *Checklist of Canadian directories, 1750–1950/Répertoire des annuaires canadiens, 1790–1950*. (National Library of Canada publication.) Ottawa, 1979.

SCOTT, HEW, *et al. Fasti ecclesiæ scoticanæ: the succession of ministers in the Church of Scotland from the Reformation*. 3 vols. in 6. Edinburgh, 1866–71. New edition. 9 vols. to date. 1915– .

"State papers – Lower Canada [1808–1818]." PAC *Report*, 1893: 1–119; 1896: 1–252. *See also* "Papiers d'État – Bas-Canada."

TANGUAY, CYPRIEN. *Dictionnaire généalogique des familles canadiennes depuis la fondation de la colonie jusqu'à nos jours*. 7 vols. Montréal, 1871–90; réimprimé Baltimore, Md., 1967, and New York, 1969. *See also* Lebœuf, *Complément*.

——— *Répertoire général du clergé canadien par ordre chronologique depuis la fondation de la colonie jusqu'à nos jours*. [2ᵉ édition.] Montréal, 1893.

THÉRIAULT, YVON. *Les publications parlementaires d'hier et d'aujourd'hui*. [2ᵉ édition.] Québec, 1982. Also published in English as *The parliamentary publications, past and present* (1983).

Toronto almanac. See ALMANACS

Toronto directory. See DIRECTORIES

TRATT, GERTRUDE ELLA NAOMI. *A survey and listing of Nova Scotia newspapers, 1752–1957, with particular reference to the period before 1867*. (Dalhousie University Libraries/School of Library Service, Occasional papers, 21.) Halifax, 1979.

TURCOTTE, GUSTAVE. *Le Conseil législatif de Québec, 1774–1933*. Beauceville, Qué., 1933.

Union list of manuscripts in Canadian repositories/Catalogue collectif des manuscrits des archives canadiennes. Revised edition. Edited by E. Grace Maurice [Hyam]. (PAC publication.) 2 vols. Ottawa, 1975. *Supplement/Supplément*. Edited by E. Grace Maurice Hyam *et al*. 4 vols. to date. 1976– .

Vital statistics from New Brunswick newspapers. . . . Compiled by Daniel F. Johnson. 20 vols. to date [1784–1863]. Saint John, N.B., 1982– . Vols. 1–5 [1784–1834] were issued by the New Brunswick Genealogical Society under the title *New Brunswick vital statistics from newspapers*, comp. D. F. Johnson *et al*. (Fredericton, 1982–84).

WALLACE, WILLIAM STEWART. *The Macmillan dictionary of Canadian biography*. Edited by William Angus McKay. 4th edition. Toronto, 1978. First published as *The dictionary of Canadian biography* (1926).

WATTERS, REGINALD EYRE. *A checklist of Canadian literature and background materials, 1628–1960. . . .* 2nd edition. Toronto and Buffalo, N.Y., 1972.

When was that? A chronological dictionary of important events in Newfoundland down to and including the year 1922; together with an appendix, "St. John's over a century ago," by the late J. W. Withers. Compiled by Harris Munden Mosdell. St John's, 1923.

York almanac. See ALMANACS

IV. STUDIES (BOOKS AND THESES)

ABBOTT, MAUDE ELIZABETH [SEYMOUR]. *History of medicine in the province of Quebec*. Toronto, 1931; Montreal, 1931.

AUDET, LOUIS-PHILIPPE. *Le système scolaire de la province de Québec* [1635–1840]. 6 vols. Québec, 1950–56.

BARTHE, JOSEPH-GUILLAUME. *Souvenirs d'un demi-siècle: ou, mémoires pour servir à l'histoire contemporaine*. Montréal, 1885.

BECK, JAMES MURRAY. *The government of Nova Scotia*. Toronto, 1957.

BELLEMARE, JOSEPH-ELZÉAR. *Histoire de Nicolet, 1669–1924*. Arthabaska, Qué., 1924. Only the first part, *La seigneurie*, was published.

BILL, INGRAHAM EBENEZER. *Fifty years with the Baptist ministers and churches of the Maritime provinces of Canada*. Saint John, N.B., 1880.

BOON, THOMAS CHARLES BOUCHER. *The Anglican Church from the Bay to the Rockies: a history of the ecclesiastical province of Rupert's Land and its dioceses from 1820 to 1950*. Toronto, 1962.

BROWN, JENNIFER STACEY HARCOURT. *Strangers in blood: fur trade company families in Indian country*. Vancouver and London, 1980.

BUCHANAN, ARTHUR WILLIAM PATRICK. *The bench and bar of Lower Canada down to 1850*. Montreal, 1925.

BUCKNER, PHILLIP ALFRED. *The transition to responsible government: British policy in British North America, 1815–1850*. Westport, Conn., and London, 1985.

[BURKE, CATHERINE, DITE DE SAINT-THOMAS]. *Les ursulines de Québec, depuis leur établissement jusqu'à nos jours*. 4 vols. Québec, 1863–66. [2e édition] (vols. 1–2 only). 1878.

CAMPBELL, ROBERT. *A history of the Scotch Presbyterian Church, St. Gabriel Street, Montreal*. Montreal, 1887.

CANNIFF, WILLIAM. *The medical profession in Upper Canada, 1783–1850: an historical narrative, with original documents relating to the profession, including some brief biographies*. Toronto, 1894; reprinted 1980.

CHABOT, RICHARD. *Le curé de campagne et la contestation locale au Québec (de 1791 aux troubles de 1837–38): la querelle des écoles, l'affaire des fabriques et le problème des insurrections de 1837–38*. Montréal, 1975.

CHAPAIS, [JOSEPH-AMABLE-]THOMAS. *Cours d'histoire du Canada* [1760–1867]. 8 vols. Québec, 1919–34. Autre édition. 8 vols. Montréal, [1944–45]; réimprimé [Trois-Rivières, Qué., 1972].

CHAUSSÉ, GILLES. *Jean-Jacques Lartigue, premier évêque de Montréal*. Montréal, 1980.

CHRISTIE, ROBERT. *A history of the late province of Lower Canada, parliamentary and political, from the commencement to the close of its existence as a separate province*. . . . 6 vols. Quebec and Montreal, 1848–55. [2nd edition.] Montreal, 1866.

CRAIG, GERALD MARQUIS. *Upper Canada: the formative years, 1784–1841*. [Toronto], 1963.

CREIGHTON, DONALD GRANT. *The commercial empire of the St. Lawrence, 1760–1850*. Toronto, 1937; reprinted under the title *The empire of the St. Lawrence*, 1956 and 1970.

CUTHBERTSON, BRIAN [CRAIG UNIACKE]. *The old attorney general: a biography of Richard John Uniacke*. Halifax, [1980].

DARROCH MILANI, LOIS. *Robert Gourlay, gadfly: the biography of Robert (Fleming) Gourlay, 1778–1863, forerunner of the rebellion in Upper Canada, 1837*. [Thornhill, Ont., 1971?]

DAVID, LAURENT-OLIVIER. *Les patriotes de 1837–1838*. Montréal, [1884]; réimprimé [1937].

DENISON, MERRILL. *Canada's first bank: a history of the Bank of Montreal*. 2 vols. Toronto and Montreal, 1966–67. Translated by Paul A. Horguelin and Jean-Paul Vinay as *La première banque au Canada: histoire de la Banque de Montréal* (2v., Toronto et Montréal, 1966–67).

DIONNE, NARCISSE-EUTROPE. *Les ecclésiastiques et les royalistes français réfugiés au Canada à l'époque de la révolution – 1791–1802*. Québec, 1905.

DOUVILLE, JOSEPH-ANTOINE-IRÉNÉE. *Histoire du collège-séminaire de Nicolet, 1803–1903, avec les listes complètes des directeurs, professeurs et élèves de l'institution*. 2 vols. Montréal, 1903.

FILTEAU, GÉRARD. *Histoire des patriotes*. 3 vols. Montréal, 1938–42. [Nouvelle édition.] 1975.

GATES, LILLIAN FRANCIS [COWDELL]. *Land policies of Upper Canada*. Toronto, 1968.

GREGG, WILLIAM. *History of the Presbyterian Church in the Dominion of Canada, from the earliest times to 1834; with a chronological table of events to the present time, and map*. Toronto, 1885.

GUILLET, EDWIN CLARENCE. *The lives and times of the Patriots; an account of the rebellion in Upper Canada, 1837–1838, and the Patriot agitation in the United States, 1837–1842*. Toronto, 1938; reprinted 1963 and 1968.

GUNN, GERTRUDE E. *The political history of Newfoundland, 1832–1864*. Toronto, 1966.

HANNAY, JAMES. *History of New Brunswick*. 2 vols. Saint John, N.B., 1909.

HARPER, JOHN RUSSELL. *Painting in Canada: a history*. [Toronto], 1966. 2nd edition. Toronto and Buffalo, N.Y., 1977.

INNIS, HAROLD ADAMS. *The fur trade in Canada: an introduction to Canadian economic history*. New Haven, Conn., and London, 1930. Revised edition. [Edited by Mary Quayle Innis *et al.*] Toronto, 1956. [Abridged edition] based on the revised edition of 1956. Foreword by Robin William Winks. 1962. Revised edition (reprint of 1956 edition with revised foreword from the 1962 edition). 1970.

JOHNSTON, CHARLES MURRAY. *The Head of the Lake; a history of Wentworth County*. Hamilton, Ont., 1958. 2nd edition. 1967.

LABARRÈRE-PAULÉ, ANDRÉ. *Les instituteurs laïques au Canada français, 1836–1900*. Québec, 1965.

LAMBERT, JAMES HAROLD. "Monseigneur, the Catholic bishop: Joseph-Octave Plessis; church, state, and society in Lower Canada: historiography and analysis." D. ès L. thesis, Université Laval, Quebec, 1981.

LAURIN, CLÉMENT. *J.-J. Girouard & les patriotes de 1837–38: portraits*. Montréal, 1973.

LAWRENCE, JOSEPH WILSON. *The judges of New Brunswick and their times*. Edited and annotated by Alfred Augustus Stockton [and William Odber Raymond]. [Saint John, N.B., 1907]; reprinted with an introduction by David Graham Bell, Fredericton, 1983 [i.e. 1985].

LEMIEUX, LUCIEN. *L'établissement de la première province ecclésiastique au Canada, 1783–1844*. Montréal et Paris, 1968.

LEVY, GEORGE EDWARD. *The Baptists of the Maritime provinces, 1753–1946*. Saint John, N.B., 1946.

LINDSEY, CHARLES. *The life and times of Wm. Lyon Mackenzie; with an account of the Canadian rebellion of 1837, and the subsequent frontier disturbances, chiefly from unpublished documents*. 2 vols. Toronto, 1862; reprinted 1971.

MACKINNON, FRANK [FRANCIS PERLEY TAYLOR]. *The government of Prince Edward Island*. Toronto, 1951; reprinted 1974.

MACNUTT, WILLIAM STEWART. *New Brunswick, a history: 1784–1867*. Toronto, 1963.

MAURAULT, [JEAN-LÉON-]OLIVIER. *Le collège de Montréal, 1767–1967*. 2e édition. Antonio Dansereau, éditeur. Montréal, 1967.

——— *La paroisse: histoire de l'église Notre-Dame de Montréal*. Montréal et New York, 1929. Édition revue et augmentée. Montréal, 1957.

MONET, JACQUES. *The last cannon shot: a study of French-Canadian nationalism, 1837–1850*. Toronto, 1969; reprinted Toronto and Buffalo, N.Y., 1976. Translated by Richard Bastien as *La première révolution tranquille: le nationalisme canadien-français (1837–1850)* (Montréal, 1981).

MORISSET, GÉRARD. *Coup d'œil sur les arts en Nouvelle-France*. Québec, 1941; réimprimé 1942.

——— *Peintres et tableaux*. 2 vols. Québec, 1936–37.

——— *La peinture traditionnelle au Canada français*. Ottawa, 1960.

MORTON, ARTHUR SILVER. *A history of the Canadian west to 1870–71, being a history of Rupert's Land (the Hudson's Bay Company's territory) and of the North-West Territory (including the Pacific slope)*. London, [1939]. 2nd edition. Edited by Lewis Gwynne Thomas. Toronto and Buffalo, N.Y., 1973.

MURDOCH, BEAMISH. *A history of Nova-Scotia, or Acadie*. 3 vols. Halifax, 1865–67.

OUELLET, FERNAND. *Le Bas-Canada, 1791–1840: changements structuraux et crise*. (Université d'Ottawa, Cahiers d'histoire, 6.) Ottawa, 1976. Translated and adapted by Patricia Claxton as *Lower Canada, 1791–1840: social change and nationalism* (Toronto, 1980).

——— *Histoire économique et sociale du Québec, 1760–1850: structures et conjoncture*. Montréal et Paris, 1966; réimprimé en 2 vols., Montréal, 1971. Translated as *Economic and social history of Quebec, 1760–1850: "structures" and "conjonctures"* ([Toronto], 1980).

PATTERSON, GRAEME HAZLEWOOD. "Studies in elections and public opinion in Upper Canada." PHD thesis, University of Toronto, 1969.

POULIOT, LÉON. *Monseigneur Bourget et son temps*. 5 vols. Montréal, 1955–77.

PROWSE, DANIEL WOODLEY. *A history of Newfoundland from the English, colonial, and foreign records*. London and New York, 1895; reprinted Belleville, Ont., 1972. 2nd edition. London, 1896. 3rd edition. With additions by James Raymond Thoms and Frank Burnham Gill. St John's, 1971.

READ, COLIN [FREDERICK]. *The rising in western Upper Canada, 1837–8: the Duncombe revolt and after*. Toronto, 1982.

RICH, EDWIN ERNEST. *The fur trade and the northwest to 1857*. Toronto, 1967; reprinted 1976.

——— *The history of the Hudson's Bay Company, 1670–1870*. (*HBRS*, 21–22.) 2 vols. London, 1958–59. [Trade edition.] 3 vols. Toronto, 1960. A copy of this work available at the PAC contains notes and bibliographical material omitted from the printed version.

Robertson's landmarks of Toronto: a collection of historical sketches of the old town of York from 1792 until 1833, and of Toronto from 1834 to [1914]. . . . Edited by John Ross Robertson. 6 vols. Toronto, 1894–1914. Vols. 1–3 reprinted Belleville, Ont., 1976, 1987, 1974.

ROY, JOSEPH-EDMOND. *Histoire de la seigneurie de Lauzon* [1608–1840]. 5 vols. Lévis, Qué., 1897–1904; réimprimé 1984 [i.e. 1985].

——— *Histoire du notariat au Canada depuis la fondation de la colonie jusqu'à nos jours*. 4 vols. Lévis, Qué., 1899–1902.

RUMILLY, ROBERT. *Histoire de Montréal*. 5 vols. Montréal, 1970–74.

——— *Papineau et son temps*. 2 vols. Montréal, 1977.

SAUNDERS, EDWARD MANNING. *History of the Baptists of the Maritime provinces*. Halifax, 1902.

SCADDING, HENRY. *Toronto of old: collections and recollections illustrative of the early settlement and social life of the capital of Ontario*. Toronto, 1873. Abridged edition, entitled *Toronto of old*. Edited by Frederick Henry Armstrong. Toronto, 1966.

SMITH, THOMAS WATSON. *History of the Methodist Church within the territories embraced in the late conference of Eastern British America, including Nova Scotia, New Brunswick, Prince Edward Island and Bermuda*. 2 vols. Halifax, 1877–90.

SULTE, BENJAMIN. *Histoire de la milice canadienne-française, 1760–1897*. Montréal, 1897.

TAFT MANNING, HELEN. *The revolt of French Canada, 1800–1835; a chapter in the history of the British Commonwealth*. Toronto, 1962.

TULCHINSKY, GERALD JACOB JOSEPH. *The river barons: Montreal businessmen and the growth of industry and transportation, 1837–53*. Toronto and Buffalo, N.Y., 1977.

UPTON, LESLIE FRANCIS STOKES. *Micmacs and colonists; Indian-white relations in the Maritimes, 1713–1867*. Vancouver, 1979.

VAN KIRK, SYLVIA. *"Many tender ties": women in fur-trade society in western Canada, 1670–1870*. Winnipeg, [1980].

WALLOT, JEAN-PIERRE. *Un Québec qui bougeait: trame socio-politique du Québec au tournant du XIXe siècle*. Québec, 1973.

WILSON, BRUCE GORDON. *The enterprises of Robert Hamilton: a study of wealth and influence in early Upper Canada, 1776–1812*. Ottawa, 1983.

V. JOURNALS

Acadiensis: Journal of the History of the Atlantic Region/Revue de l'histoire de la région atlantique. Fredericton. Published by the Department of History of the University of New Brunswick. 1 (1971–72)– . *The Acadiensis index, vols.I–XII (autumn 1971 to spring 1983)*, comp. E. L. Swanick with the assistance of David Frank, was published in 1985.

Beaver: Magazine of the North. Winnipeg. Published by the HBC. 1 (1920–21)– . *Index*: 1–outfit 284 (June 1953–March 1954). Title varies.

Le Bulletin des recherches historiques. Published usually in Lévis, Qué. Originally the organ of the Société des études historiques, it became in March 1923 the journal of the Archives de la province de Québec (now the ANQ). 1 (1895)–70 (1968). *Index*: 1–31 (1925) (4v., Beauceville, Qué., 1925–26). For subsequent years there is an index on microfiche at the ANQ-Q.

Les Cahiers des Dix. Montréal et Québec. Published by "Les Dix." 1 (1936)– .

CANADIAN CATHOLIC HISTORICAL ASSOCIATION/ SOCIÉTÉ CANADIENNE D'HISTOIRE DE L'ÉGLISE CATHOLIQUE, Ottawa. Publishes simultaneously a *Report* in English and a *Rapport* in French, the contents of which are entirely different. 1 (1933–34)– . *Index*: 1–25 (1958). Title varies: *Study sessions/Sessions d'étude*, 1966–83; in 1984 the English title became *Canadian Catholic Historical Studies*.

CANADIAN HISTORICAL ASSOCIATION/SOCIÉTÉ HISTORIQUE DU CANADA, Ottawa. *Annual report*. 1922– . *Index*: 1922–51; 1952–68. Title varies: *Historical papers/Communications historiques* from 1966.

Canadian Historical Review. Toronto. 1 (1920)– . *Index*: 1–10 (1929); 11 (1930)–20 (1939); 21 (1940)–30 (1949); 31 (1950)–51 (1970). Université Laval has also published an index: *"Canadian Historical Review," 1950–1964: index des articles et des comptes rendus de volumes*, René Hardy, compil. (Québec, 1969). A continuation of the *Review of Historical Publications relating to Canada*: 1 (1895–96)–22 (1917–18); *Index*: 1–10 (1905); 11 (1906)–20 (1915).

Canadian Historic Sites: Occasional Papers in Archaeology and History/Lieux historiques canadiens: cahiers d'archéologie et d'histoire. Ottawa. Published by Canada, National Historic Parks and Sites Branch. No.1 (1970)– .

Dalhousie Review. Halifax. Published by Dalhousie University. 1 (1921–22)– .

Historic Kingston. Kingston, Ont. Published by the Kingston Historical Society. No.1 (1952)– ; nos. 1–10 reprinted in 1 vol., Belleville, Ont., 1972. *Index*: nos.1–20 (1972).

Newfoundland Quarterly. St John's. 1 (1901–2)– . Published by the Newfoundland Quarterly Foundation from vol.78 (1982–83).

NIAGARA HISTORICAL SOCIETY, Niagara-on-the-Lake, Ont. [*Publications*.] Nos.1 (1896)–44 (1939). The first number is called *Transaction*; nos.2 (1897)–44 list titles of articles included but have no main title; nos.38 (1927)–44 are all called "Records of Niagara. . . ."

NOVA SCOTIA HISTORICAL SOCIETY, Halifax. *See* ROYAL NOVA SCOTIA HISTORICAL SOCIETY

Ontario History. Toronto. Published by the Ontario Historical Society. 1 (1899)– ; vols.1–49 (1957) reprinted Millwood, N.Y., 1975. An index to volumes 1 to 64 (1972) appears in *Index to the publications of the Ontario Historical Society, 1899–1972* (1974). Title varies: *Papers and Records* to 1946.

Revue canadienne. Montréal. 1 (1864)–80 (1922). Vols.17 (1881)–23 (1887) are also numbered nouvelle série, 1–7; vols.24 (1888)–28 (1892) are also called 3e série, 1–4 [i.e. 5]; and vols.54 (janvier–juin 1908)–80 are also numbered nouvelle série, 1–27. Subtitle varies. An index volume, *Tables générales des 53 premiers volumes de la "Revue canadienne," 1864 à 1907*, was published in 1907.

Revue d'histoire de l'Amérique française. Montréal. Published by the Institut d'histoire de l'Amérique française. 1 (1947–48)– . Index: 1–10 (1956–57); 11 (1957–58)–20 (1966–67); 21 (1967–68)–30 (1976–77).

Revue trimestrielle canadienne. Montréal. Published by the Association des anciens élèves (after 1942 the Association des diplômés de polytechnique) of the École polytechnique, Université de Montréal. 1 (1915)– . Title varies: *L'Ingénieur*, 1955– .

ROYAL NOVA SCOTIA HISTORICAL SOCIETY, Halifax

GENEALOGICAL ASSOCIATION PUBLICATIONS

1, 3, 5–6, 8, 10: *N.S. vital statistics* (Punch and Holder) [*see* section III].

OTHER PUBLICATIONS

Collections. 1 (1878)– ; vols.1–8 (1892/94) reprinted in 2 vols., Belleville, Ont., 1976–77. Index: 1–32 (1959) in 33 (1961). Vols.1–40 (1980) issued under the society's original name, the Nova Scotia Historical Society.

ROYAL SOCIETY OF CANADA/SOCIÉTÉ ROYALE DU CANADA, Ottawa. *Proceedings and Transactions/Mémoires et comptes rendus*. 1st ser., 1 (1882–83)–12 (1894); 2nd ser., 1 (1895)–12 (1906); 3rd ser., 1 (1907)–56 (1962); 4th ser., 1 (1963)–22 (1985); 5th ser., 1 (1986)– . *General index*: 1st ser.–2nd ser.; *Author index*: 3rd ser., 1–35 (1941). The Canadian Library Association has published *A subject index to the Royal Society of Canada "Proceedings and Transactions": third series, vols. I–XXXI, 1907–1937*, comp. M. A. Martin (Ottawa, 1947).

Social History, a Canadian Review/Histoire sociale, revue canadienne. Ottawa. Published under the direction of an interdisciplinary committee from various Canadian universities. No.1 (April 1968)– .

SOCIÉTÉ GÉNÉALOGIQUE CANADIENNE-FRANÇAISE, Montréal

NUMBERED PUBLICATIONS

2, 4, 6: Lebœuf, *Complément* [*see* section III].

OTHER PUBLICATIONS

Mémoires. 1 (1944–45)– . An index to volumes 1–25 (1975) has been issued as *Index onomastique des "Mémoires" de la Société généalogique canadienne-française, 1944–1975*, R.-J. Auger compil. (2v., Lac-Beauport, Qué., 1975).

CONTRIBUTORS

Contributors

ABBOTT-NAMPHY, ELIZABETH. Historian and free-lance journalist, Montreal, Quebec.
Nelson Hackett. Jean-Marie Mondelet [in collaboration with M. MacKinnon].

ABEL, KERRY. Post-doctoral fellow in history, University of Manitoba, Winnipeg, Manitoba.
Alexander Simpson.

ACHESON, THOMAS WILLIAM. Professor of history, University of New Brunswick, Fredericton, New Brunswick.
Thomas Barlow. Hugh Johnston. Thomas Leavitt. Nehemiah Merritt. John McNeil Wilmot.

ALLAIRE, GRATIEN. Professeur agrégé d'histoire, University of Alberta, Edmonton, Alberta.
Pierre-Chrysologue Pambrun.

ALLEN, ROBERT S. Deputy chief, Treaties and Historical Research Centre, Indian and Northern Affairs Canada, Ottawa, Ontario.
Robert McDouall.

ARMOUR, DAVID ARTHUR. Deputy director, Mackinac Island State Park Commission, Michigan, U.S.A.
Marguerite-Magdelaine Marcot (La Framboise).

ARTHUR, ELIZABETH. Professor emeritus of history, Lakehead University, Thunder Bay, Ontario.
James Dickson.

†AUDET, LOUIS-PHILIPPE. Ex-professeur à la retraite, Sillery, Québec.
Pierre-Antoine Dorion.

BAILEY, ALFRED GOLDSWORTHY. Professor emeritus of history, University of New Brunswick, Fredericton, New Brunswick.
James Holbrook.

BAILLARGEON, NOËL. Historien, Séminaire de Québec, Québec.
Louis-Joseph Desjardins, dit *Desplantes.*

BAKER, MELVIN. Archivist-historian, Memorial University of Newfoundland, St John's, Newfoundland.
Benjamin Bowring.

BALLSTADT, CARL P. A. Professor of English, McMaster University, Hamilton, Ontario.
David Chisholme. Alexander James Christie. James Haskins. George Menzies.

BARRETTE, ROGER. Directeur, Développement des ressources humaines, Ministère de la Main-d'œuvre et de la Sécurité du revenu du Québec, Québec.
Bonaventure Panet.

BAZIN, JULES. Ex-conservateur des bibliothèques de la ville de Montréal, Québec.
Louis Dulongpré.

BEAUREGARD, YVES. Coéditeur, *Cap-aux-Diamants*, Québec, Québec.
Claude Dénéchau.

BECK, J. MURRAY. Professor emeritus of political science, Dalhousie University, Halifax, Nova Scotia.
Samuel George William Archibald. Jotham Blanchard.

BÉDARD, MICHEL. Historien, Environnement Canada, Parcs, Québec, Québec.
Mathew Bell [in collaboration with A. Bérubé and J. Hamelin].

BEER, DONALD ROBERT. Senior lecturer in history, University of New England, Armidale, New South Wales, Australia.
Charles Theophilus Metcalfe, 1st Baron Metcalfe.

BELL, D. G. Assistant professor of law, University of New Brunswick, Fredericton, New Brunswick.
George Frederick Street Berton.

BENNETT, SUSAN L. Research and reference librarian, Ontario Agricultural Museum, Milton, Ontario.
Robert Wade.

BENSLEY, EDWARD HORTON. Honorary Osler librarian and professor emeritus of medicine, McGill University, Montreal, Quebec.
William Robertson.

BERNARD, JEAN-PAUL. Professeur d'histoire, Université du Québec à Montréal, Québec.
Jean-Baptiste-Henri Brien. Jean-Olivier Chénier. Amury Girod [in collaboration with D. Gauthier].

BERNATCHEZ, GINETTE. Historienne, Charny, Québec.
Charles Hunter. Andrew Stuart.

BERNIER, JACQUES. Professeur agrégé d'histoire, Université Laval, Québec, Québec.
Thomas Fargues.

BÉRUBÉ, ANDRÉ. Chef adjoint, Sites historiques, Environnement Canada, Parcs, Québec, Québec.
Mathew Bell [in collaboration with M. Bédard and J. Hamelin].

†BILSON, GEOFFREY. Formerly professor of history, University of Saskatchewan, Saskatoon, Saskatchewan.
Grant Powell.

BISHOP, CHARLES A. Professor of anthropology, State University of New York-Oswego, New York, U.S.A.
ʔKwah.

†BLAKELEY, PHYLLIS R. Formerly archivist emeritus, Public Archives of Nova Scotia, Halifax, Nova Scotia.
Sampson Salter Blowers. John Homer. Henry Joseph Philips. Nathan Pushee. Lewis Morris Wilkins. Sir William Robert Wolseley Winniett.

BOUCHER, NEIL J. Directeur, Centre acadien, Université Sainte-Anne, Pointe-de-l'Église, Nouvelle-Écosse.
Benoni d'Entremont.

BOUDREAU, CLAUDE. Étudiant au doctorat en géographie, Université Laval, Québec, Québec.
Joseph Bouchette [in collaboration with P. Lépine].

BOYCE, GERALD E. Teacher, Hastings County Board of Education, Belleville, Ontario.

James Hunter Samson.

†BREDIN, THOMAS F. Formerly vice-principal, St John's-Ravenscourt School, Winnipeg, Manitoba.
David Thomas Jones [in collaboration with S. M. Johnson].

BROCK, DANIEL J. Teacher, Catholic Central High School, London, Ontario.
Edward Allen Talbot.

BROCK, THOMAS L. Club historian, Royal Military College of Canada, Victoria, British Columbia.
Sir Robert Barrie.

BROWN, JENNIFER S. H. Associate professor of history, University of Winnipeg, Manitoba.
Abishabis. Duncan Cameron.

BRUCE, PAMELA. St John's, Newfoundland.
Richard Barnes. Donald Allan Fraser. Newman Wright Hoyles.

BRUNGER, ALAN G. Associate professor of geography, Trent University, Peterborough, Ontario.
John Bostwick. Thomas Alexander Stewart.

BUCKNER, PHILLIP. Professor of history, University of New Brunswick, Fredericton, New Brunswick.
Archibald Acheson, 2nd Earl of Gosford. John Gervas Hutchinson Bourne. Sir Archibald Campbell. Sir Colin Campbell. Sir Donald Campbell. Sir Charles Hamilton. Sir George Murray. Charles Jeffery Peters [in collaboration with B. Glendenning]. *Charles Edward Poulett Thomson, 1st Baron Sydenham. Matthew Whitworth-Aylmer, 5th Baron Aylmer.*

BUERGER, GEOFFREY E. Chairman, History Department, Mentor College, Mississauga, Ontario.
Thomas Williams.

BUGGEY, SUSAN. Director, Architectural History, Canadian Parks Service, Ottawa, Ontario.
Thomas McCulloch [in collaboration with G. Davies].

BUMSTED, J. M. Professor of history, University of Manitoba, Winnipeg, Manitoba.
Hugh Denoon. John Hill. Alexander McDonell (Collachie). William Rankin. William Smith. George Wright.

BURLEY, DAVID G. Assistant professor of history, University of Winnipeg, Manitoba.
Adam Ferrie. James Matthew Whyte.

BURROUGHS, PETER. Professor of history, Dalhousie University, Halifax, Nova Scotia.
George Ramsay, 9th Earl of Dalhousie.

BUSH, EDWARD F. Formerly historian, Historical Research Division, Environment Canada, Parks, Ottawa, Ontario.
John Burrows.

CAHILL, J. BARRY. Manuscripts archivist, Public Archives of Nova Scotia, Halifax, Nova Scotia.
Edward Brabazon Brenton. Snow Parker.

CAMERON, WENDY. Partner, Wordforce, Toronto, Ontario.
Peter Robinson.

CARTER, ALEXANDRA E. Administrative assistant, Public relations, Grace Maternity Hospital, Halifax, Nova Scotia.
William Eagar.

CASTONGUAY, JACQUES. Recteur, Collège militaire royal de Saint-Jean, Saint-Jean-sur-Richelieu, Québec.
Antoine-Gaspard Couillard.

CAUCHON, MICHEL. Directeur, Centre de conservation du Québec, Ministère des Affaires culturelles du Québec, Québec.
Jean-Baptiste Roy-Audy.

CHABOT, RICHARD. Chercheur autonome, Laval, Québec.
Noël-Laurent Amiot. Kenelm Conor Chandler. Cyrille-Hector-Octave Côté. Charles-Vincent Fournier. Lucien Gagnon. Louis Nau. Joseph Papineau. Jacques Paquin. François-Xavier Pigeon. Louis Proulx. Édouard-Étienne Rodier.

CHARBONNEAU, ANDRÉ. Historien, Environnement Canada, Parcs, Québec, Québec.
Elias Walker Durnford.

CHARD, DONALD F. Historic parks planner, Environment Canada, Parks, Halifax, Nova Scotia.
Sir Thomas Andrew Lumisden Strange.

CHARTRAND, RENÉ. Conseiller principal, Direction de l'interprétation, Parcs et lieux historiques nationaux, Environnement Canada, Parcs, Ottawa, Ontario.
Louis de Watteville.

CHASSÉ, BÉATRICE. Historienne, Ministère des Affaires culturelles du Québec, Québec.
Jean-Baptiste Dumouchelle.

CHASSÉ, SONIA. Directrice, Musée régional de la Côte-Nord, Sept-Îles, Québec.
Pierre Bureau. John Neilson [in collaboration with R. Girard-Wallot and J.-P. Wallot]. *Joseph Signay.*

CHAUSSÉ, GILLES. Professeur d'histoire de l'Église, Université de Montréal, Québec.
Hyacinthe Hudon. Jean-Jacques Lartigue [in collaboration with L. Lemieux]. *Jacques-Guillaume Roque.*

CHÉNÉ, LUCIE. Historienne, Sainte-Foy, Québec.
James Brown.

CHIASSON, PAULETTE M. Rédactrice-historienne, *Dictionnaire biographique du Canada/Dictionary of Canadian biography*, Les Presses de l'université Laval, Québec, Québec.
James Kerr.

CHOQUETTE, ROBERT. Professeur titulaire de sciences religieuses, Université d'Ottawa, Ontario.
William Peter MacDonald. Michael Power.

CHRISTIE, CARL A. Senior research officer, Directorate of history, Department of National Defence, Ottawa, Ontario.
Robert Roberts Loring. Thomas Merritt. Sir Phineas Riall.

CLARKE, JOHN. Professor of geography, Carleton University, Ottawa, Ontario.
Mahlon Burwell.

CLIFTON, JAMES A. Frankenthal professor of anthropology and history, University of Wisconsin, Green Bay, Wisconsin, U.S.A.
Billy Caldwell. Sou-neh-hoo-way.

CLOUTIER, JULIETTE. Archiviste, Monastère des Augustines de l'Hôpital Général de Québec, Québec.
Marie-Esther Chaloux, named *de Saint-Joseph* [in collaboration with R. Lessard].

CLOUTIER, NICOLE. Conservatrice, Art canadien ancien, Musée des beaux-arts de Montréal, Québec.
René Beauvais, dit *Saint-James.*

COGSWELL, FRED. Professor emeritus of English, University of New Brunswick, Fredericton, New Brunswick.
Walter Bates. Emily Elizabeth Shaw (Beavan).

COLLARD, ELIZABETH. Author, historian, and honorary curator, McCord Museum of Canadian History,

Montreal, Quebec.
John Griffith.

CONDON, ANN GORMAN. Associate professor of history, University of New Brunswick, Saint John, New Brunswick.
Peter Fisher.

COOKE, O. A. Senior archival officer, Directorate of history, Department of National Defence, Ottawa, Ontario.
Nathaniel Coffin. Colley Lyons Lucas Foster. Sir Richard Downes Jackson [in collaboration with N. Hillmer].

CORMIER, LOUIS-PHILIPPE. Professeur émérite de langues modernes, University of Lethbridge, Alberta.
Jean-Baptiste Perrault.

CREIGHTON, PHILIP. Chartered accountant, Toronto, Ontario.
Henry Lamb.

CUNNINGHAM, ROBERT JOHN. Local historian, Sackville, New Brunswick.
Toler Thompson.

CUTHBERTSON, BRIAN C. Head, Heritage Unit, Department of Culture, Recreation and Fitness, Halifax, Nova Scotia.
Thomas Nickleson Jeffery.

CYR, CÉLINE. Rédactrice-historienne, *Dictionnaire biographique du Canada/Dictionary of Canadian biography*, Les Presses de l'université Laval, Québec, Québec.
Michel Clouet. Michel-Louis Juchereau Duchesnay.

CYR, JEAN-ROCH. Étudiant au doctorat en histoire, Université de Montréal, Québec.
William Hanington.

DALTON, IAN ROBERT. Associate professor of electrical engineering, University of Toronto, Ontario.
Thomas Dalton.

DAVIDSON, STEPHEN ERIC. Teacher, Cavalier Drive School, Lower Sackville, Nova Scotia.
John Burton.

DAVIES, GWENDOLYN. Associate professor of English, Acadia University, Wolfville, Nova Scotia.
Sarah Herbert. Thomas McCulloch [in collaboration with S. Buggey].

DECHÊNE, LOUISE. Professeure titulaire d'histoire, Université McGill, Montréal, Québec.
George Pozer.

DE JONG, NICOLAS J. Provincial archivist, Public Archives of Prince Edward Island, Charlottetown, Prince Edward Island.
John Henry White [in collaboration with M. G. Morrow].

DESCHÊNES, GASTON. Chef, Division de la recherche, Bibliothèque de l'Assemblée nationale, Québec, Québec.
Amable Charron.

DÉSILETS, ANDRÉE. Professeure d'histoire, Université de Sherbrooke, Québec.
Marie-Françoise Huot, named *Sainte-Gertrude. John Baptist McMahon.*

DESLAURIERS, PETER. History instructor, Dawson College, and doctoral student in history, Concordia University, Montreal, Quebec.
Roderick Mackenzie. James Millar. Jules-Maurice Quesnel.

DEVER, ALAN. Television journalist, Canadian Broadcasting Corporation, Montreal, Quebec.
Michael O'Sullivan. Jean-Moïse Raymond.

DILWORTH, T. G. Professor of biology, University of New Brunswick, Fredericton, New Brunswick.
Alexander Lawrence. Thomas Nisbet.

DOUGLAS, W. A. B. Director, Directorate of history, Department of National Defence, Ottawa, Ontario.
Robert Heriot Barclay. Sir Isaac Coffin. Frederick Marryat. Daniel Pring.

DRAPER, GARY. Head, Reference and Collections Development Department, Dana Porter Library, University of Waterloo, Ontario.
William Dunlop, known as *Tiger Dunlop* [in collaboration with R. Hall].

DROUIN, FRANÇOIS. Étudiant au doctorat en histoire, Université Laval, Québec, Québec.
Pierre Canac, dit *Marquis. François Quirouet.*

DUBUC, ALFRED. Professeur titulaire d'histoire, Université du Québec à Montréal, Québec.
John Molson.

DUCHESNE, RAYMOND. Professeur d'histoire et de sociologie, Télé-Université, Université du Québec, Québec.
Pierre Chasseur.

DUCLOS, LAURETTE, S.G.M. Archiviste, Archives des Sœurs Grises, Montréal, Québec.
Marguerite Beaubien.

DUFOUR, PIERRE. Historien, Québec, Québec.
Pierre de Rastel de Rocheblave [in collaboration with M. Ouellet].

DUNLOP, ALLAN C. Associate provincial archivist, Public Archives of Nova Scotia, Halifax, Nova Scotia.
John Albro.

DUVAL, MARC. Avocat, Beauceville, Québec.
Charles-Étienne Chaussegros de Léry [in collaboration with R. Lessard].

EDMUNDS, R. DAVID. Professor of history, Texas Christian University, Fort Worth, Texas, U.S.A.
Tenskwatawa.

EDWARDS, MARY JANE. Professor of English and director, Centre for Editing Early Canadian Texts, Carleton University, Ottawa, Ontario.
Standish O'Grady.

ELLIOT, ROBERT S. Curator, History Department, New Brunswick Museum, Saint John, New Brunswick.
John Coffin.

ENNALS, PETER. Associate professor and head, Department of geography, Mount Allison University, Sackville, New Brunswick.
James Gray Bethune. John Covert.

ERICKSON, VINCENT O. Professor of anthropology, University of New Brunswick, Fredericton, New Brunswick.
Pierre Denis. Johann Ludwig Tiarks.

ERRINGTON, JANE. Assistant professor of history, Royal Military College of Canada, Kingston, Ontario.
Ann Kirby (Macaulay). John Kirby. James Macfarlane. Thomas Markland.

EVANS, CALVIN D. Area librarian, Humanities and Social Sciences Library, McGill University, Montreal, Quebec.
George Cubit. John Wills Martin. William Richard Shea.

FAHEY, CURTIS. Editor, James Lorimer & Company Ltd, Publishers, Toronto, Ontario.
William John O'Grady.

FERRON, MADELEINE. Écrivaine, Québec, Québec.

Jacques Voyer.

†FILTEAU, GÉRARD. Sillery, Québec.
Joseph Duquet.

FILTEAU, HUGUETTE. Codirectrice de la rédaction, *Dictionnaire biographique du Canada/Dictionary of Canadian biography*, Les Presses de l'université Laval, Québec, Québec.
Thomas Coffin.

FINGARD, JUDITH. Professor of history, Dalhousie University, Halifax, Nova Scotia.
Walter Bromley. John Inglis.

FINLEY, GERALD E. Professor of art history, Queen's University, Kingston, Ontario.
George Heriot.

FIRTH, EDITH G. Formerly head, Canadian History Department, Metropolitan Toronto Reference Library, Ontario.
William Cooper. Elizabeth Posthuma Gwillim (Simcoe). Anne Murray (Powell). Hannah Peters (Jarvis). Alexander Wood.

FISHER, ROBIN A. Professor of history, Simon Fraser University, Burnaby, British Columbia.
James Charles Stuart Strange.

FRASER, ROBERT LOCHIEL. Hamilton, Ontario.
William Warren Baldwin. Richard Beasley. James Martin Cawdell. William Forsyth. Christopher Alexander Hagerman. George Hillier. Peter Howard. John Mills Jackson. Jonas Jones. John McIntosh. Richard Pierpoint.

FRENCH, GOLDWIN S. Professor of religious studies, Victoria University, Toronto, Ontario.
Stephen Bamford. Samuel Heck. Joshua Marsden.

FROST, STANLEY BRICE. Director, History of McGill Project, McGill University, Montreal, Quebec.
Thomas Blackwood. Alexander Skakel.

GAGNON, SERGE. Professeur d'histoire, Université du Québec à Trois-Rivières, Québec.
Nicolas-Gaspard Boisseau. Charles-François Painchaud.

GALARNEAU, CLAUDE. Professeur titulaire d'histoire, Université Laval, Québec, Québec.
Jean-Baptiste Boucher. Félix Gatien. Charles Hindenlang. Samuel Neilson. Joseph-François Perrault. John Christopher Reiffenstein.

GALLICHAN, GILLES. Responsable, Secteur des monographies, Bibliothèque nationale du Québec, Montréal, Québec.
Amable Berthelot.

GAMELIN, ALAIN. Directeur, A. G. H. Recherchiste-conseil, Trois-Rivières, Québec.
Louis-Marie Cadieux.

GARDNER, DAVID. Free-lance actor, director, and theatre historian, Toronto, Ontario.
Frederick Brown.

GAUTHIER, DANIELLE. Historienne, Belœil, Québec.
Amury Girod [in collaboration with J.-P. Bernard].

GAUTHIER, RAYMONDE. Professeure d'histoire de l'art, Université du Québec à Montréal, Québec.
Joseph Pépin.

GIGUÈRE, GEORGES-ÉMILE. Directeur général, Fondation Robert Giguère Inc., Montréal, Québec.
Jean-Pierre Chazelle.

GILLIS, ROBERT PETER. Treasury Board Secretariat, Ottawa, Ontario.
George Hamilton (1781–1839). Charles Shirreff.

GINGERICH, ORLAND. Clergyman, Kitchener, Ontario.
Christian Nafziger

GIRARD-WALLOT, RITA. Agente de développement, Université Saint-Paul, Ottawa, Ontario.
John Neilson [in collaboration with S. Chassé and J.-P. Wallot].

GLENDENNING, BURTON. Coordinator, Historical Division, Provincial Archives of New Brunswick, Fredericton, New Brunswick.
Charles Jeffery Peters [in collaboration with P. Buckner].

GODFREY, SHELDON J. Lawyer, Toronto, Ontario.
Jacob Franks.

GOLDRING, PHILIP. Historian, Environment Canada, Parks, Ottawa, Ontario.
Andrew William Cochran. James Leith. William MacKintosh.

GOOD, E. REGINALD. Doctoral student in history, University of Saskatchewan, Saskatoon, Saskatchewan.
John Goessman. Joseph Schneider [in collaboration with P. Tiessen].

GRANT, JOHN WEBSTER. Professor emeritus of church history, Victoria University, Toronto, Ontario.
Seneca Ketchum.

GRAY, LESLIE ROBB. Formerly vice-president and secretary-treasurer, Silverwood Dairies, London, Ontario.
Christian Frederick Denke.

GREENFIELD, KATHARINE. Formerly head, Special Collections, Hamilton Public Library, Ontario.
Stephen Randal.

GREENWOOD, F. MURRAY. Associate professor emeritus of history, University of British Columbia, Vancouver, British Columbia, and legal history consultant, Montreal, Quebec.
Jonathan Sewell [in collaboration with J. H. Lambert].

GUNDY, H. PEARSON. Professor emeritus of English, Queen's University, Kingston, Ontario.
Samuel Oliver Tazewell.

HALL, ANTHONY J. Assistant professor of native studies, Laurentian University, Sudbury, Ontario.
John Aisance.

HALL, ROGER. Associate professor of history, University of Western Ontario, London, Ontario.
William Dunlop, known as *Tiger Dunlop* [in collaboration with G. Draper]. *John Galt* [in collaboration with N. Whistler].

HAMELIN, JEAN. Directeur général adjoint, *Dictionnaire biographique du Canada/Dictionary of Canadian biography*, Les Presses de l'université Laval, Québec, Québec.
Mathew Bell [in collaboration with M. Bédard and A. Bérubé].

HAREL, BRUNO, P.S.S. Archiviste, Séminaire de Saint-Sulpice, Montréal, Québec.
Louis-Charles Lefebvre de Bellefeuille. Jackson John Richards. Antoine Sattin.

†HARPER, J. RUSSELL. South Lancaster, Ontario.
James Bowman.

HÉROUX, ANDRÉE. Étudiante au doctorat en géographie, Université Laval, Québec, Québec.
Sir John Caldwell. François Languedoc.

HICKS, FRANKLYN H. Physician, Ottawa, Ontario.
William Elder.

HILLER, JAMES K. Associate professor of history, Memorial

University of Newfoundland, St John's, Newfoundland.
Benjamin Gottlieb Kohlmeister.

HILLMER, NORMAN. Senior historian, Directorate of history, Department of National Defence, Ottawa, Ontario.
Sir Richard Downes Jackson [in collaboration with O. A. Cooke].

HOLLAND, CLIVE. Historian, Scott Polar Research Institute, Cambridge, England.
Sir John Franklin. Edward Nicholas Kendall.

HOLMAN, HARRY TINSON. Adviser, Access to information, Science and Technology Canada, Ottawa, Ontario.
John Brecken.

HOLMGREN, ERIC J. Historical consultant, Edmonton, Alberta.
William Kittson.

HOWELL, COLIN D. Professor of history, St Mary's University, Halifax, Nova Scotia.
William Bruce Almon.

HUTCHINSON, GERALD M. Thorsby, Alberta.
James Evans. Thomas Hassall.

JANSON, GILLES. Responsable des archives historiques, Service des archives, Université du Québec à Montréal, Québec.
Daniel Arnoldi.

JANZEN, CAROL ANNE. Businesswoman, Kentville, Nova Scotia.
Sir Alexander Croke.

JEAN, MARGUERITE, S.C.I.M. Directrice, *Courrier Bon-Pasteur*, Sainte-Foy, Québec.
Eulalie Durocher, named *Mother Marie-Rose.*

JOHNSON, J. K. Professor of history, Carleton University, Ottawa, Ontario.
Anthony Manahan. James Newbigging.

JOHNSON, STEPHEN M. Assistant head, Glenlyon-Norfolk School, Victoria, British Columbia.
David Thomas Jones [in collaboration with T. F. Bredin]. *John M. McLeod.*

JOHNSTON, CHARLES M. Professor of history, McMaster University, Hamilton, Ontario.
Robert Lugger.

JONES, ELWOOD H. Professor of history, Trent University, Peterborough, Ontario.
William Purdy. Charles Burton Wyatt.

KAREL, DAVID. Professeur titulaire d'histoire, Université Laval, Québec, Québec.
Angelo Pienovi. Louis-Hubert Triaud.

KELSAY, ISABEL T. Free-lance historian, Media, Pennsylvania, U.S.A.
Ohtowaˀkéhson.

KEYES, JOHN. Historian, Quebec, Quebec.
William John Chapman Benson.

KIRWIN, WILLIAM. Formerly professor of English, Memorial University of Newfoundland, St John's, Newfoundland.
David Buchan.

KOS RABCEWICZ ZUBKOWSKI, LUDWIK. Président, Centre canadien d'arbitrage, de conciliation et d'amiable composition, Ottawa, Ontario.
Pierre-Dominique Debartzch.

LABERGE, ANDRÉ. Étudiant au doctorat en histoire, Université Laval, Québec, Québec.
Henry Musgrave Blaiklock.

LABRÈQUE, MARIE-PAULE R. Historienne, Acton-Vale, Québec.
John Church. Frederick George Heriot. Louis-Édouard Hubert.

LAHEY, RAYMOND J. Bishop, Diocese of St George's, Corner Brook, Newfoundland.
Michael Anthony Fleming. William Herron.

LAMBERT, JAMES H. Rédacteur-historien, *Dictionnaire biographique du Canada/Dictionary of Canadian biography*, Les Presses de l'université Laval, Québec, Québec.
Herman Witsius Ryland. Jonathan Sewell [in collaboration with F. M. Greenwood]. *Joseph-Rémi Vallières de Saint-Réal* [in collaboration with J. Monet].

LAMBERT, THÉRÈSE, C.N.D. Montréal, Québec.
Marie-Victoire Baudry, named *de la Croix.*

LAMONDE, YVAN. Professeur agrégé d'histoire, Université McGill, Montréal, Québec.
Jacques Odelin [in collaboration with L. Marcil-Lacoste].

LANDRY, PIERRE B. Conservateur adjoint, Art canadien, Musée des beaux-arts du Canada, Ottawa, Ontario.
Robert Auchmuty Sproule.

LAPOINTE-ROY, HUGUETTE. Professeure, Collège Durocher, Saint-Lambert, Québec.
Marie-Marguerite Lemaire.

LAURENCE, GÉRARD. Professeur d'information et de communication, Université Laval, Québec, Québec.
Léon Gosselin.

LEASK, MARGARET FILSHIE. Toronto, Ontario.
Stephen Humbert.

LEBEL, JEAN-MARIE. Chargé de recherche, Groupe de recherche sur la production des catéchismes, Université Laval, Québec, Québec.
John Charlton Fisher. William Kemble. Joseph Le Vasseur Borgia. Louis Martinet, dit *Bonami.*

LEBLANC, R. GILLES. Archiviste, Centre d'études acadiennes, Université de Moncton, Nouveau-Brunswick.
Charles-Dominique Auffray. Antoine Gagnon.

LEBRETON, CLARENCE. Directeur, Aquarium et Musée marin, Shippagan, Nouveau-Brunswick.
Tranquille Blanchard [in collaboration with A. Lepage].

LECHASSEUR, ANTONIO. Chercheur, Institut québécois de recherche sur la culture, Québec, Québec.
Charles-Eusèbe Casgrain.

LEGAULT, ROCH. Étudiant au doctorat en histoire, Université de Montréal, Québec.
François Vassal de Monviel [in collaboration with L. Lépine].

LEGGET, ROBERT F. Formerly director, Division of Building Research, National Research Council of Canada, Ottawa, Ontario.
John By. Henry Abraham DuVernet. Thomas Roy.

LEIGHTON, DOUGLAS. Associate professor of history, University of Western Ontario, London, Ontario.
Jean-Baptiste de Lorimier. James Winniett.

LEMIEUX, LUCIEN. Vicaire épiscopal et curé de la paroisse Sainte-Julie, Québec.
Jean-Jacques Lartigue [in collaboration with G. Chaussé]. *Pierre Viau.*

LEMOINE, LOUIS. Directeur adjoint, École secondaire Joseph-François-Perrault, Longueuil, Québec.
Marie-Charles-Joseph Le Moyne de Longueuil, Baronne de Longueuil (Grant).

LEMOINE, RÉJEAN. Historien, Groupe de ressources techniques en aménagement du Québec, Québec.
François-Hyacinthe Séguin.

LEPAGE, ANDRÉ. Contractuel, Québec, Québec.
Tranquille Blanchard [in collaboration with C. LeBreton].

LÉPINE, LUC. Archiviste-historien, Pierrefonds, Québec.
François Vassal de Monviel [in collaboration with R. Legault].

LÉPINE, PIERRE. Responsable, Secteur des cartes, Bibliothèque nationale du Québec, Montréal, Québec.
Joseph Bouchette [in collaboration with C. Boudreau].

LESLIE, JOHN F. Chief, Treaties and Historical Research Centre, Comprehensive Claims Branch, Indian and Northern Affairs Canada, Ottawa, Ontario.
James Givins.

LESSARD, RENALD. Archiviste, Archives nationales du Québec, Québec.
Marie-Esther Chaloux, named *de Saint-Joseph* [in collaboration with J. Cloutier]. *Charles-Étienne Chaussegros de Léry* [in collaboration with M. Duval]. *Louis Gugy. René Kimber* [in collaboration with J. Noël].

LEVINE, ALLAN. Teacher of history, St John's-Ravenscourt School, Winnipeg, Manitoba.
John Macallum.

LEWIS, WALTER. Assistant chief librarian, Halton Hills Public Library, Georgetown, Ontario.
William Chisholm. John Leys.

L'HEUREUX, JACQUES. Professeur titulaire de droit, Université Laval, Québec, Québec.
Hugues Heney.

LITTLE, J. I. Associate professor of history, Simon Fraser University, Burnaby, British Columbia.
William Bowman Felton.

LOCHHEAD, DOUGLAS G. Writer in residence, Mount Allison University, Sackville, New Brunswick.
Hannah Maynard Thompson (Pickard).

LORIMIER, MICHEL DE. Historien, Montréal, Québec.
Joseph-Narcisse Cardinal. Rodolphe Des Rivières. Chevalier de Lorimier.

LYSONS-BALCON, HEATHER. Associate professor of education, University of Alberta, Edmonton, Alberta.
Charles Buller. Joseph Lancaster.

MCDOUGALL, ELIZABETH ANN KERR. Research historian, Westmount, Quebec.
Edward Black. James Somerville.

MCGAHAN, ELIZABETH W. Instructor of history, University of New Brunswick, Saint John, New Brunswick.
Thomas Millidge.

MCILWRAITH, THOMAS F. Associate professor of geography, University of Toronto, Ontario.
Charles Jones.

MACINTOSH, KATHRYN TAIT. Halifax, Nova Scotia.
John Geddie.

†MACKAY, DONALD C. Halifax, Nova Scotia.
Richard Upham Marsters. Joseph Toler [in collaboration with S. A. Smith]. *William Valentine. John Wolhaupter* [in collaboration with S. A. Smith].

MCKENZIE, RUTH. Free-lance writer, editor, and researcher, Ottawa, Ontario.
Simon Ebenezer Washburn.

MACKINNON, MARGARET. Legislative counsel, Office of the Legislative Counsel, Toronto, Ontario.
Jean-Marie Mondelet [in collaboration with E. Abbott-Namphy].

MACLEAN, RAYMOND A. Formerly professor of history, St Francis Xavier University, Antigonish, Nova Scotia.
Colin P. Grant. Alexander MacDonell. Jean-Baptiste Maranda. John Young.

†MACMILLAN, DAVID S. Formerly professor of history, Trent University, Peterborough, Ontario.
Allan Gilmour.

MCNALLY, LARRY S. Science and engineering archivist, Manuscript Division, National Archives of Canada, Ottawa, Ontario.
Alfred Barrett.

MAIR, NATHAN H. Clergyman, Digby, Nova Scotia.
Robert Langham Lusher.

MANNION, JOHN. Professor of geography, Memorial University of Newfoundland, St John's, Newfoundland.
Thomas Meagher. Patrick Morris. Pierce Sweetman.

MARCIL, EILEEN REID. Historian, Charlesbourg, Quebec.
Charles Wood.

MARCIL-LACOSTE, LOUISE. Professeure de philosophie, Université de Montréal, Québec.
Jacques Odelin [in collaboration with Y. Lamonde].

MAYS, HERBERT J. Director of research administration, University of Winnipeg, Manitoba.
John McDonell.

MEALING, S. R. Professor of history, Carleton University, Ottawa, Ontario.
William Firth. Sir David William Smith.

MICHAUD, NELSON. Adjoint législatif auprès du solliciteur général du Canada, Ottawa, Ontario.
Jean-Charles Létourneau.

MILLER, CARMAN. Associate professor of history, McGill University, Montreal, Quebec.
William Allen Chipman. Adam Lymburner Macnider. William Walker.

MILLMAN, THOMAS R. Formerly archivist, Anglican Church of Canada, Toronto, Ontario.
Charles Caleb Cotton. Charles James Stewart.

MOIR, JOHN S. Professor of history, University of Toronto, Ontario.
William Jenkins. Robert McDowall.

MOMRYK, MYRON. Archivist, Manuscript Division, National Archives of Canada, Ottawa, Ontario.
Andrew Porteous.

MONET, JACQUES, S.J. President, Regis College, Toronto, Ontario.
Sir Charles Bagot. Austin Cuvillier [in collaboration with G. J. J. Tulchinsky]. *Joseph-Rémi Vallières de Saint-Réal* [in collaboration with J. H. Lambert].

MOODY, BARRY M. Associate professor of history, Acadia University, Wolfville, Nova Scotia.
Joseph Dimock. Asa McGray.

MORGAN, ROBERT J. Professor of history and director, Beaton Institute, University College of Cape Breton, Sydney, Nova Scotia.
George Robert Ainslie. Hugh Swayne.

MORRIS, JULIE M. Manuscripts archivist, Public Archives of Nova Scotia, Halifax, Nova Scotia.
Elizabeth Lichtenstein (Johnston). Nancy Purvis. [Biographies written in collaboration with W. L. Thorpe.]

MORRISON, JEAN. Supervisor, Library and Research Services, Old Fort William, Thunder Bay, Ontario.

Peter Grant. James McKenzie.

MORROW, MARIANNE G. Free-lance journalist, Charlottetown, Prince Edward Island.
John Henry White [in collaboration with N. J. de Jong].

†MORTON, W. L. Formerly professor of history, University of Manitoba, Winnipeg, Manitoba.
Pierre-Guillaume Sayer.

MURPHY, BRIAN DUNSTONE. Archivist, Manuscript Division, National Archives of Canada, Ottawa, Ontario.
James J. Langford.

MURRAY, FLORENCE B. Professor emeritus of library science, University of Toronto, Ontario.
Samuel Richardson.

NAYLOR, MARY. Westmount, Quebec.
Mark Willoughby.

NELLES, H. V. Professor of history, York University, Downsview, Ontario.
Robert Nelles.

NICKS, GERTRUDE. Associate curator-in-charge, Department of Ethnology, Royal Ontario Museum, Toronto, Ontario.
Louis Callihoo.

NOËL, FRANÇOISE. Assistant professor of history, Memorial University of Newfoundland, St John's, Newfoundland.
William Plenderleath Christie. Edme Henry.

NOËL, JOHANNE. Assistante de recherche en histoire, Sainte-Foy, Québec.
René Kimber [in collaboration with R. Lessard].

NOKES, JANE HOLLINGWORTH. Corporate archivist, Bank of Nova Scotia Archives, Toronto, Ontario.
William Lawson.

O'DEA, SHANE. Associate professor of English, Memorial University of Newfoundland, St John's, Newfoundland.
Nicholas Croke.

O'FLAHERTY, PATRICK. Professor of English, Memorial University of Newfoundland, St John's, Newfoundland.
Peter Brown. William Carson. Sir Francis Forbes. George Lilly. John Ryan.

O'GALLAGHER, MARIANNA. Historian, Sainte-Foy, Quebec.
Robert Wood [in collaboration].

OTTO, STEPHEN A. Author and consultant, Toronto, Ontario.
George Longley.

OUELLET, FERNAND. Professeur d'histoire, York University, Downsview, Ontario.
Pierre-Théophile Decoigne. John George Lambton, 1st Earl of Durham. Simon McGillivray. Joseph Masson. Philemon Wright [in collaboration with B. Thériault].

OUELLET, MARC. Chercheur autonome, Sillery, Québec.
Pierre de Rastel de Rocheblave [in collaboration with P. Dufour].

PARKER, BRUCE A. Teacher, Port Hope, Ontario.
Samuel Street.

PATTERSON, GRAEME H. Associate professor of history, University of Toronto, Ontario.
Robert Thorpe.

PEEL, BRUCE. Librarian emeritus, University of Alberta, Edmonton, Alberta.
William Connolly.

PEMBERTON, IAN. Associate professor of history, University of Windsor, Ontario.
Levius Peters Sherwood.

PFAFF, CATHERINE MCKINNON. Teacher of English, Bishop Strachan School, Toronto, Ontario.
John Cochrane [in collaboration with L. R. Pfaff].

PFAFF, LARRY ROBERT. Deputy librarian, Art Gallery of Ontario, Toronto, Ontario.
John Cochrane [in collaboration with C. M. Pfaff].

PIETERSMA, HARRY. Supervisor, Agricultural Programming, Upper Canada Village, Morrisburg, Ontario.
James Philips.

POIRIER, LUCIEN. Professeur agrégé de musique, Université Laval, Québec, Québec.
Frederick Glackemeyer. Charles Sauvageau.

POTHIER, BERNARD. Historian, Canadian War Museum, Ottawa, Ontario.
Jean-Mandé Sigogne.

POTHIER, PHILIPPE. Juge à la retraite, Saint-Hyacinthe, Québec.
Toussaint Pothier.

PRINCE, SUZANNE. Professeure de français, Collège Mérici, Québec, Québec.
Marie-Louise McLoughlin, named *de Saint-Henri.*

PRIOUL, DIDIER. Historien d'art, Sainte-Foy, Québec.
James Pattison Cockburn.

PRYKE, KENNETH G. Professor of history, University of Windsor, Ontario.
Samuel Head. William McCormick.

†PULLEN, H. F. Chester Basin, Nova Scotia.
Sir Philip Bowes Vere Broke.

PUNCH, TERRENCE M. President, Genealogical Institute of the Maritimes, and vice-president, Royal Nova Scotia Historical Society, Halifax, Nova Scotia.
John Skerry. Titus Smith. James Tobin.

RAMSEY, THOMAS A. Clergyman, Montreal, Quebec.
Edward Parkin.

RAUDZENS, GEORGE KARL. Senior lecturer in history, Macquarie University, North Ryde, New South Wales, Australia.
Sir Richard Henry Bonnycastle. Sir James Carmichael Smyth.

REA, J. E. Professor of history, University of Manitoba, Winnipeg, Manitoba.
Alexander McDonell.

READ, COLIN FREDERICK. Associate professor of history, University of Western Ontario, London, Ontario.
Jacob R. Beamer. Robert Davis. Joshua Gwillen Doan. William Putnam. Thomas Radcliff.

REANEY, JAMES. Professor of English, University of Western Ontario, London, Ontario.
John Troyer.

REID, RICHARD M. Associate professor of history, University of Guelph, Ontario.
James Johnston.

RICHARDSON, ARTHUR JOHN HAMPSON. Formerly chief, Architectural History Division, National Historic Parks and Sites Branch, Indian and Northern Affairs Canada, Ottawa, Ontario.
James Hunt. Henry Usborne.

ROBERT, JEAN-CLAUDE. Professeur d'histoire, Université du Québec à Montréal, Québec.
Barthélemy Joliette. Jean-Baptiste Thavenet.

ROBERTS, DAVID. Manuscript editor, *Dictionary of Canadian biography/Dictionnaire biographique du Canada*, University of Toronto Press, Ontario.
George Waters Allsopp. Martin Chinic. John Le Breton. Adam Lymburner. Peet Selee.

ROBERTSON, ALLEN B. Lecturer in history, Mount Saint Vincent University, Halifax, Nova Scotia.
Robert Barry.

ROBERTSON, IAN ROSS. Associate professor of history, University of Toronto, Ontario.
Frederick John Martin Collard.

ROBICHAUD, DONAT, MGR. Vicaire général et curé de la paroisse Saint-Augustin, Paquetville, Nouveau-Brunswick.
Perry Dumaresq. Vénérande Robichaux.

ROLAND, CHARLES G. Jason A. Hannah professor of the history of medicine, McMaster University, Hamilton, Ontario.
Robert Charles Horne. John Stephenson. Alexander Thom.

ROMNEY, PAUL. Private scholar, Baltimore, Maryland, U.S.A.
Joseph Cawthra. Charles Fothergill.

ROSENFELD, ROSLYN. Part-time instructor, University of New Brunswick, Fredericton, New Brunswick.
Thomas Emerson.

ROSENKRANTZ, OTTE A. Free-lance writer and journalist, London, Ontario.
John Vincent.

ROUSSEAU, LOUIS. Professeur de sciences religieuses, Université du Québec à Montréal, Québec.
Louis-François Parent.

ROWLEY, SUSAN. Researcher, Department of Anthropology, Smithsonian Institution, Washington, District of Columbia, U.S.A.
Eenoolooapik.

RUDÉ, GEORGE. Formerly professor of history, Concordia University, Montreal, Quebec.
Daniel D. Heustis. Elijah Crocker Woodman.

RUGGLE, RICHARD E. Rector, St Paul's Anglican Church, Norval, Ontario.
George Mortimer.

RUSSELL, PETER A. Resident tutor in economic history, Fircroft College, Birmingham, England.
Robert Graham Dunlop. John Johnston Lefferty.

ST-GEORGES, LISE. Étudiante au doctorat en histoire, Université de Montréal, Québec.
Louis Roy Portelance.

SAINT-PIERRE, DIANE. Assistante de recherche, Institut québécois de recherche sur la culture, Québec, Québec.
Allison Davie.

SAUTTER, UDO. Professor of history, University of Windsor, Ontario.
Johann Adam Moschell.

SENIOR, ELINOR KYTE. Assistant professor, St Francis Xavier University, Antigonish, Nova Scotia.
Francis Badgley. Louis Guy.

SENIOR, HEREWARD. Professor of history, McGill University, Montreal, Quebec.
George Perkins Bull.

†SIMARD, JEAN-PAUL. Ex-professeur d'histoire, Université du Québec à Chicoutimi, Québec.
Neil McLaren.

SIMPSON, RICHARD J. Indexer-editor, Canadian Periodical Index, Toronto, Ontario.
William Chewett.

SIOUI, GEORGES E. Étudiant au doctorat en histoire, Université Laval, Québec, Québec.
Nicolas Vincent.

SMITH, DONALD B. Associate professor of history, University of Calgary, Alberta.
Bauzhi-geezhig-waeshikum. Augustus Jones. John Jones.

SMITH, SHIRLEE ANNE. Keeper, Hudson's Bay Company Archives, Provincial Archives of Manitoba, Winnipeg, Manitoba.
John Stuart. William Williams.

SMITH, STUART ALLEN. Professor of art history, University of New Brunswick, Fredericton, New Brunswick.
Joseph Toler [in collaboration with D. C. Mackay]. *Thomas Hanford Wentworth. John Wolhaupter* [in collaboration with D. C. Mackay].

SPRAY, WILLIAM A. Vice-president (academic), St Thomas University, Fredericton, New Brunswick.
William Abrams. Hugh Munro. Francis Peabody. John Vondy. Alexander Wedderburn.

SPRY, IRENE M. Professor emeritus of economics, University of Ottawa, Ontario.
William Hemmings Cook.

STAGG, RONALD J. Professor of history, Ryerson Polytechnical Institute, Toronto, Ontario.
Jeanne-Charlotte Allamand (Berczy). Jesse Lloyd. Samuel Lount. Peter Matthews. Jordan Post. Nils von Schoultz. Joseph Shepard. Benjamin Thorne.

STANLEY, DELLA M. M. Part-time professor of history, St Mary's University and Mount Saint Vincent University, Halifax, Nova Scotia.
James Sayre.

STEARN, WILLIAM THOMAS. Senior principal scientific officer, British Museum, London, and visiting professor, University of Reading, England.
Archibald Menzies.

STEWART, J. DOUGLAS. Professor of art history, Queen's University, Kingston, Ontario.
John Solomon Cartwright [in collaboration with M. Stewart].

STEWART, MARY. Graduate student in English, Queen's University, Kingston, Ontario.
John Solomon Cartwright [in collaboration with J. D. Stewart].

SUTHERLAND, DAVID A. Associate professor of history, Dalhousie University, Halifax, Nova Scotia.
Andrew Belcher. Stephen Wastie Deblois. Charles Rufus Fairbanks. Thomas Forrester.

SYLVAIN, PHILIPPE. Professeur émérite d'histoire, Université Laval, Québec, Québec.
Charles-Auguste-Marie-Joseph de Forbin-Janson. Maria Monk.

TAYLOR, M. BROOK. Assistant professor of history, Mount Saint Vincent University, Halifax, Nova Scotia.
Charles Binns. Fade Goff. John Frederick Holland. Francis Longworth. John Small Macdonald.

TEATERO, WILLIAM. Policy analyst, Ontario Ministry of Health, Kingston, Ontario.
William Brass.

TELLIER, CORINNE. Bibliothécaire-historienne, Winnipeg, Manitoba.

Jean-Édouard Darveau.

THÉRIAULT, BENOÎT. Chercheur autonome, Hull, Québec.
Philemon Wright [in collaboration with F. Ouellet].

THIVIERGE, MARÎSE. Conseillère, Service des ressources pédagogiques, Université Laval, Québec, Québec.
John McConville.

THOMPSON, JOHN BESWARICK. Historian-writer, Low, Quebec.
William Redmond Casey.

THORPE, WENDY L. Public records archivist, Public Archives of Nova Scotia, Halifax, Nova Scotia.
Elizabeth Lichtenstein (Johnston). Nancy Purvis. [Biographies written in collaboration with J. M. Morris.]

TIESSEN, PAUL. Professor of English, Wilfrid Laurier University, Waterloo, Ontario.
Joseph Schneider [in collaboration with E. R. Good].

TREMBLAY, ROBERT. Étudiant au doctorat en histoire, Université du Québec à Montréal, Québec.
Charles-Simon Delorme.

TULCHINSKY, GERALD J. J. Professor of history, Queen's University, Kingston, Ontario.
George Auldjo. Austin Cuvillier [in collaboration with J. Monet]. *John Forsyth. George Gillespie.*

TULLOCH, JUDITH. Project historian, Environment Canada, Parks, Halifax, Nova Scotia.
Thomas Cutler. Joseph Marshall.

TURNER, LARRY. Historian, Commonwealth Historic Resource Management Ltd, Ottawa, Ontario.
William Bell.

†UPTON, L. F. S. Formerly professor of history, University of British Columbia, Vancouver, British Columbia.
Gabriel Anthony. Francis Condo. Peter Gonish. Thomas Irwin. Noel John. Joseph Malie. Andrew James Meuse. Louis-Benjamin Peminuit Paul. Francis Tomah.

VACHON, CLAUDE. Chargé de projet, Régie des rentes du Québec, Québec.
Elzéar Bédard. André-Rémi Hamel.

VAN KIRK, SYLVIA. Associate professor of history, University of Toronto, Ontario.
John McLeod. John George McTavish.

VAN VEEN, WIM J. Formerly shortwave-radio broadcaster and foreign correspondent, Toronto, Ontario.
Anthony Jacob William Gysbert Van Egmond.

VASS, ELINOR B. Acting assistant provincial archivist, Public Archives of Prince Edward Island, Charlottetown, Prince Edward Island.
John Ready.

VAUGEOIS, DENIS. Historien et éditeur, Sillery, Québec.
Ezekiel Hart.

VEILLEUX, CHRISTINE. Étudiante au doctorat en histoire, Université Laval, Québec, Québec.
John Fletcher. John Hale. Hector-Simon Huot. Norman Fitzgerald Uniacke.

VILLENEUVE, RENÉ. Conservateur adjoint, Art canadien ancien, Musée des beaux-arts du Canada, Ottawa, Ontario.
Laurent Amiot.

VINCENT, THOMAS B. Professor of English and philosophy, Royal Military College of Canada, Kingston, Ontario.
Peter John Allan. John McPherson.

VOISINE, NIVE. Professeur à la retraite, Pointe-au-Père, Québec.
Joseph-Onésime Leprohon.

WALLOT, JEAN-PIERRE. Archiviste national, Archives nationales du Canada, Ottawa, Ontario.
Charles Frederick Grece. Sir Robert Shore Milnes. John Neilson [in collaboration with S. Chassé and R. Girard-Wallot].

WEAVER, JOHN C. Professor of history, McMaster University, Hamilton, Ontario.
James Cull. George Hamilton (1788–1836).

WESTFALL, WILLIAM. Professor of history, York University, Downsview, Ontario.
Amos Ansley.

WHALEN, JAMES MURRAY. Archivist, Government Archives Division, National Archives of Canada, Ottawa, Ontario.
James Patrick Collins.

WHISTLER, NICK. Doctoral student in history, University of Cambridge, England.
John Galt [in collaboration with R. Hall].

WILBUR, RICHARD. President, Fundy Promotion Ltd, and part-time lecturer, University of New Brunswick, Saint John, New Brunswick.
Frederick William Miles.

WILLIAMS, GLYNDWR. Professor of history, University of London, England.
Alexander Roderick McLeod.

WILLIAMS, MAUREEN LONERGAN. Special collections librarian, Angus L. Macdonald Library, St Francis Xavier University, Antigonish, Nova Scotia.
Iain MacGhillEathain.

WILLIAMS, R. J. MICHAEL. Graduate student in English, University of Western Ontario, London, Ontario.
Adam Hood Burwell.

WILLIE, RICHARD A. Assistant professor of history and head, Social Science Division, Concordia College, Edmonton, Alberta.
John West.

WILSON, BRUCE G. Assistant to the director general, Public Programs Branch, National Archives of Canada, Ottawa, Ontario.
William Dickson. Alexander Hamilton. David Secord.

WILSON, J. DONALD. Professor of the history of education, University of British Columbia, Vancouver, British Columbia.
Joseph Spragg.

WINSOR, NABOTH. Clergyman, Wesleyville, Newfoundland.
William Ellis.

WITHAM, JOHN. Head, Historical Research, Environment Canada, Parks, Cornwall, Ontario.
Nicol Hugh Baird.

WOODCOCK, GEORGE. Professor emeritus of English, University of British Columbia, and former editor, *Canadian Literature*, Vancouver, British Columbia.
Samuel Black. Daniel Williams Harmon. Colin Robertson. John Tanner.

WRIGHT, HAROLD E. Coordinator, Partridge Island Research Project, Saint John, New Brunswick.
John Ward.

YOUNG, D. MURRAY. Formerly professor of history, University of New Brunswick, Fredericton, New Brunswick.
David Burpe. Henry George Clopper. Amasa Coy. Peter Fraser. Sir Martin Hunter. William Franklin Odell. Richard Simonds.

INDEX OF IDENTIFICATIONS

CATEGORIES

Agriculture

Architects

Armed forces

Artisans

Arts

Authors

Blacks

Business

Criminals

Education

Engineers

Explorers

Fur traders

Indigenous peoples

Interpreters and translators

Inventors

Journalists

Labourers and labour organizers

Legal professions

Mariners

Medicine

Miscellaneous

Office holders

Politicians

Religious

Scientists

Social reformers and philanthropists

Surveyors

Women

Index of Identifications

Like the network of cross-references within biographies, this index is designed to assist readers in following their interests through the volume. Most of the groupings are by occupations carried on either by persons within Canada or by native-born Canadians in other countries, but some have been established to help readers who approach the past from other perspectives. Thus WOMEN appear in one grouping, as do BLACKS, a reflection of the interest in their history; however, they may also be found under the occupations in which they engaged. The category INDIGENOUS PEOPLES includes Indians, listed by tribe, and Inuit. Readers interested in immigration or in the history of ethnic groups in Canada should consult the first part of the Geographical Index, where subjects are listed by their place of birth.

Some of the occupational categories require explanation so that users will be better able to find biographies of particular interest. Under AGRICULTURE is to be found a variety of people: "seigneurs" form a readily identifiable sub-group; the sub-division "developers" includes improvers, land agents, and those responsible for colonization; listed as "settlers" are individuals who pioneered in new territories; "farmers" comprise only those for whom farming was the prime occupation. Major landowners and individuals who speculated in seigneuries or other lands are to be found under "real estate" in the BUSINESS grouping. The category ARTS includes both fine and performing arts.

Although some of the engineers and doctors in this volume are military officers and so appear under ARMED FORCES, they also appear separately as ENGINEERS or under MEDICINE. Surveyors, hydrographers, and cartographers are found under SURVEYORS. Although FUR TRADERS might have appeared under BUSINESS, they are given a separate listing for the benefit of readers interested in this aspect of the economy. Under MARINERS are included civilian captains, pilots, navigators, and fishermen; naval officers appear as a sub-group of ARMED FORCES. Within OFFICE HOLDERS, the sub-division "administrators" includes high-ranking officials: governors, lieutenant governors, and administrators. Individuals who escape easy classification are grouped under MISCELLANEOUS.

Readers following a particular interest may need to consult more than one grouping. Those interested, for example, in the history of education and medicine should consult, as well as EDUCATION and MEDICINE, the category RELIGIOUS. Biographies relevant to the history of town planning, architecture, and the building trades may be listed under ENGINEERS, ARCHITECTS, ARTISANS (masons, carpenters, etc.), and BUSINESS, "real estate" (contractors). Readers pursuing legal history should turn to both LEGAL PROFESSIONS and CRIMINALS.

The DCB/DBC attempts by its assignments to encourage research in new areas as well as familiar ones, but its selection of individuals to receive biographies reflects the survival of documentation and the areas historians have chosen to investigate. The index should not, therefore, be used for quantitative judgements; it is merely a guide to what is contained in volume VII.

AGRICULTURE

Developers

Farmers

Seigneurs

Settlers

ARCHITECTS

ARMED FORCES

British

Army: officers

Army: soldiers

Militia: officers

Militia: militiamen

Navy: officers

Patriotes and rebels

ARTISANS

ARTS

Gold and silver work

Music

Painting

Photography

Sculpture

Theatre

AUTHORS

Diaries, memoirs, and biographies

Educational and scientific works

Pamphlets, essays, polemics, and sermons

Poetry, prose, and drama

Travel accounts, journals, and narratives

BLACKS

BUSINESS

Commerce

Financial institutions

Manufacturing

Natural resources

Publishing

Real estate

Service industries

Transportation

CRIMINALS

EDUCATION

Administrators

Educators

ENGINEERS

EXPLORERS

FUR TRADERS

INDIGENOUS PEOPLES

Carriers

Chipewyans

Crees

Hurons

Inuit

Iroquois

Malecites

Micmacs

Mohawks

Ojibwas

Ottawas

Shawnees

Wyandots

INTERPRETERS AND TRANSLATORS

INVENTORS

JOURNALISTS

LABOURERS AND LABOUR ORGANIZERS

LEGAL PROFESSIONS

Judges

Justices of the peace

Lawyers

Notaries

MARINERS

MEDICINE

MISCELLANEOUS

OFFICE HOLDERS

Administrators

Officials

POLITICIANS

Colonial and territorial

Appointed

Municipal

Appointed

Elected

RELIGIOUS

SCIENTISTS

SOCIAL REFORMERS AND PHILANTHROPISTS

SURVEYORS

WOMEN

GEOGRAPHICAL INDEX

CANADA

Alberta

British Columbia
Mainland
Vancouver Island

Manitoba

New Brunswick

Newfoundland and Labrador
Labrador
Newfoundland

Northwest Territories

Nova Scotia
Cape Breton Island
Mainland

Ontario
Centre
East
Niagara
North
Southwest

Prince Edward Island

Quebec
Bas-Saint-Laurent–Gaspésie/Côte-Nord
Montréal/Outaouais
Nord-Ouest/Saguenay–Lac-Saint-Jean/Nouveau-Québec
Québec
Trois-Rivières/Cantons-de-l'Est

Saskatchewan

Yukon Territory

OTHER COUNTRIES

Place of Birth

Bermuda
Channel Islands
Federal Republic of Germany
Finland
France
India
Ireland
Italy
Netherlands
Poland
Republic of Ireland
St Kitts-Nevis
Senegal
Switzerland
United Kingdom
United States of America

Career

Ghana
Tasmania
United Kingdom
United States of America
West Indies

ONTARIO

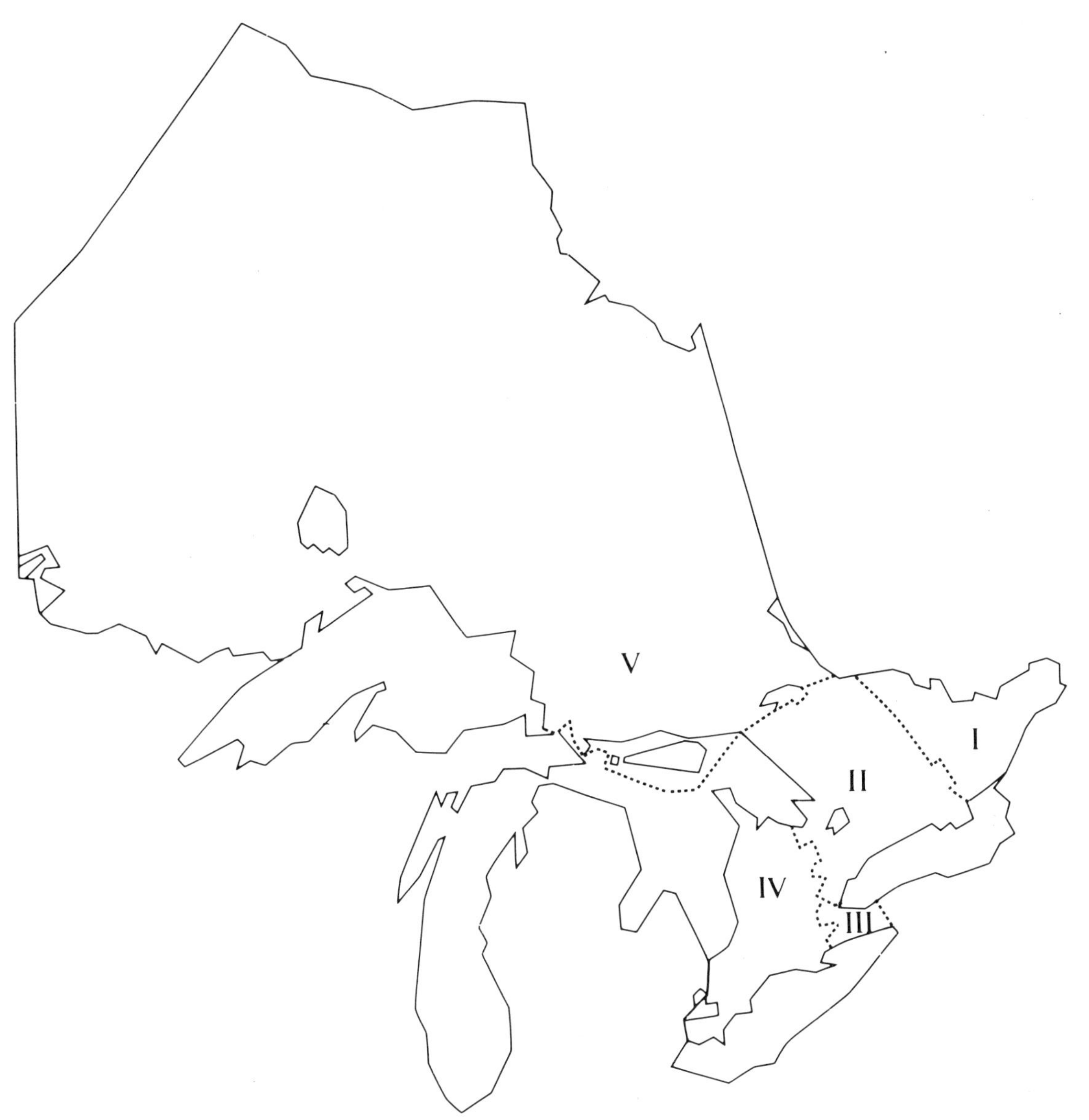

I East
II Centre
III Niagara
IV Southwest
V North

QUEBEC

I Bas-Saint-Laurent–Gaspésie/Côte-Nord
II Québec
III Trois-Rivières/Cantons-de-l'Est
IV Montréal/Outaouais
V Nord-Ouest/Saguenay–Lac-Saint-Jean/
Nouveau-Québec

Geographical Index

The Geographical Index, in two parts, provides a regional breakdown of subjects of biographies according to place of birth and according to career. Each part has two sub-sections: Canada and Other Countries.

For the purposes of this index, Canada is represented by the present provinces and territories, listed alphabetically. Five provinces are subdivided. British Columbia, Newfoundland and Labrador, and Nova Scotia each have two subdivisions. Ontario and Quebec appear in five subdivisions as shown on the maps; those for Quebec are based on the administrative regions defined by the Direction général du domaine territorial. The section Other Countries is based for the most part on modern political divisions, but overseas territories of European countries are listed separately. Only the United Kingdom is subdivided.

Place of Birth. This part of the index lists subjects of biographies by their birthplace, whether in Canada or elsewhere. Where only a strong probability of birth in a particular region exists, the name of the subject is followed by a question mark; where no such probability exists, names have not been included. It should be noted that the use of modern political divisions produces some anachronisms; a person born in Hanover, for example, appears under FEDERAL REPUBLIC OF GERMANY. To accommodate those individuals whose place of birth is known only in general terms, additional listings – e.g. IRELAND – have been provided; readers interested in Irish personalities or in immigration from Ireland should consult also REPUBLIC OF IRELAND and UNITED KINGDOM: Northern Ireland.

Career. Subjects appear here on the basis of their activity as adults. Places of education, retirement, and death have not been considered. Persons whose functions gave them jurisdiction over several regions, such as a bishop or governor, are listed according to their seat of office, but their activities as described in the biographies have also been taken into consideration. Merchants appear only in the area of the primary location of their business, unless the biographies indicate active personal involvement in other regions. Explorers are found in the areas they discovered or visited. Only individuals who were born in the territory of present-day Canada and whose lives took them elsewhere are listed in the section Other Countries; they are listed under the country or countries in which they had a career or were active.

PLACE OF BIRTH

Canada

BRITISH COLUMBIA

Mainland

NEW BRUNSWICK

NEWFOUNDLAND AND LABRADOR

Newfoundland

NORTHWEST TERRITORIES

NOVA SCOTIA

Mainland

ONTARIO

Centre

East

Niagara

Southwest

PRINCE EDWARD ISLAND

QUEBEC

Bas-Saint-Laurent–Gaspésie/ Côte-Nord

Montréal/Outaouais

Québec

Trois-Rivières/Cantons-de-l'Est

Other Countries

BERMUDA

CHANNEL ISLANDS

FEDERAL REPUBLIC OF GERMANY

FINLAND

FRANCE

INDIA

IRELAND

ITALY

NETHERLANDS

POLAND

REPUBLIC OF IRELAND

ST KITTS-NEVIS

SENEGAL

SWITZERLAND

UNITED KINGDOM

England

Northern Ireland

Scotland

Wales

UNITED STATES OF AMERICA

CAREER

Canada

ALBERTA

BRITISH COLUMBIA

Mainland

Vancouver Island

MANITOBA

NEW BRUNSWICK

NEWFOUNDLAND AND LABRADOR

Labrador

Newfoundland

NORTHWEST TERRITORIES

NOVA SCOTIA

Cape Breton Island

Mainland

ONTARIO

Centre

East

Niagara

North

Southwest

PRINCE EDWARD ISLAND

QUEBEC

Bas-Saint-Laurent–Gaspésie/Côte-Nord

Montréal/Outaouais

Nord-Ouest/Saguenay–Lac-Saint-Jean/Nouveau-Québec

Québec

Trois-Rivières/Cantons-de-l'Est

SASKATCHEWAN

YUKON TERRITORY

Other Countries

GHANA

TASMANIA

UNITED KINGDOM

England

UNITED STATES OF AMERICA

WEST INDIES

NOMINAL INDEX

VOLUME I	1000–1700
VOLUME II	1701–1740
VOLUME III	1741–1770
VOLUME IV	1771–1800
VOLUME V	1801–1820
VOLUME VI	1821–1835
VOLUME VII	1836–1850
VOLUME VIII	1851–1860
VOLUME IX	1861–1870
VOLUME X	1871–1880
VOLUME XI	1881–1890
VOLUME XII	1891–1900

As of 1988 the following volumes have been published, volumes I–XI and an *Index, volumes I to IV.*

Nominal Index

Included in this index are the names of persons mentioned in volume VII. They are listed by their family names, with titles and first names following. Wives are entered under their maiden names with their married names in parenthesis. An asterisk indicates that the person has received a biography in a volume already published, or will probably receive one in a subsequent volume. The death date or last floruit date refers the reader to the volume in which the biography will be found. Numerals in bold face indicate the pages on which a biography appears. Titles, variants, and married and religious names are fully cross-referenced.